ESSENTIALS OF
PSYCHOLOGY

SIXTH EDITION

Douglas A. Bernstein
University of South Florida

WADSWORTH
CENGAGE Learning

Australia • Brazil • Japan • Korea • Mexico • Singapore • Spain • United Kingdom • United States

Essentials of Psychology, 6th Edition
Douglas A. Bernstein

Publisher/Executive Editor: Jon-David Hague

Consulting Editor: William S. Altman

Developmental Editor: Tangelique Williams

Assistant Editor/Editorial Assistant:
  Amelia Blevins

Media Editor: Mary Noel

Senior Brand Manager: Elisabeth Rhoden

Market Development Manager: Christine Sosa

Content Project Manager: Charlene M.
  Carpentier

Art Director: Vernon Boes

Manufacturing Planner: Karen Hunt

Rights Acquisitions Specialist:
  Thomas McDonough

Production and Composition: Graphic World Inc.

Photo Researcher: Stephen Forsling

Text Researcher: Pablo D'Stair

Copy Editor: Graphic World Inc.

Text Designer: Gary Hespenheide

Cover Designer: Gary Hespenheide

Cover Image: Exactostock/SuperStock

For product information and technology assistance, contact us at
Cengage Learning Customer & Sales Support, 1-800-354-9706.

For permission to use material from this text or product,
submit all requests online at **www.cengage.com/permissions.**

Further permissions questions can be e-mailed to
permissionrequest@cengage.com.

Library of Congress Control Number: 2012944148

Student Edition:

ISBN-13: 978-1-133-95898-7

ISBN-10: 1-133-95898-2

Loose-leaf Edition:

ISBN-13: 978-1-285-05581-7

ISBN-10: 1-285-05581-0

Wadsworth
20 Davis Drive
Belmont, CA 94002-3098
USA

Cengage Learning is a leading provider of customized learning solutions with office locations around the globe, including Singapore, the United Kingdom, Australia, Mexico, Brazil, and Japan. Locate your local office at **www.cengage.com/global.**

Cengage Learning products are represented in Canada by Nelson Education, Ltd.

To learn more about Wadsworth, visit **www.cengage.com/wadsworth**

Purchase any of our products at your local college store or at our preferred online store **www.CengageBrain.com.**

Printed in Canada

1 2 3 4 5 6 7 17 16 15 14 13

For Doris

BRIEF CONTENTS

CONTENTS

6 Memory   207

7 Thought, Language, and Intelligence   247

8   Motivation and Emotion   297

9   Human Development   343

13 Treatment of Psychological Disorders   505

14 Social Psychology   543

15 Industrial and Organizational Psychology 595

16 Neuropsychology 631

FEATURES

PREFACE

Psychology is a rich and varied science, covering the breadth and depth of human behavior—everything from fleeting reflexes to enduring memories, from falling asleep to falling in love. In my experience, most students enter the introductory course thinking that psychology concerns itself mainly with personality, psychological testing, mental disorders, psychotherapy, and other aspects of clinical psychology. Many of these students are surprised, then, when they find themselves reading about such topics as the structure of the brain, optical illusions, the effect of jet lag on athletic performance, AIDS and the immune system, and prenatal risk factors, to name just a few. Yet these are all topics under the umbrella that is psychology.

For all its diversity, psychology is also a remarkably integrated discipline whose subfields are linked through common interests and related research questions. As a psychologist and scholar, I wrote this book to portray the wide range of topics that make up the science of psychology. As a teacher, I focused on the essentials of the discipline—the core concepts of psychology that I hope will be especially accessible and interesting to students. I also tried to present these topics through an integrated, active pedagogical system designed to help students get the most out of the text.

In creating the sixth edition of *Essentials of Psychology,* I remained dedicated to presenting a textbook that not only is clear and enjoyable to read but also provides features to support the learning process in all students, regardless of their academic background. Specifically, I set these goals:

- To focus on topics that represent the full range of psychology, from cell to society, without overwhelming the reader with details.
- To provide many active learning exercises that invite students to work with the book's material in ways that can help them understand and remember it.
- To help students develop their ability to think critically and scientifically by examining the ways that psychologists have solved (or tried to solve) fascinating puzzles of behavior and mental processes.
- To explain the content of psychology with an emphasis on the doing of psychology, grounding all discussions in current and classic research studies. (I help students appreciate the importance of research by exploring one study in detail in a special feature in each chapter.)

My discussion of research in psychology is also designed to remind students that although in some ways "people are people wherever you go," sociocultural factors—including gender, ethnicity, cultural background, and geography—often shape human behavior and mental processes. I repeatedly point out, therefore, that psychological research on the thinking styles, perceptual habits, psychological disorders, social pressures,

and other phenomena seen in North America or Europe, for example, may or may not apply to other cultures, or even to subcultures within Western countries.

Rather than isolating discussion of sociocultural material in boxed features, I have woven it into every chapter so that students will encounter it repeatedly as they read. I introduce the importance of sociocultural factors in Chapter 1 and continue to reinforce it through coverage of such topics as the impact of culture and experience on perception (Chapter 3), classrooms across cultures (Chapter 5), ethnic differences in IQ (Chapter 7), social and cultural factors in sexuality (Chapter 8), gender differences in stress responses (Chapter 10), personality, culture, and human development (Chapter 11), gender and cultural differences in depression and suicide (Chapter 12), and cultural factors in aggression (Chapter 14), to cite just a few examples.

What's New in This Edition?

Feedback from faculty colleagues and students suggests that the changes made in the fifth edition of *Essentials* were well received. Accordingly, in creating the sixth edition, I have sought to update and upgrade all the book's best features rather than change them for the sake of change. I hope that the result of my effort is a book that offers even more of what faculty and students want and need.

Organization

Designed for presentation in a single academic term, the book's chapter organization has been retained, and the chapters appear in the same sequence as before. However, the sixth edition now contains chapters on industrial/organizational psychology and on neuropsychology, which had been optional in the fifth edition. The order of the chapters reflects the way I teach my introductory course, but I know that your preference for chapter sequencing may not match mine. Accordingly I have again ensured that each of the sixteen chapters works as a freestanding unit so that you may assign the chapters in whatever order you wish. For example, many instructors prefer to teach the material on human development relatively late in the course, which is why it appears as Chapter 9. However, the chapter can be just as comfortably assigned earlier in the course.

A Continued Emphasis on Learning by Doing

 The added emphasis on active learning in the third edition was so popular with faculty and students that I have continued to emphasize it ever since. Three kinds of "Learn by Doing" features appear throughout the book.

- First, dozens of new or revised figure and photo captions help students understand and remember a psychological principle or phenomenon by suggesting ways they can demonstrate it for themselves. In the memory chapter, for example, a photo caption suggests that students show the photo to a friend and then ask questions about it to illustrate the operation of constructive memory. These captions are all identified with a Learn by Doing symbol.
- Second, I have placed Learn by Doing symbols in page margins at even more places where active learning opportunities occur in the narrative. At these points, I ask students to stop reading and try doing something to illustrate or highlight the psychological principle or phenomenon under discussion. For example, in the sensation and perception chapter, I ask students to focus attention on various targets as a way of appreciating the difference between overt and covert attention shifts.
- Finally, I have carried the active learning theme through to the end of each chapter, where—as part of the built-in study guide I call "Active Review"—students will find sections called "Put It in Writing" and "Personal Learning Activity." These sections invite students to (a) write about a specific chapter-related topic and (b) collect, analyze, and discuss data on a chapter-related principle or phenomenon.

Active Review

The Put It in Writing and Personal Learning Activity sections are just two aspects of my effort to add educational value to the built-in Active Review study guide. The Active Review's other features include

- A "Linkages" diagram, which helps students understand and appreciate the ways the chapter they have just read relates to other subfields of psychology.
- Twenty-item multiple-choice self-tests. I have revised some of the questions, but (as in the fifth edition) they are focused on the applications as well as the definitions of principles, concepts, and phenomena.
- The Learn by Doing section mentioned above, which highlights my emphasis on active learning.
- A "Review of Key Terms" section, which invites students to write their own definitions of the most important terms presented in the chapter. These lists have been updated to include all the key terms discussed in the new edition.

"Applying Psychology" Photos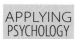

I continue to emphasize the many ways psychological theory and research results are being applied to benefit human welfare. I further highlight the diversity of applied psychology by including a number of "Applying Psychology" photos that offer memorable examples. In the learning chapter, for example,

a photo illustrates the use of classical conditioning principles in the humane control of predators that can threaten sheep ranchers' livelihoods. In the consciousness chapter, the Applying Psychology photo illustrates the value of stimulus control therapy for helping insomniacs get a better night's sleep.

Updated Content

My goal in preparing this new edition of *Essentials* was to present the latest as well as the most established results of basic and applied research on topics that are both important to psychology and of high interest to students. Following is a chapter-by-chapter summary of just some new and updated material included in the sixth edition:

Chapter 1:

- Latest figures on employment settings for psychologists
- Latest figures on graduate degrees in psychology earned by men, women, and members of ethnic minority groups
- Introduction of the concept of indigenous psychology
- Latest research methods used to evaluate claims for the effectiveness of eye movement desensitization and reprocessing (EMDR) therapy
- New information on epigenetic influences in understanding the interacting roles of heredity and environment

Chapter 2:

- Updated research on stem cells and nerve growth factors and their uses in repairing brain damage
- Latest information on techniques for studying the brain, including commercial and forensic uses
- Latest information on electrical synapses
- Latest information on the use of electrical stimulation as therapy for brain damage
- Information about how experience can change the structure of the brain
- Latest information about adolescent brain development and behavior
- Latest information on optogenetics

Chapter 3:

- New information about age-related decreases in visual acuity
- New Learn by Doing exercise to help illustrate the trichromatic theory of color vision
- New information about loss of olfaction as an early indicator of neurological disorder
- Latest information about research on pheromones in humans
- Latest information about research on acupuncture
- New information about benign paroxysmal positional vertigo
- New information about the sense of equilibrium and astronautics

- Expanded information about the effects of motivation on top-down processing
- Updated and expanded information about the effects of cell phones, texting, personal music players, and laptop computer use on attention—especially in drivers and pedestrians
- New Learn by Doing exercise on touch sensations

Chapter 4:

- Revised information on the number and labels for stages of sleep
- Updated information about nonconscious and unconscious mental processes
- Updated information about sleep disorders and treating sleep disorders
- New information about the functions of REM sleep and its effect on creativity
- New information about effects of sleep deprivation to reduce impact of trauma
- Latest information about chronotypes, and the "clock genes" that seem to drive them
- Updated information about applications of hypnosis and effects of meditation
- Updated information about neural effects of drugs, including epigenetic effects
- Latest information about the long-term effects of caffeine, nicotine, and opiates
- Latest information on the debate over medical uses of marijuana

Chapter 5:

- Latest information about the mechanisms of classical conditioning
- Latest information about the effects of reinforcers in the brain
- Updated information on applications of operant conditioning
- Updated information on the biological basis of observational learning
- Latest research on the impact of violent and prosocial television and video games
- Updated information on active learning methods in the classroom
- Latest research about e-media for delivery of college class materials
- Updated information on classrooms across cultures

Chapter 6:

- New information about hypermnesia
- Updated information about scents as memory cues
- Updated information about false memories and eyewitness testimony
- Latest research on the biological basis of memory

Chapter 7:

- Updated information on judge and jury decision making
- New section on building effective problem-solving skills
- Latest information on advances in artificial intelligence
- Latest information about creativity and its biological roots
- New information about effects of physical environment on creative thinking
- Latest information on decision making in risky situations
- Updated information on group problem solving and decision making
- Latest information about bilingualism and long-term effects on cognition
- Updated information on extraneous influences on intelligence test results
- New research on stereotype threat
- Updated information on the interaction of environmental and genetic factors in intelligence, and on group differences in IQ

Chapter 8:

- New information about how eating habits have changed over centuries
- New Learn by Doing exercise to illustrate the facial feedback hypothesis
- Latest information on lie detection
- New section on intrinsic and extrinsic sources of motivation
- Updated information about hormonal influences on eating behavior
- Updated information about neurotransmitters and eating behavior
- Latest figures on obesity and new material on its causes and on prevention efforts
- Updated material on anorexia nervosa and bulimia
- Updated information about gender differences in sexuality
- Latest information about well-being and its relation to achievement
- New coverage of the conceptual act model of emotion
- New research on situational factors in reading facial expressions

Chapter 9:

- Updated information about behavioral genetics, genetic influences on development, and the influence of environmental factors on genetic expression
- Updated information on the effects of electronic and social media on infant, child, and adolescent development
- Updated information about midlife transition and the "sandwich generation"
- New and updated information about intellectual abilities in late adulthood, including risk factors and protective or mediating influences
- Updated information about the impact of alcohol, nicotine, and other toxins on infant development

- Latest information about infant thinking and behavior during the sensorimotor stage
- Latest information about influences of nature and the environment on children's brain development
- Updated information about culture and cognitive development
- Updated information about poverty as a developmental danger
- Updated information on long-term effects of early attachment styles
- Updated information about parenting styles and their effects on child development
- Updated information on the development of infants' theory of mind
- Updated statistics on adolescent sexuality and teenage pregnancy
- Updated information about emotional development during emerging adulthood
- New and updated information about longevity

Chapter 10:

- New information about the long-term effects of stressors early in life
- New statistics on worldwide deaths due to health-damaging behaviors
- Updated information about the cognitive effects of stressors on decision making and problem solving
- Updated information about posttraumatic stress disorder
- New information about the relationship among socioeconomic status, lack of control, and premature death in lower socioeconomic groups
- Updated information about associations between social networks and happiness
- Updated information about personality and resistance to stress
- Updated information about identifying people at elevated risk for health problems
- Updated information about health beliefs and efforts to change them

Chapter 11:

- New information about empirical research on psychodynamic theory
- Updated information about applications and biological basis of the Five Factor Theory of personality
- New research on Gray's reinforcement sensitivity theory
- Updated information on personality research in nonhumans
- Updated information about the influence of genetics and epigenetics on personality traits
- Updated information about situational factors and the expression of personality traits
- Updated information about the possible impact of early attachment style in childhood and adulthood

- Updated information about the behavioral correlates of internal versus external locus of control
- Updated information about the effects of self-efficacy on achievement and well-being
- New information about the impact of positive psychology in personality
- Updated information about culture and personality
- Updated information about the latest edition of the Minnesota Multiphasic Personality Inventory (MMPI-2 RF)

Chapter 12:

- Updated information on the incidence of psychological disorders
- New information about the changes likely to appear in the forthcoming DSM5 and ICD-11, and about debates surrounding these changes
- Updated information on diagnostic reliability and validity
- Updated information about bias in psychological diagnosis
- Updated coverage of causes of psychological disorders, including epigenetics
- New information about the effects of media-driven attitudes on people's understanding and response to psychological disorders
- Updated information about culture-specific disorders
- Coverage of *cyberchondria,* a new term similar to "medical students' syndrome"
- Updated information about somatoform and dissociative disorders
- Updated statistics about the incidence of, and risk factors for, suicide
- Updated information about hallucinations in schizophrenia
- Updated statistics about the incidence of autistic spectrum disorders
- Updated information about mental illness and the law

Chapter 13:

- Updated information about the prevalence of psychological treatments in adults and children in the United States
- Updated information about research on the effectiveness of psychotherapy
- New and updated information about the evolution of evidence-based practice and empirically supported therapies
- Updated information about cultural diversity training for therapists
- Updated information about therapeutic effects of repetitive transcranial magnetic stimulation (rTMS) therapy, deep brain stimulation, and optogenic stimulation
- Updated information about effectiveness, side effects, and costs and benefits of antidepressant drugs
- Updated information about human diversity and drug treatments
- Updated information about the effectiveness of psychoactive medications for mental disorders and their value in combination with psychotherapy

- Updated information about community psychology
- New and updated information about self-help and Internet-based therapy efforts

Chapter 14:

- New Learn by Doing exercises on attitude similarity and helping behavior
- New information about factors contributing to, or mediating, feelings of empathy
- New information about how social media affect feelings of attraction
- Updated information about terror management theory
- Updated information about the speed, strength, and accuracy of first impressions and factors that influence them
- Updated information about prejudice and its possible causes
- Updated information on the contact hypothesis and the mere-exposure effect in reducing prejudice
- Updated information on factors that contribute to attraction
- Updated information on gender and conformity
- Updated statistics about aggressive behavior in the United States
- Updated information about the possible biological and social factors affecting aggression
- New information about the possible effects of prosocial media on helping behavior
- New information on neuroimaging studies in social psychology

Chapter 15:

- Expanded history of industrial and organizational psychology
- Updated employment statistics for industrial and organizational psychologists
- Updated information about factors that influence job satisfaction
- Updated statistics about workplace violence
- Updated information about leader and follower behaviors
- Updated information about leader-member exchange (LMX) theory

Chapter 16:

- Updated information about how the interconnections of modules in the brain contribute to specific abilities and behaviors
- Updated information about the effects of strokes and the latest rehabilitation approaches
- Updated information about traumatic brain injuries and memory loss
- New information about traumatic brain injuries in sports
- Updated information about consciousness disturbances
- Updated information about brain activity and prosopagnosia

- Updated information about language disorders and frontotemporal degeneration
- Updated statistics about dementia
- New and updated information about the causes and symptoms of Alzheimer's disease
- Latest information about treatments for Alzheimer's disease

Special Features

The sixth edition of *Essentials of Psychology* contains improved versions of a number of special features found in its predecessor. Designed to promote efficient learning and mastery of the material, these include, in each chapter, an integrated pedagogical system as well as Thinking Critically, Focus on Research, Linkages, and Active Review sections.

An Integrated Pedagogical System

Our integrated pedagogical system is designed to help students get the most out of their reading. Based on the PQ4R study system (discussed in Chapter 6, "Memory"), learning aids in each chapter include the following elements.

Preview Section To help students survey and question the material, each chapter opens with an outline and a brief preview statement. A question related to the key topic of each main section of the chapter appears at the beginning of each of those main sections, and these questions appear again in the Active Review, where they help to organize the chapter summary.

Margin Glossary Key terms are defined in the margin of the page where they appear, reinforcing core concepts without interrupting the flow of reading. All key terms have been revised to match those in the American Psychological Association's *Thesaurus of Psychological Index Terms* (11th ed.) and in the *APA Dictionary of Psychology*. Using key terms from these sources will help students do their own research by making it easier for them to use key-term searches in the field's most popular databases (PsycINFO & PsycARTICLES). Using these key terms will also improve students' abilities to transfer terms learned in introductory courses to their work in advanced courses. (For the sixth edition, I have continued to revise many of the phonetic guides to make it even easier for students to correctly pronounce unfamiliar key terms as well as other terms whose pronunciations are not immediately obvious.) In the Active Review section at the end of each chapter, a definition exercise encourages students to restate these core concepts in their own words.

Instructional Captions Captions for all figures, tables, photographs, and cartoons reiterate core concepts and help students learn to interpret visual information. And, as mentioned earlier, many of these captions prompt students to engage in various kinds of active learning experiences.

In Review Charts   In Review study charts summarize information in a convenient tabular format. I have placed two or three In Review charts strategically in each chapter to help students synthesize and assimilate large chunks of information—for example, on drug effects, key elements in personality theories, and stress responses and mediators. Fill-in-the-blank self-testing items at the bottom of each In Review chart further aid student learning and review of the chapter material. The answer key for these items can be found at the back of the book.

Active Review   As mentioned earlier, the built-in Active Review study guide at the end of each chapter includes

- A Linkages diagram containing questions that illustrate three of the ways that material in each chapter is connected to other chapters in the book.
- A chapter summary organized around major topic headings and the related preview questions. The summary is presented in short, easy-to-read paragraphs that focus on the topics introduced by chapter subheadings.
- A Learn by Doing feature that is designed to promote active learning. Here, students will find Put It in Writing and Personal Learning Project sections that invite them to (a) write about a specific chapter-related topic and (b) collect, analyze, and discuss some data on a chapter-related principle or phenomenon. For example, in the personality chapter, the Put It in Writing section suggests that students list a celebrity's personality traits and then summarize how various personality theories would account for the development of those traits. In the biology and behavior chapter, students are asked to write about how research on brain development might affect one's choice of an infant day-care center. These Put It in Writing suggestions might be helpful as writing-across-the-curriculum assignments.
- Personal Learning Projects that suggest ways in which students can do psychology as well as read about it. In the motivation and emotion chapter, for example, the Personal Learning Project section suggests a way for students to collect data on lie-detection skills. In the social psychology chapter, students are invited to test assumptions of evolutionary theories of mate selection by analyzing personals ads.
- A Review of Key Terms, which invites students to write their own definitions of the most important terms presented in the chapter. These lists have been updated to include all of the key terms discussed in the new edition, and (as already mentioned) all key terms now correspond to those used by the APA in its dictionary and thesaurus.
- A 20-item multiple-choice Self-Test designed to help students assess their understanding of the chapter's key points prior to taking quizzes and exams. As before, I provide an answer key at the back of the book that identifies and briefly explains each correct answer and refers students to the page on which the tested material was first discussed.

Thinking Critically

A special Thinking Critically section in each chapter helps students hone this vital skill. My approach centers on describing research on psychological phenomena in a way that reveals the logic of the scientific method, identifies possible flaws in design or interpretation, and leaves room for more questions and further research. In other words, as an author-teacher, I try to model critical thinking processes for my readers. The Thinking Critically sections are designed to make these processes more explicit and accessible by providing readers with a framework for analyzing evidence before drawing conclusions. The framework is built around five questions that the reader should find useful in analyzing not only psychological research studies but other forms of communication as well, including political speeches, advertising claims, and appeals for contributions. These five questions first appear in Chapter 1, where I introduce the importance of critical thinking, and they are repeated in every chapter's Thinking Critically section:

1. What am I being asked to believe or accept?
2. Is evidence available to support the claim?
3. Can that evidence be interpreted another way?
4. What evidence would help to evaluate the alternatives?
5. What conclusions are most reasonable?

   Using this simple yet powerful framework, I explore issues such as subliminal persuasion, recovered memories, and the origins of sexual orientation, to name just a few. Page xv includes a complete list of the Thinking Critically features.

Focus on Research

Psychological scientists have helped us better understand behavior and mental processes through their commitment to empirical research. They have posed vital questions about psychological phenomena and have designed research that can answer (or at least illuminate) those questions. In Chapter 1, I introduce readers to the methods of scientific research and to basic research designs in psychology. Every subsequent chapter features a Focus on Research section that highlights a particular research study to help students appreciate the value of research and the creativity with which psychologists have conducted it. Like the Thinking Critically sections, the Focus on Research features are organized around five questions designed to help readers organize their thinking about research questions and research results.

1. What was the researcher's question?
2. How did the researcher answer the question?
3. What did the researcher find?
4. What do the results mean?
5. What do we still need to know?

   These Focus on Research sections help students see how psychologists have used experiments, correlational studies, surveys, observations, and other designs to explore phenomena such as learned helplessness, infant cognition, evolutionary theories of helping, and human sexual behavior. A full list of the Focus on Research features appears on page xv.

Linkages

In my experience, introductory psychology students are better able to appreciate the scope of our discipline when they look at it not as a laundry list of separate topics but as an interrelated set of subfields, each of which contributes to—and benefits from—the work being done in all the others. To help students see these relationships, I have built into the book an integrating tool called Linkages. There are three elements in the Linkages program.

- *Linkages diagrams* The first element of each chapter's Active Review is a Linkages diagram, which presents a set of questions that illustrate three of the ways that material in the chapter is related to other chapters in the book. For example, the Linkages diagram in Chapter 2, "Biology and Behavior," contains questions that show how biological psychology is related to consciousness ("Does the brain shut down when I sleep?"), human development ("How do our brains change over a lifetime?"), and treatment of psychological disorders ("How do drugs help people who suffer from schizophrenia?"). These diagrams are designed to help students keep in mind how the content of each chapter fits into psychology as a whole. To introduce the concept of Linkages, the diagram in Chapter 1 appears within the body of the chapter.
- *Cross-references* The page numbers following each question in the Linkages diagrams direct the student to pages that carry further discussion of that question. There, the linking question is repeated in the margin alongside the discussion.
- *Linkages sections* One of the questions in each chapter's Linkages diagram reminds the student of the chapter's discussion of that question in a special section titled, appropriately enough, Linkages (see page xv for a complete list of Linkages sections).

These three elements combine with the text narrative to highlight the network of relationships among psychology's subfields. This Linkages program is designed to help students see the "big picture" of psychology, no matter how many chapters their instructor assigns or in what sequence.

Teaching and Learning Support Package

Many useful instructional and pedagogical materials have been developed to support the *Essentials of Psychology* textbook and the introductory course. These are designed to enhance and maximize the teaching and learning experience. This sixth edition focuses on greater integration of the supplemental package components with the text itself. New features of several supplements reflect the text's emphasis on active learning and writing across the curriculum.

For the Instructor

Instructor's Resource Manual (ISBN: 1-285-05827-6) For each chapter of the textbook, the online *Instructor's Resource Manual* includes learning objectives, a lecture outline, and numerous classroom "supplements," such as discussion, activity, and lecture suggestions and related handouts. The revised manual includes new Thinking Critically and Put It in Writing supplements similar to the exercises that appear in the textbook. The manual also includes a video guide and a pedagogical strategy section that covers active learning, critical thinking, using the Linkages feature, using the Research Focus supplements, and writing across the curriculum, as well as suggestions on how to build a syllabus. For instructors switching from the fifth to the sixth edition of the text, the manual includes a detailed transition guide for each chapter, outlining the key changes between editions.

Test Bank (ISBN: 1-285-05830-6) The online Test Bank includes 125 multiple-choice questions, 5 long-essay questions, and 5 short-answer questions per chapter. Each multiple-choice question is keyed to pages in the student text and to the learning objectives that appear in the *Instructor's Resource Manual* and that are also printed in the test bank. Each question is identified according to whether it tests simple factual recall or deeper conceptual understanding. Over 45 percent of the items have been class-tested with between 400 and 2,500 students. A statistical performance analysis is provided for those items. The computerized version allows instructors to edit questions, integrate their own questions, and generate paper or online exams.

PowerLecture® with ExamView® (ISBN: 1-285-05831-3) This one-stop lecture and class preparation tool contains ready-to-use PowerPoint slides, enabling you to assemble, edit, publish, and present custom lectures for your course. PowerLecture lets you bring together text-specific lecture outlines and art from the textbook along with videos or your own materials, culminating in a powerful, personalized, media-enhanced presentation. PowerLecture also includes the ExamView assessment and tutorial system, which guides you step by step through the process of creating tests.

Aplia
Aplia helps students understand psychology as a science through fresh and compelling content, brief engagement activities that illustrate key concepts, and thought-provoking questions.

- Engagement activities pique student interest and motivate students to learn about a concept. Short experiments, videos, and surveys provide a range of experiential learning opportunities.
- Questions about real-world situations hone students' critical-thinking skills.
- Auto-assigned, auto-graded assignments hold students accountable for the material before they come to class, increasing their effort and preparation.

- Immediate, detailed explanations for every answer enhance student comprehension.
- Gradebook analytics allow instructors to monitor and address performance on a student-by-student and topic-by-topic basis.

WebTutor™ Jump-start your course with customizable, rich, text-specific content within your Course Management System. Whether you want to Web-enable your class or put an entire course online, WebTutor delivers. WebTutor offers a wide array of resources including access to the eBook, glossaries, flashcards, quizzes, videos, Virtual Psychology Labs, and more.

ABC DVD: Introductory Psychology, Volumes 1–3
Volume 1: ISBN: 0-495-50306-1; Volume 2: ISBN: 0-495-59637-X; Volume 3: ISBN: 0-495-60490-9
ABC Videos feature short, high-interest clips from current news events as well as historic raw footage going back 40 years. Perfect for discussion starters or to enrich your lectures and spark interest in the material in the text, these brief videos provide students with a new lens through which to view the past and present, one that will greatly enhance their knowledge and understanding of significant events and open up to them new dimensions in learning. Clips are drawn from such programs as *World News Tonight, Good Morning America, This Week, PrimeTime Live, 20/20,* and *Nightline,* as well as numerous ABC News specials and material from the Associated Press Television News and British Movietone News collections.

Wadsworth Psychology: Research in Action, Volumes 1–2
Volume 1: ISBN: 0-495-60490-9; Volume 2: ISBN: 0-495-59813-5
Research in Action features the work of research psychologists to give students an opportunity to learn about cutting-edge research—not just who is doing it but also how it is done and how and where the results are being used. By taking students into the laboratories of both established and up-and-coming researchers and by showing research results being applied outside the laboratory, these videos offer insight into both the research process and the many ways that real people's lives are affected by research in the fields of psychology and neuroscience.

Wadsworth Guest Lecture Series
ISBN: 0-547-00401-X
The Guest Lecture Series features many talented teachers sharing their teaching tips and best practices on a wide range of topics, including: Rational Emotive Behavior Theory, Blogging as an Effective Tool, Demonstrations on Taste, Dramatizing Perspectives in Psychology, How to Teach Writing in Psychology, and more.

Revealing Psychology
ISBN: 0-547-01453-8
The *Revealing Psychology* Video (available on DVD) is ideal for both classroom presentation and online study. The clips include a refreshed and innovative Candid Camera–like segment depicting people in socially challenging situations, with a focus on applications of concepts and experimental variations; classic experiments in real-world context with a new look and feel; and personal profiles with interviews of real people talking about their lives in ways that illustrate social psychological principles.

For the Student

CourseMate Cengage Learning's Psychology CourseMate brings course concepts to life with interactive learning, study, and exam preparation tools that support the printed textbook. Access an integrated eBook and use learning tools including glossaries, flashcards, quizzes, videos, Virtual Psychology Labs, and more in your Psychology CourseMate. Go to CengageBrain.com to register or purchase access.

Psychology in Context: Voices and Perspectives (2nd ed.) The second edition of this exceptional reader, edited by David N. Sattler and Virginia Shabatay, may be shrink-wrapped with the text. It features engaging first-person narratives and essays by noted writers, with each article keyed to major psychological concepts.

Psychology: Fields of Application This unique reader, edited by Astrid Stec and Douglas Bernstein, explores the most prominent areas of applied psychology. Each chapter features an expert's account of one area of application, including a brief history of the area's development, examples of research and how it has been applied, and the challenges facing the field.

Succeed in College This guide is a skill-building booklet containing selected chapters from Walter Pauk's best-selling study-skills text, *How to Study in College.* The booklet is based on the recently updated *How to Succeed in College* and offers time-tested advice on note-taking, time management, and test-taking.

Writing with Style: APA Style Made Easy (4th ed.) This accessible and invaluable workbook-style reference guide, written by Lenore T. Szuchman, will help students smoothly make the transition from writing for composition classes to writing for psychology classes.

Acknowledgments

Many people provided me with the help, criticism, and encouragement I needed to create *Essentials of Psychology* and to revise it into this sixth edition. I am of course indebted to my colleagues Louis Penner, Ed Roy, and Alison Clarke-Stewart, who, as co-authors of the Bernstein, Penner, Clarke-Stewart, and Roy textbook *Psychology* provided invaluable assistance in reviewing the revised *Essentials* manuscript as it developed. I also offer sincere thanks to Professor Paul Spector of the University of South Florida, who took the lead in helping to create the chapter on industrial and organizational psychology, and to Joel Shenker, M.D., Ph.D., who took the lead in helping to create the chapter on neuropsychology. I am particularly grateful to William S. Altman of Broome Community College who worked closely with me on the revision of every chapter of this new edition. His extensive teaching experience, wisdom, and sense of humor were invaluable to me every step of the way. I am indebted, too, to a number of other colleagues for their expert help and advice on the revision of various chapters that appeared in the fifth edition of *Essentials*. These colleagues include, for Chapter 3, Joel Shenker, M.D., Ph.D., and Angela Hayden, University of Kentucky; for Chapter 5, Doug Williams, University of Winnipeg; for Chapter 6, Kathleen McDermott, Washington University; for Chapter 7, Paul Whitney, Washington State University, and Rose Mary Webb, Appalachian State University; for Chapter 8, Johnmarshall Reeve, Korea University; for Chapter 10, Catherine Stoney, National Center for Complementary and Alternative Medicine; for Chapter 12, Chris Trentacosta, Wayne State University; for Chapter 13, Vicki Phares, University of South Florida; for Chapter 15, Nathan Carter, University of Central Florida; and for Chapter 16, Joel Shenker, M.D., Ph.D.

I also want to offer heartfelt thanks to my friends and colleagues who did such a wonderful job in creating revised versions of the ancillary materials for *Essentials*. Most of these people have worked with me for years, and many of them had been graduate student instructors in the University of Illinois introductory psychology program out of which this book emerged. They include Kelly Bouas Henry, Missouri Western State College; Sandra Goss Lucas, University of Illinois; Linda Lebie, Lakeland College; Chris Armstrong, University of Illinois; and David B. Strohmetz, Monmouth University.

I also extend my deep appreciation to the *Essentials* Board of Consultants, eight dedicated instructors whose involvement in focus groups and surveys, comments on manuscript chapters, and answers to development queries shaped the first edition of this text.

Charles Blair-Broeker, *Cedar Falls High School*

Ken LeSure, *Cuyahoga Community College*

Barbara Lusk, *Collin County Community College*

Malinda Jo Muzi, *Community College of Philadelphia*

Nancy Simpson, *Trident Technical College*

Maggie Sokolik, *University of California, Berkeley*

Fred Whitford, *Montana State University*

Robert Wildblood, *Northern Virginia Community College*

I wish to thank several colleagues who helped me get the sixth edition off to a good start by reviewing and commenting on the strengths and weaknesses of the fifth edition.

Karl Blendell, *Siena College*

Elaine Cassel, *Lord Fairfax Community College*

Robin Eliason, *Piedmont Virginia Community College*

Frank Hammonds, *Troy University*

Rolf Holtz, *Troy University*

Charles J. Huffman, *Piedmont Virginia Community College*

Alishia Huntoon, *Oregon Institute of Technology*

Mary Johannesen-Schmidt, *Oakton Community College*

Sal Massa, *Marist College*

Brian Parry, *Mesa State College*

Imaura Pilotti, *New Mexico Highlands University*

William Price, *North Country Community College*

Brittney Schrick, *Southern Arkansas University*

Paul Schwartz, *Mount St. Mary College*

Albert K. Toh, *University of Arkansas, Pine Bluff*

Shannon Scott, *Texas Woman's University*

I owe an enormous debt as well to the colleagues listed below for their thoughtful reviews of the manuscripts of the first five editions as they were being developed. Their advice and suggestions for improvement were responsible for many of the good qualities you will find in this book. If you have any criticisms, they probably involve areas these reviewers warned me about!

Patricia Abbot, *D'Youville College*

Gary Altmann, *York University, United Kingdom*

Robin A. Anderson, *St. Ambrose University*

Grace Auyang, *University of Cincinnati*

Alan Baxter, *Technical Career Institutes, New York*

James Bean, *Lock Haven University*

Beth Benoit, *University of Massachusetts, Lowell, and Middlesex Community College*

Joseph J. Benz, *University of Nebraska at Kearney*

Doris A. Bitler, *George Mason University*

Winfield Brown, *Florence Darlington Technical College*

J. Peter Burton, *Santa Fe Community College*

James F. Calhoun, *University of Georgia*

Bernardo J. Carducci, *Indiana University Southeast*

Yiwei Chen, *Bowling Green State University*

Saundra Ciccarelli, *Gulf Coast Community College*

Samuel Clay, *Heartland Community College*

Dwaine Cochran, *Stetson University*

Anne M. Cooper, *St. Petersburg Junior College*

Nat DeAnda, *Los Madanos College*

Marcie N. Desrochers, *College of Charleston*

Kenneth C. Elliot, *University of Maine at Augusta*

Matthew Fanetti, *Southwest Missouri State University*

Leticia Y. Flores, *Southwest Texas State University*

John R. Foust, *Parkland College*

Laura Freberg, *California Polytechnic State University, San Luis Obispo*

Grace Galliano, *Kennesaw State University*

Christopher Gilbert, *Bristol Community College*

Craig W. Gruber, *Walt Whitman High School*

Lynn Haller, *Morehead State University*

Wen Harris, *Lane Community College*

Diane Herbert, *Hofstra University*

Debra Hollister, *Valencia Community College*

Gene Indenbaum, *SUNY Farmingdale*

John S. Klein, *Castleton State College*

Ronald Kleinknecht, *Western Washington University*

Janet L. Kottke, *California State University, San Bernardino*

Jennifer M. Lancaster, *St. Francis College*

David S. Malcolm, *Fordham University*

Joseph G. Marrone, *Siena College*

Joseph A. Mayo, *Gordon College*

David Murphy, *Waubonsee College*

Sheila M. Murphy, *Mount Wachusett Community College*

Bonnie J. Nichols, *Missouri County Community College*

Steve A. Nida, *Franklin University*

Sheila O'Brien Quinn, *Salve Regina University*

Christine Offutt Lingenfelter, *Lock Haven University*

Arthur G. Olguin, *Santa Barbara City College*

Randall E. Osborne, *Indiana University East*

Les Parrott, *Seattle Pacific University*

Ralph G. Pifer, *Sauk Valley Community College*

James S. Previte, *Victor Valley College*

Wayne J. Robinson, *Monroe Community College*

John L. Romanek, *Jefferson Community College*

Kenneth M. Rosenberg, *State University of New York, Oswego*

Elisabeth D. Sherwin, *University of Arkansas at Little Rock*

Cynthia J. Smith, *Wheeling Jesuit University*

Jane A. Smith, *Concordia University*

Mitchell Speaks, *Keene State College*

Holly Straub, *University of South Dakota*

Linda K. Swindell, *Anderson University*

Parsram S. Thakur, *Community College of Rhode Island*

Inger Thompson, *Glendale Community College*

M. Lisa Valentino, *Seminole Community College*

Mary A. Waterstreet, *St. Ambrose University*

Michael J. Wenger, *University of Notre Dame*

Gordon Whitman, *Sandhills Community College*

Jean M. Wynn, *Manchester Community College*

C. Van Youngman, *Art Institute of Philadelphia*

The process of creating *Essentials of Psychology* was greatly facilitated by the work of many dedicated people at Cengage Learning. From the sales representatives and sales managers who originally conveyed my colleagues' requests for the text to the marketing staff who worked to tell my colleagues what *Essentials* has to offer, it seems everyone at Cengage had a hand in shaping this book and now in revising it into its sixth edition. Several people in the editorial and production areas at Cengage deserve special mention, however, because they did an outstanding job in helping me develop and revise the *Essentials* manuscript and turn that manuscript into the beautiful book you are now holding. Developmental Editor Tangelique Williams was instrumental in the shaping and development of the manuscript; her editorial expertise and disciplined approach was invaluable to me. The work of our copyeditor, Jackie Simmons, revealed and corrected all my little errors and some big ones, too. Thanks to both of you for all your help. And many thanks to Mike Ederer for coordinating the myriad production tasks associated with this project and for keeping them, and me, on schedule. I also want to thank Stephen Forsling for his outstanding work in the creation of the art and photo program for this sixth edition and Charlene Carpentier for her work as Content Project Manager. Also my thanks go to Lauren Moody for her assistance in managing the print supplements. To Jon-David Hague, my Publisher, I offer my sincere thanks. Without these people, and those who worked with them, the sixth edition of *Essentials of Psychology* would not have happened.

Finally, I want to thank my wife Doris for the loving support that sustains me in my work and in my life. *Je vous aime beaucoup, ma chérie.*

DOUG BERNSTEIN

Introduction to the Science of Psychology

© imagebroker.net/SuperStock

Preview

All of the following people hold truly interesting jobs. What do you think they studied to qualify for those jobs? See if you can correctly match each person in the left column with their field of study from the right column.

People	Fields of Study
Anne Marie Apanovitch works for a major drug company, and studies which of their marketing strategies are most effective in promoting sales.	Engineering
Rebecca Snyder studies the giant pandas at Zoo Atlanta in an effort to promote captive breeding and ultimately increase the wild population of this endangered species.	Criminal Justice
Michael Moon's job at a software company is to find new ways to make Internet web sites easier for consumers to use.	Advertising
Sharon Lundgren, founder of Lundgren Trial Consulting, Inc., helps prepare witnesses to testify in court and teaches attorneys how to present their evidence in the most convincing way.	Psychology
Evan Byrne investigates the role of memory lapses, disorientation, errors, and other human factors in causing airplane crashes for the U.S. National Transportation Safety Board.	Computer Science
Captain Karen Orts, chief of mental health services at a U.S. Air Force base, provides psychotherapy to military personnel suffering combat-related stress disorders, and teaches leadership courses to commissioned and noncommissioned officers.	Zoology

Because Captain Orts offers psychotherapy, you probably guessed that she's a psychologist, but what academic field did you associate with Rebecca Snyder, who studies giant pandas? It would have been perfectly reasonable to assume that she's a zoologist, but she, too, is a psychologist. So is Michael Moon, whose work on web site design might suggest that he was a computer science major. And although Sharon Lundgren spends her time working with witnesses and conducting mock trials, she's a psychologist, not a lawyer. The fact is that all of these people are psychologists! They may not all fit your image of what psychologists do, but as you'll see in this chapter (and throughout this book), psychology is much broader and more diverse than you might have expected. We hope that reading this book will give you a fuller understanding of psychology and that you will find our field as fascinating as we do.

This chapter begins our exploration of psychology with a brief look at some of its interrelated specialty areas, or *subfields*. We then tell the story of how psychology came to be and review several theories and approaches that guide psychologists in their work.

We also point out how the activities of psychologists in virtually every subfield are affected by human diversity, especially by age, gender, ethnicity, and other individual characteristics encountered in today's multicultural societies. Finally, we consider how critical thinking, scientific methods, and ethical standards guide psychologists as they conduct research and evaluate the evidence they collect. ●

The World of Psychology: An Overview

What is psychology, and how did it grow?

Psychology is the science that seeks to understand behavior and mental processes and to apply that understanding in the service of human welfare. So although the six people we've just described are engaged in many different kinds of work, they are all psychologists because they are all involved in studying, predicting, improving, or explaining some aspect of behavior and mental processes. But even this wide variety of jobs fails to capture the full scope of psychologists' interests. As a group, psychologists around the world are interested in the behaviors and mental processes that make people who they are in every culture. Many psychologists focus on what can go wrong in behavior and mental processes, such as psychological disorders, problems in childhood development, or stress-related illnesses. Others explore the factors that lead people to be happy and satisfied with their lives, to achieve at a high level, to be creative, to help others, and to develop their full potential as human beings. This focus on the things that make life most worth living is known as **positive psychology** (e.g., Peterson, 2006; Snyder & Lopez, 2009; Uchida & Kitayama, 2009).

Subfields of Psychology

To appreciate how many things come under the umbrella of *behavior and mental processes*, think for a moment about how you would answer the question, Who are you? Would
LEARN by DOING
you describe your personality, the sharpness of your vision or hearing, your interests and goals, your job skills and accomplishments, your IQ, your cultural background, or your social skills? Perhaps you would describe a physical or psychological problem that bothers you. You could list these and dozens of other things about yourself, and every one of them would reflect some aspect of what psychologists mean by behavior and mental processes. When psychologists focus their work on particular aspects of behavior and mental processes, they enter one of psychology's many subfields. Let's take a quick look at the typical interests and activities of psychologists in these subfields now; we will focus on many of them in more detail in later chapters.

- **Cognitive psychologists** study basic mental processes such as sensation and perception (see Figure 1.1), learning and memory, judgment, decision making, and

psychology The science that seeks to understand behavior and mental processes and to apply that understanding in the service of human welfare.

positive psychology A field of research that focuses on people's positive experiences and characteristics, such as happiness, optimism, and resilience.

cognitive psychologists Psychologists whose research focuses on analysis of the mental processes underlying judgment, decision making, problem solving, imagining, and other aspects of human thought or cognition.

FIGURE 1.1
Husband and Father-In-Law

This figure is called "Husband and Father-in-Law" (Botwinick, 1961) because you can see it as two different people, **LEARN by DOING** depending on how you mentally organize the features of the drawing. The elderly "father-in-law" faces to your right and is turned slightly toward you. He has a large nose, and the dark areas represent a coat pulled up to his chin. However, the tip of his nose can also be seen as the tip of a younger man's chin. The "husband" is in profile, also looking to your right, but away from you. The old man's mouth is the young man's neck band. Both men are wearing broad-brimmed hats. Can you see them? Cognitive psychologists point out that your ability to see two different figures in the same drawing—and to choose which one to see at any given moment—means that you actively manipulate incoming information rather than just passively receiving it.

Source: J. Botwinick, "Husband and Father-In-Law: a reversible figure," from *American Journal of Psychology* 74 (pp. 312–313). Copyright © 1961 by the Board and Trustees of the University of Illinois. Used with permission of the University of Illinois Press.

FIGURE 1.2

Where Would You Put a Third Eye?
In a study of how thinking develops, children were asked to show where they would place a third eye if they could have one. Part A shows that nine-year-old children, who were still in an early stage of mental development, drew the extra eye between their existing eyes, "as a spare." Having developed more advanced thinking abilities, eleven-year-olds (Part B) drew the third eye in more creative places, such as the palm of their hand "so I can see around corners."

Source: From SHAFFER. *Developmental Psychology: Theory, Research and Application*, 1e (Box 4-2). Copyright © 1985 by Cengage Learning. Reproduced by permission. www.cengage.com/permissions.

Drawing by a nine-year-old

(A)

Drawing by an eleven-year-old

(B)

problem solving. Included in the wide range of fascinating topics they explore are such questions as whether people can forget (and then suddenly recover) traumatic memories, whether we can learn while asleep, and what role intuition and other unconscious processes play in guiding our thoughts and actions.

- **Biological psychologists,** also called *physiological psychologists* or *neuroscientists,* study topics such as the relationship of genes and brain chemistry to mental disorders, how brain cells communicate with each other in forming memories, whether certain patterns of brain activity can reveal that a person is lying, and how stress hormones weaken the body's immune system. Have you ever had the odd feeling that a new experience, such as entering an unfamiliar house, has actually happened to you before? Biological psychologists who study this experience of déjà vu (French for "already seen") suggest that it may be due to a temporary malfunction in the brain's ability to combine incoming information from the senses, creating the impression of two "copies" of a single event (Brown, 2004).

- **Personality psychologists** study individuality—the unique features of each person. Your personality traits, like your fingerprints, are different from those of any other person. Some personality psychologists use tests to describe how one individual compares with others in terms of openness to experience, emotionality, reliability, agreeableness, and sociability. Others study combinations of personality traits that may predict particular patterns of behavior. For instance, personality psychologists interested in positive psychology are identifying the characteristics of people who can remain optimistic even in the face of stress or tragedy and find happiness in life (Hutchinson, Stuart, & Pretorius, 2010; Kashdan & Rottenberg, 2010; Snyder & Lopez, 2009; Wong, 2011).

- **Developmental psychologists** study and describe changes in behavior and mental processes over the life span in order to understand their causes and effects (see Figure 1.2). They explore areas such as the development of thought, friendship patterns, parenting styles, and whether everyone must face a midlife crisis. Some of their research has been used by judges and attorneys in deciding how old a child has to be in order to serve as a reliable witness in court or to responsibly choose which divorcing parent to live with.

- **Quantitative psychologists** develop and use statistical tools to analyze vast amounts of information generated by research results from all of psychology's subfields. Later in this chapter we show how quantitative psychologists use correlation coefficients and other statistical tools to evaluate psychological tests and to estimate the relative contributions of heredity and environment in determining our intelligence. To

biological psychologists
Psychologists who analyze the biological factors influencing behavior and mental processes.

personality psychologists
Psychologists who focus on people's unique characteristics.

developmental psychologists
Psychologists who seek to understand, describe, and explore how behavior and mental processes change over the course of a lifetime.

quantitative psychologists
Psychologists who develop statistical methods for evaluating and analyzing data from psychological research.

Got a Match?

Some commercial dating services apply social psychologists' research on interpersonal attraction in an effort to pair up people whose characteristics are most likely to be compatible.

APPLYING PSYCHOLOGY

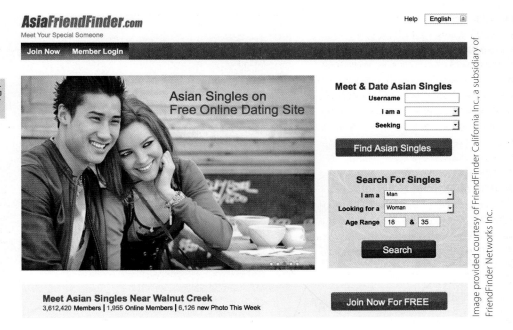

what extent are people born smart—or not so smart—and to what extent are their mental abilities affected by their environments? This is one of the hottest topics in psychology today, and quantitative psychologists are right in the middle of it.

- **Clinical, counseling, and community psychologists** study the causes of behavior disorders and offer services to help troubled people overcome these disorders. Generally, clinical psychologists have Ph.D. degrees in psychology; most provide therapy services, and many conduct research as well. A counseling psychologist might work as a mental health counselor and have either a Ph.D. or a master's degree in psychology. Community psychologists offer psychological services to the homeless and others who need help but who tend not to seek it. By working for changes in schools and other social systems, they also try to prevent poverty and other stressful conditions that so often lead to psychological disorder. All of these psychologists differ from *psychiatrists,* who are medical doctors who specialize in abnormal behavior.

- **Educational psychologists** conduct research and develop theories about teaching and learning. The results of their work are applied in programs designed to improve teacher training, refine school curricula, reduce dropout rates, and help students learn more efficiently. For example, educational psychologists support using the "jigsaw" technique, a cooperative classroom activity in which children from various ethnic groups must work together to complete a task or solve a problem. Such experiences appear to promote learning, generate mutual respect, and reduce intergroup prejudice (Aronson & Patnoe, 1997).

- **School psychologists** originally specialized in intelligence testing, diagnosing learning disabilities and other academic problems, and setting up programs to improve students' achievement and satisfaction in school. Today, they also engage in early detection of students' mental health problems and in crisis intervention following school violence (Benjamin & Baker, 2004; Crepeau-Hobson & Bianco 2011; Elliot, Reynolds, & Kratochwill, 2006; Farrell, 2010).

- **Social psychologists** study the ways that people influence one another. For example, their research on social-influence strategies has been applied in safe-sex advertising campaigns designed to halt the spread of AIDS (Noar, et al., 2011). They also explore how peer pressure affects us, what determines whom we like (or even love), and why and how prejudice forms. They have found, for example, that although we may pride ourselves on not being prejudiced, we may actually hold unconscious beliefs about certain ethnic groups that negatively affect the way we relate to people from those groups (Vanman et al., 2004).

clinical, counseling, and community psychologists Psychologists who seek to assess, understand, modify, and prevent behavior disorders.

educational psychologists Psychologists who study methods by which instructors teach and students learn and who apply their results to improve such methods.

school psychologists Psychologists who test cognitive abilities, diagnose students' academic problems, and set up programs to improve students' achievement.

social psychologists Psychologists who study how people influence one another's behavior and attitudes, especially in groups.

Forensic Psychology

Forensic psychologists may assist police and other agencies to improve techniques for offender profiling (Canter, 2011), or to devise interrogation methods that minimize the danger of obtaining false confessions (Gudjonsson & Pearse, 2011). Others study jury decision-making and how court procedures, such as allowing jurors to take notes or ask questions, affect the outcome of trials (Bornstein & Greene, 2011). Actor B. D. Wong's performance as forensic psychiatrist Dr. George Huang on *Law and Order: SVU* is so accurate that the Media Psychology division of the American Psychological Association gave the show its 2004 Golden Psi award for excellence in fictional portrayal of mental health professionals.

APPLYING PSYCHOLOGY

© NBC/Photofest

- **Industrial and organizational psychologists** study leadership, stress, competition, pay, and other factors that affect the efficiency, productivity, and satisfaction of workers and the organizations that employ them. They explore ways to increase employee motivation and help companies select the best new workers. They also look at the ways in which businesses and industrial organizations work—or fail to work—and they make recommendations to help these organizations work better. Companies all over the world apply research by industrial and organizational psychologists to foster *positive organizational behavior* through the development of employee training programs, effective goal-setting procedures, fair and reasonable evaluation methods, and systems for motivating and rewarding outstanding employee performance.

Our list of psychology's subfields is still not complete. For example, **health psychologists** study the effects of behavior on health and the impact of illness on behavior and emotion; **sport psychologists** search for the keys to maximum athletic performance; and **forensic psychologists** assist in jury selection, evaluate defendants' sanity and mental competence to stand trial, and deal with other matters involving psychology and the law. **Engineering psychologists,** also known as *human factors psychologists,* study interactions between human beings and the computers, telephones, and other machines they use. Their research has been applied in the design of computer keyboards, Internet web sites, aircraft instrument panels, controls for hospital beds and nuclear power plants, and even on-screen programming and navigation systems for TV sets and mobile phones that make them more logical, easier to use, and less likely to cause errors. **Environmental psychologists** study the effects of the environment on people's behavior and mental processes. The results of their research are applied by architects and interior designers as they plan or remodel residence halls, shopping malls, auditoriums, hospitals, prisons, offices, and other spaces to make them more comfortable and functional for the people who will occupy them. (See Table 1.1 for a summary of the typical activities and work settings of psychologists in the United States.)

Linkages within Psychology and Beyond

We have listed psychology's subfields as though they were separate, but they often overlap, and so do the activities of the psychologists working in them. When developmental psychologists study the growth of children's thinking skills, for example, their research is linked to that of colleagues in cognitive psychology. Similarly, biological psychologists have one foot in clinical psychology when they

industrial and organizational psychologists Psychologists who examine factors that influence people's performance in the workplace.

health psychologists Psychologists who study the effects of behavior on health and the impact of illness on behavior and emotion.

sport psychologists Psychologists whose research is aimed at maximizing athletic performance.

forensic psychologists Psychologists who are involved in many aspects of psychology and law.

engineering psychologists Psychologists who study and try to improve the relationships between human beings and the computers and other machines they use.

environmental psychologists Psychologists who study the relationship between people's physical environment and their behavior.

Improving Bad Designs

Consultation by human factors psychologists, who apply cognitive research to the design of equipment, would surely have improved the layout of these self-service fuel pumps. The system won't operate until you press the red spot (see enlargement at left) under the yellow "push to start" label, which is difficult to locate among all the other signs and stickers. Such user-unfriendly designs are all too common these days (e.g., Heller, 2008; Lee, 2006; Petroski, 2008a, 2008b; visit www.baddesigns.com for some amazing examples).

APPLYING PSYCHOLOGY

Photograph courtesy of www.baddesigns.com

look at how chemicals in the brain affect the risk of depression. And when social psychologists apply research on cooperation to promote group learning activities in classrooms, they link up with educational psychology. Even when psychologists work mainly in one subfield, they're still likely to draw on—and contribute to—the knowledge in other subfields.

So if you want to understand psychology as a whole, you have to understand the linkages among its subfields. To help you recognize these linkages, we highlight three of them in a diagram, similar to the one in Figure 1.3, near the end of every chapter. Each linkage is represented by a question that connects two subfields. The page numbers in parentheses tell you where you can read more about each question (look for "Linkages" symbols on those pages). There are so many linkages throughout the book that we could not include them all in our diagrams, but we hope these diagrams will remind you to look for linkages that we didn't mention. This kind of detective work can actually help you to do better on exams and quizzes, because it is often easier to remember material in one chapter by relating it to linked material in other chapters.

Planning Spaces

Environmental psychologists are often asked to consult on the design of offices. This dental office, for example, was designed to promote efficiency for the dentist and assistant, and to create a relaxing atmosphere for the patient (Ahearn, Sanders, & Turcotte, 2010).

APPLYING PSYCHOLOGY

© Masterfile

TABLE 1.1   Typical Activities and Work Settings for Psychologists

Psychology is a popular undergraduate major partly because psychologists can work in a variety of interesting jobs (Snyder, Dillow, & Hoffman, 2008). Psychology courses also provide excellent background for students planning to enter medicine, law, business, and many other fields.

Percentage of Psychologists	Work Setting	Typical Activities
30.9%	Colleges, universities, and professional schools	Teach, research, and write, often in collaboration with colleagues from other disciplines
32.1%	Mental health facilities (e.g., hospitals, clinics, counseling centers)	Test and treat children and adults
20.9%	Private practice (alone or in a group of psychologists)	Test and treat children and adults; consult with businesses and other organizations
8.1%	Business, government, and organizations	Test potential employees; assess employee satisfaction; identify and resolve conflicts; improve leadership skills; offer stress management and other employee assistance programs; improve equipment design to maximize productivity and prevent accidents
5.7%	Schools (including those for intellectually disabled and emotionally disturbed children)	Test mental abilities and other characteristics; identify children with problems; consult with parents; design and implement programs to improve academic performance
2.3%	Other	Teach prison inmates; research in private institutes; advise legislators on educational, research, or public policy; administer research funds; research effectiveness of military personnel; and so on

Source: Data from 2009 doctorate employment survey (Michalski et al., 2011).

Psychology itself is linked to other disciplines. Some of these connections occur because psychologists share interests with researchers in other fields. For example, cognitive psychologists are working with computer scientists to create artificial intelligence systems that can recognize voices, solve problems, and make decisions in ways that equal or exceed human capabilities (Condell et al., 2010; Haynes, Cohen, & Ritter, 2009; Wang, 2007). Other links occur when research in one discipline is applied in another. For example, physicians and economists are using research by psychologists to better understand the thought processes that influence (good and bad) decisions about caring for patients and choosing investments (Basu, Chapman, & Galvani, 2008; Chapman & Coups, 2006; Leiser & Azar, 2008; Leiser, Azar, & Hadar, 2008; Morgan et al.,

FIGURE 1.3

Linkages

The questions listed in this diagram highlight just three of the many ways in which psychology's subfields are linked to one another. Three additional linking questions appear in the Linkages diagram included in every chapter to come. Each diagram lists the page number on which each question is answered. When you turn to that page, you'll find a Linkages symbol in the margin where the answer is discussed. Sometimes the discussion is brief, but every chapter also contains a special Linkages feature that examines linked research in more detail. By staying alert to linkages among psychology's subfields, you'll come away from this course not only with threads of knowledge about each subfield but also with an appreciation of the fabric of psychology as a whole.

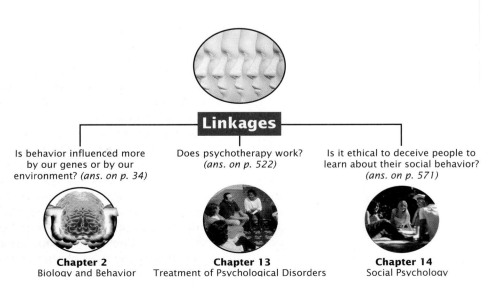

Linking Psychology and Law

Cognitive psychologists' research on the quirks of human memory has led to revised guidelines for police and prosecutors (U.S. Department of Justice, 1999). These guidelines warn that asking witnesses leading questions (e.g., "Do you remember seeing a gun?") can distort their memories, that false accusations are less likely if witnesses are told that the real criminal might not be in a lineup or in a group of photos, and that no one in a lineup should stand out from all the others (Doyle, 2005).

APPLYING PSYCHOLOGY

© Masterfile

2008; Symmonds et al., 2010). In fact, psychologist Daniel Kahneman won a Nobel Prize in economics for his work in this area. Other psychologists' research on memory has influenced how lineups are displayed to eyewitnesses attempting to identify criminals, how attorneys question eyewitnesses in court, and how judges instruct juries (Charman, Wells, & Joy, 2011; Clark, Erickson, & Breneman, 2011; Daftary-Kapur, Dumas, & Penrod, 2010; Flowe & Bessemer, 2011; Memon, Vrij, & Bull, 2004; Miles & Cottle, 2011; Steblay, Dysart, & Wells, 2011; Valentine & Maras, 2011). And psychological studies of the effects of brain disorders on elderly patients' mental abilities are shaping doctors' recommendations about when those patients should stop driving cars (Baldock et al., 2007; Bélanger, Gagnon, & Yamin, 2010; Dawson et al., 2010; Fiorentino, 2008; Rees et al., 2008; Shanmugaratnam, Kass, & Arruda, 2010).

This book is filled with examples of other ways that psychological theories and research have been applied to fields as diverse as health care, law, business, engineering, architecture, aviation, and sports.

A Brief History of Psychology

Psychology is a relatively new science, but its origins can be traced through centuries. Since at least the time of Socrates, Plato, and Aristotle in ancient Greece, philosophers have debated such psychological topics as where human knowledge comes from, the nature of mind and soul, the relationship of the mind to the body, and even the possibility of scientifically studying these matters.

Scientific psychology thus has its roots in philosophy, and especially in a philosophical view called **empiricism** (pronounced "em-PEER-ih-sihz-em"). In the 1600s, empiricists such as John Locke, George Berkeley, and David Hume challenged the long accepted claim that some of our knowledge is present at birth. Empiricists argued that our minds are more like a blank slate ("tabula rasa" in Latin) on which our experiences write a lifelong story. In other words, according to empiricism, knowledge comes to us only through our experiences and observations. Empiricism has guided psychologists in seeking knowledge about behavior and mental processes through observations governed by the rules of science, rather than speculation, for more than 130 years.

empiricism The view that knowledge comes from experience and observation.

Wilhelm Wundt (1832–1920)

In an early experiment on the speed of mental processes, Wilhelm Wundt (seated) first measured how quickly people could respond to a light by releasing a button they had been holding down. He then measured how much longer the response took when they held down one button with each hand and had to decide—based on the color of the light—which one to release. Wundt reasoned that the additional response time reflected how long it took to perceive the color and decide which hand to move. As noted in the chapter on thought, language, and intelligence, the logic behind this experiment remains a part of modern research on cognitive processes.

© INTERFOTO/Alamy

FIGURE 1.4

A Stimulus for Introspection

Look at this object and try to ignore what it is. Instead, try to describe only your conscious experience of it, such as redness, brightness, and roundness and how intense and clear these sensations and images are. If you can do this, you would have been an excellent research participant in Titchener's laboratory.

LEARN by DOING

consciousness The awareness of external stimuli and our own mental activity.

Wundt and the Structuralism of Titchener The birth date of modern scientific psychology is usually given as 1879, the year in which Wilhelm Wundt (pronounced "voont") established the first formal psychology research laboratory, at the University of Leipzig in Germany (Benjamin, 2000). Wundt was a physiologist, and like other physiologists of his day, he had been studying vision, hearing, and other sensory-perceptual systems. However, Wundt's ambitious goal was to use the methods of laboratory science to study **consciousness**—the mental experience that arises from these systems. In doing so, Wundt began psychology's transformation from the *philosophy* of mental processes to the *science* of mental processes.

Wundt wanted to describe the basic elements of consciousness, including how they are organized and how they relate to one another (Schultz & Schultz, 2002). In an attempt to study conscious experience, Wundt used *introspection*, which means "looking inward." Edward Titchener, an Englishman who studied under Wundt, later used introspection in his own laboratory at Cornell University to study sensations, feelings, and images associated with conscious experience. To understand introspection, look at the object in Figure 1.4. Try to describe not what it is but only how intensely and clearly you experience its sensations and images (such as redness, brightness, and roundness). This was the difficult task that Wundt and Titchener set for carefully trained "introspectors" in their search for the building blocks of consciousness. Titchener called his approach *structuralism* because he was trying to define the structure of consciousness. Wundt and Titchener were not the only scientific researchers in psychology, and their work was not universally accepted. Other scientific psychologists in Europe were studying the limits of sensory abilities and the capability for learning and memory. They saw the structuralists' work as too simplistic. However, introspection has taken on new life in some contemporary psychologists' research on such topics as how we solve problems and the sequence in which the brain processes information (Fox, Ericsson, & Best, 2010; Marti et al., 2010).

Gestalt Psychology Around 1912, another group of German psychologists, led by Max Wertheimer, Kurt Koffka, and Wolfgang Köhler, argued against the value of trying to break down human experience or consciousness into its component parts. They were called *Gestalt psychologists* because they pointed out that the whole shape (or *Gestalt*, in German) of conscious experience is not the same as the sum of its parts. Wertheimer noted, for example, that when two lights are placed near each other in a dark room and go on and off in just the right sequence, we experience not two lights but a single light "jumping" back and forth. This is called the *phi phenomenon*, and you've probably seen it in signs that create the impression of a series of lights racing around a display. Video provides another example. Imagine how boring it would be to browse through the thousands of still images on a DVD. Yet when those same images are shown on a screen at just the right rate, they combine to create a rich emotional experience. In other words, said the Gestaltists, consciousness should be studied as a whole, not piece by piece.

Freud and Psychoanalysis   While Wundt was conducting scientific research on consciousness in Germany, Sigmund Freud, a physician in Vienna, Austria, was exploring the unconscious. In the late 1880s, Freud began to question the assumption that biological factors were behind all behavior and mental processes, including illnesses. After interviewing his patients using hypnosis and other methods, Freud became convinced that the causes of some people's physical ailments were not physical. The real causes, he said, were deep-seated problems that the patients had pushed out of consciousness (Friedman & Schustack, 2003). He eventually came to believe that all behavior—from everyday slips of the tongue to severe forms of mental disorder—could be traced to *psychological processes,* especially to internal conflicts that he said take place without our being aware of them. He believed that many of these unconscious *psychodynamic* conflicts are created when our sexual and aggressive instincts clash with the rules set for us by society. For nearly fifty years, Freud revised and expanded his ideas into a body of work known as *psychoanalysis.* His theory included explanations of how personality and mental disorder develop as well as a set of treatment methods. Freud's ideas are by no means universally accepted, but he was a groundbreaker whose psychodynamic theories had a significant influence on psychology and many other fields.

William James and Functionalism   Psychology took root in North America not long after Wundt began his work in Germany. In the late 1870s, William James set up the first psychology laboratory in the United States, which he used mainly to conduct demonstrations for his students at Harvard University (Schultz & Schultz, 2002). The first psychology research laboratory in the United States was established in 1883, by G. Stanley Hall at Johns Hopkins University. James Mark Baldwin, Canada's first modern psychologist and a pioneer in child development research, established the first Canadian psychology research laboratory at the University of Toronto in 1889.

William James rejected both Wundt's approach and Titchener's structuralism. Influenced by Darwin's theory of evolution, James wanted to understand how sensations,

William James's Laboratory

William James (1842–1910) established this psychology demonstration laboratory at Harvard University in the late 1870s. Like the Gestalt psychologists, James saw the approach used by Wundt and Titchener as a scientific dead end; he said that trying to understand consciousness by studying its parts is like trying to understand a house by looking at individual bricks (James, 1884). He preferred instead to study the ways that consciousness functions to help people adapt to their environments. This view helped to lay the groundwork for the evolutionary approach to psychology described later.

memories, and all the other mental events that make up our ever-flowing "stream of consciousness" help us adapt to our changing environments (James, 1890, 1892). This idea was consistent with an approach to psychology called *functionalism,* which focused on the function of consciousness in guiding our ability to make decisions, solve problems, and the like. James's emphasis on the functions of mental processes encouraged other North American psychologists to look at how those processes work to our advantage and how they differ from person to person. Some of these psychologists began to measure individual differences in learning, memory, and other aspects of intelligence and to make recommendations for improving educational practices in the schools. A few even began to work with teachers on programs for children in need of special help (Kramer, Bernstein, & Phares, 2009).

John B. Watson and Behaviorism   Besides fueling James's interest in the functions of consciousness, Darwin's theory of evolution led other psychologists, especially in North America after 1900, to study animals as well as humans. If all species evolved in adaptive ways, perhaps their behavior and mental processes would follow the same, or similar, laws. Psychologists observed animal behavior in mazes and other experimental situations. From these observations, they made inferences about the animals' conscious experiences and about the general laws of learning, memory, problem solving, and other mental processes that might apply to people, too.

John B. Watson, a psychology professor at Johns Hopkins University, agreed that the behavior of animals and humans was the most important source of scientific information for psychology. In his article, "Psychology as the Behaviorist Views It," Watson argued that psychologists should ignore mental events and concern themselves only with *observable* behavior (Watson, 1913, 1919). His approach, known as *behaviorism,* did not address consciousness, as structuralism and functionalism did, let alone consider the unconscious, as the Freudian view did. Focusing on consciousness, said Watson, would prevent psychology from ever being a true science. He believed that learning is the most important cause of behavior, and famously claimed that if he had enough control over the environment, he could create learning experiences that would turn any infant into a doctor, a lawyer, or even a criminal.

American psychologist B. F. Skinner was another early champion of behaviorism. From the 1930s until his death in 1990, Skinner studied *operant conditioning,* a learning process through which rewards and punishments shape, maintain, and change behavior. Using what he called *functional analysis of behavior,* Skinner would explain, for example, how parents and teachers can unknowingly encourage children's tantrums by rewarding them with attention. He noted, too, that a virtual addiction to gambling can develop through the occasional and unpredictable rewards it brings. Skinner said that functional analysis not only reveals the learned foundations of behavior but also suggests what rewards and punishments should be changed in order to alter that behavior.

Many psychologists were drawn to Watson's and Skinner's vision of psychology as the learning-based science of observable behavior. Behaviorism dominated psychological research in North America from the 1920s through the 1960s. ("In Review: The Development of Psychology" summarizes behaviorism and the other schools of thought that have influenced psychologists over the years.)

Psychology Today   By end of the 1960s, however, more and more psychologists saw the behaviorists' lack of attention to mental processes as a serious limitation (e.g., Ericsson & Simon, 1994). As the computer age dawned, psychologists began to think about mental activity in a new way—as information processing. At the same time, progress in biotechnology began to offer psychologists new ways to study the biological bases of mental processes. Armed with ever-more sophisticated research tools, many psychologists today are trying to do what Watson thought was impossible: to study mental processes and, as shown in Figure 1.5, even watch the brain perform them. Psychology has come full circle, once again accepting consciousness, in the form of cognitive processes, as a legitimate topic for research.

FIGURE 1.5
Visualizing Brain Activity

Magnetic resonance imaging (MRI) techniques allow biological psychologists to study the brain activity accompanying various mental processes (Cooper, 2007; deCharms, 2008; Harrison et al., 2008; Johnson et al., 2008). The study illustrated here found that while reading, males (left) and females (right) show different patterns of brain activity, as indicated by the brightly colored areas (Shaywitz et al., 1995).

B. A. Shaywitz et al., 1995, NMR Research/Yale Medical School

The Development of Psychology — IN REVIEW

School of Thought	Founders	Goals	Methods
Structuralism	Edward Titchener, trained by Wilhelm Wundt	To study conscious experience and its structure	Experiments; introspection
Gestalt psychology	Max Wertheimer	To describe the organization of mental processes ("the whole is different from the sum of its parts")	Observation of sensory/perceptual phenomena
Psychoanalysis	Sigmund Freud	To explain personality and behavior; to develop techniques for treating mental disorders	Study of individual cases
Functionalism	William James	To study how the mind works in allowing an organism to adapt to the environment	Naturalistic observation of animal and human behavior
Behaviorism	John B. Watson; B. F. Skinner	To study only observable behavior and explain behavior via learning principles	Observation of the relationship between environmental stimuli and overt responses

IN REVIEW QUESTIONS

1. Darwin's theory of evolution had an especially strong influence on ___ ism and ___ ism.
2. Which school of psychological thought was founded by a European medical doctor?___
3. In the history of psychology, ___ was the first school of thought to appear.

Approaches to the Science of Psychology

Why don't all psychologists explain behavior in the same way?

We have seen that the history of psychology is, in part, the history of the differing ways in which psychologists have thought about, or "approached," behavior and mental processes. Today, psychologists no longer refer to themselves as structuralists or functionalists but the psychodynamic and behavioral approaches remain, along with some newer ones known as the *biological, evolutionary, cognitive,* and *humanistic approaches.* Some psychologists adopt just one of these approaches, but most are eclectic. This means that they blend aspects of two or more approaches in an effort to more fully understand the behavior and mental processes in their subfield (e.g., Cacioppo et al., 2000). Some approaches to psychology are more influential than others these days, but we will review the main features of all of them so you can more easily understand why different psychologists may explain the same behavior or mental process in different ways.

The Biology of Emotion
Robert Levenson, a psychologist at the University of California at Berkeley, takes a biological approach to the study of social interactions. He measures heart rate, muscle tension, and other physical reactions as couples discuss problems in their relationships. He looks for patterns of physiological activity in each partner (such as overreactions to criticism) that might be related to success or failure in resolving their problems.

Courtesy of Robert Levenson, Professor, Department of Psychology, and Director, Institute of Personality and Social Research, University of California

The Biological Approach

As its name implies, the **biological approach** assumes that behavior and mental processes are largely shaped by biological processes. Psychologists who take this approach study the psychological effects of hormones and genes and the activity of the nervous system, especially the brain. When studying memory, for example, these researchers try to identify changes taking place in the brain as information is stored there. (Figure 6.14, in the chapter on memory, shows an example of these changes.) And when studying thinking, they might look for patterns of brain activity associated with, say, making quick decisions or reading a foreign language. Research discussed in nearly every chapter of this book reflects the enormous influence of the biological approach on psychology today.

The Evolutionary Approach

Biological processes are also highlighted in an approach to psychology that is based on Charles Darwin's 1859 book *On the Origin of Species.* Darwin argued that the forms of life we see today are the result of *evolution*—of changes in life forms that occur over many generations. He said that evolution occurs through *natural selection,* which promotes the survival of the fittest individuals. Those whose behavior and appearance allow them to withstand the elements, avoid predators, and mate are able to survive and produce offspring with similar characteristics. Those less able to adjust (or *adapt*) to changing conditions are less likely to survive and reproduce. Most evolutionists today see natural selection operating at the level of genes, but the process is the same. Genes that result in characteristics and behaviors that are adaptive and useful in a certain environment will enable the creatures that inherited them to survive and reproduce, thereby passing those genes on to the next generation. According to evolutionary theory, many (but not all) of the genes that animals and humans possess today are the result of natural selection.

The **evolutionary approach** to psychology assumes that the *behavior and mental processes* of animals and humans today are largely the result of evolution through natural selection. Evolutionary psychologists see aggression, for example, as a form of territory protection, and they see gender differences in mate selection preferences as reflecting different ways of helping genes survive in future generations (Griskevicius et al., 2009; Little et al., 2010). The evolutionary approach has resulted in a growing body of research (e.g., Buss, 2009; Confer et al., 2010); in later chapters, you will see how it is applied in relation to topics such as mental disorders, temperament, interpersonal attraction, and helping.

biological approach The view that behavior is the result of physical processes, especially those relating to the brain, to hormones, and to other chemicals.

evolutionary approach A view that emphasizes the inherited, adaptive aspects of behavior and mental processes.

© Jose Luis Pelaez, Inc./Corbis

A Father's Love

Mothers are solely responsible for the care and protection of their young in almost all species of mammals. These species survive without male parenting, so why are some human fathers so active in child rearing? Do evolutionary forces make fathering more adaptive for humans? Is it a matter of learning to care? Is it a combination of both? Psychologists who take an evolutionary approach study these questions and others relating to the origins of human social behavior.

psychodynamic approach A view developed by Freud that emphasizes unconscious mental processes in explaining human thought, feelings, and behavior.

behavioral approach A view based on the assumption that human behavior is determined mainly by what a person has learned in life, especially through rewards and punishments.

cognitive approach A view that emphasizes research on how the brain takes in information, creates perceptions, forms and retrieves memories, processes information, and generates integrated patterns of action.

The Psychodynamic Approach

The **psychodynamic approach** to psychology is rooted in Freud's theory of psychoanalysis. It assumes that our behavior and mental processes reflect the constant (mostly unconscious) psychodynamic conflicts that are said to rage within us. According to Freud, these conflicts occur when the impulse to instantly satisfy our instinctive needs—such as for food, sex, or aggression—are opposed by our learned need to follow society's rules about fairness and consideration for others. Psychologists taking the psychodynamic approach might see aggression as the triumph of raw impulses over self-control. At the same time, they consider anxiety, depression, and other psychological disorders as the outward evidence of inner conflict.

Freud's original theories are not as influential today as they once were (Mischel, 2004a), but in other chapters you will see that modern versions of the psychodynamic approach still appear in various theories of personality, psychological disorders, and psychotherapy.

The Behavioral Approach

The **behavioral approach** to psychology contrasts sharply with the biological, evolutionary, and psychodynamic approaches. This approach is rooted in the behaviorism of Watson and Skinner. As we mentioned earlier, behaviorism focused entirely on observable behavior in humans and animals and on how it is learned. So strict behaviorists concentrate only on observable behavior. They want to know how life's rewards, punishments, and other learning experiences act on the "raw materials" provided by genes and evolution to shape behavior into what it is today. Whether they're trying to understand a person's aggressiveness, fear of spiders, parenting methods, or tendency to abuse drugs, behaviorists look mainly at that person's learning history. And because they believe that behavior problems develop through learning, behaviorists seek to eliminate those problems by helping people learn new and more adaptive responses.

Strict behaviorism was criticized, though, precisely because it ignored everything but observable behavior. For that reason, many behaviorists now apply their learning-based approach in an effort to understand cognitions (thoughts) as well as observable behavior. They use this *cognitive behavioral, or social-cognitive,* approach to explore topics such as how we learn our thoughts, attitudes, and beliefs and, in turn, how these learned cognitive patterns affect observable behavior.

The Cognitive Approach

The appearance of the cognitive behavioral approach was part of a more general emphasis on cognition in psychology. This **cognitive approach** focuses on how our behavior is affected by the ways we take in, mentally represent, process, and store information. Consider how the cognitive approach might guide the analysis of an incident of aggression: A person in line for movie tickets (1) *perceived* that someone had cut into the line, (2) *recalled* information stored in memory to judge that this act was inappropriate, (3) *decided* that the act was due to the other person's rudeness, (4) *labeled* the person as rude and inconsiderate, (5) *considered* several possible responses and their likely consequences, (6) *decided* that punching the other person was the best response, and then (7) *executed* that response. Psychologists who take a cognitive approach suggest that mental processes like these—some of which occur outside of awareness—can help us understand many kinds of individual and social behaviors, from decision making and problem solving to interpersonal attraction and intelligence. In the situation we just described, for example, the person's aggression would be seen as the result of poor problem solving because there were probably several better ways to deal with the problem of line cutting. The cognitive approach is especially important in the field of *cognitive science,* in which researchers from psychology, computer science, biology, engineering,

Why Is He So Aggressive?
Psychologists who take a cognitive behavioral approach suggest that children learn to be aggressive in several ways. Children might see others rewarded for acting aggressively and then might be rewarded themselves for doing the same. Aggressiveness might also be made more likely if a child constantly hears that other people can be dangerous and that aggression is the only way to deal with threats, disagreements, and other conflicts (Cooper, Gomez, & Buck, 2008; Wilkowski & Robinson, 2008).

© Mary Kate Denny/PhotoEdit

linguistics, and philosophy study intelligent systems in humans and computers. Some of their progress in creating artificial intelligence in computers is described in the chapter on thought, language, and intelligence.

The Humanistic Approach

Mental processes play a different role in the humanistic approach to psychology (also known as the *phenomenological approach*). Psychologists who favor the **humanistic approach** see behavior as determined primarily by our capacity to choose how to think and act. They don't see these choices being guided by instincts, biological processes, or rewards and punishments, but by each person's view of the world. If you perceive the world as a friendly place, you're likely to be optimistic and secure. If you perceive it as full of hostile people, you'll probably be defensive and anxious or perhaps unfriendly and aggressive. Like their cognitively oriented colleagues, psychologists taking a humanistic approach would agree that in the movie theater incident, the decision to punch the person who cut into line stemmed from a perception that aggression was justified. But unlike cognitive psychologists, humanistic psychologists try to understand how each individual's unique perceptions guided *that* person's thoughts and actions, rather than trying to find general laws governing *all* people's thoughts and actions. In fact, many who prefer the humanistic approach claim that because no two people are exactly alike, the only way to understand behavior and mental processes is to focus on how they operate in each individual. Humanistic psychologists also believe that people are essentially good, that they are in control of themselves, and that they seek to grow toward their fullest potential.

The humanistic approach began to attract attention in North America in the 1940s, mainly through the writings of Carl Rogers and Abraham Maslow. As you'll see in later chapters, their views have had a major influence on the way some psychologists think about the development of personality, how to do psychotherapy, and why people are motivated to behave as they do. In fact, some of the roots of today's growing emphasis on positive psychology can be found in the writings of Maslow and Rogers (Snyder & Lopez, 2009). Overall, however, the humanistic approach is less influential today than the biological, cognitive, behavioral, and evolutionary approaches. Many psychologists find humanistic concepts and predictions too vague to be expressed and tested scientifically (McNulty & Fincham, 2012). (All the approaches we have described are summarized in "In Review: Approaches to Psychology.")

humanistic approach A view of behavior as controlled by the decisions that people make about their lives based on their perceptions of the world.

Mary Whiton Calkins (1863–1930)
Mary Whiton Calkins studied psychology at Harvard University, where William James described her as "brilliant." Because she was a woman, though, Harvard would not grant her a doctoral degree unless she received it through Radcliffe, which was then an affiliated school for women. She refused that arrangement but went on to do research on memory, and in 1905 she became the first woman president of the American Psychological Association (APA).

Approaches to Psychology   IN REVIEW

Approach	Characteristics
Biological	Emphasizes activity of the nervous system, especially of the brain; the action of hormones and other chemicals; and genetics
Evolutionary	Emphasizes the ways that behavior and mental processes are adaptive for survival
Psychodynamic	Emphasizes internal conflicts, mostly unconscious, which usually pit sexual or aggressive instincts against environmental obstacles to their expression
Behavioral	Emphasizes learning, especially each person's experience with rewards and punishments
Cognitive	Emphasizes mechanisms through which people receive, store, retrieve, and otherwise process information
Humanistic	Emphasizes individual potential for growth and the role of unique perceptions in guiding behavior and mental processes

IN REVIEW QUESTIONS

1. Teaching people to be less afraid of heights reflects the ____ approach.
2. Charles Darwin was not a psychologist, but his work influenced the ____ approach to psychology.
3. Assuming that people inherit mental disorders suggests a ____ approach.

Human Diversity and Psychology

How does your cultural background influence your behavior?

Today, the diversity seen in psychologists' approaches to their work is matched by the diversity in their own backgrounds. This was not always the case. In the early twentieth century, most psychologists—like most members of other academic disciplines—were white, middle-class men (Walker, 1991). Even so, women and members of ethnic minorities played important roles in psychology almost from the beginning (Schultz & Schultz, 2004). Throughout this book you will find the work of their modern counterparts, whose contributions to research, service, and teaching have all increased in tandem with their growing representation in psychology. In the United States, women now constitute almost 67 percent of all psychologists holding doctoral degrees (Cook, 2011). Women are also earning 75 percent of the new doctoral degrees awarded in psychology each year. Moreover, approximately 16 percent of new doctoral degrees in psychology are being earned by members of ethnic minority groups (Michalski et al., 2011). These numbers reflect continuing efforts by psychological organizations and governmental bodies, especially in the United States and Canada, to promote the recruitment, graduation, and employment of women and ethnic minorities in psychology (Maton et al., 2006).

The Impact of Sociocultural Diversity on Psychology

As diversity among psychologists has increased, so too has their interest in the diversity of the people they study and serve. This change is significant, because psychologists once assumed that all humans were essentially alike and that whatever principles emerged from research with one group would apply to people everywhere. They were partly right, because people around the world *are* alike in many ways. They tend to live in groups; have religious beliefs; and create rules, music, dances, and games. The principles of nerve cell activity or reactions to heat or a sour taste are the same in men and women everywhere, as is their recognition of a smile. This is not true of all characteristics, however. Research has shown that people's striving for achievement, their moral values, their styles of communicating, and many other aspects of behavior and mental processes are shaped by a variety of **sociocultural factors**, including gender, ethnicity, social class, and the culture in which they grow up (Shiraev & Levy, 2010).

    Culture has been defined as the sum of all the values, rules of behavior, forms of expression, religious beliefs, occupational choices, and the like among a group of people

sociocultural factors Social identity and other background factors, such as gender, ethnicity, social class, and culture.

culture The accumulation of values, rules of behavior, forms of expression, religious beliefs, and occupational choices for a group of people who share a common language and environment.

Margaret Washburn (1871–1939)
Like Mary Whiton Calkins at Harvard, Margaret Washburn encountered sex discrimination at Columbia University, so she transferred to Cornell University and became the first woman to earn a doctorate in psychology. In 1921, she became the second woman president of the APA.

who share a common language and environment (Fiske et al., 1998). Culture is an organizing and stabilizing influence. It encourages or discourages particular behaviors and ways of thinking; it also allows people to understand others in that culture and know what to expect from them. It is a kind of group adaptation that is passed on by tradition and example (rather than by genes) from one generation to the next (Castro & Toro, 2004). Culture determines, for example, whether children's education will focus on hunting or reading, how close people stand when talking to each other, and whether or not they form lines in public places.

Cultures can differ in many ways (Cohen, 2009). They may have strict or loose rules governing social behavior. They might place great value on achievement or on self-awareness. Some seek dominance over nature; others seek harmony with it. Time is of great importance in some cultures but not in others. Psychologists have tended to focus on the differences between cultures that can be described as individualist or collectivist (Miyamoto & Wilken, 2010; Triandis & Trafimow, 2001; see Table 1.2). In *individualist* cultures, such as those typical of North America and Western Europe, people tend to focus on and value personal rather than group goals and achievement. Competitiveness to distinguish oneself from others is common, but so is a sense of isolation. By contrast, in *collectivist* cultures, such as those found in Japan and other parts of Asia, people tend to think of themselves as part of family or work groups. Cooperative effort aimed at advancing the welfare of those groups is highly valued. And although loneliness is rarely a problem, fear of rejection by the group is common. Many aspects of mainstream U.S. culture—from self-reliant movie heroes and bonuses for "top" employees to the invitation to "help yourself" at a buffet table—reflect its tendency toward an individualist orientation (see Table 1.3).

We often associate cultures with particular countries, but in reality, most countries are *multicultural*. In other words, they host many cultural groups within their borders. For instance, the United States encompasses African Americans, Hispanic Americans, Asian Americans, and American Indians as well as European Americans whose families came from Italy, Germany, Britain, Greece, Poland, Sweden, Ireland, and many other

Gilbert Haven Jones (1883–1966)
When Gilbert Haven Jones graduated from the University of Jena in Germany in 1909, he became one of the first African Americans to earn a doctorate in psychology. Many others were to follow, including J. Henry Alston, the first African American to publish research in a major U.S. psychology journal (Alston, 1920).

TABLE 1.2   Some Characteristics of Behavior and Mental Processes Typical of Individualist Versus Collectivist Cultures

Psychologists and anthropologists have noticed that cultures can create certain general tendencies in behavior and mental processes among the people living in them (Bhagat et al., 2002; Cohen, 2009; Miyamoto & Wilken, 2010). As shown here, individualist cultures tend to support placing personal goals before the goals of the extended family or work group, whereas collectivist cultures tend to encourage putting the goals of those groups ahead of personal goals. Remember, though, that these labels represent very rough categories. Cultures cannot be pigeonholed as being either entirely individualist or entirely collectivist, and not everyone raised in a particular culture always thinks or acts in exactly the same way.

Variable	Individualist	Collectivist
Personal identity	Separate from others	Connected to others
Major goals	Self-defined; be unique; reach your personal potential; compete with others	Defined by others; belong; occupy your proper place; meet your obligations to others; be like others
Criteria for self-esteem	Ability to express unique aspects of the self; ability to be self-assured	Ability to restrain the self and be part of a social unit; ability to be self-effacing
Sources of success and failure	Success comes from personal effort; failure, from external factors	Success is due to help from others; failure is due to personal faults
Major frame of reference	Personal attitudes, traits, and goals	Family, work group

TABLE 1.3   Cultural Values as Seen in Advertising

These statements appeared in advertisements in Korea and the United States. Those from Korea reflect collectivist values, whereas those from the United States emphasize a more individualist orientation (Han & Shavitt, 1994). See if you can tell which are which; then check the bottom of the next page for the answers. You might want to follow up on this exercise by identifying the cultural values appearing in the ads you see in newspapers and magazines and on billboards and television. Surf the Internet or scan international newspapers to compare the values conveyed by ads in your culture with those in ads from other cultures.

LEARN by DOING

1. "She's got a style all her own."
2. "You, only better."
3. "A more exhilarating way to provide for your family."
4. "We have a way of bringing people closer together."
5. "Celebrating a half-century of partnership."
6. "How to protect the most personal part of the environment: Your skin."
7. "Our family agrees with this selection of home furnishings."
8. "A leader among leaders."
9. "Make your way through the crowd."
10. "Your business success: Harmonizing with (company name)."

Source: Brehm, Kassin, & Fein (1999).

places. In each of these groups, individuals who identify with their cultural heritage tend to share behaviors, values, and beliefs based on their culture of origin, thus forming a *subculture*.

Most of us don't realize how strongly our culture or subculture has shaped our thoughts and actions until we come in contact with people whose culture or subculture has shaped them differently. Consider hand gestures, for example. The "thumbs-up" sign that means "everything is OK" to people in North America and Europe is considered a rude gesture in Australia, Nigeria, and Bangladesh. And although making eye contact during social introductions is usually seen as a sign of interest or sincerity in North America, it is likely to be considered rude in Japan (Axtell, 1998). Even some of the misunderstandings that occur between people in the same culture can be traced to slight, culturally-influenced differences in communication (Tannen, 2001). In the United States, for instance, women's efforts to connect with others by talking may be perceived by many men as "pointless" unless the discussion is geared to solving a particular problem. As a result, women often feel frustrated and misunderstood by men, who tend to offer well-meant but unwanted advice instead of conversation.

For decades, the impact of culture on behavior and mental processes was of concern mainly to a relatively small group of researchers working in *cross-cultural* psychology. As you will see in the chapters to come, however, psychologists in almost every subfield are now looking at how ethnicity, gender, age, sexual orientation, and many other sociocultural factors can influence the behavior and mental processes of the people they serve and the people they study. They are more aware, too, of how easily their own cultural perspective can color their research and the conclusions they draw from it. They realize, for example, that many early psychologists studied only men, as though women were somehow lesser creatures (Fiske, 2010), and studied only middle-class North Americans as though people from other cultures were less "normal" (Dueck, Ting, & Cutiongco, 2007; Hwang, 2010; Medin, Bennis, & Chandler, 2010). This awareness has led many psychological scientists to focus on *indigenous psychology,* which seeks to understand the characteristics of behavior and mental processes as they occur in many different, and often under-studied, cultural contexts (Cheung, van de Vijver, & Leong, 2011; Hwang, 2009, 2010). In other words, psychology today strives to be the science of *all* behavior and mental processes, not just of those in the cultures in which it began.

The Impact of Culture

Culture helps shape virtually every aspect of our behavior and mental processes, from how we dress to how we think to what we think is important. Because most people grow up immersed in a particular culture, they may not notice its influence on their thoughts and actions until—like these people who emigrated from Somalia to Lewiston, Maine—they encounter people whose culture has shaped them in different ways (Luna, Ringberg, & Peracchio, 2008; Markus, 2008; Masuda et al., 2008; Nisbett & Masuda, 2007; Varnum et al., 2008).

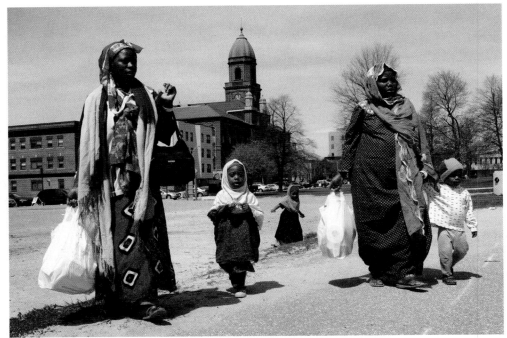

© AP Photo/Robert F. Bukaty

Thinking Critically about Psychology (or Anything Else)

How can critical thinking save you money?

In order to appreciate the effects of sociocultural factors on behavior and mental processes, psychologists had to think about their field in new ways. For one thing, they had to question the assumption that studying people of just one gender, age range, ethnic group, or culture can tell us about people in general. This kind of thinking can lead to new insights but it takes effort and it sometimes upsets those who hold more traditional views. No wonder, then, that some people prefer to simply accept what they are told, especially when it comes from a believable source (see Table 1.4). Some advertisers, politicians, and social activists hope for this kind of easy acceptance when they go after your money, your vote, or your loyalty. They want you to believe their promises or claims without careful thought on your part. In other words, they don't want you to think critically.

Critical thinking is the process of assessing claims and making judgments based on well-supported evidence (Wade, 1988). Let's consider some of the questions that arise from thinking critically about psychology (or anything else) and then review the scientific research methods that psychologists use to try to answer those questions.

Five Questions for Critical Thinking

Francine Shapiro, a clinical psychologist in northern California, had an odd experience while taking a walk one day in 1987. She had been thinking about some distressing events when she noticed that her emotional reaction to them was fading away. She realized that she'd been moving her eyes from side to side, but had these eye movements caused the emotion-reducing effect? Perhaps, because when she made these same eye movements more deliberately, the effect was even stronger. Was this a fluke, or would the same thing happen to others? To find out, she tested the eye-movement effect in

critical thinking The process of assessing claims and making judgments based on well-supported evidence.

ANSWER KEY FOR TABLE 1.3: U.S. ads are numbers 1, 2, 6, 8, and 9.

TABLE 1.4   Some Popular Myths

Ask some friends and relatives what they think about the statements listed in the left-hand column of this table. Most people will probably agree with at least one of them, even though all of them are false. Perhaps you already knew that, but don't feel too smug. At one time or another, we all accept something we are told simply because the information seems to come from a reliable source or because "everyone knows" it's true.

Myth	Fact
Many children are injured each year in the United States by razor blades, needles, or poison in Halloween candy.	Reported cases are rare, most turn out to be hoaxes, and in the only documented case of a child dying from poisoned candy, the culprit was the child's own parent (Brunvald, 1989).
If your roommate commits suicide during the school term, you automatically get A's in all your classes for that term.	No college or university anywhere has ever had such a rule.
People have been known to burst into flames and die from fire erupting within their own bodies.	In rare cases, humans have been consumed by fires that caused little or no damage to the surrounding area. However, this phenomenon has never been duplicated in a laboratory, and each alleged case of "spontaneous human combustion" has been traced to an external source of ignition (Benecke, 1999; Nickell, 2011; Nienhuys, 2001).
Most big-city police departments rely on the advice of psychics to help them solve murders, kidnappings, and missing persons cases.	Only about 35% of urban police departments ever seek psychics' advice, and that advice is virtually never more helpful than other means of investigation (Nickell, 1997; Wiseman, West, & Stemman, 1996).
Murders, suicides, animal bites, and episodes of mental disorder are more likely to occur when the moon is full.	Records of crimes, dog bites, and admissions to mental hospitals do not support this common belief (Bickis, Kelly, & Byrnes, 1995; Chapman & Morrell, 2000; Rotton & Kelly, 1985).
You can't fool a lie detector.	Lie detectors may be helpful in solving crimes, but they aren't perfect; their results can free a guilty person or send an innocent person to jail (see the chapter on motivation and emotion).
Viewers never see David Letterman walking to his desk after the opening monologue because his contract prohibits him from showing his backside on TV.	When questioned about this on the air, Letterman denied it and, to prove his point, lifted his jacket and turned a full circle in front of the cameras and studio audience (Brunvald, 1989).

friends and colleagues and then with clients who had suffered childhood sexual abuse, military combat, rape, or other traumas. She asked the clients to recall these traumas while keeping their eyes focused on her finger as she moved it back and forth in front of their faces. They said that their emotional reactions to the memories, like Shapiro's, faded. They also reported that trauma-related problems such as nightmares, fears, and emotional flashbacks decreased dramatically, often after only one session (Shapiro, 1989a). These successful case studies led Shapiro to develop a new treatment called *eye movement desensitization and reprocessing,* or *EMDR* (Leeds, 2009; Shapiro, 1991; Shapiro & Forrest, 2004). Today, Shapiro and thousands of other therapists in a number of countries are using EMDR to treat an ever-widening range of anxiety-related problems in children and adults, including phobias, posttraumatic and other stress disorders, somatoform disorders, eating disorders, alcoholism, addiction, migraine headaches, marital conflicts, and skin rashes (Abel & O'Brien, 2010; Adúriz, Bluthgen, & Knopfler, 2009; Albright & Thyer, 2010; Bloomgarden & Calogero, 2008; Cvetek, 2008; Gauvreau & Bouchard, 2008; Hase, Schallmayer, & Sack, 2008; Kemp, Drummond, & McDermott, 2010; Lawson, 2004; Manfield & Shapiro, 2004; Marcus, 2008; Marich, 2010; Phillips et al., 2009; Ribchester, Yule, & Duncan, 2010; Rodenburg et al., 2009; Russell et al., 2007;

DOONESBURY

Uncritically accepting claims for the value of astrologers' predictions, "get-rich-quick" investments, unproven therapies, or proposed government policies can be embarrassing, expensive, and sometimes dangerous. Critical thinkers carefully evaluate evidence for *and against* such claims before reaching a conclusion about them.

Shapiro, 2005; Triscari, Faraci, D'Angelo, Urso, & Catalisano, 2011; van den Hout et al., 2012; van Rood & de Roos, 2009).

Would the phenomenal growth of EMDR be enough to convince you to spend your own money on it? If not, what would you want to know about EMDR before deciding? As a cautious person, you would probably ask some of the same questions that have occurred to many scientists in psychology: Are the effects of EMDR caused by the treatment itself or by the faith that clients might have in any new and impressive treatment? And are EMDR's effects faster, stronger, and longer lasting than those of other treatments?

Questioning what we are told is an important part of a more general critical thinking process that can help us make informed decisions about psychotherapy options as well as many other things, such as which pain reliever or Internet service to choose, which college to attend, what apartment to rent, which candidate to vote for, and whether we believe that cell phones can cause cancer or that shark cartilage can cure it. One way of applying critical thinking to EMDR or any other topic is to ask the following five questions:

- **What am I being asked to believe or accept?**

In this case, you are asked to believe that EMDR reduces or eliminates anxiety-related problems.

- **Is evidence available to support the claim?**

Shapiro began her EMDR research on herself. When she found the same effects in others, coincidence became an unlikely explanation for the observed changes.

- **Can that evidence be interpreted another way?**

The dramatic effects that Shapiro's friends and clients experienced might have been due to their motivation to change or to their desire to please her, not to EMDR. And who knows? They might have eventually improved on their own without any treatment. In other words, even the most remarkable evidence cannot be accepted as confirming an assertion until all reasonable alternative explanations have been ruled out. Doing that leads to the next step in critical thinking: conducting scientific research.

- **What evidence would help to evaluate the alternatives?**

The ideal method for testing the value of EMDR would be to identify three groups of people who are identical in every way except for the anxiety treatment they receive. One group receives EMDR. The second group gets an equally motivating but useless treatment. The third group gets no treatment at all. If the EMDR group improves much more than the other two, then it is less likely that the changes following EMDR can be explained entirely by client motivation or the mere passage of time.

- **What conclusions are most reasonable?**

While the evidence available so far has not yet ruled out alternative explanations for the effects of EMDR (e.g., Hertlein & Ricci, 2004; Hughes, 2006), it does show that while its effects are no better than other treatments, they are better than no treatment at all (Bisson, 2007; Cvetek, 2008; Hughes, 2006; Ironson et al., 2002; Lilienfeld & Arkowitz, 2007; Taylor, 2004; Taylor et al., 2003; van den Hout et al., 2011; Wanders, Serra, & de Jongh, 2008). Other analyses suggest that EMDR may be no better than placebo treatments (e.g., Albright & Thyer, 2010). Accordingly, the only reasonable conclusions to be drawn at this point are that (1) EMDR remains a controversial treatment, (2) it seems to have an impact on some clients, and (3) further research is needed in order to understand it.

Does that sound wishy-washy? Critical thinking sometimes does seem to be indecisive thinking, but the reason for that is that scientific conclusions must be guided by the evidence available. In the long run, though, critical thinking opens the way to understanding. (To help you sharpen your critical thinking skills, we have included in every chapter to come a feature in which our five critical thinking questions are applied to a particularly interesting topic in psychology.) Let's now consider how psychologists translate critical thinking into scientific research.

Critical Thinking and Scientific Research

Scientific research often begins with questions based on curiosity, such as whether eye movements can reduce anxiety. Like many seemingly simple questions, this one is more complex than it first appears. Are we talking about horizontal, vertical, or diagonal eye movements? How long do they continue? How many treatment sessions should there be? Are we referring to mild or severe anxiety, and how will we measure improvement? In other words, scientists must ask specific questions in order to get meaningful answers.

Like other scientists, psychological scientists clarify their questions about behavior and mental processes by phrasing them in terms of a **hypothesis**—a specific, testable statement or proposition about something they want to study. In the case of EMDR, the hypothesis might be as follows: EMDR treatment causes a significant reduction in anxiety.

To make it easier to understand and objectively evaluate their hypotheses, scientists employ **operational definitions**, which are statements describing the exact operations or methods they will use in their research. In the hypothesis we just proposed, "EMDR treatment" might be operationally defined as a certain number of back-and-forth eye movements per second for a particular period of time. "Significant reduction in anxiety" might be operationally defined as a reduction of at least ten points on a test that measures anxiety. The kind of treatment a client is given (say, EMDR versus no treatment) and the results of that treatment (how much anxiety reduction occurred) are examples of research **variables**, the specific factors or characteristics that are altered and measured in research.

In addition to collecting evidence, scientists must also check on how good it is. Usually, the quality of evidence is evaluated in terms of two characteristics: statistical reliability and statistical validity. **Statistical reliability** (usually just called reliability) is the consistency of the evidence that is obtained. **Statistical validity** (usually just called validity) is the degree to which the evidence accurately represents the topic being studied (Mitchell, 2012). For example, if Shapiro had not been able to repeat (or *replicate*) the eye movement effects with others or if only a few clients had shown improvement, she would question the reliability of her evidence. If the clients' reports of improvement were not supported by, say, changes in their overt behavior or confirming statements by close relatives, she would doubt their validity.

The Role of Theories After examining research evidence, scientists may begin to favor certain explanations as to why these results occurred. Sometimes they organize their explanations into a **theory**, which is a set of statements designed to explain certain phenomena. Shapiro's theory about EMDR suggests that eye movements activate parts of the brain in which information about trauma or other unpleasant experiences has been stored but never fully processed. EMDR, she says, promotes the "adaptive information processing" required for the elimination of anxiety-related emotional and behavioral problems (Leeds, 2009; Shapiro & Forrest, 2004). Others (e.g., Lee, Taylor, & Drummond, 2006) suggest that EMDR may help troubled people think about stressful material in a more detached, less emotional way, perhaps as in a dream (Elofsson et al., 2008), or that EMDR may work by putting a strain on a person's memory (van den Hout et al., 2011). Because they are tentative explanations, theories must be subjected to scientific evaluation based on critical thinking about the evidence for and against them. For example, Shapiro's theory about EMDR has been criticized as vague, not well supported by evidence, and less plausible than other, simpler explanations (e.g., Carpenter, 2004; Gaudiano & Dalrymple, 2005; Herbert et al., 2000; Lohr et al., 2003). Although a psychologist's theory may be based on research results, it usually also generates predictions that stimulate additional research. These predictions will be tested by many other psychologists and the theory will be revised or even abandoned if research does not support it.

The process of creating, evaluating, and revising psychological theories does not always lead to a single "winner." You will see in later chapters that there are several possible explanations for color vision, mental disorder, prejudice, and many other aspects of behavior and mental processes. As a result, we can't offer as many final conclusions about

Taking Your Life in Your Hands?
Can microwave radiation from cell phones cause brain tumors? This question generates strong opinions, but the answer will come from research based on critical thinking. Though there is no conclusive evidence that cell phones cause tumors (Christensen et al., 2005; Hepworth et al., 2006; Inskip, Hoover, & Devesa, 2010; Kaufman, Anderson, & Issaragrisil, 2009; Schoemaker et al., 2005), some scientists see danger in short- and long-term exposure (Cardis et al., 2009; Manti et al., 2008; Sadetzki et al., 2008; Vijayalaxmi, 2008; Volkow et al., 2011) and in prenatal and early postnatal exposure (Clinical Digest, 2011; Divan et al., 2008). Research on this issue continues.

hypothesis In scientific research, a specific, testable proposition about a phenomenon.

operational definitions Statements that define phenomena or variables by describing the exact research operations or methods used in measuring or manipulating them.

variables Specific factors or characteristics that can take on different numerical values in research.

statistical reliability The degree to which test results or other research evidence occurs repeatedly.

statistical validity The degree to which evidence from a test or other research method measures what it is supposed to measure.

theory An integrated set of propositions used to explain certain phenomena, including behavior and mental processes.

psychology as you might want. The conclusions we do offer are always based on what is known so far, and we always cite the need for additional research (Greenwald, 2012). We do that because research often raises at least as many questions as it answers. For example, a certain treatment might work well for mild depression in women, but would it work as well for men or for cases of severe depression? Answering those questions would require more research.

Keep this in mind the next time you hear a talk-show guest giving simple solutions for complex problems such as obesity or anxiety, or promoting easy formulas for a happy marriage and well-behaved children. These self-proclaimed experts—called "pop" (for *popular*) psychologists by the scientific community—tend to oversimplify issues, cite evidence for their views without concern for its reliability or validity, and ignore good evidence that contradicts their pet theories. And because it's easier to understand and accept evidence presented in a simple format, without complex statistics or exceptions (Matute, Yarritu, & Vadillo, 2010), pop psychologists' assertions are especially likely to influence public opinion. Psychological scientists make far more limited and tentative statements, often delaying final judgments about behavior and mental processes until they've collected better evidence. Ironically, the frustration created by this more cautious scientific approach leads some people to doubt whether psychology is really a science at all (Lilienfeld, 2011).

It is a science, indeed. And in evaluating theories and deciding among conclusions, psychological scientists are guided not only by the research methods described in the next section, but by the *law of parsimony*, sometimes referred to by nonscientists as KISS (Keep It Simple, Stupid). The law of parsimony is based on experience in the long history of science. It suggests that when several alternative conclusions or several competing theories offer nearly equally convincing explanations of something, the correct explanation tends to be the simplest.

Throughout this book you will see examples of how the law of parsimony has helped psychological scientists sift and refine explanatory theories in search of the ones that offer the simplest yet fullest understanding of behavior and mental processes.

You will also see that research in psychological science has created an enormous body of knowledge that is being put to good use in many ways. That knowledge forms the foundation for future research that will no doubt lead to even deeper understanding. Let's look now at the scientific methods that psychologists use in their research and at some of the pitfalls that lie in their path.

Research Methods in Psychology

How do psychologists learn about people?

Like other scientists, psychologists try to achieve four main goals in their research: to *describe* a phenomenon, to *make predictions* about it, and to introduce enough *control* in their research to allow them to *explain* the phenomenon with some degree of confidence. Five research methods have proven especially useful for gathering the evidence needed to reach each of these goals. They include *observational methods, case studies, surveys, correlational studies,* and *experiments.*

Observational Methods: Watching Behavior

observational methods Procedures for systematically watching behavior in order to summarize it for scientific analysis.

naturalistic observation The process of watching without interfering as a phenomenon occurs in the natural environment.

Sometimes, the best way to describe behavior is through **observational methods,** such as **naturalistic observation,** the process of watching without interfering as behavior occurs in the natural environment (Hoyle, Harris, & Judd, 2002). This method is especially valuable when more noticeable methods might alter the behavior you want to study. For example, if you ask people to keep track of how often they exercise, they might begin to exercise more than usual, and their records would give a false impression of their typical behavior. Much of what we know about, say, gender differences in how children play and communicate with one another has come from psychologists' observations in classrooms and playgrounds. Observations of adults, too, have provided valuable insights into friendships, couple communication patterns, and even responses to terrorism (e.g., Mehl & Pennebaker, 2003a, 2003b).

Observational methods can provide a lot of good information, but they are not without problems. For one thing, people tend to act differently when they know they're being observed (and research ethics usually require that they do know). To combat this problem, researchers typically observe people long enough for them to get used to the situation and begin behaving more naturally. Still, observations can be incomplete or misleading if the observers are not well trained or if they report what they expect to see rather than what actually occurs. Further, even the best observational methods don't allow researchers to draw conclusions about what is causing the behavior being observed.

Case Studies: Taking a Closer Look

Observations are often an important part of **case studies**, which are intensive examinations of behavior or mental processes in a particular individual, group, or situation. Case studies can also include tests, interviews, and the analysis of letters, school transcripts, or other written records. Case studies are especially useful when studying something that is new, complex, or relatively rare (Sacks, 2002). Francine Shapiro's EMDR treatment, for example, first attracted psychologists' attention through case studies of its remarkable effects on her clients (Shapiro, 1989b).

Case studies have played a special role in neuropsychology, which focuses on the relationships among brain activity, thinking, and behavior. Consider the case of Dr. P., a patient described by neurologist Oliver Sacks (1985). Dr. P. was a distinguished musician who began to show odd symptoms. He could not recognize familiar people or distinguish between people and things. For instance, while he and his wife were at the neurologist's office, Dr. P. mistook his foot for his shoe. When he rose to leave, he tried to lift off his wife's head as if it were a hat and put it on his own head. He could not name common objects, but he could describe them. When handed a glove, for example, he said, "A continuous surface, infolded on itself. It appears to have … five outpouchings, if this is the word … a container of some sort." Only later, when he put it on his hand, did he exclaim, "My God, it's a glove!" (Sacks, 1985, p. 13). Using case studies such as this one, pioneers in neuropsychology have noted the symptoms suffered by people with particular kinds of brain damage or disease (Banich, 2004). Eventually, neuropsychologists were able to tie specific disorders to certain types of injuries, poisons, and other causes. In Dr. P.'s case, it was probably a large brain tumor that caused his symptoms.

© Turbo/Corbis

Little Reminders

If you asked this man what he needs to use various computer programs efficiently, he might not think to mention the notes on his monitor that list his usernames and passwords. Accordingly, researchers in human factors and in industrial and organizational psychology usually arrange to watch employees at work rather than just asking them what they do, how they do it, and how they interact with machines and fellow employees (Barriera-Viruet et al., 2006; Dempsey, McGorry, & Maynard, 2005).

case studies Research involving the intensive examination of some phenomenon in a particular individual, group, or situation.

Translating Observations Into Evidence

Observing people in natural settings can provide important clues to understanding social interaction and other aspects of behavior and mental processes (Floyd et al., 2008; Wakschlag et al., 2008). Imagine you are studying these children at play. Exactly how would you decide what behaviors would qualify as, say, "aggressive," "shy," "fearful," "cooperative," and "competitive"? Try writing a definition for each of these, and you'll see that it is harder than you might think.

LEARNby DOING

© Bill Aron/PhotoEdit

© Nancy Kaszerman/ZUMA/Corbis

Learning From Rare Cases

We can learn a great deal from studying individual cases such as Dr. Temple Grandin, whose autism has not prevented her from becoming a professor of animal science, a noted advocate for the humane treatment of livestock, a best-selling author, and a champion of the rights of people with autistic disorder. Other case studies have focused, for example, on people who can correctly identify the day of the week for any date in the past or the future or tell at a glance that, say, exactly 125 paper clips are scattered on the floor. By carefully studying such rare cases, cognitive psychologists are learning more about human mental capacities and how they might be maximized in everyone (Biever, 2009; Geddes, 2008).

surveys   Research that involves giving people questionnaires or interviews designed to describe their attitudes, beliefs, opinions, and intentions.

correlational studies   Research methods that examine relationships between variables in order to analyze trends, test predictions, evaluate theories, and suggest new hypotheses.

correlation   The degree to which one variable is related to another.

Case studies do have limitations. They may not represent people in general, and they may contain only the evidence a particular researcher considered important (Loftus & Guyer, 2002). Nonetheless, when conducted and used with care, case studies can provide valuable raw material for further research and can serve as the testing ground for new treatments, training programs, and other applications of research.

Surveys: Looking at the Big Picture

In contrast to the individual close-ups provided by case studies, surveys offer wide-angle views of large groups. In **surveys**, researchers use interviews or questionnaires to ask people about their behavior, attitudes, beliefs, opinions, or intentions. Just as politicians and advertisers rely on opinion polls to test the popularity of policies or products, psychologists use surveys to gather descriptive data on just about any behavior or mental process, from parenting practices to sexual behavior. However, the validity of survey data depends partly on the way the survey questions are asked (Bhopal et al., 2004; Wahl, Svensson, & Hydén, 2010). In one survey study at a health clinic, patients were asked how frequently they experienced headaches, stomachaches, and other symptoms of illness (Schwarz & Scheuring, 1992). If the wording of the question suggested that most people frequently experience such symptoms, the patients said that they frequently experienced them, too. But if the wording suggested that people rarely experience these symptoms, the patients said that they experienced the symptoms infrequently. A survey's validity also depends on who is surveyed. If the people surveyed don't represent the views of the population you're interested in, the survey results can be misleading (Gosling et al., 2004; Kraut et al., 2004). For example, if you were interested in Americans' views on how common ethnic prejudice is, you would come to the wrong conclusion if you surveyed only African Americans or only European Americans. To get a complete picture, you would have to survey people from all ethnic groups so that each group's opinions could be fairly represented.

Other limitations of the survey method are more difficult to avoid. For example, a poll conducted for the American Society for Microbiology (ASM) found that 92 percent of the U.S. adults surveyed said that they always wash their hands after using public toilet facilities. However, naturalistic observations of thousands of people in public restrooms across the United States revealed that the figure is closer to 77 percent (Harris Interactive, 2007). In other words, people may be unwilling to admit undesirable or embarrassing things about themselves or they may say what they believe they *should* say about an issue (Uziel, 2010). And sometimes those who respond to a survey hold views that differ from those who do not respond (Visser, Krosnick, & Lavrakas, 2000). These factors all have the potential to distort survey results and the conclusions drawn from them (Hoyle, Harris, & Judd, 2002). Still, surveys provide an efficient way to gather large amounts of data about people's attitudes, beliefs, or other characteristics.

Correlational Studies: Looking for Relationships

Data collected using observational methods, case studies, and surveys provide valuable descriptions of behavior and mental processes, but they can do more than that. The data can also be examined for what they reveal about the relationships between research variables. For example, fear surveys show that most people have fears, but correlational analysis of those surveys also shows that fear is related to age. Specifically, as people get older, they tend to have fewer fears (e.g., Kleinknecht, 1991). **Correlational studies** examine relationships between variables in order to describe research data more fully, test predictions, evaluate theories, and suggest new hypotheses about why people think and act as they do.

Correlation refers to both the strength and the direction of the relationship between two variables. A *positive correlation* means that the two variables increase together or decrease together. A *negative correlation* means that the variables move in opposite directions. For example James Schaefer observed 4,500 customers in 65 bars and found that the tempo of the jukebox music was negatively correlated with the rate at which the

Designing Survey Research

How do people feel about whether gay men and lesbians should have the legal right to marry? To appreciate the difficulties of survey research, write a question about this issue that you think is clear enough and unbiased enough to generate a valid portrait of people's views. Then ask some friends whether or not they agree that it would be a good survey question, and why.

customers drank alcohol. The slower the tempo, the faster the drinking (Schaefer et al., 1988). Does this mean that Schaefer could have worn a blindfold and predicted exactly how fast people were drinking by timing the music? Could he have plugged his ears and determined the musical tempo just by watching people's sip rates? No and no, because the accuracy of predictions made about one variable from knowing the other depends on the *strength* of the correlation. Only a perfect correlation between two variables would allow you to predict the exact value of one from knowledge of the other. The weaker the correlation, the less one variable can tell you about the other.

Psychologists describe the strength and direction of correlations with a number called a *correlation coefficient,* which can range from a high of 1.00 to a low of .00 (see the "Statistics in Psychological Research" appendix). If the correlation between two variables is *positive*—if they both move in the same direction—the correlation coefficient will have a plus sign in front of it. If there is a minus sign, the correlation is *negative,* and the two variables will move in opposite directions. The larger the correlation coefficient, the stronger the relationship between the two variables. The strongest possible relationship is indicated by either +1.00 or −1.00 (see Figure 1.6). A correlation of .00 indicates that there is virtually no relationship between variables.

Correlation coefficients can help to describe the results of correlational research and evaluate hypotheses, but psychological scientists must be extremely careful when interpreting what correlations mean. The mere fact that two variables are correlated does not guarantee that one causes an effect on the other. And even if one variable actually does cause an effect on the other, a correlation coefficient can't tell us which

A Severely Flawed Survey

Using survey methods like this, you could probably get whatever results you want! Psychologists work hard to write questions and use methods that maximize the validity of their surveys' results.

Dilbert © Scott Adams/Universal Uclick

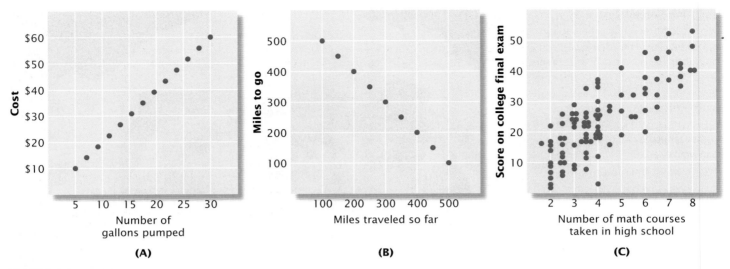

FIGURE 1.6
Three Correlations

The strength and direction of the correlation between variables can be seen in a graph called a scatterplot. Here are three examples. In Part A, we've plotted the cost of a gasoline purchase against the number of gallons pumped. The number of gallons is positively and perfectly correlated with their cost, so the scatterplot appears as a straight line and you can predict the value of either variable if you know the other. Part B shows a perfect negative correlation between the number of miles you have traveled toward a destination and the distance remaining. Again, one variable can be exactly predicted from the other. Part C illustrates a correlation of +.81 between the number of math courses students had taken in high school and their scores on a college math exam; each dot represents one student (Hays, 1981). As correlations decrease, they are represented by less and less organized scatterplots. A correlation of .00 would appear as a shapeless cloud.

variable is influencing which, or why (see Table 1.5). Consider the question of how aggression develops. Correlational studies of observational data indicate that children who are in day care for more than thirty hours a week are more aggressive than those who stay at home with a parent. Does separation from parents actually cause the heightened aggressiveness with which it is associated? It might, but psychologists must be careful about jumping to that conclusion. The most obvious explanation for the relationship found in a correlational study may not always be the correct one. Perhaps the aggressiveness seen among some children in day care has something to do with the children themselves or with what happens to them in day care, not just with separation from their parents.

One way psychologists evaluate such alternative hypotheses is to conduct further correlational studies to look for trends that support or conflict with those hypotheses (Rutter, 2007; West, 2009). Further analysis of day-care research, for example, shows that the aggressiveness seen in preschoolers who spend a lot of time in day care is the exception, not the rule. Most children don't show any behavior problems, no matter how much time they have spent in day care. This more general trend suggests that whatever effect separation has, it may be different for different children in different settings, causing some to express aggressiveness, others to display fear, and still others to find enjoyment. As described in the chapter on human development, psychologists are exploring this possibility by examining correlations between children's personality traits, qualities of different day care programs, and reactions to day care (Belsky et al., 2007; NICHD Early Child Care Research Network, 2006a).

Throughout this book you will see many more examples of how correlational studies help shed light on a wide range of topics in psychology (Rutter, 2007).

Experiments: Exploring Cause and Effect

experiment A situation in which the researcher manipulates one variable and observes the effect of that manipulation on another variable, while holding all other variables constant.

independent variable In an experiment, the variable manipulated by the researcher.

dependent variable In an experiment, the factor affected by the independent variable.

Still, to make the best choice among alternative explanations and to confirm cause-and-effect relationships between research variables, psychological scientists prefer to exert some control over those variables (Falk & Heckman, 2009). This kind of controlled research usually takes the form of an experiment. In an **experiment**, the researcher makes a change in one variable and then observes the effect of that change on another variable while holding all the other variables constant. The variable that is changed, or manipulated, by the experimenter is called the **independent variable**. The variable that is measured during this manipulation is called the **dependent variable**, because it *depends* on the independent variable (see Table 1.6). So in an experiment on the effects of TV violence, for example, the independent variable might be the amount of violence that different groups of children are allowed to watch: a

TABLE 1.5   Correlation and Causation

Look at the relationships described in the left-hand column, then ask yourself why the two variables in each case are correlated. Could one variable cause an effect on the other? If so, which is the cause, and how might it exert its effect? Could the relationship between the two variables be caused by a third one? If so, what might that third variable be? We suggest some possible explanations in the right-hand column. Can you think of others?

Correlation	Possible Explanations
The more sexual content U.S. teenagers reported watching on television, the more likely they were to begin having sex themselves in the following year (Collins et al., 2004).	Some teens' greater interest in sex may have led them to watch more sexually oriented shows and to become sexually active.
The number of drownings in the United States rises and falls during the year along with the amount of ice cream sold each month.	A third variable, the time of year, may explain the high consumption of ice cream and likelihood of water activities. (Brenner et al., 2001).
In places where beer prices are increased, the number of new cases of sexually transmitted diseases falls among young people living in those places.	If price increases cause less beer consumption, people might stay sober enough to remember to use condoms during sexual encounters. The relationship could also reflect coincidence, because prices don't always affect alcohol use. More research is required to understand this correlation.
A study found that the more antibiotics a woman has taken and the longer she has taken them, the greater is her risk of breast cancer (Velicer et al., 2004).	Long-term antibiotic use might have impaired the women's immune systems, but the cancer risk might also have been increased by the diseases being treated with antibiotics, not the drugs themselves. Obviously, much more research would be required before condemning the use of antibiotics.
The U.S. stock market rises during years when a team from the National Football Conference wins the Super Bowl and falls when an American Conference team wins.	The so-called "Super Bowl Effect" has occurred 31 times in 38 years; striking as this might seem, coincidence seems to be the most likely explanation.

TABLE 1.6   Independent and Dependent Variables

Fill in the names of the independent and dependent variables in each of these experiments (the answers are at the bottom of page 30). Remember that the experimenter manipulates the independent variable, and measures the dependent variable to determine the independent variable's effect. How did you do on this task?

1. Researchers measure the reading skills of children after they have taken either a special reading class or a standard reading class.	The independent variable is ___. The dependent variable is ___.
2. The memory of college students for German vocabulary words is tested after the students have had either a normal night's sleep or a night of no sleep.	The independent variable is ___. The dependent variable is ___.
3. Experiment title: "The effect of a daily walking program on elderly people's lung capacity."	The independent variable is ___. The dependent variable is ___.
4. People's ability to avoid "accidents" in a driving simulator is tested before, while, and after they talk on a cell phone.	The independent variable is ___. The dependent variable is ___.

lot, a little, or none at all. The **experimental group** is the group that is exposed to something of interest to the experimenter (a lot of violent TV, for example). A group that receives no such exposure or a differing amount of exposure is called the **control group**. Control groups provide baselines against which to compare the performance of the experimental group. If everything about the groups is exactly the same except for exposure to something, then any differences between groups at the end of the experiment should be due to that thing.

FOCUS ON RESEARCH   ## Studying EMDR

Let's consider how Francine Shapiro used the experimental method to explore whether her EMDR treatment was actually causing the improvements she observed in her clients. (Each chapter to follow contains a Focus on Research section like this one, which presents a different example of how researchers in psychology ask and answer questions about behavior and mental processes.)

FIGURE 1.7

A Simple Two-Group Experiment
Ideally, the only difference between the experimental and control group in experiments such as this one is whether the participants receive the treatment that the experimenter wants to evaluate. Under these ideal circumstances, at the end of the experiment any difference in the two groups' reported levels of anxiety (the dependent variable) should be attributable to whether or not they received treatment (the independent variable).

What was the researcher's question?
Like other scientists, Shapiro phrased her question about the value of EMDR in the form of a hypothesis, namely that *EMDR treatment causes a significant reduction in anxiety*. Does it?

How did the researcher answer the question?
To find out, Shapiro operationally defined "EMDR treatment" as making a certain number of back-and-forth eye movements per second for a particular period of time. And she operationally defined "significant reduction in anxiety" as a certain amount of reduction in clients' self-reported discomfort.

Shapiro then identified twenty-two people who were suffering the ill effects of traumas such as rape or military combat. These were her research participants. As shown in Figure 1.7, she assigned these participants to two groups. The experimental group received one 50-minute session of EMDR. The control group focused on their unpleasant memories for eight minutes but without moving their eyes back and forth (Shapiro, 1989b). The experimenter controlled whether EMDR treatment was given to each participant, so the presence or absence of treatment was the independent variable. The participants' anxiety level was the dependent variable. In Shapiro's experiment, having a control group allowed her to measure how much change in anxiety might be expected from exposure to bad memories without EMDR treatment.

What did the researcher find?
The results of Shapiro's experiment showed that participants receiving EMDR treatment experienced a complete and nearly immediate reduction in anxiety related to their traumatic memories. Those in the control group showed no such change.

What do the results mean?
At this point, you might be ready to believe that the treatment caused the difference. Before coming to that conclusion, though, look again at the structure, or design, of the experiment. The treatment group's session lasted 50 minutes. The control group focused on their memories for only eight minutes. Would the people in the control group have improved if they, too, had spent 50 minutes focusing on their memories? We don't know, because the experiment did not compare methods of equal length.

What do we still need to know?
Experiments have now been conducted that introduce enough control into the treatment situation to evaluate alternative explanations for the improvements seen in people treated with EMDR. Most of these studies cast doubt on whether the eye movements themselves are responsible (e.g., Albright & Thyer, 2010; Davidson & Parker, 2001; Lazarus & Lazarus, 2002; Van Deusen, 2004), but we still don't know for sure what *is* producing the

experimental group The group that receives the experimental treatment.

control group The group that receives no treatment or provides some other baseline against which to compare the performance or response of the experimental group.

ANSWER KEY TO TABLE 1.6: The independent variable (IDV) in experiment 1 is the type of reading class; the dependent variable (DV) is reading skill. In experiment 2, the IDV is the quality of sleep; the DV is the score on a memory test. In experiment 3, the IDV is amount of exercise; the DV is lung capacity. In experiment 4, the IDV is using or not using a cell phone; the DV is performance on a simulated driving task.

© AP Photo/Gene J. Puskar

Ever Since I Started Wearing This Titanium Necklace …
Placebo-controlled experiments establish cause-effect relationships between treatments and outcomes with human participants. For example, many people swear that titanium bracelets and necklaces relieve the pain of sports injuries and even arthritis (Atkinson, 2006; Galdeira, 2006; Marchman, 2008; Siber, 2005). Phiten, the leading manufacturer and marketer of titanium accessories, touts glowing testimonials and a scientific-sounding explanation of the technology behind titanium's alleged effects, but offers no evidence from placebo-controlled experiments to support their claims (Boyles, 2008; Wagg, 2008). Such experiments have already failed to support the value of "power balance" bracelets that are supposed to improve strength, flexibility, and balance (Underdown, 2011).

confound Any factor that affects the dependent variable along with, or instead of, the independent variable.

random variables Uncontrolled or uncontrollable factors that affect the dependent variable along with, or instead of, the independent variable.

randomizing A procedure through which random variables are evenly distributed in an experiment by placing participants in experimental and control groups on the basis of a coin flip or some other random process.

placebo A treatment that contains no active ingredient but produces an effect because the person receiving it believes it will.

beneficial effects that so often follow EMDR treatment (e.g., Cvetek, 2008; van den Hout et al., 2011). Considerable evidence suggests that EMDR may operate in much the same way as systematic desensitization therapy and other behavioral and cognitive behavioral treatments described in the chapter on treatment of psychological disorders. It may be that EMDR, like these other treatments, exposes people to unpleasant stimuli long enough for those stimuli to lose a lot of their emotional punch (Lilienfeld & Arkowitz, 2007; van der Does, 2006). As research on EMDR continues, it will be important for proponents and skeptics alike to avoid *confirmation bias,* the human tendency to look only for evidence that supports their own hypotheses. In fact, all scientists have a responsibility to combat confirmation bias by looking for evidence *for* and *against* even their most cherished hypotheses.

●●●●

Shapiro's (1989b) experiment reminds us to be on the lookout for flaws in experimental design and control that might affect the conclusions we can draw from research results. In fact, we have to consider anything that could confuse, or *confound,* our interpretation of those results. Any factor that might have affected the dependent variable, along with or instead of the independent variable, may be a **confound**. When confounds are present, we can't tell whether it was the independent variable or the confound that produced the results. Let's consider three sources of confounds: random variables, participants' expectations, and experimenter bias.

Random Variables   In an ideal research world, everything about experimental and control groups would be the same except for their exposure to the independent variable (such as whether or not they received treatment). In the real world, however, there are always other differences between the experimental and control groups that are due to random variables (West, 2009). **Random variables** are uncontrolled (and sometimes uncontrollable) factors, such as differences in the time of year when research takes place or differences in each participant's cultural background, personality, health, and sensitivity to stress. There are so many ways that participants might vary from each other that it's usually impossible to form groups that are matched on all of them. Instead, experimenters simply flip a coin or use some other random process to assign each research participant to experimental or control groups. These procedures, called *random assignment* or **randomizing**, tend to spread the effects of uncontrolled variables randomly (and probably about evenly) across groups. This minimizes the chance that they'll distort the results of the experiment (Shadish, Cook, & Campbell, 2002).

Participants' Expectations: The Placebo Effect   Differences in what participants think about the experimental situation can be another confound. For example, if participants expect that a treatment will help them, they may try harder to improve than those in a control group who receive no treatment or a less impressive one. Improvement created by a participant's expectations is called the *placebo effect.* Although a **placebo** (pronounced "plah-SEE-boe") contains nothing known to be helpful, it still produces benefits because a person believes it will do so (Langer et al., 2010; Stewart-Williams & Podd, 2004; Wager et al., 2004).

How can researchers estimate the strength of placebo effects in an experiment? The most common strategy is to include a special control group that receives *only* a placebo. The researchers then compare results for the experimental group, the placebo group, and a group of participants receiving no treatment. In one stop-smoking study, for example, participants in a placebo group took sugar pills that the experimenter said would help them endure the stress of giving up cigarettes (Bernstein, 1970). These participants did as well at quitting as those in the experimental group, who had received extensive treatment. This result suggested that the experimental group's success may have been due largely to the participants' expectations, not to the treatment methods. Some early studies suggested the same conclusion about the effects of EMDR, because significant anxiety reduction was observed in clients who got a version of the treatment that did not involve eye movements or even focusing on traumatic memories (Cahill, Carrigan, & Frueh, 1999; Cusack &

Spates, 1999; Rosen, 1999; Seidler & Wagner, 2006; Servan-Schreiber et al., 2006). More recent evidence suggests that EMDR can outperform placebo treatments, but the fact that its effects are not significantly better than those of other, more established treatments has led many researchers to conclude that EMDR should not be a first-choice treatment for anxiety-related disorders (Bisson, 2007; Davidson & Parker, 2001; Goldstein et al., 2000; Lilienfeld & Arkowitz, 2007; Lohr et al., 2003; Taylor, 2004; van den Hout et al., 2011).

Experimenter Bias   Another possible confound is **experimenter bias**, the unintentional effect that researchers can exert on their results. Robert Rosenthal (1966) was one of the first to demonstrate the power of experimenter bias. His participants were laboratory assistants who were asked to place rats in a maze. Rosenthal told some of the assistants that their rats were "maze-bright." He told the others that their rats were "maze-dull." In truth, both groups of rats were randomly drawn from the same population and had equal maze-learning capabilities. Still, the so-called "maze-bright" animals learned the maze significantly faster than the "maze-dull" ones. Why? Rosenthal concluded that the result had nothing to do with the rats and everything to do with the experimenters. He suggested that the assistants' expectations about their rats' supposedly superior (or inferior) capabilities caused them to slightly alter their training and handling techniques. These slight differences may have speeded (or slowed) the animals' learning. Similarly, when giving different kinds of anxiety treatments to different groups of people, experimenters who believe that one treatment will be the best might do a slightly better job with that treatment. When the results are in, such unintentional differences might make the favored treatment look better than the rest.

To prevent experimenter bias from confounding results, experimenters often use a **double-blind design**. In this design, the participants *and* those giving the treatments are unaware of ("blind" to) who is receiving a placebo and they do not know what results are to be expected of the various treatments. Only researchers who have no direct contact with participants have this information, and they do not reveal it until the end of the experiment. Double-blind studies have not yet been conducted with EMDR, which is another reason for caution in drawing conclusions about this treatment.

In summary, experiments are vital tools for examining cause-and-effect relationships between independent and dependent variables, but they are also vulnerable to error. To maximize the value of their experiments, scientists try to eliminate as many confounding variables as possible. They then repeat their work to ensure consistent results and adjust their interpretation of those results to take into account the limitations or problems that remain.

Selecting Human Participants for Research

Visitors from another planet would be wildly mistaken if they tried to describe the typical earthling after meeting only Lady Gaga, Charlie Sheen, and a trained seal. Psychologists, too, can be led astray if the participants they encounter in their research are not typical of the people or animals about which they want to draw conclusions. Accordingly, one of the most vital steps in scientific research is the selection of participants, a process called **sampling**.

If they want to make accurate statements about the behavior and mental processes of any large group, psychologists must conduct **representative sampling** of participants whose characteristics mirror the rest of that group in terms of age, gender, ethnicity, cultural background, socioeconomic status, sexual orientation, disability, and the like. In theory, a representative sample can be drawn at random from the entire population of interest. For example, psychologists could choose a representative sample of Canadians, Democrats, or any other group. Doing this would require putting hundreds of thousands—perhaps millions—of names into a computer, running a program to randomly select participants, and then tracking them down to invite them to take part in the research. This method would result in truly **random sampling**, because every member of the population to be studied would have an equal chance of being chosen. (Any selection procedure that does not offer this equal chance is said to result in **biased sampling**.)

experimenter bias A confound that occurs when an experimenter unintentionally encourages participants to respond in a way that supports the hypothesis.

double-blind design A research design in which neither the experimenter nor the participants know who is in the experimental group and who is in the control group.

sampling The process of selecting participants who are members of the population that the researcher wishes to study.

representative sampling A sample of research participants chosen from a larger population such that their age, gender, ethnicity, and other characteristics are typical of that larger population.

random sampling A group of research participants selected from a population, each of whose members had an equal chance of being chosen.

biased sampling A group of research participants selected from a population, each of whose members did not have an equal chance of being chosen.

Selecting Research Participants

Suppose that you want to study people's willingness to help each other. You have developed a way of measuring helpfulness, but now you need a sample of people to test. Think about the steps necessary to select a truly random sample, then ask yourself how you might obtain a representative sample instead. Remember that although the names are similar, *random sampling* is not the same as *randomizing*. Random sampling helps ensure that the people studied are representative of some larger group. Randomizing is used to create equivalence among various groups in experiments.

LEARN by DOING

© Jim West/The Image Works

However, random sampling is usually too expensive and time-consuming to be practical, so psychologists often find their participants in more conveniently available populations. The populations from which these *convenience samples* are drawn depend to some extent on the researcher's budget. They might include, for example, the students enrolled in a particular course, the students enrolled on a local campus, the students who are willing to sign up for a study, or visitors to web sites or Facebook groups. Ideally, this selection process will yield a sample that fairly represents the population from which it was drawn. However, scientific researchers must keep in mind that their conclusions might apply only to their samples (Kraut et al., 2004). Therefore, psychologists often conduct additional studies to determine whether their initial conclusions apply to other groups (APA Office of Ethnic Minority Affairs, 2000; Case & Smith, 2000; Gray-Little & Hafdahl, 2000). For a recap of the strategies psychologists use in their research efforts, see "In Review: Methods of Psychological Research."

Methods of Psychological Research   IN REVIEW

Method	Features	Strengths	Pitfalls
Observational methods (e.g., Naturalistic observation)	Observation of human or animal behavior in the environment in which it typically occurs	Provides descriptive data about behavior presumably uncontaminated by outside influences	Observer bias and participant self-consciousness can distort results
Case studies	Intensive examination of the behavior and mental processes associated with a specific person or situation	Provide detailed descriptive analyses of new, complex, or rare phenomena	May not provide a representative picture of phenomena
Surveys	Standard sets of questions asked of a large number of participants	Gather large amounts of descriptive data relatively quickly and inexpensively	Sampling errors, poorly phrased questions, and response biases can distort results
Correlational studies	Examine relationships between research variables	Can test predictions, evaluate theories, and suggest new hypotheses	Cannot confirm causal relationships between variables
Experiments	Manipulation of an independent variable and measurement of its effects on a dependent variable	Can establish a cause-and-effect relationship between independent and dependent variables	Confounding variables may prevent valid conclusions

IN REVIEW QUESTIONS

1. The ___ method is most likely to use a double-blind design.

2. Research on a new treatment method is most likely to begin with ___.

3. Studying language by listening to people in public places is an example of ___ research.

LINKAGES

Psychological Research and Behavioral Genetics

Is behavior influenced by our genes or by our environment?
(a link to Biology and Behavior)

One of the most fascinating and difficult challenges in psychology is finding research methods that can help us understand the ways that genes and the environment—sometimes called *nature* and *nurture*—combine to influence behavior and mental processes (Moffitt, Caspi, & Rutter, 2005). Consider Mark and John, identical twins who were both adopted at birth because their parents were too poor to care for them. John grew up with a couple who made him feel secure and loved. Mark went from orphanage to foster home to hospital and, finally, back to his biological father's second wife. In other words, these genetically identical people encountered quite different environments. Yet, when they met for the first time at the age of twenty-four, they discovered similarities that went beyond physical appearance. They used the same aftershave, smoked the same brand of cigarettes, brushed with the same imported brand of toothpaste, and liked the same sports. They had joined the military within eight days of each other, and their IQ scores were nearly identical.

How did genetic influences operate in two different environments to result in such similarities? Exploring questions such as this has taken psychologists into the field of **behavioral genetics,** the study of how genes shape behavior. They have already discovered that most behavioral tendencies can be influenced by many different genes but also by many environmental events and conditions, both before and after birth. Accordingly, research in behavioral genetics explores the relative roles of genetic and environmental factors in creating differences among people in personality, mental ability, mental disorders, and other phenomena. It also seeks to identify specific genes that contribute to hereditary influences.

Some behavioral genetics research takes the form of experiments, mainly on the selective breeding of animals (Suomi, 2004). For example, Stephen Suomi (1999) identified monkeys whose genes predisposed them to react strongly or weakly to stress. He then mated strong reactors with other strong reactors and mated weak reactors with other weak reactors. Within a few generations, descendants of the strong-reactor pairs reacted much more strongly to stressors than did the descendants of the weak-reactor pairs. Selective-breeding studies must be interpreted with caution, though, because it is not specific behaviors that are inherited. What is inherited are differing sets of physical structures and capacities that make certain behaviors more or less likely. These behavioral tendencies are often very specific, and they can be altered by environmental factors (Grigorenko, 2002; Parker et al., 2006). For example, when Suomi (1999) placed young, highly stress-reactive monkeys with unrelated "foster mothers," he discovered that the foster mothers' own stress reactivity amplified or dampened the youngsters' genetically influenced behavioral tendencies. If stress-reactive monkeys were placed with stress-reactive foster mothers, they tended to be fearful of exploring their environments and had strong reactions to stressors. But if equally stress-reactive young monkeys had calm, supportive foster mothers, they appeared eager to explore their environments and were much less upset by stressors than their peers with stress-reactive foster mothers.

Research on behavioral genetics in humans must be interpreted with even greater care. Legal, moral, and ethical considerations obviously prohibit the selective breeding of people, so most research in human behavioral genetics depends on correlational studies, not controlled experiments. Traditionally, these usually take the form of family studies, twin studies, and adoption studies (Plomin et al., 2008).

In *family studies,* researchers look at whether close relatives are more likely than distant ones to show similarities in behavior and mental processes. If increasing similarity is associated with closer family ties, the similarities might be inherited. For example, data from family studies suggest a genetic basis for schizophrenia, as Figure 1.8 shows. Remember, though, that a correlation between variables does not guarantee that one is causing the other. The appearance of similar disorders in close relatives might be due to environmental factors instead of, or in addition to, genetic ones. After all, close relatives tend to share environments as well as genes. Family studies alone cannot establish the role of genetic factors in mental disorders or other characteristics.

behavioral genetics The study of how genes and environments interact to affect behavior and mental processes.

FIGURE 1.8
Family and Twin Studies of Schizophrenia

The risk of developing schizophrenia, a severe mental disorder, is highest for the siblings and children of patients with schizophrenia and lowest for those who are not genetically related to anyone with schizophrenia. Does this mean that schizophrenia is inherited? These results are consistent with that interpretation, but the question cannot be answered through family studies alone. Studies comparing identical and nonidentical twins suggest genetic influence, but even twin studies don't eliminate the role of environmental influences. Environmental factors, such as stressors that close relatives share, could also play important roles and may even contribute to genomic imprinting, as suggested by the epigenetic perspective discussed below (Crespi, 2008; Ivleva, Thaker, & Tamminga, 2008; Singh & O'Reilly, 2009; Tandon, Keshavan, & Nasrallah, 2008).

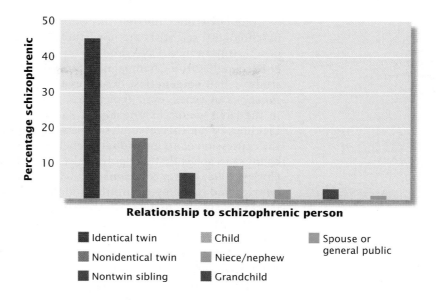

Legend:
- Identical twin
- Nonidentical twin
- Nontwin sibling
- Child
- Niece/nephew
- Grandchild
- Spouse or general public

y-axis: Percentage schizophrenic
x-axis: Relationship to schizophrenic person

Twins and Behavioral Genetics

Like other identical twins, each member of this pair has identical genes. Twin studies and adoption studies help reveal the interaction of genetic and environmental influences in human behavior and mental processes. Cases of identical twins who were separated at birth, yet have similar interests, personality traits, and mental abilities suggest that these characteristics are significantly influenced by genetic factors.

Twin studies explore the nature-nurture mix by comparing the similarities seen in identical twins with those of nonidentical pairs (Johnson et al., 2009). Twins usually share the same environment and may also be treated very much the same by parents and others. If identical twins (whose genes are the same) are more alike on some characteristics than nonidentical twins (whose genes are no more similar than those of other siblings), those characteristics may have a significant genetic component.

Adoption studies take advantage of cases in which babies are adopted very early in life. The logic of these studies is that if adopted children's characteristics are more like those of their biological parents than those of their adoptive parents, then genetics probably plays a clear role in those characteristics. In fact, the personalities of young adults who were adopted at birth do tend to be more like those of their biological parents than those of their adoptive parents. Adoption studies can be especially valuable when they focus on identical twins who, like Mark and John, were separated soon after birth. If identical twins show similar characteristics after years of living in very different environments, then the role of heredity in those characteristics is highlighted. Conversely, if identical twins show major differences after differential exposures, non-genetic factors might be more important (McGue, Osler, & Christensen, 2010). Adoption studies of intelligence tend to support the role of genetics in variations in mental ability, but they show the impact of environmental influences, too.

Remember that family, twin, and adoption studies can tell us about the relative roles of heredity and environment in creating differences among individuals, but they cannot determine the degree to which a *particular* person's behavior or characteristics are due to heredity or environment. The two factors are entwined too closely in each of us to be separated that way. In the future, though, behavioral genetics research will be shaped by the results of the Human Genome Project, which unlocked the genetic code contained in the DNA that makes each human being unique (International Human Genome Sequencing Consortium, 2001; Venter et al., 2001). This achievement has allowed behavioral geneticists and other scientists to begin pinpointing some of the many genes that contribute to individual differences in disorders such as autistic disorder, learning disabilities, hyperactivity, and Alzheimer's disease, as well as to the differences in personality and mental abilities that we see all around us (Plomin et al., 2008). Finding the DNA differences responsible for certain personal attributes and behaviors will eventually make it possible to understand exactly how heredity interacts with the environment as development unfolds. Analysis of DNA—collected by rubbing a cotton swab inside an individual's cheek—may someday be used not only in behavioral genetics research but also in clinics, where it will help psychologists more precisely diagnose clients' problems and choose the most appropriate treatments (Plomin et al., 2002).

But DNA does not tell the whole story of behavioral genetics. Biological and psychological scientists are now studying the complex interactions between people's genetic inheritance (DNA) and the environments in which their genes operate (Bollati & Baccarelli, 2010; Champagne, 2009; Champagne & Mashoodh, 2009). This field of study, called **epigenetics,** describes the ways that events within cells can alter the *functions* of genes, even though the genetic code itself—the sequence of chemicals in the DNA—remains unchanged (Gräff & Mansuy, 2008; Keverne & Curley, 2008; Lickliter, 2008). This research suggests that the cellular environment can not only affect the expression of an individual's genetic characteristics but may also create structural changes in genes that can potentially be passed on to future generations (Keverne & Curley, 2008; Lamm & Jablonka, 2008; Lickliter, 2008). Epigenetic effects—which can be triggered by many environmental influences, including diseases and stress—have been linked to individual differences in learning, memory, and brain development (Gräff & Mansuy, 2008; Keverne & Curley, 2008; Lickliter, 2008), and they may also play a role in the appearance of cognitive disorders such as Alzheimer's disease, mental disorders such as schizophrenia and depression, illnesses such as cancer, and health problems such as obesity (Gräff & Mansuy, 2008; Keverne & Curley, 2008; Pidsley & Mill, 2011). ● ● ● ●

Statistical Analysis of Research Results

What does it mean when scientists announce that a research finding is "significant"?

Observational methods, case studies, surveys, correlational studies, and experiments generate mountains of numbers—known as **data**—that represent research results and provide the basis for drawing conclusions about them (Keselman et al., 2004). These data might represent scores on intelligence tests, levels of stress hormones in blood samples, tiny differences in the time required to detect visual signals, ratings of people's personality traits, or whatever else a psychologist might be studying. Like other scientists, psychologists use descriptive and inferential *statistics* to summarize their data and interpret what they mean.

As the name implies, *descriptive statistics* are used to describe a set of data. For example, the performance of a group of students on a math test could be described statistically by the average score of the group. The difference between the performance of men and women could be described by the size of the difference between the average scores for each sex. And, as mentioned earlier, when psychologists want to describe the relationship between two variables, they use a descriptive statistic called the correlation coefficient.

Inferential statistics are mathematical procedures that help psychologists make inferences—that is, draw conclusions from their data and make assumptions about the meaning of results. Suppose, for example, that a group of trauma victims scored an average of ten points lower on an anxiety test after being treated with EMDR and that the scores of victims in a no-treatment control group dropped by an average of seven points. Does the three-point difference between these two groups reflect the impact of EMDR, or could it have been caused by random factors that made EMDR appear more powerful than it actually is? Inferential statistics allow researchers to estimate the likelihood that the difference between the average scores of the two groups reflects chance factors rather than the impact of the differing treatment they received. Other inferential statistics can help psychologists decide whether a correlation between two variables is large enough to suggest an important underlying relationship or whether it is just a fluke.

When inferential statistics reveal that a correlation coefficient or the difference between groups is larger than what would be expected by chance alone, the results are said to have reached **statistical significance.** Statistical significance alone does not guarantee final "proof," but scientists do tend to pay more attention to correlations or other research findings that are statistically significant, especially when those results have been repeated,

epigenetics The study of potentially inheritable changes in gene expression that are caused by environmental factors that do not alter a cell's DNA.

data Numbers that represent research findings and provide the basis for conclusions.

statistical significance Referring to a correlation or a difference between two groups that is larger than would be expected by chance.

or *replicated,* in separate studies. When thinking critically about research, then, part of the process of evaluating evidence about hypotheses is to ask whether a researcher's results are statistically significant and repeatable. (For more details on descriptive and inferential statistics, see the "Statistics in Psychological Research" appendix).

Ethical Guidelines for Psychologists

Do psychologists deceive people when they do research?

Some years ago, newspaper headlines claimed that hair dye causes cancer. Hairdressers were alarmed at first, then angry. The information given to the public was less than accurate. Rats—not humans—had been used in the research, and the animals developed cancer only after drinking the hair dye! Later research showed that using hair dye does not significantly increase people's cancer risk (Takkouche, Etminan, & Montes-Martinez, 2005).

Splashy headlines sell newspapers and attract advertisers, but psychological scientists have an ethical obligation not to manipulate, distort, or sensationalize their research results. The obligation to analyze and report research fairly and accurately is just one of the ethical standards that guide psychologists. Preserving the welfare and dignity of their research participants is another. So although researchers *could* measure anxiety by putting a loaded gun to people's heads or study marital conflicts by telling one partner that the other has been unfaithful, those methods could be harmful and are therefore unethical.

Whatever the research topic, psychologists' first priority is to investigate it in accordance with the highest ethical standards. They must find ways to protect their participants from harm while still gathering data that will have potential benefits for everyone. To measure anxiety, for example, a psychologist might ask people to enter a situation that is anxiety provoking but not traumatic (for example, approaching a feared animal or sitting in a dark room). And research on marital conflict usually involves observing couples as they discuss controversial issues in their relationship.

Psychologists take very seriously the obligation to minimize any immediate discomfort or risk for research participants as well as the need to protect those participants from long-term harm. They are careful to inform prospective participants about every aspect of the study that might influence their decision to participate, and they ensure that each person's involvement is voluntary. But what if the purpose of the study is to measure people's emotional reactions to being insulted? Participants might not react normally if they know ahead of time that an "insult" will be part of the experiment. When deception is necessary to create certain experimental conditions, ethical standards require the researcher to "debrief" participants as soon as the study is over by revealing all relevant information about the research and correcting any misconceptions it created.

Government regulations in the United States, Canada, and many other countries require that any research involving human participants must be approved by an Institutional Review Board (IRB) whose members have no connection with the research. If a proposed study is likely to create risks or discomfort for participants, IRB members weigh the potential benefits of the work in terms of knowledge and human welfare against any potential harm.

The obligation to protect participants' welfare also extends to animals, which are used in a small percentage of psychological research projects (American Psychological Association Committee on Animal Research and Ethics, 2009). Psychologists study animals partly because their behavior is interesting and partly because research with animals can provide information that would be impossible or unethical to collect from humans. For example, researchers can randomly assign animals to live alone and then look at how these conditions affect later social interactions. The same thing could not ethically be done with people, but animal studies offer clues about how social isolation might affect humans (see the chapter on motivation and emotion).

Caring For Research Animals
Psychologists are careful to protect the welfare of animal participants in research. They don't wish to see animals suffer. And undue stress on research animals can create reactions that can act as confounds. For example, in a study of how learning is affected by food rewards, researchers could starve animals to make them hungry enough to want the rewards. But this would introduce discomfort, which would make it impossible to separate the effects of the reward from the effects of starvation.

© Will & Deni McIntyre/Photo Researchers, Inc.

Contrary to the claims of some animal-rights activists, animals used in psychological research are not routinely subjected to extreme pain, starvation, or other inhumane conditions. Even in the small proportion of studies that require the use of electric shock, the discomfort created is mild, brief, and not harmful. High standards for the care and treatment of animal participants are outlined in the Animal Welfare Act, the National Institutes of Health's *Guide for the Care and Use of Laboratory Animals,* the National Institute of Mental Health's *Methods and Welfare Considerations in Behavioral Research with Animals,* the American Psychological Association's *Principles on Animal Use,* and other laws and regulations (APA Committee on Animal Research and Ethics, 2009). In those relatively rare studies that require animals to undergo short-lived pain or other forms of moderate stress, legal and ethical standards require that funding agencies—as well as local committees charged with monitoring animal research—first determine that the discomfort is justified by the expected benefits to human welfare.

The responsibility for conducting research in the most humane fashion is one aspect of the *Ethical Principles of Psychologists and Code of Conduct* developed by the American Psychological Association (2002b). The main purpose of these standards is to protect and promote the welfare of society and those with whom psychologists work. For example, as teachers, psychologists should give students complete, accurate, and up-to-date coverage of each topic, not a narrow and biased point of view. Further, psychologists should perform only those services and use only those techniques for which they are adequately trained. Psychologists should not reveal information obtained from clients or research participants except in the most unusual of circumstances (see the chapter on treatment of psychological disorders). Finally, they should avoid situations in which a conflict of interest might impair their judgment or harm someone else. They should not, for example, have sexual relations with their clients, students, or employees.

Despite these guidelines, doubt and controversy arise in some cases about whether a proposed experiment or a particular practice, such as deceiving participants, is ethical. The American Psychological Association has published a two-volume handbook (Knapp, 2011a, b) and a casebook (Campbell et al., 2009) to help psychologists resolve such issues. The ethical principles themselves must continually be updated to deal with complex new questions—such as how to protect the confidentiality of e-mail communications—that psychologists face in their ever-expanding range of work (American Psychological Association, 2002b; Hays, 2006; Pipes, Holstein, & Aguirre, 2005; Warmerdam et al., 2010).

Summary

The World of Psychology: An Overview

What is psychology, and how did it grow? **Psychology** is the science that seeks to understand behavior and mental processes. The broad concept of "behavior and mental processes" encompasses virtually all aspects of what it means to be human. Psychologists study a wide variety of topics, from the activity of individual nerve cells and the way we sense and perceive things, to the way we think, make decisions, and experience emotion, to the way people cooperate or compete with each other.

Most psychologists work in particular subfields within the discipline. For example, **cognitive psychologists** focus on basic psychological processes such as learning, memory, and perception. **Biological psychologists** explore the influence of brain chemistry and other physiological factors on behavior and mental processes. **Personality psychologists** focus on characteristics that set people apart from one another. **Developmental psychologists** try to understand the development of behavior and mental processes over a lifetime. **Quantitative psychologists** develop methods for statistical analysis of data. **Clinical** and **counseling psychologists** provide direct service to troubled people and conduct research on abnormal behavior. **Community psychologists** work to prevent mental disorders and extend mental health services to those who need it. **Educational psychologists** conduct and apply research on teaching and learning, whereas **school psychologists** specialize in assessing and alleviating children's academic problems. **Social psychologists** examine questions regarding how people influence one another. **Industrial and organizational psychologists** conduct research on topics such as increasing the motivation of employees and helping companies select the best new workers. **Forensic psychologists** conduct and apply psychological research in legal settings. **Health psychologists, sport psychologists, engineering psychologists,** and **environmental psychologists** work in some of psychology's many other subfields. Psychology's subfields often overlap, and psychologists often work in more than one subfield, sharing knowledge with colleagues in other subfields and contributing to knowledge in other disciplines. Psychology's roots are in philosophy, especially in **empiricism.** The modern science of psychology began to emerge in the late nineteenth century as scientists in Germany and North America established laboratories to conduct psychological research. In Germany, Wundt explored the building blocks of **consciousness;** Gestalt psychologists there later studied it as a whole. In Vienna, Freud explored the unconscious. At about the same time in the United States, James applied Darwin's theory of evolution to the exploration of human behavior. In the early twentieth century, Watson argued that to be truly scientific, psychologists should focus only on observable behavior. He founded behaviorism, which dominated psychology for decades. Today, consciousness—in the form of cognitive processes—is being studied intensively once again.

Approaches to the Science of Psychology

Why don't all psychologists explain behavior in the same way? Psychologists differ in their approaches to psychology—that is, in the assumptions, questions, and methods they believe will be most helpful in their work. Psychologists who adopt a **biological approach** examine how physiological factors shape behavior and mental processes. Darwin's theory helped stimulate the **evolutionary approach,** which emphasizes the inherited, adaptive aspects of behavior and mental processes. The **psychodynamic approach** sees behavior and mental processes as a struggle to resolve conflicts between impulses and the demands made by society to control those impulses. Psychologists who take the **behavioral approach** consider behavior to be determined primarily by learning based on experiences with rewards and punishments. The **cognitive approach** assumes that behavior can be understood through analysis of the mental processes that underlie it. The **humanistic approach** views behavior as controlled by people's decisions about their lives, based on their perceptions of the world.

Human Diversity and Psychology

How does your cultural background influence your behavior? Most of the prominent figures in psychology's history were white males, but women and members of ethnic minorities made important contributions from the start, and they continue to do so. Psychologists increasingly take into account the influence of **culture** and other **sociocultural factors** such as gender and ethnicity in shaping human behavior and mental processes.

Thinking Critically about Psychology (or Anything Else)

How can critical thinking save you money? **Critical thinking** is the process of assessing claims and making judgments on the basis of well-supported evidence. This process involves asking five questions: What am I being asked to believe or accept? Is evidence available to support the claim? Can that evidence be interpreted another way? What evidence would help to evaluate the alternatives? What conclusions are most reasonable?

Often, questions about psychological phenomena are phrased in terms of *hypotheses* about *variables* that are specified by *operational definitions.* Evidence for hypotheses must be evaluated for *statistical reliability* and *statistical validity.* After gathering evidence, scientists may organize their findings into a *theory,* a set of statements designed to explain certain phenomena. Theories must be subjected to careful evaluation.

Research Methods in Psychology

How do psychologists learn about people?

Research in psychology, as in other sciences, focuses on four main goals: description, prediction, control, and explanation. Psychologists have found several research methods especially useful in gathering the evidence needed to reach each of these goals. *Observational methods,* such as *naturalistic observation,* entail watching without interfering as behavior occurs in the natural environment. *Case studies* are intensive examinations of a particular individual, group, or situation. *Surveys* ask questions through interviews or questionnaires about behavior, attitudes, beliefs, opinions, and intentions.

Correlational studies examine the *correlation* (the relationship) between variables in order to describe data, test predictions, evaluate theories, and suggest hypotheses. In *experiments,* researchers manipulate an *independent variable* and observe the effect of that manipulation on a *dependent variable.* Participants who receive experimental treatment are in the *experimental group.* Participants in comparison conditions are in *control groups.* Experiments can reveal cause-and-effect relationships between variables, but only if researchers use *randomizing* and other strategies (such as *placebo* conditions and a *double-blind design*) to avoid being misled by *random variables, experimenter bias,* and other *confounds.*

Psychologists' research can be limited if their *sampling* procedures don't use *representative sampling* of the population they want to study and about which they want to draw conclusions. Anything other than truly *random sampling* is said to be *biased sampling* of participants. In most cases, psychologists try to select a *representative sample* of the populations that are available to them.

Statistical Analysis of Research Results

What does it mean when scientists announce that a research finding is "significant"?

Psychologists use descriptive and inferential statistical analyses to summarize and analyze *data,* which are the numbers that represent research findings and provide the basis for conclusions.

When a correlation coefficient, a difference between groups, or some other research finding is larger than would be expected by chance alone, it is said to have reached *statistical significance.*

Ethical Guidelines for Psychologists

Do psychologists deceive people when they do research?

Ethical guidelines promote the protection of human and animal participants in psychological research and set the highest standards for behavior in all other aspects of psychologists' professional lives.

LEARN by DOING

Put It in Writing

Choose one or two recent newspaper, magazine, or Internet articles describing a research study in psychology and then, based on the article alone, try to answer the five critical thinking questions we described earlier (*What am I being asked to believe or accept? Is evidence available to support the claim? Can that evidence be interpreted another way? What evidence would help to evaluate the alternatives? and What conclusions are most reasonable?*). When you have finished, write a

paragraph or two describing how well you think the popular media cover the results of scientific research in psychology and how that coverage could be improved.

Personal Learning Activity

Design an experiment on a hypothesis of your choice. First, state your hypothesis as specifically as possible, being sure to include operational definitions of the independent and dependent variables. Then tell how and where you'll

get your research participants, what the experimental and control groups will experience, and what all your research procedures will be. For example, if your hypothesis is that rock music played during studying improves students' memory for the material, then you should decide what you mean by "rock music" and "improved memory," what the experimental and control groups will hear while studying, what they will study, and how you will measure the students' memory for what they learned.

Review of Key Terms ●

Can you define each of the key terms in the chapter? Check your definitions against those on the pages shown in parentheses in the following list or in the Glossary at the end of the book.

behavioral approach (p. 15)
behavioral genetics (p. 34)
biased sampling (p. 32)
biological approach (p. 14)
biological psychologists (p. 4)
case studies (p. 25)
clinical, counseling, and community
  psychologists (p. 5)
cognitive approach (p. 15)
cognitive psychologists (p. 3)
confound (p. 31)
consciousness (p. 10)
control group (p. 29)
correlation (p. 26)
correlational studies (p. 26)
critical thinking (p. 20)
culture (p. 17)

data (p. 36)
dependent variable (p. 28)
developmental psychologists (p. 4)
double-blind design (p. 32)
educational psychologists (p. 5)
empiricism (p. 9)
engineering psychologists (p. 6)
environmental psychologists (p. 6)
epigenetics (p. 36)
evolutionary approach (p. 14)
experiment (p. 28)
experimental group (p. 29)
experimenter bias (p. 32)
forensic psychologists (p. 6)
health psychologists (p. 6)
humanistic approach (p. 16)
hypothesis (p. 23)
independent variable (p. 28)
industrial and organizational
  psychologists (p. 6)
naturalistic observation (p. 24)
observational methods (p. 24)

operational definitions (p. 23)
personality psychologists (p. 4)
placebo (p. 31)
positive psychology (p. 3)
psychodynamic approach (p. 15)
psychology (p. 3)
quantitative psychologists (p. 4)
randomizing (p. 31)
random sampling (p. 32)
random variables (p. 31)
representative sampling (p. 32)
sampling (p. 32)
school psychologists (p. 5)
social psychologists (p. 5)
sociocultural factors (p. 17)
sport psychologists (p. 6)
statistical reliability (p. 23)
statistical significance (p. 36)
statistical validity (p. 23)
surveys (p. 26)
theory (p. 23)
variables (p. 23)

Test Your Knowledge ●

Select the best answer for each of the following questions. Then check your responses against the Answer Key at the end of the book.

1. The first research laboratory in psychology was established to study ____.
   a. consciousness
   b. the unconscious
   c. perceptual processes
   d. the collective unconscious

2. Dr. Gauzz believes that low-income families who live in crowded conditions are more likely to need mental health services. Therefore, she works to eliminate overcrowded high-rises for low-income families. Dr. Gauzz is most likely a(n) ____ psychologist.
   a. developmental
   b. industrial and organizational
   c. community
   d. engineering

3. Dr. Hemmings believes that human behavior is influenced by genetic inheritance, unconscious motivations, and environmental influences. Dr. Hemmings uses a(n) ____ approach.
   a. evolutionary
   b. eclectic
   c. humanistic
   d. behavioral

4. Dr. Foreman studies what teachers actually do when they are teaching students to read. Dr. Foreman is most likely a(n) ____ psychologist.
   a. cognitive
   b. school
   c. educational
   d. community

5. Larry says that people act the way they have learned to act. He believes that if others stop rewarding a person's annoying behavior, that behavior will decrease. Larry most likely takes a(n) ____ approach to psychology.
   a. behavioral
   b. cognitive
   c. evolutionary
   d. humanistic

6. Marika just won a college scholarship because of her outstanding grades. If she is from a collectivist culture, she is most likely to say:
   a. "I've worked very hard for this honor and I appreciate the vote of confidence."
   b. "I had some tough times when I didn't think I would succeed, but this has made it all worthwhile."
   c. "I could not have won this award without the help of my teachers and family."
   d. "I am so happy that the committee recognized my hard work and perseverance and is rewarding it with this scholarship."

7. Dr. Rose, a cross-cultural psychologist, is most likely to find which behavior to be similar in all of the groups she studies?
   a. Striving for achievement
   b. Rules governing social behavior
   c. Styles of communication
   d. Recognition of a smile

8. You are watching an infomercial that claims that if you drink liquefied seaweed twice a day, you will lose ten pounds a month. As a wise consumer who knows the five critical thinking questions listed in this chapter, you would FIRST say to yourself:
   a. "I don't know whether the person making the claim about the weight-loss effects of seaweed is a doctor or not."
   b. "The only evidence they present in support of their claim is one woman's personal experience."
   c. "I'll bet you also have to exercise to lose the ten pounds."
   d. "They are asking me to believe that I can lose ten pounds a month by drinking seaweed."

9. Dr. Lucas is interested in the effect of color on people's moods. She has participants complete a mood survey in either a bright red room or a stark white one.
   A participant's score on the mood survey is her ____.
   a. descriptive statistic
   b. random variable
   c. independent variable
   d. operational definition of mood

10. Case studies are used to ____.
    a. avoid a placebo effect
    b. determine the effects of an independent variable
    c. collect descriptive data
    d. provide control in an experiment

11. Before using survey results to support a hypothesis, we must be sure about which of the following?
    a. The questions are properly worded.
    b. The sample used is representative of the population of interest.
    c. The responses are not strongly biased by efforts to appear socially acceptable.
    d. All of the above.

12. When Dr. Beren compares the performance of his experimental group and his control group, he finds the difference in their scores to be statistically significant. This means that ____.
    a. the difference is larger than would be expected by chance
    b. he used descriptive statistics
    c. his results were confounded by random variables
    d. he used a double-blind method

13. Dr. Daneli believes that memory is aided by an increase in a brain chemical called serotonin. To avoid the possibility that experimenter bias might confound the results of an experiment aimed at testing this hypothesis, she should use a(n) ____ design.
    a. operational
    b. naturalistic

c. random
d. double-blind

14. In Dr. Daneli's experiment, Group A receives serotonin before taking a memory test, whereas Group B takes the same test without receiving serotonin. In this experiment, performance on the memory test is the ____ variable.
    a. dependent
    b. independent
    c. control
    d. random

15. Angelica designed an experiment to test the effects of praise on the sharing behavior of children. Children in Group A will be praised after they share; children in Group B will only be observed. Group A is the ____ group.
    a. control
    b. experimental
    c. operational
    d. random

16. José wants to know whether growing up in an abusive family causes children to become physically violent. Which of the following research methods would create the greatest ethical problems in trying to study this question scientifically?
    a. case studies
    b. experiments
    c. observations
    d. surveys

17. Choose the strongest correlation coefficient.
    a. +.75
    b. −.99
    c. +.01
    d. −.01

18. A correlation coefficient can tell us all of the following except the ____ of a relationship between two variables.
    a. strength
    b. direction
    c. existence
    d. cause

19. Your psychology professor asks you to learn about the smoking habits of all students on your campus. The most practical yet scientific way to get participants for your study would be to find a ____.
    a. random sample of all students
    b. random sample of smokers
    c. representative sample of all students
    d. representative sample of all nonsmokers

20. Why do psychologists follow ethical guidelines?
    a. Psychologists would not want the cost of participating in an experiment to be too high in comparison with the information to be gained.
    b. The American Psychological Association has set standards for psychologists to follow when conducting research and treating clients.
    c. Stress and pain could act as confounding variables in an experiment.
    d. All of the above.

Media Resources ....

Now that you have finished reading this chapter, how about exploring some of the ideas and information that you found most interesting?

Go to **CengageBrain.com** to access Psychology CourseMate, where you will find an interactive eBook, glossaries, flashcards, quizzes, videos, Virtual Psychology Labs, and more.

If your professor has assigned Aplia:

1. Sign in to your account.
2. Complete the corresponding exercises as required by your professor.
3. When finished, click "Grade It Now" to see which areas you have mastered, which areas need more work, and detailed explanations of every answer.

Biology and Behavior

© Henrik Jonsson/iStockphoto

Preview

Before you read the next sentence, close your eyes and touch your nose. This is easy, but it is not simple. To do it, your brain used specific nerves to tell your eyelids to close. It used other nerves to tell your hand to extend a finger and then sent a series of messages that moved your arm in just the right direction until it received a message that your finger and your nose were in contact. Everything you do—including how you feel and think—is based on biological activity in your body and in your brain. This chapter describes that activity, beginning with a basic biological unit of the body, a specialized cell called the *neuron*. Collections of neurons form the systems that receive information from our senses, process that information, and biochemically translate it into behavior, thoughts, and emotions.

Biological factors are intimately related to *all* behavior and mental processes. Understanding these relationships takes us into the realm of **biological psychology**—the study of cells, genes, and organs of the body and the physical and chemical changes involved in behavior and mental processes.

Studying the biology of behavior and mental processes also involves exploring the environment's role in influencing those processes. You will see later, for example, that the experiences we have in the environment can change the chemistry and even the structure of our brains. Let's begin to consider in more detail the relationship between your body and your mind, between your brain and your behavior.

Two primary systems—the nervous system and the endocrine system—direct the activities of the body. The nervous system receives information, sends messages from one part of the body to another, and begins actions. The endocrine (pronounced "END-oh-krin") system regulates internal activity of the body with glands that secrete chemicals, called *hormones*, into the bloodstream. Hormones control energy consumption, reactions to stress, sexual functioning, and the like. These are the basic pieces of the puzzle of the body. Putting the pieces together is the next step in understanding the biology of our complex behavior. ●

Cells of the Nervous System

What are neurons, and what do they do?

The **nervous system** is a vast network of cells that tells you what is going on inside and outside your body and allows you to respond appropriately. For example, if you are jabbed with a pin, your nervous system gets the message and immediately causes you to flinch. But the nervous system can do far more than detect information and make responses. When information about the world reaches the brain, that information is *processed*—it is combined with information about past experiences and current wants and needs—to allow you to make a decision about how to respond. Our exploration of the nervous system begins at the "bottom," with a description of its individual cells. Later we consider how these cells are organized to form the structures of the human nervous system.

Neurons

The nervous system is an information-processing system with three functions: input, processing, and output (see Figure 2.1). These functions are possible partly because the nervous system is made up of cells that communicate with each other. Two major types of cells, neurons and glial cells, allow the nervous system to carry out its complex signaling tasks efficiently. The specialized cells that send and receive signals are called **neurons.**

biological psychology The study of physical and chemical changes involved in behavior and mental processes.

nervous system A network of billions of cells that detects what is going on inside or outside the body and guides appropriate responses.

neurons Specialized cells of the nervous system that send and receive messages.

FIGURE 2.1

Three Functions of the Nervous System

The nervous system's three main functions are to receive information (input), to integrate that information with past experiences (processing), and to guide actions (output). When the alarm clock goes off, this person's nervous system, like yours, gets the message, recognizes what it means, and takes action—by getting out of bed or perhaps hitting the snooze button.

1. Input
The sound of the alarm clock is conveyed to your brain by your ears.

2. Processing
Your brain knows from past experience that it is time to get up.

3. Output
Your brain directs your arm and hand muscles to reach out and shut off the alarm clock.

Paul Maguire/Shutterstock

Most of our discussion of brain cells concerns neurons, but glial cells are important, too. *Glial* means "glue," and scientists had long believed that glial cells did no more than hold neurons together. We now know, however, that **glial cells** also help neurons communicate by directing their growth, keeping their chemical environment stable, providing energy, adjusting blood flow, pruning connections among neurons, and secreting chemicals to help repair damage (Paolicelli et al., 2011; Petzold & Murthy, 2011). Further, glial cells are capable of many of the functions of neurons, including releasing chemicals that influence neurons, responding to chemicals from neurons, and changing in response to experience (Barres, 2008; Zonouzi et al., 2011). Without glial cells, neurons could not function, and malfunctions in glial cells may play a role in problems ranging from recurring pain to depression and other mental disorders (Miller, 2005a).

Every cell in the body has a skin, called an *outer membrane;* a cell body that (with the exception of red blood cells) contains a core called the *nucleus;* and tiny "engines," called *mitochondria* (pronounced "my-toh-CON-dree-uh"). Neurons are no different. A neuron's outer membrane acts like a screen, letting some substances pass in and out while blocking others. In the neuron's cell body, the nucleus (or center) carries genetic information that tells the cell what to do. And neurons' mitochondria turn oxygen and glucose into energy. This process is especially vital to brain cells, because although the brain accounts for only 2 percent of the body's weight, it uses more than 20 percent of the body's oxygen. All of this energy is required because brain cells transmit signals among themselves to an even greater extent than do cells in the rest of the body.

Neurons have special structural and chemical features that allow them to communicate with each other. While neurons come in many shapes and sizes, they all

glial cells Nervous system cells that hold neurons together and help them communicate with each other.

FIGURE 2.2
The Neuron
Part A shows fibers extending outward from the cell body of a neuron, which is a nervous system cell. These fibers are called *axons* and *dendrites*. Part B shows an enlarged drawing of the neuron's cell body. The cell body of a neuron includes an outer membrane, a nucleus, and mitochondria.

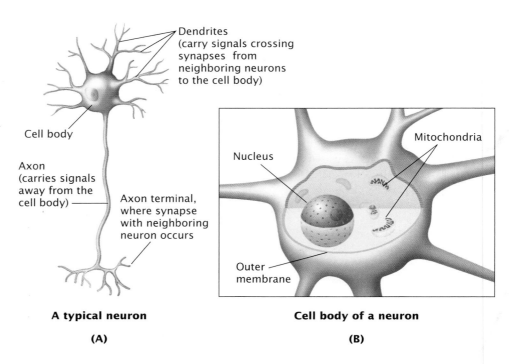

A typical neuron

(A)

Cell body of a neuron

(B)

have long, thin fibers that reach outward from the cell body like arms (see Part A in Figure 2.2). Communication between the cells can occur when these fibers are close to other neurons. The interweaving of these fibers with fibers from other neurons allows each neuron to be close to thousands or even hundreds of thousands of other neurons.

Fibers extending from the cell body are called axons and dendrites. As shown in Figure 2.2, each neuron generally has only one **axon,** whose function is to carry signals away from the cell body. An axon may have many branches along its stem, much like a tree. Axons can be short or long. In the brain, they may extend no more than a fraction of an inch, but the axon from your big toe to your spine is more than three feet long! **Dendrites** are the fibers that receive signals from the axons of other neurons and carry those signals to the cell body. As you can see in Figure 2.2, a neuron can have many dendrites, each of which usually has many branches. Remember that *axons* carry signals *away* from the cell body, and *dendrites detect* those signals.

Action Potentials

The communication signal between neurons begins with an electrochemical pulse called an **action potential,** which shoots down the axon. This is an "all-or-nothing" affair: The cell either fires its action potential at full strength or it does not fire at all. Once a cell has fired, a very short recovery time called the **refractory period** follows, during which the cell cannot fire again. Even so, neurons are able to fire as often as 1,000 times per second. The speed of an action potential ranges from about 5 to 260 miles per hour and depends on the thickness or diameter of the axon—larger ones are faster—and on the presence of myelin (pronounced "MY-a-lin"). *Myelin* is a fatty substance that wraps around some axons like a stocking and speeds up action potentials. When a neuron fires, dendrites in the next cell detect the message and send the signal to their cell body.

Synapses and Communication between Neurons

How do the dendrites detect a signal from another neuron? As shown in Figure 2.3, it works a little like the game of tag you played as a child. In this neural communication tag game, however, one neuron "sends" a tag without actually touching the next neuron. When an action potential reaches the ends of an axon's branches, it stimulates the release

axon A fiber that carries signals away from the cell body.

dendrites Fibers that receive signals from the axons of other neurons.

action potential The electrochemical impulse or message that is sent down an axon and stimulates the release of a neurotransmitter.

refractory period A short recovery time after cell firing, during which the cell cannot fire again.

1. An *action potential* shoots down the *axon*, away from the cell body.

2. A *neurotransmitter* is released into the *synapse*, where the *dendrites* of neighboring neurons detect it. See enlarged area.

3. If there is a receptor for this neurotransmitter on the dendrites, the neurotransmitter and receptor bind, creating an electrochemical signal.

4. If that signal is strong enough, it spreads down the dendrites and across the cell body of the next neuron and begins another action potential.

FIGURE 2.3

Communication between Neurons
When stimulation of a neuron reaches a certain level, the neuron fires, sending an action potential shooting to the end of its axon and triggering the release of a neurotransmitter into the synapse. This stimulates neighboring neurons and may cause them to fire their own action potentials.

neurotransmitter A chemical that transfers messages across synapses.

synapse The tiny gap between the axon of one neuron and the dendrites of another, across which they communicate.

of a **neurotransmitter.** Neurotransmitters are chemicals that act as messengers between neurons. They're stored in little "bags" called *vesicles* (pronounced "VESS-ick-els"). Neurotransmitters flow across a tiny gap, less than a millionth of an inch wide, which separates the axon of one neuron and the dendrites of another. This is the *synaptic gap,* often referred to simply as the **synapse** (see Figure 2.4). When they reach the dendrite of the next cell, neurotransmitters chemically fit, or bind, to proteins called *receptors.* Like a key fitting into the right lock, a neurotransmitter snugly binds to its own receptors but not to receptors for other neurotransmitters. Each receptor "recognizes" only one type of neurotransmitter. In the dendrite, this binding creates an electrochemical signal that is called a *postsynaptic potential* because it occurs *after* the neurotransmitter has crossed the synapse. The postsynaptic potential, in turn, passes the message to the cell body for the signaling process to continue.

Generally, more than one message must go to a cell to make it fire. Signals from groups of cells often arrive at the same postsynaptic cell at about the same time. The messages from these many cells may conflict with one another. Some messages tell the cell to fire, whereas others tell the cell not to fire. Whether it actually does fire depends on which kinds of signals are most numerous. So, axons, neurotransmitters, synapses, and dendrites allow cells of the nervous system to communicate. If these components are damaged or disordered, however, serious problems can result. For example, spinal cord injuries may cut the neural communication lines that had once allowed people to feel and move their bodies. And when the myelin surrounding some axons is destroyed by the brain disorder known as *multiple sclerosis (MS),* the result can be disruption of vision, speech, balance, and other important functions.

Most research on neural communication has focused on the chemicals that neurons respond to and release. However, we now know that some neurons "talk" to each other through direct electrical communication at specialized contact points called

FIGURE 2.4
A Synapse
This photograph taken with an electron microscope shows part of a synapse between neurons, magnified 50,000 times. The end of one neuron's axon is shaded green; the green ovals are mitochondria. The red spots are neurotransmitter-containing vesicles. The synapse itself appears as the narrow gap between the first cell's axon and the dendrite of the second cell, which is shaded blue.

gap junctions, or *electrical synapses*. At these gap junctions, neurons can transfer either neurotransmitters or electrical signals. These electrical synapses allow clusters of neurons to fire together, and the strength of their activity can change in response to experience (Haas, Zavala, & Landiesman, 2011). As a result, electrical synapses may contribute to the process of learning. They may also be involved in epilepsy, a brain disorder in which large groups of neurons fire together and produce seizures (Dere & Zlomuzica, 2012).

Neurons, Neurotransmitters, and Receptors   IN REVIEW

Part	Function	Type of Signal Carried
Axon	Carries signals away from the cell body	The action potential, an all-or-nothing electrochemical signal that shoots down the axon to vesicles at the tip of the axon, releasing neurotransmitters
Dendrite	Detects and carries signals to the cell body	The postsynaptic potential, an electrochemical signal moving toward the cell body
Synapse	An area for the transfer of signals between neurons, usually between axon and dendrite	Chemicals that cross the synapse and reach receptors on another cell or electrical impulses transferred from one cell to another
Neurotransmitter	A chemical released by one cell that binds to the receptors on another cell	A chemical message telling the next cell to fire or not to fire its own action potential
Receptor	Proteins on the cell membrane that receive chemical signals	Recognizes certain neurotransmitters, allowing it to begin a postsynaptic potential in the dendrite

IN REVIEW QUESTIONS

1. In most cases, when one neuron communicates with another, a ___ crosses the ___ between them.
2. The nervous system's main functions are to ___, ___, and ___ information.
3. The two main types of cells in the nervous system are ___ and ___.

Organization of the Nervous System

Impressive as individual neurons are (see "In Review: Neurons, Neurotransmitters, and Receptors"), we can best understand their functions by looking at how they operate in groups called **neural networks.** The billions of neurons that make up the nervous system are organized into two main parts—the *central nervous system* and the *peripheral nervous system* (see Figure 2.5). These systems work together closely to coordinate behavior and mental processes, as we'll describe later on. The **central nervous system (CNS)** consists of the brain and spinal cord, which are encased in bone for protection. Like the chief executive officer in a company, the CNS receives information, processes it, and determines what actions should result (Banich, 2009). The **peripheral nervous system (PNS)** extends throughout the body and, like an e-mail or texting service, relays information to and from the brain.

neural networks Neurons that operate together to perform complex functions.

central nervous system (CNS) The brain and spinal cord.

peripheral nervous system (PNS) The part of the nervous system that sends messages to and from the central nervous system.

The Peripheral Nervous System: Keeping in Touch with the World

How do sights and sounds reach my brain?

The peripheral nervous system sends sensory information from the eyes, ears, and other sense organs to the CNS. The PNS also carries messages from the brain and spinal cord to the muscles, glands, and other parts of the body. Unlike the CNS, it is not protected by bone. To accomplish its relay tasks, the peripheral nervous system has two subsystems— the somatic nervous system and the autonomic nervous system.

FIGURE 2.5

Organization of the Nervous System

The brain and spinal cord make up the bone-encased central nervous system (CNS), the body's central information processor, decision maker, and director of actions. The peripheral nervous system (PNS), which is not housed in bone, functions mainly to carry messages. The somatic subsystem of the PNS transmits information to the CNS from the outside world and conveys instructions from the CNS to the muscles. The autonomic subsystem conveys messages from the CNS that alter the activity of organs and glands and it sends information about that activity back to the brain.

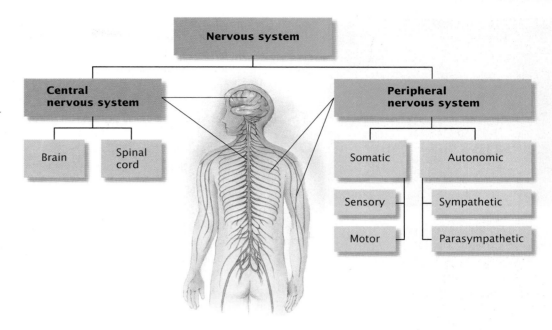

somatic nervous system The subsystem of the peripheral nervous system that transmits information from the senses to the central nervous system and carries signals from the CNS to the muscles that move the skeleton.

sensory neurons The neurons that provide the brain with information about the environment.

motor neurons The neurons that influence muscles and other organs to respond to the environment in some way.

autonomic nervous system The subsystem of the peripheral nervous system that carries messages between the central nervous system and the heart, lungs, and other organs and glands in the body.

sympathetic nervous system The subsystem of the autonomic nervous system that readies the body for vigorous activity.

parasympathetic nervous system The subsystem of the autonomic nervous system that typically influences activity related to the protection, nourishment, and growth of the body.

The Somatic Nervous System

Imagine that you're at the beach. It's hot, and the ocean smells salty. An attractive stranger approaches, catching your eye. The stranger smiles. You smile in return. The stranger continues walking away. In these few seconds, your nervous system has been busy. You feel the warmth of the sun and smell the ocean because your **somatic nervous system** takes in this sensory information and sends it to the central nervous system for processing. The CNS evaluates the warmth and the smells, sending messages through the somatic nervous system to the muscles that allow you to turn over, sit up, or put on more sunscreen. **Sensory neurons** bring information into the brain. **Motor neurons** carry information from the part of the brain that directs motion.

The Autonomic Nervous System

The **autonomic nervous system** carries messages back and forth between the CNS and the heart, lungs, and other organs and glands. For example, the autonomic nervous system takes that passing stranger's "attractive" rating from the CNS and translates it into an increase in heart rate, pupil dilation, and perhaps a little blushing. This system is called "autonomic" (pronounced "aw-toh-NOM-ic") because its activities, including digestion and sweating, for example, are generally autonomous, or independent of your control. With training and practice, some people can use a technique called *biofeedback* to bring some of their involuntary responses, such as heart rate, under conscious (CNS) control.

As shown in Figure 2.5, the autonomic system has two subsystems of its own—the *sympathetic nervous system* and the *parasympathetic nervous system*. These two subsystems work like a seesaw on a playground. Generally, the **sympathetic nervous system** readies your body for action in the face of stress. The **parasympathetic nervous system** calms you down once the crisis has passed. So the *sympathetic nervous system spends* energy, whereas the *parasympathetic nervous system preserves* energy.

The functions of the autonomic nervous system may not get star billing, but you'd miss them if they were gone. Just as a race-car driver is nothing without a good pit crew, the somatic nervous system depends on the autonomic nervous system to get its job done. For example, when you want to move your muscles, you create a demand for energy. The autonomic nervous system fills the bill by increasing sugar fuels in the bloodstream. If you decide to stand up, you need increased blood pressure so that your blood does not flow out of your brain and settle in your legs. Again, the autonomic nervous system

Is That Your Final Answer?

Is the geographically largest U.S. state (a) Montana, (b) Texas, (c) Alaska, or (d) Wyoming? Like contestants on shows such as *Who Wants to Be a Millionaire*, you must rely on your central nervous system, and especially on the information-processing power of your brain, to understand the question, recognize the correct option, and direct movements of your vocal muscles to speak your answer. (The correct choice in this case is c.)

nuclei Clusters of nerve cell bodies in the central nervous system.

fiber tracts Bundles of axons that travel together.

spinal cord The part of the central nervous system that receives information from the senses, passes these signals to the brain, and sends messages from the brain to the body.

reflexes Simple, involuntary, unlearned behaviors directed by the spinal cord without instructions from the brain.

makes the adjustment. Disorders of the autonomic nervous system can make people sweat uncontrollably or faint whenever they stand up; they can also lead to other problems, such as an inability to have sex. We examine the autonomic nervous system in more detail in the chapter on motivation and emotion.

The Central Nervous System: Making Sense of the World

How is my brain "wired"?

The amazing speed and efficiency of the central nervous system—the brain and spinal cord—have prompted many people to compare it to the central processor in a computer. But the CNS does not simply function as a high-powered computer. It certainly isn't laid out as neatly, either (Lichtman & Denk, 2011; Poldrack, 2010). The layout of the brain is more like the map of a college campus. There are clusters of offices for the administrators in one place, clusters of faculty offices in another place, and classrooms in yet another. Some of the sidewalks or hallways that connect these clusters are wide; others are narrow. There are many different but connected ways to get to the same place. Like a campus with its office clusters, the CNS has clusters of neuron cell bodies called **nuclei** (pronounced "NUKE-lee-eye"; *nuclei* is the plural of *nucleus*). The sidewalks and hallways of the CNS are axons that travel together in bundles called **fiber tracts,** or *pathways*. The axon (hallway) from any given cell (office) may merge with and leave many fiber tracts (sidewalks) and send branches out to other tracts. Let's consider a practical example of nervous system functioning to begin learning our way around the "campus" of the brain.

It is 6 A.M. and your alarm clock goes off, creating the simple case of information processing illustrated in Figure 2.1. Your ears receive sensory input in the form of sound from the alarm. The sound is converted into neural signals and sent to the brain. Your brain compares these signals with previous experiences stored in memory and correctly associates the sound with "alarm clock." Your muscle-guiding output is not yet at peak performance, though, because your brain activity has not yet reached the waking state. So, you fumble to turn off the alarm, shuffle to the kitchen, and accidentally touch the coffeemaker's heating element. Things get more lively now. Heat energy activates sensory neurons in your fingers, generating action potentials that speed along fiber tracts going into the spinal cord. Your motor neurons are reflexively activated by the CNS, causing muscles in your arm to contract and quickly withdraw your hand.

The Spinal Cord

The **spinal cord** receives signals such as pain and touch from the senses and passes those signals to the brain. Neuron fibers within the cord also carry signals downward from the brain to the muscles. Some cells of the spinal cord can direct simple behaviors without instructions from the brain. These behaviors are called **reflexes,** because the response to the incoming signal is directly "reflected" back out, as shown in Figure 2.6. Spinal reflexes, such as the one that pulled your hand away from the heat, are very fast because they include few time-consuming synaptic links. Reflexes are called *involuntary* because they occur without instructions from the brain. As reflexes occur, though, action potentials are also sent along fiber tracts to the brain. So you officially "know" you have been burned a fraction of a second after your reflex got you out of trouble.

The spinal cord is an example of a *feedback system*. When you touch something hot, a simple reflex occurs, causing one set of arm muscles to contract, and an opposing set of muscles to relax. These muscles have receptors that send information to the spinal cord to let it know how extended they are so that adjustments can be made for a smooth contracting motion. Information about the consequences of an action goes back to the source of the action for further adjustment. That's a feedback system.

FIGURE 2.6

A Reflex Pathway

Sit on a chair, cross one leg over the other, and then use the handle of a butter knife or some other solid object to gently tap your top knee, just below the joint, until you get a knee-jerk reaction. Tapping your knee at just the right spot sets off an almost instantaneous sequence of events that begins with stimulation of sensory neurons that respond to stretch. When those neurons fire, their axons, which end within the spinal cord, cause spinal neurons to fire. This, in turn, stimulates the firing of motor neurons with axons ending in your thigh muscles. The result is a contraction of those muscles and a kicking of the lower leg and foot. Information about the knee tap and about what the leg has done also goes to your cerebral cortex, but the reflex is completed without waiting for guidance from the brain.

LEARN by **DOING**

© 101dalmations/iStockphoto

The Brain

When pain messages from that hot burner reach your brain, you may become aware of more than just being burned. You might also realize that you have burned yourself twice before in the past week and become annoyed at your own carelessness. The brain is the most complex element in the central nervous system, and it is your brain's astonishing capacity for information processing that allows you to have these thoughts and feelings (Cacioppo & Decety, 2009).

The Hindbrain

You can see the major structures of the brain in Figure 2.7. The **hindbrain** lies just inside the skull and is actually a continuation of the spinal cord. Signals coming from the spinal cord reach the hindbrain first. Many vital autonomic functions, such as heart rate, blood pressure, and breathing, are controlled by nuclei in the hindbrain, particularly in an area called the **medulla oblongata** (pronounced "meh-DUH-lah ah-blon-GAH-da").

A mesh-like collection of cells called the **reticular formation** (*reticular* means "netlike") is woven through the hindbrain and into the midbrain. This network helps control arousal and attention. Cutting off fibers of the reticular system from the rest of the brain would put a person into a permanent coma. Some of the fibers that carry pain signals from the spinal cord connect in the reticular formation and immediately arouse the brain from sleep.

Axons from a small nucleus within the reticular formation, the locus coeruleus (pronounced "LOH-kus seh-ROO-lee-us"), branch extensively, making contact with as many as 100,000 other cells. The **locus coeruleus** (which means "blue spot" in Latin) is involved in directing attention (Minzenberg et al., 2008). Abnormalities in the locus coeruleus have been linked to depression, attention deficit hyperactivity disorder, sleep disorders, and posttraumatic stress disorder (Aston-Jones & Cohen, 2005).

The **cerebellum** (pronounced "sair-a-BELL-um") is also part of the hindbrain. Its primary function was long thought to be the control of finely coordinated movements, such as threading a needle (Aso et al., 2010). We now know that the cerebellum also allows the eyes to track a moving target accurately (Krauzlis & Lisberger, 1991) and that it may be the storehouse for well-rehearsed movements, such as those associated with dancing, playing a musical instrument, and athletics (McCormick & Thompson,

hindbrain The portion of the brain that lies just inside the skull and is a continuation of the spinal cord.

medulla oblongata The area of the hindbrain that controls vital autonomic functions such as heart rate, blood pressure, and breathing.

reticular formation A collection of cells and fibers in the hindbrain and midbrain that are involved in arousal and attention.

locus coeruleus A small nucleus in the reticular formation that is involved in directing attention.

cerebellum The part of the hindbrain whose main functions include controlling finely coordinated movements and storing memories about movement and may also be involved in impulse control, emotion, and language.

FIGURE 2.7

Major Structures of the Brain

This side view of a section cut down the middle of the brain reveals the forebrain, midbrain, hindbrain, and spinal cord. Many of these subdivisions do not have clear-cut borders because they are all interconnected by fiber tracts. The brain's anatomy reflects its evolution over millions of years. Newer structures (such as the cerebral cortex, which is the outer surface of the forebrain) that handle higher mental functions were built on older ones (such as the medulla oblongata) that coordinate heart rate, breathing, and other, more basic functions.

© Blend Images/Shutterstock

© The San Diego Union-Tribune/ZUMApress/Alamy

A Field Sobriety Test

The cerebellum is involved in the balance and coordination required for walking. When the cerebellum's activity is impaired by alcohol, these skills are disrupted, which is why the police ask suspected drunk drivers to walk a straight line.

1984). The cerebellum might also be involved in learning these skills (Hazeltine & Ivry, 2002) as well as in more uniquely human tasks such as language and abstract thinking (Andreasen & Pierson, 2008; Bower & Parsons, 2003). Neuroscientists believe that the cerebellum is involved in additional activities as well, including memory, emotion, language, impulse control, and other higher-order cognitive processes (e.g., Strick, Dum, & Fiez, 2009). For example, the cerebellum is important in timing (Manto, 2008), which plays a vital role in normal speech, integrating moment-to-moment feedback about vocal sounds with a sequence of precise movements of the lips and tongue (Leiner, Leiner, & Dow, 1993). Stuttering can result from a disruption of this integration and sequencing (Lu et al., 2009). Studies using some of the brain-imaging techniques we describe later have shown that the cerebellum is among the brain structures that show abnormal activity in young people who stutter (Watkins et al., 2008). In short, the cerebellum seems to be involved in both physical and cognitive agility.

Reflexes and feedback systems are important in the hindbrain. For example, if blood pressure drops, heart action reflexively increases to make up for that decrease. If you stand up quickly, your blood pressure can drop so suddenly that you feel lightheaded until the hindbrain reflexively "catches up." You'll faint if the hindbrain does not activate the autonomic nervous system to increase your blood pressure.

FIGURE 2.8

Major Structures of the Forebrain
The structures of the forebrain are covered by an outer "bark" known as the cerebral cortex. This diagram shows some of the structures that lie within the forebrain. The amygdala, the hippocampus, and portions of the cerebral cortex are part of the limbic system.

Corpus callosum: A bundle of nerve fibers that connects the left and right hemispheres of the brain.

Cerebral cortex: The outer bark that covers the forebrain and is responsible for processing complex information.

Hypothalamus: Connects to and from the autonomic nervous system and is involved in regulating hunger, thirst, and sex drive.

Thalamus

Septum

Amygdala

Hippocampus

© Juan Estey/iStockphoto

midbrain A small region between the hindbrain and the forebrain that, among other things, helps produce smooth movements.

forebrain The part of the brain responsible for the most complex aspects of behavior and mental life.

thalamus A forebrain structure that relays messages from most sense organs to higher brain areas.

hypothalamus A forebrain structure that regulates hunger, thirst, and sex drives and has many connections to and from the autonomic nervous system and other parts of the brain.

The Midbrain

A small region called the **midbrain** lies above the hindbrain. If you focus your eyes on another person and then move your head, midbrain circuits allow you to move your eyes smoothly in the direction opposite from your head movement so you never lose focus. When you swing a bat, swat a mosquito, or jump rope, part of the midbrain and its connections to the forebrain allow you to produce those movements smoothly. When a car backfires and you turn your head to look in the direction of the sound, it is again the midbrain at work. Together, the midbrain and parts of the hindbrain other than the cerebellum are called the *brainstem*.

The Forebrain

In humans, the **forebrain** controls the most complex aspects of behavior and mental life. It completely covers the hindbrain and midbrain. The outer surface of the forebrain is called the *cerebral cortex*. Some structures of the forebrain are shown in Figure 2.8.

Two structures deep within the forebrain, the *hypothalamus* and the *thalamus*, help operate basic drives, emotion, and sensation. The **thalamus** acts as a relay station for pain and sense-organ signals (except smell) from the body to the upper levels of the brain. It also processes and makes sense of these signals. The **hypothalamus** lies under the thalamus (*hypo* means "under") and helps regulate hunger, thirst, and sex drives. The hypothalamus is well connected to the autonomic nervous system and to other parts of the brain. Damage to parts of the hypothalamus upsets normal appetite, thirst, and sexual behavior.

Can you set an "internal alarm clock" to wake up in the morning at whatever time you want? If you can, it is with the help of a remarkable part of your hypothalamus called the *suprachiasmatic nuclei* that contains the brain's own clock. The suprachiasmatic (pronounced "soo-prak-eye-as-MAT-ik") nuclei operate on approximately a 24-hour cycle, controlling daily biological rhythms such as waking and sleeping as well as cycles of body temperature. Studies of the suprachiasmatic nuclei in animals suggest that having different night or morning energy times is biological and stable throughout a lifetime (Cofer et al., 1992). In humans, such differences may make some of us "morning people" and others "night people."

Other parts of the forebrain, especially the *amygdala* (pronounced "ah-MIG-duh-luh") and the *hippocampus,* help regulate memory and emotion. The **amygdala** links different kinds of sensory information in memory, such as the shape and feel of objects (Murray & Mishkin, 1985). If you close your eyes and pick up an object, your amygdala helps you recognize it. The amygdala also plays a role in fear and other emotions (Cunningham & Brosch, 2012; LeDoux, 1995; Whalen, 1998), connecting emotion to sensation. People who suffer from posttraumatic stress disorder have unusual amygdala activity (Shin, Rauch, & Pitman, 2006). The amygdala may also influence our sensitivity to other people (Corden et al., 2006). Brain scans show that the amygdala responds strongly when people view angry faces rather than neutral faces (Furmark et al., 2009). The amygdala, hippocampus, and some portions of the cerebral cortex are part of a group of brain structures called the *limbic system,* which is activated when emotions are being generated.

The **hippocampus** is involved in your ability to imagine future events (Hassabis et al., 2007; Maguire & Hassabis, 2011), but perhaps its most vital function is in helping you form new memories. For example, a patient known as R. B. suffered a stroke (an interruption of blood flow in the brain) that damaged only his hippocampus. Although his intelligence remained above average and he could recall old memories, he was almost totally unable to build new ones (Squire, 1986). Damage to the hippocampus within a day of a mildly painful event seems to erase memories of the experience. However, if the damage occurs several days after the event, the memory remains. It seems that memories are not permanently stored in the hippocampus but instead are transferred from there to somewhere else in the brain.

It isn't surprising, then, that certain aspects of memory are related to the size and level of activity in the hippocampus (Zimmerman et al., 2008). For example, having a relatively small hippocampus predicts the development of severe memory problems in the elderly (Devanand et al., 2007). Other studies suggest that some people's physical responses to stress include a reduction in the number of neurons in the hippocampus (Caspi, Sugden, et al., 2003; Frodl et al., 2004). This effect was demonstrated in a study of people who had been close to the World Trade Center on 9/11. They showed less hippocampus volume, even three years after the event, than people who had been more distant (Ganzel et al., 2008). The loss of neurons in this region may help explain the memory problems that appear in some people who have suffered depression or posttraumatic stress disorder (Bremner et al., 2003, 2004).

The hippocampus and memory also can be affected by disease. The hippocampus of a person with Alzheimer's disease, for example, has been found to be about 40 percent smaller on average than that of a person without the disease. Alzheimer's disease is a major cause of senile dementia, which involves the deterioration of cognitive capabilities.

The Cerebral Cortex

On the surface of the forebrain is the **cerebral cortex.** The total area of the cerebral cortex is between one and two square feet, but it fits into the skull because it is somewhat wrinkled and folded. (You can wad up a T-shirt and fit it into a small bowl in much the same way.) The cerebral cortex is much larger in humans than in most other animals (dolphins are an exception). It analyzes information from all the senses and controls voluntary movement, abstract thinking, and the other most complex aspects of our behavior and mental processes. The cerebral cortex looks somewhat round and has a long groove down the middle creating two halves, called *cerebral hemispheres.* The **corpus callosum,** a massive bundle of more than a million fibers, connects the two hemispheres.

amygdala A forebrain structure that links information from various systems and plays a role in emotions.

hippocampus A forebrain structure associated with the formation of new memories.

cerebral cortex The outer surface of the brain.

corpus callosum A bundle of fibers that connects the left and right cerebral hemispheres.

FIGURE 2.9

The Cerebral Cortex (Viewed from the Left Side)

The brain's ridges (gyri) and valleys (sulci) divide the cortex into four lobes: the frontal, parietal, occipital, and temporal. These terms describe where the regions are (the lobes are named for the skull bones that cover them), but the cortex is also divided in terms of function. These functional areas include the motor cortex (which controls movement), sensory cortex (which receives information from various senses), and association cortex (which integrates information). Also labeled are Wernicke's area and Broca's area, two regions that are found only on the left side of the cortex and that are vital to the interpretation and production of speech (Heim, Eickhoff, & Amunts, 2008; Peña et al., 2003; Schnur et al., 2009; Sparing et al., 2008).

(Photo ©photobank.ch/Shutterstock)

*Somatosensory cortex, auditory cortex, and visual cortex make up the sensory cortex.

sensory cortex The parts of the cerebral cortex located in the parietal, occipital, and temporal lobes that receive stimulus information from the skin, eyes, and ears, respectively.

The folds of the cerebral cortex give the surface of the human brain its wrinkled appearance, its ridges and valleys. The ridges are called *gyri* (pronounced "JI-rye"), and the valleys are known as *sulci* (pronounced "SUL-sigh") or *fissures*. As you can see in Figure 2.9, several deep sulci divide the cortex into four areas: the frontal (front), parietal (top), occipital (back), and temporal (side) lobes. The gyri and sulci provide landmarks for describing the structure of the cortex, but the *functions* of the cortex do not follow these boundaries. When divided according to function, the cortex includes areas of sensory cortex, motor cortex, and association cortex. ("In Review: Organization of the Brain" summarizes the major structures and functions of the brain.)

The Sensory and Motor Cortex

The **sensory cortex** lies in the parietal, occipital, and temporal lobes. Different regions of the sensory cortex receive information from different senses. Occipital lobe cells called the *visual cortex* receive visual information. Temporal lobe cells called the *auditory cortex* receive information from the ears. And information from the skin, such as sensations of touch, pain, and temperature, is received by cells in the parietal lobe. These skin-related areas are called the *somatosensory cortex* (*sōma* is Greek for "body"). Information about skin sensations from neighboring parts of the body comes to neighboring parts of the somatosensory cortex. It's as if the outline of a tiny person, dangling upside down, determines the location of the information (see Figure 2.10). This pattern is called the *homunculus* (Latin for "little man"). Experience can change

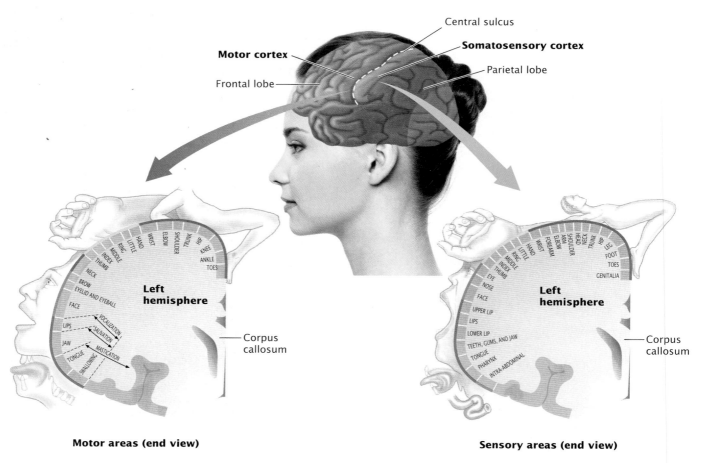

Central sulcus
Somatosensory cortex
Motor cortex
Parietal lobe
Frontal lobe

Left hemisphere
Corpus callosum

Left hemisphere
Corpus callosum

Motor areas (end view)

Sensory areas (end view)

FIGURE 2.10

Motor and Somatosensory Cortex

The areas of the cortex that move parts of the body (motor cortex) and receive sensory input from body parts (somatosensory cortex) appear in both hemispheres of the brain. Here we show cross-sections of only those on the left side, looking from the back of the brain toward the front. Areas that control movement of neighboring parts of the body, such as the foot and leg, occupy neighboring parts of the motor cortex. Areas that receive input from neighboring body parts, such as the lips and tongue, are near one another in the sensory cortex. Notice that the size of these areas is uneven; the larger the area devoted to each body part, the larger that body part appears on the "homunculus."

Note: Did you notice the error in this classic drawing? The figure of the homunculus shows the right side of its body but its left hand and the left side of its face.

Photo ©Valua Vitali/Shutterstock

motor cortex The part of the cerebral cortex that controls voluntary movement.

how the sensory cortex responds to sensory stimulation (Schaefer, Heinze, & Rotte, 2008). For example, if a limb is lost, the part of the sensory cortex that had been stimulated by that limb will now be stimulated by other regions of skin. Similarly, practicing a musical instrument will increase the number of sensory neurons that respond to touch (Candia et al., 2005; Hyde et al., 2009); the same thing happens when blind people learn to read Braille with their fingertips (Amedi et al., 2005; Pascual-Leone & Torres, 1993).

In the frontal lobe, specific neurons of the **motor cortex** control voluntary movements in specific parts of the body (Indovina & Sanes, 2001). The arrangement of the motor cortex mirrors that of the somatosensory cortex; the parts of the motor cortex that control hand movement are near parts of the sensory cortex that receive sensory information from the hands.

Seems easy, doesn't it? You have a map of your body parts in your cerebral cortex, and you activate cells in the hand region of the cortex if you want to move your hand. In fact, the process is quite complex. Recall again your sleepy reach for the coffeepot. To grasp its handle, your cortex must first translate the pot's location into a position relative to your body—to your left or right, for example. Next, the cortex must determine which muscles must be contracted to produce the desired movement toward that exact position. Groups of neurons work together to produce just the right combinations of direction and force in particular muscle groups. Making these determinations involves many interconnected areas of the cortex, and the specific neurons involved can change over time (Gallivan, Cavina-Pratesi, & Culham, 2009; W. Wang et al., 2010). Computer models of neural networks show how these complex problem-solving processes might occur (Graziano, Taylor, & Moore, 2002; Krauzlis, 2002).

Organization of the Brain

IN REVIEW

Major Division	Some Major Structures	Some Major Functions
Hindbrain	Medulla oblongata	Regulates breathing, heart rate, and blood pressure
	Reticular formation (also extends into midbrain)	Regulates arousal and attention
	Cerebellum	Controls finely coordinated movements and certain cognitive processes
Midbrain	Various nuclei	Relays sensory signals to forebrain; creates automatic responses to certain stimuli; initiates smooth movement
Forebrain	Thalamus	Interprets and relays sensory information
	Hypothalamus	Regulates hunger, thirst, and sex drives
	Amygdala	Connects sensations and emotions
	Hippocampus	Forms new memories
	Cerebral cortex	Analyzes sensory information; controls voluntary movements, abstract thinking, and other complex cognitive activity
	Corpus callosum	Transfers information between the two cerebral hemispheres

IN REVIEW QUESTIONS

1. The oldest part of the brain is the ___.
2. Cells that operate as the body's twenty-four-hour "time clock" are found in the ___.
3. Memory problems seen in Alzheimer's disease are related to shrinkage of the ___.

Association Cortex

The parts of the cortex that do not directly receive specific sensory information or control specific movements are referred to as **association cortex.** The term *association* describes these areas well, because they receive input from more than one sense or input that combines sensory and motor information. For instance, these areas associate words with images. Association cortex appears in all lobes of the brain and forms a large part of the cerebral cortex in humans. For this reason, damage to association areas can create serious problems in a wide range of mental abilities.

LINKAGES

Where are the brain's language centers? *(a link to Thought, Language, and Intelligence)*

Consider language. Language information comes from the auditory cortex for spoken language or from the visual cortex for written language. Areas of the motor cortex produce speech. Putting it all together in the complex activity known as language involves activity in association cortex. In the 1860s, a French surgeon named Paul Broca described the effects of damage to association cortex in the frontal lobe near motor areas that control face muscles. This part of the cortex is on the left side of the brain and is called *Broca's area* (see Figure 2.9). The hand and arm gestures that accompany speech are also controlled by neurons in this area (Gentilucci & Dalla Volta, 2008; Xu et al., 2009). Damage to Broca's area disrupts speech organization, a condition called *Broca's aphasia*. Victims have difficulty speaking, often making errors in grammar. Each word comes out slowly.

Other language problems result from damage to a portion of association cortex described in the 1870s by a Polish neurologist named Carl Wernicke (pronounced "VER-nick-ee"). Figure 2.9 shows that, like Broca's area, *Wernicke's area* is on the left side of the brain, but it's in the temporal lobe, near the area of the sensory cortex that receives information from the ears. Wernicke's area also receives input from the visual cortex and is involved in the interpretation of both speech and written words. Damage to Wernicke's area produces complicated symptoms. It can leave patients with the ability to speak but disrupts the ability to understand the meaning of words or to speak understandably.

association cortex The parts of the cerebral cortex that integrate sensory and motor information and perform complex cognitive tasks.

Language Areas of the Brain
Have you ever tried to write notes while you were talking to someone? You can probably write and talk at the same time because each of these language functions uses different areas of association cortex. However, stop reading for a moment and try writing one word with your left hand and a different word with your right hand. If you had trouble, it's partly because you asked the same language area of your brain to do two things at once.

LEARN by DOING

Case studies illustrate the different effects of damage to each area (Lapointe, 1990). In response to the request "Tell me what you do with a cigarette," a person with Wernicke's aphasia replied, "This is a segment of a pegment. Soap a cigarette." This speech was fluent but without meaning. In response to the same request, a person with Broca's aphasia replied, "Uh.. uh.. cigarette [pause] smoke it." This speech was meaningful but halting and awkwardly phrased. Surprisingly, when a person with Broca's aphasia sings, the words come easily and correctly. Apparently, words set to music are handled by one part of the brain and spoken words by another (Jeffries, Fritz, & Braun, 2003). Some speech therapists take advantage of this fact through "melodic intonation" therapy, which helps Broca's aphasia patients to gain fluency by speaking in a singsong manner (Norton et al., 2009). This therapy is enhanced by noninvasive electrical stimulation of the right hemisphere, an area that compensates for damage to Broca's area in the left hemisphere (Vines, Norton, & Schlaug, 2011).

It appears that written language and spoken language require the use of different areas of association cortex. So does language involving specific parts of speech (Shapiro, Moo, & Caramazza, 2006). For example, two women—H. W. and S. J. D.—each had a stroke in 1985, causing damage to different language-related parts of their association cortex. Neither woman has difficulty speaking or writing nouns, but both have difficulty with verbs (Caramazza & Hillis, 1991). S. J. D. can speak verbs but has difficulty writing them. H. W. can write verbs but cannot speak them. So she has difficulty pronouncing *watch* when it is used as a verb in the sentence "I watch TV," but she speaks the same word easily when it appears as a noun in the sentence "My watch is slow."

Association areas in the *prefrontal cortex* at the front of the brain are involved in the complex processes necessary for the conscious control of thoughts and actions and for understanding our world (Fincham & Anderson, 2006; Koechlin & Hyafil, 2007). For example, these areas of association cortex allow us to understand sarcasm or irony—that is, when someone says one thing but means the opposite. In one study, people with prefrontal cortex damage listened to sarcastic stories such as this: "Joe came to work, and instead of beginning to work, he sat down to rest. His boss noticed his behavior and said, 'Joe, don't work too hard.'" Most people immediately realized that the boss was being sarcastic, but people with prefrontal brain damage did not (Shamay-Tsoory & Tomer, 2005).

***FOCUS ON** RESEARCH*   ## The Case of the Disembodied Woman

Neurologist Oliver Sacks described the case of "Christina," a woman who had somehow lost the ability to feel the position of her own body (Sacks, 1985). This case study led to important insights about biological aspects of psychology that could not be studied through controlled experiments. It showed, for example, that the sense known as *kinesthesia* (pronounced "kin-es-THEE-see-uh") not only tells us where our body parts are but also plays an important role in our sense of self.

Christina was a healthy young woman who entered a hospital in preparation for some minor surgery. Before the surgery could be performed, however, she began to have difficulty holding onto objects. Then she had trouble moving. She would rise from bed and flop onto the floor like a rag doll. Christina seemed to have "lost" her body. She felt disembodied, like a ghost. On one occasion, for example, she became annoyed at a visitor for tapping her fingers on a tabletop. But it was Christina's fingers, not the visitor's, that were tapping. Her body was acting on its own, doing things she did not know about.

What was the researcher's question?
Christina could not walk or use her hands and arms. Why was a seemingly normal, healthy young woman falling and dropping things?

How did the researcher answer the question?
A psychiatrist at the hospital thought that Christina was suffering from *conversion disorder,* a condition in which psychological problems cause physical disabilities (see

the chapter on psychological disorders). Unconvinced, Sacks conducted a careful case study of Christina.

What did the researcher find?

It turned out that the psychiatrist was wrong. Sacks's examinations and tests revealed that Christina had lost all sensory feedback about her joints and muscle tone and the position of her limbs. She'd suffered a breakdown, or degeneration, of the sensory neurons that normally bring kinesthetic information to her brain. In other words, there was a biological reason that Christina could not walk or control her hands and arms.

What do the results mean?

In his analysis of this case, Sacks noted that the sense we have of our bodies is provided partly through our experience of seeing but also partly through *proprioception* (sensing the self). Christina herself put it this way: "Proprioception is like the eyes of the body, the way the body sees itself. And if it goes, it's like the body's blind." With great effort and determination, Christina was eventually able to regain some of her ability to move about. If she looked intently at her arms and legs, she could coordinate their movement somewhat. She was able to leave the hospital and resume many of her normal activities, but Christina never recovered her sense of self. She still feels like a stranger in her own body.

What do we still need to know?

Notice that Christina's case study did not confirm any hypotheses about kinesthesia in the way an experiment might. It did, however, focus attention on how it feels to have lost this sense. It also highlighted a rare condition that, though almost unknown when Sacks reported it, has been observed more often in recent years, especially among people taking large doses of vitamin B6, also known as *pyridoxine*. These large doses—or even smaller doses taken over a long period of time—can damage sensory neurons (Dordain & Deffond, 1994). How and why vitamin B6 does such damage still needs to be determined. Are there other causes of this kinesthetic disorder? What treatments might best combat it? These questions remain to be answered by the research of psychologists and other scientists who continue to unravel the mysteries of behavior and mental processes.   ● ● ● ●

Exploring the Brain

A variety of new brain-scanning techniques, combined with some older measures, are giving scientists ever better views of the brain and its activity (Amaro & Barker, 2006; Miller, 2003; see Table 2.1). Each technique can indirectly measure the activity of neurons firing, and each has different advantages and disadvantages. One of the earliest of these techniques, called the *electroencephalograph (EEG)*, measures general electrical activity of the brain. Electrodes are pasted on the scalp to detect the electrical fields resulting from the activity of billions of neurons (Figure 4.3 in the consciousness chapter shows how EEG can be used to record brain activity during sleep). Although this tool can associate rapidly changing electrical activity with changes in the activity of the brain, it cannot tell us exactly where the active cells are.

A newer technique, called the *PET scan* (for *positron emission tomography*), can locate brain cell activity by recording where radioactive substances become concentrated when injected into the bloodstream. It records images from the brain that indicate the location of the radioactivity as the brain performs various tasks. For instance, PET studies have revealed that specific brain regions are activated when we look at fearful facial expressions or hear fearful voices (Pourtois et al., 2005) and that neurotransmission is modified in people with posttraumatic stress disorder in the same brain regions (Murrough et al., 2011). PET scans can tell us a lot about where changes in brain activity occur, but they can't reveal details of the brain's physical structure.

A detailed structural picture of the brain can be seen using *magnetic resonance imaging, or MRI.* MRI exposes the brain to a magnetic field and measures the resulting radiofrequency waves to get amazingly clear pictures of the brain's anatomical details (see Figure 2.11). *Functional MRI, or fMRI,* combines the advantages of PET and MRI and is capable of detecting changes in blood flow and blood oxygen that reflect ongoing changes in the activity of neurons, providing a sort of "moving picture" of the brain (e.g., Shu et al., 2002). The newest techniques offer even deeper insight into brain activity, structure, and functioning. These techniques include a variant on fMRI called *diffusion tensor imaging (DTI),* which traces the activity of axon pathways, and a procedure called *transcranial magnetic stimulation (TMS)* which sets up magnetic fields outside the brain. These magnetic fields can either stimulate or disrupt neural activity (Glenberg, 2011; Lagopoulos & Malhi, 2008; López-Ibor, López-Ibor, & Pastrana, 2008). Some researchers are studying brain functions by combining fMRI and TMS (Bestmann et al., 2008). For example, when one brain region is stimulated by TMS, and changes in activity are detected by fMRI in another region, this indicates that the two regions are functionally connected. Similarly, if the ability to perform a certain behavior is affected when TMS disrupts activity in a certain brain region, this suggests that the behavior is somehow controlled or influenced by that brain region (Muggleton, 2010). TMS may also have unexpected value in the treatment of depression and migraine headaches (O'Reardon et al., 2007).

TABLE 2.1 Techniques for Studying Human Brain Function and Structure

Technique	What It Shows	Advantages	Disadvantages
EEG (electroencephalograph) Electrodes are pasted to the outside of the head.	Lines that chart the summated electrical fields resulting from the activity of billions of neurons.	Detects very rapid changes in electrical activity, allowing analysis of stages of cognitive processing.	Poor spatial resolution of the source of electrical activity; EEG is sometimes combined with magnetoencephalography (MEG), which localizes electrical activity by measuring magnetic fields associated with it.
PET (positron emission tomography) and SPECT (single-photon emission computed tomography) Radioactive substances, injected into the bloodstream, indicate activity in the brain.	An image of the amount and localization of any molecule that can be injected in radioactive form, such as neurotransmitters, drugs, or tracers for blood flow or glucose use (indicating specific changes in neuronal activity).	Allows functional and biochemical studies. Provides visual image corresponding to anatomy.	Requires exposure to low levels of radioactivity. Spatial resolution is better than EEG but poorer than MRI. Cannot follow rapid changes (faster than 30 seconds).
MRI (magnetic resonance imaging) A magnetic field measures radio frequency waves in the brain.	Traditional MRI provides high-resolution image of brain anatomy. Functional MRI (fMRI) provides images of changes in blood flow that indicate specific changes in neural activity. Diffusion tensor imaging (DTI) shows water flow in neural fibers, revealing the "wiring diagram" of neural connections in the brain.	Requires no exposure to radioactivity. Provides high spatial resolution of anatomical details (smaller than 1 mm). Provides high temporal resolution (less than one-tenth of a second).	
TMS (transcranial magnetic stimulation) Temporarily disrupts electrical activity of a small region of brain by exposing it to an intense magnetic field.	Studies normal function of a particular brain region by observing changes after TMS is applied to a specific location.	Shows which brain regions are necessary for given tasks.	Long-term safety not well established.

D. N. Levin, H. Xiaoping, K. K. Tan, S. Galhotra, C. A. Palizzare, G. T. Y. Chen, R. N. Beck, C. T. Chen, M. D. Cooper, J. F. Mullan, J. Hekmatpanah, & J. P. Spire. (1989). The Brain: Integrated three-dimensional display of MR and PET images. *Radiology, 172*: 783–789.

FIGURE 2.11

Combining a PET Scan and Magnetic Resonance Imaging

Researchers have superimposed images from PET scans and MRI to construct a three-dimensional view of the living brain. This figure shows the brain of a young girl with epilepsy. The picture of the outer surface of the brain is from the MRI; the pink area is from the PET scan and shows the source of epileptic activity. To the right of the figure are separate MRI and PET images taken at one plane, or "slice," through the brain (indicated by the line on the brain at the left).

THINKING CRITICALLY

What Can fMRI Tell Us about Behavior and Mental Processes?

A picture may be worth a thousand words, but the pictures of brain activity offered by fMRI are generating millions of them. As of 2012, over 20,000 scientific articles have reported the results of fMRI scans taken while people engaged in various kinds of thinking or experienced various emotions. Neuroscientists who use brain-imaging techniques can now be found in psychology departments around the world, and, as described in other chapters, their work is changing the research landscape in cognitive, social, and abnormal psychology. Excitement over fMRI is not confined to scientists, however. Popular and scientific magazines routinely carry fMRI pictures that appear to "show" people's thoughts and feelings as they happen, and readers see these articles as more believable than those offering the same data in less dramatic tables or graphs (Beck, 2010; McCabe & Castel, 2008). This may be one reason why so many companies these days are making money by offering brain imaging services that can supposedly improve the quality of employee selection, lie detection, political campaign strategies, product design, and diagnosis of mental disorders (Ariely & Berns, 2010; Caulfield, Rachul, & Zarzeczny, 2010; Falk, Berkman, & Lieberman, 2012; Hubert, et al., 2010; Morin, 2011). Jurors, too, find evidence from fMRI scans extremely persuasive (McCabe, Castel, & Rhodes, 2011), even though research shows that it is not an effective method for detecting deception (Adelsheim, 2011; Ganis, et al., 2011). The editor of one scientific journal summed up this trend by saying that "a picture is worth a thousand dollars" (Farah, 2009).

What am I being asked to believe or accept?

In the early 1800s, similar excitement surrounded *phrenology,* a technique that involved measuring the bumps and depressions on the skull. It was claimed that these contours reflected the size of 27 structures on the brain's surface that determine personality traits, mental abilities, talents, and other characteristics. Although wildly popular with the public (Benjamin & Baker, 2004), phrenology did not survive the critical thinking of nineteenth-century scientists, and the technique has long been discredited. Today, some scientists wonder whether fMRI is a twenty-first-century version of phrenology, at least in the sense that their colleagues might be accepting its value too readily. These scientists point out that although fMRI images can indicate where brain activity occurs as people think and experience emotion, there is no guarantee that this activity is actually *causing* the associated thoughts and feelings (Aldridge, 2005). Questions are also being raised about the assumption that particular thought processes or emotions occur in a particular brain structure or set of structures. It is easy to talk about "thinking" or "attention," but these psychological terms might not correspond to specific biological processes that can be isolated and located by *any* technology (Miller, 2010). In short, critics claim that the results of fMRI scans can be misleading and that they don't necessarily tell us much about how the mind works (Uttal, 2003). Some believe that it would be better to focus on *how* the brain produces thoughts and feelings instead of searching for their locations (Poldrack, 2010).

Is evidence available to support the claim?

When the participant in an fMRI experiment thinks or feels something, you can actually see the colors in the scanned image of the brain change, much like the color changes you see on weather radar as a rainstorm intensifies or weakens. Looking at an fMRI scan, you get a clear impression that the brain areas that "light up" when a person experiences an emotion or performs a mental task are the ones involved in that emotion or task (see Figure 1.5 in the introduction to the science of psychology chapter.

These scans are not as precise as they seem, though, because fMRI doesn't measure brain cell activity directly. The colors shown in an fMRI scan reflect the flow of blood in the brain and the amount of oxygen the blood is carrying. Changes in blood flow and blood oxygen are *related* to changes in the firing rates of neurons, but the relationship is complex (Glenberg, 2011); for example, the relationship differs from one brain region to another (Devonshire et al., 2011) and changes with age (Mohtasib et al., 2011). And changes in an fMRI signal can depend on how much neural firing was taking place before a stimulus appeared (Maandag et al., 2007; Perthen et al., 2008). Further, when brain cells process information, their firing rates may either increase or decrease (Gonsalves et al., 2005). If the increases and decreases in a particular brain region happen to cancel each other out, an fMRI scan will miss the neuronal activity taking place in that region (Glenberg, 2011). In fact, compared with the direct measurement of brain cell activity that can be done in research with animals, fMRI technology is still quite crude. It takes coordinated changes in millions of neurons to produce a detectible change in the fMRI signal.

Critics also argue that the results of fMRI research can depend too much on how experimenters choose to interpret them. In a typical fMRI experiment, participants are shown some kind of display, such as pairs of photos, and asked to perform various tasks. One task might be to press a button if the photos are exactly the same. A second task might be to press the button if objects in the photos are arranged in the same way. In this second task, a participant should press the button if one photo shows, say, a short man standing to the left of a tall woman and the other photo shows a small dog standing to the left of a giraffe. Both versions of the task require the participant to compare two images, but only the second of them requires considering whether things that look different are actually similar in some way. The fMRI scans taken during these tasks might show certain brain areas "lighting up" only during the second task. If so, the researcher would suggest that those areas are involved in recognizing *analogies,* or the similarities between apparently different things (Wharton et al., 2000). The researcher would base this conclusion on a computer program that compares fMRI scans taken during two tasks, subtracts all the "lighted" areas that are the same in both scans, and keeps only those that are different. But what the computer classifies as "different" depends on a rule that is set by the experimenter. If the experimenter programs the computer to display only big differences between the scans, not many "lit up" areas will remain after the comparison process. But if even tiny differences are allowed to count as "different," many more "lighted" areas will remain after the subtraction process. In our example, then, there could be large or small areas apparently associated with recognizing analogies, all depending on a rule set by the researcher.

These problems aside, critics wonder what it really means when fMRI research shows that certain brain areas appear activated during certain kinds of tasks or experiences. Their concern focuses on studies, such as one from the new field of *neuroeconomics,* which suggests that the neural basis of bad investment decisions is due to excessive activity in a particular area of the brain (Kuhnen & Knutson, 2005). Other studies have used fMRI to identify the neural activity associated with trust, religious belief, political liberalism or conservatism, and even love (Amodio et al., 2007; Kapogiannis et al., 2009; Krueger et al., 2007). In this last study, on "the neural basis of romantic love" (Bartels & Zeki, 2000), investigators scanned people's brains as they looked at pictures of their romantic partners and compared these scans to those taken while the same people viewed nonromantic friends. According to the "difference" rule established by the experimenters, four brain areas were more active when viewing a romantic loved one than when viewing a friend. However, these same brain regions are active in many different emotions, so does the activity tell us anything specific about the neural basis of love? Critics of fMRI would say no.

Can that evidence be interpreted another way?

Supporters of fMRI disagree with those critics. They believe that the colorful areas seen on fMRI scans can provide vital new information that will eventually allow scientists to answer important questions about behavior and mental processes. They point, for example, to fMRI research on brain mechanisms that help us to appreciate what other people are feeling—that is, to experience empathy—and to learn by watching others.

These *mirror neuron mechanisms* were discovered accidentally by scientists who had been using surgical techniques to directly record the activity of monkeys' brain cells (Caggiano et al., 2009; Rizzolatti et al., 1996). They found that neurons in an area called F5 are activated not only when a monkey plans to reach for an object, such as a peanut, but also if the monkey sees *an experimenter* reach for a peanut (Glenberg, 2011)! After fMRI scanning became available, researchers could begin looking for mirror mechanisms in the human brain, and they did so with gusto: since 2003, more than 190 studies have used fMRI to study the mirror system in humans (Molenberghs et al., 2012). And in fact, some of the mirror systems they found in humans correspond to the F5 region in monkeys (Rizolatti & Arbib, 1998) They are in other brain regions, too (Mukamel et al., 2010). One of them is *Broca's area* which, as described earlier, is an important component of our ability to speak. It makes sense that Broca's area contains a mirror mechanism, because language is a skill that we learn partly by imitation. The new fMRI findings suggest that Broca's area may also be important for many other skills that involve imitation. One study found that this area "lights up" when a guitar student learns chords by watching a professional guitarist (Buccino et al., 2004). Other fMRI research has found that mirror systems in other parts of the brain become active when a person sees someone experiencing emotion. For example, the brain area that is activated when you experience disgust (from the smell of rotten eggs, for example) is also activated if you see a video in which someone else reacts to a smell with disgust (Wicker et al., 2003).

So fMRI can be uniquely useful, say its defenders. Without it, research on mirror neurons in humans could not have taken place. And because of it, we have evidence that the experience of empathy comes about because seeing the actions and emotions of others activates the same brain regions that would be active if we were doing or feeling the same things ourselves. Some fMRI studies have also found that malfunctioning mirror mechanisms are associated with the impairments in language development, imitative skills, and empathy seen in children diagnosed with autistic disorder (Dapretto et al., 2006; Perkins et al., 2010; see the chapter on psychological disorders).

It may also be that fMRI can help answer centuries-old questions about the location of our consciousness and self-awareness (Graziano & Kastner, 2011). Studies using fMRI have suggested that these functions might be located in a region called the anterior insular cortex. This region appears to be involved in all kinds of subjective feelings and is activated by a wide range of experiences, including everything from pressure in the bowels to orgasm, from cigarette craving to maternal love, and from decision making to sudden insight (Craig, 2009; Dawes et al., 2012).

What evidence would help to evaluate the alternatives?

As technology continues to be refined, the quality of fMRI scans will continue to improve, giving us ever better images of where brain activity is taking place. But the value of this scanning technology will depend on a better understanding of what it can and cannot tell us about how brain activity is related to behavior and mental processes. We also need more evidence about correlation and causation in fMRI research. For example, one study conducted fMRI scans on compulsive gamblers as they played a simple guessing

Exploring Brain Functions with fMRI

As this participant performs a mental task, a functional magnetic resonance imaging scanner records blood flow and blood oxygen levels in her brain. The resulting computer analysis shows as "lit up" areas the parts of the brain that appear to be activated during the task, but critics doubt that fMRI scanning is as clear or accurate as its proponents suggest.

Image courtesy of Brad Sutton, Beckman Institute Biomedical Imaging Center, University of Illinois at Urbana-Champaign

game (Reuter et al., 2005). When they won the game, these people showed an unusually small amount of activity in a brain area that is normally activated by the experience of rewards, or pleasure. Noting the correlation between compulsive gambling and lower-than-normal activity in the reward area, the researchers suggested that an abnormality in the brain's reward mechanisms might be responsible for gambling addiction. But case studies also suggest that compulsive gambling appears in people taking a prescription drug that *increases* activity in reward areas—and that the gambling stops when the drug is discontinued (Abler et al., 2009; Cilia et al., 2008; Dodd et al., 2005; Ferrara & Stacy, 2008; Tippmann-Piekert et al., 2007).

As noted in the introduction to the science of psychology chapter, correlation does not guarantee causation. Is the brain activity reflected in fMRI scans causing the thoughts and feelings that take place during the scanning process? Possibly, but those thoughts and feelings might themselves be *caused by* activity elsewhere in the brain that affects the areas being scanned. The transcranial magnetic stimulation (TMS) procedures mentioned earlier might help identify causal versus correlational relationships in the brain. TMS is capable of temporarily disrupting neural activity in brain regions identified by fMRI as related to a particular kind of thought or feeling, so perhaps scientists can determine if those thoughts or feelings are temporarily disrupted when TMS occurs. Though TMS appears to be safe (López-Ibor, López-Ibor, & Pastrana, 2008), we don't yet know about its possible long-term negative side effects, so neuroscientists will have to proceed carefully in their use of this technique to explore basic questions about the mind and the brain.

Finding answers to questions like these will require continuing dialogue between those who dismiss fMRI and those who sing its praises. To make this interaction easier, a group of government agencies and private foundations has funded an fMRI Data Center (http://www.fmridc.org/f/fmridc). This facility stores information from fMRI experiments and makes it available to both critics and supporters of fMRI, who can review the research data, conduct their own analyses, and offer their own interpretations. Having access to an ever-growing database such as this will no doubt help scientists get the most out of fMRI technology and help them avoid either overstating or underestimating the meaning of fMRI research.

What conclusions are most reasonable?

When the EEG was invented nearly 100 years ago, scientists had their first glimpse of brain cell activity, as reflected in the "brain waves" traced on a long sheet of paper rolling from the EEG machine (see Figure 4.3). To many of these scientists, EEG must have seemed like a golden gateway to an understanding of the brain and its relationship to behavior and mental processes. EEG has, in fact, helped to advance knowledge of the brain, but it certainly didn't solve all of its mysteries. When all is said and done, the same will probably be true of fMRI. It is an exciting new tool, and it offers previously undreamed-of images of the structure and functioning of the brain, but it is unlikely on its own to explain just how the brain creates our behavior and mental processes. It seems reasonable to conclude, then, that those who question the use of fMRI to study psychological processes are right in calling for a careful analysis of the value of this important high-tech tool.

Although the meaning of fMRI data will remain a subject for debate, there is no doubt that brain-scanning techniques in general have opened new frontiers for biological psychology, neuroscience, and medicine. Much of our growing understanding of how and why behavior and mental processes occur is coming from research with these techniques (Poldrack, Halchenko, & Hanson, 2009). ● ● ● ●

The Divided Brain: Lateralization

A striking suggestion emerged from observations of people with damage to the language centers of the brain. Researchers noticed that damage to specific areas of the left hemisphere interfered with the ability to use or understand language. Damage to those same areas in the right hemisphere usually did not cause such problems. Could it be that the right and left hemispheres of the brain serve different functions?

This idea was not entirely new. It had long been understood that most sensory and motor pathways cross over from one hemisphere to the other as they enter or leave the brain. As a result, the left hemisphere receives information from and controls movements of the right side of the body. The right hemisphere receives input from and controls the left side of the body. Figure 2.12 shows the two hemispheres. The fact that language centers such as Broca's area and Wernicke's area almost always occur on the left side of the brain suggests that each hemisphere might be specialized to perform some functions almost independently of the other hemisphere (Stephan et al., 2003).

In the late 1800s, there was great interest in the idea that the hemispheres might be specialized, but no techniques were available for testing it. Renewed interest grew out of studies during the 1960s by Roger Sperry, Michael Gazzaniga, and their colleagues.

Split-Brain Studies   Sperry studied *split-brain* patients—people who had undergone surgery in an attempt to control the severe seizures of epilepsy. Before the surgery, their seizures began in one hemisphere and then spread throughout the brain. As a last resort, surgeons isolated the two hemispheres from each other by cutting the corpus callosum, which had connected them.

After the surgery, researchers used a special device like the one shown in Figure 2.13 to present visual images to only one side of these patients' split brains. They found that cutting the tie between the hemispheres had dramatically changed the way these people thought about and dealt with the world. For example, when the image of a spoon was presented to the left, language-oriented, side of patient N. G.'s split brain, she could say what the spoon was but when the spoon was presented to the right side of her brain, she could not describe the spoon in words. She still knew what the object was, because she could pick it out from a group of objects by feeling its shape with her left hand (controlled by the right hemisphere). When asked what she had just grasped, she replied, "A pencil." The right hemisphere recognized the object, but the patient could not say what it was because the left (language) half of her brain did not see or feel it (Sperry, 1968).

Although the right hemisphere has no control over spoken language in split-brain patients, it does have important abilities related to nonspoken language. For example, a split-brain patient's right hemisphere can guide the left hand in spelling out words with Scrabble tiles (Gazzaniga & LeDoux, 1978). Thanks to this finding, researchers

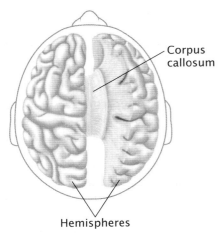

Corpus callosum

Hemispheres

FIGURE 2.12
The Brain's Left and Right Hemispheres

The brain's two hemispheres are joined by a core bundle of nerve fibers known as the corpus callosum. In this figure the hemispheres are separated so that the corpus callosum can be seen. The two cerebral hemispheres look nearly the same but perform somewhat different tasks. For one thing, the left hemisphere receives sensory input from and controls movement on the right side of the body. The right hemisphere senses and controls the left side of the body.

FIGURE 2.13

Apparatus for Studying Split-Brain Patients

When the person stares at the dot on the screen, images briefly presented on one side of the dot go to only one side of the brain. For example, a picture of a spoon presented on the left side of the screen goes to the right side of the brain. The right side of the brain can find the spoon and direct the left hand to touch it. However, the language areas on the left side of the brain did not see the spoon, so the person is unable to say what it is.

neural plasticity A property of the central nervous system that allows it to strengthen neural connections at synapses as well as to establish new connections.

concluded that split-brain patients have self-awareness and normal learning abilities in their right hemispheres. In addition, these patients' right hemispheres did better than their left hemispheres at tasks involving spatial relationships (especially drawing three-dimensional shapes) and recognizing human faces.

Having these two somewhat specialized hemispheres allows the normal brain to perform some tasks more efficiently, particularly difficult ones. This specialization seems to be present even in infancy (Dehaene-Lambertz et al., 2010), but the differences between the hemispheres should not be exaggerated. Remember, the corpus callosum usually integrates the functions of the "two brains" (Rueckert et al., 1999). As a result, the hemispheres work closely together, each making up well for whatever lack of ability the other may have (Banich, 2004; Staudt et al., 2001).

Plasticity in the Central Nervous System

The central nervous system has a remarkable property called **neural plasticity** (also known as *neuroplasticity* or simply *plasticity*), which is the ability to strengthen neural connections at synapses as well as to establish new connections (Herdener et al., 2010; Tailby et al., 2005). Plasticity depends partly on neurons and partly on glial cells (Lee & Silva, 2009), and it occurs throughout the central nervous system. Plasticity appears in the spinal cord, where simple reflexes can be modified by life experiences (Wolpaw & Chen, 2006), and also in the brain, where the connections between neurons are not only highly changeable but can change in a fraction of a second (Bikbaev & Manahan-Vaughan, 2008; Stettler et al., 2006). Plasticity in the brain is the basis of our ability to form new memories and learn new things (Ho, Lee, & Martin, 2011; Roberts et al., 2010). For example, more cells in the brain's motor cortex become involved in controlling hand movements in people who have learned to play a musical instrument. The process can be seen in brain-imaging studies; as nonmusicians get better at making rhythmic finger movements, the amount of motor cortex devoted to this task increases (Munte, Altenmuller, & Jancke, 2002). Even more amazing is that merely *imagining* practicing these movements causes changes in the motor cortex (Pascual-Leone, 2001). Athletes have long engaged in exercises in which they visualize skilled sports movements; brain-imaging research reveals that this "mental practice" can change the brain (Olsson et al., 2008). Among trained opera singers, similar changes have been observed in brain areas that control vocalization (Kleber et al., 2010). Given the impact of these specific experiences, it is no wonder that more general cultural experiences, such as growing up in a collectivist vs. individualist culture, can also affect the development of a person's brain (Park & Huang, 2010).

Repairing Brain Damage   There are limits to plasticity, though, especially when it comes to repairing damage in the brain and spinal cord. Unlike the skin or the liver, the adult central nervous system does not automatically replace damaged cells. As a result, most victims of severe stroke, Parkinson's disease, Alzheimer's disease, or spinal cord injury are permanently disabled in some way. Nevertheless, scientists are searching for ways to help a damaged central nervous system heal some of its own wounds.

One approach has been to transplant, or graft, tissue from the still-developing brain of a fetus into the brain of an adult animal. If the receiving animal doesn't reject it, the graft sends axons out into the brain and makes some functional connections. This treatment has reversed animals' learning difficulties, movement disorders, and other results of brain damage (Noble, 2000). The technique has also been used to treat a small number of people with Parkinson's disease—a disorder characterized by tremors, rigidity of the arms and legs, and poor balance (Lindvall & Hagell, 2001). The initial results have been encouraging (Mendez et al., 2005, 2008). Some patients showed improvement for several years, though improvement faded for others, and some patients suffered serious side effects (Freed et al., 2001). Brain tissue transplants in humans are controversial because they require the use of tissue from aborted fetuses. As an alternative, some scientists have tried transplanting neural tissue from another species, such as pigs, into humans (Drucker-Colin & Verdugo-Diaz, 2004). Russian physicians have even

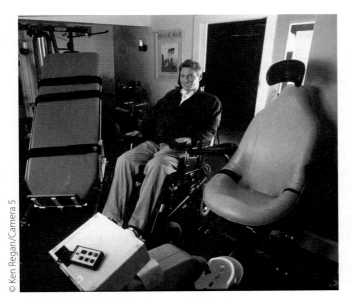

© Ken Regan/Camera 5

He Was a Super Man

After a 1995 riding accident left actor/ director Christopher Reeve paralyzed below his shoulders, he embarked on a long, intense rehabilitation regimen. He received electrical stimulation to maintain muscle tone and was strapped to a tilting table to maintain bone density. He was suspended in a harness over a treadmill while his legs were put through walking movements. In 1999, he began using a functional electrical stimulation bicycle, which sent computer-controlled electrical impulses to his legs, causing the muscles to contract and move the bike's pedals. By the end of 2002, he could move his fingers, right wrist, and upper legs. In a swimming pool, he could move his knees and upper arms. By the time of his death in 2004, he'd also regained feeling in about 70 percent of his body. Research is continuing on other exercise programs to promote recovery from spinal cord injury (Dunlop, 2008; Raineteau, 2008).

tried transplanting neural tissue from fruit flies into the brains of Parkinson's patients. The results were beneficial, and there were no immediate side effects (Saveliev et al., 1997), but the patients' bodies eventually rejected the fruit fly neurons (Korochkin, 2000).

The most promising source of new neurons now appears to be an individual's own tissues, because these cells would not be rejected. This is a revolutionary idea, because it was long believed that once humans reached adulthood, the cells of the central nervous system stopped dividing, leaving each of us with a fixed set of neurons (Rakic, 2002). Then came research showing that cell division *does* take place in the adult central nervous systems of humans, nonhuman primates, and other animals (Blakeslee, 2000; Eriksson et al., 1998; Gould et al., 1999; Steindler & Pincus, 2002). It turns out that the adult brain contains *neural stem cells,* a special kind of glial cells that are capable of dividing to form new tissue, including new neurons (Cheng, Tavazoie, & Doetsch, 2005; Sanai et al., 2004). The process of creating new neurons is called *neurogenesis.*

This discovery has created both excitement and controversy. There is excitement because stem cells raise hope that damaged tissue may someday be replaced by cells created from a person's own body. There is also controversy because stem cells are linked in many people's minds with the cloning of whole individuals and because it was at first believed that these cells could come only from human embryos, which must be destroyed in the process of harvesting the cells. The ethical storm surrounding the use of embryonic stem cells is abating, however, because researchers have demonstrated that stem cells can be harvested from bone marrow, the lining of the nose, skin cells, and other places (Vierbuchen et al., 2010), and then made to grow into brain cells. The benefits of using stem cells in treating brain disorders could be substantial (Murrell et al., 2005; Park et al., 2008; Yu et al., 2007). Patients suffering from spinal cord injuries, as well as from Parkinson's disease and Alzheimer's disease, might someday be cured by treatments that replace damaged or dying neurons with new ones, called *induced pluripotent stem cells,* grown from the patients' own stem cells (Chen, Magavi, & Macklis, 2004; Cowan et al., 2005; Horner & Gage, 2002; Mezey et al., 2003; Tsuji et al., 2010 ; Power & Rasko, 2011; Redmond et al., 2007; Takahashi & Yamanaka, 2006; Teng et al., 2002; Wernig et al., 2008; Zhao et al., 2003).

There is still a long way to go before any of these experimental strategies can be routinely used in the clinic (Lindvall & Kokaia, 2010), and in any case, successfully generating new neurons is only half the battle in helping the brain repair itself. The new cells' axons and dendrites would have to reestablish all the synaptic connections that had been lost to damage or disease. They may be able to do this (Weick, Liu, & Zhang, 2011), but the process is hampered in the central nervous system by glial cells that actively suppress new connections between newly sprouted axons and other neurons (Olson, 1997). Several central nervous system proteins, including one aptly named *Nogo,* have the same suppressant effect.

Despite these challenges, scientists are reporting exciting results in their efforts to promote healing in damaged brains and spinal cords. They have found, for example, that blocking the action of Nogo in mice and rats with spinal cord injuries allows surviving neurons to make new axonal connections and repair the damage (Harvey et al., 2009; Kastin & Pan, 2005). Other research with animals has shown that both spontaneous recovery and the effectiveness of brain-tissue transplants can be greatly enhanced by naturally occurring proteins called *growth factors,* which promote the survival of neurons (Wu et al., 2009). One of these proteins is called *nerve growth factor.* Another, called *glial cell line–derived neurotrophic factor,* or *GDNF,* actually causes neurons to produce the neurotransmitter needed to reverse the effects of Parkinson's disease (Kordower et al., 2000; Theofilopoulos et al., 2001). A third growth factor, called *brain derived neurotrophic factor,* or *BDNF,* has been used to guide the axons of transplanted neural stem cells to reestablish functional synaptic connections in the spinal cords of rats (Bonner et al., 2011). The best way to increase the amount of these growth factors in humans is still being studied. In one case, nerve growth factor was put directly into the brain of a patient with Alzheimer's disease (Seiger et al., 1993). The early results seemed encouraging, but the continuous infusion of the protein into the brain caused unacceptable side effects (Nabeshima & Yamada, 2000). Another way to deliver growth factors is through gene therapy, in which a gene for the desired growth factor is inserted into a patient's neurons (Bomze et al., 2001; Condic, 2001; Dass, Olanow, & Kordower, 2006; Tuszynski et al., 2002). Early results from the use of this treatment are encouraging (Tuszynski et al., 2005). Other scientists have begun to experiment with implantation of specially engineered neurons in order to encourage greater neuroplasticity (Boyden, 2011; Knöpfel et al., 2010; Li et al., 2011).

There are also things that patients themselves can do to promote the neural plasticity needed to restore lost central nervous system functions. Special mental and physical exercise programs appear useful in restructuring communication in the brains of stroke victims and spinal cord injury patients, thus reversing some forms of paralysis and improving some sensory and cognitive abilities (Blakeslee, 2001; Bryck & Fisher, 2012; Kao et al., 2009; Liepert et al., 2000; Taub, 2004). Christopher Reeve was an inspiring case in point. After his spinal cord injury, Reeve was told he would never again be able to move or feel his body. He refused to accept this gloomy prediction, and after years of devoted adherence to an exercise-oriented rehabilitation program, he regained some movement and in the years before his death was able to feel sensations from much of his body (Blakeslee, 2001).

LINKAGES

Human Development and the Changing Brain

How do our brains change over a lifetime? *(a link to Human Development)*

Fortunately, most of the changes that take place in the brain are not the kind associated with damage and disease. How does the human brain change as we develop throughout our lives? Researchers are using PET and fMRI scans to begin to answer that question. For example, they have found that association areas of the cerebral cortex develop later than the sensory and motor cortexes do (Casey, Galvan, & Hare, 2005). There are also some interesting correlations between changes in neural activity and the behavior of newborns and infants. Among newborns, scans show that activity is relatively high in the thalamus but low in a portion of the forebrain related to smooth movement. This finding may be related to the way newborns move. They make random, sweeping movements of the arms and legs—much like patients with Huntington's disease, who have a hyperactive thalamus and a withering of the part of the forebrain that controls smooth movement (Chugani & Phelps, 1986). During the second and third months after birth, activity increases in many regions of the cortex. This change is correlated with the disappearance of certain reflexes, such as the grasping reflex. At eight or nine months of age, infants show increased frontal cortex activity, which correlates with the apparent beginnings of cognitive activity (Chugani & Phelps, 1986).

The brain continues to mature through adolescence, showing evidence of ever-more-efficient neural communication in its major fiber tracts (Gogtay et al., 2004; Lebel & Beaulieu, 2011; Thompson et al., 2000). However, research using diffusion tensor imaging reveals that the connections between the prefrontal cortex and other areas involved in judgment and decision making are not yet fully developed (Asato et al., 2010). Some researchers suggest that these underdeveloped connections may be related to the difficulties that many teenagers have in resisting dangerous peer influences and foreseeing the negative consequences of certain actions (Grosbras et al., 2007). These ideas are supported by fMRI studies of adolescents that correlate self-reports of poor impulse control with reduced activation of the lateral prefrontal cortex (Andrews-Hanna et al., 2011).

Most of the changes we have described reflect plasticity—changes in axons and synapses—not the appearance of new cells. After birth, the number of dendrites and synapses increases. Although different areas of the cortex sprout at different rates, the number of synapses can increase tenfold in the first year after birth (Huttenlocher, 1990). In fact, by the time children are six or seven years old, their brains have more dendrites than those of adults, and they use twice as much energy. In early adolescence, the number of dendrites and neural connections actually drops, so that the adult level is reached by about the age of fourteen. During childhood, the brain overproduces neural connections

At birth

Six years old

Fourteen years old

FIGURE 2.14

Changes in Neurons of the Cerebral Cortex During Development

During childhood, the brain overproduces neural connections, establishes the usefulness of certain connections, and then "prunes" the extra connections. Overproduction of synapses, especially in the frontal cortex, may be essential for infants to develop certain intellectual abilities. The changes that occur in the brain during adolescence are particularly important, as this is when many psychiatric disorders first appear (Paus, Keshavan, & Giedd, 2008). Adolescence is also a time of adjusting to and (sometimes) resisting negative peer influences. Research suggests that functional connectivity among brain regions in early adolescence is correlated with resisting such influences (Grosbras et al., 2007).

Source: Conel (1939/1967). Reprinted by permission of the publisher from *The Postnatal Development of the Human Cerebral Cortex, Volume I–VIII* by Jesse LeRoy Conel, Cambridge, Mass.: Harvard University Press, Copyright © 1939, 1975 by the President and Fellows of Harvard College.

and then "prunes" the extra connections (Sowell et al., 2001). Figure 2.14 shows that as we grow, we develop more brainpower with less brain (Sowell et al., 2003).

As already mentioned, the brain's plasticity allows it to restructure itself to form new connections throughout life (Hua & Smith, 2004; Kozorovitskiy et al., 2005). Genes apparently determine the basic pattern of growth and the major lines of connections. However, the details of the connections depend on experience, including how stimulating and interesting the environment is. For example, researchers have compared the brains of rats raised individually with only a boring view of their cages to the brains of rats raised with toys and playmates. The cerebral cortex of the rats from the enriched environment had more and longer dendrites as well as more synapses than did the cortex of animals raised alone in bare cages (Klintsova & Greenough, 1999). Furthermore, the number of synapses increased when old animals who had been living in boring cages were moved to an enriched environment. Such changes in the brain following increased environmental stimulation may help explain why the maze-learning ability of genetically "maze-dull" rats raised in stimulating cages can equal that of genetically "maze-bright" animals.

Researchers have not yet determined whether an enriched environment stimulates the development of new connections or slows down normal pruning. Also not known is whether animals that are moved from a stimulating environment to a boring one will lose synaptic connections. If existing findings apply to humans, however, they have implications for how we raise children and treat the elderly. It is surely the case that within the limits set by genetics, interactions with the world mold the brain itself (Chang & Merzenich, 2003; Dick et al., 2011; Holtmaat et al., 2006). ● ● ● ●

The Chemistry of Behavior: Neurotransmitters

How do biochemicals affect my mood?

We have already seen that neurons in the nervous system communicate with each other through chemical messengers called neurotransmitters. The neurotransmitters they use can differ from one set of nerve cells to another. A group of neurons that communicate using the same neurotransmitter is called a *neurotransmitter system*. Let's explore where neurotransmitters operate in the brain and how they affect behavior.

Three Classes of Neurotransmitters

The process of chemical neurotransmission was first demonstrated in frogs by Otto Loewi in 1921. Since then, about 100 neurotransmitters have been identified, but they fall into three main classes: *small molecules, peptides,* and *gases.*

Small Molecules   The most important of the small-molecule chemicals that act as neurotransmitters are acetylcholine, norepinephrine, serotonin, dopamine, GABA, and glutamate. *Acetylcholine* (pronounced "uh-see-tull-KOE-leen") was the first to be identified as a neurotransmitter. Among the many neurons that communicate using acetylcholine are those active in controlling movement of the body, in making memories, and in slowing the heartbeat and activating the digestive system. No wonder, then, that disruption of acetylcholine systems can result in a wide variety of problems, including the loss of memory and other mental powers that is seen in Alzheimer's disease.

Systems of neurons that use *norepinephrine* (pronounced "nor-eppa-NEF-rin") affect arousal, wakefulness, learning, and mood. This neurotransmitter is involved when your nervous system prepares you to fight or to run away from a threat. Changes in norepinephrine systems have also been implicated in depression.

The neurotransmitter *serotonin* (pronounced "sair-oh-TOE-nin") is similar to norepinephrine in that it affects both sleep and mood. Serotonin may also be involved in the appearance of aggressive and impulsive behaviors. Unlike norepinephrine, though, the amount of serotonin in your brain can be affected by what you eat. For example, eating carbohydrates can increase serotonin, and the increase in serotonin normally reduces the desire for carbohydrates. Some researchers suspect that malfunctions in

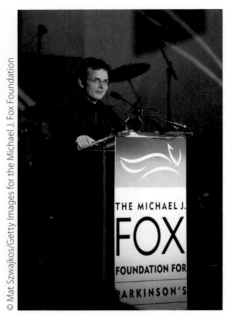

Promoting Research on Parkinson's Disease

Actor Michael J. Fox suffers from Parkinson's disease, a condition related to malfunctioning of dopamine systems in the brain. He founded the Michael J. Fox Foundation for Parkinson's Research (http://www.michaeljfox.org/) to fund more research on treating, curing, and perhaps even preventing, Parkinson's disease.

serotonin systems can result in the mood and appetite problems seen in some types of obesity, premenstrual tension, and depression, including disorders in which depressed mood, suicidal tendencies, and impulsivity appear together (Bach-Mizrachi et al., 2006; McCloskey et al., 2009; Oquendo & Mann, 2000). Antidepressant medications such as Prozac, Zoloft, and Paxil appear to relieve some of the symptoms of depression by acting on serotonin systems to maintain proper levels of this neurotransmitter.

Dopamine (pronounced "DOPE-uh-meen") is a neurotransmitter that is important for movement. Malfunctions of dopamine systems contribute to movement disorders such as Parkinson's disease and the shakiness experienced by people who have it. Parkinson's has been treated with some success using drugs that enable neurons to make more dopamine and by implanting dopamine-using neurons (Chase, 1998; Mendez et al., 2008). Permanently implanting an electrode that stimulates neurons in the brain's dopamine-influenced motor system offers an even more effective treatment but also carries a risk of surgical complications (Weaver et al., 2009). Other dopamine systems are involved in the experiencing of reward, or pleasure, which is vital in shaping and motivating behavior (Spanagel & Weiss, 1999). Animals will work very hard to receive a direct dose of dopamine to certain parts of the brain. These dopamine systems play a role in the rewarding properties of many drugs, including cocaine (Ciccocioppo, Sanna, & Weiss, 2001; Hyman, Malenka, & Nestler, 2006). Certain dopamine systems are also suspected to be partly responsible for the perceptual, emotional, and thought disturbances associated with schizophrenia, a severe mental disorder (Marenco & Weinberger, 2000).

GABA stands for gamma-amino butyric acid. Unlike most neurotransmitters, which excite neurons to fire action potentials, GABA *reduces* the likelihood that neurons will fire. In fact, it is the main neurotransmitter for slowing, or inhibiting, the brain's activity. When you fall asleep, neurons that use GABA deserve part of the credit. Drugs that cause reduced neural activity often do so by amplifying the "braking" action of GABA. For example, alcohol's effect on GABA systems is partly responsible for the impairments in thinking, judgment, and motor skills that occur when people drink too much. Malfunctions of GABA systems contribute to severe anxiety and to *Huntington's disease,* an inherited disorder that causes its victims to suffer uncontrollable movement of the arms and legs along with a progressive loss of thinking abilities. Drugs that interfere with GABA's inhibitory effects produce intense repetitive electrical discharges, known as *seizures.* Researchers suspect that impaired GABA systems contribute to *epilepsy,* another brain disorder associated with seizures and convulsive movements. Repeated or sustained seizures can result in permanent brain damage. Drug treatments can reduce the frequency and severity of seizures but do not eliminate them and may cause undesirable side effects. An alternative treatment approach may someday come from *optogenetics,* a newly developing field of neuroscience in which the genes of light-sensitive plant proteins are inserted into animal neurons (Airan et al., 2009). This procedure allows the firing of these neurons to be increased or decreased by shining a particular kind of light on them, and there is evidence that the technique is capable of stopping seizure activity in animal brain cells (Tonneson et al., 2009). If a similar strategy can be adapted for use in humans, it would provide welcome relief for millions of people with epilepsy.

Glutamate (pronounced "GLOO-tuh-mate") is used by more neurons than any other neurotransmitter, and it also helps glial cells provide energy for neurons (Rouach et al., 2008). Glutamate is particularly important because it helps the brain strengthen its synaptic connections, allowing messages to more easily cross the gap between neurons. This strengthening process is necessary for normal development and may be at the root of learning and memory (Newpher & Ehlers, 2008). Yet overactivity of glutamate synapses can cause neurons to die, and is the main cause of the brain damage that occurs when oxygen is cut off from neurons during a stroke. Blocking glutamate receptors immediately after a brain trauma can prevent permanent brain damage (Colak et al., 2003). Glutamate may also contribute to the loss of brain cells that occurs in Alzheimer's disease (Cha et al., 2001).

Peptides   Chemicals called *peptides* also act as neurotransmitters. The first of these, called *endorphins,* were discovered in the 1970s, when scientists were studying *opiates* such as morphine and heroin. Derived from poppy flowers, opiates can relieve pain, produce intense feelings of happiness, and, in high doses, bring on sleep. After marking morphine with a radioactive agent, researchers identified places where it became concentrated in the brain. They found that the opiates bind to receptors that had not been associated with any previously identified neurotransmitter. It is unlikely that the brain had developed opiate receptors just in case a person might want to use morphine or heroin, so researchers reasoned that the body must contain a substance that is similar to opiates. This hypothesis led to the search for a naturally occurring, or *endogenous,* morphine. (*Endogenous* is pronounced "en-DODGE-uh-niss"; *endorphin* is a contraction of the words *endogenous* and *morphine.*) As it turns out, there are many natural opiate-like compounds, and new ones are still being discovered. So the term *endorphin* refers to any neurotransmitter that can bind to the same receptors stimulated by opiates. Endorphins are used by neurons in several parts of the brain, including neuronal pathways that modify pain signals to the brain.

Gases   Our ideas about neurotransmitters changed radically following the discovery that *nitric oxide* and *carbon monoxide*—two toxic gases that contribute to air pollution—could act as neurotransmitters (Boehning & Snyder, 2003). When nitric oxide or carbon monoxide is released by a neuron, it spreads to nearby neurons, sending a signal that affects chemical reactions inside those neurons instead of binding to receptors on their surfaces. Nitric oxide is not stored in vesicles, as most other neurotransmitters are; it can be released from any part of the neuron. Nitric oxide appears to be one of the neurotransmitters responsible for such diverse functions as penile erection and the formation of memories—not at the same site, obviously.

In summary, neurotransmitters acting throughout the body link our biochemistry with every aspect of our behavior and mental processes. You will see other examples in the chapter on sensation and perception, where we describe some of the neurotransmitters that help convey pain messages. In the consciousness chapter, we consider how neurotransmitters are affected by alcohol and illegal drugs. In the chapter on psychological disorders, we discuss the role that neurotransmitters play in schizophrenia and depression, and in the chapter on the treatment of psychological disorders, we explore ways that prescription drugs act on neurotransmitters to alleviate the symptoms of those disorders. ("In Review: Classes of Neurotransmitters" lists the most important of these neurotransmitters and the consequences of malfunctioning neurotransmitter systems.)

Classes of Neurotransmitters   IN REVIEW

Neurotransmitter Class	Normal Function	Disorder Associated with Malfunction
Small Molecules		
Acetylcholine	Memory, movement	Alzheimer's disease
Norepinephrine	Mood, sleep, learning	Depression
Serotonin	Mood, appetite, impulsivity	Depression
Dopamine	Movement, reward	Parkinson's disease, schizophrenia
GABA	Sleep, movement	Anxiety, Huntington's disease, epilepsy
Glutamate	Memory	Damage after stroke
Peptides		
Endorphins	Pain control	No established disorder
Gases		
Nitric oxide	Memory	No established disorder

IN REVIEW QUESTIONS

1. The main neurotransmitter for slowing, or inhibiting, brain activity is ___.

2. A group of neurons that use the same neurotransmitter is called a ___.

3. Which neurotransmitter's activity causes brain damage during a stroke?

FIGURE 2.15
Some Major Glands of the Endocrine System
Each of the glands shown releases its hormones into the bloodstream. Even the hypothalamus, a part of the brain, regulates the nearby pituitary gland by secreting hormones.

(Photos: Left, © 4x6/iStockphoto; Right, © Paul Radenfeld/Digital Vision/Getty Images)

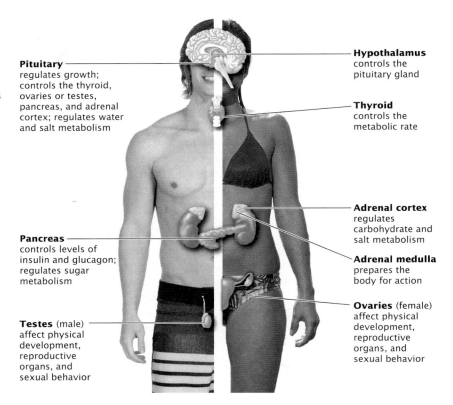

Pituitary
regulates growth; controls the thyroid, ovaries or testes, pancreas, and adrenal cortex; regulates water and salt metabolism

Hypothalamus
controls the pituitary gland

Thyroid
controls the metabolic rate

Adrenal cortex
regulates carbohydrate and salt metabolism

Pancreas
controls levels of insulin and glucagon; regulates sugar metabolism

Adrenal medulla
prepares the body for action

Ovaries (female)
affect physical development, reproductive organs, and sexual behavior

Testes (male)
affect physical development, reproductive organs, and sexual behavior

The Endocrine System: Coordinating the Internal World

How can my hormones help me in a crisis?

Neurons are not the only cells that use chemicals to communicate with one another in ways that affect behavior and mental processes. Another kind of cell with this ability is found in the **endocrine system**. Operating on orders from the brain, the endocrine system regulates growth, energy consumption, and sexual behavior, and it readies the body for action. The cells of the endocrine organs, or **glands,** communicate by secreting chemicals, much as neurons do. Figure 2.15 shows some major glands of the endocrine system. The chemicals that these glands secrete are called **hormones.**

Hormones from endocrine organs are similar to neurotransmitters. In fact, many such chemicals, including norepinephrine and the endorphins, act both as hormones and as neurotransmitters. However, whereas neurons secrete neurotransmitters into synapses, endocrine organs release their chemicals into the bloodstream, which carries them throughout the body. In this way, endocrine glands can stimulate cells with which they have no direct connection. But not all cells receive the hormonal message. Hormones, like neurotransmitters, can influence only those cells with receptors capable of receiving them. Organs whose cells have receptors for a particular hormone are called *target organs.*

Each hormone acts on many target organs, producing coordinated effects throughout the body. For example, when a woman's ovaries secrete the sex hormone *estrogen*, it activates her reproductive system, causing the uterus to grow in preparation for nurturing an embryo. It enlarges the breasts to prepare them for nursing. It stimulates the brain to increase interest in sexual activity. And it stimulates the pituitary gland to release another hormone that causes a mature egg to be released by the ovary for fertilization. In

endocrine system Cells that form organs called glands and that communicate with one another by secreting hormones.

glands Organs that secrete hormones into the bloodstream.

hormones Chemicals secreted by glands into the bloodstream, which carries them throughout the body.

males, sex organs called *testes* secrete *testosterone*, one of several sex hormones known as *androgens*. Androgens stimulate the maturation of sperm, increase a male's motivation for sexual activity, and increase his aggressiveness (Romeo, Richardson, & Sisk, 2002).

The brain, as a kind of "boss," has ultimate control over the secretion of hormones. The hypothalamus controls the pituitary gland, which in turn controls endocrine organs in the body. The brain is also a target organ for most hormones. In short, the endocrine system typically involves the brain, the pituitary gland, the endocrine organ, and the target organs (which include the brain). In fact, the brain creates some of the same hormones that are secreted in the endocrine system and uses them for neural communication (Melcangi et al., 2011). Each part in the system uses hormones to signal the next (Dubrovsky, 2005).

The secretion of each hormone is increased or decreased by other hormones. Consider stress-hormone systems, for example. When the brain interprets a situation as threatening, it stimulates the pituitary gland to release *adrenocorticotropic hormone (ACTH)*, which causes the adrenal glands to release the hormone *cortisol* into the bloodstream. Cortisol, in turn, acts on cells throughout the body, including the brain. One effect of cortisol is to activate the emotion-related limbic system, making it more likely that you will remember stressful or traumatic events. The combined effects of the adrenal hormones and the activation of the sympathetic nervous system result in the **fight-flight reaction.** The many components of this response prepare us for action in response to danger or other stress. The heart beats faster, the liver releases glucose into the bloodstream, fuels are mobilized from fat stores, and the body as a whole is placed in a state of high arousal. Without the endocrine system and the effects of its hormones on the brain, your life would not only be much less emotional but you also would be less able to escape or avoid threatening situations.

fight-flight reaction Physical reactions triggered by the sympathetic nervous system that prepare the body to fight or to run from a threatening situation.

Active Review

As noted in the introductory chapter, all of psychology's subfields are related to one another. Our discussion of developmental changes in the brain illustrates just one way that the topic of this chapter, biology and behavior, is linked to the subfield of developmental psychology, which

CHAPTER 2
Biology and Behavior

is described in the chapter on human development. The Linkages diagram shows ties to two other subfields, and there are many more ties throughout the book. Looking for linkages among subfields will help you see how they all fit together and help you better appreciate the big picture that is psychology.

LINKAGES

Does the brain shut down when we sleep? (ans. on p. 141)

How do our brains change over a lifetime? (ans. on p. 70)

How do drugs help people who suffer from schizophrenia? (ans. on p. 534)

CHAPTER 4
Consciousness

CHAPTER 9
Human Development

CHAPTER 13
Treatment of Psychological Disorders

Summary

Biological psychology focuses on the biological aspects of our being, which provide the physical basis for behavior and mental processes. Included among these aspects is the ***nervous system,*** which is composed of billions of cells that allow humans and other organisms to gain information about what is going on inside and outside the body and to respond appropriately.

Cells of the Nervous System

What are neurons, and what do they do?
Much of our understanding of the biological aspects of psychology has stemmed from research on animal and human nervous systems at levels ranging from single cells to complex organizations of cells, including the brain. The fundamental units of the

nervous system are cells called ***neurons*** and ***glial cells.*** Neurons are especially good at receiving signals from and transmitting signals to other neurons. Neurons have cell bodies and two types of fibers, called ***axons*** and ***dendrites.*** Axons usually carry signals away from the cell body, whereas dendrites usually carry signals to the cell body.

Neurons can transmit signals because of the structure of the axons and dendrites and the ***synapses,*** or gaps, between cells. A neuron can transmit, or fire, an ***action potential*** from one end of its axon to the other. The speed of the action potential is fastest in neurons covered in myelin. The very brief rest between firings is called the ***refractory period.*** When an action potential reaches the end of an axon, the axon releases a chemical called a ***neurotransmitter.*** This chemical

crosses the synapse and interacts with the postsynaptic cell at receptors, making the postsynaptic cell either more likely or less likely to fire its own action potential. Other neurons communicate more directly through electrical signals. Because neurons' fibers have many branches, each neuron can interact with thousands of other neurons. Each neuron constantly integrates signals received at its many synapses; the result of this integration determines how often the neuron fires an action potential.

The cells of the nervous system are organized into two main parts: the ***central nervous system (CNS)*** and the ***peripheral nervous system (PNS).***

The Peripheral Nervous System: Keeping in Touch with the World

How do sights and sounds reach my brain?
The peripheral nervous system has two components. The first is the ***somatic***

nervous system, which transmits information from the senses to the CNS and carries signals from the CNS to muscles that move the skeleton. It performs these tasks through sensory systems that receive information from the environment and motor systems that influence the actions of muscles and other organs. The second component of the PNS is the **autonomic nervous system,** whose subsystems, the **sympathetic nervous system** and the **parasympathetic nervous system,** carry messages back and forth between the CNS and the heart, lungs, and other organs and glands.

The Central Nervous System: Making Sense of the World

How is my brain "wired"?

The CNS is laid out in interconnected groups of neuron cell bodies called **nuclei,** whose collections of axons travel together in **fiber tracts,** or pathways. The **spinal cord** receives information from the peripheral senses and sends it to the brain; it also relays messages from the brain to the rest of the body. In addition, cells of the spinal cord can direct simple behaviors called **reflexes** without instructions from the brain. The brain's major subdivisions are the **hindbrain,** the **midbrain,** and the **forebrain.** The hindbrain includes the **medulla oblongata** and the **cerebellum.** The **reticular formation** is found in the hindbrain and the midbrain.

The forebrain is the largest and most highly developed part of the brain. Its structures include the **thalamus** and the **hypothalamus** as well as the **hippocampus,** and the **amygdala,** which form part of the limbic system. The suprachiasmatic nuclei, a part of the hypothalamus, maintain a clock that determines biological rhythms. The outer surface of the cerebral hemispheres is called the **cerebral cortex;** it is responsible for many of the higher functions of the brain, including speech and reasoning. The functional areas of the cortex consist of the **sensory cortex,** the **motor cortex,** and the **association cortex.**

The right and left hemispheres of the cerebral cortex are specialized to some degree in their functions. In most people, the left hemisphere is more active in language and logical tasks and the right hemisphere in spatial tasks. The hemispheres are connected through the **corpus callosum,** allowing them to operate in a coordinated fashion.

The brain's **neural plasticity,** the ability to strengthen neural connections at its synapses as well as to establish new synapses, forms the basis for learning and memory. Scientists are studying ways to increase plasticity and stimulate neurogenesis—the formation of new neurons—following brain damage.

A child's growing and changing intellectual abilities are based on changing synaptic connections in the brain, not on an increase in the number of brain cells. The brain produces many more synaptic connections than it needs, pruning extra connections as experience strengthens useful connections. The ability to form new synapses continues even into old age.

The Chemistry of Behavior: Neurotransmitters

How do biochemicals affect my mood?

Neurons that use the same neurotransmitter form a neurotransmitter system. There are three types of neurotransmitters: small molecules, peptides, and gases. Small molecules include acetylcholine, norepinephrine, serotonin, dopamine, GABA, and glutamate. Acetylcholine systems in the brain influence memory processes and movement. Norepinephrine is involved in arousal, mood, and learning. Serotonin is active in systems regulating mood and appetite. Dopamine systems are involved in movement and reward; Parkinson's disease and schizophrenia involve disturbances in dopamine systems. GABA is an inhibitory neurotransmitter involved in anxiety and epilepsy. Glutamate is the most common excitatory neurotransmitter; it is involved in learning and memory. In excess, though, it may cause neuronal death. Peptide neurotransmitters include the endorphins, which act like morphine by affecting pain pathways. Nitric oxide and carbon monoxide are two gases that can act as neurotransmitters.

The Endocrine System: Coordinating the Internal World

How can my hormones help me in a crisis?

Like nervous system cells, the cells of the **endocrine system** communicate by releasing a chemical that signals other cells. These chemicals, called **hormones,** are released by endocrine organs, or **glands,** and then carried by the bloodstream to remote target organs. The brain is the main controller: Through the hypothalamus, it controls the pituitary gland, which in turn controls endocrine organs in the body. The brain is also a target organ for most endocrine secretions. The target organs often produce a coordinated response to hormonal stimulation. One example is the **fight-flight reaction,** which is set off by adrenal hormones that prepare for action in times of stress.

Put It in Writing

Suppose you are asked to help a young mother choose the infant care center that will be most likely to stimulate her one-year-old son's brain development. Write a page about what biological psychology research tells you about the role of environment on brain development. Does that research provide a useful guide for choosing the best day-care center? Why or why not?

Personal Learning Activity

To get a rough measure of the role played by your brain's left hemisphere in language, try the following test. First, see how long you can balance a yardstick on the tip of your right index finger, and then try the same task with your left hand. The difference in how long you can keep the stick balanced will probably be determined by whether you are right-handed or left-handed. Now try this balancing act eight more times, alternating hands on each trial so that you use your left index finger four times and your right index finger four times. Now here's where language might come in: On two of the four trials with each hand, count backward from 100 by 3s (100, 97, 94, 91, and so on) out loud while you try to keep the stick balanced. It has been suggested that this language task might interfere with your balancing skill, especially when you are using your right hand (Kemble, Filipi, & Gravlin, 1985; Kinsbourne & Cook, 1971). Why? If the left side of your brain is more involved with language, then counting backward while balancing with your right hand requires the left hemisphere to do two things at once. When counting while balancing with the left hand, the right hemisphere is handling the balancing and the left hemisphere is dealing with the language task. Is this what happened in your case? Try the same tests on your friends and summarize the results.

Review of Key Terms

Can you define each of the key terms in the chapter? Check your definitions against those on the pages shown in parentheses in the following list or in the Glossary at the end of the book.

action potential (p. 48)
amygdala (p. 56)
association cortex (p. 59)
autonomic nervous system (p. 51)
axon (p. 48)
biological psychology (p. 46)
central nervous system (CNS) (p. 50)
cerebellum (p. 53)
cerebral cortex (p. 56)
corpus callosum (p. 56)
dendrites (p. 48)

endocrine system (p. 74)
fiber tracts (p. 52)
fight-flight reaction (p. 75)
forebrain (p. 55)
glands (p. 74)
glial cells (p. 47)
hindbrain (p. 53)
hippocampus (p. 56)
hormones (p. 74)
hypothalamus (p. 55)
locus coeruleus (p. 53)
medulla oblongata (p. 53)
midbrain (p. 55)
motor cortex (p. 58)
motor neurons (p. 51)
nervous system (p. 46)
neural networks (p. 50)

neural plasticity (p. 68)
neurons (p. 46)
neurotransmitter (p. 49)
nuclei (p. 52)
parasympathetic nervous
    system (PNS) (p. 51)
peripheral nervous system (p. 50)
reflexes (p. 52)
refractory period (p. 48)
reticular formation (p. 53)
sensory cortex (p. 57)
sensory neurons (p. 51)
somatic nervous system (p. 51)
spinal cord (p. 52)
sympathetic nervous system (p. 51)
synapse (p. 49)
thalamus (p. 55)

Test Your Knowledge

Select the best answer for each of the following questions. Then check your responses against the Answer Key at the end of the book.

1. The nucleus of a cell _____, and the mitochondria _____.
    a. produces red blood cells; turn oxygen into glucose
    b. produces red blood cells; keep a stable chemical environment

c. provides genetic information; turn oxygen into glucose
d. provides genetic information; keep a stable chemical environment

2. A nurse has mixed up some test results on neurotransmitter function for several patients at the hospital where you work. To help her out, you tell her that the depressed patient's chart will probably show malfunctions in _____ systems and the Parkinson's

patient's chart will probably show malfunctions in ____ systems.

a. dopamine; norepinephrine

b. dopamine; acetylcholine

c. serotonin; dopamine

d. acetylcholine; norepinephrine

3. Hannah had a stroke and oxygen was cut off from the neurons in her brain. This caused overactivity in ____ synapses, which led to brain damage.

a. glutamate

b. dopamine

c. acetylcholine

d. serotonin

4. Functional magnetic resonance imaging (fMRI) provides a way to ____.

a. directly measure brain cell activity

b. visualize changes in blood flow and oxygen levels in various brain areas

c. locate the causes of particular mental processes

d. locate where certain emotions take place in the brain

5. As you switch on your favorite TV medical show, a doctor charges through the emergency room doors and tells a worried spouse that her husband has a neurological problem. "The nerves that carry signals to his muscles are not functioning," the doctor says, "which means the ____ nervous system has been damaged."

a. central

b. autonomic

c. somatic

d. sympathetic

6. Kalli finishes a difficult final exam, then hurries home and flops down on her bed to relax. As Kalli relaxes, her ____ nervous system becomes less active, whereas her ____ nervous system becomes more active.

a. central; somatic

b. somatic; central

c. parasympathetic; sympathetic

d. sympathetic; parasympathetic

7. When Karena accidentally touched a hot stove, she instantly jerked her hand away. This automatic response was directed by neurons entering and leaving the ____, which is part of the ____ nervous system.

a. spinal cord; central

b. spinal cord; autonomic

c. hypothalamus; central

d. hypothalamus; autonomic

8. A neuron's action potential shoots down its axon with greater speed when the ____.

a. axon is coated in myelin

b. refractory period is longer

c. neuron's diameter is smaller

d. neuron is in the brain

9. Jessica has severe damage to her medulla. Most likely, Jessica ____.

a. is dead

b. will have memory problems

c. will have difficulty with fine motor movements

d. will not feel anything on the left side of her body

10. Damage in Lily's hindbrain caused her to lapse into a coma. The damage most likely occurred in the ____.

a. cerebellum

b. hippocampus

c. hypothalamus

d. reticular formation

11. Riley was an excellent pianist until he suffered brain damage. Now problems with fine motor skills make it impossible for him to play the piano. Riley most likely had damage to his ____.

a. cerebellum

b. hippocampus

c. hypothalamus

d. reticular formation

12. The hippocampus has been found to be significantly smaller in patients who are suffering from which of the following problems?

a. Parkinson's disease

b. Alzheimer's disease

c. depression

d. an eating disorder

13. A woman was rushed to an emergency room with severely burned hands. She had picked up an iron because she couldn't tell it was hot, and she still doesn't feel pain from her burns. The neurologist who examined her concluded that the woman's ____ system is malfunctioning.

a. sensory

b. motor

c. autonomic

d. parasympathetic

14. Reginald has suffered damage to his occipital lobe. This means that Reginald will have difficulty ____.

a. feeling pain

b. moving his body

c. seeing

d. regulating body temperature

15. Elnora wants to hit a nail with a hammer so she can hang a picture on the wall. This involves voluntary movements that are controlled by neurons in the ____ cortex, which is located in the ____ lobe.

a. motor; frontal

b. motor; parietal

c. association; temporal

d. sensory; occipital

16. Roberto, an actor, is recovering following a freak accident on the set of his latest movie. When asked about the accident, Roberto, once a confident and fluent speaker, can now only say, "Noise… acting… hurts." The part of Roberto's brain most likely involved in this type of speech problem is ____ area.

a. Broca's

b. Sperry's

c. Wernicke's

d. Sylva's

17. Joe experienced such severe seizures that doctors had to sever his corpus callosum. Following surgery, a psychologist presented the left hemisphere of Joe's brain with a picture of a car and asked Joe what he saw. Most likely, Joe could _____.
    a. correctly say "car"
    b. not identify the car in words
    c. only draw a car
    d. not understand the question
18. Edie is 80 and has suffered a paralyzing stroke. Her doctors are likely to tell her that _____.
    a. if she imagines moving her body, she can increase the number of neurons in her motor cortex
    b. the Nogo protein will help regenerate nerve cells
    c. neural stem cells will automatically repair the damage
    d. mental and physical exercise programs can help reverse some of the effects of the stroke
19. Ted is creating a study sheet to help him learn the differences between neurotransmitters and hormones. Which of the following statements on his list is *not* correct?
    a. Neurotransmitters travel through the bloodstream and hormones travel across synapses.
    b. Both hormones and neurotransmitters stimulate only those cells and organs that have receptors for them.
    c. Hormones and neurotransmitters regulate complex behaviors and mental processes.
    d. Hormones operate mainly in the endocrine system; neurotransmitters operate mainly in the nervous system.
20. When Mitch saw a woman in danger of drowning, he jumped into the water to save her. Mitch's endocrine system readied him for this exertion by releasing _____ and other stress hormones into his bloodstream.
    a. cortisol
    b. GABA
    c. glutamate
    d. BABA

Media Resources . . . .

Now that you have finished reading this chapter, how about exploring some of the ideas and information that you found most interesting?

Go to **CengageBrain.com** to access Psychology CourseMate, where you will find an interactive eBook, glossaries, flashcards, quizzes, videos, Virtual Psychology Labs, and more.

aplia™

If your professor has assigned Aplia:

1. Sign in to your account.
2. Complete the corresponding exercises as required by your professor.
3. When finished, click "Grade It Now" to see which areas you have mastered, which areas need more work, and detailed explanations of every answer.

Sensation and Perception

© Benjamin Torode/Flickr/Getty Images

Preview

You can understand this sentence because the lines and squiggles that make up its letters somehow become meaningful words. This "somehow" is what sensation and perception are all about. You translate incoming stimulation, such as the light bouncing off this page, into neural activity called *sensations*. Then you interpret these sensations as meaningful experiences called *perceptions*—in this case, as letters and words. These amazing processes are so quick and automatic that you probably take them for granted. In this chapter, we draw your attention to them. You will learn about how our sensory systems receive stimulation and how they encode that stimulation into patterns of nerve activity that the brain can decode. You will also discover how the brain interprets, or perceives, this information from your senses.

It has been years since Fred Aryee lost his right arm below the elbow in a boating accident, yet he still "feels" sensations from his missing lower arm and hand. Once, his doctor asked Aryee to reach for a cup on the table in front of him with his right arm. When asked what he felt, Aryee said, "I feel my fingers clasping the cup" (Shreeve, 1993). People like Fred may also feel intense pain that seems to be coming from a lost limb (Glummarra et al., 2007; Ramachandran, 2008). Where do these "phantom limb" sensations and perceptions come from? Fred no longer has fingers to send messages to the brain, yet he experienced his "feeling" of the cup as real. Others who have lost, say, a left arm feel that they now have two right arms (Cipriani et al., 2011). These cases remind us that the "objective reality" we assume to be the same for everyone can actually differ from person to person (Bartoshuk, Fast, & Snyder, 2005). Just as someone can feel a hand that isn't actually "there," every individual's senses actively shape information about the outside world to create a personal reality.

Psychologists find it useful to distinguish between sensation (the stimulus message coming from the senses) and perception (the process of giving meaning to that message). So you don't actually sense a cat lying on the sofa. You sense shapes and colors, the visual sensations. You then use your knowledge of the world to interpret, or perceive, these sensations as a cat. However, it's impossible to draw a clear line between sensation and perception, because the process of interpreting sensations begins in the sense organs themselves. ●

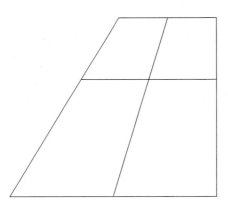

FIGURE 3.1
What do you see?

sense A system that translates data from outside the nervous system into neural activity.

sensations Raw information from the senses.

perception The process through which people take raw sensations from the environment and give them meaning using knowledge, experience, and understanding of the world.

Sensing and Perceiving the World

What is the difference between sensation and perception?

To understand how sensory systems help us create reality, we need to have some basic information about the senses. A **sense** is a system that translates outside information into activity in the nervous system. For example, your eyes convert light into neural activity that tells the brain something about the source of the light or about the objects reflecting it. Messages from the senses are called **sensations.** Sensations shape behaviors and mental processes by providing the vital link between the self and the world outside the brain.

Perception is the process of using information and your understanding of the world to turn those sensations into meaningful experiences. Perception is more than a passive process of absorbing and decoding incoming sensations. For example, look at Figure 3.1. It sends you only raw sensory information about a series of intersecting lines. But your perceptual system automatically interprets this image as a rectangle (or window frame) lying on its side. Perception is so quick and familiar that it is difficult to appreciate the processes that allow you to turn sensory signals into your experience of reality. By shaping this experience, your perceptions influence your thoughts, feelings, and actions. But before you can perceive something, you must be able to sense it.

Sensory Systems

How does information from my eyes and ears get to my brain?

Your senses gather information about the world by detecting various forms of energy, such as sound, light, heat, and physical pressure. Your eyes detect light energy, your ears detect the energy of sound, and your skin detects the energy of heat and pressure. Humans depend mainly on vision, hearing, and the skin senses to gain information about the world. Other animals depend more on smell and taste than we do. To your brain, "the world" also includes the rest of your body, so specific sensory systems provide information about the location and position of your body parts.

All senses detect information about stimuli, encode it into neural activity, and then send this encoded information to the brain. Figure 3.2 illustrates these basic steps in sensation. At each step, sensory information is "processed" in some way. So the information that arrives at one point in the system is not exactly the same information that goes to the next step.

The first step in most sensory systems involves **accessory structures,** which modify the incoming stimuli (Step 1 in Figure 3.2). For example, the lens of the eye is an accessory structure that changes incoming light by focusing it. The flexible part of the ear that extends outside your head is an accessory structure that collects sound.

The second step in sensation is **transduction,** which is the process of converting incoming energy into neural activity (Step 2 in Figure 3.2). Your cell phone receives electromagnetic energy and transduces it into sounds. In much the same way, your ears receive sound energy and transduce it into neural activity that you recognize as voices and music. Transduction takes place in structures called **neural receptors,** which are specialized cells that detect certain forms of energy. These receptors respond to incoming energy by firing an action potential and releasing neurotransmitters that send signals to neighboring cells. Sensory receptors respond best to *changes* in energy (Graziano et al., 2002). A constant level of stimulation usually produces **sensory adaptation,** or a decreasing responsiveness to the stimulus over time. This is the reason that the touch sensations you get from your glasses or wristwatch disappear shortly after you have put them on.

Sensory nerves carry information from receptors to the central nervous system—the spinal cord and the brain (Step 3 in Figure 3.2). For all the senses except smell, this information goes first to the thalamus, which does some initial processing before sending it on to the cerebral cortex (Step 4; Sherman, 2007). The most complex processing occurs in specialized areas of the sensory cortex (Step 5; Kanwisher, 2010). (For a reminder of the location of these brain structures, see Figure 2.8.)

Encoding Sensations: What Was That?

The neural activity that is created when sensory receptors transduce incoming energy acts as a coded message about the stimulus that produced the energy. So our psychological experience of a stimulus, such as its brightness or color, is based on a corresponding feature of its physical energy, as encoded by neural receptors. In other words, **encoding** translates the physical properties of a stimulus, such as its shape or intensity, into a pattern of neural activity that tells us what those physical properties are. When the brain organizes these neural patterns, you can make sense of the stimulus and decide whether you are looking at a white cat, a black dog, or a tall person.

Absolute Thresholds: Is Something Out There?

How much stimulus energy does it take to trigger a conscious perceptual experience? Not much at all. Normal human vision can detect the light equivalent to a candle flame burning in the dark 30 miles away. The minimum detectable amount of light, sound, pressure, or other physical energy has traditionally been called the *absolute threshold*. Table 3.1 lists absolute thresholds for human vision, hearing, taste, smell, and touch.

accessory structures Structures, such as the outer part of the ear, that modify a stimulus.

transduction The process of converting incoming physical energy into neural activity.

neural receptors Cells that are specialized to detect certain types of energy and convert it into neural activity.

sensory adaptation Decreasing responsiveness to an unchanging stimulus.

encoding Translation of the physical properties of a stimulus into a specific pattern of neural activity.

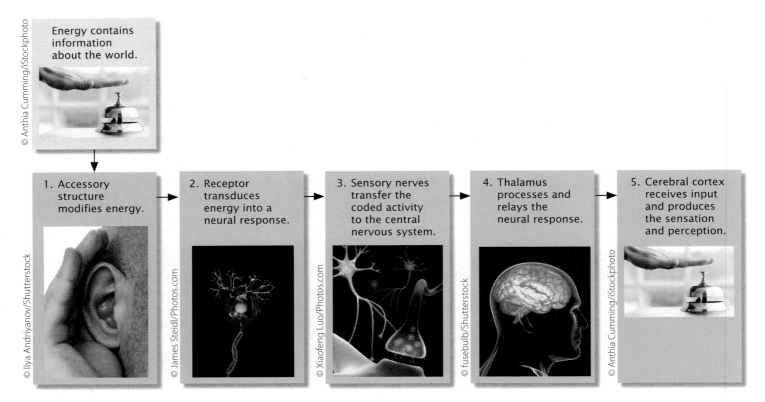

Energy contains information about the world.

1. Accessory structure modifies energy.

2. Receptor transduces energy into a neural response.

3. Sensory nerves transfer the coded activity to the central nervous system.

4. Thalamus processes and relays the neural response.

5. Cerebral cortex receives input and produces the sensation and perception.

FIGURE 3.2

Elements of a Sensory System

Objects in the world generate energy that is focused by accessory structures and detected by sensory receptors, which convert the energy into neural signals. The signals are then relayed through parts of the brain, which processes them into perceptual experiences.

absolute threshold The minimum amount of stimulus energy that can be detected 50 percent of the time.

noise The spontaneous random firing of nerve cells that occurs because the nervous system is always active.

response bias (response criterion) The internal rule a person uses to decide whether or not to report a stimulus.

Psychologists discovered these thresholds by exploring *psychophysics,* the relationship between *physical* energy in the environment and your *psychological experience* of that energy. In a typical absolute threshold experiment, you would be seated in a darkened laboratory. After your eyes got used to the darkness, the researcher would show you brief flashes of light. These flashes would differ in brightness, or stimulus intensity. Each time, you'd be asked if you saw the light. Averaged over a large number of trials, the pattern of your correct detections would probably form a curve like the one shown in Figure 3.3. As you can see, the absolute threshold is not an all-or-nothing affair. A stimulus at an intensity of three, which is below the absolute threshold in the figure, will still be detected 20 percent of the time it occurs. Because of such variability, psychophysicists redefined the **absolute threshold** as the smallest amount of energy that can be detected 50 percent of the time. Why does a supposedly "absolute" threshold vary? The two most important reasons have to do with "noise" and our response bias.

In psychophysics, the term internal **noise** describes the random firing of cells in the nervous system that continues in varying amounts whether or not you are stimulated by physical energy. If the amount of internal noise happens to be high at a particular moment, your sensory systems might mistakenly interpret the noise as an external stimulus.

The second source of variation in absolute threshold is **response bias,** also known as the **response criterion,** which reflects a person's willingness to respond to a stimulus. A person's *motivation*—wants and needs—as well as *expectations* affect response bias. For example, if you were punished for reporting that a faint light appeared when it did not, then you might be motivated to raise your response criterion. That is, you would report the light only when you were quite sure you saw it. Similarly, expecting a faint stimulus to occur lowers the response criterion. Suppose, for example, that you worked at an airport security checkpoint, examining x-ray images of people's handbags, briefcases, and luggage. The signal to be detected in this situation is a weapon. If there has been a recent terrorist attack or if the threat level has just been elevated, your airport will be on high alert. In that situation, your response criterion for saying that a questionable object on the x-ray image might be a weapon will be much lower than if terrorism were not so

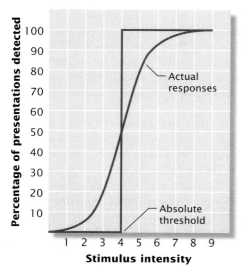

FIGURE 3.3
The Absolute Threshold
The curved line shows the relationship between the physical intensity of a signal and the chance that it will be detected. If the absolute threshold were truly absolute, or exact, all signals at or above a particular intensity would always be detected and no signals below that intensity would ever be detected (as shown by the red line). But this response pattern almost never occurs, so the "absolute" threshold is defined as the intensity at which the signal is detected 50 percent of the time.

likely. You will be more likely to detect a weapon if there is one but you'll also be more likely to mistake, say, a hairdryer for a gun.

Signal Detection Theory   Once researchers understood that the detection of a stimulus depends on the combination of its physical energy, the effects of noise, and a person's response bias, they realized that measurement of absolute thresholds could never be more precise than the 50 percent rule mentioned earlier. So they abandoned the effort to pinpoint absolute thresholds and turned instead to signal detection theory.

Signal detection theory presents a mathematical model of how your personal sensitivity and response bias combine to determine your decision about whether or not a near-threshold stimulus occurred (Green & Swets, 1966). **Sensitivity** refers to your ability to discriminate a particular stimulus from a background of competing stimuli. It is influenced by internal noise, the intensity of the stimulus, and the capacity of your sensory systems. As already mentioned, response bias is the internal rule that you use in deciding whether to report a signal. How likely is it that an airport security guard will spot a weapon in a passenger's x-rayed luggage? Signal detection theory provides a way to understand and predict such responses by guiding precise measurement of sensitivity to stimuli of any kind (MacMillan & Creelman, 2004; Swets, 1996).

Judging Differences between Stimuli   Sometimes our task is not to detect a faint stimulus but to notice small changes in a stimulus or to decide whether two stimuli are the same or different. Musicians who are tuning up for a concert must discern whether a particular note played on one instrument matches the same note played by another instrument. When you repaint part of a wall, you have to judge whether the color of the new paint matches the old color. And when you are cooking, you have to decide whether your soup tastes any spicier after you've added some pepper.

Your ability to judge differences between stimuli depends on the strength of the stimuli you are dealing with. The weaker those stimuli are, the easier it is to detect small differences between them. For example, if you're comparing the weight of two oranges, you will be able to detect a difference of as little as a fraction of an ounce. But if you are comparing two boxes weighing around 50 pounds each, you may not notice a difference unless it is a pound or more.

One of the oldest laws in psychology, named after German physiologist Ernst Weber (pronounced "VAY-ber"), describes the role of stimulus strength in our ability to detect differences. **Weber's law** states that the smallest detectable difference in stimulus energy is a constant fraction of the intensity of the stimulus. This smallest detectable difference is called the *difference threshold,* or **just-noticeable difference (JND).** According to Weber's law, if an object weighs 25 pounds, the JND is only half a pound. So if you added a small container of yogurt to a grocery bag with three gallons of milk in it, you would

signal detection theory A mathematical model of what determines a person's report of a near-threshold stimulus.

sensitivity The ability to detect a stimulus.

Weber's law A law stating that the smallest detectable difference in stimulus energy (just-noticeable difference) is a constant fraction of the intensity of the stimulus.

just-noticeable difference (JND) The smallest detectable difference in stimulus energy. Also called difference threshold.

TABLE 3.1   Some Absolute Thresholds

Absolute thresholds can be amazingly low. Here are examples of the stimulus equivalents at the absolute threshold for the five primary senses. Set up the conditions for testing the absolute threshold for sound and see if you can detect this minimal amount of auditory stimulation. If you can't hear it, the signal detection theory we discuss in this section may help explain why.

Human Sense	Absolute Threshold Is Equivalent to:
Vision	A candle flame seen at 30 miles on a clear night
Hearing	The tick of a watch under quiet conditions at 20 feet
Taste	One teaspoon of sugar in 2 gallons of water
Smell	One drop of perfume diffused into the entire volume of air in a 6-room apartment
Touch	The wing of a fly falling on your cheek from a distance of 1 centimeter

Source: Galanter (1962)

© AP Photo/Janet Hostetter

Detecting Vital Signals

According to signal detection theory, the likelihood that security screeners will detect the outline of a weapon appearing on x-ray images of luggage depends partly on the sensitivity of their visual systems and partly on their response criterion, their bias for responding to a questionable stimulus as a possible weapon. That bias, in turn, is affected by their expectations about how often weapons actually appear and by how motivated they are to look carefully for them. Airport security officials occasionally try to smuggle a simulated weapon through a checkpoint, not only to evaluate inspectors' performance but also to improve it by keeping their response criterion low enough to avoid missing real weapons (Fleck & Mitroff, 2007; McCarley et al., 2004; Wolfe et al., 2007; Wolfe & VanWert, 2010).

FIGURE 3.4
The Dimensions of a Wave
Wavelength is the distance from one peak of a wave to the next. *Frequency* is the number of complete waves, or cycles, that pass a given point in a given amount of time, such as one second. *Amplitude* is the height of a wave from baseline to peak.

wavelength The distance between peaks in a wave of light or sound.

frequency The number of complete waves, or cycles, that pass a given point per unit of time.

amplitude The distance between the peak and the baseline of a wave.

not be able to tell the difference in weight. But candy snatchers beware: It takes a change of only two-thirds of an ounce to determine that someone has been into a two-pound box of chocolates! The size of the just-noticeable difference differs from one sense to the next. The human visual system, for example, is more sensitive than the human taste system; that is why we will notice smaller differences in the brightness of a light than in, say, the saltiness of a salad.

Sensory Energy   The sensory energies of light and sound vibrate as *waves* passing through space. These waves result from reflected light or from changes in air pressure caused when vocal cords and other objects move. The eye and ear detect the waves as light and sound. Waves of light and sound can be described in terms of wavelength, frequency, and amplitude, and it is these properties that determine what is sensed and perceived. **Wavelength** is the distance from one peak of the wave to the next. Wave **frequency** is the number of complete waves, or cycles, that pass a given point in a given amount of time. **Amplitude** is the height of the wave from baseline to peak (see Figure 3.4). Different wavelengths, frequencies, and amplitudes create different visual and sound experiences. Let's now consider how these physical properties of light and sound waves become sights and sounds.

Seeing

Why do some people need eyeglasses?

Soaring eagles have the incredible ability to see a mouse move in the grass from a mile away. Cats have special "reflectors" at the back of their eyes that help them see even in very dim light. Nature has provided each species with a visual system uniquely adapted to its way of life. The human visual system is also adapted to do many things well. It combines great sensitivity with great sharpness, enabling us to see objects near and far, during the day and at night. Our night vision is not as good as that of some animals, but our color vision is excellent. Not a bad tradeoff; after all, being able to experience a sunset's splendor seems worth an occasional stumble in the dark.

Light

Light is a form of energy known as *electromagnetic radiation*. Most electromagnetic radiation, including x-rays, radio waves, television signals, Wi-Fi, and radar, is invisible to the human eye. In fact, as shown in Figure 3.5, the range, or spectrum, of *visible light* is just the tiny slice of electromagnetic radiation that vibrates at wavelengths from just under 400 nanometers to about 750 nanometers. (A *nanometer*, abbreviated *nm*, is one billionth of a meter.) It is correct to refer to light as either *light waves* or *light rays*.

Sensations of light depend on the intensity and wavelength of light waves. **Light intensity,** which refers to how much energy the light contains, determines the brightness of light while what color you sense depends mainly on **light wavelength.** At a given intensity, different wavelengths produce sensations of different colors. For instance, 440-nm light appears violet blue, and 700-nm light appears orange-ish red.

Focusing Light

The eye transduces light energy into neural activity. First, accessory structures of the eye modify incoming light rays. The light rays enter the eye by passing through the curved, transparent, protective layer called the **cornea.** As shown in Figure 3.6, the light then passes through the **pupil,** the opening just behind the cornea. The **iris,** which gives the eye its color, adjusts the amount of light allowed into the eye by constricting to reduce the size of the pupil or dilating to enlarge it. Directly behind the pupil is the **lens.** Both the cornea and lens of the eye are curved so that they bend light rays. (A camera lens works the same way.) This bending process focuses light rays coming from various angles

Wavelength in meters

| 10^{-15} | 10^{-14} | 10^{-13} | 10^{-12} | 10^{-11} | 10^{-10} | 10^{-9} | 10^{-8} | 10^{-7} | 10^{-6} | 10^{-5} | 10^{-4} | 10^{-3} | 10^{-2} | 10^{-1} | 10^{1} | 10^{2} | 10^{3} |

Cosmic rays | Gamma rays | X-rays | Ultraviolet | Visible | Infrared | Microwaves | Radar | TV FM AM Radio waves | Short waves

VISIBLE SPECTRUM

| 400 | 450 | 500 | 550 | 600 | 650 | 700 | 750 |

Wavelength in nanometers

FIGURE 3.5

The Spectrum of Electromagnetic Energy

The human eye is sensitive to only a narrow range of electromagnetic wavelengths. To detect energy outside this range, we rely on radios, cell phones, TV sets, radar detectors, infrared night-vision scopes, and other electronic instruments that can "see" this energy, just as the eye sees visible light.

light intensity A physical dimension of light waves that refers to how much energy the light contains and that determines our experience of its brightness.

light wavelength A physical dimension of light waves that refers to their length and that produces sensations of different colors.

cornea The curved, transparent, protective layer through which light rays enter the eye.

pupil An opening in the eye just behind the cornea through which light passes.

iris The part of the eye that gives it its color and adjusts the amount of light entering it.

lens The part of the eye directly behind the pupil.

retina The surface at the back of the eye onto which the lens focuses light rays.

ocular accommodation The ability of the lens to change its shape and bend light rays so objects are in focus.

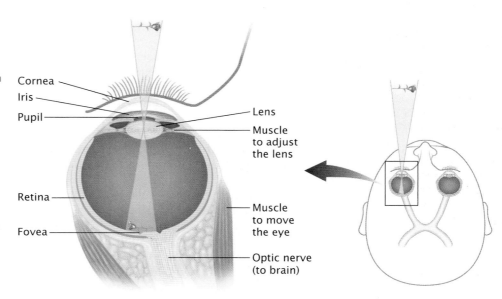

Cornea
Iris
Pupil
Lens
Muscle to adjust the lens
Retina
Muscle to move the eye
Fovea
Optic nerve (to brain)

FIGURE 3.6

Major Structures of the Eye

As shown in this top view of the eye, light rays bent by the combined actions of the cornea and the lens are focused on the retina, where the light energy is converted into neural activity. Nerve fibers from the retina combine to form the optic nerve, which leaves the back of the eye and continues to the brain.

into a sharp image on the inner surface at the back of the eye. This surface is called the **retina.** Light rays from the top of an object are focused at the bottom of the image on the retinal surface. Light rays from the right side of the object end up on the left side of the retinal image (see Figure 3.7). The brain rearranges this upside-down and reversed image so that we can see the object as it is.

The muscles that hold the lens adjust its shape so that either near or far objects can be focused on the retina. To illustrate this for yourself, try reading the next sentence while holding the book as close to your face as possible. To maintain a focused image at close range, your muscles have to tighten your lenses, making them more curved. This ability to change the shape of the lens to bend light rays is called **ocular accommodation.** As the lens loses some of its flexibility over the years, accommodation becomes more difficult. Converging light rays may come into focus either before or after they reach the retina, causing images to be blurry. This is why most older people become "farsighted," seeing distant objects clearly but needing glasses for reading or close work. A more common problem in younger people is "nearsightedness,"

LEARN by DOING

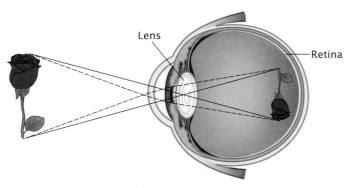

Lens

Retina

FIGURE 3.7

The Lens and the Retinal Image

To see objects as they are, your brain must rearrange the upside-down and reversed images that the lens focuses on the retina. If light rays are out of focus when they reach the retina, glasses usually correct the problem. In some older people, vision is impaired by cataracts, a condition in which a "cloudy" lens severely reduces incoming light. Cataracts can be cleared up with laser surgery or by replacing the natural lens with an artificial one (Snellingen et al., 2002).

photoreceptors Specialized cells in the retina that convert light energy into neural activity.

rods Photoreceptors in the retina that allow sight even in dim light but that cannot distinguish colors.

cones Photoreceptors in the retina that are less light sensitive than rods but that can distinguish colors.

dark adaptation The increasing ability to see in the dark as time passes.

fovea A region in the center of the retina.

optic nerve A bundle of fibers that carries visual information to the brain.

in which close objects are in focus but distant ones are blurry. This condition has a genetic component, but it can also be influenced by environmental factors such as reading habits or spending a lot of time looking at close-up images on smart-phones and computer screens (Czepita et al., 2010; Seppa, 2009). These vision problems can usually be solved with glasses or contact lenses that assist in the light-bending process. Another option is Laser-Assisted In-Situ Keratomileusis (LASIK) surgery, which reshapes and stretches the cornea (Vuori, Tervo, & Holopainen, 2009). LASIK increases the degree to which the cornea bends light rays, thus requiring the lens to do less accommodation and eliminating the need for glasses or contacts.

Converting Light into Images

The conversion of light energy into neural activity takes place in the retina, which contains neurons that are actually an extension of the brain. The word *retina* is Latin for "net," and the retina is in fact an intricate network of cells (Masland, 2001).

Rods and Cones   Specialized cells in the retina called **photoreceptors** convert light energy into neural activity. There are two main types of photoreceptors: rods and cones. **Rods** and **cones** are retinal cells that are named for their shapes and that contain chemicals that respond to light. When light strikes these chemicals, they break apart, creating a signal that can be transferred to the brain.

The process of rebuilding these light-sensitive chemicals after they break down takes a little time. This explains why you cannot see when you first come from bright sunshine into a dark room (Mahroo & Lamb, 2004). In the dark, as your rods build up their light-sensitive chemicals, your ability to see gradually increases. The increasing ability to see in the dark over time is called **dark adaptation** (Reuter, 2011). You become about 10,000 times more sensitive to light after about half an hour in a darkened room.

There are three kinds of light-sensitive chemicals in cones, and they provide the basis for color vision. Rods have only one kind of chemical, so they cannot discriminate colors. However, rods are more sensitive to light than cones, so they allow you to see in dim light, as on a moonlit night. It's only at higher light intensities that the cones, with their ability to detect colors, become most active. As a result, you might put on what looked like a matched pair of socks in a darkened bedroom only to go outside and discover that one is dark blue and the other is dark green.

Cones are concentrated in the center of the retina in a circular region called the **fovea,** which is where the eye focuses incoming light. Differences in the density of cones in the fovea can lead to differences in visual *acuity,* or ability to see details (Beirne, Zlatkova, & Anderson, 2005). Decreases in cone density over time may also be partly to blame for some age-related losses in acuity (Song et al., 2011). There are no rods in the human fovea. With increasing distance from the fovea, though, the number of cones gradually decreases and the proportion of rods gradually increases. So if you are trying to detect a weak light, such as the light from a faint star, it is better to look slightly away from where you expect to see it. This focuses the weak light on the very light-sensitive rods outside the fovea. Because cones do not work well in low light, looking directly at the star will make it seem to disappear.

From the Retina to the Brain   If the eye simply transferred to the brain the images it focused on the retina, we would experience something like a slightly blurry TV picture. Instead, the eye first sharpens visual images. How? The key lies in the interactions among cells of the retina.

Light rays pass through several layers of retinal cells before striking the rods and cones. Signals generated by the rods and cones then go back toward the surface of the retina, making connections with *bipolar cells* and *ganglion cells,* which allow the eye to begin analyzing visual information even before that information leaves the retina (Freeman, Rizzo, & Fried, 2011). Ganglion cells in the retina have axons that form the **optic nerve,**

Rods and Cones

This electron microscope view of rods (blue) and cones (aqua) shows what your light receptors look like. Rods are more light-sensitive, but they do not detect color. Cones can detect color, but they require more light in order to be activated. To experience the difference in how these cells work, try looking at an unfamiliar color photograph in a room where there is barely enough light to see. This dim light will activate your rods and allow you to make out images in the picture. But because there is not enough light to activate your cones, you will not be able to see colors in the photo.

LEARN **by** DOING

which then goes to the brain. Because there are no receptors for visual stimuli at the point where the optic nerve exits the eyeball, a **blind spot** is created, as Figure 3.8 demonstrates.

After leaving the retina, about half the optic nerve fibers cross over to the opposite side of the brain, creating a structure called the *optic chiasm.* (*Chiasm* means "cross" and is pronounced "KYE-az-um.") The fibers from the inside half of each eye (nearest to the nose) cross over. The fibers from the outside half of each eye do not. So no matter where you look, all the visual information about the right half of the visual world goes to the left hemisphere of your brain and all the visual information from the left half of the visual world goes to the right hemisphere (Roth, Lora, & Heilman, 2002).

The optic chiasm is part of the bottom surface of the brain. Beyond this chiasm, optic fibers extend into the brain itself. The axons from most of the retina's ganglion cells form synapses in the thalamus. Neurons there send the visual input to the primary visual cortex in the occipital lobe at the back of the brain. The primary visual cortex conducts initial processing of visual information and then sends that refined information to many association areas of the brain for more specialized processing (Dhruv et al., 2011; see Figure 2.9).

Certain cells in the brain's cerebral cortex are called **feature detectors** because they respond to specific characteristics of objects in the visual world (Hubel & Wiesel, 1979; Jia et al., 2010). For example, one type of feature detector specializes in responding to straight lines. Others respond to corners, to angles, or to some other feature. The combined responses of several types of feature-detecting cells allow us to sense the shapes of objects such as rectangles or triangles. Most people can also detect color. Let's explore how color vision works.

Seeing Color

Like beauty, color is in the eye of the beholder. Many animals see only shades of gray, even when they look at a rainbow, but for humans, color is an important feature of vision.

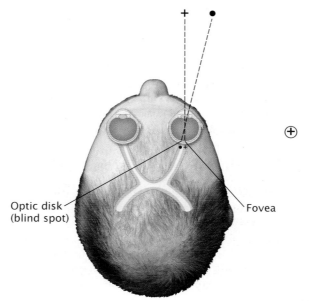

blind spot The point at which the optic nerve exits the eyeball.

feature detectors Cells in the cerebral cortex that respond to a specific feature of an object.

Optic disk (blind spot)

Fovea

FIGURE 3.8
Find Your Blind Spot

There is a blind spot where the optic nerve exits the eye. To "see" your blind spot, cover your left eye and stare at the cross inside the circle. Move the page closer and farther away, and at some point the dot to the right should disappear from view. However, the vertical lines around the dot will probably look continuous, because the brain tends to fill in visual information at the blind spot (Spillmann et al., 2006). We are normally unaware of this "hole" in our vision because the blind spot of one eye is in the normal visual field of the other eye.

LEARN **by** DOING

NONSPECTRAL HUES

These colors are not produced by any single wavelength

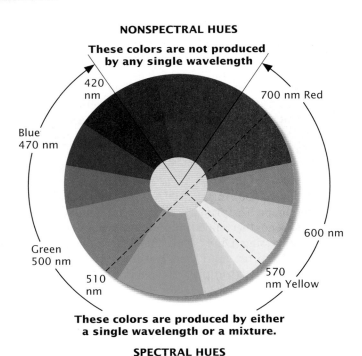

These colors are produced by either a single wavelength or a mixture.

SPECTRAL HUES

FIGURE 3.9

The Color Circle

Arranging colors according to their psychological similarities creates a color circle that predicts the result of additive mixing of two colored lights. For example, mixing equal amounts of pure green and pure red light will produce yellow, the color that lies at the midpoint of the line connecting red and green. (Note: nm stands for nanometers, the unit in which light wavelengths are measured.)

hue The essential color determined by the dominant wavelength of light.

color saturation The purity of a color.

brightness The overall intensity of the wavelengths making up light.

trichromatic theory A theory of color vision stating that information from three types of visual elements combines to produce the sensation of color.

Wavelengths and Color Sensations   At a given intensity, each wavelength of light is sensed as a certain color. However, the eye rarely (if ever) encounters pure light of a single wavelength. Sunlight, for example, is a mixture of all wavelengths of light. When sunlight passes through a droplet of water, each different wavelength of light bends to a different degree, separating into a colorful rainbow. The spectrum of color found in the rainbow illustrates an important concept: The sensation produced by a *mixture* of different wavelengths of light is not the same as the sensations produced by separate wavelengths. The sensation of a color results from features of the wavelength mixtures striking the eye. The three separate aspects of this sensation are hue, color saturation, and brightness. These labels refer to the *psychological* dimensions of what we experience when the light arrives, and they correspond roughly to the light's physical properties. **Hue,** the essential "color," is determined by the dominant wavelength in the mixture of the light. Black, white, and gray are not considered hues because they do not have a dominant wavelength. **Color saturation** is related to the purity of the color. A color is said to be more *saturated* (more pure) if just one wavelength is more intense (contains more energy) than other wavelengths. The yellow of a school bus and the red of a stop sign are saturated colors. When many other wavelengths are added in, the color is said to be *desaturated*. Pastels are colors that have been desaturated by the addition of whiteness. **Brightness** refers to the overall intensity of the wavelengths making up light.

The *color circle* shown in Figure 3.9 arranges hues according to their perceived similarities. Mix two different light wavelengths of equal intensity and the color you sense is midway between the two original colors on the color circle. This process is called *additive color mixing,* because the effects of the wavelengths are added together. Keep adding different colored lights and you eventually get white, which is the combination of all wavelengths. You are probably more familiar with a different form of color mixing, called *subtractive color mixing,* which occurs when, for example, paints are combined. Paint, like other physical objects, reflects certain wavelengths and absorbs others. Green paint is green because it absorbs all wavelengths except wavelengths perceived as green. (White objects appear white because they reflect all wavelengths.) So if you keep combining different colored paints, all of the wavelengths will eventually be subtracted, resulting in black.

Theories of Color Vision

Psychologists have long tried to explain how color vision works, but only two theories have stood the test of time: trichromatic (or "three-color") theory and opponent-process theory.

The Trichromatic Theory of Color Vision   In the early 1800s, Thomas Young proved that mixing pure versions of blue, green, and red light in different ratios could produce any other color; Hermann von Helmholtz later confirmed these findings. The Young-Helmholtz theory of color vision is called the **trichromatic theory.**

Support for trichromatic theory comes from research on cones in the retina. There are three types of cones, and each is most sensitive to particular wavelengths. *Short-wavelength* cones respond most to light in the blue range. *Medium-wavelength* cones are most sensitive to light in the green range. *Long-wavelength* cones respond best to light in the reddish-yellow range, but by tradition are known as "red" cones. No single cone by itself can signal the color of a light; it is the *ratio* of the activities of the three types of cones that determines what color will be sensed. As you can see in Figure 3.10, the exact

The Sensation of Color

The vivid array of colored powders offered by this vendor in India allows him to create virtually any combination of hue (color), saturation (purity), and brightness that a customer might request.

FIGURE 3.10

Individual Differences in Cone Types

These photographs show that people can differ widely from one another in the distribution of blue, green, and red cones in their retinas (Roorda & Williams, 1999). J. W., whose retina is shown at left, has an especially high population of red cones, whereas green cones predominate in A. N., whose retina is shown on the right. Both have normal color vision, but J. W. will be somewhat more sensitive to long wavelengths of light, whereas A.N. will be somewhat more sensitive to light of medium wavelengths.

Reprinted by permission from *Nature*. Roorda, A. & Williams, D. R. (1999). The arrangement of the three cone classes in the living human eye. *Nature, 397,* 520–522. Copyright © 1999 Macmillan Magazines Ltd.

opponent-process theory A theory of color vision stating that the visual elements that are sensitive to color are grouped into red-green, blue-yellow, and black-white pairs.

LEARN by DOING mixture of these three cone types can differ from person to person. The trichromatic theory was applied in the creation of color television screens, which contain microscopic elements of red, green, and blue. A television broadcast excites these elements to varying degrees, mixing their colors to produce many other colors. You see color mixtures, not patterns of red, green, and blue dots, because the dots are too small and close together to be seen individually. However, with a magnifying glass you may be able to see similar pixels that make up the color photos in your local newspaper.

The Opponent-Process Theory of Color Vision   Although it is essentially correct, the trichromatic theory cannot explain some aspects of color vision, such as afterimages. To see an afterimage, stare at the black dot in the flag in Figure 3.11 for thirty seconds and then look at the black dot in the white space below it. What was yellow in the original image will be blue in the afterimage. What was green before will appear red, and what was black will now appear white.

This type of observation led Ewald Hering to offer another theory of color vision, called the **opponent-process theory.** Hering suggested that color-sensitive visual elements in the eye are arranged into three kinds of pairs and that the members of each pair oppose, or inhibit, each other. Each element signals one color or the other (red or green, blue or yellow,

FIGURE 3.11

Afterimages Produced by the Opponent-Process Nature of Color Vision

Stare at the black dot in the flag for at least thirty seconds and then focus on the dot in the white space below it. The afterimage you will see can be explained by the opponent process theory of color vision. What colors appeared in the afterimage you saw?

LEARN by DOING

black or white), but never both. This theory explains color afterimages. When one member of an opponent pair is no longer stimulated, the other is activated. So in Figure 3.11, if the original image you look at is green, the afterimage will be red.

The Bottom Line on Color Vision   Together, the trichromatic and opponent-process theories encompass most of what we now know about the complex process of color vision. We see color because our three types of cones have different sensitivities to different wavelengths. We sense different colors when the three cone types are stimulated in different ratios. Because there are three types of cones, any color can be produced by mixing three pure wavelengths of light. But there is more to it than that. The cones connect to ganglion cells containing pairs of opposing elements that respond to different colors and inhibit each other. This arrangement provides the basis for afterimages. Therefore, the trichromatic theory explains color vision as it relates to rods and cones, whereas the opponent-process theory explains color vision as it relates to the ganglion cells. Both theories are needed to account for the complexity of our visual sensations of color (Jacobs, 2008).

Color vision also depends on what happens in the brain—especially in the thalamus and visual cortex—where encoded color information from the retinas is assembled and processed (Conway, 2009; Gegenfurtner & Kiper, 2003; Heywood & Kentridge, 2003). As a result, certain kinds of brain damage can weaken or destroy color vision, even though all the cones in the retina are working normally (Bouvier & Engel, 2006).

Color Blindness

Cones normally contain three kinds of chemicals, each of which responds best to a particular wavelength of light. People who have cones containing only two of these three color-sensitive chemicals are described as *color blind* (Neitz & Neitz, 2011). They are not really blind to all color, but they discriminate fewer colors than do other people, as Figure 3.12 shows. Red-green color blindness, for example, means that reds and greens appear to be the same brownish-gray color. Color blindness is more common in men than in women. ("In Review: Seeing" summarizes our discussion of vision.)

FIGURE 3.12

Are You Color Blind?

Photograph A shows how this scene appears to people whose cones have all three types of color-sensitive chemicals. The other photos simulate how colors appear to people who are missing chemicals for long wavelengths (B), short wavelengths (C), or medium wavelengths (D). If any of these photos look to you just like the one at the upper left, you may have a form of color blindness.

LEARN by DOING

(A)

(B)

(C)

(D)

Courtesy Viennot, Brettel, Mollon—MNHN, CNRS

Seeing   IN REVIEW

Aspect of Sensory System	Elements	Key Characteristics
Energy	Visible light: electromagnetic radiation with a wavelength of about 400 nm to about 750 nm	The intensity, wavelength, and complexity of light waves determine the brightness, hue, and color saturation of visual sensations.
Accessory structures of the eye	Cornea, pupil, iris, lens	Light rays are bent to focus on the retina.
Conversion of visual stimuli to neural activity	Photoreceptors (rods and cones) in the retina	Rods are more sensitive to light than cones, but cones discriminate among colors. Sensations of color depend first on the cones, which respond differently to different light wavelengths, and then on processing by ganglion cells.
Pathway to the brain	Optic nerve to optic chiasm to thalamus to primary visual cortex	Neurons in the brain respond to particular aspects of the visual stimulus, such as shape.

IN REVIEW QUESTIONS

1. The ability to see in very dim light depends on photoreceptors called ___ .
2. Color afterimages are best explained by the ___ theory of color vision.
3. Nearsightedness and farsightedness occur when images are not focused on the eye's ___ .

Hearing

How would my voice sound on the moon?

In 1969, when Neil Armstrong became the first person ever to set foot on the moon, millions of people back on earth heard his radio transmission: "That's one small step for a man, one giant leap for mankind." But if Armstrong had been foolish enough to take off his space helmet and shout, "Whoo-ee! I can moonwalk!" not even an astronaut three feet away could have heard him. Why? Because he would have been speaking into airless empty space. **Sound** is a repeating fluctuation—a rising and falling—in the pressure of a substance, such as air. Because the moon has almost no atmosphere and almost no air pressure, airborne sound cannot exist there.

Sound

Vibrations of an object produce the fluctuations in pressure that we experience as sound. When you speak, your vocal cords vibrate, causing fluctuations in air pressure that spread as sound waves. Figure 3.13 shows how these changes in air pressure can be represented as sound waveforms. The waveforms are drawn in only two dimensions, but remember that sound waves actually move through the air in all directions. This is the reason that when people talk to each other during a movie or a lecture, others all around them are distracted by the conversation.

Just as the amplitude and wavelength of light waves affect our experience of light, the characteristics of sound waves affect our experience of sound. The psychological experience we call **loudness** is determined by the amplitude, or height, of the sound wave. The greater the amplitude, the louder the sensation of sound. Loudness is described in units called *decibels* (abbreviated *dB*). By definition, 0 decibels is the minimum detectable sound for normal hearing. Every increase of 20 decibels reflects a tenfold increase in the amplitude of sound waves. So the 40-dB sounds of an office are actually 10 times as intense as a 20-dB whisper; and traffic noise of 100 dB is 10,000 times as intense as that whisper. The loudest rock bands can create sound intensity of 160 dB (Levine & Schefner, 1981).

The psychological dimension of **pitch**—how high or low a tone sounds—depends on the frequency of the sound wave. Frequency is the number of complete waves or cycles that pass a given point in one second. It is described in units called *hertz*, abbreviated

sound A repetitive fluctuation in the pressure of a medium such as air.

loudness A psychological dimension of sound determined by the amplitude of a sound wave.

pitch How high or low a tone sounds; pitch depends on the frequency of a sound wave.

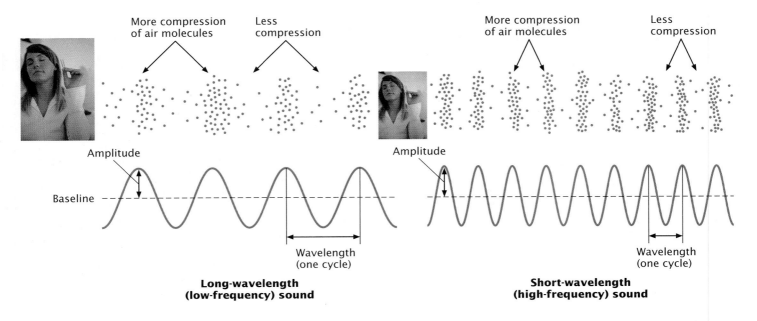

More compression of air molecules   Less compression

Amplitude

Baseline

Wavelength (one cycle)

Long-wavelength (low-frequency) sound

More compression of air molecules   Less compression

Amplitude

Wavelength (one cycle)

Short-wavelength (high-frequency) sound

FIGURE 3.13
Sound Waves and Waveforms

Sound is created when objects, such as a tuning fork, vibrate. The vibration creates alternating regions of greater and lesser compression of air molecules, which can be represented as a waveform. The point of greatest compression is the peak of the wave. The lowest point of the wave is where compression is least. In each particular substance, or *medium*, such as air, a sound's wavelength (the distance between peaks) is related to its frequency (the number of waves per second). The longer the wavelength, the lower the sound frequency. The shorter the wavelength, the higher the frequency.

Photo © Daniel Krolls/Getty Images

Hz (for Heinrich Hertz, a nineteenth-century physicist). One cycle per second is 1 Hz. High-frequency waves are sensed as sounds of high pitch. The highest note on a piano has a frequency of about 4,000 Hz, and the lowest note has a frequency of about 50 Hz. Humans can hear sounds ranging from about 20 to 20,000 Hz.

Most sounds are a mixture of many frequencies and amplitudes, and this mixture creates a sound's **timbre** (pronounced "TAM-ber"), the psychological dimension of sound quality. Complex wave patterns added to the *fundamental*, or lowest, frequency of sound determine its timbre. The extra waves allow you to tell the difference between, say, a note played on a flute and the same note played on a clarinet.

The Ear

The human ear converts sound energy into neural activity through a series of accessory structures and transduction mechanisms. The visible part of the ear on the side of the head, called the **pinna**, collects sound waves in the outer ear. (People trying to hear a faint sound may cup a hand to their ear because this action tilts the pinna forward and enlarges the area that is collecting sound. Try this for a moment, and you will notice a clear difference in the sounds you hear.) The pinna funnels sound down through the ear canal. At the end of the ear canal, the sound waves reach the **middle ear** (see Figure 3.14). There they strike the **tympanic membrane,** a tightly stretched structure also known as the **eardrum.** The sound waves set up vibrations in the tympanic membrane. The *hammer,* the *anvil,* and the *stirrup,* three tiny bones named for their shapes, amplify these vibrations and direct them onto a smaller membrane called the *oval window.*

The Inner Ear   Sound vibrations passing through the oval window enter the inner ear, reaching the **cochlea** (pronounced "KOK-lee-ah"), where transduction occurs. The cochlea is rolled into a coiled spiral. (*Cochlea* comes from the Greek word for "snail.") A

timbre The quality of a sound that identifies it.

pinna The crumpled part of the outer ear that collects sound waves.

middle ear The part of the ear that contains the hammer, anvil, and stirrup, which transmit sound from the tympanic membrane to the oval window.

tympanic membrane (eardrum) A tightly stretched membrane in the middle ear that generates vibrations that match the sound waves striking it.

cochlea A fluid-filled spiral structure in the inner ear in which auditory transduction occurs.

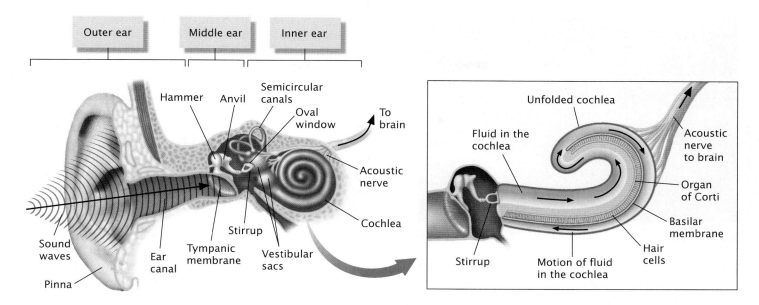

FIGURE 3.14
Structures of the Ear

The outer ear (pinna and ear canal) channels sound waves into the middle ear, where the vibrations of the tympanic membrane are amplified by the delicate bones that stimulate the cochlea. The close-up view of the cochlea shows how the vibrations of the stirrup set up vibrations in the fluid inside the cochlea. The coils of the cochlea are unrolled in this illustration to show the path of the fluid waves along the basilar membrane. Movements of the basilar membrane stimulate hair cells, which transduce the vibrations into changes in neural activity, which are sent along the acoustic nerve to the brain.

Photo © Yellowj/Shutterstock

fluid-filled tube runs down its length. The **basilar membrane** forms the floor of this tube, as you can see in Figure 3.14. When a sound wave passes through the fluid in the tube, it makes the basilar membrane rise and fall like a bed sheet on a clothesline flapping in the wind (Ren, 2002). This movement, in turn, bends *hair cells* on the membrane. These hair cells make connections with fibers from the **acoustic nerve**, a bundle of axons that goes into the brain. Bending the hair cells stimulates the acoustic nerve, also known as the *auditory nerve,* which sends encoded signals to the brain about the amplitude and frequency of the sound waves (Griesinger, Richards, & Ashmore, 2005). These signals allow you to sense loudness, pitch, and timbre.

Deafness   The middle and inner ear are among the most delicate structures in the body, and damage to them can lead to impaired hearing or deafness. One form of deafness can be caused when the bones of the middle ear fuse together, preventing accurate conduction of vibrations (Stenfelt, 2011). This condition, called *conduction deafness,* can be treated by surgery to break the bones apart or to replace the natural bones with plastic ones (Ayache et al., 2003). Hearing aids that amplify incoming sounds can also help.

Nerve deafness results when the acoustic nerve or, more commonly, the hair cells are damaged (Shepherd & McCreery, 2006). Hair-cell damage occurs gradually with age, but it can also be caused by very loud sounds, including amplified rock music (Goldstein, 2002). High-intensity sound can actually rip off the hair cells of the inner ear. Generally, any sound loud enough to produce ringing in the ears causes some damage. In humans, small amounts of damage gradually build up and can produce significant hearing loss by middle age—as many older rock musicians (and their fans) are finding out (Levine, 1999). Listening to music at high volume through the earbuds of iPods and other devices can also cause hearing loss (Petrescu, 2008; Vogel et al., 2009), which may be partly responsible for the recent increase in hearing impairments among adolescents (Shargorodsky et al., 2010).

Hair cells can be regenerated in chickens' ears (Cotanche, 1997), and a related kind of inner-ear hair cell has been regenerated in mammals (Malgrange et al., 1999). Scientists hope

basilar membrane   The floor of the fluid-filled duct that runs through the cochlea.

acoustic nerve   The bundle of axons that carries messages from the hair cells of the cochlea to the brain.

© mediaphotos/iStockphoto

Shaping the Brain

The brain region known as the primary auditory cortex is larger in trained musicians than in people whose jobs are less focused on fine gradations of sound. How much larger this area becomes is correlated with how long the musicians have studied their art. This finding reminds us that, as described in the chapter on biology and behavior, the brain can literally be shaped by experience and other environmental factors (Baumann, Meyer, & Jäncke, 2008; Lotze et al., 2003; Shahin et al., 2008).

that human hair-cell regeneration might someday be accomplished by treating damaged areas with growth factors similar to those being used to repair damaged brain cells (Shepherd et al., 2005; see the chapter on biology and behavior). Inserting genes that might stimulate the regrowth of damaged hair cells (Di Domenico et al., 2011; Husseman & Raphael, 2009; Izumikawa et al., 2005) and using stem cells to create new hair cells (Beisel et al., 2008) are two other promising approaches. If successful, these efforts could revolutionize the treatment of nerve deafness, which cannot be overcome by conventional hearing aids. In the meantime, scientists have developed an artificial cochlea that can be implanted in the human ear to stimulate the acoustic nerve (Basura, Eapen, & Buchman, 2009; Chen at al., 2010; Niparko et al., 2010; Wilson & Dorman, 2008).

Auditory Pathways to the Brain   Before sounds can be heard, the information encoded in the firing of the many axons that make up the acoustic nerve must be sent to the brain for further analysis. This transmission process begins when the acoustic nerve conveys the information to the thalamus. From there, the information is relayed to the *primary auditory cortex,* an area in the temporal lobe of the brain (see Figure 2.9). It is in the primary auditory cortex that information about sound is subjected to the most intense and complex analysis (Ciocca, 2008). Cells in the auditory cortex may have different *preferred frequencies.* That is, individual cells there respond most vigorously to sounds of a particular frequency. Each neuron in the acoustic nerve also has a "favorite," or characteristic, frequency, though each also responds to a range of frequencies, to some extent (Schnee et al., 2005). The auditory cortex examines the pattern of activity of many neurons to determine the frequency of a sound. This auditory analysis may be especially efficient in people who are deprived of visual experience because of blindness early in life (Stevens & Weaver, 2009).

Some parts of the auditory cortex are devoted to processing certain types of sounds. One part, for example, specializes in information from human speech (Belin, Zatorre, & Ahad, 2002); others are particularly responsive to sounds coming from animals, tools, or musical instruments (Lewis et al., 2005; Zatorre, 2003). Some specialization in the auditory cortex can be seen in brain scans. For example, fMRI scans of the auditory cortex look different in people who are listening to music and lyrics than to music alone (Brattico et al., 2011). Observing which brain areas become activated by which kind of sound has allowed researchers to detect whether a person is listening to words spoken by a familiar or unfamiliar voice and even to identify some details about what is being said (Formisano et al., 2008). The primary auditory cortex receives information from other senses as well. For example, it is activated when you watch someone say words (but not when the person makes other facial movements). This is the biological basis for the lip-reading that helps you hear what people say (Campbell & Capek, 2008).

Encoding Sounds

Most people can hear a wide range of sound intensities. The faintest sound that can be heard barely moves the ear's hair cells. Sounds more than a trillion times more intense can also be heard. Between these extremes, the auditory system encodes intensity in a rather simple way: The more intense the sound, the more rapid the firing of a given neuron. We're also very good at detecting differences between sound frequencies that allow us to hear differences in pitch (Shera, Guinan, & Oxenham, 2002). Information about frequency differences appears to be encoded in two ways: by their location on the basilar membrane and by the rate at which the auditory neurons fire.

As sound waves move down the basilar membrane, they reach a peak and then taper off, much like an ocean wave that crests and then dissolves. The waves produced by high-frequency sounds peak soon after they start down the basilar membrane. Waves produced by lower-frequency sounds peak farther down the basilar membrane. According to **place theory,** the greatest response by hair cells occurs at the peak of the

place theory A theory of hearing that states that hair cells at a particular place on the basilar membrane respond most to a particular frequency of sound.

wave. Because the location of the peak varies with the frequency of sound, it follows that hair cells at a particular place on the basilar membrane are most responsive to a particular frequency of sound. When cells with a particular characteristic frequency fire, we sense a sound of that frequency.

But place theory cannot explain the encoding of very low frequencies (such as deep bass notes) because none of the acoustic nerve fibers have very low preferred frequencies. However, humans can hear frequencies as low as twenty hertz, so they must be encoded somehow. The answer appears to be *frequency matching*, a process in which certain neurons in the acoustic nerve fire each time a sound wave passes. So a sound wave whose frequency is 25 cycles per second would cause those neurons to fire 25 times per second. Frequency-matching theory is sometimes called the **volley theory** of frequency encoding because the outputs of many cells can combine to create a *volley* of firing.

The nervous system apparently uses more than one way to encode the range of audible frequencies. The lowest frequencies are encoded by frequency matching. Low to moderate frequencies are encoded by frequency matching as well as by the place on the basilar membrane where the wave peaks. And high frequencies are encoded solely by the place on the basilar membrane where the wave peaks. ("In Review: Hearing" summarizes the encoding process and other aspects of the auditory system.)

Hearing   IN REVIEW

Aspect of Sensory System	Elements	Key Characteristics
Energy	Sound: pressure fluctuations of air produced by vibrations	Amplitude, frequency, and complexity of sound waves determine the loudness, pitch, and timbre of sounds.
Accessory structures of the ear	Pinna, tympanic membrane, hammer, anvil, stirrup, oval window, basilar membrane	Changes in pressure produced by the original wave are amplified.
Conversion of sound frequencies into neural activity	Hair cells in the inner ear	Frequencies are encoded by the location of the hair cells receiving the greatest stimulation (place theory) and by the combined firing rate of neurons (volley theory).
Pathway to the brain	Acoustic nerve to thalamus to primary auditory cortex	Auditory cortex examines patterns of information from the auditory nerve, allowing us to sense loudness, pitch, and timbre.

IN REVIEW QUESTIONS

1. Sound energy is converted to neural activity in an inner ear structure called the ___ .
2. Hearing loss due to damage to hair cells or the acoustic nerve is called ___ .
3. How high or low a sound sounds is called ___ and is determined by the ___ of a sound wave.

The Chemical Senses: Taste and Smell

Why can't I taste anything when I have a cold?

Some animals cannot see and some cannot hear, but all animals have some form of chemical sense. Chemical senses arise from the interaction of chemicals and receptors. **Olfactory perception,** also known as *olfaction,* or our **sense of smell,** detects chemicals that are airborne, or volatile. **Taste perception,** also known as *gustatory perception,* detects chemicals in solution that come into contact with receptors inside the mouth. These systems are connected.

Smell, Taste, and Flavor

If you have a stuffy nose, everything tastes like cardboard. Why? Because smell and taste act as two components of a single system known as *flavor* (Rozin, 1982). Most of the properties

volley theory A theory of hearing that states that the firing rate of an acoustic nerve matches a sound wave's frequency. Also called frequency-matching theory.

olfactory perception (sense of smell) The sense that detects chemicals that are airborne. Also called olfaction.

taste perception The sense that detects chemicals in solution that come into contact with receptors inside the mouth. Also called gustatory perception.

that make food taste good are actually odors detected by the olfactory system, not chemicals detected by the taste system. The scent and taste pathways converge in the *orbitofrontal cortex* of the brain (Rolls, 2006), which is how smell and taste come to seem like one sensation.

Variations in our nutritional state also affect our experience of taste and flavor and our motivation to eat particular foods (Yeomans & Mobini, 2006). If we are deprived of food or don't get enough salt, sweet or salty things taste better. Nutrition has a less direct influence on protein and fat intake. Protein and fat molecules have no particular taste or smell, so preferring or avoiding foods that contain these nutrients is based on associations between scent cues from other volatile substances in food and on the nutritional results of eating the foods (Bartoshuk, 1991; Schiffman et al., 1999).

We experience warm foods as sweeter, but temperature does not alter our experience of saltiness (Cruz & Green, 2000). Warming releases aromas that rise from the mouth into the nose and create more flavor sensations. This is why some people find hot pizza delicious and cold pizza disgusting. Spicy "hot" foods actually stimulate pain fibers in the mouth because they contain a substance called *capsaicin* (pronounced "kap-SAY-uh-sin") that stimulates pain-sensing neurons that are also stimulated by heat (Reyes-Escogido, Gonzalez-Mondragon, & Vazquez-Tzompantzi, 2011).

Our Sense of Smell

Pinching your nose prevents you from smelling odors, and putting a dilator strip on the bridge of your nose opens your nasal passages and intensifies odors (Raudenbush & Meyer, 2002). These effects occur because the nose (and the mouth, to some extent) acts as an accessory structure that collects airborne odor molecules for encoding and analysis by the olfactory system (see Figure 3.15). As odor molecules pass into the moist lining

FIGURE 3.15

The Olfactory System: the Nose and the Rose

Airborne odor molecules reach the olfactory area either through the nose or through an opening in the palate at the back of the mouth. This opening allows us to sample odors from our food as we eat. Nerve fibers pass directly from the olfactory area to the olfactory bulb in the brain, and from there signals pass to areas that are involved in emotion. This arrangement helps explain why odors often trigger strong emotional memories.

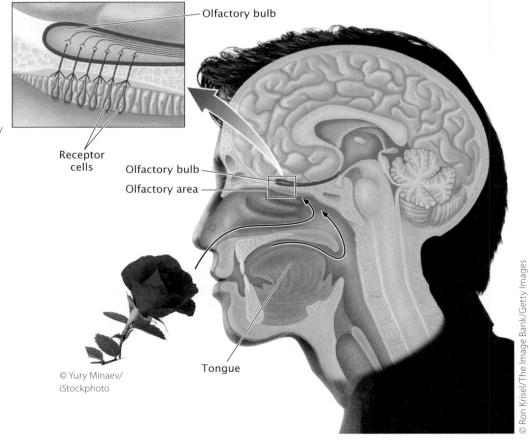

Olfactory bulb

Receptor cells

Olfactory bulb

Olfactory area

Tongue

© Yury Minaev/ iStockphoto

© Ron Krisel/The Image Bank/Getty Images

of the upper part of the nose—called the *mucous membrane*—they bind to receptors on the dendrites of olfactory neurons, causing a biochemical change. This change, in turn, leads to changes in the firing rates of these neurons, whose axons combine to form the *olfactory nerve* (Dionne & Dubin, 1994). It takes only a single molecule of an odorous substance to cause a change in the activity of an olfactory neuron, but it takes about fifty such molecules before a human will detect the odor (Reed, 2004). The number of molecules needed to trigger an olfactory sensation can vary, however. For example, women are more sensitive to odors during certain phases of their menstrual cycles (Navarrete-Palacios et al., 2003).

There are about a thousand different receptors for odors (Pinto, 2011) but there are even more possible odors in the world. Any particular odor is sensed as a particular *pattern* of responses by these odorant receptors, and humans can discriminate among tens of thousands of different odors (Kajiya et al., 2001; Zou & Buck, 2006). So a rose, a pizza, and your favorite cologne each have a different smell because they stimulate their own unique patterns of activity in your odorant receptors. Scientists are just beginning to understand exactly how this odor encoding system works (Ma, 2007). Their work has taken on special importance since the September 11, 2001, terrorist attacks in the United States. Researchers have intensified their efforts to develop an "electronic nose" capable of detecting odorants associated with guns and explosives (Thaler, Kennedy, & Hanson, 2001; Wilson & Baietto, 2011). Versions of these devices are in use at some airports. An "electronic nose" that can detect the presence of diseases that might not be evident to an examining doctor has also been developed (Chapman et al., 2011), and artificial olfactory devices are being used to examine the condition and composition of food products and the air we breathe (Marin et al., 2007).

Unlike other senses, our sense of smell does not send its messages through the thalamus. Instead, axons from olfactory neurons in the nose extend through a bony plate and directly into the brain, reaching a structure called the **olfactory bulb**, where odor processing continues (Kay & Sherman, 2007). Connections from the olfactory bulb spread throughout the brain (Zou, Li, & Buck, 2005), but they are especially plentiful in the amygdala, a part of the brain involved in emotional experience and learning (Su, Menuz, & Carlson, 2009). In humans, the amygdala is especially active in response to disgusting odors (Zald & Pardo, 1997).

The unique anatomy of the olfactory system may help account for the intense relationship between smells and emotion (Stevenson & Boakes, 2003). Associations between particular odors and experiences—especially emotional experiences—are not weakened much by time or later experiences (Lawless & Engen, 1977). So catching a whiff of the cologne once worn by a lost loved one can reactivate intense feelings of love or sadness associated with that person. Odors can also bring back accurate memories of experiences linked with them, especially positive experiences (Engen, Gilmore, & Mair, 1991; Mohr et al., 2001). These special features of the olfactory system may account for the fact that losing the sense of smell can sometimes be an early sign of brain diseases that disrupt memory and emotion (Siderowf et al., 2012; Tranel & Welsh-Bohmer, 2012). This is why doctors have developed special tests to identify even small changes in the sense of smell (Haxel et al., 2011).

Species ranging from humans to worms have remarkably similar neural mechanisms for sensing smell. And all mammals, including humans, have brain systems for detecting the source of smells by comparing the strength of sensory inputs reaching the left and right nostrils (Porter et al., 2005). Different species vary considerably, however, in their sensitivity to odor and in the degree to which they depend on it for survival. Humans have about 9 million olfactory neurons, compared with about 225 million in dogs, a species that is far more dependent on smell to identify food, territory, and receptive mates. Dogs and many other species also have an accessory olfactory system that detects pheromones. **Pheromones** (pronounced "FAIR-oh-mohns") are chemicals that are released by one creature and when detected by another can shape the second animal's behavior or physiology (Swaney & Keverne, 2009). For example, when a male snake detects a chemical on the skin of a female snake, it is stimulated to court her. Other pheromones may be

olfactory bulb A brain structure that receives messages regarding smell.

pheromones Chemicals that are released by one creature and detected by another, shaping the second creature's behavior or physiology.

released during emotional states, such as fear, thereby alerting nearby animals of possible danger (Hauser et al., 2011).

The role of pheromones in humans is much less clear (Wyatt, 2009), but it appears that some aspects of our behavior can be influenced by some sort of pheromone-like system (Berglund, Lindström, & Savic, 2006; Bhutta, 2007; Savic, Berglund, & Lindström, 2005). For example, men have been shown to behave in more sexually-oriented ways when around women who are ovulating (Haselton & Gildersleeve, 2011; Miller & Maner, 2010). Another study found that after sniffing tears that had been shed by women during negative emotional experiences, men rated photos of women to be less attractive and less sexually arousing, and they showed lower levels of testosterone (Gelstein et al., 2011). Other research shows that women make more risky decisions while playing a computer game if they are first exposed to sweat samples taken from men who had been under stress (Haegler et al., 2010).

A possible human gene for pheromone receptors has been found (Rodriguez et al., 2000), and pheromones have been shown to cause reproduction-related physiological changes in humans (Grammer, Fink, & Neave, 2005). Specifically, pheromonal signals secreted in women's perspiration can influence nearby women's menstrual cycles. As a result, women living together eventually tend to menstruate at about the same time (Stern & McClintock, 1998). Furthermore, odorants that cannot be consciously detected can nevertheless influence mood and stimulate activity in non-olfactory areas of the brain (Jacob & McClintock, 2000; Jacob et al., 2001; Savic et al., 2001).

Despite steamy ads for cologne and perfume, however, there is little or no evidence that humans give off or can detect pheromones that act as sexual attractants (Mast & Samuelsen, 2009). In one study, for example, exotic dancers reported that their income from customer tips increased during the ovulation phase of their menstrual cycles (Miller, Tyber, & Jordan, 2007), but the difference was probably not due to pheromones. During ovulation females tend to speak in a more sexually attractive manner (Pipitone & Gallup, 2008), to be more interested in erotic stimuli (Mass et al., 2008), and to be more receptive to courtship (Gueguen, 2008; Rosen & López, 2009). So it could well be that differences in their behavior, and not pheromones, were responsible for their higher tip income during ovulation (Miller, Tyber, & Jordan, 2007).

If a certain scent does enhance a person's readiness for sex, it is probably because the person has learned to associate that scent with previous sexual experiences. There are many other examples of people using olfactory information in social situations. For instance, after just a few hours of contact with their newborn babies, mothers can usually identify their infant by smell (Porter, Cernich, & McLaughlin, 1983). And if infants are breastfed, they can discriminate their own mother's odor from that of other breastfeeding women and appear to be comforted by it (Porter, 1991). Recognizing this odor may help establish the mother-infant bond discussed in the chapter on human development.

Our Sense of Taste

Our receptors for taste are in the taste buds, which are grouped together in structures called **papillae** (pronounced "puh-PILL-ee"). Normally, there are about 10,000 taste buds in a person's mouth, mostly on the tongue but also on the roof of the mouth and on the back of the throat. The human taste system detects only a few basic sensations: sweet, sour, bitter, and salty. Each taste bud responds best to one or two of these categories (Zhang et al., 2003), but it responds weakly to others, too. Research has also revealed two additional taste sensations (Rolls, 1997). One, called *umami* (which means "delicious" in Japanese), enhances other tastes and is produced by certain proteins as well as by monosodium glutamate (MSG; Beauchamp, 2009). The other, called *astringent,* is the taste produced by tannins, which are found in tea, for example. Activation of each specific basic taste activates a correspondingly different set of brain areas (Chen et al., 2011; Rolls, 2009), and causes different patterns of blood flow to the face (Kashima & Hayashi, 2011).

papillae Structures in the mouth on which taste buds are grouped.

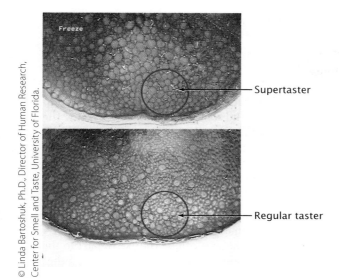

Supertaster

Regular taster

© Linda Bartoshuk, Ph.D., Director of Human Research, Center for Smell and Taste, University of Florida.

FIGURE 3.16

Are You a Supertaster?

The top photo shows papillae on the tongue of a "supertaster." If you don't mind a temporary stain on your mouth and teeth, you can look at your own papillae by painting the front of your tongue with a cotton swab soaked in blue food coloring. Distribute the dye by moving your tongue around and swallowing; then look into a magnifying mirror as you shine a flashlight on your tongue. The pink circles you see against the blue background are papillae, each of which has about six taste buds buried in its surface. Get several friends to do this test, and you will see that genes create wide individual differences in taste-bud density.

LEARN by DOING

About 25 percent of us are *supertasters*—individuals whose genes have given them an especially large number of papillae on their tongues (Bartoshuk, 2000; Hayes & Keast, 2011; see Figure 3.16). Supertasters are more sensitive than other people to bitterness, as revealed in their reactions to foods such as broccoli, soy products, and grapefruit.

Scientists are learning more and more about how foods interact with taste receptors to signal various tastes (Chandrashekar et al., 2006; Small et al., 2003; Stillman, 2002), and they are putting the information to good use. Understanding the chemistry of sweetness, for example, has led to new chemicals that fit into sweetness receptors and taste thousands of times sweeter than sugar. When used as artificial sweeteners, they offer new ways to enjoy good-tasting but low-calorie sweets. Researchers are also looking into how taste is affected by other senses such as hearing. It appears, for example, that people may experience the taste of wine differently depending on the type of music they hear while drinking it (North, 2011). ("In Review: Smell and Taste" summarizes our discussion of these senses.)

Sensing Your Body

Which is the largest organ in my body?

Some senses are not located in one place, such as in the eye or the ear. These are the *somatic senses,* also called *somatosensory systems,* and they are spread throughout the body. The **cutaneous senses** include the skin senses of touch, temperature, and pain. Another body sense, called *kinesthesia,* or *kinesthetic perception,* tells the brain where the parts of the body are. Kinesthetic perception is closely related to our sense of balance. Although balance is not strictly a somatosensory system, we describe it here.

Touch and Temperature

People can function and prosper without vision, hearing, or smell. But a person without a sense of touch would have difficulty surviving. Without this sense, you could not even swallow food, because you could not tell where it was in your mouth and throat. You receive touch sensations through your skin, which is the body's largest organ. The skin covers nearly two square yards of surface area, weighs more than twenty pounds, and has

Smell and Taste		IN REVIEW
Aspect of Sensory System	**Elements**	**Key Characteristics**
Energy	Smell: volatile chemicals Taste: chemicals in solution	The amount, intensity, and location of the chemicals determine taste and smell sensations.
Structures of taste and smell	Smell: chemical receptors in the mucous membrane of the nose Taste: taste buds grouped in papillae in the mouth	Odor and taste molecules stimulate chemical receptors.
Pathway to the brain	Olfactory bulb and taste buds	Axons from the nose and mouth bypass the thalamus and extend directly to the olfactory bulb.

IN REVIEW QUESTIONS

1. The flavor of food arises from a combination of ___ and ___.
2. Emotion and memory are linked especially closely to our sense of ___.
3. Perfume ads suggest that humans are affected by ___ that increase sexual attraction.

© Ted Foxx/Alamy

Timing is Everything
Some touch sensations depend on the timing of skin stimulation. You can experience this for yourself if you first try to feel the roughness of sandpaper by just placing your fingers on it. A much clearer sensation of roughness will appear if you slide your fingers over the surface (Hollins & Bensamaia, 2007). As you do so, the ridges that form your fingerprints vibrate in succession, activating special receptors in each ridge. Encoded messages about the timing of this sequence of activation tells the brain about the characteristics of the surface you are touching (Hartmann, 2009; Scheibert et al., 2009).

LEARN by DOING

hair virtually everywhere on it. The hairs on your skin do not sense anything, but they bend when contacted, creating pressure at their bases which stimulates touch receptors on and in the skin beneath them. Neural receptors in and just below the skin send the "touch" message to the brain (Delmas, Hao, & Rodat-Despoix, 2011).

Encoding Touch Information   The sense of touch encodes information about two aspects of an object contacting the skin: its weight and its location. The *intensity* of the stimulus—how heavy it is—is encoded both by the firing rate of individual neurons and by the number of neurons stimulated. A heavy object triggers a higher rate of firing and stimulates more neurons than a light object. The brain "knows" where the touch occurs based on the *location* of the nerves that sense the touch information.

Adapting to Touch Stimuli   Continuous, unchanging input from all your touch neurons would provide a lot of unnecessary information. Once you get dressed, you don't need to be constantly reminded that you are wearing clothes. Thanks in part to the process of sensory adaptation described earlier, you don't continue to feel your clothes against your skin.

Changes in touch (as when your belt or shoe suddenly feels loose) provide the most important sensory information. The touch sense emphasizes these changes and filters out the excess information. How? Typically, a touch neuron responds with a **LEARN by DOING** burst of firing when a stimulus is applied then quickly returns to its baseline firing rate, even though the stimulus may still be in contact with the skin. If the touch pressure increases, the neuron again responds by increasing its firing rate and then slowing down. A few neurons adapt more slowly, however, continuing to fire as long as pressure is applied. By attending to this input, you can sense a constant stimulus (try doing this by focusing on touch sensations from your clothes or shoes, or the surface you are sitting on).

Just as taste and smell interact, so do touch and vision. To experience an example of this interaction, ask someone sitting across a table from you to stroke the tabletop while **LEARN by DOING** stroking your knee under the table in exactly the same way, in exactly the same direction. If you watch the person's hand stroking the table, you will soon experience the touch sensations coming from the table, not your knee! But the person's two hands must move in synch, or the illusion will not occur (Bekrater-Bodmann et al., 2012; Kammers et al., 2009; Makin, Holmes, & Ehrsson, 2008; Press et al., 2008).

Sensing Temperature   Some of the skin's sensory neurons respond to a change in temperature but not to simple contact. "Warm fibers" and "cold fibers" respond to specific temperature changes only. However, many fibers that respond to temperature also respond to touch, so these sensations sometimes interact. For example, if you touch an object made up of alternating warm and cool sections, you'll have the sensation of intense heat (Thunberg, 1896, cited in Craig & Bushnell, 1994).

Pain

Touch can feel pleasurable, but if the intensity of touch stimulation increases too much, it can turn into a pain sensation. Pain tells you about the impact of the world on your body. It also has a distinctly negative emotional component that interrupts whatever you are doing (Eccleston & Crombez, 1999).

Pain as an Information Sense   The receptors for pain are free nerve endings that come from the spinal cord, enter the skin, and then simply end. Painful stimuli cause the release of chemicals that fit into these specialized receptors in pain neurons, causing them to fire. The axons of pain-sensing neurons release neurotransmitters not only near the spinal cord (thus sending pain information to the brain) but also near the skin (causing inflammation).

cutaneous senses   Senses including touch, temperature, pain, and kinesthetic perception that are spread throughout the body. Also called somatosensory systems.

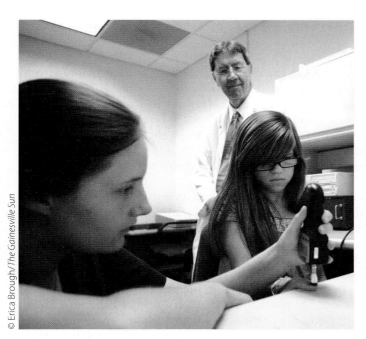

© Erica Brough/The Gainesville Sun

A Girl Who Can't Feel Pain
Ashlyn Blocker, shown here being tested at age 11, was born with a rare genetic disorder that prevented the development of pain receptors. As a result, she feels no pain if she is cut or bruised, if she bites her tongue while eating, or even if she is burned by hot soup or a hot stove. She only knows she has been injured if she sees herself bruised or bleeding, so she must find ways to protect herself from danger without the vital information provided by the pain system.

gate control theory of pain A theory suggesting the presence of a "gate" in the spinal cord that either permits or blocks the passage of pain impulses to the brain.

analgesia Reduction in the sensation of pain in the presence of a normally painful stimulus.

Two types of nerve fibers carry pain signals from the skin to the spinal cord. *A-delta fibers* carry sharp, pricking pain sensations; *C-fibers* carry dull, continuous aches and burning sensations. When you stub your toe, for example, that immediate wave of sharp, intense pain is signaled by A-delta fibers, whereas that slightly delayed wave of gnawing, dull pain is signaled by C-fibers. When pain impulses reach the spinal cord, they form synapses with neurons that relay the pain signals to the thalamus and other parts of the brain. Different pain neurons are activated by different types and degrees of painful stimulation (Ploner et al., 2002).

Emotional Aspects of Pain Specific pathways carry the emotional component of a painful stimulus to areas of the hindbrain, the reticular formation, and the cortex via the thalamus (Shackman et al., 2011). However, our overall emotional response depends greatly on our mood and how we think about the pain (Berna et al., 2010; Lumley et al., 2011). In one study, some participants were told about the kind of painful stimulus they were to receive and when to expect it. Others were not informed. Those who knew what to expect objected less to the pain, even though the sensation was reported to be equally noticeable in both groups (Mayer & Price, 1982). People can lessen their emotional responses to pain by using pain-reducing strategies such as listening to music or focusing on pictures or distracting thoughts (Buhle et al., 2012; Edwards et al., 2009; Master et al., 2009; Roy et al., 2009), especially if they expect these strategies to succeed (Bantick et al., 2002). Scientists are also developing special biofeedback systems that may someday allow patients to relieve chronic pain by reducing activity in the brain regions involved in pain perception (deCharms et al., 2005).

The Gate Control Theory of Pain   Pain is useful because it can protect you from harm. There are times, though, when enough is enough. Fortunately, the nervous system has several mechanisms for controlling the experience of pain. One theory about how these mechanisms work is called the **gate control theory of pain** (Melzack & Wall, 1965). This theory suggests that there is a "gate" in the spinal cord that either allows pain signals to reach the brain or stops them. Some details of the original theory were incorrect, but it continues to guide medical efforts at pain management (Kim et al., 2011). That's because there is evidence that natural mechanisms can indeed block pain sensations at the level of the spinal cord (DeLeo, 2006; Dickenson, 2002).

For example, input from other skin senses can come into the spinal cord at the same time the pain gets there and take over the pathways that the pain impulses would have used. This may be why we can temporarily relieve pain by rubbing the skin around a wound or using electrical stimulation or creams that produce temperature sensations (Henderson, 2008; Slavin, 2008). It also helps explain why scratching relieves itching; itchy sensations involve activity in fibers located close to pain fibers (Andrew & Craig, 2001; bin Saif et al., 2012). Unfortunately, pain gates can sometimes be "left open." Chronic pain conditions can be caused by damage or inflammation in the peripheral nervous system that sensitizes incoming pain pathways, making them more likely to send pain signals to the brain (D'Mello & Dickenson, 2008).

The brain itself can close the gate to pain impulses by sending signals down the spinal cord. These messages from the brain block incoming pain signals at spinal cord synapses. The result is **analgesia**, a reduction in pain sensation in the presence of a normally painful stimulus. Aspirin and other *analgesic* drugs can dull pain sensations, but it may also be possible to help the brain close the pain gate without them. For example, research participants who received fifteen minutes of transcranial magnetic stimulation (see Table 2.1 in the chapter on biology and behavior) found it easier to withstand a painful heat stimulus (Borckardt et al., 2007), and patients suffering from

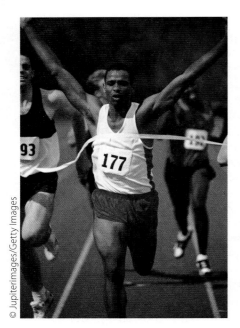

Natural Analgesia

The stress of athletic exertion causes the release of endorphins, natural painkillers that have been associated with pleasant feelings known as "runner's high" (Benedetti, 2007).

pain caused by brain damage are being helped by other brain-stimulation techniques (Arle & Shils, 2008).

Natural Analgesics As described in the chapter on biology and behavior, natural opiates called *endorphins* play a role in the brain's ability to block pain signals. Endorphins are natural painkillers that act as neurotransmitters at many levels of the pain pathway. In the spinal cord, for example, they block the synapses of the fibers that carry pain signals. Endorphins may also relieve pain when the adrenal and pituitary glands secrete them into the bloodstream as hormones. The more endorphin receptors a person has inherited, the more pain tolerance that person has (Benjamin, Wilson, & Mogil, 1999).

Several conditions can cause the body to ease its own pain. For example, endorphins are released where inflammation occurs (Cabot, 2001). A spinal cord endorphin system is activated during the late stages of pregnancy, and the more endorphins a woman spontaneously generates, the less additional analgesia she needs during childbirth (Dabo et al., 2010). An endorphin system is also activated when people believe they are receiving a painkiller, even when they are not (Wager et al., 2011; Zubieta & Stohler, 2009); this may help explain the placebo effect, as described in the introduction to the science of psychology chapter (Stewart-Williams, 2004). The resulting pain inhibition is experienced in the part of the body where the person expected it to occur, but not elsewhere (Benedetti, Arduino, & Amanzio, 1999). Physical or psychological stress can also activate natural analgesic systems. Stress-induced release of natural analgesics may account for the fact that injured soldiers and athletes sometimes continue to perform in the heat of battle or competition with no apparent pain (Colloca & Benedetti, 2005).

THINKING CRITICALLY

Does Acupuncture Relieve Pain?

Acupuncture, a widely used 3,000-year-old Asian medical treatment, is said to relieve pain (Lin & Chen, 2008). The treatment is based on the idea that body energy, called *Qi*, flows along lines called *channels* that link the internal organs to places on the surface of the skin (Vincent & Richardson, 1986; see Figure 3.17). According to this theory, there are fourteen main channels and a person's health depends on the balance of energy flowing in them. Stimulating the channels by inserting fine needles into the skin and twirling them is said to restore a balanced flow of energy. The needles produce an aching and tingling sensation called *Teh-ch'i* at the site of stimulation and they relieve pain in distant, seemingly unrelated parts of the body (Liu & Akira, 1994; Yan et al., 1992).

FIGURE 3.17
Linking Internal Organs to the Skin's Surface

These diagrams illustrate the skin locations which are said by acupuncturists to be linked to the large intestine (LI4), the lung (LU5), the gallbladder (GB34), and the stomach (ST36).

Source: From Wang, S. M., Kain, Z. N., & White, P. (2008). "Acupuncture analgesia: I. The scientific basis," *Anesthesia and Analgesia, 106*(2), 602–610. Copyright (c) 2008 Wolters Kluwer Health. Reprinted by permission.

What am I being asked to believe or accept?

Acupuncturists claim that twirling needles in the skin can relieve pain caused by everything from tooth extraction to cancer.

Is evidence available to support the claim?

There is no scientific evidence for the existence of the energy channels proposed by acupuncturists (Wang, Kain, & White, 2008). However, there *is* evidence from positron emission tomography (PET) and magnetic resonance imaging (MRI) studies that stimulating acupuncture sites changes activity in brain regions related to pain regulation and to the targets of treatment (Zhang et al., 2009). Numerous studies have also shown positive results in 50 to 80 percent of patients treated by acupuncture for various kinds of pain (Brinkhaus et al., 2006; Manheimer et al., 2005; Witt et al., 2005). One study found, for example, that acupuncture was more effective than an acupuncture-like placebo treatment in reducing the frequency of chronic migraine headaches (Li et al., 2012). A summary of eleven other headache studies found greater overall reductions in pain among patients who had been randomly assigned to receive acupuncture as compared to those randomly assigned to receive standard drug therapies (Linde et al., 2009). Adding acupuncture to a program of drugs and exercise was followed by a greater reduction in the pain of fibromyalgia, and the difference remained apparent three months after treatment (Targino et al., 2008). One study found that after receiving acupuncture, hospitalized infants needed less analgesic or sedative medications, and showed improved eating and respiration (Gentry et al., 2011). Another study found that acupuncture before surgery reduced postoperative pain and nausea, decreased the need for pain-relieving drugs, and reduced patients' stress responses (Kotani et al., 2001). Yet another found electrical-stimulation acupuncture to be more effective than either drugs or fake stimulation at reducing nausea following major breast surgery; the acupuncture group also reported the least postoperative pain (Gan et al., 2004).

Well-controlled studies of acupuncture are rare, however, and their results can be contradictory. Some studies of patients with back or neck pain, for example, have found acupuncture to be no better than placebo treatments or massage therapy (Assefi et al., 2005; Cherkin et al., 2009; Foster et al., 2007; Linde et al., 2009); others have found that acupuncture benefits only certain patients (Yuan et al., 2008).

Drugs that slow the breakdown of opiates also prolong the pain relief produced by acupuncture (He, 1987). The pain-reducing effects of acupuncture during electrical stimulation of a tooth can be reversed by naloxone, a substance that blocks the pain-killing effects of endorphins and other opiate drugs. These findings suggest that acupuncture does somehow activate the body's natural pain-killing system. Is this activation brought about only by a placebo effect? Probably not entirely, because acupuncture produces naloxone-reversible pain relief even in monkeys and rats, who obviously have no expectations about acupuncture (Kishioka et al., 1994).

Can that evidence be interpreted another way?

Yes. Evidence about acupuncture might be interpreted as simply confirming that the body's pain-killing system can be stimulated by external means. Acupuncture may merely provide one activating method (Pariente et al., 2005). There may be other methods that are even more efficient (Petrovic et al., 2005; Ulett, 2003). We already know, for example, that successful placebo treatments for human pain appear to operate by activating the endorphin system.

What evidence would help to evaluate the alternatives?

More placebo-controlled studies of acupuncture are needed, but it has been difficult to control for the placebo effect in acupuncture treatment, especially in double-blind fashion (e.g., Derry et al., 2006; Kaptchuk et al., 2006). How could a study be set up so that therapists would not know whether the treatment they are giving is acupuncture or not? What placebo treatment could look and feel like having a needle inserted and twirled in the skin? Some researchers have created single-blind placebo acupuncture using "sham" techniques in which the needles do not actually break the skin or are inserted but not twirled or are inserted in locations that should not, according to acupuncturists, have any effect on pain. In one study of "sham" techniques, research participants were indeed unable to tell whether or not they were getting genuine acupuncture (Enblom et al., 2008). So far, only a few studies have used sophisticated "sham" methods (e.g., Li et al., 2012), and some have found acupuncture to be no more effective than placebo methods (e.g., Haake et al., 2007; Linde et al., 2009). More controlled experiments should eventually reveal the degree to which placebo effects play a role in the results of acupuncture treatment.

Researchers must also learn more about what factors govern whether acupuncture will activate the endorphin system. Other important unknowns include the types of pain for which acupuncture is most effective, the types of patients who respond best, and the precise procedures that are most effective. Knowing more about the general relationship between internal pain-killing systems and external methods for stimulating them would also be valuable.

What conclusions are most reasonable?

Although acupuncture is by no means a cure-all, it appears that in some circumstances it may help to relieve pain and reduce nausea. What we still don't know is exactly why this may be and through what mechanism any genuine effects might operate. Acupuncture remains a fascinating phenomenon, a treatment used on millions of people all over the world, and a continuing source of controversy. Some critics argue that further expenditures for acupuncture research are not warranted, but it seems likely that studies will continue. The quality of these studies' methodology and the nature of their results will determine whether acupuncture finds a more prominent place in Western medicine.

●●●●

Sensing Body Position

Most sensory systems receive information from the outside world, such as the light reflected from a flower or the feeling of cool water. But as far as the brain is concerned, the rest of the body is "outside" too. You know about the position of your body and what each of its parts is doing only because sensory systems provide this information to your brain. Your sense of body movement and position is called **proprioception** (meaning "received from the self" and pronounced "pro-pree-oh-SEP-shun").

Kinesthetic Perception   In the biology and behavior chapter, we describe the case of Christina, a woman who did not recognize her own body. She had lost her **kinesthetic perception** (pronounced "kin-es-THEH-tic"), which tells us where the parts of the body are in relation to one another. To better appreciate kinesthetic perception, try this: Close your eyes; then hold your arms out in front of you and touch your two index fingers together. You probably did this easily because your kinesthetic sense told you where each finger was with respect to your body. You depend on kinesthetic information to guide all your movements, from walking to complex athletic actions. These movement patterns become simple and fluid because with practice the brain uses kinesthetic information automatically. Normally, kinesthetic information comes primarily from **proprioceptors,** which are special receptors in the joints and muscles (Proske, 2006). These receptors send information to the brain about the stretching of muscles. When the position of the bones changes, receptors in the joints set off neural activity. This encoded information goes to the spinal cord and then to the thalamus, along with sensory information from the skin. Finally, it goes to the cerebellum and to the somatosensory cortex, both of which help coordinate movements (Longo & Haggard, 2010; see Figures 2.8, 2.9, and 2.10).

LEARN by DOING

Balance   Have you ever been on a roller coaster? How did you feel when the ride ended? Your **sense of equilibrium,** sometimes called the **vestibular sense** (pronounced "ves-TIB-u-ler"), tells your brain about the position of your head (and, to some degree, the rest of your body) and about its general movements. You have probably heard it referred to as the *sense of balance.* People usually become aware of the sense of equilibrium only when they overstimulate it and become dizzy or experience motion sickness.

The organs for the vestibular sense are in the inner ear. As shown in Figure 3.14, each inner ear has two fluid-filled *vestibular sacs* that contain tiny, delicate crystals called

proprioception The sensory processes that tell us about the location of our body parts and what each is doing.

kinesthetic perception The proprioceptive sense that tells us where the parts of the body are with respect to one another.

proprioceptors Neural receptors that provide information about movement and body position.

sense of equilibrium (vestibular sense) The proprioceptive sense that provides information about the position of the head and its movements.

otoliths ("ear stones") that rest on hair endings. There are also three arc-shaped tubes, called *semicircular canals,* and they, too, are filled with fluid. Tiny hairs extend into the fluid in the canals. When your head moves, the otoliths shift in the vestibular sacs and the fluid moves in the semicircular canals, stimulating hair endings. These responses to head movement activate neurons that travel along the acoustic nerve, signaling the brain about the amount and direction of head movement (Angelaki & Cullen, 2008). If the otoliths become displaced by debris in the vestibular sacs, as they do in a condition called *benign paroxysmal positional vertigo,* or BPPV, the result is intense dizziness and spinning sensations (Fife, 2009). BPPV is treated by having the patient lie down and make specific head movements that shift debris away from the otoliths (Kerber & Helmchen, 2012).

Neural connections from the vestibular system to the cerebellum help coordinate bodily movements. Connections to the part of the autonomic nervous system that affects the digestive system help create the nausea that may follow overstimulation of the vestibular system—by a roller-coaster ride, for instance. Finally, connections to the eye muscles produce *vestibular-ocular reflexes,* which cause your eyes to move opposite to your head movements. These reflexes allow you to focus on one spot even when your head is moving. You can experience these reflexes by having a friend spin you around on a stool for a while. When you stop, try to fix your gaze on one point in the room. You'll be unable to do so, because the excitation of the vestibular system will cause your eyes to move repeatedly in the direction opposite from the way you were spinning. Our vestibular reflexes adjust to the lack of gravity in outer space (Thornton, 2011), which is why astronauts returning to earth have postural and movement difficulties until their vestibular systems readjust to gravity (Paloski, 1998). (See "In Review: Body Senses" for a summary of our discussion of touch, temperature, pain, and kinesthesia.)

Body Senses — IN REVIEW

Sense	Energy	Conversion of Physical Energy to Nerve Activity	Pathways and Characteristics
Touch	Mechanical deformation of skin	Neural receptors in the skin (may be stimulated by hair on the skin)	Nerve endings respond to changes in weight (intensity) and location of touch.
Temperature	Heat	Sensory neurons in the skin	Changes in temperature are detected by warm-sensing and cool-sensing fibers. Temperature interacts with touch.
Pain	Increases with intensity of touch or temperature	Free nerve endings in or near the skin surface	Changes in intensity cause the release of chemicals detected by receptors in pain neurons. Some fibers convey sharp pain; others convey dull aches and burning sensations.
Kinesthetic perception	Mechanical energy of joint and muscle movement	Neural receptors in muscle fibers	Information from muscle fibers is sent to the spinal cord, thalamus, cerebellum, and cortex.
Sense of equilibrium	Mechanical energy of head movement	Neural receptors in the inner ear	Information about fluid moving in the semicircular canals is sent to the brain along the acoustic nerve.

IN REVIEW QUESTIONS

1. Gate control theory offers an explanation of why we sometimes do not feel ___ .
2. Professional dancers look at the same spot as long as possible during repeated spins. They are trying to avoid the dizziness caused when the sense of ___ is overstimulated.
3. Without your sense of ___ you would not be able to swallow food without choking.

Perception

How do sensations become perceptions?

So far, we have explored how sensory information reaches the brain. Let's now consider the processes of perception that allow the brain to make sense of that information. These perceptual processes can sometimes make the difference between life and death. For

Misperceiving Reality
Measure lines A-C and A-B. They are exactly the same length, but you probably perceived A-C as longer. Why? Partly because your visual system tries to interpret all stimuli as three-dimensional, even when they are not. A three-dimensional interpretation of this drawing would lead you to see the two lines as the edges of two parallel paths, one of which ends closer to you than the other. Your eyes tell you that the two paths start at about the same point (the castle entrance), so you assume that the closer line must be the longer of the two.

LEARN by DOING

Source: Gardner (1988).

example, at a traffic circle in Scotland, fourteen fatal accidents occurred in one year, partly because drivers did not slow down as they approached the circle. After warning signs failed to solve the problem, Gordon Denton, a British psychologist, found a clever solution. He recommended that white lines be painted across the road leading to the circle, in a pattern something like this:

/ / / / / / ///

Crossing these lines, which were spaced progressively more closely, gave drivers the impression that they were speeding up, so their automatic response was to slow down (Denton, 1980). During the fourteen months after Denton's idea was implemented, there were only two fatalities at the traffic circle! Similar kinds of striping patterns are now widely used throughout Britain and on approaches to some towns and intersections in the United States. Denton's solution depended partly on his knowledge of sensation but mostly on the principles of human perception.

Some perceptual tasks take attention and effort, as when a child struggles to recognize printed letters. But as experienced readers know, a lot of the perceptual work that transforms sensory information into meaningful experiences happens automatically without conscious awareness. To illustrate the workings of these complex processes, psychologists draw attention to *perceptual failures*—cases in which we perceive stimuli incorrectly (Duguid & Goncalo, 2012; Ito, 2012; Witt, Linkenauger, & Proffitt, 2012). Just as drivers at the traffic circle incorrectly perceived themselves as speeding up, you will probably perceive the two lines in Figure 3.18 as differing in length, even though they are the same.

Organizing the Perceptual World

What determines how I perceive my world?

To further appreciate the wonder of the complicated perceptual work you do every day, imagine yourself driving on a busy road searching for Barney's Diner, an unfamiliar restaurant where you are to meet a friend. The roadside is crammed with signs of all shapes and colors, some flashing, some rotating. If you are ever to recognize the sign that says "Barney's Diner," you will have to impose some sort of organization on this overwhelming mixture of visual information. How do you do this? How do you know where one sign ends and another begins? And how do you know that an apparently tiny sign is not really tiny but just far away?

(A)

(B)

FIGURE 3.19
Reversible Images

These *reversible images* can be organized by your perceptual system in two ways. If you perceive Part A as the word "figure," the space around the letters becomes meaningless background. Now emphasize the word "ground," and what had stood out a moment ago now becomes background. In Part B, when you emphasize the white vase, the black profiles become background; if you organize the faces as the figure, what had been a vase now becomes background. We normally tend to see smaller, lower elements in a scene as figure and larger, higher elements as ground (Vecera, Vogel, & Woodman, 2002), but images like these don't allow us to use that rule of thumb.

LEARN by DOING

figure The part of the visual field that has meaning.

ground The contourless part of the visual field; the background.

figure ground discrimination The ability to organize a visual scene so that it contains meaningful figures set against a less relevant ground.

Principles of Perceptual Organization

Before you can recognize the Barney's Diner sign, your perceptual system must separate that sign from its background of lights, colors, letters, and other competing stimuli. Two basic principles—*figure ground perception* and *grouping*—guide this initial organization.

Figure and Ground   When you look at a complex scene or listen to a noisy environment, your perceptual apparatus automatically emphasizes certain features, objects, or sounds. These emphasized features become the **figure**. This part of the visual field has meaning, stands in front of the rest, and always seems to include contours or edges. These contours and edges separate the figure from the less relevant background, called the **ground** (Rubin, 1915; Zhang & von der Heydt, 2010). As you drive toward an intersection, a stop sign will become a figure that stands out clearly against the background of trees or buildings.

To experience your own **figure ground discrimination** ability, look at Figure 3.19. Notice that you can decide how to organize the stimuli in the drawings. You can repeatedly reverse figure and ground to see faces, then a vase, then faces again (3.19B) or to see the word *figure* or the word *ground* (3.19A). The fact that you can mentally manipulate these "reversible" images means that your perceptual systems are not just recording devices that passively absorb incoming sensations; you play an active part in organizing what you perceive. We also usually organize sensory stimulation into only one perceptual category at a time. This is why it is difficult to see both a vase and two faces—or the words *figure* and *ground*—at the same time.

Grouping   Why do certain parts of the world become figure and others become ground, even when nothing in particular stands out in the pattern of light that falls on the retina? The answer is that certain properties of stimuli lead you to group them together more or less automatically.

In the early 1900s, several German psychologists described the principles behind this grouping of stimuli. They argued that people perceive sights and sounds as organized wholes. These wholes, they said, are different from the sum of the individual sensations, just as a house is something other than a pile of bricks and wood and glass. Because the German word for figure or shape is *Gestalt* (pronounced "ge-SHTALT"), these researchers became known as *Gestalt psychologists*. Max Wertheimer, one of the founders of Gestalt psychology, proposed a number of principles that describe how the perceptual system "glues" raw sensations together in particular ways (Kimchi, 2003; Wertheimer, 1923):

1. *Proximity.* The closer objects or events are to one another, the more likely they are to be perceived as belonging together, as Figure 3.20(A) illustrates.
2. *Similarity.* Elements that are similar in size, color, orientation, and texture are perceived to be part of a group, as in Figure 3.20(B). This is why students wearing the same school colors at a stadium will be perceived as belonging together even if they are not seated close together.
3. *Continuity.* Sensations that appear to create a continuous form are perceived as belonging together, as in Figure 3.20(C).
4. *Closure.* We tend to mentally fill in missing parts of incomplete objects, as in Figure 3.20(D). The gaps are easy to see, but the tendency to link disconnected parts can be so strong that you may perceive faint connections that aren't actually there (Lleras & Moore, 2006).
5. *Simplicity.* We tend to group features of a stimulus in a way that provides the simplest interpretation of the world. You can see the simplicity principle in action in Figure 3.20(D), where it is simpler to see a single cube than an assortment of separate and unrelated arrows and Ys.
6. *Common fate.* Sets of objects that move in the same direction at the same speed are perceived together. So even though the individual birds in a flock are separated from each other as they fly, they will be perceived as a group.

FIGURE 3.20
Gestalt Principles of Perceptual Grouping
We tend to perceive Part A as two groups of two circles plus one single circle rather than as, say, five circles. In Part B, we see two columns of Xs and two columns of Os, not four rows of XOXO. We see the X in Part C as being made out of two continuous lines, not a combination of the odd forms shown. In Part D, we fill gaps so as to perceive a hollow cube. In Part E, we tend to pair up dots in the same oval even though they are far apart. Part F shows that connected objects are grouped together.

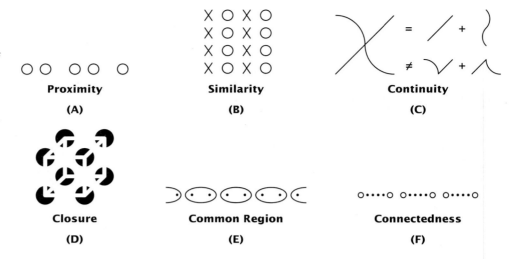

Choreographers and marching-band directors use this principle of common fate when they arrange for groups or subgroups of dancers or musicians to move in unison, causing the audience to perceive waves of motion or a single large moving object.

Stephen Palmer (1999) has identified three additional grouping principles:

1. *Synchrony.* Stimuli that occur at the same time are likely to be perceived as coming from the same source. For example, if you see a car up ahead stop violently at the same instant that you hear a crash, you will probably perceive these visual and auditory stimuli as part of the same event.
2. *Common region.* Stimuli located within some boundary tend to be grouped together. The boundary can be created by an enclosing perimeter, as in Figure 3.20(E), a region of color, or other factors.
3. *Connectedness.* Stimuli that are connected by other elements tend to be grouped together. In Figure 3.20(F), the circles connected by dotted lines seem to go together even though they are farther apart than some pairs of unconnected circles. Here, the principle of connectedness appears more important than the principle of proximity.

Neuroimaging studies are beginning to identify the brain areas that are involved in the operation of these and other principles that help us to organize our perceptions of the world (Gallace & Spence, 2011; Levinthal & Franconeri, 2011; Sayim, Westheimer, & Herzog, 2010).

Perception of Depth and Distance

We are able to experience the world in three-dimensional depth even though the visual information we receive from it is projected onto two-dimensional retinas. This is possible because of **depth perception,** our ability to perceive distance. Depth perception, in turn, is made possible by *stimulus cues* provided by the environment and also by the properties of our visual system (Anderson, 2003; Hildreth & Royden, 2011).

Stimulus Cues   To some extent, people perceive depth through the same cues that artists use to create the impression of depth and distance on a two-dimensional canvas. Figure 3.21 demonstrates several of these cues:

- One of the most important depth cues is *interposition*: Closer objects block the view of things farther away. This cue is illustrated in Figure 3.21 by the couple walking away from the camera. Because their bodies block out part of the buildings, we perceive them as being closer to us than the buildings are.

depth perception Perception of distance, allowing us to experience the world in three dimensions.

FIGURE 3.21
Stimulus Cues for Depth Perception

See if you can identify the cues of relative size, interposition, linear perspective, height in the visual field, textural gradient, and shadows that combine to create a sense of three-dimensional depth in this photograph. Notice, too, that sidewalk artist Kurt Wenner has used some of these same cues to create a dramatic illusion of depth in his drawing. (You can see more of Wenner's amazing work at http://www.kurtwenner.com/index.htm.)

LEARN by DOING

FIGURE 3.22
Light, Shadow, and Depth Perception

Shadows create three dimensional impressions of bumps on the left side of this drawing and of dents on the right side. But if you turn the book upside down, the bumps will look like dents, and the dents will look like bumps. This reversal in depth perception occurs partly because people normally assume that illumination comes from above and interpret the pattern of light and shadow accordingly (Adams, Graf, & Ernst, 2004; Cook et al., 2008).

LEARN by DOING

Image courtesy of Stephen Palmer, Department of Psychology, University of California at Berkeley (after Michael Kalloniatis, Centre for Eye Health, University of New South Wales)

- You can see the principle of *relative size* operating in Figure 3.21 by measuring the images of that same couple and comparing it to the size of the man in the foreground. If two objects are assumed to be about the same size, the object producing a larger image on the retina is perceived as closer than the one producing a smaller image.

- Another cue comes from *height in the visual field*: On the ground, objects that are more distant are usually higher in the visual field than those that are nearby. Because the building in the center of Figure 3.21 is higher than the people in the restaurant, the building appears to be farther away from you. This is one reason why objects higher in the visual field are more likely to be interpreted as the background for objects that are lower in a scene (Vecera, Vogel, & Woodman, 2002).

- The tiny figures near the center of Figure 3.21 are seen as very far away because they are near a point where the buildings on each edge of the plaza, like all parallel lines that recede into the distance, appear to converge toward a single point. This apparent *convergence* provides a cue called *linear perspective*. The closer together two converging lines are, the greater the perceived distance.

- Notice that the street in Figure 3.21 fades into a hazy background. Increased distance usually produces less clarity, and this *reduced clarity* is interpreted as a cue for greater distance. Hazy, distant objects also tend to take on a bluish tone, which is why art students are taught to add a little blue when mixing paint for deep background features.

- *Light and shadow* also contribute to the perception of three dimensions (Kingdom, 2003; Ramachandran, 1988). The buildings in Figure 3.21 are seen as three-dimensional, not flat, because of the shadows on some of their surfaces. Figure 3.22 shows a more dramatic example.

- An additional stimulus-based depth cue comes from continuous changes across the visual field, called *gradients*. For example, a textural gradient is a graduated

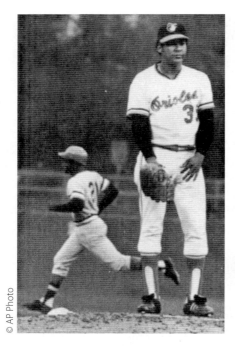

© AP Photo

A Case of Depth Misperception
The runner in this photo is actually farther away than the man on the pitcher's mound. But because he is lower, not higher, in the visual field—and because his leg can be seen as in front of, not behind, the pitcher's leg—the runner appears smaller than normal rather than farther away (Vecera, Vogel, & Woodman, 2002).

change in the texture, or "grain," of the visual field, as you can see in the plaza and the street in Figure 3.21. Texture appears more compact and less detailed as distance increases. As the texture of a surface changes across the retinal image, you perceive a change in distance.

Cues Based on Properties of the Visual System   Some depth cues result from the way human eyes are built and positioned. Recall that to bring an image into focus on the retina, the lens of the eye changes shape, or *accommodates*. Information about the muscle activity involved is relayed to the brain, and this *accommodation cue* helps create the perception of distance.

The depth cues described so far are called *monocular* cues because we can detect them with just one eye. There are also two *binocular* depth cues which are produced by the relative location of our two eyes. The first is **eye convergence**. Because each eye is located at a different place on the skull, the eyes must converge, or rotate inward, to project the same image on each retina. The closer the object, the more the eyes must converge. Eye muscles send information about this convergence to the brain, which processes it as a distance cue. You can experience this feedback from your eye muscles by holding up a finger at arm's length and then trying to keep it in focus as you move it toward your nose.

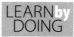

The second binocular cue occurs because each of our two eyes sees the world from a slightly different angle. The difference between these different retinal images is called **retinal disparity,** also known as *binocular disparity*. The difference, or disparity, between images decreases for objects that are far away and increases for objects that are nearby. The brain not only combines the two images of an object but also takes into account how much they differ. This information helps generate the impression of a single object that has depth as well as height and width and is located at a particular distance. Three-dimensional movies and some virtual reality systems use these *binocular cues* to create the appearance of depth in a two-dimensional stimulus. They show each eye an image of a scene as viewed from a slightly different angle.

In short, many cues—some present in the environment and in retinal images, others arising from the structure of the visual system—combine to give us a powerful and accurate sense of depth and distance.

Perception of Motion

Sometimes the most important property of an object is its motion—how fast it is going and where it is heading. Many cues about motion come from *optical flow,* or the changes that take place in retinal images across the visual field. As in the case of depth perception, you automatically translate this two-dimensional information into a three-dimensional experience. One particularly meaningful pattern of optical flow is known as **looming,** the rapid expansion in the size of an image so that it fills the retina. When an image looms, there is an automatic tendency to perceive it as an approaching object. If the expansion is as fast to the right as to the left and as fast above as below, this information signals that the object is approaching the eyes directly. In other words, duck! One reason that young children are at high risk when crossing streets alone is that they may not yet perceive the danger posed by cars and other rapidly looming objects (Wann, Poulter, & Purcell, 2011).

We are lucky that movement of the retinal image isn't the only factor contributing to motion perception. If it were, everything in sight would appear to move every time you moved your eyes and head (Ölveczky, Baccus, & Meister, 2003). This doesn't happen, because as noted earlier, the brain receives and processes information about the motion of the eyes and head (Wexler, 2005). If you look around you right now, tables, chairs, and other stationary objects will not appear to move because your brain determines that all the movement of images on your retinas is due to the movement of your eyes and head (Goltz et al., 2003). But now close one eye and wiggle your open eyeball by gently pushing your lower eyelid. Because your brain receives no signals that your eye is being moved by its own muscles, everything in the room will appear to move.

eye convergence A depth cue that results when the eyes rotate to project the image of an object on each retina.

retinal disparity A depth cue based on the difference between the retinal images received by each eye.

looming A motion cue whereby rapid expansion in the size of an image fills the available space on the retina.

Retinal Disparity and Distance
There is a smaller difference, or disparity, between each eye's view of an object when the object is far away than when it is close by. The amount of this retinal disparity helps us estimate the object's distance from us. To see for yourself how retinal disparity changes with distance, hold a pen vertically about six inches in front of your nose; then close one eye and notice where the pen is in relation to the background. Now open that eye, close the other one, and notice how much the pen "shifts." These are the two different views your eyes have of the pen. Repeat this procedure while holding the pen at arm's length. Notice that there is now less disparity or "shift," because there is less difference in the angles from which your two eyes see the pen.

LEARN by DOING

stroboscopic illusion An illusion of motion that is created when we see slightly different images or slightly displaced lights flashed in rapid succession.

perceptual constancy The perception that objects retain the same size, shape, color, and other properties despite changes in their retinal image.

When your body is moving, as in a car, the flow of visual information across the retina combines with information from the vestibular and touch senses to give you the experience of being in motion. If the car accelerates, you feel pressure from the back of the seat and feel your head tilting backward. Motion sickness may result if you perceive visual flow without appropriate sensations from other parts of the body, particularly the vestibular senses. This explains why you might feel nauseous while in a motion simulator or playing certain video games, especially those with virtual reality technology. The images suggest that you are moving through space when there is no real motion.

Other illusions of motion are more enjoyable. The most important of these occurs when still images appear, one at a time, in rapid succession, as they do on films and DVDs. Because each image differs slightly from the preceding one, the brain sees the objects in each image at one location for only a fraction of a second before they disappear and immediately reappear in a slightly different location. The entertaining result is the **stroboscopic illusion** of motion; when objects disappear and then quickly reappear nearby, the brain assumes that they have moved smoothly from one location to another. The same illusion is at work when it appears that flashing lights on a theater or casino sign are moving around the sign.

Perceptual Constancy

Suppose that one sunny day you are watching someone walking toward you along a tree-lined path. The visual sensations produced by this person are actually very strange. For one thing, the size of the image on your retinas keeps getting larger as the person gets closer. To see this for yourself, hold out a hand at arm's length and look at someone far away. The retinal image of that person will be so small that you can cover it with your hand. If you do the same thing when the person is three feet away, the retinal image will **LEARN by DOING** be too large to be covered by your hand, yet you will perceive the person as being closer now, not bigger. Similarly, as you watch the person pass from bright sunshine through the shadows of trees, your retinas receive images that shift back and forth from light to dark, but you perceive the person's coloring as staying the same.

These examples illustrate **perceptual constancy,** the perception that objects keep their size, shape, color, and other properties despite changes in their retinal image. Without this aspect of perception, you would experience the world as a place where solid objects continuously changed their properties.

Size Constancy Why does an object's perceived size stay more or less constant, regardless of changes in the size of its retinal image? One reason is that the brain perceives a change in the distance of an object and automatically adjusts the perception of size (Combe & Wexler, 2010). Specifically, the *perceived size* of an object is equal to the size of the retinal image multiplied by the perceived distance (Holway & Boring, 1941). As an object moves closer, or as we move closer to it, the size of its retinal image increases but the perceived distance decreases at the same rate. So the perceived size remains constant. If a balloon is inflated in front of your eyes, perceived distance remains constant and the perceived size (correctly) increases as the size of the retinal image increases.

Shape Constancy The principles behind shape constancy are closely related to those of size constancy. To see shape constancy at work, close this book (remember what page you're on) and tilt it toward and away from you several times. The book will **LEARN by DOING** continue to look rectangular, even though the shape of its retinal image changes dramatically as you move it. Your brain automatically combines information about retinal images and distance as movement occurs. In this case, the distance information has to do with the difference in distance between the near and far edges of the book.

Brightness Constancy Even with dramatic changes in the amount of light striking an object, our perception of the object's brightness remains relatively constant (MacEvoy &

FIGURE 3.23
Brightness Contrast

At first glance, the inner rectangle on the left probably looks lighter than the inner rectangle on the right. But carefully examine the inner rectangles alone by covering their surroundings and you will see that both are of equal intensity. The brighter surround in the right-hand figure leads you to perceive its inner rectangle as relatively darker.

LEARN by DOING — Paradiso, 2001). To see this for yourself, place a piece of charcoal in sunlight and a piece of white paper in nearby shade. The charcoal will look very dark and the paper very bright, yet a light meter would tell you that much more light energy is reflected from the sun-bathed coal than from the shaded paper. The reason is partly that the charcoal is the darkest object relative to its sunlit background and the paper is the brightest object relative to its background of shade. As shown in Figure 3.23, the brightness of an object is perceived in relation to its background.

Size Illusions

Usually the visual perceptual system works automatically and perfectly to create correct impressions of depth, distance, and size. Sometimes, though, it can fail, resulting in *size illusions* such as the ones shown in Figure 3.24. Why does the monster that is placed higher in Figure 3.24(A) look larger than the lower one even though they are exactly the same size? The converging lines in the tunnel provide depth cues telling you that the higher monster is farther away. Because the retinal image of the "distant" monster is the same size as the "closer" one, your perceptual system calculates that the more distant monster must be bigger. This is the principle of size constancy at work: When two objects have retinal images of the same size, you perceive the one that seems farther away as larger. Now look at Figure 3.24(B). The two vertical lines are the same length, but the one on the right looks longer. Why? One possible reason is that the perceived length of an object is based on what frames it. When the frame is perceived as larger, as on the right side of Figure 3.24(B), the line segment within it is perceived as larger too (Rock, 1978). In Figure 3.24(C), the inner circle at the left looks smaller than the one at the right because, like the brightness of the center rectangles in Figure 3.23, the inner circles are judged in relation to what surrounds them. Because perception is based on many principles, and can be affected by many factors (e.g., Eerland, Guadalupe, & Zwaan, 2011; Liverence & Scholl, 2011; Oberfeld & Hecht, 2011), illusions like these probably reflect the violation of more than one of them. (See "In Review: Principles of Perceptual Organization and Constancy.")

FIGURE 3.24
Three Size Illusions

These illusions are named for the scientists who described them. In Part A, a version of the Ponzo illusion, the upper monster looks bigger but is actually the same size as the lower one. In the Müller-Lyer illusion (Part B), both vertical lines are actually of equal length; in the Ebbinghaus illusion shown in Part C, both center circles are exactly the same size. To prove that you can't always believe your eyes, measure these drawings for yourself.

Ponzo illusion illustration (Part A) from *Mind Sights* by Roger N. Shepard, © 1990 by Roger N. Shepard. Reprinted by permission of Henry Holt and Company, LLC.

(A)

(B)

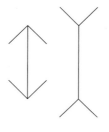
(C)

A Failure of Shape Constancy

When certain stimuli are viewed from an extreme angle, the brain's ability to maintain shape constancy can break down. Traffic engineers take this phenomenon into account in the design of road markings, as shown in these photos from a London airport. The arrow in the top photo appears to be about the same height as the lettering below it, but it isn't. The arrow had to be greatly elongated, as shown in the side view, so that approaching drivers would see its shape clearly. If the arrow had been painted to match the height of the accompanying letters, it would appear "squashed," and only half as tall as the lettering.

APPLYING
PSYCHOLOGY

Phillip Kent/www.anamorphosis.com

Principles of Perceptual Organization and Constancy   IN REVIEW

Principle	Description	Example
Figure ground discrimination	Certain objects or sounds automatically become identified as figure, whereas others become meaningless background.	You see a person standing against a building, not a building with a person-shaped hole in it.
Grouping	Properties of stimuli lead us to automatically group them together. These include proximity, similarity, continuity, closure, simplicity, common fate, synchrony, common region, and connectedness.	People who are sitting together, or who are dressed similarly, are perceived as a group.
Depth perception	The world is perceived as three-dimensional, with help from stimulus cues such as relative size, height in the visual field, interposition, linear perspective, reduced clarity, light and shadow, and gradients, and from visual system cues such as accommodation, eye convergence, and retinal disparity.	A person who looks tiny and appears high in the visual field will be perceived as being of normal size, but at a great distance.
Perceptual constancy	Objects are perceived as constant in size, shape, color, and other properties despite changes in their retinal images.	A train coming toward you is perceived as getting closer, not larger; an advertising sign is perceived as rotating, not changing shape.

IN REVIEW QUESTIONS

1. The movement we see in movies and DVDs is due to a perceptual illusion called ___ .

2. People who have lost an eye also lose the ability to use ___ depth cues, two of which are called ___ and ___ .

3. The grouping principle of ___ allows you to identify objects seen through a picket fence.

Recognizing the Perceptual World

How do I recognize familiar people?

In discussing how people organize the perceptual world, we have set the stage for addressing one of the most vital questions that perception researchers must answer: How do we recognize what objects are? If you are driving in search of Barney's Diner, exactly what happens when your eyes finally locate the pattern of light that spells out its name?

To know that you have finally found what you've been looking for, your brain must analyze incoming patterns of information and compare them with information about the target that you have stored in memory. If the brain finds a match, recognition takes place. Once you recognize a stimulus as belonging to a particular category, your perception of that stimulus may never be the same again. Look at Figure 3.25. Do you see anything familiar? If not, turn to Figure 3.26; then look at Figure 3.25 again. You should now see it in an entirely new light. The difference between your "before" and "after" experiences is the difference between the sensory world before and after a perceptual match occurs and recognition takes place.

How does this matching process occur? Some aspects of recognition begin at the "top." That is, they are guided by knowledge, expectations, and other psychological factors. This phenomenon is called **top-down processing,** because it involves high-level, knowledge-based information. Other aspects of recognition begin at the "bottom," relying on specific detailed information from the sensory receptors and assembling them into a whole. This phenomenon is called **bottom-up processing,** because it begins with basic information units that serve as a foundation for recognition.

Bottom-Up Processing

All along the path from the eye to the brain, certain cells respond to selected features of a stimulus. The stimulus is first analyzed into these *basic features,* which are then recombined to create the perceptual experience.

What are these features? As mentioned earlier, certain cells specialize in responding to lines, edges, corners, and stimuli that have specific orientations in space (Hubel & Wiesel, 1979). For example, some cells in the cerebral cortex fire only in response to a diagonal line, so they act as *feature detectors* for diagonal lines. The analysis by such feature detectors early in the sensation-perception sequence may contribute to recognition of letters or judgments of shape. Other features seem to be detected and assembled further

FIGURE 3.25
Categorizing Perceptions
What do you see here? For the identity of this figure, turn to Figure 3.26.

top-down processing Aspects of recognition guided by higher-level cognitive processes and by psychological factors such as expectations.

bottom-up processing Aspects of recognition that depend first on information about stimuli that come up to the brain from the sensory systems.

FIGURE 3.26
Another Version of Figure 3.25
Now that you can identify a dog in this figure, it should be much easier to recognize when you look back at the original version.

"Satan In the Smoke"© Mark D. Phillips/markdphillips.com

What Does It Look Like To You?
Some people see the devil's face in this photo of smoke from the World Trade Center under attack on September 11, 2001. This perception results partly from top-down processes, such as knowledge about the evil of the attack, that make it easier to see something demonic. People who don't expect to see a face in the smoke—or whose cultural background doesn't include the "devil" concept—may not see one until that interpretation is suggested. To check that possibility, show this photo to people of various religions and cultures (cover the caption). Ask if they see anything in the smoke but don't immediately tell them what to look for. How many, and which ones, identified a demonic face before you mentioned it?

LEARN**by** DOING

down the visual pathway (Kubilius, Wagemans, & de Beeck, 2011). Color and motion are sensory features that appear to be analyzed separately in different parts of the brain before full perceptual recognition takes place (Beatty, 1995; Levinthal & Franconeri, 2011; Treisman, 1999). The brain also apparently analyzes patterns of light and darkness in the visual scene. Analyzing these patterns may help us perceive textural gradients, which in turn help us to judge depth and recognize the general shape of blurry images.

Psychologists know that feature analysis is involved in pattern recognition because they have been able to determine what type of object a person is looking at (e.g., a face vs. a house) based on the pattern of activity occurring in visual processing areas of the person's brain (Haxby et al., 2001; Taylor & Downing, 2011).

Top-Down Processing

Bottom-up feature analysis can explain why you recognize the letters in a sign for Barney's Diner. But why is it that you can recognize the sign more easily if it appears where you were told to expect it rather than a block earlier? And why can you recognize it even if a few letters are missing from the sign? Top-down processing seems to be at work in those cases. In top-down processing, people rely on their knowledge to make inferences, or "educated guesses," that help them recognize objects, words, or melodies, especially when sensory information is vague or ambiguous (DeWitt & Samuel, 1990; Rock, 1983). For example, once you knew that there was a dog in Figure 3.25, it became much easier for you to perceive one. Similarly, police officers find it easy to recognize familiar people on blurry security-camera videos, but it is much more difficult for them to identify strangers (Burton et al., 1999).

Top-down processing illustrates that our experiences create **schemas,** mental representations of what we know and expect about the world. Schemas can bias our perception toward recognition of one specific pattern over another by creating a *perceptual set*—that is, a readiness to perceive a stimulus in a certain way. These expectations operate automatically, whether we are aware of them or not. For example, look again at Figure 3.20D. We see a hollow cube floating above the circles because once the closure principle has filled in the gaps, our experience tells us that the most likely interpretation of the resulting pattern of lines is a cube—even though it is not really there. Other perceptual sets are more conscious. For example, with random shooting incidents so much in the news these days, many people have become "set" to perceive ambiguous objects as weapons, especially in public places. So shoppers in a Boston mall recently called 911 after seeing what looked like the butt of a rifle sticking out of a man's backpack. The "rifle butt" was eventually identified as the handle of an umbrella, but not before the mall was evacuated and police SWAT teams arrived. Another misperceived umbrella caused a three-hour lockdown at a Carolina college after someone reported seeing a 'gunman' near campus.

Expectancy can be shaped by the *context* in which a stimulus occurs. For example, we expect to see people, not gorillas, on a city street, so when a large gorilla escaped from Boston's Franklin Park zoo in 2003, a woman who saw him at a bus stop later said, "I thought it was a guy with a big black jacket and a snorkel on" (MacQuarrie & Belkin, 2003). Context has biasing effects for sounds as well as sights. When shots are heard on a downtown street, they are often perceived as a car backfiring. The same sounds heard at a shooting range would immediately be interpreted as gunfire.

Motivation is another aspect of top-down processing that can affect perception (Balcetis & Dunning, 2006; Roye et al., 2010). For example, people tend to perceive desirable objects as being closer to them than less desirable ones (Balcetis & Dunning, 2010). They're also more likely to see objects as weapons if they feel angry or threatened (Baumann & DeSteno, 2010), and a very hungry person might at first misperceive a sign for "Burger's Body Shop" as indicating a place to eat (Radel & Clément-Guillotin, 2012). Similarly, perhaps you remember a time when an obviously incompetent referee incorrectly called a penalty on your favorite sports team. You knew the call was wrong because you clearly saw the other team's player at fault. But suppose you had been cheering for that other team. The chances are good that you would have seen the referee's call as the right one.

Top-Down and Bottom-Up Processing Together

Top-down and bottom-up processing usually work together to help us recognize the perceptual world (Förster, 2012). This interaction is beautifully illustrated by the process of reading. When the quality of the raw stimulus on the page is poor, as in Figure 3.27, top-down processes compensate to make continued reading possible. They allow you to fill in the gaps where words or letters are missing, or if they're shown backwards in a mirror, thus giving you a general idea of the meaning of the text (Duñabeitia, Molinaro, & Carreiras, 2011).

You can fill in the gaps because the world is *redundant;* it provides multiple clues about what is going on. So even if you lose or miss one stimulus in a pattern, other clues can help you recognize the pattern. There is so much redundancy in written language, for instance, that many of the words and letters you see are not needed. Fo- ex-mp-e, y-u c-n r-ad -hi- se-te-ce -it- ev-ry -hi-d l-tt-r m-ss-ng. Similarly, vision in three dimensions normally provides multiple cues to depth, making recognition of distance easy and clear. It is when many of these cues are eliminated that ambiguous stimuli create the sorts of depth illusions discussed earlier.

In hearing, too, top-down processing can compensate for ambiguous stimuli. In one experiment, participants heard strings of five words in meaningless order, such as "wet brought who socks some." There was so much background noise, however, that participants who heard this sequence could recognize only about 75 percent of the words (Miller, Heise, & Lichten, 1951). The words were then read to a second group of participants in a meaningful order (e.g., "who brought some wet socks"). The second group was able to recognize almost all of the words, even under the same noisy conditions. In fact, it took twice as much noise to reduce their performance to the level of the first group. Why? When the words were in meaningless order, only bottom-up processing was available. Recognizing one word was no help in identifying

schemas Mental representations of what we know and expect about the world.

FIGURE 3.27

Interaction of Top-Down and Bottom-Up Processing

Which obscured line do you find easier to read: the first or the second? Top-down processing should help you read the obscured text on the first line. However, in the second line, the words are not related, so top-down processing cannot operate.

LEARN by DOING

[handwritten notes:] it is very easy to read this redundant sentence

BUT NOT

better resist reading ... grammar ... (writing)

the next. Meaningful sentences, however, provided a more familiar context and allowed for some top-down processing. Hearing one word helped the listener make a reasonable guess (based on knowledge and experience) about the others. (See "In Review: Mechanisms of Pattern Recognition" for a summary of bottom-up and top-down processing.)

Mechanisms of Pattern Recognition   **IN REVIEW**

Mechanism	Description	Example
Bottom-up processing	Raw sensations from the eye or the ear are analyzed into basic features, such as edges, color, or movement; these features are then recombined at higher brain centers, where they are compared with stored information about objects or sounds.	You recognize a dog as a dog because its features—four legs, barking, panting—match your perceptual category for "dog."
Top-down processing	Knowledge of the world and experience in perceiving allow people to make inferences about the identity of stimuli, even when the quality of raw sensory information is low.	On a dark night, a small, vaguely seen blob pulling on the end of a leash is recognized as a dog because the stimulus occurs at a location where we would expect a dog to be.

IN REVIEW QUESTIONS

1. Your ability to read a battered old sign that has some letters missing is a result of ___ processing.
2. When stimulus features match the stimuli we are looking for, ___ takes place.
3. Schemas can create a ___ that makes us more likely to perceive stimuli in a particular way.

Culture, Experience, and Perception

We have been talking as if all aspects of perception work or fail in the same way for everyone everywhere. The truth is, though, that virtually all perceptual abilities are shaped to some extent by the sensory experiences we have or have not had (Boland, Chua, & Nisbett, 2008; Frankenstein et al., 2012; Goslin et al., 2012; Goto et al., 2010; McKone et al., 2010; Kitayama et al., 2003). For example, people are better at judging the size and distance of familiar objects than of unfamiliar ones. Size and shape constancy, too, depend partly on the knowledge and experience that tell us that most solid objects do not suddenly change their size or shape. The experience-based nature of perception can also be seen in brightness constancy: You perceive charcoal to be darker than a sheet of writing paper partly because no matter how much light the charcoal reflects, you *know* charcoal is black. Experience even teaches us when to ignore certain stimulus cues (Yang & Kubovy, 1999). To fully experience the depth portrayed in a painting, for example, you have to ignore ridges, scratches, dust, or other texture cues from the canvas that would remind you of its flatness. And the next time you're watching TV, notice the indistinct reflections of objects in the room that appear on the screen. You've learned to ignore these reflections, so it will take a little effort to perceive them and a lot of effort to focus on them for long.

What if you hadn't had a chance to learn or practice these perceptual skills? One way to explore this question is through case studies of people who have been blind for decades and then have had surgery that restored their sight. It turns out that these people can immediately recognize simple objects and perceive movement, but they usually have problems with other aspects of perception (Gregory, 2005; Ostrovsky et al., 2009; Robbins et al., 2010). For example, M. M. had been blind from early childhood. When his vision was restored in his forties, he adjusted well overall, but he still has difficulty with depth perception and object recognition (Fine et al., 2003).

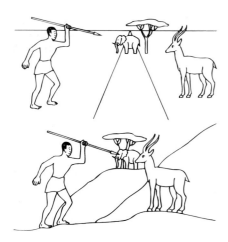

FIGURE 3.28
Culture and Depth Cues

People in various cultures were shown drawings like these and asked to judge which animal is closer to the hunter. Those in cultures that provide lots of experience with pictured depth cues choose the antelope, which is at the same distance from the viewer as the hunter. Those in cultures less familiar with such cues may choose the elephant, which, though closer on the page, is more distant when depth cues are considered.

Source: From *Journal of Social Psychology,* 52, 183–208. Reprinted with permission of the Helen Dwight Reid Educational Foundation. Published Heldref Publications, 1319 Eighteenth St., NW.,Washington, DC 20036-1802. http://heldref.org. Copyright © 1960.

Often, as people move toward or away from him, they appear to shrink or inflate. Identifying common objects can be difficult for him, and faces pose a particular challenge. To recognize individuals, he depends on features such as hair length or eyebrow shape. M. M. also has trouble distinguishing male faces from female ones and has great difficulty recognizing the meaning of facial expressions. He is unable to experience many of the perceptual illusions shown in this chapter, such as the closure illusion in Figure 3.20(D) or the size illusions in Figure 3.24. M. M.'s early blindness appears to have prevented his brain from fully developing the neural connections necessary for drawing accurate inferences about the visual world.

For the rest of us, too, the ability to experience perceptual illusions depends on our sensory history. People who grow up in significantly different sensory environments are likely to have noticeably different perceptual experiences (Caparos et al., 2012). For example, the size illusion shown in Figure 3.24(A) is strongest in the "carpentered world," where seeing straight lines is an everyday experience (Leibowitz et al., 1969). Responses to illusions such as this one are not as strong for people from rural areas of the Third World in which the visual environment contains more irregular and curved lines than straight ones (Coren & Girgus, 1978). Similarly, responses to depth cues in pictures and paintings differ in cultures that do and do not use such images to represent reality. People in the Me'n or the Nupa cultures of Africa, who have little experience with pictorial representation, have a more difficult time judging distances shown in pictures than do people in picture-oriented cultures (see Figure 3.28). These individuals also tend to have a harder time sorting pictures of three-dimensional objects into categories, even though they can easily sort the objects themselves (Derogowski, 1989). And residents of dense tropical rain forests, where most objects are seen over relatively short distances, may have some difficulty when asked to judge the distance of remote objects on an open plain (Turnbull, 1961). In other words, although the structure and principles of human perceptual systems tend to create generally similar views of the world for all of us, our perception of reality is also shaped by experience, including the experience of living in a particular culture (Chua, Boland, & Nisbett, 2005; Hedden et al., 2008).

LINKAGES

Perception and Human Development

How do infants perceive the world?
(a link to Human Development)

We have seen that perception is influenced by the knowledge and experience we gain over time, but what perceptual abilities do we start with? To learn about infants' perception, psychologists have studied two inborn patterns called *habituation* and *dishabituation*. Infants spend significantly less time looking at stimuli that are perceived to be unchanging. This is habituation. If they see a stimulus that is perceived to be new and different, they greatly increase their looking. This is dishabituation. Using the habituation/dishabituation technique, researchers have found that newborns can perceive differences in stimuli showing various amounts of black-and-white contrast but that they distinguish color differences very poorly, if at all (Adams, 1998; Bornstein, 2006; Burr, Morrone, & Fiorentini, 1996). Other studies using the same methods have shown that newborns can perceive differences in the angles of lines (Slater et al., 1991). Taken together, these studies suggest that we are born with the basic components of feature detection.

Are we also born with the ability to combine features into perceptions of whole objects? This is still a matter of debate. We know that at one month, infants concentrate their gaze on one part of an object, such as the corner of a triangle (Goldstein, 2002). By two months, though, their eyes systematically scan around the edges of the object. This change suggests that they are now perceiving the pattern, or shape, of the object, not just its component features. However, other researchers have

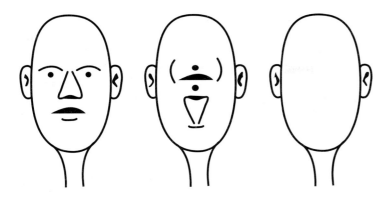

found that newborns show dishabituation (that is, they pay attention) when a familiar set of features are combined in a new way. So even newborns appear to notice and keep track of the ways some stimulus features are put together (Slater et al., 1991).

Infants may also be innately tuned to perceive at least one important complex pattern of features: the human face. In one study of newborns, patterns such as those in Figure 3.29 were moved slowly past the infants' faces (Johnson et al., 1991). The infants moved their heads and eyes to follow these patterns. But they tracked the face-like pattern shown on the left side of Figure 3.29 significantly farther than any of the nonfaces. The differences in tracking in this study and others indicates that infants can tell faces from nonfaces and are more interested in faces, or at least in face-like patterns (Cassia et al., 2008; Simion et al., 2003). Why should this be? Investigators who take an evolutionary approach suggest that interest in human faces is adaptive because it helps newborns focus on their only source of food and care. Further support for the evolutionary perspective comes from the finding that infants are also excellent at detecting potentially threatening stimuli, such as snakes (LoBue & DeLoache, 2010).

Other research on perceptual development suggests that our ability to accurately perceive depth and distance develops more slowly than our ability to recognize shapes (see Figure 3.30). For example, infants' ability to use binocular disparity and motion cues to judge depth appears to develop sometime after about three months of age (Yonas, Arterberry, & Granrud, 1987). They do not use textural gradients and linear perspective as cues to depth until they are five to seven months old (Arterberry, Craton, & Yonas, 1993; Bhatt & Bertin, 2001).

In summary, there is little doubt that many of the basic building blocks of perception are present within the first few days after birth. The basics include such depth cues as accommodation, eye convergence, and information about movement (Arterberry & Yonas, 2000; Valenza & Bulf, 2007). Maturation of the visual system adds to these basics as time goes by. Over the first few months after birth, the eye's fovea gradually develops the number of cone cells necessary for high visual acuity and perception of fine details (Goldstein, 2002). Visual experience is also necessary. Experience teaches the infant to

FIGURE 3.29
Infants' Perceptions of Human Faces

Newborns show significantly greater interest in the face-like pattern on the left than in either of the other patterns. Evidently some aspects of face perception are innate.

Source: Johnson et al. (1991). Image courtesy of Posit Science.

FIGURE 3.30
The Visual Cliff

The *visual cliff* is a glass-topped table that creates the impression of a sudden dropoff. A ten-month-old placed at what looks like the edge will calmly crawl across the shallow side to reach a parent but will hesitate and cry rather than crawl over the "cliff" (Gibson & Walk, 1960). Changes in heart rate show that infants too young to crawl also perceive the depth but are not frightened by it. Here is another example of the adaptive interaction of nature and nurture: Depth perception appears shortly after birth, but fear and avoidance of dangerous depth do not develop until an infant is old enough to crawl into trouble.

© Mark Richards/PhotoEdit

recognize unified patterns and objects and to interpret depth and distance cues and use them to move safely through the world (Bhatt & Quinn, 2011; Johnson, 2005; Quinn & Bhatt, 2005). Like so many aspects of human psychology, perception is the result of a blending of heredity and environment. From infancy onward, the perceptual system creates a personal reality.

● ● ● ●

Attention

Can you run out of attention?

Believe it or not, you still haven't found Barney's Diner! By now, you understand *how* you will recognize the right sign when you perceive it. But how can you be sure you *will* perceive it? The diner's sign will appear as one small piece of a sensory puzzle that also includes road signs, traffic lights, sirens, talk radio, and dozens of other stimuli. You can't perceive all of them at once. To find Barney's, you're going to have to be sure that the information you process includes the stimuli that will help you reach your goal. In short, you are going to have to pay attention.

Attention is the process of directing and focusing certain psychological resources to enhance perception, performance, and mental experience. We use attention to *direct* our sensory and perceptual systems toward certain stimuli, to *select* specific information for further processing, to *allocate* the mental energy required to do that processing, and to *regulate* the flow of resources necessary for performing a task or coordinating several tasks at once (Wickens & Carswell, 2006).

Psychologists have discovered three important characteristics of attention.

1. *Attention improves mental processing.* You often need to concentrate attention on a task to do your best at it.
2. *Attention takes effort.* Prolonged concentration of attention can leave you drained (McNay, McCarty, & Gold, 2001). When you're already tired, focusing attention on anything becomes more difficult.
3. *Attention is limited.* When your attention is focused on reading this book, for instance, you will have less attention left over to listen to a conversation in the next room.

Directing Attention

LEARN by DOING To experience the process of attention, try "moving it around" a bit. When you finish reading this sentence, look at something behind you, then face forward and notice the next sound you hear, then visualize your best friend, then focus on how your tongue feels. You just used attention to direct your perceptual systems toward different aspects of your external and internal environments. When you looked behind you, shifting attention involved *overt orienting*—pointing sensory systems at a particular stimulus. But you shifted attention to an image of your friend's face without having to move a muscle. This is called *covert orienting.* (We have heard a rumor that students sometimes use covert orienting to shift their attention from their lecturer to thoughts that have nothing to do with the lecture.)

How do you control, or allocate, your attention? Research shows that control over attention can be voluntary or involuntary (Yantis, 1993). *Voluntary,* or goal-directed, control over attention occurs when you purposely focus so that you can perform a task. Voluntary control reflects top-down processing because attention is guided by knowledge-based factors such as intention, beliefs, expectations, and motivation (Colzato et al., 2010; Gable & Harmon-Jones, 2010; Liuzza et al., 2011; Pacheco-Unguetti et al., 2010). As people learn certain skills, they voluntarily direct their attention to information they once ignored (Zhang, Jiang, & He, 2012). For example, experienced drivers are better than new drivers are at noticing all that

attention The process of directing and focusing certain psychological resources to enhance perception, performance, and mental experience.

FIGURE 3.31
Change Blindness

If you didn't immediately notice the difference between these photos, it was probably because you focused your attention on the similarity of their main features rather than on their specific elements. This common tendency results in blindness to a small, but obvious difference (Wilford & Wells, 2010; see page 125 for the answer). Just as we are usually unaware of our visual blind spot, we tend to be blind to inattentional blindness. We think we can see everything around us, but accidents are caused everyday because people sometimes fail to see what is right in front of their eyes (Galpin, Underwood, & Crundall, 2009). Fortunately, it may be possible to improve attentional skills through training and practice (Martens, 2011; Pollatsek, Romoser, & Fisher, 2011; Spence & Feng, 2010).

LEARN by DOING

is going on around their vehicles, including events taking place far down the road (Koustanaï, Van Elslande, & Bastien, 2012).

When some aspect of the environment—such as a loud noise—diverts your attention, control is said to be *involuntary*, or stimulus driven. Stimulus characteristics that tend to capture attention include abrupt changes in lighting or color (such as flashing signs), movement, and the appearance of unusual shapes (Folk, Remington, & Wright, 1994). Engineering psychologists' findings about which stimuli are most likely to attract—and distract—attention have been used in the design of everything from Internet web sites to operator warning devices for airliners, nuclear power plants, and other complex systems (Clay, 2000; Hervet et al., 2011; Laughery, 1999). Other psychologists use the results of attention research to help design advertisements, logos, and product packaging that grab potential customers' attention.

As already mentioned, attending to some stimuli makes us less able to attend to others. In other words, attention is *selective*. It's like a spotlight that can illuminate only a part of the external or internal environment at any particular moment. So if you focus intently on your reading or on a computer game, you may fail to perceive even dramatic changes in other parts of your environment (Hallett, Labert, & Regan, 2012). This phenomenon is called *inattentional blindness* (Mack, 2003; Mack & Rock, 1998). In one study, a researcher asked college students for directions to a campus building (Simons & Ambinder, 2005). During each conversation, two "workmen" carrying a large door passed between the researcher and the student. As the door hid the researcher from the student's view, one of the "workmen" took his place. This new person then resumed the conversation with the student as though nothing had happened. Amazingly, only half of the students noticed that they were suddenly talking to a new person! The rest had apparently been paying so much attention to the researcher's question or to the map he was showing that they did not notice what he looked like. Other studies have shown that most research participants can become so focused on their cell phone conversations or on their assigned task of counting the passes made during a basketball video that they fail to notice a clown riding by on a unicycle or a woman in a gorilla suit walking across the court (Hyman et al., 2010; Simons & Chabris, 1999). A real-world example of inattentional blindness occurred in October, 2009 when two commercial airline pilots became so involved in conversation and using their laptops that they allowed their aircraft to fly on autopilot 150 miles past its destination. Their distraction was so complete that for seventy-seven minutes, they failed to hear radioed warnings from air traffic controllers (Pasztor, 2009). Magicians take advantage of inattentional blindness when they use sudden movements or other attention-grabbing stimuli to draw our attention away from the actions that lie behind their tricks. To experience a type of inattentional blindness known as "change blindness," take a look at the photos in Figure 3.31.

Your search for Barney's Diner will be helped by your ability to overtly allocate attention to a certain part of the environment. It would be made even easier if Barney's had the only flashing sign on the road. As the most intense stimulus around you, it would attract your attention automatically. Psychologists describe this ability to search for targets rapidly and automatically as *parallel processing*. It is as if you can examine all nearby locations at once (in parallel) and rapidly detect the target no matter where it appears.

Dividing Attention

Often you can divide your attention efficiently enough to allow you to perform more than one activity at a time (Damos, 1992). You can drive a car, listen to the radio, sing along, and keep a beat by drumming on the steering wheel. However, your attention cannot be divided beyond a certain point without a loss in performance and mental-processing ability. For example, automobile drivers are much more likely to miss important signals, make errors in following directions, and react slowly to potentially

The Dangers of Distracted Driving

Talking on any kind of phone—including hands-free models—can create inattentional blindness and distractions that impair driving and may contribute to accidents (e.g., Beede & Kass, 2006; Briggs, Hole, & Land, 2011; Hyman et al., 2010; Reimer et al., 2010; Strayer & Drews, 2007). Nine U. S. states, the District of Columbia, the U.S. Virgin Islands, and many countries around the world have outlawed drivers' use of handheld cell phones. Thirty-five states, Guam, and the District of Columbia have also made it illegal for drivers to text while driving (Governors' Highway Safety Association, 2011). For the latest developments on this topic, visit http://distraction.gov.

© Michael Krinke/iStockphoto

dangerous situations when talking on a cell phone, even if it is a hands-free model (Reimer et al., 2010; Strayer & Drews, 2007). This is especially true if the conversation is an emotional one (Briggs, Hole, & Land, 2011). Distracted walking can be dangerous, too. The number of pedestrians killed or injured while listening to music on headphones more than tripled between 2004 and 2011 (Lichenstein et al., 2012). In other words, attention is a limited resource. If you try to spread it over too many targets, you "run out" of attention.

Still, it can sometimes be hard to keep your attention focused rather than divided. Look at the list of words in Figure 3.32 and as rapidly as possible call out the *color of the ink* in which each word is printed. This *Stroop task* (Stroop, 1935) is not easy, because your brain automatically processes the meanings of the familiar words in the list. These meanings then compete for attention with the responses you are supposed to give. To do well, you must focus on the ink color and not allow your attention to be divided between color and meaning. Children just learning to read have far less trouble with this task because they don't yet process the meanings of words as automatically as experienced readers do.

Although you can walk while talking or drive while listening to music, you would find it virtually impossible to read and talk at the same time. Why is it sometimes so easy and at other times so difficult to do two things at once (Connell & Lynott, 2010)? When one task is so automatic as to require little or no attention, it is usually easy to do something else at the same time (Schneider, 1985). Even when two tasks require attention, it may still be possible to perform them simultaneously if each taps into different kinds of attention (Wickens, 2002; Wickens et al., 1992). Some types of attention are devoted to perceiving incoming stimuli. Others handle making responses. This specialization allows a skilled pianist to use one kind of attention to read a new piece of music while using another kind of attention at the same time to press the correct keys. Apparently, the human brain can manage more than one type of attention and more than one spotlight of attention (Wickens, 1989). This notion of different types of attention also helps explain why an experienced driver can listen to the radio while steering safely. If two tasks require the same kind of attention, however, performance on both tasks will suffer (Just et al., 2001).

BLUE	GREEN
GREEN	ORANGE
PURPLE	ORANGE
GREEN	BLUE
RED	RED
GRAY	GRAY
RED	BLUE
BLUE	PURPLE

FIGURE 3.32

The Stroop Task

Look at this list of words and as rapidly as possible call out the *color of the ink* in which each word is printed. How did you do?

FOCUS ON RESEARCH

Attention and the Brain

What happens in the brain as people try to attend to more than one source of information at the same time?

What was the researchers' question?

If directing attention to more than one task causes extra mental work to be done, there should be evidence of that work in brain activity. One possibility is that information-processing activity in the brain should slow down. Does it? This was the question asked by one research team.

How did the researchers answer the question?

Allan J. Nash and Mercedes Fernandez (1996) examined the brain-processing speed of participants engaged in various tasks. Sixteen college students heard high and low tones and saw red and green light flashes. They were asked to respond as quickly as possible to the identified target stimulus. On some trials they were to ignore tones and respond only to one of the lights, and on other trials they were to respond to one light and keep a running count of one of the tones. In short, the participants either attended to one task (responding to a light) or split their attention between two tasks (responding to a light and counting tones). The speed of the participants' reactions to the flashing light was measured throughout the experiment.

What did the researchers find?

When attention had to be shared between information required for two tasks, reaction times were slower than they were in response to the single-attention task.

What do the results mean?

The finding that reaction times were slower on split-attention trials suggests that information processing in the brain was slower too. Further evidence for this conclusion has been provided by PET scans. They reveal increased blood flow to regions of the brain where mental processing is taking place (Corbetta et al., 1991; Just et al., 2001). When attention is focused on only one stimulus feature, increased blood flow appears only in the part of the brain where that feature is analyzed. But when attention is divided, the added supply of blood is shared between two locations.

What do we still need to know?

Still to be determined are the limits of attention, the means by which attention is shared, and the specific parts of the brain that are involved in attention, whether divided or undivided. So far, research using PET scans, surgery on laboratory animals, and case studies of humans with brain damage has shown that switching the spotlight of visual attention involves at least three different parts of the brain (e.g., Braver, Reynolds, & Donaldson, 2003; Posner & Raichle, 1994). Attention appears to be a linked set of resources that improve mental processing at several levels and locations in the brain. No single brain region has yet been identified as an "attention center" (Posner & Peterson, 1990; Sasaki et al., 2001).   ● ● ● ●

Active Review

As noted in the introductory chapter, all of psychology's subfields are related to one another. Our discussion of the development of perception illustrates just one way that the topic of this chapter, sensation and perception, is linked to the subfield of developmental psychology, which is described in

CHAPTER 3
Sensation and Perception

the chapter on human development. The Linkages diagram shows ties to two other subfields, and there are many more ties throughout the book. Looking for linkages among subfields will help you see how they all fit together and help you better appreciate the big picture that is psychology.

LINKAGES

How do infants perceive the world? *(ans. on p. 120)*

Do people perceive hallucinations as real sensory events? *(ans. on p. 484)*

Do we sometimes perceive people the same way we perceive objects? *(ans. on p. 547)*

CHAPTER 9
Human Development

CHAPTER 12
Psychological Disorders

CHAPTER 14
Social Psychology

Summary

Sensing and Perceiving the World

What is the difference between sensation and perception?
A **sense** is a system that translates information from outside the nervous system into neural activity. Messages from the senses are called **sensations. Perception** is the process through which people actively use knowledge and understanding of the world to interpret sensations as meaningful experiences.

Sensory Systems

How does information from my eyes and ears get to my brain?
Accessory structures collect and modify incoming energy from sensory stimuli. Then comes **transduction,** the process of converting that energy into neural activity. It is accomplished by sensory

neural receptors, which are neural cells specialized to detect energy of some type. **Sensory adaptation** takes place when receptors continue to receive stimulation that does not change. Except in the case of smell, sensory neural activity is transferred through the thalamus, which relays it to the cerebral cortex.

Encoding is the translation of the physical properties of a stimulus into patterns of neural activity that specifically identify those physical properties. It's the language the brain uses to describe sensations.

The minimum amount of light, sound, pressure, or other physical energy that can be detected 50 percent of the time is called the **absolute threshold.** **Internal noise** is the spontaneous random firing of cells in the nervous system that occurs whether or not you are stim-

ulated by physical energy. Your **response bias,** or **response criterion,** reflects your willingness to respond to a stimulus or ignore it. **Signal detection theory** addresses whether you will perceive a stimulus. **Sensitivity** refers to your ability to discriminate a stimulus from its background. **Weber's law** states that the smallest detectable difference in stimulus energy is a constant fraction of the intensity of the stimulus. This smallest detectable difference in a stimulus is called the difference threshold or **just-noticeable difference (JND).** The distance from one peak of a sound wave or light wave to the next is its **wavelength.** Wave **frequency** is the number of complete waves, or cycles, that pass a given point per unit of time. **Amplitude** is the height of the wave from baseline to peak.

The difference between the photos in Figure 3.31 is that the top picture includes a clump of trees just to the left of the statue.

Seeing

Why do some people need eyeglasses?
Visible light is electromagnetic radiation with a wavelength of about 400 to about 750 nanometers. **Light intensity,** or the amount of energy in light, determines its brightness. Differing **light wavelengths** are sensed as different colors.

Accessory structures of the eye include the **cornea,** the **pupil,** the **iris,** and the **lens.** Through **ocular accommodation** and other means, these structures focus light rays on the **retina,** the net-like structure of cells at the back of the eye.

Photoreceptors in the retina—**rods** and **cones**—convert light into neural activity. Rods and cones differ in shape, sensitivity to light, ability to discriminate colors, and distribution across the retina. Photoreceptors, especially rods, contribute to **dark adaptation.** The **fovea,** the area of highest acuity, has only cones, which are color sensitive. Rods are more sensitive to light but don't discriminate colors; they're distributed in areas around the fovea. From the photoreceptors, neural activity is transferred to bipolar cells and then to ganglion cells. A **blind spot** is created at the point where axons of ganglion cells leave the eye as a bundle of fibers called the **optic nerve.** Half of these fibers cross over at the optic chiasm. **Feature detectors** are cells in the cerebral cortex that respond to specific characteristics of objects in the visual field. The color of an object depends on which of the wavelengths striking it are absorbed and which are reflected. The sensation of color has three psychological dimensions: **hue, color saturation,** and **brightness.**

According to the **trichromatic** (or Young-Helmholtz) **theory,** color vision results from the fact that the eye includes three types of cones, each of which is most sensitive to short, medium, or long wavelengths. Information from the three types combines to produce the sensation of color. According to the **opponent-process** (or Hering) **theory,** there are red-green, blue-yellow, and black-white visual elements and the members of each pair inhibit each other so that only one member of a pair may produce a signal at a time. Opponent-process theory explains color afterimages.

Hearing

How would my voice sound on the moon?
Sound is a repetitive fluctuation in the pressure of a medium such as air; it travels in waves. The frequency (which is related to wavelength) and amplitude of sound waves produce the psychological experiences of **pitch** and **loudness,** respectively. **Timbre,** the quality of sound, depends on complex wave patterns added to the basic frequency of sound.

The energy from sound waves is collected and transmitted to the **cochlea** through a series of accessory structures, including the **pinna,** and components of the **middle ear,** including the **tympanic membrane,** the hammer, the anvil, the stirrup, and the oval window. Transduction occurs when sound energy stimulates hair cells on the **basilar membrane** of the cochlea, which in turn stimulate the **acoustic nerve.** Auditory information is relayed through the thalamus to the primary auditory cortex.

The intensity of a sound stimulus is encoded by the firing of auditory neurons. **Place theory** describes the encoding of high frequencies based on the place on the basilar membrane at which the sound wave peaks. Each neuron in the acoustic nerve is most sensitive to a specific frequency (its preferred frequency). According to **volley theory,** some frequencies may be matched by the firing rate of a group of neurons.

The Chemical Senses: Taste and Smell

Why can't I taste anything when I have a cold?
The chemical senses include smell (olfaction) and taste (gustatory perception). **Olfactory perception** (sense of smell) detects volatile chemicals that come into contact with olfactory receptors in the nose. Olfactory signals are sent through the olfactory nerve to the **olfactory bulb** in the brain without passing through the thalamus. **Pheromones** are odors from one creature that change the physiology or behavior of another. **Taste perception** detects chemicals that come into contact with taste receptors in **papillae** in the mouth, especially on the tongue. The basic taste sensations are sweet, sour, bitter, salty, umami, and astringent. The senses of smell and taste interact to produce flavor.

Sensing Your Body

Which is the largest organ in my body?
The **cutaneous senses,** also called somatosensory systems, include the skin senses and are related to proprioception. The skin senses detect touch, temperature, and pain. When they are mechanically stimulated, nerve endings in the skin generate touch sensations. Some nerve endings are sensitive to temperature and some respond to both temperature and touch.

Pain provides information about intense stimuli. Sharp pain is carried by A-delta fibers; dull, chronic pain is carried by C-fibers. The emotional response to pain depends on how the painful stimulus is interpreted. According to the **gate control theory of pain,** pain signals can be blocked on their way to the brain,

sometimes by messages sent from the brain down the spinal cord, resulting in **analgesia.** Endorphins act at several levels in pain systems to reduce sensations of pain.

Proprioception includes **kinesthetic perception,** which provides information about the position of body parts with respect to one another, and the **sense of equilibrium**, or **vestibular sense** (balance), which provides information about the position of the head in space. This information is provided by **proprioceptors**, which are sensory receptors for movement and body position.

Perception

How do sensations become perceptions? Perception is the knowledge-based interpretation of sensations. Much of this interpretation takes place automatically, but sometimes conscious effort is required to translate sensations into meaningful experience.

Organizing the Perceptual World

What determines how I perceive my world? Our perceptual systems automatically engage in **figure ground discrimination** to sense the difference between **figure** and **ground.** They also automatically group stimuli into patterns on the basis of the Gestalt principles of proximity, similarity, continuity, closure, texture, simplicity, common fate, and three others known as synchrony, common region, and connectedness.

Depth perception depends partly on stimulus cues and partly on the physical structure of the visual system. Stimulus cues include relative size, height in the visual field, interposition, linear perspective, reduced clarity, light and shadow, and textural gradients. Cues based on the structure of the visual system include **eye convergence** (movement of the eyes to focus on the same object), **retinal disparity** (due to each eye seeing the world from a slightly different angle), and accommodation (changes in the shapes of the lenses as objects are brought into focus).

The perception of motion results, in part, from the movement of stimuli across the retina. Expanding or **looming** stimulation is perceived as an approaching object. Movement of the retinal image is interpreted along with information about movement of the head, eyes, and other body parts to discriminate one's own movement from the movement of external objects. The **stroboscopic illusion** is a movement illusion arising when a series of slightly different still images is seen in rapid succession.

Because of **perceptual constancy,** the brightness, size, and shape of objects are seen as unchanging despite changes in the sensations received from those objects. Size constancy and shape constancy depend on the relationship between the retinal image of the object and one's knowledge-based perception of how far away the object is. Brightness constancy depends on the perceived relationship between the brightness of an object and its background.

Size illusions are distortions of reality that result when principles of perception are applied inappropriately. Many of these illusions occur when we misread depth cues or when we are overly influenced by the contexts (surroundings) in which visual stimuli appear.

Recognizing the Perceptual World

How do I recognize familiar people? Both **bottom-up processing** and **top-down processing** contribute to our recognition of the world. Our ability to recognize objects is based on our capacity to match the pattern of sensations organized by the perceptual system with a pattern stored in our memory. Bottom-up processing occurs as the brain analyzes features, or combinations of features, such as form, color, motion, and depth. Top-down processing is influenced by our knowledge, expectations,t and motivation. **Schemas** based on our past experiences can create a perceptual set; that is, a readiness or predisposition to perceive stimuli in certain ways. The context in which a stimulus appears can also create expectancies. Top-down and bottom-up processing commonly work together to create recognition. Top-down processing can fill in gaps in physical stimuli, in part because the environment provides redundant stimuli.

To the extent that the visual environments of people in different cultures differ, their perceptual experiences—and their responses to perceptual illusions—may differ as well.

The ability to perceive color, basic shape features, and possibly the human face is present at or near birth. Other abilities, such the ability to recognize forms, develop later. Depth is also perceived early, but its meaning is learned later. Perceptual abilities are modified by both experience and maturation.

Attention

Can you run out of attention? **Attention** is the process of focusing psychological resources to enhance perception, performance, and mental experience. We can shift attention overtly (by moving the eyes, for example) or covertly (without any movement of sensory systems). Attention is selective; it is like a spotlight that illuminates different parts of the external environment or specific mental processes. Control over attention can be voluntary and knowledge-based or involuntary and driven by environmental stimuli. People can sometimes attend to two tasks at once, but there are limits to how much they can divide their attention.

LEARN by DOING

Put It in Writing

Which of your five sensory systems—vision, hearing, touch, taste, or smell—do you think you could most easily do without? Which could you least easily do without? Write a page describing why you chose each of these sensory systems and listing what you would do to try to make up for the loss of each of these two systems.

Personal Learning Activity

Have you ever noticed how large the moon appears to be when it has just risen above the horizon? Some researchers suggest that the moon appears larger on the horizon than when it is overhead because the horizon moon—seen across a space filled with houses, trees, and terrain—appears to be farther away than when it is overhead (Kaufman & Kaufman, 2000). According to principles of size constancy discussed in this chapter, the greater perceived distance causes the horizon moon to be perceived as larger. This explanation has been questioned, though, because the horizon moon sometimes seems larger even when the observer cannot see the intervening terrain. The next time you see what appears to be a bigger-than-normal full moon just above the horizon, turn your back to it and then bend over and look at the moon, upside down, between your legs. Does the "moon illusion" remain, or is it destroyed when you look at the moon so that terrain appears above it rather than below it? What do you think causes the moon illusion?

Review of Key Terms

Can you define each of the key terms in the chapter? Check your definitions against those on the pages shown in parentheses in the following list or in the Glossary at the end of the book.

absolute threshold (p. 84)
accessory structures (p. 83)
acoustic nerve (p. 95)
amplitude (p. 86)
analgesia (p. 103)
attention (p. 122)
basilar membrane (p. 95)
blind spot (p. 89)
bottom-up processing (p. 116)
brightness (p. 90)
cochlea (p. 94)
color saturation (p. 90)
cones (p. 88)
cornea (p. 87)
cutaneous senses (p. 102)
dark adaptation (p. 88)
depth perception (p. 110)
encoding (p. 83)
eye convergence (p. 112)
feature detectors (p. 89)
figure (p. 109)
figure ground discrimination (p. 109)

fovea (p. 88)
frequency (p. 86)
gate control theory of pain (p. 103)
ground (p. 109)
hue (p. 90)
iris (p. 87)
just-noticeable difference (JND) (p. 85)
kinesthetic perception (p. 106)
lens (p. 87)
light intensity (p. 87)
light wavelength (p. 87)
looming (p. 112)
loudness (p. 93)
middle ear (p. 94)
neural receptors (p. 83)
noise (p. 84)
ocular accommodation (p. 87)
olfactory bulb (p. 99)
olfactory perception (sense of smell) (p. 97)
opponent-process theory (p. 91)
optic nerve (p. 88)
papillae (p. 100)
perception (p. 82)
perceptual constancy (p. 113)
pheromones (p. 99)
photoreceptors (p. 88)
pinna (p. 94)

pitch (p. 93)
place theory (p. 96)
proprioception (p. 106)
proprioceptors (p. 106)
pupil (p. 87)
response bias (response criterion) (p. 84)
retina (p. 87)
retinal disparity (p. 112)
rods (p. 88)
schemas (p. 118)
sensations (p. 82)
sense (p. 82)
sense of equilibrium (vestibular sense) (p. 106)
sensitivity (p. 85)
sensory adaptation (p. 83)
signal detection theory (p. 85)
sound (p. 93)
stroboscopic illusion (p. 113)
taste perception (p. 97)
timbre (p. 94)
top-down processing (p. 116)
transduction (p. 83)
trichromatic theory (p. 90)
tympanic membrane (eardrum) (p. 94)
volley theory (p. 97)
wavelength (p. 86)
Weber's law (p. 85)

Test Your Knowledge ....

Select the best answer for each of the following questions. Then check your responses against the Answer Key at the end of the book.

1. Sandra reads English but not Chinese. So when she looks at a Chinese newspaper, there is more ____ than ____.
   a. sensation; perception
   b. perception; sensation
   c. perception; transduction
   d. sensation; transduction

2. As Jeremy listens to music on his iPod, sound waves are converted by his auditory system into neural signals. This process is called ____.
   a. attention
   b. transduction
   c. adaptation
   d. accommodation

3. In an experiment, Dante raises his hand each time he hears a tone through a set of headphones. The tone gets quieter and quieter until he fails to hear it half the time. After repeating the same procedure many times, the researcher ends the experiment because she has found Dante's ____.
   a. absolute threshold
   b. difference threshold
   c. internal noise
   d. response criterion

4. Jane is told that she will be paid $100 for each needle she can find in a haystack. According to signal detection theory, this information should ____ Jane's ____.
   a. raise; response criterion
   b. lower; response criterion
   c. raise; sensitivity
   d. lower; sensitivity

5. Matt finishes his can of soda as he walks across campus with Brad and Andy, and now he wants to slip the empty can into one of their open backpacks. Brad's pack has several heavy textbooks in it; Andy's contains only a notebook. Weber's law suggests that to avoid detection, Matt should put the can in ____ pack because the change in weight will be ____ than a just-noticeable difference.
   a. Andy's; less
   b. Brad's; less
   c. Andy's; more
   d. Brad's; more

6. Bianca wants Bruce to see the distant star she wishes on every night. Because the star is so faint, to have him see it she should have him look ____.
   a. directly at the star
   b. slightly away from where the star is expected to be
   c. at the star's reflection in a mirror
   d. at the star when there is a full moon

7. A projection-screen TV aims green, red, and blue lights at a screen. Because the TV can show a full range of colors by combining the green, red, and blue lights in differing amounts, it best illustrates the ____ theory of color vision.
   a. convergence
   b. frequency-matching
   c. opponent-process
   d. trichromatic

8. When Sarah stubbed her toe, she immediately began to rub it. According to the gate control theory of pain, the rubbing ____.
   a. created sensations that "took over" the pain pathways
   b. released serotonin
   c. created an increase in pain tolerance
   d. shut down the brain's pain-sensing mechanisms

9. Mick has been a rock musician for fifty years. The constant loud noise from his band has caused hair-cell damage, literally ripping off hair cells from his inner ear. We would expect that Mick now has ____.
   a. extremely acute hearing
   b. conduction deafness
   c. nerve deafness
   d. normal hearing loss for someone his age

10. Jeremy developed a disease that destroyed his thalamus. The only sense that was unaffected was ____.
    a. vision
    b. hearing
    c. touch
    d. smell

11. Your blind spot is located ____.
    a. where the optic nerve leaves the eye
    b. where visual fibers cross at the optic chiasm
    c. in the center of the fovea
    d. where accommodation takes place

12. In cooking school, Natalie studied flavor. She learned that the flavor of food can be altered by ____.
    a. changing its texture
    b. changing its temperature
    c. changing its color
    d. both a and b

13. Andrea cannot yet read but Lorraine can. They are each shown a list of color names (e.g., blue, red, yellow), but each word is printed in a color that doesn't match the word. They are asked to say the color of the ink each word is printed in, not the word itself. ____ will do better at this Stroop task because ____.
    a. Andrea; she can use top-down processing
    b. Lorraine; she is older
    c. Andrea; she will not be distracted by word meanings
    d. Lorraine; word meaning will help focus on the ink color

14. Ally has lost her sense of kinesthetic perception. She will most likely be unable to ____.
   a. know that her hand is raised without looking at it
   b. identify the flavor of her ice cream cone
   c. feel the warmth of the sun on her face
   d. feel pain

15. Shanelle likes the lights that appear to race around her Christmas tree as they flash on and off in sequence. This illusion is known as ____
   a. motion parallax
   b. the stroboscopic illusion
   c. dishabituation
   d. texture gradient

16. Four swimmers practicing their synchronized swimming routine are perceived as a group because they are performing the same movements at the same speed. This is an example of ____.
   a. synchrony
   b. common fate
   c. orientation
   d. interposition

17. When you perceive an object as being closer to you because it blocks out part of the background, you are using the depth cue called ____.
   a. linear perspective
   b. interposition
   c. reduced clarity
   d. movement gradient

18. As Cliff walks out his front door, he sees a snowball coming straight at him. The retinal image of the snowball is increasing and he realizes that the snowball is approaching, not getting larger. This example illustrates ____.
   a. induced motion
   b. looming
   c. the movement gradient
   d. stroboscopic motion

19. Jeff and Larry were making chili. Jeff tasted the chili and thought it was perfectly seasoned. Then, while Jeff's back was turned, Larry added some more salt. When they sat down to eat Jeff immediately said the chili was too salty. Because he didn't know about the added salt, Jeff's perception must have been based on ____.
   a. top-down processing
   b. bottom-up processing
   c. pattern recognition
   d. selective attention

20. Although José appears to be listening as Rich talks about his new clothes, vacation plans, and exercise routine, José is thinking about the list of errands he has to run. José is ____.
   a. covertly orienting
   b. overtly orienting
   c. using parallel distributed processing
   d. using serial processing

Media Resources

Now that you have finished reading this chapter, how about exploring some of the ideas and information that you found most interesting?

Go to **CengageBrain.com** to access Psychology CourseMate, where you will find an interactive eBook, glossaries, flashcards, quizzes, videos, Virtual Psychology Labs, and more.

aplia

If your professor has assigned Aplia:

1. Sign in to your account.
2. Complete the corresponding exercises as required by your professor.
3. When finished, click "Grade It Now" to see which areas you have mastered, which areas need more work, and detailed explanations of every answer.

Consciousness

Preview

Have you ever "spaced out" while driving on a boring highway? Has your mind wandered far and wide during a dull lecture? These experiences contrast sharply with how it feels to focus your attention on playing a video game or to concentrate on a complicated recipe, but all of them represent differing versions of consciousness. In this chapter, we delve into both "normal" and altered states of consciousness. Most of the altered states—sleep, dreaming, hypnosis, meditation—differ psychologically and physiologically from normal waking consciousness. We will examine how they differ and we will also look at the effects of psychoactive drugs, which, in addition to altering consciousness, have complex physiological effects.

Keeping an Eye Out
Humans are not the only creatures capable of processing information while apparently unconscious. While ducks sleep, one hemisphere of their brains can process visual information from an eye that remains open. Birds positioned where they are most vulnerable to predators, such as at the end of a row, may spend twice as much time in this "alert" sleep than do birds in more protected positions (Rattenborg, Lima, & Amlaner, 1999).

There is an old *Sesame Street* episode in which Ernie is trying to find out whether Bert is asleep or awake. In other words, Ernie is trying to determine Bert's state of consciousness. Ernie observes that Bert's eyes are closed, and comments that Bert usually closes his eyes when he is asleep. Ernie also notes that Bert doesn't respond to pokes when he's asleep, so naturally he delivers a few. At first, Bert doesn't respond, but after being poked a few times, he awakes, very annoyed, and yells at Ernie for waking him. Ernie then informs Bert that he just wanted to let him know that it was time for his nap.

Doctors face a similar situation in dealing with the more than 30 million people each year who receive general anesthesia during surgery. These patients certainly seem unresponsive, but there's no reliable way of knowing whether they actually are unconscious (Alkire, Hudetz, & Tononi, 2008). It turns out that about two to four adults in a thousand, and about 1.1 percent of children, retain some degree of consciousness during surgical procedures (Andrade, Deeprose, & Barker, 2008; Xu, Wu, & Yue, 2009). In rare cases, patients actually are aware of surgical pain and remember the trauma. Although their surgical wounds heal, these people may be psychologically scarred by the experience and may even show symptoms of posttraumatic stress disorder (Leslie et al., 2010). To reduce the possibility of operating on someone who appears unconscious but may not be, some physicians suggest monitoring patients' brain activity during every surgery (Jameson & Sloan, 2006). Unfortunately, even this precaution may not eliminate the problem in every case (Avidan et al., 2011).

The fact that people can be aware while appearing to be unconscious makes defining consciousness quite difficult (Sarà & Pistoia, 2009). Medical doctors tend to define consciousness as awareness that is demonstrated by any ability to recall an experience (Schwender et al., 1995). In psychology, the definition is somewhat broader: **Consciousness** is generally defined as your awareness of the outside world and of your mental processes, thoughts, feelings, and perceptions (Metzinger, 2000; Zeman, 2001). Let's see how this definition applies as we explore the scope of consciousness and various states of consciousness. ●

The Scope of Consciousness

Can unconscious thoughts affect your behavior?

consciousness The awareness of external stimuli and our own mental activity.

consciousness state The characteristics of consciousness at any particular moment.

Mental activity changes constantly. The features of consciousness at any instant—what reaches your awareness, the decisions you make, and so on—make up what is called your **consciousness state** at that moment (Tassi & Muzet, 2001). Possible *states of consciousness* include coma, deep sleep, hypnosis, meditation, daydreaming, and alert wakefulness. Consciousness can also be altered by drugs and other influences.

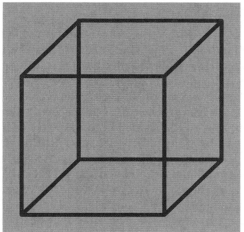

FIGURE 4.1
The Necker Cube
Each of the two squares in the Necker cube can be perceived as either the front or rear surface of the cube. Try to make the cube switch back and forth between these two orientations. Now try to hold only one orientation. You probably cannot maintain the whole cube in consciousness for longer than about three seconds before it "flips" from one orientation to the other.

conscious level The level of consciousness at which mental activities accessible to awareness occur.

nonconscious level The level of consciousness at which reside processes that are totally inaccessible to conscious awareness.

preconscious level The level of consciousness at which reside mental events that are not currently conscious but can become conscious at will.

unconscious The term used to describe a level of mental activity said by Freud to contain unacceptable sexual, aggressive, and other impulses of which an individual is unaware.

subconscious Another term that describes the mental level at which influential but normally inaccessible mental processes take place.

Consciousness States

Consciousness states can be viewed as different points along a scale or continuum of consciousness (Cavanna et al., 2011). For example, suppose you're aboard an airliner flying from New York to Los Angeles. The pilot calmly scans instrument displays while talking to an air traffic controller. In the seat next to you, a lawyer finishes her second cocktail while planning a courtroom strategy. Across the aisle, a young father gazes out the window, daydreaming, while his small daughter sleeps in his lap, dreaming dreams of her own. All these people are experiencing different states of consciousness. Some states are active and some are passive. The daydreaming father lets his mind wander, passively noticing images, memories, and other mental events that come to mind. Like the pilot, the lawyer actively directs her mental processes. In her case, though, as she evaluates various options and considers their likely outcomes, she is altering her state of consciousness by sipping alcohol.

Generally, people spend most of their time in a *waking* consciousness state. Mental processing in this state varies with changes in attention or arousal (Taylor, 2002). While reading, for example, you may temporarily ignore sounds around you. Similarly, if you're upset or bored or talking on a cell phone, you may tune out important cues from the environment, making it dangerous to perform complex activities such as driving a car.

Levels of Consciousness

The events and mental processes that you are aware of at any given moment are said to exist at the **conscious level.** For example, look at the Necker cube in Figure 4.1. If you're like most people, you can hold the cube in one orientation for only a few seconds before the other version "pops out" at you. The version that you experience at any moment is at your conscious level of awareness for that moment.

Some events, however, cannot be experienced consciously. For example, you are not directly aware of your brain regulating your blood pressure or controlling the dilation of the pupils in your eyes (Laeng, Sirois, & Gredebäck, 2012). Mental processes that control our biological functions occur at the **nonconscious level,** totally removed from conscious awareness. People can learn to alter a nonconscious process through *biofeedback training*, receiving information about their biological processes in order to control them. Usually special equipment is required, but you can approximate a biofeedback session by having a friend take your pulse at one-minute intervals while you sit quietly. First, establish a baseline pulse, then imagine a peaceful scene or think about lowering your pulse rate. Then ask your friend to softly say whether your pulse is higher or lower compared with the baseline. After four or five minutes of having this information "fed back" to you, you will probably be able to keep your pulse rate below the original baseline. Yet the pulse-regulating processes themselves remain out of consciousness.

Some mental events are not conscious but can become conscious or can influence conscious experience. These mental events make up the *cognitive unconscious* (Reber, 1992), which includes the preconscious and the subconscious. Mental events that are outside awareness but that can easily be brought into awareness are said to exist at the **preconscious level.** What did you have for dinner last night? The information you needed to answer this question probably wasn't already in your conscious awareness, but it was at the preconscious level. So when you read the question, you could answer it immediately. Similarly, when you play trivia games, you draw on your large storehouse of preconscious memories to come up with obscure facts.

Other mental activities can alter thoughts, feelings, and actions but are more difficult to bring into awareness. Sigmund Freud suggested that these **unconscious** activities, especially those involving unacceptable sexual and aggressive urges, are actively kept out of consciousness. Most psychologists do not accept Freud's view, but they still use the term *unconscious*, or **subconscious,** to describe mental activity that influences us in various ways but that occurs outside of awareness (Dijksterhuis & Nordgren, 2006).

Mental Processing without Awareness

A fascinating demonstration of mental processing without awareness was provided by an experiment with patients who had surgery under general anesthesia. After their operations but while the patients were still unconscious from the anesthesia, a recording of fifteen word pairs was played over and over for them in the recovery room. After regaining consciousness, the patients could not say what words were on the recording or even whether a recording had been played at all. However, when given one word from each of the word pairs and asked to say the first word that came to mind, the patients came up with the other member of the word pair from the recording (Cork, Kihlstrom, & Hameroff, 1992).

Even when conscious and alert, you can sometimes process and use information without being aware of it (Adams et al., 2010; Fu, Fu, & Dienes, 2008; Mudrick et al., 2011). In one study, participants watched a computer screen as an X flashed in one of four locations. The task was to indicate as quickly as possible where the X appeared. The location of the X seemed to vary randomly but was actually determined by a set of complex rules. (One such rule was "If the X moves horizontally twice in succession, its next move will be vertical.") Participants' responses became progressively faster and more accurate. Then, unknown to the participants, the rules were abandoned and the X appeared in *truly* random locations. Participants' accuracy and speed deteriorated instantly. Apparently, the participants had learned the rules without being aware of them and had applied them to improve their performance. However, even when offered $100 to state the rules that had guided the location sequence, they could not do so, nor were they sure that any such rules existed (Lewicki, 1992).

Visual processing without awareness may even occur in certain cases of blindness. When blindness is caused by damage only to the brain's primary visual cortex, pathways from the eyes are still connected to other brain areas that process visual information (Cowey, 2010b; Schmid et al., 2010). Some of these surviving connections may permit visual processing but without visual awareness—a condition called *blindsight* (Stoerig & Cowey, 1997). So though patients say they see nothing, if forced to guess, they can still locate visual targets, identify the direction of moving images, reach for objects, name the color of lights, and even discriminate happy from fearful faces (Azzopardi & Hock, 2011; Cowey, 2010a). The same blindsight phenomenon has been created in visually normal volunteers using magnetic brain stimulation to temporarily disable the primary visual cortex (Christensen et al., 2008; Ro & Rafal, 2006).

Research on *priming* also demonstrates mental processing without awareness. In a typical priming study, people tend to respond faster or more accurately to stimuli they have seen before. This is true even when they cannot consciously recall having seen those stimuli (Abrams & Greenwald, 2000; Breuer et al., 2009; Kouider & Dupoux, 2005). In one study, for example, people looked at figures like those in Figure 4.2. They had to decide which figures could actually exist in three-dimensional space and which could not. The participants were better at classifying pictures they had seen before, even when

Research shows that some surgery patients can hear, and later comply with, instructions or suggestions given while they were under anesthesia, even though they have no memory of what they were told (Bennett, Giannini, & Davis, 1985). People also have physiological responses to emotionally charged words even when they are not paying attention to them (Von Wright, Anderson, & Stenman, 1975). These and other similar studies provide evidence for the operation of subconscious mental processing (Deeprose & Andrade, 2006).

BLOOM COUNTY   **by Berke Breathed**

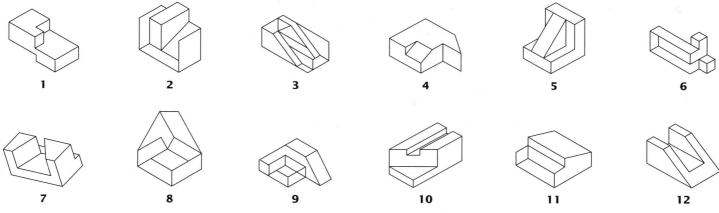

FIGURE 4.2

Stimuli Used in a Priming Experiment

Look at these figures and decide, as quickly as you can, whether each can actually exist. Priming studies show that this task would be easier for figures you have seen in the past, even if you don't recall seeing them. How did you do? The correct answers appear at the bottom of page 138.

LEARN **by** DOING

Source: From D. L. Schacter et al. , "Implicit memory for possible and impossible objects: Constraints on the construction of structural descriptions." *Journal of Experimental Psychology: Learning, Memory, and Cognition,* 17, 3–19. Copyright © 1991 by the American Psychological Association. Adapted with permission.

they couldn't remember having seen them (Schacter et al., 1991). Some priming effects are short lived, but others can last for years (Mitchell, 2006).

There is even evidence that some of the decisions and choices we make in everyday life may be guided to some extent by mental processes that occur without our awareness (Carter, Ferguson, & Hassin, 2011; Dijksterhuis et al., 2006; Galdi, Arcuri, & Gawronski, 2008; Mealor & Dienes, 2012; Ruiz-Padial & Vila, 2007). For example, your "lucky" choice of the fastest-moving supermarket checkout line might seem to have been based on nothing more than a hunch, a gut feeling, or intuition, but previous visits to that store might have given you useful information that you didn't know you had about the various clerks (Adolphs et al., 2005). In a laboratory study that supports this notion, people watched videotaped television commercials while the changing stock prices of fictional companies crawled across the bottom of the screen. Later, these people were asked to choose which of these companies they liked best. They couldn't recall anything they had seen about the companies' stock, so they had to make their choice on the basis of their gut reaction to the company names. Nevertheless, their choices were not random; they more often chose companies whose stock prices had been rising rather than those whose stock had been falling (Betch et al., 2003).

THINKING CRITICALLY

Can Subliminal Messages Change Your Behavior?

The research we have described suggests that we don't always have to be aware of information in order for it to affect us, but how strong can this influence be? In 1957, an adman named James Vicary claimed that a New Jersey theater flashed messages such as "buy popcorn" and "drink Coke" on a movie screen, too briefly to be noticed, while customers watched the movie *Picnic.* He said that these messages caused a 15 percent rise in sales of Coca-Cola and a 58 percent increase in popcorn sales. Can messages perceived at a *subliminal* level—that is, below conscious awareness—act as a form of "mind control"? Many people seem to think so. Each year, they spend millions of dollars on CDs and videos whose subliminal messages are supposed to help people lose weight, raise self-esteem, quit smoking, make more money, or achieve other goals.

What am I being asked to believe or accept?

Two types of claims have been made about subliminal stimuli. The more general one is that subliminal stimuli can influence people's behavior. The second, more specific claim is that subliminal stimuli provide an effective means of changing people's buying habits, political opinions, self-confidence, and other complex attitudes and behaviors, with or without their awareness or consent.

Is evidence available to support the claim?

Evidence that subliminal messages can affect conscious judgments comes in part from laboratory studies that present visual stimuli too briefly to be perceived consciously. In one such study, participants saw slides showing people performing ordinary acts such as washing dishes. Unknown to the participants, each slide was preceded by a subliminal exposure to a photo of "positive" stimuli (such as a child playing) or "negative" stimuli (such as a monster). Later, participants rated the people on the visible slides that had been preceded by a positive subliminal photo as being more likable, polite, friendly, successful, and reputable (Krosnick et al., 1992). The subliminal photos not only affected participants' liking of the people they saw but also shaped beliefs about their personalities.

In another study, participants were exposed to subliminal presentations of slides showing snakes, spiders, flowers, and mushrooms. Even though the slides were impossible to perceive at a conscious level, participants who were afraid of snakes or spiders showed physiological arousal (and reported feeling fear) in response to slides of snakes and spiders (Öhman & Soares, 1994).

The results of studies such as these support the notion that subliminal information can have an impact on judgments and emotion, but they say little or nothing about the value of subliminal recordings for achieving self-help goals. In fact, no laboratory evidence exists to support the effectiveness of these recordings. Their promoters offer only the reports of satisfied customers.

Can that evidence be interpreted another way?

Many claims for subliminal advertising—including the New Jersey movie theater case—have turned out to be publicity stunts using phony data (Haberstroh, 1995; Pratkanis, 1992). And testimonials from satisfied customers could be biased by what these people would like to believe about the subliminal recordings they bought. In one study designed to test this possibility, half the participants were told that they would hear recordings containing subliminal messages for improving memory. The rest were told that the subliminal messages would promote self-esteem. However, half the participants in the memory group actually got self-esteem messages, and half of the self-esteem group actually got memory messages. Regardless of which version they received, participants who thought they had heard memory enhancement messages reported improved memory; those who thought they had received self-esteem messages said their self-esteem had improved (Pratkanis, Eskenazi, & Greenwald, 1994). In other words, the effects of the recordings were determined by the listeners' expectations, not by the subliminal content of the recordings. These results suggest that customers' reports about the value of subliminal self-help recordings may reflect placebo effects based on optimistic expectations rather than the effects of subliminal messages.

What evidence would help to evaluate the alternatives?

The effectiveness of self-help recordings and other subliminal products must be evaluated through further experiments, such as the one just mentioned, that carefully control for expectations. Those who support and sell subliminal-influence methods are responsible for conducting those experiments, but as long as customers are willing to buy subliminal products on the basis of testimonials alone, scientific evaluation efforts will probably come only from those interested in protecting consumers from fraud.

What conclusions are most reasonable?

The available evidence suggests that subliminal perception occurs but that it has no potential for "mind control" (Greenwald, Klinger, & Schuh, 1995). Subliminal effects are usually small and short lived and they mainly affect simple judgments and general measures of overall arousal. The effects also tend to be related to temporary conditions such as fatigue or motivation (Bermeitinger et al., 2009). For example, a subliminal message about a beverage is more likely to influence a person who is thirsty than one who is not (Karremans, Stroebe, & Klaus, 2006). As for subliminal messages aimed at long-term behavior change, most researchers agree that such messages have no special power

ANSWERS FOR FIGURE 4.2: Figures 1, 4, 5, 7, 10, and 12 can exist in three-dimensional space.

to create needs, goals, skills, or actions (Pratkanis & Aronson, 2001; Randolph-Seng & Mather, 2009; Strahan et al., 2005). In fact, advertisements, political speeches, and other messages that we *can* perceive consciously have far stronger persuasive effects.   ● ● ● ●

FOCUS ON *RESEARCH*   # Subliminal Messages in Rock Music

Would the persuasive power of subliminal messages be increased if they were presented at normal speed but in reverse, so that we could not understand them consciously? According to numerous Internet web sites, this is exactly how satanic or drug-related messages have been hidden in the recorded music of Lady Gaga, Marilyn Manson, Eminem, Nine Inch Nails, the Rolling Stones, and hundreds of other performers. These alleged "back masked" *subliminal* messages are said to have influenced listeners to commit suicide or murder. For this claim to be true, however, the subliminal backward message would have to be perceived at some level of consciousness.

What was the researchers' question?
There is no good evidence that backward messages are actually present in most of the music cited. However, John R. Vokey and J. Don Read (1985) asked whether any backward messages that might exist could be perceived and understood while the music was playing forward. They also asked whether such a message, if perceived at all, would have any effect on the listener's behavior.

How did the researchers answer the question?
First, Vokey and Read made tape recordings of a person reading portions of the 23rd Psalm and Lewis Carroll's poem "Jabberwocky." This poem includes many nonsense words, but it follows the rules of grammar (e.g., "'Twas brillig, and the slithy toves …"). These recordings were then played backward to college students, who were asked to judge whether what they heard would have been meaningful or nonsensical if played forward.

What did the researchers find?
When the students heard the readings being played backward, they could not discriminate sense from nonsense. Nor could they tell the difference between declarative sentences and questions. They couldn't even identify the original material on which the recordings were based. In short, the participants couldn't understand the backward messages at a conscious level. Could they do so subconsciously? To find out, the researchers asked the participants to sort the backward statements they heard into one of five categories: nursery rhymes, Christian, satanic, pornographic, or advertising. They reasoned that if some sort of meaning could be subconsciously understood, the participants would be able to sort the statements nonrandomly. As it turned out, however, the participants did no better at this task than random chance would predict.

Perhaps backward messages might influence people's behavior even if the messages were not perceived consciously. To check on this possibility, Vokey and Read (1985) conducted another study. This time, they presented a backward version of a message whose sentences contained homophones (words that sound alike but have two spellings and two different meanings, such as "feat" and "feet"). When heard in the normal forward direction, such messages affect people's spelling of ambiguous words that are read aloud to them at a later time. (For example, they tend to spell out f-e-a-t rather than f-e-e-t if they had previously heard the sentence "It was a great feat of strength.") This example of priming occurs even if people do not recall having heard the message. After hearing a *backward* version of the message, however, the participants in this study did not produce the expected spelling bias.

What do the results mean?
Obviously, it wasn't possible for the participants to subconsciously understand meaning in the backward messages. Evidently, backward messages are not consciously or unconsciously understood, nor do they influence behavior (Vokey, 2002).

What do we still need to know?

Researchers would like to understand why the incorrect idea persists that backward messages can influence behavior. Beliefs and suspicions do not simply disappear in the face of contrary scientific evidence (Vyse, 2000; Winer et al., 2002). Perhaps such evidence needs to be publicized more widely in order to lay the misconceptions to rest, but it seems likely that some people so deeply want to believe in the existence and power of backward messages in rock music that such beliefs will forever hold the status of folk myths in Western culture.   ●●●●

Altered States of Consciousness

When changes in mental processes are great enough for you or others to notice significant differences in how you function, you are said to have entered an **altered state of consciousness.** In an altered state, mental processing shows distinct changes unique to that state. Cognitive processes or perceptions of yourself or the world may change and normal inhibitions or self-control may weaken (Vaitl et al., 2005).

The phrase *altered states of consciousness* recognizes waking consciousness as the most common state, a baseline against which altered states are compared. However, this is not to say that waking consciousness is universally considered more normal, proper, or valued than other states. In fact, judgments about the status and meaning of certain states of consciousness vary considerably across cultures (Ward, 1994).

Consider, for instance, *hallucinations,* which are perceptual experiences (such as hearing voices) that occur without sensory stimulation from the outside world. In the United States, hallucinations are usually viewed as so undesirable that even if they are caused by nothing more than an eye disorder people may be ashamed to seek the medical help they need to solve the problem (Menon et al., 2003). If mental patients hallucinate, they often feel stress and self-blame and may choose not to report their hallucinations (Karidi et al., 2010). Those who do report them tend to be considered more disturbed and may receive more drastic treatments than patients who keep their hallucinations to themselves (Wilson et al., 1996). Among the Moche of Peru, however, hallucinations have a culturally approved place. When someone experiences illness or misfortune, a healer conducts an elaborate ritual to find causes and treatments. During the ceremony, the healer takes mescaline, a drug that causes hallucinations. These hallucinations are thought to give the healer spiritual insight into the patient's problems (de Rios, 1989). In many other tribal cultures, too, purposeful hallucinations are respected, not rejected (Grob & Dobkin de Rios, 1992).

altered state of consciousness A condition that exists when changes in mental processes are extensive enough to produce noticeable differences in psychological and behavioral functioning.

Altered States and Cultural Values

Cultures differ in their definitions of which altered states of consciousness are approved and which are inappropriate. Here we see members of a Brazilian spirit possession cult in various stages of trance and, in Peru, a Moche curandero, or "curer," attempting to heal an ailing patient by using fumes from a potion—and a drug from the San Pedro cactus—to put himself in an altered state of consciousness.

In other words, states of consciousness differ not only in their characteristics but also in their value to members of particular cultures. In the sections that follow, we describe some of the most interesting altered states of consciousness, beginning with the most common one: sleep.

LINKAGES

Does the brain shut down when we sleep?
(a link to Biology and Behavior)

A Sleep Lab

The electroencephalograph (EEG) allows scientists to record brain activity through electrodes attached to the scalp. The development of this technology in the 1950s opened the door to the scientific study of sleep.

Sleeping and Dreaming

Does your brain go to sleep when you do?

According to ancient myths, sleepers lose control of their minds and flirt with death as their souls wander freely. Early researchers thought sleep was a time of mental inactivity, but sleep is actually an active, complex state (Hobson, 2005).

Stages of Sleep

Sleep researchers study the brain's electrical activity during sleep using an *electroencephalograph*, or *EEG*. The resulting EEG recordings, often called *brain waves*, vary in height (amplitude) and speed (frequency) as behavior or mental processes change. The brain waves of an awake, alert person are irregular, small, and closely spaced; that is, high frequency and low amplitude. A relaxed person with closed eyes shows more rhythmic brain waves occurring at slower speeds, about eight to twelve cycles per second (cps). During a normal night's sleep, your brain waves show distinctive and systematic changes in amplitude and frequency as you pass through various stages of sleep (Shatzmiller, 2010; Silber et al., 2007).

Non-REM Sleep   Imagine that you are participating in a sleep study. You're hooked up to an EEG and various monitors and a video camera watches as you sleep through the night. If you were to view the results, here's what you'd see: At first, you are relaxed; your eyes are closed, but you're awake. At this point, your muscle tone and eye movements are normal and your EEG shows the slow brain waves associated with relaxation. Then, as you drift into sleep, your breathing deepens, your heartbeat slows, and your blood pressure falls. Over the next half-hour, you descend through three stages of sleep—N1, N2, and N3—that are characterized by even slower brain waves with even higher amplitude (see Figure 4.3).

FIGURE 4.3
EEG during Sleep
EEG recordings of brain wave activity show three relatively distinct stages of sleep. Notice the regular patterns of brain waves that occur just before a person goes to sleep, followed by even slower waves as sleep becomes deeper in non-REM stages N1 through N3. In REM (rapid eye movement) sleep, the frequency of brain waves increases dramatically. In some ways the brain waves of REM sleep resemble patterns seen in people who are awake.

Source: From Horne, J. A., *Why We Sleep: The Functions of Sleep in Human and Other Mammals.* Copyright © 1988 James Horne. Reprinted by permission of Oxford University Press.).

Awake

Drowsy, relaxed

Stage N1 sleep

Stage N2 sleep

Stage N3 sleep

REM sleep

Together, these three stages are called **NREM,** or **Non-REM, sleep** because they do not include the rapid eye movements (REM) described in the next section (Iber et al., 2007). The deepest of the NREM stages, N3, is also known as *slow-wave sleep.* When you reach stage N3, it's quite difficult to wake up. If you were roused from this stage of deep sleep, you'd be groggy and confused.

REM Sleep   After thirty to forty-five minutes in stage N3, you quickly return to stage N2 and then enter a special stage in which your eyes move rapidly under your closed eyelids. This is called **REM (rapid eye movement) sleep,** or paradoxical sleep. It's called paradoxical because its characteristics contain a paradox, or contradiction. In REM sleep, your EEG resembles that of an awake, alert person, and your physiological arousal—heart rate, breathing, and blood pressure—is also similar to when you are awake. However, your muscles are nearly paralyzed. Sudden, twitchy spasms appear, especially in your face and hands, but your brain actively suppresses other movements (Blumberg & Lucas, 1994). In other words, REM sleep and NREM sleep are two distinctly different types of sleep. (Silber et al., 2007).

FIGURE 4.4
A Night's Sleep
During a typical night, a sleeper goes through this sequence of EEG stages. Notice that sleep is deepest during the first part of the night and shallower later on, when REM sleep (highlighted in orange here) becomes more prominent.

Source: Adapted by permission of the author from Cartwright, R. (1978) *A Primer on Sleep and Dreaming* (Reading, MA: Addison-Wesley).

A Night's Sleep   Most people pass through the cycle of sleep stages four to six times each night. Each cycle lasts about ninety minutes but the pattern of stages and length of the stages changes somewhat. Early in the night, most of the time is spent in NREM with only a few minutes in REM (see Figure 4.4). As sleep continues, though, it is dominated by stage N2 and REM sleep, from which sleepers finally awaken. Sleep patterns change with age. The average infant sleeps about thirteen hours a day (Galland et al., 2011). The average 70-year-old sleeps only about six hours (Roffwarg, Muzio, & Dement, 1966), and elderly people tend to wake more often during the night than younger people do (Floyd, 2002; Roenneberg et al., 2007). The composition of sleep changes, too. REM accounts for half of total sleep in newborns but less than 25 percent in young adults and even less in the elderly (Darchia, Campbell, & Feinberg, 2003). Elderly people spend more time in N1 and N2, the lighter stages of sleep (Espiritu, 2008). Individuals vary widely from these averages, though. Some people feel well rested after four hours of sleep, whereas others of similar age require ten hours to feel satisfied (Clausen, Sersen, & Lidsky, 1974).

To some extent, sleep patterns are also a matter of choice or necessity. For example, North American college students get less sleep than other people their age (Hicks, Fernandez, & Pellegrini, 2001). This trend has grown over the last 30 years as students balance academic and job responsibilities with family obligations and a variety of social and recreational activities—including those late-night sessions playing computer games, updating Facebook, or surfing the Internet. You've probably noticed the results of sleep deprivation as your classmates (or you?) struggle to stay awake during lectures.

Sleep Disorders

Most people experience sleep-related problems at one time or another (Silber, 2001). These can range from grogginess after staying up too late to occasional nights of tossing and turning to the more serious and long-term *sleep disorders* that affect as many as 70 million people in the United States alone (Institute of Medicine, 2006; Morin et al., 2009).

The most common sleep disorder is **insomnia,** in which people feel fatigue during the day because they have trouble falling asleep or staying asleep. If you have difficulty getting to sleep or staying asleep that persists for longer than one month at a time, you may be suffering from insomnia. Besides being tiring, insomnia is associated with mental distress, health problems, and impairments in daily functioning (Hamilton et al., 2007; Rajaratnam et al., 2011). Fatigue-related loss of productivity in workers has been estimated to cost an average of $1,967 a year per employee (Rosekind et al., 2010), and one study in Norway found that people with insomnia were nearly five times more likely than others to develop a permanent work disability (Sivertsen et al., 2009). Overall, people with insomnia are three times more likely to show a mental disorder than those with no sleep

NREM (non-rapid eye movement) sleep Sleep stages N1, N2, and N3; they are accompanied by gradually slower and deeper breathing; a calm, regular heartbeat; reduced blood pressure; and slower brain waves. (Stage N3 is called slow-wave sleep.)

REM (rapid eye movement) sleep The stage of sleep during which muscle tone decreases dramatically but the EEG resembles that of someone who is awake.

insomnia A sleep disorder in which a person has trouble falling asleep or staying asleep at night.

© Jupiterimages/Getty Images

Stimulus Control Therapy

Insomnia can often be reduced through a combination of relaxation techniques and stimulus control therapy, in which the person goes to bed only when sleepy and gets out of bed if sleep does not come within fifteen to twenty minutes. The goal is to have the bed become a stimulus associated with sleeping, and perhaps sex, but not with reading, eating, watching television, worrying, or anything else that is incompatible with sleep (Edinger et al., 2001).

APPLYING PSYCHOLOGY

narcolepsy A daytime sleep disorder in which a person suddenly switches from an active waking state into REM sleep.

sleep apnea A sleep disorder in which a person briefly but repeatedly stops breathing during the night.

sudden infant death syndrome (SIDS) A disorder in which a sleeping baby stops breathing, does not awaken, and dies.

complaints (Ohayon & Roth, 2003). Insomnia is especially associated with depressive and anxiety disorders (Baglioni et al., 2010). It is unclear from such correlations, however, whether insomnia causes mental disorders, mental disorders cause insomnia, or some other factor causes both.

Sleeping pills can relieve insomnia. However, they may interact dangerously with alcohol, may disturb REM sleep, and may eventually lead to increased sleeplessness (Curry, Eisenstein, & Walsh, 2006; Poyares et al., 2004). In the long run, learning-based treatments may be more helpful (Perlis et al., 2001; Stepanski & Perlis, 2000; Yang, Spielman, & Glovinsky, 2006). These include the cognitive behavior therapy methods described in the chapter on treatment of psychological disorders, and the progressive relaxation training techniques mentioned in the chapter on health, stress, and coping (Bootzin & Epstein, 2011). Both have been shown to promote better sleeping by reducing anxiety, tension, and other reactions to stress (Bernstein, Borkovec, & Hazlett-Stevens, 2000; Jacobs et al., 2004). Short daytime naps and moderate evening exercise can also help some people get to sleep more easily, sleep better, and experience better mood and performance the next day (Tanaka et al., 2001).

Narcolepsy is a disturbing daytime sleep disorder that is typically first seen in people who are between 15 and 25 years old (Dyken & Yamada, 2005; Zeman et al., 2004). People with narcolepsy abruptly enter REM sleep directly from the waking state, usually as they are laughing or experiencing some other emotional state (Ahmed & Thorpy, 2011). Because of the loss of muscle tone in REM, narcoleptics may experience *cataplexy,* meaning that they collapse and remain briefly immobile even after awakening. These attacks appear to originate in the brain's lateral hypothalamus (Nishino, 2011). The most common cause of narcolepsy appears to be the absence or deficiency of the neurotransmitter *orexin,* which is also known as *hypocretin* (Caylak, 2009; Miyagawa et al., 2008). A combination of regular naps and certain drugs can be a helpful treatment (Morganthaler et al., 2007). For example, the stimulant modafinil, taken in the morning, appears to be effective not only for narcolepsy, but also for counteracting the effects of sleep deprivation (Lavault et al., 2011). The depressant gamma hydroxybutyrate (GHB), taken at night, may also help reduce narcoleptic attacks and daytime fatigue (Boscolo-Berto et al., 2011).

People who suffer from **sleep apnea** briefly stop breathing hundreds of times each night, waking each time long enough to resume breathing. In the morning, they don't recall these awakenings, but they feel tired and tend to have headaches, learning difficulties, and reduced attention (Jackson, Howard, & Barnes, 2011). The daytime fatigue and inattention caused by sleep apnea make it a risk factor for accidents (Tregear et al., 2009). In one tragic case, two members of a train crew— both of whom had apnea—fell asleep on the job, resulting in a collision that killed two people (Pickler, 2002). Apnea has many causes, including genetic predisposition, obesity, problems with brain mechanisms that control breathing, and compression of the windpipe (Kadotani et al., 2001; Macey et al., 2002; Richards et al., 2002). Effective treatments include weight loss and use of a CPAP (or continuous positive airway pressure) mask that helps keep the breathing passages open all night (Antonescu-Turcu & Parthasarathy, 2010). In some cases surgery may be required to widen the air passageway in the upper throat (Maurer, 2010).

In cases of **sudden infant death syndrome (SIDS),** sleeping infants stop breathing and die. SIDS is the most common cause of unexpected infant death in Western countries (Hunt & Hauck, 2006). In the United States, it strikes about six of every ten thousand infants (Balayla, Azoulay, & Abenhaim, 2011), especially very low-birthweight babies, usually when they are two to four months old (Smith & White, 2006; Vernacchio et al., 2003).

Some SIDS cases may be caused by exposure to cigarette smoke, problems with brain systems that regulate breathing, or genetic factors (Courts & Madea, 2011; Klintschar & Heimbold, 2012; Machaalani, Say, & Waters, 2011; Tang, Machaalani, & Waters, 2011; Trachtenberg et al., 2012). However, the most important causes may be related to how and where infants sleep at night. SIDS rates appear to be lower in some countries where infants and parents sleep in the same bed (Gessner, Ives, & Perham-Hester, 2001; Li, Petitti, et al., 2003) but higher in others, including the United States and Ireland (McGarvey et al., 2006; Ostfeld et al., 2006). The differing risks may have to do with the kinds of bedding used or

Sudden Infant Death Syndrome (SIDS)

In SIDS cases, seemingly healthy infants stop breathing while asleep in their cribs. All the causes of SIDS are not known, but health authorities now urge parents to ensure that infants sleep on their backs, as this baby demonstrates.

sleepwalking A phenomenon that starts primarily in NREM sleep, especially in stage N3, and involves walking while asleep.

nightmares Frightening dreams that take place during REM sleep.

sleep terror disorder (night terrors) The occurrence of horrific dream images during N3 sleep, followed by a rapid awakening and a state of intense fear.

REM behavior disorder A sleep disorder in which the decreased muscle tone normally seen in REM sleep does not appear, thus allowing dreams to be acted out.

with sleeping position. Correlational evidence suggests that about half of apparent SIDS cases might actually be accidental suffocations that occur when infants sleep face down on a soft surface (Dwyer & Ponsonby, 2009; Gilbert et al., 2005; Shields et al., 2005). In the United States, for example, SIDS may be particularly common when caregivers place babies in the face-down position (Corwin et al., 2003; Hauck et al., 2002; Shields et al., 2005). The danger of the face-down position is especially great for babies who don't usually sleep in that position, who are not breastfed, or who don't sleep with a pacifier in their mouths (Li et al., 2006; Vennemann et al., 2009a, 2009b). In 1992, a new health campaign called "back to sleep" urged doctors to advise parents to be sure their babies sleep face up (Task Force on Sudden Infant Death Syndrome, 2011). Since then the number of infants dying from SIDS in the United States and United Kingdom has dropped by 50 percent (Blair et al., 2006; Daley, 2004; Moon, Calabrese, & Aird, 2008; Rasinski et al., 2003). Babies who sleep face up may also be less likely to inhale potentially toxic bacteria that grow in some foam mattresses (Jenkins & Sherbum, 2005; Weber et al., 2008).

Sleepwalking occurs in NREM sleep, usually in childhood (Guilleminault et al., 2003; Masand, Popli, & Welburg, 1995; Pilon, Montplaisir, & Zadra, 2008), but also affects up to four percent of adults (Zadra, Pilon, & Montplaisir, 2008). By morning, most sleepwalkers have forgotten their travels and their sometimes bizarre activities. One sleepwalking man had no recollection of tying his 4-month-old daughter to a clothesline in his attic (Pillmann, 2009). Sleepwalking has been associated with several possible causes, including genetic predisposition, sleep deprivation, and the side-effects of some drugs (Pressman, 2007; Seeman, 2011; Yeh et al., 2009; Zadra et al., 2008). There are no consistently effective medical treatments for sleepwalking (Harris & Grunstein, 2009), although sleepwalkers who also have sleep apnea often find relief for both conditions by wearing a CPAP mask at night (Guilleminault et al., 2005). Drugs help, but most children simply outgrow the problem. One adult sleepwalker was cured when his wife blew a whistle whenever he began a nighttime stroll (Meyer, 1975). Despite myths to the contrary, waking a sleepwalker is not harmful.

Nightmares are frightening REM dreams that occur in 4 to 8 percent of the general population. Adult women report more nightmares than men (Schredl & Reinhard, 2011), and they are especially common in people who suffer from posttraumatic stress disorder following military combat, torture, rape, or other horrific events (Hinton et al., 2009; Kryger, Roth, & Dement, 2000; Zadra & Donderi, 2000). Drugs have proved helpful in reducing the frequency of nightmares (Aurora et al., 2010), as has imagery therapy, in which people repeatedly imagine new and less frightening outcomes to their nightmares (Forbes, Phelps, & McHugh, 2001; Krakow et al., 2001). **Sleep terror disorder** (also known as **night terrors**) involves frightful dream images during stage N3 sleep (Derry et al., 2009). Sleepers often awaken from a night terror with a bloodcurdling scream and remain intensely afraid for up to 30 minutes. Yet they may not recall the episode in the morning (Snyder et al., 2008). Sleep terror disorder is especially common in children, but adults can suffer milder versions, and it appears to be partly inherited (Nguyen et al., 2008). The condition is sometimes treatable with drugs or psychotherapy (Jan et al., 2004; Sadeh 2005).

In **REM behavior disorder,** sleepers enter REM sleep without the near-paralysis that normally accompanies it (Abad & Guilleminault, 2004; Oudiette et al., 2009; Schenck, 2005). As a result, they can act out their dreams. If the dreams are violent, the disorder can be dangerous to the dreamer or those nearby (Schenck, Gittings, & Colussi-Mas, 2009). One nine-year-old boy in New York City was seriously injured when he jumped from a third-floor window while dreaming that his parents were being murdered. In another case, a man shot his wife to death while dreaming that burglars were invading their home (de Bruxelles, 2009). Although he was acquitted of murder charges, most defendants who offer a REM behavior disorder or sleepwalking defense are convicted (Lyon, 2009). REM behavior disorder, which sometimes occurs in tandem with daytime narcolepsy (Billiard, 2009; Schenck & Mahowald, 1992), can be caused by the side effects of medication (Morrison, Frangulyan, & Riha, 2011), and in one case was caused by a brain tumor (Zambelis, Paparrigopoulos, & Soldatos, 2002). REM behavior disorder is also common in patients with Parkinson's disease and is often an early sign of a degenerative brain condition that may take decades to fully develop (Claassen et al., 2010; Postuma, Gagnon, & Montplaisir, 2011). Fortunately, prescription drugs are usually effective in treating REM behavior disorder (Gagnon et al., 2006; Takeuchi et al., 2001).

Why Do People Sleep?

People need a certain amount of uninterrupted sleep to function normally. In fact, most living creatures sleep. In trying to understand why people sleep, psychologists have studied what sleep does for us and how the brain shapes the characteristics of sleep (Siegel, 2005).

Sleep as a Circadian Rhythm   Humans and almost all animals display cycles of behavior and physiology that repeat about every 24 hours (Mazzoccoli, 2011). These patterns are called **circadian rhythms** (also known as **human biological rhythms**). (*Circadian,* pronounced "sir-KAY-dee-en," comes from the Latin *circa dies,* meaning "about a day.") Longer and shorter rhythms also occur, but they are less common.

Circadian rhythms are linked to signals such as the light of day and the dark of night (Ohta, Yamazaki, & McMahon, 2005). However, most of these rhythms continue even when no time signals are available. People living for months without external light and dark cues maintain daily rhythms in sleeping and waking, eating, urination, hormone release, and other physiological functions. Under such conditions, these cycles repeat about every 24 hours (Czeisler et al., 1999).

Disruption of the sleep-wake cycle can create problems. For example, air travel across several time zones often causes **jet lag,** a pattern of fatigue, irritability, inattention, and sleeping problems that can last for several days (Akerstedt, 2007; Reilly, Atkinson, et al., 2007; Reilly, Waterhouse, et al., 2007). The traveler's body feels ready to sleep at the wrong time for the new location. It tends to be easier to stay awake longer than usual than to go to sleep earlier than usual. That is the reason that the symptoms of jet lag are usually more intense after a long eastward trip (when time is lost) than after a long westward journey (when time is gained; Doane et al., 2010; Lemmer et al., 2002). Symptoms similar to those of jet lag also appear in workers who repeatedly change between day and night shifts and in people who try to go to sleep early on a Sunday night after a weekend of later-than-usual bedtimes (Czeisler et al., 2005; Di Milia, 2006). For these people, Monday morning "blues" may actually be symptoms of a disrupted sleep-wake cycle (Yang & Spielman, 2001).

The timing of circadian sleep rhythms can vary from person to person. Most people fall into one of two patterns (Roenneberg et al., 2007)—some have a natural tendency to stay up later at night ("owls") while others normally tend to wake up earlier in the morning ("larks"). These different *chronotypes* may occur because of "clock genes," which are genetic codes that appear to determine the daily peaks and valleys in a person's sleepiness and wakefulness, hormone levels, and body temperature (Zhang et al., 2011). The action of these clock genes appears to be affected by disorders such as Alzheimer's disease, depression, and certain cancers (Kishi et al., 2011; Mazzoccoli et al., 2011; Yang et al., 2011; Yesavage et al., 2011), perhaps helping to explain why changes in sleeping habits are associated with certain illnesses.

Because our sleep-wake rhythms stay about the same even without external cues about light and dark, we must have an internal biological clock that keeps track of time. This clock is in the *suprachiasmatic nuclei* (*SCN*) of the hypothalamus (Kalsbeek et al., 2006), as shown in Figure 4.5. The SCN receives light information from a special set of photoreceptors in the eyes and then sends signals to hindbrain areas that initiate sleep or wakefulness (Reinoso-Suárez, de Andrés, & Garzón, 2011). When animals with SCN damage receive transplanted SCN cells, their circadian rhythms become like those of the donor animal (Menaker & Vogelbaum, 1993). SCN neurons also regulate the release of the hormone *melatonin.* Melatonin rises during periods of darkness, and appears to be important in maintaining circadian rhythms (Zawilska, Skene, & Arendt, 2009). Many symptoms associated with jet lag and other disruptions in sleep-wake cycles can be prevented or treated by taking melatonin (Brown et al., 2009), although for some people, such as commercial airline crewmembers, regular use is not recommended (Simons & Valk, 2009). There is some evidence, too, that sildenafil (a drug normally prescribed for

circadian rhythm (human biological rhythm) A cycle, such as waking and sleeping, that repeats about once a day.

jet lag Fatigue, irritability, inattention, and sleeping problems caused by air travel across several time zones.

FIGURE 4.5

Sleep, Dreaming, and the Brain

This diagram shows the location of some of the brain structures thought to be involved in sleep and dreaming, as well as in other altered states discussed later in the chapter. For example, one area near the suprachiasmatic nuclei acts as a "master switch" to promote sleep (Saper, Chou, & Scammell, 2001). If it is damaged, sleep may be nearly impossible. Another nearby area promotes wakefulness; individuals with damage to this area sleep virtually all the time (Salin-Pascual et al., 2001).

Photo © Daniel Laflor/iStockphoto

Suprachiasmatic nuclei
Locus coeruleus
Pineal gland
Cerebellum
Hindbrain

erectile dysfunction) can speed recovery from jet lag after eastbound (but not westbound) travel (Stephenson, 2007). It may also be possible to reduce jet lag through diet, exercise, and exposure to natural lighting conditions upon daytime arrival or to dim light upon nighttime arrival (Armstrong, 2006; Edwards, Reilly, & Waterhouse, 2009; Evans, Elliott, & Gorman, 2009).

The Value of Sleep   One way to explore what sleep does for us is to study what happens when we are prevented from sleeping. After being deprived of sleep, people don't need to make up every hour of lost sleep. Instead, they sleep about 50 percent more than usual, then wake up feeling rested. But their "recovery" night includes an unusually high percentage of REM sleep (Feinberg & Campbell, 1993). And if people are deprived *only* of REM sleep, they compensate even more directly. In one study, participants were awakened whenever their EEGs showed REM. When allowed to sleep normally the next night, they "rebounded," nearly doubling the percentage of time spent in REM (Dement, 1960). This research suggests that there is a specific need for REM sleep and that it has its own special functions. What those functions might be is still unclear, but there are several interesting possibilities.

First, REM may improve the functioning of neurons that use norepinephrine (Siegel & Rogawski, 1988), a neurotransmitter released by cells in the *locus coeruleus* (pronounced "lo-kus seh-ROO-lee-us"; see Figure 4.5). During waking hours, it affects alertness and mood. But the brain's neurons lose their sensitivity to norepinephrine if it is released continuously for too long. REM sleep deprivation causes unusually high norepinephrine levels and decreased daytime alertness (Mallick and Singh, 2011). Researchers suggest that because the locus coeruleus is almost completely inactive during REM sleep, REM helps restore sensitivity to norepinephrine and thus its ability to keep us alert (Steriade & McCarley, 1990).

REM sleep may also be a time for creating and strengthening connections between nerve cells in the brain (Diekelmann & Born, 2010). If so, it would explain why infants and children—whose brains are still developing—spend so much time in REM sleep. Evidence favoring this possibility comes from animal research showing that REM sleep helps in the creation of neural connections following new learning experiences (Frank et al., 2001; Scullin & McDaniel, 2010). There is also evidence that REM sleep deprivation slows the creation of these connections (Kim, Mahmoud, & Grover, 2005). So REM sleep may help to solidify and absorb the day's experiences and skills (Fenn, Nusbaum, & Margoliash, 2003; Fischer et al., 2002; Ishikawa et al., 2006; Sejnowski & Destexhe, 2000; Stickgold, James, & Hobson, 2000). There is evidence, too, that REM sleep may improve daytime creativity (Cai et al., 2009).

Other studies have found that information, including emotional information, is remembered better and longer when followed immediately by sleep, especially REM sleep (Djonlagic et al., 2009; Gais, Lucas, & Born, 2006; Gomez, Bootzin, & Nadel, 2006; Hu, Stylos-Allan, & Walker, 2006; Payne & Kensinger, 2010). Even 60- to 90-minute naps in which REM sleep appears can be enough to solidify the learning of visual information (Mednick, Nakayama, & Stickgold, 2003). When people are deprived of REM sleep, their performance at a skill they'd learned the day before suffers when compared with people who were either deprived of NREM sleep or had slept normally (Karni et al., 1994). However, if people are given a medication that increases the activity of acetylcholine in the brain, REM sleep deprivation does not have the same disruptive effect on learning (Aleisa, Alzoubi, & Alkadhi, 2011). This suggests that the learning impairments seen after REM sleep deprivation may be caused by its effects on brain circuits that use acetylcholine. If REM sleep deprivation can interfere with learning, could it be used to help people forget traumatic events? Some researchers have suggested that sleep deprivation immediately after a trauma might reduce the risk of posttraumatic stress disorder (Wagner et al., 2006), but others disagree (van der Helm et al., 2011). Further research will be needed to evaluate this claim.

What are the effects of total **sleep deprivation**? People who go without sleep for as long as a week usually don't suffer serious long-term effects. However, extended sleeplessness does lead to fatigue, irritability, memory problems, and inattention (Killgore, 2010; van der Kloet et al., 2012). Even short-term sleep deprivation—a common condition among busy adolescents and adults—can take its toll (Calamaro, Mason, & Ratcliffe, 2009; Caldwell, 2012; Lim & Dinges, 2010; Steptoe, Peacey, & Wardle, 2006). For example, sleep deprivation can reduce the ability of the body's immune system to fight off colds (Cohen et al., 2009), and serious mistakes in patient care are more likely when doctors work sleep-disrupting extended hospital shifts than when they work more normal hours (Lockley et al., 2007). Most fatal car crashes in the United States occur during the "fatigue hazard" hours of midnight to 6 a.m. (Coleman, 1992), and sleepiness resulting from long work shifts or other causes is a major factor in up to 25 percent of all auto accidents (Barger et al., 2005; Filtness, Reyner, & Horne, 2012; Garbarino et al., 2001; Philip et al., 2001). Fatigue has also been identified as a major cause of car accidents in Asia, South America, and Europe (Abe et al., 2010; de Pinho et al., 2006; Liu et al., 2003; Maycock, 1997; Pizza et al., 2010; Sagaspe et al., 2010). The fact that "sleepy driving" can be as dangerous as drunk driving has led at least one U.S. state (New Jersey) to expand the definition of reckless driving to include "driving while fatigued" (i.e., having had no sleep in the previous 24 hours). Fatigue also plays a role in many injuries suffered by sleepy young children at play or in day care (Boto et al., 2011). Learning and performance on IQ tests are also impaired after sleep deprivation (Gruber et al., 2010; Yoo et al., 2007), but certain parts of the cerebral cortex actually increase their activity when a sleep-deprived person faces a learning task, so we're able to compensate for a while (Drummond et al., 2000).

Scientists are looking for drugs that can combat the effects of sleep deprivation, but there seems to be no substitute for sleep itself. It appears to help restore the body and the brain for future activity and to help consolidate memories of newly learned facts (Gais et al., 2007; Korman et al., 2007; Orban et al., 2006; Racsmány, Conway, & Demeter, 2010; Rasch & Born, 2008; Walker & Stickgold, 2006). The restorative function is especially associated with NREM sleep, which would help explain why most people get their NREM sleep in the first part of the night (see Figure 4.4).

sleep deprivation A condition in which people do not get enough sleep; it may result in reduced cognitive abilities, inattention, and increased risk of accidents.

Sleep and Sleep Disorders   IN REVIEW

Types of Sleep	Characteristics	Possible Functions
NREM (non–rapid eye movement) Stage N3 is also called slow-wave sleep	Includes the deepest stages of sleep, characterized by slowed heart rate and breathing, reduced blood pressure, and low-frequency, high-amplitude brain waves	Refreshes body and brain; consolidates memory
REM (rapid eye movement) sleep	Characterized by eye movements, waking levels of heart rate, breathing, blood pressure, and brain waves, but near-paralysis in muscles	Restores sensitivity to norepinephrine, thus improving waking alertness; creates and solidifies nerve cell connections; consolidates memories and new skills

Sleep Disorders	Characteristics	Possible Causes
Insomnia	Difficulty (lasting at least a month) in falling asleep or staying asleep	Worry, anxiety
Narcolepsy	Sudden switching from a waking state to REM sleep	Absence or deficiency in orexin (hypocretin)
Sleep apnea	Frequent episodes of interrupted breathing while asleep	Genetic predisposition, obesity, faulty breathing-related brain mechanisms, windpipe compression
Sudden infant death syndrome (SIDS)	Interruption of an infant's breathing, resulting in death	Genetic predisposition, faulty breathing-related brain mechanisms, exposure to cigarette smoke
Sleepwalking	Engaging in walking or other waking behaviors during NREM sleep	Genetic predisposition, drug side effects, and sleep deprivation
Nightmares	Frightening dreams during REM sleep	Stressful or traumatic events or experiences
Sleep terror disorder (night terrors)	Frightening dream images during NREM sleep	Stressful or traumatic events or experiences
REM behavior disorder	Lack of paralysis during REM sleep allows dreams to be enacted, sometimes with harmful consequences	Malfunction of brain mechanism normally creating REM paralysis

IN REVIEW QUESTIONS

1. Jet lag occurs because of a disruption in a traveler's ___ .

2. The importance of NREM sleep is suggested by its appearance ___ in the night.

3. The safest sleeping position for babies is ___ .

Dreams and Dreaming

We have seen that the brain is active in all sleep stages (for a summary of our discussion, see "In Review: Sleep and Sleep Disorders"). Some of this brain activity during sleep is experienced as the story-like sensations and perceptions known as **dreaming.** Dreams may be as short as a few seconds or last for many minutes. They may be organized or chaotic, realistic or fantastic, peaceful or exciting (Schredl, 2010).

Some dreaming occurs during NREM sleep, but most dreams—and the most bizarre and vivid dreams—happen during REM (Dement & Kleitman, 1957; Eiser, 2005). Even when they seem to make no sense, dreams may contain a certain amount of logic. For example, people can tell the difference between written dream reports whose sentences had been randomly rearranged and those that had been left alone (Stickgold, Rittenhouse, & Hobson, 1994). And although dreams often involve one person transforming into another or one object turning into another object, it is rare that objects become people or vice versa (Cicogna et al., 2006).

Daytime activities may influence the content of dreams (Blagrove et al., 2011). In one study, an unusually high number of animal characters appeared in the dreams reported by people who had just attended an animal rights conference (Lewis, 2008). In another, people with health problems reported more dreams that included illness or injury (King & DiCicco, 2007), and several studies have found that dream images of violence, terrorism, and disaster became more common in the days and weeks following the September 11, 2001, terrorist attacks in the United States (Bulkeley & Kahan, 2008). Sounds and odors can influence dreams, too. In one study, sleeping research participants were exposed to the

dreaming The production during sleep of story-like sequences of images, sensations, and perceptions that last from several seconds to many minutes; it occurs mainly during REM sleep.

smell of roses or rotten eggs. Those who had smelled the roses reported happier dreams than those who had smelled the rotten eggs (Schredly et al., 2010). It is also sometimes possible for people to intentionally direct their dream content. This is called **lucid dreaming,** because the sleeper is aware of dreaming while it occurs (Kahn & Gover, 2010).

Research leaves little doubt that everyone dreams during every night of normal sleep (Bertolo et al., 2003; Nir & Tononi, 2010; Saurat et al., 2011; Voss et al., 2011). Whether you remember a dream depends on how you sleep and wake up. You'll remember more if you awaken abruptly and lie quietly while writing or recording your recollections.

Why do we dream? Theories abound (Antrobus, 2001; Domhof, 2001; Eiser, 2005). Some see dreaming as a process through which all species with complex brains analyze and consolidate information that is personally important or has survival value (Payne & Nadel, 2004; Porte & Hobson, 1996; Zadra, Desjardins, & Marcotte, 2006). This view is supported by the fact that dreaming appears to occur in most mammals, as indicated by the appearance of REM sleep. For example, after researchers disabled the neurons that cause REM sleep paralysis, sleeping cats ran around and attacked or seemed alarmed by unseen objects, presumably the images from dreams (Winson, 1990).

According to Freud (1900), dreams are a disguised form of *wish fulfillment,* a way to satisfy unconscious urges or resolve unconscious conflicts that are too upsetting to deal with consciously. For example, a person's sexual desires might appear in a dream as the rhythmic motions of a horseback ride. Conflicting feelings about a parent might appear as a dream about a fight. Seeing his patients' dreams as a "royal road to a knowledge of the unconscious," Freud interpreted their meaning as part of his psychoanalytic therapy methods (see the chapter on the treatment of psychological disorders).

In contrast, the *activation-synthesis theory* describes dreams as the meaningless by-products of REM sleep (Eiser, 2005; Hobson, 1997). According to this theory, hindbrain arousal during REM sleep creates random messages that *activate* the brain, especially the cerebral cortex. Dreams result as the cortex connects, or *synthesizes,* these messages as best as it can, using stored memories and current feelings to organize this random brain activity into something more coherent. From this perspective, dreams represent the brain's attempt to make sense of meaningless stimulation during sleep (Bernstein & Roberts, 1995; Tierney, 2009).

Even if dreams arise from random brain activity, their content may still have psychological significance (Bulkeley & Domhoff, 2010). Some psychologists believe that dreams give people a chance to review and address some of the problems they face during waking hours (Cartwright, 1993). This view is supported by evidence suggesting that people's current concerns can affect both the content of their dreams and the way in which dreams are organized and recalled (Domhoff, 1996, 1999; Domhoff & Schneider, 2008; Stevens, 1996). However, neuroimaging studies show that while we are in REM sleep, brain areas involved in emotion tend to be overactivated, whereas those areas controlling logical thought tend to be suppressed (Miyauchi et al., 2009). In fact, as we reach deeper sleep stages and then enter REM sleep, logical thinking subsides and unusual perceptions increase (Fosse, Stickgold, & Hobson, 2001). This is probably why dreams rarely provide realistic, logical solutions to our problems (Blagrove, 1996).

© Rudyanto Wijaya/iStockphoto

Inducing Hypnosis

In the late 1700s, Austrian physician Franz Anton Mesmer used a forerunner of hypnosis to treat physical disorders. His procedure, known as mesmerism, included elaborate trance-induction rituals, but we now know that hypnosis can be induced far more easily, often simply by staring at an object, as this woman did.

lucid dreaming Being aware that a dream is a dream while it is occurring.

hypnosis A phenomenon that is brought on by special techniques and is characterized by varying degrees of responsiveness to suggestions for changes in a person's behavior and experiences.

Hypnosis

Can you be hypnotized against your will?

The word *hypnosis* comes from the Greek word *hypnos,* meaning "sleep." However, hypnotized people are not sleeping. Even those who say afterward that their bodies felt "asleep" also report that their minds were active and alert. **Hypnosis** has been defined as an altered state of consciousness that is brought on by special techniques and produces responsiveness to suggestions for changes in experience and behavior (Kirsch, 1994a). Most hypnotized people do not feel forced to follow the hypnotist's instructions. They simply see no reason to refuse (Hilgard, 1965). In fact, the more that people want to cooperate with the hypnotist, the more likely it is they will experience hypnosis (Lynn et al., 2002). People cannot be hypnotized against their will.

Experiencing Hypnosis

Hypnosis often begins with suggestions that the person feels relaxed and sleepy. The hypnotist may then gradually focus the person's attention on a particular and often monotonous set of stimuli, such as a swinging pendant. The hypnotist suggests that the individual should ignore everything else and imagine certain feelings.

There are special tests to measure **hypnotic susceptibility,** the degree to which people respond to hypnotic suggestions (Kumar & Farley, 2009). Different tests can yield somewhat different results (Barnes, Lynn, & Pekala, 2009), but in general, they show that about 10 percent of adults are difficult or impossible to hypnotize (Hilgard, 1982). At the other extreme are people whose hypnotic experiences are so vivid that they can't tell the difference between images the hypnotist asked them to imagine and images projected on a screen (Bryant & Mallard, 2003). Hypnotically susceptible people typically differ from others in having a better ability to focus attention and ignore distractions (Crawford, Brown, & Moon, 1993; Iani et al., 2006). They also tend to have more active imaginations (Spanos, Burnley, & Cross, 1993), a tendency to fantasize (Lynn & Rhue, 1986), a capacity for processing information quickly and easily (Dixon, Brunet, & Laurence, 1990), a tendency to be suggestible (Kirsch & Braffman, 2001), and positive attitudes and expectations about hypnosis (Benham et al., 2006; Fassler, Lynn, & Knox, 2008).

The results of hypnosis can be fascinating. People told that their eyes are locked shut may struggle unsuccessfully to open them. They may appear deaf or blind or insensitive to pain. They may seem to forget their own names. Some appear to remember forgotten things. Others show *age regression,* apparently recalling or reenacting their childhoods (see Figure 4.6). These hypnotic effects can be extended for hours or days through *posthypnotic suggestions,* which are instructions about how to behave after hypnosis has ended (such as smiling whenever someone says "Paris"). Some individuals show *posthypnotic amnesia,* an inability to recall what happened while they were hypnotized, even after being told what happened (Sutcher, 2008; Wark, 2008).

Ernest Hilgard (1965, 1992) described the main changes that people display during hypnosis. First, hypnotized people *tend not to begin actions on their own,* waiting instead for the hypnotist's instructions. One participant said, "I was trying to decide if my legs were crossed, but I couldn't tell, and didn't quite have the initiative to move to find out" (Hilgard, 1965). Second, hypnotized people tend to ignore all but the hypnotist's voice and whatever it points out: Their *attention is redistributed.* Third, hypnosis *enhances the ability to fantasize.* Participants more vividly imagine a scene or relive a memory. Fourth, hypnotized people *readily take on roles.* They more easily act as though they were people of a different age or sex than nonhypnotized people do. Fifth, hypnotized individuals show *reduced reality testing.* They tend not to question whether statements are true and they are more willing to accept distortions of reality. So a hypnotized person might shiver in a warm room if a hypnotist says it is snowing.

Explaining Hypnosis

Hypnotized people look and act differently from nonhypnotized people (Hilgard, 1965). Do these differences indicate an altered state of consciousness?

Advocates of **state theories of hypnosis** say that they do. They point to the notable changes in brain activity that occur during hypnosis (Egner, Jamieson, & Gruzelier, 2005; Mohr, Binkofski, et al., 2005; Pyka et al., 2011; Raij et al., 2005) and to the dramatic effects that hypnosis can produce, including insensitivity to pain and the disappearance of warts (Noll, 1994). They also note that there are slight differences in the way hypnotized and nonhypnotized people carry out suggestions. In one study, hypnotized people and those pretending to be hypnotized were told to run their hands through their hair whenever they heard the word "experiment" (Orne, Sheehan, & Evans, 1968). The pretenders did so only when the hypnotist said the cue word. Hypnotized participants complied no matter who said it. Another study found that hypnotized people complied more often than pretenders with a posthypnotic suggestion to mail postcards to the experimenter (Barnier & McConkey, 1998).

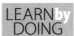

FIGURE 4.6
Hypnotic Age Regression
Here are the signatures of two adults before hypnotically induced age regression (top of each pair) and while age regressed (bottom of each pair). The lower signature in each pair looks less mature, but was the change due to hypnosis? To find out, ask a friend to sign a blank sheet of paper, first as usual, and then as if he or she were five years old. If the two signatures look significantly different, what does this say about the cause of certain age-regression effects?

LEARN by DOING

Source: Reprinted by permission of the author from Hypnotic Susceptibility by Ernest R. Hilgard. Copyright © 1965. Published by Harcourt, Brace, Jovanovich, Inc.

hypnotic susceptibility The degree to which a person responds to hypnotic suggestion.

state theories of hypnosis Theories proposing that hypnosis creates an altered state of consciousness.

FIGURE 4.7

Reports of Pain in Hypnosis

This graph compares the intensity of pain reported by three groups of participants while one of their hands was immersed in ice water. The orange line represents nonhypnotized participants. The blue line represents hypnotized participants who were told they would feel no pain. The purple line shows the reports of hypnotized participants who were told they would feel no pain but were asked to press a key if "any part of them" felt pain. The key pressing by this "hidden observer" suggests that under hypnosis, the experience of pain was dissociated from conscious awareness.

Source: From Hilgard, E. R., *Divided Consciousness: Multiple Controls in Human Thought and Action,* (John Wiley, 1977). Reprinted by permission of the author.

However, there are also several **nonstate theories of hypnosis.** Supporters of *role theory,* for example, maintain that hypnosis is not a special state of consciousness. They point out that some of the changes in brain activity associated with hypnosis can also be created without hypnosis (McGeown et al., 2012; Mohr, Binkofski, et al., 2005). They suggest that hypnotized people are merely complying with the demands of the situation and acting in accordance with a special social role (Kirsch, 1994b). From this perspective, hypnosis provides a socially acceptable reason to follow someone's suggestions, much as a checkup at your doctor's office provides a socially acceptable reason to remove your clothing on request. Support for role theory comes from several sources. First, nonhypnotized people sometimes display behaviors that are usually associated with hypnosis. For example, contestants on television game shows and reality shows do lots of odd, silly, disgusting, or even dangerous things without first being hypnotized. Second, laboratory studies show that motivated but nonhypnotized volunteers can duplicate many aspects of hypnotic behavior, from arm rigidity to age regression (Dasgupta et al., 1995; Mazzoni et al., 2009; Orne & Evans, 1965). Other studies have found that people rendered blind or deaf by hypnosis can still see or hear, even though their actions and beliefs suggest that they cannot (Bryant & McConkey, 1989). Still others indicate that people's responses to hypnotic suggestions can vary from one occasion to the next, depending on situational factors (Fassler, Lynn, & Knox, 2008).

Hilgard's (1992) *dissociation theory* blends role and state theories. He suggested that hypnosis is not a single specific state but a general condition that temporarily reorganizes or breaks down our normal control over thoughts and actions (Holmes et al., 2005). Hypnosis, he said, may activate a process called *dissociation,* meaning a split in consciousness (Hilgard, 1979). Dissociation allows body movements normally under voluntary control to occur on their own and normally involuntary processes (such as overt reactions to pain) to be controlled voluntarily. This relaxation of control is possible because of a social agreement between the hypnotized person and the hypnotist to share control. In other words, people usually decide for themselves how to act or what to attend to, perceive, or remember. During hypnosis, the hypnotist is given permission to control some of these experiences and actions. Compliance with a social role may tell part of the story, Hilgard said, but hypnosis also leads to significant changes in mental processes.

Support for Hilgard's theory comes from brain-imaging studies showing that the ability to dissociate certain mental processes is greater in people who are more hypnotically susceptible (Bob, 2008; Egner, Jamieson, & Gruzelier, 2005). Dissociation was also demonstrated behaviorally by asking hypnotized participants to immerse a hand in ice water (Hilgard, Morgan, & MacDonald, 1975). They were told that they would feel no pain but were asked to press a key with their other hand if "any part of them" felt pain. The results are shown in Figure 4.7. The participants' oral reports indicated almost no pain, but their key-pressing told a different story. Hilgard concluded that a "hidden observer" was reporting on pain that was reaching these people but that had been separated, or dissociated, from conscious awareness (Hilgard, 1977).

Much remains to be learned about the nature of hypnosis. However, traditional distinctions between state and role theories have become less important as researchers focus on larger questions, such as why people are susceptible to hypnosis and the biological, social, and cognitive factors that underlie hypnosis (e.g., Lynn & Kirsch, 2006; Raz, Fan, & Posner, 2005).

Applications of Hypnosis

Whatever hypnosis is, it has proven useful, especially in relation to pain (Patterson, 2010). Functional magnetic resonance imaging (fMRI) studies of hypnotized pain patients show reduced activity in brain regions that normally process the emotional aspects of pain (Vanhaudenhuyse et al., 2009). For some people, hypnosis can block the pain of dental work (Gow, 2010), childbirth (Landolt & Milling, 2011), burns (Askay et al., 2007), and surgery (Hammond & Coidon, 2008). For others, hypnosis has been shown to relieve

nonstate theories of hypnosis Theories, such as role theory, proposing that hypnosis does not create an altered state of consciousness.

chronic pain from arthritis, nerve damage, migraine headaches, and cancer (Stewart, 2005). Hypnotic suggestion can also help eliminate diarrhea (Tan, Hammond, & Joseph, 2005), reduce nausea and vomiting due to chemotherapy (Richardson et al., 2007), limit surgical bleeding (Gerschman, Reade, & Burrows, 1980), and speed postoperative recovery (Astin, 2004). Hypnosis has even been effective in reducing stress-related hair loss (Willemsen & Vanderlinden, 2008).

Other applications of hypnosis are more controversial (Loftus & Davis, 2006). For example, hypnotic age regression is sometimes used in an attempt to help people recover lost memories. However, the memories of past events reported by age-regressed individuals are not as accurate as those of nonhypnotized individuals (Lynn, Myers, & Malinoski, 1997). Similarly, it is doubtful that hypnosis can help witnesses recall the details of a crime. In fact, their positive expectations about the value of hypnosis may lead them to unintentionally distort or reconstruct memories of what they saw and heard (Garry & Loftus, 1994; Wells & Olson, 2003). Being hypnotized may also make witnesses more confident about their reports, even if those reports are not accurate.

Meditation, Health, and Stress

LINKAGES

Does meditation relieve stress?
(a link to Health, Stress, and Coping)

M*editation* provides a set of techniques intended to create an altered state of consciousness characterized by inner peace and tranquility (Chiesa & Serretti, 2009; Walsh & Shapiro, 2006). Techniques to achieve a meditative state differ, depending on belief and philosophy (e.g., Eastern meditation, Sufism, yoga, or prayer). However, in the most common meditation methods, attention is focused on just one thing until the meditator stops thinking about anything else and experiences nothing but "pure awareness" (Benson, 1975; Perlman et al., 2010). In this way, the individual becomes more fully aware of the present moment rather than being caught up in the past or the future.

To organize their attention, meditators may focus on the sound or tempo of their breathing or slowly repeat a soothing word or phrase, called a mantra. During a typical meditation session, breathing, heart rate, muscle tension, blood pressure, and oxygen consumption decrease, whereas blood flow in the brain to the thalamus and frontal lobes increases (Cahn & Polich, 2006; Newberg et al., 2001; Wallace & Benson, 1972). The effects of meditation on the brain are complex (Austin, 2006; Hölzel et al., 2011). During most forms of meditation, EEG activity is similar to that seen in a relaxed, eyes-closed, waking state (see Figure 4.3). Meditation is also associated with increases in dopamine (Kjaer et al., 2002), a neurotransmitter involved in the experience of reward or pleasure, and fMRI scans show that during meditation, activity increases in brain areas involved in concentrated attention (Brefczynski-Lewis et al., 2007; Hölzel et al., 2011). Neuroimaging studies have shown, too, that meditation is associated with increased connectivity among brain cells (Luders et al., 2011; Moyer et al., 2011).

© Masons News Service

Surgery under Hypnosis
Bernadine Coady, of Wimblington, England, has a condition that makes general anesthesia dangerous for her. In April 1999, she faced a foot operation that would have been extremely painful without anesthesia. She arranged for a hypnotherapist to help her through the procedure, but when he failed to show up, she was forced to rely on self-hypnosis as her only anesthetic. She said she imagined the pain as "waves lashing against a sea wall ... [and] going away, like the tide." Coady's report that the operation was painless is believable because, in December 2000, she had the same operation on her other foot, again using only self-hypnosis for pain control (Morris, 2000).

APPLYING PSYCHOLOGY

Some people claim that meditation improves their awareness and understanding of themselves and their environment. It has also been associated with better immune system functioning, reductions in high blood pressure, anxiety, and insomnia, longer survival among heart patients, and enhanced performance in everything from work to tennis (Dakwar & Levin, 2009; Davidson et al., 2003; Lee et al., 2009; MacLean et al., 2010; Oman, Hedberg, & Thoreson, 2006; Paul-Labrador et al., 2006; Vidrine et al., 2009; Zeidan et al., 2010). More generally, meditators' scores on personality tests indicate increases in overall mental health, happiness, self-esteem, and social openness (Hofmann, Grossman, & Hinton, 2011; Janowiak & Hackman, 1994; Sakairi, 1992; Tang et al., 2007). Exactly how meditation produces these benefits is unclear, though its activation of dopamine brain systems may tell an important part of the story. Whatever the mechanism, it is probably not unique to meditation. Many of the benefits associated with meditation have also been reported in association with other techniques, such as biofeedback, hypnosis, tai chi, or just relaxing (Bernstein et al., 2000; Beyerstein, 1999; Wang, Collet, & Lau, 2004).

●●●●

Psychoactive Drugs

How do drugs affect the brain?

The altered states we have discussed so far serve a biological need (sleep) or rely on the chemistry of the brain and body (hypnosis and meditation). Other altered states are brought on by outside agents, namely drugs. Every day most people in the world use drugs that alter brain activity and consciousness (Levinthal, 2001). For example, 80 to 90 percent of people in North America use caffeine, the stimulant found in coffee, tea, and many popular energy drinks. A *drug* is a chemical that is not required for normal physiological functioning yet has an effect on the body. You may say that you "need" a cup of coffee in the morning, but you'll still wake up without it; accordingly, the caffeine in coffee is defined as a drug. Drugs whose effects on the brain alter consciousness and other psychological processes are called **psychoactive drugs** (Julien, 2008). The study of psychoactive drugs is called **psychopharmacology.**

Psychopharmacology

Most psychoactive drugs affect the brain by altering the interactions between neurotransmitters and their receptors, as described in the chapter on biology and behavior. To create their effects, these drugs must cross the **blood-brain barrier,** a feature of blood vessels in the brain that prevents some substances from entering brain tissue (Urquhart & Kim, 2009). If a drug can pass this barrier, its psychoactive effects depend on several factors, such as with which neurotransmitter systems the drug interacts, how the drug affects those neurotransmitters and their receptors, and the psychological functions normally affected by the brain systems that use those neurotransmitters.

Drugs can affect neurotransmitters or their receptors through several mechanisms. As mentioned in the biology and behavior chapter, neurotransmitters fit into their own receptors (see Figure 4.8). Some drugs, such as morphine, are similar enough to a particular neurotransmitter to fool its receptors. These drugs, called **agonists,** bind to receptors and imitate, or mimic, the effects of the normal neurotransmitter. Other drugs, called **antagonists,** are similar enough to a neurotransmitter to occupy its receptors but cannot mimic its effects. When they bind to receptors, they prevent the normal

psychoactive drugs Chemical substances that act on the brain to create psychological effects.

psychopharmacology The study of psychoactive drugs and their effects.

blood-brain barrier A characteristic of blood vessels in the brain that prevents some substances from entering brain tissue.

agonists Drugs that bind to a receptor and mimic the effects of the neurotransmitter that normally fits that receptor.

antagonists Drugs that bind to a receptor and prevent the normal neurotransmitter from binding.

FIGURE 4.8
Agonists and Antagonists
In Part A, a molecule of neurotransmitter interacts with a receptor on a neuron's dendrite by fitting into and stimulating it. Part B shows a drug molecule acting as an agonist, affecting the receptor in the same way a neurotransmitter would. Part C depicts an antagonist drug molecule blocking a natural neurotransmitter from reaching and acting on the receptor.

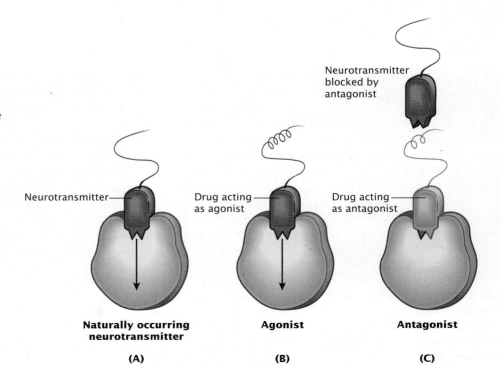

neurotransmitter from binding. Still other drugs work by increasing or decreasing the release of a specific neurotransmitter. Finally, some drugs work by speeding or slowing the *removal* of a neurotransmitter from synapses.

Predicting a psychoactive drug's effects on behavior is complicated. For one thing, most of these drugs interact with many neurotransmitter systems. Also, the nervous system may compensate for a given drug's effects. For instance, repeated exposure to a drug that blocks receptors for a certain neurotransmitter often leads to an increase in the number of receptors available to accept that neurotransmitter.

The Varying Effects of Drugs

The chemical properties that give drugs their medically desirable main effects, such as pain relief, often create undesirable side effects as well.

Drug Abuse   One side effect may be the potential for abuse. **Drug abuse** (sometimes called *substance abuse*) is a pattern of use that causes serious social, legal, or interpersonal problems for the user (American Psychiatric Association, 2000). Of course, as a culture changes, which drugs cause a person social and legal problems may also change, as Figure 4.9 illustrates.

Substance abuse can lead to psychological or physical dependence. People displaying *psychological dependence* on a drug will continue to use it even though it has harmful effects. They need the drug for a sense of well-being and become preoccupied with getting the drug if it is no longer available. However, they can still function without the drug. Psychological dependence can occur with or without addiction, also known as *physical dependence*. **Addiction** is a physiological state in which there is not only a strong craving for the drug but also in which using the drug becomes necessary to prevent the unpleasant experience of **drug withdrawal** (sometimes called a *withdrawal syndrome*). Withdrawal symptoms vary depending on the drug, but they often include an intense desire for the drug and physical effects generally opposite to those of the drug itself. Eventually, drug users may develop **drug tolerance,** a condition in which increasingly larger drug doses are required to produce the same effect. With the development of drug tolerance, many addicts need the drug just to prevent the negative effects of not taking it. However, most researchers believe that a craving for the positive effects of drugs is what keeps addicts coming back to them (Ciccocioppo, Martin-Fardon, & Weiss, 2004; Everitt & Robbins, 2005; George et al., 2001).

drug abuse (substance abuse) The use of psychoactive drugs in ways that deviate from cultural norms and cause serious problems for the user.

addiction Development of a physical need for a psychoactive drug.

drug withdrawal A set of symptoms associated with ending the use of an addictive substance.

drug tolerance A condition in which increasingly larger drug doses are needed to produce a given effect.

The William H. Helfand Collection/The New York Academy of Medicine

© Thinkstock

FIGURE 4.9
Changing Views of Drugs
The legal and social status of a drug can vary across cultures and over time (Weiss & Moore, 1990). For example, in the United States cocaine was once a respectable, commercially available drug; today it is illegal. And alcohol, which is legal in the United States and many other nations, is banned in countries such as Kuwait, Iran, and Saudi Arabia.

It may be tempting to think of "addicts" as being different from the rest of us, but we should never underestimate the ease with which drug dependence can develop in anyone, including ourselves. Physical dependence can develop gradually, without our awareness. In fact, scientists believe that the changes in the brain that underlie addiction may be similar to those that occur during learning (Koob & Kreek, 2007; Nestler, 2001; Ross & Peselow, 2009). All addictive drugs stimulate the brain's "pleasure centers," regions that are sensitive to the neurotransmitter dopamine. Activity of neurons in these areas creates intensely pleasurable feelings, including those associated with a good meal, "runner's high," gambling, or sex (Haber & Knutson, 2010; Reuter et al., 2005). When addictive drugs affect dopamine regulation in these "pleasure centers," they, too, produce tremendously rewarding effects in most people (Boyd, 2006; Cannon, 2005; Diana, 2011; Maldonado, Valverde, & Berrendero, 2006). In fact, the changes created in the brain by drug addiction can remain long after drug use ends (Diana, Spiqa, & Acquas, 2006), which is one reason that people who succeed in giving up addictive drugs may still be in danger of relapse months or even years later. The risk of relapse is also elevated because of epigenetic effects (see the chapter on introduction to the science of psychology); for some people, exposure to addictive drugs changes gene expression such that the pleasure a drug creates becomes more intense as use continues (Wong, Mill, & Fernandes, 2011).

Expectations and Drug Effects   Drug effects are not determined by biochemistry alone (Crombag & Robinson, 2004). The *expectations* we learn through experience with drugs and/or drug users also play a role (Pollo & Benedetti, 2009; Siegel, 2005). So just expecting to drink alcohol, for example, can create neural activity in the same brain areas that are affected by actually drinking it (Gundersen et al., 2008). Several experiments have shown that research participants who consume nonalcoholic drinks that they *think* contain alcohol are likely to behave in line with their expectations about alcohol's effects. So they tend to feel drunk and to become more aggressive, more interested in violent and sexual material, and more easily sexually aroused (Darkes & Goldman, 1993; George & Marlatt, 1986; Lang et al., 1975; Lansky & Wilson, 1981). And because they know that alcohol impairs memory, these participants are more vulnerable to developing false memories about a crime they witnessed on videotape (Assefi & Garry, 2003). The effects of expectancy are not limited to alcohol. Other research shows that people may feel and act "high" after smoking a cigarette that they believe contains marijuana, even though it doesn't (Metrik et al., 2009).

Expectations about drug effects develop in part as people watch other people, especially their parents, react to drugs (Cranford et al., 2010; Sher et al., 1996), and these expectations can influence how much of a drug they themselves consume. What they see can differ from one individual and culture to the next, so drug effects vary considerably throughout the world (Lin, Smith, & Ortiz, 2001; MacAndrew & Edgerton, 1969). In the United States, for example, drinking alcohol is commonly associated with uninhibited behavior, including impulsiveness, anger, violence, and sexual promiscuity. These effects are not seen in all cultures, however. In Bolivia's Camba culture, people sometimes engage in extended bouts of drinking a brew that is 89 percent alcohol (178 proof). During these binges, the Camba repeatedly pass out, wake up, and start drinking again—all the while maintaining friendly social relations.

In short, the effects of psychoactive drugs are complex and variable. Let's now consider several major categories of psychoactive drugs that people use primarily to produce altered states of consciousness. They include depressant drugs, stimulating drugs, opiates, and hallucinogenic drugs.

CNS Depressant Drugs

Drugs such as alcohol and barbiturates are called **CNS depressant drugs** because they reduce or depress activity in the central nervous system (CNS), mainly in the brain. They do so partly by increasing the effects of the neurotransmitter GABA. As described in the chapter on biology and behavior, GABA reduces the activity of neurons in various brain

CNS depressant drugs Psychoactive drugs that inhibit the functioning of the central nervous system.

circuits. So if a drug increases the amount of GABA available, activity in those circuits will be lower than usual, creating feelings of relaxation, drowsiness, and sometimes depression (Hanson & Venturelli, 1995).

Alcohol The most common CNS depressant drug by far is alcohol. In the United States, more than 100 million people drink it, and alcohol is equally popular worldwide (Leigh & Stacy, 2004; Swendsen et al., 2012). Alcohol affects several neurotransmitters, including glutamate, serotonin, and GABA (Daglish & Nutt, 2003; Enoch, 2003; Vinod et al., 2006). The effect on GABA is especially significant. In fact, animal studies show that the intoxicating effects of alcohol can be blocked by drugs that prevent it from interacting with GABA receptors (Suzdak et al., 1986).

Alcohol also enhances the effect of endorphins, the body's natural painkillers. The fact that endorphins produce a sense of well-being may explain why people initially feel "high" when drinking alcohol. It may also explain why drugs that block endorphins are better than placebos at reducing alcohol cravings and relapse rates in recovering alcoholics (Rösner et al., 2010). Alcohol's pleasurable effects are partly due to its interaction with the dopamine systems that are part of the brain's reward mechanisms (Morikawa & Morrisett, 2010). Prolonged alcohol use can have lasting effects on the brain's ability to regulate dopamine levels (Tiihonen et al., 1995). Dopamine agonists reduce alcohol cravings and the effects of alcohol withdrawal (Swift et al., 2010).

Alcohol affects specific brain regions. It depresses activity in the locus coeruleus, an area that, as described in our discussion of sleep, normally helps activate the cerebral cortex (Koob & Bloom, 1988). The resulting reduction in cortical activity, in turn, tends to cause cognitive changes and a loosening of control over normally inhibited behaviors (Casbon et al., 2003). Some drinkers begin talking loudly, acting silly, or telling others what they think of them. Emotional reactions range from giddy happiness to despair. Normally shy people may become impulsive or violent (Giancola & Corman, 2007). Alcohol also impairs the hippocampus, making it more difficult to process information and form new memories (Matsumoto & Matsumoto, 2008). The effects on the hippocampus may be permanent; brain-imaging studies have shown that the hippocampus is smaller in heavy drinkers than in nondrinkers (Beresford et al., 2006). Alcohol's suppression of the cerebellum causes poor motor coordination, including

Drinking and Driving Don't Mix
Though practice makes it seem easy, driving a car is a complex information processing task. As described in the chapter on thought, language, and intelligence, such tasks require constant vigilance, quick decisions, and skillful execution of responses. Alcohol can impair all these processes, as well as the ability to judge the degree of impairment—thus making drinking and driving a deadly combination that results in almost 11,000 deaths each year in the United States alone (National Highway Traffic Safety Administration, 2010).

© Luis Santana/Photos.com

difficulty in walking (Rogers et al., 1986). Excessive use can permanently damage the cerebellum (Manto, 2012). Alcohol's ability to depress hindbrain mechanisms required for breathing and heartbeat can make overdoses fatal.

As mentioned earlier, some effects of alcohol—such as anger and aggressiveness—depend on both biochemical factors and learned expectations (Goldman, Darkes, & Del Boca, 1999; Kushner et al., 2000). But other effects—especially disruptions in motor coordination, speech, and thought—result from biochemical factors alone. These biological effects depend on the amount of alcohol the blood carries to the brain. It takes the liver about an hour to break down one ounce of alcohol (the amount in one typical drink), so alcohol has milder effects if consumed slowly (Zakhari, 2006). Faster drinking or drinking on an empty stomach speeds absorption of alcohol into the blood and heightens its effects. Even after allowing for differences in average male and female body weight, researchers have found metabolic differences that make male bodies able to tolerate somewhat greater amounts of alcohol. So a given quantity of alcohol may have a stronger effect on a woman than on a man (York & Welte, 1994). Overindulgence by either sex results in unpleasant physical hangover effects that cannot be prevented or relieved by aspirin, bananas, vitamins, coffee, eggs, exercise, fresh air, honey, pizza, herbal remedies, more alcohol, or any of the dozens of other "surefire" hangover cures you may have heard about (Pittler, Verster, & Ernst, 2005).

Genetics also seems to play a role in determining the biochemical effects of alcohol (Edenberg, 2007; Scholz, Franz, & Heberlein, 2005). Evidence suggests that some people have a genetic predisposition toward alcohol dependence (Kimura & Higuchi, 2011), though the genes involved have not yet been identified. Other groups (the Japanese, for example) may have inherited metabolic characteristics that enhance the adverse effects of alcohol, possibly inhibiting the development of alcohol abuse (Iwahashi et al., 1995).

Barbiturates Sometimes called "downers" or sleeping pills, *barbiturates* are highly addictive. In small doses, their psychoactive effects include relaxation, mild pleasure, loss of muscle coordination, and reduced attention. Higher doses cause deep sleep, but continued use actually distorts sleep patterns (Zammit, 2007), so long-term use of barbiturates as sleeping pills may be unwise. Overdoses can be fatal. Withdrawal symptoms are among the most severe for any drug and can include intense agitation, violent outbursts, seizures, hallucinations, and even sudden death.

GHB *Gamma hydroxybutyrate (GHB)* is a naturally occurring substance similar to the neurotransmitter GABA (Drasbek, Christensen, & Jensen, 2006; Wong, Gibson, & Snead, 2004). As mentioned earlier, it is sometimes used by physicians in the treatment of narcolepsy. However, a laboratory-manufactured version of GHB (also known as "G") has become a popular "club drug" known for creating relaxation, feelings of elation, loss of inhibitions, and increased sex drive (Schuman-Oliver et al., 2011). Unfortunately, it can also cause nausea and vomiting, headaches, memory loss, dizziness, loss of muscle control or paralysis, breathing problems, loss of consciousness, and even death—especially when combined with alcohol or other drugs (Miotto et al., 2001; Stillwell, 2002). As with other CNS depressants, long-term use of GHB can lead to dependence (Carter et al., 2006). Dependent users who abruptly stop taking the drug may experience withdrawal symptoms that can include seizures, hallucinations, agitation, coma, or death (Van Noorden et al., 2009).

CNS Stimulating Drugs

Whereas depressants slow down central nervous system activity, **CNS stimulating drugs** speed it up. Amphetamines, cocaine, caffeine, and nicotine are all examples of CNS stimulating drugs.

Amphetamines Often called "uppers" or "speed," *amphetamines* increase the release of norepinephrine and dopamine into synapses, affecting sleep, learning, and mood (Bonci et al., 2003; Kolb et al., 2003). Amphetamines also slow the removal of both substances at synapses, leaving more of them there, ready to work. The increased activity at these

CNS stimulating drugs Psychoactive drugs that increase behavioral and mental activity.

© PA Photos/Landov

Deadly Drug Use

Singer Whitney Houston's death in 2012 was due in part to her chronic use of cocaine. She joined a long list of celebrities (including Amy Winehouse, Chris Farley, and Righteous Brother Bobby Hatfield) and an even longer list of ordinary people whose lives have been destroyed by the abuse of alcohol, cocaine, or other addictive drugs.

neurotransmitters' receptors results in alertness, arousal, and appetite suppression. These effects are amplified by the fact that amphetamines also reduce activity of the inhibitory neurotransmitter GABA (Vlachou & Markou, 2010). Amphetamines' rewarding properties are probably associated with their effect on dopamine activity, because taking dopamine antagonists reduces amphetamine use (Higley et al., 2011).

People who abuse amphetamines usually begin taking these drugs in an effort to lose weight, stay awake, or "get high." Repeated use leads to anxiety, insomnia, heart problems, brain damage, movement disorders, confusion, paranoia, nonstop talking, and psychological and physical dependence (Rusyniak, 2011). In some cases, the symptoms of amphetamine abuse are almost identical to those of paranoid schizophrenia (Salo, Ravizza, & Fassbender, 2011), a serious mental disorder linked to dopamine malfunction.

Cocaine   Like amphetamines, *cocaine* increases norepinephrine and dopamine activity and decreases GABA activity, so it produces many amphetamine-like effects (Ciccarone, 2011; Vlachou & Markou, 2010). Cocaine's particularly powerful and rapid effect on dopamine activity may underlie its remarkably addictive nature (Wise & Kiyatkin, 2011). In fact, most drugs with rapid onset and short duration are more addictive than others (Kato, Wakasa, & Yamagita, 1987), which helps explain why *crack*—a purified, fast-acting, highly potent, smokable form of cocaine—is especially addictive (Falck, Wang, & Carlson, 2007). In the United States, about 5.3 million people over the age of 12 have used cocaine and about 1.1 million have used crack at least once in the last year (Substance Abuse and Mental Health Services Administration, 2009).

Cocaine stimulates self-confidence, a sense of well-being, and optimism. Continued use, though, brings nausea, overactivity, insomnia, paranoia, a sudden depressive "crash," hallucinations, sexual dysfunction, and seizures (Lacayo, 1995). Overdoses, especially overdoses of crack cocaine, can be deadly. Even small doses can cause a fatal heart attack or stroke (Maraj, Figueredo, & Lynn, 2010). Using cocaine during pregnancy harms the fetus (e.g., Hurt et al., 1995) and is associated with lasting cognitive and behavioral problems for the child (Salisbury et al., 2009). However, many of the severe, long-term behavioral problems seen in "cocaine babies" may have as much to do with poverty and neglect after birth as with the mother's cocaine use beforehand (Ackerman, Riggins, & Black, 2010). Early intervention can reduce the effects of both cocaine and the hostile environment that confronts most cocaine babies (Mayes et al., 2003; Singer et al., 2004).

Caffeine   *Caffeine* may be the world's most popular drug. It is found in chocolate, in many soft drinks, in tea and in coffee, which is consumed in greater quantities worldwide than any other beverage except water (Butt & Sultan, 2011). A typical cup of coffee has 58 to 259 mg of caffeine, and even "decaffeinated" coffee may contain up to 15.8 mg (McCusker, Goldberger, & Cone, 2003; McCusker et al., 2006). Energy drinks have up to 505 mg per can (Reissig, Strain, & Griffiths, 2011). Caffeine reduces drowsiness, can enhance cognitive performance, including problem solving and vigilance (Snel & Lorist, 2011), increases the capacity for physical work, and raises urine production (Warburton, 1995). At high doses it causes anxiety and tremors. People can develop tolerance to caffeine, and it can be physically addictive (Ogawa & Ueki, 2007; Strain et al., 1994). Withdrawal symptoms—including headache, fatigue, anxiety, shakiness, and craving—appear on the first day of abstinence and last about a week (Silverman et al., 1992). Caffeine may make it harder for women to become pregnant, and it can affect the embryos of coffee or tea drinkers who do become pregnant (Al-Saleh et al., 2010). So heavy caffeine use may increase the risk of miscarriage, stillbirth, or having a low-birthweight baby (Kuczkowski, 2009). Moderate daily use may cause slight increases in blood pressure (Geleijnse, 2008), but otherwise it appears to have few, if any, negative effects (Kleemola et al., 2000; Lopez-Garcia et al., 2008; Winkelmayer et al., 2005). There is even some evidence that caffeine consumption may be associated with a decreased risk of developing Alzheimer's disease (Marques et al., 2011).

Nicotine   A powerful autonomic nervous system stimulant, *nicotine* is the main psychoactive ingredient in tobacco. It enhances the action of acetylcholine (Penton &

Lester, 2009) and increases the availability of glutamate, the brain's primary excitatory neurotransmitter (Liechti & Markou, 2008). It also activates the brain's dopamine-related pleasure systems (Balfour, 2002; McGehee et al., 1995). Nicotine has many psychoactive effects, including elevated mood and improved memory and attention (Domino, 2003; Ernst et al., 2001).

Like heroin and cocaine, nicotine can be physically addictive (White, 1998), and teenagers who smoke cigarettes are much more likely to go on to use illegal addictive drugs (Mayet et al., 2011). Nicotine doesn't create the "rush" characteristic of many drugs of abuse, but quitting smoking usually causes withdrawal symptoms, including craving, irritability, anxiety, reduced heart rate, and lower activity in the brain's reward pathways (Epping-Jordan et al., 1998; Hughes, Higgins, & Bickel, 1994). Nicotine withdrawal also impairs activity in brain regions involved in complex thinking tasks, which may explain the cognitive dysfunctions some people experience when they stop smoking (Froeliger et al., 2011).

Some people are more vulnerable to nicotine addiction than others (Hiroi & Scott, 2009). The tendency to become physically dependent on nicotine appears to be at least partly inherited (Russo et al., 2011), so some smokers appear to develop only a psychological dependence on nicotine (Robinson & Pritchard, 1995). In either case, there is no doubt that smoking tobacco can be a difficult habit to break (Crane, 2007). Quitting is worthwhile, though: Although smoking is a major risk factor for death from cancer, heart disease, and respiratory disorders, smokers who quit before the age of 35 have long term mortality rates similar to those who never smoked (Centers for Disease Control and Prevention, 2008, 2011a).

MDMA The stimulant "ecstasy," or *MDMA* (short for methylenedioxymetham-phetamine), is a popular drug on college campuses in the United States (Strote, Lee, & Wechsler, 2002). MDMA acts on dopamine pathways in the brain (Schenk, Gittings, & Colussi-Mas, 2011), so it leads to some of the same effects as those produced by cocaine and amphetamines (Steele, McCann, & Ricaurte, 1994). These include a sense of well-being, increased sex drive, and a feeling of greater closeness to others. Unfortunately, MDMA may also cause dry mouth, hyperactivity, jaw muscle spasms that may result in "lockjaw," elevated blood pressure, fever, dangerously abnormal heart rhythms, and visual hallucinations (Baylen & Rosenberg, 2006). The hallucinations may appear because MDMA is a serotonin agonist that also increases serotonin release (Green, Cross, & Goodwin, 1995). On the day after using MDMA—also known as "XTC," "clarity," "essence," "E," and "Adam"—people often report muscle aches, fatigue, depression, and poor concentration.

Even though it does not appear to be physically addictive, MDMA is a dangerous, potentially deadly drug, especially when taken by women (Liechti, Gamma, & Vollenweider, 2001; National Institute on Drug Abuse, 2000). It permanently damages the brain (Sarkar & Schmued, 2010), killing serotonin-sensitive neurons as well as neurons that use dopamine. As you might expect, the danger of brain damage increases with higher doses and continued use. MDMA also impairs memory (Reneman et al., 2001; Rodgers, 2000; Zakzanis & Young, 2001), and users may develop the symptoms of panic disorder, which include intense anxiety and a sense of impending death (see the chapter on psychological disorders). When given to pregnant animals, MDMA produces permanent behavioral changes in their offspring (Thompson et al., 2009). Research on humans and nonhumans indicates that many of the MDMA's effects remain even after its use is discontinued (Kalechstein et al., 2007; Smith, Tivarus, et al., 2006).

Opiates

The **opiates** (opium, morphine, heroin, and codeine) are unique in their capacity for inducing sleep and relieving pain (Julien, 2008). *Opium,* which comes from the poppy plant, relieves pain, and creates feelings of euphoria and relaxation (Cowan et al., 2001). One of its most active ingredients, *morphine,* was first isolated in the early 1800s. It is used worldwide for pain relief. Percodan and Demerol are some common morphine-like drugs. *Heroin* is made from morphine but is three times more powerful, causing intensely pleasurable reactions. Opiates have complex effects on consciousness (Gruber, Silveri, & Yurgelun-Todd, 2007). Drowsy, cloudy feelings occur because opiates depress activity

opiates Psychoactive drugs that produce both sleep-inducing and pain-relieving effects.

in some areas of the cerebral cortex. They also create excitation in other parts, causing some users to experience euphoria, or elation (Bozarth & Wise, 1984). Opiates exert many of their effects by stimulating the receptors normally stimulated by endorphins, the body's own painkillers. This action "tricks" the brain into an exaggerated activation of its painkilling and mood-altering systems (Julien, 2008).

Opiates are highly addictive, largely because of their actions on the dopamine reward system but also partly because they affect both glutamate and GABA receptors in a way that changes how nerve cells communicate with each other (Dacher & Nugent, 2011). It may be, then, that opiates alter neurons so that they come to require the drug (Christie, 2008). Beyond the hazard of addiction itself, heroin addicts risk death through overdoses, contaminated drugs, or AIDS contracted through sharing needles (Hser et al., 2001).

Hallucinogenic Drugs

Hallucinogenic drugs, also called *psychedelic drugs,* create a loss of contact with reality and alter other aspects of emotion, perception, and thought. They can cause distortions in body image (the user may feel gigantic or tiny), loss of identity (confusion about who one actually is), dreamlike fantasies, and hallucinations. Because these effects resemble many severe forms of mental disorder, hallucinogenic drugs are also called *psychotomimetics* ("mimicking psychosis").

LSD   One of the most powerful hallucinogenic drugs is *lysergic acid diethylamide,* or *LSD.* It was first synthesized from a rye fungus by Swiss chemist Albert Hofmann. In 1938, after Hofmann accidentally ingested a tiny amount of the substance, he discovered the drug's strange effects in the world's first LSD "trip" (Julien, 2008). LSD hallucinations can be quite bizarre. Time may seem distorted, sounds may cause visual sensations, and users may feel as if they have left their bodies. LSD's hallucinatory effects have been attributed partly to its ability to stimulate a specific type of serotonin receptor in the forebrain (Halberstadt & Geyer, 2011). This is supported by evidence that serotonin antagonists greatly reduce LSD's hallucinatory effects (Passie et al, 2008). LSD also stimulates a subtype of dopamine receptors whose activation leads to hallucinations and delusions (Minuzzi et al., 2005).

The effects of LSD on a particular person are unpredictable. Unpleasant hallucinations and delusions can occur during a person's first—or two hundredth—LSD experience. Although LSD is not addictive, tolerance to its effects does develop. Some users suffer lasting side effects, including severe short-term memory loss, paranoia, violent outbursts, nightmares, and panic attacks (Gold, 1994). Distortions in visual sensations can remain for years after heavy use has ended (Iaria et al., 2010). Sometimes "flashbacks" can occur, in which a person suddenly returns to an LSD-like state of consciousness weeks or even years after using the drug.

Ketamine   *Ketamine* is an anesthetic used by veterinarians to ease pain in animals (Hirota, 2006; Robakis & Hirsch, 2006), but because it also has hallucinogenic effects, it is being stolen and sold as a recreational drug known as "Special K." Its effects include dissociative feelings that create what some users describe as an "out-of-body" or "near-death" experience. Ketamine intoxication can create thought problems similar to those seen in schizophrenia (Neill et al., 2011), and long-term use causes lasting memory impairments (Venâncio et al., 2011), probably because the drug damages memory-related brain structures such as the hippocampus (Jevtovic-Todorovic et al., 2001).

Marijuana   A mixture of crushed leaves, flowers, and stems from the hemp plant (*Cannabis sativa*) makes up *marijuana.* The active ingredient is *tetrahydrocannabinol,* or *THC* (Fisar, 2009). When inhaled, THC is absorbed in minutes by many organs, including the brain (Martin-Santos et al., 2010), and it continues to affect consciousness for a few hours (O'Leary et al., 2002). THC tends to collect in fatty deposits of the brain and reproductive organs, where it can remain for weeks. Low doses of marijuana may initially create restlessness and hilarity, followed by a dreamy, carefree relaxation, an

© Stockbyte/Thinkstock

Another Drug Danger
Oxycodone, a morphine-like drug prescribed by doctors under the label OxyContin, has become popular among recreational substance abusers. It was designed as a timed-release painkiller, but when people crush OxyContin tablets and then inject or inhale the drug, they get a much stronger and potentially lethal dose, especially when they are also using other drugs such as alcohol or cocaine (Cone et al., 2004). Deaths from OxyContin abuse have been on the rise in the United States in recent years (Centers for Disease Control and Prevention, 2011b).

hallucinogenic drugs Psychoactive drugs that alter consciousness by producing a temporary loss of contact with reality and changes in emotion, perception, and thought.

expanded sense of space and time, more vivid sensations, food cravings, and subtle changes in thinking (Kelly et al., 1990).

There is an ongoing debate about the dangers and potential benefits of marijuana. Proponents note that, unlike tobacco, marijuana does not harm lung functions (Sidney, Feng, & Kertesz, 2011). Its dangers are suggested by the fact that a mild withdrawal syndrome has been reported in rats; in humans, withdrawal from marijuana may be accompanied by increases in anxiety, depression, irritability, restlessness, and aggressiveness (Allsop et al., 2011; Levin et al., 2010). Further, marijuana interacts with the same dopamine and opiate receptors as heroin (Lopez-Moreno et al., 2008; Lynskey et al., 2003; Spano et al., 2007), leading some researchers to speculate that, like tobacco, marijuana might be a "gateway" to the use of more addictive drugs (Mayet et al., 2012). Other researchers caution that the interpretation of these results is not clear cut, because even though the rewarding effects of sex and chocolate occur by activating these same receptors, those pleasures are not generally viewed as gateways to drug addiction.

Regardless of whether marijuana is addicting or leads to the use of opiates, it can create a number of problems, including in the cardiovascular and immune systems (Hall & Degenhardt, 2009; Jayanthi et al., 2010; McHale & Hunt, 2008; Pope et al., 2001). Marijuana also disrupts memory formation, making it difficult to carry out mental or physical tasks and, despite users' impressions, it actually reduces creativity (Bourassa & Vaugeois, 2001; Pope & Yurgelun-Todd, 1996). Because marijuana disrupts muscle coordination, driving while under its influence can be dangerous (Asbridge, Hayden, & Cartwright, 2012; Hall & Degenhardt, 2009). In fact, motor impairment continues well after the subjective effects of the drug have worn off. Marijuana easily reaches a developing fetus and therefore should not be used by pregnant women (Fried, Watkinson, & Gray, 1992; Spano et al., 2007); a woman's use of marijuana during pregnancy has been associated with behavioral problems in her offspring (Day, Leech, & Goldschmidt, 2011). Finally, long-term use can lead to psychological dependence (Stephens, Roffman, & Simpson, 1994) as well as to impairments in reasoning and memory that last for months or years after marijuana use stops (Bolla et al., 2002; Crean, Crane, & Mason, 2011; Solowij et al., 2002). These effects are especially strong in people who start using marijauna before the age of 15 (Fontes et al., 2011). Research has also shown that adults who frequently used marijuana scored lower than nonusers with equal IQs on a twelfth-grade academic achievement test (Block & Ghoneim, 1993). Heavy use by teenagers has been associated with smaller than normal volume in brain areas involved in emotion and memory as well as with the later appearance of anxiety, depression, and other even more serious symptoms of mental disorder (Moore et al., 2007; Patton et al., 2002; Yücel et al., 2008; Zammit et al., 2002).

Marijuana may have considerable value in some domains, however. Doctors have successfully used it in the treatment of asthma, glaucoma, epilepsy, chronic pain, and nausea from cancer chemotherapy; it may even help in treating some types of cancer (Abrams et al., 2007; Bowles et al., 2011; Gorter et al., 2005; Leung, 2011; Parolaro et al., 2002; Rog et al., 2005; Tramer et al., 2001). But critics say medical legalization of marijuana is premature until more controlled research is available to establish its medicinal value. They point out, too, that even though patients tend to prefer marijuana-based drugs, other medications may be equally effective and less dangerous (e.g., Campbell et al., 2001; Fox et al., 2004; Hall & Degenhardt, 2003). Nevertheless, in Canada, it is legal to grow and use marijuana for medicinal purposes, and the same is true in seventeen U.S. states and the District of Columbia, despite federal laws to the contrary and the threat of federal intervention to enforce those laws. The American Medical Association has rejected the idea of medical uses for marijuana, but scientists are intent on objectively studying its potential value in the treatment of certain diseases as well as its possible dangers. Their work is being encouraged by the National Institute of Medicine (Joy, Watson, & Benson, 1999), and drug companies are working on new cannabis-based medicines (Altman, 2000; Tuller, 2004). The United Nations, too, has recommended that governments worldwide sponsor additional work on the medical uses of marijuana (Wren, 1999).

Further complicating the scientific and legal controversy surrounding marijuana is the recent emergence of several forms of "legal pot." These synthetic substances, such as "spice" and "K2," are being marketed as marijuana alternatives, and because their chemical makeup differs from the THC molecules they mimic, they are not yet illegal (Drug Enforcement Administration, 2010). Nevertheless, these compounds and their effects are not well understood, and so potential new dangers arise for users each time a new one is synthesized.

("In Review: Major Classes of Psychoactive Drugs" summarizes our discussion of these substances.)

Major Classes of Psychoactive Drugs — IN REVIEW

Drug	Trade/Street Name	Main Effects	Potential for Physical/Psychological Dependence
CNS Depressant Drugs			
Alcohol	"booze"	Relaxation, anxiety reduction, sleep	High/high
Barbiturates	Seconal, Tuinal, Nembutal ("downers")	Relaxation, anxiety reduction, sleep	High/high
GHB	"G," "jib," "scoop," "GH buddy"	Relaxation, euphoria	High/high
CNS Stimulating Drugs			
Amphetamines	Benzedrine, Dexedrine, Methadrine ("speed," "uppers," "ice")	Alertness, euphoria	Moderate/high
Cocaine	"coke," "crack"	Alertness, euphoria	Moderate to high/high
Caffeine		Alertness	Moderate/moderate
Nicotine	"smokes," "coffin nails"	Alertness	High (?)/high
MDMA	"ecstasy," "clarity"	Hallucinations	Low/(?)
Opiates			
Opium		Euphoria	High/high
Morphine	Percodan, Demerol	Euphoria, pain control	High/high
Heroin	"junk," "smack"	Euphoria, pain control	High/high
Hallucinogenic Drugs			
LSD/ketamine	"acid"/"special K"	Altered perceptions, hallucinations	Low/low
Marijuana (cannabis)	"pot," "dope," "reefer," "weed"	Euphoria, relaxation	Low/moderate

IN REVIEW QUESTIONS

1. Physical dependence on a drug is a condition more commonly known as ___ .
2. Drugs that act as antagonists ___ the interaction of neurotransmitters and receptors.
3. Drug effects are determined partly by what we learn to ___ the effects to be.

Active Review

As noted in the introductory chapter, all of psychology's subfields are related to one another. Our discussion of meditation, health, and stress illustrates just one way that the topic of this chapter, consciousness, is linked to the subfield of health psychology, which is described in the chapter on health, stress, and

CHAPTER 4
Consciousness

coping. The Linkages diagram shows ties to two other subfields, and there are many more ties throughout the book. Looking for linkages among subfields will help you see how they all fit together and help you better appreciate the big picture that is psychology.

LINKAGES

Do forgotten memories remain in consciousness? *(ans. on p. 233)*

Does meditation relieve stress? *(ans. on p. 152)*

Can subconscious processes alter our reaction to people? *(ans. on p. 555)*

CHAPTER 6
Memory

CHAPTER 10
Health, Stress, and Coping

CHAPTER 14
Social Psychology

Summary

Consciousness can be defined as awareness of the outside world and of one's own thoughts, feelings, perceptions, and other mental processes.

The Scope of Consciousness

Can unconscious thoughts affect your behavior?

A person's ***consciousness state*** is constantly changing. When the changes are particularly noticeable, they are called ***altered states of consciousness***. Examples of altered states include sleep, hypnosis, meditation, and some drug-induced conditions. Cultures differ in the value they place on particular states of consciousness.

Differing levels of consciousness are described as variations in awareness of your own mental functions. The

preconscious level includes mental activities that are outside awareness but that can easily be brought to the ***conscious level***. ***Subconscious*** and ***unconscious*** mental activity is said to involve thoughts, memories, and processes that are more difficult to bring to awareness. Mental processes that cannot be brought into awareness are said to occur at the ***nonconscious level***.

Awareness is not always required for mental operations. For example, research on priming shows that people's responses to stimuli speed up and improve as stimuli are repeated, even when there

is no conscious memory of which stimuli are old and which are new. And some decisions that seem intuitive may be guided by information that is outside of awareness.

Sleeping and Dreaming

Does your brain go to sleep when you do?

Sleep is an active and complex state. Different stages of sleep are defined on the basis of changes in brain activity (as measured by an electroencephalograph, or EEG) and physiological arousal.

Sleep normally begins with stage N1 sleep and progresses gradually through stage N2 to stage N3 sleep. The deepest stage of this ***NREM (non-rapid eye movement)*** sleep is also called slow-wave sleep.

After passing back to stage N2, people enter **REM (rapid eye movement) sleep,** or paradoxical sleep. The sleeper passes through these stages several times each night, gradually spending more time in stage N2 and REM sleep later in the night.

Sleep disorders can disrupt the natural rhythm of sleep. Among the most common is **insomnia,** a condition in which one has trouble falling asleep or staying asleep. **Narcolepsy** produces sudden daytime sleeping episodes. In cases of **sleep apnea,** people briefly but repeatedly stop breathing during sleep. **Sudden infant death syndrome (SIDS)** may be due to brain abnormalities or accidental suffocation. **Sleepwalking** happens most frequently during childhood. **Nightmares** and **sleep terror disorder (night terrors)** involve different kinds of frightening dreams. **REM behavior disorder** is potentially dangerous because it allows people to act out REM dreams. The cycle of waking and sleeping is a natural **circadian rhythm** or **human biological rhythm,** controlled by the suprachiasmatic nuclei of the brain. **Jet lag** can be one result of disrupting the normal sleep-wake cycle.

The purpose of sleep is still unclear. NREM sleep may aid bodily rest and repair. REM sleep may help maintain activity in brain areas that provide daytime alertness or it may allow the brain to "check circuits," eliminate useless information, and solidify learning from the previous day. **Sleep deprivation** leads to fatigue, irritability, and inattention and is a major factor in poor decision-making, learning and memory difficulties, and traffic accidents.

Dreaming is the production of story-like sequences of images, sensations, and perceptions that occur during sleep. Most dreams occur during REM sleep. Evidence from research on **lucid dreaming** suggests that people may be able to control their own dreams. Some claim that dreams are the meaningless by-products of brain activity, but our recall of dreams may still have psychological significance.

Hypnosis

Can you be hypnotized against your will?

Hypnosis is a well-known but still poorly understood phenomenon. Tests of **hypnotic susceptibility** suggest that some people cannot be hypnotized and that others are hypnotized easily. Hypnotized people tend to focus attention on the hypnotist and passively follow instructions. They become better at fantasizing and role taking. They may exhibit apparent age regression, experience posthypnotic amnesia, and obey posthypnotic suggestions.

State theories of hypnosis see hypnosis as a special state of consciousness. **Nonstate theories of hypnosis** such as role theory suggest that hypnosis creates a special social role that frees people to act in unusual ways. *Dissociation theory* combines aspects of role and state theories, suggesting that hypnotized individuals enter into a social contract with the hypnotist to allow normally integrated mental processes to become dissociated and to share control over these processes.

Hypnosis is useful in the control of pain and the reduction of nausea associated with cancer chemotherapy. Meditation is a set of techniques designed to create an altered state of consciousness characterized by inner peace and increased awareness. The consistent practice of meditation has been associated with reductions in stress-related problems such as anxiety and high blood pressure.

Psychoactive Drugs

How do drugs affect the brain?

Psychoactive drugs affect the brain, changing consciousness and other psychological processes. **Psychopharmacology** is the field that studies drug effects and their mechanisms. Psychoactive drugs exert their effects primarily by influencing specific neurotransmitter systems and hence certain brain activities. To reach brain tissue, drugs must cross the **blood-brain barrier.** Drugs that mimic the receptor effects of a neurotransmitter are called **agonists**; drugs that block the receptor effects of a neurotransmitter are called **antagonists**. Some drugs alter the release or removal of specific neurotransmitters, thus affecting the amount of neurotransmitter available for receptor effects.

Adverse effects such as **drug abuse** often accompany the use of psychoactive drugs. Psychological dependence, **addiction** (physical dependence), **drug tolerance,** and symptoms of **drug withdrawal** (withdrawal syndrome) may result. Drugs that produce dependence share the property of directly stimulating certain dopamine-sensitive areas of the brain known as pleasure centers. The consequences of using a psychoactive drug depend both on how the drug affects neurotransmitters and on the user's expectations.

Alcohol and barbiturates are examples of **CNS depressant drugs.** They reduce activity in the central nervous system, often by enhancing the action of inhibitory neurotransmitters. They have considerable potential for producing both psychological and physical dependence.

CNS stimulating drugs, such as amphetamines and cocaine, increase behavioral and mental activity mainly by increasing the action of dopamine and norepinephrine. These drugs can produce both psychological and physical dependence. Caffeine, one of the world's most popular stimulants, may also create dependence. Nicotine is a potent stimulant. And MDMA, which has both stimulant and hallucinogenic properties, is one of several psychoactive drugs that can permanently damage brain tissue.

Opiates such as opium, morphine, and heroin are highly addictive drugs that induce sleep and relieve pain.

LSD and marijuana are examples of **hallucinogenic drugs,** or psychedelic drugs. They alter consciousness by producing a temporary loss of contact with reality and changes in emotion, perception, and thought.

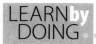

Put It in Writing
Watch a prime-time television program and make notes on the role played in the story by alcohol, nicotine, cocaine, or other psychoactive drugs. Think about what you saw and write a one-page paper describing the messages the show gave viewers about drugs. Did it directly or indirectly approve or disapprove of drug use? Did it lead viewers to expect particular effects from particular drugs? Conclude by considering what effects these drug-related messages might have on viewers, especially young children.

Personal Learning Activity
For the next two weeks, keep a notepad or voice recorder by your bed and write down or record your dreams as soon as you awaken. During this same period, use a diary or calendar to jot down significant events, problems, and emotional reactions in your waking life. Then compare the two sets of information. Do you see any correlation? For example, did any of your life events appear in your dreams? Did any dreams contain wished-for solutions to the problems or challenges you were facing at the time? What do you think your own data might say about the meaning of dreams in general?

Review of Key Terms

Can you define each of the key terms in the chapter? Check your definitions against those on the pages shown in parentheses in the following list or in the Glossary at the end of the book.

addiction (p. 154)
agonists (p. 153)
altered state of consciousness (p. 140)
antagonists (p. 153)
blood-brain barrier (p. 153)
circadian rhythm (human biological rhythm) (p. 145)
CNS depressant drugs (p. 155)
CNS stimulating drugs (p. 157)
conscious level (p. 135)
consciousness (p. 134)

consciousness state (p. 134)
dreaming (p. 148)
drug abuse (substance abuse) (p. 154)
drug tolerance (p. 154)
drug withdrawal (p. 154)
hallucinogenic drugs (p. 160)
hypnosis (p. 149)
hypnotic susceptibility (p. 150)
insomnia (p. 142)
jet lag (p. 145)
lucid dreaming (p. 149)
narcolepsy (p. 143)
nightmares (p. 144)
nonconcious level (p. 135)
nonstate theories of hypnosis (p. 151)
NREM (non-rapid eye movement) sleep (p. 142)

opiates (p. 159)
preconcious level (p. 135)
psychoactive drugs (p. 153)
psychopharmacology (p. 153)
REM behavior disorder (p. 144)
REM (rapid eye movement) sleep (p. 142)
sleep apnea (p. 143)
sleep deprivation (p. 147)
sleep terror disorder (night terrors) (p. 144)
sleepwalking (p. 144)
state theories of hypnosis (p. 150)
subconscious (p. 135)
sudden infant death syndrome (SIDS) (p. 143)
unconscious (p. 135)

Test Your Knowledge

Select the best answer for each of the following questions. Then check your responses against the Answer Key at the end of the book.

1. Tyrrell is undergoing biofeedback training to help him regulate his blood pressure, a bodily function typically regulated at which level of consciousness?
   a. Nonconscious
   b. Preconscious
   c. Subconscious
   d. Unconscious

2. Dr. Eplort is staying in a cave for several months with no external light cues and no way to keep time. He goes to sleep when he feels sleepy and gets up when he is awake. Dr. Eplort will most likely sleep ___.
   a. fewer hours than he did before
   b. more hours than he did before
   c. about the same as he did before
   d. on a varying and unpredictable schedule

3. Zandra knew nothing about art, and during her first semester on campus she had not noticed the framed Rembrandt prints in the hallway of her classroom building. But when she took an art appreciation class the next semester, she found that the paintings she liked best were those same Rembrandt images. Her preference was most likely affected by ___.
   a. the prosopagnosia effect
   b. supraliminal perception
   c. priming
   d. visual masking

4. Edie has purchased a tape that contains subliminal messages designed to help her lose weight. According to the Thinking Critically section in this chapter, Edie's success in losing weight most likely depends on ___.
   a. the content of the subliminal messages
   b. her expectation that the subliminal messages will help
   c. how relaxed the subliminal messages make her feel
   d. the number of times the subliminal messages occur

5. Mitch noticed that after his friends smoked marijuana, they soon began giggling, acting silly, and singing "We're Off to See the Wizard." After he smoked marijuana himself for the first time, he found himself doing the very same things. Mitch's specific responses to marijuana were most likely due to ___.
   a. an altered state of consciousness
   b. reversion to a preconscious state
   c. priming
   d. learned expectations

6. The telephone rang several hours after Leroy fell asleep. It takes Leroy a while to locate the phone, and he is so groggy when he answers that in the morning, he can't remember who called or what was said. When the phone rang, Leroy was most likely in ___ sleep.
   a. stage N1
   b. stage N2
   c. stage N3
   d. REM

7. Alan's wife is concerned because he often gets out of bed during the night and acts out his dreams. One night he boxed with an invisible opponent, and last night he was fighting a phantom bull. Alan most likely would be diagnosed as having ___.
   a. sleep apnea
   b. narcolepsy
   c. REM behavior disorder
   d. sleep terror disorder

8. The "back to sleep" program, which advises parents to have their babies sleep face up, has greatly reduced the incidence of ___ in the United States.
   a. SIDS
   b. sleep terror disorder
   c. REM behavior disorder
   d. insomnia

9. Dr. Franklin was flying from Los Angeles to Paris, where he was to give a speech shortly after arrival. To minimize the effects of jet lag, his physician would most likely recommend that Dr. Franklin should ___.
   a. be sure to sleep eight hours a night for at least a week before his trip
   b. take melatonin
   c. stay awake for 24 hours before departure, then sleep throughout the flight
   d. reverse his sleep-wake cycle for a week before departure

10. Sleep research suggests that REM sleep may be important for all of the following *except* ___.
   a. improving the functioning of neurons that use norepinephrine
   b. developing, checking, and expanding the brain's nerve connections
   c. restoring the body's and brain's energy stores for the next day's activity
   d. establishing memories of emotional information

11. According to the activation-synthesis theory, dreams ___.
   a. help our brains analyze and consolidate information
   b. satisfy unconscious urges and resolve unconscious conflicts
   c. are hallucinations
   d. are meaningless, random byproducts of REM sleep

12. Lavonne, a hypnotist, wanted to present a dramatic demonstration of hypnosis. Which of the following people should she select as her hypnotic subject?
   a. Alex, who is easily distracted.
   b. Bobbi, who doesn't believe in hypnosis.
   c. Carl, who is good at focusing his attention.
   d. Dellena, whose imagination is limited.

13. Hypnosis has been especially effective in ___.
   a. connecting with past lives
   b. improving memory
   c. pain control
   d. lowering cholesterol

14. Norman has been meditating for over a year. By now, according to this chapter, we would expect Norman to ___.
   a. be less anxious
   b. need less sleep to feel refreshed
   c. have a better memory
   d. daydream more

15. Candice was given morphine to ease the pain of back surgery. Her doctor explained that morphine occupies the same receptors and has the same effect as endorphins, the body's natural painkillers. In other words, morphine is an endorphin ___.
   a. agonist
   b. antagonist
   c. reuptake blocker
   d. placebo

16. Vincent has been using heroin for some time, and now he finds that he needs larger amounts of the drug to achieve the same effect he used to get from smaller doses. Vincent is experiencing ___.
   a. drug tolerance
   b. learned expectations
   c. withdrawal
   d. synaptic potential

17. Which of the following is true about alcohol?
   a. A given amount of alcohol will affect a man more than a woman.
   b. Alcohol's effects are the same whether it is consumed slowly or quickly.
   c. There are no genetic predispositions toward alcohol abuse.
   d. Dopamine agonists reduce alcohol cravings.

18. A young man experiencing hallucinations is brought to a hospital emergency room. Which of the following drugs could his doctor rule out as a likely cause of the hallucinations?
    a. MDMA
    b. Cocaine
    c. Caffeine
    d. LSD
19. Abel took a drug to reduce the pain in his broken arm. The drug Abel took to reduce his pain would be classified as a(n) ____.
    a. depressant
    b. opiate
    c. hallucinogen
    d. stimulant

20. Yeh is doing research for a term paper about legalizing the use of marijuana in the United States. If her research is accurate, she is likely to learn all of the following *except* which one?
    a. Marijuana has been used successfully in treating asthma, glaucoma, chronic pain, and nausea from chemotherapy.
    b. Marijuana increases memory function and creativity.
    c. It is legal to grow and use marijuana for medicinal purposes in Canada.
    d. Doctors have found that marijuana may help treat some types of cancer.

Media Resources

Now that you have finished reading this chapter, how about exploring some of the ideas and information that you found most interesting?

Coursemate Go to **CengageBrain.com** to access Psychology CourseMate, where you will find an interactive eBook, glossaries, flashcards, quizzes, videos, Virtual Psychology Labs, and more.

aplia

Aplia If your professor has assigned Aplia:
1. Sign in to your account.
2. Complete the corresponding exercises as required by your professor.
3. When finished, click "Grade It Now" to see which areas you have mastered, which areas need more work, and detailed explanations of every answer.

Learning

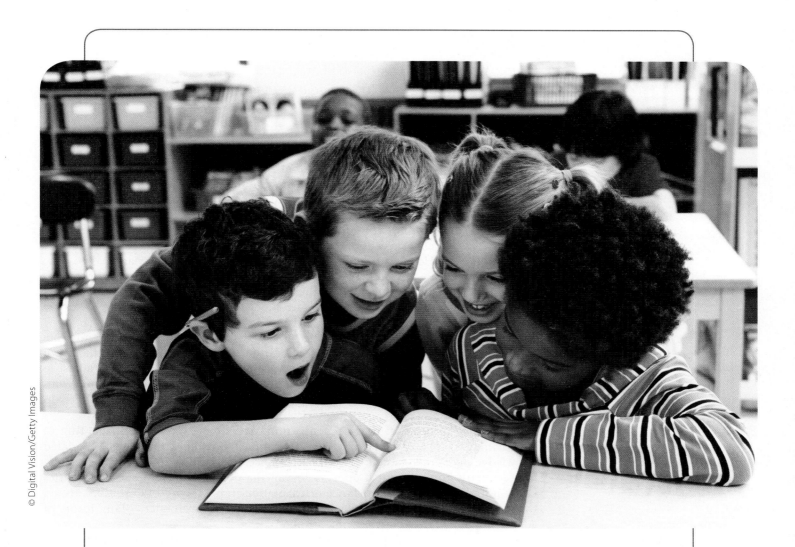

© Digital Vision/Getty Images

Preview

Live and learn. This simple phrase captures the idea that learning is a lifelong process that affects our behavior every day. Understanding how learning takes place is an important part of understanding ourselves. Sometimes learning involves one event signaling another, as when we learn to associate wailing sirens with ambulances. Other times learning depends on what happens after we do something—whether we receive praise or punishment, for example. But learning is more than these kinds of associations. What we think and how we feel about life's signals and consequences also have an impact on what we learn to do and not to do. Blend in practice and feedback about our behavior, mix well, and you have all the ingredients of the learning process.

Like most newborn babies, Jeffrey cried until he was fed. He awakened at 3 A.M. nearly every morning, hungry and crying for food. And as she had done every day since he was born, his mother would put on her slippers and walk down the tiled hallway to his bedroom. After a quick change of his diaper came the feeding. By the time he was four months old, Jeffrey would cry for about a minute and then quietly wait a few more minutes for his mother to arrive for his feeding. One particular morning, as his mother was halfway down the hall, she stopped in her tracks as she felt a sneeze coming. She pinched her nostrils together and the urge to sneeze passed. However, she noticed that Jeffrey had begun to cry again. This was unusual. She began to walk again and he quieted. Her scientific curiosity aroused, she walked a few steps, then stopped, then started, then stopped. She discovered that Jeffrey stopped crying when he heard her footsteps but resumed crying when the sound of footsteps stopped.

Jeffrey had learned a lot in the four months since his birth. He could anticipate events and predict outcomes based on the meaning of certain sounds. Like the rest of us, he showed an ability to learn about relationships in the environment and adjust to them. This adjustment to changes in the environment is called *adaptation*. Along with adaptation come expectations and predictions about what is and what is not likely to occur in our world.

The entire process of development, from birth to death, involves adapting to increasingly complex, ever-changing environments using continuously updated knowledge and skills gained through experience. This ability to adapt is especially impressive in humans, but it appears to varying degrees in every species. Charles Darwin highlighted the importance of adaptation in his theory of evolution, noting that individuals who do not adapt may not survive to reproduce. Many forms of adaptation follow the principles of learning.

Learning is a relatively permanent change in behavior or knowledge due to experience. We are born with some behaviors and knowledge, we acquire others automatically as we grow (through maturation), and we learn still others. In fact, learning plays a central role in most aspects of human behavior. If you want to know who you are and how you became the person you are today, examining what and how you have learned is a good place to start.

This chapter describes what psychologists now know about the fundamental principles of learning. These include a form of learning called *operant conditioning* in which rewards and punishments affect the frequency of observable behavior. There is also *classical conditioning*, a form of learning in which specific signals come to trigger behavior. In addition, cognitive processes underlie some of the most complex forms of learning, such as the ability to learn from watching others. Some learning takes place consciously, as when you study for an exam, but as mentioned later, you learn many things without being aware that you are doing so (Ward, 2011). Let's begin by considering classical conditioning. ●

learning The modification of preexisting behavior and understanding.

Classical Conditioning: Learning Signals and Associations

How did Russian dogs teach psychologists about learning?

At the first notes of the national anthem, an athlete's heart may start to pound because those sounds signal that the game is about to begin. A flashing red light on the instrument panel might raise your heart rate, too, because it means that something is wrong with your car. People are not born with these reactions. They have learned them by observing relationships, or *associations,* between events in the world. The experimental study of this kind of learning was begun, almost by accident, by Ivan Petrovich Pavlov.

Pavlov's Discovery

Pavlov is one of the best-known figures in psychology, but he was not a psychologist. He was a Russian physiologist who won the Nobel Prize in 1904 for his research on the digestive system of dogs. In the course of this research, Pavlov noticed a strange phenomenon. His dogs sometimes salivated, or drooled, when no food was present. For instance, they salivated when they saw the assistant who normally brought their food, even if he was empty-handed.

Pavlov devised a simple experiment to determine why salivation occurred without an obvious physical cause, such as food. First he performed an operation to divert a dog's saliva into a container so that the amount of salivation could be measured. Next he placed the dog in an apparatus similar to the one shown in Figure 5.1. The experiment had three phases.

In the first phase, Pavlov and his associates confirmed that when meat powder was placed in the dog's mouth, the dog automatically salivated (Anrep, 1920). They also confirmed that the dog did not automatically salivate in response to a musical tone. The researchers had now established the two basic components of Pavlov's experiment: (1) a quick automatic response called a *reflex*; and (2) a neutral stimulus that does not trigger that reflex.

In the second phase of Pavlov's experiment, the tone was sounded and then meat powder was placed in the dog's mouth. The dog salivated. This pairing of the tone and the meat powder was repeated several times. The tone always preceded the arrival of the meat powder, but had the dog learned that relationship? It had.

FIGURE 5.1
Apparatus for Measuring Conditioned Responses
Pavlov used this laboratory apparatus to precisely measure the amount of saliva flowing from a dog's mouth.

© Bettmann/CORBIS

In the third phase of the experiment, the tone was sounded but no meat powder was presented. The dog still salivated. The tone alone was now enough to trigger salivation. You may have seen a similar process if you regularly open pet food with an electric can opener. The sound of the opener probably brings your pet running (and salivating) because that sound means that food is on its way.

Pavlov's experiment demonstrated what we now call **classical conditioning.** In this procedure, a neutral stimulus is repeatedly paired with a stimulus that already triggers an automatic reflexive response. As a result of this pairing, the previously neutral stimulus itself comes to trigger a response that is similar to that reflex. Figure 5.2 shows the basic elements of classical conditioning. The stimulus that naturally elicits a response without conditioning, such as the meat powder in Pavlov's experiment, is called the **unconditioned stimulus (UCS).** The automatic, unlearned, reflexive response to this stimulus is called the **unconditioned response (UCR),** in this case, salivation. After being paired with the unconditioned stimulus (meat powder), the previously neutral stimulus becomes the **conditioned stimulus (CS)** and the response it comes to trigger is a learned or **conditioned response (CR).**

PHASE 1: Before conditioning has occurred

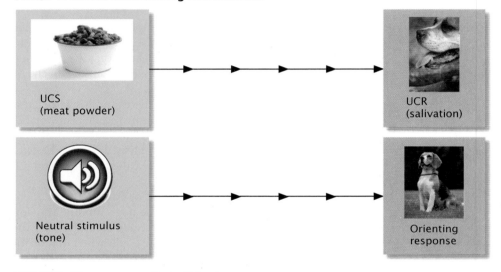

PHASE 2: The process of conditioning

PHASE 3: After conditioning has occurred

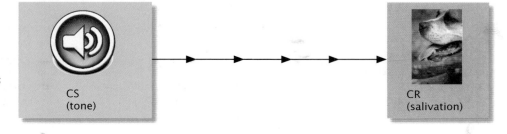

FIGURE 5.2
Classical Conditioning

Before classical conditioning, putting meat powder on a dog's tongue produces salivation but the sound of a tone—a neutral stimulus—brings only orienting responses such as turning toward the sound. During the process of conditioning, the tone is repeatedly paired with the meat powder. After classical conditioning, the tone alone is a conditioned stimulus, producing salivation.

Photo credits: Dog food bowl © Joshua Blake/ iStockphoto; tone © Redshinestudio/Shutterstock; salivating dog © Donna Wilding/Design Pics/ Alamy; alert dog © Mark Raycroft/Minden Pictures/Getty Images.

FIGURE 5.3

Changes over Time in the Strength of a Conditioned Response

As the conditioned stimulus (CS) and the unconditioned stimulus (UCS) are repeatedly paired during initial conditioning, the strength of the conditioned response (CR) increases. If the CS is then repeatedly presented without the UCS, the CR weakens—and eventually disappears—through a process called extinction. If the CS is presented again later on, a weaker version of the CR will reappear (Rescorla, 2004). This phenomenon, called spontaneous recovery, is only temporary, though. Unless the UCS is again paired with the CS, the recovered CR soon disappears.

classical conditioning A procedure in which a neutral stimulus is paired with a stimulus that triggers a reflexive response until the neutral stimulus alone comes to trigger a similar response.

unconditioned stimulus (UCS) A stimulus that triggers a response without conditioning.

unconditioned response (UCR) The automatic, unlearned, reflexive reaction to a stimulus.

conditioned stimulus (CS) An originally neutral stimulus that now triggers a conditioned response.

conditioned response (CR) The response triggered by the conditioned stimulus.

extinction The gradual disappearance of a conditioned response.

reconditioning The relearning of a conditioned response following extinction.

spontaneous recovery The temporary reappearance of a conditioned response after extinction.

stimulus generalization A process in which a conditioned response is triggered by stimuli similar to the original conditioned stimulus.

Conditioned Responses over Time: Extinction and Spontaneous Recovery

If you have ever been bitten by a barking dog, you might have learned to feel distress whenever you hear a dog's bark. The more bad experiences you have had with dogs, the stronger will be your learned distress in response to barking sounds. In the language of classical conditioning, continued pairings of a conditioned stimulus (CS/bark) with an unconditioned stimulus (UCS/bite) strengthen the conditioned response (CR/distress). The curve on the left side of Figure 5.3 shows an example: Repeated associations of a tone (CS) with meat powder (UCS) caused Pavlov's dogs to increase their salivation (CR) to the tone alone.

What if the tone (CS) is repeatedly sounded but the meat powder (UCS) is no longer given? As you might expect, if the unconditioned stimulus is not paired with the conditioned stimulus at least now and then, the conditioned response will gradually disappear. This loss of the conditioned response is known as **extinction** (see the center section of Figure 5.3). The term is not entirely accurate, though. *Extinction* suggests that like the dinosaurs, the conditioned response has been wiped out, never to return. However, many kinds of evidence support the conclusion that extinction merely suppresses a conditioned response (Miller & Laborda, 2011). For instance, if the CS (tone) and the UCS (meat powder) are again paired after the conditioned response has been extinguished, that conditioned response will return to its original strength after as few as one or two trials. This quick relearning of a conditioned response after extinction is called **reconditioning.** Reconditioning takes much less time than the original conditioning, so it appears that extinction does not entirely erase the association between the conditioned stimulus and the conditioned response (Bouton, 1993, 2002; Myers & Davis, 2007).

The right side of Figure 5.3 provides more evidence for this conclusion. After a conditioned response has been extinguished it will temporarily reappear if the conditioned stimulus occurs again, even in a different situation (Neumann & Kitlertsirivatana, 2010). This is called **spontaneous recovery,** the temporary reappearance of a conditioned response after extinction (and without further CS-UCS pairings). In general, the longer the time between extinction and the reappearance of the CS, the stronger the recovered conditioned response (Devenport, 1998; Rescorla, 2005). Unless the UCS is again paired with the CS, extinction will reoccur and will further suppress the conditioned response (Leung & Westbrook, 2008). Still, even after many years, spontaneous recovery can create a ripple of emotion—a conditioned response—when we hear a song or catch a scent associated with a long-lost lover or a departed relative.

Stimulus Generalization and Discrimination

Once a conditioned stimulus is able to trigger a conditioned response, stimuli similar to the conditioned stimulus will also trigger some version of that response. This phenomenon, called **stimulus generalization,** is illustrated by the fact that a person

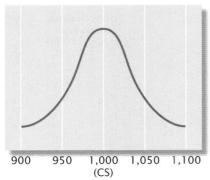

FIGURE 5.4
Stimulus Generalization

The strength of a conditioned response (CR) is greatest when the original conditioned stimulus (CS) occurs. However, some version of the CR is also triggered by stimuli that closely resemble the CS. Here, the CS is the sound of a buzzer at a frequency of 1,000 hertz (Hz), and the CR is salivation. Notice that the CR generalizes well to stimuli at 990 or 1,010 Hz but that it gets weaker and weaker as the buzzer sounds less and less similar to the CS.

stimulus discrimination A process through which people learn to differentiate among similar stimuli and respond appropriately to each one.

who was bitten by one particular dog may now show some fear of all dogs. Usually, the greater the similarity between a new stimulus and the original conditioned stimulus, the stronger the conditioned response will be. If the person was bitten by a small, curly-haired dog, fear responses would be strongest to other small dogs with similar types of hair. Figure 5.4 shows an example involving sounds.

Stimulus generalization has some obvious advantages. For example, it is important for survival that if you get sick after drinking sour-smelling milk, you now avoid dairy products that have a similar odor. Generalization would be a problem if it had no limits, however. You would probably be justifiably frightened if you found a lion in your living room, but imagine how disruptive it would be if your fear response generalized so widely that you were panicked by the sight of lions on TV or even by the word "lion" in a book.

Stimulus generalization does not run wild because it is usually balanced by a process called **stimulus discrimination.** Through stimulus discrimination, we learn to make distinctions among similar stimuli. Many parents find that the sound of their own baby whimpering soon becomes a conditioned stimulus, triggering a conditioned response that wakes them up. That conditioned response may not occur if a visiting friend's baby whimpers.

The Signaling of Significant Events

Early research suggested that classical conditioning involves nothing more than automatic associations that allow one stimulus (the conditioned stimulus, or CS) to substitute for another (the unconditioned stimulus, or UCS) in triggering a reflex. However, classical conditioning is not that simplistic. For example, a rat's unconditioned, reflexive response to a mild shock (UCS) will be flinching and jumping. But the animal's conditioned response to the sound of a tone (CS) that always precedes shock will not be to flinch and jump but to freeze—much as it would if threatened by a predator (Domjan, 2005). In other words, classical conditioning allows the rat to prepare for an upcoming shock. Many psychologists now believe that classical conditioning provides a means through which people, and some other animals, develop expectations and other *mental representations* of the relationships between events in their environment and expectancies about when such events will occur (Rescorla, 1988; Shanks, 1995; Sternberg & McClelland, 2012). These representations aid in adaptation and survival. When two events repeatedly take place together, we can predict that one will occur based on what we know about the other. Baby Jeffrey predicted his feeding from hearing his mother's footsteps. You have learned that a clear blue sky means dry weather, that too little sleep makes you irritable, that you can reach someone on the telephone by pressing certain buttons, and that yelling orders motivates some people and angers others.

What determines whether conditioned responses are learned? In general, these responses develop when one event *signals* the appearance of another. Other important factors are the timing, predictability, and intensity of the CS and UCS; the amount of attention that is devoted to them; and how easily the signals can be associated with other stimuli.

Timing   If your instructor always dismisses class at 9:59 and a bell rings at 10:00, the bell cannot prepare you for the dismissal. It comes too late to be a useful signal. For the same reason, classical conditioning works best when the conditioned stimulus comes before the unconditioned stimulus. This arrangement makes sense for adaptation and survival. Usually, the presence of food, predators, or other significant stimuli is most reliably signaled by smells, sounds, or other events that come just before their appearance (Einhorn & Hogarth, 1982). So it is logical that the brain should be "wired" to form associations most easily between things that occur at about the same time. How close together do they have to be? There is no single "best" interval for every situation. Classical conditioning can occur in some cases when the interval between the CS and the UCS is less than a second and in other cases when that interval is longer than a minute. It all depends on the particular CS, UCS, and UCR that are involved (Longo, Klempay, & Bitterman, 1964; Ross & Ross, 1971). However, classical conditioning will always be weaker if the interval between the CS and the UCS is longer than what is ideal for the stimuli and responses in a given situation.

Predictability It is not enough for the CS merely to come before the UCS. Suppose your dogs, Moxie and Fang, have very different personalities. When Moxie growls, she sometimes bites, but sometimes she doesn't. Fang growls only before biting. Your conditioned fear response to Moxie's growl will probably occur slowly, because her growl does not reliably signal the danger of a bite. However, you are likely to quickly develop a classically conditioned fear response to Fang's growl. It always means that you are in danger of being bitten. Classical conditioning proceeds most rapidly when the CS *always* signals the UCS and only the UCS. Even if both dogs provide the same number of pairings of the CS (growl) and the UCS (bite), it is only with Fang that the CS *reliably* predicts the UCS (Rescorla, 1968).

Intensity A conditioned response will be learned more rapidly if the UCS is strong. For example, a CS that acts as a predictive signal will be more rapidly associated with a strong shock (UCS) than with a weak one. As with the importance of timing and predictability, the effect of UCS strength on classical conditioning makes adaptive sense. It's more important to be prepared for major events than for minor ones.

© Rubberball/SuperStock

Taste Aversions

Humans can develop classically conditioned taste aversions, even to preferred foods. For example, Ilene Bernstein (1978) gave one group of cancer patients Mapletoff ice cream an hour before they received nausea-provoking chemotherapy. A second group ate this same kind of ice cream on a day they did not receive chemotherapy. A third group got no ice cream. Five months later, the patients were asked to taste several ice cream flavors. Those who had never tasted Mapletoff and those who had not eaten it in association with chemotherapy chose it as their favorite. Those who had eaten Mapletoff before receiving chemotherapy found it distasteful.

Attention An association between a pair of stimuli is most predictably learned when there are no other potentially distracting stimuli present (Jones & Haselgrove, 2011). In Pavlov's laboratory, just one conditioned stimulus, a tone, was linked to just one unconditioned stimulus, meat powder. In the natural environment, a wide variety of stimuli might be present just before a UCS occurs. Suppose you are at the beach. You're eating a hot dog, reading a magazine, listening to Nicki Minaj, digging your toes in the warm sand, and enjoying the smell of suntan lotion when you are surprised by the sting of a buzzing wasp. Which of these stimuli is most likely to become a conditioned stimulus that might later trigger discomfort? It depends partly on where you were focusing your attention at the moment you were stung. Because your attention was focused on the music or your reading, you might not have noticed the buzzing sound that preceded the sting (UCS). The stimulus you most closely attended to—the one you most fully perceived—is most likely to become a CS. In general, loud tones, bright lights, and other intense stimuli tend to get extra attention, so they are the ones most rapidly associated with an unconditioned stimulus. As long as it remains a reliable predictive signal, however, even a low intensity CS will produce a reliable CR if repeatedly paired with a UCS (Jakubowska & Zielinski, 1978).

Biopreparedness Certain kinds of signals or events are especially likely to become associated with other signals or events (Logue, 1985). So which beach stimulus becomes a conditioned stimulus for fear will depend not only on attention but also on whether the stimulus is a sight, a sound, or a taste and what kind of unconditioned stimulus follows it. The apparently natural tendency for certain events to become linked suggests that organisms are "biologically prepared" to develop certain conditioned associations (Öhman & Soares, 1993, 1998). This *biopreparedness* is seen in infants as young as 14 months of age (LoBue & DeLoache, 2010).

The most dramatic example of the biopreparedness phenomenon is seen in conditioned taste aversions. In one study, rats were either shocked or made nauseous in the presence of a light, a buzzer, and flavored water. The rats formed only certain conditioned associations. Animals that had been shocked developed a conditioned fear response to the light and the buzzer but not to the flavored water. Those that had been made nauseous developed a conditioned avoidance of the flavored water, but they showed no particular response to the light or buzzer (Garcia & Koelling, 1966). These results reflect an adaptive process. Nausea is more likely to be caused by something we eat or drink than by a noise or a light. So nausea is more likely to become a conditioned response to an internal stimulus, such as a flavor, than to an external stimulus. In contrast, the sudden pain of a shock is more likely to have been caused by an external stimulus, so it makes evolutionary sense that the organism should be "tuned" to associate shock or sudden pain with a sight or sound. In our beach example, it is more likely that you would have associated the pain of that wasp sting with the sight of the insect than with the taste of your hot dog.

Conditioned taste aversion shows that for certain kinds of stimuli, classical conditioning can occur even when there is a long delay between the CS (taste) and the UCS (sickness). The nausea caused by eating spoiled food may be delayed for minutes or hours, but people who have experienced food poisoning may never again eat the food that made them ill. Organisms that are biologically prepared to link taste signals with illness, even a delayed illness, are more likely to survive than organisms not so prepared.

Evidence from several sources suggests other ways in which animals and people are innately prepared to learn aversions to certain stimuli. For example, experiments with animals suggest that they are prone to learn the types of associations that are most common in or most relevant to their environments (Wilcoxon, Dragoin, & Kral, 1971). Birds are strongly dependent on their vision in searching for food and may develop taste aversions on the basis of visual stimuli. Coyotes and rats, more dependent on their sense of smell, tend to develop aversions related to odor. In humans, preparedness results in far more cases of conditioned fear of harmless dogs or snakes than of potentially more dangerous objects, such as electrical outlets or knives (Öhman & Mineka, 2001, 2003). We are also particularly likely to learn fear responses to people who are "different," such as members of other ethnic groups (Olsson et al., 2005).

Higher Order Conditioning   Once we learn that a conditioned stimulus (CS) signals the arrival of an unconditioned stimulus (UCS), the CS may operate as if it actually were that UCS. For instance, suppose that a child endures a painful medical procedure (UCS) at the doctor's office and the pain becomes associated with the doctor's white coat. The white coat might then become a conditioned stimulus (CS) that can trigger a conditioned fear response. Once the white coat is able to set off a conditioned fear response, the coat may take on some properties of an unconditioned stimulus. So, if the child later sees a white-coated pharmacist at the drugstore, that once-neutral store can become a conditioned stimulus for fear because it signals the appearance of a white coat, which in turn signals pain. When a conditioned stimulus (the white coat) acts like an unconditioned stimulus, creating conditioned stimuli (the drugstore) out of events associated with it, the process is called **higher order conditioning.**

This process serves as an adaptive "early warning system." It prepares us for threatening events (UCS) that are signaled not only by a CS but also by associated events that precede—and thus predict—that CS. But higher order conditioning can also cause problems. For example, the high blood pressure seen in medical patients who are known as *white-coat hypertensives* (Ugajin et al., 2005) does not reflect a physical disorder. It occurs simply because the sight of a doctor or nurse has become a conditioned stimulus for fear. Medical staff must be alert to such cases if they are to avoid giving blood pressure medication to patients who don't need it.

The Power of Higher Order Conditioning
Cancer patients may feel queasy when they enter a chemotherapy room because they have associated the room with nausea-producing treatment. Through higher order conditioning, almost anything associated with the room can also become a conditioned stimulus for nausea. One cancer patient who was flying out of town on a business trip became nauseated just by seeing her hospital from the air.

higher order conditioning A process through which a conditioned stimulus comes to signal another conditioned stimulus that is already associated with an unconditioned stimulus.

Some Applications of Classical Conditioning

The principles of classical conditioning are summarized in "In Review: Basic Processes of Classical Conditioning." These principles have proven useful in many areas, including in recent efforts to use insects to help detect explosive material. In one study, for example, after the taste of sugar water was associated with the smell of a chemical used in certain explosives, wasps quickly developed a conditioned response to the smell alone. When several of these trained insects were placed in a plastic tube and brought near the target chemical, they displayed an immediate attraction to it (Rains, Utley, & Lewis, 2006). Researchers hope that it may someday be possible to use these so-called Wasp Hounds and other similar devices to detect explosives or drugs concealed in airline passengers' luggage (Tomberlin, Rains, & Sanford, 2008). Classical conditioning principles have also been applied in overcoming fears and understanding certain aspects of drug addiction (Xue et al., 2012).

Phobias   *Phobias* are intense, irrational fears of objects or situations—such as public speaking—that are not dangerous or that are less dangerous than the fear response would suggest. Classical conditioning often plays a role in the development of phobias (Bouton, Mineka, & Barlow, 2001; Waters, Henry, & Neumann, 2009). As mentioned earlier, a person frightened by a dog may learn a fear that is so intense and generalized that it leads the person to avoid all dogs and all situations in which dogs might be encountered. Classically conditioned fears can be extremely long lasting, especially when they are based on experiences with strong unconditioned stimuli. Combat veterans and victims of violent crime, terrorism, or other traumatic events may show intense fear responses to trauma-related stimuli for many years afterward.

Classical conditioning has also been used to treat phobias (see the chapter on treatment of psychological disorders). Joseph Wolpe (1958) was a pioneer in this effort. He showed that irrational fears could be relieved through *systematic desensitization,* a procedure that associates a new response, such as relaxation, with a feared stimulus. To treat a thunderstorm phobia, for instance, a therapist might first teach the client to relax deeply and then associate that relaxation with increasingly intense sights and sounds of thunderstorms presented on videotape (Öst, 1978). Because, as Wolpe (1958) noted, a person cannot be relaxed and afraid at the same time, the new conditioned response (relaxation) to thunderstorms replaces the old one (fear).

Basic Processes of Classical Conditioning   IN REVIEW

Process	Description	Example
Acquisition	A neutral stimulus and an unconditioned stimulus (UCS) are paired. The neutral stimulus becomes a conditioned stimulus (CS), eliciting a conditioned response (CR).	A child learns to fear (conditioned response) the doctor's office (conditioned stimulus) by associating it with the reflexive emotional reaction (unconditioned response) to a painful injection (unconditioned stimulus).
Stimulus generalization	A conditioned response is elicited not only by the conditioned stimulus but also by stimuli similar to the conditioned stimulus.	A child fears most doctors' offices and places that smell like them.
Stimulus discrimination	Generalization is limited so that some stimuli similar to the conditioned stimulus do not elicit the conditioned response.	A child learns that his mother's doctor's office is not associated with the unconditioned stimulus.
Extinction	The conditioned stimulus is presented alone, without the unconditioned stimulus. Eventually the conditioned stimulus no longer elicits the conditioned response.	A child visits the doctor's office several times for a checkup but does not receive a shot. Fear may eventually cease.

IN REVIEW QUESTIONS

1. If a person with a conditioned fear of spiders is also frightened by the sight of creatures that look somewhat like spiders, the person is demonstrating stimulus ____ .

2. Because of ____ , we are more likely to learn a fear of snakes than a fear of cars.

3. Feeling sad upon hearing a song associated with a long-lost relationship illustrates ____ .

© Rich Kirchner/NHPA/Photoshot

Predator Control through Conditioning

In the western United States, some ranchers lace a sheep carcass with enough lithium chloride to make wolves and coyotes nauseous (Pfister et al., 2003). The predators associate nausea with the smell and taste of sheep and afterward stay away from the ranchers' flocks. A similar program in India has greatly reduced the human death toll from tiger attacks. Stuffed dummies are connected to a shock generator and placed in areas where tigers have killed people. When the animals approach the dummies, they receive a shock (UCS). After learning to associate shock with the human form (CS), the tigers tend to avoid people (CR).

APPLYING PSYCHOLOGY

Manuscripts and Archives, Yale University Library

FIGURE 5.5

Thorndike's Puzzle Box

This photograph shows the kind of puzzle box used in Thorndike's research. His cats learned to open the door and reach food by stepping on a pedal, but the learning occurred gradually. Some cats actually took longer to get out of the box on one trial than on a previous trial.

habituation Reduced responsiveness to a repeated stimulus.

Drug Addiction   When people repeatedly use heroin or other addictive drugs, their responses to the drugs become weaker. This reduction in responsiveness to a repeated stimulus is called **habituation.** According to Richard Solomon's (1980) *opponent-process theory,* habituation is the result of two processes that balance each other, like a seesaw. The first process is a quick, automatic, involuntary response—essentially an unconditioned response (UCR) to the drug. The second—or opponent—process is a response that follows and counteracts the first. When a person is taking addictive drugs, this opponent response can be learned, or conditioned (McDonald & Siegel, 2004). So if the unconditioned response to a drug injection includes an increase in body temperature, the conditioned response will include an opponent process that reduces body temperature somewhat, creating the sensation of "chills." As the addict continues drug injections day after day, the learned opponent process ("chills") gets stronger and occurs sooner. As this CR strengthens, the rise in temperature caused by the drug gets smaller, resulting in habituation. In the same fashion, the intense pleasure first experienced as an unconditioned response to the drug begins to be weakened over time by an unpleasant opponent process (CR) that becomes faster and stronger. The addict begins to take larger drug doses in an effort to achieve the "high" once created by smaller doses. As described in the chapter on consciousness, people who display this pattern are said to have developed a *tolerance* for the drug.

The location where a drug is usually taken and the rituals that precede an injection (such as preparing the syringe) can become conditioned stimuli that trigger conditioned opponent-process responses even before the drug enters the bloodstream. These stimuli signal that the drug is coming, and the body begins to brace itself. But what if a person takes the drug in a new location or doesn't follow the usual ritual? According to opponent-process theory, in the absence of these conditioned environmental stimuli, the conditioned responses that normally dampen the user's unconditioned responses to the drug will not be as strong. As a result, the drug dose the addict took in the usual way yesterday might cause a potentially fatal overdose today (Melchior, 1990; Siegel et al., 1982; Siegel, 2005).

Instrumental and Operant Conditioning: Learning the Consequences of Behavior

How do reward and punishment work?

Classical conditioning is an important form of learning, but you also learn many associations between responses and the stimuli that *follow* them, between behavior and its consequences. A child learns to say "please" and gets a piece of candy. A headache sufferer takes a pill and escapes pain. A dog "shakes hands" and earns a treat. Such actions are called *goal-directed* if the response is made with the outcome in mind, while they are called *habits* if the response occurs simply because the action has previously been rewarded in a similar situation (Balleine & Dickinson, 1998). The capacity for goal-directed action appears in children around the age of three (Klossek, Russell, & Dickinson, 2008), and develops early in the lives of other species, too (Hall et al., 2000).

From the Puzzle Box to the Skinner Box

While Pavlov was exploring classical conditioning in Russia, Edward L. Thorndike, an American psychologist, was studying the consequences of behavior and animal intelligence, including the ability to solve problems. For example, he placed a hungry cat in a *puzzle box* like the one in Figure 5.5. The cat had to learn some response—such as stepping on a pedal—to unlock the door and get food. During the first few trials in the puzzle box, the cat explored and prodded until it finally hit the pedal. The

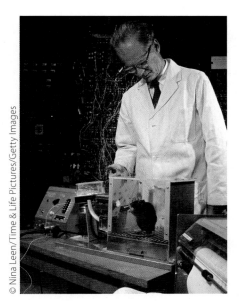

FIGURE 5.6
B. F. Skinner (1904–1990)

In the operant conditioning chamber shown here, the rat can press a bar to obtain food pellets from a tube. Operant and instrumental conditioning are similar in most respects, but they do differ in one way. Instrumental conditioning is measured by how long it takes for a response (such as a bar press) to occur. Operant conditioning is measured by the rate at which responses occur. In this chapter, the term operant conditioning refers to both.

law of effect A law stating that if a response made in the presence of a particular stimulus is rewarded, the same response is more likely to occur when that stimulus is encountered again.

operant conditioning A process in which responses are learned on the basis of their rewarding or punishing consequences.

operant A response that has some effect on the world.

reinforcer A stimulus event that increases the probability that the response immediately preceding it will occur again.

positive reinforcers Stimuli that strengthen a response if they follow that response.

negative reinforcers The removal of unpleasant stimuli.

reinforcement The process through which a particular response is made more likely to recur.

animal eventually solved the puzzle, but very slowly. It did not appear to understand, or suddenly gain insight into, the problem (Thorndike, 1898). After many trials, though, the cat solved the puzzle quickly each time it was placed in the box. What was it learning? Thorndike argued that any response (such as pacing or meowing) that did not produce a satisfying effect (opening the door) gradually became weaker, whereas any response (pressing the pedal) that did have a satisfying effect gradually became stronger. The cat's learning, said Thorndike, is governed by the **law of effect.** According to this law, if a response made to a particular stimulus is followed by a satisfying effect (such as food or some other reward), that response is more likely to occur the next time the stimulus is present. In contrast, responses that produce discomfort are less likely to be performed again. Thorndike described this kind of learning as *instrumental conditioning* because responses are strengthened when they are instrumental in producing rewards (Thorndike, 1905).

About thirty years after Thorndike published his work, B. F. Skinner extended and formalized many of Thorndike's ideas. Skinner (1938) noted that during instrumental conditioning, an organism learns a response by *operating on* the environment. So he used the term **operant conditioning** to refer to the learning process in which behavior is changed by its consequences, specifically by rewards and punishments. To study operant conditioning, Skinner devised some new tools. One of these was a small chamber that, despite Skinner's objections, came to be known as the *Skinner box* (see Figure 5.6).

Basic Components of Operant Conditioning

The chamber Skinner designed allowed researchers to arrange relationships between a particular response and its consequences. If an animal pressed a lever in the chamber, for example, it might receive a food pellet. The researchers could then analyze how consequences affect behavior. It turned out that stimulus generalization, stimulus discrimination, extinction, spontaneous recovery, and other phenomena seen in classical conditioning also appear in operant conditioning. However, research in operant conditioning also focused on concepts known as operants, reinforcers, and discriminative conditioned stimuli.

Operants and Reinforcers Skinner coined the term *operant,* or *operant response,* to distinguish the responses in operant conditioning from those in classical conditioning. In classical conditioning, the conditioned response does not affect whether or when the stimulus occurs. Pavlov's dogs salivated when a tone sounded. The salivation had no effect on the tone or on whether food was presented. In contrast, an **operant** has some effect on the world. It is a response that operates on the environment. When a dog stands whimpering by the front door and is then taken for a walk, it has made an operant response that influences when it will be able to go outside.

A **reinforcer** is a stimulus that increases the probability that the operant behavior will occur again. There are two main types of reinforcers: positive and negative. **Positive reinforcers** strengthen a response if they are presented after that response occurs. The food that hungry pigeons received after pecking a response key in Skinner's training chamber was a positive reinforcer. Receiving the food increased the birds' key pecking. For people, positive reinforcers can include food, smiles, money, and other desirable outcomes. Presentation of a positive reinforcer after a response is called *positive reinforcement.* **Negative reinforcers** are the *removal* of unpleasant stimuli, such as pain or noise. For example, the disappearance of a headache after you take a pain reliever acts as a negative reinforcer that makes you more likely to take that pain reliever in the future. When a response is strengthened by the removal of an unpleasant stimulus such as pain, the process is called *negative reinforcement.*

Notice that **reinforcement** always increases the likelihood of the behavior that precedes it, whether the reinforcer is adding something pleasant or removing something unpleasant. Figure 5.7 shows this relationship.

FIGURE 5.7
Positive and Negative Reinforcement

Remember that behavior is strengthened through positive reinforcement when something pleasant or desirable occurs following the behavior. Behavior is strengthened through negative reinforcement when the behavior results in the removal or termination of something unpleasant. To see how these principles apply in your own life, list two examples of situations in which your behavior was affected by positive reinforcement and two in which you were affected by negative reinforcement.

LEARNby DOING

Photo credits: Top row photos © Maria R. T. Deseo/ PhotoEdit; Bottom row photos © Jonathan Sammartino.

POSITIVE REINFORCEMENT

| **Behavior** You put coins into a vending machine. | **Presentation of a pleasant or positive stimulus** You receive a bag of chips. | **Frequency of behavior increases** You put coins in vending machines in the future. |

NEGATIVE REINFORCEMENT

| **Behavior** In the middle of a boring date, you say you have a headache. | **Termination of an unpleasant stimulus** The date ends early. | **Frequency of behavior increases** You use the same tactic on future boring dates. |

Escape and Avoidance Conditioning   The effects of negative reinforcement can be seen in both escape conditioning and avoidance conditioning. **Escape conditioning** occurs when we learn responses that stop an unpleasant stimulus. The left-hand panel of Figure 5.8 shows an example from an animal laboratory, but escape conditioning operates in humans, too. Not only do we learn to take pills to stop pain, but some parents learn to stop their child's annoying demands for a toy by agreeing to buy it. And television viewers learn escape annoying commercials by muting the sound.

When an animal or a person responds to a signal in a way that *avoids* an aversive stimulus before it arrives, **avoidance conditioning** has occurred (see the right-hand sections of Figure 5.8). Avoidance conditioning is an important influence on everyday behavior. We go to work even when we would rather stay in bed, we stop at red lights even when we are in a hurry, we apologize for our mistakes even before they are discovered, and we stay away from feared or dangerous places. Each of these behaviors helps us avoid a negative consequence, such as lost pay, a traffic ticket, a scolding, or anxiety or injury.

Avoidance conditioning represents a marriage of classical and operant conditioning. If, as shown in Figure 5.8, a buzzer predicts shock (an unconditioned stimulus), the buzzer becomes a conditioned stimulus (CS). Through classical conditioning, the buzzer (now a CS) triggers a conditioned fear response (CR). Like the shock itself, conditioned fear is an unpleasant internal sensation. The animal then learns the instrumental response of jumping the barrier. The instrumental response (jumping) is reinforced because it reduces fear.

Once learned, avoidance is a difficult habit to break, because avoidance responses continue to be reinforced by fear reduction (Solomon, Kamin, & Wynne, 1953). So even without the shock, animals may keep jumping over the barrier when the buzzer sounds because they never discover that avoidance is no longer necessary. The same is often true of people. Those who avoid escalators out of fear never get a chance to find out that they are safe. Others avoid potentially embarrassing social situations, but doing so also prevents them from learning how to be successful in those situations.

The study of avoidance conditioning has not only expanded our understanding of negative reinforcement but also has led some psychologists to consider more complex cognitive processes in operant learning. These psychologists suggest, for example, that

escape conditioning   The process of learning responses that stop an aversive stimulus.

avoidance conditioning   The process of learning particular responses that avoid an aversive stimulus.

Escape conditioning

Avoidance conditioning

FIGURE 5.8
A Shuttle Box
A shuttle box has two sections that are usually separated by a barrier; its floor is an electric grid. Shock can be administered through the grid to either section. The left-hand panel shows escape conditioning, in which an animal learns to get away from a mild shock by jumping over the barrier when the electricity is turned on. The next two panels show avoidance conditioning. Here, the animal has learned to avoid shock altogether by jumping over the barrier when it hears a warning buzzer just before shock occurs.

Source: From Hintzman, D. L. *Divided consciousness: Multiple controls in human thought and action.* Reprinted by permission of the author.

discriminative conditioned stimuli
Stimuli that signal whether reinforcement is available if a certain response is made.

in order for people to learn to avoid an unpleasant event (such as getting fired or paying a fine), they must have established an expectancy or other mental representation of that event. The role of such mental representations is emphasized in the cognitive theories of learning described later in this chapter.

Discriminative Conditioned Stimuli and Stimulus Control   The consequences of our behavior often depend on the situation we are in. Most people know that a flirtatious comment about someone's appearance may be welcomed on a date but not at the office. And even if you have been rewarded for telling jokes, you are not likely to do so during a funeral. In the language of operant conditioning, situations serve as **discriminative conditioned stimuli,** which are stimuli that signal whether reinforcement is available if a certain response is made. *Stimulus discrimination* occurs when an organism learns to make a particular response in the presence of one stimulus but not another. The response is then said to be under *stimulus control*. Stimulus discrimination allows people or animals to learn what is appropriate (reinforced) and inappropriate (not reinforced) in particular situations. For example, bears searching for food in Yosemite National Park campgrounds tend to break into minivans; it appears that they've learned that minivans are more likely than other vehicles to contain the goodies they are after (Breck, Lance, & Seher, 2009).

Stimulus generalization also occurs in operant conditioning. That is, an animal or person will perform a response in the presence of a stimulus that is similar to (but not exactly like) a stimulus that has signaled reinforcement in the past. The more similar the new stimulus is to the old one, the more likely it is that the response will be performed. Suppose you ate a wonderful meal at a restaurant called "Captain Jack's," which was decorated to look like the inside of a sailing ship. You might later be attracted to other restaurants with nautical names or with interiors that look something like the one where you had that great meal.

Stimulus generalization and stimulus discrimination complement each other. In one study, for example, pigeons received food for pecking at a response key, but only when they saw certain kinds of artwork (Watanabe, Sakamoto, & Wakita, 1995; see Figure 5.9). As a result, these birds learned to *discriminate* the works of the impressionist painter Claude Monet from those of the cubist painter Pablo Picasso. Later, when the birds were shown new paintings by other impressionist and cubist artists, they were able to *generalize* from the original artists to other artists who painted in the same style, as if they had learned the conceptual categories of "impressionism" and "cubism." We humans learn to place people and objects into even more finely detailed categories, such as "honest," "dangerous," or "tax deductible." We discriminate one stimulus from another and then through generalization respond similarly to all those we perceive to be in a particular category. This ability to respond in a similar way to all members of a category can save us considerable time and effort, but it can also lead to the development of unwarranted prejudice against certain groups of people (see the chapter on social psychology).

Photo courtesy of Bruce E. Hesse, Ph.D., Department of Psychology and Child Development, California State University, Stanislaus

FIGURE 5.9

Stimulus Discrimination

Pigeons reinforced for responding to the work of a particular painter learned to tell the difference between his paintings and those of other artists (Watanabe, Sakamoto, & Wakita, 1995).

Forming and Strengthening Operant Behavior

Your daily life is full of examples of operant conditioning. You go to movies, parties, classes, and jobs primarily because doing so brings reinforcement. What is the effect of the type or timing of your reinforcers? How do you learn new behaviors? How can you get rid of old ones?

Shaping Let's say you want to train your dog, Sugar, to sit and "shake hands." You figure that positive reinforcement should work, so you decide to give Sugar a treat every time she sits and shakes hands. But there's a problem with this plan. As smart as Sugar is, she may never make the desired response on her own, so you might never be able to give the reinforcer. The way around this problem is to shape Sugar's behavior. **Shaping** is the process of reinforcing *successive approximations*—that is, responses that come successively closer to the desired behavior. For example, you might first give Sugar a treat whenever she sits down. Next, you might reinforce her only when she sits and partially lifts a paw. Finally, you might reinforce only complete paw lifting. Eventually, you would require Sugar to perform the entire sit-lift-shake sequence before giving the treat. Shaping is a powerful tool. Animal trainers have used it to teach chimpanzees to roller-skate, dolphins to jump through hoops, and pigeons to play Ping-Pong (Coren, 1999).

Secondary Reinforcement Operant conditioning often begins with the use of **primary reinforcers,** which are events or stimuli—such as food or water—that satisfy needs that are basic to survival. The effects of primary reinforcers are powerful and automatic. But constantly giving Sugar food as a reward can disrupt training, because she will stop to eat after every response. Also, once she gets full, food will no longer act as an effective reinforcer. To avoid these problems, animal trainers, parents, and teachers rely on the principle of secondary reinforcement.

Secondary reinforcers are previously neutral stimuli that take on reinforcing properties after being paired with stimuli that are already reinforcing. In other words, they are rewards that people or animals learn to like (Seo & Lee, 2009). If you say "Good girl!" just before feeding Sugar, those words will become reinforcing after a few pairings. "Good girl!" can then be used alone, without food, to reinforce Sugar's behavior. It helps if the words are again paired with food every now and then. Does this remind you of classical conditioning? It should, because the primary reinforcer (food) is an unconditioned stimulus. If the words "Good girl!" become a reliable signal for food, they will act as a conditioned stimulus (CS). For this reason, secondary reinforcers are sometimes called *conditioned reinforcers.*

The power of operant conditioning can be greatly increased by using secondary reinforcers. Consider the secondary reinforcer we call money. Some people will do almost anything for it despite the fact that it tastes terrible and won't quench your thirst. Its reinforcing power lies in its association with the many rewards it can buy. Smiles and other forms of social approval (such as the words "Good job!") are also important secondary reinforcers for human beings. However, secondary reinforcers can vary widely from person to person and culture to culture. Tickets to a rock concert may be an effective secondary reinforcer for some people but not for others. A ceremony honoring outstanding job performance might be strongly reinforcing in an individualist culture, but the same experience might be embarrassing for a person in a collectivist culture, where group cooperation is given greater value than personal distinction (Miller, 2001). When carefully chosen, however, secondary reinforcers can build or maintain behavior, even when primary reinforcement is absent for long periods.

shaping The reinforcement of responses that come successively closer to some desired response.

primary reinforcers Events or stimuli that satisfy physiological needs basic to survival.

secondary reinforcers Rewards that people or animals learn to like.

Delay and Size of Reinforcement   Much of our behavior is learned and maintained because it is regularly reinforced. But many of us overeat, smoke, drink too much, or procrastinate, even though we know these behaviors are bad for us. We may want to eliminate them, but they are hard to change. We seem to lack self-control. If behavior is controlled by its consequences, why do we do things that are ultimately self-defeating?

Part of the answer lies in the timing of reinforcers. For example, the good feelings (positive reinforcers) that follow excessive drinking are immediate. But because hangovers and other negative consequences are usually delayed, their effects on future drinking are weakened. In other words, operant conditioning is stronger when reinforcers appear soon after a response occurs (Rachlin, 2000). Under some conditions, delaying a positive reinforcer for even a few seconds can decrease the effectiveness of positive reinforcement. The size of the reinforcer is also important. In general, conditioning is faster when the reinforcer is large than when it is small.

Reinforcement Schedules   When a *continuous reinforcement schedule* is in effect, a reinforcer is delivered every time a particular response occurs. This schedule can be helpful when teaching someone a new skill, but it can be impractical in the long run. Imagine how inefficient it would be, for example, if an employer had to deliver praise or pay following every little task employees performed all day long. In most cases, reinforcement is given only some of the time, on a *partial,* or *intermittent, reinforcement schedule.* Intermittent schedules are described in terms of when and how reinforcers are given. "When" refers to the number of responses that have to occur, or the amount of time that must pass, before a reinforcer will occur. "How" refers to whether the reinforcer will be delivered in a predictable or unpredictable way.

Getting the Hang of It
Learning to eat with a spoon is, as you can see, a hit-and-miss process at first. However, this child will learn to hit the target more and more often as the food reward gradually shapes a more efficient (and far less messy) pattern of behavior.

1. *Fixed-ratio (FR) schedules* provide reinforcement following a fixed number of responses. Rats might receive food after every tenth time they press the lever in a Skinner box (FR 10) or after every twentieth time (FR 20). Technicians working at computer help centers might be allowed to take a break after every fifth call they handle, or every tenth.

2. *Variable-ratio (VR) schedules* also call for reinforcement after a certain number of responses, but that number varies. As a result, it is impossible to predict which particular response will bring reinforcement. On a VR 30 schedule, for example, a rat will be reinforced after an *average* of thirty lever presses. This means that the reward sometimes comes after ten presses, sometimes after fifteen, and other times after fifty or more. Gambling offers humans a similar variable-ratio schedule. Casino slot machines pay off only after a frustratingly unpredictable number of button-pushes, averaging perhaps one in twenty.

3. *Fixed-interval (FI) schedules* provide reinforcement for the first response that occurs after some fixed time has passed since the last reward. On an FI 60 schedule, for instance, the first response after sixty seconds has passed will be rewarded, regardless of how many responses have been made during that interval. Some radio stations make use of fixed-interval schedules. Listeners who have won a call-in contest might have to wait at least ten days before they are eligible to win again.

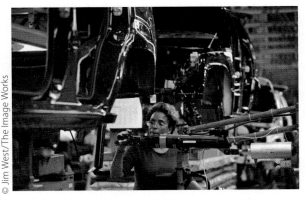

Reinforcement Schedules on the Job
Make a list of all the jobs you have ever held, along with the reinforcement schedule on which you received your pay for each. Which of the four types of schedules (fixed ratio, fixed interval, variable ratio, or variable interval) was most common, and which was most satisfying to you?

LEARN by DOING

4. *Variable-interval (VI) schedules* reinforce the first response after some period of time, but the amount of time varies unpredictably. So on a VI 60 schedule, the first response that occurs after an *average* of 60 seconds is reinforced, but the actual time between reinforcements might vary anywhere from 1 to 120 seconds or more. Police in Illinois and California have used a VI schedule to encourage seat belt use and careful driving. They stopped drivers at random times and awarded prizes to those who were buckled up and driving safely (Associated Press, 2007; Mortimer et al., 1988). Kindergarten teachers use VI schedules when they give rewards to children who are in their seats when a chime sounds at random intervals.

Results of Four Partial Reinforcement Schedules
These curves illustrate the patterns of behavior typically seen under different reinforcement schedules. The steeper the curve, the faster the response rate was. The thin diagonal lines crossing the curves show when reinforcement was given. In general, the rate of responding is higher under ratio schedules than under interval schedules.

Source: Adapted from Skinner (1961).

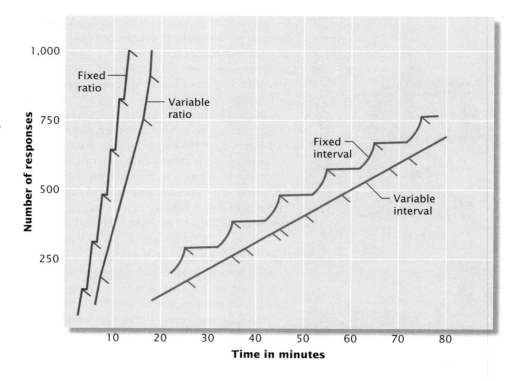

As shown in Figure 5.10, different **reinforcement schedules** produce different patterns of responding (Skinner, 1961). Both fixed-ratio and variable-ratio schedules produce especially high response rates overall. The reason, in both cases, is that the frequency of reward depends directly on the rate of responding.

Fixed-interval and variable-interval schedules generally produce lower response rates than ratio schedules. This makes perfect sense. Under a fixed-interval schedule, for example, it does not matter how many responses you make between one reward and the next. You will only be reinforced for the first response you make after a specified amount of time has passed. Because the timing of the reinforcement is so predictable, the rate of responding typically drops immediately after reinforcement and then increases as the time for another reward approaches. When teachers schedule quizzes on the same day each week, most students will study just before each quiz and then cease studying almost immediately afterward. Variable-interval schedules produce a slower, but steadier, response rate. Because one can never be sure how long it will be before the next response will be reinforced, rewards will be maximized by responding at a regular, but not frantic, pace. This is why students whose teachers give unannounced "pop" quizzes on an unpredictable schedule are likely to study on a steady, regular basis just in case a quiz might occur at the next class (Kouyoumdjian, 2004). Variable-interval schedules also encourage the transformation of a goal-directed action (e.g., steady studying to do well on one professor's "pop" quizzes) into a habit that gains momentum from reinforcement and becomes, for example, a more general studying style (Nevin et al., 2001).

Schedules and Extinction   Ending the relationship between an operant response and its consequences weakens that response. In fact, failure to reinforce a response eventually extinguishes it. The response occurs less and less often and eventually may disappear. If you keep sending text messages to someone who never replies, you eventually stop trying. But extinction in operant conditioning does not erase learned relationships (Delamater, 2004). If a discriminative stimulus for reinforcement reappears some time after an operant response has been extinguished, that response may recur (spontaneously recover). And if it is reinforced again, the response will quickly return to its former level, as though extinction had never happened.

reinforcement schedules   In operant conditioning, rules that determine how and when certain responses will be reinforced.

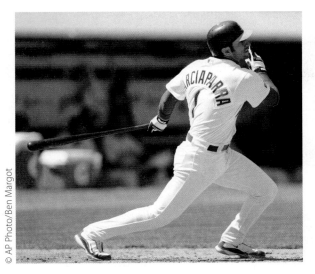

Superstition and Partial Reinforcement

Partial reinforcement helps sustain superstitious athletic rituals—such as a fixed sequence of actions prior to hitting a golf ball or shooting a free throw in basketball. If the ritual has preceded success often enough, failure to execute it may upset the player and disrupt performance. Former Oakland Athletics' infielder Nomar Garciaparra tugged, loosened, and retightened each batting glove after every pitch. Those who watch sports have their superstitious rituals, too. One Pittsburgh Steelers football fan we know insists on wearing the same outfit while watching every game and eats a particular brand of lime-flavored corn chips because he believes this will assure victory.

partial reinforcement effect
A phenomenon in which behaviors learned under a partial reinforcement schedule are more difficult to extinguish than those learned on a continuous reinforcement schedule.

punishment The presentation of an aversive stimulus or the removal of a pleasant one following some behavior.

In general, behaviors learned under a partial reinforcement schedule are far more difficult to extinguish than those learned on a continuous reinforcement schedule. This phenomenon is called the **partial reinforcement effect.** Imagine, for example, that you are in a gambling casino, standing near a broken candy machine and a broken slot machine. You might deposit money in the broken candy machine once, but this behavior will probably stop (extinguish) very quickly. The candy machine should deliver its goodies on a continuous reinforcement schedule, so you can easily tell that it is not going to provide a reinforcer. But you know that slot machines give rewards on an unpredictable, intermittent schedule. So, you might put in coin after coin, unsure of whether the machine is broken or is simply not paying off at the moment.

Partial reinforcement helps explain why superstitious behavior is so resistant to extinction (Vyse, 2000). Suppose you had been out for a run just before hearing that you passed an important exam. The run did nothing to cause this outcome. The reward followed it through sheer coincidence. Still, for some people, this kind of *accidental reinforcement* can strengthen the behavior that appeared to "cause" good news (Mellon, 2009; Pronin et al., 2006). These people might decide that it is "lucky" to go running after taking an exam. Similarly, someone who wins the lottery or a sports bet while wearing a particular shirt may begin wearing the "lucky shirt" more often (Hendrick, 2003). Of course, if the person wears the shirt often enough, something good is bound to follow every now and then, thus further strengthening the superstitious behavior on a sparse partial schedule.

Why Reinforcers Work

What makes a reinforcer reinforcing? Research by biological psychologists suggests that reinforcers may exert particular effects on the brain. In a classic study on this point, James Olds and Peter Milner (1954) discovered that mild electrical stimulation of certain areas of the brain's hypothalamus can be a powerful reinforcer. Hungry rats will ignore food if they can press a lever that stimulates these "pleasure centers" (Olds, 1973). It has since been discovered that activation of brain systems that use the neurotransmitter dopamine is associated with the pleasure of many stimuli, including food, music, sex, and highly addictive drugs such as cocaine (Berns et al., 2001; Blood & Zatorre, 2001; Chase & Clark, 2010; Ciccocioppo, Sanna, & Weiss, 2001; Hewig et al., 2010; Reuter et al., 2005; Tobler, Fiorillo, & Schultz, 2005). Actions that produce unexpected rewards, such as gambling, also produce spikes in dopamine levels in the brain (Waelti, Dickinson, & Schultz, 2001). In fact, the same brain reward areas are activated whether we are receiving money or food rewards (Kim, Shimojo, & O'Doherty, 2011). In short, complex and widespread patterns of brain activity are involved in our response to reinforcers, allowing us to enjoy them, to learn to want them, and to learn how to get them (Dreher et al., 2010; Montague, Hyman, & Cohen, 2004; Pessiglione et al., 2006; Robinson et al., 2005).

Punishment

Positive and negative reinforcement increase the frequency of a response, either by presenting something pleasurable or by removing something that is unpleasant. In contrast, positive and negative **punishment** *reduce* the frequency of an operant behavior by presenting an unpleasant stimulus or removing a pleasant one (in other words, by increasing discomfort or reducing pleasure). Shouting "No!" and swatting your cat when it scratches your furniture is an example of positive punishment, because it *presents* an aversive stimulus following a response. Taking away a child's TV privileges because of rude behavior is called negative punishment because it *removes* a pleasurable stimulus (see Figure 5.11).

Punishment is often confused with negative reinforcement, but the two are quite different. Just remember that reinforcement of any type always *strengthens* behavior, whereas punishment always *weakens* behavior. If shock is *turned off* when a rat presses a

FIGURE 5.11

Two Kinds of Punishment

In positive punishment, an aversive, or unpleasant, stimulus follows a behavior. In negative punishment, sometimes called penalty, a pleasant stimulus is removed following a behavior. In either case, punishment decreases the chances that the behavior will occur in the future. Now you decide: When a toddler reaches toward an electric outlet and her father says "NO!" and gently taps her hand, is that punishment or negative reinforcement? If you said punishment, you're right, because it will reduce the likelihood of her touching outlets in the future.

Photo credits, clockwise from top left: © Rob Wilkinson/Alamy; © Rob Byron/Shutterstock; © akit/iStockphoto; © Fotosearch/SuperStock; © Tetra Images/Getty Images; © Exactostock/ Superstock.

POSITIVE PUNISHMENT

| **Behavior** You touch a hot iron. | **Presentation of an unpleasant stimulus** Your hand is burned. | **Frequency of behavior decreases** You no longer touch hot irons. |

NEGATIVE PUNISHMENT (Penalty)

| **Behavior** You're careless with your ice cream cone. | **Removal of a pleasant stimulus** The ice cream falls on the ground. | **Frequency of behavior decreases** You're not as careless with the next cone. |

lever, negative reinforcement occurs. It increases the probability that the rat will press the lever when shock occurs again. But if shock is *turned on* when the rat presses the lever, punishment occurs. The rat will be less likely to press the lever again.

Although punishment can change behavior, it has some drawbacks (Gershoff & Bitensky, 2007). First, it does not "erase" an undesirable behavior. It merely suppresses the behavior temporarily. In fact, people often repeat punished acts when they think they can do so without getting caught. Second, punishment can produce unwanted side effects. If you punish a child for swearing, the child may associate the punisher with the punishment and end up fearing you. Third, punishment is often ineffective unless it is given immediately after the undesirable behavior and each time that behavior occurs. If a child gets into the cookie jar and enjoys a few cookies before being discovered and punished, the effect of the punishment will be greatly reduced. Fourth, physical punishment can become aggression, even abuse, if given in anger or with an object other than a hand (Zolotor et al., 2008). Fifth, because children tend to imitate what they see, frequent punishment may lead them to behave aggressively themselves (Eriksen & Jensen, 2006; Lansford & Dodge, 2008; Taylor et al., 2010). Finally, punishment lets people know they have done something wrong, but it doesn't specify what they should do instead. An "F" on a term paper means that the assignment was poorly done, but the grade alone tells the student nothing about how to improve.

When used properly, however, punishment can be a valuable tool (Baumrind, Larzelere, & Cowan, 2002). As shown in Figure 5.12, for example, it can help children who suffer from certain developmental disorders or who purposely injure themselves (Flavell et al., 1982). Punishment is used more frequently in some cultures and subcultures than in others (Runyan et al., 2010), and it is especially effective when a few guidelines are followed.

- Specify why punishment is being given, in order to prevent the development of a general fear of the punisher.
- Emphasize that the behavior, not the person, is being punished.
- Make the punishment immediate and noticeable enough to eliminate the undesirable response, without being abusive. A half-hearted "Quit it" may actually reinforce a child's misbehavior, because almost any attention is rewarding to some children.

FIGURE 5.12

Life-Saving Punishment

This child suffered from chronic ruminative disorder, a condition in which he vomited everything he ate. At left, the boy was approximately one year old and had been vomiting for four months. At right is the same child thirteen days after punishment with electric shock had eliminated the vomiting response; his weight had increased 26 percent. He was physically and psychologically healthy when tested six months, one year, and two years later (Lang & Melamed, 1969).

APPLYING PSYCHOLOGY

© Lang and Melamed, 1969

And once a child gets used to mild punishment, the parent may resort to punishment that is far more severe than would have been necessary if stern, but moderate, punishment had been used in the first place. (You may have witnessed this *escalation effect* in grocery stores or restaurants where children ignore their parents' initially weak efforts to stop their misbehavior.)

• Identify and positively reinforce more appropriate responses.

When these guidelines are not followed, the beneficial effects of punishment may be wiped out or may be only temporary. As prison systems demonstrate, punishment alone does not usually lead to rehabilitation because the punishment of confinement is not usually supplemented by efforts to teach and reinforce noncriminal lifestyles. Following their release, about two-thirds of U.S. prison inmates are rearrested for felonies or serious misdemeanors within three years, and about 50 percent will go back to prison (Cassel & Bernstein, 2007; U.S. Department of Justice, 2002).

Some Applications of Operant Conditioning

Although the principles of operant conditioning were originally worked out with animals in the laboratory, they are valuable for understanding human behavior in an endless variety of everyday situations. ("In Review: Reinforcement and Punishment" summarizes some key concepts of operant conditioning.) Effective use of reinforcements and punishments by parents, teachers, and peers is vital to helping children learn what is and is not appropriate behavior at the dinner table, in the classroom, or at a birthday party. People learn how to be "civilized" in their culture partly through experiencing positive and negative responses from others. And differing patterns of rewards and punishments for boys and girls underlie the development of behavior that fits culturally approved *gender roles,* a topic explored in more detail in the chapter on human development.

The scientific study of operant conditioning has been applied in many practical ways. For example, operant reinforcement of car-pooling has been successful in reducing the number of cars on the road during big city rush hours (Ben-Elia & Ettema, 2011), and rewarding children for trying foods they once disliked has helped them learn to enjoy those foods (Cooke et al., 2011). Programs that combine the use of rewards and extinction (or carefully administered punishment) have helped improve the behavior of countless people with mental disorders, intellectual disability, and brain injuries, as well as pre-schoolers with behavioral and emotional disorders (e.g., Alberto, Troutman, & Feagin, 2002; Dickerson, Tenhula, & Green-Paden, 2005;

Learning Cultural Values

The use of alcohol varies considerably from culture to culture, in part because some cultures reward it more than others. In Japan, for example, drinking alcohol after work is considered appropriate and is even encouraged. In some Islamic cultures, any use of alcohol is actively discouraged and may even be illegal.

Martin & Pear, 2010). These programs include establishing goal behaviors, choosing reinforcers and punishers, and developing a systematic plan for applying them to achieve desired changes. Many self-help books also incorporate the principles of positive reinforcement, recommending self-reward following each small victory in people's efforts to lose weight, stop smoking, avoid procrastination, or reach other goals (e.g., Grant & Kim, 2002; Rachlin, 2000).

When people cannot alter the consequences of a behavior, discriminative conditioned stimuli may help change their behavior. For example, many smokers find it easier to quit if they temporarily avoid bars and other places where there are powerful discriminative conditioned stimuli for smoking. Stimulus control can also help alleviate insomnia. Many insomniacs tend to use their beds for activities such as watching television, writing letters, reading magazines, worrying, and so on. Soon the bedroom becomes a discriminative stimulus for so many activities that relaxation and sleep become less and less likely. *Stimulus control therapy* encourages these people to use their beds only for sleeping, and perhaps sex, making it more likely that they will sleep better when in bed (Perlis et al., 2011).

Reinforcement and Punishment — IN REVIEW

Concept	Description	Example or Comment
Positive reinforcement	Increasing the frequency of a behavior by following it with the presentation of a positive reinforcer—a pleasant, positive stimulus or experience	You say "Good job!" after someone works hard to perform a task.
Negative reinforcement	Increasing the frequency of a behavior by following it with the removal of an unpleasant stimulus or experience	You learn to use the mute button on the TV remote control to remove the sound of an obnoxious commercial.
Escape conditioning	Learning to make a response that removes an unpleasant stimulus	A little boy learns that crying will cut short the time that he must stay in his room.
Avoidance conditioning	Learning to make a response that avoids an unpleasant stimulus	You slow your car to the speed limit when you spot a police car, thus avoiding being stopped and reducing the fear of a fine; very resistant to extinction.
Punishment	Decreasing the frequency of a behavior by either presenting an unpleasant stimulus (positive punishment) or removing a pleasant one (negative punishment)	You swat the dog after it steals food from the table or you take a favorite toy away from a child who misbehaves. A number of cautions should be kept in mind before using punishment.

IN REVIEW QUESTIONS

1. Taking a pill can relieve headache pain, so people learn to do so through the process of ___ reinforcement.
2. The "walk" sign that tells people it is safe to cross the street is an example of a ___ stimulus.
3. Response rates tend to be higher under ___ schedules of reinforcement than under ___ schedules.

LINKAGES

How are learned associations stored in memory? (a link to Memory)

Networks of Learning

Associations between conditioned stimuli and reflexes or between responses and their consequences play an important role in learning, but how are they actually stored in the brain? No one yet knows for sure, but associative network models provide a good way of thinking about the process. As suggested in the chapter on memory, the associations we form among stimuli and events are represented in complex networks of connections among neurons in the brain. Consider the word "dog." As shown in Figure 5.13, each person's experience builds many associations to this word, and the strength of each association will reflect the frequency with which "dog" has been mentally linked to the other objects, events, and ideas in that person's life.

Using what they know about the laws of learning and the way neurons communicate and alter their connections, psychologists have developed computer models of how these associations are established (Messinger et al., 2001). An important feature of these *parallel distributed processing* models is the idea of distributed memory or distributed knowledge. These models suggest, for example, that your knowledge of "dog" does not lie in a single spot, or node, in your brain. Instead, that knowledge is distributed throughout the network of associations that connect the letters D, O, and G, along with other dog- related experiences. In addition, as shown in Figure 5.13, each of the interconnected nodes that make up your knowledge of "dog" is connected to many other nodes as well. So the letter D will be connected to "daisy," "danger," and many other concepts.

Neural network models of learning focus on how these connections develop through experience (Hanson & Burr, 1990). For example, suppose you are learning a new word in a foreign language. Each time you read the word and associate it with its English equivalent, you strengthen the neural connections between the sight of the letters forming that word and all of the nodes activated when its English equivalent is brought to mind. Neural network, or *connectionist*, models of learning predict how much the strength of each linkage grows (in terms of the likelihood of neural communication between the two connected nodes) each time the two words are experienced together.

The details of various theories about how these connections grow are very complex, but a theme common to many of them is that the weaker the connection between two items, the greater the increase in connection strength when they are experienced together. So in a classical conditioning experiment, the connections between the nodes that characterize the conditioned stimulus and those that characterize the unconditioned stimulus will show the greatest increase in strength during the first few learning trials. Notice that this prediction nicely matches the typical learning curve shown in Figure 5.3 (Rescorla & Wagner, 1972).

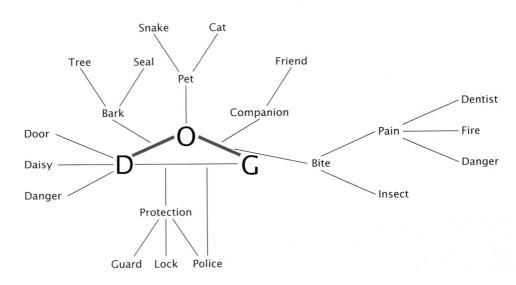

FIGURE 5.13
An Associative Network
Here is an example of a network of associations to the word "dog." Network theorists suggest that the connections shown here represent patterns of connections among nerve cells in the brain.

Neural network models have yet to fully explain the learning of complex tasks, and they cannot easily account for how people adapt when the "rules of the game" are suddenly changed and old habits must be unlearned and replaced. Nevertheless, further research on neural network models is likely to produce a better understanding of what we mean by *associations* (Boden, 2006; Coutanche & Thompson-Schill, 2012; Goldblum, 2001; Houghton, 2005).   ● ● ● ●

Cognitive Processes in Learning

Can people learn to be helpless?

In the first half of the twentieth century, psychologists in North America tended to look at learning through the lens of behaviorism. As we mentioned earlier, they did acknowledge that mental representations, expectancies, and other cognitive processes can be involved in learning, but they nevertheless concentrated on studying the formation or modification of associations between observable stimuli and observable responses. Their research resulted in a rich set of learning principles based on classical and operant conditioning experiments.

In recent decades, however, there has been an increasing and more specific interest in exploring other, more complex forms of learning, and the cognitive processes associated with them. These forms of learning include the development of concepts, of skill at communication, navigation, and tool use, and of abilities and behavior patterns formed by watching what others do (Blaisdell, Sawa, & Leising, 2006; Wasserman, 1993). Researchers in an area known as *comparative cognition* are exploring the extent to which the cognitive processes involved in these more complex forms of learning are seen in nonhumans as well as humans. How, they wonder, can food-storing birds hide, and then later retrieve, thousands of individual food items they need to survive over the winter? Their search might look random, but there is evidence that these birds form memories not only of where they have hidden something, but what they hid and when they hid it (Clayton & Dickinson, 1998; Suddendorf & Corballis, 2007). And although tool use was once thought to be a uniquely human form of adaptation, research by animal behaviorists has shown that chimpanzees, crows, sea otters, and other nonhuman animals have learned to use tools, too (e.g., Cheke et al., 2011; Goodall, 1964). It may well be, then, that nonhumans can form mental representations, have expectations, and make generalizations that go beyond simply associating a particular response with a reward in an instrumental conditioning experiment (Asen & Cook, 2012; Blaisdell, Sawa, & Leising, 2006).

These processes are most certainly at work in humans, as shown in cognitive psychologists' research on phenomena such as learned helplessness, latent learning, cognitive maps, insight, and observational learning.

Learned Helplessness

Babies learn that crying attracts attention. Children learn how to make the TV louder. Adults learn what actions lead to success or failure in the workplace. On the basis of this learning people come to expect that certain actions on their part will have certain consequences. But sometimes events are beyond our control. What happens when our actions have no effect on events, and especially when our escape or avoidance behaviors fail? If these circumstances last long enough, one result may be **learned helplessness,** a tendency to give up on efforts to control the environment (Overmier, 2002; Seligman, 1975).

Learned helplessness was first demonstrated in animals. As described earlier, dogs in a shuttle box will learn to jump over a partition to escape a shock (see Figure 5.8). But if the dogs first receive shocks that they cannot escape, they later do not even try to escape when the shock is turned on in the shuttle box (Overmier & Seligman, 1967). It is as if the animals had learned that "shock happens, and there is nothing I can do about it." Do people learn the same lesson?

learned helplessness A process in which a person or animal stops trying to exert control after experience suggests that no control is possible.

FOCUS ON *RESEARCH*   # The "I Can't Do It" Attitude

What lessons do abused and neglected children learn about their ability to get what they need from the environment? Do they learn that even their best efforts result in failure? Do they give up even trying? Why would a student with above average ability tell a counselor, "I can't do math"? How do people develop an "I can't do it" attitude?

What was the researcher's question?

Can lack of control over the environment lead to helplessness in humans? Donald Hiroto (1974) conducted an experiment to test the hypothesis that people develop learned helplessness either after experiencing lack of control or after simply being told that their control is limited.

How did the researcher answer the question?

Hiroto (1974) randomly assigned research participants to one of three groups. One group heard a series of thirty bursts of loud, obnoxious noise and, like dogs receiving inescapable shock, had no way to stop it. A second group could control the noise by pressing a button to turn it off. The third group heard no noise at all. After this preliminary phase, all three groups were exposed to eighteen additional bursts of noise, each preceded by a red warning light. During this second phase, all participants could prevent the noise if they pushed a lever quickly enough. However, they didn't know whether to push the lever left or right on any given trial. Before these new trials began, the experimenter told half the participants in each group that avoiding or escaping the noise depended on their skill. The other half were told that their success would be a matter of chance.

What did the researcher find?

The people who had previously experienced lack of control now failed to control noise on about four times as many trials as did those who had earlier been in control (50 percent versus 13 percent). This finding was similar to that of the research with dogs and inescapable shock. When the dogs were later placed in a situation in which they could escape or avoid shock, they did not even try. Humans, too, seem to use prior experiences to guide later efforts to try, or not to try, to control their environment.

Expectation of control, whether accurate or not, also had an effect on behavior. In Hiroto's study, those participants who expected that skill could control the noise exerted control on significantly more trials than did those who expected chance to govern the result. This outcome occurred regardless of whether the participants had experienced control before.

What do the results mean?

These results support Hiroto's hypothesis that people, like animals, tend to make less effort to control their environment when prior experience suggests that those efforts will be of no use. But unlike animals, humans need only be *told* that they have no control or are powerless in order for this same effect to occur.

Hiroto's (1974) results appear to reflect a general phenomenon. When prior experience leads people to *believe* that there is nothing they can do to change their lives or control their destiny, they may stop trying to improve their lot (Faulkner, 2001; LoLordo, 2001; Peterson, Maier, & Seligman, 1993). Instead, they may passively endure painful situations. Has this ever happened to you?

What do we still need to know?

Further research is needed on when and how learned helplessness affects people's thoughts, feelings, and actions. For example, could learned helplessness explain why some battered women remain with abusive partners? We do know that learned helplessness experiences are associated with the development of a generally pessimistic way of thinking that can produce depression and other mental disorders (Peterson & Seligman, 1984). People with this *pessimistic explanatory style* see the good things that happen to them as temporary and due to chance and the bad things as permanent and due to internal factors such as lack of ability. This explanatory style has, in fact, been associated with poor grades, inadequate sales performance, health problems, and other negative outcomes (Bennett & Elliott, 2002; Seligman & Schulman, 1986; Taylor, 2002). The exact mechanisms responsible for this connection are still unknown, but understanding how pessimistic (or optimistic) explanatory styles can lead to negative (or positive) consequences remains an important focus of research (e.g., Brennan & Charnetski, 2000). Research is also focusing on how best to minimize learned helplessness and maximize learned optimism in areas such as education, parenting, and psychotherapy (e.g., Jackson, Sellers, & Peterson, 2002).   ● ● ● ●

Latent Learning and Cognitive Maps

Decades ago, Edward Tolman studied cognitive processes in learning by watching rats try to find their way to food that was waiting for them at the end of a complex maze. At first, the rats took many wrong turns. Over time, though, they made fewer and fewer mistakes. The behavioral interpretation of this result was that the rats learned a long chain of turning responses that were reinforced by food. Tolman disagreed and offered evidence for a cognitive interpretation.

In one of Tolman's studies, three groups of rats were placed in the same maze once a day for several days (Tolman & Honzik, 1930). For Group A, food was placed at the end of the maze on each trial. As shown in Figure 5.14, these rats gradually improved their performance. Group B also ran the maze once a day, but there was never any food waiting for them. The animals in Group B continued to make many errors. Neither of these results is surprising.

The third group of rats, Group C, was the critical one. For the first ten days, they received no reinforcement for running the maze and continued to make many mistakes. On the eleventh day, food was placed at the end of the maze for the first time. What do you think happened? On the day after receiving reinforcement, these rats made almost no mistakes (again, see Figure 5.14). In fact, their performance was as good as that of the group that had been reinforced every day. The single reinforcement trial on day 11 produced a dramatic change in their performance the next day.

Tolman argued that these results support two conclusions. First, because the rats in Group C improved their performance the first time they ran the maze after being

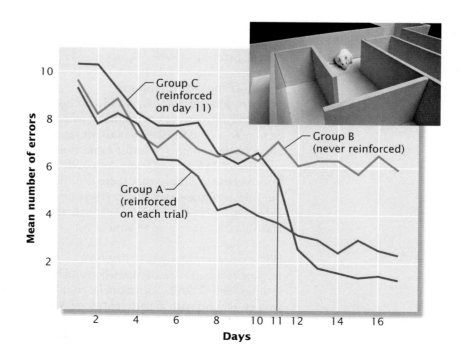

reinforced, the reinforcement on day 11 could not have significantly affected their *learning* of the maze. Rather, the reinforcement simply changed their subsequent *performance*. They must have learned the maze earlier as they wandered around making mistakes on their way to the end of the maze. These rats demonstrated **latent learning**—learning that is not evident when it first occurs. (Latent learning occurs in humans, too; for example, after years of experience in your neighborhood, you could probably tell a visitor that the corner drugstore is closed on Sundays, even if you had never tried to go there on a Sunday yourself.) Second, the rats' sudden improvement in performance after the first reinforcement trial could have occurred only if the rats had earlier developed a cognitive map of the maze. A **cognitive map** is a mental representation of some physical arrangement—in this case, a maze.

Tolman concluded that cognitive maps develop naturally through experience, even in the absence of any overt response or reinforcement. Research on learning in the natural environment has supported this view. We develop mental maps of shopping malls and city streets even when we receive no direct reward for doing so (Tversky & Kahneman, 1991). Having such a map allows you to tell that neighborhood visitor exactly how to get to the corner drugstore from where you are standing.

Insight and Learning

Wolfgang Köhler was a psychologist whose work on the cognitive aspects of learning happened almost by accident. He was visiting Tenerife, an island in the Atlantic Ocean, when World War I broke out in 1914. As a German in territory controlled by Germany's enemy, Britain, Köhler was confined there until the war ended in 1918. He used this time to study problem solving in a colony of local chimpanzees (Köhler, 1924).

For example, Köhler would put a chimpanzee in a cage and place a piece of fruit where the chimp could see it but not reach it. He sometimes hung the fruit too high to be reached or placed it on the ground too far outside the animal's cage to be retrieved. Many of the chimps overcame these obstacles easily. If the fruit was out of reach beyond the cage, some chimps looked around, found a long stick, and used it to rake in the fruit. Surprised that the chimpanzees could solve these problems, Köhler tried more difficult tasks. Again, the chimps quickly got to the fruit.

Three aspects of Köhler's observations convinced him that animals' problem solving does not have to depend on trial and error and the gradual association of responses with consequences. First, once a chimpanzee solved one type of problem, it would immediately do the same thing in a similar situation. In other words, it acted as if it understood the problem. Second, Köhler's chimpanzees rarely tried a solution that did not work. Apparently, the solution was not discovered randomly but "thought out" ahead of time and then acted out successfully. Third, the chimps often reached a solution quite suddenly. When confronted with a piece of fruit hanging from a string, for instance, a chimp would jump for it several times, then it would stop jumping, look up, and pace back and forth. Finally, it would run over to a wooden crate, place it directly under the fruit, and climb on top of it to reach the fruit. Once, when there were no other objects in the cage, a chimp went over to Köhler, dragged him by the arm until he stood beneath the fruit, and then started climbing up his back!

Köhler believed that the only explanation for these results was that the chimpanzees had experienced **insight,** a sudden understanding of the problem as a whole. Was he right? Possibly, but what Köhler saw as sudden insight might not have been so sudden. Other psychologists found that previous trial-and-error experience with objects, such as boxes and sticks, is necessary for "insight" in chimps (Birch, 1945). In fact, some psychologists argue that all known cases of "insight" by humans and nonhumans alike include a long history of experience with the objects that are used to solve the problem (Epstein et al., 1984; Kounios et al., 2006; Wynne, 2004). Others have suggested true insight seems to result from a "mental trial-and-error process" in which people (and perhaps certain other animals) envision a course of action, mentally simulate its results, compare it with the imagined outcome of other alternatives, and settle on the course of action most likely to aid complex problem solving and decision making (Klein, 1993).

latent learning Learning that is not demonstrated at the time it occurs.

cognitive map A mental representation of the environment.

insight A sudden understanding of what is required to solve a problem.

So although Köhler's work helped highlight the importance of cognitive processes in learning, questions remain about whether it demonstrated true insight in chimps.

Observational Learning: Learning by Imitation

People and animals learn a lot from personal experience, but they can also learn by observing what others do and what happens to them when they do it (e.g., Akins & Zentall, 1998; Mattar & Gribble, 2005). Learning by watching others—a process called **observational learning,** or **social learning**—is efficient and adaptive. We don't have to find out for ourselves that a door is locked or an iron is hot if we have just seen someone else try the door or suffer a burn.

The biological basis for observational learning may lie partly in the activity of brain systems that help us predict what will happen when other people do something like walk on the thin ice of a recently frozen pond (Burke et al., 2010). It is also based partly on the operation of the brain's *mirror neurons* (Fogassi et al., 2005; Mukamel et al., 2010), which fire not only when we do something or experience something but also when we see someone else do or experience the same thing. This mirrored pattern of activity in our own brains makes it almost as though we are actually performing the observed action or having the observed experience. Mirror neurons are activated, for example, when we feel disgust upon seeing someone react to the taste of sour milk. They also probably fire when we imitate the correct pronunciation of foreign words or follow someone's example in using an unfamiliar tool.

Children are particularly influenced by the adults and peers who act as *models* for appropriate behavior. In a classic experiment, Albert Bandura showed nursery school children a film starring an adult and a large, inflatable, bottom-heavy Bobo doll (Bandura, 1965). The adult in the film punched the doll in the nose, kicked it, threw things at it, and hit its head with a hammer while saying things like "Sockeroo!" There were different endings to the film. Some children saw an ending in which the aggressive adult was called a "champion" by a second adult and rewarded with candy and soft drinks. Some saw the aggressor scolded and called a "bad person." Some saw a neutral ending in which there was neither reward nor punishment. After the film, each child was allowed to play alone with a Bobo doll. The way they played in this and similar studies led to some important conclusions about learning and the role of cognitive factors in it.

observational learning (social learning) Learning by watching the behavior of others.

Learning by Imitation
Much of our behavior is learned by imitating others, especially those who serve as role models. To appreciate the impact of social learning in your life, list five examples of how your own actions, speech, appearance, or mannerisms have come to match those of a parent, a sibling, a friend, a teacher, or even a celebrity.

LEARN**by** DOING

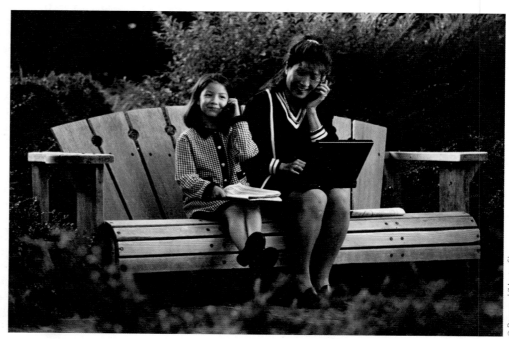

© Rommel/Masterfile

FIGURE 5.15

Observational Learning

Bandura found that after observing an aggressive model, many children imitate the model's acts precisely, especially if the model's aggression was rewarded.

Source: Ross, L. A. et al. (1963). Imitation of film-mediated aggressive models. *Journal of Abnormal and Social Psychology, 66,* 3–11.

Aggressive model rewarded

Aggressive model punished

Nonaggressive model

No model

Bandura found that children who saw the adult rewarded for aggression showed the most aggressive acts in play (see Figure 5.15). They had received *vicarious conditioning,* a kind of observational learning through which a person is influenced by watching or hearing about the consequences of others' behavior. The children who had seen the adult punished for aggressive acts showed less aggression, but they still learned something. When later offered rewards for imitating all the aggressive acts they had seen in the film, these children displayed just as many of these acts as the children who had watched the adult being rewarded. Observational learning can occur even when there are no vicarious consequences; many children in the neutral condition also imitated the model's aggression.

Like direct reward and punishment, observational learning is a powerful force in the *socialization* process through which children learn about which behaviors are—and are not—appropriate in their culture (Bandura, 1999; Caldwell & Millen, 2009). For example, children show long-term increases in their willingness to help and share after seeing a demonstration of helping by a friendly, impressive model (Schroeder et al., 1995). Fears, too, can be learned partly by the sight of fearfulness in others (Askew & Field, 2008; Broeren et al., 2011; Burstein & Ginsburg, 2010) and seeing other people behave dishonestly may lead observers to do the same (Gino, Ayal, & Ariely, 2009).

THINKING CRITICALLY

Does Watching Violence on Television Make Children More Violent?

If observational learning is important, then surely movies, video games, and television—and the violence they so often portray—must teach children a great deal. Psychologists have spent a great deal of time studying these media, and especially the possible effects of televised violence. It is estimated that the average child in the United States spends about four hours each day watching television (Annenberg Public Policy Center, 2000; Christakis & Garrison, 2009; Tandon et al., 2011). Much of what children see is violent. In addition to the real-life violence portrayed on the news

(Van der Molen, 2004), prime-time entertainment programs in the United States present an average of five acts of simulated violence per hour. Some Saturday morning cartoons include more than twenty per hour (American Psychological Association, 1993; Gerbner, Morgan, & Signorielli, 1994). As a result, the average child will have witnessed at least 8,000 murders and more than 100,000 other acts of televised violence before finishing elementary school and twice that number by age 18 (Annenberg Public Policy Center, 1999; Kunkel et al., 1996; Parents Television Council, 2006).

Psychologists have long speculated that watching so much violence might be emotionally arousing, making viewers more likely to react violently to frustration (Huston & Wright, 1989). In fact, there is evidence that exposure to media violence can trigger or amplify viewers' aggressive thoughts and feelings, thus increasing the likelihood that they will act aggressively (Anderson & Dill, 2000; Bushman, 1998). Televised violence might also provide models that viewers imitate, particularly if the violence is carried out by the "good guys" (Huesmann et al., 2003). Finally, prolonged viewing of violent TV programs might desensitize viewers, making them less distressed when they see others suffer, less likely to help them, and less disturbed about inflicting pain on others (Aronson, 1999; Bushman & Anderson, 2009; Smith & Donnerstein, 1998). Concern over the influence of violence on television has led to the development of a violence-blocking V-Chip for new television sets in the United States.

What am I being asked to believe or accept?

Many have argued that watching violence on television actually causes violent behavior in viewers (Anderson et al., 2003; Anderson & Bushman, 2002b; Bushman & Huesmann, 2000; Eron et al., 1972; Huesmann, 1998). In 1993, a National Academy of Sciences report concluded that "overall, the vast majority of studies, whatever their methodology, showed that exposure to television violence resulted in increased aggressive behavior, both contemporaneously and over time" (Reiss & Roth, 1993, p. 371). An American Psychological Association Commission on Violence and Youth reached the same conclusion (American Psychological Association, 1993).

Is evidence available to support the claim?

Three types of evidence back up the claim that watching violent television programs increases violent behavior. First, there are anecdotes and case studies. Children have poked one another in the eye after watching the Three Stooges appear to do so on television and adults have claimed that watching TV shows prompted them to commit murders or other violent acts like those seen on the shows (Werner, 2003).

Second, many correlational studies have found a strong link between watching violent television programs and later acts of aggression and violence (Christakas & Zimmerman, 2007; Johnson, Cohen et al., 2002). One such study tracked people from the time they were six or seven until they reached their early twenties. Those who watched more violent television as children were significantly more aggressive as adults (Huesmann et al., 1997, 2003) and more likely to engage in criminal activity (Huesmann, 1995). They were also more likely to use physical punishment on their own children, who themselves tended to be much more aggressive than average. These latter results were found not only in the United States but also in Israel, Australia, Poland, the Netherlands, and even Finland, where the number of violent TV shows is very small (Centerwall, 1990; Huesmann & Eron, 1986).

Finally, the results of numerous experiments support the view that TV violence increases aggression among viewers (American Psychological Association, 1993; Paik & Comstock, 1994; Reiss & Roth, 1993). In one study, groups of boys watched either violent or nonviolent programs in a controlled setting and then played floor hockey (Josephson, 1987). Boys who had watched the violent shows were more likely than those who had watched nonviolent programs to behave aggressively on the hockey floor. This effect was greatest for boys who had the most aggressive tendencies to begin with. More extensive experiments in which children are exposed for long periods to carefully controlled types of television programs also suggest that exposure to large amounts of violent activity on television results in aggressive behavior (Eron et al., 1972).

Can that evidence be interpreted another way?

To some, this evidence leaves no doubt that media violence causes increases in aggressive and violent behavior, especially in children (Anderson et al., 2003). Others suggest that the evidence is not conclusive and is open to some qualifications and alternative interpretations (e.g., Browne & Hamilton-Giachritsis, 2005; Ferguson, 2010; Freedman, 2002; Thakkar, Garrison, & Christakis, 2006), or that increases in youth violence are due to other factors (Ferguson, San Miguel, & Hartley, 2009).

Anecdotal reports and case studies are certainly open to different interpretations. If people face imprisonment or execution for their violent acts, how believable are their claims that their actions were triggered by television programs? How many other people might say that the same programs made them less likely to be violent? Anecdotes alone do not provide a good basis for drawing solid scientific conclusions.

What about the correlational evidence? A correlation between two variables does not necessarily mean that one caused the other. Both might be caused by a third factor. At least one possible "third factor" might account for the observed relationship between watching TV violence and acting aggressively: Certain people may prefer both to watch more violent TV programs and to behave aggressively toward others. In other words, personality may partly account for the observed correlations (e.g., Aluja-Fabregat & Torrubia-Beltri, 1998; Steinberg & Monahan, 2011).

As for the results of controlled experiments on the effects of televised violence, some researchers suggest that those effects may be short lived and may not apply beyond the experimental situation (Anderson, Lindsay, & Bushman, 1999; Browne & Hamilton-Giachritsis, 2005; Freedman, 2002). Who is to say, for example, whether an increase in aggressive acts during a hockey game has any later bearing on a child's tendency to commit an act of violence?

What evidence would help to evaluate the alternatives?

By their nature, correlational studies of the role of TV violence in violent behavior can never be conclusive. As we've pointed out, a third, unidentified causal variable could always be responsible for the results. More important would be further evidence from controlled experiments in which equivalent groups of people were given different long-term "doses" of TV violence and its effects on their subsequent behavior were observed for many years. Such experiments could also explore the circumstances under which different people (for example, children versus adults) are affected by various forms of violence. However, conducting studies such as these would create an ethical dilemma. If watching violent television programs really does cause violent behavior, are psychologists justified in creating conditions that might lead some people to be more violent? If such violence occurred, would the researchers be responsible to the victims and to society? If some participants commit violent acts, should the researchers continue the experiment to establish a pattern or should they terminate the participation of those individuals? Difficulty in answering questions such as these is partly responsible for the use of short-term experiments and correlational designs in this research area, as well as for some of the remaining uncertainty about the effects of television violence.

One approach to this problem might be to conduct experiments in which children watch television shows that portray cooperative rather than violent behavior. If exposure to such *prosocial* programming were followed by significant increases in viewers' own prosocial behavior, it would strengthen—though still not prove—the argument that what children see on television can have a causal impact on their actions. Recent experiments have already shown that people who played prosocial video games were later more helpful than those who had played neutral games (Greitemeyer & Osswald, 2010), and showed greater empathy and less pleasure at others' misfortunes (Greitemeyer, Osswald, & Brauer, 2010; Um et al., 2011).

What conclusions are most reasonable?

The evidence collected so far makes it reasonable to conclude that watching TV violence is one cause of violent behavior, especially in some children and especially in boys (Anderson & Bushman, 2002a; Browne & Hamilton-Giachritsis, 2005; Bushman & Anderson, 2001;

"I have HAD it with you two and your violent video games!"

The violence that may affect children's aggressive behavior is not always limited to what they see on television and video games.

Huesmann et al., 1997; Robinson et al., 2001; Smith & Donnerstein, 1998). Playing violent video games may be another (Anderson et al., 2008; Anderson, Shibuya et al., 2010; Polman, Orobio de Castro, & van Aken, 2008). Some research suggests that violent video games may lead players to dehumanize other people, making them mere "targets" and releasing acts of real violence (e.g., Greitemeyer & McLatchie, 2011).

But a cause-and-effect relationship between watching TV violence or playing violent games and acting violently is not inevitable and may not always be long lasting (Browne & Hamilton-Giachritsis, 2005; Ferguson & Kilburn, 2009, 2010; Ferguson et al., 2010; Savage, 2004; Savage & Yancey, 2008). Further, there are many circumstances in which the effect does not occur (Charleton, Gunter, & Coles, 1998; Ferguson, 2009; Freedman, 1992, 2002). Parents, peers, and other environmental influences as well as personality factors may dampen or amplify the effect of watching televised violence or playing violent video games (Markey & Markey, 2010). So may the nature of the games themselves; aggressive behavior may be more strongly associated with games that feature competitiveness, difficulty, and a fast pace (Adachi & Willoughby, 2011). In addition, not every viewer interprets violence in the same way, and not everyone is equally vulnerable to its possible effects (Ferguson, 2002, 2009; Feshbach & Tangney, 2008; Kirsh, 2011; Wood, Wong, & Chachere, 1991). The most vulnerable may be young boys, especially those who are the most aggressive or violence-prone in the first place, a trait that could well have been acquired by observing the behavior of parents or peers (Ferguson et al., 2010; Kirsh, 2011).

Still, the fact that violence on television and in video games *can* have a causal impact on violent behavior is reason for serious concern. This issue continues to influence public debate about what should and should not be aired on television and offered by video game manufacturers.   ● ● ● ●

Using Research on Learning to Help People Learn

What should teachers learn about learning?

The study of how people learn obviously has important implications for improved teaching in our schools and for helping people develop skills (Bjork & Linn, 2006; Halpern & Hakel, 2003; Li, 2005; Newcombe et al., 2009).

Active Learning

The importance of cognitive processes in learning is apparent in instructional methods that emphasize *active learning* (Bonwell & Eison, 1991). These methods take many forms, including, for example, small-group problem-solving tasks, discussion of "one-minute essays" written in class, use of student response devices ("clickers") or just "thumbs up" or "thumbs down" gestures to indicate agreement or disagreement with the instructor's lecture, and multiple-choice questions that give students feedback about their understanding of the previous fifteen minutes of a lecture (Goss Lucas & Bernstein, 2005). Students typically find classes that include active learning experiences to be interesting and enjoyable (Bruff, 2009; Moran, 2000; Murray, 2000). In addition, active learning methods help students go beyond memorizing isolated facts. These methods encourage students to think more deeply, to consider how new material relates to what they already know, and to apply it in new situations. This kind of thinking also makes the material easier to remember, which is why we have included so many opportunities for you to actively learn, rather than just passively read, the material in this book.

Studies of students in elementary schools, high schools, community colleges, and universities have found that compared with instructional techniques that are more passive, active learning approaches result in better test performance and greater class participation (e.g., Altman, 2007; Deslauriers, Schelew, & Wieman, 2011; Hake, 1998; Karpicke & Blunt, 2011; Kellum, Carr, & Dozier, 2001; Meyers & Jones, 1993; Saville et al., 2006). In one study, a fifth-grade teacher spent some days calling only on students whose hands were raised. On other days, all students were required to answer every question by holding up a card with their response written on it. Scores on next-day quizzes and biweekly tests showed that students remembered more of the material covered on the active learning days than on the "passive" days (Gardner, Heward, & Grossi, 1994). In another study of two consecutive medical school classes taught by the same instructor, scores on the final exam were significantly higher when students learned mainly through small-group discussions and case studies than when they were taught mainly through lectures (Chu, 1994). Similarly, among adults being taught to use a new computer program, active learning with hands-on practice was more effective than passively watching a demonstration video (Kerr & Payne, 1994). Finally, high school and college students who passively listened to a physics lecture received significantly lower scores on a test of lecture content than did those who participated in a virtual reality lab that allowed them to interact with the physical forces covered in the lecture (Brelsford, 1993). Results like these have fueled the development of other science education programs that place students in virtual laboratory environments in which they actively manipulate materials and test hypotheses (e.g., Horwitz & Christie, 2000).

Despite the enthusiasm generated by active learning methods, rigorous experimental research is still needed to compare their short- and long-term effects with those of more traditional methods in teaching various kinds of course content (Alexander, Eaton, & Egan, 2010; Fiorella & Mayer, 2012; Moran, 2006). At least one study has shown that college students who learned about pathogens or electromechanical devices through the use of interactive computerized "adventure games" did not perform as well on exams as students who learned the same material using more conventional methods (Adams et al., 2011). Other studies have found standard textbooks superior to e-books and podcasts for delivering primary text material in college courses (Daniel & Woody, 2010; Woody, Daniel, & Baker, 2010). It may turn out that traditional teaching methods (including interesting lectures and engaging textbooks) are effective tools for presenting basic course material, but that active learning methods—including repeated testing and self-testing—may be superior to passive ones for helping students to retain, recall, and apply new information.

© Hank Morgan/Science Photo Library/Photo Researchers, Inc.

Virtual Surgery

Using a virtual reality system, this medical student can actively learn and practice eye surgery skills before working with real patients. Computer-based human body simulators are also giving new doctors active learning experience in emergency room diagnosis and treatment; heart, lung, and abdominal surgery; and other medical skills (Aggarwal, Cheshire, & Darzi, 2008; Ganai et al., 2007; Groopman, 2005; Heinrichs et al., 2008; Kanno et al., 2008; Kato, 2010; Katsavelis et al., 2007; Prabhudesai et al., 2008; Seymour, 2008; Tsang et al., 2008).

Skill Learning

The complex action sequences, or *skills,* that people learn to perform in everyday life develop through learning processes that include feedback and lots of practice (Ackerman, 2007). In fact, *practice*—the repeated performance of a skill—is critical to mastery (Howe, Davidson, & Sloboda, 1998). For perceptual-motor skills such as playing pool or piano, both physical and mental practice are beneficial (Druckman & Bjork, 1994). To be most effective, practice should continue past the point of correct performance until the skill can be performed automatically, with little or no attention. Feedback about the correctness of the response is also necessary. As with any learning process, the feedback should come soon enough to be effective but not so quickly that it interferes with the learner's efforts to learn independently.

Large amounts of guidance may produce very good performance during practice, but too much guidance may hurt later performance (Kluger & DeNisi, 1998; Wickens, 1992). For instance, coaching students about correct responses in math may impair their ability later to retrieve the correct response from memory on their own. Independent practice at retrieving previously learned responses or information requires more effort, but it is critical for skill development (Ericsson & Charness, 1994). There is little or no evidence to support "sleep learning" or similar schemes designed to make learning effortless (Druckman & Bjork, 1994). In short, "no pain, no gain."

Reciprocal Teaching

Ann Brown and her colleagues (1992) demonstrated the success of reciprocal teaching, in which children take turns teaching each other. This technique, which is similar to the cooperative arrangements seen in Japanese education, has become increasingly popular in North American schools (Palincsar, 2003; Spörer, Brunstein, & Kieschke, 2009).

Classrooms across Cultures

Many people have expressed concern that schools in the United States are not doing a very good job. A recent report by the Center on Education Policy found, for example, that nearly half of public schools in the U.S. failed to meet Federal standards for adequate yearly progress (Usher, 2011). Further, the average performance of U.S. students on tests of reading, math, and other basic academic skills has tended to fall short of that of youngsters in other countries, especially Asian countries (Mullis et al., 2007; National Center for Education Statistics, 2000, 2002; Program for International Student Assessment, 2004, 2005). In one early comparison study, Harold Stevenson (1992) followed a sample of pupils in Taiwan, Japan, and the United States from the first grade, in 1980, to the eleventh grade, in 1991. In the first grade, the Asian students scored no higher than their U.S. peers on tests of mathematical aptitude and skills and they did not enjoy math more. However, by the fifth grade, the U.S. students had fallen far behind. Corresponding differences were seen in reading skills. More recent studies have found similar results (Mullis et al., 2004, 2007).

Some possible causes of these differences were found in the classroom itself (Rindermann & Ceci, 2009). In a typical U.S. classroom, teachers talked to students as a group, then students worked at their desks independently. Reinforcement or other feedback about performance on their work was usually delayed until the next day or not provided at all. In contrast, the typical Japanese classroom placed greater emphasis on cooperative work among students (Kristof, 1997). Teachers provided more immediate feedback on a one-to-one basis. And there was an emphasis on creating teams of students with varying abilities, an arrangement in which faster learners help teach slower ones. However, before concluding that the differences in performance are the result of social factors alone, we must consider another important distinction: The Japanese children practiced more. They spent more days in school during the year and, on average, spent more hours doing homework.

Psychologists and educators are considering how various principles of learning can be applied to improve education. For example, anecdotal and experimental evidence suggests that some of the most successful educational techniques are those that apply basic principles of operant conditioning, offering frequent testing, positive reinforcement for correct performance, and immediate corrective feedback following mistakes (Oppel, 2000; Roediger, McDaniel, & McDermott, 2006).

Further, research in cognitive psychology suggests that students will retain more of what they learn if they study in several sessions distributed over time rather than in a single "cramming" session on the night before a test (e.g., Cepeda et al., 2008, 2009; Kramár et al., 2012; Pashler, Rohrer, & Cepeda, 2006; Rawson & Dunlosky, 2011). To encourage this kind of *distributed practice*, researchers say, teachers should give enough exams and quizzes (some unannounced, perhaps) that students will be reading and studying more or less continuously. And because learning is aided by repeated opportunities to use new information, these exams and quizzes should cover material from throughout the term, not just the material from recent classes (Karpicke, 2012; Karpicke & Smith, 2012). These recommendations are not necessarily popular with students, but there is good evidence that they promote long-term retention of course material (e.g., Bjork, 2001; Bjork & Linn, 2006).

Active Review

As noted in the introductory chapter, all of psychology's subfields are related to one another. Our discussion of associative network models illustrates just one way that the topic of this chapter, learning, is linked to the subfield of memory, which is described in the chapter by

CHAPTER 5
Learning

that name. The Linkages diagram shows ties to two other subfields, and there are many more ties throughout the book. Looking for linkages among subfields will help you see how they all fit together and help you better appreciate the big picture that is psychology.

LINKAGES

How are learned associations stored in memory? *(ans. on p. 189)*

CHAPTER 6
Memory

Who teaches boys to be men and girls to be women? *(ans. on p. 371)*

CHAPTER 9
Human Development

Are psychological disorders learned behaviors? *(ans. on p. 460)*

CHAPTER 12
Psychological Disorders

Summary

Individuals adapt to changes in the environment through the process of *learning,* which is the modification, through experience, of preexisting behavior and understanding.

Classical Conditioning: Learning Signals and Associations

How did Russian dogs teach psychologists about learning?
One form of learning is *classical conditioning.* It occurs when a previously neutral *conditioned stimulus,* or *CS* (such as a tone), is repeatedly paired with an *unconditioned stimulus,* or *UCS* (such as meat powder on a dog's tongue), which naturally brings about an *unconditioned response,* or *UCR* (such as salivation). Eventually the conditioned stimulus will elicit a response, known as

the *conditioned response,* or *CR,* even when the unconditioned stimulus is not presented.

The strength of a conditioned response grows as CS-UCS pairings continue. If the UCS is no longer paired with the CS, the conditioned response eventually disappears; this is *extinction.* After extinction, the conditioned response may reappear if the CS is presented after some time; this is *spontaneous recovery.* In addition, if the conditioned and unconditioned stimuli are paired once or twice after extinction, *reconditioning* occurs; that is, the conditioned response regains much of its original strength.

Because of *stimulus generalization,* conditioned responses occur to stimuli that are similar, but not identical, to conditioned stimuli. Generalization is limited by *stimulus discrimination,*

which prompts conditioned responses to some stimuli but not to others.

Classical conditioning involves learning that the CS is an event that predicts the occurrence of another event, the UCS. Many psychologists see the conditioned response as a means through which animals and people develop mental representations of the relationships between events. Classical conditioning works best when the conditioned stimulus precedes the unconditioned stimulus by intervals ranging from less than a second to a minute or more, depending on the stimuli involved. Conditioning is also more likely when the CS reliably signals the UCS. In general, the speed of conditioning increases as the intensity of the UCS increases. Which particular stimulus is likely to become a CS linked to a subsequent UCS depends partly on which stimulus was being attended to when the UCS occurred; more intense stimuli are more likely to attract attention. *Higher order conditioning* occurs when one conditioned stimulus signals a conditioned stimulus that is already associated with an unconditioned stimulus. Some stimuli become associated more easily than others; taste aversions provide illustrations that organisms seem to be biologically prepared to learn certain associations.

Classical conditioning plays a role in the development and treatment of phobias. *Habituation* is reduced responsiveness to a repeated stimulus. According to Solomon's opponent-process theory, habituation is the result of two processes that balance each other. The first process is a relatively automatic, involuntary response—essentially a UCR. The second, or opponent, process is a learned or conditioned response that follows and counteracts the first. These conditioned responses may help explain the development of drug tolerance and some cases of drug overdoses.

Instrumental and Operant Conditioning: Learning the Consequences of Behavior

How do reward and punishment work? Learning occurs not only through associating stimuli but also through associating behavior with its consequences. Thorndike's *law of effect* holds that any response that produces satisfaction becomes more likely to occur again and that any response that produces discomfort becomes less likely to recur. Thorndike referred to this type of learning as instrumental conditioning. Skinner called the process *operant conditioning.*

An *operant* is a response that has some effect on the world. A *reinforcer* increases the probability that the operant preceding it will occur again. There are two types of reinforcers: *positive reinforcers,* desirable stimuli that strengthen a response if they are presented after that response occurs, and *negative reinforcers,* which are the removal of an unpleasant stimulus following some response. Both kinds

of reinforcers strengthen the behaviors that precede them. When behavior is strengthened by a positive reinforcer, the process is called positive reinforcement. When behavior is strengthened by a negative reinforcer, the process is called negative reinforcement. *Escape conditioning* results when a behavior stops an unpleasant stimulus. *Avoidance conditioning* results when behavior prevents an unpleasant stimulus from occurring; it reflects both classical and operant conditioning. Behaviors learned through avoidance conditioning are hard to extinguish. *Discriminative conditioned stimuli* signal whether reinforcement is available for a particular behavior.

Complex responses can be learned through *shaping,* which involves reinforcing successive approximations of the desired response. *Primary reinforcers* are innately rewarding; *secondary reinforcers* are rewards that people or animals learn to like because of their association with primary reinforcers. In general, operant conditioning proceeds more quickly when the delay in receiving reinforcement is short rather than long and when the reinforcer is large rather than small. Reinforcement may be delivered on a continuous reinforcement schedule or on one of four types of partial, or intermittent, *reinforcement schedules:* fixed-ratio (FR), variable-ratio (VR), fixed-interval (FI), and variable-interval (VI) schedules. Ratio schedules lead to a rapid rate of responding. Behavior learned through partial reinforcement is very resistant to extinction; this phenomenon is called the *partial reinforcement effect.* Partial reinforcement is involved in superstitious behavior, which results when some action is followed by, but does not actually cause, a reinforcer. Research in neuroscience suggests that reinforcers

act as rewards largely because of their ability to create activity in "pleasure centers" in the hypothalamus as well as in other brain areas that use the chemical dopamine.

Punishment decreases the frequency of a behavior by following it either with an unpleasant stimulus (*positive punishment*) or with the removal of a pleasant one (*negative punishment*). Punishment can be useful when performed properly, but it can have drawbacks. It only suppresses behavior; fear of punishment may generalize to the person doing the punishing; it is ineffective when delayed; it can be physically harmful and may teach aggressiveness; and it teaches only what not to do, not what should be done to obtain reinforcement.

The principles of operant conditioning have been applied in many areas, from teaching social skills to treating sleep disorders.

Cognitive Processes in Learning

Can people learn to be helpless? Cognitive processes—how people represent, store, and use information—play an important role in learning. *Learned helplessness* appears to result when people believe that their behavior has no effect on the world. Both animals and humans display *latent learning.* They also form *cognitive maps* of their environments, even in the absence of any reinforcement for doing so. Experiments on *insight* also suggest that cognitive processes play an important role in learning. The process of learning by watching others is called *observational learning,* or *social learning.* Some observational learning occurs through vicarious conditioning, in which a person is influenced by seeing or hearing about the consequences of others' behavior. Observational learning is more likely to occur when the observed model's behavior is seen to be rewarded. It is a powerful source of socialization.

Using Research on Learning to Help People Learn

What should teachers learn about learning? Research on how people learn has implications for improved teaching and for the development of a wide range of skills. The degree to which learning principles such as immediate reinforcement are used in teaching varies considerably from culture to culture. The importance of cognitive processes in learning is seen in active learning methods designed to encourage people to think deeply about and apply new information instead of just memorizing isolated facts. Observational learning, practice, and corrective feedback play important roles in the learning of skills.

LEARN by DOING

Put It in Writing
Imagine that you have just been hired as the principal of a high school where students' attendance and test performance has been poor and the dropout rate has been high. At a meeting with your teachers, you explain that the principles of classical and operant conditioning could be used to improve the situation. Write a one-page paper describing how these principles could be used to increase students' class attendance, study skills, and test performance. Be sure to label all the concepts and principles you use (such as "conditioned stimulus," "positive reinforcement," "conditioned response," "discriminative conditioned stimulus," "shaping," and the like).

Personal Learning Activity
Select a pair of friends or relatives who are about the same age and intelligence and try teaching each of them something that is new to them but that you know well—perhaps the words to a song, a popular dance, or how to operate a digital camera, tie a tie, hit a tennis ball, or use a skateboard. Teach one person simply by telling or showing what you want him or her to learn, but for the second person, work out a set of active learning methods. (Recall that active learning requires the learner to get involved in the learning process by doing something other than just listening to a lesson.) Keep a record of which student does better at this learning task and how long it takes each of them to learn. Which method was more efficient? Which student enjoyed the learning process more? Did your results confirm or conflict with research on active learning in the classroom?

Review of Key Terms

Can you define each of the key terms in the chapter? Check your definitions against those on the pages shown in parentheses in the following list or in the Glossary at the end of the book.

avoidance conditioning (p. 180)
classical conditioning (p. 173)
cognitive map (p. 193)
conditioned response (CR) (p. 173)
conditioned stimulus (CS) (p. 173)
discriminative conditioned stimuli (p. 181)
escape conditioning (p. 180)
extinction (p. 173)
habituation (p. 178)
higher order conditioning (p. 176)
insight (p. 193)
latent learning (p. 193)
law of effect (p. 179)
learned helplessness (p. 190)
learning (p. 170)
negative reinforcers (p. 179)
observational learning (social learning) (p. 194)
operant (p. 179)
operant conditioning (p. 179)
partial reinforcement effect (p. 185)
positive reinforcers (p. 179)
primary reinforcers (p. 182)
punishment (p. 185)
reconditioning (p. 173)
reinforcement (p. 179)
reinforcement schedules (p. 184)
reinforcer (p. 179)
secondary reinforcers (p. 182)
shaping (p. 182)
spontaneous recovery (p. 173)
stimulus discrimination (p. 174)
stimulus generalization (p. 173)
unconditioned response (UCR) (p. 172)
unconditioned stimulus (UCS) (p. 172)

Test Your Knowledge ·

Select the best answer for each of the following questions. Then check your responses against the Answer Key at the end of the book.

1. Which saying best reflects learning?
   a. "A watched pot never boils."
   b. "A stitch in time saves nine."
   c. "Once burned, twice shy."
   d. "If you will it, it is no dream."

2. In a classical conditioning experiment, a puff of air was blown into Ralph's eye and he reflexively blinked. The experimenter then began flashing a green light just before presenting the puff of air. After many pairings of the green light and the puff of air, Ralph began to blink as soon as the green light appeared, whether or not the air puff followed. In this experiment, the green light is the
   a. unconditioned stimulus.
   b. conditioned stimulus.
   c. conditioned response.
   d. unconditioned response.

3. Suppose that the experimenter in the previous question continues presenting the green light but never again follows it with the puff of air. Ralph will soon ____ through the process of ____.
   a. blink faster; reconditioning
   b. stop blinking; extinction
   c. blink slower; stimulus control
   d. stop blinking; spontaneous recovery

4. Kim has gone out with both Alan and Brad this week. Even though she said she hates rock concerts, Alan took her to one, and she came home with a headache. Brad took her to a movie she had been wanting to see. According to ____, Kim would be more likely to date Brad in the future.
   a. the law of effect
   b. Premack's principle
   c. classical conditioning theory
   d. all of the above

5. After being bitten by a dog at a young age, Najla became fearful of all dogs. Now, when Najla sees a dog, her heart races and she feels like running away. Najla has developed ____ through ____ conditioning.
   a. habituation; operant
   b. habituation; classical
   c. a phobia; operant
   d. a phobia; classical

6. The idea that knowledge is located in many areas throughout the brain rather than in one particular place is a basic assumption of ____.
   a. neural network theories
   b. classical conditioning
   c. observational learning
   d. stimulus generalization

7. Because of birth defects, Justin, a four-year-old, has had to have a number of surgical operations. As a result, just seeing a doctor or nurse in a surgical mask makes Justin fearful and tearful. At Halloween this year, Justin had the same reaction to children wearing masks. This is an example of ____.
   a. stimulus generalization
   b. stimulus discrimination
   c. vicarious learning
   d. observational learning

8. Laverne lost control and ate an entire coconut cream pie. Later that day she got the flu, complete with nausea and vomiting. After this experience, Laverne associated coconut cream pie with being sick, and now she can't even stand the smell of it. This is an example of ____, which supports the concept of ____.
   a. escape conditioning; spontaneous recovery
   b. discriminative conditioning; biopreparedness
   c. taste aversion; biopreparedness
   d. latent learning; spontaneous recovery

9. When baby Sally cries after being put to bed, her parents check to see that she is all right but otherwise ignore her. After several evenings of this treatment, Sally's bedtime crying stopped. This is an example of ____.
   a. extinction
   b. habituation
   c. higher order conditioning
   d. shaping

10. Manuel has learned that every time he cleans his room, his mother makes his favorite dessert. This is an example of ____.
    a. classical conditioning
    b. operant conditioning
    c. negative reinforcement
    d. extinction

11. Loretta gets a backache every day, but if she sits in a hot bath, the pain goes away. So she decides to take a hot bath every day. She has learned to do this through ____.
    a. positive reinforcement
    b. negative reinforcement
    c. stimulus discrimination
    d. shaping

12. Doug hates to hear children misbehaving in the grocery store, so he always shops late at night when children are not present. Doug's choice of shopping time is an example of ____.
    a. escape conditioning
    b. avoidance conditioning
    c. shaping
    d. secondary reinforcement

13. Ten minutes before a movie starts, the theater is filled with people who are talking and laughing. As soon as the lights

go out, everyone becomes quiet. Sudden darkness serves as a ____ in this example of operant conditioning.
a. positive reinforcer
b. negative reinforcer
c. punishment
d. discriminative conditioned stimulus

14. Craig wanted to teach his dog, JoJo, to sit up and beg using operant conditioning principles. He started by giving JoJo a treat when she was sitting. Next, he gave her a treat only if she was sitting and had raised one paw, and so on. This is an example of ____.
a. stimulus discrimination
b. stimulus generalization
c. negative reinforcement
d. shaping

15. When Jamey has washed the dinner dishes on five evenings, his parents take him to the movies. Susan's dad occasionally gives her a dollar after she washes the dishes. Jamey is on a ____ reinforcement schedule, and Susan is on a ____ schedule.
a. fixed interval; variable interval
b. fixed ratio; variable ratio
c. variable ratio; fixed interval
d. variable interval; fixed ratio

16. Which of the following is a potential problem with using punishment to change behavior?
a. It can produce unwanted side effects.
b. Frequent punishment can teach children to behave aggressively.
c. It signals that inappropriate behavior occurred but doesn't indicate what should be done instead.
d. These are all potential problems with using punishment.

17. Whenever Javier asked his next-door neighbor to turn down her loud music, she ignored him. Later, when a new neighbor moved in next door and began playing loud music, Javier did not even bother to complain. His case demonstrates ____.
a. latent learning
b. learned helplessness
c. observational learning
d. trial and error

18. When Kenzi got a flat tire not far from campus, he walked down the street to a service station he drove by every day but had never visited. The fact that he immediately knew where it was illustrates ____.
a. insight learning
b. observational learning
c. latent learning
d. vicarious learning

19. After watching a number of people petting and playing with a dog, Najla decides that dogs aren't as scary as she'd thought. The next day, at her neighbors' house, she pets their dog. Najla's fear has been reduced through ____.
a. classical conditioning
b. operant conditioning
c. spontaneous recovery
d. observational learning

20. Whether the skill you want to learn involves a foreign language, the words of a speech, or a golf swing, the most important thing you can do is ____.
a. delay feedback until you have almost reached perfection
b. read all you can about the task you want to learn
c. engage in all the practice you can
d. work in a group

Media Resources ....

Now that you have finished reading this chapter, how about exploring some of the ideas and information that you found most interesting?

Coursemate Go to **CengageBrain.com** to access Psychology CourseMate, where you will find an interactive eBook, glossaries, flashcards, quizzes, videos, Virtual Psychology Labs, and more.

aplia

Aplia If your professor has assigned Aplia:

1. Sign in to your account.
2. Complete the corresponding exercises as required by your professor.
3. When finished, click "Grade It Now" to see which areas you have mastered, which areas need more work, and detailed explanations of every answer.

Memory

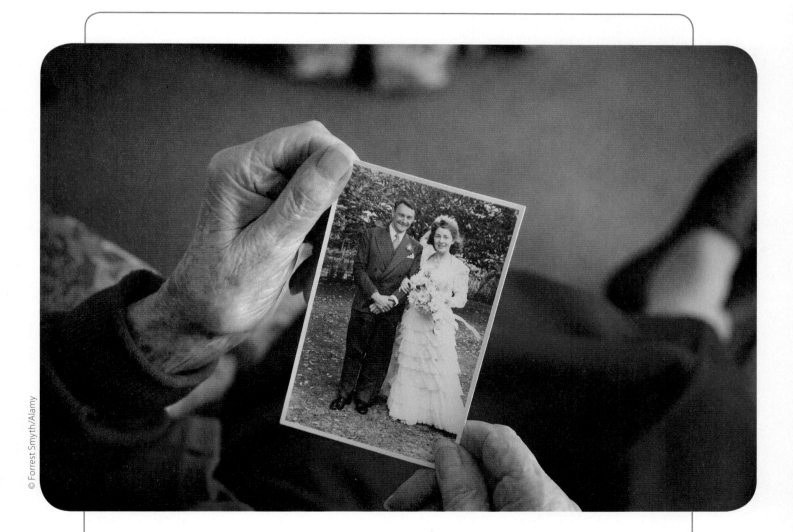

Preview

Have you ever forgotten where you parked your car? Have you ever had a name on the tip of your tongue but couldn't quite recall it? Researchers in the field of memory explore these common experiences. They have found that memory is a complex system. You use different kinds of memory for storing different types of information, such as personal experiences, specific skills, and abstract concepts. They have also found that once information is stored in memory, recalling it can sometimes be difficult. In this chapter, you'll learn about some techniques that can help you to retrieve memories. Psychologists have used what they've learned about memory to create study techniques that really work!

"I'll make him an offer he can't refuse." "I'll be back." "Trust no one." "Life is like a box of chocolates." "I see dead people." "Show me the money." "Is that your final answer?" Do you remember where you heard these words? They are memorable lines from *The Godfather, The Terminator, The X-Files, Forrest Gump, The Sixth Sense, Jerry Maguire*, and *Who Wants to Be a Millionaire*. Can you say who Private Ryan was and why he needed to be saved? And do you know which classic film character said "Play it again, Sam"? (If you don't, ask someone who knows about old movies.) The most common answer to the latter question is Rick, the café owner played by Humphrey Bogart in *Casablanca*. Bogart never actually said this often-quoted line, though many people are sure they "remember" it.

Your memory stores vast amounts of useful and not-so-useful information from all of your experiences. This chapter will help you understand the nature of memory—how you form memories, how memory errors happen, and how you forget. ●

The Nature of Memory

How does information turn into memories?

Memory is a funny thing. You might be able to remember the name of your first-grade teacher but not the name of someone you met five minutes ago. Mathematician John Griffith estimated that in an average lifetime, a person stores roughly five hundred times as much information as can be found in all the volumes of the *Encyclopaedia Britannica* (Hunt, 1982). Keep in mind, however, that although we retain a great deal of information, we also lose a great deal (Wixted, 2004). Consider Joshua Foer. In his book, *Moonwalking with Einstein: The Art and Science of Remembering Everything*, Foer (2011) describes his journey from forgetful science writer to U.S. Memory Champion but says that he still sometimes can't recall where he left his car keys. Memory is made up of many different abilities, some of which may be better than others from person to person and from time to time.

Memory plays a critical role in your life. Without it, you wouldn't know how to shut off your alarm, take a shower, get dressed, recognize objects, or communicate. You would be unaware of your own likes and dislikes. You would have no idea of who you are. The impressive capacity of human memory depends on the operation of a complex mental system.

Basic Memory Processes

In February 2002, prison warden James Smith lost his set of master keys to the Westville Correctional Facility. As a result, 2,559 inmates were kept under partial lockdown for eight days while the Indiana Department of Correction spent $53,000 to change locks in the affected areas. As it turned out, the warden had put the keys in his pocket when he went home, forgot he had done so, and reported the keys "missing" when they were not in their usual place in his office the next day (Associated Press, 2002). What went wrong? There

FIGURE 6.1

Basic Memory Processes

Remembering something requires, first, that the information be encoded—put in a form that can be placed in memory. It must then be stored and, finally, retrieved, or recovered. If any of these processes fails, forgetting will occur.

Encoding Put information into memory	Storage Maintain in memory	Retrieval Recover from memory
Types of memory codes ■ Acoustic ■ Visual ■ Semantic	**Types of long-term memory** ■ Episodic ■ Procedural ■ Semantic	**Types of retrieval** ■ Recall ■ Recognition

© MilsiArt/Shutterstock © ruigsantos/Shutterstock © cobalt88/Shutterstock

encoding The process of putting information into a form that the memory system can accept and use.

auditory memory (acoustic memory) Mental representations of stimuli as sounds.

visual memory Mental representations of stimuli as pictures.

semantic memory Memory for generalized knowledge about the world.

storage The process of maintaining information in the memory system over time.

retrieval The process of finding information stored in memory.

recall Retrieving information stored in memory without much help from retrieval clues.

recognition Retrieving information stored in memory with the help of retrieval clues.

are several possibilities. Memory depends on three basic processes: encoding, storage, and retrieval (see Figure 6.1). Our absent-minded warden might have had problems with any one of these processes.

First, information must be put into memory, a step that requires encoding. **Encoding** is a process that puts information to be remembered into a form that our memory system can accept and use. We use *memory codes* to translate information from the senses into mental representations of that information. Codes for **auditory memory** (also known as **acoustic memory**) represent information as sequences of sounds, such as a tune or a rhyme. Codes for **visual memory** represent information as pictures, such as the image of your best friend's face. Codes for **semantic memory** represent the general meaning of an experience. So if you see a billboard that reads "Huey's Going-Out-of-Business Sale," you might encode the sound of the words as if they had been spoken (acoustic encoding), the image of the letters as they were arranged on the sign (visual encoding), or the fact that you recently saw an ad for Huey's (semantic encoding). The type of encoding we use influences what we remember. Semantic encoding might allow you to remember the fact that an unfamiliar car was parked in your neighbors' driveway just before their house was robbed. If little or no other encoding took place, however, you might not be able to remember the make, model, or color of the car.

The second basic memory process is storage. **Storage** refers to the holding of information in your memory over time. When you recall a vacation you took in childhood or find that you can use a pogo stick many years after you last played with one, you are depending on the storage capacity of your memory.

The third memory process—**retrieval**—occurs when you find information stored in memory and bring it into consciousness. Retrieving stored information such as your address or telephone number is usually so fast and effortless that it seems automatic. The search-and-retrieval process becomes more noticeable, however, when you read a quiz question but cannot quite recall the answer. Retrieval involves both recall and recognition. To **recall** information, you have to retrieve it from memory without much help; this is what is required when you answer an essay test question or play *Jeopardy!* In **recognition,** retrieval is aided by clues, such as the response alternatives given on multiple-choice tests and the questions on *Who Wants to Be a Millionaire*. Accordingly, recognition tends to be easier than recall.

Types of Memory

When was the last time you made a phone call? Who was the first president of the United States? How do you keep your balance on skates? Answering each of these questions involves different aspects of memory. To answer the first question, you must remember a particular event in your life. To answer the second one, you have to recall general knowledge that is unlikely to be tied to a specific event. And the answer to the third question is easier to demonstrate than to describe. So how many types of memory are there? No one is sure, but most research suggests that there are at least three. Each type of memory is named for the kind of information it handles: episodic, semantic, and procedural (Rajaram & Barber, 2008).

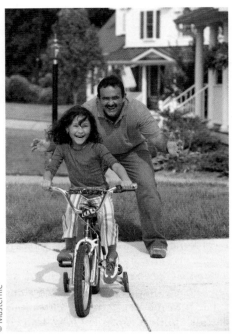

© Masterfile

How Does She Do That?

As she practices, this youngster is developing procedural memories of how to ride a bike that may be difficult to put into words. To appreciate the special nature of procedural memory, try writing a step-by-step description of exactly how to tie a shoe.

LEARN by DOING

episodic memory Memory for events in one's own past.

procedural knowledge (procedural memory) A type of memory containing information about how to do things.

explicit memory Information retrieved through a conscious effort to remember something.

implicit memory The unintentional recollection and influence of prior experiences.

levels-of-processing model of memory A model that suggests that memory depends on the degree or depth to which we mentally process information.

maintenance rehearsal A memorization method that involves repeating information over and over to keep it in memory.

Any memory of a specific event that happened while you were present is an **episodic memory** (Ezzyat & Davcachi, 2010; Tulving, 2005). It is a memory of an episode in your life. What you had for dinner yesterday, what you did last summer, or whether you've already told someone a story are episodic memories (Gopie & MacLeod, 2009). Semantic memory contains generalized knowledge of the world—such as the fact that twelve items make a dozen—that does not involve memory of a specific event. So if you were asked "Are wrenches pets or tools?" you could answer using your semantic memory; you don't have to remember a specific episode in which you learned that wrenches are tools. As a general rule, people report episodic memories by saying, "I remember when …" whereas they report semantic memories by saying, "I know that …" (Tulving, 2000). Memory of how to do things, such as riding a bike, folding a map, or playing golf, is called **procedural memory,** or **procedural knowledge** (Cohen & Squire, 1980). Procedural knowledge often consists of a sequence of movements that are difficult or impossible to put into words. As a result, teachers of music, dance, cooking, woodworking, and other skills usually prefer to first show their students what to do rather than describe how to do it.

Many activities require all three types of memory. Consider the game of tennis. Knowing the official rules or the number of sets needed to win a match involves semantic memory. Remembering who served last requires episodic memory. And knowing how to hit the ball involves procedural memory.

Recalling these three kinds of memories can be either intentional or unintentional. When you deliberately try to remember something, such as where you went on your last vacation, the information you retrieve is an **explicit memory** (Masson & McLeod, 1992). In contrast, **implicit memory** involves the unintentional recollection and influence of prior experiences (McDermott, 2002; Mulligan, 2012; Yee, Ahmed, & Thompson-Schill, 2012). For example, if you were to read this chapter twice, implicit memories from your first reading would help you to read it more quickly the second time. For the same reason, you can solve a puzzle faster if you have solved it in the past. This improvement of performance—often called *priming*—is automatic, and it occurs without conscious effort. In fact, people are often unaware that their actions have been influenced by previous events (see the chapter on consciousness). Have you ever found yourself disliking someone you just met but you didn't know why? The person might have triggered an implicit memory of a similar-looking person who once treated you badly. In such cases, we are usually unaware of any connection between the two individuals (Lewicki, 1992). Because some influential events cannot be recalled even when people try to do so, implicit memory has been said to involve "retention without remembering" (Roediger, Guynn, & Jones, 1995).

Models of Memory

We remember some information far better than other information. Suppose your friends throw a surprise party for you. When you enter the room, you might barely notice the flash of a camera. Later, you cannot recall it at all. And you might forget in a few seconds the name of a person you met at the party. But if you live to be a hundred, you will never forget where the party took place or how surprised and pleased you were. Why do some things stay in memory forever, whereas others barely make an impression? Four *models* of memory each provide a somewhat different explanation. Let's see what the levels-of-processing, transfer-appropriate processing, parallel distributed processing, and information-processing models have to say about memory.

Levels of Processing   The **levels-of-processing model of memory** suggests that memory depends on the extent to which you encode and process information when you first encounter it (Craik & Lockhart, 1972). Consider, for example, the task of remembering a phone number you just heard on the radio. If you were unable to write it down, you would probably repeat the number over and over to yourself until you could find a pen or get to your phone. This repetition process is called **maintenance rehearsal.** It can be effective for encoding information temporarily, but what if you need to remember something for hours, months, or years? In that case, you would be better off using **elaborative rehearsal,** a process in which you relate new material to information you already have stored in memory. For example, instead of trying to remember a new person's name by simply repeating it to yourself, you could try thinking about how the name is related to something you know well. So if you are introduced to a man named Jim Crews, you might think, "He is as tall as my Uncle Jim, who always wears a crew cut."

Study after study has shown that using elaborative rehearsal rather than maintenance rehearsal improves memory (Jahnke & Nowaczyk, 1998). According to the levels-of-processing model of memory, the reason is that when you use elaborative rehearsal you process material more "deeply" (Lockhart & Craik, 1990; Roediger & Gallo, 2001; Roediger, Gallo, & Geraci, 2002). The more you think about new information, organize it, and relate it to something you already know, the "deeper" the processing and the better your memory of the information becomes. Teachers use this idea when they ask students not only to define a new word but also to use it in a sentence. Figuring out how to use the new word takes deeper processing than merely defining it does. (The next time you come across an unfamiliar word in this book, don't just read its definition. Try to use the word in a sentence by coming up with an example of the concept that is related to your knowledge and experience.)

LEARN by DOING

Transfer-Appropriate Processing   Level of processing is not the only factor that affects memory (Baddeley, 1992). The **transfer-appropriate processing model of memory** suggests that another critical factor is the match between how we try to retrieve information and how we originally encoded it. For example, what do you think would happen to your performance on an exam if your instructor told you it would be in a multiple-choice format but then surprised you with an essay test? In a study about just such a situation, half the students in a class were told that their next exam would contain multiple-choice questions. The rest were told to expect essay questions. Only half the students actually got the type of exam they expected. These students did much better on the exam than those who took an unexpected type of exam. Apparently, in studying for the exam each group used encoding strategies that were most appropriate to the type of exam they expected. Students who tried to retrieve the information in a way that didn't match their encoding method had a harder time (d'Ydewalle & Rosselle, 1978). Results such as these indicate that how well the encoding method aligns with the retrieval task is just as important as the depth of processing (Bauch & Otten, 2012; Mulligan & Picklesimer, 2012).

Parallel Distributed Processing   A third way of thinking about memory is based on **parallel distributed processing (PDP) models of memory** (Rumelhart & McClelland, 1986). These models suggest that new experiences do more than provide specific facts that are stored and later retrieved one at a time. Those facts are also combined with what you already know so that each new experience changes your overall understanding of the world and how it operates. For example, when you first arrived on campus, you learned lots of specific facts, such as where classes are held, what time the library closes, and where to get the best pizza. Over time, these and many other facts about student life form a network of information that creates a more general understanding of how the whole system works. The development of this network makes experienced students not only more knowledgeable than new students but also more sophisticated. It allows them to, say, allocate their study time in order to do well in their most important courses and to plan a schedule that doesn't conflict with work commitments and maybe even avoids early morning classes—and certain professors.

PDP models of memory see each unit of knowledge as connected to every other unit. The connections between units become stronger as they are experienced together more frequently. In other words, your knowledge about the world is distributed across a network of associations that all operate at the same time, in parallel. Your PDP network allows you to quickly and efficiently draw inferences and generalizations about the world, including how you can get information that is not already in your knowledge base. For

elaborative rehearsal A memorization method that relates new information to information already stored in memory.

transfer-appropriate processing model of memory A model that suggests that memory depends on how the encoding process matches up with what is later retrieved.

parallel distributed processing (PDP) models of memory Memory models in which new experiences are seen as changing one's overall knowledge base.

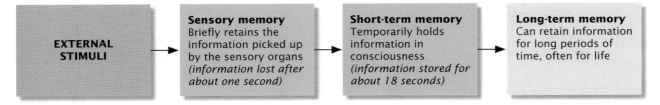

| EXTERNAL STIMULI | → | **Sensory memory**
Briefly retains the information picked up by the sensory organs *(information lost after about one second)* | → | **Short-term memory**
Temporarily holds information in consciousness *(information stored for about 18 seconds)* | → | **Long-term memory**
Can retain information for long periods of time, often for life |

FIGURE 6.2
Three Stages of Memory
This traditional information-processing model describes the three stages in the memory system.

example, because of your network of associations, just seeing the word "chair" allows you to know immediately what a chair looks like, what it's used for, where it tends to be located, who might buy one, and how—such as through an Internet search—you can find one for sale (Sparrow, Liu & Wegner, 2011). PDP models of memory explain this process very effectively.

Sensory Memory at Work
In a darkened room, ask a friend to hold a small flashlight and move it very slowly in a circle. You will see a moving point of light. If it appears to have a "tail," like a comet, that is your sensory memory of the light before it fades. Now ask your friend to move the light faster. You should now see a complete circle of light, because as the light moves, its impression on your sensory memory does not have time to fade before the circle is completed. A similar process allows us to see "sparkler circles."

LEARN by DOING

information-processing model of memory A model that suggests that information must pass through sensory memory, short-term memory, and long-term memory in order to become firmly embedded in memory.

Information Processing The **information-processing model of memory** is probably the most influential and comprehensive memory model (Roediger, 1990). It suggests that for information to be firmly implanted in memory, it must pass through three stages of mental processing: sensory memory, short-term memory, and long-term memory (Atkinson & Shiffrin, 1968; see Figure 6.2).

In *sensory memory,* information from the senses—sights or sounds, for example—is held very briefly before being lost. But if information in sensory memory is attended to, analyzed, and encoded as a meaningful pattern, we say that it has been *perceived* (see the chapter on sensation and perception). Perceived information in sensory memory can now enter *short-term memory.* That information will disappear in less than twenty seconds, if nothing further is done with it. With additional processing, however, the information may be encoded into *long-term memory,* where it may remain indefinitely.

The act of reading illustrates all three stages of memory processing. As you read any sentence in this book, light energy reflected from the page reaches your eyes, where it is converted to neural activity and registered in your sensory memory. If you pay attention to these visual stimuli, your perception of the patterns of light can be held in short-term memory. This stage of memory holds the early parts of the sentence so that they can be integrated and understood as you read the rest of the sentence. As you read, you constantly recognize words by matching your perceptions of them with the patterns and meanings you have stored in long-term memory. In other words, all three stages of memory are necessary for you to understand a sentence.

Contemporary views of the information-processing model emphasize these constant interactions among sensory, short-term, and long-term memory. For example, sensory memory can be thought of as that part of your knowledge base (or long-term memory) that is momentarily activated by information sent to the brain via the sensory nerves. And short-term memory can be thought of as that part of your knowledge base that is the focus of attention at any given moment (Cowan, 2011; Wagner, 1999). Like perception, memory is an active process, and what is already in long-term memory influences how new information is encoded (Cowan, 1988). To understand this interaction better, try the exercise in Figure 6.3.

Which model offers the best explanation? The answer is that more than one model may be required to understand memory. Psychologists find it useful to think of memory as both a sequential process, as suggested by the information-processing model, and as a parallel process, as suggested by parallel distributed processing models. "In Review: Models of Memory" summarizes each of the four memory models we have described.

FIGURE 6.3

The Role of Long-Term Memory in Understanding New Information

Read the paragraph shown here, then turn away and try to recall as much of it as you can. It probably didn't make much sense, and it was probably difficult to remember. But if you read it again after checking the footnote on page 214, the meaning will not only be clearer but it will now be much easier to remember (try it again!). Why? Because knowing the title of the paragraph allows you to retrieve from long-term memory what you already know about the topic (Bransford & Johnson, 1972).

Source: Howard (1983).

The procedure is actually quite simple. First, you arrange items into different groups. Of course, one pile may be sufficient, depending on how much there is to do. If you have to go somewhere else due to lack of facilities that is the next step; otherwise, you are pretty well set. It is important not to overdo things. That is, it is better to do too few things at once than too many. In the short run, this may not seem important, but complications can easily arise. A mistake can be expensive as well. At first, the whole procedure will seem complicated. Soon, however, it will become just another facet of life. It is difficult to foresee any end to the necessity for this task in the immediate future, but then, one never can tell. After the procedure is completed, one arranges the materials into different groups again. Then they can be put into their appropriate places. Eventually they will be used once more, and the whole cycle will then have to be repeated. However, that is part of life.

Models of Memory — IN REVIEW

Model	Assumptions
Levels of processing	The more deeply material is processed, the better our memory of it.
Transfer-appropriate processing	Retrieval is improved when we try to recall material in a way that matches how the material was encoded.
Parallel distributed processing (PDP)	New experiences add to and alter our overall knowledge base; they are not separate, unconnected facts. Networks of associations allow us to draw inferences and make generalizations about the world.
Information-processing	Information is processed in three stages: sensory memory, short-term memory, and long-term memory.

IN REVIEW QUESTIONS

1. **The value of elaborative rehearsal over maintenance rehearsal has been cited as evidence for the ___ model of memory.**

2. **Deliberately trying to remember something means using your ___ memory.**

3. **Playing the piano uses ___ memory.**

Storing New Memories

What am I most likely to remember?

Storing information is critical to memory because we can retrieve only information that has been stored. According to the information-processing model, sensory memory, short-term memory, and long-term memory each provide a different type of storage. Let's take a closer look at these three memory systems in order to better understand how they work—and sometimes fail.

Sensory Memory

sensory memory A type of memory that is very brief but lasts long enough to connect one impression to the next.

To recognize incoming information, the brain must analyze and compare it with what is already stored in long-term memory. This process is very quick, but it still takes time. The major function of **sensory memory** is to hold information long enough for it to be processed further (Nairne, 2003). This "holding" function is the job of the **sensory registers,** which act as temporary storage bins. There is a separate register for each of the senses. Each register can store a nearly complete representation of a sensory stimulus, but it can do so only briefly, often for less than one second (Eysenck & Keane, 2005).

Sensory memory helps us experience a constant flow of information, even if that flow is interrupted. To see this for yourself, move your head and eyes slowly from left to right. It may seem as though your eyes are moving smoothly, like a movie camera scanning a scene, but that's not what is happening. Your eyes fixate at one point for about one-fourth of a second and then rapidly jump to a new position. You perceive smooth motion because you hold the scene in your visual sensory register (also known as your **iconic memory**) until your eyes fixate again. Similarly, when you listen to someone speak, your auditory sensory register allows you to experience a smooth flow of information, even though there are actually short silences between or within words.

The fact that sensory memories fade quickly if they are not processed further is actually an adaptive characteristic of the memory system (Baddeley, 1998). You simply cannot deal with all of the sights, sounds, odors, tastes, and touch sensations that come to your sense organs at any given moment. Using **selective attention,** you focus your mental resources on only some of the stimuli around you, thus controlling what information is processed further in short-term memory.

Short-Term Memory and Working Memory

The sensory registers allow your memory system to develop a representation of a stimulus. However, they can't perform the more thorough analysis needed if the information is going to be used in some way. That function is accomplished by short-term memory and working memory.

Short-term memory (STM) is the part of your memory system that stores limited amounts of information for up to about eighteen seconds. When you check the building directory to see which floor your new dentist's office is on, and then keep that number in mind as you press the correct elevator button, you are using short-term memory. **Working memory** is the part of the memory system that allows us to mentally work with, or manipulate, the information being held in short-term memory. When you mentally calculate what time you have to leave home in order to have lunch on campus, return a library book, and still get to class on time, you are using working memory.

Short-term memory is actually a component of working memory, and together these memory systems allow us to do many kinds of mental work (Baddeley, 2003). Suppose you're buying something for eighty-three cents. You go through your change and pick out two quarters, two dimes, two nickels, and three pennies. To do this you use both short-term memory and working memory to remember the price, retrieve the rules of addition 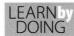 from long-term memory, and keep a running count of how much change you have so far. Now try to recall how many windows there are on the front of the house or apartment where you grew up. In answering this question, you probably formed a mental image of the building. You used one kind of working-memory process to form that image and then you maintained the image in short-term memory while you "worked" on it by counting the windows. So working memory has at least two components: *maintenance* (holding information in short-term memory) and *manipulation* (working on that information).

Encoding in Short-Term Memory   Encoding information in short-term memory is much more elaborate and varied than encoding in the sensory registers (Brandimonte, Hitch, & Bishop, 1992; Logie, 2011). Acoustic encoding (by sound) seems to dominate. This conclusion comes from research on the mistakes people make when encoding information in short-term memory, which tend to involve the substitution of similar sounds. For instance, Robert Conrad (1964) showed people strings of letters and asked them to repeat the letters immediately. Among their most common mistakes was the replacement of the correct letter with another that sounded like it. So if the correct letter was *C*, it was often replaced with a *D*, *P*, or *T*. The participants made

---

sensory registers Memory systems that briefly hold incoming information.

iconic memory The sensory register for visual information.

selective attention The process of focusing mental resources on only part of the stimulus field.

short-term memory (STM) A stage of memory in which information normally lasts less than twenty seconds; a component of working memory.

working memory Memory that allows us to mentally work with, or manipulate, information being held in short-term memory.

The title of the paragraph in Figure 6.3 is "Washing Clothes."

these mistakes even though the letters were presented visually, without any sound. Studies in several cultures have also shown that items are more difficult to remember if they sound similar. For example, native English speakers do less well when they try to remember a string of letters like *ECVTGB* (which all have similar sounds) than when trying to remember one like *KRLDQS* (in which there are different sounds).

Encoding in short-term memory is not always acoustic, however. Information in short-term memory also can be encoded visually, semantically, and even kinesthetically (in terms of physical movements; Best, 1999). In one study, deaf people were shown a list of words and then asked to immediately write down as many as they could remember (Shand, 1982). When these participants made errors, they wrote words expressed through similar *hand movements* in American Sign Language rather than words that *sounded* similar to the correct words. Apparently, these individuals had encoded the words on the basis of the movements they would use when making the signs for them.

9 2 5
8 6 4 2
3 7 6 5 4
6 2 7 4 1 8
0 4 0 1 4 7 3
1 9 2 2 3 5 3 0
4 8 6 8 5 4 3 3 2
2 5 3 1 9 7 1 7 6 8
8 5 1 2 9 6 1 9 4 5 0
9 1 8 5 4 6 9 4 2 9 3 7

FIGURE 6.4

The Capacity of Short-Term Memory

Here is a test of your immediate memory span (Howard, 1983). Ask someone to read to you the numbers in the top row at the rate of about one per second, then try to repeat them back in the same order. Then try the next row and the one after that, until you make a mistake. Your immediate memory span is the maximum number of items you can repeat back perfectly.

LEARN by DOING

Source: From Cognitive Psychology: Memory, Language, and Thought by Darlene V. Howard. Copyright © 1983 by Darlene V. Howard. Reprinted by permission of the author.

Storage Capacity of Short-Term Memory   How much information can you hold in short-term memory? The simple test presented in Figure 6.4 will help you determine your **immediate memory span,** which is the largest number of items you can recall perfectly after one presentation. If your memory span is like most people's, you can repeat six or seven items from the test in this figure. Further, you should come up with about the same result whether you use digits, letters, words, or virtually anything else (Pollack, 1953). George Miller (1956) noticed that many studies using a variety of tasks showed the same limit on the ability to process information. This "magic number," which is seven plus or minus two, appears to be the immediate memory span or capacity of short-term memory, at least for most adults in laboratory settings. In addition, the "magic number" refers not only to discrete elements, such as words or digits, but also to *chunks,* meaningful groupings of information that are produced by a process called **chunking** (Gilchrist & Cowan, 2012; Mathy & Feldman, 2012).

To see the difference between discrete elements and chunks, read the following letters to a friend, pausing at each dash: *FB-IAO-LM-TVQ-VCB-MW.* The chances are very good that your friend will not be able to repeat this string of letters perfectly. Why? There are fifteen letters, which exceeds most people's immediate memory span. Now, give your friend the test again, but group the letters like this: *FBI-AOL-MTV-QVC-BMW.* Your friend will probably repeat the string easily. Although the same fifteen letters are involved, they will be processed as only five meaningful chunks of information.

LEARN by DOING

The Power of Chunking   Chunks of information can be quite complex. If you heard someone say, "The boy in the red shirt kicked his mother in the shin," you could probably repeat the sentence perfectly. Yet it contains twelve words and forty-three letters. How can you repeat the sentence so effortlessly? The answer is that you are able to build bigger and bigger chunks of information (Ericsson & Staszewski, 1989). In this case, you might represent "the boy in the red shirt" as one chunk of information rather than as six words or nineteen letters. Similarly, "kicked his mother" and "in the shin" represent separate chunks of information.

Learning to use bigger and bigger chunks of information can improve short-term memory. In fact, children's short-term memories improve partly because they gradually become able to hold more chunks in memory and also because they get better at grouping information into chunks (Cowan, 2010; Servan-Schreiber & Anderson, 1990). Adults also can greatly increase the capacity of their short-term memory by using more efficient chunking (Zhang & Luck, 2011). For example, after extensive training, one college student increased his immediate memory span from seven to eighty digits (Neisser, 2000a), and experienced waiters often use chunking techniques to remember the details of numerous dinner orders without taking notes (Bekinschtein, Cardozo, & Manes, 2008). So although the capacity of short-term memory is more or less constant (from five to nine chunks of meaningful information), the size of those chunks can vary tremendously.

immediate memory span The maximum number of items a person can recall perfectly after one presentation of the items.

chunking Organizing individual stimuli so that they will be perceived as larger units of meaningful information.

FIGURE 6.5

Forgetting in Short-Term Memory

This graph shows the percentage of items recalled after various intervals during which rehearsal was prevented. Notice that forgetting was virtually complete after a delay of eighteen seconds.

Source: Data from Peterson & Peterson (1959).

Brown-Peterson distractor technique A method for determining how long unrehearsed information remains in short-term memory.

long-term memory (LTM) The stage of memory that researchers believe has an unlimited capacity to store new information.

Duration of Short-Term Memory   Why don't you remember every phone number you ever called or every conversation you ever had? The answer is that unless you do something to retain it, information in short-term memory is soon forgotten. This feature of short-term memory is adaptive because it gets rid of a lot of useless information; indeed, there are rare cases of people whose inability to forget interferes with their ability to concentrate (Parker, Cahill, & McGaugh, 2006; Storm, 2011). But losing information from short-term memory can also be inconvenient. You may have discovered this if you ever looked up a phone number, got distracted before you could call it, and then forgot the number.

How long does information remain in short-term memory if you don't keep rehearsing it? John Brown (1958) and Lloyd and Margaret Peterson (1959) devised the **Brown-Peterson distractor technique** to measure the duration of short-term memory when no rehearsal is allowed. In this procedure, participants are presented with a group of three letters, such as *GRB*. They then count backward by threes from some number until they get a signal. Counting serves as a distraction that prevents the participants from rehearsing the letters. At the signal, they stop counting and try to recall the letters. By varying the number of seconds spent counting backward, the experimenter can determine how much forgetting takes place over time. As you can see in Figure 6.5, information in short-term memory is forgotten rapidly: After only eighteen seconds, participants can remember almost nothing. Evidence from other such experiments also suggests that unrehearsed information can be held in short-term memory for no more than about eighteen seconds. However, if the information is rehearsed or processed further in some other way, it may be encoded into long-term memory.

Long-Term Memory

When people talk about memory, they're usually referring to long-term memory. **Long-term memory (LTM)** is the part of the memory system where encoding and storage capabilities can produce memories that last a lifetime.

Encoding in Long-Term Memory   Some information is encoded into long-term memory even if we make no conscious effort to memorize it (Ellis, 1991; Hoffman, Bein, & Maril, 2011). However, putting information into long-term memory is often the result of more elaborate and more conscious processing that usually involves *semantic encoding*. As we mentioned earlier, semantic encoding often leaves out details in favor of the more general underlying meaning of the information.

In a classic study, Jacqueline Sachs (1967) demonstrated the dominance of semantic encoding in long-term memory. Her participants first listened to tape recordings of people speaking. She then showed them sets of similar sentences and asked them to say which contained the exact wording heard on the tape. Participants did well at this task when tested immediately, using mainly short-term memory. However, after twenty-seven seconds, they couldn't be sure which of two sentences they had heard. For example, they could not remember whether they had heard "He sent a letter about it to Galileo, the great Italian scientist" or "A letter about it was sent to Galileo, the great Italian scientist." They didn't do as well after the delay because they had to recall information from long-term memory, where they had encoded the general meaning of what they had heard, but not the exact wording.

Perhaps you are thinking, "So what?" After all, the two sentences mean the same thing. Unfortunately, when people encode the general meaning of information they hear or read, they can make mistakes about the details (Brewer, 1977). For example, after listening to a list of words such as *cold, white, ice, winter, frosty, blizzard, frozen, drift, flurries, parka, shovel, skis, sled,* and *flakes,* people often remember having heard the related word "snow" even though it was not presented (Gallo, 2006; Roediger & McDermott, 1995). This kind of false memory can be a problem when recalling exact words is important—such as in the courtroom, during business negotiations, and in agreements between students and teachers about course requirements. Later in this chapter, we show that such mistakes occur partly because people encode into long-term

FIGURE 6.6
Encoding into Long-Term Memory
Which is the correct image of a U.S. penny? (See page 218 for answers.)

Source: From R. S. Nickerson and M. J. Adams, "Long-Term Memory for a Common Object," *Cognitive Psychology,* Volume 11, 287–307. Copyright © 1979 Elsevier. Reprinted by permission.

(A)　　　**(B)**　　　**(C)**　　　**(D)**　　　**(E)**

memory not only the general meaning of information but also what they think and assume about that information (McDermott & Chan, 2006). Indeed, anyone who has watched Judge Judy knows that people's flawed memories make it vital in everyday life to "get it in writing."

Counterfeiters depend on the fact that people encode the general meaning of visual stimuli rather than specific details. For example, look at Figure 6.6 and find the correct drawing of a U.S. penny (Nickerson & Adams, 1979). Research shows that most people from the United States are unsuccessful at this task. People from other countries do poorly at recognizing their country's coins, too (Jones, 1990). This research has prompted the U.S. Department of the Treasury to begin using more distinctive drawings on the paper currency it distributes.

Storage Capacity of Long-Term Memory　The capacity of long-term memory is extremely large. In fact, many psychologists believe that it is literally unlimited (Matlin, 1998). There is no way to prove this, but we do know that people store vast quantities of information in long-term memory that can be remembered remarkably well after long periods of time (Seamon, Punjabi, & Busch, 2010). For example, people are amazingly accurate at recognizing the faces of their high school classmates after having not seen them for over twenty-five years (Bruck, Cavanagh, & Ceci, 1991). They also do surprisingly well on tests of a foreign language or algebra fifty years after having formally studied these subjects (Bahrick & Hall, 1991; Bahrick et al., 1994; Bowers, Mattys, & Gage, 2009).

But long-term memories are also subject to distortion. Do you remember where were you were and what you were doing when you heard about the 9/11 terrorist attacks on the United States? You may be quite sure that you do, but if you are like the students tested in one study, your memories of 9/11 may not be entirely correct (Hirst et al., 2009; Talarico & Rubin, 2003). Most of the students whose memories had been substantially distorted over time were unaware that this distortion had occurred. In fact, they were very confident

A Remarkable Memory
Using only his long-term memory, Franco Magnani created amazingly accurate paintings of his hometown in Italy even though he had not seen it for more than 30 years (Sacks, 1992). People like Magnani display *eidetic imagery,* commonly called *photographic memory.* About 5 percent of school-age children have eidetic imagery, but it is extremely rare in adults (Haber, 1979). You can test yourself for eidetic imagery by drawing a detailed picture or map of a place that you know well but have not seen recently, then comparing your version with a photo or map of the same place. How did you do?

© Franco Magnani, www.francomagnani.com

Magnani's painting

© Exploratorium, www.exploratorium.edu, photo by Susan Schwartzenberg

Photo of the same scene

FIGURE 6.7
A Serial-Position Curve
This curve shows the probability of recalling items that appear at various serial positions in a list. Generally, the first several items and the last several items are most likely to be recalled (Silverman, 2012).

that their reports were accurate. Later, we will see that such overconfidence can also appear in courtroom testimony by eyewitnesses to crime.

Distinguishing between Short-Term and Long-Term Memory

Some psychologists argue that short-term memory and long-term memory have different features and obey different laws (Cowan, 1988; Talmi et al., 2005). ("In Review: Storing New Memories" summarizes the characteristics of these systems.) Evidence that information is transferred from short-term memory to a distinct storage system comes primarily from experiments on recall.

You can conduct your own recall experiment by reading aloud a list of words at a slow pace (about one word every two seconds). After reading the list just once, look away and write down as many of the words as you can, in any order. Here is a list you can use: *desk, frame, carburetor, flag, grill, book, urn, candle, briefcase, screen, tree, soup, ocean, castle, monster, bridge.* Did you notice anything about which words you remembered and which ones you forgot? If you are like most people, your recall depended partly on where each word appeared on the list—its serial position. As shown in the serial-position curve in Figure 6.7, memory researchers have found that recall tends to be very good for the first two or three words in a list. This result is called the **primacy effect.** The probability of recall decreases for words in the middle of the list and then rises dramatically for the last few words. The ease of recalling words near the end of the list is called the **recency effect.** The primacy effect may reflect the rehearsal that puts early words into long-term memory. The recency effect may occur because the last few words are still in short-term memory when you try to recall the list (Glanzer & Cunitz, 1966; Koppenaal & Glanzer, 1990).

Storing New Memories			IN REVIEW
Storage System	**Function**	**Capacity**	**Duration**
Sensory memory	Briefly holds representations of stimuli from each sense for further processing	Large: absorbs all sensory input from a particular stimulus	Less than one second
Short-term and working memory	Hold information in awareness and manipulate it to accomplish mental work	Five to nine distinct items or chunks of information	About 18 seconds
Long-term memory	Stores new information indefinitely	Unlimited	Unlimited

IN REVIEW QUESTIONS

1. If you looked up a phone number but forgot it before you could call it, the information was probably lost from ___ memory.
2. The capacity of short-term memory is about ___ to ___ items.
3. Encoding is usually ___ in short-term memory and ___ in long-term memory.

primacy effect A characteristic of memory in which recall is particularly good for the first two or three items in a list.

recency effect A characteristic of memory in which recall is particularly good for the last few items in a list.

retrieval cues Stimuli that allow or help people to recall information.

Drawing A shows the correct penny image.

Retrieving Memories

How do I retrieve stored memories?

Most people have trouble remembering things at one time or another. Have you ever been unable to recall the name of a musical group or movie star, only to think of it the next day? Remembering requires not only the encoding and storing of information but also the ability to bring it into consciousness. In other words, you have to be able to *retrieve* it.

Retrieval Cues and Encoding Specificity

Retrieval cues are stimuli that help you retrieve information from long-term memory. As mentioned earlier, these cues make recognition tasks (such as multiple-choice tests) easier than recall tasks (such as essay exams).

The effectiveness of retrieval cues depends on the extent to which they tap into information that was encoded at the time of learning (Tulving, 1983). This rule is known as the **encoding specificity principle.** Because long-term memories are often encoded in terms of their general meaning, cues that trigger the meaning of the stored information tend to work best. Imagine that you have learned a long list of sentences. One of them was either (1) "The man lifted the piano" or (2) "The man tuned the piano." Now suppose that on a later recall test, you were given the retrieval cue "something heavy." This cue would probably help you to remember the first sentence (because you probably encoded something about the weight of a piano as you read it) but not the second sentence (because it has nothing to do with weight). Similarly, the cue "makes nice sounds" would probably help you recall the second sentence but not the first (Barclay et al., 1974; Goh & Lu, 2012).

Context and State Dependence

Have you ever taken a test in a classroom other than the one where you learned the material for that test? If so, was your performance affected? Research has shown that people tend to recall more of what they have learned when they're in the place where they learned it (Smith & Vela, 2001). Why? Because if they have encoded features of the environment where the learning occurred, these features can later act as retrieval cues (Richardson-Klavehn & Bjork, 1988). Smells are especially effective retrieval cues (Toffolo, Smeets, & van den Hout, 2012). In one experiment, people studied a series of photos while in the presence of a particular odor. Later, they reviewed a larger set of photos and tried to recognize the ones they had seen earlier. Half of the people were exposed to the original odor while taking the recognition test. The rest were tested in the presence of another odor. Those who smelled the same odor during learning and testing did significantly better on the recognition task than those who were tested in the presence of a different odor. The matching odor served as a powerful retrieval cue (Cann & Ross, 1989).

Context-specific memory, also known as **context-specific learning,** refers to memories that are helped or hindered by similarities or differences in environmental context. Police and prosecutors sometimes ask eyewitnesses to revisit the scene of a crime because they hope that being there will provide retrieval cues that can improve the accuracy of eyewitness testimony (e.g., Campos & Alonso-Quecuty, 2006). This context-specificity effect is not always strong (Smith, Vela, & Williamson, 1988), but some students do find it helpful to study for a test in the classroom where the test will be given.

Sometimes we also encode information about how we felt during a learning experience, and this information, too, can act as a retrieval cue. When our internal state influences retrieval, we have a **state-dependent memory,** also known as **state-dependent learning.** For example, if people learn new material while under the influence

encoding specificity principle A principle stating that the ability of a cue to aid retrieval depends on how well it taps into information that was originally encoded.

context-specific memory (context-specific learning) Memories that are helped or hindered by similarities or differences between the contexts in which they are learned and recalled.

state-dependent memory (state-dependent learning) Memory that is helped or hindered by similarities or differences in a person's internal state during learning versus recall.

Context-Dependent Memories
Many people attending a reunion at their old high school find that being in the building again provides context cues that help bring back memories of their school days. Visit your elementary school or high school and see if it helps you to remember things you'd forgotten. Be sure to look into specific rooms where you had classes or assemblies, and check out the restroom and your old locker, too.

LEARN by DOING

© Steve Skjold/Alamy

of marijuana, they tend to recall it better if they are tested on the material while under the influence of marijuana (Eich et al., 1975). Similar effects have been found with alcohol and other psychoactive drugs (Eich, 1989; Overton, 1984), although memory is best when people aren't using any drugs during encoding or retrieval. Mood states, too, can affect memory (Eich & Macaulay, 2000). College students are more likely to remember pleasant events when they're feeling good at the time of recall (Bower, 1981; Eich & Macaulay, 2006). Negative events are more likely to be recalled when people are feeling sad or angry (Lewinsohn & Rosenbaum, 1987). These *mood congruency* effects are strongest when people try to recall personally meaningful episodes (Eich & Metcalfe, 1989). The more meaningful the experience, the more likely it is that the memory has been colored by their mood. (See "In Review: Factors Affecting Retrieval from Long-Term Memory.")

Factors Affecting Retrieval from Long-Term Memory   IN REVIEW

Process	Effect on Memory
Encoding specificity	Retrieval cues are effective only to the extent that they tap into information that was originally encoded.
Context-specific memory	Retrieval is most successful when it occurs in the same environment where the information was originally learned.
State-dependent memory	Retrieval is most successful when people are in the same physiological or psychological state as when they originally learned the information.

IN REVIEW QUESTIONS

1. Stimuli called ___ help you recall information stored in long-term memory.
2. If it is easier to remember something in the place where you learned it, you have ___ learning.
3. The tendency to remember the last few items in a list is called the ___ effect.

Retrieval from Semantic Memory

The retrieval situations we have discussed so far are relevant to episodic memory—our memory for events. But how do we retrieve information from semantic memory, where we store our general knowledge about the world? Researchers studying this question typically ask participants general knowledge questions, such as (1) Are fish minerals? (2) Is a beagle a dog? (3) Do birds fly? and (4) Does a car have legs? As you might imagine, most people answer such questions correctly. But by measuring how long it takes to answer them, psychologists gain important clues about how semantic memory is organized and how we retrieve information from it.

Semantic Networks   One view of semantic memory suggests that virtually everything we know about, including concepts such as "bird" or "animal," is represented in a dense network of associations (Churchland, 1989). Figure 6.8 presents just a tiny part of what our *semantic memory network* might look like. In general, semantic network theories suggest that information is retrieved from memory through the principle of **spreading activation** (Medin, Ross, & Markman, 2001). In other words, when you think about some concept, it becomes activated in the network and this activation begins to "spread" down all the paths that are related to it. So if you are asked if a robin is a bird, the concepts of both "robin" and "bird" will become activated and the spreading activation from each will intersect somewhere in these paths. When they do, you know what answer to give.

Some associations in the network are stronger than others, as illustrated by the thicker lines between some concepts in Figure 6.8. For instance, you probably have a stronger association between "bat" and "wings" than between "bat" and "mammal." Spreading activation travels faster along stronger paths than along weaker ones. As a result, you'd probably respond more quickly to "Can a bat fly?" than to "Is a bat a mammal?"

Because of the tight organization of semantic networks and the speed at which activation spreads through them, we can gain access to an enormous body of knowledge about the

spreading activation In semantic network theories of memory, a principle that explains how information is retrieved.

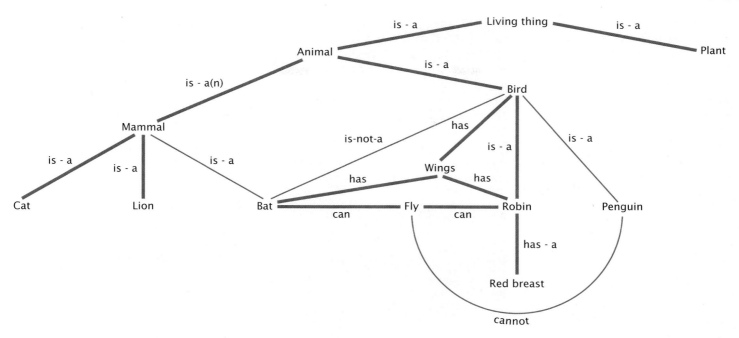

FIGURE 6.8
Semantic Memory Networks
This drawing represents just a small part of a network of semantic associations. Semantic network theories of memory suggest that networks like these allow us to retrieve specific pieces of previously learned information, draw conclusions about how concepts are related, and make new inferences about the world.

world quickly and effortlessly. We can retrieve not only facts we have learned from others but also knowledge that allows us to draw our own conclusions and inferences (Matlin, 1998). For example, imagine answering these two questions: (1) Is a robin a bird? and (2) Is a robin a living thing? You can probably answer the first question "directly," because you probably learned this fact at some point in your life. However, you may never have consciously thought about the second question, so answering it requires some inference. Figure 6.8 illustrates the path to that inference. Because you know that a robin is a bird, a bird is an animal, and animals are living things, you infer that a robin must be a living thing. As you might expect, however, it takes slightly longer to answer the second question than the first.

Retrieving Incomplete Knowledge   Figure 6.8 shows that concepts such as "bird" or "living thing" are represented in semantic memory as unique sets of features or attributes. As a result, there may be times when you can retrieve some features of a concept from your semantic network but not enough of them to identify the concept. For example, you might know that there is an animal that has wings, can fly, and is not a bird and yet you might not be able to retrieve its name (Connor, Balota, & Neely, 1992). When this happens, you are retrieving *incomplete knowledge*. (The animal in question is a bat.)

You've probably experienced a particular example of incomplete knowledge called the *tip-of-the-tongue phenomenon*. In a typical experiment on this phenomenon, participants listen to dictionary definitions and then are asked to name the word being defined (Brown & McNeill, 1966). If they can't recall the correct word, they are asked if they can recall any feature of it, such as its first letter or how many syllables it has. People are surprisingly good at this task, indicating that they are able to retrieve at least some knowledge of the word (Brennen et al., 1990). Most people experience the tip-of-the-tongue phenomenon about once a week; older people tend to experience it more often than younger people (Brown, 1991; Brown & Nix, 1996).

Constructing Memories

How accurate are my memories?

Our memories are affected by what we experience but also by what we already know about the world in general and about the particular culture and family in which we live (Ross & Wang, 2010; Schacter, Norman, & Koutstaal, 1998; Simpson, Rholes, & Winterheld, 2010).

Constructive Memory

Here is a photo of the office used in the Brewer & Treyens (1981) study. Ask a friend to examine it for a minute or so (cover this caption). Then close the book and ask whether each of the following items appeared in the office: chair, wastebasket, bottle, typewriter, coffeepot, and book. If your friend reports having seen a wastebasket or a book, you will have demonstrated constructive memory.

LEARNby **DOING**

Courtesy Professor William F. Brewer. From Brewer, W. F., & Treyens, J. C. (1981). Role of schemata in memory for places. *Cognitive Psychology, 13*, 207–230.

We use that existing knowledge to organize the new information we encounter and we fill in gaps in that information as we encode and retrieve it (Sherman & Bessenoff, 1999). These processes are called *constructive memory.*

In one study of constructive memory, undergraduates were asked to wait for several minutes in a graduate student's office (Brewer & Treyens, 1981). Later, they were asked to recall everything that was in the office. Most of the students mistakenly "remembered" seeing books, even though there were none. Apparently, the general knowledge that graduate students read many books influenced the participants' memory of what was in the room (Roediger, Meade, & Bergman, 2001). In another study, participants read one of two versions of a story about a man and woman at a ski lodge. One version ended with the man proposing marriage to the woman. The second version was identical until the end, when instead of proposing, the man sexually assaulted the woman. A few days after reading the story, all the participants were asked what they remembered from it. Those who had read the "proposal" version recalled nice things about the man, such as that he wanted the woman to meet his parents. Those who read the "assault" version recalled negative things, such as that the man liked to drink a lot. However, neither kind of information had actually been part of the original story. The participants had "recalled" memories of the man that they had constructed in accordance with their overall impression of him (Carli, 1999).

FOCUS ON *RESEARCH* # I Could Swear I Heard It!

By constructing our own versions of what we have seen and heard, we may remember an event differently from the way it actually happened. These errors, called *false memories,* can occur in relation to anything from the objects present in a room to the identity of an armed robber (Clancy et al., 2000).

What was the researchers' question?

How easy is it for people to form false memories? Henry Roediger and Kathleen McDermott (1995) addressed this question in an experiment to test for false memories as people recalled lists of words that had been read to them.

How did the researchers answer the question?

On each of sixteen trials, college students heard a different list of words. Each list related to a particular theme. For example, the "cold" list contained fifteen words such as *sleet, slush, frost, white, snow,* and so on. Yet the list's theme word—in this case, *cold*—was not included. In half of these trials, the students were simply asked to recall as many words as possible from the list they had just heard. But in the other half, the students did math problems instead of trying to recall the words. Once all sixteen lists had been presented, the students were given a new list of words and asked to say which of them they recognized as having been on the lists they had heard earlier. Some of the words on this new list were theme words, such as *cold,* that had not been presented earlier. Would the students "remember" hearing these theme words on the list even though they hadn't? And if so, how confident would they be about their "memory" of these words?

What did the researchers find?

The students falsely, but confidently, recognized the theme words from twelve of the sixteen lists. In fact, theme words were falsely recognized as often as listed words were correctly recognized. As you might expect, the chance of accurately recognizing the listed words was greater when the students had been allowed to recall them shortly after hearing them. However, false memory of never-presented theme words occurred in both conditions.

What do the results mean?

The results of this study suggest that the participants could not always distinguish words they had heard from those they had not heard. Why? The never-presented theme words "belonged" with the lists of presented words and apparently were "remembered" because they fit logically into the gaps in the students' memories. In short, the students' knowledge of words that *should* have been included on the lists created a "memory" that they *were* presented.

What do we still need to know?

Studies such as this one make it clear that memory is constructive and that memory distortion and inaccuracy are commonplace (Arndt, 2012; Otgaar, Peters, & Howe, 2012; Otgaar et al., 2012; Schmolck, Buffalo, & Squire, 2000; Scoboria et al., 2012; Zhu et al., 2012). With appropriate feedback, people may be able to recognize and correct false memories (Clark et al., 2012; Fazio & Marsh, 2010; Leding, 2012), but exactly how the distortion process works and why false memories seem so real is still unclear. Perhaps the more frequently we recall an event, as when students were allowed to rehearse some lists, the stronger our belief is that we have recalled it accurately. There is also evidence that merely thinking about certain objects or events or hearing sounds or seeing photos associated with them appears to make false memories of them more likely (Garry & Gerrie, 2005; Henkel, Franklin, & Johnson, 2000). And there are times when, after watching someone else do something, we form the false memory that we have done that same thing ourselves (Lindner et al., 2010). This phenomenon may involve the activity of mirror neurons, which we discuss in the chapter on biology and behavior. Questions about how false memories are created lead to even deeper questions about the degree to which our imperfect memory processes might distort our experiences of reality. Is there an objective reality, or do we each experience our own version of reality?   ● ● ● ●

Constructive Memory and PDP Models

Parallel distributed processing models of memory offer one way of explaining how semantic and episodic information become integrated in constructive memories. As mentioned earlier, PDP models suggest that newly learned facts alter our general knowledge of the world. In these network models, learned associations between specific

© AP Photo

PDP Models and Constructive Memory

If you hear that "our basketball team won last night," your schema about basketball might prompt you to encode, and later retrieve, the fact that the players were men. Such spontaneous, though often incorrect, generalizations associated with PDP models of memory help explain the appearance of constructive memories.

schemas Mental representations of categories of objects, places, events, and people.

facts come together. Let's say, for example, that your own network "knows" that your friend Joe is a male European American business major. It also "knows" that Claudia is a female African American student, but it has never learned her major. Now suppose that every other student you know is a business major. In this case, the connection between "students you know" and "business majors" would be so strong that you would conclude that Claudia is a business major, too. You would be so confident in this belief that it would take overwhelming evidence for you to change your mind (Rumelhart & McClelland, 1986). In other words, you would have constructed a memory about Claudia.

PDP networks also produce *spontaneous generalizations.* So if your friend tells you that she just bought a new car, you would know without asking that like all other cars you have experienced, it has four wheels. This is a spontaneous generalization from your knowledge base. Spontaneous generalizations are obviously helpful, but they can also create significant errors if the network is based on limited or biased experience with a class of objects or people.

If it occurs to you that ethnic prejudice can result from spontaneous generalization errors, you're right (Greenwald & Banaji, 1995). Researchers are actually encouraged by this aspect of PDP networks, though, because it accurately reflects human thought and memory. Virtually all of us make spontaneous generalizations about males, females, European Americans, African Americans, the young, the old, and many other categories (Rudman et al., 1999). Is prejudice, then, a process that we have no choice in or control over? Not necessarily. Relatively unprejudiced people tend to recognize that they are making generalizations and consciously try to ignore or suppress them (Amodio et al., 2004).

Schemas   PDP models also help us understand constructive memory by explaining the operation of the schemas that guide it. As described in the chapters on social psychology and on thought, language, and intelligence, **schemas** are mental representations of categories of objects, places, events, and people. For example, most North Americans have a schema for *baseball game,* so simply hearing these words is likely to activate whole clusters of information in long-term memory, including the rules of the game and images of players, bats, balls, a green field, summer days, and perhaps hot dogs and stadiums. The generalized knowledge contained in schemas provides a basis for making inferences about new information during the encoding stage. So, if you hear that a baseball player was injured, your schema about baseball might prompt you to encode the incident as game related, even though the cause was not mentioned. Later, you are likely to recall the injury as having occurred during a game (see Figure 6.9 for another example).

FIGURE 6.9

The Effect of Schemas on Recall

In a classic experiment, people were shown figures like these, along with labels designed to activate certain schemas (Carmichael, Hogan, & Walter, 1932). For example, when showing the top figure, the experimenter said either "This resembles eyeglasses" or "This resembles a dumbbell." When the participants were later asked to draw these figures from memory, their drawings tended to resemble the items mentioned by the experimenter. In other words, their memory had been altered by the schema-activating labels.

	Group 1		Group 2	
Figure shown to participants	Label given	Figure drawn by participants	Label given	Figure drawn by participants
○—○	Eyeglasses	○○	Dumbbell	○—○
⋈	Hourglass	⋈	Table	⋈
7	Seven	7	Four	4
⊐—	Gun	⟋⟍	Broom	⪫

LINKAGES

How accurate is eyewitness testimony?
(a link to Sensation and Perception)

Memory and Perception in the Courtroom

There are few situations in which accurate retrieval of memories is more important—and constructive memory is more dangerous—than when an eyewitness testifies in court about a crime. Let's consider the accuracy of eyewitness memory and how it can be distorted.

The presence of an eyewitness can be a key factor in deciding to prosecute an alleged criminal (Flowe, Mehta, & Ebbesen, 2011), and in the courtroom it is the most compelling evidence a lawyer can provide. Nevertheless, eyewitnesses often make mistakes (Brewer & Wells, 2011; Roediger, Wixted, & DeSoto, in press; Wells, Memon, & Penrod, 2006; Wright et al., 2009). In 1984, for example, North Carolina college student Jennifer Thompson confidently identified Ronald Cotton as the man who had raped her at knifepoint. Mainly on the basis of Thompson's testimony, Cotton was convicted of rape and sentenced to life in prison. He was released eleven years later, when DNA evidence revealed that he was innocent (and identified another man as the rapist). The eyewitness/victim's certainty had convinced a jury, but her memory had been faulty (O'Neill, 2000).

Like the rest of us, eyewitnesses can remember only what they perceive, and they can perceive only what they attend to (Backman & Nilsson, 1991). Further, their perceptions can be affected by physiological arousal and many other factors (Hope et al., 2012; Megreya, Memon, & Havard, 2012). Witnesses are asked to report as accurately as possible what they saw or heard, but no matter how hard they try to be accurate, there are limits to how valid their reports can be (Fahsing, Ask, & Granhag, 2004; Kassin, Rigby, & Castillo, 1991). For example, hearing new information about a crime (including in the form of a lawyer's question) can alter a witness's memory (Belli & Loftus, 1996; Wells & Quinlivan, 2009; Wright et al., 2009). Experiments show that when witnesses are asked "How fast were the cars going when they *smashed into* each other?" they are likely to recall a higher speed than when asked "How fast were the cars going when they hit each other?" (Loftus & Palmer, 1974; see Figure 6.10). There is also evidence that an object mentioned during questioning about an incident is often mistakenly remembered as having been there during the incident (Broaders & Goldin-Meadow, 2010; Roediger, Meade, & Bergman, 2001). So if a lawyer says that a screwdriver was lying on the ground when it was not, witnesses may recall with great certainty having seen it (Ryan & Geiselman, 1991). This *misinformation effect* can occur in several ways (Loftus & Hoffman, 1989). In some cases, hearing new information can make it harder to retrieve the original memory (Tversky & Tuchin, 1989). In others, the new information may be integrated into the old memory, making it impossible to

FIGURE 6.10

The Impact of Questions on Eyewitness Memory

After seeing a filmed traffic accident, people were asked, "About how fast were the cars going when they (smashed into, hit, or contacted) each other?" As shown here, the witnesses' responses were influenced by the verb used in the question. "Smashed" was associated with the highest average speed estimates. A week later, people who heard the "smashed" question remembered the accident as being more violent than did people in the other two groups (Loftus & Palmer, 1974).

Question	Verb	Estimated mph
About how fast were the cars going when they _____ each other?	smashed into	40.8
	hit	34.0
	contacted	30.8

Original information

External information: About how fast were the cars going when they SMASHED INTO each other?

The "memory"

distinguish from what was originally seen (Loftus, 1992). In still others, an eyewitness report might be influenced by the person's assumption that if a lawyer or police officer says an object was there or that something happened, it must be true (Chan, Thomas, & Bulevich, 2009).

Jurors' belief in a witness's testimony often depends at least as much on how the witness presents evidence as it does on the content or relevance of that evidence (Leippe, Manion, & Romanczyk, 1992). For example, many jurors are particularly impressed by witnesses who give lots of details about what they saw. Extremely detailed testimony from prosecution witnesses is especially likely to lead to guilty verdicts, even when the details reported are irrelevant (Bell & Loftus, 1989). When a witness reports details, such as the color of the criminal's shoes, jurors might assume that the witness had paid especially close attention or has a particularly good memory. This assumption seems reasonable, but there are limits on how much people can pay attention to, particularly when they are emotionally aroused and the crime happens quickly. Witnesses whose attention was drawn to details such as shoe color might not have accurately perceived the criminal's facial features (Backman & Nilsson, 1991; Perfect, Andrade, & Syrett, 2012). So the fact that an eyewitness reports many details doesn't guarantee that all of them were remembered correctly.

Jurors also tend to believe witnesses who are confident about their testimony (Leippe, Manion, & Romanczyk, 1992). Unfortunately, research shows that witnesses' confidence is frequently much higher than their accuracy (Devilly et al., 2007; Luna & Martín-Luengo, 2012; Wells, Olson, & Charman, 2002). In some cases, repeated exposure to misinformation and the repeated recall of that misinformation can lead witnesses to feel certain about their testimony even when—as in the Jennifer Thompson case—it may not be correct (Foster et al., 2012; Frenda, Nichols, & Loftus, 2011; Lamb, 1998; Mitchell & Zaragoza, 1996; Roediger, Jacoby, & McDermott, 1996).

The weaknesses inherent in eyewitness memory can be amplified by the use of police lineups and certain other criminal identification procedures (Brewer & Wells, 2011; Haw & Fisher, 2004; Laudan, 2012; Wells, Memon, & Penrod, 2006; Wells & Olson, 2003; Wells, Steblay, & Dysart, 2012). In one study, for example, participants watched a videotaped crime and then tried to identify the criminal from a set of photographs (Wells & Bradfield, 1999). None of the photos showed the person who had committed the crime, but some participants nevertheless identified one of them as the criminal they saw on tape. When these mistaken participants were led to believe that they had correctly identified the criminal, they became even more confident in the accuracy of their false identification (Semmler, Brewer, & Wells, 2004; Wells, Olson, & Charman, 2003). These incorrect but confident witnesses became more likely than other participants to claim that it had been easy for them to identify the criminal from the photos because they had had a good view of him and had paid careful attention to him.

Since 1973, at least 140 people, including Ronald Cotton, have been released from U.S. prisons after DNA tests or other evidence revealed that they had been falsely convicted—mostly on the basis of faulty eyewitness testimony (Death Penalty Information Center, 2012). DNA evidence freed Charles Fain, who had been convicted of murder and spent almost 18 years on death row in Idaho (Bonner, 2001). Maryland officials approved $900,000 in compensation for Bernard Webster, who served 20 years in prison for rape before DNA revealed that he was innocent (Associated Press, 2003). Frank Lee Smith, too, would have been set free after the sole eyewitness at his murder trial retracted her testimony, but he had already died of cancer while awaiting execution in a Florida prison. Research on memory and perception helps explain how these miscarriages of justice can occur, and it is also guiding efforts to prevent such errors in the future. The U.S. Department of Justice has acknowledged the potential for errors in eyewitness evidence as well as the dangers of asking witnesses to identify suspects from lineups and photo arrays. The result is *Eyewitness Evidence: A Guide for Law Enforcement* (U.S. Department of Justice, 1999), the first-ever guide for police and prosecutors involved in obtaining eyewitness evidence.

This is exactly the sort of biased police lineup that *Eyewitness Evidence: A Guide for Law Enforcement* (U.S. Department of Justice, 1999) is designed to avoid. Based on research in memory and perception, this guide recommends that no suspect should stand out from all the others in a lineup, that witnesses should not assume that the real criminal is in the lineup, and that they should not be encouraged to "guess" when making an identification.

"Thank you, gentlemen—you may all leave except for No. 3."

The guide warns that asking witnesses leading questions about what they saw can distort their memories. It also suggests that witnesses should examine photographs of possible suspects one at a time and points out that false identifications are less likely if witnesses viewing suspects in a lineup are told that the real perpetrator might not be included (Beresford & Blades, 2006; Humphries, Holliday, & Flowe, 2012; Quinlivan et al., 2012; Wells & Olson, 2003; Wells et al., 2000). Research on other methods for improving the accuracy of eyewitness testimony continues on several fronts (e.g., Ahola, 2012; Camp, Wesstein, & Bruin, 2012; Clark, 2012a, 2012b; Newman & Loftus, 2012; Wixted & Mickes, 2012). ● ● ● ●

Forgetting

What causes me to forget things?

The frustrations of forgetting—where you left your cell phone, the answer to a test question, an anniversary—are apparent to most people nearly every day (Neisser, 2000b). Let's look more closely at the nature of forgetting and what causes it.

How Do We Forget?

Hermann Ebbinghaus, a German psychologist, began the systematic study of memory and forgetting in the late 1800s, using only his own memory as his laboratory. He read aloud a list of nonsense syllables (such as *POF, XEM,* and *QAL*) at a constant pace and then tried to recall them.

Ebbinghaus devised a special **relearning method** to measure how much he forgot over time. He compared the number of repetitions (or trials) it took him to learn a list of items and the number of trials needed to relearn that same list later. Any reduction in the number of relearning trials represents the *savings* from one learning to the next. If it took Ebbinghaus ten trials to learn a list and another ten trials to relearn

relearning method A method for measuring forgetting.

FIGURE 6.11
Ebbinghaus's Curve of Forgetting

List 30 words, selected at random from a dictionary, and spend a few minutes memorizing them. After an hour has passed, write down as many words as you can remember, but don't look at the original list again. Test yourself again eight hours later, a day later, and two days later. Now look at the original list and see how well you did on each recall test. Ebbinghaus found that most forgetting occurs during the first nine hours after learning, especially during the first hour. If this was not the case for you, why do you think your results were different?

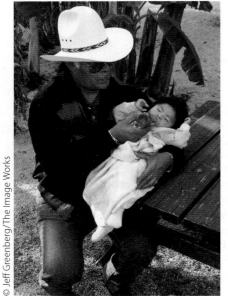

© Jeff Greenberg/The Image Works

It's All Coming Back To Me
This grandfather hasn't fed an infant for decades, but his memory of how to do it is not entirely gone. He showed some "savings"; it took him less time to relearn the skill than it took him to learn it initially. In fact, sometimes previously forgotten information is later recalled in exquisite, accurate detail, a phenomenon called *hypermnesia* (Erdelyi, 2010).

decay theory A description of forgetting as the gradual disappearance of information from memory.

interference The process through which storage or retrieval of information is impaired by the presence of other information.

it, there would be no savings. Forgetting would have been complete. If it took him ten trials to learn the list and only five trials to relearn it, there would be a savings of 50 percent.

Ebbinghaus's research produced two lasting discoveries. One is the shape of the forgetting curve shown in Figure 6.11. Even when psychologists substitute words, sentences, and stories for nonsense syllables, the forgetting curve shows the same large initial drop in memory, followed by a more moderate decrease over time (Slamecka & McElree, 1983; Wixted, 2004). Of course, we remember sensible stories better than nonsense syllables, but the shape of the curve is the same no matter what type of material is involved (Davis & Moore, 1935). Even the forgetting of events from daily life tends to follow Ebbinghaus's forgetting curve (Thomson, 1982).

Ebbinghaus also discovered just how long-lasting "savings" in long-term memory can be. Psychologists now know from the method of savings that information about everything from algebra to bike riding is often retained for decades (Matlin, 1998). So although you may forget something you have learned if you do not use the information, it is very easy to relearn the material if the need arises, indicating that the forgetting was not complete (Hall & Bahrick, 1998).

Why Do We Forget?

We have seen how forgetting occurs, but *why* does it happen? In principle, one of two processes can be responsible (Best, 1999). One process is described by **decay theory**, which suggests that information gradually disappears from memory. Decay occurs in memory in much the same way that the inscription on a ring or bracelet wears away and fades over time. Forgetting might also occur because of interference. Through **interference**, either the storage or the retrieval of information is impaired by the presence of other information (Healy et al., 2010; Robertson, 2012). Interference might occur because one piece of information actually displaces other information, pushing it out of memory. It might also occur because one piece of information makes storing or recalling other information more difficult.

The memory for an item in short-term memory decreases consistently over the course of about eighteen seconds if it isn't rehearsed or thought about. So decay appears to play the main role in forgetting in short-term memory. But interference through displacement can also be operating. Like the top of a desk, short-term memory can hold only so much. Once it is full, adding additional items tends to make others "fall off" and become unavailable (Haberlandt, 1999). Displacement is one reason why the phone number you just looked up is likely to drop out of short-term memory if you read another number immediately afterward. Rehearsal prevents displacement by continually reentering the same information into short-term memory.

PROACTIVE INTERFERENCE EXPERIMENT

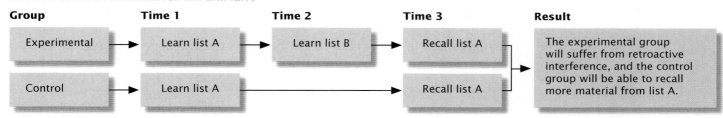

Group	Time 1	Time 2	Time 3	Result
Experimental	Learn list A	Learn list B	Recall list B	The experimental group will suffer from proactive interference, and the control group will be able to recall more material from list B.
Control		Learn list B	Recall list B	

RETROACTIVE INTERFERENCE EXPERIMENT

Group	Time 1	Time 2	Time 3	Result
Experimental	Learn list A	Learn list B	Recall list A	The experimental group will suffer from retroactive interference, and the control group will be able to recall more material from list A.
Control	Learn list A		Recall list A	

FIGURE 6.12

Procedures for Studying Interference
To remember the difference between the two types of interference, note that prefixes *pro* and *retro* indicate directions in time. Pro means "forward," and retro means "backward." In proactive inhibition, previously learned material "comes forward" to interfere with new learning; in retroactive inhibition, occurs when new information "goes back" to interfere with the recall of past learning.

retroactive inhibition A cause of forgetting whereby new information placed in memory interferes with the ability to recall information already in memory.

proactive inhibition A cause of forgetting whereby previously learned information interferes with the ability to remember new information.

FIGURE 6.13

Retrieval Failures and Forgetting
Tulving and Psotka (1971) found that people's ability to recall a list of items was strongly affected by the number of other lists they learned before being tested on the first one.

Source: From Tulvin and Psotka, "Retroactive Inhibition in Free Recall: Inaccessibility of Information Available in the Memory Store," *Journal of Experimental Psychology* Vol. 87 (pp. 1–8). Copyright © 1971 by the American Psychological Association. Adapted with permission.

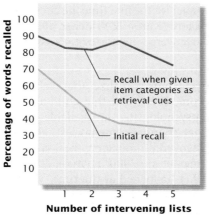

Forgetting from long-term memory appears to be more directly tied to interference. Sometimes the interference is due to **retroactive inhibition,** in which learning new information interferes with our ability to recall older information (Miller & Laborda, 2011; Wixted, 2005). Interference can also occur because of **proactive inhibition**, a process by which old information interferes with our ability to learn or remember new information (Wright, Katz, & Ma, 2012). Retroactive inhibition would help explain why studying French vocabulary this term might make it more difficult to remember the Spanish words you learned last term. And because of proactive inhibition, the French words you are learning now might make it harder to learn German vocabulary next term. Figure 6.12 outlines the types of experiments used to study the influence of each form of interference in long-term memory.

Does interference push information out of memory or does it merely make it harder to retrieve the information? To find out, Endel Tulving and Joseph Psotka (1971) presented people with lists of words that represented a particular category. For example, there was a "buildings" list (e.g., *hut, cottage, cabin, hotel*) and a geographical features list (e.g., *cliff, river, hill, volcano*). Some people learned a list and then recalled as many of its words as possible. Other groups learned one list and then learned up to five additional lists before trying to recall the first one.

The results were dramatic. As the number of additional lists increased, the number of words that people could recall from the original list decreased. This finding reflected strong retroactive inhibition; the new lists were interfering with recall of the first one. Then the researchers gave a second test, but this time they provided a retrieval cue by telling the category of the words (such as "types of buildings") to be recalled. Now the number of additional lists had almost no effect on the number of words recalled from the original list, as Figure 6.13 shows. These results indicate that the words from the first list were still in long-term memory: They had not been pushed out, but the participants couldn't remember them without appropriate retrieval cues. In short, faulty retrieval caused the original forgetting. Putting more and more information in long-term memory may be like putting more and more items in a suitcase or a refrigerator. Although none of the items disappears, it becomes increasingly difficult to find the one you are looking for (Malmberg et al., 2012).

Some theorists have suggested that all forgetting from long-term memory is due to retrieval failure (Ratcliff & McKoon, 1989). Does this mean that everything in long-term memory remains there for life, even if you cannot always (or ever) recall it? No one knows for sure yet, but as described in the next section, this question lies at the heart of some highly controversial court cases.

THINKING CRITICALLY   Can Traumatic Memories Be Repressed, Then Recovered?

In 1989, Eileen Franklin told California police that when she looked into her young daughter's eyes one day, she suddenly remembered seeing her father kill her childhood friend more than 20 years earlier. On the basis of her testimony about this memory, her father, George Franklin, Sr., was sent to prison for murder (Loftus & Ketcham, 1994).

What am I being asked to believe or accept?

Other cases in the 1990s also resulted in imprisonment as adult children claimed to have recovered childhood memories of physical or sexual abuse at the hands of their parents. The juries in these trials accepted the assertion that all memory of shocking events can be *repressed,* or pushed into an inaccessible corner of the mind where subconscious processes keep it out of awareness for decades yet potentially subject to accurate recall (Hyman, 2000). Jurors are not the only ones who believe in this **repressed memory** phenomenon. Some years ago a large American news organization reported that the United States had illegally used nerve gas during the war in Vietnam. This story was based, in part, on a Vietnam veteran's account of recovered memories of having been subjected to a nerve gas attack.

What evidence is available to support the claim?

First, as discussed in the chapter on consciousness, a lot of mental activity occurs outside of awareness (Kihlstrom, 1999). Second, research on implicit memory shows that our behavior can be influenced by information of which we are not aware (Betch et al., 2003; Kouider & Dupoux, 2005; Schacter, Chiu, & Ochsner, 1993). Third, research on *motivated forgetting* suggests that people may sometimes be able to suppress information willfully, so that it is no longer accessible on a later memory test (Anderson & Green, 2001; Anderson & Levy, 2009; Bailey & Chapman, 2012). Even suppressing one's emotional reactions to events can interfere with memories of those events (Richards & Gross, 2000). And people appear more likely to forget unpleasant rather than pleasant events (Erdelyi, 1985). One psychologist kept a detailed record of his daily life over a six-year period. When he later tried to recall these experiences, he remembered more than half of the positive events but only a third of the negative ones (Waagenaar, 1986). In another study, 38 percent of women who had been brought to a hospital when they were children because of sexual abuse did not report the incident when they were interviewed as adults (Williams, 1994). Fourth, retrieval cues can help people recall memories that had previously been inaccessible to conscious awareness (Andrews et al., 2000; Landsdale & Laming, 1995). For example, these cues have helped soldiers remember for the first time the circumstances under which they had been wounded many years before (Karon & Widener, 1997). Finally, there is the confidence with which people report recovered memories; they say they are just too vivid to be anything but real.

Can that evidence be interpreted another way?

Skeptical psychologists realize that subconscious memory and retrieval processes exist (Kihlstrom, 1999), and that child abuse and other traumas are all too common. But to these psychologists, the available evidence is not strong enough to support the conclusion that traumatic memories can be repressed and then accurately recalled. Any given "recovered" memory, they say, may actually be a distorted or constructed memory (Clancy et al., 2000; Hyman, 2000; Loftus, 1998). Our recall of past events is affected by what happened at the time, what we knew beforehand, and everything we have experienced since. The people in the study mentioned earlier who "remembered" nonexistent books in an office inadvertently used their prior knowledge of what is usually

repressed memory A painful memory that is said to be kept out of consciousness by psychological processes.

in graduate students' offices to construct a false memory of seeing books. Similarly, that Vietnam veteran's "recovered memory" of a nerve gas attack appears to have had no basis in fact; the news organization that published the story later retracted it.

As we saw in the Focus on Research section, false memories—distortions of actual events and the recall of events that didn't actually happen—can be just as vivid as real, accurate memories, and people can be just as confident about them (Brainerd & Reyna, 2005; Brainerd et al., 2003; Loftus, 2004; Nourkova, Bernstein, & Loftus, 2004; Roediger & McDermott, 2000). Most of us have experienced everyday versions of false memories. It is not unusual to "remember" turning off the coffeemaker or mailing the rent check, only to discover later that we didn't. Researchers have demonstrated that false memories can occur in relation to more emotional events, too. For example, a teenager named Chris was given descriptions of four incidents from his childhood and asked to write about each of them every day for five days (Loftus, 1997a). One of these incidents—being lost in a shopping mall at age five—never really happened. Yet Chris eventually "remembered" this event, and even added many details about the mall and the stranger whose hand he was supposedly found holding. He also rated this (false) memory as being more vivid than two of the other three (real) incidents he wrote about. Similar results occurred with about half of 77 child participants in other case studies (Porter, Yuille, & Lehman, 1999).

The same pattern of results has appeared in formal experiments about planting emotion-laden false memories (Hyman & Pentland, 1996; Loftus & Pickrell, 1995). Researchers have been able to create vivid and striking (but completely false) memories of events that people thought they experienced when they were one day old (DuBreuil, Garry, & Loftus, 1998). And some people will begin to avoid a certain food after researchers create in them a false memory of having been ill after eating that food as a child (Bernstein & Loftus, 2009a; Geraerts et al., 2008a). In other experiments, children who were repeatedly asked about a nonexistent trauma (getting a hand caught in a mousetrap) eventually developed a clear and unshakable false memory of experiencing it (Ceci et al., 1994). Results like these have led to concern that inaccurate reports and false memories might be made more likely by the use of repeated questioning and anatomically correct dolls during interviews with children about whether they have been touched inappropriately by an adult (Poole, Bruck, & Pipe, 2011).

Studies have found that people who are prone to fantasy, who easily confuse real and imagined stimuli, and who tend to have lapses in attention and memory are more likely than others to develop false memories and possibly more likely to report the recovery of repressed memories (Fuentemilla et al., 2009; McNally, 2003; McNally et al., 2000a, 2000b, 2005; Porter et al., 2000; Wilson & French, 2006). Two other studies have found that women who have suffered physical or sexual abuse are more likely to falsely remember words on a laboratory recall test (Bremner, Shobe, & Kihlstrom, 2000; Zoellner et al., 2000). This tendency appears strongest among abused women who show signs of posttraumatic stress disorder (Bremner, Shobe, & Kihlstrom, 2000). Another study found that the tendency to have false memories during a word recall task was greater in women who reported recovered memories of sexual abuse than in nonabused women or in those who had always remembered the abuse they suffered (Clancy et al., 2000).

Why would anyone "remember" a trauma that did not actually occur? Elizabeth Loftus (1997b) suggests that popular books about repressed memory may lead people to believe that anyone who experiences guilt, depression, low self-esteem, overemotionality, or virtually any other psychological problem is harboring repressed memories of abuse. This message may be reinforced and elaborated by certain therapists, particularly those who specialize in using guided imagination, hypnosis, and other methods to "help" clients recover repressed memories (Lindsay et al., 2004; McHugh, 2009; Pendergrast, 1996). In so doing, these therapists may influence their clients to construct false memories by encouraging them to imagine experiencing events that might never have actually occurred or that occurred only in a dream (Mazzoni & Loftus, 1996; Olio, 1994). As one client described her therapy, "I was rapidly losing the ability to differentiate between my imagination and my real memory" (Loftus & Ketcham, 1994, p. 25). To such therapists, a client's failure to recover memories of abuse or refusal to accept that they exist is evidence of denial of the truth (Loftus, 1997a; Tavris, 2003).

The possibility that recovered memories might actually be false memories has led to dismissed charges or not-guilty verdicts for defendants in some repressed memory cases.

In other cases, previously convicted defendants have been released. (George Franklin's conviction was overturned, but only after he spent five years in prison.) Concern over the potential damage resulting from false memories prompted the establishment in 1992 of the False Memory Syndrome Foundation, an organization of families affected by abuse accusations stemming from allegedly repressed memories. More than a hundred of these families (including George Franklin's) have filed lawsuits against hospitals and therapists. In 1994, California winery executive Gary Ramona received $500,000 in damages from two therapists who had "helped" his daughter recall his alleged sexual abuse of her. A more recent suit led to a $2 million judgment against a Minnesota therapist whose client discovered that her "recovered" memories of childhood abuse were false; similar cases in Wisconsin brought $1 million and $5 million judgments against therapists. And an Illinois case resulted in a $10.6 million settlement and the suspension of the license of the psychiatrist who had "found" his patient's lost memories (Heller, 2011; Loftus, 1998).

What evidence would help to evaluate the alternatives?

Evaluating reports of recovered memories would be easier if we had more information about whether it is possible for people to repress memories of traumatic events. If it is possible, we also need to know how common it is and how accurate recovered memories might be. So far, we know that some people apparently forget intense emotional experiences but that most people's memories of them are vivid and long lasting (Alexander et al., 2005; Goodman et al., 2003; Henckens et al., 2009; McGaugh, 2003; Pope et al., 1998; Porter & Peace, 2007). Some of these memories are called *flashbulb memories* because they preserve particular experiences in great detail (Brown & Kulik, 1977; McGaugh, 2003). In other words, evidence suggests that negative emotional information is retained as long, and as accurately, as any other information (Nørby, Lange, & Larsen, 2010). In fact, many people who live through trauma are *unable* to forget it, though they wish they could (Henig, 2004). In the sexual abuse study mentioned earlier, for example (Williams, 1994), 62 percent of the victims recalled as adults the trauma that had been documented in their childhoods. A similar study of a different group of adults found that about 92 percent of them recalled the abuse that had been documented in their childhoods (Alexander et al., 2005; Goodman et al., 2003). The true recall figures might actually be even higher in such studies, because some people who remember abuse may not wish to talk about it. In any case, additional studies like these— studies that track the fate of memories in known abuse cases—would not only help estimate the prevalence of this kind of forgetting but also might offer clues as to the kinds of people and events most likely to be associated with it.

It would also be valuable to know more about the processes through which repression might occur. Is there a mechanism that specifically pushes traumatic memories out of awareness and then keeps them at a subconscious level for long periods? Despite some

Exploring Memory Processes

Elizabeth Loftus (at center) is shown here with her students. Loftus and other cognitive psychologists have demonstrated mechanisms through which false memories can be created. They have shown, for example, that false memories appear even in research participants who are told about them and asked to avoid them (McDermott & Roediger, 1998). Their work has helped focus scientific scrutiny on reports of recovered memories, especially those arising from contact with therapists who assume that most people have repressed memories of abuse.

Courtesy of Elizabeth Loftus, University of California, Irvine

suggestive results (Anderson & Green, 2001; Anderson & Levy, 2009; Anderson, Ochsner et al., 2004; DePrince & Freyd, 2004), cognitive psychologists have so far not found reliable evidence for such a mechanism (Bulevich et al., 2006; Geraerts et al., 2006; Loftus, 1997a; McNally, 2003; McNally, Clancy, & Schacter, 2001; McNally et al., 2000a; Pope et al., 1998).

LINKAGES

Do forgotten memories remain in the subconscious?
(a link to Consciousness)

What conclusions are most reasonable?

An objective reading of the research evidence suggests that the recovery of traumatic memories is at least possible but that the implantation of false memories is also possible—and has been demonstrated repeatedly in controlled experiments. With this in mind, it is not easy to decide whether any particular case is an instance of recovered memory or false memory, especially when there is no objective corroborating evidence to guide the decision.

The intense conflict between those who uncritically accept claims of recovered memories and those who are more wary about the accuracy of such claims reflects a fundamental disagreement about evidence (Tavris, 2003). To many therapists who deal daily with victims of sexual abuse and other traumas, clients' reports constitute stronger proof of recovered memories than do the results of laboratory experiments. Client reports are viewed with considerably more skepticism by psychologists who engage in, or rely on, empirical research on the processes of memory and forgetting (Loftus, 2003, 2004; Pope, 1998). They would like to have additional sources of evidence, including from research on brain activity "signatures" that might someday distinguish true memories from false ones (e.g., Bernstein & Loftus, 2009b; Cabeza et al., 2001; Rissman, Greely, & Wagner, 2010; Sederberg et al., 2007; Slotnick & Schacter, 2004).

So people's responses to claims of recovered memory may be determined by the relative weight that they assign to reports of personal experiences versus evidence from controlled experiments. Still, the apparent ease with which false memories can be created should lead judges, juries, and the general public to exercise great caution before accepting unverified memories of traumatic events as the truth. At the same time, we should not automatically reject the claims of people who appear to have recovered memories (Geraerts et al., 2007; McNally & Geraerts, 2009). Perhaps the wisest course is to use all the scientific and circumstantial evidence available to carefully and critically examine claims of recovered memories while keeping in mind the possibility that constructive memory processes might have influenced those memories (Alison, Kebbell, & Lewis, 2006; Geraerts et al., 2007). This careful scientific approach is vital if we are to protect the rights of those who report recovered memories as well as those who face accusations arising from them (Geraerts et al., 2008b).   ● ● ● ●

Biological Bases of Memory

How does my brain change when I store a memory?

Many psychologists who study memory focus on explicit and implicit mental processes (e.g., Rubin et al., 2011; Schott et al., 2005). Others explore the physical, electrical, and chemical changes that take place in the brain or the pupils of the eyes when people encode, store, and retrieve information (Abraham, 2006; Fields, 2005; Goldinger & Papesh, 2012; Jonides, Lacey, & Nee, 2005; Kuhl, Bainbridge, & Chun, 2012; Linden et al., 2012; Touzani, Puthanveettil, & Kandel, 2007).

The Biochemistry of Memory

As described in the chapter on biology and behavior, communication among brain cells takes place at the synapses between axons and dendrites using chemicals called *neurotransmitters* that are released at the synapses. The formation and storage of new memories are associated with at least two kinds of changes in synapses.

The first kind of change occurs when stimulation from the environment promotes the formation of *new* synapses. Scientists can now actually see this process occur. As shown in Figure 6.14, repeatedly sending signals across a particular synapse increases the number of special little branches, called *spines,* that appear on the receiving cell's dendrites (Hofer et

FIGURE 6.14
Building Memories

These models are based on electron microscope images of synapses in the brain. The model on the left shows that before signals were repeatedly sent across the synapse, just one spine (shown in white) appears on this part of the dendrite. Afterward, as shown in the other model, there are two spines, which helps improve communication across the synapse. The creation and changing of many individual synapses in the brain appears to underlie the formation and storage of new memories.

Source: Toni et al. (1999).

Courtesy of Professor Dominique Muller

al., 2009; Lang et al., 2004; Nägerl et al., 2008; Roberts et al., 2010; Stepanyants & Escobar, 2011). The second kind of change occurs as new experiences change the operation of *existing* synapses. For example, when two neurons fire at the same time and together stimulate a third neuron, that other neuron will later be more responsive than before to stimulation by either neuron alone (Sejnowski, Chattarji, & Stanton, 1990). This process of "sensitizing" synapses is called *long-term potentiation* (Fidzinski et al., 2012; Li et al., 2003; Lisman, Yasuda, & Raghavachari, 2012; Mozzachiodi et al., 2008). Other patterns of electrical stimulation can weaken synaptic connections, a process called *long-term depression* (Malenka, 1995). Changes in the sensitivity of synapses could account for the development of conditioned responses and other types of learning and for the operation of working memory (Mongillo, Barak, & Tsodyks, 2008; Olson et al., 2006; Whitlock et al., 2006).

In the hippocampus (see Figure 6.15), these changes appear to occur at synapses that use the neurotransmitter *glutamate* (Malenka & Nicoll, 1999). Other neurotransmitters,

FIGURE 6.15
Brain Structures Involved in Memory

Combined neural activity in many parts of the brain allows us to encode, store, and retrieve memories. The complexity of the biological bases of these processes is underscored by research showing that different aspects of a memory—such as the sights and sounds of some event—are stored in different parts of the cerebral cortex.

Photo © Daniel Laflor/iStockphoto

such as *acetylcholine*, also play important roles in memory formation (e.g., Furey, Pietrini, & Haxby, 2000; Li et al., 2003). The memory problems seen in Alzheimer's patients are related to a lack of neurons that use acetylcholine and send fibers to the hippocampus and the cortex (Muir, 1997). Drugs that interfere with the action of acetylcholine impair memory, and drugs that increase the amount of acetylcholine in synapses can improve memory somewhat in aging animals and humans (Pettit, Shao, & Yakel, 2001; Sirvio, 1999).

In summary, research has shown that the formation of memories is associated with changes in many individual synapses that, together, strengthen and improve the communication in networks of neurons.

LINKAGES

Where are memories stored?
(a link to Biology and Behavior)

Brain Structures and Memory

Are the biochemical processes involved in memory concentrated in certain brain regions, or are they distributed throughout the brain? Research suggests that memory involves both specialized regions where various types of memories are formed and widespread areas for storage (Takashima et al., 2006).

The Impact of Brain Damage   Studies of how brain injuries affect memory provide evidence about which parts of the brain are involved in various kinds of memory. For example, damage to the hippocampus, nearby parts of the cerebral cortex, and the thalamus often results in **anterograde amnesia,** a loss of memory for any event occurring after the injury. People who suffer this kind of damage are unable to form new memories (Zhuang et al., 2011).

The case of Henry Molaison (H. M.) provides a striking example of anterograde amnesia (Milner, 1966). When H. M. was 27 years old, part of his hippocampus was removed in order to stop his severe epileptic seizures. After the operation, his long-term and short-term memory appeared normal, but something was wrong. Two years later, he still believed that he was 27. When his family moved into a new house, he couldn't remember the new address or how to get there. When his uncle died, he grieved in a normal way, but soon afterward he began to ask why his uncle had not visited him. He had to be repeatedly reminded of the death and, each time, H. M. began the mourning process all over again. The surgery had apparently destroyed the mechanism that transfers information from short-term to long-term memory. Until his death in 2008, H. M. lived in a nursing home, where his only long-term memories were from 50 years earlier, before the operation. He was still unable to recall events and facts he had experienced since then—not even the names of people he saw every day (Corkin, 2002; Hathaway, 2002; Squire, 2009).

Although patients with damage to the hippocampus cannot form new episodic memories, they may still be able to form implicit memories. For example, H. M.'s performance on a complicated puzzle improved steadily over several days of practice, just as it does with normal people, and eventually it became virtually perfect. But each time he tried the puzzle, he insisted that he had never seen it before (Cohen & Corkin, 1981). Even people without a hippocampus can form certain kinds of memories. For example, Clive Wearing, a pianist whose hippocampus was destroyed by a viral infection, has only a few seconds of short-term memory, but he can still play pieces he'd learned before the infection. He can also learn new ones, though he has no memory of doing so (Sacks, 2007). The same is true of P.M., a cellist with a similar condition (Esfahani, Kopp, & Finke, 2012). So although the hippocampus is crucial in the formation of new episodic memories, it appears that implicit memory, procedural memory, and working memory are governed by other regions of the brain (Budson, 2009; Schott et al., 2005; Squire, 1992; Touzani, Puthanveettil, & Kandel, 2007).

Retrograde amnesia involves loss of memory for events prior to a brain injury (Kapur, 1999). Often, a person with this type of amnesia can't remember anything that took place in the months or years before the injury. In 1994, head injuries from a car crash left 36-year-old Perlene Griffith-Barwell with retrograde amnesia so severe that she forgot virtually everything she had learned about everything and everyone she had known over the previous 20 years. She thought she was still 16 and did not recognize her husband, Malcolm, or her four children. She said, "The children were sweet, but they didn't seem like mine," and she "didn't feel anything" for Malcolm. Her memories of the previous 20 years

anterograde amnesia A loss of memory for events that occur after a brain injury.

retrograde amnesia A loss of memory for events that occurred prior to a brain injury.

A Famous Case of Retrograde Amnesia

After Ralf Schumacher slammed his race car into a wall during the United States Grand Prix in June of 2004, he sustained a severe concussion that left him with no memory of the crash. Retrograde amnesia is relatively common following concussions, so if you ride a bike or a motorcycle, wear that helmet!

© Paul Gilham/Getty Images

never fully returned. She is divorced, but at last report, she was living with her children, working in a bank, and planning to remarry (Echo News, 2000; Weinstein, 1999).

Unlike Perlene, most victims of retrograde amnesia gradually recover their memories (Riccio, Millin, & Gisquet-Verrier, 2003). The most distant events are recalled first, then the person gradually regains memory for events leading up to the injury. Recovery is seldom complete, however, and the person may never remember the last few seconds before the injury. One man received a severe blow to the head after being thrown from his motorcycle. Upon regaining consciousness, he claimed that he was 11 years old. Over the next three months, he slowly recalled more and more of his life. He remembered when he was 12, 13, and so on—right up until the time he was riding his motorcycle the day of the accident. But he was never able to remember what happened just before the accident (Baddeley, 1982). Those final events were probably encoded into short-term memory, but apparently they were never transferred into long-term memory (Dudai, 2004).

Other conditions that suppress neural activity in the brain can also disrupt the transfer of information from short-term to long-term memory. These conditions include anesthetic drugs, poisoning by carbon monoxide or other toxins, and strong electrical impulses such as those in the electroconvulsive therapy that is sometimes used to treat cases of severe depression (see the chapter on treatment of psychological disorders).

Multiple Storage Areas Obviously, the hippocampus does not permanently store long-term memories (Bayley, Hopkins, & Squire, 2003; Rosenbaum et al., 2000). If it did, H. M. would not have retained memories from the years before part of his hippocampus was removed. The hippocampus and thalamus send nerve impulses to the cerebral cortex, and it is in and around the cortex that long-term semantic and episodic memories are probably stored—but not just in one place (Levy, Bayley, & Squire, 2004; Maviel et al., 2004; Miceli et al., 2001; Ranganath, 2010). As described in the chapter on biology and behavior, different regions of the cortex receive messages from different senses. Specific aspects of an experience are probably stored in or near these regions. For example, damage to the auditory association cortex disrupts memory for sounds (Colombo et al., 1990). A memory, however, involves more than one sensory system. Even in the simple case of a rat remembering a maze, the experience of the maze involves vision, smell, movements, and emotions, each of which may be stored in different regions of the brain (Gallagher & Chiba, 1996). So memories are both localized and distributed. Certain brain areas store specific aspects of each remembered event, but many brain systems are involved in experiencing a whole event (Brewer et al., 1998; Kensinger & Corkin, 2004). For example, the cerebellum (see Figure 6.15) is involved in the storage of procedural knowledge, such as dance steps and other movements.

What happens in the brain as we retrieve memories? Brain imaging studies show that the hippocampus and various regions of the cerebral cortex are active during memory retrieval (Cabeza et al., 2001; Davachi, Mitchell, & Wagner, 2003; McDermott, Szpunar, & Christ, 2009). There is also evidence to suggest that retrieving memories of certain experiences, such as a conversation or a tennis game, reactivates the sensory and motor regions of the brain that had been involved during the event itself (Danker & Anderson, 2010; Nyberg et al., 2001). Research shows, too, that when people or animals recall a stored emotional (fear-related) memory, that memory may have to be stored again. During this biological restorage process known as *reconsolidation*, it may be either strengthened or distorted (Dudai, 2004; Eisenberg et al., 2003; Inda, Muravieva, & Alberini, 2011; Kuhbandner, Spitzer, & Pekrun, 2011; Lee, Everitt, & Thomas, 2004; Nader & Hardt, 2009; Nader, Schafe, & Le Doux, 2000; Schiller et al., 2010).

Cognitive neuroscientists are trying to determine whether different patterns of brain activity are associated with the storage and retrieval of accurate versus inaccurate memories (Bäuml & Samenieh, 2012; Bernstein & Loftus, 2009b; Gonsalves & Paller, 2000; Slotnick & Schacter, 2004; Urbach et al., 2005). Another new line of work concerns the ability to think about the future (Atance & O'Neill, 2001; Szpunar, 2010). Scientists have found, for example, that patients with amnesia due to damage to the medial temporal lobe are not only unable to recollect the past but they also cannot vividly envision future events, such as their next birthday party (Hassabis et al., 2007; Maguire & Hassabis, 2011). It appears from neuroimaging studies that the same brain regions involved in remembering are important for envisioning, too (Addis et al., 2007; Szpunar, Watson, & McDermott, 2007; Szpunar, Chan, & McDermott, 2009).

Improving Your Memory

How can I remember more information?

Some questions remain about what memory is and how it works, but the results of memory research offer many valuable guidelines to help people improve their memories (Adesope & Nesbit, 2012; Hu & Ericsson, 2012; Neisser, 2000a). For example, the physiological arousal that accompanies walking and other exercise appears to promote the storage and retrieval of memories (Lin et al., 2012; Salas, Minakata, & Kelemen, 2011; Schaefer et al., 2010), and as noted in the consciousness chapter, a good night's sleep can help consolidate the memories you formed during the day (Payne et al., 2012; Rudoy et al., 2009; Scullin & McDaniel, 2010; Simmons, 2012). More specific memory enhancement strategies are based on the elaboration of incoming information and especially on linking new information to what you already know.

Mnemonic Strategies

One way to improve your memory is to use mnemonic strategies (pronounced "nee-MON-ik"). **Mnemonic strategies** are ways to put information into an organized framework in order to remember it more easily. To remember the names of the Great Lakes, for example, you could use the acronym HOMES (for Huron, Ontario, Michigan, Erie, and Superior). Verbal organization is the basis for many mnemonic strategies. You can link items by weaving them into a story, a sentence, or a rhyme. To help customers remember where they left their cars, some large parking lots have replaced traditional section designations such as "A1" or "G8" with the names of colors, months, or animals. Customers can then tie the location of their cars to information already in long-term memory—for example, "I parked in the month of my mother's birthday." And which do you think would be easier to remember: 1-800-438-4357 or 1-800-GET-HELP? Obviously, the more meaningful "get help" number is more memorable (Topolinski, 2011), and there are Web sites that can help you translate any phone number into words or a phrase.

One simple but powerful mnemonic strategy is called the *method of loci* (pronounced "LOW-sigh"), or the "method of places." To use this method, first think about a set of familiar locations. Use your home, for example. You might imagine walking through the

mnemonic strategies Methods for organizing information in order to remember it.

"YOU SIMPLY ASSOCIATE EACH NUMBER WITH A WORD, SUCH AS 'TABLE' AND 3,476,029."

© S. Harris/ScienceCartoonsPlus.com

Mnemonic Strategies
You can improve your memory by using mnemonic strategies, but make sure they are easy to remember!

front door, around all four corners of the living room, and through each of the other rooms. Next, imagine that each item you want to remember is in one of these locations. Creating vivid or unusual images of how the items appear in each location seems to be particularly effective (Kline & Groninger, 1991). For example, tomatoes smashed against the front door or bananas hanging from the bedroom ceiling might be helpful in recalling these items on a grocery list. Whenever you want to remember a new list, you can create new images using the same locations in the same order.

Guidelines for More Effective Studying

The success of mnemonic strategies demonstrates again the importance of relating new information to knowledge already stored in memory. All mnemonic systems require that you have a well-learned body of knowledge (such as locations) that can be used to provide a framework, or context, for organizing incoming information (Hilton, 1986).

When you want to remember complex material, such as a textbook chapter, the same principle applies (Palmisano & Herrmann, 1991). You can improve your memory for text material by first creating an outline or other overall context for learning, rather than by just reading and rereading (Glover et al., 1990). Repetition may *seem* effective because it keeps material in short-term memory, but for retaining information over long periods, repetition alone tends to be ineffective, no matter how much time you spend on it (Bjork, 1999; Bjorklund & Green, 1992). In short, "work smarter, not harder."

In addition, spend your time wisely. **Distributed practice** is much more effective than **massed practice** for learning and retaining new information. If you are going to spend 10 hours studying for a test, you will be much better off studying for ten 1-hour blocks, separated by periods of sleep and other activity. "Cramming" for one 10-hour block will not be as successful (Rohrer & Pashier, 2007). By scheduling more study sessions, you will stay fresh and be able to think about the material from a new perspective during each session. This method will remind you of the previously studied material, and help you elaborate on the material, as in elaborative rehearsal, and thus remember it better (Benjamin & Tullis, 2010; Cepeda et al., 2009).

You should also practice retrieving what you have learned by testing yourself repeatedly. For example, instead of simply re-reading a section of a chapter, close the book and try to jot down the section's main points from memory. Many laboratory and classroom studies have found that students' exam performance is significantly better after self-testing than after merely reading and rereading the material they are trying to learn (Bugg & McDaniel, 2012; Hartwig & Dunlosky, 2012; Karpicke, 2009, 2012; Karpicke & Bauernschmidt, 2011; Karpicke & Smith, 2012; Nunes & Weinstein, 2012; Pyc & Rawson, 2010; Rawson & Dunlosky, 2011; Roediger et al., 2011; Roediger & Karpicke, 2006). This is why we have included self-tests following each "In Review" table and at the end of every chapter of this book.

distributed practice Learning new information in many study sessions that are spaced across time.

massed practice Trying to learn complex new information in a single long study period.

Reading a Textbook   More specific advice for remembering textbook material comes from a study that examined how successful and unsuccessful college students approached their reading (Whimbey, 1976). Unsuccessful students tended to read the material straight through. They did not slow down when they reached a difficult section. They kept going even when they did not understand what they were reading. In contrast, successful college students monitored their understanding, reread difficult sections, and periodically stopped or reviewed what they had learned. (This book's "In Review" features are designed to help you do that.) In short, effective learners engage in a deep level of processing. They are active learners. They think of each new fact in relation to other material, and they develop a context in which many new facts can be organized effectively.

Research on memory suggests two specific guidelines for reading a textbook. First, make sure that you understand what you are reading before moving on (Herrmann & Searleman, 1992). Second, try the *PQ4R method* (Thomas & Robinson, 1972). PQ4R stands for six activities to engage in when you read a chapter: *preview, question, read, reflect, recite,* and *review*. These activities are designed to increase the depth to which you process the information you read and should be done as follows:

1. *Preview.* Begin by skimming the chapter. Look at the section headings and any boldfaced or italicized terms. Get a general idea of what material will be discussed, the way it is organized, and how its topics relate to one another and to what you already know. Some people find it useful to survey the entire chapter once and then survey each major section a little more carefully before reading it in detail.
2. *Question.* Before reading each section, ask yourself what content will be covered and what information you should be getting from it.
3. *Read.* Read the text, but think about the material as you read. Are the questions you raised earlier being answered? Do you see the connections between and among the topics?
4. *Reflect.* As you read, think of your own examples—and create visual images—of the concepts and phenomena you encounter. Ask yourself what the material means and consider how each section relates to other sections in the chapter and other chapters in the book (this book's Linkages features are designed to promote this kind of reflection).
5. *Recite.* At the end of each section, recite the major points. Resist the temptation to be passive and say, "Oh, I'll remember that." Be active. Put the ideas into your own words by reciting them aloud to yourself (MacLeod et al., 2010) or by summarizing the material in a mini-lecture to a friend or study partner.
6. *Review.* When you reach the end of the chapter, review all of its material. You should now see connections not only within each section but also among sections. The objective is to see how the material is organized. Once you grasp that organization, the individual facts will be far easier to remember.

By following these procedures, you will learn and remember the material better. You will also save yourself considerable time.

Lecture Notes   Students and employees often have to learn and remember material from lectures or other presentations. Taking notes will help, but effective note taking is a learned skill that improves with practice (Pauk & Owens, 2010). Research on memory suggests some simple strategies for taking and using notes effectively.

Recognize first that in note taking, more is not necessarily better. Taking detailed notes on everything requires that you pay close attention to unimportant as well as important content, leaving little time for thinking about the material. Note takers who concentrate on expressing the major ideas in relatively few words remember more than those who try to catch every detail (Pauk & Owens, 2010). In short, the best way to take notes is to think about what is being said. Draw connections with other material in the presentation. Then summarize the major points clearly and concisely (Kiewra, 1989).

Once you have a set of lecture notes, review them as soon as possible after the lecture so that you can fill in missing details. (Remember: Most forgetting from long-term memory occurs during the first hour after learning.) When the time comes for serious study, use your notes as if they were a chapter in a textbook. Write a detailed outline. Think about how various points are related. Once you have organized the material, the details will make more sense and will be much easier to remember. ("In Review: Improving Your Memory" summarizes tips for studying.)

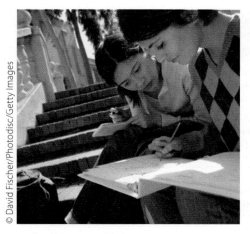

Understand and Remember
Research on memory suggests that students who simply read their textbooks won't remember as much as those who read for understanding using strategies such as the PQ4R method. Further, memory for the material is likely to be better if you read and study it over a number of weeks rather than in one marathon session on the night before a test.

APPLYING PSYCHOLOGY

Improving Your Memory   IN REVIEW

Goal	Helpful Techniques
Remembering lists of items	• Use mnemonic strategies. • Look for meaningful acronyms. • Try the method of loci.
Remembering textbook material	• Follow the PQ4R system. • Allocate your time to allow for distributed practice. • Read actively, not passively. • Test yourself repeatedly as you read.
Taking lecture notes	• Take notes, but record only the main points. • Think about the overall organization of the material. • Review your notes as soon after the lecture as possible in order to fill in missing points.
Studying for exams	• Write a detailed outline of your lecture notes rather than passively reading them.

IN REVIEW QUESTIONS

1. Using mnemonic strategies and the PQ4R system to better remember course material are examples of the value of _____ rehearsal.

2. "Cramming" illustrates _____ practice that usually leads to _____ long-term retention than _____ practice.

3. To minimize forgetting, you should review lecture notes _____ after a lecture ends.

Active Review

As noted in the introductory chapter, all of psychology's subfields are related to one another. Our discussion of eyewitness testimony illustrates just one way that the topic of this chapter, memory, is linked to the subfield of sensation and perception, as discussed in

CHAPTER 6
Memory

the chapter by that name. The Linkages diagram shows ties to two other subfields, and there are many more ties throughout the book. Looking for linkages among subfields will help you see how they all fit together and help you better appreciate the big picture that is psychology.

LINKAGES

Where are memories stored? *(ans. on p. 235)*

How accurate is eyewitness testimony *(ans. on p. 225)*

Why does memory improve during childhood *(ans. on p. 356)*

CHAPTER 2
Biology and Behavior

CHAPTER 3
Sensation and Perception

CHAPTER 9
Human Development

Summary

The Nature of Memory

How does information turn into memories?
Human memory depends on a complex mental system. There are three basic memory processes. ***Encoding*** transforms stimulus information into some type of mental representation. Codes for ***auditory (*** or ***acoustic) memory*** represent information as sounds, codes for ***visual memory*** represent information as images, and codes for semantic memory represent information as general meanings. ***Storage*** maintains information in the memory system over time. ***Retrieval*** is the process of gaining access to previously stored information.

Most psychologists agree that there are at least three types of memory. ***Episodic memory*** refers to memory for

specific events in a person's life. ***Semantic memory*** refers to generalized knowledge about the world. ***Procedural memory,*** or ***procedural knowledge,*** refers to information about how to do things. Research on memory focuses on ***explicit memory,*** the information we retrieve through a conscious effort to remember something, and ***implicit memory,*** the unintentional recollection and influence of prior experiences.

Four models of memory have guided most research. The ***levels-of-processing model of memory*** suggests that the most important determinant of memory is how extensively information is encoded or processed when it is first received. In general, ***elaborative rehearsal*** is more effective than ***maintenance rehearsal*** in learning new information, because it

represents a deeper level of processing. According to the ***transfer-appropriate processing model of memory,*** the critical determinant of memory is not how deeply information is encoded but whether the processes used during retrieval match those used during encoding. ***Parallel distributed processing (PDP) models of memory*** suggest that new experiences not only provide specific information but also become part of (and alter) a whole network of associations. The ***information-processing model of memory*** suggests that for information to become firmly embedded in memory, it must pass through three stages of processing: sensory memory, short-term memory, and long-term memory.

Storing New Memories

What am I most likely to remember?
Sensory memory maintains information about incoming stimuli in the ***sensory registers,*** such as in ***iconic memory,*** for a very brief time. ***Selective attention,***

which focuses mental resources on only part of the stimulus field, controls what information in the sensory registers is actually perceived and transferred to short-term memory.

Working memory is a system that allows us to store, organize, and manipulate information in order to think, solve problems, and make decisions. The storage, or maintenance, component of working memory is referred to as **short-term memory (STM).** Various memory codes can be used in short-term memory, but acoustic codes seem to be used in most verbal tasks. Studies of the **immediate memory span** indicate that the capacity of short-term memory is approximately seven meaningful groupings of information, created by **chunking.** Studies using the **Brown-Peterson distractor technique** show that information in short-term memory is usually forgotten in about eighteen seconds if it is not rehearsed.

Long-term memory (LTM) normally results from semantic encoding, which means that people tend to encode the general meaning of information, not the surface details, into long-term memory. The capacity of long-term memory to store new information is extremely large and perhaps unlimited. The appearance of a **primacy effect** and a **recency effect** suggests that short-term and long-term memory may be distinct systems.

Retrieving Memories

How do I retrieve stored memories?
Retrieval cues help people remember things that they would otherwise not be able to recall. The effectiveness of retrieval cues follows the **encoding specificity principle:** Cues help retrieval only if they match some feature of the information that was originally encoded. All else being equal, memory may be better when we attempt to retrieve information in the same environment in which it was learned; this is called **context-specific memory,** or **context-specific learning.** When our internal state can affect retrieval, we have a **state-dependent memory,** or **state-dependent learning.** Researchers usually study retrieval from semantic memory by examining how long it takes people to answer general knowledge questions. It appears that ideas are represented as associations in a dense semantic memory network and that the retrieval of information occurs by a process of **spreading activation.** Each concept in the network is represented as a unique collection of features or attributes. The tip-of-the-tongue phenomenon illustrates the retrieval of incomplete knowledge.

Constructing Memories

How accurate are my memories?
In the process of constructive memory, people use generalized knowledge, or **schemas,** to fill in gaps in the information they encode and retrieve. PDP models provide one explanation of how people make spontaneous generalizations about the world.

Eyewitnesses can remember only what they perceive, and they can perceive only what they attend to. As a result, eyewitness testimony is often much less accurate than witnesses—and jurors—think it is.

Forgetting

What causes me to forget things?
In his research on long-term memory and forgetting, Ebbinghaus devised a **relearning method** to measure the amount of time that is saved when previously learned material is learned again after a delay. He found that most forgetting from long-term memory occurs during the first hour after learning and that savings can be extremely long lasting. **Decay theory** and **interference** describe two mechanisms of forgetting. There is evidence of both decay and interference in short-term memory; it appears that most forgetting from long-term memory is due to interference caused by either **retroactive inhibition** or **proactive inhibition.** There is considerable controversy over the possibility of **repressed memory** of traumatic events, especially about whether recovered memories of such events are more likely to be true recollections or false, constructed ones.

Biological Bases of Memory

How does my brain change when I store a memory?
Research has shown that memories can result from new synapses forming in the brain and improved communication at existing synapses. Studies of **anterograde amnesia, retrograde amnesia,** and other consequences of brain damage provide information about the brain structures involved in memory. For example, the hippocampus and thalamus are known to play a role in the formation of memories. These structures send nerve impulses to the cerebral cortex, and it is there that memories are probably stored. Memories appear to be both localized and distributed throughout the brain.

Improving Your Memory

How can I remember more information?
Mnemonic strategies are methods that can be used to remember things better. One of the simplest but most powerful mnemonic strategies is the method of loci. It is useful because it provides a

context for organizing material effectively. Another key memory strategy is to space out your study sessions over time. This *distributed practice* is much more effective than *massed practice* ("cramming"), in which you try to learn a lot of

information all at once. The key to remembering textbook material is to read actively rather than passively. One way to do this is to follow the PQ4R method: preview, question, read, reflect, recite, and review. Similarly, to take lecture notes or to study them effectively, organize the points in a meaningful outline and think about how each main point relates to the others.

LEARN by DOING

Put It in Writing
Write a paragraph describing your views on the accuracy of eyewitness's memories of crimes. Be sure to mention what evidence leads you to think as you do about this topic. For example, indicate whether you tend to give more weight to the testimony of witnesses who seem very sure of their stories or to the results of scientific research on constructed and distorted memories. Be sure to say why you prefer one kind of evidence over another and whether you think the debate over the accuracy of eyewitness testimony will ever be resolved to everyone's satisfaction. If you wish, go on to write another paragraph describing your views on, and the evidence for and against, claims of recovered memories of childhood abuse.

Personal Learning Activity
When you study for your next quiz or exam, try using some of the memory tips contained in this chapter. Use one or more mnemonic devices to help you to remember lists of information, and try the PQ4R method with the next chapter you read. Did these memory-enhancing methods make it easier for you to study and to do well on your next quiz or exam? Why or why not?

Review of Key Terms

Can you define each of the key terms in the chapter? Check your definitions against those on the pages shown in parentheses in the following list or in the Glossary at the end of the book.

auditory memory (acoustic memory) (p. 209)
anterograde amnesia (p. 235)
Brown-Peterson distractor technique (p. 216)
chunking (p. 215)
context-specific memory (context-specific learning) (p. 219)
decay theory (p. 228)
distributed practice (p. 238)
elaborative rehearsal (p. 211)
encoding (p. 209)
encoding specificity principle (p. 219)
episodic memory (p. 210)
explicit memory (p. 210)

iconic memory (p. 214)
immediate memory span (p. 215)
implicit memory (p. 210)
information-processing model of memory (p. 212)
interference (p. 228)
levels-of-processing model of memory (p. 210)
long-term memory (LTM) (p. 216)
maintenance rehearsal (p. 210)
massed practice (p. 238)
mnemonic strategies (p. 237)
parallel distributed processing (PDP) models of memory (p. 211)
primacy effect (p. 218)
proactive inhibition (p. 229)
procedural memory (procedural knowledge) (p. 210)
recall (p. 209)
recency effect (p. 218)
recognition (p. 209)

relearning method (p. 227)
repressed memory (p. 230)
retrieval (p. 209)
retrieval cues (p. 218)
retroactive inhibition (p. 229)
retrograde amnesia (p. 235)
schemas (p. 224)
selective attention (p. 214)
semantic memory (p. 209)
sensory memory (p. 213)
sensory registers (p. 214)
short-term memory (STM) (p. 214)
spreading activation (p. 220)
state-dependent memory (state-dependent learning) (p. 219)
storage (p. 209)
transfer-appropriate processing model of memory (p. 211)
visual memory (p. 209)
working memory (p. 214)

Test Your Knowledge

Select the best answer for each of the following questions. Then check your responses against the Answer Key at the end of the book.

1. Ludwig had an extraordinary memory for sound. Even when he lost his hearing in his later years, he was still able to create beautiful music. This demonstrates his well-developed ____ codes.
   a. acoustic
   b. visual
   c. semantic
   d. auditory

2. Henry is talking about his high school graduation ceremony. He remembers that his parents and grandparents were there and that afterward they gave him a laptop computer. Henry's memory of this event is both ____ and ____.
   a. semantic; explicit
   b. episodic; explicit
   c. semantic; implicit
   d. episodic; implicit

3. Riesa was uncomfortable when she was introduced to her roommate's cousin. She was not aware of it, but the cousin reminded her of a hated classmate in elementary school. This incident provides an example of the operation of ____ memory.
   a. procedural
   b. semantic
   c. implicit
   d. explicit

4. Raquel was still studying ten minutes before her test. As she entered the classroom, she kept repeating the last sentence she had read: "Henry VIII had six wives." She was using ____ to keep this information in mind.
   a. elaborative rehearsal
   b. maintenance rehearsal
   c. mnemonic strategies
   d. spreading activation

5. In a memory study, half the students in a class were told to expect multiple-choice questions on their upcoming exam and the other half was told to expect essay questions. Students did better if they got the type of exam they expected, which is consistent with the ____ model of memory.
   a. levels-of-processing
   b. transfer-appropriate processing
   c. parallel distributed processing
   d. information-processing

6. Reepal listens as her father describes a party the family is planning. She also smells popcorn from the kitchen, hears the radio playing, notices flashes of lightning outside, and feels too warm in her sweater. Yet Reepal is able to transfer the information about the party to her short-term memory, primarily because of ____.
   a. elaborative rehearsal
   b. implicit memory cues
   c. selective attention
   d. transfer-appropriate processing

7. Larry was thrilled when he met the girl of his dreams at the mall. She told him her phone number before she left, but if Larry doesn't use any rehearsal methods, he will remember the number for only about ____.
   a. one second
   b. eighteen seconds
   c. one minute
   d. five minutes

8. Remembering your bank account number (2171988) as your birthday (February 17, 1988) is an example of ____.
   a. chunking
   b. the Brown-Peterson distractor technique
   c. the PQ4R method
   d. the method of loci

9. Lisbeth's mother once told her to remember that "the nail that stands out will get pounded down." But when Lisbeth tried to tell a friend about this saying, she remembered it as "if you stand out too much you'll get in trouble." Her problem in recalling the exact words is probably due to the fact that encoding in long-term memory is usually ____.
   a. acoustic
   b. visual
   c. semantic
   d. state dependent

10. Raul went to a lecture on the structure of DNA but forgot his notebook and pen. He tried to remember as much of it as possible so that he could make some notes later. Research by Ebbinghaus suggests that Raul will forget most of the lecture within about ____ after it ends.
    a. eighteen seconds
    b. a minute
    c. an hour
    d. twenty-four hours

11. Nesta had made a list of twenty CDs that she wanted to check out of the library, but she forgot to bring it with her. Nesta is most likely to remember the CDs that were at the ____ of the list.
    a. beginning
    b. middle
    c. end
    d. beginning and end

12. Janetta has been studying for tomorrow's test while drinking strong caffeinated coffee. A friend tells Janetta that her test score can improve improved if she takes advantage of state-dependent memory by ____.
    a. drinking strong, caffeinated coffee just before the test
    b. doing the rest of her studying where the test will be given
    c. avoiding any kind of coffee just before the test
    d. using mnemonic strategies to remember key terms

13. Molly, a high school student, knows that she knows the name of her kindergarten teacher, but she can't quite remember it when asked. This experience is called ____.
    a. constructive memory block
    b. sensory memory impairment
    c. the tip-of-the-tongue phenomenon
    d. the tip-of-the-nose phenomenon

14. When asked if there was a fever thermometer in her doctor's office, Careen says she remembers seeing one, even though it wasn't actually there. This is an example of ____, which is influenced by ____.
    a. the tip-of-the-tongue phenomenon; schemas
    b. the tip-of-the-tongue phenomenon; selective attention
    c. constructive memory; schemas
    d. constructive memory; selective attention

15. The use of DNA evidence has had what effect on the U.S. legal system's view of eyewitness testimony?
    a. It has tended to back up eyewitness testimony.
    b. It has demonstrated that eyewitness testimony, though not always accurate, is much better than anyone thought it was.
    c. It has revealed that eyewitness testimony has put many people in prison for crimes they did not commit.
    d. It has had little effect.

16. Robin memorized the names of all of the U.S. presidents when she was 10. Two years later, she had forgotten most of them, so she was pleasantly surprised that she could learn them a second time much more quickly than the first. This faster relearning time is an example of what Ebbinghaus called ____.
    a. mnemonic strategies
    b. state dependence
    c. savings
    d. context dependence

17. Berean studied French during his first year at college and then started learning Spanish in his second year. Now he is having difficulty remembering his Spanish vocabulary because the French words keep popping into his mind. This is an example of ____.
    a. retrograde amnesia
    b. anterograde amnesia
    c. proactive inhibition
    d. retroactive inhibition

18. When her brother said he had gotten a job in a bookstore, Danielle immediately assumed it would be a large room with books along the walls, a magazine section, a children's section, and cash registers near the door. But he had been hired by an online store, so Danielle was wrong. Her mistaken assumptions occurred because of ____, which is/are predicted by the ____ model of memory.
    a. spontaneous generalizations; PDP
    b. spontaneous generalizations; information-processing
    c. constructive memory; depth of processing
    d. semantic memory; transfer-appropriate

19. Jerry, a factory worker, suffered a brain injury when a steel beam fell on his head. Jerry cannot remember anything that has happened since the accident. Jerry is experiencing ____ amnesia.
    a. retrograde
    b. anterograde
    c. proactive
    d. retroactive

20. Loretta wanted to remember a list of important memory researchers, so she pictured them all visiting her apartment. She imagined Elizabeth Loftus playing video games in the living room, Hermann Ebbinghaus napping in the bathtub, Henry Roediger and Kathleen McDermott dancing in the kitchen, and so on. Loretta is using the memory strategy called ____.
    a. the method of loci
    b. procedural memorization
    c. encoding cues
    d. context dependence

Media Resources ●

Now that you have finished reading this chapter, how about exploring some of the ideas and information that you found most interesting?

Go to **CengageBrain.com** to access Psychology CourseMate, where you will find an interactive eBook, glossaries, flashcards, quizzes, videos, Virtual Psychology Labs, and more.

If your professor has assigned Aplia:

1. Sign in to your account.
2. Complete the corresponding exercises as required by your professor.
3. When finished, click "Grade It Now" to see which areas you have mastered, which areas need more work, and detailed explanations of every answer.

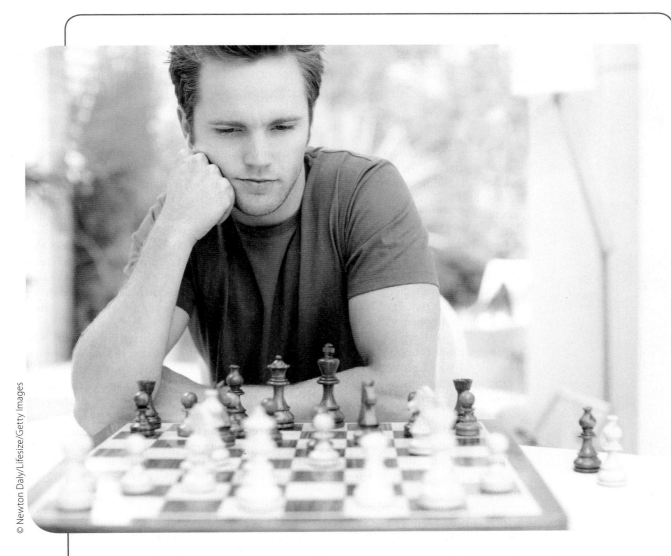

© Newton Daly/Lifesize/Getty Images

7

Thought, Language, and Intelligence

Preview

"Say what you mean, and mean what you say." This is good advice, but following it isn't always easy, partly because our thoughts don't always come to us in clear, complete sentences. We have to construct those sentences—using the language we've learned—from the words, images, ideas, and other mental material in our minds. Often, the material's complexity makes it difficult to accurately express what we're thinking. We all manage to do it, but with varying degrees of success. In this chapter, we explore what thoughts are, what language is, and how people translate one into the other. We also consider how thinking guides decision making and problem solving and how psychologists measure individual differences in these and other cognitive abilities that are commonly described as *intelligence*.

Dr. Joyce Wallace, a New York City physician, was having trouble figuring out what was the matter with a 43-year-old patient, "Laura McBride." Laura reported pain in her stomach and abdomen, aching muscles, irritability, occasional dizzy spells, and fatigue (Rouéché, 1986). The doctor's first hypothesis was iron-deficiency anemia, a condition in which there is not enough oxygen-carrying hemoglobin in the blood. There was some evidence to support that hypothesis. A physical examination revealed that Laura's spleen was somewhat enlarged, and blood tests showed low hemoglobin and high production of red blood cells, suggesting that her body was attempting to compensate for the loss of hemoglobin. However, other tests revealed normal iron levels. Perhaps she was losing blood through internal bleeding, but other tests ruled that out. Had Laura been vomiting blood? She said no. Blood in the urine? No. Abnormally heavy menstrual flow? No.

As Dr. Wallace puzzled over the problem, Laura's condition worsened. She reported more intense pain, cramps, shortness of breath, and severe loss of energy. Her blood was becoming less and less capable of sustaining her, but if it was not being lost, what was happening to it? Finally, the doctor looked at a smear of Laura's blood on a microscope slide. What she saw indicated that a poison was destroying Laura's red blood cells. What could it be? Laura spent most of her time at home, and her teenage daughters, who lived with her, were perfectly healthy. Dr. Wallace asked herself, "What does Laura do that the girls do not?" She repairs and restores paintings. Paint. Lead! She might be suffering from lead poisoning! When the next blood test showed a lead level seven times higher than normal, Dr. Wallace knew she had found the answer at last.

To unravel this medical mystery, Dr. Wallace relied on her intelligence, part of which can be seen in her ability to think, solve problems, and make judgments and decisions. She put these vital cognitive abilities to use in weighing the pros and cons of various hypotheses and in reaching decisions about what tests to order and how to interpret them. In consulting with the patient and other physicians, she relied on another remarkable human cognitive ability known as *language*. Let's take a look at what psychologists have discovered about these complex mental processes, how to measure them, and how to compare people in terms of intelligence. We begin by examining a general framework for understanding human thinking and then go on to look at some specific cognitive processes. ●

Basic Functions of Thought

What good is thinking, anyway?

Thinking involves five main operations or functions: describing, elaborating, deciding, planning, and guiding action. Figure 7.1 shows how these functions can be organized into a circle of thought.

The Circle of Thought

Consider how the circle of thought operated in Dr. Wallace's case. It began when she received the information about Laura's symptoms that enabled her to *describe* the problem. Next, Dr. Wallace *elaborated* on this information by using her knowledge, experience, and powers of reasoning to consider what disorders might cause such symptoms. Then she made a *decision* to investigate a possible cause, such as anemia. To pursue this decision, she formulated a *plan*—and then *acted* on that plan. But the circle of thought did not stop there. Information from the blood test provided new descriptive information, which Dr. Wallace elaborated further to reach another decision, create a new plan, and guide her next action. Each stage in the circle of thought was also influenced by her overall intention—in this case, to find and cure her patient's problem.

The processes making up the circle of thought usually occur so quickly and are so complex that slowing them down for careful analysis might seem impossible. Some psychologists approach this difficult task by studying thought processes as if they were part of a computer-like information-processing system. An **information-processing system** receives information, represents the information with symbols, and then manipulates those symbols (e.g., Anderson, Bothell et al., 2004). In an information-processing model, **thinking** is defined as the manipulation of mental representations. Figure 7.2 shows how an information-processing model might describe the sequence of mental events that make up one trip around the circle of thought.

information-processing system
Mechanisms for receiving information, representing it with symbols, and manipulating it.

thinking The manipulation of mental representations.

FIGURE 7.1
The Circle of Thought
The circle of thought begins as our sensory systems receive information from the world. Our perceptual system describes and elaborates this information, which is represented in the brain in ways that allow us to make decisions, formulate plans, and guide our actions. As those actions change our world, we receive new information, which begins another journey around the circle of thought.

Photo © Umberto Shtanzman/Shutterstock

FIGURE 7.2

An Information-Processing Model
Some stages in the information-processing model depend heavily on both short-term and long-term memory and require some attention—that limited supply of mental resources required for information processing to be carried out efficiently (Oberauer & Hein, 2012).

"Automatic" Thinking

The sensory, perceptual, decision-making, response-planning, and action components of the circle of thought can occur so rapidly that—as when playing a fast-paced video game—we may only be aware of the incoming information and our quick response to it. In such cases, our thinking processes become so well practiced that they are virtually automatic (Charlton & Starkey, 2011).

concepts Categories of objects, events, or ideas that have common properties.

In the first stage, information about the world reaches your brain through the senses we discussed in the chapter on sensation and perception. This stage does not require attention. In the second stage, you must perceive and recognize the information—processes that do require attention. Also in this stage, you consciously elaborate information using the short-term and working-memory processes described in the memory chapter. These processes allow you to think about new information in relation to knowledge that is already stored in your long-term memory. Once the information has been elaborated in this way, you must decide what to do with it. This third stage—decision making—demands attention, too. Your decision might be to store the information or to take some action. If the decision is to act, it is at this stage that you plan what to do. In the fourth and fifth stages, the action is carried out. Your action usually affects the environment, providing new information that is "fed back" to the system for processing in the ongoing circle of thought.

Mental Representations: The Ingredients of Thought

What are thoughts made of?

Just as measuring, stirring, and baking are only part of the story of cookie making, describing the processes of thinking tells only part of the story behind the circle of thought. Psychologists usually describe the ingredients of thought as information. But that is like saying that you make cookies with "stuff." What specific forms can information take in our minds? Cognitive psychologists have found that information can be mentally represented in many ways, including as concepts, propositions, schemas, scripts, mental models, images, and cognitive maps. Let's explore these ingredients of thought and how people manipulate them as they think.

Concepts

When you think about anything—dogs, happiness, sex, movies, pizza—you are manipulating a basic ingredient of thought called concepts. **Concepts** are categories of objects, events, or ideas with common properties. Some concepts, such as "round" and "red," are visual and concrete. Concepts such as "truth" and "justice" are more abstract and harder to define. To have a concept is to recognize the properties, or features, that tend to be shared by members of a category. For example, the concept of "bird" includes such properties as having feathers, laying eggs, and being able to fly. The concept of "scissors" includes such properties as having two blades, a connecting hinge, and a pair of finger holes. Concepts allow you to relate each object or event you encounter to a category that you already know. Using concepts, you can say, "No, that is not a dog," or "Yes, that is a car." Concepts also make it possible for you to think logically. If you have the concepts "whale" and "bird," you can decide whether a whale is a bird without having either creature in the room with you.

Types of Concepts   Some concepts—called *formal concepts*—clearly define objects or events by a set of rules and properties, so that every member of the concept has all of the concept's defining properties and nonmembers do not. For instance, the concept "square" can be defined as "a shape with four equal sides and four right-angle corners." Any object that does not have all of these features is simply not a square. Formal concepts are often used to study concept learning in the laboratory because the members of these concepts can be neatly defined (Trabasso & Bower, 1968).

Now stop reading for a moment and make a list of the features that define the concepts "home" or "game." You might have said that "home" is the place where you live and that a "game" is a competition between players. However, some people define "home" as the place where they were born, and almost everyone thinks of solitaire as a card game even though it involves only one player. These are just two examples of *natural concepts*. Unlike formal concepts, natural concepts don't have a fixed set of defining features. Instead, natural concepts have a set of typical or *characteristic* features, and members don't need to have all of them. For example, the ability to fly is a characteristic feature of the natural concept "bird," but an ostrich is still a bird even though it can't fly. It is a bird because it has enough other characteristic features of "bird" (such as feathers and wings). Having just one bird property is not enough, though. A snake lays eggs and a bat can fly, but neither animal is a bird. It is usually a combination of properties that defines a concept. In most situations outside the laboratory, people are thinking about natural rather than formal concepts. These natural concepts include object categories, such as "bird" or "house." They also include abstract idea categories, such as "honesty" or "justice," and goal-related categories, such as "things to pack for my vacation" (Barsalou, 1993).

The boundaries of a natural concept are fuzzy, so some members are better examples of it than others. A robin, a chicken, an ostrich, and a penguin are all birds. But a robin is a better example of the bird concept than the others, because it is closer to what most people have learned to think of as a typical bird. A member of a natural concept that possesses all or most of its characteristic features is called a **prototype.** The robin is a *prototypical* bird. The more prototypical of a concept something is, the more quickly you can decide whether it is an example of the concept. This is the reason people can answer just a little more quickly when asked "Is a robin a bird?" than when asked "Is a penguin a bird?" Because prototypes are fundamental to the way we perceive and understand the world, understanding the nature of people's prototypes can have great practical value. For example, smokers—particularly young male smokers—are at greater risk for long-term cigarette use if their prototype for "smoker" includes traits such as "smart and independent" (Piko, Bak, & Gibbons, 2007). This is why health psychologists' anti-smoking programs often include efforts to create in smokers' minds a more negative prototype of the "typical smoker."

Propositions

We often combine concepts in units known as propositions. A **proposition** is a mental representation that expresses a relationship between concepts. Propositions can be true or false. Suppose you hear someone say that your friend Heather broke up with her boyfriend Jason. Your mental representation of this event will include a proposition that links your concepts of "Heather" and "Jason" in a particular way. This proposition could be diagrammed (using unscientific terms) as follows: Heather → dumped → Jason.

The arrows indicate that this statement is a proposition rather than a sentence. Propositions can be expressed as sentences, but they are actually general ideas that can be conveyed in any number of specific ways. In this case, the words "Jason was dumped

LEARNby DOING

prototype A member of a natural concept that possesses all or most of its characteristic features.

proposition A mental representation that expresses a relationship between concepts.

by Heather" and "Heather is not willing to date Jason anymore" would all express the same proposition. If you later discovered that it was Jason who caused the breakup, the diagram of your proposition about the event would change to reflect this new information, shown here as reversed arrows: Heather ← dumped ← Jason.

Schemas, Scripts, and Mental Models

Sets of propositions are often so closely associated that they form more complex mental representations called *schemas*. As mentioned in the chapters on sensation and perception, memory, and human development, **schemas** are generalizations that we develop about categories of objects, places, events, and people. Our schemas help us understand the world. If you borrow a friend's car, your "car" schema will give you a good idea of where the accelerator and brake are, and how to raise and lower the windows. Schemas also generate expectations about objects, places, events, and people—telling us that stereo systems have speakers, that picnics occur in the summer, that rock concerts are loud, and so on.

You Can't Judge a Book by Its Cover
Does this person look like a millionaire to you? Our schemas tell us what to expect about objects, places, events, and people, but those expectations can sometimes be wrong. This was dramatically illustrated in October 1999 when Gordon Elwood died. The Medford, Oregon, man, who dressed in rags and collected cans, left over $9 million to charity (McMahon, 2000).

Scripts   Schemas about familiar activities, such as going to a restaurant, are known as **scripts** (Anderson, 2000). Your "restaurant" script represents the sequence of events you can expect when you go out to eat (See Figure 7.3). That script tells you what to do when you are in a restaurant and helps you understand stories involving restaurants (Whitney, 2001). Scripts also shape your interpretation of events. For example, on your first day of high school, you no doubt assumed that the person standing at the front of the class was a teacher, not a security guard or a janitor.

© Rolf Bruderer/Masterfile   © iStockphoto   © MonkeyBusiness Images/ Shutterstock   © Phil Date/Shutterstock

FIGURE 7.3

Following a Script: Eating at a Restaurant

Schemas about what happens in restaurants and how to behave in them take the form of scripts, represented here in four "scenes." Scripts guide our actions in all sorts of familiar situations and also help us understand descriptions of events occurring in those situations (e.g., "Our service was really slow").

Source: Whitney (2001).

FIGURE 7.4
Applying a Mental Model

Try to imagine the path that the ball will follow when it leaves the curved tube. In one study, most people drew the incorrect (curved) path indicated by the dotted line, rather than the correct (straight) path indicated by the dashed line (McCloskey, 1983). Their error was based on the construction of a faulty mental model of the behavior of physical objects.

LEARN by DOING

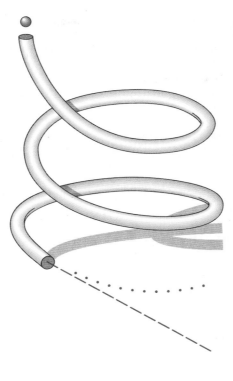

If our scripts are violated, however, it is easy to misinterpret events. In one case, a heart attack victim in London lay for nine hours in the hallway of an apartment building after an ambulance crew smelled alcohol on his breath and assumed he was "sleeping it off." The crew's script for what happens in the poorer sections of big cities told them that someone slumped in a hallway is drunk, not sick. Because script-violating events are unexpected, our reactions to them tend to be slower and less effective than our reactions to expected events. Your "grocery shopping" script, for example, probably includes pushing a cart, putting items in it, going to the checkout stand, paying, and leaving. But suppose you are at the back of the store when a robber near the entrance fires a gun and shouts at the manager to open the safe. People sometimes ignore these script-violating events, interpreting gunshots as a car backfiring and shouted orders as "someone fooling around" (Raisig et al., 2010). Others simply freeze, unsure of what to do or not realizing that they could call the police on their cell phones.

FIGURE 7.5
Manipulating Images

Are these pairs of objects the same or different? To decide, you will have to rotate one member of each pair. Manipulating mental images, like manipulating actual objects, takes time, so the speed of your decision will depend on how far you have to mentally rotate one object to line it up with the other for comparison. (The top pair matches; the bottom pair does not.)

LEARN by DOING

Source: From Shepard, R. N., & Metzler, J., "Mental rotation of three-dimensional objects." *Science* vol 171 (pp. 701–703). Copyright © 1971 American Association for the Advancement of Science. Reprinted with permission.

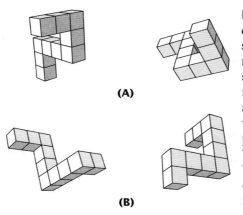

(A)

(B)

Mental Models The relationships among concepts can be organized not only as schemas and scripts but also as **mental models** (Johnson-Laird, 1983). For example, suppose someone tells you, "My living room has blue walls, a white ceiling, and an oval window across from the door." You will mentally represent this information as propositions about how the concepts "wall," "blue," "ceiling," "white," "door," "oval," and "window" are related. However, you will also combine these propositions to create in your mind a three-dimensional model of the room. As more information about the world becomes available, either from existing memories or from new information we receive, our mental models become more complete.

Accurate mental models are excellent guides for thinking about, and interacting with, many of the things we encounter every day (Johnson-Laird, 2010). If our mental models are incorrect, however, we are likely to make mistakes (e.g., Michael, Garry, & Kirsch, 2012; see Figure 7.4). For example, college students conduct more effective online searches while shopping or consulting academic databases if their mental models of search engines recognize that those search engines require precise search terms. Students who think that human operators read and interpret the meaning of the search terms they enter are less likely to use precise terms and thus less likely to get useful results (Holman, 2011; Roth et al., 2010; Uther, 2008; Zang, 2008). Similarly, people who hold an incorrect mental model of how physical illness is cured might stop taking their antibiotic medication when their symptoms begin to disappear, well before the bacteria causing those symptoms have been eliminated (Medin, Ross, & Markman, 2001). Others overdose on medication because according to their faulty mental model, "if taking three pills a day is good, taking six would be even better."

schemas Generalizations about categories of objects, places, events, and people.

scripts Mental representations of familiar sequences of activity.

Images and Cognitive Maps

Think about how your best friend would look in a clown suit. The mental picture you just got illustrates that thinking often involves the manipulation of **images**—mental representations of visual information. We can manipulate these images in a way that is similar to manipulating the objects themselves (Reed, 2000; Trickett, Trafton, & Schunn, 2009; see Figure 7.5). Our ability to think using images extends beyond the

Ingredients of Thought		IN REVIEW
Ingredient	**Description**	**Examples**
Concepts	Categories of objects, events, or ideas with common properties; basic building blocks of thought	"Square" (a formal concept); "game" (a natural concept)
Propositions	Mental representations that express relationships between concepts; can be true or false	Assertions such as "The cow jumped over the moon."
Schemas	Sets of propositions that create generalizations and expectations about categories of objects, places, events, and people	A schema might suggest that all grandmothers are elderly, have gray hair, and bake a lot of cookies.
Scripts	Schemas about familiar activities and situations that guide behavior in those situations	You pay before eating in fast-food restaurants and after eating in fancier restaurants.
Mental models	Representations of how concepts relate to each other in the real world; can be correct or incorrect	Mistakenly assuming that airflow around an open car will send thrown objects upward, a driver tosses a lighted cigarette butt overhead, causing it to land in the back seat.
Images	Mental representations of visual information	Hearing a description of your blind date creates a mental picture of him or her.
Cognitive maps	Mental representations of familiar parts of the world	You can get to class by an alternate route even if your usual route is blocked by construction.

IN REVIEW QUESTIONS

1. Thinking is the manipulation of ___.
2. Arguments over what is "fair" occur because "fairness" is a ___ concept.
3. Your ___ of "hotel room" would lead you to expect yours to include a bathroom.

mental models Sets of propositions that represent people's understanding of how things look and work.

images Mental representations of visual information.

cognitive map A mental model that represents familiar parts of the environment.

reasoning The process by which people generate and evaluate arguments and reach conclusions about them.

manipulation of stimuli such as those in Figure 7.5. We also create mental images that serve as mental models of descriptions we hear or read (Mazoyer et al., 2002). For example, you probably created an image a minute ago when you read about that blue-walled room.

The same thing happens when someone gives you directions to a new pizza place in town. In this case, you scan your **cognitive map**—a mental model of familiar parts of your world—to find the location. In doing so, you use a mental process similar to the visual process of scanning a Google map (Anderson, 2000; Hölscher, Tenbrink, & Wiener, 2011; Taylor & Tversky, 1992). Manipulating images on a different cognitive map would help you if a power failure left your home pitch dark. Even though you couldn't see a thing, you could still find a flashlight or a candle because your cognitive map would show the floor plan, furniture placement, door locations, and other physical features of your home. You would not have this mental map in a hotel room or an unfamiliar house; there, you would have to walk slowly, arms outstretched, to avoid wrong turns and painful collisions. In the chapter on learning we describe how experience shapes cognitive maps that help animals navigate mazes and people navigate shopping malls. ("In Review: Ingredients of Thought" summarizes the ways we mentally represent information.)

Pitfalls in Logical Reasoning
"Elderly people cannot be Antarctic explorers; this is an elderly man; therefore, he cannot be an Antarctic explorer." The logic is correct, but because the first statement is wrong, so is the conclusion. In 1929, Norman Vaughan reached the South Pole as part of Richard Byrd's team of Antarctic explorers. Here he is in 1994, at the age of 88, after climbing Antarctica's Mount Vaughan, a mountain named for him.

Thinking Strategies

Do people always think logically?

We have seen that our thinking capacity is based largely on our ability to manipulate mental representations—the ingredients of thought—much as a baker manipulates the ingredients of cookies. The baker's food-processing system combines and transforms these ingredients into a delicious treat. Our information-processing system combines, transforms, and elaborates mental representations in ways that allow us to engage in reasoning, problem solving, and decision making. Let's begin our discussion of these thinking strategies by considering **reasoning:** the process through which we generate and evaluate arguments, as well as reach conclusions about them.

Formal Reasoning

Astronomers tell us that the temperature at the core of the sun is about 27 million degrees Fahrenheit. How do they know this? They can't put a temperature probe inside the sun, so their estimate is based on *inferences* from other things that they know about the sun and about physical objects in general. For example, telescopic observations allowed astronomers to calculate the energy coming from one small part of the sun. They then used what geometry told them about the surface area of spheres to estimate the sun's total energy output. Further calculations told them how hot a body would have to be to generate that much energy.

In other words, astronomers' estimates of the sun's core temperature are based on **formal reasoning** (also called *logical reasoning*)—the process of following a set of rigorous steps for reaching valid, or correct, conclusions. Some of these steps included applying specific mathematical formulas to existing data in order to generate new data. Such formulas are examples of **algorithms**—systematic methods that always reach a correct solution to a problem if a correct solution exists.

The astronomers also followed the rules of **logic,** a set of statements that provide a formula for drawing valid conclusions about the world. For example, each step in the astronomers' thinking took the form of if-then propositions: if we know how much energy comes from one part of the sun's surface and if we know how big the whole surface is, then we can calculate the total energy output. You use the same logical reasoning processes when you conclude, for example, that if your friend José is two years older than you are, then his twin brother, Juan, will be two years older, too. This kind of reasoning is called *deductive reasoning,* because it takes a general rule (e.g., twins are the same age) and applies it to deduce conclusions about specific cases (e.g., José and Juan).

Most of us try to use logical or deductive reasoning to reach valid conclusions and avoid invalid ones. However, even when our logic is perfect, we can make mistakes if we base our reasoning on false assumptions. Likewise, correct assumptions combined with faulty logic can lead to errors. Do you think the following example leads to a valid conclusion?

Assumption 1:	*All women want to be mothers.*
Assumption 2:	*Jill is a woman.*
Conclusion:	*Jill wants to be a mother.*

If you said that the first assumption is not necessarily correct, you're right. Now consider this example:

Assumption 1:	*All gun owners are people.*
Assumption 2:	*All criminals are people.*
Conclusion:	*All gun owners are criminals.*

Here, the assumptions are correct but the logic is faulty. According to the rules of logic, if "all As are B" and "all Cs are B," it does not follow that "all As are C." So it is true that all gun owners are people and that all criminals are people, but it does not follow that all gun owners are criminals.

Psychologists have discovered that both kinds of pitfalls we just described can lead people to make errors in logical reasoning. This finding is one reason that misleading advertisements or speeches can still attract sales and votes (Cialdini, 2007).

formal reasoning A set of rigorous procedures for reaching valid conclusions.

algorithms Systematic procedures that cannot fail to produce a correct solution to a problem.

logic A system of formulas for drawing valid conclusions.

informal reasoning The process of evaluating a conclusion based on the evidence available to support it.

Formal reasoning follows the rules of logic, but there are no foolproof rules for informal reasoning, as this fool demonstrates.

Informal Reasoning

Using the rules of formal logic to deduce answers about specific cases is an important kind of reasoning, but it is not the only kind. A second kind, **informal reasoning,** comes into play when we are trying to assess the *believability* of a conclusion based on the evidence available to support it. Informal reasoning is also known as *inductive reasoning,* because its goal is to induce a general conclusion to appear on the basis of specific facts or examples. Psychologists use informal reasoning when they design experiments and other research methods whose results will provide evidence for (or against) their theories. Judges and jurors use informal reasoning when weighing evidence for the guilt or innocence of a defendant (Baker, ten Brinke, & Porter, 2012; Bornstein & Greene, 2011; Kassin, Bogart, & Kerner, 2012; Vidmar, 2011). And air crash investigators use it in their efforts to discover and eliminate the causes of aviation accidents.

Formal reasoning is guided by algorithms, or formulas, but there are no foolproof methods for informal reasoning. For instance, how many white swans would you have to see before concluding that all swans are white? Fifty? A hundred? A million? Formal logic would require that you observe every swan in existence. A more practical approach is to base your conclusion on the number of observations that some mental rule of thumb leads you to believe is enough. In other words, you would take a mental shortcut to reach a conclusion that is probably, but not necessarily, correct (there are, in fact, black swans). Such mental shortcuts are called **heuristics** (pronounced "hyoor-IST-ix").

Heuristics can be helpful, but they can also bias our thinking and cause errors. Suppose your rule of thumb is to vote for all the candidates in a particular political party instead of researching the views of each individual. You might end up helping to elect someone with whom you strongly disagree on some issues. The origins and development of heuristics, and the extent to which they are responsible for important errors in judgment and decision making is still being studied and debated by cognitive psychologists (e.g., Deng & Sloutsky, 2012; Dube, Rotello, & Heit, 2010; Hilbert, 2012; Keil, Lockhart, & Schlegel, 2010; Keysar, Hayakawa, & An, 2012; Strough, Karns, & Schlosnagle, 2011; Weaver, Vandello, & Bosson, 2012). Nevertheless, Amos Tversky and Daniel Kahneman (1974; 1993) have described three potentially problematic heuristics that often affect people's judgments. These are the *anchoring heuristic* (also known as *anchoring bias*), the *representativeness heuristic,* and the *availability heuristic.*

The Anchoring Bias   People use the **anchoring bias** (or **anchoring heuristic**) when they estimate the probability of some event by adjusting their existing estimate rather than starting from scratch on the basis of new information (Furnham & Boo, 2011; Rottenstreich & Tversky, 1997). This strategy sounds reasonable, but their existing estimate biases their final judgment. So even if new information suggests that their first estimate is way off, people may not adjust that estimate enough. It is as if they have dropped a "mental anchor" that keeps them from drifting too far from their original judgment. Suppose you think that the chance of being mugged in Los Angeles is 90 percent, but then you see evidence that the figure is closer to 1 percent. You might reduce your estimate, but only to 80 percent, so your new estimate is still quite inaccurate. The anchoring heuristic presents a challenge for defense attorneys in U.S. criminal courts because the prosecution presents its evidence first. Once this evidence has created the impression that a defendant is guilty, some jurors mentally anchor to that impression

heuristics   Mental shortcuts or rules of thumb.

anchoring bias (anchoring heuristic)   A shortcut in the thought process that involves adding new information to existing information to reach a judgment.

representativeness heuristic   A mental shortcut that involves judging whether something belongs in a given class on the basis of its similarity to other members of that class.

and may not be swayed much by defense evidence to the contrary (Greene & Loftus, 1998; Hogarth & Einhorn, 1992). In a similar way, first impressions of people are not easily shifted by later evidence (see the chapter on social psychology).

The Representativeness Heuristic   People use the **representativeness heuristic** when they conclude that something belongs in a certain class based on how similar it is to other items in that class. For example, consider this personality sketch:

Tom W. is of high intelligence although lacking in true creativity. He has a need for order and clarity and for neat and tidy systems in which every detail finds its appropriate place. His writing is rather dull and mechanical, occasionally enlivened by somewhat corny puns and by flashes of imagination of the sci-fi type. He has a strong drive for competence. He seems to have little feeling and little sympathy for other people and does not enjoy interacting with others. Self-centered, he nonetheless has a deep moral sense.

Do you think Tom is majoring in computer science or psychology? Research by Kahneman and Tversky (1973; Tversky & Kahneman, 1974) showed that most people would choose *computer science.* But this answer would probably be wrong. True, the description given is more similar to the prototypical computer science major than to the prototypical psychology major. However, there are many more psychology majors than computer science majors in the world. So there are probably more psychology majors than computer science majors who match this description. In fact, almost any personality sketch is more likely to describe a psychology major than a computer science major.

The representativeness heuristic affects many real-life judgments and decisions. For example, when jurors hear an expert witness presenting technical or scientific evidence, they are supposed to consider only the validity of the evidence itself, not the characteristics of the person presenting it. However, they're more likely to be persuaded by the evidence if the witness looks and acts in ways that are representative of the "expert" category (Bornstein & Greene, 2011; McAuliff, Kovera, & Nuñez, 2008). (See the chapter on social psychology for more on the role of communicator characteristics in persuasion.)

The Availability Heuristic   People use the **availability heuristic** when they judge the likelihood of an event or the correctness of a hypothesis by how easy it is to think of that event or hypothesis (Tversky & Kahneman, 1974). In other words, they tend to choose the hypothesis or predict the event that is most mentally "available," much as they might select the box of cereal that happens to be at the front of the supermarket shelf. Although the availability heuristic tends to work well, it too can lead to biased judgments—especially when the mental availability of events doesn't match their actual frequency (Morewedge, Gilbert, & Wilson, 2005). For example, news reports about shark attacks and urban shootings lead many people to overestimate how often these memorable but relatively rare events actually occur (Courtenay, Smith, & Gladstone, 2012; Ungemach, Chater, & Stewart, 2009). As a result, people may suffer undue anxiety over swimming in the ocean or being in certain cities (Bellaby, 2003). Similarly, many students stick with their first responses to multiple-choice test questions because it is especially easy to recall those galling occasions on which they changed a right answer to a wrong one. Research shows, though, that an answer that is changed in light of further reflection is more likely to be correct than incorrect (Kruger, Wirtz, & Miller, 2005; Skinner, 2009).

The three heuristics we have presented represent only a few of the many mental shortcuts that people use more or less automatically in making judgments in daily life (Todd & Gigerenzer, 2007), and they describe only some of the biases and limitations that operate in human reasoning. Other biases and limitations are described in the following sections, as we consider two important goals of thinking: problem solving and decision making.

Problem Solving

What's the best way to solve a problem?

Suppose that you're lost, you don't have a cell phone or a GPS, and there's nobody around to ask for directions. You have a *problem.* The circle of thought suggests that the most

availability heuristic A mental shortcut through which judgments are based on information that is most easily brought to mind.

Simply knowing about problem-solving strategies, such as decomposition, is not enough. As described in the chapter on motivation and emotion, people must believe that the effort required is worth the rewards it can bring.

Calvin and Hobbes
by Bill Watterson

efficient approach to solving it would be to first diagnose the problem in the elaboration stage, then formulate a plan for solving it, then execute the plan, and finally evaluate the results to determine whether the problem remains (Bransford & Stein, 1993). But people's problem-solving efforts are not always so systematic. This is one reason why medical tests are sometimes given unnecessarily, diseases are sometimes misdiagnosed, and auto parts are sometimes replaced when there is nothing wrong with them (Mamede et al., 2010).

Strategies for Problem Solving

When you're trying to get from one place to another, the best path may not necessarily be a straight line. In fact, obstacles may require going in the opposite direction to get around them. So it is with problem solving. Sometimes the best strategy doesn't involve mental steps aimed straight at your goal. Psychologists have identified a variety of strategies that people use when solving a problem (Marewski & Schooler, 2011). For example, when a problem is especially difficult, it can sometimes be helpful to allow it to "incubate" by setting it aside for a while. A solution that once seemed out of reach may suddenly appear after you have been thinking about other things. The benefits of *incubation* probably arise from forgetting incorrect ideas that may have been blocking the path to a correct and possibly creative solution (Kohn & Smith, 2009; McCaffrey, 2012; Storm, 2011; Storm & Angello, 2010). Other effective problem-solving strategies are more direct.

One of these strategies is called *means-end analysis.* It involves continuously asking where you are in relation to your final goal and then deciding on the means by which you can get one step closer to that goal (Newell & Simon, 1972). In other words, rather than trying to solve the problem all at once, you identify a subgoal that will take you toward a solution (this process is also referred to as *decomposition*). After reaching that subgoal, you identify another one that will get you even closer to the solution, and you continue this step-by-step process until the problem is solved. Some students apply this approach to the problem of writing a major term paper. The task might seem overwhelming at first, but their first subgoal is simply to write an outline of what they think the paper should cover. When the outline is complete, they decide whether a paper based on it will satisfy the assignment. If it will, the next subgoal might be to search the library and the Internet for information about each section. If they decide that this information is adequate, the next subgoal would be to write a rough draft of the introduction, and so on.

A second strategy in problem solving is to *work backward.* Many problems are like a tree. The trunk is the information you are given; the solution is a twig on one of the branches. If you work forward by taking the "givens" of the problem and trying to find the solution, it's easy to branch off in the wrong direction. Sometimes the more efficient approach is to start at the twig end and work backward (Galotti, 1999). Consider the problem of planning a climb to the summit of Mount Everest. The best strategy is to figure out, first, what equipment and supplies are needed at the highest camp on the night before the attempt to reach the summit, then how many people are needed to stock that camp the day before, then how many people are needed to supply those who must stock the camp, and so on until a plan for the

Working Backward to Forge Ahead
Whether you are organizing a family vacation or preparing to sail alone around the world, as 16-year-old Laura Dekker did, working backward from the final goal through all the steps necessary to reach that goal is a helpful approach to solving complex problems.

entire expedition is established. People often overlook the working-backward strategy because it runs counter to the way they have learned to think. It is hard to imagine that the first step in solving a problem could be to assume that you have already solved it. It is partly because of failure to apply this strategy that climbers sometimes die on Everest (Krakauer, 1997).

A third problem-solving strategy is trying to find *analogies,* or similarities, between today's problem and others you have encountered before. A supervisor may discover that a seemingly hopeless problem between co-workers can be resolved by the same compromise that worked during a recent family squabble. Of course, to take advantage of analogies, you must first recognize the similarities between current and previous problems. Then you will be in a position to recall the solution that worked before. Unfortunately, most people are surprisingly poor at seeing the similarities between new and old problems (Anderson, 2000). They tend to concentrate on the surface features that make problems appear different.

FOCUS ON RESEARCH

Problem-Solving Strategies in the Real World

How do people use the problem-solving strategies we have described to solve real-world problems? To explore this question, researchers have reconstructed problem-solving strategies associated with major inventions and scientific discoveries (Klahr & Simon, 1999; Weber, 1992).

What was the researcher's question?

On December 17, 1903, Wilbur and Orville Wright successfully flew the first heavier-than-air flying machine. Gary Bradshaw (1993a, 1993b) was interested in identifying the problem-solving strategies that led to this momentous event. He found that 49 individuals or teams had worked on the problem of heavier-than-air flight, but only the Wright brothers were successful. In fact, it took them only four years to develop the airplane, whereas others worked for decades without success. Bradshaw asked himself how the Wright brothers solved the problem of creating a heavier-than-air flying machine when so many others had failed?

How did the researcher answer the question?

Bradshaw compared the written records left by all the individuals and teams who had worked on an airplane design. Using this *comparative case study* method, he was able to see patterns in the ways they approached the flying machine problem.

What did the researcher find?

Bradshaw found several factors that might have contributed to the Wright brothers' success. First, as bachelors, they had a lot of spare time to work on their designs. Second, they owned a bicycle shop, so they were familiar with lightweight but sturdy structures. Third, they were brothers who had a good working relationship. And finally, as mechanics, they were good with their hands. Were any of these features directly responsible for their successful invention of the airplane?

Perhaps, but Bradshaw's use of the comparative case study method revealed that everyone else working on the problem of flight shared at least one of these features with the Wright brothers. For instance, an engineer named Octave Chanute was good with his hands and familiar with lightweight, sturdy structures. And two other pairs of brothers had worked together to try to invent a flying machine.

However, Bradshaw found one feature that was unique to the Wright brothers' approach. Of all the inventors working on the problem, only the Wrights spent considerable time and energy testing aircraft components before field-testing complete machines. This feature was important because even the best designs of the day flew for only a few seconds—far too briefly to reveal what was working and what was not. As a result, inventors had to guess about what to fix and often ended up with an "improved" model that was worse than the previous one.

What do the results mean?

Bradshaw's comparative case study method suggested that the problem-solving strategy of decomposition was the basis for the Wright brothers' success. By testing components, they were able to collect the information they needed to develop an efficient propeller, improve the shape of the wings for maximum lift, and refine other vital components of their aircraft.

What do we still need to know?

Decomposition is a strategy often seen in the laboratory, and as demonstrated by the case of the Wright brothers, it is a potentially important aspect of major inventions and discoveries beyond the laboratory. But is decomposition, or means-end analysis, used in other real-world settings as well? To find out, researchers will need to conduct additional studies of the mental strategies people use as they attempt to solve problems ranging from how to install a new computer to how to efficiently search the Internet.   ● ● ● ●

Obstacles to Problem Solving

The failure of the Wright brothers' competitors to use decomposition is just one example of the obstacles that problem solvers encounter every day. Difficulties frequently occur at the start, during the diagnosis stage, when a person forms and then tests hypotheses about a problem.

As a case in point, consider this true story: In September 1998, John Gatiss was in the kitchen of his rented house in Cheltenham, England, when he heard a faint "meowing" sound. Worried that a kitten had become trapped somewhere, he called for the fire brigade to rescue the animal. The sound seemed to be coming from the electric stove, so the rescuers dismantled it, disconnecting the power cord in the process. The sound stopped, but everyone assumed that wherever the kitten was, it was now too frightened to meow. The search was reluctantly abandoned and the stove was reconnected. Four days later, however, the meowing began anew. This time, Gatiss and his landlord called the Royal Society for the Prevention of Cruelty to Animals (RSPCA), whose inspectors heard the kitten in distress and asked the fire brigade to come back. They spent the next three days searching for the cat. First, they dismantled parts of the kitchen walls and ripped up the floorboards. Next, they called in plumbing and drainage specialists, who used cables tipped with fiber-optic cameras to search remote cavities where a kitten might hide. Rescuers then brought in a disaster search team, which tried to find the kitten with acoustic and ultrasonic equipment normally used to locate victims trapped under earthquake debris. Not a sound was heard. Increasingly concerned about how much longer the kitten could survive, the fire brigade tried to coax it from hiding with the finest-quality fish, but to no avail. Suddenly, there was a burst of "purring" that, to everyone's surprise (and the landlord's dismay), was traced by the ultrasonic equipment to the clock in the electric stove! Later, the landlord commented that everyone assumed Gatiss's original hypothesis was correct—that the "meowing" came from a cat trapped in the kitchen. "I just let them carry on. If there is an animal in there, you have to do what it takes. The funniest thing was that it seemed to reply when we called out to it" (*London Daily Telegraph*, 1998).

How could fifteen fire-rescue workers, three RSPCA inspectors, four drainage workers, and two acoustics experts waste eight days and cause thousands of dollars in damage to a house in pursuit of a nonexistent kitten? The answer lies in the fact that they, like the rest of us, were prone to the four main obstacles to efficient problem solving described in the following sections.

Multiple Hypotheses   Often we begin to solve a problem with only a hazy notion of which hypotheses to test. Suppose you heard a strange sound in your kitchen. It could be caused by several different things, but which hypotheses should you test, and in what order?

People have a difficult time working with more than two or three hypotheses at a time (Mehle, 1982). The limited capacity of short-term memory may be part of the reason (Halford et al., 2005). As discussed in the memory chapter, a person can hold only about seven chunks of information in short-term memory. Because a single hypothesis, let alone two or three, might include more than seven chunks, it may be difficult or impossible to keep them all in mind at once. Further, the availability and representativeness heuristics may lead people to choose the hypothesis that comes most easily to mind and seems most likely to fit the circumstances (Tversky & Kahneman, 1974). That hypothesis may be wrong, though, meaning that the correct hypothesis is never considered (Bilalić, McLeod, & Gobet, 2010). Mr. Gatiss diagnosed what he heard as distressed meowing because it sounded more like a kitten than a clock and because it was easier to imagine an animal trapped behind the stove than a suddenly faulty clock inside it.

Mental Sets   Sometimes people are so blinded by one hypothesis or strategy that they stick with it even when better alternatives should be obvious. This is a clear case of the anchoring heuristic at work. Once Gatiss reported hearing a "trapped kitten," his description created an assumption that everyone else accepted and no one challenged. Figure 7.6 shows a problem-solving situation in which such errors often appear. The first problem in the figure is to come up with 21 quarts of liquid by using 3 jars that have capacities of 8, 35, and 3 quarts, respectively. Before you read any further, try to solve this problem and all the others listed in Figure 7.6.

How did you do? You probably figured out that the solution to the first problem is to fill Jar B to its capacity of 35 quarts, and then use its contents to fill Jar A to its capacity of 8 quarts, leaving 27 quarts in Jar B. Finally, you pour from Jar B to fill Jar C twice, leaving 21 quarts in Jar B [27 − (2 × 3) = 21]. You probably found that a similar solution worked for each problem. In fact, by the time you reached Problem 7, you might have developed a **mental set,** a tendency for old patterns of problem solving to persist (Luchins, 1942; Sweller & Gee, 1978). If so, your mental set probably caused you to use the same old formula (B − A − 2C) even though a simpler one (A + C) would have worked just as well. Figures 7.7 and 7.9 show another way in which mental sets can restrict our perception of the possible solutions to a problem.

Another restriction on problem solving may come from experience with objects. Once people become familiar with using an object for one purpose, they may be blinded to other ways of using it. Long experience may produce **functional fixedness,** a tendency to use familiar objects in familiar rather than creative ways (German & Barrett, 2005). Figure 7.8 provides an example. An incubation strategy often helps to break mental sets.

Ignoring Negative Evidence   On September 26, 1983, Lt. Col. Stanislav Petrov was in command of a secret facility that analyzed information from Russian early-warning satellites. Suddenly alarms went off as computers found evidence that five U.S. missiles were being launched toward Russia. Tension between the two countries was high at the time, so based on the availability heuristic, Petrov hypothesized that a nuclear attack was under way. He was about to alert his superiors to launch a counterattack on the United States when it occurred to him that if this were a real nuclear attack, it would involve many more than five missiles. Fortunately for everyone, he realized that the "attack" was a false alarm (Hoffman, 1999). As this near-disaster shows, the *absence* of symptoms or events can sometimes provide important evidence for or against a hypothesis. Compared with evidence that is present, however, symptoms or events that do not occur are less likely to be noticed (Hunt & Rouse, 1981). People have a difficult time using the absence of evidence to help eliminate hypotheses from consideration (Hyman, 2002). In the "trapped kitten" case, when the "meowing" stopped for several days after the stove was unplugged and reconnected, rescuers assumed that the animal was frightened into silence. They ignored the possibility that their hypothesis was incorrect in the first place.

Confirmation Bias   Anyone who has had a series of medical tests knows that diagnosis is not a one-shot affair. Instead, physicians choose their first hypothesis on the basis of observed symptoms—perhaps the most dramatic or obvious ones—and then order tests or evaluate additional symptoms to confirm or eliminate that hypothesis (Kwan et al., 2012; Trillin, 2001). This process can be distorted by a **confirmation bias:** Humans have a strong bias to confirm rather than reject the hypothesis they have chosen, even in the face of strong evidence against the hypothesis (Aronson, Wilson, & Akert, 2005; Groopman, 2007; Mendel et al., 2011). In other words, people are quite willing to perceive and accept data that support their hypothesis, but they tend to ignore information that is inconsistent with it (Groopman, 2000). Confirmation bias may be seen as a form of the anchoring heuristic. Once you've "anchored" to your first hypothesis, you may be

Quantity	Jar A	Jar B	Jar C
1. 21 quarts	8	35	3
2. 10 quarts	6	18	1
3. 19 quarts	5	32	4
4. 21 quarts	20	57	8
5. 18 quarts	8	40	7
6. 6 quarts	7	17	2
7. 15 quarts	12	33	3

FIGURE 7.6
The Jar Problem
The task here is to come up with the number of quarts of water shown in the first column by using jars with the capacities shown in the next three columns. Each line represents a different problem and you have an unlimited supply of water for each one. Try to solve all seven problems without looking at the answers in the text.

LEARN by DOING

FIGURE 7.7
The Nine-Dot Problem
Draw four straight lines that run through all nine dots on the page without lifting your pen or pencil from the paper. Figure 7.9 shows how to go beyond mental sets to solve this problem.

LEARN by DOING

mental set   The tendency for old patterns of problem solving to persist.

functional fixedness   The tendency to think about familiar objects in familiar ways.

confirmation bias   The tendency to pay more attention to evidence in support of one's hypothesis about a problem than to evidence that refutes that hypothesis.

FIGURE 7.8

An Example of Functional Fixedness

Before reading further, look at this image and ask yourself how you would fasten together two strings that are hanging from the ceiling but are too far apart for you to grasp at the same time. Several tools are available, yet most people don't think of attaching, say, a hammer to one string and swinging it like a pendulum until it can be reached while holding the other string. This solution is not obvious because we tend to fixate on the hammer's function as a tool rather than as a weight. People are more likely to solve this problem if the tools are scattered around the room. If the hammer is in a toolbox, its function as a tool is emphasized, and functional fixedness becomes nearly impossible to break.

LEARNby**DOING**

© Bill Altman

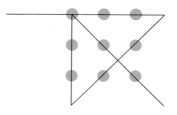

FIGURE 7.9

A Creative Solution to the Nine-Dot Problem

Many people find problems like this difficult because mental sets create artificial limits on the range of solutions. In this case, the mental set involves the tendency to draw within the frame of the dots. As shown here, however, there are other possibilities.

unwilling to abandon it. The would-be rescuers of John Gatiss's "trapped kitten" were so intent on their efforts to pinpoint its location that they never stopped to question its existence. Similarly, as described in the chapter on social psychology, we tend to look for and pay extra attention to information that is consistent with our first impressions of other people. This tendency can create positive or negative bias in, say, a teacher's views of children's cognitive abilities or an interviewer's judgments of a job candidate's skills (Jussim & Eccles, 1992; Reich, 2004). Confirmation bias can also serve to perpetuate and intensify differences of opinion. People tend to get their news from media outlets that support their own political views, and they pay more attention to areas of discord than to areas of agreement when talking to individuals who hold differing views (Wojcieszak & Price, 2010). With this phenomenon in mind, some psychologists have developed programs designed to reduce the confirmation bias that can impair communication on "hot button" issues (Lilienfeld, Ammirati, & Landfield, 2009).

Building Problem-Solving Skills   How do experts in any field avoid some of the obstacles that normally limit problem solving? What do they bring to a situation that a beginner does not? Knowledge based on experience is particularly important (Mayer, 1992). One way that they develop this knowledge is through deliberate practice, solving progressively more difficult problems and forming ever more accurate mental models over a long period of time (Campitelli & Gobet, 2008, 2011; Plant & Stanton, 2012). Using that knowledge, experts frequently proceed by looking for similarities or analogies between current and past problems. Their experience makes experts better than beginners at identifying the common principles that underlie seemingly different problems. Experts' superior ability to link information about a new problem to what they already know (Anderson, 1995) also allows them to organize information about a problem into manageable and memorable chunks, a process described in the chapter on memory (Jaušovec & Jaušovec, 2012). By chunking many elements of a problem into a smaller number of units, experts are better than beginners at visualizing problems clearly and efficiently (Reingold et al., 2001). Their experience also helps experts to stay calm while working on a problem, thus reducing the emotion-related disruptions in cognitive skills often seen in nonexperts under stress (Decety, Yang, & Cheng, 2010; Worthy et al., 2011).

It is no wonder, then, that experts are often better problem solvers than beginners, but their expertise also carries a danger: Extensive experience may create mental sets. Top-down, knowledge-driven processes can bias experts toward seeing what they expect or want to see and prevent them from seeing a problem in new ways (Groopman, 2007).

As in the case of the "trapped kitten," confirmation bias sometimes prevents experts from appreciating that a proposed solution is incorrect. Several studies have shown that although experts may be more confident in their solutions (Payne, Bettman, & Johnson, 1992), they are not always more accurate than others in such areas as medical diagnosis, accounting, pilot judgment, and predicting political events (Sibbald, Panisko, & Cavalcanti, 2011;

Solving Problems   IN REVIEW

Steps	Pitfalls	Remedies
Define the problem.	Inexperience: the tendency to see each problem as unique.	Gain experience and practice in seeing the similarity between present problems and previous problems.
Form hypotheses about solutions.	Availability heuristic: the tendency to recall the hypothesis or solution that is most available to memory.	Force yourself to write down and carefully consider many different hypotheses.
	Anchoring bias, or mental set: the tendency to anchor on the first solution or hypothesis and not adjust your beliefs in light of new evidence or failures of the current approach.	Break the mental set, stop, and try a fresh approach.
Test hypotheses.	The tendency to ignore negative evidence.	In evaluating a hypothesis, consider the things you should see (but don't) if the hypothesis is true.
	Confirmation bias: the tendency to seek only evidence that confirms your hypothesis.	Look for disconfirming evidence that, if found, would show your hypothesis to be false.

IN REVIEW QUESTIONS

1. People stranded without water could use their shoes to collect rain, but they may not do so because of an obstacle to problem solving called ___.
2. Because of the ___ heuristic, once sellers set a value on their house, they may refuse to take much less for it.
3. If you tackle a massive problem one small step at a time, you are using an approach called ___.

Stiegler et al., 2012; Tetlock, 2006; Wickens et al., 1992). In other words, there is a fine line between using past experience and being trapped by it. Experience alone does not ensure excellence at problem solving, and practice may not make perfect. (For a summary of problem solving and its pitfalls, see "In Review: Solving Problems.")

Problem Solving by Computer

Researchers have created artificial limbs, retinas, cochleas, and even hearts to help people with disabilities move, see, hear, and live more normally. They are also developing artificial brains, in the form of computer systems that not only see, hear, and manipulate objects but also reason and solve problems. These systems are the product of research in **artificial intelligence (AI),** a field that seeks to develop computers that imitate the processes of human perception and thought (Chappell et al., 2012; Fekete, 2010; O'Reilly, 2006; Zamani, 2010).

Symbolic Reasoning and Computer Logic   Chess-playing artificial intelligence systems have won games against the world's best chess masters. This result is not surprising, because chess is a clearly defined, logical game at which computers can perform effectively. However, it is precisely their reliance on logic and formulas that accounts for the shortcomings of today's artificial intelligence systems (Allen & Wallach, 2011; Dowe & Hernández-Orallo, 2012). For example, these systems are successful only in narrowly defined fields, not in general problem solving. This limitation stems from the fact that AI systems are based on logical symbolic manipulations that depend on if-then rules. Unfortunately, it is difficult to tell a computer how to recognize the "if" condition in the real world (Dreyfus & Dreyfus, 1988). Consider this simple if-then rule: "If it is a clock, then set it." Humans recognize all kinds of clocks because they have the natural concept of "clock," but computers are still not very good at forming natural concepts. Doing so requires putting into the same category many examples that have very different physical features, from your bedside digital alarm clock to London's Big Ben. The fact that computers cannot yet do this allows

artificial intelligence (AI) The field that studies how to program computers to imitate the products of human perception, understanding, and thought.

Artificial Intelligence

Artificial intelligence systems such as IBM's Deep Blue have been able to win chess games against the world's best competitors, and AI researchers hope to have the same success someday against champion players of the ancient Chinese board game called Go (Harré et al., 2011). Still, even the most sophisticated computers cannot perceive and think about the world in general anywhere near as well as humans can. Some observers believe that this situation will eventually change as progress in computer technology—and a deepening understanding of human cognitive processes—leads to dramatic breakthroughs in artificial intelligence.

online businesses to protect themselves from potentially dangerous computer programs that pose as human customers. So when ordering something online, you may be shown a set of distorted, odd-looking letters and numbers and then be asked to type them. By doing so, you are proving that you are a human being, not a computer.

Neural Network Models Recognizing the problems posed by the need to teach computers to form natural concepts, many researchers in AI have moved toward a connectionist, or neural network, approach. This approach uses computers to simulate the information processing taking place at many different but interconnected locations in the brain. Neural network models have helped researchers develop computers that are able to recognize voices, understand speech, read print, guide missiles, and perform many other complex tasks (Ashcraft, 2006). Some of the newest of these computer systems are even capable of recognizing and expressing certain basic emotions (e.g., D'Mello & Graesser, 2010; Velik, 2010; Yang & Wang, 2011).

Applications of connectionist research in AI are all around us. It is being used to improve the speech recognition software that allows us to interact with our smart phones and GPS navigation systems through voice commands (Nasoz, Lisetti, & Vasilakos, 2010; Sabah, 2011). Apple has even attempted to create a sense of humor for Siri, the assistance service in its latest iPhone (Fowler, Sherr, & Troianovski, 2011). Other AI systems help people with disabilities and medical conditions to remain more independent (Boger & Mihailidis, 2011; Chittaro et al., 2011; Dewsbury & Linskell, 2011; Najjar et al., 2010). Still others have been used to improve on human decision making; AI systems have been found superior to humans in making decisions in areas ranging from judging meat quality and running credit checks to detecting credit card fraud, and diagnosing and prescribing treatment for various medical conditions (Başçiftçi & Hatay, 2011; Chen et al., 2012; Faisal, Taib, & Ibrahim, 2012; Keleş, Keleş, & Yavuz, 2011; McNelis, 2004; Rabunal & Dorado, 2006; Wong et al., 2012). "Intelligent" Internet search engines such as Google are also based on neural network models, as are the systems that guide you to the news items, films, books, and other material that your previous online activity suggests will be of greatest interest to you (Al Masum Shaikh, Prendinger, & Ishizuka, 2010). Artificial intelligence systems are also at the heart of interactive learning programs which not only present course material but adjust the content and pace of instruction to match each student's abilities and understanding (Bakardjieva & Gercheva, 2011; Corbett et al., 2010; Garner, Tsui, & Lukose, 2009; Gaudioso, Montero, & Hernandez-del-Olmo, 2012; Hsu, & Ho, 2012; Iglesias et al., 2009; Lin et al., 2009; McLaren, DeLeeuw, & Mayer, 2011; Pedrazzoli, 2010). Some researchers are even hoping to develop computers that can grade papers and evaluate other complex student work (Cheng, 2010; Collins, Deck, & McCrickard, 2008; Nehm Ha, & Mayfield, 2012; Nehm & Haertig, 2012).

Unfortunately, however, most computer models of neural networks still fall well short of the capacities of the human perceptual system. For example, computers are slow to learn how to classify visual patterns, which has led to disappointment in efforts to develop computerized face recognition systems capable of identifying terrorists and other criminals in public places (Feder, 2004; Fleuret et al., 2011). But even though neural networks are far from perfect "thinking machines," they are sure to play an important role in psychologists' efforts to build ever more intelligent systems and to better understand the principles of human problem solving (Gamez, 2008; Schapiro & McClelland, 2009).

One approach to overcoming the limitations of both computers and humans is to have them work together in ways that create a better outcome than either could achieve alone. In medical diagnosis, for example, the human's role is to establish the presence and nature of a patient's symptoms. The computer then combines this information in a completely unbiased way to identify the most likely diagnosis (Roy et al., 2009; Swets, Dawes, & Monahan, 2000). This kind of human-machine teamwork can also help in the assessment of psychological problems (Kramer, Bernstein, & Phares, 2013).

Creative Thinking

One of the greatest challenges in the development of artificial intelligence will be to program devices that can think and solve problems as creatively as humans. Consider the case that opened this chapter. It was Dr. Wallace's knowledge of the chemicals in paint—which has no obvious connection to human body chemistry—that led her to figure out what was causing Laura McBride's illness. Computers are still not nearly as good as humans are at recognizing that information from one area can be used to solve a problem in a seemingly unrelated area. The ability to blend knowledge from many different domains is only one aspect of the creative thinking that humans display every day. People demonstrate **creativity** by producing original but useful solutions to all sorts of challenges (Simonton, 1999, 2004, 2012; Sternberg & Grigorenko, 2004a). How do we know when people are thinking creatively? Psychologists have defined *creativity* as mental activity that can be inferred from performance on certain tests, as well as from the writings, computer programs, artwork, and other products resulting from the creative process (Sternberg & Dess, 2001). To measure creativity, some psychologists have generated tests of **divergent thinking**—the ability to think along many paths to generate multiple solutions to a problem (Diakidoy & Spanoudis, 2002). The Consequences Test is an example. It contains items such as "Imagine all of the things that might possibly happen if all national and local laws were suddenly abolished" (Guilford, 1959). Divergent-thinking tests are scored by counting the number of sensible responses that a person can give to each item and how many of these responses differ from those given by most people.

Only sensible responses to creativity tests are counted, because creativity involves divergent thinking that is appropriate for a given problem or situation. To be productive rather than just weird, a creative person must be firmly anchored in reality, understand society's needs, and learn from the experience and knowledge of others (Sternberg & Lubart, 1992). Theresa Amabile has identified three kinds of cognitive and personality characteristics necessary for creativity (Amabile, 1996; Amabile, Hennessey, & Grossman, 1986):

1. *Expertise* in the field of endeavor, which is directly tied to what a person has learned. For example, a painter or composer must know the paints, techniques, or instruments available.
2. A set of *creative skills,* including persistence at problem solving, capacity for divergent thinking, ability to break out of old problem-solving habits (mental sets), and willingness to take risks. Amabile believes that training can influence many of these skills, some of which are closely linked to the strategies for problem solving discussed earlier.
3. The *motivation* to pursue creative work for internal reasons, such as satisfaction, rather than for external reasons, such as prize money. In fact, Amabile and her colleagues found that external rewards can deter creativity. They asked groups of children and adults to produce creative projects such as paintings or stories. Some were simply asked to work on these projects. Others were told that the projects would be judged for creativity and excellence and that rewards would be given or winners announced. Experts, who had no idea which products were created by which group, judged those from the "reward" group to be significantly less creative. Similar effects have been found in other studies (Byron & Khazanchi, 2012; Deci, Koestner, & Ryan, 1999, 2001; Murayama et al., 2010), though under some circumstances, rewarding people's creativity can strengthen it—in much the same way that positive reinforcement strengthens any other behavior (Eisenberger & Rhoades, 2001; Eisenberger & Shanock, 2003).

Is creativity inherited? To some extent, perhaps it is (Kéri, 2009; Lykken, 1998a), but evidence suggests that the social, economic, and political environment in which a person grows and lives also influences creative behavior (Amabile, 2001; Nakamura & Csikszentmihalyi, 2001). Do you have to be smart to be creative? Creativity does appear to require a certain degree of intelligence (Sternberg, 2001). For example, longitudinal studies have shown that individuals identified as particularly smart in adolescence were up to eight times more likely than other people to show creativity as adults by patenting inventions or producing scientific publications (Park, Lubinski, & Benbow, 2008; Wai, Lubinski, & Benbow,

creativity The capacity to produce original solutions or novel compositions.

divergent thinking The ability to generate many different solutions to a problem.

© James Brittain/VIEW/Corbis

Thinking Outside the Box

Psychological scientists are finding that people tend to think less creatively while in confined spaces or when their movements are restricted (Ambrosini, Sinigaglia, & Costantini, 2012; Goldin-Meadow & Beilock, 2010; Leung et al., 2012). Perhaps the boundaries that limit physical movement create psychological boundaries that—like the mental sets and functional fixedness discussed earlier—limit the options we consider when solving problems and developing new ideas. With this possibility in mind, many businesses today work with environmental psychologists to design workplaces that avoid the physical confinements of traditional office cubicles.

convergent thinking The ability to apply the rules of logic and what one knows about the world to narrow down the possible solutions to a problem.

utility In decision making, any subjective measure of value.

expected value The total benefit to be expected of a decision if it were repeated on several occasions.

2005). But you don't have to be a genius to be creative (Simonton, 1984, 2002; Sternberg, 2001). In fact, although correlations between scores on creativity tests and intelligence tests are almost always positive, they are relatively modest (Kim, 2008; Simonton, 1999). This finding is not surprising, because creativity involves divergent thinking about many solutions to a problem. As described later, high scores on most intelligence tests require **convergent thinking,** which uses logic and knowledge to narrow down the number of possible solutions to a problem. One result of research on this topic has been to see intelligence and creativity in the same person as contributing to the broader trait of *wisdom* (Baltes & Smith, 2008; Callahan, 2011; Sternberg, 2001; Sternberg, 2010; Sternberg & O'Hara, 1999).

The biological aspects of creativity are being investigated through the use of fMRI technology, which can identify the amount and location of brain activity that accompanies creative thinking (Chermahini & Hommel, 2010; Dietrich & Kanso, 2010). Other researchers are exploring the possibility of teaching creativity (Gupta et al., 2012; Jarosz, Colflesh, & Wiley, 2012; Kohn, Paulus, & Korde, 2011; Polman & Emich, 2011). If it is successful, their work may someday enable all of us to think more creatively about life's problems, and perhaps about life in general (Glăveanu, 2012).

Decision Making

How can I become a better decision maker?

Paper or plastic? Do I watch TV or study for the test? Should I get out of this relationship? Is it time to start thinking about a nursing home for Mom? Life is full of decisions. Some are quick and easy to make; others are painfully difficult and require considerable time, planning, and mental effort. Even carefully considered decisions can lead to undesirable outcomes, though, because the world is an uncertain place. Decisions made when the outcome is uncertain are called *risky decisions* or *decisions under uncertainty.* Chance aside, psychologists have discovered reasons why human decisions sometimes lead to unsatisfactory outcomes (Chandler & Pronin, 2012; Gifford, 2011). Let's consider some of these reasons.

Evaluating Options

Suppose that you have to decide whether to pursue an academic major you love but that is unlikely to lead to steady employment or to choose a less interesting major that almost guarantees a high-paying job. The fact that each option has positive and negative features greatly complicates decision making. Deciding which car to buy, which college to attend, or even how to spend the evening are all examples of choices that require you to weigh several options. Such choices are often based on the positive or negative value, or **utility,** that you place on each feature of each option. Listing the pros and cons of each option is a helpful way of keeping them all in mind as you think about your decisions. You also have to estimate the probabilities and risks associated with the possible outcomes of each choice. For example, you must consider how likely it is that job opportunities in your chosen major will have faded by the time you graduate. In studying risky decision making, psychologists begin with the assumption that the best decision maximizes *expected value.* The **expected value** of a decision is the average benefit you could expect to receive if the decision were repeated on several occasions.

Biases and Flaws in Decision Making

Most people think of themselves as logical and rational, but in making decisions about everything from giving up smoking to investing in the stock market, they don't always

Analyzing your choices and the possible outcomes of each takes some time and effort, but the results are usually worth it. Like Dilbert's boss, many people prefer to make decisions more impulsively, and although their decisions sometimes turn out well, they often don't (Gladwell, 2005; Myers, 2004; Rubenwolf & Spörrle, 2011).

act in ways that maximize expected value (Farmer, Patelli, & Zovko, 2005; Shiller, 2001; Tessari et al., 2011). Why not?

Gains, Losses, and Probabilities   For one thing, our pain over losing a certain amount is usually greater than the pleasure we feel after gaining the same amount (Kermer et al., 2006). This phenomenon is called *loss aversion* (Dawes, 1998; McGraw et al., 2010; Tversky & Kahneman, 1991). Because of loss aversion, you might go to more trouble to collect a $100 debt than to win a $100 prize. In addition, the value of a gain may not depend on the amount of the gain but on what you start with. Suppose you could have a $10 gift certificate from a restaurant but you would have to drive 10 miles to pick it up. This gain has the same monetary value as having an extra $10 added to your paycheck. However, most people tend to behave as if the difference between $0 and $10 is greater than the difference between, say, $300 and $310. So a person who won't drive across town after work to earn a $10 bonus on next week's paycheck might gladly make the same trip to pick up a $10 gift certificate. Understanding these biases and how they affect people's purchasing patterns and other economic decisions has proven so important that Daniel Kahneman received the 2002 Nobel Prize in economics for his research in this area.

People are also biased in how they think about probability. For example, we tend to overestimate the probability of rare events and to underestimate the probability of frequent ones (Kahneman & Tversky, 1984). This bias tends to be especially strong in relation to risky decisions (Glaser et al., 2012; Huber, 2012) and helps explain why people gamble in casinos and enter lotteries. The odds are against them and the decision to gamble has a negative expected value, but because people overestimate the probability of winning, they associate a positive expected value with gambling. In one study, not even a course that highlighted gambling's mathematical disadvantages could change university students' gambling behavior (Williams & Connolly, 2006). The tendency to overestimate rare events is amplified by the availability heuristic: vivid memories of rare gambling successes and the publicity given to lottery winners encourage people to recall gains rather than losses.

Sometimes our bias in estimating probability costs more than money. For example, many people underestimate the risk of HIV and other infections and continue to engage in unprotected sex (Specter, 2005). And after the September 11, 2001, terrorist attacks on the United States, the risks of flying seemed so high that many more people than usual decided to travel by car instead. Yet driving is more dangerous overall than flying, so the decision to drive might actually have increased these people's risk of death, especially if stress associated with the attacks made these drivers less careful (Su et al., 2008). With more cars on the road, there were 353 more traffic fatalities in the last three months of 2001 than there were during the same period in previous years (Gigerenzer, 2004). Similar bias in risk perception leads many people to buy a big, heavy sport utility vehicle that makes them feel safe, even though the chances of serious injury in an SUV are actually greater than in a minivan or family sedan (Gladwell, 2004). Their heightened sense of safety may even lead some SUV drivers to drive less carefully, which further increases their risk of injury (Bener et al., 2008; Thomas & Walton, 2007).

A Highly Unlikely Outcome
Casinos and lotteries attract business by creating memorable images of big winners. They know that people's gambling and ticket buying will be influenced by the availability heuristic and the tendency to overestimate the probability of rare events. Did you ever notice that casino and lottery ads and websites never show or talk about the millions of players who lost money or whose tickets were worthless (McMullan & Miller, 2009)?

Another bias in estimating probability is called the *gambler's fallacy:* People believe that the probability of future events in a random process will change depending on past events. This belief is false. For example, if you flip a coin and it comes up heads ten times in a row, what is the likelihood of tails on the next flip? Although some people think otherwise, the chance that it will come up tails on the eleventh flip is still 50 percent, just as it was for the first ten flips. Yet many gamblers continue feeding a slot machine that has not paid off much for hours, because they believe it is "due."

Poor decision making can also stem from the human tendency to be unrealistically confident in the accuracy of our predictions. Baruch Fischoff and Donald MacGregor (1982) devised a clever way to study this bias. People were asked whether they believed a certain event would occur and then were asked to say how confident they were about their prediction. For example, they were asked whether a particular sports team would win an upcoming game. After the events were over, the accuracy of the people's forecasts was compared with their level of confidence. Sure enough, their confidence in their predictions was consistently greater than their accuracy. Investors, too—including professional stockbrokers—are usually confident about what to buy and sell even though many of their decisions turn out to be bad ones (Puetz & Ruenzi, 2011). Overconfidence operates even when people make predictions concerning the accuracy of their own memories (Bjork, 1998). The moral of the story is to be wary when people express confidence that a forecast or decision is correct. They will be wrong more often than they think.

How Biased Are We?   Almost everyone makes decisions that they later regret, but these outcomes may not entirely be due to biased thinking about gains, losses, and probabilities. Some decisions are not intended to maximize expected value but rather to satisfy other goals, such as minimizing expected loss, producing a quick and easy resolution, or preserving a moral principle (Arkes & Ayton, 1999; Galotti, 2007; McCaffery & Baron, 2006). Often decisions depend not just on how likely we are to gain or lose a particular amount of something but also on what that something is. A decision that could cost or save a human life may be made differently than one that could cost or gain a few dollars, even though the probabilities of each outcome are exactly the same in both cases.

Even the "goodness" or "badness" of decisions is often difficult to measure. Many decisions depend on personal values (utilities), which can vary from person to person

Justice is Served
Decision making can be affected by many factors, including motivational states such as hunger (Bos, van Baaren, & Dijksterhuis, 2011; Eskine, Kacinik, & Prinz, 2011; Symmonds et al., 2010; Zhong & DeVoe, 2010). One study found, for example, that judges' courtroom decisions tended to be more lenient just after they had eaten, and became progressively harsher as the judges got hungrier (Danziger, Levav, & Avnaim-Pessoa, 2011).

and from culture to culture (Weber & Morris, 2010; Yates, 2010). People in individualist cultures, for example, may tend to assign high utilities to attributes that promote personal goals, whereas people in collectivist cultures might place greater value on attributes that bring group harmony and the approval of family and friends (Markus, Kitayama, & Heiman, 1996; Varnum et al., 2010).

Group Processes in Problem Solving and Decision Making

LINKAGES

Do groups solve problems more effectively than individuals?
(a link to Social Psychology)

Problem solving and decision making often take place in groups. The factors that influence an individual's problem solving and decision making continue to operate when the individual is in a group, but group interactions also shape the outcome.

When groups are trying to make a decision, for example, they usually begin by considering the preferences or opinions stated by various members. Not all of these views have equal influence. Views that are shared by the greatest number of group members will have the greatest impact on the group's final decision (Tindale & Kameda, 2000). This means that extreme proposals or opinions will usually have less effect on group decisions than those that are more representative of the majority's views.

This is not always the case, though. Through a process called *group polarization*, discussions sometimes result in decisions that are more extreme than group members would make individually (Baron, Branscombe, & Byrne, 2008). Two mechanisms appear to underlie group polarization. First, most arguments presented during the discussion favor the majority view and most criticisms are directed at the minority view. In fact, confirmation bias leads group members to seek additional information that supports the majority position (Minson & Mueller, 2012; Schulz-Hardt et al., 2000). In this atmosphere, those who favor the majority view find it reasonable to adopt an even stronger version of it (Kassin, Fein, & Markus, 2010). Second, once some group members begin to agree that a particular decision is desirable, other members may try to associate themselves with it, perhaps by suggesting an even more extreme version (Kassin, Fein, & Markus, 2010).

Are people better at problem solving and decision making when they work in groups or on their own? This is one of the questions about human thinking that is studied by social psychologists. In a typical experiment, a group of people is asked to solve a problem like the one in Figure 7.6 or to decide the guilt or innocence of the defendant in a fictional court case. Each person is asked to work alone and then to join with the others to try to agree on a decision. These studies have found that when problems have solutions that can be easily demonstrated to everyone, groups will usually outperform individuals at solving them (Laughlin, 1999). When problems have less obvious solutions, groups may be somewhat better at solving them than their average member but usually no better than their most talented member (Hackman, 1998). And because of phenomena such as *social loafing* and *groupthink* (discussed in the social psychology chapter), people working in a group are often less productive than people working alone (Cheshire & Antin, 2010; Williams & Sommer, 1997).

Other research suggests that a critical element in successful group problem solving is the sharing of individual members' unique information and expertise (e.g., Kohn, Paulus, & Choi, 2011; Puvathingal & Hantula, 2012; Stasser, Stewart, & Wittenbaum, 1995). For example, when asked to diagnose an illness, groups of physicians were much more accurate when they pooled their knowledge (Larson et al., 1998). However, *brainstorming,* a popular strategy that supposedly encourages group members to generate new and innovative solutions to a problem, may actually produce fewer or less creative ideas than are generated by individuals working alone (Baumeister & Bushman, 2008; Kohn & Smith, 2011). This result may occur because comments from other group members may interfere with some members' ability to think clearly and creatively (Nijstad, Stroebe, & Lodewijkx, 2003). Further, some participants in a brainstorming session may be reluctant to offer an idea, even a good one, for fear it will be rejected or

One disadvantage of brainstorming sessions is that running comments and bizarre ideas from some group members can interfere with the creative process in others (Nijstad, Stroebe, & Lodewijkx, 2003).

ridiculed by the group (Kerr & Tindale, 2004; Mojzisch & Schulz-Hardt, 2010). To prevent these problems, some brainstorming groups are specifically instructed to come up with as many ideas as possible, without regard for quality or anything else, just to assure that as many ideas as possible are considered (Paulus, Kohn, & Arditti, 2011). Following these procedures has been shown to elevate the level of performance by brainstorming groups significantly above what is typically found in such groups (Nemeth et al., 2004). Other researchers arrange for brainstorming groups to meet electronically using computer-based communication systems that allow group members to offer suggestions without being identified or interrupted yet still give everyone access to the ideas of all the other members. The levels of trust and the patterns of communication that develop in these groups appear comparable to those seen in face-to-face groups (Wilson, Straus, & McEvily, 2006), and because electronic brainstorming allows people to think more clearly and express themselves without fear, these groups may actually perform as well or better than those that meet in person (Englemann, Tergan, & Hesse, 2010; Nijstad, Stroebe, & Lodewijkx, 2003).

As they work to solve a problem, group members experience their own thoughts as concepts, propositions, images, or other mental representations. How does each member share these private events to help the group perform its task? The answer lies in the use of language. ●●●●

Language

How do babies learn to talk?

Our language abilities are usually well integrated with our memory, thinking, and other cognitive abilities (Boroditsky & Gaby, 2010). This integration allows us to use language to express everything from simple requests to abstract principles. We can speak about our thoughts and memories, think about what people tell us, and interact with each other in meaningful ways (Majid et al., 2011). We can create stories that pass on cultural information and traditions from one generation to the next. In fact, as described in the chapter on biology and behavior, our brains process language so effectively that it is only when strokes or other forms of damage interfere with the brain's language areas that we are reminded that language is a very special kind of cognitive ability (Bedny et al., 2011; Kohnert, 2004; Stephens, Silbert, & Hasson, 2010).

Let's consider the components of language, how and why language ability changes over time (Adank, Hagoort, & Bekkering, 2010; Rabaglia & Salthouse, 2011) and how these changes affect our learning and ability to function in society (Parsons et al., 2011; Rozin, Berman, & Royzman, 2010; Schoon et al., 2010).

A **language** has two basic elements: symbols such as words and a set of rules called **grammar** for combining those symbols. With their knowledge of approximately 50,000 to 100,000 words (Miller, 1991), humans can create and understand an infinite number of sentences. Yet all of the sentences ever spoken are created from just a few dozen categories of sounds. The power of language comes from the way these rather unimpressive raw materials are organized according to certain rules.

language Symbols (and a set of rules for combining them) that are used as a means of communicating.

grammar A set of rules for combining the symbols, such as words, used in a given language.

© Marilyn Conway/Photographer's Choice/Getty Images

Getting Ready to Talk

Long before they say their first words, babies are getting ready to talk. Laboratory studies show that even six-month-olds tend to look longer at faces whose lip movements match the sounds of spoken words. This tendency reflects babies' abilities to focus on, recognize, and discriminate the sounds of speech, especially in their native language. These abilities are crucial to the development of language (Lewkowicz & Hansen-Tift, 2012; Mayberry, Lock, & Kazmi, 2002).

Learning to Speak: Stages of Language Development

Children the world over develop language with impressive speed; the average six-year-old already has a vocabulary of about 13,000 words (Pinker, 1994). But acquiring language involves more than just learning vocabulary. We also have to learn how words are combined and how to produce and understand sentences. Psychologists who study the development of language have found that the process begins in the earliest days of a child's life and follows some predictable steps (Parise & Csibra, 2012; Saffran, Senghas, & Trueswell, 2001).

The First Year   In their first year, infants become more and more attuned to the sounds that will be important in acquiring their native language (Gerken, 1994; Lee, Davis, & MacNeilage, 2010; Peña, Pittaluga, & Mehler, 2010; Weker et al., 1996). In fact, this early experience with language appears to be vital. Without it, language development can be impaired (Mayberry & Lock, 2003). The first year is also the time when babies begin to produce particular kinds of **infant vocalizations,** called **babblings,** patterns of meaningless sounds that first resemble speech. These alternating consonant and vowel sounds (such as "bababa," "dadada," and "mamimamima") appear at about four months of age, once the infant has developed the necessary coordination of the tongue and mouth. Though meaningless to the baby, babblings are a delight to parents. Infants everywhere begin with the same set of babbling sounds, but at about nine months of age, they begin to produce only the sounds that occur in the language they hear the most. At about the same time, their babbling becomes more complex and begins to sound like "sentences" in the babies' native language (Goldstein, King, & West, 2003). Infants who hear English, for example, begin to shorten some of their vocalizations to "da," "duh," and "ma." They use these sounds to convey joy, anger, interest, and other messages in specific contexts and with obvious purpose (Blake & de Boysson-Bardies, 1992).

By ten to twelve months of age, babies can understand several words—certainly more words than they can say (Fenson et al., 1994). Proper names and object words—such as *mama, daddy, cookie, doggy,* and *car*—are among the earliest words they understand. These are also the first words children are likely to say when they begin to talk at around twelve months of age (some talk a little earlier and some a little later). Infants acquire nouns for simple object categories (*dog, flower*) before they acquire more general nouns (*animal, plant*) or more specific names (*collie, rose*) (Rosch et al., 1976).

Of course, these early words do not sound exactly like adult language. English-speaking babies usually reduce them to a shorter, easier form, like "duh" for *duck* or "mih" for *milk.* Children make themselves understood, however, by using gestures, voice tones, facial expressions, and endless repetitions. Once they have a word for an object, they may "overextend" it to cover more ground. So they might use *doggy* to refer to cats, bears, and horses; they might use *fly* for all insects and perhaps for other small things such as raisins and M&Ms (Clark, 1983, 1993). Children make these "errors" because their vocabularies are limited, not because they fail to notice the difference between dogs and cats or because they want to eat flies (Fremgen & Fay, 1980; Rescorla, 1981). Being around people who don't understand these overextensions encourages children to learn and use more precise words (Markman, 1994). During this period, children build up their vocabularies one word at a time. They also use their limited vocabulary one word at a time. They cannot yet put words together into sentences, but they are getting ready to do so. Their language skills will blossom during the years from two to four, and the richness of the vocabulary they eventually develop will be influenced by the richness of the language that they hear and the encouragement they receive for their earliest efforts to communicate using both words and gestures (Goldstein & Schwade, 2008; Rowe & Goldin-Meadow, 2009).

infant vocalizations Early sounds, such as babblings, made by babies.

babblings Repetitions of syllables; the first sounds infants make that resemble speech.

The Second Year   The **one-word stage** of speech lasts for about six months. Then, some time around eighteen months of age, children's vocabularies expand dramatically (Gleitman & Landau, 1994). They may learn several new words each day, and by the age of two, most youngsters can use 50 to well over 100 words. They also start using two-word combinations to form efficient little sentences. These two-word sentences are called "telegraphic" because, like telegrams or text messages, they are brief and to the point, leaving out anything that is not absolutely essential. So if she wants her mother to give her a book, a 20-month-old might first say, "Give book," then "Mommy give," and if that does not work, "Mommy book." The child also uses rising tones to indicate a question ("Go out?") and emphasizes certain words to indicate location ("Play *park*") or new information ("*Big* car").

Three-word sentences come next in the development of language. They are still telegraphic but they are more nearly complete: "Mommy give book." The child's sentences now begin to have the subject-verb-object form typical of adult sentences. Other words and word endings begin appearing, too. In English, these include the suffix *-ing,* the prepositions *in* and *on,* the plural *-s,* and irregular past tenses such as "It broke," and "I ate" (Brown, 1973; Dale, 1976). Children learn to use the suffix *-ed* for the past tense ("I walked"), but they often overapply this rule to irregular verbs that they had previously used correctly, saying, for example, "It breaked," "It broked," or "I eated" (Marcus, 1996). Children also expand their sentences with adjectives, although at first they make some mistakes. For example, they are likely to use both *less* and *more* to mean "more" (Smith & Sera, 1992).

The Third Year and Beyond   By age three or so, children begin to use auxiliary verbs ("Adam is going") and to ask questions using what, where, who, and why. They begin to put together clauses to form complex sentences ("Here's the ball I was looking for"). By age five, children have acquired most of the grammatical rules of their native language.

How Is Language Acquired?

Despite all that has been learned about the steps children follow in acquiring language, mystery and debate still surround the question of just how they do it. We know that children pick up the specific content of language from the speech they hear around them: English children learn English; French children learn French. But how do children come to follow the rules of grammar?

LINKAGES

How do we learn to speak?
(a link to Human Development)

Conditioning, Imitation, and Rules   Perhaps children learn grammar because their parents reward them for using it. This idea sounds reasonable, but observational research suggests that positive reinforcement (which we describe in the learning chapter) is not the main character in the story of language acquisition. Parents are usually more concerned about what is said than about its grammatical form (Hirsch-Pasek, Treiman, & Schneiderman, 1984). So when the little boy with chocolate crumbs on his face says, "I not eat cookie," his mother is more likely to respond, "Yes, you did" than to ask the child to say, "I did not eat the cookie" and then praise him for his grammatical correctness.

Learning through imitation appears to be more influential. Children learn grammar most rapidly when adult models demonstrate the correct form in the course of conversation (Zimmerman et al., 2009). For example:

Child: *Mommy fix.*
Mother: *Okay, Mommy will fix the truck.*
Child: *It breaked.*
Mother: *Yes, it broke.*

But if children learn grammar by imitation, why do children who at one time said "I went" later say "I goed"? Adults don't use this form of speech, so neither imitation nor reward can account for its sudden appearance. It appears more likely that children analyze for themselves the underlying patterns in the language they hear around them and then learn the rules governing those patterns (Bloom, 1995).

one-word stage A stage of language development during which children tend to use one word at a time.

Animal Language?

Several chimpanzees and gorillas have been taught to use American Sign Language (ASL), as demonstrated here by Nim Chimpsky (who was named after Noam Chomsky). Are nonhuman primates' accomplishments with ASL the same as human language abilities? Probably not (Povinelli & Bering, 2002; Rendall, Cheney, & Seyfarth, 2000; Zuberbühler, 2005). Still, research suggests that with the right tools and training, these animals can communicate using abstract symbols (Gillespie-Lynch et al., 2011; Lyn et al., 2011; Lyn, Russell, & Hopkins, 2010; Pedersen & Fields, 2009).

© Susan Kuklin/Photo Researchers, Inc.

Biological Bases for Language Acquisition   The ease with which children the world over discover these patterns and develop language has led some to argue that language acquisition is at least partly innate, or automatic. Noam Chomsky (1965) has proposed that we are born with a built-in universal grammar, a mechanism that allows us to identify the basic dimensions of language (Baker, 2002; Chomsky, 1986; Nowak, Komarova, & Niyogi, 2001). According to Chomsky, a child's universal grammar might tell the child that word order is important to the meaning of a sentence. In English, for example, word order tells us who is doing what to whom (the sentences "Heather teased Jason" and "Jason teased Heather" contain the same words, but they have different meanings). In Chomsky's view, then, we don't entirely learn language—we develop it as genetic predispositions interact with experience (Senghas & Coppola, 2001). So a child's innate assumption that word order is important to grammar would change if the child heard language in which word order did not have much effect on the meaning of a sentence.

Some theorists disagree with Chomsky, arguing that the development of language reflects the development of more general sensory, perceptual, and cognitive skills, not just innate, language-specific mechanisms (e.g., Bates, 1993; Gogate & Hollich, 2010; Goldstein et al., 2010). In other words, they say, we probably don't inherit a single, specific "grammar gene" (White, 2006). Still, other evidence supports the existence of biological factors in language acquisition (Peltola et al., 2012). For example, the unique properties of the human mouth and throat, the language-related brain regions described in the chapter on biology and behavior, and genetic research all suggest that humans are innately "prewired," or biologically programmed, for language (Buxhoeveden et al., 2001; Dehaene-Lambertz et al., 2010; Lai et al., 2001). In fact, researchers are even beginning to uncover genetic mechanisms behind some speech and language disorders (e.g., Bates et al., 2011; Fisher, 2005). In addition, there appears to be a period in childhood during which we can learn language more easily than at any other time (Ridley, 2000). The existence of this *critical period* is supported by evidence from tragic cases in which children spent their early years isolated from human contact and the sound of adult language. Even after years of therapy and language training, these individuals are not able to combine ideas into sentences (Rymer, 1993). Such cases suggest that in order to acquire the complex features of language, we must be exposed to speech before a certain age.

Learning a Second Language
As these international students are discovering, people who learn a second language as adults do so more slowly, and with less proficiency, than younger people (Johnson & Newport, 1989; Patkowski, 1994) and virtually never learn to speak it without an accent (Lenneberg, 1967). Still, the window of opportunity for learning a second language remains open long after the end of the critical period in childhood during which first-language acquisition must occur (Hakuta, Bialystok, & Wiley, 2003).

Bilingualism   Does trying to learn two languages at once, even before the critical period for language learning is over, impair the learning of either? Research suggests just the opposite. Like some children in any situation, the early language of children from a bilingual environment may be confused or delayed, but they eventually show enhanced performance in each language (Bialystok & Craik, 2010; de Houwer, 1995; Garcia-Sierra et al., 2011). Early exposure to more than one language appears to help the brain maintain flexibility in recognizing the sounds and patterns of speech that monolingual children normally lose.

There is also some evidence that balanced bilinguals—those who have roughly equal mastery of two languages in childhood enjoy some more general advantages in cognitive flexibility, concept formation, and creativity. It is as if each language offers a slightly different perspective on thinking and this dual perspective makes the brain more flexible (Bialystok & Craik, 2010; Cushen & Wiley, 2011; Kovács & Mehler, 2009; Krizman et al., 2012; Poulin-Dubois et al., 2011). Bilinguals have an easier time than other people do in learning a third language later in life, even if the grammar of the new language is very different from the ones they already know (Kaushanskaya, 2009). The flexibility of thought developed by bilingual children also seems to provide a sort of *cognitive reserve* in old age, which may protect against the loss of cognitive abilities that is sometimes associated with aging, and may even delay the onset of Alzheimer's disease (Bialystok, Craik, & Luk, 2012; Craik, Bialystok, & Freedman, 2010; Luk et al., 2011).

Testing Intelligence

How is intelligence measured?

People who are good at using and understanding language and skilled at thinking, problem solving, and decision making are likely to be seen as *intelligent.* But intelligence is not limited to these abilities alone. Over the years, psychologists studying people in various cultures around the world have proposed that the concept of "intelligence" is a broad umbrella that can include many different kinds of attributes and abilities, from rapidly processing information to having a good sense of direction or displaying polished social skills (Berry & Bennett, 1992; Eysenck, 1986; Gardner, 1999; Hunt, 1983; Kush, Spring, & Barkand, 2012; Meyer & Salovey, 1997; Sternberg, 1996; Sternberg, Lautrey, & Lubart, 2003).

So what exactly is intelligence? Psychologists have never been able to agree on a precise answer to this question, but the vast majority of them tend to agree that **intelligence** includes three main characteristics: (1) abstract thinking or reasoning abilities, (2) problem-solving abilities, and (3) the capacity to acquire knowledge (Gottfredson, 1997a; Snyderman & Rothman, 1987).

Standard tests of intelligence measure some of these characteristics, but they don't address all of them. Accordingly, some psychologists argue that these tools are not able to capture all that should be tested if we want to get a complete picture of someone's intelligence in its broadest sense. Others say that broadening the definition of intelligence too much will make it meaningless. Still others suggest dropping the term altogether in favor of the more descriptive and less emotionally charged concept of *cognitive ability.* To better understand the controversy, let's take a look at how standard intelligence tests were created, what they are designed to measure, and how well they do their job. Later, we will consider some alternative intelligence tests that have been proposed by those who find fault with traditional ones.

A Brief History of Intelligence Tests

The story of modern intelligence tests begins in 1904, when the French psychologist Alfred Binet was appointed to a government committee whose job was to identify, study,

intelligence   The possession of knowledge, the ability to efficiently use that knowledge to reason about the world, and the ability to use that reasoning adaptively in different environments.

and provide special educational programs for children who were not doing well in school. As part of his work, Binet developed a set of mental tasks that provided the model for today's intelligence tests. Binet assumed that reasoning, thinking, and problem solving all depend on intelligence, so he chose tasks that would highlight individual differences in children's ability to do these things (Binet & Simon, 1905). Children taking Binet's test were asked to unwrap a piece of candy, repeat numbers or sentences from memory, identify familiar objects, and the like (Rogers, 1995).

Binet also assumed that children's cognitive abilities increase with age. So after trying out test items on children of various ages, he categorized each item according to how old a child had to be to get the item right. For example, a "six-year-old item" was one that a large majority of six-year-olds could answer correctly but that five-year-olds could not. In other words, Binet's test contained a set of *age-graded* items (Binet & Simon, 1908). It measured a child's "mental level," later called **mental age**, by determining the age level of the most advanced items that the child could consistently answer correctly. Children whose mental age equaled their actual age, or *chronological age,* were considered to be of "regular" intelligence (Schultz & Schultz, 2000).

At about the time Binet published his test, Lewis Terman at Stanford University began to develop an English-language version that has come to be known as the **Stanford-Binet Intelligence Scale** (Terman, 1906, 1916). Table 7.1 gives examples of the kinds of items included on the test. Terman added items to measure the intelligence of adults and revised the scoring scale. He divided mental age by chronological age and multiplied the result by 100. He called this figure the **intelligence quotient,** or **IQ.** So a child whose mental age and chronological age were equal would have an IQ of 100, which is considered "average" intelligence. A ten-year-old who scored at the mental age of twelve would have an IQ of $12/10 \times 100 = 120$. From this method of scoring came the term *IQ test,* a name now widely used for any test designed to measure intelligence on an objective, standardized scale.

The method used to score the Stanford-Binet allowed testers to rank people based on their IQs. This goal was important to Terman and others who promoted the test in the United States. Terman believed that IQ tests could pinpoint who did and who did not have a suitable "amount" of intelligence. These beliefs were controversial and in some instances

mental age A score corresponding to the age level of the most-advanced items a child could answer correctly on Alfred Binet's first intelligence test.

Stanford-Binet Intelligence Scale A test for determining a person's intelligence quotient, or IQ.

intelligence quotient (IQ) A number that was originally determined by dividing mental age by chronological age and multiplying the result by 100. It now reflects the degree to which a person's score on an intelligence test differs from the average score of others in his or her age group.

TABLE 7.1 The Stanford-Binet Intelligence Scale

Here are samples of the types of items included on Lewis Terman's original Stanford-Binet Intelligence Scale. As in Alfred Binet's test, an age level was assigned to each item.

Age	Task
2	Place geometric shapes into corresponding openings; identify body parts; stack blocks; identify common objects.
4	Name objects from memory; complete analogies (e.g., fire is hot; ice is ___); identify objects of similar shape; answer simple questions (e.g., "Why do we have schools?").
6	Define simple words: explain differences (e.g., between a fish and a horse); identify missing parts of a picture; count out objects.
8	Answer questions about a simple story; identify absurdities (e.g., in statements like "John had to walk with crutches because he hurt his arm"); explain similarities and differences among objects; tell how to handle certain situations (e.g., finding a stray puppy).
10	Define more difficult words; give explanations (e.g., about why people should be quiet in a library); list as many words as possible; repeat six-digit numbers.
12	Identify more difficult verbal and pictured absurdities; repeat five-digit numbers in reverse order; define abstract words (e.g., sorrow); fill in a missing word in a sentence.
14	Solve reasoning problems; identify relationships among points of the compass; find similarities in apparently opposite concepts (e.g., "high" and "low"); predict the number of holes that will appear when folded paper is cut and then opened.
Adult	Supply several missing words for incomplete sentences; repeat six-digit numbers in reverse order; create a sentence using several unrelated words (e.g., forest, businesslike, and dismayed); describe similarities between concepts (e.g., "teaching" and "business").

led to prejudice and discrimination as enthusiasm for testing outpaced understanding of what was being tested. For example, in 1917, as the United States moved closer to entering World War I, a team of psychologists was asked to develop group-administered tests that could identify the cognitive ability of army recruits. Scores on these tests were used to guide the assignment of each recruit to the most appropriate military job. Soldiers who could speak and read English were tested on mental tasks that required verbal skills, such as defining words, whereas the rest were asked to visualize objects and perform other nonverbal tasks. Unfortunately, the verbal tests contained items that were unfamiliar to many recruits. Further, tests were often given under stressful conditions in crowded rooms where instructions were not always audible or (for those who did not speak English) understandable. As a result, almost half of the soldiers tested appeared to have a mental age of thirteen or lower (Yerkes, 1921), leading testers to draw seriously incorrect conclusions about their lack of intelligence—especially in the cases of those who did not speak English (Brigham, 1923). Later, David Wechsler (1939, 1949) developed intelligence tests that were designed to correct some of the weaknesses of earlier ones.

Intelligence Tests Today

Today's editions of the Wechsler tests and the Stanford-Binet are among the most widely used of all individually administered intelligence tests. The Wechsler Adult Intelligence Scale (WAIS-IV; Wechsler, 2008) includes fifteen subtests. Some of the subtests require verbal skills, and include such items as remembering a series of digits, solving arithmetic problems, defining vocabulary words, and understanding and answering general-knowledge questions. Other subtests have little or no verbal content, and include tasks that require understanding the relationships between objects and manipulation of various materials—tasks such as assembling blocks, solving mazes, arranging pictures to form a story, and completing unfinished pictures. Testers using the WAIS-IV can combine the results of the subtests in various ways to calculate an overall IQ, as well as "index" scores that reflect a person's mental processing speed, memory ability, perceptual skills, and understanding of verbal information. The latest edition of the Wechsler Intelligence Scale for Children (WISC-IV; Wechsler, 2003) yields four similar index scores and an overall IQ (see Figure 7.10).

FIGURE 7.10

Performance Items Similar to Those on the Wechsler Intelligence Scale for Children (WISC-IV)

The WISC-IV includes ten standard and five supplemental subtests, grouped into four clusters. The *perceptual reasoning* cluster includes tasks, such as those shown here, that involve assembling blocks, solving mazes, and reasoning about pictures. Tests in the *verbal comprehension* cluster require defining words, explaining the meaning of sentences, and identifying similarities between words. Tests in the *working memory* cluster ask children to recall a series of numbers, put a random sequence of numbers into logical order, and the like. The *processing speed* cluster tests children's ability to search for symbols on a page and to decode simple coded messages.

Source: Sample item from the Wechsler Intelligence Scale for Children, Fourth Edition (WISC-IV). Copyright © 2003 NCS Pearson, Inc. Reproduced with permission. All rights reserved. "Wechsler Intelligence Scale for Children" and "WISC" are trademarks, in the U.S. and/or other countries, of Pearson Education, Inc. or its affiliates.

Copyright © 1949, 1955, 1974, 1981, 1991, and 1997 by Harcourt Assessment, Inc. Reproduced with permission. All rights reserved. "Wechsler" is a trademark of Harcourt Assessment, Inc. registered in the United States of America and/or other jurisdictions.

Picture completion
What part is missing from this picture?

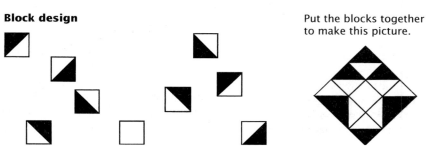

Block design

Put the blocks together to make this picture.

FIGURE 7.11

The Distribution of IQ in the Population

When the IQs in the general population are plotted on a graph, a bell-shaped curve appears. The average IQ of any given age group is 100. Half of the scores are higher than 100 and half are below 100. Approximately 68 percent of the IQs of any age group fall between 84 and 116; about 16 percent fall below 84, and about 16 percent fall above 116.

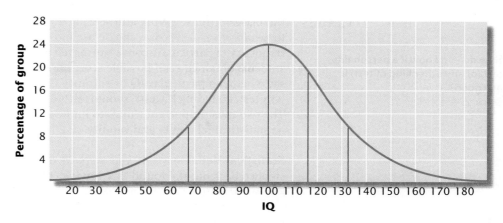

The latest edition of the Stanford-Binet (SB5) also contains subtests (Roid, 2003). However, the SB5 subtests are designed to measure five different abilities: *fluid reasoning* (e.g., completing verbal analogies, such as "hot is to cold as ___ is to low"), *knowledge* (e.g., defining words, detecting errors in pictures), *quantitative reasoning* (e.g., solving math problems), *visual-spatial processing* (e.g., assembling a puzzle), and *working memory* (e.g., repeating a sentence). Each of these five abilities is measured by one verbal and one nonverbal subtest, so it is possible to calculate a score for each of the five abilities, a total score on all the verbal tests, a total score on all the nonverbal tests, and an overall score for all ten tests combined.

Calculating IQ

IQ is no longer calculated by dividing mental age by chronological age and multiplying by 100. If you take an intelligence test today, the points you earn for each correct subtest or age-level answer are added up. Your total score is then compared with the scores earned by other people. The average score obtained by people at each age level is given the IQ value of 100. Other scores are given IQ values that reflect how much each score differs from the average. So if you do better on the test than the average person in your age group, you will receive an IQ above 100. How far above depends on how much better than average you do. Similarly, a person scoring below the age-group average will have an IQ below 100. This procedure is based on a well-supported assumption about many characteristics: most people's scores fall in the middle of the range of possible scores, creating a bell-shaped curve that approximates the normal distribution (see Figure 7.11). Half of those tested score below 100, the average for any given age group. The other half score above 100. In short, your IQ reflects your relative standing within a population of your age.

Evaluating Intelligence Tests

How good are IQ tests?

We have said that no intelligence test can accurately measure all aspects of what various people think of as intelligence. So what does your IQ say about you? Can it predict your performance in school or on the job? Is it a fair summary of your cognitive abilities? To scientifically answer questions such as these, we have to measure the quality of the tests that yield IQs, using the same criteria that apply to tests of personality, language skills, driving, or anything else. Let's review these criteria and then see how they are used to evaluate IQ tests.

A **test** is a systematic procedure for observing behavior in a standard situation and describing it with the help of a numerical scale or system of categories (Cronbach, 1990). Tests are *standardized,* meaning that they present the same tasks, under similar conditions, to each person who takes them. Standardization helps ensure that test results will not be significantly affected by factors such as who gives and scores the test. Because

test A systematic observation of behavior in a standard situation, described by a numerical scale or category.

LINKAGES

How do you know if a personality test (or any other kind of test) is any good?
(a link to Personality)

the biases of those giving and scoring a test are minimized, a standardized test is said to be *objective*. Test scores can be used to calculate **norms,** which are descriptions of the frequency of particular scores. Norms tell us, for example, what percentage of high school students obtained each possible score on a college entrance exam. They also allow us to say whether a particular IQ or entrance-exam score is above or below the average score. Any test, including IQ tests, should fairly and accurately measure a person's performance. The two most important things to know about when determining the value of a test are its statistical reliability and validity.

Statistical Reliability   If you stepped on a scale, checked your weight, stepped off, stepped back on, and found that your weight had increased by twenty pounds, you would know it was time to buy a new scale. A good scale, like a good test, must have **statistical reliability;** in other words, the results must be repeatable or stable. The test must measure the same thing in the same way every time it is used. Let's suppose you receive a very high score on a test of reasoning, but when you take the same test the next day, you get a very low score. Your reasoning ability probably didn't change much overnight, so the test is probably unreliable. The higher the reliability of a test, the less likely it is that its results will be affected by temperature, hunger, or other random and irrelevant changes in the environment or the test taker.

Statistical Validity   Most scales reliably measure your weight, giving you about the same reading day after day. But what if you use these readings as a measure of your height? This far-fetched example illustrates that a reliable scale reading can be incorrect, or invalid, if it is misinterpreted. The same is true of tests. Even the most reliable test might not provide a correct, or valid, measure of intelligence, of anxiety, of typing skill, or of anything else if those are not the things the test really measures. In other words, we can't say that a test itself is "valid" or "invalid." Instead, **statistical validity** refers to the degree to which test scores are interpreted appropriately and used properly (American Educational Research Association, American Psychological Association, & National Council on Measurement in Education, 1999; Messick, 1989). As in our scale example, a test can be valid for one purpose but invalid for another.

Researchers evaluate the statistical reliability of a test by obtaining two sets of scores on the same test from the same people. They then calculate a correlation coefficient between the two sets of scores (see the introductory chapter). When the correlation is high and positive (usually above +.80), the test is considered reliable. Evaluating a test's statistical validity usually means calculating a correlation coefficient between test scores and something else. What that "something else" is depends on what the test is designed to measure. Suppose, for example, you wanted to know if a creativity test is valid for identifying creative people. You could do so by computing the correlation between people's scores on the creativity test and experts' judgments about the quality of those same people's artistic creations. If the correlation is high, the test has high validity as a measure of creativity.

The Statistical Reliability and Validity of Intelligence Tests

The statistical *reliability* of intelligence tests is generally evaluated on the basis of their stability, or consistency. The statistical *validity* of intelligence tests is usually based on their accuracy in guiding statements and predictions about people's cognitive abilities.

Statistical Reliability   IQs obtained before the age of seven are only moderately correlated with scores on intelligence tests given later (Fagan & Detterman, 1992; Fagan, Holland, & Wheeler, 2007; Rose & Feldman, 1995). There are two key reasons. First, the test items used with very young children are different from those used with older children. Second, cognitive abilities change rapidly in the early years (see the chapter on human development). During the school years, IQs tend to remain stable (Allen & Thorndike, 1995; Mayer & Sutton, 1996). So for teenagers and adults, the reliability of intelligence tests is high, as seen in correlation coefficients that are generally between + .85 and + .95 (Deary et al., 2000, 2004).

norms Descriptions of the frequency of particular scores on a test.

statistical reliability The degree to which test results or other research evidence occur repeatedly.

statistical validity The degree to which test scores are interpreted appropriately and used properly.

If only measuring intelligence were this easy!

Of course, a person's score may vary from one occasion to another if there are significant changes in the person's motivation, anxiety, health, or other factors. Overall, though, modern IQ tests usually provide exceptionally consistent results, especially compared with most other kinds of mental tests.

Statistical Validity   If everyone agreed on exactly what intelligence is (having a good memory, for example), we could evaluate the statistical validity of IQ tests simply by correlating people's IQs with their performance on various tasks (in this case, memory tasks). IQ tests whose scores correlated most highly with scores on memory tests would be the most valid measures of intelligence. But because psychologists do not fully agree on a single definition of intelligence, they don't have a single standard against which to compare intelligence tests. Therefore, the validity of intelligence tests is best examined by correlating IQ test scores with a variety of performance measures. Because intelligence is always displayed in the course of specific tasks and specific social, educational, and work situations, psychologists assess the validity of intelligence tests for specific purposes.

The results of their research suggest that intelligence test scores are most valid for assessing aspects of intelligence that are related to schoolwork, such as abstract reasoning and understanding verbal material. Their validity—as measured by correlating IQs with high school grades—is reasonably good, about +.50 (Brody & Erlichman, 1998). Scores on tests that focus more specifically on reasoning skills show even higher correlations with school performance (Kuncel, Hezlett, & Ones, 2004; Lohman & Hagen, 2001). For example, the correlation between people's intelligence test scores and the level of education they achieve ranges from +.60 to +.80 (e.g., Colom & Flores-Mendoza, 2007; Judge, Ilies, & Dimotakis, 2010; Lynn & Mikk, 2007).

There is also evidence that employees who score high on verbal and mathematical reasoning tests tend to perform better at work than those who earn lower scores (Arneson, Sackett, & Beatty, 2011; Borman, Hanson, & Hedge, 1997; Johnson & Neal, 1998; Kuncel & Hezlett, 2010; Pulakos et al., 2002), especially if their jobs require complex reasoning and judgment skills (Gottfredson, 1997b; Schmidt & Hunter, 2004). Later we describe a study that kept track of people for 70 years and found that those who had high IQs as children tended to be well above average in terms of academic and financial success in adulthood (Cronbach, 1996; Oden, 1968; Terman & Oden, 1947). IQs also appear to be highly correlated with performance on routine tasks such as reading medicine labels and using a telephone book (Gottfredson, 1997b, 2004).

So by the standard measures for judging psychological tests, scores on intelligence tests have good reliability and good validity for predicting success in school and in many life situations and occupations (Firkowska-Mankiewicz, 2011; Sackett, Borneman, & Connelly, 2008). However, IQ is not a perfect measure of how "smart" a person is. For example, the average intelligence of children appears to have risen in recent decades, but some psychologists suggest that this may be partly due to the use of deviation scores instead of the old MA/CA × 100 formula for calculating IQ (McDonald, 2010). Further because intelligence tests do not measure the full array of cognitive abilities, a particular test score tells only part of the story, and even that part may be distorted. Many factors other than cognitive ability, including self control and reactions to the testing situation, can influence test performance (Chapell et al., 2005; Duckworth, Quinn, & Tsukayama, 2012; Onyper et al., 2011). So if children are suspicious of strangers and adults, and fear making mistakes, they may become anxious and fail even to try answering certain questions, thus artificially lowering their IQs (Fagan, 2000). Scores may also be depressed artificially if individuals are not motivated to take a particular test (Duckworth et al., 2011).

Claude Steele and his colleagues have suggested that some people's test-related anxiety stems from a phenomenon known as *stereotype threat* (Steele & Aronson, 2000). According to Steele, concern over negative stereotypes about the cognitive abilities of the group to which they belong can impair the performance of some women and some members of ethnic minorities. As a result, the test scores they earn, in laboratory settings at least, underestimate those abilities (Blascovich et al., 2001; Cadinu et al., 2005; Mazerolle et al., 2012; Murphy, Steele, & Gross, 2007; Schmader, 2010; Schmader, Johns, & Forbes, 2008). However, research on the performance of females and minority group members on high-stakes tests such as the SAT has yielded mixed results. Some studies suggest that stereotype threat can lead to reduced scores on these tests—possibly by impairing test preparation and test-taking strategies (Appel, Kronberger, & Aronson, 2011; Davis, Aronson, & Salinas, 2006; Lesko & Corpus, 2006; Mangels et al., 2012; Martiny et al., 2012; Rydell et al., 2010; Scherbaum et al., 2011; Taylor & Walton, 2011; Walton & Spenser, 2009). Other studies find no such effects or only a weak effect (Cullen, Hardison, & Sackett, 2004; Cullen, Waters, & Sackett, 2006; Fischer & Massey, 2007; Grand et al., 2011; Sackett, Hardison, & Cullen, 2004; Stricker & Ward, 2004). It may be that some people—such as girls whose parents reject gender stereotypes—are more resistant to stereotype threat than others (Tomasetto, Alparone, & Cadinu, 2011). In any case, the extent to which stereotype threat impairs performance on cognitive abilities tests in real-world settings remains uncertain (Stoet & Geary, 2012).

"Summarizing" a person with a score on an IQ test does run the risk of oversimplifying reality and making errors, but remember that intelligence tests can also *prevent* errors. Specifically, they can reduce the chances that inaccurate stereotypes, false preconceptions, and faulty generalizations will influence important educational and employment decisions. For example, if boredom or lack of motivation makes a child appear mentally slow at school, a test of cognitive abilities conducted under the right conditions is likely to reveal the child's potential. Intelligence tests can also help to identify children who do need special educational attention. So despite their limitations, IQ tests can minimize the likelihood of assigning children to remedial work they do not need or to advanced work they cannot yet handle.

IQ as a Measure of Inherited Ability

Alfred Binet believed that intelligence could be improved with training and practice at mental tasks. Lewis Terman saw it as an inherited characteristic. Both were partly right. Years of research have led psychologists to conclude that intelligence is *developed ability*. This means that intelligence is influenced partly by genetics and partly by educational, cultural, and other environmental factors and experiences that shape the knowledge, reasoning, and other skills that intelligence tests measure (Atran, Medin, & Ross, 2005; Garlick, 2003; Hunt, 2012; Nisbett et al., 2012; Plomin & Spinath, 2004; Rattan, Good, & Dweck, 2012; Tsethlikai, 2011).

To explore the influence of genetics on individual differences in IQs, psychologists have compared the correlations in scores between people who share varying degrees of similarity in genetic makeup and environment. For example, they have examined the IQs of identical twins (pairs with exactly the same genes) who were separated when very young and raised in different environments. They have also examined the scores of identical twins raised together. In other studies, they have compared individual children's IQs before and after environmental changes such as adoption. (Research designs used in these *behavioral genetics* studies are described in the introductory chapter.)

These studies find, first, that genetic factors are strongly related to IQ. In one study, when identical twins who were separated at birth and adopted by different families were tested many years later, the correlation between their scores was moderately high and positive, at least +.60 (Bouchard, 1999). If one twin earned a high score on an intelligence test, the other probably did, too; if one was low, the other was likely to be low as well. In another study, children who had been adopted soon after birth were tested after years of living in their adopted homes. Those whose biological parents were from higher socioeconomic groups (where higher IQs are more common) had higher IQs than those whose biological parents came from lower socioeconomic groups, regardless of the socioeconomic status of the adopted homes (Capron & Duyme, 1989, 1996). These findings are supported by data from the Colorado Adoption Project (Cardon & Fulker, 1993; Cardon et al., 1992), and they suggest that a genetic component of the children's cognitive abilities continued to exert an influence in the adoptive environment (McGue & Bouchard, 1998).

However, studies of IQ correlations also highlight the importance of the environment (Scarr, 1998). Consider any two people—twins, siblings who are not twins, or unrelated children—brought up together in a foster home. No matter what the degree of genetic

FIGURE 7.12

Correlations of IQ

The correlation in IQ between pairs increases with increasing similarity in heredity or environment.

Source: Bouchard & McGue (1981).

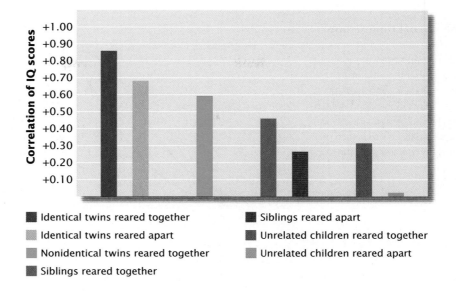

■ Identical twins reared together

■ Identical twins reared apart

■ Nonidentical twins reared together

■ Siblings reared together

■ Siblings reared apart

■ Unrelated children reared together

■ Unrelated children reared apart

similarity in these pairs, the correlation between their IQs is higher if they share the same home than if they are raised in different homes, as Figure 7.12 shows (Scarr & Carter-Saltzman, 1982).

The role of environmental influences is also seen in adoption studies (van IJzendoom & Juffer, 2005). Generally, when children from relatively impoverished backgrounds are adopted into homes offering a more enriching intellectual environment—including interesting materials and experiences and a supportive, responsive adult—they show twelve- to eighteen-point increases in their IQs (Capron & Duyme, 1989; Nisbett et al., 2012; Weinberg, Scarr, & Waldman, 1992; Zhai, Brooks-Gunn, & Waldfogel, 2011; Zhai, Raver, & Jones, 2012).

Programs designed to enhance young children's school readiness and academic ability have also been associated with improved scores on tests of intelligence and academic success (Bulotsky-Shearer, Dominguez, & Bell, 2012; McWayne et al., 2012 Neisser et al., 1996). The same is true of enrichment programs that focus on musical training and improving memory capacity (Jaeggi et al., 2011; Moreno et al., 2011, Morrison, & Chein, 2011; Schellenberg, 2004, 2005, 2006, 2011a, 2011b; Shipstead, Redick, & Engle, 2012; Studer-Luethi et al., 2012). These early intervention programs may be partly responsible for the steady increase children's average IQs mentioned earlier (Flynn, 1999; Neisser, 1998).

Some researchers have concluded that the influences of genetic and environmental factors on intelligence appear to be about equal. Others see a somewhat larger role for genetic factors (Deary, 2012; Deary et al., 2012; Herrnstein & Murray, 1994; Loehlin, 1989; Petrill et al., 1998; Plomin, 1994), and they are working to identify specific groups of genes that might be associated with variations in cognitive abilities (Posthuma & de Geus, 2006). However, the effects of genetics and the environment are intertwined in complex ways, so the influence of either factor may change across developmental stages and in particular situations (Tucker-Drob et al., 2011). It is also important to understand that any estimates of the relative contributions of heredity and environment apply only to groups, not to individuals. It would be inaccurate to say that 50 percent of your IQ is inherited and 50 percent learned. It is more accurate to say that about half of the variability in the IQs of a group of people can be attributed to genetic influences. The other half can be attributed to other influences, including shared and nonshared environmental influences and measurement error. (As discussed in the appendix, *variability* is the degree to which scores spread out around an average score.)

Group Differences in IQ

Much of the controversy over the roles played by genes and the environment in intelligence has been sparked by efforts to explain differences in the average IQs of particular groups

FIGURE 7.13

A Representation of Ethnic Group Differences in IQ

The average IQ of Asian Americans is about four to six points higher than the average IQ of European Americans, who average twelve to fifteen points higher than African Americans and Hispanic Americans. Notice, however, that the variation *within* each of these groups is much greater than the variation *among* them.

Averages

—— African Americans and Hispanic Americans
—— European Americans
—— Asian Americans

of people. For example, the average scores of Asian Americans are typically the highest among various ethnic groups, followed, in order, by European Americans, Hispanic Americans, and African Americans (e.g., Fagan, 2000; Herrnstein & Murray, 1994; Lynn, 2006; Taylor & Richards, 1991). Similar patterns appear on a number of other tests of cognitive ability and achievement (e.g., Bobko, Roth, & Potosky, 1999; Jencks & Phillips, 1998; Koretz, Lynch, & Lynch, 2000; Nisbett, 2005; Rushton & Jenson, 2005; Sackett et al., 2001). Further, the average IQs of people from high-income areas in the United States and elsewhere are consistently higher than those of people from low-income communities with the same ethnic makeup (Jordan, Huttenlocher, & Levine, 1992; McLoyd, 1998; Rowe, Jacobson, & Van den Oord, 1999).

To understand these differences and where they come from, we must remember two things. First, group scores are just that; they do not describe individuals. So even though the average IQ of Asian Americans is higher than the average IQ of European Americans, there will still be many European Americans who score well above the Asian American average and large numbers of Asian Americans who score below the European American average (see Figure 7.13). Second, inherited characteristics are not necessarily fixed. As already mentioned, living in a favorable environment can improve a child's intellectual performance somewhat (Humphreys, 1984). There is also evidence that living in an impoverished environment can impair the development of cognitive skills (Turkheimer et al., 2003).

LINKAGES

How does motivation affect IQ?
(a link to Motivation and Emotion)

Socioeconomic Differences   We have already mentioned that there is a positive correlation between socioeconomic status (SES) and scores on IQ and other cognitive ability tests (e.g. Marks, 2011; Sackett et al., 2009). Why should this be? Four factors seem to account for it. First, parents' jobs and status depend on characteristics related to their own intelligence. And this intelligence is partly determined by a genetic component that, in turn, contributes to their children's cognitive ability level. Second, parents' income affects their children's environment in ways that can increase or decrease the children's IQs (Bacharach & Baumeister, 1998). Third, motivational differences may play a role. Parents in upper- and middle-income families tend to provide more financial and psychological support for their children's motivation to succeed and excel in academic endeavors (Erikson et al., 2005; Nelson-LeGall & Resnick, 1998). As a result, children from middle- and upper-income families may exert more effort in testing situations and therefore obtain higher scores (Bradley-Johnson, Graham, & Johnson, 1986; Robbins et al., 2004; Zigler & Seitz, 1982). Fourth, because colleges, universities, and businesses usually select people with higher scores on various cognitive ability tests, those with higher IQs—who tend to do better on such tests—may have greater opportunities to earn more money (Sackett et al., 2001).

Ethnic Differences   Some have argued that the average differences in IQ among various ethnic groups in the United States and other developed countries are due at least partly to heredity (Rowe, 2005; Rushton & Jensen, 2005). However, the existence of hereditary differences among individuals *within* groups does not indicate whether differences *between* groups result from similar genetic causes. Notice again in Figure 7.13 that variation within ethnic groups is much greater than variation among the mean scores of those groups (Zuckerman, 1990).

We must also take into account the large differences among the environments in which the average African American, Hispanic American, Asian American, and European American child grows up. To take only the most blatant evidence, the latest U.S. Census Bureau figures show that 27.5 percent of African American families and 26.7 percent of Hispanic American families live below the poverty level, compared with 12.1 percent of Asian American families and 10 percent of European American families (Short, 2011). Compared with European Americans, African American children are more likely to have parents with less extensive educational backgrounds and to have less access to good nutrition, health care, and schools (Evans, 2004; Wilson, 1997). All of these conditions are likely to pull down scores on intelligence tests (Brooks-Gunn, Klebanov, & Duncan, 1996; Englund, Luckner, & Whaley, 2004; Lemos et al., 2011; Sangwan, 2001). Cultural factors may also contribute to differences among the average scores of various ethnic groups. For example, those differing averages may partly reflect differences in the degree to which parents in each group tend to encourage their children's academic achievement (Al-Fadhli & Kersen, 2010; Ryan et al., 2010; Steinberg, Dornbusch, & Brown, 1992).

In short, it appears that some important nongenetic factors serve to decrease the average scores of African American and Hispanic American children. Whatever heredity might contribute to children's performance, it may be possible for them to improve, given the removal of negative environmental conditions. ("In Review: Influences on IQ" summarizes our discussion of environmental and genetic factors affecting performance on intelligence tests.)

Influences on IQ   IN REVIEW

Source or Effect	Description	Examples of Evidence for Effect
Genetics	Genes appear to play a significant role in IQ test performance.	The IQs of siblings who share no common environment are positively correlated. There is a greater correlation between scores of identical twins than between those of nonidentical twins.
Environment	Environmental conditions interact with genetic inheritance. Nutrition, medical care, sensory and intellectual stimulation, interpersonal relations, and influences on motivation are all significant features of the environment.	IQs have risen among children who are adopted into homes that offer a stimulating, enriching environment. Correlations between IQs of twins reared together are higher than for those reared apart.

IN REVIEW QUESTIONS

1. Intelligence is influenced by both ___ and ___.

2. Children living in poverty tend to have ___ IQs than those in middle-income families.

3. IQs of children whose parents encourage learning tend to be ___ than those of children whose parents do not.

THINKING CRITICALLY

Are Intelligence Tests Unfairly Biased against Certain Groups?

We have seen that intelligence tests can have great value but also that IQ can be negatively affected by poverty, inferior educational opportunities, and other environmental factors. So there is understandable concern among psychologists and the general public that members of ethnic minorities and other environmentally disadvantaged groups have not had an equal chance to develop the knowledge and skills that are required to achieve high IQs.

What am I being asked to believe or accept?

Some critics claim that, indeed, standard intelligence tests are not fair. They argue that a disproportionately large number of people in some ethnic minority groups score low on intelligence tests for reasons that are unrelated to cognitive ability, job potential, or other criteria that the tests are supposed to predict (Helms, 1992, 1997; Kwate, 2001; Neisser et al., 1996). They say that using intelligence tests to make decisions about people—such as assigning them to particular jobs or special classes—causes members of certain groups to be unfairly deprived of equal employment or educational opportunities.

Is evidence available to support the claim?

Research reveals several possible sources of bias in intelligence test scores. First, noncognitive factors can influence a person's performance on IQ tests and may put certain groups at a disadvantage. We have seen, for example, that children from some ethnic and socioeconomic groups may be less motivated than other children to perform well on standardized tests. They may also be less comfortable in the testing situation and less likely to trust adult testers (Steele, 1997). So the differences in test scores may partly reflect motivational or emotional differences among various groups, not intellectual ones.

Second, many intelligence test items are still drawn from the vocabulary and experiences of the dominant middle-class culture in the United States. As a result, these tests often measure achievement in acquiring knowledge valued by that culture. Not all cultures value the same things, however (Nisbett, 2003; Serpell, 1994; Sternberg & Grigorenko, 2004b). For example, a study of Cree Indians in northern Canada revealed that Cree words and phrases meaning "competent" included *good sense of direction*. At the "incompetent" end of the scale was the phrase *lives like a white person* (Berry & Bennett, 1992). A European American might not perform well on a Cree intelligence test based on these criteria. In fact, as illustrated in Figure 7.14, poor performance on a culture-specific test is probably due more to unfamiliarity with culture-based concepts than to lack of cognitive ability.

Third, some tests may reward those who interpret questions as expected by the test designer. Conventional intelligence tests have clearly defined "right" and "wrong" answers. Yet a person may interpret test questions in a manner that is "intelligent" or "correct" but that produces a "wrong" answer. For example, when one child was asked, "In what way are a pen and a pencil alike?" he replied, "They can both poke holes in paper." The fact that you don't give the answer that the test designer was looking for does not mean that you *can't*. When Liberian rice farmers were asked to sort objects, they tended to put a knife in the same group as vegetables. This was the clever way to do it, they said, because the knife is used to cut vegetables. When asked to sort the objects as a "stupid" person would, the farmers grouped the cutting tools together, the vegetables together, and so on, as most North Americans would (Segall et al., 1990).

Can that evidence be interpreted another way?

The same evidence might be interpreted as showing that although traditional intelligence tests do not provide a pure measure of inherited cognitive ability, they do

FIGURE 7.14

An Intelligence Test?

How did you do on this "intelligence test"? If, like most people, you are unfamiliar with the material being tested by these rather obscure questions, your score was probably low. Would it be fair to say, then, that you are not very intelligent?

LEARN by DOING

Take a minute to answer each of these questions, and check your answers against the key on page 286.

1. What fictional detective was created by Leslie Charteris?

2. What dwarf planet travels around the sun every 248 years?

3. What vegetable yields the most pounds of produce per acre?

4. What was the infamous pseudonym of broadcaster Iva Toguri d'Aquino?

5. What kind of animal is Dr. Dolittle's Pushmi-Pullyu?

provide a fair test of whether a person is likely to succeed in school or in certain jobs. When some people have had more opportunity than others to develop their abilities, the difference will be reflected in higher IQs. From this point of view, intelligence tests are fair measures of the cognitive abilities people have developed while living in a society that, unfortunately, contains some unfair elements. In other words, the tests may be accurately detecting knowledge and skills that are not represented equally in all groups. That doesn't mean that the tests discriminate *unfairly* among those groups (Sackett, Borneman, & Connelly, 2008).

To some observers, concern over cultural bias in intelligence tests stems from a tendency to think of IQs as measures of innate ability. These psychologists suggest instead that intelligence tests are measuring ability that is developed and expressed in a cultural context—much as athletes develop the physical skills needed to play certain sports (Lohman, 2004). Eliminating language and other cultural elements from intelligence tests, they say, would eliminate a vital part of what the term *intelligence* means in any culture (Sternberg, 2004). This may be the reason that "culture-fair" tests do not predict academic achievement as well as conventional intelligence tests do (Aiken, 1994; Lohman, 2005). Perhaps familiarity with the culture reflected in intelligence tests is just as important for success at school or work in that culture as it is for success on the tests themselves. After all, the ranking among groups on measures of academic achievement is similar to the ranking for average IQs (Sue & Okazaki, 1990).

What evidence would help to evaluate the alternatives?

If the problem of test bias is really a reflection of differences between various groups' opportunities to develop their cognitive skills, it will be important to learn more about how to reduce those differences. Making "unfair" cultures fairer by enhancing the skill development opportunities of traditionally disadvantaged groups should lead to smaller differences between groups on tests of cognitive ability (Martinez, 2000). It will also be important to find better ways to encourage members of disadvantaged groups to take advantage of those opportunities (Sowell, 2005).

At the same time, alternative tests of cognitive ability must also be explored, particularly those that include assessment of problem-solving skills and other abilities not measured by most intelligence tests (e.g., Shaunessy, Karnes, & Cobb, 2004; Sternberg & Kaufman, 1998). If new tests show smaller between-group differences than traditional tests but have equal or better predictive validity, many of the issues discussed in this section will have been resolved. So far, efforts in this direction have not been successful.

What conclusions are most reasonable?

The effort to reduce unfair cultural biases in tests is well founded, but "culture-fair" tests will be of little benefit if they fail to predict academic or occupational success as well as conventional tests do (Anastasi & Urbina, 1997; Sternberg, 1985). Whether one considers this situation good or bad, fair or unfair, it is important for people to have the information and skills that are valued by the culture in which they live and work. So using tests that are designed to predict success in such areas seems reasonable as long as the tests accurately measure a person's skills and access to culturally valued information.

In other words, there is probably no value-free, experience-free, or culture-free way to measure the concept known as intelligence. The reason is that the concept is defined in terms of the behaviors that a culture values and that are developed through experience in that culture (Sternberg, 1985, 2004). This conclusion has led some researchers to worry less about how cultural influences might "contaminate" tests of cognitive abilities and to focus instead on how to help people develop the abilities that are required for success in school and society. As mentioned earlier, if more attention were focused on combating poverty, poor schools, inadequate nutrition, lack of health care, and other conditions that result in lower average IQs and reduced economic opportunities for certain groups of people, many of the reasons for concern about test bias might be eliminated. ●●●●

Diversity in Intelligence

Is there more than one type of intelligence?

Intelligence test scores can tell us some things—and predict some things—about people, but we have seen that they don't tell the whole story of intelligence. Let's see how diverse intelligence can be by looking at some nontraditional aspects of intelligence and at some people whose intellectual abilities are unusually high or low.

Practical and Creative Intelligence

According to Robert Sternberg (1988b, 1999), a complete theory of intelligence must deal with three different types of intelligence: analytic, creative, and practical. *Analytic intelligence,* the kind that is measured by traditional intelligence tests, would help you solve a physics problem; *creative intelligence* is what you would use to compose music; and you would draw on *practical intelligence* to figure out what to do if you were stranded on a lonely road during a blizzard. Sternberg's *triarchic theory* of intelligence deals with all three types of intelligence.

Sternberg recognizes the importance of analytic intelligence for success in academics and other areas, but he argues that universities and companies should not select people solely on the basis of tests of this kind of intelligence (Sternberg, 1996; Sternberg & Williams, 1997). Why? Because the tasks posed by tests of analytic intelligence are often of little interest to the people taking them and typically have little relationship to these people's daily experiences. In contrast, the practical problems people face every day are generally of personal interest and are related to more common life experiences (Sternberg et al., 1995). It is no wonder, then, that children who do poorly in school and on intelligence tests may also show high degrees of practical intelligence. Some Brazilian street children, for example, can do the math required for their street businesses despite having failed mathematics in school (Carraher, Carraher, & Schliemann, 1985).

Sternberg and his colleagues have developed new intelligence tests designed to assess analytic, practical, and creative intelligence (see Figure 7.15). They offer evidence that scores on these tests can predict success at some jobs at least as well as standard intelligence tests (Leonhardt, 2000; Sternberg & Kaufman, 1998; Sternberg et al., 1995; Sternberg and the Rainbow Project Coordinators, 2006), but other researchers have questioned this interpretation (Brody, 2003; Gottfredson, 2003).

Multiple Intelligences

Many people with only average scores on intelligence tests have exceptional ability in specific areas. Even those with very low IQs have been known to show incredible ability in narrowly defined skills. One such child, whose IQ was only 50, could instantly and correctly state the day of the week for any date between 1880 and 1950 (Scheerer, Rothmann, & Goldstein, 1945). He could also play melodies on the piano by ear and sing Italian operatic pieces he had heard. He could spell—forward or backward—any word spoken to him and could memorize long speeches. However, he had no understanding of what he was doing.

Cases such as this are part of the evidence that led Howard Gardner to suggest that everyone possesses a number of intellectual potentials, or "intelligences," each of which involves a somewhat different set of aptitudes (Gardner, 1993, 2002). Biology, he says, provides raw capacities for *multiple intelligences*; cultures provide symbolic systems (such as language) that enable people to use their raw capacities. According to Gardner, the various intelligences normally interact but can function with some independence and individuals may develop certain intelligences further than others, often in response to the opportunities and demands found in their culture.

ANSWERS TO FIGURE 7.14: (1) Simon Templar (2) Pluto (3) Cabbage (4) Tokyo Rose (5) A two-headed llama

FIGURE 7.15

Testing for Practical and Creative Intelligence

Robert Sternberg argues that traditional IQ tests measure mainly analytic intelligence. Here are sample items from tests he developed that measure practical and creative intelligence as well. The answers are given at the bottom of the next page. How did you do?

Source: From Robert J. Sternberg, "Testing for Practical and -Creative Intelligence," *New York Times*, November 8, 1997. Reprinted by permission of the author.

PRACTICAL

1. Think of a problem that you are currently experiencing in real life. Briefly describe the problem, including how long it has been present and who else is involved (if anyone). Then describe three different practical things you could do to try to solve the problem. *(Students are given up to 15 minutes and up to 2 pages.)*

2. Choose the answer that provides the **best** solution, given the specific situation and desired outcome.

   John's family moved to Iowa from Arizona during his junior year in high school. He enrolled as a new student in the local high school two months ago but still has not made friends and feels bored and lonely. One of his favorite activities is writing stories. What is likely to be the most effective solution to this problem?

   A. Volunteer to work on the school newspaper staff.

   B. Spend more time at home writing columns for the school newsletter.

   C. Try to convince his parents to move back to Arizona.

   D. Invite a friend from Arizona to visit during Christmas break.

3. This question asks you to use information about everyday things. Read the question carefully and choose the best answer.

   Mike wants to buy two seats together and is told there are pairs of seats available only in Rows 8, 12, 49, and 95–100. Which of the following is not one of his choices for the total price of the two tickets?

   ```
   D:  $5 (Rows 31–100)
   C: $10 (Rows 21–30)
   B: $15 (Rows 11–20)
   A: $20 (Rows 1–10)
        FIELD
   ```

   A. $10. **B.** $20. **C.** $30. **D.** $40.

CREATIVE

1. Suppose you are the student representative to a committee that has the power and the money to reform your school system. Describe your ideal school system, including buildings, teachers, curriculum, and any other aspects you feel are important. *(Students are given up to 15 minutes and up to 2 pages.)*

2. Each question has a "Pretend" statement. You must suppose that this statement is true. Decide which word goes with the third underlined word in the same way that the first two underlined words go together.

   Colors are audible.

   flavor is to <u>tongue</u> as <u>shade</u> is to

   A. ear. **B.** light. **C.** sound. **D.** hue.

3. First, read how the operation is defined. Then, decide what is the correct answer to the question.

   *There is a new mathematical operation called **flix.** It is defined as follows:*

   $$A \text{ flix } B = A + B, \text{ if } A > B$$

   but $\quad A \text{ flix } B = A \times B, \text{ if } A < B$

   and $\quad A \text{ flix } B = A / B, \text{ if } A = B$

   How much is 4 flix 7?

   A. 28. **B.** 11. **C.** 3. **D.** −11.

The specific intelligences that Gardner (1999) proposes are (1) *linguistic* intelligence (reflected in good vocabulary and reading comprehension); (2) *logical-mathematical* intelligence (as indicated by skill at arithmetic and certain kinds of reasoning); (3) *spatial* intelligence (seen in the ability to visualize the relationships among objects in the environment); (4) *musical* intelligence (as in abilities involving rhythm, tempo, and sound identification); (5) *body-kinesthetic* intelligence (reflected in skill at dancing, athletics, and eye-hand coordination); (6) *intrapersonal* intelligence (displayed by self-understanding); (7) *interpersonal* intelligence (seen in the ability to understand and interact with others); and (8) *naturalistic* intelligence (the ability to see patterns in nature). Other researchers have suggested that people also possess *emotional* intelligence, which involves the capacity to perceive, use, understand, and manage their emotions (Meyer & Salovey, 1997; Salovey & Grewal, 2005). Gardner says that standard IQ tests sample only the first three of these diverse intelligences, mainly because they are the forms of intelligence most valued in school. Gardner's view of intelligence is appealing, partly because it supports the flattering idea that almost everyone is especially intelligent in at least one way. However, his critics argue that including athletic or musical skill as part of intelligence dilutes the usefulness of the concept, especially as it is applied to performance in school and in many kinds of jobs. They also point out that Gardner's theory lacks the empirical evidence necessary to challenge other, more established theories of intelligence (Klein, 1997; Waterhouse, 2006a, 2006b). The ultimate value of the theory and of methods for assessing multiple intelligences will be determined by further research.

Unusual Intelligence

Psychologists' understanding of intelligence has been advanced by studying people whose cognitive abilities are unusual—especially the gifted and the intellectually disabled (Robinson, Zigler, & Gallagher, 2000).

Giftedness   People who show remarkably high levels of accomplishment in particular areas are often referred to as gifted (Subotnik, Olszewski-Kubilius, & Worrell, 2011). Giftedness is typically measured by school achievement. A child's potential for high achievement is usually measured by intelligence tests, but researchers warn that it is risky to predict academic potential from a single measure, such as IQ (Hagen, 1980; Lohman & Hagen, 2001; Thorndike & Hagen, 1996).

For one thing, not all people with unusually high IQs become famous and successful in their chosen fields, although they are more likely than others to do so. One of the best-known studies of the intellectually gifted was conducted by Lewis Terman and his colleagues (Oden, 1968; Sears, 1977; Terman & Oden, 1947, 1959). This study began in 1921 with the identification of more than 1,500 boys and girls whose IQs were very high—most higher than 135 by age ten. Periodic interviews and tests over the next seventy years revealed that few, if any, became world-famous scientists, inventors, authors, artists, or composers. But only 11 failed to graduate from high school, and more than two-thirds graduated from college—this at a time when completing a college education was relatively rare, particularly for women. Ninety-seven went on to earn Ph.D.'s; 92, law degrees; and 57, medical degrees. In 1955, their median family income was well above the national average (Terman & Oden, 1959).

In general, they were physically and mentally healthier than the general population and appeared to have led happier lives (Cronbach, 1996). Several more recent studies also show that people with higher IQs tend to live longer (Deary & Batty, 2011; Deary et al., 2004; Deary, Weiss, & Batty, 2010; Der, Batty, & Deary, 2009; Gottfredson, 2004; Hagger-Johnson et al., 2012; Hart et al., 2003; Koenen et al., 2009; Leon et al., 2009; Weiss et al., 2009), perhaps because they have the reasoning and problem-solving skills that lead them to take better care of themselves and avoid danger (Breslau, Lucia, & Alvarado,

ANSWERS TO FIGURE 7.15. Practical (2) A, (3) B. Creative: (2) A, (3) A.

2006; Calvin et al., 2011; Deary & Der, 2005b; Gottfredson & Deary, 2004; Hall et al., 2009; see the Focus on Research section in the chapter on health, stress, and coping).

In other words, higher IQs tend to predict greater success in life (Lubinski et al., 2006; Simonton & Song, 2009; Wai, Lubinski, & Benbow, 2005), but an extremely high IQ does not guarantee special distinction. Some research suggests that gifted children are not fundamentally different kinds of people. They just have more of the same basic cognitive abilities seen in all children (Dark & Benbow, 1993; Singh & O'Boyle, 2004). Other work suggests that gifted people may be different in other ways, too, such as having unusually intense curiosity or motivation to master certain tasks or areas of intellectual endeavor (Lubinski et al., 2001; Nicpon & Pfeiffer, 2011; von Stumm, Hell, & Chamorro-Premuzic, 2011; Winner, 2000). Whatever the case, there is broad support for the idea that giftedness is something that can and should be encouraged and developed (Dai, Swanson, & Cheng, 2011; Subotnik, Olszewski-Kubilius, & Worrell, 2011).

Intellectual Disability   People whose IQs are lower than about 70 and who fail to display the skills at daily living, communication, and other tasks that are expected of those their age were once described as mentally retarded (American Psychiatric Association, 1994). They are now more often referred to as mentally challenged or as having a developmental disability, an intellectual disability, or a developmental delay (Schalock et al., 2009). People in this very broad category differ greatly in their cognitive abilities and in their ability to function independently in daily life (see Table 7.2).

Some cases of intellectual disability have a clearly identifiable cause. The best-known example is *Down syndrome,* which occurs when an abnormality during conception results in an extra copy of chromosome 21 (Hattori et al., 2000; Shin et al., 2009). Children with Down syndrome typically have IQs in the range of 40 to 55, though some may score higher than that. There are also several inherited causes of intellectual disability. The most common of these is *fragile X syndrome,* a defect on chromosome 23 (known as the *X chromosome*). Intellectual disability can also result from environmental causes, such as exposure to German measles (rubella), alcohol, or other toxins before birth; oxygen deprivation during birth; and head injuries, brain tumors, and infectious diseases (such as meningitis or encephalitis) in childhood (U.S. Surgeon General, 1999).

Psychosocial intellectual disability refers to the 30 to 40 percent of (usually mild) cases of intellectual disability that have no obvious genetic or environmental cause (American Psychiatric Association, 1994). These cases appear to result from a complex and as yet unknown interaction between heredity and environment that researchers are continuing to explore (Croen, Grether, & Selvin, 2001; Spinath, Harlaar et al., 2004).

psychosocial intellectual disability
Cases of mild intellectual disability for which no environmental or genetic cause can be found.

TABLE 7.2   Categories of Intellectual Disability

These categories are approximate. Especially at the upper end of the scale, many people with an intellectual disability can be taught to handle tasks well beyond what their IQs might suggest. Furthermore, IQ is not the only diagnostic criterion for intellectual disability. Many people with IQs lower than 70 can function adequately in their everyday environment and so would not be classified as having an intellectual disability.

Level of Intellectual Disability	IQ Range	Characteristics
Mild	50–70	A majority of all intellectually disabled people. Usually show no physical symptoms of abnormality. Individuals with higher IQs can marry, maintain a family, and work in unskilled jobs. Abstract reasoning is difficult for those with the lower IQs of this category. Capable of some academic learning to a sixth-grade level.
Moderate	35–49	Often lack physical coordination. Can be trained to take care of themselves and to acquire some reading and writing skills. Abilities of a 4- to 7-year-old. Capable of living outside an institution with their families.
Severe	20–34	Only a few can benefit from any schooling. Can communicate vocally after extensive training. Most require constant supervision.
Profound	Below 20	Mental age less than 3. Very limited communication. Require constant supervision. Can learn to walk, utter a few simple phrases, and feed themselves.

Photo by Fraser Hale. Copyright St. Petersburg Times. Reprinted with permission

The Eagle Has Landed

In February 2000, Richard Keebler, 27, became an Eagle Scout in the Boy Scouts of America. His achievement was notable not only because a mere 6 percent of all Scouts ever reach this rank but also because Keebler has Down syndrome. As we come to better understand the potential of people with intellectual disabilities and not just their limitations, their opportunities and roles in society will continue to expand.

People who have mild intellectual disability differ from other people in three important ways (Campione, Brown, & Ferrara, 1982):

1. They perform certain mental operations more slowly, such as retrieving information from long-term memory. When asked to repeat something they have learned, they are not as quick as a person of normal intelligence.
2. They know fewer facts about the world. It is likely that this deficiency is a consequence of the problem listed next.
3. They are not very good at using certain mental strategies that may be important in learning and problem solving. For example, they do not remember to rehearse material that must be held in short-term memory, even though they know how to do so.

Despite such difficulties, the cognitive abilities of intellectually disabled people can be improved to some extent. One program that emphasized positive parent-child communications began when the children were as young as two and a half years old. It helped children with Down syndrome to eventually master reading skills at a second-grade level, providing the foundation for further achievement (Rynders & Horrobin, 1980; Turkington, 1987). However, designing effective programs for children who are intellectually disabled is complicated by the fact that learning does not depend on cognitive skills alone. It also depends on social and emotional factors, including where children learn. Much debate has focused on *mainstreaming* and *inclusive education,* which involve teaching children with disabilities, including those who are intellectually disabled, in regular classrooms alongside children without disabilities. A number of studies comparing the cognitive and social skills of children who have been mainstreamed and those who were separated show few significant differences overall. However, it does appear that students at higher ability levels may gain more from being mainstreamed than their less mentally able peers. There are also advantages for them in terms of self-esteem, friendships, and social support (Cole et al., 1991; Hardiman, Guerin, & Fitzsimons, 2009; Huck, Kemp, & Carter, 2010; Mills et al., 1998; Pati, 2011; Vianello & Lanfranchi, 2011).

Active Review

As noted in the introductory chapter, all of psychology's subfields are related to one another. Our discussion of group problem solving illustrates just one way that the topic of this chapter—thought, language, and intelligence—is linked to the subfield of social psychology, which is described in the chapter by that

CHAPTER 7
Thought, Language, and Intelligence

name. The Linkages diagram shows ties to two other subfields, and there are many more ties throughout the book. Looking for linkages among subfields will help you see how they all fit together and help you better appreciate the big picture that is psychology.

LINKAGES

Where are the brain's language centers? *(ans. on p. 59)*

How does motivation affect IQ scores? *(ans. on p. 282)*

Do groups solve problems more effectively than individuals? *(ans. on p. 269)*

CHAPTER 2
Biology and Behavior

CHAPTER 8
Motivation and Emotion

CHAPTER 14
Social Psychology

Summary

Basic Functions of Thought

What good is thinking, anyway?
The five core functions of thought are describing, elaborating, deciding, planning, and guiding action. Many psychologists think of the components of this circle of thought as constituting an ***information-processing system*** that receives, represents, transforms, and acts on incoming stimuli. ***Thinking,*** then, is defined as the manipulation of mental representations by this system.

Mental Representations: The Ingredients of Thought

What are thoughts made of?
Mental representations take the form of concepts, propositions, schemas, scripts, mental models, images, and cognitive maps. ***Concepts*** are categories of objects, events, or ideas with common properties. They may be formal or natural. Formal concepts are precisely defined by the presence or absence of certain features. Natural concepts are fuzzy; no fixed set of defining properties determines membership in a natural concept. A member of a natural concept that displays all or most of the concept's characteristic features is called a ***prototype.***

Propositions are assertions that state how concepts are related. Propositions can be true or false. ***Schemas*** serve as generalized mental representations of concepts and generate expectations about them. ***Scripts*** are schemas about familiar sequences of events or activities. Experience creates accurate or inaccurate ***mental models*** that help guide our understanding of and interaction with the world. Mental ***images*** may also be manipulated when people think. ***Cognitive maps*** are mental representations of familiar parts of one's world.

Thinking Strategies

Do people always think logically?
By combining and transforming mental representations, our information-processing system makes it possible for us to engage in ***reasoning,*** to solve problems, and to make decisions. ***Formal reasoning*** seeks valid conclusions through the application of rigorous

procedures. It is guided by *algorithms,* systematic methods that always reach a correct result (if there is one). To reach a sound conclusion, people should consider both the truth and falsity of their assumptions and whether the argument follows the rules of *logic.* Unfortunately, people are prone to logical errors.

People use *informal reasoning* to assess the validity of a conclusion based on the evidence supporting it. Errors in informal reasoning often stem from the use of *heuristics,* which are mental shortcuts or rules of thumb. Three important heuristics are the *anchoring bias* or *anchoring heuristic* (estimating the probability of an event by adjusting an earlier estimate), the *representativeness heuristic* (basing conclusions about whether something belongs in a certain class on how similar it is to other items in that class), and the *availability heuristic* (estimating probability by how available an event is in memory).

Problem Solving

What's the best way to solve a problem?
Steps in problem solving include diagnosing the problem and then planning, executing, and evaluating a solution. Especially when solutions are not obvious, problem solving can be aided by incubation and the use of strategies such as means-end analysis (also called decomposition), working backward, and finding analogies.

Many of the difficulties that people experience in solving problems arise when they are dealing with hypotheses. People do not easily consider multiple hypotheses. Because of *mental sets,* they may stick to one hypothesis even when it is incorrect, and because of *functional fixedness,* they may miss opportunities to use familiar objects in unusual ways.

People may be reluctant to revise or change hypotheses on the basis of new data, partly because *confirmation bias* focuses their attention on evidence that supports their hypotheses. They may also fail to use the absence of symptoms or events as evidence in solving problems. Problem solving ability can be improved through deliberate practice.

Some specific problems can be solved by computer programs developed by researchers in the field of *artificial intelligence (AI).* There are two approaches to AI. One focuses on programming computers to imitate the logical manipulation of symbols that occurs in human thought; the other (involving connectionist, or neural network, models) attempts to imitate the connections among neurons in the human brain.

Tests of *divergent thinking* are used to measure differences in *creativity.* In contrast, intelligence tests require *convergent thinking.* Although creativity and intelligence are not highly correlated, creative behavior requires a certain amount of intelligence, along with expertise in a creative field, skill at problem solving and divergent thinking, and motivation to pursue a creative endeavor for its own sake.

Decision Making

How can I become a better decision maker?
Decisions are sometimes difficult because there are too many alternatives and too many features of each alternative to consider all at once. Furthermore, decisions often involve comparisons of subjective *utility,* not of objective value. Decision making is also complicated by the fact that the world is unpredictable, which makes decisions risky.

People should act in ways that maximize the *expected value* of their decisions. They often fail to do so because losses are perceived differently from gains of equal size and because people tend to overestimate the probability of rare events, underestimate the probability of frequent events, and feel overconfident about the accuracy of their forecasts. The gambler's fallacy leads people to believe that events in a random process are affected by previous events. People also make decisions aimed at goals other than maximizing expected value; these goals may be determined by personal and cultural factors.

Group decisions tend to show group polarization, the selection of more extreme outcomes than would have been chosen by the average group member. Group performance in problem solving and decision making can be effective, but depending on the problem and the people involved, it may be less efficient than when individuals work alone.

Language

How do babies learn to talk?
Language consists of words or word symbols and rules for their combination—a *grammar.* Children develop grammar according to an orderly pattern. *Infant vocalizations,* such as *babblings,* come first, then a *one-word stage* of speech, and then two-word sentences. Next come three-word sentences and certain grammatical forms that appear in a somewhat predictable order. Once children learn certain regular verb forms and plural endings, they may overgeneralize rules. Children acquire most of the grammatical rules of their native language by the time they are five years old.

Both conditioning and imitation play a role in a child's acquisition of language, but neither can provide a complete explanation of how children acquire grammar. Humans may be biologically programmed to learn language. In any event, it appears that language must be learned during a certain critical period if normal language is to occur.

Testing Intelligence

How is intelligence measured?
Intelligence refers to information-processing skills, problem-solving skills, and the capacity to adapt to changing environments. Binet's pioneering test of intelligence included questions that required reasoning and problem solving at varying levels of difficulty, comparing children's ***mental age*** to their chronological age. Terman developed a revision of Binet's test that became known as the ***Stanford-Binet Intelligence Scale***; it included items designed to assess the intelligence of adults as well as that of children, and it became the model for IQ tests. Early intelligence tests in the United States required not just cognitive ability but also knowledge of U.S. culture. Wechsler's intelligence tests remedied some of the deficiencies of earlier tests. Made up of verbal and nonverbal subtests, these tests allow testers to obtain scores for different aspects of cognitive ability.

In schools, the Stanford-Binet and Wechsler tests are among the most popular individually administered intelligence tests. Both include subtests and provide subscores as well as an overall score. A person's ***intelligence quotient,*** or ***IQ,*** is no longer the result of dividing mental age by actual age and multiplying by 100. It reflects instead how much the person's performance on the test deviates from the average performance of people in the same age group. An average performance is assigned an IQ of 100.

Evaluating Intelligence Tests

How good are intelligence tests?
Tests are standardized, so the performance of different people can be compared; they also produce scores that can be compared with ***norms.*** A good test must have ***statistical reliability,*** which means that the results for each person are consistent, or stable. ***Statistical validity*** refers to the degree to which test scores are interpreted appropriately and used properly.

Intelligence tests are quite reliable and do a reasonable job of predicting academic and occupational success. However, these tests assess only some of the abilities that might be considered aspects of intelligence, and they may favor people who are most familiar with middle-class culture. Nonetheless, this familiarity is important for academic and occupational success in that culture.

Both genes and the environment influence IQs, and their effects interact. Genetic influences are reflected in the high correlation between IQs of identical twins raised in separate households and in the similarity between the IQs of children adopted at birth and those of their biological parents. The influence of the environment is revealed by the higher correlation of IQ between siblings who share the same environment than between those who do not and by the effects of environmental changes such as adoption.

Different socioeconomic and ethnic groups have somewhat different average IQs. These differences appear to be due in part to noncognitive factors, such as differences in motivation, family support, educational opportunity, and other environmental conditions. An enriched environment sometimes raises preschool children's IQs. Despite their limitations, intelligence tests can help educators identify a student's strengths and weaknesses and offer the curriculum that will best serve that student.

Diversity in Intelligence

Is there more than one type of intelligence?
Sternberg sees three types of intelligence: analytic, practical, and creative. He says that scores on tests of practical intelligence predict job success as well as traditional intelligence test scores do. According to Gardner, biology equips us with the capacities for several intelligences that can function with some independence—specifically, linguistic, logical-mathematical, spatial, musical, body-kinesthetic, intrapersonal, interpersonal, and naturalistic intelligences. Knowledge about cognitive abilities has been expanded by research on giftedness and intellectual disability. People with very high IQs tend to be successful in life but are not necessarily geniuses. People are considered intellectually disabled if their IQs are below about 70 and if their communication and daily living skills are less than expected of people their age. In cases of ***psychosocial intellectual disability,*** no genetic or environmental causes are evident. People who have an intellectual disability process information more slowly, know fewer facts, and are deficient at knowing and using mental strategies when compared to people of normal intelligence. Special teaching programs can, to some extent, improve the cognitive abilities of some people who have an intellectual disability.

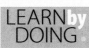

LEARN by DOING

Put It in Writing
Try writing your own definition of *intelligence*. Make a list of at least seven behaviors or characteristics that you feel represent intelligence and then decide how they could best be tested in children and adults from your own culture and other cultures. Describe the kinds of difficulties you encountered in making your list and designing your assessment devices.

Personal Learning Activity
Consider a problem that you are facing at the moment or one that someone you know is facing. In accordance with the problem-solving section of this chapter, write down all the alternative solutions you can think of to solve this problem, then list the pros and cons of each option. Which alternative comes out on top? Does the alternative that seems best on paper also strike you as the best solution to try? Why or why not?

Review of Key Terms

Can you define each of the key terms in the chapter? Check your definitions against those on the pages shown in parentheses in the following list or in the Glossary at the end of the book.

algorithms (p. 255)
anchoring bias (anchoring heuristic) (p. 256)
artificial intelligence (AI) (p. 263)
availability heuristic (p. 257)
babblings (p. 271)
cognitive map (p. 254)
concepts (p. 250)
confirmation bias (p. 261)
convergent thinking (p. 266)
creativity (p. 265)

divergent thinking (p. 265)
expected value (p. 266)
formal reasoning (p. 255)
functional fixedness (p. 261)
grammar (p. 270)
heuristics (p. 256)
images (p. 254)
infant vocalizations (p. 271)
informal reasoning (p. 255)
information-processing system (p. 249)
intelligence (p. 274)
intelligence quotient (IQ) (p. 275)
language (p. 270)
logic (p. 255)
mental age (p.275)
mental models (p. 254)
mental set (p. 261)

norms (p. 278)
one-word stage (p. 272)
proposition (p. 251)
prototype (p. 251)
psychosocial intellectual disability (p. 289)
reasoning (p. 254)
representativeness heuristic (p. 256)
schemas (p. 252)
scripts (p. 252)
Stanford-Binet Intelligence Scale (p. 275)
statistical reliability (p. 278)
statistical validity (p. 278)
test (p. 277)
thinking (p. 249)
utility (p. 266)

Test Your Knowledge

Select the best answer for each of the following questions. Then check your responses against the Answer Key at the end of the book.

1. Thinking is defined as the manipulation of ___.
   a. concepts
   b. mental models
   c. heuristics
   d. mental representations
2. While trying to describe an unusual bird he saw on his walk, Jarrod asks his friend to "think of a robin, but with blue tips on the wings and a tuft of hair on the head. That's what it looked like." Because "bird" is a ___ concept, Jarrod began with the image of a robin, which is the ___ of "bird." He hoped that his description would allow his friend to develop a ___ of the bird he saw.
   a. formal; concept; prototype
   b. natural; image; concept
   c. natural; prototype; mental model
   d. visual; mental model; script

3. Clint is frustrated. His uncle has been winning at checkers all night. During the next game he is going to base his strategy on an algorithm, not a heuristic. What problem will this strategy cause?
   a. Clint still may not win the game.
   b. Clint and his uncle may be playing the same game of checkers for a long time.
   c. Clint will be ignoring overall probabilities.
   d. The representativeness heuristic will bias Clint's choice of strategy.
4. Alicia agreed to go to dinner and a movie with Adam but was surprised and angry when Adam expected her to pay for her half of the evening's expenses. Adam and Alicia apparently had different ___ for what is supposed to happen on a date.
   a. mental models
   b. propositions
   c. images
   d. scripts

5. Stephanie has worked for hours on a biochemistry problem without success. She decides to put it aside and work on her psychology homework in the hope that a solution might occur to her while she is thinking about something else. Stephanie is trying the ___ strategy to solve her problem.
   a. decomposition
   b. incubation
   c. working backward
   d. analogies

6. Ebony wanted to leave a note for her husband but couldn't find a pen, so she wrote the note with her lipstick. Ebony was able to overcome the obstacle to problem solving called ___.
   a. absence of information
   b. multiple hypotheses
   c. confirmation bias
   d. functional fixedness

7. Dr. Sand is sure that Ahmed has appendicitis and as a result he pays more attention to test results that are consistent with appendicitis than to results that suggest a different problem. Dr. Sand has fallen victim to ___.
   a. functional fixedness
   b. a mental model
   c. confirmation bias
   d. the availability heuristic

8. While playing a dominos game, Richard drew a tile at random and got a "double blank," which costs the most points during the first two rounds. At the start of the third round, he says, "There is no way I will draw the double blank tile next time!" Richard is being influenced by ___.
   a. the gambler's fallacy
   b. loss aversion
   c. a disregard of negative evidence
   d. confirmation bias

9. The fact that children learning language sometimes make errors, such as saying "I goed" instead of "I went," has been used to suggest which of the following?
   a. There is a critical period in language development.
   b. Children are born with a knowledge of grammar.
   c. Children do not learn language entirely through imitation.
   d. Speech is learned mainly through imitation.

10. Children who spend their early years isolated from human contact and the sound of adult language are unable to develop adult language skills despite extensive training efforts later. This phenomenon provides evidence for the notion that ___.
   a. there is a critical period in language development
   b. children are born with a language acquisition device
   c. there are no fixed stages in language acquisition
   d. speech is acquired only through imitation

11. Binet's intelligence test was developed to ___.
   a. identify children who needed special educational programs
   b. help the armed forces make appropriate assignments of recruits
   c. identify which immigrants were mentally defective and thus should not be allowed into the United States
   d. help employers decide which employees were most appropriate for the available jobs

12. "All monsters are ugly. The Creature from the Black Lagoon is a monster. Therefore, the Creature is ugly." Together, these three statements are an example of ___.
   a. a premise
   b. a proposition
   c. a natural concept
   d. formal reasoning

13. Jonah's parents are told that their son has an IQ of 100. According to the intelligence test scoring method used today, this means that Jonah ___.
   a. has a mental age that is higher than his chronological age
   b. scored higher than half the children in his age group
   c. is considered to be a gifted child
   d. shows about average skill at divergent thinking

14. Like all other applicants to medical school, Lavinia took the MCAT admission test. Later, researchers compared all the successful applicants' medical school grades with their MCAT scores. The researchers were obviously trying to measure the MCAT's ___.
   a. statistical reliability
   b. standardization
   c. statistical validity
   d. norms

15. When Jerrica first took the Handy Dandy Intelligence test, her score was 140. When she took the same test six weeks later, her score was only 102. If other people showed similarly changing score patterns, the Handy Dandy Intelligence test would appear to lack ___.
   a. statistical reliability
   b. statistical validity
   c. standardization
   d. norms

16. Research shows that today's standardized intelligence tests ___.
   a. have good reliability and reasonably good validity for predicting success in school
   b. do not do a good job of predicting success on the job
   c. are not correlated with performance on "real-life" tasks
   d. measure the full array of cognitive abilities

17. There are two sets of twins in the Mullis family. Louise and Lanie are identical twins; Andy and Adrian are not. According to research on heredity and intelligence, which pair of twins is likely to show the most similarity in IQs?
    a. Andy and Adrian, because they are male siblings.
    b. Andy and Adrian, because they are fraternal twins.
    c. Louise and Lanie, because they are female siblings.
    d. Louise and Lanie, because they are identical twins.

18. Rowena is mildly intellectually disabled, but she is attending regular classes at a public school. Rowena most likely ___ and she will ___ from being mainstreamed.
    a. knows fewer facts about the world than others; benefit
    b. knows fewer facts about the world than others; not benefit
    c. learns just as fast as other children, but forgets it faster; not benefit
    d. has little or no potential for employment; benefit

19. Betsey took an intelligence test that included items requiring her to say what she would do if she were stranded in a large city with no money and how she would teach music to children who had no musical instruments. This test was most likely based on ___.
    a. Sternberg's triarchic theory of intelligence
    b. Gardner's concept of multiple intelligences
    c. Terman's giftedness theory
    d. The Wechsler Adult Intelligence Scale

20. Theresa Amabile identified cognitive and personality characteristics necessary for creativity. Which of the following is not one of these characteristics?
    a. A capacity for focusing on the most important element in a problem, which is tied to convergent thinking.
    b. Expertise in the field of endeavor, which is tied to learning.
    c. A set of creative skills, including the capacity for divergent thinking.
    d. The motivation to pursue creative work for internal reasons.

Media Resources

Now that you have finished reading this chapter, how about exploring some of the ideas and information that you found most interesting?

Coursemate Go to **CengageBrain.com** to access Psychology CourseMate, where you will find an interactive eBook, glossaries, flashcards, quizzes, videos, Virtual Psychology Labs, and more.

Aplia If your professor has assigned Aplia:

1. Sign in to your account.
2. Complete the corresponding exercises as required by your professor.
3. When finished, click "Grade It Now" to see which areas you have mastered, which areas need more work, and detailed explanations of every answer.

Motivation and Emotion

© Bob Daemmrich/Alamy

Motivation and Emotion

The link between motivation and emotion can be seen in many situations. For example, being motivated to win the U.S. National Spelling Bee creates strong emotions, as we see in this winning contestant. And the link works both ways. Often, emotions create motivation, as when anger leads a person to become aggressive toward a child or when love leads a person to provide for that child.

Preview

When your clock goes off in the morning, do you jump out of bed, eager to face the day, or do you bury your head in the blankets? Once you're at your job or on campus, do you always do your best, or do you work just hard enough to get by? Are you generally happy? Do you sometimes worry or feel sad? In this chapter, we explore the physical, mental, and social factors that motivate behavior in areas ranging from eating to sexuality to achievement. We also examine what emotions are and how they are expressed.

Think of a famous person you admire—maybe a business or technology innovator like Steve Jobs, an inspiring leader like Martin Luther King, an athlete like Maria Sharapova, or an entertainer like Adele. As with these people, success probably came to the person you chose only after years of intense effort and unwavering determination. Why do some people work so hard in the face of daunting challenges and tough competition to rise to the top of their fields? For that matter, why do any of us try to excel, to perform acts of kindness, to look for food, to take dancing lessons, to go bungee jumping, to become violent, or to act in any other particular way? Why do some people go all out to reach a goal whereas others make only half-hearted efforts and quit at the first obstacle?

Questions about "why" behavior occurs are questions about **motivation,** the processes that give behavior its energy, direction, intensity, and persistence (Figner & Weber, 2011; Reeve, 2009). Like the study of *how* people and other animals behave and think, the puzzle of *why* they do so has intrigued psychologists for many decades. Part of the motivation for behavior is to feel certain emotions, such as the joy of finishing a race or becoming a parent. Motivation also affects emotion, as when hunger makes you more likely to become angry if people annoy you. In this chapter, we review several aspects of motivation and the features and value of emotions. ●

Concepts and Theories of Motivation

Where does motivation come from?

Suppose that a woman works two jobs, never goes to parties, wears old clothes, drives an old car, eats food left behind by others, ignores charity appeals, and keeps her house at sixty degrees all winter. Why does she do these things? You could suggest a separate explanation for each of these behaviors, or you could suggest a **motive,** a reason or purpose that provides a single explanation for all of them. That unifying motive might be the woman's desire to save as much money as possible. This example illustrates that motivation itself cannot be directly observed. We have to infer, or presume, that motivation is present based on what we can observe.

Sources of Motivation

Human motivation stems from five main sources. First, we can be motivated by *physiological factors,* such as when the activity of certain hormones or certain areas of the brain influences sexual interest. Second, our behavior can be motivated by *needs*, such as the need for food, water, or sleep. *Emotional factors* provide a third source of motivation. Panic, fear, anger, love, envy, and hatred can influence behavior ranging from selfless giving to brutal murder (Terburg, Aarts, & van Honk, 2012; van de Ven, Zeelenberg, & Pieters, 2011). *Cognitive factors* are a fourth source of motivation. These include your perceptions of the world, your beliefs about what you can and cannot do, the amount of choice or control you think you have in particular situations, and your expectations about how others will respond to the behaviors you are considering (Damisch, Stoberock,

motivation The influences that account for the initiation, direction, intensity, and persistence of behavior.

motive A reason or purpose for behavior.

& Mussweiler, 2010; Johnson & Fujita, 2012; Laurin, Kay, & Fitzsimons, 2012; Leotti & Delgado, 2011; Witt, Linkenauger, & Proffitt, 2012). For example, many of the contestants who try for stardom on talent shows such as *American Idol* seem utterly confident in their ability to sing despite the fact that they are obviously and painfully wrong. Finally, motivation can stem from *social and environmental factors* (Neville, 2012). These include the influence of parents, teachers, siblings, friends, television, and other sociocultural forces. Have you ever bought a jacket, tried a new hairstyle, or gotten a tattoo, not because you really liked it but because it was in fashion at the time? And think about all those times when the deadlines and demands set for you by teachers or parents or bosses led you to spend your time doing things that you might not otherwise have done. These are just a few examples of how social factors can affect almost all human behavior.

No single source of motivation can fully explain all aspects of why people behave as they do, but psychologists have combined them in various ways to formulate four main theories of motivation. These include the instinct doctrine, drive reduction theory, arousal theory, and incentive theory. Each of these theories has proven helpful in accounting for some aspects of behavior.

Instinct Doctrine and Its Descendants

In the early 1900s, many psychologists explained motivation in terms of the **instinct doctrine,** which highlights the instinctive nature of behavior. **Instinctive behaviors** are automatic, involuntary, and unlearned behavior patterns consistently "released" or triggered by particular stimuli (Tinbergen, 1989). For example, the male stickleback fish instantly attacks when it sees the red underbelly of another male. Such behaviors in nonhuman species were originally called *fixed-action patterns* because they are unlearned, genetically coded responses to specific "releaser" stimuli.

William McDougall (1908) argued that human behavior, too, is instinctive. He began by listing eighteen human instinctive behaviors that included self-assertion, reproduction, pugnacity (eagerness to fight), and gregariousness (sociability). Within a few years, McDougall and other theorists had named more than 10,000 instinctive behaviors, prompting one critic to suggest that his colleagues had "an instinct to produce instincts" (Bernard, 1924). The problem was that instincts had become meaningless labels that described behavior without explaining it. Saying that people gamble because of a gambling instinct or work hard because of a work instinct explains nothing about why these behaviors appear in some people and not others or about how they develop. Applying the instinct doctrine to human motivation also seemed problematic because people display few, if any, instinctive fixed-action patterns.

Today, psychologists continue to investigate the role played by inborn tendencies in human motivation. Their work has been stimulated partly by research on a number of human behaviors that are present at birth. Among these are the sucking, grasping, and other reflexes discussed in the human development chapter as well as certain facial expressions, such as grimacing at bitter tastes (Steiner et al., 2001). Further, as discussed in the chapter on learning, humans appear to be biologically prepared to learn to fear snakes and other potential dangers (Öhman & Mineka, 2003). But psychologists' thinking about instinctive behavior is more sophisticated now than it was a century ago. They recognize that even though certain behaviors reflect inborn motivational tendencies, those behaviors may or may not actually appear, depending on each individual's experience. So although we might be biologically "programmed" to learn to fear snakes, that fear won't develop if we never see a snake. In other words, motivation can be influenced by inherited tendencies, but that doesn't mean that all motivated behavior is genetically determined.

Psychologists who take an evolutionary approach to behavior suggest that a wide range of behavioral tendencies have evolved because over the centuries they were adaptive for individual survival in particular circumstances. Those who possessed and expressed these adaptive predispositions were more likely than others to live to produce children. We are descendants of these human survivors, so to the extent that their behavioral predispositions were transmitted genetically, we should have inherited similar predispositions. Evolutionary psychologists also argue that many aspects of human social behavior—including helping, aggression, and the choice of sexual or marriage

instinct doctrine A view that behavior is motivated by automatic, involuntary, and unlearned responses.

instinctive behaviors Innate, automatic dispositions to respond in particular ways to specific stimuli.

partners—are motivated by inborn factors, especially by the desire to maximize our genetic contribution to the next generation (Buss, 2004b). We may not be consciously aware of this desire (Geary, 2000), so you're more likely to hear someone say "I can't wait to have children" than to hear them say "I want to pass on my genes."

By emphasizing the evolutionary roots of human behavior, modern versions of the instinct doctrine focus on the ultimate, long-term reasons behind much of what we do. The theories of motivation discussed next highlight influences that act as more immediate causes of behavior (Alcock, 2001).

Drive Reduction Theory

Like the instinct doctrine, the drive reduction theory of motivation emphasizes internal factors, but it focuses mainly on how these factors operate to maintain homeostasis. **Homeostasis** (pronounced "ho-me-oh-STAY-sis") is the tendency to make constant adjustments to maintain body temperature, blood pressure, and other physiological systems at a steady level, or *equilibrium*—much as a thermostat functions to maintain a constant temperature in a house.

According to **drive reduction theory,** any imbalances in homeostasis create **needs,** which are biological requirements for well-being. In responding to needs, the brain tries to restore homeostasis by creating a psychological state called **drive**—a feeling that prompts an organism to take action to fulfill the need and thus return to a balanced state. For example, if you have had nothing to drink for some time, the chemical balance of your bodily fluids will be disturbed, creating a physiological need for water. One consequence of this need is a drive—thirst—that motivates you to find and drink water. After you drink, the need for water is met, so the drive to drink is reduced. In other words, drives push people to satisfy needs, thus reducing the drives that have been created. This cycle is shown in Figure 8.1.

Early drive reduction theorists described two types of drives. **Primary drives** stem from physiological needs, such as the need for food or water. People do not have to

homeostasis The tendency for physiological systems to remain stable by constantly adjusting themselves in response to change.

drive reduction theory A theory that motivation arises from imbalances in homeostasis.

needs Biological requirements for well-being.

drive A psychological state that arises from an imbalance in homeostasis and prompts action to fulfill a need.

primary drives Drives that arise from basic biological needs.

FIGURE 8.1

Drive Reduction Theory and Homeostasis

The mechanisms of homeostasis regulate your body temperature and food and water intake, among other things. For example, when you don't have enough nutrients in your bloodstream, an unbalanced equilibrium is created and your body develops a need for food. This biological disturbance leads to your drive to find something to eat, perhaps by ordering a pizza. After eating satisfies your need for food, your equilibrium is restored.

Photos *(clockwise from top):* © Hywit Dimyadi/ Shutterstock; © Vincenzo Lombardo/Photodisc/ Getty Images; © amana productions inc/Getty Images; © iStockphoto/Thinkstock; © Lana K/Shutterstock

Need: a biological disturbance

Unbalanced equilibrium

Drive: a psychological state that provides motivation to satisfy need

PIZZERIA
RISTORANTE

Equilibrium restored

Behavior that satisfies need and reduces drive

learn these basic needs or the primary drives to satisfy them (Hull, 1951). Other drives, however, are learned through experience. These learned **secondary drives** motivate us to act as if we have unmet basic needs. For example, as people learn to associate money with the ability to buy things that satisfy primary drives for food, shelter, and so on, having money becomes a secondary drive. Having too little money then motivates many behaviors—from hard work to stealing—to obtain more funds (Nordgren & Chou, 2011).

Arousal Theory

Drive reduction theory can account for a wide range of motivated behaviors but not for all of them. Consider curiosity, for example. Monkeys, dogs, cats, and rats will work hard simply to enter a new environment, especially if it is complex and full of novel objects to explore and manipulate (Loewenstein, 1994). And most humans, too, can't resist checking out whatever is new and unusual. We go to the mall opening, watch builders work, surf the Internet, and travel the world just to see what there is to see. People also go out of their way to ride roller coasters, skydive, drive race cars, and do countless other things that do not reduce any known drive (Bergman & Kitchen, 2009; Hsee, Yang, & Wang, 2010; Hughes, 2007; Kaulfuss & Mills, 2008; Zuckerman, 1996).

In fact, these behaviors create an increase in **physiological arousal**—the body's general level of activation. Physiological arousal is reflected in heart rate, muscle tension, brain activity, blood pressure, and other bodily systems (Plutchik & Conte, 1997). It is usually lowest during deep sleep, but physiological arousal can also be lowered by meditation, relaxation techniques, and various depressant drugs. Increases in arousal tend to occur in response to hunger, thirst, stimulant drugs, and stimuli that are intense, sudden, new, or unexpected. Because people sometimes try to reduce their arousal and sometimes try to increase it, some psychologists have suggested that motivation is tied to the regulation of physiological arousal.

Specifically, **arousal theory** suggests that we are motivated to behave in ways that keep or restore an ideal, or *optimal level,* of arousal (Hebb, 1955). Too much arousal can hurt performance, as when test anxiety interferes with some students' ability to recall what they have studied. Overarousal can also cause athletes to "choke" so badly that they miss an easy catch or a simple shot (Smith et al., 2000; Wright et al., 1995). Underarousal, too, can cause problems, as you probably know if you have ever tried to work, drive, or study when you are sleepy. So we try to increase arousal when it is too low and decrease it when it is too high. In simpler terms, we seek excitement when we're bored and relaxation when we're stressed or overstimulated.

In general, we perform best and may feel best when physiological arousal is moderate (Teigen, 1994), but people differ in the exact level of arousal that is optimal for them (Zabel et al., 2009; Zuckerman, 1984). These differences in optimal arousal may stem from inherited differences in the nervous system (Bardo, Donohew, & Harrington, 1996; Berns et al., 2001; Derringer et al., 2010; Eysenck, 1990a) and may motivate boldness, shyness, and many other personality traits and behavioral tendencies.

Incentive Theory

Instinct, drive reduction, and arousal theories of motivation all focus on internal processes that prompt people to behave in certain ways. In contrast, **incentive theory** emphasizes the role of external stimuli that motivate behavior. According to this view, people are pulled toward behaviors that bring positive incentives (maximizing pleasure) and are pushed away from behaviors associated with negative incentives (minimizing pain). For example, as described in the learning chapter, operant conditioning occurs because we're more likely to repeat actions that are followed by positive outcomes rather than by negative ones. According to incentive theory, the differences in behavior from one person to another or from one situation to another can be traced to the incentives available and the value a person places on those incentives at the time. If you expect that some behavior (such as buying a lottery ticket or apologizing for a mistake) will lead to a

Arousal and Personality
People whose ideal, or optimal, level of arousal is high are more likely to smoke, drink alcohol, engage in frequent sexual activity, listen to loud music, eat "hot" foods, and do other things that are stimulating, novel, and risky (Farley, 1986; Zuckerman, 1993). Those whose optimal level of arousal is lower tend to take fewer risks and behave in ways that are less stimulating. As discussed in the personality chapter, differences in optimal arousal may help shape other characteristics, such as whether we tend to be introverted or extraverted.

secondary drives Stimuli that take on the motivational properties of primary drives through learning.

physiological arousal A general level of activation reflected in several physiological systems.

arousal theory A theory that people are motivated to maintain what is an optimal level of arousal for them.

incentive theory A theory that people are pulled toward behaviors that offer positive incentives and pushed away from behaviors associated with negative incentives.

valued outcome (winning money or reducing guilt), you will be motivated to engage in that behavior (Bastian, Jetten, & Fasoli, 2011; Cooke et al., 2011).

The value of incentives can be influenced by inborn physiological factors such as hunger and thirst as well as by cognitive and social factors (Chein et al., 2011; DeVoe & Iyengar, 2010; Saunders & Lynn, 2010). As an example of physiological influences, consider that food is a more motivating incentive when you are hungry than when you're full. As for cognitive and social influences, notice that the value of some things we eat—such as communion wafers or diet shakes—isn't determined by hunger or flavor but by what our culture has taught us about spirituality, health, or attractiveness. Perhaps you have also noticed that what early drive reduction theorists called *primary drives* reappear in incentive theory as unlearned influences on an incentive's value. *Secondary drives* reappear as learned influences on the value of incentives.

Intrinsic and Extrinsic Motivation

Suppose that you decide to learn a new language, write a book, start an exercise program, or volunteer at a homeless shelter. Like almost everything else we do, these decisions can be based on intrinsic motivation or extrinsic motivation (Deci et al., 2001; Ryan & Deci, 2000). **Intrinsic motivation** would lead you to do these things simply to experience the pleasure and satisfaction of doing them, and especially to enjoy the feelings of competence and autonomy (independence) they bring (Przybylski et al., 2011). When intrinsically motivated to do something, you're likely to explain your behavior by saying, "I enjoy it" or "It's interesting." But you might do those same things because of **extrinsic motivation**, in which case your actions would be aimed at achieving some external goal, such as pleasing or impressing other people, qualifying for a better job, alleviating a health problem, or making money. In such cases, you would probably explain your behavior in a different way, perhaps by saying, "It's a good way to get a raise" or "My parents insisted." And, of course, there are many cases in which behavior is based on both intrinsic and extrinsic motivation. For example, many people decide to get in shape not only to experience a sense of accomplishment and autonomy but also to become more physically attractive to others.

It isn't always easy to tell whether someone's behavior is based on intrinsic or extrinsic motivation, and sometimes we may not be sure what motivates our own behavior. Psychologists have discovered some clues, however (Vansteenkiste et al., 2009). For example, when people are intrinsically motivated—doing things mainly for the sake of doing them—they tend to show greater energy, persistence, and creativity, more enjoyment, and better learning than when they are motivated mainly by extrinsic rewards such as money or grades (Ryan & Deci, 2000). So you are more likely to understand this chapter, think actively about its contents, and enjoy reading it if you're motivated by intrinsic, rather than extrinsic, factors (Vansteenkiste et al., 2005). This is one reason that students who take courses because they *want* to often do better—and enjoy class more—than those who take courses because they *have* to.

What happens if a person who is intrinsically motivated to engage in some activity—painting or singing or woodworking, say—begins to receive an extrinsic reward for it? If the extrinsic motivation added to the intrinsic motivation, you might expect to see super-high motivation and performance, but that is not what typically happens. Instead, the longer people receive extrinsic rewards for doing something that had been intrinsically motivated, the less intrinsic motivation they show later on (Deci, Koester, & Ryan, 1999; Kohn, 1993; Lepper, Greene, & Nisbett, 1973; Murayama et al., 2010).

So although creating extrinsic motivation in the form of rewards and punishments is a vital tool in shaping all kinds of behavior, there are also situations in which it can create some hidden costs (Lepper & Greene, 1978). In addition to reducing intrinsic motivation, extrinsic rewards can interfere with learning. If you have been learning French just for fun, but are now offered a lot of money for doing well in the course, the fun might disappear and the arousal associated with worrying about the next test might impair your performance. Even if it doesn't, the prospect of getting that reward might change what and how you learn. Because extrinsically motivated students tend to focus on test scores, final grades, and other external rewards rather than on trying to really understand and apply course material, they tend to be passive learners (Vansteenkiste

© Kolbz/iStockphoto

The Hidden Cost of Reward

We might expect that when people receive money, trophies, prizes, and other extrinsic rewards for doing something, they would be more motivated to continue doing it. As described in the learning chapter, this may be true as long as the rewards continue, but external rewards can undermine intrinsic motivation, and may result in poorer performance over time (Pulfrey, Buchs, & Butera, 2011). The adverse effect of extrinsic motivation on intrinsic motivation has been called *the hidden cost of reward* (Lepper & Greene, 1978).

et al., 2005). As described in the learning and memory chapters, passive learners may be at a disadvantage because they depend on superficial reading and rote memorization rather than repeated self-testing, and other more active learning methods.

Yet another hidden cost of relying on extrinsic motivation in education is that it can undermine students' capacity to be independent learners (Lepper, 1983; Ryan, 1993). After years of receiving rewards for doing well on tests, students may become dependent on them. Over time, the process of learning becomes little more than the process of studying for tests. Questions about whether, when, and how long to study come to be regulated by the testing schedule rather than by interest, curiosity, or independent self-regulation. As a result, when students ask teachers if the final exam will cover the entire course, they may really be asking when they can stop trying to remember what they learned for previous exams.

Fortunately, extrinsic rewards do not always bring hidden costs (Cameron, 2001; Deci et al., 1999). Researchers have found that these costs are most likely to appear when the rewards are both expected (announced in advance) and tangible (money, food, or prizes). The costs are less likely when rewards are unexpected and intangible, such as in the form of a sincere compliment from a respected teacher, colleague, or manager. Unfortunately, expected and tangible rewards are exactly the kinds that are most commonly used in schools and workplaces (Kohn, 1993).

"In Review: Sources, Theories, and Types of Motivation" summarizes our discussion of the basic concepts and principles of motivation. These concepts and principles have helped to guide research on motivated behaviors such as eating, sex, and work, which we consider in the sections that follow.

intrinsic motivation Engaging in behavior simply for the feelings of pleasure, satisfaction, or sense of competence or independence it brings.

extrinsic motivation Engaging in behavior in order to obtain an external reward or avoid a penalty or other undesirable consequence.

Sources, Theories, and Types of Motivation   IN REVIEW

SOURCES OF MOTIVATION

Source	Examples
Physiological factors	Activity of hormones or brain cells
Needs	Food, water, or sleep
Emotional factors	Feelings, such as happiness, sadness, fear, anger, surprise, or disgust
Cognitive factors	Perceptions and beliefs about yourself and the consequences of your actions
Social and environmental factors	Influence of other people or situations

THEORIES OF MOTIVATION

Theory	Main Points
Instinct doctrine	Innate biology produces instinctive behaviors.
Drive reduction	Behavior is guided by biological needs and learned ways of reducing drives that arise from those needs.
Arousal	People seek to maintain an optimal level of physiological arousal, which differs from person to person. Maximum performance occurs at optimal arousal levels.
Incentive	Behavior is guided by the lure of rewards and the threat of punishment. Cognitive factors influence expectations of the value of various rewards and the likelihood of attaining them.

TYPES OF MOTIVATION

Type	Examples
Intrinsic	Doing things for the sake of enjoyment, satisfying curiosity, or feeling competent or independent
Extrinsic	Doing things to get money, prizes, or other external rewards

IN REVIEW QUESTIONS

1. The fact that some people like roller coasters and other scary amusement park rides has been cited as evidence for the ____ theory of motivation.

2. Evolutionary theories of motivation are modern outgrowths of theories based on ____.

3. The value of incentives can be affected by ___, ___, and ___ factors.

Eating

What makes me start eating and stop eating?

At first glance, eating seems to be a simple example of homeostasis and drive reduction theory at work. You're motivated to eat when you get hungry. Much as a car needs gasoline, you need fuel from food, so you eat. But what bodily mechanism acts as a "gauge" to signal the need for food? What determines which foods you eat, and how you know when to stop? The answers to these questions involve complex interactions between the brain and the rest of the body (Pinel, Lehman, & Assand, 2002).

Signals for Hunger and Satiation

A variety of mechanisms operate to create **hunger,** the general state of wanting to eat, and **satiation** (pronounced "say-she-EH-shun"), the satisfaction of hunger. Satiation leads to **satiety** (pronounced "seh-TYE-a-tee"), a state in which we no longer want to eat.

Signals from the Gut The stomach would seem to be a logical source of signals for hunger and satiation. You have probably felt hunger pangs from an "empty" stomach and felt "stuffed" after overeating. It is true that the stomach contracts during hunger pangs and that increased pressure within the stomach can reduce appetite (Cannon & Washburn, 1912; Houpt, 1994). However, people who have lost their stomachs due to illness still get hungry and they still eat normal amounts of food (Janowitz, 1967). So cues from the stomach itself can affect eating, but they appear to operate mainly when you are very hungry or very full. The small intestine is also involved in the regulation of eating (Maljaars et al., 2008). It is lined with cells that detect the presence of nutrients and send neural signals to the brain about the need to eat (Capasso & Izzo, 2008).

Signals from the Blood Still, the most important signals about the body's fuel level and nutrient needs are sent to the brain from the blood. The brain's ability to "read" blood-borne signals about the body's nutritional needs was discovered when researchers deprived rats of food for a long period and then injected some of the rats with blood from rats that had just eaten. When offered food, the injected rats ate little or nothing (Davis et al., 1969). Something in the injected blood of the well-fed animals apparently signaled the hungry rats' brains that there was no need to eat. What was that satiety signal? Research has shown that the brain constantly monitors both the level of food nutrients absorbed into the bloodstream from the stomach and the level of hormones released into the blood in response to those nutrients (Korner & Leibel, 2003).

The nutrients that the brain monitors include *glucose* (the main form of sugar used by body cells), *fatty acids* (from fats), and *amino acids* (from proteins). When the level of blood glucose drops, eating increases sharply (Chaput & Tremblay, 2009; Mogenson, 1976). The brain also monitors hormone levels to regulate hunger and satiety. For example, when a lack of nutrients is detected by the stomach, the hormone *ghrelin* is released into the bloodstream and acts as a "start eating" signal when it reaches the brain (Cummings et al., 2002; Wren, 2001). When glucose levels rise, the pancreas releases *insulin,* a hormone that most body cells need in order to use the glucose they receive. Insulin itself may also provide a satiety signal by acting directly on brain cells (Brüning et al., 2000; Schwartz et al., 2000).

The hormone *leptin* (from the Greek word for "thin") also appears to provide a satiety signal to the brain (Barzilai et al., 1997; Farooqi et al., 2001; Margetic et al., 2002; Spiegelman & Flier, 2001). Unlike glucose and insulin, whose satiety signals help us know when to end a particular meal, leptin appears to be involved mainly in the long-term regulation of body fat (Huang & Li, 2000). The process works like this: cells that store fat normally have genes that produce leptin. As the fat supply in these cells increases, leptin is released into the blood, helping to reduce food intake (Tamashiro & Bello, 2008). Mice with defects in these genes make no leptin and are obese (Bouret, Draper, & Simerly, 2004; Zhang et al., 1994). When these animals are given leptin injections, though, they rapidly lose weight and body fat but not muscle tissue (Forbes et al., 2001). Leptin injections can

hunger The general state of wanting to eat.

satiation The satisfaction of a need such as hunger.

satiety The condition of no longer wanting to eat.

also produce the same changes in normal animals (Fox & Olster, 2000; Priego et al., 2010). Some cases of obesity in humans, too, have been linked to problems in leptin regulation (Considine et al., 1996; Müller et al., 2009). These research results initially raised hope that leptin might be a "magic bullet" for treating human obesity, but this is not the case. Although injections of leptin can help those rare individuals whose fat cells make no leptin (Baicy et al., 2007; Kelesidis et al., 2010), this treatment is far less effective in people who are obese because they overeat a high-fat diet (Gura, 1999; Heymsfield et al., 1999). In these far more common cases of obesity, the brain appears to have become less sensitive to leptin's satiety signals (Ahima & Flier, 2000; Lin et al., 2000; Lustig et al., 2004).

Hunger and the Brain

LINKAGES

How does the brain know when we are hungry?
(a link to Biology and Behavior)

Many parts of the brain contribute to the control of eating. However, research has focused on regions of the hypothalamus that may play primary roles in detecting and reacting to the blood's signals about the need to eat. The hypothalamus influences both how much food is taken in and how quickly its energy is used, or metabolized.

Some regions of the hypothalamus detect ghrelin, leptin, and insulin; these regions generate signals that either increase hunger and reduce energy expenditure or reduce hunger and increase energy expenditure. At least twenty neurotransmitters convey these signals to networks in various parts of the hypothalamus and in the rest of the brain (Cota et al., 2006; Woods et al., 2000).

Activity in a part of the neural network that passes through the *ventromedial nucleus* in the hypothalamus tells an animal that there is no need to eat. So if a rat's ventromedial nucleus is stimulated, the animal will stop eating (Kent et al., 1994). However, if the ventromedial nucleus is destroyed, the animal will eat much more than usual and maintain a much higher body weight.

In contrast, the *lateral hypothalamus* contains networks that tell an animal to start eating. So when the lateral hypothalamus is stimulated, rats begin to eat huge quantities, even if they have just had a large meal (Stanley et al., 1993). When the lateral hypothalamus is destroyed, however, rats stop eating almost entirely.

Decades ago, these findings led to the suggestion that these two hypothalamic regions interact to maintain some homeostatic level, or *set point,* based on food intake, body weight, or other eating-related signals (Powley & Keesey, 1970). According to set-point theory, each individual has a "fat thermostat" that is set by genetics, either at birth or shortly thereafter, to maintain a certain body weight (Keesey, 1980; Keesey & Powley, 1975). So normal animals eat until their set point is reached, then stop eating until desirable intake falls below the set point (Cabanac & Morrissette, 1992).

This theory turned out to be too simplistic. More recent research shows that the brain's control of eating involves more than just the interaction of a pair of "stop-eating" and "start-eating" areas (Winn, 1995). For example, the *paraventricular nucleus* in the hypothalamus also plays an important role. As with the ventromedial nucleus, stimulating the paraventricular nucleus reduces food intake. Damaging it causes animals to become obese (Leibowitz, 1992). In addition, hunger—and the eating of particular types of food—is related to the effects of various neurotransmitters on certain neurons in the brain. One of these neurotransmitters, called *neuropeptide Y,* stimulates increased eating of carbohydrates (Kishi & Elmquist, 2005; Kuo et al., 2007). Another one, *serotonin,* suppresses carbohydrate intake. *Galanin* motivates eating of high-fat food (Krykouli et al., 1990), and *enterostatin* reduces it (Lin et al., 1998). *Endocannabinoids* stimulate eating in general, especially the eating of tasty foods (DiPatrizio, Astarita et al., 2011; DiPatrizio & Simansky, 2008; Mahler et al., 2007). They affect the same hypothalamic receptors as the active ingredient in marijuana does, which may account for "the munchies," a sudden hunger that marijuana use often creates (Cota et al., 2003; Di Marzo et al., 2001). *Peptide YY3–36* causes a feeling of fullness and reduced food intake (Batterham et al., 2002, 2003).

In other words, several brain regions and many brain chemicals regulate hunger and food selection. These internal regulatory processes are themselves affected by the physical environment (e.g., what foods are available), by learning experiences with particular foods, and, for humans, by social and cultural traditions about eating.

© Richard Howard

One Fat Mouse

After surgical damage to its ventromedial nucleus, this mouse ate enough to triple its body weight. Results such as this initially led many psychologists to conclude that food intake is regulated by a combination of "start-eating" signals from the lateral hypothalamus and "stop-eating" signals from the ventromedial nucleus. We now know that the regulation process is far more complex and involves more than just these two brain regions.

© Chad Zuber/Shutterstock

Bon Appetit!

The definition of delicacy differs from culture to culture. While most people in the United States are unlikely to sit down to a plate of grasshoppers or mealworms, over 80 percent of the world's population enjoy eating insects (Dicke & van Huis, 2011; Ekpo, 2011; Gahukar, 2011; Goodyear, 2011), which are an excellent source of protein and essential amino acids (Melo et al., 2011). To appreciate your own food culture, make a list of foods that are traditionally valued by your family or cultural group but that people from other groups do not (or might even be unwilling to) eat.

LEARN by DOING

Flavor, Sociocultural Experience, and Food Selection

For example, eating is powerfully affected by the *flavor* of food—the combination of its taste and smell. In general, people eat more when differently flavored foods are served, as in a multicourse meal, than when only one food is served (Berry, Beatty, & Klesges, 1985; Remick, Polivy, & Pliner, 2009). Apparently the flavor of a food becomes less enjoyable as more of it is eaten (Swithers & Hall, 1994). In one study, participants rated how much they liked four kinds of food, then they ate one of the foods and rated all four again. The participants gave the food they had just eaten a lower rating the second time, whereas their liking increased for all the other foods (Johnson & Vickers, 1993).

The appearance and smell of certain foods also affect eating. These signals come to elicit conditioned physiological responses—including the secretion of saliva, digestive juices, and insulin—in anticipation of eating those foods (see the learning chapter for more on conditioned responses). So merely seeing a pizza on television may prompt you to order one. And if a delicious-looking cookie comes your way, you don't have to be hungry to start eating it. In fact, many people who have just pronounced themselves "full" after a huge holiday meal still manage to find room for an appetizing dessert. In other words, humans eat not just to satisfy nutritional needs but also because of *appetite*, the desire to experience enjoyment (Lundy, 2008; Stroebe et al., 2008; Zheng et al., 2009).

Eating is stimulated by other kinds of signals, too. Do you usually eat while reading or watching television? If so, you may find that merely settling down with a book or your favorite show can trigger the desire to have a snack, even if you have just finished dinner! This happens partly because situations associated with eating in the past can become signals that stimulate eating in the future (Epstein et al., 2009). People also learn social rules and cultural traditions that influence eating. In North American culture, having lunch at noon, munching popcorn at movies, and eating hot dogs at ball games are common examples of how certain social situations can stimulate the eating of particular items at particular times. How much you eat may also depend on what others do. Politeness or custom might prompt you to try foods you would otherwise have avoided. Generally, the mere presence of others, especially friends and family, but even strangers, tends to increase the amount we eat and how long we spend eating (De Castro, 1990, 1994; Redd & de Castro, 1992). Most people consume 60 to 75 percent more food when they are with others than when eating alone (Clendenen, Herman, & Polivy, 1995), and the same effect has been observed in other species, from monkeys to chickens (Galloway et al., 2005; Keeling & Hurink, 1996). If others stop eating, we may do the same even if we're still hungry—especially if we want to impress them with our self-control (Herman, Roth, & Polivy, 2003). And people who are trying to diet are more likely to relapse when they're with others who are eating without restraint (Grilo, Shiffman, & Wing, 1989).

Celebrations, holidays, vacations, and even daily family interactions often revolve around food and what some call a *food culture* (Rozin, 2007). Food use and selection varies widely across cultures. For example, chewing coca leaves is popular in the Bolivian highlands but illegal in the United States (Burchard, 1992). Many westerners regard insects called palm weevils as disgusting (Springer & Belk, 1994), but they are a delicacy for people in Papua New Guinea (Paoletti, 1995), and the beef those same westerners enjoy is morally repugnant to devout Hindus in India. Even within the same culture, different groups may have sharply contrasting food traditions. Squirrel brains won't be found on most dinner tables in the United States, but some people in the rural South consider them to be a tasty treat. In short, eating serves functions beyond nutrition—functions that help to remind us of who we are and with whom we identify.

Unhealthy Eating

Problems in the processes that regulate hunger and eating may cause *eating disorders* such as anorexia nervosa or bulimia and can result in a level of food intake that leads to obesity.

obesity A condition in which a person is severely overweight.

Obesity   The World Health Organization (WHO, 2002) defines **obesity** as a condition in which a person's body mass index, or BMI, is greater than 30 (Yanovski & Yanovski,

2002). You can determine BMI by dividing your weight by the square of your height. So someone who is 5 feet 2 inches and weighs 164 pounds would be classified as obese, as would someone 5 feet 10 inches who weighs 207 pounds. BMI calculators are available at web sites such as http://www.nhlbisupport.com/bmi/. People whose BMI is 25 to 29.9 are considered to be overweight but not obese. (Keep in mind, though, that a given volume of muscle weighs more than the same volume of fat, so very muscular individuals may have an elevated BMI without being overweight.)

Using the BMI criterion, about 34 percent of adults in the United States are obese, as are about 16 percent of children and adolescents (Bell et al., 2011; Ogden et al., 2012). These percentages are even higher among the poor and members of some ethnic minority groups (Kumanyika, 2008; Skelton et al., 2009). Obesity has become so common that commercial jets have to burn excess fuel to carry heavier loads, the United States Coast Guard has reduced the number of passengers that boats are allowed to carry, the parents of obese young children have trouble finding car safety seats to fit them, and the funeral industry has had to offer larger than normal coffins and purchase wider hearses (Associated Press, 2011; Dannenberg, Burton, & Jackson, 2004; Nolin, 2011; St. John, 2003; Trifiletti et al., 2006). Though the problems of overweight and obesity are especially severe in the United States, they are growing worldwide. An analysis of data from 106 countries in Asia, Europe, South America, and Africa—comprising about 88 percent of the world's population—found that 23.2 percent of adults are overweight and another 10 percent are obese. Projections based on present trends suggest that by 2030, there will be over one *billion* obese people living in these countries (Kelly et al., 2008).

Obesity is a risk factor for physical health problems such as Type 2 diabetes, respiratory disorders, high blood pressure, certain cancers, liver and gall bladder disease, osteoarthritis, heart attack, and stroke (Baker, Olsen, & Sørensen, 2007; Bell et al., 2011; Bibbins-Domingo et al., 2007; Centers for Disease Control and Prevention, 2009b; Franks et al., 2010; Reeves et al., 2007). In the United States alone, obesity is blamed for about 300,000 deaths each year and for a predicted shortening of life expectancy in the twenty-first century (Adams et al., 2006; de Gonzalez et al., 2010; Flegel et al., 2005; Olshansky et al., 2005; Shimazu et al., 2009). The medical and other costs of obesity in the workplace have been estimated at over $73.1 billion per year (Finkelstein et al., 2010). Obesity, especially in adolescence, is also associated with the development of anxiety and depression (Anderson et al., 2007; Baumeister & Härter, 2007; Bell et al., 2011; BeLue, Francis, & Colaco, 2009; Gariepy, Nitka, & Schmitz, 2010; Kasen et al., 2008; Zhao et al., 2009), though it is not yet clear whether the relationship is causal, and if it is, which condition might be causing which problem (Atlantis & Baker, 2008; Kivimäki et al., 2009; Scott et al., 2008).

Art Imitates Life?
To see how changes in people's expectations about food and eating might be reflected in works of art, Brian Wansink (shown here) and his brother Craig analyzed 52 paintings of the Last Supper. They found that the size of the plates and food portions shown in the paintings have steadily increased over the past one thousand years (Wansink & Wansink, 2010). In other words, "supersizing" is not a new phenomenon!

Courtesy of Cornell University, Photo by Jason Koski

The precise reasons for this obesity epidemic are unknown, but possible causes include big portion sizes in restaurants—especially fast food outlets—the prevalence of high-fat foods, and reductions in physical activity (e.g., Adachi-Mejia et al., 2007; Mozaffarian et al., 2011; Slentz et al., 2004; Wansink & Wansink, 2010). These are important factors, because body weight is determined by a combination of food intake and energy output (Keesey & Powley, 1986). Obese people get more energy from food than their body metabolizes, or "burns up." The excess energy, measured in calories, is stored as fat. Obese people tend to eat above-average amounts of high-calorie tasty foods but below-average amounts of less tasty foods (Kauffman, Herman, & Polivy, 1995). Further, they may be less active than lean people, a pattern that often begins in childhood (Jago et al., 2005; Marshall et al., 2004; Strauss & Pollack, 2001). Spending long hours watching television or playing computer games is a major cause of the inactivity seen in overweight children (Adachi-Mejia et al., 2007; Cleland et al., 2008; Eisenmann et al., 2008).

In short, inadequate physical activity combined with overeating—especially of the high-fat foods so prevalent in most Western cultures—has a lot to do with obesity (Arsenault et al., 2010). But not everyone who is inactive and eats a high-fat diet becomes obese, and some obese people are as active as lean people, so other factors must also be involved (Blundell & Cooling, 2000; Parsons, Power, & Manor, 2005). Some people probably have a genetic predisposition toward obesity (Bochukova et al., 2010; Bouchard et al., 2007; Frayling et al., 2007; Loos et al., 2006; Su et al., 2008). For example, although most obese people have the genes to make leptin, they may not be sensitive to its weight-suppressing effects, perhaps because of differing genetic codes for leptin receptors in the hypothalamus. Brain-imaging studies also suggest that obese people's brains may be slower to "read" satiety signals coming from their blood, thus causing them to continue eating when leaner people would have stopped (Morton et al., 2006; Thorens, 2008). They may also be more sensitive to the rewards of eating (Stice et al., 2011). These genetic factors, along with the presence of viruses associated with the common cold and other infectious diseases (Dhurandhar et al., 2000; Vasilakopoulou & le Roux, 2007), may help explain obese people's tendency to eat more, accumulate fat, and feel hungrier than lean people.

Other explanations for obesity focus on factors such as learning from the examples set by parents who overeat (Hood et al., 2000), too little parental control over what and how much children eat (Cooper & Warren, 2011; Johnson & Birch, 1994), impulsivity (Churchill, Jessop, & Sparks, 2008), or over-responsiveness to tempting foods, especially high fat "comfort foods" (Hofmann et al., 2010; Troisi & Gabriel, 2011). Many people tend to eat more when under stress, a reaction that may be especially extreme among those who become obese (Dallman et al., 2003; Friedman & Brownell, 1995).

For most people, especially for people who are obese, it's a lot easier to gain weight than to lose it and keep it off (Jain, 2005; McTigue et al., 2003). The problem arises partly because our evolutionary ancestors—like nonhuman animals in the wild today—could not always be sure that food would be available. Those who survived lean times were the ones whose genes created tendencies to build and maintain fat reserves (e.g., Hara et al., 2000; Wells, 2009). These "thrifty genes" are adaptive in famine-plagued environments, but they can be harmful and even deadly in affluent societies in which overeating is unnecessary and in which doughnut shops and fast food restaurants are on every corner (DiLeone, 2009). Further, if people starve themselves to lose weight, their bodies may burn calories more slowly. This drop in metabolism saves energy and fat reserves and slows weight loss (Leibel, Rosenbaum, & Hirsch, 1995). Restricted eating also enhances activation of the brain's "pleasure centers" when a hungry person even looks at energy-rich foods (Siep et al., 2009), thus making restraint that much more difficult. It is no wonder, then, that health and nutrition experts warn that obese people (and others) should not try to lose a great deal of weight quickly by dramatically cutting food intake (Carels et al., 2008).

Researchers are constantly looking for safe and effective medications for the treatment of obesity (Cheung, 2011; Gray et al., 2012; Park, Lee, & Daily, 2011; Powell, Apovian, & Aronne, 2011). The drugs available today are designed to either suppress appetite or increase fat burning (Fernstrom & Choi, 2008; Gilbert et al., 2012; Kolonin et al., 2004; Loftus et al., 2000; Smith et al., 2010; Thomas et al., 2011; Witkamp, 2011), and millions of people are already taking them (Neovius & Narbro, 2008). An even more

Unhappy Meals

A report from the Feeding Infants and Toddlers Study found that toddlers in the United States prefer French fries to any other vegetable, that one in five babies eats candy every day, and that 44 percent of babies consume sugary drinks (Fox et al., 2004). Children's preference for high-fat fast food is so well learned that when children in one experiment were given identical foods wrapped either in plain paper or in paper bearing the logo of a popular fast food restaurant, they rated the restaurant-branded food as tasting better (Robinson et al., 2009). Changing these habits and preferences will not be easy, but the need to do so is obvious and urgent. Take a look at the nutrition information on packages of your favorite foods. If the fat and sugar content seems excessive, make a list of some alternative choices that might make your eating habits healthier.

LEARN by DOING

anorexia nervosa An eating disorder characterized by self-starvation and dramatic weight loss.

radical approach to the problem of obesity is *bariatric surgery* (Ben-David & Rossidis, 2011; Eldar et al., 2011; Moldovan & David, 2011; Vetter, Dumon, & Williams, 2011), which restructures the stomach and intestines so that less food energy is absorbed and stored (Hamad, 2004; Vetter et al., 2009). Bariatric surgery is being performed on about 100,000 people a year in the United States (Santry, Gillen, & Lauderdale, 2005), and it is becoming increasingly popular, both in the United States and around the world (Burns et al., 2010; Jen et al., 2010; Nguyen et al., 2011; Sarwer & Dilks, 2012; Silberhumer et al., 2011). Still, due to its costs and risks—postoperative mortality rates range from 0.1 to 2 percent (Morino et al., 2007; Skroubis et al., 2011; Steele et al., 2011)—bariatric surgery is recommended only for extreme and life-threatening cases of obesity. Its long-term effects are not yet fully understood (Maciejewski et al., 2011; Sjöström et al., 2012).

Though they might seem to offer relatively quick and easy options, neither medication nor surgery alone is likely to solve the problem of obesity. In fact, no single anti-obesity treatment is likely to be a safe, effective solution that works for everyone. To achieve the kind of gradual weight loss that is most likely to last, obese people are advised to make lifestyle changes in addition to (or instead of) seeking medical solutions. These changes can be as simple as limiting the number of available foods, eating from smaller plates, buying lower fat foods in smaller packages, and fasting one day a week (Levitsky, Iyer, & Pacanowski, 2012; Levitsky & Pacanowski, 2011; Wansink, 2010). The most effective weight-loss programs include components designed to reduce food intake, change eating habits and attitudes toward food, and increase energy expenditure through regular exercise (Bell et al., 2011; Shamah et al., 2012; Stice & Shaw, 2004; Wadden et al., 2001). Exercise is especially important because it burns calories while raising metabolism instead of lowering it, as reducing food intake alone does (Binzen, Swan, & Manore, 2001; Curioni & Lourenço, 2005; Wadden et al., 2005). Some people pursue these programs individually, others work in groups, and still others enroll in medical weight loss treatments carried out under the supervision of specialists known as bariatric physicians (Wadden et al., 2001, 2009).

Of course, the ultimate remedy for the obesity epidemic is prevention, which will require convincing parents and other caregivers to promote exercise and healthy eating habits in their children from an early age (De Craemer et al., 2012; Kuhl, Clifford, & Stark, 2012; Lent et al., 2012; Summerbell et al., 2012).

Anorexia Nervosa   In stark contrast to the problem of obesity is the eating disorder known as **anorexia nervosa**. It is characterized by some combination of self-starvation, self-induced vomiting, excessive exercise, and laxative use that results in weight loss to below 85 percent of normal (Kaye et al., 2000). Anorexia affects about 0.5 to 1 percent of young people in the United States, and it is a significant problem in many other industrialized nations as well (Currin, 2005; Hoek, 2006; Hudson et al., 2007). About 95 percent of those who suffer from anorexia are young females. People with anorexia often feel hungry, and many are obsessed with food and its preparation yet they refuse to eat. Anorexic self-starvation causes serious, often irreversible, physical damage, including reduction in bone density that increases the risk of fractures (Grinspoon et al., 2000). The health dangers may be especially high in anorexic dancers, gymnasts, and other female athletes, who are at risk for stress fractures and heart problems (Davis & Kapstein, 2006; Sherman & Thompson, 2004; Van Durme, Goossens, & Braet, 2012). It is estimated that from 4 to 30 percent of those suffering severe anorexia eventually die of starvation, biochemical imbalances, or suicide; their death rate is twelve times higher than the death rate for other young women (Arcelus et al., 2011; Crow et al., 2009; Millar et al., 2005; National Association of Anorexia Nervosa and Associated Disorders, 2002).

The appearance of anorexia has been attributed to a combination of factors, including genetic predispositions, hormonal and other biochemical imbalances, social influences, and psychological characteristics (Bulik et al., 2006; Jacobi et al., 2004; Klump et al., 2009; Procopio & Marriott, 2007; Ribases et al., 2005; Terracciano et al., 2009; Treat & Viken, 2010; Vink et al., 2001; Wasylkiw, MacKinnon, MacLellan, 2012). Psychological factors that may contribute to the problem include a self-punishing, perfectionistic personality and a culturally reinforced obsession with thinness and attractiveness (American Psychological

© the food passionates/Corbis

© Jack Guez/AFP/Getty Images

Thin Is In

In Western cultures today, thinness is a much-sought-after ideal, especially among young women. This ideal is seen in fashion models as well as in Miss America pageant winners, whose body mass index has decreased from the "normal" range of 20 to 25 in the 1920s to an "undernourished" 18.5 in recent years (Rubinstein & Caballero, 2000; Voracek & Fisher, 2002). In the United States, 35 percent of normal-weight girls—and 12 percent of underweight girls!—begin dieting when they are as young as nine or ten. Correlational studies suggest that the efforts of many of these children to lose weight may have come in response to criticism from family members (Barr Taylor et al., 2006a; Schreiber et al., 1996); for some the result is anorexia. To combat the problem, some fashion shows have established a minimum BMI for all models and Israel bans the use of underweight models in advertising (New Israeli Law, 2012).

bulimia An eating disorder that involves eating massive quantities of food, then eliminating it by self-induced vomiting or laxatives.

Association Task Force on the Sexualization of Girls, 2007; Cooley et al., 2008; Dittmar, Halliwell, & Ive, 2006; Dohnt & Tiggermann, 2006; Grabe, Ward, & Hyde, 2008; Juarascio et al., 2011; Klaczynski, Daniel, & Keller, 2009; Steinglass et al., 2012; Treat & Viken, 2010; Wilksch & Wade, 2010). People with anorexia appear to develop a fear of being fat, which they take to dangerous extremes (de Castro & Goldstein, 1995). Many continue to view themselves as fat or misshapen even as they are wasting away.

Drugs, hospitalization, and psychotherapy are all used to treat anorexia (Herpertz et al., 2011). In many cases, treatment brings recovery and the maintenance of normal weight (Brewerton & Costin, 2011a,b; Carter et al., 2011; Goldstein et al., 2011; Lock, 2011; Steinglass et al., 2012), but more effective treatment and early intervention methods are still needed. Prevention programs now being tested with college women and preteen girls at high risk for developing anorexia are showing promising results (e.g., Barr Taylor et al., 2006b; Black Becker et al., 2008; Halliwell, Easun, & Harcourt, 2011).

Bulimia   Like anorexia, the eating disorder called bulimia (pronounced "bu-LEE-mee-uh") involves an intense fear of being fat, but the person may be thin, normal in weight, or even overweight. **Bulimia** (also referred to as *bulimia nervosa*) involves eating huge amounts of food (say, several boxes of cookies, a half-gallon of ice cream, and a bucket of fried chicken) and then getting rid of the food through self-induced vomiting or strong laxatives. These "binge-purge" episodes may occur as often as twice a day (Weltzin et al., 1995).

Bulimia shares many features with anorexia (Fairburn et al., 2008). For instance, most bulimics are female, and like anorexia, bulimia usually begins with a desire to be slender. However, bulimia and anorexia are quite different disorders (Eddy et al., 2008). For one thing, most people with bulimia see their eating habits as problematic, whereas most people with anorexia do not. In addition, bulimia is usually not life threatening (Thompson, 1996). It has consequences, however, that include dehydration, nutritional problems, and intestinal damage (Abraham & Kellow, 2011; Cremonini et al., 2009; Li et al., 2011; Mehler, 2011). Many people with bulimia develop dental problems from the acids associated with vomiting (Chi et al., 2010; Schlueter et al., 2012). Frequent vomiting and the insertion of objects to cause it can also damage the throat.

Estimates of the prevalence of bulimia in the United States range from 1 to 3 percent of adolescent and college-age women (National Institutes of Health, 2001; Swanson et al., 2011; U.S. Surgeon General, 1999); a figure that has remained relatively stable since the early 1990s (Crowther et al., 2008). The combination of factors that contribute to bulimia includes perfectionism, high achievement orientation, low self-esteem, stress, a culturally encouraged preoccupation with being thin, and depression and other emotional problems (de Souza, Mussap, & Cummins, 2010). Problems in the brain's satiety mechanisms may also be involved (Crowther et al., 2001; Smith et al., 2007; Steiger et al., 2001; Stice, 2001; Stice & Fairburn, 2003; Stice, Marti, & Durant, 2011; Zalta & Keel, 2006). Treatment for bulimia, which typically includes individual or group psychotherapy and sometimes antidepressant drugs, can help most people with bulimia eat more normally (Brewerton & Costin, 2011a, b; Herpertz et al., 2011; Mitka, 2011; Steinhausen & Weber, 2009; Trunco et al., 2011; Zeeck et al., 2011).

For a summary of the processes involved in hunger and eating, see "In Review: Major Factors Controlling Hunger and Eating."

Sexual Behavior

How often does the average person have sex?

Unlike food, sex is not necessary for an individual's survival, but it is obviously vital for improving the chances that an individual's genes will be represented in the next generation. The various factors that shape sexual motivation and behavior differ in strength across species. These factors can include physiology, evolutionary forces, learned behavior, and physical and social environments. For example, one species of desert bird

Major Factors Controlling Hunger and Eating   IN REVIEW

Theory	Stimulate Eating	Inhibit Eating
Biological factors	Hormones released into the bloodstream provide signals that stimulate eating. Signals in the blood such as ghrelin and glucose affect neurons in the hypothalamus and stimulate eating, including hungers for specific kinds of foods, such as fats and carbohydrates. The lateral nucleus of the hypothalamus may be a "hunger center" that monitors these hormonal signals in the blood.	Hormones released into the bloodstream provide signals that inhibit eating. Signals in the blood such as leptin and insulin affect neurons in the hypothalamus and inhibit eating. The ventromedial nucleus of the hypothalamus may be a "satiety center" that monitors these hormonal signals in the blood.
Nonbiological factors	Sights and smells of particular foods elicit eating because of prior associations. Family customs and social occasions often include norms for eating in particular ways.	Values in contemporary U.S. society encourage thinness and thus can inhibit eating.

IN REVIEW QUESTIONS

1. People may eat when they are "full," suggesting that eating is not controlled by ___ alone.

2. People with an eating disorder called ___ know that they have a problem; those with a disorder called ___ tend not to.

3. The best strategy for lasting weight loss includes regular ___ as well as improved eating habits.

requires adequate sex hormones, a suitable mate, and a particular environment before it engages in sexual behavior. As long as the dry season lasts, it shows no interest in sex, but within ten minutes of the first rainfall, the birds vigorously court and copulate.

Rainfall is obviously much less influential as a sexual trigger for humans. In fact, people show an amazing diversity of *sexual scripts,* the step-by-step sequences of thoughts and events that lead to sexual behavior (Simon & Gagnon, 1986). Surveys of college-age men and women have identified 122 specific acts, 34 different tactics, and 237 stated reasons surrounding their efforts to have sex (Greer & Buss, 1994; Meston & Buss, 2007). What actually happens during sex? The matter is exceedingly difficult to address scientifically, partly because most people are reluctant to allow researchers to observe their sexual behavior. Many won't even answer questions about their sexual practices. Yet having valid information about the nature of human sexual behavior is a vital first step for psychologists and other scientists who study such topics as individual differences in sexuality, gender differences in sexual motivation and behavior, sources of sexual orientation, disturbances of sexual functioning, and pathways through which AIDS and other sexually transmitted diseases reach new victims. This information can also help people think about their own sexual behavior in relation to trends in the general population.

FOCUS ON RESEARCH

Tell Me About Your Sex Life

The first extensive studies of sexual behavior in the United States were completed in the 1950s and 1960s by Alfred Kinsey (Kinsey, Pomeroy, & Martin, 1948; Kinsey et al., 1953) and William Masters and Virginia Johnson (1966). In the Kinsey studies, volunteers answered questions about their sexual practices, whereas Masters and Johnson actually recorded volunteers' **sexual arousal,** their physiological responses during natural or artificial sexual stimulation in a laboratory. Together, these pioneering studies broke new ground in the exploration of human sexuality. However, the people who volunteered for them were probably not a representative sample of the adult population. So the results and the conclusions drawn from them might not apply to people in general. Further, the data are now so old that they may not reflect sexual practices today. Unfortunately, the results of more recent surveys, such as reader polls in *Cosmopolitan* and other magazines, are also flawed because the samples they use are not representative (Davis & Smith, 1990).

sexual arousal Physiological arousal that arises from sexual contact or erotic thoughts.

What was the researchers' question?

Is it possible to gather data about sexual behavior that are more representative and therefore more applicable to people in general? A team of researchers at the University of Chicago believe it is, so they undertook the National Health and Social Life Survey, the first extensive survey of sexual behavior in the United States since the Kinsey studies (Laumann et al., 1994).

How did the researchers answer the question?

This survey included important design features that had been neglected in most other surveys of sexual behavior. First, the study did not depend on self-selected volunteers. The researchers sought out a particular sample of 3,432 people who ranged in age from 18 to 59. Second, the sample was carefully constructed so as to reflect the sociocultural diversity of the U.S. population in terms of gender, ethnicity, socioeconomic status, geographical location, and the like. Third, unlike previous surveys that had relied on mail-in responses from participants, the Chicago study was based on face-to-face interviews. This approach made it easier to ensure that the participants understood each question and allowed them to explain their responses. To encourage honesty, the researchers let participants answer some of the survey's questions anonymously by placing written responses in a sealed envelope.

What did the researchers find?

For one thing, the researchers found that people in the United States have sex less often and with fewer partners than many had assumed. For most, sex occurs about once a week and almost always with the partner with whom they share a stable relationship. About a third of the participants reported having had sex only a few times (or not at all) in the preceding year. And, in contrast to various celebrities' splashy tales of dozens, even hundreds, of sexual partners per year, the average male survey participant had had only six sexual partners in his entire life. The average female respondent reported a lifetime total of two. Further, the survey data suggested that people in committed, one-partner relationships had the most frequent and the most satisfying sex. And although a wide variety of specific sexual practices were reported, the overwhelming majority of heterosexual couples said that they tend to engage mainly in penis-vagina intercourse. Many of these findings are consistent with the results of more recent surveys conducted by other researchers (e.g., National Center for Health Statistics, 2007).

What do the results mean?

The Chicago survey challenges some of the cultural and media images of sexuality in the United States. In particular, it suggests that people in the United States may be more sexually conservative than one might think on the basis of magazine reader polls and the testimony of guests on daytime talk shows.

What do we still need to know?

Many questions remain. The Chicago survey did not ask about some of the more controversial aspects of sexuality, such as the effects of pornography or the role in sexual activity of sexual fetishes such as shoes or other clothing. Had the researchers asked about such topics, their results might have painted a different picture. Further, because the Chicago survey focused on people in the United States, it told us little or nothing about the sexual practices, traditions, and values of people in the rest of the world.

The Chicago team has continued to conduct interviews and the results are beginning to fill in the picture about sexual behavior in the United States and around the world (Youm & Laumann, 2002). They have found, for example, that nearly one-quarter of U.S. women prefer to achieve sexual satisfaction without partners of either sex. And although people in the United States tend to engage in a wider variety of sexual behaviors than do those in Britain, people in the United States appear to be less tolerant of disapproved sexual practices (Laumann & Michael, 2000; Michael et al., 1998). They have found, too, that although sexual activity declines with advancing age, it by no means disappears. Between 26 and 33 percent of people in the 75 to 95 age group—especially men—reported that they were still sexually active (Hyde et al., 2010; Lindau & Gavrilova, 2010; Lindau et al., 2007).

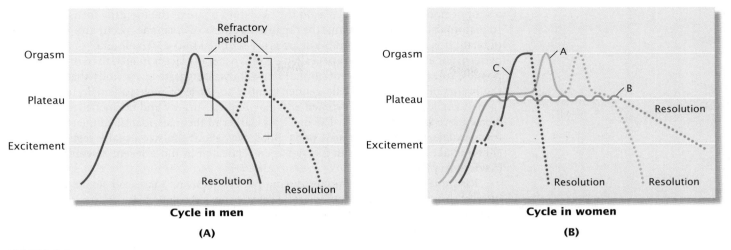

FIGURE 8.2
The Sexual Response Cycle
Masters and Johnson (1966) found that men show one primary pattern of sexual response, depicted in Part A, and that women display at least three different patterns from time to time—labeled A, B, and C in Part B.

Other researchers have found a number of consistent gender differences in sexuality (Basson, 2001; Schmitt et al., 2012). For example, men are more likely than women to mistake another person's friendliness for sexual interest (Perilloux, Easton, & Buss, 2012). This may be because men tend to have a stronger interest in and desire for sex than women, whereas women are more likely than men to associate sexual activity with love and to be affected by cultural and situational influences on sexual attitudes and behavior (Basson, 2001, 2002, 2003; Baumeister & Stillman, 2006; Diamond, 2008; Peplau, 2003; Petersen & Hyde, 2010). Some researchers point out, though, that many of these differences are actually quite small and not necessarily significant (Conley et al., 2011).

The results of even the best survey methods—like those of the best of all other research methods—usually raise as many questions as they answer. When do people become interested in sex, and why? How do they choose to express these desires, and why? What determines their sexual likes and dislikes? How do learning and sociocultural factors modify the biological forces that seem to provide the raw material of human sexual motivation? These are some of the questions about human sexual behavior that a survey cannot easily or accurately explore (Benson, 2003).   ● ● ● ●

The Biology of Sex

Observations in Masters and Johnson's laboratory led to important findings about the **sexual response cycle,** the pattern of physiological arousal before, during, and after sexual activity (see Figure 8.2). Masters and Johnson (1966) found that men show one primary pattern of sexual response and that women display at least three different patterns from time to time. In both men and women, the first, or *excitement,* phase begins with sexually stimulating input from the environment or from one's own thoughts. Further stimulation leads to intensified excitement in the second, or *plateau,* phase. If stimulation continues, the person reaches the third, or *orgasmic,* stage. Although orgasm lasts only a few seconds, it provides an intensely pleasurable release of physical and psychological tension. The *resolution* phase follows, during which the person returns to a state of relaxation. At this point, men enter a *refractory period,* during which they are temporarily unable to be aroused. Women are capable of immediately repeating the cycle if stimulation continues.

People's motivation to engage in sexual activity has biological roots in **sex hormones.** The female sex hormones are **estrogens** and **progestational hormones** (also called **progestins**); the main ones are *estradiol* and *progesterone.* The male hormones are **androgens;** the principal example is *testosterone.* Each sex hormone flows in the blood of both sexes, but males have relatively more androgens and women have relatively more estrogens and progestins.

Sex hormones have both *organizing* and *activating* effects on the brain. The organizing effects are permanent changes in the brain that influence the brain's response to hormones. The activating effects are temporary behavioral changes that last only as long as the level of

sexual response cycle The pattern of arousal before, during, and after sexual activity.

sex hormones Chemicals in the blood that organize and motivate sexual behavior.

estrogens Feminine hormones that circulate in the bloodstream.

progestational hormones (progestins) Feminine hormones that circulate in the bloodstream.

androgens Masculine hormones that circulate in the bloodstream.

a sex hormone is elevated, such as in the ovulation phase of the monthly menstrual cycle. In mammals, including humans, the organizing effects of hormones occur around the time of birth. It is then that certain brain areas are sculpted into a "female-like" or "male-like" pattern. For example, a brain area called *BnST* is generally larger in men than in women. Its possible role in some aspects of human sexuality was suggested by a study that compared the brains of men with a male gender identity to those of male-to-female transsexuals (genetic males who feel like women and may request surgery and hormone treatments to create more feminine bodies). The BnST was larger in the male-identified men than in the transsexuals. In fact, the transsexuals' BnST was about the size usually seen in women (Zhou et al., 1995). This result has not been replicated in more recent research, however (Savic & Aryer, 2011).

Rising levels of sex hormones during puberty activate increased sexual desire and interest in sexual behavior. Generally, estrogens stimulate females' sexual interest, especially their interest in more masculine-looking men, and increase the accuracy of their judgments of men's sexual orientation (Burleson, Gregory, & Trevarthen, 1995; Durante et al., 2012; Roney & Simmons, 2008; Rule et al., 2011). Androgens raise males' sexual interest (Davidson, Camargo, & Smith, 1979), but they may also do so in females (Sherwin & Gelfand, 1987). The activating effects of hormones are also seen in reduced sexual motivation and behavior among people whose hormone-secreting ovaries or testes have been removed for medical reasons. Injections of hormones help restore these people's sexual interest and activity (Sherwin, Gelfand, & Brender, 1985).

Generally, hormones affect sexual desire, not the physical ability to have sex (Wallen & Lovejoy, 1993). This fact may explain why castration (removal of the testes) does not prevent sex crimes by male offenders. Men with low testosterone levels due to medical problems or castration show less sexual desire, but they still have erections in response to erotic stimuli (Kwan et al., 1983). So a sex offender treated by chemical or physical castration would be less likely to seek out sex, but he would still respond as before to his favorite sexual stimuli (Wickham, 2001).

Social and Cultural Factors in Sexuality

Human sexuality is shaped not only by hormones but also by a lifetime of learning and thinking. For example, children learn some of their sexual attitudes and behaviors as part of the development of *gender roles,* as described in the human development chapter. The specific attitudes and behaviors they learn depend partly on the nature of gender roles in their culture (Baumeister, 2000; Hyde & Durik, 2000; Peplau, 2003; Petersen & Hyde, 2010).

There are also differences in what women and men find sexually arousing. For example, in many cultures, men are far more interested in and responsive to erotic visual images than women are (Herz & Cahill, 1997; Petersen & Hyde, 2010; Symons, 1979). A biological basis for this difference was investigated in a study that scanned the brain activity of males and females while they looked at erotic photographs (Hamann et al., 2004). As expected, the men showed greater activity in the amygdala and hypothalamus than the women did. But even though there were gender differences in brain activity, the male and female participants rated the photos as equally attractive and sexually arousing. In another study, when men reported sexual arousal in response to erotic films, they showed signs of physiological arousal, too. For women, self-reports of sexual arousal were not strongly correlated with signs of physiological arousal (Chivers et al., 2004). Further, though men and women both show more sexual arousal to more intensely erotic films, the level of women's arousal may not depend as much as men's does on whether the actors are males or females (Chivers, Seto, & Blanchard, 2007). A third study found that women were aroused by a wider range of sexual stories than men were (Suschinsky & Lalumière, 2011).

These are just a few examples of the fact that sexuality is a product of a complex mixture of factors. Each person's learning history, cultural background, and perceptions of the world interact so deeply with such a wide range of physiological processes that—as in many other aspects of human behavior and mental processes—it is impossible to separate their influence on sexuality. Nowhere is this point clearer than in the case of sexual orientation.

Sexual Orientation

Sexual orientation refers to the nature of a person's enduring emotional, romantic, or sexual attraction to others (American Psychological Association, 2002a; Ellis & Mitchell, 2000). The most common sexual orientation is **heterosexuality,** in which the attraction is to members of the opposite sex. When attraction focuses on members of one's own sex, the orientation is called **homosexuality,** more specifically, gay (for men) and lesbian (for women). **Bisexuality** refers to the orientation of people who are attracted to members of both sexes. Sexual orientation involves feelings that may or may not be translated into corresponding patterns of sexual behavior (Pathela et al., 2006). For example, some people whose orientation is gay, lesbian, or bisexual may have sex only with opposite-sex partners. Similarly, people whose orientation is heterosexuality may have had one or more same-sex encounters.

Gays, lesbians, and bisexuals are often the victims of discrimination and even hate crimes, so many of them are reluctant to let their sexual orientation be known (Hightow-Weidman et al., 2011; Lau & Stotzer, 2011; Meyer, 2003; Mishna et al., 2009; Poteat, O'Dwyer, & Mereish; 2011). It is difficult, therefore, to obtain an accurate picture of the mix of heterosexual, gay, lesbian, and bisexual orientations in a population. In the Chicago sex survey mentioned earlier, 1.4 percent of women and 2.8 percent of men identified themselves as exclusively gay or lesbian (Laumann et al., 1994). These figures are much lower than the 10 percent found earlier in Kinsey's studies. However, the Chicago survey's face-to-face interviews did not allow respondents to give anonymous answers to questions about sexual orientation. Some researchers suggest that if anonymous responses to those questions had been permitted, the prevalence figures for gay, lesbian, and bisexual orientations would have been higher (Bullough, 1995). In fact, studies that have allowed anonymous responding estimate that gay, lesbian, and bisexual people make up between 2 and 21 percent of the population in the United States, Canada, and Western Europe (Aaron et al., 2003; Bagley & Tremblay, 1998; Binson et al., 1995; Hayes et al., 2012; Savin-Williams, 2006; Sell, Wells, & Wypij, 1995).

THINKING CRITICALLY

What Shapes Sexual Orientation?

The question of where sexual orientation comes from is a topic of intense debate in scientific circles, on talk shows, in Internet chat rooms, and in everyday conversations.

What am I being asked to believe or accept?

Some people believe that genes exert a major influence on our sexual orientation. According to this view, we do not learn or choose a sexual orientation but rather are born with a strong predisposition to develop a particular orientation.

Is evidence available to support the claim?

In 1995, a report by a respected research group suggested that one kind of sexual orientation—namely, that of gay men—is associated with a particular gene on the X chromosome (Hu et al., 1995). This finding was not supported by later studies (Rice et al., 1999), but a growing body of evidence from research in behavioral genetics suggests that genes might indeed influence sexual orientation in humans (Kendler et al., 2000; Pillard & Bailey, 1998). One study examined pairs of monozygotic male twins (whose genes are identical), pairs of dizygotic, or nonidentical, twins (whose genes are no more alike than those of any pair of brothers), and pairs of adopted brothers (who are genetically unrelated). To participate in this study, at least one brother in each pair had to be gay. As it turned out, the other brother was also gay or bisexual in 52 percent of the identical twin pairs but in only 22 percent of the nonidentical pairs and in just 11 percent of the adoptive pairs (Bailey & Pillard, 1991). Similar findings have been reported for male identical twins raised apart. In such cases, a shared sexual orientation cannot be due to the effects of a shared environment (Whitam, Diamond, & Martin, 1993). The few available studies of female sexual orientation have yielded similar results (Bailey & Benishay, 1993; Bailey, Dunne, & Martin, 2000).

Other evidence for the role of biological factors in sexual orientation comes from research on the impact of sex hormones. In adults, differences in the levels of these

heterosexuality Sexual desire or behavior that is focused on members of the opposite sex.

homosexuality Sexual desire or behavior that is focused on members of one's own sex.

bisexuality Sexual desire or behavior that is focused on members of both sexes.

A Committed Relationship, with Children

Like heterosexual relationships, gay and lesbian relationships can be brief and stormy or stable and long lasting (Kurdek, 2005). These gay men are committed to each other for the long haul, as evidenced by their decision to adopt two children together. The strong role of biological factors in sexual orientation is seen in research showing that these children's orientation will not be influenced much, if at all, by that of their adoptive parents (Anderssen, Amlie, & Ytteroy, 2002; Patterson, 2004, 2009; Pennington & Knight, 2011; Stacey & Biblarz, 2001; Tasker & Golombok, 1995).

hormones are not generally associated with differences in sexual orientation. However, hormonal differences during prenatal development might be involved in the shaping of sexual orientation (Lalumière, Blanchard, & Zucker, 2000; Lippa, 2003; Williams et al., 2000), and the influences may differ for men and for women (Mustanski et al., 2002). For example, one study found that women—but not men—who had been exposed to high levels of androgens during their fetal development were much more likely to report bisexual or homosexual behaviors or fantasies than were their relatives of the same sex who had not been exposed (Hines, Brook, & Conway, 2004; Meyer-Bahlburg et al., 2008).

Another line of research focuses on the possibility that previous pregnancies might permanently affect a woman's hormones in ways that influence the sexual orientation of her next child (Blanchard, 2001). Some evidence for this hypothesis comes from a study showing that the more older biological brothers a man has, the higher is the probability he will have a homosexual orientation (Blanchard & Lippa, 2007; Bogaert, Blanchard, & Crosthwait, 2007). These results appear to reflect mainly hormonal rather than mainly environmental influences, because the number of *nonbiological* (adopted) brothers that the men had was not predictive of their sexual orientation. Further, because sexual orientation in women appeared not to be predicted by the number and gender of their older biological siblings, it was at first thought that the hormonal consequences of carrying male fetuses might only influence males' sexual orientation. The picture is not that simple, though. Other researchers have found that women's sexual orientation, too, is related to the number of older biological brothers they have (McConaghy et al., 2006), and still others have reported a relationship between men's sexual orientation and the number of older biological sisters they have (Francis, 2008; Vasey & VanderLaan, 2007). We don't yet know exactly how prenatal hormonal influences might operate to affect sexual orientation, but studies of nonhuman animals have found that such influences alter the structure of the hypothalamus, a brain region known to underlie some aspects of sexual functioning (Swaab & Hofman, 1995).

Finally, a biological basis for sexual orientation is suggested by the fact that sexual orientation is not predicted by environmental factors. For example, the sexual orientation of children's caregivers has little or no effect on those children's own orientation. Several studies have shown that children adopted by homosexual parents are no more or less likely to display a homosexual orientation than are children raised by heterosexual parents (Anderssen, Amlie, & Ytteroy, 2002; Bailey et al., 1995; Tasker & Golombok, 1995).

Can that evidence be interpreted another way?

Like all correlational data, correlations between genetics and sexual orientation are open to alternative interpretations. As discussed in the introductory chapter, a correlation describes the strength and direction of the relationship between two variables, but it does not guarantee that one variable actually influences the other. Consider again the data showing that the brothers who shared the most genes (identical twins) were also most likely to share a gay orientation. What they shared was probably not a "gay gene" but rather a set of genes that influenced the boys' activity levels, emotionality, aggressiveness, and the like. One example is gender conformity/nonconformity in childhood, the tendency for children to either conform or not conform to the behaviors, interests, and appearance that are typical for their gender in their culture (Bailey, Dunne, & Martin, 2000; Knafo, Iervolino, & Plomin, 2005). Such general aspects of their temperaments or personalities in childhood—and other people's reactions to them—could influence the emergence in later life of a particular sexual orientation (Bem, 2000). In other words, sexual orientation could arise as a reaction to the way people respond to a genetically determined but nonsexual aspect of personality. The influence of prenatal hormone levels could also influence sexual orientation by shaping aggressiveness or other nonsexual aspects of behavior.

It is also important to look at behavioral genetics evidence for what it can tell us about the role of *environmental* factors in sexual orientation. When we read a study showing that 52 percent of the time, both members of identical-twin pairs have a gay, lesbian, or bisexual orientation, it is easy to ignore the fact that the sexual orientation of the twin pair members *differed* in 48 percent of the cases. Viewed in this way, the results suggest that genes do not tell the entire story of sexual orientation. In other words, it is not determined by unlearned, genetic forces alone. As described in the chapter on biology and behavior, the brains and bodies we inherit are quite responsive to environmental influences. In fact, the behaviors we engage in and the experiences we have often result in physical changes in the brain and elsewhere (Wang et al., 1995). For example, physical changes occur in the brain's synapses as we form new memories. So differences seen in the brains of adults with differing sexual orientations could be the effect, not the cause, of their behavior or experiences.

What evidence would help to evaluate the alternatives?

Much more evidence is needed regarding the role of genes in shaping sexual orientation. We also have a lot to learn about the extent to which genes and hormones shape physical and psychological characteristics that lead to various sexual orientations. In studying these topics, researchers will want to learn more about the genetic makeup, mental style, and behavioral characteristics of people with different sexual orientations. Are there personality characteristics associated with particular sexual orientations? If so, do those characteristics have a strong genetic component? To what extent are heterosexuals, gays, lesbians, and bisexuals similar—and different—in terms of biases, coping skills, developmental histories, and the like (Bailey, Dunne, & Martin, 2000)? The more we learn about sexual orientation in general, the easier it will be to interpret data relating to its origins.

Yet even classifying sexual orientation is not simple, because people do not always fall into sharply defined categories (Savin-Williams, 2006; Thompson & Morgan, 2008; Worthington, et al., 2008). Should a man who identifies himself as gay be considered bisexual because he occasionally has heterosexual daydreams? What sexual orientation label would be appropriate for a 40-year-old woman who experienced a few lesbian encounters in her teens but has engaged in exclusively heterosexual sex since then? Progress in understanding the origins of sexual orientation would be enhanced by a generally accepted system for describing and defining all facets of exactly what is meant by the term *sexual orientation* (Klein, 1990; Stein, 1999).

What conclusions are most reasonable?

The evidence available so far suggests that genetic factors, probably operating via prenatal hormones, create differences in the brains of people with different sexual orientations. However, the manner in which a person expresses a genetically influenced sexual orientation will be profoundly shaped by what that person learns through social and cultural experiences (Bancroft, 1994). In short, as is true of other psychological phenomena, sexual orientation reflects the complex interplay of both genetic and nongenetic mechanisms—of both nature and nurture.   ● ● ● ●

Achievement Motivation

Why do some people try harder than others to succeed?

The next time you visit someone's home or office, notice the mementos displayed there. Perhaps there are framed diplomas and awards, trophies and ribbons, and photos of children and grandchildren. These badges of achievement affirm that a person has accomplished tasks that merit approval or establish worth. Much of human behavior is motivated by a desire for approval, admiration, and a sense of achievement—in short, for esteem—from others and from within. In this section, we examine two of the most common avenues to esteem: achievement in general and achievement in one's work.

Need for Achievement

achievement motivation (need for achievement) The degree to which a person establishes specific goals, cares about meeting them, and experiences satisfaction by doing so.

Many athletes who already hold world records still train intensely; many people who have built multimillion-dollar businesses still work fourteen-hour days. What motivates these people? One answer is **achievement motivation** (also called the **need for achievement**)— the desire to do well in relation to some standard of excellence (McClelland et al., 1953;

FIGURE 8.3

Assessing Achievement Motivation

This picture is similar to those included in the Thematic Apperception Test, or TAT (Morgan & Murray, 1935). The strength of people's achievement motivation is inferred from the stories they tell about TAT pictures. A response like "The boy is thinking about playing his violin in concert at Carnegie Hall," would be seen as reflecting high achievement motivation.

Murray, 1938). People with high achievement motivation seek to master tasks—such as sports, business ventures, occupational skills, intellectual puzzles, or artistic creation—and feel intense satisfaction from doing so. They work hard at striving for excellence, enjoy themselves in the process, and take great pride in achieving at a high level. For individuals with low achievement motivation, standards of excellence tend to create avoidance as well as anxiety, worry, and the anticipation of shame (Bjornebekk, Gjesme, & Ulriksen, 2011).

Individual Differences How do people with strong achievement motivation differ from others? To find out, researchers gave children a test to measure their need for achievement (Figure 8.3 shows a test for adults) and then asked them to play a ring-toss game. Most of the children who scored low on the need-for-achievement test stood either so close to the ring-toss target that they couldn't fail or so far away that they could not succeed. In contrast, children scoring high on the need-for-achievement test stood at a moderate distance from the target, making the game challenging but not impossible (McClelland, 1958).

Experiments with adults and children suggest that people with high achievement needs tend to set challenging but realistic goals. They actively seek success, take risks when necessary, can wait for rewards, and are intensely satisfied when they do well (Mayer & Sutton, 1996). Yet if they feel they have tried their best, people with high achievement motivation are not too upset by failure. Those with low achievement motivation also like to succeed, but instead of joy, success tends to bring them relief at having avoided failure (Winter, 1996). Indeed, there is some evidence that the differing emotions—such as anticipation versus worry—that accompany the efforts of people with high and low achievement motivation can affect how successful those efforts will be (Pekrun et al., 2009).

Differences in achievement motivation also appear in the kinds of goals people seek in achievement-related situations (Corker & Donnellan, 2012; Molden & Dweck, 2000; Morisano et al., 2010). Some tend to adopt *learning goals*, which are focused on developing competence (Dweck, 1999; Pintrich, 2003). When these people play golf, take piano lessons, work on puzzles or problems, go to school, and engage in other achievement-oriented activities, they do so mainly to get better at those activities (Spinath & Steinmayr, 2012). They realize that they may not yet have the skills necessary to achieve at a high level, so they tend to learn by watching others and to struggle with problems on their own rather than immediately asking for help (Mayer & Sutton, 1996). They will seek help if they feel they really need it, but people with learning goals are likely to ask for explanations, hints, and other forms of task-related information, not for quick, easy answers that remove the challenge from the situation (Roussel, Elliot, & Feltman, 2011). In contrast, people who adopt *performance goals* are usually more concerned with demonstrating to others the competence they believe they already possess. They tend to seek information about how well they have performed compared with others rather than about how to improve their performance (Butler, 1998). When they seek help, it is usually to ask for the "right answer" rather than for tips on how to find the answer themselves. Because their primary goal is to display competence, people with performance goals tend to avoid new challenges if they are not confident that they will be successful, and they tend to quit in response to failure (Grant & Dweck, 2003; Weiner, 1980). Those with learning goals tend to be more persistent and less upset when they don't immediately perform well (Niiya, Crocker, & Bartmess, 2004).

Development of Achievement Motivation Achievement motivation develops in early childhood under the influence of both genetic and environmental factors. As described in the personality chapter, children inherit general behavioral tendencies, such as impulsiveness and emotionality, and these tendencies may support or undermine the development of achievement motivation. The motivation to achieve is also shaped by what children learn from watching and listening to others, especially their parents and teachers (Hughes et al., 2012; Kim, Schaller, & Kim, 2010). Evidence for the influence of parental teachings about achievement comes from a study in which young boys were given a task so difficult that they were sure to fail. Fathers whose sons scored low on achievement motivation tests often became annoyed as they watched their boys work on the task, discouraged them from continuing, and interfered or even completed the task themselves (Rosen & D'Andrade, 1959). A much different response pattern emerged

Helping Them Do Their Best

Learning-oriented goals are especially appropriate in classrooms, where students typically have little knowledge of the subject matter. This is why most teachers tolerate errors and reward gradual improvement. They do not usually encourage performance goals, which emphasize doing better than others and demonstrating immediate competence (Reeve, 1996). Still, to help students do their best in the long run, teachers may also promote performance goals. The proper combination of both kinds of goals may be more motivating than either kind alone (Barron & Harackiewicz, 2001; Byron & Khazanchi, 2012).

among parents of children who scored high on tests of achievement motivation. Those parents tended to (1) encourage the child to try difficult tasks, especially new ones; (2) give praise and other rewards for success; (3) encourage the child to find ways to succeed rather than merely complaining about failure; and (4) prompt the child to go on to the next, more difficult challenge (McClelland, 1985).

The ways in which children learn to think about themselves is another important factor in achievement motivation. Those who are optimistic, confident in their abilities, expect to succeed, and think of achievement situations as challenges rather than threats are more likely to develop high achievement motivation than children who are pessimistic about their abilities, threatened by achievement situations and expect to fail (Ames & Ames, 1984; Dweck, 1999; Law, Elliot, & Murayama, 2012; Weiner, 1985).

These cognitive habits affect children's behavior in achievement situations, but the habits are themselves affected by the outcome of previous achievement efforts. Strong achievement motivation is more likely to develop in children who have experienced the pride that follows success at facing challenges and meeting standards of excellence. Achievement motivation is likely to be lower in those who have experienced embarrassment or shame following unsuccessful achievement efforts—especially if their failures have been met with ridicule (Stipek, 1983).

Cultural factors can also influence the development of achievement motivation. For example, subtle messages about a culture's view of the importance and value of achievement

Children raised in environments that support the development of strong achievement motivation tend not to give up on difficult tasks—even if all the king's horses and all the king's men do!

"Maybe they didn't try hard enough."

often appear in the books children read, the stories they hear, and the programs they see on television (Hong & Lin-Siegler, 2011). Does the story's main character work hard and overcome obstacles, thus creating expectations of a payoff for persistence? Or does a lazy main character drift aimlessly and then win the lottery, suggesting that rewards come randomly, regardless of effort? And if the main character succeeds, is it the result of personal effort, as is typical of stories in individualist cultures? Or is success based on ties to a cooperative and supportive group, as is typical of stories in collectivist cultures? These themes appear to act as blueprints for reaching one's goals. It is not surprising, then, that ideas about achievement motivation differ from culture to culture. In one study, individuals from Saudi Arabia and from the United States were asked to comment on short stories describing people succeeding at various tasks. Saudis tended to see the people in the stories as having succeeded because of the help they got from others, whereas Americans tended to attribute success to the internal characteristics of each story's main character (Zahrani & Kaplowitz, 1993).

In short, achievement motivation is strongly influenced by social and cultural learning experiences and by the beliefs about oneself that these experiences help create. People who come to believe in their ability to achieve are more likely to do so than those who expect to fail (Dweck, 1998; Greven et al., 2009; Wigfield & Eccles, 2000).

Achievement and Success in the Workplace

In the workplace, there is usually more concern with employees' motivation to work hard during business hours than with their general level of achievement motivation. In fact, employers tend to set up jobs in accordance with their ideas about how intrinsic and extrinsic motivations combine to shape employees' performance (Riggio, 1989). Employers who see workers as lazy, dishonest, and lacking in ambition tend to offer highly structured, heavily supervised jobs. They give the employees little say in deciding what to do or how to do it. These employers assume that workers are motivated mainly by extrinsic rewards—especially money or job security. So they are often surprised when some employees are dissatisfied with their jobs and show little motivation to work hard, in spite of good pay and benefits (Diener & Seligman, 2004; Igalens & Roussel, 1999).

If good pay and benefits alone don't bring job satisfaction and the desire to excel on the job, what does? In Western cultures low worker motivation appears to come largely from negative thoughts and feelings about having little or no control over the work environment (Rosen, 1991). Compared with those in highly structured jobs, workers tend to be happier, more satisfied, and more productive if they are (1) encouraged to participate in decisions about how work should be done; (2) given problems to solve, without being told how to solve them; (3) taught more than one skill; (4) given individual responsibility; and (5) given public recognition, not just money, for good performance (Fisher, 2000).

Allowing people to set and achieve clear goals is one way to increase both job performance and job satisfaction (Abramis, 1994; Locke & Latham, 2002). Goals that most effectively maintain work motivation have several features (Katzell & Thompson, 1990). First, they are personally meaningful. When a memo from a high-level administrator tells employees that their goal should be to increase production, they tend to feel unfairly burdened and not particularly motivated to meet the goal. Second, effective goals tend to be those that are challenging, but not impossible. Moderately difficult goals provide the best arena for testing one's skills and experiencing emotions such as pride and satisfaction when the goals are met (Trope, 1975, 1983). Third, goals that involve interpersonal competition tend to be effective, especially for workers with high achievement motivation. For example, some auto makers have teams of designers compete, not necessarily for money, but for the honor of having "their" new model chosen to be manufactured and sold throughout the world. Similarly, students with high achievement motivation often improve their academic performance by forming study groups whose members compete for the best grades. For such people, knowing that others are vying to achieve the same goal as they are tends to create strong intrinsic motivation, even when there are few if any extrinsic rewards at stake (Harackiewicz & Elliot, 1993; Harackiewicz, Sansone, & Manderlink, 1985). Fourth, effective goals are specific and concrete (Locke & Latham, 2002). The goal of "doing better" is usually

Goal Setting and Achievement Motivation

Clear and specific goals motivate the most persistent achievement efforts on the job and in other areas, too (Locke & Latham, 2002). These people are more likely to stick with their exercise program if they are pursuing the goal of "losing twenty pounds" or "doing aerobics three times a week" rather than the vague goal of "getting in shape." Similarly, you are more likely to keep reading this chapter if your goal is to "read the motivation section of the motivation and emotion chapter today" than if it is to "do some studying." Clarifying your goal makes it easier to know when you have reached it and when it is time to take a break. Without clear goals, a person can be more easily distracted by fatigue, boredom, or frustration and more likely to give up before completing a task.

well-being (subjective well-being)
A cognitive judgment of satisfaction with life, the frequent experiencing of positive moods and emotions, and the relatively infrequent experiencing of unpleasant moods and emotions.

not a strong motivator. A specific target, such as increasing sales by 10 percent, is a far more motivating goal. It is there for all to see, and it is easy to determine whether, and when, the goal has been reached. Finally, goals are most effective if management supports the workers' own goal setting, offers special rewards for reaching goals, and gives encouragement for renewed efforts after failure (Kluger & DeNisi, 1998).

To summarize, motivating jobs offer personal challenges, independence, and both intrinsic and extrinsic rewards. They provide enough satisfaction for people to feel excitement and pleasure in working hard. They inspire workers to be passionate about their work, not merely driven by it (Burke & Fiksenbaum, 2009). For employers, the rewards are more productivity, less absenteeism, and fewer resignations (Ilgen & Pulakos, 1999).

Achievement and Well-Being

Some people believe that the more they achieve and the more money and other material goods they gain as a result, the happier they will be. Do you agree? Researchers studying *positive psychology* (Seligman et al., 2005; Sheldon & King, 2001) have become interested in the systematic study of what it actually takes to achieve happiness, or, more formally, well-being (Diener, in press; McNulty & Fincham, 2012; Seligman et al., 2005; Sheldon & King, 2001). **Well-being** (also known as **subjective well-being**) is a combination of a cognitive judgment of satisfaction with life, the frequent experiencing of positive moods and emotions, and the relatively infrequent experiencing of unpleasant moods and emotions (Diener, 2008; Eid & Larsen, 2008; Fredrickson & Losada, 2005; Urry et al., 2004).

Research on well-being indicates that, as you might expect, people living in extreme poverty or in war-torn or politically chaotic countries are less happy than people in better circumstances (Diener et al., 2010; Morrison, Tay, & Diener, 2011). And people everywhere react to good or bad events with corresponding changes in mood. As described in the chapter on health, stress, and coping, for example, severe or long-lasting stressors—such as the death of a loved one—can lead to psychological and physical problems. But although events do have an impact, the depressing or elevating effects of major changes, such as being promoted or fired or even being imprisoned, seriously injured, or disabled tend not to last as long or be as intense as we might think they would (Abrantes-Pais, et al., 2007; Mathieu & Gosling, 2012). In other words, how happy you are may have less to do with what happens to you than you might expect (Aknin, Norton, & Dunn, 2009; Côté, Gyurak, & Levenson, 2010; Kahneman & Deaton, 2010; Kahneman et al., 2006; Lyubomirsky, 2001; Sheppes et al., 2011; Urry & Gross, 2010).

Most event-related changes in mood subside within days or weeks, and most people then return to their previous level of happiness (Suh, Diener, & Fujita, 1996). Even when events create permanent changes in circumstances, most people adapt by changing their expectancies and goals, not by radically and permanently changing their baseline level of happiness (e.g., Smith et al., 2009; Sussman & Shafir, 2011). For example, people may be thrilled after getting a big salary increase, but as they get used to having more money, the thrill fades, and they may eventually feel just as underpaid as before. In fact, although there are exceptions (Fujita & Diener, 2005; Lucas, 2007), most people's level of well-being tends to be remarkably stable throughout their lives. This stable baseline may be related to temperament, or personality, and it has been likened to the homeostatic processes that maintain body temperature or weight (Lykken, 1999). And like many other aspects of temperament, our baseline level of happiness may be influenced by genetics. Twin studies have shown, for example, that individual differences in happiness are more strongly associated with inherited personality characteristics than with environmental factors such as money, popularity, or physical attractiveness (Lykken, 1999; Tellegen et al., 1988).

Beyond inherited tendencies, the things that appear to matter most in generating happiness are having close social ties (such as friends and a satisfying marriage or partnership) and social support in general, being religious, having relatively high status and respect within a group, fitting in with one's culture, and having the resources necessary to make progress toward one's goals (Adams, 2012; Anderson et al., 2012; Boyce et al., 2010; Diener, 2000; Fischer & Boer, 2011; Fulmer et al., 2010; Mehl et al., 2010; Mogilner, 2010; Myers, 2000; Oishi & Schimmack, 2010; Oishi, Schimmack, & Diener,

2012; Tay & Diener, 2011). So you don't have to be a smart, rich, physically attractive high achiever to be happy, and it turns out that most people in Western cultures are relatively happy (Diener & Diener, 1995; Gow et al., 2005; Stone et al., 2010).

These results are consistent with the views expressed over many centuries by philosophers, psychologists, and wise people in all cultures (e.g., Ekman et al., 2005). As discussed in the personality chapter, for example, Abraham Maslow (1970) noted that when people in Western cultures experience unhappiness and psychological problems, those problems can often be traced to a *deficiency orientation*. He said that these people tend to seek happiness by trying to acquire the goods and status they don't have—but think they need—rather than by appreciating life itself and the material and nonmaterial riches they already have. Others have amplified this point, suggesting that our efforts to get more money, status, power, or other things we think will bring happiness may actually contribute to unhappiness if what we get is never "enough" (Bauer et al., 2012; Diener & Seligman, 2004; Gruber, Mauss, & Tamir, 2011; Luthar & Latendresse, 2005; Quoidbach et al., 2010). Indeed, the old saying that "life is a journey, not a destination" suggests that we are more likely to find happiness by experiencing full engagement in what we are *doing*—a state that some positive psychologists call *flow* (Hektner, Schmidt, & Csikszentmihalyi, 2007)—rather than by focusing on what we are or are not *getting*.

Relations and Conflicts among Motives

Which motives move me most?

It is far too early to tell whether research on well-being will help channel people's achievement motivation toward a more balanced set of goals, but there is no doubt that people will continue striving to meet whatever needs they perceive to be important. What are those needs?

Maslow's Hierarchy

Maslow (1970) suggested that human behavior is influenced by a hierarchy, or ranking, of five classes of needs, or motives (see Figure 8.4). He said that needs at the lowest level of the hierarchy must be at least partially satisfied before people can be motivated by the ones at higher levels. From the bottom to the top of Maslow's hierarchy, these five motives are as follows:

1. *Physiological,* such as the need for food, water, oxygen, and sleep.
2. *Safety,* such as the need to be cared for as a child and to have a secure income as an adult.
3. *Belongingness and love,* such as the need to be part of groups and to participate in affectionate sexual and nonsexual relationships.
4. *Esteem,* such as the need to be respected as a useful, honorable individual.
5. *Self-actualization,* which means reaching one's full potential. People motivated by this need explore and enhance relationships with others; follow interests for intrinsic pleasure rather than for money, status, or esteem; and are concerned with issues affecting all people, not just themselves.

Maslow's hierarchy has been very influential over the years, partly because the needs associated with basic survival and security do generally take precedence over those related to self-enhancement or personal growth (Baumeister & Leary, 1995; Oishi et al., 1999). But critics see the hierarchy as too simplistic (Hall, Lindzey, & Campbell, 1998; Kenrick et al., 2010; Neher, 1991). It doesn't predict

FIGURE 8.4
Maslow's Hierarchy of Motives
Abraham Maslow saw human motives as organized in a hierarchy in which motives at lower levels come before those at higher levels. According to this view, self-actualization is the essence of mental health, but Maslow recognized that only rare individuals, such as Mother Teresa or Martin Luther King, Jr., approach full self-actualization. Take a moment to consider which level of Maslow's hierarchy you are focused on at this point in your life. Which level do you ultimately hope to reach?

LEARN by DOING

Source: Adapted from Maslow (1943).

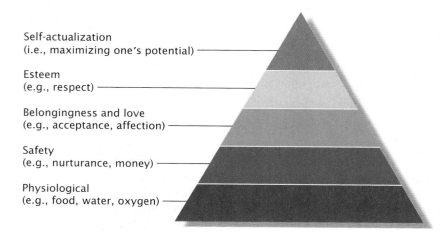

Self-actualization
(i.e., maximizing one's potential)

Esteem
(e.g., respect)

Belongingness and love
(e.g., acceptance, affection)

Safety
(e.g., nurturance, money)

Physiological
(e.g., food, water, oxygen)

or explain, for example, the motivation of people who starve themselves to draw attention to political or moral causes. Further, people may not have to satisfy one kind of need before addressing others; we can seek to satisfy several needs at once. Finally, the ordering of needs within the survival/security and enhancement/growth categories differs from culture to culture, suggesting that there may not be a single, universal hierarchy of needs.

To address some of the problems in Maslow's theory, Clayton Alderfer (1969) proposed *existence, relatedness, growth (ERG) theory,* which places human needs into just three categories: *existence needs* (such as for food and water), *relatedness needs* (e.g., for social interactions and attachments), and *growth needs* (such as for developing one's capabilities). Unlike Maslow, Alderfer doesn't assume that these needs must be satisfied in a particular order. Instead, he sees needs in each category as rising and falling from time to time and from situation to situation. When a need in one area is fulfilled (or even if it is frustrated), a person will be motivated to pursue some other needs. For example, if a breakup frustrates relatedness needs, a person might focus on existence or growth needs by eating more or volunteering to work late.

Conflicting Motives and Stress

LINKAGES

Can motivational conflicts cause stress? (a link to Health, Stress, and Coping)

As in the case of hunger strikes, in which the desire to promote a cause is pitted against the desire to eat, human motives can sometimes conflict. The usual result is some degree of discomfort. For example, imagine that you are alone and bored on a Saturday night and you think about going out for a snack. What are your motives? Hunger might play a part, and so might the prospect of the increased physiological arousal that a change of scene will provide. Even sexual motivation might be involved, as you consider the chances of meeting someone exciting in the convenience store. But safety-related motives may also kick in: Is your neighborhood safe enough for you to go out alone? Even an esteem motive might come into play, making you hesitate to be seen on your own on a weekend night (Krieglmeyer et al., 2010).

These are just a few of the motives that may shape a trivial decision. When the decision is more important, the number and strength of motivational pushes and pulls are often greater, creating far more internal conflict and indecision. There are four basic types of motivational conflicts (Elliot, 2008; Miller, 1959):

1. *Approach-approach conflicts.* When we must choose only one of two desirable activities—say, going to a movie or to a concert—an *approach-approach conflict* exists.
2. *Avoidance-avoidance conflicts.* An *avoidance-avoidance conflict* arises when we must select one of two undesirable alternatives. Someone forced either to sell the family home or to declare bankruptcy faces an avoidance-avoidance conflict.
3. *Approach-avoidance conflicts.* If someone you dislike had tickets to your favorite group's sold-out concert and invited you to come along, what would you do? When a particular event or activity has both attractive and unattractive features, an *approach-avoidance* conflict is created.
4. *Multiple approach-avoidance conflicts.* Suppose you must choose between two jobs. One offers a high salary with a well-known company but requires long working hours and relocation to a miserable climate. The other boasts advancement opportunities, fringe benefits, and a better climate, but it doesn't pay as much and involves an unpredictable work schedule. This is an example of a *multiple approach-avoidance conflict,* in which two or more alternatives each have both positive and negative features. Such conflicts are especially difficult to resolve, partly because the features of each option may not be easy to compare. For example, how many dollars a year does it take to compensate you for living in a bad climate?

The difficulties associated with resolving each of these conflicts can create stress, a topic explored in the chapter on health, stress, and coping (Krosch, Figner, & Weber, 2012). During motivational conflicts, people are often tense, irritable, and more vulnerable than usual to physical and psychological problems. These reactions are especially likely when no choice is obviously "right," when varying motives have approximately equal strength, and when a choice can have serious consequences (as in decisions about marrying, splitting up, or placing an elderly parent in a nursing home). Some people may spend a long time agonizing over these conflicts, whereas others may make a choice quickly, impulsively, and thoughtlessly, simply to end the discomfort of uncertainty. Even after resolving the conflict on the basis of careful thought, people may continue to experience stress responses, such as worrying about whether they made the right decision or blaming themselves for bad choices. These and other consequences of conflicting motives sometimes lead to depression or other serious disorders.

The emotions associated with motivational conflicts provide just one example of the close links between motivation and emotions. Motivation can intensify emotions, as when hunger leads a normally calm person to angrily complain about slow service at a restaurant. But emotions can also create motivation. Happiness, for example, is an emotion that people want to feel (e.g., Bryant & Veroff, 2006), so they engage in whatever behaviors—studying, artwork, investing, beachcombing—they think will achieve it. Similarly, as an emotion that most people want to avoid, anxiety motivates many behaviors, from leaving the scene of an accident to staying away from poisonous snakes. But sometimes, as when facing a stressful job interview or agreeing to a painful medical procedure, people are motivated to endure anxiety or other unpleasant emotions because they believe that doing so will eventually lead to a desired goal (Tamir, 2009). Let's take a closer look at emotions.   ●●●●

A Stressful Conflict

Think back to when you were deciding which college to attend. Was the decision easy and obvious or did it create a motivational conflict? If there was a conflict, was it an approach-approach, approach-avoidance, or multiple approach-avoidance conflict? What factors were most important in deciding how to resolve the conflict, and what emotions and signs of stress did you experience during and after the decision-making process?

LEARN by DOING

The Nature of Emotions

How do feelings differ from thoughts?

Everyone seems to agree that joy, sorrow, anger, fear, love, and hate are emotions. However, it is often hard to identify the shared features that make these experiences emotions rather than, say, thoughts or impulses.

Defining Characteristics and Dimensions

Most psychologists in Western cultures tend to see emotions as organized psychological and physiological reactions to significant life events (Izard, 1993). These reactions are partly private, or *subjective,* experiences and partly measurable patterns of behavior and physiological arousal. The subjective experience of emotions has several characteristics:

1. Emotions are usually *temporary.* In other words, they tend to have relatively clear beginnings and ends and a relatively short duration. Moods, by contrast, tend to last longer.
2. Emotional experience can be *positive,* as in joy, or *negative,* as in sadness. It can also be a mixture of both, as in the bittersweet feelings of watching one's child leave for the first day of kindergarten (Larsen et al., 2004).
3. Emotions can vary in intensity. You can feel pleased, happy, or ecstatic. You can also feel mildly disappointed, sad, or deeply depressed (Shidlovski & Hassin, 2011).
4. Emotional experience is triggered partly by thoughts, especially by a *mental assessment* of how a situation relates to your goals. The same event can bring on different emotions depending on what it means to you. An exam score of 75 percent may thrill you if your best previous score had been 50 percent, but it may upset you if you had never before scored below 90 percent.
5. Emotional experience *alters thought processes,* often by directing attention toward some things and away from others. Negative emotions tend to narrow attention, and positive emotions tend to broaden it (Ford et al., 2010; Fredrickson et al., 2008). Anxiety about terrorism, for example, narrows our attention to focus on potential threats in airports and other public places (Craske, 1999; Yovel & Mineka, 2005).
6. Emotional experience brings on an *action tendency,* a motivation to behave in certain ways. Grieving parents' anger, for example, might motivate them to try to harm their child's killer. But for John Walsh, whose son was kidnapped and

Winners and Losers
Emotional experiences depend in part on our interpretation of situations and how those situations relate to our goals. A single event—the announcement of the results of this wrestling match—triggered drastically different emotional reactions in the contestants, depending on whether they perceived it as making them the winner or the loser.

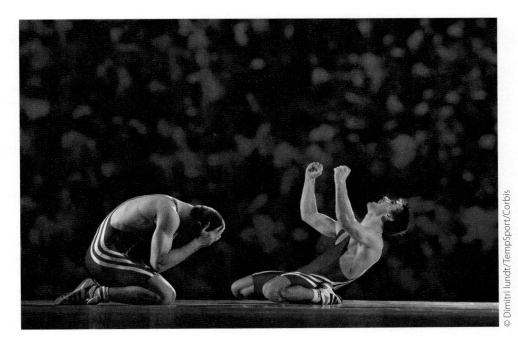

© Dimitri Iundt/TempSport/Corbis

murdered, grief led him to help prevent such crimes by creating *America's Most Wanted*, a TV show dedicated to bringing criminals to justice.

7. Emotional experiences are *passions* that you feel, whether you want to or not. You do have some control over emotions, though, because they depend partly on how you interpret situations (Gross, 2001). For example, you can reduce your emotional reaction to having a car accident by reminding yourself that no one was hurt and that you are insured. Still, you can't just *decide* what emotions you experience; instead, you "fall in love" or "explode in anger" or are "overcome by grief."

In other words, the subjective aspects of emotions are experiences that are both triggered by the thinking self and felt as happening to the self. The extent to which we are "victims" of our passions versus rational controllers of our emotions is a central dilemma of human existence.

The objectively measurable aspects of emotions include learned and innate *expressive displays* and *physiological responses*. Expressive displays—such as a smile or a frown—communicate feelings to others. Physiological responses—changes in heart rate, for example—provide the biological adjustments needed to perform actions generated by the emotional experience. If you throw a temper tantrum, for instance, your heart must deliver additional oxygen and fuel to your muscles.

In summary, **emotions** are temporary experiences with positive, negative, or mixed qualities. People experience emotions with varying intensity as happening to the self, generated in part by a mental assessment of situations, and accompanied by both learned and innate physical responses. Through emotions, whether they mean to or not, people communicate their internal states and intentions to others. Emotions often disrupt thinking and behavior, but they also trigger and guide thinking and organize, motivate, and sustain behavior and social relations (Izard, 2007).

Where do our emotions come from? There are two main sources: our biology and our thoughts. Let's consider what psychological scientists have discovered about how these sources operate, separately and together, to create emotional experiences.

The Biology of Emotions

The biological systems described in the chapter on biology and behavior play a major role in emotions. In the *central nervous system*, numerous brain areas are involved in the generation of emotions as well as in our experience of those emotions (Barrett & Wager,

emotions Temporary positive or negative experiences that are felt as happening to the self, that are generated partly by interpretation of situations, and that are accompanied by learned and innate physical responses.

2006; Szameitat et al., 2010). The *autonomic nervous system* gives rise to many of the physiological changes associated with emotional arousal.

Brain Mechanisms   Although many questions remain, researchers have described three main aspects of how emotions are processed in the brain. First, it appears that activity in the *limbic system,* especially in the *amygdala,* is central to emotions (Kensinger & Corkin, 2004; Phelps & LeDoux, 2005; see Figure 2.8 in the chapter on biology and behavior). Normal functioning in the amygdala appears critical to the ability to learn emotional associations, recognize emotional expressions, detect personally relevant information, and perceive emotionally charged words (Anderson & Phelps, 2001; Cunningham & Brosch, 2012; Suslow et al., 2006; Whalen et al., 2004). For example, victims of a disease that destroys only the amygdala are unable to judge other people's emotional states by looking at their faces (Adolphs, Tranel, & Damasio, 1998).

A second aspect of the brain's involvement in emotions is seen in its control over our emotional and nonemotional facial expressions (Rinn, 1984; Szameitat et al., 2010). Take a moment to look in a mirror, and put on your best fake smile. The voluntary facial movements you just made, like all voluntary movements, are controlled by the brain's *pyramidal motor system,* a system that includes the motor cortex. However, a smile that expresses genuine happiness is involuntary. That kind of smile, like the other facial movements associated with emotions, is governed by the *extrapyramidal motor system,* which depends on areas beneath the cortex. Brain damage can disrupt either system. People with pyramidal motor system damage show normal facial expressions during genuine emotion, but they cannot fake a smile. In contrast, people with damage to the extrapyramidal system can pose facial expressions at will, but they remain straight-faced even when feeling genuine joy or profound sadness (Hopf, Muller, & Hopf, 1992).

A third aspect of the brain's role in emotions is revealed by research on the two sides, or hemispheres, of the cerebral cortex. For example, after suffering damage to the right, but not the left, hemisphere, people no longer laugh at jokes, even though they can still understand their words, the logic (or illogic) underlying them, and their punch lines (Critchley, 1991). Further, when people are asked to name the emotions shown in slides of facial expressions, blood flow increases in the right hemisphere more than in the left hemisphere (Gur, Skolnic, & Gur, 1994). But smiling while experiencing a positive emotion is correlated with greater activity in the *left* side of the brain (Davidson et al., 1990). When an area of one patient's left hemisphere was stimulated, she began to smile, then laugh (Fried et al., 1998). She attributed her emotional expression to the situation ("You guys are just so funny ... standing around"). Similarly, brain-imaging studies conducted while sports fans watched their favorite team in action have revealed greater activation in the left hemisphere when the team is winning and more activation in the right hemisphere when the team is losing (Park et al., 2009). And there's evidence that the experience of anger or depression is associated with greater brain activity on the right side than on the left (Carver & Harmon-Jones, 2009; Herrington et al., 2010).

The fact that different brain areas appear to be involved in displaying and experiencing positive and negative emotions (Harmon-Jones, 2004; Harmon-Jones & Sigelman, 2001; Heller, 1993) makes it difficult to map the exact roles the two hemispheres play in emotion (Bourne, 2010; Root, Wong, & Kinsbourne, 2006; Vingerhoets, Berckmoes, & Stroobant, 2003). Generally, however, most aspects of emotions—the experiencing of negative emotion, the perception of any emotion exhibited in faces or other stimuli, and the facial expression of any emotion—depend more on the right hemisphere than on the left (Heller, Nitschke, & Miller, 1998; Kawasaki et al., 2001).

If the right hemisphere is relatively dominant in emotions, which side of the face would you expect to be somewhat more involved in expressing emotions? If you said the left side, you are correct, because, as described in the chapter on biology and behavior, movements of each side of the body are controlled by the opposite side of the brain.

Mechanisms of the Autonomic Nervous System   The autonomic nervous system (ANS) triggers many of the physiological changes that accompany emotions (Vernet, Robin, &

CNS

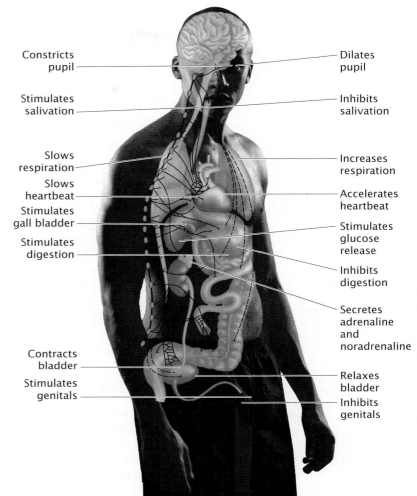

Parasympathetic functions | Sympathetic functions

- Sympathetic ganglion
- Norepinephrine released
- Target organ
- Acetylcholine released
- Parasympathetic ganglion

Parasympathetic functions:
- Constricts pupil
- Stimulates salivation
- Slows respiration
- Slows heartbeat
- Stimulates gall bladder
- Stimulates digestion
- Contracts bladder
- Stimulates genitals

Sympathetic functions:
- Dilates pupil
- Inhibits salivation
- Increases respiration
- Accelerates heartbeat
- Stimulates glucose release
- Inhibits digestion
- Secretes adrenaline and noradrenaline
- Relaxes bladder
- Inhibits genitals

FIGURE 8.5

The Autonomic Nervous System

Emotional responses involve activation of the autonomic nervous system, which is organized into sympathetic and parasympathetic subsystems. Which of the bodily responses shown here do you associate with emotional experiences?

LEARN by DOING

Photo © Peter Kindersley/Brand X Pictures/Getty Images

parasympathetic nervous system The subsystem of the autonomic nervous system that typically influences activity related to the protection, nourishment, and growth of the body.

sympathetic nervous system The subsystem of the autonomic nervous system that readies the body for vigorous activity.

fight-flight reaction (fight-or-flight syndrome) Physical reactions triggered by the sympathetic nervous system that prepare the body to fight or flee a threatening situation.

Dittmar, 1995; see Figure 8.5). If your hands get cold and clammy when you are nervous, it is because the ANS has increased perspiration and decreased the blood flow in your hands.

As described in the chapter on biology and behavior, the ANS carries information between the brain and most organs of the body—the heart and blood vessels, the digestive system, and so on. Each of these organs is active on its own, but input from the ANS can increase or decrease that activity. By doing so, the ANS coordinates the functioning of these organs to meet the body's general needs and prepare the body for change (Porges, Doussard, & Maita, 1995). If you are aroused to take action, such as running to catch a bus, you need more glucose to fuel your muscles. The ANS frees needed energy by stimulating the secretion of glucose-generating hormones and promoting blood flow to the muscles.

Figure 8.5 shows that the autonomic nervous system is organized into two parts: the sympathetic nervous system and the parasympathetic nervous system. Emotions can activate either part, both of which send axon fibers to each organ in the body. Generally, the sympathetic and parasympathetic fibers have opposite effects on these *target organs*. Axons from the **parasympathetic nervous system** release the neurotransmitter *acetylcholine* onto target organs, leading to activity related to the protection, nourishment, and growth of the body. Axons from the **sympathetic nervous system** release a different neurotransmitter, *norepinephrine,* onto target organs, helping prepare the body for vigorous activity. When one part of the sympathetic system is stimulated, other parts are activated "in sympathy" with it (Gellhorn & Loofbourrow, 1963). The result is the **fight-flight reaction** (also called the **fight-or-flight syndrome**), a pattern of increased heart rate and blood pressure, rapid or irregular breathing, dilated pupils, perspiration, dry mouth, increased blood sugar, "goose bumps," and other changes that help prepare the body to confront or run from a threat.

You cannot consciously experience the brain mechanisms that alter the activity of your autonomic nervous system. This is why most people cannot exert direct, conscious control over blood pressure or other aspects of ANS activity. However, you can do things that have indirect effects on the ANS. For example, to create autonomic arousal of your sex organs, you might imagine an erotic situation. To raise your blood pressure, you might hold your breath or strain your muscles. And to lower your blood pressure, you can lie down, relax, and think calming thoughts.

Theories of Emotion

Are emotions in the heart, in the head, or both?

Are the physiological responses associated with emotions enough to create an emotional experience? Or are those responses the *result* of emotional experiences that begin in the brain? And how do our mental interpretations of events affect our emotional reactions to them? For over a century now, psychologists have worked at finding the answers to these questions. In the process, they have developed a number of theories that explain emotions mainly in terms of biological or cognitive factors. The main biological theories are those of William James and Walter Cannon. The most prominent cognitive theories are those of Stanley Schachter and Richard Lazarus. Let's review these theories, along with some research designed to evaluate them.

James's Peripheral Theory

Suppose you are camping in the woods when a huge bear wanders through your campsite. You might be afraid and run for your life, but would you run because you're afraid or are you afraid because you run? This was the example and the question posed by William James, one of the first psychologists to offer a formal account of how physiological responses relate to emotional experience. He argued that you are afraid because you run. Your running and the physiological responses associated with it, he said, follow directly from your perception of the bear.

At first, James's claim sounds ridiculous; it would be silly to run from something unless you already feared it. James concluded otherwise after examining his own mental processes. He decided that once you strip away all physiological responses—such as changes in heart rate, breathing, and other peripheral nervous system activity—nothing remains of the experience of an emotion (James, 1890). Without these responses, he said, you would feel no fear, because it is the experiencing of physiological responses that creates fear and other emotions. The same argument was made by Carle Lange, a Danish physician, so James's view is sometimes called the *James-Lange theory* of emotion. It is also known as a *peripheral theory* of emotion, because it emphasizes activity in the peripheral nervous system, not in the central nervous system, as the main cause of emotional experience.

Observing Peripheral Responses   According to James, the first step in the creation of an emotional experience occurs when perception affects the cerebral cortex. The brain interprets a situation and automatically directs a particular set of physiological changes, such as increased heart rate, sinking stomach, perspiration, and certain patterns of blood flow. It is when we become *aware* of this pattern of bodily changes, said James, that we experience an emotion. According to this view, each particular emotion is created by a particular pattern of physiological responses.

Notice that according to James's theory, emotional experience is not generated by the brain alone. There is no special "emotion center" in the brain where the firing of neurons creates a direct experience of emotion. If this theory is accurate, it might account for the

Do You Feel It, Too?

To get an idea of how facial expressions can alter as well as communicate emotion, try your best to imitate the expression shown in this photograph. Did this create in you the same feelings and autonomic responses that the other person appears to be experiencing?

LEARN by DOING

difficulty we sometimes have in knowing our true feelings: we must figure out what emotions we feel by perceiving small differences in specific physiological response patterns (Katkin, Wiens, & Öhman, 2001).

Evaluating James's Theory   Research shows that certain emotional states are indeed associated with particular patterns of autonomic changes (Damasio et al., 2000; Dunn et al., 2010; Harrison et al., 2010; Keltner & Buswell, 1996; Sinha & Parsons, 1996). For example, blood flow to the hands and feet increases in association with anger and decreases in association with fear (Levenson, Ekman, & Friesen, 1990). So fear involves "cold feet"; anger does not. A pattern of activity associated with disgust includes increased muscle activity but no change in heart rate. And when people mentally relive different kinds of emotional experiences, they show different patterns of autonomic activity (Ekman, Levenson, & Friesen, 1983). These emotion-specific patterns of physiological activity have been found in widely different cultures (Levenson et al., 1992). Further, people who are more keenly aware of physiological changes in their bodies are likely to experience emotions more intensely than those who are less aware of such changes (Schneider, Ring, & Katkin, 1998; Wiens, Mezzacappa, & Katkin, 2000). It has even been suggested that the "gut feelings" that cause us to approach or avoid certain situations might be the result of physiological changes that are perceived without conscious awareness (Bechara et al., 1997; Damasio, 1994; Katkin, Wiens, & Öhman, 2001; Winkielman & Berridge, 2004).

Different patterns of autonomic activity are also related to specific emotional facial expressions. In one study, research participants were asked to make a series of facial movements that, when combined, would create the appearance of sadness, fear, happiness, anger, or some other emotion (Levenson, Ekman, & Friesen, 1990). Making these movements led to autonomic changes that resembled those normally accompanying emotions. In addition, almost all of the participants reported feeling the emotion associated with the expression they had created, even though they couldn't see their own expressions and didn't realize that they had made an "emotional" face.

Other studies have confirmed these results (Schnall & Laird, 2003) and have also shown that emotional feelings can be eased by relaxing facial muscles (Duclos & Laird, 2001). Even our ability to understand emotional information seems to be due in part to the facial movements we make in response to that information. For example, when people's faces are immobilized by injections of botulinum toxin-A (Botox) they find it more difficult to understand the meaning of emotional reading material (Havas et al., 2010).

A variation on James's theory, called the *facial feedback hypothesis,* suggests that involuntary facial movements provide enough information about activity in the rest of the body to create an emotional experience (Ekman & Davidson, 1993). If so, it would help to explain how posed facial expressions create the emotions normally associated with them. Try taking advantage of this notion in your own life. The next time you want to cheer yourself up, it might help to smile—even though you don't feel like it (Fleeson, Malanos, & Achille, 2002)!

Lie Detection   The idea that different patterns of physiological activity are associated with different emotions forms the basis for the lie detection industry. If people experience anxiety or guilt when they lie, specific patterns of physiological activity accompanying these emotions should be detectable on instruments, called *polygraphs,* that record heart rate, breathing rate, perspiration, and other autonomic responses (Granhag & Stromwall, 2004; Iacono & Patrick, 2006).

To identify the perpetrator of a crime using the *control question test,* a polygraph tester might ask questions specific to the crime, such as "Did you stab someone on May 31, 2012?" Responses to such *relevant questions* are then compared with responses to *control questions,* such as "Have you ever lied to get out of trouble?" Innocent people might have lied at some time in the past and might feel guilty when asked about it, but they should have no reason to feel guilty about what they did on May 31, 2012. Accordingly, an innocent person should have a stronger emotional response to control questions than to relevant questions (Rosenfeld, 1995). Another approach, called the *directed*

© Guy Bell/Alamy

Searching for the Truth

Polygraph tests have limited accuracy, and so do the alternative lie-detection methods designed to improve on them (Ganis et al., 2011; Karim et al., 2009; Porter & Brinke, 2010). However, they may intimidate people who believe that they are foolproof. In one small town police station which had no polygraph, a burglar confessed to his crime when a kitchen colander was placed on his head and attached by wires to a copy machine (Shepherd, Kohut, & Sweet, 1989).

lie test, compares a person's physiological reactions when asked to lie about something and when telling what is known to be the truth. Finally, the *guilty knowledge test* seeks to determine whether a person reacts in a notable way to information about a crime that only the guilty party would know (Ben-Shakhar, Bar-Hillel, & Kremnitzer, 2002).

Most people do have emotional responses when they lie, but statistics about the accuracy of polygraphs vary widely. Some studies suggest that polygraphs detect 90 percent of guilty, lying individuals (Gamer et al., 2006; Honts & Quick, 1995; Kircher, Horowitz, & Raskin, 1988; Raskin, 1986), while others find that polygraphs mislabel as many as 40 percent of truthful, innocent people as guilty liars (Ben-Shakhar & Furedy, 1990; Saxe & Ben-Shakhar, 1999). The inconsistency occurs partly because the results of a polygraph test are not determined entirely by whether a person is telling the truth. What people think about the act of lying and about the value of the test can also influence the accuracy of its results. For example, people who believe that lying is acceptable and who don't believe in the power of polygraphs are not likely to display emotion-linked physiological responses while lying during the test. However, an innocent person who believes in such tests and who thinks that "everything always goes wrong" might show a large fear response when asked about a crime, thus wrongly indicating "guilt" (Lykken, 1998b).

So although polygraphs can catch some liars, most researchers agree that a guilty person can "fool" a polygraph lie detector and that some innocent people can be mislabeled as guilty (Ruscio, 2005). After reviewing the relevant research literature, a panel of distinguished psychologists and other scientists in the United States expressed serious reservations about the value of polygraph tests in detecting deception and argued against their use as evidence in court or in employee screening and selection (Committee to Review the Scientific Evidence on the Polygraph, 2003). Scientists are working on several alternative lie-detecting techniques, including those that focus on brain activity, impose high cognitive demands during interrogation interviews, spring surprising questions, or ask people to draw pictures about their experiences. Such alternative measures do not depend on a link between deception and autonomic nervous system responses (Bhatt et al., 2009; Broaders & Goldin-Meadow, 2010; Leal & Vrij, 2010; Leal et al., 2010; Lee et al., 2009; Liang et al., 2012; Memon et al., 2010; Porter et al., 2011; Vrij, Granhag, & Porter, 2010; Vrij, Granhag, et al., 2011; Vrij, Leal, Grahang, et al., 2009; Vrij, Leal, Mann, et al., 2010; Vrij, Mann, et al., 2010; Warmelink et al., 2011; Wright, Berry, & Bird, 2012).

Cannon's Central Theory

James said that the experience of emotions depends on feedback from physiological responses occurring outside the brain, but Walter Cannon disagreed (Cannon, 1927). According to Cannon, you feel fear at the sight of a wild bear even before you start to run because emotional experience starts in the brain—specifically, in the thalamus, the brain structure that relays information from most sense organs to the cortex.

According to Cannon's *central theory* of emotions (called the *Cannon-Bard theory,* in recognition of Philip Bard's contribution), information about emotional situations goes first to the thalamus. The thalamus then sends signals to the autonomic nervous system and—at the same time—to the cerebral cortex, where the emotion becomes conscious. So when you see a bear, the brain receives sensory information about it, interprets that information as a bear, and instantly creates the experience of fear while at the same time sending messages to your heart, lungs, and legs to get you out of the situation. According to Cannon's theory, then, there is a *direct* experience of emotion in the central nervous system, whether or not the brain receives feedback about responses in other parts of the body.

Updating Cannon's Theory   Research conducted since Cannon's time indicates that the thalamus is not the "seat" of emotion, as he had suggested. Still, the thalamus does participate in some aspects of emotional processing (Lang, 1995). For example, studies of humans and laboratory animals show that the emotion of fear is generated by connections from the thalamus to the amygdala (Anderson & Phelps, 2000; LeDoux, 1995). The implication is that strong emotions can sometimes bypass the cortex without requiring conscious thought to activate them. This process helps explain why people find it so difficult to overcome an intense fear, or phobia, even though they may consciously know the fear is irrational.

An updated version of Cannon's theory suggests that in humans and other animals, activity in specific brain areas is experienced as either enjoyable or aversive and produces the feelings of pleasure or discomfort associated with emotion. In humans, these areas have extensive connections throughout the brain (Fossati et al., 2003). As a result, the representation of emotions in the brain probably involves activity in widely distributed neural circuits, not just in a narrowly localized emotion "center" (Derryberry & Tucker, 1992; West et al., 2010).

Cognitive Theories of Emotion

Suppose you are about to be interviewed for your first job or go out on a blind date or take your first ride in a hot-air balloon. In such situations, it is not always easy to be sure of what you are feeling. Is it fear, excitement, anticipation, worry, happiness, dread, or what? Stanley Schachter suggested that the emotions we experience every day are shaped partly by how we interpret the arousal we feel. His cognitive theory of emotions is known as the *Schachter-Singer theory* in recognition of the contributions of Jerome Singer. The theory took shape in the early 1960s, when many psychologists were raising questions about the validity of James's theory of emotion. Schachter argued that the theory was essentially correct, but required a few modifications (Cornelius, 1996).

According to the Schachter-Singer theory, emotions result from a combination of feedback from the body's responses and our interpretation of what caused those responses. So cognitive interpretation comes into play twice, first when you perceive the situation that leads to bodily responses, and again when you interpret those responses as a particular emotion. Schachter said that a given pattern of physiological responses can be interpreted in many different ways and so might give rise to many different emotions. According to Schachter, then, the emotion you experience when that bear approaches your campsite might be fear, excitement, astonishment, or surprise, depending on how you label your bodily reactions to seeing it (Schachter & Singer, 1962).

Schachter also said that how we label arousal depends on **attribution,** the process of identifying the cause of some event. We attribute our physiological arousal to different emotions depending on the information we have about the situation. For example, if you are watching the final seconds of a close ball game, you might attribute your racing heart, rapid breathing, and perspiration to excitement. But you might attribute the same

attribution The process of explaining the cause of some event.

Labeling Arousal
Schachter's cognitive theory of emotion predicts that these people will attribute their physiological arousal to the game they are watching and will label their emotion as "excitement." Further, as described in the chapter on health, stress, and coping, the emotions they experience will also depend partly on their cognitive interpretation of the outcome (Lazarus & Folkman, 1984). Those who see their team's defeat as a disaster will experience more negative emotions than those who think of it as a challenge to improve.

physiological reactions to anxiety if you are waiting for a big exam to begin. Schachter predicted that our emotional experiences will be less intense if we attribute arousal to a nonemotional cause. So if you notice your heart pounding before an exam but say to yourself, "Sure my heart's pounding—I just drank five cups of coffee!" then you should feel "wired" from caffeine rather than afraid or worried. This prediction has received some support (Mezzacappa, Katkin, & Palmer, 1999; Sinclair et al., 1994), but other aspects of Schachter's theory have not.

Few researchers today fully accept the Schachter-Singer theory, but it did stimulate an enormous amount of valuable research, including research on **excitation transfer theory.** This theory focuses on a phenomenon in which physiological arousal from one experience carries over to affect emotions in an independent situation (Eskine, Kacinik, & Prinz, 2012; Reisenzein, 1983; Zillmann, 1984). For example, people who have been aroused by physical exercise become angrier when provoked and experience more intense sexual feelings around an attractive person than do people who have been less physically active (Allen et al., 1989). Physiological arousal from fear, like arousal from exercise, can also enhance emotions, including sexual feelings. One study of this transfer took place in Canada, near a deep river gorge. The gorge could be crossed either by a shaky swinging bridge or by a more stable wooden structure. A female researcher asked men who had just crossed each bridge to respond to a questionnaire which included pictures from the TAT, the projective test described in Figure 8.3. The amount of sexual content in the stories these men wrote about the pictures was much higher among those who met the woman after crossing the more dangerous bridge compared to those who had crossed the stable bridge. Furthermore, they were more likely to rate the researcher as attractive and to attempt to contact her afterward (Dutton & Aron, 1974). When the person giving out the questionnaire was a male, however, the type of bridge crossed had no impact on sexual imagery. You might be wondering whether the men who crossed the dangerous bridge were simply more adventurous than other men regarding both bridge crossing and heterosexual encounters. To check this possibility, the researchers repeated the study, but with one change. This time, the woman approached the men farther down the trail, long after physiological arousal from the bridge crossing had subsided. Now the apparently adventurous men were no more likely than others to rate the woman as attractive. So it was probably excitation transfer, not differing amounts of adventurousness, that produced the original result.

Schachter focused on the way we interpret our bodily responses to events. Other cognitive theorists have argued that it is our interpretations of the events themselves that are most important in shaping emotional experiences. For example, as we mentioned earlier, a person's emotional reaction to receiving exam results can depend partly on whether the score is seen as a sign of improvement or as a disaster. According to Richard Lazarus's (1966, 1991) *cognitive appraisal theory* of emotion, these differing reactions can be best explained by how we think exam scores, job interviews, blind dates, bear sightings, and other events will affect our personal well-being. According to Lazarus, the process of cognitive appraisal, or evaluation, begins when we decide whether or not an event matters to us; that is, do we even care about it? If we don't, as might be the case when an exam doesn't count toward our grade, we are unlikely to have an emotional experience when we get the results. If the event is relevant to our health, well-being, status, self-esteem, goals, or finances (or those of a loved one) we will probably have a significant emotional reaction to it. That reaction will be positive or negative, said Lazarus, depending on whether we interpret the event as advancing our personal goals or as threatening to harm us or block our progress. The *specific* emotion we experience depends on our individual goals, needs, personal and cultural standards, expectations, and experiences. As a result, a second-place finisher in a marathon race might experience bitter disappointment at having "lost," whereas someone at the back of the pack may be thrilled just to have completed the race alive. (Imada & Ellsworth, 2011; Larsen et al., 2004; O'Brien & Ellsworth, 2011).

More recently, researchers have developed cognitive theories of emotion that depart from Schachter's in some new directions. In the *conceptual act model* of emotion, for instance, *core affect*—pleasant or unpleasant feelings—is distinguished from *emotion*.

excitation transfer theory The theory that physiological arousal stemming from one situation is carried over to and enhances emotional experience in an independent situation.

According to this model, emotion results when we impose on a feeling a *category label* (e.g., guilt, shame, anger, or resentment) that our cultural and language training has taught us to use (Barrett et al., 2007; Barrett & Kensinger, 2010; Barrett, Mesquita, & Gendron, 2011). For instance, if you succeed at an important task and attribute the success to your own efforts, then you'll likely feel pride. But, if you attribute that same success to the help of another person, then you'll more likely feel gratitude. Similarly, if you fail at an important task and attribute your failure to your own mistakes or lack of effort, then you'll probably feel guilt or shame. If you attribute that same failure to the interference of another person, then you are more likely to feel anger. Models like this one are valuable because they incorporate research on language and culture in an effort to better understand the labeling processes involved in human emotional experience.

"In Review: Theories of Emotion" summarizes key elements of the theories we have discussed. Research on these theories suggests that both bodily responses (including facial responses) and the cognitive interpretation of those responses add to emotional experience. So does cognitive appraisal of events themselves. In addition, the brain can apparently generate emotional experience independent of physiological arousal. So emotions are probably both in the heart and in the head (including the face). The most basic emotions—fear and anger, for example—probably occur directly within the brain, whereas the many more complex shades of emotions—such as hope, pride, shame, guilt, and disappointment—probably arise from attributions, categorization, and other cognitive interpretations of physiological responses (Barrett et al., 2007).

The issue of which, if any, component of emotion is primary remains a topic of lively debate. Each of the emotion theories we have discussed has helped psychological scientists better understand how the various components interact to produce emotional experience. Cognitive appraisal theories have been especially useful in studying and treating stress-related emotional problems (see the chapters on health, stress, and coping; psychological disorders; and treatment of psychological disorders).

Theories of Emotions — IN REVIEW

Theory	Source of Emotions	Example
James-Lange	Emotions are created by awareness of specific patterns of peripheral (autonomic) responses.	Anger is associated with increased blood flow in the hands and feet; fear is associated with decreased blood flow in these areas.
Cannon-Bard	The brain generates direct experiences of emotions.	Stimulation of certain brain areas can create pleasant or unpleasant emotions.
Cognitive (Schachter-Singer, Lazarus)	Cognitive interpretation of events and of physiological reactions to events shapes emotional experiences.	Autonomic arousal can be experienced as anxiety or excitement, depending on how it is labeled. A single event can lead to different emotions, depending on whether it is perceived as threatening or challenging.

IN REVIEW QUESTIONS

1. Research showing that there are pleasure centers in the brain has been cited in support of the ___ theory of emotions.

2. The use of polygraphs in lie detection is based on the ___ theory of emotions.

3. The process of attribution is most important to ___ theories of emotions.

Communicating Emotion

Which emotional expressions are innate and which are learned?

So far, we have described emotions and how people experience them. Let's now consider how people communicate emotions to one another.

One way they do this is, of course, through words. Some people describe their feelings relatively simply, and mainly in terms of pleasantness or unpleasantness; others include information about the intensity of their emotions (Barrett, 1995; Barrett et al., 2001, 2007). In general, women are more likely than men to talk about their emotions and the complexity of their feelings (Barrett et al., 2000; Kring & Gordon, 1998). Humans

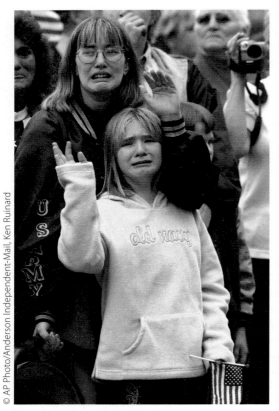

also communicate emotion through touch (Thompson & Hampton, 2011), body movement and posture (de Gelder et al., 2004; Hadjikhani & de Gelder, 2003), tone of voice (Simon-Thomas et al., 2009), and especially through facial movements and expressions.

Imagine a woman watching television. You can see her face but not what she sees on the screen. She might be deep in complex thought, perhaps comparing her investment decisions with those of the experts being interviewed on CNBC. Or she might be thinking of nothing at all as she loses herself in a rerun of *Seinfeld*. In other words, you can't tell much about what she is thinking just by looking at her. But if the TV program creates an emotional experience, you will be able to make a reasonably accurate guess about which emotion she is feeling based on her facial expressions. The human face can create thousands of different expressions, and people—especially females—are good at detecting them (Becker et al., 2011; McClure, 2000; Zajonc, 1998). Observers can see even very small facial movements: a twitch of the mouth can carry a lot of information (Ambadar, Schooler, & Cohn, 2005; Ekman, 2009). Are emotional facial expressions innate or are they learned? And how are they used in communicating emotion?

Innate Expressions of Emotion

Charles Darwin noticed that some facial expressions seem to be universal (Darwin, 1872). He proposed that these expressions are genetically determined, passed on biologically from one generation to the next. The facial expressions seen today, said Darwin, are those that have been most effective over the centuries for telling others something about how a person is feeling, and thus what they are likely to say and do next (Shariff & Tracey, 2011). If someone is scowling with teeth clenched, for example, you will probably assume that the person is angry, and you won't choose that particular moment to ask for a loan (Marsh, Ambady, & Kleck, 2005).

What Are They Feeling?
People's emotions are usually "written on their faces." Jot down what emotions you think these people are feeling, and then look at the answer shown at the bottom of page 336 to see how well you "read" their emotions.

Infants provide one source of evidence that some facial expressions are innate. Newborns do not have to be taught to grimace in pain, to smile in pleasure, or to blink when startled (Balaban, 1995). Even blind infants, who cannot imitate adults' expressions, show the same emotional expressions as do sighted infants (Goodenough, 1932). These emotional facial expressions help to provide caregivers with accurate information about babies' conditions and needs (Izard et al., 1980; Huebner & Izard, 1988).

Another line of evidence for innate facial expressions comes from studies showing that for the most basic emotions, people in all cultures show similar facial responses to similar emotional stimuli (Hejmadi, Davidson, & Rozin, 2000; Matsumoto &

The Universal Smile
The idea that some emotional expressions are inborn is supported by the fact that the facial movement pattern we call a smile is related to happiness, pleasure, and other positive emotions in cultures throughout the world.

FIGURE 8.6
Elements of Ceremonial Facial Masks That Convey Threat

Certain geometric patterns are common to threatening masks in many cultures. "Scary" Halloween pumpkins tend to include these patterns, too. When people in various cultures were asked which member of each of these pairs was more threatening, they consistently chose those containing triangular and diagonal elements (shown here on the left). Cover this caption, then ask a few friends to try the same task. How many of them chose the elements on the left as being more threatening?

LEARN by DOING

Willingham, 2006; Zajonc, 1998). Participants in these studies looked at photographs of people's faces and then tried to name the emotion each person was feeling. The pattern of facial movements we call a smile, for example, is universally related to positive emotions. Sadness is almost always accompanied by slackened muscle tone and a "long" face. Likewise, in almost all cultures, people contort their faces in a similar way when shown something they find disgusting. And a furrowed brow is frequently associated with frustration or unpleasantness (Ekman, 1994).

Anger is also linked with a facial expression recognized by almost all cultures. One study examined the ceremonial masks seen in 18 Western and non-Western cultures (Aronoff, Barclay, & Stevenson, 1988). In all these cultures, angry, threatening masks contained similar elements, such as triangular eyes and diagonal lines on the cheeks. In particular, angular and diagonal elements carry the impression of threat (see Figure 8.6).

Social and Cultural Influences on Emotional Expression

Not all basic emotional expressions are innate or universal (Ekman, 1993; Jack et al., 2012). Some are learned through contact with a particular culture, and all of them, even innate expressions, are flexible enough to change as necessary in the social situations in which they occur (Fernández-Dols & Ruiz-Belda, 1995). For example, facial expressions become more intense and change more frequently when people are imagining social scenes as opposed to solitary scenes (Fridlund et al., 1990). Similarly, facial expressions in response to odors tend to be more intense when others are watching than when people are alone (Jancke & Kaufmann, 1994).

Further, although some basic emotional facial expressions are recognized by all cultures (Hejmadi, Davidson, & Rozin, 2000), even these can be interpreted differently depending on body language and environmental cues. For example, research participants interpreted a particular expression as disgust when it appeared on the face of a person who was holding a dirty diaper, but that same expression was seen as anger when it was digitally superimposed on a person in a fighting stance (Aviezer et al., 2008).

There is a certain degree of cultural variation when it comes to recognizing some emotions (Russell, 1995). In one study, Japanese and North Americans agreed about which facial expressions signaled happiness, surprise, and sadness, but they frequently disagreed about which faces showed anger, disgust, and fear (Matsumoto & Ekman, 1989). Members of cultures such as the Fore of Papua New Guinea agree even less with people in Western cultures on the labeling of facial expressions (Russell, 1994). People from different cultures may also differ in the way they interpret emotions expressed by tone of voice, or by a combination of vocal and facial cues (Mesquita & Frijda, 1992; Tanaka et al., 2010). An example is provided by a study showing that Taiwanese participants were best at recognizing a sad tone of voice, whereas Dutch participants were best at recognizing happy tones (Van Bezooijen, Otto, & Heenan, 1983).

People learn how to express certain emotions in ways specified by cultural rules. Suppose you say, "I just bought a new car," and all your friends stick their tongues out at you. In North America, this display probably means they are envious or resentful. But in some regions of China, it expresses surprise. Even smiles can vary as people learn to use them to communicate certain feelings. Paul Ekman and his colleagues categorized seventeen types of smiles, including "false smiles," which fake enjoyment, and "masking smiles," which hide unhappiness. They called the smile that occurs with real happiness the *Duchenne smile* (pronounced "do-SHEN"), after the French researcher who first noticed a difference between spontaneous, happy smiles and posed smiles. A genuine Duchenne smile includes contractions of the muscles around the eyes (creating a distinctive wrinkling of the skin in these areas) as well as contractions of the muscles that raise the lips and cheeks. Few people can successfully contract the muscles around the eyes during a posed smile, so this feature can be used to distinguish "lying smiles" from genuine ones (Frank, Ekman, & Friesen, 1993).

Learning about Emotions   The effects of learning are seen in a child's growing range of emotional expressions. Although infants begin with a set of innate emotional responses, they soon learn to imitate facial expressions and use them to express a wide range of emotions. In time, these expressions become more precise and personalized, so that a particular expression conveys a clear message to anyone who knows that person well.

If facial expressions become too personalized, however, no one will know what the expressions mean and they will fail to bring responses from others. Operant shaping, described in the chapter on learning, probably helps keep emotional expressions within certain limits. If you could not see other people's facial expressions or observe their responses to yours, you might show fewer, or less intense, facial signs of emotion. In fact, as congenitally blind people grow older, their facial expressions tend to become less animated (Izard, 1977; Matsumoto & Willingham, 2009).

As children grow, they learn an *emotion culture*—rules that govern what emotions are appropriate in what circumstances and what emotional expressions are allowed (Chen, Kennedy, & Zhou, 2012). These rules can vary between genders and from culture to culture (LaFrance, Hecht, & Paluck, 2003; Matsumoto et al., 2005; Tsai, Levenson, & McCoy, 2006). For example, TV news cameras showed that men in the U.S. military being deployed to a war zone tended to keep their emotions in check as they said goodbye to wives, girlfriends, and parents. However, many male soldiers in Italy—where mother-son ties are particularly strong—wailed with dismay and wept openly as they left. In a laboratory study, when viewing a distressing movie with a group of peers, Japanese students exerted much more control over their facial expressions than did North American students. When they watched the film while alone, however, the Japanese students' faces showed the same emotional expressions as those of the North American students (Ekman, Friesen, & Ellsworth, 1972).

Social Referencing   Facial expressions, tone of voice, body postures, and gestures can do more than communicate emotion. They can also influence other people's behavior, especially people who are not sure what to do (Blechert et al., 2012; Howell & Shepperd, 2012; Parkinson, Phiri, & Simons, 2012; Skarratt, Cole, & Kingstone, 2010). An inexperienced chess player, for instance, might reach out to move the queen, catch sight of a spectator's pained expression, and infer that another move would be better. Poker players often rely on their opponents' tell-tale facial expressions for cues about whether to bet, and how much (Schlicht et al., 2010). The process of letting another person's emotional state guide our own behavior is called *social referencing* (Campos, 1980). This process begins early; even three-month-old infants will look in the direction in which an adult's eyes have moved (Hood, Willen, & Driver, 1998).

The visual-cliff studies described in the sensation and perception chapter have been used to create an uncertain situation for infants. To reach its mother, an infant in these experiments must cross the visual cliff. If the apparent drop-off is very small or very large, there is no doubt about what to do. One-year-olds crawl across in the first case and stay put in the second case. However, if the apparent drop-off is just large enough (say, two feet) to create uncertainty, the infant relies on its mother's facial expressions to decide what to do. In one study, mothers were asked to make either a fearful or a joyful face. When the mothers made a fearful face, no infant crossed the glass floor. But when they made a joyful face, most infants crossed (Sorce et al., 1981). Here is yet another example of the adaptive value of sending, and receiving, emotional communications.

The photo on page 334 shows the wife and daughter of a U.S. Army soldier waving goodbye as his unit departs for training prior to deployment in a war zone. Their emotions probably included sadness, anxiety, worry, dread, uncertainty, hope, and perhaps anger.

Active Review

As noted in the introductory chapter, all of psychology's subfields are related to one another. Our discussion of motivational conflicts and stress illustrates just one way that the topic of this chapter, motivation and emotion, is linked to the subfield of health psychology, discussed in the chapter on health, stress, and coping.

CHAPTER 8
Motivation and Emotion

The Linkages diagram shows ties to two other subfields, and there are many more ties throughout the book. Looking for linkages among subfields will help you see how they all fit together and help you better appreciate the big picture that is psychology.

LINKAGES

How does the brain know when we're hungry?
(ans. on p. 305)

CHAPTER 2
Biology and Behavior

Can motivational conflicts cause stress?
(ans. on p. 323)

CHAPTER 10
Health, Stress, and Coping

Why do some people take more risks than others?
(ans. on p. 432)

CHAPTER 11
Personality

Summary

Motivation refers to factors that influence the initiation, direction, intensity, and persistence of behavior. Emotions and motivation are often linked: motivation can influence emotions, and people are often motivated to seek certain emotions.

Concepts and Theories of Motivation

Where does motivation come from?
Focusing on a *motive* often reveals a single theme within apparently diverse behaviors. The many sources of motivation fall into five categories: physiological factors, needs, emotional factors, cognitive factors, and social factors.

An early argument held that motivation is based on *instinctive behaviors*—automatic, involuntary, and unlearned action patterns consistently "released" by particular stimuli. Modern versions of this *instinct doctrine* are seen in evolutionary accounts of helping, aggression, mate selection, and other aspects of social behavior. *Drive reduction theory* is based on *homeostasis*, a tendency to maintain equilibrium in a physical or behavioral process. When disruption of equilibrium creates *needs* of some kind, people are motivated to reduce the resulting *drives* by behaving in some way that satisfies the needs and restores balance. *Primary drives* are unlearned; *secondary drives* are learned. According to the *arousal theory* of motivation, people are motivated to behave in ways that maintain a level of *physiological arousal* that is optimal for their functioning. Finally, *incentive theory* highlights behaviors that are motivated by attaining desired stimuli (positive incentives) and avoiding undesirable ones (negative incentives).

When behavior is based mainly on *intrinsic motivation* it occurs simply for the pleasure and satisfaction that it brings. Behavior based mainly on *extrinsic motivation* is aimed at an external goal such as a winning a prize or avoiding a penalty.

Eating

What makes me start eating and stop eating?
Eating is controlled by a complex mixture of learning, culture, and biochemistry. The desire to eat *(hunger)* and the satisfaction *(satiation)* of that desire *(satiety)* that leads us to stop eating, depend on signals from the gut and from blood-borne substances such as glucose, fatty acids, amino acids, insulin, and

leptin. Activity in the ventro-medial nucleus of the hypothalamus results in satiety, whereas activity in the lateral hypothalamus results in hunger. Other areas of the hypothalamus, such as the paraventricular nucleus, are also involved. Further, several neurotransmitters act in various regions of the hypothalamus to motivate the eating of certain types of foods. Eating may also be influenced by the flavor of food and by the pleasure it can bring. Food selection is influenced by many factors, including social contexts and cultural traditions.

Obesity has been linked to overconsumption of certain kinds of foods, low energy metabolism, genetic factors, and even viruses. People suffering from **anorexia nervosa** starve themselves. Those who suffer from **bulimia** engage in binge eating, followed by purging through self-induced vomiting or laxatives.

Sexual Behavior
How often does the average person have sex?
Sexual motivation and behavior result from a rich interplay of biology and culture. Sexual stimulation produces a **sexual response cycle,** a predictable physiological pattern of **sexual arousal** before, during, and after sexual activity. **Sex hormones,** which include male hormones **(androgens)** and female hormones **(estrogens** and **progestational hormones,** or **progestins)**, occur in different relative amounts in both sexes. They can have organizing effects, which create physical differences in the brain, and activating effects, which temporarily increase the desire for sex.

Gender-role learning, educational experiences, media influences, and family dynamics are examples of cultural factors that can bring about variations in sexual attitudes and behaviors. Sexual

orientation—**heterosexuality, homosexuality** (gay or lesbian), or **bisexuality**—is increasingly viewed as a sociocultural variable that affects many other aspects of behavior and mental processes. Although undoubtedly shaped by a lifetime of learning, sexual orientation appears to have strong biological roots.

Achievement Motivation
Why do some people try harder than others to succeed?
People gain esteem from achievement in many areas, including the workplace. The motive to succeed is called **achievement motivation,** or the **need for achievement**. Individuals with high achievement motivation strive for excellence, persist despite failures, and set challenging but realistic goals.

Workers are most satisfied when they are working toward their own goals and getting concrete feedback. Jobs that offer clear and specific goals, a variety of tasks, individual responsibility, and other intrinsic rewards are the most motivating. People tend to have a characteristic level of happiness, or **well-being,** that is not necessarily related to the attainment of money, status, or other material goals.

Relations and Conflicts among Motives
Which motives move me most?
People's behavior reflects many motives, some of which may be in conflict. Maslow proposed a hierarchy of five types of human motives, from meeting basic physiological needs to attaining

self-actualization. Motives at the lowest levels, according to Maslow, must be at least partially satisfied before people can be motivated by higher-level goals. Alderfer's three-level version does not assume that needs must be met in a particular order.

Four types of motivational conflict have been identified: approach-approach, avoidance-avoidance, approach-avoidance, and multiple approach-avoidance conflicts. These conflicts act as stressors, and people caught in them often experience physical and psychological problems.

The Nature of Emotions
How do feelings differ from thoughts?
Emotions are temporary experiences with negative or positive qualities that are felt with some intensity as happening to the self, are generated in part by interpretation of a situation, and are accompanied by both learned and innate physical responses.

Several brain mechanisms are involved in emotions, including the amygdala in the limbic system. The expression of emotions through involuntary facial movement is controlled by the extrapyramidal motor system. Voluntary facial movements are controlled by the pyramidal motor system. The brain's right and left hemispheres play somewhat different roles in emotions. In addition to specific brain mechanisms, both the **sympathetic nervous system** and the **parasympathetic nervous system,** which are divisions of the autonomic nervous system, are involved in physiological changes that accompany emotional activation. The **fight-flight reaction (or fight-or-flight syndrome)**, for example, follows from activation of the sympathetic nervous system.

Theories of Emotion

Are emotions in the heart, in the head, or both?
James said that peripheral physiological responses are the primary source of emotions and that awareness of these responses creates emotional experience. James's peripheral theory is supported by evidence that, at least for several basic emotions, physiological responses are distinguishable enough for emotions to be generated in this way. Distinct facial expressions are linked to particular patterns of physiological change.

Cannon's central theory of emotions proposes that emotional experience is independent of bodily responses and that there is a direct experience of emotions based on activity of the central nervous system. Updated versions of this theory suggest that various parts of the central nervous system may be involved in different emotions and different aspects of emotional experience. Some pathways in the brain, such as the pathway from the thalamus to the amygdala, allow strong emotions to occur before conscious thought can take place. Specific parts of the brain appear to be responsible for the feelings of pleasure or pain in emotions.

Cognitive theories of emotions include the Schachter-Singer theory. It suggests that physiological responses are primary sources of emotion but that interpretation of these responses in light of the situation is required to label the emotion. This interpretation process depends on **attribution**. Attributing arousal from one situation to stimuli in another situation is explained by **excitation transfer theory**, which suggests that physiological arousal stemming from one situation can intensify the emotion experienced in a second situation. Other cognitive theorists such as Lazarus have argued that emotional experience is significantly affected by how we interpret events themselves, not just by how we interpret physiological responses to those events.

Communicating Emotion

Which emotional expressions are innate, and which are learned?
In humans, emotions can be communicated by words, voice tones, postures, bodily movements, and facial movements and expressions. Darwin suggested that certain facial expressions of emotions are innate and universal and that these expressions evolved because they effectively communicate one creature's emotional condition to other creatures. Some facial expressions of basic emotions do appear to be innate, and certain facial movements are universally associated with certain emotions.

Other emotional expressions are learned, and even innate expressions are modified by learning and social contexts. As children grow, they learn an emotion culture, the rules of emotional expression appropriate to their culture.

Accordingly, the same emotion may be communicated by different facial expressions in different cultures. Especially in ambiguous situations, one person's emotional expressions may serve to guide another person's behavior, a phenomenon called **social referencing.**

Put It in Writing

Write a page or two about what goals you hope to achieve in life, what motivates you to strive for them, and how important it is for you to reach them. In light of our discussion about achievement and well-being, consider the question of whether reaching your goals will make you happy and contented or leave you always wanting more.

Personal Learning Activity

Make a video of a session in which you ask a friend four questions, such as "Who was the best teacher you ever had?" "What's the strangest thing that ever happened to you?" "What is your most surprising talent?" or "Where would you most like to live?" Ask your friend to give truthful answers to two of these questions but to lie as convincingly as possible while answering the other two. Now show the video to a group of people and ask them to say which answers are true and which are lies. How well did your participants do? If they are like most people, they probably were right about half the time on this lie detection task (DePaulo, 1994). Did the participants' accuracy differ depending on whether or not they knew the person on the video? If so, why do you think this was so?

Review of Key Terms

Can you define each of the key terms in the chapter? Check your definitions against those on the pages shown in parentheses in the following list or in the Glossary at the end of the book.

achievement motivation (need for achievement) (p. 317)
androgens (p. 313)
anorexia nervosa (p. 309)
arousal theory (p. 301)
attribution (p. 331)
bisexuality (p. 315)
bulimia (p. 310)
drive (p. 300)
drive reduction theory (p. 300)

emotions (p. 325)
estrogens (p. 313)
excitation-transfer theory (p. 332)
extrinsic motivation (p. 303)
fight-flight reaction (fight-or-flight syndrome) (p. 327)
heterosexuality (p. 315)
homeostasis (p. 300)
homosexuality (p. 315)
hunger (p. 304)
incentive theory (p. 301)
instinct doctrine (p. 299)
instinctive behaviors (p. 299)
intrinisic motivation (p.303)
motivation (p. 298)
motive (p. 298)

needs (p. 300)
obesity (p. 306)
parasympathetic nervous system (p. 327)
physiological arousal (p. 301)
primary drives (p. 300)
progestational hormones (progestins) (p. 313)
satiation (p. 304)
satiety (p. 304)
secondary drives (p. 301)
sex hormones (p. 313)
sexual arousal (p. 311)
sexual response cycle (p. 313)
sympathetic nervous system (p. 327)
well-being (subjective well-being) (p. 321)

Test Your Knowledge

Select the best answer for each of the following questions. Then check your responses against the Answer Key at the end of the book.

1. Although most researchers do not believe in instinct theories of motivation, psychologists who advocate ___ theory argue that many aspects of human behavior are motivated by efforts to pass on our genes to the next generation.
   a. drive reduction
   b. evolutionary
   c. arousal
   d. incentive
2. Steve is cold, so he turns up the thermostat in his house. As soon as it starts to get too warm, the thermostat shuts off the furnace. This process is similar to the biological concept of ___.
   a. homeostasis
   b. secondary drive
   c. incentive
   d. arousal
3. Lisbeth and Harriet work as instructors in an exercise class. After class, Lisbeth prefers to go home and read quietly, whereas Harriet is ready to party. Which theory of motivation *best* explains the difference between these two women?
   a. Drive reduction
   b. Instinct
   c. Evolutionary
   d. Arousal
4. Monica wants her daughter to get high grades, so she offers her $10 for each A that she earns and $5 for each B. Monica appears to believe in the ___ theory of motivation.
   a. drive reduction
   b. incentive
   c. evolutionary
   d. arousal

5. Ahmed is desperate to lose weight. To keep from eating, he buys an electrical device that allows him to stimulate various areas of his brain. Which areas should he stimulate if he wants his brain to help him reduce food intake?
   a. Ventromedial nucleus and paraventricular nucleus
   b. Lateral hypothalamus and ventromedial nucleus
   c. Lateral hypothalamus and paraventricular nucleus
   d. Thalamus and pineal gland
6. Ronia is on a diet—again! She is *most* likely to eat less food if she ___.
   a. eats only with friends, never alone
   b. eats only one or two kinds of food at each meal
   c. changes her food culture
   d. focuses on the flavor of what she eats
7. Dr. Stefan is working in the emergency room when a very dehydrated young woman comes in. She is of normal weight, but a medical exam reveals nutritional imbalances and intestinal damage. The woman is *most* likely suffering from ___.
   a. anorexia nervosa
   b. bulimia
   c. lateral hypothalamic disorder
   d. ventromedial disorder
8. The University of Chicago's National Health and Social Life Survey found that people in the United States ___.
   a. are more sexually active than previously thought
   b. have sex more often if they are not in an exclusive relationship
   c. have sex less often and with fewer people than previously thought
   d. do not enjoy sex very much
9. According to the Thinking Critically section of this chapter, sexual orientation is *most* likely influenced by ___.
   a. prenatal hormones
   b. genetic factors
   c. sociocultural learning
   d. all of the above

10. Edwina wants her son, Egbert, to develop high achievement motivation and to be successful in life. According to research on the need for achievement, Edwina should do all of the following *except* ___.
    a. encourage Egbert to try difficult tasks
    b. encourage Egbert to avoid failure at all costs
    c. give praise and rewards for success
    d. read achievement-oriented stories to him

11. Liang wants his employees to work hard. As a psychologist specializing in motivation, you tell Liang that the *best* way to increase employees' performance is to ___.
    a. increase their pay and benefits
    b. allow them to set their own goals
    c. remind them regularly of the need to do better
    d. keep all tasks as simple as possible

12. According to Maslow, which of the following would you *most* likely do first if you were shipwrecked on a desert island?
    a. Look for food and fresh water
    b. Look for firewood
    c. Start keeping a diary
    d. Build a place to live

13. Jill would like to send her son to an expensive private school, but this would create a financial hardship for her. Jill is faced with a(n) ___ motivational conflict.
    a. approach-approach
    b. avoidance-avoidance
    c. approach-avoidance
    d. multiple approach-avoidance

14. Which of the following is *not* a characteristic associated with emotions? They ___.
    a. tend to last a relatively short time
    b. can be triggered by thoughts
    c. are always intense
    d. can motivate behavior

15. When people are afraid to do something, they are said to have "cold feet." The fact that fear is associated with decreased blood flow to the feet and hands supports ___ theory of emotion.
    a. James's peripheral
    b. Cannon's central
    c. Schachter's cognitive
    d. Lazarus's cognitive

16. After she finished a vigorous workout, Lydia saw Thaddeus walk into the gym and instantly fell in love. This is an example of ___, which is consistent with ___ theory of emotion.
    a. social referencing; James's
    b. social referencing; Schachter's
    c. excitation transfer; James's
    d. excitation transfer; Schachter's

17. When Yatsira saw someone trying to open her car door while she was stopped at a light, her heart raced and at the exact same time she felt fear. This is *most* consistent with ___ theory of emotion.
    a. James's
    b. Cannon's
    c. Schachter's
    d. Lazarus's

18. As Jarrod got older, he learned that he could not express his anger by throwing his toys. Jarrod is learning ___.
    a. to use facial feedback
    b. Darwin's universal rules
    c. to use social referencing
    d. his emotion culture

19. Suppose that some friendly space aliens landed in your backyard. They tell you they want to learn how to communicate their emotions so that humans will understand them. What should you focus on teaching them?
    a. Body postures
    b. Facial movements
    c. Hand gestures
    d. Voice inflections

20. Sam is unsure how to react to a comment from one of his friends, so he glances at his girlfriend, Diane, to see what her reaction is. In doing so, he is using ___.
    a. facial feedback
    b. social referencing
    c. attribution
    d. excitation transfer

Media Resources

Now that you have finished reading this chapter, how about exploring some of the ideas and information that you found most interesting?

Coursemate Go to **CengageBrain.com** to access Psychology CourseMate, where you will find an interactive eBook, glossaries, flashcards, quizzes, videos, Virtual Psychology Labs, and more.

aplia

Aplia If your professor has assigned Aplia:
1. Sign in to your account.
2. Complete the corresponding exercises as required by your professor.
3. When finished, click "Grade It Now" to see which areas you have mastered, which areas need more work, and detailed explanations of every answer.

Human Development

© Catherine Yeulet/Photos.com

Preview

Infancy, childhood, adolescence, adulthood, and old age. These words can be read in seconds, but the stages they represent take a lifetime to play out. The story of development is different for each of us, but there are some common threads, too, and developmental psychologists are exploring them. In this chapter, we describe what they have discovered so far about how people change and grow over the course of their lives.

When he was eight years old, Jelani Freeman came home from school to find that his mentally ill mother was gone. She never came back. His father, whom he had never met, was in prison, so social workers arranged for him to live in a foster home. Over the next ten years he lived in six of them, in a series of slum neighborhoods in Rochester, NY. A couple of attempts were made to reunite him with his mother, but because of her mental condition, these reunions did not last long. His final placement, for a year and a half, was with an older sister who took him in on a foster-care basis, but told him he would have to leave when he turned 18. In his teenage years, his grades slipped and so did his school attendance, and when he asked a high school counselor about taking a college entrance examination, she told him the exam was for students who value education. But Jelani took the test anyway and did well enough to get into college in Buffalo, NY, taking out loans, finding financial aid, and working at several part-time jobs. After graduation he won an internship at the United States Senate in Washington, DC and then went on to complete a master's degree in history and then a law degree. What allowed Jelani to succeed, when the odds were so heavily against him from the beginning?

Developmental psychologists try to find answers to questions like these. They ask how and why some children are more resilient to stress than others, why some develop into well-adjusted, socially competent, caring individuals while others become murderers or why some adolescents go on to win honors in college and others drop out of high school (El-Sheikh, Hinnant, & Erath, 2011; Goodman, Miller, & West-Olatunji, 2011; Miller et al., 2011; Moffitt et al., 2011; Phillips & Morse, 2011; Raine & Liu, 1998; Reijntjes et al., 2010). They seek to explain how genetics and the environment affect development through infancy, childhood, and adolescence; to analyze the extent to which development is a product of what we arrive with at birth—our inherited, biological *nature*—and the extent to which it is a product of what the world provides—the *nurture* of the environment (Blair & Raver, 2012; Lewkowicz & Ghazanfar, 2012; Luby et al., 2012; Sandman, Davis, & Glynn, 2012). They explore the times when certain kinds of behavior first appear, how those behaviors change with age, and whether the changes are sudden or gradual. They look into how development in one area, such as moral reasoning, relates to development in other areas, such as aggressive behavior. Developmental psychologists attempt to discover whether everyone develops at the same rate and if not, whether slow starters ever catch up to early bloomers. They also study the development that occurs over the years of adulthood and try to determine how these changes are related to earlier abilities and the events of life. In short, **developmental psychology** is concerned with the course and causes of developmental changes over a person's entire lifetime (Heckhausen, Wrosch, & Schulz, 2010).

This chapter focuses on many of these changes, beginning with the physical and biological changes that take place from the moment of conception to the moment of birth. ●

Courtesy of Jelani Freeman

Beating the Odds
Despite a severely disadvantaged childhood, Jelani Freeman—shown here with Hillary Rodham Clinton—managed to graduate from law school and begin a career in the U.S. State Department. How did he do it? One important factor appeared at age 16, when he met an adult mentor who gave him a part time job in her office. She also took him to church and helped him fight the temptation to earn money by selling drugs. Most of all she let him know that she cared about him and was there to help him whenever he needed it. Studying the interplay of genetic and environmental factors that influence positive and negative life trajectories is an important aspect of developmental psychology.

developmental psychology The psychological specialty that documents the course of people's social, emotional, moral, and intellectual development over the life-span.

Exploring Human Development

What does "genetic influence" mean?

Philosophical arguments about how nature and nurture affect development can be traced back through centuries. In essays published in the 1690s, the British empiricist philosopher John Locke argued for the importance of nurture. He believed that what happens in childhood has a profound and permanent effect on the individual. Empiricists saw the newborn as a blank slate, or *tabula rasa*. Adults write on that slate, said Locke, as they teach children about the world and how to behave in it. About seventy years later, French philosopher Jean-Jacques Rousseau argued just the opposite, claiming that children are capable of discovering how the world operates and how they should behave without instruction from adults. According to Rousseau, children should be allowed to grow as nature commands, with little guidance or pressure from parents.

The first American psychologist to investigate the role of nature in behavior systematically was Arnold Gesell (pronounced "geh-ZELL"). In the early 1900s, Gesell observed many children of all ages. He found that motor skills, such as standing and walking, picking up a cube, and throwing a ball, develop in a fixed sequence of stages in all children, as illustrated in Figure 9.1. Gesell argued that the order of the stages and the ages at which they appear are determined by nature and are relatively unaffected by nurture. Only under extreme conditions, such as famine, war, or poverty, he claimed, are children thrown off their biologically programmed timetable. This type of natural growth or change, which unfolds in a fixed sequence relatively independent of the environment, is called **maturation.** The broader term *development* encompasses not only maturation but also the behavioral and mental processes that are influenced by learning.

John B. Watson disagreed with Gesell's views. He argued that the environment, not nature, molds and shapes development. As described in the introductory chapter,

FIGURE 9.1
Motor Development

When did you start walking? The left end of each bar indicates the age at which 25 percent of infants were able to perform a particular behavior; 50 percent of the babies were performing the behavior at the age indicated by the vertical line in the bars; the right end indicates the age at which 90 percent could do so (Frankenberg & Dodds, 1967). Although different infants, especially in different cultures, achieve milestones of motor development at slightly different ages, all infants—regardless of their ethnicity, social class, or temperament—achieve them in the same order.

Photos (from bottom): © Design Pics/Kelly Redinger/Getty Images; © Elyse Lewin/The Image Bank/Getty Images; © Mastering_Microstock/Shutterstock; © Liz Banfield/Workbook Stock/Getty Images; © Rayes/Lifesize/Getty Images; © Ryan McVay/Riser/Getty Images; © KidStock/Blend Images/Getty Images

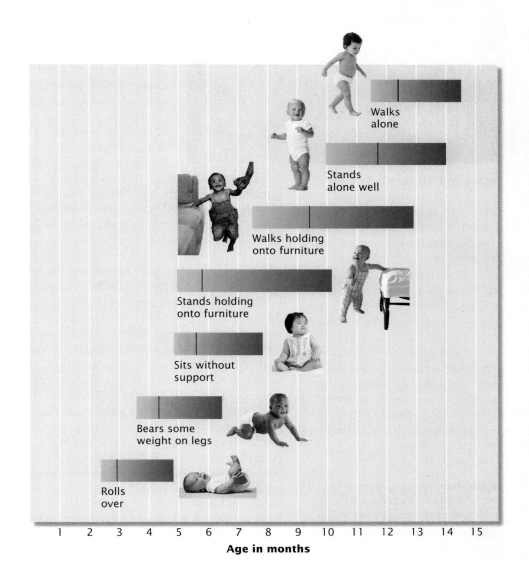

Walks alone

Stands alone well

Walks holding onto furniture

Stands holding onto furniture

Sits without support

Bears some weight on legs

Rolls over

1 2 3 4 5 6 7 8 9 10 11 12 13 14 15

Age in months

Watson founded the behaviorist approach to psychology. In the early 1900s he began conducting experiments with children. From these experiments Watson inferred that children learn *everything,* from skills to fears. In his words, "There is no such thing as an inheritance of capacity, talent, temperament, mental constitution and characteristics. These things … depend on training that goes on mainly in the cradle" (Watson, 1925, pp. 74–75).

It was the Swiss psychologist Jean Piaget (pronounced "pee-ah-ZHAY") who first suggested that nature and nurture work together and that their influences are inseparable and interactive. Through a series of books published from the 1920s until his death in 1980, Piaget's ideas influenced the field of developmental psychology more than those of any other person before or since (Flavell, 1996).

Understanding Genetic Influence

Most developmental psychologists now accept Piaget's idea that both nature and nurture contribute to development. Guided by research in **behavioral genetics,** the study of how genes affect behavior, they explore how genes and the environment influence specific aspects of development (Loehlin, 2010). Their studies have demonstrated that nature and nurture jointly contribute to development in two ways. First, nature and nurture operate together to make all people *similar* in some respects. For example, nature influences all of us to achieve milestones of motor development in the same order and at roughly the same rate. But supportive nurture, in the form of proper nutrition and exercise, is also necessary to allow normal maturation to unfold. Second, nature and nurture operate together to make each person *unique.* The nature of inherited genes and the nurture of diverse family and cultural environments produce differences among individuals in athletic abilities, intelligence, speech patterns, personality, and many other dimensions (Benjamin & Taylor, 2010; Bleidorn et al., 2010; Boutwell et al., 2011; Brendgen et al., 2008; Ducci & Goldman, 2008; Gregory et al., 2009; Haddad et al., 2008; Hopwood et al., 2011; Malouff, Rooke, & Schutte, 2008; Nigg, Nikolas, & Burt, 2010; South & Krueger, 2008).

Nature and Nurture Entwined
The combined effects of nature and nurture are illustrated in this family photo of Eli and Peyton Manning and their father, Archie Manning. The effect of nature on their athleticism could be seen in the fact that both boys weighed over 12 pounds at birth and were built like athletes, even as toddlers. The influence of nurture on their success—Peyton is quarterback of the Denver Broncos and Eli is quarterback of the New York Giants—came about partly through the fact that their father was quarterback of the New Orleans Saints. Their family life revolved around sports; they were tossing a football at the age of 3—and honing their skills with help from their father's coaching.

Behavioral geneticists are concerned with the *differences* between individuals or groups of individuals, not with the characteristics of a single individual. Consider height. Whether raised together or apart, identical twins (who have identical genes) are much more similar in height than fraternal twins (who share no more genes than other siblings) or unrelated individuals. This finding suggests that height is more strongly influenced by genes than by the environment. Does this mean that a person who is six feet tall grew four of those feet because of genes and the other two feet because of environment? No. It means that more of the variability in height that we see among people can be explained by differences in their genetics than by differences in their environments. In fact, genes do account for about 80 to 95 percent of the variability in height. So if a person is taller or shorter than average, genetic factors are probably the primary cause (Lettre, 2011). We say "probably" because genetic influences on height refer only to the origins of average individual differences in the population. So even though the differences in people's heights are due mainly to genetic factors, a particular person's shorter than normal height could be due mainly to an early illness or other growth-stunting environmental factors.

To see how behavioral genetics applies to psychological characteristics, suppose a researcher discovered that a certain personality trait is 50 percent heritable. This finding would mean that approximately half of the *differences between people* on that trait can be explained by genetic factors. It would not mean that each person inherits half of the trait and gets the other half from environmental influences. In other words, the results of behavioral genetics research allow us to draw general conclusions about the influence of nature and nurture on certain characteristics, but those conclusions do not necessarily apply to the origins of a *particular person's* characteristics. Keep in mind, too, that the effects of genes on our traits and behaviors are not always simple or fixed. Complex traits such as intelligence and personality are influenced by many genes as well as by

maturation Natural growth or change triggered by biological factors independent of the environment.

behavioral genetics The study of the effect of genes on behavior.

many environmental factors (Davies et al., 2011; Hare et al., 2012; Vinkhuyzen et al., 2012; Yang et al., 2011). So genetic influence means just that: *influence* (Bakermans-Kranenburg & Van Ijzendoorn, 2011; Malouff, Rooke, & Schutte, 2008; Plomin et al., 2002; South & Krueger, 2008). Genes can affect a trait without completely determining whether that trait will actually appear in a particular individual.

Genes and the Environment

The relative contributions of nature and nurture differ for specific aspects of development, but their influences on all human characteristics are forever intertwined (Perovic & Radenovic, 2011). They are also mutually influential. Just as the environment encourages or discourages the expression of an individual's inherited characteristics, those inherited characteristics determine the individual's environment to some extent. In short, heredity creates predispositions that interact with the immediate environment, including family, teachers, books, and computers (Caspi et al., 2002). This interaction is what produces developmental outcomes (Champagne; 2010, Curley et al., 2011; Lahey et al., 2011; Lewkowicz, 2011; Tucker-Drob & Harden, 2012a, 2012b). Let's now consider how it all begins.

Beginnings

Why should pregnant women stay away from tobacco and alcohol?

Nowhere are the intertwined contributions of heredity and environment clearer than during the eventful nine months before birth, when a single fertilized egg develops into a functioning newborn infant.

Prenatal Development

The process of development begins when sperm from a father-to-be fertilizes the egg of a mother-to-be and forms a brand-new cell. Most human cells contain 46 **chromosomes**, arranged in 23 matching pairs. Each chromosome is made up of thousands of **genes**, the biochemical units of heredity that govern the development of an individual. Genes, in turn, are composed of **DNA (deoxyribonucleic acid)**. The DNA in genes provides coded messages that serve as blueprints for constructing every aspect of a physical human being, including eye color, height, blood type, inherited disorders, and the like. All of this information fits in less space than the period that ends this sentence.

New cells in the body are constantly being produced by the division of existing cells. Most of the body's cells divide through a process called *mitosis*, in which the cell's chromosomes duplicate themselves so that each new cell contains copies of the 23 pairs of chromosomes in the original cell.

A different kind of cell division, called *meiosis*, occurs in the formation of a male's sperm cells and a female's egg cells. In meiosis, the chromosome pairs are not copied, but are randomly split and rearranged, leaving each new sperm and egg cell with just one member of each chromosome pair, or 23 *single* chromosomes. No two of these special new cells are quite the same, and none contains an exact copy of the person who produced it. So, at conception, when a male's sperm penetrates and *fertilizes* the female's ovum, a truly new cell is formed. The fertilized cell, called a *zygote*, carries the usual 23 pairs of chromosomes, but half of each pair comes from the mother and half from the father. The zygote represents a unique heritage—a complete genetic code for a new person that combines randomly selected aspects from both parents. The zygote divides first into copies of itself; then it continues to divide into the billions of specialized cells that form a complete new human being.

Stages of Prenatal Development   The first two weeks after conception are called the *germinal stage* of development. By the end of this stage, the cells of the dividing zygote have formed an **embryo**. In the *embryonic stage* of development, the embryo quickly

A Fetus at Twelve Weeks
In this photo of a fetus at three months after conception, the umbilical cord and placenta are clearly visible. At this point in prenatal development, the fetus can kick its legs, curl its toes, make a fist, turn its head, squint, open its mouth, swallow, and take a few "breaths" of amniotic fluid.

chromosomes Structures in every biological cell that contain genetic information in the form of genes.

genes Hereditary units, located on chromosomes, that contain biological instructions inherited from both parents, providing the blueprint for physical development.

DNA (deoxyribonucleic acid) The molecular structure of a gene that provides the genetic code.

embryo The developing individual from two weeks to two months after fertilization.

© Lennart Nilsson/Albert Bonniers Forlag AB, Behold Man, Little Brown and Company/Scanpix forms a heart, nervous system, stomach, esophagus, and ovaries or testes. By two months after conception, when the embryonic stage ends, the embryo looks decidedly human, with eyes, ears, nose, jaw, mouth, and lips. The tiny arms have elbows, hands, and stubby fingers and the legs have knees, ankles, and toes.

The seven-month period remaining until birth is called the *fetal stage* of prenatal development. During this stage, the various organs grow and start to function. By the end of the third month, the **fetus** can kick, make a fist, turn its head, open its mouth, swallow, and frown. In the sixth month, the eyelids, which have been sealed, open. The fetus is now capable of making sucking movements and has taste buds, eyebrows, eyelashes, and a well-developed grasp.

By the end of the seventh month, the organ systems, though immature, are all functional. In the eighth and ninth months, fetuses can respond to light and touch and can hear what is going on outside. They can remember a particular sound or melody heard a month earlier (Dirix et al., 2009; Granier-Deferre et al., 2011), and when hearing an unpleasant sound, they may respond with movements like those of a crying newborn (Gingras, Mitchell, & Grattan, 2005). They can also learn. When they hear their mother's familiar voice, their heart beats a little faster, but it slows if they hear a stranger (Kisilevsky et al., 2003).

Prenatal Risks   During prenatal development, a spongy organ called the *placenta* appears and attaches itself to the mother's uterus through an *umbilical cord*. (The cord is detached at birth, but you can see where yours was by looking at your navel.) The placenta sends nutrients from the mother to the developing baby and carries away wastes. It also screens out many potentially harmful substances, including most bacteria. This screening is imperfect, however: gases, viruses, nicotine, alcohol, and other drugs can pass through. Severe damage can occur if the baby's mother takes certain drugs, is exposed to certain toxic substances such as mercury, or has certain illnesses while organs are forming in the embryonic stage (Koger, Schettler, & Weiss, 2005).

Harmful external substances that invade the womb and result in birth defects are called **teratogens**. Teratogens are especially damaging in the embryonic stage, because it is a **critical period** in prenatal development, a time during which certain kinds of growth must occur if development is to proceed normally. If the heart, eyes, ears, hands, and feet do not appear during the embryonic stage, they cannot form later on. If they form incorrectly, the defects will be permanent. So even before a mother knows she is pregnant, she may accidentally damage her embryo by exposing it to teratogens. For example, a baby whose mother had rubella (German measles) during the third or fourth week after conception has a 50 percent chance of being born blind, deaf, intellectually disabled, or having a malformed heart. If the mother had rubella later in the pregnancy, after the infant's eyes, ears, brain, and heart have formed, the likelihood of these defects is much lower. Later, during the fetal stage, teratogens affect the baby's size, behavior, intelligence, and health rather than the formation of organs and limbs.

Defects due to teratogens are most likely to appear when the negative effects of nature and nurture combine. The worst-case scenario is one in which a genetically vulnerable infant receives a strong dose of a damaging substance during a critical period of prenatal development (Huizink, Mulder, & Buitelaar, 2004; Van den Bergh & Marcoen, 2004).

Of special concern are the effects of drugs on infants' development (e.g., Eroglu et al., 2008; Forcelli, & Heinrichs, 2008; Gendle et al., 2004; James et al., 2007; Jones, 2006; Weiss, St. Jonn-Seed, & Harris-Muchell, 2007). Pregnant women who use substances such as cocaine create a substantial risk for their fetuses, which do not yet have the enzymes necessary to break down the drugs. "Cocaine babies" or "crack babies" may be born premature, underweight, tense, and fussy (Tronick et al., 2005). They may also suffer delayed physical growth and motor development (Richardson, Goldschmidt, & Larkby, 2007; Shankaran et al., 2011) and are more likely to have behavioral and learning problems (Accornero et al., 2011; Bada et al., 2007; Lewis et al., 2011; Richardson et al., 2011; Singer et al., 2001; Singer et al., 2002; Tan-Laxa et al., 2004). They may display slower-than-normal cognitive processing, too (Mayes et al., 2005), but other aspects of their cognitive abilities are not necessarily different from those of any baby born into an

fetus The developing individual from the third month after conception until birth.

teratogens Harmful substances, such as alcohol and other drugs, that can cause birth defects.

critical period An interval during which certain kinds of growth must occur if development is to proceed normally.

impoverished environment (Behnke et al., 2006; Frank et al., 2001; Jones, 2006). How well these children ultimately do in school depends on how supportive that environment turns out to be (Ackerman, Riggins, & Black, 2010; Bennett, Bendersky, & Lewis, 2008; Messinger et al., 2004).

Alcohol is another dangerous teratogen, because it interferes with infants' brain development (Sayal et al., 2009). Almost half the children born to expectant mothers who abuse alcohol will develop **fetal alcohol syndrome,** a pattern of defects that includes intellectual disability and malformations of the face (Davis, Desrocher, & Moore, 2011; Jenkins & Culbertson, 1996). Pregnant women who drink as little as a glass or two of wine a day can harm their infants' intellectual functioning (Roussotte et al., 2012; Willford, Leech, & Day, 2006). Those who engage in bouts of heavy drinking triple the odds that their child will develop alcohol-related problems by the age of 21 (Baer et al., 2003; Landgren et al., 2010). The effects of prenatal exposure to alcohol may be even more severe when combined with the effects of other environmental toxins, such as air pollution (Arruda et al., 2011; Mancinelli, Binetti, & Ceccanti, 2007).

Smoking can also affect the developing fetus. Smokers' babies often suffer from respiratory problems, allergies, irritability, and attention problems, and they are at greater risk for nicotine addiction, insulin resistance, and behavioral problems in adolescence and adulthood (Buka, Shenassa, & Niaura, 2003; Ekblad et al., 2011; Espy et al., 2011; Hay et al., 2011; Huijbregts et al., 2011; Linnet et al., 2005; Liu, 2011; Stéphan-Blanchard et al., 2010; Stroud et al., 2009; Tanaka & Miyake, 2011; Thiering et al., 2011; Verhagen et al., 2011; Wakschlag et al., 2006). Worse, they may be born prematurely, and they are usually underweight.

The risk of low birth weight and later complications is also increased for children whose mothers were under significant stress or got the flu during the first six months of pregnancy (Beijers et al., 2010; Brown et al., 2005; Entringer et al., 2011; Khashan et al., 2008). Babies who are premature and/or underweight—for whatever reason—are likely to have cognitive, emotional, and behavioral problems that continue throughout their lives (Bhutta et al., 2002; Doyle & Anderson, 2010; Evrard et al., 2011; Ginzel et al., 2007; Jefferis, Power, & Hertzman, 2002; Kerstjens et al., 2011; Nosarti et al., 2012; Rogers et al., 2012; Sansavini et al., 2011; Woythaler, McCormick, & Smith, 2011).

Fortunately, mental or physical problems resulting from all harmful prenatal factors affect fewer than 10 percent of the babies born in Western nations. The vast majority of fetuses arrive at the end of their nine-month gestation averaging a healthy seven pounds and ready to continue a normal course of development in the world.

The Newborn

Determining what newborns can see, hear, or do is one of the most fascinating and frustrating challenges for researchers in developmental psychology. Babies are extremely difficult to study because they sleep about 70 percent of the time. When they are not sleeping, they are drowsy, crying, awake and active, or awake and inactive. It is only when they are in this latter state, which is infrequent and lasts only a few minutes, that psychological scientists can assess the infants' abilities.

To do so, they show infants objects or pictures and record where they look and for how long. They film the infants' eye movements and pupil dilations, and note changes in heart rates, sucking rates, brain waves, bodily movements, and skin conductance (a measure of perspiration that accompanies emotion) when objects are shown or sounds are made. From studies using these techniques, researchers have pieced together a fair picture of what infants can see and hear (Kellman & Arterberry, 2006; Laeng, Sirois, & Gredebäck, 2012).

Vision and Other Senses Infants can see at birth, but their vision is blurry. Researchers estimate that newborns have 20/300 eyesight. In other words, an object 20 feet away looks only as clear as it would if viewed from 300 feet by an adult with normal vision. The reason infants' vision is so limited is that their eyes and brains still need time to grow and develop. Newborns' eyes are smaller than those of adults, and the cells in the fovea—the

A Rare Multiple Birth
When Nadya Suleman delivered eight babies on January 26, 2009, it was only the second time that octuplets have been known to survive for more than a few hours. The infants remained at severe risk for a considerable time, though, because they were premature and underweight (the heaviest was 3 pounds, 4 ounces, and the lightest only 1 pound, 8 ounces).

fetal alcohol syndrome A pattern of defects found in babies born to women who abused alcohol during pregnancy.

A Baby's-Eye View of the World
The top photograph simulates what a mother looks like to her infant at three months of age. Although their vision is blurry, infants particularly seem to enjoy looking at faces.

Source: Nelson, C. A. (1987). The recognition of facial expressions in the first two years of life: Mechanisms of development. *Child Development, 58*, 889–909.

area in each eye on which images are focused—are fewer and far less sensitive. Their eye movements are slow and jerky. And pathways connecting the eyes to the brain are still inefficient, as is the processing of visual information within the brain.

Although infants cannot see small objects across the room, they can see large objects up close—the distance at which most interactions with caregivers take place. Infants look longest at moving objects, especially those that have large elements, clear contours, and a lot of contrast—all of which are features of the human face (Farroni et al., 2005; Turati, 2004).

Newborns actively use their senses to explore the world around them. At first, they attend to sights and sounds for only short periods. Gradually, their attention spans lengthen and their exploration becomes more systematic. In the first two months, they focus only on the edges of objects, but after two months of age, they scan whole objects (Banks & Salapatek, 1983). Then, when they see an object, they get all the information they can from it before going on to something new (Hunter & Ames, 1988). Newborns stare at human faces longer than at other figures (Valenza et al., 1996). They are particularly interested in eyes, as shown in their preference for faces that are looking directly at them (Farroni et al., 2002).

At two or three days of age, newborns can hear soft voices and notice differences between tones about one note apart on the musical scale (Aslin, Jusczyk, & Pisoni, 1998). In addition, they turn their heads toward sounds (Clifton, 1992). But their hearing is not as sharp as that of adults' until well into childhood. This condition is not merely a hearing problem; it also reflects an inability to listen selectively to some sounds over others (Bargones & Werner, 1994). As infants grow, they develop sensory capacities and the skill to use them.

Infants pay special attention to speech. When they hear someone talking, they open their eyes wider and search for the speaker. Infants also prefer certain kinds of speech. They like rising tones spoken by women or children (Sullivan & Horowitz, 1983). They also like high-pitched, exaggerated, and expressive speech. In other words, they like to hear the "motherese," or "baby talk," used by most adults in all cultures when talking to babies. They even seem to learn language faster when they hear baby talk (Thiessen, Hill, & Saffran, 2005).

Newborns also like certain smells and tastes more than others. When given something sweet to drink, they suck longer and slower, pause for shorter periods, and smile and lick their lips (Ganchrow, Steiner, & Daher, 1983). When they smell their mother's breast, newborns become quiet, open their eyes, and try to suck (Doucet et al., 2007, 2009). Within a few days after birth, breastfed babies prefer the odor of their own mother's breast milk to that of another mother (Porter et al., 1992).

Reflexes and Motor Skills In the first weeks and months after birth, babies show involuntary, unlearned reactions called **reflexes.** These swift, automatic movements occur in response to external stimuli. Figure 9.2 illustrates the *grasping reflex,* one of more than 20 reflexes that have been observed in newborn infants. Another is the *rooting reflex,* whereby the infant turns its mouth toward a finger or nipple that touches its cheek. And the newborn exhibits the *sucking reflex* in response to anything that touches its lips. Many of these reflexive behaviors evolved because they help infants survive. The absence of reflexes in a newborn signals problems in brain development. So does a failure of reflexes to disappear during the first three or four months, when brain development allows the infant to control muscles voluntarily.

Voluntary control permits the development of motor skills, allowing the infant to roll over, sit up, crawl, stand, and walk. Until a few years ago, most developmental psychologists accepted Gesell's view that except under extreme environmental conditions, these motor abilities occur spontaneously as the central nervous system and muscles mature. Research demonstrates, however, that maturation does not tell the whole story, even in normal environments (Thelen, 1995).

Consider the fact that many babies today aren't learning to crawl on time— or at all. Why? One reason has to do with the "Back to Sleep" campaign, which was launched in 1995 in an effort to prevent sudden infant death syndrome (see the chapter on consciousness). This public health campaign urges parents to put babies to sleep on their

reflexes Simple, involuntary, unlearned behaviors directed by the spinal cord without instructions from the brain.

FIGURE 9.2
Reflexes in the Newborn
When a finger is pressed into a newborn's palm, the grasping reflex causes the infant to hold on tightly enough to suspend its entire weight. And when a newborn is held upright over a flat surface, the stepping reflex leads to walking movements.

backs rather than face down. The campaign has been successful, but researchers have discovered that many babies who were never placed on their tummies went directly from sitting to toddling, skipping the crawling stage but reaching all other motor milestones on schedule (Kolata & Markel, 2001). In contrast, the "Prone to Play" campaign, which began in 2001, advised parents to place their babies in a prone (face down) position when awake in order to encourage play and learning. Babies of parents who followed this advice did show earlier than expected skill at rolling, crawling on their abdomens, and crawling on all fours, but their ability to walk did not appear unusually early (Kuo et al., 2008).

Observation of infants as they learn to crawl has shown that it does not happen suddenly. It takes the development of enough muscle strength to support the abdomen—and some active experimentation. Six infants in one study tried various crawling techniques—moving backward, moving one limb at a time, using the arms only, and so on (Freedland & Bertenthal, 1994). After a week or two of trial and error, all six infants arrived at the same method: moving the right arm and left leg together, then the left arm and right leg. This pattern turned out to be the most efficient way of getting around quickly without tipping over. Such observations suggest that as maturation increases infants' strength, they try out various motor patterns and select the ones that work best (Nelson, 1999).

In other words, motor development results from a combination of maturation and experience. It is not the result of an entirely automatic sequence that is genetically etched in the brain. Yet again, we see that nature and nurture influence each other. The brain controls developing behavior, but its own development is affected by experience, including efforts to build motor skills.

Infancy and Childhood: Cognitive Development

How do babies think?

In less than 10 years, a tiny infant becomes a person who can read a book, write a poem, and argue logically for a new computer. What leads to the dramatic shifts in thinking, knowing, and remembering that occur between early infancy and later childhood? Researchers studying *cognitive development* try to answer this question.

The Development of Knowledge: Piaget's Theory

Foremost among these researchers was Jean Piaget, who dedicated his life to a search for the origins of intelligence and the factors that lead to changes in knowledge over the life span. Piaget was the first to chart the journey from the simple reflexes of the newborn to the complex understandings of the adolescent. Although his theory turned out to be incomplete (and in some respects incorrect), his ideas about cognitive development are still guiding research (Fischer & Hencke, 1996; Shayer, 2008; Zittoun et al., 2007).

Intensive observations of infants (including his own) and extensive interviews with children led Piaget to propose that cognitive development proceeds in a series of distinct stages, or periods. He believed that all children's thinking goes through the same stages, in the same order, without skipping. (Table 9.1 outlines these stages.) According to Piaget, infants' thinking is different from children's thinking, which is different from adolescents' thinking. He said that children are not just miniature adults and that they are not less intelligent than adults, they just think in completely different ways at different stages of development. In other words, entering each stage involves a *qualitative* change from whatever preceded it, much as a caterpillar is transformed into a butterfly.

Building Blocks of Development   To explain how infants and children move to ever higher stages of understanding and knowledge, Piaget introduced the concept of *schemas* as the basic units of knowledge, the building blocks of intellectual development. As noted in other chapters, **schemas** are the generalizations that form as people experience the

schemas Mental representations of what we know and expect about the world.

TABLE 9.1   Piaget's Periods of Cognitive Development

According to Piaget, a predictable set of features characterizes each period of children's cognitive development. The ages associated with the stages are approximate; Piaget realized that some children move through the stages slightly faster or slower than others.

Period	Abilities and Achievements
Sensorimotor	
Birth–2 years	Infants discover aspects of the world through their sensory impressions, motor activities, and coordination of the two. They learn to differentiate themselves from the external world. They learn that objects exist even when they are not visible and that these objects are independent of the infants' own actions. Infants gain some appreciation of cause and effect.
Preoperational	
2–4 years	Children cannot yet manipulate and transform information in logical ways, but they now can think in images and symbols.
4–7 years	They become able to represent something with something else, acquire language, and play games of pretend. Intelligence at this stage is said to be intuitive because children cannot make general, logical statements.
Concrete operational	
7–11 years	Children can understand logical principles that apply to concrete external objects. They can appreciate that certain properties of an object remain the same, despite changes in appearance, and they can sort objects into categories. They can appreciate the perspective of another viewer. They can think about two concepts (such as longer and wider) at the same time.
Formal operational	
Over 11 years	Only adolescents and adults can think logically about abstractions, can speculate, and can consider what might or what ought to be. They can work in probabilities and possibilities. They can imagine other worlds, especially ideal ones. They can reason about purely verbal or logical statements. They can relate any element or statement to any other, manipulate variables in a scientific experiment, and deal with proportions and analogies. They can reflect on their own activity of thinking.

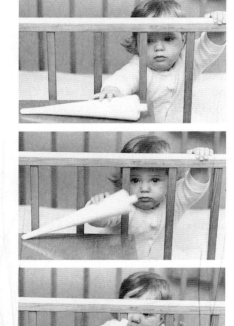

© George S. Zimbel 2009

FIGURE 9.3
Accommodation
Because the bars of the crib are in the way, this child discovers that her schema for grasping and pulling objects toward her will not work. So she adjusts, or accommodates, her schema to achieve her goal.

world. Schemas, in other words, organize past experiences and provide a framework for understanding future experiences.

At first, infants form simple schemas. For example, a sucking schema combines their experiences of sucking into images of what objects can be sucked on (bottles, fingers, pacifiers) and what kinds of sucking can be done (soft and slow, speedy and vigorous). Later, children form more complex schemas, such as a schema for tying a knot or making a bed. Still later, adolescents form schemas about what it is to be in love.

Two related processes guide this development: assimilation and accommodation. In **assimilation,** infants and children take in information about new objects by trying out existing schemas and finding schemas that the new objects will fit. They *assimilate* the new objects into their existing schemas. So when an infant is given a squeaker toy, he will suck on it, thus assimilating it into the sucking schema he has developed with his bottle and pacifier. In the same way, a toddler who sees a butterfly for the first time may assimilate it into her "birdie" schema because, like a bird, it's colorful and it flies. Now suppose an older toddler encounters a large dog. How she assimilates this new experience depends on her existing schema of dogs. If she has had positive experiences with the family dog, she will have a positive schema, and, expecting the dog to behave like her pet, she will greet it happily. In other words, past experiences affect what and how children think about new ones.

Sometimes, like Cinderella's stepsisters squeezing their oversized feet into the glass slipper, people distort information about a new object to make it fit an existing schema. When squeezing won't work, though, people are forced to change, or *accommodate*, their schemas to the new objects. In **accommodation,** the person tries out familiar schemas on a new object, finds that the schemas cannot be made to fit the object, and changes the schemas so that they will fit (see Figure 9.3). So when the infant discovers that the squeaker toy is more fun when it makes a noise, he accommodates his sucking schema and starts munching on the squeaker instead. When the toddler realizes that butterflies are not birds because they don't have beaks and feathers, she accommodates her "birdie" schema to include two kinds of "flying animals"—birds and butterflies. And if the child with the positive "doggie" schema meets a snarling stray, she discovers that her original schema does not extend to all dogs and refines it to distinguish between friendly dogs and aggressive ones.

Sensorimotor Development

Piaget (1952) called the first stage of cognitive development the **sensorimotor stage,** a time when mental activity is confined to schemas about sensory functions, such as seeing and hearing, and schemas about motor skills, such as grasping and sucking. Piaget believed that during the sensorimotor stage, infants can form schemas only of objects and actions that are present—things they can see, hear, or touch. They cannot think about absent objects, he said, because they cannot act on them. For infants, then, thinking is doing. They do not lie in the crib thinking about their mother or their teddy bear, because they are not yet able to form schemas that are *mental representations* of objects and actions that are not present.

The sensorimotor stage ends when infants do become able to form such mental representations. At that point, they can think about objects or actions when the objects are not visible or the actions are not occurring. This milestone, according to Piaget, frees the child from the here and now of the sensory environment. It allows for the development of thought. One sign of this milestone is the child's ability to find a hidden object. This behavior reflects the infant's knowledge that an object exists even if it cannot be seen, touched, or sucked. Piaget called this knowledge **object permanence.**

Piaget believed that before infants acquire knowledge of object permanence, they do not search for objects that are placed out of sight. For infants, out of sight is literally out of mind. He said that evidence of object permanence begins to appear when infants are four to eight months old. At this age, for the first time, they can recognize a familiar object even if part of it is hidden: they know it's their bottle even if they can see only the nipple peeking out from under the blanket. Infants now have some primitive mental representations of objects. If an object is completely hidden, however, they will not search for it.

Several months later, infants will search briefly for a hidden object, but their search is random and ineffective. Not until they are about 18 to 24 months old, said Piaget, do infants appear able to picture and follow events in their minds. They look for the object in places other than where they saw it last, sometimes in entirely new places. According to Piaget, their concept of object permanence is now fully developed. They have a mental representation of the object that is completely separate from their immediate perception of it.

Preoperational Development

According to Piaget, the **preoperational stage** follows the sensorimotor stage of development. During the first half of this period, children between the ages of two and four begin to understand, create, and use *symbols* that represent things that aren't present. They draw, pretend, and talk.

Using and understanding symbols opens up a new world for two- to four-year-olds. At two, for the first time, children are able to play "pretend." They make their fingers "walk" or "shoot" and use a spoon to make a bridge. By the age of three or four, children can symbolize complex roles and events as they play "house," "doctor," or "superhero." They also can use drawing symbolically: pointing to their scribble, they might say, "This is Mommy and Daddy and me going for a walk."

During the second half of the preoperational stage, according to Piaget, four- to seven-year-olds begin to make intuitive guesses about the world as they try to figure out how things work. However, Piaget observed that they cannot tell the difference between imagination and reality. For example, children in this age range might claim that dreams are real and take place outside of themselves as "pictures on the window," "a circus in the

THE FAMILY CIRCUS   By Bil Keane

"I think the moon likes us. It keeps on followin' us."

During the second half of the preoperational period, according to Piaget, children believe that inanimate objects are alive and have intentions, feelings, and consciousness.

assimilation The process of taking in new information about objects by using existing schemas on objects that fit those schemas.

accommodation The process of modifying schemas when they do not work on new objects.

sensorimotor stage According to Piaget, the first stage of cognitive development, when the infant's mental activity is confined to sensory perception and motor skills.

object permanence The knowledge that an object exists even when it is not in view.

preoperational stage According to Piaget, the second stage of cognitive development, during which children begin to understand, create, and use symbols that represent things that are not present.

© Tony Freeman/PhotoEdit

Testing for Conservation

If you know a child who is between the ages of four and seven, get parental permission to test the child for what Piaget called *conservation*. Show the child two identical glasses filled with identical amounts of water and ask which glass contains more water. The child will probably say they are the same. Now pour the contents of one glass into a third glass that is taller and thinner than the others and again ask which glass has more water. If the child still says that they are the same, this is evidence of conservation. If the child says the taller glass has more water, conservation has not yet developed—at least not for this task. The older the child, the more likely it is that conservation will appear, but some children display conservation much earlier than Piaget thought was possible.

LEARN by DOING

conservation The ability to recognize that the important properties of substances or objects, such as quantity, volume, or weight, remain constant despite changes in shape, length, or position.

concrete operations According to Piaget, the third stage of cognitive development, during which children can learn to count, measure, add, and subtract.

formal operations According to Piaget, the fourth stage of cognitive development, characterized by the ability to engage in hypothetical thinking.

room," or "something from the sky." And they believe that inanimate objects are alive and have intentions, feelings, and consciousness: "Clouds go slowly because they have no legs"; "Flowers grow because they want to"; and "Empty cars feel lonely." Children in the preoperational period are also *egocentric,* meaning that they assume that their own view of the world is shared by everyone else. (This helps explain why they stand between you and the TV screen and assume you can still see it or ask "What's this?" as they look at a picture book in the back seat of the car you're driving.)

Children's thinking at this stage is so dominated by what they can see and touch for themselves that they do not realize something is the same if its appearance is changed. In one study, preoperational children thought that a cat wearing a dog mask was actually a dog because that's what it looked like (DeVries, 1969). These children do not yet have what Piaget called **conservation,** the ability to recognize that important properties of a substance or a person remain the same despite changes in shape or appearance.

In a test of conservation, Piaget showed children water from each of two equal-sized glasses being poured into either a tall, thin glass or a short, wide one. They were then asked if one glass contained more water than the other. Children at the preoperational stage of development said that one glass (usually the taller one) contained more. They were dominated by the evidence of their eyes. If the glass looked bigger, then they thought it contained more.

Children at this stage do not understand the logic of *reversibility*—that if you just poured the water from one container to another, you can pour it back into the original container and it will be the same amount. Nor do they understand the concept of *complementarity*—that one glass is taller but narrower and the other is shorter but wider. They focus on only one dimension at a time—the most obvious or important one—and make their best guess. In fact, Piaget named this stage *preoperational* because children at this stage do not yet understand logical mental *operations* such as reversibility and complementarity.

Concrete and Formal Operational Thought   At around the age of six or seven, Piaget observed, children do develop conservation. When this happens, they enter what he called the stage of **concrete operations.** Now, he said, they can count, measure, add, and subtract. Their thinking is no longer dominated by the appearance of things. They can use simple logic and perform simple mental manipulations and mental operations on things. They can sort objects into classes (such as tools, fruit, and vehicles) or series (such as largest to smallest) by systematic searching and ordering.

Still, concrete operational children can perform their logical operations only on real, concrete objects, such as sticks, glasses, tools, and fruit—not on abstract concepts, such as justice or freedom. They can reason only about what is, not about what is *possible.* The ability to think logically about abstract ideas comes in the next stage of cognitive development, as children enter adolescence. This new stage of **formal operations** is marked by the ability to engage in hypothetical thinking, including the imagining of logical consequences. For example, adolescents who have reached this level can consider various strategies for finding a part-time job and recognize that some methods are more likely to succeed than others. They can form general concepts and understand the impact of the past on the present and the present on the future. They can question social institutions, think about the world as it might be and ought to be, and consider the consequences and complexities of love, work, politics, and religion. They can think logically and systematically about symbols and propositions.

Piaget explored adolescents' formal operational abilities by asking them to perform science experiments that involved forming and investigating hypotheses. Research indicates that only about half the people in Western cultures ever reach the formal operational level necessary to succeed in Piaget's experiments (Kuhn & Franklin, 2006). People who have not studied science and math at a high school level are less likely to do well in those experiments (Keating, 1990). In adulthood, people are more likely to use formal operations for problems based on their own occupations; this is one reason that people who think logically at work may still become victims of a home-repair or investment scam (Cialdini, 2001).

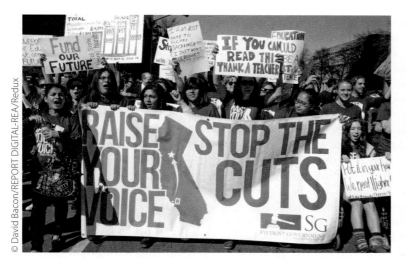

Thinking about the Future
Once they have reached the formal operational stage, many young people become involved in politics because, for the first time, they can think about the consequences of differing approaches to government and which approach might support their emerging ideals.

Modifying Piaget's Theory

Piaget's observations and demonstrations of children's cognitive development are vivid and fascinating. He was right in pointing out that significant shifts in children's thinking occur with age and that thinking becomes more systematic, consistent, and integrated as children get older. His idea that children are active explorers and constructors of knowledge, not passive recipients of input from the environment, influenced our contemporary views of child development. Piaget's work also inspired other psychologists to test his findings and theory with experiments of their own. The results of these experiments suggest that Piaget's theory needs some modification.

New Views of Infants' Cognitive Development   Since Piaget's time, psychologists have found new ways to measure what is going on in infants' minds. They use infrared photography to record infants' eye movements, time-lapse photography to detect slight hand movements, special equipment to measure infants' sucking rates, and computer technology to track and analyze it all. Their research shows that infants know a lot more—and know it sooner—than Piaget ever thought they did (Franchak & Adolph, 2012; Onishi & Baillargeon, 2005; Roseberry et al., 2011).

For example, it turns out that infants in the sensorimotor stage are doing more than just sensing and moving; they are thinking, judging people's reliability, and developing preferences as well (Cacchione, Möhring, & Bertin, 2011; Carey, 2009; Poulin-Dubois, Brooker, & Polonia, 2011; Sakkalou & Gattis, 2012; Saxe, Tzelnic, & Carey, 2007; Sobel & Kirkham, 2006; Téglás et al., 2011). And they aren't just experiencing isolated sights and sounds but combining these experiences (Hunnius, & Bekkering, 2010; Parise & Csibra, 2012; Vouloumanos et al., 2009). In one study, for example, infants were shown two different videotapes at the same time, while the soundtrack for only one of them came from a speaker placed between the two TV screens. The infants tended to look at the video that matched the soundtrack—for example, at a toy bouncing in synch with a tapping sound, at Dad's face when his voice was on the audio, or at an angry face when an angry voice was heard (Soken & Pick, 1992). Infants remember, too (Rovee-Collier & Cuevas, 2009). Babies as young as two to three months of age can recall a mobile that was hung over their crib a few days before (Rovee-Collier, 1999; see Figure 9.4).

Young babies even seem to have a sense of object permanence. Piaget required infants to demonstrate object permanence by making effortful responses, such as removing a cover that had been placed over an object. Today, researchers recognize that finding a hidden object under a cover requires several abilities: mentally representing the hidden object, figuring out where it might be, and pulling off the cover. Piaget's tests did not allow for the possibility that infants know a hidden object still exists but don't yet have the skill to find it. When researchers have created situations in which infants merely have to stare to indicate that they know where an object is hidden, even infants under the age of one have demonstrated this cognitive ability, especially when the object is a familiar one (Baillargeon, 2008; Bertenthal, Longo, & Kenny, 2007; Hespos & Baillargeon, 2001; Keen & Berthier, 2004; Shinskey & Munakata, 2005). And when experimenters simply turn off the lights in a room, infants as young as five months of age may reach for now-unseen objects in the dark (Clifton on et al., 1991).

Developmental psychologists generally agree that infants develop some mental representations earlier than Piaget suggested. However, they disagree about whether this knowledge is "programmed" in infants (Spelke et al., 1992), whether it develops quickly through interactions with the world (Baillargeon, 1995, 2008), or whether it is constructed by combining old schemas into new ones (Fischer & Bidell, 1991).

FIGURE 9.4
Infant Memory

This infant has learned to move a mobile by kicking her left foot, which is connected to the mobile by a ribbon. Even a month later, the baby will show recognition of this particular mobile by kicking more vigorously when she sees it than when she sees another one.

Courtesy of Carolyn Rovee-Collier

LINKAGES

Why does memory improve during childhood?
(a link to Memory)

information processing model
A view of cognitive development which focuses on the processes of taking in, remembering or forgetting, and using information.

New Views of Developmental Stages   Contemporary researchers have also shown that changes from one developmental stage to the next are less consistent and global than Piaget thought. For example, three-year-olds can sometimes make the distinction between physical and mental events; they know the characteristics of real dogs versus pretend dogs (Woolley, 1997). And they are not always egocentric. In one study, children of this age knew that a white card, which looked pink to them because they were wearing rose-colored glasses, looked white to someone who was not wearing the glasses (Liben, 1978). Preoperational children can even succeed at conservation tasks if they are allowed to count the number of objects or have been trained to focus on relevant dimensions such as number, height, and width (Gelman & Baillargeon, 1983).

Taken together, these studies suggest that children's knowledge and mental strategies develop at different ages in different areas and in "pockets" rather than at global levels of understanding (Sternberg, 1989). Knowledge in particular areas is demonstrated sooner in children who are given specific experience in those areas or who are faced with very simple questions and tasks. In other words, children's reasoning depends not only on their general level of development but also on (1) how easy the task is; (2) how familiar they are with the objects involved; (3) how well they understand the language being used; and (4) what experiences they have had in similar situations (Siegal, 1997). Research has also shown that the level of a child's thinking varies from day to day and may even shift when the child solves the same problem twice in the same day (Siegler, 1994; 2006).

Information Processing During Childhood

An alternative to Piaget's theory of cognitive development is based on the concept of information processing described in the chapters on memory and thought, language, and intelligence. The **information processing model** describes cognitive activities in terms of how people take in information, use it, and remember it. Developmental psychologists taking this approach focus on gradual quantitative changes in children's mental capacities rather than on qualitative advances or stages in development.

As children get older, their information processing skills gradually get better (Coyle et al., 2011; Munakata, 2006). Older children have longer attention spans. They take in information and shift their attention from one task to another more rapidly. (This is how they manage to do their homework while watching TV.) They are also more efficient in processing information once it is received (Miller & Vernon, 1997). Children's memory storage capacity also improves (Riggs et al., 2006; Schneider & Bjorklund, 1998). Preschoolers can keep only two or three pieces of information in mind at the same time; older children can hold four or five. And compared with younger children, older children are better at choosing problem-solving strategies that fit the task they are facing (Schwenck, Bjorklund, & Schneider, 2009; Siegler, 2006).

We don't yet know exactly what causes these increases in children's attention, information processing, and memory capacities. A full explanation will undoubtedly include both nature—specifically, maturation of the brain (Bell & Wolfe, 2007; Munakata, Snyder, & Chatham, 2012; Richmond & Nelson, 2007), and nurture—including attention training and increased familiarity with the information that is to be processed and memorized (Bryck & Fisher, 2012; Immordino-Yang, Christodoulou, & Singh, 2012; Wass, Porayska-Pomsta, & Johnson, 2011). Researchers have noticed that children's cognitive abilities improve dramatically when they are dealing with familiar rather than unfamiliar material. In one experiment, Mayan children in Mexico lagged behind their age-mates in the United States on standard memory tests of pictures and nouns. But they did a lot better when researchers gave them a more familiar task, such as recalling miniature objects in a model of a Mayan village (Rogoff & Waddell, 1982).

Better memorization strategies may also help account for the improvement in children's memories. To a great extent, children learn these strategies in school. They learn how to memorize and how to study. They learn to repeat information over and over to help fix it in memory, to place information into categories, and to use other memory aids to help them remember.

After about age seven, schoolchildren are also better at remembering more complex and abstract information. Their memories are more accurate, extensive, and well organized. The knowledge they have accumulated allows them to draw more inferences and integrate new information into a more complete network of facts. (See "In Review: Milestones of Cognitive Development in Infancy and Childhood.")

Milestones of Cognitive Development in Infancy and Childhood   IN REVIEW

Age*	Achievement	Description
3–4 months	Maturation of senses	Immaturities that limit the newborn's vision and hearing are overcome.
	Voluntary movement	Reflexes disappear, and infants begin to gain voluntary control over their movements.
12–18 months	Mental representation	Infants can form images of objects and actions in their minds.
	Object permanence	Infants understand that objects exist even when out of sight.
18–24 months	Symbolic thought	Young children use symbols to represent things that are not present in their pretend play, drawing, and talk.
4 years	Intuitive thought	Children reason about events, real and imagined, by guessing rather than by engaging in logical analysis.
6–7 years	Concrete operations; Conservation	Children can apply simple logical operations to real objects. For example, they recognize that important properties of a substance, such as number or amount, remain constant despite changes in shape or position.
7–8 years	Information processing	Children can remember more information; they begin to learn strategies for memorization.

IN REVIEW QUESTIONS

1. Research in cognitive development suggests that children form mental representations ___ than Piaget thought they did.
2. Recognizing that changing the shape of clay doesn't change the amount of clay is evidence of a cognitive ability called ___.
3. The appearance of object permanence signals the end of the ___ period.

*These ages are approximate; they indicate the order in which children first reach these milestones of cognitive development rather than the exact ages.

Development and Memory

LINKAGES

What happens to our memories of infancy?
(a link to Memory)

The ability to remember facts, figures, pictures, and objects improves as we get older and more expert at processing information. But take a minute right now and try to recall anything that happened to you when you were, say, one year old. Most people can accurately recall a few memories from age five or six but remember virtually nothing from before the age of three (Bauer, 2006; Bruce, Dolan, & Phillips-Grant, 2000; Davis, Gross, & Hayne, 2008).

Psychologists have not yet found a fully satisfactory explanation for this "infantile amnesia." Some have suggested that young children lack the memory encoding and storage processes described in the chapter on memory. Yet children of two or three can clearly recall experiences that happened weeks or even months earlier (Bauer, 2006; Cleveland & Reese, 2008). Others suggest that infantile amnesia occurs because very young children lack a sense of self. Because they don't even recognize themselves in the mirror, they may not have a framework for organizing memories about what happens to them (Howe, 2003, 2011). However, this explanation would hold for only the first two years or so, because after that children do recognize their own faces and even their recorded voices (Legerstee, Anderson, & Schaffer, 1998).

Another possibility is that early memories, though "present," are implicit rather than explicit. As mentioned in the memory chapter, *implicit memories* form automatically and can affect our emotions and behavior even when we do not consciously recall them. However, children's implicit memories of their early years, like the *explicit memories* that they create on purpose, are quite limited. One study found that when 10-year-old children were shown photographs of preschool classmates they hadn't seen in five years, the children had little implicit or explicit memory of them (Newcombe & Fox, 1994). In contrast, adults can correctly identify 90 percent of photographs of high-school classmates they have not seen for 30 years (Bahrick, Bahrick, & Wittlinger, 1975).

Other explanations of infantile amnesia suggest that our early memories are lost because in early childhood we don't yet have the language skills to talk about—and thus solidify—those memories. This possibility was explored in a study in which two- to three-year-old children played with a machine that supposedly could shrink toys (Simcock & Hayne, 2002). Six months later, they were asked what they remembered about this event. If they had not yet developed language at the time they played with the machine, the children could say little or nothing about the experience when asked about it later. However, most of these same children could correctly identify pictures of the machine and act out what they had done with it. It appears that they had memories of the event that could be recalled nonverbally but not in words (Richardson & Hayne, 2007). Another possibility is that early experiences tend to be fused into *generalized event representations,* such as "going to Grandma's" or "playing at the beach," so it becomes difficult to remember any specific event.

Some researchers believe that adults have difficulty accessing early memories because when they were very young children they lacked the emotional knowledge necessary for interpreting, representing, organizing, and retrieving information about the events they experienced (Wang, 2008). Still other researchers believe that infantile amnesia is due partly to the ways that people are asked about their early memories and that specialized questioning techniques might allow retrieval of early memories that are normally unavailable (Jack & Hayne, 2007).

Research on hypotheses such as these may someday unravel the mystery of infantile amnesia (Nelson & Fivush, 2004; Newcombe et al., 2000; Wang, 2006).   ● ● ● ●

Culture and Cognitive Development

To explain cognitive development, Piaget focused on the physical world of objects. Russian psychologist Lev Vygotsky (pronounced "vah-GOT-skee") focused on the social world of people. He viewed cognitive abilities as the product of cultural history. The child's mind, said Vygotsky, grows through contact with other minds. It is through interaction with parents, teachers, and other representatives of their culture that children acquire the ideas of that culture (Vygotsky, 1991).

Vygotsky's followers have studied the effects of the social world on children's cognitive development—especially how participation in social routines affects children's developing knowledge of the world (Gauvain, Beebe, & Zhao, 2011). In Western societies, those routines include shopping, eating at McDonald's, going to birthday parties, and attending religious services. In other cultures they might include helping to make pottery, going hunting, and weaving baskets (Larson & Verma, 1999). Quite early, children develop mental representations, called *scripts,* for these activities (see the chapter on thought, language, and intelligence). By the time they are three, children can describe routine activities quite accurately (Nelson, 1986). Scripts, in turn, affect children's knowledge and understanding of cognitive tasks (Saxe, 2004). For example, in cultures in which pottery making is important, children display conservation about the mass of objects sooner than children do in other cultures (Gardiner & Kosmitzki, 2005).

Children's cognitive abilities are also influenced by the language of their culture (Chen, Kennedy, & Zhou, 2012; Salillas & Wicha, 2012). Korean and Chinese children, for instance, show exceptional ability at adding and subtracting large numbers (Miller et al., 1995). As third-graders, they do three-digit problems in their heads (such as 702 minus 125) that their peers in the United States labor over or fail to solve. The difference seems traceable in part to the clear and explicit words that Asian languages use for the numbers from 11 to 19. In English, the meaning of the words *eleven* and *twelve,* for instance, is not as clear as the Asian *ten-one* and *ten-two.* Moreover, Asians use the abacus and the metric system of measurement, both of which are structured around the number 10. Korean math textbooks emphasize this tens structure by presenting the ones digits in red, the tens in blue, and the hundreds in green. Above all, for children in Asian cultures, educational achievement, especially in mathematics, is encouraged at home and strongly encouraged in school (Naito & Miura, 2001). In short, children's cognitive development is affected in ways large and small by the culture they live in (Broesch et al., 2011; Gauvain et al., 2011).

Individual Variations in Cognitive Development

Even within a single culture, some children are mentally advanced, whereas others lag behind their peers. Why? As already suggested, heredity is an important factor, but experience also plays a role. To explore how significant that role is, psychologists have studied the cognitive development of children raised in many different environments.

Cognitive development is seriously delayed if children are raised in environments where they are deprived of the everyday sights, sounds, and feelings provided by pictures and books, by conversation and loving interaction with family members, and even by television, radio, and the Internet. Children subjected to this kind of severe deprivation show significant impairment in intellectual development by the time they are two or three years old. "Genie" was one such child. When rescued at age 14, she weighed only fifty-nine pounds. The only things she could say were "stop it" and "no more." Investigators discovered that she had spent her life confined to a small bedroom, harnessed to a potty chair during the day and caged in a crib at night. She had not been permitted to hear or make many sounds. Although scientists and therapists worked intensively with Genie in the years after her rescue, she never learned to speak in complete sentences, and she remains in an adult care facility (James, 2008).

Cognitive development may also be impaired by less extreme conditions of deprivation, including the neglect, malnourishment, noise, and chaos that occur in some homes (Berger, Paxson, & Waldfogel, 2009; Hungerford et al., 2012; Tucker-Drob et al., 2011; Turkheimer et al., 2003; Yoshikawa, Aber, & Beardslee, 2012). One study of the effects of poverty found that by the time they were five years old, children raised in poverty scored nine points lower on IQ tests than did children in families whose incomes were at twice the poverty level—even after the researchers had controlled for other variables, such as family structure and parents' education (Duncan, Brooks-Gunn, & Klebanov, 1994). These differences continue as poor children enter school (Cushon et al., 2011). Children who remain in poverty have lower IQs and poorer school achievement (Duncan, Morris, & Rodrigues, 2011; McLoyd, 1998; Siegler, 2003). They also have more learning disabilities (Bigelow, 2006), are less engaged in school (Teachman, 2008), and score lower on neurocognitive tests (Farah et al., 2006). One study of more than 10,000 children found that the economic status of the family into which a child is born is a much better predictor of the child's cognitive development than are physical risk factors such as low birth weight (Jefferis, Power, & Hertzman,

Babies at Risk

The cognitive development of infants raised in this understaffed Russian orphanage will be permanently impaired if they are not given far more stimulation in the orphanage or, better yet, adopted into a loving family before they're six months of age (Becket et al., 2006; Kreppner et al., 2007). It's likely that they'll suffer from reduced brain metabolism and reduced activity in regions associated with higher cognitive functions, memory, and emotion (McLaughlin et al., 2011; Nelson, 2007).

© Josef Polleross/The Image Works

When Does Stimulation Become Overstimulation?

A child's cognitive development is enhanced by a stimulating environment, but can there be too much stimulation? In the face of an avalanche of electronic media aimed specifically at babies and toddlers, some people are beginning to wonder (Zimmerman & Christakis, 2007; Zimmerman, Christakis, & Neltzoff, 2007). These stimulating media include computer "lapware," such as this baby is enjoying, videos and DVDs for even the tiniest infants, and, of course, television programs such as *Teletubbies*. We don't yet know how all this well-intentioned electronic stimulation is affecting young children, but there is some evidence that passively watching videos may not promote learning in infants and toddlers (DeLoache et al., 2010), and the American Academy of Pediatrics (2011) recommends that children under the age of two should remain "screen free" because they don't yet understand what they're seeing.

© LWA/Dann Tardif/Getty Images

2002). It is no wonder then that lower average IQs are seen in countries where higher numbers of children are living in poverty (Weiss, 2007).

In families with incomes above the poverty line, children's cognitive development is related to their surroundings and experiences, as well. Parents can often make the difference between a child's getting A's or getting C's. To help children achieve those A's, adults can expose them from the early years to a variety of interesting materials and experiences—though not so many that the child is overwhelmed (Cook, Goodman, & Schulz, 2011; Evans et al., 2010; van Schijndel et al., 2010). Children's cognitive development is also enhanced when parents read and talk to them, encourage and help them explore, and actively teach them (Gottfried, 1997; Raikes et al., 2006)—in short, when they provide both support and challenge for their children's talents (Yeung, Linver, & Brooks-Gunn, 2002).

To improve the cognitive skills of children who do not get these kinds of stimulation, developmental psychologists have provided some children with extra lessons, educational materials, and contact with caring adults (DuBois et al., 2011; van der Kooy-Hofland et al., 2012). In the United States, the most comprehensive effort of this sort is Project Head Start, a federally funded preschool program for poor children. Many smaller, more intensive programs are offered by state and local agencies. Such programs do enhance children's cognitive abilities (Love et al., 2005; Pianta et al., 2009; Ramey, Ramey, & Lanzi, 2006; Tucker-Drob, 2012; Welsh et al., 2010), and some effects can last into adulthood (Campbell, Pungello et al., 2001, 2012). Music lessons can also promote children's cognitive development, especially verbal memory (Ho, Cheung, & Chan, 2003; Moreno et al., 2011; Schellenberg, 2004). Internet access, too, has been related to improved reading scores and school grades among poor children (Jackson et al., 2006). Even electronic games, although they are no substitute for adult attention, can provide opportunities for school-age children to develop problem-solving skills (Blumberg, Rosenthal, & Randall, 2008; de Freitas & Griffiths, 2007), hone spatial skills that can help improve their performance in math and science (Canada & Goering, 2008; Green & Bavelier, 2003; Greenfield, 1994), and possibly even enhance their physical fitness (Hayes & Silberman, 2007; Trout & Christie, 2007). There are limits, however. An excess of computer gaming has been associated with reduced academic achievement as well as with some physical and behavioral problems (Desai et al., 2010; Weis & Cerankosky, 2010).

Infancy and Childhood: Social and Emotional Development

How do infants become attached to their caregivers?

Life for the child is more than learning about objects, doing math problems, and getting good grades. It is also about social relationships and emotional reactions. From the

Playing Their Way to Fitness?
Some researchers claim that people can improve their physical fitness by using video games that simulate athletic activity (Baumann, 2007; Grieser et al., 2012; Light, 2008; Penko & Barkley, 2010; Worley, Rogers, & Kraemer, 2011). Others have found that the amount of exercise involved in playing these games is not enough to keep people fit or help stem the rising tide of childhood obesity (Graves et al., 2008; Owens et al., 2011).

first months onward, infants are sensitive to those around them (Geangu et al., 2010; Mumme & Fernald, 2003), and they are both attracted by and attractive to other people—especially parents and other caregivers.

During the first hour or so after birth, mothers gaze into their infants' eyes and give them gentle touches (Klaus & Kennell, 1976). This is the first opportunity for the mother to display her *bond* to her infant—an emotional tie that begins even before the baby is born (Feldman et al., 2007). Psychologists once believed that this immediate contact was critical—that the mother-infant bond would never be strong if the opportunity for early interaction was missed. Research has revealed, however, that although newborns separated from their mothers may show signs of distress (Morgan, Horn, & Bergman, 2011) such interaction is not a requirement for a close relationship (Myers, 1987). Mothers and fathers, whether biological or adoptive, gradually form close attachments to their infants by interacting with them day after day.

As the mother gazes at her baby, the baby is gazing back. By the time infants are two days old, they recognize—and like—their mother's face. They will suck more vigorously in order to see an image of her face than to see a stranger's (Walton, Bower, & Bower, 1992). Soon, they begin to respond to the mother's facial expressions as well. By the time they are a year old, children use their mothers' emotional expressions to guide their own behavior in uncertain situations (Hertenstein & Campos, 2004; Saarni, 2006). If the mother looks frightened when a stranger approaches, for example, the child is more likely to avoid the stranger. Research on infants' brain activity suggests that they pay particular attention to signs of fear and other negative emotions in adults (Carver & Vaccaro, 2007; Leppänen & Nelson, 2012). This tendency helps to explain why, as described in the chapter on learning, observation of other people's reactions can sometimes lead to the development of fears and even phobias.

Infants communicate feelings as well as recognize them. Before they can speak, infants use gestures to show their caregivers that they are feeling happy, mad, sad, scared, sleepy, or cold (Vallotton, 2008).

Individual Temperament

From the moment infants are born, they differ from one another. Some are happy, active, and vigorous; they splash, thrash, and wriggle. Others lie still most of the time. Some infants approach new objects with enthusiasm; others turn away or fuss. Some infants whimper; others kick, scream, and wail. Characteristics such as these make up the infant's temperament. **Temperament** refers to the infant's individual style and frequency of expressing needs and emotions; it is constitutional, biological, and genetically based. Although temperament mainly reflects nature's contribution to the beginning of an individual's personality, it can also be affected by the prenatal environment, including—as noted earlier—the mother's smoking, drug use, and stress levels during pregnancy (Blair et al., 2011; Davis et al., 2011; Sandman et al., 2011, 2012). The stress experienced by the mother after her baby's birth also affects the baby's temperament. For example, breastfed infants who ingest more of the stress-related hormone cortisol tend to have more fearful temperaments (Glynn et al., 2007). And if mothers of babies with negative temperaments continue to experience stress, the babies tend to express even more negative emotion during the next five years (Pesonen et al., 2008).

Alexander Thomas and Stella Chess (1977) found three main temperament patterns. *Easy babies,* the most common kind, get hungry and sleepy at predictable times, react to new situations cheerfully, and seldom fuss. *Difficult babies* are irregular and irritable. Those in the third group, *slow-to-warm-up babies,* react warily to new situations but eventually come to enjoy them.

Traces of early temperamental characteristics weave their way from birth throughout childhood and into adulthood (Jong et al., 2010; Komsi et al., 2008; Rothbart, 2011; Slutske et al., 2012). Easy infants usually stay easy (Zhou et al., 2004) and tend not to develop

temperament An individual's basic, natural disposition that is evident from infancy.

© Daniel M. Nagy/Shutterstock

Forming a Bond

Mutual eye contact, exaggerated facial expressions, and shared "baby talk" are an important part of the early social interactions that promote an enduring bond of attachment between parent and child.

conduct problems (Lahey et al., 2008); difficult infants often remain difficult, sometimes developing attention and aggression problems in childhood (Else-Quest et al., 2006; Miner & Clarke-Stewart, 2008). Timid toddlers tend to become shy preschoolers, restrained and inhibited eight-year-olds, somewhat anxious teenagers, and shy and cautious young adults (Caspi, Harrington et al., 2003; Rothbart, 2011). These individuals tend marry at a later age than their more outgoing peers (Caspi, Elder, & Bem, 1988). However, in temperament, as in cognitive development, nature interacts with nurture (Jaffari-Bimmel et al., 2006; Kiff, Lengua, & Zalewski, 2011). Events and influences that occur between infancy and adulthood can help to stabilize an individual's temperament or shift its development in one direction or the other.

One source of influence suggested by Thomas and Chess (1977) is the degree to which an infant's temperament matches the parents' personal styles and what they want and expect from their baby. When the match is a good one, parents tend to support and encourage the infant's behavior, thus increasing the chances that temperamental qualities will be stable. Consider the temperament patterns of Chinese American and European American children. At birth, Chinese American infants are calmer, less changeable, less excitable, and more easily comforted when upset than European American infants (Kagan et al., 1994). This tendency toward self-control is powerfully reinforced by the Chinese culture. Compared with European American parents, Chinese parents are less likely to reward and stimulate infants' babbling and smiling and more likely to maintain close control of their young children. The children, in turn, are more dependent on their mothers and less likely to play by themselves. They are less vocal, noisy, and active than European American children (Smith & Freedman, 1983), and as preschoolers they show far more impulse control, including the ability to wait their turn (Sabbagh et al., 2006).

These temperamental differences between children in different ethnic groups illustrate the combined contributions of nature and nurture. Mayan infants, for example, are relatively inactive from birth. The Zinacantecos, a Mayan group in southern Mexico, reinforce this innate predisposition toward restrained motor activity by tightly wrapping their infants and by nursing at the slightest sign of movement (Greenfield & Childs, 1991). This combination of genetic predisposition and cultural reinforcement is adaptive. Quiet infants do not kick off their covers at night, which is important in the cold highlands where they live. Inactive infants are able to spend long periods on their mothers' backs as the mothers work. And infants who do not begin to walk until they can understand some language do not wander into the open fire at the center of the house. This adaptive interplay of innate and cultural factors in the development of temperament operates in all cultures.

Nature and nurture combine to influence individual differences within cultures, too. A variety of studies show that children are more likely to display aggressiveness, anxiety, depression, or academic and social problems if they have suffered the "double whammy" of starting life with a difficult temperament and then being raised in a harsh, insensitive, unsupportive, or anxiety-provoking family environment (Miner & Clarke-Stewart, 2008; Paulussen-Hoogeboom et al., 2008; Stright, Gallagher, & Kelley, 2008). For example, children who had both timid temperaments and mothers who were unsupportive, negative, or depressed were more likely to remain fearful, to be socially withdrawn, to have more negative moods, and to have difficulty controlling their negative emotions (Feng et al., 2008; Gilissen et al., 2008; Hane et al., 2008). However, if a difficult or shy baby is lucky enough to have patient parents who allow their baby to respond to new situations and changes in daily routines at a more relaxed pace, the baby is likely to become less difficult or shy over time.

The Infant Grows Attached

attachment A deep, affectionate, close, and enduring relationship with a person with whom a baby has shared many experiences.

attachment theory The idea that children form a close attachment to their earliest caregivers and that this attachment pattern can affect aspects of the children's later lives.

As infants and caregivers respond to one another in the first year, the infant begins to form an **attachment**—a deep, affectionate, close, and enduring relationship—to these important figures. **Attachment theory** was first developed by John Bowlby, a British psychoanalyst who drew attention to the importance of attachment after he observed children who had been orphaned in World War II. These children's depression and other emotional scars led Bowlby to propose a theory about the importance of developing a strong attachment to one's primary caregivers—a tie that normally keeps infants close to those caregivers and, therefore, safe (Bowlby, 1973). Soon after Bowlby first described his theory, researchers in the United States began to investigate how such attachments are formed and what happens when they fail to form or are broken by loss or separation. The most dramatic of these studies was conducted with monkeys by Harry Harlow.

Motherless Monkeys—and Children   Harlow (1959) separated newborn monkeys from their mothers and raised them in cages containing two artificial mothers. One "mother" was made of wire with a rubber nipple from which the infant could get milk (see Figure 9.5). It provided food but no physical comfort. The other artificial mother had no nipple but was made of soft, comfortable terry cloth. If attachments form entirely because caregivers provide food, the infants would be expected to prefer the wire mother. In fact, they spent most of their time with the terry cloth mother. And when they were frightened, the infants immediately ran to their terry cloth mother and clung to it. Harlow concluded that the monkeys were motivated by the need for comfort. The terry cloth mother provided feelings of softness and cuddling, which were things the infants needed when they sensed danger.

Harlow also investigated what happens when attachments do not form. He isolated some monkeys from all social contact from birth. After a year of this isolation, the monkeys showed dramatic disturbances. When visited by normally active, playful monkeys, they withdrew to a corner, huddling or rocking. These monkeys' problems continued into adulthood. As adults, they were unable to have normal sexual relations. When some of the females became pregnant through artificial means, their maternal behaviors were woefully inadequate. In most cases, these mothers ignored their infants. When the infants became distressed, the mothers physically abused and sometimes even killed them.

Tragically, humans who spend their first few years without a consistent caregiver react in a similar manner. Like Harlow's deprived monkeys, children at Romanian and Russian orphanages staffed by neglectful caregivers did not develop attachments to those caregivers; they were withdrawn and engaged in constant rocking (Holden, 1996; Zeanah et al., 2005, 2009). These effects tend to remain even after the children are adopted. In one study, researchers observed the behavior of four-year-old children who had been in a Romanian orphanage for at least eight months before being adopted (Chisholm, 1997). Compared with children who had been adopted before they were four months old, the late-adopted children were found to have many more serious problems. Depressed or withdrawn, they stared blankly, demanded attention, and could not control their tempers. Although they interacted poorly with their adoptive mothers, they were friendly with strangers, usually trying to cuddle and kiss them. At age six, a third of late-adopted children still showed no preference for their parents or any tendency to look to them when stressed (Rutter, O'Connor, & ERA Study Team, 2004). Other studies have found that children who spent their first year in such orphanages displayed antisocial behavior and other long-term social and behavioral problems (Hawk & McCall, 2011). Neuroscientists suggest that the dramatic problems seen in isolated monkeys and chimpanzees—as well as in humans—are the result of developmental brain dysfunction and damage brought on by a lack of touch and body movement in infancy, and by the absence of early play, conversation, and other social experiences in childhood (Kalcher-Sommersguter et al., 2011; Prescott, 1996; Rutter, O'Connor, & ERA Study Team, 2004; Wiik et al., 2011; Wismer, Fries et al., 2005, 2008).

Forming an Attachment   Fortunately, most infants do have a consistent caregiver, usually the mother, to whom they can form an attachment. They learn to recognize her and are able to distinguish her from a stranger at an early age. Some infants vocalize more to their mothers than to a stranger when they are only three months old. By the age of six or seven months, infants show signs of preferring the mother to anyone else. They crawl after her, call out to her, hug her, climb into her lap, protest when she leaves, and brighten when she returns (Ainsworth & Marvin, 1995). After an attachment has formed, separation from the mother for even thirty minutes can be a stressful experience

FIGURE 9.5
Wire and Terry Cloth "Mothers"
These are the two types of artificial mothers used in Harlow's research. Although baby monkeys received milk from the wire mother, they spent most of their time with the terry cloth version, and they clung to it when frightened.

Source: Baillargeon (1992).

(Cassidy, 2008). Babies who recognize and prefer their mothers even earlier—at three months—may be especially bright. One study found that such babies eventually achieve higher-than-average grades in high school, score higher on college entrance exams, and complete more years of education (Roe, 2001).

Infants also develop attachments to their fathers, but usually a little later (Arsalidou et al., 2010; Lamb, 1997). Father-infant interaction is also less frequent than mother-infant interaction, and most studies show that it has a somewhat different nature (Lamb & Lewis, 2010). Mothers tend to feed, bathe, dress, cuddle, and talk to their infants, whereas fathers are more likely to play with, jiggle, and toss them, especially sons.

Variations in Attachment The amount of closeness and contact the infant seeks with either mother or father depends to some extent on the infant. Babies who are ill, tired, or slow to warm up may require more closeness. Closeness also depends to some extent on the parent. An infant whose parent has been absent or unresponsive is likely to need more closeness than one whose parent is accessible and responsive.

Researchers have studied the differences in infants' **attachment behavior** in a special situation that simulates the natural comings and goings of parents and infants—the so-called *Strange Situation* (Ainsworth et al., 1978). Testing occurs in an unfamiliar playroom where the infant interacts with the mother and an unfamiliar woman in brief episodes: the infant plays with the mother and the stranger, the mother leaves the baby with the stranger for a few minutes, the mother and the stranger leave the baby alone in the room briefly, and the mother returns.

Videos of these sessions show that most infants display a *secure attachment* to the mother (Thompson, 2006). In the unfamiliar room, the infant uses the mother as a home base, leaving her side to explore and play but returning to her periodically for comfort or contact. Securely attached children can tolerate the brief separation from their mothers, but they are always happy to see them return, and they are always receptive to the mothers' offers of contact. These mother-child pairs tend to have harmonious interactions from the earliest months, and the mothers themselves tend to be sensitive and responsive (DeWolff & van IJzendoorn, 1997).

Some infants, however, form *insecure attachments*. If the relationship is *avoidant,* the infant avoids or ignores the mother when she approaches or when she returns after the brief separation. If the relationship is *ambivalent,* the infant is upset when the mother leaves, but when she returns the child acts angry and rejects the mother's efforts at contact; when picked up, the child squirms to get down. If the relationship is *disorganized,* the infant's behavior is inconsistent, disturbed, and disturbing; the child may begin to cry again after the mother has returned and provided comfort or may reach out for the mother while looking away from her (Moss et al., 2004).

The nature of a child's attachment to caregivers can have long-term and far-reaching effects (Ahrens, Ciechanowski, & Katon, 2012; NICHD Early Child Care Research Network, 2006b; Vess, 2012). For example, an infant's secure attachment continues into young adulthood—and probably throughout life—unless it is disrupted by the loss of a parent, abuse by a family member, chronic depression in the mother, or some other severe negative event (Hamilton, 2000; Mattanah, Hancock, & Brand, 2004; Waters et al., 2000; Weinfield, Sroufe, & Egeland, 2000). A secure attachment to the mother is also reflected in relationships with other people. Children who are securely attached receive more positive reactions from other children when they are toddlers (Fagot, 1997) and have better relations with peers in middle childhood and adolescence (Berlin, Cassidy, & Appleyard, 2008; Dykas & Cassidy, 2011; Lucas-Thompson & Clarke-Stewart, 2007; McElwain, Booth-LaForce, & Wu, 2011; McElwain et al., 2008; Thompson, 2006). Securely attached children also require less contact, guidance, and discipline from their teachers, and are less likely to seek excessive attention, to act impulsively or aggressively, to express frustration, to become distracted, or to display helplessness (Carlson, Sroufe, & Egeland, 2004; Fearon et al., 2010; Groh et al., 2012; NICHD Early Child Care Research Network, 2006; Sroufe et al., 2005; Warren et al., 2010). Their teachers like them more, expect more of them, and rate them as more competent (Diener et al., 2008).

attachment behavior Actions such as crying, smiling, vocalizing, and gesturing that help bring an infant into closer proximity to its caretaker.

Patterns of child care and attachment vary widely in different parts of the world (Rothbaum, Morelli, & Rusk, 2010). In northern Germany, for example, where parents are quite strict, the proportion of infants who display avoidant attachments is much higher than in the United States (Grossman et al., 2008; Spangler, Fremmer-Bombik, & Grossman, 1996). Kibbutz babies in Israel, who sleep in infant houses away from their parents, are relatively likely to show insecure attachments and other related problems (Aviezer et al., 1999). In Japan, where mothers are expected to be completely devoted to their children and are seldom apart from them, even at night, children develop an attachment relationship that emphasizes harmony and union (Rothbaum, Pott et al., 2000). These attachment patterns differ from the secure type that is most common in the United States: with their parents' encouragement, U.S. children balance closeness and proximity with exploration and autonomy.

In all countries, the likelihood that children will develop a secure attachment depends on the mother's attentiveness; if the mother is sensitive and responsive to the baby's needs and signals, a secure attachment is more likely; if she is rejecting or neglecting, the child's attachment is more likely to be insecure (Bakermans-Kranenburg, van IJzendoorn, & Juffer, 2008; Nievar & Becker, 2008).

THINKING CRITICALLY Does Day Care Harm the Emotional Development of Infants?

About 60 percent of U.S. mothers with children work outside of the home. How might this daily separation affect their children, especially the infants (Clarke-Stewart & Allhusen, 2005)? Some have argued that putting infants in day care with a nanny or child care center damages the quality of mother-child relations and increases the babies' risk for psychological problems later on (Gallagher, 1998).

What am I being asked to believe or accept?
The claim is that daily separations created by day care damage the formation of an attachment between the mother and infant and harm the infant's emotional development.

Is evidence available to support the claim?
There is clear evidence that separation from the mother is painful for young children. If separation lasts a week or more, children who have formed an attachment to their mother tend to protest, then become apathetic and mournful (Robertson & Robertson, 1971). But day care does not involve such lasting separations. Research has shown that infants who are in day care do form attachments to their mothers. In fact, they prefer their mothers to their daytime caregivers (Lamb & Ahnert, 2006).

Are these attachments as secure as the attachments formed by infants whose mothers do not work outside the home? Researchers have examined this question by comparing how infants react to brief separations from their mothers in the Strange Situation. A review of about 20 studies done in the 1980s revealed that infants in full-time day care were somewhat more likely to be classified as insecurely attached. About 36 percent of them were classified as insecure; only 29 percent of the infants who were not in full-time day care were counted as insecure (Clarke-Stewart, 1989). These results appeared to support the suggestion that day care harms infants' attachments to their mothers.

Can that evidence be interpreted another way?
Perhaps factors other than day care could explain the difference between infants in day care and those at home with their mothers. One such factor could be the method that was used to assess attachment. Infants in these studies were judged insecure if they did not run to their mothers after a brief separation in the Strange Situation. But maybe infants who experience daily separations from their mothers during day care feel more comfortable in the Strange Situation and therefore seek out less closeness with their mothers. A second factor concerns the possible differences between the infants' mothers. Perhaps mothers who value independence in themselves and in their children are more

© Bob Mahoney/The Image Works

The Effects of Day Care

Parents are understandably concerned that leaving their infants in a day-care center all day long might interfere with the mother-infant attachment or with other aspects of their children's development. Research shows that most infants in day care do form healthy bonds with their parents but that if children spend many hours in day care between infancy and kindergarten, they are more likely to have behavior problems in school, such as talking back to the teacher or getting into fights with other children (NICHD Early Child Care Research Network, 2001, 2006b). Some employers try to help parents build attachments with their infants by providing on-site day care or allowing employees to keep their babies in their offices while working (Armour, 2008). These policies help parents and their children stay in contact throughout the day, but take a minute to list some of the problems the policies might create in the workplace.

LEARN by DOING

socialization The process by which parents, teachers, and others teach children the skills and social norms necessary to be well-functioning members of society.

likely to be working and to place their children in day care, whereas mothers who emphasize closeness with their children are more likely to stay home.

What evidence would help evaluate the alternatives?

Finding insecure attachment to be more common among the infants of working mothers does not, by itself, demonstrate that day care is harmful. To judge the effects of day care, we must consider other measures of emotional adjustment as well. If infants in day care showed consistent signs of impaired emotional relations in other situations (at home, for example) and with other caregivers (such as the father), this evidence would support the argument that day care harms children's emotional development. We should also statistically control for differences in the behavior and attitudes of parents who do and do not put their infants in day care and then look for differences in their children.

In fact, this research design has already been employed. In 1990, the U.S. government funded a study of infant day care in ten sites around the country. The psychological and physical development of more than 1,300 randomly selected infants was tracked from birth through age three. The results available so far show that when factors such as parents' education, income, and attitudes were statistically controlled, infants in day care were no more likely to have emotional problems or to be insecurely attached to their mothers than infants not in day care. However, in cases in which infants were in poor-quality day care with insensitive, unresponsive caregivers, and in which mothers were insensitive to their babies' needs at home, the infants were less likely to develop a secure attachment to their mothers (Belsky et al., 2007; NICHD Early Child Care Research Network, 2005, 2006a).

What conclusions are most reasonable?

Based on available evidence, the most reasonable conclusion appears to be that day care by itself does not lead to insecure attachment. But if that day care is of poor quality, it can worsen a risky situation at home and increase the likelihood that infants will have problems forming a secure attachment to their mothers. The U.S. government study is still under way, and the children's progress is being followed into adolescence.   ● ● ● ●

Relationships with Parents and Peers

Erik Erikson (1968) saw the first year of life as a time when infants develop a feeling of trust (or mistrust) about the world. According to his theory, an infant's first year represents the first of eight stages of lifelong psychosocial development (see Table 9.2). Each stage focuses on an issue, or "crisis," that is especially important at that time of life. Erikson believed that the ways that people resolve these crises shape their personalities and social relationships. Resolving a crisis in a positive way provides the foundation for characteristics such as trust, independence, initiative, or industry. But if the crisis is not resolved positively, according to Erikson, the person will be psychologically troubled and cope less effectively with later crises. In Erikson's theory, trusting caregivers during infancy forms the bedrock for all future social and emotional development.

After children have formed strong emotional attachments to their parents, their next psychological task is to develop a more independent relationship with them. In Erikson's theory, this task is reflected in the second stage (again, see Table 9.2). Children begin to exercise their wills, to develop some independence from their parents, and to begin activities on their own. According to Erikson, children who are not allowed to exercise their wills or start their own activities will feel uncertain about doing things for themselves and guilty about seeking independence. The extent to which parents allow or encourage their children's independence is related to their parenting style.

Parenting Styles   Most parents try to channel children's impulses into socially accepted outlets and teach them the skills and rules needed to function in their society. This process is called **socialization**.

TABLE 9.2   Erikson's Stages of Psychosocial Development

In each of Erikson's stages of development, a different psychological issue presents a new crisis for the person to resolve. The person focuses attention on that issue and by the end of the period has worked through the crisis and resolved it either positively, in the direction of healthy development, or negatively, hindering further psychological development.

Age	Central Psychological Issue or Crisis
First Year	**Trust versus mistrust**
	Infants learn to trust that their needs will be met by the world, especially by the mother—or they learn to mistrust the world.
Second year	**Autonomy versus shame and doubt**
	Children learn to exercise will, make choices, and control themselves—or they become uncertain and doubt that they can do things by themselves.
Third to fifth year	**Initiative versus guilt**
	Children learn to initiate activities and enjoy their accomplishments, acquiring direction and purpose—or, if they are not allowed initiative, they feel guilty for their attempts at becoming independent.
Sixth year through puberty	**Industry versus inferiority**
	Children develop a sense of industry and curiosity and are eager to learn—or they feel inferior and lose interest in the tasks before them.
Adolescence	**Identity versus role confusion**
	Adolescents come to see themselves as unique and integrated persons with an ideology—or they become confused about what they want out of life.
Early adulthood	**Intimacy versus isolation**
	Young people become able to commit themselves to another person—or they develop a sense of isolation and feel they have no one in the world but themselves.
Middle age	**Generativity versus stagnation**
	Adults are willing to have and care for children and to devote themselves to their work and the common good—or they become self-centered and inactive.
Old age	**Integrity versus despair**
	Older people enter a period of reflection, becoming assured that their lives have been meaningful and becoming ready to face death with acceptance and dignity—or they are in despair about their unaccomplished goals, failures, and ill-spent lives.

parenting styles The varying patterns of behavior—ranging from permissive to authoritarian—that parents display as they interact with and discipline their children.

authoritarian parents Parents who are firm, punitive, and unsympathetic.

permissive parents Parents who give their children complete freedom and lax discipline.

authoritative parents Parents who reason with their children and are firm but understanding.

uninvolved parents (rejecting-neglecting parents) Parents who invest as little time, money, and effort in their children as possible.

European American parents tend to employ one of four distinct **parenting styles** (Baumrind, 1991; Maccoby & Martin, 1983). **Authoritarian parents** tend to be strict, punishing, and unsympathetic. They value obedience from children and try to curb the children's wills and shape their children's behavior to meet a set standard. They do not encourage independence. They are detached and seldom praise their youngsters. In contrast, **permissive parents** give their children complete freedom and provide little discipline. **Authoritative parents** fall between these two extremes. They reason with their children, encouraging give and take. They allow children increasing responsibility as they get older and better at making decisions. They are firm but understanding. They set limits but also encourage independence. Their demands are reasonable, rational, and consistent. **Uninvolved parents** (also known as **rejecting-neglecting parents**) are indifferent to their children. They invest as little time, money, and effort in their children as possible, focusing on their own needs before their children's. These parents often fail to monitor their children's activities, particularly when the children are old enough to be out of the house alone.

Research shows that these parenting styles are consistently related to young children's social and emotional development (Eisenberg, Fabes, & Spinrad, 2006; Erath et al., 2011; Parke & Buriel, 2006; Paulussen-Hoogeboom et al., 2008; Thompson, 2006). Authoritarian parents tend to have children who are unfriendly, distrustful, and withdrawn. The children of permissive parents tend to be immature, dependent, and unhappy; they are likely to have tantrums or to ask for help when they encounter even slight difficulties.

Children raised by authoritative parents tend to be friendly, cooperative, self-reliant, and socially responsible (Ginsburg et al., 2009).

Other researchers have found that authoritative parenting styles are associated with additional positive outcomes, including better school achievement, greater popularity, and better psychological adjustment to parental divorce (Hetherington & Clingempeel, 1992; Hinshaw et al., 1997; Steinberg et al., 1994). In contrast, children of authoritarian parents are more likely to cheat, to display aggression and other behavioral problems, and to be less likely to experience guilt or accept blame after doing something wrong (Eisenberg, Fabes, & Spinrad, 2006; Paulussen-Hoogeboom et al., 2008).

The results of all these parenting studies are interesting and important, but they are limited in several ways. First, they are based on correlations, which, as discussed in the introductory chapter, do not prove causation. Finding consistent correlations between parents' and children's behavior does not establish that the parents are *causing* the differences seen in their children. Socialization is a two-way street: Parents' behavior is shaped by their children as well as the reverse. Children's temperament, size, and appearance may influence the way parents treat them (Bugental & Grusec, 2006; Ganiban et al., 2011; Lipscomb et al., 2011). Some developmental psychologists even suggest that it is not the parents' socialization practices that influence children but rather how the children perceive the discipline they receive—as stricter or more lenient than what an older sibling received, for example (Reiss et al., 2000).

A second limitation of parenting studies is that the correlations between parenting styles and children's behavior, though statistically significant, are usually not terribly large (Ho, Bluestein, & Jenkins, 2008), and therefore do not apply to every child in every family. In fact, research shows that the effects of parents' socialization can differ depending on their children's temperament. The gentle parental guidance that has a noticeable effect on a child with a fearful temperament might have far less impact on a child whose temperament is less fearful (Kochanska, Aksan, & Joy, 2007). Similarly, harsh authoritarian parenting seems to disrupt emotion regulation and the development of conscience in children who are temperamentally fearful (Feng et al., 2008; Schwartz & Bugental, 2004; Kochanska, 1997).

Parenting Styles and Culture   Yet another limitation of parenting studies is that most of them were conducted with European American families. Is the impact of various parenting styles different in other ethnic groups and other cultures? Possibly. Parents in Latino cultures in Mexico, Puerto Rico, and Central America and in Asian cultures in China and India, for example, tend to be influenced by a collectivist tradition in which family and community interests are emphasized over individual goals. Children in these cultures are expected to respect and obey their elders and to do less of the questioning, negotiating, and arguing that is encouraged—or at least allowed—in many middle-class European and European American families (Greenfield, Suzuki, & Rothstein-Fisch, 2006; Parke & Buriel, 2006). In short, their parenting style tends to be relatively authoritarian. When parents from these cultures immigrate to the United States, they bring their authoritarian parenting style with them. There is evidence, though, that the authoritarian discipline often seen in Asian American, Hispanic American, and African American families does not have the same negative consequences for young children's behavior as it does in European American families (Chao & Tseng, 2002; Slade & Wissow, 2004). The difference is likely due to the fact that different disciplinary styles have different meanings in different cultures and subcultures (Ho, Bluestein, & Jenkins, 2008). Chinese American parents, for example, use authoritarian discipline to "govern" (*guan*) and provide "training" (*chiao shun*) for their children so that they will know what is expected of them (Chao, 2001). By contrast, European American parents are more likely to use authoritarian discipline to keep children in line and break their wills. In countries such as India and Kenya, where physical punishment tends to be an accepted form of discipline, punishment is associated with less aggression and anxiety than in Thailand and China, where it is rarely used (Lansford et al., 2005). These findings remind us that it is important to evaluate parenting styles in their cultural context. There is no single, universally "best" style of parenting (Parke & Buriel, 2006).

Relationships with Peers   Social development over the years of childhood spans an ever-enlarging social world that broadens to include siblings, playmates, and classmates. Psychologists have observed that from a remarkably early age—as young as one year—children are interested in the behavior of other children (usually their siblings) and that by the time they are a year and a half old, they know how to hurt or comfort other children (Rubin, Bukowski, & Parker, 2006).

It takes time for children to learn how to interact with other children. Two-year-olds in Western cultures are only able to exchange or fight over toys. By the time they are three, they can use toys to get a response from peers. At age four, children converse about the toys they are playing with, and at the end of the preschool period, they are able to share toys and tasks cooperatively. This kind of play is important because it shows children how to communicate what they are feeling and gives them the chance to form their first friendships (Dunn & Hughes, 2001; Rubin, Bukowski, & Parker, 2006).

In the school years, peer interaction becomes more complex and structured as children play games with rules, play on teams, tutor each other, and cooperate—or compete—in achieving goals. The school years are also the time when friends become important and friendships become long lasting (Hartup & Stevens, 1997). At this age, the most important aspects of friendship are companionship and fun; psychological intimacy does not enter the picture until children become teenagers (Parker et al., 2001).

Children's Friendships
Although relationships with peers may not always be this friendly, they are often among the closest and most positive in a child's life. Friends are more interactive than nonfriends; they smile and laugh together more, pay closer attention to equality in their conversations, and talk about mutual goals. Having at least one close friend in childhood predicts good psychological functioning later on (Laursen et al., 2007; Parker et al., 2001).

Social Skills

The changes in peer interactions and relationships over the years of childhood reflect children's increasing social competence and understanding. Social skills, like cognitive skills, must be learned (Rubin et al., 2006).

One important social skill is the ability to engage in sustained, responsive interactions with peers. These interactions require cooperation, sharing, and taking turns—behaviors that first appear in the preschool years. A second social skill that children learn is the ability to detect and correctly interpret other people's emotional signals. Much as children's school performance depends on processing academic information, their social performance depends on processing emotional information about other people (Slomkowski & Dunn, 1996). A related set of social skills involves the ability to feel what another person is feeling, or something close to it (*empathy*), and to respond with comfort or help if the person is in distress.

Children whose social skills allow them to understand another person's perspective, appreciate how that person might be feeling, and offer sympathy, cooperation, and help tend to be the most popular members of a peer group (Izard et al., 2001; Rubin et al., 2006). Children without these skills tend to be rejected or neglected; they may become bullies or the victims of bullies. Parents, other adults, and even older siblings can help their children develop these skills by engaging them in lots of "pretend" play and other prosocial activities and by encouraging them to express their emotions constructively (Eisenberg, Fabes, & Spinrad, 2006; Ladd, 2005; Lopes et al., 2005).

FOCUS ON RESEARCH ## Exploring Developing Minds

Children's ability to make sense of other people's behavior depends on their ability to understand the thinking that underlies other people's actions. Critical to this understanding is the recognition that what other people think is sometimes incorrect. For more than 20 years, researchers have argued that children under four years of age cannot understand other people's mental states because they do not yet have a "theory of mind." This argument was based on studies in which children were asked questions about other people's beliefs (e.g., Baron-Cohen, Leslie, & Frith, 1985). In one study, children were shown a simple little drama starring two dolls, "Sally" and "Anne." First, Sally puts a marble in her basket and then leaves the stage. While Sally is away, Anne takes the marble out of Sally's basket and puts it into her own box. Then Sally returns to get her marble, and the child is asked where Sally will look for it. To correctly predict that Sally will look in the basket where she last saw the marble, the children in this study would have to recognize that Sally has a false belief about its location. Even though they know where the marble really is, they will have to be able to "read Sally's mind," realize what she must be thinking, and say "she'll look in her basket." However, most children under the age of four ignore the fact that Sally thinks the marble is still in her basket and say that she'll look in Anne's box.

What was the researcher's question?

Renee Baillargeon (pronounced "by-ar-ZHAN") wondered, though, whether the inability of these young children to recognize what others are thinking reflected a true lack of a "theory of mind" or was the result of using research methods that were not sensitive enough to detect its existence. So her research question was whether more specialized methods might reveal that even children under four can understand that other people's behavior is affected by their mental states, including false beliefs and false perceptions.

How did the researcher answer the question?

Instead of requiring children to answer questions about other people's behavior, Baillargeon used a more creative and potentially more sensitive method to probe young children's knowledge. She reasoned that infants' tendency to look longer at certain events indicates that those events violate their expectations about the world, so she showed infants various events and then carefully measured the amount of time they spent looking at them.

Baillargeon used this method to measure the ability of 15-month-old infants to predict where a woman would look for a toy, depending on whether she had a true or a false belief about the toy's location (Onishi & Baillargeon, 2005). Each infant first watched the woman play with a toy watermelon slice for a few seconds, then hide it inside a green box. Next, the woman watched the toy being moved from the green box to a yellow box. Then she left the scene, and while she was gone the toy was put back into the green box. When she came back, she looked for the toy by reaching either into the green box or the yellow box. Baillargeon reasoned that if the infants expected the woman to search for the toy on the basis of her false belief that it was still in the yellow box, they would look longer at her if she violated their expectation by searching in the green box instead. This would suggest that they were thinking "Hey, how could she know the toy had been moved? I expected her to look where she last saw it!" But if, as earlier studies had suggested, the infants really had no "theory of mind," they would ignore the woman's false belief and expect her to look in the green box, where they knew the toy now lay. If the woman did that, they would not pay any special attention to her action.

What did the researcher find?

The results of this study showed that, contrary to what would be expected from previous research, the infants did look longer when the woman looked for the toy in the green box.

What do the results mean?

These results, and those from other more recent studies (Fabricius et al., 2010; Hedger & Fabricius, 2011; Kovács, Teglas, & Endress, 2010; Sakkalou & Gattis, 2012; Senju et al., 2011) support the view that despite lots of earlier research evidence to the contrary, children under the age of four do have a "theory of mind." When evaluated using appropriate research methods, these young children demonstrate an ability to recognize that other people's beliefs and perceptions can be false, that those beliefs and perceptions can differ from the child's own, and that these mental states affect the other person's behavior.

What do we still need to know?

Among other things, it would be good to know more about the extent of infants' understanding of mental states. Does it appear in other situations? Baillargeon has begun to explore this question. In one study, infants viewed a scene in which a woman looked for a doll with blue pigtails. She could look in either a plain box or in a box that had a blue tuft of hair sticking out from under its lid (Song & Baillargeon, 2008). The infants knew that the doll was in the plain box, but they stared longer when the woman looked in that box first; this suggested that they expected her to be misled by the blue tuft of hair and to falsely perceive it as belonging to the doll. In another study, Baillargeon investigated whether infants know that new information can correct an adult's false belief (Song et al., 2008). In this case, infants watched an adult hide a ball in a box while another adult watched. After the first adult left the scene, the second adult moved the ball from the box to a cup. When the first adult returned, the second adult told her "The ball is in the cup!" Infants stared longer if the adult searched for the ball in the box despite this corrective information. Those who saw her reach for the cup did not pay special attention, suggesting that they expected her to do so once her false belief had been corrected.

What other mental states can infants understand (Palmquist & Jaswal, 2012)? Do they also realize that other people's behavior can be influenced by goals, intentions, emotions, and even by the fairness or unfairness of a situation (LoBue, Nichida et al., 2011; Sloane, Baillargeon, & Premack, 2012; Warneken et al., 2011)? How soon after birth does a "theory of mind" develop? These are among the dozens of additional questions that remain for future research in this fascinating area of developmental psychology (Woodward, 2009).   ●●●●

LINKAGES

Who teaches boys to be men and girls to be women? (a link to Learning)

Gender Roles

An important aspect of understanding other people is knowing about social roles, including those linked to being male or female. All cultures establish expectations about **sex roles**—also known as **gender roles**—which are the general patterns of work, appearance, and behavior associated with being a man or a woman (Blakemore, Berenbaum, & Liben, 2009). Gender roles appear in every culture, but they are more pronounced in some cultures than in others. One analysis revealed, for example, that where smaller differences in social status exist between males and females, gender-role differences are smaller as well (Wood & Eagly, 2002). In North America, some roles—such as homemaker and firefighter—have traditionally been tied to gender, although these traditions are weakening. Research by Deborah Best suggests that although children show gender-role expectations earliest in Muslim countries (where the differences in roles are perhaps most extreme), children in all 25 countries she studied eventually developed them (Best, 1992; Williams & Best, 1990).

Gender roles appear and persist because they are deeply rooted in both nature and nurture (Knafo & Spinath, 2011). Small physical and behavioral differences between the sexes appear early on and tend to increase over the years. For example, girls tend to speak and write earlier and to be better at grammar and spelling than boys (Halpern, 2012). Girls are also able to read emotional signals at younger ages than boys (Dunn et al., 1991) and to ask for help as well as offer it (Benenson & Koulnazarian, 2008; Bornstein et al., 2008). Their play also tends to be more orderly. Boys tend to be more skilled than girls at manipulating objects, constructing three-dimensional forms, and mentally manipulating complex figures and pictures (Choi & Silverman, 2003; Newhouse, Newhouse, & Astur, 2007). They are more physically active and aggressive and are more inclined to hit obstacles or people (Baillargeon et al., 2007; Card et al., 2008; Ostrov, 2006). They play in larger groups and spaces and enjoy noisier, more strenuous physical games (Fabes, Martin, & Hanish, 2003; Rose & Rudolph, 2006).

Biological Factors   A biological contribution to these male-female differences is suggested by several lines of evidence. First, studies show sex differences in anatomy, hormones, and brain organization and functioning that are related to sex-typed patterns of behavior (Auyeung et al., 2009; Geary, 1999; Ruble, Martin, & Berenbaum, 2006). Second, cross-cultural research reveals consistent gender patterns at an early age, even in the face of differing socialization practices (Baillargeon et al., 2007; Simpson & Kenrick, 1997). Third, research with nonhuman primates finds sex differences that parallel those seen in human children. Young female animals prefer playing with dolls, and young males prefer playing with a toy car, for example (Alexander & Hines, 2002; Williams & Pleil, 2008). Fourth, research in behavioral genetics shows that genes exert a moderate influence on the appearance of gender-typed behaviors (Iervolino et al., 2005).

gender roles (sex roles) Patterns of work, appearance, and behavior that a society associates with being male or female.

Learning Gender Roles

In every culture, socialization by parents and others typically encourages the interests, activities, and other characteristics traditionally associated with a child's own gender.

Social Factors   There is no doubt, though, that socialization also influences gender roles, partly by exaggerating whatever sex differences may already exist (Hyde, 2005, 2007). From the moment they are born, boys and girls are treated differently (Lobue & DeLoache, 2011). Adults usually play more gently with, and talk more to, infants they believe to be girls than infants they believe to be boys (Culp, Cook, & Housley, 1983). They often give their daughters dolls and tea sets, their sons trucks and tools. They tend to encourage boys to achieve, compete, and explore; to control their feelings; to be independent; and to assume personal responsibility. They more often encourage girls to be expressive, nurturing, reflective, dependent, domestic, obedient, and unselfish (Blakemore et al., 2009; Ruble, Martin, & Berenbaum, 2006). In short, parents, teachers, and television role models consciously or accidentally pass on their ideas about "appropriate" behaviors for boys and girls (Else-Quest et al., 2010; Parke & Buriel, 2006; Ruble et al., 2006).

They also convey information about gender-appropriate interests (Wood & Eagly, 2012). For example, sixth-grade girls and boys express equal interest in science and earn the same grades. Yet parents underestimate their daughters' interest in science, believe that science is difficult for them, and are less likely to give them scientific explanations when working on a physics task (Tenenbaum & Leaper, 2003) or visiting a science museum (Crowley et al., 2001; Leinhardt & Knutson, 2004). They do not encourage their daughters to select science courses in school (Tenenbaum, 2009). Additionally, even though girls have the same aptitudes as boys (Schmidt, 2011), they may choose not to enter technical fields in which they either feel, or have been taught, they do not belong (Diekman et al., 2010; Good, Rattan, & Dweck, 2012).

Children also pick up ideas about gender-appropriate behavior from their peers (Martin & Fabes, 2001; Rose & Rudolph, 2006). For example, boys tend to be better than girls at computer or video games (Greenfield, 1994). However, this difference stems partly from the fact that boys encourage and reward each other for skilled performance at these games more than girls do (Law, Pellegrino, & Hunt, 1993). Children are also more likely to play with children of the same sex and in gender-typical ways on the playground than they are in private, at home, or in the classroom (Luria, 1992; Martin & Ruble, 2009). An analysis of 143 studies of sex differences in aggression showed that boys acted significantly and consistently more aggressively than girls, but especially so when they knew they were being watched (Hyde, 1986). Among girls, aggression is less obvious; it is usually "relational aggression" that shows up in nasty words or social exclusion, not punching (Benenson et al., 2011; Crick et al., 2004).

In short, social and cultural training tends to support and amplify any biological predispositions that distinguish boys and girls. Gender roles reflect a mix of nature and nurture.

Parents' efforts to deemphasize gender roles in their children's upbringing may be helping to reduce the size of sex differences in areas such as verbal and quantitative skills. And their efforts may be changing children's ideas about gender roles. One recent study found that 4- to 8-year-old children tended to think of gender roles as personal choices rather than social imperatives (Conry-Murray, & Turiel, 2012). However, evolutionary psychologists suggest that some sex differences are unlikely to change much; for example, males' greater ability to visualize the rotation of objects in space and females' greater ability to read facial expressions (Quinn & Liben, 2008). Evolutionary psychologists see these differences as deeply rooted reflections of gender-related hunting versus child-rearing duties that were adaptive eons ago for the survival of both sexes (Buss, 2004a; Geary, 2010). Others have suggested that such differences result from prenatal exposure to male or female hormones that shape brain development in different ways (Halpern, 2012; Vuoksimaa et al., 2010). Still others see gender differences as reflecting social inequality, not just biological destiny (Wood & Eagly, 2002). Whatever the cause of gender differences, it is important to remember that most of them are quite small (Ardila et al., 2011; Hyde, 2005). (Gender roles and other elements of early development are summarized in "In Review: Social and Emotional Development During Infancy and Childhood.")

Social and Emotional Development during Infancy and Childhood IN REVIEW

Age	Relationships With Parents	Relationships With Other Children	Social Understanding
Birth–2 years	Infants form an attachment to the primary caregiver.	Play focuses on toys, not on other children.	Infants respond to emotional expressions of others.
2–4 years	Children become more independent and no longer need their parents' constant attention.	Toys are a way of eliciting responses from other children.	Young children can recognize emotions of others.
4–10 years	Parents actively socialize their children.	Children begin to cooperate, compete, play games, and form friendships with peers.	Children learn social rules (such as politeness) and roles (such as being a male or female).

IN REVIEW QUESTIONS

1. As part of their social development, children learn ___, which tell them what patterns of appearance and behavior are associated with being male or female.

2. Teaching children to talk quietly in a restaurant is part of the process called ___.

3. Strict rules and the threat of punishment are typical of ___ parenting.

Adolescence

What threatens adolescents' self-esteem?

The years of middle childhood usually pass smoothly as children busy themselves with schoolwork, hobbies, friends, and clubs. But in adolescence, things change dramatically. All adolescents undergo significant changes in size, shape, and physical capacities. In Western cultures, many adolescents also experience huge changes in their social lives, reasoning abilities, and views of themselves.

Changes in Body, Brain, and Thinking

A sudden spurt in physical growth is a visible signal that adolescence has begun. This growth spurt peaks at about age 12 for girls and at about age 14 for boys (Tanner, 1978; see Figure 9.6). Suddenly, adolescents find themselves in new bodies. At around the peak of the growth spurt, menstruation begins in females and live sperm are produced in males. This condition of being able to reproduce is called **puberty.**

These dramatic changes in teenagers' bodies are accompanied by significant changes in their brains, especially in parts of the frontal lobes known as the prefrontal cortex (Kuhn, 2006; Spear, 2000; see Figure 2.9 in the chapter on biology and behavior). These areas are vital to the ability to think flexibly, to act appropriately in challenging situations, and to juggle multiple pieces of information. They are also involved in skills such as planning and organization, controlling impulses, and allocating attention.

In Western cultures, the changes taking place during *early adolescence,* from age 11 to 14 or so, can be disorienting. Adolescents—especially early-maturing girls—may experience bouts of depression, insomnia, and other psychological problems (Johnson et al., 2006; Mendle, Turkheimer, & Emery, 2007; Ohring, Graber, & Brooks-Gunn, 2002). This is also the time when eating disorders are first likely to appear (Wilson et al., 1996) and when the incidence of attempted and completed suicides begins to rise (Centers for Disease Control and Prevention, 2012). As sex hormones and pleasure-related brain systems become more active, sexual interest stirs and the prospect of smoking, drinking alcohol, and taking other drugs becomes more appealing (Patton et al., 2004; Reyna & Farley, 2006). Opportunities to do these things increase, because adolescents tend to spend more time with peers than with family, to be more influenced by peers, and to take more risks and seek out more novel sensations than either younger children or adults do (Gardner & Steinberg, 2005; Harden, Quinn, & Tucker-Drob, 2012; Steinberg, 2007, 2008).

Much of this risk-taking seems to be due to the different rates at which parts of the adolescent brain develop. The areas of prefrontal cortex involved in planning and impulse control do not complete their development until long after the emotional and reward-related areas of the limbic system do (Casey, Getz, & Galvan, 2008; Chein et al., 2011; Dreifus, 2009;

puberty The condition of being able, for the first time, to reproduce.

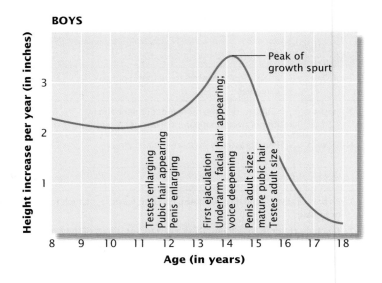

FIGURE 9.6

Physical Changes in Adolescence
At about ten and a half years of age, girls begin their growth spurt, and by age twelve, they are taller than their male peers. When boys, at about twelve and a half years of age, begin their growth spurt, they usually grow faster and for a longer period of time than girls. Adolescents may grow as much as five inches a year. The development of sexual characteristics accompanies these changes in height. The ages at which these changes occur vary considerably across individuals, but the sequence of changes is the same.

Kim & Lee, 2011; Steinberg, 2007, 2008; Vetter-O'Hagen & Spear, 2012). So, as one researcher put it, the teenage brain is like a car with a good accelerator but a weak brake (Ritter, 2007). Adolescents can make rational decisions and appreciate the difference between right and wrong, but when confronted with stressful or emotional decisions, they are likely to act impulsively, without fully understanding or analyzing the consequences of their actions. Of course, a certain amount of adolescent risk-taking and sensation-seeking is normal. In fact, adolescents who engage in moderate risk-taking tend to be more socially competent than those who take either no risks or extreme risks (Spear, 2000).

Some of the problems of adolescence appear as young people begin to face challenges to their *self-esteem*—their sense of being worthy, capable, and deserving of respect (Harter, 2012). Adolescents are especially vulnerable if other stressors occur at the same time (DuBois et al., 1992; Kling et al., 1999). The switch from elementary school to middle school is particularly challenging (Eccles, Lord, & Buchanan, 1996; Wigfield et al., 2006). Declining grades are especially likely among students who were already having trouble in school or who don't have confidence in their own abilities (Eccles & Roeser, 2003; Rudolph et al., 2001). But grades do not affect self-esteem in all teens; many base their self-esteem primarily on what others think of them or on other social factors that might affect their feelings of self-worth (Crocker & Wolfe, 2001).

The changes and pressures of adolescence are often played out at home. Many teenagers become discontented with their parents' rules and values, leading to arguments over everything from taking out the garbage to who left the gallon of milk on top of the refrigerator. They want more control over their lives, whether it involves going to the mall or getting tattoos or body piercings—especially if they think that their friends enjoy such control (Daddis, 2011). Serious conflicts may lead adolescents—especially those who do not feel close to their parents—to serious problems, including running away, pregnancy, stealing, taking drugs, or even suicide (Blum, Beuhring, & Rinehart, 2000; Goldstein, Davis-Kean, & Eccles, 2005; Klahr et al., 2011). Fortunately, although the bond with parents weakens during the transition from early to mid-adolescence, most adolescents and young adults maintain reasonably good relationships with their parents (McGue et al., 2005; Moore, 2005; van Wel, ter Bogt, & Raaijmakers, 2002). In fact, research suggests that although most parents and teachers seem to believe that adolescence is a time of "storm and stress" in Western cultures (Hines & Paulson, 2007), more than half of today's teens find early adolescence relatively trouble free (Arnett, 1999, 2007); only about 15 percent of the adolescents studied experience serious turmoil.

Love and Sex in Adolescence   Surveys suggest that nearly half of 15-year-olds and 70 percent of 18-year-olds in North America have romantic relationships (Carver, Joyner, & Udry, 2003; Collins & Steinberg, 2006). About 46 percent of adolescents between ages 15 and

Digital Connections

Compared to adults and children, adolescents spend more time online and communicating electronically to stay in touch with people in their social networks (Reich, Subrahmanyam, & Espinoza, 2012; Valkenburg & Peter, 2007a, 2009). About a third of them believe that online communication is more effective than in-person conversation for disclosing intimate personal information. This technology is relatively new, so we do not yet know what (if any), long-term effects the constant use of social media might have on adolescents' cognitive functioning and academic performance, or whether it has positive or negative effects on the size of young people's social networks, their feelings of well-being, or their closeness to friends (Junco & Cotton, 2011; Pea et al., 2012; Pollet, Roberts, & Dunbar, 2011).

Mothers Too Soon?

More than half of the U.S. adolescents who become pregnant elect to keep their babies and become single mothers. These young women and their children are likely to face special academic, social, and other problems. For this reason, support programs for teenage mothers have been developed, and a number of them have reported some success in three areas: alleviating the mothers' symptoms of depression, increasing the mothers' parenting capabilities, and achieving the mothers' educational goals (Cox et al., 2008; Sadler et al., 2007).

19 say they have had sexual intercourse, nearly half have engaged in oral sex, and over 10 percent have tried anal sex (Adolescent Sexual Behavior, 2012; Melby, 2008; Kaiser Family Foundation, 2005; National Center for Chronic Disease Prevention and Health Promotion, 2002; Trends, 2010).

Teens who have sex differ from those who do not in a number of ways (Huibregtse et al., 2011). They hold less conventional attitudes and values and they are more likely to smoke, use alcohol and other drugs (National Center on Addiction and Substance Abuse, 2004), be aggressive, and have attention problems in school (Schofield et al., 2008). They also spend more unsupervised time after school (Cohen & Steele, 2002), they are more likely to belong to peer groups with socially deviant behavioral norms (diNoia & Schinke, 2008), and they are more likely to have sexually active best friends (Jaccard, Blanton, & Dodge, 2005). Their parents tend to be less educated, less likely to exert control over them, and less likely to be supportive or talk openly with them (Price & Hyde, 2011). The typical pairing of sexually active heterosexual teens is a "macho" male and a "girly" female (Udry & Chantala, 2003). Adolescents who displayed poor self-control skills as children are the ones most likely to take greater sexual risks, such as having multiple partners and not using condoms (Atkins, 2008; Raffaelli & Crockett, 2003). It has been suggested that sexual content in movies, television, and other media may encourage adolescents' sexual activity, but with only mixed research results available so far, it is too early to draw firm conclusions about this possibility (Agbo-Quaye & Robertson, 2010; Collins et al., 2011; Morgan, 2011; Steinberg & Monahan, 2011).

Too often, sexual activity leads to declining interest in academic achievement and in school generally (Frisco, 2008), as well as to sexually transmitted diseases, and unplanned and unwanted pregnancies. Teenage girls have the highest rates of sexually transmitted diseases (such as gonorrhea, chlamydia, human papillomavirus, and pelvic inflammatory disease) of any age group (Forhan et al., 2009; Malhotra, 2008; Ross, 2002). About half of the 19 million cases of sexually transmitted diseases reported each year occur in adolescents (Malhotra, 2008); these cases include about one fourth of all teenage girls (Contemporary Sexuality, 2008; Hampton, 2008). One-fifth of all AIDS cases start in adolescence.

Though teenage pregnancy rates have recently fallen to new lows (Ventura & Hamilton, 2011), nearly 18 percent of teenage girls in the United States still get pregnant before they reach age 19 and about 415,000 of them become teenage mothers (Malhotra, 2008; Martin et al., 2009; Martin et al., 2011; Perper & Manlove, 2009). The teens most likely to become pregnant are those with little confidence in themselves or in their educational futures (Chandra et al., 2008; Young et al., 2004). A teenage pregnancy can create problems for the mother, the baby, and others in the family. For one thing, the mother

is less likely to complete high school (Perper, Peterson, & Manlove, 2010). The education of younger sisters may be affected, too, because they may have to take time away from school work to help care for the baby. These siblings are also at increased risk for drug and alcohol use and for becoming pregnant themselves (East & Jacobson, 2001; Monstad, Propper, & Salvanesvc, 2011). The baby is less likely than an older mother's child to survive its first year (Phipps, Blume, & DeMonner, 2002). This danger occurs partly because teenage parents tend to be less positive and stimulating with their children than older parents and are more likely to abuse them (Brooks-Gunn & Chase-Lansdale, 2002). The children of teenage parents are also more likely to develop behavior problems and to do poorly in school than children whose parents are older (Hoffman, 2008; Moffitt, 2002).

© Bill Aron/PhotoEdit

Hanging Out, Separately

Ethnic identity is that part of our personal identity that reflects the racial, religious, or cultural group to which we belong. Ethnic identity often leads people to interact mainly with others who share that same identity. To what extent is this true of you? You can get a rough idea by jotting down the ethnicity of all the people you chose to spend time with over the past week or so.

LEARN by DOING

ethnic identity The part of a person's identity that reflects the racial, religious, or cultural group to which that person belongs.

identity crisis The phase during which an adolescent attempts to develop an integrated self-image as a unique person by pulling together self-knowledge acquired during childhood.

Identity and Development of the Self

In many less economically developed nations today, as in the United States in the nineteenth century, early adolescence ends at around age 15. This age marks the onset of adulthood—a time when work, parenting, and grown-up responsibilities begin. In modern North America, the transition from childhood to adulthood often lasts well into the twenties. Adolescents spend a lot of time being students or trainees. This lengthened adolescence has created special problems—among them, the matter of finding or forming an identity.

Forming a Personal and Ethnic Identity Preschool children asked to describe themselves often mention a favorite or habitual activity: "I watch TV" or "I play in the yard." At eight or nine, children identify themselves by giving facts such as their sex, age, name, physical appearance, and likes and dislikes. They may still describe themselves in terms of what they do, but they now include how well they do it compared with other children. Then, at about age eleven, children begin to describe themselves in terms of social relationships, personality traits, and other general, stable psychological characteristics such as "smart" or "friendly" (Sakuma, Endo, & Muto, 2000; Shaffer, 1999). By the end of adolescence, self-descriptions emphasize personal beliefs, values, and moral standards (Harter, 2012). These changes in the way children and adolescents describe themselves suggest changes in the way they think about themselves (Davis-Kean, Jager, & Collins, 2009). As they become more self-conscious, they gradually develop a personal identity as unique individuals.

Their personal identity may be affected by their **ethnic identity**—the part of identity that reflects the racial, religious, or cultural group to which the person belongs (French et al., 2006; Quintana, 2010). In melting-pot nations such as the United States, some members of ethnic minorities may identify with their ethnic group—Chinese, Mexican, or Italian, for example—even more than with their national citizenship. Children are aware of ethnic cues such as skin color before they reach the age of three. Minority-group children notice these cues earlier than other children and prefer to play with children from their own group (Milner, 1983). In high school, most students hang out with members of their own ethnic group. They tend not to know classmates in other ethnic groups well, seeing them more as members of those groups than as individuals (Steinberg, Dornbusch, & Brown, 1992). A positive ethnic identity contributes to self-esteem, partly because seeing their own group as superior makes people feel good about themselves and is associated with more positive attitudes about education (Fiske, 1998; Fuligni, Witkow, & Garcia, 2005). Adolescents with a strong ethnic identity are more likely to do well academically and less likely to become delinquents, especially if they are from ethnic minorities (Adelabu, 2008; Bruce & Waelde, 2008; Fuligni, Witkow, & Garcia, 2005). As described in the chapter on social psychology, the same processes that create ethnic identity can also sow the seeds of ethnic prejudice, but such prejudice is not inevitable. Adolescents who regularly interact with members of other ethnic groups usually develop more mature ethnic identities and express more favorable attitudes toward people of other ethnicities (Phinney, Ferguson, & Tate, 1997; Phinney, Jacoby, & Silva, 2007).

Facing the Identity Crisis Identity formation is the central task of adolescence in Erikson's theory of psychosocial development. According to Erikson (1968), events of late adolescence—graduating from high school, going to college, and forming new relationships—challenge the adolescent's self-concept and trigger an **identity crisis** (see Table 9.2). In this crisis, the adolescent must develop the self-image of a unique person by pulling together self-knowledge acquired earlier. According to Erikson, if infancy, childhood, and early adolescence brought trust, autonomy, initiative, and industry, adolescents will resolve the identity crisis positively and develop feelings of self-confidence and competence. However, if infancy and childhood resulted in feelings of mistrust, shame, guilt, and inferiority, adolescents will be confused about their identity and goals.

In Western cultures there is some limited empirical support for Erikson's ideas about the identity crisis. In late adolescence, young people do consider alternative identities

(Roberts, Walton, & Viechtbauer, 2006; Waterman, 1982). They may "try out" being rebellious, studious, or detached as they attempt to resolve questions about sexuality, self-worth, industriousness, and independence, but late adolescence is also a time when many people become more aware of their obligations to their families (Fuligni & Pedersen, 2002). By the time they are 21, about half of the adolescents studied have resolved the identity crisis in a way that is consistent with their self-image and the historical era in which they are living. They enter young adulthood with self-confidence. They are basically the same people they were when they entered adolescence, but they now have more mature attitudes and behavior, more consistent goals and values, and a clearer idea of who they are (Savin-Williams & Demo, 1984). For those who fail to resolve identity issues—either because they avoided the identity crisis by accepting the identity their parents set for them or because they postponed dealing with the crisis and remain uncommitted and lacking in direction—there are often problems ahead (Lange & Byrd, 2002).

Moral Development

Adolescents are able to develop an identity partly because, according to Piaget's theory, they have entered the stage of *formal operations,* which allows them to think logically and reason about abstract concepts. Adolescents often find themselves applying these advanced cognitive skills to questions of morality.

Kohlberg's Stages of Moral Reasoning   To examine how people think about morality, Lawrence Kohlberg asked them to resolve moral dilemmas and to describe the reasoning behind their choices. Perhaps the most famous of these is the "Heinz dilemma," in which people must decide whether a man named Heinz should steal a rare and unaffordable drug in order to save his wife's life.

By posing moral dilemmas such as this one, Kohlberg found that the reasons given for moral choices change systematically and consistently with age (Kohlberg & Gilligan, 1971). Young children make moral judgments that differ from those of older children, adolescents, or adults. Kohlberg proposed that moral reasoning develops in six stages, which are summarized in Table 9.3. These stages, he said, are not tightly linked to a

---

TABLE 9.3   Kohlberg's Stages of Moral Reasoning

Kohlberg's stages of moral reasoning describe differences in how people think about moral issues. Some researchers have suggested that the changes seen from stage to stage are partly attributable to developments in the brain that allow greater cognitive complexity and empathy (van den Bos et al., 2011). Here are some examples of answers that people at different stages of development might give to the "Heinz dilemma" described in the text. This dilemma is more realistic than you might think. In 1994, a man was arrested for robbing a bank after being turned down for a loan to pay for his wife's cancer treatments.

Stage	What is Right?	Should Heinz Steal the Drug?
Preconventional		
1.	Obeying and avoiding punishment from a superior authority	"Heinz should not steal the drug because he will be jailed."
2.	Making a fair exchange, a good deal	"Heinz should steal the drug because his wife will repay him later."
Conventional		
3.	Pleasing others and getting their approval	"Heinz should steal the drug because he loves his wife and because she and the rest of the family will approve."
4.	Doing your duty, following rules and social order	"Heinz should steal the drug for his wife because he has a duty to care for her," or "Heinz should not steal the drug because stealing is illegal."
Postconventional		
5.	Respecting rules and laws but recognizing that they may have limits	"Heinz should steal the drug because life is more important than property."
6.	Following universal ethical principles such as justice, reciprocity, equality, and respect for human life and rights	"Heinz should steal the drug because of the principle of preserving and respecting life."

person's chronological age. Instead, there is a range of ages for reaching each stage, and not everyone reaches the highest level.

Stage 1 and Stage 2 moral judgments, which are most typical of children under the age of nine, tend to be selfish in nature. Kohlberg called this the **preconventional level** of moral reasoning because it is not based on the conventions or rules that usually guide social interactions in society. People at this level of **moral development** are mainly concerned with avoiding punishment or following rules when it is to their own advantage. At the **conventional level** of moral reasoning, Stages 3 and 4, people care about other people. They think that morality consists of following rules and conventions such as duty to the family, to marriage vows, and to the country. The moral reasoning of children and adolescents from nine to nineteen is most often at this level. Stages 5 and 6 represent the highest level of moral reasoning, which Kohlberg called the **postconventional level** because it occurs after conventional reasoning. Moral judgments at this level are based on personal standards or universal principles of justice, equality, and respect for human life, not just on the demands of authority figures or society. People who have reached this level view rules and laws as arbitrary but respect them because they protect human welfare. They believe that individual rights can sometimes justify violating these laws if the laws become destructive. People do not usually reach this level until sometime in young adulthood—if at all. Studies of Kohlberg's stages have generally supported the sequence he proposed (Turiel, 2006).

Limitations of Kohlberg's Stages   Do Kohlberg's stages appear across cultures? In general, yes. Forty-five studies in 27 cultures from Alaska to Zambia showed that people do tend to make upward progress through Kohlberg's stages, without reversals, although stages 5 and 6 did not always appear (Gibbs et al., 2007; Snarey, 1987; Snarey & Hooker, 2006; Turiel, 2006; Wainryb, 2006). Stage 6 is seen only rarely in extraordinary individuals. Further, the moral judgments made in some cultures do not always fit neatly into Kohlberg's stages. For example, some people in collectivist cultures, such as Papua New Guinea, Taiwan, and Israeli kibbutzim, explained their answers to moral dilemmas by pointing to the importance of the community. And people in India included in their moral reasoning the importance of acting in accordance with one's caste (social class) and with maintaining personal purity (Shweder et al., 1994). As in other areas of cognitive development, culture plays a significant role in shaping moral judgments (Abarbanell & Hauser, 2010; Rai & Fiske, 2011).

Gender may also play a role. Carol Gilligan (1982, 1993) has suggested that Kohlberg's research documented mainly the abstract, impersonal concept of justice typically seen in males. When Gilligan asked people about moral conflicts, the majority of men focused on justice, but only half of the women did. The other half focused on caring. This finding supports Gilligan's belief that for North American females, the moral ideal is to protect enduring relationships and fulfill human needs. This difference between men and women has not been found consistently, however (Jaffee & Hyde, 2000). In fact, it appears that males and females are capable of using either approach to moral reasoning (Johnston, 1988). The tendency for females to focus on caring more than males do and for males to focus on justice more than females do appears most clearly when they are resolving real-life moral issues that they have personally experienced (Jaffe & Hyde, 2000). However when asked about hypothetical moral dilemmas, there is no substantial difference in how males and females reason (Jaffe & Hyde, 2000; Raaijmakers, Engels, & Van Hoof, 2005; Walker, 2006).

Taken together, the results of research in different countries and with both genders suggest that moral ideals are not absolute and universal. Moral development is apparently an adaptation to the moral world and the specific situations in which people find themselves (Bersoff, 1999; Sweet et al., 2010; Wainryb & Psaupathi, 2008). Formal operational reasoning may be necessary for people to reach the highest level of moral reasoning, but formal operational reasoning alone is not sufficient. To some extent, at the highest levels, moral reasoning is a product of culture and history, of situations, and of people's emotions and goals in those situations (Almås et al., 2010; Amit & Greene, 2012; Feinberg et al., 2012; Gino, Norton, & Ariely, 2010; Hussar & Horvath, 2011; Krebs & Denton, 2005; Teper, Inzlicht, & Page-Gould, 2011; Turiel, 2006).

preconventional level Moral reasoning that is not based on the conventions or rules that guide social interactions in a society.

moral development The growth of an individual's understanding of the concepts of right and wrong.

conventional level Moral reasoning that reflects a concern about other people as well as the belief that morality consists of following rules and conventions.

postconventional level Moral reasoning that reflects moral judgments based on personal standards or universal principles of justice, equality, and respect for human life.

Adulthood

What developmental changes occur in adulthood?

Development does not end with adolescence. Adults, too, go through transitions and experience physical, cognitive, and social changes. It has been suggested that adulthood emerges as early as age 18 (Arnett, 2000), but for our purposes, adulthood can be divided into three periods: *early adulthood* (ages 20 to 39), *middle adulthood* (ages 40 to 65), and *late adulthood* (beyond age 65).

Physical Changes

In early adulthood, physical growth continues. Shoulder width, height, and chest size increase and people continue to develop their athletic abilities. By their mid-thirties nearly everyone shows some hearing impairment, but for most people, the years of early adulthood are the prime of life.

In middle adulthood, other physical changes slowly emerge. The most common of these involve the further loss of sensory sharpness (Fozard et al, 1977). People become less sensitive to light, less accurate at perceiving differences in distance, and slower and less able at seeing details. Increased farsightedness is common among people in their forties, and they may need glasses to correct for it. In their late forties or early fifties, women generally experience **menopause,** the shutdown of reproductive capability. Estrogen and progesterone levels drop and the menstrual cycle eventually ceases.

Most people are well into late adulthood before their bodily functions show noticeable impairment. However, inside the body, bone mass is dwindling and the risk of heart disease is increasing. Men shrink about an inch in height and women about two inches as their posture changes and cartilage disks between the spinal vertebrae become thinner. Older adults tend to go to sleep earlier but may find it harder to sleep through the night without awakening to use the bathroom (Park et al., 2002). Hardening of the arteries and a buildup of fat deposits on the artery walls may lead to heart disease. The digestive system slows down and becomes less efficient. Both digestive disorders and heart disease sometimes result from problems of diet—too little fluid, too little fiber, too much fat— and inactivity. In addition, the brain shrinks during late adulthood. The few reflexes that remained after infancy, such as the knee-jerk reflex, weaken or disappear. The flow of blood to the brain slows. As in earlier years, many of these changes can be delayed or diminished by a healthy diet and exercise (Brach et al., 2003; Larson et al., 2006; Seeman & Chen, 2002).

Cognitive Changes

Adulthood is marked by increases as well as decreases in cognitive abilities. Reaction times become slower and more variable (Deary & Der, 2005a), and although abilities that involve intensive information processing begin to decline in early adulthood, those that depend on accumulated knowledge and experience increase and don't begin to decline until old age, and some individuals never experience this decline. In fact, older adults may function as well as or better than younger adults in situations that tap their long-term memories and well-learned skills (Campbell, Hasher, & Thomas, 2010; Worthy et al., 2011). The experienced teacher may deal with an unruly child more skillfully than the new teacher, and the senior lawyer may understand the implications of a new law better than the recent graduate. Their years of accumulating and organizing information can make older adults practiced, skillful, and wise.

Early and Middle Adulthood Until age 60 at least, important cognitive abilities improve. During this period, adults do better on tests of vocabulary, comprehension, and general knowledge—especially if they use these abilities in their daily lives or engage in enriching activities such as travel or reading (Park, 2001). Young and middle-aged adults learn new information and new skills and remember old information and hone old skills. In fact, it is in their forties through their early sixties that people tend to put in the best

menopause The cessation of a woman's reproductive capacity.

performance of their lives on complex mental tasks such as reasoning, verbal memory, and vocabulary (Schaie & Willis, in press).

The nature of thought may also change during adulthood. Adult thought is often more complex and adaptive than adolescent thought (Labouvie-Vief, 1992). Unlike adolescents, adults see both the possibilities and the problems in every course of action—in deciding whether to start a new business, back a political candidate, move to a new place, or change jobs. Middle-aged adults are more expert than adolescents or young adults at making rational decisions and at relating logic and abstractions to actions, emotions, social issues, and personal relationships (Tversky & Kahneman, 1981). As they appreciate these relationships, their thought becomes more global, more concerned with broad moral and practical issues (Labouvie-Vief, 1982). It has been suggested that the achievement of these new kinds of thinking reflects a stage of cognitive development that goes beyond Piaget's formal operational stage (Lutz & Sternberg, 1999). In this stage, people's thinking becomes *dialectical,* which means they understand that knowledge is relative, not absolute. They realize that what is seen as wise today might have been thought foolish in times past. They see life's contradictions as an inevitable part of reality, and they tend to weigh various solutions to problems rather than just accepting the first one that springs to mind (Grossmann et al., 2010). Although age does not necessarily produce wisdom, researchers in one study found that college-educated older adults scored higher on a measure of wisdom than current college students, and that the wisest of them felt that they had grown wiser by learning from life experiences (Ardelt, 2010).

Late Adulthood   It is not until late in adulthood, after the age of 65 or so, that some intellectual abilities decline noticeably (Craik & Salthouse, 2008; Salthouse, 2011, 2012a, 2012b). Generally, these are abilities that require intense mental effort, such as rapid and flexible manipulation of ideas and symbols, and active thinking and reasoning (Baltes, 1993, 1994; Bugg et al., 2006; Finkel et al., 2003; Gilmore, Spinks, & Thomas, 2006; see Figure 9.7). Older adults do just as well as younger ones at tasks they know well, such as naming familiar objects (Radvansky, 1999). However, when asked to perform an unfamiliar task or solve a complex problem they have not seen before, older adults are generally slower and less effective than younger ones (Craik & Rabinowitz, 1984). When faced with complex problems, older people apparently suffer from having too much information to sift through (Gazzaley et al., 2005). They have trouble considering, choosing, and executing solutions (Arenberg, 1982; Peters et al., 2007). As people age, they grow less efficient at organizing the elements of a problem and at holding and

FIGURE 9.7
Mental Abilities over the Life Span
Mental abilities collectively known as "fluid" intelligence—speed and accuracy of information processing, for example—begin to decline quite early in adult life (Tucker-Drob, 2011). Changes in these biologically based aspects of thinking are usually not noticeable until late adulthood, however. "Crystallized" abilities learned over a lifetime— such as reading, writing, comprehension of language, and profes-sional skills—decline too, but later and at a slower pace (Finkel et al., 2007; Li et al., 2004).

Source: Adapted from Baltes (1994).

Crystallized intelligence
Fluid intelligence

Staying Alert, Staying Active, Staying Alive

Sisters Alcantara, Claverine, and Nicolette of the School Sisters of Notre Dame convent were in their eighties or nineties when this photo was taken. They stayed alert by reading, solving puzzles, playing cards, and participating in vocabulary quizzes. The nuns at this convent are participating in a study of aging and the brain.

mentally manipulating more than one idea at a time. They have difficulty doing tasks that require them to divide their attention between two activities and are slower at shifting their attention back and forth between those activities (Verhaeghen, 2011; Wasylyshyn, Verhaeghen, & Sliwinski, 2011; Wecker et al., 2005). If older adults have enough time, though, and if they can separate the two activities and choose appropriate problem solving strategies, they can perform just as well as younger adults (Hawkins, Kramer, & Capaldi, 1993; Lemaire, 2010).

Usually, the loss of intellectual abilities is slow and need not cause severe problems (Bashore & Ridderinkhof, 2002). A study of older adults in Sweden (Nilsson, 1996) showed, for example, that their memory problems were largely confined to *episodic memory* (e.g., remembering what they had for lunch yesterday) rather than *semantic memory* (remembering general information, such as the capital of Italy). In other words, everyday abilities that involve verbal processes are likely to remain intact into advanced old age (Freedman, Aykan, & Martin, 2001; Schaie & Willis, in press).

The decline in cognitive abilities in old age, as well as the rate of that decline, is partly a matter of genetics (Finkel et al., 2009; Kremen & Lyons, 2011; Reynolds et al., 2005), but other factors are important too. The risk of cognitive decline is significantly lower for people who are healthy and psychologically flexible and who have a high level of education, income, and occupation. Cognitive decline is slower among those who eat a healthy diet (Morris et al., 2006), live in an intellectually stimulating atmosphere with mentally able spouses or companions (Albert et al., 1995; Chodosh et al., 2002; Shimamura et al., 1995) and who had high IQ and activity levels in adolescence (Fritsch et al., 2005; Morris et al., 2006; Yaffe et al., 2009). Continued mental exercise—such as doing puzzles, painting, and having intellectually stimulating conversations with friends—can also help older adults think and remember effectively and creatively (Hall et al., 2009; Schooler, 2007; Verghese et al., 2003, 2006; Wilson, Beckett et al., 2002; Wilson et al., 2012). Practice at memory and other information processing tasks may even lead to some improvement in skills that had been impaired by old age and disuse (Erickson et al., 2007; Gross & Rebok, 2011; Kramer & Willis, 2002; Pollatsek, Romoser, & Fisher, 2012; Rapp, Brenes, & Marsh, 2002; Tranter & Koutstaal, 2008; Villers-Sidani et al., 2010). Maintaining physical fitness through dancing or other forms of aerobic exercise has been associated with better maintenance of skills on a variety of mental tasks, including those involving reaction time, reasoning, and divided attention (Abbott et al., 2004; Baker et al., 2010; Erickson et al., 2011; McAuley, Kramer, & Colcombe, 2004; Smith et al., 2010; Weuve et al., 2004). And a life full of organized activities and opportunities to interact with a lots of different people—not just family members—seems best for preventing decline in cognitive abilities (Hertzog et al., 2009; Keller-Cohen et al., 2004).

The greatest threat to cognitive abilities in late adulthood is Alzheimer's disease. As the disease progresses, parts of the brain begin to deteriorate, leaving even the brightest minds incapable (Dauwels et al., 2010; Pengas et al., 2010). People with Alzheimer's become emotionally flat, then disoriented, then mentally vacant. They usually die prematurely. The average duration of the disease, from onset to death, is seven years. But the age of onset and rate of decline depends on a number of factors, such as intelligence (Fritsch et al., 2005; Rentz et al., 2004), gender (Molsa, Marttila, & Rinne, 1995; Wilson, Scherr, et al., 2007), personality (Duberstein et al., 2011), motivation (Boyle et al., 2012), education (Mortimer, Snowdon, & Markesbery, 2003; Wilson, Scherr, et al., 2007), vulnerability to stress (Wilson et al., 2011), physical activity (Buchman et al., 2012), and vascular health (Reitz et al., 2010). Overall, women tend to deteriorate more slowly than men, and people of either gender who are highly intelligent, well-educated, open to experience, secure, confident, and conscientious tend to deteriorate more slowly than people who do not have these characteristics (Wilson et al., 2007b).

Social Changes

Adulthood is a time when changes occur in social relationships and positions. These changes do not come in neat, predictable stages but instead follow various paths, depending on individual experiences. Transitions—such as divorcing, being fired, going back to school, remarrying, losing a spouse to death, being hospitalized, getting arrested, moving back home, or retiring—are just a few of the turning points that can redirect a person's life path and lead to changes in personality (Caspi & Shiner, 2006; Roberts, Helson, & Klohnen, 2002).

Early Adulthood   Men and women in Western cultures usually enter the adult world in their twenties. The process may begin with a period of *emerging adulthood* during which they explore life's possibilities through education, dating, and travel before they settle into stable adult roles and responsibilities (Arnett, 2000; 2011; Roisman et al., 2004). They decide on an occupation (or at least take a job) and become preoccupied with their careers (Srivastava et al., 2003). They also become more agreeable—warm, generous, and helpful (Srivastava et al., 2003); more controlled and confident; more socially dominant, conscientious, and emotionally stable; and less angry and alienated (Roberts, Caspi, & Moffitt, 2001; Roberts, Walton, & Viechtbauer, 2006; Roberts & Mroczek, 2008). Nevertheless, by age 25 about 20 percent of young adults are still living with their parents, and just under half are still financially dependent (Cohen et al., 2003). It is in their twenties, too, that many young adults become more concerned with matters of romantic love. Having reached the sixth of Erikson's stages of psychosocial development listed in Table 9.2 (intimacy versus isolation), they begin to focus on forming mature relationships based on sexual intimacy, friendship, or mutual intellectual stimulation. The result may be marriage or some other committed relationship.

Just how willing and able people are to make intimate commitments may depend on their earlier attachment relationships (Birnbaum et al., 2006; Nosko et al., 2011; Oriña et al., 2011; Roisman, 2007; Treboux, Crowell, & Waters, 2004). Researchers have discovered that young adults' views of intimate relationships parallel the patterns of infant attachment that we described earlier (Broussard & Cassidy, 2010; Campbell et al., 2005; Horowitz, Rosenberg, & Bartholomew, 1993). If their view reflects a secure attachment, they tend to feel valued and worthy of support and affection; they develop closeness easily. They have relationships characterized by joy, trust, and commitment. If their view reflects an insecure attachment, however, they tend to be preoccupied with relationships and may feel misunderstood, underappreciated, and worried about being abandoned. Their relationships are often negative, obsessive, and jealous. Alternatively, they may be aloof and unable to trust or to commit themselves to a partner; they may be more prone to infidelity (DeWall et al., 2011). Overall, young adults whose parents have been accepting and supportive tend to develop warm and supportive romantic relationships (Conger et al., 2000; Hatton et al., 2009; Overbeek et al., 2007; Salvatore et al., 2011).

For many young adults, the experience of becoming parents represents entry into a major new developmental phase often accompanied by personal, social, and occupational changes (Palkovitz, Copes, & Woolfolk, 2001). This milestone usually comes earlier for young adults from lower income backgrounds, who are more likely to be in full-time employment and less likely to be living at home (Cohen et al., 2003). Often, satisfaction with the marriage or partnership declines once a baby is born (Doss et al., 2009; Gilbert, 2006), and about half of all marriages break under the strain (National Center for Health Statistics, 2001). Young mothers may experience particular dissatisfaction—especially if they resent the constraints infants bring, if they see their careers as important, if the infants are temperamentally difficult, if the partnerships are not strong, or if their partners are not supportive (Cowan & Cowan, 2000, 2009; Harwood, McLean, & Durkin, 2007; Hogan & Msall, 2002; Jokela, 2010; Shapiro, Gottman, & Carrere, 2000). When the father does not do his share of caring for the baby, both mothers and fathers are dissatisfied (Levy-Shiff, 1994). The ability of young parents to provide adequate care for their babies is related to their own attachment histories. New mothers whose attachments to their own mothers were secure tend to be more responsive to their infants and the infants, in turn, are more

Building Monuments

Middle adulthood tends to be a time when people become deeply committed to building something that lasts, perhaps by raising children and grandchildren, or through achievements outside the home (Hebblethwaite & Norris, 2011; Son & Wilson, 2011; Tabuchi & Gondo, 2011).

generativity The concern of adults in midlife with generating something enduring.

The "Sandwich" Generation

During their midlife transition, many people feel "sandwiched" between generations—pressured by the social, emotional, and financial needs of their children on one side and the needs of their aging parents on the other (Chassin et al., 2010; Keene & Prokos, 2007; Pines et al., 2011; Ugwu, 2010; Wujcik, 2008).

likely to develop secure attachments to them (Adam, Gunnar, & Tanaka, 2004; Behrens, Hesse, & Main, 2007; van IJzendoorn, 1995).

The challenges of young adulthood are complicated by the nature of family life today (Halpern, 2005: Howe, 2012). Forty years ago, about half of North American households consisted of married couples in their twenties and thirties—a breadwinner husband and a homemaker wife—raising at least two children together. This description now applies to only about one fifth of households (Lofquist et al., 2012). Today, more people are cohabiting instead of getting married (Fry & Cohn, 2011); parents are older because young adults are delaying marriage and waiting longer to have children. Many are having children without marrying (Hertz, 2006). About 40 percent of births are to unmarried women (Child Trends, 2011). Most of these women become pregnant "the old-fashioned way," but some take advantage of technological advances that allow them to conceive through in vitro fertilization (Hahn & DiPietro, 2001; Parke et al., 2012). Many gay men and lesbians are becoming parents too. Some estimates suggest that at least four million families in the United States are headed by openly gay or lesbian adults who became parents by retaining custody of children born in a previous heterosexual marriage, by adopting children, or by having children through artificial insemination or surrogacy (Goldberg, 2010; Patterson, 2002).

Nearly half of all marriages in the United States end in divorce, creating yet another set of challenges for adults (Clarke-Stewart & Brentano, 2006; U.S. Census Bureau, 2012). People who divorce face many unanticipated stressors, including money problems, changes in living circumstances and working hours, loneliness, anxiety, and, for custodial parents, a dramatic increase in housework and child-care tasks (Amato, 2010; Clarke-Stewart & Brentano, 2006). In short, the changes seen in families and family life over the past several decades have made it more challenging than ever to successfully navigate the years of early adulthood.

Middle Adulthood   At around age 40, people go through a *midlife transition* during which they may rethink and modify their lives and relationships. Many feel invigorated and liberated; some may feel upset and have a "midlife crisis" (Beck, 1992; Levinson et al., 1978). The contrast between youth and middle age may be especially upsetting for men who matured early in adolescence and were sociable and athletic rather than intellectual (Block, 1971). Women who chose a career over a family now hear the biological clock ticking out their last childbearing years. Women who have had children, however, become more independent and confident and more oriented toward achievement and events outside the family (Helson & Moane, 1987). For both men and women, the emerging sexuality of their teenage children, the emptiness of the nest as children leave home, or the declining health of a parent may precipitate a crisis.

Following the midlife transition, the middle years of adulthood are often a time of satisfaction and happiness (Mroczek & Spiro, 2005). Many people become concerned with producing something that will outlast them (Sheldon & Kasser, 2001; Zucker, Ostrove, & Stewart, 2002). Erikson called this concern the crisis of **generativity** because people are focused on producing or generating something. Making this kind of social investment tends to be associated with better adult adjustment (Snarey, 1994; Wilt et al., 2010). If people do not resolve this crisis, he suggested, they stagnate.

In their fifties, most people become grandparents (Smith & Drew, 2002), though they may find it hard to believe they are no longer young (Karp, 1991). At this age, spending lots of time caring for young grandchildren can be stressful and may increase the risk of heart disease, depression, and reduced life satisfaction (Hayslip, King & Jooste, 2008; Lee, Colditz et al., 2003). Overall, the degree of happiness and healthiness people experience during middle adulthood depends on how much control they feel they have over their work, finances, marriages, children, and sex lives as well as on their personality characteristics, how many years of education they completed, and what kind of jobs they have (Azar, 1996; Griffin, Mroczek, & Spiro, 2006).

"When I was your age, I was an adult."

Most people in their sixties want their offspring to be independent, so they may have mixed feelings toward children who continue to need financial support during an extended period of "emerging adulthood" (Kloep & Hendry, 2010; Pillemer & Suitor, 2002).

Late Adulthood   Most people between 65 and 75 years of age think of themselves as middle-aged, not old (Kleinspehn-Ammerlahn, Kotter-Grühn, & Smith, 2008). They are active and influential politically and socially, and they often are physically vigorous. Ratings of life satisfaction and self-esteem are, on average, as high in old age as during any other period of adulthood (Ben-Zur, 2002; Charles, Mather, & Carstensen, 2003; Hamarat et al., 2002; Stone, 2010). Men and women who have been employed usually retire from their jobs during this period. They adjust most easily to retirement if they are prepared for it, and view it as a choice (Adams & Rau, 2011; Moen et al., 2000; Swan, 1996). Retirement doesn't necessarily mean giving up on life. In fact, psychologists are now studying the ways in which the current generation of retirees has transformed retirement into a more active, engaged stage of life (Shultz & Wang, 2011).

Today, more people than ever are reaching old age. In fact, those over 75 make up the fastest-growing segment of the population, a group that is 25 times larger than it was a century ago. Today, 100,000 people in the United States are over 100, and the Census Bureau predicts that number will rise to 834,000 by 2050 (Volz, 2000). Old age is not necessarily a time of loneliness and desolation, but it is a time when people generally become more inward looking, cautious, and conforming (Reedy, 1983). It is a time when people develop coping strategies that increasingly take into account the limits of their control; people in this age group begin to accept what they cannot change, such as chronic health problems (Urry & Gross, 2010).

Compared to younger adults, older people's memories contain a larger proportion of positive events (Brassen et al., 2012; Charles, 2011; Mather & Carstensen, 2005), and they report less anger in response to interpersonal conflicts (Charles & Carstensen, 2008). In late adulthood, people find relationships more satisfying, supportive, and fulfilling than they did earlier in life. As they sense that time is running out, they value positive interactions and become selective about their social partners. So although they interact with others less frequently, older adults enjoy these interactions more (Carstensen, 1997). As long as they have a network of at least three close relatives or friends, they are usually content (Litwin & Shiovitz-Ezra, 2006).

The many changes associated with adolescence and adulthood are summarized in "In Review: Milestones of Adolescence and Adulthood."

Death and Dying

With the onset of old age, people become aware that death is approaching. They watch as their friends disappear. They may feel their health failing, their strength waning, and their intellectual capabilities declining. A few years or a few months before death, people may experience a gradual decline or a sharper **terminal drop** in mental functioning (Gerstorf et al., 2011; MacDonald, Hultsch, & Dixon; 2011; Wilson et al., 2007a).

The awareness of impending death brings about the last psychological crisis, according to Erikson's theory. During this stage, people evaluate their lives and accomplishments and see them as meaningful (leading to a feeling of integrity) or meaningless (leading to a feeling of despair). They tend to become more philosophical and reflective. They attempt to put their lives into perspective. They revisit old memories, resolve past conflicts, and integrate past events. They may also become more interested in the religious and spiritual side of life. This "life review" may trigger anxiety, regret, guilt, and despair; the risk of suicide does increase with age (Anderson & Conwell, 2002). But it may also help people face their own deaths and the deaths of friends and relatives with a feeling of peace and acceptance (Steinhauser et al., 2008; Torges, Stewart, & Nolen-Hoeksema, 2008).

Even the actual confrontation with death does not have to bring despair and depression. When death finally is imminent, old people strive for a death with dignity, love, affection, physical contact, and no pain (Schulz, 1978). As they think about death, they are comforted by their religious faith, their achievements, and the love of their friends and family.

terminal drop A sharp decline in mental functioning that tends to occur in late adulthood, a few months or years before death.

Still Going Strong

At the age of 82, actor and Academy Award–winning director Clint Eastwood is a famous example of the many people whose late adulthood is healthy and vigorous. And he is not slowing down. His acting remains as riveting as ever, and the films he directs continue to attract huge audiences and critical acclaim.

Longevity Facing death with dignity and openness helps people complete the life cycle with a sense of life's meaningfulness, but most of us want to live as long as possible. How can we do so? A great deal of what helps us live long lives may be genetic (Chung et al., 2010; Dykiert et al., 2012), and gender-related. Women live longer than men, on average. Longevity is also related to personality characteristics such as conscientiousness as a child (Friedman & Martin, 2011) and curiosity as an adult (Boyle et al., 2009; Swan & Carmelli, 1996). People with higher IQs and faster reaction times tend to live longer, too (Deary & Der, 2005b), as do those who typically experienced happiness, enthusiasm, contentment, and other forms of *positive affect* during adulthood (Carstensen et al., 2011; Cohen & Pressman, 2006; Ong, 2010; Pressman & Cohen, 2007). Certain age-related life events—such as whether women have children later in life or whether men have experienced hair loss—can act as environmental cues which affect people's perceptions of their ages and the aging process (Hsu, Chung, & Langer, 2010). In one study, adults who had more positive self-perceptions when they were in their fifties and sixties lived seven and a half years longer than those with less positive self-perceptions. This factor was more predictive of longevity than were health problems such as high blood pressure, high cholesterol, smoking, lack of exercise, or being overweight (Levy et al., 2002). Remaining more socially engaged and having a network of good friends, even more than close family ties, is also related to longer life (Giles et al., 2005; Poon, 2008; Shankar et al., 2011). Further, people who don't smoke, don't drink heavily, restrict their caloric intake, engage in regular physical and mental exercise, and have a sense of control over important aspects of their lives are likely to live longer (Infurna, Gerstorf, & Zarit, 2011; Kahlbaugh et al., 2011; Krause & Shaw, 2000; Manini et al., 2006; Poon, 2008; Sun et al., 2010; Yaffe et al., 2001). So eat your veggies, stay physically fit, and continue to think actively—not just to live longer later but also to live better now.

Milestones of Adolescence and Adulthood IN REVIEW

Age	Physical Changes	Cognitive Changes	Social Events and Psychological Changes
Early adolescence (11–15 years)	Puberty brings reproductive capacity and marked bodily changes.	Formal operations and principled moral reasoning become possible for the first time. (This occurs only for some people.)	Social and emotional changes result from growing sexual awareness; adolescents experience mood swings, physical changes, and conflicts with parents.
Late adolescence (16–19 years)	Physical growth continues.	Formal operations and principled moral reasoning become more likely.	An identity crisis accompanies graduation from high school.
Early adulthood (20–39 years)	Physical growth continues.	Increases continue in knowledge, problem-solving ability, and moral reasoning.	People choose a job and often a mate; they may become parents.
Middle adulthood (40–65 years)	Size and muscle mass decrease; fat increases; eyesight declines; reproductive capacity in women ends.	Thought becomes more complex, adaptive, and global.	Midlife transition may lead to change; for most, the middle years are satisfying.
Late adulthood (over 65 years)	Height decreases; organs become less efficient.	Reasoning, mathematical ability, comprehension, novel problem solving, and memory may decline.	Retirement requires adjustments; people look inward; awareness of death precipitates life review.

IN REVIEW QUESTIONS

1. The greatest threat to cognitive abilities in late adulthood is ___ disease.

2. Adolescents' ___ identity may be more defining than their national citizenship.

3. Not stealing because "I might get caught" reflects the ___ stage of moral reasoning.

Active Review

As noted in the introductory chapter, all of psychology's subfields are related to one another. Our discussion of infantile amnesia illustrates just one way that the topic of this chapter, human development, is linked to the subfield of memory, which is discussed in the chapter on

CHAPTER 9
Human Development

memory. The Linkages diagram shows ties to two other subfields, and there are many more ties throughout the book. Looking for linkages among subfields will help you see how they all fit together and help you better appreciate the big picture that is psychology.

LINKAGES

What happens to our memories of infancy?
(ans. on p. 357)

CHAPTER 6
Memory

How do we learn to speak?
(ans. on p. 272)

CHAPTER 7
Thought, Language, and Intelligence

Are childhood traits related to how long we live?
(ans. on p. 406)

CHAPTER 10
Health, Stress, and Coping

Summary

Developmental psychology is the study of the course and causes of systematic, sequential, age-related changes in mental abilities, social relationships, emotions, and moral understanding over the life-span.

Exploring Human Development

What does "genetic influence" mean? A central question in developmental psychology concerns the relative influences of nature and nurture. Gesell stressed nature in his theory of development, proposing that development is *maturation*—the natural unfolding of abilities with age. Watson took the opposite view, claiming that development is learning, as shaped by the external environment. In his theory of cognitive development, Piaget described how

nature and nurture work together. Today we accept the notion that both nature and nurture affect development and ask not whether but how and to what extent each contributes. Research in *behavioral genetics* shows that complex traits, such as intelligence and personality, are influenced by many genes as well as by many environmental factors.

Beginnings

Why should pregnant women stay away from tobacco and alcohol? Development begins with the union of an ovum and a sperm to form a zygote, which develops into an *embryo. Genes*, which consist of **DNA** (*deoxyribonucleic acid*), make up the

chromosomes that are in each body cell. The embryonic stage is a *critical period* for development, a time when certain organs must develop properly or they never will. The development of organs at this stage is permanently affected by harmful *teratogens* such as tobacco, alcohol, or other drugs. After the embryo develops into a *fetus*, adverse conditions may harm the infant's size, behavior, intelligence, or health. Babies born to women who drink heavily are at risk for *fetal alcohol syndrome*.

Newborns have limited but effective senses of vision, hearing, taste, and smell. They exhibit many *reflexes*—swift, automatic responses to external stimuli. Motor development proceeds as the nervous system matures and muscles grow and as the infant experiments with and selects the most efficient movement patterns.

Infancy and Childhood: Cognitive Development

How do babies think?

Cognitive development refers to the development of thinking, knowing, and remembering. According to Piaget, *schemas* are modified through the complementary processes *of assimilation* (fitting new objects or events into existing schemas) and *accommodation* (changing schemas when new objects will not fit existing schemas). During the *sensorimotor stage,* infants progress from using only their senses and simple reflexes to forming mental representations of objects and actions. As a result, the child becomes capable of thinking about objects that are not present. The ability to recognize that objects continue to exist even when they are hidden from view is what Piaget called *object permanence*. During the *preoperational stage,* children can use symbols, but they do not have the ability to think logically and rationally. Their understanding of the world is intuitive. When children develop the ability to think logically about concrete objects, they enter the period of *concrete operations*. At this time they can solve simple problems and have a knowledge *of conservation,* recognizing that, for example, the amount of a substance is not altered when its shape changes. The stage of *formal operations* begins in adolescence and allows thinking and logical reasoning about abstract ideas.

Today, developmental psychologists believe that new levels of cognition do not appear in sharply separated stages of global understanding but emerge more gradually and that children's reasoning can be affected by factors such as task difficulty and degree of familiarity with the objects and language involved.

Psychologists who explain cognitive development in terms of the *information processing model* have documented age-related improvements in children's attention, their abilities to explore and focus on features of the environment,

and their memories. "Infantile amnesia" leaves us with virtually no memory of events from before the age of three. Several explanations have been suggested, but this phenomenon is not yet fully understood.

The specific content of cognitive development, including the development of scripts, depends on the cultural context in which children live. How fast children develop cognitive abilities depends to some extent on how stimulating and supportive their environments are. Children growing up in poverty are likely to have delayed or impaired cognitive abilities.

Infancy and Childhood: Social and Emotional Development

How do infants become attached to their caregivers?

From the early months onward, infants and their caregivers respond to each other's emotional expressions. Most infants can be classified as having easy, difficult, or slow-to-warm-up *temperaments*. Whether they retain these temperamental styles depends to some extent on their parents' expectations and demands. According to *attachment theory,* infants form a deep, long-lasting emotional *attachment* to their mothers or other primary caregivers. Their *attachment behavior* may reflect secure or insecure attachment. The process *of socialization* begins as parents teach their children the skills and rules needed in their culture, using *parenting styles* described as *authoritarian, permissive, authoritative,* or *uninvolved (rejecting-neglecting)*. Among European American parents, those with authoritative styles tend to have more competent and cooperative children. Patterns of

parental socialization depend on cultural and other circumstances.

Over the childhood years, interactions with peers evolve into cooperative and competitive encounters; friendships become more important. Changes in children's relationships are based in part on their growing social competence. Children become increasingly able to interpret and understand social situations and emotional signals. They also learn social rules and roles, including those related to gender. *Gender roles,* also known as *sex roles,* are based both on biological differences between the sexes and on implicit and explicit socialization by parents, teachers, and peers.

Adolescence

What threatens adolescents' self-esteem?

Adolescents undergo significant changes not only in size, shape, and physical capacity but also, typically, in their social lives, reasoning abilities, and views of themselves. *Puberty* brings about physical changes that lead to psychological changes. Early adolescence is a period of shaky self-esteem. It is also a time when conflict with parents is likely to arise and when closeness with friends and conformity to peer group norms are likely to emerge. Later adolescence focuses on finding an answer to the question, "Who am I?" Events such as graduating from high school and going to college challenge the adolescent's self-concept, precipitating an *identity crisis*. To resolve this crisis, the adolescent must develop an integrated self-image as a unique person, an image that often includes *ethnic identity. Moral development* progresses from *preconventional* to *conventional* and (possibly) *postconventional levels*. Principled moral judgment—shaped by gender and culture— becomes possible for the first time.

Adulthood

What developmental changes occur in adulthood?
Physical, cognitive, and social changes occur throughout adulthood. During middle adulthood, changes begin that include decreased sharpness of the senses, increased risk of heart disease, and declining fertility (***menopause*** in women). Nevertheless, most people do not experience major health problems until late adulthood.

The cognitive changes that occur in early and middle adulthood are generally positive, including improvements in reasoning and problem-solving ability. In late adulthood, some intellectual abilities decline—especially those involved in tasks that are unfamiliar, complex, or difficult. Other abilities, such as recalling facts or making wise decisions, tend not to decline.

In their twenties, young adults make choices about occupations and form intimate commitments. By the end of their thirties, they settle down and decide what is important. They become concerned with ***generativity***—with producing something that will outlast them. Sometime around age forty, adults experience a midlife transition, which may or may not be a crisis. The forties and fifties are often a time of satisfaction. In their sixties, people contend with the issue of retirement. They generally become more inward looking, cautious, and conforming. In their seventies, eighties, and beyond, people confront their own mortality. They may become more philosophical and reflective as they review their lives. A few years or months before death, many experience a sharp decline in mental functioning known as ***terminal drop***. Still, they strive for a death with dignity, love, and no pain.

Death is inevitable, but healthy diets, exercise, conscientiousness and curiosity, and a sense of control over one's life are associated with living longer and happier lives. Older adults feel better and live longer if they receive attention from other people, maintain an open attitude toward new experiences, and keep their minds active.

LEARN by DOING

Put It in Writing
Write a short paper describing some aspects of your development over the past five years. Include comments on physical changes as well as changes in your thoughts, feelings, and behavior. Then imagine yourself five years from now and describe what further changes you expect in your physical condition, lifestyle, relationships, ideas, emotional state, and behavior. Compare the changes that have taken place in your life with those we have described in this chapter for the average person of your age.

Personal Learning Activity
Ask several of your friends about the way their parents raised them, especially about how strict or permissive they were. Take notes on these interviews and then try to categorize your friends' parents as authoritarian, permissive, authoritative, or uninvolved. (You might try categorizing your own parents as well.) Was it easy to decide which category to use in each case? Do you think that additional categories are necessary to describe parenting styles? Do you think that your friends' personalities reflect the characteristics associated with the parenting styles described in this chapter?

Review of Key Terms

Can you define each of the key terms in the chapter? Check your definitions against those on the pages shown in parentheses in the following list or in the Glossary at the end of the book.

accommodation (p. 353)
assimilation (p. 352)
attachment (p. 362)
attachment behavior (p. 364)
attachment theory (p. 362)
authoritarian parents (p. 367)
authoritative parents (p. 367)
behavioral genetics (p. 346)

chromosomes (p. 347)
concrete operations (p. 354)
conservation (p. 354)
conventional level (p. 378)
critical period (p. 348)
developmental psychology (p. 344)
DNA (deoxyribonucleic acid) (p. 347)
embryo (p. 347)
ethnic identity (p. 376)
fetal alcohol syndrome (p. 349)
fetus (p. 348)
formal operations (p. 354)
gender roles (sex roles) (p. 371)
generativity (p. 383)

genes (p. 347)
identity crisis (p. 376)
information processing model (p. 356)
maturation (p. 346)
menopause (p. 379)
moral development (p. 378)
object permanence (p. 353)
parenting styles (p. 367)
permissive parents (p. 367)
postconventional level (p. 378)
preconventional level (p. 378)
preoperational stage (p. 353)
puberty (p. 373)
reflexes (p. 350)

schemas (p. 351)
sensorimotor stage (p. 353)
socialization (p. 366)

temperament (p. 361)
teratogens (p. 348)
terminal drop (p. 384)

uninvolved (rejecting-neglecting)
parents (p. 367)

Test Your Knowledge

Select the best answer for each of the following questions. Then check your response against the Answer Key at the end of the book.

1. Ralph read an article that described intelligence as 50 percent heritable. Ralph can reasonably conclude that
   a. half of his intelligence came from his genes and half from his environment.
   b. about half of the variation in intelligence among groups of people can be accounted for by genetic influences.
   c. about half of a person's intelligence can be changed by environmental influences.
   d. about half the population got their intelligence from their genes alone.
2. When she became pregnant, Alyse was advised to quit smoking, but she didn't. Her baby is likely to be born ___.
   a. mentally retarded
   b. with facial deformities
   c. underweight
   d. with an irritable temperament
3. When they brought their newborn, Tyrone, home from the hospital, his parents always laid him on his back, especially at night. As Tyrone grew, he began to roll over, sit up, pull himself up on furniture, and walk. He skipped the crawling stage. Tyrone's physical development is the result of ___.
   a. behavioral genetics alone
   b. maturation alone
   c. environmental influences alone
   d. maturation and environmental influences
4. Keshawn is one month old. He is most likely to look longest at ___.
   a. small figures on the wallpaper
   b. a ribbon hanging above his crib
   c. colorful figures
   d. a nearby human face
5. At six months of age, Jacob still demonstrates the grasping and rooting reflexes. This could signal that Jacob
   a. has advanced motor skills.
   b. has muscles that cannot support his body.
   c. has a problem with brain development.
   d. needs less environmental stimulation than the average baby.
6. When two-year-old Jesse sees a scuba diver emerge on the beach, he says "Big fish!" According to Piaget, Jesse used ___ to try to understand the new stimulus of a scuba diver.
   a. assimilation
   b. accommodation
   c. object permanence
   d. conservation

7. Adriana is crying because her teddy bear, Boyd, has fallen off the table and landed face down. She insists that her mother put a bandage on Boyd's nose. According to Piaget's theory, Adriana is most likely in the stage of ___ cognitive development.
   a. sensorimotor   c. concrete operational
   b. preoperational   d. formal operational
8. Renee Baillargeon's research focused on infants' understanding about the mental states of other people and how those states affect behavior. Baillargeon found that infants under the age of four
   a. looked longer at "possible" events that they had experienced many times.
   b. looked longer at events that violated their expectations about other people's beliefs.
   c. do not yet have a "theory of mind" and thus are unable to anticipate what others might do.
   d. can recognize the effects of people's true beliefs but are unable to recognize the effects of false beliefs.
9. According to research on information processing and memory, when you try to recall your first birthday, you are likely to
   a. recall a general schema of "birthday" as well as details about your first one.
   b. be unable to recall anything about your first birthday due to infantile amnesia.
   c. recall information about your first birthday if you are shown pictures of yourself taken that day.
   d. recall information about the birthday if you hear a tape recording of your party.
10. Tara is a difficult baby. She is irritable, sleeps at irregular intervals, and cries at unpredictable times. According to research on temperament, Tara will most likely
    a. outgrow her difficult temperament and become an easier child.
    b. remain difficult in childhood and may display aggressiveness.
    c. develop a dependent relationship with her parents.
    d. become independent and especially successful in school.
11. Harlow's research with infant monkeys and artificial mothers demonstrated that
    a. the monkeys became attached to the "mothers" that fed them.
    b. the monkeys became attached to the "mothers" that provided contact comfort.
    c. attachment is entirely innate and has no learned component.
    d. "mothering" is instinctive and has no learned component.

12. When young Habib's mother drops him off at the day care center, he always cries when she leaves. When his mother returns and lifts him up, Habib tries to squirm away. Habib is demonstrating a(n) ___ attachment to his mother.
    a. secure
    b. anxious insecure
    c. avoidant insecure
    d. ambivalent insecure

13. Sam and Alex are 16 and want to drive to a rock concert in a big city that is five hours away. Sam's parents explain that it is too dangerous for him to drive that distance and to be in a major city without an adult. They offer to drive him and Alex to the concert. Alex's parents tell him that it is no problem if he wants to drive their car and stay in the city overnight. According to Baumrind's research, Sam's parents are displaying a(n) ___ style of parenting, whereas Alex's parents are displaying a(n) ___ style.
    a. authoritative; authoritarian
    b. authoritarian; authoritative
    c. authoritative; permissive
    d. authoritarian; permissive

14. Pat is seven years old and lives in the Midwestern United States. Pat learned to speak early and writes well. Pat is able to "read" people's emotional reactions by watching their faces. From this information we can conclude that Pat is most likely ___.
    a. female
    b. male
    c. African American
    d. Asian American

15. Ludmilla recently graduated from high school but can't decide whether to attend a local community college or work full time. She doesn't know what career she would like to pursue, and she is also uncertain whether she should stay with her current boyfriend. According to Erikson, Ludmilla is most likely experiencing the psychosocial crisis characterized by ___,
    a. trust versus mistrust
    b. initiative versus guilt
    c. identity versus role confusion
    d. integrity versus despair

16. Louise is 16 and having a difficult time with adolescence. She became sexually active two years ago and doesn't worry about using condoms or other safe sex practices. Louise is most likely to
    a. hold conventional attitudes and values and feel ashamed of herself.
    b. avoid smoking and drinking alcohol.
    c. have average or better grades at school.
    d. have parents who are not highly educated.

17. Jeanine and Helen are in a drugstore when Jeanine suggests that they steal some candy. Helen says that they should not steal the candy because they might get caught and put into jail. According to Kohlberg's theory, Helen is at the ___ stage of moral reasoning.
    a. preconventional
    b. conventional
    c. postconventional
    d. universal

18. In the past ten years Vernon has gained weight, especially around the middle. He also now needs glasses. If he is typical of most people his age, Vernon has most likely reached ___.
    a. adolescence
    b. early adulthood
    c. middle adulthood
    d. late adulthood

19. Verna is 50 years old. Based on developmental research, we would assume that Verna
    a. has less general knowledge than younger people.
    b. has a more limited vocabulary than younger people.
    c. understands that knowledge is relative, not absolute.
    d. is experiencing a slow but steady decay of all of her cognitive skills.

20. Patrice is 80 years old and has recently been unable to understand what she reads. She can't make sense of her checkbook, even though she was once an expert accountant. Her health is deteriorating, and her strength is waning. Patrice is most likely experiencing ___.
    a. cognitive dissonance
    b. terminal drop
    c. the crisis of initiative versus guilt
    d. androgyny

Media Resources •••

Now that you have finished reading this chapter, how about exploring some of the ideas and information that you found most interesting?

Coursemate Go to **CengageBrain.com** to access Psychology CourseMate, where you will find an interactive eBook, glossaries, flashcards, quizzes, videos, Virtual Psychology Labs, and more.

aplia

Aplia If your professor has assigned Aplia:
1. Sign in to your account.
2. Complete the corresponding exercises as required by your professor.
3. When finished, click "Grade It Now" to see which areas you have mastered, which areas need more work, and detailed explanations of every answer.

Health, Stress, and Coping

10

© Kzenon/Shutterstock

Preview

People in North America are living longer than ever. In fact, those over 75 constitute the fastest-growing age group in the United States. Will you eventually join them? To some extent, the answer lies in your genes, but how long you live is also determined in large measure by how you behave, how you think, and what stressors you face. Health care psychologists explore how illness and death are related to these behavioral, psychological, and social factors, and they apply their research to preventing illness and promoting health. They develop programs to help people make lifestyle changes that can lower their risk of illness and premature death. And they study how stress affects people's mental and physical health. The immune system's response to stress is particularly important. In this chapter, you will learn about several kinds of stressors, how people respond to them, and the relationship between stress reactions and illness. You will also discover what you can do to protect your own health and change risky behaviors that may affect it.

In Bangor, Maine, where snow and ice have paralyzed the community, Angie's headache gets worse as her four-year-old daughter and six-year-old son start bickering again. The daycare center and elementary school are closed, so Angie must stay home from her job at the grocery store. She probably couldn't have gotten there anyway, because the buses have stopped running. During the latest storm, the power went out, and the house is now almost unbearably cold; the can of spaghetti Angie opens is nearly frozen. Worry begins to creep into her head: "If I can't work, how will I pay for rent and daycare?" Her parents have money problems, too, so they can't offer financial help, and her ex-husband rarely makes his child support payments. On top of everything else, Angie is coming down with the flu.

How do people manage such adversity, and what are its consequences for them? Psychologists who study questions such as these have established a specialty known as **health care psychology** (also called **health psychology**), "a field within psychology devoted to understanding psychological influence on how people stay healthy, why they become ill, and how they respond when they do get ill" (Taylor, 1999, p.4). ●

Health Psychology

What do health care psychologists do?

The themes underlying health care psychology date back to ancient times. For thousands of years, in many cultures around the world, people have believed that their mental state, their behavior, and their health are linked. Today, there is scientific evidence to support this belief (Antoni & Lutgendorf, 2007; Schneiderman, 2004; Taylor, 2002). Stress affects health through its impact on psychological and physical processes. Research has also associated anger, hostility, pessimism, depression, and hopelessness with physical illnesses. Traits such as optimism are associated with good health. Similarly, poor health has been linked to behavioral factors such as lack of adequate sleep or exercise, eating too much fat and sugar, smoking, and abuse of alcohol and other drugs (Freedman et al., 2006; Mente et al., 2009; van Dam et al., 2008; Vollset, Tverdal, & Gjessing, 2006). Good health has been associated with behaviors such as regular exercise and following medical advice.

Health psychology has become increasingly prominent in North America, in part because of changing patterns of illness. Until the middle of the twentieth century, acute infectious diseases such as influenza, tuberculosis, and pneumonia were the major causes of illness and death in the United States and Canada. With these deadly diseases now tamed, chronic illnesses—such as coronary heart disease, cancer, and diabetes—have

health care psychology (health psychology) A field focused on understanding how psychological factors affect health and illness and which interventions help maintain health and combat illness.

joined stroke, accidents, and injury as the leading causes of disability and death (Heron, 2007). Compared with acute diseases, these chronic diseases develop more slowly and are more strongly associated with people's psychological makeup, lifestyle, and environment (Centers for Disease Control and Prevention, 2008; see Table 10.1). The psychological and behavioral factors that contribute to illness can be changed by intervention programs that promote exercising, healthy eating, and quitting smoking (e.g., Bazzano et al., 2003; Kraus et al., 2002). In fact, about half the deaths in the United States today are due to preventable health-risk behaviors (Greenland et al., 2003; Khot et al., 2003; Mokdad et al., 2004). Worldwide, the number of deaths caused by health-damaging behaviors is expected to double by 2015 (World Health Organization, 2008).

Yet as few as 3 percent of people in the United States follow a lifestyle that includes maintaining a healthy weight, getting regular exercise, eating a healthy diet, getting eight hours of sleep, and not smoking (Reeves & Rafferty, 2005). One goal of health psychology is to help people understand the role they can play in controlling their own health and life expectancy (Nash et al., 2003; Nicassio, Meyerowitz, & Kerns, 2004). For example, health care psychologists have been active in educating people about the warning signs of cancer, heart disease, and other serious illnesses; encouraging them to engage in self-examinations; and emphasizing the importance of seeking medical attention while lifesaving treatment is still possible. Health care psychologists also study and help people understand the role stress plays in physical health and illness. And clinical health care psychologists help individuals cope as effectively as possible with cancer, diabetes, heart disease, and many other kinds of serious and chronic illness.

Understanding Stress and Stressors

How do psychological stressors affect physical health?

You have probably heard that death and taxes are the only two things guaranteed in life. If there is a third, it surely must be stress. Stress is woven into the fabric of life. No matter how wealthy, powerful, attractive, or happy you might be, stress happens. It comes in many forms: a difficult exam, an automobile accident, a trauma of some kind, standing in a long line, reading about frightening world events, or just having a day when everything goes wrong. Some stress experiences, such as waiting to be with that special person, can be stimulating, motivating, and even desirable, but when circumstances begin to exceed our ability to cope with them, the result can be stress that creates physical, psychological, and behavioral problems. Stress in the workplace, for example, costs U.S. businesses

TABLE 10.1 Behaviors that Affect Some of the Leading Causes of Death in the United States

This table shows five of the leading causes of death in the United States today and behavioral factors that contribute to their development (Jemal et al., 2005; Kochanek et al., 2011).

Cause of Death	Excessive Alcohol Consumption	Tobacco Smoking	Unhealthy Diet	Inadequate Exercise	Inadequate Sleep
Heart disease	x	x	x	x	x
Cancer	x	x	x		
Chronic lung diseases		x			x
Stroke	x	x	x	?	x
Accidents and injury	x	x			x

Source: Data from National Vital Statistics Reports, Centers for Disease Control and Prevention (Kochanek, 2011).

more than $150 billion each year due to employee absenteeism, reduced productivity, and health care costs (Chandola, Brunner, & Marmot, 2006; Sauter et al., 1999; Schwartz, 2004; Spector, 2002).

Stress is the negative emotional and physiological process that occurs as individuals try to adjust to or deal with stressors. **Stressors**, in turn, are events and situations (such as exams or accidents) that disrupt or threaten to disrupt people's daily functioning and sense of well-being. **Stress reactions** are the physical, psychological, and behavioral responses (such as nausea, anxiety, or avoidance) that occur in the face of stressors (Taylor, 2002).

Some of us are more strongly affected by stressors than others, and we may be more strongly affected on some occasions than on others. Why? As described in more detail later, several *mediating factors* influence the relationship between people and their environments. These mediating factors include (1) the extent to which we can *predict* and *control* our stressors; (2) how we *interpret* the threat involved; (3) the *social support* we get; and (4) our *skills* for coping with stress. Mediating factors can either minimize or magnify a stressor's impact. In other words, as shown in Figure 10.1, stress is not a specific event but a transaction between people and their environments. It is a *process* in which the nature and intensity of our responses depend on what stressors occur and how they are affected by factors such as the way we think about them and how much confidence we have in our coping skills and resources.

Psychological Stressors

Most stressors have both physical and psychological components. Because these components overlap, it's often difficult to separate them for analysis. For example, students are challenged by psychological demands to do well in their courses as well as by physical fatigue resulting from a heavy load of classes and maybe a job and family responsibilities, too. So although we focus here on psychological stressors, remember that physical stressors almost always accompany them (Rios & Zautra, 2011).

Any event that forces a person to change or adapt can be a psychological stressor. Even pleasant events can be stressful. For example, a vacation is supposed to be relaxing and a wedding is supposed to be wonderful, but both can also be exhausting. And a promotion that brings higher pay can also bring new pressures (Schaubroeck, Jones, & Xie, 2001). Still, circumstances that are unpleasant, threatening, and difficult to cope with usually produce the most adverse psychological and physical effects (e.g., Kiecolt-Glaser et al., 2005). These circumstances include catastrophic events, life changes and strains, chronic stressors, and daily hassles.

Catastrophic events are sudden, unexpected, potentially life-threatening experiences or traumas. Physical or sexual assault, military combat, natural disasters, terrorist attacks, and accidents fall into this category. *Life changes* and *strains* include divorce, illness in the family, difficulties at work, moving to a new house, and other circumstances that create demands to which people must adjust (see Table 10.2). *Chronic stressors*—those that continue over a long period of time—include such circumstances as living under the threat of terrorism, having a serious illness (or caring for someone who does), being unable to earn a decent income, living in a high-crime urban neighborhood, being the victim of discrimination, and even enduring years of academic pressure (Castle et al., 2011; Fuller-Rowell, Evans, & Ong, 2012; Lederbogen et al., 2011; Lovell, Moss, & Wetherell, 2012;

stress The process of adjusting to circumstances that disrupt or threaten to disrupt a person's daily functioning.

stressors Events or situations to which people must adjust.

stress reactions Physical and psychological responses to stressors.

FIGURE 10.1

The Process of Stress

Stressful events, stress reactions, and stress mediators are all important components of the stress process. Notice that the process involves many two-way relationships. For example, if a person has effective coping skills, stress responses will be less severe. Having milder stress responses can act as a "reward" that strengthens those skills. Further, as coping skills (such as refusing unreasonable demands) improve, certain stressors (such as a boss's unreasonable demands) may become less frequent.

Potential Stressors	Stress mediators	Stress responses
Life changes and strains Catastrophic events Daily hassles Chronic stressors	Cognitive appraisal Predictability Control Coping resources and methods Social support	Physical Psychological • Emotional • Cognitive • Behavioral

Coping With Catastrophe

Catastrophic events such as terrorism, explosions, hurricanes, and plane crashes are stressors that can be psychologically devastating for victims, their families, and rescue workers. Health psychologists and other professionals provide on-the-spot counseling and follow-up sessions to help people deal with the consequences of trauma.

© Reuters/Marco Dormino/Minustah/Landov

TABLE 10.2   The Undergraduate Stress Questionnaire
Here are some items from the Undergraduate Stress Questionnaire (Crandall, Priesler, & Aussprung, 1992), which asks students to indicate whether various stressors have occurred in their lives during the previous week.
Has this stressful event happened to you at any time during the last week? If it has please check the space next to it. If it has not, please leave it blank.
1. _____ Assignments in all classes due the same day
2. _____ Having roommate conflicts
3. _____ Lack of money
4. _____ Trying to decide on major
5. _____ Can't understand your professor
6. _____ Stayed up late writing a paper
7. _____ Sat through a boring class
8. _____ Went into a test unprepared
9. _____ Parents getting divorced
10. _____ Incompetence at the registrar's office

Source: Crandall, Priesler, & Aussprung (1992).

Pieterse & Carter, 2010). Finally, *daily hassles* involve irritations, pressures, and annoyances that may not be major stressors by themselves but whose effects add up to become significant (Almeida, 2005; Evans & Wener, 2006). The frustrations of daily commuting in heavy traffic, for example, can become so intense for some drivers that they display a pattern of aggression called "road rage."

Measuring Stressors

Which stressors are the most harmful? To study stress more precisely, psychologists have tried to measure the impact of particular stressors. In 1967, Thomas Holmes and Richard Rahe (pronounced "ray") pioneered the effort to find a standard way of measuring the stress in a person's life. Working on the assumption that both positive and negative changes produce stress, they asked a large number of people to rate—in terms of *life-change units,* or *LCUs*—the amount of change and demand for adjustment caused by events such as divorcing, being fired, retiring, losing a loved one, or becoming pregnant. On the basis of these ratings, Holmes and Rahe (1967) created the *Social Readjustment Rating Scale,* or *SRRS.* People taking the SRRS receive a stress score equal to the sum of the LCUs for all the stressful events they've recently experienced. Numerous studies have shown that people scoring high on the SRRS and other life-change scales are more likely to suffer physical illness, mental disorder, or other problems than those with lower scores (e.g., Monroe, Thase, & Simons, 1992).

Other researchers wondered, though, whether life changes alone tell the whole story about the impact of stressors. Accordingly, some investigators have used face-to-face interviews to more precisely measure stressors and their impact (e.g., Dohrenwend et al., 1993). Others developed scales such as the *Life Experiences Survey,* or *LES* (Sarason, Johnson, & Siegel, 1978), which measure not just which life events occurred but also people's perceptions of how positive or negative the events were and how well they were able to cope with the events. The LES also allows respondents to write in and rate any stressors they have experienced that are not on the printed list. This individualized approach can capture the differing impact and meaning that certain experiences might have for men compared with women and for members of various cultural groups. Divorce, for example, may have different meanings to people of different religious backgrounds. And members of some ethnic groups may experience stressors, such as prejudice and discrimination, that are not felt by other groups (Flores et al., 2010; Lewis et al., 2006; Matthews et al., 2005; Merritt et al., 2006; Yip, Gee, & Takeuchi, 2008).

The timing of stressors matters, too; those that occur early in life can have especially enduring consequences. For example, experiencing the stress of poverty, trauma, or other adversities during early childhood is associated with an increased risk of developing heart disease, arthritis, certain cancers, and other health problems in adulthood, even for people who by then had achieved middle or upper class socioeconomic status (Chan et al., 2011; Lehman et al., 2005; Rooks et al., 2012). These long-lasting effects occur partly because early life stressors can alter the functioning of the brain as well as the cardiovascular and immune systems, and may set the stage for poor stress-coping abilities (Taylor, 2010).

Stress Responses

How do people react to stressors?

Physical and psychological stress reactions often occur together, especially as stressors become more intense. Furthermore, one type of stress response can set off a stress response in another dimension. For example, a physical stress reaction such as mild chest pains might trigger the psychological stress response of worrying about a heart attack. Still, it's useful to consider each category of stress responses one at a time.

Physical Responses

fight-flight reaction Physical reactions triggered by the sympathetic nervous system that prepare the body to fight or to run from a threatening situation.

general adaptation syndrome (GAS) A three-stage pattern of responses triggered by the effort to adapt to stressors.

If you have experienced a near-accident or some other sudden, frightening event, you know that the physical responses to stressors include rapid breathing, increased heartbeat, sweating, and, a little later, shakiness. These reactions make up a general pattern known as the **fight-flight reaction**. As described in the chapters on biology and behavior and on motivation and emotion, the fight-flight reaction prepares the body to either face or flee an immediate threat. Once the danger passes, fight-flight responses subside (Gump et al., 2005).

When stressors last longer or recovery from stressors is slow, however, the fight-flight reaction is only the beginning of a longer sequence of events. Observation of animals and humans led Hans Selye (pronounced "SELL-yay") to suggest that this extended sequence of physical stress responses occurs in a consistent pattern. He called this sequence the **general adaptation syndrome**, or **GAS** (Selye, 1956, 1976). The GAS occurs in three stages (see Figure 10.2), and it is activated by efforts to adapt to any physical or psychological stressor.

FIGURE 10.2

The General Adaptation Syndrome

Hans Selye found that physical reactions to stressors include an initial alarm reaction followed by resistance and then exhaustion. During the alarm reaction, the body's resistance to stress temporarily drops below normal as it absorbs a stressor's initial impact. Resistance increases and then levels off in the resistance stage, but it ultimately declines if the exhaustion stage is reached.

Source: Adapted from Selye (1975).

The first stage, called the *alarm reaction,* involves some version of the fight-flight reaction. The alarm reaction to a mild stressor, such as an overheated room, might be no more than changes in heart rate, respiration, and perspiration that help the body regulate its temperature. More severe stressors prompt more dramatic alarm reactions, rapidly mobilizing the body's adaptive energy, much as a burglar alarm alerts the police to take action (Kiecolt-Glaser et al., 1998).

Alarm reactions are controlled by the sympathetic nervous system through organs and glands that make up the *sympatho-adreno-medullary (SAM) system.* As shown on the right side of Figure 10.3, stressors trigger a process that begins when the brain's hypothalamus activates the sympathetic branch of the autonomic nervous system (ANS), which stimulates the medulla (inner part) of the adrenal glands. The adrenals, in turn, secrete *catecholamines* (pronounced "kat-uh-KOH-luh-meens")—especially adrenaline and noradrenaline—which circulate in the bloodstream, activating the liver, kidneys, heart, lungs, and other organs. This causes increases in blood pressure, muscle tension, blood sugar, and pupil size, along with other physical changes that provide the energy and resources needed to cope with stressors. Even brief exposure to a stressor can produce major changes in these coordinated regulatory body systems (Stoney et al., 2002).

As shown on the left side of Figure 10.3, stressors also activate the *hypothalamic-pituitary-adrenocortical (HPA) system,* in which the hypothalamus stimulates the pituitary gland in the brain. The pituitary, in turn, secretes hormones such as adrenocorticotropic hormone (ACTH). Among other things, ACTH stimulates the cortex (outer surface) of the adrenal glands to secrete *corticosteroids*; these hormones release the body's energy supplies and fight excessive inflammation. The pituitary gland also triggers the release of *endorphins,* which are some of the body's natural painkillers.

Together, these stress systems generate the energy needed to cope with an emergency. The more stressors there are and the longer they last, the more resources the body must spend in responding to them. If the stressors persist, the *resistance stage* of the GAS begins. Here, obvious signs of the initial alarm reaction fade as the body settles in to resist the stressor on a long-term basis. The drain on adaptive energy is less during the resistance stage compared with the alarm stage, but the body is still working hard to cope with stress.

This continued campaign of biochemical resistance is costly. It slowly but surely uses up the body's reserves of adaptive energy. The body then enters the third GAS stage, known as *exhaustion.* In extreme cases, such as prolonged exposure to freezing temperatures, the result is death. More commonly, the exhaustion stage brings signs of physical wear and tear. Especially hard hit are the organ systems that were weak to begin with or that were heavily involved in the resistance process. For example, if adrenaline and cortisol (which help fight stressors during the resistance stage) remain elevated for an extended time, the result can be damage to the heart and blood vessels; suppression of the body's disease-fighting immune system; and vulnerability to illnesses such as heart disease, high blood pressure, arthritis, colds, and flu (e.g., Robles, Glaser, & Kiecolt-Glaser, 2005). Selye referred to illnesses caused or worsened by stressors as **diseases of adaptation.**

diseases of adaptation Illnesses caused or worsened by stressors.

FIGURE 10.3
Organ Systems Involved in the General Adaptation Syndrome

Stressors produce a variety of physiological responses that begin in the brain and spread to organs throughout the body. For example, the pituitary gland triggers the release of painkilling endorphins. It also stimulates the release of corticosteroids, which help resist stress but also tend to suppress the immune system. Some of these substances may interact with sex hormones to create different physical stress responses and coping methods in men and women (Taylor, Klein et al., 2000; Taylor et al., 2006).

Photo © Michael Sharkey/Taxi/Getty Images

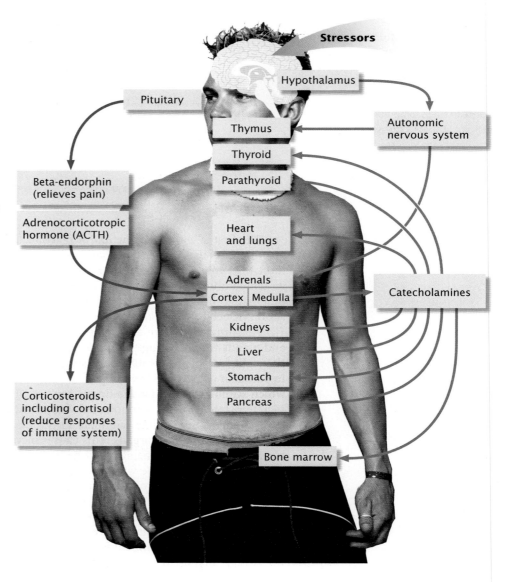

Psychological Responses

Selye's research focused mainly on the physiological aspects of stress responses, but stressors also create a variety of psychological responses, including changes in emotion and cognition (thinking) and accompanying changes in behavior.

Emotional Changes   The physical stress responses we have described are usually accompanied by emotional stress responses. If someone pulls out a gun and demands your money, you will most likely experience physiological changes, such as a spike in heart rate, but you'll also feel some strong emotion—probably fear, maybe anger. In describing stress, people tend to say, "I was angry and frustrated!" rather than "My heart rate increased and my blood pressure went up." In other words, they tend to mention changes in the emotions they experienced.

In most cases, emotional stress reactions fade soon after the stressors are gone or coped with effectively. Even severe emotional stress responses ease eventually. However, if stressors continue for a long time or if lots of them occur in a short time, emotional stress reactions may persist. When people don't have a chance to recover their emotional equilibrium, they feel tense, irritable, short-tempered, or anxious and they may experience increasingly intense feelings of fatigue, depression, and hopelessness. These reactions can become severe enough to be diagnosed as major depressive disorder, generalized anxiety disorder, or other stress-related problems discussed in the chapter on psychological disorders.

Cognitive Changes   In the busy, noisy intensive care unit of a London hospital, a doctor misplaced a decimal point while calculating the amount of morphine a one-day-old premature baby should receive. The child died of a massive overdose (Davies, 1999). Reductions in the ability to concentrate, think clearly, or remember accurately are typical cognitive stress reactions (Beilock & Carr, 2005; Cavenett & Nixon, 2006; Liston, McEwen, & Casey, 2009; Morgan et al., 2006). These problems appear partly because of *ruminative thinking,* the repeated intrusion of thoughts about stressful events (Lyubomirsky & Nolen-Hoeksema, 1995). Ruminative thoughts about relationship problems, for example, can seriously interfere with studying for a test. A related phenomenon is *catastrophizing,* which means dwelling on and overemphasizing the possible negative consequences of events. During exams, college students who are anxious about tests are likely to say to themselves, "I'm falling behind" or "Everyone is doing better than I am." As catastrophizing or ruminative thinking impairs memory and other aspects of cognitive functioning, resulting feelings of anxiety and other emotional arousal add to the total stress response, further hampering performance (Beilock et al., 2004).

Overarousal created by stressors can also interfere with our ability to adapt to new or difficult situations (Schwabe & Wolf, 2011) because one effect of overarousal is to narrow the scope of attention. When people don't attend to the entire situation and don't consider enough solutions to complex problems (Craske, 1999), they may make one or more of the problem-solving errors described in the chapter on thought, language, and intelligence. People under stress are more likely to cling to *mental sets,* which are well-learned (but not always efficient) approaches to problems. Stress may also intensify *functional fixedness,* the tendency to use objects for only one purpose. Victims of hotel fires, for example, sometimes die trapped in their rooms because in the stress of the moment, it did not occur to them to use a piece of furniture to break open a window (Renner & Beversdorf, 2010).

Stressors may also impair decision making (Blanchette & Richards, 2010; Mather & Lighthall, 2012). Under stress, people who normally consider all aspects of a situation before making a decision may act impulsively and sometimes foolishly. High-pressure salespeople take advantage of this stress response by creating time-limited offers or by telling indecisive customers that others are waiting to buy the item they are considering (Cialdini, 2001).

Behavioral Responses   Clues about people's physical and emotional stress reactions come from changes in how they look, act, or talk. Strained facial expressions, a shaky voice, tremors, and jumpiness are common behavioral stress responses.

Even more obvious behavioral stress responses appear as people try to escape or avoid stressors (Atalay & Meloy, 2011). They may turn to alcohol, overeat (especially high-fat "comfort" foods) and either sleep too much or skimp on sleep in favor of late-night socializing. These tactics may provide some temporary relief, but they can also have negative health consequences (Cohen et al., 2009; Frone, 2008; Hamer, Molloy, & Stamatakis, 2008; King et al., 2008). In the face of severe or long-lasting stress, some people quit their jobs, drop out of school, or even attempt suicide. In the month after Hurricane Katrina struck the U.S. Gulf Coast in 2005, for example, more than double the normal number of calls were placed from the affected area to the National Suicide Prevention Hotline, and stress-related mental health problems remained long after the storm's immediate effects abated (Breed, 2006; Kessler et al., 2008; Roberts et al., 2010). Unfortunately, as discussed in the chapter on learning, escape and avoidance tactics deprive people of the opportunity to learn more adaptive ways of coping with stressful events and situations, including college (Cooper et al., 1992). Aggression is another common behavioral response to

Stress for $500, Alex

The negative effects of stress on memory, thinking, decision making, and other cognitive functions are often displayed by players on TV game shows such as *Jeopardy!, Who Wants to Be a Millionaire, and Survivor.* Under the intense pressure of time, competition, and the scrutiny of millions of viewers, contestants may make mistakes that seem ridiculous to those calmly watching at home.

© Amanda Edwards/Getty Images

stressors. All too often, this response is directed at members of one's own family (Hellmuth & McNulty, 2008; Polusny & Follette, 1995). So areas devastated by hurricanes and other natural disasters are likely to see not only an increase in suicides but also significant increases in reports of domestic violence (Curtis, Miller, & Berry, 2000).

LINKAGES

When do stress responses become mental disorders?
(a link to Psychological Disorders)

Stress and Psychological Disorders

Physical and psychological stress responses sometimes appear together in patterns known as *burnout* and *posttraumatic stress disorder*. **Burnout** is an increasingly intense pattern of physical and psychological dysfunction in response to a continuous flow of stressors or to chronic stress (Maslach, 2003). As burnout nears, previously reliable workers or once-attentive spouses become indifferent, disengaged, impulsive, or accident prone. They miss work frequently, oversleep, perform their jobs poorly, abuse alcohol or other drugs, and become irritable, suspicious, withdrawn, and depressed (Fahrenkopf et al., 2008; Taylor, 2002). Burnout is particularly common among those who do "people work," such as teachers, doctors, and nurses, and those who perceive themselves as being treated unjustly by employers (Barnard & Curry, 2012; Elovainio, Kivimäki, & Vahtera, 2002; Hoobler & Brass, 2006; Schultz & Schultz, 2002).

Posttraumatic stress disorder (PTSD) is a different pattern of severe negative reactions to a traumatic event. Among its characteristics are anxiety, irritability, jumpiness, inability to concentrate or work productively, sexual dysfunction, flash-backs, intrusive thoughts and images, and difficulty in social and family relationships. PTSD sufferers also experience sleep disturbances, intense startle responses to noise or other sudden stimuli, long-term suppression of their immune systems, and elevated risk of coronary heart disease (e.g., Goenjian et al., 2001; Guthrie & Bryant, 2005; Hagenaars et al., 2010; Johnson, Westermeyer et al., 2002; Kawamura, Kim, & Asukai, 2001; Kubzansky et al., 2009; Rutkowski et al., 2010). Neuroimaging studies reveal that PTSD symptoms are accompanied by noticeable changes in brain functioning and even in brain structure (Kitayama et al., 2005). The most common feature of PTSD is reexperiencing the trauma through nightmares or vivid memories. In rare cases, *flashbacks* occur in which the person behaves for minutes, hours, or days as if the trauma were occurring again.

burnout A pattern of physical and psychological dysfunctions in response to continuous stressors.

posttraumatic stress disorder (PTSD) A pattern of adverse reactions following a traumatic event, commonly involving reexperiencing the event through nightmares or vivid memories.

Life Hanging in the Balance
Symptoms of burnout and posttraumatic stress disorder (PTSD) often plague firefighters, police officers, emergency medical personnel, and others who are repeatedly exposed to time pressure, trauma, danger, and other stressors (Fullerton, Ursano, & Wang, 2004; Perrin et al., 2007). PTSD can also occur following a single catastrophic event, such as the earthquake and tsunami which caused devastation in Japan in 2011.

Posttraumatic stress disorder is usually associated with events such as war, rape, terrorism, assault, or abuse in childhood (e.g., Dohrenwend et al., 2006; Galea, Ahern, et al., 2002; Galea, Resnick, et al., 2002; Goldberg & Garno, 2005; Shalev & Freedman, 2005; Shalev et al., 2006), but researchers believe that some PTSD symptoms can be triggered by any major stressor, such as a car accident, being stalked, or living in a community that is threatened by terrorism or serial killers (Diamond et al., 2010; Kangas, Henry, & Bryant, 2005; Marshall, Miles, & Stewart, 2010; Schulden et al., 2006). PTSD usually appears immediately following a trauma, but full expression of its symptoms may not appear until weeks later (Andrews et al., 2007; Gilboa-Schechtman & Foa, 2001; Port, Engdahl, & Frazier, 2001). Many people affected by PTSD require professional help, although some seem to recover without it (Bradley et al., 2005; Perkonigg et al., 2005). For most, improvement takes time; for nearly all, the support of family and friends is vital to recovery (Foa et al., 2005). For some people, though, PTSD never appears, even after severe trauma (Breslau et al., 2005). In fact, some people report enhanced psychological growth after surviving a trauma (Zoellner & Maercker, 2006). Researchers are working to discover what protective factors operate in these individuals and whether those factors can be strengthened through PTSD treatment and prevention programs (Bonanno et al., 2007; Bonanno & Mancini, 2008; Caccioppo, Reis, & Zautra, 2011; Cornum et al., 2011; Haskett et al., 2006; Kolassa et al., 2010; Reivich, Seligman, & McBride, 2011; Shalev et al., 2012; Tedeschi & McNally, 2011).

© Dan Chung/Guardian/Camera Press/Redux

Stress is also thought to play a role in the development of many other psychological disorders, including depression, certain anxiety disorders, and schizophrenia (e.g., Cutrona et al., 2005). This point is emphasized in the chapter on psychological disorders, especially in relation to the *diathesis-stress model* of psychopathology. This model suggests that certain individuals may be predisposed to develop certain disorders but that whether or not these disorders actually appear depends on the frequency, nature, and intensity of the stressors the people encounter.   ● ● ● ●

Stress Mediators

Why doesn't everyone react to stressors in the same way?

The ways that particular people interact with particular stressors can be seen in many areas of life. The stress of combat, for example, is partly responsible for the errors in judgment and decision-making that lead to "friendly fire" deaths and injuries in almost every military operation (Adler, 1993). But not everyone in combat makes these mistakes. Why does stress disrupt the performance of some individuals and not others? And why does one individual survive and even thrive under the same circumstances that lead another to break down, give up, and burn out?

The answer may lie in *psychobiological models,* which recognize the importance of psychological as well as biological factors in the stress process (Cyranowski et al., 2011; Folkman et al., 2000; Ganzel, Morris, & Wethington, 2010; Kidd, Hamer, & Steptoe, 2011; Lazarus & Folkman, 1984; Suls & Rothman, 2004; Taylor, 2002). These models emphasize that (as shown in Figure 10.1) the impact of stressors depends not only on the stressors themselves but also on several important mediating factors (Bonanno, 2005; Kemeny, 2003).

How Stressors Are Perceived

As described in the chapter on sensation and perception, our view of the world depends partly on how we interpret sensory information. Similarly, our physical and psychological reactions to stressors depend somewhat on how we think about them, a process known as *cognitive appraisal.* A potential stressor usually has a stronger negative impact on people who perceive it as a threat than on people who see it as a challenge (Lazarus, 1999; Maddi & Khoshaba, 2005). This may be why people who are deeply engaged in and passionate about their stressful jobs are less likely than their coworkers to suffer burnout (Vallerand et al., 2010).

Evidence for the effects of cognitive factors on stress responses comes from surveys and experiments (e.g., Abelson et al., 2005; Sonnentag, Binnewies, & Mojza, 2010; Sonnentag, 2012). In one of the first laboratory demonstrations of these effects, Richard Lazarus gave differing instructions to three groups of students who were about to watch a film showing bloody industrial accidents (Lazarus et al., 1965). One group (the "intellectualizers") was instructed to remain mentally detached from the gruesome scenes; a second group (the "denial" group) was instructed to think of the scenes as unreal; and a third group (the "unprepared" group) was not told anything about the film. As Figure 10.4 shows, the intensity of physiological arousal during the film, as measured by sweat gland activity, depended on how the viewers were instructed to think about the film. The unprepared students were more upset than either of the other two groups. In a more recent study, students who were first trained to see the threatening aspects of information showed more emotional arousal to a stressful video than those who had been trained to see information as nonthreatening (Wilson et al., 2006). Similarly, physical and psychological symptoms associated with the stress of airport noise, of being diagnosed with a serious illness, of learning about toxins in local soil, or of living with terrorism threats are more common in people who engage in more catastrophic thinking about these problems (Bryant & Guthrie, 2005; Lerner et al., 2003; Matthies, Hoeger, & Guski, 2000; Speckhard, 2002). Those who hold a more optimistic outlook in general tend to show milder stress responses and better health outcomes (de Moor et al., 2006; Taylor, Kemeny et al., 2000; Taylor et al., 2003).

The influence of cognitive factors weakens somewhat as stressors become extreme. For example, patients who have a sense of control over chronic pain are more likely than other patients to remain physically active, but this difference does not hold if the pain is severe (Jensen & Karoly, 1991). Still, even the impact of major stressors, such as a natural disaster

FIGURE 10.4

Cognitive Influences on Stress Responses

Richard Lazarus and his colleagues found that students' physiological stress reactions to a film showing bloody industrial accidents were affected by the way they thought about what they saw. Those who had been instructed to remain detached from the film (the "intellectualizers") or to think of it as unreal (the "denial" group) were less upset—as measured by sweat gland activity—than those in an "unprepared" group. These results were among the first to show that people's cognitive appraisals of stressors can affect their responses to those stressors.

Source: Adapted from Lazarus, Opton, Nornikos, and Rankin, "The principle of short-circuiting of threat: Further evidence" *Journal of Personality,* 33:4. Copyright © 1965 John Wiley and Sons. Reprinted with permission.

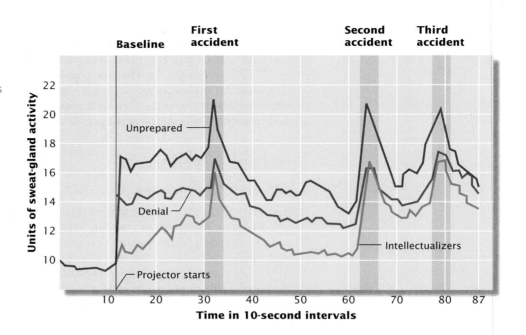

or a divorce, may be less severe for those who think of them as challenges to be overcome. In other words, many stressful events are not inherently stressful; their impact depends partly on how people perceive them. An important part of this appraisal is the degree to which the stressors are perceived to be predictable and controllable, or at least manageable.

Predictability and Control

Why is the threat of terrorism so terrorizing? For one thing, knowing that a stressor might occur but being uncertain whether or when it will occur tends to increase the stressor's impact (Lerner et al., 2003; Sorrentino & Roney, 2000). In other words, *unpredictable* stressors tend to have more impact than those that are predictable (Lazarus & Folkman, 1984; Pham, Taylor, & Seeman, 2001), especially when the stressors are intense and relatively brief. For example, people whose spouses have died suddenly tend to display more immediate disbelief, anxiety, and depression than those who have had weeks or months to prepare for the loss (Schulz et al., 2001; Swarte et al., 2003). However, predictability does not provide total protection against stressors. Research with animals shows that predictable stressors can be even more damaging than unpredictable ones if they occur over long periods of time (Abbott, Schoen, & Badia, 1984).

The *perception of control* also mediates the effects of stressors. If people feel they have some control over stressors, those stressors usually have less impact (e.g., Johnson & Krueger, 2005; Smith et al., 2008). For example, studies of several thousand employees in the United States, Sweden, and the United Kingdom have found that those who felt they had little or no control over their work environment were more likely to suffer heart disease and other health problems than workers with a high degree of perceived control (Bosma et al., 1997; Cheng et al., 2000; Spector, 2002). And at many hospitals, it is now standard procedure to help patients manage or control the stress of emergency treatment or the side effects of surgery by providing preparatory information about what to expect during and after a medical procedure, teaching relaxation skills, and allowing patients to control the administration of their pain medication. These strategies have all been shown to help people heal faster and go home sooner (Broadbent et al., 2003; Chamberlin, 2000; Gordon et al., 2005; Kiecolt-Glaser et al., 1998; Ludwig-Rosenthal & Neufelf, 1988).

Simply *believing* that a stressor is controllable (even if it isn't) can also reduce its impact. This effect was demonstrated in a study in which participants with panic disorder inhaled a mixture of oxygen and carbon dioxide that typically causes a panic attack (Sanderson, Rapee, & Barlow, 1989). Half the participants were led to believe (falsely) that they could control the concentration of the mixture. Compared with those who believed that they had no control, significantly fewer of the "in-control" participants experienced full-blown panic attacks during the session, and their panic symptoms were fewer and less severe.

People who feel they have no control over negative events appear especially prone to physical and psychological problems. They often experience feelings of helplessness and hopelessness that in turn may promote depression or other mental disorders (Sarin, Abela, & Auerbach, 2005; Whang et al., 2009). It's even been suggested that a perceived lack of control partly explains why people in lower socioeconomic groups are at somewhat elevated risk for early death (Stringhini et al., 2010; Trumbetta et al., 2010).

Coping Resources and Coping Methods

People usually suffer fewer ill effects from a stressor if they have adequate coping resources and effective coping methods. *Coping resources* include, among other things, the money and time to deal with stressful events. For example, the physical and psychological responses you experience if your car breaks down tend to be more negative if you are broke and pressed for time than if you have the money for repairs and the freedom to take a day off from work.

Effective coping methods can also reduce the impact of stressors (Cote & Pepler, 2002). Most of these methods can be classified as either problem-focused or emotion-focused. *Problem-focused* coping methods involve efforts to change or eliminate a source of stress, whereas *emotion-focused* techniques attempt to control the negative emotional consequences of stressors (Folkman et al., 1986). Some people use both kinds of coping. For example, you might deal with the problem of noise from a nearby factory by forming a community action group to push for tougher noise-reduction laws and at the same time calm your anger when noise occurs by mentally focusing on the group's efforts to improve the situation (Folkman & Moskowitz, 2000; Hatfield et al., 2002). Susan Folkman and Richard Lazarus (1988) devised a widely used questionnaire to assess the specific ways in which people cope with stressors; Table 10.3 shows some examples from their questionnaire.

Particularly when a stressor is difficult to control, it is sometimes helpful to fully express and think about the emotions you are experiencing in relation to the stressful event

---

TABLE 10.3   Ways of Coping

Coping is defined as cognitive and behavioral efforts to manage specific demands that people perceive as taxing their resources (Folkman et al., 1986). This table illustrates two major approaches to coping measured by Folkman and Lazarus's (1988) Ways of Coping Questionnaire: problem-focused and emotion-focused. Ask yourself which approach you usually take when faced with stressors. Now rank the coping skills under each major approach in terms of how often you tend to use each. Do you rely on just one or two? Or do you adjust your coping strategies to fit different kinds of stressors?

LEARN by DOING

Coping Skills	Example
Problem-focused coping	
Confronting	"I stood my ground and fought for what I wanted."
Seeking social support	"I talked to someone to find out more about the situation."
Planful problem solving	"I made a plan of action and I followed it."
Emotion-focused coping	
Self-controlling	"I tried to keep my feelings to myself."
Distancing	"I didn't let it get to me; I tried not to think about it too much."
Positive reappraisal	"I changed my mind about myself."
Accepting responsibility	"I realized I brought the problem on myself."
Escape/avoidance (wishful thinking)	"I wished that the situation would go away or somehow be over with."

Source: Adapted from Folkman et al. (1986).

(Langens & Schüler, 2007; Niederhoffer & Pennebaker, 2002; Stanton & Low, 2012; Tamir & Mitchell, 2012). In one program designed to promote this kind of emotional expression, also known as *emotional disclosure,* people spend thirty to sixty minutes a day for several days writing or talking about their thoughts and feelings about past or present stressors. Laboratory studies have shown this emotional coping strategy to significantly reduce psychological and physical stress responses (Petrie et al., 2004; Willmott et al., 2011). Its benefits have also been observed outside the laboratory in many individuals whose religious beliefs or philosophy of life allow them to bring meaning to events—such as having cancer, enduring the death of a loved one, or suffering a devastating natural disaster—that might otherwise seem to be senseless tragedies (Heppner et al., 2006; Powell, Shahabi, & Thoreson, 2003; Tallman, Altmaier, & Garcia, 2007). Some individuals who use humor to help them cope also show better adjustment and milder physiological reactivity to stressful events (Martin, 2001; Moran, 2002).

Social Support

Has a good friend comforted or reassured you during troubled times? If so, you have experienced the value of *social support* in easing the impact of stressful events. Social support consists of emotional, tangible, or informational resources provided by other people. These people might help eliminate a stressor (by, say, fixing your car), suggest how to deal with the stressor (by recommending a good mechanic), or reduce a stressor's impact by providing companionship and reassurance (Sarason, Sarason, & Gurung, 1997). The people you can depend on for support make up your network of **social support** (Burleson, Albrecht, & Sarason, 1994).

The stress-reducing effects of social support have been documented in people dealing with a wide range of stressors, including cancer, stroke, military combat, loss of loved ones, natural disasters, arthritis, AIDS, and even ethnic discrimination (e.g., Antoni & Lutgendorf, 2007; Boden-Albala et al., 2005; Foster, 2000; Jason, Witter, & Torres-Harding, 2003; Penner, Dovidio, & Albrecht, 2001; Savelkoul et al., 2000; Weihs, Enright, & Simmens, 2008). Social support can have health benefits, too. For example, students who get emotional support from friends show better immune system functioning than those with less-adequate social support (Cohen & Herbert, 1996). This may be why people with strong social support are less vulnerable to colds and flu during exams and other periods of high academic stress (Kop et al., 2005; Pressman et al., 2005; Taylor, Dickerson, & Klein, 2002). Having strong social support is also associated with faster recovery from surgery or illness, possibly because helpful friends and

You've Got A Friend
Even when social support cannot eliminate stressors, it can help people, such as these cancer survivors, feel less anxious, more optimistic, more capable of control, and more willing to try new ways of dealing with stressors (Trunzo & Pinto, 2003). Those who provide support may feel better, too (Brown et al., 2003).

APPLYING PSYCHOLOGY

family members encourage patients to follow medical advice (Brummett et al., 2005; Grassi et al., 2000; Krohne & Slangen, 2005; Taylor, 2002). People in stronger social networks—especially those filled with happy people—tend to be happier than those in weaker networks and may even enjoy better mental functioning in old age (Barnes et al., 2004; Fowler & Christakis, 2008; Gleibs et al., 2011). According to some researchers, having inadequate social support can be as dangerous as smoking, obesity, or lack of exercise in that it nearly doubles a person's risk of dying from disease, suicide, or other causes (House, Landis, & Umberson, 1988a, 1988b; Kiecolt-Glaser & Newton, 2001; Rutledge et al., 2004).

Exactly how social support brings about its positive effects is not entirely clear. James Pennebaker (1995, 2000) has suggested that social support may help prevent illness by providing the person under stress with an opportunity to express pent-up thoughts and emotions. Pennebaker and other researchers suggest that keeping important things to yourself is itself a stressor (e.g., Dalgleish, Hauer, & Kuyken, 2008; Srivastava et al., 2009). In a laboratory experiment, for example, participants who were asked to deceive an experimenter showed elevated physiological arousal (Pennebaker & Chew, 1985). Further,

social support The friends and social contacts on whom one can depend for help and support.

if the spouses of people who die as the result of an accident or suicide do not or cannot confide their feelings to others they're especially likely to develop physical illness during the year following the death (Pennebaker & O'Heeron, 1984). Disclosing (even anonymously) the stresses and traumas one has experienced is associated with enhanced immune functioning, reduced physical symptoms, and decreased use of health services (Broderick, Junghaenel, & Schwartz, 2005; Campbell & Pennebaker, 2003; Epstein, Sloan, & Marx, 2005; Sloan, Marx, & Epstein, 2005; Pachankis & Goldfried, 2010). This may explain why support groups for a wide range of problems such as bereavement, overeating, and alcohol and drug abuse tend to promote participants' physical health (Taylor et al., 2002).

Research in this area is made more challenging by the fact that the relationship between social support and the impact of stressors is not a simple one. For one thing, the quality of social support can influence the ability to cope with stress, but the reverse may also be true: your ability to cope may determine the quality of the social support you receive (McLeod, Kessler, & Landis, 1992). People who complain endlessly about stressors but never do anything about them may discourage social support whereas those with an optimistic, action-oriented approach may attract support.

Second, *social support* refers not only to your relationships with others but also to the recognition that others care and will help (Demaray & Malecki, 2002). Some relationships in a seemingly strong social network can be stormy, fragile, or shallow, resulting in interpersonal conflicts that can have an adverse effect on health (Ben-Ari & Gil, 2002; Malarkey et al., 1994).

Third, having too much support or the wrong kind of support can be as bad as not having enough (Reynolds & Perrin, 2004). Dangerous behaviors such as smoking or overeating, for example, can be harder to give up if one's social support consists largely or entirely of smokers or overeaters (Christakis & Fowler, 2007). People whose friends and family overprotect them from stressors may have fewer opportunities to learn effective coping strategies. They may also lose confidence in the strategies they have, and thus put less energy into their coping efforts. If the efforts of people in a social support network become annoying, disruptive, or interfering, they can actually increase stress and intensify psychological and physical problems (De Vogli, Chandola, & Marmot, 2007; Gleason et al., 2008; Newsom et al., 2008; Ruiz et al., 2006). It has even been suggested that among people under intense stress, the benefits of having a large social support network may be offset by the dangers of catching a cold or the flu from people in that network (Hamrick, Cohen, & Rodriguez, 2002).

Finally, the value of social support may depend on the kind of stressor being encountered. So although having a friend nearby might reduce the impact of some stressors, it might amplify the impact of others. In one study, participants who were about to make a speech experienced the task as more threatening—and showed stronger physical and psychological stress responses—when a friend was with them than when they were waiting alone (Stoney & Finney, 2000).

Stress, Personality, and Gender

The impact of stress on health appears to depend not only on how people think about particular stressors but also to some extent on how they think about and react to the world in general. For instance, stress-related health problems tend to be especially common among people whose "disease-prone" personalities lead them to (1) try to ignore stressors when possible; (2) perceive stressors as long-term, catastrophic threats that they brought on themselves; and (3) be pessimistic about their ability to overcome stressors (e.g., Penninx et al., 2001; Peterson et al., 1998; Roy et al., 2010; Segerstrom et al., 1998; Suinn, 2001).

Other cognitive styles, such as those characteristic of "disease-resistant" personalities, help insulate people from the ill effects of stress. These people tend to think of stressors as temporary challenges to be overcome, not catastrophic threats. And they don't constantly blame themselves for causing these stressors. One particularly important component of the "disease-resistant" personality seems to be *dispositional optimism,* the belief or expectation that things will work out positively (Folkman & Moskowitz, 2000; Pressman & Cohen, 2005; Rosenkranz et al., 2003; Taylor, Kemeny et al., 2000). Optimistic people tend to live longer (Giltay et al., 2004, 2006) and to have more resistance than pessimists to colds and other infectious diseases (Boyce & Wood, 2011; Cohen et al., 2003a, 2003b; Kivimäki et al., 2005; Pressman & Cohen, 2005; Segerstrom & Sephton, 2010), which helps explain why optimistic students experience fewer physical symptoms at the end of the academic term (Aspinwall & Taylor, 1992; Ebert, Tucker, & Roth, 2002). Optimistic coronary bypass surgery patients tend to heal faster and stay healthier than pessimists (Scheier et al., 1989, 1999), perceive their quality of life following coronary surgery to be higher (Fitzgerald et al., 1993), and respond better to treatments for post-operative depression (Tindle et al., 2012) than do patients with less optimistic outlooks. And among HIV-positive men, dispositional optimism has been associated with lower psychological distress, fewer worries, and lower perceived risk of acquiring full-blown AIDS (Johnson & Endler, 2002; Taylor et al., 1992). These effects appear due in part to optimists' tendency to use challenge-oriented, problem-focused coping strategies that attack stressors directly, in contrast to pessimists' tendency to use emotion-focused coping strategies, such as denial and avoidance (Bosompra et al., 2001; Brenes et al., 2002; Moskowitz et al., 2009). They also tend to be happier than pessimists, a tendency associated not only with less intense and less dangerous physiological responses to stressors but also with greater success in life (e.g. Lyubomirsky, King, & Diener, 2005; Steptoe, Wardle, & Marmot, 2005).

Gender may also play a role in responses to stressors (Goldstein et al., 2010; Mather & Lighthall, 2012; St. Claire, Hayward, & Rogers, 2010). In a review of 200 studies of stress responses and coping methods, Shelley Taylor and her colleagues found that males under stress tended to get angry, avoid stressors, or both, whereas females were more likely to help others and to make use of social support (Taylor, Klein et al., 2000; Taylor et al., 2002). Further, in the face of equally intense stressors, men's physical responses tend to be more intense than women's (Stoney & Matthews, 1988). This is not true in every case, of course (Smith et al., 2008), but why should gender differences show up at all? Though the learning of gender roles that is discussed in the human development chapter surely plays a part (Eagly & Wood, 1999), Taylor proposes that women's "tend and befriend" style differs from the "fight-flight" pattern so often seen in men partly because of gender differences in how hormones combine under stress. Consider, for example, oxytocin (pronounced "ox-see-TOH-sin"), a hormone released in both sexes in response to social stressors (Poulin, Holman, & Buffone, 2012; Taylor et al., 2006; Uvnas-Moberg, Arn, & Magnusson, 2005). Taylor suggests that oxytocin interacts differently with male and female sex hormones: in men it amplifies physical responses to stress but reduces those responses in women (Light et al., 2005). This gender difference could lead to the more intense emotional and behavioral stress responses typical of men, and it might be partly responsible for men's greater vulnerability to heart disease and other stress-related illnesses (Kajantie & Phillips, 2006). If that is the case, gender differences in stress responses may help explain why women in industrialized societies live an average of 5 to 10 years longer than men (Hoyert, Kung, & Smith, 2005; Kajantie, 2008). The role of gender-related hormones in responding to stress is supported by the fact that there are few (if any) gender differences in children's responses to stress. Those differences begin to appear only around adolescence, when sex hormone differences become pronounced (Allen & Matthews, 1997).

LINKAGES

Are childhood traits related to how long we live?
(a link to Human Development)

FOCUS ON RESEARCH

Personality and Health

The way people think and act in the face of stressors, the ease with which they attract social support, and their tendency to be optimists or pessimists are but a few aspects of *personality*.

What was the researchers' question?

Are there other personality characteristics that protect or threaten people's health? This was the question asked by Howard Friedman and his associates (Friedman, 2000; Friedman et al., 1995a, 1995b). In particular, they attempted to identify aspects of personality that increase the likelihood that people will die prematurely from heart disease, high blood pressure, or other chronic diseases.

How did the researchers answer the question?

Friedman suspected that an answer might lie in the results of the Terman Life Cycle Study of Intelligence. As described in the chapter on thought, language, and intelligence, the study was originally designed to measure the long-term development of 1,528 gifted California children (856 boys and 672 girls) who were nicknamed the "Termites," after Louis Terman, the research team leader (Terman & Oden, 1947).

Starting in 1921, and every five to ten years thereafter, the team gathered information about the Termites' personality traits, social relationships, stressors, health habits, and many other variables. The data were collected through questionnaires and interviews with the Termites themselves as well as with their teachers, parents, and other family members. By the early 1990s, about half of the Termites had died. It was then that Friedman realized that the Terman Life Cycle Study could shed light on the relationship between personality and health, because the personality traits identified in the Termites could be related to how long they lived. So he examined the Termites' death certificates, noting the dates and causes of death, and then looked for associations between their personalities and the length of their lives.

What did the researchers find?

Friedman and his colleagues found that one of the most important predictors of long life was a dimension of personality known as *conscientiousness,* or social dependability (described in the personality chapter). Termites who in childhood had been seen as truthful, prudent, reliable, hard working, and humble tended to live longer than those whose parents and teachers had identified them as impulsive and lacking in self-control.

Friedman also examined the Terman Life Cycle Study for what it suggested about the relationship between health and social support. In particular, he compared Termites whose parents had divorced or who had been in unstable marriages themselves with those who grew up in stable homes and who had stable marriages. He discovered that people who had experienced parental divorce during childhood or who themselves had unstable marriages died an average of four years earlier than those whose close social relationships had been less stressful.

What do the results mean?

Did these differences in personality traits and social support actually cause some Termites to live longer than others? Friedman's research is based mainly on correlational analyses, so it was difficult for the investigators to draw conclusions about what caused the relationships they observed. Still, Friedman and his colleagues searched the Terman data for clues to mechanisms through which personality and other factors might have exerted a causal influence on how long the Termites lived (Peterson et al., 1998). For example, they evaluated the hypothesis that conscientious, dependable Termites who lived socially stable lives might have followed healthier lifestyles than those who were more impulsive and socially stressed. They found that people in the latter group did, in fact, tend to eat less healthy diets and were more likely to smoke, drink to excess, or use drugs. But health behaviors alone did not fully account for their shorter average life spans. Another possible explanation is that conscientiousness and stability in social relationships reflect a general attitude of caution that goes beyond eating right and avoiding substance abuse. Friedman found some support for this idea in the Terman data. Termites who were impulsive or low on conscientiousness were somewhat more likely to die from accidents or violence than those who were less impulsive.

What do we still need to know?

The Terman Life Cycle Study does not provide final answers about the relationship between personality and health. However, it has generated some important clues and a number of intriguing hypotheses to be evaluated in research with more representative samples of participants. Some of that research has already taken place and tends to confirm Friedman's findings about conscientiousness (Hampson et al., 2006; Kern & Friedman, 2008; Roberts et al., 2009; Terracciano et al. 2008). Further, Friedman's decision to reanalyze a set of data on psychosocial development as a way of exploring issues in health care psychology stands as a fine example of how a creative researcher can pursue answers to complex questions that are difficult or impossible to study via controlled experiments.   ● ● ● ●

Our discussion of personality and other factors that can alter the impact of stressors should make it obvious that what is stressful for a given individual is not determined fully and simply by predispositions, coping styles, or situations (see "In Review: Stress Responses and Stress Mediators"). Even more important are interactions between the person and the situation, the mixture of each individual's coping resources with the specific characteristics of the situations encountered.

Stress Responses and Stress Mediators   IN REVIEW

Category	Examples
Responses	
Physical	The fight-flight reaction involves increased heart rate, respiration, and muscle tension as well as sweating and dilated pupils. Activation of SAM and HPA systems releases catecholamines and corticosteroids. Organ systems involved in prolonged resistance to stressors eventually break down.
Psychological	*Emotional* examples include anger, anxiety, depression, and other emotional states. *Cognitive* examples include inability to concentrate or think logically, ruminative thinking, and catastrophizing. *Behavioral* examples include aggression and escape/avoidance tactics (including suicide attempts), and health-risk behaviors.
Mediators	
Appraisal	Thinking of a difficult new job as a challenge will create less discomfort than focusing on the threat of failure.
Predictability	A tornado that strikes without warning may have a more devastating emotional impact than a long-predicted hurricane.
Control	Repairing a disabled spacecraft may be less stressful for the astronauts doing the work than for their loved ones on earth, who can do nothing to help.
Coping resources and methods	Having no effective way to relax after a hard day may prolong tension and other stress responses.
Social support	Having no one to talk to about a rape or other trauma may amplify the negative impact of the experience.

IN REVIEW QUESTIONS

1. The friends and family we can depend on to help us deal with stressors are called our ____ network.
2. Fantasizing about winning money is a(n) ____-focused way of coping with financial stress.
3. Sudden, extreme stressors may cause psychological and behavioral problems known as ____ .

The Physiology and Psychology of Health and Illness

How does stress affect your immune system?

Several studies mentioned so far show that people under stress are more likely than less-stressed people to develop infectious diseases. Other research shows that they are also more likely to experience flare-ups of the latent viruses responsible for oral herpes (cold sores) or genital herpes (Cohen & Herbert, 1996). In the following sections we focus on some of the ways that these and other illnesses are related to the impact of stress on the immune system and the cardiovascular system.

LINKAGES
● ● ● ● ● ● ● ●

Can stress give you the flu?
(a link to Biology and Behavior)

Stress, Illness, and the Immune System

On March 19, 1878, at a seminar at the Académie de Médecine in Paris, Louis Pasteur showed his distinguished audience three chickens. One bird had been raised normally and was healthy. A second bird had been intentionally infected with bacteria but given no other treatment; it was also healthy. The third chicken that Pasteur presented was dead. It had been infected with the same bacteria as the second bird but it had also been physically stressed by being exposed to cold temperatures; as a result, the bacteria had killed it (Kelley, 1985).

© Boehringer Ingelheim International GmbH/ photo Lennart Nilsson, The Incredible Machine, National Geographic Society/Scanpix

The Body's Internal Defense System
A patrolling immune system cell sends out an extension known as a pseudopod to engulf and destroy a bacterial cell before alerting more defenders. These immune cells are able to squeeze out of the bloodstream and enter organs, where they destroy foreign cells.

Research conducted since Pasteur's time has greatly expanded our knowledge about how stressors affect the body's reaction to disease. **Psychoneuroimmunology** is the field that examines the interaction of psychological and physiological processes that strengthen or weaken the body's ability to defend itself against disease (Ader, 2001).

The Immune System and Illness   The body's first line of biological defense against invading substances and microorganisms is the **immune system.** The immune system is perhaps as complex as the nervous system, and it contains as many cells as the brain (Guyton, 1991). Some of these cells are in organs such as the thymus and spleen, whereas others circulate in the bloodstream, entering tissues throughout the body. Components of the immune system kill or inactivate foreign or harmful substances in the body, such as viruses and bacteria (Simpson, Hurtley, & Marx, 2000). **Inflammation** (seen externally as swelling and redness around a wound) is another immune system response that helps to fight infectious agents and promote the healing of injuries. However, if this inflammatory response is prolonged or excessive it can promote or worsen asthma, coronary artery disease, diabetes, some cancers, and other chronic conditions (Chiang et al., 2012; Cohen et al., 2012).

If our immune systems are impaired, we are left more vulnerable to colds, mononucleosis, and many other infectious diseases (Potter & Zautra, 1997). The human immunodeficiency virus (HIV) disables the immune system, leading to AIDS and leaving the HIV-infected person defenseless against other infections or cancers. The immune system can also become overactive, with devastating results. Many chronic, progressive diseases—including arthritis, diabetes, and lupus erythematosus—are now recognized as *autoimmune disorders*. In these cases, cells of the immune system begin to attack and destroy normal body cells (Oldenberg et al., 2000).

An important aspect of the human immune system is the action of the white blood cells, called *leukocytes* (pronounced "LU-koh-sites"). These cells are formed in the bone marrow and serve as the body's mobile defense units. Leukocytes are called to action when foreign substances are detected. Among the varied types of leukocytes are *B-cells,* which produce *antibodies* to fight foreign toxins; *T-cells,* which kill other cells; and *natural killer cells,* which destroy a variety of foreign organisms and are particularly important in fighting viruses and tumors. The brain can influence the immune system indirectly by altering the secretion of adrenal hormones, such as cortisol, that modify the circulation of T-cells and B-cells. The brain can also influence the immune system directly by connecting with the immune organs, such as the thymus, where T-cells and B-cells are stored (Felten et al., 1991; Maier & Watkins, 2000).

The Immune System and Stress

A wide variety of stressors can lead to suppression of the immune system. The effects are especially strong in the elderly (Penedo & Dahn, 2004), but they occur in everyone (Kiecolt-Glaser & Glaser, 2001; Kiecolt-Glaser et al., 2002). One study showed that as first-year law students participated in class, took exams, and experienced other stressful aspects of law school, they showed a decline in several measures of immune functioning (Segerstrom et al., 1998). Similarly, decreases in natural killer cell activity have been observed in both men and women following the deaths of their spouses (Irwin et al., 1987), and a variety of immune system impairments have been found in people suffering the effects of prolonged marital conflict, divorce, unemployment, lack of social support, loneliness, or extended periods of caring for elderly relatives (Cacioppo et al., 1998; Cohen et al., 2007; Kiecolt-Glaser & Glaser, 1992; Kiecolt-Glaser et al., 2003, 2005; Sbarra, Law, & Portley, 2011; Vitaliano, Zhang, & Scanlan, 2003).

The relationship between stress and the immune system can be critical to people who are HIV positive but do not have AIDS. Because their immune systems are already fragile, further stress-related impairments could be life threatening. Research indicates that psychological stressors are associated with the progression of HIV-related illnesses (e.g., Antoni et al., 2000; Gore-Felton & Koopman, 2008). Unfortunately, people with

psychoneuroimmunology The field that examines the interaction of psychological and physiological processes affecting the body's ability to defend itself against disease.

immune system The body's first line of biological defense against invading substances and microorganisms.

inflammation An immune system response that combats infectious agents and helps to heal injuries.

HIV (and AIDS) face a particularly heavy load of immune-suppressing psychological stressors, including uncertainty about the future. A lack of perceived control and resulting depression and anxiety can further magnify their stress responses (e.g., Sewell et al., 2000).

Stress, Illness, and the Cardiovascular System

Earlier we mentioned the role of the sympatho-adreno-medullary (SAM) system in mobilizing the body's defenses during times of threat. Because the SAM system is linked to the cardiovascular system, its repeated activation in response to stressors has been linked to the development of coronary heart disease (CHD), high blood pressure (hypertension), and stroke (Chida & Steptoe, 2009; Krantz & McCeney, 2002). For example, adults in a nationwide sample who reported the strongest and longest-lasting worry about terrorism after the 9/11 attacks on New York City and Washington, D.C. were three times more likely than less worried people to develop heart problems over the next three years. Even those who reported the most intense temporary distress right after 9/11 were at elevated risk of developing heart problems over those same three years (Holman et al., 2008).

The link between CHD and physical stress responses appears especially close in people whose stress responses are especially strong (Andre-Petersson et al., 2001; Ming et al., 2004; Treiber et al., 2001). For example, among healthy young adult research participants, those whose blood pressure rose most dramatically in response to a mild stressor or a series of stressors were the ones most likely to develop hypertension later in life (Light et al., 1999; Matthews et al., 2004).

THINKING **CRITICALLY**

Does Hostility Increase the Risk of Heart Disease?

Health care psychologists see hostility as characterized by suspiciousness, resentment, frequent anger, antagonism, and distrust of others (Krantz & McCeney, 2002; Williams, 2001). The identification of hostility as a risk factor for coronary heart disease and heart attack may be an important breakthrough in understanding these illnesses, which remain among the chief causes of death in the United States and most other Western nations. But is hostility as dangerous as health care psychologists suspect?

What am I being asked to believe or accept?

Many researchers claim that individuals who display hostility—especially when it is accompanied by irritability and impatience—increase their risk for coronary heart disease and heart attack (e.g., Bleil et al., 2004; Boyle et al., 2004; Bunde & Suls, 2006; Day & Jreige, 2002; Krantz & McCeney, 2002; Smith et al., 2007). This risk, they say, is independent of other risk factors such as heredity, diet, smoking, and drinking alcohol.

Is evidence available to support the claim?

There is evidence that hostility and heart disease are related, but scientists are still not sure about what causes the relationship. Some suggest that the risk of coronary heart disease and heart attack is elevated in hostile people because these people tend to be unusually reactive to stressors, especially when challenged. During interpersonal conflicts, for example, people predisposed to hostile behavior display not only overt hostility but also unusually large increases in blood pressure, heart rate, and other aspects of autonomic reactivity (Brondolo et al., 2003; Suls & Wan, 1993). In addition, it takes hostile individuals longer than normal to get back to their resting levels of autonomic functioning (Gerin et al., 2006). Like a driver who damages a car's engine by pressing the accelerator and applying the brakes at the same time, these "hot reactors" may create excessive wear and tear on the heart's arteries as their increased heart rate forces blood through tightened vessels (Johnston, Tuomisto, & Patching, 2008). Increased sympathetic nervous system activation not only puts stress on the coronary arteries but also leads to surges of stress-related hormones from the adrenal glands. High levels of these hormones are associated with increases in cholesterol and other fatty substances that are deposited in arteries and contribute to coronary heart disease (Bierhaus et al., 2003; Stoney & Hughes, 1999; Stoney, Bausserman, et al., 1999; Stoney, Niaura, et al., 1999). Cholesterol levels do appear

You Can't Fire Me—I Quit!
For a time, researchers believed that anyone who displayed the pattern of aggressiveness, competitiveness, and nonstop work known as Type A behavior was at increased risk for heart disease (Friedman & Rosenman, 1974). More recent research, however, has led to the hypothesis that the danger lies not in these characteristics alone but in hostility, which is seen in some, but not all, Type A people.

to be elevated in the blood of hostile people (Dujovne & Houston, 1991; Engebretson & Stoney, 1995).

Hostility may affect heart disease risk less directly as well, through its impact on social support. Some evidence suggests that hostile people get fewer benefits from social support (Lepore, 1995). Failing to use this support—and possibly offending potential supporters in the process—may intensify the impact of stressful events on hostile people. The result may be increased anger, antagonism, and, ultimately, additional stress on the cardiovascular system.

Can that evidence be interpreted another way?

Studies suggesting that hostility causes coronary heart disease are not true experiments. Researchers cannot manipulate the independent variable by creating hostility in randomly selected people in order to assess its effects on heart health. Accordingly, we have to consider other possible explanations of the observed relationship between hostility and heart disease.

For example, some researchers suggest that higher rates of heart problems among hostile people are not due entirely to the impact of hostility on blood pressure, heart rate, and hormone surges. It may also be that a genetically determined tendency toward autonomic reactivity increases the likelihood of both hostility and heart disease (Cacioppo et al., 1998; Krantz et al., 1988). If this is the case, then the fact that hostility and coronary heart disease often appear in the same people might reflect not just the effects of hostility but also a third factor—autonomic reactivity—that contributes to both of them.

It has also been suggested that hostility may be only one of many traits linked to heart disease. Depressiveness, hopelessness, pessimism, anger, and anxiety may be involved, too (Frasure-Smith & Lespérance, 2005; Kubzansky, Davidson, & Rozanski, 2005; Nicholson, Fuhrer, & Marmot, 2005; Roy et al., 2010; Suls & Bunde, 2005).

What evidence would help to evaluate the alternatives?

Research on the role these other traits may play in heart disease will be vital, and some of that work has already been done. One way to test whether hostile people's higher rates of heart disease are related specifically to their hostility or to a more general tendency toward intense physiological arousal is to examine how these individuals react to stress when they are not angry. Some researchers have done this by observing the physiological reactions of hostile people during the stress of surgery. One study found that even under general anesthesia, such people show unusually strong autonomic reactivity (Krantz & Durel, 1983). Because these patients were not conscious, it appears that oversensitivity to stressors, not hostile thinking, caused their exaggerated stress responses. This possibility is supported by research showing that individuals who have strong blood pressure responses to stressors also show different patterns of brain activity during stress than other people do (Gianaros et al., 2005).

What conclusions are most reasonable?

Most studies continue to find that among generally healthy people, those who are hostile—especially men—are at greater risk for heart disease and heart attacks than other people (Chida & Steptoe, 2009; Haukkala et al., 2010; Krantz & McCeney, 2002; Stansfeld & Marmot, 2002). However, the picture is probably more complex than researchers first thought; it appears that many interacting factors affect the relationship between hostility and heart problems (Sloan et al., 2010).

A more elaborate psychobiological model may be required—one that takes into account that (1) some individuals may be biologically predisposed to react to stress with hostility and increased cardiovascular activity, each of which can contribute to heart disease; (2) hostile people help create and maintain stressors through aggressive thoughts and actions, which can provoke others to be aggressive; and (3) hostile people are more likely than others to smoke, drink alcohol to excess, overeat, fail to exercise, and engage in other heart-damaging behaviors (Kiecolt-Glaser, 2010).

We must also keep in mind that the relationship between heart problems and hostility may not be universal. Although this relationship appears to hold for women as well as men and for individuals in various ethnic groups (e.g., Davidson, Hall, & MacGregor, 1996; Nakano & Kitamura, 2001; Olson et al., 2005; Powch & Houston, 1996; Yoshimasu et al., 2002), final conclusions must await further research that examines the relationship between hostility and heart disease in other cultures (Finney, Stoney, & Engebretson, 2002). ● ● ● ●

Promoting Healthy Behavior

Who is most likely to adopt a healthy lifestyle?

Health care psychologists are deeply involved in the development of smoking cessation programs, in campaigns to discourage young people from taking up smoking, in anti-alcoholism efforts, in the prevention of skin cancer through sun safety education, in promoting regular exercise, in encouraging health-care workers to wear protective masks and follow other safety practices, and in the fight against the spread of HIV and AIDS (e.g., Albarracín et al., 2008; Buller, Buller, & Kane, 2005; Durantini et al., 2006; Grant & Hofmann, 2011; Lally et al., 2010; Leitzmann et al., 2007; Lichtenstein, Zhu, & Tedeschi, 2010; Lombard et al., 2010; Morisky et al., 2006; Stice, Shaw, & Nathan, 2006; Tybur et al., 2011). They are also working to identify individuals who are at elevated risk for disease because of genetic predispositions or exposure to stressors early in life.

In addition, health care psychologists help promote early detection of disease. Encouraging women to perform breast self-examinations and men to do testicular self-examinations are just two examples of health care psychology programs that can save thousands of lives each year (Taylor, 2002). Health care psychologists have also explored the reasons why some people fail to follow public health recommendations or doctors' orders that are vital to the control of diabetes, heart disease, lung cancer, AIDS, high blood pressure, and various childhood diseases (Bartlett, 2002; Gardner et al., 2010; Gonzalez et al., 2004; Griffin & Harris, 2011; Sieverding, Decker, & Zimmermann, 2010). Understanding these reasons and finding ways to encourage better adherence to medical advice could speed recovery, prevent unnecessary suffering, and save many lives (Barclay et al., 2007; Howell & Shepperd, 2012; Rhodes, Warburton, & Bredin, 2009; Simpson et al., 2006).

Efforts to reduce, eliminate, or prevent behaviors that pose health risks and to encourage healthy behaviors are called **health promotion** (Smith, Orleans, & Jenkins, 2004). For example, health care psychologists have developed programs that teach children as young as nine to engage in healthy behaviors and avoid health-risk behaviors. School systems now offer a variety of these programs, including those that give children and adolescents the skills necessary to turn down cigarettes, drugs, and unprotected sex. Health care psychologists have also brought their healthy lifestyle campaigns into workplaces and some are involved in creating video games designed to promote better health (Peng, 2009; Thompson et al., 2010). They teach stress-management techniques, too (Langenberg et al., 2000; Tuomilehto et al., 2001). These programs can create savings in future medical treatment costs (Blumenthal et al., 2002; Schneiderman et al., 2001) and better health for those who participate (Lisspers et al., 2005; Orth-Gomér et al., 2009).

Even modest lifestyle changes can have profound effects. In one major long-term study, adults who engaged in mild exercise for 15 minutes a day had an average life expectancy that was three-years longer than those who weren't physically active; every additional 15 minutes of daily physical activity was associated with a further 4 percent reduction in mortality (Wen et al., 2011). Increased exercise is also associated with reduced health risks among children and adolescents (Ekelund et al., 2012).

© Digital Vision/Getty Images

Doctor's Orders

Despite physicians' instructions, many patients fail to take their blood pressure medication and continue to eat an unhealthy diet. Noncompliance with medical advice is especially common when cultural values and beliefs conflict with that advice. Aware of this problem, health psychologists are developing culture-sensitive approaches to health promotion and disease prevention (Kazarian & Evans, 2001).

health promotion The process of altering or eliminating behaviors that pose risks to health and, at the same time, fostering healthier behavior patterns.

Health Beliefs and Health Behaviors

Health care psychologists are also trying to understand the social, educational, and cognitive factors that lead people to engage in health-endangering behaviors and that can interfere with efforts to adopt healthier lifestyles (Berkman, Falk, & Lieberman, 2011; Chiou, Yang, & Wan, 2011; Erskine, Gerogiou, & Kvavilashvli, 2010; Evans & Kutcher, 2010; Fitzsimons & Finkel, 2011; Klepp, Kelder, & Perry, 1995; Moffitt et al., 2011; Nestler & Egloff, 2009; Peters et al., 2010; Rubin, 2011). Their research has led to intervention programs that seek to change these patterns of thinking or at least take them into account (Churchill & Jessop, 2011; Freimuth & Hovick, 2012; Knauper et al., 2011; Kwan et al., 2012; Logel & Cohen, 2011; Petrie & Weinman, 2012). In one study, for example, women who avoid thinking about the risks of breast cancer were more likely to get a mammogram screening after receiving health information that was tailored to their cognitive styles (Williams-Piehota et al., 2005).

This cognitive approach to health care psychology can be seen in various *health-belief models*. Irwin Rosenstock (1974) developed one of the most influential and extensively tested of these models (e.g., Aspinwall & Duran, 1999). He based his model on the assumption that people's decisions about health-related behaviors (such as smoking) are guided by four main factors:

1. Perceiving a *personal threat* of risk for getting a specific illness. (Do you believe that *you* will get lung cancer from smoking?)
2. Perceiving the seriousness of the illness and the consequences of having it. (How serious do you think lung cancer is? What will happen to you if you get it?)
3. Believing that changing a particular behavior will reduce the threat. (Will stopping smoking prevent *you* from getting lung cancer?)
4. Comparing the *perceived costs* of changing a health-risk behavior and the *benefits expected* from making that change. (Will the reduced risk of getting cancer in the future be worth the discomfort and loss of pleasure from not smoking?)

According to this health-belief model, the people most likely to quit smoking would be those who believe that they are at risk for getting cancer from smoking, that cancer is serious and life threatening, and that the benefits of reducing cancer risks are greater than the costs of quitting (McCaul et al., 2006).

Other cognitive factors are emphasized in other health-belief models (Ng et al., 2012). For example, people generally do not try to quit smoking unless they believe they can succeed. So *self-efficacy,* the belief that you are able to perform some behavior, is an additional consideration in making decisions about health behaviors (Armitage, 2005; Bandura, 1992; Dijkstra, DeVries, & Bakker, 1996). A related factor is the *intention* to engage in a healthy behavior (Albarracín et al., 2001; Schwarzer, 2001; Webb & Sheeran, 2006).

Health-belief models have been useful in predicting a variety of health behaviors, including exercise (McAuley, 1992), safe-sex practices (Fisher, Fisher, & Rye, 1995), adherence to doctors' orders (Bond, Aiken, & Somerville, 1992), and having routine vaccinations and mammograms (Brewer et al., 2007; Champion & Huster, 1995).

As described in the chapter on thought, language, and intelligence, humans tend to underestimate the likelihood of common outcomes and to overestimate the likelihood of rare events. When this tendency causes people to ignore the dangers of smoking and other health-risk behaviors, the results can be disastrous.

© Steve Kelley, *The Times-Picayune,* New Orleans. Reprinted by permission.

Changing Health Behaviors: Stages of Readiness

Changing health-related behaviors depends not only on a person's health beliefs but also on that person's readiness to change. According to James Prochaska and his colleagues, successful change occurs in five stages (Prochaska, DiClemente, & Norcross, 1992; Schumann et al., 2005):

1. *Precontemplation:* The person does not perceive a health-related problem and has no intention of changing anytime soon.
2. *Contemplation:* A problem behavior has been identified and the person is seriously thinking about changing it.
3. *Preparation:* The person has a strong intention to change and has made specific plans to do so.
4. *Action:* The person is engaging successfully in behavior change.
5. *Maintenance:* The healthy behavior has continued for at least six months and the person is using newly learned skills to prevent relapse, or "backsliding."

These stages may actually overlap somewhat; for example, some "precontemplators" might actually be starting to contemplate change (Herzog & Blagg, 2007). The road from precontemplation through maintenance can be a bumpy one (Prochaska, 1994). Usually, people relapse and go through the stages repeatedly until they finally achieve stability in the healthy behavior they desire (Polivy & Herman, 2002). Smokers, for example, typically require three to four cycles through the stages over several years before they finally reach the maintenance stage (Piasecki, 2006).

Programs for Coping with Stress and Promoting Health

Improving people's stress-coping skills is an important part of health care psychologists' health promotion work (e.g., Keogh, Bond, & Flaxman, 2006; Sbarra, Smith, & Mehl, 2012). Let's consider a few specific procedures and programs associated with this effort.

Planning to Cope   Just as people with extra money in the bank have a better chance of weathering a financial crisis, those with effective coping skills have a better chance of escaping some of the more harmful effects of intense stress. Like family money, the ability to handle stress appears to come naturally—perhaps even genetically—to some people (Caspi et al., 2010), but coping strategies can also be learned. Programs for teaching these strategies include several stages, which are summarized in Table 10.4.

Bear in mind, though, that no single method of coping with stressors is right for everyone or every stressor. For example, denying the existence of an uncontrollable

TABLE 10.4   Steps for Coping with Stress

Many successful programs for systematically coping with stress guide people through several steps and are aimed at removing stressors that can be changed and improving responses to stressors that cannot be changed (Taylor, 2002).

APPLYING PSYCHOLOGY

Step	Task
1. Assessment	Identify the sources and effects of stress.
2. Goal setting	List the stressors and stress responses to be addressed. Designate which stressors can and cannot be changed.
3. Planning	List the specific steps to be taken to cope with stress.
4. Action	Implement coping plans.
5. Evaluation	Determine the changes in stressors and stress responses that have occurred as a result of coping methods.
6. Adjustment	Alter coping methods to improve results if necessary.

stressor may be fine in the short run but may lead to problems if no other coping method is used. Similarly, people who rely entirely on active, problem-focused coping might handle controllable stressors well but find themselves nearly helpless in the face of uncontrollable ones (Murray & Terry, 1999). The most successful stress managers may be those who can adjust their coping methods to the demands of changing situations, differing stressors, and cultural traditions (Chen, 2012; Chen & Miller, 2012; Fischer et al., 2010; Kashdan & Rottenberg, 2010; Sheppes et al., 2011; Taylor, 2002).

LINKAGES

How can people manage stress?
(a link to Treatment of Psychological Disorders)

Developing Coping Strategies   Strategies for coping with stress can be cognitive, emotional, behavioral, or physical. *Cognitive coping strategies* involve changing the way we think. These changes include thinking more calmly, rationally, and constructively in the face of stressors and may lead to a more hopeful outlook. For example, students with heavy course loads may experience anxiety, confusion, discouragement, lack of motivation, and the desire to run away from it all. Frightening, catastrophizing thoughts (such as "What if I fail?") magnify these stress responses. Cognitive coping strategies replace catastrophic thinking with thoughts that cast stressors as challenges, not threats (Ellis & Bernard, 1985). This substitution process is called *cognitive restructuring* (Lazarus, 1971; Meichenbaum, 1977). It involves first identifying upsetting thoughts (such as "I'll never figure this out!") and then developing and practicing more constructive thoughts to use when under stress (such as "All I can do is the best I can"). Cognitive coping doesn't eliminate stressors, of course, but it can help us to perceive them as less threatening and therefore less disruptive (Antoni et al., 2000; Chesney et al., 2003).

Finding social support is an effective *emotional coping strategy.* As mentioned earlier, feeling that you are cared about and valued by others can be a buffer against the ill effects of stressors, which can lead to enhanced immune functioning (Kiecolt-Glaser & Newton, 2001) and quicker recovery from illness (Taylor, 2002).

Behavioral coping strategies involve changing behavior in order to minimize the negative impact of stressors. Time management is one example. If it seems that you are always pressed for time, try developing a time management plan. The first step is to use a calendar or day planner to record how you spend each hour of each day in a typical week. Next, analyze the information you have recorded. Locate when and how you might be wasting time and how you might use your time more efficiently. Then set out a schedule for the coming week and stick to it. Make adjustments in subsequent weeks as you learn more realistic ways to manage your time. Time management can't create more time, but it can help control catastrophizing thoughts by providing reassurance that there is enough time for everything and a plan for handling all that you have to do.

LEARN by DOING

Physical coping strategies can be used to alter the undesirable physical responses that occur before, during, or after the appearance of stressors. The most common physical coping strategy is some form of drug use. Prescription medications are sometimes an appropriate coping aid, especially when stressors are severe and acute, such as the sudden death of one's child. However, people who rely on prescribed or nonprescription drugs, including alcohol, to help them face stressors may come to believe that their ability to cope is due to the drug, not to their own skill. This belief can make people more and more psychologically dependent on the drug. Further, the drug effects that blunt stress responses may also interfere with the ability to apply other coping strategies. The resulting loss of perceived control over stressors may make those stressors even more threatening and disruptive.

Nonchemical methods of reducing physical stress reactions and improving stress coping include progressive relaxation training (Bernstein, Borkovec, & Hazlette-Stevens, 2000; Scheufele, 2000), physical exercise (Anshel, 1996), biofeedback (Nestoriuc, Rief, & Martin, 2008; Sarafino & Goehring, 2000), yoga (Kiecolt-Glaser et al., 2010), meditation, and tai chi (Carlson et al., 2003; Davidson et al., 2003; Li et al., 2001), among others (Taylor, 2002).

"In Review: Methods for Coping with Stress" summarizes our discussion of methods for coping with stress.

© Medioimages/Photodisc/Getty Images

Dealing with Chemotherapy
Progressive relaxation training (Jacobson, 1938) involves briefly tensing groups of muscles throughout the body, one at a time, then releasing the tension and focusing on the resulting feelings of relaxation. It can be used to ease a variety of health-related problems, including the anxiety, physiological arousal, and nausea associated with cancer chemotherapy (Bernstein, Borkovec, & Hazlette-Stevens, 2000).

APPLYING PSYCHOLOGY

Methods for Coping with Stress IN REVIEW

Type Of Coping Method	Examples
Cognitive	Thinking of stressors as challenges rather than as threats; avoiding perfectionism
Emotional	Seeking social support; getting advice
Behavioral	Implementing a time-management plan; where possible, making life changes to eliminate stressors
Physical	Progressive relaxation training; exercise; meditation

IN REVIEW QUESTIONS

1. Catastrophizing thoughts are best overcome through ___ coping strategies.

2. The first step in coping with stress is to ___ the sources and effects of your stressors.

3. True or false: It is best to rely on only one good coping strategy. ___ .

Active Review

As noted in the introductory chapter, all of psychology's subfields are related to one another. Our discussion of how stressors can lead to the development of mental disorders illustrates just one way that the topic of this chapter—health, stress, and coping—is linked to the subfield of abnormal psychology,

CHAPTER 10
Health, Stress, and Coping

which is described in the chapter on psychological disorders. The Linkages diagram shows ties to two other subfields, and there are many more ties throughout the book. Looking for linkages among subfields will help you see how they all fit together and help you better appreciate the big picture that is psychology.

LINKAGES

Can stress give you the flu? *(ans. on p. 408)*

When do stress responses become mental disorders? *(ans. on p. 400)*

How does stress affect group decision-making? *(ans. on p. 585)*

CHAPTER 2
Biology and Behavior

CHAPTER 12
Psychological Disorders

CHAPTER 14
Social Psychology

Summary

Health Psychology

What do health care psychologists do?
Recognition of the link between stress and illness and of the role of behaviors such as smoking in increasing the risk of illness prompted the development of **health care psychology** (or **health psychology**). Health care psychologists work to understand how psychological factors are related to physical disease and to help people behave in ways that prevent or minimize disease and promote health.

Understanding Stress and Stressors

How do psychological stressors affect physical health?
Stress is an ongoing, interactive process that takes place as people adjust to and cope with their environment. **Stressors** are physical

or psychological events or situations to which people must adjust. Psychological stressors include catastrophic events, life changes and strains, chronic stressors, and daily hassles. Stressors can be measured by tests such as the Social Readjustment Rating Scale (SRRS) and the Life Experiences Survey (LES), but scores on such tests provide only a partial picture of the stress in a person's life. **Stress reactions** are physical and psychological responses to stressors.

Stress Responses

How do people react to stressors?
Physical and psychological stress responses can

occur alone or in combination, and the appearance of one can often stimulate others.

Physical stress responses include changes in heart rate, respiration, and many other processes that are part of a pattern known as the **general adaptation syndrome**, or **GAS.** The GAS has three stages: alarm (or **fight-flight reaction**), resistance, and exhaustion. The GAS helps people resist stress, but if activated for too long it can lead to impairment of immune system functions as well as to physical illnesses; Selye called such illnesses **diseases of adaptation**.

Psychological stress responses can be emotional, cognitive, or behavioral. Anxiety, anger, and depression are among the most common emotional stress reactions. Cognitive stress reactions include ruminative thinking, catastrophizing, and disruptions in the ability to think clearly, remember accurately, and solve problems efficiently. Behavioral stress responses include irritability, aggression, absenteeism, engaging in health-damaging behaviors, and even suicide attempts. Severe or long-lasting stressors can lead to **burnout** or to psychological disorders such as **posttraumatic stress disorder (PTSD)**.

Stress Mediators

Why doesn't everyone react to stressors in the same way?

The key to understanding stress appears to lie in observing how particular people interact with specific stressors. Stressors are likely to have greater impact if an individual perceives them as threats or if they are unpredictable, uncontrollable, or unmanageable. The people most likely to react strongly to a stressor are those whose coping resources, coping methods, and **social support** are inadequate or perceived as inadequate.

The Physiology and Psychology of Health and Illness

How does stress affect your immune system? **Psychoneuroimmunology** is the field that examines the interaction of psychological and physiological processes that affect the body's ability to defend itself against disease. When a person is under stress, some of the hormones released from the adrenal glands, such as cortisol, reduce the effectiveness of the cells of the **immune system** (T-cells, B-cells, and natural killer cells), which use **inflammation** and other responses in combating foreign invaders, such as viruses and cancer cells.

People who are hostile appear to be at greater risk for heart disease than other people. The heightened reactivity to stressors that these people experience may damage their cardiovascular systems.

Promoting Healthy Behavior

Who is most likely to adopt a healthy lifestyle?

The process of altering or eliminating health-risk behaviors and encouraging healthy behaviors is called **health promotion**. People's health-related behaviors are partly guided by their beliefs about health risks and what they can do about them.

The process of changing health-related behaviors appears to involve several stages, including precontemplation, contemplation, preparation, action, and maintenance. Understanding which stage people are in and helping them move through these stages is an important task in health care psychology.

To cope with stress, people must identify the stressors affecting them and develop a plan for coping with these stressors. Important coping skills include cognitive restructuring, acting to minimize the number or intensity of stressors, and using progressive relaxation training and other techniques for reducing physical stress reactions.

LEARN by DOING

Put It in Writing

What is stress like for you? To help you understand the role of stress in your life, write a page or two describing a stressful incident that you had to face in the recent past. Identify what the stressors were and classify each of them as physical or psychological. List your physical, emotional, cognitive, and behavioral responses to these stressors, noting how long the responses lasted. Include a brief summary of how you coped with these stressors and how successful your coping efforts were. Some research suggests that writing about stressful experiences can help people deal with those experiences. Did this writing project have any such benefits for you? For more about writing and health, visit http://homepage.psy.utexas.edu/homepage/faculty/pennebaker/Home2000/WritingandHealth.html.

Personal Learning Activity

To get an idea of the differences in people's methods for coping with stress, create a one-paragraph story about a stressful situation (such as losing a job, having one's home destroyed by fire, working for an obnoxious boss, or being overburdened by schoolwork). Now show this description to ten people and ask each of them to tell you how they would cope with the situation if it happened to them. Classify each of their coping methods as problem focused or emotion focused. Did you notice any relationships between the kind of coping responses these people chose and their personal characteristics, such as age, gender, ethnicity, or experience with stress? If so, why do you think those relationships appeared?

Review of Key Terms ·

Can you define each of the key terms in the chapter? Check your definitions against those on the pages shown in parentheses in the following list or in the Glossary at the end of the book.

burnout (p. 400)
diseases of adaptation (p. 397)
fight-flight reaction (p. 396)

general adaptation syndrome
  (GAS) (p. 396)
health care psychology (health
  psychology) (p. 392)
health promotion (p. 412)
immune system (p. 409)
inflammation (p. 409)
posttraumatic stress disorder
  (PTSD) (p. 400)

psychoneuroimmunology (p. 409)
social support (p. 404)
stress (p. 394)
stress reactions (p. 394)
stressors (p. 394)

Test Your Knowledge ·

Select the best answer for each of the following questions. Then check your response against the Answer Key at the end of the book.

1. Health research statistics show that your great-grandparents' generation was most likely to die from ___ diseases, whereas your own generation is most likely to die from ___ diseases.
   a. infectious; infectious
   b. chronic; chronic
   c. infectious; chronic
   d. chronic; infectious

2. Stephanie married a wonderful guy, moved to a new city, and took a great new job, all in the same month. We would expect her to ___.
   a. display physical and/or psychological stress responses
   b. experience little stress, because these are all desirable changes
   c. experience little stress, because these are not chronic stressors
   d. experience physical stress responses only

3. Doug lives next to a family that includes several teenagers. He is forever reminding them not to run across his front lawn. Their loud music often keeps him awake at night, and their cars are parked so that it is hard for him to back out of his driveway. These stressors can best be classified as ___.
   a. life changes and strains
   b. traumatic
   c. catastrophic
   d. daily hassles

4. Aaron's sympathetic nervous system is engaged in the fight-flight reaction. Which stage of the general adaptation syndrome (GAS) is he experiencing?
   a. Alarm
   b. Resistance
   c. Exhaustion
   d. Precontemplative

5. Bill and Ellen's car breaks down and it takes two hours for help to arrive. According to Shelley Taylor's research on stress and gender, Bill is likely to ___, and Ellen is likely to ___.
   a. get angry; get angry, too
   b. be supportive of Ellen; be supportive of Bill
   c. get angry; seek and offer support
   d. seek and offer support; get angry

6. Enrico finds that no matter what else he is doing, he can't stop thinking about all the stressful events in his life. Enrico is experiencing ___.
   a. catastrophizing
   b. ruminative thinking
   c. functional fixedness
   d. cognitive restructuring

7. Caitlin just failed her high school math test. She says to herself, "Mom is going to be furious with me! She will probably ground me, which means I won't be able to go to the prom. If I don't go to the prom, I will be a social outcast, and no one will talk to me. I'll never have any friends or find a partner, and no one will ever love me!" This is an example of ___.
   a. cognitive restructuring
   b. catastrophizing
   c. posttraumatic stress disorder
   d. the fight-or-flight syndrome

8. Dr. Zarro finds that one of her patients, Juan, has a disease-resistant personality. This means that Juan is likely to ___.
   a. ignore his stressors
   b. be optimistic
   c. blame himself for his stressors
   d. ruminate about his stressors

9. Shane, a veteran, occasionally experiences flashbacks involving vivid recollections of his wartime experiences. Flashbacks are associated with ___.
   a. generalized anxiety disorder
   b. posttraumatic stress disorder
   c. the general adaptation syndrome
   d. the fight-flight reaction

10. When Robin didn't get the promotion he had been hoping for, he tries to laugh it off. He goes out with friends and jokingly tells them that it is all for the best because the promotion would have forced him to buy a lot of new clothes. Robin is using ___ coping strategies.
    a. problem-focused
    b. social-focused
    c. emotion-focused
    d. posttraumatic

11. Postsurgical patients who are allowed to adjust their own levels of pain medication tend to use less medication than patients who must ask for it. This phenomenon is consistent with research showing that ___.
    a. social support can mediate stress
    b. predictable stressors are easier to manage
    c. the perception of control reduces the impact of stressors
    d. thinking of stressors as threats amplifies their effects

12. Laton, the head of human resources at his company, knows that the employees have stressful jobs. He schedules group picnics and lunches to help employees get better acquainted. Laton is trying to ease the employees' stressors by ___.
    a. promoting cognitive restructuring
    b. improving social support
    c. increasing employees' sense of control
    d. helping employees think of their stressors as challenges rather than threats

13. The Focus on Research section of this chapter described the relationship between personality and life expectancy. Researchers have found ___.
    a. no significant relationship between the two
    b. that conscientiousness was associated with longer life
    c. that social relationships had no impact on longevity
    d. that impulsiveness was associated with longer life

14. Porter has a flu virus. Research on the immune system shows that Porter's ___ will be working to fight off this virus.
    a. B-cells
    b. T-cells
    c. natural killer cells
    d. macrophages

15. Fred is at high risk for coronary heart disease. As his friend, you tell him that current research suggests that he could lower his risk if he ___.
    a. takes up fishing as a hobby
    b. works at being less hostile
    c. reduces his workload
    d. restructures his thinking about stress

16. When Larry is diagnosed with arthritis, he is very upset. His stress reactions are likely to be reduced *most* if Larry ___.
    a. goes to a spa to try to ignore the situation
    b. keeps his worries to himself
    c. focuses all his attention on worrying about his medical condition
    d. joins an arthritis support group

17. According to Rosenstock's health-belief model, which of the following would *most* help Bridgit decide to quit smoking?
    a. Perceiving a personal threat of getting cancer from her smoking
    b. Knowing that smoking causes cancer
    c. Knowing that quitting can lower people's risk of cancer
    d. Carefully reading the statistics on smoking and health in general

18. Amanda is severely overweight. She knows that for her health's sake, she needs to limit her caloric intake, but she loves to eat and has made no specific plans to go on a diet. Amanda is at the ___ stage of readiness to change a health-risk behavior.
    a. precontemplation
    b. contemplation
    c. preparation
    d. maintenance

19. Sayumi is trying to control her stress. In response to a hurtful comment from a friend, Sayumi thinks to herself, "Don't jump to conclusions; he probably didn't mean it the way it sounded," instead of "That jerk! Who does he think he is?" Sayumi is using the coping strategy of ___.
    a. cognitive restructuring
    b. emotional restructuring
    c. catastrophizing
    d. contemplation

20. Loretta, a marriage counselor, finds her job very stressful. She has found that physical coping strategies help her the most. This means that Loretta most likely ___.
    a. constantly reminds herself about the good she is doing
    b. organizes a support group for therapists
    c. practices progressive relaxation every evening
    d. works on her time-management plan

Media Resources

Now that you have finished reading this chapter, how about exploring some of the ideas and information that you found most interesting?

Coursemate Go to **CengageBrain.com** to access Psychology CourseMate, where you will find an interactive eBook, glossaries, flashcards, quizzes, videos, Virtual Psychology Labs, and more.

Aplia If your professor has assigned Aplia:

1. Sign in to your account.
2. Complete the corresponding exercises as required by your professor.
3. When finished, click "Grade It Now" to see which areas you have mastered, which areas need more work, and detailed explanations of every answer.

Personality

© John Lund/Blend Images/Getty Images

Preview

If you've ever been stuck in heavy traffic, you have probably noticed differences in how drivers deal with the situation. Some are tolerant and calm; others become so cautious that they worsen the congestion; still others react with such impatience and anger that they may trigger a shouting match or cause an accident. Variations in how people handle traffic jams and other frustrating situations reflect just one aspect of their *personalities*—the consistent patterns of thinking, feeling, and behaving that make each person different from (and in some ways similar to) others. In this chapter, we examine four views of personality and review some of the personality tests psychologists have developed to measure and compare people's personalities. We also look at how our personalities interact with the situations in which we find ourselves. For example, being late for an important meeting might change the way in which you would normally handle being in a traffic jam. We also describe some of the ways that personality theory and research are being applied in areas such as diagnosing psychological disorders and screening potential employees.

Founder of Psychoanalytic Theory
Here is Sigmund Freud with his daughter, Anna, who became a psychoanalyst herself and eventually developed a revised version of her father's theories.

personality The pattern of psychological and behavioral characteristics by which each person can be compared and contrasted with other people.

Take out your wallet, look through it, and select the four most important things you carry with you. One person we know picked a driver's license, a credit card, a friend's phone number, and a witty prediction from a fortune cookie. The driver's license describes his physical traits. The credit card represents information about his buying history and responsibility in paying debts. His friends provide support, affection, and intimacy. And the fortune cookie prediction says something about his **LEARN by DOING** wishes, beliefs, or hopes. In other words, the selected items form a crude personality sketch.

There is no universally accepted definition, but psychologists generally view **personality** as the unique pattern of enduring thoughts, feelings, and actions that characterize a person. Personality research, in turn, seeks to understand how and why our consistent patterns of thinking, emotion, and behavior make each of us different in some ways and alike in others (Carver & Connor-Smith, 2010).

To gain a full understanding of just one individual's personality, a researcher would have to learn about many things, including the person's developmental experiences and cultural influences, genetic and other biological characteristics, perceptual and other information-processing habits and biases, typical patterns of emotional expression, and social skills. Psychologists also want to know about personality in general, such as how it develops and changes across the life span. They ask why some people are usually optimistic whereas others are usually pessimistic and whether people respond consistently or inconsistently from one situation to the next.

The specific questions psychologists ask and the methods they use to investigate personality often depend on which of the four main approaches to personality they take. These are the *psychodynamic, trait, social-cognitive,* and *humanistic* approaches. ●

The Psychodynamic Approach

How did paralyzed patients lead Freud to psychoanalysis?

Some people think that personality reveals itself in behavior alone. A person with an "obnoxious personality," for example, shows it by acting obnoxiously. But is that all there is to personality? Not according to Sigmund Freud. As a physician in Vienna, Austria, during the 1890s, Freud specialized in treating "neurotic" disorders. These were physical

Conscious

Preconscious

EGO

Unconscious

SUPEREGO   **ID**

FIGURE 11.1

A Freudian View of Personality Structure

According to Freud, some parts of the personality are conscious, whereas others are unconscious. Between these levels is the preconscious, which Freud saw as the home of memories and other material that we are not usually aware of but that we can easily bring into consciousness.

Source: Adapted from Liebert & Spiegler (1994). *Photos (clockwise from left)*: © Eduardo Fuentes Guevara/iStockphoto; © Ana de Sousa/Shutterstock; © Jaimie Duplass/Shutterstock.

psychoanalytic theory Freud's view that human behavior and personality are determined largely by psychological factors, many of which are unconscious.

psychodynamic approach A view developed by Freud that emphasizes unconscious mental processes in explaining human thought, feelings, and behavior.

id According to Freud, a personality component containing basic instincts, desires, and impulses with which all people are born.

pleasure principle The operating principle of the id, which guides people toward whatever feels good.

ego According to Freud, the part of the personality that makes compromises and mediates conflicts between and among the demands of the id, the superego, and the real world.

reality principle The operating principle of the ego, which takes into account the constraints of the social world.

superego According to Freud, the component of personality that tells people what they should and should not do.

ailments, such as blindness or paralysis, for which there was no physical cause. Often, hypnosis could alleviate or remove these ailments. One patient sleepwalked on legs that were paralyzed during the day. Such cases led Freud to believe in *psychic determinism,* the idea that personality and behavior are determined more by psychological factors than by biological conditions or current events (Carducci, 2009). He proposed that people may not know why they feel, think, or act the way they do because they are partly controlled by the unconscious portion of the personality—the part of which they are normally unaware (Friedman & Schustack, 2009; Funder, 2007). From these ideas Freud created **psychoanalytic theory,** a theory of personality that also led to a way of treating psychological disorders. Freud's theory became the basis of the **psychodynamic approach** to personality, which assumes that various unconscious psychological processes interact to determine our thoughts, feelings, and behavior (Schultz & Schultz, 2009).

The Structure of Personality

Freud believed that people are born with basic needs or instincts—not only for food and water but also for sex and aggression (Schultz & Schultz, 2009). He believed that needs for love, knowledge, security, and the like arise from these more fundamental desires. He said that each of us has to find ways of meeting our needs in a world that often frustrates our efforts. Our personalities develop, said Freud, as we struggle with this task and are reflected in the way we satisfy a wide range of urges.

Id, Ego, and Superego Freud described the personality as having three major components: the id, the ego, and the superego (Cervone & Pervin, 2010; see Figure 11.1). The **id** represents the inborn, unconscious portion of the personality where life and death instincts reside. The *life instincts* promote positive, constructive behavior; the *death instincts* are responsible for human aggression and destructiveness (Olson & Hergenhahn, 2011). The id operates on the **pleasure principle,** seeking immediate satisfaction of both kinds of instincts, regardless of society's rules or the rights and feelings of others. The hungry person who pushes to the front of the line at Burger King would be satisfying an id-driven impulse.

As parents, teachers, and others place ever greater restrictions on the expression of id impulses, a second part of the personality, called the *ego* (or "self"), emerges from the id. The **ego** is responsible for organizing ways to get what a person wants in the real world, as opposed to the fantasy world of the id. Operating on the **reality principle,** the ego makes compromises as the id's demands for immediate satisfaction run into the practical realities of the social world. The ego would influence that hungry person at Burger King to wait in line and think about what to order rather than risk punishment by pushing ahead.

As children gain experience with the rules and values of society, they tend to adopt them. This process of *internalizing* parental and cultural values creates the third component of personality. It is called the **superego,** and it tells us what we should and should not do. The superego becomes our moral guide, and it is just as relentless and unreasonable as the id in its demands to be obeyed. The superego would make the person at Burger King feel guilty for even thinking about violating culturally approved rules about waiting in line.

Conflicts and Defenses Freud described the inner clashes among id, ego, and superego as *intrapsychic,* or *psychodynamic, conflicts.* He believed that each individual's personality is shaped by the number, nature, and outcome of these conflicts. Freud said that the ego's main job is to prevent the anxiety or guilt that would arise if we became conscious of socially unacceptable id impulses, especially those that would violate the superego's rules (Westen et al., 2008). Sometimes the ego guides sensible actions, as when people ask for help once they realize they have a drinking problem. However, the ego also uses **defense mechanisms,** which are unconscious tactics that protect against anxiety and guilt by either preventing threatening material from surfacing or disguising it when it does (Coifman et al., 2007; Cramer, 2009; Cramer & Jones, 2007; Rokach, 2008; see Table 11.1).

TABLE 11.1   Ego Defense Mechanisms

According to Freud, defense mechanisms prevent anxiety or guilt in the short run, but they sap energy. Further, using them to avoid dealing with the source of problems can make those problems worse in the long run. Try listing some incidents in which you or someone you know might have used each of the defenses described here. What questions would a critical thinker ask to determine whether these behaviors were unconscious defense mechanisms or actions motivated by conscious intentions?   **LEARN by DOING**

Defense Mechanism	Description
Repression	Unconsciously pushing threatening memories, urges, or ideas from conscious awareness: a person may experience loss of memory of unpleasant events.
Rationalization	Attempting to make actions or mistakes seem reasonable: the reasons or excuses given (e.g., "I spank my children because it is good for them") sound rational, but they are not the real reasons for the behavior.
Projection	Unconsciously attributing one's own unacceptable thoughts or impulses to another person: instead of recognizing that "I hate him," a person may feel that "He hates me."
Reaction formation	Defending against unacceptable impulses by acting opposite to them: sexual interest in a married co-worker might appear as strong dislike instead.
Sublimation	Converting unacceptable impulses into socially acceptable actions and perhaps symbolically expressing them: sexual or aggressive desires may appear as artistic creativity or devotion to athletic excellence.
Displacement	Deflecting an impulse from its original target to a less threatening one: anger at one's boss may be expressed through hostility toward a clerk, a family member, or even a pet.
Denial	Simply discounting the existence of threatening impulses: a person may vehemently deny ever having had even the slightest degree of physical attraction to a person of the same sex.
Compensation	Striving to make up for unconscious impulses or fears: a business executive's extreme competitiveness might be aimed at compensating for unconscious feelings of inferiority.

Which of Freud's ego defense mechanisms is operating here? (Check the answer at the bottom of page 428).   **LEARN by DOING**

defense mechanisms Unconscious tactics that either prevent threatening material from surfacing or disguise it when it does.

psychosexual development Periods of personality development in which, according to Freud, internal and external conflicts focus on particular issues.

oral stage The first of Freud's psychosexual stages, in which the mouth is the center of pleasure.

Stages of Personality Development

Freud proposed that during childhood, personality evolves through several stages of **psychosexual development.** Failure to resolve the conflicts that appear at any of these stages can leave a person *fixated*—that is, unconsciously preoccupied with the area of pleasure associated with that stage. Freud believed that the stage at which a person became fixated in childhood can be seen in the person's adult personality characteristics.

The Oral Stage In Freud's theory, a child's first year or so is called the **oral stage** because the mouth—which infants use to eat and to explore everything from toys to their own hands and feet—is the center of pleasure during this period. Personality problems arise, said Freud, when oral needs are either neglected or overindulged. For example, early or late weaning from breastfeeding or bottle feeding may leave a child fixated at the

© Big Cheese Photo RF/Jupiterimages

The Oral Stage

According to Freud, personality develops in a series of psychosexual stages. At each stage, a different part of the body becomes the primary focus of pleasure. This baby would appear to be in the oral stage.

anal stage The second of Freud's psychosexual stages, in which the focus of pleasure shifts from the mouth to the anus.

phallic stage The third of Freud's psychosexual stages, in which the focus of pleasure shifts to the genital area.

Oedipal complex The notion that young boys' impulses involve sexual feelings for the mother and the desire to eliminate the father.

Electra complex The notion that young girls develop an attachment to the father and compete with the mother for the father's attention.

latency period The fourth of Freud's psychosexual stages, in which sexual impulses become dormant and the child focuses on education and other matters.

genital stage The fifth and last of Freud's psychosexual stages, when sexual impulses reappear at the conscious level during adolescence.

oral stage. The resulting adult characteristics may range from overeating or childlike dependence (late weaning) to the use of "biting" sarcasm (early weaning).

The Anal Stage   The **anal stage** occurs during the second year, when the child's ego develops to cope with parental demands for socially appropriate behavior. For example, in most Western cultures, toilet training clashes with the child's freedom to have bowel movements at will. Freud said that if toilet training is too harsh or begins too early, it can produce an anal fixation that leads, in adulthood, to stinginess or excessive neatness (symbolically withholding feces). If toilet training is too late or too lax, however, the result could be a kind of anal fixation that is reflected in adults who are disorganized or impulsive (symbolically expelling feces).

The Phallic Stage   According to Freud, between the ages of three and five the focus of pleasure shifts to the genital area. Because he emphasized the psychosexual development of boys, Freud called this period the **phallic stage** (*phallus* is another word for penis). It is during this stage, he claimed, that the boy experiences sexual feelings for his mother and a desire to eliminate, or even kill, his father, with whom the boy competes for the mother's affection. Freud called this set of impulses the **Oedipal complex** because it reminded him of the plot of the classical Greek play *Oedipus Rex.* (In the play, Oedipus unknowingly kills his father and marries his mother.) The boy's fantasies create so much fear, however, that the ego represses his incestuous desires and leads him to "identify" with his father and try to be like him. In the process, the child's superego begins to develop.

According to Freud, a girl begins the phallic stage with a strong attachment to her mother. However, when she realizes that boys have penises and girls don't, she supposedly develops *penis envy* and transfers her love to the father. (This sequence has been called the **Electra complex** because it echoes the plot of *Electra,* another classical Greek play, but Freud never used this term.) To avoid her mother's disapproval, the girl identifies with and imitates her, thus forming the basis for her own superego.

Freud believed that unresolved conflicts during the phallic stage create a fixation that is reflected in many kinds of adult problems. These problems can include difficulties with authority figures and an inability to maintain a stable love relationship.

The Latency Period   As the phallic stage draws to a close and its conflicts are coped with by the ego, there is an interval of psychological peace. During this **latency period,** which lasts through childhood, sexual impulses stay in the background as the youngster focuses on education, same-sex peer play, and the development of social skills.

The Genital Stage   During adolescence, when sexual impulses reappear at the conscious level, the genitals again become the focus of pleasure. Thus begins what Freud called the **genital stage,** which lasts for the rest of the person's life. The quality of relationships and the degree of fulfillment experienced during this final stage, he claimed, are influenced by how intrapsychic conflicts were resolved during the earlier stages.

Variations on Freud's Personality Theory

Freud's ideas—especially those concerning infantile sexuality and the Oedipal complex—were (and still are) controversial. Even many of Freud's followers did not entirely agree with him. Some of these followers are known as *neo-Freudian* theorists because they employed many aspects of Freud's theory, but developed their own approaches. Others are known as *ego psychologists* because their theories focus more on the ego than on the id (Hergenhahn & Olson, 2007; Larsen & Buss, 2010).

Neo-Freudian Theorists   Carl Jung (pronounced "YOONG") was the most prominent of Freud's early followers to chart his own theoretical course. In developing his ideas about *analytic psychology,* Jung (1916) argued that people are born with a general life force that (in addition to a sex drive) includes a drive for creativity, for growth-oriented resolution of conflicts, and for the productive blending of basic impulses with real-world demands. Jung did not identify specific stages in personality development. He suggested instead that people gradually develop differing degrees of *introversion* (a tendency to reflect on one's own experiences) or *extraversion* (a tendency to focus on the social world) along with differing tendencies to rely on specific psychological functions, such as thinking or feeling. The combination of these tendencies and functions, said Jung (1933), creates personalities that show distinctive and predictable patterns of behavior.

Alfred Adler, once a loyal follower of psychoanalysis, came to believe that the power behind the development of personality comes not from id impulses but from an innate desire to overcome infantile feelings of helplessness and gain some control over the environment. Other prominent neo-Freudians emphasized social relationships in the development of personality. Some, including Erik Erikson, Erich Fromm, and Harry Stack Sullivan, argued that once biological needs are met, the attempt to meet social needs (to feel protected, secure, and accepted, for example) is the main force that shapes personality. According to these theorists, the strategies that people use to meet social needs, such as dominating other people or being dependent on them, become core features of their personalities.

The first feminist personality theorist, Karen Horney (pronounced "HORN-eye"), challenged Freud's view that women's lack of a penis causes them to envy men and feel inferior to them. Horney (1937) argued that it is men who envy women. Realizing that they cannot bear children, males see their lives as having less meaning and substance than women's. Horney called this condition *womb envy,* and she felt that it led men to belittle women. She believed that when women feel inferior, it is because of cultural factors—such as the personal and political restrictions that men have placed on them—not because of penis envy (Hergenhahn & Olson, 2011; Larsen & Buss, 2005).

Contemporary Psychodynamic Theories

Today, some of the most influential psychodynamic approaches to personality focus on *object relations*—that is, on how early relationships, particularly with parents, affect how people perceive and relate to other people later in life (Cervone & Pervin, 2010). According to object relations theorists, early relationships between infants and their love objects (usually the mother and other primary caregivers) are vital influences on the development of personality (Greenberg & Mitchell, 1983; Klein, 1975; Kohut, 1984; Sohlberg & Jansson, 2002). These relationships, they say, shape our thoughts and feelings about social relationships in later life (Westen et al., 2008).

A close cousin of object relations theory is called *attachment theory* because it focuses specifically on the early attachment process that we describe in the chapter on human development. Ideally, infants form a secure bond, or attachment, to their mothers, gradually tolerate separation from this "attachment object," and eventually develop the ability to relate to others as independent, secure individuals (Ainsworth & Bowlby, 1991). Attachment theorists have studied how variations in the nature of this early bond are related to differences in people's personalities, self-images, identities, security, and social relationships in adolescence, adulthood, and even old age (Mattanah, Hancock, & Brand, 2004; Oliver, Wright, & Kendall, 2011; Shaver & Mikulincer, 2011; Simpson, Collins, & Salvatore, in press; Simpson, Rholes, & Winterheld, 2010). One study, for example, found that insecure attachment during infancy was associated with less happy romantic relationships later on (Tomlinson et al., 2010). Others have found that people who had had insecure attachments showed much stronger physiological reactions to interpersonal conflicts than did people whose attachments had been secure (Powers et al., 2006), and that people with insecure early attachments were less likely than those with secure attachments to be helpful when encountering a person in distress (Mikulincer & Shaver, 2005). Further evidence along these lines comes from a long-term study of children diagnosed with severe heart disease. The children whose mothers had

---

The defense mechanism illustrated in the cartoon on page 426 is displacement.

not been securely attached to their own mothers tended to show greater evidence of anxiety and other emotional difficulties in the years following the diagnosis than did those whose mothers had been more securely attached (Berant, Mikulincer, & Shaver, 2008). In short, attachment theorists suggest that people who miss the opportunity to become securely attached may suffer significant disturbances in their later relationships (Shaver & Mikulincer, 2011), including in relationships with their own children.

Evaluating the Psychodynamic Approach

Freud's personality theory is probably the most comprehensive and influential psychological theory ever proposed. His ideas have shaped a wide range of psychotherapy techniques (see the chapter on treatment of psychological disorders) and stimulated the development of several personality assessments, including the projective personality measures described later in this chapter. Research on cognitive processes supports some of Freud's ideas. For example, people do employ several of the defense mechanisms Freud described (Shahar et al., 2010), although these may not always operate at an unconscious level. There's also evidence that our thoughts and actions can be influenced by events and experiences that we don't recall (Bargh & Morsella, 2010; Dijksterhuis et al., 2008; Kihlstrom, 2008) and possibly by emotions we don't consciously experience (Williams et al., 2009). Some researchers believe that unconscious processes can also affect our health (Goldenberg et al., 2008; Krieger et al., 2010).

However, Freud's theories have several weaknesses. For one thing, his conclusions about personality are based almost entirely on case studies of a few individuals. As discussed in the introductory chapter, conclusions drawn from case studies may not apply to people in general. Freud's sample of cases was certainly not representative of people in general. Most of his patients were upper-class Viennese women who not only had psychological problems but were raised in a society that considered the discussion of sex to be uncivilized. Second, Freud's theory reflected Western European and North American cultural values, which may or may not be helpful in understanding people in other cultures (Schultz & Schultz, 2009). For example, the concepts of ego and self that are so central to Freud's personality theory are based on the self-oriented values of individualist cultures. These values may be less central to personality development in collectivist cultures, such as those of Asia and South America (Morling & Kitayama, 2008).

Freud's conclusions may have been distorted by other biases as well. Some Freud scholars believe he might have (perhaps unconsciously) modified reports of what happened during therapy to better fit his theory (Esterson, 2001; Schultz & Schultz, 2009). He may also have asked leading questions that influenced patients to "recall" events from their childhoods that never happened (Carducci, 2009). Today, as described in the memory chapter, there are similar concerns that some patients who recover allegedly repressed memories about childhood sexual abuse may actually be reporting false memories implanted by their therapists (Laney & Loftus, 2010).

Freud's focus on male psychosexual development and his notion that females envy male anatomy have also been attacked. In the tradition of Horney, some contemporary neo-Freudians have proposed theories that focus specifically on the psychosexual development of women (Sayers, 1991; Yonke & Barnett, 2001).

Finally, as judged by modern standards, Freud's theory is not very scientific. His definitions of id, ego, unconscious conflict, and other concepts lack the precision required for scientific measurement and testing (Carver & Scheier, 2008). Further, his belief that unconscious desires drive most human behavior ignores evidence showing that much of that behavior goes beyond impulse gratification. For example, the conscious drive to attain personal, social, and spiritual goals is an important determinant of behavior, as is learning from others.

Some of the weaknesses in Freudian theory have been addressed by those who seek to subject psychodynamic principles and theories to empirical tests (e.g., Betan et al., 2005; Roffman & Gerber, 2008; Wegner, Wenzlaff, & Kozak, 2004; Westen, 2005), but the psychodynamic approach to personality remains less popular today than it was in past decades (Feist & Feist, 2009; Friedman & Schustack, 2009).

The Trait Approach

What personality traits are most basic?

You could probably describe the personality of someone you know well with just a few statements. For example, you might say,

He's a really caring person, and very outgoing. He's generous with his time, and he works very hard at everything he does. Yet sometimes I think he also lacks self-confidence. He always gives in to other people's demands because he wants to be accepted by them.

In other words, most people describe others by referring to the kind of people they are ("outgoing"); to the thoughts, feelings, and actions that are most typical of them ("caring," "lacks self-confidence"); or to their needs ("wants to be accepted"). Together, these statements describe **personality traits**—the tendencies that help direct how a person usually thinks and behaves (Cervone & Pervin, 2010).

The trait approach to personality makes three main assumptions:

1. Personality traits are relatively stable, and therefore predictable, over time. So a gentle person tends to stay that way day after day, year after year (Cervone & Pervin, 2010).
2. Personality traits are relatively stable across situations, and they can explain why people act in predictable ways in many different situations. A person who is competitive at work will probably also be competitive on the tennis court or at a party (Roberts, Woods, & Caspi, 2008).
3. People differ in how much of a particular personality trait they possess; no two people are exactly alike on all traits. The result is an endless variety of unique personalities.

In short, psychologists who take the **trait approach** see personality as a combination of stable internal characteristics that people display consistently over time and across situations (Pervin, Cervone, & John, 2005). Trait theorists seek to measure the relative strength of the many personality characteristics that they believe are present in everyone (see Figure 11.2).

Early Trait Theories

Today's trait theories of personality are largely based on the work of Gordon Allport, Raymond Cattell, and Hans Eysenck. Allport spent 30 years searching for the traits that combine to form personality. When he looked at the nearly 18,000 dictionary terms that can be used to describe human behavior (Allport & Odbert, 1936; John, Naumann, & Soto, 2008), he noticed clusters of terms that refer to the same thing. For example, *hostile, nasty,* and *mean* all convey a similar meaning. To better understand this clustering, think of a close relative and jot down all the personality traits that describe this person. If you are like most people, you were able to capture your relative's personality using only a few trait labels. Allport believed that the set of labels that describe a particular person reflects that person's *central traits*—those that are usually obvious to others and that organize and control behavior in many different situations. Central traits are roughly equivalent to the descriptive terms used in letters of recommendation (*reliable* or *distractible,* for example) that are meant to tell what can be expected from a person most of the time (Schultz & Schultz, 2009). Allport also believed that people possess *secondary traits*—those that are more specific to certain situations and control far less behavior. "Dislikes crowds" is an example of a secondary trait.

Allport's research helped lay the foundation for modern research on personality traits. His focus on the uniqueness of each personality made it difficult to draw conclusions about the

Scores for Bob:
Industry: High
Generosity: Moderate
Nervousness: Low
Extraversion: Low
Aggression: Low-Moderate

Scores for Ted:
Industry: High
Generosity: Low
Nervousness: High
Extraversion: High
Aggression: Moderate-High

FIGURE 11.2

Two Personality Profiles

Trait theory describes personality in terms of the strength of particular dimensions, or traits. Here are trait profiles for Bob, a computer engineer, and Ted, a stock trader. Compared with Ted, Bob is about equally industrious, more generous, and less nervous, extraverted, and aggressive. Just for fun, score yourself to indicate how strong you think you are on each of the listed traits. Trait theorists suggest that it should be easy for you to do this, because virtually everyone displays a certain amount of almost any personality characteristic.

LEARN by DOING

Source: From McCrae & John, "An Introduction to the five-factor model and its applications," *Journal of Personality* vol 60 (pp. 175–215). Copyright © 1992 John Wiley and Sons, Inc. Reprinted with permission. *Photos:* (L) © gyn9037/ Shutterstock; (R) © Monkey Business Images/ Shutterstock.

personality traits A set of stable characteristics that people display over time and across situations.

trait approach A perspective on personality that views it as the combination of stable characteristics that people display over time and across situations.

five-factor personality model (Big Five model) A view based on studies using factor analysis that suggests the existence of five basic components of human personality: openness, conscientiousness, extraversion, agreeableness, and neuroticism.

structure of personality in general (Barenbaum & Winter, 2008), but some researchers today continue to employ a modern version of Allport's approach (e.g., Caldwell, Cervone, & Rubin, 2008).

In contrast, British psychologist Raymond Cattell was interested in the personality traits that people share. He used a mathematical technique called *factor analysis* to study which traits are correlated with one another. Factor analysis can reveal, for example, whether people who are moody are also likely to be anxious, rigid, and unsociable. Cattell found sixteen clusters of traits that he believed make up the basic dimensions, or factors, of personality (Cattell, Eber, & Tatsuoka, 1970).

The Five-Factor Personality Model

Building on the work of Allport and Cattell, factor analytic research by many of today's trait theorists suggests that personality is organized around just five basic dimensions (McCrae & Costa, 2004, 2008). The dimensions of this **five-factor (or Big Five) personality model** have been given slightly different labels by different researchers, but the most widely used names are *openness, conscientiousness, extraversion, agreeableness,* and *neuroticism* (see Table 11.2). The fact that some version of the Big Five factors reliably appears in many countries and cultures—including Canada, China, the Czech Republic, Germany, Greece, Finland, India, Japan, Korea, the Philippines, Poland, Turkey, and Zimbabwe (Allik & McCrae, 2004; Ashton et al., 2004; Heine & Buchtel, 2009; McCrae et al., 2004; McCrae & Costa, 2006; Saucier et al., 2005; Yamagata et al., 2006)—provides evidence that these factors may indeed represent the most important components of human personality (De Fruyt et al., 2009; McCrae, Terracciano, & Profiles of Cultures Project, 2005). Researchers using MRI scanning have suggested that a biological basis for each of these factors might someday be found in specific regions of the brain (DeYoung et al., 2010).

Many trait theorists consider the emergence of the five-factor personality model to be a major breakthrough in examining the personalities of all people, regardless of where they live or the nature of their economic, social, and cultural backgrounds (Carver & Scheier, 2004; John, Naumann, & Soto, 2008). The model also allows researchers to precisely describe the similarities and differences in people's personalities and to explore how these factors are related to everything from personality disorders and political

TABLE 11.2 Dimensions of the Five-Factor Personality Model

Here is a list of the adjectives that define the Big Five personality factors. You can more easily remember these factors by noting that the first letters of their names spell the word *ocean*.

Dimension	Defining Descriptors
Openness	Artistic, curious, imaginative, insightful, original, wide interests, unusual thought processes, intellectual interests
Conscientiousness	Efficient, organized, planful, reliable, thorough, dependable, ethical, productive
Extraversion	Active, assertive, energetic, outgoing, talkative, gesturally expressive, gregarious
Agreeableness	Appreciative, forgiving, generous, kind, trusting, noncritical, warm, compassionate, considerate, straightforward
Neuroticism	Anxious, self-pitying, tense, emotionally unstable, impulsive, vulnerable, touchy, prone to worry

Source: Adapted from McCrae & John (1992).

© uwesSERENGETI/Alamy

Animal Personalities

The idea that personality can be described in terms of five main dimensions seems to hold for some animals as well as humans. The five animal dimensions differ from (but are still related to) human traits. For example, hyenas differ among themselves in terms of dominance, excitability, agreeableness (toward people), sociability (toward each other), and curiosity. Some of these same traits have been observed in a wide variety of other species, including sheep, langurs, orangutans, chipmunks, and chimpanzees (Bell & Sih, 2007; King, Weiss, & Farmer, 2005; Konecná et al., 2008; Martin & Réale, 2008; Michelena et al., 2009; Weinstein, Capitanio, & Gosling, 2008; Weiss, King, & Perkins, 2006). Dog and cat lovers often report such traits in their pets, too (Gosling, Kwan, & John, 2003; Lee, Ryan, & Kreiner, 2007; Ley, Bennett, & Coleman, 2009). Researchers have even begun to develop personality tests for nonhuman primates, dogs, and other animals (Freeman, Gosling, & Schapiro, in press; Gosling & Jones, 2012).

LINKAGES

Why do some people take more risks than others?
(a link to Motivation and Emotion)

beliefs to substance abuse, academic and occupational performance, happiness, physical well-being, driving skill, and even voting behavior (e.g., Adrian et al., 2011; Boyce & Wood, 2011; Boyce et al., 2010; Brummett et al., 2006; Chiaburu et al., 2011; Cuperman & Ickes, 2009; Diener, 2000; Friedman, Kern, & Reynolds, 2010; Hughes et al., 2012; Lynam & Widiger, 2001; Noftle & Robins, 2007; Noftle & Shaver, 2006; Poropat, 2009; Roberts & Bogg, 2004; Roberts et al., 2009; Van Hiel & Merviedle, 2004; Vianello, Robusto, & Anselmi, 2010; Vecchione et al., 2011).

Biological Trait Theories

While some personality theorists study the basic dimensions of personality, others explore the biological factors that shape and influence those dimensions (DeYoung et al., 2010; Terracciano et al., 2010).

Eysenck's Biological Trait Theory   The biological basis for personality was emphasized in the work of British psychologist Hans Eysenck (pronounced "EYE-sink"). Like other trait theorists who helped lay the groundwork for the five-factor personality model, Eysenck used factor analysis to study personality. His research led him to focus on two main personality dimensions known as *introversion-extraversion* and *emotionality-stability* (Eysenck, 1990a, 1990b; Deary & Bedford, 2011):

1. ***Introversion-extraversion.*** Extraverts are sociable and outgoing, enjoy parties and other social activities, take risks, and love excitement and change. Introverts tend to be quiet, thoughtful, and reserved, enjoying solitary pursuits and avoiding excitement and social involvement.
2. ***Emotionality-stability*** (also often called ***neuroticism***). At one extreme of this dimension are people who exhibit such characteristics as moodiness, restlessness, worry, anxiety, and other negative emotions. People at the opposite end are calm, even-tempered, relaxed, and emotionally stable.

According to Eysenck, personality can be described in terms of where a person falls along these two dimensions. For example, an introverted but stable person is likely to be controlled and reliable. An introverted but emotional person is likely to be rigid and anxious (see Figure 11.3). Eysenck's personality dimensions do seem to be related to particular behaviors. For example, college students' levels of neuroticism, extraversion, and psychoticism (a third dimension described by Eysenck) have been shown to be related to the students' passion for Internet use and how much they reveal about themselves online (Tosun & Lajunen, 2009, 2010)

Eysenck argued that the variations in personality characteristics that we see among individuals can be traced to inherited differences in their nervous systems, especially in their brains. These biological differences, he said, create differences in people's typical levels of physiological arousal and in their sensitivity to stress and other environmental stimulation. For example, people who inherit a nervous system that normally operates below some ideal level of arousal will always be on the lookout for excitement, change, and social contact in order to increase their arousal. As a result, they will be *extraverted*. In contrast, people whose nervous system is normally "overaroused" will tend to avoid excitement, change, and social contact in order to reduce arousal to their ideal level. In short, they will be *introverted*. What about the emotionality-stability dimension? Eysenck said that people who fall toward the stability side have nervous systems that are relatively insensitive to stress; those who are more emotional have nervous systems that react more strongly to stress.

Gray's Reinforcement Sensitivity Theory   Jeffrey Gray, another British psychologist, agrees with Eysenck about the two basic dimensions of personality but offers a different explanation of the biological factors underlying them (Corr, 2002; DeYoung et al., 2010; Gray, 1991; Gray & McNaughton, 2002). According to Gray's *reinforcement sensitivity theory,* differences among people along the dimensions of introversion-extraversion and

FIGURE 11.3

Eysenck's Personality Dimensions

According to Eysenck, varying degrees of emotionality-stability and introversion-extraversion combine to produce predictable trait patterns. The traits appearing in the four sections created by crossing these two personality dimensions roughly define the four basic temperaments identified centuries ago by the ancient Greek physician Hippocrates: melancholic (sad), choleric (hot-tempered), phlegmatic (slow and lethargic), and sanguine (optimistic). Which section of the figure do you think best describes your personality traits? How about those of a friend or a relative? Did you find it any easier to place other people's personalities in a particular section than it was to place your own personality? If so, why do you think that might be?

LEARN by DOING

Source: From H.J. Eysenck and S. Rachman, *The Causes and Cures of Neurosis: An Introduction to Modern Behavior Therapy Based on Learning Theory and the Principle of Conditioning.* Copyright © 1965 by Edits. Reprinted with permission.

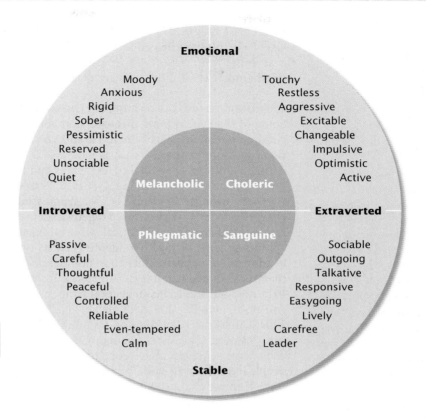

emotionality-stability originate in the brain regions that influence how sensitive people are to different kinds of events. These regions are called the behavioral approach system and the flight or freeze system (Pickering & Gray, 1999). The *behavioral approach system,* or *BAS,* affects people's sensitivity to rewards and their motivation to seek these rewards. The BAS has been called a "go" system because it is responsible for how impulsive or uninhibited a person is. The *flight or freeze system,* or *FFS,* affects how sensitive people are to punishment (Smillie, Pickering, & Jackson, 2006). The FFS is a "stop" system that is responsible for how fearful or inhibited a person is (Bijttebier et al., 2009). Gray sees extraverts as having a sensitive reward system (BAS) and an insensitive punishment system (FFS). Introverts are just the opposite: they are relatively insensitive to rewards but highly sensitive to punishment. Emotionally unstable people are much more sensitive to both rewards and punishments than are those who are emotionally stable.

Gray's theory has its critics (e.g., Jackson, 2003; Matthews, 2008), but it is now more widely accepted than Eysenck's theory—primarily because it is supported by data from other researchers (e.g., Revelle, 2008) and because it is consistent with what neuroscientists have learned about brain structures and neurotransmitters and how they operate (Buckholtz et al., 2008; Joseph et al., 2009; Read et al., 2010; Reuter et al., 2006).

THINKING CRITICALLY

Are Personality Traits Inherited?

Gray's reinforcement sensitivity theory is one of several biologically oriented explanations of the origins of personality traits (e.g., Depue, 2007). A related approach explores the role of genetics in these traits (e.g., Loehlin, 2011; Terracciano et al., 2010). For example, consider a pair of identical twins who had been separated at five weeks of age and did not meet again for 39 years. Both men drove Chevrolets, chain-smoked the same brand of cigarettes, had divorced a woman named Linda, were remarried to a woman named Betty, had sons named James Allan, had dogs named Toy, enjoyed similar hobbies, and had served as sheriff's deputies (Tellegen et al., 1988).

What am I being asked to believe or accept?

Cases like this have helped focus the attention of behavioral geneticists on the possibility that some core aspects of personality might be partly or even largely inherited (Ekehammar et al., 2010; Kreuger & Johnson, 2008; Yamagata et al. 2006).

Is evidence available to support the claim?

Some of the evidence for this assertion comes from the many familiar cases in which children seem to "have" their parents' or grandparents' bad temper, generosity, or shyness. More systematic studies have also found moderate but significant correlations between children's personality test scores and those of their parents and siblings (Davis, Luce, & Kraus, 1994; DeYoung, Quilty, & Peterson, 2007; Loehlin et al., 1998).

Even stronger evidence comes from studies conducted around the world that compared identical twins raised together, identical twins raised apart, nonidentical twins raised together, and nonidentical twins raised apart (Larsen & Buss, 2010). Whether they are raised apart or together, identical twins (who have exactly the same genes) tend to be more alike in personality than nonidentical twins (whose genes are no more similar than those of other siblings). This research also shows that identical twins are more alike than nonidentical twins in general temperament, such as how active, sociable, anxious, and emotional they are (Borkenau et al., 2002, 2006; Pickering & Gray, 1999; Wolf et al., 2004; Yamagata et al., 2006), and where they fall on various other personality dimensions (e.g., Johnson et al., 2009; Riemann & Kandler, 2010). On the basis of such twin studies, behavioral geneticists have concluded that about 50 percent of the differences among people in terms of personality traits are due to genetic factors (Caspi, Roberts, & Shiner, 2005; Kreuger et al., 2008).

Can that evidence be interpreted another way?

Family resemblances in personality could reflect inheritance or social influence. So an obvious alternative interpretation of this evidence might be that family similarities come not from common genes but from a common environment (Rentfrow, 2010). Children learn many rules, skills, and behaviors by watching parents, siblings, and others; perhaps they learn their personalities as well (Funder, 2007). And the fact that nontwin siblings are less alike than twins may well result from what is called a *nonshared environment* (Plomin, 2004). Nonshared factors include, for example, a child's place in the family birth order, differences in the way parents treat each of their children, and accidents, illnesses, or events that alter a particular child's life or health (Loehlin, 2010). Nontwins are more likely than twins, especially identical twins, to be affected by these nonshared environmental factors.

What evidence would help to evaluate the alternatives?

One way to evaluate the idea that personality is inherited would be to locate genes that are associated with certain personality characteristics (Ebstein, 2006). Genetic differences have already been tentatively associated with certain behavior disorders, but most behavioral genetics researchers doubt that there are direct links between particular genes and particular personality traits (Caspi, Roberts, & Shiner, 2005; Kreuger & Johnson, 2008).

Another way to evaluate the role of genes in personality is to study people in infancy, before the environment has had a chance to exert its influence. If the environment were entirely responsible for personality, newborns should be essentially alike. However, as discussed in the chapter on human development, infants show immediate differences in activity level, sensitivity to the environment, the tendency to cry, and interest in new stimuli (Rothbart & Derryberry, 2002). These differences in *temperament* suggest biological and perhaps genetic influences.

To evaluate the relative contributions of nature and nurture beyond infancy, psychologists have examined the personality characteristics of adopted children. If adopted children are more like their biological than their adoptive parents, this suggests the influence of heredity in personality. If they are more like their adoptive families, a strong role for environmental factors in personality is suggested. In actuality, adopted children's personalities tend to resemble the personalities of their biological parents and

Family Resemblance
Do children inherit personality traits in the same direct way as they inherit facial features, coloration, and other physical characteristics? Research in behavioral genetics suggests that personality is the joint product of genetically influenced behavioral tendencies and the environmental conditions each child encounters.

siblings more closely than they do those of the families in which they are raised (Kreuger & Johnson, 2008).

Further research will determine more clearly which aspects of the environment are most important in shaping personality (Turkheimer & Waldron, 2000). So far, the evidence suggests that personality is not influenced very strongly by elements of the shared environment—such as socioeconomic status—that equally affect all children in the same family. However, nonshared environmental influences, at home and elsewhere, appear to be very important in personality development (Kendler & Neale, 2009). We need to know more about the exact impact on personality development of nonshared environmental factors that may be different for twins and nontwin siblings.

What conclusions are most reasonable?

Even those researchers, such as Robert Plomin, who support genetic theories of personality caution that we should not replace "simple-minded environmentalism" with the equally incorrect view that personality is almost completely biologically determined (Loehlin, 2010). It is pointless to talk about heredity *versus* environment as causes of personality, because nature and nurture always intertwine to exert joint and simultaneous influences (Kreuger & Johnson, 2008). For example, we know that genetic factors affect the environment in which people live (e.g., their families) and how they react to that environment, but as discussed in the chapter on introducing psychology, research in epigenetics has shown that environmental factors can influence which of a person's genes are activated (or "expressed") and how much those genes affect the person's behavior (Champagne & Mashoodh, 2009; Kreuger & Johnson, 2008).

With this caution in mind, we would be well advised to draw only tentative conclusions about the origins of personality differences. The evidence available so far suggests that genetic influences do appear to contribute significantly to the differences among people in many personality traits (DeYoung et al., 2007; Vernon et al., 2008). As noted earlier, however, there is no evidence of a specific gene for any specific personality trait (Kreuger & Johnson, 2008). The genetic contribution to personality most likely comes as genes influence people's nervous systems and general predispositions toward certain temperaments (Alliey-Rodriquez et al., 2011; Blom et al., 2011; Ebstein, 2006). Temperamental factors (e.g., emotionality and sociability) then interact with environmental factors, such as family experiences, to produce specific features of personality (Caspi, Roberts, & Shiner, 2005). For example, a child's ability to control or regulate emotions appears to be strongly determined by heredity. Children who are less able to regulate their emotions might play less with other children, withdraw more from social interactions, and thereby fail to learn important social skills (Spinrad et al., 2006). These experiences and tendencies, in turn, might foster the self-consciousness and shyness seen in introverted personalities. Genes also appear to influence people's emotional responses to specific events, such as how they respond to socioeconomic adversity or other negative environmental conditions (Cole et al., 2011).

Notice, though, that genetic predispositions toward particular personality characteristics may or may not be expressed in behavior, depending on whether the environment supports or stifles them. Changes in genetically predisposed traits are not only possible but may actually be quite common as children grow (Cacioppo et al., 2000). So even though there is a strong genetic basis for shyness, many children learn to overcome this tendency and become quite outgoing (Leary, 2001). In summary, rather than inheriting specific traits, people appear to inherit the behavioral and emotional raw materials out of which their personalities are shaped by the world.   ●●●●

Evaluating the Trait Approach

The trait approach, and especially the five-factor personality model, tends to dominate contemporary research in personality. Yet there are several problems and weaknesses associated with this approach.

Trait theories seem better at describing people than at understanding them. It is easy to say, for example, that Marilyn is nasty because she has a strong hostility trait; but other factors, such as the way people treat her, could also be responsible. In other words, trait theories say a lot about how people behave, but they don't always explain why (Mischel, 2004a, 2004b). Nor do trait theories say much about how traits are related to the thoughts and feelings that precede, accompany, and follow behavior. Do introverts and extraverts decide to act as they do? Can they behave otherwise? And how do they feel about their actions and experiences? Some personality psychologists are linking their research with that of cognitive psychologists in an effort to better understand how thoughts and emotions influence, and are influenced by, personality traits (Jackson et al., 2012; Shoda & LeeTiernan, 2002). And as noted earlier, other psychologists are studying the role played by genes, brain structures, and neurotransmitters in the individual differences we see among people's personality traits (e.g., Goldberg & Weinberger, 2009; Loehlin & Martin, 2011).

The trait approach has also been criticized for offering a short list of traits that provides, at best, a fixed and rather shallow description of personality that fails to capture how traits combine to form a complex and dynamic individual (Boag, 2011; Funder, 2007). There are questions, too, about whether there really are exactly five core dimensions of personality. Some evidence suggests, for example, that there might be a sixth dimension known as *honesty and humility* (Lee, Ogunfowora, & Ashton, 2005). Whatever the number turns out to be, some personality researchers doubt that these dimensions are exactly the same in all cultures (De Raad et al., 2010; Heine & Buchtel, 2009). Finally, even if some version of the five-factor personality model proves to be correct and universal, its factors are not all-powerful. Situations, too, affect behavior. For instance, eating sweet-tasting food can (at least temporarily) lead people to describe themselves as more agreeable and helpful to others (Meier et al., 2011). And people high in extraversion are not always sociable. Whether they behave sociably depends, in part, on where they are and who else is present.

In fairness, early trait theorists such as Allport acknowledged the importance of situations in influencing behavior, but it is only recently that consideration of interactions between people and situations has become an important part of trait-based approaches to personality. This change is largely the result of research conducted by psychologists who have taken a social-cognitive approach to personality, which we describe next.

The Social-Cognitive Approach

Do we learn our personalities?

To social-cognitive researchers, psychodynamic theories place too much emphasis on unconscious forces in personality and trait theories presume more consistency in people's behavior than there really is. In contrast, researchers who take a **social-cognitive approach** see personality as the full set of behaviors that people have acquired through *learning* and that they then display in particular situations (Mischel & Shoda, 2008). Some aspects of this approach reflect the view of traditional behaviorists, namely that all behavior is learned through classical and operant conditioning (see the chapter on learning). However, the social-cognitive approach expands that view by emphasizing (1) the role played by *learned patterns of thinking* in guiding behavior; and (2) the fact that personality is learned in social situations as people observe and interact with other people (Bandura & Walters, 1963; Cervone & Pervin, 2010). The social-cognitive approach is sometimes called the *social-learning approach* because it defines personality as the sum of the behaviors and cognitive habits that develop as people learn through experience in the social world. Social-cognitive theorists are interested in how our thinking affects our behavior as well as how our behavior and its consequences affect our thinking and our future actions (Mischel & Shoda, 2008; Shoda & Mischel, 2006).

Prominent Social-Cognitive Theories

The most prominent social-cognitive theories were developed by Julian Rotter, Albert Bandura, and Walter Mischel.

Rotter's Expectancy Theory   Julian Rotter (1982) argued that learning creates cognitions known as *expectancies* and that these expectancies guide behavior. According to Rotter,

social-cognitive approach The view that personality reflects learned patterns of thinking and behavior.

a person's decision to engage in a behavior is determined by (1) what the person expects to happen following the behavior; and (2) the value the person places on the outcome. For example, people spend a lot of money on new clothes for job interviews because past learning leads them to expect that doing so will help get them the job and they place a high value on having the job. To Rotter, then, behavior is shaped by the positive or negative consequences it brings and by the expectancy that a particular behavior will be rewarded or punished (Mischel, Shoda, & Smith, 2004).

Personality researchers influenced by Rotter have suggested that in addition to learning expectancies about particular behaviors in particular situations, we also learn more general expectancies, especially about how life's rewards and punishments are controlled (e.g., Phares, 1976). Some people (called *internals*) come to expect that events are controlled mainly by their own efforts. These people assume, for example, that what they achieve and the rewards they receive are determined by what they themselves do. Others (*externals*) tend to expect events to be controlled by external forces over which they have no control. So when externals succeed, they tend to believe that their success was based on chance or luck.

Research on differences in generalized expectancies does show that they are correlated with differences in behavior. For example, when threatened by a hurricane or other natural disaster, internals—in accordance with their belief that they can control what happens to them—are more likely than externals to buy bottled water and make other preparations (Sattler, Kaiser, & Hittner, 2000). Internals tend to work harder than externals at staying physically healthy and as a result may be healthier (Stürmer, Hasselbach, & Amelang, 2006). For instance, children with an internal control orientation are less likely than externals to become obese in later life (Gale, Batty, & Deary, 2008). Internals are less likely to drink alcohol or if they do drink, are less likely to drive while intoxicated (Cavaiola & Desordi, 2000). They are also more careful with money and better than externals at bargaining or negotiating (Lim, Teo, & Loo, 2003; Shalvi, Simone, & Ritov, 2010). As college students, internals tend to be better informed about their courses and about what they need to do to get a high grade than externals are. This may help to account for why internals tend to get better grades and graduate sooner (Dollinger, 2000; Hall, Smith, & Chia, 2008).

Bandura and Reciprocal Determinism   In his social-cognitive theory, Albert Bandura (1999, 2011) sees personality as shaped by the ways that thoughts, behavior, and the environment interact and influence one another. He points out that whether people learn through direct experience with rewards and punishments or through watching what happens to others, their behavior creates changes in their environment. Observing these changes, in turn, affects how they think, which then affects their behavior, and so on in a constant web of mutual influence that Bandura calls *reciprocal determinism* (see Figure 11.4).

An especially important cognitive element in this system of mutual influence is perceived **self-efficacy**, the learned expectation of success. Bandura says that what we do and what we try to do are largely controlled by our perceptions or beliefs about our chances of success at a particular task or problem. People with a high degree of perceived self-efficacy believe that they can successfully perform a behavior regardless of past failures or current obstacles. So the higher your perceived self-efficacy is in a particular situation or task, the greater your actual accomplishments in that situation or task are likely to be (Greven et al., 2009; Joët, Usher, & Bressoux, 2011; Richardson, Abraham, & Bond, 2012; Zimmerman & Schunk, 2003). For example, research in 26 countries found that students' self-efficacy in mathematics was significantly related to their mathematical achievement (Williams & Williams, 2010). (Perhaps you recall the classic children's story *The Little Engine That Could*: Trying to get up a steep hill, the scared little engine starts by saying "I think I can, I think I can" and ends up saying "I know I can, I know I can." And it did.)

Self-efficacy interacts with expectancies about the outcome of behavior in general and the result of this interplay helps shape a person's psychological well-being (Srimathi & Kiran, 2011). So if a person has low self-efficacy and believes that people

self-efficacy According to Bandura, the learned expectation of success in given situations.

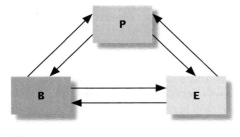

■ B = Behavior

■ E = The external environment

■ P = Personal factors, such as thoughts, feelings, and biological events

FIGURE 11.4
Reciprocal Determinism
Bandura's notion of reciprocal determinism suggests that thoughts, behavior, and the environment are constantly affecting each other. For example, a person's hostile thoughts might lead to hostile behavior, which generates even more hostile thoughts. At the same time, the hostile behavior offends others, thus creating a threatening environment that causes the person to think and act in even more negative ways. As increasingly negative thoughts alter the person's perceptions of the environment, that environment seems to be more threatening than ever (e.g., Bushman et al., 2005).

Source: From A. Bandura, "The Assessment and Predictive Generality of Self-Precepts of Efficacy," *Journal of Behavior Therapy and Experimental Psychiatry* vol 13 (pp. 195–199). Copyright © 1982 Elsevier. Reprinted with permission.

have little effect on the world, apathy may result. But if a person with low self-efficacy believes that *other* people are enjoying the benefits of their efforts, the result may be self-criticism and depression.

Mischel's Cognitive/Affective Theory   Social-cognitive theorists argue that learned beliefs, feelings, and expectancies characterize each individual and make that individual different from other people. Walter Mischel calls these characteristics *cognitive person variables.* He believes that they outline the dimensions along which individuals differ (Mischel, 2009; Mischel & Shoda, 2008).

According to Mischel, the most important cognitive person variables are:

1. *Encodings:* the person's beliefs about the environment and other people
2. *Expectancies:* including self-efficacy and what results the person expects will follow from various behaviors
3. *Affects:* feelings and emotions
4. *Goals and values:* the things a person believes in and wants to achieve
5. *Competencies and self-regulatory plans:* the things the person can do and the ability to thoughtfully plan behaviors (Shoda & Mischel, 2006).

To predict how a person might behave in a particular situation, says Mischel, we need to know about these cognitive person variables and about the features of that situation. In short, the person and the situation interact to produce behavior. Mischel's ideas have been called an "if-then" theory because he proposes that *if* people encounter a particular situation, *then* they will engage in the characteristic behaviors (called *behavioral signatures*) that they typically show in this situation (Smith et al., 2009).

Mischel was once highly critical of the trait approach to personality, but now he sees his own theory as generally consistent with it. In fact, the concept of behavioral signatures is quite similar to the concept of traits. However, Mischel still argues that trait theorists underestimate the power of situations to alter behavior and do not pay enough attention to the cognitive and emotional processes that underlie people's overt actions. Despite their remaining differences, most advocates of the trait and social-cognitive approaches are now focusing on the similarities between their views (Cervone, 2005; Funder, 2008). This search for similarities has helped clarify the relationship between personal and situational variables and how they affect behavior under various conditions. Many of the conclusions that have emerged are consistent with Bandura's concept of reciprocal determinism:

1. Personal dispositions (which include traits and cognitive person variables) influence behavior only in relevant situations. The trait of anxiousness, for example, may predict anxiety, but mainly in situations in which an anxious person feels threatened.
2. Personal dispositions can lead to behaviors that alter situations that in turn promote other behaviors. For example, a hostile child can trigger aggression in others and thus start a fight.

The Impact of Situations
Like the rest of us, Dwayne "The Rock" Johnson behaves differently in different situations, including when acting in his movies or wrestling, and when not "on stage". Mischel's theory of personality emphasizes that the interactions between particular people and specific situations are vitally important in determining behavior.

© Universal Pictures/Photofest

© Axel Schmidt/AFP/Getty Images

3. People choose to be in situations that are in accord with their personal dispositions. Introverts, for instance, are likely to choose quiet environments, whereas extraverts tend to seek out livelier, more social circumstances (Beck & Clark, 2009).

4. Personal dispositions are more important in some situations than in others. Where many different behaviors would be appropriate—at a picnic, for example—what people do can usually be predicted from their dispositions (extraverts will probably play games and socialize while introverts will probably watch from the sidelines). However, in situations such as a funeral, where fewer options are socially acceptable, personal dispositions will not differentiate one person from another; everyone is likely to be quiet and somber.

Today, social-cognitive theorists are attempting to discover how person variables develop, how they relate to stress and health, and how they interact with situational variables to affect behavior.

Evaluating the Social-Cognitive Approach

The social-cognitive approach to personality is valuable because it blends behavioral learning theories with concepts from cognitive psychology and applies them to such socially important topics as aggression, the effects of mass media on children, and the development of techniques that enhance personal control over behavior. Social-cognitive principles have also been translated into cognitive-behavioral treatment procedures (O'Donohue, Fisher, & Hayes, 2003; see the chapter on treatment of psychological disorders).

The social-cognitive approach has not escaped criticism, however. Psychodynamic theorists point out that social-cognitive theories leave no role for unconscious thoughts and feelings in determining behaviors (e.g., Westen et al., 2008). Some advocates of trait theory complain that social-cognitive theorists have focused more on explaining why traits are unimportant than on why situations are important and argue that they have failed to identify what it is about specific situations that brings out certain behaviors (Funder, 2008). The social-cognitive approach has also been faulted for offering only a set of limited theories that share certain common assumptions about the nature of personality, rather than presenting a general theory of personality (Feist & Feist, 2009). Finally, some critics feel that the social-cognitive approach cannot capture the complexities, richness, and uniqueness that are inherent in human personality (Carver & Scheier, 2004). For these critics, a far more attractive alternative is offered by the humanistic approach to personality.

The Humanistic Psychology Approach

Is everyone basically good?

The **humanistic psychology approach** to personality focuses on mental capabilities that set humans apart: self-awareness, creativity, planning, decision making, and responsibility. Those who adopt the humanistic approach see human behavior as motivated mainly by an innate drive toward growth that prompts each of us to fulfill our own unique potential and thus to achieve an ideal condition known as **self-actualization** (Goldstein, 1939). And like the planted seed whose natural potential is to become a flower, people are seen as naturally inclined toward goodness, creativity, love, and joy. Humanistic psychologists also believe that to explain people's actions, it is more important to understand their view of the world than their instincts, traits, or learning experiences. To humanists, every individual's worldview is a bit different, and it is this unique *phenomenology* (pronounced "feh-nah-men-AHL-oh-gee"), or way of perceiving and interpreting the world, that shapes personality and guides behavior (Kelly, 1980). Because of its emphasis on the importance of looking at people's perceptions, this approach to personality is also sometimes called the *phenomenological approach.*

humanistic psychology approach The view that personality develops in accordance with each person's unique perceptions of the world.

self-actualization The reaching of one's fullest potential; the complete realization of a person's talents, faculties, and abilities.

Prominent Humanistic Theories

The most prominent humanistic theories of personality are those of Carl Rogers and Abraham Maslow.

Rogers's Self Theory   In his extensive writings, Carl Rogers (1961, 1970, 1980) emphasized the **actualizing tendency**, which he described as an innate inclination toward growth and fulfillment that motivates all human behavior (Raskin & Rogers, 2001). To Rogers, personality is the expression of that actualizing tendency as it unfolds in each person's uniquely perceived reality (Allen, 2006; Feist & Feist, 2009).

The centerpiece of Rogers's theory is the *self,* the part of experience that a person identifies as "I" or "me." According to Rogers, those who accurately experience the self— with all its preferences, abilities, fantasies, shortcomings, and desires—are on the road to self-actualization. The progress of those whose experiences of the self become distorted, however, is likely to be slowed or stopped.

Rogers saw personality development beginning early, as children learn to need the approval, or *positive regard,* of others. Evaluations by parents, teachers, and others soon begin to affect children's self-evaluations. When evaluations by others are in agreement with a child's self-evaluations, the child reacts in a way that matches, or is *congruent* with, self-experience. The child not only feels the other person's positive regard but also evaluates the self as "good" for having earned approval. This positive self-experience becomes part of the **self-concept**, which is the way one thinks of oneself. Unfortunately, things may not always go so smoothly. If a pleasurable self-experience is evaluated negatively by others, the child must either do without their positive regard or reevaluate the experience. So a little boy who is teased by his father for playing with dolls might adopt a distorted self-experience—deciding, perhaps, that "I don't like dolls" or that "Feeling good is bad."

In other words, Rogers suggested that personality is shaped partly by the actualizing tendency and partly by other people's evaluations. In this way, people come to like what they are "supposed" to like and to behave as they are "supposed" to behave. This socialization process helps people get along in society, but it often requires that they suppress their self-actualizing tendencies and distort their experiences. Rogers argued that psychological discomfort, anxiety, or mental disorder can result when the feelings people experience or express are *incongruent,* or at odds, with their true feelings.

Incongruence is likely, Rogers said, when parents and teachers lead children to believe that their personal worth depends on displaying the "right" attitudes, behaviors, and values. These **conditions of worth** are created whenever *people* are evaluated instead of their behavior. For example, parents who find their child drawing on the wall are not likely to say, "I love you, but I don't approve of this behavior." They are more likely to shout, "Bad boy!" or "Bad girl!" This reaction suggests that the child is lovable and worthwhile only when well behaved. As a result, the child's self-experience is not "I like drawing on the wall but Mom and Dad don't approve," but instead, "Drawing on the wall is bad and I am bad if I like it, so I don't like it." The child may eventually show overly neat and tidy behaviors that do not reflect the real self but rather are part of an ideal self that was dictated by the parents.

As with Freud's concept of superego, conditions of worth are first set up by external pressure but eventually become part of the person's belief system. To Rogers, then, rewards and punishments are important in personality development not just because they shape behavior but also because they so easily create distorted self-perceptions and incongruence (Roth et al., 2009).

Maslow's Growth Theory   Like Rogers, Abraham Maslow (1954, 1971) viewed personality as the expression of a basic human tendency toward growth and self-actualization. In fact, Maslow believed that self-actualization is not just a human capacity but a human need; as described in the chapter on motivation and emotion,

"Just remember, son, it doesn't matter whether you win or lose—unless you want Daddy's love."

Parents aren't usually this obvious about creating conditions of worth, but according to Rogers, the message gets through in many more subtle ways.

actualizing tendency An innate inclination toward growth and fulfillment that motivates all human behavior.

self-concept The way one thinks of oneself.

conditions of worth According to Rogers, circumstances in which an individual experiences positive regard from others only when displaying certain behaviors or attitudes.

Seeking Self-Actualization
According to Rogers, conditions of worth can make it harder for children to become aware of and accept those aspects of themselves that conflict with their parents' values. Many people find that their progress toward self-actualization is enhanced by associating with those whose positive regard for them does not depend on their displaying any particular set of behaviors.

he placed self-actualization as the highest in a hierarchy of needs. Yet, said Maslow, people are often distracted from seeking self-actualization because they are focusing on needs that are lower in the hierarchy.

Maslow saw most people as controlled by a *deficiency orientation,* a preoccupation with perceived needs for material things. Ultimately, he said, deficiency-oriented people come to see life as a meaningless exercise in disappointment and boredom and they may begin to behave in problematic ways. For example, in an attempt to satisfy the need for love, many people focus on what love can give them (security), not on what they can give to someone else. This deficiency orientation may lead a person to be jealous and to focus on what is missing in relationships; as a result, the person will never truly experience love or security.

In contrast, people with a *growth orientation* draw satisfaction from what they have, what they are, and what they can do, instead of focusing on what's missing. This orientation opens the door to what Maslow called *peak experiences,* in which people feel joy, and even ecstasy, in the mere fact of being alive, being human, and knowing that they are utilizing their fullest potential.

Evaluating the Humanistic Approach

The humanistic approach to personality is consistent with the way many people view themselves. It focuses on immediate experience and emphasizes each person's uniqueness. The best-known application of the humanistic approach is the client-centered therapy of Carl Rogers, which is discussed in the chapter on treatment of psychological disorders. The humanistic approach has also inspired other therapies as well as short-term personal-growth experiences such as sensitivity training and encounter groups that are designed to help people become more aware of themselves and the way they relate to others (e.g., Cain & Seeman, 2002). Rogers' perspective has also been incorporated into interventions designed to help people live healthier lives, including by giving up smoking and increasing their physical activity (Suarez & Mullins, 2008). Further, the humanistic approach is consistent with the rapidly growing field of *positive psychology,* which, as described in the chapter on motivation and emotion, focuses on well-being and other positive aspects of human thought and feelings (Diener, Oishi, & Lucas, 2009; Fredrickson & Cohn, 2008; Peterson, 2006a, 2006b; Snyder & Lopez, 2006).

Yet to some, the humanistic approach is naive, romantic, and unrealistic. Are all people as inherently good and "growth oriented" as this approach suggests? Critics wonder about that, and they also fault humanists for paying too little attention to the role of inherited characteristics, learning, situational influences, and unconscious motivation in shaping personality. Further, the idea that personality development is directed only by an innate growth potential is seen by many as an oversimplification. So, too, is the humanistic assumption that all human problems stem from blocked self-actualization. Personality researchers also see many humanistic concepts as too vague to be tested empirically. Accordingly, the humanistic approach has not been popular among those who conduct empirical research to learn about personality (Cervone & Pervin, 2010). That may begin to change, though, as an explosion of research in positive psychology leads to new humanistically oriented theories that better lend themselves to empirical evaluation (e.g., Burton et al., 2006; Cohn et al., 2009; Fredrickson & Cohn, 2008; Waugh, Fredrickson, & Taylor, 2008; Waugh et al., 2008).

Finally, humanists' tendency to define ideal personality development in terms of personal growth, independence, and self-actualization has been criticized for

Photo by Scott Huffman

The Joys of a Growth Orientation
According to Maslow's theory of personality, the key to personal growth and fulfillment lies in focusing on what we have, not on what we lack or have lost. Liz Heywood, a successful horse trainer, author, activist, and speaker, has never let the loss of her left leg slow her down.

emphasizing culture-specific concepts about mental health that may not apply outside North America and other Western individualist cultures (Heine & Buchtel, 2009). As discussed in the next section, the foundations of humanistic self theories may be in direct conflict with the values of non-Western collectivist cultures.

"In Review: Major Approaches to Personality" summarizes key features of the humanistic approach and those of the other approaches we have described. Which approach is most accurate? There is no simple answer to that question, partly because each approach emphasizes different aspects of personality. Accordingly, it has been suggested that a full understanding of the origins and development of personality will come only by recognizing the roles of all the factors that various approaches have shown to be important. Some psychologists are working on theoretical models that take this promising integrative approach (Mayer, 2005; McAdams & Pals, 2006).

Major Approaches to Personality		IN REVIEW
Approach	**Basic Assumptions about Behavior**	**Typical Research Method**
Psychodynamic	Determined by largely unconscious intrapsychic conflicts	Case studies
Trait	Determined by traits or needs	Analysis of tests for basic personality dimensions
Social-cognitive	Determined by learning, cognitive factors, and specific situations	Analysis of interactions between people and situations
Humanistic	Determined by innate growth tendency and individual perception of reality	Studies of relationships between perceptions and behavior

IN REVIEW QUESTIONS

1. Tests that measure the five-factor model's dimensions of personality are based on the ___ approach to personality.
2. The role of learning is most prominent in the ___ approach to personality.
3. Object relations and attachment theories are modern variants on ___ personality theories.

LINKAGES

Does culture determine personality?
(a link to Human Development)

Personality, Culture, and Human Development

In many Western cultures, people encourage others to "stand up for yourself" or to "blow your own horn" in order to "get what you have coming to you." In middle-class North America, the values of achievement and personal distinction are taught to children, particularly male children, very early in life (Kitayama, Duffy, & Uchida, 2007). North American children are encouraged to feel special, to have self-esteem, and to feel good about themselves, partly because these characteristics are associated with happiness, popularity, and superior performance in school. Whether self-esteem is the cause or the result of these good outcomes (Baumeister et al., 2003), children who learn and display these values tend to receive praise for doing so.

As a result of this cultural training, many people in North America and Europe develop personalities that are largely based on a sense of high self-worth. In a study by Hazel Markus and Shinobu Kitayama (1997), for example, 70 percent of a sample of U.S. students believed that they were superior to their peers. In addition, 60 percent believed that they were in the top 10 percent on a wide variety of personal attributes! This tendency toward self-enhancement is evident as early as age four.

Many Western personality theorists see a sense of independence, uniqueness, and self-esteem as fundamental to mental health. As noted in the chapter on human development, for example, Erik Erikson included the emergence of personal identity and self-esteem as part of normal psychosocial development. Middle-class North Americans who fail to value and strive for independence, self-promotion, and unique personal achievement may be seen as having a personality disorder, some form of depression, or other psychological problems.

Are these ideas based on universal truths about personality development or do they reflect the values of the cultures that generated them? It's certainly clear that people in many non-Western cultures develop personal orientations that are quite different from those of North Americans and Europeans (Heine & Buchtel, 2009; Markus & Kitayama; 2010). In China and Japan, for example, an independent, unique self is not emphasized nearly as much as it is in North America (Kitayama et al., 2009). Children there are encouraged to develop and maintain pleasant, respectful relations with others and not to stand out from the crowd, because doing so might make others seem inferior by comparison. So whereas children in the United States hear that "the squeaky wheel gets the grease" (meaning that you don't get what you want unless you ask for it), Japanese children are warned that "the nail that stands up gets pounded down" (meaning that it is not a good idea to draw attention to yourself). From a very young age, they are taught to be modest, to play down the value of personal contributions, and to appreciate the joy and value of group work (Kitayama & Uchida, 2003).

In contrast to the *independent* self system common in individualist cultures such as Great Britain, Switzerland, and the United States, cultures with a more collectivist orientation (such as Brazil, China, Japan, and Nigeria) promote an *interdependent* self system through which people see themselves as a fraction of the social whole. Each person has little or no meaningful definition without reference to the group. These differences in self systems may produce differences in what gives people a sense of well-being and satisfaction (Tsai, Knutson, & Fung, 2006). For example, in the United States, a sense of well-being is usually associated with having *positive* attributes, such as intelligence, creativity, competitiveness, persistence, and so on. In Japan and other Asian countries, feelings of well-being are more likely to be associated with having no *negative* attributes (Eliot et al., 2001). Studies of thousands of people all over the world indicate that in collectivist

The goal of esteem building is clear these days in many children's activities at school and in some team sports, too, which are designed either to eliminate competition or (as in this case) assure that everyone feels like winners. The same goal is reflected in day-care centers, summer camps, and other children's programs with names such as Starkids, Little Wonders, Superkids, and Precious Jewels.

"We lost!"

Culture and Personality

In individualist cultures, most children learn early that personal distinction is valued by parents, teachers, and peers. In collectivist cultures, having a strong sense of self-worth may be seen as less important. In other words, the features of "normal" personality development vary from culture to culture. Make a list of the core values you've learned. Which of them are typical of individualist cultures, which are typical of collectivist cultures, and which reflect a combination of both?

LEARN**by**
DOING

© Jeff Greenberg/PhotoEdit

cultures, life satisfaction is associated with having social approval and harmonious relations with others. In individualist cultures, life satisfaction is associated with having high self-esteem and good feelings about one's own life (Uchida et al., 2001).

Because cultural factors shape ideas about how the ideal personality develops, it's important to evaluate various approaches to personality in terms of how well they apply to cultures other than the one in which they were developed (Church, 2001; Cross & Markus, 1999; Nye et al., 2008). Their applicability to males and females must be considered as well. Even within North American cultures, for example, there are gender differences in the development of self-esteem. Females tend to show an interdependent self system, achieving their sense of self and self-esteem from attachments to others. By contrast, males' self-esteem tends to develop in relation to personal achievement, in a manner more in keeping with an independent self system (Cross & Madson, 1997). Cross-gender and cross-cultural differences in the nature and determinants of a sense of self highlight the widespread effects of gender and culture on the development of many aspects of human personality (Acerbi, Engquist, & Ghirlanda, 2009; Matsumoto, Yoo, & Nakagawa, 2008; Zakriski, Wright, & Underwood, 2005).   ● ● ● ●

FOCUS ON RESEARCH ## Personality Development over Time

Psychologists have long been interested in how people's personalities differ, but they also want to know the origins of those differences. Some search for the source of personality differences by looking at infants' differing temperaments. As noted in the chapter on human development, temperament is reflected in the unlearned, generalized patterns of emotional expression and other behavior that humans display from birth (Buss, 1997).

What was the researchers' question?

Can young children's temperaments predict their personality characteristics and behaviors as adults?

How did the researchers answer the question?

To try to answer this question, Avshalom Caspi and his colleagues conducted a longitudinal study that assessed the same people at several different times in their lives (Caspi, 2000; Caspi et al., 1997; Caspi et al., 1995; Caspi, Harrington et al., 2003; Caspi & Silva, 1995). The research sample included all the children born in Dunedin, New Zealand, between April 1972 and March 1973—a total of about 1,000 people. When these children were three years old, research assistants observed them in a standard situation and rated them on a number of dimensions, including the degree to which they showed explosive or uncontrolled behavior, interacted easily with others, or acted withdrawn and unresponsive. These observations were used to place each child into one of five temperament categories: *undercontrolled* (irritable, impatient, emotional), *inhibited* (shy, fearful, easily distracted), *confident* (eager to perform, responsive to questions), *reserved* (withdrawn, uncomfortable), and *well adjusted* (friendly, well controlled). The children were observed and categorized again when they were five, seven, and nine years old. If it occurs to you that seeing a child at one point in life might bias an observer's ratings of that child later on, you are right. To ensure that ratings would not be influenced by this kind of observer bias, the researchers arranged for different people to make the ratings at each point in time. These ratings indicated that the children's temperaments stayed about the same over the years from age three to age nine.

When the research participants were twenty-one, they were interviewed about their involvement in risky and unhealthy behaviors, such as excessive drinking, violent criminal activities, unprotected sex, and unsafe driving habits. To avoid bias, the interviewers were given no information about the participants' childhood temperaments. At age twenty-six, the participants took a standard personality test and were rated by friends on the Big Five personality dimensions.

What did the researchers find?

Several significant differences were found in the personality test results of the five original temperament groups. For example, the average test scores of 26-year-olds who had been classified as "undercontrolled" in childhood showed that they were more alienated, uninhibited, and stressed than the other temperament groups. Further, people who had been classified as "confident" or "well adjusted" as children tended to be better adjusted and more extraverted at twenty-six than people who had been classified as "inhibited" or "reserved." These findings held true for males and females alike.

There were also small but significant correlations between childhood temperament and risky behavior in young adulthood. For example, "undercontrolled" children were about twice as likely as others to develop personalities that are associated with violence, excessive drinking, and other health-endangering behaviors (Caspi, Harrington et al., 2003).

What do the results mean?

The results of this research provide support for a hypothesis long endorsed by personality psychologists, namely that we can make relatively accurate predictions about people's personalities and behaviors as adults if we know about their temperaments as children (e.g., Glenn et al., 2007). But as critical thinkers, we must be careful not to overstate the strength of these results. Although the correlations between temperament and personality and between temperament and various problematic behaviors were statistically significant, they were also relatively small. In other words, not all children classified as "undercontrolled" at age three turned out to be aggressive or violent at eighteen. So it is more accurate to say that personality may be influenced and shaped by temperament but not completely determined by it (Clark & Watson, 2008; Roberts, Walton, & Viechtbauer, 2006).

What do we still need to know?

Valuable as it is, this study leaves a number of unanswered questions about the relationship between temperament and personality (Roberts & DelVecchio, 2000). For example, why is there a connection between temperament as a child and personality as an adult? The link is probably a complex one involving both nature and nurture (Hampson, 2008). Caspi and his colleagues (1989) offered one explanation that draws heavily on social-cognitive theories, especially Bandura's notion of reciprocal determinism. They proposed that long-term consistencies in behavior result from the mutual influence that temperament and environmental events have on one another. For example, people may put themselves in situations that reinforce their temperament. So undercontrolled people might choose to spend time with people who accept (and even encourage) rude or impolite behavior. When such behavior does bring negative reactions, the world seems that much more hostile and the undercontrolled people become even more aggressive and negative. Caspi and his colleagues see the results of their studies as evidence that this process of mutual influence between personality and situations can continue over a lifetime (Caspi, Harrington et al., 2003).   ● ● ● ●

Assessing Personality

How do psychologists measure personality?

There are four basic methods of assessing and describing personality (Funder, 2007): *life outcomes* (such as records of education, income, or marital status), *situational tests* (observations of behavior in situations designed to measure personality), *observer ratings* (judgments about a person made by friends or family; Oltmanns & Turkheimer, 2009), and *self-reports* (responses to interviews and personality test items). Data gathered through these methods assist in employee selection, in the diagnosis of psychological disorders, in making predictions about a convict's or mental patient's dangerousness, and in other situations involving risky decisions (Kramer, Bernstein, & Phares, 2013; Meyer et al., 2001).

Life outcomes, observer ratings, and situational tests make it possible to directly assess many aspects of personality and behavior, including how often, how effectively, and how consistently various actions occur (Funder, 2012). *Interviews* provide information about personality from the person's own point of view. Some interviews are *open-ended,* meaning that questions are tailored to the intellectual level, emotional state, and special needs of the person being assessed. Others are *structured,* meaning that the interviewer asks a fixed set of questions about specific topics in a particular order. Structured interviews are routinely used in personality research because they are sure to cover matters of special interest to the researcher.

Personality tests offer a way to gather self-report information that is more standardized and economical than interviews. To be useful, however, a personality test must be reliable and valid. As described in the chapter on thought, language, and intelligence, *reliability* refers to how stable or consistent the results of a test are; *validity* reflects the degree to which test scores are interpreted appropriately and used properly in making inferences about people. The many personality tests available today are traditionally classified as either *projective* or *nonprojective.*

Projective Personality Measures

Projective personality measures contain items or tasks that are ambiguous, meaning that they can be perceived in many different ways. People taking projective tests might be asked to draw a house, a person, a family, or a tree; to fill in the missing parts of incomplete pictures or sentences; to say what they associate with particular words; or to report what they see in a drawing or picture. Projective techniques are sometimes used in personality research, but they are far more popular among psychodynamically oriented clinical psychologists, who use them to assess their clients' personality characteristics and psychological disorders (Garb et al., 2005). These psychologists believe that people's responses to projective tests are guided by unconscious needs, motives, fantasies, conflicts, thoughts, and other hidden aspects of personality.

One widely used projective test, called the *Thematic Apperception Test,* or *TAT,* is described in the chapter on motivation and emotion as a measure of need for achievement. Henry Murray and Christina Morgan developed this test to assess the needs they saw as the basis of personality. Another well-known projective test, the *Rorschach Inkblot Test,* features a series of ten inkblots similar to the one in Figure 11.5. The respondent is asked to tell what the blot might be and then to explain why.

Those who support projective testing claim that using ambiguous test items makes it difficult for respondents to detect what is being measured and what the "best" answers would be. They argue, therefore, that these tests can measure aggressive and sexual impulses and other personality features that people might be able to conceal in their responses to a nonprojective personality measure. Advocates of projective measures also point to specific cases in which projective tests have shown acceptable reliability and validity, such as in the assessment of achievement motivation with the TAT (Grønnerød, 2003; Meyer, Mihura, & Smith, 2005; Schultheiss, 2008; Schultheiss & Rohde, 2002).

Nonetheless, most researchers agree that projective personality measures, especially the Rorschach, are substantially less reliable and valid than the nonprojective personality

© Charlotte Miller

FIGURE 11.5

The Rorschach Inkblot Test

People taking the Rorschach test are shown ten patterns similar to this one and asked to tell what the blot looks like and why. Jot down what you see in this blot and why, and then compare your responses to those of some friends. Most methods of scoring this test focus on (1) what part of the blot the person responds to; (2) what details, colors, or other features determine each response; (3) the content of responses (such as seeing animals, maps, or body parts); and (4) the popularity or commonness of the responses.

LEARN by DOING

projective personality measures Tests made up of relatively unstructured stimuli in which responses are seen as reflecting the individuals' unconscious needs, fantasies, conflicts, thought patterns, and other aspects of personality.

measures described next (Garb et al., 2005; Hunsley, Lee, & Wood, 2003; Wood et al., 2010). In fact, because of their generally poor ability to predict behavior, projective measures often add little information about people beyond what might be inferred from interviews or other sources (Hunsley, Lee, & Wood, 2003).

Nonprojective Personality Measures

Nonprojective personality measures, also known as *objective personality measures*, ask clear questions about a person's thoughts, feelings, or behavior (such as "Do you like to go to parties?"). The answers are used to draw conclusions about the individual's personality. These self-report tests are usually set up in a multiple-choice or true-false format that allows them to be given to many people at once, much like the academic tests used in many classrooms. A different approach has been taken by personality researchers who assess personality characteristics on the basis of computerized analysis of people's writing style, including how formal it is and how often they use particular kinds of words and phrases (e.g., Yarkoni, 2010). As in the classroom, nonprojective personality measures can be scored by machine and then compared with the responses of other people. So before interpreting your score on a nonprojective personality measure of extraversion, for example, a psychologist would compare it to a *norm*, or the average score of thousands of others of your age and gender. You would be considered unusually extraverted only if you scored well above that norm.

Some nonprojective personality measures focus on one particular trait, such as optimism (Carver & Scheier, 2002). Others measure a small group of related traits, such as empathy and social responsibility (Penner & Orom, 2009). Still other nonprojective tests measure the strength of a wider variety of traits to reveal general psychological functioning. For example, the third edition of the *Neuroticism Extraversion Openness Personality Inventory,* or *NEO-PI-3* (McCrae, Harwood & Kelly, 2011) is designed to measure the Big Five personality traits described earlier. Table 11.3 shows how the test's results are presented. The NEO-PI-3 is quite reliable (Costa & McCrae, 2008), and people's scores on its various scales have been successfully used to predict a number of criteria, including performance on specific jobs and overall career success (Conte & Gintoft, 2005; Zhao & Seibert, 2006), social status (Anderson et al., 2001), and the likelihood that a person will engage in criminal activities or risky sexual behaviors (Miller et al., 2004).

nonprojective personality measures Tests that list clear, specific questions, statements, or concepts to which people are asked to respond.

TABLE 11.3   Sample Summary of Results From the NEO-PI-3

The NEO-PI-3 assesses the Big Five personality dimensions. In this example of the results a person might receive, the five factors scored are (from the top row to the bottom row) neuroticism, extraversion, openness, agreeableness, and conscientiousness. Because people with different NEO profiles tend to have different psychological problems, this test has been used to aid in the diagnosis of personality disorders (Trull & Sher, 1994).

Compared with the responses of other people, your responses suggest that you can be described as:		
☐ Sensitive, emotional, and prone to experience feelings that are upsetting.	☒ Generally calm and able to deal with stress but you sometimes experience feelings of guilt, anger, or sadness.	☐ Secure, hardy, and generally relaxed even under stressful conditions.
☐ Extraverted, outgoing, active, and high-spirited. You prefer to be around people most of the time.	☐ Moderate in activity and enthusiasm. You enjoy the company of others but you also value privacy.	☒ Introverted, reserved, and serious. You prefer to be alone or with a few close friends.
☐ Open to new experiences. You have broad interests and are very imaginative.	☐ Practical but willing to consider new ways of doing things. You seek a balance between the old and the new.	☒ Down-to-earth, practical, traditional, and pretty much set in your ways.
☐ Compassionate, good-natured, and eager to cooperate and avoid conflict.	☒ Generally warm, trusting, and agreeable, but you can sometimes be stubborn and competitive.	☐ Hardheaded, skeptical, proud, and competitive. You tend to express your anger directly.
☒ Conscientious and well organized. You have high standards and always strive to achieve your goals.	☐ Dependable and moderately well organized. You generally have clear goals but are able to set your work aside.	☐ Easygoing, not very well organized, and sometimes careless. You prefer not to make plans.

FIGURE 11.6

The MMPI-2-RF: Clinical Scales and Sample Profiles

A score of 50 on the clinical scales of the MMPI-2-RF is average. Scores at or above 65 mean that the person's responses on that scale are more extreme than at least 95 percent of the normal population. The red line on this chart represents the MMPI-2-RF profile of a 26 year-old married man. It is characteristic of a person who is about average in most ways, but who believes that other people are against him, are "out to get him" or are a threat to him. The clinical scales abbreviated in the figure are as follows:

RCd: Demoralization—General unhappiness and dissatisfaction

RC1: Somatic Complaints—Diffuse physical health complaints

RC2: Low Positive Emotions—Lack of positive emotional responsiveness

RC3: Cynicism—Beliefs that express distrust and a generally low opinion of others

RC4: Antisocial Behavior—Rule breaking and irresponsible behavior

RC6: Ideas of Persecution—Beliefs that others pose a threat to oneself

RC7: Dysfunctional Negative Emotions— Maladaptive anxiety, anger, irritability

RC8: Aberrant Experiences—Unusual perceptions or thoughts

RC9: Hypomanic Activation—Over-activation, aggression, impulsivity, and grandiosity

Source: Excerpted from the MMPI®-2 (Minnesota Multiphasic Personality Inventory®-2) Manual for Administration, Scoring, and Interpretation, Revised Edition. Copyright (c) 2001 by the Regents of the University of Minnesota. All rights reserved. Used by permission of the University of Minnesota Press. "MMPI-2" and "Minnesota Multiphasic Personality Inventory-2" are trademarks owned by the Regents of the University of Minnesota.

Restructured Clinical

	RCd	RC1	RC2	RC3	RC4	RC6	RC7	RC8	RC9
Raw Score:	4	1	1	6	4	4	4	1	9
T Score:	51	42	38	49	49	70	46	47	45
Response %:	100	100	100	100	100	100	100	100	100

The highest and lowest T scores possible on each scale are indicated by a "---"; MMPI-2-RF T scores are non-gendered.

When the goal of personality assessment is to diagnose psychological disorders, the most commonly used nonprojective measure is the *Minnesota Multiphasic Personality Inventory,* better known as the *MMPI* (Butcher, 2006). The original 566-item true-false test, developed during the 1930s at the University of Minnesota by Starke Hathaway and J. C. McKinley, has been revised and updated to become the MMPI-2-RF (restructured form; Ben-Porath & Tellegen, 2008).

The MMPI is organized into groups of items called *clinical scales*. Certain patterns of responses to the items on these scales have been associated with people who display particular psychological disorders or personality characteristics. It also contains several *validity scales*. Responses to these scales detect whether respondents are distorting their answers, misunderstanding the items, or being uncooperative. For example, someone who responds "true" to items such as "I never get angry" may not be giving honest answers to the test as a whole.

To interpret the meaning of MMPI results, a person's scores on the clinical scales are plotted as a *profile* (see Figure 11.6). This profile is then compared with the profiles of people who are known to have certain personality characteristics or problems. It is presumed that people taking the MMPI share characteristics with people whose profiles are most similar to their own. So although a high score on a particular clinical scale, such as depression, might suggest a problem in that area, interpreting the MMPI usually focuses on the overall pattern in the clinical scale scores—particularly on the combination of two or three scales on which a person's scores are unusually high.

There is considerable evidence for the reliability and validity of MMPI clinical scales (Forbey & Ben-Porath, 2008), but even the latest editions of the test are far from perfect measurement tools (Carr, Moretti, & Cue, 2005; Rouse, 2007; Selbom & Bagby, 2010). A particular pattern of MMPI scale scores does not guarantee the presence of a particular disorder (Leising & Zimmerman, 2011). The validity of MMPI interpretations may be particularly suspect when—because of cultural factors—the perceptions, values, and experiences of the test taker differ significantly from those of the test developers and the people with whom the respondent's results are compared. So although an MMPI profile might look like that of someone with a mental disorder, the profile might actually reflect the culture-specific way the person interpreted the test items, not a psychological problem (Butcher, 2004; Groth-Marnat,

LINKAGES

Can personality tests be used to diagnose mental disorders?

(a link to Psychological Disorders)

1997). Even though the MMPI-2-RF uses comparison norms that represent a more culturally diverse population than did those of the original MMPI, psychologists must still be cautious when interpreting the profiles of people who identify with minority subcultures (Butcher, 2004; Cheung, van de Vijver, & Leong, 2011; Church, 2010).

"In Review: Personality Measures" summarizes the characteristics of projective and nonprojective personality tests and some of their advantages and disadvantages.

Personality Measures   IN REVIEW

Type of Test	Characteristics	Advantages	Disadvantages
Projective	Ambiguous stimuli create maximum freedom of response; scoring is relatively subjective	"Correct" answers not obvious; designed to tap unconscious impulses; flexible use	Reliability and validity lower than those of nonprojective tests
Nonprojective	Written format; quantitatively scored	Efficiency, standardization	Subject to deliberate distortion

IN REVIEW QUESTIONS

1. Projective personality measures are based on the ___ approach to personality.
2. The NEO-PI-3 and the MMPI-2-RF are examples of ___ tests.
3. Most personality researchers use ___ tests in their work.

Personality Tests and Employee Selection

How good are nonprojective personality measures at selecting people for jobs? Most industrial and organizational psychologists see them as valuable tools for selecting good employees. Tests such as the MMPI (and even some projective measures) are sometimes used to help guide hiring decisions (Matyas, 2004), but large organizations usually choose nonprojective measures that are designed to measure the Big Five personality dimensions or related characteristics (Costa, 2001; Kuncel, Ones, & Sackett, 2010). Several researchers have found significant relationships between scores on the Big Five dimensions and measures of job performance and effective leadership (Hirschfeld et al., 2008; Kieffer, Schinka, & Curtiss, 2004; Lim & Ployhart, 2004; Motowidlo, Brownlee, & Schmit, 2008; Silverthorne, 2001). A more general review of studies involving thousands of people has shown that nonprojective personality measures are of value in helping businesses reduce theft, absenteeism, and other disruptive employee behaviors (Berry, Sackett, & Wiemann, 2007; Hogan, 2006; Iliescu, Ilie, & Ispas, 2011; Kuncel et al., 2010).

Still, personality tests are not perfect predictors of workplace behavior. Many of them measure traits that may be too general to predict specific aspects of job performance (Berry, Sackett, & Wiemann, 2007; Furnham, 2001). In fact, features of the work situation are often better predictors of employee behavior than are personality measures (Mumford et al., 2001). Further, some employees see personality measures as an invasion of their privacy. They worry that test results in their personnel files might later be misinterpreted and hurt their chances for promotion or for employment by other companies. Lawsuits have resulted in a ban on the use of personality tests in the selection of U.S. federal employees. Concerns about privacy and other issues surrounding personality testing have led the American Psychological Association and related organizations to publish joint ethical standards relating to procedures for the development, distribution, and use of all psychological tests (American Educational Research Association, American Psychological Association, & National Council on Measurement in Education, 1999; American Psychological Association, 2002b). The goal is not only to improve the reliability and validity of tests but also to ensure that their results are properly used and do not infringe on individuals' rights (Turner et al., 2001).

Active Review

As noted in the introductory chapter, all of psychology's subfields are related to one another. Our discussion of personality, culture, and human development illustrates just one way that the topic of this chapter, personality, is linked to the subfield of developmental psychology, which

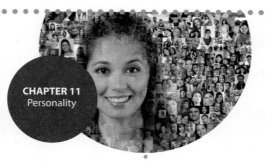

CHAPTER 11
Personality

is described in the chapter on human development. The Linkages diagram shows ties to two other subfields, and there are many more ties throughout the book. Looking for linkages among subfields will help you see how they all fit together and help you better appreciate the big picture that is psychology.

LINKAGES

How do you know if a personality test (or any other kind of test) is any good?
(ans. on p. 278)

CHAPTER 7
Thought, Language, and Intelligence

Does culture determine personality?
(ans. on p. 442)

CHAPTER 9
Human Development

Can therapy change personality?
(ans. on p. 520)

CHAPTER 13
Treatment of Personality Disorders

Summary

Personality refers to the unique pattern of psychological and behavioral characteristics by which each person can be compared and contrasted with other people. The four main theoretical approaches to personality are the psychodynamic, trait, social-cognitive, and humanistic approaches.

The Psychodynamic Approach

How did paralyzed patients lead Freud to psychoanalysis?
The *psychodynamic approach,* pioneered by Freud, assumes that personality arises out of unconscious psychological processes that interact to determine our thoughts, feelings, and behavior. According to Freud's *psychoanalytic theory,* personality has three components—the *id,* which operates according to the *pleasure principle;* the *ego,* which operates according to the *reality principle;* and the *superego,* which internalizes society's rules and values. The ego uses *defense mechanisms* to prevent unconscious conflicts among these components from

becoming conscious and causing anxiety or guilt.

Freud proposed that the focus of conflict changes as the child passes through stages of *psychosexual development*. These include the *oral stage,* the *anal stage,* the *phallic stage* (during which the *Oedipal complex* or the *Electra complex* occurs), the *latency period,* and the *genital stage.*

Many of Freud's followers developed new theories that differed from his. Among these theorists were Jung, Adler, and Horney. They tended to downplay the role of instincts and the unconscious, emphasizing instead the importance of conscious processes, ego functions, and social and cultural factors. Horney also challenged the male-oriented nature of Freud's original theory.

Current psychodynamic theories reflect the neo-Freudians' emphasis on family and social relationships. According to object relations and attachment

theorists, personality development depends mainly on the nature of early interactions between individuals and their caregivers.

The psychodynamic approach is reflected in many forms of psychotherapy, but critics fault the approach for its lack of a scientific base and for its view of human behavior as driven by forces that are difficult or impossible to measure.

The Trait Approach

What personality traits are most basic?
The *trait approach* assumes that personality is made up of stable internal *personality traits* that appear at varying strengths in different people and guide their thoughts, feelings, and behavior. Allport believed that personality is created by a small set of central traits and a larger number of secondary traits in each individual. Allport studied unique

patterns of traits, whereas later researchers such as Cattell used factor analysis to explore common traits or core dimensions of personality. Most recently, these factor analyses have identified five basic dimensions of personality, collectively referred to as the *five-factor,* or *Big Five, personality model.* These dimensions—openness, conscientiousness, extraversion, agreeableness, and neuroticism—have been found in many different cultures and may arise partly from inherited differences in temperament and other biological factors that provide the raw materials from which each personality is molded by experience. These biological factors are the focus of trait theories proposed by Eysenck and by Gray.

The trait approach has been criticized for being better at describing personality than at explaining it, for failing to consider mechanisms that motivate behavior, and for underemphasizing the role of situational factors. Nevertheless, the trait approach—particularly the five-factor personality model—currently dominates the field.

The Social-Cognitive Approach

Do we learn our personalities? The *social-cognitive approach* assumes that personality is a set of unique patterns of thinking and behavior that a person acquires through learning and then displays in particular situations. The social-cognitive approach has expanded on traditional behavioral approaches by emphasizing the role of cognitive factors, such as observational learning, in personality development.

Rotter's theory focuses on expectancies that guide behavior, and it generated interest in assessing general beliefs about whether rewards occur because of personal efforts (internal control) or chance (external control). Bandura believes that personality develops largely through cognitively mediated learning, including

observational learning. He sees personality as reciprocally determined by interactions among cognition, environmental stimuli, and behavior. *Self-efficacy*—the belief in one's ability to accomplish a given task—is an important determinant of behavior. Mischel emphasizes the importance of situations and their interactions with cognitive person variables in determining behavior. According to Mischel, we must look at both cognitive person variables and situational variables in order to understand human consistencies and inconsistencies.

The social-cognitive approach has led to new forms of psychological treatment and many other applications. However, critics of this approach consider even its latest versions to be incapable of capturing all the unlearned factors that some psychologists see as important in personality.

The Humanistic Approach

Is everyone basically good? The *humanistic psychology approach,* also called the *phenomenological approach,* is based on the assumption that personality is determined by the unique ways that each individual views the world. These perceptions form a personal version of reality and guide people's behavior as they strive to reach *self-actualization,* their fullest potential. Rogers believed that personality development is driven by an innate *actualizing tendency,* but also that one's *self-concept* is shaped by social evaluations. He proposed that the *conditions of worth* parents and others impose interfere with personal growth and can lead to psychological

problems. Maslow saw self-actualization as the highest in a hierarchy of needs. Personality development is healthiest, he said, when people have a growth orientation rather than a deficiency orientation.

The humanistic approach has been used in certain forms of psychotherapy, in parent training, and in group experiences designed to enhance personal growth. This approach has considerable popularity, but it has been faulted for being too idealistic, for failing to explain personality development, for being vague and unscientific, and for underplaying cultural differences in "ideal" personalities.

Many people in the individualist cultures of North America and Europe are taught to believe in the importance of self-worth and personal distinction. This independent self system contrasts with the interdependent self system that is often fostered in collectivist cultures, in which the self is defined mainly in relation to family or other groups. Contrasting definitions of the self in different cultures and among males versus females tend to exert differing influences on the development of personality.

Research suggests that temperament in childhood may influence personality development into adulthood.

Assessing Personality

How do psychologists measure personality? Personality is usually assessed through some combination of life outcomes, observer ratings, situational tests, and self-reports. To be useful, personality assessments must be both reliable and valid.

Based on psychodynamic theories, *projective personality measures* present ambiguous stimuli in an attempt to tap unconscious personality characteristics. Two popular projective tests are the TAT and the Rorschach. In general, projective personality measures are less reliable and valid than nonprojective personality measures.

Nonprojective personality measures, also known as objective measures, usually present clear, direct items; their scores can be compared with group norms. The NEO-PI-3 and the MMPI-2-RF are examples of nonprojective personality measures.

Nonprojective personality measures are often used to identify which people are best suited for certain occupations. Although such tests can be helpful in this regard, those who use them must be aware of the tests' limitations and take care not to violate the rights of test respondents.

Put It in Writing

Choose a well-known person who interests you. It could be a rock star; an actor; a television personality; a political, religious, or business figure; or even a famous criminal. Write a one-paragraph description of this individual's personality traits as they seem to you. Then write a page or two about how you think the development of these traits would be explained by psychodynamic, biological trait, social-cognitive, and humanistic personality theories.

Personal Learning Activity

To get an idea of the problems involved in scoring projective personality tests, try creating your own projective test that contains pictures, drawings, or other stimuli that can be interpreted in many different ways. Administer your test to some friends and record their responses to each stimulus. How will you decide what your friends' responses tell you about their personalities? Do you think your conclusions about their personalities were affected mainly by their test responses or by what you already knew about them? Now give your test to someone you don't know. Was it easier or harder to draw conclusions about this person's personality? How will you know if your conclusions about this new person are correct, or valid?

Review of Key Terms

Can you define each of the key terms in the chapter? Check your definitions against those on the pages shown in parentheses in the following list or in the Glossary at the end of the book.

actualizing tendency (p. 440)
anal stage (p. 427)
conditions of worth (p. 440)
defense mechanisms (p. 426)
ego (p. 425)
Electra complex (p. 427)

five-factor personality model (Big Five model) (p. 431)
genital stage (p. 427)
humanistic psychology approach (p. 439)
id (p. 425)
latency period (p. 427)
nonprojective personality measures (p. 447)
Oedipal complex (p. 427)
oral stage (p. 426)
personality (p. 424)
personality traits (p. 431)
phallic stage (p. 427)

pleasure principle (p. 425)
projective personality measures (p. 446)
psychoanalytic theory (p. 425)
psychodynamic approach (p. 425)
psychosexual development (p. 426)
reality principle (p. 425)
self-actualization (p. 439)
self-concept (p. 440)
self-efficacy (p. 437)
social-cognitive approach (p. 436)
superego (p. 425)
trait approach (p. 431)

Test Your Knowledge

Select the best answer for each of the following questions. Then check your responses against the Answer Key at the end of the book.

1. When psychologists talk about the unique pattern of enduring psychological and behavioral characteristics by which each person can be compared and contrasted with other people, they are referring to ____.
   a. motivation
   b. personality
   c. reciprocal determinism
   d. conditions of worth

2. As Jared is jostled by a passerby he thinks, "I'd like to hit that guy!" Freud would say that this impulse comes from Jared's ____, which operates on the ____ principle.
   a. id; pleasure
   b. id; reality
   c. ego; pleasure
   d. ego; reality

3. Nine-year-old Jeffrey has just bounded into the room with his latest artistic creation. He chatters about his friends at school and how much he likes reading and working math problems. According to Freud, Jeffrey is most likely in the ____ stage of psychosexual development.
   a. oral
   b. anal
   c. phallic
   d. latency

4. Elizabeth's therapist suggests that Elizabeth's inability to trust her boyfriend could stem from her parents' neglecting her when she was a child. This therapist most likely follows the ____ theory of personality.
   a. reciprocal deterministic
   b. social-cognitive
   c. humanistic
   d. object relations

5. Oscar strives to be the best at everything he does. He believes that he is successful because he is intelligent, works hard, and never gives up. Oscar most likely has a(n) ____ self system.
   a. independent
   b. interdependent
   c. reciprocal
   d. growth-oriented

6. Which of the following is *not* a common criticism of Freud's psychodynamic approach to personality?
   a. His sample of patients was small and unrepresentative of the general population.
   b. His theory reflects Western European and North American cultural values.
   c. The theory was not developed scientifically and thus is subject to bias.
   d. The theory was not comprehensive and has had little influence on psychology.

7. Rajeem believes that he is unique because no one else has exactly the same combination of internal characteristics (such as high intelligence, low sociability, average creativity) that he does. In other words, Rajeem believes in the ____ approach to personality.
   a. psychodynamic
   b. trait
   c. social-cognitive
   d. humanistic

8. A politician is described by her critics as dishonest, intelligent, industrious, extraverted, aggressive, generous, and charming. This method of describing personality most closely matches ____ model of personality.
   a. Eysenck's biological trait
   b. Rotter's expectancy
   c. Allport's trait
   d. the five-factor

9. Tamerika has been described as high in openness, low in conscientiousness, high in extraversion, high in agreeableness, and high in neuroticism. This description reflects ____ model of personality
   a. Eysenck's biological trait
   b. Rotter's expectancy
   c. Allport's trait
   d. the five-factor

10. David is very sociable and tends to seek out situations in which other people are appreciative of his work and his jokes. He is usually happy and loves to try new activities, such as bungee jumping. According to Gray, David has an active ____ system.
    a. external control
    b. internal control
    c. behavioral approach
    d. flight or freeze system

11. According to the Thinking Critically section of this chapter, research on the question of whether or not personality is inherited concludes that ____.
    a. there are specific genes for specific personality traits
    b. there are genetic predispositions toward particular personality characteristics
    c. the environment is the strongest influence on personality development
    d. personality is essentially determined by the age of six months

12. Sandy believes that if she works hard, she will be rewarded. So when she gets a D on her psychology test, she decides that she didn't study hard enough. When she wins the "Outstanding Senior of the Month" award, she believes that she earned it. According to one type of social-cognitive personality theory, Sandy would be described as ____.
    a. internal
    b. external
    c. deficiency oriented
    d. growth oriented

13. Darma was standing in line at a movie theater, thinking about how her boyfriend had dumped her, when she was accidentally shoved from behind. She shouted "Hey! Back off, you jerks!" This prompted angry comments from the people behind her, which made Darma even angrier, so she refused to move forward in line. This case is an example of ____.
    a. conditions of worth
    b. growth orientation
    c. reciprocal determinism
    d. internal locus of control

14. At college basketball games, Melinda jumps up and down and yells and screams continuously. Otherwise, however, she is a quiet person who chooses peaceful environments without much social stimulation. She finds that when she is around other people, they often become quiet, too. Melinda's personality can best be explained by ____ theory.
    a. psychodynamic
    b. Allport's trait
    c. Rotter's expectancy
    d. Mischel's person-situation

15. Rolf believes that his children's personalities are shaped by the way he rewards and punishes them. His wife, Jena, believes that the children were born with an innate drive toward growth and that their personalities are shaped by their unique perceptions of the world. Rolf's beliefs most closely match the ____ approach to personality, and Jena's most closely match the ____ approach.
    a. psychodynamic; trait
    b. social-cognitive; trait
    c. social-cognitive; humanistic
    d. psychodynamic; humanistic

16. When Lizzie finger-paints on the wall, her mother gets angry and shouts, "You are a very bad girl!" Rogers would say that Lizzie's mother is creating ____.
    a. growth-oriented development
    b. deficiency-oriented development
    c. conditions of worth
    d. psychodynamic conflicts

17. Ruben is preoccupied with what is missing from his life. He has a good job and just got a raise, but he still feels underpaid. He has a great wife, but he wishes she were more attractive. He bought a new car, but he just saw a better one that has become his latest obsession. Maslow would say that Ruben is controlled by ____.
    a. growth orientation
    b. deficiency orientation
    c. conditions of worth
    d. self-actualization

18. Which of the following techniques would a psychodynamic psychologist be most likely to use to assess personality?
    a. Behavioral observations
    b. Nonprojective personality measures
    c. Measurements of physiological activity
    d. Projective personality measures

19. Paul is an undercontrolled eight-year-old who regularly has tantrums. The longitudinal study described in this chapter's Focus on Research section would suggest that, when Paul is an adult, he will most likely ____.
    a. join the military or live in some other highly structured environment
    b. have outgrown his lack of control
    c. be more aggressive than most other men
    d. keep jobs longer than most other men

20. Peggy is responsible for hiring new employees for her company. To guide her selections, she decides to use ____, which have been shown to have value in screening out employees who are likely to be unreliable or dishonest.
    a. structured interviews
    b. nonprojective personality measures
    c. projective personality measures
    d. life outcome measures

Media Resources

Now that you have finished reading this chapter, how about exploring some of the ideas and information that you found most interesting?

Go to **CengageBrain.com** to access Psychology CourseMate, where you will find an interactive eBook, glossaries, flashcards, quizzes, videos, Virtual Psychology Labs, and more.

Aplia If your professor has assigned Aplia:
1. Sign in to your account.
2. Complete the corresponding exercises as required by your professor.
3. When finished, click "Grade It Now" to see which areas you have mastered, which areas need more work, and detailed explanations of every answer.

Psychological Disorders

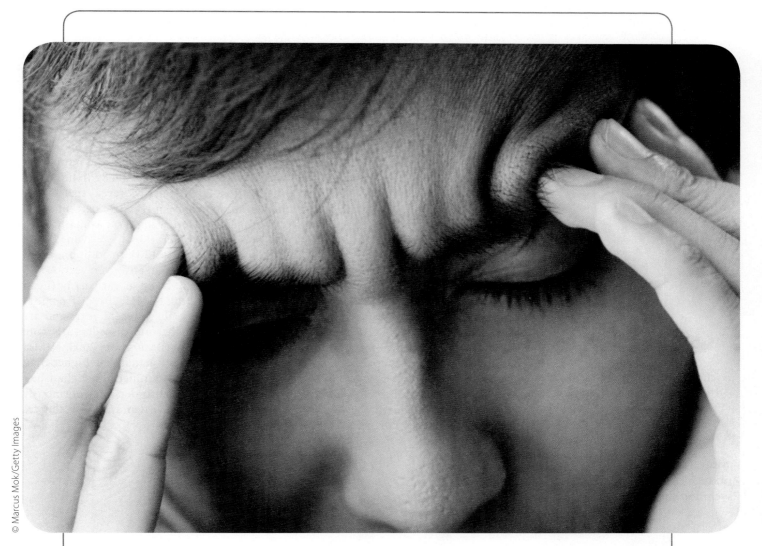

© Marcus Mok/Getty Images

Preview

Do you know someone who collects odd objects, or believes in things that most people don't, or dresses in strange or even shocking ways? Is this person crazy or just eccentric? When does oddness become abnormality? When does sadness become depression? What are psychological disorders? In this chapter, we describe the major categories of psychological disorders, discuss some of their possible causes, consider how they have been explained over the centuries, and examine their role in the insanity defense.

José is a 55-year-old electronics technician. A healthy and vigorous father of two adult children, he was forced to take medical leave because of a series of sudden, uncontrollable panic attacks in which dizziness, a racing heart, sweating, and other terrifying symptoms made him fear that he was about to die. José is suffering from a psychological disorder, also called a *mental disorder* or *psychopathology*. **Psychopathology** involves patterns of thought, emotion, and behavior that are maladaptive, disruptive, or uncomfortable either for the person affected or for others.

Psychological disorders appear in every country in the world, and the number of people who are affected is staggering (Kessler et al., 2012; King et al., 2008; Moffitt et al., 2010; Stein et al., 2008; World Health Organization, 2009). Surveys reveal that in any given year in the United States alone, about 60 million people, or about 26 percent of the adult population, have displayed some form of mental disorder and that as many as 46 percent have experienced a disorder at some point in their lives (Kessler & Wang, 2008; National Institute of Mental Health [NIMH], 2012n; see Figure 12.1). In addition, about 13 percent of U.S. children display a significant mental disorder in any given year. About three-quarters of adult disorders first appear by age 24; half begin as early as 14 (Egan & Asher, 2005; Kessler & Wang, 2008; Merikangas et al., 2010; NIMH, 2012o; Twenge et al., 2010). These rates of mental disorder have remained steady in recent years and are seen in all segments of U.S. society. As described later, though, some disorders are more prevalent in males or in females or in certain ethnic groups (Beals et al., 2005; NIMH 2012a, 2012l; Peterson et al., 1993). The overall prevalence may actually be higher than the survey percentages suggest, because major studies have examined fewer than half of all known psychological disorders. In short, psychological disorders are enormously costly in terms of human suffering, wasted potential, economic burden, and lost resources (Insel, 2008; Kessler, 2012; Kessler, Chiu et al., 2008). ●

psychopathology Patterns of thinking and behaving that are maladaptive, disruptive, or uncomfortable for the affected person or for others.

FIGURE 12.1
Annual Incidence of Specific Psychological Disorders

Several large-scale surveys of adults in the United States revealed that nearly 30 percent of them experience some form of mental disorder in any given year and that almost half of them have displayed a disorder at some time in life. The data shown here summarize these findings by category of disorder. The same general patterns appear among the more than 400 million people worldwide who suffer from some form of psychological disorder (Kessler et al., 2012; King et al., 2008; Moffitt et al., 2010; NIMH, 2012a, 2012k, 2012l, 2012m; World Health Organization, 2009).

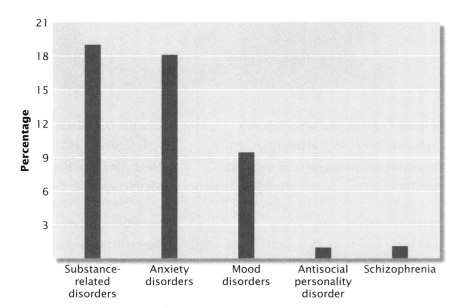

Defining Psychological Disorders

How do psychologists define abnormal behavior?

A California woman's husband dies. In her grief, she stays in bed all day, weeping, refusing to eat, at times holding "conversations" with him. In India, a Hindu holy man on a pilgrimage rolls along the ground for more than 1,000 miles of deserts and mountains, in all kinds of weather, until he reaches the sacred place he seeks. In London, an artist randomly scratches parked cars as part of his "creative process" (Telegraph Correspondent, 2005). One third of U.S. adults believe in UFOs, fourteen percent say they have seen one (Associated Press, 2007), and hundreds claim to have been abducted by space aliens (Clancy, 2005). These examples and countless others raise the question of where to draw the line between normality and abnormality, between eccentricity and mental disorder.

What Is Abnormal?

The criteria for judging whether people's thinking, emotions, or behaviors are abnormal have been called the "three D's": deviance, distress, and dysfunction. Each criterion has value but also some flaws.

Deviance   If we define *normality* as what most people do, then the criterion for abnormality becomes *statistical infrequency,* or that which is deviant, meaning unusual or rare. By this criterion, the few people who believe that space aliens steal their thoughts would be judged as abnormal; the many people who worry about becoming victims of crime or terrorism would not. But statistical infrequency alone is a poor criterion for abnormality because it would define as abnormal any rare quality or characteristic, including creative genius or world-class athletic ability. Further, the infrequency criterion implies that conformity with the majority is normal, so equating rarity with abnormality may result in the oppression of nonconformists who express unusual or unpopular views or ideas. Finally, just how rare must a behavior be in order to call it "abnormal"? The dividing line is not easy to locate.

A related criterion for abnormality is the violation of social norms, the cultural rules that tell us how we should and shouldn't behave in various situations, especially in relation to others. According to this *norm violation* criterion, when people behave in ways that are unusual enough or disturbing enough to violate social norms, they may be described as abnormal. However, norm violation alone is an inadequate measure of abnormality. For one thing, some norm violations are better characterized as eccentric or illegal than as abnormal. People who seldom bathe or who stand too close during conversation violate social norms, but are they abnormal or merely annoying? Further, whose norms are we talking about? Social norms vary across cultures, subcultures, and historical eras, so certain behaviors that qualify as abnormal in one part of the world might be perfectly acceptable elsewhere (Giosan, Glovsky, & Haslam, 2001; Phelan et al., 2000).

Distress   Abnormality can also be described in terms of *personal suffering.* In fact, experiencing distress is the criterion that people often use in deciding that their psychological problems are severe enough to require treatment. But personal suffering alone is not an adequate criterion for abnormality. For one thing, it does not take into account the fact that people are sometimes distressed about characteristics (such as being gay or lesbian) that are not mental disorders. Second, some people display serious psychological disorders but experience little or no distress. Those who sexually abuse children, for example, create far more distress in victims and their families than they suffer themselves.

Dysfunction   A final criterion for abnormality is *impaired functioning,* which means having difficulty in fulfilling appropriate and expected roles in family, social, and work-related situations (Üstün & Kennedy, 2009). For example, it is normal for people to

Is This Person Abnormal?
Whether unusual individuals are labeled "abnormal" and perhaps given treatment for psychological disorders depends on a number of factors, including how abnormality is defined by the culture in which they live, who is most directly affected by their behavior, and how much distress they suffer or cause.

© Huang Yongxian/Xinhua/Eyevine/Redux

© Mark A. Johnson/Alamy

Situational Factors in Defining Abnormality

Men in Delhi, India, can take advantage of outdoor urinals like this one. In some countries, it is even acceptable for men to urinate against buildings on city streets. In the United States and many other places, though, males who urinate anywhere other than the relative privacy of a men's room are considered to be deviant and might even be arrested for indecent exposure. In other words, situational factors can determine whether a particular behavior is labeled "normal" or "abnormal." Make a list of the reasons you would give for, or against, calling these men "abnormal." Which criteria for abnormality did you use?

LEARN by DOING

experience sadness at one time or another, but if their sadness becomes so intense or long-lasting that it interferes with their ability to hold a job or care for their children, it is likely to be considered abnormal. It isn't quite fair, though, to call someone abnormal just because they are dysfunctional. Their dysfunction might be caused by physical illness, by an overwhelming but temporary family problem, or by a variety of things other than a psychological disorder. Further, some people who display significant psychological disorders are still able to function reasonably well at school, at work, or at home.

Behavior in Context: A Practical Approach

Obviously, no single criterion fully defines abnormality. So mental health practitioners and researchers tend to adopt a *practical approach* that combines aspects of all the criteria we've described. They consider the *content* of behavior (that is, what the person does), the sociocultural *context* in which the person's behavior occurs, and the *consequences* of the behavior for that person and for others.

They also recognize that the definition of behavior that is "appropriate," "expected," and "functional" depends on age, gender, culture, and the particular situation and historical era in which people live. For example, a short attention span and unemployment are considered normal in a two-year-old but inappropriate and problematic in an adult. In some countries, expressing certain emotions is considered more appropriate for women than for men. So kisses, tears, and long embraces are common when women in North America greet each other after a long absence; men tend to simply shake hands or hug briefly. And because of cultural differences, hearing a dead relative's voice calling from the afterlife would be more acceptable in certain American Indian tribes than among, say, the families of suburban Toronto. Situational factors are important as well. Falling to the floor and "speaking in tongues" is considered appropriate and even desirable during the worship services of some religious groups; but the same behavior would be seen as inappropriate (and possibly a sign of disorder) in a college classroom. Finally, judgments about behavior are shaped by changes in social trends and cultural values. At one time, the American Psychiatric Association listed homosexuality as a mental disorder, but it dropped this category from its official list of disorders in 1973. In taking this step, it was responding to changing views of sexual orientation prompted in part by the political and educational efforts of gay and lesbian rights groups.

In summary, it is difficult (and probably impossible) to define a specific set of behaviors that everyone, everywhere, will agree constitutes abnormality. Instead, the practical approach sees abnormality as including those patterns of thought, behavior, and emotion that lead to suffering and significantly impair people's ability to function as expected within their culture (Nordsletten, & Mataix-Cols, 2012; Wakefield, 1992).

Explaining Psychological Disorders

What causes abnormality?

It is one thing to define psychological disorders; it is quite another to explain them. Centuries ago, explanations of abnormal behavior focused on gods or demons. Disordered people were seen either as innocent victims of evil spirits or as social or moral deviants suffering supernatural punishment. In Europe during the late Middle Ages, for example, it was widely believed that people who engaged in threatening or unusual behavior were controlled by the devil or other evil beings. Supernatural explanations of psychological disorders are still invoked today in many cultures around the world, including certain ethnic and religious subcultures in North America (Glazer et al., 2004; Legare & Gelman, 2008). Other explanations have focused on mental incompetence, weak character, personal choices, illness or other physical problems, faulty learning, and difficult social conditions.

Explanations of psychological disorders tend to influence a society's attitudes and responses toward the people who display them (Blease, 2012; Fontaine, 2009). Where disorder is seen as a sign that a person is evil, that person may be the target of anger and punishment, but in societies in which the cause of disorder is thought to be demonic

An Exorcism

The exorcism being performed by this Buddhist monk in Thailand is designed to cast out the evil forces that are seen as causing this child's disorder. Supernatural explanations of mental disorder remain influential among religious groups in many cultures and subcultures around the world (Fountain, 2000). Awareness of this influence in the United States and Europe has increased recently after cases in which people have died during exorcism rituals (e.g., Christopher, 2003; Radford, 2005).

© Jean Leo Dugast/Sygma/Corbis

possession, the person may be the object of sympathy and might be offered an exorcism ceremony. If abnormality is viewed as a personal decision to behave in odd ways, those who do so are likely to be avoided, isolated, and ignored, but if psychological problems are assumed to be caused by illness or learned habits, troubled people are likely to receive drugs or to be offered programs designed to teach more appropriate behaviors. The view of psychological disorders that is most prevalent in a given society is often driven by the ways in which those disorders are portrayed in the news and entertainment media (Lewison et al., 2012; Sarrett, 2011).

The Biopsychosocial Approach

Today, most mental health researchers in Western cultures attribute the appearance of psychopathology to three main causes: biological factors, psychological processes, and sociocultural contexts. For many decades, there was controversy over which of these three causes was most important, but it is now widely agreed that they can all be important. Most researchers have adopted a **biopsychosocial approach** in which mental disorders are seen as caused by the combination and interaction of biological, psychological, and sociocultural factors, each of which contributes in varying degrees to particular problems in particular people (Andrews, 2008; Kendler et al., 2011; Krueger & Markon, 2006; Nolen-Hoeksema & Watkins, 2011; Page et al., 2010).

Biological Factors   The biological factors thought to be involved in causing mental disorders include physical illnesses and disruptions or imbalances of bodily processes. This view of psychological disorders has a long history. For example, Hippocrates, a physician in ancient Greece, said that psychological disorders result from imbalances among four *humors,* or bodily fluids (blood, phlegm, black bile, and yellow bile). In ancient Chinese cultures, psychological disorders were seen as arising from an imbalance of *yin* and *yang,* the dual forces of the universe flowing in the physical body.

As the biologically oriented view gained prominence in Western cultures after the Middle Ages, special hospitals for the insane were established throughout Europe. Treatment in these early *asylums* consisted mainly of physical restraints, laxative purges, bleeding of "excess" blood, and induced vomiting. Cold baths, fasts, and other physical discomforts were also used in efforts to "shock" patients back to normality.

The biologically oriented view, sometimes called the *medical model,* also gave rise to the concept of abnormality as *mental illness.* Today the medical model is now

biopsychosocial approach Viewing mental disorders as resulting from a combination of biological, psychological, and sociocultural factors.

Visiting Bedlam

As shown in William Hogarth's portrayal of "Bedlam" (slang for a hospital in London formerly known as St. Mary Bethlehem), most asylums of the 1700s were little more than prisons. Notice the well-dressed visitors. In those days, the public could buy tickets to look at mental patients, much as people go to the zoo today.

"The Interior of Bedlam," from A Rake's Progress by William Hogarth, 1763

more properly called the *neurobiological model* because it explains psychological disorders in terms of particular disturbances in the anatomy and chemistry of the brain and in other biological processes, including genetic influences (e.g., Kendler, 2005; Plomin & McGuffin, 2003; Williams, 2008). Neuroscientists and others who employ a neurobiological model investigate these disorders as they would investigate any physical illness, seeing problematic symptoms stemming primarily from an underlying illness that can be diagnosed, treated, and cured. This model is widely accepted in Western cultures today; most people tend to seek medical doctors and hospitals for the diagnosis and treatment of psychological disorders (Wang et al., 2006).

Psychological Processes   The biological factors we have described are constantly influencing and being influenced by a variety of psychological processes, such as our wants, needs, and emotions; our learning experiences; and our way of looking at the world. The roots of the **psychological model** of mental disorders can be found in ancient Greek literature and drama dealing with *psyche,* or mind, and especially with the problems people experience as they struggle to resolve inner conflicts or to overcome the effects of stressful events.

These ideas took center stage in the late 1800s, when Sigmund Freud challenged the assumption that psychological disorders had only physical causes. As described in the chapter on personality, Freud viewed psychological disorders as resulting mainly from the effects of unresolved, mostly unconscious clashes between people's inborn impulses and the limits placed on those impulses by the environment. These conflicts, he said, begin early in childhood. Today's versions of this *psychodynamic approach* focus less on instinctual urges and more on the role of attachment and other early interpersonal relationships, but they retain the basic idea that internal conflicts can cause psychological disorders (Bienenfeld, 2005; Levy & Ablon, 2009; Schultz & Schultz, 2005).

LINKAGES

Are psychological disorders learned behaviors? (a link to Learning)

psychological model   A view in which mental disorder is seen as arising from psychological processes.

Other theories discussed in the personality chapter suggest other psychological processes that contribute to the appearance of mental disorders. For example, *social-cognitive* theorists, also known as *social-learning* theorists, see most psychological disorders as the result of past learning and current situations. These theorists say that just as people learn to avoid touching hot stoves after being burned by one, bad experiences in school or a dental office can "teach" people to fear such places. Social-cognitive theorists also emphasize the effects of expectancies and other mental processes (e.g., Johnson-Laird, Mancini, & Gangemi, 2006). They see depression, for example, as stemming from negative events, such as losing a job, and from learned patterns of thoughts about these events, such as "I never do anything right."

According to the *humanistic,* or phenomenological, approach to personality, behavior disorders appear when a person's natural tendency toward healthy growth is blocked, usually by a failure to be aware of and to express true feelings. When this happens, the person's perceptions of reality become distorted. The greater the distortion, the more serious the psychological disorder.

LINKAGES

How do societies define what is abnormal? (a link to Social Psychology)

Sociocultural Context   Together, neurobiological and psychological factors can go a long way toward explaining many forms of mental disorder. Still, they focus mainly on causes residing within the individual. The **sociocultural perspective** on disorder emphasizes the importance of examining the individual's environment, including the social and cultural factors that form the context of abnormal behavior. Looking for causes of disorders in this *sociocultural context* means paying attention to **sociocultural factors** such as gender, age, and marital status; the physical, social, and economic situations in which people live; and the cultural values, traditions, and expectations in which they are immersed (Appignanesi, 2009; Lim, 2006; Sue & Sue, 2008). Sociocultural context influences not only what is and is not labeled "abnormal" but also who displays what kind of disorder.

Consider gender, for instance. The greater tolerance in many cultures for the open expression of emotional distress among women but not men may contribute to the fact that women report higher rates of depression than men do (Whiffen, 2006; Wupperman & Neumann, 2006). Similarly, the view held in many cultures that excessive alcohol consumption is less appropriate for women than for men is a sociocultural factor that may set the stage for rates of alcohol abuse that are higher in men than women (Helzer et al., 1990; Timko, Finney, & Moos, 2005).

Sociocultural factors also influence the form that abnormality takes (Kyrios et al., 2001). For example, depression is considered a *culture-general* disorder because it appears virtually everywhere in the world. However, specific symptoms tend to differ depending on a person's cultural background (Falicov, 2003; Hopper & Wanderling, 2000; Whaley & Hall, 2009). In Western cultures, where the emotional and physical components of disorders are generally viewed separately, symptoms of depression tend to revolve around despair and other signs of emotional distress (Kleinman, 1991). But in China and certain other Asian cultures where emotional and physical experiences tend to be viewed as one, depressed people are as likely to report stomach or back pain as to complain of sadness (Nakao & Yano, 2006; Weiss et al., 2009; Ryder et al., 2008).

There are also *culture-specific* forms of disorder. For instance, Puerto Rican and Dominican Hispanic women sometimes experience *ataques de nervios* ("attacks of nerves"), a unique way of reacting to stress that includes heart palpitations, shaking, shouting, nervousness, depression, and possibly fainting or seizure-like episodes (Baer et al., 2003; Keough, Timpano, & Schmidt, 2009; Lizardi, Oquendo, & Graver, 2009). In Asia, Khmer refugees sometimes suffer from panic-related fainting spells known as *kyol goeu* (Hinton, Um, & Ba, 2001). And genital retraction syndromes are occasionally observed in a number of places around the world. In Southeast Asia, southern China, and Malaysia, men suffering from *koro* fear that their penis will shrivel, retract into the body, and cause death (Dzokoto & Adams, 2005; Garlipp, 2008). In females the fear relates to shriveling of the breasts.

In short, sociocultural factors create differing social roles, stressors, opportunities, and experiences for people who differ in age, gender, and cultural traditions. They also help shape the disorders and symptoms to which certain categories of people are prone. Any attempt to fully explain psychological disorders must take these sociocultural factors into account.

sociocultural perspective Explaining mental disorders in ways that emphasize the role of factors such as gender and age, physical situations, cultural values and expectations, and historical era.

sociocultural factors Characteristics or conditions that can influence the appearance and form of maladaptive behavior.

The Diathesis-Stress Model as an Integrative Explanation

The biopsychosocial approach is currently the most comprehensive and influential way of explaining psychological disorders. It is prominent partly because it encompasses so many important causal factors, including biological imbalances, genetically inherited characteristics, brain damage, psychological traits, socioculturally influenced learning experiences, stressful life events, and many more.

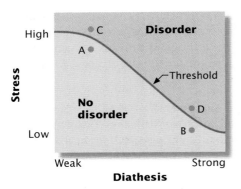

FIGURE 12.2
Diathesis, Stress, and Disorder
The diathesis-stress model's explanations suggest that psychological disorders can result from many combinations of predisposition and stress. Point D shows disorder stemming from a strong predisposition and relatively little stress. At Point C, disorder resulted from a weak predisposition but a lot of stress. Points A and B represent blends of diathesis and stress that are not potent enough to trigger disorder.

But how do all these factors actually interact to create disorder? Most researchers who study psychopathology believe that inherited characteristics, biological processes, learning experiences, and sociocultural forces combine to create a predisposition, or *diathesis* (pronounced "dye-ATH-uh-sis"), for psychological disorders. Whether or not a person eventually develops symptoms of disorder, they say, depends on the nature and amount of stress the person encounters (Elwood et al., 2009; Turner & Lloyd, 2004). For example, a person may have inherited a biological tendency toward depression or may have learned depressing patterns of thinking, but these predispositions might not result in a depressive disorder unless the person is faced with a severe financial crisis or suffers the loss of a loved one. If major stressors don't occur or if the person has good stress-coping skills, depressive symptoms may never appear or may be relatively mild (Canli et al., 2006).

So according to the **diathesis-stress model**, biological, psychological, and sociocultural factors can predispose us toward disorder, but it takes a certain amount of stress to actually trigger it. For those with a strong diathesis, relatively mild stress might be enough to create a problem. Those whose predisposition is weaker might not show signs of disorder until stress becomes extreme or prolonged (see Figure 12.2). Another way to think about the diathesis-stress model is in terms of *risk:* The more risk factors for a disorder a person has—whether they take the form of genetic tendencies, personality traits, cultural traditions, or stressful life events—the more likely it is that the person will display a form of psychological disorder associated with those risk factors.

Table 12.1 shows how a particular case of psychopathology might be explained by various biopsychosocial factors and how it might be summarized in terms of diathesis and stress. Later, you'll see these same biopsychosocial factors combined within a diathesis-stress framework to explain a number of other psychological disorders.

Classifying Psychological Disorders

How many psychological disorders have been identified?

Although definitions of abnormality differ within and across cultures, there does seem to be a set of behavior patterns that roughly defines the range of most abnormality in most cultures. The majority of these behavior patterns qualify as disorders because

diathesis-stress model The notion that psychological disorders arise when a predisposition for a disorder combines with sufficient amounts of stress to trigger symptoms.

TABLE 12.1 **Explaining Psychopathology**	
Here are the factors that would be highlighted by the biopsychosocial approach in the case of José, the man described at the beginning of this chapter. At the bottom is a summary of how these factors might be combined within a diathesis-stress framework.	
Explanatory Domain	**Possible Contributing Factors**
Neurobiological/medical	José may have a genetic tendency toward anxiety, an endocrine dysfunction, a neurotransmitter imbalance, a brain tumor, or some other biological disorder.
Psychological: psychodynamic	José has unconscious conflicts and desires. Instinctual impulses are breaking through ego defenses into consciousness, causing panic.
Psychological: social-cognitive	José interprets physical stress symptoms as signs of serious illness or impending death. His panic is rewarded by stress reduction when he stays home from work.
Psychological: humanistic	José fails to recognize his genuine feelings about work and his place in life, and he fears expressing himself.
Sociocultural	A culturally based belief that "a man should not show weakness" amplifies the intensity of stress reactions and delays José's decision to seek help.
Diathesis-stress summary	José has a biological (possibly genetic) predisposition to be overly responsive to stressors. The stress of work and extra activity exceeds his capacity to cope and triggers panic as a stress response.

they result in impaired functioning, a main criterion of the practical approach to defining abnormality. It has long been the goal of those who study abnormal behavior to classify these patterns into a set of precise diagnostic categories. Ideally, establishing these categories should make it easier to diagnose which disorder a particular person is displaying and thus which treatment method would be most appropriate.

Diagnoses are also important for research on the causes of psychopathology. If researchers can accurately classify people into particular disorder categories, they will have a better chance of spotting genetic features, biological abnormalities, cognitive processes, and environmental experiences that people in the same category might share. Finding that people in one category share a set of features that differs from those shared by people in other categories could provide clues about which features are related to the development of each disorder.

In 1952 the American Psychiatric Association published the first edition of what has become the "official" North American diagnostic classification system, the *Diagnostic and Statistical Manual of Mental Disorders (DSM)*. Each edition of the *DSM* has included more categories. The current editions, the *DSM-IV* and the *DSM-IV-TR* (text revision), include more than 300 specific diagnostic labels (American Psychiatric Association, 1994, 2000). The *DSM-IV-TR* is due to be replaced by the *DSM-5* in 2013. Mental health professionals outside North America diagnose mental disorders using classification systems that appear in the tenth edition of the World Health Organization's *International Classification of Diseases (ICD-10)* and its companion volume, the International Classification of Functioning, Disability, and Health (ICF). The ICD-10 is scheduled to be replaced by the ICD-11 by 2015. To facilitate international communication and cross-cultural research with respect to psychopathology, efforts are under way to remove any inconsistencies between the DSM and the ICD (Cottler & Grant, 2007; Kupfer & Regier, 2010; Löwe et al., 2008; Widiger et al., 2006). (The latest information about the upcoming editions of the *DSM* and the *ICD* is available at http://www.dsm5.org/Pages/Default.aspx and http://www.who.int/classifications/icd/revision/en/index.html.)

A Classification System: The *DSM-IV-TR*

The *DSM-IV-TR* describes the patterns of thinking, emotion, and behavior that define various mental disorders. For each disorder, the *DSM-IV-TR* provides specific criteria outlining the conditions that must be present before a person is given that diagnostic label. In keeping with the biopsychosocial approach, diagnosticians can use the *DSM-IV-TR* to evaluate troubled people on five dimensions, or *axes*. (*Axes* is the plural of *axis* and is pronounced "AX-eez"). Together, these axes provide a broad picture of each person's biological and psychological problems and of any sociocultural context factors that might contribute to them. As shown in Table 12.2, mental disorders such as schizophrenia or depression are recorded on Axis I, whereas evidence of personality disorders or intellectual disability is noted on Axis II. Any medical conditions that might be important in understanding the person's cognitive, emotional, or behavioral problems are listed on Axis III. On Axis IV, the diagnostician notes any psychosocial or environmental problems (such as the loss of a loved one, physical or sexual abuse, discrimination, unemployment, poverty, homelessness, inadequate health care, or conflict with religious or cultural traditions) that are important for understanding the person's psychological problems. Finally, on Axis V, the person is rated (from 100 down to 1) on current psychological, social, and occupational functioning. Here is a sample *DSM-IV-TR* diagnosis for someone who received labels on all five axes:

Axis I:	Major depressive disorder, single episode
Axis II:	Avoidant personality disorder
Axis III:	Alcoholic cirrhosis of the liver
Axis IV:	Problems with primary support group (death of spouse)
Axis V:	Global assessment of functioning 50

TABLE 12.2 The Diagnostic and Statistical Manual of Mental Disorders (DSM) of The American Psychiatric Association

Axis I of the fourth edition (*DSM-IV-TR*) lists the major categories of mental disorders. Personality disorders and intellectual disability are listed on Axis II.

Axis I (Clinical Syndromes)

1. ***Disorders usually first diagnosed in infancy, childhood, or adolescence.*** Problems such as hyperactivity, childhood fears, conduct disorders, frequent bed-wetting or soiling, and other problems in normal social and behavioral development. Includes autistic spectrum disorders (severe impairment in social, behavioral, and language development) as well as learning disorders.

2. ***Delirium, dementia, and amnesic and other cognitive disorders.*** Problems caused by physical deterioration of the brain due to aging, disease, drugs or other chemicals, or other possible unknown causes. These problems can appear as an inability to "think straight" (delirium) or as loss of memory and other intellectual functions (dementia).

3. ***Substance-related disorders.*** Psychological, behavioral, physical, social, or legal problems caused by dependence on or abuse of a variety of chemical substances, including alcohol, heroin, cocaine, amphetamines, painkillers, hallucinogens, marijuana, and tobacco.

4. ***Schizophrenia and other psychotic disorders.*** Severe conditions characterized by abnormalities in thinking, perception, emotion, movement, and motivation that greatly interfere with daily functioning. Problems involving false beliefs (delusions).

5. ***Affective disorders*** (also called ***mood disorders***). Severe disturbances of mood, especially depression, overexcitement (mania), or alternating episodes of each extreme (bipolar disorder).

6. ***Anxiety disorders.*** Specific fears (phobias), panic attacks, generalized feelings of dread, rituals of thought and action (obsessive-compulsive disorder) aimed at controlling anxiety, and problems caused by traumatic events, such as rape or military combat.

7. ***Somatoform disorders.*** Physical symptoms such as paralysis and blindness that have no physical cause. Unusual preoccupation with physical health or with nonexistent physical problems (hypochondriasis, somatization disorder, somatoform pain disorder).

8. ***Factitious disorders.*** False mental disorders that are intentionally produced to satisfy some psychological need.

9. ***Dissociative disorders.*** Psychologically caused problems of consciousness and self-identification—e.g., loss of memory (amnesia) or the development of more than one identity (dissociative identity disorder).

10. ***Sexual and gender identity disorders.*** Problems of (a) finding sexual arousal through unusual objects or situations (like shoes or exposing oneself); (b) unsatisfactory sexual activity (sexual dysfunction); or (c) identifying with the opposite gender.

11. ***Eating disorders.*** Problems associated with eating too little (anorexia nervosa) or binge eating followed by self-induced vomiting (bulimia).

12. ***Sleep disorders.*** Severe problems involving the sleep-wake cycle, especially an inability to sleep well at night or to stay awake during the day.

13. ***Impulse control disorders.*** Compulsive gambling, stealing, or fire setting.

14. ***Adjustment disorders.*** Failure to adjust to or deal well with such stressors as divorce, financial problems, family discord, or other unhappy life events.

Axis II (Personality Disorders and Intellectual Disability)

1. ***Personality disorders.*** Diagnostic labels given to individuals who may or may not receive an Axis I diagnosis but who show lifelong behavior patterns that are unsatisfactory to them or that disturb other people. These patterns may involve unusual suspiciousness, unusual ways of thinking, self-centeredness, shyness, overdependency, excessive concern with neatness and detail, or overemotionality, among others.

2. ***Intellectual disability (mental retardation).*** This label is applied to individuals whose measured IQ is less than about 70 *and* who fail to display the skills of daily life, communication, and other tasks expected of people their age.

Source: Reprinted with permission from the *Diagnostic and Statistical Manual of Mental Disorders*, Text Revision, Fourth Edition. Copyright © 2000. American Psychiatric Association.

Neurosis and *psychosis* are no longer listed in the *DSM-IV-TR*, because they are not specific enough. However, some mental health professionals still sometimes use these terms as shorthand descriptions. *Neurosis* refers to conditions in which some form of anxiety is the major characteristic. *Psychosis* refers to conditions involving more extreme problems that leave people "out of touch with reality" or unable to function on a daily basis. The disorders once listed under these headings now appear in various Axis I categories in the *DSM-IV-TR*.

Further changes in the diagnostic system will surely appear in the *DSM-5* (Beutler & Malik, 2002; Helzer & Hudziak, 2002; Maj et al., 2002; McHugh, 2005). For example,

Anxiety and Depression

People who experience anxiety disorders—particularly panic disorder, generalized anxiety disorder, or posttraumatic stress disorder—are likely to display some other mental disorder as well, most often depression (Kaufman & Charney, 2000; Roy-Byrne et al., 2000). Accordingly, the next edition of the *DSM* may include *mixed anxiety/depression*, a new category to describe people whose symptoms of anxiety and depression combine to impair their daily functioning (Das-Munshi et al., 2008).

because it is common for certain disorders, such as anxiety and depression, to appear together, *DSM-5* will probably include some diagnostic labels that designate "mixed" disorders (Das-Munshi et al., 2008; First, 2011). Among other possible changes is a new category of disorders characterized primarily by obsessive-compulsive symptoms, including hoarding and hair-pulling (Hollander, Braum, & Simeon, 2008; Huprich, 2009; Mataix-Cols et al., 2010). It has also been proposed that *DSM-5* should include in its addictions category excessive involvement with sex, eating, shopping, gambling, and gaming, as well as texting, e-mailing, and other Internet activities (Kafka, 2010; Mitzner, Whelan, & Meyers, 2011; Moser, 2011; Young, 2009).

Another popular proposal is to organize the *DSM-5* around symptom clusters or symptom dimensions rather than around specific diagnostic categories (Widiger & Lowe, 2008). The idea behind this *dimensional approach* would be to create a set of symptom "building blocks" that could be combined in many different ways so as to better recognize and describe the precise nature of each person's problems (Bell, Sowers, & Thompson, 2008; Hankin et al., 2005; Krueger & Markon, 2006; Krueger, Watson, & Barlow, 2005; Markon, Krueger, & Watson, 2005; Samuel & Widiger, 2006; Widiger & Samuel, 2005). Other proposals for the *DSM-5* include basing diagnoses on the results of brain imaging and the analysis of people's genetic characteristics (Kiviniemi, 2008; Kupfer, & Regier, 2011), and on factors related to a person's stage of development (Bell, 2011; Beynon, 2011; Egger & Emde, 2010; Knoll, Bulik, & Hebebrand, 2011).

Not everyone is happy with the proposed changes. Critics worry that some of the proposals being considered for *DSM-5* will have unintended negative consequences (First, 2011; Frances, 2009, 2010; Spitzer, 2009). For example, it might become too easy for shopping, texting, and other behaviors that are quite common in the general population to be labeled as addictions and thus greatly increase the number of individuals who qualify for a psychiatric diagnosis (e.g., First, 2011; Frances, 2009, 2010; Spitzer, 2009). Skeptics point out that such changes could create "false epidemics" of mental disorder and result in the "medicalization of normality." And although the American Psychiatric Association claims that the changes being proposed are well-supported by empirical research (Schatzberg et al., 2009), there are many who have doubts about that (Babor, 2011; First, 2011; Moser, 2011; von Gontard, 2011; Widiger, 2011).

Other critics say that *DSM-5* will just continue the long tradition of focusing diagnosis only on people's weaknesses and problems while ignoring their character strengths, virtues, prosocial values, and other psychological resources upon which they can potentially build during treatment. Some researchers in the field of *positive psychology* have even offered comprehensive lists of human strengths and values from which diagnosticians can choose (Baumgardner & Crothers, 2009; Park, Peterson, & Seligman, 2004; Peterson, 2006b).

Evaluating the Diagnostic System

How good is the current diagnostic system? One way to evaluate the *DSM-IV-TR* is to consider *interrater reliability,* the degree to which different mental health professionals agree on what diagnostic label a particular person should have. Reviews of research show that the reliability of the *DSM-IV-TR* is acceptable or high for some disorders but not others. For instance, interrater agreement is strong on Axis I categories such as anxiety disorders, affective disorders, some childhood disorders, and schizophrenia (Brown et al., 2001; Jakobsen et al., 2005; Keenan et al., 2007; Simpson et al., 2002), but is much lower for other categories, such as somatoform disorders and Axis II personality disorders (Mayou et al., 2005; Shedler & Westen, 2004; Westen, Shedler, & Bradley, 2006; Wollert, 2007). Overall, interrater agreement appears highest when diagnosis is based on structured interviews that systematically address each area of functioning and provide uniform guidelines for interpreting people's responses (Brown et al., 2001; Rogers, 2003; Widiger & Sanderson, 1995).

Do diagnostic labels give accurate information that guides correct inferences about people? This *validity* question is difficult to answer because accuracy can be judged in different ways. A diagnosis could be evaluated, for example, on how well it predicts a person's behavior or perhaps on whether the person is helped by treatment that has helped others in the same diagnostic category. Still, evidence does support the validity of most criteria in the *DSM-IV-TR* (Deep-Soboslay et al., 2006; Keenan & Wakschlag, 2004; Kim-Cohen et al., 2005; Langenbucher & Nathan, 2006; Simon & von Korff, 2006; Vieta & Phillips, 2007). Validity is likely to improve even more as diagnostic labels— and the diagnostic system—are refined in the *DSM-5* to reflect what researchers are learning about the characteristics, causes, courses, and cultural factors involved in various disorders.

The diagnostic system is far from perfect, however (Beutler & Malik, 2002; Kendell & Jablensky, 2003; Krueger & Markon, 2006; Nestadt et al., 2005). First, people's problems often do not fit neatly into a single category. For example, a person may suffer both anxiety and depression. Second, the same symptom (such as difficulty sleeping) can appear as part of more than one disorder. Third, although the *DSM-IV-TR* provides many useful diagnostic criteria, some of them—such as "clinically significant impairment"—are open to a certain amount of interpretation. When mental health professionals must decide for themselves whether a particular person's symptoms are severe enough to warrant a particular diagnosis, personal bias can creep into the system (Kim & Ahn, 2002; Widiger & Clark, 2000). All of these factors may lead to misdiagnosis in some cases. Concern over this possibility has grown as the nations of North America and Western Europe have become increasingly multicultural. Diagnosticians in these countries are encountering more and more people whose cultural backgrounds they may not fully understand and whose behavior they may misinterpret (Broekman et al., 2011; Crowther, Lipworth, & Kerridge, 2011).

Some people whose behavior differs enough from cultural norms to cause annoyance feel that society should tolerate their "neurodiversity" instead of giving them a diagnostic label (Harmon, 2004; Kapp, 2011; Langan, 2011; Mackenzie & Watts, 2011). In the same vein, Thomas Szasz (pronounced "zaws") and other critics have argued that the entire process of labeling people instead of describing problems is dehumanizing because it ignores people's strengths and the features that make each individual unique (Caplan, 1995; Kutchins & Kirk, 1997; McElvaney, 2011; Perry, 2011; Snyder & Lopez, 2006, 2007; Szasz, 2003; Wampold, Ahn, & Coleman, 2001). Calling people "schizophrenics" or "alcoholics," Szasz said, may actually encourage the behaviors associated with these labels, undermine the confidence of clients and therapists about a person's chances for improvement, and may even force people—especially those who hold noncomformist or politically unpopular views—to undergo treatment (Dickinson & Hurley, 2012; Doyle & Marco, 2011; Horley, 2011; Szasz, 1972, 2009). Though most mental health professionals disagree with Szasz on this last point, his arguments are worth noting because psychiatric diagnosis has indeed been used in the past, and even in some countries today, to suppress social dissent or unpopular beliefs and lifestyles.

In summary, it is unlikely that any diagnostic system will ever satisfy everyone. No shorthand label can fully describe a person's problems or predict exactly how that person will behave. All that can be reasonably expected of a diagnostic system is that it provides informative general descriptions of the types of problems displayed by people who have been placed in various categories (First et al., 2004).

THINKING CRITICALLY ## Is Psychological Diagnosis Biased?

Some researchers and clinicians worry that problems with the reliability and validity of the diagnostic system are due partly to bias in its construction and use. They point out, for example, that if the criteria for diagnosing a certain disorder were based on research that focused on only one gender, one ethnic group, or one age group, those criteria might not apply to other groups. Moreover, diagnosticians, like other people, hold expectations and make assumptions about males versus females and about individuals from differing cultures or ethnic groups. These cognitive biases could color their judgments and might lead them to apply diagnostic criteria in ways that are slightly but significantly different from one case to the next (Bjorklund, 2006; Caetano, 2011; During et al., 2011; Hartung & Widiger, 1998; Lewis-Fernández et al., 2010; Poland & Caplan, 2004).

What am I being asked to believe or accept?

Here we focus on ethnicity as a possible source of bias in diagnosing psychopathology. It is of special interest because there is evidence that like social class and gender, ethnicity is an important sociocultural factor in the development of mental disorder. The assertion to be considered is that clinicians in the United States base their diagnoses partly on a client's ethnic background and more specifically that bias affects these clinicians' diagnoses of African Americans.

Is evidence available to support the claim?

Several facts suggest the possibility of ethnic bias in psychological diagnosis. For one thing, African Americans receive the diagnosis of schizophrenia more frequently than European Americans do (Barnes, 2004; Kilbourne et al., 2004; Minsky et al., 2003). And certain kinds of odd symptoms tend to be diagnosed as a mood disorder in European Americans but as schizophrenia in African Americans (Gara et al., 2012; Neighbors et al., 2003; Schwartz & Feisthamel, 2009). Further, relative to their presence in the general population, African Americans are overrepresented in public mental hospitals, where the most serious forms of disorder are seen, and underrepresented in private hospitals and outpatient clinics, where less severe problems are treated (Barnes, 2004; Snowden & Cheung, 1990; U.S. Surgeon General, 1999). African Americans are also more likely than European Americans to be discharged from mental hospitals without a definite diagnosis, suggesting that clinicians have more difficulty in diagnosing their disorders (Sohler & Bromet, 2003). Emergency room physicians, too, appear less likely to recognize psychiatric disorders in African American patients than in patients from other groups (Kunen et al., 2005).

There is also evidence that members of ethnic minorities, including African Americans, are underrepresented in research on psychopathology (Iwamasa, Sorocco, & Koonce, 2002). This lack of minority representation may leave clinicians less aware of sociocultural factors that could influence diagnosis. For example, they might more easily misinterpret an African American's unwillingness to trust a European American diagnostician as evidence of paranoid symptoms (Whaley, 2001, 2011).

Can that evidence be interpreted another way?

Differences among ethnic groups in diagnosis or treatment do not automatically indicate bias based on ethnicity. Perhaps there are real differences in psychological functioning among different ethnic groups. If African Americans are exposed to more risk factors for disorder, including poverty, violence, and other major stressors than other groups are, they could be especially vulnerable to more serious forms of mental disorder (Plant & Sachs-Ericsson, 2004; Turner & Lloyd, 2004). And poverty, not diagnostic bias, could be responsible for the fact that African Americans are more often seen at less expensive public hospitals than at more expensive private ones. Finally, there is no guarantee that diagnostic criteria would be significantly different if more African Americans had been included in psychopathology research samples.

What evidence would help to evaluate the alternatives?

So do African Americans actually display more signs of mental disorder than other groups do, or do diagnosticians just perceive them as more disordered? One way of approaching this question is to conduct experiments in which diagnosticians assign labels to clients on the basis of case histories, test scores, and the like. In some studies, the cases are selected so that pairs of clients show about the same amount of disorder but one member of the pair is described as European American and the other as African American. In other studies, the same case materials, described as representing either African American or European American clients, are presented to different diagnosticians. Bias in diagnosis would be suggested if, for example, the clinicians saw patients who were described as African American as more seriously disordered than others.

Most studies of this type have found little or no ethnic bias (e.g., Angold et al., 2002; Garb, 1997; Kales et al., 2005a, 2005b; Littlewood, 1992). These results are difficult to interpret, however, because the diagnosticians might have been aware of the purpose of the study and so might have gone out of their way to be unbiased (Abreu, 1999; Gushue, 2004). In fact, researchers *have* found evidence of some diagnostic bias against African Americans when clinicians were unaware of the purpose of the research (e.g., Baskin, Bluestone, & Nelson, 1981; Jones, 1982). But bias can result in underdiagnosis as well as overdiagnosis. One review of research found that African American children exhibited more signs of hyperactivity disorder than European American children did, yet were given that diagnosis less often (Miller, Nigg, & Miller, 2009). In another study, socially disruptive African American youngsters were less likely than disruptive European American adolescents to be diagnosed with conduct disorder (Pottick et al., 2007). These results suggest that some diagnosticians might believe that a certain amount of overactivity, inattention, and misbehavior is to be expected of African Americans and that this behavior is therefore "normal" for them.

Bias has also appeared in studies aimed at identifying the factors that influence clinicians' judgments following extensive interviews with patients. For example, one hospital study found that in arriving at their diagnoses, psychiatrists were more likely to attribute hallucinations and paranoid thinking to African American patients than to non–African American patients and they were more likely to attribute symptoms of depressive disorders to non–African Americans (Trierweiler et al., 2000). Another study showed that after being diagnosed with schizophrenia, African Americans were more likely than Caucasian Americans to be hospitalized, even when symptoms were about equally severe (Rost et al., 2011).

As noted earlier, some of these differences could reflect ethnic differences in the rate of disorder in the population. However, when people were interviewed in their own homes as part of large-scale mental health surveys, the diagnosis of schizophrenia was given only slightly more often to African Americans than to European Americans (Robins & Regier, 1991; Snowden & Cheung, 1990). So the presence of ethnic bias is suggested, at least for some diagnoses, for patients who are evaluated in mental hospitals but not necessarily for those who are interviewed in their own homes (Trierweiler et al., 2000, 2005).

What conclusions are most reasonable?

Just as the *DSM-IV-TR* is imperfect, so are the people who use it. As described in the chapters on social psychology and on thought, language, and intelligence, cognitive biases and stereotypes affect human thinking to some extent in virtually every social situation. It is not surprising, then, that they operate in diagnosis as well. Diagnostic bias does not necessarily reflect deliberate discrimination, however. Like the processes of prejudice discussed in the social psychology chapter, diagnostic bias based on ethnicity can operate unconsciously, without the diagnostician's being aware of it (Abreu, 1999; Boysen, 2009). So no matter how precisely researchers specify the criteria for assigning diagnostic labels, biases and stereotypes are likely to threaten the objectivity of the diagnostic process (Poland & Caplan, 2004; Trierweiler et al., 2000).

Minimizing diagnostic bias requires a better understanding of it. Diagnosticians should focus more intently than ever on the fact that their concepts of "normality" and "abnormality" are affected by sociocultural values that a given client might not share (Kales et al., 2006; Landrine, 1991; Trierweiler et al., 2005; Whaley & Hall, 2009). They must also become more aware that the same cognitive shortcuts and biases that affect everyone else's thinking and decision making can impair their own clinical judgments (Lopez, 1989). In fact, future research on memory, problem solving, decision making, social attributions, and other aspects of culture and cognition may turn out to hold the key to reducing bias in the diagnosis of psychological disorders. Meanwhile, perhaps the best way to counteract clinicians' cognitive shortcomings is to teach them to base their diagnoses solely on standard diagnostic criteria and decision rules rather than relying on their (potentially biased) clinical impressions (Akin & Turner, 2006; Kramer, Bernstein, & Phares, 2013).   ● ● ● ●

We don't have space to cover all of the *DSM-IV-TR* categories, so we will focus on several of the most prevalent and socially significant examples. As you read, try not to catch "medical student's disease." Just as medical students often think that they have the symptoms of every illness they read about, some psychology students worry that certain aspects of their behavior (or that of a relative or friend) might reflect a mental disorder. A related phenomenon has recently been labeled *cyberchondria* (Harding et al., 2008; Hart & Björgvinsson, 2010; Vasconcellos-Silva et al., 2010) because people's worries so often stem from their unguided use of the Internet to learn about psychiatric disorders (Al-Shammary et al., 2007; Muse et al., 2012; Trotter & Morgan, 2008; White & Horvitz, 2009). Just remember that everyone has problems sometimes. Before deciding that you or someone you know has a serious disorder or needs psychological help, consider whether the content, context, and functional impairment associated with the behavior would qualify it as abnormal according to the criteria of the practical approach.

Anxiety Disorders

What is a phobia?

If you've ever been tense before an exam, a date, or a job interview, you have some idea of what anxiety feels like. An increased heart rate, sweating, rapid breathing, dry mouth, and a sense of dread are all common features of anxiety. Brief episodes of moderate anxiety are a normal part of life for most people. But when anxiety is so intense and long-standing that it disrupts a person's daily functioning, it is called an **anxiety disorder** (Kessler & Wang, 2008).

Types of Anxiety Disorders

Here, we discuss four types of anxiety disorders: *phobia, generalized anxiety disorder, panic disorder,* and *obsessive-compulsive disorder.* Another type, called *posttraumatic stress disorder,* is described in the chapter on health, stress, and coping. Together, these are the most common psychological disorders in North America; about 29 percent of the adults and 25 percent of children and adolescents in the United States will have an anxiety disorder at some point in their lives (Kessler et al., 2009; NIMH, 2012a, 2012b).

Phobia   An intense, irrational fear of an object or situation that is not likely to be dangerous is called a **phobia.** Even though people who experience phobias may realize that their fears are groundless, their efforts to avoid some object or situation greatly interfere with daily life. Thousands of phobias have been described; some of them are listed in Table 12.3.

The *DSM-IV-TR* includes diagnostic categories for specific phobia, social phobia, and agoraphobia. **Specific phobias** are fear and avoidance of heights, blood, animals, automobile or air travel, and other specific stimuli and situations. In the United States and other developed nations, they are the most prevalent of the anxiety disorders, affecting 9 to 15 percent of adults and children (Burstein et al., 2011; Hollander & Simeon, 2008; Kessler, Demler et al., 2005; Kessler & Wang, 2008; National Institute of Mental Health, 2012 c, 2012d). These figures are at least as high in other countries (Bener, Ghuloum, & Dafeeah, 2011; Iancu & Ram, 2011). Here is an example:

> Mr. L., a 50-year-old office worker, became terrified whenever he had to drive over a bridge. For years, he avoided bridges by taking roundabout ways to and from work and he refused to be a passenger in anyone else's car, in case they used a bridge. Even these inconvenient strategies failed when Mr. L. was transferred to a job requiring frequent automobile trips, many of which were over bridges. He refused the transfer and lost his job.

Social phobias involve anxiety about being criticized by others or acting in a way that is embarrassing or humiliating. The anxiety is so intense and persistent that it impairs the person's normal functioning. Common social phobias include fear of public speaking or performance ("stage fright"), fear of eating in front of others, and fear of using public rest rooms (Baptista et al., 2012; Gallego et al., 2011; Ginzburg et al., 2011; Gren-Landell et al., 2009; Kleinknecht, 2000). *Generalized social phobia* is a particularly severe form of social phobia in which fear occurs in virtually all social situations (Jacobs et al., 2009;

TABLE 12.3   Some Phobias

Phobia, the Greek word for "morbid fear," refers to *Phobos,* the Greek god of terror. The names of most phobias begin with the Greek word for the feared object or situation.

Name	Feared Stimulus
Acrophobia	Heights
Aerophobia	Flying
Claustrophobia	Enclosed places
Cynophobia	Dogs
Entomophobia	Insects
Gamophobia	Marriage
Gephyrophobia	Crossing a bridge
Hematophobia	Blood
Kenophobia	Empty rooms
Melissophobia	Bees
Ophidiphobia	Snakes
Xenophobia	Strangers

anxiety disorder A condition in which intense feelings of fear and dread are long-standing or disruptive.

phobia An anxiety disorder that involves strong, irrational fear of an object or situation that does not objectively justify such a reaction.

specific phobias Phobias that involve fear and avoidance of specific stimuli and situations such as heights, blood, and certain animals.

social phobias Strong, irrational fears related to social situations.

Mineka & Zinbarg, 2006; Noyes & Hoehn-Saric, 2006). Sociocultural factors can alter the form of social phobias. For example, in Japan, where cultural training emphasizes group-oriented values and goals, a common social phobia is *taijin kyofusho,* fear of embarrassing those around you (Essau et al., 2012; Kleinknecht, 1994).

Agoraphobia is a strong fear of being away from a safe place, such as home; of being away from a familiar person, such as a spouse or close friend; or of being in crowds or in other situations that are difficult to leave. People who suffer from agoraphobia prefer to stay at home, thus avoiding the intense anxiety associated with shopping, driving, or using public transportation. Many individuals who display agoraphobia have a history of panic attacks, which we describe later (Fava et al., 2008). In Western cultures, agoraphobia is more often reported by women, many of whom are totally homebound by the time they seek help. Although agoraphobia occurs less frequently than specific phobias (affecting only about 1.4 percent of adults and about 2.4 percent of children and adolescents in the United States), it is the phobia that most often leads people to seek treatment—mainly because it so severely disrupts everyday life (National Institute of Mental Health, 2012c, 2012d, 2012e, 2012f).

Generalized Anxiety Disorder   Strong and long-lasting anxiety that is not focused on any particular object or situation marks **generalized anxiety disorder**. Because the problem occurs in virtually all situations and because the person cannot pinpoint its source, this disorder is sometimes called *free-floating anxiety* and is essentially a disorder of worry (Fisher & Wells, 2009). For weeks at a time, the person feels anxious and preoccupied, sure that some disaster is about to occur. The person becomes jumpy and irritable and cannot sleep soundly. Fatigue, inability to concentrate, and physiological signs of anxiety are also common. Generalized anxiety disorder affects about 3 percent of adults in the United States in any given year and about 6 percent of the population at some point in their lives (Hollander & Simeon, 2008; Kessler & Wang, 2008; NIMH, 2012g). It is more common in women, often accompanying other problems such as depression or substance abuse (Wittchen & Hoyer, 2001).

Panic Disorder   For some people, anxiety takes the form of **panic disorder**. Like José, whom we met at the beginning of this chapter, people suffering from panic disorder experience recurrent, terrifying *panic attacks* that seem to come without warning or obvious cause. These attacks are marked by intense heart palpitations, pressure or pain in the chest, sweating, dizziness, and feeling faint. Often, victims believe they are having a heart attack. They may worry so much about having panic episodes that they limit their activities to avoid possible embarrassment (Kinley et al., 2009). As noted earlier, the fear of experiencing panic attacks may lead to agoraphobia as the person begins to fear and avoid places where help won't be available should panic recur (Grant et al., 2006; National Institute of Mental Health, 2006). Panic disorder may last for years, during which periods of improvement may be followed by recurrence. As many as 30 percent of the U.S. population have experienced at least one panic attack within the past year, but full-blown panic disorder is seen in only about 2 to 3 percent of the population in any given year (Hollander & Simeon, 2008; Kessler, Chiu et al., 2006; NIMH, 2012h, 2012i). Here is one example:

> *Geri, a 32-year-old nurse, had her first panic attack while driving on a freeway. Afterward, she would not drive on freeways. Her next attack occurred while she was with a patient and a doctor in a small examining room. A sense of impending doom flooded over her, and she burst out of the office and into the parking lot, where she felt immediate relief. From then on, fear of another attack made it impossible for her to tolerate any close quarters, including crowded shopping malls. She eventually quit her job because of terror of the examining rooms.*

Obsessive-Compulsive Disorder   Anxiety is also at the root of **obsessive-compulsive disorder (OCD)**, which affects about 1 percent of the U.S. population in any given year and about 2 to 3 percent of the world population at some time in their lives (Kessler

agoraphobia   A strong fear of being alone or away from the safety of home.

generalized anxiety disorder   A condition that involves long-lasting anxiety that is not focused on any particular object or situation.

panic disorder   Anxiety in the form of severe panic attacks that come without warning or obvious cause.

obsessive-compulsive disorder (OCD)   An anxiety disorder in which a person becomes obsessed with certain thoughts or feels a compulsion to do certain things.

© R. Ashrafov/Shutterstock

A Cleaning Compulsion
Obsessive-compulsive disorder is diagnosed when a culturally expected degree of cleanliness turns into an obsessive preoccupation with germs and a life-disrupting compulsion to clean things. Learning and stress appear to play the major role in shaping and triggering this and other anxiety disorders, but biological factors, including genetically inherited characteristics and problems in certain neurotransmitter systems, may result in an oversensitive nervous system and a predisposition toward anxiety.

obsessions Persistent, upsetting, and unwanted thoughts that interfere with daily life and may lead to compulsions.

compulsions Repetitive behaviors that interfere with daily functioning but are performed in an effort to prevent dangers or events associated with obsessions.

& Wang, 2008; Matthews, 2009; NIMH, 2012j; Ruscio et al., 2010). People displaying OCD are plagued by persistent, upsetting, and unwanted thoughts—called **obsessions**—that often focus on the possibility of infection, contamination, or doing harm to themselves or others. They don't actually carry out harmful acts, but the obsessive thoughts motivate repetitive behaviors—called **compulsions**—that the person believes will prevent infection, aggressive acts, or other events associated with the obsessions (Noyes & Hoehn-Saric, 2006). Common compulsions include rituals such as checking locks; repeating words or numbers; counting things; or arranging objects "just so." Obsessions and compulsions are much more intense than the familiar experience of having a thought or tune running "in the back of your mind" or rechecking a door to see that it is locked. In OCD, the obsessions and compulsions are intense, disturbing, and often strange intrusions that can severely impair daily activities (Morillo, Belloch, & Garcia-Soriano, 2007). The *DSM-IV-TR* defines compulsions as taking up more than one hour a day. Many of those who display OCD recognize that their thoughts and actions are irrational, but they still experience severe anxiety if they try to interrupt their obsessions or give up their compulsive rituals.

Causes of Anxiety Disorders

As with all the forms of psychopathology we will consider, the exact causes of anxiety disorders are a matter of some debate. However, there is good evidence that biological, psychological, and social factors all contribute (Coelho & Purkis, 2009; Williams et al., 2005). The exact nature and combination of causal factors varies from one anxiety disorder to the next. For example, the brain regions involved in panic disorder are not identical to those involved in obsessive-compulsive, social, or other forms of anxiety disorder (Young, Wu, & Menon, 2012; Zhou et al., 2010), and the learning experiences that contribute to specific phobias may differ from those that contribute to agoraphobia.

Biological Factors   Most anxiety disorders appear to run in families (Bolton et al., 2006; Grabe et al., 2006; Stewart et al., 2007), suggesting that these disorders are influenced by a genetic predisposition (Fyer et al., 2006). This influence is seen in the fact that if one identical twin has an anxiety disorder, the other twin (who shares the same genes) is more likely to also have an anxiety disorder than is the case in nonidentical twin pairs (Bolton et al., 2006; Kendler, Jacobson et al., 2002). Some inherited predispositions may be rather specific. One study found that identical twins are more likely than other siblings to share phobias about small animals and social situations but not about heights or enclosed spaces (Skre et al., 2000). The degree of genetic influence in anxiety disorders is moderate, however (Hollander & Simeon, 2008), and varies among disorders. For instance, genes appear to play a stronger role in early-onset panic disorder and generalized anxiety disorder than in specific phobias (Bolton et al., 2006; Distel et al., 2008; Neumeister et al., 2004).

Many researchers are trying to identify the specific genes or gene combinations involved in anxiety disorders. For example, a number of genes have been suggested as contributing to OCD, including two variations of the SLlC6A4 gene (Saiz et al., 2008). This work is difficult, though, because the mere presence of a gene doesn't necessary predict the appearance of a disorder. Rather, as described in our discussion of *epigenetics* in the introductory chapter, genes are often "switched on" or "switched off" by environmental triggers (Uddin et al., 2010). The genes or gene combinations that may be involved in anxiety disorders may exert their influence through their effects on the brain's neurotransmitter systems, which are discussed in the chapter on biology and behavior. For instance, excessive activity of norepinephrine circuits in certain parts of the brain has been linked with panic disorder, and dysregulation of serotonin has been associated with obsessive-compulsive disorder and social phobia (Lanzenberger et al., 2007). The role of these neurotransmitters is also suggested by the fact that medications that affect them are often effective in the treatment of OCD and other anxiety disorders (Bartz & Hollander, 2006).

Psychological and Environmental Factors   Biological predispositions combine with environmental stressors and psychological factors—especially cognitive processes and learning—to bring about most anxiety disorders (Hudson & Rapee, 2009; Leppänen & Nelson, 2012; Mineka & Zinbarg, 2006; Moses & Barlow, 2006; Nugent et al., 2011; Wilcox et al., 2008). To see the effects of environmental stressors, one need only look at the dramatic rise in cases of posttraumatic stress disorder following natural disasters or terrorist attacks (Galea, Ahern et al., 2002; Galea, Resnick et al., 2002; Hoven et al., 2005). Abuse or other traumatic experiences in childhood are also associated with increased risk of developing an anxiety disorder, particularly panic disorder (Brook & Schmidt, 2008; Safren et al., 2002). The impact of learning can be seen in families in which parents don't socialize much, tend to be suspicious of others, and exaggerate life's everyday dangers. These parents might unwittingly promote social anxiety in their children—especially in those born with a tendency toward shyness or anxiety (Eley et al., 2010)—by being overly protective and controlling, and thus influencing them to interpret social situations as threatening (Essex et al., 2010).

Learned ways of thinking play their part, too. Many people suffering from anxiety disorders exaggerate dangers in their environment, thereby creating an unrealistic expectation that bad things are going to happen (Brook & Schmidt, 2008; Cisler & Koster, 2010; Ouimet, Gawronski, & Dozois, 2009). This expectation leads them to dwell on and be constantly on the lookout for negative events (Vroling & de Jong, 2010; Wells & Matthews, 2006; Wong & Moulds, 2009). In addition, they tend to underestimate their own capacity for dealing with threatening events, thus triggering anxiety and desperation when feared events do occur (Beck & Emery, 1985). Their lack of perceived control, in turn, can lead these people to avoid or overreact to threatening situations (Wells & Matthews, 2006; White et al., 2006). Consider the development of panic attacks. They may seem to come out of nowhere, but in fact subtle symptoms of physical arousal may set the stage (Meuret et al., 2011). It is the person's sensitivity to and cognitive interpretation of those symptoms that can determine whether or not the attack actually develops (Domschke et al., 2010; Hollander & Simeon, 2008; Lim & Kim, 2005). In fact, experiments have shown that panic attacks are less likely in panic disorder patients who believe they can control the source of their discomfort (Rapee et al., 1992; White et al., 2006). These and other research results suggest that cognitive factors play an important role in panic disorder as well as in specific phobias, social phobias, generalized anxiety disorder, and OCD (Kolassa et al., 2009; Purdon, 2009; White et al., 2006).

Anxiety Disorders and Learning

LINKAGES

Can we learn to become "abnormal"?
(a link to Learning)

Money troubles, illness, final exams, unhappy relationships, and other problems often create upsetting thoughts. And upsetting thoughts create worry and anxiety, especially for people who are under stress or feel incapable of dealing with their problems. As these thoughts become more persistent, anxiety increases. If doing something such as cleaning the kitchen temporarily relieves the anxiety, that action may be strengthened through the process of negative reinforcement (see the chapter on learning). But cleaning can't eliminate the obsessive thoughts, so when they return, the cleaning may begin again. Eventually, cleaning or other actions may become compulsive, endlessly repeated rituals that keep the person trapped in a vicious circle of anxiety (Barlow, 1988). Based on this kind of analysis, social-cognitive theorists see obsessive-compulsive disorder as a learned pattern sparked by distressing thoughts and maintained by operant conditioning (Abramowitz et al., 2006).

They also see phobias as based in part on the principles of learning, especially classical conditioning and observational learning. The object of the phobia becomes a conditioned aversive stimulus through association with a traumatic event that acts as an unconditioned stimulus (Olatunji, 2006; Stein, 2006). Fear of dogs, for example, may result from a dog attack. Observing or hearing about other people's bad experiences can produce the same result: most people who fear flying have never been in a plane crash. Fears can even develop after seeing scary movies or TV shows (Askew, Kessock-Philip, & Field, 2008; Cook & Mineka, 1990). Once the fear is learned, avoidance of the feared object

Biological Preparedness

Being predisposed to learn to fear snakes and other potentially dangerous stimuli makes evolutionary sense. Like other animals, humans who rapidly learn a fear response to objects or situations that they see frightening their parents or peers are more likely to survive to pass on their genes to the next generation. Are there things you are especially afraid of? If so, list them and make a note of how you think these fears developed. How many of them appear to have "survival value"?

LEARN by DOING

or situation prevents the person from finding out that the fear is exaggerated. This cycle of avoidance helps explain why many fears don't disappear on their own (Lovibond et al., 2009).

Why are phobias involving snakes and spiders so common, even though people are seldom harmed by them? And why are there so few cases of phobias about electrical shocks, even though lots of people receive accidental shocks? The answer may be that people are *biologically prepared* to learn to fear and avoid things that had the potential to harm their evolutionary ancestors (Canu, 2008; Öhman & Mineka, 2001, 2003; Skre et al., 2000). This idea is supported by laboratory research (Hamm, Vaitl, & Lang, 1989). In one study, a group of Swedish psychologists created conditioned fear reactions to certain stimuli by associating photographs of those stimuli with electrical shocks (Öhman, Dimberg, & Öst, 1985). Their volunteer participants developed approximately equal conditioned anxiety reactions to photos of houses, human faces, and snakes. Later, however, when the participants were shown the photos alone, their conditioned reaction to snakes remained long after their response to houses and faces had faded. Similar results have also occurred in experiments with monkeys (Mühlberger et al., 2006; Zinbarg & Mineka, 1991). This evidence suggests that genetic predispositions and learning combine to promote the appearance of anxiety disorders and also to influence their responsiveness to treatment (Armfield, 2006; Bryant et al., 2010; Leyro, Zvolensky, & Bernstein, 2010; Mineka & Zinbarg, 2006; Nugent et al., 2011; Xie et al., 2009). ● ● ● ●

Somatoform Disorders

Can mental disorder cause blindness?

A young athlete was suffering fainting spells that prevented her from competing in track and field events. Doctors found no physical problems, and it was only after a program of stress management that her symptoms disappeared and she was able to rejoin her team (Lively, 2001). Sometimes people show symptoms of a *somatic,* or bodily, disorder even though there is nothing physically wrong. When psychological problems take somatic form, they are called **somatoform disorders.** The classic example of a somatoform disorder is **conversion disorder,** a condition in which a person appears to be (but is not) blind, deaf, paralyzed, or insensitive to pain in various parts of the body. (An earlier term for this disorder was *hysteria.*) Conversion disorders are rare, accounting for only about 1 to 2 percent of diagnoses, and are more common among women than men (American Psychiatric Association, 2000; Eifert, Zvolensky, & Louis, 2008; Feinstein, 2011). Although they can occur at any point in life, they usually appear in adolescence or early adulthood.

Conversion disorders differ from true physical disabilities in several ways. First, they tend to appear when a person is under severe stress. Second, they often help reduce that stress by enabling the person to avoid unpleasant situations. Third, the symptoms may be neurologically impossible or improbable, as Figure 12.3 illustrates. Finally, the person may show remarkably little concern about what most people would think was a rather serious problem. One college student, for example, experienced visual impairment that began each Sunday evening and became total blindness by Monday morning. Her vision would begin to return on Friday evenings and was fully restored in time for weekend social activities. She expressed no particular concern over her condition (Holmes, 1991). In such cases, the sensory systems remain intact, but the person appears to be unaware of the sensory information that the brain is still processing (Ballmaier & Schmidt, 2005; Blake, 1998; Bryant & Das, 2012; Grosz & Zimmerman, 1970; Harvey, Stanton, & David, 2006).

Another type of somatoform disorder is **hypochondriasis** (pronounced "hye-poh-kon-DRY-a-sis"), a strong, unjustified fear that one has or might get cancer, heart disease, AIDS, or some other serious medical problem. In some ways, hypochondriasis is like an anxiety disorder in that it includes elements of phobia, panic, and obsessive-compulsive disorder (Olantunji, 2008). Some people with hypochondriasis fear that they

somatoform disorders Psychological problems in which a person shows the symptoms of a physical disorder for which there is no physical cause.

conversion disorder A somatoform disorder in which a person appears to be (but actually is not) blind, deaf, paralyzed, or insensitive to pain.

hypochondriasis A strong, unjustified fear of physical illness.

(A)   **(B)**

FIGURE 12.3
Glove Anesthesia

In a form of conversion disorder called *glove anesthesia,* lack of feeling stops abruptly at the wrist (Part B). But as indicated by the overlapping colors in Part A, the nerves of the hand and arm blend, so if they were actually impaired, part of the arm would also lose sensitivity. Other neurologically impossible symptoms of conversion disorder include sleepwalking at night on legs that are "paralyzed" during the day.

somatization disorder A somatoform disorder in which there are numerous physical complaints without verifiable physical illness.

somatoform pain disorder
A somatoform disorder marked by complaints of severe, often constant pain with no physical cause.

body dysmorphic disorder
A somatoform disorder characterized by intense distress over imagined abnormalities of the skin, hair, face, or other areas of the body.

dissociative disorders Conditions involving sudden and usually temporary disruptions in a person's memory, consciousness, or identity.

will contract a terrible disease; the majority are convinced that they already have one. The fear prompts frequent visits to doctors and reports of numerous symptoms. Their preoccupation with illness often leads people with hypochondriasis to become "experts" on their most feared diseases, sometimes by endlessly searching health-related Internet websites (Taylor & Asmundson, 2008). In a related condition called **somatization disorder**, individuals make dramatic but vague reports about a multitude of physical problems rather than any specific illness. **Somatoform pain disorder** is marked by complaints of severe, often constant pain (typically in the neck, chest, or back) with no physical cause. In **body dysmorphic disorder,** the person is intensely distressed about an imagined abnormality of the skin, hair, face, or other bodily area. They may become preoccupied with the imagined deformity or imperfection, avoid social contacts, become dysfunctional, and even seek unnecessary corrective surgery (Veale, 2009).

A number of biological, psychological, and social factors have been suggested as contributing to somatoform disorders. Some cases, for example, may be related to childhood experiences in which a person learns that symptoms of physical illness bring special attention and care (Abramowitz & Braddock, 2006; Barsky et al., 1994; Feinstein, 2011). Others, including conversion disorder, may be triggered by severe stressors (Ballmaier & Schmidt, 2005; Ovsiew, 2006; Spiegel, 1994). Cognitive factors come into play, too. When given information about their health, people who display hypochondriasis are strongly biased to focus on threat-confirming information but to ignore reassuring information (Eifert, Zvolensky, & Louis, 2008). Abnormal serotonin functioning has also been associated with hypochondriasis, and various combinations of neurochemical and social skill deficits appear to accompany conversion disorder and body dysmorphic disorder (Brodino et al., 2008; Eifert, Zvolensky, & Louis, 2008).

Based on such findings, many researchers have adopted a diathesis-stress approach to explaining somatoform disorders. The results of their work suggest that certain people may have biological and psychological traits that make them especially vulnerable to somatoform disorders, particularly when combined with a history of physical illness (Suls & Howren, 2012). Among these traits are self-consciousness and oversensitivity to physical sensations. If such people experience a number of long-lasting stressors, intense emotional conflicts, or severe traumas, they are more likely than others to display physical symptoms in association with negative emotional arousal (Abramowitz & Braddock, 2006; Siti, 2004).

Sociocultural factors may also shape some somatoform disorders. In many Asian, Latin American, and African cultures, it is not unusual for people to experience severe headaches and other physical symptoms in association with psychological or interpersonal conflicts (Weiss et al., 2009). In North America such conflicts are more likely to be accompanied by anxiety or depression (Brislin, 1993). Genetic factors appear to play only a minor role in somatoform disorders.

Dissociative Disorders

What disorders create sudden memory loss?

Have you ever been driving all day on a boring highway and suddenly realized that you had almost no memory of what happened during the past half-hour? This common experience does not signal a mental disorder, but when disruptions in a person's memory, consciousness, or identity are more intense and long-lasting, they are known as **dissociative disorders.** These disruptions can come on gradually, but they usually occur suddenly and last from a few hours to many years. Consider the case of 18-year-old "Jane Doe," who was found lying in the fetal position outside a New York City youth shelter in October, 2009. She claimed to have no memory of her name, where she came from, or

"Would it be possible to speak with the personality that pays the bills?"

By dropping the label *multiple personality disorder,* the DSM-IV downplayed the idea that some people harbor multiple personalities that can easily be "contacted" through hypnosis or drugs. The new label, *dissociative identity disorder,* suggests, instead, that a dissociation, or separation, between one's memories and other aspects of identity can be so dramatic that people experiencing it may come to believe that they have more than one personality (Gleaves, May, & Cardena, 2001; Kong, Allen, & Gilsky, 2008; Spiegel, 1994).

fugue reaction (dissociative fugue) A psychological disorder involving sudden loss of memory and the assumption of a new identity in a new locale.

dissociative amnesia A psychological disorder marked by a sudden loss of memory for one's own name, occupation, or other identifying information.

dissociative identity disorder (DID) A dissociative disorder in which a person appears to have more than one identity, each of which behaves in a different way.

how she got where she was (Moore, 2009). After her picture was shown on national television, a viewer identified her as Kacie Peterson.

Kacie displayed a disorder known as a **fugue reaction** or **dissociative fugue** (pronounced "fewg"), which is characterized by sudden wandering and loss of memory for (or confusion about) personal identity. In some cases, the person adopts an entirely new identity. A related disorder called **dissociative amnesia** also involves sudden loss of memory about personal information but the person does not leave home or create a new identity. These conditions are rare, but they tend to attract intense publicity because they are so dramatic.

The most famous dissociative disorder is **dissociative identity disorder (DID)**, known in earlier editions of the *DSM* (and still commonly called) *multiple personality disorder (MPD).* A person with DID appears to have more than one identity, each of which speaks and acts in a different way. Each personality seems to have its own memories, wishes, and (often conflicting) impulses. Here is a case example:

Mary, a pleasant and introverted 35-year-old social worker, was referred to a psychiatrist for hypnotic treatment of chronic pain. At an early interview she mentioned the odd fact that though she had no memory of using her car after coming home from work, she often found that it had been driven 50 to 100 miles overnight. It turned out that she also had no memory of large parts of her childhood. Mary rapidly learned self-hypnosis for pain control, but during one hypnotic session, she suddenly began speaking in a hostile manner. She told the doctor her name was Marian and that it was "she" who had been taking long evening drives. She also called Mary "pathetic" for "wasting time" trying to please other people. Eventually, six other identities emerged, some of whom told of having experienced parental abuse in childhood. (Spitzer et al., 1994)

During the 1970s, there was a minor "epidemic" of DID, as well as an increase in the number of alternative personalities per case; some patients reported over forty of them (Castelli, 2009). This upsurge in DID may have occurred because clinicians were looking for it more carefully or because the conditions leading to it became more prevalent, but it may have also been influenced by movies such as *Sybil* and by tell-all books written by people who had been diagnosed with DID (Kihlstrom, 2005). These media influences may have increased the status of DID as a socioculturally approved method of expressing distress (Hacking, 1995).

There is a great deal of controversy over how dissociative disorders develop. Psychodynamic theorists see massive repression of traumatic events as the basis for creating "new personalities" who act out otherwise unacceptable impulses or recall otherwise unbearable memories (Maldonado & Spiegel, 2008; Ross, 1997). Social-cognitive theorists focus on the fact that everyone is capable of behaving in different ways depending on circumstances (e.g., rowdy in a bar, quiet in a museum). In rare cases, they say, this variation can become so extreme that a person feels like and is perceived by others as a "different person." Further, sudden memory loss or unusual behavior may be rewarded if they allow a person to escape unpleasant situations, responsibilities, or punishment for misbehavior (Lilienfeld & Lynn, 2003; Lilienfeld et al., 2009). Among other possible contributing factors are habitual errors in thinking and memory, difficulties in controlling attention, and problems in the daily sleep-wake cycle (Lynn et al., 2012; van der Kloet et al., 2012).

Research available so far suggests four conclusions. First, memory loss and other forms of dissociation are genuine phenomena and (as seen in fugue reactions) can sometimes be extreme. Second, many people displaying DID have experienced events they would like to forget or avoid. The majority (some clinicians believe all) have suffered severe, unavoidable, persistent abuse in childhood (Foote et al., 2006; Kihlstrom, 2005). Third, like Mary, most of these people appear to be skilled at self-hypnosis, through which they can induce a trance-like dissociative state. Fourth, most found that they could escape the trauma of abuse (at least temporarily) by creating "new personalities" to deal with stress (Spiegel, 1994; van der Hart et al., 2005).

However, not all abused children display DID, and there is evidence that some cases of DID may indeed be triggered by media stories or by therapists who expect to see alternative personalities and use hypnosis and other methods that encourage clients to display them (Lindsay et al., 2004; McHugh, 2009; Rieber, 2006). For example, it now appears that "Sybil's" famous story about having 16 personalities was untrue (Nathan, 2011). This evidence has led some skeptics to question the very existence of multiple personalities (Acocella, 1998; Lynn et al., 2012; Merckelbach, Devilly, & Rassin, 2002). They point to research showing, for example, that people who display DID may be more aware than they think they are of the memories and actions of each apparent identity (Allen, 2002; Allen & Iacono, 2001; Canaris, 2008).

Research on the existence and effects of repressed memories (discussed in the memory chapter) is sure to have an impact on our understanding of (and the controversy over) the causes of dissociative identity disorder. ("In Review: Anxiety, Somatoform, and Dissociative Disorders" presents a summary of our discussion of these topics.)

Anxiety, Somatoform, and Dissociative Disorders — IN REVIEW

Disorder	Subtypes	Major Symptoms
Anxiety disorders	Phobias	Intense, unreasonable, and disruptive fear of objects or situations.
	Generalized anxiety disorder	Excessive anxiety not focused on a specific situation or object; free-floating anxiety.
	Panic disorder	Repeated attacks of intense fear involving physical symptoms such as faintness, dizziness, and nausea.
	Obsessive-compulsive disorder	Persistent ideas or worries accompanied by ritualistic behaviors performed to neutralize anxiety-driven thoughts.
Somatoform disorders	Conversion disorder	A loss of physical ability (e.g., sight, hearing) that is related to psychological factors.
	Hypochondriasis	Preoccupation with or belief that one has a serious illness in the absence of any physical evidence.
	Somatization disorder	Wide variety of somatic complaints that occur over several years and are not the result of a known physical disorder.
	Somatoform pain disorder	Preoccupation with pain in the absence of physical reasons for the pain.
Dissociative disorders	Dissociative amnesia	Sudden loss of memory
	Fugue reaction (dissociative fugue)	Sudden loss of memory that may result in a person relocating and assuming a new identity.
	Dissociative identity disorder (multiple personality disorder)	Appearance within the same person of two or more distinct identities, each with a unique way of thinking and behaving.

IN REVIEW QUESTIONS

1. Concern that it may be triggered by media stories or therapists' suggestions has made ___ the most controversial of the dissociative disorders.
2. A person who sleepwalks but is not able to walk when awake is showing signs of ___.
3. Panic disorder sometimes leads to another anxiety disorder called ___.

Affective Disorders

How common is depression?

Everyone's mood, or *affect,* tends to rise and fall from time to time. However, when people experience long periods of extreme moods such as wild elation or deep depression, when they shift from one extreme to another, and especially when their moods are not consistent with the events around them, they are said to show an **affective disorder** (also called a **mood disorder**). We describe two main types: depressive disorders and bipolar disorders.

Depressive Disorders

Depression can range from occasional, normal "down" periods to episodes severe enough to require hospitalization. A person suffering **major depression** (also called **major depressive disorder**) feels sad and overwhelmed, typically losing interest in activities and relationships and taking pleasure in nothing (Getzfeld, 2006; Rapaport et al., 2005; Sloan,

affective disorder (mood disorder) A condition in which a person experiences extremes of moods for long periods, shifts from one extreme mood to another, and experiences moods that are inconsistent with events.

major depression (major depressive disorder) A condition in which a person feels sad and hopeless for weeks or months, often losing interest in all activities and taking pleasure in nothing.

Strauss, & Wisner, 2001). Despite the person's best efforts, anything from conversation to bathing can become an unbearable, exhausting task. Changes in eating habits resulting in weight loss or weight gain often accompany major depression. There may also be disturbed sleeping or excessive sleeping. Problems in working, concentrating, making decisions, and thinking clearly are also common, as are symptoms of an accompanying anxiety disorder or physical illness (Andreescu et al., 2007; Suls, & Howren, 2012; Zimmerman, McDermut, & Mattia, 2000). In extreme cases, depressed people may express false beliefs, or **delusions**, worrying, for example, that government agents are planning to punish them. Major depression may come on suddenly or gradually. It may consist of a single episode, or of repeated periods of depression (Klein, 2010). These episodes can last weeks or months; the average length of the first episode is four to nine months (Durand & Barlow, 2006). Exaggerated feelings of inadequacy, worthlessness, hopelessness, or guilt are common in major depression (Klein, 2010). Here is a case example:

> Mr. J. was a fifty-one-year-old industrial engineer.... Since the death of his wife five years earlier, he had been suffering from continuing episodes of depression marked by extreme social withdrawal and occasional thoughts of suicide.... He drank, and when thoroughly intoxicated would plead to his deceased wife for forgiveness. He lost all capacity for joy. . . . Once a gourmet, he now had no interest in food and good wine ... and could barely manage to engage in small talk. As might be expected, his work record deteriorated markedly. Appointments were missed and projects haphazardly started and left unfinished. (Davison & Neale, 1990, p. 221)

Depression is not always so extreme (de Graff et al., 2010). In a less severe pattern of depression, called **dysthymic disorder**, the person shows the sad mood, lack of interest, and loss of pleasure associated with major depression but less intensely and for a longer period. (The duration must be at least two years in adults and one year in children to qualify as dysthymic disorder.) Mental and behavioral disruptions are also less severe. People exhibiting dysthymic disorder rarely require hospitalization.

Major depression occurs at some time in the lives of about 17 percent of people in North America and Europe; in any given year, about 9.5 percent of these populations are experiencing the disorder (Edwards & Glick, 2008; Hasin et al., 2005; Kessler & Wang, 2008). Unfortunately, depression is becoming more common, both in the United States and elsewhere. The World Health Organization estimates that if current trends continue, depression will become the second leading cause of disability and premature death in developed countries (Kessler, 2012; Moussavi et al., 2007; World Health Organization, 2012; World Health Organization Mental Health Survey Consortium, 2004). The incidence of the disorder varies considerably across cultures and subcultures, however. For example, it occurs at much higher rates in urban Ireland than in urban Spain, or in China (Judd et al., 2002; Lee et al., 2007), and at higher rates in countries with the highest average incomes (Kessler, 2012). There are gender differences in some cultures, too. In North America and Europe, women are two to three times more likely than men to experience major depression (Kessler & Wang, 2008), but this difference does not appear in the less economically developed countries of the Middle East, Africa, and Asia (Ayuso-Mateos et al., 2001; Culbertson, 1997; World Health Organization, 2003). Depression can occur at any age, but it peaks in late adolescence or young adulthood and again in old age (Cross-National Collaborative Group, 2002; Durand & Barlow, 2006; Fassler & Dumas, 1997; Richards, 2011; Sowdon, 2001).

Depression often occurs in combination with other psychological disorders and medical conditions; it is especially likely to be diagnosed along with posttraumatic stress disorder, obsessive-compulsive disorder, and other anxiety disorders, as well as with substance use disorders, physical disabilities, and obesity, and during recovery from heart attack (Mitra et al., 2005; O'Brien, 2006; Rosen-Reynoso et al., 2011). Some researchers believe that the overlap between anxiety and depression is significant enough that the two should be combined into a single category in *DSM-5*, or, as mentioned earlier, that a new diagnosis of mixed anxiety/depression should be created (Miller & Holden, 2010; Moses & Barlow, 2006).

Suicide and Depression   Suicide is associated with a variety of psychological disorders, but it is most closely tied to depression and other affective disorders (Balázs et al., 2006;

delusions False beliefs, such as those experienced by people suffering from schizophrenia or severe depression.

dysthymic disorder A pattern of depression in which the person shows the sad mood, lack of interest, and loss of pleasure associated with major depression but to a lesser degree and for a longer period.

Holma et al., 2010). In fact, thinking about suicide is a symptom of depressive disorders. When suicidal thoughts combine with hopelessness about the future, which is another depressive symptom, a suicide attempt is much more likely to occur. Indeed, the rate of suicide among those with major depression is 3.4 percent overall, but 7 percent for males and as high as 15 percent for those who have been hospitalized for depression (Brown et al., 2000; Dawe, 2008; Morris, Ciesla, & Garber, 2008; Pompili et al., 2008; Van Orden et al., 2010).

In 2009, the year for which the most recent data are available, about 36,000 people in the United States committed suicide, and ten to twenty times that many attempted it (Centers for Disease Control and Prevention, 2009). This put the suicide rate at 11 per 100,000 people, making suicide the tenth leading cause of death in the United States that year. The suicide rate is as high as 25 per 100,000 in some northern and eastern European countries and Japan and as low as 6 per 100,000 in countries with stronger religious prohibitions against suicide, such as Greece, Italy, Ireland, and the nations of the Middle East (Lamar, 2000; Ono et al., 2008; Phillips, Li, & Zhang, 2002; World Health Organization, 2003).

Suicide rates differ considerably depending on sociocultural factors such as age, gender, and ethnicity (Baca-Garcia et al., 2010; Castle et al., 2011; Centers for Disease Control and Prevention, 2002b; NIMH, 2009; Oquendo et al., 2001). In the United States, suicide is most common among people 65 and older, especially males (Centers for Disease Control and Prevention, 2004; Warner, 2010). However, since 1950, suicide among adolescents has tripled. And though the rate has begun to level off in the last decade (Centers for Disease Control and Prevention, 2006), it is still the third leading cause of death, after accidents and homicides, among 15- to 24-year-olds (Centers for Disease Control and Prevention, 2002a, 2006). Suicide is the second leading cause of death among college students; about 10,000 try to kill themselves each year and about 1,000 actually do so. These figures are much higher than for young people in general but much lower than for the elderly (NIMH, 2009). Women attempt suicide three times as often as men, but men are four times as likely to actually kill themselves (Centers for Disease Control and Prevention, 2006). The gender difference is even greater among people who have been diagnosed with depression. In this group, the male suicide rate of 65 per 100,000 is ten times higher than the rate for women (Blair-West et al., 1999; Centers for Disease Control and Prevention, 1999b). The suicide rate for men who are 85 or older is 55 per 100,000; which is more than ten times higher than for women in this age group (Centers for Disease Control and Prevention, 2004).

Suicide rates also differ across ethnic groups. Among males in the United States, for example, the overall rate for American Indians is 15.1 per 100,000, compared with 13.9 for European Americans, 5.7 for Asian Americans, 4.9 for Hispanic Americans, and 5.0 for African Americans. The same pattern of ethnic differences appears among women, though the actual rates are much lower (NIMH, 2009).

Predicting who will commit suicide is difficult. For one thing, suicidal thoughts are not uncommon. About 3 percent of all adults and as many as 10 percent of college students report having had such thoughts during the past year (Brener, Hassan, & Barrios, 1999; Dawe, 2008; Kessler, Berglund, Borges et al., 2005). Still, the results of hundreds of research studies provide some predictive guidelines (Smyth & MacLachian, 2005). In the United States, at least, suicide is most likely among European American males, especially those who are older than 45, single or divorced, and living alone. Extended unemployment increases the suicide risk for this group (Joska & Stein, 2008; Inoue et al., 2006). The risk is also heightened among people diagnosed with an affective disorder, anxiety disorder, or schizophrenia (Boardman & Healy, 2001; Khan et al., 2002; Rihmer, 2001). Among the elderly, suicide is most common in males who suffer depression over health problems (e.g., Brown, Bongar, & Cleary, 2004). The risk is higher, too, in people who have made a specific plan, given away possessions, and are impulsive (Centers for Disease Control and Prevention, 2004; Kohli et al., 2010). Certain genetic risk factors, combined with a history of child abuse may further increase the likelihood of a suicide attempt (Murphy et al., 2011). A previous suicide attempt may not always be a good predictor of eventual suicide, because such attempts may have been help-seeking gestures, not failed efforts to die (Nock & Kessler, 2006). In fact, although about 10 percent of unsuccessful attempters try again and succeed, most people who commit suicide had made no prior attempts (Clark & Fawcett, 1992).

It is often said that people who talk about suicide will never try it. This is a myth (Shneidman, 1987). Those who say they are thinking of suicide are much more likely than other people to try suicide. In fact, most suicides are preceded by some kind of warning, whether direct ("I think I'm going to kill myself") or vague ("Sometimes I wonder if life is worth living"). Failure to recognize or respond to warning signs is a common phenomenon, even among psychologists (Fowler, 2012; Valuck et al., 2007). So although not everyone who threatens suicide follows through, if you suspect that someone you know is thinking about suicide, encourage the person to contact a mental health professional or a crisis hotline. If the danger is immediate, make the contact yourself and ask for advice about how to respond. Many suicide attempts—including those triggered by other suicides in the same town or school—can be prevented by social support and other forms of help for people at high risk (Centers for Disease Control and Prevention, 2004; Mann et al., 2005). For more information, visit suicide-related websites, such as that of the American Association of Suicidology (www.suicidology.org).

Bipolar Disorders

The alternating appearance of two emotional extremes, or poles, characterizes the **bipolar disorders**. In these disorders, episodes of depression alternate with **mania**, which is an extremely agitated and usually elated emotional state. During periods of mania, people tend to be overly optimistic, boundlessly energetic, certain of having extraordinary powers and abilities, and bursting with all sorts of ideas. They are irritated by anyone who tries to reason with them or "slow them down," and they may make impulsive and unwise decisions, including spending their life savings on foolish schemes; they can even become a danger to themselves or to others (Goldberg & Burdick, 2008; Kessler, Berglund, & Demier et al., 2005; National Institute of Mental Health, 2006).

There are two versions of bipolar disorder, known as bipolar I and bipolar II. In *bipolar I disorder,* episodes of mania may alternate with periods of deep depression (Ghaemi, 2008). Sometimes periods of relatively normal mood separate these extremes (Tohen et al., 2003). This pattern has also been called *manic depression.* Compared with major depression, bipolar disorder is rare. It occurs in only about 1 percent of adults, and it affects men and women about equally. Another 1 percent of adults display *bipolar II disorder,* in which major depressive episodes alternate with episodes known as *hypomania,* which are less severe than the manic phases seen in bipolar I disorder (Merikangas et al., 2007). Either version can severely disrupt a person's ability to work or maintain social relationships (Kessler, Berglund, Demler, et al., 2005; NIMH, 2006).

Slightly more common is a pattern of milder mood swings known as **cyclothymic personality** (also called **cyclothymic disorder**), the bipolar equivalent of dysthymic disorder. Like major depression, bipolar disorders are extremely disruptive to a person's ability to work or maintain social relationships (Goldberg, Harrow, & Grossman, 1995; Van Meter, Youngstrom, & Findling, 2012), and they are often accompanied by anxiety disorders or substance abuse (Andreescu et al., 2007; Freeman, Freeman, & McElroy, 2002; Ghaemi, 2008). "In Review: Affective Disorders" summarizes the main types of affective disorders.

Causes of Affective Disorders

Research on the causes of affective disorders has focused on biological, psychological, and sociocultural risk factors. The more of these risk factors people have, the more likely they are to experience an affective disorder.

bipolar disorder A condition in which a person alternates between the two emotional extremes of depression and mania.

mania An elated, active emotional state.

cyclothymic personality (cyclothymic disorder) An affective disorder characterized by an alternating pattern of mood swings that is less extreme than that of bipolar disorder.

Affective Disorders   IN REVIEW

Type	Typical Symptoms	Related Features
Major depression (major depressive disorder)	Deep sadness, feelings of worthlessness, changes in eating and sleeping habits, loss of interest and pleasure	Lasts weeks or months; may occur in repeating episodes; severe cases may include delusions
Dysthymic disorder	Similar to major depression but less severe and longer lasting	Hospitalization usually not necessary
Bipolar disorder	Alternating extremes of mood from deep depression to mania and back	Manic episodes include impulsivity, unrealistic optimism, high energy, severe agitation
Cyclothymic personality (cyclothymic disorder)	Similar to bipolar disorder, but less severe	Hospitalization usually not necessary

IN REVIEW QUESTIONS

1. The risk of suicide is associated with ___ more than with any other disorder.
2. Cyclothymic personality is the bipolar version of ___.
3. Women are ___ likely than men to try suicide, but men are ___ likely to succeed.

LINKAGES

Are some psychological disorders inherited? (a link to Biology and Behavior)

Biological Factors   The role of genetics in affective disorders is suggested by the results of twin studies and family studies (Fullerton et al., 2010; Goodwin & Jamison, 2007; Hayden & Nurnberger, 2006; Kendler et al., 2006). For example, bipolar disorder is much more likely to be seen in both members of genetically identical twin pairs than in nonidentical twins (Smoller, 2008). Family studies also show that those who are closely related to people with bipolar disorder are more likely than others to develop the disorder themselves (Althoff et al., 2005; Serretti et al., 2009). Major depression, too, is more likely to occur in both members of identical twins than in both members of nonidentical twins (Kendler et al., 2009; Levinson, 2006). Findings such as these suggest that genetic influences tend to be stronger for affective disorders (especially for bipolar I disorder and severe, early-onset depression) than for most other disorders.

Researchers have already identified certain genetic variations that affect vulnerability to affective disorders (e.g., Joska & Stein, 2008; McMahon et al., 2010; Smoller, 2008; Young et al., 2008). These include genes on chromosome 13 that are involved in the operation of the neurotransmitter serotonin (Hariri et al., 2005; Jacobs et al., 2006; Wilhelm et al., 2006). Still, it is important to recognize that genetic variations alone probably do not cause affective disorders. Rather, genes appear to act in combination with other biological, psychological, and environmental factors. For example, a version of the serotonin transporter gene appears to increase the likelihood of depression when the individual is exposed to high levels of life stress (Caspi et al., 2010). Researchers in the field of epigenetics are investigating how genes associated with affective disorders can be "turned on" or "turned off" by environmental factors (Butcher, Mineka, & Hooley, 2010; Levinson et al., 2007).

Other biological factors that may contribute to affective disorders include structural abnormalities or malfunctions in regions of the brain involved in mood, imbalances in the brain's neurotransmitter systems, malfunctioning of the endocrine system, disruption of biological rhythms, and underdevelopment in the frontal lobes, hippocampus, or other brain areas (Alloy & Abramson, 2010; Alloy et al., 2011; Butcher et al., 2010; Jans et al., 2007; Langan & McDonald, 2009; Munn et al., 2007; Shankman et al., 2007; Staley et al., 2006; Strakowski, DelBello, & Adler, 2005). All of these conditions may themselves be influenced by genetics (Caspi et al., 2010).

The brain regions involved in mood are many, including the prefrontal cortex, the hippocampus, the amygdala, and other components of the limbic system (Blumberg et al., 2003; MacQueen et al., 2003). There are so many of these regions, in fact, and so many different pathways through which their activity can be disrupted, that particular affective disorders may reflect problems in particular brain regions (Davidson et al., 2002; Elliott et al., 2002). Some of these same brain regions, and many of the same genes, may also be involved in anxiety disorders, which helps account for the fact that affective and anxiety disorders often occur together (Middledorp et al., 2005).

Treating SAD

Seasonal affective disorder (SAD) can often be relieved by exposure to full-spectrum light for as little as a couple of hours a day (Terman & Terman, 2005).

As for the role of neurotransmitters, norepinephrine, serotonin, and dopamine were implicated in affective disorders decades ago, when scientists discovered that drugs capable of altering these substances also relieved affective disorders. However, the precise nature of the relationship between neurotransmitters and affective disorders is still not fully understood. So despite what antidepressant drug advertisements might suggest, no one really knows exactly what "chemical imbalance" exists in the brains of depressed people (Sharp & Cowen, 2011).

Affective disorders have also been related to malfunctions of the endocrine system, especially the subsystem involved in the body's responses to stress. For example, research shows that as many as 70 percent of depressed people secrete abnormally high levels of the stress hormone cortisol (Dinan, 2001; Posener et al., 2000). Studies of identical twins also suggest that higher levels of cortisol are associated with depression (Dinan, 2001; Wichers et al., 2008).

The cycles of mood swings seen in bipolar disorders and in recurring episodes of major depression suggest that affective disorders may be related to stressful triggering events (Hammen, 2005; Keller & Nesse, 2006). They may also be related to disturbances in the body's biological clock, which is described in the chapter on consciousness (Goodwin & Jamison, 1990; Monteleone & Maj, 2008). This second possibility seems especially likely in the 15 percent of depressed people who consistently experience a calendar-linked pattern of depressive episodes known as *seasonal affective disorder (SAD)*. During months of shorter daylight, these people slip into severe depression, accompanied by irritability and excessive sleeping (Durand & Barlow, 2006; Vyssoki et al., 2012). Their depression tends to lift as daylight hours lengthen (Faedda et al., 1993). Disruption of biological rhythms is also suggested by the fact that many depressed people tend to have trouble sleeping, partly because during the day their biological clocks may be telling them it is the middle of the night. Resetting the biological clock through methods such as sleep deprivation or light stimulation has relieved depression in many cases (Lavoie et al., 2009; Lewy et al., 2006; Wu et al., 2009).

Psychological and Social Factors   Researchers have come to recognize that the biological factors involved in affective disorders always operate in combination with psychological and social factors (Jacobs, 2004). As mentioned earlier, the very nature of depressive symptoms can depend on the culture in which a person lives. Biopsychosocial explanations for affective disorders also emphasize the impact of social isolation, anxiety, negative thinking; other psychological and emotional responses triggered by stressful events such as trauma; and the impact of cultural factors (Monroe & Reid, 2009; Rice et al., 2006; Stepanikova, Nie, & He, 2010; Steunenberg et al., 2006). For example, the higher rate of depression among females—especially poor ethnic-minority single mothers—has been attributed to their greater exposure to stressors of all kinds (Brown & Moran, 1997; Miranda & Green, 1999; Nolen-Hoeksema, 2006; Whiffen, 2006). Environmental stressors affect men, too, which may be one reason that gender differences are smaller in countries in which men and women face equally stressful lives (Bierut et al., 1999).

A number of social-cognitive theories suggest that the way people think about their stressors can affect the likelihood of affective disorders. One of these theories is based on the *learned helplessness* research described in the chapter on learning. Just as animals become inactive and appear depressed when they have no control over negative events (El Yacoubi et al., 2003), humans may experience depression as a result of feeling incapable of controlling their lives, especially the stressors confronting them (Alloy et al., 2008; Klein & Seligman, 1976; Seligman, 1991). But most of us have limited control, so why aren't we all depressed? The ways that people learn to think about events in their lives may hold the key. For example, Aaron Beck's cognitive theory of depression suggests that depressed people develop mental habits of (1) blaming themselves when things go wrong; (2) focusing on and exaggerating the negative side of events; and (3) jumping to overly generalized, pessimistic conclusions. Such cognitive habits, says Beck, are errors that lead to depressing thoughts and other symptoms of depression (Beck, 2008; Evans et al., 2005; Joormann, Teachman, & Gotlib, 2009). Depressed people, in fact, do tend to think about significant negative events in ways that are likely to increase or prolong their depression (Gotlib & Hammen, 1992; Gotlib et al., 2004; Morris, Ciesla & Garber, 2008; Strunk, Lopez, & DeRubeis, 2006).

Severe, long-lasting depression is especially likely among people who blame their lack of control or other problems on a permanent, generalized lack of personal competence rather than on a temporary condition or some external cause (Seligman et al., 1988). This *negative attributional style* may be another important cognitive factor in depression (Alloy et al., 2006; Ball et al., 2008; Hankin, Fraley, & Abela, 2005; Hunt & Forand, 2005). Are depressed people's unusually negative beliefs about themselves actually helping to cause their depression or are they merely symptoms of it? A number of studies have assessed the attributional styles of large samples of nondepressed people and then kept in touch with them to see whether individuals with negative self-beliefs are more likely to become depressed when stressors occur. These longitudinal studies suggest that a negative attributional style is, in fact, a risk factor for depression, not just a result of being depressed (Alloy et al., 2006; Evans et al., 2005; Keenan et al., 2008). In one study, for example, adolescents who held strong negative self-beliefs were more likely than other youngsters to develop depression when faced with stress later in life (Lewinsohn, Joiner, & Rohde, 2001).

Social-cognitive theorists also suggest that whether depression continues or worsens depends in part on how people respond once they start to feel depressed. People who continuously dwell on negative events, on why they occur, and even on being depressed are likely to feel more and more depressed (Just & Alloy, 1997; McMurrich & Johnson, 2008; Rimes & Watkins, 2005; Sarin, Abela, & Auerbach, 2005). According to Susan Nolen-Hoeksema (1990, 2001), this *ruminative style* is especially characteristic of women and may help explain gender differences in the frequency of depression. When men start to feel sad, she says, they tend to use a *distracting style*. In other words, they engage in activity that distracts them from their concerns and helps bring them out of their depressed mood (Hankin & Abramson, 2001; Just & Alloy, 1997; Nolen-Hoeksema, Morrow, & Fredrickson, 1993).

Notice that social-cognitive explanations of depression are consistent with the diathesis-stress approach to disorder (Hankin & Abramson, 2001). These explanations suggest that certain cognitive styles serve as a predisposition (or diathesis) that makes a person vulnerable to depression, which is made even more likely by stressors. As suggested in the chapter on health, stress, and coping, the depressing effects of these stressors are likely to be magnified by lack of social support, inadequate coping skills, and the presence of other stressful conditions, such as poverty (e.g., Belik et al., 2007; Nikulina, Widom, & Czaja, 2011; Stice, Ragan, & Randall, 2004).

Given the number and complexity of biological, psychological, social, and situational factors potentially involved in causing affective disorders, the diathesis-stress approach appears to be an especially appropriate guide to future research (Kendler, Gardner, & Prescott, 2006). Indeed, some researchers are integrating the various factors into predictive and causal models. For instance, Kenneth Kendler and his colleagues have described specific sets of risk factors for depression in women that appear at five developmental stages, including childhood, early adolescence, late adolescence, adulthood, and in the year preceding the diagnosis of depression (Kendler, Gardner, & Prescott, 2006).

In the final analysis, it may turn out that each subtype of affective disorder is caused by a unique combination of factors. The challenge for researchers is to identify these subtypes and map out their causal ingredients (Eshel & Roiser, 2010).

Schizophrenia

Is schizophrenia the same as "split personality"?

schizophrenia A pattern of severely disturbed thinking, emotion, perception, and behavior that constitutes one of the most serious and disabling of all mental disorders.

Schizophrenia (pronounced "skit-so-FREE-nee-uh") is a pattern of severely disturbed thinking, emotion, perception, and behavior that seriously impairs the ability to communicate and relate to others and disrupts most other aspects of daily functioning

(Freedman, 2003; Green & Horan, 2010; Hooley, 2010). It is one of the most severe and disabling of all mental disorders. Schizophrenia's core symptoms are seen virtually everywhere in the world, in about 1 to 2 percent of the population (American Psychiatric Association, 2000; National Institute of Mental Health, 2006). In the United States, it appears about equally in various ethnic groups, but like most disorders, it tends to be diagnosed more frequently in economically disadvantaged populations. It is seen about equally in men and women, although in women it may appear later in life, be less severe, and respond better to treatment (Aleman, Kahn, & Selten, 2003; American Psychiatric Association, 2000).

Schizophrenia tends to develop in adolescence or early adulthood. In about three out of four cases, symptoms appear gradually over a period of years; in other cases, the onset is more rapid. Longitudinal studies suggest that about 40 percent of people diagnosed with schizophrenia improve with treatment and are able to function reasonably well; the rest continue to display symptoms that permanently impair their functioning (Harrow & Jobe, 2005; Jobe & Harrow, 2010) and, especially for those with a drug abuse problem, may lead to homelessness (Timms, 2005).

One of the best predictors of the outcome of schizophrenia is *premorbid adjustment,* which refers the level of functioning a person had achieved before schizophrenia symptoms first appeared. Improvement is more likely in those who had reached higher levels of education and occupation and who had established supportive relationships with family and friends (Keshavan et al., 2005; Rabinowitz et al., 2002).

Symptoms of Schizophrenia

The main problems seen in people displaying schizophrenia relate to thinking—both how they think and what they think (Heinrichs, 2005). Indeed, the very word *schizophrenia,* or "split mind," refers to the oddities of schizophrenic thinking, including a splitting of normally integrated mental processes, such as thoughts and feelings. So the person may giggle while talking about sad events and claiming to feel unhappy. Contrary to common usage, schizophrenia does not refer to the "split personality" seen in dissociative identity disorder (multiple personality disorder).

Schizophrenic thought and language are often disorganized, as illustrated in the following letter that arrived in the mail several years ago:

> *Dear Sirs:*
>
> *Pertaining to our continuing failure to prosecute violations of minor's rights to sovereign equality which are occurring in gestations being compromised by the ingestation of controlled substances, ... the skewing of androgyny which continues in female juveniles even after separation from their mother's has occurred, and as a means of promulflagitating my paying Governor Hickel of Alaska for my employees to have personal services endorsements and controlled substance endorsements, ... the Iraqi oil being released by the United Nations being identified as Kurdistanian oil, and the July, 1991 issue of the Siberian Review spells President Eltsin's name without a letter y.*

People with schizophrenia may create *neologisms,* or new words, that are usually nonsensical and have meaning only to the person speaking them. The word "promulflagitating" in the preceding letter is one example. The letter also illustrates *loose associations,* the tendency for one thought to be logically unconnected or only loosely connected to the next. In the most severe cases, thought becomes just a jumble known as *word salad.* For example, one patient was heard to say, "Upon the advisability of held keeping, environment of the seabeach gathering, to the forest stream, reinstatement to be placed, poling the paddleboat, of the swamp morass, to the forest compensation of the dunce" (Lehman, 1967, p. 627).

The content of schizophrenic thinking is also disturbed. Often it includes a bewildering assortment of *delusions* (false beliefs), especially *delusions of persecution.* Some patients believe that space aliens or government agents are trying to steal their internal organs, and they may interpret everything from TV commercials to casual hand gestures as part of the plot. Delusions that such common events are somehow related to oneself are called *ideas of reference. Delusions of grandeur* may also appear; one young man was convinced that the president of the United States was trying to contact him for advice. Other types of delusions include *thought broadcasting,* in which patients believe that their thoughts can be heard by others; *thought blocking* or *thought withdrawal,* the belief that someone is either preventing thoughts or "stealing" them as they appear; and *thought insertion,* the belief that other people's thoughts are appearing in one's own mind. Some patients believe that their behavior is being controlled by others; in one case, a man claimed that the CIA had placed a control device in his brain. Such delusions tend to be deeply entrenched and resistant to change, no matter how strong the evidence against them (Minzenberg et al., 2008; Woodward et al., 2006).

LINKAGES

Do people perceive hallucinations as real sensory events? (a link to Sensation and Perception)

Hallucinations, or false perceptions, are common in schizophrenia, often emerging as voices. These voices may sound like an overheard conversation or they may urge the person to do or not to do things. Sometimes they comment on, narrate, or (most often) criticize the person's actions. Hallucinations can also involve the experience of nonexistent sights, smells, tastes, and touch sensations. The brain areas activated during hallucinations are related to those that respond to real sights and sounds (Alerman & Larøi, 2008; Shergill et al., 2000; Simons et al., 2010).

People with schizophrenia often report that they cannot focus their attention. They may feel overwhelmed by stimulation as they try to attend to everything at once. Various perceptual disorders may also appear. The person may feel detached from the world and see other people as flat cutouts. The body may feel like a machine or parts of it may seem to be dead or rotting. Emotional expression is often muted—a pattern called *flat affect*. But when people with schizophrenia do display emotion, it is often exaggerated or inappropriate (Kring et al., 2011; Kring & Caponigro, 2010), For example, they may cry for no apparent reason or fly into a rage in response to a simple question.

Some people with schizophrenia are quite agitated, constantly fidgeting, grimacing, or pacing the floor in ritualized patterns. Others become so withdrawn that they move very little. Lack of motivation and poor social skills, deteriorating personal hygiene, and an inability to function in everyday situations are other common characteristics of schizophrenia.

Categorizing Schizophrenia

The *DSM-IV-TR* lists five major subtypes of schizophrenia: paranoid, disorganized, catatonic, undifferentiated, and residual. These subtypes are summarized in Table 12.4.

Researchers have also made other useful distinctions among various forms of schizophrenia. One of these distinctions involves the presence of positive vs. negative symptoms. Disorganized thoughts, delusions, and hallucinations are sometimes called *positive symptoms* of schizophrenia, because they appear as undesirable *additions* to a person's mental life (Iancu et al., 2005; Smith et al., 2006). In contrast, the absence of pleasure and motivation, lack of emotion, social withdrawal, reduced speech, and other deficits seen in schizophrenia are sometimes called *negative symptoms,* because they appear to *subtract* elements from normal mental life (Batki et al., 2008). Many patients exhibit both positive and negative symptoms, but when the negative symptoms are stronger, schizophrenia generally has a more severe course, including long-term disability and relative lack of response to treatment (e.g., Kirkpatrick et al., 2006; Milev et al., 2005; Prikryl et al., 2006).

Yet another way of categorizing schizophrenia symptoms focuses on whether they are *psychotic* (e.g., hallucinations or delusions), *disorganized* (e.g., incoherent speech, chaotic behavior, or inappropriate affect), or *negative* (e.g., lack of speech or motivation). The fact that, like positive and negative symptoms, these dimensions of schizophrenia are to some extent independent from one another suggests to some researchers that each symptom cluster or dimension may ultimately be traceable to different causes. For this reason, schizophrenia is often referred to as the *schizophrenia spectrum,* in recognition of the fact that each cluster may develop differently and require different treatments (Tsuang, Stone, & Faraone, 2000). The schizophrenia spectrum also includes other diagnoses that share features with schizophrenia. For example, people diagnosed with *schizoaffective disorder*

hallucinations False or distorted perceptions of objects or events.

Catatonic Stupor
The symptoms of schizophrenia often occur in characteristic patterns. This woman's lack of motivation and other negative symptoms of schizophrenia are severe enough that she appears to be in a catatonic stupor. Such patients may become rigid or, as in this case, show a waxy flexibility that allows them to be "posed" in virtually any position. Diagnosticians using the traditional subtype system would probably label her as displaying catatonic schizophrenia.

TABLE 12.4 Subtypes of Schizophrenia

These traditional categories of schizophrenia convey some useful information, but subtype labels are not always accurate. Some symptoms of schizophrenia appear in more than one subtype, and people first placed in one subtype might later display characteristics of another. These concerns, plus the fact that different subtypes in the *DSM-IV-TR* may not be linked to different causal factors, have led to the suggestion that some or all of these subtype labels be eliminated in *DSM-5* (Bruijnzeel & Tandon, 2011; Miller & Holden, 2010).

Type	Frequency	Prominent Features
Paranoid schizophrenia	40 percent of people with schizophrenia; usually appears after age 25–30	Delusions of grandeur or persecution; anger; anxiety; argumentativeness; extreme jealousy; onset often sudden; signs of impairment may be subtle
Disorganized schizophrenia	5 percent of all people with schizophrenia; high prevalence in homeless population	Delusions, hallucinations, incoherent speech, facial grimaces, inappropriate laughter/giggling, neglected personal hygiene, loss of bladder/bowel control
Catatonic schizophrenia	8 percent of all people with schizophrenia	Disordered movement, alternating between total immobility (stupor) and wild excitement. In stupor, the person does not speak or attend to communication
Undifferentiated schizophrenia	40 percent of all people with schizophrenia	Patterns of disordered behavior, thought, and emotion that do not fall easily into any other subtype
Residual schizophrenia	Varies	Applies to people who have had prior episodes of schizophrenia but are not currently displaying symptoms

show symptoms of both schizophrenia and depression. *Schizophreniform disorder* is characterized by schizophrenia-like symptoms that do not last as long as those typically seen in schizophrenia.

Causes of Schizophrenia

The search for causes of schizophrenia has been more intense than for any other psychological disorder. The findings so far confirm one thing for certain: as with other disorders, biological, psychological, and sociocultural factors combine to cause or worsen all forms of schizophrenia (Sullivan, Kendler, & Neale, 2003; Tandon, Nasrallah, & Keshaven, 2009).

Biological Factors Research in behavioral genetics shows that schizophrenia runs in families (Dubertret et al., 2004; Gottesman et al., 2010; Kasper & Papadimitriou, 2009). If one person in a family is diagnosed with schizophrenia, the risk that another family member will receive the same diagnosis increases in proportion with their genetic similarity (Kasper & Papadimitriou, 2009). Even if they are adopted by families in which there is no schizophrenia, the children of parents with schizophrenia are ten times more likely to develop schizophrenia than adopted children whose biological parents do not have schizophrenia (Kety et al., 1994; Tienari et al., 2003). But even though identical twins have virtually identical genes, the appearance of schizophrenia in one of them does not guarantee that the other will be diagnosed as well. In fact, the rate of shared diagnosis is only about 50 percent, which suggests that genetics alone cannot explain the disorder. Further, it is unlikely that a single gene transmits schizophrenia (Minzenberg et al., 2008; Plomin & McGuffin, 2003; Pogue-Geile, & Yokley, 2010). Rather, several genes on several chromosome pairs are probably involved, and probably combine with nongenetic factors to cause the disorder. Researchers in the field of epigenetics are studying how environmental factors alter the expression of genes associated with schizophrenia (Akbarian, 2010; Pogue-Geile, & Yokley, 2010).

The search for biological factors in schizophrenia also focuses on a number of abnormalities in the structure, functioning, and chemistry of the brain that tend to appear in people with schizophrenia (e.g., Andrews et al., 2006; Grace, 2010; Karlsgodt, Daqiang, & Cannon, 2010; Lynall et al., 2010; Meyer-Lindenberg, 2010; Neves-Pereira et al., 2005; Rasmussen et al., 2010; van Haren et al., 2012). For example, brain imaging studies have compared schizophrenia patients with other mental patients (Salgado-Pineda et al., 2010). Many patients with schizophrenia (especially those who display mostly negative symptoms) have less tissue in areas of the brain that are involved in emotional expression, thinking, and information processing—functions that are disordered in schizophrenia (Arango et al., 2012; Ettinger et al., 2007; Goto, Yang, & Otani, 2010; Javitt & Kantrowitz, 2009; Javitt, Kantrowitz, & Lajtha, 2009; Rimol, Hartberg et al., 2010, Rimol, Nesvåg et al.,2012; Ursu et al., 2011). There is also evidence that worsening symptoms are associated with continued tissue loss in these areas (Ho et al., 2003). Patients with mainly positive symptoms tend to have essentially normal-looking brains (Andreasen, 1997).

Researchers are also investigating the possibility that abnormalities in brain chemistry—especially in neurotransmitter systems that use dopamine—play a role in causing or intensifying the symptoms of schizophrenia (Javitt & Kantrowitz, 2009; Tan et al., 2007). Because drugs that block the brain's dopamine receptors often reduce the hallucinations, disordered thinking, and other positive symptoms of schizophrenia, some investigators speculate that schizophrenia results from excess dopamine. Other research suggests that excessive activity in dopamine systems may be related to the appearance of these positive symptoms (Buchsbaum et al., 2006; Winterer, 2006). However, the relationship between dopamine and schizophrenia may be more complex than that (Albert et al., 2002; Carlsson & Lecrubier, 2004; Grace, 2010). For example, it may be that changes in the ratio of dopamine to other neurochemicals, particularly in the region of the thalamus, are involved in the difficulties experienced by people with schizophrenia in distinguishing genuine sights and sounds from those produced by neural "noise" within the brain (Buchsbaum et al., 2006; Winterer, 2006).

Some researchers are integrating genetic and environmental explanations for schizophrenia by looking for *neurodevelopmental* abnormalities (e.g., Meyer et al., 2005; Rapoport, Addington, & Frangou, 2005). Perhaps, they say, some forms of schizophrenia arise from disruptions in brain development during the period from before birth through childhood, when the brain is growing and its various functions are maturing (King, St-Hilaire, & Heidkamp, 2010; Walker et al., 2010). For instance, prenatal exposure to physical trauma, flu, or other infections is associated with increased risk for developing schizophrenia (AbdelMalik et al., 2003; Brown & Derkits, 2010; Brown et al., 2004, 2005; Subotnik et al., 2006). It may be that the expression of a genetically transmitted predisposition for brain abnormality is enhanced by environmental stressors such as maternal drug use during pregnancy, complications during birth, and childhood malnutrition (Sørensen et al., 2003; National Institute of Mental Health, 2008b). Neurodevelopmental factors may help explain why children of parents with schizophrenia tend to show cognitive and intellectual problems associated with brain abnormalities (Ashe, Berry, & Boulton, 2001; Cannon et al., 1994; Harvey, 2010; McGlashan & Hoffman, 2000; Neumann et al., 1995).

Psychological and Sociocultural Factors　Psychological processes and sociocultural influences can contribute to the appearance of schizophrenia and influence its course (Kealy, 2005; Vahia & Cohen, 2009). Among the factors cited are dysfunctional cognitive habits, the stress of urban living, the stigma of being labeled with a severe mental disorder, being an immigrant, and exposure to stressful family communication patterns (Henry, von Hippel, & Shapiro, 2010; Mueser & Jeste, 2009; van Os et al., 2008). For example, criticism by family members—sometimes called *expressed emotion*—is associated with more severe symptoms (Nomura et al., 2005; Polanczyk et al., 2010). And if individuals with schizophrenia live with relatives who are critical, unsupportive, or emotionally overinvolved, they're especially likely to relapse following initial improvement (Hooley, 2004). Family members' negative attitudes may be a source of stress that actually increases the chances that disruptive or odd behaviors will persist or worsen (Rosenfarb et al., 1995). Keep in mind, though, that the strange and often disturbing behavior of a family member with schizophrenia can place tremendous strain on the rest of the family, making it harder for them to remain helpful and supportive (Kymalainen et al., 2006; Rosenfarb, Bellack, & Aziz, 2006). In any case, patients who are helped to cope with potentially damaging family influences tend to have better long-term outcomes (Bustillo et al., 2001; Velligan et al., 2000).

Vulnerability Theory   All the causal theories of schizophrenia we have outlined are consistent with the diathesis-stress approach, which assumes that stress activates a person's predisposition for disorder (Stahl, 2007). ("In Review: Schizophrenia" summarizes these theories, as well as the symptoms of schizophrenia.) In fact, a diathesis-stress framework forms the basis for the *vulnerability theory* of schizophrenia (Cornblatt & Erlenmeyer-Kimling, 1985; Zubin & Spring, 1977). This theory suggests that (1) vulnerability to schizophrenia is mainly biological; (2) different people have differing degrees of vulnerability; (3) vulnerability is influenced partly by genetic influences on development and partly by abnormalities that arise from environmental risk factors; and (4) psychological components, such as exposure to poor parenting, a high-stress environment, or inadequate coping skills, may help determine whether schizophrenia actually appears and may also influence its course (van Os, Kenis, & Rutten, 2010; Walker & Diforio, 1998; Wearden et al., 2000).

Many different blends of vulnerability and stress can lead to schizophrenia. People whose genetic characteristics or prenatal experiences leave them vulnerable to developing schizophrenia may be especially likely to do so if they are later exposed to learning experiences, family conflicts, or other stressors that trigger and maintain schizophrenic patterns of thought and action. Those same experiences and stressors would not be expected to lead to schizophrenia in people who are less vulnerable to developing the disorder. In other words, schizophrenia is a highly complex disorder—probably a spectrum of related disorders (Kirkpatrick et al., 2001; Lenzenweger, McLachlan, & Rubin, 2007)—whose origins appear to lie in numerous biological, psychological, and sociocultural domains, some of which are yet to be discovered (Gilmore, 2010).

Schizophrenia   IN REVIEW

Aspect	Key Features
Common Symptoms	
Disorders of thought	Disturbed content, including delusions; disorganization, including loose associations, neologisms, and word salad
Disorders of perception	Hallucinations or false perceptions; poorly focused attention
Disorders of emotion	Flat affect; inappropriate tears, laughter, or anger
Possible Causes	
Biological	Genetics; abnormalities in brain structure; abnormalities in dopamine systems; neurodevelopmental problems
Psychological and sociocultural	Learned maladaptive behavior; disturbed patterns of family communication

IN REVIEW QUESTIONS

1. The ___ approach forms the basis of the vulnerability theory of schizophrenia.

2. Hallucinations are ___ symptoms of schizophrenia; lack of emotion is a ___ symptom.

3. Patients with schizophrenia who were able to finish school are ___ likely to show improvement.

Personality Disorders

Which personality disorder often leads to crime?

Personality disorders are long-standing, inflexible ways of behaving that are not so much severe mental disorders as dysfunctional styles of living (Clarkin, 2006). These disorders affect all areas of functioning and, beginning in childhood or adolescence, create problems for those who display them and for others (Cohen, 2008; Millon & Davis, 1996). Some psychologists view personality disorders as interpersonal strategies (Kiesler, 1996) or as extreme, rigid, and maladaptive expressions of personality traits (Widiger, 2008).

The ten personality disorders found on Axis II of the *DSM-IV-TR* are grouped into three clusters that share certain features (see Table 12.5). The *odd-eccentric* cluster (Cluster A) includes paranoid, schizoid, and schizotypal personality disorders. People diagnosed as having *schizotypal personality disorder,* for example, display some of the peculiarities seen in schizophrenia but are not disturbed enough to be labeled as having schizophrenia. The *dramatic-erratic* cluster (Cluster B) includes the histrionic, narcissistic, borderline, and antisocial personality disorders. The main characteristics of *narcissistic personality disorder,* for example, are an exaggerated sense of self-importance, extreme sensitivity to criticism, a constant need for attention, and a tendency to arrogantly overestimate personal abilities and achievements. Finally, the *anxious-fearful* cluster (Cluster C) includes dependent, obsessive-compulsive, and avoidant personality disorders. *Avoidant personality disorder,* for example, is similar to social phobia in the sense that people labeled with this disorder tend to be "loners" with a long-standing pattern of avoiding social situations and of being particularly sensitive to criticism or rejection.

The most serious, costly, and intensively studied personality disorder is **antisocial personality disorder**. It is marked by a long-term pattern of irresponsible, impulsive, unscrupulous, and sometimes criminal behavior, beginning in childhood or early

personality disorders Long-standing, inflexible ways of behaving that become styles of life that create problems, usually for others.

antisocial personality disorder A long-term, persistent pattern of impulsive, selfish, unscrupulous, even criminal behavior.

TABLE **12.5**   **Personality Disorders**

Here are brief descriptions of the ten personality disorders listed on Axis II of the *DSM-IV-TR*. Only six of them are likely to remain in *DSM-5*: borderline, obsessive-compulsive, avoidant, schizotypal, antisocial, and narcissistic.

	Type	Typical Features
Cluster A (odd-eccentric)	Paranoid	Suspiciousness and distrust of others, all of whom are assumed to be hostile
	Schizoid	Detachment from social relationships; restricted range of emotion
	Schizotypal	Detachment from and great discomfort in social relationships; odd perceptions, thoughts, beliefs, and behaviors
Cluster B (dramatic-erratic)	Histrionic	Excessive emotionality and preoccupation with being the center of attention, emotional shallowness, overly dramatic behavior
	Narcissistic	Exaggerated ideas of self-importance and achievements, preoccupation with fantasies of success, arrogance
	Borderline	Lack of stability in interpersonal relationships, self-image, and emotion; impulsivity; angry outbursts; intense fear of abandonment; recurring suicidal gestures
	Antisocial	Shameless disregard for and violation of other people's rights
Cluster C (anxious-fearful)	Dependent	Helplessness, excessive need to be taken care of, submissive and clinging behavior, difficulty in making decisions
	Obsessive-compulsive	Preoccupation with orderliness, perfection, and control
	Avoidant	Inhibition in social situations, feelings of inadequacy, oversensitivity to criticism

99065636

A Classic Case of Antisocial Personality Disorder

Alfred Jack Oakley meets women through personal ads, claiming to be a millionaire movie producer, pilot, and novelist. In reality, he is a penniless con artist who uses his smooth-talking charm to gain the women's trust so he can steal from them. In January 2000, after being convicted of stealing a Florida woman's Mercedes, Oakley complimented the prosecutor's skills and the jury's wisdom and claimed remorse. The judge appeared to see through this ploy ("I don't believe there is a sincere word that ever comes out of your mouth"), but it was still effective enough to get Oakley probation instead of jail time!

adolescence (Washburn et al., 2007). In the nineteenth century, the pattern was called *moral insanity* because the people displaying it appear to have no morals or common decency. Later, people in this category were called *psychopaths* or *sociopaths* (Coid & Ullrich, 2010; Hare & Newmann, 2009). The current "antisocial personality" label used in *DSM-IV-TR* more accurately portrays them as troublesome but not "insane" by the legal standards we discuss later (Skeem et al., 2011). About 3 percent of men and about 1 percent of women in the United States fall into this diagnostic category (American Psychiatric Association, 2000; Hodgins, 2007).

At their least troublesome, these people are a nuisance. They are often charming, intelligent "fast talkers" who borrow money and fail to return it; they are arrogant, selfish manipulators who "con" people into doing things for them, usually by lying and taking advantage of the decency and trust of others. At their most troublesome, people with this disorder are criminals, sometimes violent ones. Persistent violent offenders, most of whom have antisocial personality disorder, make up less than 5 percent of the male population, but they commit over 50 percent of violent crimes (Hodgins, 2007). A hallmark of those displaying antisocial personality is a lack of anxiety, remorse, or guilt, whether they have wrecked a borrowed car or killed an innocent person (Gray et al., 2003; Hare & Newmann, 2009).

No method has yet been found for permanently altering the behavior of these people (Rice, 1997). Research suggests that the best hope for dealing with them is to identify their antisocial personalities early, before the most treatment-resistant traits are fully developed (Compton et al., 2005; Crawford, Cohen, & Brooks, 2001; Diamantopoulou, Verhulst, & van der Ende, 2010). Fortunately, these individuals tend to become less active and dangerous after the age of 40 or so (Stoff, Breiling, & Maser, 1997). If, as sometimes happens, people with milder forms of antisocial personality disorder also have a certain degree of conscientiousness, they may become successful in socially acceptable roles, often in the world of politics or business (Mullins-Sweatt, et al., 2010).

There are numerous theories about the causes of antisocial personality disorder. Some research suggests a genetic predisposition (Arseneault et al., 2003; Larsson, Andershed, & Lichtenstein, 2006), possibly in the form of abnormal brain development, impaired neurological functioning, deficits in the ability to encode or recall emotional information, or chronic underarousal of both the autonomic and central nervous systems (Craig et al., 2009; Crozier et al., 2008; Dolan & Fullam, 2006; Kiehl et al., 2006; Narayan et al., 2007; Raine et al., 2005; van Goozen et al., 2007; Visser et al., 2010, Yang et al., 2009). This underarousal may render people less sensitive to punishment and more likely to seek excitement than is normally the case (Birbaumer et al., 2005; Fowles & Dindo, 2009; Gao et al., 2010). Broken homes, rejection by parents, poor discipline, lack of good parental models, lack of attachment to early caregivers, impulsivity, conflict-filled childhoods, and poverty have all been suggested as psychological and sociocultural factors that contribute to the development of antisocial personality disorder (Caspi et al., 2004; Lahey et al., 1995; Lyman & Gudonis, 2005; Raine, Brennan, & Mednick, 1994; Tremblay et al., 1994). The biopsychosocial approach suggests that antisocial personality disorder results when these psychosocial and environmental conditions combine with a genetic predisposition to low arousal and the sensation seeking and impulsivity associated with it (Beach, et al., 2010; Diamantopoulou, Verhulst, & van der Ende, 2010; Gray et al., 2003).

FOCUS ON RESEARCH

Exploring Links between Child Abuse and Antisocial Personality Disorder

One of the most prominent environmental factors associated with the more violent forms of antisocial personality disorder is the experience of abuse in childhood (MacMillan et al., 2001). However, most of the studies that have found a relationship between childhood abuse and antisocial personality disorder were based on potentially biased reports (Monane, Leichter, & Lewis, 1984; Rosenbaum & Bennett, 1986). People with antisocial personalities—especially those with criminal records—are likely to make up stories of abuse in order to shift the blame for their behavior onto others. Even if their reports were accurate, however, most of these studies didn't compare the abuse histories of antisocial people with those of a control group from similar backgrounds who did not become antisocial. This research design flaw makes it almost impossible to separate the effects of reported child abuse from the effects of poverty or other factors that might also have contributed to the development of antisocial personality disorder.

What was the researcher's question?
Can childhood abuse cause antisocial personality disorder? To help answer this question and to correct some of the flaws in earlier studies, Cathy Widom (1989) used a *prospective* research design, first finding cases of childhood abuse and then looking for the effects of that abuse on adult behavior.

How did the researcher answer the question?
Widom began by identifying 416 adults whose backgrounds included official records of their having been physically or sexually abused before the age of eleven. She then explored the stories of these people's lives as told in police and school records as well as in a two-hour diagnostic interview. To reduce experimenter bias and distorted reporting, Widom ensured that the interviewers did not know the purpose of the study and that the respondents were told only that the study's purpose was to talk to people who had grown up in an urban area of the midwestern United States in the late 1960s and early 1970s. Widom also selected a comparison group of 283 people who had no histories of abuse but who were similar to the abused sample in terms of age, gender, ethnicity, hospital of birth, schools attended, and area of residence. Her goal was to obtain a nonabused control group that had been exposed to approximately the same environmental risk factors and socioeconomic conditions as the abused children.

What did the researcher find?
First, Widom (1989) tested the hypothesis that exposure to abuse in childhood is associated with criminality and/or violence in later life. She found that 26 percent of the abused youngsters went on to commit juvenile crimes, 29 percent were arrested as adults, and 11 percent committed violent crimes. These percentages were significantly higher than the figures for the nonabused group. The correlations between criminality and abuse were higher for males than for females and higher for African Americans than for European Americans. And overall, victims of physical abuse were more likely to commit violent crimes as adults than were victims of sexual abuse.

Next, Widom tested the hypothesis that childhood abuse is associated with the development of antisocial personality disorder (Luntz & Widom, 1994). She found that the abused group did show a significantly higher rate of antisocial personality disorder (13.5 percent) than the comparison group (7.1 percent). The apparent role of abuse in antisocial personality disorder was particularly pronounced in men, and it remained strong even when other factors—such as age, ethnicity, and socioeconomic status—were accounted for in the statistical analyses. One other factor—failure to graduate from high school—was also strongly associated with the appearance of antisocial personality, whether or not childhood abuse had occurred.

What do the results mean?
Widom's research supported earlier studies in finding an association between childhood abuse and criminality, violence, and antisocial personality disorder. Further, although her study did not permit a firm conclusion that abuse alone causes antisocial personality disorder, the data from its prospective design added strength to the argument that abuse may be an important causal factor (Widom, 2000). This interpretation is supported by the results of research by other investigators (Dudeck et al., 2007; Jaffee et al., 2004; McGrath, Nilsen, & Kerley, 2011). Finally, Widom's work offers yet another reason (as if more reasons were needed) why it is so important to prevent the physical and sexual abuse of children. The long-term consequences of such abuse can be tragic not only for its immediate victims but also for those victimized by the criminal actions and antisocial behavior of some abused children as they grow up (Weiler & Widom, 1996; Widom, Czaja, & Dutton, 2008).

What do we still need to know?

Widom's results suggest that child abuse can have a broad range of effects, all of which can derail normal childhood development. It is not yet clear, though, how abuse combines with other risk factors such as genetics or differences in neurocognitive functioning. More research is obviously needed to discover whether antisocial personality disorder stems from abuse itself, from one of the factors accompanying it, or from some specific combination of known and still-unknown risk factors (Beach et al., 2010). The importance of combined and interacting risk factors is suggested by the fact that abuse is often part of a larger pool of experiences, such as exposure to deviant models, social rejection, and poor supervision. For instance, child abuse might increase the likelihood of encountering stressful events later in life (Horwitz et al., 2001), thus creating a general vulnerability to a variety of psychological disorders, including antisocial personality disorder (Scott, Smith, & Ellis, 2010). Until we understand how all these potentially causal pieces fit together, we will not fully understand the role childhood abuse plays in the chain of events leading to antisocial personality disorder.

We need to know more, too, about why such a small percentage of the abused children in Widom's sample displayed violence, criminal behavior, and antisocial personality disorder. These results raise the question of which genetic characteristics or environmental experiences serve to protect children from at least some of the devastating effects of abuse (Flores, Cicchetti, & Rogosch, 2005; Rind, Tromovitch, & Bauserman, 1998; Widom et al., 2007). As described in the chapter on human development, some clues have already been found (Caspi et al., 2002; Kim-Cohen & Gold, 2009; Wills et al., 2001), but a better understanding of what these protective elements are might go a long way toward the development of programs to prevent antisocial personality disorder.   ●●●●

Some Other Psychological Disorders

How do children's disorders differ from adults' disorders?

The disorders described so far represent some of the most prevalent and socially disruptive psychological problems. Several others are mentioned in other chapters. In the chapter on consciousness, for example, we discuss insomnia, night terrors, and other sleep disorders; intellectual disability is covered in the chapter on thought, language, and intelligence; and posttraumatic stress disorder is described in the chapter on health, stress, and coping. Here we consider two other significant psychological problems: disorders of childhood and substance-related disorders.

Psychological Disorders of Childhood

The physical, cognitive, emotional, and social changes that occur in childhood—and the stress associated with them—can create or worsen psychological disorders in children. Stress can do the same in adults, but childhood disorders are not just miniature versions of adult psychopathology. Because children's development is still incomplete and because their capacity to cope with stress is limited, children are often vulnerable to special types of disorders. The *DSM-IV-TR* lists over two dozen Axis I disorders seen in infants, children, and adolescents, but the majority of childhood behavior problems can be placed in two broad categories: externalizing disorders and internalizing disorders (Phares, 2008).

The *externalizing,* or *undercontrolled,* category includes behaviors that disturb people in the child's environment. Lack of control shows up as *conduct disorders* in about 2 to 9 percent of children and adolescents, mostly boys, and appears most frequently at around 11 or 12 years of age (Merikangas et al., 2010; Nock et al., 2006). Conduct disorders are characterized by a relatively stable pattern of aggression, disobedience, destructiveness, inappropriate sexual activity, academic failure, and other problematic behaviors (Frick & Nigg, 2012; Kalb & Loeber, 2003; Petitclerc & Tremblay, 2009). Often these behaviors involve criminal activity, pursued without remorse or empathy for victims, and they may signal the development of antisocial personality disorder (Lahey et al., 2005; Lyman & Gudonis, 2005; Pardini, Frick, & Moffitt, 2010).

© Cherry-Merry/Shutterstock

Active or Hyperactive?

Normal behavior for children in one culture might be considered hyperactive in other cultures. Do people in the same culture disagree on what is hyperactive? To find out, ask two or three friends to join you in observing a group of children at a playground, a schoolyard, a park, or some other public place. Ask your friends to privately identify which children they would label as "hyperactive" and then count how many of their choices agree with yours and with others in your group.

LEARN by DOING

There may be a genetic predisposition toward externalizing disorders (Larsson, Andershed, & Lichtenstein, 2006; Slutske et al., 2012; Van Hulle et al., 2009). For example, many children who display conduct disorder have parents who display antisocial personality disorder (Gelhorn et al., 2005). Children who are temperamentally inclined toward high activity levels and lack of concern for other people's feelings are at greater risk for externalizing disorders (Anastassiou-Hadjicharalambous & Warden, 2008; Mesman & Koot, 2000; Pardini et al., 2010). There is no doubt, though, that parental and peer influences as well as academic problems at school combine with genetic factors to shape the antisocial behavior of these children (Brody et al., 2011; Giles et al., 2011; Hanish et al., 2005; Jaffee et al., 2012; Lahey et al., 2011; Leve, Kim, & Pears, 2005; Scourfield et al., 2004; Weitzman, Rosenthal, & Liu, 2011).

Another kind of externalizing problem, *attention deficit hyperactivity disorder* (*ADHD*), is seen in up to 8 percent of children and in about 4 percent of adults, mainly boys and men (Bloom & Cohen, 2007; Merikangas et al., 2010). An ADHD diagnosis is given to children who are more impulsive, more inattentive, or both, than other children their age (Nigg, 2001; Wolraich et al., 2005). Many of these children also have great difficulty sitting still or otherwise controlling their physical activity. They appear to be less able than other children to recognize emotions in others and to regulate their own emotions (Da Fonseca et al., 2009; Musser et al., 2011). Their impulsiveness and lack of self-control contribute to significant impairments in learning and to an astonishing ability to annoy and exhaust those around them. Children diagnosed with ADHD also tend to perform poorly on tests of attention, memory, decision making, and other information-processing tasks. As a result, ADHD is being increasingly viewed as a neurological condition rather than just "bad behavior" (Halperin & Schulz, 2006; Konrad et al., 2006; Krain & Castellanos, 2006).

Like so many other disorders, ADHD appears to result from the interaction of a genetic predisposition and environmental influences (Hart et al., 2010; Nigg, 2010; Nigg, Nikolas, & Burt, 2010; Nikolas, Klump, & Burt, 2011). The genes involved may be those that regulate dopamine, a neurotransmitter important in the functioning of the attention system (Bush, 2010; Gilden & Marusich, 2009; Waldman & Gizer, 2006). Other factors, such as brain damage, poisoning from lead or other household substances, and low birth weight may also play causal roles (Hudziak et al., 2005; Linnet et al., 2003; Mick et al., 2002; Nigg, 2010; Nikolas & Burt, 2010). In some cases, problems in parenting may increase the risk for ADHD (Clarke et al., 2002). Exactly how all these factors might combine is still not clear.

Also uncertain is exactly what constitutes hyperactivity. Cultural standards about acceptable activity levels in children vary, so a "hyperactive" child in one culture might be considered merely "active" in another. In fact, when mental health professionals from four cultures used the same rating scale to judge hyperactivity in a videotaped sample of children's behavior, the Chinese and Indonesians rated the children as significantly more hyperactive than did their U.S. and Japanese colleagues (Jacobson, 2002; Mann et al., 1992). And as mentioned earlier, there is evidence that African American children are diagnosed with ADHD only about two thirds as often as European American children even when they have at least as many symptoms (Miller, Nigg, & Miller, 2009). Such findings remind us that sociocultural factors can be important determinants of what is expected or acceptable and thus what is considered abnormal.

The second broad category of child behavior problems involves *internalizing*, or *overcontrol*. Children in this category experience significant distress, especially depression and anxiety, and may be socially withdrawn (Luby, 2010). Those displaying *separation anxiety disorder*, for example, constantly worry that they will be lost, kidnapped, or injured or that some harm may come to a parent, usually the mother (Orgilés et al., 2009, 2011). The child clings desperately to the parent, and becomes upset or sick at the prospect of separation (Brand et al., 2011; Kossowsky et al., 2012). Refusal to go to school, sometimes called "school phobia," is often the result (Bahali, & Tahiroğlu, 2010; Doobay, 2008; Iwata, Hazama, & Nakagome, 2012). Children who are temperamentally shy or withdrawn are at higher risk for internalizing disorders, but these disorders are also associated with environmental factors, including rejection or bullying by peers, and (especially for girls) being raised by a single parent (Darwich, Hymel, & Waterhouse, 2012; Phares, 2008; Prinstein & La Greca, 2002).

A few childhood disorders, such as *pervasive developmental disorders*, do not fall into either the externalizing or internalizing category. Children diagnosed with these disorders show severe deficits in communication and impaired social relationships. They also often show repetitive patterns of behavior (such as spinning objects) and unusual preoccupations and interests (American Psychiatric Association, 2000). The disorders in this group, which will be known officially as *autistic spectrum disorders* in *DSM-5*, share many of these core symptoms, although the severity of the symptoms may differ (Çeponien et al., 2003; Constantino & Todd, 2003). Estimates of the prevalence of autistic spectrum disorders vary—depending on where and how data were collected—from 22 to 60 children per 10,000 (a rate of about 0.3 percent to 0.6 percent).The most recent data suggest rates nearer the high end of this range (Durkin et al., 2010; Saracino et al., 2010; Williams et al., 2008; Zaroff & Um, 2012). Autistic spectrum disorders are diagnosed four times as often in boys than in girls, and more often in European American children than in other groups (Kogan et al., 2009).

Some of these children have *autistic disorder*, which can be the most severe disorder of the group. The earliest signs of autistic disorder usually occur within the first 30 months after birth; these babies show little or no evidence of forming an attachment to their caregivers. Language development is seriously disrupted in most of these children; half of them never learn to speak at all. However, those who display "high functioning autism" or a less severe autistic spectrum disorder called *Asperger's disorder* are able to function adaptively and, in some cases, independently as adults (e.g., Grandin, 1996; Pexman et al., 2011; Shore, 2003).

Possible biological roots of autistic disorder include genetic factors (Freitag, 2007; Gupta & State, 2007; Hallmayer et al., 2011; St. Pourcain et al., 2010; Vorstman et al., 2006; Weiss & Arking, 2009) or neurodevelopmental abnormalities that affect language and communication (Baron-Cohen, Knickmeyer, & Belmonte, 2005; Belmonte et al., 2004; Grossberg & Seidman, 2006; Minshew & Williams, 2007). Researchers studying these biological factors are especially interested in the activity of *mirror neurons* in the brain. As described in the chapter on biology and behavior, these neurons are activated when we see other people's actions, such as smiling, frowning, or showing disgust. Because they are in the areas of our own brain that control these same actions, activity in mirror neurons helps us to understand how the other person might be feeling and to empathize with those feelings. The functioning of mirror neurons appears disturbed in people with autism, which may help explain why these individuals seem to operate with little appreciation for what others might be thinking or feeling (Welsh et al., 2009; Williams et al., 2006). This explanation has not been confirmed, however, (Yang-Teng et al., 2010), and other possible causal factors are also being investigated, including the effects of drugs, environmental chemicals, and infectious agents. Hypotheses that autistic disorder is caused by cold and unresponsive parents, or by vaccinations, have been rejected by the results of scientific research (Dietert, Dietert, & DeWitt, 2011; Doja & Roberts, 2006).

Disorders of childhood differ from adult disorders not only because the patterns of behavior are distinct but also because their early onset disrupts development. To take just one example, children whose separation anxiety causes spotty school attendance may not only fall behind academically but also may fail to form the relationships with other children that promote normal social development (Wood, 2006). Some children never make up for this deficit. They may drop out of school and risk a life of psychiatric disorders, poverty, crime, and violence (Bahali, & Tahiroğlu, 2010; Doobay, 2008). Moreover, children depend on others to get help for their psychological problems, but all too often those problems may go unrecognized or untreated. For some, the long-term result may be adult forms of mental disorder. This is particularly tragic because early diagnosis and appropriate intervention can lead to significant improvement in childhood disorders (Ingersoll, 2011; Kurita, 2012).

Substance-Related Disorders

substance-related disorders
Problems involving the use of psychoactive drugs for months or years in ways that harm the user or others.

Childhood disorders, especially externalizing disorders, often lead to substance-related disorders in adolescence and adulthood. The *DSM-IV-TR* defines **substance-related disorders** as the use of psychoactive drugs for months or years in ways that harm the user or others. These disorders, to be called *substance use and addictive disorders* in DSM-5, create major political, economic, social, and health problems worldwide. The substances involved most often are alcohol and other depressants (such as barbiturates), opiates (such as heroin), stimulants (such as cocaine or amphetamines), and hallucinogenic drugs (such as LSD). About half of the world's population uses at least one psychoactive substance, and about two thirds of people in the United States report that alcohol or drug addiction has affected them, their families, or their close friends (Leamon, Wright, & Myrick, 2008; Swendsen et al., 2012).

One effect of using some substances (including alcohol, heroin, and amphetamines) is **addiction**, a physical need for the substance. The *DSM-IV-TR* calls addiction *physiological dependence.* Even when the use of a drug does not create physical addiction, some people may overuse, or *abuse*, it because the drug gives them temporary self-confidence, enjoyment, or relief from tension. The *DSM-IV-TR* defines *substance abuse* as a pattern of use that causes serious social, legal, or interpersonal problems. In other words, people can become psychologically dependent on psychoactive drugs without becoming physiologically addicted to them. But people who are psychologically dependent on a drug often have problems that are at least as serious as those of people who are addicted and that may be even more difficult to treat. In the consciousness chapter, we describe how consciousness is affected by a wide range of psychoactive drugs. Here, we focus more specifically on the problems associated with the use and abuse of alcohol, heroin, and cocaine.

Alcohol Use Disorders   According to national surveys in the United States, 3.1 percent of the adult population abuse alcohol or are dependent on it in any given year, and 14 percent of adults have had these problems at some time in their lives (Kessler & Wang, 2008; Leamon, Wright, & Myrick, 2008). *Alcohol abuse* is characterized by a pattern of continuous or intermittent drinking that may lead to *alcohol dependence,* an addiction that almost always causes severe social, physical, and other problems (U.S. Department of Health and Human Services Office of Applied Studies, 2003). Males outnumber females in this category by a ratio of about three to one, although the problem is on the rise among women and teenagers of both genders (Grucza et al., 2008). Abuse is greater among European Americans and American Indians than among African Americans and Hispanics; it is lowest among Asians (Chassin, Pitts, & Prost, 2002; Grant et al., 2004; Substance Abuse and Mental Health Services Administration, 2007). Prolonged overuse of alcohol can result in life-threatening liver damage, impaired cognitive abilities, vitamin deficiencies that can lead to severe and permanent memory loss, and a host of other physical ailments (Hommer et al., 2001; Pfefferbaum et al., 2001).

Alcohol dependence and abuse, commonly referred to as **alcoholism**, are serious problems. They are involved in 40 to 50 percent of all automobile accidents, murders, and rapes (Butcher et al., 2010). Alcohol abuse also figures prominently in child abuse and in elevated rates of hospitalization and absenteeism from work (Freisthler, 2011; Keller et al., 2009; Lawder et al., 2011; Lidwall & Marklund, 2011; National Institute on Alcohol Abuse and Alcoholism, 2001). Children growing up in families in which one or both parents abuse alcohol are at increased risk for developing a host of psychological disorders, including substance-related disorders (Hoffmann & Cerbone, 2002; Jones, 2007; Odgers et al., 2008). And as described in the chapter on human development, children of mothers who abused alcohol during pregnancy may be born with fetal alcohol syndrome. In short, alcohol abuse and dependence carry a staggering cost in terms of personal suffering, medical expenditures, lost productivity, and shortened lifespans.

The biopsychosocial approach suggests that alcohol abuse stems from a combination of genetically influenced characteristics (including inherited aspects of temperament such as impulsivity, a taste for novelty, and emotionality) and what people learn in their social and cultural environments (Donovan & Molina, 2011; Elkins et al., 2006; Kanazawa & Hellberg, 2010; King et al., 2012; Leeman et al., 2012; Lovallo et al., 2006; Ray et al., 2010; van Beek et al., 2012). For example, the children of people with alcoholism are more likely than others to develop alcoholism themselves, and if the children are identical twins, both are at increased risk for alcoholism, even when raised apart (Volk et al., 2007). It

addiction Development of a physical need for a psychoactive drug.

alcoholism A pattern of drinking that may lead to addiction and that almost always causes severe social, physical, and other problems.

is still unclear just what might be inherited or which genes are involved. One possibility involves inherited abnormalities in the brain's neurotransmitter systems or in the body's metabolism of alcohol (Martinez et al., 2005; Nurnberger et al., 2001; Petrakis et al., 2004). Males with alcoholism do tend to be less sensitive than other people to the effects of alcohol—a factor that may contribute to greater consumption (Pollack, 1992; Schuckit, 1998; Vetter-O'Hagen, Carlinskaya, & Spear, 2009). Now that the human genome has been decoded, researchers are focusing on specific chromosomes as the possible location of genes that predispose people to—or protect them from—the development of alcoholism (Beirut et al., 2011; Cheng et al., 2004; National Institute on Alcohol Abuse and Alcoholism, 2000, 2001; Wall et al., 2005). However, the genetics of addiction are highly complex; there is probably not a single gene for alcoholism (Crabbe, 2002; Higuchi, Matsushita, & Kashima, 2006). As with other disorders, alcoholism arises as many genes interact with each other and with environmental events, including parental influences (Duncan et al., 2006; Kaufman et al., 2007; Kendler, Gardner, & Dick, 2011; Philbert et al., 2009; Young-Wolff, Enoch, & Prescott, 2011). For example, one study found that boys whose fathers had alcoholism were at elevated risk for alcoholism, but not if the father's genetically identical *twin* had alcoholism (Jacob et al., 2003). In these cases, something in the boys' nonalcoholic family environment had apparently moderated whatever genetic tendency toward alcoholism they might have inherited.

Youngsters typically learn to drink by watching their parents and their peers (Abar, 2012). The observations help shape their expectations, such as that alcohol will make them feel good and help them cope with stressors (Schell et al., 2005). But alcohol use can become abuse and perhaps addiction if drinking is a person's main coping strategy (National Institute on Alcohol Abuse and Alcoholism, 2001). The importance of learning is supported by evidence that alcoholism is more commonly reported among ethnic and cultural groups in which frequent drinking tends to be socially approved, such as the Irish and English, than among religious or ethnic groups in which all but moderate drinking tends to be discouraged, such as Jews, Italians, and Chinese (Gray & Nye, 2001; Koenig, Haber, & Jacob, 2011; Ryan & Hout, 2011; Schwartz et al., 2011; Wilson et al., 1996). Moreover, different forms of social support for drinking can result in different consumption patterns within a cultural group (Biron, Banberger, & Noyman, 2011; McKay et al., 2011). For example, one study found significantly more drinking among Japanese men living in Japan (where social norms for male drinking are most permissive) compared with Japanese men living in Hawaii or California, where excessive drinking is less strongly supported (Kitano et al., 1992).

Heroin and Cocaine Dependence   Like people with alcoholism, those who are addicted to heroin or cocaine suffer many serious health problems as a result of both the drugs themselves and the poor eating and health habits related to use of those drugs. The risk of death from overdose, contaminated drugs, AIDS (contracted through shared needles), or suicide is also always present. Drug dependence tends to be more prevalent among males, especially young males (Compton et al., 2007; Warner et al., 1995).

Addiction to heroin and cocaine appears in about 4 percent of the adult population in the United States (Compton et al., 2005) and is mainly a biological process brought about by the physical effects of the drugs (Kalivas & Volkow, 2005; Phillips et al., 2003). Explaining why people first use these drugs is more complicated. Beyond the obvious and immediate pleasure these drugs provide, the causes of initial drug use are less well established than the reasons for alcohol abuse. Some research has identified structural abnormalities in the brains of people who become addicted to stimulant drugs (Ersche et al., 2012). Another line of research suggests that there might be a genetic tendency toward behavioral compulsions that predisposes some people to abuse many kinds of drugs (Crabbe, 2002; Fernández-Serrano et al., 2012; Koob & Volkow, 2010; Kreek et al., 2005). One study supporting this idea found a link between alcoholism in biological parents and drug abuse in the sons they had given up for adoption (Cadoret et al., 1995). The same study also found a link between antisocial personality traits in biological parents and antisocial acts—including drug abuse—in the sons they had put up for adoption.

A number of psychological and environmental factors have been proposed as promoting initial drug use (Alessi et al., 2002; Brems & Namyniuk, 2002; Hoffmann & Cerbone, 2002). These include seeing parents use drugs, being abused in childhood, using drugs to cope with stressors or to ease anxiety or depression, associating drug use with pleasant experiences, seeking popularity, caving in to peer pressure, and thrill seeking (Alessi et al., 2002; Baker et al., 2004; Dube et al., 2003; Ferguson & Meehan, 2011; García-Montes et al., 2009; Putnam, 2003; Reed, Anthony, & Breslau, 2007; Rudolph et al., 2011; Singh, Thornton, & Tonmyr, 2011; Tucker et al., 2011). Research has not yet established why continued drug use occurs in some people and not in others, but, again, it is likely that a biological predisposition interacts with psychological processes and stressors that play out their roles in specific social and cultural contexts (Hammen, 2009; Hicks et al., 2011; Kreek et al., 2005; Munafo, 2011).

Mental Illness and the Law

Can insanity protect criminals from punishment?

Have you wondered why the word *insanity* doesn't appear in our definition of *mental disorder* or in the *DSM-IV-TR* categories we have described? The reason is that *insanity* is a legal term, not a psychiatric diagnosis (Torry & Billick, 2010). For example, John Hinckley, Jr., was found *not guilty by reason of insanity* for his attempted assassination of President Ronald Reagan in 1981. This verdict reflected U.S. laws and rules that protect people with severe psychological disorders when they are accused of crimes (Cassel & Bernstein, 2007). Many other countries around the world have similar laws (Ahn-Redding, 2008).

This protection takes two forms. First, under certain conditions, people designated as mentally ill may be protected from prosecution. If at the time of trial individuals accused of crimes are unable to understand the proceedings and charges against them or help their attorneys to prepare a defense, they are declared *mentally incompetent* to stand trial. When that happens, defendants are sent to a mental institution for treatment until they are judged to be mentally competent (Zapf & Roesch, 2011). If they are still not competent after some specified period—two years, in many cases—defendants may be ruled permanently ineligible for trial and either committed to a mental institution or released. Release is rare, however, because most defendants who are unable to meet competency standards have mental disorders that are serious enough to pose a danger to themselves or others.

Second, the mentally ill may be protected from punishment. In most U.S. states, defendants may be judged not guilty by reason of insanity if at the time of the crime mental illness prevented them from (1) understanding what they were doing; (2) knowing that what they were doing was wrong; and (3) resisting the impulse to do wrong. The first two of these criteria relate to a person's ability to think clearly and are called the *M'Naghton rule,* for the defendant in the 1843 case that established it. The third criterion, which relates to the defendant's emotional state during a crime, is known as the *irresistible impulse test.* All three criteria were combined in a rule proposed by the American Law Institute in 1962—a rule that is now followed in about one third of U.S. states.

After the Hinckley verdict, the U.S. Congress passed the Insanity Defense Reform Act, which eliminated the irresistible impulse criterion from the definition of insanity in federal cases. About 75 percent of the U.S. states have passed similar or related reform laws (Giorgi-Guarnieri et al., 2002); in about half the states, these laws require the use of some version of the narrower M'Naghton rule (American Psychiatric Association, 2003). Whatever criteria are used, when defendants plead insanity, judges and juries must decide whether or not these people should be held responsible for criminal acts. Defendants who are judged not guilty by reason of insanity and who still display a psychological disorder are usually required to receive treatment, typically through

© AP Photo/Brett Coomer, Pool

Assessment of Mental Competence

Andrea Yates admitted to drowning her five children in the bathtub of her Houston, Texas, home in 2001. She had twice tried to kill herself in previous years, and she was reportedly depressed at the time of the murders. Accordingly, she pleaded not guilty by reason of insanity. The first legal step in deciding her fate was to confine her in a mental institution to assess her mental competency to stand trial. Following the testimony of psychologists who examined her, she was found competent and ultimately sentenced to life in prison. Her conviction was overturned on appeal, though, and at a second trial in 2006, she was found not guilty by reason of insanity and committed to a mental hospital.

APPLYING PSYCHOLOGY

commitment to a hospital, until judged to be cured or no longer dangerous. Thirteen U.S. states have laws allowing jurors to find defendants *guilty but mentally ill*. These defendants are supposed to receive treatment while in prison, though they seldom do (Cassel & Bernstein, 2007).

Critics of insanity rules complain that these rules allow criminals to "get away with murder." Actually, such outcomes are rare. Insanity pleas occur in only 1 out of every 200 felony cases in the United States, and they are successful in only 2 of every 1,000 attempts (American Psychiatric Association, 2003; Silver, Cirincione, & Steadman, 1994). Even the few defendants found not guilty by reason of insanity in the United States may be hospitalized for at least as long as they would have spent in prison had they been found guilty (Roesch, Zapf, & Hart, 2010). Those with the most severe disorders may never be released. John Hinckley, Jr., has been in Saint Elizabeth's Hospital in Washington, D.C., since 1982, and in spite of his annual efforts to be released and court approval for longer visits with his mother outside the hospital, he is unlikely to be freed anytime soon.

In summary, society is constantly seeking the proper balance between protecting the rights of defendants and protecting society from dangerous criminals. In the process, the sociocultural values that shape our views about what is abnormal also influence judgments about the extent to which abnormality should relieve people of responsibility for criminal behavior (O'Connell, 2011).

Active Review

As noted in the introductory chapter, all of psychology's subfields are related to one another. Our discussion of how mental disorders might be learned illustrates just one way that the topic of this chapter, psychological disorders, is linked to the subfield of learning, which is

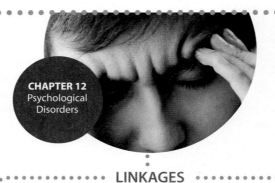

CHAPTER 12
Psychological Disorders

discussed in the chapter by that name. The Linkages diagram shows ties to two other subfields, and there are many more ties throughout the book. Looking for linkages among subfields will help you see how they all fit together and help you better appreciate the big picture that is psychology.

LINKAGES

Are some psychological disorders inherited?
(ans. on p. 480)

Can we learn to become abnormal?
(ans. on p. 472)

Can personality tests be used to diagnose mental disorders?
(ans. on p. 448)

CHAPTER 2
Biology and Behavior

CHAPTER 5
Learning

CHAPTER 11
Personality

Summary

Psychopathology involves patterns of thinking, feeling, and behaving that are maladaptive, disruptive, or distressing, either for the person affected or for others.

Defining Psychological Disorders
How do psychologists define abnormal behavior?
Some psychological disorders show considerable similarity across cultures, but the definition of abnormality is largely determined by social and cultural factors. The criteria for judging abnormality include deviance (statistical infrequency and norm violations), distress (personal suffering), and dysfunction. Each of these criteria is flawed to some extent. The practical approach, which considers the content, context, and consequences of behavior, emphasizes the question of whether individuals show impaired functioning

in fulfilling the roles appropriate for particular people in particular settings, cultures, and historical eras.

Explaining Psychological Disorders
What causes abnormality?
At various times and places, abnormal behavior has been attributed to the action of gods or the devil. Mental health professionals in Western cultures rely on a *biopsychosocial approach,* which attributes mental disorders to the interaction of biological, psychological, and *sociocultural factors*. Biological factors, such as brain chemistry, are highlighted by the medical or *neurobiological model* of disorder. The *psychological model* focuses on processes such as inner conflicts, maladaptive

learning experiences, or blocked personal growth. The *sociocultural perspective* helps explain disorder by focusing on the social relations, social support and cultural and subcultural factors that form the context of abnormality. The *diathesis-stress model* suggests that biological, psychological, and sociocultural characteristics create predispositions for disorder that are translated into symptoms in the face of sufficient amounts of stress.

Classifying Psychological Disorders
How many psychological disorders have been identified?
The dominant system for classifying abnormal behavior in North America is the fourth edition of the *Diagnostic and Statistical Manual of Mental Disorders* (*DSM-IV* and *DSM-IV-TR*) of

the American Psychiatric Association. It includes more than 300 specific categories of mental disorder that can be described using five dimensions, or axes. Diagnosis helps identify the features, causes, and most effective methods of treating various psychological disorders. Research on the reliability and validity of the *DSM-IV-TR* shows that it is a useful but not perfect classification system.

Anxiety Disorders

What is a phobia?
Long-standing and disruptive patterns of anxiety characterize **anxiety disorders.** The most prevalent type of anxiety disorder is **phobia,** a category that includes **specific phobias**, **social phobias**, and **agoraphobia**. Other anxiety disorders are **generalized anxiety disorder,** which involves nonspecific anxiety; **panic disorder,** which brings unpredictable attacks of intense anxiety; and **obsessive-compulsive disorder (OCD),** which is characterized by uncontrollable repetitive thoughts called **obsessions** and ritualistic actions called **compulsions**.

The most influential explanations of anxiety disorders suggest that they may develop when a biological predisposition for strong anxiety reactions combines with fear-enhancing thought patterns and learned anxiety responses. Many anxiety disorders appear to develop in accordance with the principles of classical and operant conditioning and with those of observational learning. People may be biologically prepared to learn fear of certain objects and situations.

Somatoform Disorders

Can mental disorder cause blindness?
Somatoform disorders appear as physical problems that have no apparent physical cause or as intense preoccupation with physical illness or deformity. They include **conversion disorder,** which involves problems such as blindness, deafness, and paralysis that have no apparent physical cause; **hypochondriasis,** an unjustified concern over being or becoming ill; **somatization disorder,** in which the person complains of numerous unconfirmed physical complaints; **somatoform pain disorder,** in which pain is felt in the absence of a physical cause; and **body dysmorphic disorder,** in which there is intense distress over imagined abnormalities of the skin, hair, face, or other bodily areas.

Dissociative Disorders

What disorders create sudden memory loss?
Dissociative disorders involve rare conditions such as **fugue reactions** and **dissociative amnesia**, both of which involve sudden and severe memory loss, and **dissociative identity disorder (DID),** or multiple personality disorder, in which a person appears to have two or more identities. There is considerable controversy about the origins of dissociative identity disorder.

Affective Disorders

How common is depression?
Affective disorders, also known as **mood disorders**, are quite common and involve extreme moods that may be inconsistent with events. **Major depression (major depressive disorder)** is marked by feelings of inadequacy, worthlessness, and guilt; in extreme cases, **delusions** may also occur. **Dysthymic disorder** includes similar but less severe symptoms that persist for a long period. Suicide is often related to these disorders. Alternating periods of depression and **mania** characterize **bipolar disorders;** there are more intense manic phases in bipolar I disorder than in bipolar II disorder. These disorders are also known as manic depression. **Cyclothymic personality** or **cyclothymic disorder,** an alternating pattern of less extreme mood swings, is a slightly more common variant.

Affective disorders have been attributed to biological causes such as genetic inheritance, disruptions in neurotransmitter and endocrine systems, and irregularities in biological rhythms. These interact with stressors and psychological factors such as maladaptive patterns of thinking. A predisposition toward some of these disorders may be inherited, although their appearance is probably determined by a diathesis-stress process.

Schizophrenia

Is schizophrenia the same as "split personality"?
Schizophrenia is perhaps the most severe and puzzling disorder of all. Among its symptoms are problems in thinking, perception (often including **hallucinations**), attention, emotion, movement, motivation, and daily functioning. Positive symptoms of schizophrenia include hallucinations or disordered speech; negative symptoms can include withdrawal, immobility, and the absence of affect.

Genetic influences, neurotransmitter problems, abnormalities in brain structure and functioning, and neurodevelopmental abnormalities are biological factors implicated in schizophrenia. Psychological factors such as maladaptive learning experiences and disturbed family interactions can affect the severity and course of this disorder. Diathesis-stress explanations, including vulnerability theory, provide a promising framework for research into the multiple causes of schizophrenia.

Personality Disorders
Which personality disorder often leads to crime?
Personality disorders are long-term patterns of maladaptive behavior that are not always associated with discomfort for the person with the disorder but may be disturbing to others. These include odd-eccentric types (paranoid, schizoid, and schizotypal personality disorders), anxious-fearful types (dependent, obsessive-compulsive, and avoidant personality disorders), and dramatic-erratic types (histrionic, narcissistic, borderline, and antisocial personality disorders). **Antisocial personality disorder** is marked by impulsive, irresponsible, and unscrupulous behavior patterns that often begin in childhood. Childhood abuse may be related to the appearance of this potentially dangerous personality disorder.

Some Other Psychological Disorders
How do children's disorders differ from adults' disorders?
Childhood psychological disorders can be categorized as externalizing conditions (such as conduct disorders or attention deficit hyperactivity disorder) and internalizing disorders, in which children show overcontrol and experience distress (as in separation anxiety disorder).

Pervasive developmental disorders do not fall into either category and include the autistic spectrum disorders. In autistic disorder, which can be the most severe of these, children show no interest in or attachment to others.

Substance-related disorders involving alcohol and other drugs affect millions of people. **Addiction** to and psychological dependence on these substances contribute to disastrous personal and social problems, including physical illnesses, accidents, and crime. Genetic factors probably create a predisposition for **alcoholism,** but learning, cultural traditions, and other nonbiological processes are also important. Stress reduction, imitation, thrill seeking, and social maladjustment have been proposed as important factors in drug addiction, as has genetic predisposition; but the exact causes of initial use of these drugs are unknown.

Mental Illness and The Law
Can insanity protect criminals from punishment?
"Insanity" is a legal term, not a psychiatric diagnosis. Current rules protect people accused of crimes from prosecution or punishment if they are declared mentally incompetent at the time of their trials or if they were legally insane at the time of their crimes. Defendants judged not guilty by reason of insanity and who still display a psychological disorder are usually required to receive treatment until they are judged to be cured or no longer dangerous. Those found guilty but mentally ill are supposed to receive treatment in prison.

Put It in Writing
Think about something you have seen someone do recently that you considered truly abnormal. Now write a page describing what happened and the specific rules or criteria—such as statistical infrequency, norm violation, personal suffering, or impaired functioning—that you used in deciding that this person's behavior qualifies as abnormal. Include a statement about whether you think this person should be treated for his or her behavior problem and why. Predict the degree to which this behavior would be considered abnormal by other people in your culture. Finally, tell whether and why people in other cultures might have a different view of the case.

Personal Learning Activity
To what extent do people agree on what is abnormal? To find out, ask at least 20 friends, family members, teachers, classmates in other courses, casual acquaintances, and maybe even some strangers to read your description of the behavior you diagnosed as abnormal in the Put It in Writing exercise. (Show them only the description, not your comments.) Ask these people to tell you whether they think the behavior is normal, merely odd, or seriously abnormal and whether they think the person is in need of treatment. Analyze the results in terms of how many of these people agreed with your diagnosis and with one another. Did you notice any trends in their responses based on age, gender, educational status, or cultural background? What do your results say about how easy or difficult it is to precisely define abnormality?

Review of Key Terms ·······················

Can you define each of the key terms in the chapter? Check your definitions against those on the pages shown in parentheses in the following list or in the Glossary at the end of the book.

addiction (p. 494)
affective disorder (mood disorder) (p. 476)
agoraphobia (p. 470)
alcoholism (p. 494)
antisocial personality disorder (p. 488)
anxiety disorder (p. 469)
biopsychosocial approach (p. 459)
bipolar disorder (p. 479)
body dysmorphic disorder (p. 474)
compulsions (p. 471)
conversion disorder (p. 473)

cyclothymic personality (cyclothymic disorder) (p. 479)
delusions (p. 477)
diathesis-stress model (p. 462)
dissociative amnesia (p. 475)
dissociative disorders (p. 474)
dissociative identity disorder (DID) (p. 475)
dysthymic disorder (p. 477)
fugue reaction (dissociative fugue) (p. 475)
generalized anxiety disorder (p. 470)
hallucinations (p. 484)
hypochondriasis (p. 473)
major depression (major depressive disorder) (p. 476)
mania (p. 479)
obsessions (p. 471)

obsessive-compulsive disorder (OCD) (p. 470)
panic disorder (p. 470)
personality disorders (p. 488)
phobia (p. 469)
psychological model (p. 460)
psychopathology (p. 456)
schizophrenia (p. 482)
social phobias (p. 469)
sociocultural factors (p. 461)
sociocultural perspective (p. 461)
somatization disorder (p. 474)
somatoform disorders (p. 473)
somatoform pain disorder (p. 474)
specific phobias (p. 469)
substance-related disorders (p. 493)

Test Your Knowledge ·····················

Select the best answer for each of the following questions. Then check your responses against the Answer Key at the end of the book.

1. According to the statistics on psychopathology, ____ percent of people in the United States experience a mental disorder in their lifetimes.
   a. less than 5 percent
   b. approximately 25 percent
   c. almost 50 percent
   d. over 75 percent

2. Babette, a successful opera singer, believes that aliens could snatch her at any time if she isn't wearing her lucky charm. She is constantly worried and insists that the stage be rimmed with foil to ward off evil spirits. According to which criterion of abnormality would Babette *not* be considered abnormal?
   a. Statistical
   b. Norm violation
   c. Practical
   d. Personal suffering

3. Herman murdered a man who bumped into him in a bar. In order to be found not guilty by reason of insanity, the jury would have to find that he ____.
   a. was under the influence of alcohol when he committed the crime
   b. is currently insane
   c. was insane when he committed the crime
   d. knew the crime was wrong but did it anyway

4. Roberta and Rhonda are identical twins who inherited identical predispositions for depression. Roberta has lived an easy life and has not developed any depressive symptoms. Rhonda, who has been divorced and lost several jobs over the years, has been diagnosed with major depression. The difference between these twins is most consistent with the ____ approach to abnormality.
   a. neurobiological
   b. psychological
   c. sociocultural
   d. diathesis-stress

5. Dr. Kramer is evaluating a patient brought in for psychiatric treatment. In his report he indicates that his global assessment of the patient's functioning is about 30 on a 100-point scale. Dr. Kramer is using ____ to evaluate the patient.
   a. the M'Naghton rule
   b. norm violation criteria
   c. insanity criteria
   d. the *DSM-IV-TR*

6. Kat stopped going to classes because of worry that she will embarrass herself by saying something silly. She takes her meals to her dorm room so that no one will see her eat. According to the *DSM-IV-TR*, Kat is probably displaying ____.
   a. agoraphobia
   b. simple phobia
   c. generalized anxiety disorder
   d. social phobia

7. Terraba had a difficult time driving to work. Every time she went over a bump she had to drive back around to make sure that she had not run over anything. This occurred ten or twelve times each day, so Terraba was always late for everything. Terraba appears to be suffering from ____.
   a. specific phobia
   b. panic attacks
   c. obsessive-compulsive disorder
   d. generalized anxiety disorder

8. Conversion disorder is characterized by ____.
   a. impairment of movement or sensory ability with no apparent physical cause
   b. severe pain with no apparent physical cause
   c. fear of becoming seriously ill
   d. frequent, vague complaints of physical symptoms

9. Tomas has been suffering severe back pain for several weeks, but extensive medical tests reveal no physical problem. Tomas appears to be displaying ____.
   a. somatoform pain disorder
   b. hypochondriasis
   c. paranoid schizophrenia
   d. somatization disorder

10. When Jennifer, a newspaper reporter, disappeared while covering a crime story that put her under constant threat, everyone assumed she had been kidnapped. But she was found several months later, now married and calling herself Emily, working as a waitress in a city 1,000 miles from her home. She had no memory of her previous life, even after being reunited with her parents. Jennifer would most likely be diagnosed as displaying ____.
    a. fugue reaction
    b. dissociative identity disorder
    c. dissociative amnesia
    d. schizophrenia

11. Over the past three months, Barb has been feeling very sad; she has been sleeping as much as 15 hours a day and has gained thirty pounds. Debbie, too, feels very low, but she can barely sleep and has lost both her appetite and 15 pounds. Both Barb and Debbie have symptoms of ____.
    a. obsessive-compulsive disorder
    b. major depression
    c. bipolar disorder
    d. hypochondriasis

12. Suicide is closely tied to depression. Studies of suicide in the United States have found that ____.
    a. people who talk about suicide typically don't attempt suicide
    b. older males who are living alone are the most likely to commit suicide
    c. suicide rates are about the same across ethnic groups and gender
    d. depressed women almost never actually attempt suicide

13. Carlisle has been very depressed. He can't face his responsibilities and often spends days at a time in bed. A psychologist who adopts the social-cognitive approach would be most likely to see this depression as caused by Carlisle's____.
    a. attributional style
    b. brain chemicals
    c. unconscious conflicts
    d. blocked growth tendencies

14. As you sit down next to a messy-looking man on a bus, he says, "Ohms vibrate orange and dishwrings obvious dictionary." As he continues talking in this manner, you begin to suspect that he is displaying ____, a ____ symptom of ____.
    a. anxiety; negative; obsessive-compulsive disorder
    b. thought disorder; positive; schizophrenia
    c. thought disorder; negative; schizophrenia
    d. flat affect; negative; depression

15. Juan can't explain why, but he worries constantly that something terrible is going to happen to him. This vague feeling of impending doom is associated with a diagnosis of ____.
    a. conversion disorder
    b. specific phobia
    c. social phobia
    d. generalized anxiety disorder

16. Forty-year-old Richard believes that he was ordered by God to save the world. He is suspicious of other people because he thinks they want to prevent him from fulfilling his mission. He is unable to keep a job because he is angry and argumentative most of the time. Richard would most likely be diagnosed as displaying ____.
    a. affective disorder
    b. dissociative identity disorder
    c. paranoid schizophrenia
    d. catatonic schizophrenia

17. Al is charming and intelligent, but he has always been irresponsible, impulsive, and unscrupulous. None of his girlfriends knows he is dating other women. He borrows money from friends and doesn't pay them back. He doesn't care about anyone else, including his family. Al would probably be diagnosed as displaying ____ personality disorder.
    a. antisocial
    b. narcissistic
    c. passive-aggressive
    d. inadequate

18. Cathy Widom's research study, discussed in the Focus on Research section of this chapter, found that there was a relationship between antisocial personality disorder and ___.
    a. narcissistic personality disorder
    b. schizophrenia
    c. high intelligence
    d. being abused in childhood

19. Angelo drinks alcohol until he passes out. Unable to hold a job or take care of himself, Angelo is diagnosed as having a substance-related disorder. Research on alcoholism suggests that Angelo's problems are caused by ___.
    a. a single inherited gene
    b. a culture that did not tolerate drinking
    c. having parents with alcoholism
    d. a combination of genetic and environmental factors

20. Aaron is an infant who shows no signs of attachment to his parents. He dislikes being held and doesn't smile or laugh. Aaron's symptoms are most consistent with ___.
    a. infantile schizophrenia
    b. autistic disorder
    c. antisocial personality disorder
    d. an externalizing disorder of childhood

Media Resources

Now that you have finished reading this chapter, how about exploring some of the ideas and information that you found most interesting?

Go to **CengageBrain.com** to access Psychology CourseMate, where you will find an interactive eBook, glossaries, flashcards, quizzes, videos, Virtual Psychology Labs, and more.

If your professor has assigned Aplia:

1. Sign in to your account.
2. Complete the corresponding exercises as required by your professor.
3. When finished, click "Grade It Now" to see which areas you have mastered, which areas need more work, and detailed explanations of every answer.

Treatment of Psychological Disorders

Preview

In old Hollywood movies, such as *The Dark Past* or *The Three Faces of Eve*, troubled people find instant cures when a psychotherapist helps them discover an unconscious memory that holds the key to their psychological disorder. Somewhat more realistic versions of psychotherapy have been presented in movies and television shows such as *Good Will Hunting, The Sopranos,* and *In Treatment*. Yet even these portrayals do not convey what psychotherapy is really like, and even the best of them tell only part of the story of how psychological disorders can be treated. In this chapter we describe a wide range of treatment options, including methods based on psychodynamic, humanistic, behavioral, and biological theories of psychological disorders. We also consider research on the effectiveness of treatment and methods for preventing disorders.

I n the chapter on psychological disorders, we describe José, an electronics technician who had to take medical leave from his job because of his panic attacks. After four months of diagnostic testing turned up no physical problems, José's physician suggested that he see a psychologist. José resisted at first, insisting that his condition was not "just in his head," but he eventually began psychological treatment. Within a few months, his panic attacks had ceased and José had returned to all his old activities. After the psychologist helped him reconsider his workload, José decided to take early retirement from his job in order to pursue more satisfying work at his home-based computer business.

José's case is by no means unique. During any given year in the United States alone, about 15 percent of adults and about 21 percent of children and adolescents are receiving some form of treatment for psychological disorders, including substance abuse problems (Costello, Copeland, & Angold, 2011; McGorry et al., 2011). In fact, you probably know someone who has received treatment for a psychological disorder (Connor-Greene, 2001). The treatment can be expensive in the short-run, but saves money in the long-run because it typically reduces clients' need for later mental and physical health services (American Psychological Association, 2009; Insel, 2008; Jordan et al., 2008; Schoenbaum, Sherbourne, & Wells, 2005). The most common targets of treatment in adults are problems involving anxiety, mood, impulse control, substance abuse, or some combination of these (Antony & Barlow, 2010). Many people also seek treatment for problems that are not officially diagnosed as disorders, such as relationship conflicts or difficulties associated with grief, divorce, retirement, or other life transitions. The most common treatment targets in children are hyperactivity, oppositional behavior, anxiety, and affective disorders (Mash & Wolfe, 2012). ●

Basic Features of Treatment

What features do all treatment techniques have in common?

Psychotherapy is the treatment of psychological disorders through psychological methods. All types of psychotherapy share certain basic features. These common features include a *client* or *patient,* a professionally trained *therapist* or other agent who works to help the client, and a *special therapeutic relationship* between the client and the therapist. In addition, all forms of treatment are based on some *theory* about the causes of the client's problems (Antony & Barlow, 2010). The presumed causes can range from magic spells to infections, and everything in between (Corey, 2008). These theories form the basis of *treatment procedures* for dealing with the client's problems. So traditional healers combat supernatural forces with ceremonies and prayers, medical doctors treat chemical imbalances with drugs, and psychologists focus on altering psychological processes through psychotherapy.

psychotherapy The treatment of psychological disorders through talking and other psychological methods.

Medieval Treatment Methods

Methods used to treat psychological disorders have always been related to the presumed causes of those disorders. In medieval times, when abnormal behavior was associated with demonic possession, physician-priests tried to make the victim's body an uncomfortable place for evil spirits. In this depiction, demons are shown fleeing as an afflicted person's head is placed in an oven.

Stock Montage

People can receive treatment as inpatients or outpatients. *Inpatients* are treated while living in a hospital or other institution. They enter these institutions—voluntarily or involuntarily—because their impairments are severe enough to create a threat to their own well-being or that of others. Depending on their level of functioning, inpatients may stay in the hospital for a few days or weeks or (in rare cases) several years. Their treatment almost always includes prescription drugs. *Outpatients* receive psychotherapy and/or prescription drugs while living in the community. Outpatients tend to have fewer and less severe symptoms of disorder than inpatients, and function better in social and occupational situations (Hybels et al., 2008; Pottick et al., 2008).

Those who provide psychological treatment are a diverse group (Robiner, 2006). **Psychiatrists** are medical doctors who complete specialty training in the treatment of mental disorders. Like other physicians, they are authorized to prescribe drugs for the relief of psychological problems. **Psychologists** who offer psychotherapy have usually completed a doctoral degree in clinical or counseling psychology, often followed by additional specialized training. Except in Louisiana and New Mexico, and in the U.S. military and the Indian Health Service, psychologists in the United States are not authorized to prescribe drugs (Heiby, DeLeon, & Anderson, 2008). Other therapy providers include *clinical social workers, marriage and family therapists,* and *licensed professional counselors,* all of whom typically hold master's degrees in their respective fields. They provide treatment in many settings, including hospitals, clinics, and private practice. *Psychiatric nurses, substance abuse counselors,* members of the clergy working as *pastoral counselors,* and a host of *paraprofessionals* also provide therapy services, often as part of a hospital or outpatient treatment team (Kramer, Bernstein, & Phares, 2013).

The overall goal of treatment is to help troubled people change their thinking, feelings, and behavior in ways that relieve discomfort, promote happiness, and improve functioning as parents, students, employees, and the like. More specific goals and the methods chosen to reach them are included in a treatment plan that the therapist and client develop together. The details of this plan depend on the nature of the client's problems, preferences, financial circumstances, and the time available for treatment (Johnson, 2003). They also depend on the therapist's training and qualifications, theoretical leanings, methodological preferences, and the degree to which the therapist is

psychiatrists Medical doctors who have completed special training in the treatment of mental disorders.

psychologists Among therapists, those with advanced training in clinical or counseling psychology.

© Geraint Lewis/Alamy

Freud's Consulting Room
During psychoanalytic sessions, Freud's patients lay on this couch, free associating or describing dreams and events in their lives, while he sat in the chair behind them. (The couch is now on display at the Freud Museum in London, which you can visit online at www.freud.org.uk.) According to Freud, even apparently trivial actions may carry messages from the unconscious. Forgetting a dream or missing a therapy appointment might reflect a client's unconscious resistance to treatment. Even accidents may be meaningful. Freud might have said that a waiter who spilled hot soup on an older male customer was acting out unconscious aggressive impulses against a father figure.

psychoanalysis A method of psychotherapy that seeks to help clients gain insight into and work through unconscious thoughts and emotions presumed to cause psychological problems.

guided by the results of experimental research on treatment. Let's consider several forms of psychotherapy, each of which is based on psychodynamic, humanistic, behavioral, or cognitive behavioral explanations of mental disorder.

Although we describe different approaches in separate sections, keep in mind that the majority of mental health professionals describe themselves as *eclectic* therapists. In other words, they might lean toward one set of treatment methods, but when working with particular clients or particular problems they may employ other methods as well (Cook et al., 2010; Magnavita, 2006; Goldfried, Glass, & Arnkoff, 2011).

Psychodynamic Psychotherapy

How did Freud get started as a therapist?

The field of formal psychotherapy began in the late 1800s when, as described in the personality chapter, Sigmund Freud established the psychodynamic approach to personality and mental disorders. Freud's method of treatment, **psychoanalysis**, was aimed at understanding unconscious conflicts and how they affect clients. Almost all forms of psychotherapy reflect some of Freud's ideas, including (1) his one-to-one treatment method; (2) his search for relationships between an individual's life history and current problems; (3) his emphasis on thoughts, emotions, and motivations in treatment; and (4) his focus on the client-therapist relationship. We'll describe Freud's original methods first and then consider some more recent treatments that are rooted in his psychodynamic approach.

Classical Psychoanalysis

Classical psychoanalysis developed mainly out of Freud's medical practice. He was puzzled by patients who suffered from "hysterical" ailments, such as blindness, paralysis, or other disabilities that had no physical cause (see our discussion of *conversion disorders* in the chapter on psychological disorders). Freud tried to cure these patients with hypnotic suggestions, but he found this method to be only partially and temporarily successful. Later, he asked hypnotized patients to recall events that might have caused their symptoms. Eventually, however, he stopped using hypnosis and merely had patients lie on a couch and report whatever thoughts, memories, or images came to mind. Freud called this process *free association*.

Freud's "talking cure" produced surprising results. He was struck by how many patients reported childhood memories of sexual abuse, usually by a parent or other close relative (Esterson, 2001). Although these allegations were probably accurate (DeMause, 1987), Freud eventually concluded that his patients' memories of abuse were actually unconscious childhood wishes and fantasies that resulted in hysterical symptoms. So psychoanalysis came to focus on exploring the unconscious and resolving the conflicts raging within it.

Classical psychoanalytic treatment helps a client gain insight into problems through the use of free association, dream analysis, and analysis of the client's reactions to the therapist (called *transference*). Clients are first encouraged to recognize unconscious thoughts and emotions. Then they are encouraged to discover, or *work through*, the many ways those unconscious elements continue to motivate maladaptive thinking and behavior in everyday life. The treatment may require as many as three to five sessions per week, usually over several years. Generally, the psychoanalyst remains compassionate but neutral as the client slowly develops insight into how past conflicts have shaped current problems (Gabbard, 2004).

Contemporary Variations on Psychoanalysis

Classical psychoanalysis is still practiced, but not as much as it was several decades ago (Kaner & Prelinger, 2007; Wolitzky, 2011). This decline is due in part to the growth of several alternative forms of treatment, including several variations on classical psychoanalysis developed by neo-Freudian theorists (e.g., Roseborough, 2006; Russ, 2006; Safran, 2012). As noted in the personality chapter, these theorists placed less emphasis than Freud

A Play Therapy Session

Modern versions of psychodynamic treatment include fantasy play and other techniques that make the approach more useful with children. A child's behavior and comments while playing with puppets representing family members, for example, are seen as a form of free association that the therapist hopes will reveal important unconscious material, such as fear of abandonment (Booth & Lindaman, 2000; Carlson, Watts, & Maniacci, 2006). Some therapists encourage child clients to play video games during therapy sessions. This allows them to observe the children's behaviors, draw inferences about their attitudes, and enhance the therapeutic relationship (Ceranoglu, 2010a, 2010b).

APPLYING PSYCHOLOGY

did on the past and on unconscious impulses driven by the id. They focused instead on the role played by social relationships in clients' problems and on how the power of the ego can be harnessed to solve them (Gray, 2005). Psychotherapists who adopt various neo-Freudian treatment methods tend to take a much more active role than classical analysts do, in particular by directing the client's attention to evidence of certain conflicts in social relationships.

Many of these methods have come to be known as *short-term psychodynamic psychotherapy* because they aim to provide benefits in far less time than is required in classical psychoanalysis (Levenson, 2003; Messer & Kaplan, 2004; Rawson, 2006). However, virtually all modern psychodynamic therapies still focus attention on unconscious as well as conscious aspects of mental life, on the impact of internal conflicts, and on transference analysis as key elements in treatment (Safran, 2012). In a particularly popular short-term psychodynamic approach known as *object relations therapy,* the powerful need for human contact and support takes center stage (Greenberg & Mitchell, 2006). Object relations therapists believe that most of the problems for which clients seek treatment ultimately stem from their relationships with others, especially their mothers or other early caregivers. (The term *object* usually refers to a person who has emotional significance for the client.) Accordingly, these therapists work to create a nurturing relationship in which the client's problems can be understood and corrected (Kahn & Rachman, 2000; Wallerstein, 2002). This relationship provides a "second chance" for the client to receive the support that might have been missing in infancy and to counteract some of the consequences of maladaptive early attachment patterns. For example, object relations therapists take pains to show that they will not abandon their clients, as might have happened to these people in the past. *Interpersonal therapy* is rooted partly in neo-Freudian theory as well (Sullivan, 1954). Often used in cases of depression, it focuses on helping clients explore and overcome the problematic effects of interpersonal events that occur after early childhood, such as the loss of a loved one, conflicts with a parent or a spouse, job loss, or social isolation (Mufson et al., 2004; Stuart & Robertson, 2003; Weissman, Markowitz, & Kierman, 2007).

With their focus on interpersonal relationships rather than instincts, their emphasis on clients' potential for self-directed problem solving, and their reassurance and emotional supportiveness, contemporary variants on classical psychoanalysis have helped the psychodynamic approach retain its influence among some mental health professionals (Kaner & Prelinger, 2007; Maroda, 2010; Safran, 2012; Shedler, 2010; Stiles et al., 2006).

Humanistic Psychotherapy

Why won't some therapists give advice?

Whereas some therapists revised Freud's ideas, others developed radical new therapies based on the humanistic approach to personality, which we describe in the personality chapter. *Humanistic psychologists,* sometimes called *phenomenologists,* view people as capable of consciously controlling their own actions and taking responsibility for their decisions. Most humanistic therapists believe that human behavior isn't motivated by inner conflicts but by an innate drive toward growth that is guided by the way people perceive their world. Disordered behavior, they say, reflects a blockage in natural growth brought on by distorted perceptions or lack of awareness about feelings. Accordingly, humanistic therapy operates on the following assumptions:

1. Treatment is an encounter between equals, not a "cure" given by an expert. It's a way to help clients restart their natural growth and feel and behave in more genuine ways.

2. Clients will improve on their own, given the right therapeutic conditions. These ideal conditions promote clients' awareness, acceptance, and expression of their feelings and perceptions.
3. Ideal conditions in therapy can best be established through a therapeutic relationship in which clients are made to feel accepted and supported as human beings, no matter how problematic or undesirable their behavior may be. The client's experience of this relationship brings beneficial changes. (Notice that this assumption is shared with object relations and some other forms of brief psychodynamic therapy.)
4. Clients must remain responsible for choosing how they will think and behave.

Of the many humanistically oriented treatments in use today, the most influential are client-centered therapy, developed by Carl Rogers (1951), and Gestalt therapy, developed by Frederick and Laura Perls (Cain & Seeman, 2002; Patterson, 2000; Woldt & Toman, 2005).

Client-Centered Therapy

Carl Rogers was trained in psychodynamic therapy methods during the 1930s, but he soon began to question their value. He especially disliked being a detached expert whose task is to "figure out" the client. Eventually convinced that a less formal approach would be more effective, Rogers allowed his clients to decide what to talk about, and when, without direction, judgment, or interpretation by the therapist (Raskin & Rogers, 2005). This approach, now called **client-centered therapy** or **person-centered therapy**, relies on the creation of a relationship that reflects three intertwined therapist attitudes: unconditional positive regard, empathy, and congruence.

Unconditional Positive Regard   The attitude Rogers called **unconditional positive regard** consists of treating the client as a valued person, no matter what. This attitude is communicated through the therapist's willingness to listen without interrupting and to accept what is said without evaluating it. The therapist doesn't have to approve of everything the client says or does but must accept it as reflecting that client's view of the world. Because Rogerian therapists trust clients to solve their own problems, they rarely give advice (Merry & Brodley, 2002). Doing so, said Rogers, would send clients an unspoken message that they are incompetent, making them less confident and more dependent on help.

Empathy   In addition, client-centered therapists try to see the world as the client sees it. In other words, the therapist tries to develop **empathy**, an emotional understanding of what the client might be thinking and feeling. Like other skillful interviewers, they engage in active listening—making eye contact with the client, nodding in recognition as the client speaks, and giving other signs of careful attention. They also use *reflection*, a paraphrased summary of the client's words that emphasizes the feelings and meanings that appear to go along with them. Reflection confirms that the therapist has understood what the client has said, conveys the therapist's interest in hearing it, and helps the client to be more aware of the thoughts and feelings being expressed. Here is an example:

Client: *This has been such a bad day. I've felt ready to cry any minute, and I'm not even sure what's wrong!*

Therapist: *You really do feel so bad. The tears just seem to well up inside, and I wonder if it is a little scary to not even know why you feel this way.*

Notice that, in rephrasing the client's statements, the therapist reflected back not only the obvious feelings of sadness but also the fear in the client's voice. Most clients respond to empathic reflection by elaborating on their feelings. This client went on to say, "It *is* scary, because I don't like to feel in the dark about myself. I have always prided myself on being in control."

client-centered therapy (person-centered therapy) A type of therapy in which the client decides what to talk about, and when, without direction, judgment, or interpretation from the therapist.

unconditional positive regard In client-centered therapy, the therapist's attitude that expresses caring for and acceptance of the client as a valued person.

empathy In client-centered therapy, the therapist's attempt to appreciate how the world looks from the client's point of view.

Empathic listening tends to be so effective in promoting self-understanding and awareness that it is used across a wide range of therapies (Corsini & Wedding, 2005; Miller & Rollnick, 2002). Even beyond the realm of therapy, people who are thought of as easy to talk to are usually "good listeners" who reflect back the important messages they hear from others.

Congruence   Rogerian therapists also try to convey **congruence** (sometimes called *genuineness*) by acting in ways that are consistent with their feelings during therapy. For example, if they are confused by what a client has said, they say so instead of trying to pretend that they always understand everything. When the therapist's unconditional positive regard and empathy are genuine, the client is able to see that relationships can be built on openness and honesty. Ideally, this experience will help the client become more congruent, or genuine, in other relationships.

Gestalt Therapy

Another form of humanistic treatment was developed by Frederick S. (Fritz) Perls and his wife, Laura Perls. A European psychoanalyst, Frederick Perls was greatly influenced by Gestalt psychology, which focused on the idea that people actively organize their perceptions of the world. As a result, he believed that (1) people create their own versions of reality; and (2) people's natural psychological growth continues only as long as they perceive, remain aware of, and act on their true feelings. Growth stops and symptoms of mental disorder appear, said Perls, when people are not aware of all aspects of themselves (Perls, 1969; Perls, Hefferline, & Goodman, 1951).

Like client-centered therapy, **Gestalt therapy** seeks to create conditions in which clients can become more unified, self-aware, and self-accepting and thus ready to grow again. However, Gestalt therapists use more direct and dramatic methods than do Rogerians. Often working with groups, Gestalt therapists prod clients to become aware of feelings and impulses that they have disowned and to discard feelings, ideas, and values that are not really their own. For example, the therapist or other group members might point out inconsistencies between what clients say and how they behave. Gestalt therapists pay particular attention to clients' gestures and other forms of "body language" that appear to conflict with what the clients are saying (Kepner, 2001). The therapist may also ask clients to engage in imaginary dialogues with other people, with parts of their own personalities, and even with objects (Elliott, Watson, & Goldman, 2004a, 2004b). Like a shy person who can be socially outgoing only while at a costume party, clients often find that these dialogues help them get in touch with and express their feelings (Woldt & Toman, 2005).

Over the years, client-centered and other forms of humanistic therapy have declined in popularity (Watson, 2011), but Carl Rogers's contributions to psychotherapy remain significant and influential (Cook, Biyanova, & Coyne, 2009). In particular, many other treatment approaches have incorporated his emphasis on the importance of the therapeutic relationship in bringing about change (Kirschenbaum & Jourdan, 2005). Gestalt therapy, too, remains on the therapy scene; some psychologists now combine Perls' techniques with concepts from Eastern philosophy to help clients develop greater self-awareness and self-acceptance (Barnard & Curry, 2011; Schanche et al., 2011).

Behavior Therapy and Cognitive Behavior Therapy

Can we learn to conquer fears?

Psychodynamic and humanistic approaches to therapy assume that if clients gain insight or self-awareness about underlying problems, the symptoms created by those problems will disappear. Behavior therapists emphasize a different kind of self-awareness: they help clients think about psychological problems as *learned behaviors* that can be changed without first searching for hidden meanings or unconscious causes (Miltenberger, 2011; Spiegler & Guevremont, 2009). For example, suppose you have a

© Roger Ressmeyer/Corbis

Client-Centered Therapy
Carl Rogers believed that people in successful client-centered therapy become more self-confident, more aware of their feelings, more accepting of themselves, more comfortable and genuine with other people, more reliant on self-evaluation than on the judgments of others, and more effective and relaxed.

APPLYING PSYCHOLOGY

congruence In client-centered therapy, a consistency between the way therapists feel and the way they act toward clients.

Gestalt therapy An active form of humanistic treatment that seeks to create conditions in which clients can become more unified, more self-aware, and more self-accepting.

panic attack every time you leave home and find relief only when you return. Making excuses when friends invite you out temporarily eases your anxiety but does nothing to solve the problem. Could you reduce your fear without first searching for its underlying meaning? Behavior therapists say yes. So instead of focusing on the possible meaning of your anxiety, they would begin by helping you identify the learning principles that have served to create and maintain it. They would then guide you in learning more adaptive responses in anxiety-provoking situations.

These goals are based on the behavioral approach to psychology in general and on the social-cognitive approach to personality and disorder in particular. As described in the personality chapter, social-cognitive theorists see learning as the basis of both normal personality and most behavior disorders. According to this perspective, disordered behavior and thinking are examples of the maladaptive actions and thoughts that the client has developed through the processes described in the chapter on learning. For example, behavior therapists believe that fear of being in open spaces, in crowds, or away from home (agoraphobia) stems from classically conditioned associations between being away from home and having panic attacks. The problem is partly maintained, they say, through operant conditioning: Staying home and making excuses for doing so is rewarded by reduced anxiety.

Some behavior therapists also emphasize that fears and other problems are maintained by what we think about situations and about ourselves. As discussed later, these *cognitive behavior* therapists focus their treatment efforts on changing maladaptive thoughts as well as problematic behaviors. In short, behavior therapists believe that if problems can be created through prior learning experiences, they can be eliminated through new learning experiences. So whether phobias and other problems are based on events in childhood or were learned more recently, behavior therapists address them by arranging for their clients to have beneficial new experiences.

The notion of applying learning principles in order to change troublesome overt behavior has its roots in the work of John B. Watson, Ivan Pavlov, and others who studied the learned nature of fear in the 1920s. It also stems from B. F. Skinner's research on the impacts of reward and punishment on behavior. In the late 1950s and early 1960s, researchers began to use classical conditioning, operant conditioning, and observational learning techniques in a systematic way to create treatment programs designed to eliminate fears, improve the behavior of disruptive schoolchildren and mental patients, and deal with many other problems (Fishman, Rego, & Muller, 2011). By 1970, behavioral treatment had become a popular alternative to psychodynamic and humanistic methods (Miltenberger, 2011). The most notable features of behavioral treatment include the following:

1. Development of a productive therapist-client relationship. As in other therapies, this relationship enhances clients' confidence that change is possible and makes it easier for them to speak openly and to cooperate in and benefit from treatment (Creed & Kendall, 2005; Lejuez et al., 2005).

2. A careful listing of the behaviors and thoughts to be changed (Umbreit et al., 2006). This assessment and the establishment of specific treatment goals sometimes replace the formal diagnosis used in some other therapy approaches. So, instead of treating "depression" or "obsessive-compulsive disorder," behavior therapists work to change the specific thoughts, behaviors, and emotional reactions that lead people to receive these diagnostic labels.

3. A therapist who acts as a teacher/assistant by providing learning-based treatments, giving "homework" assignments, and helping the client make specific plans for dealing with problems rather than just talking about them (Kazantizis et al., 2010).

4. Continuous monitoring and evaluation of treatment, and constant adjustments to any procedures that do not seem to be effective (Farmer & Nelson-Gary, 2005). Because ineffective procedures are soon altered or abandoned, behavioral treatment tends to be one of the briefer forms of therapy.

behavior therapy Treatments that use classical conditioning principles to change behavior.

behavior modification Treatments that use operant conditioning methods to change behavior.

Behavioral treatment can take many forms. By tradition, those that rely mainly on classical conditioning principles are usually referred to as **behavior therapy**. Those that focus on operant conditioning methods are usually called **behavior modification**, or *applied behavior analysis* (Miltenberger, 2011). Behavioral treatment that focuses on changing thoughts as well as overt behaviors is called **cognitive behavior therapy**. These methods, especially cognitive behavior therapy, have become increasingly influential in recent years (Antony & Barlow, 2010).

Techniques for Modifying Behavior

LINKAGES

Can people learn their way out of a disorder? *(a link to Learning)*

The most commonly used behavioral treatment methods include systematic desensitization therapy, modeling, positive reinforcement, extinction, aversion conditioning, and punishment.

Systematic Desensitization Therapy   Joseph Wolpe (1958) developed one of the first behavioral methods for helping clients to overcome phobias and other forms of anxiety. In his **systematic desensitization therapy**, the client remains relaxed while visualizing a series of anxiety-provoking stimuli. Wolpe believed that this process gradually weakens the learned association between anxiety and the feared object until the fear disappears.

Wolpe first helped his clients learn to relax, often using the *progressive relaxation training* procedures described in the chapter on health, stress, and coping. While relaxed, clients would be asked to imagine the easiest item on a *desensitization hierarchy*, a list of increasingly fear-provoking situations. As treatment progressed, clients imagined each item in the hierarchy, one at a time, moving to a more difficult item only after learning to imagine the previous one without distress. For example, a client who feared flying might begin by imagining airline ads in the newspaper, then imagine people on a TV show boarding an airliner, then imagine boarding a flight, being seated during takeoff, and so on. Wolpe found that once clients could remain calm as they imagined being in feared situations, they were better able to deal with those situations in real life later on.

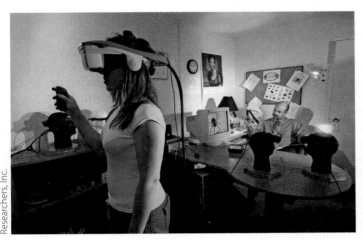

Virtual Desensitization

This client fears spiders. She is wearing a virtual reality display that, under the therapist's careful control, creates the visual experience of seeing spiders of various sizes at varying distances. After learning to tolerate these realistic images without anxiety, clients are better able to fearlessly face the situations they once avoided.

APPLYING PSYCHOLOGY

It turns out, though, that desensitization can be especially effective when it slowly and carefully presents clients with real, rather than imagined, hierarchy items (Bouton, 2000; Choy, Fyer, & Lipsitz, 2007; Marks, 2002; Tryon, 2005). This in vivo, or "real life," desensitization was once difficult to arrange or control, especially in treating fear of heights, highway driving, or flying for example. Today, however, *virtual reality graded exposure* makes it possible for clients to "experience" vivid, precisely graduated versions of feared situations without actually being exposed to the real thing. In one early study of this approach, clients who feared heights wore a virtual reality helmet that gave the impression of standing on bridges of gradually increasing heights, on outdoor balconies on higher and higher floors, and in a glass elevator as it slowly rose 49 stories (Rothbaum et al., 1995). The same virtual reality technology has been used successfully in the treatment of fears caused by spiders, dentistry, air travel, social interactions, public speaking, and posttraumatic stress disorder (Anderson, Rothbaum, & Hodges, 2003; Dittman, 2005; Glantz, Rizzo, & Graap, 2003; Maltby, Kirsch, & Mayers, 2002; North, North, & Burwick, 2008; Powers et al., 2010; Rothbaum, 2006; Safir & Wallach, 2012; Wiederhold & Wiederhold, 2005; Winerman, 2005).

cognitive behavior therapy
Learning-based treatment methods that help clients change the way they think as well as the way they behave.

systematic desensitization therapy
A behavioral method for treating anxiety in which clients visualize a graduated series of anxiety-provoking stimuli while remaining relaxed.

modeling   A behavior therapy method in which desirable behaviors are demonstrated for clients.

Modeling   In **modeling** treatments, clients learn important skills by watching other people perform desired behaviors (Bidwell & Rehfeldt, 2004). For example, modeling can teach fearful clients how to respond fearlessly and confidently. In one case study, a therapist showed a spider-phobic client how to calmly kill spiders with a fly swatter and then assigned her to practice this skill at home with rubber spiders (MacDonald & Bernstein, 1974). This combination of fearless demonstrations and firsthand practice, called *participant modeling,* is one of the most powerful treatments for fear (e.g., Bandura, Blanchard, & Ritter, 1969; Zinbarg & Griffith, 2008).

Modeling is also a major part of *assertiveness training* and *social skills training*, which help clients learn how to deal with people more comfortably and effectively. Social skills

© Thierry Berrod/Mona Lisa Production/Photo Researchers, Inc.

training has been used to help children interact more effectively with peers, to help social-phobic singles make conversation on dates, to reduce loneliness in adults, and to help rebuild mental patients' ability to have normal conversations with people outside a hospital setting (Al-Kubaisy & Jassim, 2003; Dowd, 2005; Lin et al., 2008; Masi et al., 2011). In **assertiveness training,** the therapist helps clients learn to express their feelings and stand up for their rights in social situations (Alberti & Emmons, 2008; Ballou, 1995; Patterson, 2000). Assertiveness training is often done in groups and involves both modeling and role playing of specific situations (Duckworth, 2009). For example, group assertiveness training has helped wheelchair-bound adults and students with learning disabilities to more comfortably handle the socially awkward situations in which they sometimes find themselves (Eamon, 2008).

Positive Reinforcement   Behavior therapists also use **positive reinforcement** to alter problematic behaviors and teach new skills in cases ranging from childhood tantrums and juvenile delinquency to schizophrenia and substance abuse (Lussier et al., 2006; Virués-Ortega, 2010). Employing operant conditioning principles, they set up *contingencies,* or rules, that specify the behaviors to be strengthened through reinforcement. In one pioneering study, children with autistic disorder, who typically speak very little, were given grapes, popcorn, or other items they liked in return for saying "please," "thank you," and "you're welcome" while exchanging crayons and blocks with a therapist. After the therapist modeled the desired behavior by saying the appropriate words at the appropriate times, the children began to say these words on their own. Their use of language also began to appear in other situations, and, as shown in Figure 13.1, the new skills were still evident six months later (Matson et al., 1990).

When working with severely disturbed or intellectually disabled clients in institutions or with juveniles who display emotional or behavioral disorders in residential facilities, behavior therapists sometimes establish a **token economy program**, which is a system for reinforcing desirable behaviors with points or coin-like tokens that can be exchanged later for snacks, access to television, or other rewards (Kazdin, 2008; LePage et al., 2003; Matson & Boisjoli, 2009; Seegert, 2003). The goal is to shape more adaptive behavior patterns that will continue outside the institution (Miltenberger, 2011).

assertiveness training A set of methods for helping clients learn to express their feelings and stand up for their rights in social situations.

positive reinforcement Presenting a positive reinforcer (reward) after a desired response.

token economy program A system for improving the behavior of clients in institutions by rewarding desirable behaviors with tokens that can be exchanged for various rewards.

FIGURE 13.1

Positive Reinforcement for a Child with Autistic Disorder

During each pretreatment baseline period, a child with autistic disorder rarely said "please," "thank you," or "you're welcome," but he began to make such statements once the therapist demonstrated them, then reinforced the child for saying them. Did modeling and reinforcement actually cause the change? Probably, because each type of response did not start to increase until the therapist began demonstrating it.   APPLYING PSYCHOLOGY

Source: From Matson, J., Sevin, J., Fridley, and Love, S., "Increasing Spontaneous Language in Autistic Children," *Journal of Applied Behavior Analysis,* 23 (pp. 227–233). Copyright © 1990. Reprinted with the permission of the Society for the Experimental Analysis of Behavior.

Treating Fear through Flooding
Flooding is designed to extinguish anxiety by allowing it to occur without the harmful consequences the person dreads. These clients' fear of flying is obvious here, just before takeoff, but it is likely to diminish during and after an uneventful flight. Like other behavioral treatments, flooding is based on the idea that phobias and other psychological disorders are learned and can thus be "unlearned." Some therapists prefer more gradual exposure methods similar to those of in vivo desensitization, which start with situations that are lower on the client's fear hierarchy (Back et al., 2001; Fava et al., 2001; Fritzler, Hecker, & Losee, 1997).

APPLYING PSYCHOLOGY

extinction The gradual disappearance of a conditioned response.

flooding An exposure technique for reducing anxiety that keeps a client in a feared but harmless situation.

implosive therapy An exposure technique in which clients are helped to imagine being kept in a feared but harmless situation.

aversion conditioning A method for reducing unwanted behaviors by using classical conditioning principles to create a negative response to some stimulus.

punishment The presentation of an aversive stimulus or the removal of a pleasant one following some behavior.

Extinction   Just as reinforcing desirable behaviors can make them more likely to occur, failing to reinforce undesirable behaviors can make them less likely to occur, a process known as **extinction**. Treatment methods that use extinction change behavior slowly but offer a valuable way of reducing inappropriate behavior in children and adolescents and in intellectually disabled or seriously disturbed adults (Yan-Xue et al., 2012). For example, a client who gets attention by disrupting a classroom, damaging property, or violating hospital rules might be placed in a quiet, boring "time out" room for a few minutes to eliminate reinforcement for misbehavior (Kaminski et al., 2008; Kazdin, 2008).

Extinction is also the basis of a fear-reduction treatment called **flooding**, in which clients are kept in a feared but harmless situation and are not permitted to use their normally rewarding escape strategies (O'Donohue, Fisher, & Hayes, 2003). **Implosive therapy** is a related method in which the therapist helps the client to vividly imagine being in the feared situation by describing it at length and in great detail. A client undergoing flooding or implosive therapy might be overwhelmed with fear at first, but after an extended period of exposure to the feared stimulus (a frog, say) without experiencing pain, injury, or any other dreaded result, the association between the feared stimulus and the fear response gradually weakens and the conditioned fear response is extinguished (Hauner et al., 2012; Öst et al., 2001; Powers et al., 2010). In one early study, 20 clients who feared needles were exposed for two hours to the sight and feel of needles, including by having mild finger pricks, harmless injections, and blood samplings (Öst, Hellström, & Kåver, 1992). Afterward, all but one of these clients were able to have a blood sample drawn without experiencing significant anxiety. Because they continuously expose clients to feared stimuli, flooding, implosive therapy, and other similar methods are also called *exposure techniques*.

Aversion Therapy   Some unwanted behaviors, such as excessive gambling or using addictive drugs, can become so habitual and temporarily rewarding that they must be made less attractive if a client is to have any chance of giving them up. Methods for reducing the appeal of certain stimuli are known as *aversion therapy*. The name reflects the fact that these methods rely on a classical conditioning process called **aversion conditioning** to associate shock, nausea, or other physical or psychological discomfort with undesirable stimuli, thoughts, or actions (e.g., Bordnick et al., 2004).

Because aversion conditioning is unpleasant and uncomfortable, because it may not work with all clients (Flor et al., 2002), and because its effects are often temporary, most behavior therapists use this method relatively rarely, only when it is the best treatment choice, and only long enough to allow the client to learn more appropriate alternative behaviors.

Punishment   Sometimes the only way to eliminate a dangerous or disruptive behavior is to punish it with an unpleasant but harmless stimulus, such as a shouted "No!" or a mild electric shock. Unlike aversion conditioning, in which the unpleasant stimulus occurs along with the behavior that is to be eliminated (a classical conditioning approach), **punishment** is an operant conditioning technique; it presents the unpleasant stimulus *after* the undesirable behavior occurs.

Before using electric shock or other forms of punishment, behavior therapists are required by ethical and legal guidelines to ask themselves several important questions: Have all other methods failed? Would the client's life be in danger without treatment? Has an ethics committee reviewed and approved the procedures? Has the adult client or a child client's parent or guardian agreed to the treatment (Kazdin, 2008)? When the answer to these questions is yes, punishment can be an effective, sometimes life-saving, treatment—as in the case illustrated in Figure 5.12 in the chapter on learning. Like extinction and aversion conditioning, though, punishment works best when

© Westend61/Getty Images

it is used just long enough to eliminate undesirable behavior and is combined with other behavioral methods designed to reward more appropriate behavior (Hanley et al., 2005).

Cognitive Behavior Therapy

Like psychodynamic and humanistic therapists, most behavior therapists recognize that depression, anxiety, and many other behavior disorders can stem from how clients think about themselves and the world. And like other therapists, most behavior therapists try to change clients' troublesome ways of thinking, not just their overt behavior. Unlike other therapists, however, behavior therapists rely on learning principles to help clients change the way they think. Their methods are known collectively as *cognitive behavior therapy* (Antony & Barlow, 2010; Beck, Freeman, & Davis, 2007). Suppose, for example, that a client has good social skills but suffers intense anxiety around other people. In a case like this, social skills training would obviously be unnecessary. Instead, the behavior therapist would use cognitive behavioral methods designed to help the client identify habitual thoughts (such as "I shouldn't draw attention to myself") that create awkwardness and discomfort in social situations. Once these cognitive obstacles are brought to light, the therapist describes new and more adaptive ways of thinking and encourages the client to learn and practice them. As these cognitive skills develop (e.g., "I have as much right to give my opinion as anyone else"), it becomes easier and more rewarding for clients to let these new thoughts guide their behavior (Beck, 2005).

Rational-Emotive Behavior Therapy   One prominent form of cognitive behavior therapy is **rational-emotive behavior therapy (REBT)**, which was developed by Albert Ellis (1962, 1993, 1995, 2004a, 2004b, 2011). REBT aims first at identifying unrealistic and self-defeating thoughts, such as "I must be loved or approved of by everyone" or "I must always be competent to be worthwhile." After the client learns to recognize such thoughts and to see how they can cause problems, the therapist uses suggestions, encouragement, and logic to help the client replace maladaptive thoughts with more realistic and beneficial ones. The client is then given "homework" assignments to try these new ways of thinking in everyday situations. Here is part of an REBT session with a woman who suffered from panic attacks. She has just said that it would be "terrible" if she had an attack in a restaurant and that people "should be able to handle themselves!"

Therapist: *The reality is that ... "shoulds" and "musts" are the rules that other people hand down to us, and we grow up accepting them as if they are the absolute truth, which they most assuredly aren't.*

Client: *You mean it is perfectly okay to, you know, pass out in a restaurant?*

Therapist: *Sure!*

Client: *But ... I know I wouldn't like it to happen.*

Therapist: *I can certainly understand that. It would be unpleasant, awkward, inconvenient. But it is illogical to think that it would be terrible, or ... that it somehow bears on your worth as a person.*

Client: *What do you mean?*

Therapist: *Well, suppose one of your friends calls you up and invites you back to that restaurant. If you start telling yourself, "I might panic and pass out and people might make fun of me and that would be terrible," ... you might find you are dreading going to the restaurant, and you probably won't enjoy the meal very much.*

Client: *Well, that is what usually happens.*

Therapist: *But it doesn't have to be that way.... The way you feel, your reaction ... depends on what you choose to believe or think, or say to yourself. (Masters et al., 1987)*

rational-emotive behavior therapy (REBT) A treatment designed to identify and change illogical, self-defeating thoughts that lead to anxiety and other symptoms of disorder.

Albert Ellis
Rational-emotive behavior therapy (REBT) focuses on altering the self-defeating thoughts that Ellis believed underlie people's behavior disorders. Ellis argued, for example, that students do not get upset because they fail a test but because they have learned to believe that failure is a disaster that indicates they are worthless. Many of Ellis's ideas have been incorporated into various forms of cognitive behavior therapy, and they helped Ellis himself to deal rationally with the health problems he encountered prior to his death in 2007 (Ellis, 1997).

Cognitive behavior therapists use many techniques related to REBT to help clients learn to think in more adaptive ways (Hertel & Mathews, 2011; Lang et al., 2012; Lau et al., 2011; Macleod & Mathews, 2012; Wiers et al., 2011). Techniques aimed at replacing upsetting thoughts with alternative thinking patterns are described by behaviorists as *cognitive restructuring* (Dobson & Hamilton, 2009). They help clients plan calming thoughts to use during exams, tense conversations, and other anxiety-provoking situations. These thoughts might include "OK, stay calm, you can handle this. Just focus on the task, and don't worry about being perfect." Sometimes, these techniques are expanded to include *stress inoculation training,* in which clients imagine being in a stressful situation and then practice newly learned cognitive skills to remain calm (Meichenbaum, 2009; Sheehy & Horan, 2004).

Beck's Cognitive Therapy   Behavior therapists seek a different kind of cognitive restructuring when they use Aaron Beck's **cognitive therapy** (Beck, 1976, 1995, 2005, 2011; Clark & Beck, 2012). Beck's treatment approach is based on the idea that certain psychological problems—especially those related to depression and anxiety but also those related to personality disorders and schizophrenia (Beck et al., 2007; Beck et al., 2008)—can be traced partly to errors in logic and false beliefs. These include *catastrophizing* (e.g., "If I fail my driver's test the first time, I'll never pass it, and that'll be the end of my social life"), *all-or-none thinking* (e.g., "Everyone ignores me"), and *personalization* (e.g., "I know those people are laughing at me"). Beck refers to these errors and beliefs as *cognitive distortions* (Beck, Freeman, & Davis, 2007). They occur so quickly and automatically that the client never stops to consider that they might not be true.

Cognitive therapy takes an active, organized, problem-solving approach in which therapists first help clients learn to identify the errors in logic, false beliefs, and other cognitive distortions that precede anxiety, depression, conduct problems, eating disorders, and other psychological problems (Beck & Rector, 2005; Fairburn, 2008; Hendricks & Thompson, 2005; Hollon & DiGiuseppe, 2011). Then, much as in the five-step critical thinking system illustrated throughout this book, these thoughts and beliefs are considered as hypotheses to be tested, not as "facts" to be uncritically accepted (Hollon & DiGiuseppe, 2011). In other words, the therapist and client become a team of "investigators" as they plan ways to test beliefs such as "I'm no good around the house." For example, they might agree on tasks that the client will attempt as "homework"—such as cleaning the basement, hanging a picture, or cutting the grass. Success at accomplishing even one of these tasks provides concrete evidence to challenge a false belief about incompetence that has supported feelings of depression or anxiety, thus helping to reduce them (Beck et al., 1992; Mullin, 2000).

As described in the chapter on psychological disorders, however, depression, anxiety, and some other disorders may not entirely be due to specific thoughts or beliefs about specific situations. Sometimes they stem from a more general cognitive style that leads people to expect that the worst will always happen to them and to assume that negative events occur because they are completely and permanently incompetent and worthless (Beck & Alford, 2009). So cognitive behavior therapists also work with clients to develop more generally optimistic ways of thinking and to reduce their tendency to blame themselves for negative outcomes (Persons, Davidson, & Tompkins, 2001). In some cases, cognitive restructuring is combined with skill training, techniques for managing anxiety, and practice in using logical thinking, all of which are designed to help clients experience success and develop confidence in situations in which they had previously expected to fail (Bryant et al., 2008).

Group, Family, and Couples Therapy

How does group psychotherapy differ from individual therapy?

cognitive therapy An organized problem-solving approach in which the therapist actively collaborates with clients to help them notice how certain negative thoughts precede anxiety and depression.

The one-on-one methods of psychodynamic, humanistic, and behavioral treatment we have described are often adapted for use with groups of clients or with family units (Burlingame & Baldwin, 2011; Kaslow, 2011).

Group Psychotherapy

Group psychotherapy refers to the treatment of several clients under the guidance of a therapist who encourages helpful interactions among group members. Many groups are organized around one type of problem (such as alcoholism) or one type of client (such as adolescents). In most cases, six to twelve clients meet with their therapist at least once a week for about two hours. All group members agree to hold confidential everything that occurs within these sessions.

Group psychotherapy offers features that are not found in individual treatment (Marmarosh, Holtz, & Schottenbauer, 2005; Yalom, 2005). First, it allows the therapist to observe clients interacting with one another. Second, groups encourage their members to talk about themselves and explore their feelings. As they listen to each other, clients often feel less alone because they realize that other people are struggling with difficulties at least as severe as their own. This realization tends to raise each client's expectations for improvement, a factor that is important in all forms of treatment. Third, group members can boost one another's self-confidence and self-acceptance as they come to trust and value one another. Fourth, clients learn from one another. They share ideas for solving problems and give one another honest feedback about their attitudes and behavior. Fifth, perhaps through mutual modeling, the group experience makes clients more sensitive to other people's needs, motives, and messages. Finally, group psychotherapy allows clients to try out new skills in a supportive environment. So although the procedures and techniques employed in group psychotherapy may reflect one or more of the theoretical orientations we have described in relation to individual therapy (Bieling, McCabe, & Antony, 2006), the impact of the treatment is thought to be enhanced by the nature and strength of the group itself.

Family and Couples Therapy

As its name implies, **family therapy** involves treatment of two or more individuals from the same family. One of these, often a troubled adolescent or child, is the initially identified client. Whether family therapy is based on psychodynamic, humanistic, or cognitive behavioral approaches, the family is usually considered as a functioning unit known as a *family system*. As with group psychotherapy, the family therapy format gives the therapist a chance to see how the initially identified client interacts with others, thus providing a basis for discussion of topics that are important to each family member. And as with group psychotherapists, family therapists usually have special training that helps them understand how the problems of individual family members affect and are affected by problems in the complex interactions taking place within the family system as a whole (Kaslow, 2011; Nichols, 2007; Williams, 2005). Ultimately, the client in family therapy is the family itself, and treatment involves as many members as possible (Novick & Novick, 2005). In fact, the goal of family therapy is not just to ease the identified client's problems but also to create greater harmony and balance within the family by helping each member understand family interaction patterns and the problems they create (Blow & Timm, 2002).

group psychotherapy Psychotherapy involving six to twelve unrelated individuals.

family therapy A type of treatment involving two or more clients from the same family.

couples therapy A form of therapy that focuses on improving communication between partners.

FIGURE 13.2
Some "Rules for Talking" in Couples Therapy
Many forms of couples therapy help partners improve communication by establishing rules such as the ones listed here. Think about your own experience in relationships or your observations of heterosexual or homosexual couples as they interact, and then write down some rules you would add to this list. Why do you think it would be important for couples to follow the rules on your list?

LEARN by DOING

- Always begin wih something positive when stating a problem.
- Maintain a focus on the present or the future; don't review all previous examples of the problem or ask "why" questions such as "Why do you always...?"
- Talk about observable events; don't make inferences about them (e.g., say "I get angry when you interrupt me" rather than "Stop trying to make me feel stupid").

© Nancy Sheehan/PhotoEdit

In **couples therapy**, improving communication between partners is one of the most important targets of treatment (Christensen et al., 2004; Gurman, 2008; Long & Andrews, 2011). Discussions in couples therapy sessions typically focus on identifying the miscommunication or lack of communication that interferes with the couples' happiness and intimacy. Often the sessions revolve around learning to abide by certain "rules for talking" (see Figure 13.2). For some therapists, helping couples become closer also means helping them express emotions more honestly and be more accepting of one another (Shadish & Baldwin, 2005; Wood et al., 2005). One version of couples therapy focuses on strengthening the bond between partners by teaching them how to deal with their unsolvable problems and recover from their fights by making at least five times as many positive statements as negative ones (Gottman, Driver, & Tabares, 2002). Some therapists even offer preventive treatment to couples who are at risk for relationship problems (Gottman, Gottman, & Declaire, 2006; Laurenceau et al., 2004). ("In Review: Approaches to Psychological Treatment" summarizes key features of the main approaches to treatment that we have discussed so far.)

Approaches to Psychological Treatment   IN REVIEW

Dimension	Classical Psychoanalytic	Contemporary Psychodynamic	Humanistic	Behavioral/Cognitive Behavioral
Nature of the human being	Driven by sexual and aggressive urges	Driven by the need for human relationships	Has free will, choice, and capacity for self-actualization	Is a product of social learning and conditioning; behaves on the basis of experience
Therapist's role	Neutral; helps client explore meaning of free associations and other material from the unconscious	Active; develops relationship with client as a model for other relationships	May be active or nondirective; facilitates client's growth	Active, action oriented; teacher/ trainer helps client replace undesirable thoughts and behaviors
Focus	Unresolved unconscious conflicts from the distant past	Understanding the past but focusing on current relationships	Here and now; focus on immediate experience	Current behavior and thoughts; may not need to know original causes to create change
Goals	Psychosexual maturity through insight; strengthening of ego functions	Correcting effects of early attachment failures; developing satisfying intimate relationships	Expanded awareness; fulfillment of potential; self-acceptance	Changes in thinking and behavior in particular classes of situations; better self-management
Typical methods	Free association; dream analysis, analysis of transference	Analysis of interpersonal relationships, including the client-therapist relationship	Reflection-oriented interviews convey unconditional positive regard, empathy, and congruence; exercises to promote self-awareness	Systematic desensitization, flooding, implosive therapy, modeling, assertiveness and social skills training, positive reinforcement, extinction, aversion conditioning, punishment, cognitive restructuring

IN REVIEW QUESTIONS

1. Object relations therapy and interpersonal therapy are both contemporary examples of the ___ approach to psychological treatment.

2. Imagining increasingly fear-provoking stimuli while relaxed is a ___ treatment method called ___.

3. Reflection is an interviewing technique associated mainly with the ___ approach to treatment.

Evaluating Psychotherapy

How effective is psychotherapy?

Some years ago, a consumer magazine's survey suggested that most clients believe that psychotherapy is effective (Consumer Reports, 1995; Seligman, 1996), but confirming that effectiveness through scientific research has proven to be challenging and controversial (David & Montgomery, 2011; Fontao & Hoffmann, 2011; Kazdin, 2011; Lambert, 2011; Levy & Ablon, 2009; McHugh & Barlow, 2010; Norcross, 2011; Wampold, Hollon, & Hill, 2011).

LINKAGES

Can therapy change personality?
(a link to Personality)

The value of psychotherapy was first widely questioned in 1952, when British psychologist Hans Eysenck reviewed studies in which thousands of clients had received

FIGURE 13.3

An Analysis of Psychotherapy's Effects

These curves show the results of a large-scale analysis of the effects of psychotherapy. Notice that on average, people who received therapy were better off than 80 percent of troubled people who did not. The overall effectiveness of psychotherapy has also been confirmed in an analysis of 90 treatment outcome studies (Shadish et al., 2000) and in other research reviews (Nathan & Gorman, 2007; Weisz & Kazdin, 2010). *Source:* Data from Smith, Glass, & Miller (1980).

either traditional psychodynamic therapy, various other therapies, or no treatment. To the surprise and dismay of many therapists, Eysenck (1952) found that the percentage of clients who improved following any kind of psychotherapy was actually lower than among people who received no treatment.

Critics argued that Eysenck was wrong (e.g., Bergin, 1971; de Charms, Levy, & Wertheimer, 1954; Luborsky, 1972). They claimed that he had ignored studies supporting the value of psychotherapy and had misinterpreted the data. In fact, when some of these critics reviewed treatment successes and failures themselves, they concluded that psychotherapy tends to be *more* helpful than no treatment (e.g., Bergin, 1971).

Debate over Eysenck's findings and the contradictory reports that followed them highlight several reasons why it is so hard to answer the apparently simple question of whether psychotherapy works. For one thing, there is the problem of how to measure improvement in psychotherapy. Should we focus on psychological test results, behavioral observations, interviews, or a combination of all three? Different measurements may tell somewhat different stories about improvement, making it difficult for researchers to compare or combine the results of different studies and draw conclusions about the overall effectiveness of treatment (Achenbach, 2011; Cuijpers et al., 2010; De Los Reyes, 2011; Wampold et al., 2011).

The question of effectiveness is further complicated by the broad range of clients, therapists, and treatments involved in psychotherapy. Clients differ in the problems they present, in their motivation to solve those problems, and in the amount of stress and social support present in their environments (Petrie & Weinman, 2012; Price & Anderson, 2012). Therapists differ, too, not only in skill, experience, and personality but also in which of the hundreds of available treatment procedures they decide to use and for how long (Barkham et al., 2006; Norcross, Beutler, & Levant, 2005; Wampold, 2005). In addition, differences in the nature and quality of the client-therapist relationship from one case to another can significantly alter the course of treatment, the clients' belief in the procedures, and their willingness to cooperate (Bedics et al., 2012; Kazdin & Durbin, 2012; Lambert & Barley, 2001; Levin, Henderson, & Ehrenreich-May, 2012; Norcross, 2002; Walling et al., 2012; Westra et al., 2012; Zuroff & Blatt, 2006). Because clients' responses to psychotherapy can be influenced by all of these factors, results from any particular treatment evaluation study might not tell us much about how well different therapists using different methods would do with other kinds of clients and problems (Kazdin, 1994; Roth & Fonagy, 2005; Staines & Cleland, 2012).

In short, the question of whether psychotherapy "works" is difficult (if not impossible) to answer scientifically in a way that applies to all therapies for all disorders. However, several research reviews (Antony & Barlow, 2010; Lambert, 2011; Nathan & Gorman, 2007; Norcross, 2011; Weisz & Kazdin, 2010) have demonstrated that, in general, psychotherapy does work (see Figure 13.3).

THINKING CRITICALLY

Are All Forms of Therapy Equally Effective?

As you might imagine, most therapists agree that psychotherapy is effective and most believe that the theoretical approach and treatment methods *they* use work better than those of other therapists (Mandelid, 2003).

What am I being asked to believe or accept?

They can't all be right, of course, and some researchers claim that all of them are wrong. These researchers argue that the success of psychotherapy doesn't have much to do with theories about the causes of behavior disorder, or even with the specific treatment methods used in treatment. All approaches, they say, are equally effective. This has been called the "Dodo Bird Verdict," named after the *Alice in Wonderland* creature who when called on to judge who had won a race answered, "Everybody has won and all must have prizes" (Duncan, 2002; Luborsky, Singer, & Luborsky, 1975).

Is evidence available to support the claim?

Some evidence does suggest that there are no significant differences in the overall effectiveness of psychodynamic, humanistic, and behavioral therapies. Statistical analyses that combine the results of a large number of therapy studies show that the three approaches are associated with about the same degree of success (Luborsky et al., 2002; Luborsky, Rosenthal, & Diguer, 2003; Shadish et al., 2000; Weisz, McCarty, & Valeri, 2006).

Can that evidence be interpreted another way?

Those who question the Dodo Bird Verdict say that evidence in its favor is based on statistical methods that cannot detect genuine differences among treatments (Barlow, 2010). Statistical analyses that average the results of many different studies might not reveal important differences in the impact of particular treatments for particular problems (Ehlers et al., 2010). Suppose, for example, that Therapy A works better than Therapy B in treating anxiety but that Therapy B works better than Therapy A in cases of depression. If you combined the results of treatment studies with both kinds of clients, the average effects of each therapy would be about the same, making it appear that the two treatments are about equally effective. Differences among the effects of specific treatment procedures might also be overshadowed by the beneficial *common factors* shared by almost all forms of therapy—such as the support of the therapist, the hope and expectancy for improvement that therapy creates, and the trust that develops between client and therapist (Greenberg, Constantino, & Bruce, 2006; Kazantzis, Lampropoulos, & Deane, 2005; Vocisano et al., 2004). Therapists whose personal characteristics can motivate clients to change might promote that change no matter what specific therapeutic methods they use (Norcross, 2002).

What evidence would help to evaluate the alternatives?

Debate is likely to continue over whether, on average, all forms of psychotherapy are about equally effective, but to many researchers, this is the wrong question. They argue that it's pointless to compare the effects of psychodynamic, humanistic, and behavioral methods in general. It is more important, they say, to address what Gordon Paul called the "ultimate question" about psychotherapy: "What treatment, by whom, is most effective for this individual with that specific problem, under what set of circumstances?" (Paul, 1969).

What conclusions are most reasonable?

Statistical analyses show that various treatment approaches appear about equally effective overall. But this does not mean that every psychotherapy experience will be equally helpful. Potential clients must realize that the success of their treatment can still be affected by how severe their problems are, by the quality of the therapeutic relationship they form with a therapist, by their motivation to change, and by the appropriateness of the therapy methods chosen for their problems (Goldfried & Davila, 2005; Haque & Waytz, 2012; Hatfield et al., 2010). ●●●●

LINKAGES

Does psychotherapy work? *(a link to Introduction to the Science of Psychology)*

evidence-based practice The selection of treatment methods based mainly on empirical evidence of their effectiveness.

Like those seeking treatment, many clinical psychologists are eager for more specific scientific evidence about the effectiveness of particular therapies for particular kinds of clients and disorders. These empirically oriented clinicians are concerned that, all too often, therapists' choices of therapy methods depend more heavily on personal preferences or current trends than on scientific evidence of effectiveness (Kazdin, 2011; Lilienfeld, 2011; McHugh, Murray, & Barlow, 2009). They believe that advocates of any treatment—whether it is object relations therapy or systematic desensitization—must demonstrate that its benefits are the result of the treatment itself and not just of the passage of time, the effects of repeated assessment, the client's motivation and personal characteristics, or other confounding factors (Chambless & Hollon, 1998). In other words, these clinicians advocate **evidence-based practice**, in which practitioners make decisions about which methods to use based mainly on the results of empirical evidence about the effectiveness of those methods. A movement toward evidence-based practice has also appeared in the medical and dental professions (Borry, Schotsmans, & Dierickx, 2006; Niederman & Richards, 2005).

Empirically oriented clinicians also want to see evidence that the benefits of treatment are clinically significant. To be *clinically significant,* therapeutic changes must be great enough to make the feelings and actions of treated clients similar to those of people who have not experienced these clients' disorders (Crits-Christoph et al., 2008; Kazdin, 2011; Kendall & Choudhury, 2003). The need to demonstrate clinical significance has become more important than ever as increasingly cost-conscious clients and their health insurance companies decide whether and how much to pay for various psychotherapy services (Levant, 2005; Makeover, 2004; Nelson & Steele, 2006). The most scientific way to evaluate treatment effects is through studies in which clients are randomly assigned to various treatments or control conditions and their progress is measured objectively.

FOCUS ON RESEARCH

Which Therapies Work Best for Which Problems?

To help clinicians select treatment methods on the basis of this kind of empirical evidence, the Society of Clinical Psychology (a division of the American Psychological Association) created a task force in 1993, called the Task Force on Promotion and Dissemination of Psychological Procedures.

What was the researchers' question?

The question addressed by this task force was "What therapies have proven themselves most effective in treating various kinds of psychological disorders?"

How did the researchers answer the question?

Working with other empirically oriented clinical psychologists, this task force examined thousands of studies that evaluated the psychotherapy methods used for treating mental disorders, marital distress, and health-related behavior problems in children, adolescents, and adults (Baucom et al., 1998; Chambless & Ollendick, 2001; Compas et al., 1998; DeRubeis & Crits-Christoph, 1998; Foley, 2004; Kazdin & Weisz, 1998; Kendall & Chambless, 1998).

What did the researchers find?

The task force found that a number of treatments—known as **empirically supported therapies**, or **ESTs**—had been validated by controlled experimental research (Chambless & Ollendick, 2001; DeRubeis & Crits-Christoph, 1998; Kendall & Chambless, 1998; Norcross, 2001, 2002). These therapies were called "efficacious and specific" and "well-established" if they had been found superior to no treatment or to some alternative treatment in at least two randomized clinical trials, or RCTs. RCTs are experiments in which clients are randomly assigned to different treatment or control conditions. Also included in this "well established" category were treatments supported by scientific measures in a large number of carefully conducted case studies. Treatments were called "probably efficacious" if they had been supported by at least one RCT or by a smaller number of rigorously evaluated case studies. Finally, treatments were labeled "possibly efficacious" if they had been supported only by a mixture of data from single-case studies or other nonexperimental designs (Chambless & Ollendick, 2001).

About ten years later, another APA task force was asked to update experimental research on treatment effectiveness and to integrate that knowledge with what clinical expertise can tell us about treating clients from various sociocultural backgrounds in real-world treatment settings. The goal was to reach agreement among researchers *and* clinicians about which specific treatments, and which specific clinical practices, are most likely to lead to improvements in clients' mental health. The result of this second group's work was the establishment of guidelines for *evidence-based practice (EBP) in psychology* (APA Presidential Task Force on Evidence-Based Practice, 2006). Table 13.1 contains some examples of what the EBP task force found.

empirically supported therapies (ESTs) Treatments for psychological disorders whose effectiveness has been validated by controlled experimental research.

TABLE 13.1 Examples of Evidence-Based Practice Therapies That Work for Selected Disorders

Treatments listed here as having "strong" research support are those that meet the criteria originally defined as "well established" in the original APA Task Force Report (Chambless et al., 1998). Those listed as having "modest" research support are comparable to those defined earlier as "probably efficacious." Therapies appear in the "controversial research support" column either because outcome research on them has produced mixed results or because the reason that they work is still uncertain. For more information on evidence-based practice and research-supported psychological treatments, visit http://www.div12.org/PsychologicalTreatments/index.html. Information on evidence-based therapies for children and adolescents can be found at: http://effectivechildtherapy.com/sccap/. There are also reviews of empirical research aimed at identifying potentially harmful therapies (Barlow, 2010; Lilienfeld, 2007; Norcross, Koocher, Fala, & Wexler, 2010).

Problem	Strong Research Support	Modest Research Support	Controversial Research Support
Major depression	Behavior therapy/behavior activation Cognitive behavior therapy Cognitive therapy Interpersonal therapy Problem-solving therapy	Acceptance and commitment therapy Short-term psychodynamic therapy Behavioral couples therapy	
Specific phobia	Exposure therapies Cognitive behavior therapy		Psychoanalytic treatment
Panic disorder		Applied relaxation	
Generalized anxiety disorder	Cognitive and behavior therapies		
Obsessive-compulsive disorder	Exposure and response prevention Cognitive therapy		
Posttraumatic stress disorder	Prolonged exposure Cognitive processing therapy	Stress inoculation	Eye movement desensitization and reprocessing (EMDR)
Schizophrenia	Social skills training Cognitive behavior therapy Assertive community treatment Family psychoeducation Social learning/token economy programs	Cognitive adaptation training Illness management and recovery	
Alcohol abuse and dependence	Motivational interviewing Motivational enhancement therapy (MET) MET plus cognitive behavior therapy Behavioral couples therapy	Moderate drinking therapy Prize-based contingency management	
Substance abuse and dependence in general; Mixed substance abuse/dependence	Motivational interviewing Motivational enhancement therapy (MET) MET plus cognitive behavior therapy Prize-based contingency management	Friends care program	
Borderline personality disorder	Dialectical behavior therapy	Mentalization-based treatment Schema-focused therapy	Transference-focused therapy

Source: http://www.div12.org/PsychologicalTreatments/index.html.

What do the results mean?

The authors of the original report on empirically supported therapies, the authors of the more recent EBP guidelines, and psychologists who support their efforts argue that by relying on analysis of experimental research and other high-quality clinical studies, they have scientifically evaluated various treatments. They have generated a list of methods from which consumers—and clinicians who want to conduct an evidence-based practice—can choose with confidence when dealing with specific disorders (Antony & Barlow, 2010; Kazdin, 2011; Nathan & Gorman, 2007). They also suggest that many of the *treatment manuals* that guided therapists in psychotherapy outcome experiments can help other clinicians deliver evidence-based therapies exactly as they were intended (Addis & Krasnow, 2000; Wallace & vanRanson, 2011).

Not everyone agrees with the conclusions or recommendations of the two APA task forces (see Norcross, 2011). Critics note, first, that treatments missing from the latest list of effective therapies haven't necessarily been discredited. Some of those treatments might not yet have been studied thoroughly enough or validated in relation to the efficacy criteria selected by the task force (Lantz, 2004; Westen & Morrison, 2001). These critics also have doubts about the value of some of those criteria. They point to research showing that had the first task force used different outcome criteria, it might have reached different (and perhaps less optimistic) conclusions about the value of some empirically supported treatments (Bradley et al., 2005; Thompson-Brenner, Glass, & Westen, 2003). Critics argue further that the first list of effective therapies was based on research that may not be relevant to clinicians working in the real world of clinical practice. They note that experimental studies of psychotherapy have focused mainly on relatively brief treatments for highly specific disorders, even though most clients' problems tend to be far more complex (Westen & Bradley, 2005). These studies also focused on the therapeutic procedures used rather than on the characteristics and interactions of therapists and clients (Cornelius-White, 2002; Westen et al., 2004). This emphasis on procedure is a problem, critics say, because the outcome of therapy in these experiments might have been strongly affected by client-therapist factors, such as whether the random pairing of clients and therapists resulted in a match or a mismatch on certain personal characteristics. In real clinical situations, clients and therapists are not usually paired up at random (Goldfried & Davila, 2005; Hill, 2005). Finally, because therapists participating in experimental research were required to follow standard treatment manuals, they were not free to adapt treatment methods to the needs of particular clients, as they normally would do (Addis & Krasnow, 2000; Garfield, 1998). Perhaps, say critics, when there is less experimental control over the treatment situation, all therapies really are about equally effective, as suggested by the statistical analyses of outcome research we mentioned earlier (Shadish et al., 2000; Smith, Glass, & Miller, 1980). In short, these critics reject the idea of creating lists of effective therapies as useful guides.

The APA's evidence-based task force was created partly in response to these concerns, and its practice guidelines are based on results not just from randomized clinical trials but also from less rigorous studies of therapy and the therapeutic relationship and from clinicians' experiences in real-world treatment settings (Norcross, 2011).

What do we still need to know?

The effort to develop evidence-based practice in clinical psychology represents an important step in responding to Paul's (1969) "ultimate question" about psychotherapy: "What treatment, by whom, is most effective for this individual with that specific problem, under what set of circumstances?" We still have a long way to go to answer all aspects of this question, but empirically oriented clinical psychologists are determined to do so (Norcross & Wampold, 2011; Wolfe, 2012; Youn, Kraus, & Castonguay, 2012).

There remains a significant divide, though, between those who would base treatment decisions mainly on the outcome of controlled experimental research and those who feel that the guidance provided by research results must be interpreted and adjusted in light of clinical judgment and experience. The work of the evidence-based task force shows that clinical researchers and clinical practitioners are looking for common ground. It remains to be seen if they will be able to bridge the gap between them in a way that makes the best use of both domains of knowledge in the service of clients' welfare (e.g., Barlow, 2006; Becker et al., 2009; Castonguay & Beutler, 2005; Fago, 2009; Hershenberg, Drabick, & Vivian, 2012). ● ● ● ●

Though the combinations of treatment methods and therapist and client characteristics that are best suited to solving particular psychological problems have not yet been mapped out, a few notable trends have emerged. For example, when differences in the effectiveness of different treatments occur in comparative studies of adult psychotherapy, they tend to reveal a small to moderate advantage for behavioral and cognitive behavioral methods—especially in the treatment of phobias and certain other anxiety disorders (Antony & Barlow, 2010; Butler et al., 2006; Chaker, Hofmann, & Hoyer, 2010; Craske & Barlow, 2008; Eddy et al., 2004; Hollon, Stewart, & Strunk, 2006; Houben, Wiers, & Jansen, 2011; Mochizuki-Kawai et al., 2010; Schnurr et al., 2007; Tolin, 2010), and in the prevention and treatment of eating disorders (Hendricks & Thompson, 2005; Stice & Shaw, 2004; Wilson et al., 2010). The same overall trend holds true in the treatment of child and adolescent clients (Carr, 2009; Kazak et al., 2010; Kendall et al., 2008; Weisz, Doss, & Hawley, 2005). Cognitive methods appear to be less effective, however, at dealing with the emergence of severe disorders such as schizophrenia (Morrison et al., 2012). As for psychodynamic methods, there is still a great deal of controversy. As shown in Table 13.1, interpersonal therapy and short-term psychodynamic therapy have received strong and modest support, respectively, for the treatment of depression, but some studies have found this approach to be no more effective overall than placebo or other comparison conditions (Shedler, 2010; Smit et al., 2012).

The client-therapist relationship seems to play a significant role in the success of many forms of treatment (Karver et al., 2006; Norcross, 2011; Uwe, 2005; Zuroff & Blatt, 2006). Certain people seem to be particularly effective in forming productive human relationships. Even without formal training, these people can sometimes be as helpful as professional therapists because of personal qualities that are inspiring, healing, and soothing to others (Hill & Lent, 2006; Ronnestad & Ladany, 2006). These qualities may help account for the success of many kinds of therapy.

In summary, the Dodo Bird Verdict is probably incorrect, and it is certainly incomplete. Although different treatments can be equally effective in addressing some disorders, empirical research shows that for other disorders certain therapies are more effective than others. That research provides valuable guidelines for matching treatments to disorders, but it doesn't guarantee success. The outcome of any given case will also be affected by characteristics of the client, characteristics of the therapist, and the nature of the therapeutic relationship that develops between them (e.g., Hill, 2005; Sherer & Schreibman, 2005). The challenge now is to combine research on empirically supported therapy methods with research on the common factors they share and create a picture of the effectiveness of psychotherapy methods that is based on both sets of data (Messer, 2004; Westen & Bradley, 2005). Such a comprehensive view would be a useful guide for clinicians practicing today and an ideal training model for the clinicians of tomorrow.

Given what is known so far, potential clients should choose a treatment approach and a therapist based on (1) suggestions from empirical research about the best treatment for their particular problem; (2) the treatment approach, methods, and goals the person finds most comfortable and appealing; (3) information about the potential therapist's "track record" of clinically significant success with a particular method for treating problems similar to those the person faces; and (4) the likelihood of forming a productive relationship with the therapist. This last consideration assumes special importance when the client and the therapist do not share similar social or cultural backgrounds.

Sociocultural Factors in Therapy

Sociocultural differences between clients and therapists—in religious faith, gender, age, ethnicity, sexual orientation, socioeconomic background, and the like—can sometimes create miscommunication or mistrust (Seeley, 2006). If it does, their working relationship and the clients' motivation to change may both be impaired (Jones, Botsko, & Gorman, 2003; Pachankis & Goldfried, 2004; Vasquez, 2007; Wintersteen, Mensinger, & Diamond, 2005). Suppose, for example, that a therapist suggests that a client's insomnia is a reaction to stress but the client is sure that it comes as punishment for having offended a long-dead ancestor. That client may not easily accept a treatment based on the principles of stress management (Wohl, 1995). Similarly, a therapist who believes that people should confront and overcome life's problems might run into trouble when treating clients whose cultural or religious training encourages the calm acceptance of these problems (Sue et al., 2009). In such cases, the result may be much like two people singing a duet

© Rhoda Sidney/PhotoEdit

Preparing for Therapy

Special pretreatment orientation programs may be offered to clients who, because of sociocultural factors, are unfamiliar with the rules and procedures of psychotherapy. These programs provide a preview of what psychotherapy is, how psychotherapy can help, and what the client is expected to do to make it more effective (Reis & Brown, 2006; Swartz, Zuckoff et al., 2007).

using the same music but different lyrics (Martinez et al., 2005; Martinez-Taboas, 2005).

In the United States, cultural clashes may be partly to blame for the underuse of or withdrawal from mental health services by recent immigrants and by African Americans, Asian Americans, Hispanic Americans, American Indians, and members of other minority populations (Chakraborty et al., 2011; Dingfelder, 2005; Duran et al., 2005; Gone, 2004; Neighbors et al., 2007; Pieterse et al., 2012; Sanders et al., 2004; Thurston & Phares, 2008; Wang et al., 2005). Accordingly, efforts are under way to ensure that sociocultural differences do not impede the delivery of treatment to anyone who wants or needs it (Cabral & Smith, 2011; Richards & Bergin, 2000). Virtually every mental health training program in North America is recruiting more students from traditionally underserved minority groups. This will surely create a more diverse workforce of psychologists and give clients more options in selecting a therapist (e.g., Meredith & Baker, 2007; Rogers & Molina, 2006; Vasquez & Jones, 2006). In the meantime, many minority clients are likely to encounter a therapist from a differing background, so researchers have also examined the value of matching therapeutic techniques with clients' culturally based expectations and preferences (Jones, Botsko, & Gorman, 2003; Kaczorowski et al., 2011; Li & Kim, 2004; Muñoz & Mendelson, 2005).

Today, psychotherapists are more sensitive than ever to the cultural values of particular groups and the difficulties that can impair intercultural communication (Fields, 2010; Hays & Iwamasa, 2006; Hwang, 2006; Martinez et al., 2005; Sue et al., 2009). Some U.S. states now require clinical psychologists to complete courses on the role of cultural factors in therapy before they can qualify for licenses (Rehm & DeMers, 2006). Similar cultural diversity training is also required for all graduate students in clinical and counseling psychology training programs accredited by the American Psychological Association (Commission on Accreditation, 2008; Kersting, 2004; Smith, Constantine et al., 2006). Cultural diversity training focuses not just on clients' ethnicity, but also on other sociocultural factors such as sexual orientation, gender, spirituality, age, socioeconomic status, and physical challenges. This training helps clinicians and graduate students appreciate, for example, that it is considered impolite in some cultures to make eye contact with a stranger. Armed with this information, a therapist is more likely to realize that clients from those cultures are not necessarily depressed, lacking in self-esteem, or overly submissive just because they look at the floor during an interview.

There is no guarantee that cultural diversity training for therapists will improve treatment results (Shin et al., 2005), but there is some evidence that it can help (e.g., Constantine, 2002; Razali, Aminah, & Umeed, 2002; Sue et al., 2009). And although it is unrealistic to expect all therapists to be equally effective with clients of all sociocultural backgrounds, cultural diversity training offers a way to improve their *cultural competence,* an extension of Carl Rogers's concept of empathy. When therapists appreciate the client's view of the world, it is easier for them to set goals that are in harmony with that view (Dyche & Zayas, 2001; Pedersen & Draguns, 2002; Stuart, 2004). Minimizing misunderstanding and miscommunication is one of the many ethical obligations that therapists assume when working with clients (Tomes, 1999). Let's consider some others.

Rules and Rights in the Therapeutic Relationship

Psychotherapy can be an intensely emotional experience, and the relationship established with a therapist can profoundly influence a client's life. Professional ethics and common sense require the therapist to ensure that this relationship does not harm the client. For example, the American Psychological Association's *Ethical Principles of Psychologists and Code of Conduct* forbids a sexual relationship between therapist and client during treatment and for at least two years afterward because of the severe harm it can cause the client (American Psychological Association, 2002b; Bersoff, 2008; Campbell et al.,

2009). Even after two years have passed, therapists may not ethically pursue a sexual relationship with a former client unless they can demonstrate that the relationship is not exploitative or otherwise harmful to that client. Laws in some U.S. states prohibit therapists from *ever* having a sexual relationship with a former client, and these stricter laws take precedence over the APA's code of conduct.

The APA's ethical standards also require therapists to keep strictly confidential everything a client says in therapy. Confidentiality is one of the most important features of a successful therapeutic relationship. It allows the client to reveal unpleasant or embarrassing impulses, behaviors, or events without fear that this information will be repeated to anyone else. Professionals do sometimes consult with one another about a client, but each is required not to reveal information to outsiders (including members of an adult client's family) without the client's consent. The APA's code of ethics even includes standards for protecting confidentiality for the growing number of clients who seek psychological services via *telehealth* or *e-health* channels, which include telephone, Skype or other video conferencing platforms, e-mail, or Internet links (Aguilera & Munoz, 2011; Andersson, 2009; American Psychological Association, 2002b; Mohr et al., 2005; Ruskin et al., 2004; Yuen et al., 2012). One of these standards requires therapists to inform clients that others might be able to gain access to their electronic communication and that no formal client-therapist relationship exists in e-mail exchanges (Van Allen & Roberts, 2011).

Professional standards about confidentiality are backed up in most U.S. states and in federal courts by laws that recognize that information revealed in therapy—like information given to a priest, a lawyer, or a physician—is privileged communication. This means that a therapist can refuse—even in court—to answer questions about a client or to provide personal notes or recordings from therapy sessions. Only under special circumstances can therapists be legally required to violate confidentiality (Donner et al., 2008). These circumstances include those in which (1) a client is so severely disturbed or suicidal that hospitalization is needed; (2) a client uses his or her mental condition and history of therapy as part of his or her defense in a civil or criminal trial; (3) the therapist must defend against a client's charge of malpractice; (4) a client reveals information about sexual or physical abuse of a child; and (5) the therapist believes a client may commit a violent act against a specific person.

Biological Treatments

Is electric shock still used to treat psychological disorders?

So far, we have described psychological approaches to the treatment of mental disorders. But biological treatments are also available, primarily through psychiatrists and other medical doctors, who often work in cooperation with psychologists. Today, biological treatments for psychological problems mainly involve the prescribing of psychoactive drugs. In the mid-1900s, however, the most common biological treatment for severe psychological problems was the use of electric shock to create seizures.

Electroconvulsive Shock Therapy

In the 1930s, a Hungarian physician named Ladislaus von Meduna used a drug to induce convulsions in people with schizophrenia. He believed—incorrectly—that because schizophrenia and epilepsy rarely occur in the same person, epileptic-like seizures might combat schizophrenia. In 1938, Italian physicians Ugo Cerletti and Lucio Bini created seizures by passing an electric current through the brains of patients with schizophrenia. During the next twenty years or so, this procedure, called **electroconvulsive shock therapy** (**ECT**), became a routine treatment for schizophrenia, depression, and sometimes mania. Many patients improved at first, but their problems often reappeared. The benefits of ECT also had to be weighed against side effects such as memory loss, confusion, speech disorders, and, in some cases, death due to cardiac arrest (Lickey & Gordon, 1991; Shiwach, Reid, & Carmody, 2001).

The Medical History Museum of the University of Zurich

Hospital Restraints
Here are examples of the chains, straitjackets, belts, and covered bathtubs that were used to restrain disruptive patients in North American and European mental hospitals in the 1800s and well into the 1900s. These devices were gentle compared with some of the methods endorsed in the late 1700s by Benjamin Rush. Known as the father of American psychiatry, Rush advocated curing patients by frightening or disorienting them—for example, by placing them in a coffin-like box that was then briefly immersed in water. *Source:* The Museum of the History of Medicine of the University of Zurich, accessed online at http://www.nobelprize.org/nobel_prizes/medicine/laureates/1949/moniz-article.html.

© Will McIntyre/Photo Researchers, Inc.

Electroconvulsive Shock Therapy
Approximately 100,000 individuals in the United States receive ECT each year (Payne & Prudic, 2009). Because of its dramatic and potentially dangerous nature, ECT remains a controversial treatment (Breggin, 2007). Critics want it outlawed, but proponents say the benefits of ECT for certain patients outweigh its potential dangers.

In an effort to make ECT safer, doctors now give patients an anesthetic so that they are unconscious before the shock is delivered, along with a muscle relaxant to prevent bone fractures during convulsions. Also, the shock now lasts only about half a second and is usually delivered to only one side of the brain (Weiner & Falcone, 2011). Finally, in contrast to the dozens of treatments administered decades ago, patients now receive only about six to twelve shocks, one approximately every two days (Shorter & Healy, 2007).

Although scientists are still trying to determine how and why ECT works (Greenberg & Kellner, 2005; Perrin et al., 2012; Shorter & Healy, 2007), it is being performed more frequently in the United States than coronary bypass operations, appendectomies, and tonsillectomies (Mathew, Amiel, & Sackeim, 2005). ECT is administered mainly to patients suffering severe depression (and occasionally to manic patients) who do not respond to medication (de Macedo-Soares et al., 2005; Payne & Prudic, 2009; Weiner & Falcone, 2011). It can be effective in such cases—especially when followed up with medication—and it does not appear to cause brain damage, even when administered repeatedly (e.g., Kellner et al., 2005, 2006; Payne & Prudic, 2009; Sackeim et al., 2009; Sackeim et al., 2001).

Nevertheless, researchers are looking for even safer methods of inducing seizures. Among the techniques being investigated are *magnetic seizure therapy (MST)*, which administers timed pulses of magnetic energy (Lisanby, 2004), and a related but less intense procedure called *repetitive transcranial magnetic stimulation (rTMS*; Jorge et al., 2008; O'Reardon et al., 2007). It appears that rTMS can be effective in treating severe depression as well as auditory hallucinations, while creating only relatively mild side effects (Slotema et al., 2010).

Deep brain stimulation (DBS) does not cause seizures but requires the placement of electrodes in the brain to provide continuous pulses of electricity to a particular target area. Some researchers suggest that DBS may be of value in severe cases of depression and obsessive-compulsive disorder that are unresponsive to other treatments (George et al., 2010; Goodman et al., 2010; Hamani et al., 2012; Hardesty & Sackeim, 2007; Martiny, Lunde, & Bech, 2010; Malone et al., 2009). Researchers are also beginning to explore the therapeutic use of *optogenic stimulation*, which uses light to induce or control neural activity in particular brain regions (Covington et al., 2010).

Psychoactive Drugs

The use of ECT declined after the 1950s, in part because psychoactive drugs had begun to emerge as more convenient and effective treatment alternatives. In the chapters on biology and behavior and on consciousness, we discuss the effects of psychoactive drugs on neurotransmitter systems, autonomic activity, emotions, thinking, and behavior. Here, we describe their role in combating schizophrenia, depression, mania, and anxiety.

Neuroleptic Drugs **Neuroleptic drugs**, also called *antipsychotics,* dramatically reduce the intensity of psychotic symptoms such as hallucinations, delusions, paranoid suspiciousness, disordered thinking, and confused speech in many mental patients, especially those with schizophrenia. The most widely used antipsychotic drugs are the *phenothiazines* (pronounced "fee-noh-THIGH-uh-zeens"), of which the first, chlorpromazine (marketed as Thorazine in the United States and as Largactil in Canada and the United Kingdom), has been especially popular. Another neuroleptic drug, haloperidol (Haldol), is about as effective as the phenothiazines, but it creates less sedation (Julien, 2005). Patients who do not respond to one type of neuroleptic may respond to the other (Schatzberg, Cole, & DeBattista, 2007). Between 60 and 70 percent of psychiatric patients receiving these drugs show improvement, though fewer than 30 percent respond well enough to live successfully on their own (Rothschild, 2010).

Neuroleptic drugs have side effects ranging from dry mouth and dizziness to symptoms similar to those of Parkinson's disease, including muscle rigidity, restlessness, tremors, and slowed movement. Some of these side effects can be treated with medication, but at least 25 percent of patients who take chlorpromazine or haloperidol for several years develop an irreversible movement disorder. This disorder, called *tardive dyskinesia*

electroconvulsive shock therapy (ECT) A brief electric shock administered to the brain, usually to reduce severe depression that does not respond to drug treatments.

neuroleptic drugs Drugs that relieve the symptoms of schizophrenia and other severe psychological disorders.

(*TD*), causes uncontrollable, repetitive actions, often including twitching of the face, flailing of the arms and legs, and thrusting of the tongue (Miller, McEvoy, et al., 2005).

A newer generation of antipsychotic drugs, called *atypical neuroleptics*, includes clozapine (Clozaril), which has effects like those of the phenothiazines but is less likely to cause movement disorders except at high doses (Louzá & Bassitt, 2005; Rochon et al., 2005). Although no more effective overall than the phenothiazines, clozapine has helped many patients who did not respond to the phenothiazines or haloperidol (Rabinowitz et al., 2001; Rothschild, 2010). Unfortunately, taking clozapine carries a slight risk of developing a fatal blood disease called *agranulocytosis* (Ginsberg, 2006), which means that weekly blood tests are required to detect early signs of this disease. These tests greatly increase the cost and inconvenience of using clozapine (Meltzer, 1997), so it is usually prescribed only for patients who have not responded well to other medications and are willing to have their blood drawn frequently.

Several other atypical neuroleptics have been introduced recently, including risperidone (Risperdal), olanzapine (Zyprexa), quetiapine (Seroquel), ziprasidone (Geodon), and, most recently, aripiprazole (Abilify). These medications are expensive, but they have fewer side effects than clozapine and they do not seem to cause agranulocytosis (Schatzberg et al., 2007). Like clozapine, they also appear to reduce the "negative" symptoms of schizophrenia, such as lack of emotion, social withdrawal, and reduced speech (e.g., Fleischhacker & Widschwendter, 2006; Kane et al., 2003; Kapur, Sridhar, & Remington, 2004; Potkin et al., 2003; Wang et al., 2010). There is some doubt, though, whether these newest atypical neuroleptics are significantly more effective than older drugs, partly because 60 to 80 percent of patients may stop taking them because of weight gain, nervous tics, and other bothersome side effects (Lieberman et al., 2005; Miyamoto et al., 2005; Swartz, Perkins et al., 2007).

antidepressant drugs Drugs that reduce symptoms of depression.

Antidepressant Drugs   Soon after antipsychotic drugs appeared, they were joined by **antidepressant drugs**, a class of medications that is now widely prescribed for relieving the symptoms of depression (Schatzberg et al., 2007; Thomson Healthcare, 2007). There are several types of antidepressant drugs. The *monoamine oxidase inhibitors* (*MAOIs*) are used to treat many cases of depression, especially with clients who also experience anxiety and panic (Julien, 2008). *Tricyclic antidepressants* (*TCAs*) are another popular type. The TCAs have been prescribed more frequently than MAOI drugs because they seem to work somewhat better and have fewer side effects. However, overdoses of TCAs can be fatal, as can combining TCAs with the use of alcohol (Nutt, 2005a).

The most prominent of several newer antidepressant drugs is fluoxetine (Prozac). Introduced in 1986, fluoxetine quickly became the most widely used antidepressant drug in North America (Brambilla et al., 2005). Its popularity is due to the fact that it is about as effective as older drugs and in most cases has fewer and milder side effects—mainly weight gain, sexual dysfunction, and gastrointestinal problems (Nutt, 2005a; Patten et al., 2005). An improved version of Prozac, R-fluoxetine, has now been developed (Norman & Olver, 2004), and other, even newer antidepressants also show promise (Gibbons et al., 2012). These include bupropion (Wellbutrin), venlafaxine (Effexor), nefazodone (Serzone), escitalopram (Lexapro), and duloxetine (Cymbalta) (Brambilla et al., 2005; Hirschfeld & Vornik, 2004; Schatzberg et al., 2007; Zimmerman et al., 2005). The antipsychotic medication *aripiprazole* (Abilify) has also shown benefits in treating clients whose depression does not respond to antidepressant medications (Baldwin, 2011).

About 50 to 60 percent of patients who take antidepressant drugs experience improved mood, greater physical activity, increased appetite, and better sleep (Hollon, Thase, & Markowitz, 2002). All of these drugs appear to be about equally effective (Gartlehner et al., 2011), although Escitalopram (Lexapro) seems to be particularly beneficial to clients with severe depression (Montgomery et al., 2007). Unfortunately, only about 10 to 20 percent of people suffering the most severe psychotic depression show this same amount of improvement (Fournier et al., 2010). Mental health professionals have generally assumed that the effects of antidepressant drugs are due to the chemical action of their active ingredients, but there is some doubt about this. An analysis of

© Mario Tama/Getty Images

A Natural Cure?

St. John's wort, an herbal remedy, has become a popular nonprescription treatment for depression. One of its active ingredients, *hypericin*, may affect neurotransmitters in the brain much as Prozac or Zoloft does. One double-blind, placebo-controlled study showed St. John's wort to be no more effective than a placebo for treating major depression (Hypericum-Depression Trial Study Group, 2002), though others have shown it to be as effective as Prozac in cases of milder depression (e.g., Hammerness, Basch, & Ulbricht, 2003; Szegedi et al., 2005). Final conclusions about the safety and effectiveness of St. John's wort must await the results of further research.

clinical trial data submitted to the U.S. Food and Drug Administration by the makers of six widely prescribed antidepressant drugs showed that in 57 percent of the trials, antidepressant drugs did only a little better than placebo medications ("sugar pills") at relieving depression (Kirsch et al., 2002; Kirsch, Scoboria, & Moore, 2002). A more recent study found similar results when comparing the effects of newer antidepressants and placebos (Kirsch, 2009). Defenders of antidepressant medications argue that even relatively small effects are better than none (e.g., Baldwin, 2011), whereas critics contend that those effects are too small to matter, especially when viewed in light of these drugs' high cost and potential adverse side effects (Breggin, 2008; Kirsch, 2010; Wampold et al., 2005).

Lithium and Anticonvulsants   The mineral salt lithium carbonate, when taken regularly, prevents both the depression and the mania associated with bipolar disorder in some patients (Geddes et al., 2004; Schatzberg et al., 2007). Without lithium, the typical patient with bipolar disorder has a manic episode about every fourteen months and a depressive episode about every seventeen months (American Psychiatric Association, 2000); with lithium, attacks of mania occur as rarely as every nine years (Geddes et al., 2004; Ketter, 2010). The lithium dosage must be exact and carefully controlled, however, because taking too much can cause vomiting, nausea, tremor, fatigue, slurred speech, and, with severe overdoses, coma or death (Johnson, 2002). Combining lithium with other mood stabilizing drugs, such as carbamazepine, has shown enhanced benefits but also more adverse side effects (Baethge et al., 2005).

In recent years, anticonvulsant drugs such as divalproex and lamotrigine (Epival/Depakote; Lamictal) have been used as alternatives to lithium in treating mania (e.g., Daban et al., 2006; Delbello et al., 2006). These drugs cause fewer side effects, are less dangerous at higher doses, and are easier to regulate than lithium (Ketter, 2010; Schatzberg et al., 2007). However, their long-term benefits in reducing mania and the risk of suicide are not as well established, so lithium is still considered the treatment of choice against which others are measured (Calabrese et al., 2005; Capriani et al., 2005; Carney & Goodwin, 2005; Ketter, 2010; McAllister-Williams, 2006).

Tranquilizing Drugs (Anxiolytics)   During the 1950s, a new class of drugs called *tranquilizers* was shown to reduce mental and physical tension and the symptoms of anxiety. The first of these drugs, meprobamate (Miltown or Equanil), acts somewhat like barbiturate sleeping pills, meaning that overdoses can cause sleep and even death. Because they do not pose this danger, the *benzodiazepines*—particularly chlordiazepoxide (Librium) and diazepam (Valium)—became the worldwide drug treatment of choice for anxiety (Stevens & Pollack, 2005). Today, these and other anti-anxiety drugs, now called **tranquilizing drugs**, or **anxiolytics** (pronounced "ang-zee-oh-LIT-ix"), are the most widely prescribed and used of all legal drugs (Stevens & Pollack, 2005). Anxiolytics have an immediate calming effect and are quite useful in treating the symptoms of generalized anxiety and posttraumatic stress disorder.

One of the benzodiazepines, alprazolam (Xanax), has become especially popular for the treatment of panic disorder and agoraphobia (Verster & Volkerts, 2004). But benzodiazepines can have bothersome side effects, such as sleepiness, lightheadedness, and impaired memory and thinking. Combining these drugs with alcohol can be fatal, and continued use can lead to tolerance and physical dependence (Chouinard, 2004). Further, suddenly discontinuing benzodiazepines after heavy or long-term use can cause severe withdrawal symptoms, including seizures and anxiety attacks (Lemoine et al., 2006).

The tranquilizing drug called buspirone (BuSpar) provides an alternative anxiety treatment that eliminates some of the problems associated with the benzodiazapines (Stahl, 2002; Wagner et al., 2003). Its effects do not occur for days or weeks after treatment begins, but buspirone can ultimately equal diazepam in reducing generalized anxiety (Gorman, 2003; Rickels & Rynn, 2002). Further, it does not seem to promote dependence, it causes less interference with thinking, and it does not interact dangerously with alcohol.

tranquilizing drugs (anxiolytics)
Drugs that reduce tension and symptoms of anxiety.

Because anxiety is often accompanied by depression, antidepressant drugs such as fluoxetine (Prozac), paroxetine (Paxil), clomipramine (Anafranil), fluvoxamine (Luvox), and sertraline (Zoloft) are also used in treating anxiety-related problems such as panic disorder, social phobia, obsessive-compulsive disorder, and posttraumatic stress disorder (e.g., Gorman, 2003; Julien, 2005; Nutt, 2005b; Rickels et al., 2003). Table 13.2 lists the effects and side effects of some of the psychoactive drugs we have described.

TABLE 13.2 A Sampling of Psychoactive Drugs Used for Treating Psychological Disorders

Psychoactive drugs have been successful in dramatically reducing the symptoms of many psychological disorders. Critics point out that drugs can have troublesome side effects, however, and that they may create dependence, especially after years of use (e.g., Breggin, 2008). They note, too, that drugs do not "cure" mental disorders (National Institute of Mental Health, 1995), that their effects are not always strong (Kirsch et al., 2002), and that temporary symptom relief may make some patients less likely to seek a permanent solution to their psychological problems.

Chemical Name	Trade Name	Effects and Side Effects
For Schizophrenia: Neuroleptic Drugs (Antipsychotics)		
Chlorpromazine Haloperidol	Thorazine Haldol	Reduce hallucinations, delusions, incoherence, jumbled thought processes; but may cause movement-disorder side effects, including tardive dyskinesia
Clozapine	Clozaril	Reduces psychotic symptoms; causes no movement disorders but carries some risk of serious blood disease
Risperidone	Risperdal	Reduces positive and negative psychotic symptoms without risk of blood disease
Ziprasidone	Geodon	Reduces positive and negative psychotic symptoms without causing weight gain
Aripiprazole	Abilify	Reduces positive and negative psychotic symptoms without weight gain and with few side effects; Can also be effective in some cases of depression
For Affective (Mood) Disorders: Antidepressant Drugs and Mood Elevators		
Tricyclics		
Imipramine	Tofranil	Act as antidepressants but also have anti-panic action; cause sleepiness and other moderate side effects; potentially dangerous if taken with alcohol
Amitriptyline	Elavil, Amitid	
Other Antidepressant Drugs		
Fluoxetine	Prozac	
Clomipramine	Anafranil	
Fluvoxamine	Luvox	All have antidepressant, anti-panic, and anti-obsessive action
Sertraline	Zoloft	
Escitalopram	Lexapro	
Other Drugs		
Lithium carbonate	Carbolith, Lithizine	Calms mania and reduces mood swings of bipolar disorder; overdose harmful, potentially deadly
Divalproex	Depakote	Effective against mania with fewer side effects
Lamotrigine	Lamictal	Effective in delaying relapse in bipolar disorder; most benefits associated with depression
For Anxiety Disorders: Tranquilizing Drugs (Anxiolytics)		
Benzodiazepines		
Chlordiazepoxide Diazepam	Librium Valium	Act as potent anxiolytics for generalized anxiety, panic, stress; extended use may cause physical dependence and withdrawal syndrome if abruptly discontinued
Alprazolam	Xanax	Also has antidepressant effects; often used in agoraphobia; has high dependence potential
Clonazepam	Klonopin	Often used in combination with other anxiolytics for panic disorder
Other Anti-Anxiety Agents		
Buspirone	BuSpar	Has slow-acting anti-anxiety action; no known dependence problems

Human Diversity and Drug Treatment

Drug treatments are designed to benefit everyone in the same way, but it turns out that the same psychoactive drug dose can have significantly different effects in each sex and in people from various ethnic groups (e.g., Esel et al., 2005; Lambert & Norman, 2008; Seeman, 2004; Vemuri et al., 2011). For example, Caucasians must take significantly higher doses than Asians of the benzodiazepines, haloperidol, clozapine, lithium, and possibly the tricyclic antidepressants in order to obtain equally beneficial effects (Hull et al., 2001; Ng et al., 2005). In addition, African Americans may show a faster response to tricyclic antidepressants than European Americans and may respond to lower doses of lithium (Chaudhry et al., 2008). There is also some evidence that, compared with European Americans, African Americans and Hispanic Americans might require higher doses of antipsychotic drugs to get the same benefits (Citrome et al., 2005). Some of these ethnic differences are thought to be related to genetically regulated differences in drug metabolism (Kato & Serretti, 2010; Zhang, Lencz, & Malhotra, 2010), whereas others may be due to dietary practices and other sociocultural factors (Bakare, 2008).

Males and females may respond in about the same way to tricyclic antidepressants (Wohlfarth et al., 2004), but women may maintain higher blood levels of these and other therapeutic drugs and may show better response to neuroleptics (Hildebrandt et al., 2003; Salokangas, 2004). They also may be more vulnerable to neuroleptics' adverse side effects, such as tardive dyskinesia (Yarlagadda et al., 2008), but less prone to the cholesterol-related side effects of medications for bipolar disorder (Vemuri et al., 2011). These gender differences in drug response appear less related to estrogen than to other hormonal or body-composition differences between men and women, such as the ratio of body fat to muscle (Dawkins & Potter, 1991; Salokangas, 2004). Continued research on these and other dimensions of human diversity will undoubtedly lead to more effective and safer drug treatments for everyone (Thompson & Pollack, 2001; Vemuri et al., 2011).

Drugs and Psychotherapy

Despite their widespread success in the treatment of psychological disorders, psychoactive drugs do have some drawbacks. As we have seen, some of them can result in physical or psychological dependence, and their side effects can range from minor problems such as the thirst and dry mouth caused by some antidepressant drugs to movement disorders such as tardive dyskinesia caused by some neuroleptics. Although the most serious of these side effects are relatively rare, some are irreversible, and it is impossible to predict in advance who will develop them. For example, although a clear causal link has not yet been confirmed (Gibbons et al., 2005; Simon et al., 2006; Wheeler et al., 2008), the U.S. National Institute of Mental Health (NIMH) and regulatory agencies in Canada and Britain have issued warnings about the danger of suicidal behavior in children and adolescents who are given Prozac and similar antidepressant drugs (Bridge et al., 2007; Breggin, 2008; Gualtieri & Johnson, 2006; Hammad, Laughren, & Racoosin, 2006; National Institute of Mental Health, 2004; Olfson, Marcus, & Shaffer, 2006; Stone et al., 2009). There is also concern about whether psychoactive drugs are as effective as they appear to be, especially in research sponsored by the drug companies that make them (Heres et al., 2006; Moncrieff & Kirsch, 2005; Kirsch, 2010; Turner et al., 2008). These considerations may be partly responsible for dampening the enthusiasm that once led many clinical psychologists to seek drug prescription privileges (Greenberg, 2010).

So which is better: drugs or psychotherapy? A considerable amount of research is being conducted to address this question. Although occasionally a study shows that one form of treatment or the other is more effective, neither drugs nor psychotherapy has been shown to be clearly superior overall for treating problems such as anxiety disorders and major depressive disorder (Smits, O'Cleirigh, & Otto, 2006; Stewart & Harkness, 2012; Thase et al., 2007). For example, several studies of treatment for severe depression have found that behavior therapy, cognitive behavior therapy, and interpersonal

There is widespread concern that psychiatrists, and especially general practitioners, rely too heavily on drugs to deal with psychological problems, partly because of drug ads that fuel consumer demand (Albee, 2002; Breggin, 2008; Olfson et al., 2006; Zuvekas, Vitiello, & Nordquist, 2006). In one case, for example, increasing doses of medication failed to stop a patient with paranoid schizophrenia from repeatedly escaping from a mental hospital. The problem was solved without drugs, though, after a psychologist discovered that the man's escapes were motivated by his fear of calling his mother on "bugged" hospital phones, and he was allowed to use a telephone at a nearby shopping mall (Rabasca, 1999).

"I medicate first and ask questions later."

psychotherapy can be as effective as antidepressant drugs (Butler et al., 2006; DeRubeis et al., 2005; Dimidjian et al., 2006; Hollon, Thase, & Markowitz, 2002; March et al., 2004; Stewart & Harkness, 2012). The effects of cognitive behavior therapy have also equaled drug effects in the treatment of phobias (Clark et al., 2003; Davidson et al., 2004; Otto et al., 2000; Thom, Sartory, & Jöhren, 2000), panic disorder (Barlow, 2007; Mitte, 2005a), generalized anxiety disorder (Mitte, 2005b), and obsessive-compulsive disorder (Kozak, Liebowitz, & Foa, 2000). Further, the dropout rate from psychotherapy may be lower than from drug therapies, and the benefits of many kinds of psychotherapy may last longer than those of drug treatments (e.g., Casacalenda, Perry, & Looper, 2002; Hollon, Stewart, & Strunk, 2006; Hollon, Thase, & Markowitz, 2002; Stewart & Harkness, 2012; Thom, Sartory, & Jöhren, 2000).

What about combining drugs and psychotherapy? Research suggests that doing so can sometimes be helpful (Addington, Piskulic, & Marshall, 2010; Geyer, 2010; Hofmann et al., 2006; Miklowitz, 2007; Winston, Been, & Serby, 2005). Combined treatment is recommended in cases of bipolar disorder (Miklowitz, 2008; Otto, Bruce, & Deckersbach, 2005; Vieta et al., 2011) and produces slightly better results than either psychotherapy or drugs alone in people suffering from severe, long-term depression (Hegerl, Plattner, & Moller, 2004). The combination of drugs and psychotherapy has been also shown to be more effective than either method alone in treating attention deficit hyperactivity disorder, childhood anxiety disorders, obsessive-compulsive disorder, alcoholism, stammering, eating disorders, compulsive sexual behavior, posttraumatic stress disorder, and panic disorder (Barlow, 2007; Flament, Bissada, & Spettigue, 2012; Keller et al., 2000; March et al., 2004; Roy-Byrne et al., 2005; Sheerin, Seim, & Spates, 2012; Walkup et al., 2008). The combined approach may be especially useful for clients who are initially too distressed to benefit much from psychotherapy. A related approach, already shown to be successful with clients who had been taking drugs for panic disorder and depression, is the use of psychotherapy to prevent relapse and to make further progress as drug treatment is discontinued (e.g., Dobson et al., 2008; Klein et al., 2004; Lam et al., 2003). Preliminary evidence also suggests that a drug called D-cycloserine might be helpful in preventing the reappearance of fears being extinguished through exposure techniques or other forms of behavior therapy (Choy, Fyer, & Lipsitz, 2007; Davis et al., 2005, 2006; Hofmann et al., 2006; Norberg, Krystal, & Tolin, 2008). And when combined with cognitive behavior therapy, D-cycloserine also shows promise for treating obsessive-compulsive disorder (Storch et al., 2010).

However, many other studies have found little advantage in combining drugs and psychotherapy (e.g., Davidson et al., 2004; Nemeroff et al., 2003; Spiegel & Bruce, 1997). One early study compared the effects of a form of in vivo desensitization called *gradual exposure* and an anti-anxiety drug (Xanax) in the treatment of agoraphobia. Clients who received gradual exposure alone showed better short- and long-term benefits than those who received either the drug alone or a combination of the drug and gradual exposure (Echeburua et al., 1993). Other studies, too, have found that combining drugs and psychotherapy may produce surprisingly little added benefit (e.g., Elkin, 1994; Spiegel & Bruce, 1997).

Perhaps the most conservative strategy for treating most cases of anxiety and depression is to begin with cognitive or interpersonal psychotherapy (which have no major negative side effects) and then add or switch to drug treatment if psychotherapy alone is ineffective (Jacobs et al., 2004; Schatzberg et al., 2005). Often clients who do not respond to one method will be helped by the other (Heldt et al., 2006). Someday research may offer better guidelines about which clients should be treated with psychotherapy alone, medication alone, or a combination of the two (Hollon et al., 2005; Practice Guidelines, 2011).

LINKAGES

How do psychoactive drugs work?
(a link to Biology and Behavior)

Biology, Behavior, and the Treatment of Psychological Disorders

Human feelings, thoughts, and actions—whether normal or abnormal—are ultimately the result of biological processes, especially those involving neurotransmitters and their receptors in the brain. Because different neurotransmitters are especially prominent in particular circuits or regions of the brain, altering the functioning of particular neurotransmitter systems will have relatively specific psychological and behavioral effects.

Let's consider some of the ways that therapeutic psychoactive drugs affect neurotransmitters and their receptors. Some therapeutic drugs cause neurons to fire, whereas others reduce, or inhibit, firing. For example, benzodiazepines (e.g., Valium and Xanax) exert their anti-anxiety effects by helping the inhibitory neurotransmitter GABA bind to receptors and thus suppress neuron firing. This increased inhibitory effect acts as a sort of braking system that slows the activity of GABA-sensitive neurons involved in the experience of anxiety. However, benzodiazepines also slow the action of all neural systems that use GABA, including those associated with motor activity and mental processing, which are spread throughout the brain. The result is the decreased motor coordination and clouded thinking that appear as the side effects of the benzodiazepines. Research suggests that it might soon be possible to develop drugs that will bind only to certain kinds of GABA receptors and thus greatly reduce these side effects (Gorman, 2005).

LINKAGES

How do drugs help people who suffer from schizophrenia? *(a link to Biology and Behavior)*

Other therapeutic drugs are receptor antagonists (see Figure 4.8 in the consciousness chapter), acting to block the receptor site normally used by a particular neurotransmitter. The phenothiazines and haloperidol, for example, exert their antipsychotic effects by blocking receptors for dopamine, a neurotransmitter that is important for movement, as described in the chapter on biology and behavior. Blocking dopamine seems to normalize the jumbled thinking of many schizophrenia patients, but it can create severe disorders— including tardive dyskinesia—in the movement systems that are also controlled by dopamine.

Some psychoactive drugs exert their therapeutic influence by increasing the amount of a neurotransmitter available to act on receptors. This effect usually occurs because the drug slows a process called *reuptake*, through which the neurotransmitter would normally return to the brain cell from which it was released. The tricyclic antidepressants, for example, operate by slowing the reuptake of norepinephrine. Prozac, Anafranil, and some other antidepressant drugs are called *selective serotonin reuptake inhibitors (SSRIs)* because they slow the reuptake of serotonin. Others, such as Effexor, slow the reuptake of both serotonin and norepinephrine.   ● ● ● ●

Community Psychology

How can we prevent psychological disorders?

It has long been argued that even if psychologists and psychiatrists knew exactly how to treat every psychological problem, there would never be enough mental health professionals to help everyone in need (Albee, 1968, 2006). A study by the World Health Organization found, for example, that even individuals with severe mental health problems often do not receive the psychological services they need (Wang et al., 2007). The study revealed, too, that the treatment situation is especially dire in poorer countries where only about 11 percent of psychologically troubled individuals had received treatment for their disorders. In "high income" countries such as the United States and Belgium, the figure was about 60 percent (see also Gonzalez et al., 2010). Even in "high income" countries, though, mental health problems are more common among individuals who are poor, so the people who most need psychological treatment are often the ones least likely to receive it (van Oort et al., 2011).

Recognition of this treatment access problem helped fuel the rise of **community psychology**, which seeks to treat people in their local communities, raise people's awareness and understanding of mental health problems, and work for social changes that can prevent psychological disorders (Jorm, 2012; Nelson & Prilleltensky, 2004).

One aspect of community psychology, the *community mental health movement,* appeared during the 1960s as an attempt to make treatment available to people in their own communities. As antipsychotic drugs became available and as concern grew that patients were not improving (and might be getting worse) after years of confinement in mental hospitals, thousands of these patients were released. The plan was for them to receive drugs and other mental health services in newly funded community mental health centers. This *deinstitutionalization* process spared patients the boredom and isolation of the hospital environment, but the mental health services available in the community never matched the need for them (Leff, 2006). Some former hospital patients and many people whose disorders might once have sent them to mental hospitals are now living in halfway houses and other community-based facilities where they receive *psychosocial rehabilitation*. These community support services are not designed to "cure" them but to help them cope with their problems and develop the social and occupational skills necessary for semi-independent living (Coldwell & Bender, 2007; Cook et al., 2005; Talbott, 2004). But too many others with severe psychological disorders did not receive or respond to rehabilitation and are to be found enduring the dangers of homelessness on city streets or of confinement in jails and prisons (Luhrmann, 2008; Smith & Sederer, 2009; Teplin et al., 2005).

Community psychology also attempts to prevent psychopathology by addressing unemployment, poverty, overcrowded substandard housing, and other stressful social situations that may put vulnerable people at greater risk for some disorders (Fagan et al., 2009; Fuller-Rowell, Evans, & Ong, 2012; Komro, Flay, & Biglan, 2011; Nikulina, Widom, & Czaja, 2011; Van Hulst et al., 2011; Xue et al., 2005; Yoshikawa, Aber, & Beardsleee, 2012). Less ambitious but perhaps even more significant are efforts to detect psychological problems in their earliest stages and keep those problems from becoming worse (e.g., Bond & Hauf, 2004; President's New Freedom Commission on Mental Health, 2003; Sanders et al., 2000). Some examples include encouraging positive lifestyle changes (Walsh, 2011), prevention of depression and suicide and posttraumatic stress disorder (Cuijpers et al., 2008; Gates et al., 2012; Gillham et al., 2007; Horowitz & Garber, 2006;

© Geri Engberg/The Image Works

Community Mental Health Efforts

Professional and nonprofessional staff members at community mental health centers provide traditional therapy and mental health education as well as walk-in facilities and hotlines for people who are suicidal or in crisis because of rape or domestic violence. They also offer day treatment to former mental patients, many of whom are homeless.

APPLYING PSYCHOLOGY

community psychology An approach to minimizing or preventing psychological disorders by promoting social change and community mental health programs.

Lynch et al., 2005; Shalev et al., 2012; Spence, Sheffield, & Donovan, 2005); programs (including Project Head Start) that help preschoolers whose backgrounds hurt their chances of doing well in school and put them at risk for failure and delinquency (Foster et al., 2006; Reid, Webster-Stratton, & Baydar, 2004; Shaw et al., 2006); and identification of children who are at risk for disorder because of parental divorce, poverty, or because they are rejected or victimized at school (e.g., Cappella et al., 2012; Frey et al., 2005; Lochman & Wells, 2004; Martinez & Forgatch, 2001). Other interventions are designed to head off conduct problems, anxiety disorders, or schizophrenia in children and adults (McGilloway et al., 2012; McGorry et al., 2002; Neil & Christensen, 2009; Rapee et al., 2005); to prevent domestic violence, dating violence, and child abuse (Duggan et al., 2004; Miller et al., 2012; Whitaker et al., 2006), and to promote health consciousness in ethnic minority communities (Borg, 2002).

Active Review

As noted in the introductory chapter, all of psychology's subfields are related to one another. Our discussion of the psychopharmacology of drug treatment illustrates just one way that the topic of this chapter, treatment of psychological disorders, is linked to the subfield of biological

CHAPTER 13
Treatment of Psychological Disorders

psychology, which is described in the chapter on biology and behavior. The Linkages diagram shows ties to two other subfields, and there are many more ties throughout the book. Looking for linkages among subfields will help you see how they all fit together and help you better appreciate the big picture that is psychology.

LINKAGES

How do psychoactive drugs work?
(ans. on p. 534)

Can people learn their way out of a disorder?
(ans. on p. 513)

How can people manage stress?
(ans. on p. 415)

CHAPTER 2
Biology and Behavior

CHAPTER 5
Learning

CHAPTER 10
Health, Stress, and Coping

Summary

Basic Features of Treatment

What features do all treatment techniques have in common?
Psychotherapy is usually based on psychodynamic, humanistic, or behavioral theories of personality and behavior disorder. Many therapists employ elements of more than one approach. The biological approach uses drugs and other physical treatment methods.

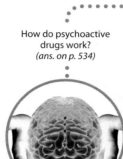

All forms of treatment include a client, a therapist, a theory of behavior disorder, a set of treatment procedures suggested by the theory, and a special relationship between the client and therapist. Therapy may be offered to inpatients and outpatients in many different settings by ***psychologists, psychiatrists***, and other helpers. The goal of treatment is to help people change their thinking, feelings,

and behavior so that they will be happier and function better.

Psychodynamic Psychotherapy

How did Freud get started as a therapist?
Psychodynamic psychotherapy began with Freud's ***psychoanalysis***, which seeks to help clients gain insight into unconscious conflicts and impulses and then to explore how those factors have created disorders. Exploration of the unconscious is aided by the use of free association, dream interpretation, and related methods. Some variations

on psychoanalysis retain most of Freud's principles but are typically shorter in duration and tend to stress social and interpersonal factors, such as early relationships with caregivers.

Humanistic Psychotherapy

Why won't some therapists give advice?
Humanistic psychotherapy helps clients become more aware of discrepancies between their feelings and their behavior. According to the humanistic approach, these discrepancies are at the root of behavior disorders and can be resolved by the client once they are brought to light in the context of a genuine, trusting relationship with the therapist. Therapists using Rogers's ***client-centered therapy***, also known as ***person-centered therapy***, help mainly by adopting

attitudes toward the client that express **unconditional positive regard**, **empathy**, and **congruence** to create a nonjudgmental atmosphere. Therapists employing the **Gestalt therapy** of Fritz and Laura Perls use more active techniques than Rogerian therapists, often pointing out inconsistencies between what clients say and how they behave.

Behavior Therapy

Can we learn to conquer fears?
Behavior therapy and **behavior modification** apply learning principles to eliminate undesirable behavior patterns and strengthen more desirable alternatives. The methods they employ include **systematic desensitization therapy**, **modeling**, **assertiveness training** and social skills training, **positive reinforcement** (sometimes within a **token economy program**), **extinction** techniques (such as **flooding** or **implosive therapy**), **aversion conditioning**, and **punishment**.

Many behavior therapists also employ **cognitive behavior therapy** to help clients alter the way they think as well as the way they behave. Among the specific cognitive behavioral methods are **rational-emotive behavior therapy (REBT)**, cognitive restructuring, stress inoculation training, and **cognitive therapy**.

Group, Family, and Couples Therapy

How does group psychotherapy differ from individual therapy?
Therapists of all theoretical persuasions offer **group psychotherapy**, **family therapy**, and **couples therapy**. These forms of treatment take advantage of relationships in the group, family, or couple to enhance the effects of treatment.

Evaluating Psychotherapy

How effective is psychotherapy?
Research has found that clients who receive psychotherapy are better off than most clients who receive no treatment but that no single approach is uniformly better than all others for all clients and problems. Still, some methods appear effective enough in the treatment of particular disorders to have been listed as **empirically supported therapies** (**ESTs**) that can guide **evidence-based practice**. The outcome of treatment is also affected by the characteristics of the client and the therapist and the relationship that develops between them. Several factors, including personal preferences, must be considered when choosing a form of treatment and a therapist. The effects of cultural differences in the values and goals of therapist and client have also attracted increasing attention. In all forms of treatment and under all but the most exceptional circumstances, the client's rights include the right to confidentiality.

Biological Treatments

Is electric shock still used to treat psychological disorders?
Biological treatment methods seek to relieve psychological disorders by physical or pharmaceutical means. **Electroconvulsive shock therapy** (**ECT**) involves passing an electric current through the patient's brain, usually in an effort to relieve severe depression. Today, the most prominent form of biological treatment involves psychoactive drugs, including those with antipsychotic (**neuroleptic**), **antidepressant**, or **tranquilizing** (**anxiolytic**) effects. Psychoactive medications appear effective in many cases, but critics point out that a number of undesirable side effects are associated with these drugs. Drugs may be no more effective than some forms of psychotherapy for many people. Combining drugs and psychotherapy may help in some cases and in the treatment of certain disorders, but their joint effect may be no greater than the effect of either one alone.

Community Psychology

How can we prevent psychological disorders?
The realization that there will never be enough therapists to treat all who need help prompted the development of **community psychology**. Community mental health programs and efforts to prevent mental disorders are the two main elements of community psychology.

Put It in Writing

Imagine that you have decided to get help for depression, anxiety, or some other psychological problem. Using what you have learned in this chapter, write a page describing what approach to treatment you would prefer and why. Tell whether you would choose that approach for all kinds of problems or whether your choice would depend on the nature of the problem. Finally, list the characteristics of your ideal therapist and say why you think those characteristics might lead to successful treatment.

Personal Learning Activity

To get a better idea of how practicing therapists choose their treatment methods, ask a local psychologist, psychiatrist, or counselor (at your student counseling center, perhaps) to see you for a short research interview. Ask what treatment approach and methods this therapist prefers, how that preference developed, and what convinces him or her to continue using these methods. Write a summary of what you learned in this interview, and don't forget to include your impressions of whether this therapist's choice of treatment methods depends mainly on personal experience, empirical research evidence, or a combination of both.

Review of Key Terms

Can you define each of the key terms in the chapter? Check your definitions against those on the pages shown in parentheses in the following list or in the Glossary at the end of the book.

antidepressant drugs (p. 529)
assertiveness training (p. 514)
aversion conditioning (p. 515)
behavior modification (p. 512)
behavior therapy (p. 512)
client-centered therapy (person-centered therapy) (p. 510)
cognitive behavior therapy (p. 513)
cognitive therapy (p. 517)

community psychology (p. 535)
congruence (p. 511)
couples therapy (p. 518)
electroconvulsive shock therapy (ECT) (p. 528)
empathy (p. 510)
empirically supported therapies (ESTs) (p. 522)
evidence-based practice (p. 521)
extinction (p. 515)
family therapy (p. 518)
flooding (p. 515)
Gestalt therapy (p. 511)
group psychotherapy (p. 518)
implosive therapy (p. 515)

modeling (p. 513)
neuroleptic drugs (p. 528)
positive reinforcement (p. 514)
psychiatrists (p. 507)
psychoanalysis (p. 508)
psychologists (p. 507)
psychotherapy (p. 506)
punishment (p. 515)
rational-emotive behavior therapy (REBT) (p. 516)
systematic desensitization therapy (p. 513)
token economy program (p. 514)
tranquilizing drugs (anxiolytics) (p. 530)
unconditional positive regard (p. 510)

Test Your Knowledge

Select the best answer for each of the following questions. Then check your responses against the Answer Key at the end of the book.

1. Claudia's therapist asks her to talk about whatever thoughts, memories, or ideas come into her mind. He asks her not to "edit" any of her thoughts. This technique is called ____ and is part of ____ therapy.
   a. reflection; psychodynamic
   b. reflection; humanistic
   c. free association; psychodynamic
   d. free association; humanistic

2. Vicki tells Dr. Denter, her therapist, that she is very happy in her marriage. Dr. Denter points out that as she says this, she is clenching her fist. He asks her to have a dialogue with herself by "becoming" her fist and saying what it would say to her. Dr. Denter is most likely a ____ therapist.
   a. Gestalt
   b. psychodynamic
   c. behavior
   d. cognitive

3. Melinda is a licensed clinical psychologist, which means she probably has ____.
   a. a doctoral degree in psychology
   b. a psychodynamic approach to therapy
   c. the right to prescribe drugs in all but two U.S. states
   d. a medical degree

4. A primary aim of classical psychoanalysis is to ____.
   a. help clients get in touch with their current feelings
   b. help clients gain insight into their unconscious conflicts
   c. replace clients' problematic behaviors with more desirable behaviors
   d. teach clients new ways of thinking

5. Dr. Margent listens as her client, Eric, talks at length about his problems at work, including the fact that he hates the job, often sneaks out early, sometimes ignores his manager's instructions, and generally avoids working hard. Dr. Margent doesn't interrupt or criticize him but often rephrases what he says to be sure she understands it. Dr. Margent is using methods most closely associated with ____ therapy.
   a. psychodynamic
   b. behavioral
   c. client-centered
   d. cognitive-behavioral

6. Carl's therapist is helping him overcome his fear of heights by imagining increasingly frightening images while he is relaxed. The therapist is using methods known as ____.
   a. assertion training
   b. systematic desensitization therapy
   c. flooding
   d. modeling

7. Shanobi is tearfully telling a friend that she is depressed and does not know why. Her friend says, "You seem so unhappy, and maybe a bit scared, too." The friend's response is most like which method used in client-centered therapy?
   a. sympathy
   b. empathy
   c. reflection
   d. actualization

8. Rebecca is convinced that she will never get the promotion she wants because she "is just not good at job interviews." Her therapist asks her to close her eyes and say the first thing that comes into her mind as she thinks about her job. He also asks Rebecca for details of the dreams she has been having lately. Rebecca's therapist appears to prefer the ____ approach to treatment.
   a. behavioral
   b. cognitive behavioral
   c. Gestalt
   d. psychodynamic

9. Brandon complains that he has an intense need to touch all four walls of any room he enters for the first time. His therapist suggests that Brandon might have learned this compulsive behavior because it helped him avoid anxiety. The therapist appears to favor the ____ approach to treatment.
   a. psychodynamic
   b. humanistic
   c. behavioral
   d. neurobiological

10. Your friend Rallo is considering entering psychotherapy, but he wonders if it will help. Based on the research you read about in this chapter, you tell Rallo that ____.
    a. therapy does not help the average client
    b. therapy helps the average client
    c. humanistic therapies are most effective overall
    d. there is no experimental research on the effectiveness of therapy

11. According to the American Psychological Association's *Ethical Principles of Psychologists and Code of Conduct*, a therapist may reveal information learned about a client during therapy if ____.
    a. the client's employer requests this information in confidence
    b. the client drops out of therapy
    c. the client is suicidal and needs immediate hospitalization
    d. the therapist feels it will do no harm

12. Juanita is trying to influence her state legislature to pass laws that will help prevent psychological problems caused by malnutrition, overcrowding, and homelessness. She is most likely a ____ psychologist.
    a. behavioral
    b. community
    c. humanistic
    d. psychodynamic

13. Rafer's intense fear of spiders greatly interferes with his job as a forest ranger. His therapist suggests that he stay in a room full of harmless spiders until he feels no further anxiety. This therapy technique is known as ____.
    a. flooding
    b. punishment
    c. systematic desensitization therapy
    d. aversion conditioning

14. Sally constantly tells herself that she is "worthless" and "will never succeed at anything." Her therapist helps her practice new thoughts such as "I'm as good as the next person" and "I am going to try my best." Her therapist is using the technique of ____, which is part of ____ therapy.
    a. free association; psychodynamic
    b. reflection; humanistic
    c. stress inoculation; behavioral
    d. cognitive restructuring; cognitive behavior

15. Lucinda is experiencing severe depression that leaves her unable to enjoy life. She has not responded to psychotherapies or medication. Lucinda would be a candidate for ___.
    a. neuroleptic drugs
    b. ECT
    c. aversion conditioning
    d. cognitive restructuring

16. Therapeutic drugs can work in many ways, but *not* by ___.
    a. increasing the amount of neurotransmitters released in the brain
    b. decreasing the amount of neurotransmitters released in the brain
    c. blocking the action of neurotransmitters in the brain
    d. changing the kind of neurotransmitters released by neurons in the brain

17. An important common element in the success of many forms of psychotherapy is ___.
    a. the client-therapist relationship
    b. randomly assigning therapists to clients
    c. having a therapist trained in a variety of therapeutic methods
    d. having appropriate assessment methods to measure outcomes

18. When prescribing neuroleptic drugs for schizophrenia, psychiatrists must consider that patients may ___.
    a. become addicted to them
    b. become insensitive to them after an extended period of time
    c. develop side effects such as tardive dyskinesia
    d. experience hallucinations after extensive use

19. Jon's therapist has prescribed anxiolytics for him. Jon is probably being treated for ___.
    a. depression
    b. an anxiety disorder
    c. schizophrenia
    d. somatoform disorder

20. Which of the following is *not* an advantage of group psychotherapy?
    a. It allows the therapist to observe clients interacting with one another.
    b. Clients learn from one another.
    c. Clients improve more quickly.
    d. Clients feel less alone.

Media Resources··

Now that you have finished reading this chapter, how about exploring some of the ideas and information that you found most interesting?

Go to **CengageBrain.com** to access Psychology CourseMate, where you will find an interactive eBook, glossaries, flashcards, quizzes, videos, Virtual Psychology Labs, and more.

aplia

If your professor has assigned Aplia:

1. Sign in to your account.
2. Complete the corresponding exercises as required by your professor.
3. When finished, click "Grade It Now" to see which areas you have mastered, which areas need more work, and detailed explanations of every answer.

Social Psychology

© Rubberball/Getty Images

Preview

If you are like most people, there is probably at least one thing you do in private that you would never do when someone else is around. The tendency to behave differently when others are present is just one aspect of social psychology. This chapter describes many other ways that the presence and behavior of other people affect our own thoughts and actions and how we, in turn, affect the thoughts and actions of others. It explores how perception, learning, memory, thinking, and emotion occur in relation to other people; how people think about themselves and others; why we may like one person but dislike another; how people form and change attitudes; and why and how we judge other people, sometimes in biased ways. Social pressure, ranging from unspoken social rules to commands for obedience, is another concern of social psychologists. The chapter also reviews some of the helpful, cooperative, competitive, and aggressive ways in which people behave toward one another in the workplace and in other social situations. Finally, it considers group decision making and other group processes.

The death toll in the September 11, 2001, terrorist attacks on the World Trade Center and the Pentagon was almost 3,000, and many thousands more have perished since then in hundreds of suicide bombings and other attacks all over the world. Almost all of the questions that can be asked about terrorism relate to human behavior. For example, what could lead people to kill themselves and thousands of innocent people in the name of political or religious beliefs? Why do firefighters, police officers, emergency medical workers, and other first responders enter burning buildings to save the lives of others while risking, and, in some cases, losing, their own? Why did some of the people who were about to flee the World Trade Center return to their offices after hearing an announcement telling them to do so? Is there any reason to hope that the hatred, distrust, and extremism that underlie terrorist attacks can someday be reduced or eliminated?

We may never have final answers to such questions as these, but some partial answers may lie in the study of **social psychology**, the scientific investigation of how people's thoughts and feelings influence their behavior toward others and how the behavior of others influences people's own thoughts, feelings, and behavior. In this chapter, we focus on several topics in social psychology, including **social cognition**, the mental processes associated with how people perceive and react to other individuals and groups (Fiske & Taylor, 2008), and group and interpersonal behaviors such as conformity, aggression, and helping. One important aspect of social cognition is how it affects the way we see ourselves. ●

Social Influences on the Self

How do we compare ourselves with others?

Each of us lives in both a personal and a social world. This means that although you experience your thoughts and feelings as your own, they have been strongly influenced by other people.

The thoughts, feelings, and beliefs about what characteristics you have and who you are make up your **self-concept**. Although your self-concept is unique to you, it is a product of your social and cultural environment. In the chapters on human development and personality, we describe how each individual develops within a cultural context and how collectivist and individualist cultures emphasize different core values and encourage contrasting definitions of the self. As you will see in this chapter, culture also provides the context for **self-esteem**, the evaluations you make of your worth as a human being (Baumeister, 2010). Let's look at how self-esteem develops.

social psychology The subfield of psychology that explores the effects of the social world on the behavior and mental processes of individuals and groups.

social cognition Mental processes associated with people's perceptions of and reactions to other people.

self-concept The way one thinks of oneself.

self-esteem The evaluations people make about their worth as human beings.

Social Comparison

People spend a lot of time thinking about themselves, trying to evaluate their own perceptions, opinions, values, abilities, and so on (Epstude & Mussweiler, 2009). Self-evaluation involves two distinct types of questions: those that can be answered objectively, and those that cannot (Festinger, 1954). You can determine your height or weight by measuring it, but for other types of questions—about your creativity or attractiveness, for example—there are no objective criteria. According to Leon Festinger's theory of **social comparison**, people evaluate themselves in relation to others. When you use others as a basis for evaluating how intelligent, athletic, interesting, or attractive you are, you engage in social comparison (Dijkstra, Gibbons, & Buunk, 2010; Freund & Kasten, 2012).

Who serves as your basis of comparison? Festinger said that people usually look to others who are similar to themselves. For example, if you are curious about how good you are at swimming or science, you'll probably compare yourself with people who are at about your own level of experience and ability, not with Olympic champions or Nobel Prize winners (Major, Sciacchtinano, & Crocker, 1993). The categories of people you feel you belong to and usually compare yourself with are called your **reference groups**.

The performance of individuals in your reference groups can affect your self-esteem (Chambers & Windschitl, 2009). If being good at science is important to you, for example, knowing that someone in your reference group always scores much higher than you on science tests can lower your self-esteem. To protect their self-esteem and make themselves feel better, people sometimes compare themselves with those who are not as good, a strategy called *downward social comparison*. They may also sometimes engage in *upward social comparison,* in which they compare themselves with people who are doing much better than they are (Locke, 2010). At first glance, this might not seem sensible, but upward social comparison can create optimism about improving our own situations (Wheeler & Suls, 2007). We may tell ourselves "If they can do it, so can I!" (Buunk, Peiró, & Griffioen, 2007). Or we might tell ourselves that the superior performer is not really similar enough to be in our reference group or even that the ability in question is not that important to us (Alicke et al., 1997; Dijkstra, Gibbons, & Buunk, 2010).

FOCUS ON RESEARCH

Self-Esteem and the Ultimate Terror

Why is self-esteem so important to so many people? An intriguing answer to this question comes from the *terror management theory* proposed by Jeff Greenberg, Tom Pyszczynski, and Sheldon Solomon. This theory is based on the notion that humans are the only creatures capable of thinking about the future and realizing that we will all eventually die. Terror management theory suggests that humans cope with anxiety, including the terror that thoughts about death might bring, by developing a variety of self-protective psychological strategies. One strategy is to establish and maintain high self-esteem (Greenberg, Solomon, & Arndt, 2008; Pyszczynski et al., 2010).

What was the researchers' question?
In a series of experiments, Greenberg and his colleagues (1992) asked whether high self-esteem serves as a buffer against anxiety—specifically, the anxiety brought on by thoughts about death and pain.

How did the researchers answer the question?
About 150 students at several North American universities participated in these studies, each of which followed a similar format. The first step was to temporarily alter the participants' self-esteem. To do so, the researchers gave the students feedback about a personality or intelligence test they had taken earlier in the semester. Half the participants received positive feedback designed to increase their self-esteem. The other half received feedback that was neutral—it was neither flattering nor unflattering. (Measurements showed that the positive feedback actually did create higher self-esteem than the neutral feedback.) In the next phase of each experiment, the researchers used either a film about

social comparison Using other people as a basis of comparison for evaluating oneself.

reference groups Categories of people with whom individuals compare themselves.

death or the (false) threat of a mild electric shock to provoke some anxiety in half the participants in the positive-feedback group and half the participants in the neutral-feedback group. The amount of anxiety created was measured by the participants' self-reports or by monitoring galvanic skin resistance (GSR), a measure of perspiration in the skin that reflects anxiety-related physiological arousal (Dawson, Schell, & Filion, 2000).

What did the researchers find?

Self-reports and GSR measures revealed that participants in all three experiments were significantly less upset by an anxiety-provoking experience (the death film or the threat of shock) if they had first received esteem-building feedback about their previous test performance. Other studies have reported similar findings (Schmeichel et al., 2009).

What do the results mean?

The researchers concluded that their results support the notion that self-esteem can act as a buffer against anxiety and other negative feelings. This conclusion would help explain why people are so eager to maintain or enhance their self-esteem (Leary, 2010; Loughnan et al., 2011): we don't like to feel anxious, and increased self-esteem reduces most people's anxiety.

What do we still need to know?

These results certainly support terror management theory, but by themselves they're not broad enough to confirm all of its assumptions. For example, the theory also predicts that when people are sensitized to the threat of death, they will seek to protect themselves by suppressing thoughts of death and by doing things that increase the approval and support of others in their society (Baka, Derbis, & Maxfield, 2012; Fransen, Smeesters, & Ferris, 2011; Goncalves Portelinha et al., 2012). Consistent with this prediction, people have been found to make larger contributions to charity after being made more aware of their own mortality (Jonas et al., 2002; Wade-Benzoni et al., 2012). Similarly, dramatic increases in volunteering for charity work occurred after the terrorist attacks of 9/11 (Penner, Brannick, et al., 2005).

But not everyone reacts with prosocial behavior when sensitized to the threat of death. The greatest increase in prosocial behavior following reminders about death appears in people who value prosocial behavior (Joireman & Durell, 2007). In other people, those same reminders may be followed by a *reduction* in humanitarian concerns (Hirschberger, 2009). Social psychologists would like to know more about how people's values and personality characteristics are related to the strategies they adopt when dealing with the threat of death.

Researchers also wonder whether terror management theory offers the best explanation of why high self-esteem reduces anxiety. Perhaps people value self-esteem not because it makes them less afraid of death but simply because it is a flattering indicator (a sort of "sociometer") of their acceptance by others (Leary, 2010). According to sociometer theory, people want to have high self-esteem because it tells them that they are liked and accepted. Perhaps the goal of acceptance evolved because people who were excluded from the protective circle of their group were not likely to survive to reproduce. Compared with terror management theory, sociometer theory is certainly a simpler and more plausible explanation of the desire for high self-esteem, but is it the best explanation? Both theories make similar predictions about the effects of self-esteem on anxiety, so it will take additional research to evaluate their relative merits. ●●●●

Social Identity Theory

LEARN by DOING Take a moment to complete the following sentence: I am a(n) _____. Did you fill the blank with something like "good athlete" or "honor student," or did you insert something like "woman" or "Hispanic American?" The first type of response reflects *personal identity*, something about one's individuality, while the second reflects **social identity**, the beliefs we hold about the groups to which we belong. Our social identity is therefore a part of our self-concept (Abrams & Hogg, 2010; Forsyth & Burnette, 2010).

social identity The beliefs we hold about the groups to which we belong.

Our social identity permits us to feel part of a larger whole (Bryant & Cummins, 2010). We see its importance in the pride people feel when a member of their family graduates from college or when a local team wins a big game (Burris, Branscombe, & Klar, 1997). In wars between national, ethnic, or religious groups, individuals sacrifice and sometimes die for the sake of their group identity. A group identity is also one reason people donate money to those in need, support friends in a crisis, and display other forms of prosocial behavior. Many factors may affect the strength of our group identity. For instance, thinking about the challenges and difficulties our own group has overcome tends to strengthen our identification with that group (Ersner-Hershfield et al., 2010). As we shall see later, however, defining ourselves in terms of a group identity can foster an "us versus them" mentality that sets the stage for prejudice, social discrimination, intergroup conflict, and even terrorism (Abrams & Hogg, 2010).

Social Perception

Do we perceive people and objects in similar ways?

LINKAGES

Do we sometimes perceive people the same way we perceive objects?
(a link to Sensation and Perception)

There's a story about a company president who was having lunch with a man being considered for an executive position. When the man salted his food without first tasting it, the president decided not to hire him. The reason, she explained, was that the company had no room for a person who acted before collecting all relevant information. The candidate lost his chance because of the president's **social perception**, the processes through which people interpret information about others, form impressions of them, and draw conclusions about the reasons for their behavior. In this section, we examine how and why social perception influences our thoughts, feelings, and actions.

The Role of Schemas

The ways in which we perceive people follow many of the same laws that govern how we perceive objects, including the Gestalt principles discussed in the chapter on sensation and perception (Macrae & Quadflieg, 2010). Consider Figure 14.1. Consistent with Gestalt principles, most people would describe it as "a square with a notch in one side," not as eight straight lines (Woodworth & Schlosberg, 1954). The reason is that they interpret new information using the mental representations, or **schemas**, that they already have about squares (Fiske & Taylor, 2008). In other words, they interpret this diagram as a square with a slight modification.

We have schemas about people, too, and they can affect our perceptions. For one thing, schemas influence what we pay attention to and what we ignore. We tend to process information about another person more quickly if it confirms our beliefs about that person's gender or ethnic group, for example, than if it violates those beliefs (Betz & Sekaquaptewa, 2012; Carlston, 2010). Schemas also influence what we remember about others (Carlston, 2010). In one study, if people thought a woman they saw in a videotape was a waitress, they recalled that she had a beer with dinner and owned a TV set. Those who thought she was a librarian remembered that she was wearing glasses and liked classical music (Cohen, 1981). Finally, schemas affect our judgment about the actions of others (Moskowitz, 2005). For instance, people may be less likely to blame a defendant in a rape case if their schema about rape victims includes the myth that their appearance or behavior makes them partially responsible for being attacked (Eyssel & Bohner, 2011).

In other words, our schemas about people influence our perceptions of them through the top-down processing that is discussed in the chapter on sensation and perception. And just as schemas help us read sentences that contain words with missing letters, they also allow us to efficiently "fill in the blanks" about people. Our schemas tell us, for example, that someone wearing a store uniform or name tag is likely to know where merchandise is located, so we usually approach that person for assistance. Accurate schemas help us categorize people quickly and respond appropriately in social situations, but if schemas are incorrect they can create false expectations and errors in judgment about people that can lead to narrow-mindedness and even prejudice.

FIGURE 14.1
A Schema-Plus-Correction
People who see an object like this tend to use a preexisting mental representation (their schema of a square) and then correct or modify it in some way (here, with a notch).

social perception The processes through which people interpret information about others, draw inferences about them, and develop mental representations of them.

schemas Generalizations about categories of objects, places, events, and people.

May I Help You?
Schemas help us quickly categorize people and respond appropriately to them, but schemas can also create narrow-mindedness and, as we shall see later, social prejudice. If this woman does not fulfill your schema—your mental representation—of how carpenters are supposed to look, you might be less likely to ask her advice on your home improvement project. One expert carpenter who manages the hardware department of a large home improvement store told us that most customers walk right past her in order to ask the advice of one of her less-experienced male clerks.

First Impressions

Our schemas about people act as lenses that alter our first impressions of them. Those impressions, in turn, affect both our later perceptions of their behavior and our reactions to it. First impressions are formed quickly, usually change slowly, and typically have a long-lasting influence. No wonder they're so important in the development of social relations (Brehm, Kassin, & Fein, 2005). How do people form impressions of other people? And why are these impressions so resistant to change?

Forming Impressions   Think about your first impression of a close friend. It was probably formed quickly, because existing schemas create a tendency to automatically assume 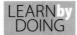 a great deal about a person on the basis of limited information (Funder, 2012; Smith & Quellar, 2001). One study found that people could make judgments about a person's trustworthiness and competence after seeing the person's face for only a tenth of a second (Willis & Todorov, 2006). First impression judgments become much more accurate after as little as one minute of exposure to a new person (Ames et al., 2010), and although our judgments of more attractive people tend to be more accurate—perhaps because we spend more time looking at them (Lorenzo, Biesanz, & Human, 2010; Stirrat & Perrett, 2010)—we are not influenced by appearance alone. We're often swayed, too, by a person's handshake or use of language (Bernieri & Petty, 2011; Douglas & Sutton, 2010). And a distinctive or unusual name, for example, might cause us to draw inferences about the person's religion, ethnicity, food preferences, or temperament (Gebauer, Leary, & Neberich, 2011). Clothing or hairstyle might lead us to make assumptions about political views or taste in music (Gillath et al., 2012). These inferences and assumptions may or may not be accurate. How many turned out to be true in your friend's case?

One schema has a particularly strong influence on first impressions: We tend to assume that the people we meet have attitudes and values similar to our own (Srivastava, Guglielmo, & Beer, 2010). So all else being equal, we're inclined to like other people. However, even a small amount of negative information can change our minds. Why? The main reason is that most of us don't expect other people to act negatively toward us. When unexpected negative behaviors do occur, they capture our attention and lead us to believe that these behaviors reflect something negative about the other person (Taylor, Peplau, & Sears, 2006). As a result, negative information attracts more attention and carries more weight than positive information in shaping first impressions (Lount et al., 2008).

Lasting Impressions   Does your friend seem the same to you today as when you first met? First impressions can change, but the process is usually slow. One reason is that negative first impressions may cause us to avoid certain people, thus reducing our exposure to new information that might change our view of them (Denrell, 2005). Further, most people want to keep their social environment simple and easy to understand (Kassin, Markus, & Fein, 2011). We cling to our beliefs about the world, often using our schemas to preserve a reality that fits our expectations. Holding on to existing impressions appears to be part of this effort. If your friend recently violated your expectations by being impatient, your view of her probably did not change much,

Noticeable features or actions help shape our impressions of others. Those impressions may or may not be correct (Biesanz et al., 2011; Human & Biesanz, 2012; Vartanian et al., 2012).

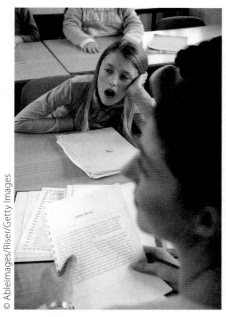

© Ableimages/Riser/Getty Images

Self-Fulfilling Prophecies in the Classroom

If teachers inadvertently spend less time helping children who at first seem "dull," those children may not learn as much, thus fulfilling the teachers' expectations. If this girl has not impressed her teacher as being very bright, how likely do you think it is that she will be called on during class?

self-fulfilling prophecy A process in which an initial impression causes us to bring out behavior in another that confirms the impression.

attribution The process of explaining the causes of people's behavior, including our own.

fundamental attribution error A bias toward attributing the behavior of others to internal factors.

if at all. In fact, you may have preserved your impression of her by thinking something like "She's not herself today." In other words, impressions change slowly because the meaning we give to new information about people is shaped by what we already know or believe about them (Kenrick, Neuberg, & Cialdini, 2010).

Self-Fulfilling Prophecies   Another reason first impressions tend to be stable is that we often do things that cause others to confirm our impressions (Madon et al., 2011). If teachers expect particular students to do poorly in mathematics, those students may sense this expectation, exert less effort, and perform below their ability level in that teacher's class, and perhaps in later years (de Boer, Bosker, & van der Werf, 2010; Michael, Garry, & Kirsch, 2012). And if mothers expect their young children to abuse alcohol eventually, those children may be more likely to do so than the children of mothers who didn't convey that expectation (Madon et al., 2006). When, without our awareness, schemas cause us to subtly lead people to behave in line with our expectations, a **self-fulfilling prophecy** is at work.

Self-fulfilling prophecies also help maintain our judgments about groups. If you assume that people in a certain social group are snobby, you might be defensive or even hostile when you encounter them. If they react to your behavior with hostility and anger, their behavior would fulfill your prophecy and strengthen the impression that created it (Kenrick, Neuberg, & Cialdini, 2010).

Explaining Behavior: Attribution

So far, we have examined how people form impressions about other people's characteristics. But our perceptions of others also include our explanations of their behavior. People tend to form ideas about why people (including themselves) behave as they do and about what behavior to expect in the future (Brehm, Kassin, & Fein, 2005; Shafto, Goodman, & Frank, 2012). Psychologists use the term **attribution** to describe the process we go through to explain the causes of behavior (including our own).

Suppose a classmate borrows your lecture notes but fails to return them. You could attribute this behavior to many causes, from an emergency situation to selfishness. Which of these explanations you choose is important, because it will help you *understand* your classmate's behavior, *predict* what will happen if this person asks to borrow something in the future, and decide how to *control* the situation should it arise again. Similarly, whether a person attributes a partner's nagging to temporary stress or to loss of affection can influence whether that person will work on the relationship or end it.

People usually attribute behavior in a particular situation to either internal causes (characteristics of the person) or external causes (characteristics of the situation). For example, if you thought your classmate's failure to return your notes was due mainly to lack of consideration or laziness, you would be making an *internal attribution*. If you thought that the oversight was due mainly to preoccupation with a family crisis, you would be making an *external attribution*. Similarly, if you failed an exam, you could explain it by concluding that you're not very smart (internal attribution) or that your work schedule left you too little time to study (external attribution). The attribution that you make might determine how much you study for the next exam or even whether you decide to stay in school.

Errors in Attribution

Most people are usually logical in their attempts to explain behavior (Kenrick, Neuberg, & Cialdini, 2010). However, they are also prone to *attributional errors* that can distort their view of behavior (Baumeister & Bushman, 2011).

The Fundamental Attribution Error   North American psychologists have paid special attention to the **fundamental attribution error**, a tendency to over-attribute the behavior of others to internal factors (Fiske & Taylor, 2008). Imagine that you receive an e-mail that contains lots of errors in spelling and grammar. If you are like most people,

© Zute Lightfoot/Alamy

Why Are They Helping?
Attributional biases are more common in some cultures than in others. In one study, students in an individualist culture were more likely than those in a collectivist culture to explain acts of helping as being due to internal causes such as kindness or the enjoyment of helping (Miller & Bersoff, 1994).

you'll probably attribute these errors to an internal cause and infer that the writer isn't very smart, or at least not very careful (Vignovic & Thompson, 2010). In doing so, however, you might be ignoring possible external factors, such as the possibility that the writer didn't have time to proofread the message or is not a native English speaker.

The *ultimate attribution error* is a related attributional bias. Here, we attribute the positive actions of people from a different ethnic or social group to external causes, such as easy opportunities, whereas we attribute their negative actions to internal causes, such as dishonesty (Pettigrew, 1979). The ultimate attribution error also causes people to see good deeds done by those in their own group as due to kindness or other internal factors and bad deeds as stemming from external causes, such as unemployment or a bad economy. In this way, the ultimate attribution error helps create and maintain people's negative views of other groups and positive views of their own group (Fiske, 1998).

These attributional biases may not be universal (Miyamoto & Kitayama, 2002; Norenzayan & Lee, 2010). For example, research suggests that the fundamental attribution error and the ultimate attribution error are less likely to appear among people in collectivist cultures such as India, China, Japan, and Korea than among people in the individualist cultures of North America and Europe (Heine, 2010). And even within individualist cultures, some people hold a stronger individualist orientation than others. So some people in these cultures are more likely than others to make attribution errors (Miller, 2001; Vandello & Cohen, 1999).

Other Attributional Errors   People are less likely to make internal attributions when explaining their own behavior. In fact, people tend to show the **actor-observer effect**: that is, we often attribute other people's behavior to internal causes but attribute our own behavior to external factors, especially when our behavior is inappropriate or inadequate (Baumeister, 1998). For example, when Australian students were asked why they sometimes drive too fast, they focused on circumstances, such as being late, but saw other people's dangerous driving as a sign of aggressiveness or immaturity (Harré, Brandt, & Houkamau, 2004). Similarly, when you're driving too slowly, the reason is that you are looking for an address, not that you are a big loser like that jerk who crawled along in front of you yesterday.

The actor-observer effect occurs mainly because people have different kinds of information about their own behavior and the behavior of others. When *you* are in a situation—giving a speech, perhaps—the information most available to you is likely to be external and situational, such as the temperature of the room and the size of the audience. You also have a lot of information about other external factors, such as the amount of time you had to prepare your talk or the upsetting conversation you had this morning. If your speech is disorganized and boring, you can easily attribute it to one or all of these external causes. But when you observe someone else, the most obvious information in the situation is *that person*. You don't know what happened to the person last night or this morning, so you're likely to attribute the quality of the performance to stable, internal characteristics (Moskowitz, 2005).

Of course, people don't always attribute their own behavior to external forces. In fact, whether they do so often depends on whether the outcome is positive or negative. In one study, when people were asked to explain their good and bad online shopping experiences, they tended to take personal credit for positive outcomes (such as finding bargains) but blamed the computer for problems such as receiving the wrong merchandise (Moon, 2003). In other words, these people showed a **self-serving bias**, the tendency to take personal credit for success but to blame external causes for failure (Brice & Gunia, 2010). This bias has been found in almost all cultures, but as with the fundamental attribution error, it is usually more pronounced among people from

actor-observer effect The tendency to attribute other people's behavior to internal causes while attributing one's own behavior to external causes.

self-serving bias The tendency to attribute one's successes to internal characteristics while blaming one's failures on external causes.

individualistic Western cultures than among those from collectivist Eastern cultures (Mezulis et al., 2004).

The self-serving bias occurs, in part, because people are motivated to maintain their self-esteem, and ignoring negative information about themselves is one way to do so. If you just failed an exam, it's painful to admit that the exam was fair. Like the other attributional biases we have discussed, self-serving bias helps people think about their failures and shortcomings in ways that protect their self-esteem (Shepperd, Malone, & Sweeny, 2008). These self-protective cognitive biases can help us temporarily escape unpleasant thoughts and feelings, but they may also create a distorted view of reality that can lead to other problems. One such problem is *unrealistic optimism*, the tendency to believe that good things (such as financial success or having a gifted child) are likely to happen to you but that bad things (such as accidents or illness) are not (Klein et al., 2010). Unrealistic optimism tends to persist even when there is strong evidence against it, and can lead to potentially harmful behaviors. For example, people who are unrealistically optimistic about their health may not bother to exercise, may ignore information about how to prevent heart disease, or may underestimate the risks of engaging in unsafe sex (Dillard, McCaul, & Klein, 2006; Radcliffe & Klein, 2002; Taylor et al., 1992). ("In Review: Some Biases in Social Perception" summarizes the common cognitive biases discussed here.)

Some Biases in Social Perception IN REVIEW

Bias	Description
Importance of first impression	Ambiguous information is interpreted in line with a first impression and the initial schema is recalled better and more vividly than any later correction to it. Actions based on this impression may bring out behavior that confirms it.
Fundamental attribution error	The tendency to over-attribute the behavior of others to internal factors.
Actor-observer bias	The tendency to attribute our own behavior to external causes and to attribute the behavior of others to internal factors.
Self-serving bias	The tendency to attribute one's successes to internal factors and one's failures to external factors.
Unrealistic optimism	The tendency to believe that good things will happen to us but that bad things will not.

IN REVIEW QUESTIONS

1. The fundamental attribution error appears to be somewhat less likely to occur among people in ___ cultures.

2. First impressions form ___, but change ___.

3. If you believed that immigrants' successes are due to government help but that their failures are due to laziness, you would be committing the ___ error.

Attitudes

Do attitudes always determine behavior?

Our views about health, safety, or any other topic reflect our attitudes. An **attitude** is our tendency to think, feel, or act in positive or negative ways about the world around us. We can hold attitudes about almost anything, but they are usually focused on other people, such as a spouse, on groups of people, such as the elderly, on social or political issues such as abortion or term limits, or on events and activities such as art exhibitions or sports (Fabrigar & Wegener, 2010). Attitudes help guide how we react to other people, which causes and politicians we support, which products we choose to buy, and countless other daily decisions.

attitude A tendency toward a particular cognitive, emotional, or behavioral reaction to objects in one's environment.

© Muellek Josef/Shutterstock

A Reminder about Poverty

The more accessible an attitude is, the more likely it is to predict behavior (Fabrigar & Wegner, 2010). Photographs such as this one are used by fund-raising organizations to remind us of the kind thoughts and charitable feelings we have toward needy people and other worthy causes. As a result, we may be more likely to behave in accordance with the cognitive and affective components of our attitudes and make a donation to these causes. Browse through some newspapers, magazines, and popular websites and calculate the percentage of such photos you find in ads for charitable organizations.

LEARN by DOING

The Structure of Attitudes

Attitudes have three components (Fabrigar, MacDonald, & Wegener, 2005). The *cognitive* component is our set of beliefs about the attitude object. The emotional, or *affective,* component includes our feelings about the object. And the *behavioral* component is the way we act toward the object. If these three components were always in harmony, we would be able to predict people's behavior toward the homeless, for example, on the basis of the thoughts or feelings they express, and vice versa.

The three components may not be in harmony, though (Fabrigar & Wegener, 2010). There are people who feel sympathy for the homeless and believe that they deserve attention, but never actually do anything to help them. What factors determine whether people's behavior will be consistent with the cognitive and affective components of their attitudes? First, behavior is more likely to be consistent with attitude when people feel the attitude is important and relevant to their lives (Kenrick, Neuberg, & Cialdini, 2007; Skitka, Bauman, & Sargis, 2005). Second, attitude-behavior consistency is more likely when the behavioral component of the attitude is in line with a *subjective norm,* our view of how the important people in our lives want us to act. If there's a conflict between what we want to do and what a subjective norm tells us we should do, we may end up behaving in ways that are inconsistent with our attitudes (Ajzen & Gilbert-Cote, 2008). For example, someone who believes in protecting the rights of gay men and lesbians might not campaign for those rights because doing so would upset valued family members or co-workers. Third, attitude-consistent behavior is more likely when people have *perceived control,* a belief that they can actually perform the behavior (Fishbein & Ajzen, 2010). The cognitive and emotional components of your attitude toward the homeless might be positive, but if you don't believe you can do anything to help them, you are not likely to even try. Fourth, *direct experience* with the attitude object increases the likelihood of attitude-consistent behavior (Glasman & Albarracín, 2006). So you might be more likely to actively support and perhaps even participate in efforts to help the homeless if you know a homeless person on your campus than if you have only read about their problems.

Forming Attitudes

People's attitudes about objects begin to appear in early childhood and continue to emerge throughout life. How do these attitudes form? Genetics may influence some attitudes to an extent (Albarricín & Vargas, 2010), but social learning—what children learn from their parents and others—appears to play the major role in attitude formation. Children learn not only the names of objects but also what they should believe and feel about them and how they should act toward them. For example, a parent may teach a child not only that snakes are reptiles but also that they should be feared and avoided. So as children learn concepts such as "reptile" or "work," they learn attitudes about those concepts, too (Bohner & Schwarz, 2001).

Classical and operant conditioning can also shape attitudes (Baron, Byrne, & Branscombe, 2006). Advertisers pair up enjoyable music or sexy images with the products they want to sell (Pratkanis & Aronson, 2001; Walther & Langer, 2008), and parents, teachers, and peers reward children for stating particular views. The *mere-exposure effect* is influential as well. All else being equal, more frequent exposure to an object produces a more positive attitude toward it (Winkielman & Cacioppo, 2004). In one study, for example, after European American college students were repeatedly exposed to pictures of Asians and Blacks, their liking for new pictures of Asians and Blacks increased (Zebrowitz, White, & Wieneke, 2008). This mere-exposure effect helps explain why commercials and political ads are aired over and over and why some rock bands won't include new songs in a live concert until their fans have repeatedly heard and come to like the recorded versions.

Changing Attitudes

The nearly $170 billion a year spent on advertising in the United States alone provides just one example of how people constantly try to change our attitudes. There are many others,

Central route

Persuasive message → High elaboration → Careful processing of information → Degree of attitude change depends on quality of arguments

Peripheral route

Persuasive message → Low elaboration → Careful processing does not occur → Attitude change depends on presence of persuasion cues

FIGURE 14.2

The Elaboration Likelihood Model of Attitude Change

The central route to attitude change involves carefully processing and evaluating a message's content (high elaboration). The peripheral route involves little processing and evaluation of message content (low elaboration) and relies instead on persuasion cues such as the attractiveness of the person making the argument (Cacioppo, Petty, & Crites, 1993).

including the persuasive messages of groups concerned with abortion or gun control or recycling—and don't forget about friends and family members who want you to think the way they do.

Two Routes to Attitude Change Whether a persuasive message succeeds in changing attitudes depends mainly on three factors: (1) the person communicating the message; (2) the content of the message; and (3) the person receiving it (Albarracín & Vargas, 2010). The **elaboration likelihood model** of attitude change provides a framework for understanding when and how these factors affect attitude change (Petty & Briñol, 2010). As shown in Figure 14.2, the model is based on the idea that persuasive messages can change people's attitudes through one of two main routes.

The first is called the *peripheral route* because when it is activated, we devote little attention to the central content of the persuasive message. We tend to be affected instead by peripheral, or surrounding, persuasion cues, such as the confidence, attractiveness, or other characteristics of the person who delivers the message. These persuasion cues influence attitude change even though they may have nothing to do with the logic or accuracy of the message itself. Commercials in which movie stars or other attractive non-experts endorse pain relievers or denture cleaners encourage the peripheral route to attitude change.

By contrast, when the *central route* is activated, the core content of the message becomes more important than the communicator's characteristics in determining attitude change. A person following the central route uses logical steps—such as those outlined in the Thinking Critically sections of this book—to analyze the content of the persuasive message, including the validity of its claims, whether it leaves out important information, alternative interpretations of evidence, and so on.

What determines which route people will follow? One factor is a person's *need for cognition*, the desire to think things through (Douglas, Sutton, & Stathi, 2010). People with a strong need for cognition are more likely than others to follow a central route to attitude change. Personal involvement with a message's content is another important factor. People are more likely to activate the central route when thinking about topics that are personally relevant (Bohner, Erb, & Siebler, 2008). Suppose, for example, that you hear someone arguing for the cancellation of all student loans in Chile. This message might persuade you through the peripheral route if it comes from someone who looks attractive and sounds intelligent. However, if the message proposes eliminating student loans at your own school, you're more likely to follow the central route. You might still be persuaded, but only if the logic of the message is clear and convincing. This is why celebrity endorsements tend to be more effective when the products being advertised are relatively unimportant to the audience.

Persuasive messages are not the only means of changing attitudes. Another approach is to get people to act in ways that are inconsistent with their attitudes in the hope that they will adjust those attitudes to match their behavior. Often, such adjustments do occur, and Leon Festinger proposed a theory to explain why.

Cognitive Dissonance Theory According to his **cognitive dissonance theory**, people want their thoughts, beliefs, and attitudes to be in harmony with one another

elaboration likelihood model
A model of attitude change suggesting that people can change their attitudes through a central route (by considering an argument's content) or through a peripheral route (by relying on irrelevant persuasion cues).

cognitive dissonance theory
A theory that attitude change is driven by efforts to reduce tension caused by inconsistencies between attitudes and behaviors.

High justification (low dissonance)

Low justification (high dissonance)

FIGURE 14.3

Cognitive Dissonance and Attitude Change

According to cognitive dissonance theory, the $20 that people were given to say that a boring task was enjoyable provided them with a clear justification for lying. Having been paid to lie, they should experience little dissonance between what they said and what they felt about the task. And in fact their attitude toward the task was not positive. However, people who received only $1 had little justification to lie so they reduced their dissonance mainly by displaying a more positive attitude toward the task.

Source: Festinger & Carlsmith (1959).

and with their behavior (Festinger, 1957). People experiencing inconsistency, or *dissonance*, among these elements, become anxious and are motivated to make them more consistent (Festinger, 1957; Harmon-Jones, 2010; Olson & Stone, 2005). For example, someone who believes that "smoking is dangerous" but who must also admit that "I smoke" would be motivated to reduce the resulting dissonance. Because it is often difficult to change well-established behavior, people usually reduce cognitive dissonance by changing attitudes that are inconsistent with the behavior. So rather than quit smoking, the smoker might decide that smoking is not so dangerous after all.

In one of the first studies of cognitive dissonance, Festinger and his colleague Merrill Carlsmith asked people to turn pegs in a pegboard, a very dull task (Festinger & Carlsmith, 1959). Later, some of these people were asked to persuade a person who was waiting to participate in the study that the task was "exciting and fun." Some were told that they would be paid $1 to tell this lie. Others were promised $20. After they had talked to the waiting person, their attitudes toward the dull task were measured. Figure 14.3 shows and explains the surprising results. The people who were paid just $1 to lie liked the dull task more than those who were paid $20 (Festinger & Carlsmith, 1959).

Hundreds of other experiments have also found that when people publicly engage in behaviors that are inconsistent with their privately held attitudes, they're likely to change their attitudes to be consistent with their behavior (Cooper, Mirabile, & Scher, 2005). Attitude-behavior inconsistency is likely to change attitudes when (1) the inconsistency causes some distress or discomfort in a person; and (2) changing attitudes will reduce that discomfort. But why should attitude-behavior inconsistency cause discomfort in the first place? There is considerable debate among attitude researchers about this question (Harmon-Jones, Amodio, & Harmon-Jones, 2009). Currently, the most popular of several possible answers is that discomfort results when people's positive self-concept (e.g., "I am honest") is threatened by recognizing that they have done something inconsistent with that self-concept. For example, if they have encouraged another person to do something that they themselves didn't believe in or that they themselves wouldn't do, this inconsistency makes most people feel uncomfortable. So they change their attitudes to reduce or eliminate the discomfort (Stone & Fernandez, 2008). In other words, if people can persuade themselves that they really believe in what they've said or done, the inconsistency disappears, their positive self-concept is restored, and they can feel good about themselves again. One study suggests that people can experience the same result, at least for a little while, just by washing their hands (Lee & Schwarz, 2010). Perhaps this cleansing represents a fresh start and creates a greater sense of moral superiority (Zhong, Strejcek, & Sivanathan, 2010).

The circumstances that lead to cognitive dissonance may be different in the individualist cultures of Europe and North America than in collectivist cultures such as those in Japan and China. In individualist cultures, dissonance typically arises from behaving in a manner inconsistent with one's own beliefs because this behavior causes self-doubt. But in collectivist cultures, dissonance typically arises when such behavior causes people to worry about what others think of them (Kitayama et al., 2004). Cultural values also help shape dissonance-reducing strategies. For example, people from individualistic cultures can reduce the unpleasant feelings that accompany dissonance by affirming their value as unique individuals, whereas people from collectivist cultures can reduce the same kind of feelings by affirming the value of the groups to which they belong (Hoshino-Browne et al., 2005). ("In Review: Forming and Changing Attitudes" summarizes some of the main processes through which attitudes are formed and changed.)

Forming and Changing Attitudes   IN REVIEW

Type of Influence	Description
Social learning and conditioning	Attitudes are usually formed through observing how others behave and speak about an attitude object as well as through classical and operant conditioning.
Elaboration likelihood model	People change attitudes through either a central or peripheral route, depending on factors such as personal involvement.
Cognitive dissonance	Holding inconsistent cognitions can motivate attitude change.

IN REVIEW QUESTIONS

1. According to the elaboration likelihood model, people are more likely to pay close attention to the content and logic of a persuasive message if the ___ route to attitude change has been activated.

2. Holding attitudes that are similar to those of your friends illustrates the importance of ___ in attitude formation.

3. According to cognitive dissonance theory, we tend to reduce conflict between attitudes and behaviors by changing our ___.

Prejudice and Stereotypes

How does prejudice develop?

All of the principles behind impression formation, attribution, and attitudes come together in prejudice and stereotypes. **Stereotypes** are the perceptions, beliefs, and expectations a person has about members of a particular group. They are schemas about entire groups of people (Dovidio & Gaertner, 2010). Usually, they involve the false assumption that all members of a group share the same characteristics. The characteristics that make up the stereotype can be positive, but more often they are negative. The most prevalent and powerful stereotypes focus on observable personal attributes, particularly ethnicity, gender, and age (Operario & Fiske, 2001).

LINKAGES

Can subconscious processes alter our reaction to people?
(a link to Consciousness)

The stereotypes people hold can be so ingrained that their effects on behavior can be automatic and unconscious (Dovidio et al., 2009; Stepanikova, Triplett, & Simpson, 2011). In one study, for example, European American and African American participants played a video game in which white or black men suddenly appeared on a screen holding an object that might be a weapon (Correll et al., 2002; see Figure 14.4). The participants had to immediately "shoot" armed men but not unarmed ones. Under this time pressure, participants' errors were not random. If they "shot" an unarmed man, he was more likely to be black; when they failed to "shoot" an armed man, he was more likely to be white. These differences appeared in both European American and African American participants, but were most pronounced among those who held the strongest cultural stereotypes about blacks.

stereotypes False assumptions that all members of some group share the same characteristics.

prejudice A positive or negative attitude toward people in certain groups.

social discrimination Differential treatment of people in certain groups; the behavioral component of prejudice.

Stereotyping often leads to **prejudice,** which is a positive or negative attitude toward an individual based simply on that individual's membership in some group (Maio et al., 2010). The word *prejudice* means "prejudgment." Many theorists believe that prejudice, like other attitudes, has cognitive, affective, and behavioral components. The cognitive component of prejudice is stereotyped thinking. The affective component includes people's hatred, admiration, anger, and other feelings about stereotyped groups. The behavioral component of prejudice involves **social discrimination**, which is differing treatment of individuals who belong to different groups. Prejudiced thinking can be quite complex. For instance, most people are prejudiced in favor of attractive people in general, but in a competitive situation they tend to be prejudiced against the best-looking individuals of the same sex (Agthe, Spörrle, & Maner, 2010, 2011).

FIGURE 14.4

The Impact of Stereotypes on Behavior

When these men suddenly appeared on a video screen, participants were supposed to "shoot" them, but only if they appeared to be armed (Correll et al., 2002). Stereotypes about whether white men or black men are more likely to be armed significantly affected the errors made by participants in firing their video game "weapons." Similar results appeared in a sample of police officers, although they were not as quick as civilians were to "shoot" an unarmed black man (Correll et al. 2007). Cover these photos with a pair of index cards, then ask a few friends to watch as you show each photo, one at a time, for just an instant, before covering it again. Then ask your friends to say whether either man appeared to be armed. Was one individual more often seen as armed? If so, which one?

LEARN by **DOING**

Theories of Prejudice and Stereotyping

Prejudice and stereotyping may occur for several reasons. Let's consider three explanatory theories, each of which has been supported by research and accounts for many instances of stereotyping and prejudice.

Motivational Theories   Prejudice meets certain needs and increases the sense of security for some people. This idea was first proposed by Theodor W. Adorno and his associates more than 60 years ago (Adorno et al., 1950), and it is still seen as a major cause of prejudice (Altemeyer & Hunsberger, 2005; Duckitt & Sibley, 2010; Hehman et al., 2012; Huang et al., 2011). Researchers suggest that prejudice is especially likely among people who display a personality trait called *authoritarianism*. Authoritarianism is composed of three main elements: (1) acceptance of conventional or traditional values; (2) willingness to unquestioningly follow the orders of authority figures; and (3) an inclination to act aggressively toward individuals or groups identified by authority figures as threats to the person's values or well-being. In fact, people with an authoritarian orientation tend to view the world as a threatening place (Cohrs & Ibler, 2009). One way to protect themselves from the threats they perceive all around them is to strongly identify with people like themselves—their *ingroup*—and to reject, dislike, and maybe even punish people who are members of *outgroups,* groups that are different from their own (Thomsen, Green, & Sidanius, 2008). Looking down on and discriminating against members of these outgroups—gay men and lesbians, African Americans, or Muslims, for example—may help authoritarian people feel safer and better about themselves (Duckitt, 2006).

Another motivational explanation of prejudice involves the concept of social identity discussed earlier. Recall that whether or not they display authoritarianism, most people are motivated to identify with their ingroup and tend to see it as better than other groups (Abrams & Hogg, 2010). As a result, members of an ingroup often see all members of outgroups as less attractive and less socially acceptable than members of the ingroup and may thus treat them badly (Jackson, 2002). In other words, prejudice may result when people's motivation to enhance their own self-esteem causes them to disrespect other people.

Cognitive Theories   Stereotyping and prejudice may also result from the thought processes that people use in dealing with the world. There are so many other people, so many situations in which we meet them, and so many behaviors that others might display that we cannot possibly attend to and remember them all. Therefore, when people encounter other people, especially for the first time, they must use schemas and other cognitive shortcuts to organize and make sense of their social world (Buck & Plant, 2011; Brescoll, Dawson, & Uhlmann, 2010; Carlston, 2010). Often these cognitive processes provide accurate and useful summaries of what to expect from other people, but sometimes they lead to inaccurate stereotypes (Lewis et al., 2012).

For example, one effective way to deal with social complexity is grouping people into *social categories*. Rather than remembering every detail about everyone we have ever encountered, we tend to put other people into categories such as doctor, senior citizen, Republican, student, Italian, and the like (Gaertner, Dovidio, & Houlette, 2010). To further simplify perception of these categories, we tend to see group members as quite similar to one another. In fact, members of one ethnic group may find it harder to distinguish among specific faces in other ethnic groups than in their own (Anthony, Cooper, & Mullen, 1992; Michel et al., 2006). People also tend to assume that all members of a different group hold the same beliefs and values and that those beliefs and values differ from those of their own group (Gaertner, Dovdio, & Houlette, 2010; Waytz & Young, 2011). And because particularly noticeable stimuli tend to draw a lot of attention, rude behavior by even a few members of an easily identified ethnic group may lead people to see an *illusory correlation* between rudeness and ethnicity (Meiser & Hewstone, 2006). As a result, they may incorrectly believe that all members of that group are rude. Finally, many people—especially those at lower levels of cognitive ability—seem to have a need for *cognitive closure*, meaning that they prefer to decide quickly and once and for all what they

© Jessica Rinaldi/Reuters/Landov

Schemas and Stereotypes

The use of schemas to assign certain people to certain categories can be helpful when deciding who is a customer and who is a store employee, but it can also lead to inaccurate stereotypes. After 9/11, many people began to think of all Muslims as potential terrorists and to discriminate against them. This false assumption and the problems it has created for Muslims in the United States was one of the many side effects of the terrorist attacks.

think about everyone in a particular group (Hodson & Busseri, 2012; Roets & Hiel, 2011). Satisfying this need saves them the time and effort it would take to consider individuals as individuals (Rubin, Paolini, & Crisp, 2010).

Learning Theories   Like other attitudes, prejudice can be learned. Some prejudice is learned as a result of personal conflicts with members of particular groups, but people also develop negative attitudes toward groups with whom they have had little or no contact. Learning theories suggest that children can pick up prejudices just by watching and listening to parents, peers, and others (Castelli, Zogmaister, & Tomelleri, 2009; Rutland, Killen, & Abrams, 2010). Evolutionary forces may even have created a kind of biopreparedness (described in the learning chapter) that makes us especially likely to affiliate with our own group and to learn to fear people who are strangers or who look different from us (Kelly et al., 2007; Lewis & Bates, 2010; Olson et al., 2001). The media also portray certain groups in ways that teach stereotypes and prejudice (Brehm, Kassin, & Fein, 2005; Jost & Hamilton, 2005). For example, one study found that European American characters in popular television shows tend to behave more negatively toward African American characters than toward other European Americans. This study also found that watching these shows can elevate viewers' prejudice against African Americans in general (Weisbuch, Pauker, & Ambady, 2009). No wonder so many young children already know about the supposed negative characteristics of certain groups long before they ever meet members of those groups (Baron & Banaji, 2006; Degner & Wentura, 2010).

Reducing Prejudice

The cognitive and learning theories of prejudice and stereotyping suggest that members of one group are often ignorant of, or misinformed about, the characteristics of people in other groups (Dovidio, Gaertner, & Kawakami, 2010). However, simply providing accurate information to prejudiced people and encouraging them to be less prejudiced can actually increase prejudice (Legault, Gutsell, & Inzlicht, 2011). Encouraging people to ignore ethnic differences does not seem to reduce prejudiced attitudes, either (Apfelbaum et al., 2010).

The **contact hypothesis** provides a more promising approach. It states that stereotypes and prejudice toward a group will decrease as contact with that group increases (Greenwald, 2010). Before 1954, most black and white schoolchildren in the United States knew very little about one another because they went to separate schools. Then the Supreme Court declared that segregated public schools should be prohibited. In doing so, the court created a real-life test of the contact hypothesis.

Did the desegregation of U.S. schools confirm that hypothesis? In a few schools, integration was followed by a decrease in prejudice, but in many places, either no change occurred or prejudice actually increased (Pettigrew et al., 2011). However, these results did not necessarily disprove the contact hypothesis. In-depth studies of schools with successful desegregation suggested that contact alone was not enough. Integration usually reduced prejudice only when certain social conditions were created (Pettigrew et al., 2011). First, members of the two groups had to be of roughly equal social and economic status. Second, school authorities had to promote cooperation and interdependence between ethnic groups by having members of the two groups work together on projects that required reliance on one another to achieve success. Third, the contact between group members had to occur on a one-to-one basis. It was only when *individuals* got to know each other that the errors contained in stereotypes became apparent. Finally, the members of each group had to be seen as typical and not unusual in any significant way. When these four conditions were met, the children's attitudes toward one another became more positive (Deeb et al., 2011).

A teaching strategy called the *jigsaw technique* helps create these conditions (Aronson & Patnoe, 2011). The strategy calls for children from several ethnic groups to work in teams to complete a task, such as writing a report about a famous person in

contact hypothesis The idea that stereotypes and prejudice toward a group will diminish as contact with the group increases.

Fighting Ethnic Prejudice
Negative attitudes about members of
ethnic groups are often based on negative
personal experiences or on the negative
experiences and attitudes people hear
about from others. Cooperative contact
between equals can help promote mutual
respect and reduce ethnic prejudice
(Fischer, 2011; Hodson, 2011; Vezzali &
Giovannini, 2011).

history. Each child learns a separate piece of information about this person, such as place of birth or greatest achievement, then provides this information to the team (Aronson, 1990). Studies show that children from various ethnic groups who take part in the jigsaw technique and other cooperative learning experiences display substantial reductions in prejudice while also facilitating learning (Aronson &Patnoe, 2011; Doymus, Karacop, & Simsel, 2010). The success reported in these studies has greatly increased the popularity of cooperative learning exercises in U.S. classrooms. Such exercises may not eliminate all aspects of ethnic prejudice in children, but they seem to be a step in the right direction.

Can friendly, cooperative, interdependent contact reduce the more entrenched forms of prejudice seen in adults? It may (Hodson, 2011). One study found that the prejudicial attitudes of first-year college students weakened more if their roommate was from a different ethnic group rather than from the students' own ethnic group (Shook & Fazio, 2008). Another showed that when equal-status adults from different ethnic groups work jointly toward a common goal, bias and distrust can be reduced, particularly among those in ethnic majority groups (Tropp & Pettigrew, 2005). This is especially true if they come to see themselves as members of the same group rather than as belonging to opposing groups (Gaertner, Dovidio, & Houlette, 2010). The challenge to be met in creating such cooperative experiences in the real world is that the participants must be of equal status, a challenge made more difficult in many countries by the status differences that still exist between ethnic groups (Kenworthy et al., 2006).

In the final analysis, contact can provide only part of the solution to the problems of stereotyping, prejudice, and social discrimination. To reduce ethnic prejudice, we must develop additional techniques to address the social cognitions and perceptions that lie at the core of bigotry and hatred toward people who are different from ourselves (Amodio & Devine, 2009; Bigler & Liben, 2007). Altering these mental processes will be difficult because, as we saw earlier, they can operate both consciously and unconsciously, causing even those who do not see themselves as prejudiced to discriminate against individuals who are different (Banaji, Lemm, & Carpenter, 2001; Uleman, Blader, & Todorov, 2005). However, recent research suggests that it may be possible to change even unconscious forms of stereotyping and prejudice (Gervais & Norenzayan, 2012; Kawakami, Dovidio, & van Kamp, 2005; Luguri, Napier, & Dovidio, 2012; Plaks et al., 2012; Todd, Bodenhausen, & Galinsky, 2011).

Proximity and Liking
Research on environmental factors in
attraction suggests that, barring bad first
impressions, the more often we make
contact with someone—as neighbors,
classmates, or co-workers, for example—the
more we tend to like that person (Preciado
et al., 2012). Does this principle apply in your
life? To find out, think about how and where
you met each of your closest friends. If you
can think of cases in which proximity
did not lead to liking, what
do you think interfered with
the formation of friendship?

LEARN**by**
DOING

Interpersonal Attraction

What factors affect who likes whom?

Research on prejudice suggests some of the reasons why people may come to dislike or even hate other people. An equally fascinating aspect of social cognition is why people like or love other people. Folklore tells us that "opposites attract" but also that "birds of a feather flock together." Each statement is partly true, but neither is entirely accurate in all cases. We begin our coverage of interpersonal attraction by discussing the factors that draw people toward one another. We then examine how liking sometimes develops into more intimate relationships.

Keys to Attraction

Whether you like someone or not depends partly on situational factors and partly on personal characteristics.

The Environment   One of the most important determinants of attraction is simple physical proximity (Clark & Lemay, 2010). As long as you do not initially dislike a person, your liking for that person will increase with additional contact (Brehm, Kassin, & Fein, 2005). This proximity phenomenon—another example of the *mere-exposure effect* mentioned earlier—helps account for why next-door neighbors are usually more likely to become friends than people who live farther from one another. Chances

"HE'S PERFECT. WE HAVE LOADS OF THE SAME APPS."

Similarity can take many forms. How many apps do you and your closest friends have in common?

LEARN **by** DOING

are, most of your friends are people you met as neighbors, co-workers, or classmates (Reis et al., 2011).

The circumstances under which people first meet also influence attraction. You are much more likely to be attracted to a stranger if you meet in comfortable, rather than uncomfortable, physical conditions (IJzerman & Semin, 2009). Similarly, if you receive a reward in the presence of a stranger, the chances are greater that you will like that stranger, even if the stranger is not the one giving the reward (Clark & Pataki, 1995). In one study, for example, an experimenter judged one person's creativity while another person watched. Compared with those who received a negative evaluation, participants who were evaluated positively tended to like the observer more (Griffitt & Guay, 1969). At least among strangers, then, liking can occur through associating someone with something pleasant.

Similarity   People also tend to like those they perceive as similar to themselves on variables such as appearance, age, religion, smoking or drinking habits, being a "morning" or "evening" person, or their use of language (Clark & Lemay, 2010; Ireland et al., 2011; MacKinnon, Jordan, & Wilson, 2011). Similarity in attitudes is another important influence on attraction (Brehm, Kassin, & Fein, 2005; Taylor, Peplau, & Sears, 2006).

An especially good predictor of liking is similarity in attitudes about mutual acquaintances, because in general, people prefer relationships that are *balanced*. As illustrated in Figure 14.5, if Meagan likes Abigail, the relationship is balanced as long as they agree on their evaluation of a third person, regardless of whether they like or dislike that third person. However, the relationship will be imbalanced if Meagan and Abigail disagree on their evaluation of a third person.

One reason why we like people whose attitudes are similar to our own is that we expect such people to think highly of us (Condon & Crano, 1988). It's hard to say, though, whether attraction is a cause or an effect of similarity. For example, you might like someone because his attitudes are similar to yours, but it is also possible that as a result of liking him, your attitudes will become more similar to his (Davis & Rusbult, 2001). Even if your own attitudes do not change, you may change your perceptions of the liked person's attitudes such that those attitudes now seem more similar to yours (Brehm, 1992).

Physical Attractiveness   Physical characteristics are another important factor in attraction, particularly in the early stages of a relationship (Leary, 2010; Platek & Singh, 2010). From preschool through adulthood, physical attractiveness is a key to popularity

FIGURE 14.5
Balanced and Imbalanced Relationships
Here are some common examples of balanced and imbalanced relationships among three people. The plus and minus signs refer to liking and disliking, respectively. Balanced relationships are comfortable and harmonious; imbalanced ones often bring conflict.

Photos: Meagan: © Palmer Kane LLC/Shutterstock; Abigail: © rphotos/Photos.com; Samantha: © Will Rennick/iStockphoto.

Balanced relationships   **Imbalanced relationships**

© Jozsef Szasz-Fabian/Shutterstock

Attraction Online

As more people begin and carry out their friendships and intimate relationships online (Stout, 2010), psychologists have begun to investigate how social media affect attraction and interaction (Crosier, Webster, & Dillon, 2012; Finkel et al., 2012; Forest & Wood, 2012; Lam & Riedl, 2012; McLaughlin & Vitak, 2012, Sheer, 2011; Spence, 2011; Wilson, Gosling, & Graham, 2012). It appears, for example, that uncertainty contributes to attraction in online relationships. In one study, women were more attracted to a man if they didn't know whether or not he liked their Facebook profiles (Whitchurch, Wilson, & Gilbert, 2011).

with members of both sexes (Finkel & Baumeister, 2010). Consistent with the **matching hypothesis** of interpersonal attraction, however, people tend to date, marry, or form other committed relationships with those who are similar to themselves in physical attractiveness (Finkel & Baumeister, 2010). One possible reason for this is that although people tend to be most attracted to those with the greatest physical appeal, they also want to avoid being rejected by such individuals. So it may be compromise, not preference, that leads people to pair off with those who are roughly equivalent to themselves in physical attractiveness (Kavanagh, Robins, & Ellis, 2010).

Intimate Relationships and Love

There is much about intimate relationships that psychologists do not and may never understand, but they are learning all the time (Reis & Aron, 2008). For example, evolutionary psychologists suggest that men and women employ different strategies to ensure the survival of their genes and that each gender looks for different attributes in a potential mate (Buss, 2008; Neuberg, Kenrick, & Schaller, 2010; Salmon, 2012). The physical appearance of a partner tends to be more important to men than to women, while a partner's intelligence tends to be more important to women than to men (Buss, 2008; see Figure 14.6). Women also tend to be more influenced than men are by a potential mate's economic and social status. In one study, for instance, women rated men as being far more attractive when the men were seen to own a luxury automobile rather than an ordinary one. Men's ratings of women's attractiveness was not related to the kind of car she owned (Dunn & Searle, 2010).

Intimate Relationships   Eventually, people who are attracted to each other usually become *interdependent*, which means that one person's thoughts, emotions, and behaviors affect the thoughts, emotions, and behaviors of the other (Clark & Lemay, 2010). Interdependence is one of the defining characteristics of intimate relationships (Agnew et al., 1998).

Another key component of successful intimate relationships is *commitment*, which is the extent to which each person is psychologically attached to the relationship and wants to remain in it (Amodio & Showers, 2005). People feel committed to a relationship when they are satisfied with the rewards they receive from it, when they have invested significant tangible and intangible resources in it, and when they have few attractive alternative relationships available to them (Bui, Peplau, & Hill, 1996; Lydon, Fitzsimons, & Naidoo, 2003).

Analyzing Love   Although some people think love is simply a strong form of liking, research suggests that romantic love and liking are quite separate emotions, at least in the sense that they are associated with differing patterns of brain chemistry and brain activity (Emanuele et al., 2006; Fletcher & Overall, 2010). And although romantic love and sexual desire are often experienced together, they too seem to be separate emotions associated with different patterns of physiological arousal (Diamond, 2004). Further, most theorists agree that there are several different types of love (Berscheid, 2010). One widely accepted view distinguishes between passionate (romantic) love and companionate love (Berscheid, 2011). *Passionate love* is intense, arousing, and marked by both strong physical attraction and deep emotional attachment. Sexual feelings are intense, and thoughts of the other intrude on each person's awareness frequently. *Companionate love* is less arousing but psychologically more intimate. It is marked by mutual concern for the welfare of the other and a willingness to disclose personal information and feelings (Berscheid, 2010). People who experience companionate love seem especially satisfied with their lives (Brehm, Kassin, & Fein, 2005; Hendrick & Hendrick, 2003; Kim & Hatfield, 2004).

Robert Sternberg (2009) has offered an even broader analysis of love. According to his *triangular theory*, the three basic components of love are passion, intimacy, and commitment (see Figure 14.7). Various combinations of these components result in various types of love. For example, Sternberg suggests that *romantic love* involves a high

matching hypothesis   The notion that people are most likely to form committed relationships with those who are similar to themselves in physical attractiveness.

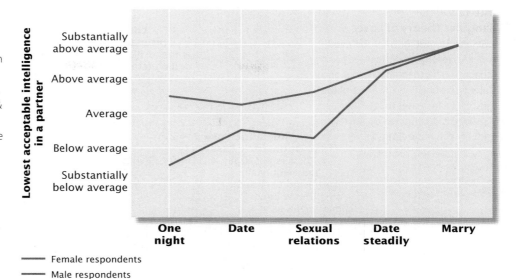

FIGURE 14.6

Sex Differences in Date and Mate Preferences

Evolutionary psychologists suggest that men and women have developed different strategies for selecting sexual partners (Buss, 2004b; Kenrick, Neuberg, & Cialdini, 2005; Li & Kenrick, 2006; Schmitt, 2003). These psychologists say that women became more selective than men because they can have relatively few children and want a partner who is best able to help support those children. So when asked about the intelligence of people they would choose for one-night stands, dating, and sexual relationships, women preferred much smarter partners than men did. Only when the choices concerned steady dating and marriage did the men's preference for bright partners equal that of the women (Eastwick & Finkel, 2008). Critics suggest, however, that these sex differences reflect learned social norms and expected gender-specific behaviors (Eagly & Wood, 1999; Miller, Putcha-Bhagavatula, & Pedersen, 2002).

Source: From Kenrick, D. T., Groth, G., Trost, M., & Sadalla, E. K., "Integrating Evolutionary and Social Exchange Perspectives on Relationships: Effects of Gender, Self-Appraisal, and Involvement Level on Mate Selection," *Journal of Personality and Social Psychology*. Copyright © 1993 by the American Psychological Association. Reprinted with permission.

degree of passion and intimacy yet lacks substantial commitment to the other person. *Companionate love* is marked by a great deal of intimacy and commitment but little passion. *Consummate love* is the most complete and satisfying. It is the most complete because it includes a high level of all three components. It is the most satisfying because the relationship is likely to fulfill many of the needs of each partner. More recently, Sternberg advanced a "duplex theory" of love by pairing his triangular theory with a second one that focuses on love as a story. This second theory is based on the fact that in Western cultures, at least, it appears that the success of a relationship depends not just on its perceived characteristics but also on the degree to which those characteristics fit each partner's ideal story of love, such as that of a prince and princess, or a pair of business partners, for example (Sternberg, 2009).

Cultural factors have a strong influence on the way people think about love and marriage. In North America and Western Europe, for example, the vast majority of people believe that they should love the person they marry. By contrast, in India and Pakistan, about half the people interviewed in a survey said they would marry someone they did not love if that person had other qualities that they desired (Levine et al., 1995). In Russia, only 40 percent of respondents said that they married for love. Most reported marrying because of loneliness, shared interests, or an unplanned pregnancy (Baron & Byrne, 1994). Many such cultural differences in the role of love in marriage are likely to continue, but others seem to be disappearing (Hatfield & Rapson, 2006).

Strong and Weak Marriages   Research on successful and unsuccessful marriages suggests that premarital attitudes, feelings, and perceptions can predict marital success. For example, couples who are strongly committed to each other; have a close, intimate relationship; similar attitudes; and realistic views of each other's strengths and weaknesses when they were dating are more likely than other couples to remain married (Hill & Peplau, 1998; Lee, Rogge, & Reis, 2010; Neff & Karney, 2005; Schoebi, Karney, & Bradbury, 2011). And as discussed in the chapter on human development, people who had a secure bond to parents or other caregivers in infancy are more likely to make deep commitments in adult relationships, including marriage (Holland & Roisman, 2010; Oriña et al., 2011; Simpson, Collins, & Salvatore, 2011).

After the wedding, women—but not men—generally tend to be more satisfied with their marriages when the partners talk a lot about the relationship (Acitelli, 1992). Partners in successful marriages also tend to share each other's view of themselves and the other, even if that view is a negative one (Swann, De La Ronde, & Hixon,

FIGURE 14.7

A Triangular Theory of Love

According to Sternberg (2009), different types of love result when the three basic components in his triangular theory occur in different combinations. The size of the triangle of love increases as love increases, and its shape is determined by the relative strength of each basic component.

Source: From R. J. Sternberg & M. L. Barnes, "Triangulating Love," in The Psychology of Love. Copyright © Yale University Press. Reprinted with permission.

Liking =
Intimacy Alone
(true friendship without passion or long-term commitment)

Romantic Love =
Intimacy + Passion
(lovers physically and emotionally attracted to each other but without commitment, as in a summer romance)

INTIMACY

Companionate Love = Intimacy + Commitment
(long-term committed friendship such as a marriage in which the passion has faded)

Consummate Love =
Intimacy + Passion + Commitment
(a complete love consisting of all three components—an ideal difficult to attain)

PASSION

COMMITMENT

Infatuation =
Passion Alone
(passionate, obsessive love at first sight without intimacy or commitment)

Fatuous Love =
Passion + Commitment
(commitment based on passion but without time for intimacy to develop—shallow relationship such as a whirlwind courtship)

Empty Love =
Commitment Alone
(decision to love another without intimacy or passion)

When there is a lot of conflict in a marriage, it usually affects both spouses, but wives tend to suffer more mental and physical health problems overall than husbands do (Wanic & Kulik, 2011).

1994). But rose-colored glasses can help, too. Having an unrealistically idealized view of one's partner seems to contribute to the long-term satisfaction reported by some couples (Murray et al., 2011). Marital satisfaction also tends to be high among couples who see their relationship as fair and equitable, who are willing to make sacrifices to help each other, and who treat the marriage as a willingly shared partnership rather than a contractual agreement for the exchange of assets, services, or favors (Clark et al., 2010; De Maris, 2007; Kolgan et al., 2010). After the birth of a first child, for example, many wives find that they have much more work than they had anticipated. If their husbands do not share this work to the degree the wives expected, or if the distribution of effort is seen by the wives as being unfair, marital satisfaction tends to decrease (Doss et al., 2009; McNulty & Karney, 2004; Mikula, Riederer, & Bodi, 2011).

One particularly interesting line of research suggests that even brief observations of married couples' interactions can predict whether they will divorce and when (Madhyastha, Hamaker, & Gottman, 2011). Among couples who divorced relatively soon after marriage, the partners tended to express both positive and negative feelings toward one another, but they were unable to control the way they expressed these feelings, especially the negative ones. Communication became increasingly hurtful and eventually broke down (Driver et al., 2003). A different picture emerged, however, in couples who divorced after many years of marriage. These people did not necessarily express negative emotions toward one another. Indeed, older adults tend to adopt a more forgiving communication style which emphasizes sensitivity to their partners' emotional states (Fingerman & Charles, 2010). But many late-divorcing couples simply become less and less likely to communicate *any* feelings. This increasing emotional distance between the spouses can create a sense of isolation that eventually leads to divorce (Gottman & Levenson, 2002). These findings can help us understand why people in a long (and apparently strong) marriage might suddenly announce that they are divorcing—and why they may remain friends afterward. These people may still like each other but no longer love each other (Gottman & Levenson, 2000; Huston et al., 2001).

Social Influence

What social rules shape our behavior?

So far, we have considered social cognition, the mental processes associated with people's perceptions of, and reactions to, other people. Let's now explore *social influence,* the process through which individuals and groups directly and indirectly influence a person's thoughts, feelings, and behavior. Research has shown, for example, that suicide rates increase following well-publicized suicides (Chen et al., 2010; Collings & Kemp, 2010) and that murder rates increase after well-publicized homicides (Jamieson, Jamieson, & Romer, 2003). Do these correlations mean that media coverage of violence triggers similar violence? As described in the chapter on learning, televised violence can play a causal role in aggressive behavior, but there are other reasons to believe that murders or suicides stimulate imitators when they become media events. For one thing, many of the people who kill themselves after a widely reported suicide are similar to the original victim in some respect (Cialdini, 2008). For example, after German television reported a story about a young man who committed suicide by jumping in front of a train, there was a dramatic increase in the number of young German men who committed suicide in the same way (Schmidtke & Hafner, 1988). This phenomenon—known as "copycat" violence—illustrates the effects of social influence.

Social Norms

The most common yet subtle form of social influence is communicated through social norms. **Social norms** are learned, socially-based rules that tell people what they should or should not do in various situations (Hogg, 2010). Parents, teachers, members of the clergy, peers, and other agents of culture transmit these social norms (Schmidt & Tomasello, 2012). Because of the power of social norms, people often follow them automatically. In North America and the United Kingdom, for example, social norms tell us that we should get in line to buy a movie ticket rather than crowd around the box office window. They also lead us to expect that others will do the same. By informing people of what is expected of them and others, social norms make social situations clearer, more predictable, and more comfortable (Schultz et al., 2007).

One particularly powerful social norm is *reciprocity,* the tendency to respond to others as they have acted toward you (Cialdini & Griskevicius, 2010). Restaurant servers often take advantage of this social norm by leaving some candy with the bill. Customers who receive this gift tend to reciprocate by leaving a larger tip than customers who don't get candy (Strohmetz et al., 2002). The reciprocity norm probably exists in every culture, but other social norms are not universal (Adam, Shirako, & Maddux, 2010; Miller, 2001). For instance, people around the world differ greatly in terms of the physical distance they keep between themselves and others while talking. People from South America usually stand much closer to each other than do people from North America. And as suggested in the chapter on psychological disorders, behavior that is considered normal and friendly in one culture may be seen as offensive or even abnormal in another.

The social influence exerted by social norms creates orderly social behavior, but social influence can also lead to a breakdown in order. For example, **deindividuation** is a psychological state in which a person becomes "submerged in the group" and loses the sense of individuality (Baumeister & Bushman, 2011). When people experience deindividuation, they become emotionally aroused and feel intense closeness with their group. This increased awareness of group membership may lead people to follow the group's social norms, even if those norms promote antisocial behavior (Spears et al., 2001). Normally mild-mannered adults may throw rocks at police during political protests, and youngsters who would not ordinarily commit hate crimes have done so as part of gangs. Such behavior—whether physical or verbal—becomes more extreme as

social norms Learned, socially-based rules that prescribe what people should or should not do in various situations.

deindividuation A psychological state occurring in group members that results in loss of individuality and a tendency to do things not normally done when alone.

Deindividuation

Robes, hoods, and group rituals help create deindividuation in these members of the Ku Klux Klan by focusing their attention on membership in their organization and its values. The hoods also hide their identities, which reduces their sense of personal responsibility and accountability and makes it easier for them to engage in hate crimes and other cowardly acts of bigotry. Deindividuation operates in other groups, too, ranging from lynch mobs and terrorist cells to political protesters, urban rioters, and even members of so-called "flash mobs." Through deindividuation, people appear to become "part of the herd," and they may do things that they might not do on their own (Spears et al., 2001).

© David Leeson/The Image Works

people feel less identifiable, as they often do in crowds, in dark environments, or online (Naquin, Kurtzberg, & Belkin, 2010; Stout, 2010; Zhong, Bohns, & Gino, 2010). An analysis of newspaper accounts of lynchings in the United States over a 50-year period showed that larger lynch mobs were more savage and vicious than smaller ones (Mullen, 1986). Deindividuation provides an example of how, given the right circumstances, quite normal people can engage in destructive, even violent behavior.

Conformity and Compliance

When people change their behavior or beliefs to match those of other members of a group, they are said to conform. **Conformity** occurs as a result of unspoken group pressure, real or imagined (Hogg, 2010). You probably have experienced group pressure when everyone around you stands to applaud a performance that you thought was not particularly great. You may conform by standing as well, though no one told you to do so; the group's behavior creates a silent but influential pressure to follow suit. **Compliance**, in contrast, occurs when people adjust their behavior because of a request. The request can be clear and direct, such as "Please do me a favor," or it can be more subtle, as when someone simply looks at you in a way that lets you know that the person needs a favor.

Conformity and compliance are usually generated by spoken or unspoken social norms. In a classic experiment, Muzafer Sherif (1937) charted the formation of a group norm by taking advantage of a visual illusion: if you look at a fixed point of light in a pitch-dark room, the light will appear to move. Estimates of how far the light seems to move tend to stay the same over time if an observer is alone. But when Sherif tested several people at once, asking each person to say aloud how far the light moved on repeated trials, their estimates tended to converge; they had established a group norm. Even more important, when individuals who had been in the group were later tested alone, they continued to be influenced by this norm.

In another classic experiment, Solomon Asch (1956) explored what people do when faced with a norm that is obviously wrong. The participants in this experiment saw a standard line like the one in Figure 14.8(A); then they saw a display like that in Figure 14.8(B). Their task was to pick out the line in the display that was the same length as the one they had first been shown.

Each participant performed this task in a small group of people who posed as fellow participants but who were actually the experimenter's assistants. There were

conformity Changing one's behavior or beliefs to match those of others, generally as a result of real or imagined (though unspoken) group pressure.

compliance Adjusting one's behavior because of a direct request.

Standard line

(A)

Test lines

(B)

FIGURE 14.8

Types of Stimulus Lines Used in Experiments by Asch

Participants in Asch's experiments saw a new set of lines like these on each trial. The middle line in Part B matches the one in Part A, but when several of Asch's assistants claimed that a different line matched, so did many of the participants. Try re-creating this experiment with four friends. Secretly ask three of them to say that the test line on the left matches the standard line, then show this drawing to all four. Did the fourth person conform to the group norm? If not, do you think it was something about the person, the length of the incorrect line chosen, or both that led to nonconformity? Would conformity be more likely if the first three people had chosen the test line on the right? (Read on for more about this possibility.)

LEARN by DOING

two conditions. In the control condition, the real participant responded first. In the experimental condition, the participant did not respond until after the other people did. The experimenter's assistants chose the correct response on 6 trials, but on the other 12 trials they all gave the same, obviously incorrect response. So on 12 trials, each participant was confronted with a "social reality" created by a group norm that conflicted with the physical reality created by what the person could clearly see. Only 5 percent of the participants in the control condition ever made a mistake during this easy perceptual task. However, among participants who heard the assistants' incorrect responses before giving their own, about 70 percent made at least one error by conforming to the group norm. An analysis of 133 studies conducted in 17 countries reveals that conformity in Asch-type situations has declined somewhat in the United States since the 1950s but that it still occurs (Cialdini et al., 2001).

Why Do People Conform?   Why did so many people in Asch's experiment give incorrect responses when they were capable of near-perfect performance? One possibility, called *public conformity,* is that they didn't really believe in their responses but gave them simply because it was the socially desirable thing to do. Another possibility is that the participants experienced *private acceptance.* Perhaps they used the other people's responses as a guide, became convinced that their own perceptions were wrong, and actually changed their minds. Which possibility is more likely? Morton Deutsch and Harold Gerard (1955) reasoned that if people still conformed even when the other group members couldn't hear their response, then Asch's findings must reflect private acceptance, not just public conformity. Actually, although conformity does decrease when people respond privately, it doesn't disappear (Deutsch & Gerard, 1955). So people sometimes say things in public that they don't believe in, but hearing other people's responses also appears to influence their private beliefs (Moscovici, 1985).

Why are group norms so powerful? Research suggests several influential factors (Cialdini & Griskevicius, 2010). First, people are motivated to be correct, and group norms provide information about what is right and wrong. Second, people want others to like them, so they may seek favor by conforming to the social norms that those others have established (Hewlin & Faison, 2009). Third, conforming to group norms may increase a person's sense of self-worth, especially if the group is valued or prestigious (Cialdini & Goldstein, 2004). The process may occur without our awareness (Lakin & Chartrand, 2003). For example, observations of interviews by former talk show host Larry King revealed that he tended to imitate the speech patterns of high-status guests but not low-status ones (Gregory & Webster, 1996). Finally, social norms affect the distribution of social rewards and punishments (Cialdini, 2008). From childhood on, people in many cultures learn that going along with group norms is good and earns rewards. (These positive outcomes presumably help compensate for not always saying or doing exactly what we please.) People also learn that breaking a norm may bring punishments ranging from scoldings for small transgressions to imprisonment for violation of social norms that have been translated into laws.

When Do People Conform?   People do not always conform to group influence. In the Asch studies, for example, nearly 30 percent of the participants did not go along with the assistants' obviously wrong judgments. Countless experiments have probed the question of what combinations of people and circumstances do and do not lead to conformity.

Ambiguity, or uncertainty, is important in determining how much conformity will occur. As the features of a situation become less clear, people rely more and more on others' opinions and conformity to a group norm becomes increasingly likely (Cialdini & Goldstein, 2004). You can demonstrate this aspect of conformity on any street corner. First, create an ambiguous situation by having several people look at the sky or the top of a building. When passersby ask what is going on, be sure everyone excitedly reports seeing something interesting but fleeting—perhaps a faint flashing light or a tiny, shiny high-flying object. If you are especially successful, conforming newcomers will begin persuading other passersby that there is something fascinating to be seen.

LEARN by DOING

© Nabeel Turner/Getty Images

© OSSERVATORE ROMANO/Reuters/Corbis

Mass Conformity

The faithful who gather at Mecca, at the Vatican, and at other holy places around the world exemplify the power of religion and other social forces to produce conformity to group norms.

If ambiguity contributes so much to conformity, though, why did so many of Asch's participants conform to a judgment that was clearly wrong? The answer has to do with the *unanimous* nature of the group's judgment and the number of people expressing that judgment. Specifically, people experience intense pressure to conform as long as all the other group members agree with each other. If even one other person in the group disagrees with the majority view, conformity drops greatly. When Asch (1951) arranged for just one assistant to disagree with the others, fewer than 10 percent of the real participants conformed. Once unanimity is broken, it becomes much easier to disagree with the majority, even if the other nonconformist does not agree with the person's own view (Baumeister & Bushman, 2011).

Conformity also depends on the *size of the majority.* Asch (1955) demonstrated this phenomenon by varying the number of assistants in the group from one to fifteen. Conformity to incorrect social norms grew as the number of people in the group increased. However, most of the growth in conformity occurred as the size of the majority rose from one to about three or four members. This effect probably occurs because pressure to conform has already reached a peak after someone has heard three or four people agree. Hearing more people confirm the majority view has little additional social impact (Latané, 1981).

Conformity can also occur through *minority influence,* by which a minority of group members influences the behavior or beliefs of the majority (Hogg, 2010). This phenomenon is less common than majority influence, but when members of a numerical minority are established group members, agree with one another, and persist in their views, they can be influential (Hogg, 2010; Mucchi-Faina & Pagliaro, 2008). Perhaps because the views of a numerical minority are examined especially carefully by the rest of the group (Martin & Hewstone 2003), minority-influenced change often takes a while. Even then, the amount of change tends to be small (Alvaro & Crano, 1997; Crano & Chen, 1998) and is most likely to occur when those in the minority are perceived by the majority to be loyal group members (Crano & Seyranian, 2009).

Does gender affect conformity? Early research suggested that women conform more than men, but the gender difference stemmed mainly from the fact that the tasks used in those studies were often more familiar to men than to women. This fact is important because people are especially likely to conform when they are faced with an unfamiliar situation (Kassin, Fein & Markus, 2011). Those studies also usually required people to make their responses aloud so that everyone knew if they had conformed or not. When the experimental tasks are equally familiar to both genders and when people can make their responses privately, no male-female differences in conformity are found. Accordingly, it has been suggested that gender differences in public conformity are based not on a genuine difference in reactions to social pressure but rather on men's desire to be seen as strong and independent and women's desire to be seen as cooperative (Hogg, 2010; Kenrick, Neuberg, & Cialdini, 2010).

Creating Compliance   In the experiments just described, the participants experienced psychological pressure to conform to the views or actions of others even though no one specifically asked them to do so. In contrast, *compliance* involves changing what you say or do because of a direct request.

How is compliance brought about? Many people believe that the direct approach is always best: if you want something, ask for it. But salespeople, political strategists, social psychologists, and other experts have learned that often the best way to get something is to ask for something else. Three examples of this strategy are the foot-in-the-door technique, the door-in-the-face technique, and the lowball technique (Cialdini & Griskevicius, 2010).

The *foot-in-the-door technique* works by getting a person to agree to small requests and then working up to larger ones. In the original experiment on this strategy, homeowners were asked to do one of two things. Some were asked to allow a large, unattractive "Drive Carefully" sign to be placed on their front lawns. About 17 percent of the people approached in this way complied with the request. In the foot-in-the-door condition, however, homeowners were first asked only to sign a petition supporting laws aimed at reducing traffic accidents. Several weeks later, when a different person asked these same homeowners to put the "Drive Carefully" sign on their lawns, 55 percent of them complied (Freedman & Fraser, 1966).

Why should granting small favors lead to the granting of larger ones? First, people are usually far more likely to comply with a request that doesn't cost much in time, money, effort, or inconvenience. Second, complying with a small request makes people think of themselves as being committed to the cause or issue involved (Burger & Guadagno, 2003). This occurs through the processes of self-perception and cognitive dissonance discussed earlier (Cialdini & Griskevicius, 2010). In the study just described, participants who signed the petition might have thought, "I must care enough about traffic safety to do something about it." Compliance with the higher-cost request (displaying the sign) increased because it was consistent with these people's self-perceptions and past actions (Burger & Guadagno, 2003).

The foot-in-the-door technique can be amazingly effective. Steven Sherman (1980) created a 700 percent increase in the rate at which people volunteered to work for a charity simply by first getting them to say that in a hypothetical situation they would volunteer if asked. For some companies, the foot in the door is a request that potential customers merely answer a few questions; the request to buy something comes later. Others offer a small gift, or "door opener," as salespeople call it. Acceptance of the gift not only gives the salesperson a foot in the door but also may activate the reciprocity norm: many people who get something for free feel obligated to reciprocate by buying something, especially if the request to do so is delayed for a while (Cialdini & Griskevicius, 2010; Guadagno et al., 2001).

The *door-in-the-face technique* offers a second effective way of obtaining compliance (Cialdini, 2008). This strategy begins with a request for a favor that is likely to be refused. The person making the request then concedes that this favor was too much to ask and substitutes a lesser alternative, which is what the person really wanted in the first place! Because the person appears willing to compromise and because the second request seems small in comparison with the first one, it is more likely to be granted than if it had been made at the outset. The door-in-the-face strategy is at the heart of bargaining among political groups and between labor and management (Ginges et al., 2007).

The third method, called the *lowball technique,* is commonly used by car dealers and other businesses (Cialdini, 2001). The first step in this strategy is to get people to say that they will do something, such as purchase a car. Once this commitment is made, the cost of fulfilling it is increased, often because of an "error" in computing the car's price. Why do buyers end up paying much more than originally planned for "lowballed" items? Apparently, once people commit themselves to do something, they feel obligated to follow through, especially when the initial commitment was made in public and when the person who obtained that commitment also makes the higher-cost request (Burger & Cornelius, 2003).

© EdBockStock/Shutterstock

Promoting Compliance

Have you ever been asked to sign a petition favoring some political, social, or economic cause? Supporters of these causes know that people who comply with this small request are the best people to contact later with requests to do more. Complying with larger requests is made more likely because it's consistent with the signer's initial commitment to the cause. If you were contacted after signing a petition, did you agree to donate money or become a volunteer?

APPLYING PSYCHOLOGY

From the film Obedience © 1968 by Stanley Milgram, © renewed 1993 by Alexandra Milgram, and distributed by Alexander Street Press. Permission granted by Alexandra Milgram

FIGURE 14.9

Studying Obedience in the Laboratory

In this photograph from Milgram's original experiment, a man is being strapped into a chair with electrodes on his arm. Although participants in the experiment didn't know it, the man was actually the experimenter's assistant and received no shock.

Obedience

How far will people go in obeying authority?

Compliance involves a change in behavior in response to a request. In the case of **obedience**, the behavior change comes in response to a *demand* from an authority figure (Sanderson, 2010). In the 1960s, Stanley Milgram developed a laboratory procedure at Yale University to study obedience. For his first experiment, he used newspaper ads to find 40 male volunteer participants. They ranged in age from 20 to 50, lived in the local community, and included professionals, white-collar businessmen, and unskilled workers (Milgram, 1963).

Imagine you are one of the people who answered the ad. When you arrive for the experiment, you join a 50-year-old man who has also volunteered and has been scheduled for the same session. The experimenter explains that the purpose of the experiment is to examine the effects of punishment on learning. One of you—the "teacher"—will help the "learner" remember a list of words by administering an electric shock whenever the learner makes a mistake. Then the experimenter turns to you and asks you to draw one of two cards out of a hat. Your card says, "TEACHER." You think to yourself that this must be your lucky day.

Now the learner is taken into another room and strapped into a chair, and, as illustrated in Figure 14.9, electrodes are attached to his arm. You are shown a shock generator with 30 switches. The experimenter explains that the switch on the far left administers a mild, 15-volt shock and that each succeeding switch increases the shock by 15 volts. The one on the far right delivers 450 volts. The far left section of the shock generator is labeled "Slight shock." Looking across the panel, you see "Moderate shock," "Very strong shock," and at the far right, "Danger—severe shock." The last two switches are ominously labeled "XXX." The experimenter explains that you, the teacher, will begin by reading a list of word pairs to the learner. Then you will go through the list again, presenting just one word of each pair. The learner will have to say which word went with it. After the first mistake, you are to throw the switch to deliver 15 volts of shock. Each time the learner makes another mistake, you are to increase the shock by 15 volts.

You begin, following the experimenter's instructions. But after the learner makes his fifth mistake and you throw the switch to give him 75 volts, you hear a loud moan. At 90 volts, the learner cries out in pain. At 150 volts, he screams and asks to be let out of the experiment. You look to the experimenter, who says, "Proceed with the next word."

No shock was actually delivered in Milgram's experiments. The learner was always an employee of the experimenter, and the moans and other sounds of pain came from a prerecorded tape. But you do not know that. What would you do in this situation? Suppose you continue and eventually deliver 180 volts. The learner screams that he cannot stand the pain any longer and starts banging on the wall. The experimenter says, "You have no other choice; you must go on." Would you continue? Would you keep going even when the learner begged to be let out of the experiment and then fell silent? Would you administer 450 volts of potentially deadly shock to an innocent stranger just because an experimenter demanded that you do so? Figure 14.10 shows that only 5 participants in Milgram's experiment stopped before 300 volts and that 26 out of 40 (65 percent) went all the way to the 450-volt level. The decision to continue was difficult and stressful for the participants. Many protested repeatedly. But each time the experimenter told them to continue, they did so. Here is a partial transcript of what a typical participant said:

[After throwing the 180-volt switch]: *He can't stand it. I'm not going to kill that man in there. Do you hear him hollering? He's hollering. He can't stand it. What if something happens to him? I'm not going to get that man sick in there. He's hollering in there. Do you know what I mean? I mean, I refuse to take responsibility. He's getting hurt in there…. Too many left here. Geez, if he gets them wrong. There are too many of them left. I mean, who is going to take responsibility if anything happens to that gentleman?*

[After the experimenter accepts responsibility]: *All right….*

[After administering 240 volts]: *Oh, no, you mean I've got to keep going up the scale? No sir, I'm not going to kill that man. I'm not going to give him 450 volts.*

obedience Changing behavior in response to a demand from an authority figure.

FIGURE 14.10
Results of Milgram's Obedience Experiment

When Milgram asked a group of college students and a group of psychiatrists to predict how participants in his experiment would respond, they estimated that fewer than 2 percent would go all the way to 450 volts. In fact, 65 percent of the participants did so. What do you think you would have done in this situation?

Source: From S. Milgram, "Behavioral Study of Obedience," *Journal of Abnormal and Social Psychology* Vol. 67:4 (p. 376). Used with the permission of Alexandra Milgram.

From the film Obedience © 1968 by Stanley Milgram, © renewed 1993 by Alexandra Milgram, and distributed by Alexander Street Press. Permission granted by Alexandra Milgram.

[After the experimenter says, "The experiment requires that you go on"]: *I know it does, but that man is hollering in there, sir.*

This participant administered shock up to 450 volts (Milgram, 1974).

Factors Affecting Obedience

Milgram had not expected so many people to deliver such apparently intense shocks. Was there something about his procedure that produced this high level of obedience? To find out, Milgram and other researchers varied the original procedure in a number of ways and discovered that the degree of obedience was affected by several aspects of the situation and procedure.

Experimenter Status and Prestige Perhaps the experimenter's status as a Yale University professor helped produce high levels of obedience in Milgram's original experiment (Blass & Schmitt, 2001). To test this possibility, Milgram rented an office in a rundown building in Bridgeport, Connecticut. He then placed a newspaper ad for research sponsored by a private firm. There was no mention of Yale. In all other ways, the experimental procedure was identical to the original.

Under these less impressive circumstances, the level of obedience dropped, but not as much as Milgram expected: 48 percent of the participants continued to the maximum level of shock, compared with 65 percent in the original study. Milgram concluded that people are willing to obey orders to do great harm to another person even when the authority making the demand is not especially reputable or prestigious.

The Behavior of Other People To study how the behavior of fellow participants might affect obedience, Milgram (1965) created a situation in which there appeared to be three teachers. Teacher 1 (in reality, a research assistant) read the words to the learner. Teacher 2 (another research assistant) stated whether or not the learner's response was correct. Teacher 3 (the actual participant) was to deliver shock when the learner made mistakes. At 150 volts, when the learner began to complain that the shock was too painful, Teacher 1 refused to participate any longer and left the room. The experimenter asked him to come back, but he refused. The experimenter then instructed Teachers 2 and 3 to continue by themselves. The experiment continued for several more trials. However, at 210 volts, Teacher 2 said that the learner was suffering too much and also refused to participate further. The experimenter then told Teacher

© John Chiasson/Getty Images

Proximity and Obedience

Milgram's research showed that close physical proximity to an authority figure is one of several factors that can enhance obedience to authority (Rada & Rogers, 1973). This proximity principle is used in the military, where no one is ever far away from the authority of a higher-ranking person.

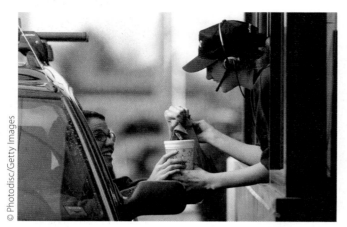

May I Take Your Order?

In February 2004, the managers of four fast food restaurants in Boston, Massachusetts, received calls from someone claiming to be a police detective on the trail of a robbery suspect. The caller said the suspect might be one of the restaurant's employees and told the managers to strip search all of them for evidence of guilt. The calls turned out to be hoaxes, but every manager obeyed this bizarre order, apparently because it appeared to come from a legitimate authority. In two similar cases, residents of a special needs school were given unnecessary electric shock treatments on the telephoned orders from a hoaxer, and hospital nurses obeyed medical treatment orders given by a teenager who claimed to be a doctor (Associated Press, 2007a; Kenrick, Neuberg, & Cialdini, 2010).

3 (the actual participant) to continue the procedure. In this case, only 10 percent of the participants (compared with 65 percent in the original study) continued to deliver shock all the way up to 450 volts. In other words, as research on conformity would suggest, the presence of others who disobey appears to be the most powerful factor in reducing obedience.

The Behavior of the Learner   A recent reanalysis of data from Milgram's obedience studies (Packer, 2008) found that although the supposedly shocked learner's increasingly intense expressions of pain had no effect on whether the participants disobeyed the experimenter, the learner's stated desire to be released from the experiment did affect disobedience. In fact, among those participants who refused to continue to shock the learner, almost 37 percent of them disobeyed at the 150 volt level, which was when the learner first said he wanted to be released from the experiment. So it appears that perceiving a victim's pain does not reduce obedience to authority but being reminded of a victim's right to be released from the experiment does.

Personality Characteristics   Were the participants in Milgram's original experiment heartless creatures who would have given strong shocks even if there had been no pressure on them to do so? Quite the opposite; most of them were nice people who were influenced by experimental situations to behave in apparently antisocial ways. In a later demonstration of the same phenomenon, college students playing the role of prison guards behaved with aggressive heartlessness toward other students who were playing the role of prisoners (Zimbardo, 1973). A more recent illustration of this phenomenon occurred among some soldiers who were assigned to guard or interrogate prisoners in Afghanistan and Iraq.

Still, not everyone is equally obedient to authority. For example, people who display what we described earlier as *authoritarianism* are more likely than others to obey an experimenter's instructions to shock the learner (Blass, 2000; Dambrun & Valnetine, 2010). Further support for this idea comes from findings that German soldiers who may have obeyed orders to kill Jews during World War II displayed more authoritarianism than other German men of the same age and background (Steiner & Fahrenberg, 2000). In contrast, a recent study that repeated Milgram's experimental procedures (Burger, 2009) found that the participants who were less likely to obey orders to harm the learner were also the ones who were concerned about others and predisposed to have *empathy*—that is, to understand or experience another person's emotional state (Davis, 1994).

Evaluating Obedience Research

Milgram's obedience studies were conducted 50 years ago. How relevant are they today? Consider this fact: The U.S. Federal Aviation Administration attributes some fatal commercial airline accidents to a phenomenon it calls "captainitis." This phenomenon occurs when the captain of an aircraft makes an obvious error but the copilot is unwilling to challenge the captain's authority by pointing out the mistake (Gladwell, 2008; Kanki & Foushee, 1990). Obedience to authority may also have operated on 9/11, when some people returned to their offices in the World Trade Center after hearing an ill-advised public address announcement telling them to do so. Most of these people died as a result.

These tragic events suggest that Milgram's findings are still relevant and important (Blass, 2004). Similar kinds of obedience have been observed in experiments conducted in many countries, from Europe to the Middle East, with female as well as male participants, and even in lifelike virtual environments (Burger, 2009; Dambrun & Valentine, 2010). In short, people may be as likely to obey orders today as they were when Milgram conducted his research (Blass, 2004, 2009; Burger, 2009). Nevertheless, there is still debate over the ethics and meaning of Milgram's work.

LINKAGES

Is it ethical to deceive people to learn about their social behavior? *(a link to Introduction to the Science of Psychology)*

Questions About Ethics   Although the "learners" in Milgram's experiment suffered no discomfort, the participants did. Milgram (1963) observed participants "sweat, stutter, tremble, groan, bite their lips, and dig their fingernails into their flesh" (p. 375). Against the potential harm inflicted by Milgram's experiments stand the potential gains. For example, people who learn about Milgram's work often take his findings into account when deciding how to act in social situations (Sherman, 1980). But even if social value has come from Milgram's studies, a question remains: Was it ethical for Milgram to treat his participants as he did?

In the years before his death in 1984, Milgram defended his experiments (e.g., Milgram, 1977). He argued that the way he dealt with his participants after the experiment prevented any lasting harm. For example, he explained to them that the learner did not experience any shock; in fact, the learner came in and chatted with each participant. On a later questionnaire, 84 percent of the participants said that they had learned something important about themselves and that the experience had been worthwhile. Milgram argued, therefore, that the experience was actually a positive one. Still, the committees charged with protecting human participants in research today would be unlikely to approve Milgram's experiments as they were originally done, and less controversial ways to study obedience have now been developed (Blass, 2004; Elms, 2009).

Questions About Meaning   Do Milgram's dramatic results mean that most people are putty in the hands of authority figures and that most of us would blindly follow inhumane orders from our leaders? Some critics have argued that Milgram's results cannot be interpreted in this way because his participants knew they were in an experiment and may simply have been playing a cooperative role. If so, the social influence processes identified in his studies may not explain obedience in the real world today (Berkowitz, 1999).

In fact, it has been proposed that what looks like blind obedience in Milgram's experiments might be better explained by the *social identity theory* we described earlier (Reicher, Haslam, & Smith, 2012). According to this interpretation, when participants administered what they thought were severe shocks it could have been because they identified more strongly with the experimenter and the scientific community he represented than with the person they were supposedly shocking. When the research was not associated with Yale and when others refused to continue, participants might have identified more with the learner than with the experimenter and so were less willing to continue. This line of reasoning offers quite a different perspective on why people sometimes follow brutal orders. These people may simply see themselves and their leaders as part of the same group and their willingness to follow orders reflects the conscious pursuit of that group's goals. This alternative explanation of Milgram's results has yet to be directly tested, but that will surely happen in the near future.

Most psychologists believe, however, that Milgram demonstrated a basic truth about human behavior—namely, that under certain circumstances people are capable of unspeakable acts of brutality toward other people (Benjamin & Simpson, 2009). Sadly, examples abound. And one of the most horrifying aspects of human inhumanity—whether it is the Nazis' campaign of genocide against Jews 70 years ago or the campaigns of terror under way today—is that the perpetrators are not necessarily demented, sadistic fiends. Most of them are normal people who have been prompted by economic, political, or religious influences and the persuasive power of their leaders to behave in a demented and fiendish manner (Skitka, 2010). (For a summary of Milgram's results, plus those of studies on conformity and compliance, see "In Review: Types of Social Influence.")

In short, inhumanity can occur even without pressure to obey. A good deal of people's aggressiveness toward other people appears to come from within. Let's consider human aggressiveness and some of the circumstances that influence its expression.

Types of Social Influence

IN REVIEW

Type	Definition	Key Findings
Conformity	A change in behavior or beliefs to match those of others	In cases of ambiguity, people develop a group norm and then adhere to it.
		Conformity occurs because people want to be right, because they want to be liked by others, and because conformity to group norms is usually reinforced.
		Conformity usually increases with the ambiguity of the situation as well as with the unanimity and size of the majority.
Compliance	Adjusting one's behavior because of a direct request	Compliance increases with the foot-in-the-door technique, which begins with a small request and works up to a larger one.
		The door-in-the-face procedure can also be used. After making a large request that is denied, the person substitutes a less extreme alternative that was desired all along.
		The lowball approach also elicits compliance. An oral commitment for something is first obtained, then the person claims that only a higher-cost version of the original request will suffice.
Obedience	A change in behavior in response to an explicit demand, typically from an acknowledged authority figure	People may inflict great harm on others when an authority demands that they do so.
		Even when people obey orders to harm another person, they often agonize over the decision.
		People are most likely to disobey orders to harm someone else when they see another person disobey.

IN REVIEW QUESTIONS

1. Joining the end of a ticket line is an example of ___, whereas forming two lines when a theater employee requests it is an example of ___.
2. Seeing someone disobey a questionable order makes people ___ likely to obey the order themselves.
3. Pricing your used car for more than you expect to get then agreeing to reduce it to make a sale is an example of the ___ approach to gaining compliance.

Aggression

Are people born aggressive?

Aggressive behavior, more commonly known as **aggression**, is any action intended to harm another person (Bushman & Huesmann, 2010). It is all too common. About 1.6 million violent crimes are committed each year in the United States alone, including nearly 90,000 rapes and about 15,000 murders (U.S. Census Bureau, 2012). In fact, homicide is the third leading cause of death for people in the United States between the ages of 15 and 24 (Heron, 2007). One of the most disturbing aspects of these figures is that about 85 percent of all murder victims knew their assailants and that over 70 percent of rapists were romantic partners, friends, relatives, or acquaintances of their victims (U.S. Department of Justice, 2007). Further, as many as one-third of married people and a significant proportion of dating couples in the United States have engaged in aggressive acts toward each other that range from pushing, shoving, and slapping to beatings and the threatened or actual use of weapons (Cornelius & Resseguie, 2007; Durose et al., 2005).

Why Are People Aggressive?

Sigmund Freud proposed that aggression is an instinctive biological urge that builds up in everyone and must be released. Evolutionary psychologists offer a different view, suggesting that in prehistoric times, aggression helped people compete for mates, thus ensuring the survival of their genes in the next generation (Liddle, Shackelford, & Weekes–Shackelford, 2012; Malamuth & Addison, 2001). Through natural selection, they say, aggressive tendencies have been passed on through countless generations.

Evolutionary theories of aggression are popular, but even evolutionary theorists recognize that "nature" alone cannot fully account for aggression. "Nurture," in the form of environmental factors, also plays a role in when and why people are aggressive. We know this partly because there are large differences in aggression from culture to culture. The murder rate in Venezuela, for example, is more than nine times higher than it is in the United States, and the U.S. murder rate is about three times as high as the rate in Canada or the United Kingdom (United Nations Office on Drugs and Crime, 2010). These data suggest that even if aggressive *impulses* are universal, the appearance of aggressive

aggressive behavior (aggression)
An act that is intended to harm another person.

behavior reflects the influence of both nature and nurture, including the degree to which people learn to control aggressive tendencies (Bushman & Huesmann, 2010; Denson, DeWall, & Finkel, 2012). No equation can predict exactly when people will be aggressive, but research has revealed a number of important biological, learning, and environmental factors that combine in various ways to produce aggression in various situations.

Genetic and Biological Mechanisms   There is strong evidence for hereditary influences on aggression, especially in nonhuman animals (Bushman & Huesmann, 2010). In one study, the most aggressive members of a large group of mice were interbred and then the most aggressive of their offspring were interbred. After this procedure was followed for 25 generations, the resulting animals would immediately attack any mouse put in their cage. Continuous inbreeding of the least aggressive members of the original group produced animals that were so nonaggressive that they would refuse to fight even when attacked (Lagerspetz & Lagerspetz, 1983). Research that rated the aggressiveness of human twins who had been raised together or apart suggests that there is a genetic component to aggression in people as well (Hudziak et al., 2003; Vierikko et al., 2006). However, other research suggests that people do not necessarily inherit the tendency to be aggressive. Instead, they may inherit certain aspects of temperament, such as impulsiveness, or certain aspects of brain chemistry that in turn make aggression more likely (Alia-Klein et al., 2009; Eisenberger et al., 2007; Hennig et al., 2005).

Several parts of the brain influence aggression (Anderson & Bushman, 2002a). One of these is the limbic system, which includes the amygdala, the hypothalamus, and related areas. Damage to these structures may produce *defensive aggression,* which includes heightened aggressiveness toward stimuli that are not usually threatening or a decrease in the responses that normally inhibit aggression (Coccaro, 1989; Siever, 2008). The cerebral cortex may also be involved in aggression (e.g., Pietro et al., 2000; Séguin & Zelazo, 2005). Hormones such as *testosterone*—the masculine hormone that is present in both sexes—may also play an important role in aggression (Bushman & Huesmann, 2010). Aggressive behavior increases or decreases dramatically with the amount of testosterone in the human bloodstream. This may be because people with high levels of testosterone have more difficulty controlling their impulses (Mehta & Beer, 2010). Criminals who commit violent crimes have higher levels of testosterone than those whose crimes are nonviolent, and murderers with higher levels of testosterone are more likely than others to have planned their crimes before committing them (Dabbs, Riad, & Chance, 2001).

Testosterone's most significant and durable influence may be through its impact on early brain development. One natural test of this hypothesis occurred when pregnant women were given testosterone in an attempt to prevent miscarriage. As a result, their children were exposed to high doses of testosterone during prenatal development. Figure 14.11 shows that these children grew up to be more aggressive than their same-sex siblings who were not exposed to testosterone during prenatal development (Reinisch, Ziemba-Davis, & Sanders, 1991). Another study found that men who had been exposed to high levels of testosterone before birth were more likely than other men to be aggressive toward their female partners (Cousins, Fugere, & Franlin, 2009). Still other research has linked low levels of the neurotransmitter serotonin with high levels of impulsive aggression in both humans and nonhuman animals (Bushman & Bartholow, 2010; Carver, Johnson, & Joormann, 2008). It is not yet clear, though, whether the low serotonin level is a cause or a consequence of aggression (Kassin, Fein, & Markus, 2008).

Aggression can also be influenced by drugs that affect the central nervous system. For example, even relatively small amounts of alcohol can greatly increase some people's aggressiveness (deWall, Bushman, et al., 2010; Giancola et al., 2010). Canadian researchers have found that in almost 70 percent of the acts of aggression they studied, the aggressors had been drinking alcohol. And the more alcohol the aggressors consumed, the more aggressive they were (Wells, Graham, & West, 2000). No one knows exactly why alcohol increases aggression, but research suggests that the drug may affect areas of the brain that normally inhibit aggressive responses (Bartholow & Heinz, 2006; Graham et al., 2006; Lau, Pihl, & Peterson, 1995).

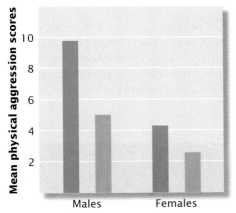

■ Participants exposed to high doses of testosterone during prenatal development

■ Unexposed participants

FIGURE 14.11

Testosterone and Aggression

In the study illustrated here, the children of women who had taken testosterone during pregnancy to prevent miscarriage became more aggressive than the mothers' other children of the same sex who had not been exposed to testosterone during prenatal development. This outcome appeared in both males' and females' development (Reinisch, Ziemba-Davis, & Sanders, 1991).

Learning and Cultural Mechanisms   Biological factors may increase or decrease the likelihood of aggression, but cross-cultural research makes it clear that learning also plays a role. Aggressive behavior is much more common in individualist than in collectivist cultures, for example (Oatley, 1993). Cultural differences in the expression of aggression appear to stem partly from differing cultural values (Cohen, 1998). For example, the Utku (an Inuit culture) view aggression in any form as a sign of social incompetence. In fact, the Utku word for "aggressive" also means "childish" (Oatley, 1993). The effects of culture on aggression can also be seen in the fact that the amount of aggression in a given culture changes over time as cultural values change (Matsumoto, 2000).

In addition, people can learn aggressive responses by watching other people (Bingheimer, Brennan, & Earls, 2005; Bushman & Huesmann, 2010). Children, in particular, learn and perform many of the aggressive responses they see modeled by others. Bandura's Bobo-doll experiments, which are described in the chapter on learning, provide impressive demonstrations of the power of observational learning. The significance of observational learning is also highlighted by studies described in that chapter on the effects of televised violence. For example, the amount of violent content eight-year-olds watch on television predicts aggressiveness in these children even 15 years later (Bushman & Huesmann, 2010; Huesmann et al., 2003). Fortunately, not everyone who sees aggression becomes aggressive. Individual differences in temperament, the modeling of nonaggressive behavior by parents, and other factors can reduce the effects of violent television. Nevertheless, observational learning, including the learning that comes through exposure to violent television and violent video and computer games, can play a significant role in the development and display of aggressive behavior (Adachi & Willoughby, 2011; Anderson & Murphy, 2003; Bushman & Anderson, 2001; Greitemeyer & McLatchie, 2011; Konijn, Bijvank, & Bushman, 2007). In contrast, exposure to music with prosocial lyrics and prosocially oriented video games has been associated with less aggressive thoughts and actions and with higher levels of prosocial behavior (Greitemeyer, 2010, 2011).

Reward or punishment can also alter the frequency of aggressive acts. People become more aggressive when rewarded for aggressiveness and less aggressive when punished for aggression (Bushman & Bartholow, 2010). In short, a person's life experiences, including culturally transmitted teachings, combine with daily rewards and punishments to influence whether, when, and how aggressive acts occur (Bettencourt et al., 2006; Bushman & Bartholow, 2010).

Following Adult Examples

Learning to express aggression is especially easy for children who live in countries plagued by war or sectarian violence because they see aggressive acts modeled for them all too often.

© Mario Tama/Getty Images

When Are People Aggressive?

In general, people are more likely to be aggressive when they are both physically aroused and experiencing a strong emotion such as anger (Bushman, & Bartholow, 2010). People tend either to lash out at those who make them angry or to displace, or redirect, their anger toward children, pets, or other defenseless targets. However, aggression can also be made more likely by other forms of emotional arousal. One emotion that has long been considered to be a major cause of aggression is *frustration*, which occurs when we are prevented from reaching some goal.

Frustration and Aggression   Suppose that a friend interrupts your studying for an exam by asking to borrow a book. If things have been going well that day and you are feeling confident about the exam, you will probably be friendly and helpful. But what if you are feeling frustrated because your friend's visit was the fifth interruption in the last hour? Under these emotional circumstances, you may react aggressively, perhaps snapping at your startled visitor for bothering you.

Your aggressiveness in this situation would be predicted by the **frustration-aggression hypothesis**, which suggests that frustration leads to aggression (Dollard et al., 1939). Research on this hypothesis has shown that it is too simple and too general, however. For one thing, frustration sometimes produces depression and withdrawal, not aggression (Berkowitz, 1998). In addition, not all aggression is preceded by frustration (Berkowitz, 1994).

After many years of research, Leonard Berkowitz suggested two modifications designed to increase the accuracy of the frustration-aggression hypothesis. First, he proposed that it may be stress in general, not just frustration, that is involved in aggression. Stress, he said, produces a readiness for aggression that may or may not be translated into aggressive behavior (Berkowitz, 1998). Once this readiness exists, however, aggression can be more easily triggered by environmental stimuli. The triggering stimuli might be guns or knives, televised scenes of people arguing, violent song lyrics, or other cues associated with aggression. In other words, neither stress alone nor environmental cues alone are enough to set off aggression. When combined, however, they often do. Support for this aspect of Berkowitz's theory has been quite strong (Bushman & Huesmann, 2010).

Second, Berkowitz argues that the direct cause of most kinds of aggression is negative feelings, or *negative affect* (Berkowitz, 1998). Research suggests that the more negative affect people experience, regardless of what caused it, the stronger is their readiness to be aggressive. Participants in one study experienced negative affect caused by the pain of immersing their hands in ice water. They became more aggressive than participants in a control group whose hands were in water of room temperature (Berkowitz, 1998).

Generalized Arousal   Imagine that you've just jogged three miles. You are hot, sweaty, and out of breath, but you aren't angry. Still, the physiological arousal caused by jogging may increase the probability that you will become aggressive if, say, a passerby shouts an insult (Zillmann, 1988). Why? The answer lies in a phenomenon described in the chapter on motivation and emotion: arousal from one experience may carry over to a new situation, producing what is called *excitation transfer*. So the physiological arousal caused by jogging may intensify your reaction to an insult (Harrison, 2003).

By itself, however, arousal does not lead to aggression. It is most likely to produce aggression when a situation presents some reason, opportunity, or target for aggression (Zillmann, 2003). In one study, for example, people engaged in two minutes of vigorous exercise. Then they had the opportunity to deliver electric shock to another person. The participants chose to give high levels of shock only if they had first been insulted (Zillmann, Katcher, & Milavsky, 1972). Apparently, the arousal resulting from the exercise made aggression more likely; the insult "released" it. These findings are in keeping with the notion that aggression is caused not by internal impulses alone or by particular situations alone but by the interaction of the two (Ferguson & Dyck, 2012; Klinesmith, Kasser, & McAndrew, 2006).

frustration-aggression hypothesis
A proposition stating that frustration always leads to some form of aggressive behavior.

THINKING CRITICALLY # Does Pornography Cause Aggression?

In both men and women, sexual stimulation produces strong, generalized physiological arousal, especially in the sympathetic nervous system. If arousal in general can make a person more likely to be aggressive (given a reason, opportunity, and target), could stimuli that create sexual arousal be dangerous? In particular, does viewing or reading pornographic material make people more likely to be aggressive? Prior to the mid-1980s, several scholars had concluded that there was no evidence for an overall relationship between any type of antisocial behavior and mere exposure to pornographic material (Donnerstein, 1984). However, in 1986 the U.S. Attorney General's Commission on Pornography reexamined the question and concluded that pornography is dangerous.

What am I being asked to believe or accept?

Specifically, the commission proposed that there is a cause-effect link between exposure to erotic material and several forms of antisocial behavior, including sexually related violent crimes.

Is evidence available to support the claim?

The commission cited several types of evidence in support of its conclusion. First, there was the testimony of men convicted of sex crimes. Rapists, for example, are unusually heavy users of pornography, and they often say that they were aroused by erotic material immediately before committing a rape (Silbert & Pines, 1984). Similarly, child molesters often view child pornography immediately before committing their crimes (Marshall, 1989).

The commission also cited experimental evidence that men who are most aroused by aggressive themes in pornography are also the most potentially sexually aggressive. One study, for example, showed that men who said they could commit a rape became sexually aroused by scenes of rape and less aroused by scenes of mutually consenting sex; this was not true for men who said they could never commit a rape (Malamuth & Check, 1983).

Perhaps the strongest evidence cited by the commission, however, came from excitation transfer studies. In one experiment, male participants were told that a person in another room (actually an employee of the experimenter) would be performing a learning task and that they were to administer an electric shock every time the person made a mistake. The intensity of shock could be varied (as in the Milgram studies, no shock actually reached the employee), but participants were told that changing the intensity would not affect the speed of learning. So the shock intensity (and presumed pain) that they chose to administer was considered to be a measure of aggression. Before the learning trials began, some participants watched a film in which several men had sex with the same woman. These participants' aggressiveness during the learning experiment was greater than that of men who did not watch the film (Donnerstein, 1984).

Can that evidence be interpreted another way?

The commission's interpretation of all this evidence was questioned for several reasons. First, critics argued that some of the evidence should be given little weight. In particular, how much should we rely on what convicted sex offenders say? Their testimony may reflect self-serving attempts to lay the blame for their crimes on pornography. These reports cannot establish that exposure to pornography causes aggression. In fact, it may be that pornography partially *satisfies* sex offenders' aggressive impulses rather than creating them (Aronson, Wilson, & Akert, 2005). Similarly, the fact that potential rapists are most aroused by rape-oriented material may show only that they prefer violence-oriented pornography, not that such materials created their impulse to rape.

What about the evidence from excitation transfer studies? To interpret these studies, you need to know that the pornography that led to increased aggression contained violence as well as sex. The sexual activity depicted was painful for or unwanted by the woman. So the higher levels of aggression that followed viewing these films could have been due to the transfer of sexual arousal, the effects of observing violent behavior, or the effects of seeing sex combined with violence (Donnerstein, Slaby, & Eron, 1995).

Several careful experiments have found that highly arousing sexual themes do not produce aggression in and of themselves. When men in excitation transfer studies experience pleasant arousal by viewing a film depicting nudity or mutually consenting sexual activity, they are actually less aggressive than when they viewed no film or a neutral film (Lord, 1997). In short, excitation transfer studies might be interpreted as showing that aggressiveness is influenced by portrayals of sexual violence but not by watching other kinds of sexually arousing material.

What evidence would help to evaluate the alternatives?

Two types of evidence are needed to better understand the effects of pornography on aggression. First, because pornography can include sexual acts, aggressive acts, or both, the effects of each of these components must be more carefully examined. Second, factors affecting men's reactions to pornography, particularly pornography that involves violence, must be more clearly understood. Work is in progress on each of these fronts.

Whether specifically paired with sexual activity or not, aggressive themes do appear to increase subsequent aggression (Bushman & Anderson, 2001). Research has focused on *aggressive pornography*, which contains both sexual themes and scenes of violence against women (Malamuth, Addison, & Koss, 2000). In laboratory experiments, males have been shown to administer stronger electric shocks to females after viewing aggressive pornographic films than after viewing nonpornographic films. Yet there was no parallel increase in aggression against other men, suggesting that aggressive pornography creates an increase in aggressiveness that is specifically directed toward women (Aronson, Wilson, & Akert, 2005). Similarly, viewing aggressive pornography in which a rape victim appears to be aroused by the aggression usually leads men to become less sympathetic toward the victim and more tolerant of aggressive acts toward women (Donnerstein & Linz, 1995). Sexually explicit films that do not contain violence have no effects on attitudes toward rape (Linz, Donnerstein, & Penrod, 1987).

Are all men who are exposed to aggressive pornography equally likely to become rapists? The evidence available so far suggests that the answer is no (Seto, Maric, & Barbaree, 2001). Whether aggressive pornography alters men's behavior and attitudes toward women depends to some extent on the men. For example, one study of about 2,700 men in the United States collected data on their sexual aggressiveness, their use of pornography, their history of sexual promiscuity, and their feelings of hostility toward women (Malamuth, 1998). Among men low in promiscuity and hostility, viewing pornography had little or no impact on sexual aggression, but among men who were high in promiscuity and hostility, pornography dramatically increased the chances that these men would engage in sexual aggression. In fact, 72 percent of the men who were high in all three factors—use of pornography, promiscuity, and hostility—had actually engaged in sexually aggressive acts (see Figure 14.12). Viewing pornography appears to have similar effects on convicted sex offenders who have been placed on probation or released on parole, and the effects are especially pronounced among those who had committed the most serious sex crimes (Kingston et al., 2008).

What conclusions are most reasonable?

The attorney general's commission appeared to ignore numerous studies showing that the relationship between sexual arousal and aggression is neither consistent nor simple (Seto, Marick, & Barbaree, 2001). Analysis of this relationship reveals that it is important to distinguish between pornography in general and aggressive pornography in particular. Aggressive pornography can lead to violence against women, especially in men who are already inclined to abuse and exploit them. So there is reason for concern over the impact of sexual violence commonly seen on television and in movies, especially in "slasher" films. Remarkably, such films are sometimes given less restrictive ratings ("R" or even "PG-13") than films that are nonviolent but erotic.

The effects of nonaggressive pornography are more complicated. For most men, it has little or no impact on their behavior toward women. But among men who are inclined to abuse and exploit women, exposure to a lot of pornography might increase the chances that they would act on their abusive impulses (Malamuth, Addison, & Koss, 2000; Seto, Marick,

Percentage who engaged in sexual aggression

- 80
- 70
- 60
- 50
- 40
- 30
- 20
- 10

Hostile, promiscuous men   Nonhostile, nonpromiscuous men

Small amount of pornography watched
Large amount of pornography watched

FIGURE 14.12

Pornography and Sexual Aggression
By itself, extensive exposure to pornography does not increase most men's sexual aggressiveness. Such aggressiveness is much more likely, however, among men who not only view or read a lot of pornography but also are hostile toward women and are sexually promiscuous (Malamuth, 1998).

Rape
Murder
Other violent crime

FIGURE 14.13

Temperature and Aggression

Studies from around the world indicate that aggressive behaviors are most likely to occur during the hottest months of the year. These studies support the hypothesis that environmental factors can affect aggression.

Source: From C. A. Anderson, and K. P. Anderson, "Temperature and Aggression: Paradox, Controversy, and a (Fairly) Clear Picture," *in Human Aggression,* edited by R. G. Green and E. Donnerstein. Copyright © 1998 Elsevier. Reprinted with permission.

environmental psychology
The study of the effects of the physical environment on people's behavior and mental processes.

prosocial behavior (helping behavior)
Any act that is intended to benefit another person.

altruism An unselfish concern for another's welfare.

& Barbaree, 2001). In summary, pornography is probably not, by itself, a major cause of violence against women. In combination with other factors, however, pornography—especially aggressive pornography—can play a role in sexual aggression. • • • •

Environmental Influences on Aggression The link between stress, arousal, and the likelihood of aggressive behavior suggests that stressful environmental conditions can create enough arousal to make aggressive behavior more likely (Bushman & Bartholow, 2010). This possibility is one of the research topics in **environmental psychology**, the study of the relationship between people's physical environment and their behavior (Bell et al., 2000). One aspect of the environment that clearly affects social behavior is the weather, especially temperature. High temperatures are a source of stress: as Figure 14.13 indicates, murder and other violent crimes are most likely to occur during the hottest months of the year (Anderson et al., 2000; Bushman, Wang, & Anderson, 2005). Athletes tend to behave more aggressively in hotter weather, and even hearing words associated with high temperatures—such as "boiling" or "roasting"—is associated with increased aggressiveness (Dewall & Bushman, 2009; Larrick et al., 2011).

Aggressiveness is also associated with noisy environments, especially if the noise is unpredictable and irregular (Bushman & Bartholow, 2010), and with living in crowded and unpleasant conditions such as those often found in prisons and some psychiatric hospitals (Baumeister & Bushman, 2011; Yuma, 2010).

Altruism and Prosocial Behavior

What motivates people to help one another?

Acts of terrorism provide horrifying examples of human behavior at its worst. But like all tragedies, they draw responses that provide inspiring examples of human behavior at its best. For example, Michael Benfante and John Cerqueira were working in the World Trade Center on 9/11 when one of the hijacked planes struck their building. They headed for a stairwell, but they did not just save themselves. Although it slowed their own escape, they chose to carry Tina Hansen, a wheelchair-bound co-worker, down 68 flights of stairs to safety. Acts of selflessness and sacrifice were common that day and in the days and weeks and months that followed. Police officers, medical personnel, search-and-rescue specialists, and just ordinary people came to New York from all over the United States to help clear wreckage, look for survivors, and recover bodies. More than $1 billion in donations to the Red Cross and other charity organizations poured in to help victims, and volunteering in general more than tripled in the weeks following the attacks (Penner, Dovidio, et al., 2005).

All of these actions are examples of **prosocial behavior,** also known as **helping behavior,** which is defined as any act that is intended to benefit another person. Helping can range from picking up dropped packages to donating a kidney. Closely related to prosocial behavior is **altruism,** an unselfish concern for another's welfare (Penner, Dovidio, et al., 2005). Let's consider some of the reasons behind helping and altruism, along with some of the conditions under which people are most likely to thelp others.

Why Do People Help?

The tendency to help others begins early in life, although at first it is not automatic. Children have to learn to be helpful (Eisenberg & Fabes, 1998). In most cultures, very young children usually help others only when they are asked to do so or are offered a reward (Grusec, Davidov, & Lundell, 2002). Still, observational studies have shown that many children as young as 18 months will spontaneously help a friend, a family member, or even a stranger (Dunfield & Kuhlmeier, 2010; Hepach, Vaish, & Tomasello, 2012; Knafo et al., 2008; Over & Carpenter, 2009). As they grow older, children use helping to gain social approval and their efforts at assisting others become more elaborate. The role of social influence in the development of helping is seen as children follow the examples set by people around them (McCullough & Tabak, 2010). In addition, children are usually praised and given other rewards for helpfulness but are scolded for selfishness. Eventually most children come to believe that being helpful is good and that they are good when they are helpful. By the late teens, people often assist others even when no one is watching and no one will know that they did so (Grusec, Davidov, & Lundell, 2002). There are three major theories about why people help even when they cannot expect any external rewards for doing so.

A Young Helper
Even before their second birthday, some children offer help to those who are hurt or crying by snuggling, patting, or offering food or even their own teddy bears. Their helpful actions are shaped by the norms established by their families and the broader culture (Grusec & Goodnow, 1994).

Arousal: Cost-Reward Theory   The **arousal: cost-reward theory** proposes that people find the sight of a victim distressing and anxiety-provoking and that this experience motivates them to do something to reduce the unpleasant arousal (Dovidio et al., 2006; Piliavin et al., 1981). Before rushing to a victim's aid, however, the bystander will first evaluate two aspects of the situation: the costs associated with helping and the costs (to the bystander and the other person) of not helping. Whether or not the bystander actually helps depends on the outcome of this evaluation (Dovidio et al., 1991). If the costs of helping are low (as in picking up someone's dropped grocery bag) and the costs of not helping are high (as when the other person is physically unable to do this alone), the bystander will almost certainly help. However, if the costs of helping are high (as when the task is to load a heavy box into a car) and the costs of not helping are low (as when the other person is obviously strong enough to do the job alone), the bystander is unlikely to offer help. One of the strengths of the arousal: cost-reward theory is that it is broad enough to explain several factors that affect assistance.

The first of these factors is the *clarity of the need for help* (McCullough & Tabak, 2010). In a laboratory study of this factor, undergraduate students waiting alone in a campus building saw what appeared to be an accident involving a window washer. The man screamed as he and his ladder fell to the ground, then he clutched his ankle and groaned in pain. All the students looked out of the window to see what had happened, but only 29 percent of them did anything to help. Other students witnessed the same "accident" but with one important added element: the man said he was hurt and needed help. In this case, more than 80 percent of the participants came to his aid (Yakimovich & Saltz, 1971). Why so many? Apparently, this one additional cue eliminated any uncertainty about whether assistance was needed. The man's more obvious need for assistance served to raise the perceived costs of not helping him, thus making helping more likely.

If this laboratory study seems unrealistic, consider the March 2000 case of a 62-year-old woman in Darby, Pennsylvania. She was walking to the grocery store when she was pushed from behind by an attacker. She fended him off and then did her shopping as usual. It was only when she got home and her daughter saw the handle of a knife protruding from her back that she realized that the assailant had stabbed her! No one in the grocery store said anything to her about the knife, let alone offered to help. Why? The most likely explanation is that the woman did nothing to suggest that assistance was necessary.

The *presence of others* also has a strong influence on the tendency to help. Somewhat surprisingly, however, their presence tends to make assistance less likely (Garcia et al., 2002). In October, 2011, a two-year-old girl who had been injured in a hit-and-run accident in Foshan, China lay bleeding in the street as more than a dozen people passed by without offering assistance ("Chinese Girl", 2011). Two years earlier, 12 people in Richmond, California, simply watched as a 15-year-old girl was beaten and gang-raped outside her high school homecoming dance ("Dozen People Watched," 2009). And in June of 2007, in a Wichita, Kansas convenience store, a 27-year-old woman who had been stabbed after an argument lay ignored by passersby as she bled to death. Surveillance video shows five other shoppers stepping over her, including one who stopped only long enough to take a picture with a cell phone (Associated Press, 2007b). Whenever such cases are publicized, journalists and social commentators express dismay about the cold, uncaring attitudes that seem to exist among people who live in big cities.

That description may apply to some people, but research stimulated by such cases has revealed a social phenomenon that offers a different explanation of why all those passersby took no action to help. This phenomenon, called the **bystander effect**, makes an individual less likely to help in an emergency when there are many other people present

arousal: cost-reward theory
A theory attributing people's prosocial behavior to their efforts to reduce unpleasant arousal in the face of someone's need or suffering, while also considering the costs involved.

bystander effect   A phenomenon in which the chances that someone will help in an emergency decrease as the number of people present increases.

(McCullough & Tabak, 2010). Why does the bystander effect occur? One explanation is that each witness assumes someone else will take responsibility for helping the victim. This *diffusion of responsibility* among all the witnesses leaves each witness feeling less obligated to help and thus lowers the perceived cost of not helping (Dovidio et al., 2006; Dovidio & Penner, 2001). So if you're ever in need of help, especially in a crowd, it is important not only to actually ask for help, but also to tell a specific onlooker to take specific action (e.g., "You, in the yellow shirt, please call an ambulance!").

The degree to which the presence of other people will suppress the tendency to help may depend on who those other people are. When they are strangers, perhaps poor communication interferes with assistance. Many people have difficulty speaking to strangers, particularly in an emergency, and without speaking, they have difficulty knowing what the others intend to do. According to this logic, if people are with friends rather than strangers, they should be less embarrassed, more willing to discuss the problem, and more likely to help.

In a study designed to test this idea, an experimenter left a research participant in a waiting room, either alone, with a friend, with a stranger, or with a stranger who was actually the experimenter's assistant (Latané & Rodin, 1969). The experimenter then stepped behind a curtain into an office. For a few minutes, she could be heard opening and closing the drawers of her desk, shuffling papers, and so on. Then there was a loud crash and she screamed, "Oh, my god—my foot, I—I can't move it. Oh, my ankle—I can't get this—thing off me." Then the participant heard her groan and cry.

Would the participant go behind the curtain to offer assistance? Once again, people were most likely to help if they were alone. When one other person was present, participants were more likely to communicate with one another and offer help if they were friends than if they were strangers. When the stranger was the experimenter's assistant—who had been instructed not to help—very few participants offered to help. Other studies have confirmed that bystanders' tendency to help increases when they know one another (Rutkowski, Gruder, & Romer, 1983).

Research suggests that the *personality of the helper* also plays a role in helping. Some people are simply more likely to help than others. Consider, for example, the Christians who risked their lives to save Jews from the Nazi Holocaust during World War II. Researchers

No Diffusion of Responsibility Here
Although people are sometimes callous and indifferent to the plight of others in emergencies, they are sometimes just the opposite. This September, 2011 photo shows bystanders lifting a burning car to reach a motorcyclist who had been trapped underneath it after a collision. In light of our previous discussion, make a list of the social, personality, cultural, and situational factors that might have prevented diffusion of responsibility in this case and led these people to risk their lives to pull the injured man to safety.

LEARN by DOING

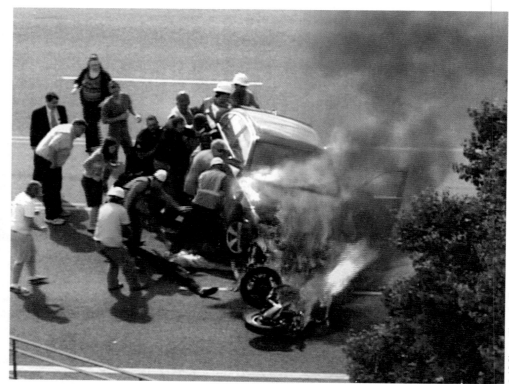

interviewed these rescuers many years later and compared their personalities with those of people who had a chance to save Jews but did not do so (Fagin-Jones & Midlarsky, 2007; Oliner & Oliner, 1988). The rescuers were found to have more empathy, more concern about others, a greater sense of responsibility for their own actions, and greater confidence that their efforts would succeed. Louis Penner and his associates (Penner, 2002; Penner & Finkelstein, 1998) have found that these kinds of personality traits predict a broad range of helping, from how quickly bystanders intervene in an emergency to how much time volunteers spend helping AIDS patients. Consistent with the arousal: cost-reward theory, these personality characteristics are correlated with people's estimates of the costs of helping and not helping. For example, empathic individuals usually estimate the costs of not helping as high, and people who are confident about their ability to help usually rate the costs of helping as low (Penner et al., 1995).

Valuable as it is, the arousal: cost-reward theory cannot account for all aspects of helping. For instance, it cannot easily explain why environmental factors affect prosocial behavior. Research conducted in several countries has shown that people in urban areas are generally less helpful than those in rural areas (Aronson, Wilson, & Akert, 2005; Dovidio et al., 2006). Why? The explanation probably has more to do with the stressors found in cities than with city living itself. One study of 24 U.S. cities showed that the greater a city's size and density (number of people per square mile), the less likely people were to help others. Helping was also much less likely in cities where stressful economic conditions were greatest (Levine, Reysen, & Ganz, 2008). Previous studies of cities in the United States, the United Kingdom, the Middle East, and Africa had also found that people's tendency to help was more strongly related to the population density where they lived than to the overall size of their city (Hedge & Yousif, 1992; Levine et al., 1994; Yousif & Korte, 1995). The higher the density, the less likely people were to help others. Why should stress make people less helpful? Two explanations have been suggested. The first is that stressful environments create bad moods—and generally speaking, people in bad moods are less likely to help (Forgas, Dunn, & Granland, 2008; Salovey, Mayer, & Rosenhan, 1991). A second possibility is that noise, crowding, and other urban stressors create too much stimulation. To reduce this stimulation, people may pay less attention to their surroundings, including less attention to individuals who need help.

Empathy-Altruism Helping Theory   There are also situations in which matters of cost are not the major cause of a decision to help or not help. A second approach to explaining prosocial behavior considers some of these situations. This second approach is embodied in **empathy-altruism helping theory**, which maintains that people are more likely to engage in altruistic, or unselfish, assistance—even at a high cost—if they feel empathy toward the person in need (Batson, 1998, 2010). In one experiment illustrating this phenomenon, students listened to a recorded interview in which a young woman told how her parents had died in an automobile accident, leaving no life insurance (Batson et al., 1997). She said that she was trying to take care of her younger brother and sister while going to college but that time and money were so tight that she might have to quit school or give up her siblings for adoption. None of this was true, but the participants were told that it was. Before hearing the recording, half the participants were given information about the woman that would increase their empathy for her; the other half were not. After listening to the recording, all participants were asked to help the woman raise money for herself and her siblings. Consistent with the empathy-altruism helping theory, more participants in the empathy group offered to help than did those in the control group.

Were the students who offered help in this experiment being utterly unselfish or could there have been other reasons for their apparent altruism? This is a hotly debated question. Some researchers dispute the claim that this study illustrated truly altruistic helping. They suggest instead that people help in such situations for more selfish reasons, such as relieving the distress they experienced after hearing of the woman's problems (Maner et al., 2002). The final verdict on this question is not yet in.

Evolutionary Theory   The evolutionary approach to psychology offers a third way to explain prosocial behavior. According to this approach, many human social behaviors are

Creating Empathy

The amount of empathy a person feels for you can depend on several factors, including the words you choose when asking for help (Guéguen & Lamy, 2011), whether you physically touch the other person while asking (Schirmer et al., 2011), whether you're a member of the same social ingroup (Cikara, Botvinik, & Fiske, 2011; Cikara, Bruneau, & Saxe, 2011), and whether the person sees you as a potential threat (Agthe, Spörrle, & Maner, 2010; van de Ven, Zeelenberg, & Pieters, 2010). The person's actual or perceived socioeconomic status can also be influential (Ma, Wang, & Han, 2011; Rucker, Dubois, & Galinsky, 2011; Stellar et al., 2012).

empathy-altruism helping theory
A theory suggesting that people help others because they feel empathy toward them.

a reflection of actions that contributed to the survival of our prehistoric ancestors (Maner & Kenrick, 2010). At first glance, it might not seem reasonable to apply evolutionary theory to prosocial behavior and altruism, because helping others at the risk of our own well-being does not appear adaptive. If we die while trying to save others, it will be their genes, not ours, that will survive. In fact, according to Darwin's concept of the "survival of the fittest," helpers—and their genes—should have disappeared long ago. Today's evolutionary theorists suggest, however, that Darwin's thinking about natural selection focused too much on the survival of the fittest *individuals* and not enough on the survival of their genes in *others*. Accordingly, the concept of survival of the fittest has been replaced by the concept of *inclusive fitness*, the survival of one's genes in future generations (Hamilton, 1964; West & Gardner, 2010). Because we share genes with our relatives, helping—or even dying for—a cousin, a sibling, or (above all) our own child increases the likelihood that at least some of our genetic characteristics will be passed on to the next generation through the beneficiary's future reproduction (Rachlin & Jones, 2008). So *kin selection,* or helping a relative survive, may produce genetic benefits for the helper even if it provides no personal benefits (Krebs, 2011).

There is considerable evidence that kin selection occurs among birds, squirrels, and other animals. The more closely the animals are related, the more likely they are to risk their lives for one another. Studies in a wide variety of cultures show the same pattern of prosocial behavior among humans (Krebs, 2011). For example, people in the United States are three times as likely to donate a kidney to a relative as to a nonrelative (Borgida, Conner, & Monteufel, 1992). (See "In Review: Prosocial Behavior" for a summary of the major reasons why people help and the conditions under which they are most likely to do so.)

Prosocial Behavior		IN REVIEW
Theory	**Basic Premise**	**Important Variables**
Arousal: cost-reward	People help others in order to reduce the unpleasant arousal caused by another person's distress. They attempt to minimize the costs of doing this.	Factors that affect the costs of helping and of not helping
Empathy-altruism	People sometimes help others for unselfish reasons if they feel empathy for a person in need. They are motivated by a desire to increase another person's well-being.	The amount of empathy that one person feels for another
Evolutionary	People help relatives because it increases the chances that the helper's genes will survive in future generations.	The biological relationship between the helper and the recipient of help

IN REVIEW QUESTIONS

1. If you could save only one person from a burning house, the ___ theory of prosocial behavior would predict that it would be your own child rather than, say, a grandparent.

2. Are you more likely to receive help in a nearly empty bus or in a crowded bus terminal?

3. People who have empathy for others are ___ likely to be helpful.

cooperation Any type of behavior in which people work together to attain a goal.

competition Any type of behavior in which individuals try to attain a goal while denying others access to that goal.

conflict What occurs when a person or group believes that another person or group interferes with the attainment of a goal.

Cooperation, Competition, and Conflict

Helping is one of several ways that people *cooperate* with one another. **Cooperation** is any type of behavior that involves people working together to attain a goal (Penner, Dovidio, et al., 2005). For example, several law students might form a study group to help one another pass the bar exam. But people also compete with others for limited resources. Those same students might later try to outdo one another to be chosen for a single job opening at a top law firm. **Competition** exists whenever individuals try to reach a goal while denying others access to that goal. Finally, there is **conflict**, which occurs when a person or group believes that another person or group interferes with the attainment of a goal. When the law students become attorneys and represent opposing parties in a trial, they will be in conflict with one another. One way that psychologists have learned about all three of these phenomena is by studying social dilemmas (Kassin, Fein, & Markus, 2011). **Social dilemmas** are situations in which an action that is most rewarding for the individual will, if widely adopted, create problems for everyone (Aronson, Wilson, & Akert, 2010). For instance, during a drought, individual homeowners are better off in the short run by watering their lawns as often as necessary to keep them from dying, but if everyone ignores local water restrictions, there will be no drinking water for anyone in the long run. Social dilemmas reflect conflicts between the interests of the individual and those of the group and between short-term and long-term interests (Schroeder, 1995). Are people from collectivist cultures (which emphasize cooperation) less likely to act competitively or selfishly in social dilemma situations? In general, they may be, but interpersonal conflict in such situations still appears to some extent in all cultures (Smith & Bond, 1999).

Group Processes

What makes a good leader?

Although Western industrialized cultures tend to emphasize individuals over groups, the fact remains that most important decisions and efforts by governments and businesses in those cultures and elsewhere are made by groups, not individuals (Hackman & Katz, 2010). Sometimes groups function very well. Perhaps you recall the extraordinary teamwork of emergency workers and volunteers that led to dramatic rescues of people trapped by flood waters after Hurricane Sandy struck the Northeast coast of the United States in 2012. At other times, though, groups malfunction, resulting in poor performance and bad and sometimes disastrous decisions. To begin to understand why, let's consider some of the social psychological processes that often occur in groups to alter the behavior of individuals and the quality of their collective efforts.

The Presence of Others

The term **social facilitation** describes circumstances in which the presence of other people can improve performance (Aiello & Douthitt, 2001). This improvement does not always occur, however. In fact, having other people present sometimes hurts performance, a process known as **social interference.** For decades, these results seemed contradictory; then Robert Zajonc (pronounced "ZYE-onze") suggested that both effects could be explained by one process: arousal.

The presence of other people, said Zajonc, increases a person's general level of arousal or motivation (Zajonc, 1965). Why? One reason is that being watched by others increases our sense of being evaluated, producing worry that in turn increases emotional arousal (Penner & Craiger, 1992; Uziel, 2007). Arousal increases the tendency to perform those behaviors that are most *dominant*—the ones you know best. This tendency can either help or hinder performance. When you are performing an easy, familiar task, such as riding a bike, increased arousal due to the presence of others should allow you to ride even faster than normal. But when a task is hard or unfamiliar—such as trying new dance steps or playing a newly learned piano piece in front of an audience—the most dominant responses may be incorrect and cause performance to suffer. In other words, the impact of other people on performance depends on whether the task is easy or difficult. It can depend, too, on how people interpret the performance situation. For example, they tend to do better if they see the performance as a chance to show off their skill rather than as an attempt to avoid looking incompetent (Feinberg & Aiello, 2010).

What if a person is not merely in the presence of others but is working with them on some task? In these situations, people often exert less effort than when performing alone, a phenomenon called **social loafing** (Forsyth & Burnette, 2010). Whether the task is pulling on a rope, clapping as loudly as possible, or working together on a class project, people tend to work harder when alone than with others (Price, Harrison, & Gavin, 2006;

social dilemmas Situations in which actions that produce rewards for one individual will produce negative consequences for all if they are adopted by everyone.

social facilitation A phenomenon in which the presence of others improves a person's performance.

social interference A reduction in performance due to the presence of other people.

social loafing Exerting less effort when performing a group task than when performing the same task alone.

© Ahmad Yusni/EPA/Landov

Social Facilitation

Premier athletes like Victoria Azarenka, shown here winning the 2012 women's singles championship at the Australian Open, are able to perform at their best even though large crowds are present. In fact, the crowds probably help them do well, because the presence of others tends to increase arousal, which enhances the performance of familiar and well-learned skills, such as tennis strokes. However, arousal created by an audience tends to interfere with the performance of unfamiliar and poorly developed skills. This is one reason that professional athletes who show flawless grace in front of thousands of fans are likely to freeze up or blow their lines in front of a small production crew when trying for the first time to tape a TV ad or a public service announcement.

task-motivated leaders Leaders who provide close supervision, lead by giving directions, and generally discourage group discussion.

relationship-motivated leaders Leaders who provide loose supervision, ask for group members' ideas, and are generally concerned with subordinates' feelings.

van Dick et al., 2009). Research in industrial and organizational psychology suggests that social loafing is most likely when large groups work on the same task (making each member's contribution harder to evaluate), when the group is not closely knit, and when members feel they are not being rewarded according to their performance (Hoigaard & Ingvaldeson, 2006; Pearsall, Christian, & Ellis, 2010). Social loafing is less likely when group members like each other and identify with the group and its goals (Hoigaard, Säfvenbom, & Tonnessen, 2006). It is also reduced when harder-working members of a group punish the social loafers with criticism or other negative consequences (Barclay, 2006).

In Western cultures, social loafing appears in groups of all sorts, from volunteer committees to search parties. It is much less likely among people in collectivist cultures such as those in China and Japan (Kassin, Fein, & Markus, 2011). In fact, in collectivist cultures, working in a group usually produces *social striving*—defined as greater individual effort when working in a group (Matsumoto, 2000). This difference in the effects of group membership on individual efforts probably reflects the high value that collectivist cultures place on coordinated and cooperative group activities. Social loafing is not unknown in collectivist cultures, though, especially in situations where people see others in their group doing it (Hong, Wyer, & Fong, 2008).

Group Leadership

The role of group leaders is especially important when social loafing and other obstacles threaten to impair the effectiveness of group efforts. A good leader can help a group pursue its goals, but a bad one can get in the way of a group's functioning (Forsyth & Burnette, 2010). What makes a good leader? Psychologists once thought that the personalities of good and bad leaders were about the same, but we now know that certain personality traits often distinguish effective from ineffective leaders. For example, researchers have found that, in general, effective leaders are intelligent, conscientious, success oriented, flexible, and confident (Chemers, Watson, & May, 2000; Foti & Hauenstein, 2007; Ones, Viswesvaran, & Dilchert, 2005).

Having particular personality traits does not guarantee good leadership ability, however. People who are effective leaders in one situation may be ineffective in another (Chemers, 2000; Ng, Ang, & Chan, 2008). This is because effective leadership also depends on the characteristics of the group members, the task at hand, and, most important, the interaction between these factors and the leader's style (Van Kleef et al., 2010; Yun, Faraj, & Sims, 2005).

For many years, leadership research focused on two main types of leaders. The first, called **task-motivated leaders,** provide close supervision, lead by giving orders, and generally discourage group discussion (Yukl & Van Fleet, 1992). Their style may make them unpopular. The second, called **relationship-motivated leaders,** provide loose supervision, ask for group members' ideas, and are generally concerned with subordinates' feelings. They are usually well liked by the group, even when they must discipline a group member (Kassin, Fein, & Markus, 2011). More recently, additional leadership styles have been identified. One of these styles is seen in *transactional leaders,* whose actions depend on the actions of those they lead. They reward those who behave as the leader wishes and they correct or punish those who don't. There are also *transformational* or *charismatic leaders* (Hogg, 2010). These people concentrate on creating a vision of the group's goals, inspiring others to pursue that vision, and giving their followers reason to respect and admire them.

Do men or women make better leaders? Research by Alice Eagly and her colleagues at first found that, overall, men and women are equally capable leaders (e.g., Eagly & Carli, 2007). It also looked as though men tend to be more effective when success requires a task-motivated leader, and that women tend to be more effective when success requires a more relationship-motivated leader. In other words, it appeared that people of each gender tend to be most effective when they are acting in a manner consistent with gender-role traditions (Eagly & Karau, 1991; Eagly, Karau, & Makhijani, 1995). Perhaps the reason was that some people did not like female leaders who act in a "masculine" manner or occupy leadership positions traditionally held by men (Eagly, Makhijani, & Klonsky, 1992).

A somewhat different picture of gender and leadership has emerged from Eagly's more recent research. For one thing, she found that females are generally more likely than males to display a transformational leadership style. Further, when women display a transactional style, they tend to be more encouraging than transactional male leaders, focusing more on using rewards rather than punishments to modify group members' behaviors. Finally, and in contrast to earlier findings, Eagly's results now suggest that women may be slightly more effective leaders overall than men (Ayman, Korabik, & Morris, 2009; Eagly & Sczesny, 2009).

Groupthink

The emphasis on group decisions in most large organizations is based on the belief that several people working together will make better decisions than will individuals working alone. As noted in the chapter on thought, language, and intelligence, this belief is generally correct, yet under certain circumstances groups have been known to make amazingly bad decisions (Forsyth & Burnette, 2010). Consider, for example, the fact that, in 1986, administrators at the National Aeronautics and Space Administration (NASA) ignored engineers' warnings about the effects of cold weather and decided to launch the space shuttle *Challenger*. The spacecraft exploded 73 seconds after liftoff, killing all aboard. After analyzing these and other disastrous decisions, Irving Janis (1989) proposed that they can be attributed to a phenomenon called *groupthink*. **Groupthink** occurs, he said, when group members are unable to realistically evaluate the options available to them or to fully consider the potential negative consequences of the option they are about to choose.

LINKAGES

How does stress affect group decision making? *(a link to Health, Stress, and Coping)*

Groupthink is particularly likely when four conditions exist: (1) the decision is not based on all the facts at hand; (2) group members all share certain biases; (3) members who express disagreement with the majority view are punished or even ejected from the group; and (4) the group leader puts pressure on the members to reach agreement. Some social psychologists believe that bad group decisions can be explained by processes other than groupthink (e.g., Baron, 2005; Hackman & Katz, 2010), but because groupthink does sometimes occur, other researchers have worked on developing techniques to help groups avoid it (Galinsky & Kray, 2004; Kray & Galinsky, 2003; Packer, 2009).

One way to avoid groupthink is to teach group members to imagine all the negative outcomes of each course of action they are considering. Another is to designate someone to play the "devil's advocate," a person who constantly challenges the group's emerging decision and forces everyone to consider all the facts and other decisions that are possible (Risen, 1998). Yet another technique is to encourage diverse opinions by allowing people to express them anonymously. For example, group members might communicate by e-mail on networked computers that hide the sender's identity. Research suggests that allowing groups to discuss decision options without knowing who is saying what stimulates logical debate and makes it easier for people to disagree with the group (O'Brien, 1991).

LINKAGES

Can we "see" prejudice in the brain? *(a link to Biology and Behavior)*

Biological and Social Psychology

Research in social psychology was once thought to be entirely separate from research on the biological processes that underlie social behavior (Heatherton & Wheatley, 2010). Social psychologists believed it was impossible to reduce complex social psychological processes to the firing of neurons or the secretion of hormones. For their part, biological psychologists, more commonly known as *neuroscientists,* viewed the study of social psychology as having little, if any, relevance to the understanding of, say, behavioral genetics or the functioning of the nervous system. Recently, however, scientists in both subfields have begun to take a closer look at each other's research and at how their subfields are linked. The result has been the emergence of a new specialty

groupthink A pattern of thinking that renders group members unable to evaluate realistically the wisdom of various options and decisions.

called **social neuroscience** or *social cognitive neuroscience* (Lieberman, 2010). This new specialty focuses on the influence of social processes on biological processes and on the influence of biological processes, including genetics, on social psychological phenomena (e.g., Bielsky et al., 2005; Mikolajczak et al., 2010; Robinson, Fernald, & Clayton, 2008; Thompson et al., 2006).

There are many reasons to believe that this approach will be valuable. For example, the chapter on health, stress, and coping contains numerous examples of how social stressors can have health-related biological consequences. Health psychologists have also found that the availability and quality of a person's social support network can affect biological processes ranging from blood pressure to the healing of wounds (Gouin et al., 2008, 2010; Kiecolt-Glaser, 2009). So the psychological pain of social rejection can appear not only in words ("she broke my heart," or "he hurt my feelings") but also in activation of brain regions that normally process physical pain (Eisenberger, 2012). The social environment can even affect the way our genes express themselves (Cole, 2009). In addition, as discussed in the chapter on psychological disorders, some problems in social behavior can result from the interaction of environmental stressors with genetic influences. One study compared the amount of antisocial behavior displayed by men who either had or had not suffered the stress of parental abuse in childhood. Antisocial behavior was much more common among men who had been abused, but this behavior was most common among abused men who also had inherited characteristics associated with antisocial behaviors (Caspi et al., 2002).

Researchers are beginning to identify the biological aspects of many social processes. One example can be seen in studies of how the amygdala—a brain structure involved in emotion—is related to the stereotyping and prejudice discussed earlier in this chapter (Amodio & Lieberman, 2009). Researchers found that European Americans who were prejudiced against African Americans showed significantly more amygdala activity when looking at pictures of black people than when looking at pictures of white people (Cunningham et al., 2004; Hart et al., 2000; Phelps et al., 2000). Using fMRI to study people's emotional reactions to other people's distress, some researchers have found patterns of brain activity that were quite different depending on whether the individual experienced empathy for a distressed person or simply observed the person's distress (Corradi-Dell'Acqua, Hofstetter, & Vuilleumier, 2011; Decety, 2012). Others have identified a relationship between people's ability to take the perspectives of others and the development of their brains from childhood through adolescence (van den Bos et al., 2011). Studies such as these are shedding light on the biological aspects of empathy, and they may eventually lead to a broader understanding of the factors influencing people's motivation to help each other (Decety, 2012; Poulin, Holman, & Buffone, 2012).

In short, social cognitive neuroscience shows great promise for creating a better understanding of the linkages among social, cognitive, and biological phenomena as well as a better understanding of complex social and physiological processes. ● ● ● ●

social neuroscience A specialty that focuses on the influence of social processes on biological processes and on the influence of biological processes on social psychological phenomena.

Active Review

As noted in the introductory chapter, all of psychology's subfields are related to one another. Our discussion of social neuroscience illustrates just one way that the topic of this chapter, social psychology, is linked to the subfield of biological psychology, which is discussed in the chapter

CHAPTER 14
Social Psychology

on biology and behavior. The Linkages diagram shows ties to two other subfields, and there are many more ties throughout the book. Looking for linkages among subfields will help you see how they all fit together and help you better appreciate the big picture that is psychology.

LINKAGES

Can we "see" prejudice in the brain?
(ans. on p. 585)

CHAPTER 2
Biology and Behavior

Do groups solve problems more effectively than individuals?
(ans. on p. 269)

CHAPTER 7
Thought, Language, and Intelligence

How do societies define what is normal?
(ans. on p. 461)

CHAPTER 12
Psychological Disorders

Summary

Social cognition, the mental processes through which people perceive and react to others, is one aspect of *social psychology,* the study of how people influence and are influenced by other people. Through social cognition, each person creates a unique perception of reality.

Social Influences on the Self

How do we compare ourselves with others?

People's social and cultural environments affect their thoughts and feelings about themselves, including their *self-concept* and their *self-esteem.* When people have no objective criteria by which to judge themselves, they look to others as the basis for *social comparison.* Such comparison can affect self-evaluation or self-esteem. Categories of people that are regularly used for social comparison are known as *reference groups.*

A person's *social identity* is formed from beliefs about the groups to which the person belongs. Social identity

affects the beliefs we hold about ourselves, our self-concept. Social identity permits people to feel that they are part of a larger group, generating loyalty and sacrifice from group members but also potentially creating bias and social discrimination toward people who are not members of the group.

Social Perception

Do we perceive people and objects in similar ways?

Social perception concerns the processes by which people interpret information about others, form impressions of them, and draw conclusions about the reasons for their behavior. *Schemas,* the knowledge about people and social situations that we carry into social interactions, affect what we pay attention to, what we

remember, and how we judge people and events.

First impressions are formed easily and quickly, in part because people apply existing schemas to their perceptions of others. First impressions change slowly because once we form an impression about another person, we try to maintain it. Schemas, however, can create *self-fulfilling prophecies,* leading us to act in ways that bring out behavior in others that is consistent with our expectations of them.

Attribution is the process of explaining the causes of people's behavior, including our own. Observers tend to attribute behavior to causes that are either internal or external to the actor. Attributions are also affected by biases that systematically distort our view of behavior. The most common attributional biases are the *fundamental attribution error* (and its cousin, the ultimate attribution error), the *actor-observer effect,* and the *self-serving bias.* Personal and cultural factors can affect the extent to which people exhibit these biases.

Attitudes

Do attitudes always determine behavior?

An *attitude* is the tendency to respond positively or negatively to a particular object. Attitudes affect a wide range of behaviors. Most social psychologists see attitudes as composed of three components: cognitive components (beliefs), affective components (feelings), and behavioral components (actions). However, it is often difficult to predict a specific behavior from a person's beliefs or feelings about an object. Cognitive theories suggest that the likelihood of attitude-behavior consistency depends on the importance of the attitude, subjective social norms, perceived control over the behavior, and prior direct experience with the attitude object.

Attitudes can be learned through modeling as well as through classical or operant conditioning. They are also subject to the mere-exposure effect: all else being equal, people develop greater liking for a new object the more often they are exposed to it.

The effectiveness of a persuasive message in changing attitudes is influenced by the characteristics of the person who communicates the message, by its content, and by the audience receiving it. The *elaboration likelihood model* suggests that attitude change can occur through either the peripheral or the central route, depending on a person's ability to carefully consider an argument and their motivation to do so. Accordingly, different messages will produce attitude change under different circumstances. Another approach is to change a person's behavior in the hope that attitudes will be adjusted to match the behavior. *Cognitive dissonance theory* holds that if inconsistency between attitude and behavior creates discomfort related to a person's self-concept, the attitude may change in order to reduce the conflict.

Prejudice and Stereotypes

How does prejudice develop?

Stereotypes often lead to *prejudice* and *social discrimination*. Motivational theories of prejudice suggest that some people have a need to dislike people who differ from themselves. This need may stem from the trait of authoritarianism as well as from a strong social identity with one's ingroup. In either case, feeling superior to members of outgroups helps these people feel better about themselves. As a result, ingroup members tend to discriminate against outgroups. Cognitive theories suggest that people categorize others into groups in order to reduce social complexity. Learning theories maintain that stereotypes, prejudice, and discriminatory behaviors can be learned from parents, peers, and the media. The *contact hypothesis* proposes that intergroup contact can reduce prejudice and lead to more favorable attitudes toward the stereotyped group, but only if the contact occurs under specific conditions, such as equal status between groups.

Interpersonal Attraction

What factors affect who likes whom?

Interpersonal attraction is affected by many variables. Physical proximity is important because it allows people to meet. The situation in which they meet is important because positive or negative aspects of the situation tend to be associated with the other person. Characteristics of the other person are also important. Attraction tends to be greater when two people share similar attitudes and personal characteristics. Physical appearance plays a role in attraction; initially, attraction is strongest to those who are most physically attractive. But for long-term relationships, the *matching hypothesis* applies: people tend to choose others whose physical attractiveness is about the same as theirs.

Two key components of successful intimate relationships are interdependence and mutual commitment. Sternberg's triangular theory suggests that love is a function of three components: passion, intimacy, and commitment. Varying combinations of these three components create qualitatively different types of love. Marital satisfaction depends on communication, the perception that the relationship is equitable, the couple's ability to deal effectively with conflict and anger, and agreement on important issues in the marriage.

Social Influence

What social rules shape our behavior?

Social norms establish the rules for what should and should not be done in a particular situation. One particularly powerful norm is reciprocity, the tendency to respond to others as they have acted toward us. *Deindividuation* is a psychological state in which people temporarily lose their individuality, their normal inhibitions are relaxed, and they may perform aggressive or illegal acts that they would not do otherwise.

When behavior or beliefs change as the result of unspoken or implicit group pressure, **conformity** has occurred. When the change is the result of a request, **compliance** has occurred. People tend to follow the normative responses of others, and groups create norms when none already exist. People sometimes display public conformity without private acceptance; at other times, the responses of others have an impact on private beliefs. People conform because they want to be right, because they want to be liked, and because they tend to be rewarded for conformity. People are most likely to conform when the situation is unclear as well as when others in the group are in unanimous agreement. Up to a point, conformity usually increases as the number of people holding the majority view grows larger. Effective strategies for creating compliance include the foot-in-the-door technique, the door-in-the-face procedure, and the lowball approach.

Obedience

How far will people go in obeying authority? **Obedience** involves complying with an explicit demand from an authority figure. Research by Milgram indicates that obedience is likely even when obeying an authority appears to result in pain and suffering for another person. Obedience declines when the status of the authority figure declines, when others are observed to disobey, and if a victim asks to be released. Some people are more likely to obey orders than others. Because participants in Milgram's studies experienced considerable stress, the experiments have been questioned on ethical grounds. Nevertheless, his research showed that people do not have to be psychologically disordered to inflict pain on others.

Aggression

Are people born aggressive? **Aggressive behavior** (**aggression**) is an act intended to harm another person.

Freud saw aggression as due partly to instincts. More recent theories attribute aggressive tendencies to genetic and evolutionary factors, brain dysfunctions, and hormonal influences. Learning is also important; people learn to display aggression by watching others and by being rewarded for aggressive behavior. There are wide cultural differences in the occurrence of aggression.

A variety of emotional factors play a role in aggression. The **frustration-aggression hypothesis** suggests that frustration can lead to aggression, particularly in the presence of cues that invite or promote aggression. Arousal from sources unrelated to aggression, such as exercise, can also make aggressive responses more likely, especially if aggression is already a dominant response in that situation. Research in **environmental psychology** suggests that factors such as high temperature and crowding increase the likelihood of aggressive behavior, particularly among people who are already angry.

Altruism and Prosocial Behavior

What motivates people to help one another? Humans often display **prosocial behavior (helping behavior)** and **altruism**. There are three major theories of why people help others. According to the **arousal: cost-reward theory**, people help in order to reduce the unpleasant arousal they experience when others are in distress. Their specific reaction to a suffering person depends on the costs associated with helping or not helping. Helping is most likely when the need for help is clear and when diffusion

of responsibility is not created by the presence of other people—a phenomenon called the **bystander effect**. Environmental and personality factors also affect willingness to help others. The **empathy-altruism helping theory** suggests that helping can be truly unselfish if the helper feels empathy for the person in need. Finally, evolutionary theory suggests that humans have an innate tendency to help others, especially relatives, because doing so increases the likelihood that family genes will survive.

Cooperation is any type of behavior in which people work together to attain a goal; **competition** exists whenever individuals try to attain a goal while denying others access to that goal. Interpersonal or intergroup **conflict** occurs when one person or group believes that another stands in the way of reaching some goal. Psychologists study conflict by observing behavior in **social dilemmas**, situations in which behavior that benefits individuals in the short run may spell disaster for an entire group in the long run.

Group Processes

What makes a good leader? People's behavior is affected by the mere presence of other people. By enhancing one's most likely behavior in a situation, the presence of others sometimes creates **social facilitation** (which improves performance) and sometimes creates **social interference** (which impairs performance). When people work in groups, they often exert less effort than when alone, a phenomenon called **social loafing**. Effective group leaders tend to score high on emotional stability, agreeableness, and conscientiousness. In general, they are also intelligent, success oriented, flexible, and confident. *Task-motivated leaders* provide close supervision, lead by giving orders, and generally discourage group discussion. *Relationship-motivated leaders* provide loose supervision, ask for group members' ideas, and are generally concerned with subordinates' feelings.

Transactional leaders focus on rewarding or correcting group members' performance, and transformational leaders tend to lead by example, thus inspiring good performance.

When *groupthink* occurs, decisions are not based on all the facts, group members share certain biases, dissenting members' views are rejected, and the

group leader pressures members to reach agreement.

A new specialty called *social neuroscience* focuses on the influence of social processes on biological processes and on the influence of biological processes on social psychological phenomena.

LEARN by DOING

Put It in Writing
Suppose that a survey reveals that first-graders from various ethnic groups in a local school hold prejudiced attitudes toward one another. Imagine that you have been hired to develop a program to help these children become less prejudiced and more accepting of members of other ethnic groups. Write a one-page description of two or three classroom activities that would help you accomplish this goal and tell why you think they would work. Do you think these activities could be

successful in eliminating all prejudiced thinking in the children? Why or why not?

Personal Learning Activity
Research mentioned in this chapter suggests that the physical appearance of a partner tends to be more important to men, whereas a partner's intelligence tends to be more important to women. If that is true, what qualities would you hypothesize that men versus women will say they are looking for when they place ads for a partner in a personal column or

dating web site? Develop a research plan to test your hypothesis and then collect some data by reading and analyzing personal ads in your local newspaper or on a web site for singles. Was your hypothesis supported? Did gender differences in the content of the ads appear more often, less often, or about equally in ads placed by heterosexuals, homosexuals, and bisexuals? Write a brief report of your findings, and summarize what you think they can and cannot say about the factors that attract people to each other.

Review of Key Terms

Can you define each of the key terms in the chapter? Check your definitions against those on the pages shown in parentheses in the following list or in the Glossary at the end of the book.

actor-observer effect (p. 550)
aggressive behavior (aggression) (p. 572)
altruism (p. 578)
arousal: cost-reward theory (p. 579)
attitude (p. 551)
attribution (p. 549)
bystander effect (p. 579)
cognitive dissonance theory (p. 553)
competition (p. 582)
compliance (p. 564)
conflict (p. 582)
conformity (p. 564)
contact hypothesis (p.557)

cooperation (p. 582)
deindividuation (p. 563)
elaboration likelihood model (p. 553)
empathy-altruism helping theory (p. 581)
environmental psychology (p. 578)
frustration-aggression hypothesis (p. 575)
fundamental attribution error (p. 549)
groupthink (p. 585)
matching hypothesis (p. 560)
obedience (p. 568)
prejudice (p. 555)
prosocial behavior (helping behavior) (p. 578)
reference groups (p. 545)
relationship-motivated leaders (p. 584)
schemas (p. 547)
self-concept (p. 544)

self-esteem (p. 544)
self-fulfilling prophecy (p. 549)
self-serving bias (p. 550)
social cognition (p. 544)
social comparison (p. 545)
social dilemmas (p. 583)
social discrimination (p. 555)
social facilitation (p. 583)
social identity (p. 546)
social interference (p. 583)
social loafing (p. 583)
social neuroscience (p. 586)
social norms (p. 563)
social perception (p. 547)
social psychology (p. 544)
stereotypes (p. 555)
task-motivated leaders (p. 584)

Test Your Knowledge

Select the best answer for each of the following questions. Then check your responses against the Answer Key at the end of the book.

1. Jack was accepted to a top graduate school in social psychology after completing college with honors and having his senior research paper published. As he reads the biographies of Leon Festinger, Theodor Adorno, Elliot Aronson, and other famous social psychologists, he thinks about all of the things each of them accomplished and contrasts that with his own career, which is just beginning. Jack is engaging in ___.
   a. social facilitation
   b. social interference
   c. upward social comparison
   d. social discrimination

2. One of the assumptions of terror management theory is that ___.
   a. having high self-esteem helps reduce the impact of thoughts about death
   b. people who engage in terrorism have antisocial personalities
   c. it is better to dwell on negative thoughts than avoid them
   d. people cope better with terrifying thoughts when they do not seek social support

3. When Rowland first met Jacob, Jacob wasn't feeling well and threw up on Rowland's shoes. According to research on first impressions, we would expect Rowland to ___.
   a. feel sorry for Jacob and thus have a positive first impression of him
   b. develop a negative impression of Jacob because of the negative first experience with him
   c. have an initial negative impression that will become positive later, no matter what Jacob does
   d. have a positive first impression of Jacob because he is a male

4. Gena is in a bad mood because she is convinced that she won't like her blind date, Pat. When Pat arrives, he is outgoing and considerate, but Gena is short-tempered and rude to him. Soon Pat becomes irritable and ends the date early. Gena's prediction that she wouldn't have a good time came true mainly because of ___.
   a. cognitive dissonance
   b. prejudice
   c. a self-fulfilling prophecy
   d. the fundamental attribution error

5. "I earned an A on my history test because I studied hard and I'm smart, but I failed my philosophy test because its questions were poorly worded and the teacher doesn't like me." This statement is an example of ___.
   a. the actor-observer effect
   b. the fundamental attribution error
   c. a self-fulfilling prophecy
   d. a self-serving bias

6. Richard is listening to a student government leader suggest that professors on campus should stop giving grades. Richard is most likely to be convinced if the speaker ___.
   a. introduces a famous celebrity who supports this idea
   b. circulates a petition in support of the idea
   c. presents evidence that eliminating grades will not hurt students' job prospects
   d. is personable and funny

7. Rachel and Matteus listen to a boring lecture. Afterward, Rachel is offered $100 and Matteus is offered $1 to tell the lecturer's next class that the lecture was interesting and fun. Both agree to do so. According to cognitive dissonance theory, we would expect real attitude change about the lecture to occur in ___.
   a. Rachel, but not Matteus
   b. Matteus, but not Rachel
   c. both Rachel and Matteus
   d. neither Rachel nor Matteus

8. In an attempt to reduce prejudice between ethnic groups at Lincoln School, the principal asks members of all groups to help build a new playground. Prejudice would be most likely to decrease as a result if ___.
   a. teams from each ethnic group competed to see which could work the fastest
   b. one member of each group was appointed to a committee to lead the project
   c. members of all the groups worked together in teams to complete various parts of the playground
   d. members of each ethnic group wore the same kind of T-shirt

9. Rhona, a pretty woman with conservative political views, has just moved into an apartment building on campus. All else being equal, which neighbor will Rhona probably like the most?
   a. Jill, whose hair color, height, and weight are similar to Rhona's
   b. Shauna, president of the Young Conservatives club
   c. Patrice, president of the Young Liberals club
   d. Yolanda, who comes from Rhona's home town

10. Giorgio and Louisa share their thoughts, hopes, and daily worries. They plan to stay married throughout their lifetime, and they enjoy an active and satisfying sex life. According to Sternberg's theory, Giorgio and Louisa are experiencing ___ love.
    a. consummate
    b. companionate
    c. temporary
    d. romantic

11. When her best friend stopped by with a Christmas gift, Jen was upset because she had nothing to give in return. Jen was uncomfortable because she ___.
    a. experienced deindividuation
    b. engaged in social loafing
    c. made the ultimate attribution error
    d. could not follow the reciprocity norm

12. In Harper Lee's novel *To Kill a Mockingbird,* an angry mob tries to lynch a prisoner. The prisoner's attorney, Atticus Finch, and his young daughter, "Scout," talk to the crowd, calling people by name, and reminding them that they know their families. Soon the mob disperses, no longer a faceless crowd but a group of identifiable individuals. Atticus and Scout disrupted the phenomenon of ____.
   a. diffusion of responsibility
   b. deindividuation
   c. situational ambiguity
   d. social facilitation

13. Shawn's teacher doesn't keep track of her students' performance when they work in groups, so Shawn does not put as much effort into his group project as he does into his individual project. Shawn is exhibiting ____.
   a. a self-serving bias
   b. social facilitation
   c. social loafing
   d. diffusion of responsibility

14. Keyonna thought that the play she had just seen was boring, but everyone else seemed to like it. At the closing curtain, the audience gave the actors a standing ovation. Keyonna stood up and applauded too, even though she didn't believe the actors deserved it. Keyonna's behavior in this situation is an example of ____.
   a. conformity
   b. compliance
   c. obedience
   d. a self-fulfilling prophecy

15. Colleen knows she should take a day off from work to study for a big exam, but she also knows her boss won't like it. So she first asks for the entire week off. When the boss refuses, she asks for the one day off instead and he agrees. Colleen used the ____ approach to gain her boss's compliance.
   a. foot-in-the-door
   b. door-in-the-face
   c. lowball
   d. peripheral

16. Which of the following is not a major factor in determining whether or not a person will obey an order?
   a. The status of the authority figure giving the order.
   b. The personality characteristics of the person receiving the order.
   c. The presence of another person who disobeys the order.
   d. The gender of the person given the order.

17. Leonard is upset because he just can't get his new iPhone to work. When his roommate comes home and accidentally knocks over Leonard's glass of lemonade, Leonard becomes abusive, screaming at his roommate and throwing books and pillows at him. This is an example of the ____ theory of aggression.
   a. frustration-aggression
   b. generalized arousal
   c. authoritarian
   d. biological

18. While shopping, Lenora falls and breaks her ankle. She is most likely to receive help from a stranger if she ____.
   a. is in a quiet area where only a few people saw her fall
   b. is in the midst of a large crowd
   c. is in a large city
   d. doesn't ask for help

19. Which of the following summarizes the evolutionary view of prosocial behavior?
   a. People feel good when they help others.
   b. People help others in order to improve the chance that some of their genes will survive in future generations.
   c. People are motivated to protect others if the costs of helping are outweighed by the benefits.
   d. People are helpful because it improves everyone's chances of survival.

20. When groups fail to consider all the facts and all their options, when they share similar biases, and when they are pressured to reach an agreement, they may make poor decisions because of a phenomenon called ____.
   a. deindividuation
   b. groupthink
   c. social facilitation
   d. social interference

Media Resources

Now that you have finished reading this chapter, how about exploring some of the ideas and information that you found most interesting?

Go to **CengageBrain.com** to access Psychology CourseMate, where you will find an interactive eBook, glossaries, flashcards, quizzes, videos, Virtual Psychology Labs, and more.

aplia

If your professor has assigned Aplia:

1. Sign in to your account.
2. Complete the corresponding exercises as required by your professor.
3. When finished, click "Grade It Now" to see which areas you have mastered, which areas need more work, and detailed explanations of every answer.

Industrial and Organizational Psychology

© Christopher Robbins/Digital Vision/Getty Images

Preview

If you've ever had a full-time or part-time job, you know that work involves more than just doing certain tasks and collecting a paycheck.
Many job-related experiences—including the characteristics of coworkers and supervisors, the nature of the work, and the pleasures and stressors found in the workplace—have significant effects on employees and the organizations that hire them. Understanding the impact of these experiences is just one aspect of the subfield known as *industrial and organizational (I/O) psychology*. In this chapter, we explore this growing subfield by reviewing how I/O psychologists conduct their research and how they apply that research to improve the performance and welfare of workers and the organizations that employ them.

Suppose that you are the manager of a large department store. You want to hire someone to head up the cosmetics department but you're not sure how to find the best person for the job. How can you attract applicants with the necessary skills? How will you know which of them would be the best choice? Should you rely on interviews with the candidates or should you also give them some psychological tests? Perhaps you decide to do both, but how do you choose the interview questions and tests? How should you interpret the results? And, what happens after you've made your hiring decision? Do you have procedures available to train, motivate, supervise, and reward employees so that they perform at their best and are happy in their work? For answers to such questions, many human resources managers and other company executives seek the help of *industrial and organizational (I/O) psychologists.* We briefly mentioned I/O psychology in the introductory chapter; here we describe it in more detail, including a summary of what I/O psychologists do and some of the ways their work has benefited organizations and employees. ●

An Overview of Industrial and Organizational Psychology

What do industrial and organizational psychologists do?

Psychology is the science of behavior and mental processes. The subfield of **industrial and organizational (I/O) psychology** is the science of behavior and mental processes in the workplace. I/O psychologists conduct scientific research on all sorts of people-oriented workplace topics, such as what personality traits predict good performance under stress, what social factors cause conflict in work groups, and how people feel about the organizations in which they work. I/O psychologists are also hands-on practitioners who help organizations apply research findings to problems such as matching employees to jobs and improving cooperation in workplace teams. The link between scientific research and professional practice can be especially strong in I/O psychology, because the workplace provides both a natural laboratory for studying psychological questions and a setting in which research-based answers can be applied and evaluated.

I/O psychologists address two main goals in their research and practice. First, they *promote effective job performance* by employees, which leads to better performance by the organization as a whole. Second, they contribute to human welfare by *improving the health, safety, and well-being of employees.* This second goal is important in itself, but it is also related to the first one. Effective organizations are those whose employees are not only capable of performing their jobs well but are also healthy and well adjusted in the workplace.

industrial and organizational (I/O) psychology The science of behavior and mental processes in the workplace.

Entering I/O Psychology

Some graduates pursue careers in I/O psychology after completing a master's degree program, but salaries and opportunities are better for those with a Ph.D. For example, virtually all I/O psychologists who are hired as college or university professors have completed a doctoral degree. Master's or doctoral training in I/O psychology is available at more than 100 universities in the United States, about 10 in Canada, and more than 80 in other countries.

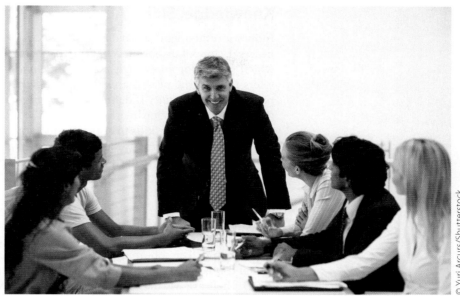

© Yuri Arcurs/Shutterstock

I/O psychology emerged early in the 1900s as psychologists began to apply laboratory findings about topics such as learning, memory, and motivation to solve practical problems in the workplace. In fact, some of the first I/O psychologists studied under experimental psychologists. For example, Hugo Münsterberg and James McKeen Cattell studied under Wilhelm Wundt in Germany, and Elsie Oschrin Bregman was a student of Edward L. Thorndike at Columbia University (Katzell & Austin, 1992; Koppes, 1997; Landy, 1992). Research and applications in I/O psychology continue to be influenced by laboratory research in many of psychology's subfields, including cognitive psychology, personality, motivation and emotion, health psychology, and especially social psychology. And many I/O psychologists study work-related behavior in the laboratory as well as in the workplace (Parasuraman, 2011). The work of I/O psychologists is also shaped by findings in fields beyond psychology, including business management, marketing, engineering, and medicine.

Like psychologists in other subfields, I/O psychologists hold graduate degrees in their specialty. The popularity of I/O psychology has grown rapidly in recent decades, both in North America and throughout the industrialized world (Spector, 2003). About 51 percent of I/O psychologists work in the private sector. Another 36 percent are professors in college or university departments of psychology, business, or related fields. About 7 percent are research scientists in the public sector, including in government agencies, and about 6 percent work in other areas (Khanna & Medsker, 2010). Let's consider some of the specific kinds of work that I/O psychologists do in these various settings.

Assessing People, Jobs, and Job Performance

How do industrial and organizational psychologists match employees to jobs?

If you apply for a job with a large corporation or government agency, you will probably be given one or more standardized tests of personality or mental ability, as well as assessments of your knowledge and skills to help determine whether you have the "right stuff" for the job you seek. These assessment programs are usually designed by I/O psychologists. In fact, the most typical request that I/O psychologists receive from organizations is to develop or conduct some sort of assessment procedure. Accordingly, the creation and evaluation of new and better assessment devices is one of the main areas for scientific research in I/O psychology.

Knowledge, Skills, Abilities, and Other Characteristics

Industrial and organizational assessments are often used to describe the human attributes necessary for doing jobs successfully. Those attributes are referred to collectively as *KSAOs*, which stands for *knowledge, skill, ability, and other personal characteristics. Knowledge* refers to what the person already knows. *Skill* refers to how good a person is at doing a particular task. *Ability* is defined as the person's more general capacities in areas such as thinking, physical coordination, and the like. Skills and abilities are closely related; some researchers consider skills to be the products of inherent abilities (Muchinsky, 2003). *Other personal characteristics* can be almost anything else about a person, including attitudes, personality traits, physical characteristics, preferences, values, and the like.

Job Analysis

How do organizations know which KSAOs are important for which jobs? The answer lies in **job analysis,** in which I/O psychologists collect information about particular jobs and job requirements. This job-analysis information is then used to guide decisions about whom to hire and what kind of training is needed to succeed at a particular job (Brannick & Levine, 2002). There are two major approaches to job analysis. The *job-oriented approach* describes the tasks involved in doing a job, such as wiring circuit boards, creating a computer database, or driving a truck. In organizations that emphasize teamwork, the job-oriented approach to job analysis might also include asking each team member to describe their coworkers' tasks as well as their own (Brannick, Levine, & Morgeson, 2007). The *person-oriented approach* describes the KSAOs needed to do those job tasks (see Table 15.1). Some job analyses take one approach or the other, but many provide information about both tasks and KSAOs. A job-analysis report can be a relatively brief and superficial description, a microscopically detailed examination, or anything in between. The approach taken and the level of detail included in a job analysis depend mainly on how the report will be used. When the analysis will guide the hiring of employees, it should contain enough detail to make clear what needs to be done in a particular job. Having these details spelled out also helps the organization establish and maintain fair hiring practices. The person-oriented approach is the most useful one for these purposes, because it describes the KSAOs the employer should be looking for in the new employee.

Job analysis can also help organizations recognize the need to train employees, and it can even establish the kind of training required. Suppose you have five job openings, but when you test candidates for hiring or promotion, too few of them have the KSAOs that a job analysis says are necessary for success in these positions. Obviously, some training will be needed, and because the job analysis lists specific KSAOs, you can use that analysis to determine exactly what the training should include. Suppose a job analysis reveals that people in a particular computer sales position have to be familiar with the Linux operating system. You would need to provide Linux training for all individuals hired for that position unless they already knew that operating system.

job analysis The process of collecting information about jobs and job requirements that is used to guide hiring and training decisions.

TABLE 15.1 Knowledge, Skill, Ability, and Other Personal Characteristics (KSAOs)

Here are examples of the kinds of KSAOs required for successful performance by people working in two different jobs. Just for fun, try writing KSAOs for your job as a student and for your teacher's job, too.

Job Title	Knowledge	Skill	Ability	Other
Secretary	Knowledge of office procedures	Skill in using a word-processing program	Ability to communicate with others	Willingness to follow instructions
Plumber	Knowledge of county building codes	Skill in using a wrench	Good hand-eye coordination	Willingness to work in dirty environments

Questionnaires which ask current employees to describe their jobs are the most common tool for job analysis. Other methods include asking specially trained job analysts to observe people as they do their jobs or even to perform those jobs themselves (Dierdorff & Wilson, 2003). If the goals of job analysis include comparing one job with another, I/O psychologists might use an instrument such as the *Position Analysis Questionnaire,* or *PAQ* (McCormick, Jeanneret, & Mecham, 1972). The 189 items on the PAQ can describe almost any job in terms of a particular set of characteristics, or dimensions, such as the degree to which a job involves communicating with people, lifting heavy objects, doing mental arithmetic, or the like. The results of thousands of job analyses have been collected in the U.S. Department of Labor's Occupational Information Network, or O*NET (Peterson et al., 2001). This computer database contains analyses of approximately 1,100 groups of jobs, including the KSAOs and tasks involved in each, and how each job fits into the larger organizational picture. O*NET is an excellent source of information about occupations for anyone who is in the process of choosing a career; you can access it online at http://www.onetonline.org/.

LINKAGES

What methods are used to select good employees? *(a link to Personality)*

Measuring Employee Characteristics

I/O psychologists use a wide variety of instruments to measure a person's knowledge, skill, ability, and other characteristics. These instruments range from simple paper-and-pencil tests (an arithmetic test for a sales clerk, for example) to several days of hands-on activities that simulate the tasks required of a midlevel manager. Some assessments are used to select new employees, others are designed to choose employees for promotion, and still others are meant to determine how well employees are doing their jobs at the moment. The three main methods used to measure employee characteristics are psychological tests, job applicant interviews, and assessment center exercises.

Psychological Tests   The tests that I/O psychologists most often use to measure general mental ability and skill are the standard intelligence tests described in the chapter on thought, language, and intelligence. These tests are relatively inexpensive and easy to administer, and they do a reasonably good job at predicting people's performance in a wide variety of occupational tasks (Bertau, Anderson, & Salgado, 2005; Jansen & Vinkenburg, 2006; Kuncel & Hezlett, 2010; Rooy, et al., 2006; Salgado et al., 2003). In addition, job applicants might be asked to participate in *situational judgment tests* (SJTs), in which they read about or watch videos of simulated workplace situations, such as a conflict between co-workers. The applicants are then asked to rate which of several responses to that situation would be best or to describe what they would do if confronted with that same situation (Sackett & Lievens, 2008). The information provided by SJTs supplements cognitive and personality tests and provides an additional perspective from which to predict an applicant's eventual job performance (Lievens, Peeters, & Schollaert, 2008). Tests of job-relevant knowledge—such as basic accounting principles or stock-trading rules—may also be used to confirm that an individual has the information necessary to succeed at a particular job. Finally, personality tests measure a wide variety of other employee characteristics. As described in the personality chapter, some of these tests provide information about personality dimensions that may be relevant to hiring decisions. For example, a person's score on *conscientiousness* (i.e., reliability and industriousness) has been linked to job performance across many occupations (Dudley et al., 2006; Thoreson et al., 2003). Some employers also use personality-related *integrity tests* which ask about moral values, tendencies, temptations, and history that might make employees more likely to steal or engage in other disruptive acts (Alliger & Dwight, 2000; Berry, Sackett, & Wiemann, 2007; Ones & Viswesvaran, 2001; Wanek, Sackett, & Ones, 2003). Unfortunately, it is relatively easy to give false or misleading responses on these tests and there is evidence that applicants may do so (van Hooft & Born, 2012; Zickar, Gibby, & Robie, 2004).

Job Applicant Interviews   *Job applicant interviews* are designed to determine a job applicant's suitability for a job. They are popular with employers and tend to be

A Matter of Degree

When hiring employees for some jobs, organizations often rely on credentials rather than knowledge tests. For example, an undergraduate degree in any major may be enough to qualify for some white-collar jobs because people assume that college graduates have enough general knowledge and "mental horsepower" to succeed. For jobs in medicine, law, accounting, engineering, and other specialty fields, candidates' knowledge is assumed if they have completed a particular degree program or earned a particular license. These assumptions are usually correct, but credentials alone do not always guarantee competence.

assessment center An extensive set of exercises designed to determine an individual's suitability for a particular job.

preferred by employees, too (Hausknecht, Day, & Thomas, 2004). Interviews usually take place in person, though some are conducted by telephone, videoconferencing, or even e-mail. As mentioned in the personality chapter, interviews can be structured or unstructured (open ended). In a *structured interview,* the interviewer prepares a list of specific topics or even specifically worded questions to be covered in a particular order (Campion, Palmer, & Campion, 1997; Chapman & Zweig, 2005). In *unstructured interviews,* the course of the conversation is more spontaneous and variable. Following some interviews, especially structured ones, the candidate's responses will be rated on a set of dimensions, such as product knowledge, clarity of expression, poise, or the like. After other interviews, the interviewer's subjective impression of the candidate is used to make a yes-or-no judgment about the candidate's suitability for the job.

Research consistently shows that structured interviews are far more effective than unstructured interviews in leading to good hiring decisions (e.g., Huffcutt & Arthur, 1994; Wiesner & Cronshaw, 1988). The difference is due largely to the fact that structured interviews focus specifically on job-related knowledge and skills—especially interpersonal skills—whereas unstructured interviews do not (Huffcutt et al., 2001). Further, lack of structure makes it easier for personal bias to enter the hiring picture; ratings from an unstructured interview might have more to do with the interviewer's personal bias about a candidate than with the candidate's objective qualifications.

Assessment Centers   An **assessment center** is an extensive set of exercises designed to determine an individual's suitability for a particular job. Performance is usually judged by a team of raters (Spychalski et al., 1997). Assessment centers are often used to hire or promote managers, but they can be employed in relation to other positions as well. A typical assessment center consists of two to three days of exercises that simulate various aspects of a job. The *in-basket test* is a typical assessment center exercise for managers. Candidates are seated at a desk and asked to imagine that they have just taken over a new management job. On the desk is the "previous manager's" overflowing in-basket, containing correspondence, memos, phone messages, and other items. The candidate's task is to go through all this material and write on the back of each item what action should be taken to deal with it and how soon. Later, experts read what the candidate has written and assign an appropriateness score to each action. For example, candidates who prioritize tasks well—taking immediate action on critical matters and delaying action on less important ones—would receive higher scores than those who, say, deal with each task in the order in which it is encountered, regardless of its importance.

Other assessment center exercises measure interpersonal skills. The job candidate might be asked to play the role of a manager who is working with others to solve a problem or who must discipline a problem employee. As in the in-basket test, each candidate is given a score on the knowledge, skills, abilities, and other job-relevant characteristics displayed during each exercise.

The evaluation team reviews and discusses the candidate's total score on the assessment center exercises and reaches a group decision about the person's suitability for a particular position. There is considerable evidence to support the value of assessment centers (Arthur et al., 2003; Jansen & Vinkenburg, 2006; Meriac et al., 2008). For example, the assessment center scores earned by first-year college students predicted their performance as teachers several years after graduation (Shechtman, 1992). Assessment centers have also successfully predicted the performance of police officers, pilots, and managers, among others (Dayan, Kasten, & Fox, 2002; Lievens et al., 2003; McEvoy & Beatty, 1989). Assessment centers can be expensive and time-consuming, though. Further, performance scores on assessment centers correlate relatively strongly with applicants' performance on interviews and cognitive tests. With these factors in mind some researchers suggest using assessment centers only as a second step in the selection process, and only for applicants whose interview and test scores are neither high enough nor low enough to guide a final hiring decision (Dayan, Fox, & Kasten, 2008).

Measuring Job Performance

Almost all employees of medium to large organizations receive an annual **job performance** appraisal, which, much like a student's report card, provides an evaluation of how well they are doing in various aspects of their work. Organizations use these appraisals to guide decisions about salary raises and bonuses for employees and about whether to keep, promote, or fire particular individuals. The appraisals are also used to give employees feedback on the quality and quantity of their work (Rynes, Gerhart, & Parks, 2005). This feedback function of job performance appraisals is important because it helps employees recognize what they are doing right and what they need to do differently to reach their own goals and promote the goals of the organization.

Establishing Performance Criteria   One of the most important roles for I/O psychologists in designing job performance appraisal systems is to help establish *criteria,* or benchmarks, that define what the organization means by "good" or "poor" performance (see Table 15.2). These criteria can be theoretical or actual. A *theoretical criterion* is a statement of what we mean by good (or poor) performance, in theory. A theoretical criterion for good teaching, for example, might be "promotes student learning." This criterion certainly sounds reasonable, but notice that it does not specify how we would measure it in order to decide whether a particular teacher is actually promoting student learning. So we also need an *actual criterion,* which specifies what we should measure to determine whether the theoretical criterion has been met. An actual criterion for good teaching might be defined in terms of students' performance on a standardized test of what their teacher has taught them. If, on average, the students reach or exceed some particular score, the teacher will have satisfied one of the school district's criteria for good teaching.

Keep in mind, though, that the match between theoretical criteria and actual criteria is never perfect. The actual criterion chosen should provide a sensible way to assess the theoretical criterion, but the actual criterion may be flawed. For one thing, actual criteria are usually incomplete. There is probably more to good teaching than just ensuring that students earn a particular score on a particular test. The teacher may have done a great (or poor) job at teaching material that did not happen to be covered on that test. Second, the actual criterion can be affected by factors other than the employee's performance. Perhaps students' scores on a standardized test were affected partly by the work of a good (or poor) teacher they had before their current teacher was hired. I/O psychologists are sensitive to these problems, and they usually recommend that job performance appraisals be based on several actual criteria, not just one.

job performance A measure of how well employees are doing in various aspects of their work, usually recorded in an annual appraisal.

TABLE 15.2   Examples of Theoretical and Actual Criteria

Here are some theoretical and actual criteria for several kinds of jobs. Notice that theoretical criteria tend to be rather vague, so for purposes of job performance appraisals, they must be backed up by actual criteria. By evaluating employees on how well they have reached actual criteria, organizations can decide whether the theoretical criteria have been met and they can act accordingly. Think about the kinds of jobs you have had in your life or that you might like to have and try to develop your own set of fair, appropriate theoretical and actual criteria for performance in these jobs.

LEARN by DOING

Job	Theoretical Criterion	Actual Criterion
Architect	Design buildings	Number of buildings designed
Car salesperson	Sell cars	Number of cars sold per month
Police officer	Fight crime	Number of arrests made per month
Roofer	Install roofs	Square feet of shingles installed per month
Scientist	Make scientific discoveries	Number of articles published in scholarly journals

Methods of Performance Appraisal

The information used in job performance appraisals can come from objective measures and subjective measures.

Objective Measures   *Objective measures* of job performance include counting the frequency of particular behaviors or the results of those behaviors. The number of calls made by a telemarketer, the number of computers shipped out by a factory worker, and the total value of items sold each month by a shoe store employee are just three examples of objective measures of job performance. Objective measures of problematic behaviors might include the number of days employees are absent, how often they are late, or the number of complaints filed against them (Roth, Huffcutt, & Bobko, 2003). Objective appraisal measures are especially valuable because they provide a close link between theoretical and actual performance criteria. If the theoretical criterion for good performance as a salesperson is to sell a company's products, the most closely linked actual criterion would be an objective count of the number of those products sold per month.

Objective methods of job performance are not right for all jobs, however, because some performance criteria cannot be evaluated by counting things. For example, it would make no sense to evaluate a teacher's job performance by counting the number of students taught per year. Teachers usually have no control over their class size, and in any case, an enrollment count tells us nothing about what the students learned. Similarly, a salesperson might have sold twenty cars last month, but it would also be important to know how this was accomplished. If the person used unethical or high-pressure tactics that angered customers and harmed the organization's reputation, the sales count tells only part of the story of this employee's performance. In other words, except for the simplest jobs, objective measures may fail to assess all the aspects of performance that are of interest to an organization.

Subjective Measures   I/O psychologists sometimes recommend that objective performance measures be supplemented or sometimes even replaced by subjective measures. *Subjective measures* of job performance tend to focus on a supervisor's judgments about various aspects of an employee's work (Rynes, Gerhart, & Parks, 2005). Typically, the supervisor records these judgments on a graphic rating form or a behavior-focused rating form.

Graphic rating forms list several criterion-related dimensions of job performance and provide a space for the supervisor to rate each employee's performance on each dimension, using a scale ranging from, say, 1 to 10 or from *poor* to *excellent* (see Figure 15.1). These graphic ratings can be valuable, but they reflect the supervisor's subjective judgment. So, as in unstructured interviews, factors other than the employee's performance can influence the results (Peretz & Fried, 2012; Wong & Kwong, 2005). For example, most graphic ratings reflect *leniency error,* meaning that supervisors tend to use only the top of the scale. As a result, almost all employees in most organizations receive ratings that are "satisfactory" or better. Many supervisors also show errors based on the *halo effect,* meaning that they tend to give the same rating on every dimension of job performance. So if Tasha receives an "outstanding" rating on one dimension, such as promptness, she will probably be rated at or near "outstanding" on all the others. Similarly, if Jack is rated as only "satisfactory" on one scale, such as product knowledge, he will probably get "satisfactory" ratings on the rest of them.

To some extent, these "errors" reflect reality. After all, most people try to do their jobs well and may do about equally well (or equally poorly) in various aspects of their work (Balzer & Sulsky, 1992; Solomonson & Lance, 1997). However, when using graphic rating forms, supervisors may not carefully discriminate between those aspects of job performance that are satisfactory from those that need improvement. Further, many

FIGURE 15.1

A Graphic Rating Form Used in Subjective Job Performance Appraisal

Supervisors often use graphic rating forms like this one in subjective job performance appraisals. The ratings are based on the supervisor's personal experience with the employee and on subjective impressions of that employee's work.

Rate employee on each dimension on the left by checking the appropriate box corresponding to the level of performance for the past year.

Dimension

Customer service	☐ Poor	☐ Fair	☐ Satisfactory	☐ Above satisfactory	☐ Outstanding
Management of time	☐ Poor	☐ Fair	☐ Satisfactory	☐ Above satisfactory	☐ Outstanding
Professional appearance	☐ Poor	☐ Fair	☐ Satisfactory	☐ Above satisfactory	☐ Outstanding
Teamwork	☐ Poor	☐ Fair	☐ Satisfactory	☐ Above satisfactory	☐ Outstanding
Work quality	☐ Poor	☐ Fair	☐ Satisfactory	☐ Above satisfactory	☐ Outstanding
Work quantity	☐ Poor	☐ Fair	☐ Satisfactory	☐ Above satisfactory	☐ Outstanding

tend to "go easy" on their employees, especially if they like them, if they want to curry favor with them for some reason, or if they want to appear "politically correct" (Ferris et al., 1994; Harber et al., 2012; Heilman & Haynes, 2008; Judge & Cable, 2011; Tziner, Murphy, & Cleveland, 2005). This kind of bias can result in favoritism in which supervisors intentionally inflate ratings beyond what an employee's performance deserves (Fried & Tiegs, 1995; Rynes, Gerhart, & Parks, 2005). Supervisors who are biased against certain employees based on gender, ethnicity, or other factors may give those employees undeservedly low ratings (Heilman & Haynes, 2008; Stauffer & Buckley, 2005).

To help minimize the errors and bias associated with graphic rating forms, industrial and organizational psychologists developed *behavior-focused rating forms,* which ask supervisors to rate employees on specific behaviors rather than on general dimensions of performance (Smith & Kendall, 1963). These forms contain lists of *critical incidents* that illustrate different levels of performance—from "extremely effective" to "extremely ineffective"—on important job dimensions (Flanagan, 1954). A critical incident list relating to customer relations, for example, might include "listens patiently," "tries to reach a compromise," "coldly states store policy," and "angrily demands that complaining customers leave." Once these behavior-focused forms are constructed, supervisors choose which incidents are most typical of each employee.

Behavior-based rating forms help supervisors and their employees come to a better understanding of what is meant by "good" and "poor" performance. However, these forms don't appear to eliminate the impact of supervisor bias and error (Bernardin & Beatty, 1984; Latham et al., 1993). Accordingly, some employers assess employees' job performance on the basis of ratings by peers and subordinates as well as supervisors. These "360-degree" ratings are designed to provide a broader and potentially less biased picture of an employee's performance (Oh & Berry, 2009). (See "In Review: Assessing People, Jobs, and Job Performance" for a summary of these topics.)

Assessing People, Jobs, and Job Performance — IN REVIEW

Target Of Assessment	Typical Purpose	What Is Assessed	Examples
Employees	Employee selection	Knowledge, skill, ability, and other personal characteristics (KSAOs)	Tests of ability, achievement, or personality; structured or unstructured interviews; assessment centers requiring simulated job tasks
Jobs	Matching employees to jobs; identifying training needs	Job tasks and personal attributes needed for the job	Job-oriented analysis (identifies required tasks); person-oriented analysis (identifies KSAOs required for success)
Job performance	Feedback on performance; decisions about retention, salary adjustments, or promotion	Work activities and/or products; supervisors' reports	Evaluating employees' work in relation to theoretical and actual criteria as measured by objective (counting) or subjective (rating) methods

IN REVIEW QUESTIONS

1. Lists of critical incidents are contained in ____-focused employee rating forms.

2. A potential employer might use a two-day ____ to measure your skill at the job you want.

3. In general, ____ interviews are more useful in employee selection than ____ interviews.

Recruiting and Selecting Employees

How do organizations find good employees?

So far, we've described some of the assessment methods that I/O psychologists have developed to help organizations hire, train, and evaluate employees. Let's now consider the role of I/O psychology in finding candidates for employment and in selecting the right people for each job.

Recruitment Processes

It is generally agreed that people are an organization's most valuable assets because it is people who are ultimately responsible for achieving an organization's goals. It is no wonder, then, that there is intense competition among organizations to recruit the "best and brightest" employees. It is a disciplined competition, however. There is no point in hiring this year's top ten accounting graduates if your organization needs only two new accountants. So the first step in effective recruiting is to determine what employees are needed and then go after the best people to fill those needs.

Determining employment needs means more than just counting empty chairs, though. Analyses by I/O psychologists help organizations determine how many people are needed in each position at the moment and how many will be needed in the future. Suppose, for example, that a computer company anticipates a 20 percent growth in business over the next five years. That growth will require a 20 percent increase in the number of customer service representatives, but how many new representatives should be hired each month? An I/O psychologist's analysis would help answer this question by taking into account not only the growth projections but also estimates of how many representatives quit their jobs each year and whether the existing ratio of customer service employees to customers is too high, too low, or just about right for efficient operation. In making recommendations about recruitment plans, I/O psychologists must also consider the intensity of demand for employees in various occupations. More active recruitment plans will be necessary to attract the best people in high-demand areas (see Table 15.3).

Once employment needs are established and the competitive landscape has been explored, the next step in recruitment is to persuade people with the right kinds of knowledge, skill, ability, and other characteristics to apply for the jobs to be filled. Common methods for identifying and attracting candidates include posting jobs on Monster.com or other recruitment web sites; newspaper advertising; interviewing graduating seniors on college campuses; seeking referrals from current employees; working with employment agencies, recruitment consultants, and private "head-hunting" firms; and accepting walk-in applications from job seekers who appear on their

TABLE 15.3　Fast-Growing Occupations

Here are the 20 fastest growing occupations listed in the U.S. Bureau of Labor Statistics Occupational Outlook Handbook (U.S. Bureau of Labor Statistics, 2012). I/O psychologists must take such trends into account when making recommendations about where to make the strongest efforts at recruiting new employees. More information about these job categories is available in the Occupational Outlook Handbook, 2012-2013 Edition (U.S. Bureau of Labor Statistics, 2012) and on the Bureau of Labor Statistics website at http://www.bls.gov/oco/.

Occupation	Percent Employment Change, 2010–2020
Personal and home care aides	70.5
Home health aides	69.4
Biomedical engineers	61.7
Helpers—brickmasons, blockmasons, stonemasons, and tile and marble setters	60.1
Helpers—carpenters	55.7
Veterinary technologists and technicians	52.0
Reinforcing iron and rebar workers	48.6
Physical therapist assistants	45.7
Helpers—pipelayers, plumbers, pipefitters, and steamfitters	45.4
Meeting, convention, and event planners	43.7
Diagnostic medical sonographers	43.5
Occupational therapy assistants	43.3
Physical therapist aides	43.1
Glaziers	42.4
Interpreters and translators	42.2
Medical secretaries	41.3
Market research analysts and marketing specialists	41.2
Marriage and family therapists	41.2
Brickmasons and blockmasons	40.5
Physical therapists	39.0

own. The recruitment methods used for any particular job will depend on how easy or difficult it is to attract high-quality applicants and on the importance of the position in the organization. For relatively low-level positions requiring few skills, it may be possible to rely on walk-in applicants to fill available positions. Much more effort and several different recruitment methods may be required in order to attract top-notch candidates for higher-level jobs that demand extensive experience and skill.

Selection Processes

Selecting the right employee for a particular job is generally a matter of using the results of tests, interviews, and assessment centers to find the best fit between each candidate's characteristics and the tasks and characteristics that a job analysis has identified as necessary for successful performance. This matching strategy would suggest that a candidate who is better at written communication than at computer skills would do better in, say, the public relations department than at the computer help desk.

Is this strategy always the best way to select employees? Usually it is, but I/O psychologists help ensure that the characteristics that are supposed to predict success at particular jobs are, in fact, associated with success. To do this, they conduct *validity studies,* which are research projects designed to determine how well a particular test, interview, or other assessment method predicts the employee's actual job performance (Chan, 2005). For example, on the basis of a job analysis conducted years ago, a department store might require applicants for sales clerk positions to pass a test of mental arithmetic. A validity study could determine whether performance on that test is actually related to sales clerks' performance. The easiest way to conduct this study would be to ask a representative sample of the store's sales clerks to take the arithmetic test, then compute the correlation between their test scores and some objective or subjective performance criterion, such as monthly sales figures or a supervisor's ratings. If those who score highest on the test also do best at their job, the arithmetic test can be seen as valid for predicting job performance. If not, it may be that for clerks using today's computerized sales terminals, mental arithmetic is no longer as important to job success as it was in the past.

A large body of results from I/O psychology research is available to tell organizations which types of tests and other assessments are most valid in predicting performance in which types of jobs. These results save organizations a great deal of time and money because they eliminate the need to conduct their own validity studies for each assessment device they use in selecting employees for every job they want to fill.

Legal Issues in Recruitment and Selection

The United States and many other industrialized countries have established the principle that an organization's hiring, firing, and promotion processes should not discriminate against anyone based on characteristics that have nothing to do with job performance. This principle has been translated into laws designed to protect all employees and job candidates against unfair discrimination. U.S. laws—including the Civil Rights Act, the Americans with Disabilities Act, and the Age Discrimination in Employment Act— have also created special safeguards for several *protected classes,* including women, Asians, Blacks, Hispanics, American Indians, and other groups whose members have been unfairly discriminated against in the past. Together, these laws make it illegal for employers in the United States to discriminate in hiring or promotion on the basis of a candidate's age, ethnicity, gender, national origin, disability, or religion. Some states, cities, and counties—and some other countries—also forbid discrimination on the basis of sexual orientation.

In 1978, I/O psychologists helped the U.S. government create its *Uniform Guidelines on Employee Selection Procedures,* a document that outlines the procedures organizations must use to ensure fairness in hiring and promotion. The most important element of these guidelines is the requirement that personnel decisions be based solely on job-related criteria. This means that in choosing new employees, for example, organizations should hire people whose knowledge, skill, ability, and other characteristics match the KSAO requirements previously established by the job-analysis process described earlier. The guidelines also state that organizations should use only test scores and other assessment data that validation studies have established as good predictors of job performance.

Training Employees

What kind of training do employees need?

Every year, organizations in the industrialized world spend billions on training their employees (Thompson et al., 2002); the figure is more than $126 billion each year in the U.S. alone (Paradise, 2007). I/O psychologists are directly involved in establishing the need for training, designing training methods and content, and evaluating the outcome of training efforts (Salas et al., 2012). Some I/O psychologists actually conduct training programs, but in most cases these programs are delivered by professional trainers and/or by experts on the training topics involved.

Ensuring Equal Opportunity
Affirmative action (AA) is an important element of the U.S. government's *Uniform Guidelines on Employee Selection Procedures*. A major goal of AA was to encourage organizations to actively seek out job applicants from underrepresented minority groups and in the process ensure that qualified minority candidates are not overlooked. Critics claim, though, that AA establishes quota systems in which certain percentages of people from particular groups must be hired or promoted even if they are not all well qualified. AA has thus become an increasingly controversial aspect of employment law.

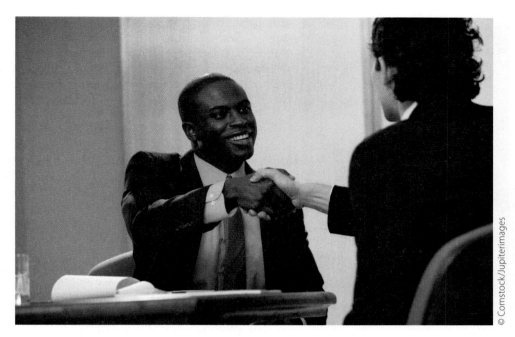

© Comstock/Jupiterimages

Assessing Training Needs

To help organizations identify which employees need what kind of training, I/O psychologists typically carry out a *training needs assessment* that takes into account the organization's job categories, work force, and goals (Blanchard & Thacker, 2007; Goldstein, 1993; Salas et al., 2012). One aspect of this assessment involves looking at job-analysis reports. As mentioned earlier, the need for training is indicated when job analyses reveal that certain jobs require knowledge, skills, or abilities that employees do not have or that should be strengthened. A second aspect of a training needs assessment is to give employees a chance to describe the training they would like to have. This information often emerges from *personal development plans* created by employees and their supervisors. These plans usually include an evaluation of the person's strengths and weaknesses. The weaknesses identified suggest where training might be useful, especially for employees who are motivated to improve their skills (Klein, Noe, & Wang, 2006). For example, if the supervisor notes that an individual is awkward when making presentations, a course in public speaking might be worthwhile. Finally, I/O psychologists will look at the goals of the organization. If those goals include reducing workplace accidents or improving communication with international customers, then training in safety procedures or foreign-language skills would be in order.

Designing Training Programs

In designing organizational training programs, I/O psychologists are always mindful of the basic principles that govern the learning and remembering of new information and skills. These principles, which are described in the learning and memory chapters, guide efforts to promote *transfer of training, feedback, training in general principles, overlearning,* and *sequencing.*

Transfer of Training   The most valuable training programs teach knowledge and skills that will generalize, or transfer, to the workplace. If employees don't apply what they have learned so as to improve their job performance, the training effort will have been wasted. Because promoting *transfer of training* is not always easy, I/O psychologists work hard to develop written materials and active learning exercises that not only clarify the link between training and application but also give employees some experience at applying new knowledge and skills in simulated work situations. So trainees might first

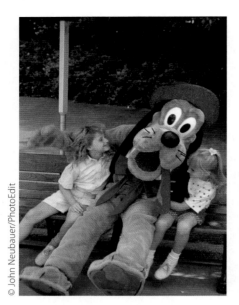

© John Neubauer/PhotoEdit

Staying Goofy

Training programs for employees who portray cartoon characters at major theme parks emphasize the general principle that the organization's goal is to create a fantasy world for customers. This aspect of training helps the employees understand why it is important to follow the rule of remaining in character at all times. A carefully cultivated fantasy world would be disrupted if children were to see "Mickey Mouse" or "Bugs Bunny" holding his headgear under his arm while smoking a cigarette! 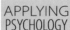 APPLYING PSYCHOLOGY

complete reading assignments, attend lectures, and watch videos illustrating effective approaches to dealing with customer complaints or defusing an office conflict. Then they might form groups to role-play using these approaches in a variety of typical workplace scenarios. These experiences enhance transfer of training, especially when the trainees' newly learned skills are supported and rewarded by their coworkers and supervisors (Kontoghiorghes, 2004).

Feedback   People learn new skills faster when they receive *feedback* on their performance (Smither, London, & Reilly, 2005). In organizational training, this feedback usually comes from the trainer and/or other trainees. It takes the form of positive reinforcement following progress, constructive suggestions following errors or failure, and constant encouragement to continue the effort to learn. For example, after one trainee has role-played a new way to deal with an irate customer or a disgruntled employee, the trainer might play a videotape of the effort so that everyone can offer comments, compliments, and suggestions for improvement.

Training in General Principles   People tend to learn better and remember more of what they learn when they can see new information in a broader context—in other words, when they have some insight into how the information or skill they are learning fits into a bigger picture (Baldwin & Ford, 1988). The Linkages sections in this book are designed specifically to promote this kind of learning. In organizational settings, the "big picture" approach takes the form of *training in general principles,* which teaches not only how to do things in particular ways but also why it is important to do so. When training new customer service agents at a hotel, a bank, or an airline, for example, trainers often provide an orientation to the basic characteristics of these businesses, including how competitive they are. Understanding their company's need to survive intense competition will help employees recognize the importance of courtesy training in determining whether a customer remains a customer or goes elsewhere.

Overlearning   Practice makes perfect in all kinds of teaching and training. I/O psychologists emphasize the need for employees to practice using the information and skills learned in a training program until they reach a high level of performance. In fact, many training programs encourage employees to continue practicing until they are not only highly competent but are also able to perform the skill or use the information automatically without having to think much about it. This *overlearning* is seen in many everyday situations, most notably among experienced drivers, who can easily get from one place to another without paying much attention to the mechanics of steering, braking, and turning. Athletes and musicians, too, practice until their skills seem to unfold on their own. In the workplace, overlearning can save time and improve efficiency. For example, members of an experienced medical team can perform surgery using skills and information that, through overlearning, have become second nature to them. They do not have to stop and think about how critical tasks must be done; they simply do them (Driskell, Willis, & Copper, 1992).

Sequencing   Is it better to cram organizational training into one or two long, intense sessions over a single weekend or to schedule it in several shorter sessions over a longer period of time? Intense, *massed training* is certainly less expensive and less disruptive to employees' work schedules than *distributed training.* However, I/O psychologists know that, as described in the memory chapter, people don't retain as much after massed practice ("cramming") as they do after distributed practice (Bjork, 1999; Donovan & Radosevich, 1999). Among other problems, massed training, like massed practice, can create boredom, inattention, and fatigue, all of which interfere with the learning and retention of new material. As most students can appreciate, an employee might remain motivated and interested during a one-hour training session but will probably be exhausted and inattentive by the end of an eight-hour training marathon. With this in mind, organizational training programs are set up using a distributed schedule whenever possible.

Evaluating Training Programs

Did a training program produce enough benefits to the organization to make it worth the time and money it cost? Should it be repeated? If so, should it be refined in some way? I/O psychologists are prepared to conduct research on these important evaluation questions (Salas et al., 2012). As described in the introductory chapter, controlled experiments offer a way to draw reasonably strong cause-effect conclusions about the impact of a training program. In such experiments, a sample of employees who need training would be randomly selected and then randomly assigned either to receive training or to spend an equivalent amount of time away from their jobs pursuing some alternative activity. The value of the training program could then be measured in terms of the size of the difference in job performance between the trained (experimental) group and the untrained (control) group. However, organizations rarely ask for experimental research on their training programs. Most of them merely hope that what seemed to be valuable training did, in fact, deliver information and skills that employees will remember and use to improve their job performance. Accordingly, evaluation tends to focus on nonexperimental designs using criteria such as employees' reactions to training, what they remember about it, and the changes in behavior that follow it.

Evaluation Criteria   The first kind of evaluation criteria, called *training-level criteria,* includes data collected immediately after a training session. Trainees are typically asked to fill out questionnaires about how much they liked the training and how valuable they felt it was. Training sessions that receive low ratings on enjoyment, value, and effectiveness are not likely to be repeated, at least not in the same format. But just as some effective teachers may not be immediately appreciated by their students, some effective training programs may receive low post-session ratings. A complete evaluation should consider other criteria as well.

A second class of evaluation criteria, called *trainee-learning criteria,* includes information about what trainees actually learned from the training program. These criteria are usually measured by a test similar to a college final exam that is designed to determine each trainee's knowledge and skill in the areas covered by the training. In some cases, alternative forms of this test are given to the trainees before and after training to assess how much improvement has taken place.

Finally, *performance-level criteria* measure the degree to which the knowledge and skills learned in training transferred to the employees' workplace behavior. If employees now know how to do a better job on the assembly line or at the hotel's front desk but do not apply this knowledge to improve their performance, the training program has not been successful. Organizations often evaluate training on the basis of criteria such as number or quality of products produced, frequency of customer complaints, and the like. Significant improvements following training might be a result of that training, but because so few organizations conduct controlled experimental evaluations of training, drawing this conclusion is usually risky. The improvement might have had less to do with the training than with some other uncontrolled factor, such as a downturn in the economy that motivated employees to work harder in an effort to keep their jobs.

I/O psychologists recommend evaluating training programs on as many criteria as possible, because the apparent value of training can depend on which criteria you consider (Sitzmann et al., 2008). A program that looks great on one criterion might be dismal on another. In particular, many programs that get high employee ratings on enjoyment, value, and other training-level criteria fail to show effectiveness in terms of increased productivity, efficiency, or other performance-level criteria (Alvarez, Salas, & Garofano, 2004; May & Kahnweiler, 2000). For example, one training program that was designed to improve employees' interviewing skills received high ratings from the trainees, who showed improved interviewing during training. Unfortunately, these skills did not transfer to real interview situations (Campion & Campion, 1987). ("In Review: Recruiting, Selecting, and Training Employees" summarizes our discussion of these topics.)

Recruiting, Selecting, and Training Employees IN REVIEW

Process	Methods
Recruitment	Perform hiring needs assessment; place ads on web sites and in newspapers; contact employment agencies; conduct campus interviews; solicit nominations from current employees; accept walk-in applications
Selection	Measure candidates' knowledge, skill, ability, and other personal characteristics using interviews, tests, and assessment centers; conduct validation studies to ensure that these KSAO criteria predict job success
Training	Conduct training needs assessment; design training to promote transfer of training, feedback, understanding of general principles, overlearning, and distributed training; evaluate training in terms of employee ratings of the experience and improvement in employee performance

IN REVIEW QUESTIONS

1. Employees tend to remember more from a training program when it is set up on a ___ rather than a ___ schedule.

2. Depending on walk-in applications is usually acceptable when hiring ___-level employees.

3. Assuring that your hiring criteria actually predict employees' job performance requires a ___.

Employee Motivation

What motivates employees to do their best?

In the chapter on motivation and emotion, we define *motivation* as the reason people behave as they do. It includes biological, emotional, cognitive, and social factors that influence the direction, intensity, and persistence of behavior (Reeve, 1996; Spector, 2003). These factors are as important in the workplace as they are anywhere else (Nye et al., 2012). We can see motivation affecting the *direction* of work-related behavior in people's decisions about whether to work and what kind of job to seek. The effect of motivation on the *intensity* of work can be seen in how often an employee misses work, shows up late, works overtime, or goes beyond the call of duty. Motivation is also reflected in a worker's *persistence* at a task. Some employees give up as soon as difficulties arise, perhaps not bothering to pursue information if it is hard to find. Others keep trying, using every strategy possible until their efforts are successful.

Let's consider three theories that have been used by I/O psychologists to better understand employee motivation. One theory focuses on general factors that can affect behavior in the workplace and all other areas of life, too. The others highlight factors that are more specifically associated with motivation in the workplace.

ERG Theory

In the motivation and emotion chapter we describe Abraham Maslow's (1943, 1970) theory in which human behavior is seen as based on a hierarchy of needs or motives. These range from such basic biological needs as food and water to higher needs, such as esteem and self-actualization (see Figure 8.4). Maslow believed that people must at least partially satisfy needs at the lower levels of the hierarchy before they will be motivated by higher-level goals. This is not always true, though. Hunger strikers, for example, ignore their need for food in order to pursue a protest that brings them closer to self-actualization.

To address some of the problems in Maslow's theory, Clayton Alderfer (1969) proposed **existence, relatedness, growth (ERG) theory,** which places human needs into three rather than five categories. *Existence needs* are things such as food and water that are necessary for survival. *Relatedness needs* include the need for social contact, especially having satisfying interactions with and attachments to others. *Growth needs* are those involving the development and use of a person's capabilities. These three categories of needs range from the most concrete (existence) to the most abstract (growth), but

existence, relatedness, growth (ERG) theory A theory of motivation that focuses on employees' needs at the levels of existence, relatedness, and growth.

ERG theory does not suggest that they must be satisfied in any particular order. Instead, the strength of people's needs in each category is seen as rising and falling from time to time and from situation to situation. If a need in one area is fulfilled or frustrated, a person will be motivated to pursue some other needs. For example, after a relationship breakup frustrates relatedness needs, a person might focus on existence or growth needs by eating more or volunteering to work late. Similarly, losing a job frustrates growth needs, so a laid-off employee might focus on relatedness needs by seeking the social support of friends. Finally, a person obsessed with work-related growth needs might ignore those friends until after a big project is completed and it is time to party.

I/O psychologists apply ERG theory in the workplace by helping organizations to recognize that employees may not be as motivated to pursue job-related growth needs if other need categories are frustrated or unfulfilled. As we describe later, for example, many organizations now allow flexible working hours in the hope that employees will be more motivated on the job once they can more easily satisfy family-oriented relatedness needs.

Expectancy Theory

A second approach to employee motivation is similar in many respects to Julian Rotter's (1954, 1982) expectancy theory, which is discussed in the personality chapter. It seeks to explain how cognitive processes affect the impact of salary, bonuses, and other rewards on employees' behavior (Vroom, 1964). The main assumption of **expectancy theory** in the workplace is that employees behave in accordance with (1) what results they expect their actions to bring; and (2) how much they value those results. For example, the motivation to put out extra effort will increase if (1) employees expect a bonus for doing so; and (2) the bonus is valued enough to be worth the effort. Both expectancy and value are a matter of individual perception, though, so it is difficult to use expectancy theory to predict employee motivation by considering outcomes alone. If some workers don't believe that a supervisor will actually provide a bonus for extra work or if certain individuals are not strongly focused on money, the prospect of a bonus may not be equally motivating for all employees.

Workplace tests provide strong support for expectancy theory. One review of 77 studies showed that how hard employees work and the quality of their work are strongly related to their expectancies about rewards and the value they place on those rewards (Van Eerde & Thierry, 1996). In other words, people tend to work hard when they believe it will be worth it to do so. Part of the task of industrial and organizational psychologists is to help organizations make employees feel that the effort needed for high performance is worthwhile.

Goal-Setting Theory

A third approach to employee motivation, called **goal-setting theory,** focuses on the idea that workplace behavior is affected partly by people's general needs and expectations, but also by their intentions to achieve specific goals. These goals can be short term, such as finishing a report by the end of the week, or long term, such as earning a promotion within the next two years. A basic prediction of goal-setting theory is that employees will be motivated to choose, engage in, and persist at behaviors that take them closer to their goals.

Goal-setting theory has proven quite useful in motivating employees. There is evidence that arranging for employees to spend some time setting specific goals can lead to better job performance (Locke & Latham, 1990). Many organizations encourage their employees to engage in goal-setting activities (Yearta, Maitlis, & Briner, 1995), but I/O psychologists remind managers that some goals are more useful than others. The most motivating goals tend to be those that are (1) chosen, or at least accepted, by employees; (2) difficult enough to be challenging but not so difficult as to be impossible; and (3) specific enough (e.g., "increase sales by 10 percent") to allow employees to keep track of their progress and know when they have succeeded (Latham, 2004; Locke, 2000; Wegge & Haslam, 2005).

expectancy theory A theory of workplace motivation in which employees are seen as acting in accordance with expected results and with how much they value those results.

goal-setting theory A theory of workplace motivation focused on the idea that employees' behavior is shaped by their intention to achieve specific goals.

In an ideal workplace, the goals of employees and employers are aligned. When they are not, a worker's motivation can suffer.

Job Satisfaction

Is pay the most important factor in job satisfaction?

Success in achieving workplace goals is one of many factors that can affect **job satisfaction,** the degree to which people like or dislike their jobs. Like other attitudes described in the chapter on social psychology, job satisfaction is made up of cognitive, emotional, and behavioral components (Schleicher, Watt, & Greguras, 2004). The cognitive component of job satisfaction includes *beliefs* about the job, such as "this job is too demanding" or "this job always presents new challenges." The emotional component includes positive or negative *feelings* about the job, such as boredom, excitement, anxiety, or pride. The behavioral component of job satisfaction is reflected in how people act in relation to their work, perhaps showing up early and staying late or maybe taking every opportunity to avoid work by calling in "sick."

Measuring Job Satisfaction

I/O psychologists assess employees' attitudes about their jobs in general (a *global approach*) and about various aspects of it (a *facet approach*; see Table 15.4). In most cases, job satisfaction is measured using questionnaires. Some questionnaires, such

---

TABLE 15.4   Facets of Job Satisfaction

Here are the results of a Gallup poll in which workers in the United States reported on their attitudes toward various facets of their jobs. Notice that workers tend to have differing attitudes about differing facets. For example, workers can be satisfied with their co-workers and supervisors but not satisfied with their salaries. How do you feel about your own job as "student?" Try listing those aspects of "studenting" that give you the most satisfaction, then take a poll among your student friends to see which aspects of their studentship give them the most satisfaction.

LEARN by DOING

Facet	Percent Satisfied
Relationships with co-workers	94
Physical safety conditions of work	92
Flexibility of hours	90
Amount of work	88
Job security	87
Supervisor	84
Recognition received at work	81
Amount of vacation time	79
Salary	75
Promotion opportunities	68
Health insurance	64
Retirement plan	62

job satisfaction The degree to which people like or dislike their jobs.

FIGURE 15.2
Pay Satisfaction Subscale from the Job Satisfaction Survey

Here are just four items from the pay satisfaction subscale of the Job Satisfaction Survey (Spector, 1985). As its name implies, this subscale focuses on employees' attitudes about the pay they receive in their jobs. Other subscales assess attitudes toward other job facets, such as promotion opportunities, benefits, co-workers, and supervisors.

Source: Copyright © 1994 Paul E. Spector. All rights reserved. Reprinted with permission.

as the Job in General Scale (Ironson et al., 1989), take a global approach. Others, such as the Job Satisfaction Survey (Spector, 1985), are designed to assess attitudes about several job facets, including pay, promotion, benefits, co-workers, and supervision (see Figure 15.2).

Factors Affecting Job Satisfaction

Satisfaction with a job in general or with its various aspects can vary widely from one person to the next, even when people do the same job in the same organization (Bond & Bunce, 2003; Schleicher, Watt, & Greguras, 2004; Staw & Cohen-Charash, 2005). In other words, some employees may like jobs or aspects of jobs that others hate. I/O psychologists have studied several environmental and personal factors that can influence people's job satisfaction (Chudzikowski et al., 2009; Sonnentag, 2012). Among the environmental factors are the requirements of the job, how much it pays, and how it affects workers' lives outside of the workplace. Among the personal factors are workers' attachment styles, gender, age, and ethnicity (e.g., Richards & Schat, 2011).

Job Requirements   Some jobs, such as those of assembly line workers, involve performing the same, relatively simple tasks again and again throughout the work day. Other jobs, such as those in management, are more complex, requiring workers to perform a different set of tasks each day, often in response to unpredictable requests or demands. Is the complexity of a job related to workers' job satisfaction? In general, yes. People tend to be more satisfied with jobs that are more complex (Fried & Ferris, 1987; Melamed, Fried, & Froom, 2001). As described in the chapter on motivation and emotion, this higher satisfaction may relate to the fact that more complex jobs tend to be more interesting, more challenging, and more likely to create a sense of responsibility and control in setting and achieving goals (Maynard, Joseph, & Maynard, 2006). However, not everyone responds to complex jobs in the same way (Jex et al., 2002). A complex job may create dissatisfaction among people who don't have the knowledge, skills, abilities, or other characteristics to do it successfully (Hackman & Oldham, 1980). Even individuals who have the necessary knowledge and skills may be dissatisfied with a complex job if their personality characteristics lead them to prefer simpler, less intellectually demanding work (Loher et al., 1985).

Salary   Many workers feel underpaid, but as discussed in the motivation and emotion chapter, higher salaries alone do not necessarily lead to higher levels of job satisfaction (Igalens & Roussel, 1999). One study of recent college graduates found a correlation of only +.17 between starting salary and overall job satisfaction (Brasher & Chen, 1999). A main reason for this low correlation is that a substantial salary may not compensate for other unsatisfactory aspects of a job, such as poor working conditions, lack of respect from supervisors, or the like. In fact, knowing that salary and pay raise decisions are made in a fair way can be more important to job satisfaction than the amount of money employees receive (Liao & Rupp, 2005; Simons & Roberson, 2003). As a result, students working at low-paying jobs may be more satisfied than executives who earn six-figure salaries. The student's satisfaction may come from knowing that everyone doing the same job is getting the same pay, whereas the executive may experience *relative deprivation,* the perception that others are unfairly receiving more benefits for the same or lesser effort (see the social psychology chapter).

Work-Family Conflict   The number of two-career couples and single-parent families is on the increase in the industrialized world (e.g., Demo, Allen, & Fine, 2000; Weinraub, Horvath, & Gringlas, 2002). With this increase comes increasing conflict between the demands of a job and the demands of family life (Eby et al., 2005; O'Driscoll, Brough, & Kalliath, 2006; ten Brummelhuis & Bakker, 2012). One common example is the conflict that occurs when the need to care for a sick child or attend a child's school play interferes with a parent's work responsibilities. For both men and women, the amount of conflict between the demands of job and family is strongly and consistently related to job satisfaction (Baltes & Heydens-Gahir, 2003; Ford, Heinen, & Langkamer, 2007; Lapierre & Allen, 2006). In cooperation with I/O psychologists, many organizations are dealing with this source of job dissatisfaction by instituting *family-friendly work policies* that help employees balance work and family responsibilities. One of these policies, called *flextime,* allows parents to work an eight-hour day but frees them from the standard nine-to-five schedule. One parent can come to work at, say, 9:30 a.m. after taking the children to school and then stay on the job beyond 5:00 p.m. to complete an eight-hour day. The other parent can start work at, say, 7:30 a.m. and then leave early to pick up the children from school.

Gender, Age, and Ethnicity   The many studies that have compared job satisfaction in men and women have found few, if any, differences—even when the men and women

Minimizing Work-Family Conflict
To help working couples deal with the demands of work and family obligations, many organizations have adopted family-friendly programs and policies, including workplace daycare services and the availability of flexible work schedules (flextime). These programs and policies have been associated with higher levels of job satisfaction and less absenteeism among employees with children (Baltes et al., 1999; Scandura & Lankau, 1997). *Fortune* magazine publishes an annual issue listing the best U.S. companies to work for. Look through this year's issue to see what kinds of family-friendly policies these companies have created.

LEARN by DOING

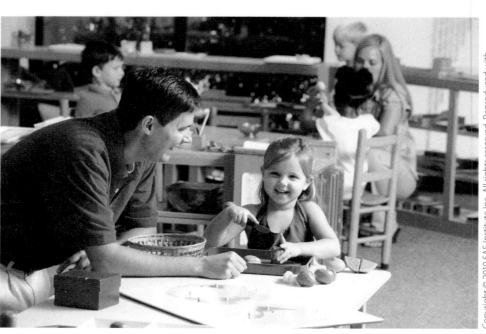

compared were doing quite different jobs (e.g., Greenhaus, Parasuraman, & Wormley, 1990; Moncrief et al., 2000). Job satisfaction is related to age, though. Older workers tend to be more satisfied than younger ones (Brush, Moch, & Pooyan, 1987), but the picture may be a bit more complicated than that (Clark, Oswald, & Warr, 1996; Hedge, Borman, & Lammlein, 2006). For example, among people who enter the world of work immediately after high school or community college, job satisfaction may at first be quite high but may soon begin to decline, especially among males. Satisfaction ratings then tend to increase slowly but steadily from about age 30 until retirement. This pattern may occur because young workers with relatively little education may find themselves in jobs that not only are poorly paid but also offer few of the features associated with job satisfaction, such as complexity, control over time, opportunity to set goals and tasks, and the like (White & Spector, 1987).

Some studies of workers in the United States have found slightly higher job satisfaction among whites than among nonwhites (e.g., Jones & Schaubroeck, 2004; Tuch & Martin, 1991), but others have found no differences (e.g., Brush, Moch, & Pooyan, 1987). In fact, when comparisons are made across groups doing the same jobs, ethnicity does not appear to be a major factor in job satisfaction. Culture can have an influence, though (Benton & Overtree, 2012). For example, one study found that job satisfaction among workers in the United States tends to be related to internal factors, such as feeling stimulated and challenged by their jobs, while satisfaction among workers in China may be related more to external factors such as being offered new opportunities or satisfying the requests of their employers (Chudzikowski et al., 2009).

THINKING CRITICALLY   Is Job Satisfaction Genetic?

In the chapter on motivation and emotion, we mention that people's overall level of happiness, or subjective well-being, may be determined partly by genetic influences. Could those same influences operate in the workplace in relation to job satisfaction?

What am I being asked to believe or accept?

Richard Arvey and his colleagues (1989) have suggested that differences in job satisfaction reflect genetic predispositions toward liking or not liking a job.

Is evidence available to support the claim?

People's temperament and personality are certainly influenced by genetics. Research in I/O psychology shows that these genetically influenced personality characteristics are related to people's job satisfaction. In one study, for example, hostility and other personality traits measured in adolescence were found to be significantly related to job satisfaction up to 50 years later (Judge, Heller, & Mount, 2002; Staw, Bell, & Clausen, 1986; Watson & Slack, 1993). These data suggest that job satisfaction is at least indirectly shaped by inherited predispositions.

However, Arvey and his colleagues (1989) conducted what may be the only direct investigation of the role of genetics in job satisfaction. They selected 34 pairs of genetically identical twins who had been separated and raised in different environments. They then arranged for these people to complete a job satisfaction questionnaire. The questionnaire responses showed a strong positive correlation between the twins' job satisfaction; if one twin was satisfied, the other one tended to be satisfied, too. If one was dissatisfied, the other twin tended to be dissatisfied as well. The researchers suggested that because the members of each twin pair had been raised in different environments, genetic factors were at least partly responsible for creating the observed similarity in job satisfaction ratings.

Can that evidence be interpreted another way?

These results suggest a strong genetic influence, but they could have been affected by factors other than a genetic predisposition to be satisfied or dissatisfied with a job. For example, although the twins grew up in different home environments, their

Genes may play a role in job satisfaction, but other factors are surely at work as well.

work environments might have been quite similar, and it may have been those similar work environments that produced similar satisfaction ratings. Why would separated twins have similar work environments? For one thing, the innate abilities, interests, behavioral tendencies, or physical characteristics that identical twins might share could have led them into similar kinds of jobs. Some pairs might have selected jobs that tend to be satisfying, whereas other pairs might have taken jobs that tend to be less satisfying. A pair of bright, athletic, or musically talented twins might have found it possible to have complex, interesting, and challenging jobs and to enjoy a high level of satisfaction. A less fortunate set of twins may have been unable to qualify for the kind of job they might want and may have settled for more routine work that leaves them feeling dissatisfied. In other words, it may be that genes don't shape job satisfaction itself but do help shape characteristics that influence people's access to satisfying work.

What evidence would help to evaluate the alternatives?

One way to assess the impact of job characteristics on the high correlation in twins' job satisfaction ratings is to look at the nature of the twins' jobs. When Arvey and his colleagues (1989) did this, they found that the twins did tend to hold jobs that were similar in several ways, including overall job complexity and some of the skills required. A more complete assessment of the jobs and job environments would be needed, however, to determine the strength of these nongenetic factors in creating positively correlated job satisfaction ratings.

It will also be important to look for specific genes that might be associated with job satisfaction. Research has already linked job satisfaction with two specific genetic markers associated with the activity of the neurotransmitters dopamine and serotonin (Song, Li, & Arvey, 2011), and this line of research will undoubtedly continue.

What conclusions are most reasonable?

Research in I/O psychology suggests that individual differences in job satisfaction are probably related to workers' characteristics, some of which are influenced by genetics. However, the precise mechanisms through which genetics might affect job satisfaction are not yet clear (Ilies & Judge, 2003). It is most likely that job satisfaction, like so many other aspects of behavior and mental processes, is shaped by both genetic and environmental influences. So there is no single reason why people differ in terms of job satisfaction. How satisfied we are with our work can be predicted to some extent by job characteristics and to some extent by personal characteristics (Gerhart, 2005), but the outcome in a given case is ultimately a matter of who does what job in what organization.   ●●●●

Consequences of Job Satisfaction

Organizations spend a lot of time, money, and effort to try to maintain a reasonable level of job satisfaction among their employees. They do so, if for no other reason, because job satisfaction is linked to a variety of positive consequences for individuals, their co-workers, and their organizations (Harter et al., 2010). Dissatisfaction with a job can lead to numerous negative consequences.

Job Performance   Research shows that people who are satisfied with their jobs tend to be more motivated, work harder, and perform better than employees who are dissatisfied (e.g., Fisher, 2003; Judge et al., 2001). The positive correlation between job satisfaction and performance makes sense, and though a correlation alone cannot confirm that satisfaction is causing good performance, it is certainly consistent with that conclusion (Harrison, Newman, & Roth, 2006). It's possible, though, that people who perform better feel more satisfied with their jobs as a result (Jacobs & Solomon, 1977).

Organizational Citizenship Behavior   Job satisfaction is also associated with **organizational citizenship behavior (OCB),** a willingness to go beyond formal job requirements in order to help co-workers and/or the organization (Borman et al., 2001; Ilies, Scott, & Judge, 2006; Moorman & Byrne, 2005; Organ, Podsakoff, & MacKenzie, 2006). As in the case of job performance, it is difficult to determine whether job satisfaction causes increased organizational citizenship behavior or whether engaging in OCB causes increased job satisfaction. Further, organizational citizenship behavior may reflect factors other than job satisfaction, such as personality characteristics (Chiaburu et al., 2011). And some cases of OCB might occur as part of a strategy designed to get a pay raise or promotion or reach some other personal goal. In one study, for example, employees who believed it would help their chances for promotion engaged in high levels of OCB before being promoted, then reduced their OCB afterward (Hui, Lam, & Law, 2000).

Turnover   Every organization must deal with a certain amount of *turnover*, or loss of employees. Some turnover is involuntary, as in cases of disability or dismissal, but much of it is voluntary (Harman et al., 2007). Some employees simply quit, and they tend to be employees whose job satisfaction is low (e.g., Griffeth, Hom, & Gaertner, 2000). However, in order to avoid unemployment, few dissatisfied workers quit until and unless they have found another job (Kammeyer-Mueller et al., 2005). So the relationship between job dissatisfaction and turnover is strongest when people are able to find other jobs (Trevor, 2001). When alternative employment is unavailable, even dissatisfied workers tend to stay put.

Absenteeism   You might expect that absenteeism, like voluntary turnover, would be strongly related to low job satisfaction. However, the correlation between job satisfaction and attendance is surprisingly weak (Farrell & Stamm, 1988). True, there is a tendency for dissatisfied employees to be absent more frequently than those who are satisfied, but other factors, including personal or family illness, work-family conflicts, and the financial consequences of missing work are far more important in determining who shows up and who doesn't (Dalton & Mesch, 1991; Erickson, Nichols, & Ritter, 2000).

Aggression and Counterproductive Work Behavior   Job dissatisfaction is one cause of workplace aggression as well as of theft and other forms of *counterproductive work behavior (CWB)*. Assaults or murders involving co-workers or supervisors are rare (Barling, Dupre, & Kelloway, 2009; LeBlanc, Dupre, & Barling, 2006), but theft, computer hacking, and other forms of CWB by employees and former employees are commonplace. Employee theft in the United States alone costs organizations billions of dollars each year (Brown, 2010; Gatewood & Feild, 2001). In fact, employees steal more from their employers than do shoplifters (Hollinger et al., 1996; Rob, 2012). The direct and indirect costs of other forms of counterproductive work behavior, such as sabotage, working slowly, or doing jobs incorrectly, are staggering. But the true cost of CWB can be hard to determine because so much of it goes unnoticed (Bennett & Robinson, 2000).

As illustrated in Figure 15.3, it is often stress in the workplace that leads to job dissatisfaction and negative emotions, such as anger and anxiety (e.g., Spector, Fox, & Domalgaski, 2006). These emotions, in turn, can result in CWB, especially among employees who feel they have been treated unfairly or have little or no control over stressors (Aquino, Tripp, & Bies, 2006; Fox, Spector, & Miles, 2001; Penney & Spector, 2005; Whitman et al., 2012). Why does lack of control matter? As described in the chapter on health, stress, and coping, when people feel they have control over the

LINKAGES

How do stressors affect job performance? *(a link to Health, Stress, and Coping)*

organizational citizenship behavior (OCB) A willingness to go beyond formal job requirements in order to help co-workers and/or the organization.

FIGURE 15.3

Job Satisfaction and Counterproductive Work Behavior

Workplace stressors can lead to job dissatisfaction, which leads to negative emotions and counterproductive work behavior, especially among employees who feel mistreated and unable to control stressors.

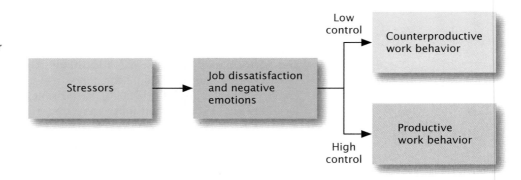

work situation, they are more likely to perceive stressors as challenges to be overcome and to try constructive means of doing so. Suppose, for example, that a supervisor suddenly assigns a difficult task to an employee, who must complete it by the next day or face serious consequences. If the employee senses enough control over the situation to complete the task on time, this stressful assignment is likely to be perceived as a challenge to be mastered. If the employee doesn't have that sense of control and believes it is impossible to meet the deadline, this stressful assignment will probably create dissatisfaction and negative emotions such as resentment. This person is at elevated risk for engaging in counterproductive work behavior directed at the supervisor, the organization, or other employees.

LINKAGES

What causes workplace aggression?
(a link to Social Psychology)

Aggression in the Workplace

In the chapter on social psychology, we describe a number of biological, psychological, and environmental factors that appear to be responsible for creating and/or triggering human aggression and violence. These factors operate in the workplace, too, but aggression between or against workers differs in some ways from violence outside of the workplace (Hershcovis et al., 2007).

About 70 percent of workplace homicides are committed against employees by strangers (U.S. Department of Justice, 2011). Despite well-publicized cases of disgruntled employees killing co-workers or supervisors, employees actually commit only about 21 percent of workplace homicides and less than 10 percent of workplace assaults (U.S. Department of Justice, 2011). Convenience store clerks, taxi drivers, and others who deal directly with the public, handle money, and work alone at night are the employees at greatest risk to be victims of workplace aggression (LeBlanc, Dupre, & Barling, 2006). Most aggression against these people is *instrumental aggression,* meaning that the aggressor's intent is not necessarily to injure but to achieve a goal such as getting money or other valuables (Merchant & Lundell, 2001). Though the perpetrator often uses a weapon to intimidate the employee, these aggressive incidents do not usually result in physical injury.

Most cases of injury in the workplace occur in the course of aggressive assaults on doctors, nurses, and other health care workers, sales clerks, bartenders, and food servers by patients or customers (Büssing & Höge, 2004; LeBlanc & Barling, 2004). Often these injuries occur under stressful circumstances—such as during emergency room treatment—in which pain, anger, fatigue, and frustration lead to an impulsive, emotional, aggressive outburst. In contrast to instrumental aggression, the perpetrator's intent in these cases is to injure the employee victim.

Aggression in the workplace is typically verbal, and the result is usually resentment and hurt feelings, not bruised bodies (Barling, Dupre, & Kelloway, 2009; Grubb et al., 2005). Like road-rage incidents, employee-to-employee aggression is often the by-product of an impulsive outburst under time pressure or other stressful conditions, such as workplace injustices or abusive supervision (Berry, Ones, & Sackett, 2007; Inness, Barling, & Turner, 2005). Sometimes, though, this form of aggression reflects a continuing attempt by one employee to control others through intimidation or bullying (Bies, Tripp, & Kramer, 1997; Grubb et al., 2005). ● ● ● ●

Occupational Health Psychology

How can workplace accidents be prevented?

In the chapter on health, stress, and coping, we defined *health psychology* as a field devoted to understanding psychological factors in how people stay healthy, why they become ill, and how they respond when they do get ill (Taylor, 2002). **Occupational health psychology** is concerned with psychological factors that affect the health, safety, and well-being of employees in the workplace. I/O psychologists help promote the goals of occupational health psychology by consulting with organizations about ways to reduce threats to employees posed by undue stress, accidents, and hazards. Their success in this enterprise is reflected in the fact that today, most workplaces are safer and healthier than employees' own homes (National Safety Council, 2004).

Physical Conditions Affecting Health

Many physical conditions in the workplace have the potential to cause illness and injury (Lund et al., 2006). Accordingly, in the United States, the Occupational Safety and Health Administration (OSHA) establishes regulations designed to minimize employees' exposure to hazards arising from infectious agents, toxic chemicals, dangerous machinery, and the like. For example, to guard against the spread of AIDS, U.S. doctors, dentists, nurses, and other health care workers have been asked to follow a set of safety procedures called *universal precautions,* which include wearing disposable gloves when drawing blood, giving injections, or performing dental procedures and discarding needles and other sharp objects into special sealed containers.

These procedures can be effective in reducing the spread of disease, but because of heavy workloads and lack of encouragement from supervisors, health care workers do not always follow them (McDiarmid & Condon, 2005). I/O psychologists play a role in this aspect of occupational health psychology by promoting organizational support for following proper safety procedures and by designing safety training that employees will actually use in the workplace (Smith-Crowe, Burke, & Landis, 2003). They also help protect employees' health by creating reminders to be careful on the job and by consulting with organizations to minimize stressors that can lead to illness or injury.

One of these stressors comes in the form of jobs that require performing specific movements in the same way over long periods of time, such as turning a screwdriver or making cut after cut in pieces of plastic. Eventually, these movements can create *repetitive strain injuries,* in which joints become inflamed, sometimes producing permanent damage. The most familiar of these injuries is *carpal tunnel syndrome,* a condition of the wrist that produces pain, numbness, and weakness in the fingers. Although typically associated with using a computer keyboard or mouse, carpal tunnel syndrome can be caused by many other activities involving the fingers and wrist. Psychologists have been involved in two approaches to preventing repetitive strain injuries. First, as described in the introductory chapter, those working in *engineering psychology* (also called *human factors*) consult with industrial designers to create tools and equipment that are less physically stressful to use. As a result, people who perform typing tasks for many hours each day now usually place a pad in front of their keyboard that provides support and helps keep their wrists from twisting. Second, I/O psychologists are working with organizations to ensure that employees whose jobs require repetitive actions be allowed to take breaks that are long enough and frequent enough to rest the body parts at risk for strain injuries. These psychologists are also working with employees to ensure that they follow the recommended break schedule.

Work Schedules, Health, and Safety

The arrangements mentioned earlier that allow employees to adjust their working hours are but one part of a more general trend away from the traditional nine-to-five workday. As many organizations expand their hours of service, including to 24 hours a day, seven days a week, more and more employees are on the job during what once would have

© Lanica Klein/Photos.com

Doing It Over and Over
Performing the same movements on the job hour after hour and day after day can lead to *repetitive strain injuries.* This employee's keyboard movements resulted in a painful and potentially disabling condition called *carpal tunnel syndrome.* Wearing a wrist brace can reduce the pain somewhat, but I/O and engineering psychologists know that improved wrist support for keyboard users can help prevent the problem in the first place. To appreciate the impact of psychologists' consultation efforts, browse some online computer equipment catalogs, such as geeks.com or tigerdirect.com, and calculate the percentage of keyboards, mice, and other devices that have been designed to minimize the possibility of repetitive strain injuries.

LEARN by DOING

occupational health psychology
A field concerned with psychological factors that affect the health, safety, and well-being of employees.

© Walter Hodges/CORBIS

Staying Sharp

I/O psychologists' research on the negative impact of extended work shifts has led to organizational and U.S. government rules requiring rest breaks at fixed intervals for commercial airline pilots, long-haul bus and truck drivers, and others whose jobs require constant attention to complex tasks and systems. The rules also limit the total number of hours these employees can work in any 24-hour period.

APPLYING PSYCHOLOGY

been considered "odd hours." They may work at night or on weekends and follow shift patterns once associated mainly with hospitals, law enforcement, and factories. Others are working more than eight hours a day but less than five days a week, and in the face of staffing cutbacks, still others may be working more than 40 hours a week. Whether undertaken by choice or by assignment, these nontraditional work schedules can create stress and fatigue that can adversely affect employees' health.

Rotating Shift Work   The negative effects of such schedules can be especially great among employees who change work shifts from week to week, rotating from evenings to days to nights, for example (Demerouti et al., 2004). As described in the chapter on consciousness, these shift changes disrupt employees' *circadian rhythms* of eating, sleeping, and wakefulness, resulting in a number of unpleasant mental and physical symptoms. A major problem with working night shifts, for example, is fatigue, irritability, and reduced cognitive sharpness resulting from difficulty in getting to sleep or staying asleep during the day (Daus, Sanders, & Campbell, 1998). Some shift workers also experience upset stomachs and other symptoms of digestive distress (Rouch et al., 2005). These problems may be far less troubling for workers whose night shift assignments last long enough that they can get used to their "backward" schedule (Barton & Folkard, 1991), but rotating shift work can also be disruptive to employees' social relationships and may create work-family conflicts (Barnes-Farrell et al., 2008). Absenteeism, too, may increase, especially among younger workers who are new to shift work, and there is some evidence that burnout and earlier retirement are more common among workers on rotating shifts than among those on fixed schedules (Shen & Dicker, 2008).

Long Shifts and Long Weeks   Many organizations today are establishing longer-than-normal work shifts. For example, some have set up 10-hour shifts that allow employees to work 40 hours in four days, thus creating an extra day off. Others have replaced three 8-hour work shifts with a more efficient system of two 12-hour shifts that allows workers even more time off. There is evidence that many employees like these arrangements and that longer shifts can lead to greater job satisfaction and better job performance (Baltes et al., 1999).

However, extended workdays may create health and performance problems for some workers in some jobs (Lamberg, 2004). This possibility is suggested by research on drivers of intercity buses. Those who drove longer routes that required being on the road for up to 14 hours a day with few rest breaks tended to use stimulants to stay alert, drink alcohol to counteract the stimulants after arrival, and experience sleep disturbances, various physical symptoms, and anxiety and fatigue. They were also more likely than drivers with shorter shifts to be involved in accidents (Raggatt, 1991).

There are also dangers in requiring employees to work more than 48 hours per week, especially when those employees would prefer not to do so. These involuntary extensions of the work week have been associated with a number of employee health problems, particularly heart disease (Sparks et al., 1997). Accordingly, nations of the European Union have adopted regulations setting work weeks at a maximum of 48 hours. So far, there are no such governmental regulations in the United States.

Stress, Accidents, and Safety

Though most accidents occur outside the workplace, workplace safety is still a major focus of organizations and, therefore, of I/O psychologists (Barling & Frone, 2004). In just one recent year, 5,734 workers were killed and 4.2 million others were injured on the job in the United States alone (U.S. Bureau of Labor Statistics, 2007). Motor vehicle accidents account for nearly half of workplace fatalities. Falls and equipment accidents account for about another third of these deaths.

Longer-than-normal work shifts and extended work weeks are just one source of the occupational stress contributing to the fatigue, inattention, cognitive impairment, sleepiness, and other problems that elevate the risk of workplace accidents (Caldwell, 2012). I/O psychologists have identified many other individual and organizational factors that contribute to stress-related accidents. These include, for example, lack of clear instructions, heavy workloads, concern about job security, sexual harassment or ethnic discrimination, burnout, and workplace bullying (Berdahl & Moore, 2006; Hoel, Faragher, & Cooper, 2004; Schabracq, 2003; Schaufeli & Buunk, 2003; Schneider, Hitlan, & Radhakrishnan, 2000; Sparks, Faragher, & Cooper, 2001). Accidents are also more likely when the *climate of safety* in the workplace is poor, meaning that there is a lack of safety training, too little supervisory emphasis on following safety rules, and a tendency for workers to ignore those rules (Griffin & Neal, 2000). Accidents are least common in organizations that create a *total safety culture* by providing adequate safety training for employees, conducting thorough and frequent safety inspections, and ensuring that supervisors consistently communicate the need for and value of safety (Geller, 2011; Newnam, Griffin, & Mason, 2008; Wallace, Popp, & Mondore, 2006).

Work Groups and Work Teams

Do groups need supervision to work well?

work group At least two people who interact with one another as they perform the same or different workplace tasks.

work team A work group in which the members' specialized activities are coordinated and interdependent as they work toward a common goal.

A great deal of workplace activity is accomplished by groups of individuals working together. I/O psychologists have been at the forefront of efforts to help organizations maximize the effectiveness and efficiency of work groups and work teams (Barsade & Gibson, 2012; Kleingeld, van Mierlo, & Arends, 2011; Ormiston & Wong, 2012; Shuffler, DiazGranados, & Salas, 2011; Shteynberg & Galinsky, 2011). A **work group** is defined as at least two people who interact with one another as they perform the same or different tasks. The four servers waiting on customers during the dinner shift at a restaurant would be an example of a work group. A **work team** is a special kind of work

Medical Teamwork

The doctors, nurses, and technicians who join forces to perform surgery are a perfect example of a work team. Everyone on the surgical team is devoted to the same goal of completing a successful operation, but each performs a somewhat different task in a coordinated way under the direction of the surgeon, who acts as the team leader.

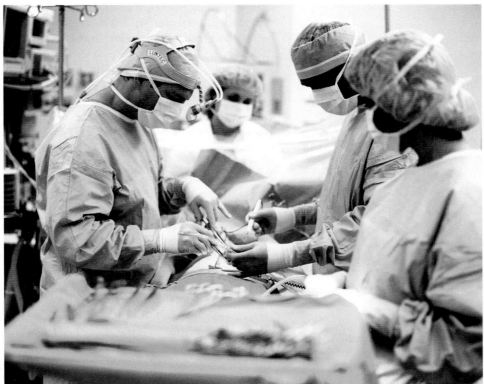

group in which (1) each member's activities are coordinated with and depend on the activities of other members; (2) each member has a specialized role; and (3) members are working to accomplish a common goal (West, Borrill, & Unsworth, 1998). The entire staff on duty during the restaurant's dinner shift would be considered a work team. All members of the team are working on the same task with the same goal in mind—namely, to successfully serve customers as quickly and efficiently as possible. Further, each team member has a specialized role: greeters seat customers, servers take orders and deliver the food prepared by the cooks, and managers monitor progress, direct employees, and fill in at various tasks as needed. Whether it involves food service, brain surgery, automobile repair, or other workplace activities, an effective work team performs like the proverbial well-oiled machine.

Autonomous Work Groups

In most organizations, work groups and work teams operate in a traditional way, meaning that as in the case of a restaurant or grocery store, all workers report to a manager who directs and supervises their activities. However, a growing number of organizations today are establishing **autonomous work groups (AWGs)** that manage themselves and do not report to anyone for routine daily supervision. Instead, once AWGs are given a work assignment, it is up to them to determine how best to accomplish their goal and then work together to achieve it. The classic example of AWGs can be seen in the manufacturing sector. Automobiles and other consumer products were once built on long assembly lines by large numbers of workers who each performed only one small part of the process before passing the product on to another worker, who performed the next step. In AWGs however, each member rotates among jobs, such that everyone is involved in every aspect of assembly from time to time. The team members also design and order their own tools, conduct their own product inspections to ensure quality and performance, and even participate in hiring and firing decisions. Many brands of automobiles and other large pieces of equipment are now assembled in AWG factories that feature a series of workstations where perhaps half a dozen employees assemble the entire product or a substantial portion of it.

AWGs have been shown to have benefits for employees and for organizations. In one comparison study, employees in AWG factories reported higher levels of job satisfaction than did employees of traditional factories (Cordery, Mueller, & Smith, 1991). Further, the productivity of AWGs has been shown to be at least as good as and sometimes better than traditional arrangements despite the fact that AWG facilities don't need as many supervisors, and thus cost less to run (Banker et al., 1996; Glassop, 2002; Hoegl & Parboteeah, 2006; Stewart, 2006).

Group Leadership

Workplace groups almost always have leaders. Even in AWGs, leaders usually emerge (Taggar, Hackett, & Saha, 1999), although the leadership roles may sometimes be shared by more than one person (Uhl-Bien, Marion, & McKelvey, 2007). And AWGs are themselves embedded in organizations that operate through a leadership hierarchy (Kaiser, Hogan, & Craig, 2008). At each level, designated leaders direct or supervise the activities of others, set group and organizational objectives, figure out how individual employees can best contribute to those objectives, and make sure employees perform the tasks assigned to them. Let's consider some of the characteristics of good leaders, how good leaders behave, and how they relate to various members of their work groups and work teams.

What Makes a Good Leader?   One way to study leadership is to look at lots of leaders to see whether particular kinds of knowledge, skill, ability, or other personal characteristics are associated with those who are effective and those who are ineffective. Much of what social and I/O psychologists have learned about the KSAOs of effective leaders comes from their research on managers (e.g., Peterson et al., 2003; Zaccarco, 2007). That research suggests that some characteristics are seen by almost everyone as necessary for good leadership. For example, a large study of leadership effectiveness in 62 countries

autonomous work groups (AWGs)
Self-managed employee groups that do not report to anyone for routine daily supervision.

found that being intelligent, trustworthy, and team-oriented were universally rated as important traits of good leaders (House et al., 1999). These results are supported by other studies showing that intelligence is consistently important for competent managerial performance (Chemers, Watson, & May, 2000; Judge, Colbert, & Ilies, 2004). In other words, smarter leaders tend to be better leaders. Good leaders also tend to score high on agreeableness, emotional stability, extraversion, and conscientiousness (Silverthorne, 2001). The value of other leadership traits can depend on social, cultural, and situational factors (Chemers, 2000; Gibson & McDaniel, 2010; Hoyt, Simon, & Innella, 2011; Livingston et al., 2012). For instance, a willingness to take risks tends to be seen as a positive leadership trait in some countries and as a negative trait in others (House et al., 1999). Further, a leader's success may sometimes depend more on the loyalty, organizational citizenship behaviors, and other "followership" traits of the particular people they lead than on their leadership style (Popper, 2011).

How Do Good Leaders Behave?   Another way to study leadership is to explore the things that effective and ineffective leaders do. The foundation for this research was provided by the Ohio State Leadership Studies, which began in 1945. The first step in this extensive program was to collect 1,800 critical incidents of effective and ineffective leader behavior. An example of "effective" leadership might be a situation in which a manager suggested that a troubled employee transfer to a less demanding job; an example of "ineffective" leadership might be a situation in which a manager shouted at an employee who questioned the leader's decision. These and other studies have revealed that specific kinds of leader behaviors can have profound effects on group members and organizations. For example, one study found that army platoons led by active and involved leaders were especially effective under combat conditions (Bass et al., 2003). The Ohio State researchers identified two dimensions on which leaders typically vary. The first, called *consideration,* is the degree to which a leader shows concern for the welfare of employees, including friendly and supportive behavior that makes the workplace more pleasant. The second dimension, called *initiating structure,* is the degree to which a leader coordinates employee efforts by assigning tasks and clarifying expectations so that group members know what is required of them to perform well.

The relationship-motivated leaders described in the social psychology chapter tend to be high on the consideration dimension while the task-motivated leaders described there tend to be high on the initiating-structure dimension. Where managers fall on each of these dimensions of leadership style can have important effects on employees (Eagly, Johannesen-Schmidt, & van Engen, 2003; Judge, Piccolo, & Ilies, 2004; Keller, 2006; Zaccarco, 2007). In one study, workers in a truck-manufacturing plant were asked to rate their immediate supervisors on the dimensions of consideration and initiating structure (Fleishman & Harris, 1962). These ratings were then related to the number of complaints these employees filed against their supervisors and the rate at which they quit their jobs (voluntary turnover). There were more grievances and much higher turnover among employees whose supervisors had been rated low on consideration than among those whose supervisors had been rated high on consideration. More grievances were also filed by employees whose supervisors were high on initiating structure, but there is more to that part of the story. The highest rates of grievance and turnover occurred among employees whose supervisors were not only high on initiating structure but also low on consideration. As long as supervisors were high on consideration, they could be high on initiating structure without creating a lot of grievances and turnover. In other words, it is possible for a leader to be firm but fair, thus promoting maximum performance with a minimum of complaints and employee losses.

Leader-Member Interactions   Are leadership styles like the relatively stable traits described in the personality chapter? Do they create consistent leadership behaviors toward all group members in all situations? Some leaders might fit this description, but **leader-member exchange (LMX) theory** suggests that as leaders gain experience with their groups over time, most of them tend to adopt different styles with two different kinds of subordinates (Dansereau, Graen, & Haga, 1975; Naidoo et al., 2011).

leader-member exchange (LMX) theory A theory suggesting that leaders tend to supervise ingroup and outgroup employees in different ways.

Leaders tend to offer the most consideration and best treatment to subordinates who make up the employee *ingroup*. These individuals tend to be the best performers and are seen by the leader as competent, trustworthy, loyal, and dependable (Bauer & Green, 1996). As such, ingroup members' opinions and requests tend to carry more weight with the leader than do those of *outgroup* employees, who are seen by the leader as less competent, less reliable, and potentially expendable. Ingroup members may also benefit from having "inside" information from the leader, more helpful mentoring, and perhaps even inflated performance evaluations (Duarte, Goodson, & Klich, 1993; Scandura & Schriesheim, 1994). Leaders give outgroup employees less opportunity to influence decisions and tend to supervise them by giving high structure and low consideration (Dansereau, Graen, & Haga, 1975). More than 80 studies of leader-member interaction patterns support the existence of employee ingroups and outgroups. They also confirm the tendency for ingroup members to experience more job satisfaction and less occupational stress and to more often engage in organizational citizenship behaviors (Gerstner & Day, 1997; Ilies, Nahrgang, & Morgeson, 2007; Schyns, 2006). By comparison, the job satisfaction and performance of outgroup members is likely to suffer, especially if they feel that the organizational climate is unjust (Hooper & Martin, 2007).

Traditional leadership models are based on situations in which there is face-to-face interaction among team members and leaders. Do these models apply equally well to "virtual teams" whose members communicate electronically (Zigurs, 2003)? Industrial and organizational psychologists are beginning to investigate this question (e.g. Huang, Kahai, & Jestice, 2010; Ocker et al., 2011; Shuffler et al., 2010; Xiao et al., 2008), and the results of their research on *e-leadership* will undoubtedly expand our understanding of leadership as it operates in today's increasingly technology-driven workplaces.

FOCUS ON *RESEARCH*   # Can People Learn to Be Charismatic Leaders?

Some people's leadership abilities are so effective that they are described as *charismatic* (pronounced "kare-iz-MAT-ic"). A *charismatic leader* is one who inspires followers to embrace a vision of success and make extraordinary efforts to achieve things they would not have done on their own (Bass & Riggio, 2006; Erez et al., 2008). Charismatic leaders such as Martin Luther King, Jr., and Sir Winston Churchill captured the imaginations of their followers. Dr. King led the fight for civil rights in the 1960s, inspiring countless thousands of followers to overcome entrenched opposition and personal danger to achieve the long-sought goal of equality under the law for African Americans. Prime Minister Churchill rallied the British people to resist and overcome the effects of Nazi air attacks during the darkest days of 1940 and throughout World War II. It has long been assumed that charismatic leadership is a by-product of a charismatic personality, not something that one can learn.

What was the researchers' question?
I/O psychologists wonder, though, whether that assumption is correct. Might it be possible to train leaders to be charismatic and if so, how would such training affect the job satisfaction and performance of those leaders' employees? Julian Barling, Tom Weber, and E. Kevin Kelloway (1996) addressed these questions by designing and evaluating a charisma-building training program for corporate managers.

How did the researchers answer the question?
Their study was conducted in 20 branches of a large Canadian banking corporation. The managers of these branches were randomly assigned to either a charisma training group or a control group that received no training. Two weeks before training began and five months after it was completed, the people working for each manager filled out a questionnaire on which they rated their manager's charisma. They also reported on their own level of job satisfaction. The financial performance of each branch office was measured before and after training, too.

Charisma training was delivered in five sessions over a three-month period. At the first session, managers met as a group to spend an entire day learning what makes charismatic leaders charismatic and practicing these behaviors in order to increase their own charisma. In the next four sessions, managers worked individually with one of the researchers, receiving additional training, getting feedback on performance, and setting goals for further progress.

What did the researchers find?

All the results indicated that this training program had a positive impact on managers' charisma. First, branch employees' ratings showed that managers in the training group were now more charismatic. There was a small decline in charisma for those in the control group. Second, employees who worked for the managers who had received charisma training reported higher levels of job satisfaction after training was over than did those who worked for the untrained managers. Finally, the financial performance of the trained managers' branches increased, whereas that of the untrained group decreased somewhat.

What do the results mean?

This charisma training program may not have produced a Martin Luther King, Jr., or a Winston Churchill, but its impact supports the notion that charisma can be taught, at least to some extent (Frese, Beimel, & Schoenborn, 2003). The trained managers became more charismatic and more effective than their untrained colleagues, suggesting that charisma involves behavior that can be learned by people with many different personality characteristics.

What do we still need to know?

The findings of this study are encouraging, but we should be cautious in interpreting them. For one thing, the changes seen in the trained managers might have been due to factors other than the training itself. As described in the introductory chapter, improvements following almost any treatment may be due partly or largely to placebo effects or other factors that create positive expectations among research participants. If the managers expected to be better at their jobs as a result of training and if their subordinates expected them to be better managers, it could have been these expectations rather than the training that caused the behavior changes and/or the increased charisma ratings. Even the improved financial performance could have been the result of expectation-driven efforts by managers and employees to do better, efforts that had nothing to do with the training itself. Interpreting the results of this experiment would have been easier if members of the untrained group had participated in some sort of placebo program that, like the charisma training, would have raised their expectations and those of their employees.

Even if the training program actually was responsible for the improvements seen, it would be important to know whether its effects would last beyond the five-month follow-up period. If it does have long-term effects, it would then be important to evaluate charisma training with leaders in other kinds of organizations and at other levels of leadership. It will take time and a lot of research to explore these matters, but if charisma can indeed be taught, we may someday see candidates for political office lining up to learn it. ●●●●

A Charismatic Leader
Apple founder Steve Jobs was considered by many to exemplify the kind of leader whose charisma inspires followers to accomplish what they might not otherwise have done.

Active Review

As noted in the introductory chapter, all of psychology's subfields are related to one another. Our discussion of aggression in the workplace illustrates just one way that the topic of this chapter, industrial and organizational psychology, is linked to the subfield of social psychology,

CHAPTER 15
Industrial and Organizational Psychology

which is covered in the chapter by that name. The Linkages diagram shows ties to two other subfields, and there are many more ties throughout the book. Looking for linkages among subfields will help you see how they all fit together and help you better appreciate the big picture that is psychology.

LINKAGES

How do stressors affect job performance?
(ans. on p. 617)

What methods are used to select good employees?
(ans. on p. 599)

What causes workplace aggression?
(ans. on p. 618)

CHAPTER 10
Health, Stress, and Coping

CHAPTER 11
Personality

CHAPTER 14
Social Psychology

Summary

An Overview of Industrial and Organizational Psychology

What do industrial and organizational psychologists do?
Industrial and organizational (I/O) psychology is the science of behavior and mental processes in the workplace. I/O psychologists study the psychology of the workplace and apply psychological research to enhance the performance of employees and organizations and improve the health, safety, and well-being of employees. I/O psychology grew out of experimental psychology early in the twentieth century as psychologists began to apply laboratory research to workplace problems.

Assessing People, Jobs, and Job Performance

How do industrial and organizational psychologists match employees to jobs?
The development and evaluation of methods for assessing employees, jobs, and job performance is one of the main areas for scientific research in I/O psychology. The human attributes necessary for doing jobs successfully are referred to collectively as KSAOs, which stands for knowledge, skill, ability, and other personal characteristics.
A **job analysis** is the assessment of jobs and job requirements. It may be job oriented (describing job tasks), person oriented (describing the KSAOs necessary to perform job tasks),

or both. Organizations use job analysis information for many purposes, including employee hiring and training.

The three main methods used to measure employee characteristics are psychological tests, job applicant interviews, and assessment centers. Tests can focus on employees' knowledge, ability, skill, and other characteristics, such as personality traits. A job applicant interview is designed to determine an applicant's suitability for a job. It can be structured or unstructured, but structured interviews are far more effective in selecting successful employees than unstructured interviews, in which questions are not organized ahead of time. An *assessment center* is an extensive battery of exercises used to determine whether a person is suited for a particular job.

Most organizations give an annual *job performance* appraisal to all employees. Much like a school report card, these appraisals describe how well a person is doing in several job domains. Performance is measured in relation to general (theoretical) criteria as well as in relation to more specific (actual) criteria.

Objective measures of job performance rely on counting behaviors or the results of behaviors. These measures are valuable, but they are not appropriate for evaluating performance in jobs that have little or no objectively measurable output. Subjective measures can be used in any job situation, but because they rely on supervisor ratings of performance, these measures may be distorted by judgment bias or error.

Recruiting and Selecting Employees

How do organizations find good employees?

I/O psychologists frequently use assessment tools to help hire people who will be best able to succeed in particular jobs. The first step in effective recruiting is to determine what employees are needed and then attract applicants to fill those needs, using employment agencies, Internet and print advertising, and campus visits; encouraging nominations from current employees; and accepting walk-in applications.

The I/O approach to hiring uses scientific principles to match jobs to the KSAOs of applicants. Establishing the KSAO requirements of a job helps determine which employee assessment tools will be most appropriate, and validation studies may be used to confirm that particular scores on the chosen assessments actually predict success on the job. Many industrialized countries have established laws and regulations that bar

discrimination in hiring, firing, or promotion based on ethnicity, age, gender, or any other characteristics that have nothing to do with job performance.

Training Employees

What kind of training do employees need?

I/O psychologists help organizations establish the need for training, design training methods and content, and evaluate the outcome of training. Using a training needs assessment, organizations determine what training employees need in order to perform their jobs safely and well. Training needs assessments can focus on what KSAOs are required for specific jobs, on what training employees say they need, and on the objectives of the organization, such as improving production and decreasing accidents.

The design of training programs is guided by research on the processes through which people acquire new information and skills. These principles are translated into employee training that emphasizes transfer of training (applying new skills to the workplace), feedback (providing reinforcement for progress and guidance and encouragement following errors), training in general principles (providing "big picture" information to show the relevance of training), overlearning (practicing new skills until they become automatic), and sequencing (distributing training over time to improve learning and retention). A training program can be evaluated in terms of how trainees felt about the training (training-level criteria), what trainees actually learned during training (trainee learning criteria), and/or the

degree to which trainees used what was learned during training in doing their jobs (performance-level criteria).

Employee Motivation

What motivates employees to do their best?

Motivation in the workplace refers to factors that influence the direction, intensity, and persistence of employees' behavior. Three theories of motivation have special workplace applications. *Existence, relatedness, growth (ERG) theory* divides human needs into existence needs (e.g., for food and water), relatedness needs (e.g., social contact), and growth needs (the development and use of one's capabilities). It suggests that the strength of each type of need affects workers' motivation to do their jobs well. According to *expectancy theory,* employees work hard if they perceive it to be in their best interest to do so. *Goal-setting theory* describes workers' motivation as stemming mainly from their desire to achieve short- and long-term goals. According to this theory, organizations should help employees set clear, specific goals that are challenging but not impossible.

Job Satisfaction

Is pay the most important factor in job satisfaction?

Job satisfaction is a cluster of attitudes that reflect the degree to which people like their jobs. It is usually assessed using questionnaires that ask employees to say how they feel about their jobs in general (the global approach) or about pay, supervision, or other specific job components (the facet approach). I/O psychologists have studied several environmental and personal factors that can influence people's job satisfaction. Among the environmental factors are the requirements of the job, how much it pays, and how it affects workers' lives outside the workplace. Among the personal factors are workers' gender, age, and ethnicity. For the most part, complex jobs tend to be more satisfying than simple jobs. Salary itself may be a less important factor in job satisfaction than the fairness of the salary system. Excessive work-family conflict can reduce job satisfaction. Because of temperament and experience, some individuals may have a tendency to be more satisfied with their jobs than others.

Job satisfaction has been associated with better job performance and with *organizational citizenship behavior (OCB),* but it isn't clear whether satisfaction is a cause or an effect of these attributes. Job dissatisfaction is clearly at work in causing people to quit their jobs (turnover), but it has a smaller effect on absenteeism. Job dissatisfaction can also lead to aggression and counterproductive work behavior (CWB) such as theft or sabotage. CWB is especially likely among dissatisfied employees who work under conditions of high stress and low perceived control.

Occupational Health Psychology
How can workplace accidents be prevented?
Occupational health psychology is concerned with psychological factors that affect the health, safety, and well-being of employees. A number of physical conditions in the workplace can affect health, including infectious agents, toxic chemicals, dangerous machinery, and stressors such as the need to perform repetitive actions.

Work schedules, too, can have an impact on health and well-being. Rotating shift work, extended shifts, and longer-than-normal work weeks have been associated with a variety of problems ranging from fatigue and sleeping problems to substance abuse and increased risk of heart disease. Reducing workplace accidents can be accomplished not only by reducing occupational stressors but also by promoting a climate of safety. Workplace accidents are least frequent in organizations that provide rigorous safety training, conduct frequent safety inspections, and encourage adherence to safety procedures.

Work Groups and Work Teams
Do groups need supervision to work well?
A *work group* is a collection of people who interact on the job, whereas a *work team* is a group in which members depend on one another as they work at specialized yet coordinated tasks aimed at accomplishing a common goal. Unlike traditional, closely supervised work teams, *autonomous work groups (AWGs)* are assigned tasks and then given the freedom to manage themselves, solve their own problems, and even influence hiring and firing decisions, all of which tend to result in greater job satisfaction among team members.

Leaders direct or supervise the activities of others, set group and organizational objectives, and ensure that employees perform their assigned tasks. Certain characteristics tend to be universally seen as desirable leadership attributes; others may not be seen as ideal in all cultures. Two dimensions of leadership style—consideration and initiating structure—have been found to have strong effects on employees' performance and job satisfaction. *Leader-member exchange (LMX) theory* suggests that leaders adopt different styles toward ingroup and outgroup employees. Charismatic leaders have the ability to influence and inspire employees to accomplish things they would not have done on their own. Charisma in leaders tends to promote job satisfaction in employees, and there is evidence that some aspects of charisma can be taught.

Put It in Writing
Think about a job you have had—perhaps the one you have now—and write a paragraph describing what you like about it and what you don't like about it. Then read what you have written and ask yourself whether the factors that affect your job satisfaction correspond to those we described as affecting employee satisfaction in general.

Personal Learning Activity
Arrange to visit the human resources (personnel) department of a local department store, factory, or other business organization where you can talk to an I/O psychologist or other staff member about how new employees are recruited and selected. Find out how many of the six recruitment tools we mentioned are being used by the organization and ask about how the results of tests, interviews, and assessment centers are used in making decisions about hiring, training, and promotions. Summarize what you learned in a two-page report, including your view of how well the organization seems to be applying the results of research in industrial and organizational psychology.

Review of Key Terms

Can you define each of the key terms in the chapter? Check your definitions against those on the pages shown in parentheses in the following list or in the Glossary at the end of the book.

assessment center (p. 600)
autonomous work groups (AWGs)
   (p. 622)

existence, relatedness, growth (ERG)
   theory (p. 610)
expectancy theory (p. 611)
goal-setting theory (p. 611)
industrial and organizational (I/O)
   psychology (p. 596)
job analysis (p. 598)
job performance (p. 601)
job satisfaction (p. 612)

leader-member exchange (LMX) theory
   (p. 623)
occupational health psychology (p. 619)
organizational citizenship behavior
   (OCB) (p. 617)
work group (p. 621)
work team (p. 621)

Test Your Knowledge

Select the best answer to each of the following questions. Then check your responses against the Answer Key at the end of the book.

1. I/O psychologists ____.
   a. conduct research on behavior and mental processes in the workplace
   b. focus mainly on improving the efficiency of employees
   c. focus mainly on the development of intelligence and personality tests
   d. work mainly for government agencies

2. Donald Crump's new business has grown so quickly that he needs to hire more employees. The first thing that Mr. Crump should do is ____.
   a. interview all applicants
   b. create psychological profiles of the best applicants
   c. conduct a job analysis of each open position
   d. identify the salary for each position

3. You have been hired to conduct a job analysis at a local fast food chain. After completing your analysis, you conclude that the job requires cooking hamburgers. What type of job analysis have you performed?
   a. Job oriented
   b. Person oriented
   c. Analysis oriented
   d. Performance oriented

4. Jobs require individuals with specific knowledge, skill, ability, and other personal characteristics. These KSAOs are identified by a detailed study called a ____.
   a. job assessment study
   b. job analysis
   c. KSAO-ometry
   d. computer-aided assessment

5. Attributes or characteristics necessary to successfully perform a job are called ____.
   a. compensable factors
   b. critical factors
   c. KSAOs
   d. essential functions

6. Larry Recruiter is interviewing potential employees at an on-campus job fair. To find the most appropriate candidate for his job opening, Larry should use ____ interviews.
   a. unstructured
   b. panel
   c. structured
   d. inferential

7. A large company is most likely to select high-level managers using mainly ____.
   a. assessment centers
   b. unstructured interviews
   c. letters of recommendation
   d. personality tests

8. Performance appraisal information can be used for ____.
   a. employee development
   b. decisions about pay increases
   c. evaluating the need for new training
   d. all of the above

9. Consider the job of "student." Which of the following is a theoretical criterion for this job?
   a. The number of A's earned in a three-year period
   b. The total value of scholarships obtained over a three-year period
   c. Engaging in scholarly activities
   d. The number of clubs joined

10. Which of the following reflects a subjective measure of a teacher's job performance?
    a. The average of student ratings on a course evaluation questionnaire
    b. The average size of the teacher's classes
    c. The number of courses taught
    d. The frequency of being late for class

11. Ruth is evaluating all of the employees in her department. To be as fair as possible, she uses behavior-focused ratings. This means that Ruth will ____.
    a. interview each employee in an unstructured way.
    b. give each employee global ratings in areas such as efficiency and honesty.
    c. rate employees on their handling of critical incidents in their job.
    d. observe each employee's performance for one day.

12. Organizations hope that employees will apply to their jobs what they learn during training. This process is called ____.
    a. response discrimination
    b. transfer of training
    c. application management
    d. training to learn

13. ____ training is more efficient, but ____ training is more effective in the long run.
    a. Part; whole
    b. Whole; part
    c. Massed; distributed
    d. Distributed; massed

14. Which of the following aspects of employee training is *not* usually done by I/O psychologists?
    a. Conducting a training needs assessment
    b. Delivering the training
    c. Designing the training
    d. Evaluating the training

15. The need for water is an example of a ____ need in Maslow's hierarchy of needs theory and of a(n) ____ need in Alderfer's ERG theory of employee motivation.
    a. physiological; relatedness
    b. safety; existence
    c. safety; growth
    d. physiological; existence

16. According to the ____ approach to job satisfaction, people can be satisfied with some aspects of their jobs and dissatisfied with other aspects of their jobs.
    a. global
    b. facet
    c. ERG
    d. expectancy

17. If Eric is satisfied with his job, he most likely ____.
    a. earns a lot of money
    b. feels that his company's promotion and salary decisions are fair
    c. has a job that does not require complex thinking
    d. works alone with few distractions

18. Which of the following statements about counterproductive work behavior (CWB) is correct?
    a. Employees steal more from their employers than do shoplifters
    b. Dissatisfied employees are much more likely to be absent from work than satisfied employees
    c. Employees are more likely to engage in CWB if they feel in control of their work
    d. Assaulting a co-worker is as common as stealing from a co-worker

19. Five students in an advertising class jointly prepare a 60-second commercial, each taking a separate production role. The quality of the commercial determines the project grade for all five students. These five students constitute a ____.
    a. work group but not a work team
    b. work team
    c. group-think
    d. nominal group

20. Which leadership theory emphasizes the relationship between the leader and individual group members rather than between the leader and the group as a whole?
    a. Leader-member exchange theory
    b. Vroom-Yetton model
    c. Leader behavior theory
    d. Path-goal theory

Media Resources

Now that you have finished reading this chapter, how about exploring some of the ideas and information that you found most interesting?

Go to **CengageBrain.com** to access Psychology CourseMate, where you will find an interactive eBook, glossaries, flashcards, quizzes, videos, Virtual Psychology Labs, and more.

aplia

If your professor has assigned Aplia:

1. Sign in to your account.
2. Complete the corresponding exercises as required by your professor.
3. When finished, click "Grade It Now" to see which areas you have mastered, which areas need more work, and detailed explanations of every answer.

Neuropsychology

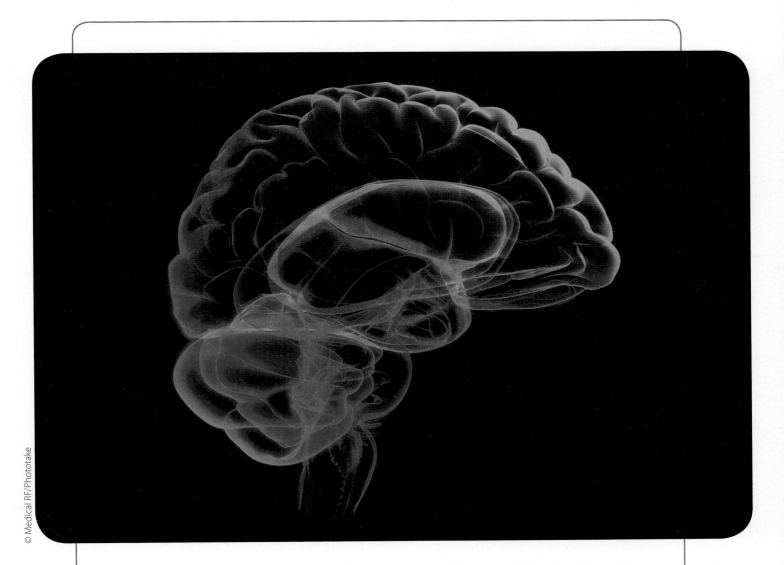

© Medical RF/Phototake

Preview

Our eyes, in cooperation with our brains, allow most of us to see the world in three-dimensional depth and in full color, but there are people who suffer conditions that leave them unaware of half of that world. Even though their eyes work properly, when these people look at a nice round pizza, they see only half a pizza. They are not suffering from a mental illness of the kind described in the chapter on psychological disorders, but they most definitely have a problem somewhere in their brains. Understanding what the problem is, exactly where it is, and how it affects a person's behavior and mental processes takes us into the realm of *neuropsychology,* the focus of this chapter. We describe the history of neuropsychology and some basic features of brain functions that are of particular interest to neuropsychologists. We also review the events and diseases that can result in brain damage or dysfunction, and we consider the tools that neuropsychologists use to try to pinpoint the location of such problems. Finally, we describe the symptoms of several kinds of neuropsychological disorders that can result from disruptions in the normal functioning of the brain.

Something was wrong with Max. He put away his car keys, his wallet, and a pair of dress shoes in their usual places, but when he tried looking for them later, he had no idea where they were. "You're just getting forgetful," his wife teased. But at breakfast one day, he used a piece of bacon to stir his coffee. Then, mistaking a candle on the table for a glass of orange juice, he tried to drink it, and he used a pancake as a napkin, wiping his mouth with it before placing it carefully on his lap. He seemed puzzled by these mistakes. His wife took him to a doctor. Suppose you were that doctor. How could you determine what was wrong with Max? There would be many possibilities to consider. Perhaps something is amiss in his brain. Or maybe he is choosing to do silly things to annoy his wife for some reason. But if he isn't acting oddly on purpose, just where does the problem lie? It might reside somewhere in his memory systems, but it might involve attention or some other psychological function, too. The problem might also be something less specific. Perhaps he's just been working too hard or is having a reaction to a medication or some sort of dietary deficiency. He might even be suffering from depression or from an unrecognized infection that is affecting his ability to remember and concentrate. ●

Foundations of Neuropsychology

What is neuropsychology and how did it develop?

Neuropsychology is the subfield of psychology whose goal is to explore and understand the relationship between brain processes, human behavior, and psychological functioning. *Neuropsychologists* are interested in how brain processes and disruptions of those processes affect a wide range of human abilities, including cognitive functioning (such as language, memory, attention, mathematical ability, and visual-spatial skills), motor functioning (such as walking or threading a needle), emotional functioning (such as the ability to express emotions and understand other people's emotional expressions), and social functioning (such as daily interactions with others). They are also interested in how dysfunctions in the brain relate to changes in personality and the appearance of psychological disorders such as depression.

The field of neuropsychology rests on two main assumptions. The first is that many complicated mental tasks, such as memory or decision making, involve many subtasks that can be tested and studied separately (Lezak, Loring, & Howieson, 2004). For example, as described in earlier chapters, the ability to form a new memory usually

neuropsychology The subfield of psychology whose goal is to explore and understand the relationship between brain processes, human behavior, and psychological functioning.

requires a person to be awake, to pay attention, to receive sensations, to perceive those sensations, to form mental representations of that information, to be motivated to remember the information, and to have the language or other verbal skills necessary to express the information when it is retrieved from memory. If any of these subtasks fail, a person's memory could also fail in any number of everyday situations. With this assumption about subtasks in mind, neuropsychologists must not only figure out which complicated mental tasks a person can and cannot do but also identify the failure of one or more subtasks that may be at the root of the problem.

Neuropsychology's second main assumption is that different psychological processes are controlled by different brain regions or by different combinations of brain regions (Fodor, 1983; Heilman & Valenstein, 2003). Neuropsychologists use this assumption to draw conclusions about each patient they examine. After deciding what psychological processes are impaired, they work backward to infer what brain region or combinations of regions may not be working properly. This "working backward" approach is valuable because many kinds of brain damage or disease are too subtle to be identified by physical examination or by various brain scanning procedures (Nadeau & Crosson, 1995). This approach also helps to clarify which areas of known brain damage may be causing symptoms, and which may not be.

Using these two main assumptions, some neuropsychologists conduct research on how the human brain controls and organizes separate parts of complicated mental activities. These scientists, known as *experimental neuropsychologists,* most often study people with brain damage, but they sometimes do research on people with normal brains, too. Their aim is to add to our knowledge of brain functioning among people in general. *Clinical neuropsychologists* use this knowledge to try to understand the problems that appear in particular individuals such as Max. They look for the best way to examine each person so as to determine the likelihood of brain damage or dysfunction, identify what psychological processes are impaired and exactly how they are impaired, and determine which processes are still operating properly (Heilman & Valenstein, 2003; Lezak, Loring, & Howieson, 2004; Scott, 2006). Most clinical neuropsychologists are found in hospitals and other health care settings, where they work with physicians to test people with brain damage (Johnson-Greene & Collins, 2011).

For example, Max's physician decided to have him tested by a clinical neuropsychologist. She showed Max a long series of simple line drawings of common objects and asked him to name each one. Experimental neuropsychological research on thousands of people provided *norms* that told her what kind of performance she could expect on this test from people of Max's age and educational background. She could then compare his performance with these norms. As it turned out, Max's responses were not normal. Looking at the drawing of a pencil, he said he saw "a long narrow protrusion of some kind." He called a paperclip "an object curling into itself." For eyeglasses he said, "That's two circular devices suspended together." Clearly he was not naming things well—but why? Could his vision be bad? No, because he could accurately describe the drawings and he could correctly read words, even when they were in small print. He could also produce reasonably accurate copies of the drawings, even though he could not always name them. These findings meant that he had sensed and perceived the drawings' shapes and angles and spatial relationships. Did Max have a general problem with memory, as his wife had suggested? To test that idea, the neuropsychologist read him lists of words and later asked him to recall them. He did about as well on this memory test as most people his age and level of education, so his memory seemed normal. The neuropsychologist next considered whether Max was no longer able to understand the concepts represented in the drawings. But this possibility was ruled out when he was able to give perfect responses when asked to define what is meant by a pencil, a paperclip, eyeglasses, and other objects shown in the drawings. So he knew what these objects were, and, in fact, when examples of them were placed into his hands while he was blindfolded, he could instantly name them. So Max could recognize these objects through his sense of touch, but not through his sense of vision.

Why? The neuropsychologist concluded that Max still had normal function within brain areas that process basic visual sensations but that something was wrong in the brain regions that normally convert those sensations into recognizable visual perceptions.

This problem is called a *visual agnosia,* and it can occur when parts of the temporal lobes on both sides of the brain don't work properly (Devinsky, Farah, & Barr, 2008). Max's physician used that information to focus his medical care on those brain regions.

Max's case illustrates several important features of what neuropsychologists have learned about how the brain operates. Let's review some of what they have discovered and how these discoveries occurred.

A Brief History of Neuropsychology

Max's case shows **localization of function**, the idea that a specific psychological function can be affected by damage to a specific brain area. This concept might seem obvious to you, especially if you have read about the brain in the chapters on biology and behavior, sensation and perception, and consciousness. But this "commonsense" notion was born amid considerable debate.

For centuries, philosophers and scientists had been speculating about the role of different brain areas in different psychological functions (Eling, 2008; Kaitaro, 2001). Early in the 1800s, for example, the dominant view was that the brain worked more or less as a single organ, such that no particular part was any more important than any other part in the control of mental life. An anatomist named Franz Gall disagreed with this view, suggesting instead that particular brain areas controlled particular aspects of cognitive functioning (Livianos-Aldana, Rojo-Moreno, & Sierra-Sanmiguel, 2007; Zola-Morgan, 1995). This suggestion actually turned out to be correct, and his legacy would be more widely honored except for the fact that Gall also mistakenly believed that brain areas, like muscles, get larger and stronger as people use them. He also believed that each brain area was associated with certain behavior patterns or personality traits, such as honesty or love or aggressiveness. Further, Gall claimed that as brain areas grew larger, there would be corresponding bumps in the skull just above them. He created a map showing which brain areas were supposedly controlling which traits, and used it to assess people's psychological makeup by measuring the bumps on the surface of their skulls. Gall's approach, known as *phrenology,* was a hit with the public because it appeared to be a simple way to measure personality (Benjamin & Baker, 2004). But assessing personality by feeling people's skulls was a far-fetched and easily refuted notion that led Gall's scientific colleagues to dismiss virtually everything he said about the brain's role in psychology. In fact, the ridicule heaped on phrenology spread to any and all theories about localization of function.

In 1861, though, everything changed. In that year, a famous and widely respected French surgeon, Paul Broca, examined a patient whose leg had gangrene, a serious deep-tissue infection. In this era before antibiotics, gangrene often required a surgeon to amputate the affected limb, which is the reason that Broca was consulted. It so happened that many years earlier, this patient had had a *stroke*—also called a **cerebrovascular accident,** or *CVA*—a condition in which one of the blood vessels to the brain is blocked, causing permanent damage to the brain. The stroke left him unable to say anything but the word *tan,* which became the staff's nickname for him. Despite his speech difficulties, Tan could apparently understand language because he easily followed verbal commands. Before anything could be done about Tan's gangrene, he died, and Broca ordered an autopsy. It showed a small **lesion,** or area of damage, in the left frontal lobe of Tan's brain (see Figure 16.1). Broca wondered whether this lesion was related to Tan's speech problems and if so, how such a small lesion could cause such a major and specific problem. Not long afterward, Broca requested an autopsy on another patient who had had language problems similar to Tan's and discovered a brain lesion in the same place as Tan's.

If lesions in this spot were somehow linked to these patients' speech disorders, it would support the previously dismissed idea of localization of function. Indeed, it would suggest that a particular brain area is involved in controlling a particular function, namely speech (Broca, 1861, 1865). This was precisely what Broca hypothesized when he shared his observations in a lecture to the Anthropological Society of Paris. And because, unlike Gall, Broca had such high status in the scientific community, his endorsement of localization of function made it respectable again. In fact, it created an upsurge of scholarly interest in localization of brain function that is still seen today. The resulting

localization of function The idea that specific psychological functions can be affected by damage to specific brain areas.

cerebrovascular accident (stroke) A loss of blood supply to some part of the brain, resulting in disruption of some aspect of behavior or mental processes.

lesion A damaged area in the brain.

FIGURE 16.1

Tan's Brain

When Tan died, surgeon Paul Broca discovered severe damage in the left frontal lobe of the cerebral cortex, just in front of the primary motor cortex. Now called *Broca's area*, it is involved with the ability to produce normal speech.

Left   Right

FIGURE 16.2

Alexia without Agraphia

This is a classic example of a disconnection syndrome. Brain damage (in darker blue) has occurred in the left occipital lobe and part of the corpus callosum. As a result, no visual information can enter the left hemisphere. The left-hemisphere brain regions that create writing are intact, so the patient can write. But because feedback from the visual system cannot get back to the language-processing systems of the left hemisphere, the patient cannot read what he or she has written.

explosion of brain research that occurred in the last century and a half has not only confirmed localization but has also established that localization is more complex than anyone in Broca's time would ever have guessed.

Modules and Networks

More recent theories about localization of function have introduced the idea that the brain is organized into discrete regions called *modules,* each of which performs its own unique kind of analysis of the information it receives (Fodor, 1983; Sternberg, 2011). According to this *modularity* view, each module, located in a unique brain area, acts somewhat like a circuit board in a computer. That is, a module does not itself "control" any one particular function, but it adds a needed piece to complete a larger puzzle that allows speech or some other particular function to occur. The analysis performed by a particular module can be used in many kinds of brain functions. And each brain function—whether it is detecting the edges of an object or making a decision about something—is accomplished through the support of a different team, or *network,* of modules (Mesulam, 1990). It is as if the brain were the head of a company with a vast array of employees, each with a specific skill, which can be organized and reorganized from one moment to the next into many different work teams that can perform many different tasks. So, some of the same brain areas can participate in many different psychological tasks, though the exact combinations of areas, or the timing of their participation, may differ from one function to another.

Speaking and understanding language, for example, involves a network of modules in several different brain areas (Friederici, 2011). This means that damage to any part of the network can affect a person's language ability in some way, but the exact effect will depend on which part of the network is damaged. In Tan's case, the lesion in his left frontal lobe affected his ability to speak but left him with the ability to understand what was said to him.

The brain regions underlying language are a particularly good example of a network that utilizes several modules. One of the interesting consequences of a system that is organized in this way is the potential for a *disconnection syndrome.* As described later, a syndrome is a pattern of symptoms, and in this case it occurs when various modules in a network are prevented from interacting even when the modules themselves are intact (Geschwind, 1968). A classic example is *alexia without agraphia,* which literally means inability to read while still being able to write (Imtiaz, Nirodi, & Khaleeli, 2001). The brain damage shown in Figure 16.2 could produce this kind of disconnection syndrome. Here, there is damage to the left occipital lobe, causing loss of vision, but only for what is on the right side of the visual field. The patient can still see the left side of the world. However, there is also damage to the corpus callosum, a structure that connects the left and right hemispheres of the brain. The damaged area of the corpus callosum normally allows visual information from the left side of the world to cross from the right hemisphere into the left hemisphere, but now this pathway is blocked. Because the language-producing regions of the left hemisphere are intact, people with this kind of damage can still talk and write normally, but when they look at what they write, they can see only the part that lies in their left visual fields. That information goes to the right hemisphere but because it cannot cross into the left hemisphere, where most language functions reside, these people have difficulty reading the very letters they have written. In effect, the visual processing of the words is disconnected from the brain regions that are needed to extract the meaning of those words.

Lesion Analysis

Much as Broca did so long ago, experimental neuropsychologists today still study the intricacies of localization of function by observing the results of brain damage. This aspect of their work is sometimes called *lesion analysis* (Aharonov et al., 2003). To get an idea of how lesion analysis works, suppose that a man with normal mathematical ability has a stroke that damages his left parietal lobe (see Figure 2.9 in the chapter on biology and behavior for the location of this area). Afterward, like other people with similar brain damage, he can no longer do mathematical calculations. Do these observations confirm that the ability to do math is localized in the left parietal lobe in human brains? Not necessarily. Critical thinking suggests other possibilities, too.

For example, we have already seen that complex psychological functions often require the cooperation of several different modules in several different parts of the brain. So although mathematical ability may suffer after damage to the left parietal lobe, it might also be affected by damage to other regions in a "mathematics" network. Experimental neuropsychologists explore this possibility by studying changes in the math ability seen in large numbers of people with damage to many different regions of the brain. If they find that math ability is affected by left parietal lobe damage but not by damage anywhere else, they would be more confident in asserting that mathematical disability is localized in that area. If they find that damage in other areas also affects math ability, they would realize that this ability may depend on a widely distributed set of brain areas.

But lesion analysis must also address the question of just what function it is that has been damaged. For example, doing a mathematical calculation might require you to use several kinds of abilities, such as recognizing numbers and symbols, remembering the rules of addition or multiplication, holding several numbers in your memory as you do calculations, and being able to read or hear the math problem and report your answer. So if a brain lesion makes it hard for you to talk, you would not be able to answer the question "how much is two and two." But this doesn't mean there is anything wrong with your mathematical ability.

To help figure out exactly what problems a patient with brain damage actually has, experimental neuropsychologists look at a complex mental task, such as reading or doing math, and try to identify all the abilities that a person's brain must combine to succeed at that task. They then try to determine which of these abilities are actually separate, or *dissociated,* perhaps because they are based in different brain modules in particular brain regions. One way to establish a dissociation between abilities is to study which components of a mental task are affected by which kinds of brain damage. An important example of dissociated abilities is described in the chapter on biology and behavior: damage to a particular area in the left frontal lobe disrupts a person's ability to speak fluently but leaves the person able to understand what others say. Damage to a different area in the left temporal lobe does the opposite, leaving the person able to speak easily but unable to understand what others are saying. We discuss these conditions again later in this chapter. ("In Review: Foundations of Neuropsychology" summarizes milestones in the history of neuropsychology.)

Foundations of Neuropsychology   IN REVIEW

Principle	Main Figure or Era	Key Idea(s)
Localization of function	Franz Gall, early 1800s Paul Broca, late 1800s	The notion that specific psychological functions depend on specific brain areas.
Modularity	Late 1900s	A revision of localization in which each brain area performs different, unique computations, which contribute to various psychological functions.
Networks	Late 1900s	A perspective suggesting that different complex psychological functions rely on unique combinations of brain modules.
Lesion analysis	1800s and 1900s	An approach to experimental neuropsychology in which psychological functions are linked to particular brain areas by studying patients with damage to those areas and comparing these people with people who have damage elsewhere or no damage.

IN REVIEW QUESTIONS

1. A person who studies individual patients to determine what kind of brain damage each one happens to have is called a ___.

2. The case of "Tan" helped to establish the principle of ___.

3. In alexia without agraphia, the brain areas that control reading and writing are intact but cannot interact. This condition is called a ___.

Neuropsychological Assessment

So far we have discussed how the brain is organized and how neuropsychologists go about studying the ways in which its functioning is related to behavior and behavior problems. Let's now consider how they decide when a person has such problems. Consider memory, for example. Everyone forgets things sometimes, even such familiar things as your best friend's phone number, the name of your roommate's brother, or where you left your car keys. But where is the dividing line between normal forgetfulness and forgetfulness that is excessive or problematic?

LINKAGES

What psychological tests are used in diagnosing neuropsychological disorders? *(a link to Thought, Language, and Intelligence)*

To answer this question, neuropsychologists typically conduct a **neuropsychological assessment** in which they give patients tests designed to assess a wide range of mental functions, such as general intelligence, memory, reading, motor coordination, naming pictures, finding targets in a visual display, and the like. Some neuropsychologists prefer to use a set of assessments tailored to each patient (Blakesley et al., 2009). In this way they hope to measure the specific problems that a given patient is most likely to have. In another approach, patients are given a predetermined set of tests that are designed to complement one another and to comprehensively address all aspects of psychological functioning (Kane, 1991). Many such standardized test batteries have been carefully prepared and validated. Among the best known examples are the *Halstead-Reitan Battery,* the *Wechsler Adult Intelligence Scale,* and the *Luria-Nebraska Neuropsychological Batteries.* Standardized batteries offer the advantage of giving each patient the same tests in the same way, but they don't allow the neuropsychologist to tailor the testing to focus on a patient's particular problems or unique situation. Accordingly, most clinical neuropsychologists start with a standard test battery and then administer additional tests that are particularly relevant to each case.

By giving many different tests, the clinical neuropsychologist can get a glimpse into many different aspects of a person's psychological functioning as well as measure each area separately. Analyzing the overall pattern of results may help pinpoint where the difficulties in the brain may lie. But the results of neuropsychological assessment, like the results of personality testing, intelligence testing, or academic assessment, must be interpreted with caution. Many factors, such as age, education, and cultural background, for example, can affect a person's performance on neuropsychological tests. With this in mind, each patient's performance on these tests must be compared with established averages, or norms. These norms are based on the test performance of thousands of people of the patient's own age, educational level, and cultural background who have no known brain damage. Norms also give clinical neuropsychologists an idea of how often normal people's scores vary from the average and by how much. Having this information helps them establish whether a score that looks deviant at first glance is actually as unusual as it seems. Norms might also reveal that even a small deviation from the average is very unusual and indicative of a potential problem.

Training for Neuropsychology

A considerable part of a clinical neuropsychologist's training is focused on learning about the many different kinds of neuropsychological tests available, about exactly how to give them and score them, and about how to combine and interpret their results so as to reach the most accurate conclusions about patients' problems and the likely source of those problems (Boake, Yeates, & Donders, 2002). Neuropsychologists typically train in graduate school, earning a Ph.D. degree in clinical psychology with a special focus on neuropsychology and the many topics related to it. Before they can get a license to practice on their own, however, they must complete an internship. The internship usually includes a year or more of neuropsychological practice performed under the close supervision and mentoring of a licensed clinical neuropsychologist, typically in a university hospital setting. Licensed clinical neuropsychologists are usually hired by health facilities where there is a need for testing patients for possible brain damage. Many neuropsychologists are employed directly by hospitals; others join specialty clinics where they work closely with physicians who focus on the diagnosis and treatment of brain disorders. Some may

neuropsychological assessment Testing a patient's intelligence, memory, reading, motor and sensory functions in an effort to locate problems in the brain responsible for neuropsychological symptoms.

work in highly specialized facilities that offer programs focusing only on patients who have had a cerebrovascular accident or brain trauma. Experimental neuropsychologists are usually employed as professors in a university setting, where they teach, conduct their own research, and participate in testing patients.

Mechanisms of Brain Dysfunction

What are the main causes of brain damage and dysfunction?

We have been talking a lot about brain damage, and perhaps you are wondering how brains get hurt.

Cerebrovascular Accidents

As you may have guessed by now, cerebrovascular accidents (CVAs) are a common source of brain damage. What is a cerebrovascular accident, exactly? The problem arises because the brain receives all the oxygen, sugar (glucose), and other nutrients it needs from the rich supply of blood flowing through it (see Figure 16.3). But brain cells cannot store much of this energy, so they must have a supply of fresh blood at all times (Acker & Acker, 2004). If a vessel bringing blood into some part of the brain becomes blocked, the tissue in that part of the brain will die and whatever function that part of the brain normally performs will be disrupted or destroyed (Biller, Love, & Schenk, 2008). When someone's behaviors or mental processes are affected by loss of the blood supply in some part of the brain, the person is said to have had a CVA. Even very tiny CVAs can cause disabling symptoms if they take place in vital brain areas, but strokes in less vital areas might cause no symptoms at all. There are even rare cases in which a CVA may be beneficial, as in the case of a man whose lifelong stammering problem disappeared after a CVA (Bakheit, Frost, & Ackroyd, 2011).

FIGURE 16.3

The Brain's Blood Supply

Blood reaches the brain either through the carotid arteries on either side of the neck or through vertebral arteries entering through the base of the skull. Once in the brain, these arteries branch into the anterior cerebral artery, the middle cerebral artery, and the posterior cerebral artery. Each artery provides blood to specific brain areas. As a result, a blockage in each particular blood vessel damages a specific, predictable part of the brain. Review the chapter on biology and behavior to remind yourself of what functions are associated with each area of the cerebral cortex. Then make a list of the functions that would most likely be affected by blockage in each of the arteries shown in this figure.

LEARN**by** DOING

Source: From Freberg, L. *Discovering Biological Psychology*, 2nd ed. (p. 34). Copyright © 2006 Cengage Learning. Photo © JupiterImages/Photos.com

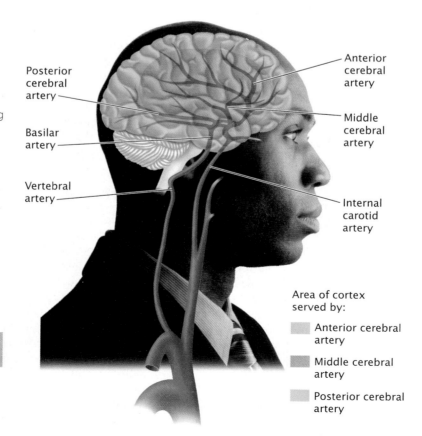

Posterior cerebral artery

Basilar artery

Vertebral artery

Anterior cerebral artery

Middle cerebral artery

Internal carotid artery

Area of cortex served by:

Anterior cerebral artery

Middle cerebral artery

Posterior cerebral artery

Normally, though, CVAs can be quite dangerous (Feigin, 2003; Rothwell, 2003; Truelsen & Bonita, 2003; Wolf, 2003). In fact, they are the third most common cause of death in the developed world (Di Carlo, 2009). They tend to occur as people get older, but young adults and even children have been known to have them. Unlike heart attacks, in which the blood supply to the heart muscle is disrupted, a CVA usually involves little or no pain because there are no pain receptors in brain tissue. So a stroke victim may not immediately realize that anything is wrong (Jenkinson, Preston, & Ellis, 2011). The resulting delay in seeking medical attention can be dangerous, because treatments that can help reduce or reverse the effects of a cerebrovascular accident must be given as soon as possible after the stroke occurs (Chaudhary, Pandey, & Gammete, 2011).

Like explosions that break windows a block away, CVAs affect not only the area in which brain tissue has died but also the area surrounding it. Fortunately, if cells around a CVA have not actually died, they may start working again (Liebeskind, 2010). As a result, some people experience some recovery of the functions that were lost when the stroke occurred. The amount of recovery depends on many factors, including the quality and speed of medical treatment, where and how large the CVA is, the health of the remaining blood vessels and brain tissue, the location of the salvageable tissue, the degree to which the remaining nervous system can reorganize along its original lines, and what kinds of rehabilitation programs are undertaken after the CVA (Cramer, 2008; Frizzell, 2005; Heiss & Teasel, 2006; Hillis et al., 2008; Kelley & Borazanci, 2009). To help the brain heal itself, some scientists are experimenting with the use of chemicals or stem cells to stimulate the growth of new brain cells and blood vessels (England et al., 2012; Yu et al., 2012). As described in the chapter on biology and behavior, though, restoring lost functions is not as simple as restoring the cell population in damaged brain areas. The new cells must somehow be influenced to reestablish the right connections with other brain cells (Kalluri & Dempsey, 2008; Liu et al., 2009).

Traumatic Brain Injury

Another major cause of brain damage is **traumatic brain injury,** also known as **trauma** (Heegaard, 2007). Trauma creates a sudden impact on the brain, as when a person's head is struck by a baseball bat, a bullet, or some other object or when the head suddenly moves or stops moving, as when a person is thrown violently against a

traumatic brain injury (trauma) An impact on the brain caused by a blow or sudden violent movement of the head.

Traumatic Brain Injury in Sports
Traumatic brain injuries known as *concussions* are a risk in football and other contact sports (Gilchrist et al., 2011; Hamalainen, 2012; O'Rourke, 2011). The short-term effects of a concussion may include nausea, confusion, and problems with vision and memory. The long-term effects can be even more problematic (DeKosky, Ikonomovic, & Gandy, 2010). Some players develop symptoms similar to those of Alzheimer's disease (Hamalainen, 2012). Others suffer depression, and some develop a form of amyotrophic lateral sclerosis, or Lou Gehrig's disease (Bartholet, 2012). Ideally, the development of more protective helmets and more restrictive rules about helmet-to-helmet contact will reduce the number of concussions among football players at every level, from high school to the NFL.

© James Boulette/iStockphoto

head restraint during an automobile accident. Traumatic events such as these can cause damage because the brain is not firmly attached to the skull. Instead, it floats within it, suspended in a bath of **cerebrospinal fluid.** So when the skull is struck or the head suddenly and violently accelerates or decelerates, the brain will slide in one direction inside its bony case and then bounce backward. As the soft globe of brain bounces back and forth and bumps up against bone, nerve fibers in many places may stretch and tear (Meaney & Smith, 2011).

The amount of brain damage resulting from trauma depends greatly on the amount of force involved in such situations. Further, unlike in CVAs, in which only the area in and around a disrupted blood supply is likely to be affected, the damage and disruption caused by traumatic brain injury may be widespread. So whereas stroke patients may show very specific kinds of neuropsychological deficits, sometimes with striking dissociations between functions that are lost and those that are preserved, people with head injuries may display deficits that are far more diffuse, harder to specify, and involve more aspects of functioning (Wade, 2004), including cognitive and psychiatric problems (Diehl, 2009; Stern et al., 2011; Whyte et al., 2011). Perhaps as a result, we know much more about the neuropsychological symptom patterns that follow CVAs than we do about those following traumatic brain injuries.

Neurodegenerative Diseases

Unlike the sudden symptoms that result from brain damage caused by cerebrovascular accident and trauma, other brain problems develop gradually. These more slowly developing symptoms often appear because **neurodegenerative diseases** are causing *neurodegeneration,* the gradual process of damage to brain cells (Mayeux, 2003). Three of the most prominent examples of neurodegenerative diseases are Alzheimer's disease, Parkinson's disease, and frontotemporal degeneration. Each type of neurodegenerative disease affects a particular kind of brain cell, or cells in a particular part of the brain, causing them to be the first to stop working properly (Cummings, 2003), and leaving the victim without the mental or physical functions those cells had once supported. The pattern of symptoms resulting from each neurodegenerative disease is different enough that neuropsychological assessment of a patient can usually lead to a diagnosis of which disease is affecting that patient (Brun, 2007; Hickey et al., 2008; Miller, 2007).

Some kinds of neurodegeneration appear to be caused by infections, nutritional deficiencies, or genetic abnormalities, but despite intense research, we still do not know the ultimate causes of most such diseases. "In Review: Mechanisms of Brain Dysfunction" summarizes the major causes of brain injury and dysfunction.

Mechanisms of Brain Dysfunction			**IN REVIEW**
Brain Problem	**Onset**	**Underlying Process**	**Symptoms**
Cerebrovascular Accident (stroke)	Sudden	Blocked blood flow in some part of the brain	Specific to the area of the brain that is destroyed
Traumatic Brain Injury (trauma)	Sudden	Brain slides back and forth inside the skull	Often nonspecific, diffuse
Neurodegenerative Disease (neurodegeneration)	Gradual	A subset of neuron cell types becomes diseased and stops working properly	Specific to the types of brain cells affected

IN REVIEW QUESTIONS

1. The brain floats in a bath of ___ inside the skull.

2. The brain needs a constant flow of fresh ___ all the time.

3. Cerebrovascular accidents rank as the number ___ cause of death in the developed world.

cerebrospinal fluid A clear liquid that surrounds and buffers the brain against vibration.

neurodegenerative diseases Conditions in the brain that result in the gradual loss of nerve cells and of the cognitive or other functions in which those cells are normally involved.

Neuropsychological Disorders

What disorders can be caused by brain damage or dysfunction?

Let's now take a closer look at the **syndromes**, or patterns of symptoms, that clinical neuropsychologists typically see in patients who have been affected by CVAs, traumas, or neurodegenerative diseases. These syndromes are referred to as *neuropsychological disorders*, and they include amnestic disorders, consciousness disturbances, perceptual disturbances, disorders of language and communication, movement disorders, and disorders involving dementia.

LINKAGES

What disorders are caused by damage to brain areas involved in memory?
(a link to Memory)

Amnestic Disorders

Amnestic disorders are those that involve memory loss (often referred to as *amnesia*). Quite often, a specific concern about memory problems is what brings people to clinical neuropsychologists for evaluation. These people are concerned partly because they rely heavily on memory and therefore any threat to its integrity can be extremely upsetting. But patients also tend to highlight memory problems because we all have a tendency to interpret almost any psychological deficit as being related to memory (Lezak, Loring, & Howieson, 2004). As in Max's case, for example, people who begin having trouble naming objects may assume they are "forgetting" words, even though the problem could actually be one of language or visual recognition. Many older individuals, too, seek neuropsychological assessment because of worry that even minor forgetfulness might be an early sign of Alzheimer's disease (we discuss Alzheimer's in the section on dementia). However, memory loss can occur in other neuropsychological syndromes, too (Lucas, 2005).

For example, the ability to create new long-term memories can be impaired by damage in the brain's medial temporal lobes ("medial" means toward the middle of the brain) especially in the hippocampus (Ando et al., 2008; de Haan et al., 2006; Pauli et al., 2006; Rosenbaum et al., 2008). Consider the famous case of Henry Molaison, a patient known for much of his life as "H.M." to protect his identity (Scoville & Milner, 1957; Squire, 2009). In 1953, at the age of 27, he had brain surgery to remove parts of both his left and right temporal lobes, including parts of the hippocampus on both sides. The surgery was successful at controlling his severe epileptic seizures, but it left him with a dense amnestic syndrome that persisted until his death in 2008 (Squire, 2009; see Figure 16.4). Although Mr. Molaison was able to recall most details of his life from before the surgery, he had difficulty forming new memories afterward. In other words, as discussed in the memory chapter, he had **anterograde amnesia.** When he met someone new, he was unable to recall the meeting, so the person seemed to be a stranger no matter how many times they met again. Similarly, the new terms he heard over the years—such as "computer," "videotape," "cell phone," and "Jacuzzi"—never made it into his vocabulary. He wasn't even able to remember that time was passing, so he had few clues that he was getting older; to a great extent, he was mentally stuck in the 1950s.

Yet many of Mr. Molaison's other mental capacities remained largely intact, providing a striking example of the dissociation that can occur between abilities lost and those retained after brain damage. His language function remained good; he recognized objects; he thought and reasoned; he remained intelligent, pleasant, and sociable; and he carried on very normal-sounding conversations. Still, he was well aware of his memory problem. He put it as follows (Corkin, 2002):

> *Right now, I'm wondering, have I done or said something amiss? You see, at this moment everything looks clear to me, but what happened just before? That's what worries me. It's like waking from a dream. I just don't remember.*

Henry Molaison was carefully studied for years, and the lessons learned from him have prompted research on memory loss in other people after medial temporal lobe damage. This research has yielded some surprises. When other people have amnesia caused by damage to the hippocampus, just like H.M., they also have difficulty remembering the new experiences or events of their lives. But, also like H.M., it turns out that these

syndrome A pattern of symptoms associated with a particular neuropsychological disorder.

amnestic disorders Neuropsychological disorders that involve memory loss.

anterograde amnesia A loss of memory for events that occur after a brain injury.

FIGURE 16.4

H. M.'s Brain Surgery

H. M. underwent surgery that removed the hippocampus, the amygdala, and part of the association cortex from both temporal lobes. As shown in these MRI scans comparing an intact brain with H. M.'s brain after surgery, H. M. had some hippocampus (H) but no entorhinal cortex (EC). In this image, (V) refers to the lateral ventricle, (f) refers to the fornix, (PH) refers to the parahippocampal cortex, and (Cer) refers to the cerebellum.

Coronal sections of typical person's brain   Coronal sections of H. M.'s brain

Photos courtesy Dr. Suzanne Corkin, Massachusetts Institute of Technology. Copyright © 1997 Society for Neuroscience. J. Neurosci., May 15, 1997, 17(10):3964-3979

Korsakoff's psychosis An amnestic condition in people whose thiamine (vitamin B1) level is depleted by inadequate nutrition or alcoholism.

confabulation A characteristic of some neuropsychological disorders in which patients report false memories.

consciousness disturbances Neuropsychological disorders in which there are impairments in the ability to be conscious, or accurately aware, of the world.

reticular formation A collection of cells and fibers in the hindbrain and midbrain that are involved in arousal and attention.

individuals can still learn new skills and habits as a result of their new experiences. When they do a task over and over, they get better at it, meaning that they do form some kind of a memory. Nonetheless, they have no awareness of this learning and do not recall the experiences that led to it (see Figure 16.5).

Anterograde amnesia and other amnestic syndromes can be caused by events other than surgery in the hippocampus and medial temporal lobe. For example, certain brain infections, such as herpes encephalitis (Ando et al., 2008; Baringer, 2008), tend to damage these same parts of the brain and create an amnestic syndrome similar to that of H.M. Cerebrovascular accidents, too, can sometimes damage these regions, though they usually occur on just one side of the brain, so amnestic syndromes are less often seen (Woods, Schoene, & Kneisley, 1982). Finally, as described later, these regions and the memory functions they normally perform can also be impaired by Alzheimer's disease (Wolk et al., 2010).

The hippocampus is not the only structure involved in memory. For example, as described in the chapter on biology and behavior, the thalamus processes information from all the senses except smell and sends it on to the cerebral cortex for further processing. But some areas of the thalamus are also part of the brain's limbic system, an interconnected set of structures that includes the hippocampus (see Figure 16.6). Memory

FIGURE 16.5
Memory without Awareness
People with amnesia from medial temporal lobe damage may still learn from the experiences that they otherwise cannot recall. This stimulus shows a degraded version of a drawing. Using stimuli similar to these, participants with amnesia first saw a very degraded version, then one less so, then less, and so on until they could name the item. Patients with amnesia were able to name items earlier if they had seen them before, even when they could not recall having seen them.

Source: From Snodgrass, J. G., and Feenan, K. "Priming effects in picture fragment completion: support for the perceptual closure hypothesis." *Journal of Experimental Psychology: General* vol. 119 (p.280). Copyright © 2006 Cengage Learning.

delirium Periods of abnormally impaired and/or abnormally elevated levels of consciousness.

loss can occur when strokes in the thalamus damage these limbic system connections (Nishio et al., 2011).

A certain part of the thalamus, called the medial dorsal (middle top) section, is seldom damaged by traumatic brain injury or cerebrovascular accident, but it is often damaged by **Korsakoff's psychosis** (Butters, 1981). This is a condition in which a person's thiamine (vitamin B1) is depleted by inadequate nutrition or alcoholism. Running low on thiamine is dangerous because it is needed to process glucose (sugar) for energy. Nerve cells of the medial dorsal thalamus are especially dependent on this function of thiamine (Marti, Singleton, & Hiller-Sturmhofel, 2003), and if thiamine deficiency is severe, nerve cells there are more likely to be stressed, to become inflamed, or to die than are cells in other brain regions (Kumar, 2010; Vemuganti et al., 2006; Visser et al., 1999). The result is anterograde amnesia with an additional unusual feature: patients with Korsakoff's psychosis are prone to **confabulation**—in other words, they create false memories, both spontaneously and in response to questions (Borsutzky et al., 2008; Butters, 1981; Kessels et al., 2008). These individuals believe that they have had experiences that they have not actually had, and they "recall" them as if they were real. Research with other confabulating patients suggests that this condition may also occur following damage to the inferior medial prefrontal system (Nieuwenhuis & Takashima, 2011). Other amnestic syndromes do not usually produce confabulation, so when clinical neuropsychologists test patients with severe anterograde amnesia and find confabulation, too, they often suspect a medial dorsal thalamic amnesia or inferior medial prefrontal amnesia.

Consciousness Disturbances

Sometimes, problems in the brain can create **consciousness disturbances,** which impair people's ability to be conscious, or accurately aware, of the world around them (Bruno et al., 2011). One such problem occurs when there is disruption or damage to the **reticular formation,** also known as the *reticular activating system,* or *RAS.* The RAS is a long, tube-like structure that begins in the base of the brain and extends upward, eventually splitting into two halves that reach into both sides of the thalamus. As its name implies, the RAS normally serves to increase and decrease arousal in the rest of the brain and helps create our daily cycles of wakefulness and sleep (Izac & Eeg, 2006). If the RAS is severely damaged, the result can be an unconscious state known as a *coma* (Rosenberg, 2009). People with lesser amounts of RAS damage may enter a *persistent vegetative state* (*PVS*; Bekinschtein et al., 2005; Rosenberg, 2009) or a *minimally conscious state (MCS;* Gosseries et al., 2011). Unlike patients in comas, people suffering PVS or MCS may open their eyes and appear to wake up during the day and close their eyes and appear to sleep at night. They may also show a wider array of automatic movements than do coma patients. For example, when food is put in the mouth of someone in a PVS or MCS, chewing movements may occur, and sounds and touches may sometimes trigger facial expressions. But although EEG and PET scans sometimes show isolated activity in some areas of these individuals' brains—including activity in speech-processing areas in response to familiar sounds (Cruse et al., 2011; Heiss, 2012)—most patients appear unaware or only vaguely aware of their environment. The chances for recovery are often poor following significant damage to the RAS.

Even if the RAS is working properly to stimulate the rest of the brain, consciousness can be impaired if there are widespread disruptions in the functioning of both sides of the cerebral cortex, where other aspects of awareness are controlled (Stevens & Bhardwaj, 2006). Impairment of both sides of the cortex is most commonly caused by drugs, such as alcohol or sleeping pills, but other causes include fever, seizures, chemical imbalances in the blood, hormonal disorders, or infections that have spread to the blood (Posner et al., 2007).

Other consciousness disturbances have more complex and variable effects. People with **delirium,** for example, enter alternating periods of abnormally impaired conscio-usness and abnormally elevated levels of consciousness (Gofton, 2011). The

FIGURE 16.6
The Limbic System
A number of closely connected structures form the limbic system, which controls many aspects of motivation and emotion.

Source: From Freberg, L. *Discovering Biological Psychology*, 2nd ed. (p. 42). Copyright © 2006 Cengage Learning. Photo © Monika Gete/Flickr/ Getty Images.

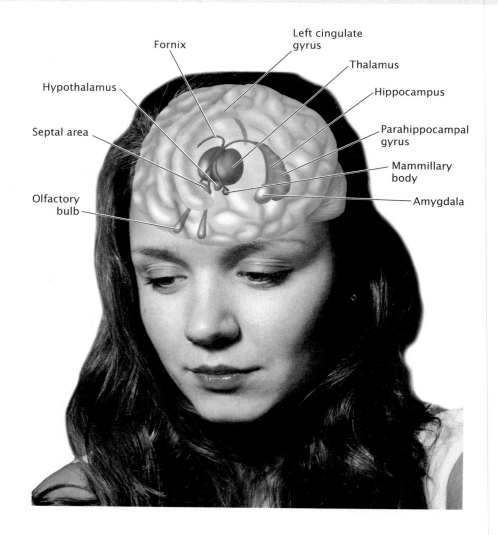

impairments in consciousness appear in many mental functions, usually including poor attention, poor memory, and disorientation. Elevated consciousness may appear as hallucinations (hearing sounds or seeing things that are not really there) or as periods of mental agitation for no apparent reason (Henker, 1979). Indeed, a key feature of delirium is the waxing and waning, the rising and falling, of consciousness (Posner et al., 2007) and a distorted recollection of experiences (Duppils & Wikblad, 2007; Fornaro et al., 2007). These patients may appear sleepy and "out of it" one minute and then far too attentive the next, as shown by reactions to every little sight and sound. Common causes of delirium include cerebrovascular accidents, traumatic brain injury, encephalitis, lesions in the frontal and temporal lobes, fever, poisons, infections that have reached the bloodstream, and the side effects of medication (Bassetti, 2007; Ramirez-Bermudez et al., 2006). Delirium can sometimes create a medical emergency (Bassetti, 2007; Pandharipande, Jackson, & Ely, 2005), though it may not be correctly diagnosed in emergency rooms (Press et al., 2009). Most of the time the psychological effects of delirium are not permanent, and the condition usually goes away when its underlying medical cause has been corrected or disappears on its own (Skrobik, 2009).

Neuropsychological assessment of people in delirium is difficult (Milisen et al., 2006). Their attention and awareness can vary, sometimes dramatically, over the course of testing. So not only can one patient with delirium behave very differently from the next, but the same patient can also look very different at different times. In general, performance on almost any test is very poor, probably because patients with delirium cannot pay attention long enough or well enough to cooperate with the testing process.

Indeed, their typical pattern of performance on neuropsychological tests is that there is no pattern—everything may look impaired.

Still other consciousness disturbances don't involve problems in people's level of consciousness but in the nature, or content, of their consciousness. For example, a person may have a CVA that causes total paralysis of one side of the body, but the person may have no awareness that there is anything wrong (Starkstein, Jorge, & Robinson, 2010). This condition is called *anosognosia* (pronounced "a-nose-ag-NOSE-ya"),which means an absence of knowledge of disease (Langer, 2009). In such cases, it appears that brain damage causes not only an impairment in functioning but also decreased ability to know about that impairment. This makes sense, because the brain is the organ that we use to figure out when something is wrong. So if you have pain in your arm, sensory neurons "tell" the brain about it. But if the brain itself is hurt, it has nowhere to send its message.

Anosognosia can occur in association with a variety of problems, from paralysis to blindness to amputation of a limb (McGlynn & Schacter, 1989). It is also sometimes seen in association with neurodegenerative dementias (Rosen, 2011). Anosognosia is particularly likely after damage to the right side of the brain (Vocat et al., 2010). It is also relatively common, occurring, for example, in more than 25 percent of all CVA patients (Starkstein et al., 1992). An unfortunate result is that these patients may not be motivated to get the prompt medical attention needed to limit the amount of damage that a CVA can cause. Anosognosia may fade over time or it may persist. When it does persist, it impairs patients' cooperation with rehabilitative treatments. They don't understand that there is anything wrong, so they don't see the treatment as necessary. There may be ways to improve awareness of neurological deficits, though. In one case, a man was unaware of the sudden and bizarre involuntary movements he had been making for several years. He could not see these movements, even when looking at himself in a mirror, but when doctors arranged for him to see himself on videotape, he instantly saw the problem (Shenker et al., 2004).

THINKING CRITICALLY Can Someone Be Partially Paralyzed and Not Know It?

In anosognosia, patients deny any neurological deficit because they have no understanding that a problem exists. This phenomenon was first described long ago in relation to cerebrovascular accidents that caused *hemiparesis,* a weakness or partial paralysis that affects just one side of the body (Babinski, 1914). It has occurred following other neurological problems, too. Skeptics have argued that people with hemiparesis are still fully capable of knowing that they are partially paralyzed but that this knowledge would be so upsetting that they simply cannot admit it, even to themselves. Perhaps, this skeptical argument goes, anosognosia reflects not true unawareness but instead the operation of an unconscious mental process similar to the ego defense mechanisms that Freud called denial and repression (Nardone et al., 2007; see the chapter on personality).

What am I being asked to believe or accept?

Arguing against these skeptics are those who say that anosognosia occurs because the brain damage that causes hemiparesis also damages the parts of the brain that would allow the person to know that something is wrong. As a result, patients who seem unaware of hemiparesis or other problems are, in fact, truly unaware of them (Heilman, Barrett, & Adair, 1998; McGlynn & Schacter, 1989).

Is evidence available to support the claim?

Those who believe that anosognosia is genuine unawareness point out that if it were the result of an ego defense mechanism, it would operate in a general way to deny any and all potentially upsetting deficits. Yet evidence from neurological examinations shows that some hemiparesis patients, for example, are aware that an arm is weak but not that a leg is weak (Berti, Ladavas, & Corti, 1996; Bisiach et al., 1986). Others are aware that they have a speech disturbance but not weakness in a limb (Bisiach et al., 1986; Breier et al., 1995), and some patients are aware of blindness yet remain unaware of limb paralysis (Prigatano et al., 2011).

Another problem with the ego defense mechanism argument is that anosognosia occurs much more often after right-hemisphere brain damage, which causes left-side hemiparesis, than it does when left-hemisphere brain damage causes right-side hemiparesis. It would seem that weakness on either side should be about equally upsetting and equally likely to cause anosognosia. In fact, because most people are right-handed, weakness on the right side might be even more upsetting and therefore *more* likely to result in psychologically motivated denial.

Additional evidence against the ego defense mechanism hypothesis comes from research showing that anosognosia can occur even when there is no threat of permanent paralysis. In a procedure pioneered by June Wada (Strauss & Wada, 1983), participants being evaluated for possible brain surgery had an anesthetic injected into one side of their brain at a time (Adair et al., 1995; Gilmore et al., 1992). This *Wada technique* temporarily "turns off" either the left hemisphere or the right hemisphere without causing any permanent brain damage. When the right hemisphere was "turned off" in this way, participants became paralyzed on the left side of their bodies. When they were asked about their experience, they recalled most details correctly, but most of them displayed anosognosia—that is, they said that they did not notice any weakness or paralysis. When the left hemisphere was anesthetized, though, patients not only became weak on the right side but also later reported awareness of the paralysis. These data are hard to explain as being due to ego defense mechanisms, because once participants had recovered from their left-side paralysis, why would they be motivated to deny that it had occurred?

Can that evidence be interpreted another way?

One problem with the Wada technique is that it is difficult to compare what patients are experiencing at the time the left and right hemispheres are actually anesthetized. The problem is that because speech areas are on the left side, people are usually unable to speak when their left hemispheres are "turned off." This doesn't happen on the right side, so the only way to do a direct comparison of the experience of left-versus right-hemisphere inactivation is to ask the patient questions after the anesthetic has worn off. If it were possible to talk to people during the left-hemisphere inactivation, perhaps they would show anosognosia because at that particular moment there could be enough distress to motivate denial.

This interpretation is supported by research conducted decades ago with patients who had suffered CVAs that caused hemiparesis (Weinstein & Kahn, 1955). Interviews with these patients' families revealed that the patients who had tended to cope with stress through denial before their cerebrovascular accidents were the ones most likely to deny their hemiparesis afterward. Patients who did not show anosognosia were described by their families as less likely to have previously used denial as a coping mechanism. These data suggest that denial of hemiparesis is just an exaggeration of a person's established stress-coping tendencies.

What evidence would help to evaluate the alternatives?

The results of this and other family report studies might be affected by *retrospective bias* (Heilman, Barrett, & Adair, 1998). That is, once they know that their relative is denying hemiparesis, family members might be more likely to recall similar episodes of denial in the relative's past and forget about episodes in which the patient had coped with stress in other ways. Similarly, if their relative isn't denying the symptoms caused by a stroke, perhaps family members will be less likely to recall incidents in which the patient did use denial in stressful situations.

One way around the problem of retrospective bias would be to do a *prospective* study in which a large group of individuals is identified, assessed for their typical stress-coping tendencies, and then contacted on a regular basis for many years. The ego defense mechanism hypothesis would be supported in such a study if the people in the group that was most likely to use denial as a coping mechanism are also the ones most likely to display anosognosia following a CVA.

What conclusions are most reasonable?

It is probably true that some individuals who suffer neurological deficits may use denial or other psychological defense mechanisms to avoid facing their distressing problems, but given the neurological evidence we have reviewed, it seems reasonable to conclude that many cases of anosognosia reflect a true lack of awareness of neurological deficit. ●●●●

Perceptual Disturbances

As described in the chapter on sensation and perception, the brain must analyze the information we receive from our eyes, ears, and other senses in order to organize, recognize, interpret, and understand it if we are to make sense of the world. These vital perceptual functions depend on the normal operation of specific regions of the brain. For example, visual information passes from the eyes to and through the thalamus and then to particular areas in the occipital lobe of the cerebral cortex, where the information is analyzed further. From there, visual information is sent along two separate but parallel pathways. Along each of these pathways are a series of connected cortical regions that perform specialized analyses that allow us to experience different aspects of visual perception (Ungerleider & Mishkin, 1982; see Figure 16.7). The pathway leading down toward the temporal lobe has been called the "what" system because the cortical regions along this pathway help us to decide what it is that we are seeing—a dog or a car, for example. The pathway leading up toward to the parietal lobe has been called the "where" system because it processes information about the location of objects and where those objects are in relation to one another. This system helps us understand, for example, that the dog is sitting in the car. Damage to our perceptual systems can result in **perceptual disturbances.**

For example, damage to the "what" pathway causes a condition called *visual agnosia* (Barton, 2011). As in the case of Max, individuals with visual agnosia can see objects in the world, they can describe them, and they can even draw them, but they no longer know what the objects are based on their appearance (Rubens & Benson, 1971). So a patient with visual agnosia can correctly define the word "apple" and, based on how it feels, correctly state that the neurologist has placed an apple in the person's hand. In other words, these patients still know what apples and other objects are, but they have

perceptual disturbances
Neuropsychological disorders in which there are impairments in the ability to organize, recognize, interpret, and make sense of incoming sensory information.

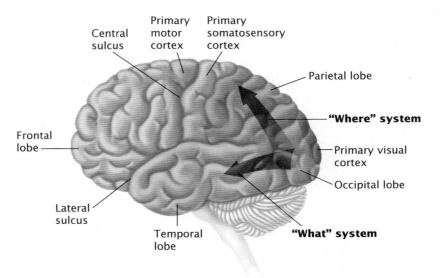

FIGURE 16.7
"What" Versus "Where" Visual Pathways
Research suggests that visual information reaching the primary visual cortex is sent along two separate but parallel systems. The "where" system focuses on an object's location in space and how it is moving. The "what" system determines the identity of the object.

lost the ability to link visual images of these objects to the part of the brain where that knowledge is stored.

Visual agnosia may leave patients unable to name anything they see, but the problem may also occur only in relation to certain categories of objects (Bauer & Demery, 2003). For example, some people have visual agnosia only for manufactured objects such as a car or a book or a drinking glass but can still correctly identify on sight a tree, a dog, or any other living thing (Riddoch et al., 2008). In other cases of visual agnosia, the person may be able to name on sight only manufactured objects (Kurbat, 1997; Riddoch et al., 2008; Thomas & Forde, 2006). These case observations suggest that information about natural versus manufactured objects must be processed in different ways by different brain areas. Visual agnosia can be even more specific. For example, there appears to be a special brain system dedicated to visual recognition of faces (Farah, 1996). When this aspect of the "what" system is damaged, the result is *prosopagnosia* (pronounced "proh-suh-pag-NOH-zhuh"), a condition in which a person can no longer recognize faces, even familiar ones, including his or her own face in a photograph or mirror (Barton et al., 2004; Bentin et al., 2007; Heutink et al., 2012; Stephan & Caine, 2009). The facial recognition system appears to depend on temporal lobe structures. Most people who develop prosopagnosia have damage to these areas on both sides of the brain (Valdés-Sosa et al., 2011), but sometimes a lesion on the right side alone is enough to produce a facial recognition syndrome (Barton et al., 2002). Patients with prosopagnosia may not be able to say whether a face is familiar, but they may show greater changes in brain activity when looking at people they know than at people they don't know. This difference suggests that some sort of unconscious recognition may still be taking place (Simon et al., 2011).

In a different kind of face-related perceptual disturbance, people can still recognize faces, but they believe that a parent, a spouse, or some other familiar person has been replaced by an "imposter." This false belief, known as *Capgras syndrome* or *Capgras delusion* (pronounced "KAHP-grah") in recognition of the French psychiatrist who first reported it (Capgras & Reboul-Lachaux, 1923), tends to occur after temporal lobe damage. The damage appears to create a disconnection between brain areas that recognize faces from those that allow us to have a sense of familiarity (Ramachandran, 1998). Capgras delusions are usually permanent, though there is at least one case in which the condition was cured by antiseizure medication (Shenker, 2010).

What happens when there is damage to the "where" system? As you might expect, this kind of damage creates problems in the visual perception of objects in space and how they are related to one another. A particularly interesting example is called *simultanagnosia* (Wolpert, 1924), a condition in which a person can see parts of a visual scene but has difficulty perceiving the whole scene. In a sense, a person with simultanagnosia can see the "trees" but cannot see the "forest." So if simultanagnosia patients were to look at the pattern shown in Figure 16.8, they could see all the Ts but not the larger letter H formed by the smaller letters.

One patient described her perceptions as follows (Shenker, 2005):

Examiner: *What do you see?*
   Patient: I see T, T, T, T, … Do I keep going?
Examiner: *Anything else?*
   Patient: T, T, T, T … lots of T's.
Examiner: *Are there any other letters?*
   Patient: No.
Examiner: *Is there an H?*
   Patient: No, just T's.
Examiner: *Is there a big letter?*
   Patient: No, I don't see one.
Examiner: *Is there a big letter H?*
   Patient: No.

FIGURE 16.8
A "Global-Local" Stimulus
People with simultanagnosia have difficulty seeing an H in this stimulus but see the Ts easily. Try showing this pattern to several friends. Unless any of them are suffering a similar neuropsychological disorder, you should be able to confirm that they will report seeing both the little Ts and the larger letter H.

FIGURE 16.9
Examples of Neglect on a Drawing Test
When shown an object and asked to draw it, patients with hemineglect often leave out details from the neglected side of the object.

Examiner: Do the little letters together form the shape of a big letter H?

Patient: I don't see how.

Examiner: (outlines the H with finger) Do you see how this is a big H?

Patient: I don't see an H.

Simultanagnosia has been associated with damage or dysfunction on both sides of the brain in the upper part of the parietal lobes (Barton, 2011). Damage to the "where" system in a different region of the parietal lobes can cause a condition known as *hemineglect*. This condition, which usually occurs after a CVA, involves difficulty in seeing, responding to, or acting on information coming from either the right or (more often) the left side of the world (Heilman, Watson, & Valenstein, 2003). The side of space that is neglected is usually opposite the side where the parietal lobe lesion is located. A person with hemineglect may ignore food on one side of a dinner plate, fail to put makeup on one side of the face, or pay no attention to voices coming from one side of the room. As shown in Figure 16.9, when asked to draw a picture of, say, a flower or a clock, the person may complete only half a drawing—the half on the side of space to which the person is still paying attention.

One of the most fascinating aspects of hemineglect is that it is cannot be explained as being due to a lack of sensation on one side or the other. For patients with left hemineglect, it is as if the concept of "leftness" is lost and so the left side of things is simply ignored (Bisiach, Capitani, & Tansini, 1979). This ignoring process is easy to demonstrate in some patients. The neuropsychologist simply holds up one hand on each side of the patient's visual field and then asks the patient to say when any fingers are wiggling. In some cases of hemineglect, patients will be able to correctly report when fingers are wiggling on the right *or* on the left, as long as the wiggling is only on one side. When there is wiggling on both sides, though, these patients may report seeing it only on the side to which they pay attention. These cases demonstrate that some hemineglect patients are capable of seeing both sides of space; they don't have a pure sensory problem. They are simply more likely to pay attention to one side of the world and ignore the other. The tendency to do so can be reduced, though. In one study, patients showed increased awareness of the normally neglected side of space while listening to music that put them in a more positive emotional state (Soto et al., 2009).

Other patients with hemineglect do also have sensory problems. They may be blind in their left visual fields, for example. It may seem surprising, but neuropsychologists can show that even in these patients, the tendency to ignore one side of space cannot be explained by their sensory loss. For example, patients with left hemineglect may not respond to the sound of a voice coming from the left. Is it because of a problem in their left ears? No, because the sound was heard by their right ears, too. Also, left hemineglect patients may ignore the left side of an object, even if the entire object appears in their right visual fields.

FOCUS ON RESEARCH

Studying Hemineglect

Proving that hemineglect cannot be explained by sensory problems alone can be tricky. After all, in many cases of hemineglect the brain damage that caused it also caused a loss of sensation from the same side. Also, most tests for hemineglect rely on giving a person some kind of sensory information to respond to. How can one show that hemineglect is not due to a sensory problem if you can only test for it by having people respond to the sensations they receive?

What was the researcher's question?
Edoardo Bisiach (Bisiach, Luzzatti, & Perani, 1979) reasoned that if hemineglect were truly a problem of understanding that a particular side of space exists then this problem should persist even for a scene that is not viewed directly but is instead put together using one's imagination only.

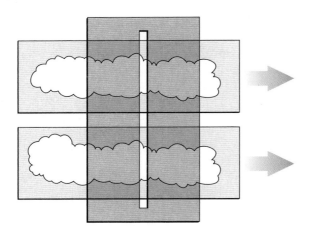

FIGURE 16.10

Studying Hemineglect

Here are examples of the cloudlike shapes used by Edoardo Bisiach and his colleagues (1979) to explore whether hemineglect is a sensory problem. Hemineglect patients could see only vertical slices of these shapes as the patterns passed behind a narrow vertical slit. So to "see" these shapes as whole patterns and to decide whether pairs of patterns were the same or different, they had to build an image of each pattern in their minds.

How did the researchers answer the question?

Bisiach tested patients who had both right-hemisphere lesions and left-sided hemineglect. He created randomly shaped stimuli that looked a bit like clouds. The stimuli were passed behind a vertical slit so that as each moved across the slit, patients could see only a small slice of it at a time (see Figure 16.10). In other words, the only way to "see" the whole stimulus was to imagine all the slices assembled in the mind's eye. Patients were shown two of these passing images at a time, one passing by the top part of the slit and the other passing by the bottom part of the slit. On some trials, the two stimuli were identical. On other trials, only their left sides were different, and on still others only their right sides were different. The patients' task was to decide whether the two stimuli were the same or different.

What did the researchers find?

Patients with left-sided hemineglect were able to determine when the stimuli were different if the right sides were different. But the patients could not detect differences between the stimuli if the left sides were different.

What do the results mean?

Because of the slit, the patients could not see the left and right sides of the images at the same time. This means that their failure to notice differences on only the left side did not result because they couldn't see the left side of space. Instead, these results appear to suggest that hemineglect occurs when patients ignore stimulation that is on a particular side of space, even when they are assembling that stimulation through memory and imagination.

What do we still need to know?

Different kinds of hemineglect are produced by damage in different parts of the brain (Watson & Heilman, 1979). So it is not clear whether Bisiach's patients, who had damage in their parietal lobes, are representative of all hemineglect patients. Notice, too, that the stimuli in Bisiach's study were all visual. Would the same results appear in research using imagined touches or sounds, for example? These are questions to be answered by further research on the fascinating topic of hemineglect. ●●●●

LINKAGES

How does damage to language areas affect language abilities? *(a link to Biology and Behavior)*

Language Disorders and the Brain

Disruptions in the functioning of brain regions that normally support speaking, reading, writing, and understanding language result in corresponding **language disorders,** or *aphasias.* Careful, detailed neuropsychological assessments can identify the precise nature of these aphasias (Goodglass & Kaplan, 1982). In this section, we describe several subtypes of aphasias, each of which is associated with damage or dysfunction in a particular area of the brain's language centers.

Most aphasias occur as a result of damage to the left side of the brain, often from CVAs or trauma but sometimes from a neurodegenerative disease process called *primary progressive aphasia (PPA;* Gorno-Tempini et al., 2011). Most cases of PPA are due to a disease process called *frontotemporal degeneration (FTD),* which gradually kills nerve cells in the forward section of the brain's temporal or frontal lobes—often more on one side than the other (Davies & Kipps, 2011; see Figure 16.11). The result is similar to a CVA because FTD tends to affect a fairly specific brain area, but unlike the sudden symptoms of a CVA, FTD symptoms develop gradually over a period of years. If FTD is focused on the language-related regions of the brain's left hemisphere, the result is PPA. Let's consider where these brain regions are, what they normally do, and what else can happen when their functioning is disrupted.

The brain has several "language areas," as described in the chapter on biology and behavior. These interconnected regions work together as a network, and all of them must

language disorders (aphasias)
Neuropsychological disorders in which there are disruptions in the ability to speak, read, write, and understand language.

FIGURE 16.11

Frontotemporal Degeneration

In frontotemporal degeneration, a relatively limited part of the brain can become extremely shrunken, as shown here.

Broca's aphasia A language disorder in which there is a loss of fluent speech.

Wernicke's aphasia A language disorder in which there is a loss of ability to understand written or spoken language and to produce sensible speech.

work properly in order for us to use and understand language. For example, it appears that *Broca's area* is vital to our ability to translate thoughts into words or writing that will be clear and meaningful to others. People who suffer damage to Broca's area (see Figure 16.12) display **Broca's aphasia,** which is seen mainly in the loss of language fluency (Burns & Fahy, 2010). That is, they are no longer able to smoothly and easily express themselves. Instead, they speak in a halting, sputtering manner and only with great effort and often with much frustration. There may be other symptoms as well, including a change in the kinds of words that individuals produce (Benson & Geschwind, 1971). Most of the words that patients with Broca's aphasia can still speak or write are those that refer to concrete objects, such as *book* or *pillow* or *water,* rather than those that refer to abstract ideas, such as *justice* or *literature* or *weather.* These patients also tend to use mainly concrete nouns and verbs, leaving out the more abstract articles, adjectives, and adverbs they once spoke or wrote. This change in word usage results in a "telegraphic" speaking style that recalls a bygone era when people sending telegrams had to pay for each word in a message. A patient with Broca's aphasia who once would have said "Please give me the spoon" might now say simply "Give spoon." Sometimes patients with Broca's aphasia make mistakes when naming objects. Such naming errors are called *paraphasias,* and in Broca's aphasia they tend to be *phonemic paraphasias,* or errors in the way a word should sound. So a person with Broca's aphasia might look at a pen and call it a *peb.* Finally, people with Broca's aphasia may also have some difficulty understanding what they see and hear (Caplan, 2003a, 2003b). Patients with *agrammatism,* for example, may not understand that the sentences "The boy hit the girl," and "The girl was hit by the boy," express the same meaning.

People with damage to *Wernicke's area* (see Figure 16.12) display a different set of problems (Goodglass & Kaplan, 1982) because this area is involved in the ability to understand the meaning of sensory information. These people have difficulty understanding what they read or what others are saying (Goodglass & Kaplan, 1982). In fact, because everything everyone says sounds like nonsense to a person with **Wernicke's aphasia,** the world must seem like a suddenly strange and even unfriendly place where everyone *else* has a problem. Further, although people with Wernicke's aphasia can still speak fluently and effortlessly, what they say is far from normal. Most notably, they display *semantic paraphasias,* which are naming errors in which they may use words that have the wrong meaning. So when trying to name a pen they may call it a book. In contrast to people with Broca's aphasia, those with Wernicke's aphasia tend to use lots of adverbs, adjectives, and articles but relatively few nouns and verbs. As a result these people's speech sounds rather empty of content. For example, when attempting to

FIGURE 16.12

The Wernicke-Geschwind Model of Aphasia

The Wernicke-Geschwind model of aphasia accounts for many (but not all) of the findings associated with the major aphasias. The pathways shown in part A transmit information when a participant is instructed to repeat a spoken word. The image shown in part B traces the flow of information when the person is asked to read a written word out loud.

Source: From Freberg, L. *Discovering Biological Psychology*, 2nd ed. (p. 396). Copyright © 2006 Cengage Learning. Photo © Cameron Whitman/iStockphoto.

Repeating a spoken word
(A)

Reading a word out loud
(B)

describe a picture of a woman and her children in the kitchen, a patient with Wernicke's aphasia may say "Over here is the top of the rest for the other rapid sheesh of many red sitters." This kind of output, combined with naming errors, can make the speech of a person with Wernicke's aphasia sound so disorganized that it may be mistaken for the "word salad" associated with some cases of severe schizophrenia (Sambunaris & Hyde, 1994; see the chapter on psychological disorders). Yet because they do not recognize all the mistakes they are making or appreciate the oddness of their speech, people with Wernicke's aphasia are often puzzled and upset when others do not seem to understand them or respond to them correctly.

Most language disorders are associated with damage in the brain's left hemisphere, but communication problems can also occur when the right hemisphere is damaged. In general, people with right-hemisphere damage can still speak words fairly normally and can understand fairly well the words that they hear and see. However, they may lose the ability to use tone of voice to express meaning or to use other people's tone of voice to help them understand what those people mean (Ross & Monnot, 2008). This problem, called *aprosodia,* can take several forms (Ross, 1981, 2006). For example, damage to the right frontal lobe can cause an *expressive aprosodia,* in which people speak in such a dull monotone that they may be forced to say something like "I am angry" in order to get their emotional meaning across (Ghacibeh & Heilman, 2003). Yet they may still be able to correctly understand and use cues from other people's tone of voice. By contrast, people with damage to the right temporal and parietal regions may have a *receptive aprosodia,* which means that they can use tone of voice correctly when they speak but have difficulty understanding the meaning of other people's tone of voice. So if someone were to sarcastically say "Well, that was really smart," meaning just the opposite, a person with receptive aprosodia may miss the sarcasm, pay attention only to the words themselves, and say "Thanks!"   ● ● ● ●

Movement Disorders

The brain's motor pathways are "wired" to our muscles in ways that allow us to move our limbs and body, but the knowledge of how to move in ways that effectively accomplish our goals is not built into that system. Using a fork, pedaling a bicycle, sucking on a

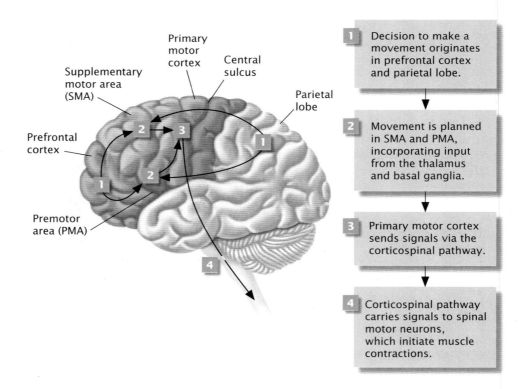

1 Decision to make a movement originates in prefrontal cortex and parietal lobe.

2 Movement is planned in SMA and PMA, incorporating input from the thalamus and basal ganglia.

3 Primary motor cortex sends signals via the corticospinal pathway.

4 Corticospinal pathway carries signals to spinal motor neurons, which initiate muscle contractions.

FIGURE 16.13
The Initiation of Voluntary Movement
A network of brain regions is involved in initiating voluntary movements.

FIGURE 16.14
An Example of Apraxic Motor Behavior

When imitating the movements involved in using a common object, an individual with apraxia may mistakenly use an arm or a leg to represent that object. So instead of showing how they would move in order to use a tool, they act as if their limb is the tool itself.

Source: From Banich M. T. *Cognitive Neuroscience and Neuropsychology,* 2nd ed. (p. 179). Copyright © 2004 Cengage Learning.

Correct pantomime

(A)

Apraxic behavior

(B)

straw, or swinging a hammer are just a few examples of the thousands of coordinated movements that each of us has had to learn from experience. A network of special brain systems control these learned motor skills by instructing the brain's motor control centers to make the movements needed for each action sequence (Goldenberg, 2009; see Figure 16.13). These brain systems tell the motor system what combinations of movements to make for a specific kind of task. Damage to part of this special network can result in **movement disorders,** or **apraxias,** in which learned motor skills are disrupted (McClain & Foundas, 2004).

There are two main types of apraxia (Heilman & Gonzalez-Rothi, 2003). In *ideational apraxia,* the individual movements needed to perform a task are all correctly executed but in the wrong order. So although a person with ideational apraxia can still open a tube of toothpaste, wet a toothbrush, squeeze paste onto the brush, insert the brush, and do a good job of brushing, the person might begin to brush before putting toothpaste on the brush or might squeeze the toothpaste tube first and then unscrew the cap.

A more common problem is *ideomotor apraxia,* which involves difficulties not in the sequence of skilled movements but in performing them (Wheaton, 2007). So a person with ideomotor apraxia will execute each step in tooth brushing in its proper order but may have difficulty in making the movements necessary to hold onto the brush and may be unable to make the arm and hand motions required to actually do the brushing. In one kind of ideomotor apraxia, the person may use a finger or other body part as if it were a tool, perhaps brushing with the finger or using it to try to turn a screw. In such cases, patients cannot seem to figure out how to use the brush or screwdriver or other tools they once employed with skillful ease (see Figure 16.14).

Dementia

We have already seen that in cases of delirium, people show reduced or heightened levels of consciousness and that many psychological abilities may all fail at once. But these multiple deficits are usually reversible, such that when the toxin or other cause of delirium disappears, the deficits do, too. In conditions known as **dementia,** however, there is no waxing and waning of consciousness; wakefulness and alertness remain normal but many other mental functions are impaired (Dekosky et al., 2008). To receive a diagnosis of dementia, a person must have developed a notable impairment of memory as well as impairment in some other area of psychological function, such as perceptual

movement disorders (apraxias) Neuropsychological disorders in which there are impairments in the ability to perform or coordinate previously normal motor skills.

dementia Neuropsychological disorders in which there are significant and disruptive impairments in memory as well as in perceptual ability, language, or learned motor skills.

ability, language, or learned motor skills. In addition, the impairments must be significant enough to cause problems in the person's ability to function at work, in social situations, or in everyday life tasks such as driving, cooking, or balancing a checkbook. In most cases, dementia is gradual and progressive. It has been estimated that about 34.4 million people worldwide have dementia (Wimo, Winblad, & Jönsson, 2010).

A condition known as *mild cognitive impairment (MCI)* may precede the appearance of some kinds of dementia (Petersen, 2011). In *amnestic MCI,* for example, patients display much-below-average memory skills on neuropsychological tests but no other deficits, and they may have adapted well enough to the memory loss that it has not caused a significant disruption in daily functioning. People with amnestic MCI often get worse, though, and about 2 to 10 percent of them each year progress to the point at which they receive a diagnosis of dementia (Mitchell & Shiri-Feshki, 2009; Petersen et al., 1999). Identifying people with amnestic MCI is important because at this relatively early stage of memory loss it may still be possible to use medication and a low-fat "Mediterranean" diet to stabilize memory and slow the development of full-fledged dementia (Farlow, 2009; Solfrizzi et al. 2011).

Dementia is usually caused by a progressive neurodegenerative disease, and the most common of these, accounting for about 60 to 80 percent of all cases, is **Alzheimer's disease** (Alzheimer's Association, 2009; Fratiglioni & Qiu, 2009). About 5.4 million people have Alzheimer's disease in the United States alone, where its economic costs—currently estimated at more than $183 billion a year—are projected to rise to $1.1 trillion by 2050. Its costs in human suffering are incalculable (Alzheimer's Association, 2011). The percentage of people with Alzheimer's disease doubles about every five years after the age of 60. As a result, about 13 percent of people over age 65 suffer from this disease, and the chances of developing Alzheimer's disease increase dramatically at age 75 and again at 85 (Alzheimer's Association, 2009, 2011). With more people than ever living longer and longer lives, current estimates suggest that by the year 2050 Alzheimer's disease will affect 11 to 16 million people in the United States (Alzheimer's Association, 2011; Brookmeyer et al., 2011).

Alzheimer's disease was first described in 1907 by a German neurologist, Alois Alzheimer (Devi & Quitschke, 1999). He told of a 51-year-old woman called Auguste D. who before her death displayed what Alzheimer described as "early onset senility." When he examined her brain after she died, he found two types of microscopic abnormalities. The first were degenerated nerve cells that had twisted into misshapen *tangles.* The second were clumps of protein deposits, called *amyloid plaques,* lying around the outside of dead and dying nerve cells. To this day, the ultimate diagnosis of Alzheimer's disease depends on the appearance of these tangles and plaques (Nelson, Braak, & Markesbery, 2011).

Today we know that the brain areas where neurofibrillary tangles are most numerous in Alzheimer patients are precisely the areas that fail to work properly and cause most of these patients' symptoms. As for amyloid plaque, we all develop some of it as we get older, and although it can be toxic to nerve cells, it may cause no more harm than other signs of aging, such as hair loss or wrinkles. In Alzheimer's disease patients, though, amyloid plaque is abnormally abundant and some researchers believe that this excessive plaque causes the brain damage that results in Alzheimer's symptoms (Hardy, 2006; Swerdlow & Khan, 2009). Other scientists suggest that damage to the energy-producing mitochondria in brain cells may be the trigger that eventually leads to the damage seen in Alzheimer's disease (Swerdlow, 2011).

The search for the cause of Alzheimer's continues. Researchers studying the brains of deceased Alzheimer's patients have found that the anatomical basis of the disease mainly involves neurons that use the neurotransmitter *acetylcholine* (Perry, 1980). They have discovered, too, that Alzheimer's symptoms are especially related to dysfunction in the parietal and medial temporal lobes on both sides of the brain (Cummings, 2004; Jacobs et al., 2012; see Figure 16.15). Because the parietal lobes are important for locating objects in space, Alzheimer's disease patients have difficulty drawing certain kinds of shapes and may easily get lost as they drive or walk around. Many Alzheimer's patients are endangered every day by wandering away from home or from the care facility in which they are living (Rolland et al., 2007). Because the left parietal lobe contains brain areas

Alzheimer's disease Dementia resulting from a neurodegenerative disease characterized by the loss of cognitive functions.

FIGURE 16.15

Brain Atrophy in Alzheimer's Disease
Alzheimer's disease causes some brain cells to stop working and eventually die, whereas other brain cells may be unaffected. Where brain cells die off, the cortex shrinks, leaving gaping spaces.

important for language, patients with Alzheimer's disease may also develop *anomia,* a condition in which it becomes hard to name objects even if they know what the objects are. The left parietal lobe usually also contains brain areas that are important for learned skills such as using a hammer or a spoon, so these kinds of functions can also become impaired enough to lead to apraxia. And because the medial temporal lobes contain the hippocampus, patients with Alzheimer's disease become unable to form new memories. Old memories, the ones already formed and stored elsewhere, usually remain accessible until the disease has progressed further. So, as in the case of H.M., Alzheimer's disease patients may remember details from their early adulthood yet they may not remember a conversation they had yesterday. Finally, because the temporal lobes are also important for the ability to interpret visual sensations, patients with Alzheimer's disease sometimes develop visual agnosia, an inability to recognize the objects they see.

Drugs such as dimebolin (Dimebon), galantamine (Reminyl), and rivastigmine (Exelon) have been shown to be somewhat effective at slowing the progress of Alzheimer's disease and are well tolerated by patients (Burns et al., 2009; Doody et al., 2008; Small & Dubois, 2007). Certain antidepressant medications may have similar benefits (Hashioka et al., 2009), and antipsychotic drugs may reduce some of the behavioral and psychological symptoms of Alzheimer's disease (Oshima, 2008). These drugs do not offer a cure, though (Tayeb et al, 2011). Until more effective treatments are available, health professionals can do little more than prescribe the medications available and encourage Alzheimer's patients to combat cognitive decline by staying physically and mentally active (Archer, 2011; Ballard, Kahn et al., 2011; Reitz, Brayne, & Mayeux, 2011; Sattler et al., 2011), and eating a low-fat diet (Solfrizzi et al., 2011).

There is a final type of dementia in which memory loss and other psychological deficits are not caused by Alzheimer's or any other kind of neurodegenerative disease. This condition, called **vascular dementia,** is brought about by restrictions in the brain's blood supply (O'Brien, 2011). We have already mentioned that when a blood vessel in the brain is blocked, the brain cells die in the tissue that normally receives oxygen and nutrients from that blood vessel (Caplan, 2005). Sometimes this loss of blood supply occurs in very tiny blood vessels, resulting in the death of only a tiny amount of brain tissue. Such tiny injuries may not cause symptoms when they first occur, especially if vital areas are not affected (Fisher, 1982); but if many small injuries occur repeatedly, more and more brain tissue is lost (e.g., Hallam et al., 2008) and the cumulative effect can be an impairment of memory and other psychological functions (Fisher, 1989).

The prevalence of vascular dementia is second only to the dementia caused by Alzheimer's disease, accounting for about 17 percent of all cases among people 71 and older (Alzheimer's Association, 2009). The two conditions may occur in the same individual (O'Brien, 2011), but the symptoms of vascular dementia may differ from those associated with Alzheimer's disease (Knopman, 2006). Vascular dementia patients show memory loss, including difficulty in remembering recent events, but in contrast to Alzheimer's disease, the hippocampus is usually relatively unaffected. So, vascular dementia patients should still be able to form new memories. Why, then, do these people have difficulty remembering new material? The answer often is that they have more of a problem in retrieving recent memories than in forming them. This subtle difference highlights the importance of careful neuropsychological assessment. Differences between vascular dementia and other impairments have also been found on behavioral tests (Milan et al., 2008), as well as in the appearance in vascular dementia patients of deficits such as aphasia, apraxia, and dyslexia (Topakian & Aichner, 2008).

A proper testing protocol can help establish the exact cause of a dementia. This information is vital, because specialized new medications are becoming available that can stop or slow the progression of particular dementias (Tayeb et al., 2011). It is important for physicians to know exactly what form of dementia they are dealing with in each case, so that they can prescribe the correct medication and help families plan for the problems that dementia is likely to bring (Liefer, 2009). Choosing the right drug at the right time can help patients have a higher quality of life for a longer period and can delay for years the need for nursing home care (Geldmacher et al., 2003).

vascular dementia A form of dementia caused by multiple restrictions of the brain's blood supply.

Accordingly, it would be ideal if Alzheimer's disease and other dementias could be diagnosed even before their symptoms appear. Scientists are working to develop early diagnostic tests based on molecular and brain imaging (Ballard, Gauthier et al., 2011), EEG analysis of brain waves (Gasser et al., 2008), refined neuropsychological assessment batteries (De Santi et al., 2008), and observation of behavioral changes (Caputo et al., 2008). One study found, for example, that patients who displayed three or more subtle neurological abnormalities, such as difficulty with balance, were more likely than others to show cognitive decline over the next eight years (Inzitari et al., 2008). Another found that the inability to smell certain types of odors may be an early sign of Alzheimer's disease or dementia related to frontotemporal degeneration (FTD), and still others have found that losing the ability to appreciate sarcasm may signal the presence of FTD (Kipps et al., 2009; McLaughlin & Westervelt, 2008).

Giving the right prescription at the right time is of little use, though, if, as often happens in cases of dementia, the patients forget—or are unable or unwilling—to take their medication on the proper schedule. To address this compliance problem, pharmaceutical companies have begun to offer some of their dementia medications in transdermal patches which, when applied to the skin, automatically provide the correct daily drug dose (Small & Dubois, 2007).

Progress in the development of new medications and early diagnostic tests leads many researchers to hope that instead of just stopping or slowing the progress of dementia, it may someday be possible to reverse its course, allowing some patients to once again enjoy more normal cognitive functioning (Lacor, 2007). And as discussed in the human development chapter, the appearance of dementia may be delayed or prevented in those who spend their lives engaged in stimulating mental activity, interactions with friends, and healthy eating and exercise (Fratiglioni & Qiu, 2009).

("In Review: Major Neuropsychological Problems" summarizes the various dysfunctions discussed here.)

Major Neuropsychological Problems   IN REVIEW

Syndrome	Patient Has Difficulty...	Area(s) of Brain Malfunction
Apraxia	Making learned skilled movements even if not weak or confused.	Usually left cerebral hemisphere parietal or frontal lobes
Visual agnosia	Attaching meaning to visual sensations.	Temporal lobes, often bilateral
Anosognosia	Becoming aware of the loss of neurological function.	Usually right cerebral hemisphere
Hemineglect	Paying attention to one side of space.	Usually right parietal lobe
Aphasia	Using language as a communication system.	Usually left cerebral hemisphere
Aprosodia	Using tone of voice as a communication tool.	Usually right cerebral hemisphere
Dementia	With memory and with at least one other psychological ability that is severe enough to impair functioning.	Variable, depending on the cause of the dementia

IN REVIEW QUESTIONS

1. A patient who has become forgetful but has no problems in other areas of cognitive function may be said to have ___.

2. A dementia patient whose hippocampus is relatively intact and can still form new memories probably has ___ dementia.

3. A patient with thiamine deficiency who is forgetful but makes up memories and believes they are real probably has ___.

Active Review

As noted in the introductory chapter, all of psychology's subfields are related to one another. Our discussion of language disorders illustrates just one way that the topic of this chapter, neuropsychology, is linked to the subfield of biological psychology, which is described in

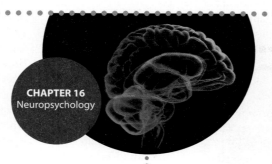

CHAPTER 16
Neuropsychology

the chapter on biology and behavior. The Linkages diagram shows ties to two other subfields, and there are many more ties throughout the book. Looking for linkages among subfields will help you see how they all fit together and help you better appreciate the big picture that is psychology.

LINKAGES

How does damage to language areas affect language abilities?
(ans. on p. 650)

CHAPTER 12
Biology and Behavior

What disorders are caused by damage to brain areas involved in memory?
(ans. on p. 641)

CHAPTER 6
Memory

What psychological tests are used in diagnosing neurological disorders?
(ans. on p. 637)

CHAPTER 7
Thought, Language, and Intelligence

Summary

Neuropsychology is the subfield of psychology whose goal is to explore and understand the relationship between brain processes, human behavior, and psychological functioning.

Foundations of Neuropsychology

What is neuropsychology and how did it develop?

There are two main assumptions in neuropsychology. The first is that complicated mental tasks such as memory involve many subtasks that can be studied separately. The second is that different psychological processes are controlled by different brain regions or different combinations of brain regions. Experimental neuropsychologists use these assumptions as they conduct research on how the brain controls and organizes human mental activity. Clinical neuropsychologists

use the results of neuropsychological research to try to understand the nature and location of brain disorders in individual patients.

Neuropsychology's early history focused on debates over *localization of function*, the idea that specific psychological functions are governed by specific parts of the brain. Early evidence for this notion was dismissed by serious scientists but by the 1860s it began to be accepted, and it now forms the basis for much of what we know about neuropsychological functioning. Recent theories of localization center on the idea that the brain is organized into modules, each of which performs its own unique analysis of information and each of which works together with varying combinations of other modules throughout the brain to perform all aspects of behavior and

mental processing. Experimental neuropsychologists today use lesion analysis to try to understand the complexities of localization of function; they look at how damage *(lesions)* in particular places in the brain relate to the appearance of particular problems.

Clinical neuropsychologists use *neuropsychological assessment* to help determine the nature of a patient's neuropsychological problems and even to suggest where in the brain the problem may lie. These tests may consist of a standardized group of instruments, such as the Halstead-Reitan Battery, or they may be an individualized combination of tests chosen by the neuropsychologist with a particular patient in mind. In most cases, a standard battery is followed by some additional individualized tests. To develop their skills, clinical neuropsychologists typically earn a Ph.D. in clinical psychology with a focus on neuropsychology and then complete a postdoctoral internship.

Mechanisms of Brain Dysfunction

What are the main causes of brain damage and dysfunction?
One of the main causes of brain damage and dysfunction is a ***cerebrovascular accident (stroke),*** which occurs when the blood supply to a part of the brain is blocked, causing the death of brain cells in that region and the loss of that brain region's ability to perform its normal control over some aspect of behavior or mental processing. Cerebrovascular accidents can be disabling and sometimes deadly. Damage and dysfunction can also result from ***traumatic brain injury (trauma),*** a sudden impact on the brain caused by a blow to the head, sudden and violent head movements, or other events that literally shake the brain inside the skull. The amount of damage and dysfunction following such events depends mainly on the amount of force involved and the degree to which the impact is cushioned by the action of ***cerebrospinal fluid***. Finally, neurodegeneration is the gradual process of damage to brain cells caused by ***neurodegenerative diseases*** such as Alzheimer's, Parkinson's, and frontotemporal degeneration, or by infections, nutritional deficiencies, or genetic abnormalities.

Neuropsychological Disorders

What disorders can be caused by brain damage or dysfunction?
The ***syndromes,*** or patterns of symptoms, associated with cerebrovascular accident, trauma, and neurodegenerative diseases appear as several kinds of neuropsychological disorders.

The hallmark of ***amnestic disorders*** is some significant disruption or loss of memory, as seen in conditions such as ***anterograde amnesia,*** in which new memories do not form, and ***Korsakoff's psychosis,*** in which memory distortions and ***confabulations*** are caused by a lack of thiamine. ***Consciousness disturbances*** are characterized by impairment in a person's normal awareness of the world. These conditions can range from loss of consciousness, as in coma or persistent vegetative state or a minimally conscious state (which may result from damage to the ***reticular formation***), to ***delirium,*** in which the patient alternates between reduced and elevated degrees of consciousness. In cases of anosognosia, a person may be paralyzed on one side of the body but have no awareness of the problem. When people suffer ***perceptual disturbances,*** they may become unable to understand what objects or certain categories of objects are by looking at them (visual agnosia), may be unable to recognize faces (prosopagnosia), or may have difficulty assembling the parts of a visual scene into a coherent whole (simultanagnosia). Patients suffering from a perceptual disorder called hemineglect ignore one half of the world. ***Language disorders*** usually result from damage to language areas on the left side of the brain and take the form of aphasias, in which the ability to speak or understand language is disrupted. The many forms of aphasia include ***Broca's aphasia,*** in which people can no longer speak fluently, and ***Wernicke's aphasia,*** which makes it difficult for people to understand what they read or hear (individuals with Wernicke's aphasia can speak fluently, but their speech makes little or no sense). Damage in the right side of the brain can result in aprosodia, the loss of ability to use tone of voice to express one's meaning or to understand the meaning of other people's speech. ***Movement disorders***, also known as ***apraxias,*** involve the inability to perform various motor skills or to perform those skills in the correct order.

Patients with ***dementia*** suffer gradually more significant and usually irreversible loss of many mental functions, including impairment of memory, perception, language, and motor skills. It is usually caused by progressive neurodegenerative diseases such as ***Alzheimer's disease,*** though it may also be caused by restrictions of the brain's blood supply, called ***vascular dementia.*** A condition known as mild cognitive impairment may precede the appearance of some forms of dementia.

Put It in Writing
People who have anterograde amnesia retain memories of people and events before their brains were injured but they cannot form new memories. Imagine that someone you know had anterograde amnesia. Write a page or so describing some of the everyday problems this person would have and how you would try to help him or her to function as normally as possible.

Personal Learning Activity
Contact a local nursing home or rehabilitation facility and ask for permission to spend part of a day visiting some of the people who live there. (The residents will probably enjoy the company.) Chat with as many of the residents as you can and take note of any obvious neuropsychological problems, as indicated by the way each person acts, speaks, and moves. Later, write a description of each person you met and, based on what you read in this chapter, speculate on what factors (e.g. cerebrovascular accident, trauma, neurodegenerative disease) might be responsible for any problems you noticed. Conclude by describing your personal reactions to the experience.

Review of Key Terms

Can you define each of the key terms in the chapter? Check your definitions against those on the pages shown in parentheses in the following list or in the Glossary at the end of the book.

Alzheimer's disease (p. 654)
amnestic disorders (p. 641)
anterograde amnesia (p. 641)
Broca's aphasia (p. 651)

cerebrospinal fluid (p. 640)
cerebrovascular accident (stroke) (p. 634)
confabulation (p. 642)
consciousness disturbances (p. 642)
delirium (p. 643)
dementia (p. 653)
Korsakoff's psychosis (p. 642)
language disorders (aphasias) (p. 650)
lesion (p. 634)
localization of function (p. 634)

movement disorders (apraxias) (p. 653)
neurodegenerative diseases (p. 640)
neuropsychological assessment (p. 637)
neuropsychology (p. 632)
perceptual disturbances (p. 647)
reticular formation (p. 642)
syndrome (p. 641)
traumatic brain injury (trauma) (p. 639)
vascular dementia (p. 655)
Wernicke's aphasia (p. 651)

Test Your Knowledge

Select the best answer for each of the following questions. Then check your responses against the Answer Key at the end of the book.

1. Dr. Boar is an experimental neuropsychologist, whereas Dr. Yemas is a clinical neuropsychologist. This means that Dr. Boar's work will most likely involve ____; and Dr. Yemas' work will most likely involve ____.
   a. adding to the knowledge about general brain function; applying knowledge of brain function to specific patients
   b. adding to the knowledge about general brain function; adding to the knowledge about general brain function
   c. applying knowledge of brain function to specific patients; adding to the knowledge about general brain function
   d. applying knowledge of brain function to specific patients; applying knowledge of brain function to specific patients

2. The idea that feeling the bumps on a person's head can tell you about that person's psychological makeup, originated from the idea that ____.
   a. much-used areas of the brain shrink because they become more efficient at processing
   b. the brain is a homogenous organ that works in a unified fashion
   c. different areas of the brain perform different functions
   d. both a and b

3. Broca's area ____.
   a. is not related to a specific place in the brain but is used as a general descriptor for people experiencing any language impairment
   b. was identified when people experiencing language difficulties were found to have lesions in the left frontal part of the brain
   c. is a brain module used in all language functions in the brain
   d. directs the network responsible for language within the brain

4. When an experimental neuropsychologist performs lesion analysis, this means that she is ____.
   a. looking for the one brain module that is responsible for the patient's neurological problem
   b. looking for a dissociation between abilities
   c. performing brain surgery to look at particular lesions in the brain
   d. looking for general information about how normal brains work

5. Damian was having extreme difficulty remembering anything. His mother, worried about his memory, took him to the doctor to find out if his memory lapses were normal. The neuropsychologist evaluating Damian will most likely give him ____.
   a. a battery of psychometric tests and compare his scores with established norms
   b. a battery of psychometric tests and compare his scores with those of people with memory disorders
   c. an individualized set of psychometric tests, which will be normed only for Damian
   d. a clinical interview in which he asks Damian to identify changes in his own memory functioning

6. Jerry suddenly was unable to speak and felt "funny." His doctor's diagnosis was that Jerry had suffered a cerebro-vascular accident. This means that ____.
   a. Jerry had experienced some type of brain trauma
   b. Jerry was experiencing pain in his brain
   c. a blood vessel in Jerry's brain was blocked
   d. parts of Jerry's brain temporarily stopped functioning

7. When Roselle was diagnosed with a neurodegenerative disease, she didn't understand what was happening. Her doctor explained that ____.
   a. some blood vessels in her brain were blocked, killing brain tissue
   b. the nerve cells of her brain had become too easily excitable
   c. her brain had bumped against bone, causing microscopic tears
   d. diseased brain neurons had stopped functioning correctly

8. Mickey cannot remember people he just met, but he still remembers his childhood. He also remembers that he was at the fateful Cubs baseball game when Steve Bartman interfered with the outfielder's catching of a fly ball. However, Mickey has never been to Chicago and was not at that game, despite what he believes he remembers. Mickey will most likely be diagnosed ___.
   a. with Alzheimer's disease
   b. as having had a cerebrovascular accident
   c. with a brain infection such as herpes encephalitis
   d. with Korsakoff's psychosis

9. When Betty was told that her mother was experiencing delirium, it was explained that this means that her mother ___.
   a. probably would remain in a persistent vegetative state
   b. could have both impaired and elevated levels of consciousness from time to time
   c. had a problem caused by being very upset and nervous
   d. would be likely to show signs of brain trauma

10. Rachel did not seek medical care when she had a cerebrovascular accident because her brain was damaged in such a way that she had no knowledge of the damage. In other words, Rachel experienced ___.
   a. aphasia
   b. anterograde amnesia
   c. anosognosia
   d. a deficiency in thiamine

11. When a patient experiences visual agnosia, it is often due to damage to the "what" pathway. This damage is most likely to be in the ___ lobe.
   a. thalamic
   b. parietal
   c. temporal
   d. frontal

12. Tracy was diagnosed with prosopagnosia. This means that Tracy will be unable to identify ___.
   a. an apple she is holding
   b. manufactured objects
   c. the sound of a familiar voice
   d. people's faces

13. When Robin experienced a cerebrovascular accident, she had significant damage to her right parietal lobe. She now ignores everything in the left side of space. Robin is showing symptoms of ___.
   a. hemineglect
   b. simultanagnosia
   c. aphasia
   d. anosognosia

14. A study described in the Focus on Research section of this chapter was able to establish that patients with hemineglect ___.
   a. ignore one side of space in a manner that is not explained by sensory loss
   b. are no longer able to imagine scenes under any circumstances
   c. can use only concrete visual stimuli
   d. do not experience sensory deficits

15. Alex had a language problem. He could speak, but not in a normal manner. He could use only a limited number of simple and concrete words. For example, when he wanted his wife to purchase applesauce when she went to the grocery store, he was only able to say, "Applesauce buy." A neuropsychologist would most likely look for damage to ___ in Alex's brain.
   a. Wernicke's area
   b. Broca's area
   c. the occipital lobe
   d. the corpus callosum

16. Allana also had a language problem. Her speech also was not normal. However, when she wanted her husband to purchase applesauce from the grocery store, she said "From flowing flowery in a with the shrubs buy over the other." We know that Allana is not schizophrenic, so we would infer that she has damage to ___.
   a. Wernicke's area
   b. Broca's area
   c. the occipital lobe
   d. corpus callosum

17. A neurological deficit in which people have difficulty reading the letters that they themselves wrote is known as ___.
   a. anosognosia
   b. aprosodia
   c. alexia without agraphia
   d. corpus callosumania

18. Alfreda said to her husband, "I am very angry with you." However, she said it in a monotone that did not really suggest she was expressing anger. It was as though she had e-mailed him this information. A neuropsychologist would suspect Alfreda is experiencing ___.
   a. hemineglect
   b. simultanagnosia
   c. Alzheimer's disease
   d. aprosodia

19. Fred's problem in remembering things was slowly becoming more apparent. In addition, he had to stop playing golf because he could no longer swing his club correctly. Yet he remained alert and attentive. His wife brought him to a neuropsychologist because Fred, a skilled accountant, could no longer even balance their checkbook. Fred most likely will be diagnosed with ___.
   a. dementia
   b. delirium
   c. aphasia
   d. apraxia

20. Research on Alzheimer's disease has found that ___.
   a. the number of people diagnosed with Alzheimer's disease decreases after age 80
   b. memory loss is the only significant symptom
   c. patients with Alzheimer's have a different brain pathology than those experiencing normal aging
   d. the disease begins with dysfunction in the dopamine neurotransmitter network

Media Resources

Now that you have finished reading this chapter, how about exploring some of the ideas and information that you found most interesting?

Go to **CengageBrain.com** to access Psychology CourseMate, where you will find an interactive eBook, glossaries, flashcards, quizzes, videos, Virtual Psychology Labs, and more.

If your professor has assigned Aplia:

1. Sign in to your account.
2. Complete the corresponding exercises as required by your professor.
3. When finished, click "Grade It Now" to see which areas you have mastered, which areas need more work, and detailed explanations of every answer.

APPENDIX
Statistics in Psychological Research

Understanding and interpreting the results of psychological research depend on *statistical analyses,* the methods for describing and drawing conclusions from data. The introductory chapter introduced some terms and concepts associated with these analyses. *Descriptive statistics* are the numbers that psychologists use to describe and present their data. *Inferential statistics* are the mathematical procedures they use to draw conclusions from data and to make inferences about what the data mean. Here, we present more details about these statistical analyses that will help you to evaluate research results.

Describing Data

To illustrate our discussion, let's imagine a hypothetical experiment about the effects of rewards on performance. The experimenter presents a set of mathematics problems to two groups of people. Each group must solve the problems within a fixed time. For each correct answer, the low-reward group is paid ten cents. The high-reward group gets one dollar. The hypothesis to be tested is the **null hypothesis**, the assertion that the independent variable manipulated by the experimenter will have no effect on the dependent variable measured by the experimenter. In this case, the null hypothesis is that the size of the reward (the independent variable) will not affect performance on the mathematics task (the dependent variable).

Assume that the experimenter has obtained a sample of participants, assigned them randomly to the two groups, and done everything possible to avoid the influence of confounding variables and other research problems discussed in the introductory chapter. The experiment has been run, and the researcher now has the data, a list of the number of correct answers given by each participant in each group. Now comes the first task of statistical analysis. We must describe the data in a way that makes them easy to understand.

The Frequency Histogram

The simplest way to describe the data is to draw up something like Table 1, in which all the numbers are simply listed. After examining the table, you might notice that the high-reward group seems to have done better than the low-reward group. But the difference is not immediately obvious. It might be even harder to see if more participants had been involved or if the scores included three-digit numbers. A more satisfactory way of presenting the same data is in a picture-like graphic known as a **histogram** (see Figure 1).

Construction of a histogram is simple. First, divide the scale for measuring the dependent variable (in this case, the number of correct solutions) into a number of categories, or "bins." The bins in our example are 1–2, 3–4, 5–6, 7–8, and 9–10. Next, sort the raw data into the appropriate bin. (For example, the score of a participant who had 5 correct answers would go into the 5–6 bin, a score of 8 would go into the 7–8 bin, and so on.) Finally, for each bin, count the number of scores in that bin, and draw a bar up to the height of that number on the vertical axis of the graph. The set of bars makes up the frequency histogram. Figure 1 shows a histogram comparing the scores of the high-reward group and the low-reward group. Now the difference between groups that was

null hypothesis A testable statement that the independent variable manipulated by an experimenter will have no effect on the dependent variable being measured by the experimenter.

histogram A pictorial presentation of how often each possible score on a dependent variable occurs in a set of research data.

TABLE 1   A Simple Data Set

Here are the test scores obtained by thirteen participants performing under low-reward conditions and thirteen participants performing under high-reward conditions.

Low Reward	High Reward
4	6
6	4
2	10
7	10
6	7
8	10
3	6
5	7
2	5
3	9
5	9
9	3
5	8

Low reward

High reward

■ 1–2   ■ 5–6   ■ 9–10
■ 3–4   ■ 7–8

FIGURE 1
A Histogram
The height of each bar of a histogram represents the number of scores falling within each range of score values. The pattern formed by these bars gives a visual image of how research results are distributed.

difficult to see in Table 1 becomes clearly visible. More people in the high-reward group obtained high scores than in the low-reward group.

Histograms and other "pictures" of data are useful for visualizing and better understanding the "shape" of research data. But in order to analyze data statistically, we need to use other ways of handling the numbers that make up these graphic presentations. For example, before we can tell whether two histograms are different statistically or just visually, the data they represent must be summarized using descriptive statistics.

Descriptive Statistics

The four basic categories of descriptive statistics do the following: (1) count the number of observations made; (2) summarize the typical value of a set of data; (3) summarize the spread, or variability, in a set of data; and (4) express the correlation between two sets of data, using the correlation coefficient described in the introductory chapter.

N   The easiest statistic to compute, abbreviated as *N*, simply describes the number of observations that make up the data set. In Table 1, for example, $N = 13$ for each group, or 26 for the entire data set. Simple as it is, *N* plays a very important role in more sophisticated statistical analyses.

Measures of Central Tendency   It is apparent in Figure 1 that there is a difference in the pattern of scores between the two groups. But how much of a difference? What is the typical value, or *central tendency,* that represents each group's performance? There are three measures that capture this typical value: the mode, the median, and the mean. The *mode* is the value or score that occurs most frequently in the data set. The *median* is the halfway point in a set of data; half the scores fall above the median, and half fall below it. The *mean* is the arithmetic average. To find the mean, add the values of all the scores and divide by the number of scores *(N)*.

Measures of Variability   The variability (or spread or dispersion) of a set of data is often just as important as its central tendency. This variability can be quantified by measures

© Cengage Learning

Statistics can be valuable for describing research results, but critical thinking demands that we evaluate them carefully before drawing conclusions about what they mean. Knowing this pointy-haired executive's tendency toward uncritical thinking, you can bet that Dogbert's impressive-sounding restatement of the definition of median will win him an extension of his pricey consulting contract.

known as the *range* and the *standard deviation*. The range is simply the difference between the highest and the lowest values in a data set. For the data in Table 1, the range for the low-reward group is $9 - 2 = 7$; for the high-reward group, the range is $10 - 3 = 7$. The standard deviation, or SD, describes the average difference between each score and the mean of the data set.

The Normal Distribution   In most subfields in psychology, when researchers collect many measurements and plot their data in histograms, the pattern that results often resembles that shown for the low-reward group in Figure 1. That is, the majority of scores tend to fall in the middle of the distribution, whereas fewer and fewer scores occur as one moves toward the extremes. As more and more data are collected, and as smaller and smaller bins are used (perhaps containing only one value each), the histogram tends to smooth out until it resembles the bell-shaped curve known as the **normal distribution**, or normal curve, which is shown in Figure 2. When a distribution of scores follows a truly normal curve, its mean, median, and mode all have the same value. Furthermore, if the curve is normal, we can use its standard deviation to describe how any particular score stands in relation to the rest of the distribution.

The distribution of IQ scores shown in Figure 2 provides an example. They are distributed in a normal curve, with a mean, median, and mode of 100 and a standard deviation (SD) of 16. In such a distribution, half of the population will have an IQ above 100, and half will have one below 100. The shape of the true normal curve is such that 68 percent of the area under it lies within 1 standard deviation above and below the mean. In terms of IQ, this means that 68 percent of the population has an IQ somewhere between 84 (100 minus 16) and 116 (100 plus 16). Of the remaining 32 percent of the

normal distribution A smooth, bell-shaped curve representing a set of data in which most scores occur in the middle of the possible range, with fewer and fewer scores occurring toward the extremes of the range.

FIGURE 2
The Normal Distribution
Many kinds of research data approximate the shape of the normal curve, in which most scores fall toward the center of the range.

population, half falls more than 1 SD above the mean, and half falls more than 1 SD below the mean. Thus, 16 percent of the population has an IQ above 116, and 16 percent scores below 84.

The normal curve is also the basis for percentiles. A **percentile** score indicates the percentage of people or observations that fall at or below a given score in a normal distribution. In Figure 2, for example, the mean score (which is also the median) lies at a point below which 50 percent of the scores fall. Thus, the mean of a normal distribution is at the 50th percentile. What does this mean for IQ? If you score 1 SD above the mean, your score is at a point above which only 16 percent of the population falls. This means that 84 percent of the population (100 percent minus 16 percent) must be below that score. So this IQ score is at the 84th percentile. A score at 2 SDs above the mean is at the 97.5 percentile, because 97.5 percent of the scores are below it in a normal distribution.

Scores may also be expressed in terms of their distance in standard deviations from the mean, producing what are called **standard scores**. A standard score of 1.5, for example, is 1.5 standard deviations from the mean.

Inferential Statistics

It can be hard to understand the meaning of research results summarized in descriptive statistics alone. Is a correlation between college grade-point averages and the eating of certain foods large enough to support the hypothesis that diet is important for mental functioning? Is the difference in the effects of two different kinds of psychotherapy large enough to recommend one over the other? The answers to questions such as these are based largely on the results of analyses that use inferential statistics.

Consider again the descriptive statistics from our rewards experiment. They tell us that the performances of the high- and low-reward groups differ, but there is some uncertainty. Is the difference large enough to be important? Does it represent a real effect or a fluke? The researcher would like to have some measure of confidence that the difference between groups did not occur by chance alone. **Inferential statistics** use certain rules to estimate the likelihood that a particular correlation or a particular difference between groups was due to chance. If that likelihood is small enough, the researcher can usually conclude that the correlation or difference is *statistically significant*.

Differences between Means: The t Test

One of the most important tools of inferential statistics is the *t* test. It allows the researcher to ask how likely it is that the difference between two means occurred by chance rather than because of the independent variable. When the *t* test or another inferential statistic says that the probability of chance effects is small enough (usually less than 5 percent), the results are said to be statistically significant. Conducting a *t* test of statistical significance requires the use of three descriptive statistics.

The first component of the *t* test is the size of the observed effect, the difference between the means. Recall that the mean is calculated by summing a group's scores and dividing by the number of scores. In the example shown in Table 1, the mean of the high-reward group is 94/13, or 7.23, and the mean of the low-reward group is 65/13, or 5. Thus the difference between the means for the high- and low-reward groups is $7.23 - 5 = 2.23$.

Second, the standard deviation of scores in each group must be known. If the scores in the groups are quite variable, their standard deviations will be large, indicating that chance may have played a large role in producing the results. If the scores within each group are all very similar, however, their standard deviations will be small, which suggests that the participants in each group reacted in about the same way to the rewards they were given. Thus, the difference between groups is more likely to be significant when each group's standard deviation is small. In Table 1, some people in the low-reward group actually did better on the math test than some in the high-reward group. If variability is high enough that the scores of two groups overlap, the difference between group means, though large, may not be statistically significant.

percentile A way of stating what percentage of scores in a data set fall at or below a certain score.

standard score A way of stating how many standard deviations separate a particular score from the mean of all the scores in a data set.

inferential statistics A form of statistical analysis designed to provide a measure of confidence about how likely it is that a certain result appeared by chance.

Third, we need to take the sample size, N, into account. The larger the number of participants or observations, the more likely it is that a given difference between means is significant. This is so because with larger samples, random factors within a group will have less impact on the group's mean. The unusual performance of a few people who were sleepy or anxious or hostile, for example, will likely be canceled out by the scores of the more representative majority of people. The same effect of sample size can be seen in coin tossing. If you toss a coin 5 times, you might not be too surprised if heads come up 80 percent of the time. But if you get 80 percent heads after 100 tosses, you might begin to suspect that this is probably not due to chance alone. Some other effect, perhaps some bias in the coin, is probably producing the results. For the same reason, a relatively small correlation coefficient—between diet and grades, say—might be statistically significant if it was based on 50,000 students. As the number of participants increases, it becomes less likely that the correlation reflects the influence of a few oddball cases.

To summarize, as the difference between the means gets larger, as N increases, and as standard deviations get smaller, t increases. This increase in t raises the researcher's confidence in the significance of the difference between means.

Beyond the t Test

Many experiments in psychology are considerably more complex than simple comparisons between two groups. They often involve three or more experimental and control groups. Some experiments also include more than one independent variable. For example, suppose we were interested not only in the effect of reward size on performance but also in the effect of problem difficulty. We might then create six groups whose members would perform easy, moderate, or difficult problems under low- or high-reward conditions.

In an experiment like this, the results might be due to the size of the reward, the difficulty of the problem, or the combined effects (known as the *interaction*) of the two. Analyzing the size and source of these effects is typically accomplished through procedures known as *analysis of variance*. The details of analysis of variance are beyond the scope of this book, but note that, as in the t test, the statistical significance of each effect is influenced by differences between means, standard deviation, and sample size.

For more detailed information about how analysis of variance and other inferential statistics are used to understand and interpret the results of psychological research, consider taking courses in research methods and statistical or quantitative methods.

ANSWER KEY
Multiple-Choice Self-Test Questions

Chapter 1 Introduction to the Science of Psychology

1A The first research laboratory in psychology was established to study consciousness *(p. 10)*. **2C** A community psychologist would believe that low-income families who live in crowded conditions are more likely to need mental health services *(p. 5)*. **3B** Someone who believes that human behavior is influenced by genetic inheritance, unconscious motivations, and environmental influences exemplifies the multiple perspectives of the eclectic approach *(p. 13)*. **4C** An educational psychologist studies what teachers actually do when they are teaching students to read *(p. 5)*. **5A** Behaviorists say that people think and behave in ways that have previously been rewarded *(p. 15)*. **6C** In collectivist cultures, people tend to think of themselves as part of a family or work group *(p. 18)*. **7D** Recognition of a smile is a behavior that cross-cultural psychologists find to be similar around the world *(p. 17)*. **8D** "What am I being asked to believe or accept?" is the first of five critical thinking questions discussed in this chapter *(p. 22)*. **9D** An operational definition defines a variable so that it can be measured. In this case the score on the mood survey is the operational definition of mood *(p. 23)*. **10C** Case studies are used to collect descriptive data *(pp. 25–26)*. **11D** Before using survey results to support a hypothesis, we must be sure that the questions are properly worded, the sample used is representative of the population of interest, and the responses are not biased by efforts to appear "socially acceptable" *(p. 26)*. **12A** When research results are statistically significant it means that the probability that the results occurred by chance is extremely small *(p. 36)*. **13D** To avoid the possibility that experimenter bias may confound the results of an experiment aimed at testing a hypothesis, a researcher should use a double-blind study *(p. 32)*. **14A** In an experiment, the outcome behavior being measured (such as memory) is the dependent variable *(p. 28)*. **15B** In an experiment, the group that receives the "treatment" or intervention is the experimental group *(p. 29)*. **16B** Using a true experiment to try to scientifically study this problem would pose the greatest ethical problems for Jose because it is not ethical to purposely create abusive conditions for children *(p. 37)*. **17B** The number closest to 1.00 is the strongest correlation coefficient *(pp. 27–28)*. **18D** A correlation coefficient can tell us the strength, direction, and existence of a relationship between two variables, but not its cause *(pp. 27–28)*. **19C** To select participants for a study such as smoking habits of a group of students, you would use a representative sample *(pp. 32–33)*. **20D** All are good reasons for ethical behavior *(pp. 37–38)*.

Chapter 2 Biology and Behavior

1C The nucleus of a cell provides genetic information, and the mitochondria turn oxygen and glucose into energy *(p. 47)*. **2C** Malfunctions of serotonin systems contribute to depression, and malfunctions in dopamine systems contribute to Parkinson's disease *(pp. 71–72)*. **3A** Overactivity of glutamate, which occurs when oxygen is cut off from neurons in the brain, can result in a stroke *(p. 72)*. **4B** Functional magnetic resonance imaging (fMRI) combines the advantages of PET and MRI and is capable of detecting changes in blood flow and blood oxygen that reflect ongoing changes in the activity of neurons *(p. 62)*. **5C** The somatic system carries information to and from the central nervous system *(p. 51)*. **6D** The sympathetic nervous system is less active, and the parasympathetic system is more active, now that Kalli is relaxing *(pp. 51–52)*. **7A** Some simple behaviors like reflexes occur automatically via the spinal cord and without instructions from the other portion of the central nervous system, the brain *(pp. 52–53)*. **8A** A neuron's action potential shoots down its axon with greater speed when the axon is coated in myelin *(p. 48)*. **9A** The medulla oblongata, located in the hindbrain, helps to regulate heart rate, blood pressure, and breathing *(p. 53)*. **10D** If the reticular formation fibers in Lily's hindbrain were damaged, she would go into a coma *(p. 53)*. **11A** The cerebellum is that part of the hindbrain that controls finely coordinated movements *(pp. 53–54)*. **12B** Defects in the hippocampus have been found in people with Alzheimer's disease *(p. 56)*. **13A** The sensory system provides information about the environment *(pp. 57–58)*. **14C** The sensory cortex in the occipital lobe receives information concerning vision *(p. 57)*. **15A** Voluntary movements are controlled by neurons in the motor cortex, located in the frontal lobe *(p. 58)*. **16A** Damage to Broca's area creates difficulties in speaking *(p. 59)*. **17A** The left hemisphere of the brain is specialized for language *(pp. 67–68)*. **18A** Brain imaging research reveals that imagining movements causes changes in the motor cortex *(p. 68)*. **19A** Neurons release neurotransmitters into synapses and endocrine organs secrete hormones into the blood stream *(pp. 48–49, 74–75)*. **20A** Glands release hormones such as cortisol into the bloodstream *(p. 74)*.

Chapter 3 Sensation and Perception

1A Perception is the process of using information and your understanding of the world so that messages from the senses become meaningful experiences *(p. 82)*. **2B** Transduction is the process of converting incoming energy into neural activities *(p. 83)*. **3A** The described procedure defines absolute threshold *(p. 84)*. **4B** Expecting a stimulus to occur lowers the response criterion *(pp. 84–85)*. **5B** According to Weber's law, the lighter the objects being compared, the smaller the weight difference needed to detect a change in weight *(pp. 85–86)*. **6B** When a star is faint, it is more easily seen by looking slightly away from where the star is expected to be *(p. 88)*. **7D** The trichromatic theory proposes that combining three primary colors can produce any other color *(pp. 90–91)*. **8A** According to the gate control theory, input from other skin senses can come into the spinal cord at the same time the pain gets there and "take over" the pathways that the pain impulses would have used *(p. 103)*. **9C** Constant loud noise causes hair cell damage, literally ripping off hair cells from his inner ear, resulting in nerve deafness *(p. 95)*. **10D** Unlike other senses, our sense of smell does not send its messages through the thalamus *(p. 99)*. **11A** Your blind spot is located where the optic nerve leaves the eyeball *(pp. 88–89)*. **12B** Temperature can contribute to food's flavor *(pp. 97–98)*. **13C** The Stroop task is difficult because one must divide attention between the meaning of the word and the color of the word. Without knowing the meaning of the word, there is no divided attention *(p. 124)*. **14A** Kinesthesia gives us knowledge of the position of our body parts *(p. 101)*. **15B** Stroboscopic motion is an illusion in which lights or images flashed in rapid succession are perceived as moving *(p. 113)*. **16B** People moving at the same speed, in a sense having a "common fate," are perceived as a group *(pp. 109–110)*. **17B** Interposition is the depth perception cue that operates on this basis *(p. 110)*. **18B** Looming is a motion cue such that objects increasingly fill the retinal space as they get closer *(p. 112)*. **19B** Bottom-up processing involves basic sensory feature analysis, including the sensation of changes in salt level *(pp. 116–117)*. **20A** Covert orienting involves a shift of attention that isn't easily observed *(p. 122)*.

Chapter 4 Consciousness

1A Mental processing of bodily processes, such as the brain regulating blood pressure, occur at the nonconscious level, and some people are able to learn to control these processes through biofeedback *(p. 135)*. **2C** Dr. Eplort will most likely sleep about the same as he did before *(p. 145)*. **3C** Zandra's preference for the Rembrandt paintings was most likely affected by priming *(pp. 116–117)*. **4B** Edie's success depends on her expectation that the messages will help her *(pp. 137–139).* **5D** Mitch's responses to marijuana were most likely due to learned expectations *(p. 155).* **6C** Leroy was most likely in stage N3, deep slow-wave sleep *(pp. 141–142).* **7C** Alan is most likely suffering from REM behavior disorder, a condition that allows dreams to be acted out *(pp. 144–145).* **8A** SIDS (sudden infant death syndrome) has been greatly reduced in the United States by the "back to sleep" program, which advises parents to have their babies sleep face up *(p. 144).* **9B** Disruptions of your circadian rhythm can make you grouchy and less productive. Melatonin has been used to maintain these circadian rhythms *(p. 145).* **10C** It is non-REM sleep that researchers believe is important for restoring the body and brain's energy stores for the next day's activity; the other three responses are functions of REM sleep *(pp. 146–147).* **11D** According to the activation-synthesis theory, dreams are meaningless, random byproducts of REM sleep *(p. 149).* **12C** People susceptible to hypnosis are able to focus and redistribute their attention on the hypnotist *(p. 150).* **13C** Hypnosis has been used to help people reduce nausea from chemotherapy, surgical bleeding, and pain *(pp. 151–152).* **14A** Research on meditation has shown that meditators report a decrease in stress-related problems and anxiety *(p. 152).* **15A** Agonists are drugs that bind to a receptor and mimic the effects of the neurotransmitter that normally fits that receptor *(p. 153).* **16A** Drug tolerance is a condition in which increasingly larger drug doses are required to produce the same effect *(p. 154).* **17D** Since alcohol's physiological effects involve dopamine, dopamine agonists can reduce cravings and withdrawal effects *(p. 156).* **18C** Caffeine is a stimulant, which does not cause hallucinations *(p. 158).* **19B** Opiates relieve pain and cause sleep *(pp. 159–160).* **20B** Marijuana disrupts memory function and reduces creativity *(pp. 160–161).*

Chapter 5 Learning

1C The expression "Once burned, twice shy" reflects a change in knowledge (or behavior) due to experience *(p. 170).* **2B** After repeated pairings with a stimulus that already triggers a reflexive response, the conditioned stimulus alone elicits the reflexive-like response *(pp. 171–172).* **3B** Extinction is the gradual disappearance of a conditioned response when the UCS is eliminated *(p. 173).* **4A** The law of effect predicts that Kim will be more likely to date Brad because he is associated with a positive outcome, her enjoyment of the movie *(p. 179).* **5D** Najla has developed a phobia through classical conditioning *(p. 177).* **6A** The idea that knowledge is located in many areas throughout the brain rather than in one particular place is a basic assumption of neural network theories *(pp. 189–190).* **7A** Stimulus generalization is a process in which a conditioned response is triggered by stimuli similar to the original conditioned stimulus *(pp. 173–174).* **8C** For survival reasons, people are biologically prepared to link taste signals with illness *(pp. 175–176).* **9A** Extinction occurs because the behavior is no longer being rewarded *(pp. 184–185).* **10B** Operant conditioning involves learning that behaviors have consequences *(p. 179).* **11B** Negative reinforcement strengthens behavior that is followed by the removal of an unpleasant event or stimulus *(p. 179).* **12B** Once avoidance conditioning is learned, avoidance can be a difficult habit to break *(pp. 180–181).* **13D** A discriminative conditioned stimulus signals that a reward will occur if a certain response is given *(p. 181).* **14D** Shaping is the process of reinforcing successive approximations to the target behavior *(p. 182).* **15B** Jamey must exhibit a fixed number of behaviors while Susan must work a variable amount of time *(pp. 183–184).* **16D** They are all problems with using punishment *(pp. 185–187).* **17B** Learned helplessness occurs when people learn they are unable to control circumstances or outcomes *(pp. 190–192).* **18C** Latent learning is learning that is not demonstrated when it is first learned *(pp. 192–193).* **19D** Najla has learned from the experience of watching others pet a dog *(p. 192).* **20C** Group work is not really helpful for everything. Practice is. It's more likely to be active learning. *(pp. 198–199).*

Chapter 6 Memory

1A Acoustic codes represent information as sequences of sounds, such as a tune or a rhyme *(p. 209).* **2B** Episodic memory is a person's recall of a specific event that happened while that person was present; explicit memory involves the processes through which people try to remember something *(pp. 209–210).* **3C** Implicit memories are not purposefully recalled but do influence behavior *(p. 210).* **4B** Maintenance rehearsal is a method of keeping information in short-term memory by repeating it *(p. 210).* **5B** The transfer-appropriate

processing model of memory suggests that a critical factor in memory is how the encoding process matches up with what is later retrieved *(p. 211).* **6C** Selective attention allows Reepal to focus on the most important information *(p. 214).* **7B** Unrehearsed information stays in short-term memory for about eighteen seconds *(p. 214).* **8A** Chunking involves grouping information into meaningful units that can be stored *(p. 215).* **9C** Semantic memory contains general knowledge not linked to a specific event *(p. 209).* **10C** Ebbinghaus found that most forgetting occurs during the first nine hours after learning, and especially during the first hour *(pp. 227–228).* **11D** The serial position curve predicts that first items (primacy effect) and last items (recency effect) will be best remembered. *(p. 218).* **12A** State-dependent memory is memory that is helped or hindered by similarities or differences in a person's internal state during learning versus recall *(pp. 219–220).* **13C** The tip-of-the-tongue phenomenon represents the retrieval of incomplete knowledge *(p. 221).* **14C** In the process of constructive memory, people use generalized knowledge, or schemas, to fill in gaps in the information they encode and retrieve *(pp. 221–223).* **15C** Recent use of DNA evidence has revealed that many people in prison for serious crimes did not commit those crimes *(pp. 225–227).* **16C** As Ebbinghaus discovered, relearning takes much less time than original learning. This difference represents the savings from one learning to the next learning *(pp. 227–228).* **17C** Proactive inhibition occurs when old information disrupts the learning of new information *(p. 229).* **18A** Spontaneous generalizations are produced by PDP networks *(p. 224).* **19B** Anterograde amnesia is the inability to form new long-term memories following a brain injury *(p. 235).* **20A** The method of loci involves mentally placing objects in various spots in a familiar location (locus) *(pp. 237–238).*

Chapter 7 Thought, Language, and Intelligence

1D Thinking is part of an information processing system that manipulates mental representations *(p. 249).* **2C** A natural concept has no fixed set of defining characteristics but a prototype possesses most of its characteristic features *(p. 251).* **3B** Basing his strategy on an algorithm would require Clint to evaluate every possible move and countermove *(pp. 255–256).* **4D** Scripts are mental representations of familiar sequences of activity *(pp. 252–253).* **5B** Setting aside a difficult problem, hoping for a solution to occur while working on something else, is called incubation *(pp. 257–258).* **6D** Functional fixedness occurs when a person fails to use a familiar object in a novel way to solve a problem *(p. 261).* **7C** Confirmation bias is a strong tendency to confirm rather than refute the preferred hypothesis, even in the face of strong evidence against the hypothesis *(pp. 261–262).* **8A** The gambler's fallacy has led Richard to believe that the probability of a random event will change over time *(p. 268).* **9C** Incorrect words or word endings are not likely to have been reinforced. They are overgeneralizations of a language rule the child has learned *(p. 272).* **10A** A critical period is a limited window of opportunity for language learning. If the critical period is missed, normal language development will not occur *(p. 273).* **11A** Alfred Binet designed the first test to identify children with special educational needs *(p. 275).* **12D** Formal reasoning is based on the rules of logic *(pp. 254–255).* **13B** The average score obtained by people at each age level is assigned the IQ value of 100 with half of the scores lower than 100 and half higher than 100 *(p. 277).* **14C** If the scores from this preemployment test predict future performance on the job, the test is statistically valid for the purpose of employee selection *(p. 278).* **15A** A statistically reliable test yields consistent and stable scores over time *(p. 278).* **16A** IQ tests appear to be most valid for assessing aspects of intelligence that are related to school work *(p. 279).* **17D** The highest correlation is likely to be found between the identical twins' scores *(pp. 280–281).* **18A** Individuals with mild intellectual disability will have most difficulty with academic material and abstract reasoning but are able to learn new material *(pp. 289–290).* **19A** This test was most likely based on Sternberg's triarchic theory of intelligence, which proposes three types of intelligences: creative, analytic, and practical *(pp. 286–287).* **20A** Creative people are internally motivated, have a set of creative skills, use divergent thinking, and have expertise in the field of pursuit *(pp. 265–266).*

Chapter 8 Motivation and Emotion

1B The evolutionary approach suggests that adaptive behaviors that promote the survival of the species reflect inborn motivations to pass on genes *(pp. 299–300).* **2A** Homeostasis is the tendency to maintain physiological systems at a steady, stable level by adjusting to changes (p. 300). **3D** Arousal theory states that people are motivated to behave in ways that maintain an individual, optimal level of arousal (p. 301). **4B** Incentive theory states that behavior is goal directed to obtain positive stimuli and avoid negative stimuli (pp. 301–302). **5A** When stimulated, the ventromedial nucleus tells Ahmed that there is no need to eat (p. 305). **6B** Research shows that we tend to eat less when given only one food than when given several choices of food (p. 306). **7B** Although people with bulimia can maintain normal weight, they may experience dehydration and other symptoms (p. 310). **8C** The Chicago survey found that people in the United States have sex less frequently and with fewer partners than was earlier believed (pp. 311–312). **9D** According to the Thinking Critically section of this chapter, sexual orientation is most likely influenced by prenatal hormones, genetic factors and sociocultural learning (pp. 315–317). **10B** Edwina should encourage her son to try difficult tasks, praise his efforts, and help him learn from his mistakes (pp. 318–319). **11B** Studies have shown that allowing people to set and achieve clear goals is one way to increase job performance (p. 320). **12A** Physiological needs, including those for food and water, come first in Maslow's hierarchy (p. 322). **13C** An approach-avoidance conflict arises when we must decide whether to do something that has both positive and negative consequences. (p. 323). **14C** Emotions can vary in intensity from ecstatic to mildly pleased (p. 324). **15A** James's theory states that we experience emotions only by perceiving our physiological response to an event (pp. 328–329). **16D** Excitation transfer occurs when arousal from an experience carries over to a different situation. This is consistent with Schachter's theory of emotion (pp. 331–332). **17B** Cannon's theory maintains that emotional experience originates in the thalamus and simultaneously triggers physiological arousal and cognitive awareness (pp. 330–331). **18D** As children grow up, they learn an emotional culture, which are rules that govern what emotions are appropriate, in what situations, and what expressions are allowed (p. 336). **19B** Human emotions are communicated mainly through facial movements and expressions (p. 333). **20B** In allowing Diane's emotional state to guide his behavior, Sam is using social referencing (p. 336).

Chapter 9   Human Development

1B Behavioral genetics is concerned with the differences between groups of individuals, not with the characteristics of a single individual (p. 346). **2C** Smokers' babies are usually underweight (p. 349). **3D** Tyrone's physical development is the result of maturation and environmental influences (pp. 350–351). **4D** Newborns visually prefer novelty and shapes that resemble human faces (p. 350). **5C** With normal brain development, grasping and rooting reflexes should have disappeared by 6 months of age (p. 350). **6A** Assimilation is the process of taking in information that adds to an existing schema (pp. 352–353). **7B** Adriana is probably four to six years old; she is in the preoperational stage (pp. 353–354). **8B** Babies stare longer when they see events that violate their expectations about other people's beliefs. (pp. 369–370). **9B** We are unlikely to recall anything about our first year due to infantile amnesia (pp. 357–358). **10B** Difficult babies tend to remain difficult into childhood (pp. 361–362). **11B** Harlow's attachment studies demonstrate that infant monkeys form attachments based on contact comfort needs (pp. 363). **12D** With ambivalent insecure attachment, the child sometimes prefers and sometimes rejects the primary caregiver (p. 364). **13C** Authoritative parents are sympathetic but firm; permissive parents give lots of freedom (pp. 366–368). **14A** Girls tend to speak and write earlier and are able to read emotional signals at younger ages than boys (p. 371). **15C** Ludmilla is still confused about her identity (pp. 376–377). **16D** Teens who have sex tend to have parents who are less educated and less likely to exert control over them than teens who do not have sex (p. 375). **17A** People at the Stage 1 (preconventional) level of moral reasoning are concerned with avoiding punishment (p. 377). **18C** These changes occur mainly in middle adulthood (pp. 379–380). **19C** Up until at least age sixty, people's thinking becomes dialectical, which means they understand that knowledge is relative, not absolute (p. 380). **20B** Terminal drop is the decline in mental functioning that occurs in the months or years preceding death (p. 384).

Chapter 10   Health, Stress, and Coping

1C Your great-grandparents' generation was most likely to die from infectious diseases, whereas your own generation is most likely to die from chronic diseases (pp. 393–394). **2A** The more stressors Lila has, the more physical, psychological, and behavioral responses she will probably experience (p. 396). **3D** Daily hassles involve irritations, pressures, and annoyances that may not be major stressors by themselves but whose effects add up to become significant (pp. 395). **4A** The first stage of the GAS, the alarm reaction, involves some version of the fight-flight reaction (pp. 396–397). **5C** Males under stress tended to get angry, avoid stressors, or both, whereas females are more likely to help others and to make use of their social support network (p. 406). **6B** Rumination is continuously thinking about negative events and it tends to intensify negative emotional states (p. 399). **7B** Catastrophizing involves the exaggeration of negative consequences (p. 399). **8B** People with disease-resistant personalities tend to think of stressors as temporary challenges to be overcome, not catastrophic threats (pp. 405–406). **9B** Flashbacks are associated with posttraumatic stress disorder (p. 400). **10C** Emotion-focused coping strategies include denial and avoidance (p. 403). **11C** Perceived control over stressful events helps reduce their negative effects (p. 402). **12B** Laton is trying to improve the employees' social support (pp. 404–405). **13B** People who are impulsive or low on conscientiousness are more likely to die from accidents or violence (pp. 406–408). **14C** Natural killer cells of the immune system have antiviral properties and help prevent tumors (p. 409). **15B** Hostility is a risk factor in heart disease (pp. 410–412). **16D** Social support is a mediating factor on stress (pp. 404–405). **17A** Personalizing the risk of danger to the individual should increase the likelihood of behavioral change (p. 413). **18B** Being aware of a problem behavior and thinking about changing it occur during the contemplation stage of readiness to alter a health-related behavior (p. 414). **19A** Sayumi is using the coping strategy of cognitive restructuring, or changing her thinking about an event or person (p. 415). **20C** Progressive relaxation trains a person to physically relax muscles, thus reducing heart rate and blood pressure (p. 415).

Chapter 11   Personality

1B Personality is defined as a person's unique pattern of enduring psychological and behavioral characteristics (p. 424). **2A** The id contains the life and death instincts, is impulsive and pleasure seeking (p. 425). **3D** During the latency period, which lasts from about age five until puberty, an individual's focus is on education and social development (p. 427). **4D** Object relations theory sees today's problems as reflecting the impact of early relationships with caregivers and other significant people in a child's life (p. 428). **5A** Oscar's belief reflects an independent self system often seen in individualist cultures (p. 443). **6D** Although based on a small, culturally biased sample and not scientifically derived, Freud's theory is comprehensive and has profoundly affected psychology (p. 429). **7B** Trait theory assumes that personality traits are relatively stable, consistent, and predictable (p. 430). **8C** Allport believed that personality can be described using about seven central traits (pp. 430). **9D** Trait theorists have identified five main factors that make up personality (p. 431). **10C** According to Gray, people with an active behavioral approach system tend to experience positive emotions (pp. 432–433). **11B** Twin studies suggest that there are genetic predispositions toward particular personality traits and temperament (pp. 433–435). **12A** Internals expect outcomes and events to be controlled mainly by their own efforts (p. 437). **13C** Reciprocal determinism is a mutually influential interaction among cognitive patterns, the environment, and behavior (p. 437). **14D** According to Mischel, person variables and situation variables are important in explaining particular behaviors (pp. 438–439). **15C** Social-cognitive theories describe personality as patterns of thought and behavior that are learned though experience in social situations (p. 436). **16C** Conditions of worth are created when "people" are evaluated instead of their behavior (p. 440). **17B** A preoccupation with perceived need for material things and a devaluation of what one does have, reflects a deficiency orientation (p. 441). **18D** Unconscious needs, motives, and conflicts supposedly guide responses to the relatively unstructured stimuli of projective personality measures (p. 446). **19C** Research has found that those rated as ill-tempered as children are more likely to be aggressive in adulthood (pp. 444–445). **20B** Nonprojective personality measures are often used by potential employers to screen out employees who are likely to be unreliable or dishonest (p. 449).

Chapter 12 Psychological Disorders

1C Approximately 46 percent of the population in the United States have experienced a mental disorder at some point in their lives (p. 456). **2C** The practical approach defines abnormality based on the content, context, and consequence of behavior (p. 458). **3C** To be found not guilty by reason of insanity, the jury would have to find that Herman was insane at the time he committed the crime (p. 496). **4D** The diathesis-stress approach attributes abnormal behavior to the interaction of stress with biological, environmental, and psychological predispositions (p. 461). **5D** The global assessment of functioning is one evaluation axis of the DSM IV (p. 463). **6D** Social phobias involve anxiety about being criticized by others or acting in a way that is embarrassing or humiliating (p. 469). **7C** OCD involves an obsession with particular thoughts or images, which motivates repetitive, uncontrollable behaviors called compulsions (pp. 470–471). **8A** Conversion disorder involves functional impairment with no physical cause (p. 473). **9A** Severe pain in the absence of any physical problem is symptomatic of somatoform pain disorder (p. 474). **10A** Fugue reaction is disorder that includes a sudden loss of personal memory and the adoption of a new identity in a new place (p. 475). **11B** Sleep changes and weight gain or loss are typical of major depression (pp. 476–477). **12B** Depressed women, certain ethnic groups, males over forty-five and living alone, and those who talk about suicide do tend to be at elevated risk for committing suicide (pp. 478–479). **13A** Attribution is the process of explaining the causes of one's own and others' behavior; social-cognitive theorists see a depressive attributional style as partly responsible for depression (p. 482). **14B** Schizophrenia is characterized by abnormality in thinking, writing, speaking, affect, perception and attention, and personal identity. Positive symptoms are undesirable additions to a person's mental life (p. 484). **15D** Strong and long-lasting anxiety that is not focused on any particular object or situation marks generalized anxiety disorder (p. 470). **16C** The most common symptoms of paranoid schizophrenia include delusions of grandeur or persecution, which are often accompanied by anger, anxiety, or jealousy (p. 483). **17A** People diagnosed with antisocial personality disorder display impulsive, selfish, unscrupulous behavior and have few morals or deep feelings for others (pp. 488–489). **18D** The more violent forms of antisocial personality disorder are associated with the experience of abuse in childhood (pp. 489–491). **19D** Studies have shown that genetics and what people learn in their social and cultural environment play a role in alcoholism (p. 494). **20B** Children with autistic disorder usually show little attachment, poor eye contact, and asocial behavior (p. 493).

Chapter 13 Treatment of Psychological Disorders

1C As a part of psychodynamic therapy, the client reports all feelings, thoughts, memories, and images that come to mind in free association (p. 508). **2A** Gestalt therapy uses role playing, among other techniques, to help clients become more self-aware and self-accepting (p. 511). **3A** Licensed clinical psychologists generally hold a doctoral degree in clinical or counseling psychology (p. 507). **4B** Psychoanalysis focuses on revealing and working through unconscious conflicts (p. 508). **5C** Client-centered therapists use reflection, a paraphrased summary of the client's words that emphasizes the feelings and meanings that appear to go along with them (p. 510). **6B** Systematic desensitization therapy is a behavioral method for treating anxiety in which clients visualize a graduated series of anxiety-provoking stimuli while remaining relaxed (p. 513). **7C** By paraphrasing what Shanobi has said, her friend is responding in a manner consistent with reflection (pp. 510–511). **8D** Psychodynamic therapists seek to help clients gain insight by recognizing and understanding unconscious thoughts and emotions (p. 508). **9C** Behavioral therapists see compulsive behaviors as learned habits (pp. 511–512). **10B** Although there is much controversy about the effectiveness of therapy, there are therapies that have been empirically found to help clients. And overall, those seeking therapy get better more often than those who do not (pp. 520–521). **11C** Confidentiality is a critical aspect of therapy that can be violated only under special circumstances, as when the therapist believes the client's life is in danger (p. 528). **12B** Community psychologists are concerned with promoting social changes that prevent psychological problems (pp. 535–536). **13A** Flooding is a behavior therapy technique that places a client in a feared but harmless situation to extinguish the fear (p. 515). **14D** Cognitive restructuring, which is a part of cognitive behavior therapy, seeks to replace stress-producing thoughts with more constructive ones. (p. 517). **15B** ECT involves passing electric current through the brain to treat depression when other treatments have failed (pp. 528–529). **16D** Therapeutic psychoactive drugs may alter the functioning of particular neurotransmitter systems but they cannot change the type of neurotransmitters released into the brain (pp. 529–532). **17A** One of the most important elements of success with any therapy is the client-therapist relationship, which involves trust, disclosure, and empathy (p. 506). **18C** Neuroleptics are those that can reduce psychotic symptoms, but some of these drugs can cause severe side effects (p. 529). **19B** Anxiolytics are drugs that reduce anxiety and tension (p. 532). **20C** Simultaneous treatment of several clients has many positive features, but client improvement is not more rapid with this technique than with others (p. 518).

Chapter 14 Social Psychology

1C Jack is engaging in upward social comparison, comparing himself to others like himself, but who are at higher levels of accomplishment (p. 545). **2A** An experiment conducted by Greenberg et al. revealed that participants were significantly less upset by an anxiety-provoking experience if they had first received esteem-building feedback about their previous test performance (pp. 545–546). **3B** The first impression is formed quickly and is difficult to change (p. 548). **4C** The change in her date's behavior was probably due to a self-fulfilling prophecy (p. 549). **5D** A self-serving bias is the tendency to take credit for success and blame external causes for failures (p. 550). **6C** Richard will more likely be persuaded by evidence from the presenter (central route) since he is personally involved in the content of the presenter's message (p. 553). **7B** The amount of money Matteus received was too small to justify lying about what he thought about the lecture, so he changed his attitude toward the lecture, thus making his attitude consistent with his behavior (p. 554). **8C** The contact hypothesis suggests that stereotypes and prejudices can be reduced through cooperation and interdependence (p. 557). **9B** People tend to like others who have attitudes similar to their own, especially attitudes about other people (p. 559). **10A** Intimacy, commitment, and passion are characteristic of consummate love (pp. 560–561). **11D** A particularly powerful norm is reciprocity, the tendency to respond to others as they have acted toward you (p. 563). **12B** Deindividuation occurs when people in a group temporarily lose their individuality and behave in ways they otherwise would not (p. 563). **13C** Shawn is exhibiting social loafing by not putting in as much effort as other group members (pp. 583–584). **14A** Conformity results from unspoken group pressure (p. 564). **15B** Colleen used the door-in-the-face procedure, first asking for an unrealistic favor, then a smaller one (p. 567). **16D** The gender of the person giving the order is not a major factor determining whether someone will obey the order (pp. 569–570). **17A** According to frustration-aggression hypothesis, frustration produces a readiness to respond aggressively, which can later be environmentally triggered (p. 575). **18A** The presence of others actually tends to suppress helping behavior so the fewer people who witness Lenora's fall, the better chance she will have that one of them will help her (pp. 579–580). **19B** According to the evolutionary view, people display helping behaviors to improve the chances that some of their genes will survive in future generations (p. 582). **20B** Groupthink impairs a group's ability to realistically evaluate options and their own decisions (p. 585).

Chapter 15 Industrial and Organizational Psychology

1A I/O psychologists conduct research on behavior and mental processes in the workplace (p. 596). **2C** The information from a job analysis of the position is used to guide decisions about whom to hire (p. 598). **3A** A job-oriented approach describes the tasks involved in doing a job (p. 598). **4B** A job analysis identifies the KSAOs required for a specific position (p. 598). **5C** KSAOs are attributes or characteristics necessary to successfully perform a job (p. 598). **6C** Research has consistently shown that structured interviews are far more effective than unstructured interviews in leading to good hiring decisions (p. 600). **7A** Assessment centers are used primarily to determine an individual's suitability for a position and are often used to hire or promote managers (p. 600). **8D** Performance appraisals are used for all of these purposes (pp. 601). **9C** A theoretical criterion is a general statement of what we mean by good or poor performance (p. 601). **10A** Subjective measures of job performance take the form of judgments about various aspects of an employee's work (p. 602). **11C** A critical incident provides an example of what is considered to be effective or ineffective behavior by an employee *(p. 603)*. **12B** The most valuable training programs are those that teach knowledge or skills that can be applied or transferred to the workplace *(p. 607)*. **13C** Massed training is less expensive and disruptive to employees' work schedules but people do not retain as much after massed training as they do after distributed training *(p. 608)*. **14B** I/O psychologists usually conduct a training needs assessment, design the training, and evaluate the training, but do not usually deliver the training *(p. 606)*. **15D** In Maslow's theory the need for water is a physiological need; in Alderfer's theory it is an existence need *(p. 610)*. **16B** The facet approach to job satisfaction presumes that employees can be satisfied with some aspects of their jobs, but dissatisfied with others *(p. 612)*. **17B** Knowing that salary and pay raise decisions are made in a fair way can be more important to job satisfaction than to the amount of money employees receive *(p. 614)*. **18A** Employees steal more from their employers than do shoplifters *(p. 617)*. **19B** A work team is a special kind of workgroup in which the members' activities depend on one another; each person has a specialized task, and everyone is working toward a common goal *(p. 621)*. **20A** Leader-member exchange theory suggests that most leaders tend to adopt different styles with different kinds of subordinates *(p. 623)*.

Chapter 16 Neuropsychology

1A The experimental neuropsychologist's aim is to add to our knowledge of brain functioning among people in general, whereas the clinical neuropsychologist's aim is to use this knowledge to try to understand the problems that appear in particular individuals *(p. 633)*. **2C** Phrenology originated from the idea that particular brain areas, indicated by corresponding bumps in the skull just above them, controlled particular aspects of mental life *(p. 634)*. **3B** Broca's area was identified when people experiencing language difficulties were found to have left frontal brain lesions *(p. 634)*. **4A** Lesion analysis is research conducted by experimental neuropsychologists in an attempt to understand localization of function by looking at the results of brain damage *(pp. 635–636)*. **5A** The neuropsychologist evaluating Damian will most likely give him a battery of psychometric tests and compare his scores to established norms *(p. 637)*. **6C** A cardiovascular accident is the loss of blood supply to some part of the brain, resulting in disruption of some aspect of behavior or mental processes *(p. 638)*. **7D** Neurodegenerative disease affects a particular kind of brain cell, or cells in a particular part of the brain, causing them to be the first to stop working properly *(p. 640)*. **8D** Patients with Korsakoff's psychosis are prone to creating false memories *(p. 643)*. **9B** People with delirium enter alternating periods of abnormally impaired consciousness and abnormally elevated levels of consciousness *(p. 644)*. **10C** Anosognosia is a disorder of consciousness in which a person has difficulty becoming aware of the loss of neurological function *(p. 645)*. **11C** The pathway leading toward the ventrolateral temporal lobe has been called the "what" system because the cortical regions along this pathway help us to decide what it is that we are seeing *(p. 647)*. **12D** Prosopagnosia is a condition in which a person can no longer recognize faces, even their own *(p. 648)*. **13A** Hemineglect is a condition, usually occurring after a cardiovascular accident, that involves difficulty in seeing, responding to, or acting on information coming from either the right, or more often, the left side of the world *(p. 649)*. **14A** In the study cited, patients exhibiting hemineglect were not found to have visual deficits that explained their symptoms *(pp. 649–650)*. **15B** People who suffer damage to Broca's area display Broca's aphasia, which is seen mainly in the loss of language fluency *(p. 651)*. **16A** People with Wernicke's aphasia can still speak fluently and effortlessly, but what they say sounds like gibberish *(p. 651)*. **17C** Alexia without agraphia is a neurological deficit in which people have difficulty reading the letters that they themselves wrote *(p. 635)*. **18D** Alfreda is most likely experiencing aprosodia, a condition whereby she has lost the ability to use tone of voice to express meaning *(pp. 651–652)*. **19A** Dementia is a neuropsychological disorder in which there are significant and disruptive impairments in memory, as well as in perceptual ability, language, or learned motor skills *(p. 654)*. **20C** Research on Alzheimer's disease has found that patients with Alzheimer's have a different brain pathology than those experiencing normal aging *(pp. 654–655)*.

ANSWER KEY
Answers to In Review Questions

The questions at the bottom of each chapter's In Review charts are listed here, followed in parentheses by the correct answers. The questions are grouped under each chapter's title and by the name and page number of the In Review chart in which they appear.

Chapter 1   Introduction to the Science of Psychology

The Development of Psychology *(p. 13)*

1. Darwin's theory of evolution had an especially strong influence on ____ ism and ____ism. *(functionalism; behaviorism)*
2. Which school of psychological thought was founded by a European medical doctor? ____ *(Psychoanalysis)*
3. In the history of psychology, ____ was the first school of thought to appear. *(structuralism)*

Approaches to Psychology *(p. 17)*

1. Teaching people to be less afraid of heights reflects the ____ approach. *(behavioral)*
2. Charles Darwin was not a psychologist, but his work influenced the ____ approach to psychology. *(evolutionary)*
3. Assuming that people inherit mental disorders suggests a ____ approach. *(biological)*

Methods of Psychological Research *(p. 33)*

1. The ____ method is most likely to use a double-blind design. *(experimental)*
2. Research on a new treatment method is most likely to begin with ____. *(case studies)*
3. Studying language by listening to people in public places is an example of ____ research. *(naturalistic observation)*

Chapter 2   Biology and Behavior

Neurons, Neurotransmitters, and Receptors *(p. 50)*

1. For one neuron to communicate with another, a ____ has to cross the ____ between them. *(neurotransmitter; synapse)*
2. The nervous system's main functions are to ____, ____, and ____ information. *(receive; process; act on)*
3. The two main types of cells in the nervous system are ____ and ____. *(neurons; glial cells)*

Organization of the Brain *(p. 59)*

1. The oldest part of the brain is the ____. *(hindbrain)*
2. Cells that operate as the body's twenty-four-hour "time clock" are found in the ____. *(hypothalamus)*
3. Memory problems seen in Alzheimer's disease are related to shrinkage of the ____ *(hippocampus)*

Classes of Neurotransmitters *(p. 73)*

1. The main neurotransmitter for slowing, or inhibiting, brain activity is ____. *(GABA)*
2. A group of neurons that use the same neurotransmitter is called a ____. *(neurotransmitter system)*
3. Which neurotransmitter's activity causes brain damage during a stroke? ____ *(glutamate)*

Chapter 3   Sensation and Perception

Seeing *(p. 93)*

1. The ability to see in very dim light, depends on photoreceptors called ____. *(rods)*
2. Color afterimages are best explained by the ____ theory of color vision. *(opponent-process)*
3. Nearsightedness and farsightedness occur when images are not focused on the eye's ____. *(retina)*

Hearing *(p. 97)*

1. Sound energy is converted to neural activity in an inner ear structure called the ____. *(cochlea [or basilar membrane])*
2. Hearing loss due to damage to hair cells or the auditory nerve is called ____. *(nerve deafness)*
3. How high or low a sound sounds is called ____ and is determined by the ____ of a sound wave. *(pitch; frequency)*

Smell and Taste *(p. 101)*

1. The flavor of food arises from a combination of ____ and ____. *(taste; smell)*
2. Emotion and memory are linked especially closely to our sense of ____. *(smell)*
3. Perfume ads suggest that humans are affected by ____ that increase sexual attraction. *(pheromones)*

Body Senses *(p. 107)*

1. Gate control theory offers an explanation of why we sometimes do not feel ____. *(pain)*
2. Professional dancers look at the same spot as long as possible during repeated spins. They are trying to avoid the dizziness caused when the sense of ____ is overstimulated. *(equilibrium)*
3. Without your sense of ____, you would not be able to swallow food without choking. *(touch)*

Principles of Perceptual Organization and Constancy *(p. 115)*

1. The movement we see in movies, videos, and DVDs is due to a perceptual illusion called ____. *(the stroboscopic illusion)*
2. People who have lost an eye also lose the ability to use ____ depth cues, two of which are called ____ and ____. *(binocular; eye convergence; retinal disparity)*
3. The grouping principle of ____ allows you to identify objects seen through a picket fence. *(closure)*

Mechanisms of Pattern Recognition *(p. 119)*

1. Your ability to read a battered old sign that has some letters missing is a result of ____ processing. *(top-down)*
2. When stimulus features match the stimuli we are looking for, ____ takes place. *(recognition)*
3. Schemas can create a ____ that makes us more likely to perceive stimuli in a particular way. *(perceptual set)*

Chapter 4 Consciousness

Sleep and Sleep Disorders (p. 148)

1. Jet lag occurs because of a disruption in a traveler's ____. (*circadian rhythms [or human biological rhythms or sleep-wake cycle]*)
2. The importance of non-REM sleep is suggested by its appearance ____ in the night. (*early*)
3. The safest sleeping position for babies is ____. (*face up*)

Major Classes of Psychoactive Drugs (p. 162)

1. Physical dependence on a drug is a condition more commonly known as ____. (*addiction*)
2. Drugs that act as antagonists ____ the interaction of neurotransmitters and receptors. (*block*)
3. Drug effects are determined partly by what we learn to ____ the effects to be. (*expect*)

Chapter 5 Learning

Basic Processes of Classical Conditioning (p. 177)

1. If a person with a conditioned fear of spiders is triggered by the sight of other creatures that look like spiders, the person is demonstrating stimulus ____. (*generalization*)
2. Because of ____, we are more likely to learn a fear of snakes than a fear of cars. (*biopreparedness*)
3. Feeling sad upon hearing a song associated with a long-lost relationship illustrates ____. (*spontaneous recovery*)

Reinforcement and Punishment (p. 188)

1. Taking a pill can relieve headache pain, so people learn to do so through the process of ____ reinforcement. (*negative*)
2. The "walk" sign that tells people it is safe to cross the street is an example of a ____ stimulus. (*discriminative conditioned*)
3. Response rates tend to be higher under ____ schedules of reinforcement than under ____ schedules. (*ratio; interval*)

Chapter 6 Memory

Models of Memory (p. 213)

1. The value of elaborative rehearsal over maintenance rehearsal has been cited as evidence for the ____ model of memory. (*levels-of-processing*)
2. Deliberately trying to remember something means using your ____ memory. (*explicit*)
3. Playing the piano uses ____ memory. (*procedural*)

Storing New Memories (p. 218)

1. If you looked up a phone number but forgot it before you could call it, the information was probably lost from ____ memory. (*short-term*)
2. The capacity of short-term memory is about ____ to ____ items. (*five; nine*)
3. Encoding is usually ____ in short-term memory and ____ in long-term memory. (*acoustic; semantic*)

Factors Affecting Retrieval from Long-Term Memory (p. 220)

1. Stimuli called ____ help you recall information stored in long-term memory. (*retrieval cues*)
2. If it is easier to remember something in the place where you learned it, you have ____ learning. (*context-dependent*)
3. The tendency to remember the last few items in a list is called the ____ effect. (*recency*)

Improving Your Memory (p. 240)

1. Using mnemonic strategies and the PQ4R system to better remember course material are examples of the value of ____ rehearsal. (*elaborative*)

2. "Cramming" illustrates ____ practice that usually leads to ____ long-term retention than ____ practice. (*massed; poorer [or less]; distributed*)
3. To minimize forgetting, you should review lecture notes ____ after a lecture ends. (*immediately [or as soon as possible]*)

Chapter 7 Thought, Language, and Intelligence

Ingredients of Thought (p. 254)

1. Thinking is the manipulation of ____. (*mental representations*)
2. Arguments over what is "fair" occur because "fairness" is a ____ concept. (*natural*)
3. Your ____ of "hotel room" would lead you to expect yours to include a bathroom. (*schema*)

Solving Problems (p. 263)

1. People stranded without water could use their shoes to collect rain, but they may not do so because of an obstacle to problem solving called ____. (*functional fixedness*)
2. Because of the ____ heuristic, once sellers set a value on their house, they may refuse to take much less for it. (*anchoring*)
3. If you tackle a massive problem one small step at a time, you are using an approach called ____. (*decomposition or means-end analysis*)

Influences on IQ (p. 283)

1. Intelligence is influenced by both ____ and ____. (*heredity; environment*)
2. Children living in poverty tend to have ____ IQs than those in middle-class families. (*lower*)
3. IQs of children whose parents encourage learning tend to be ____ than those of children whose parents do not. (*higher*)

Chapter 8 Motivation and Emotion

Sources, Theories, and Types of Motivation (p. 303)

1. The fact that some people like roller coasters and other scary amusement park rides has been cited as evidence for the ____ theory of motivation. (*arousal*)
2. Evolutionary theories of motivation are modern outgrowths of theories based on ____. (*the instinct doctrine*)
3. The value of incentives can be affected by ____, ____, and ____ factors. (*physiological [or biological]; cognitive; social*)

Major Factors Controlling Hunger and Eating (p. 311)

1. People may eat when they are "full," suggesting that eating is not controlled by ____ alone. (*hunger*)
2. People with an eating disorder called ____ know that they have a problem; those with a disorder called ____ tend not to. (*bulimia; anorexia nervosa*)
3. The best strategy for lasting weight loss includes regular ____, as well as improved eating habits. (*exercise*)

Theories of Emotions (p. 333)

1. Research showing that there are pleasure centers in the brain has been cited in support of the ____ theory of emotions. (*Cannon-Bard [or central]*)
2. The use of polygraphs in lie detection is based on the ____ theory of emotions. (*James-Lange [or peripheral]*)
3. The process of attribution is most important to ____ theories of emotions. (*cognitive*)

Chapter 9 Human Development

Milestones of Cognitive Development in Infancy and Childhood (p. 357)

1. Research in cognitive development suggests that children form mental representations ____ than Piaget thought they did. (*earlier*)

2. Recognizing that changing the shape of clay doesn't change the amount of clay is evidence of a cognitive ability called ____. (*conservation*)
3. The appearance of object permanence signals the end of the ____ period. (*sensorimotor*)

Social and Emotional Development during Infancy and Childhood (*p. 373*)

1. As part of their social development, children learn ____, which tell them what patterns of appearance and behavior are associated with being male or female. (*gender roles*)
2. Teaching children to talk quietly in a restaurant is part of the process called ____. (*socialization*)
3. Strict rules and the threat of punishment are typical of ____ parenting. (*authoritarian*)

Milestones of Adolescence and Adulthood (*p. 385*)

1. The greatest threat to cognitive abilities in late adulthood is ____ disease. (*Alzheimer's*)
2. Adolescents' ____ identity may be more defining than their national citizenship. (*ethnic*)
3. Not stealing because "I might get caught" reflects the ____ stage of moral reasoning. (*preconventional*)

Chapter 10 Health, Stress, and Coping

Stress Responses and Stress Mediators (*p. 408*)

1. The friends and family we can depend on to help us deal with stressors are called our ____ network. (*social support*)
2. Fantasizing about winning money is a(n) ____-focused way of coping with financial stress. (*emotion*)
3. Sudden, extreme stressors may cause psychological and behavioral problems known as ____. (*posttraumatic stress disorder*)

Methods for Coping with Stress (*p. 416*)

1. Catastrophizing thoughts are best overcome through ____ coping strategies. (*cognitive*)
2. The first step in coping with stress is to ____ the sources and effects of your stressors. (*identify*)
3. True or false: It is best to rely on only one good coping strategy. ____ (*False*)

Chapter 11 Personality

Major Approaches to Personality (*p. 442*)

1. Tests that measure the five factor model's dimensions of personality are based on the ____ approach to personality. (*trait*)
2. The role of learning is most prominent in the ____ approach to personality. (*social-cognitive*)
3. Object relations and attachment theories are modern variants on ____ personality theories. (*psychodynamic*)

Personality Measures (*p. 449*)

1. Projective personality measures are based on the ____ approach to personality. (*psychodynamic*)
2. The NEO-PI-3 and the MMPI-2-RF are examples of ____ tests. (*nonprojective*)
3. Most personality researchers use ____ tests in their work. (*nonprojective*)

Chapter 12 Psychological Disorders

Anxiety, Somatoform, and Dissociative Disorders (*p. 476*)

1. Concern that it may be triggered by media stories or therapists' suggestions has made ____ the most controversial of the dissociative disorders. (*dissociative identity disorder*)
2. A person who sleepwalks but is not able to walk when awake is showing signs of ____. (*conversion disorder*)

3. Panic disorder sometimes leads to another anxiety disorder called ____. (*agoraphobia*)

Affective Disorders (*p. 480*)

1. The risk of suicide is associated with ____ more than with any other disorder. (*depression*)
2. Cyclothymic personality is the bipolar version of ____. (*dysthymic disorder*)
3. Women are ____ likely than men to try suicide, but men are ____ likely to succeed. (*more; more*)

Schizophrenia (*p. 487*)

1. The ____ approach forms the basis of the vulnerability theory of schizophrenia. (*diathesis-stress*)
2. Hallucinations are ____ symptoms of schizophrenia; lack of emotion is a ____ symptom. (*positive; negative*)
3. Patients with schizophrenia who were able to finish school are ____ likely to show improvement. (*more*)

Chapter 13 Treatment of Psychological Disorders

Approaches to Psychological Treatment (*p. 520*)

1. Object relations therapy and interpersonal therapy are both contemporary examples of the ____ approach to psychological treatment. (*psychodynamic*)
2. Imagining increasingly fear-provoking stimuli while relaxed is a ____ treatment method called ____. (*behavioral; systematic desensitization*)
3. Reflection is an interviewing technique associated mainly with the ____ approach to treatment. (*humanistic [or nondirective]*)

Chapter 14 Social Psychology

Some Biases in Social Perception (*p. 551*)

1. The fundamental attribution error appears to be somewhat less likely to occur among people in ____ cultures. (*collectivist*)
2. First impressions form ____, but change ____. (*quickly; slowly*)
3. If you believed that immigrants' successes are due to government help but that their failures are due to laziness, you would be committing the ____ error. (*ultimate attribution error*)

Forming and Changing Attitudes (*p. 555*)

1. According to the elaboration likelihood model, people are more likely to pay close attention to the content and logic of a persuasive message if the ____ route to attitude change has been activated. (*central*)
2. Holding attitudes that are similar to those of your friends illustrates the importance of ____ in attitude formation (*learning*)
3. According to cognitive dissonance theory, we tend to reduce conflict between attitudes and behaviors by changing our ____. (*attitudes*)

Types of Social Influence (*p. 572*)

1. Joining the end of a ticket line is an example of ____, whereas forming two lines when a theater employee requests it is an example of ____. (*conformity; compliance*)
2. Seeing someone disobey a questionable order makes people ____ likely to obey the order themselves. (*less*)
3. Pricing your used car for more than you expect to get, then agreeing to reduce it to make a sale, is an example of the ____ approach to gaining compliance. (*door-in-the-face*)

Prosocial Behavior (*p. 582*)

1. If you could save only one person from a burning house, the ____ theory of prosocial behavior would predict that it would be your own child rather than, say, a grandparent. (*evolutionary*)

2. Are you more likely to receive help in a nearly empty bus or a crowded bus terminal? ____. *(A nearly empty bus)*
3. People who have empathy for others are ____ likely to be helpful. *(more)*

Chapter 15 Industrial/Organizational Psychology

Assessing People, Jobs, and Job Performance *(p. 604)*

1. Lists of critical incidents are contained in ____-focused employee rating forms. *(behavior)*
2. A potential employer might use a two-day ____ to measure your skill at the job you want. *(assessment center)*
3. In general, ____ interviews are more useful in employee selection than ____ interviews. *(structured; unstructured)*

Recruiting, Selecting, and Training Employees *(p. 610)*

1. Employees tend to remember more from a training program when it is set up on a ____ rather than a ____ schedule. *(distributed; massed)*
2. Depending on "walk-in" applications is usually acceptable when hiring ____ level employees. *(low [or entry])*
3. Ensuring that your hiring criteria actually predict employees' job performance requires a ____. *(validation study)*

Chapter 16 Neuropsychology

Foundations of Neuropsychology *(p. 636)*

1. A person who studies individual patients to determine what kind of brain damage each one happens to have is called a ____. *(clinical neuropsychologist)*
2. The case of "Tan" helped to establish the principle of ____. *(localization of function)*
3. In alexia without agraphia, the brain areas that control reading and writing are intact but cannot interact. This condition is called a ____. *(disconnection syndrome)*

Mechanisms of Brain Dysfunction *(p. 640)*

1. The brain floats in a bath of ____ inside the skull. *(cerebrospinal fluid)*
2. The brain needs a constant flow of fresh ____ all the time. *(blood)*
3. Cerebrovascular accidents rank as the number ____ cause of death in the developed world. *(three)*

Major Neuropsychological Problems *(p. 656)*

1. A patient who has become forgetful but has no problems in other areas of cognitive function may be said to have ____. *(mild cognitive impairment)*
2. A dementia patient whose hippocampus is relatively intact and can still form new memories probably has ____ dementia. *(vascular)*
3. A patient with thiamine deficiency who is forgetful but makes up memories and believes they are real probably has ____. *(Korsakoff's psychosis)*

REFERENCES

Aaron, D. J., Chang, Y.-F., Markovic, N., & LaPorte, R. E. (2003). Estimating the lesbian population: A capture-recapture approach. *Journal of Epidemiology and Community Health, 57,* 207–209.

Abad, V. C., & Guilleminault, C. (2004). Review of rapid eye movement behavior sleep disorders. *Current Neurology and Neuroscience Reports, 4,* 157–163.

Abar, C. C. (2012). Examining the relationship between parenting types and patterns of student alcohol-related behavior during the transition to college. *Psychology of Addictive Behaviors, 26*(1), 20–29. doi:10.1037/a0025108.

Abarbanell, L., & Hauser, M. D. (2010). Mayan morality: An exploration of permissible harms. *Cognition, 115*(2), 207–224. doi:10.1016/j.cognition.2009.12.007.

Abbott, B. B., Schoen, L. S., & Badia, P. (1984). Predictable and unpredictable shock: Behavioral measures of aversion and physiological measures of stress. *Psychological Bulletin, 96,* 45–71.

Abbott, R. D., White, L. R., Ross, G. W., Masaki, K. H., Curb, J. D., & Petrovitch, H. (2004). Walking and dementia in physically capable elderly men. *Journal of the American Medical Association, 292,* 1447–1453.

AbdelMalik, P., Husted, J., Chow, E. W., & Bassett, A. S. (2003). Childhood head injury and expression of schizophrenia in multiply affected families. *Archives of General Psychiatry, 60,* 231–236.

Abe, T., Komada, Y., Nishida, Y., Hayashida, K., & Inoue, Y. (2010). Short sleep duration and long spells of driving are associated with the occurrence of Japanese drivers' rear-end collisions and single-car accidents. *Journal of Sleep Research, 19*(2), 310–316.

Abel, N. J., & O'Brien, J. M. (2010). EMDR treatment of comorbid PTSD and alcohol dependence: A case example. *Journal of EMDR Practice and Research, 4*(2), 50–59. doi:10.1891/1933-3196.4.2.50.

Abelson, J. L., Liberzon, I., Young, E. A., & Khan, S. (2005). Cognitive modulation of the endocrine stress response to a pharmacological challenge in normal and panic disorder subjects. *Archives of General Psychiatry, 62,* 668–675.

Abler, B., Hahlbrock, R., Unrath, A., Gron, G., & Kassubek, J. (2009). At-risk for pathological gambling: Imaging neural reward processing under chronic dopamine agonists. *Brain,132,* 2396–2402.

Abraham, S., & Kellow, J. (2011). Exploring eating disorder quality of life and functional gastrointestinal disorders among eating disorder patients. *Journal of Psychosomatic Research, 70*(4), 372–377.

Abraham, W. C. (2006). Memory maintenance: The changing nature of neural mechanisms. *Current Directions in Psychological Science, 15,* 5–8.

Abramis, D. J. (1994). Work role ambiguity, job satisfaction, and job performance: Meta-analyses and review. *Psychological Reports, 75,* 1411–1433.

Abramowitz, J. S., & Braddock, A. E. (2006). Hypochondriasis: Conceptualization, treatment, and relationship to obsessive-compulsive disorder. *Psychiatric Clinics of North America, 29,* 503–519.

Abrams, R. L., & Greenwald, A. G. (2000). Parts outweigh the whole (word) in unconscious analysis of meaning. *Psychological Science, 11,* 118–124.

Abrams, D., & Hogg, M. A. (2010). Social identity and self-categorization In J. F. Dovidio, M. Hewstone, P. Glick, & V. M. Esses (Eds.), *The SAGE handbook of prejudice, stereotyping and discrimination.* London: Sage.

Abrams, D. I., Jay, C. A., Shade, S. B., Vizoso, H., Reda, H., Press, S., Kelly, M. E., Rowbotham, M. C., & Petersen, K. L. (2007). Cannabis in painful HIV-associated sensory neuropathy. *Neurology, 68,* 515–521.

Abrantes-Pais, F. de N., Friedman, J. K., Lovallo, W. R., & Ross, E. D. (2007). Psychological or physiological: Why are tetraplegic patients content? *Neurology, 69,* 261–267.

Abreu, J. M. (1999). Conscious and unconscious African American stereotypes: Impact on first impression and diagnostic ratings by therapists. *Journal of Consulting and Clinical Psychology, 67,* 387–393.

Accornero, V. H., Anthony, J. C., Morrow, C. E., Xue, L., Mansoor, E., Johnson, A. L., & .. Bandstra, E. S. (2011). Estimated effect of prenatal cocaine exposure on examiner-rated behavior at age 7 years. *Neurotoxicology and Teratology, 33*(3), 370–378. doi:10.1016/j.ntt.2011.02.014.

Acerbi, A., Enquist, M., & Ghirlanda, S. (2009). Cultural evolution and individual development of openness and conservatism. *Proceedings of the National Academy of Sciences, 106,* 18931–18935.

Achenbach, T. M. (2011). Definitely more than measurement error: But how should we understand and deal with informant discrepancies? *Journal of Clinical Child and Adolescent Psychology, 40,* 80–86.

Acitelli, L. K. (1992). Gender differences in relationship awareness and marital satisfaction among young married couples. *Personality and Social Psychology Bulletin, 18,* 102–110.

Acker, T., & Acker, H. (2004). Cellular oxygen sensing need in CNS function: Physiological and pathological implications. *Journal of Experimental Biology, 207*(Pt. 18), 3171–3188.

Ackerman, J. P., Riggins, T., & Black, M. M. (2010). A review of the effects of prenatal cocaine exposure among school-aged children. *Pediatrics, 125,* 554–565.

Ackerman, P. L. (2007). New developments in understanding skilled performance. *Current Directions in Psychological Science, 16,* 235–239.

Acocella, J. (1998, April 6). The politics of hysteria. *New Yorker,* pp. 64–79.

Adachi, P. J., & Willoughby, T. (2011). The effect of violent video games on aggression: Is it more than just the violence? *Aggression and Violent Behavior 16,* 55–62. doi:10.1016/j.avb.2010.12.002.

Adachi-Mejia, A. M., Longacre, M. R., Gibson, J. J., Beach, M. L., Titus-Ernstoff, L. T., & Dalton, M. A. (2007). Children with a TV in their bedroom at higher risk for overweight. *International Journal of Obesity, 31,* 644–651.

Adair, J. C., Gilmore, R. L., Fennell, E. B., Gold, M., & Heilman, K. M. (1995). Anosognosia during intracarotid barbiturate anesthesia: Unawareness or amnesia for weakness. *Neurology, 45*(2), 241–243.

Adam, E. K., Gunnar, M. R., & Tanaka, A. (2004). Adult attachment, parent emotion, and observed parenting behavior: Mediator and moderator models. *Child Development, 75,* 110–122.

Adam, H., Shirako, A., & Maddux, W. W. (2010). Cultural Variance in the Interpersonal Effects of Anger in Negotiations. *Psychological Science (Sage Publications Inc.), 21*(6), 882–889. doi:10.1177/0956797610370755.

Adams, D. M., Mayer, R. E., MacNamara, A., Koenig, A., & Wainess, R. (2011). Narrative games for learning: Testing the discovery and narrative hypotheses. *Journal Of Educational Psychology,* doi:10.1037/a0025595.

Adams, G. A., & Rau, B. L. (2011). Putting off tomorrow to do what you want today planning for retirement. *American Psychologist, 66*(3), 180–192. doi:10.1037/a0022131.

Adams, K. F., Schatzkin, A., Harris, T. B., Kipnis, V., Mouw, T., Ballard-Barbash, R., et al. (2006). Overweight, obesity, and mortality in a large prospective cohort of persons 50 to 71 years old. *New England Journal of Medicine, 355,* 763–778.

Adams, N. (2012). Skinner's Walden Two: An anticipation of positive psychology? *Review of General Psychology, 16*(1), 1–9. doi:10.1037/a0026439

Adams, R. J. (1998). Human newborn color vision: Measurement with chromatic stimuli varying in excitation purity. *Journal of Experimental Child Psychology, 68*(1), 22–34.

Adams, W. J., Graf, E. W., & Ernst, M. O. (2004). Experience can change the "light from above" prior. *Nature Neuroscience, 7,* 1057–1058.

Adank, P., Hagoort, P., & Bekkering, H. (2010). Imitation improves language comprehension. *Psychological Science, 21*(12), 1903–1909. doi:10.1177/0956797610389192.

Addington, J., Piskulic, D., & Marshall, C. (2010). Psychosocial Treatments for Schizophrenia. *Current Directions in Psychological Science, 19*(4), 260–263. doi:10.1177/0963721410377743.

Addis, D. R., Wong, A. T., & Schacter, D. L. (2007). Remembering the past and imagining the future: common and distinct neural substrates during event construction and elaboration. *Neuropsychologia, 45,* 1363–1377.

Addis, M. E., & Krasnow, A. D. (2000). A national survey of practicing psychologists' attitudes toward psychotherapy treatment manuals. *Journal of Consulting and Clinical Psychology, 68,* 331–339.

Adelabu, D. H. (2008). Future time perspective, hope, and ethnic identity among African American adolescents. *Urban Education, 43,* 347–360.

Adelsheim, C. (2011). Functional magnetic resonance detection of deception: Great as fundamental research, inadequate as substantive evidence. *Mercer Law Review, 62*(3), 885–908.

Ader, R. (2001). Psychoneuroimmunology. *Current Directions in Psychological Science, 10,* 94–98.

Adesope, O. O., & Nesbit, J. C. (2012). Verbal redundancy in multimedia learning environments: A meta-analysis. *Journal of Educational Psychology, 104*(1), 250–263. doi:10.1037/a0026147

Adler, T. (1993, March). Bad mix: Combat stress, decisions. *APA Monitor,* p. 1.

Adolphs, R., Tranel, D., & Damasio, A. R. (1998). The human amygdala in social judgment. *Nature, 393*(6684), 470–474.

Adolphs, R., Tranel, D., Koenigs, M., & Damasio, A. R. (2005). Preferring one taste over another without recognizing either. *Nature Neuroscience, 8,* 860–861.

Adorno, T. W., Frenkel-Brunswik, E., Levinson, D. J., & Sanford, R. N. (1950). *The authoritarian personality.* New York: Harper & Row.

Aduriz, M.E., Bluthgen, C. & Knopfler, C. (2009). Helping child flood victims using group EMDR intervention in Argentina: Treatment outcome and gender differences. *International Journal of Stress Management. 16,* 138–153.

Aggarwal, R., Cheshire, N., & Darzi, A. (2008). Endovascular simulation-based training. *Surgeon, 6*(4), 196–197.

Agnew, C. R., Van Lange, P. A. M., Rusbult, C. E., & Langston, C. A. (1998). Cognitive interdependence: Commitment and the mental representation of close relationships. *Journal of Personality and Social Psychology, 74,* 939–954.

Aguiler, A., & Munoz, R. F. (2011). Text messaging as an adjunct to CBT in low-income populations: A usability and feasibility pilot study. *Professional Psychology: Research and Practice, 42,* 472–478.

Aharonov, R., Segev, L., Meilijson, I., & Ruppin, E. (2003). Localization of function via lesion analysis. *Neural Computation, 15*(4), 885–913.

Ahearn, D. J., Sanders, M. J., & Turcotte, C. (2010). Ergonomic design for dental offices. *Work: Journal of Prevention, Assessment & Rehabilitation, 35*(4), 495–503.

Ahima, R. S., & Flier, J. S. (2000). Leptin. *Annual Review of Physiology, 62,* 413–437.

Ahmed. I. & Thorpy, M. (2010). Clinical features, diagnosis and treatment of narcolepsy. *Clinics in Chest Medicine, 31*(2), 371–381.

Ahn-Redding, H. (2008). *The insanity defense the world over.* Lanham, MD: Lexington Books. Aiello, J. R., & Douthitt, E. A. (2001). Social facilitation from Triplett to electronic performance monitoring. *Group Dynamics, 5,* 163–180.

Ahola, A. (2012). How reliable are eyewitness memories? Effects of retention interval, violence of act, and gender stereotypes on observers' judgments of their own memory regarding witnessed act and perpetrator. *Psychology, Crime & Law, 18*(5), 491–503. doi:10.1080/1068316X.2010.509316

Aiken, L. R. (1994). *Psychological testing and assessment* (8th ed.). Boston: Allyn & Bacon.

Ainsworth, M. D. S., Blehar, M. D., Waters, E., & Wall, S. (1978). *Patterns of attachment: A psychological study of the Strange Situation.* Hillsdale, NJ: Erlbaum.

Ainsworth, M. D. S., & Bowlby, J. (1991). An ethological approach to personality development. *American Psychologist, 46,* 333–341.

Ainsworth, M. D. S., & Marvin, R. S. (1995). On the shaping of attachment theory and research: An interview with Mary D. S. Ainsworth (Fall 1994). *Monographs of the Society for Research in Child Development, 60,* 3–21.

Ajzen, I., & Gilbert-Cote, N. (2008). Attitudes and the prediction of behavior. In W. Crano & R. Prislin (Eds.), *Attitudes and attitude change* (pp. 289–311). New York: Psychology Press.

Akbarian, S. (2010). The molecular pathology of schizophrenia: Focus on histone and DNA modifications. *Brain Research Bulletin, 83,* 103–107. doi:10.1016/j.brainresbull.2009.08.018

Akerstedt, T. (2007). Altered sleep/wake patterns and mental performance. *Physiology and Behavior, 90,* 209–218.

Akin, W. M., & Turner, S. M. (2006). Toward understanding ethnic and cultural factors in the interviewing process. *Psychotherapy: Theory, Research, Practice, Training, 43,* 50–64.

Akins, C. K., & Zentall, T. R. (1998). Imitation in Japanese quail: The role of reinforcement of demonstrator responding. *Psychonomic Bulletin and Review, 5,* 694–697.

Albarracín, D., Durantini, M. R., Allison, E., Gunnoe, J. B., & Leeper, J. (2008). Beyond the most willing audiences: A meta-intervention to increase exposure to HIV-prevention programs by vulnerable populations. *Health Psychology, 27,* 638–644.

Albarracín, D., Johnson, B. T., Fishbein, M., & Muellerleile, P. A. (2001). Theories of reasoned action and planned behavior as models of condom use: A meta-analysis. *Psychological Bulletin, 127,* 142–161.

Albee, G. W. (1968). Conceptual models and manpower requirements in psychology. *American Psychologist, 23,* 317–320.

Albee, G. W. (2002). Just say no to psychotropic drugs! *Journal of Clinical Psychology, 58,* 635–648.

Albee, G. W. (2006). Historical overview of primary prevention of psychopathology. *Journal of Primary Prevention, 27,* 449–456.

Albert, K. A., Hemmings, H. C., Adamo, A. I. B., Potkin, S. G., Akbarian, S., Sandman, C. A. (2002). Evidence for decreased DARPP-32 in the prefrontal cortex of patients with schizophrenia. *Archives of General Psychiatry, 59,* 705–712.

Albert, M. S., Savage, C. R., Blazer, D., Jones, K., Berkman, L., & Seeman, T. (1995). Predictors of cognitive change in older persons: MacArthur studies of successful aging. *Psychology and Aging, 10,* 578–589.

Alberti, R., & Emmons, M. (2008). *Your perfect right: Assertiveness and equality in your life and relationships* (9th ed.). Atascadero, CA: Impact Publishers.

Alberto, P. A., Troutman, A. C., & Feagin, J. R. (2002). *Applied behavior analysis for teachers* (6th ed.). Englewood Cliffs, NJ: Prentice Hall.

Alcock, J. (2001). *Animal behavior: An evolutionary approach* (7th ed.). Sunderland, MA: Sinauer.

Alderfer, C. P. (1969). An empirical test of a new theory of human needs. *Organizational Behavior and Human Performance, 4,* 142–175.

Aldridge, J. W. (2005). Interpreting correlation as causation? *Science, 308*(5724), 954.

Aleman, A., Kahn, R. S., & Selten, J.-P. (2003). Sex differences in the risk of schizophrenia: Evidence from meta-analysis. *Archives of General Psychiatry, 60,* 565–571.

Alerman, A., & Larøi, F. (2008). *Hallucinations: The science of idiosyncratic perception.* Washington, DC: American Psychological Association.

Aleisa, A. M., Alzoubi, K. H., & Alkadhi, K. A. (2011). Post-learning REM sleep deprivation impairs long-term memory: Reversal by acute nicotine treatment. *Neuroscience Letters, 499*(1), 28–31.

Alessi, S. M., Roll, J. M., Reilly, M. P., & Johanson, C.-E. (2002). Establishment of a diazepam preference in human volunteers following a differential-conditioning history of placebo versus diazepam choice. *Experimental and Clinical Psychopharmacology, 10,* 77–83.

Alexander, G., Eaton, I., & Egan, K. (2010). Cracking the code of electronic games: Some lessons for educators. *Teachers College Record, 112*(7), 1830–1850.

Alexander, G. M., & Hines, M. (2002). Sex differences in response to children's toys in non-human primates (*Cercopithecus aethiops sabaeus*). *Evolution and Human Behavior, 23,* 467–479.

Alexander, K. W., Quas, J. A., Goodman, G. S., Ghetti, S., Edelstein, R. S., Redlich, A. D., et al. (2005). Traumatic impact predicts long-term memory for documented child sexual abuse. *Psychological Science, 16,* 33–40.

Alexander Pollatsek, A., Romoser, M. R. E., & Fisher, D. L. (2012). Identifying and remediating failures of selective attention in older drivers. *Current Directions in Psychological Science, 21,* 3–7, doi:10.1177/0963721411429459

Alicke, M., LoSchiavo, F. M., Zerbst, J., & Zhang, S. (1997). The person who outperforms me is a genius: Maintaining perceived competence in upward social comparisons. *Journal of Personality and Social Psychology, 73,* 781–789.

Alison, L., Kebbell, M., & Lewis, P. (2006). Considerations for experts in assessing the credibility of recovered memories of child sexual abuse: The importance of maintaining a case-specific focus. *Psychology, Public Policy, and Law, 12,* 419–441.

Alkire, M. T., Hudetz, A. G., & Tononi, G. (2008). Consciousness and anesthesia. *Science, 322,* 876–880.

Al-Kubaisy, T. F., & Jassim, A. L. (2003). The efficacy of assertive training in the acquisition of social skills in Iraqi social phobics. *Arab Journal of Psychiatry, 14,* 68–72.

Allen, B. P. (2006). *Personality theories: Development, growth, and diversity* (5th ed.). Boston, MA: Pearson.

Allen, J. B., Kenrick, D. T., Linder, D. E., & McCall, M. A. (1989). Arousal and attraction: A response-facilitation alternative to misattribution and negative-reinforcement models. *Journal of Personality and Social Psychology, 57,* 261–270.

Allen, J. J. B. (2002). The role of psychophysiology in clinical assessment: ERPs in the evaluation of memory. *Psychophysiology, 39,* 261–280.

Allen, J. J. B., & Iacono, W. G. (2001). Assessing the validity of amnesia in dissociative identity disorder: A dilemma for the DSM and the courts. *Psychology, Public Policy and Law, 7,* 311–344.

Allen, M. T., & Matthews, K. A. (1997). Hemodynamic responses to laboratory stressors in children and adolescents: The influences of age, race and gender. *Psychophysiology, 34,* 329–339.

Allen, S. R., & Thorndike, R. M. (1995). Stability of the WPPSI-R and WISC-III factor structure using cross-validation of covariance structure models. *Journal of Psychoeducational Assessment, 13,* 3–20.

Alliger, G. M., & Dwight, S. A. (2000). A meta-analytic investigation of the susceptibility of integrity tests to faking and coaching. *Educational and Psychological Measurement, 60,* 59–72.

Allik, J., & McCrae, R. R. (2004). Toward a geography of personality traits: Patterns of profiles across 36 cultures. *Journal of Cross-Cultural Psychology, 35,* 13–28.

Alloy, L. B., & Abramson, L. Y. (2010). The role of the Behavioral Approach System (BAS) in bipolar spectrum disorders. *Current Directions in Psychological Science, 19*(3), 189–194. doi:10.1177/0963721410370292

Alloy, L. B., Abramson, L. Y., Cogswell, A., Hughes, M. E., & Iacoviello, B. M. (2008). Cognitive vulnerability to depression: Implications for prevention. In M. T. Tsuang, W. S. Stone, & M. J. Lyons (Eds.) *Recognition and prevention of major mental and substance use disorders* (pp. 97–113). Arlington, VA: American Psychiatric Publishing.

Alloy, L. B., Abramson, L. Y., Whitehouse, W. G., Hogan, M. E., Panzarella, C., & Rose, D. T. (2006). Prospective incidence of first onsets and recurrences of depression in individuals at high and low cognitive risk for depression. *Journal of Abnormal Psychology, 115,* 145–156.

Alloy, L. B., Bender, R. E., Whitehouse, W. G., Wagner, C. A., Liu, R. T., Grant, D. A., & ... Abramson, L. Y. (2011). High Behavioral Approach System (BAS) sensitivity, reward responsiveness, and goal-striving predict first onset of bipolar spectrum disorders: A prospective behavioral high-risk design. *Journal of Abnormal Psychology,121,* 339–351. doi:10.1037/a0025877

Allport, G. W., & Odbert, H. S. (1936). Trait names: A psycholexical study. *Psychological Monographs, 47*(1, Whole No. 211).

Allsop, D. J., Norberg, M. M., Copeland, J., Fu, S., & Budney, A. J. (2011). The Cannabis Withdrawal Scale development: Patterns and predictors of cannabis withdrawal and distress. *Drug and Alcohol Dependence, 119*(1–2), 123–129.

Almeida, D. M. (2005). Resilience and vulnerability to daily stressors assessed via diary methods. *Current Directions in Psychological Science, 14,* 64–68.

Al-Saleh, I., El-Doush, I., Grisellhi, B., & Coskun, S. (2010). The effect of caffeine consumption on the success rate of pregnancy as well various performance parameters of in-vitro fertilization treatment. *Medical Science Monitor, 16*(12), CR598–605.

Al-Shammary, N., Awan, S., Butt, K., & Yoo, J. (2007). Internet use before consultation with a health professional. *Primary Health Care, 17*(10), 18–21.

Alston, J. H. (1920). Spatial condition of the fusion of warmth and cold in heat. *American Journal of Psychology, 31,* 303–312.

Altemeyer, B., & Hunsberger, B. (2005). Fundamentalism and authoritarianism. In R. Paloutzian & C. Park (Eds.), *Handbook of the psychology of religion and spirituality* (pp. 378–393). New York: Guilford Press.

Althoff, R. R., Faraone, S. V., Rettew, D. C., Morley, C. P., & Hudziak, J. J. (2005). Family, twin, adoption, and molecular genetic studies of juvenile bipolar disorder. *Bipolar Disorders, 7,* 598–609.

Altman, L. K. (2000, April 10). Company developing marijuana for medical uses. *New York Times.* Retrieved December 13, 2004, from http://www.mapinc.org/drugnews/v00/n474/a01.html.

Aluja-Fabregat, A., & Torrubia-Beltri, R. (1998). Viewing of mass media violence, perception of violence, personality and academic achievement. *Personality and Individual Differences, 25,* 973–989.

Alvarez, K., Salas, E., & Garofano, C. M. (2004). An integrated model of training evaluation and effectiveness. *Human Resource Development and Review, 3,* 385–416.

Alvaro, E. M., & Crano, W. D. (1997). Indirect minority influence: Evidence for leniency in source evaluation and counterargumentation. *Journal of Personality and Social Psychology, 72,* 949–964.

Alzheimer's Association. (2009). 2009 Alzheimer's disease facts and figures. *Alzheimer's & Dementia: The Journal of the Alzheimer's Association, 5*(3), 234–70.

Amabile, T. M. (1996). *Creativity in context: Update to "The Social Psychology of Creativity."* Boulder, CO: Westview.

Amabile, T. M. (2001). Beyond talent: John Irving and the passionate craft of creativity. *American Psychologist, 56,* 333–336.

Amabile, T. M., Hennessey, B. A., & Grossman, B. S. (1986). Social influences on creativity: The effects of contracted-for reward. *Journal of Personality and Social Psychology, 50,* 14–23.

Amaro, E., Jr., & Barker, G. J. (2006). Study design in fMRI: Basic principles. *Brain and Cognition, 60,* 220–232.

Ambadar, Z., Schooler, J. W., & Cohn, J. F. (2005). Deciphering the enigmatic face. *Psychological Science, 16,* 403–410.

Ambrosini, E., Sinigaglia, C., & Costantini, M. (2012). Tie my hands, tie my eyes. *Journal of Experimental Psychology: Human Perception and Performance, 38*(2), 263–266. doi:10.1037/a0026570

Amedi, A., Merabet, L. B., Bermpohl, F., & Pascual-Leone, A. (2005). The occipital cortex in the blind. *Current Directions in Psychological Science, 14,* 306–311.

American Educational Research Association, American Psychological Association, & National Council on Measurement in Education. (1999). *Standards for educational and psychological testing.* Washington, DC: American Educational Research Association.

American Psychiatric Association. (1994). *Diagnostic and statistical manual of mental disorders* (4th ed.). Washington, DC: American Psychiatric Association.

American Psychiatric Association. (2000). *Diagnostic and statistical manual of mental disorders* (4th ed., text rev.). Washington DC: Author.

American Psychiatric Association. (2003). *The insanity defense.* Retrieved May 26, 2004, from http://www.psych.org/public_info/insanity.cfm.

American Psychological Association. (1993). *Violence and youth: Psychology's response.* Washington: DC: American Psychological Association.

American Psychological Association. (2002a). *Answers to your questions about sexual orientation and homosexuality.* Retrieved December 13, 2004, from http://www. apa.org/pubinfo/answers.html#whatis.

American Psychological Association. (2002b). Ethical principles of psychologists and code of conduct. *American Psychologist, 57,* 1060–1073.

American Psychological Association. (2009). Medical cost offset. In *Resources for practicing psychologists: The practice directorate.* Retrieved April 23, 2009, from http://www.apa.org/ practice/offset3.html.

American Psychological Association Committee on Animal Research and Ethics. (2009). *Research with animals in psychology.* Retrieved from http://www.apa.org/ science/animal2.html.

American Psychological Association Presidential Task Force on Evidence-Based Practice. (2006). Evidence-based practice in psychology. *American Psychologist, 61,* 271–285.

American Psychological Association Task Force on the Sexualization of Girls. (2007). *Report of the APA Task Force on the Sexualization of Girls.* Washington, DC: American Psychological Association.

Ames, D. R., Kammrath, L. K., Suppes, A., & Bolger, N. (2010). Not so fast: The (not-quite-complete) dissociation between accuracy and confidence in thin-slice impressions. *Personality and Social Psychology Bulletin, 36,* 264–277.

Ames, R., & Ames, C. A. (1984). Introduction. In R. Ames & C. A. Ames (Eds.), *Research on motivation in education: Student motivation* (Vol. 1, pp. 1–11). Orlando, FL: Academic Press.

Amodio, D. M., & Lieberman, M. D (2009). Pictures in our heads: Contributions of fMRI to the study of prejudice and stereotyping. In T. D. Nelson, (Ed.), *Handbook of prejudice, stereotyping, and discrimination* (pp. 347–365). New York: Psychology Press.

Amodio, D. M., & Devine, P. G. (2009). On the functions of implicit prejudice and stereotyping: Insights from social neuroscience. In R. E. Petty, R. H. Fazio, & P. Briñol (Eds.), *Attitudes: Insights from the new wave of implicit measures* (pp. 192–229). Hillsdale, NJ: Erlbaum.

Amodio, D. M., Harmon-Jones, E., Devine, P. G., Curtin, J. J., Hartley, S. L., & Covert, A. E. (2004). Neural signals for the detection of unintentional race bias. *Psychological Science, 15,* 88–93.

Amodio, D. M., Jost, J. T., Master, S. L., & Yee, C. M. (2007). Neurocognitive correlates of liberalism and conservatism. *Nature Neuroscience, 10,* 1246–1247.

Amodio, D. M., & Showers, C. J. (2005). "Similarity breeds liking" revisited: The moderating role of commitment. *Journal of Social and Personal Relationships, 22,* 817–836.

Anastasi, A., & Urbina, S. (1997). *Psychological testing* (7th ed.). Upper Saddle River, NJ: Prentice Hall.

Anastassiou-Hadjicharalambous, X., & Warden, D. (2008). Physiologically indexed and self perceived affective empathy in conduct-disordered children high and low on callousunemotional traits. *Child Psychiatry and Human Development, 39,* 503–517.

Anderson, C., Kraus, M. W., Galinsky, A. D., & Keltner, D. (2012). The local-ladder effect: Social status and subjective well-being. *Psychological Science, 23,* 764. doi: 10.1177/0956797611434537

Anderson, J. R. (1995). *Learning and memory: An integrated approach.* New York: Wiley.

Anderson, M. C., & Levy, B. J. (2009). Suppressing unwanted memories. *Current Directions in Psychological Science, 18,* 189–194.

Anderson, A., & Conwell, Y. (2002). Doctors study why elderly so prone to suicide. *American Journal of Geriatric Psychiatry.* Retrieved June 7, 2009, from http://www. stopgettingsick.com/templates/news_template.cfm/6086.

Anderson, A. K., & Phelps, E. A. (2000). Expression without recognition: Contributions of the human amygdala to emotional communication. *Psychological Science, 11,* 106–111.

Anderson, A. K., & Phelps, E. A. (2001). Lesions of the human amygdala impair enhanced perception of emotionally salient events. *Nature, 411,* 305–309.

Anderson, B. L. (2003). The role of occlusion in the perception of depth, lightness, and opacity. *Psychological Review, 110*(4), 785–801.

Anderson, C. A., Shibuya, A., Ihori, N., Swing, E. L., Bushman, B. J., Sakamoto, A., & Saleem, M. (2010). Violent video game effects on aggression, empathy, and prosocial behavior in Eastern and Western countries: A meta-analytic review. *Psychological Bulletin, 136*(2), 151–173. doi:10.1037/a0018251.

Anderson, C. A., Anderson, K. B., Dorr, N., DeNeve, K. M., & Flanagan, M. (2000). Temperature and aggression. In M. Zanna (Ed.), *Advances in experimental social psychology* (Vol. 32, pp. 63–133). New York: Academic Press.

Anderson, C. A., Berkowitz, L., Donnerstein, E., Huesmann, L. R., Johnson, J. D., Linz, D., et al. (2003). The influence of media violence on youth. *Psychological Science in the Public Interest, 4,* 81–110.

Anderson, C. A., & Bushman, B. J. (2002a). Human aggression. *Annual Review of Psychology, 53,* 27–51.

Anderson, C. A., & Bushman, B. J. (2002b). Media violence and the American public revisited. *American Psychologist, 57,* 448–450.

Anderson, C. A., & Dill, K. E. (2000). Video games and aggressive thoughts, feelings, and behavior in the laboratory and in life. *Journal of Personality and Social Psychology, 78,* 772–790.

Anderson, C. A., Lindsay, J. J., & Bushman, B. J. (1999). Research in the psychological laboratory: Truth or triviality? *Current Directions in Psychological Science, 8,* 3–9.

Anderson, C. A., & Murphy, C. R. (2003). Violent video games and aggressive behavior in young women. *Aggressive Behavior, 29,* 423–429.

Anderson, C. A., Sakamoto, A., Gentile, D. A., Ihori, N., Shibuya, A. Yukawa, S., Naito, M., & Kobayashi, K. (2008). Longitudinal effects of violent video games on aggression in Japan and the United States. *Pediatrics, 122,* 1067–1072.

Anderson, J. R. (2000). *Cognitive psychology and its implications* (5th ed). New York: Worth.

Anderson, J. R., Bothell, D., Byrne, M. D., Douglass, S., Lebiere, C., & Qin, Y. (2004). An integrated theory of the mind. *Psychological Review, 111,* 1036–1060.

Anderson, M. C., & Green, C. (2001). Suppressing unwanted memories by executive control. *Nature, 410,* 366–369.

Anderson, M. C., Ochsner, K. N., Kuhl, B., Cooper, J., Robertson, E., Gabrieli, S. W., et al. (2004). Neural systems underlying the suppression of unwanted memories. *Science, 303,* 232–235.

Anderson, P., Rothbaum, B. O., & Hodges, L. F. (2003). Virtual reality exposure in the treatment of social anxiety. *Cognitive and Behavioral Practice, 10*(3), 240–247.

Anderson, S. E., Cohen, P., Naumova, E. N., Jacques, P. F., & Must, A. (2007). Adolescent obesity and risk for subsequent major depressive disorder and anxiety disorder: Prospective evidence. *Psychosomatic Medicine 69,* 740–747.

Anderssen, N., Amlie, C., & Ytteroy, E. A. (2002). Outcomes for children with lesbian or gay parents: A review of studies from 1978 to 2000. *Scandinavian Journal of Psychology, 43,* 335–351.

Andersson, G., Carlbring, P., & Grimlund, A. (2008). Predicting treatment outcome in Internet versus face-to-face treatment of panic disorder. *Computers in Human Behavior, 24,*1790–1801.

Andersson, G. (2009). Using the Internet to provide cognitive behaviour therapy. *Behaviour Research and Therapy, 47,* 175–180.

Ando, Y., Kitayama, H., Kawaguchi, Y., & Koyanagi, Y. (2008). Primary target cells of herpes simplex virus type 1 in the hippocampus. *Microbes & Infection, 10*(14/15), 1514–1523.

Andrade, J., Deeprose, C., & Barker, I. (2008). Awareness and memory function during paediatric anaesthesia. *British Journal of Anaesthesia, 100,* 389–396.

Andreasen, N. C., & Pierson, R. (2008). The role of the cerebellum in schizophrenia. *Biological Psychiatry, 64,* 81–88.

Andreescu, C., Lenze, E. J., Dew, M. A., Begley, A. E., Mulsant, B. H., et al. (2007). Effect of comorbid anxiety on treatment response and relapse risk in late-life depression. *British Journal of Psychiatry, 190,* 344–349.

Andre-Petersson, L., Engstroom, G., Hagberg, B., Janzon, L., Steen, G., Lane, D. A., et al. (2001). Adaptive behavior in stressful situations and stroke incidence in hypertensive men: Results from prospective cohort study "Men Born in 1914" in Malmo, Sweden. *Stroke, 32,* 1712–1720.

Andrew, D., & Craig, A. D. (2001). Spinothalamic lamina I neurons selectively sensitive to histamine: A central neural pathway for itch. *Nature Neuroscience, 4,* 72–77.

Andrews, B., Brewin, C., Ochera, J., Morton, J., Bekerian, D. A., Davies, G. M., & Mollon, P. (2000). The timing, triggers, and quality of recovered memories in therapy. *British Journal of Clinical Psychology, 39,* 11–26.

Andrews, B., Brewin, C. R., Philpott, R., & Stewart, L. (2007). Delayed-onset posttraumatic stress disorder: A systematic review of the evidence. *American Journal of Psychiatry, 164,* 1319–1326.

Andrews, J., Wang, L., Csernansky, J. G., Gado, M. H., & Barch, D. M. (2006). Abnormalities of thalamic activation and cognition in schizophrenia. *American Journal of Psychiatry, 163,* 463–469.

Andrews, L. B. (2008). The psychiatric interview and mental status examination. In R. E. Hales, S. C. Yudofsky, & G. O. Gabbard (Eds) *Textbook of psychiatry.* (pp. 3–17). Washington, DC: American Psychiatric Publishing.

Andrews-Hanna, J. R., Mackiewicz Seghete, K. L., Claus, E. D., Burgess, G. C., Ruzic, L., & Banich, M. T. (2011). Cognitive control in adolescence: neural underpinnings and relation to self-report behaviors. *PLoS One 6*(6):e21598.

Angelaki, D. E., & Cullen, K. E. (2008). Vestibular system: The many faces of a multimodal sense. *Annual Review of Neuroscience, 31,* 125–150.

Angold, A., Erkanli, A., Farmer, E. M. Z., Fairbank, J. A., Burns, B. J., Keeler, G., & Costello, E. J. (2002). Psychiatric disorder, impairment, and service use in rural African American and white youth. *Archives of General Psychiatry, 59,* 893–901.

Annenberg Public Policy Center. (1999). *The 1999 state of children's television report: Programming for children over broadcast and cable television.* Washington, DC: Annenberg Public Policy Center.

Annenberg Public Policy Center. (2000). *Media in the home: The fifth annual survey of parents and children 2000.* Washington, DC: Annenberg Public Policy Center.

Anrep, G. V. (1920). Pitch discrimination in the dog. *Journal of Physiology, 53,* 367–385.

Anshel, M. (1996). Coping styles among adolescent competitive athletes. *Journal of Social Psychology, 136,* 311–323.

Antony, M. M., & Barlow, D. H. (2010). *Handbook of assessment and treatment planning for psychological disorders* (2nd ed.). New York: Guilford.

Antonescu-Turcu, A. & Parthasarathy, S. (2010). CPAP and bi-level PAP therapy: new and established roles. *Respiratory Care, 55*(9), 1216–1229.

Antoni, M. H., Cruess, D. G., Cruess, S., Lutgendorf, S., Kumar, M., Ironson, G., et al. (2000). Cognitive-behavioral stress management intervention effects on anxiety, 24-hr urinary norepinephrine output, and t-cytotoxic/suppressor cells over time among symptomatic HIV-infected gay men. *Journal of Consulting and Clinical Psychology, 68,* 31–45.

Antoni, M. H., & Lutgendorf, S. (2007). Psychosocial factors and disease progression in cancer. *Current Directions in Psychological Science, 16,* 42–46.

Antrobus, J. (2001). Rethinking the fundamental process of dream and sleep mentation production: Defining new questions that avoid the distraction of REM versus NREM comparisons. *Sleep and Hypnosis, 3,* 1–8.

APA Office of Ethnic Minority Affairs. (2000). *Guidelines for research in ethnic minority communities.* Washington, DC: American Psychological Association.

Apfelbaum, E. P., Pauker, K., Sommers, S. R., & Ambady, N. (2010). In blind pursuit of racial equality? *Psychological Science, 21*(11), 1587–1592. doi:10.1177/0956797610384741.

Appel, M., Kronberger, N., & Aronson, J. (2011). Stereotype threat impairs ability building: Effects on test preparation among women in science and technology. *European Journal of Social Psychology, 41*(7), 904-913. doi:10.1002/ejsp.835.

Appignanesi, L. (2009). *Mad, bad, and sad: A history of women and mind doctors.* New York, NY: W. W. Norton.

Aquino, K., Tripp, T. M., & Bies, R. J. (2006). Getting even or moving on? Power, procedural justice, and types of offense as predictors of revenge, forgiveness, reconciliation, and avoidance in organizations. *Journal of Applied Psychology, 91,* 653–668.

Arango, C., Rapado-Castro, M., Reig, S., Castro-Fornieles, J., González-Pinto, A., Otero, S., & Desco, M. (2012). Progressive brain changes in children and adolescents with first-episode psychosis. *Archives Of General Psychiatry, 69*(1), 16–26.

Arcelus, J., Mitchell, A., Wales, J., & Nielsen, S. (2011). Mortality rates in patients with anorexia nervosa and other eating disorders. A meta-analysis of 36 studies. *Archives Of General Psychiatry, 68*(7), 724–731.

Archer, T. T. (2011). Physical exercise alleviates debilities of normal aging and Alzheimer's disease. *Acta Neurologica Scandinavica, 123*(4), 221–238. doi:10.1111/j.1600-0404.2010.01412.x.

Ardelt, M. (2011). Are older adults wiser than college students? A comparison of two age cohorts. *Journal of Adult Development, 17,* 193–207.

Ardila, A., Rosselli, M., Matute, E., & Inozemtseva, O. (2011). Gender differences in cognitive development. *Developmental Psychology, 47*(4), 984–990. doi:10.1037/a0023819.

Arenberg, D. (1982). Changes with age in problem solving. In F. I. M. Craik & S. Trehub (Eds.), *Aging and cognitive processes* (pp. 221–236). New York: Plenum.

Ariely, D., & Berns, G. S. (2010). Neuromarketing: the hope and hype of neuroimaging in business. *Nature Reviews Neuroscience, 11*(4), 284–292. doi:10.1038/nrn2795.

Arkes, H. R., & Ayton, P. (1999). The sunk cost and Concorde effects: Are humans less rational than lower animals? *Psychological Bulletin, 125,* 591–600.

Arle, J. E., & Shils, J. L. (2008). Motor cortex stimulation for pain and movement disorders. *Neurotherapeutics, 5*(1), 37–49.

Armfield, J. M. (2006). Cognitive vulnerability: A model of the etiology of fear. *Clinical Psychology Review, 26,* 746–768.

Armitage, C. J. (2005). Can the theory of planned behavior predict the maintenance of physical activity? *Health Psychology, 24,* 235–245.

Armour, S. (2008, March 31). Day care's new frontier: Your baby at your desk. *USA Today.*

Armstrong, L. E. (2006). Nutritional strategies for football: Counteracting heat, cold, high altitude, and jet lag. *Journal of Sports Sciences, 24*(7), 723–740.

Arndt, J. (2012). The influence of forward and backward associative strength on false recognition. *Journal of Experimental Psychology. Learning, Memory & Cognition, 38*(3), 747–756. doi:10.1037/a0026375

Arneson, J. J., Sackett, P. R., & Beatty, A. S. (2011). Ability-performance relationships in education and employment settings: Critical tests of the more-is-better and the good-enough hypotheses. *Psychological Science, 22*(10), 1336-1342. doi:10.1177/0956797611417004.

Arnett, J. J. (2011). Emerging adulthood(s): The cultural psychology of a new life stage. In L. A. Jensen (Ed.), *Bridging cultural and developmental psychology: New syntheses in theory, research, and policy.* New York: Oxford University Press.

Arnett, J. J. (1999). Adolescent storm and stress, reconsidered. *American Psychologist, 54,* 317–326.

Arnett, J. J. (2000). Emerging adulthood: A theory of development from the late teens through the twenties. *American Psychologist, 55,* 469–480.

Arnett, J. J. (2007). Suffering, selfish, slackers? Myths and reality about emerging adults. *Journal of Youth & Adolescence, 36*(1), 23–29.

Aronoff, J., Barclay, A. M., & Stevenson, L. A. (1988). The recognition of threatening stimuli. *Journal of Personality and Social Psychology, 54,* 647–655.

Aronson, E., Wilson, T., & Akert, R. (2010). *Social psychology* (7th ed.). Upper Saddle River, NJ: Prentice Hall.

Aronson, E. (1990). Applying social psychology to desegregation and energy conservation. *Personality and Social Psychology Bulletin, 16,* 118–132.

Aronson, E. (1997). *The jigsaw classroom.* New York: Longman.

Aronson, E. (1999). *The social animal* (8th ed.). New York: Worth/Freeman.

Aronson, E., & Patnoe, S. (1997). *The jigsaw classroom: Building cooperation in the classroom* (2nd ed.). New York: Addison Wesley Longman.

Aronson, E. & Patnoe, S. (2011). *Cooperation in the classroom: The jigsaw method* (3rd ed.). London: Pinter & Martin, Ltd.

Aronson, E., Wilson, T. D., & Akert, R. M. (2005). *Social psychology* (5th ed.). Upper Saddle River, NJ: Prentice Hall.

Arruda, M., Guidetti, V., Galli, F., de Albuquerque, R., & Bigal, M. (2011). Prenatal exposure to tobacco and alcohol are associated with chronic daily headaches at childhood: A population-based study. *Arquivos de Neuro-Psiquiatria, 69*(1), 27–33. doi:10.1590/S0004-282X2011000100007.

Arsalidou, M., Barbeau, E. J., Bayless, S. J., & Taylor, M. J. (2010). Brain responses differ to faces of mothers and fathers. *Brain & Cognition, 74*(1), 47–51. doi:10.1016/j.bandc.2010.06.003.

Arsenault, B. J., Rana, J. S., Lemieux, I., Despres, J.-P., et al. (2010). Physical inactivity, abdominal obesity and risk of coronary heart disease in apparently healthy men and women. *International Journal of Obesity, 34,* 340–347.

Arseneault, L., Moffitt, T. E., Caspi, A., Taylor, A., et al. (2003). Strong genetic effects on crosssituational antisocial behavior among 5-year-old children according to mothers, teachers, examiner-observers, and twins' self-reports. *Journal of Child Psychology and Psychiatry, 44,* 832–848.

Arterberry, M. E., Craton, L. G., & Yonas, A. (1993). Infants' sensitivity to motion-carried information for depth and object properties. In C. Granrud (Ed.), *Visual perception and cognition in infancy. Carnegie Mellon symposia on cognition* (pp. 215–234). Hillsdale, NJ: Erlbaum.

Arterberry, M. E., & Yonas, A. (2000). Perception of three-dimensional shape specified by optic flow by 8-week-old infants. *Perception and Psychophysics, 62*(3), 550–556.

Arthur, W., Jr., Day, E. A., McNelly, T. L., & Edens, P. S. (2003). A meta-analysis of the criterion-related validity of assessment center dimensions. *Personnel Psychology, 56,* 125–154.

Arvey, R. D., Bouchard, T. J., Segal, N. L., & Abraham, L. M. (1989). Job satisfaction: Environmental and genetic components. *Journal of Applied Psychology, 74,* 187–192.

Asato, M. R., Terwilliger, R., Woo, J., & Luna, B. (2010). White matter development in adolescence: A DTI study. *Cerebral Cortex, 5,* 5. doi:10.1093/cercor/bhp282.

Asbridge, M., Hayden, J.A., & Cartwright, J.L. (2012). Acute cannabis consumption and motor vehicle collision risk: Systematic review of observational studies and meta-analysis. BMJ, 344, e536.

Asch, S. E. (1951). Effects of group pressure upon the modification and distortion of judgments. In H. Guetzkow (Ed.), *Groups, leadership, and men* (pp. 177–190). Pittsburgh, PA: Carnegie Press.

Asch, S. E. (1955). Opinions and social pressure. *Scientific American, 193,* 31–35.

Asch, S. E. (1956). Studies of independence and conformity: A minority of one against a unanimous majority. *Psychological Monographs, 70,* 1–70.

Asen, Y., & Cook, R. G. (2012). Discrimination and Categorization of Actions by Pigeons. *Psychological Science (Sage Publications Inc.), 23*(6), 617–624. doi:10.1177/0956797611433333

Ashcraft, M. H. (2006). *Cognition* (4th ed.). Upper Saddle River, NJ: Prentice Hall.

Ashe, P. C., Berry, M. D., & Boulton, A. A. (2001). Schizophrenia, a neurodegenerative disorder with neurodevelopmental antecedents. *Progress in Neuro-Psychopharmacology and Biological Psychiatry, 25,* 691–707.

Ashton, M. C., Lee, K., Perugini, M., Szarota, P., de Vries, R. E., Di Blas, L., et al. (2004). A six-factor structure of personality-descriptive adjectives: Solutions from psycholexical studies in seven languages. *Journal of Personality and Social Psychology, 86,* 356–366.

Askay, S. W., Patterson, D. R., Jensen, M. P., & Sharar, S. R. (2007). A randomized controlled trial of hypnosis for burn wound care. Rehabilitation *Psychology, 52*(3), 247–253.

Askew, C., & Field, A. P. (2008). The vicarious learning pathway to fear 40 years on. *Clinical Psychology Review, 28,* 1249–1265.

Askew, C., Kessock-Phillip, H., & Field, A. P. (2008). What happens when verbal threat information and vicarious learning combine. *Behavioural and Cognitive Psychotherapy, 36,* 491–505.

Aslin, R. N., Jusczyk, P. W., & Pisoni, D. B. (1998). Speech and auditory processing during infancy: Constraints on and precursors to language. In W. Damon (Ed.), *Handbook of child psychology* (5th ed., pp. 147–198). New York: Wiley.

Aso, K., Hanakawa, T., Aso, T., & Fukuyama, H. (2010). Cerebro-cerebellar interactions underlying temporal information processing. *Journal of Cognitive Neuroscience, 4,* 4.

Aspinwall, L. G., & Duran, R. E. F. (1999). Psychology applied to health. In A. M. Stec & D. A. Bernstein (Eds.), *Psychology: Fields of application* (pp. 17–38). Boston: Houghton Mifflin.

Aspinwall, L. G., & Taylor, S. E. (1992). Modeling cognition adaptation: A longitudinal investigation of the impact of individual differences and coping on college adjustment and performance. *Journal of Personality and Social Psychology, 63,* 989–1003.

Assefi, N. P., Sherman, K. J., Jacobsen, C., Goldberg, J., Smith, W. R., & Buchwald, D. (2005). A randomized clinical trial of acupuncture compared with sham acupuncture in fibromyalgia. *Annals of Internal Medicine, 143,* 10–19.

Assefi, S. L., & Garry, M. (2003). Absolut® memory distortions: Alcohol placebos influence misinformation effect. *Psychological Science, 14,* 77–80.

Associated Press. (2002, March 9). Odds and ends. *Naples Daily News.* Retrieved August 27, 2003, from http://www.nctimes.net/news/2002/20020313/ wwww.html.

Associated Press. (2007, December 17). Excellent driving, now pull over: California cops to reward motorists with $5 Starbucks cards.

Associated Press. (2007a). Officials investigating prank call that led to shock treatments at special needs school. December 18.

Associated Press. (2007b). Kansas store video captures five shoppers stepping over dying stabbing victim. July 3.

Associated Press. (2007). Poll: One-Third of Americans Believe in Ghosts, UFOs. Retrieved from http://www.foxnews.com/story/0,2933,305277,00.html

Associated Press. (2011). Obesity rise prompts Washington ferry capacity change. *The Daily Astorian.* Retrieved from http://www.dailyastorian.com/business/obesity-rise-prompts-washington-ferry-capacity-change/article_6859103c-2cc9-11e1-b9c0-001871e3ce6c.html

Astin, J. A. (2004). Mind-body therapies for the management of pain. *Clinical Journal of Pain, 20,* 27–32.

Aston-Jones, G., & Cohen, J. D. (2005). An integrative theory of locus coeruleus-norepinephrine function: Adaptive gain and optimal performance. *Annual Review of Neuroscience, 28,* 403–450.

Atalay, A., & Meloy, M. G. (2011). Retail therapy: A strategic effort to improve mood. *Psychology & Marketing, 28,* 638–660. doi:10.1002/mar.20404

Atance, C. M., & O'Neill, D. K. (2001). Episodic future thinking. *Trends in Cognitive Science, 5,* 533–539.

Atkins, R. (2008). The association of childhood personality on sexual risk taking during adolescence. *Journal of School Health, 78*(11), 594–600.

Atkinson, J. (2006, August). Shake it off. *GQ: Gentlemen's Quarterly, 76*(8), 87–92.

Atkinson, R. C., & Shiffrin, R. M. (1968). Human memory: A proposed system and its control processes. In K. Spence (Ed.), *The psychology of learning and motivation* (Vol. 2, pp. 89–195). New York: Academic Press.

Atlantis, E., & Baker, M. (2008). Obesity effects on depression: Systematic review of epidemiological studies. *International Journal of Obesity, 32,* 881–891.

Atran, S., Medin, D. L., & Ross, N. O. (2005). The cultural mind: Environmental decision making and cultural modeling within and across populations. *Psychological Review, 112,* 744–776.

Aurora, R. N., Zak, R. S., Auerbach, S. H., Casey, K. R., Chowdhuri, S., Karippot, A., Maganti, R. K., Ramar, K., Kristo, D. A., Bista, S. R., Lamm, C. I., Morgenthaler, T. I., & Standards of Practice Committee, American Academy of Sleep Medicine. (2010). Best practice guide for the treatment of nightmare disorder in adults. *Journal of Clinical Sleep Medicine, 6*(4):389–401.

Austin, J. (2006). *Zen-Brain reflections.* Cambridge, MA, US: MIT Press.

Auyeung B., Baron-Cohen, S., Ashwin, E., Knickmeyer, R., Taylor, K., Hackett, G., & Hines, M. (2009). Fetal testosterone predicts sexually differentiated childhood behavior in girls and in boys. *Psychological Science, 20,* 144–148.

Avidan, M. S., Jacobsohn, E., Glick, D., Burnside, B. A., Zhang, L., Villafranca, A., Karl, L., Kamal, S., Torres, B., O'Connor, M., Evers, A.S., Gradwohl, S., Lin, N., Palanca, B. J., and Mashour, G. A., for the BAG-RECALL Research Group. (2011). Prevention of intraoperative awareness in a high-risk surgical population. *New England Journal of Medicine, 365*(7), 591–600.

Aviezer, O., Sagi, A., Joels, T., & Ziv, Y. (1999). Emotional availability and attachment representations in kibbutz infants and their mothers. *Developmental Psychology, 35,* 811–821.

Axtell, R. (Ed.). (1998). *Gestures: The do's and taboos of body language around the world.* Hoboken, NJ: Wiley.

Ayache, D., Corre, A., Can Prooyen, S., & Elbaz, P. (2003). Surgical treatment of otosclerosis in elderly patients. *Otolaryngological Head and Neck Surgery, 129,* 674–677.

Ayman, R. , Korabik, K., & Morris, S. (2009). Is transformational leadership always perceived as effective? Male subordinates' devaluation of female transformational leaders. *Journal of Applied Social Psychology, 39,* 852–879.

Ayuso-Mateos, J. L., Vazquez-Barquero, J. L., Dowrick, C., Lehtinen, V., Dalgard, O. S., Casey, P., et al. (2001). Depressive disorders in Europe: Prevalence figures fromt he ODIN study. *British Journal of Psychiatry, 179,* 308–316.

Azar, B. (1996, November). Project explores landscape of midlife. *APA Monitor,* p. 26.

Azzopardi, P., & Hock, H. S. (2011). Illusory motion perception in blindsight. *Proceedings Of The National Academy Of Sciences Of The United States Of America, 108*(2), 876–881. doi:10.1073/pnas.1005974108.

Babinski, J. (1914). Contribution a l'etude dies troubles mentaux dans l'hemiplegie organique cerebrale (anosognosia). *Reveu Neurologie (Paris), 27,* 845–847.

Babor, T. F. (2011). Substance, not semantics, is the issue: Comments on the proposed addiction criteria for DSM-V. *Addiction, 106*(5), 870–872. doi:10.1111/j.1360-0443.2010.03313.x.

Baca-Garcia, E., Perez-Rodriguez, M. M., Keyes, K. M., Oquendo, M. A., et al. (2010). Suicidal ideation and suicide attempts in the United States, 1991–1992 and 2001–2002. *Molecular Psychiatry, 15,* 250–259.

Bacharach, V. R., & Baumeister, A. A. (1998). Direct and indirect effects of maternal intelligence, maternal age, income, and home environment on intelligence of preterm, low-birth-weight children. *Journal of Applied Developmental Psychology, 19,* 361–375.

Bach-Mizrachi, H., Underwood, M. D., Kassir, S. A., Bakalian, M. J., Sibille, E., Tamir, H., et al. (2006). Neuronal tryptophan hydroxylase mRNA expression in the human dorsal and median raphe nuclei: Major depression and suicide. *Neuropsychopharmacology: Official Publication of the American College pf Neuropsychopharmacology, 31,* 814–824.

Back, S. E., Dansky, B. S., Carroll, K. M., Foa, E. B., & Brady, K. T. (2001). Exposure therapy in the treatment of PTSD among cocaine-dependent individuals: Description of procedures. *Journal of Substance Abuse Treatment, 21,* 35–45.

Backman, L., & Nilsson, L. (1991). Effects of divided attention on free and cued recall of verbal events and action events. *Bulletin of the Psychonomic Society, 29,* 51–54.

Bada, H. S., Das, A., Bauer, C. R., Shankaran, S., Lester, B., LaGasse, L., et al. (2007). Impact of prenatal cocaine exposure on child behavior problems through school age. *Pediatrics, 119,* 348–359.

Baddeley, A. (1982). *Your memory: A user's guide.* New York: Macmillan.

Baddeley, A. (1992). Working memory. *Science, 255,* 556–559.

Baddeley, A. (1998). *Human memory: Theory and practice.* Boston: Allyn & Bacon.

Baddeley, A. D. (2003). Working memory: Looking back and looking forward. *Nature Reviews Neuroscience, 4,* 829–839.

Baer, J. S., Sampson, P. D., Barr, H. M., Connor, P. D., & Streissguth, A. P. (2003). A 21-year longitudinal analysis of the effects of prenatal alcohol exposure on young adult drinking. *Archives of General Psychiatry, 60,* 377–385.

Baethge, C., Baldessarini, R. J., Mathiske-Schmidt, K., Hennen, J., Berghofer, A., et al. (2005). Long-term combination therapy versus monotherapy with lithium and carbamazepine in 46 bipolar I patients. *Journal of Clinical Psychiatry, 66,* 174–182.

Bagley, C., & Tremblay, P. (1998). On the prevalence of homosexuality and bisexuality, in a random survey of 750 men aged 18–27. *Journal of Homosexuality, 36,* 1–18.

Baglioni, C., Spiegelhalder, K., Lombardo, C., & Riemann, D. (2010). Sleep and emotions: A focus on insomnia. *Sleep Medicine Reviews, 14,* 227–238. Epub 2010 Feb 6.

Bahali, K., & Tahiroğlu, A. (2010). Okul Reddi: Klinik Özellikler, Tani ve Tedavi. (Turkish). *Current Approaches in Psychiatry / Psikiyatride Guncel Yaklasimlar, 2*(3), 362–383.

Bahrick, H. P., Bahrick, P. O., & Wittlinger, R. P. (1975). Fifty years of memory for names and faces: A cross-cultural approach. *Journal of Experimental Psychology: General, 104,* 54–75.

Bahrick, H. P., & Hall, L. K. (1991). Lifetime maintenance of high school mathematics content. *Journal of Experimental Psychology: General, 120,* 20–33.

Bahrick, H. P., Hall, L. K., Noggin, J. P., & Bahrick, L. E. (1994). Fifty years of language maintenance and language dominance in bilingual Hispanic immigrants. *Journal of Experimental Psychology: General, 123,* 264–283.

Baicy, K., London, E. D., Monterosso, J. Wong, M.-L., Delibasi, T., Sharma, A., & Licinio, J. (2007). Leptin replacement alters brain response to food cues in genetically leptin-deficient adults. *Proceedings of the National Academies of Science, 104,* 18276–18279.

Bailey, J. M., & Benishay, D. S. (1993). Familial aggregation of female sexual orientation. *American Journal of Psychiatry, 150,* 272–277.

Bailey, J. M., Bobrow, D., Wolfe, M., & Mikach, S. (1995). Sexual orientation of adult sons of gay fathers. *Developmental Psychology, 31*(1), 124–129.

Bailey, J. M., Dunne, M. P., & Martin, N. G. (2000). Genetic and environmental influences on sexual orientation and its correlates in an Australian twin sample. *Journal of Personality and Social Psychology, 78,* 524–536.

Bailey, J. M., & Pillard, R. C. (1991). A genetic study of male sexual orientation. *Archives of General Psychiatry, 48,* 1086–1096.

Bailey, K., & Chapman, P. (2012). When can we choose to forget? An ERP study into item-method directed forgetting of emotional words. *Brain & Cognition, 78*(2), 133–147. doi:10.1016/j.bandc.2011.11.004.

Baillargeon, R. (1992). A model of physical reasoning in infancy. In C. Rovee-Collier & L. P. Lipsett (Eds.), *Advances in infancy research.* Norwood, NJ: Ablex.

Baillargeon, R. (1995). Physical reasoning in infancy. In M. S. Gazzaniga (Ed.), *The cognitive neurosciences* (pp. 181–204). Cambridge, MA: MIT Press.

Baillargeon, R. (2008). Innate ideas revisited: For a principle of persistence in infants' physical reasoning. *Perspectives on Psychological Science, 3*(1), 2–13.

Baillargeon, R. H., Zoccolillo, M., Keenan, K., Cote, S., et al. (2007). Gender differences in physical aggression: A prospective population-based survey of children before and after 2 years of age. *Developmental Psychology, 43,* 13–26.

Baillargeon, R. H., Zoccolillo, M., Keenan, K., Côté, S., Pérusse, D., Wu, H.-X., Boivin, M., & Tremblay, R. E. (2007). Gender differences in physical aggression: A prospective population-based survey of children before and after 2 years of age. *Developmental Psychology, 43,* 13–26.

Baka, L., Derbis, R., & Maxfield, M. (2012). The anxiety-buffering properties of cultural and subcultural worldviews: Terror management processes among juvenile delinquents. *Polish Psychological Bulletin, 43,* 1–11. doi:10.2478/v10059-012-0001-x.

Bakardjieva, T., & Gercheva, G. (2011). Knowledge Management and e-Learning—An Agent-Based Approach. *World Academy Of Science, Engineering & Technology,* 663–666.

Bakare, M. O. (2008). Effective therapeutic dosage of antipsychotic medications in patients with psychotic symptoms: Is there a racial difference? *BMC Research Notes, 1,* 25.

Baker, A., ten Brinke, L., & Porter, S. (2012). Will get fooled again: Emotionally intelligent people are easily duped by high-stakes deceivers. *Legal and Criminological Psychology.* doi:http://dx.doi.org/10.1111/j.2044-8333.2012.02054.x

Baker, L. D., Frank, L. L., Foster-Schubert, K., Green, P. S., et al. (2010). Effects of aerobic exercise on mild cognitive impairment: A controlled trial. *Archives of Neurology, 67,* 71–79.

Baker, J. L., Olsen, L. W., & Sørensen, T. I. A. (2007). Childhood body-mass index and the risk of coronary heart disease in adulthood. *The New England Journal of Medicine, 357,* 2229–2237.

Baker, M. C. (2002). *The atoms of language: The mind's hidden rules of grammar.* New York: Basic Books.

Baker, T. B., Piper, M. E., McCarthy, D. E., & Majeskie, M. R. (2004). Addiction motivation reformulated: An affective processing model of negative reinforcement. *Psychological Review, 111,* 33–51.

Bakermans-Kranenburg, M. J., & Van Ijzendoorn, M. H. (2011). Differential susceptibility to rearing environment depending on dopamine-related genes: New evidence and a meta-analysis. *Development And Psychopathology, 23*(1), 39–52. doi:10.1017/S0954579410000635.

Bakermans-Kranenburg, M. J., van IJzendoorn, M. H., & Juffer, F. (2008). Less is more: Meta-analytic arguments for the use of sensitivity-focused interventions. In F. Juffer, M. J. Bakermans-Kranenburg, & M. H. van IJzendoorn (Eds.), *Promoting positive parenting: An attachment-based intervention* (pp. 59–74). New York: Taylor & Francis Group/Lawrence Erlbaum Associates.

Bakheit, A. O., Frost, J. J., & Ackroyd, E. E. (2011). Remission of life-long stammering after posterior circulation stroke. *Neurocase (Psychology Press), 17*(1), 41–45. doi:10.1080/13554794.2010.497153.

Balaban, M. T. (1995). Affective influences on startle in five-month-old infants: Reactions to facial expressions of emotion. *Child Development, 66*(1), 28–36.

Balayla, J., Azoulay, L., & Abenhaim, H. A. (2011). Maternal marital status and the risk of stillbirth and infant death: a population-based cohort study on 40 million births in the United States. *Women's Health Issues, 21*(5), 361–365.

Balázs, J., Benazzi, F., Rihmer, Z., Annamaria, A., Akiskal, K. K., et al. (2006). The close link between suicide attempts and mixed (bipolar) depression: Implications for suicide prevention. *Journal of Affective Disorders, 91*, 133–138.

Balcetis, E., & Dunning, D. (2006). See what you want to see: Motivational influences on visual perception. *Journal of Personality and Social Psychology, 91*, 612–625.

Baldock, M. R. J., Mathias, J., McLean, J., & Berndt, A. (2007). Visual attention as a predictor of on-road driving performance of older drivers. *Australian Journal of Psychology, 59*(3), 159–168.

Baldwin, D. S. (2011). Where is the room for improvement in the drug treatment of depression and anxiety? *Human Psychopharmacology: Clinical and Experimental, 26*, 1–3.

Baldwin, T. T., & Ford, J. K. (1988). Transfer of training: A review and directions for future research. *Personnel Psychology, 41*, 63–105.

Balfour, D. J. (2002). The neurobiology of tobacco dependence: A commentary. *Respiration, 69*, 7–11.

Ball, H. A., McGuffin, P., & Farmer, A. E. (2008). Attributional style and depression. *British Journal of Psychiatry, 192*, 275–278.

Ballard, C., Gauthier, S., Corbett, A., Brayne, C., Aarsland, D., & Jones, E. (2011). Alzheimer's disease. *Lancet, 377*(9770), 1019–1031.

Ballard, C., Khan, Z., Clack, H., & Corbett, A. (2011). Nonpharmacological treatment of Alzheimer disease. *Canadian Journal of Psychiatry, 56*(10), 589–595.

Balleine, B. W., & Dickinson, A. (1998). Goal-directed instrumental action: contingency and incentive learning and their cortical substrates. *Neuropharmacology, 37*, 407–419.

Ballmaier, M., & Schmidt, R. (2005). Conversion disorder revisited. *Functional Neurology, 20*, 105–113.

Ballou, M. (1995). Assertiveness training. In M. Ballou (Ed.), *Psychological interventions: A guide to strategies* (pp. 125–136). Westport, CT: Praeger.

Baltes, B. B., Briggs, T. E., Huff, J. W., Wright, J. A., & Neumann, G. A. (1999). Flexible and compressed workweek schedules: A meta-analysis of their effects on work-related criteria. *Journal of Applied Psychology, 84*, 496–513.

Baltes, B. B., & Heydens-Gahir, H. A. (2003). Reduction of work–family conflict through the use of selection, optimization, and compensation behaviors. *Journal of Applied Psychology, 88*, 1005–1018.

Baltes, P. B. (1993). The aging mind: Potential and limits. *The Gerontologist, 33*, 580–594.

Baltes, P. B. (1994, August). *Life-span developmental psychology: On the overall landscape of human development.* Address presented at the annual meeting of the American Psychological Association, Los Angeles.

Baltes, P. B., & Smith, J. (2008). The fascination of wisdom: Its nature, ontogeny, and function. *Perspectives on Psychological Science, 3*, 56–64.

Balzer, W. K., & Sulsky, L. M. (1992). Halo and performance appraisal research: A critical examination. *Journal of Applied Psychology, 77*, 975–985.

Banaji, M., Lemm, K. M., & Carpenter, S. J. (2001). The social unconscious. In A. Tesser & N. Schwarz (Eds.), *Blackwell handbook of social psychology: Intraindividual processes* (pp. 134–158). Oxford, UK: Blackwell.

Bancroft, J. (1994). Homosexual orientation: The search for a biological basis. *British Journal of Psychiatry, 164*, 437–440.

Bandura, A. (1965). Influence of a model's reinforcement contingencies on the acquisition of imitative responses. *Journal of Personality and Social Psychology, 1*, 589–595.

Bandura, A. (1992). Self-efficacy mechanism in psychobiologic functioning. In R. Schwarzer (Ed.), *Self-efficacy: Thought control of action* (pp. 355–394). Washington, DC: Hemisphere.

Bandura, A. (1999). Social cognitive theory of personality. In L. Pervin & O. John (Eds.), *Handbook of personality: Theory and research* (2nd ed., pp. 154–196). New York: Guilford.

Bandura, A., Blanchard, E. B., & Ritter, B. (1969). The relative efficacy of desensitization and modeling approaches for inducing behavioral, affective, and attitudinal changes. *Journal of Personality and Social Psychology, 13*, 173–199.

Bandura, A., Ross, D., & Ross, S. A. (1963). Imitation of film-mediated aggressive models. *Journal of Abnormal and Social Psychology, 66*, 3–11.

Bandura, A., & Walters, R. H. (1963). *Social learning and personality development.* New York: Holt, Rinehart & Winston.

Banich, M. T. (2004). *Cognitive neuroscience and neuropsychology.* Boston: Houghton Mifflin.

Banich, M. T. (2009). Executive function: The search for an integrated account. *Psychological Science, 18*, 89–94.

Banker, R. D., Field, J. M., Schroeder, R. G., & Sinha, K. K. (1996). Impact of work teams on manufacturing performance: A longitudinal field study. *Academy of Management Journal, 39*, 867–890.

Banks, M. S., & Salapatek, P. (1983). Infant visual perception. In P. H. Mussen (Ed.), *Handbook of child psychology: Vol. 2. Infancy and developmental psychobiology* (pp. 435–571). New York: Wiley.

Bantick, S. J., Wise, R. G., Ploghaus, A., Clare, S., Smith, S. M., & Tracey, I. (2002). Imaging how attention modulates pain in humans using functional MRI. *Brain, 125*, 310–319.

Baptista, C., Loureiro, S., de Lima Osório, F., Zuardi, A., Magalhães, P. V., Kapczinski, F., & Crippa, J. S. (2012). Social phobia in Brazilian university students: Prevalence, under-recognition and academic impairment in women. *Journal of Affective Disorders, 136*(3), 857–861. doi:10.1016/j.jad.2011.09.022.

Barclay, J. R., Bransford, J. D., Franks, J. J., McCarrell, N. S., & Nitsch, K. (1974). Comprehension and semantic flexibility. *Journal of Verbal Learning and Verbal Behavior, 13*, 471–481.

Barclay, P. (2006). Reputational benefits for altruistic punishment. *Evolution and Human Behavior, 27*, 325–344.

Barclay, T. R., Hinkin, C. H., Castellon, S. A., Mason, K. I., Reinhard, M. J., Marion, S. D., et al. (2007). Age-associated predictors of medication adherence in HIV-positive adults: health beliefs, self-efficacy, and neurocognitive status. *Health Psychology, 26*, 40–49.

Bardo, M. T., Donohew, R. L., & Harrington, N. G. (1996). Psychobiology of novelty-seeking and drug-seeking behavior. *Behavioral Brain Research, 77*(1–2), 23–43.

Barenbaum, N., & Winter, D. (2008). History of modern personality theory and research. In O. John, R. Robins, & L. Pervin (Eds.), *Handbook of personality: Theory and research* (3rd ed., pp. 3–28). New York: Guilford.

Barger, L. K., Cade, B. E., Ayas, N. T., Cronin, J. W., Rosner, B., Speizer, F. E., et al. (2005). *New England Journal of Medicine, 352*, 125–134.

Bargh, J. A. & Morsella, E (2010). Unconscious behavioral guidance systems. In C. Agnew, D. Carlston, W. G Graziano, & J. R. Kelly, (Eds.) *Then a miracle occurs: Focusing on behavior in social psychological theory and research* (pp. 89-118). New York, NY: Oxford University Press.

Bargones, J. Y., & Werner, L. A. (1994). Adults listen selectively; infants do not. *Psychological Science, 5*, 170–174.

Baringer, J. R. (2008). Herpes simplex infections of the nervous system. *Neurology Clinics, 26*, 657–674.

Barkham, M., Connell, J., Stiles, W. B., Miles, J. N. V., Margison, F., Evans, C., et al. (2006). Dose-effect relations and responsive regulation of treatment duration: The good enough level. *Journal of Consulting and Clinical Psychology, 74*, 160–167.

Barling, J., Dupré, K. E., & Kelloway, E. K. (2009). Predicting workplace aggression and violence. *Annual Review of Psychology, 60*, 671–692.

Barling, J., & Frone, M. R. (Eds.). (2004). *The psychology of workplace safety.* Washington, DC: APA Books.

Barling, J., Weber, T., & Kelloway, E. K. (1996). Effects of transformational leadership training on attitudinal and financial outcomes: A field experiment. *Journal of Applied Psychology, 81*, 827–832.

Barlow, D. H. (2010). The dodo bird–again–and again. *The Behavior Therapist, 33*, 15–16.

Barlow, D. H. (2007). *Clinical handbook of psychological disorders.* New York: Guilford.

Barlow, D. H., Gorman, J. M., Shear, M. K., & Woods, S. W. (2000). Cognitive-behavioral therapy, imipramine, or their combination for panic disorder: A randomized controlled trial. *Journal of the American Medical Association, 283*, 2529–2536.

Barlow, D. H. (2006). Psychotherapy and psychological treatments: The future. *Clinical Psychology: Science and Practice, 13*, 216–220.

Barlow, D. H. (1988). *Anxiety and its disorders: The nature and treatment of panic and anxiety.* New York: Guilford.

Barnard, L., & Curry, J. (2012). The relationship of clergy burnout to self-compassion and other personality dimensions. *Pastoral Psychology, 61*, 149–163. doi:10.1007/s11089-011-0377-0

Barnard, L. K., & Curry, J. F. (2011). Self-compassion: Conceptualizations, correlates, & interventions. *Review of General Psychology, 15*(4), 289–303. doi:10.1037/a0025754.

Barnes, A. (2004). Race schizophrenia, and admission to state psychiatric hospitals. *Administration and Policy in Mental Health, 31*, 241–252.

Barnes, L. L., Mendes de Leon, C. F., Wilson, R. S., Bienias, J. L., & Evans, D. A. (2004). Social resources and cognitive decline in a population of older African Americans and whites. *Neurology, 63*, 2322–2326.

Barnes, S. M., Lynn, S. J., & Pekala, R. J. (2009). Not all group hypnotic suggestibility scales are created equal: Individual differences in behavioral and subjective responses. *Consciousness and Cognition, 18*, 255–265.

Barnes-Farrell, J. L., Davies-Schuls, K., McGonagle, A., Walsh, B., Di Milia, L., Fischer, F. M., Hobbs, B. B., Kaliterna, L., & Tepas, D. (2008). What aspects of shiftwork influence off-shift well-being of healthcare workers? *Applied Ergonomics, 39*, 589–596.

Barnier, A. J., & McConkey, K. M. (1998). Posthypnotic responding away from the hypnotic setting. *Psychological Science, 9*, 256–262.

Baron, A. S., & Banaji, M. R. (2006). The development of implicit attitudes. *Psychological Science 17*, 53–58.

Baron, R. A., & Byrne, D. (1994). *Social psychology: Understanding human interaction* (7th ed.). Boston: Allyn & Bacon.

Baron, R. A., Byrne, D., & Branscombe, N. R. (2006). *Social psychology* (11th ed.). Boston: Allyn & Bacon.

Baron-Cohen, S., Knickmeyer, R. C., & Belmonte, M. K. (2005). Sex differences in the brain: Implications for explaining autism. *Science, 310*, 819–823.

Baron-Cohen, S., Leslie, A. M., & Frith, U. (1985). Does the autistic child have a "theory of mind"? *Cognition, 21*, 37–46.

Barr Taylor, C., Bryson, S., Celio Doyle, A. A., Luce, K. H., Cunning, D., Abascal, L. B., et al. (2006a). The adverse effect of negative comments about weight and shape from family and siblings on women at high risk for eating disorders. *Pediatrics, 118*, 731–738.

Barr Taylor, C., Bryson, S., Luce, K. H., Cunning, D., Celio Doyle, A. A., Abascal, L. B., et al. (2006b). Prevention of eating disorders in at-risk college-age women. *Archives of General Psychiatry, 63,* 881–888.

Barres, B. A. (2008). The mystery and magic of glia: A perspective on their roles in health and disease. *Neuron, 60*(3), 430–440.

Barrett, L. F. (1995). Valence focus and arousal focus: Individual differences in the structure of affective experience. *Journal of Personality and Social Psychology, 69,* 153–166.

Barrett, L. F., Gross, J., Christensen, T. C., & Benvenuto, M. (2001). Knowing what you're feeling and knowing what to do about it: Mapping the relation between emotion differentiation and emotion regulation. *Cognition and Emotion, 15,* 713–724.

Barrett, L. F., Lane, R. D., Sechrest, L., & Schwartz, G. E. (2000). Sex differences in emotional awareness. *Personality and Social Psychology Bulletin, 26,* 1027–1035.

Barrett, L. F., Mesquita, B., & Gendron, M. (2011). Context in emotion perception. *Current Directions in Psychological Science, 20*(5) 286–290. doi:10.1177/0963721411422522.

Barrett, L. F., Mesquita, B., Ochsner, K. N., & Gross, J. J. (2007). The experience of emotion. *Annual Review of Psychology, 58,* 373–403.

Barrett, L. F., & Wager, T. D. (2006). The structure of emotion. *Current Directions in Psychological Science, 15,* 79–83.

Barriera-Viruet, H., Sobeih, T. M., Daraiseh, N., & Salem, S. (2006). Questionnaires vs observational and direct measurements: A systematic review. *Theoretical Issues in Ergonomics Science, 7*(3), 261–284.

Barron, K. E., & Harackiewicz, J. M. (2001). Achievement goals and optimal motivation: Testing multiple goal models. *Journal of Personality and Social Psychology, 80,* 706–722.

Barsade, S. G., & Gibson, D. E. (2012). Group affect: Its influence on individual and group outcomes. *Current Directions In Psychological Science, 21,* 119–123. doi:10.1177/0963721412438352.

Barsalou, L. W. (1993). Flexibility, structure, and linguistic vagary in concepts: Manifestations of a compositional system of perceptual symbols. In A. F. Collins, S. E. Gathercole, M. A. Conway, & P. E. Morris (Eds.), *Theories of memory* (pp. 29–102). Hillsdale, NJ: Erlbaum.

Barsky, A. J., Wool, C., Barnett, M. C., & Cleary, P. D. (1994). Histories of childhood trauma in adult hypochondriacal patients. *American Journal of Psychiatry, 151,* 397–401.

Bartels, A., & Zeki, S. (2000). The neural basis of romantic love. *Neuroreport, 11,* 3829–3834.

Bartholow, B. D., & Heinz, A. (2006). Alcohol and aggression without consumption: Alcohol cues, aggressive thoughts, and hostile perception bias. *Psychological Science, 17,* 30–37.

Bartholet, J. (2012). The collision syndrome. *Scientific American, 306*(2), 66-71.

Bartlett, J. A. (2002). Addressing the challenges of adherence. *Journal of Acquired Immune Deficiency Syndrome, 29* (Suppl. 1), S2–S10.

Barton, J. J. (2011). Disorder of higher visual function. *Current Opinion in Neurology, 24*(1), 1–5.

Barton, J. J., Cherkasova, M. V., Press, D. Z., Intriligator, J. M., & O'Connor, M. (2004). Perceptual functions in prosopagnosia. *Perception, 33*(8), 939–956.

Barton, J., & Folkard, S. (1991). The response of day and night nurses to their work schedules. *Journal of Occupational Psychology, 64,* 207–218.

Barton, J. J., Press, D. Z., Keenan, J. P., & O'Connor, M. (2002). Lesions of the fusiform face area impair perception of facial configuration in prosopagnosia. *Neurology, 58*(1), 71–78.

Bartoshuk, L. M. (1991). Taste, smell, and pleasure. In R. C. Bollef (Ed.), *The hedonics of taste* (pp. 15–28). Hillsdale, NJ: Erlbaum.

Bartoshuk, L. M. (2000). Comparing sensory experiences across individuals: Recent psychophysical advances illuminate genetic variation in taste perception. *Chemical Senses, 25,* 447–460.

Bartoshuk, L. M., Fast, K., & Snyder, D. J. (2005). Differences in our sensory worlds: Invalid comparisons with labeled scales. *Current Directions in Psychological Science, 14,* 122–125.

Bartz, J. A., & Hollander, E. (2006). Is obsessive-compulsive disorder an anxiety disorder? *Progress in Neuro-Psychopharmacology & Biological Psychiatry, 30,* 338–352.

Barzilai, N., Wang, J., Massilon, D., Vuguin, P., Hawkins, M., & Rossetti, L. (1997). Leptin selectively decreases visceral adiposity and enhances insulin action. *Journal of Clinical Investigation, 100,* 3105–3110.

Başçiftçi, F., & Hatay, Ö. (2011). Reduced-rule based expert system by the simplification of logic functions for the diagnosis of diabetes. *Computers In Biology & Medicine, 41*(6), 350–356. doi:10.1016/j.compbiomed.2011.03.012.

Bashore, T. R., & Ridderinkhof, K. R. (2002). Older age, traumatic brain injury, and cognitive slowing: Some convergent and divergent findings. *Psychological Bulletin, 128,* 151–198.

Baskin, D., Bluestone, H., & Nelson, M. (1981). Ethnicity and psychiatric diagnosis. *Journal of Clinical Psychology, 37,* 529–537.

Bass, B. M., Avolio, B. J., Jung, D. I., & Berson, Y. (2003). Predicting unit performance by assessing transformational and transactional leadership. *Journal of Applied Psychology, 88,* 207–218.

Bass, B. M., & Riggio, R. E. (2006). *Transformational leadership* (2nd ed.). Mahwah, NJ: Erlbaum.

Bassetti, C. L. (2007). Differential diagnosis and management of non-psychiatric acute confusional states. *Schweizer Archiv für Neurologie und Psychiatrie, 158*(8), 368–378.

Basson, R. (2003). Commentary on "In the mood for sex—The value of androgens." *Journal of Sex and Marital Therapy, 29,* 177–179.

Basson, R. (2002). Women's sexual desire—disordered or misunderstood? *Journal of Sex and Marital Therapy, 28,* 17–28.

Basson, R. (2001). Human sex-response cycles. *Journal of Sex and Marital Therapy, 27,* 33–43.

Bastian, B., Jetten, J., & Fasoli, F. (2011). Cleansing the soul by hurting the flesh: The guilt-reducing effect of pain. *Psychological Science, 22*(3), 334–335. doi:10.1177/0956797610397058.

Basu, S., Chapman, G. B., & Galvani, A. P. (2008). Integrating epidemiology, psychology, and economics to achieve HPV vaccination targets. *Proceedings of the National Academy of Sciences, 105*(48), 19018–19023.

Basura, G. J., Eapen, R., & Buchman, C. A. (2009). Bilateral cochlear implantation: Current concepts, indications, and results. *Laryngoscope, 119,* 2395–2401.

Bates, E. (1993, March). *Nature, nurture, and language development.* Paper presented at the biennial meeting of the Society for Research in Child Development, New Orleans.

Bates, T. C., Luciano, M., Medland, S. E., Montgomery, G. W., Wright, M. J., & Martin, N. G. (2011). Genetic variance in a component of the Language Acquisition Device: ROBO1 polymorphisms associated with phonological buffer deficits. *Behavior Genetics, 41*(1), 50–57. doi:10.1007/s10519-010-9402-9.

Batki, S. L., Leontieva, L., Dimmock, J. A., & Ploutz-Snyder, R. (2008). Negative symptoms are associated with less alcohol use, craving, and "high" in alcohol dependent patients with schizophrenia. *Schizophrenia Research, 105,* 201–207.

Batson, C. D. (2010). Empathy-induced altruistic motivation. In M. Mikulincer & P. Shaver (Eds.), *Prosocial motives, emotions, and behavior: The better angels of our nature* (pp. 15–34). Washington, DC: American Psychological Association.

Batson, C. D. (1998). Altruism and prosocial behavior. In D. Gilbert, S. T. Fiske, & G. Lindzey (Eds.), *Handbook of social psychology* (Vol. 2, 4th ed., pp. 282–316). Boston: McGraw-Hill.

Batson, C. D., Sager, K., Garst, E., & Kang, M. (1997). Is empathy-induced helping due to self-other merging? *Journal of Personality and Social Psychology, 73,* 495–509.

Batterham, R. L., Cohen, M. A., Ellis, S. M., Le Roux, C. W., Withers, D. J., Frost, G. S., et al. (2003). Inhibition of food intake in obese subjects by peptide YY3-36. *New England Journal of Medicine, 349,* 941–948.

Batterham, R. L., Cowley, M. A., Small, C. J., Herzog, H., Cohen, M. A., Dakin, C. L., et al. (2002). Gut hormone PYY3–36 physiologically inhibits food intake. *Nature, 418,* 650–654.

Bauch, E. M., & Otten, L. J. (2012). Study-test congruency affects encoding-related brain activity for some but not all stimulus materials. *Journal of Cognitive Neuroscience, 24*(1), 183–195. doi:10.1162/jocn_a_00070

Baucom, D. H., Shoham, V., Mueser, K. T., Daiuto, A. D., & Stickle, T. R. (1998). Empirically supported couple and family interventions for marital distress and adult mental health problems. *Journal of Consulting and Clinical Psychology, 66,* 53–88.

Bauer, M. A., Wilkie, J. B., Kim, J. K., & Bodenhausen, G. V. (2012). Cuing consumerism: Situational materialism undermines personal and social well-being. *Psychological Science, 23*(5), 517–523. doi:10.1177/0956797611429579

Bauer, P. J. (2006). Event memory. In W. Damon & R. M. Lerner (Series Eds.) & D. Kuhn & R. Siegler (Vol. Eds.), *Handbook of child psychology: Vol. 2. Cognition, perception, and language* (6th ed., pp. 373–345). New York: Wiley.

Bauer, R. M., & Demery, J. A. (2003). Agnosia. In K. M. Heilman & E. Valenstein (Eds.), *Clinical neuropsychology* (4th ed.). New York: Oxford.

Bauer, T. N., & Green, S. G. (1996). Development of leader-member exchange: A longitudinal test. *Academy of Management Journal, 39,* 1538–1567.

Baumann, J., & DeSteno, D. (2010). Emotion guided threat detection: Expecting guns where there are none. *Journal Of Personality And Social Psychology, 99*(4), 595–610. doi:10.1037/a0020665.

Baumann, M. (2007). Slimming down with Wii sports. *Information Today, 24*(4), 47.

Baumann, S., Meyer, M., & Jäncke, L. (2008). Enhancement of auditory-evoked potentials in musicians reflects an influence of expertise but not selective attention. *Journal of Cognitive Neuroscience, 20*(12), 2238–2249.

Baumeister, H., & Härter, M. (2007). Mental disorders in patients with obesity in comparison with healthy probands. *International Journal of Obesity, 31,* 1155–1164.

Baumeister, R., & Bushman, B. (2008). *Social psychology and human nature.* Belmont, CA: Wadsworth.

Baumeister, R. F. (2010). The self. In R. Baumeister & E. Finkel (Eds.) *Advanced social psychology: The state of the science* (pp. 139–176). New York, NY: Oxford.

Baumeister, R. F. (1998). The self. In D. Gilbert, S. T. Fiske, & G. Lindzey (Eds.), *Handbook of social psychology* (Vol. 1, 4th ed., pp. 680–740). Boston: McGraw-Hill.

Baumeister, R. F. (2000). Gender differences in erotic plasticity: The female sex drive as socially flexible and responsive. *Psychological Bulletin, 126,* 347–374.

Baumeister, R. J. & Bushman, B. J. (2011). *Social psychology and human nature* (2nd Ed.) Belmont, CA: Cengage.

Baumeister, R. F., Campbell, J. D., Krueger, J. I., & Vohs, K. D. (2003). Does high self-esteem cause better performance, interpersonal success, happiness, or healthier lifestyles? *Psychological Science in the Public Interest, 4,* 1–44.

Baumeister, R. F., & Leary, M. R. (1995). The need to belong: Desire for interpersonal attachments as a fundamental human motivation. *Psychological Bulletin, 117*(3), 497–529.

Baumeister, R. F., & Stillman, T. (2006). Erotic plasticity: Nature, culture, gender, and sexuality. In McAnulty, R. D., Burnette, M. M. (Eds.), *Sex and sexuality: Vol 1. Sexuality today: Trends and controversies* (pp. 343–359). Westport, CT, US: Praeger Publishers/Greenwood Publishing Group.

Baumgardner, S. R., & Crothers, M. K. (2009). *Positive psychology.* Upper Saddle River, NJ: Prentice Hall/Pearson.

Bäuml, K. T., & Samenieh, A. (2012). Selective memory retrieval can impair and improve retrieval of other memories. *Journal of Experimental Psychology: Learning, Memory, and Cognition, 38*(2), 488–494. doi:10.1037/a0025683

Baumrind, D. (1971). Current patterns of parental authority. *Developmental Psychology Monographs, 4*(1, part 2).

Baumrind, D. (1991). Effective parenting during the early adolescent transition. In P. A. Cowan & E. M. Hetherington (Eds.), *Family transition* (pp. 111–163). Hillsdale, NJ: Erlbaum.

Baumrind, D., Larzelere, R. E., & Cowan, P. A. (2002). Ordinary physical punishment: Is it harmful? Comment on Gershoff. *Psychological Bulletin, 128,* 580–589.

Baylen, C. A., & Rosenberg, H. (2006). A review of the acute subjective eff ects of MDMA/ecstasy. *Addiction, 101,* 933–947.

Bayley, P. J., Hopkins, R. O., & Squire, L. R. (2003). Successful recollection of remote autobiographical memory by amnesic patients with medial temporal lobe lesions. *Neuron, 38,* 135–144.

Bazzano, L. A., He, J., Ogden, L. G., Loria, C. M., & Whelton, P. K. (2003). Dietary fiber intake and reduced risk of coronary heart disease in US men and women. *Archives of Internal Medicine, 163,* 1897–1904.

Beach, S. R. H., Brody, G. H., Gunter, T. D., Packer, H., Wernett, P., & Philibert, R. A. (2010). Child maltreatment moderates the association of MAOA with symptoms of depression and antisocial disorder. *Journal of Family Psychology, 24*(1), 12–20. doi:10.1037/a0018074.

Beals, J., Novins, D. K., Whitesell, N. R., Spicer, P., Mitchell, C. M., & Manson, S. M. (2005). Prevalence of mental disorders and utilization of mental health services in two American Indian reservation populations: Mental health disparities in a national context. *American Journal of Psychiatry, 162,* 1723–1732.

Beatty, J. (1995). *Principles of behavioral neuroscience.* Dubuque: Brown and Benchmark.

Beauchamp, G. K. (2009). Sensory and receptor responses to umami: An overview of pioneering work. *American Journal of Clinical Nutrition, 90,* S723–S727.

Bechara, A., Damasio, H., Tranel, D., & Damasio, A. R. (1997). Deciding advantageously before knowing the advantageous strategy. *Science, 275,* 1293–1295.

Beck, A. T. (1976). *Cognitive therapy and the emotional disorders.* New York: International Universities Press.

Beck, A. T. (1995). Cognitive therapy: A 30-year retrospective. In S. O. Lilienfeld (Ed.), *Seeing both sides: Classic controversies in abnormal psychology* (pp. 303–311). Pacific Grove, CA: Brooks/Cole. (Original work published 1991.)

Beck, A. T. (2005). The Current State of Cognitive Therapy: A 40-Year Retrospective. *Archives of General Psychiatry, 62,* 953–959. doi:10.1001/archpsyc.62.9.953

Beck, A. T. (2008). The evolution of the cognitive model of depression and its neurobiological correlates. *American Journal of Psychiatry, 165,* 969–977.

Beck, A. T., & Alford, B. A. (2009). *Depression: Causes and treatment.* Philadelphia, PA: University of Pennsylvania Press.

Beck, A. T., & Dozois, D. A. (2011). Cognitive Therapy: Current Status and Future Directions. *Annual Review of Medicine, 62,* 397–409. doi:10.1146/annurev-med-052209-100032

Beck, A. T., & Emery, G. (1985). *Anxiety disorders and phobias: A cognitive perspective.* New York: Basic Books.

Beck, A. T., Freeman, A., & Davis, D. D. (2007). *Cognitive therapy of personality disorders.* New York: Guilford.

Beck, A. T., & Rector, N. A. (2005). Cognitive approaches to schizophrenia: Theory and therapy. *Annual Review of Clinical Psychology, 1,* 577–606.

Beck, A. T., Rector, N. A., Stolar, N., & Grant, P. (2008). *Schizophrenia: Cognitive theory, research, and therapy.* New York: Guilford.

Beck, A. T., Sokol, L., Clark, D., Berchick, R., & Wright, F. (1992). A crossover study of focused cognitive therapy for panic disorder. *American Journal of Psychiatry, 149,* 778–783.

Beck, D. M. (2010). The appeal of the brain in the popular press. *Perspectives on Psychological Science, 5*(6), 762–766. doi:10.1177/1745691610388779.

Beck, J. S. (2005). *Cognitive therapy for challenging problems: What to do when the basics don't work.* New York: Guilford.

Beck, L. A., & Clark, M. S. (2009). Choosing to enter or avoid diagnostic social situations. *Psychological Science, 20,* 1175–1181.

Beck, M. (1992, December 7). The new middle age. *Newsweek,* 50–56.

Becker, C., Bull, S., Smith, L. M., Ciao, A. C. (2008). Effects of being a peer-leader in an eating disorder prevention program: can we further reduce eating disorder risk factors? *Eating Disorders, 16*(5), 444–459.

Becker, C. B., Stice, E., Shaw, H., & Woda, S. (2009). Use of empirically supported interventions for psychopathology: Can the participatory approach move us beyond the research-to-practice gap? *Behaviour Research and Therapy, 47,* 265–274.

Beckett, C., Maughan, B., Rutter, M., Castle, J., Colvert, E., Groothues, C., et al. (2006). Do the effects of early severe deprivation on cognition persist into early adolescence? Findings from the English and Romanian adoptees study. *Child Development, 77,* 696–711.

Becker, D. V., Anderson, U. S., Mortensen, C. R., Neufeld, S. L., & Neel, R. (2011, July 11). The face in the crowd effect unconfounded: Happy faces, not angry faces, are more efficiently detected in single- and multiple-target visual search tasks. *Journal of Experimental Psychology: General.* Advance online publication. doi:10.1037/a0024060.

Bedics, J. D., Atkins, D. C., Comtois, K., & Linehan, M. M. (2012). Weekly therapist ratings of the therapeutic relationship and patient introject during the course of dialectical behavioral therapy for the treatment of borderline personality disorder. *Psychotherapy, 49,* 231–240. doi:10.1037/a0028254

Bedny, M., Pascual-Leone, A., Dodell-Feder, D., Fedorenko, E., & Saxe, R. (2011). Language processing in the occipital cortex of congenitally blind adults. *PNAS*

Proceedings of the National Academy of Sciences of the United States of America, 108(11), 4429–4434. doi:10.1073/pnas.1014818108.

Beede, K. E., & Kass, S. J. (2006). Engrossed in conversation: Th e impact of cell phones on simulated driving performance. *Accident Analysis and Prevention, 38,* 415–421.

Behnke, M., Eyler, F. D., Warner, T. D., Garvan, C. W., Hou, W., & Wobie, K. (2006). Outcome from a prospective, longitudinal study of prenatal cocaine use: Preschool development at 3 years of age. *Journal of Pediatric Psychology, 31*(1), 41–49.

Behrens, K. Y., Hesse, E., & Main, M. (2007). Mothers' attachment status as determined by the Adult Attachment Interview predicts their 6-year-olds' reunion responses: A study conducted in Japan. *Developmental Psychology, 43,* 1553–1567.

Beijers, R., Jansen, J., Riksen-Walraven, M., & de Weerth, C. (2010). Maternal prenatal anxiety and stress predict infant illnesses and health complaints. *Pediatrics, 126*(2), e401–e409.

Bender, D., & Lösel, F. (2011). Bullying at school as a predictor of delinquency, violence and other anti-social behaviour in adulthood. *Criminal Behaviour and Mental Health, 21,* 99–106.

Beilock, S. L., & Carr, T. H. (2005). When high-powered people fail: Working memory and "choking under pressure" in math. *Psychological Science, 16,* 101–105.

Beilock, S. L., Kulp, C. A., Holt, L. E., & Carr, T. H. (2004). More on the fragility of performance: Choking under pressure in mathematical problem solving. *Journal of Experimental Psychology: General, 133,* 584–600.

Beirne, R. O., Zlatkova, M. B., & Anderson, R. S. (2005). Changes in human short-wavelength-sensitive and achromatic resolution acuity with retinal eccentricity and meridian. *Visual Neuroscience, 22,* 79–86.

Beisel, K., Hansen, L., Soukup, G., & Fritzsch, B. (2008). Regenerating cochlear hair cells: Quo vadis stem cell. *Cell and Tissue Research, 333*(3), 373–379.

Bekinschtein, T. A., Cardozo, J., & Manes, F. F. (2008). Strategies of Buenos Aires waiters to enhance memory capacity in a real-life setting. *Behavioural Neurology, 20,* 65–70.

Bekinschtein, T., Tiberti, C., Niklison, J., Tamashiro, M., Ron, M., Carpintiero, S., et al. (2005). Assessing level of consciousness and cognitive changes from vegetative state to full recovery. *Neuropsychological Rehabilitation, 15*(3–4), 307–322.

Bekrater-Bodmann, R., Foell, J., Diers, M., & Flor, H. (2012). The perceptual and neuronal stability of the rubber hand illusion across contexts and over time. *Brain Research, 1452130–139.* doi:10.1016/j.brainres.2012.03.001.

Bélanger, A., Gagnon, S., & Yamin, S. (2010). Capturing the serial nature of older drivers' responses towards challenging events: A simulator study. *Accident Analysis & Prevention, 42*(3), 809–817. doi:10.1016/j.aap.2009.07.010.

Belik, S., Cox, B. J., Murray, B. S., Asmundson, G. J. G., & Sareen, J. (2007). Traumatic events and suicidal behavior: Results from a National Mental Health Survey. *Journal of Nervous and Mental Disease, 195,* 342–350.

Belin, P., Zatorre, R. J., & Ahad, P. (2002). Human temporal-lobe response to vocal sounds. *Brain Research and Cognitive Brain Research, 13,* 17–26.

Bell, A. M., & Sih, A. (2007). Exposure to predation generates personality in threespined sticklebacks (*Gasterosteus aculeatus*). *Ecology Letters, 10,* 828–834.

Bell, A. S. (2011). A critical review of ADHD diagnostic criteria: What to address in the DSM-V. *Journal of Attention Disorders, 15*(1), 3–10. doi:10.1177/1087054710365982.

Bell, B. E., & Loftus, E. F. (1989). Trivial persuasion in the courtroom: The power of (a few) minor details. *Journal of Personality and Social Psychology, 56,* 669–679.

Bell, C. C., Sowers, W., & Thompson, K. S. (2008). American Association of Community Psychiatrists' views on general features of DSM-I.V. *Psychiatric Services, 59,* 687–690.

Bell, J. J., Rogers, V. W., Dietz, W. H., Ogden, C. L., Schuler, C. C., & Popovic, T. T. (2011). CDC grand rounds: Childhood obesity in the United States. *JAMA: Journal Of The American Medical Association, 305*(10), 988–991.

Bell, M. A., & Wolfe, C. D. (2007). Changes in brain functioning from infancy to early childhood: Evidence from EEG power and coherence working memory tasks. *Developmental Neuropsychology, 31*(1), 21–38.

Bell, P. A., Greene, T. C., Fisher, J. D., & Baum, A. (2000). *Environmental psychology* (5th ed.). Belmont, CA: Wadsworth.

Bellaby, P. (2003). Communication and miscommunication of risk: Understanding UK parents' attitudes to combined MMR vaccination. *British Medical Journal, 327,* 725–728.

Belli, R. F., & Loftus, E. F. (1996). The pliability of autobiographical memory: Misinformation and the false memory problem. In D. C. Rubin (Ed.), *Remembering our past: Studies in autobiographical memory* (pp. 157–179). New York: Cambridge University Press.

Belmonte, M. K., Cook, E. H., Jr, Anderson, G. M., Rubenstein, J. L., Greenough, W. T., Beckel-Mitchener, A., et al. (2004). Autism as a disorder of neural information processing: Directions for research and targets for therapy. *Molecular Psychiatry, 9,* 646–663.

Belsky, J., Vandell, D. L., Burchinal, M., Clarke-Stewart, K. A., McCartney, K., Owen, M. T., & The NICHD Early Child Care Research Network. (2007). Are there long-term effects of early child care? *Child Development, 74,* 681–701.

BeLue, R., Francis, L. A., & Colaco, B. (2009). Mental health problems and overweight in a nationally representative sample of adolescents: effects of race and ethnicity. *Pediatrics, 123,* 697–702.

Bem, D. J. (2000). Exotic becomes erotic: Interpreting the biological correlates of sexual orientation. *Archives of Sexual Behavior, 29*(6), 531–548.

Ben-Ari, A., & Gil, S. (2002). Traditional support systems: Are they sufficient in a culturally diverse academic environment? *British Journal of Social Work, 32,* 629–638.

Ben-David, K., & Rossidis, G. (2011). Bariatric surgery: Indications, safety and efficacy. *Current Pharmaceutical Design, 17*(12), 1209–1217.

Benecke, M. (1999). Spontaneous human combustion: Thoughts of a forensic biologist. *Skeptical Inquirer, 22,* 47–51.

Benedetti, F. G. (2007). Placebo and endogenous mechanisms of analgesia. *Handbook of Experimental Pharmacology,177,* 393–413.

Benedetti, F., Arduino, C., & Amanzio, M. (1999). Somatotopic activation of opioid systems by target-directed expectations of analgesia. *Journal of Neuroscience, 19,* 3639–3648.

Ben-Elia, E., & Ettema, D. (2011). Changing commuters' behavior using rewards: A study of rush-hour avoidance. *Transportation Research Part F: Traffic Psychology and Behaviour, 14*(5), 354-368. doi:10.1016/j.trf.2011.04.003.

Benenson, J., Markovits, H., Thompson, M., & Wrangham, R. (2011). Under threat of social exclusion, females exclude more than males. *Psychological Science, 22*(4), 538–544.

Benenson, J. F., & Koulnazarian, M. (2008). Sex differences in help-seeking appear in early childhood. *British Journal of Developmental Psychology, 26,* 163–169.

Bener, A., Al Maadidb, M. G. A., Özkanc, T., Al-Bastb, D. A. E., Diyabb, K. N., & Lajunenc, T. (2008). The impact of four-wheel drive on risky driver behaviours and road traffic accidents. *Transportation Research Part F: Traffic Psychology and Behaviour, 11,* 324–333.

Bener, A. A., Ghuloum, S. S., & Dafeeah, E. E. (2011). Prevalence of common phobias and their socio-demographic correlates in children and adolescents in a traditional developing society. *African Journal of Psychiatry, 14*(2), 140–145. doi:10.4314/ajpsy.v14i2.6.

Benham, G., Woody, E. Z., Wilson, K. S., & Nash, M. R. (2006). Expect the unexpected: Ability, attitude, and responsiveness to hypnosis. *Journal of Personality and Social Psychology, 91,* 342–350.

Benjamin, L. T., Jr., & Simpson, J. A. (2009). The power of the situation: The impact of Milgram's obedience studies on personality and social psychology. *American Psychologist, 64,* 12–19.

Benjamin, K., Wilson, S. G., & Mogil, J. S. (1999). Sex differences in supraspinal morphine analgesia are dependent on genotype. *Journal of Pharmacology and Experimental Therapeutics, 289,* 1370–1375.

Benjamin, A. S., & Tullis, J. (2010). What makes distributed practice effective? *Cognitive Psychology, 61*(3), 228-247. doi:10.1016/j.cogpsych.2010.05.004.

Benjamin, L. T., Jr. (2000). The psychology laboratory at the turn of the 20th century. *American Psychologist, 55,* 318–321.

Benjamin, L. T., Jr., & Baker, D. (2004). *From séance to science: A history of the profession of psychology in America.* Belmont, CA: Wadsworth.

Benjamin, S., & Taylor, W. D. (2010). Nature and nurture: Genetic influences and gene-environment interactions in depression. *Current Psychiatry Reviews, 6*(2), 82–90. doi:10.2174/157340010791196484.

Bennett, D. S., Bendersky, M., & Lewis, M. (2008). Children's cognitive ability from 4 to 9 years old as a function of prenatal cocaine exposure, environmental risk, and maternal verbal intelligence. Developmental Psychology, *44,* 919–928.

Bennett, H. L., Giannini, J. A., & Davis, H. S. (1985). Nonverbal response to intraoperational conversation. *British Journal of Anaesthesia, 57,* 174–179.

Bennett, K. K., & Elliott, M. (2002). Explanatory style and health: Mechanisms linking pessimism to illness. *Journal of Applied Social Psychology, 32,* 1508–1526.

Bennett, R. J., & Robinson, S. L. (2000). Development of a measure of workplace deviance. *Journal of Applied Psychology, 85,* 349–360.

Ben-Porath, Y. S., & Tellegen, A. (2008). *Minnesota multiphasic personality inventory-2-RF.* San Antonio, TX: Pearson Assessment.

Ben-Shakhar, G., & Furedy, J. J. (1990). *Theories and applications in the detection of deception: A psychophysiological and international perspective.* New York: Springer-Verlag.

Ben-Shakhar, G., Bar-Hillel, M., & Kremnitzer, M. (2002). Trial by polygraph: Reconsidering the use of the guilty knowledge technique in court. *Law & Human Behavior, 26,* 527–541.

Benson, E. (2003). Sex: The science of sexual arousal. *Monitor on Psychology, 34,* 50.

Benson, H. (1975). *The relaxation response.* New York: Morrow.

Benton, J. M., & Overtree, C. E. (2012). Multicultural office design: A case example. *Professional Psychology: Research and Practice, 43,* 265–269. doi:10.1037/a0027443.

Bentin, S., DeGutis, J. M., D'Esposito, M., & Robertson, L. C. (2007). Too many trees to see the forest: Performance, event-related potential, and functional Magnetic Resonance Imaging manifestations of integrative congenital prosopagnosia. *Journal of Cognitive Neuroscience, 19*(1), 132–146.

Ben-Zur, H. (2002). Coping, affect and aging: The roles of mastery and self-esteem. *Personality & Individual Differences, 32*(2), 357–372.

Berant, E., Mikulincer, M., & Shaver, P. R. (2008). Mothers' attachment style, their mental health, and their children's emotional vulnerabilities: A 7-year study of children with congenital heart disease. *Journal of Personality, 76,* 31–65.

Berdahl, J. L., & Moore, C. (2006). Workplace harassment: Double jeopardy for minority women. *Journal of Applied Psychology, 91,* 426–436.

Beresford, J., & Blades, M. (2006). Children's identification of faces from lineups: The effects of lineup presentation and instructions on accuracy. *Journal of Applied Psychology, 91,* 1102–1113.

Berger, L. M., Paxson, C., & Waldfogel, J. (2009). Income and child development. *Children and Youth Services Review, 31,* 978–989.

Bergin, A. E. (1971). The evaluation of therapeutic outcomes. In A. E. Bergin & S. L. Garfield (Eds.), *Handbook of psychotherapy and behavior change: An empirical analysis* (pp. 217–270). New York: Wiley.

Berglund, H., Lindstrom, P., & Savic, I. (2006). Brain response to putative pheromones in lesbian women. *Proceedings of the National Academy of Sciences, 103,* 8269–8274.

Bergman, T., J., Kitchen, D. M. (2009). Comparing responses to novel objects in wild baboons (*Papio ursinus*) and geladas (*Theropithecus gelada*). *Animal Cognition, 12*(1), 63–73.

Berkowitz, L. (1994). Is something missing? Some observations prompted by the Cognitive-neoassociationist view of anger and emotional aggression. In L. R. Huesmann (Ed.), *Human aggression: Current perspectives* (pp. 35–60). New York: Plenum.

Berkman, E. T., Falk, E. B., & Lieberman, M. D. (2011). In the trenches of real-world self-control: Neural correlates of breaking the link between craving and smoking. *Psychological Science, 22*(4), 498–506. doi:10.1177/0956797611400918.

Berkowitz, L. (1998). Affective aggression: The role of stress, pain, and negative affect. In R. G. Geen & E. Donnerstein (Eds.), *Human aggression* (pp. 49–72). San Diego: Academic Press.

Berkowitz, L. (1999). Evil is more than banal: Situationism and the concept of evil. *Personality and Social Psychology Review, 3,* 246–253.

Berlin, L. J., Cassidy, J., & Appleyard, K. (2008). The influence of early attachments on other relationships. In J. Cassidy & P. R. Shaver (Eds.), *Handbook of attachment* (2nd ed., pp. 333–347). New York: Guilford Press.

Bermeitinger, C., Goelz, R., Johr, N., Neumann, M., Ecker, U. K. H., & Doerr, R. (2009). The hidden persuaders break into the tired brain. *Experimental Social Psychology, 45*(2), 320–326.

Berna, C., Leknes, S., Holmes, E. A., Edwards, R. R., Goodwin, G. M., & Tracey, I. (2010). Induction of Depressed Mood Disrupts Emotion Regulation Neurocircuitry and Enhances Pain Unpleasantness. *Biological Psychiatry, 67*(11), 1083–1090. doi:10.1016/j.biopsych.2010.01.014.

Bernard, L. L. (1924). *Instinct.* New York: Holt, Rinehart & Winston.

Bernardin, H. J., & Beatty, R. W. (1984). *Performance appraisal: Assessing human behavior at work.* Boston: Kent.

Bernat, J. A., Calhoun, K. S., Adams, H. E., & Zeichner, A. (2001). Homophobia and physical aggression toward homosexual and heterosexual individuals. *Journal of Abnormal Psychology, 110,* 179–187.

Bernieri, F. J., & Petty, K. N. (2011). The influence of handshakes on first impression accuracy. *Social Influence, 6,* 78–87. doi:10.1080/15534510.2011.566706.

Berns, G. S., McClure, S. M., Pagnoni, G., & Montague, P. R. (2001). Predictability modulates human brain response to reward. *Journal of Neuroscience, 21,* 2793–2798.

Bernstein, D. A. (1970). The modification of smoking behavior: A search for effective variables. *Behaviour Research and Therapy, 8,* 133–146.

Bernstein, D. A., Borkovec, T. D., & Hazlett-Stevens, H. (2000). *Progressive relaxation training: A manual for the helping professions* (2nd ed.). New York: Praeger.

Bernstein, D. M., & Loftus, E. F. (2009a). The consequences of false memories for food preferences and choices. *Perspectives on Psychological Science, 4,* 135–139.

Bernstein, D. M., & Loftus, E. F. (2009b). How to tell if a particular memory is true or false. *Perspectives in Psychological Science, 4,* 370–374.

Bernstein, D. M., & Roberts, B. (1995). Assessing dreams through self-report questionnaires: Relation with past research and personality. *Dreaming: Journal of the Association for the Study of Dreams, 5,* 13–27.

Bernstein, I. L. (1978). Learned taste aversions in children receiving chemotherapy. *Science, 200,* 1302–1303.

Berry, C. M., Ones, D. S., & Sackett, P. R. (2007). Interpersonal deviance, organizational deviance, and their common correlates: A review and meta-analysis. *Journal of Applied Psychology, 92,* 409–423.

Berry, C. M., Sackett, P. R., & Wiemann, S. (2007). A review of recent developments in integrity test research. *Personnel Psychology, 60,* 271–301.

Berry, J. W., & Bennett, J. A. (1992). Cree conceptions of cognitive competence. *International Journal of Psychology, 27,* 73–88.

Berry, S. L., Beatty, W. W., & Klesges, R. C. (1985). Sensory and social influences on ice cream consumption by males and females in a laboratory setting. *Appetite, 6,* 41–45.

Berscheid, E. (2011). Love and compassion: Caregiving in adult close relationships. In S. Brown, M. Brown, & L. Penner (Eds.), *Self-interest and beyond: Toward a new understanding of human caregiving.* New York: Oxford University Press.

Berscheid, E. (2010). Love in the fourth dimension. *Annual Review of Psychology, 61,* 1–26. Bersoff, D. N. (2008). *Ethical conflicts in psychology* (4th ed.). Washington, DC: American Psychological Association.

Bersoff, D. M. (1999). Why good people sometimes do bad things: Motivated reasoning and unethical behavior. *Personality and Social Psychology Bulletin, 25,* 28–39.

Bertau, C., Anderson, N., & Salgado, J. F. (2005). The predictive validity of cognitive ability tests: A UK meta-analysis. *Journal of Occupational and Organizational Psychology, 78,* 387–409.

Bertenthal, B. I., Longo, M. R., & Kenny, S. (2007). Phenomenal permanence and the development of predictive tracking in infancy. *Child Development, 78*(1), 350–363.

Berti, A., Ladavas, E., & Corti, M. D. (1996). Anosognosia for hemiplegia, neglect dyslexia, and drawing neglect: Clinical findings and theoretical implications. *Journal of the International Neuropsychological Association, 2,* 426–440.

Bertolo, H., Paiva, T., Pessoa, L., Mestre, T., Marques, R., & Santos, R. (2003). Visual dream content, graphical representation and EEG alpha activity in congenitally blind subjects. *Brain Research. Cognitive Brain Research, 15*(3), 277–284.

Best, D. (1992, June). *Cross-cultural themes in developmental psychology.* Paper presented at workshop on cross-cultural aspects of psychology. Western Washington University, Bellingham.

Best, J. B. (1999). *Cognitive psychology* (5th ed.). Belmont, CA: Brooks/Cole.

Bestmann, S., Ruff, C. C., Blankenburg, F., Weiskopf, N., Driver, J., & Rothwell, J. C. (2008). Mapping causal interregional influences with concurrent TMS-fMRI. *Experimental Brain Research, 191*(4), 383–402.

Betan, E., Heim, A. K., Conklin, C. Z., & Westen, D. (2005). Countertransference phenomena and personality pathology in clinical practice: An empirical investigation. *American Journal of Psychiatry, 162,* 890–898.

Betch, T., Hoffman, K., Hoffrage, U., & Plessner, H. (2003). Intuition beyond recognition: When less familiar events are liked more. *Experimental Psychology, 50,* 49–54.

Bettencourt, B. A., Talley, A., Benjamin, A. J., & Valentine, J. (2006). Personality and aggressive behavior under provoking and neutral conditions: A meta-analytic review. *Psychological Bulletin. 132,* 751–777.

Betz, D., & Sekaquaptewa, D. (2012) My fair physicist? Feminine math and science role models demotivate young girls. *Social Psychological and Personality Science.* doi:dx.doi.org/10.1177/1948550612440735.

Beutler, L. E., & Malik, M. L. (Eds.). (2002). *Rethinking DSM: A psychological perspective.* Washington, DC: American Psychological Association.

Beynon, C. (2011). Diagnosing the use of illegal drugs by older people—Comments on the proposed changes to DSM-V. *Addiction, 106*(5), 884–885. doi:10.1111/j.1360-0443.2010.03283.x.

Beyerstein, B. L. (1999). Pseudoscience and the brain: Tuners and tonics for aspiring superhumans. In S. Della Sala (Ed.), *Mind myths: Exploring popular assumptions about the mind and brain* (pp. 59–82). Chichester, UK: Wiley.

Bhatt, R. S., & Bertin, E. (2001). Pictorial cues and three-dimensional information processing in early infancy. *Journal of Experimental Child Psychology, 80,* 315–332.

Bhatt, R. S., & Quinn, P. C. (2011). How does learning impact development in infancy? The case of perceptual organization. *Infancy, 16*(1), 2–38.

Bhatt, S., Mbwana, J., Adeyemo, A., Sawyer, A. Hailu, A., & VanMeter, J. (2009). Lying about facial recognition: An fMRI study. *Brain and Cognition, 69,* 382–390.

Bhopal, R., Vettini, A., Hunt, S., Wiebe, S., Hanna, L., & Amos, A. (2004). Review of prevalence data in, and evaluation of methods for cross cultural adaptation of, UK surveys on tobacco and alcohol in ethnic minority groups. *British Medical Journal, 328,* 76.

Bhutta, A. T., Cleves, M. A., Casey, P. H., Cradock, M. M., & Anand, K. J. S. (2002). Cognitive and behavioral outcomes of school-aged children who were born preterm. *Journal of the American Medical Association, 288,* 728–737.

Bhutta, M. F. (2007). Sex and the nose: Human pheromonal responses. *Journal of the Royal Society of Medicine, 100*(6), 268–274.

Bialystok, E., & Craik, F. M. (2010). Cognitive and linguistic processing in the bilingual mind. *Current Directions in Psychological Science, 19*(1), 19–23. doi:10.1177/0963721409358571.

Bialystok, E., Craik, F. M., & Luk, G. (2012). Bilingualism: consequences for mind and brain. *Trends in Cognitive Sciences,* 16(4), 240–250. doi:10.1016/j.tics.2012.03.001.

Bibbins-Domingo, K., Coxson, P., Pletcher, M. J., Lightwood, J., & Goldman, L. (2007). Adolescent overweight and future adult coronary heart disease. *The New England Journal of Medicine, 357,* 2371–2379.

Bickis, M., Kelly, I. W., & Byrnes, G. (1995). Crisis calls and temporal and lunar variables: A comprehensive study. *Journal of Psychology, 129,* 701–711.

Bidwell, M. A., & Rehfeldt, R. A. (2004). Using video modeling to teach a domestic skill with an embedded social skill to adults with severe mental retardation. *Behavioral Interventions, 19,* 263–274.

Bieling, P. J., McCabe, R. E., & Antony, M. M. (2006). *Cognitive-behavioral therapy in groups.* New York: Guilford.

Bielsky, I. F., Hu, S.-B., Ren, X., Terwilliger, E. F., & Young, L. J. (2005). The V1a Vasopressin receptor is necessary and sufficient for normal social recognition: A gene replacement study. *Neuron, 47,* 503–513.

Bienenfeld, D. (2005). *Psychodynamic theory for clinicians.* New York: Lippincott Williams & Wilkins.

Bierhaus, A., Wolf, J., Andrassy, M., Rohleder, N., Humpert, P. M., Petrov, D., et al. (2003). A mechanism converting psychosocial stress into mononuclear cell activation. *Proceedings of the National Academy of Sciences, 100,* 1920–1925.

Bierut, L. J., Agrawal, A., Bucholz, K. K., Doheny, K. F., Laurie, C., Pugh, E. (2011). A genome-wide association study of alcohol dependence. *PNAS, 107,* 5082–5087. doi:10.1073/pnas.0911109107

Bierut, L. J., Heath, A. C., Bucholz, K. K., Dinwiddie, S. H., Madden, P. A., Statham, D. J., et al. (1999). Major depressive disorder in a community-based twin sample: Are there different genetic and environmental contributions for men and women? *Archives of General Psychiatry, 56,* 557–563.

Bies, R. J., Tripp, T. M., & Kramer, R. M. (1997). At the breaking point: Cognitive and social dynamics of revenge in organizations. In R. A. Giacalone & J. Greenberg (Eds.), *Antisocial behavior in organizations* (pp. 18–36). Thousand Oaks, CA: Sage.

Biesanz, J. C., Human, L. J., Paquin, A., Chan, M., Parisotto, K. L., Sarracino, J., & Gillis, R. L. (2011). Do we know when our impressions of others are valid? Evidence for realistic accuracy awareness in first impressions of personality. *Social Psychological and Personality Science, 2,* 452–459. doi:10.1177/1948550610397211.

Biever, C. (2009, January 3). Interview: Inside the savant mind. *New Scientist, 200*(2688), 40–41.

Bigelow, B. J. (2006). There's an elephant in the room: The impact of early poverty and neglect on intelligence and common learning disorders in children and adolescents, and their parents. *Developmental Disabilities Bulletin, 34,* 177–215.

Bigler, R., & Liben, L. (2007). Developmental intergroup theory: Explaining and reducing children's social stereotyping and prejudice. *Current Directions in Psychological Science, 16,* 162–166.

Bijttebier, P., Beck, I., Claes, L., & Vandereycken, W. (2009). Gray's reinforcement sensitivity theory as a framework for research on personality-psychopathology associations. *Clinical Psychology Review, 5,* 421–430.

Bikbaev, A., & Manahan-Vaughan, D. (2008). Relationship of hippocampal theta and gamma oscillations to potentiation of synaptic transmission. *Frontiers in Neuroscience, 2*(1), 56–63.

Bilalić, M., McLeod, P., & Gobet, F. (2010). The mechanism of the *Einstellung* (set) effect: Apervasive source of cognitive bias. *Current Directions in Psychological Science, 19,* 111–115.

Biller, J., Love, B. B., & Schenk, M.J. (2008). Ischemic Cerebrovascular Disease. In W. G. Bradley, R. B. Daroff, G. M. Fenichel, & J. Jamkovic (Eds). *Bradley: Neurology in Clinical Practice, 5th Edition.* Philadelphia, PA: Butterworth, Heinemann, Elsevier.

Billiard, M. (2009). REM sleep behavior disorder and narcolepsy. *CNS and Neurological Disorders—Drug Targets, 8,* 264–270.

bin Saif, G. A., Papoiu, A. P, Banari, L. L., McGlone, F. F., Kwatra, S. G., Chan, Y. H., & Yosipovitch, G. G. (2012). The pleasurability of scratching an itch: A psychophysical and topographical assessment. *British Journal of Dermatology, 166*(5), 981–985. doi:10.1111/j.1365–2133.2012.10826.x.

Binet, A., & Simon, T. (1905). Methodes nouvelles pour le diagnostic du niveau intellectuel des anormaux. *L'Annee Psychologique, 11,* 191–244.

Binet, A., & Simon, T. (1908). The development of intelligence in the child. *L'Annee Psychologique, 14,* 1–94.

Bingheimer, J. B., Brennan, R. T., & Earls, F. J. (2005). Firearm violence exposure and serious violent behavior. *Science, 308,* 1323–1326.

Binzen, C. A., Swan, P. D., & Manore, M. M. (2001). Post exercise oxygen consumption and substrate use after resistance exercise in women. *Medicine and Science in Sports and Exercise, 33,* 932–938.

Birbaumer, N., Veit, R., Lotze, M., Erb, M., Hermann, C., Grodd, W., & Flor, H. (2005). Deficient fear conditioning in psychopathy: A functional magnetic resonance imaging study. *Archives of General Psychiatry, 62,* 799–805.

Birch, H. G. (1945). The relation of previous experience to insightful problem solving. *Journal of Comparative Psychology, 38,* 367–383.

Birnbaum, G. E., Reis, H. T., Mikulincer, M., Gillath, O., & Orpaz, A. (2006). When sex is more than just sex: Attachment orientations, sexual experience, and relationship quality. *Journal of Personality & Social Psychology, 91,* 929–943.

Biron, M., Bamberger, P. A., & Noyman, T. (2011). Work-related risk factors and employee substance use: Insights from a sample of Israeli blue-collar workers. *Journal of Occupational Health Psychology, 16*(2), 247–63. doi:10.1037/a0022708

Bisiach, E., Capitani, E., & Tansini, E. (1979). Detection from left and right hemifields on single and double simultaneous stimulation. *Perceptual and Motor Skills, 48*(3, Pt. 1), 960.

Bisiach, E., Luzzatti, C., & Perani, D. (1979). Unilateral neglect, representational schema and consciousness. *Brain, 102*(3), 609–618.

Bisiach, E., Vallar, G., Perani, D., Papagano, C., & Berti, A. (1986). Unawareness of disease following lesions of the right hemisphere: Anosognosia for hemiplegia and anosognosia for hemianopia. *Neuropsychologia, 24,* 471–482.

Bisson, J. I. (2007). Eye movement desensitisation and reprocessing reduces PTSD symptoms compared with fluoxetine at six months post-treatment. *Evidence-Based Mental Health, 10*(4), 118.

Bjork, R. A. (1999). Assessing our own competence: Heuristics and illusions. In D. Gopher & A. Koriat (Eds.), *Attention and performance XVII. Cognitive regulation of performance: Interaction of theory and application* (pp. 435–459). Cambridge: MIT Press.

Bjork, R. A. (2001, March). How to succeed in college: Learn how to learn. *American Psychological Society Observer, 14,* 9.

Bjork, R. A., & Linn, M. C. (2006, March). The science of learning and the learning of science: Introducing desirable difficulties. *American Psychological Society Observer, 19,* 29, 39.

Bjorklund, D. F., & Green, B. L. (1992). The adaptive nature of cognitive immaturity. *American Psychologist, 47,* 46–54.

Bjorklund, P. (2006). No man's land: Gender bias and social constructivism in the diagnosis of borderline personality disorder. *Issues in Mental Health Nursing, 27,* 3–23.

Bjornebekk, G., Gjesme, T., & Ulriksen, R. (2011). Achievement motives and emotional processes in children during problem-solving: Two experimental studies of their relation to performance in different achievement goal conditions. *Motivation and Emotion, 35,* 351–367.

Blagrove, M. (1996). Problems with the cognitive psychological modeling of dreaming. *Journal of Mind and Behavior, 17,* 99–134.

Blagrove, M., Fouquet, N. C., Henley-Einion, J. A., Pace-Schott, E. F., Davies, A. C., Neuschaffer, J. L., & Turnbull, O. H. (2011). Assessing the Dream-Lag Effect for REM and NREM Stage 2 Dreams. *PLoS One, 6*(10), e26708.

Blair, C., & Raver, C. (2012). Child development in the context of adversity: Experiential canalization of brain and behavior. *American Psychologist,* doi:10.1037/a0027493.

Blair, M. M., Glynn, L. M., Sandman, C. A., & Davis, E. (2011). Prenatal maternal anxiety and early childhood temperament. *Stress: The International Journal on the Biology of Stress, 14*(6), 644–651.

Blair, P. S., Sidebotham, P., Berry, P. J., Evans, M., & Fleming P. J. (2006). Major epidemiological changes in sudden infant death syndrome: A 20-year population-based study in the UK. *Lancet, 367,* 314–319.

Blair-West, G. W., Cantor, C. H., Mellsop, G. W., & Eyeson-Annan, M. L. (1999). Lifetime suicide risk in major depression: Sex and age determinants. *Journal of Affective Disorders, 53,* 171–178.

Blaisdell, A. P., Sawa, K., & Leising, K. J. (2006). Causal reasoning in rats. *Science, 311,* 1020–1022.

Blake, J., & de Boysson-Bardies, B. (1992). Patterns in babbling: A cross-linguistic study. *Journal of Child Language, 19,* 51–74.

Blake, R. (1998). What can be "perceived" in the absence of visual awareness? *Current Directions in Psychological Science, 6,* 157–162.

Blakeslee, S. (2000, January 4). A decade of discovery yields a shock about the brain. *New York Times*.

Blakeslee, S. (2001, August 28). Therapies push injured brains and spinal cords into new paths. *New York Times*.

Blakesley, R. E., Mazumdar ,S., Dew, M. A., Houck, P. R., Tang, G., Reynolds, C. F. 3rd, & Butters, M. A. (2009). Comparisons of methods for multiple hypothesis testing in neuropsychological research. *Neuropsychology, 23*(2), 255–264.

Blakemore, J. E. O., Berenbaum, S. A. & Liben, L. S. (2009). *Gender development*. New York: Taylor & Francis.

Blanchard, P. N., & Thacker, J. W. (2007). *Effective training: Systems, strategies, and practices*. Upper Saddle River, NJ: Pearson Prentice Hall.

Blanchard, R., & Lippa, R. A. (2007). Birth order, sibling sex ratio, handedness, and sexual orientation of male and female participants in a BBC Internet Research Project. *Archives of Sexual Behavior, 36*(2), 163–176.

Blanchette, I., & Richards, A. (2010). The influence of aff ect on higher level cognition: A review of research on interpretation, judgement, decision making and reasoning. *Cognition and Emotion, 24*, 561–595.

Blascovich, J., Spencer, S. J., Quinn, D., & Steele, C. (2001). African Americans and high blood pressure: The role of stereotype threat. *Psychological Science, 12*, 225–229.

Blass, T. (2000). The Milgram paradigm 35 years later: Some things we know about obedience to authority. In T. Blass (Ed.), *Current perspectives on the Milgram paradigm* (pp. 35–59). Mahwah, NJ: Erlbaum.

Blass, T. (2004). *The man who shocked the world: The life and legacy of Stanley Milgram*. New York: Basic Books.

Blass, T. (2009). From New Haven to Santa Clara: A historical perspective on the Milgram obedience experiments. *American Psychologist, 64*, 37–45.

Blass, T., & Schmitt, C. (2001). The nature of perceived authority in the Milgram paradigm: Two replications. *Current Psychology: Developmental, Learning, Personality, Social, 20*, 115–121.

Blease, C. (2012). Mental health illiteracy? Perceiving depression as a disorder. *Review of General Psychology, 16*(1), 59–69. doi:10.1037/a0026494.

Blechert, J., Sheppes, G., Di Tella, C., Williams, H., & Gross, J. J. (2012). See what you think: Reappraisal modulates behavioral and neural responses to social stimuli. *Psychological Science, 23*(4), 346–353. doi:10.1177/0956797612438559

Bleidorn, W., Kandler, C., Hülsheger, U. R., Riemann, R., Angleitner, A., & Spinath, F. M. (2010). Nature and nurture of the interplay between personality traits and major life goals. *Journal Of Personality And Social Psychology, 99*(2), 366–379. doi:10.1037/a0019982.

Bleil, M. E., McCaffery, J. M., Muldoon, M. F., Sutton-Tyrrell, K., & Manuck, S. B. (2004). Anger-related personality traits and carotid artery atherosclerosis in untreated hypertensive men. *Psychosomatic Medicine, 66*, 633–639.

Block, J. (2001). Millennial contrarianism: The Five-Factor approach to personality description 5 years later. *Journal of Research in Personality, 35*, 98–107.

Block, J. A. (1971). *Lives through time*. Berkeley: Bancroft Books.

Block, R. I., & Ghoneim, M. M. (1993). Effects of chronic marijuana use on human cognition. *Psychopharmacology, 110*(1–2), 219–228.

Bohner, G., Erb, H.-P., & Siebler, F. (2008) Information processing approaches to persuasion: Integrating assumptions from the dual- and single-processing perspectives. In W. B. Crano & R. Prislin (Eds.), *Attitudes and persuasion* (pp. 161–188). New York: Psychology Press.

Blom, R. M., Samuels, J. F., et al., (2011). Association between a serotonin transporter promoter polymorphism (5HTTLPR) and personality disorder traits in a community sample. *Journal of Psychiatric Research, 45*, 1153–1159.

Blood, A. J., & Zatorre, R. J. (2001). Intensely pleasurable responses to music correlate with activity in brain regions implicated in reward and emotion. *Proceedings of the National Academy of Sciences, 98*, 11818–11823.

Bloom, B., & Cohen, R. A. (2007). *Summary health statistics for U.S. children: National Health Interview Survey, 2006*. Washington, D C: National Center for Health Statistics.

Bloom, L. (1995). *The transition from infancy to language: Acquiring the power of expression*. New York: Cambridge University Press.

Bloomgarden, A., & Calogero, R. M. (2008). A randomized experimental test of the efficacy of EMDR treatment on negative body image in eating disorder inpatients. *Eating Disorders, 16*(5), 418–427.

Blow, A. J., & Timm, T. M. (2002). Promoting community through family therapy: Helping clients develop a network of significant social relationships. *Journal of Systematic Therapies, 21*, 67–89.

Blum, R. W., Beuhring, T., & Rinehart, P. M. (2000). *Protecting teens: Beyond race, income and family structure*. Minneapolis, MN: Center for Adolescent Health, University of Minnesota.

Blumberg, F. C., Rosenthal, S. F., & Randall, J. D. (2008, July). Impasse-driven learning in the context of video games. *Computers in Human Behavior, 24*(4), 1530–1541.

Blumberg, H. P., Leung, H.-C., Skudlarski, P., Lacadie, C. M., Fredericks, C. A., Harris, B. C., et al. (2003). A functional magnetic resonance imaging study of bipolar disorder: State- and trait-related dysfunction in ventral prefrontal cortices. *Archives of General Psychiatry, 60*, 601–609.

Blumberg, M. S., & Lucas, D. E. (1994). Dual mechanisms of twitching during sleep in neonatal rats. *Behavioral Neuroscience, 108*(6), 1196–1202.

Blumenthal, J. A., Babyak, M., Wei., J., O'Conner, C., Waugh, R., Eisenstein, E., et al. (2002). Usefulness of psychosocial treatment of mental stress-induced myocardial ischemia in men. *American Journal of Cardiology, 89*, 164–168.

Blundell, J. E., & Cooling, J. (2000). Routes to obesity: Phenotypes, food choices, and activity. *British Journal of Nutrition, 83*, S33–S38.

Boag, S. (2011). Explanation in personality psychology: "Verbal magic" and the five-factor model. *Philosophical Psychology, 24*, 223–243.

Boake, C., Yeates, K. O., & Donders, J. (2002). Association of postdoctoral programs in clinical neuropsychology: Update and new directions. *Clinical Neuropsychology, 16*(1), 1–6.

Boardman, A. P., & Healy, D. (2001). Modeling suicide risk in affective disorders. *European Psychiatry, 16*, 400–405.

Bob, P. (2008). Pain, dissociation and subliminal self-representations. *Consciousness and Cognition, 17*, 355–369.

Bobko, P., Roth, P. L., & Potosky, D. (1999). Derivation and implications of a meta-analytic matrix incorporating cognitive ability, alternative predictors, and job performance. *Personnel Psychology, 52*, 561–590.

Bochukova, E. G., Huang, N., Keogh, J., Henning, E., et al. (2010). Large, rare chromosomal deletions associated with severe early-onset obesity. *Nature, 463*, 666–670.

Boden, M. A. (2006). *Computer models of mind*. Cambridge, UK: Cambridge University Press.

Boden-Albala, B., Litwak, E., Elkind, M. S., Rundek, T., & Sacco, R. L. (2005). Social isolation and outcomes post stroke. *Neurology, 64*, 1888–1892.

Boehning, D., & Snyder, S. H. (2003). Novel neural modulators. *Annual Review of Neuroscience, 26*, 105–131.

Bogaert, A. F., Blanchard, R., & Crosthwait, L. (2007). Interaction of birth order, handedness, and sexual orientation in the Kinsey interview data. *Behavioral Neuroscience, 121*(5), 845–853.

Boger, J., & Mihailidis, A. (2011). The future of intelligent assistive technologies for cognition: Devices under development to support independent living and aging-with-choice. *Neurorehabilitation, 28*(3), 271–280. doi:10.3233/NRE-2011-0655.

Bohner, G., & Schwarz, N. (2001). Attitudes persuasion and behavior. In A. Tesser & N. Schwarz (Eds.), *Blackwell handbook of social psychology: Intraindividual processes* (pp. 413–435). Oxford, UK: Blackwell.

Boland, J. E.,Chua, H. F., & Nisbett, R. E. (2008). Culture, class, and cognition: Evidence from Italy. In K. Rayner, D. Shen, X. Bai (Eds.). *Cognitive and cultural influences on eye movements*. (pp. 363–378). Tianjin, China: Tianjin People's Publishing House.

Bolla, K. I., Brown, K., Eldreth, D., Tate, K., & Cadet, J. L. (2002). Dose-related neurocognitive effects of marijuana use. *Neurology, 59*, 1337–1343.

Bollati, V., & Baccarelli, A. (2010). Environmental epigenetics. *Heredity, 105*(1), 105–112.

Bolton, D., Eley, T. C., O'Connor, T. G., Perrin, S., & Rabe-Hesketh, S., et al. (2006). Prevalence and genetic and environmental influences on anxiety disorders in 6-year-old twins. *Psychological Medicine, 36*, 335–344.

Bomze, H. M., Bulsara, K. R., Iskandar, B. J., Caroni, P., & Skene, J. H. (2001). Spinal axon regeneration evoked by replacing two growth cone proteins in adult neurons. *Nature Neuroscience, 4*, 38–43.

Bonanno, G. A. (2004). Loss, trauma, and human resilience: Have we underestimated the human capacity to thrive after extremely aversive events? *American Psychologist, 59*, 20–28.

Bonanno, G. A. (2005). Resilience in the face of potential trauma. *Current Directions in Psychological Science, 14*, 135–138.

Bonanno, G. A., Galea, S., Bucciarelli, A., & Vlahov, D. (2007). What predicts psychological resilience after disaster? The role of demographics, resources, and life stress. *Journal of Consulting and Clinical Psychology, 75*, 671–682.

Bonanno, G. A., & Mancini, A. D. (2008). The human capacity to thrive in the face of potential trauma. *Pediatrics, 121*, 369–375.

Bonci, A., Bernardi, G., Grillner, P., & Mercuri, N. B. (2003). The dopamine-containing neuron: Maestro or simple musician in the orchestra of addiction? *Trends in Pharmacological Science, 24*, 172–177.

Bond, F. W., & Bunce, D. (2003). The role of acceptance and job control in mental health, job satisfaction, and work performance. *Journal of Applied Psychology, 88*, 1057–1067.

Bond, G., Aiken, L., & Somerville, S. (1992). The Health Beliefs Model and adolescents with insulin-dependent diabetes mellitus. *Health Psychology, 11*, 190–198.

Bond, L. A., & Hauf, A. M. C. (2004). Taking stock and putting stock in primary prevention: Characteristics of effective programs. *Journal of Primary Prevention, 24*, 199–221.

Bonner, J. F., Connors, T. M., Silverman, W. F., Kowalski, D. P., Lemay, M. A., & Fischer, I. (2011) Grafted neural progenitors integrate and restore synaptic connectivity across the injured spinal cord. *J Neurosci 31*(12):4675–4686.

Bonner, R. (2001, August 24). Death row inmate is freed after DNA test clears him. *New York Times*.

Bonwell, C. C., & Eison, J. A. (1991). *Active learning: Creating excitement in the classroom*. Washington, DC: George Washington University.

Booji, L, Tremblay, R. E. & Benkelfat, C. (2010). Brain serotonin synthesis in adult males characterized by physical aggression during childhood: A 21-year longitudinal study PLoS ONE, 5 ArtID e11255.

Booth, P. B. & Lindaman, S. L. (2000). Theraplay as a short-term treatment for enhancing attachment in adopted children. In H. G. Kaduson & C. E.Schaefer (Eds.) *Short Term Play Therapy for Children*. New York: The Guilford Press.

Bootzin, R. R. & Epstein D. R. (2011). Understanding and treating insomnia. *Annual Review of Clinical Psychology, 7*, 435–458.

Bordnick, P. S., Elkins, R. L., Orr, T. E., Walters, P., & Thyer, B. A. (2004). Evaluating the relative effectiveness of three aversion therapies designed to reduce craving among cocaine abusers. *Behavioral Interventions, 19*, 1–24.

Borg, M. B., Jr. (2002). The Avalon Garden Men's Association: A community health psychology case study. *Journal of Health Psychology, 7*, 345–357.

Borgida, E., Conner, C., & Monteufel, L. (1992). Understanding living kidney donors: A behavioral decision-making perspective. In S. Spacapan & S. Oskamp (Eds.), *Helping and being helped* (pp. 183–212). Newbury Park, CA: Sage.

Borkenau, P., Riemann, R., Angleitner, A., & Spinath, F. M. (2002). Similarity of childhood experiences and personality resemblance in monozygotic and dizygotic twins: A test of the equal environments assumption. *Personality & Individual Differences, 33,* 261–269.

Borkenau, P., Riemann, R., Spinath, F. M., & Angleitner, A. (2006). Genetic and environmental influences on person [MUL] situation profiles. *Journal of Personality, 74,* 1451–1479.

Borman, W. C., Hanson, M. A., & Hedge, J. W. (1997). Personnel selection. *Annual Review of Psychology, 48,* 299–337.

Borman, W. C., Penner, L. A., Allen T. D., & Motowidlo, S. (2001). Personality predictors of citizenship performance. *International Journal of Selection and Assessment, 9,* 52–69.

Bornstein, M. H., Putnick, D. L., Heslington, M., Gini, M., et al. (2008). Mother-child emotional availability in ecological perspective: Three countries, two regions, two genders. *Developmental Psychology, 44,* 666–680.

Bornstein, B. H. & Greene, E. (2011). Jury decision making: Implications for and from psychology. *Current Directions in Psychological Science, 20*(1), 63–77. doi:10.1177/0963721410397282.

Bornstein, M. H. (2006). Hue categorization and color naming: physics to sensation to perception. In N. J. Pitchford & C. P. Biggum (Eds.), *Progress in Color Studies: Volume II. Psychological Aspects.* Amsterdam: John Benjamins.

Boroditsky, L., & Gaby, A. (2010). Remembrances of times east: Absolute spatial representations of time in an Australian Aboriginal community. *Psychological Science, 21*(11), 1635–1639. doi:10.1177/0956797610386621.

Borry, P., Schotsmans, P., & Dierickx, K. (2006). Evidence-based medicine and its role in ethical decision-making. *Journal of Evaluation in Clinical Practice, 12,* 306–311.

Borsutzky, S., Fujiwara, E., Brand, M., & Markowitsch, H. J. (2008). Confabulations in alcoholic Korsakoff patients. *Neuropsychologia, 46*(13), 3133–3143.

Bos, M. W., van Baaren, R. B., & Dijksterhuis, A. (2011). Food for thought? *Neuropsychoeconomics Conference Proceedings,* 26.

Boscolo-Berto, R., Viel, G., Montagnese, S., Raduazzo, D. I., Ferrara, S. D., & Dauvilliers. Y. (2011). Narcolepsy and effectiveness of gamma-hydroxybutyrate (GHB): A systematic review and meta-analysis of randomized controlled trials. *Sleep Medicine Reviews,* Nov 3, 2011 [Epub ahead of print].

Bosma, H., Marmot, M. G., Hemingway, H., Nicholson, A. C., Brunner, E., & Stansfeld, S. A. (1997). Low job control and risk of coronary heart disease in Whitehall II (prospective cohort) study. *British Medical Journal, 314,* 558–565.

Bosompra, K., Ashikaga, T., Worden, J. K., & Flynn, B. S. (2001). Is more optimism associated with better health? Findings from a population-based survey. *International Quarterly of Community Health Education, 20,* 29–58.

Boto, L. R., Crispim, J. N., de Melo, I. S., Juvandes, C., Rodrigues, T., Azeredo, P., & Ferreira R. (2011). Sleep deprivation and accidental fall risk in children. *Sleep Medicine,* November 4, 2011 [Epub ahead of print].

Botwinick, J. (1961). Husband and father-in-law: A reversible figure. *American Journal of Psychology, 74,* 312–313.

Bouchard, L., Tremblay, A., Bouchard, C., & Perusse, L. (2007). Contribution of several candidate gene polymorphisms in the determination of adiposity changes: Results from the Quebec family study. *International Journal of Obesity, 31,* 891–899.

Bouchard, T. J. (1999). Genes, environment, and personality. In S. J. Ceci & W. M. Williams (Eds.), *The nature-nurture debate: The essential readings* (pp. 97–103). Malden, MA: Blackwell.

Bouchard, T. J., & McGue, M. (1981). Familial studies of intelligence: A review. *Science, 212*(4498), 1055–1059.

Boucher, K. L., Rydell, R. J., Van Loo, K. J., & Rydell, M. T. (2012). Reducing stereotype threat in order to facilitate learning. *European Journal of Social Psychology, 42*(2), 174–179. doi:10.1002/ejsp.871.

Bourassa, M., & Vaugeois, P. (2001). Effects of marijuana use on divergent thinking. *Creativity Research Journal, 13,* 411–416.

Bouret, S. G., Draper, S. J., & Simerly, R. B. (2004). Trophic action of leptin on hypothalamic neurons that regulate feeding. *Science, 304,* 108–110.

Bourne, V. J. (2010). How are emotions lateralised in the brain? Contrasting existing hypotheses using the Chimeric Faces Test. *Cognition and Emotion, 24,* 903–911. doi:10.1080/02699930903007714.

Bouton, M. E. (1993). Context, time, and memory retrieval in the interference paradigms of Pavlovian learning. *Psychological Bulletin, 114,* 80–99.

Bouton, M. E. (2000). A learning theory perspective on lapse, relapse, and the maintenance of behavior change. *Health Psychology, 19,* 57–63.

Bouton, M. E. (2002). Context, ambiguity, and unlearning: Sources of relapse after behavioral extinction. *Biological Psychiatry, 52,* 976–986.

Bouton, M., Mineka, S., & Barlow, D. (2001). A modern learning theory perspective on the etiology of panic disorder. *Psychological Review, 107,* 4–32.

Boutwell, B. B., Franklin, C. A., Barnes, J. C., & Beaver, K. M. (2011). Physical punishment and childhood aggression: The role of gender and gene–environment interplay. *Aggressive Behavior, 37*(6), 559-568. doi:10.1002/ab.20409.

Bouvier, S. E., & Engel, S. A. (2006). Behavioral deficits and cortical damage loci in cerebral achromatopsia. *Cerebral Cortex, 16*(2), 183–191.

Bower, G. H. (1981). Mood and memory. *American Psychologist, 36,* 129–148.

Bower, J. M., & Parsons, L. M. (2003). Rethinking the "lesser brain." *Scientific American, 289,* 50–57.

Bowers, J. S., Mattys, S. L., & Gage, S. H. (2009). Preserved implicit knowledge of a forgotten childhood language. *Psychological Science, 20,* 1064–1069.

Bowlby, J. (1973). *Attachment and loss: Vol. 2. Separation.* New York: Basic Books.

Bowles, D. W., O'Bryant, C. L., Camidge, D. R., & Jimeno, A. (2011). The intersection between cannabis and cancer in the United States. *Critical Reviews in Oncology/Hematology.* October 19, 2011 [Epub ahead of print].

Boyd, S. T. (2006). The endocannabinoid system. *Pharmacotherapy, 26*(12 Pt. 2), 218S–221S.

Boyce, C. J., Brown, G. A., & Moore, S. C. (2010). Money and happiness: Rank of income, not income, affects life satisfaction. *Psychological Science, 21*(4), 471–475. doi:10.1177/0956797610362671.

Boyce, C. J., & Wood, A. M. (2011). Personality prior to disability determines adaptation: Agreeable individuals recover lost life satisfaction faster and more completely. *Psychological Science, 22*(11), 1397–1402. doi:10.1177/0956797611421790.

Boyden, E. S. (2011, July 1). The birth of optogenetics: An account of the path to realizing tools for controlling brain circuits with light. *The Scientist: Magazine of the Life Sciences.* Retrieved from http://the-scientist.com/2011/07/01/the-birth-of-optogenetics/.

Boyle, P. A., Barnes, L. L., Buchman, A. S., & Bennett, D. A. (2009). Purpose in life is associated with mortality among community-dwelling older persons. *Psychosomatic Medicine, 71,* 574–579.

Boyles, S. (2008, October 14). Phiten necklace: Red Sox secret weapon? Some athletes are true believers in the power of titanium. Retrieved January 15, 2009, from http://www.webmd.com/pain-management/news/20081014/phiten-necklace-red-sox-secret-weapon.

Boyle, S. H., Williams, R. B., Mark, D. B., Brummett, B. H., Siegler, I. C., Helms, M. J., & Barefoot, J. C. (2004).Hostility as a predictor of survival in patients with coronary artery disease. *Psychosomatic Medicine, 66,* 629–632.

Boysen, G. A. (2009). A review of experimental studies of explicit and implicit bias among counselors. *Journal of Multicultural Counseling and Development, 37,* 240–249.

Bozarth, M. A., & Wise, R. A. (1984). Anatomically distinct opiate receptor fields mediate reward and physical dependence. *Science, 224,* 516–518.

Brach, J. S., FitzGerald, S., Newman, A. B., Kelsey, S., Kuller, L., VanSwearingen, J. M., & Kriska, A. M. (2003). Physical activity and functional status in community-dwelling older women. *Archives of Internal Medicine, 163,* 2565–2571.

Bradley, R., Greene, J., Russ, E., Dutra, L., & Westen, D. (2005). A multidimensional meta-analysis of psychotherapy for PTSD. *American Journal of Psychiatry, 162,* 214–227.

Bradley-Johnson, S., Graham, D. P., & Johnson, C. M. (1986). Token reinforcement on WISC-R performance for white, low-socioeconomic, upper and lower elementary-school-age students. *Journal of School Psychology, 24,* 73–79.

Bradshaw, G. L. (1993a). Why did the Wright brothers get there first? Part 1. *Chemtech, 23*(6), 8–13.

Bradshaw, G. L. (1993b). Why did the Wright brothers get there first? Part 2. *Chemtech, 23*(7), 16–22.

Brainerd, C. J., & Reyna, V. F. (2005). *The science of false memory.* New York: Oxford University Press.

Brainerd, C. J., Reyna, V. F., Wright, R., & Mojardin, A. H. (2003). Recollection rejection: False memory editing in children and adults. *Psychological Review, 110,* 762–784.

Brambilla, P., Cipriani, A., Hotopf, M., & Barbul, C. (2005). Side-effect profile of fluoxentine in comparison with other SSRIs, tricyclic, and newer antidepressants: A meta-analysis of clinical trial data. *Pharmacopsychiatry, 38,* 69–77.

Brand, S., Wilhelm, F. H., Kossowsky, J., Holsboer-Trachsler, E., & Schneider, S. (2011). Children suffering from separation anxiety disorder (SAD) show increased HPA axis activity compared to healthy controls. *Journal of Psychiatric Research, 45*(4), 452–459. doi:10.1016/j.jpsychires.2010.08.014

Brandimonte, M. A., Hitch, G. J., & Bishop, D. V. M. (1992). Influence of short-term memory codes on visual image processing: Evidence from image transformation tasks. *Journal of Experimental Psychology: Learning, Memory, and Cognition, 18,* 157–165.

Brannick, M., & Levine, E. (2002). *Job analysis.* Thousand Oaks: CA: Sage.

Brannick, M. T., Levine, E. L., & Morgeson, F. P. (Eds.) (2007). *Job and work analysis, second edition: Methods, research, and applications for human resource management.* Thousand Oaks, CA: Sage.

Bransford, J. D., & Johnson, M. K. (1972). Contextual prerequisites for understanding: Some investigations of comprehension and recall. *Journal of Verbal Learning and Verbal Behavior, 11,* 717–726.

Bransford, J. D., & Stein, B. S. (1993). *The ideal problem solver* (2nd ed.). New York: Freeman.

Brasher, E. E., & Chen, P. Y. (1999). Evaluation of success criteria in job search: A process perspective. *Journal of Occupational and Organizational Psychology, 72,* 57–70.

Brassen, S., Gamer, M., Peters, J., Gluth, S., & Büchel, C. (2012, May 4). Don't look back in anger! Responsiveness to missed chances in successful and nonsuccessful aging. *Science, 336*(6081), 612–614. Published online first: http://www.sciencemag.org/content/336/6081/612.short.

Brattico, E., Alluri, V., Bogert, B., Jacobsen, T., Vartiainen, N., Nieminen, S., and Tervaniemi, M. (2011). A functional MRI study of happy and sad emotions in music with and without lyrics. *Frontiers in Psychology,* Epub December 1, 2011.

Braver, T. S., Reynolds, J. R., & Donaldson, D. I. (2003). Neural mechanisms of transient and sustained cognitive control during task switching. *Neuron, 39,* 713–726.

Bray, G. A., & Tartaglia, L. A. (2000). Medicinal strategies in the treatment of obesity. *Nature, 404,* 672–677.

Breck, S. W., Lance, N., & Seher, V. (2009). Selective foraging for antrhopogenic resources by black bears: Minivans in Yosemite National Park. *Journal of Mammology, 90*(5), 1041–1044.

Breed, A. G. (2006, January 28). Stress from Katrina is called "recipe for suicide." *Naples Daily News,* p. 4A.

Brefczynski-Lewis, J. A., Lutz, A., Schaefer, H. S., Levinson, D. B., & Davidson, R. J. (2007). Neural correlates of attentional expertise in long-term meditation practitioners. *Proceedings of the National Academies of Science, 104,* 11483–11488.

Breggin, P. R. (2007). *Brain-disabling treatments in psychiatry: Drugs, electroshock, and the psychopharmaceutical complex* (2nd ed.). New York: Springer Publishing.

Breggin, P. R. (2008). *Medication madness: True stories of mayhem, murder, and suicide caused by psychiatric drugs.* New York: St. Martin's Press.

Brehm, S. (1992). *Intimate relationships.* New York: McGraw-Hill.

Brehm, S., Kassin, S., & Fein, S. (1999). *Social psychology* (4th ed., Table 6.4). Boston: Houghton Mifflin.

Brehm, S., Kassin, S., & Fein, S. (2005). *Social psychology* (6th ed.). Boston, MA: Houghton-Mifflin.

Breier, J. I., Adair, J. C., Gold, M., Fennell, E. B., Gilmore, R. L., & Heilman, K. M. (1995). Dissociation of anosognosia for hemiplegia and aphasia during left-hemisphere anesthesia. *Neurology, 45,* 65–67.

Brelsford, J. W. (1993). Physics education in a virtual environment. In *Proceedings of the 37th Annual Meeting of the Human Factors and Ergonomics Society.* Santa Monica, CA: Human Factors.

Bremner, J. D., Shobe, K. K., & Kihlstrom, J. F. (2000). False memories in women with self-reported childhood sexual abuse. *Psychological Science, 11,* 333–337.

Bremner, J. D., Vythilingam, M., Vermetten, E., Caccarino, V., & Charney, D. S. (2004). Deficits in hippocampal and anterior cingulate functioning during verbal declarative memory encoding in midlife major depression. *American Journal of Psychiatry, 161,* 637–645.

Bremner, J. D., Vythilingam, M., Vermetten, E., Southwick, S. M., McGlashan, T., Nazeer, A., et al. (2003). MRI and PET study of deficits in hippocampal structure and function in women with childhood sexual abuse and posttraumatic stress disorder. *American Journal of Psychiatry, 160,* 924–932.

Brems, C., & Namyniuk, L. (2002). The relationship of childhood abuse history and substance use in an Alaska Sample. *Substance Use and Misuse, 37,* 473–494.

Brendgen, M., Boivin, M., Vitaro, F., Bukowski, W. M., Dionne, G., Tremblay, R. E., & Pérusse, D. (2008). Linkages between children's and their friends' social and physical aggression: Evidence for a gene-environment interaction? *Child Development, 79*(1), 13–29.

Brener, N. D., Hassan, S. S., & Barrios, L. C. (1999). Suicidal ideation among college students in the United States. *Journal of Consulting and Clinical Psychology, 67,* 1004–1008.

Brenes, G. A., Rapp, S. R., Rejeski, W. J., & Miller, M. E. (2002). Do optimism and pessimism predict physical functioning? *Journal of Behavioral Medicine, 25,* 219–231.

Brennan, F. X., & Charnetski, C. J. (2000). Explanatory style and Immunoglobulin A (IgA). *Integrative Physiological & Behavioral Science, 35,* 251–255.

Brennen, T., Baguley, T., Bright, J., & Bruce, V. (1990). Resolving semantically induced tip-of-the-tongue states for proper nouns. *Memory & Cognition, 18,* 339–347.

Brenner, R. A., Trumble, A. C., Smith, G. S., Kessler, E. P., & Overpeck, M. D. (2001). Where children drown, United States, 1995. *Pediatrics, 108,* 85–89.

Brescoll, V. L., Dawson, E., & Uhlmann, E. L. (2010). Hard won and easily lost: The fragile status of leaders in gender-stereotype-incongruent occupations. *Psychological Science, 21*(11), 1640–1642. doi:10.1177/0956797610384744.

Breslau, N., Lucia, V. C., & Alvarado, G. F. (2006). Intelligence and other predisposing factors in exposure to trauma and posttraumatic stress disorder: A follow-up study at age 17 years. *Archives of General Psychiatry, 63,* 1238–1245.

Breslau, N., Reboussin, B. A., Anthony, J. C., & Storr, C. L. (2005). The structure of posttraumatic stress disorder: Latent class analysis in 2 community samples. *Archives of General Psychiatry, 62,* 1343–1351.

Breuer, A. T., Masson, M. E., Cohen, A. L., & Lindsay, D. S. (2009). Long-term repetition priming of briefly identified objects. *Journal of Experimental Psychology: Learning, Memory, and Cognition, 35,* 487–498.

Brewer, J. B., Zhao, Z., Desmond, J. E., Glover, G. H., & Gabriel, J. D. E. (1998). Making memories: Brain activity that predicts how well visual experience will be remembered. *Science, 281,* 1185–1187.

Brewer, N., & Wells, G. L. (2011). Eyewitness identification. *Current Directions In Psychological Science, 20*(1), 24–27. doi:10.1177/0963721410389169.

Brewer, N. T., Chapman, G. B., Gibbons, F. X., Gerrard, M., McCaul, K. D., & Weinstein, N. D. (2007). *Health Psychology, 26,* 136–145.

Brewer, W. F. (1977). Memory for the pragmatic implications of sentences. *Memory & Cognition, 5,* 673–678.

Brewer, W. F., & Treyens, J. C. (1981). Role of schemata in memory for places. *Cognitive Psychology, 13,* 207–230.

Brewerton, T. D., & Costin, C. (2011a). Long-term outcome of residential treatment for anorexia nervosa and bulimia nervosa. *Eating Disorders: The Journal of Treatment & Prevention, 19*(2), 132–144. doi:10.1080/10640266.2011.551632

Brewerton, T. D., & Costin, C. (2011b). Treatment results of anorexia nervosa and bulimia nervosa in a residential treatment program. *Eating Disorders: The Journal of Treatment & Prevention, 19*(2), 117–131. doi:10.1080/10640266.2011.551629

Bridge, J. A., Iyengar, S., Salary, C. B., Barbe, R. P., Birmaher, B., Pincus, H. A., et al. (2007). Clinical response and risk for reported suicidal ideation and suicide attempts in pediatric antidepressant treatment: A meta-analysis of randomized controlled trials. *Journal of the American Medical Association, 297,* 1683–1696.

Briggs, G. F., Hole, G. J, & Land, M. F. (2011). Emotionally involving telephone conversations lead to driver error and visual tunnelling. *Transportation Research Part F: Traffic Psychology and Behaviour, 14*(4), 313–323. doi:10.1016/j.trf.2011.02.004.

Brigham, C. C. (1923). *A study of American intelligence.* Princeton, NJ: Princeton University Press.

Bright, J. I., Baker, K. D., & Neimeyer, R. A. (1999). Professional and paraprofessional group treatments for depression: A comparison of cognitive-behavioral and mutual support interventions. *Journal of Consulting and Clinical Psychology, 67,* 491–501.

Brinkhaus, B., Witt, C. M., Jena, S., Linde, K., Streng, A., Wagenpfeil, S., et al. (2006). Acupuncture in patients with chronic low back pain: A randomized controlled trial. *Archives of Internal Medicine, 166,* 450–457.

Brislin, R. (1993). *Understanding culture's influence on behavior.* Fort Worth: Harcourt, Brace, Jovanovich.

Broadbent, E., Petrie, K. J., Alley, P. G., & Booth, R. J. (2003). Psychological stress impairs early wound repair following surgery. *Psychosomatic Medicine, 65,* 865–869.

Broaders, S. C., & Goldin-Meadow, S. (2010). Truth is at hand: How gesture adds information during investigative interviews. *Psychological Science, 21*(5), 623–628. doi:10.1177/0956797610366082.

Broca, P. (1861). Remargues sur le siege de la faculte de la porle articulee, suives d'une observation d'aphemie (perte de parole). *Bulletin Societie Anatomie, 36,* 330–357.

Broca, P. (1865). Sur la faculté du langage articulé. *Bulletin Societe Anthropologie Paris, 6,* 337–393.

Broderick, J. E., Junghaenel, D. U., & Schwartz, J. E. (2005). Written emotional expression produces health benefits in fibromyalgia patients. *Psychosomatic Medicine, 67,* 326–34.

Brodino, N., Lanati, N., Barale, F., Martinelli, V., Politi, P., et al. (2008). Decreased NT-3 plasma levels and platelet serotonin content in patients with hypochondriasis. *Journal of Psychosomatic Research, 65,* 435–439.

Brody, G. H., Beach, S. R. H., Chen, Y., Obasi, E., Philibert, R. A., Kogan, S. M. (2011). Perceived discrimination, serotonin tranporter linked polymorphic region status, and the development of conduct problems. *Development and Psychopathology, 23,* 617–627. doi:10.1017/S0954579411000046.

Brody, N. (2003). Construct validation of the Sternberg Triarchic Abilities Test: Comment and reanalysis. *Intelligence, 31,* 319–330.

Brody, N., & Ehrlichman, H. (1998). *Personality psychology: The science of individuality.* Upper Saddle River, NJ: Prentice Hall.

Broekman, B. P., Niti, M., Nyunt, M., Ko, S., Kumar, R., & Ng, T. (2011). Validation of a brief seven-item response bias-free Geriatric Depression Scale. *The American Journal of Geriatric Psychiatry, 19*(6), 589–596. doi:10.1097/JGP.0b013e3181f61ec9.

Broeren, S., Lester, K. J., Muris, P., & Field, A. P. (2011). They are afraid of the animal, so therefore I am too: Influence of peer modeling on fear beliefs and approach-avoidance behaviors towards animals in typically developing children. *Behaviour Research and Therapy, 49*(1), 50–57. doi:10.1016/j.brat.2010.11.001.

Broesch, T., Callaghan, T., Henrich, J., Murphy, C., & Rochat, P. (2011). Cultural variations in children's mirror self-recognition. *Journal Of Cross-Cultural Psychology, 42*(6), 1018–1029. doi:10.1177/0022022110381114.

Brondolo, E., Rieppi, R., Erickson, S. A., Bagiella, E., Shapiro, P. A., McKinley, P., & Sloan, R.P. (2003). Hostility, interpersonal interactions, and ambulatory blood pressure. *Psychosomatic Medicine, 65,* 1003–1011.

Brook, C. A., & Schmidt, L. A. (2008). Social anxiety disorder: A review of environmental factors. *Neuropsychiatric Disease and Treatment, 4,* 123–143.

Brookmeyer, R., Evans, D. A., Hebert, L., Langa, K. M., Heeringa, S. G., Plassman, B. L., & Kukull, W. A. (2011). National estimates of the prevalence of Alzheimer's disease in the United States. *Alzheimer's & Dementia, 7*(1), 61–73. doi:10.1016/j.jalz.2010.11.007.

Brooks-Gunn, J., & Chase-Lansdale, P. L. (2002). Adolescent parenthood. In M. H. Bornstein (Ed.), *Handbook of parenting* (2nd ed.). Mahwah, NJ: Erlbaum.

Broussard, E. R., & Cassidy, J. (2010). Maternal perception of newborns predicts attachment organization in middle adulthood. *Attachment & Human Development, 12*(1/2), 159–172. doi:10.1080/14616730903282464.

Brown, A. (2010). Reduce Employee Theft Be proactive. Not reactive. *Alaska Business Monthly, 26*(1), 68–69.

Brown, A. S., & Derkits, E. J. (2010). Prenatal infection and schizophrenia: A review of epidemiologic and translational studies. *American Journal of Psychiatry, 167,* 261–280.

Brown, A. L., Campione, J. C., Webber, L. S., & McGilly, K. (1992). Interactive learning environments: A new look at assessment and instruction. In B. Gifford & M. C. O'Connor (Eds.), *Changing assessments: Alternative views of aptitude, achievement, and instruction* (pp. 121–212). Boston: Kluwer.

Brown, A. S. (1991). A review of the tip-of-the-tongue experience. *Psychological Bulletin, 109,* 204–233.

Brown, A. S. (2004). *The déjà vu experience.* New York: Psychology Press.

Brown, A. S., & Nix, L. A. (1996). Age-related changes in the tip-of-the-tongue experience. *American Journal of Psychology, 109,* 79–91.

Brown, A. S., Begg, M. D., Gravenstein, S., Schaefer, C. A., Wyatt, R. J., Bresnahan, M., et al. (2005). Serologic evidence of prenatal influenza in the etiology of schizophrenia. *Obstetrical and Gynecological Survey, 60,* 77–78.

Brown, A. S., Schaefer, C. A., Quesenberry, C. P., Jr., Liu, L., Babulas, V. P., & Susser, E. S. (2005). Maternal exposure to toxoplasmosis and risk of schizophrenia in adult offspring. *American Journal of Psychiatry, 162,* 767–773.

Brown, G. K., Beck, A. T., Steer, R. A., & Grisham, J. R. (2000). Risk factors for suicide in psychiatric outpatients: A 20-year prospective study. *Journal of Consulting and Clinical Psychology, 68,* 371–377.

Brown, G. M., Pandi-Perumal, S. R., Trakht, I., & Cardinali, D. P. (2009). Melatonin and its relevance to jet lag. *Travel Medicine and Infectious Disease, 7*(2):69–81.

Brown, G. W., & Moran, P. M. (1997). Single mothers, poverty and depression. *Psychological Medicine, 27,* 21–33.

Brown, J. (1958). Some tests of the decay theory of immediate memory. *Quarterly Journal of Experimental Psychology, 10,* 12–21.

Brown, L. M., Bongar, B., & Cleary, K. M. (2004). A profile of psychologists' views of critical risk factors for completed suicide in older adults. *Professional Psychology: Research and Practice, 35,* 90–96.

Brown, R. A. (1973). *First language*. Cambridge: Harvard University Press.

Brown, R., & Kulik, J. (1977). Flashbulb memories. *Cognition, 5,* 73–99.

Brown, R., & McNeill, D. (1966). The "tip-of-the-tongue" phenomenon. *Journal of Verbal Learning and Verbal Behavior, 5,* 325–337.

Brown, S. L., Nesse, R. M., Vinokur, A. D., & Smith, D. M. (2003). Providing social support may be more beneficial than receiving it: Results from a prospective study of mortality. *Psychological Science, 14,* 320–327.

Brown, T., DiNardo, P. A., Lehman, C., & Campbell, L. A. (2001). Reliability of DSM-IV anxiety and mood disorders: Implications for classification of emotional disorders. *Journal of Abnormal Psychology, 110,* 49–58.

Browne, K. D., & Hamilton-Giachritsis, C. (2005). The influence of violent media on children and adolescents: A public health approach. *Lancet, 365,* 702–710.

Bruce, D., Dolan, A., & Phillips-Grant, K. (2000). On the transition from childhood amnesia to the recall of personal memories. *Psychological Science, 11,* 360–364.

Bruce, E., & Waelde, L. C. (2008). Relationships of ethnicity, ethnic identity, and trauma symptoms to delinquency. *Journal of Loss & Trauma, 13,* 395–405.

Bruck, M., Cavanagh, P., & Ceci, S. J. (1991). Fortysomething: Recognizing faces at one's 25th reunion. *Memory and Cognition, 19,* 221–228.

Bruijnzeel, D., & Tandon, R. (2011). The concept of schizophrenia: From the 1850's to the DSM-5. *Psychiatric Annals, 41*(5), 289–295. doi:10.3928/00485713-20110425-08.

Bruff, D. (2009). *Teaching with classroom response systems: Creating active learning environments.* San Francisco: Jossey-Bass.

Brummett, B. H., Babyak, M. A., Williams, R. B., Barefoot, J. C., Costa, P. T., & Siegler, I. C. (2006). NEO personality domains and gender predict levels and trends in body mass index over 14 years during midlife *Journal of Research in Personality, 40,* 222–236.

Brummett, B. H., Mark, D. B., Siegler, I. C., Williams, R. B., Babyak, M. A., Clapp-Channing, N. E., & Barefoot, J. C. (2005). Perceived social support as a predictor of mortality in coronary patients: Effects of smoking, sedentary behavior, and depressive symptoms. *Psychosomatic Medicine, 67,* 40–45.

Brun, A. (2007). Identification and characterization of frontal lobe degeneration: Historical perspective on the development of FTD. *Alzheimer Disease & Associated Disorders, 21*(4), S3–S4.

Bruning, J. C., Gautam, D., Burks, D. J., Gillette, J., Schubert, M., Orban, P. C., & ... Kahn, C. (2000). Role of Brain Insulin Receptor in Control of Body Weight and Reproduction. *Science, 289*(5487), 2122.

Bruno, M. A., Vanhaudenhuyse, A., Thibaut, A., Moonen, G., & Laureys, S. (2011). From unresponsive wakefulness to minimally conscious PLUS and functional locked-in syndromes: recent advances in our understanding of disorders of consciousness. *Journal of Neurology, 258*(7), 1373–1384.

Brunvald, J. H. (1989). *Curses! Broiled again! The hottest urban legends going.* New York: Norton.

Brush, D. H., Moch, M. K., & Pooyan, A. (1987). Individual demographic differences and job satisfaction. *Journal of Occupational Behaviour, 8,* 139–155.

Bryant, J., & Cummins, R, G. (2010). The effects of outcome of mediated and live sporting events on sports fans' self- and social identities. In H. L. Hundley & A. Billings (Eds.), *Examining identity in sports media* (pp. 217–238). Thousand Oaks, CA: Sage.

Bryant, F. B., & Veroff, J. (2006). *The process of savoring: A new model of positive experience.* Mahwah, NJ: Erlbaum.

Bryant, R. A., & Das, P. (2012). The neural circuitry of conversion disorder and its recovery. *Journal Of Abnormal Psychology, 121*(1), 289–296. doi:10.1037/a0025076.

Bryant, R. A., Felmingham, K. L., Falconer, E. M., Benito, L. P., Dobson-Stone, C., Pierce, K. D. (2010). Preliminary evidence of the short allele of the serotonin transporter gene predicting poor response to cognitive behavior therapy in posttraumatic stress disorder. *Biological Psychiatry, 67,* 1217–1219. doi:10.1016/j.biopsych.2010.03.016.

Bryant, R. A., & Guthrie, R. M. (2005). Maladaptive appraisals as a risk factor for posttraumatic stress. *Psychological Science, 16,* 749–752.

Bryant, R. A., & Mallard, D. (2003). Seeing is believing: The reality of hypnotic hallucinations. *Consciousness and Cognition, 12,* 219–230.

Bryant, R. A., & McConkey, K. M. (1989). Hypnotic blindness: A behavioral and experiential analysis. *Journal of Abnormal Psychology, 98,* 71–77.

Bryant, R. A., Moulds, M. L., Guthrie, R. M., Dang, S. T., Mastrodomenico, J., Nixon, R. D. V., et al. (2008). A randomized controlled trial of exposure therapy and cognitive restructuring for posttraumatic stress disorder. *Journal of Consulting and Clinical Psychology, 76,* 695–703.

Bryck, R. L., & Fisher, P. A. (2012). Training the brain: Practical applications of neural plasticity from the intersection of cognitive neuroscience, developmental psychology, and prevention science. *American Psychologist, 67*(2), 87–100. doi:10.1037/a0024657.

Buccino, G., Vogt, S., Ritzl, A., Fink, G. R., Zilles, K., Freund, H. J., et al. (2004). Neural circuits underlying imitation learning of hand actions: An event-related fMRI study. *Neuron, 42,* 323–334.

Buchman, A.S. Boyle, P. A., Yu, L., Shah, R. C., Wilson, R. S., & Bennett, D. A. (2012) Total daily physical activity and the risk of AD and cognitive decline in older adults. *Neurology, 78*(17), 1323-1329. doi:10.1212/WNL.0b013e3182535d35 Published online before print. Retrieved from http://www.neurology.org/content/78/17/1323.abstract?etoc.

Buchsbaum, M. S., Christian, B. T., Lehrer, D. S., Narayanan, T. K., Shi, B., et al. (2006). D2/D3 dopamine receptor binding with (F–18) fallypride in thalamus and cortex of patients with schizophrenia. *Schizophrenia Research, 85,* 232–244.

Buck, D. M., & Plant, E. (2011). Interorientation interactions and impressions: Does the timing of disclosure of sexual orientation matter? *Journal Of Experimental Social Psychology, 47*(2), 333–342. doi:10.1016/j.jesp.2010.10.016.

Buckholtz, J. W., Callicott, J. H., Kolachana, B., Hariri, A. R., Goldberg, T. E., Genderson, M., Egan, M. F., Mattay, V. S., Weinberger, D. R., & Meyer-Lindenberg, A. (2008). Genetic variation in MAOA modulates ventromedial prefrontal circuitry mediating individual differences in human personality. *Molecular Psychiatry, 13,* 313–324.

Bugg, J. M., & McDaniel, M. A. (2012). Selective benefits of question self-generation and answering for remembering expository text. *Journal of Educational Psychology,* doi:10.1037/a0028661

Bulotsky-Shearer, R. J., Dominguez, X., & Bell, E. R. (2012). Preschool classroom behavioral context and school readiness outcomes for low-income children: A multilevel examination of child- and classroom-level influences. *Journal of Educational Psychology, 104*(2), 421–438. doi:10.1037/a0026301

Burns, M. S. & Fahy, J. (2010). Broca's area: rethinking classical concepts from a neuroscience perspective. *Topics in Stroke Rehabilitation, 17*(6), 401–410.

Bush, G. (2010). Attention-defi cit/hyperactivity disorder and attention networks. *Neuropsychopharmacology, 35,* 278–300.

Büssing, A., & Höge, A. (2004). Aggression and violence against home care workers. *Journal of Occupational Health Psychology, 9,* 206–219.

Bugental, D. B., & Grusec, J. E. (2006). Socialization processes. In W. Damon & R. M. Lerner (Series Eds.) & N. Eisenberg (Vol. Ed.), *Handbook of child psychology: Vol. 3. Social, emotional, and personality development* (6th ed.). New York: Wiley.

Bugg, J. M., Zook, N. A., DeLosh, E. L., Davalos, D. B., & Davis, H. P. (2006). Age differences in fluid intelligence: Contributions of general slowing and frontal decline. *Brain and Cognition, 62*(1), 9–16.

Buhle, J. T., Stevens, B., L., Friedman, J. J., & Wager, T. D. (2012). Distraction and placebo: Two separate routes to pain control. *Psychological Science.* doi:10.1177/0956797611427919.

Bui, K.-V. T., Peplau, L. A., & Hill, C. T. (1996). Testing the Rusbult model of relationship commitment and stability in a 15-year study of heterosexual couples. *Personality and Social Psychology Bulletin, 22,* 1244–1257.

Buka, S. L., Shenassa, E. D., & Niaura, R. (2003). Elevated risk of tobacco dependence among offspring of mothers who smoked during pregnancy: A 30-year prospective study. *American Journal of Psychiatry, 160,* 1978–1984.

Bulevich, J. B., Roediger, H. L., Balota, D. A., & Butler, A. C. (2006). Failures to find suppression of episodic memories in the think/no-think paradigm. *Memory and Cognition, 34,* 1569–1577.

Bulik, C. M., Sullivan, P. F., Tozzi, F., Furberg, H., Lichtenstein, P., & Pedersen, N. L. (2006). Prevalence, heritability, and prospective risk factors for anorexia nervosa. *Archives of General Psychiatry, 63,* 305–312.

Bulik, C. M., Sullivan, P. F., Wade, T. D., & Kendler, K. S. (2000). Twin studies of eating disorders: A review. *International Journal of Eating Disorders, 27,* 1–20.

Bulkeley, K. & Domhoff, G. W. (2010). Detecting meaning in dream reports: An extension of a word search approach. *Dreaming, 20*(2), 77–95.

Bulkeley, K., & Kahan, T. L. (2008). The impact of September 11 on dreaming. *Consciousness and Cognition, 17,* 1248–1256.

Buller, D. B., Buller, M. K., & Kane, I. (2005). Web-based strategies to disseminate a sun safety curriculum to public elementary schools and state-licensed child-care facilities. *Health Psychology, 24,* 470–476.

Bullough, V. L. (1995, August). Sex matters. *Scientific American,* 105–106.

Bulotsky-Shearer, R. J., Dominguez, X., & Bell, E. R. (2012). Preschool classroom behavioral context and school readiness outcomes for low-income children: A multilevel examination of child- and classroom-level influences. *Journal of Educational Psychology, 104,* 421.

Bunde, J., & Suls, J. (2006). A quantitative analysis of the relationship between the Cook-Medley hostility scale and traditional coronary artery disease risk factors. *Health Psychology, 25,* 493–500.

Burchard, R. E. (1992). Coca chewing and diet. *Current Anthropology, 33*(1), 1–24.

Burger, J. M. (2009). Replicating Milgram: Would people still obey today? *American Psychologist, 64,* 1–11.

Burger, J. M., & Cornelius, T. (2003). Raising the price of agreement: Public commitment and the lowball compliance procedure. *Journal of Applied Social Psychology, 33,* 923–934.

Burger, J. M., & Guadagno, R. E. (2003). Self-concept clarity and the foot-in-the-door procedure. *Basic and Applied Social Psychology, 25,* 79–86.

Burlingame, G. M., & Baldwin, S. (2011). Group therapy. In J. C. Norcross, G. R. VandenBos, & D. K. Freedheim (Eds.), *History of psychotherapy: Continuity and change* (pp. 505–515). Washington, D.C.: American Psychological Association.

Burke, C. J., Tobler, P. N., Baddeley, M., & Schultz, W. (2010). Neural mechanisms of observational learning. *Proceedings Of The National Academy Of Sciences Of The United States Of America, 107*(32), 14431–14436.

Burke, R. J., & Fiksenbaum, L. (2009). Work motivations, work outcomes, and health: Passion versus addiction. *Journal of Business Ethics, 84*(Suppl. 2), 257–263.

Burleson, B. R., Albrecht, T. L., & Sarason, I. G. (Eds.). (1994). *Communication of social support: Messages, interactions, relationships, and community.* Thousand Oaks, CA: Sage.

Burleson, M. H., Gregory, W. L., & Trevarthen, W. R. (1995). Heterosexual activity: Relationship with ovarian function. *Psychoneuroendocrinology, 20*(4), 405–421.

Burns, A., Bernabei, R., Bullock, R., Jentoft, A. J. C., Frölich, L., Hock, C., Raivio, M., Triau, E. Vandewoude, M. Wimo, A., Came, E. Van Baelen, B., Hammond, G. L., van Oene, J. C., & Schwalen, S. (2009). Safety and efficacy of galantamine

(Reminyl) in severe Alzheimer's disease (the SERAD study): a randomised, placebo-controlled, double-blind trial. *Lancet Neurology, 8*(1), 39–47.

Burns, E. M., Naseem, H., Bottle, A., Lazzarino, A., Aylin, P., Darzi, A., & Faiz, O. (2010). Introduction of laparoscopic bariatric surgery in England: Observational population cohort study. *BMJ: British Medical Journal (Overseas & Retired Doctors Edition), 341*(7772), 546. doi:10.1136/bmi.c4296.

Burns, K. C., & Friedman, S. L. (2012). The benefits of emotional expression for math performance. *Cognition and Emotion, 26*(2), 245–251. doi:10.1080/02699931.2011.577564.

Burr, D. C., Morrone, C., & Fiorentini, A. (1996). Spatial and temporal properties of infant colour vision. In F. Vital-Durand, J. Atkinson, & O. J. Braddick (Eds.), *Infant vision* (pp. 63–77). Oxford: Oxford University Press.

Burris, C. T., Branscombe, N. R., & Klar, Y. (1997). Maladjustment implications of self and group gender-role discrepancies: An ordered-discrepancy model. *European Journal of Social Psychology, 27*, 75–95.

Burstein, M., & Ginsburg, G. S. (2010). The effect of parental modeling of anxious behaviors and cognitions in school-aged children: An experimental pilot study. *Behaviour research and Therapy, 48*(6), 506–515. doi:10.1016/j.brat.2010.02.006.

Burstein, M., He, J.-P., Kattan, G., Albano, A., M., Avenevoli, S., & Merikangas, K. R. (2011). Social phobia and subtypes in the national comorbidity survey-adolescent supplement: Prevalence, correlates, and comorbidity. *Journal Of The American Academy Of Child & Adolescent Psychiatry, 50*, 870–880. doi:10.1016/j.jaac.2011.06.005

Burton, K. D., Lydon, J. E., D'Alessandro, D. U., & Koestner, R. (2006). The differential effects of intrinsic and identified motivation on well-being and performance: Prospective, experimental, and implicit approaches to self-determination theory. *Journal of Personality and Social Psychology, 91*, 750–762.

Buschman, T. J., Siegel, M., Roy, J. E., & Miller, E. K. (2011). Neural substrates of cognitive capacity limitations. *Proceedings of the National Academy of Sciences of the United States of America, 108*(27), 11252–11255. doi:10.1073/pnas.1104666108

Bush, G. (2010). Attention-deficit/hyperactivity disorder and attention networks. *Neuropsychopharmacology, 35*, 278–300.

Bushman, B. J., & Huesmann, L. R. (2010). Aggression. In S. T. Fiske, D. T. Gilbert, & G. Lindzey (Eds.), *Handbook of social psychology* (5th ed., Vol. 2, pp. 833–863). Hoboken, NJ: Wiley.

Bushman, B. J., Wang, M. C., & Anderson, C. A. (2005). Is the curve relating temperature to aggression linear or curvilinear? Assaults and temperature in Minneapolis reexamined. *Journal of Personality and Social Psychology, 89*, 62–66.

Bushman, B., & Bartholow, B. D. (2010). Aggression In R. Baumeister & E. Finkel (Eds.) *Advanced social psychology: The state of the science* (pp. 303–340). New York, NY: Oxford.

Bushman, B. J. (1998). Priming effects of media violence on the accessibility of aggressive constructs in memory. *Personality and Social Psychology Bulletin, 24*, 537–545.

Bushman, B. J., & Anderson, C. A. (2001). Media violence and the American public: Scientific facts versus media misinformation. *American Psychologist, 56*, 477–489.

Bushman, B. J., & Anderson, C. A. (2009). Comfortably numb: Desensitizing effects of violent media on helping others. *Psychological Science, 20*, 273–277.

Bushman, B. J., & Huesmann, L. R. (2000). Effects of televised violence on aggression. In D. Singer & J. Singer (Eds.), *Handbook of children and the media* (pp. 223–254). Thousand Oaks, CA: Sage.

Bushman, B. J., Bonacci, A. M., Pedersen, W. C., Vasquez, E. A., & Miller, N. (2005). Chewing on it can chew you up: Effects of rumination on triggered displaced aggression. *Journal of Personality and Social Psychology, 88*, 969–983.

Buss, D. M. (2008). *Evolutionary psychology: The new science of the mind* (3rd ed.). Boston: Allyn & Bacon.

Buss, A. H. (1997). Evolutionary perspectives on personality traits. In R. Hogan, J. Johnson, & S. Briggs (Eds.), *Handbook of personality psychology* (pp. 345–366). San Diego: Academic Press.

Buss, D. M. (2004a). *Evolutionary psychology: The new science of the mind* (2nd ed.). Boston: Allyn & Bacon.

Buss, D. M. (2004b). *The evolution of desire: Strategies of human mating*. New York: Basic Books.

Buss, D. M. (2009). The great struggles of life: Darwin and the emergence of evolutionary psychology. *American Psychologist, 64*, 140–148.

Bustillo, J. R., Lauriello, J., Horan, W. P., & Keith, S. J. (2001). The psychosocial treatment of schizophrenia: An update. *American Journal of Psychiatry, 158*, 163–175.

Butcher, J. N. (2006). *MMPI-2: A practitioner's guide*. Washington, DC: American Psychological Association.

Butcher, J. N. (2004). Personality assessment without borders: Adaptation of the MMPI-2 across cultures. *Journal of Personality Assessment, 83*(2), 90–104.

Butcher, J. N., Mineka, S., & Hooley, J. M. (2010). *Abnormal psychology* (14th ed.). Boston: Allyn & Bacon.

Butler, A. C., Chapman, J. E., Forman, E. M., & Beck, A. T. (2006). The empirical status of cognitive-behavioral therapy: A review of meta-analyses. *Clinical Psychology Review, 26*, 17–31.

Butler, R. (1998). Information seeking and achievement motivation in middle childhood and adolescence: The role of conceptions of ability. *Developmental Psychology, 35*, 146–163.

Butt, M. S., & Sultan, M. T. (2011). Coffee and its consumption: benefits and risks. *Critical Reviews in Food Science and Nutrition, 51*(4), 363–373.

Butters, N. (1981). The Wernicke-Korsakoff syndrome: A review of psychological, neuropathological and etiological factors. *Currents in Alcohol, 8*, 205–232.

Buunk, A. P., Peiró, J. M., & Griffioen, C. (2007). A positive role model may stimulate career-oriented behavior. *Journal of Applied Social Psychology, 37*, 1489–1500.

Buxhoeveden, D. P., Switala, A. E., Roy, E., Litaker, M., & Casanova, M. F. (2001). Morphological differences between minicolumns in human and nonhuman primate cortex. *American Journal of Physical Anthropology, 115*, 361–371.

Byron, K., & Khazanchi, S. (2012). Rewards and creative performance: A meta-analytic test of theoretically derived hypotheses. *Psychological Bulletin, 138*(4), 809–830. doi:10.1037/a0027652

Cabanac, M., & Morrissette, J. (1992). Acute, but not chronic, exercise lowers the body weight set-point in male rats. *Physiology and Behavior, 52*(6), 1173–1177.

Cabeza, R., Rao, S. M., Wagner, A. D., Mayer, A. R., & Schacter, D. L. (2001). Can medial temporal lobe regions distinguish true from false? An event-related functional MRI study of veridical and illusory recognition memory. *Proceedings of the National Academy of Sciences, 98*, 4805–4810.

Cabot, P. J. (2001). Immune-derived opioids and peripheral antinociception. *Clinical and Experimental Pharmacology and Physiology, 28*, 230–232.

Cabral, R. R., & Smith, T. B. (2011). Racial/ethnic matching of clients and therapists in mental health services: A meta-analytic review of preferences, perceptions, and outcomes. *Journal of Counseling Psychology, 58*(4), 537–554. doi:10.1037/a0025266.

Cacchione, T., Möhring, W., & Bertin, E. (2011). What is it about Picasso? Infants' categorical and discriminatory abilities in the visual arts. *Psychology of Aesthetics, Creativity, and the Arts, 5*(4), 370–378. doi:10.1037/a0024129.

Cacioppo, J. T., & Decety, J. (2009). What are the brain mechanisms on which psychological processes are based? *Perspectives on Psychological Science, 4*, 10–18.

Cacioppo, J. T., Berntson, G. G., Sheridan, J. F., & McClintock, M. K. (2000). Multilevel integrative analyses of human behavior: Social neuroscience and the complementing nature of social and biological approaches. *Psychological Bulletin, 126*, 829–843.

Cacioppo, J. T., Petty, R. E., & Crites, S. L. (1993). Attitude change. In V. S. Ramachandran (Ed.), *Encyclopedia of human behavior* (pp. 261–270). San Diego: Academic Press.

Cacioppo, J. T., Reis, H. T., & Zautra, A. J. (2011). Social resilience: The value of social fitness with an application to the military. *American Psychologist, 66*(1), 43–51. doi:10.1037/a0021419.

Cacioppo, J. T., Poehlmann, K. M., Kiecolt-Glaser, J. K., Malarkey, W. B., Burleson, M. H., Berntson, G. G., & Glaser, R. (1998). Cellular immune responses to acute stress in female caregivers of dementia patients and matched controls. *Health Psychology, 17*, 182–189.

Cadinu, M., Maass, A., Rosabianca, A., & Kiesner, J. (2005). Why do women underperform under stereotype threat? *Psychological Science, 16*, 572–578.

Cadoret, R. J., Yates, W. R., Troughton, E., Woodworth, G., & Stewart, M. A. (1995). Adoption study demonstrating two genetic pathways to drug abuse. *Archives of General Psychiatry, 52*, 42–52.

Caetano, R. (2011). There is potential for cultural and social bias in DSM-V. *Addiction, 106*(5), 885–887. doi:10.1111/j.1360-0443.2010.03308.x.

Caggiano, V., Fogassi, L., Rizzolatti, G., Thier, P., & Casile, A. (2009). Mirror neurons differentially encode the peripersonal and extrapersonal space of monkeys. *Science, 324*, 403–406.

Cahill, S. P., Carrigan, M. H., & Frueh, B. C. (1999). Does EMDR work? And if so, why?: A critical review of controlled outcome and dismantling research. *Journal of Anxiety Disorders, 13*, 5–33.

Cahn, B. R., & Polich, J. (2006). Meditation states and traits, EEG, ERP, and neuroimaging studies. *Psychological Bulletin, 132*, 180–211.

Cai, D. J., Mednick, S. A., Harrison, E. M., Kanady, J. C., & Mednick, S. C. (2009). REM, not incubation, improves creativity by priming associative networks. *Proceedings of theNational Academy of Sciences, 106*, 10130–10134.

Cain, D. J., & Seeman, J. (Eds.). (2002). *Humanistic psychotherapies: Handbook of research and practice*. Washington, DC: APA Books.

Calabrese, J. R., Shelton, M. D., Rapport, D. J., Youngstrom, E. A., Jackson, K., Bilali, S., et al. (2005). A 20-month, double-blind, maintenance trial of lithium versus divalproex in rapid-cycling bipolar disorder. *American Journal of Psychiatry, 162*, 2152–2161.

Calamaro, C. J., Mason, T. B. A., & Ratcliff e, S. J. (2009). Adolescents living the 24/7 lifestyle: Effects of caffeine and technology on sleep duration and daytime functioning. *Pediatrics,123*, e1005–e1010.

Caldwell, C. A., & Millen, A. E. (2009). Social learning mechanisms and cumulative cultural evolution: Is imitation necessary? *Psychological Science, 20*, 1478–1483.

Caldwell, J. A. (2012). Crew schedules, sleep deprivation, and aviation performance. *Current Directions in Psychological Science, 21*(2), 85–89. doi:10.1177/0963721411435842

Caldwell, T. L., Cervone, D., & Rubin, L. H. (2008). Explaining intra-individual variability in social behavior through idiographic assessment: The case of humor. *Journal of Research in Personality 42*, 1229–1242.

Callahan, C. M. (2011). The "multiples" of Howard Gardner, Joseph Renzulli, and Robert Sternberg. *Gifted Child Quarterly, 55*(4), 300–301. doi:10.1177/0016986211421871.

Calvin, C. M., Batty, G., Lowe, G. O., & Deary, I. J. (2011). Childhood intelligence and midlife inflammatory and hemostatic biomarkers: The National Child Development Study (1958) cohort. *Health Psychology, 30*(6), 710–718. doi:10.1037/a0023940.

Cameron, J. (2001). Negative effects of reward on intrinsic motivation: A limited phenomenon: Comment on Deci, Koestner, and Ryan. *Review of Educational Research, 71*, 29–42.

Camp, G., Wesstein, H., & Bruin, A. H. (2012). Can questioning induce forgetting? Retrieval-induced forgetting of eyewitness information. *Applied Cognitive Psychology, 26*(3), 431–435. doi:10.1002/acp.2815

Campbell, F. A., Pungello, E. P., Burchinal, M., Kainz, K., Pan, Y., Wasik, B. H., Barbarin, O. A., Sparling, J. J., & Ramey, C. T. (2012). Adult outcomes as a function of an early childhood educational program: An Abecedarian Project follow-up. *Developmental Psychology, 48,* 1033–1043. doi:10.1037/a0026644

Campbell, F. A., Pungello, E. P., Miller-Johnson, S., Burchinal, M., & Ramey, C. T. (2001). The development of cognitive and academic abilities: Growth curves from an early childhood educational experiment. *Developmental Psychology, 37,* 231–242.

Campbell, K. L, Hasher, L., & Thomas, R. C. (2010). Hyper-binding: A unique age effect. *Psychological Science, 21,* 399–405. doi:10.1177/0956797609359910.

Campbell, L., Simpson, J. A., Boldry, J., & Kashy, D. A. (2005). Perceptions of conflict and support in romantic relationships: The role of attachment anxiety. *Journal of Personality and Social Psychology, 88,* 510–531.

Campbell, L., Vasquez, M., Behnke, S., & Kinscherff, R. (2009). *APA ethics code commentary and case illustrations.* Washington, DC: American Psychological Association.

Campbell, R., & Capek, C. (2008). Seeing speech and seeing sign: Insights from a fMRI study. *International Journal of Audiology, 47*(Suppl. 2), S3–S9.

Campbell, R. S., & Pennebaker, J. W. (2003). The secret life of pronouns: Flexibility in writing style and physical health. *Psychological Science, 14,* 60–65.

Campion, M. A., & Campion, J. E. (1987). Evaluation of an interviewee skills training program in a natural field experiment. *Personnel Psychology, 40,* 676–691.

Campion, M. A., Palmer, D. K., & Campion, J. E. (1997). A review of structure in the selection interview. *Personnel Psychology, 50,* 655–702.

Campione, J. C., Brown, A. L., & Ferrara, R. A. (1982). Mental retardation and intelligence. In R. J. Sternberg (Ed.), *Handbook of human intelligence* (pp. 392–490). Cambridge: Cambridge University Press.

Campitelli, G., & Gobet, F. (2008). The role of practice in chess: A longitudinal study. *Learning & Individual Differences, 18*(4), 446–458. doi:10.1016/j.lindif.2007.11.006.

Campos, L., & Alonso-Quecuty, M. L. (2006). Remembering a criminal conversation: Beyond eyewitness testimony. *Memory, 14,* 27–36.

Campos, J. J. (1980). Human emotions: Their new importance and their role in social referencing. *Research and Clinical Center for Child Development, 1980–81 Annual Report,* 1–7.

Canada, D., & Goering, D. (2008). Deep thoughts on the river crossing game. *Mathematics Teacher, 101*(9), 632–639.

Canaris, J. (2008). An analysis of the efficacy of extinction as an intervention in the modification of switching in patients with dissociative identity disorder. *Disseration Abstracts International: Section B: Sciences and Engineering,* p. 3255.

Candia, V., Rosset-Llobet, J., Elbert, T., & Pascual-Leone, A. (2005). Changing the brain through therapy for musicians' hand dystonia. *Annals of the New York Academy of Sciences, 1060,* 335–342.

Canli, T., Qui, M., Omura, K., Congdon, E., Haas, B. W., Amin, Z., et al. (2006). Neural correlates of epigenesist. *Proceedings of the National Academy of Sciences, 103,* 16033–16038.

Cann, A., & Ross, D. A. (1989). Olfactory stimuli as context cues in human memory. *American Journal of Psychology, 102,* 91–102.

Cannon, C. P. (2005). The endocannabinoid system: A new approach to control cardiovascular disease. *Clinical Cornerstone, 7*(2–3), 17–26.

Cannon, T. D., Zorrilla, L. E., Shtasel, D., Gur, R. E., Gur, R. C., Marco, E. J., Moberg, P., & Price, A. (1994). Neuropsychological functioning in siblings discordant for schizophrenia and healthy volunteers. *Archives of General Psychiatry, 51,* 651–661.

Cannon, W. B. (1927). *Bodily changes in pain, hunger, fear and rage—An account of recent researches into the function of emotional excitement.* New York: Appleton.

Cannon, W. B., & Washburn, A. L. (1912). An explanation of hunger. *American Journal of Physiology, 29,* 444–454.

Canter, D. V. (2011). Resolving the offender "profiling equations" and the emergence of an investigative psychology. *Current Directions in Psychological Science, 20*(1), 5–10. doi:10.1177/0963721410396825.

Canu, W. H. (2008). An experimental learning activity demonstrating normal and phobic anxiety. *Teaching of Psychology, 35,* 22–25.

Caparos, S., Ahmed, L., Bremner, A. J., de Fockert, J. W., Linnell, K. J., & Davidoff, J. (2012). Exposure to an urban environment alters the local bias of a remote culture. *Cognition, 122*(1), 80–85. doi:10.1016/j.cognition.2011.08.013.

Capasso, R., Izzo, A. A. (2008). Gastrointestinal regulation of food intake: General aspects and focus on anandamide and oleoylethanolamide. *Journal of Neuroendocrinology, 20*(Suppl. 1), 39–46.

Capgras, J., & Reboul-Lachaux, J. (1923). Illusion des « sosies » dans un delire systematise chronique ["Doppelganger" delusion in chronic persistent delirium]. *Bulletin de la Société Clinique de Médicine Mentale, 2,* 6–16.

Caplan, D. (2003a). Aphasic syndromes. In K. M. Heilman & E. Valenstein (Eds.), *Clinical neuropsychology* (4th ed.). New York: Oxford.

Caplan, D. (2003b). Syntactic aspects of language disorders. In K. M. Heilman & E. Valenstein (Eds.), *Clinical neuropsychology* (4th ed.). New York: Oxford University Press.

Caplan, L. R. (2005). Stroke. *Review of Neurological Disorders, 2,* 223–225.

Caplan, P. J. (1995). *They say you're crazy. How the world's most powerful psychiatrists decide who's normal.* Reading, MA: Addison-Wesley.

Cappella, E., Hamre, B. K., Kim, H. Y., Henry, D. B., Frazier, S. L., Atkins, M. S., & Schoenwald, S. K. (2012). Teacher consultation and coaching within mental health practice: Classroom and child effects in urban elementary schools. *Journal of Consulting and Clinical Psychology.* doi:10.1037/a0027725.

Capriani, A., Pretty, H., Hawton, K., & Geddes, J. R. (2005). Lithium in the prevention of suicidal behavior and all-cause mortality in patients with mood disorders: A systematic review of randomized trials. *American Journal of Psychiatry, 162,* 1805–1819.

Capron, C., & Duyme, M. (1989). Assessment of effects of socio-economic status on IQ in a full cross-fostering study. *Nature, 340,* 552–553.

Capron, C., & Duyme, M. (1996). Effect of socioeconomic status of biological and adoptive parents on WISC-R subtest scores of their French adopted children. *Intelligence, 22,* 259–276.

Caputo, M., Monastero, R., Mariani, E., Santucci, A., Mangialasche, F., Camarda, R., Senin, U., & Mecocci, P. (2008). Neuropsychiatric symptoms in 921 elderly subjects with dementia: a comparison between vascular and neurodegenerative types. *Acta Psychiatrica Scandinavica, 117*(6), 455–464.

Caramazza, A., & Hillis, A. E. (1991). Lexical organization of nouns and verbs in the brain. *Nature, 349,* 788–790.

Card, N. A., Stucky, B. D., Sawalani, G. M., & Little, T. D. (2008). Direct and indirect aggression during childhood and adolescence: A meta-analytic review of gender differences, intercorrelations, and relations to maladjustment. *Child Development, 79,* 1185–1229.

Cardis, E., et al. (2010). Brain tumour risk in relation to mobile telephone use: Results of the INTERPHONE international case-control study. *International Journal of Epidemiology, 39,* 675–694. doi:10.1093/ije/dyq079.

Cardon, L. R., & Fulker, D. W. (1993). Genetics of specific cognitive abilities. In R. Plomin & G. McClearn (Eds.), *Nature, nurture, and psychology* (pp. 99–120). Washington, DC: American Psychological Association.

Cardon, L. R., Fulker, D. W., DeFries, J. C., & Plomin, R. (1992). Multivariate genetic analysis of specific cognitive abilities in the Colorado Adoption Project at age 7. *Intelligence, 16,* 383–400.

Carducci, B. (2009). *The psychology of personality.* Malden, MA: Wiley-Blackwell.

Carels, R. A., Young, K. M., Coit, C., Clayton, A. M., Spencer, A., & Hobbs, M. (2008). Can following the caloric restriction recommendations from the Dietary Guidelines for Americans help individuals lose weight? *Eating Behaviors, 9,* 328–335.

Carey, S. (2009). *The origin of concepts.* New York: Oxford University Press.

Carlbring, P., & Smit, F. (2008). Randomized trial of Internet-delivered self-help with telephone support for pathological gamblers. *Journal of Consulting and Clinical Psychology, 76,* 1090–1094.

Carli, L. L. (1999). Cognitive reconstruction, hindsight, and reactions to victims and perpetrators. *Personality and Social Psychology Bulletin, 25,* 966–979.

Carlson, E. A., Sroufe, L. A., & Egeland, B. (2004). Th econstruction of experience: A longitudinal study of representation and behavior. *Child Development, 75,* 66–83.

Carlson, E. A., Sroufe, L. A., & Egeland, B. (2004). The construction of experience: A longitudinal study of representation and behavior. *Child Development, 75,* 66–83.

Carlson, J., Watts, R. E., & Maniacci, M. (2006). Play therapy. In J. Carlson, R. E. Watts, & M. Maniacci (Eds.), *Adlerian therapy: Theory and practice* (pp. 227–248). Washington, DC: American Psychological Association.

Carlson, L. E., Speca, M., Patel, K. D., & Goodey, E. (2003). Mindfulness-based stress reduction in relation to quality of life, mood, symptoms of stress, and immune parameters in breast and prostate cancer outpatients. *Psychosomatic Medicine, 65,* 571–581.

Carlsson, A., & Lecrubier, Y. (Eds.). (2004). *Progress in dopamine research schizophrenia.* New York: Taylor & Francis.

Carlston, D. (2010). Social cognition. In R. Baumeister & E. Finkel (Eds.) *Advanced social psychology: The state of the science* (pp. 63–99). New York, NY: Oxford.

Carmichael, L. L., Hogan, H. P., & Walter, A. A. (1932). An experimental study of the effect of language on the reproduction of visually perceived form. *Journal of Experimental Psychology, 15,* 73–86.

Carney, S. M., & Goodwin, G. M. (2005). Lithium—A continuing story in the treatment of bipolar disorder. *Acta Psychiatricia Scandinavica, 111,* 7–12.

Carpenter, J. T. (2004). EMDR as an integrative psychotherapy approach: Experts explore the paradigm prism. *Psychotherapy Research, 14,* 135–136.

Caspi, A., Hariri, A. R., Holmes, A., Uher, R., & Moffi tt, T. E. (2010). Genetic sensitivity to the environment: The case of the serotonin transporter gene and its implications for studying complex diseases and traits. *American Journal of Psychiatry, 167,* 509–527. doi:10.1176/appi.ajp.2010.09101452

Carr, A. (2009). The effectiveness of family therapy and systemic interventions for child-focused problems. *Journal of Family Therapy, 31,* 3–45.

Carr, G. D., Moretti, M. M., & Cue, B. J. H. (2005). Evaluating parenting capacity: Validity problems with the MMPI-2, PAI, CAPI, and ratings of child adjustment. *Professional Psychology: Research and Practice, 36,* 188–196.

Carraher, T. N., Carraher, D., & Schliemann, A. D. (1985). Mathematics in the streets and in the schools. *British Journal of Developmental Psychology, 3,* 21–29.

Carstensen, L. (1997, August). *Psychology and the aging revolution: Changes in social needs and social goals across the lifespan.* Paper presented at the annual convention of the American Psychological Association.

Carstensen, L. L.,Turan, B., Scheibe, S., Ram, N., Ersner-Hershfield, H., Samanez-Larkin, G. R. Brooks, K. P., & Nesselroade, J. R. (2011). Emotional experience improves with age: Evidence based on over 10 years of experience sampling. *Psychology and Aging, 26,* 21–33.

Carter, F. A., Jordan, J., McIntosh, V. W., Luty, S. E., McKenzie, J. M., Frampton, C. A., & ... Joyce, P. R. (2011). The long-term efficacy of three psychotherapies for anorexia nervosa: A randomized, controlled trial. *International Journal of Eating Disorders, 44*(7), 647–654. doi:10.1002/eat.20879

Carter, L. P., Richards, B. D., Mintzer, M. Z., & Griffiths, R. R. (2006). Relative abuse liability of GHB in humans: A comparison of psychomotor, subjective, and cognitive effects of supratherapeutic doses of triazolam, pentobarbital, and GHB. *Neuropsychopharmacology, 31*(11), 2537–2551.

Carter, M. M., Hollon, S. D., Carson, R., & Shelton, R. C. (1995). Effects of a safe person on induced distress following a biological challenge in panic disorder with agoraphobia. *Journal of Abnormal Psychology, 104,* 156–163.

Carter, T. J., Ferguson, M. J., & Hassin, R. R. (2011). A single exposure to the American flag shifts support toward Republicanism up to 8 months later. *Psychological Science, 22*(8), 1011–1018. doi:10.1177/0956797611414726.

Cartwright, R. D. (1978). *A primer on sleep and dreaming.* Reading, MA: Addison-Wesley.

Cartwright, R. D. (1993). Who needs their dreams? The usefulness of dreams in psychotherapy. *Journal of the American Academy of Psychoanalysis, 21*(4), 539–547.

Carver, C., & Scheier, M. (2004). *Perspectives on personality* (5th ed.). Boston, MA: Pearson.

Carver, C. S., & Connor-Smith, J. (2010). Personality and coping. *Annual Review of Psychology, 61,* 679–704.

Carver, C. S., & Harmon-Jones, E. (2009). Anger is an approach-related aff ect: Evidence and implications. *Psychological Bulletin, 135,* 183–204.

Carver, C. S., Johnson, S. L., & Joormann, J. (2008). Serotonergic function, two-mode models of self-regulation, and vulnerability to depression: What depression has in common with impulsive aggression. *Psychological Bulletin, 134,* 912–943.

Carver, C. S., & Scheier, M. F. (2002). The hopeful optimist. *Psychological Inquiry, 13,* 288–290.

Carver, C. S., & Scheier, M. F. (2008). *Perspectives on personality* (6th ed.). Boston: Allyn & Bacon.

Carver, K., Joyner, K., & Udry, J. R. (2003). National estimates of adolescent romantic relationships. In P. Florsheim (Ed.), *Adolescent romantic relations and sexual behavior: Theory, research, and practical implications* (pp. 23–56). Mahwah, NJ: Erlbaum.

Carver, L. J., & Vaccaro, B. G. (2007). 12-month-old infants allocate increased neural resources to stimuli associated with negative adult emotion. *Developmental Psychology, 43,* 54–69.

Casbon, T. S., Curtin, J. J., Lang, A. R., & Patrick, C. J. (2003). Deleterious effects of alcohol intoxication: Diminished cognitive control and its behavioral consequences. *Journal of Abnormal Psychology, 112,* 476–487.

Case, L., & Smith, T. B. (2000). Ethnic representation in a sample of the literature of applied psychology. *Journal of Consulting and Clinical Psychology, 68,* 1107–1110.

Casey, B. J., Galvan, A., & Hare, T. A. (2005). Changes in cerebral functional organization during cognitive development. *Current Opinion in Neurobiology, 15,* 239–244.

Casey, B. J., Getz, S., & Galvan, A. (2008, March). The adolescent brain. *Developmental Review, 28*(1), 62–77.

Caspi, A. (2000). The child is the father of man: Personality continuities from childhood to adulthood. *Journal of Personality and Social Psychology, 78,* 158–172.

Caspi, A., Elder, G. H., & Bem, D. J. (1988). Moving away from the world: Life-course patterns of shy children. *Developmental Psychology, 24,* 824–831.

Caspi, A., Harrington, H., Milne, B., Amell, J. W., Theodore, R. F., & Moffitt, T. E. (2003). Children's behavioral styles at age 3 are linked to their adult personality traits at age 26. *Journal of Personality, 71,* 495–513.

Caspi, A., & Shiner, R. L. (2006). Personality development. In W. Damon & R. M. Lerner (Series Eds.) & N. Eisenberg (Vol. Ed.), *Handbook of child psychology: Vol. 3. Social, emotional, and personality development* (6th ed., pp. 300–365). New York: Wiley.

Caspi, A., & Silva, P. A. (1995). Temperamental qualities at age 3 predict personality traits in young adulthood: Longitudinal evidence from a birth cohort. *Child Development, 66,* 468–498.

Caspi, A., Begg, D., Dickson, N., Harrington, H., Langley, J., Moffitt, T. E., & Silva, P. A. (1997). Personality differences predict health-risk behaviors in young adulthood: Evidence from a longitudinal study. *Journal of Personality and Social Psychology, 73,* 1052–1063.

Caspi, A., Bem, D. J., & Elder, G. H., Jr. (1989). Continuities and consequences of interactional styles across the life course. *Journal of Personality, 57,* 375–406.

Caspi, A., Hariri, A. R., Holmes, A., Uher, R., & Moffitt, T. E. (2010). Genetic sensitivity to the environment: the case of the serotonin transporter gene and its implications for studying complex diseases and traits. *Am J Psychiatry, 167*(5), 509–527.

Caspi, A., Harrington, H., Milne, B., Amell, J. W., Theodore, R. F., & Moffitt, T. E. (2003). Children's behavioral styles at age 3 are linked to their adult personality traits at age 26. *Journal of Personality, 71,* 495–513.

Caspi, A., Henry, B., McGee, R. O., Moffitt, T. E., & Silva, P. A. (1995). Temperamental origins of child and adolescent behavior problems: From age 3 to Age 15. *Child Development, 66,* 55–68.

Caspi, A., McClay, J., Moffitt, T. E., Mill, J., Martin, J., Craig, I. W., et al. (2002). Role of genotype in the cycle of violence in maltreated children. *Science, 297,* 851–854.

Caspi, A., Moffitt, T. E., Morgan, J., Rutter, M., Taylor, A., Arseneault, L., et al. (2004). Maternal expressed emotion predicts children's antisocial behavior problems: Using monozygotic-twin differences to identify environmental effects on behavioral development. *Developmental Psychology, 40,* 149–161.

Caspi, A., Roberts, B. W., & Shiner, R. L. (2005). Personality development: Stability and change. *Annual Review of Psychology, 56,* 453–484.

Caspi, A., Sugden, K., Moffitt, T. E., Taylor, A., Craig, I. W., Harrington, H., et al. (2003). Influence of life stress on depression: Moderation by a polymorphism in the 5-HTT gene. *Science, 301,* 386–389.

Cassel, E., & Bernstein, D. A. (2007). *Criminal behavior* (2nd ed.). Mahwah, NJ: Erlbaum.

Cassia, V. M., Valenza, E., Simion, F., & Leo, I. (2008). Congruency as a non-specific perceptual property contributing to newborns' face preference. *Child Development, 79*(4), 807–820.

Cassidy, J. (2008). The nature of the child's ties. In J. Cassidy & P. R. Shaver (Eds.), *Handbook of attachment: Theory, research, and clinical applications* (2nd ed., pp. 3–22). New York: Guilford Press.

Castelli, J. (2009). Life after MPD/DID: An article on multiple personality disorder and child abuse. *Mental Health Matters.* Retrieved from http://www.mental-health-matters. com/index.php?option=com_content&view=article&id=364: life-aft er-mpddid-anarticle-on-multiple-personality-disorder-and-child-abuse&catid=77:dissociativeidentity&Itemid=2086.

Castelli, L., Zogmaister, C., & Tomelleri, S. (2009). Th e transmission of racial attitudes within the family. *Developmental Psychology, 45,* 586–591.

Castle, K., Conner, K., Kaukeinen, K., & Tu, X. (2011). Perceived racism, discrimination, and acculturation in suicidal ideation and suicide attempts among black young adults. *Suicide & Life-Threatening Behavior, 41,* 342–351. doi:10.1111/j.1943-278X.2011.00033.x

Castonguay, L. G., & Beutler, L. E. (Eds.) (2005). *Principles of therapeutic change that work.* New York: Oxford University Press.

Castro, L., & Toro, M. A. (2004).The evolution of culture: From primate social learning to human culture. *Proceedings of the National Academy of Sciences, 101,* 10235–10240.

Cattell, R. B., Eber, H. W., & Tatsuoka, M. (1970). *Handbook for the sixteen personality factor questionnaire (16PF).* Champaign, IL: Institute for Personality Testing.

Caulfield, T., Rachul, C., & Zarzeczny, A. (2010). "Neurohype" and the name game: Who's to blame?. *AJOB Neuroscience, 1*(2), 13–15. doi:10.1080/21507741003699355.

Cavaiola, A. A., & Desordi, E. G. (2000). Locus of control in drinking driving offenders and nonoffenders. *Alcoholism Treatment Quarterly, 18,* 63–73.

Cavanna, A. E., Shah, S., Eddy, C. M., Williams, A., & Rickards, H. (2011). Consciousness: A neurological perspective. *Behavioural Neurology, 24*(1), 107–116.

Cavenett, T., & Nixon, D. V. (2006). The effect of arousal on memory for emotionally-relevant information: A study of skydivers. *Behaviour Research and Therapy, 44,* 1461–1469.

Caylak, E. (2009). Th e genetics of sleep disorders in humans: Narcolepsy, restless legs syndrome, and obstructive sleep apnea syndrome. *American Journal of Medical Genetics A, 149A,* 2612–2626.

Ceci, S. J., Huffman, M. L. C., Smith, E., & Loftus, E. F. (1994). Repeatedly thinking about a non-event: Source misattributions among preschoolers. *Consciousness and Cognition, 3,* 388–407.

Centers for Disease Control and Prevention. (1999b). *Suicide deaths and rates per 100,000.* Retrieved December 7, 2004, from http://www.cdc.gov/ncipc/data/us9794/suic.htm.

Centers for Disease Control and Prevention. (2002a). *Suicide and self-inflicted injury.* Retrieved June 30, 2009, from http://www.cdc.gov/nchs/fastats/suicide.htm.

Centers for Disease Control and Prevention. (2004). Web-based injury statistics query and reporting system (WISQARS). Retrieved December 7, 2004, from http://www.cdc.gov/ ncipc/wisquars.

Centers for Disease Control and Prevention. (2006). WISQARS website and "Fatal Injury Reports." Retrieved February 8, 2006, from http://www.cdc.gov/ncipc/wisqars/.

Centers for Disease Control and Prevention. (2008). Deaths: Final Data for 2005. *National Vital Statistics Reports, 56,* 1–121.

Centers for Disease Control and Prevention. (2009a). *Preventing teen pregnancy: An update in 2009.* Retrieved from http://www.cdc.gov/reproductivehealth/AdolescentReproHealth/AboutTP.htm#b.

Centers for Disease Control and Prevention. (2009b). Preventing teen pregnancy: An update in 2009. Retrieved June 10, 2009, from http://www.cdc.gov/reproductivehealth/AdolescentReproHealth/AboutTP.htm#b.

Centers for Disease Control and Prevention. (2010). Trends in the prevalence of sexual behaviors: National Youth Risk Behavior Survey: 1991–2009. Retrieved September 14, 2012 from http://www.cdc.gov/healthyyouth/yrbs/pdf/us_sexual_trend_yrbs.pdf

Centers for Disease Control and Prevention. (2011a). Quitting smoking among adults—United States, 2001–2010. *Morbidity and Mortality Weekly, 60,* 1513–1519.

Centers for Disease Control And Prevention. (2011b). Drug Overdose Deaths—Florida, 2003–2009. *Morbidity and Mortality Weekly Report, 60,* 869–905.

Centers for Disease Control and Prevention. (2012). Youth suicide. Retrieved July 24, 2012 from http://www.cdc.gov/violenceprevention/pub/youth_suicide.html on July 24, 2012.

Centerwall, L. (1990). Controlled TV viewing and suicide in countries: Young adult suicide and exposure to television. *Social Psychiatry and Social Epidemiology, 25,* 149–153.

Cepeda, N. J., Coburn, N., Rohrer, D., Wixted, J. T., Mozer, M. C., & Pashler, H. (2009). Optimizing distributed practice: Theoretical analysis and practical implications. *Experimental Psychology, 56*(4), 236–246. doi:10.1027/1618–3169.56.4.236

Cepeda, N. J., Coburn, N. C., Roher, D., Wixted, J. T., et al. (2009). Optimizing distributed practice theoretical analysis and practical implications. *Experimental Psychology, 56,* 236–246.

Cepeda, N. J., Vul, E., Rohrer, D., Wixted, J. T., & Pashler, H. (2008). Spacing effects in learning: A temporal ridgeline of optimal retention. *Psychological Science, 19,* 1095–1102.

Çeponien, R., Lepisto, T., Shesakova, A., Vanhala, R., Alku, P., Naatanen, R., & Yaguchi, K. (2003). Speech-sound-selective auditory impairment in children with autism: They can perceive but do not attend. *Proceedings of the National Academy of Sciences, 100,* 5567–5572.

Ceranoglu, T. (2010b). Video games in psychotherapy. *Review of General Psychology, 14*(2), 141–146. doi:10.1037/a0019439.

Ceranoglu, T. (2010a). Star Wars in psychotherapy: video games in the office. *Academic Psychiatry: The Journal of the American Association of Directors of Psychiatric Residency Training and the Association for Academic Psychiatry, 34*(3), 233–236.

Cervone, D. (2005). Personality architecture: Within-person structures and processes. *Annual Review of Psychology, 56,* 423–452.

Cervone, D. & Pervin, L. (2010). *Personality: Theory and research.* (11th ed) Danvers MA: Wiley.

Cha, J. H., Farrell, L. A., Ahmed, S. F., Frey, A., Hsiao-Ashe, K. K., Young, A. B., et al. (2001). Glutamate receptor dysregulation in the hippocampus of transgenic mice carrying mutated human amyloid precursor protein. *Neurobiological Disorders, 8,* 90–102.

Chaker, S., Hofmann, S. G., & Hoyer, J. (2010). Can a one-weekend group therapy reduce fear of blushing? Results of an open trial. *Anxiety, Stress & Coping, 23*(3), 303–318. doi:10.1080/10615800903075132.

Chakraborty, A., King, M., Leavey, G., & McKenzie, K. (2011). Perceived racism, medication adherence, and hospital admission in African-Caribbean patients with psychosis in the United Kingdom. *Social Psychiatry & Psychiatric Epidemiology, 46*(9), 915–923. doi:10.1007/s00127-010-0261-8.

Chamberlin, J. (2000). Easing children's psychological distress in the emergency room. *Monitor on Psychology, 31,* 40–42.

Chambers, J. R., & Windschitl, P. D. (2009). Evaluating one performance among others: The influence of rank and degree of exposure to comparison referents. *Personality and Social Psychology Bulletin, 35,* 776–792.

Chambless, D. L., Baker, M. J., Baucom, D. H., Beutler, L. E., Calhoun, K. S., Crits-Christoph, P., et al. (1998). Update on empirically validated therapies, II. *The Clinical Psychologist, 51,* 3–16.

Chambless, D. L., & Hollon, S. D. (1998). Defining empirically supported therapies. *Journal of Consulting and Clinical Psychology, 66,* 7–18.

Chambless, D. L., & Ollendick, T. H. (2001). Empirically supported psychological treatments. *Annual Review of Psychology, 52,* 685–716.

Champagne, F. A. (2010). Early adversity and developmental outcomes: Interaction between genetics, epigenetics, and social experiences across the life span. *Perspectives on Psychological Science, 5*(5), 564–574. doi:10.1177/1745691610383494.

Champagne, F. A. (2009). Beyond nature vs. nurture: Philosophic insights from molecular biology. *Association for Psychological Science Observer, 22,* 3, 27–28.

Champagne, F. A., & Mashoodh, R. (2009). Genes in context: Gene-environment interplay and the origins of individual diff erences in behavior. *Current Directions in Psychological Science, 18,* 127–131.

Chan, D. (2005). Current directions in personnel selection research. *Current Directions in Psychological Science, 14,* 220–223.

Chan, J. C. K., Thomas, A. K., & Bulevich, J. B. (2009). Recalling a witnessed event increases eyewitness suggestibility: The reversed testing effect. *Psychological Science, 20,* 66–73.

Chan, M., Chen, E, Hibbert, A. S., Wong, J. H. K., Miller, G. E. (2011)Implicit measures of early-life family conditions: relationships to psychosocial characteristics and cardiovascular disease risk in adulthood. *Health Psychology, 30,* 570–578.

Chandler, J. J., & Pronin, E. (2012). Fast thought speed induces risk taking. *Psychological Science, 23*(4), 370–374. doi:10.1177/0956797611431464.

Chandola, T., Brunner, E., & Marmot, M. (2006). Chronic stress at work and the metabolic syndrome: Prospective study. *British Medical Journal, 332,* 521–525.

Chandra, A., Martino, S., Collins, R., Elliott, M., et al. (2008). Does watching sex on television predict teen pregnancy? Findings from a national longitudinal survey of youth. *Pediatrics, 122,* 1047–1054.

Chandrashekar, J., Hoon, M. A., Ryba, N. J., & Zuker, C. S. (2006). The receptors and cells for mammalian taste. *Nature, 444*(7117), 288–294.

Chang, E. F., & Merzenich, M. M. (2003). Environmental noise retards auditory cortical development. *Science, 300,* 498–502.

Chao, R. K. (2001). Extending research on the consequences of parenting style for Chinese Americans and European Americans. *Child Development, 72,* 1832–1843.

Chao, R. K., & Tseng, V. (2002). Parenting of Asians. In M. H. Bornstein (Ed.), *Handbook of parenting: Vol. 4. Social conditions and applied parenting* (2nd ed., pp. 59–93). Mahwah, NJ: Erlbaum.

Chapman, D. Z., & Zweig, D. I. (2005). Developing a nomological network for interview structure: Antecedents and consequences of the structured selection interview. *Personnel Psychology, 58,* 673–702.

Chapman, E. A., Thomas, P. S., Stone, E., Lewis, C., and Yates, D. H. (2011). A breath test for malignant mesothelioma using an electronic nose. *The* European Respiratory Journal, Epub December 19, 2011.

Chapman, G. B., & Coups, E. J. (2006). Emotions and preventive health behavior: Worry, regret, and influenza vaccination. *Health Psychology, 25*(1), 82–90.

Chapman, S., & Morrell, S. (2000). Barking mad? Another lunatic hypothesis bites the dust. *British Medical Journal, 321,* 1561–1563.

Chapell, M. S., Blanding, Z. B., Silverstein, M. E., Takahashi, M., et al. (2005). Test anxiety and academic performance in undergraduate and graduate students. *Journal of Educational Psychology, 97,* 268–274.

Chappell, J., Demery, Z. P., Arriola-Rios, V., & Sloman, A. (2012). How to build an information gathering and processing system: Lessons from naturally and artificially intelligent systems. *Behavioural Processes, 89*(2), 179–186. doi:10.1016/j.beproc.2011.10.001.

Chaput, J.-P., & Tremblay, A. (2009). The glucostatic theory of appetite control and the risk of obesity and diabetes. *International Journal of Obesity, 33,* 46–53.

Charles, S. T. (2011). Emotional experience and regulation in later life. In K. W. Schaie & S. L. Willis (Eds.), *Handbook of the Psychology of Aging* (7th ed., pp. 295–310). San Diego, CA: Academic Press/Elsevier Science.

Charles, S. T., & Carstensen, L. L. (2008). Unpleasant situations elicit different emotional responses in younger and older adults. *Psychology and Aging, 23,* 495–504.

Charles, S. T., Mather, M., & Carstensen, L. L. (2003). Aging and emotional memory: The forgettable nature of negative images for older adults. *Journal of Experimental Psychology: General, 132,* 310–324.

Charlton, S. G., & Starkey, N. J. (2011). Driving without awareness: The effects of practice and automaticity on attention and driving. *Transportation Research: Part F, 14*(6), 456–471. doi:10.1016/j.trf.2011.04.010

Charleton, T., Gunter, B., & Coles, D. (1998). Broadcast television as a cause of aggression? Recent findings from a naturalistic study. *Emotional and Behavioral Difficulties, 3,* 5–13.

Chase, H., & Clark, L. (2010). Gambling severity predicts midbrain response to near-miss outcomes. *The Journal Of Neuroscience: The Official Journal Of The Society For Neuroscience, 30*(18), 6180–6187.

Chase, T. N. (1998). The significance of continuous dopaminergic stimulation in the treatment of Parkinson's disease. *Drugs, 55*(Suppl. 1), 1–9.

Charman, S. D., Wells, G. L., & Joy, S. W. (2011). The dud effect: Adding highly dissimilar fillers increases confidence in lineup identifications. *Law and Human Behavior, 35*(6), 479–500. doi:10.1007/s10979-010-9261-1.

Chassin, L., Macy, J. T., Seo, D., Presson, C. C., & Sherman, S. J. (2010). The association between membership in the sandwich generation and health behaviors: A longitudinal study. *Journal of Applied Developmental Psychology, 31*(1), 38–46. doi:10.1016/j.appdev.2009.06.001.

Chassin, L., Pitts, S. C., & Prost, J. (2002). Binge drinking trajectories from adolescence to emerging adulthood in a high-risk sample: Predictors and substance abuse outcomes. *Journal of Consulting and Clinical Psychology, 70,* 67–78.

Chaudhary, N., Pandey, A. S., Gemmete, J. J. (2011). Intervention in acute cerebral ischaemic stroke: a review of the role of pharmacological therapies and intra-arterial mechanical thrombectomy devices. *Postgraduate Medical Journal, 87*(1032), 714–723.

Chaudhry, I. B., Neelam, K., Duddu, V., & Husain, N. (2008). Ethnicity and psychopharmacology. *Journal of Psychopharmacology, 22,* 673–680.

Chein, J., Albert, D., O'Brien, L., Uckert, K., & Steinberg, L. (2011). Peers increase adolescent risk taking by enhancing activity in the brain's reward circuitry. *Developmental Science, 14*(2), F1–F10. doi:10.1111/j.1467-7687.2010.01035.x

Chein, J. M., & Schneider, W. (2012). The brain's learning and control architecture. *Current Directions in Psychological Science, 21*(2), 78–84. doi:10.1177/0963721411434977

Chein, J., Albert, D., O'Brien, L., Uckert, K., & Steinberg, L. (2011). Peers increase adolescent risk taking by enhancing activity in the brain's reward circuitry. *Developmental Science, 14,* F1–F10.

Cheke, L. G., Bird C. D., Clayton N. S. (2011). Tool-use and instrumental learning in the Eurasian jay (Garrulus glandarius), *Animal Cognition, 14,* 441–455.

Chemers, M. M. (2000). Leadership research and theory: A functional integration. *Group Dynamics, 4,* 27–43.

Chemers, M. M., Watson, C. B., & May, S. T. (2000). Dispositional affect and leadership effectiveness: A comparison of self-esteem, optimism, and efficacy. *Personality and Social Psychology Bulletin, 26,* 267–277.

Chen, E. (2012). Protective factors for health among low-socioeconomic-status individuals. *Current Directions in Psychological Science, 21,* 189–193. doi:10.1177/0963721412438710

Chen, E., & Miller, G. E. (2012). "Shift-and-persist" strategies: Why low socioeconomic status isn't always bad for health. *Perspectives on Psychological Science, 7,* 135–158. doi:10.1177/1745691612436694

Chen, J., Magavi, S. S. P., & Macklis, J. D. (2004). Neurogenesis of corticospinal motor neurons extending spinal projections in adult mice. *Proceedings of the National Academy of Sciences, 101,* 16357–16362.

Chen, J. K., Chuang, A. Y., McMahon, C., Hsieh, J. C., Tung, T. H., and LI, L. P. (2010). Music training improves pitch perception in prelingually deafened children with cochlear implants. *Pediatrics, 125*(4), e793–800.

Chen, S. H., Kennedy, M., Zhou, Q. (2012). Parents' Expression and Discussion of Emotion in the Multilingual Family: Does Language Matter? *Perspectives on Psychological Science, 7,* 365–383, doi:10.1177/1745691612447307

Chen, X., Gabitto, M., Peng, Y., Ryba, N. J., Zuker, C. S. (2011). A gustotopic map of taste qualities in the mammalian brain. *Science, 333*(6047), 1262–1266.

Chen, Y., Hsu, C., Liu, L., & Yang, S. (2012). Constructing a nutrition diagnosis expert system. *Expert Systems With Applications, 39*(2), 2132–2156. doi:10.1016/j.eswa.2011.07.069.

Chen, Y., Tsai, P, Chen, P, Fan, C., Hung, G. C. & Cheng, A. T. A. (2010). Effect of media reporting of the suicide of a singer in Taiwan: The case of Ivy Li. *Social Psychiatry and Psychiatric Epidemiology, 45,* 363–369.

Cheng, A. T. A., Gau, S.-F., Chen, T. H. H., Chang, J.-C., & Chang, Y.-T. (2004). A 4-year longitudinal study on risk factors for alcoholism. *Archives of General Psychiatry, 61,* 184–191.

Cheng, L.-C., Tavazoie, M., & Doetsch, F. (2005). Stem cells: From epigenetics to microRNAs. *Neuron, 46,* 363–367.

Cheng, S. (2010). Intelligent cognition-based systems approach to multiple-criteria computerized essay assessment. *Systems Research And Behavioral Science, 27*(6), 680–696. doi:10.1002/sres.1001.

Cheng, Y., Kawachi, I., Coakley, E. H., Schwartz, J., & Colditz, G. (2000). Association between psychosocial work characteristics and health functioning in American women: Prospective study. *British Medical Journal, 320,* 1432–1436.

Cherkin, D. C., Sherman, K. J., Avins, A. L., Erro, J. H., et al. (2009). A randomized trial comparing acupuncture, simulated acupuncture, and usual care for chronic low back pain. *Archives of Internal Medicine, 169,* 858–866.

Chermahini, S., & Hommel, B. (2010). The (b)link between creativity and dopamine: Spontaneous eye blink rates predict and dissociate divergent and convergent thinking. *Cognition, 115*(3), 458–465. doi:10.1016/j.cognition.2010.03.007.

Cheshire, C., & Antin, J. (2010). None of us is as lazy as all of us. *Information, Communication & Society, 13*(4), 537–555. doi:10.1080/13691181003639858.

Chesney, M. A., Chambers, D. B., Taylor, J. M., Johnson, L. M., & Folkman, S. (2003). Coping effectiveness training for men living with HIV: Results from a randomized clinical trial testing a group-based intervention. *Psychosomatic Medicine, 65*, 1038–1046.

Cheung, B. (2011). Drug treatment for obesity in the post-sibutramine era. *Drug Safety: An International Journal of Medical Toxicology and Drug Experience, 34*(8), 641–650. doi:10.2165/11592040-000000000-00000

Cheung, F. M., van de Vijver, F. R., & Leong, F. L. (2011). Toward a new approach to the study of personality in culture. *American Psychologist, 66*(7), 593–603. doi:10.1037/a0022389.

Chi, A., Neville, B., Krayer, J., & Gonsalves, W. (2010). Oral manifestations of systemic disease. *American Family Physician, 82*(11), 1381–1388.

Chiaburu, D. S., Oh, I.-S., Berry, C. M., Li, N., & Gardner, R. G. (2011). The five-factor model of personality traits and organizational citizenship behaviors: A meta-analysis. *Journal of Applied Psychology, 96*(6), 1140–1166. doi:10.1037/a0024004.

Chiang, J. J., Eisenberger, N. I., Seeman, T. E., & Taylor, S. E. (2012). Negative and competitive social interactions are related to heightened proinflamatory cytokine activity. *Proceedings of the National Academy of Sciences*, online, Jan 23, 2012.

Chida, Y., & Steptoe, A. (2009). The association of anger and hostility with future coronary heart disease. *Journal of the American College of Cardiology, 53*, 936–946.

Chiesa, A., & Serretti, A. (2009). A systematic review of neurobiological and clinical features of mindfulness meditations. *Psychological Medicine, 40*, 1249–1252. Epub 2009 Nov 27.

Chinese Girl, 2, Run Over by Van, Ignored by At Least 18 Passers-By. (2011, October 18). Retrieved from http://www.foxnews.com/world/2011/10/18/chinese-girl-2-run-over-by-van-ignored-by-at-least-18-bystanders/?test=latestnews#ixzz1jlKunr8o.

Chiou, W., Yang, C., & Wan, C. (2011). Ironic effects of dietary supplementation: Illusory invulnerability created by taking dietary supplements licenses health-risk behaviors. *Psychological Science, 22*(8), 1081–1086. doi:10.1177/0956797611416253.

Chisholm, K. (1997, June). Trauma at an early age inhibits ability to bond. *APA Monitor*, 11.

Chittaro, L., Carchietti, E., De Marco, L., & Zampa, A. (2011). Personalized emergency medical assistance for disabled people. *User Modeling And User-Adapted Interaction, 21*(4-5), 407–440. doi:10.1007/s11257-010-9092-2.

Chivers, M. L., Rieger, G., Latty, E., & Bailey, J. M. (2004). A sex difference in the specificity of sexual arousal. *Psychological Science, 15*, 736–744.

Chivers, M. L., Seto, M. C., & Blanchard, R. (2007). Gender and sexual orientation differences in sexual response to sexual activities versus gender of actors in sexual films. *Journal of Personality and Social Psychology, 93*, 1108–1121.

Chodosh, J., Reuben, D. B., Albert, M. S., & Seeman, T. E. (2002). Predicting cognitive impairment in high-functioning community-dwelling older persons: MacArthur studies of successful aging. *Journal of the American Geriatrics Society, 50*(6), 1051–1060.

Choi, J., & Silverman, I. (2003). Processes underlying sex differences in route-learning strategies in children and adolescents. *Personality and Individual Differences, 34*, 1153–1166.

Chomsky, N. (1965). *Aspects of the theory of syntax.* Cambridge, MA: MIT Press.

Chomsky, N. (1986). *Knowledge of language: Its nature, origin, and use.* New York: Praeger.

Chouinard, G. (2004). Issues in the clinical use of benzodiazepines: Potency, withdrawal, and rebound. *Journal of Clinical Psychiatry, 65*(Suppl. 5), 7–21.

Choy, Y., Fyer, A. J., & Lipsitz, J. D. (2007). Treatment of specific phobia in adults. *Clinical Psychology Review, 27*, 266–286.

Christakis, D. A., & Garrison, M. M. (2009). Preschool-aged children's television viewing in child care settings. *Pediatrics, 124*, 1627–1632.

Christakas, D. A., & Zimmerman, F. J. (2007). Violent television viewing during preschool is associated with antisocial behavior during school age. *Pediatrics, 120*, 993–999.

Christakis, N. A., & Fowler, J. R. (2007). The spread of obesity in a large social network over 32 years. *New England Journal of Medicine, 357*, 370–379.

Christensen, A., Atkins, D. C., Berns, S., Wheeler, J., Baucom, D. H., & Simpson, L. E. (2004). Traditional versus integrative behavioral couple therapy for significantly and chronically distressed married couples. *Journal of Consulting and Clinical Psychology, 72*, 176–191.

Christensen, H. C., Schüz, J., Kosteljanetz, M., Poulsen, H. S., Boice, J. D., Jr., McLaughlin, J. K., & Johansen, C. (2005). Cellular telephones and risk for brain tumors: A population-based, incident case-control study. *Neurology, 64*, 1189–1195.

Christensen, M. S., Kristiansen, L., Rowe, J. B., & Nielsen, J. B. (2008). Action-blindsight in healthy subjects after transcranial magnetic stimulation. *Proceedings of the National Academies of Science, 105*, 1353–1357.

Christie, M. J. (2008). Cellular neuroadaptations to chronic opioids: Tolerance, withdrawal and addiction. *Journal of Pharmacology, 154*(2). 384–396.

Christopher, K. (2003). Autistic boy killed during exorcism. *Skeptical Inquirer, 27*(6), 11.

Chu, J. (1994). Active learning in epidemiology and biostatistics. *Teaching and Learning in Medicine, 6*, 191–193.

Chua, H. F., Boland, J. E., & Nisbett, R. E. (2005). Cultural variation in eye movements during scene perception. *Proceedings of the National Academy of Sciences, 102*, 12629–12633.

Chudzikowski, K., Demel, B., Mayrhofer, W., Briscoe, J. P., Unite, J., Milikić, B., & .. Zikic, J. (2009). Career transitions and their causes: A country-comparative perspective. *Journal Of Occupational & Organizational Psychology, 82*(4), 825–849.

Chugani, H. T., & Phelps, M. E. (1986). Maturational changes in cerebral function in infants determined by 18FDG positron emission tomography. *Science, 231*, 840–843.

Chung, W., Dao, R., Chen, L., & Hung, S. (2010). The role of genetic variants in human longevity. *Ageing Research Reviews, 9* Suppl 1, S67–S78

Church, A. T. (2010). Current perspectives in the study of personality across cultures. *Perspectives on Psychological Science, 5*(4), 441–449. doi:10.1177/1745691610375559.

Church, A. T. (2001). Personality measurement in cross-cultural perspective. *Journal of Personality, 69*(6), 979–1006.

Churchill, S., & Jessop, D. (2011). Too impulsive for implementation intentions? Evidence that impulsivity moderates the effectiveness of an implementation intention intervention. *Psychology & Health, 26*(5), 517–530. doi:10.1080/08870441003611536.

Churchill, S., Jessop, D., & Sparks, P. (2008). Impulsive and/or planned behaviour: Can impulsivity contribute to the predictive utility of the theory of planned behaviour? *British Journal of Social Psychology, 47*, 631–646. doi:10.1348/014466608X284434.

Churchland, P. M. (1989). *A neurocomputational perspective: The nature of mind and the structure of science.* Cambridge, MA: MIT Press.

Cialdini, R. (2007). *Influence: Sciences and Practice* (5th ed.). New York: Allyn & Bacon.

Cialdini, R. B. (2001). *Influence: Science and practice* (4th ed.). Boston: Allyn & Bacon.

Cialdini, R. B., & Goldstein, N. J. (2004). Social influence: Compliance and conformity. *Annual Review of Psychology, 55*, 591–621.

Cialdini, R. C. (2008). *Influence: Science and practice* (5th ed). Boston, MA: Allyn & Bacon.

Cialdini, R. C., & Griskevicius (2010). Social Influence In R. Baumeister & E. Finkel (Eds.) *Advanced social psychology: The state of the science* (pp. 385–418). New York, NY: Oxford.

Ciccarone, D. (2011). Stimulant abuse: Pharmacology, cocaine, methamphetamine, treatment, attempts at pharmacotherapy. *Primary Care, 38*(1), 41–58.

Ciccocioppo, R., Martin-Fardon, R., & Weiss, F. (2004). Stimuli associated with a single cocaine experience elicit long-lasting cocaine-seeking. *Nature Neuroscience, 7*, 495–496.

Ciccocioppo, R., Sanna, P. P., & Weiss, F. (2001). Cocaine-predictive stimulus induces drug-seeking behavior and neural activation in limbic brain regions after multiple months of abstinence: Reversal by D1 antagonists. *Proceedings of the National Academy of Sciences, 98*, 1976–1981.

Cicogna, P. C., Occhioneroa, M., Natalea, V., & Espositoa, M. J. (2006). Bizarreness of size and shape in dream images. *Consciousness and Cognition, 16*, 381–390.

Cikara, M., Botvinick, M. M., & Fiske, S. T. (2011). Us versus them: Social identity shapes neural responses to intergroup competition and harm. *Psychological Science, 22*(3), 306–313. doi:10.1177/0956797610397667.

Cikara, M., Bruneau, E. G., & Saxe, R. R. (2011). Us and them: Intergroup failures of empathy. *Current Directions in Psychological Science 20*(3) 149–153. doi:10.1177/0963721411408713.

Cilia, R., Siri, C., Marotta, G., Isaias, I. U., De Gaspari, D., Canesi, M., Pezzoli, G., & Antonini, A. (2008). Functional abnormalities underlying pathological gambling in Parkinson disease. *Archives of Neurology, 65*, 1604–1611.

Ciocca, V. (2008). The auditory organization of complex sounds. *Frontiers in Bioscience, 13*, 148–169.

Cipriani, G., Picchi, L., Vedovello. M., Nuti, A., & Fiorino, M. D. (2011). The phantom and the supernumerary phantom limb: historical review and new case. *Neuroscience Bulletin, 27*(6), 359–365.

Cisler, J. M., & Koster, E. H. W. (2010). Mechanisms of attentional biases toward threat in anxiety disorders: An integrative review. *Clinical Psychology Review, 30*, 203–216.

Citrome, L., Jaffe, A., Levine, J., & Lindenmayer, J. (2005). Dosing of quetiapine in schizophrenia: How clinical practice differs from registration studies. *Journal of Clinical Psychiatry, 66*, 1512–1516.

Claassen, D. O., Josephs, K. A., Ahlskog, J. E., & Silber, M. H., Tippmann-Peikert, M., & Boeve, B. F. (2010). REM sleep behavior disorder preceding other aspects of synucleinopathies by up to half a century. *Neurology, 75*(6), 494–499.

Clancy, S. A. (2005). *Abducted: How people come to believe they were kidnapped by aliens.* Cambridge, MA: Harvard University Press.

Clancy, S. A., Schacter, D. L., McNally, R. J., & Pittman, R. K. (2000). False recognition in women reporting recovered memories of sexual abuse. *Psychological Science, 11*, 26–31.

Clark, M. S., & Lemay, E. A., Jr. (2010). Close relationships. In S. T. Fiske, D. T. Gilbert, & G. Lindzey (Eds.), *Handbook of social psychology* (5th ed., Vol. 2, pp. 898–940). Hoboken, NJ: Wiley.

Clark, A., Nash, R. A., Fincham, G., & Mazzoni, G. (2012). Creating non-believed memories for recent autobiographical events. *Plos ONE, 7*(3), doi:10.1371/journal.pone.0032998

Clark, A., Oswald, A., & Warr, P. (1996). Is job satisfaction U-shaped in age? *Journal of Occupational and Organizational Psychology, 69*, 57–81.

Clark, D. A., & Beck, A. T. (2012). *The anxiety and worry workbook: The cognitive behavioral solution.* New York: Guilford Press.

Clark, D. C., & Fawcett, J. (1992). Review of empirical risk factors for evaluation of the suicidal patient. In B. Bongar (Ed.), *Suicide: Guidelines for assessment, management, and treatment* (pp. 16–48). New York: Oxford University Press.

Clark, E. V. (1983). Meanings and concepts. In P. H. Mussen, J. H. Flavell, & E. M. Markman (Eds.), *Handbook of child psychology: Vol. 3. Cognitive development* (4th ed., pp. 787–840). New York: Wiley.

Clark, E. V. (1993). *The lexicon in acquisition.* Cambridge: Cambridge University Press. Clark, L. A., & Watson, D. (2008). Temperament: An organizing paradigm for trait psychology. In O. John, R. Robins, & L. Pervin (Eds.), *Handbook of personality: Theory and research* (3rd ed., pp. 265–286). New York: Guilford.

Clark, L. A., & Watson, D. (2008). Temperament: An organizing paradigm for trait psychology. In O. P. John, R. W. Robins, & L. A. Pervin (Eds.), *Handbook of personality: Theory and research* (3rd ed., pp. 265–286). New York: Guilford Press.

Clark, M. S., Lemay, E. P. Jr., Graham, S. M., Pakaki, S. P., & Finkel, E. J. (2010). Ways of giving benefits in marriage: Norm use, relationship satisfaction, and attachment-related variability. *Psychological Science, 21*(7), 944–951. doi:10.1177/0956797610373882.

Clark, M. S., & Pataki, S. P. (1995). Interpersonal processes influencing attraction and relationships. In A. Tesser (Ed.), *Advanced social psychology* (pp. 283–332). New York: McGraw-Hill.

Clark, S. E. (2012a). Costs and benefits of eyewitness identification reform: Psychological science and public policy. *Perspectives in Psychological Science, 7*(3), 238–259. doi:10.1177/1745691612439584

Clark, S. E. (2012b). Eyewitness identification reform: Data, theory, and due process. *Perspectives on Psychological Science, 7*(3), 279–283. doi:10.1177/1745691612444136

Clark, S. E., Erickson, M. A., & Breneman, J. (2011). Probative value of absolute and relative judgments in eyewitness identification. *Law and Human Behavior, 35*(5), 364–380. doi:10.1007/s10979-010-9245-1.

Clarke, L., Ungerer, J., Chahoud, K., Johnson, S., Stiefel, I. (2002). Attention deficit hyperactivity disorder is associated with attachment insecurity. *Clinical Child Psychology and Psychiatry, 7*, 179–198.

Clarke-Stewart, A., & Allhusen, V. (2005). *What we know about childcare.* Cambridge, MA: Harvard University Press.

Clarke-Stewart, A., & Brentano, C. (2006). *'Til divorce do us part: Causes and consequences of marital separation for children and adults.* New Haven, CT: Yale University Press.

Clarke-Stewart, K. A. (1989). Infant day care: Maligned or malignant? *American Psychologist, 44*, 266–273.

Clarkin, J. F. (2006). Conceptualization and treatment of personality disorders. *Psychotherapy Research, 16*, 1–11.

Clausen, J., Sersen, E., & Lidsky, A. (1974). Variability of sleep measures in normal subjects. *Psychophysiology, 11*, 509–516.

Clay, R. A. (2000). Often, the bells and whistles backfire. *Monitor on Psychology, 31*, 64–65.

Clayton N. S., & Dickinson A. (1998) Episodic-like memory during cache recovery by scrub-jays. *Nature, 395*, 272–278.

Cleland, V., Crawford, D., Baur, L. A., Hume1, C., Timperio, A., & Salmon, J. (2008). A prospective examination of children's time spent outdoors, objectively measured physical activity and overweight. *International Journal of Obesity, 32*, 1685–1693.

Clendenen, V. I., Herman, C. P., & Polivy, J. (1995). Social facilitation of eating among friends and strangers. *Appetite, 23*, 1–13.

Cleveland, E. S., & Reese, E. (2008). Children remember early childhood: Long-term recall across the offset of childhood amnesia. *Applied Cognitive Psychology, 22*(1), 127–142.

Clifton, R. K. (1992). The development of spatial hearing in human infants. In L. A. Werner & E. W. Rubel (Eds.), *Developmental psychoacoustics* (pp. 135–157). Washington, DC: American Psychological Association.

Clifton, R. K., Rochat, P., Litovsky, R., & Perris, E. (1991). Object representation guides infants' reaching in the dark. *Journal of Experimental Psychology: Human Perception and Performance, 17*, 323–329.

Clinical Digest. Early exposure to mobile phones affects children's behaviour. (2011). *Nursing Standard, 25*(21), 17.

Coccaro, E. F. (1989). Central serotonin and impulsive aggression. *British Journal of Psychiatry, 155*, 52–62.

Coelho, C. M., & Purkis, H. (2009). The origins of specific phobias: Influential theories and current perspectives. *Review of General Psychology, 13*, 335–348.

Cofer, L. F., Grice, J., Palmer, D., Sethre-Hofstad, L., & Zimmermann, K. (1992, June 20–22). *Evidence for developmental continuity of individual differences in morningness-eveningness.* Paper presented at the annual meeting of the American Psychological Society, San Diego, CA.

Cohen, G. L., & Steele, C. M. (2002). A barrier of mistrust: How negative stereotypes affect cross-race mentoring. In J. Aronson (Ed.), *Improving academic achievement: Impact of psychological factors on education* (pp. 303–327). San Diego, CA: Academic Press.

Cohen, A. (2009). Many forms of culture. *American Psychologist, 64*, 194–204.

Cohen, C. E. (1981). Person categories and social perception: Testing some boundaries of the processing effects of prior knowledge. *Journal of Personality and Social Psychology, 40*, 441–452.

Cohen, D. (1998). Culture, social organization, and patterns of violence. *Journal of Personality and Social Psychology, 75*, 408–419.

Cohen, F., Kemeny, M. E., Zegans, L. S., Johnson, P., Kearney, K. A., & Strites, D. P. (2007). Immune function declines with unemployment and recovers after stressor termination. *Psychosomatic Medicine, 69*, 225–234.

Cohen, N. J., & Corkin, S. (1981). The amnesic patient H. M.: Learning and retention of a cognitive skill. *Neuroscience Abstracts, 7*, 235.

Cohen, N. J., & Squire, L. R. (1980). Preserved learning and retention of pattern analyzing skills in amnesia: Dissociation of knowing how and knowing that. *Science, 210*, 207–210.

Cohen, P. (2008). Child development and personality disorder. *Psychiatric Clinics of North America, 31*, 477–493.

Cohen, P., Kasen, S., Chen, H., Hartmark, C., & Gordon, K. (2003). Variations in patterns of developmental transitions in the emerging adulthood period. *Developmental Psychology, 39*, 657–669.

Cohen, S., & Herbert, T. B. (1996). Health psychology: Psychological factors and physical disease from the perspective of human psychoneuroimmunology. *Annual Review of Psychology, 47*, 113–142.

Cohen, S., & Pressman, S. D. (2006). Positive affect and health. *Current Directions in Psychological Science, 15*, 122–125.

Cohen, S., Doyle, W. J., Alper, C. M., Janicki-Deverts, D., & Turner, R. B. (2009). Sleep habits and susceptibility to the common cold. *Archives of Internal Medicine, 169*, 62–67.

Cohen, S., Doyle, W. J., Turner, R. B., Alper, C. M., & Skoner, D. P. (2003a). Emotional style and susceptibility to the common cold. *Psychosomatic Medicine, 65*, 652–657.

Cohen, S., Doyle, W. J., Turner, R., Alper, C. M., & Skoner, D. P. (2003b). Sociability and susceptibility to the common cold. *Psychological Science, 14*, 389–395.

Cohen, S., Janicki-Deverts, D., Doyle, W. J., Miller, G. E., Frank, E., Rabin, B. S., & Turner, R. B. (2012). Chronic stress, glucocorticoid receptor resistance, inflammation, and disease risk. *Proceedings of the National Academy of Sciences of the United States of America, 109*, 5995–5999. doi:10.1073/pnas.1118355109

Cohn, M. A., Fredrickson, B. L., Brown, S. L., Mikels, J. A., & Conway, A. M. (2009). Happiness unpacked: Positive emotions increase life satisfaction by building resilience. *Emotion, 9*, 361–368.

Cohrs, J. C., & Ibler, S. (2009). Authoritarianism, threat, and prejudice: An analysis of mediation and moderation. *Basic and Applied Social Psychology, 31*, 81–94.

Coid, J. & Ullrich, S. (2010). Antisocial personality disorder is on a continuum with psychopathy. *Comprehensive Psychiatry, 51*, 426–433.

Coifman, K. G., Bonanno, G. A., Ray, R. D., & Gross, J. J. (2007). Does repressive coping promote resilience? Affective-autonomic response discrepancy during bereavement. *Journal of Personality & Social Psychology, 92*(4), 745–758.

Colak, A., Soy, O., Uzun, H., Aslan, O., Barut, S., Belce, A., et al. (2003). Neuroprotective effects of GYKI 52466 on experimental spinal cord injury in rats. *Journal of Neurosurgery, 98*, 275–281.

Coldwell, C. M., & Bender, W. S. (2007). The effectiveness of assertive community treatment for homeless populations with severe mental illness: A meta-analysis. *American Journal of Psychiatry, 164*, 393–399.

Cole, K. N., Mills, P. E., Dale, P. S., & Jenkins, J. R. (1991). Effects of preschool integration for children with disabilities. *Exceptional Children, 58*, 36–45.

Cole, S. W. (2009). Social regulation of human gene expression. *Current Directions in Psychological Science, 18*, 132–137.

Cole, S. W., Arevalo, J. M. G. Manu, K., Telzer, E. H., Kiang, L., Bower, J. E., Irwin, M. R. & Fuligni, A. J. (2011). Antagonistic pleiotropy at the human IL6 promoter confers genetic resilience to the pro-inflammatory effects of adverse social conditions in adolescence *Developmental Psychology, 47*, 1173–1180.

Coleman, D. (1992). Why do I feel so tired? Too little, too late. *American Health, 11*(4), 43–46.

Collings, S. C., & Kemp, C. G (2010). Death knocks, professional practice, and the public good: The media experience of suicide reporting in New Zealand., *Social Science and Medicine, 71*, 244–248.

Collins, D., Deck, A., & McCrickard, M. (2008). Computer aided instruction: A study of student evaluations and academic performance. *Journal of College Teaching & Learning, 5*(11), 49–58.

Collins, R. L., Martino, S. C., Elliott, M. N., & Miu, A. (2011). Relationships between adolescent sexual outcomes and exposure to sex in media: Robustness to propensity-based analysis. *Developmental Psychology, 47*(2), 585–591. doi:10.1037/a0022563.

Collins, R. L., Elliott, M. N., Berry, S. H., Kanouse, D. E., Kunkel, D., Hunter, S. B., et al. (2004). Watching sex on television predicts adolescent initiation of sexual behavior. *Pediatrics, 114*, e280–e289.

Collins, W. A., & Steinberg, L. (2006). Adolescent development in interpersonal context. In W. Damon & R. M. Lerner (Series Eds.) & N. Eisenberg (Vol. Ed.), *Handbook of child psychology: Vol. 3, Social, emotional, and personality development* (pp. 1003–1068). Hoboken, NJ: Wiley.

Colloca, L., & Benedetti, F. (2005). Placebos and painkillers: Is mind as real as matter? *Nature Reviews Neuroscience, 6*, 545–552.

Colom, R., & Flores-Mendoza, C. E. (2007). Intelligence predicts scholastic achievement irrespective of SES factors: Evidence from Brazil. *Intelligence, 35*, 243–251.

Colombo, M., D'Amato, M. R., Rodman, H. R., & Gross, C. G. (1990). Auditory association cortex lesions impair auditory short-term memory in monkeys. *Science, 247*, 336–338.

Colzato, L. S., Beest, I., van den Wildenberg, W. M., Scorolli, C., Dorchin, S., Meiran, N., & Hommel, B. (2010). God: Do I have your attention? *Cognition, 117*(1), 87–94. doi:10.1016/j.cognition.2010.07.003.

Combe, E., & Wexler, M. (2010). Observer movement and size constancy. *Psychological Science, 21*(5), 667–675. doi:10.1177/0956797610367753.

Commission on Accreditation. (2008). *Guidelines and principles for accreditation of programs in professional psychology.* Washington, DC: American Psychological Association.

Committee to Review the Scientific Evidence on the Polygraph. (2003). *The polygraph and lie detection.* Washington, DC: National Academies Press.

Compas, B. E., Haaga, D. A. F., Keefe, F. J., Leitenberg, H., & Williams, D. A. (1998). Sampling of empirically supported psychological treatments from health psychology: Smoking, chronic pain, cancer, and bulimia nervosa. *Journal of Consulting and Clinical Psychology, 66*, 89–112.

Compton, W. M., Conway, K. P., Stinson, F. S., Colliver, J. D., & Grant, B. F. (2005). Prevalence, correlates, and comorbidity of DSM-IV antisocial personality syndromes and alcohol and specific drug use disorders in the United States: Results from the national epidemiologic survey on alcohol and related conditions. *Journal of Clinical Psychiatry, 66*, 677–685.

Compton, W. M., Thomas, Y. F., Stinson, F. S., & Grant, B. F. (2007). Prevalence, correlates, disability, and comorbidity of DSM-IV drug abuse and dependence in the United States: Results from the National Epidemiologic Survey on Alcohol and Related Conditions. *Archives of General Psychiatry, 164*, 566–576.

Condell, J., Wade, J., Galway, L., McBride, M., Gormley, P., Brennan, J., & Somasundram, T. (2010). Problem solving techniques in cognitive science. *Artificial Intelligence Review, 34*(3), 221–234. doi:10.1007/s10462-010-9171-0.

Condic, M. L. (2001). Adult neuronal regeneration induced by transgenic integrin expression. *Journal of Neuroscience, 21*, 4782–4788.

Condon, J. W., & Crano, W. D. (1988). Inferred evaluation and the relationship between attitude similarity and interpersonal attraction. *Journal of Personality and Social Psychology, 54*, 789–797.

Cone, E. J., Fant, R. V., Rohay, J. M., Caplan, Y. H., Ballina, M., Reder, R. F., et al. (2004). Oxycodone involvement in drug abuse deaths: II. Evidence for toxic multiple drug-drug interactions. *Journal of Analytical Toxicology, 28*, 616–624.

Conel, J. L. (1939/1967). *The postnatal development of the human cerebral cortex* (Vols. 1, 8). Cambridge, MA: Harvard University Press.

Confer, J. C., Easton, J. A., Fleischman, D. S., Goetz, C. D., Lewis, D.M.G., Perilloux, C., & Buss, D. M. (2010). Evolutionary psychology: Controversies, questions, prospects, and limitations. *American Psychologist, 65*, 110–126.

Conger, R. D., Cui, M., Bryant, C. M., & Elder, G. H. (2000). Competence in early adult romantic relationships: A developmental perspective on family influences. *Journal of Personality and Social Psychology, 79*(2), 224–237.

Conley, T. D., Moors, A. C., Matsick, J. L., Ziegler, A., & Valentine, B. A. (2011). Women, men, and the bedroom: Methodological and conceptual insights that narrow, reframe, and eliminate gender differences in sexuality. *Current Directions In Psychological Science, 20*(5), 296–300. doi:10.1177/0963721411418467.

Connell, L., & Lynott, D. (2010). Look but don't touch: Tactile disadvantage in processing modality-specific words. *Cognition, 115*(1), 1–9. doi:10.1016/j.cognition.2009.10.005.

Conner, K. O., Copeland, V., Grote, N. K., Koeske, G., Rosen, D., Reynolds, C., & Brown, C. (2010). Mental health treatment seeking among older adults with depression: The impact of stigma and race. *The American Journal of Geriatric Psychiatry, 18*(6), 531–543.

Connor, L. T., Balota, D. A., & Neely, J. H. (1992). On the relation between feeling of knowing and lexical decision: Persistent subthreshold activation of topic familiarity? *Journal of Experimental Psychology: Learning, Memory, and Cognition, 18*, 544–554.

Connor-Greene, P. A. (2001). Family, friends, and self: The real-life context of an abnormal psychology class. *Teaching of Psychology, 28*, 210–212.

Conrad, R. (1964). Acoustic confusions in immediate memory. *British Journal of Psychology, 55*, 75–84.

Conry-Murray, C., & Turiel, E. (2012). Jimmy's baby doll and Jenny's truck: Young children's reasoning about gender norms. *Child Development, 83*(1), 146–158. doi:10.1111/j.1467-8624.2011.01696.x.

Considine, R., V., Sinha, M. K., Heiman, M. L., Kriauciunas, A., et al. (1996). Serum immunoreactive-leptin concentrations in normal-weight and obese humans. *New England Journal of Medicine, 334*(5), 292–295.

Constantine, M. G. (2002). Predictors of satisfaction with counseling: Racial and ethnic minority clients' attitudes toward counseling and ratings of their counselors' general and multicultural competence. *Journal of Counseling Psychology, 49*, 255–263.

Constantino, J. N., & Todd, R. D. (2003). Autistic traits in the general population: A twin study. *Archives General Psychiatry, 60*, 524–530.

Consumer Reports. (1995, November). Mental health: Does therapy help? *Consumer Reports*, pp. 734–739.

Conte, J. M., & Gintoft, J. N. (2005). Polychronicity, big five personality dimensions, and sales performance. *Human Performance, 18*, 427–444.

Contemporary Sexuality. (2008, May). CDC: One in four teens has an STI. *Contemporary Sexuality, 42*(5), 11–12.

Conway, B. R. (2009). Color vision, cones, and color-coding in the cortex. *Neuroscientist, 15*, 274–290.

Cook, C., Goodman, N. D., & Schulz, L. E. (2011). Where science starts: Spontaneous experiments in preschoolers' exploratory play. *Cognition, 120*(3), 341–349. doi:10.1016/j.cognition.2011.03.003.

Cook, J. A., Leff, H. S., Blyler, C. R., Gold, P. B., Goldberg, R. W., Mueser, K. T., et al. (2005). Results of a multisite randomized trial of supported employment interventions for individuals with severe mental illness. *Archives of General Psychiatry, 62*, 505–512.

Cook, J. M., Biyanova, T., & Coyne, J. C. (2009). Influential psychotherapy figures, authors, and books: An Internet survey of over 2,000 psychotherapists. *Psychotherapy: Theory, Research, Practice, Training, 46*, 42–51. doi:10.1037/a0015152

Cook, J. M., Biyanova, T., Elhai, J., Schnurr, P. P., & Coyne, J. C. (2010). What do psychotherapists really do in practice? An Internet study of over 2,000 practitioners. *Psychotherapy: Theory, Research, and Practice, 47*, 260–267.

Cook, K. J. (Ed.) (2011). *Employment & Earnings, 58* (1). Retrieved from http://www.bls.gov/opub/ee/empearn201101.pdf.

Cook, M., & Mineka, S. (1990). Selective associations in the observational conditioning of fear in rhesus monkeys. *Journal of Experimental Psychology: Animal Behavior Processes, 16*, 372–389.

Cook, N. D., Yutsudo, A., Fujimoto, N., & Murata, M. (2008). Factors contributing to depth perception: Behavioral studies on the reverse perspective illusion. *Spatial Vision, 21*(3–5), 397–405.

Cooke, L. J., Chambers, L. C., Añez, E. V., Croker, H. A., Boniface, D., Yeomans, M. R., & Wardle, J. (2011). Eating for Pleasure or Profit: The Effect of Incentives on Children's Enjoyment of Vegetables. *Psychological Science, 22*(2), 190–196. doi:10.1177/0956797610394662.

Cooley, E., Toraya, T., Wanga, M. C., & Valdeza, N. N. (2008). Maternal effects on daughters' eating pathology and body image. *Eating behaviors, 9*, 52–61.

Cooper, A., Gomez, R., & Buck, E. (2008). The relationships between the BIS and BAS, anger and responses to anger. *Personality and Individual Differences, 44*(2), 403–413.

Cooper, J., Mirabile, R., & Scher, S. J. (2005). Actions and attitudes: The theory of cognitive dissonance. In T. Brock & M. Green (Eds.), *Persuasion: Psychological insights and perspectives* (2nd ed., pp. 63–79). Thousand Oaks, CA: Sage Publications, Inc.

Cooper, L. N. (2007). On the problem of consciousness. *Neural Networks, 20*(9), 1057–1058.

Cooper, M. L., Russell, M., Skinner, J. B., Frone, M. R., & Mudar, P. (1992). Stress and alcohol use: The moderating effects of gender, coping, and alcohol expectancies. *Journal of Abnormal Psychology, 101*, 139–152.

Corbett, A., Kauffman, L., MacLaren, B., Wagner, A., & Jones, E. (2010). A cognitive tutor for genetics problem solving: Learning gains and student modeling. *Journal of Educational Computing Research, 42*(2), 219–239. doi:10.2190/EC.42.2.e.

Corbetta, M., Miezin, F. M., Dobmeyer, S., Shulman, G. L., & Petersen, S. E. (1991). Selective and divided attention during visual discriminations of shape, color, and speed: Functional anatomy by positron emission tomography. *Journal of Neuroscience, 11*, 2383–2402.

Corden, B., Critchley, H. D., Skuse, D., & Dolan, R. J. (2006). Fear recognition ability predicts differences in social cognitive and neural functioning in men. *Journal of Cognitive Neuroscience, 18*, 889–897.

Cordery, J. L., Mueller, W. S., & Smith, L. M. (1991). Attitudinal and behavioral effects of autonomous group working: A longitudinal field study. *Academy of Management Journal, 34*, 464–476.

Coren, S. (1999). Psychology applied to animal training. In A. Stec & D. Bernstein (Eds.), *Psychology: Fields of application*. Boston: Houghton Mifflin.

Coren, S., & Girgus, J. S. (1978). *Seeing is deceiving: The psychology of visual illusions.* Hillsdale, NJ: Erlbaum.

Corey, G. (2008). *Theory and practice of counseling and psychotherapy* (8th ed.). Belmont, CA: Brooks/Cole.

Cork, R. C., Kihlstrom, J. F., & Hameroff, S. R. (1992). Explicit and implicit memory dissociated by anesthetic technique. *Society for Neuroscience Abstracts, 22*, 523.

Corkin, S. (2002). What's new with the amnesic patient H. M.? *Nature Reviews. Neuroscience, 3*(2), 153–160.

Cornblatt, B., & Erlenmeyer-Kimling, L. E. (1985). Global attentional deviance in children at risk for schizophrenia: Specificity and predictive validity. *Journal of Abnormal Psychology, 94*, 470–486.

Cornelius, R. R. (1996). *The science of emotion.* Upper Saddle River, NJ: Prentice Hall.

Cornelius, T. L., & Resseguie, N. (2007). Primary and secondary prevention programs for dating violence: A review of the literature. *Aggression and Violent Behavior, 12*, 364–375.

Cornelius-White, J. H. D. (2002). The phoenix of empirically supported therapy relationships: The overlooked person-centered bias. *Psychotherapy: Theory, Research, Practice, Training, 39*, 219–222.

Cornum, R., Matthews, M. D., & Seligman, M. E., P. (2011). Comprehensive soldier fitness: Building resilience in a challenging institutional context. *American Psychologist, 66*(1), 4–9. doi:10.1037/a0021420.

Corr, P. J. (2002). J. A. Gray's reinforcement sensitivity theory: Tests of the joint subsystem hypothesis of anxiety and impulsivity. *Personality and Individual Differences, 33*, 511–532.

Corradi-Dell'Acqua, C., Hofstetter, C., & Vuilleumier, P. (2011). Felt and seen pain evoke the same local patterns of cortical activity in insular and cingulate cortex. *Journal of Neuroscience, 31*, 17996–18006. doi:10.1523/JNEUROSCI.2686-11.2011.

Correll, J., Park, B., Judd, C. M., & Wittenbrink, B. (2002). The police officer's dilemma: Using ethnicity to disambiguate potentially threatening individuals. *Journal of Personality and Social Psychology, 83*, 1314–1329.

Correll, J., Park, B., Judd, C. M., Wittenbrink, B., et al. (2007). Across the thin blue line: Police officers and racial bias in the decision to shoot. *Journal of Personality and Social Psychology, 92*, 1006–1023.

Corsini, R. J., & Wedding, W. (Eds.). (2005). *Current psychotherapies* (7th ed.). Belmont, CA: Thomson Brooks/Cole.

Corwin, M. J., Lesko, S. M., Heeren, T., Vezina, R. M., Hunt, C. E., Mandell, F., et al. (2003). Secular changes in sleep position during infancy: 1995–1998. *Pediatrics, 111*, 52–60.

Costa, P. (2001, June). *New insights on personality and leadership provided by the five-factor model.* Paper presented at Annual Convention of American Psychological Society, Toronto, Canada.

Costa, P. T., Jr., & McCrae, R. R. (in press). The Revised NEO Personality Inventory. In S. R. Briggs, J. Cheek. & E. Donahue (Eds.), *Handbook of adult personality inventories.* New York: Plenum.

Costa, P., & McCrae, R. (2008). The NEO inventories. In R. P. Archer & S. R. Smith, (Eds), *Personality assessment* (pp. 213–245). New York: Routledge/Taylor & Francis.

Costello, E. J., Copeland, W., & Angold, A. (2011). Trends in psychopathology across the adolescent years: What changes when children become adolescents, and when adolescents become adults? *Journal of Child Psychology and Psychiatry, 52*, 1015–1025.

Cota, D., Marsicano, G., Lutz, B., Vicennati, V., Stalla, G. K., Pasquali, R., & Pagotto, U. (2003). Endogenous cannabinoid system as a modulator of food intake. *International Journal of Obesity, 27*, 289–301.

Cota, D., Proulx, K., Smith, K. A. B., Kozma, S. C., Thomas, G., Woods, S. C., et al. (2006). Hypothalamic mTOR signaling regulates food intake. *Science, 312,* 927–930.

Cotanche, D. A. (1997). Hair cell regeneration in the avian cochlea. *Annals of Otology, Rhinology, and Laryngology Supplement, 168,* 9–15.

Cote, J. K., & Pepler, C. (2002). A randomized trial of a cognitive coping intervention for acutely ill HIV-positive men. *Nursing Research, 51,* 237–244.

Côté, S., Gyurak, A., & Levenson, R. W. (2010). The ability to regulate emotion is associated with greater well-being, income, and socioeconomic status. *Emotion, 10*(6), 923–933. doi:10.1037/a0021156

Cottler, L. B., & Grant, B. F. (2007). Characteristics of nosologically informative data sets that address key diagnostic issues facing the DSM-V and ICD-11 substance use disorders workgroups. In J. B. Saunders, M. A. Schuckit, P. J. Sirovatka, & Reiger, D. A. (Eds.), *Diagnostic issues in substance use disorders: Refining the research agenda for DSM-V. Advancing the research agenda for DSM-V.* (pp. 285–302). Washington, DC: American Psychiatric Association.

Courtenay, G., Smith, D. R., & Gladstone, W. (2012). Occupational health issues in marine and freshwater research. *Journal of Occupational Medicine & Toxicology, 7*(1), 1–11. doi:10.1186/1745-6673-7-4.

Courts, C. & Madea, B. (2011). Significant association of TH01 allele 9.3 and SIDS. *Journal of Forensic Sciences, 56*(2), 415–417.

Cousins, A. J., Fugère, M. A., & Franklin, M. (2009). Digit ratio (2D:4D), mate guarding, and physical aggression in dating couples. *Personality and Individual Differences, 46,* 709–713.

Coutanche, M. N., & Thompson-Schill, S. L. (2012). Reversal without remapping: What we can (and cannot) conclude about learned associations from training-induced behavior changes. *Perspectives On Psychological Science, 7*(2), 118–134. doi:10.1177/1745691611434211

Covington, H., Lobo, M., Maze, I., Vialou, V., Hyman, J., Zaman, S., & .. Nestler, E. (2010). Antidepressant effect of optogenetic stimulation of the medial prefrontal cortex. *The Journal of Neuroscience: The Official Journal of the Society for Neuroscience, 30*(48), 16082–16090.

Cowan, C. A., Atienza, J., Melton, D. A., & Eggan, K. (2005). Nuclear reprogramming of somatic cells after fusion with human embryonic stem cells. *Science, 309,* 1369–1373.

Cowan, C. P., & Cowan, P. A. (2000). *When partners become parents: The big life change for couples.* Hillsdale, NJ: Erlbaum.

Cowan, D. T., Allan, L. G., Libretto, S. E., & Griffiths, P. (2001). Opiod drugs: A comparative survey of therapeutic and "street" use. *Pain, 2,* 193–203.

Cowan, N. (2011). The focus of attention as observed in visual working memory tasks: Making sense of competing claims. *Neuropsychologia, 49,* 1401–1406.

Cowan, N. (2010). The magical mystery four: How is working memory capacity limited, and why? *Current Directions in Psychological Science, 19*(1) 51–57. doi:10.1177/0963721409359277.

Cowan, N. (1988). Evolving concepts of memory storage, selective attention, and their mutual constraints within the human information-processing system. *Psychological Bulletin, 104,* 163–191.

Cowan, P. A., & Cowan, C. P. (2009). How working with couples fosters childrens development: From prevention science to public policy. In M. Schulz, M. K. Pruett, P. Kerig, & R. D. Parke (Eds.), *Strengthening couple relationships for optimal child development* (pp. 211–228). Washington, DC: American Psychological Association.

Cowey, A. (2010a). The blindsight saga. *Experimental Brain Research, 200*(1), 3–24.

Cowey, A. (2010b). Visual system: how does blindsight arise? *Current Biology, 20*(17), R702–R704.

Cox, J. E., Buman, M., Valenzuela, J., Joseph, N. P., Mitchell, A., & Woods, E. R. (2008). Depression, parenting attributes, and social support among adolescent mothers attending a teen tot program. *Journal of Pediatric & Adolescent Gynecology, 21*(5), 275–281.

Coyle, T. R., Pillow, D. R., Snyder, A. C., & Kochunov, P. (2011). Processing speed mediates the development of general intelligence (g) in adolescence. *Psychological Science, 22*(10), 1265–1269. doi:10.1177/0956797611418243.

Crabbe, J. C. (2002). Alcohol and genetics: new models. *American Journal of Medical Genetics, 114,* 969–974.

Craig, A. D. (2009). How do you feel—now? The anterior insula and human awareness. *Nature Reviews Neuroscience, 10*(1), 59–70.

Craig, A. D., & Bushnell, M. C. (1994). The thermal grill illusion: Unmasking the burn of cold pain. *Science, 265,* 252–254.

Craik, F., Bialystok, E., & Freedman, M. (2010). Delaying the onset of Alzheimer disease: bilingualism as a form of cognitive reserve. *Neurology, 75*(19), 1726–1729.

Craik, F. I. M., & Lockhart, R. S. (1972). Levels of processing: A framework for memory research. *Journal of Verbal Learning and Verbal Behavior, 11,* 671–684.

Craik, F. I. M., & Rabinowitz, J. C. (1984). Age differences in the acquisition and use of verbal information. In H. Bouma & D. G. Bouwhuis (Eds.), *Attention and performance* (Vol. 10, pp. 471–499). Hillsdale, NJ: Erlbaum.

Craik, F. I. M., & Salthouse, T. A. (2008). *The handbook of aging and cognition* (3rd ed.). New York: Psychology Press.

Cramer, P. (2009). The development of defense mechanisms from pre-adolescence to early adulthood: Do IQ and social class matter? A longitudinal study. *Journal of Research in Personality, 43,* 464–471.

Cramer, P., & Jones, C. J. (2007). Defense mechanisms predict differential lifespan change in self-control and self-acceptance. *Journal of Research in Personality, 41*(4), 841–855.

Cramer, S. C. (2008). Repairing the human brain after stroke: I. Mechanisms of recovery. *Annals of Neurology, 63*(3), 272–287.

Crandall, C. S., Preisler, J. J., & Aussprung, J. (1992). Measuring life event stress in the lives of college students: The Undergraduate Stress Questionnaire (USQ). *Journal of Behavioral Medicine, 15,* 627–662.

Crane, R. (2007). The Most Addictive Drug, the Most Deadly Substance: Smoking Cessation Tactics for the Busy Clinician. *Primary Care: Clinics in Office Practice, 34*(1), 117–135.

Cranford, J. A., Zucker, R. A., Jester, J. M., Puttler, L. I., & Fitzgerald, H. E. (2010). Parental alcohol involvement and adolescent alcohol expectancies predict alcohol involvement in male adolescents. *Psychology of Addictive Behaviors, 24*(3), 386–396.

Crano. W. D., & Seyranian, V. (2009). How minorities prevail: The context/comparisonleniency contract model. *Journal of Social Issues, 65,* 335–363.

Crano, W. D., & Chen, X. (1998). The leniency contract and persistence of majority and minority influence. *Journal of Personality and Social Psychology, 74,* 1437–1450.

Craske, M. G. (1999). *Anxiety disorders: Psychological approaches to theory and treatment.* Boulder, CO: Westview Press.

Craske, M. G., & Barlow, D. H. (2008). Panic disorder and agoraphobia. In D. H. Barlow (Ed.), *Clinical handbook of psychological disorders: A step-by-step treatment manual* (4th ed., pp. 1–64). New York: Guilford.

Crawford, H. J., Brown, A. M., & Moon, C. E. (1993). Sustained attentional and disattentional abilities: Differences between low and highly hypnotizable persons. *Journal of Abnormal Psychology, 102*(4), 534–543.

Crawford, T. N., Cohen, P., & Brooks, J. S. (2001). Dramatic-erratic personality disorder symptoms: II. Developmental pathways from early adolescence to adulthood. *Journal of Personality Disorders, 15,* 336–350.

Crean, R. D., Crane, N. A., & Mason, B. J. (2011). An evidence based review of acute and long-term effects of cannabis use on executive cognitive functions. *Journal of Addiction Medicine, 5*(1), 1–8.

Creed, T. A., & Kendall, P. C. (2005). Therapist alliance-building behavior within a cognitive-behavioral treatment for anxiety in youth. *Journal of Counseling and Clinical Psychology, 73,* 498–505.

Cremonini, F., Camilleri, M., Clark, M., Beebe, T., Locke, G., Zinsmeister, A., & ... Talley, N. (2009). Associations among binge eating behavior patterns and gastrointestinal symptoms: A population-based study. *International Journal of Obesity (2005), 33*(3), 342–353.

Crepeau-Hobson, F., & Bianco, M. (2011). Identification of gifted students with learning disabilities in a Response-to-Intervention era. *Psychology in the Schools, 48*(2), 102–109. doi:10.1002/pits.20528.

Crespi, B. (2008). Genomic imprinting in the development and evolution of psychotic spectrum conditions. *Biological Reviews, 83*(4), 441–493.

Crick, N. R., Ostrov, J. M., Appleyard, K., Jansen, E. A., & Casas, J. F. (2004). Relational aggression in early childhood: "You can't come to my birthday party unless. . ." In M. Putallaz & K. L. Bierman (Eds.), *Aggression, antisocial behavior, and violence among girls: A developmental perspective* (pp. 71–89). New York: Guilford Press.

Critchley, E. M. (1991). Speech and the right hemisphere. *Behavioural Neurology, 4*(3), 143–151.

Crits-Christoph, P., Gibbons, M. B. C., Ring-Kurtz, S., Gallop, R., Stirman, S., Present, J., Temes, C., & Goldstein, L. (2008). Changes in positive quality of life over the course of psychotherapy. *Psychotherapy: Theory, Research, Practice, Training, 45,* 419–430.

Crocker, J., & Wolfe, T. (2001). Contingencies of self-worth. *Psychological Review, 108,* 593–623.

Croen, L. A., Grether, J. K., & Selvin, S. (2001). The epidemiology of mental retardation of unknown cause. *Pediatrics, 107,* 86.

Crombag, H. S., & Robinson, T. E. (2004). Drugs, environment, brain, and behavior. *Current Directions in Psychological Science, 13,* 107–111.

Cronbach, L. J. (1990). *Essentials of psychological testing* (5th ed.). New York: Harper & Row.

Cronbach, L. J. (1996). Acceleration among the Terman males: Correlates in midlife and after. In C. P. Benbow & D. J. Lubinski (Eds.), *Intellectual talent: Psychometric and social issues* (pp. 179–191). Baltimore: Johns Hopkins University Press.

Crosier, B. S., Webster, G. D., & Dillon, H. M. (2012). Wired to connect: Evolutionary psychology and social networks. *Review of General Psychology, 16,* 230–239. doi:10.1037/a0027919.

Cross, S. E., & Madson, L. (1997). Models of the self: Self-construals and gender. *Psychological Bulletin, 122,* 5–37.

Cross, S. E., & Markus, H. R. (1999). The cultural constitution of personality. In L. Pervin & O. John (Eds.), *Handbook of personality research* (2nd ed., pp. 378–398). New York: Guilford.

Cross-National Collaborative Group. (2002). The changing rate of major depression: Cross-national comparisons. *Journal of the American Medical Association, 268,* 3098–3105.

Crow, S. J., Peterson, C. B., Swanson, S. A., Raymond, N. C., et al. (2009). Increased mortality in bulimia nervosa and other eating disorders. *American Journal of Psychiatry, 166,* 1342–1346.

Crowley, K., Callanan, M. A., Tenenbaum, H. R., & Allen, E. (2001). Parents explain more often to boys than to girls during shared scientific thinking. *Psychological Science, 12,* 258–261.

Crowther, H., Lipworth, W., & Kerridge, I. (2011). Evidence-based medicine and epistemological imperialism: narrowing the divide between evidence and illness. *Journal of Evaluation In Clinical Practice, 17*(5), 868–872. doi:10.1111/j.1365-2753.2011.01723.x.

Crowther, J. H., Armey, M., Luce, K. H., Dalton, G. R., & Leahey, T. (2008). The point prevalence of bulimic disorders from 1990 to 2004. *International Journal of Eating Disorders, 41*(6), 491–497.

Crowther, J. H., Sanftner, J., Bonifazi, D. Z., & Shepherd, K. L. (2001). The role of daily hassles in binge eating. *International Journal of Eating Disorders, 29,* 449–454.

Crozier, J. C., Dodge, K. A., Fontaine, R. G., Lansford, J. E., et al. (2008). Social information processing and cardiac predictors of adolescent antisocial behavior. *Journal of Abnormal Psychology, 117,* 253–267.

Cruse, D., Chennu, S., Chatelle, C., Bekinschtein, T. A., Fernández-Espejo, D., Pickard, J. D., Laureys, S., Owen, A. M. (2011). Bedside detection of awareness in the vegetative state: a cohort study. *Lancet, 378*(9809), 2088–2094.

Cruz, A., & Green, B. G. (2000). Thermal stimulation of taste. *Nature, 403,* 889–892.

Cuijpers, P., Li, J., Hofmann, S. G., & Andersson, G. (2010). Self-reported versus clinician-rated symptoms of depression as outcome measures in psychotherapy research on depression: A meta-analysis. *Clinical Psychology Review, 30,* 768–778.

Cuijpers, P., van Straten, A., Smit, F., Mihalopoulos, C., & Beekman, A. (2008). Preventing the onset of depressive disorders: A meta-analytic review of psychological interventions. *American Journal of Psychiatry, 165,* 1272–1280.

Culbertson, F. M. (1997). Depression and gender. An international review. *American Psychologist, 52,* 25–31.

Cullen, M. J., Hardison, C. M., & Sackett, P. R. (2004). Using SAT-grade and ability-job performance relationships to test predictions derived from stereotype threat theory. *Journal of Applied Psychology, 89,* 220–230.

Cullen, M. J., Waters, S. D., & Sackett, P. R. (2006). Testing stereotype threat theory predictions for math-identified and non-math-identified students by gender. *Human Performance, 19*(4), 421–440.

Culp, R. E., Cook, A. S., & Housley, P. C. (1983). A comparison of observed and reported adult-infant interactions: Effects of perceived sex. *Sex Roles, 9,* 475–479.

Cummings, D. E., Weigle, D. S., Frayo, R. S., Breen, P. A., Ma, M. K., Dellinger, E. P., & Purnell, J. Q. (2002). Plasma ghrelin levels after diet-induced weight loss or gastric bypass surgery. *New England Journal of Medicine, 346,* 1623–1630.

Cummings, J. L. (2003). Toward a molecular neuropsychiatry of neurodegenerative diseases. *Annals of Neurology, 54*(2), 147–154.

Cummings, J. L. (2004). Alzheimer's disease. *New England Journal of Medicine, 351,* 56–67.

Cunningham, W. A., & Brosch, T. (2012). Motivational salience: Amygdala tuning from traits, needs, values, and goals. *Current Directions In Psychological Science, 21*(1), 54–59. doi:10.1177/0963721411430832.

Cunningham, W. A., Johnson, M. K., Raye, C. L., Gatenby, J. C., Gore, J. C., & Banaji, M. R. (2004). Separable neural components in the processing of black and white faces. *Psychological Science, 15,* 806–813.

Cuperman, R., & Ickes, W. (2009). Big Five predictors of behavior and perceptions in initial dyadic interactions: Personality similarity helps extraverts and introverts but hurts "disagreeables." *Journal of Personality and Social Psychology, 97,* 667–684.

Curioni, C. C., & Lourenço, P. M. (2005). Long-term weight loss after diet and exercise: A systematic review. *International Journal of Obesity, 29,* 1168–1174.

Curley, J. P., Jensen, C. L., Mashoodh, R. R., & Champagne, F. A. (2011). Social influences on neurobiology and behavior: Epigenetic effects during development. *Psychoneuroendocrinology, 36*(3), 352–371. doi:10.1016/j.psyneuen.2010.06.005.

Currin, L., Schmidt, U., Treasure, J., & Jick, H. (2005). Time trends in eating disorder incidence. *British Journal of Psychiatry, 186,* 132–135.

Curry, D. T., Eisenstein, R. D., & Walsh, J. K. (2006). Pharmacologic management of insomnia: Past, present, and future. *Psychiatric Clinics of North America, 29,* 871–893.

Curtis, T., Miller, B. C., & Berry, E. H. (2000). Changes in reports and incidence of child abuse following natural disasters. *Child Abuse & Neglect, 24,* 1151–1162.

Cusack, K., & Spates, C. R. (1999). The cognitive dismantling of eye movement desensitization and reprocessing (EMDR) treatment of posttraumatic stress disorder (PTSD). *Journal of Anxiety Disorders, 13,* 87–99.

Cushen, P. J., & Wiley, J. (2011). Aha! Voila! Eureka! Bilingualism and insightful problem solving. *Learning & Individual Differences, 21*(4), 458–462. doi:10.1016/j.lindif.2011.02.007.

Cushon, J. A., Vu, L. H., Janzen, B. L., & Muhajarine, N. (2011). Neighborhood poverty impacts children's physical health and well-being over time: Evidence from the Early Development Instrument. *Early Education & Development, 22,* 183–205. doi:10.1080/10409280902915861

Cutrona, C. E., Russell, D. W., Brown, P. A., Clark, L. A., Hessling, R. M., & Gardner, K. A. (2005). Neighborhood context, personality, and stressful life events as predictors of depression among African American women. *Journal of Abnormal Psychology, 114,* 3–15.

Cvetek, R. (2008). EMDR treatment of distressful experiences that fail to meet the criteria for PTSD. *Journal of EMDR Practice and Research, 2*(1), 2–14.

Cyranowski, J. M., Hofkens, T. L., Swartz, H. A., & Gianaros, P. J. Thinking about a close relationship differentially impacts cardiovascular stress responses among depressed and nondepressed women. *Health Psychology, 30,* 276–284, 2011.

Czeisler, C. A., Duffy, J. F., Shanahan, T. L., Brown, E. N., Mitchell, J. F., Rimmer, D. W., et al. (1999). Stability, precision, and near 24-hour period of the human circadian pacemaker. *Science, 284,* 2177–2181.

Czeisler, C. A., Walsh, J. K., Roth, T., Hughes, R. J., Wright, K. P., Kingsbury, L., et al. (2005). Modafinil for excessive sleepiness associated with shift-work sleep disorder. *New England Journal of Medicine, 353,* 476–486.

Czepita, D, Mojsa, A., Ustianowska, M., Czepita, M., and Lachowicz, E. (2010). Reading, writing, working on a computer or watching television, and myopia. *Klinica Oczna, 112*(10–12), 293–295.

Daban, C., Martínez-Arán, A., Torrent, C., Sánchez-Moreno, J., Goikolea, J. M., Benabarre, A., et al. (2006). Cognitive functioning in bipolar patients receiving lamotrigine: Preliminary results. *Journal of Clinical Psychopharmacology, 26,* 178–181.

Dabbs, J. M., Jr., Riad, J. K., & Chance, S. E. (2001). Testosterone and ruthless homicide. *Personality and Individual Differences, 31,* 599–603.

Dabo, F., Nyberg, F., Qin Zhou, Sundström-Poromaa, I., & Akerud, H. (2010). Plasma levels of beta-endorphin during pregnancy and use of labor analgesia. *Reproductive Sciences, 17*(8), 742–747.

Dacher, M. & Nugent, F. S. (2011). Opiates and plasticity. *Neuropharmacology, 61*(7), 1088–1096.

Daddis, C. (2011). Desire for increased autonomy and adolescents' perceptions of peer autonomy: "Everyone else can; why can't I?" *Child Development, 82,* 1310–1326.

Daftary-Kapur, T., Dumas, R., & Penrod, S. D. (2010). Jury decision-making biases and methods to counter them. *Legal & Criminological Psychology, 15*(1), 133–154. doi:10.1348/135532509X465624.

Da Fonseca, D., Seguier, V., Santos, A., Poinso, F., & Deruelle, C. (2009). Emotion understanding in children with ADHD. *Child Psychiatry and Human Development, 40,* 111–121.

Daglish, M. R., & Nutt, D. J. (2003). Brain imaging studies in human addicts. *European Neuropsychopharmacology, 13,* 453–458.

Dai, D., Swanson, J., & Cheng, H. (2011). State of research on giftedness and gifted education: A survey of empirical studies published during 1998-2010 (April). *Gifted Child Quarterly, 55*(2), 126–138. doi:10.1177/0016986210397831.

Dakwar, E., & Levin, F. R. (2009). The emerging role of meditation in addressing psychiatric illness, with a focus on substance use disorders. *Harvard Review of Psychiatry, 17,* 254–267.

Dale, P. S. (1976). *Language and the development of structure and function.* New York: Holt, Rinehart & Winston.

Daley, K. C. (2004). Update on sudden infant death syndrome. *Current Opinion in Pediatrics, 16,* 227–232.

Dalgleish, T., Hauer, B., & Kuyken, W. (2008). The mental regulation of autobiographical recollection in the aftermath of trauma. *Current Directions in Psychological Science, 17,* 259–263.

Dallman, M. F., Pecoraro, N., Akana, S. F., La Fleur, S. E., Gomez, F., Houshyar, H., et al. (2003). Chronic stress and obesity: A new view of "comfort food." *Proceedings of the National Academies of Science, 100,* 11696–11701.

Dalton, D. R., & Mesch, D. J. (1991). On the extent and reduction of avoidable absenteeism: An assessment of absence policy provisions. *Journal of Applied Psychology, 76,* 810–817.

Damasio, A. R. (1994). *Descartes' error.* New York: Putnam.

Damasio, A. R., Grabowski, T. J., Bechara, A., Damasio, H., Ponto, L. L. B., Parvizi, J., & Hichwa, R. D. (2000). Subcortical and cortical brain activity during the feeling of self-generated emotions. *Nature Neuroscience, 3,* 1049–1056.

Dambrun, M., & Valentiné, E., (2010). Reopening the study of extreme social behaviors: Obedience to authority within an immersive video environment, *European Journal of Social Psychology, 40,* 760–773.

Damisch, L., Stoberock, B., & Mussweiler, T. (2010). Keep your fingers crossed! How superstition improves performance. *Psychological Science, 21*(7), 1014–1020. doi:10.1177/0956797610372631.

Damos, D. (1992). *Multiple task performance.* London: Taylor & Francis.

Daniel, D. B., & Woody, W. D. (2010). They hear, but do not listen: Retention for podcasted material in a classroom context. *Teaching of Psychology, 37*(3), 199–203. doi:10.1080/00986283.2010.488542.

Danker, J. F., & Anderson, J. R. (2010). The ghosts of brain states past: Remembering reactivates the brain regions engaged during encoding. *Psychological Bulletin, 136,* 87–102.

Dannenberg, A. L., Burton, D. C., & Jackson, R. J. (2004). Economic and environmental costs of obesity: The impact on airlines. *American Journal of Preventive Medicine, 27,* 264–264.

Dansereau, F., Jr., Graen, G., & Haga, W. J. (1975). A vertical dyad linkage approach to leadership with formal organizations. *Organizational Behavior and Human Performance, 13,* 46–78.

Danziger, S., Levav, J., & Avnaim-Pessoa, L. (2011). Extraneous factors in judicial decisions. *PNAS Proceedings of the National Academy of Sciences of the United States of America, 108*(17), 6889–6892. doi:10.1073/pnas.1018033108.

Dapretto, M., Davies, M. S., Pfeifer, J. H., Scott, A. A., Sigman, M., Bookheimer, S. Y., et al. (2006). Understanding emotions in others: Mirror neuron dysfunction in children with autism spectrum disorders. *Nature Neuroscience, 9,* 28–30.

Darchia, N., Campbell, I. G., & Feinberg, I. (2003). Rapid eye movement density is reduced in the normal elderly. *Sleep, 26,* 973–977.

Dark, V. J., & Benbow, C. P. (1993). Cognitive differences among the gifted: A review and new data. In D. K. Detterman (Ed.), *Current topics in human intelligence* (Vol. 3, pp. 85–120). Norwood, NJ: Ablex.

Darkes, J., & Goldman, M. S. (1993). Expectancy challenge and drinking reduction. *Journal of Clinical and Consulting Psychology, 61,* 344–353.

Darwich, J., Hymel, S., & Waterhouse, T. (2012). School avoidance and substance use among lesbian, gay, bisexual, and questioning youths: The impact of peer victimization and adult support. *Journal Of Educational Psychology,* doi:10.1037/a0026684.

Darwin, C. E. (1872). *The expression of the emotions in man and animals.* London: John Murray.

Dasgupta, A. M., Juza, D. M., White, G. M., & Maloney, J. F. (1995). Memory and hypnosis: A comparative analysis of guided memory, cognitive interview, and hypnotic hypermnesia. *Imagination, Cognition, and Personality, 14*(2), 117–130.

Das-Munshi, J., Goldberg, D., Bebbington, P. E., Bhugra, D. K., Brugha, T. S., Dewey, M. E., et al. (2008). Public health significance of mixed anxiety and depression: beyond current classification. *British Journal of Psychiatry, 192,* 171–177.

Dass, B., Olanow, C. W., & Kordower, J. H. (2006). Gene transfer of trophic factors and stem cell grafting as treatments for Parkinson's disease. *Neurology, 66,* S89–103.

Dauwels, J., Vialatte, F., Musha, T., & Cichocki, A. (2010). A comparative study of synchrony measures for the early diagnosis of Alzheimer's disease based on EEG. *NeuroImage, 49*, 668–693.

Daus, C. S., Sanders, D. N., & Campbell, D. P. (1998). Consequences of alternative work schedules. In C. L. Cooper & I. T. Robertson (Eds.), *International review of industrial and organizational psychology 1998* (pp. 185–223). Chichester, UK: Wiley.

Davachi, L., Mitchell, J. P., & Wagner, A. D. (2003). Multiple routes to memory: Distinct medial temporal lobe processes build item and source memories. *Proceedings of the National Academy of Sciences, 100*, 2157–2162.

David, D., Montgomery, G. H. (2011). The scientific status of psychotherapies: A new evaluative framework for evidence-based psychosocial interventions. *Clinical Psychology: Science and Practice, 18*, 89–99.

Davidson, R. J., Pizzagalli, D., Nitschke, J. B., & Putnam, K. (2002). Depression: Perspectives from aff ective neuroscience. *Annual Review of Psychology, 53*, 545–574.

Davidson, J. M., Camargo, C. A., & Smith, E. R. (1979). Effects of androgen on sexual behavior in hypogonadal men. *Journal of Clinical Endocrinological Metabolism, 48*, 955–958.

Davidson, J. R., Foa, E. B., Huppert, J. D., Keefe, F. J., Franklin, M. E., Compton, J. S., et al. (2004). Fluoxetine, comprehensive cognitive behavioral therapy, and placebo in generalized social phobia. *Archives of General Psychiatry, 61*, 1005–1013.

Davidson, K., Hall, P., & MacGregor, M. (1996). Gender differences in the relation between interview-derived hostility scores and resting blood pressure. *Journal of Behavioral Medicine, 19*, 185–201.

Davidson, P. R., & Parker, K. C. (2001). Eye movement desensitization and reprocessing (EMDR): A meta-analysis. *Journal of Consulting and Clinical Psychology, 69*, 305–316.

Davidson, R. J., Ekman, P., Saron, C., Senulis, J., & Friesen, W. V. (1990). Approach-withdrawal and cerebral asymmetry: Emotional expression and brain physiology: I. *Journal of Personality and Social Psychology, 58*, 330–341.

Davidson, R. J., Kabat-Zinn, J., Schumacher, J., Rosenkranz, M., Muller, D., Santorelli, S. F., et al. (2003). Alterations in brain and immune function produced by mindfulness meditation. *Psychosomatic Medicine, 65*, 564–570.

Davies, R. R. & Kipps, C. M. (2011). Lobar atrophy in frontotemporal dementia: diagnostic and prognostic implications. *Current Alzheimer Research, 8*(3), 261–265.

Davis, C., & Kapstein, S. (2006). Anorexia nervosa with excessive exercise: A phenotype with close links to obsessive-compulsive disorder. *Psychiatry Research, 142*, 209–217.

Davis, C., III, Aronson, J., & Salinas, M. (2006). Shades of threat: Racial identity as a moderator of stereotype threat. *Journal of Black Psychology, 32*(4), 399–417.

Davies, G. G., Tenesa, A. A., Payton, A. A., Yang, J. J., Harris, S. E., Liewald, D. D., & Deary, I. J. (2011). Genome-wide association studies establish that human intelligence is highly heritable and polygenic. *Molecular Psychiatry, 16*(10), 996–1005. doi:10.1038/mp.2011.85.

Davis, E., Glynn, L. M., Waffarn, F., & Sandman, C. A. (2011). Prenatal maternal stress programs infant stress regulation. *Journal of Child Psychology and Psychiatry, 52*(2), 119–129. doi:10.1111/j.1469-7610.2010.02314.x.

Davis, J. A., & Smith, T. W. (1990). *General social surveys, 1972–1990: Cumulative codebook.* Chicago: National Opinion Research Center.

Davis, J. D., Gallagher, R. J., Ladove, R. F., & Turansky, A. J. (1969). Inhibition of food intake by a humoral factor. *Journal of Comparative and Physiological Psychology, 67*, 407–414.

Davis, J. L., & Rusbult, C. (2001). Attitude alignment in close relationships. *Journal of Personality and Social Psychology, 81*, 65–84.

Davis, K., Desrocher, M., & Moore, T. (2011). Fetal Alcohol Spectrum Disorder: A review of neurodevelopmental findings and interventions. *Journal of Developmental and Physical Disabilities, 23*(2), 143–167. doi:10.1007/s10882-010-9204-2.

Davis, M. H. (1994). *Empathy: A social psychological approach.* Madison, WI: Brown and Benchmark.

Davis, M. H., Luce, C., & Kraus, S. J. (1994). The heritability of characteristics associated with dispositional empathy. *Journal of Personality, 60*, 369–391.

Davis, M., Myers, K. M., Ressler, K. J., & Rothbaum, B. O. (2005). Facilitation of extinction of conditioned fear by D-cycloserine. *Current Directions in Psychological Science, 14*, 214–219.

Davis, M., Ressler, K., Rothbaum, B. O., & Richardson, R. (2006). Effects of D-cycloserine on extinction: Translation from preclinical to clinical work. *Biological Psychiatry, 60*, 369–375.

Davis, N., Gross, J., & Hayne, H. (2008). Defining the boundary of childhood amnesia. *Memory, 16*(5), 465–474.

Davis, R. A., & Moore, C. C. (1935). Methods of measuring retention. *Journal of General Psychology, 12*, 144–155.

Davis-Kean, P. E., Jager, J., & Collins, W. A. (2009). The self in action: An emerging link between self-beliefs and behaviors in middle childhood. *Child Development Perspectives, 3*, 184–188.

Davison, G. C., & Neale, J. M. (1990). *Abnormal psychology* (5th ed.). New York: Wiley.

Dawe, I. C. (2008). Suicide and homicide. In R. L. Glick, J. S. Berlin, A. B. Fishkind, & S. L. Zeller (Eds.). *Emergency psychiatry: Principles and practice* (pp. 149–159). Philadelphia: Wolters Kluwer Health/Lippincott Williams & Wilkins.

Dawes, C. T., Loewen, P., Schreiber, D., Simmons, A. N., Flagan, T., McElreath, R., & ... Paulus, M. P. (2012). Neural basis of egalitarian behavior. *Proceedings Of The National Academy Of Sciences Of The United States Of America, 109*(17), 6479–6483. doi:10.1073/pnas.1118653109

Dawes, R. M. (1998). Behavioral decision making and judgment. In D. Gilbert, S. T. Fiske & G. Lindzey (Eds.), *Handbook of social psychology* (Vol. 1, 4th ed., pp. 497–549). Boston: McGraw-Hill.

Dawkins, K., & Potter, W. (1991). Gender differences in pharmacokinetics and pharmacodynamics of psychotropics: Focus on women. *Psychopharmacology Bulletin, 27*, 417–426.

Dawson, J. D., Uc, E. Y., Anderson, S. W., Johnson, A. M., & Rizzo, M. (2010). Neuropsychological Predictors of Driving Errors in Older Adults. *Journal of the American Geriatrics Society, 58*(6), 1090–1096. doi:10.1111/j.1532-5415.2010.02872.x.

Dawson, M., Schell, A. M., & Filion, D. L. (2000). The electodermal system. In J. Cacioppo, L. Tassinary, & G. Bernston (Eds.), *Handbook of psychophysiology* (2nd ed., pp. 200–222). New York: Cambridge University Press.

Day, A. L., & Jreige, S. (2002). Examining Type A behavior pattern to explain the relationship between job stressors and psychosocial outcomes. *Journal of Occupational Health Psychology, 7*, 109–120.

Day, N. L., Leech, S. L., & Goldschmidt, L. (2011). The effects of prenatal marijuana exposure on delinquent behaviors are mediated by measures of neurocognitive functioning. *Neurotoxicology and Teratology, 33*(1), 129–136.

Dayan, K., Fox, S., & Kasten, R. (2008). The preliminary employment interview as a predictor of assessment center outcomes. *International Journal of Selection and Assessment, 16*, 102–111.

Dayan, K., Kasten, R., & Fox, S. (2002). Entry-level police candidate assessment center: An efficient tool or a hammer to kill a fly? *Personnel Psychology, 55*, 827–849.

Deary, I. J. (2012). Intelligence. *Annual Review of Psychology, 63*(1), 453–482. doi:10.1146/annurev-psych-120710-100353.

Deary, I. J., & Batty, G. (2011). Intelligence as a predictor of health, illness; and death. In R. J. Sternberg, S. Kaufman, R. J. Sternberg, S. Kaufman (Eds.), *The Cambridge handbook of intelligence* (pp. 683–707). New York, NY: Cambridge University Press.

Deary, I. J., & Der, G. (2005a). Reaction time, age, and cognitive ability: Longitudinal findings from age 16 to 63 years in representative population samples. *Aging, Neuropsychology, and Cognition, 12*, 187–215.

Deary, I. J., & Der, G. (2005b). Reaction time explains IQ's association with death. *Psychological Science, 16*(1), 64–69.

Deary, I. J., Weiss, A., & Batty, G. (2010). Intelligence and personality as predictors of illness and death: How researchers in differential psychology and chronic disease epidemiology are collaborating to understand and address health inequalities. *Psychological Science in the Public Interest, 11*(2), 53–79. doi:10.1177/1529100610387081.

Deary, I. J., Whalley, L. J., Lemmon, H., Crawford, J. R., & Starr, J. M. (2000). The stability of individual differences in ability from childhood to old age: Follow up of the 1932 Scottish mental survey. *Intelligence, 28*, 49–55.

Deary, I. J., Whiteman, M. C., Starr, J. M., Whalley, L. J., & Fox, H. C. (2004). The impact of childhood intelligence on later life: Following up the Scottish mental surveys of 1932 and 1947. *Journal of Personality and Social Psychology, 86*, 130–147.

Deary, I. J., Yang, J., Davies, G., Harris, S. E., Tenesa, A., Liewald, D., & .. Visscher, P. M. (2012). Genetic contributions to stability and change in intelligence from childhood to old age. *Nature, 481*(7384), 212–215.

Deary, I. J., & Bedford, A. (2011). Some origins and evolution of the EPQ-R (short form) neuroticism and extraversion items. *Personality and Individual Differences, 50*, 1213–1217.

Death Penalty Information Center. (2012, March 29). Facts about the death penalty. Retrieved from http://www.deathpenaltyinfo.org/documents/FactSheet.pdf.

de Boer, H., Bosker, R. J., & van der Werf, M. P. C. (2010). Sustainability of teacher expectation bias effects on long-term student performance. *Journal of Educational Psychology, 102*, 168–179.

de Bruxelles, S. (2009, November 18). Sleepwalker accidentally killed wife during nightmare, prosecutors say. *(London) Times.*

de Castro, J. M., & Goldstein, S. J. (1995). Eating attitudes and behaviors pre- and postpubertal females: Clues to the etiology of eating disorders. *Physiology and Behavior, 58*(1), 15–23.

De Castro, J. M. (1990). Social facilitation of duration and size but not rate of the spontaneous meal intake of humans. *Physiology and Behavior, 47*, 1129–1135.

Decety, J., Yang, C., & Cheng, Y. (2010). Physicians down-regulate their pain empathy response: An event-related brain potential study. *Neuroimage, 50*(4), 1676–1682. doi:10.1016/j.neuroimage.2010.01.025.

de Charms, R., Levy, J., & Wertheimer, M. (1954). A note on attempted evaluations of psychotherapy. *Journal of Clinical Psychology, 10*, 233–235.

de Charms, R. C. (2008). Applications of real-time fMRI. *Nature Reviews Neuroscience, 9*(9), 720–729.

de Charms, R. C., Maeda, F., Glover, G. H., Ludlow, D., Pauly, J. M., Soneji, D., et al. (2005). Control over brain activation and pain learned by using real-time functional MRI. *Proceedings of the National Academy of Sciences, 102*, 18626–18631.

Deci, E. L., Koestner, R., & Ryan, R. M. (1999). A meta-analytic review of experiments examining the effects of extrinsic rewards on intrinsic motivation. *Psychological Bulletin, 125*, 627–668.

Deci, E. L., Koestner, R., & Ryan, R. M. (1999). The undermining effect is a reality after all—Extrinsic rewards, task interest, and self-determination: Reply to Eisenberger, Pierce, and Cameron (1999) and Lepper, Henderlong, and Gingras (1999). *Psychological Bulletin, 125*, 692–700.

Deci, E. L., Koestner, R., & Ryan, R. M. (2001). A meta-analytic review of experiments examining the effects of extrinsic rewards on intrinsic motivation. *Psychological Bulletin, 125*, 627–668.

De Craemer, M., De Decker, E., De Bourdeaudhuij, I., Vereecken, C., Deforche, B., Manios, Y., & Cardon, G. (2012). Correlates of energy balance-related behaviours in preschool children: a systematic review. *Obesity Reviews: An Official Journal of The International Association For The Study of Obesity, 13 Suppl 1*, 13–28. doi:10.1111/j.1467-789X.2011.00941.x

Deeb, I., Segall, G., Birnbaum, D., Ben-Eliyahu, A., & Diesendruck, G. (2011). Seeing isn't believing: The effect of intergroup exposure on children's essentialist beliefs about ethnic categories. *Journal of Personality and Social Psychology, 101*(6), 1139–1156. doi:10.1037/a0026107.

Deeprose, C., & Andrade, J. (2006). Is priming during anesthesia unconscious? *Consciousness and Cognition, 15*, 1–23.

Deep-Soboslay, A., Akil, M., Martin, C. E., Bigelow, L. B., Herman, M. M., et al. (2006). Reliability of psychiatric diagnosis in postmortem research. *Biological Psychiatry, 57*, 96–101.

Degner, J., & Wentura, D. (2010). Automatic prejudice in childhood and early adolescence. *Journal of Personality and Social Psychology, 98*, 356–374.

de Gonzalez, A., Hartge, P., Cerhan, J. R., Flint, A. J., Hannan, L., MacInnis, R. J., & .. Hoppin, J. A. (2010). Body-mass index and mortality among in 1.46 million White adults. *New England Journal Of Medicine, 363*(23), 2211–2219. doi:10.1056/NEJMoa1000367.

Dehaene-Lambertz, G. G., Montavont, A. A., Jobert, A. A., Allirol, L. L., Dubois, J. J., Hertz-Pannier, L. L., & Dehaene, S. S. (2010). Language or music, mother or Mozart? Structural and environmental influences on infants' language networks. *Brain and Language, 114*(2), 53–65. doi:10.1016/j.bandl.2009.09.003.

de Freitas, S., & Griffiths, M. (2007). Online gaming as an educational tool in learning and training. *British Journal of Educational Technology, 38*(3), 535–537.

De Fruyt, F., De Bolle, M., McCrae, R. R., Terracciano, A. & Costa, P. T., Jr. (2009). Assessing the universal structure of personality in early adolescence: The NEO-PI-R and NEO-PI-3 in 24 cultures. *Assessment, 16*, 301–311.

de Gelder, B., Snyder, J., Greve, D., Gerard, G., & Hadjikhani, N. (2004). Fear fosters flight: A mechanism for fear contagion when perceiving emotion expressed by a whole body. *Proceedings of the National Academy of Sciences, 101*, 16701–16706.

de Graaf, L. E., Huibers, M. J. H., Cuijpers, P., & Arntz, A. (2010). Minor and major depression in the general population: Does dysfunctional thinking play a role? *Comprehensive Psychiatry, 51*, 266–274.

de Haan, M., Mishkin, M., Baldeweg, T., & Vargha-Khadem, F. (2006). Human memory development and its dysfunction after early hippocampal injury. *Trends in Neurosciences, 29*(7), 374–381.

Dehaene-Lambertz, G. G., Montavont, A. A., Jobert, A. A., Allirol, L. L., Dubois, J. J., Hertz-Pannier, L. L., & Dehaene, S. S. (2010). Language or music, mother or Mozart? Structural and environmental influences on infants' language networks. *Brain & Language, 114*(2), 53–65. doi:10.1016/j.bandl.2009.09.003.

de Houwer, A. (1995). Bilingual language acquisition. In P. Fletcher & B. MacWhinney (Eds.), *The handbook of child language* (pp. 219–250). Cambridge, MA: Blackwell.

DeKosky, S. T., Ikonomovic, M. D., & Gandy, S. (2010). Traumatic brain injury: Football, warfare, and long-term effects. *The New England Journal Of Medicine, 363*(14), 1293–1296. doi:10.1056/NEJMp1007051.

DeKosky, S. T., Kaufer, D. I., Hamilton, R. L., Wolk, D. A., Lopez, O. L. (2008). The Dementias. In W. G. Bradley, R. B. Daroff, G. M. Fenichel, & J. Jamkovic (Eds). *Bradley: Neurology in Clinical Practice, 5th Edition*. Philadelphia, PA: Butterworth, Heinemann, Elsevier.

Delamater, A. R. (2004). Experimental extinction in Pavlovian conditioning: Behavioural and neuroscience perspectives. *Quarterly Journal of Experimental Psychology, 57B*, 97–132.

Delaney, P. F., Sahakyan, L., Kelley, C. M., & Zimmerman, C. A. (2010). Remembering to forget : The amnesic effect of daydreaming. *Psychological Science, 21*(7), 1036–1042. doi:10.1177/0956797610374739.

Delbello, M. P., Kowatch, R. A., Adler, C. M., Stanford, K. E., Welge, J. A., Barzman, D. H., et al. (2006). A double-blind randomized pilot study comparing quetiapine and divalproex for adolescent mania. *Journal of the American Academy of Child & Adolescent Psychiatry, 45*, 305–313.

DeLeo, J. A. (2006). Basic science of pain. *Journal of Bone and Joint Surgery (American), 88*(Suppl. 2), 58–62.

Delmas, P., Hao, J. & Rodat-Despoix, L. (2011). Molecular mechanisms of mechanotransduction in mammalian sensory neurons. *Nature Review Neuroscience, 12*(3), 139–153.

DeLoache, J. S., Chiong, C., Sherman, K., Islam, N., Vanderborght, M., Troseth, G. L., & O'Doherty, K. (2010). Do babies learn from baby media? *Psychological Science, 21*(11), 1570–1574. doi:10.1177/0956797610384145.

De Los Reyes, A. (2011). More than measurement error: Discovering meaning behind informant discrepancies in clinical assessments of children and adolescents, *Journal of Clinical Child and Adolescent Psychology, 40*, 1–9.

De Maris, A. (2007). The role of relationship inequity in marital disruption. *Journal of Social and Personal Relationships, 24*, 177–195.

DeMause, L. (1987). Schreber and the history of childhood. *The Journal of Psychohistory, 15*, 423–430.

de Macedo-Soares, M. B., Moreno, R. A., Rigonatti, S. P., & Lafer, B. (2005). Efficacy of electroconvulsive therapy in treatment-resistant bipolar disorder: A case series. *Journal of ECT, 21*, 31–34.

Demaray, M. K., & Malecki, C. K. (2002). Critical levels of perceived social support associated with student adjustment. *School Psychology Quarterly, 17*, 213–241.

Dement, W. (1960). The effect of dream deprivation. *Science, 131*, 1705–1707.

Dement, W., & Kleitman, N. (1957). Cyclic variations in EEG during sleep and their relation to eye movements, body motility and dreaming. *Electroencephalography and Clinical Neurophysiology, 9*, 673–690.

Demerouti, E., Geurts, S. A. E., Bakker, A. B., & Euwema, M. (2004). The impact of shiftwork on work-home conflict, job attitudes, and health. *Ergonomics, 47*, 987–1002.

Demo, D. H., Allen, K. R., & Fine, M. A. (Eds.). (2000). *Handbook of family diversity*. New York: Oxford University Press.

de Moor, J. S., de Moor, C. A., Basen-Engquist, K., Kudelka, A., Bevers, M. W., & Cohen, L. (2006). Optimism, distress, health-related quality of life, and change in cancer antigen 125 among patients with ovarian cancer undergoing chemotherapy. *Psychosomatic Medicine, 68*, 555–562.

Dempsey, P. G., McGorry, R. W., & Maynard, W. S. (2005). A survey of tools and methods used by certified professional ergonomists. *Applied Ergonomics, 36*(4), 489–503.

Deng, W., & Sloutsky, V. M. (2012). Carrot eaters or moving heads: Inductive inference is better supported by salient features than by category labels. *Psychological Science, 23*(2), 178–186. doi:10.1177/0956797611429133.

Denrell, J. (2005). Why most people disapprove of me: Experience sampling in impression formation. *Psychological Review, 112*, 951–978.

Denson, T.F., DeWall, C.N., & Finkel, E.J. (2012). Self-control and aggression. *Current Directions in Psychological Science, 21*, 20–25.

Denton, G. (1980). The influence of visual pattern on perceived speed. *Perception, 9*, 393–402.

DePaulo, B. M. (1994). Spotting lies: Can humans learn to do better? *Current Directions in Psychological Science, 3*, 83–86.

de Pinho, R. S., da Silva-Júnior, F. P., Bastos, J. P., Maia, W. S., de Mello, M. T., de Bruin, V. M., & de Bruin, P. F. (2006). Hypersomnolence and accidents in truck drivers: A cross-sectional study. *Chronobiology International, 23*(5):963–971.

DePrince, A. P., & Freyd, J. J. (2004). Forgetting trauma stimuli. *Psychological Science, 15*, 488–492.

Depue, R. A. (2009). Neurobehavioral dimensions in personality and personality disorders. In S. J. Wood, N. B. Allen, & C. Pantelis (Eds.), *The neuropsychology of mental illness* (pp. 300–315) New York: Cambridge University Press.

Der, G., Batty, G. D., & Deary, I. J. (2009). Th e association between IQ in adolescence and a range of health outcomes at 40 in the 1979 U.S. National Longitudinal Study of Youth. *Intelligence, 37*, 573–580.

De Raad, B., Barelds, D. P. H., Levert, E., Ostendorf, F., et al. (2010). Only three factors of personality description are fully replicable across languages: A comparison of 14 trait taxonomies. *Journal of Personality and Social Psychology, 98*, 160–173.

Dere, E., & Zlomuzica, A. (2012) The role of gap junctions in the brain in health and disease. *Neurosci Biobehav Rev 36* (1):206–217.

de Rios, M. D. (1992). Power and hallucinogenic states of consciousness among the Moche: An ancient Peruvian society. In C. A. Ward (Ed.), *Altered states of consciousness and mental health: A cross cultural perspective*. Newbury Park, CA: Sage.

Derogowski, J. B. (1989). Real space and represented space: Cross-cultural perspectives. *Behavior and Brain Sciences, 12*, 51–73.

Derringer, J., Krueger, R. F., Dick, D. M., Saccone, S., Grucza, R. A., Agrawal, A., & .. Bierut, L. J. (2010). Predicting sensation seeking from dopamine genes: A candidate-system approach. *Psychological Science, 21*(9), 1282–1290. doi:10.1177/0956797610380699.

Derry, C. J., Derry, S., McQuay, H. J., & Moore, R. A. (2006). Systematic review of systematic reviews of acupuncture published 1996–2005. *Clinical Medicine, 6*, 381–386.

Derry, C. P., Harvey, A. S., Walker, M. C., Duncan, J. S., & Berkovic, S. F. (2009). NREM arousal parasomnias and their distinction from nocturnal frontal lobe epilepsy: A video EEG analysis. *Sleep, 32*(12), 1637–1644.

Derryberry, D., & Tucker, D. M. (1992). Neural mechanisms of emotion. *Journal of Consulting and Clinical Psychology, 60*, 329–338.

DeRubeis, R. J., & Crits-Christoph, P. (1998). Empirically supported individual and group psychological treatments for adult mental disorders. *Journal of Consulting and Clinical Psychology, 66*, 37–52.

DeRubeis, R. J., Hollon, S. D., Amsterdam, J. D., Shelton, R. C., Young, P. R., Salomon, R. M., et al. (2005). Cognitive therapy vs medications in the treatment of moderate to severe depression. *Archives of General Psychiatry, 62*, 409–416.

Desai, R., Krishnan-Sarin, S., Cavallo, D., & Potenza, M. (2010). Video-gaming among high school students: health correlates, gender differences, and problematic gaming. *Pediatrics, 126*(6), e1414-e1424.

De Santi, S., Pirraglia, E., Barr, W., Babb, J., Williams, S., Rogers, K., Glodzik, L. Brys, M., Mosconi, L., Reisberg, B., Ferris, S., & de Leon, M. J. (2008). Robust and conventional neuropsychological norms: Diagnosis and prediction of age-related cognitive decline. *Neuropsychology, 22*, 469–484.

Deslauriers, L., Schelew, E., & Wieman, C. (2011). Improved Learning in a Large-Enrollment Physics Class. *Science, 332*(6031), 862–864. doi:10.1126/science.1201783.

de Souza, M., Mussap, A. J., & Cummins, R. A. (2010). Primary and secondary control over eating behaviors. *Eating Behaviors*, doi:10.1016/j.eatbeh.2010.05.002.

Deutsch, M., & Gerard, H. B. (1955). A study of normative and informative social influences on individual judgments. *Journal of Abnormal and Social Psychology, 51*, 629–636.

Devanand, D. P., Pradhaban, G., Liu, X., Khandji, A., De Santi, S., Segal, S., et al. (2007). Hippocampal and entorhinal atrophy in mild cognitive impairment: Prediction of Alzheimer's disease. *Neurology, 68*, 828–836.

Devenport, L. D. (1998). Spontaneous recovery without interference: Why remembering is adaptive. *Animal Learning and Behavior, 26*, 172–181.

Devi, G., & Quitschke, W. (1999). Alois Alzheimer, neuroscientist (1864–1915). *Alzheimer Disease and Associated Disorders, 13*(3), 132–137.

Devilly, G. J., Varker, T., Hansen, K., & Gist, R. (2007). An analogue study of the effects of psychological debriefing on eyewitness testimony. *Behaviour Research and Therapy, 45,* 1245–1254.

Devinsky, O., Farah, M. J., & Barr ,W. B. (2008). Chapter 21 Visual agnosia. In P. J. Vinken & G. W. Bruyn (Eds). *Handbook of Clinical Neurology, 88,* 417–27.

DeVoe, S. E., & Iyengar, S. S. (2010). Medium of exchange matters: What's fair for goods is unfair for money. *Psychological Science, 21*(2), 159–162. doi:10.1177/0956797609357749.

De Vogli, R., Chandola, T., & Marmot, M. G. (2007). Negative aspects of close relationships and heart disease. *Archives of Internal Medicine, 167,* 1951–1957.

Devonshire, I. M., Papadakis, N. G., Port, M., Berwick, J., Kennerley, A. J., Mayhew, J. E., & Overton, P. G. (2011) Neurovascular coupling is brain region-dependent. *Neuroimage.*

DeVries, R. (1969). Constancy of generic identity in the years three to six. *Monographs of the Society for Research in Child Development, 34*(3), 1–67.

DeWall, C., Lambert, N. M., Slotter, E. B., Pond, R. r., Deckman, T., Finkel, E. J., & Fincham, F. D. (2011). So far away from one's partner, yet so close to romantic alternatives: Avoidant attachment, interest in alternatives, and infidelity. *Journal of Personality and Social Psychology, 101*(6), 1302–1316. doi:10.1037/a0025497.

DeWall C. N., & Bushman, B. J. (2009). Hot under the collar in a lukewarm environment: Words associated with hot temperature increase aggressive thoughts and hostile perceptions *Journal of Experimental Social Psychology, 45,* 1045–1047.

DeWall, C. N., Bushman, B. J., Giancola, P. R., & Webster, G. D. (2010)., The big, the bad, and the boozed-up: Weight moderates the effect of alcohol on aggression. *Journal of Experimental Social Psychology, 46,* 619–623. doi:10.1016/j.jesp.2010.02.008.

DeWitt, L. A., & Samuel, A. G. (1990). The role of knowledge-based function in music perception. *Journal of Experimental Psychology: General, 119,* 123–144.

DeWolff, M. S., & van IJzendoorn, M. H. (1997). Sensitivity and attachment: A meta-analysis on parental antecedents of infant attachment. *Child Development, 68,* 571–591.

Dewsbury, G., & Linskell, J. (2011). Smart home technology for safety and functional independence: The UK experience. *Neurorehabilitation, 28*(3), 249–260. doi:10.3233/NRE-2011-0653.

DeYoung, C. G., Hirsh, J. B., Shane, M. S., Papademetris, X., et al. (2010). Testing predictions from personality neuroscience: Brain structure and the Big Five. *Psychological Science, 21,* 820–828.

DeYoung, C. G., Quilty, L. C., & Peterson, J. B. (2007). Between facets and domains: 10 aspects of the Big Five. *Journal of Personality and Social Psychology, 93*(5), 880–896.

DeYoung, C. G., Hirsh, J. B., Shane, M. S., Papademetris, X. Rajeevan, N. & Gray, J. R. (2010). Testing predictions from personality neuroscience: Brain structure and the big five. *Psychological Science, 21*(6), 820–828. doi:10.1177/0956797610370159.

Dhruv, N. T, Tailby, C., Sokol, S. H., and Lennie, P. (2011). Multiple adaptable mechanisms early in the primate visual pathway. *Journal of Neuroscience, 31*(42), 15016–15025.

Dhurandhar, N. V., Israel, B. A., Kolesar, J. M., Mayhew, G. F., Cook, M. E., & Atkinson, R. L. (2000). Increased adiposity in animals due to a human virus. *International Journal of Obesity, 24,* 989–996.

Diakidoy, I. N., & Spanoudis, G. (2002). Domain specificity in creativity testing: A comparison of performance on a general divergent-thinking test and a parallel, content-specific test. *Journal of Creative Behavior, 36,* 41–61.

Diamantopoulou, S., Verhulst, F. C., & van der Ende, J. (2010). Testing developmental pathways to antisocial personality problems. *Journal of Abnormal Child Psychology, 38,* 91–103.

Diamond, G. M., Lipsitz, J. D., Fajerman, Z., & Rozenblat, O. (2010). Ongoing traumatic stress response (OTSR) in Sderot, Israel. *Professional Psychology: Research and Practice, 41,* 19–25.

Diamond, L. M. (2004). Emerging perspectives on distinctions between romantic love and sexual desire. *Current Directions in Psychological Science, 13,* 116–119.

Diamond, L. M. (2008). *Sexual fluidity: Understanding women's love and desire.* Cambridge, MA: Harvard University Press.

Diana, M. (2011). The dopamine hypothesis of drug addiction and its potential therapeutic value. *Frontiers in Psychiatry, 2,* 64.

Diana, M., Spiga, S., & Acquas, E. (2006). Persistent and reversible morphine withdrawal– induced morphological changes in the nucleus accumbens. *Annals of the New York Academy of Sciences, 1074,* 446–457.

Di Carlo, A. (2009). Human and economic burden of stroke. *Age and Aging, 38,* 4–5.

Dick, D. M., Meyers, J. L., Latendresse, S. J., Creemers, H. E., Lansford, J. E., Pettit, G. S., & Huizink, A. C. (2011). CHRM2, Parental monitoring, and adolescent externalizing behavior: Evidence for gene-environment interaction. *Psychological Science, 22*(4), 481–489. doi:10.1177/0956797611403318.

Dicke, M., & Van Huis, A. (2011, February 19). The Six-Legged Meat of the Future. *Wall Street Journal—Eastern Edition.* p. C3.

Dickenson, A. H. (2002). Gate control theory of pain stands the test of time. *British Journal of Anaesthesia, 88*(6), 755–757.

Dickerson, F. B., Tenhula, W. N., & Green-Paden, L. D. (2005). The token economy for schizophrenia: Review of the literature and recommendations for future research. *Schizophrenia Research, 75,* 405–416.

Dickinson, T., & Hurley, M. (2012). Exploring the antipathy of nursing staff who work within secure healthcare facilities across the United Kingdom to young people who self-harm. *Journal of Advanced Nursing, 68*(1), 147–158. doi:10.1111/j.1365-2648.2011.05745.x.

Di Domenico, M., Ricciardi, C., Martone, T., Mazzarella, N., Cassandro, C., Chiarella, G., D'Angelo, L., and Cassandro, E. (2011). Towards gene therapy for deafness. *Journal of Cellular Physiology, 226*(10), 2494–2499.

Diehl, K. A. (2009). Complex case: Head trauma, dissociation and possible development of multiple personalities. *Personality And Mental Health, 3*(4), 295–301. doi:10.1002/pmh.95.

Diekelmann, S. & Born, J. (2010). The memory function of sleep. *Nature Reviews, Neuroscience, 11*(2), 114-126. *Drug and Alcohol Dependence, 99*(1–3), 1–10.

Diekman, A. B., Brown, E. R., Johnston, A. M., & Clark, E. K. (2010). Seeking congruity between goals and roles: A new look at why women opt out of science, technology, engineering, and mathematics careers. *Psychological Science, 21*(8), 1051–1057. doi:10.1177/0956797610377342.

Diener, E., Oishi, S., & Lucas, R. E. (2009). Subjective well-being: The science of happiness and life satisfaction. In C. R. Snyder & S. J. Lopez (Eds.), *Oxford handbook of positive psychology.* Oxford: Oxford University Press.

Diener, E. (in press). The validity of life satisfaction measures. (We have a copy of the manuscript for this article, but don't actually know if it was submitted anywhere).

Diener, E. (2008). *Happiness: Unlocking the mysteries of psychological wealth.* Hoboken, NJ: Wiley.

Diener, E. (2000). Subjective well-being: The science of happiness and a proposal for a national index. *American Psychologist, 55,* 34–43.

Diener, E., & Diener, C. (1995). Most people are happy. *Psychological Science, 7,* 181–185.

Diener, E., & Seligman, M. E. P. (2004). Beyond money: Towards an economy of well-being. *Psychological Science in the Public Interest, 5,* 1–31.

Diener, E., Ng, W., Harter, J., & Arora, R. (2010). Wealth and happiness across the world: Material prosperity predicts life evaluation, whereas psychosocial prosperity predicts positive feeling. *Journal of Personality and Social Psychology, 99,* 52–61.

Dierdorff , E. C., & Wilson, M. A. (2003). A meta-analysis of job analysis reliability. *Journal of Applied Psychology, 88,* 635–646.

Dierdorff, E. C., & Ellington, K. J. (2008). It's the nature of the work: Examining behavior-based sources of work-family conflict across occupations. *Journal of Applied Psychology, 93,* 883–892.

Dietert, R. R., Dietert, J. M., & DeWitt, J. C. (2011). Environmental risk factors for autism. *Emerging Health Threats, 4,* 1–11. doi:10.3402/ehtj.v4i0.7111.

Dietrich, A., & Kanso, R. (2010). A review of EEG, ERP, and neuroimaging studies of creativity and insight. *Psychological Bulletin, 136*(5), 822–848. doi:10.1037/a0019749.

Dijksterhuis, A., Bos, M. W., Nordgren, L. F., & van Baaren, R. B. (2006). On making the right choice: The deliberation-without-attention effect. *Science, 311,* 1005–1007.

Dijksterhuis, A., & Nordgren, L. F. (2006). A theory of unconscious thought. *Perspectives on Psychological Science, 1,* 95–109.

Dijksterhuis, A., Preston, J., Wegner, D. M., & Aarts, H. (2008). Effects of subliminal priming of self and God on self-attribution of authorship for events. *Journal of Experimental Social Psychology, 44,* 2–9.

Dijkstra, A., DeVries, H., & Bakker, M. (1996). Pros and cons of quitting, self-efficacy, and the stages of change in smoking cessation. *Journal of Consulting and Clinical Psychology, 64,* 758–763.

Dijkstra, P., Gibbons, F. X. & Buunk, A. P. (2010) Social comparison theory In J. Maddux & J. Tangney (Eds.) *Social psychological foundations of clinical psychology* (pp. 195–211). New York, NY: Guilford Press.

Dillard, A. J., McCaul, K. D., & Klein, W. M. P. (2006). Unrealistic optimism in smokers: Implications for smoking myth endorsement and self-protective motivation. *Journal of Health Communication, 11,* 93–102.

Di Marzo, V., Goparaju, S. K., Wang, L., Liu, J., Batkai, S., Jarai, Z., et al. (2001). Leptin-regulated endocannabinoids are involved in maintaining food intake. *Nature, 410,* 822–825.

Dimidjian, S., Hollon, S. D., Dobson, K. S., Schmaling, K. B., Kohlenberg, R. J., Addis, M. E., et al. (2006). Randomized trial of behavioral activation, cognitive therapy, and antidepressant medication in the acute treatment of adults with major depression. *Journal of Consulting and Clinical Psychology, 74,* 658–670.

Di Milia, L. (2006). Shift work, sleepiness, and long distance driving. *Transportation Research, 9,* 278–285.

Dinan, T. G. (2001). Novel approaches to the treatment of depression by modulating the hypothalamic-pituitary-adrenal axis. *Human Psychopharmacology: Clinical and Experimental, 16,* 89–93.

Dingfelder, S. F. (2005, January). Closing the gap for Latino patients. *Monitor on Psychology,* 58–61.

diNoia, J., & Schinke, S. P. (2008). HIV risk-related attitudes, interpersonal influences, and intentions among at-risk urban, early adolescent girls. *American Journal of Health Behavior, 32*(5), 497–507.

Dionne, V. E., & Dubin, A. E. (1994). Transduction diversity in olfaction. *Journal of Experimental Biology, 194,* 1–21.

DiPatrizio, N. V., Astarita, G., Schwartz, G., Xiaosong, L., & Piomelli, D. (2011). Endocannabinoid signal in the gut controls dietary fat intake. *Proceedings Of The National Academy Of Sciences Of The United States Of America, 108*(31), 12904–12908. doi:10.1073/pnas.1104675108.

DiPatrizio, N. V., & Simansky, K. J. (2008). Activating parabrachial cannabinoid CB-sub-1 receptors selectively stimulates feeding of palatable foods in rats. *Journal of Neuroscience, 28*(39), 9702–9709.

Dirix, C. E. H., Nijhuis, J. G., Jongsma, H. W., & Hornstra, G. (2009). Aspects of fetal learning and memory. *Child Development, 80,* 1251–1258.

Distel, M. A., Vink, J. M., Willemsen, G., Middeldorp, C. M., Merckelbach, H. G. J., & Boomsma, D. I. (2008). Heritability of self-reported fear. *Behavioral Genetics, 38,* 24–33.

Dittmann, M. (2004, June). Alternative health care gains steam. *Monitor on Psychology*, 42–44.

Dittmann, M. (2005, July/August). When health fears hurt health. *Monitor on Psychology*, 100–103.

Dittmar, H., Halliwell, E., & Ive, S. (2006). Does Barbie make girls want to be thin? The effect of experimental exposure to images of dolls on the body image of 5- to 8-year-old girls. *Developmental Psychology, 42*, 283–292.

Divan, H., Kheifets, L., Obel, C., & Olsen, J. (2008). Prenatal and postnatal exposure to cell phone use and behavioral problems in children. *Epidemiology, 19*(4), 523–529.

Dixon, M., Brunet, A., & Laurence, J.-R. (1990). Hypnotizability and automaticity: Toward a parallel distributed processing model of hypnotic responding. *Journal of Abnormal Psychology, 99*, 336–343.

Djonlagic, I., Rosenfeld, A., Shohamy, D., Myers, C., et al. (2009). Sleep enhances category learning. *Learning and Memory, 16*, 751–755.

D'Mello, R., & Dickenson, A. H. (2008). Spinal cord mechanisms of pain. *British Journal of Anesthesiology, 101*(1), 8–16.

D'Mello, S. K., & Graesser, A. (2010). Multimodal semi-automated affect detection from conversational cues, gross body language, and facial features. *User Modeling And User-Adapted Interaction, 20*(2), 147–187. doi:10.1007/s11257-010-9074-4.

Dobson, & Hamilton, K. E. (2009). Cognitive restructuring: Behavioral tests of negative cognitions. In W. T. O'Donohue & J. E. Fisher (Eds.), *General principles and empirically supported techniques of cognitive behavior therapy* (pp. 194–198). Hoboken, NJ: Wiley and Sons.

Dobson, K. S., Hollon, S. D., Dimidjian, S.,Schmaling, K. B., Kohlenberg, R. J., Gallop, R. J., Rizvi, S. L., Gollan, J. K., Dunner, D. L., & Jacobson, N. S. (2008). Randomized trial of behavioral activation, cognitive therapy, and antidepressant medication in the prevention of relapse and recurrence in major depression. *Journal of Consulting and Clinical Psychology, 76*, 468–477.

Dodd, M. L., Klos, K. J., Bower, J. H., Geda, Y. E., Josephs, K. A., & Ahlskog, J. E. (2005). Pathological gambling caused by drugs used to treat Parkinson disease. *Archives of Neurology, 62*, 1377–1381.

Dohnt, H., & Tiggermann, M. (2006). The contribution of peer and media influences to the development of body satisfaction and self-esteem in young girls: A prospective study. *Developmental Psychology, 42*, 929–936.

Dohrenwend, B. P., Raphael, K. G., Schwartz, S., Stueve, A., & Skodol, A. (1993). The structured event probe and narrative rating method for measuring stressful life events. In L. Goldenberger & S. Breznitz (Eds.), *Handbook of stress: Theoretical and clinical aspects* (2nd ed.). New York: The Free Press.

Dohrenwend, B. P., Turner, J. B., Turse, N. A., Adams, B. G., Koenen, K. C., & Marshall, R. (2006). The psychological risks of Vietnam for U.S. veterans: A revisit with new data and methods. *Science, 313*, 979–982.

Doja, A., & Roberts, W. (2006). Immunizations and autism: a review of the literature. *The Canadian Journal of Neurological Sciences. Le Journal Canadien des Sciences Neurologiques, 33*, 341–346.

Dolan, M., & Fullam, R. (2006). Memory for emotional events in violent offenders with antisocial personality disorder. *Personality and Individual Differences, 38*, 1657–1667.

Dollard, J., Doob, L., Miller, N., Mowrer, O. H., & Sears, R. R. (1939). *Frustration and aggression.* New Haven, CT: Yale University Press.

Dollinger, S. J. (2000). Locus of control and incidental learning: An application to college students. *College Student Journal, 34*, 537–540.

Domhoff, G. W. (1996). *Finding meaning in dreams: A quantitative approach.* New York: Plenum.

Domhoff, G. W. (1999). Drawing theoretical implications from descriptive empirical findings on dream content. *Dreaming, 9*, 201–210.

Domhoff, G. W. (2001). A new neurocognitive theory of dreams. *Dreaming: Journal of the Association for the Study of Dreams, 11*, 13–33.

Domhoff, G. W., & Schneider, A. (2008). Studying dream content using the archive and search engine on DreamBank.net. *Consciousness and Cognition, 17*, 1238–1247.

Domino, E. F. (2003). Effects of tobacco smoking on electroencephalographic, auditory evoked and event related potentials. *Brain and Cognition, 53*, 66–74.

Domjan, M. (2005). Pavlovian conditioning: A functional perspective. *Annual Review of Psychology, 56*, 179–206.

Domschke, K., Stevens, S., Pfleiderer, B., & Gerlach, A. L. (2010). Interoceptive sensitivity in anxiety and anxiety disorders: An overview and integration of neurobiological findings. *Clinical Psychology Review, 30*, 1–11.

Donner, M. B., VandeCreek, L., Gonsiorek, J. C., & Fisher, C. B. (2008). Balancing confidentiality: Protecting privacy and protecting the public. *Professional Psychology: Research and Practice, 39*, 369–376.

Donnerstein, E. (1984). Pornography: Its effects on violence against women. In N. M. Malamuth & E. Donnerstein (Eds.), *Pornography and sexual aggression.* New York: Academic Press.

Donnerstein, E., & Linz, D. (1995). The mass media: A role in injury causation and prevention. *Adolescent Medicine: State of the Art Reviews, 6*, 271–284.

Donnerstein, E., Slaby, R. G., & Eron, L. D. (1995). The mass media and youth aggression. In L. Eron, J. Gentry, & P. Schlegel (Eds.), *Reason to hope: A psychosocial perspective on violence and youth* (pp. 219–250). Washington, DC: American Psychological Association.

Donovan, J. E., & Molina, B. S. (2011). Childhood risk factors for early-onset drinking. *Journal of Studies on Alcohol and Drugs, 72*(5), 741–751.

Donovan, J. J., & Radosevich, D. J. (1999). A meta-analytic review of the distribution of practice effect: Now you see it, now you don't. *Journal of Applied Psychology, 84*, 795–805.

Doobay, A. F. (2008). School refusal behavior associated with separation anxiety disorder: A cognitive-behavioral approach to treatment. *Psychology in The Schools, 45*(4), 261–272.

Doody, R. S., Gavrilova, S. I., Sano, M., Thomas, R. G., Aisen, P. S., Bachurin, S. O., Seely, L., & Hung, D. (2008). Effect of dimebon on cognition, activities of daily living, behaviour, and global function in patients with mild-to-moderate Alzheimer's disease: a randomised, double-blind, placebo-controlled study. *Lancet, 372*(9634), 207–215.

Dordain, G., & Deffond, D. (1994). Pyridoxine neuropathies: Review of the literature. *Therapie, 49*(4), 333–337.

Doss, B. D., Rhoades, G. K., Stanley, S. M., & Markman, H. J. (2009). The effect of the transition to parenthood on relationship quality: An 8-year prospective study. *Psychological Bulletin, 96*, 601–619.

Doucet, S., Soussignan, R., Sagot, P., & Schaal, B. (2009). The secretion of areolar (Montgomery's) glands from lactating women elicits selective, unconditional responses in neonates. *PLoS ONE 4*, e7579.

Doucet, S., Soussignan, R., Sagot, P., & Schaal, B. (2007). The "smellscape" of mother's breast: Effects of odor masking and selective unmasking on neonatal arousal, oral, and visual responses. *Developmental Psychobiology, 49*,129–138.

Douglas, K. M., & Sutton, R. M. (2010). By their words ye shall know them: Language abstraction and the likeability of describers. *European Journal of Social Psychology, 40*, 366–-374. doi:10.1002/ejsp.634.

Douglas, K. M., Sutton, R. M., & Stathi, S. (2010). Why I am less persuaded than you: People's intuitive understanding of the psychology of persuasion. *Social Influence, 5*(2), 133–148. doi:10.1080/15534511003597423.

Dovidio, J. F., & Gaertner, S. L. (2010). Intergroup bias. In S. T. Fiske, D. T. Gilbert, & G. Lindzey (Eds.), *Handbook of social psychology* (5th ed., Vol. 2, pp. 1084–1121). Hoboken, NJ: Wiley.

Dovidio, J. F., Gaertner, S. L., & Kawakami, K. (2010). Racism. In J. F. Dovidio, M. Hewstone, P. Glick, & V. M. Esses (Eds.), *The SAGE handbook of prejudice, stereotyping and discrimination* (pp. 312–327). London: Sage.

Dovidio, J. F., Kawakami, K., Smoak, N., & Gaertner, S. L. (2009). The roles of implicit and explicit processes in contemporary prejudice. In R. E. Petty, R. H. Fazio, & P. Brinol (Eds.), *Attitudes: Insights from the new implicit measures* (pp. 165–192). New York: Psychology Press.

Dovidio, J., Piliavin, J., Schroeder, D., & Penner, L. (2006). *The social psychology of prosocial behavior.* Mahwah, NJ: Lawrence Erlbaum.

Dovidio, J. F., & Penner, L. A. (2001). Helping and altruism. In G. Fletcher & M. Clark (Eds.), *Blackwell handbook of social psychology: Interpersonal processes* (pp. 162–195). Boston: Blackwell.

Dovidio, J. F., Piliavin, J. A., Gaertner, S. L., Schroeder, D. A., & Clark, R. D., III. (1991). The arousal: cost-reward model and the process of intervention: A review of the evidence. In M. Clark (Ed.), *Review of personality and social psychology: Vol. 12. Prosocial behavior* (pp. 86–118). Newbury Park, CA: Sage.

Dowd, J. T. (2005). *Teaching social skills to youth.* Boys Town, Nebraska: Boys Town Press.

Dowe, D. L., & Hernández-Orallo, J. (2012). IQ tests are not for machines, yet. *Intelligence, 40*(2), 77–81. doi:10.1016/j.intell.2011.12.001.

Doyle, J. (2005). *True witness: Cops, courts, science, and the battle against misidentification.* New York: Palgrave Macmillan.

Doyle, L., & Anderson, P. (2010). Adult outcome of extremely preterm infants. *Pediatrics, 126*(2), 342–351.

Doyle, P. J., & Marco, C. A. (2011). The effect of labeling on employee perceptions of residents living on Alzheimer's disease specialized care units. *Journal of The American Medical Directors Association, 12*(8), 547–550. doi:10.1016/j.jamda.2010.12.002.

Doymus, K., Karacop, A., & Simsek, U. (2010). Effects of jigsaw and animation techniques on students' understanding of concepts and subjects in electrochemistry. *Educational Technology Research and Development, 58*, 671–691.

Dozen people watched gang rape, police say. (2009, October 27). *Associated Press.* Retrieved from http://www.youtube.com/watch?v=vwxiCVVGnZ8.

Drasbek, K. R., Christensen, J., & Jensen, K. (2006). Gamma-hydroxybutyrate—a drug of abuse. *Acta Neurologica Scandinavica, 114*, 145–156.

Dreher, J.-C., Kohn, P., Kolachana, B., Weinberger, D. R., & Berman, K. F. (2010). Variation in dopamine genes influences responsivity of the human reward system. *Proceedings of the National Academy of Sciences, 106*, 617–622.

Dreifus, C. (November 30, 2009). Developmental psychologist says teenagers are different. *New York Times.* Retrieved from: http://www.nytimes.com/2009/12/01/science/01conv.html.

Dreyfus, H. L., & Dreyfus, S. E. (1988). Making a mind versus modeling the brain: Intelligence back at a branchpoint. In S. R. Graubard (Ed.), *The artificial intelligence debate* (pp. 15–44). Cambridge: MIT Press.

Driskell, J. E., Willis, R., & Copper, C. (1992). Effect of overlearning on retention. *Journal of Applied Psychology, 77*, 615–622.

Driver, J., Tabares, A., Shapiro, A., Nahm, E. Y., & Gottman, J. M. (2003). Interactional patterns in marital success and failure: Gottman laboratory studies. In F. Walsh (Ed.), *Normal family processes: Growing diversity and complexity* (3rd ed., pp. 493–513). New York: Guilford.

Drucker-Colin, R., & Verdugo-Diaz, L. (2004). Cell transplantation for Parkinson's disease: Present status. *Cellular and Molecular Neurobiology, 24*, 301–316.

Druckman, D., & Bjork, R. A. (1994). *Learning, remembering, believing: Enhancing human performance.* Washington, DC: National Academy Press.

Drug Enforcement Adminstration, US Department of Justice. (2010). Herbal high-legal synthetic cannabinoids produce illicit marijuana effects: Spice, k2 and other "legal" products sold as marijuana alternatives. Available at: www.wyptac.org/upload/DEA%20K2%20Fact%20Sheet.pdf. Accessed May 31, 2011.

Drummond, S. P., Brown, G. G., Gillin, J. C., Stricker, J. L., Wong, E. C., & Buxton, R. B. (2000). Altered brain response to verbal learning following sleep deprivation. *Nature, 403*, 655–657.

DuBois, D. L., Portillo, N., Rhodes, J. E., Silverthorn, N., & Valentine, J. C. (2011). How effective are mentoring programs for youth? A systematic assessment of the evidence. *Psychological Science in the Public Interest, 12*(2), 57–91. doi:10.1177/1529100611414806.

Duckworth, A. L., Quinn, P. D., & Tsukayama, E. (2012). What No Child Left Behind leaves behind: The roles of IQ and self-control in predicting standardized achievement test scores and report card grades. *Journal of Educational Psychology, 104*(2), 439–451. doi:10.1037/a0026280

Duckworth, M. P. (2009). Assertiveness skills and the management of related factors. In W. T. O'Donohue & J. E. Fisher (Eds.), *General principles and empirically supported techniques of cognitive behavior therapy* (pp. 124–132). Hoboken, NJ: Wiley and Sons.

Duguid, M. M., & Goncalo, J. A. (2012). Living large: The powerful overestimate their own height. *Psychological Science, 23*(1), 36–40. doi:10.1177/0956797611422915

Dunfield, K. A., & Kuhlmeier, V. A. (2010). Intention-mediated selective helping in infancy. *Psycholoigcal Science, 21*, 523–527. doi:10.1177/0956797610364119.

Dunn, M. J., & Searle, R. (2010). Effect of manipulated prestige-car ownership on both sex attractiveness ratings. *British Journal Of Psychology, 101*(1), 69–80. doi:10.1348/000712609X417319.

Duarte, N. T., Goodson, J. R., & Klich, N. R. (1993). How do I like thee? Let me appraise the ways. *Journal of Organizational Behavior, 14*, 239–249.

Dube, C., Rotello, C. M., & Heit, E. (2010). Assessing the belief bias effect with ROCs: It's a response bias effect. *Psychological Review, 117*(3), 831–863. doi:10.1037/a0019634.

Dube, S. R., Felitti, V. J., Dong, M., Chapman, D. P., Giles, W. H., & Anda, R. F. (2003). Childhood abuse, neglect, and household dysfunction and the risk of illicit drug use: the adverse childhood experiences study. *Pediatrics, 111*, 564–572.

Dubertret, C., Hanoun, N., Ades, J., Hamon, M., & Gorwood, P. (2004). Family-based association studies between 5-HT-sub(5A) receptor gene and schizophrenia. *Journal of Psychiatric Research, 38*, 371–376.

DuBois, D. L., Felner, R. D., Brand, S., Adan, A. M., & Evans, E. G. (1992). A prospective study of life stress, social support, and adaptation in early adolescence. *Child Development, 63*, 542–557.

DuBreuil, S. C., Garry, M., & Loftus, E. F. (1998). Tales from the crib: Memories of infancy. In S. J. Lynn & K. M. McConkey (Eds.), *Truth in memory* (pp. 137–160). New York: Guilford.

Dubrovsky, B. O. (2005). Steroids, neuroactive steroids and neurosteroids in psychopathology. *Progress in Neuropsychopharmacology and Biological Psychiatry, 29*, 169–192.

Ducci, F., & Goldman, D. (2008). Genetic approaches to addiction: Genes and alcohol. *Addiction, 103*(9), 1414–1428.

Duckitt, J. & Sibley, C. G. (2010). Right-wing authoritarianism and social dominance orientation differentially moderate intergroup effects on prejudice. *European Journal of Personality, 24*, 583–601.

Duckitt, J. (2006). Differential effects of right-wing authoritarianism and social dominance orientation on outgroup attitudes and their mediation by threat from and competitiveness to outgroups. *Personality and Social Psychology Bulletin, 32*, 684–696.

Duckworth, A., Quinn, P. D., Lynam, D. R., Loeber, R., & Stouthamer-Loeber, M. (2011). Role of test motivation in intelligence testing. *PNAS Proceedings of the National Academy of Sciences of the United States of America, 108*(19), 7716–7720. doi:10.1073/pnas.1018601108.

Duclos, S. E., & Laird, J. D. (2001). The deliberate control of emotional experience through control of expressions. *Cognition and Emotion, 15*, 27–56.

Dudai, Y. (2004). The neurobiology of consolidations, or, how stable is the engram? *Annual Review of Psychology, 55*, 51–86.

Dudeck, M., Spitzer, C., Stopsack, M., Freyberger, H. J., & Barnow, S. (2007). Forensic inpatient male sexual offenders: The impact of personality disorders and childhood sexual abuse. *Journal of Forensic Psychiatry and Psychology, 18*, 494–506.

Dudley, N. M., Orvis, K. A., Lebiecki, J. E., & Cortina, J. M. (2006). A meta-analytic investigation of conscientiousness in the prediction of job performance: Examining the intercorrelations and the incremental validity of narrow traits. *Journal of Applied Psychology, 91*, 40–57.

Dueck, A., Ting, S., & Cutiongco, R. (2007). Constantine, Babel, and Yankee Doodle: Whose indigeneity? Whose psychology? *Pastoral Psychology, 56*(1), 55–72. doi:10.1007/s11089-007-0082-1.

Duggan, A., Fuddy, L., Burrell, L., Higman, S. M., McFarlane, E., Windham, A., et al. (2004). Randomized trial of a statewide home visiting program to prevent child abuse: Impact in reducing parental risk factors. *Child Abuse and Neglect, 28*, 623–643.

Dujovne, V., & Houston, B. (1991). Hostility-related variables and plasma lipid levels. *Journal of Behavioral Medicine, 14*, 555–564.

Duñabeitia, J. A., Molinaro, N., & Carreiras, M. (2011). Through the looking-glass: Mirror reading. *NeuroImage, 54*, 3004–3009. doi:10.1016/j.neuroimage.2010.10.079.

Duncan, A. E., Scherrer, J., Fu, Q., Bucholz, K. K., Heath, A. C., et al. (2006). Exposure to paternal alcoholism does not predict development of alcohol-use disorders in off spring: Evidence from an offspring-of-twins study. *Journal of Studies on Alcohol, 67*, 649–656.

Duncan, B. L. (2002). The legacy of Saul Rosenzweig: The profundity of the dodo bird. *Journal of Psychotherapy Integration, 12*(1), 32–57.

Duncan, G. J., Morris, P. A., & Rodrigues, C. (2011). Does money really matter? Estimating impacts of family income on young children's achievement with data from random-assignment experiments. *Developmental Psychology, 47*, 1263–1279.

Duncan, G. J., Brooks-Gunn, J., & Klebanov, P. K. (1994). Economic deprivation and early childhood development. *Child Development, 65*, 296–318.

Dunlop, S. (2008). Activity-dependent plasticity: Implications for recovery after spinal cord injury. *Trends in Neurosciences, 31*(8), 410–418.

Dunn, B. D., Galton, H. C., Morgan, R., Evans, D., Oliver, C., Meyer, M., & Dalgleish, T. (2010). Listening to your heart: How interoception shapes emotion experience and intuitive decision making. *Psychological Science, 21*(12), 1835–1844. doi:10.1177/0956797610389191.

Dunn, J., Brown, H., Slomkowski, C., Tesla, C., & Youngblade, L. (1991). Young children's understanding of other people's feelings and beliefs: Individual differences and their antecedents. *Child Development, 62*, 1352–1366.

Dunn, J., & Hughes, C. (2001). "I got some swords and you're dead!": Violent fantasy, antisocial behavior, friendship, and moral sensibility in young children. *Child Development, 72*, 491–505.

Duppils, G. S., & Wikblad, K. (2007). Patients' experiences of being delirious. *Journal of Clinical Nursing, 16*(5), 810–818.

Duran, B., Oetzel, J., Lucero, J., Jiang, Y., Novins, D. K., Manson, S., et al. (2005). Obstacles for rural American Indians seeking alcohol, drug, or mental health treatment. *Journal of Consulting and Clinical Psychology, 73*, 819–829.

Durand, M. V., & Barlow, D. H. (2006). *Essentials of abnormal psychology.* Belmont, CA: Wadsworth.

Durante, K.M., Griskevicius, V.,Simpson, J.A., Cantú, S.M., & Li, N.P. (2012). Ovulation leads women to perceive sexy cads as good dads. *Journal of Personality and Social Psychology, 103*, 292–305. doi:10.1037/a0028498

Durantini, M. R., Albarracin, D., Mitchell, A. L., Earl, A. N., & Gillette, J. C. (2006). Conceptualizing the influence of social agents of behavior change: A meta-analysis of the effectiveness of HIV-prevention interventionists for different groups. *Psychological Bulletin, 132*, 212–248.

During, E. H., Elahi, F. M., Taleb, O., Moro, M., & Baubet, T. (2011). A critical review of dissociative trance and possession disorders: Etiological, diagnostic, therapeutic, and nosological issues. *Canadian Journal of Psychiatry, 56*(4), 235–242.

Durkin, K. (2010). Videogames and young people with developmental disorders. *Review Of General Psychology, 14*(2), 122–140. doi:10.1037/a0019438

Durkin, M. S., Maenner, M. J., Meaney, F., Levy, S. E., DiGuiseppi, C., Nicholas, J. S., & Schieve, L. A. (2010). Socioeconomic inequality in the prevalence of autism spectrum disorder: Evidence from a U.S. cross-sectional study. *Plos ONE, 5*(7), 1–8. doi:10.1371/journal.pone.0011551.

Durose, M. R., Harlow, C. W., Langan, P. A., Motivans, M., Rantala, R. R., & Smith, E. L. (2005). *Family violence statistics.* Washington, DC: Bureau of Justice Statistics.

Dutton, D. G., & Aron, A. P. (1974). Some evidence for heightened sexual attraction under conditions of high anxiety. *Journal of Personality and Social Psychology, 30*, 510–517.

Dweck, C. S. (1999). *Self-theories: Their role in motivation, personality, and development.* Philadelphia: Psychology Press.

Dweck, C. S. (1998). The development of early self-conceptions: Their relevance for motivational processes. In J. Heckhausen & C. S. Dweck (Eds.), *Motivation and self-regulation across the life span.* New York: Cambridge University Press.

Dwyer, T., & Ponsonby, A. L. (2009). Sudden infant death syndrome and prone sleeping position. *Annals of Epidemiology, 19*, 245–249.

Dyche, L., & Zayas, L. H. (2001). Cross-cultural empathy and training the contemporary psychotherapist. *Clinical Social Work Journal, 29*, 245–258.

d'Ydewalle, G., & Rosselle, H. (1978). Text expectations in text learning. In M. M. Gruneberg, P. E. Morris, & R. N. Sykes (Eds.), *Practical aspects of memory.* Orlando, FL: Academic Press.

Dykas, M. J., & Cassidy, J. (2011). Attachment and the processing of social information across the life span: Theory and evidence. *Psychological Bulletin, 137*(1), 19–46. doi:10.1037/a0021367.

Dyken, M. E., & Yamada, T. (2005). Narcolepsy and disorders of excessive somnolence. *Primary Care, 32*, 389–413.

Dykiert, D., Bates, T. C., Gow, A. J., Penke, L., Starr, J. M., & Deary, I. J. (2012). Predicting mortality from human faces. *Psychosomatic Medicine, 74*, 560–566. Published online: doi:10.1097/PSY.0b013e318259c33f

Dzokoto, V. A., & Adams, G. (2005). Understanding genital-shrinking epidemics in West Africa: Koro, Juju, or mass psychogenic illness? *Culture, Medicine, and Psychiatry, 29*, 53–78.

Eagly, A. H., & Sczesny, S. (2009). Stereotypes about women, men, and leaders: Have times changed? In M. Barreto, M. Ryan, & M. Schmitt (Eds.), *The glass ceiling in the 21st century: Understanding barriers to gender equality* (pp. 21–47). Washington, DC: American Psychological Association.

Eagly, A., & Carli, L. (2007) *Through the labyrinth: The truth about how women become leaders.* Boston, MA: Harvard Business School Press.

Eagly, A. H., Johannesen-Schmidt, M. C., & van Engen, M. L. (2003). Transformational, transactional, and laissez-faire leadership styles: A meta-analysis comparing women and men. *Psychological Bulletin, 129*, 569–591.

Eagly, A. H., & Karau, S. J. (1991). Gender and the emergence of leaders: A meta-analysis. *Journal of Personality and Social Psychology, 60*, 685–710.

Eagly, A. H., Karau, S. J., & Makhijani, M. G. (1995). Gender and the effectiveness of leaders: A meta-analysis. *Psychological Bulletin, 117*, 125–145.

Eagly, A. H., Makhijani, M. G., & Klonsky, B. G. (1992). Gender and evaluation of leaders: A meta-analysis. *Psychological Bulletin, 111*, 3–22.

Eagly, A. H., & Wood, W. (1999). The orgins of sex diffrences in human behavior: Evolved dispositions versus social roles. *American Psychologist, 54*, 408–423.

Eamon, M. K. (2008). *Empowering vulnerable populations: Cognitive-behavioral interventions.* Chicago, IL: Lyceum Books.

East, P. L., & Jacobson, L. J. (2001). The younger siblings of teenage mothers: A follow-up of their pregnancy risk. *Developmental Psychology, 37,* 254–264.

Eastwick, P. W., & Finkel, E. J. (2008). Sex differences in mate preferences revisited: Do people know what they initially desire in a romantic partner? *Journal of Personality and Social Psychology, 94,* 245–264.

Ebert, S. A., Tucker, D. C., & Roth, D. L. (2002). Psychological resistance factors as predictors of general health status and physical symptom reporting. *Psychology Health & Medicine, 7,* 363–375.

Ebstein, R. B. (2006). The molecular genetic architecture of human personality: Beyond self-report questionnaires. *Molecular Psychiatry, 11,* 427–445.

Eby, L. T., Casper, W. J., Lockwood, A., Bordeaux, C., & Brinley, A. (2005). Work and family research in IO/OB: Content analysis and review of the literature (1980–2002). *Journal of Vocational Behavior, 66,* 124–197.

Eccles, J., Lord, S., & Buchanan, C. M. (1996). School transitions in early adolescence: What are we doing to our young people? In J. A. Graber, J. Brooks-Gunn, & A. C. Peterson (Eds.), *Transitions through adolescence: Interpersonal domains and context* (pp. 251–284). Mahwah, NJ: Erlbaum.

Eccles, J. S., & Roeser, R. W. (2003). Schools as developmental contexts. In G. Adams & D. Beizonsky (Eds.), *Blackwell handbook of adolescence* (pp. 129–148). Malden, MA: Blackwell.

Eccleston, C., & Crombez, G. (1999). Pain demands attention: A cognitive-affective model of the interruptive function of pain. *Psychological Bulletin, 125,* 356–366.

Echeburua, E., de Corral, P., Garcia Bajos, E., & Borda, M. (1993). Interactions between self-exposure and alprazolam in the treatment of agoraphobia without current panic: An exploratory study. *Behavioural and Cognitive Psychotherapy, 21,* 219–238.

Echo News. (2000). Car crash mum tells of fight to rebuild her life. March 17. Retrieved from May 17, 2009, at http://archive.echo-news.co.uk/2000/3/17/206088.html.

Eddy, K. T., Dorer, D. J., Franko, D. L., Tahilani, K., Thompson-Brenner, H., & Herzog, D. B. (2008). Diagnostic crossover in anorexia nervosa and bulimia nervosa: Implications for DSM-V. *American Journal of Psychiatry, 165,* 245–250.

Eddy, K. T., Dutra, L., Bradley, R., & Westen, D. (2004). A multidimensional meta-analysis of psychotherapy and pharmacotherapy for obsessive-compulsive disorder. *Clinical Psychology Review, 24,* 1011–1030.

Edenberg, H. J. (2007). The genetics of alcohol metabolism: Role of alcohol dehydrogenase and aldehyde dehydrogenase variants. *Alcohol Research and Health. 30,* 5–13.

Edinger, J. D., Wohlgemuth, W. K., Radtke, R. A., Marsh, G. R., & Quillian, R. E. (2001). Cognitive behavioral therapy for treatment of chronic primary insomnia. *American Medical Association, 285,* 1856–1864.

Edwards, R. R., Campbell, C., Jamison, R. N., & Wiech, K. (2009). Th e neurobiological underpinnings of coping with pain. *Psychological Science, 18,* 237–241.

Edwards, B. J., Reilly, T., & Waterhouse, J. (2009). Zeitgeber-effects of exercise on human circadian rhythms: What are alternative approaches to investigating the existence of a phase-response curve to exercise? *Biological Rhythm Research, 40*(1), 53–69.

Edwards, C. D., & Glick, R. (2008). Depression. In R. L. Glick, J. S. Berlin, A. B. Fishkind, & S. L. Zeller (Eds.). *Emergency psychiatry: Principles and practice.* (pp. 175–187). Philedalphia: Wolters Kluwer/Lippincott, Williams & Wilkins.

Eerland, A., Guadalupe, T., & Zwaan, R. (2011). Leaning to the left makes the Eiffel Tower seem smaller: posture-modulated estimation. *Psychological Science, 22*(12), 1511–1514.

Egan, K., & Asher, J. (2005). *Mental illness extracts heavy toll, beginning in youth* [Press release]. National Institute of Mental Health. Retrieved from http://www.nimh.nih.gov/press/ mentalhealthstats.cfm

Egger, H. L., & Emde, R. N. (2010). Developmentally sensitive diagnostic criteria for mental health disorders in early childhood: The Diagnostic and Statistical Manual of Mental Disorders—IV, the Research Diagnostic Criteria—Preschool Age, and the Diagnostic Classification of Mental Health and Developmental Disorders of Infancy and Early Childhood—Revised. *American Psychologist,* doi:10.1037/a0021026.

Egner, T., Jamieson, G., & Gruzelier, J. (2005). Hypnosis decouples cognitive control from conflict monitoring processes of the frontal lobe. *Neuroimage, 27,* 969–978.

Ehlers, A., Bisson, J., Clark, D. M., Creamer, M., et al. (2010). Do all psychological treatments really work the same in posttraumatic stress disorder? *Clinical Psychology Review, 30,* 269–276.

Eich, E. (1989). Theoretical issues in state dependent memory. In H. L. Roediger & F. I. M. Craik (Eds.), *Varieties of memory and consciousness.* Hillsdale, NJ: Erlbaum.

Eich, E., & Macaulay, D. (2000). Are real moods required to reveal mood-congruent and mood-dependent memory? *Psychological Science, 11,* 244–248.

Eich, E., & Metcalfe, J. (1989). Mood dependent memory for internal versus external events. *Experimental Psychology: Learning, Memory, and Cognition, 15,* 443–455.

Eich, J. E., Weingartner, H., Stillman, R. C., & Gillin, J. C. (1975). State dependent accessibility of retrieval cues in the retention of a categorized list. *Journal of Verbal Learning and Verbal Behavior, 14,* 408–417.

Eid, M., & Larsen, R. J. (Eds.) (2008). *The science of subjective well-being.* New York, NY: Guilford Press.

Eifert, G. H., Zvolensky, M. J., & Louis, A. (2008). Somatoform disorders: Nature, psychological processes, and treatment strategies. In J. E. Maddux & B. A. Winstead (Eds.). *Psychopathology: Foundations for a contemporary understanding* (2nd ed., pp. 307–325). New York: Routledge/Taylor & Francis Group.

Einhorn, H., & Hogarth, R. (1982). Prediction, diagnosis and causal thinking in forecasting. *Journal of Forecasting, 1,* 23–36.

Eisenberg, M., Kobilo, T., Berman, D. E., & Dudai, Y. (2003). Stability of retrieved memory: Inverse correlation with trace dominance. *Science, 301,* 1102–1104.

Eisenberg, N., & Fabes, R. A. (1998). Prosocial development. In W. Damon & N. Eisenberg (Eds.), *Handbook of child psychology: Vol. 3. Social, emotional, and personality development* (5th ed., pp. 701–778). New York: Wiley.

Eisenberg, N., Fabes, R. A., & Spinrad, T. L. (2006). Prosocial development. In W. Damon & R. M. Lerner (Series Eds.) & N. Eisenberg (Vol. Ed.), *Handbook of child psychology: Vol. 3. Social, emotional, and personality development* (6th ed.). New York: Wiley.

Eisenberger, R., & Rhoades, L. (2001). Incremental effects of reward on creativity. *Journal of Personality and Social Psychology, 81,* 728–741.

Eisenberger, R., & Shanock, L. (2003). Rewards, intrinsic motivation, and creativity: A case study of conceptual and methodological isolation. *Creativity Research Journal, 15,* 121–130.

Eisenberger, N.I. (2012). Broken hearts and broken bones: A neural perspective on the similarities between social and physical pain. *Current Directions in Psychological Science, 21,* 42–47.

Eisenberger, N. I., Way, B. M., Taylor, S. E., Welch, W. T., & Lieberman, M. D. (2007). *Biological Psychiatry, 61,* 1100–1108.

Eisenmann, J. C., Bartee, R. T., Smith, D. T., Welk, G. J., & Fu, Q. (2008). Combined influence of physical activity and television viewing on the risk of overweight in US youth. *International Journal of Obesity, 32,* 613–618.

Eiser, A. S. (2005). Physiology and psychology of dreams. *Seminars in Neurology, 25,* 97–105.

Ekblad, M., Gissler, M., Lehtonen, L., & Korkeila, J. (2011). Relation of Prenatal Smoking Exposure and Use of Psychotropic Medication up to Young Adulthood. *American Journal of Epidemiology, 174*(6), 681–690.

Else-Quest, N. M., Hyde, J. S., & Linn, M. C. (2010). Cross-national patterns of gender diff erences in mathematics: A meta-analysis. *Psychological Bulletin, 136,* 103–127.

Ekelund, U., Luan, J., Sherar, L. B., Esliger, D. W., Griew, P., & Cooper, A. (2012). Moderate to vigorous physical activity and sedentary time and cardiometabolic risk factors in children and adolescents. *JAMA: Journal Of The American Medical Association, 307*(7), 704–712.

Ekehammar, B., Akrami, N., Hedlund, L. E. , Yoshimura, K.; Ono, Y., Ando, J., & Yamagata, S. (2010). The generality of personality heritability: Big-Five trait heritability predicts response time to trait items. *Journal of Individual Differences, 31,* 209–214.

Ekman, P. (1993). Facial expression and emotion. *American Psychologist, 48,* 384–392.

Ekman, P. (1994). Strong evidence for universals in facial expressions: A reply to Russell's mistaken critique. *Psychological Bulletin, 115*(2), 268–287.

Ekman, P. (2009). Lie catching and micro expressions. In C. W. Martin (Ed.), *The philosophy of deception* (pp. 118–138). New York: Oxford University Press.

Ekman, P., & Davidson, R. J. (1993). Voluntary smiling changes regional brain activity. *Psychological Science, 4*(5), 342–345.

Ekman, P., Davidson, R. J., Ricard, M., & Alan, W. B. (2005). Buddhist and psychological perspectives on emotions and well-being. *Current Directions in Psychological Science, 14,* 59–63.

Ekman, P., Friesen, W. V., & Ellsworth, P. (1972). *Emotion in the human face: Guidelines for research and a review of findings.* New York: Pergamon Press.

Ekman, P., Levenson, R. W., & Friesen, W. V. (1983). Autonomic nervous system activity distinguishes among emotions. *Science, 221,* 1208–1210.

Ekpo, K. E. (2011). Nutritional and biochemical evaluation of the protein quality of four popular insects consumed in Southern Nigeria. *Archives of Applied Science Research, 3*(6), 24–40.

Eldar, S., Heneghan, H., Brethauer, S., & Schauer, P. (2011). Bariatric surgery for treatment of obesity. *International Journal of Obesity (2005), 35 Suppl 3,* S16–S21. doi:10.1038/ijo.2011.142

Eley, T. C., Napolitano, M., Lau, J. Y. F., & Gregory, A. M. (2010). Does childhood anxiety evoke maternal control? A genetically informed study. *The journal of child psychology and psychiatry, 51:7,* 772–779. doi:10.1111/j.1469-7610.2010.02227.x.

Eling, P. (2008). Cerebral localization in the Netherlands in the nineteenth century: Emphasizing the work of Aletta Jacobs. *Journal of the History of the Neurosciences, 17*(2), 175–194.

Eliot, A. J., Chirkov, V. I., Kim, Y., & Shelldon, K. M. (2001). A cross-cultural analysis of avoidance (relative to approach) personal goals. *Psychological Science, 12,* 505–510.

Elkin, I. (1994). The NIMH treatment of depression collaborative research program: Where we began and where we are. In A. E. Bergin & S. L. Garfield (Eds.), *Handbook of psychotherapy and behavior change* (pp. 114–139). New York: Wiley.

Elkins, I. J., King, S. M., McGue, M., & Iacono, W. G. (2006). Personality traits and the development of nicotine, alchohol, and illicit drug disorders: Prospective links from adolescence to young adulthood. *Journal of Abnormal Psychology, 115,* 26–39.

Elliot, S. N., Reynolds, C. R., & Kratochwill, T. R. (2006). *School psychology: Essentials of theory and practice.* Hoboken, NJ: Wiley.

Elliott, R., Rubinsztein, J. S., Sahakian, B. J., & Dolan, R. J. (2002). The neural basis of moodcongruent processing biases in depression. *Archives of General Psychiatry, 59,* 597–604.

Elliott, R., Watson, J. C., & Goldman, R. N. (2004a). Empty chair work for unfinished interpersonal issues. In R. Elliott & J. Watson (Eds.), *Learning emotion-focused therapy: The process-experiential approach to change* (pp. 243–265). Washington, DC: American Psychological Association.

Elliott, R., Watson, J. C., & Goldman, R. N. (2004b). Two-chair work for conflict splits. In R. Elliott & J. Watson (Eds.), *Learning emotion-focused therapy: The process-experiential approach to change* (pp. 219–241). Washington, DC: American Psychological Association.

Ellis, A., & Bernard, M. E. (1985). *Clinical applications of rational-emotive therapy.* New York: Plenum.

Ellis, A. (1962). *Reason and emotion in psychotherapy.* New York: Lyle Stuart.

Ellis, A. (1993). Reflections on rational-emotive therapy. *Journal of Consulting and Clinical Psychology, 61,* 199–201.

Ellis, A. (1995). Rational emotive behavior therapy. In R. J. Corsini & D. Wedding (Eds.), *Current psychotherapies* (5th ed., pp. 162–196). Itasca, IL: Peacock.

Ellis, A. (2004a). Why I (really) became a therapist. *Journal of Rational-Emotive and Cognitive Behavior Therapy, 22*(2), 73–77.

Ellis, A. (2004b). Why rational emotive behavior therapy is the most comprehensive and effective form of behavior therapy. *Journal of Rational-Emotive and Cognitive Behavior Therapy, 22*(2), 85–92.

Ellis, A. (2011). *Rational emotive behavior therapy.* Washington, D.C.: American Psychological Association.

Ellis, A. L., & Mitchell, R. W. (2000). Sexual orientation. In L. T. Szuchman & F. Muscarella (Eds.), *Psychological perspectives on human sexuality* (pp. 196–231). New York: Wiley.

Ellis, N. R. (1991). Automatic and effortful processes in memory for spatial location. *Bulletin of the Psychonomic Society, 29,* 28–30.

Elms, A. C. (2009). Obedience lite. *American Psychologist, 64,* 32–36.

Elofsson, U. O. E., von Schèele, B., Theorell, T., & Söndergaard, H. P. (2008). Physiological correlates of eye movement desensitization and reprocessing. *Journal of Anxiety Disorders, 22*(4), 622–634.

Elovainio, M., Kivimäki, M., & Vahtera, J. (2002). Organizational justice: Evidence on a new psychosocial predictor of health. *American Journal of Public Health, 92,* 105–108.

Else-Quest, N. M., Hyde, J. S., Goldsmith, H. H., & Van Hulle, C. A. (2006). Gender differences in temperament: A meta-analysis. *Psychological Bulletin, 132,* 33–72.

El-Sheikh, M., Hinnant, J., & Erath, S. (2011). Developmental trajectories of delinquency symptoms in childhood: The role of marital conflict and autonomic nervous system activity. *Journal of Abnormal Psychology, 120*(1), 16–32. doi:10.1037/a0020626.

Elwood, L. S., Hahn, K. S., Olatunji, B., O., & Williams, N. L. (2009). Cognitive vulnerabilities to the development of PTSD: A review of four vulnerabilities and the proposal of an integrative vulnerability model. *Clinical Psychology Review, 29,* 87–100.

El Yacoubi, M., Bouali, S., Popa, D., Naudon, L., Leroux-Nicollet, I., Hamon, M., et al. (2003). Behavioral, neurochemical, and electrophysiological characterization of a genetic mouse model of depression. *Proceedings of the National Academy of Sciences, 100,* 6227–6232.

Emanuele, E., Politi, P., Bianchi, M., Minoretti, P., Bertona, M., & Geroldi, D. (2006). Raised plasma nerve growth factor levels associated with early-stage romantic love. *Psychoneuroendocrinology, 31,* 288–294.

Enblom, A., Hammar, M., Steineck, G., & Börjeson, S. (2008). Can individuals identify if needling was performed with an acupuncture needle or a non-penetrating sham needle? *Complementary Therapies in Medicine, 16*(5), 288–294.

Engebretson, T. O., & Stoney, C. M. (1995). Anger expression and lipid concentrations. *International Journal of Behavioral Medicine, 2,* 281–298.

Engen, T., Gilmore, M. M., & Mair, R. G. (1991). Odor memory. In T. V. Getchell et al. (Eds.), *Taste and smell in health and disease.* New York: Raven Press.

England, T. J., Abaei, M., Auer, D. P., Lowe, J., Jones, D. R., Sare, G., Walker, M., & Bath, P. M. (2012). Granulocyte-colony stimulating factor for mobilizing bone marrow stem cells in subacute stroke: The stem cell trial of recovery enhancement after stroke 2 randomized controlled trial. *Stroke, 43*(2), 405–411.

Englemann, T., Tergan, S., & Hesse, F. (2010). Evoking knowledge and information awareness for enhancing computer-supported collaborative problem solving. *Journal of Experimental Education, 78*(2), 268–290.

Englund, M. M., Luckner, A. E., Whaley, G. L., & Egeland, B. (2004). Children's achievement in early elementary school: Longitudinal effects of parental involvement, expectations, and quality of assistance. *Journal of Educational Psychology, 96*(4), 723–730.

Enoch, M. A. (2003). Pharmacogenomics of alcohol response and addiction. *American Journal of Pharmacogenomics, 3,* 217–232.

Entringer, S., Epel, E. S., Kumsta, R., Lin, J., Hellhammer, D. H., Blackburn, E. H., & Wadhwa, P. D. (2011). Stress exposure in intrauterine life is associated with shorter telomere length in young adulthood. *PNAS Proceedings of the National Academy of Sciences of the United States of America, 108*(34), E513–E518. doi:10.1073/pnas.1107759108.

Epping-Jordan, M. P., Watkins, S. S., Koob, G. F., & Markou, A. (1998). Dramatic decreases in brain reward function during nicotine withdrawal. *Nature, 393,* 76–79.

Epstein, E. M., Sloan, D. M., & Marx, B. P. (2005). Getting to the heart of the matter: Written disclosure, gender, and heart rate. *Psychosomatic Medicine, 67,* 413–419.

Epstein, L. H., Temple, J. L., Roemmich, J. N., & Bouton, Mark E. (2009). Habituation as a determinant of human food intake. *Psychological Review, 116,* 384–407.

Epstein, R., Kirshit, C. E., Lanza, R. P., & Rubin, C. L. (1984). "Insight" in the pigeon: Antecedents and determinants of an intelligent performance. *Nature, 308,* 61–62.

Epstude, K., & Mussweiler, T. (2009). What you feel is how you compare: How comparisons influence the social induction of affect. *Emotion, 9,* 1–14.

Erath, S. A., El-Sheikh, M., Hinnant, J. B., Cummings, E. M. (2011). Skin conductance level reactivity moderates the association between harsh parenting and growth in child externalizing behavior. *Developmental Psychology, 47,* 693–706.

Erdelyi, M. (2010). The ups and downs of memory. *American Psychologist, 65*(7), 623–633. doi:10.1037/a0020440.

Erdelyi, M. H. (1985). *Psychoanalysis: Freud's cognitive psychology.* San Francisco: Freeman.

Erez, A., Misangyi, V. F., Johnson, D. E., LePine, M. A., & Halverson, K. C. (2008). Stirring the hearts of followers: Charismatic leadership as the transferal of affect. *Journal of Applied Psychology, 93,* 602–616.

Erickson, K. I., Voss, M. W., Prakash, R., Basak, C., Szabo, A., Chaddock, L., & Kramer, A. F. (2011). Exercise training increases size of hippocampus and improves memory. *Proceedings of the National Academy of Sciences of the United States of America, 108*(7), 3017–3022. doi:10.1073/pnas.1015950108.

Erickson, K. I., Colcombe, S. J., Wadhwa, R., Scalf, P. E., Kim, J. S., et al. (2007). Training-induced plasticity in older adults: Effects of training on hemispheric asymmetry. *Neurobiology of Aging, 28,* 272–283.

Erickson, R. J., Nichols, L., & Ritter, C. (2000). Family influences on absenteeism: Testing an expanded process model. *Journal of Vocational Behavior, 57,* 246–272.

Ericsson, K. A., & Charness, N. (1994). Expert performance: Its structure and acquisition. *American Psychologist, 49,* 725–747.

Ericsson, K. A., & Simon, H. A. (1994). *Protocol analysis: Verbal reports as data* (Rev. ed.). Cambridge, MA: MIT Press.

Ericsson, K. A., & Staszewski, J. (1989). Skilled memory and expertise: Mechanisms of exceptional performance. In D. Klahr & K. Kotovsky (Eds.), *Complex information processing: The impact of Herbert A. Simon.* Hillsdale, NJ: Erlbaum.

Eriksen, S., & Jensen, V. (2006). All in the family? Family environment factors in sibling violence. *Journal of Family Violence, 21*(8), 497–507.

Erikson, E. H. (1968). *Identity: Youth and crisis.* New York: Norton.

Eriksson, P. S., Perfilieva, E., Bjork-Eriksson, T., Alborn, A. M., Nordborg, C., Peterson, D. A., & Gage, F. H. (1998). Neurogenesis in the adult human hippocampus. *Nature Medicine, 4,* 1313–1317.

Ernst, M., Matochik, J. A., Heishman, S. J., Van Horn, J. D., Jons, P. H., Henningfield, J. E., & London, E. D. (2001). Effect of nicotine on brain activation during performance of a working memory task. *Proceedings of the National Academy of Sciences, 98,* 4728–4733.

Eroglu, E., Gökçil, Z., Bek, S., Ulas, U. H., & Odabasi, Z. (2008). Pregnancy and teratogenicity of antiepileptic drugs. *Acta Neurologica Belgica, 108*(2), 53–57.

Eron, L. D., Huesmann, L. R., Lefkowitz, M. M., & Walder, L. O. (1972). Does television violence cause aggression? *American Psychologist, 27*(4), 253–263.

Ersche, K. D., Jones, P., Williams, G. B., Turton, A. J., Robbins, T. W., & Bullmore, E. T. (2012). Abnormal brain structure implicated in stimulant drug addiction. *Science, 335*(6068), 601–604. doi:10.1126/science.1214463.

Erskine, J. K., & Georgiou, G. J. (2010). Effects of thought suppression on eating behaviour in restrained and non-restrained eaters. *Appetite, 54*(3), 499–503. doi:10.1016/j.appet.2010.02.001.

Ersner-Hershfield, H., Galinsky, A. D., Kray, L. J., & King, B. G. (2010). Company, country, connections: Counterfactual origins increase organizational commitment, patriotism, and social investment. *Psychological Science, 21*(10), 1479–1486. doi:10.1177/0956797610382123.

Esel, E., Ozsay, S., Tutus, A., Sofiuoglu, S., Kartaici, S., Bayram, F., et al. (2005). Effects of anti-depressant treatment and of gender on serum leptin levels in patients with major depression. *Progress in Neuro-Psychopharmacology and Biological Psychiatry, 29,* 565–570.

Eshel, N., & Roiser, J. P. (2010). Reward and punishment processing in depression. *Biological Psychiatry, 68,* 118–124.

Eskine, K. J., Kacinik, N. A., & Prinz, J. J. (2011). A bad taste in the mouth: Gustatory disgust influences moral judgment. *Psychological Science, 22*(3), 295–299. doi:10.1177/0956797611398497.

Eskine, K. J., Kacinik, N. A., & Prinz, J. J. (2012). Stirring images: Fear, not happiness or arousal, makes art more sublime. *Emotion,* doi:10.1037/a0027200

Espiritu, J. R. D. (2008). Aging-Related Sleep Changes. *Clinics in Geriatric Medicine, 24*(1), 1–14.

Espy, K. A., Fang, H., Johnson, C., Stopp, C., Wiebe, S. A., & Respass, J. (2011). Prenatal tobacco exposure: Developmental outcomes in the neonatal period. *Developmental Psychology, 47,* 153–169.

Essau, C. A., Sasagawa, S., Chen, J., & Sakano, Y. (2012). Taijin kyofusho and social phobia symptoms in young adults in England and in Japan. *Journal of Cross-Cultural Psychology, 43*(2), 219–232. doi:10.1177/0022022110386372.

Essex, M. J., Klein, M. H., Slattery, M. J., Goldsmith, H. H., & Kalin, N. H. (2010). Early risk factors and developmental pathways to chronic high inhibition and social anxiety disorder in adolescence. *American Journal of Psychiatry, 167,* 40–46.

Esterson, A. (2001). The mythologizing of psychoanalytic history: Deception and self-deception in Freud's account of the seduction theory episode. *History of Psychiatry, 12,* 329–352.

Ettinger, U., Picchioni, M., Landau, S., Matsumoto, K., van Haren, N. E., Marshall, N., et al. (2007). Magnetic resonance imaging of the thalamus and adhesio interthalamica in twins with schizophrenia. *Archives of General Psychiatry, 64,* 401–409.

Evans, G. W., Ricciuti, H. N., Hope, S., Schoon, I., et al. (2010). Crowding and cognitive development: The mediating role of maternal responsiveness among 36-month-old children. *Environment and Behavior, 42,* 135–148.

Evans, J., Heron, J., Lewis, G., Araya, R., & Wolke, D. (2005). Negative self-schemas and the onset of depression in women: Longitudinal study. *British Journal of Psychiatry, 186,* 302–307.

Evans, G. W. (2004). The environment of childhood poverty. *American Psychologist, 59,* 77–92.

Evans, G. W., & Wener, R. E. (2006). Rail commuting duration and passenger stress. *Health Psychology, 25,* 408–412.

Evans, G. W., & Kutcher, R. (2010). Loosening the link between childhood poverty and adolescent smoking and obesity: The protective effects of social capital. *Psychological Science, 22*(1), 3–7. doi:10.1177/0956797610390387.

Evans, J., Heron, J., Lewis, G., Araya, R., & Wolke, D. (2005). Negative self-schemas and the onset of depression in women: Longitudinal study. *British Journal of Psychiatry, 186,* 302–307.

Evans, J. A., Elliott, J. A., & Gorman, M. R. (2009). Dim nighttime illumination accelerates adjustment to timezone travel in an animal model. *Current Biology, 19*(4), R156–R157.

Everitt, B. J., & Robbins, T. W. (2005). Neural systems of reinforcement for drug addiction: From actions to habits to compulsion. *Nature Neuroscience, 8,* 1481–1489.

Evrard, D., Charollais, A., Marret, S., Radi, S., Rezrazi, A., & Mellier, D. (2011). Cognitive and emotional regulation developmental issues in preterm infants 12 and 24 months after birth. *European Journal of Developmental Psychology, 8*(2), 171–184. doi:10.1080/17405620903504538.

Eysenck, H. J. (1952). The effects of psychotherapy: An evaluation. *Journal of Consulting Psychology, 16,* 319–324.

Eysenck, H. J. (1986). What is intelligence? In R. J. Sternberg & D. K. Detterman (Eds.), *What is intelligence? Contemporary viewpoints on its nature and definition.* Norwood, NJ: Ablex.

Eysenck, H. J. (1990a). Biological dimensions of personality. In L. A. Pervin (Ed.), *Handbook of personality: Theory and research* (pp. 244–276). New York: Guilford.

Eysenck, H. J. (1990b). Genetic and environmental contributions to individual differences: The three major dimensions of personality. *Journal of Personality, 58,* 245–261.

Eysenck, H. J., & Rachman, S. (1965). *The causes and cures of neurosis: An introduction to modern behavior therapy based on learning theory and the principle of conditioning.* San Diego: Knapp.

Eysenck, M. W., & Keane, M. T. (2005). *Cognitive psychology: A student's handbook* (5th ed.). East Sussex, UK: Psychology Press.

Eyssel, F. & Bohner, G. (2011) Schema effects of rape myth acceptance on judgments of guilt and blame in rape cases: The role of perceived entitlement to judge. *Journal of Interpersonal Violence, 26,* 1579–1605.

Ezzyat, Y., & Davachi, L. (2010). What constitutes an episode in episodic memory? *Psychological Science, 22*(2), 243–252. doi:10.1177/0956797610393742.

Fabes, R. A., Martin, C. L., & Hanish, L. D. (2003). Young children's qualities in same-, other-, and mixed-sex peer groups. *Child Development, 74,* 921–932.

Fabricius, W. V., Boyer, T. W., Weimer, A. A., & Carroll, K. (2010). True or false: Do 5-year-olds understand belief? *Developmental Psychology, 46*(6), 1402–1416. doi:10.1037/a0017648.

Fabrigar, L. R., MacDonald, T. K., & Wegener, D. T. (2005). The structure of attitudes. In D. Albarracín, B. T. Johnson, & M. P. Zanna (Eds.), *Handbook of attitudes* (pp. 79–124). Mahwah, NJ: Erlbaum.

Fabrigar, L. R. & Wegener, D. T. (2010). Attitude structure In R. Baumeister & E. Finkel (Eds.) *Advanced social psychology The state of the science* (pp. 177–216). New York, NY: Oxford.

Faedda, G., Tondo, L., Teicher, M., Baldessarini, R., Gelbard, H., & Floris, G. (1993). Seasonal mood disorders: Patterns of seasonal recurrence in mania and depression. *Archives of General Psychiatry, 50,* 17–23.

Fagan, A. A., Hanson, K., Hawkins, J. D., & Arthur, M. S. (2009). Translational research in action: Implementation of the Communities That Care prevention system in 12 communities. *Journal of Community Psychology, 37,* 809–829.

Fagan, J. F. (2000). A theory of intelligence as processing. *Psychology, Public Policy, and Law, 26,* 168–179.

Fagan, J. F., & Detterman, D. K. (1992). The Fagan Test of Infant Intelligence: A technical summary. *Journal of Applied Developmental Psychology, 13,* 173–193.

Fagan, J. F., Holland, C. R., & Wheeler, K. (2007). The prediction, from infancy, of adult IQ and achievement. *Intelligence, 35,* 225–231.

Fagin-Jones, S., & Midlarsky, E. (2007). Courageous altruism: Personal and situational correlates of rescue during the Holocaust. *The Journal of Positive Psychology, 2,* 136–147.

Fago, David P. (2009). Comment: The evidence-based treatment debate: Toward a dialectical rapprochement. *Psychotherapy: Theory, Research, Practice, Training, 46,* 15–18.

Fagot, B. I. (1997). Attachment, parenting, and peer interactions of toddler children. *Developmental Psychology, 33,* 489–499.

Fahrenkopf, A. M., Sectish, T. C., Barger, L. K., Sharek, P. J., Lewin, D., Chiang, V. W., Edwards, S., Wiedermann, B. L., & Landrigan, C. P. (2008). Rates of medication errors among depressed and burnt out residents: prospective cohort study. *British Medical Journal, 336,* 488–491.

Fahsing, I. A., Ask, K., & Granhag, P. A. (2004). Th e man behind the mask: Accuracy and predictors of eyewitness off ender descriptions. *Journal of Applied Psychology, 89,* 722–729.

Fairburn, C. G. (Ed.). (2008). *Cognitive behavior therapy and eating disorders.* New York: Guilford.

Faisal, T., Taib, M., & Ibrahim, F. (2012). Adaptive Neuro-Fuzzy Inference System for diagnosis risk in dengue patients. *Expert Systems With Applications, 39*(4), 4483–4495. doi:10.1016/j.eswa.2011.09.140.

Falck, R. S., Wang, J., & Carlson, R. G. (2007). Crack cocaine trajectories among users in a midwestern American city. *Addiction, 102,* 1421–1431.

Falicov, C. J. (2003). Culture, society, and gender in depression. *Journal of Family Therapy, 25,* 371–387.

Falk, A., & Heckman, J. J. (2009). Lab experiments are a major source of knowledge in the social sciences. *Science, 326,* 535–538.

Falk, E., Berkman, E., & Lieberman, M. (2012). From neural responses to population behavior: neural focus group predicts population-level media effects. *Psychological Science, 23*(5), 439–445.

Farah, M. J. (1996). Is face recognition "special"? Evidence from neuropsychology. *Behavioral Brain Research, 76*(1–2), 181–189.

Farah, M. J. (2009). A picture is worth a thousand dollars. *Journal of Cognitive Neuroscience, 21,* 623–624.

Farah, M. J., Shera, D. M., Savage, J. H., Betancourt, L., Giannetta, J. M., Brodsky, N. L., Malmud, E. K., & Hurt, H. (2006). Childhood poverty: Specific associations with neurocognitive development. *Brain Research, 1110,* 166–174.

Farley, F. (1986). The big T in personality. *Psychology Today, 20,* 44–52.

Farmer, J. D., Patelli, P., & Zovko, I. I. (2005). The predictive power of zero intelligence in financial markets. *Proceedings of the National Academy of Sciences, 102,* 2254–2259.

Farmer, R. F., & Nelson-Gray, R. (2005). *Personality-guided behavior therapy.* Washington, DC: American Psychological Association.

Farooqi, I. S., Keogh, J. M., Kamath, S., Jones, S., Gibson, W. T., Trussel, R., et al. (2001). Metabolism: Partial leptin deficiency and human adiposity. *Nature, 414,* 34–35.

Farrell, D., & Stamm, C. L. (1988). Meta-analysis of the correlates of employee absence. *Human Relations, 41,* 211–227.

Farrell, P. (2010). School psychology: Learning lessons from history and moving forward. *School Psychology International, 31*(6), 581–598. doi:10.1177/0143034310386533.

Farroni, T., Csibra, G., Simion, F., & Johnson, M. H. (2002). Eye contact detection in humans from birth. *Proceedings of the National Academy of Sciences, 99,* 9602–9605.

Farroni, T., Johnson, M. H., Menon, E., Zulian, L., Faraguna, D., & Csibra, G. (2005). Newborns' preference for face-relevant stimuli: Effects of contrast polarity. *Proceedings of the National Academy of Sciences, 102,* 17245–17250.

Farlow, M. R. (2009). Treatment of mild cognitive impairment (MCI). *Current Alzheimer Research, 6*(4), 362–367.

Fassler, D. G., & Dumas, L. S. (1997). *Help me, I'm sad: Recognizing, treating, and preventing childhood depression.* New York: Viking Press.

Fassler, O., Lynn, S. J., & Knox, J. (2008). Is hypnotic suggestibility a stable trait? *Consciousness and Cognition, 17,* 240–253.

Faulkner, M. (2001). The onset and alleviation of learned helplessness in older hospitalized people. *Aging & Mental Health, 5,* 379–386.

Fava, G. A., Grandi, S. Rafanelli, C., Ruini, C., Conti, S., & Bellurado, P. (2001). Long-term outcome of social phobia treated by exposure. *Psychological Medicine, 31,* 899–905.

Fava, G. A., Rafanelli, C., Tossani, E., & Grandi, S. (2008). Agoraphobia is a disease: A tribute to Sir Martin Roth. *Psychotherapy and Psychosomatics, 77,* 133–138.

Fazio, L. K., & Marsh, E. J. (2010). Correcting false memories. *Psychological Science, 21*(6), 801–803, doi:10.1177/0956797610371341.

Fearon, R. P., Bakermans-Kranenburg, M. J., Van IJzendoorn, M. H., Lapsley, A.-M., & Roisman, G. I. (2010). The significance of insecure attachment and disorganization in the development of children's externalizing behavior: A meta-analytic study. *Child Development, 81,* 435–456.

Feder, B. J. (2004, May 31). Technology strains to find menace in the crowd. *The New York Times,* p. C1.

Feigin, V. L. (2003). Stroke epidemiology: A review of population based studies of incidence, prevalence, and case-fatality in the late 20th century. *Lancet Neurology, 2*(1), 43–53.

Feinberg, J. M., & Aiello, J. R. (2010). The effect of challenge and threat appraisals under evaluative presence. *Journal of Applied Social Psychology, 40,* 2071–2104.

Feinberg, L., & Campbell, I. G. (1993). Total sleep deprivation in the rat transiently abolishes the delta amplitude response to darkness: Implications for the mechanism of the "negative delta rebound." *Journal of Neurophysiology, 70*(6) 2695–2699.

Feinberg, M., Willer, R., Antonenko, O., & John, O. (2012). Liberating reason from the passions: overriding intuitionist moral judgments through emotion reappraisal. *Psychological Science, 23,* 788–795.

Feinstein, A. (2011). Conversion disorder: advances in our understanding. *CMAJ: Canadian Medical Association Journal, 183*(8), 915–920. doi:10.1503/cmaj.110490

Feist, J., & Feist, G. J. (2009). *Theories of personality* (7th ed.). New York: McGraw-Hill.

Fekete, T. (2010). Representational systems. *Minds And Machines, 20*(1), 69–101. doi:10.1007/s11023-009-9166-2.

Feldman, R., Weller, A., Zagoory-Sharon, O., & Levine, A. (2007). Evidence for a neuroendocrinological foundation of human affiliation: Plasma oxytocin levels across pregnancy and the postpartum period predict mother-infant bonding. *Psychological Science, 18,* 965–970.

Feldman Barrett, L., & Kensinger, E. A. (2010). Context is routinely encoded during emotion perception. *Psychological Science (Sage Publications Inc.), 21*(4), 595–599. doi:10.1177/0956797610363547

Felten, D. L., Cohen, N., Ader, R., Felten, S. Y., Carlson, S. L., & Roszman, T. L. (1991). Central neural circuits involved in neural-immune interactions. In R. Ader (Ed.), *Psychoneuroimmunology* (2nd ed.). New York: Academic Press.

Feng, X., Shaw, D. S., Kovacs, M., Lane, T., O'Rourke, F. E., & Alarcon, J. H. (2008). Emotion regulation in preschoolers: The roles of behavioral inhibition, maternal affective behavior, and maternal depression. *Journal of Child Psychology and Psychiatry, 49,* 132–141.

Fenn, K. M., Nusbaum, H. C., & Margoliash, D. (2003). Consolidation during sleep of perceptual learning of spoken language. *Nature, 425,* 614–616.

Fenson, L., Dale, P. S., Reznick, J. S., & Bates, E. (1994). Variability in early communicative development. *Monographs of the Society for Research in Child Development, 59*, 173.

Ferguson, C. J. (2002). Media violence: Miscast causality. *American Psychologist, 57*, 446–447.

Ferguson, C. J. (2009). Violent video games: Dogma, fear, and pseudoscience. *Skeptical Inquirer, 33*, 38–43.

Ferguson, C. J. (2010). Blazing angels or resident evil? Can violent video games be a force for good? *Review of General Psychology, 14*, 122–140.

Ferguson, C. J., & Dyck, D. (2012). Paradigm change in aggression research: The time has come to retire the General Aggression Model. *Aggression & Violent Behavior, 17*, 220–228. doi:10.1016/j.avb.2012.02.007

Ferguson, C. J., & Kilburn, J. (2009). The public health risks of media violence: A meta-analytic review. *Journal of Pediatrics, 154*, 759–763.

Ferguson, C. J., & Kilburn, J. (2010). Much ado about nothing: Th e misestimation and overinterpretation of violent video game eff ects in Eastern and Western nations: Comment on Anderson et al. (2010). *Psychological Bulletin, 136*, 174–178.

Ferguson, C. J., & Meehan, D. C. (2011). With friends like these…: Peer delinquency influences across age cohorts on smoking, alcohol and illegal substance use. *European Psychiatry, 26*(1), 6–12. doi:10.1016/j.eurpsy.2010.09.002

Ferguson,C. J., Olson, C. K., Kutner, L. A., & Warner, D. E. (2010). Violent video games, catharsis seeking, bullying, and delinquency: A multivariate analysis of eff ects. *Crime and Delinquency, 56*, 1–21.

Ferguson, C. J., San Miguel, C., & Hartley, R. D. (2009). A multivariate analysis of youth violence and aggression: The influence of family, peers, depression, and media violence. *Journal of Pediatrics, 155*(6), 904–908.

Fernández-Dols, J.-M., & Ruiz-Belda, M.-A. (1995). Are smiles a sign of happiness? Gold medal winners at the Olympic Games. *Journal of Personality and Social Psychology, 69*, 1113–1119.

Fernández-Serrano, M., Perales, J., Moreno-López, L., Pérez-García, M., & Verdejo-García, A. (2012). Neuropsychological profiling of impulsivity and compulsivity in cocaine dependent individuals. *Psychopharmacology, 219*(2), 673–683. doi:10.1007/s00213-011-2485-z

Fernstrom, J. D., & Choi, S. (2008). The development of tolerance to drugs that suppress food intake. *Pharmacology & Therapeutics, 117*, 105–122. doi:10.12016/j.pharmthera.2007.09.001

Ferrara, J. M., & Stacy, M. (2008). Impulse-control disorders in Parkinson's disease. *CNS Spectrums, 13*(8), 690–698.

Ferris, G. R., Judge, T. A., Rowland, K. M., & Fitzgibbons, D. E. (1994). Subordinate influence and the performance evaluation process: Test of a model. *Organizational and Human Decision Processes, 58*, 101–135.

Feshbach, S., & Tangney, J. (2008). Television viewing and aggression: Some alternative perspectives. *Perspectives on Psychological Science, 3*(5), 387–389.

Festinger, L. (1954). A theory of social comparison processes. *Human Relations, 7*, 117–140.

Festinger, L. (1957). *A theory of cognitive dissonance.* Evanston, IL: Row, Petersen.

Festinger, L., & Carlsmith, J. M. (1959). Cognitive consequences of forced compliance. *Journal of Abnormal and Social Psychology, 58*, 203–210.

Fidzinski, P., Wawra, M., Bartsch, J., Heinemann, U., & Behr, J. (2012). High-frequency stimulation of the temporoammonic pathway induces input-specific long-term potentiation in subicular bursting cells. *Brain Research, 1430*:1–7. doi:10.1016/j.brainres.2011.10.040

Fields, A. J. (2010). Multicultural research and practice: Th eoretical issues and maximizing cultural exchange. *Professional Psychology: Research and Practice, 41*, 196–201.

Fields, R. D. (2005). Making memories stick. *Scientific American, 292*, 74–81.

Fife, T. D. (2009). Benign paroxysmal positional vertigo. *Seminars in Neurology, 29*(5), 500–508.

Figner, B., & Weber, E. U. (2011). Who takes risks when and why?: Determinants of risk taking. *Current Directions in Psychological Science, 20*(4), 211–216. doi 10.1177/0963721411415790

Filtness, A. J., Reyner, L. A., & Horne, J. A. (2012). Driver sleepiness—Comparisons between young and older men during a monotonous afternoon simulated drive. *Biological Psychology, 89*(3), 580–583. doi:10.1016/j.biopsycho.2012.01.002

Fincham, J. M., & Anderson, J. R. (2006). Distinct roles of the anterior cingulated and the prefrontal cortex in the acquisition and performance of a cognitive skill. *Proceedings of the National Academy of Sciences, 103*, 12941–12946.

Fine, I., Wade, A. R., Brewer, A. A., May, M. G., Goodman, D. F., Boynton, G. M., et al. (2003). Long-term deprivation affects visual perception and cortex. *Nature Neuroscience, 6*, 915–916.

Fingerman, K. L., & Charles, S. T. (2010). It takes two to tango: Why older people have the best relationships. *Current Directions in Psychological Science, 19*(3), 172–176. doi:10.1177/0963721410370297.

Finkel, D., Reynolds, C. A., McArdle, J. J., Hamagami, F., & Pedersen, N. L. (2009). Genetic variance in processing speed drives variation in aging of spatial and memory abilities. *Developmental Psychology, 45*, 820–834.

Finkel, D., Reynolds, C. A., McArle, J. J., Gatz, M., & Pedersen, N. L. (2003). Latent growth curve analyses of accelerating decline in cognitive abilities in late adulthood. *Developmental Psychology, 39*, 535–550.

Finkel, D., Reynolds, C. A., McArdle, J. J., & Pedersen, N. L. (2007). Age changes in processing speed as a leading indicator of cognitive aging. *Psychology and Aging, 22*(3), 558–568.

Finkel, E. & Baumeister, R. F. (2010). Attraction and rejection In R. Baumeister & E. Finkel (Eds.) *Advanced social psychology: The state of the science* (pp. 419–459). New York, NY: Oxford.

Finkel, E. J., Eastwick, P. W., Karney, B. R., Reis, H. T., & Sprecher, S. (2012). Online dating: A critical analysis from the perspective of psychological science. *Psychological Science in the Public Interest, 13*, 3–66. doi:10.1177/1529100612436522.

Finkelstein, E. A., DiBonaventura, M., Burgess, S. M., & Hale, B. C. (2010). The costs of obesity in the workplace. *Journal Of Occupational & Environmental Medicine, 52*(10), 971–976. doi:10.1097/JOM.0b013e3181f274d2.

Finney, M. L., Stoney, C. M., & Engebretson, T. O. (2002). Hostility and anger expression in African American and European American men is associated with cardiovascular and lipid reactivity. *Psychophysiology, 39*, 340–349.

Fiorella, L., & Mayer, R. E. (2012). Paper-based aids for learning with a computer-based game. *Journal of Educational Psychology,* doi:10.1037/a0028088

Fiorentino, D. D. (2008). Cognition, but not sensation, mediates age-related changes in the ability to monitor the environment. *Psychology & Aging, 23*(3), 665–670.

Firkowska-Mankiewicz, A. (2011). Adult careers: Does childhood IQ predict later life outcome?. *Journal of Policy and Practice in Intellectual Disabilities, 8*(1), 1–9. doi:10.1111/j.1741-1130.2011.00281.x.

First, M. B. (2011). DSM-5 proposals for mood disorders: A cost-benefit analysis. *Current Opinion in Psychiatry, 24*, 1–9. doi:10.1097/YCO.0b013e328340b594.

First, M. B., Pincus, H. A., Levine, J. B., Williams, J. B. W., Ustun, B., & Peele, R. (2004). Clinical utility as a criterion for revising psychiatric diagnoses. *American Journal of Psychiatry, 161*, 946–954.

Fisar, Z. (2009). Phytocannabinoids and endocannabinoids. *Current Drug Abuse Review, 2*, 51–75.

Fischer, K. W., & Bidell, T. (1991). Constraining nativist inferences about cognitive capacities. In S. Carey & R. Gelman (Eds.), *The epigenesis of mind: Essays on biology and cognition* (pp. 199–235). Hillsdale, NJ: Erlbaum.

Fischer, K. W., & Hencke, R. W. (1996). Infants' construction of actions in context: Piaget's contribution to research on early development. *Psychological Science, 7*, 204–209.

Fischer, M. J. (2011). Interracial contact and changes in the racial attitudes of White college students. *Social Psychology of Education, 14*, 547–574. doi:10.1007/s11218-011-9161-3.

Fischer, M. J., & Massey, D. S. (2007). The effects of affirmative action in higher education. *Social Science Research, 36*(2), 531–549.

Fischer, P., Ai, A. L., Aydin, N., Frey, D., & Haslam, S. A. (2010). The relationship between religious identity and preferred coping strategies: An examination of the relative importance of interpersonal and intrapersonal coping in Muslim and Christian faiths. *Review of General Psychology, 14*(4), 365–381. doi:10.1037/a0021624.

Fischer, R., & Boer, D. (2011). What is more important for national well-being: Money or autonomy? A meta-analysis of well-being, burnout, and anxiety across 63 societies. *Journal Of Personality & Social Psychology, 101*(1), 164-184.

Fischer, S., Hallschmid, M., Elsner, A. L., & Born, J. (2002). Sleep forms memory for finger skills. *Proceedings of the National Academy of Sciences, 99*, 11987–11991.

Fischoff, B., & MacGregor, D. (1982). Subjective confidence in forecasts. *Journal of Forecasting, 1*, 155–172.

Fishbein, M., & Ajzen, I. (2010). *Predicting and changing behavior: The reasoned action approach.* New York: Psychology Press.

Fisher, C. D. (2000). Mood and emotion while working: Missing pieces of job satisfaction? *Journal of Organizational Behavior, 21*, 185–202.

Fisher, C. D. (2003). Why do lay people believe that satisfaction and performance are correlated? Possible sources of a commonsense theory. *Journal of Organizational Behavior, 24*, 753–777.

Fisher, C. M. (1982). Lacunar strokes and infarcts: A review. *Neurology, 32*(8), 871–876.

Fisher, C. M. (1989). Binswanger's encephalopathy: A review. *Journal of Neurology, 236*(2), 65–79.

Fisher, P. L., & Wells, A. (2009). Psychological models of worry and generalized anxiety disorder. In M. M. Antony & M. B. Stein (Eds.), *Oxford handbook of anxiety and related disorders* (pp. 225–237). New York: Oxford University Press.

Fisher, S. E. (2005). Dissection of molecular mechanisms underlying speech and language disorders. *Applied Psycholinguistics, 26*, 111–128.

Fisher, W. A., Fisher, J. D., & Rye, B. J. (1995). Understanding and promoting AIDS-preventive behavior: Insights from the theory of reasoned action. *Health Psychology, 14*, 255–264.

Fishman, D. B., Rego, S. A., & Muller, K. L. (2011). Behavioral theories of psychotherapy. In J. C. Norcross, G. R. VandenBos, & D. K. Freedheim (Eds.), *History of psychotherapy: Continuity and change* (pp. 101–140). Washington, D.C.: American Psychological Association.

Fiske, A. P., Kitayama, S., Markus, H. R., & Nisbett, R. E. (1998). The cultural matrix of social psychology. In D. T. Gilbert, S. T. Fiske, & G. Lindzey (Eds.), *Handbook of social psychology* (Vol. 2, 4th ed., pp. 915–981). Boston: McGraw-Hill.

Fiske, S., & Taylor, S. (2008). *Social cognition, from brains to culture.* New York: McGraw-Hill.

Fiske, S. T. (1998). Stereotyping, prejudice, and discrimination. In D. Gilbert, S. T. Fiske, & G. Lindzey (Eds.), *Handbook of social psychology* (Vol.2, 4th ed., pp. 357–414). Boston: McGraw-Hill.

Fiske, S. T. (2010). Venus and Mars or down to Earth: Stereotypes and realities of gender differences. *Perspectives on Psychological Science, 5*(6), 688–692. doi:10.1177/1745691610388768.

Fitzgerald, T. E., Tennen, H., Affleck, G. S., & Pransky, G. (1993). The relative importance of dispositional optimism and control appraisals in quality of life after coronary artery bypass surgery. *Journal of Behavioral Medicine, 16*, 25–43.

Fitzsimons, G. M., & Finkel, E. J. (2011). Outsourcing self-regulation. *Psychological Science, 22*(3), 369–375. doi:10.1177/0956797610397955.

Flament, M., Bissada, H., & Spettigue, W. (2012). Evidence-based pharmacotherapy of eating disorders. *International Journal of Neuropsychopharmacology, 15,* 189–207.

Flanagan, J. C. (1954). The critical incident technique. *Psychological Bulletin, 51,* 327–358.

Flavell, J. E., Azrin, N., Baumeister, A., Carr, E., Dorsey, M., Forehand, R., et al. (1982). The treatment of self-injurious behavior. *Behavior Therapy, 13,* 529–554.

Flavell, J. H. (1996). Piaget's legacy. *Psychological Science, 7,* 200–203.

Fleck, M. S., & Mitroff, S. R. (2007). Rare targets are rarely missed in correctable search. *Psychological Science, 18*(11), 943–947.

Fledderus, M., Bohlmeijer, E. T., Pieterse, M. E., & Schreurs, K. M. G. (2012). Acceptance and commitment therapy as guided self-help for psychological distress and positive mental health: A randomized controlled trial. *Psychological Medicine, 42* 485–495.

Fleeson, W., Malanos, A. B., & Achille, N. M. (2002). An intraindividual process approach to the relationship between extraversion and positive affect: Is acting extraverted as "good" as being extraverted? *Journal of Personality & Social Psychology, 83,* 1409–1422.

Flegal, K. M., Graubard, B. I., Williamson, D. F., & Gail, M. H. (2005). Excess deaths associated with underweight, overweight, and obesity. *Journal of the American Medical Association, 293,* 1861–1867.

Fleischhacker, W. W., & Widschwendter, C. G. (2006). Treatment of schizophrenia patients: Comparing new-generation antipsychotics to each other. *Current Opinion in Psychiatry, 19,* 128–134.

Fleishman, E. A., & Harris, E. F. (1962). Patterns of leadership behavior related to employee grievances and turnover. *Personnel Psychology, 15,* 43–56.

Fletcher, G. & Overall, N. C. (2010) Intimate relationships In R. Baumeister & E. Finkel (Eds.) *Advanced social psychology: The state of the science* (pp. 461–494). New York, NY: Oxford.

Fleuret, F., Li, T., Dubout, C., Wampler, E. K., Yantis, S., & Geman, D. (2011). Comparing machines and humans on a visual categorization test. *PNAS Proceedings of the National Academy of Sciences of the United States of America, 108*(43), 17621–17625. doi:10.1073/pnas.1109168108.

Flor, H., Birbaumer, N., Herman, C., Ziegler, S., & Patrick, C. J. (2002). Aversive Pavlovian conditioning in psychopaths: Peripheral and central correlates. *Psychophysiology, 39,* 505–518.

Flores, E., Tschann, J. M., Dimas, J. M., Pasch, L. A., & de Groat, C. L. (2010). Perceived racial/ethnic discrimination, posttraumatic stress symptoms, and health risk behaviors among Mexican American adolescents. *Journal of Counseling Psychology, 57,* 264–273.

Flores, E., Cicchetti, D., & Rogosch, F. A. (2005). Predictors of resilience in maltreated and nonmaltreated Latino children. *Developmental Psychology, 41,* 338–351.

Flowe, H., & Bessemer, A. (2011). The effects of target discriminability and criterion placement on accuracy rates in sequential and simultaneous target-present lineups. *Psychology, Crime & Law, 17*(7), 587–610. doi:10.1080/10683160903397540.

Flowe, H. D., Mehta, A., & Ebbesen, E. B. (2011). The role of eyewitness identification evidence in felony case dispositions. *Psychology, Public Policy, And Law, 17*(1), 140–159. doi:10.1037/a0021311.

Floyd, J. A. (2002). Sleep and aging. *Nursing Clinics of North America, 37,* 719–731.

Floyd, M. F., Spengler, J. O., Maddock, J. E., Gobster, P. H., & Suau, L. (2008). Environmental and social correlates of physical activity in neighborhood parks: An observational study in Tampa and Chicago. *Leisure Sciences, 30*(4), 360–375.

Flynn, J. T. (1999). Searching for justice: The discovery of IQ gains over time. *American Psychologist, 54,* 5–20.

Foa, E. B., Cahill, S. P., Boscarino, J. A., Hobfoll, S. E., Lahad, M., McNally, R. J., et al. (2005). Social, psychological, and psychiatric interventions following terrorist attacks: Recommendations for practice and research. *Neuropsychopharmacology, 30,* 1806–1817.

Fodor, J. A. (1983). Modularity of mind: An essay on faculty psychology. Cambridge, MA: MIT Press.

Foer, J. (2011). *Moonwalking with Einstein: The Art and Science of Remembering Everything.* New York: Penguin Press.

Fogassi, L., Ferrari, P. F., Gesierich, B., Rozzi, S., et al. (2005). Parietal lobe: From action organization to intention understanding. *Science, 308,* 662–667.

Foley, J. M. (2004). Empirically supported treatment endeavour: A successful future or inevitable debacle? *Clinical Psychologist, 8,* 29–38.

Folk, C. L., Remington, R. W., & Wright, J. H. (1994). The structure of attentional control: Contingent attentional capture by apparent motion, abrupt onset, and color. *Journal of Experimental Psychology: Human Perception and Performance, 20,* 317–329.

Folkman, S., & Lazarus, R. (1988). *Manual for the ways of coping questionnaire.* Palo Alto, CA: Consulting Psychologists Press.

Folkman, S., Lazarus, R., Dunkel-Shetter, C., DeLongis, A., & Gruen, R. (1986). Dynamics of a stressful encounter: Cognitive appraisal, coping, and encounter outcomes. *Journal of Personality and Social Psychology, 50,* 992–1003.

Folkman, S., Lazarus, R. S., Dunkel-Schetter, C., DeLongis, A., & Gruen, R. J. (2000). The dynamics of a stressful encounter. In E. T. Higgins & A. W. Kruglanski (Eds.), *Motivational science: Social and personality perspectives* (pp. 111–127). Hove, UK: Psychology Press.

Folkman, S., & Moskowitz, J. T. (2000). Stress, positive emotion, and coping. *Current Directions in Psychological Science, 9,* 115–118.

Fontaine, K. L. (2009). *Mental health nursing.* Upper Saddle River, NJ: Pearson/ Prentice Hall.

Fontao, M., & Hoffmann, K. (2011). Psychosocial treatment in group format with people diagnosed with schizophrenia: Results and limitations of empirical research. *Psychosis, 3*(3), 226–234. doi:10.1080/17522439.2010.548100.

Fontes, M. A., Bolla, K. I., Cunha, P. J., Almeida, P. P., Jungerman, F., Laranjeira, R. R., Bressan, R. A., & Lacerda, A. L. (2011). Cannabis use before age 15 and subsequent executive functioning. *British Journal of Psychiatry, 198*(6), 442–447.

Foote, B., Smolin, Y., Kaplan, M., Legatt, M. E., & Lipschitz, D. (2006). Prevalence of dissociative disorders in psychiatric outpatients. *American Journal of Psychiatry, 163,* 623–629.

Forbes, D., Phelps, A., & McHugh, T. (2001). Treatment of combat-related nightmares using imagery rehearsal: A pilot study. *Journal of Traumatic Stress, 14,* 433–442.

Forbes, C. E., & Schmader, T. (2010). Retraining attitudes and stereotypes to affect motivation and cognitive capacity under stereotype threat. *Journal of Personality and Social Psychology, 99*(5), 740-754. doi:10.1037/a0020971.

Forbey, J. D., & Ben-Porath, Y. S. (2008). Empirical correlates of the MMPI-2 Restructures Clinical (RC) scales in a nonclinical setting. *Journal of Personality Assessment, 90,* 136–141.

Forcelli, P. A., & Heinrichs, S. C. (2008). Teratogenic effects of maternal antidepressant exposure on neural substrates of drug-seeking behavior in offspring. *Addiction Biology, 13*(1), 52–62.

Ford, B. Q., Tamir, M., Brunyé, T. T., Shirer, W. R., Mahoney, C. R., & Taylor, H. A. (2010). Keeping your eyes on the prize: Anger and visual attention to threats and rewards. *Psychological Science, 21*(8), 1098–1105. doi:10.1177/0956797610375450.

Ford, M. T., Heinen, B. A., & Langkamer, K. L. (2007). Work and family satisfaction and conflict: A meta-analysis of cross-domain relations. *Journal of Applied Psychology, 92,* 57–80.

Forest, A. L., & Wood, J. V. (2012). When social networking is not working: Individuals with low self-esteem recognize but do not reap the benefits of self-disclosure on Facebook. *Psychological Science, 23,* 295–302. doi:10.1177/0956797611429709.

Forgas, J. P., Dunn, E., & Granland, S. (2008). Are you being served. . . ? An unobtrusive experiment of affective influences on helping in a department store. *European Journal of Social Psychology, 38,* 333–342.

Forhan, S. E., Gottlieb, S. L., Sternberg, M. R., Xu, F., et al. (2009). Prevalence of sexually transmitted infections among female adolescents aged 14 to 19 in the United States. *Pediatrics, 124,* 1505–1512.

Formisano, E., De Martino, F., Bonte, M., & Goebel, R. (2008). "Who" is saying "what?" Brain-based decoding of human voice and speech. *Science, 322*(5903), 970–973.

Fornaro, M., Gabrielli, F., Rasore, F., Pompei, F., & Fornaro, P. (2007). Phenomenological, subjective experience and neurobiological aspects of delirium. *Minerva Psichiatrica, 48*(3), 365–372.

Förster, J. (2012). GLOMOsys: The how and why of global and local processing. *Current Directions in Psychological Science, 21*(1), 15–19. doi:10.1177/0963721411429454.

Forsyth, D. & Burnette, J. (2010). Group processes In R. Baumeister & E. Finkel (Eds.) *Advanced social psychology: The state of the science* (pp. 495–534). New York, NY: Oxford.

Fossati, P., Hevenor, S. J., Graham, S. J., Grady, C., Keightley, M. L., Craik, F., & Mayberg, H. (2003). In search of the emotional self: An FMRI study using positive and negative emotional words. *American Journal of Psychiatry, 160,* 1938–1945.

Fosse, R., Stickgold, R., & Hobson, J. A. (2001). Brain-mind states: Reciprocal variation in thoughts and hallucinations. *Psychological Science, 12,* 30–36.

Foster, E. M., Jones, D., & the Conduct Problems Prevention Research Group. (2006). Can a costly intervention be cost-effective? An analysis of violence prevention. *Archives of General Psychiatry, 63,* 1284–1291.

Foster, J. L., Huthwaite, T., Yesberg, J. A., Garry, M., & Loftus, E. F. (2012). Repetition, not number of sources, increases both susceptibility to misinformation and confidence in the accuracy of eyewitnesses. *Acta Psychologica, 139*(2), 320–326. doi:10.1016/j.actpsy.2011.12.004

Foster, M. D. (2000). Positive and negative responses to personal discrimination: Does coping make a difference? *Journal of Social Psychology, 140,* 93–106.

Foster, N. E., Thomas, E., Barlas, P., Hill, J. C., Young, J., Mason, E., & Hay, E. M. (2007). Acupuncture as an adjunct to exercise based physiotherapy for osteoarthritis of the knee: Randomised controlled trial. *British Medical Journal, 335,* 436.

Foti, R. J., & Hauenstein, N. M. A. (2007). Pattern and variable approaches in leadership emergence and effectiveness. *Journal of Applied Psychology, 92,* 347–355.

Fournier, J. C., DeRubeis, R. J., Hollon, S. D., Dimidjian, S., et al. (2010). Antidepressant drug effects and depression severity: A patient-level meta-analysis. *Journal of the American Medical Association, 303,* 47–53.

Fowler, G. A., Sherr, I., & Troianovski, A. (2011, October 15). Are Smartphones Becoming Smart Alecks?. *Wall Street Journal—Eastern Edition.* pp. A1–A12.

Fowler, J. (2012). Suicide risk assessment in clinical practice: Pragmatic guidelines for imperfect assessments. *Psychotherapy, 49*(1), 81–90. doi:10.1037/a0026148.

Fowler, J. R., & Christakis, N. A. (2008). Dynamic spread of happiness in a large social network: Longitudinal analysis over 20 years in the Framingham Heart Study. *British Medical Journal, 337,* a2533.

Fowles, D. C., & Dindo, L. (2009). Temperament and psychopathy: A dual-pathway model. *Current Directions in Psychological Science, 18,* 179–183.

Fox, A. S., & Olster, D. H. (2000). Effects of intracerebroventricular leptin administration on feeding and sexual behaviors in lean and obese female zucker rats. *Hormones and Behavior, 37,* 377–387.

Fox, M. C., Ericsson, K. A., & Best, R. (2010). Do procedures for verbal reporting of thinking have to be reactive? A meta-analysis and recommendations for best reporting methods. *Psychological Bulletin, 137*(2), 316–344. doi:10.1037/a0021663.

Fox, M. K., Pac, S., Devaney, B., & Jankowski, L. (2004). Feeding infants and toddlers study: What foods are infants and toddlers eating? *Journal of the American Dietetic Association, 104*(Suppl 1), s22–30.

Fox, S., Spector, P. E., & Miles, D. (2001). Counterproductive work behavior (CWB) in response to job stressors and organizational justice: Some mediator and moderator tests for autonomy and emotions. *Journal of Vocational Behavior, 59*, 291–309.

Fozard, J., Wolf, E., Bell, B., Farland, R., & Podolsky, S. (1977). Visual perception and communication. In J. Birren & K. Schaie (Eds.), *Handbook of the psychology of aging*. New York: Van Nostrand Reinhold.

Frances, A. (2009). A warning sign on the road to DSM-V: Beware of its unintended consequences. *Psychiatric Times, 26*, 1–9.

Frances, A. (2010). Alert to the research community: Be prepared to weigh in on DSM-V. *Psychiatric Times, 27*, 1–5.

Franchak, J. M., & Adolph, K. E. (2012). What infants know and what they do: Perceiving possibilities for walking through openings. *Developmental Psychology*, doi:10.1037/a0027530.

Francis, A. M. (2008). Family and sexual orientation: The family-demographic correlates of homosexuality in men and women. *Journal of Sex Research, 45*(4), 371–377.

Frank, D. A., Augustyn, M., Knight, W. G., Pell, T., & Zuckerman, B. (2001). Growth, development, and behavior in early childhood following prenatal cocaine exposure: A systematic review. *Journal of the American Medical Association, 285*, 1613–1625.

Frank, M. G., Ekman, P., & Friesen, W. V. (1993). Behavioral markers and recognizability of the smile of enjoyment. *Journal of Personality and Social Psychology, 64*(1), 83–93.

Frankenberg, W. K., & Dodds, J. B. (1967). The Denver developmental screening test. *Journal of Pediatrics, 71*, 181–191.

Frankenstein, J., Mohler, B. J., Bülthoff, H. H., & Meilinger, T. (2012). Is the map in our head oriented north? *Psychological Science, 23*(2), 120–125. doi:10.1177/0956797611429467.

Franks, P. W., Hanson, R. L., Knowler, W. C., Sievers, M. L., et al. (2010). Childhood obesity, other cardiovascular risk factors, and premature death. *New England Journal of Medicine, 362*, 485–493.

Fransen, M. L., Smeesters, D., & Fennis, B. M. (2011). The role of social presence in mortality salience effects. *Journal of Business Research, 64*, 29–33. doi:10.1016/j.jbusres.2009.09.016

Frasure-Smith, N., & Lespérance, F. (2005). Depression and coronary heart disease. *Current Directions in Psychological Science, 14*, 39–43.

Fratiglioni, L., & Qiu, C. (2009). Prevention of common neurodegenerative disorders in the elderly. *Experimental Gerontology, 44*(1–2), 46–50.

Frayling, T. M., Timpson, N. J., Weedon, M. N., Zeggini, E., Freathy R. M., Lindgren, C. M., Perry, J. R. B., Elliott, K. S., Lango, H., Rayner, N. W., Shields, B., Harries, L. W., Barrett, J. C., Ellard, S., Groves, C. J., Knight, B., Patch, A.-M., Ness, A. R., Ebrahim, S., Lawlor, D. A., Ring, S. M., Ben-Shlomo, Y., Jarvelin, M.-R., Sovio, U., Bennett, A. J., Melzer, D., Ferrucci, L., Loos, R. J. F., Barroso, I., Wareham, N. J., Karpe, F., Owen, K. R., Cardon, L. R., Walker, M., Hitman, G. A., Palmer, C. N. A., Doney, A. S. F., Morris, A. D., Davey-Smith, G. D., The Wellcome Trust Case Control Consortium, Hattersley, A. T., & McCarthy, M. I. (2007). A common variant in the FTO gene is associated with body mass index and predisposes to childhood and adult obesity. *Science, 316*, 889–894.

Fredrickson, B. L., & Cohn, M. A. (2008). Positive emotions. In M. Lewis, J. M. Haviland-Jones, L. Barrett, M., Lewis, J. M. Haviland-Jones, L. Barrett (Eds.), *Handbook of emotions* (3rd ed.) (pp. 777–796). New York, NY US: Guilford Press.

Fredrickson, B. L., Cohn, M. A., Coffey, K. A., Pek, J., & Finkel, S. M. (2008). Open hearts build lives: Positive emotions, induced through loving-kindness meditation, build consequential personal resources. *Journal of Personality and Social Psychology, 95*(5), 1045–1062.

Fredrickson, B. L., & Losada, M. F. (2005). Positive affect and the complex dynamics of human flourishing. *American Psychologist, 60*, 678–686.

Freed, C. R., Greene, P. E., Breeze, R. E., Tsai, W. Y., DuMouchel, W., Kao, R., et al. (2001). Transplantation of embryonic dopamine neurons for severe Parkinson's disease. *New England Journal of Medicine, 344*, 710–719.

Freedland, R. L., & Bertenthal, B. I. (1994). Developmental changes in interlimb coordination: Transition to hands-and-knees crawling. *Psychological Science, 5*, 26–32.

Freedman, D. M., Ron, E., Ballard-Barbash, R., Doody, M. M., & Linet, M. S. (2006). Body mass index and all-cause mortality in a nationwide U.S. cohort. *International Journal of Obesity, 30*, 822–829.

Freedman, J. L. (1992). Television violence and aggression: What psychologists should tell the public. In P. Suedfeld & P. E. Tetlock (Eds.), *Psychology and social policy*. New York: Hemisphere.

Freedman, J. L. (2002). *Media violence and its effect on aggression: Assessing the scientific evidence*. Toronto, Ontario, Canada: University of Toronto Press.

Freedman, J. L., & Fraser, S. C. (1966). Compliance without pressure: The foot-in-the-door technique. *Journal of Personality and Social Psychology, 4*, 195–202.

Freedman, R. (2003). Schizophrenia. *New England Journal of Medicine, 349*, 1738–1749.

Freedman, V. A., Aykan, H., & Martin, L. G. (2001). Aggregate changes in severe cognitive impairment among older Americans: 1993 and 1998. *Journal of Gerontology, 56B*, S100–S111.

Freeman, D., Rizzo, J., & Fried, S. (2011). Encoding visual information in retinal ganglion cells with prosthetic stimulation. *Journal of Neural Engineering, 8*(3), 035005.

Freeman, H., Gosling. S. D., & Schapiro, S. J. (in press). Methods for assessing personality in non-human primates. In A. Weiss, J King, & L. Murray (Eds.), *Personality and Behavioral Syndromes in Nonhuman Primates*. New York: Springer

Freeman, M. P., Freeman, S. A., & McElroy, S. L. (2002). The comorbidity of bipolar and anxiety disorders: Prevalence, psychobiology, and treatment issues. *Journal of Affective Disorders, 68*, 1–23.

Freimuth, V. S., & Hovick, S. R. (2012). Cognitive and emotional health risk perceptions among people living in poverty. *Journal of Health Communication, 17*, 303–318. doi:10.1080/10810730.2011.626505

Freisthler, B. (2011). Alcohol use, drinking venue utilization, and child physical abuse: Results from a pilot study. *Journal of Family Violence, 26*, 185–193. doi:10.1007/s10896-010-9352-2

Freitag, C. M. (2007). The genetics of autistic disorders and its clinical significance: A review of the literature. *Molecular Psychiatry, 12*, 2–22.

Fremgen, A., & Fay, D. (1980). Overextensions in production and comprehension: A methodological clarification. *Journal of Child Language, 7*, 205–211.

French, S. E., Seidman, E., Allen, L., & Aber, J. L. (2006). The development of ethnic identity during adolescence. *Developmental Psychology, 42*, 1–10.

Frenda, S. J., Nichols, R. M., & Loftus, E. F. (2011). Current issues and advances in misinformation research. *Current Directions In Psychological Science (Sage Publications Inc.), 20*(1), 20–23. doi:10.1177/0963721410396620.

Frese, M., Beimel, S., & Schoenborn, S. (2003). Action training for charismatic leadership: Two evaluations of studies of a commercial training module on inspirational communication of a vision. *Personnel Psychology, 56*, 671–697.

Freud, S. (1900). The interpretation of dreams. In J. Strachey (Ed.), *The standard edition of the complete psychological works of Sigmund Freud* (Vol. 8). London: Hogarth Press.

Freund, P., & Kasten, N. (2012). How smart do you think you are? A meta-analysis on the validity of self-estimates of cognitive ability. *Psychological Bulletin, 138*, 296–321. doi:10.1037/a0026556.

Frey, K. S., Hirschstein, M. K., Snell, J. L., Edstrom, L. V. S., MacKenzie, E. P., & Broderick, C. J. (2005). Reducing playground bullying and supporting beliefs: An experimental trial of the steps to respect program. *Developmental Psychology, 41*, 479–491.

Frick, P., & Nigg, J. (2012). Current issues in the diagnosis of attention deficit hyperactivity disorder, oppositional defiant disorder, and conduct disorder. *Annual Review of Clinical Psychology, 8*, 77–107.

Fridlund, A., Sabini, J. P., Hedlund, L. E., Schaut, J. A., Shenker, J. I., & Knauer, M. J. (1990). Audience effects on solitary faces during imagery: Displaying to the people in your head. *Journal of Nonverbal Behavior, 14*(2), 113–137.

Fried, I., Wilson, C. L., MacDonald, K. A., & Behnke, E. J. (1998). Electric current stimulates laughter. *Nature, 391*, 650.

Fried, P. A., Watkinson, B., & Gray, R. (1992). A follow-up study of attentional behavior in 6-year-old children exposed prenatally to marijuana, cigarettes, and alcohol. *Neurotoxicity and Teratology, 14*(5), 299–311.

Fried, Y., & Ferris, G. R. (1987). The validity of the job characteristics model: A review and meta-analysis. *Personnel Psychology, 40*, 287–322.

Friederici, A, D. (2011). The brain basis of language processing: from structure to function. *Physiological Reviews, 91*(4), 1357–1392.

Friedman, H. S., & Schustack, M. (2009). *Personality: Classic theories and modern research* (4th ed.). Boston: Allyn & Bacon.

Friedman, H. S., & Martin, L. R. (2011). *The Longevity Project: Surprising discoveries for health and long life from the landmark eight-decade study.* New York: Hudson Street Press.

Friedman, H. S., Kern, M. L. & Reynolds, C. A. (2010). Personality and health, subjective well-being, and longevity. *Journal of Personality, 78*, 179–216.

Friedman, H. S. (2000). Long-term relations of personality and health: Dynamisms, mechanisms, tropisms. *Journal of Personality, 68*, 1089–1107.

Friedman, H. S., & Schustack, M. W. (2003). *Personality: Classic theories and modern research*. Boston: Allyn & Bacon.

Friedman, H. S., Tucker, J. S., Schwartz, J. E., Martin, L. R., Tomlinson-Keasey, C., Wingard, D. L., & Criqui, M. H. (1995a). Childhood conscientiousness and longevity: Health behaviors and cause of death. *Journal of Personality and Social Psychology, 68*, 696–703.

Friedman, H. S., Tucker, J. S., Schwartz, J. E., Tomlinson-Keasey, C., Martin, L. R., Wingard, D. L., & Criqui, M. H. (1995b). Psychosocial and behavioral predictors of longevity: The aging and death of the "Termites." *American Psychologist, 50*, 69–78.

Friedman, M. A., & Brownell, K. D. (1995). Psychological correlates of obesity: Moving to the next research generation. *Psychological Bulletin, 117*(1), 3–20.

Friedman, M., & Rosenman, R. H. (1974). *Type A behavior and your heart*. New York: Knopf.

Frisco, M. L. (2008). Adolescents' sexual behavior and academic attainment. *Sociology of Education, 81*(3), 284–311.

Fritsch, T., Smyth, K. A., McClendon, M. J., Ogrocki, P. K., Santillan, C., et al. (2005). Associations between dementia/mild cognitive impairment and cognitive performance and activity levels in youth. *Journal of the American Geriatrics Society, 53*, 1191–1196.

Fritzler, B. K., Hecker, J. E., & Losee, M. C. (1997). Self-directed treatment with minimal therapist contact: Preliminary findings for obsessive-compulsive disorder. *Behaviour Research and Therapy, 35*, 627–631.

Frizzell, J. P. (2005). Acute stroke: Pathophysiology, diagnosis, and treatment. *AACN Clinical Issues, 16*(4), 421–440.

Frodl, T., Meisenzahl, E. M., Zill, P., Baghai, T. Rujescu, D. Leinsinger, G., et al. (2004). Reduced hippocampal volumes associated with the long variant of the serotonin transporter polymorphism in major depression. *Archives of General Psychiatry, 61*, 177–183.

Froeliger, B., Modlin, L., Wang, L., Kozink, R. V., & McClernon, F. J. (2011). Nicotine withdrawal modulates frontal brain function during an affective Stroop task. *Psychopharmacology*, October 12, 2011 [Epub ahead of print].

Frone, M. R. (2008). Are work stressors related to employee substance use? The importance of temporal context assessments of alcohol and illicit drug use. *Journal of Applied Psychology, 93,* 199–206.

Fry, R., & Cohn, D. (2011). Living together: The economics of cohabitation. *Social & Demographic Trends.* Washington, DC: Pew Research Center. Retrieved from: Fuligni, A. J., Witkow, M., & Garcia, C. (2005). Ethnic identity and the academic adjustment of adolescents from Mexican, Chinese, and European backgrounds. *Developmental Psychology, 41,* 799–811.

Fu, Q., Fu, X., & Dienes, Z. (2008). Implicit sequence learning and conscious awareness. *Consciousness and Cognition, 17,* 185–202.

Fuentemilla, L., Camara, E., Munte, T. F., Kramer, U. M., et al. (2009). Individual differences in true and false memory retrieval are related to white matter brain microstructure. *Journal of Neuroscience, 29,* 8698–8703.

Fujita, F., & Diener, E. (2005). Life satisfaction set point: Stability and change. *Journal of Personality and Social Psychology, 88,* 158–164.

Fuligni, A. J., & Pedersen, S. (2002). Family obligation and the transition to young adulthood. *Developmental Psychology, 38*(5), 856–868.

Fuligni, A. J., Witkow, M., & Garcia, C. (2005). Ethnic identity and the academic adjustment of adolescents from Mexican, Chinese, and European backgrounds. *Developmental Psychology, 41,* 799–811.

Fuller-Rowell, T. E., Evans, G. W., & Ong, A. D., (2012). Poverty and health: The mediating role of perceived discrimination. *Psychological Science, 23,* 734–739. doi:10.1177/0956797612439720

Fullerton, J. M., Donald, J. A., Mitchell, P. B., & Schofield, P. R. (2010). Two-dimensional genome scan identifies multiple genetic interactions in bipolar affective disorder. *Biological Psychiatry, 67,* 478–486.

Fullerton, C. S., Ursano, R. J., & Wang, L. (2004). Acute stress disorder, posttraumatic stress disorder, and depression in disaster or rescue workers. *American Journal of Psychiatry, 161,* 1370–1376.

Fulmer, C. A., Gelfand, M. J., Kruglanski, A. W., Kim-Prieto, C., Diener, E., Pierro, A., & Higgins, E. (2010). On "feeling right" in cultural contexts: How person-culture match affects self-esteem and subjective well-being. *Psychological Science 21*(11), 1563–1569. doi:10.1177/0956797610384742

Funder, D. (2008). Persons, situations, and person-situation interactions. In O. John, R. Robins, & L. Pervin (Eds.), *Handbook of personality: Theory and research* (3rd ed., pp. 568–582). New York: Guilford.

Funder, D. C. (2007). *The personality puzzle* (4th ed.). New York: W.W. Norton.

Funder, D. C. (2012). Accurate personality judgment. *Current Directions in Psychological Science, 21,* 177–182. doi:10.1177/0963721412445309

Furey, M. L., Pietrini, P., & Haxby, J. V. (2000). Cholinergic enhancement and increased selectivity of perceptual processing during working memory. *Science, 290,* 2315–2319.

Furmark, T., Henningsson, S., Appel, L., Ahs, F., Linnman, C., Pissiota, A., et al. (2009). Genotype over-diagnosis in amygdala responsiveness: Affective processing in social anxiety disorder. *Journal of Psychiatry and Neuroscience, 34*(1), 30–40.

Furnham, A. (2001). Personality and individual differences in the workplace: Person-organization-outcome fit. In R. Hogan & B. Roberts (Eds.), *Personality psychology in the workplace* (pp. 223–251). Washington, DC: American Psychological Association.

Furnham, A., & Boo, H. (2011). A literature review of the anchoring effect. *Journal of Socio-Economics, 40*(1), 35–42. doi:10.1016/j.socec.2010.10.008.

Fyer, A. J., Hamilton, S. P., Durner, M., Haghighi, F., et al. (2006). A third-pass genome scan in panic disorder: Evidence for multiple susceptibility loci. *Biological Psychiatry, 60,* 388–401.

Gabbard, G. O. (2004). *Long-term psychodynamic psychotherapy: A basic text.* Washington DC: American Psychiatric Association.

Gable, P., & Harmon-Jones, E. (2010). The blues broaden, but the nasty narrows: Attentional consequences of negative affects low and high in motivational intensity. *Psychological Science 21*(2) 211–215. doi:10.1177/0956797609359622.

Gaertner, S. L., Dovidio, J. F., & Houlette, M. (2010). Social categorization. In J. F. Dovidio, M. Hewstone, P. Glick, & V. M. Esses (Eds.), *The SAGE handbook of prejudice, stereotyping, and discrimination* (pp. 526–543) London: Sage.

Gagnon, J. F., Postuma, R. B., Mazza, S., Doyon, J., & Montplaisir, J. (2006). Rapid-eye-movement sleep behaviour disorder and neurodegenerative diseases. *Lancet Neurology, 5,* 424–432.

Gahukar, R. T. (2011). Entomophagy and human food security. *International Journal of Tropical Insect Science, 31*(3), 129–144. doi:10.1017/S1742758411000257.

Gais, S., Albouy, G., Boly, M., Dang-Vu, T. T., Darsaud, A., Desseilles, M., Rauchs, G., Schabus, M., Sterpenich, V., Vandewalle, G., Maquet, P., & Peigneux, P. (2007). Sleep transforms the cerebral trace of declarative memories. *Proceedings of the National Academies of Science, 104,* 18778–18783.

Gais, S., Lucas, B., & Born, J. (2006). Sleep after learning aids memory recall. *Learning & Memory, 13,* 259–262.

Galanter, E. (1962). Contemporary psychophysics. In R. Brown (Ed.), *New directions in psychology* (Vol. 1). New York: Holt, Rinehart, Winston.

Galdeira, K. (2006, October). Phiten power. *Hawaii Business, 52*(4), 52–54.

Galdi, S., Arcuri, L., & Gawronski, B. (2008). Automatic mental associations predict future choices of undecided decision-makers. *Science, 321,* 1100–1102.

Gale, C., R., Batty, G., & Deary, I. J. (2008). Locus of control at age 10 years and health outcomes and behaviors at age 30 years: The 1970 British cohort study. *Psychosomatic Medicine, 70,* 397–403.

Galea, S., Ahern, J., Resnick H., Kilpatrick D., Bucuvalas M., Gold, J., & Vlahov, D. (2002). Psychological sequelae of the September 11 terrorist attacks in New York City. *New England Journal of Medicine, 346,* 982–987.

Galea, S., Resnick, H., Ahern, J., Gold, J., Bucuvalas, M., Kilpatrick, D., et al. (2002). Post-traumatic stress disorder in Manhattan, New York City, after the September 11th terrorist attacks. *Journal of Urban Health, 79,* 340–353.

Galinsky, A. D., & Kray, L. J. (2004). From thinking about what might have been to sharing what we know: The effects of counterfactual mind-sets on information sharing in groups. *Journal of Experimental Social Psychology, 40,* 606–618.

Gallace, A., & Spence, C. (2011). To what extent do Gestalt grouping principles influence tactile perception? *Psychological Bulletin, 137*(4), 538–561. doi:10.1037/a0022335.

Gallagher, M. (1998, January 26). Day careless. *National Review, 50*(1), 37–43.

Gallagher, M., & Chiba, A. A. (1996). The amygdala and emotion. *Current Opinions in Neurobiology, 6*(2), 221–227.

Galland, B. C., Taylor, B. J., Elder, D. E., & Herbison, P. (2011). Normal sleep patterns in infants and children: A systematic review of observational studies. *Sleep Medicine Reviews,* July 22, 2011 [Epub ahead of print]Gallego, M., Gerardus Emmelkamp, P., van der Kooij, M., & Mees, H. (2011). The effects of a Dutch version of an Internet-based treatment program for fear of public speaking: A controlled study. *International Journal of Clinical Health & Psychology, 11*(3), 459–472.

Gallego, M., Gerardus Emmelkamp, P., van der Kooij, M., & Mees, H. (2011). The effects of a Dutch version of an Internet-based treatment program for fear of public speaking: A controlled study. *International Journal of Clinical Health & Psychology, 11*(3), 459–472.

Gallivan, J. P. Cavina-Pratesi, C., & Culham, J. C. (2009). Is that within reach? fMRI reveals that the human superior parieto-occipital cortex encodes objects reachable by the hand. *The Journal of Neuroscience, 29,* 4381–4391.

Gallo, D. A. (2006). *Associative illusions of memory.* New York: Psychology Press.

Galloway, A. T., Addessi, E., Fragaszy, D. M., & Visalberghi, E. (2005). Social facilitation of eating familiar food in tufted capuchins (*Cebus appella*): Does it involve behavioral coordination? *International Journal of Primatology, 26,* 181–189.

Galotti, K. M. (1999). Making a "major" real-life decision: College students choosing an academic major. *Journal of Educational Psychology, 91,* 379–387.

Galotti, K. M. (1999). *Cognitive psychology in and out of the laboratory* (2nd ed.). Belmont, CA: Brooks/Cole.

Galpin, A., Underwood, G., & Chapman, P. (2008). Sensing without seeing in comparative visual search. *Consciousness and Cognition, 17,* 672–687.

Gamer, M., Rill, H.-G., Vossel, G., & Gödert, H. W. (2006). Psychophysiological and vocal measures in the detection of guilty knowledge. *International Journal of Psychophysiology, 60,* 76–87.

Gamez, D. (2008). Progress in machine consciousness. *Consciousness and Cognition, 17,* 887–910.

Gan, T. J., Jiao, K. R., Zenn, M., & Georgiade, G. (2004). A randomized controlled comparison of electro-acupoint stimulation or ondansetron versus placebo for the prevention of post-operative nausea and vomiting. *Anesthesia and Analgesia, 99,* 1070–1075.

Ganai, S., Donroe, J. A., St. Louis, M. R., Lewis, G. M., & Seymour, N. E. (2007). Virtual-reality training improves angled telescope skills in novice laparoscopists. *American Journal of Surgery, 193*(2), 260–265.

Ganchrow, J. R., Steiner, J. E., & Daher, M. (1983). Neonatal facial expressions in response to different qualities and intensities of gustatory stimuli. *Infant Behavior and Development, 6,* 189–200.

Ganiban, J. M., Ulbricht, J., Saudino, K. J., Reiss, D., & Neiderhiser, J. M. (2011). Understanding child-based effects on parenting: Temperament as a moderator of genetic and environmental contributions to parenting. *Developmental Psychology, 47,* 676–692.

Ganis, G., Rosenfeld, J., Meixner, J., Kievit, R. A., & Schendan, H. E. (2011). Lying in the scanner: Covert countermeasures disrupt deception detection by functional magnetic resonance imaging. *Neuroimage, 55*(1), 312–319. doi:10.1016/j.neuroimage.2010.11.025.

Ganzel, B. L., Morris, P. A., & Wethington, E. (2010). Allostasis and the human brain: Integrating models of stress from the social and life sciences. *Psychological Review, 117,* 134–174.

Ganzel, B. L., Kim, P., Glover, G. H., & Temple, E. (2008). Resilience after 9/11: Multimodal neuroimaging evidence for stress-related change in the healthy adult brain. *NeuroImage, 40*(2), 788–795.

Gao, Y., Raine, A., Venables, P. H., Dawson, M. E., & Mednick, S. A. (2010). Association of poor childhood fear conditioning and adult crime. *American Journal of Psychiatry, 167,* 56–60.

Gara, M. A., Vega, W. A., Arndt, S. Escamilla, M., Fleck, D. E., Lawson, W. B., Lesser, I., Neighbors, H. W., Wilson, D. R., Arnold, L. M., & Strakowski, S. M. (2012). Influence of patient race and ethnicity on clinical assessment in patients with affective disorders. Published online first: *Arch Gen Psychiatry.* 2012;69:593–600. doi:10.1001/archgenpsychiatry.2011.2040 Retrieved from: http://archpsyc.jamanetwork.com/article.aspx?articleid=1151017

Garb, H. N. (1997). Race bias, social class bias, and gender bias in clinical judgment. *Clinical Psychology: Science and Practice, 4,* 99–120.

Garb, H. N., Wood, J. M., Lilienfeld, S. O., & Nezworski, T. (2005). Roots of the Rorschach controversy. *Clinical Psychology Review, 25,* 97–118.

Garbarino, S., Nobili, L., Beelke, M., De Carli, F., & Ferrillo, F. (2001). The contributing role of sleepiness in highway vehicle accidents. *Sleep: Journal of Sleep Research and Sleep Medicine, 24,* 203–206.

Garcia, J., & Koelling, R. A. (1966). Relation of cue to consequences in avoidance learning. *Psychonomic Science, 4,* 123–124.

Garcia, S. M., Weaver, K., Moskowitz, G. B., & Darley, J. M. (2002). Crowded minds: The implicit bystander effect. *Journal of Personality and Social Psychology, 83,* 843–853.

García-Montes, J. M., Zaldívar-Basurto, F., López-Ríos, F., & Molina-Moreno, A. (2009). The role of personality variables in drug abuse in a Spanish university population. *International Journal of Mental Health & Addiction, 7*(3), 475–487. doi:10.1007/s11469-007-9144-y

Garcia-Sierra, A., Rivera-Gaxiola, M., Percaccio, C. R., Conboy, B. T., Romo, H., Klarman, L., & Kuhl, P. K. (2011). Bilingual language learning: An ERP study relating early brain responses to speech, language input, and later word production. *Journal of Phonetics, 39*(4), 546–557. doi:10.1016/j.wocn.2011.07.002.

Gardner, B., Davies, A., McAteer, J., & Michie, S. (2010). Beliefs underlying UK parents' views towards MMR promotion interventions: A qualitative study. *Psychology, Health & Medicine, 15*(2), 220–230. doi:10.1080/13548501003623963.

Gardiner, H. W., & Kosmitzki, C. (2005). *Lives across cultures: Cross-cultural human development* (3rd ed.). Needham Heights, MA: Allyn & Bacon.

Gardner, H. (1993). *Multiple intelligences: The theory in practice.* New York: Basic Books.

Gardner, H. (1999). Are there additional intelligences? The case for naturalist, spiritual, and existential intelligences. In J. Kane (Ed.), *Education, information and transformation: Essays on learning and thinking* (pp. 111–131). Englewood Cliffs, NJ: Prentice Hall.

Gardner, H. (2002). *Learning from extraordinary minds.* Mahwah, NJ: Erlbaum.

Gardner, M. (1988). *The second Scientific American book of mathematical puzzles and diversions.* Chicago: University of Chicago Press.

Gardner, M., & Steinberg, L. (2005). Peer influence on risk taking, risk preference, and risky decision making in adolescence and adulthood: An experimental study. *Developmental Psychology, 41,* 625–635.

Gardner, R., Heward, W. L., & Grossi, T. A. (1994). Effects of response cards on student participation and academic achievement: A systematic replication with inner-city students during whole-class science instruction. *Journal of Applied Behavior Analysis, 27,* 63–71.

Garfield, S. L. (1998). Some comments on empirically supported treatments. *Journal of Consulting and Clinical Psychology, 66,* 121–125.

Gariepy, G., Nitka, D., & Schmitz, N. (2010). The association between obesity and anxiety disorders in the population: A systematic review and meta-analysis. *International Journal of Obesity, 34,* 407–419.

Garlick, D. (2003). Integrating brain science research with intelligence research. *Current Directions in Psychological Science, 12,* 185–188.

Garlipp, P. (2008). Koro–a culture-bound phenomenon: Intercultural psychiatric implications. *German Journal of Psychiatry, 11,* 21–28.

Garner, B. J., Tsui, E., & Lukose, D. (2009). Artificial intelligence (AI) in blended learning. *Knowledge-Based Systems, 22*(4), 247–248. doi:10.1016/j.knosys.2009.03.001.

Garry, M., & Gerrie, M. P. (2005). When photographs create false memories. *Current Directions in Psychological Science, 14,* 321–325.

Garry, M., & Loftus, E. (1994). Pseudomemories without hypnosis. *International Journal of Clinical and Experimental Hypnosis, 42,* 363–373.

Gartlehner, G., Hansen, R., Morgan, L., Thaler, K., Lux, L., Van Noord, M., & Lohr, K. (2011). Comparative benefits and harms of second-generation antidepressants for treating major depressive disorder: an updated meta-analysis. *Annals of Internal Medicine, 155*(11), 772–785.

Gasser, U. S., Rousson, V., Hentschel, F., Sattel, H., & Gasser, T. (2008). Alzheimer disease versus mixed dementias: An EEG perspective. *Clinical Neurophysiology, 119*(10), 2255–2259.

Gates, M. A., Holowka, D. W., Vasterling, J. J., Keane, T. M., Marx, B. P., & Rosen, R. C. (2012). Posttraumatic stress disorder in veterans and military personnel: Epidemiology, screening, and case recognition. *Psychological Services.* doi:10.1037/a0027649.

Gatewood, R. D., & Feild, H. S. (2001). *Human resource selection* (5th ed.). Fort Worth, TX: Harcourt.

Gaudiano, B. A., & Dalrymple, K. L. (2005). EMDR variants, pseudoscience, and the demise of empirically supported treatments? *PsycCRITIQUES, 50,* 8.

Gaudioso, E., Montero, M., & Hernandez-del-Olmo, F. (2012). Supporting teachers in adaptive educational systems through predictive models: A proof of concept. *Expert Systems With Applications, 39*(1), 621–625. doi:10.1016/j.eswa.2011.07.052.

Gauvain, M., Beebe, H., & Zhao, S. (2011). Applying the cultural approach to cognitive development. *Journal of Cognition and Development, 12,* 121–133.

Gauvreau, P., & Bouchard, S. (2008). Preliminary evidence for the efficacy of EMDR in treating generalized anxiety disorder. *Journal of EMDR Practice and Research, 2*(1), 26–40.

Gazzaley, A., Cooney, J. W., Rissman, J., & D'Esposito, M. (2005). Top-down suppression deficit underlies working memory impairment in normal aging. *Nature Neuroscience 8,* 1298–1300.

Gazzaniga, M. S., & LeDoux, J. E. (1978). *The integrated mind.* New York: Plenum.

Geangu, E., Benga, O., Stahl, D., & Striano, T. (2010). Contagious crying beyond the first days of life. *Infant Behavior & Development, 33*(3), 279–288. doi:10.1016/j.infbeh.2010.03.004.

Geary, D. C. (2010). *Male, female: The evolution of human sex differences* (2nd ed.). Washington, DC: American Psychological Association.

Geary, D. C. (2000). Evolution and proximate expression of human paternal investment. *Psychological Bulletin, 126,* 55–77.

Gebauer, J., Leary, M., & Neberich, W. (2011). Unfortunate first names: Effects of name-based relational devaluation and interpersonal neglect. *Social Psychological and Personality Science.* doi:http://dx.doi.org/10.1177/1948550611431644.

Geddes, J. R., Burgess, S., Hawton, K., Jamison, K., & Goodwin, G. M. (2004). Long-term lithium therapy for bipolar disorder: Systematic review and meta-analysis of randomized controlled trials. *American Journal of Psychiatry, 161,* 217–222.

Geddes, L. (2008, June 7). Are autistic savants made not born? *New Scientist, 198*(2659), 10.

Gegenfurtner, K. R., & Kiper, D. C. (2003). Color vision. *Annual Review of Neuroscience, 26,* 181–206.

Geleijnse, J. M. (2008). Habitual coffee consumption and blood pressure: An epidemiological perspective. *Vascular Health Risk Management, 4,* 963–970.

Geldmacher, D. S., Provenzano, G., McRae, T., Mastey, V., & Ieni, J. R. (2003). Donepezil is associated with delayed nursing home placement in patients with Alzheimer's disease. *Journal of the American Geriatric Society, 51,* 937–944.

Gelhorn, H. L., Stallings, M. C., Young, S. E., Corley, R. P., Rhee, S. H., & Hewitt, J. K. (2005). Genetic and environmental influences on conduct disorder: symptom, domain and full-scale analyses. *Journal of Child Psychology and Psychiatry, 46,* 580–591.

Gellhorn, E., & Loofbourrow, G. N. (1963). *Emotions and emotional disorders.* New York: Harper & Row.

Gelman, R., & Baillargeon, R. (1983). A review of some Piagetian concepts. In P. H. Mussen (Ed.), *Handbook of child psychology* (Vol. 3, pp. 167–230). New York: Wiley.

Gelstein, S., Yeshurun, Y., Rozenkrantz, L., Shushan, S., Frumin, I., Roth, Y., and Sobel, N. (2011). Human tears contain a chemosignal. *Science, 331*(6014), 226–230.

Gendle, M. H., White, T. L., Strawderman, M., Mactutus, C. F., Booze, R. M., Levitsky, D. A., & Strupp, B. J. (2004). Enduring effects of prenatal cocaine exposure on selective attention and reactivity to errors: Evidence from an animal model. *Behavioral Neuroscience, 118,* 290–297.

Gentilucci, M., & Dalla Volta, R. (2008). Spoken language and arm gestures are controlled by the same motor control system. *Quarterly Journal of Experimental Psychology, 61*(6), 944–957.

Gentry, K. R., McGinn, K. L., Kundu, A., & Lynn, A. M. (2011). Acupuncture therapy for infants: a preliminary report on reasons for consultation, feasibility, and tolerability. *Paediatric Anaesthesia.* Epub December 6, 2011.

George, M. S., Lisanby, S. H., Avery, D., McDonald, W. M., et al. (2010). Daily left prefrontal transcranial magnetic stimulation therapy for major depressive disorder: A shamcontrolled randomized trial. *Archives of General Psychiatry, 67,* 507–516.

George, M. S., Anton, R. F., Bloomer, C., Teneback, C., Drobes, D. J., Lorberbaum, J. P., et al. (2001). Activation of prefrontal cortex and anterior thalamus in alcoholic subjects on exposure to alcohol-specific cues. *Archives of General Psychiatry, 58,* 345–352.

George, W. H., & Marlatt, G. A. (1986). The effects of alcohol and anger on interest in violence, erotica, and deviance. *Journal of Abnormal Psychology, 95,* 150–158.

Geraerts, E., Bernstein, D. M., Merckelbach, H., Linders, C., Raymaekers, L., & Loftus, E. F. (2008a). Lasting false beliefs and their behavioral consequences. *Psychological Science, 19,* 749–753.

Geraerts, E., Lindsay, D. S., Merckelbach, H., Jelicic, M., Raymaekers, L., Arnold, M. M., & Schooler, J. W. (2008b). Cognitive mechanisms underlying recovered-memory experiences of childhood sexual abuse. *Psychological Science, 20,* 92–98.

Geraerts, E., Schooler, J. W., Merckelbach, H., Jelicic, M., Hauer, B. J. A., & Ambadar, Z. (2007). The reality of recovered memories: Corroborating continuous and discontinuous memories of childhood sexual abuse, *Psychological Science, 18,* 564–568.

Geraerts, E., Smeets, E., Jelicic, M., Merckelbach, H., & van Heerden, J. (2006). Retrieval inhibition of trauma-related words in women reporting repressed or recovered memories of childhood sexual abuse. *Behaviour Research and Therapy, 44,* 1129–1136.

Gerbner, G., Morgan, M., & Signorielli, N. (1994). *Television violence profile no. 16: The turning point.* Philadelphia: Annenberg School for Communication.

Gerhart, B. (2005). The (affective) dispositional approach to job satisfaction: Sorting out the policy implications. *Journal of Organizational Behavior, 26,* 79–97.

Gerin, W., Davidson, K. W., Christenfeld, N. J. S., Goyal, T., & Schwartz, J. E. (2006). The role of angry rumination and distraction in blood pressure recovery from emotional arousal. *Psychosomatic Medicine, 68,* 64–72.

Gerken, L. (1994). Child phonology: Past research, present questions, future directions. In M. A. Gernsbacher (Ed), *Handbook of psycholinguistics* (pp. 781–820). San Diego, CA: Academic Press.

German, T. P., & Barrett, H. C. (2005). Functional fixedness in a technologically sparse culture. *Psychological Science, 16*(1), 1–5.

Gerschman, J. A., Reade, P. C., & Burrows, G. D. (1980). Hypnosis and dentistry. In G. D. Burrows & L. Dennerstein (Eds.), *Handbook of hypnosis and psychosomatic medicine.* New York: Elsevier.

Gershoff, E. T., Grogan-Kaylor, A., Lansford, J. E., Chang, L., Zelli, A., Deater-Deckard, K., & Dodge, K. A. (2010). Parent discipline practices in an international sample: Associations with child behaviors and moderation by perceived normativeness. *Child Development, 81,* 487–502.

Gershoff, E. T., & Bitensky, S. H. (2007). The case against corporal punishment of children: Converging evidence from social science research and international human rights law and implications for U.S. public policy. *Psychology, Public Policy, and Law, 13,* 231–272.

Gerstner, C. R., & Day, D. V. (1997). Meta-analytic review of leader–member exchange theory: Correlates and construct issues. *Journal of Applied Psychology, 82,* 827–844.

Gerstorf, D., Ram, N., Hoppmann, C., Willis, S. L., & Schaie, K. (2011). Cohort differences in cognitive aging and terminal decline in the Seattle Longitudinal Study. *Developmental Psychology, 47*(4), 1026–1041. doi:10.1037/a0023426.

Gervais, W. M., & Norenzayan, A. (2012). Reminders of secular authority reduce believers' distrust of atheists. *Psychological Science, 23,* 483–491. doi:10.1177/0956797611429711.

Geschwind, N. (1968). Disconnexion syndromes in animals and man. *Brain, 88,* 237–294.

Gessner, B. D., Ives, G. C., & Perham-Hester, K. A. (2001). Association between sudden infant death syndrome and prone sleep position, bed sharing, and sleeping outside an infant crib in Alaska. *Pediatrics, 108,* 923–927.

Getzfeld, A. R. (2006). *Essentials of abnormal psychology.* New York: Wiley.

Geyer, M. A. (2010). New opportunities in the treatment of cognitive impairments associated with schizophrenia. *Current Directions in Psychological Science, 19*(4), 264–269. doi:10.1177/0963721410378359.

Ghacibeh, G A. & Heilman, K. M. (2003). Progressive affective aprosodia and prosoplegia. *Neurology, 60*(7), 1192–1194.

Ghaemi, S. N. (2008). *Mood disorders* (2nd ed.). Philadelphia: Wolters Kluwer Health/Lippincott, Williams & Wilkins.

Gianaros, P. J., May, J. C., Siegle, G. J., & Jennings, J. R. (2005). Is there a functional neural correlate of individual differences in cardiovascular reactivity? *Psychosomatic Medicine, 67,* 31–39.

Giancola, P. R., Josephs, R. A., Parrott, D. J., & Duke, A. A. (2010). Alcohol myopia revisited: Clarifying aggression and other acts of disinhibition through a distorted lens. *Perspectives on Psychological Science, 5,* 265–278.

Giancola, P. R., & Corman, M. D. (2007). Alcohol and aggression: A test of the attention-allocation model. *Psychological Science, 18,* 649–655.

Gibbons, R. D., Hur, K., Bhaumik, D. K., & Mann, J. J. (2005). The relationship between antidepressant use and rate of suicide. *Archives of General Psychiatry, 62,* 165–172.

Gibbons, R. D., Hur, K., Brown, C. H., Davis, J. M., & Mann, J. J. (2012). Benefits from antidepressants: Synthesis of 6-week patient-level outcomes from double-blind placebo-controlled randomized trials of fluoxetine and venlafaxine. *Arch Gen Psychiatry. 69,* 572–579. doi:10.1001/archgenpsychiatry.2011.2044

Gibbs, J. C., Basinger, K. S., Grime, R. L., & Snarey, J. R. (2007). Moral judgment development across cultures: Revisiting Kohlberg's universality claims. *Developmental Review, 27,* 443–500.

Gibson, C. B., & McDaniel, D. M. (2010). Moving beyond conventional wisdom: Advancements in cross-cultural theories of leadership, conflict, and teams. *Perspectives on Psychological Science, 5*(4) 450–462. doi:10.1177/1745691610375560.

Gibson, E. J., & Walk, R. D. (1960). The visual cliff. *Scientific American, 202,* 64–71.

Gifford, R. (2011). The dragons of inaction: Psychological barriers that limit climate change mitigation and adaptation. *American Psychologist, 66*(4), 290–302. doi:10.1037/a0023566.

Gigerenzer, G. (2004). Dread risk, September 11, and fatal traffic accidents. *Psychological Science, 15,* 286–287.

Gilbert, D. T. (2006). *Stumbling on happiness.* New York: Knopf.

Gilbert, D. T., & Wilson, T. D. (1998). Miswanting: Some problems in the forecasting of future affective states. In J. P. Forgas (Ed.), *Feeling and thinking: The role of affect in social cognition* (pp. 178–197). New York: Cambridge University Press.

Gilbert, J., Gasteyger, C., Raben, A., Meier, D., Astrup, A., & Sjödin, A. (2012). The effect of tesofensine on appetite sensations. *Obesity (Silver Spring, Md.), 20*(3), 553–561. doi:10.1038/oby.2011.197.

Gilbert, R., Salanti, G., Harden, M., & See, S. (2005). Infant sleeping position and the sudden infant death syndrome: A systematic review of observational studies and historical review of recommendations from 1940 to 2002. *International Journal of Epidemiology, 34,* 874–887.

Gilchrist, J., Thomas, K. E., Xu, L., McGuire, L. C., & Coronado, V. (2011). Nonfatal traumatic brain injuries related to sports and recreation activities among persons aged 19 years—United States, 2001–2009. *JAMA: Journal Of The American Medical Association, 306*(21), 2318–2320.

Giles, L. C., Glonek, G. F., Luszcz, M. A., & Andrews, G. R. (2005). Effect of social networks on 10-year survival in very old Australians: The Australian Longitudinal Study of Aging. *Journal of Epidemiology and Community Health, 59,* 574–579.

Gilboa-Schechtman, E., & Foa, E. B. (2001). Patterns of recovery from trauma: The use of intraindividual analysis. *Journal of Abnormal Psychology, 110,* 392–400.

Gilchrist & Cowan, N. (2012). Chunking. In: V.S. Ramachandran (Ed.) *Encyclopedia of Human Behavior,* 2nd Ed, vol. 1, pp 476-483. San Diego: Academic Press.

Gilden, D. L., & Marusich, L. R. (2009). Contraction of time in attention-deficit hyperactivity disorder. *Neruopsychology, 23,* 265–269.

Giles, L., Davies, M., Whitrow, M., Warin, M., & Moore, V. (2011). Maternal depressive symptoms and child care during toddlerhood relate to child behavior at age 5 years. *Pediatrics, 128,* e78–e84.

Gilissen, R., Bakermans-Kranenburg, M. J., van IJzendoorn, M. H., & van der Veer, R. (2008). Parent-child relationship, temperament, and physiological reactions to fear-inducing film clips: Further evidence for differential susceptibility. *Journal of Experimental Child Psychology, 99,* 182–195.

Gillath, O., Bahns, A. J., Ge, F., & Crandall, C. S. (2012). Shoes as a source of first impressions. *Journal of Research in Personality, 46,* 423–430. doi:10.1016/j.jrp.2012.04.003.

Gillespie-Lynch, K., Greenfield, P. M., Lyn, H., & Savage-Rumbaugh, S. (2011). The role of dialogue in the ontogeny and phylogeny of early symbol combinations: A cross-species comparison of bonobo, chimpanzee, and human learners. *First Language, 31*(4), 442–460. doi:10.1177/0142723711406882.

Gillham, J. E., Reivich, K. J., Freres, D. R., Chaplin, T. M., Shatté, A. J., Samuels, B., et al. (2007). School-based prevention of depressive symptoms: A randomized controlled study of the effectiveness and specificity of the Penn Resiliency Program. *Journal of Consulting and Clinical Psychology, 75,* 9–19.

Gilligan, C. (1982). *In a different voice: Psychological theory and women's development.* Cambridge, MA: Harvard University Press.

Gilligan, C. (1993). Adolescent development reconsidered. In A. Garrod (Ed.), *Approaches to moral development: New research and emerging themes.* New York: Teachers College Press.

Gilmore, G. C., Spinks, R. A., & Thomas, C. W. (2006). Age effects in coding tasks: Componential analysis and test of the sensory deficit hypothesis. *Psychology and Aging, 21,* 7–18.

Gilmore, J. H. (2010). Understanding what causes schizophrenia: A developmental perspective. *American Journal of Psychiatry, 167,* 8–10.

Gilmore, R. L., Heilman, K. M., Schmidt, R. P., Fennell, E. M., & Quisling, R. (1992). Anosognosia during Wada testing. *Neurology, 42*(4), 925–927.

Giltay, E. J., Geleijnse, J. M., Zitman, F. G., Hoekstra, T., & Schouten, E. G. (2004). Dispositional optimism and all-cause and cardiovascular mortality in a prospective cohort of elderly Dutch men and women. *Archives of General Psychiatry, 61,* 1126–1135.

Giltay, E. J., Kamphuis, M. H., Kalmijn, S., Zitman, F. G., & Kromhout, D. (2006). Dispositional optimism and the risk of cardiovascular death: The Zutphen elderly study. *Archives of Internal Medicine, 166,* 431–436.

Ginges, J., Atran, S., Medin, D., & Shikaki, K. (2007). Sacred bounds on rational resolution of violent political conflict. *Proceeedings of the National Academy of Sciences, 104,* 7357–7360.

Gingras, J. L., Mitchell, E. A., & Grattan, K. E. (2005). Fetal homologue of infant crying. *Archives of Disease in Childhood: Fetal and Neonatal Edition, 90,* F415–F418.

Gino, F., Ayal, S., & Ariely, D. (2009). Contagion and diff erentiation in unethical behavior: Theeffect of one bad apple on the barrel. *Psychological Science, 20,* 393–398.

Gino, F., Norton, M. I., & Ariely, D. (2010). The counterfeit self: The deceptive costs of faking it. *Psychological Science, 21*(5), 712–720. doi:10.1177/0956797610366545.

Ginsburg, K. R., Durbin, D. R., Garcia-Espana, J. F., Kalicka, E. A., & Winston, F. K. (2009). Associations between parenting styles and teen driving, safety-related behaviors, and attitudes. *Pediatrics, 124,* 1040–1051.

Ginsberg, D. L. (2006). Fatal agranulocytosis four years after clozapine discontinuation. *Primary Psychiatry, 13,* 32–33.

Ginzburg, D. M., Bohn, C., Stangier, U., & Steil, R. (2011). Kognitive therapie der paruresis. *Verhaltenstherapie, 21*(2), 125–131. doi:10.1159/000329001.

Ginzel, K. H., Maritz, G. S., Neuberger, M., Pauly, J. R., Polito, J. R., Schulte-Hermann, R., Slotkin, T. A., & Marks, D. F. (2007). Nicotine for the fetus, the infant and the adolescent? *Journal of Health Psychology, 12*(2), 215–224.

Giorgi-Guarnieri, D., Janofsky, J., Keram, E., Lawsky, S., Merideth, P., Mossman, D., et al. (2002). AAPL practice guideline for forensic psychiatric evaluation of defendants raising the insanity defense. *Journal of the American Academy of Psychiatry and the Law, 30*(Suppl. 2), S1–S40.

Giosan, C., Glovsky, V., & Haslam, N. (2001). The lay conception of "mental disorder": A cross-cultural study. *Transcultural Psychiatry, 38,* 317–332.

Gladwell, M. (2008). *Outliers: The story of success.* New York: Little Brown.

Gladwell, M. (2005). *Blink: The power of thinking without thinking.* New York: Little, Brown.

Gladwell, M. (2004, January 12). Big and bad. *New Yorker,* 28–33.

Glantz, K., Rizzo, A., & Graap, K. (2003). Virtual reality for psychotherapy: Current reality and future possibilities. *Psychotherapy: Theory, Research, Practice, and Training, 40,* 55–67.

Glanzer, M., & Cunitz, A. (1966). Two storage mechanisms in free recall. *Journal of Verbal Learning and Verbal Behavior, 5,* 351–360.

Glaser, C., Trommershäuser, J., Mamassian, P., & Maloney, L. T. (2012). Comparison of the distortion of probability information in decision under risk and an equivalent visual task. *Psychological Science, 23*(4), 419–426. doi:10.1177/0956797611429798.

Glasman, L. R., & Albarracín, D. (2006). Forming attitudes that predict future behavior: A meta-analysis of the attitude-behavior relation. *Psychological Bulletin, 132,* 778–822.

Glassop, L. I. (2002). The organizational benefits of teams. *Human Relations, 55,* 225–249.

Glăveanu, V. (2012). Habitual creativity: Revising habit, reconceptualizing creativity. *Review of General Psychology, 16*(1), 78-92. doi:10.1037/a0026611.

Glazer, M., Baer, R. D., Weller, S., de Alba, J. E. G., & Liebowitz, S. W. (2004). Susto and soul loss in Mexicans and Mexican Americans. *Cross-Cultural Research: The Journal of Comparative Social Science, 38,* 270–288.

Gleason, M. E. J., Iida, M., Shrout, P. E., & Bolger, N. (2008). Receiving support as a mixed blessing: Evidence for dual effects of support on psychological outcomes. *Journal of Personality and Social Psychology, 94,* 824–838.

Gleaves, D. H., May, M. C., & Cardena, E. (2001). An examination of the diagnostic validity of dissociative identity disorder. *Clinical Psychology Review, 21,* 577–608.

Gleibs, I. H., Haslam, C., Jones, J. M., Alexander Haslam, S. S., McNeill, J., & Connolly, H. (2011). No country for old men? The role of a 'Gentlemen's Club' in promoting social engagement and psychological well-being in residential care. *Aging & Mental Health, 15*(4), 456–466. doi:10.1080/13607863.2010.536137.

Gleitman, L., & Landau, B. (1994). *The acquisition of the lexicon.* Cambridge: MIT Press.

Glenn, A. L., Raine, A., Venables, P. H., & Mednick, S. A. (2007). Early temperamental and psychophysiological precursors of adult psychopathic personality. *Journal of Abnormal Psychology, 116*(3), 508–518.

Glenberg, A. M. (2011). Introduction to the Mirror Neuron Forum. *Perspectives on Psychological Science, 6*(4), 363–368. doi:10.1177/1745691611412386.

Glover, J. A., Krug, D., Dietzer, M., George, B. W., & Hannon, M. (1990). "Advance" advance organizers. *Bulletin of the Psychonomic Society, 28,* 4–6.

Glummarra, M. J., Gibson, S. J., Georgiou-Karistianis, N., & Bradshaw, J. L. (2007). Central mechanisms in phantom limb perception: The past, present and future. *Brain Research Reviews, 54*(1), 219–232.

Glynn, L. M., Davis, E. P., Schetter, C. D., Chicz-DeMet, A., Hobel, C. J., & Sandman, C. A. (2007). Postnatal maternal cortisol levels predict temperament in healthy breastfed infants. *Early Human Development, 83,* 675–681.

Goenjian, A. K., Molina, L., Steinberg, A. M., Fairbanks, L. A., Alvarez, M. L., Goenjian, H. A., & Pynoos, R. S. (2001). Posttraumatic stress and depressive reactions among Nicaraguan adolescents after hurricane Mitch. *American Journal of Psychiatry, 158,* 788–794.

Gofton, T. E. (2011). Delirium: a review. *Canadian Journal of Neurological Sciences, 38*(5), 673–680.

Gogate, L. J., & Hollich, G. (2010). Invariance detection within an interactive system: A perceptual gateway to language development. *Psychological Review, 117*(2), 496–516. doi:10.1037/a0019049.

Gogtay, N., Giedd, J. N., Lusk, L., Hayashi, K. M., Greenstein, D., Vaituzis, A. C., Nugent, T. F., III, Herman, D. H., Clasen, L. S., Toga, A. W., Rapoport, J. L., & Thompson, P. M. (2004). Dynamic mapping of human cortical development during childhood through early adulthood. *Proceedings of the National Academy of Sciences, 101,* 8174–8179.

Goh, W. D., & Lu, S. X. (2012). Testing the myth of the encoding–retrieval match. *Memory & Cognition, 40*(1), 28–39. doi:10.3758/s13421-011-0133-9.

Gold, M. S. (1994). The epidemiology, attitudes, and pharmacology of LSD use in the 1990s. *Psychiatric Annals, 24*(3), 124–126.

Goldberg, A. E. (2010). *Lesbian and gay parents and their children: Research on the family life cycle.* Washington, DC: American Psychological Association Press.

Goldberg, J. F., & Burdick, K. E. (Eds.) (2008). *Cognitive dysfunction in bipolar disorder.* Washington, DC: American Psychiatric Association Publishing.

Goldberg, J. F., & Garno, J. L. (2005). Development of posttraumatic stress disorder in adult bipolar patients with histories of severe childhood abuse. *Journal of Psychiatric Research, 39,* 595–601.

Goldberg, J. F., Harrow, M., & Grossman, L. S. (1995). Course and outcome in bipolar affective disorder: A longitudinal follow-up study. *American Journal of Psychiatry, 152,* 379–384.

Goldberg, T. E. & Weinberger, D. R. (2009). *The genetics of cognitive neuroscience.* Cambridge, MA: MIT Press.

Goldblum, N. (2001). *The brain-shaped mind: A neural-network view: What the brain can tell us about the mind.* Cambridge: Cambridge University Press.

Goldenberg, G. (2009). Apraxia and the parietal lobes. *Neuropsychologia, 47*(6), 1449–1459.

Goldfried, M. R., & Davila, J. (2005). The role of relationship and technique in therapeutic change. *Psychotherapy: Theory, Research, Practice, Training, 42,* 421–430.

Goldfriend, M. R., Glass, C. R., & Arnkoff, D. B. (2011). Integrative approaches to psychotherapy. In J. C. Norcross, G. R. VandenBos, & D. K. Freedheim (Eds.), *History of psychotherapy: Continuity and change* (pp. 269–296). Washington, D.C.: American Psychological Association.

Goldin-Meadow, S., & Beilock, S. L. (2010). Action's influence on thought: The case of gesture. *Perspectives on Psychological Science, 5*(6), 664–674. doi:10.1177/1745691610388764.

Goldinger, S. D., & Papesh, M. H. (2012). Pupil dilation reflects the creation and retrieval of memories. *Current Directions in Psychological Science, 21*(2) 90–95. doi:10.1177/0963721412436811.

Goldman, M. S., Darkes, J., & Del Boca, F. K. (1999). Expectancy meditation of biopsychosocial risk for alcohol use and alcoholism. In I. Kirsch (Ed.), *How expectancies shape experience* (pp. 233–262). Washington, DC: American Psychological Association.

Goldstein, J. M., Jerram, M., Abbs, B., Whitfield-Gabrieli, S., & Makris, N. (2010). Sex diff erences in stress response circuitry activation dependent on female hormonal cycle. *Journal of Neuroscience, 30,* 431–438.

Goldstein, M., Peters, L., Baillie, A., McVeagh, P., Minshall, G., & Fitzjames, D. (2011). The effectiveness of a day program for the treatment of adolescent anorexia nervosa. *International Journal of Eating Disorders, 44*(1), 29–38. doi:10.1002/eat.20789.

Goldstein, A. J., de Beurs, E., Chambless, D. L., & Wilson, K. A. (2000). EMDR for panic disorder with agoraphobia: Comparison with waiting list and credible attention-placebo control conditions. *Journal of Consulting and Clinical Psychology, 68*(6), 947–956.

Goldstein, E. B. (2002). *Sensation and perception* (6th ed.). Pacific Grove CA: Wadsworth.

Goldstein, I., & Rosen, R. C. (Eds.). (2002). Guest editors' introduction: Female sexuality and sexual dysfunction. *Archives of Sexual Behavior, 31,* 391.

Goldstein, I. L. (1993). *Training in organizations: Needs assessment, development, and evaluation* (3rd ed.). Monterey, CA: Brooks/Cole.

Goldstein, K. (1939). *The organism.* New York: American Book.

Goldstein, M. H., King, A. P., & West, M. J. (2003). Social interaction shapes babbling: Testing parallels between birdsong and speech. *Proceedings of the National Academy of Sciences, 100,* 8030–8035.

Goldstein, M. H., Schwade, J., Briesch, J., & Syal, S. (2010). Learning while babbling: Prelinguistic object-directed vocalizations indicate a readiness to learn. *Infancy, 15*(4), 362–391. doi:10.1111/j.1532-7078.2009.00020.x.

Goldstein, M. H., & Schwade, J. A. (2008). Social feedback to infants' babbling facilitates rapid phonological learning. *Psychological Science, 19,* 515–523.

Goldstein, S. E., Davis-Kean, P. E., & Eccles, J. S. (2005). Parents, peers, and problem behavior: A longitudinal investigation of the impact of relationship perceptions and characteristics on the development of adolescent problem behavior. *Developmental Psychology, 41,* 401–413.

Goltz, H. C., DeSouza, J. F. X., Menon, R. S., Tweed, D. B., & Vilis, T. (2003). Interaction of retinal image and eye velocity in motion perception. *Neuron, 39,* 569–576.

Gomez, R. L., Bootzin, R. R., & Nadel, L. (2006). Naps promote abstraction in language-learning infants. *Psychological Science, 17,* 670–674.

Goncalves Portelinha, I., Verlhiac, J., Meyer, T., & Hutchison, P. (2012). Terror management and biculturalism: When the salience of cultural duality affects worldview defense in the face of death. *European Psychologist, 17,* 237–245. doi:10.1027/1016-9040/a000111.

Gone, J. (2004). Mental health services for Native Americans in the 21st century United States. *Professional Psychology: Theory and Practice, 35,* 10–18.

Gonsalves, B., & Paller, K. A. (2000). Neural events that underlie remembering something that never happened. *Nature Neuroscience, 3,* 1316–1321.

Gonsalves, B. D., Kahn, I., Curran, T., Norman, K. A., & Wagner, A. D. (2005). Memory strength and repetition suppression: Multimodal imaging of medial temporal cortical contributions to recognition. *Neuron, 47,* 751–761.

Gonzalez, H. M., Vega, W. A., Williams, D. R., Tarraf, W., et al. (2010). Depression care in the United States: Too little for too few. *Archives of General Psychiatry, 67,* 37–46.

Gonzalez, J. S., Penedo, F. J., Antoni, M. H., Duran, R. E., McPherson-Baker, S., Ironson, G., et al. (2004). Social support, positive states of mind, and HIV treatment adherence in men and women living with HIV/AIDS. *Health Psychology, 23,* 413–418.

Good, C., Rattan, A., & Dweck, C. S. (2012). Why do women opt out? Sense of belonging and women's representation in mathematics. *Journal of Personality and Social Psychology, 102*(4), 700–717. doi:10.1037/a0026659.

Goodall, J. (1964). Tool-using and aimed throwing in a community of free-living chimpanzees. *Nature, 201,* 1264-1266.

Goodenough, F. L. (1932). Expression of the emotions in a blind-deaf child. *Journal of Abnormal and Social Psychology, 27,* 328–333.

Goodglass, H., & Kaplan, E. (1982). *The assessment of aphasia and related disorders* (2nd ed.). Philadelphia: Lea & Febiger.

Goodman, W. K., Foote, K. D., Greenberg, B. D., Ricciuti, N., et al. (2010). Deep brain stimulation for intractable obsessive compulsive disorder: Pilot study using a blinded, staggered-onset design. *Biological Psychiatry, 67,* 535–542.

Goodman, G. S., Ghetti, S., Quas, J. A., Edelstein, R. S., Alexander, K. W., Redlich, A. D., et al. (2003). A prospective study of memory for child sexual abuse: New findings relevant to the repressed-memory controversy. *Psychological Science, 14,* 113–118.

Goodman, R. D., Miller, M., & West-Olatunji, C. A. (2011). Traumatic stress, socioeconomic status, and academic achievement among primary school students. *Psychological Trauma: Theory, Research, Practice, and Policy,* doi:10.1037/a0024912.

Goodwin, F. K., & Jamison, K. R. (Eds.). (2007). *Manic-depressive illness: Bipolar disorders and recurrent depression* (2nd Edition). New York: Oxford University Press.

Goodyear, D. (2011). GRUB. *New Yorker, 87*(24), 38–46.

Gopie, N., & MacLeod, C. M. (2009). Destination memory: Stop me if I've told you this before. *Psychological Science (Wiley-Blackwell), 20*(12), 1492–1499. doi:10.1111/j.1467-9280.2009.02472.x.

Gordon, D. B., Dahl, J. L., Miaskowski, C., McCarberg, B., Todd, K. H., Paice, J. A., et al. (2005). American Pain Society recommendations for improving the quality of acute and cancer pain management: American Pain Society Quality of Care Task Force. *Archives of Internal Medicine, 165,* 1574–1580.

Gore-Felton, C., & Koopman, C. (2008). Behavioral mediation of the relationship between psychosocial factors and HIV disease progression. *Psychosomatic Medicine 70,* 569–574.

Gorman, J. M. (2003). Treating generalized anxiety disorder. *Journal of Clinical Psychiatry, 64*(Suppl. 2), 24–29.

Gorman, J. M. (2005). Benzodiazepines: Taking the good with the bad and the ugly. *CNS Spectrums, 10,* 14–15.

Gorno-Tempini, M. L., Hillis, A. E., Weintraub, S., Kertesz, A., Mendez, M., Cappa, S. F., Ogar, J. M., Rohrer, J. D., Black, S., Boeve, B. F., Manes, F., Dronkers, N. F, Vandenberghe, R., Rascovsky, K., Patterson, K., Miller, B. L, Knopman, D. S., Hodges, J. R., Mesulam, M. M., & Grossman, M. (2011). Classification of primary progressive aphasia and its variants. *Neurology. 76*(11), 1006–1114.

Gorter, R. W., Butorac, M., Cobian, E. P., & van der Sluis, W. (2005). Medical use of cannabis in the Netherlands. *Neurology, 64,* 917–919.

Goslin, J., Dixon, T., Fischer, M. H., Cangelosi, A., & Ellis, R. (2012). Electrophysiological examination of embodiment in vision and action. *Psychological Science, 23*(2), 152–157. doi:10.1177/0956797611429578.

Gosling, S. D. (2001). From mice to men: What can we learn about personality from animal research? *Psychological Bulletin, 127,* 45–86.

Gosling, S. D., Kwan, V. S. Y., & John, O. P. (2003). A dog's got personality: A cross-species comparative approach to personality judgments in dogs and humans. *Journal of Personality and Social Psychology, 85,* 1161–1169.

Gosling, S. D., Vazire, S., Srivastava, S., & John, O. P. (2004). Should we trust web-based studies? A comparative analysis of six preconceptions about Internet questionnaires. *American Psychologist, 59,* 93–104.

Gosling, S.D. & Jones, A.C. (2012) Dog personality questionnaire. Available at https://survey.psy.utexas.edu/API/dpq4.php.

Goss Lucas, S., & Bernstein, D. A. (2005). *Teaching psychology: A step by step guide.* Mahwah, NJ: Erlbaum.

Gosseries, O., Bruno, M. A., Chatelle, C., Vanhaudenhuyse, A., Schnakers, C., Soddu, A., & Laureys, S. (2011). Disorders of consciousness: what's in a name? *NeuroRehabilitation. 28*(1), 3–14.

Gotlib, I. H., & Hammen, C. L. (1992). *Psychological aspects of depression: Toward cognitive interpersonal integration.* Chichester, England: Wiley.

Goto, S. G., Ando, Y., Huang, C., Yee, A., & Lewis, R. S. (2010). Cultural differences in the visual processing of meaning: Detecting incongruities between background and foreground objects using the N400. *Social Cognitive and Affective Neuroscience, 5*(2–3), 242–253.

Goto, Y., Yang, C. R., & Otani, S. (2010). Functional and dysfunctional synaptic plasticity in prefrontal cortex: Roles in psychiatric disorders. *Biological Psychiatry, 67,* 199–207.

Gottesman, I. I., Laursen, T. M., Bertelsen, A., & Mortensen, P. B. (2010). Severe mental disorders in off spring with 2 psychiatrically ill parents. *Archives of General Psychiatry, 67,* 252–257.

Gottfredson, L. S. (1997a). Mainstream science on intelligence: An editorial with 52 signatories, history, and bibliography. *Intelligence, 24,* 13–23.

Gottfredson, L. S. (1997b). Why g matters: The complexity of everyday life. *Intelligence, 24,* 79–132.

Gottfredson, L. S. (2004). Intelligence: Is it the epidemiologists' elusive "fundamental cause" of social class inequalities in health? *Journal of Personality and Social Psychology, 86,* 174–199.

Gottfredson, L. S., & Deary, I. J. (2004). Intelligence predicts health and longevity, but why? *Current Directions in Psychological Science, 13,* 1–4.

Gottfredson, L. S. (2003). Dissecting practical intelligence theory: Its claims and evidence. *Intelligence, 31,* 343–397.

Gottfried, A. W. (1997, June). Parents' role is critical to children's learning. *APA Monitor, 24.*

Gottman, J. M., Driver, J., & Tabares, A. (2002). Building the sound marital house: An empirically derived couple therapy. In A. S. Gurman & N. S. Jacobson (Eds.), *Clinical handbook of couple therapy* (3rd ed., pp. 373–399). New York: Guilford Press.

Gottman, J. M., Gottman, J. S., & Declaire, J. (2006). *Ten lessons to transform your marriage.* New York: Crown Press.

Gottman, J. M., & Levenson, R. W. (2000). The timing of divorce: Predicting when a couple will divorce over a 14-year period. *Journal of Marriage and the Family, 62,* 737–745.

Gottman, J. M., & Levenson, R. W. (2002). A two-factor model for predicting when a couple will divorce: Exploratory analyses using 14-year longitudinal data. *Family Process, 41,* 83–96.

Gouin, J.-P., Kiecolt-Glaser, J. K., Malarkey, W. B., & Glaser, R. (2008). The influence of anger expression on wound healing. *Brain, Behavior, and Immunity, 22,* 699–708.

Gould, E., Beylin, A., Tanapat, P., Reeves, A., & Schors, T. J. (1999). Learning enhances adult neurogenesis in the hippocampal formation. *Nature Neuroscience, 2,* 260–265.

Governer's Highway Safety Association. (2011, December). *Cell phone and texting laws.* Retrieved from http://www.ghsa.org/html/stateinfo/laws/cellphone_laws.html.

Gow, A. J., Whiteman, M. C., Pattie, A., Whalley, L., Starr, J., & Deary, I. J. (2005). Lifetime intellectual function and satisfaction with life in old age: Longitudinal cohort study. *British Medical Journal, 331,* 141–142.

Gow, M. A. (2010). Dental extractions and immediate implant placements using hypnosis in place of traditional local anaesthetics. *Contemporary Hypnosis, 27(4),* 268–277.

Grabe, H. J., Ruhrmann, S., Ettelt, S., Buhtz, F., Hochrein, A., Schulze-Rauschenbach, S., et al. (2006). Familiality of obsessive-compulsive disorder in nonclinical and clinical subjects. *American Journal of Psychiatry, 163,* 1986–1992.

Grabe, S., Ward, L. M., & Hyde, J. S. (2008). The role of the media in body image concerns among women: A meta-analysis of experimental and correlational studies. *Psychological Bulletin, 134,* 460–476.

Grace, A. A. (2010). Ventral hippocampus, interneurons, and schizophrenia: A new understanding of the pathophysiology of schizophrenia and its implications for treatment and prevention. *Current Directions in Psychological Science, 19(4),* 232–237. doi:10.1177/0963721410378032.

Gräff, J., & Mansuy, I. M. (2008). Epigenetic codes in cognition and behaviour. *Behavioural Brain Research, 192(1),* 70–87.

Graham, K., Osgood, D. W., Wells, S., & Stockwell, T. (2006). To what extent is intoxication associated with aggression in bars? A multilevel analysis. *Journal of Studies on Alcohol, 67,* 382–390.

Grammer, K., Fink, B., & Neave, N. (2005). Human pheromones and sexual attraction. *European Journal of Obstetrics, Gynecology, and Reproductive Biology, 118,* 135–142.

Grand, J. A., Ryan, A., Schmitt, N., & Hmurovic, J. (2011). How far does stereotype threat reach? The potential detriment of face validity in cognitive ability testing. *Human Performance, 24(1),* 1–28. doi:10.1080/08959285.2010.518184.

Grandin, T. (1996). *Thinking in pictures: And other reports from my life with autism.* New York: Vintage Press.

Granhag, P.-A., & Stromwall, L. (2004). *The detection of deception in forensic contexts.* New York: Cambridge University Press.

Granier-Deferre, C., Bassereau, S., Ribeiro, A., Jacquet, A.-Y., & DeCasper, A. J. (2011). A melodic contour repeatedly experienced by human near-term fetuses elicits a profound cardiac reaction one month after birth. *PLoS One, 6,* e17304.

Grant, A. M., & Hofmann, D. A. (2011). It's not all about me : Motivating hand hygiene among health care professionals by focusing on patients. *Psychological Science, 22(12),* 1494–1499. doi:10.1177/0956797611419172.

Grant, B. F., Dawson, D. A., Stinson, F. S., Chou, S. P., Dufour, M. C., & Pickering, R. P. (2004). The 12-month prevalence and trends in DSM-IV alcohol abuse and dependence: United States, 1991–1992 and 2001–2002. *Drug and Alcohol Dependence, 74,* 223–234.

Grant, B. F., Hasin, D. S., Stinson, F. S., Dawson, D. A., Goldstein, R. B., Smith, S., Huang, B., & Saha, T. D. (2006). The epidemiology of DSM-IV panic disorder and agoraphobia in the United States: Results from the National Epidemiology survey on alcohol and related conditions. *Journal of Clinical Psychiatry, 67(3),* 363–374.

Grant, H., & Dweck, C. S. (2003). Clarifying achievement goals and their impact. *Journal of Personality and Social Psychology, 85,* 541–553.

Grant, J. E., & Kim, S. W. (2002). *Stop me because I can't stop myself: Taking control of impulsive behavior.* New York: McGraw-Hill.

Grassi, L., Rasconi, G., Pedriali, A., Corridoni, A., & Bevilacqua, M. (2000). Social support and psychological distress in primary care attenders. *Psychotherapy and Psychosomatics, 69,* 95–100.

Graves, L., Stratton, G., Ridgers, N. D., & Cable, N. T. (2008). Energy expenditure in adolescents playing new generation computer games. *British Journal of Sports Medicine, 42(7),* 592–594.

Gray, J. A., & McNaughton, N. (2000). *The neuropsychology of anxiety: An enquiry into the functions of the septohippocampal system* (2nd ed.). New York: Oxford University Press.

Gray, J. A. (1991). Neural systems, emotions, and personality. In J. Madden, IV (Ed.), *Neurobiology of learning, emotion, and affect* (pp. 272–306). New York: Raven Press.

Gray, L., Cooper, N., Dunkley, A., Warren, F., Ara, R., Abrams, K., & ... Sutton, A. (2012). A systematic review and mixed treatment comparison of pharmacological interventions for the treatment of obesity. *Obesity Reviews: An Official Journal of The International Association For The Study of Obesity, 13(6),* 483–498. doi:10.1111/j.1467-789X.2011.00981.x

Gray, N., & Nye, P. S. (2001). American Indian and Alaska Native substance abuse: Co-morbidity and cultural issues. *American Indian and Alaska Native Mental Health Research, 10,* 67–84.

Gray, N. S., MacCulloch, M. J., Smith, J., Morris, M., & Snowden, R. J. (2003). Forensic psychology: Violence viewed by psychopathic murderers. *Nature, 423,* 497.

Gray, P. (2005). *The ego and analysis of defense.* Northvale, NJ: Aronson.

Gray-Little, B., & Hafdahl, A. R. (2000). Factors influencing racial comparisons of self-esteem: A quantitative review. *Psychological Bulletin, 126,* 26–54.

Graziano, M. S., & Kastner, S. (2011) Human consciousness and its relationship to social neuroscience: A novel hypothesis. *Cogn Neurosci 2(2):*98–113.

Graziano, M. S., Taylor, C. S., & Moore, T. (2002). Complex movements evoked by microstimulation of precentral cortex. *Neuron, 34,* 841–851.

Green, C. S., & Bavelier, D. (2003). Action video game modifies visual selective attention. *Nature, 423,* 534–537.

Green, D. M., & Swets, J. A. (1966). *Signal detection theory and psychophysics.* New York: Wiley.

Green, M. F., & Horan, W. P. (2010). Social cognition in schizophrenia. *Current Directions in Psychological Science, 19(4),* 243–248. doi:10.1177/0963721410377600.

Green, R. A., Cross, A. J., & Goodwin, G. M. (1995). Review of the pharmacology and clinical pharmacology of 3,4-methylenedioxymethamphetamine (MDMA or "ecstasy"). *Psychopharmacology, 119,* 247–260.

Greenberg, J. R., & Mitchell, S. A. (1983). *Object relations in psychoanalytic theory.* Cambridge, MA: Harvard University Press.

Greenberg, J. R., & Mitchell, S. A. (2006). *Object relations in psychoanalytic theory.* Cambridge, MA: Harvard University Press.

Greenberg, J., Solomon, S., & Arndt, J. (2008). A basic but uniquely human motivation: Terror management theory. In J. Shah & W. Gardner (Eds.), *Handbook of motivation science* (pp. 114–134). New York: Guilford Press.

Greenberg, J., Solomon, S., Pyszczynski, T., & Rosenblatt, A. (1992). Why do people need self-esteem? Converging evidence that self-esteem serves an anxiety-buffering function. *Journal of Personality and Social Psychology, 63,* 913–922.

Greenberg, R. M., & Kellner, C. H. (2005). Electroconvulsive therapy: A selected review. *American Journal of Geriatric Psychiatry, 13,* 268–281.

Greenberg, R. P., Constantino, M. J., & Bruce, N. (2006). Are patient expectations still relevant for psychotherapy process and outcome? *Clinical Psychology Review, 26,* 657–678.

Greenfield, P. M. (1994). Video games as cultural artifacts. *Journal of Applied Developmental Psychology, 15,* 3–12.

Greenfield, P. M., & Childs, C. P. (1991). Developmental continuity in biocultural context. In R. Cohen & A. W. Siegel (Eds.), *Context and development* (pp. 135–159). Hillsdale, NJ: Erlbaum.

Greenfield, P. M., Suzuki, L. K., & Rothstein-Fisch, C. (2006). Cultural pathways through human development. In W. Damon & R. M. Lerner (Series Eds.) & K. A. Renninger & I. E. Sigel (Vol. Eds.), *Handbook of child psychology: Vol. 4. Child psychology in practice* (6th ed.). New York: Wiley.

Greenhaus, J. H., Parasuraman, S., & Wormley, W. M. (1990). Effects of race on organizational experiences, job performance evaluations, and career outcomes. *Academy of Management Journal, 33,* 64–86.

Greenland, P., Knoll, M. D., Stamler, J., Neaton, J. D., Dyer, A. R., Garside, D. B., & Wilson, P. W. (2003). Major risk factors as antecedents of fatal and nonfatal coronary heart disease events. *Journal of the American Medical Association, 290,* 891–897.

Greenwald, A. G. (2012). There is nothing so theoretical as a good method. *Perspectives on Psychological Science, 7(2),* 99–108. doi:10.1177/1745691611434210

Greenwald, A. G. (2010). Under what conditions does intergroup contact improve intergroup harmony? In M. Gonzales, C. Tavris, & J. Aronson (Eds.) *The scientist and the humanist: A festschrift in honor of Elliot Aronson* (pp. 269–283). New York, NY, Psychology Press, New York, NY.

Greenwald, A. G., & Banaji, M. R. (1995). Implicit social cognition: Attitudes, self-esteem, and stereotypes. *Psychological Review, 102,* 4–27.

Greenwald, A. G., Klinger, M. R., & Schuh, E. S. (1995). Activation by marginally perceptible ("subliminal") stimuli: Dissociation of unconscious from conscious cognition. *Experimental Psychology: General, 124(1),* 22–42.

Greer, A. E., & Buss, D. M. (1994). Tactics for promoting sexual encounters. *Journal of Sex Research, 31(3),* 185–201.

Gregory, A. M., Light-Häusermann, J., Rijsdijk, F., & Eley, T. C. (2009). Behavioral genetic analyses of prosocial behavior in adolescents. *Developmental Science, 12(1),* 165–174.

Gregory, R. L. (2005). Seeing after blindness. *Nature Neuroscience, 6,* 909–910.

Gregory, S. W., & Webster, S. (1996). A nonverbal signal in voices of interview partners effectively predicts communication accommodation and social status perceptions. *Journal of Personality and Social Psychology, 70,* 1231–1240.

Greitemeyer, T. (2011). Effects of prosocial media on social behavior: When and why does media exposure affect helping and aggression? *Current Directions in Psychological Science, 20*(4), 521–255. doi:10.1177/0963721411415229.

Greitemeyer, T. (2010). Exposure to music with prosocial lyrics reduces aggression: First evidence and test of the underlying mechanism. *Journal Of Experimental Social Psychology,* doi:10.1016/j.jesp.2010.08.005.

Greitemeyer, T., & McLatchie, N. (2011). Denying humanness to others: A newly discovered mechanism by which violent video games increase aggressive behavior. *Psychological Science, 22*(5), 659–665. doi:10.1177/0956797611403320.

Greitemeyer, T., & Osswald, S. (2010). Effects of prosocial video games on prosocial behavior. *Journal of Personality and Social Psychology, 98,* 211–221.

Greitemeyer, T., Osswald, S., & Brauer, M. (2010). Playing prosocial video games increases empathy and decreases shadenfreude. *Emotion, 10*(6), 796–802. doi:10.1037/a0020194.

Gren-Landell, M., Tillfors, M., Furmark, T., Bohlin, G., Andersson, G., & Svedin, C. G. (2009). Social phobia in Swedish adolescents: Prevalence and gender differences. *Social Psychiatry and Psychiatric Epidemiology, 44,* 1–7.

Greven, C. U., Harlaar, N., Kovas, Y., Chamorro-Premuzic, T., & Plomin, R. (2009). More than just IQ: School achievement is predicted by self-perceived abilities—but for genetic rather than environmental reasons. *Psychological Science, 20,* 753–762.

Greven, C. U., Harlaar, N., Kovas, Y., Chamorro-Premuzic, T., & Plomin, R. (2009). More than just IQ: School achievement is predicted by self-perceived abilities—but for genetic rather than environmental reasons. *Psychological Science, 20,* 753–762.

Grieser, J. D., Gao, Y., Ransdell, L., & Simonson, S. (2012). Determining intensity levels of selected Wii Fit activities in college aged individuals. *Measurement in Physical Education & Exercise Science, 16*(2), 135–150. doi:10.1080/109136 7X.2012.665268.

Griesinger, C. B., Richards, C. D., & Ashmore, J. F. (2005). Fast vesicle replenishment allows indefatigable signalling at the first auditory synapse. *Nature, 435,* 212–215.

Griffin, P. W., Mroczek, D. K., & Spiro, A. (2006). Variability in aff ective change among aging men: Longitudinal fi ndings from the VA Normative Aging Study. *Journal of Research in Personality, 40,* 942–965.

Griffin, D. W., & Harris, P. R. (2011). Calibrating the response to health warnings: Limiting both overreaction and underreaction with self-affirmation. *Psychological Science, 22,*(5), 572–578. doi:10.1177/0956797611405678.

Griffeth, R. W., Hom, P. W., & Gaertner, S. (2000). A meta-analysis of antecedents and correlates of employee turnover: Update, moderator tests, and research implications for the next millennium. *Journal of Management, 26,* 463–488.

Griffin, M. A., & Neal, A. (2000). Perceptions of safety at work: A framework for linking safety climate to safety performance, knowledge, and motivation. *Journal of Occupational Health Psychology, 5,* 347–358.

Griffitt, W. B., & Guay, P. (1969) "Object" evaluation and conditioned affect. *Journal of Experimental Research in Personality, 4,* 1–8.

Grigorenko, E. L. (2002). In search of the genetic engram of personality. In D. Cervone & W. Mischel (Eds.), *Advances in personality science* (pp. 29–82). New York: The Guilford Press.

Grilo, C., Shiffman, S., & Wing, R. (1989). Relapse crises and coping among dieters. *Journal of Consulting And Clinical Psychology, 57*(4), 488–495.

Grinspoon, S., Thomas, E., Pitts, S., Gross, E., Mickley, D., Killer, K., et al. (2000). Prevalence and predictive factors for regional osteopenia in women with anorexia nervosa. *Annals of Internal Medicine, 133,* 790–794.

Griskevicius, V., Tybur, J. M., Gangestad, S. W., Perea, E. F., Shapiro, J. R., & Kenrick, D. T. (2009). Aggress to impress: Hostility as an evolved context-dependent strategy. *Journal of Personality and Social Psychology, 96,* 980–994.

Grob, C., & Dobkin de Rios, M. (1992). Adolescent drug use in cross-cultural perspective. *Journal of Drug Issues, 22*(1), 121–138.

Groh, A. M., Roisman, G. I., van IJzendoorn, M. H., Bakermans-Kranenburg, M. J., & Fearon, R. P. (2012). The significance of insecure and disorganized attachment for children's internalizing symptoms: A meta-analytic study. *Child Development, 83,* 591–610.

Grønnerød, C. (2003). Temporal stability in the Rorschach method. *Journal of Personality Assessment, 80,* 272–293.

Groopman, J. (2000, January 24). Second opinion. *The New Yorker,* pp. 40–49.

Groopman, J., (2005, May 2). A model patient. *The New Yorker,* 48–54.

Groopman, J. (2007, January 29). What's the trouble? *The New Yorker,* 36–41.

Grosbras, M. H., Jansen, M., Leonard, G., McIntosh, A., et al. (2007). Neural mechanisms of resistance to peer influence in early adolescence. *Journal of Neuroscience, 27,* 8040–8045.

Grosbras, M. H., Jansen, M., Leonard, G., McIntosh, A., Osswald, K., Poulsen, C., et al. (2007). Neural mechanisms of resistance to peer influence in early adolescence. *Journal of Neuroscience, 27*(30), 8040–8045.

Gross, A. L., & Rebok, G. W. (2011). Memory training and strategy use in older adults: Results from the ACTIVE study. *Psychology and Aging, 26,* 503–517.

Gross, J. J. (2001). Emotion regulation in adulthood: Timing is everything. *Current Directions in Psychological Science, 10,* 214–219.

Grossberg, S., & Seidman, D. (2006). Neural dynamics of autistic behaviors: Cognitive, emotional, and timing substrates. *Psychological Review, 113,* 483–525.

Grossmann, I., Na, J., Varnum, M. E. W., Park, D. C., et al. (2010). Reasoning about social conflicts improves into old age. *Proceedings of the National Academy of Sciences, 107,* 7246–7250.

Grossmann, K., Grossmann, K. E., Kindler, H., & Zimmermann, P. (2008). A wider view of attachment and exploration: The influence of mothers and fathers on the development of psychological security from infancy to young adulthood. In J. Cassidy & P. R. Shaver (Eds.), *Handbook of attachment: Theory, research, and clinical applications* (2nd ed., pp. 857–879). New York: Guilford Press.

Grosz, H. I., & Zimmerman, J. (1970). A second detailed case study of functional blindness: Further demonstration of the contribution of objective psychological data. *Behavior Therapy, 1,* 115–123.

Grubb, P. L., Roberts, R. K., Swanson, N. G., Burnfield, J. L., & Childress, J. H. (2005). Organizational factors and psychological aggression: Results from a nationally representative sample of US companies. In V. Bowie, B. S. Fisher, & C. L. Cooper (Eds.), *Workplace violence: Issues, trends, strategies* (pp. 37–59). Portland, OR: Willan Publishing.

Gruber, R., Laviolette, R., Deluca, P., Monson, E., et al. (2010). Short sleep duration is associated with poor performance on IQ measures in healthy school-age children. *Sleep Medicine, 11,* 289–294. Epub 2010 Feb 13.

Gruber, S. A., Silveri, M. M., & Yurgelun-Todd, D. A. (2007). Neuropsychological consequences of opiate use. *Neuropsychology Review, 17,* 299–315.

Gruber, J., Mauss, I. B., & Tamir, M. (2011). A dark side of happiness? How, when, and why happiness is not always good. *Perspectives On Psychological Science, 6*(3), 222–233. doi:10.1177/1745691611406927.

Grucza, R. A., Bucholz, K. K., Rice, J. P., & Beirut, L. J. (2008). Secular trends in the lifetime prevalence of alcohol dependence in the United States: A re-evaluation. *Alcoholism: Clinical and Experimental Research, 32,* 763–770.

Grusec, J. E., Davidov, M., & Lundell, L. (2002). Prosocial and helping behavior. In P. K. Smith & C. H. Hart (Eds.), *Blackwell handbook of childhood social development* (pp. 457–474). Malden, MA: Blackwell.

Grusec, J. E., & Goodnow, J. J. (1994). Impact of parental discipline methods on the child's internalization of values. *Developmental Psychology, 30,* 4–19.

Guadagno, R. E., Asher, T., Demaine, L. J., & Cialdini, R. B. (2001). When saying yes leads to saying no: Preference for consistency and the reverse foot-in-the-door effect. *Personality and Social Psychology Bulletin, 27,* 859–867.

Gualtieri, C. T., & Johnson, L. G. (2006). Antidepressant side effects in children and adolescents. *Journal of Child and Adolescent Psychopharmacology, 16,* 147–157.

Gudjonsson, G. H. & Pearse, J. (2011). Suspect interviews and false confessions. *Current Directions in Psychological Science, 20*(1), 33–37. doi:10.1177/ 0963721410396824.

Gueguen, N. (2008). The receptivity of women to courtship solicitation across the menstrual cycle: A field experiment. *Biological Psychology, 80*(3), 321–324.

Guéguen, N., & Lamy, L. (2011). The effect of the word "love" on compliance to a request for humanitarian aid: An evaluation in a field setting. *Social Influence, 6*(4), 249–258. doi: http://dx.doi.org/10.1080/15534510.2011.627771.

Guilford, J. P. (1959). Traits of creativity. In H. H. Anderson (Ed.), *Creativity and its cultivation* (pp. 142–161). New York: Harper & Row.

Guilleminault, C., Kirisoglu, C., Bao, G., Arias, V., et al. (2005). Adult chronic sleep-walking and its treatment based on polysomnography. *Brain, 128,* 1062–1069.

Guilleminault, C., Palombini, L., Pelayo, R., & Chervin, R. D. (2003). Sleepwalking and sleep terrors in prepubertal children: What triggers them? *Pediatrics, 111,* 17–25.

Guimon, J. (2004). Evidence-based research studies on the results of group therapy: A critical review. *European Journal of Psychiatry, 18*(Suppl.), 49–60.

Gump, B. B., Reihman, J., Stewart, P., Lonky, E., & Darvill, T. (2005). Terrorism and cardiovascular responses to acute stress in children. *Health Psychology, 24,* 594–600.

Gundersen, H., Specht, K., Gruner, R., Ersland, L., & Hugdahl, K. (2008). Separating the effects of alcohol and expectancy on brain activation: An fMRI working memory study. *Neuroimage, 42,* 1587–1596.

Gupta, A. R., & State, M. W. (2007). Recent advances in the genetics of autism. *Biological Psychiatry, 61,* 429–437.

Gupta, N., Jang, Y., Mednick, S. C., & Huber, D. E. (2012). The road not taken: Creative solutions require avoidance of high-frequency responses. *Psychological Science, 23*(3), 288–294. doi:10.1177/0956797611429710.

Gur, R. C., Skolnic, B. E., & Gur, R. E. (1994). Effects of emotional discrimination tasks on cerebral blood flow: Regional activation and its relation to performance. *Brain and Cognition, 25*(2), 271–286.

Gura, T. (1999). Leptin not impressive in clinical trial. *Science, 286,* 881–882.

Gurman, A. S. (Ed.). (2008). *Clinical handbook of couple therapy* (4th ed.). New York: Guilford.

Gushue, G. V. (2004). Race, color-blind racial attitudes, and judgments about mental health: A shifting standards perspective. *Journal of Counseling Psychology, 51,* 398–407.

Guthrie, R. M., & Bryant, R. A. (2005). Auditory startle response in firefighters before and after trauma exposure. *American Journal of Psychiatry, 162,* 283–290.

Guyton, A. C. (1991). *Textbook of medical physiology* (8th ed.). Philadelphia: Saunders.

Haake, M., Müller, H.-H., Schade-Brittinger, C., Basler, H. D., Schäfer, H., Maier, C., Endres, H. G., Trampisch, H. J., & Molsberger, A. (2007). German acupuncture trials (GERAC) for chronic low back pain: Randomized, multicenter, blinded, parallel-group trial with 3 groups. *Archives of Internal Medicine, 167,* 1892–1898.

Haas, J. S., Zavala, B., & Landisman, C. E. (2011) Activity-dependent long-term depression of electrical synapses. *Science 334* (6054):389–393.

Haber, R. N. (1979). Twenty years of haunting eidetic imagery: Where's the ghost? *The Behavioral and Brain Sciences, 2,* 583–629.

Haber, S. N., & Knutson, B. (2010). The reward circuit: Linking primate anatomy and human imaging. *Neuropsychopharmacology, 35,* 4–26.

Haberlandt, K. (1999). *Human memory: Exploration and application*. Boston: Allyn & Bacon.

Haberstroh, J. (1995). *Ice cube sex: The truth about subliminal advertising*. South Bend, IN: Cross Cultural Publications/Crossroads.

Hacking, I. (1995). *Rewriting the soul: Multiple personality and the sciences of memory*. Princeton, NJ: Princeton University Press.

Hackman, J. R. (1998). Why don't teams work? In R. S. Tindale, J. Edwards, & E. J. Posavac (Eds.), *Applications of theory and research on groups to social issues*. New York: Plenum.

Hackman, R., & Katz, N. (2010). In S. T. Fiske, D. T. Gilbert, & G. Lindzey (Eds.), *Handbook of social psychology* (5th ed., Vol. 2, pp. 1208–1252). Hoboken, NJ: Wiley.

Hackman, J. R., & Oldham, G. R. (1980). *Work redesign*. Reading, MA: Addison-Wesley.

Haddad, S. K., Reiss, D., Spotts, E. L., Ganiban, J., Lichtenstein, P., & Neiderhiser, J. M. (2008). Depression and internally directed aggression: Genetic and environmental contributions. *Journal of the American Psychoanalytic Association, 56*(2), 515–550.

Hadjikhani, N., & de Gelder, B. (2003). Seeing fearful body expressions activates the fusiform cortex and amygdale. *Current Biology, 13*, 2201–2205.

Haegler, K., Zernecke, R., Kleemann, A. .M., Albrecht, J., Pollatos, O., Brückmann, H., and Wiesmann, M. (2010). No fear no risk! Human risk behavior is affected by chemosensory anxiety signals. *Neuropsychologia, 48*(13), 3901–3908.

Hagen, E. P. (1980). *Identification of the gifted*. New York: Teachers College Press.

Hagenaars, M. A., Brewin, C. R., van Minnen, A., Holmen, E. A., & Hoogduin, K. A. L. (2010). Intrusive images and intrusive thoughts as different phenomena: Two experimental studies. *Memory, 18* (1), 76–84. doi:10.1080/09658210903476522.

Hagger-Johnson, G., Mõttus, R., Craig, L. A., Starr, J. M., & Deary, I. J. (2012). Pathways from childhood intelligence and socio-economic status to late-life cardiovascular disease risk. *Health Psychology*, doi:10.1037/a0026775.

Hahn, C.-S., & DiPietro, J. A. (2001). In vitro fertilization and the family: Quality of parenting, family functioning, and child psychosocial adjustment. *Developmental Psychology, 37*, 37–48.

Hake, R. R. (1998). Interactive-engagement vs. traditional methods: A six-thousand-student survey of mechanics test data for introductory physics courses. *American Journal of Physics, 66*, 64–74.

Hakuta, K., Bialystok, E., & Wiley, E. (2003). Critical evidence: A test of the critical-period hypothesis for second language acquisition. *Psychological Science, 14*, 31–38.

Halberstadt AL, & Geyer MA. (2011). Multiple receptors contribute to the behavioral effects of indoleamine hallucinogens. *Neuropharmacology, 61*(3), 364–381.

Halford, G. S., Baker, R., McCredden, J. E., & Bain, J. D. (2005). How many variables can humans process? *Psychological Science, 16*(1), 70–76.

Hall, C. B., Lipton, R. B., Sliwinski, M., Katz, M. J., et al. (2009). Cognitive activities delay onset of memory decline in persons who develop dementia. *Neurology, 73*, 356–361.

Hall, C., Smith, K., & Chia, R. (2008). Cognitive and personality factors in relation to timely completion of a college degree. *College Student Journal, 42*, 1087–1098.

Hall, C. S., Lindzey, G., & Campbell, J. P. (1998). *Theories of personality* (4th ed.). New York: Wiley.

Hall, L. K., & Bahrick, H. P. (1998). The validity of metacognitive predictions of widespread learning and long-term retention. In G. Mazzoni & T. Nelson (Eds.), *Metacognition and cognitive neuropsychology: Monitoring and control processes* (pp. 23–36). Mahwah, NJ: Erlbaum.

Hall, W., & Degenhardt, L. (2003). Medical marijuana initiatives: Are they justified? How successful are they likely to be? *CNS Drugs, 17*, 689–697.

Hall, W.G. Moore Arnold, H., & Myers, K. P. (2000). The acquisition of an appetite. *Psychological Science, 11*, 101–105.

Hallam, B. J., Brown, W. S., Ross, C., Buckwalter, J. G., Bigler, E. D., Tschanz, J. T., Norton, M. C., Welsh-Bohmer, K. A., & Breitner, J. C. S. (2008). Regional atrophy of the corpus callosum in dementia. *Journal of the International Neuropsychological Society, 14*(3), 414–423.

Hallett, C., Lambert, A., & Regan, M. A. (2012). Text messaging amongst New Zealand drivers: Prevalence and risk perception. *Transportation Research: Part F, 15*(3), 261–271. doi:10.1016/j.trf.2011.12.002.

Halliwell, E., Easun, A., & Harcourt, D. (2011). Body dissatisfaction: Can a short media literacy message reduce negative media exposure effects amongst adolescent girls? *British Journal Of Health Psychology, 16*(2), 396–403. doi:10.1348/135910710X515714.

Hallmayer, J., Cleveland, S., Torres, A., Phillips, J., Cohen, B., Torigoe, T., & Risch, N. (2011). Genetic heritability and shared environmental factors among twin pairs with autism. *Archives Of General Psychiatry, 68*(11), 1095–1102. doi:10.1001/archgenpsychiatry.2011.76.

Halloran, M. J., & Kashima, E. S. (2004). Social identity and worldview validation: The effects of ingroup identity primes and mortality salience on value endorsement. *Personality and Social Psychology Bulletin, 30*, 915–925.

Halperin, J. M., & Schulz, K. P. (2006). Revisiting the role of the prefrontal cortex in the pathophysiology of attention-deficit/hyperactivity disorder. *Psychological Bulletin, 132*, 560–581.

Halpern, D. F. (2012). *Sex differences in cognitive abilities* (4th ed.). New York: Psychology Press.

Halpern, D. F. (2005). Psychologyret at the intersection of work and family: Recommendations for employers, working families, and policymakers. *American Psychologist, 60*, 397–409.

Halpern, D. F., & Hakel, M. D. (2003). *Applying the science of learning to university teaching and beyond: New directions for teaching and learning*. San Francisco: Jossey-Bass.

Hamad, G. G. (2004). The state of the art in bariatric surgery for weight loss in the morbidly obese patient. *Clinics in Plastic Surgery, 31*, 591–600.

Hamalainen, K. (2012). Head to head. *Science World, 68*(8), 14.

Hamani, C., Machado, D. C., Hipólide, D. C., Dubiela, F. P., Suchecki, D., Macedo, C. E., & Nobrega, J. N. (2012). Deep brain stimulation reverses anhedonic-like behavior in a chronic model of depression: Role of serotonin and brain derived neurotrophic factor. *Biological Psychiatry, 71*(1), 30–35. doi:10.1016/j.biopsych.2011.08.025.

Hamann, S., Herman, R. A., Nolan, C. L., & Wallen, K. (2004). Men and women differ in amygdala response to sexual stimuli. *Nature Neuroscience, 7,* 411–416.

Hamarat, E., Thompson, D., Steele, D., Matheny, K., & Simons, C. (2002). Age differences in coping resources and satisfaction with life among middle-aged, young-old, and oldest-old adults. *Journal of Genetic Psychology, 163*(3), 360–367.

Hamer, M., Molloy, G. J., & Stamatakis, E. (2008). Psychological distress as a risk factor for cardiovascular events. *Journal of the American College of Cardiology, 52*, 2156–2162.

Hamilton, C. E. (2000). Continuity and discontinuity of attachment from infancy through adolescence. *Child Development, 71*, 690–694.

Hamilton, N. A., Gallagher, M. W., Preacher, K. J., Stevens, N., Nelson, C. A., Karlson, C., & McCurdy, D. (2007). Insomnia and well-being. *Journal of Consulting and Clinical Psychology, 75*, 939–946.

Hamilton, W. D. (1964). The evolution of social behavior: Parts I and II. *Journal of Theoretical Biology 7*, 1–52.

Hamm, A. O., Vaitl, D., & Lang, P. J. (1989). Fear conditioning, meaning, and belongingness: A selective association analysis. *Journal of Abnormal Psychology, 98*, 395–406.

Hammen, C. (2005). Stress and depression. *Annual Review of Clinical Psychology, 1,* 293–319.

Hammen, C. (2009). Adolescent depression: Stressful interpersonal contexts and risk for recurrence. *Current Directions in Psychological Science, 18*, 200–204.

Hammad, T. A., Laughren, T., & Racoosin, J. (2006). Suicidality in pediatric patients treated with antidepressant drugs. *Archives of General Psychiatry, 63*, 332–339.

Hammerness, P., Basch, E., & Ulbricht, C. (2003). St. John's wort: A systematic review of adverse effects and drug interactions for the consultation psychiatrist. *Journal of Consultation Liaison Psychiatry, 44*(4), 271–282.

Hammond, D. C. (2008). Hypnosis as sole anesthesia for major surgeries: Historical & contemporary perspectives. *American Journal of Clinical Hypnosis, 51*(2), 101–121.

Hampson, S. E. (2008). Mechanisms by which childhood personality traits influence adult well-being. *Current Directions in Psychological Science, 17*, 264–268.

Hampson, S. E., Goldberg, L. R., Vogt, T. M., & Dubanoski, J. P. (2006). Forty years on: Teachers' assessments of children's personality traits predict self-reported health behaviors and outcomes at midlife. *Health Psychology, 25*, 57–64.

Hampton, T. (2008). Researchers seek ways to stem STDs. *Journal of the American Medical Association, 299*(16), 1888–1889.

Hamrick, N., Cohen, S., & Rodriguez, M. S. (2002). Being popular can be healthy or unhealthy: Stress, social network diversity, and incidence of upper respiratory infection. *Health Psychology, 21*, 294–298.

Han, S., & Shavitt, S. (1994). Persuasion and culture: Advertising appeals in individualist and collectivist societies. *Journal of Experimental Social Psychology, 30*, 326–350.

Hane, A. A., Cheah, C., Rubin, K. H., & Fox, N. A. (2008). The role of maternal behavior in the relation between shyness and social reticence in early childhood and social withdrawal in middle childhood. *Social Development, 17*, 795–811.

Hanish, L. D., Martin, C. L., Fabes, R. A., Seonard, S., & Herzoh, M. (2005). Exposure to externalizing peers in early childhood: Homophily and peer contagion processes. *Journal of Abnormal Child Psychology, 33*, 267–281.

Hankin, B. L., & Abramson, L. Y. (2001). Development of gender differences in depression: An elaborated cognitive vulnerability-transactional stress theory. *Psychological Bulletin, 127*, 773–796.

Hankin, B. L., Fraley, R. C., & Abela, J. R. Z. (2005). Daily depression and cognitions about stress: Evidence for a traitlike depressogenic cognitive style and the prediction of depressive symptoms in a prospective daily diary study. *Journal of Personality and Social Psychology, 88*, 673–685.

Hankin, B. L., Fraley, R. C., Lahey, B. B., & Waldman, I. D. (2005). Is depression best viewed as a continuum or discrete category? A taxometric analysis of childhood and adolescent depression in a population-based sample. *Journal of Abnormal Psychology, 114*, 96–110.

Hanley, G. P., Piazza, C. C., Fisher, W. W., & Maglieri, K. A. (2005). On the effectiveness of and preference for punishment and extinction components of function-based interventions. *Journal of Applied Behavior Analysis, 38*, 51–65.

Hanson, G., & Venturelli, P. J. (1995). *Drugs and society* (4th ed.). Boston: Jones & Bartlett.

Hanson, S. J., & Burr, D. J. (1990). What connectionist models learn: Learning and representations in connectionist networks. *Behavioral and Brain Sciences, 13*, 471–518.

Haque, O., & Waytz, A. (2012). Dehumanization in medicine: Causes, solutions, and functions. *Perspectives on Psychological Science, 7*(2), 176–186. doi:10.1177/1745691611429706.

Hara, K., Kubota, N., Tobe, K., Terauchi, Y., Miki, H., Komeda, K., et al. (2000). The role of PPARg as a thrifty gene both in mice and humans *British Journal of Nutrition, 84*(Suppl. 2), S235–S239.

Harackiewicz, J. M., & Elliot, A. J. (1993). Achievement goals and intrinsic motivation. *Journal of Personality and Social Psychology, 65*, 904–915.

Harackiewicz, J. M., Sansone, C., & Manderlink, G. (1985). Competence, achievement orientation, and intrinsic motivation: A process analysis. *Journal of Personality and Social Psychology, 48*, 493–508.

Harber, K. D., Gorman, J. L., Gengaro, F. P., Butisingh, S., Tsang, W., & Ouellette, R. (2012). Students' race and teachers' social support affect the positive feedback bias in public schools. *Journal Of Educational Psychology*, doi:10.1037/a0028110.

Harden, K., Quinn, P. D., & Tucker-Drob, E. M. (2012). Genetically influenced change in sensation seeking drives the rise of delinquent behavior during adolescence. *Developmental Science*, 15(1), 150–163. doi:10.1111/j.1467-7687. 2011.01115.x.

Hardesty, D. E., & Sackeim, H. A. (2007). Deep brain stimulation in movement and psychiatric disorders. *Biological Psychiatry, 61*, 831–835.

Hardiman, S., Guerin, S., & Fitzsimons, E. (2009). A comparison of the social competence of children with moderate intellectual disability in inclusive versus segregated school settings. *Research in Developmental Disabilities*, 30(2), 397–407. doi:10.1016/j.ridd.2008.07.006.

Harding, K. J., Skritskaya, N., Doherty, E., & Fallon, B. A. (2008). Advances in understanding illness anxiety. *Current Psychiatry Reports, 10*(4), 311–317.

Hare, R. D., & Newmann, C. S. (2009). Psychopathy: Assessment and forensic implications. *Canadian Journal of Psychiatry, 54*, 791–802.

Hare, E., Contreras, J., Raventos, H., Flores, D., Jerez, A., Nicolini, H., & Escamilla, M. (2012). Genetic structure of personality factors and bipolar disorder in families segregating bipolar disorder. *Journal of Affective Disorders, 136*(3), 1027–1033. doi:10.1016/j.jad.2011.04.057.

Hariri, A. R., Drabant, E. M., Munoz, K. E., Kolachana, B. S., Mattay, V. S., Egan, M. F., et al. (2005). A susceptibility gene for affective disorders and the response of the human amygdala. *Archives of General Psychiatry, 62*, 146–152.

Harlow, H. F. (1959, June). Love in infant monkeys. *Scientific American,* pp. 68–74.

Harman, W. S., Lee, T. W., Mitchell, T. R., Felps, W., & Ownes, B. P. (2007). The psychology of voluntary turnover. *Current Directions in Psychological Science, 16*, 51–54.

Harmon, A. (2004, May 9). Neurodiversity forever: The disability movement turns to brains. *New York Times,* p.1.

Harmon-Jones, E. (2004). On the relationship of frontal brain activity and anger: Examining the role of attitude toward anger. *Cognition and Emotion, 18*, 337–361.

Harmon-Jones, E., Amodio, D. M., & Harmon-Jones, C. (2009). Action-based model of dissonance: A review, integration, and expansion of conceptions of cognitive conflict. In M. Zanna (Ed.), *Advances in experimental social psychology* (Vol. 41, pp. 119–166). San Diego, CA: Academic Press.

Harmon-Jones, E. (2010). Decisions, action, and neuroscience: A contemporary perspective on cognitive dissonance. In M. Gonzales, C. Tavris, & J. Aronson (Eds.) *The scientist and the humanist: A festschrift in honor of Elliot Aronson* (pp. 109–131). New York, NY, Psychology Press.

Harmon-Jones, E., & Sigelman, J. (2001). State anger and prefrontal brain activity: Evidence that insult-related relative left prefrontal activation is associated with experienced anger and aggression. *Journal of Personality and Social Psychology, 80*, 797–804.

Harré, M. S., Bossomaier, T. T., Gillett, A. A., & Snyder, A. A. (2011). The aggregate complexity of decisions in the game of Go. *European Physical Journal B— Condensed Matter, 80*(4), 555–563. doi:10.1140/epjb/e2011-10905-8.

Harré, N., Brandt, T., & Houkamau, C. (2004). An examination of the actor-observer effect in young drivers' attributions for their own and their friends' risky driving. *Journal of Applied Social Psychology, 34*, 806–824.

Harris, M., & Grunstein, R. R. (2009). Treatments for somnambulism in adults: Assessing the evidence. *Sleep Medicine Reviews, 13*, 295–297.

Harris Interactive. (2007). Handwashing survey fact sheet. Retrieved January 22, 2009, from http://www.asm.org/ASM.

Harrison, B. J., Pujol, J., López-Soià, M., Hernández-Ribas, R., Deus, J., Ortiz, H., Soriano-Mas, C., Yücel, M., Pantelis, C., & Cardoner, N. (2008). Consistency and functional specialization in the default mode brain network. *Proceedings of the National Academy of Sciences, 105*(28), 9781–9786.

Harrison, D. A., Newman, D. A., & Roth, P. L. (2006). How important are job attitudes? Meta-analytic comparisons of integrative behavioral outcomes and time sequences. *Academy of Management Journal, 49*, 305–325.

Harrison, K. (2003). Fitness and excitation. In J. Bryant, & D. Roskos-Ewoldsen (Eds.), *Communication and emotion: Essays in honor of Dolf Zillmann* (pp. 473–489). Mahwah, NJ: Erlbaum.

Harrison, N., Gray, M., Gianaros, P., & Critchley, H. (2010). The embodiment of emotional feelings in the brain. *The Journal Of Neuroscience: The Official Journal Of The Society For Neuroscience, 30*(38), 12878–12884.

Harrow, M., & Jobe, T. H. (2005). Longitudinal studies of outcome and recovery in schizophrenia and early interventions: Can they make a difference? *Canadian Journal of Psychiatry, 50*, 879–880.

Hart, A. J., Whalen, P. J., Shin, L. M., McInerney, S. C., Fischer, H., & Rauch, S. L. (2000). Differential response in the human amygdala to racial outgroup vs. ingroup face stimuli. *Neuroreport, 11*, 2351–2355.

Hart, C. L., Taylor, M. D., Smith, G. D., Whalley, L. J., Starr, J. M., Hole, D. J., et al. (2003). Childhood IQ, social class, deprivation, and their relationships with mortality and morbidity risk in later life: Prospective observational study linking the Scottish mental survey of 1932 and the midspan studies. *Psychosomatic Medicine, 65*, 877–883.

Hart, J., & Björgvinsson, T. (2010). Health anxiety and hypochondriasis: Description and treatment issues highlighted through a case illustration. *Bulletin of The Menninger Clinic, 74*(2), 122–140.

Hart, S. A., Petrill, S. A., Willcutt, E., Thompson, L. A., Schatschneider, C., Deater-Deckard, K., & Cutting, L. E. (2010). Exploring how symptoms of attention-deficit/hyperactivity disorder are related to reading and mathematics performance: General genes, general environments. *Psychological Science, 21*(11), 1708–1715. doi:10.1177/0956797610386617.

Harter, J. K., Schmidt, F. L., Asplund, J. W., Killham, E. A., & Agrawal, S. (2010). Causal impact of employee work perceptions on the bottom line of organizations. *Perspectives On Psychological Science*, 5(4), 378–389. doi:10.1177/1745691610374589.

Harter, S. (2012). *The construction of the self* (2nd ed.). New York: Guilford Press.

Hartmann, M. J. (2009). Active touch, exploratory movements, and sensory prediction. *Integrative and Comparative Biology*, 49(6), 681–690.

Hartung, C. M., & Widiger, T. A. (1998). Gender differences in the diagnosis of mental disorders: Conclusions and controversies of *DSM-IV. Psychological Bulletin, 123*, 260–278.

Hartup, W. W., & Stevens, N. (1997). Friendships and adaptation in the life course. *Psychological Bulletin, 121*, 355–370.

Hartwig, M. K., & Dunlosky, J. (2012). Study strategies of college students: Are self-testing and scheduling related to achievement? *Psychonomic Bulletin & Review, 19*(1), 126–134. doi:10.3758/s13423-011-0181-y.

Harvey, P. A., Lee, D. H. S., Qian, F., Weinreb, P. H., & Frank, E. (2009). Blockade of Nogo receptor ligands promotes functional regeneration of sensory axons after dorsal root crush. *Journal of Neuroscience, 29*, 6285–6295.

Harvey, P. D. (2010). Cognitive functioning and disability in schizophrenia. *Current Directions in Psychological Science, 19*(4), 249–254. doi:10.1177/0963721410378033.

Harvey, S. B., Stanton, B. R., & David, A. S. (2006). Conversion disorder: Towards a neurobiological understanding. *Neuropsychiatric Disease and Treatment, 2*, 13–20.

Harwood, T. M., & L'Abate, L. (2010). *Self-help in mental health: A critical review*. New York: Springer.

Harwood, K., McLean, N., & Durkin, K. (2007). First-time mothers' expectations of parenthood: What happens when optimistic expectations are not matched by later experiences? *Developmental Psychology, 43*, 1–12.

Hase, M., Schallmayer, S., & Sack, M. (2008). EMDR reprocessing of the addiction memory: Pretreatment, posttreatment, and 1-month follow-up. *Journal of EMDR Practice and Research, 2*(3), 170–179.

Haselton, M. G., & Gildersleeve, K. (2011). Can men detect ovulation? *Current Directions in Psychological Science, 20*(2), 87–92. doi:10.1177/0963721411402668.

Hashioka, S., McGeer, P. L., Monji, A., & Kanba, S. (2009). Anti-Inflammatory Effects of Antidepressants: Possibilities for Preventives Against Alzheimer's Disease. *Central Nervous System Agents in Medicinal Chemistry, 9*(1), 12–19.

Hasin, D. S., Goodwin, R. D., Stinson, F. S., & Grant, B. F. (2005). Epidemiology of major depressive disorder: Results from the national epidemiologic survey on alcoholism and related conditions. *Archives of General Psychiatry, 62*, 1097–1106.

Haskett, M. E., Nears, K., Sabourin Ward, C., & McPherson, A. V. (2006). Diversity in adjustment of maltreated children: Factors associated with resilient functioning. *Clinical Psychology Review, 26*, 796–812.

Hassabis, D., Kumaran, D., Vann, S. D., & Maguire, E. A. (2007). Patients with hippocampal amnesia cannot imagine new experiences. *Proceedings of the National Academy of Sciences of The United States of America, 104*(5), 1726–1731. doi:10.1073/pnas.0610561104.

Hatfield, D., McCullough, L., Frantz, S. B., & Krieger, K. (2010). Do we know when our clients get worse? an investigation of therapists' ability to detect negative client change. *Clinical Psychology & Psychotherapy, 17*(1), 25–32.

Hatfield, E., & Rapson, R. L. (2006). Passionate love, sexual desire, and mate selection: Cross-cultural and historical perspectives. In P. Noller & J. Feeney (Eds.), *Close relationships: Functions, forms and processes* (pp. 227–243). Hove, England: Psychology Press/Taylor & Francis.

Hatfield, J., Job, R. F. S., Hede, A. J., Carter, N. L., Peploe, P., Taylor, R., & Morrell, S. (2002). Human response to environmental noise: The role of perceived control. *International Journal of Behavioral Medicine, 9*, 341–359.

Hathaway, W. (2002, December 22). Henry M: The day one man's memory died. *Hartford Courant.*

Hatton, H., Conger, R. D., Larsen-Rife, D., & Ontai, L. (2009). An integrative and developmental perspective for understanding romantic relationship quality during the transition to parenthood. In M. S. Schulz, M. K. Pruett, P. K. Kerig, & R. D. Parke (Eds.), *Strengthening couple relationships for optimal child development: Lessons from research and intervention.* Washington, DC: American Psychological Association Press.

Hattori, M., Fujiyama A., Taylor, T. D., Watanabe, H., Yada, T., Park, H. S., et al. (2000). The DNA sequence of human chromosome 21. *Nature, 405*, 311–319.

Hauck, F. R., Moore, C. M., Herman, S. M., Donovan, M., Kalelkar, M., Christoffel, K. K., et al. (2002). The contributions of prone sleeping to the racial disparity in sudden infant death syndrome: The Chicago Infant Mortality Study. *Pediatrics, 110*, 772–780.

Haukkala, A., Konttinen, H., Laatikainen, T., Kawachi, I., & Uutela, A. (2010). Hostility, anger control, and anger expression as predictors of cardiovascular disease. *Psychosomatic Medicine, 72*, 556–562.

Hauner, K., Mineka, S., Voss, J., & Paller, K. (2012). Exposure therapy triggers lasting reorganization of neural fear processing. *Proceedings of the National Academy of Sciences of the United States of America, 109*, 9203–9208.

Hauser, R., Wiergowski, M., Kaliszan, M., Gos, T., Kernbach-Wighton, G., Studniarek, M., Jankowski, Z., and Namieśnik, J. (2011). Olfactory and tissue markers of fear in mammals including humans. *Medical Hypotheses, 77*(6), 1062–1067.

Hausknecht, J. P., Day, D. V., & Thomas, S. C. (2004). Applicant reactions to selection procedures: An updated model and meta-analysis. *Personnel Psychology, 57*, 639–683.

Havas, D. A., Glenberg, A. M., Gutowski, K. A., Lucarelli, M. J., & Davidson, R. J. (2010). Cosmetic use of botulinum toxin-A affects processing of emotional language. *Psychological Science, 21*(7), 895–900. doi:10.1177/0956797610374742.

Haw, R. M., & Fisher, R. P. (2004). Effects of administrator-witness contact on eyewitness identification accuracy. *Journal of Applied Psychology, 89*, 1106–1112.

Hawk, B. N., & McCall, R. B. (2011). Specific extreme behaviors of postinstitutionalized Russian adoptees. *Developmental Psychology, 47*, 732–738.

Hawkins, H. L., Kramer, A. R., & Capaldi, D. (1993). Aging, exercise, and attention. *Psychology and Aging, 7*, 643–653.

Haxby, J. V., Gobbini, M. I., Furey, M. L., Ishai, A., et al. (2001). Distributed and overlapping representations of faces and objects in ventral temporal cortex. *Science, 293*, 2425–2430.

Haxel, B. R., Bertz-Duffy, S., Faldum, A., Trellakis, S., Stein, B., Renner, B., Kobal, G., Letzel, S., Mann, W. J., and Muttray, A. (2011). The Candy Smell Test in clinical routine. *American Journal of Rhinology and Allergy, 25*(4), e145–e148.

Hay, D. F., Mundy, L., Roberts, S., Carta, R., Waters, C. S., Perra, O., & van Goozen, S. (2011). Known risk factors for violence predict 12-month-old infants' aggressiveness with peers. *Psychological Science, 22*(9), 1205–1211. doi:10.1177/0956797611419303.

Hayden, E. P., & Nurnberger, J. I. (2006). Molecular genetics of bipolar disorder. *Genes, Brain & Behavior, 5*, 85–95.

Hayes, E., & Silberman, L. (2007). Incorporating video games into physical education. *JOPERD: The Journal of Physical Education, Recreation & Dance, 78*(3), 18–24.

Hayes, J., Chakraborty, A. T., McManus, S., Bebbington, P., Brugha, T., Nicholson, S., & King, M. (2012). Prevalence of same-sex behavior and orientation in England: Results from a national survey. *Archives of Sexual Behavior, 41*(3), 631–639. doi:10.1007/s10508-011-9856-8

Hayes, J. E. & Keast, R. S. (2011). Two decades of supertasting: Where do we stand? *Physiology & Behavior, 104*(5), 1072–1074.

Haynes, S. R., Cohen, M. A., & Ritter, F. E. (2009). Designs for explaining intelligent agents. *International Journal of Human-Computer Studies, 67*(1), 90–110.

Hays, K. F. (2006). Being fit: The ethics of practice diversification in performance psychology. *Professional Psychology: Research and Practice, 37*, 223–232.

Hays, P. A., & Iwamasa, G. Y. (Eds.). (2006). *Culturally responsive cognitive-behavioral therapy: Assessment, practice, and supervision.* Washington, DC: American Psychological Association.

Hays, W. L. (1981). *Statistics* (3rd ed). New York: Holt, Rinehart & Winston.

Hayslip, B., King, J. K., & Jooste, J. L. (2008). Grandchildren's difficulties and strengths impact the mental health of their grandparents. In B. Hayslip & P. Kaminski (Eds.), *Parenting the custodial grandchild: Implications for clinical practice* (pp. 53–74). New York: Springer.

Hazeltine, E., & Ivry, R. B. (2002). Neuroscience: Can we teach the cerebellum new tricks? *Science, 296*, 1979–1980.

He, L. F. (1987). Involvement of endogenous opioid peptides in acupuncture analgesia. *Pain, 31*, 99–121.

Healey, M., Campbell, K. L., Hasher, L., & Ossher, L. (2010). Direct evidence for the role of inhibition in resolving interference in memory. *Psychological Science, 21*(10), 1464–1470. doi:10.1177/0956797610382120.

Heatherton, T. F. & Wheatley, T. (2010). Social neuroscience.). In R. Baumiester & E. Finkel (Eds.) *Advanced social psychology: The state of the science* (pp. 575–612). New York, NY: Oxford.

Hebb, D. O. (1955). Drives and the C. N. S. (conceptual nervous system). *Psychological Review, 62*, 243–254.

Hebblethwaite, S., & Norris, J. (2011). Expressions of generativity through family leisure: Experiences of grandparents and adult grandchildren. *Family Relations: An Interdisciplinary Journal of Applied Family Studies, 60*(1), 121–133. doi:10.1111/j.1741-3729.2010.00637.x.

Heckhausen, J., Wrosch, C., & Schulz, R. (2010). A motivational theory of life-span development. *Psychological Review, 117*, 32–60.

Hedden, T., Ketay, S., Aron, A., Markus, H. R., & Gabrieli, J. D. E. (2008). Cultural influences on neural substrates of attentional control. *Psychological Science 19*, 12–17.

Hedge, J. W., Borman, W. C., & Lammlein, S. E. (2006). *The aging workforce: Realities, myths, and implications for organizations.* Washington, DC: American Psychological Association.

Hedger, J. A., & Fabricius, W. V. (2011). True belief belies false belief: Recent findings of competence in infants and limitations in 5-year-olds, and implications for theory of mind development. *Review of Philosophy and Psychology, 2*(3), 429–447. doi:10.1007/s13164-011-0069-9.

Heegaard, W. (2007). Traumatic brain injury. *Emergency Medicine Clinics of North America, 25*(3), 655–678.

Hegerl, U., Plattner, A., & Moller, H. J. (2004). Should combined pharmaco- and psychotherapy be offered to depressed patients? A qualitative review of randomized clinical trials from the 1990s. *European Archives of Psychiatry and Clinical Neuroscience, 254*, 99–107.

Hehman, E., Gaertner, S. L., Dovidio, J. F., Mania, E. W., Guerra, R., Wilson, D. C., & Friel, B. M. (2012). Group status drives majority and minority integration preferences. *Psychological Science, 23*, 46–52. doi:10.1177/0956797611423547.

Heiby, E. M., DeLeon, P. H., & Anderson, T. (2008). A debate on prescription privileges for psychologists. In D. N. Bersoff (Ed.), *Ethical conflicts in psychology* (4th ed., pp. 370–375). Washington, DC: American Psychological Association.

Heilman, K. M., Barrett, A. M., & Adair, J. C. (1998). Possible mechanisms of anosognosia: A defect in self-awareness. *Philosophical Transactions of the Royal Society of London: Series B. Biological Sciences, 353*(1377), 1903–1909.

Heilman, K. M., & Gonzalez-Rothi, L. (2003). Apraxia. In K. M. Heilman & E. Valenstein (Eds.), *Clinical neuropsychology* (4th ed.). New York: Oxford University Press.

Heilman, K. M., & Valenstein, E. (Eds.). (2003). *Clinical neuropsychology* (4th ed.). New York: Oxford University Press.

Heilman, K. M., Watson, R. T., & Valenstein, E. (2003). Neglect and related disorders. In K. M. Heilman & E. Valenstein (Eds.), *Clinical neuropsychology* (4th ed.). New York: Oxford University Press.

Heilman, M. E., & Haynes, M. C. (2008). Subjectivity in the appraisal process: A facilitator of gender bias in work settings. In E. Borgida & S. T. Fiske (Eds.), *Beyond common sense: Psychological science in the courtroom* (pp. 127–155). Malden: Blackwell Publishing.

Heim, S., Eickhoff, S. B., & Amunts, K. (2008). Specialisation in Broca's region for semantic, phonological, and syntactic fluency? *NeuroImage, 40*(3), 1362–1368.

Heine, S. J. (2010) Cultural psychology In R. Baumeister & E. Finkel (Eds.) *Advanced social psychology: The state of the science* (pp. 665–696). New York, NY: Oxford.

Heine, S. J., & Buchtel, E. A. (2009). Personality: The universal and the culturally specific. *Annual Review of Psychology, 60*, 369–394.

Heine, S. J., Harihara, M., & Niiya, Y. (2002). Terror management in Japan. *Asian Journal of Social Psychology, 5*, 187–196.

Heinrichs, R. W. (2005). The primacy of cognition in schizophrenia. *American Psychologist, 60*, 229–242.

Heinrichs, W. L., Youngblood, P., Harter, P. M., & Dev, P. (2008). Simulation for team training and assessment: Case studies of online training with virtual worlds. *World Journal of Surgery, 32*(2), 161–170.

Heiss, W. D. (2012). PET in coma and in vegetative state. *European Journal of Neurology, 19*(2), 207–211.

Heiss, W. D., & Teasel, R. W. (2006). Brain recovery and rehabilitation. *Stroke, 37*(2), 314–316.

Hejmadi, A., Davidson, R. J., & Rozin, P. (2000). Exploring Hindu Indian emotion expressions: Evidence for accurate recognition by Americans and Indians. *Psychological Science, 11*, 183–187.

Hektner, J. M., Schmidt, J. A., & Csikszentmihalyi, M. (2007). *Experience sampling method: Measuring the quality of everyday life.* Thousand Oaks, CA: Sage Publications, Inc.

Heldt, E., Manfro, G. G., Kipper, L., Blaya, C., Isolan, L., & Otto, M. W. (2006). One-year follow-up of pharmacotherapy-resistant patients with panic disorder treated with cognitive-behavior therapy: Outcome and predictors of remission. *Behaviour Research and Therapy, 44*, 657–665.

Heller, M. (2011, March 12). Parents make history with $1M false memory award. Retrieved from http://www.onpointnews.com/NEWS/Parents-Make-History-With-$1M-False-Memory-Award.html.

Heller, S. (2008). *Design disasters: Great designers, fabulous failure, and lessons learned.* New York: St. Martin's Press.

Heller, W. (1993). Neuropsychological mechanisms of individual differences in emotion, personality, and arousal. *NeuroPsychology, 7*(4), 486–489.

Heller, W., Nitschke, J. B., & Miller, G. A. (1998). Lateralization in emotion and emotional disorders. *Current Directions in Psychological Science, 7*, 26–32.

Hellmuth, J. C., & McNulty, J. K. (2008). Neuroticism, marital violence, and the moderating role of stress and behavioral skills. *Journal of Personality and Social Psychology, 95*, 166–180.

Helms, J. E. (1992). Why is there no study of cultural equivalence in standardized cognitive ability testing? *American Psychologist, 47*, 1083–1101.

Helms, J. E. (1997). The triple quandary of race, culture, and social class in standardized cognitive ability testing. In D. P. Flanagan, J. L. Genshaft, & P. L. Harrison (Eds.), *Contemporary intellectual assessment: Theories, tests, and issues* (pp. 517–532). New York: Guilford Press.

Helson, R., & Moane, G. (1987). Personality change in women from college to midlife. *Journal of Personality and Social Psychology, 53*, 176–186.

Helzer, J. E., Canino, G. J., Yeh, E., Bland, R. C., Lee, C. K., Hwu, H., & Newman, S. (1990). Alcoholism—North America and Asia: A comparison of population surveys with the diagnostic interview schedule. *Archives of General Psychiatry, 47*, 313–319.

Helzer, J. E., & Hudziak, J. J. (Eds.). (2002). *Defining psychopathology in the 21st century: DSM-V and beyond.* Washington DC: American Psychiatric Publishing, Inc.

Henckens, M. J. A. G., Hermans, E. J., Pu, Z., Joels, M., & Fernandez, G. (2009). Stressed memories: How acute stress affects memory formation in humans. *Journal of Neuroscience, 29*, 10111–10119.

Henderson, J. M. (2008). Peripheral nerve stimulation for chronic pain. *Current Pain and Headache Reports, 12*(1), 28–31.

Hendrick, B. (2003, May 8). Exam day rituals help students feel lucky. *Naples Daily News.*

Hendrick, C., & Hendrick, S. S. (2003). Romantic love: Measuring cupid's arrow. In S. J. Lopez & C. R. Snyder (Eds.), *Positive psychological assessment: A handbook of models and measures* (pp. 235–249). Washington, DC: American Psychological Association.

Hendricks, P. S., & Thompson, J. K. (2005). An integration of cognitive-behavioral therapy and interpersonal psychotherapy for bulimia nervosa: A case study using the case formulation method. *International Journal of Eating Disorders, 37*, 171–174.

Henig, R. (2004, April 4). The quest to forget. *New York Times*, p. 32.

Henkel, L. A., Franklin, N., & Johnson, M. K. (2000). Cross-modal source monitoring, confusion between perceived and imagined events. *Journal of Experimental Psychology: Learning, Memory and Cognition, 26*, 321–335.

Henker, F. O. (1979). Acute brain syndromes. *Journal of Clinical Psychiatry, 40*(3), 117–120.

Hennig, J., Reuter, M., Netter, P., Burk, C., & Landt, O. (2005). Two types of aggression are differentially related to serotonergic activity and the A779C TPH polymorphism. *Behavioral Neuroscience, 119*, 16–25.

Henry, J. D., von Hippel, C., & Shapiro, L. (2010). Stereotype threat contributes to social difficulties in people with schizophrenia. *British Journal Of Clinical Psychology, 49*(1), 31–41.

Hepach, R., Vaish, A., & Tomasello, M. (2012). Young children are intrinsically motivated to see others helped. *Psychological Science.* Published online before print July 31, 2012, doi:10.1177/0956797612440571.

Heppner, P. P., Heppner, M. J., Lee, D., Wang, Y.-W., Park, H., & Wang, L. (2006). Development and validation of a collectivist coping styles inventory. *Journal of Counseling Psychology, 53,* 107–125.

Hepworth, S. J., Schoemaker, M. J., Muir, K. R., Swerdlow, A. J., van Tongeren, M. J. A., & McKinney, P. A. (2006). Mobile phone use and risk of glioma in adults: Case control study. *British Medical Journal, 332,* 883–887.

Herbert, J. D., Lilienfeld, S. O., Lohr, J. M., Montgomery, R. W., O'Donohue, W. T., Rosen, G. M., & Tolin, D. F. (2000). Science and pseudoscience in the development of eye movement desensitization and reprocessing: Implications for clinical psychology. *Clinical Psychology Review, 20,* 945–971.

Herdener, M., Esposito, F., di Salle, F., Boller, C., et al. (2010). Musical training induces functional plasticity in human hippocampus. *Journal of Neuroscience, 30,* 1377–1384.

Heres, S., Davis, J., Maino, K., Jetzinger, E., Kissling, W., & Leucht, S. (2006). Why olanzapine beats risperidone, risperidone beats quetiapine, and quetiapine beats olanzapine: An exploratory analysis of head-to-head comparison studies of second-generation antipsychotics. *American Journal of Psychiatry, 163,* 185–194.

Hergenhahn, B. R., & Olson, M. (2007). *Introduction to theories of personality* (7th ed.). Upper Saddle River, NJ: Prentice Hall.

Hergenhahn, B. R., H. (2011). An introduction to theories of personality (8th edition). Upper Saddle River: Prentice Hall.

Heron, M. P. (2007). Deaths: Leading causes for 2004. *National Vital Statistics Reports, 56*(5), 1–96.

Herrington, J. D., Heller, W., Mohanty, A., Engels, A. S., et al. (2010). Localization of asymmetric brain function in emotion and depression. *Psychophysiology, 11,* 11.

Herman, C. P., Roth, D. A., & Polivy, J. (2003). Effects of the presence of others on food intake: A normative interpretation. *Psychological Bulletin, 129,* 873–886.

Herpertz, S., Hagenah, U., Vocks, S., von Wietersheim, J., Cuntz, U., Zeeck, A., & Wagstaff, K. (2011). The diagnosis and treatment of eating disorders. *Deutsches Ärzteblatt International, 108*(40), 678–685.

Herrmann, D. J., & Searleman, A. (1992). Memory improvement and memory theory in historical perspective. In D. Herrmann, H. Weingartner, A. Searlman, & C. McEvoy (Eds.), *Memory improvement: Implications for memory theory.* New York: Springer-Verlag.

Herrnstein, R. J., & Murray, C. (1994). *The bell curve: Intelligence and class structure in American life.* New York: Free Press.

Hershcovis, M. S., Turner, N., Barling, H., Arnold, K. A., Dupré, K. E., Innes, M., LeBlanc, M. M., & Sivanathan, N. (2007). Predicting workplace aggression: A meta-analysis. *Journal of Applied Psychology, 92,* 228–238.

Hershenberg, R., Drabick, D. G., & Vivian, D. (2012). An opportunity to bridge the gap between clinical research and clinical practice: Implications for clinical training. *Psychotherapy, 49,* 123–134. doi:10.1037/a0027648

Hertel, P. T., & Mathews, A. (2011). Cognitive bias modification: Past perspectives, current findings, and future applications. *Perspectives on Psychological Science, 6*(6), 521–536. doi:10.1177/1745691611421205.

Hertenstein, M. J., & Campos, J. J. (2004). The retention effects of an adult's emotional displays on infant behavior. *Child Development, 75,* 585–613.

Hertlein, K., & Ricci, R. J. (2004). A systematic research synthesis of EMDR studies: Implementation of the platinum standard. *Trauma, Violence, and Abuse, 5,* 285–300.

Hertz, R. (2006). *Single by chance, mothers by choice.* New York: Oxford University Press.

Hertzog, C., Kramer, A. F., Wilson, R. S., & Lindenberger, U. (2009). Enrichment effects on adult cognitive development: Can the functional capacity of older adults be preserved and enhanced? *Psychological Science in the Public Interest, 9,* 1–65.

Hervet, G., Guérard, K., Tremblay, S., Chtourou, M. S. (2011) Is banner blindness genuine? Eye tracking internet text advertising. *Applied Cognitive Psychology, 25*(5), 708–716. doi:10.1002/acp.1742.

Herz, R. S., & Cahill, E. D. (1997). Differential use of sensory information in sexual behavior as a function of gender. *Human Nature, 8,* 275–286.

Herzog, D. B., Dorer, D. J., Keel, P. K., Selwyn, S. E., Ekeblad, E. R., Flores, A. T., et al. (1999). Recovery and relapse in anorexia and bulimia nervosa: A 7.5-year follow-up study. *Journal of the American Academy of Child and Adolescent Psychiatry, 38,* 829–837.

Herzog, T. A., & Blagg, C. O. (2007). Are most precontemplators contemplating smoking cessation? Assessing the validity of the stages of change. *Health Psychology, 26,* 222–231.

Hespos, S. J., & Baillargeon, R. (2001). Infants' knowledge about occlusion and containment events: A surprising discrepancy. *Psychological Science, 12,* 141–147.

Hetherington, E. M., & Clingempeel, W. G. (1992). Coping with marital transitions. *Monographs of the Society for Research in Child Development, 57*(2–3), 1–14.

Heutink, J., Brouwer, W., Kums, E., Young, A., & Bouma, A. (2012). When family looks strange and strangers look normal: a case of impaired face perception and recognition after stroke. *Neurocase, 18*(1), 39-49.

Hewig, J., Kretschmer, N., Trippe, R. H., Hecht, H., et al. (2010). Hypersensitivity to reward in problem gamblers. *Biological Psychiatry, 67,* 781–783.

Hewlin, J., & Faison, P. (2009). Wearing the cloak: Antecedents and consequences of creating facades of conformity. *Journal of Applied Psychology, 94,* 727–741.

Heymsfield, S. B., Greenberg, A. S., Fujioa, K., Dixon, R. M., Kushner, R., Hunt, T., et al. (1999). Recombinant leptin for weight loss in obese and lean adults. *Journal of the American Medical Association, 282,* 1568–1575.

Heywood, C. A., & Kentridge, R. W. (2003). Achromatopsia, color vision, and cortex. *Neurology Clinics, 21,* 483–500.

Hickey, C., Chisholm, T., Passmore, M. J., O'Brien, J. D., & Johnston, J. (2008). Differentiating the dementias. Revisiting synucleinopathies and tauopathies. *Current Alzheimer Research, 5*(1), 52–60.

Hicks, B. M., Schalet, B. D., Malone, S. M., Iacono, W. G., & McGue, M. (2011). Psychometric and genetic architecture of substance use disorder and behavioral disinhibition measures for gene association studies. *Behavior Genetics, 41*(4), 459–475. doi:10.1007/s10519-010-9417-2

Hicks, R. A., Fernandez, C., & Pelligrini, R. J. (2001). The changing pattern of sleep habits of university students: An update. *Perceptual and Motor Skills, 93,* 648.

Hightow-Weidman, L. B., Phillips, G., Jones, K. C., Outlaw, A. Y., Fields, S. D., & Smith, J. C. (2011). Racial and sexual identity-related maltreatment among minority YMSM: Prevalence, perceptions, and the association with emotional distress. *AIDS Patient Care And Stds, 25*(Sup1), S39–S45. doi:10.1089/apc.2011.9877.

Higley, A. E., Kiefer, S. W., Li, X., Gaál, J., Xi, Z. X., & Gardner, E. L. (2011). Dopamine D(3) receptor antagonist SB-277011A inhibits methamphetamine self-administration and methamphetamine-induced reinstatement of drug-seeking in rats. *European Journal of Pharmacology, 659*(2–3), 187–192.

Higuchi, S., Matsushita, S., & Kashima, H. (2006). New findings on the genetic influences on alcohol use and dependence. *Current Opinion in Psychiatry, 19,* 253–265.

Hilbert, M. (2012). Toward a synthesis of cognitive biases: How noisy information processing can bias human decision making. *Psychological Bulletin, 138*(2), 211–237. doi:10.1037/a0025940.

Hildebrandt, M. G., Steyerberg, E. W., Stage, K. B., Passchier, J., Kragh-Soerensen, P., and the Danish University Antidepressant Group. (2003). Are gender differences important for the clinical effects of antidepressants? *American Journal of Psychiatry, 160,* 1643–1650.

Hildreth, E. C., & Royden, C. S. (2011). Integrating multiple cues to depth order at object boundaries. *Attention, Perception, and Psychophysics, 73*(7), 2218-2235.

Hilgard, E. R. (1965). *Hypnotic susceptibility.* New York: Harcourt, Brace & World.

Hilgard, E. R. (1977). *Divided consciousness: Multiple controls in human thought and action.* New York: Wiley.

Hilgard, E. R. (1979). *Personality and hypnosis: A study of imaginative involvement.* Chicago: University of Chicago Press.

Hilgard, E. R. (1982). Hypnotic susceptibility and implications for measurement. International *Journal of Clinical and Experimental Hypnosis, 30,* 394–403.

Hilgard, E. R. (1992). Divided consciousness and dissociation. *Consciousness and Cognition, 1,* 16–31.

Hilgard, E. R., Morgan, A. H., & MacDonald, H. (1975). Pain and dissociation in the cold pressor test: A study of "hidden reports" through automatic key-pressing and automatic talking. *Journal of Abnormal Psychology, 84,* 280–289.

Hill, C. (2005). Therapist techniques, client involvement, and the therapeutic relationship: Inextricably intertwined in the therapy process. *Psychotherapy: Theory, Research, Practice, Training, 42,* 431–442.

Hill, C. E., & Lent, R. W. (2006). A narrative and meta-analytic review of helping skills training: Time to revive a dormant area of inquiry. *Psychotherapy: Theory, Research, Practice, Training, 43,* 154–172.

Hill, C. T., & Peplau, L. A. (1998). Premarital predictors of relationship outcomes: A 15-year follow-up of the Boston Couples Study. In T. N. Bradbury (Ed.), *The developmental course of marital dysfunction* (pp. 237–278). New York: Cambridge University Press.

Hillis, A. E., Gold, L., Kannan, V., Cloutman, L., Kleinman, J. T., Newhart, M., Heidler-Gary, J., Davis, C., Aldrich, E., Llinas, R., & Gottesman, R. F. (2008). Site of the ischemic penumbra as a predictor of potential for recovery of functions. *Neurology, 71*(3), 184–189.

Hilton, D. (2002). Thinking about causality: Pragmatic, social and scientific rationality. In P. E. Carruthers, S. Stich, & M. Siegal (Eds.), *The cognitive basis of science* (pp. 211–231). New York: Cambridge University Press.

Hilton, H. (1986). *The executive memory guide.* New York: Simon & Schuster.

Hines, A. R., & Paulson, S. E. (2007). Parents' and teachers' perceptions of adolescent storm and stress: Relations with parenting and teaching styles. *Family Therapy, 34*(2), 63–80.

Hines, M., Brook, C., & Conway, G. (2004). Androgen and psychosexual development: Core gender identity, sexual orientation, and recalled childhood gender role behavior in women and men with congenital adrenal hyperplasia (CAH). *Journal of Sex Research, 41*(1), 75–81.

Hinshaw, S. P., Zupan, B. A., Simmel, C., Nigg, J. T., & Melnick, S. (1997). Peer status in boys with and without attention-deficit hyperactivity disorder: Predictions from overt and covert antisocial behavior, social isolation, and authoritative parenting beliefs. *Child Development, 68,* 880–896.

Hinton, D. E., Hinton, A. L., Pich, V., Loeum, J. R., & Pollack, M. H. (2009). Nightmares among Cambodian refugees: The breaching of concentric ontological security. *Culture Medicine and Psychiatry, 33,* 219–265.

Hinton, D., Um, K., & Ba, P. (2001). Kyol goeu ("wind overload") Part I: A cultural syndrome of orthostatic panic among Khmer refugees. *Transcultural Psychiatry, 38,* 403–432.

Hiroi, N., & Scott, D. (2009). Constitutional mechanisms of vulnerability and resilience to nicotine dependence. *Molecular Psychiatry, 14,* 653–667.

Hirota, K. (2006). Special cases: Ketamine, nitrous oxide and xenon. *Best Practice and Research: Clinical Anaesthesiology, 20*(1), 69–79.

Hiroto, D. S. (1974). Locus of control and learned helplessness. *Journal of Experimental Psychology, 102,* 187–193.

Hirschberger, G. (2009). Compassionate callousness: A terror management perspective on prosocial behavior. In M. Mikulincer & P. Shaver (Eds.), *Prosocial motives, emotions, and behavior: The better angels of our nature,* 201–219. Washington, DC: American Psychological Association.

Hirschfeld, R. J., Jordan, M. H., Thomas, C. H., & Field, H. S. (2008). Observed leadership potential of personnel in a team setting: big five traits and proximal factors as predictors. *International Journal of Selection and Assessment, 16,* 385–402.

Hirschfeld, R. M. A., & Vornik, L. A. (2004). Newer antidepressants: Review of efficacy and safety of escitalopram and duloxetine. *Journal of Clinical Psychiatry, 65*(Suppl. 4), 46–52.

Hirsch-Pasek, K., Treiman, R., & Schneiderman, M. (1984). Brown and Hanlon revisited: Mothers' sensitivity to ungrammatical forms. *Journal of Child Language, 11*, 81–88.

Hirst, W., Phelps, E. A., Buckner, R. L., Budson, A. E., Cuc, A., Gabrieli, J. E., & ... Vaidya, C. J. (2009). Long-term memory for the terrorist attack of September 11: Flashbulb memories, event memories, and the factors that influence their retention. *Journal of Experimental Psychology: General, 138*(2), 161–176. doi:10.1037/a0015527

Ho, B.-C., Andreasen, N. C., Nopoulos, P., Arndt, S., Magnotta, V., & Flaum M. (2003). Progressive structural brain abnormalities and their relationship to clinical outcome: A longitudinal magnetic resonance imaging study early in schizophrenia. *Archives of General Psychiatry, 60*, 585–594.

Ho, C., Bluestein, D. N., & Jenkins, J. M. (2008). Cultural differences in the relationship between parenting and children's behavior. *Developmental Psychology, 44*, 507–522.

Ho, V., Lee, J., & Martin, K. (2011). The cell biology of synaptic plasticity. *Science, 334*(6056), 623–628.

Ho, Y.-C., Cheung, M., & Chan, A. S. (2003). Music training improves verbal but not visual memory: Cross-sectional and longitudinal explorations in children. *Neuropsychology, 17*, 439–450.

Hobson, J. (1997). Dreaming as delirium: A mental status analysis of our nightly madness. *Seminar in Neurology, 17*, 121–128.

Hobson, J. A. (2005). Sleep is of the brain, by the brain and for the brain. *Nature, 437*, 1254–1256.

Hodgins, S. (2007). Persistent violent offending: What do we know? *British Journal of Psychiatry, 190* (supplement), s12–s14.

Hodson, G. (2011). Do ideologically intolerant people benefit from intergroup contact? *Current Directions in Psychological Science, 20*(3), 154–159. doi:10.1177/0963721411409025.

Hodson, G., & Busseri, M. A. (2012). Bright minds and dark attitudes: Lower cognitive ability predicts greater prejudice through right-wing ideology and intergroup conflict. *Psychological Science,* Published online in advance of publication. doi:10.1177/0956797611421206.

Hoegl, M., & Parboteeah, K. P. (2006). Autonomy and teamwork in innovative projects. *Human Resource Management, 45*, 67–79.

Hoek, H. W. (2006). Incidence, prevalence and mortality of anorexia nervosa and other eating disorders. *Current Opinion in Psychiatry, 19*(4), 389–394.

Hoel, H., Faragher, B., & Cooper, C. L. (2004). Bullying is detrimental to health, but all bullying behaviors are not necessarily equally damaging. *British Journal of Guidance and Counseling, 32*, 367–387.

Hofer, S. B., Mrsic-Flogel, T. D., Bonhoeffer, T., & Hübener, M. (2009). Experience leaves a lasting structural trace in cortical circuits. *Nature, 457*, 313–317.

Hoffman, D. (1999, February 11). When the nuclear alarms went off, he guessed right. *International Herald Tribune*, p. 2.

Hoffman S.D. (2008). *Kids having kids: Economic costs and social consequences of teen pregnancy*. Washington, DC: Urban Institute Press.

Hoffmann, J. P., & Cerbone, F. G. (2002). Parental substance use disorder and the risk of adolescent drug abuse: An event history analysis. *Drug and Alcohol Dependence, 66*, 255–264.

Hofmann, W., can Koningsbruggen, G. M., Stroebe, W., Ramanathan, S., & Aarts, H. (2010). As pleasure unfolds: Hedonic responses to tempting food. *Psychological Science, 21*(12), 1863–1870. doi:10.1177/0956797610389186.

Hoffman, Y., Bein, O., & Maril, A. (2011). Explicit memory for unattended words: The importance of being in the "no". *Psychological Science, 22*(12), 1490–1493.

Hofmann, S. G., Grossman, P., & Hinton, D. E. (2011). Loving-kindness and compassion meditation: Potential for psychological interventions. *Clinical Psychology Review, 31*(7), 1126–1132. doi:10.1016/j.cpr.2011.07.003.

Hofmann, S. G., Meuret, A. E., Smits, J. A., Simon, N. M., Pollack, M. H., Eisenmenger, K., et al. (2006). Augmentation of exposure therapy with D-cycloserine for social anxiety disorder. *Archives of General Psychiatry, 63*, 298–304.

Hogan, D. P., & Msall, M. E. (2002). Family structure and resources and the parenting of children with disabilities and functional limitations. In J. G. Borkowski, S. L. Ramey, & M. Bristol-Power (Eds.), *Parenting and the child's world* (pp. 311–328). Mahwah, NJ: Erlbaum.

Hogarth, R. M., & Einhorn, H. J. (1992). Order effects in belief updating: The belief adjustment model. *Cognitive Psychology, 24*, 1–55.

Hogg, M. A. (2010). Influence and leadership In S. T. Fiske, D. T. Gilbert, & G. Lindzey (Eds.), *Handbook of social psychology* (5th ed., Vol 2, pp. 1166–1207). Hoboken, NJ: Wiley.

Hoigaard, R., & Ingvaldsen, R. P. (2006). Social loafing in interactive groups: The effects of identifiability on effort and individual performance in floorball. *Athletic Insight: The Online Journal of Sport Psychology, 8*. Retrieved March 19, 2009, from http://www.athleticinsight.com/Vol8Iss2/Loafing.htm.

Hoigaard, R., Säfvenbom, R., & Tonnessen, F. E. (2006). The relationship between group cohesion, group norms, and perceived social loafing in soccer teams. *Small Group Research, 37*, 217–232.

Holden, C. (1996). Small refugees suffer the effects of early neglect. *Science, 274*, 1076–1077.

Holland, A. S., & Roisman, G. I. (2010). Adult attachment security and young adults' dating relationships over time: Self-reported, observational, and physiological evidence. *Developmental Psychology, 46*, 552–557.

Hollander, E., Braum, A., Simeon, D. (2008). Should OCD leave the anxiety disorders in DSM-V? The case for obsessive-compulsive-related disorders. *Depression and Anxiety, 25*, 317–329.

Hollander, E., & Simeon, D. (2008). Anxiety disorders. In R. E. Hales, S. C., Yudofsky, & G. O. Gabbard (Eds.), *Textbook of psychiatry* (pp. 505–567). Alexandria, VA: American Psychiatric Association.

Hollinger, R. C., Dabney, D. A., Lee, G., Hayes, R., Hunter, J., & Cummings, M. (1996). *1996 national retail security survey final report*. Gainesville: University of Florida.

Hollins, S. S. & Bensmaia, S. J. (2007). The coding of roughness. *Canadian Journal of Experimental Psychology, 61*, 184–195.

Hollon, S. D., & DiGiuseppe, R. (2011). Cognitive theories of psychotherapy. In J. C. Norcross, G. R. VandenBos, & D. K. Freedheim (Eds.), *History of psychotherapy: Continuity and change* (pp. 203–241). Washington, DC: American Psychological Association.

Hollon, S. D., Jarrett, R. B., Nienberg, A. A., Thase, M. E., Trivendi, M., et al. (2005). Psychotherapy and medication in the treatment of adult and geriatric depression: Which monotherapy or combined therapy? *Journal of Clinical Psychiatry, 66*, 455–468.

Hollon, S. D., Stewart, M. O., & Strunk, D. (2006).Enduring effects for cognitive behavior therapy in the treatment of depression and anxiety. *Annual Review of Psychology, 57*, 285–315.

Hollon, S. D., Thase, M. E., & Markowitz, J. C. (2002). Treatment and prevention of depression. *Psychological Science in the Public Interest, 3*, 39–77.

Holma, K. M., Melartin, T. K., Haukka, J., Holma, I.A.K., Sokero, T. P., & Isometsa, E. T. (2010). Incidence and predictors of suicide attempts in DSM-IV major depressive disorder: A five-year prospective study. *American Journal of Psychiatry, 167*, 801–808.

Holman, E. A., Silver, R. C., Poulin, M., Andersen, J., Gil-Rivas, V., & McIntosh, D. N. (2008). Terrorism, acute stress, and cardiovascular health: A 3-year national study following the September 11th attacks. *Archives of General Psychiatry, 65*, 73–80.

Holman, L. (2011). Millennial students' mental models of search: Implications for academic librarians and database developers. *Journal of Academic Librarianship, 37*(1), 19–27.

Holmes, D. S. (1991). *Abnormal psychology*. New York: HarperCollins.

Holmes, E. A., Brown, R. J., Mansell, W., Fearon, R. P., Hunter, E. C. M., Frasquilho, F., & Oakley, D. A. (2005). Are there two qualitatively distinct forms of dissociation? A review and some clinical implications. *Clinical Psychology Review, 25*(1), 1–23.

Holmes, T. H., & Rahe, R. H. (1967). The Social Readjustment Rating Scale. *Journal of Psychosomatic Research, 11*, 213–218.

Hölscher, C., Tenbrink, T., & Wiener, J. M. (2011). Would you follow your own route description? Cognitive strategies in urban route planning. *Cognition, 121*(2), 228–247. doi:10.1016/j.cognition.2011.06.005.

Holtmaat, A., Wilbrecht, L., Knott, G. W., Welker, E., & Svoboda, K. (2006). Experience-dependent and cell-type-specific spine growth in the neocortex. *Nature, 441*, 979–983.

Holway, A. H., & Boring, E. G. (1941). Determinants of apparent visual size with distance variant. *American Journal of Psychology, 54*, 21–37.

Hölzel, B. K., Lazar, S. W., Gard, T., Schuman-Olivier, Z., Vago, D. R., & Ott, U. (2011). How does mindfulness meditation work? Proposing mechanisms of action from a conceptual and neural perspective. *Perspectives on Psychological Science, 6*(6), 537–559.

Hommer, D. W., Momenan, R., Kaiser, E., & Rawlings, R. R. (2001). Evidence for a gender-related effect of alcoholism on brain volumes. *American Journal of Psychiatry, 158*, 198–204.

Hong, H., & Lin-Siegler, X. (2011). How learning about scientists' struggles influences students' interest and learning in physics. *Journal Of Educational Psychology*, doi:10.1037/a0026224.

Hong, Y., Wyer, R., & Fong, C.P.S (2008). Chinese working in groups: Effort dispensability versus normative influence. *Asian Journal of Social psychology, 11*, 187–195.

Honts, C. R., & Quick, B. D. (1995). The polygraph in 1996: Progress in science and the law. *North Dakota Law Review, 71*, 997–1020.

Hoobler, J. M., & Brass, D. J. (2006). Abusive supervision and family undermining as displaced aggression. *Journal of Applied Psychology, 91*, 1125–1133.

Hood, B. M., Willen, J. D., & Driver, J. (1998). Adult's eyes trigger shifts of visual attention in human infants. *Psychological Science, 9*, 131–134.

Hood, M. Y., Moore, L. L., Sundarajan-Ramamurti, A., Singer, M., Cupples, L. A., & Ellison, R. C. (2000). Parental eating attitudes and the development of obesity in children: The Framingham children's study. *International Journal of Obesity, 24*, 1319–1325.

Hooley, J. M. (2010). Social factors in schizophrenia. *Current Directions in Psychological Science, 19*(4), 238–242. doi:10.1177/0963721410377597.

Hooley, J. M. (2004). Do psychiatric patients do better clinically if they live with certain kinds of families? *Current Directions in Psychological Science, 13*, 202–205.

Hooper, D. T., & Martin, R. (2007). Measuring perceived LMX variability within teams and its impact on procedural justice climate. In A. Glendon, B. M. Thompson, B. Myors, A. Glendon, B. M. Thompson, B. Myors (Eds.) , *Advances in organisational psychology* (pp. 249–267). Bowen Hills, QLD Australia: Australian Academic Press.

Hope, L., Lewinski, W., Dixon, J., Blocksidge, D., & Gabbert, F. (2012). Witnesses in action : The effect of physical exertion on recall and recognition. *Psychological Science*. Advance online publication. doi:10.1177/0956797611431463.

Hopf, H. C., Muller, F. W., & Hopf, N. J. (1992). Localization of emotional and volitional facial paresis. *Neurology, 42*(10), 1918–1923.

Hopper, K., & Wanderling, J. (2000). Revisiting the developed versus developing country distinction in course and outcome in schizophrenia: Results from ISoS, the WHO Collaborative Followup Project. *Schizophrenia Bulletin, 26,* 835–846.

Hopwood, C. J., Donnellan, M., Blonigen, D. M., Krueger, R. F., McGue, M., Iacono, W. G., & Burt, S. (2011). Genetic and environmental influences on personality trait stability and growth during the transition to adulthood: A three-wave longitudinal study. *Journal Of Personality And Social Psychology, 100*(3), 545–556. doi:10.1037/a0022409.

Horley, J. (2011). On the tyranny of professional labelling. *Psychotherapy & Politics International, 9*(2), 127–133. doi:10.1002/ppi.244.

Horner, P. J., & Gage, F. H. (2002). Regeneration in the adult and aging brain. *Archives of Neurology, 59,* 1717–1720.

Horney, K. (1937). *Neurotic personality of our times.* New York: Norton.

Horowitz, J. L., & Garber, J. (2006). The prevention of depressive symptoms in children and adolescents: A meta-analytic review. *Journal of Consulting and Clinical Psychology, 74,* 401–415.

Horowitz, L. M., Rosenberg, S. E., & Bartholomew, K. (1993). Interpersonal problems, attachment styles, and outcome in brief dynamic psychotherapy. *Journal of Consulting and Clinical Psychology, 61,* 549–560.

Horwitz, A. V., Widom, C. S., McLaughlin, J., & White, H. R. (2001). Th e impact of childhood abuse and neglect on adult mental health: A prospective study. *Journal of Health and Social Behavior, 42,* 184–201.

Horwitz, P., & Christie, M. A. (2000). Computer-based manipulatives for teaching scientific reasoning: An example. In M. J. Jacobson & R. B. Kozuma (Eds.), *Innovations in science and mathematics education: Advanced designs for technologies of learning* (pp. 163–191). Mahwah, NJ: Erlbaum.

Hoshino-Browne, E., Zanna, A. S., Spencer, S. J., Zanna, M. P., Kitayama, S., & Lackenbauer, S. (2005). On the cultural guises of cognitive dissonance: The case of Easterners and Westerners. *Journal of Personality and Social Psychology, 89,* 294–310.

Houben, K., Wiers, R., & Jansen, A. (2011). Getting a grip on drinking behavior: Training working memory to reduce alcohol abuse. *Psychological Science, 22*(7), 968–975.

Houghton, G. (2005). *Connectionist models in cognitive psychology.* New York: Psychology Press.

Houpt, T. R. (1994). Gastric pressure in pigs during eating and drinking. *Physiology and Behavior, 56*(2), 311–317.

House, J. S., Landis, K. R., & Umberson, D. (1988a). Social relationships and health. *Science, 241,* 540–545.

House, J. S., Landis, K. R., & Umberson, D. (1988b). Structures and processes of social support. *Annual Review of Sociology, 14,* 293–318.

House, R. J., Hanges, P. J., Ruiz-Quintanilla, S. A., Dorfman, P. W., Javidan, M., Dickson, M., et al. (1999). Cultural influences on leadership and organizations: Project GLOBE. In W. H. Mobley, M. J. Gessner, & V. Arnold (Eds.), *Advances in global leadership* (Vol. 1, pp. 171–233). Stamford, CT: JAI.

Hoven, C. W., Duarte, C. S., Lucas, C. P., Wu, P., Mandell, D. J., Goodwin, R. D., et al. (2005). Psychopathology among New York city public school children 6 months after September 11. *Archives of General Psychiatry, 62,* 545–552.

Howard, D. V. (1983). *Cognitive psychology.* New York: Macmillan.

Howe, M. J. A., Davidson, J. W., & Sloboda, J. A. (1998). Innate talent: Reality or myth? *Behavioral and Brain Sciences, 21,* 399–442.

Howe, M. L. (2011). *Nature of early memory: An adaptive theory of the genesis and development of memory.* Oxford, England: Oxford University Press.

Howe, M. L. (2003). Memories from the cradle. *Current Directions in Psychological Science, 12,* 62–65.

Howe, T. (2012). *Marriage and families in the 21st century.* Malden, MA: Wiley-Blackwell.

Howell, J. L., & Shepperd, J. A. (2012). Reducing information avoidance through affirmation. *Psychological Science, 23*(2), 141–145. doi:10.1177/0956797611424164.

Howell, J. L., & Shepperd, J. A. (2012). Reducing information avoidance through affirmation. *Psychological Science, 23,* 141–145. doi:10.1177/0956797611424164.

Hoyert, D. L., Kung, H.-C., & Smith, B. L. (2005). Deaths: Preliminary data for 2003. *National Vital Statistics Reports, 53,* 1–48.

Hoyle, R. H., Harris, M. J., & Judd, C. M. (2002). *Research methods in social relations.* Belmont, CA: Wadsworth.

Hoyt, C. L., Simon, S., & Innella, A. N. (2011). Taking a turn toward the masculine: The impact of mortality salience on implicit leadership theories. *Basic and Applied Social Psychology, 33,* 374–381. doi:10.1080/01973533.2011.614173.

Hsee, C. K., Yang, A., X., & Wang, L. (2010). Idleness aversion and the need for justifiable busyness. *Psychological Science, 21*(7), 926–930. doi:10.1177/0956797610374738.

Hser, Y. I., Hoffman, V., Grella, C. E., & Anglin, M. D. (2001). A 33-year follow-up of narcotics addicts. *Archives of General Psychiatry, 58,* 503–508.

Hsu, C., & Ho, C. (2012). The design and implementation of a competency-based intelligent mobile learning system. *Expert Systems With Applications, 39*(9), 8030–8043. doi:10.1016/j.eswa.2012.01.130.

Hsu, L. M., Chung, J., & Langer, E. J. (2010). The influence of age-related cues on health and longevity. *Perspectives on Psychological Science, 5*(6), 632–648. doi:10.1177/1745691610388762.

Hu, P., Stylos-Allan, M., & Walker, M. P. (2006). Sleep facilitates consolidation of emotional declarative memory. *Psychological Science, 17,* 891–898.

Hu, S., Patatucci, A. M. L., Patterson, C., Li, L., Fulker, D. W., Cherny, S. S., et al. (1995). Linkage between sexual orientation and chromosome Xq28 in males but not females. *Nature Genetics, 11,* 248–256.

Hu, Y., & Ericsson, K. (2012). Memorization and recall of very long lists accounted for within the Long-Term Working Memory framework. *Cognitive Psychology, 64*(4), 235–266. doi:10.1016/j.cogpsych.2012.01.001.

Hua, J. Y., & Smith, S. J. (2004). Neural activity and the dynamics of central nervous system development. *Nature Neuroscience, 7,* 327–332.

Huang, J. Y., Sedlovskaya, A., Ackerman, J. M., & Bargh, J. A. (2011). Immunizing against prejudice: Effects of disease protection on attitudes toward out-groups. *Psychological Science, 22*(12), 1550–1556. doi:10.1177/0956797611417261.

Huang, L., & Li, C. (2000). Leptin: A multifunctional hormone. *Cell Research, 10,* 81–92.

Huang, R., Kahai, S., & Jestice, R. (2010). The contingent effects of leadership on team collaboration in virtual teams. *Computers In Human Behavior, 26*(5), 1098–1110. doi:10.1016/j.chb.2010.03.014.

Hubel, D. H., & Wiesel, T. N. (1979). Brain mechanisms of vision. *Scientific American, 241,* 150–162.

Huber, O. (2012). Risky decisions: Active risk management. *Current Directions in Psychological Science, 21*(1), 26–30. doi:10.1177/0963721411422055.

Hubert, M., Hubert, M., Hansen, F., & Kenning, P. (2010). Net emotional response strength and fMRI. *Neuropsychoeconomics Conference Proceedings,* 21.

Huck, S., Kemp, C., & Carter, M. (2010). Self-concept of children with intellectual disability in mainstream settings. *Journal of Intellectual and Developmental Disability, 35*(3), 141–154. doi:10.3109/13668250.2010.489226.

Hudson, J. I., Hiripi, E., Pope, H. G., Jr, & Kessler, R. C. (2007). The prevalence and correlates of eating disorders in the National Comorbidity Survey replication. *Biological Psychiatry, 61,* 348–358.

Hudson, J. L., & Rapee, R. M. (2009). Familial and social environments in the eitology and maintenance of anxiety disorders. In M. M. Antony & M. B. Stein (Eds.) *Oxford handbook of anxiety and related disorders* (pp. 173–189). New York: Oxford University Press.

Hudson, W. (1960). Pictorial depth in perception in subcultural groups in Africa. *Journal of Social Psychology, 52,* 183–208.

Hudziak, J. J., Derks, E. M., Althoff, R. R., Rettew, D. C., & Boomsma, D. I. (2005). The genetic and environmental contributions to attention deficit hyperactivity disorder as measured by the Conners' Rating Scales—Revised. *American Journal of Psychiatry, 162,* 1614–1620.

Hudziak, J. J., van Beijsterveldt, C. E. M., Bartels, M., Rietveld, M. J. H., Rettew, D. C., Derks, E. M., et al. (2003). Individual differences in aggression: Genetic analyses by age, gender, and informant in 3-, 7-, and 10-year-old Dutch twins. *Behavior Genetics, 33,* 575–589.

Huebner, R. R., & Izard, C. E. (1988). Mothers responses to infants facial expressions of sadness, anger, and physical distress. *Motivation and Emotion, 12,* 185–196.

Huesmann, L. R. (1995). *Screen violence and real violence: Understanding the link.* Auckland, NZ: Media Aware.

Huesmann, L. R. (1998). The role of social information processing and cognitive schema in the acquisition and maintenance of habitual aggressive behavior. In R. G. Geen & E. Donnerstein (Eds.), *Human aggression.* San Diego: Academic Press.

Huesmann, L. R., & Eron, L. D. (1986). *Television and the aggressive child: A cross-national comparison.* Hillsdale, NJ: Erlbaum.

Huesmann, L. R., Moise, J., Podolski, C., & Eron, L. (1997, April). *Longitudinal relations between early exposure to television violence and young adult aggression: 1977–1992.* Paper presented at the annual meeting of the Society for Research in Child Development, Washington, DC.

Huesmann, L. R., Moise-Titus, J., Podolski, C., & Eron, L. D. (2003). Longitudinal relations between children's exposure to TV violence and their aggressive and violent behavior in young adulthood: 1977–1992. *Developmental Psychology, 39,* 201–221.

Huffcutt, A. I., & Arthur, W. (1994). Hunter and Hunter (1984) revisited: Interview validity for entry-level jobs. *Journal of Applied Psychology, 79,* 184–190.

Huffcutt, A. I., Conway, J. M., Roth, P. L., & Stone, N. J. (2001). Identification and meta-analytic assessment of psychological constructs measured in employment interviews. *Journal of Applied Psychology, 86,* 897–913.

Hughes, B. M. (2006). Lies, damned lies, and pseudoscience: The selling of eye movement desensitization and reprocessing (EMDR). *PsycCritiques, 51,* 10.

Hughes, D., Rowe, M., Batey, M., & Lee, A. (2012). A tale of two sites: Twitter vs. Facebook and the personality predictors of social media usage. *Computers in Human Behavior, 28,* 561–569. doi:10.1016/j.chb.2011.11.001.

Hughes, J. N., Wu, J., Kwok, O., Villarreal, V., & Johnson, A. Y. (2012). Indirect effects of child reports of teacher–student relationship on achievement. *Journal of Educational Psychology, 104*(2), 350–365. doi:10.1037/a0026339.

Hughes, J. R., Higgins, S. T., & Bickel, W. K. (1994). Nicotine withdrawal versus other drug withdrawal syndromes: Similarities and dissimilarities. *Addiction, 89*(11), 1461–1470.

Hughes, R. N. (2007). Neotic preferences in laboratory rodents: Issues, assessment and substrates. *Neuroscience & Biobehavioral Reviews, 31*(3), 441–464.

Hui, C., Lam, S. S. K., & Law, K. K. S. (2000). Instrumental values of organizational citizenship behavior for promotion: A field quasi-experiment. *Journal of Applied Psychology, 85,* 822–828.

Huibregtse, B., Bornovalova, M., Hicks, B., McGue, M., & Iacono, W. (2011). Testing the role of adolescent sexual initiation in later-life sexual risk behavior: a longitudinal twin design. *Psychological Science, 22*(7), 924–933.

Huijbregts, S. J., van Berkel, S. R., Swaab-Barneveld, H., & van Goozen, S. M. (2011). Neurobiological and behavioral stress reactivity in children prenatally exposed to tobacco. *Psychoneuroendocrinology, 36*(6), 913–918. doi:10.1016/j.psyneuen.2010.12.008.

Huizink, A. C., Mulder, E. J. H., & Buitelaar, J. K. (2004). Prenatal stress and risk for psychopathology. *Psychological Bulletin, 130,* 115–142.

Hull, C. L. (1951). *Essentials of behavior.* New Haven, CT: Yale University Press.

Hull, S. A., Cornwell, J., Harvey, C., Eldridge, S., & Bare, P. O. (2001). Prescribing rates for psychotropic medication amongst east London general practices: Low rates where Asian populations are greatest. *Family Practice, 18,* 167–173.

Human, L. J., & Biesanz, J. C. (2012). Accuracy and assumed similarity in first impressions of personality: Differing associations at different levels of analysis. *Journal of Research in Personality, 46*, 106–110. doi:10.1016/j.jrp.2011.10.002.

Humphreys, K. (2004). *Circles of recovery: Self-help organizations for addictions.* New York: Cambridge University Press.

Humphries, J. E., Holliday, R. E., & Flowe, H. D. (2012). Faces in motion: Age-related changes in eyewitness identification performance in simultaneous, sequential, and elimination video lineups. *Applied Cognitive Psychology, 26*(1), 149–158. doi:10.1002/acp.1808.

Hungerford, A., Wait, S. K., Fritz, A. M., & Clements, C. M. (2012). Exposure to intimate partner violence and children's psychological adjustment, cognitive functioning, and social competence: A review. *Aggression & Violent Behavior, 17*, 373–382. doi:10.1016/j.avb.2012.04.002.

Hunnius, S., & Bekkering, H. (2010). The early development of object knowledge: A study of infants' visual anticipations during action observation. *Developmental Psychology, 46*(2), 446–454. doi:10.1037/a0016543.

Hunsley, J., Lee, C. M., & Wood, J. M. (2003). Controversial and questionable assessment techniques. In S. O. Lilienfeld & S. J. Lynn (Eds.), *Science and pseudoscience in clinical psychology* (pp. 39–76). New York: Guilford Press.

Hunt, C. E., & Hauck, F. R. (2006). Sudden infant death syndrome. *Canadian Medical Association Journal, 174*, 1861–1869.

Hunt, E. (1983). On the nature of intelligence. *Science, 219*, 141–146.

Hunt, E. (2012). What makes nations intelligent? *Perspectives on Psychological Science, 7*(3), 284–306. doi:10.1177/1745691612442905.

Hunt, M. (1982). *The universe within.* New York: Simon & Schuster.

Hunt, M., & Forand, R. (2005). Cognitive vulnerability to depression in never depressed subjects. *Cognition and Emotion, 19*, 763–770.

Hunt, R., & Rouse, W. B. (1981). Problem solving skills of maintenance trainees in diagnosing faults in simulated power plants. *Human Factors, 23*, 317–328.

Hunter, M. A., & Ames, E. W. (1988). A multifactor model of infants' preferences for novel and familiar stimuli. In C. Rovee-Collier & L. P. Lipsitt (Eds.), *Advances in infancy research* (Vol. 5, pp. 69–91). Norwood, NJ: Ablex.

Huprich, S. K. (2009). What should become of depressive personality in DSM-V? *Harvard Review of Psychiatry, 17*, 41–59.

Hurt, H., Brodsky, N. L., Betancourt, L., & Braitman, L. E. (1995). Cocaine-exposed children: Follow-up through 30 months. *Journal of Developmental and Behavioral Pediatrics, 16*(1), 29–35.

Hussar, K. M., & Horvath, J. C. (2011). Do children play fair with mother nature? Understanding children's judgments of environmentally harmful actions. *Journal of Environmental Psychology, 31*(4), 309–313. doi:10.1016/j.jenvp.2011.05.001.

Husseman, J., & Raphael, Y. (2009). Gene therapy in the inner ear using adenovirus vectors. *Advances in Otorhinolaryngology, 66*, 37–51.

Huston, A. C., & Wright, J. C. (1989). The forms of television and the child viewer. In G. Comstock (Ed.), *Public communication and behavior* (Vol. 2, pp. 103–159). San Diego: Academic Press.

Huston, T. L., Caughlin, J. P., Houts, R. M., Smith, S. E., & George, L. J. (2001). The connubial crucible: Newlywed years as predictors of marital delight, distress, and divorce. *Journal of Personality and Social Psychology, 80*, 237–252.

Hutchinson, A. K., Stuart, A. D., & Pretorius, H. G. (2010). Biological contributions to well-being: The relationships amongst temperament, character strengths and resilience. *SAJIP: South African Journal of Industrial Psychology, 36*(2), 1–10. doi:10.4102/sajip.v36i2.844.

Huttenlocher, P. R. (1990). Morphometric study of human cerebral cortex development. *Neuropsychologia, 28*, 517–527.

Hwang, K. (2010). Way to capture theory of indigenous psychology. *Psychological Studies, 55*(2), 96–100. doi:10.1007/s12646-010-0024-3.

Hwang, K. (2009). The development of indigenous counseling in contemporary Confucian communities. *The Counseling Psychologist, 37*(7), 930–943. doi:10.1177/0011000009336241.

Hwang, W.-C. (2006). The psychotherapy adaptation and modification framework: Application to Asian Americans. *American Psychologist, 61*, 702–715.

Hybels, C. F., Pieper, C. F., Blazer, D. G., & Steffens, D. C. (2008). The course of depressive symptoms in older adults with comorbid major depression and dysthymia. *American Journal of Geriatric Psychiatry, 16*, 300–309.

Hyde, J. S. (1986). Gender differences in aggression. In J. S. Hyde & M. C. Linn (Eds.), *The psychology of gender: Advances through meta-analysis.* Baltimore: Johns Hopkins University Press.

Hyde, J. S. (2005). The gender similarities hypothesis. *American Psychologist, 60*, 581–592.

Hyde, J. S., & Durik, A. M. (2000). Gender differences in erotic plasticity–Evolutionary or sociocultural forces? Comment on Baumeister (2000). *Psychological Bulletin, 126*, 375–379.

Hyde, K. L., Lerch, J., Norton, A., Forgeard, M., Winner, E., Evans, A. C., & Schlaug, G. (2009). Musical training shapes structural brain development. *The Journal of Neuroscience, 29*, 3019–3025.

Hyde, Z., Flicker, L., Hankey, G. J., Almeida, O. P., McCaul, K. A., Chubb, S., & Yeap, B. B. (2010). Prevalence of sexual activity and associated factors in men aged 75 to 95 years. *Annals Of Internal Medicine, 153*(11), 693–702.

Hyman, I. E., Jr. (2000). The memory wars. In U. Neisser & I. E. Hyman, Jr. (Eds.), *Memory observed* (2nd ed., pp. 374–379). New York: Worth.

Hyman, I. E., Jr.; Boss, S. M.; Wise, B. M.; McKenzie, K. E.; & Caggiano, J. M. (2010). Did you see the unicycling clown? Inattentional blindness while walking and talking on a cell phone. *Applied Cognitive Psychology, 24*, 597–607. doi:10.1002/acp.1638

Hyman, I. E., Jr., & Pentland, J. (1996). The role of mental imagery in the creation of false childhood memories. *Journal of Memory and Language, 35*, 101–117.

Hyman, R. (2002). Why and when are smart people stupid? In R. J. Sternberg (Ed.), *Why smart people can be so stupid* (pp. 1–23). New Haven, CT: Yale University Press.

Hyman, S. E., Malenka, R. C., & Nestler, E. J. (2006). Neural mechanisms of addiction: The role of reward-related learning and memory. *Annual Review of Neuroscience, 29*, 565–598.

Hypericum Depression Trial Study Group. (2002). Effect of *Hypericum perforatum* (St. John's wort) in major depressive disorder: A randomized, controlled trial. *Journal of the American Medical Association, 287*, 1.

Iacono, W. G., & Patrick, C. J. (2006). Polygraph ("lie detector") testing: Current status and emerging trends. In I. B. Weiner & A. K. Hess (Eds.), *The handbook of forensic psychology* (3rd ed., pp. 552–588). Hoboken, NJ: Wiley.

Iancu, I., Poreh, A., Lehman, B., Shamir, E., & Kotler, M. (2005). The positive and negative symptoms questionnaire: A self-report in schizophrenia. *Comprehensive Psychiatry, 46*, 61–66.

Iancu, I. I., & Ram, E. E. (2011). P01-455 - Shyness and social phobia in Israeli Jewish versus Arab students. *European Psychiatry, 26459*. doi:10.1016/S0924-9338(11)72166-6.

Iani, C., Ricci, F., Ghem, E., & Rubichi, S. (2006). Hypnotic suggestion modulates cognitive conflict: The case of the flanker compatibility effect. *Psychological Science, 17*, 721–727.

Iaria, G., Fox, C. J., Scheel, M., Stowe, R. M., & Barton, J. J. (2010). A case of persistent visual hallucinations of faces following LSD abuse: a functional Magnetic Resonance Imaging study. *Neurocase, 16*(2), 106–18.

Iber, C., Ancoli-Israel, S., Chesson, A., & Quan, S. F. (2007). *The AASM Manual*

Iervolino, A. C., Hines, M., Golombok, S. E., Rust, J., & Plomin, R. (2005). Genetic and environmental influences on sex-typed behavior during the preschool years. *Child Development, 76*, 826–840.

Igalens, J., & Roussel, P. (1999). A study of the relationships between compensation package, work motivation, and job satisfaction. *Journal of Organizational Behavior, 20*, 1003–1025.

Iglesias, A., Martínez, P., Aler, R., & Fernández, F. (2009). Learning teaching strategies in an adaptive and intelligent educational system through reinforcement learning. *Applied Intelligence, 31*(1), 89-106. doi:10.1007/s10489-008-0115-1.

IJzerman, H., & Semin, G. R. (2009). Th e thermometer of social relations: Mapping social proximity on temperature. *Psychological Science, 20*, 1214–1220.

Ilgen, D. R., & Pulakos, E. D. (Eds.). (1999). *The changing nature of performance: Implications for staffing, motivation, and development.* San Francisco, CA: Jossey-Bass.

Ilies, R., & Judge, T. A. (2003). On the heritability of job satisfaction: The mediating role of personality. *Journal of Applied Psychology, 88*, 750–759.

Ilies, R., Nahrgang, J. D., & Morgeson, F. P. (2007). Leader-member exchange and citizenship behaviors: A meta-analysis. *Journal of Applied Psychology, 92*, 269–277.

Ilies, R., Scott, B. A., & Judge, T. A. (2006). The interactive effects of personal traits and experienced states on intraindividual patterns of citizenship behavior. *Academy of Management Journal, 49*, 561–575.

Iliescu, D., Ilie, A., & Ispas, D., (2011). Examining the Criterion-Related Validity of the Employee Screening Questionnaire: A Three-Sample Investigation *International Journal of Selection and Assessment, 19*, 222–228.

Imada, T., & Ellsworth, P. C. (2011). Proud Americans and lucky Japanese: Cultural differences in appraisal and corresponding emotion. *Emotion, 11*(2), 329–345. doi:10.1037/a0022855.

Immordino-Yang, M.H., Christodoulou, J.A., & Singh, V. (2012). Rest is not idleness: Implications of the brain's default mode for human development and education. *Perspectives on Psychological Science, 7*, 352–364. doi:10.1177/1745691612447308.

Imtiaz, K. E., Nirodi, G., & Khaleeli, A. A. (2001). Alexia without agraphia: A century later. *International Journal of Clinical Practice, 55*(3), 225–226.

Inda, M., Muravieva, E. V., & Alberini, C. M. (2011). Memory retrieval and the passage of time: From reconsolidation and strengthening to extinction. *Journal Of Neuroscience, 31*(5), 1635–1643. doi:10.1523/JNEUROSCI.4736-10.201.

Indovina, I., & Sanes, J. N. (2001). On somatotopic representation centers for finger movements in human primary motor cortex and supplementary motor area. *Neuroimage, 13*, 1027–1034.

Ingersoll, B. (2011). Recent advances in early identification and treatment of autism. *Current Directions in Psychological Science, 20*(5), 335–339. doi:10.1177/0963721411418470.

Inness, M., Barling, J., & Turner, N. (2005). Understanding supervisor-targeted aggression: A within-person, between-jobs design. *Journal of Applied Psychology, 90*, 731–739.

Inoue, K., Tanii, H., Fukunaga, T., Abe, S., Kaiya, H., Nata, M., & Okazaki, Y. (2006). Letter to the editor: Significant correlation of yearly suicide rates with the rate of unemployment among men results in a rapid increase of suicide in Mie Prefecture, Japan. *Psychiatry and Clinical Neurosciences, 60*, 781–782.

Insel, T. R. (2008). Assessing the economic cost of serious mental illness. *American Journal of Psychiatry, 165*, 663–665.

Inskip, P., Hoover, R., & Devesa, S. (2010). Brain cancer incidence trends in relation to cellular telephone use in the United States. *Neuro-Oncology, 12*(11), 1147–1151.

Institute of Medicine. (2006, April 5). *Sleep disorders and sleep deprivation: An unmet public health problem* [Press release]. Retrieved September 26, 2006, from http://www.iom.edu/ CMS/3740/23160/33668.aspx.

International Human Genome Sequencing Consortium. (2001). Initial sequencing and analysis of the human genome. *Nature, 409*, 860–921.

Inzitari, M., Pozzi, C., Ferrucci, L., Chiarantini, D., Rinaldi, L. A., Baccini, M., Pini, R., Masotti, G., Marchionni, N., & Di Bari, M. (2008). Subtle neurological abnormalities as risk factors for cognitive and functional decline, cerebrovascular events, and mortality in older community-dwelling adults. *Archives of Internal Medicine, 168,* 1270–1276.

Ireland, M. E., Slatcher, R. B., Eastwick, P. W., Scissors, L. E., Finkel, E. J., & Pennebaker, J. W. (2011). Language style matching predicts relationship initiation and stability. *Psychological Science, 22*(1), 39–44. doi:10.1177/0956797610392928.

Ironson, G., Freund, B., Strauss, J. L., & Williams J. (2002). Comparison of two treatments for traumatic stress: A community-based study of EMDR and prolonged exposure. *Journal of Clinical Psychology, 58,* 113–128.

Ironson, G. H., Smith, P. C., Brannick, M. T., Gibson, W. M., & Paul, K. B. (1989). Constitution of a Job in General scale: A comparison of global, composite, and specific measures. *Journal of Applied Psychology, 74,* 193–200.

Irwin, M., Daniels, M., Smith, T., Bloom, E., & Weiner, H. (1987). Impaired natural killer cell activity during bereavement. *Brain, Behavior, and Immunity, 1,* 98–104.

Ishikawa, A., Kanayama, Y., Matsumura, H., Tsuchimochi, H., Ishida, Y., & Nakamura, S. (2006). Selective rapid eye movement sleep deprivation impairs the maintenance of long-term potentiation in the rat hippocampus. *European Journal of Neuroscience, 24,* 243–248.

Ito, H. (2012). Cortical shape adaptation transforms a circle into a hexagon: A novel afterimage illusion. *Psychological Science, 23*(2), 126–132. doi:10.1177/0956797611422236.

Ivleva, E., Thaker, G., & Tamminga, C. (2008). Comparing genes and phenomenology in the major psychoses: Schizophrenia and bipolar 1 disorder. *Schizophrenia Bulletin, 34*(4), 734–742.

Iwahashi, K., Matsuo, Y., Suwaki, H., Nakamura, K., & Ichikawa, Y. (1995). CYP2E1 and ALDH2 genotypes and alcohol dependence in Japanese. *Alcoholism Clinical and Experimental Research, 19*(3), 564–566.

Iwamasa, G. Y., Sorocco, K. H., & Koonce, D. A. (2002). Ethnicity and clinical psychology: A content analysis of the literature. *Clinical Psychology Review, 22,* 932–944.

Iwata, M., Hazama, G., & Nakagome, K. (2012). Depressive state due to isolated adrenocorticotropic hormone deficiency underlies school refusal. *Psychiatry & Clinical Neurosciences, 66*(3), 243–244. doi:10.1111/j.1440-1819.2012.02322.x

Izac, S. M., & Eeg, T. R. (2006). Basic anatomy and physiology of sleep. *American Journal of Electroneurodiagnostic Technology, 46*(1), 18–38.

Izard, C., Fine, S., Schultz, D. Mostow, A., Ackerman, B., & Youngstrom, E. (2001). Emotion knowledge as a predictor of social behavior and academic competence in children at risk. *Psychological Science, 12,* 18–23.

Izard, C. E. (2007). Basic emotions, natural kinds, emotion schemas, and a new paradigm. *Perspectives on Psychological Science, 2,* 260–280.

Izard, C. E. (1993). Four systems for emotion activation: Cognitive and noncognitive development. *Psychological Review, 100,* 68–90.

Izard, C. E., Huebner, R. R., Risser, D., McGinnes, G., & Dougherty, L. (1980). The young infant's ability to reproduce discrete emotion expressions. *Developmental Psychology, 16,* 132–140.

Izard, C. E. (1977). *Human emotions.* New York: Plenum.

Izumikawa, M., Minoda, R., Kawamoto, K., Abrashkin, K. A., Swiderski, D. L., Dolan, D. F., et al. (2005). Auditory hair cell replacement and hearing improvement by Atoh1 gene therapy in deaf animals. *Nature, 11,* 271–276.

Jaccard, J., Blanton, H., & Dodge, T. (2005). Peer influences on risk behavior: An analysis of the effects of a close friend. *Developmental Psychology, 41,* 135–147.

Jack, F., & Hayne, H. (2007). Eliciting adults' earliest memories: Does it matter how we ask the question? *Memory, 15*(6), 647–663.

Jack, R. E., Garrod, O. G. B., Yu, H., Caldarac, R., & Schyns, P. G. (2012). Facial expressions of emotion are not culturally universal. www.pnas.org/cgi/doi/10.1073/pnas.1200155109.

Jackson, B., Sellers, R. M., & Peterson, C. (2002). Pessimistic explanatory style moderates the effect of stress on physical illness. *Personality & Individual Differences, 32,* 567–573.

Jackson, C. J. (2003). Gray's Reinforcement Sensitivity Theory: A psychometric critique. *Personality and Individual Differences, 34,* 533–544.

Jackson, J. J., Thoemmes, F., Jonkmann, K., Lüdtke, O., & Trautwein, U. (2012). Military training and personality trait development: Does the military make the man, or does the man make the military? *Psychological Science, 23,* 270–277. doi:10.1177/0956797611423545.

Jackson, J. W. (2002). The relationship between group identity and intergroup prejudice is moderated by sociostructural variation. *Journal of Applied Social Psychology, 32,* 908–933.

Jackson, L. A., von Eye, A., Biocca, F. A., Barbatsis, G., Zhao, Y., & Fitzgerald, H. E. (2006). Does home internet use influence the academic performance of low-income children? *Developmental Psychology, 42,* 429–435.

Jackson, M. L., Howard, M. E., & Barnes, M. (2011). Cognition and daytime functioning in sleep-related breathing disorders. *Progress in Brain Research, 190,* 53–68.

Jacob, S., & McClintock, M. K. (2000). Psychological state and mood effects of steroidal chemosignals in women and men. *Hormones and Behavior, 37,* 57–78.

Jacob, S., Kinnunen, L. H., Metz, J., Cooper, M., & McClintock, M. K. (2001). Sustained human chemosignal unconsciously alters brain function. *Neuroreport, 12,* 2391–2394.

Jacob, T., Waterman, B., Heath, A., True, W., Bucholz, K. K., Haber, R., et al. (2003). Genetic and environmental effects on offspring alcoholism: New insights using an offspring-of-twins design. *Archives of General Psychiatry, 60,* 1265–1272.

Jacobi, C., Hayward, C., de Zwaan, M., Kraemer, H. C., & Agras, W. S. (2004). Coming to terms with risk factors for eating disorders: Application of risk terminology and suggestions for a general taxonomy. *Psychological Bulletin, 130,* 19–65.

Jacobs, B. L. (2004). Depression: The brain finally gets into the act. *Current Directions in Psychological Science, 13,* 103–106.

Jacobs, G. D., Pace-Schott, E. F., Stickgold, R., & Otto, M. W. (2004). Cognitive behavior therapy and pharmacotherapy for insomnia: A randomized controlled trial and direct comparison. *Archives of Internal Medicine, 164,* 1888–1896.

Jacobs, G. H. (2008). Primate color vision: A comparative perspective. *Vision Neuroscience, 25*(5–6), 619–631.

Jacobs, H. I., Van Boxtel, M. P., Heinecke, A., Gronenschild, E. H., Backes, W. H., Ramakers, I. H., Jolles, J., & Verhey, F. R. (2012). Functional integration of parietal lobe activity in early Alzheimer disease. *Neurology, 78*(5), 352–360.

Jacobs, M., Snow, J., Geraci, M., Vythilingam, M., Blair, R. J. R., et al. (2009). Association between level of emotional intelligence and severity of anxiety in generalized social phobia. *Journal of Anxiety Disorders, 22,* 1487–1495.

Jacobs, N., Kenis, G., Peeters, F., Derom, C., Vlietinck, R., & van Os, J. (2006). Stress-related negative affectivity and genetically altered serotonin transporter function: Evidence of synergism in shaping risk of depression. *Archives of General Psychiatry, 63,* 989–996.

Jacobs, R., & Solomon, T. (1977). Strategies for enhancing the prediction of job performance from job satisfaction. *Journal of Applied Psychology, 62,* 417–421.

Jacobson, E. (1938). *Progressive relaxation.* Chicago: University of Chicago Press.

Jacobson, K. (2002). ADHD in cross-cultural perspective: Some empirical results. *American Anthropologist, 104,* 283–286.

Jaeggi, S. M., Buschkuehl, M., Jonides, J., & Shah, P. (2011). Short- and long-term benefits of cognitive training. *PNAS Proceedings of the National Academy of Sciences of the United States of America, 108*(25), 10081–10086. doi:10.1073/pnas.1103228108.

Jaffari-Bimmel, N., Juffer, F., van IJzendoorn, M. H., Bakermans-Kranenburg, M. J., & Mooijaart, A. (2006). Social development from infancy to adolescence: Longitudinal and concurrent factors in an adoption sample. *Developmental Psychology, 42*(6), 1143–1153.

Jaffee, S., & Hyde, J. S. (2000). Gender differences in moral orientation: A meta-analysis. *Psychological Bulletin, 126,* 703–726.

Jaffee, S. R., Caspi, A., Moffitt, T. E., & Taylor, A. (2004). Physical maltreatment to antisocial child: Evidence of an environmentally mediated process. *Journal of Abnormal Psychology, 113,* 44–55.

Jaffee, S. R., Hanscombe, K. B., Haworth, C. A., Davis, O. P., & Plomin, R. (2012). Chaotic homes and children's disruptive behavior: A longitudinal cross-lagged twin study. *Psychological Science, 23,* 643–650. doi:10.1177/0956797611431693

Jago, R., Baranowski, T., Baranowski, J. C., Thompson, D., & Greaves, K. A. (2005). BMI from 3–6 y of age is predicted by TV viewing and physical activity, not diet. *International Journal of Obesity, 29,* 557–564.

Jahnke, J. C., & Nowaczyk, R. H. (1998). *Cognition.* Upper Saddle River, NJ: Prentice Hall. Jain, A. (2005). Treating obesity in individuals and populations. *British Medical Journal, 331,* 1387–1390.

Jakobsen, K. D., Frederiksen, J. N., Hansen, T., Jansson, L., et al. (2005). Reliability of clinical ICD-10 schizophrenia diagnoses. *Nordic Journal of Psychiatry, 59,* 209–212.

Jakubowska, E., & Zielinski, K. (1978). Stimulus intensity effects on the acute extinction of the CER in rats. *Acta Neurobiologica Experimentalis, 38,* 1–10.

James, L., Barnes, T. R. E., Lelliott, P., Taylor, D., & Paton, C. (2007). Informing patients of the teratogenic potential of mood stabilizing drugs: A case note review of the practice of psychiatrists. *Journal of Psychopharmacology, 21*(8), 815–819.

James, S. D., (2008, May 7). Wild child speechless after tortured life. Retrieved from http://abcnews.go.com/Health/story?id=4804490&page=1#.T6_6k1Iuh8E.

James, W. (1890). *Principles of psychology.* New York: Holt.

James, W. (1892). *Psychology: Briefer course.* New York: Holt.

Jameson, L. C., & Sloan, T. B. (2006). Using EEG to monitor anesthesia drug effects during surgery. *Journal of Clinical Monitoring and Computers, 20,* 445–472.

Jamieson, P., Jamieson, K. H., & Romer, D. (2003). The responsible reporting of suicide in print journalism. *American Behavioral Scientist, 46,* 1643–1660.

Jan, J. E., Freeman, R. D., Wasdell, M. B., & Bomben, M. M. (2004). 'A child with severe night terrors and sleep-walking responds to melatonin therapy'. *Developmental Medicine and Child Neurology, 46*(11), 789.

Jancke, L., & Kaufmann, N. (1994). Facial EMG responses to odors in solitude and with an audience. *Chemical Senses, 19*(2), 99–111.

Janis, I. L. (1989). *Crucial decisions: Leadership in policy making and crisis management.* New York: Free Press.

Janowiak, J. J., & Hackman, R. (1994). Meditation and college students' self-actualization and rated stress. *Psychological Reports, 75*(2), 1007–1010.

Janowitz, H. D. (1967). Role of gastrointestinal tract in the regulation of food intake. In C. F. Code (Ed.), *Handbook of physiology: Alimentary canal 1.* Washington, DC: American Physiological Society.

Jans, L. A. W., Riedel, W. J., Markus, C. R., & Blokland, A. (2007). Serotonergic vulnerability and depression: Assumptions, experimental evidence and implications. *Molecular Psychiatry, 12,* 522–543.

Jansen, P. G., & Vinkenburg, C. J. (2006). Predicting managerial career success from assessment center data: A longitudinal study. *Journal of Vocational Behavior, 68,* 253–266.

Jarosz, A., Colflesh, G., and Wiley, J. (2012). Uncorking the muse: Alcohol intoxication facilitates creative problem solving. *Consciousness and Cognition, 21*(1), 487–493 DOI: 10.1016/j.concog.2012.01.002

Jason, L. A., Witter, E., & Torres-Harding, S. (2003). Chronic fatigue syndrome, coping, optimism and social support. *Journal of Mental Health, 12,* 109–118.

Jaušovec, N., & Jaušovec, K. (2012). Working memory training: Improving intelligence—Changing brain activity. *Brain & Cognition, 79*(2), 96–106. doi:10.1016/j.bandc.2012.02.007.

Javitt, D. C., Kantowitz, J., & Lajtha, A. (Eds.) (2009). *Handbook of neurochemistry and molecular neurobiology: Schizophrenia* (3rd ed.). New York: Springer.

Jayanthi, S., Buie, S., Moore, S., Herning, R. I., et al. (2010). Heavy marijuana users show increased serum apolipoprotein C-III levels: Evidence from proteomic analyses. *Molecular Psychiatry, 15,* 101–112.

Jefferis, B. M. J. H., Power, C., & Hertzman, C. (2002). Birth weight, childhood socioeconomic environment, and cognitive development in the 1958 British birth cohort study [Electronic version]. *British Medical Journal, 325,* 305.

Jeffries, K. J., Fritz, J. B., & Braun, A. R. (2003). Words in melody: An H(2)15O PET study of brain activation during singing and speaking. *Neuroreport, 14,* 749–754.

Jen, H. C., Rickard, D. G., Shew, S. B., Maggard, M. A., Slusser, W. M., Dutson, E. P., & DeUgarte, D. A. (2010). Trends and outcomes of adolescent bariatric surgery in California, 2005–2007. *Pediatrics, 126*(4), 773.

Jencks, C., & Phillips, M. (Eds.). (1998). *The black-white test score gap.* Washington, DC: Brookings Institution Press.

Jenkins, M. R., & Culbertson, J. L. (1996). Prenatal exposure to alcohol. In R. L. Adams, O. A. Parsons, J. L. Culbertson, & S. J. Nixon (Eds.), *Neuropsychology for clinical practice: Etiology, assessment, and treatment of common neurological disorders* (pp. 409–452). Washington, DC: American Psychological Association.

Jenkins, R. O., & Sherbum, R. E. (2005). Growth and survival of bacteria implicated in sudden infant death syndrome on cot mattress materials. *Journal of Applied Microbiology, 99,* 573–579.

Jenkinson, P. M., Preston, C., & Ellis, S. J. (2011). Unawareness after stroke: a review and practical guide to understanding, assessing, and managing anosognosia for hemiplegia. *Journal of Clinical and Experimental Neuropsychology, 33*(10), 1079–1093.

Jensen, M., & Karoly, P. (1991). Control beliefs, coping efforts, and adjustment to chronic pain. *Journal of Consulting and Clinical Psychology, 59,* 431–438.

Jevtovic-Todorovic, V., Wozniak, D. F., Benshoff, N. D., & Olney, J. W. (2001). A comparative evaluation of the neurotoxic properties of ketamine and nitrous oxide. *Brain Research, 895,* 264–267.

Jex, S. M., Adams, G. A., Elacqua, T. C., & Bachrach, D. G. (2002). Type A as a moderator of stressors and job complexity: A comparison of achievement strivings and impatience-irritability. *Journal of Applied Social Psychology, 32,* 977–996.

Jobe, T. H., & Harrow, M. (2010). Schizophrenia course, long-term outcome, recovery, and prognosis. *Current Directions in Psychological Science, 19*(4), 220–225. doi:10.1177/0963721410378034.

Jo°t, G., Usher, E. L., & Bressoux, P. (2011). Sources of self-efficacy: An investigation of elementary school students in France. *Journal of Educational Psychology, 103*(3), 649–663. doi:10.1037/a0024048.

John, O., Naumann, L., & Soto, C. (2008). Paradigm shift to the integrative big five trait taxonomy: History, measurement, and conceptual issues, In O. John, R. Robins, & L. Pervin (Eds.), *Handbook of personality: Theory and research* (3rd ed. pp., 114–158). New York: Guilford.

Johnson, B. T., Maio, G. R., & Smith-McLallen, A. (2005). Communication and attitude change: Causes, processes, and effects. In D. Albarracín, B. T. Johnson, & M. P. Zanna (Eds.), *Handbook of attitudes* (pp. 617–669). Mahwah, NJ: Erlbaum.

Johnson, D. R., Westermeyer, J., Kattar, K., & Thuras, P. (2002). Daily charting of posttraumatic stress symptoms: A pilot study. *Journal of Nervous & Mental Disease, 190,* 683–692.

Johnson, E. O., Roth, T., Schultz, L., & Breslau, N. (2006). Epidemiology of DSM-IV insomnia in adolescence: Lifetime prevalence, chronicity, and an emergent gender difference. *Pediatrics, 117,* 247–256.

Johnson, G. (2002). Comments on lithium toxicity. *Australian and New Zealand Journal of Psychiatry, 36,* 703.

Johnson, H. J., Barnard-Brak, L., Saxon, T. F., & Johnson, M. K. (2012). An experimental study of the effects of stereotype threat and stereotype lift on men and women's performance in mathematics. *Journal of Experimental Education, 80*(2), 137–149. doi:10.1080/00220973.2011.567312.

Johnson, I. R., & Fujita, K. (2012). Change we can believe in: Using perceptions of changeability to promote system-change motives over system-justification motives in information search. *Psychological Science, 23*(2), 133–140. doi:10.1177/0956797611423670.

Johnson, J., & Vickers, Z. (1993). Effects of flavor and macronutrient composition of food servings on liking, hunger and subsequent intake. *Appetite, 21*(1), 25–39.

Johnson, J. G., Cohen, P., Smailes, E. M., Kasen, S., & Brook, J. S. (2002). Television viewing and aggressive behavior during adolescence and adulthood. *Science, 295,* 2468–2471.

Johnson, J. M., & Endler, N. S. (2002). Coping with human immunodeficiency virus: Do optimists fare better? *Current Psychology: Developmental, Learning, Personality, Social, 21,* 3–16.

Johnson, J. S., & Newport, E. L. (1989). Critical period effects in second language learning. *Cognitive Psychology, 21,* 60–99.

Johnson, M. A., Dziurawiec, S., Ellis, H., & Morton, J. (1991). Newborns' preferential tracking of face-like stimuli and its subsequent decline. *Cognition, 4,* 1–19.

Johnson, S. L. (2003). *Therapist's guide to clinical intervention: The 1-2-3's of treatment planning.* San Diego, CA: Academic Press.

Johnson, S. L., & Birch, L. L. (1994).Parents' and children's adiposity and eating style. *Pediatrics, 94,* 653–656.

Johnson, W., Jung, R. E., Colom, R., & Haier, R. J. (2008). Cognitive abilities independent of IQ correlate with regional brain structure. *Intelligence, 36*(1), 18–28.

Johnson, W., McGue, M., & Krueger, R. F. (2005). Personality stability in late adulthood: A behavioral genetic analysis. *Journal of Personality, 73,* 523–551.

Johnson, W., Turkheimer, E., Gottesman, I. I., & Bouchard, T. J., Jr. (2009). Beyond heritability: Twin studies in behavioral research. *Current Directions in Psychological Science, 18,* 217–220.

Johnson, W. R., & Neal, D. (1998). Basic skills and the black-white earnings gap. In C. Jencks & M. Phillips (Eds.), *The black-white test score gap* (pp. 480–497). Washington, DC: Brookings Institute Press.

Johnson-Greene, D. & Collins, K. C. (2011). Characteristics of American Psychological Association Division 40 (clinical neuropsychology) Fellows. *Clinical Neuropsychology, 25*(8), 1378–1385.

Johnson-Laird, P.N. (2010). Mental models and human reasoning. *Proceedings of the National Academy of Sciences, 107,* 18243–18250.

Johnson-Laird, P. N. (1983). *Mental models: Toward a cognitive science of language, inference, and consciousness.* Cambridge, MA: Harvard University Press.

Johnson-Laird, P. N., Mancini, F., & Gangemi, A. (2006). A hyper-emotion theory of psychological illnesses. *Psychological Review, 113,* 822–841.

Johnston, D. W., Tuomisto, M. T., & Patching, G. R. (2008). The relationship between cardiac reactivity in the laboratory and in real life. *Health Psychology, 27,* 34–42.

Johnston, K. (1988). Adolescents' solutions to dilemmas in fables: Two moral orientations. In C. Gilligan, J. V. Ward, J. M. Taylor, & B. Bardige (Eds.), *Mapping the moral domain: A contribution to psychological theory and education.* Cambridge: Harvard University Press.

Joireman, J., & Durell, B. (2007). Self-transcendent values moderate the impact of mortality salience on support for charities. *Personality and Individual Differences, 43,* 779–789.

Jokela, M. (2010). Characteristics of the first child predict the parents' probability of having another child. *Developmental Psychology, 46,* 915–926.

Jonas, E., Schimel, J., Greenberg, J., & Pyszczynski, T. (2002). The Scrooge effect: Evidence that mortality salience increases prosocial attitudes and behavior. *Personality and Social Psychology Bulletin, 28,* 1342–1353.

Jones, A. (2007). Maternal alcohol abuse/dependence, children's behavior problems, and home environment: Estimates from the national longitudinal survey of youth using propensity score matching. *Journal of Studies on Alcohol and Drugs, 68*(2), 266–275.

Jones, E. E. (1982). Psychotherapists' impressions of treatment outcome as a function of race. *Journal of Clinical Psychology, 38,* 722–731.

Jones, G. V. (1990). Misremembering a common object: When left is not right. *Memory & Cognition, 18,* 174–182.

Jones, H. E. (2006). Drug addiction during pregnancy. *Current Directions in Psychological Science, 15,* 126–130.

Jones, J. R., & Schaubroeck, J. (2004). Mediators of the relationship between race and organizational citizenship behavior. *Journal of Managerial Issues, 16,* 505–527.

Jones, M. A., Botsko, M., & Gorman, B. S. (2003). Predictors of psychotherapeutic benefit of lesbian, gay, and bisexual clients: The effects of sexual orientation matching and other factors. *Psychotherapy: Theory, Research, Practice, Training, 40,* 289–301.

Jones, P. M., & Haselgrove, M. (2011) Overshadowing and associability change. *Journal of Experimental Psychology: Animal Behavior Processes, 37,* 287–299.

Jones, P. R. (2011). Reducing the impact of stereotype threat on women's math performance: Are two strategies better than one? *Electronic Journal of Research in Educational Psychology, 9*(2), 587–616.

Jong, J., Kao, T., Lee, L., Huang, H., Lo, P., & Wang, H. (2010). Can temperament be understood at birth? The relationship between neonatal pain cry and their temperament: A preliminary study. *Infant Behavior & Development, 33*(3), 266–272. doi:10.1016/j.infbeh.2010.02.001.

Jonides, J., Lacey, S. C., & Nee, D. E. (2005). Processes of working memory in mind and brain. *Current Directions in Psychological Science, 14,* 2–5.

Joormann, J., Teachman, B. A., & Gotlib, I. H. (2009). Sadder and less accurate? False memory for negative material in depression. *Journal of Abnormal Psychology, 118,* 412–417.

Jordan, N., Grissom, G., Alonzo, G., Dietzen, L., & Sangsland, S. (2008). Economic benefit of chemical dependency treatment to employers. *Journal of Substance Abuse Treatment, 34,* 311–319.

Jordan, N. C., Huttenlocher, J., & Levine, S. C. (1992). Differential calculation abilities in young children from middle- and low-income families. *Developmental Psychology, 28,* 644–653.

Jorge, R. E., Moser, D. J., Acion, L., & Robinson, R. G. (2008). Treatment of vascular depression using repetitive transcranial magnetic stimulation. *Archives of General Psychiatry, 65,* 268–276.

Jorm, A. F. (2012). Mental health literacy: Empowering the community to take action for better mental health. *American Psychologist, 67*(3), 231–243. doi:10.1037/a0025957.

Joseph, J. E., Liu, X., Jiang, Y., Lynam, D., & Kelly, T. (2009). Neural correlates of emotional reactivity in sensation seeking. *Psychological Science, 20,* 215–223.

Josephson, W. L. (1987). Television violence and children's aggression: Testing the priming, social script, and disinhibition predictions. *Journal of Personality and Social Psychology, 53,* 882–890.

Joska, J. A., & Stein, D. J. (2008). Mood disorders. In R. E. Hales, S. C. Yudofsky, & G. O. Gabbard (Eds.), *Textbook of psychiatry* (pp. 457–503). Washington, DC: American Psychiatric Publishing.

Jost, J. T., & Hamilton, D. L. (2005). *Stereotypes in our culture.* In J. F. Dovidio, P. Glick, & L. Rudman (Eds.), *On the nature of prejudice: Fifty years after Allport* (pp. 208–224). Malden, MA: Blackwell Publishing.

Joy, J. E., Watson, S. J., Jr., & Benson, J. A., Jr. (1999). *Marijuana and medicine: Assessing the science base.* Washington, DC: National Academy Press.

Juarascio, A., Forman, E., Timko, C., Herbert, J., Butryn, M., & Lowe, M. (2011). Implicit internalization of the thin ideal as a predictor of increases in weight, body dissatisfaction, and disordered eating. *Eating Behaviors, 12*(3), 207–213.

Judd, F. K., Jackson, H. J., Komiti, A., Murray, G., Hodgins, G., Fraser, C. (2002). High prevalence disorders in urban and rural communities. *Australian and New Zealand Journal of Psychiatry, 36,* 104–113.

Judge, T. A., Ilies, R., & Dimotakis, N. (2010). Are health and happiness the product of wisdom? The relationship of general mental ability to educational and occupational attainment, health, and well-being. *Journal of Applied Psychology, 95,* 454–468.

Judge, T. A., & Cable, D. M. (2011). When it comes to pay, do the thin win? The effect of weight on pay for men and women. *Journal of Applied Psychology, 96,* 95–112. doi:10.1037/a0020860.

Judge, T. A., Colbert, A. E., & Ilies, R. (2004). Intelligence and leadership: A quantitative review and test of theoretical propositions. *Journal of Applied Psychology, 89,* 542–552.

Judge, T.A., Heller, D., & Mount, M.K. (2002). Five-factor model of personality and job satisfaction: A meta-analysis. *Journal of Applied Psychology, 87,* 530–541.

Judge, T. A., Piccolo, R. F., & Ilies, R. (2004). The forgotten ones? The validity of consideration and initiating structure in leadership research. *Journal of Applied Psychology, 89,* 36–51.

Judge, T. A., Thoresen, C. J., Bono, J. E., & Patton, G. K. (2001). The job satisfaction-job performance relationship: A qualitative and quantitative review. *Psychological Bulletin, 127,* 376–407.

Julien, R. M. (2005). *A primer of drug action* (10th ed.). New York: Worth.

Julien, R. M. (2008). *A primer of drug action* (11th ed.). New York: Worth.

Junco, R., & Cotten, S. R. (2011). Perceived academic effects of instant messaging use. *Computers & Education, 56*(2), 370–378. doi:10.1016/j.compedu.2010.08.020.

Jung, C. G. (1916). *Analytical psychology.* New York: Moffat.

Jung, C. G. (1933). *Psychological types.* New York: Harcourt, Brace and World.

Jussim, L., & Eccles, J. S. (1992). Teacher expectations: II. Construction and reflection of student achievement. *Journal of Personality and Social Psychology, 63,* 947–961.

Just, M. A., Carpenter, P. A., Keller, T. A., Emery, L., Zajac, H., & Thulborn, K. R. (2001). Interdependence of nonoverlapping cortical systems in dual cognitive tasks. *Neuroimage, 14,* 417–426.

Just, N., & Alloy, L. B. (1997). The response styles theory of depression: Tests and an extension of the theory. *Journal of Abnormal Psychology, 106,* 221–229.

Kaczorowski, J. A., Williams, A., Smith, T. F., Fallah, N., Mendez, J. L., & Nelson-Gray, R. (2011). Adapting clinical services to accommodate needs of refugee populations. *Professional Psychology: Research and Practice, 42*(5), 361–367. doi:10.1037/a0025022.

Kadotani, H., Kadotani, T., Young, T., Peppard, P. E., Finn, L., Colrain, I. M., et al. (2001). Association between apolipoprotein E epsilon4 and sleep-disordered breathing in adults. *Journal of the American Medical Association, 285,* 2888–2890.

Kafka, M. P. (2010). Hypersexual disorder: A proposed diagnosis for DSM-V. *Archives of Sexual Behavior, 39*(2), 377–400. doi:10.1007/s10508-009-9574-7.

Kagan, J. R., Snidman, N., Arcus, D., & Resnick, J. S. (1994). *Galen's prophecy: Temperament in human nature.* New York: Basic Books.

Kahn, D. & Gover, T. (2010). Consciousness in dreams. *International Review of Neurobiology, 92,* 181–195.

Kahn, E., & Rachman, A. W. (2000). Carl Rogers and Heinz Kohut: A historical perspective. *Psychoanalytic Psychology, 17,* 294–312.

Kahneman, D., & Deaton, A. (2010). High income improves evaluation of life but not emotional well-being. *Proceedings Of The National Academy Of Sciences Of The United States Of America, 107*(38), 16489–16493. doi:10.1073/pnas.1011492107.

Kahneman, D., & Tversky, A. (1973). On the psychology of prediction. *Psychological Review, 80,* 237–251.

Kahneman, D., & Tversky, A. (1984). Choices, values, and frames. *American Psychologist, 29,* 341–356.

Kahneman, D., Krueger, A. B., Schkade, D., Schwarz, N., & Stone, A. A. (2006). Would you be happier if you were richer? A focusing illusion. *Science, 312,* 1908–1910.

Kaiser, R. B., Hogan, R., & Craig, S. B. (2008). Leadership and the fate of organizations. *American Psychologist, 63,* 96–110.

Kaiser Family Foundation. (2005). *U.S. teen sexual activity.* Retrieved from http://www.kff.org/youthhivstds/upload/U-S-Teen-Sexual-Activity-Fact-Sheet.pdf

Kaitaro, T. (2001). Biological and epistemological models of localization in the nineteenth century: From Gall to Charcot. *Journal of Historical Neuroscience, 10*(3), 262–276.

Kajantie, E. (2008). Physiological stress response, estrogen, and the male-female mortality gap. *Current Directions in Psychological Science, 17,* 348–352.

Kajantie, E. J., & Phillips, D. I. W. (2006). The effects of sex and hormonal status on the physiological response to acute psychosocial stress. *Psychoneuroendocrinology, 31,* 151–178.

Kajiya, K., Inaki, K., Tanaka, M., Haga, T., Kataoka, H., & Touhara, K. (2001). Molecular bases of odor discrimination: Reconstitution of olfactory receptors that recognize overlapping sets of odorants. *Journal of Neuroscience, 21,* 6018–6025.

Kalb, L. M., & Loeber, R. (2003). Child disobedience and noncompliance: A review. *Pediatrics, 111,* 641–652.

Kalcher-Sommersguter, E., Preuschoft, S., Crailsheim, K., & Franz, C. (2011). Social competence of adult chimpanzees (Pan troglodytes) with severe deprivation history: I. An individual approach. *Developmental Psychology, 47*(1), 77–90. doi:10.1037/a0020783.

Kalechstein, A. D., De La Garza, R., II, Mahoney, J. J., III, Fantegrossi, W. E., & Newton, T. F. (2007). MDMA use and neurocognition: A meta-analytic review. *Psychopharmacology* (Berlin), *189,* 531–537.

Kales, H. C., Neighbors, H. W., Blow, F. C., Taylor, K. K., et al. (2005a). Race, gender, and psychiatrists' diagnosis and treatment of major depression among elderly patients. *Psychiatric Services, 56,* 721–728.

Kales, H. C., Neighbors, H. W., Valenstein, M., Blow, F. C., et al. (2005b). Effect of race and sex on primary care physicians' diagnosis and treatment of late-life depression. *Journal of the American Geriatrics Society, 53,* 777–784.

Kales, H. C., DiNardo, A. R., Blow, F. C., McCarthy, J. F., et al. (2006). International medical graduates and the diagnosis and treatment of late-life depression. *Academic Medicine, 81,* 171–175.

Kalivas, P. W., & Volkow, N. D. (2005). The neural basis of addiction: A pathology of motivation and choice. *American Journal of Psychiatry, 162,* 1403–1413.

Kalluri, H. S., & Dempsey, R. J. (2008). Growth factors, stem cells, and stroke. *Neurosurgery Focus, 24*(3–4), E14.

Kalsbeek, A., Palm, I. F., La Fleur, S. E., Scheer, F. A., Perreau-Lenz, S., Ruiter, M., et al. (2006). SCN outputs and the hypothalamic balance of life. *Journal of Biological Rhythms, 21,* 458–469.

Kaminski, J. W., Valle, L. A., Filene, J. H., & Boyle, C. L. (2008). A meta-analytic review of components associated with parent training program effectiveness. *Journal of Abnormal Child Psychology, 36,* 567–589.

Kammers, M. P. M., de Vignemont, F., Verhagen, L., & Dijkerman, H. C. (2009). The rubber hand illusion in action. *Neuropsychologia, 47*(1), 204–211.

Kammeyer-Mueller, J. D., Wanberg, C. R., Glomb, T. M., & Ahlburg, D. (2005). The role of temporal shifts in turnover processes: It's about time. *Journal of Applied Psychology, 90,* 644–658.

Kanazawa, S., & Hellberg, J. U. (2010). Intelligence and substance use. *Review Of General Psychology, 14*(4), 382–396. doi:10.1037/a0021526.

Kane, J. M., Eerdekens, M., Lindenmayer, J.-P., Keith, S. J., Lesem, M., & Karcher, K. (2003). Long-acting injectable risperidone: Efficacy and safety of the first long-acting atypical antipsychotic. *American Journal of Psychiatry, 160,* 1125–1132.

Kane, R. L. (1991). Standardized and flexible batteries in neuropsychology: an assessment update. *Neuropsychology Review, 2*(4), 281–339.

Kaner, A., & Prelinger, E. (2007). *The craft of psychodynamic psychotherapy* (2nd ed.). Lanham, MD: Jason Aronson Publishers.

Kangas, M., Henry, J. L., & Bryant, R. A. (2005). Predictors of posttraumatic stress disorder following cancer. *Health Psychology, 24,* 579–585.

Kanki, B. J., & Foushee, H. C. (1990). Crew factors in the aerospace workplace. In S. Oskamp & S. Spacepan (Eds.), *People's reactions to technology* (pp. 18–31). Newbury Park, CA: Sage.

Kanno, T., Mitsugi, M., Sukegawa, S., Hosoe, M., & Furuki, Y. (2008). Computer-simulated bi-directional alveolar distraction osteogenesis. *Clinical Oral Implants Research, 19*(12), 1211–1218.

Kanwisher, N. (2010). Functional specificity in the human brain: A window into the functional architecture of the mind. *Proceedings Of The National Academy Of Sciences Of The United States Of America, 107*(25), 11163–11170. doi:10.1073/pnas.1005062107.

Kao, T., Shumsky, J. S., Murray, M., & Moxon, K. A. (2009). Exercise induces cortical plasticity after neonatal spinal cord injury in the rat. *Journal of Neuroscience, 29,* 7549–7557.

Kapogiannis, D., Barbey, A. K., Su, M., Zamboni, G., Krueger, F., & Grafman, J. (2009). Cognitive and neural foundations of religious belief. *Proceedings of the National Academy of Sciences, 106,* 4876–4881.

Kapp, S. K. (2011). Navajo and autism: The beauty of harmony. *Disability & Society, 26*(5), 583–595. doi:10.1080/09687599.2011.589192.

Kaptchuk, T. J., Stason, W. B., Legedza, A. R. T., Schnyer, R. N., et al. (2006). Sham device vs. inert pill: Randomised controlled trial of two placebo treatments. *British Medical Journal, 332,* 391–397.

Kapur, N. (1999). Syndromes of retrograde amnesia: A conceptual and empirical synthesis. *Psychological Bulletin, 125,* 800–825.

Kapur, S., Sridhar, N., & Remington, G. (2004). The newer antipsychotics: Underlying mechanisms and the new clinical realities. *Current Opinion in Psychiatry, 17*(2), 115–121.

Karama, S., Colom, R., Johnson, W., Deary, I. J., Haier, R., Waber, D. P., & ... Evans, A. C. (2011). Cortical thickness correlates of specific cognitive performance accounted for by the general factor of intelligence in healthy children aged 6 to 18. *Neuroimage, 55*(4), 1443–1453. doi:10.1016/j.neuroimage.2011.01.016

Karim, A., Schneider, M., Lotze, M., Veit, R., Sauseng, P., Braun, C., & Birbaumer, N. (2010). The truth about lying: inhibition of the anterior prefrontal cortex improves deceptive behavior. *Cerebral Cortex (New York, N.Y.: 1991), 20*(1), 205–213.

Karni, A., Meyer, G., Adams, M., Turner, R., & Ungerleider, L. G. (1994). The acquisition and retention of a motor skill: A functional MRI study of long-term motor cortex plasticity. *Abstracts of the Society for Neuroscience, 20,* 1291.

Karlsgodt, K. H., Daqiang, S., & Cannon, T. D. (2010). Structural and functional brain abnormalities in schizophrenia. *Current Directions in Psychological Science, 19*(4), 226–231. doi:10.1177/0963721410377601.

Karon, B. P., & Widener, A. J. (1997). Repressed memories and World War II: Lest we forget. *Professional Psychology: Research and Practice, 28*(4), 338–340.

Karp, D. A. (1991). A decade of reminders: Changing age consciousness between fifty and sixty years old. In B. B. Hess & E. W. Markson (Eds.), *Growing old in America* (pp. 67–92). New Brunswick, NJ: Transaction.

Karpicke, J. D. (2009). Metacognitive control and strategy selection: Deciding to practice retrieval during learning. *Journal of Experimental Psychology: General, 138,* 469–486.

Karpicke, J. D., & Blunt, J. R. (2011). Retrieval practice produces more learning than elaborative studying with concept mapping. *Science, 331*(6018), 772–775. doi:10.1126/science.1199327.

Karpicke, J. D. (2012). Retrieval-Based Learning: Active Retrieval Promotes Meaningful Learning. *Current Directions In Psychological Science (Sage Publications Inc.), 21*(3), 157–163. doi:10.1177/0963721412443552.

Karpicke, J. D., & Bauernschmidt, A. (2011). Spaced retrieval: Absolute spacing enhances learning regardless of relative spacing. *Journal of Experimental Psychology: Learning, Memory, and Cognition, 37*(5), 1250–1257. doi:10.1037/a0023436.

Karpicke, J. D., & Smith, M. A. (2012). Separate mnemonic effects of retrieval practice and elaborative encoding. *Journal Of Memory And Language,* doi:10.1016/j.jml.2012.02.004

Karpicke, J. D., & Smith, M. A. (2012). Separate mnemonic effects of retrieval practice and elaborative encoding. *Journal of Memory and Language,* doi:10.1016/j.jml.2012.02.004

Karremans, J. C., Stroebe, W., & Claus, J. (2006). Beyond Vicary's fantasies: The impact of subliminal priming and brand choice. *Journal of Experimental Social Psychology, 42,* 792–798.

Karver, M. S., Handelsman, J. B., Fields, S., & Bickman, L. (2006). Meta-analysis of therapeutic relationship variables in youth and family therapy: The evidence for different relationship variables in the child and adolescent treatment outcome literature. *Clinical Psychology Review, 26,* 50–65.

Kasen, S., Cohen, P., Chen, H., & Must, A. (2008). Obesity and psychopathology in women: A three decade prospective study. *International Journal of Obesity, 32,* 558–566.

Kashdan, T. B., & Rottenberg, J. (2010). Psychological flexibility as a fundamental aspect of health. *Clinical Psychology Review, 30,* 467–480.

Kashdan, T. B., & Rottenberg, J. (2010). Psychological flexibility as a fundamental aspect of health. *Clinical Psychology Review, 30*(7), 865–878. doi:10.1016/j.cpr.2010.03.001.

Kashima, H. & Hayashi, N. (2011). Basic taste stimuli elicit unique responses in facial skin blood flow. *PLoS One, 6*(12), e28236.

Kaskutas, L. A., Bond, J., & Avalos, L. A. (2009). 7-year trajectories of Alcoholics Anonymous attendance and associations with treatment. *Addictive Behaviors, 34,* 1029–1035.

Kaslow, F. W. (2011). Family therapy. In J. C. Norcross, G. R. VandenBos, & D. K. Freedheim (Eds.), *History of psychotherapy: Continuity and change* (pp. 497–504). Washington, D.C.: American Psychological Association.

Kasper, S., & Papadimitriou, G. N. (Eds.) (2009). *Schizophrenia* (2nd ed.). New York: Informa Health Care.

Kassin, S. M., Bogart, D., & Kerner, J. (2012). Confessions that corrupt: Evidence from the DNA exoneration case files. *Psychological Science, 23*(1), 41–45. doi:10.1177/0956797611422918.

Kassin, S. M., Fein, S., & Markus, H. R. (2010). *Social psychology* (8th ed.). Belmont, CA: Wadsworth.

Kassin, S. M., Rigby, S., & Castillo, S. R. (1991). The accuracy-confidence correlation in eyewitness testimony: Limits and extensions of the retrospective self-awareness effect. *Journal of Personality and Social Psychology, 61,* 698–707.

Kassin, S., Fein, S., & Markus, H. (2008). *Social Psychology.* Boston, MA: Houghton-Mifflin.

Kastin, A. J., & Pan, W. (2005). Targeting neurite growth inhibitors to induce CNS regeneration. *Current Pharmaceutical Design, 11,* 1247–1253.

Katkin, E. S., Wiens, S., & Öhman, A. (2001). Nonconscious fear conditioning, visceral perception, and the development of gut feelings. *Psychological Science, 12,* 366–370.

Kato, M., & Serretti, A. (2010). Review and meta-analysis of antidepressant pharmacogenetic findings in major depressive disorder. *Molecular Psychiatry, 15,* 473–500. Epub 2008 Nov 4.

Kato, P. M. (2010). Video games in health care: Closing the gap. *Review Of General Psychology, 14*(2), 113–121. doi:10.1037/a0019441.

Katsavelis, D., Siu, K.-S., Brown-Clerk, B., Lee, I. H., Oleynikov, D., & Stergiou, N. (2007). Learning robotic surgical skills with a virtual reality environment. *Journal of Sport & Exercise Psychology, 29,* S91–S92.

Katzell, R. A., & Austin, J. T. (1992). From then to now: The development of industrial-organizational psychology in the United States. *Journal Of Applied Psychology, 77*(6), 803–835. doi:10.1037/0021-9010.77.6.803.

Katzell, R. A., & Thompson, D. E. (1990). Work motivation: Theory and practice. *American Psychologist, 45,* 144–153.

Kauffman, N. A., Herman, C. P., & Polivy, J. (1995). Hunger-induced finickiness in humans. *Appetite, 24,* 203–218.

Kaufman, D. W., Anderson, T. E., & Issaragrisil, S. (2009). Risk factors for leukemia in Thailand. *Annals of Hematology, 88*(11), 1079–1088. doi:10.1007/s00277-009-0731-9.

Kaufman, J., & Charney, D. (2000). Comorbidity of mood and anxiety disorders. *Depression and Anxiety, 12*(Suppl. 1), 69–76.

Kaufman, J., Yang, B.-Z., Douglas-Palumberi, H., Crouse-Artus, M., Lipschitz, D., Krystal, J. H., & Gelernter, J. (2007). Genetic and environmental predictors of early alcohol use. *Biological Psychiatry, 61,* 1228–1234.

Kaufman, L., & Kaufman, J. H. (2000). Explaining the moon illusion. *Proceedings of the National Academy of Sciences, 97,* 500–505.

Kaulfuss, P., Mills, D. S. (2008). Neophilia in domestic dogs (*Canis familiaris*) and its implication for studies of dog cognition. *Animal Cognition, 11*(3), 553–556.

Kaushanskaya, M. (2009). Th e bilingual advantage in novel word learning. *Psychonomic Bulletin and Review, 16,* 705–710.

Kavanagh, P. S., Robins, S. C., & Ellis, B. J. (2010). The mating sociometer: A regulatory mechanism for mating aspirations. *Journal of Personality and Social Psychology, 99,* 120–132.

Kawakami, K., Dovidio, J. F., & van Kamp, S. (2005). Kicking the habit: Effects of nonstereotypic association training and correction processes on hiring decisions. *Journal of Experimental Social Psychology, 41,* 68–75.

Kawamura, N., Kim, Y., & Asukai, N. (2001). Suppression of cellular immunity in men with a past history of posttraumatic stress disorder. *American Journal of Psychiatry, 158,* 484–486.

Kawasaki, H., Adolphs, R., Kaufman, O., Damasio, H., Damasio, A. R., Granner, M., et al. (2001). Single-neuron responses to emotional visual stimuli recorded in human ventral prefrontal cortex. *Nature Neuroscience, 4,* 15–16.

Kay, L. M., & Sherman, S. (2007). An argument for an olfactory thalamus. *Trends In Neurosciences, 30*(2), 47–53. doi:10.1016/j.tins.2006.11.007.

Kaye, W. H., Klump, K. L., Frank, G. K., & Strober, M. (2000). Anorexia and bulimia nervosa. *Annual Review of Medicine, 51,* 299–313.

Kazak, A. E., Hoagwood, K., Weisz, J. R., Hood, K., Kratochwill, T. R., Vargas, L. A., & Banez, G. A. (2010). A meta-systems approach to evidence-based practice for children and adolescents. *American Psychologist, 65*(2), 85–97. doi:10.1037/a0017784.

Kazantzis, N., Lampropoulos, G. K., & Deane, F. P. (2005). A national survey of practicing psychologists' use and attitudes toward homework in psychotherapy. *Journal of Consulting and Clinical Psychology, 73,* 742–748.

Kazarian, S. S., & Evans, D. R. (Eds.). (2001). *Handbook of cultural health psychology.* New York: Academic Press.

Kazdin, A. E. (2011). Evidence-based treatment research: Advances, limitations, and next steps. *American Psychologist, 66,* 685–698.

Kazdin, A. E. (1994). Methodology, design, and evaluation in psychotherapy research. In A. E. Bergin & S. L. Garfield (Eds.), *Handbook of psychotherapy and behavior change* (4th ed., pp. 19–71). New York: Wiley.

Kazdin, A. E. (2008). *Behavior modification in applied settings* (6th ed.). Long Grove, IL: Waveland Press.

Kazdin, A. E., & Durbin, K. A. (2012). Predictors of child–therapist alliance in cognitive–behavioral treatment of children referred for oppositional and antisocial behavior. *Psychotherapy, 49,* 202–217. doi:10.1037/a0027933

Kazdin, A. E., & Weisz, J. R. (1998). Identifying and developing empirically supported child and adolescent treatments. *Journal of Consulting and Clinical Psychology, 66,* 19–36.

Kealy, E. M. (2005). Variations in the experience of schizophrenia: A cross-cultural review. *Journal of Social Work Research and Evaluation, 6,* 47–56.

Keating, D. P. (1990). Adolescent thinking. In S. S. Feldman & G. R. Elliott (Eds.), *At the threshold: The developing adolescent* (pp. 4–89). Cambridge, MA: Harvard University Press.

Keeling, L. J., & Hurink, J. F. (1996). Social facilitation acts more on the consummatory phase on feeding behaviour. *Animal Behaviour, 52,* 11–15.

Keen, R. E., & Berthier, N. E. (2004). Continuities and discontinuities in infants' representation of objects and events. In R. V. Kail (Ed.), *Advances in child development and behavior* (Vol. 32, pp. 243–279). San Diego, CA: Elsevier/Academic Press.

Keenan, K., Hipwell, A., Feng, X., Babinski, D., Hinze, A., et al. (2008). Subthreshold symptoms of depression in preadolescent girls are stable and predictive of depressive disorders. *Journal of the American Academy of Child and Adolescent Psychiatry, 47,* 1433–1442.

Keenan, K., & Wakschlag, L. S. (2004). Are oppositional defiant and conduct disorder symptoms normative behaviors in preschoolers? A comparison of referred and nonreferred children. *American Journal of Psychiatry, 161,* 356–358.

Keenan, K., Wakschlag, L. S., Danis, B., Hill, C., Humphries, M., Daux, J., & Radiah, D. (2007). Further evidence of reliability and validity of DSM-IV ODD and CD in preschool children. *Journal of the American Academy of Child and Adolescent Psychiatry, 46,* 457–468.

Keene, J. R., & Prokos, A. H. (2007). The sandwiched generation: Multiple caregiving responsibilities and the mismatch between actual and preferred work hours. *Sociological Spectrum, 27*(4), 365–387.

Keesey, R. E. (1980). A set-point analysis of the regulation of body weight. In A. J. Stunkard (Ed.), *Obesity* (pp. 144–165). Philadelphia: Saunders.

Keesey, R. E., & Powley, T. L. (1986). The regulation of body weight. *Annual Review of Psychology, 37,* 109–133.

Keesey, R. E., & Powley, T. L. (1975). Hypothalamic regulation of body weight. *American Scientist, 63,* 558–565.

Keil, F. C., Lockhart, K. L., & Schlegel, E. (2010). A bump on a bump? Emerging intuitions concerning the relative difficulty of the sciences. *Journal of Experimental Psychology: General, 139*(1), 1–15. doi:10.1037/a0018319.

Keleş, A., Keleş, J., & Yavuz, U. (2011). Expert system based on neuro-fuzzy rules for diagnosis breast cancer. *Expert Systems With Applications, 38*(5), 5719–5726. doi:10.1016/j.eswa.2010.10.061.

Kelesidis, T., Kelesidis, L., Chou, S., & Mantzoros, C. S. (2010). The role of leptin in human physiology: Emerging clinical applications. *Annals of Internal Medicine, 152,* 93–100.

Keller, M. B., McCullough, J. P., Klein, D. N., Arnow, B., et al. (2000). A comparison of nefazodone, the cognitive behavioral-analysis system of psychotherapy, and their combination for the treatment of chronic depression. *New England Journal of Medicine, 342,* 1462–1470.

Keller, M. B., McCullough, J. P., Klein, D. N., Arnow, B., Dunner, D. L., Gelenberg, A. J., et al. (2000). A comparison of nefazodone, the cognitive behavioral-analysis system of psychotherapy, and their combination for the treatment of chronic depression. *New England Journal of Medicine, 342,* 1462–1470.

Keller, M. C., & Nesse, R. M. (2006). The evolutionary significance of depressive symptoms: Different adverse situations lead to different depressive symptom patterns. *Journal of Personality and Social Psychology, 91,* 316–330.

Keller, R. T. (2006). Transformational leadership, initiating structure, and substitutes for leadership: A longitudinal study of research and development project team performance. *Journal of Applied Psychology, 91*, 202–210.

Keller, S. S., Crow, T., Foundas, A., Amunts, K., & Roberts, N. (2009). Broca's area: Nomenclature, anatomy, typology, and asymmetry. *Brain and Language, 109*, 29–48. Epub 2009 Jan 19.

Keller-Cohen, D., Toler, A., Miller, D., Fiori, K., & Bybee, D. (2004, August). *Social contact and communication in people over 85.* Paper presented at the convention of the American Psychological Association, Honolulu, HI.

Kelley, R. E., & Borazanci, A. P. (2009). Stroke rehabilitation. *Neurology Research, 31*, 832–840.

Kelley, K. W. (1985). Immunological consequences of changing environmental stimuli. In G. P. Moberg (Ed.), *Animal stress.* Bethesda, MD: American Physiological Society.

Kellman, P. J., & Arterberry, M. E. (2006). Infant visual perception. In W. Damon & R. M. Lerner (Series Eds.) & D. Kuhn & R. Siegler (Vol. Eds.), *Handbook of child psychology: Vol. 2. Cognition, perception, and language* (6th ed.). New York: Wiley.

Kellner, C. H., Fink, M., Knapp, R., Petrides, G., Husain, M., Rummans, T., et al. (2005). Relief of expressed suicidal intent by ECT: A consortium for research in ECT study. *American Journal of Psychiatry, 162*, 977–982.

Kellner, C. H., Knapp, R. G., Petrides, G., Rummans, T. A., Husain, M. M., Rasmussen, K., et al. (2006). Continuation electroconvulsive therapy vs pharmacotherapy for relapse prevention in major depression. *Archives of General Psychiatry, 63*, 1337–1344.

Kellum, K. K., Carr, J. E., & Dozier, C. L. (2001). Response-card instruction and student learning in a college classroom. *Teaching of Psychology, 28*, 101–104.

Kelly, D. J., Quinn, P. C., Slater, A. M., Lee, K., Ge, L., & Pascalis, O. (2007). The other-race effect develops during infancy: Evidence of perceptual narrowing. *Psychological Science 18*, 1084–1089.

Kelly, G. A. (1980). A psychology of the optimal man. In A. W. Landfield & L. M. Leitner (Eds.), *Personal construct psychology: Psychotherapy and personality.* New York: Wiley.

Kelly, J. F. (2003). Self-help for substance-use disorders: History, effectiveness, knowledge gaps and research opportunities. *Clinical Psychology Review, 23*(5), 639–663.

Kelly, T., Yang, W., Chen, C.-S., Reynolds, K., & He, J. (2008). Global burden of obesity in 2005 and projections to 2030. *International Journal of Obesity, 32*, 1431–1437.

Kelly, T. H., Foltin, R. W., Emurian, C. S., & Fischman, M. W. (1990). Multidimensional behavioral effects of marijuana. *Progress in Neuro-Psychopharmacology and Biological Psychiatry, 14*, 885–902.

Keltner, D., & Buswell, B. N. (1996). Evidence for the distinctiveness of embarrassment, shame, and guilt: A study of recalled antecedents and facial expressions of emotion. *Cognition and Emotion, 10*, 117–125.

Kemble, E. D., Filipi, T., & Gravlin, L. (1985). Some simple classroom experiments on cerebral lateralization. *Teaching of Psychology, 12*, 81–83.

Kemeny, M. E. (2003). The psychobiology of stress. *Current Directions in Psychological Science, 12*, 124–129.

Kemp, M., Drummond, P., & McDermott, B. (2010). A wait-list controlled pilot study of eye movement desensitization and reprocessing (EMDR) for children with post-traumatic stress disorder (PTSD) symptoms from motor vehicle accidents. *Clinical Child Psychology and Psychiatry, 15*(1), 5–25. doi:10.1177/1359104509339086.

Kendall, P. C., & Chambless, D. L. (Eds.). (1998). Special section: Empirically supported psychological therapies. *Journal of Consulting and Clinical Psychology, 66*, 3–167.

Kendall, P. C., & Choudhury, M. S. (2003). Children and adolescents in cognitive-behavioral therapy: Some past efforts and current advances, and the challenges in our future. *Cognitive Therapy and Research, 27*, 89–104.

Kendall, P. C., Hudson, J. L., Gosch, E., Flannery-Schroeder, E., & Suveg, C. (2008). Cognitive-behavioral therapy for anxiety disordered youth: A randomized clinical trial evaluating child and family modalities. *Journal of Consulting and Clinical Psychology, 76*, 282–297.

Kendell, R., & Jablensky, A. (2003). Distinguishing between the validity and utility of psychiatric diagnoses. *American Journal of Psychiatry, 160*, 4–12.

Kendler, K. S., Fisk, A., Gardner, C. O., & Gatz, M. (2009). Delineation of two genetic pathways to major depression. *Biological Psychiatry, 65*, 808–811.

Kendler, K. S., & Neale, M. C. (2009). "Familiality" or heritability? *Archives of General Psychiatry, 66*, 452–453.

Kendler, K. S. (2005). "A gene for . . .": The nature of gene action in psychiatric disorders. *American Journal of Psychiatry, 162*, 1243–1252.

Kendler, K. S., Eaves, L. J., Loken, E. K., Pedersen, N. L., Middeldorp, C. M., Reynolds, C., & .. Gardner, C. O. (2011). The impact of environmental experiences on symptoms of anxiety and depression across the life span. *Psychological Science, 22*(10), 1343–1352. doi:10.1177/0956797611417255.

Kendler, K. S., Gardner, C. C., & Dick, D. M. (2011). Predicting alcohol consumption in adolescence from alcohol-specific and general externalizing genetic risk factors, key environmental exposures and their interaction. *Psychological Medicine: A Journal of Research in Psychiatry and the Allied Sciences, 41*(7), 1507–1516. doi:10.1017/S003329171000190X

Kendler, K. S., Gardner, C. O., & Prescott, C. A. (2006). Toward a comprehensive developmental model for major depression in men. *American Journal of Psychiatry, 163*, 115–124.

Kendler, K. S., Gatz, M., Gardner, C. O., & Pedersen, N. L. (2006). A Swedish national twin study of lifetime major depression. *American Journal of Psychiatry, 163*, 109–114.

Kendler, K. S., Jacobson, K. C., Myers, J., & Prescott, C. A. (2002). Sex differences in genetic and environmental risk factors for irrational fears and phobias. *Psychological Medicine, 32*, 209–217.

Kendler, K. S., Thornton, L. M., Gilman, S. E., & Kessler, R. C. (2000). Sexual orientation in a U.S. national sample of twin and non-twin sibling pairs. *American Journal of Psychiatry, 157*, 1843–1846.

Kenrick, D. T., Griskevicius, V., Neuberg, S. L., & Schaller, M. (2010). Renovating the pyramid of needs: Contemporary extensions built upon ancient foundations. *Perspectives On Psychological Science, 5*(3), 292–314. doi:10.1177/1745691610369469.

Kenrick, D. T., Groth, G., Trost, M., & Sadalla, E. K. (1993). Integrating evolutionary and social exchange perspectives on relationships: Effects of gender, self-appraisal, and involvement level on mate selection. *Journal of Personality and Social Psychology, 64*, 951–969.

Kenrick, D., Neuberg, S., & Cialdini, R. (2005). *Social psychology: Unraveling the mystery* (3rd ed.). Boston, MA: Pearson.

Kenrick, D., Neuberg, S., & Cialdini, R. (2007). *Social psychology: Goals in interaction* (4th ed.). Upper Saddle River, NJ: Pearson.

Kensinger, E. A., & Corkin, S. (2004). Two routes to emotional memory: Distinct neural processes for valence and arousal. *Proceedings of the National Academy of Sciences, 101*, 3310–3315.

Kent, S., Rodriguez, F., Kelley, K. W., & Dantzer, R. (1994). Reduction in food and water intake induced by microinjection of interleukin-1b in the ventromedial hypothalamus of the rat. *Physiology and Behavior, 56*(5), 1031–1036.

Kenworthy, J. B., Turner, R. N., Hewstone, M., & Voci, A. (2006). Intergroup contact: When does it work, and why. In J. Dovidio, P. Glick, & L. Rudman (Eds.), *On the nature of prejudice: Fifty years after Allport.* Boston, MA: Blackwell.

Keogh, E., Bond, F. W., & Flaxman, P. E. (2006). Improving academic performance and mental health through a stress management intervention: Outcomes and mediators of change. *Behaviour Research and Therapy, 44*, 339–357.

Keough, M. E., Timpano, K. R., & Schmidt, N. B. (2009). Ataques de nervios: Culturally-bound and distinct from panic attacks? *Depression and Anxiety, 26*, 16–21.

Kepner, J. (2001). Touch in Gestalt body process psychotherapy: Purpose, practice, and ethics. *Gestalt Review, 5*, 97–114.

Kerber, K. A. and Helmchen, C. (2012). Benign paroxysmal positional vertigo: New opportunities but still old challenges. *Neurology, 78*, 154–156.

Keri, S. (2009). Genes for psychosis and creativity: A promoter polymorphism of the neuregulin 1 gene is related to creativity in people with high intellectual achievement. *Psychological Science, 20*, 1070–1073.

Kermer, D. A., Driver-Linn, E., Wilson, T. D., & Gilbert, D. T. (2006). Loss aversion is an affective forecasting error. *Psychological Science, 17*, 649–653.

Kern, M. L., & Friedman, H. S. (2008). Do conscientious individuals live longer? A quantitative review. *Health Psychology, 27*, 505–512.

Kerr, M. P., & Payne, S. J. (1994). Learning to use a spreadsheet by doing and by watching. *Interacting with Computers, 6*, 3–22.

Kerr, N. L., & Tindale, R. S. (2004). Group performance and decision making. *Annual Review of Psychology, 55*, 623–655.

Kersting, K. (2004, September). Cross-cultural training: 30 years and going strong. *Monitor on Psychology,* 48–49.

Kerstjens, J. M., de Winter, A. F., Bocca-Tjeertes, I. F., ten Vergert, E. J., Reijneveld, S. A., & Bos, A. F. (2011). Developmental delay in moderately preterm-born children at school entry. *The Journal of Pediatrics, 159*(1), 92–98. doi:10.1016/j.jpeds.2010.12.041.

Keselman, H. J., Othman, A. R., Wilcox, R. R., & Fradette, K. (2004). The new and improved two-sample *t* test. *Psychological Science, 15*, 47–51.

Keshavan, M. S., Diwadkar, V. A., Montrose, D. M., Rajarethinam, R., & Sweeny, J. A. (2005). Premorbid indicators and risk for schizophrenia: A selective review and update. *Schizophrenia Research, 79*, 45–57.

Kessels, R. P. C., Kortrijk, H. E., Wester, A. J., & Nys, G. M. S. (2008). Confabulation behavior and false memories in Korsakoff 's syndrome: Role of source memory and executive functioning. *Psychiatry and Clinical Neurosciences, 62*(2), 220–225.

Kessler, R., Avenevoli, S., Costello, E., Georgiades, K., Green, J., Gruber, M., & Merikangas, K. (2012). Prevalence, persistence, and sociodemographic correlates of DSM-IV disorders in the National Comorbidity Survey Replication Adolescent Supplement. *Archives Of General Psychiatry, 69*(4), 372–380.

Kessler, R. C. (2012). The costs of depression. *Psychiatry Clinics of North America, 35*, 1–14. doi:10.1016/j.psc.2011.11.005

Kessler, R. C., Berglund, P., Borges, G., Nock, M., & Wang, P. S. (2005). Trends in suicide ideation, plans, gestures, and attempts in the United States, 1990–1992 to 2001–2003. *Journal of the American Medical Association, 293*, 2487–2495.

Kessler, R. C., Berglund, P., Demler, O., Jin, R., & Walters, E. E. (2005). Lifetime prevalence of and age of onset distributions of DSM-IV disorders in the national comorbidity survey replication. *Archives of General Psychiatry, 62*, 593–602.

Kessler, R. C., Chiu, W. T., Jin, R., Ruscio, A. M., Shear, K., & Walters, E. E. (2006). The epidemiology of panic attacks, panic disorder, and agoraphobia in the National Comorbidity Survey Replication. *Archives of General Psychiatry, 63*, 415–424.

Kessler, R. C., Demler, O., Frank, R. G., Olfson, M., Pincus, H. A., et al. (2005). Prevalence and treatment of mental disorders, 1990 to 2003. *New England Journal of Medicine, 352*, 2515–2523.

Kessler, R. C., Galea, S., Gruber, M. J., Sampson, N. A., Ursano, R. J., & Wessely, S. (2008). Trends in mental illness and suicidality after Hurricane Katrina. *Molecular Psychiatry, 13*, 374–384.

Kessler, R. C., Ruscio, A., Shear, K., & Wittchen, H.-U. (2009). Epidemiology of anxiety disorders. In M. M. Antony & M. B. Stein (Eds.), *Oxford handbook of anxiety and related disorders* (pp. 19–33). New York: Oxford University Press.

Kessler, R. C., & Wang, P. S. (2008). The descriptive epidemiology of commonly occurring mental disorders in the United States. *Annual Review of Public Health, 29*, 115–129.

Ketter, T. A. (2010). *Handbook of diagnosis and treatment of bipolar disorders.* Arlington, VA: American Psychiatric Publishing.

Kety, S. S., Wender, P. H., Jacobsen, B., Ingraham, L. J., Jansson, L., Faber, B., & Kinney, D. K. (1994). Mental illness in the biological and adoptive relatives of schizophrenic adoptees. *Archives of General Psychiatry, 51*, 442–455.

Keverne, E. B., & Curley, J. P. (2008). Epigenetics, brain evolution and behaviour. *Frontiers in Neuroendocrinology, 29*(3), 398–412.

Keysar, B., Hayakawa, S. L., & An, S. (2012). The foreign-language effect: Thinking in a foreign tongue reduces decision biases. *Psychological Science, 23*(6), 661–668. doi:10.1177/0956797611432178.

Khader, P. H., Pachur, T., Meier, S., Bien, S., Jost, K., & Rösler, F. (2011). Memory-based Decision-making with heuristics: Evidence for a controlled activation of memory representations. *Journal of Cognitive Neuroscience, 23*(11), 3540–3554.

Khan, A., Leventhal, R. M., Khan, S., & Brown, W. A. (2002). Suicide risk in patients with anxiety disorders: A meta-analysis of the FDA database. *Journal of Affective Disorders, 69*, 183–190.

Khanna, C., & Medsker, G. J. (2010). 2009 *Income and employment survey results for the Society for Industrial and Organizational Psychology.* Retrieved from the Society for Industrial & Organizational Psychology, Inc. website: http://www.siop.org/2009SIOPIncomeSurvey.pdf.

Khashan, A. S., McNamee, R., Abel, K. M., Pedersen, M. G., Webb, R. T., Kenny, L. C., Mortensen, P. B., & Baker, P. N. (2008). Reduced infant birthweight consequent upon maternal exposure to severe life events. *Psychosomatic Medicine, 70*, 688–694.

Khot, U. N., Khot, M. B., Bajzer, C. T., Sapp, S. K., Ohman, E. M., Brener, S. J., et al. (2003). Prevalence of conventional risk factors in patients with coronary heart disease. *Journal of the American Medical Association, 290*, 898–904.

Kidd, T., Hamer, M., & Steptoe, A. (2011). Examining the association between adult attachment style and cortisol responses to acute stress. *Psychoneuroendocrinology, 36*, 771–779. doi:10.1016/j.psyneuen.2010.10.014

Kiecolt-Glaser, J. K. (2009). Psychoneuroimmunology psychology's gateway to the biomedical future. *Perspectives in Psychological Science, 4*, 367–369.

Kiecolt-Glaser, J. K. (2010). Stress, food, and inflammation: Psychoneuroimmunology and nutrition at the cutting edge. *Psychosomatic Medicine, 72*, 365–369.

Kiecolt-Glaser, J. K., & Glaser, R. (1992). Psychoneuroimmunology: Can psychological interventions modulate immunity? *Journal of Consulting and Clinical Psychology, 60*, 569–575.

Kiecolt-Glaser, J. K., & Glaser, R. (2001). Stress and immunity: Age enhances the risks. *Current Directions in Psychological Science, 10*, 18–21.

Kiecolt-Glaser, J. K., Loving, T. J., Stowell, J. R., Malarkey, W. B., Lemeshow, S., Dickinson, S. L., et al. (2005). Hostile marital interactions, proinflammatory cytokine production, and wound healing. *Archives of General Psychiatry, 62*, 1377–1384.

Kiecolt-Glaser, J. K., McGuire, L., Robles, T. F., & Glaser, R. (2002). Psychoneuro-immunology: Psychological influences on immune function and health. *Journal of Consulting & Clinical Psychology, 70*, 537–547.

Kiecolt-Glaser, J. K., & Newton, T. L. (2001). Marriage and health: His and hers. *Psychological Bulletin, 127*, 472–503.

Kiecolt-Glaser, J. K., Page, G. G., Marucha, P. T., MacCallum, R. C., & Glaser, R. (1998). Psychological influences on surgical recovery: Perspectives from psychoneuroimmunology. *American Psychologist, 11*, 1209–1218.

Kiecolt-Glaser, J. K., Preacher, K. J., MacCallum, R. C., Atkinson, C., Malarkey, W. B., & Glaser, R. (2003). Chronic stress and age-related increases in the proinflammatory cytokine IL-6. *Proceedings of the National Academy of Sciences, 100*, 9090–9095.

Kieffer, K. M., Schinka, J. A., & Curtiss, G. (2004). Person-environment congruence and personality domains in the prediction of job performance and work quality. *Journal of Counseling Psychology, 51*, 168–177.

Kiehl, K. A., Bates, A. T., Laurens, K. R., Hare, R. D., & Liddle, P. F. (2006). Brain potentials implicate temporal lobe abnormalities in criminal psychopaths. *Journal of Abnormal Psychology, 115*, 443–453.

Kiesler, D. J. (1996). *Contemporary interpersonal theory and research.* New York: Wiley.

Kiewra, K. A. (1989). A review of note-taking: The encoding storage paradigm and beyond. *Educational Psychology Review, 1*, 147–172.

Kiff, C. J., Lengua, L. J., & Zalewski, M. (2011). Nature and nurturing: Parenting in the context of child temperament. *Clinical Child And Family Psychology Review, 14*(3), 251–301. doi:10.1007/s10567-011-0093-4.

Kihlstrom, J. F. (1999). The psychological unconscious. In L. Pervin & O. John (Eds.), *Handbook of personality* (pp. 424–442). New York: Guilford.

Kihlstrom, J. F. (2005). Dissociative disorders. *Annual Review of Clinical Psychology, 1*, 227–253.

Kihlstrom, J. F. (2008). The psychological unconscious. In O. John, R. Robins, & L. Pervin (Eds.), *Handbook of personality: Theory and research* (3rd ed. pp., 583–602). New York: Guilford.

Kilbourne, A. M., Haas, G. L., Musant, B. H., Bauer, M. S., & Picnus, H. A. (2004). Concurrent psychiatric diagnosis by age and race among persons with bipolar disorder. *Psychiatric Services, 55*, 931–933.

Killgore, W. D. (2010). Effects of sleep deprivation on cognition. *Progress in Brain Research, 185*, 105–129.

Kim, E. Y., Mahmoud, G. S., & Grover, L. M. (2005). REM sleep deprivation inhibits LTP in vivo in area CA1 of rat hippocampus. *Neuroscience Letters, 388*, 163–167.

Kim, H., Shimojo, S. and O'Doherty, J. P. (2011). Overlapping responses for the expectation of juice and money rewards in human ventromedial prefrontal cortex *Cerebral Cortex, 21*, 769–776.

Kim, J., & Hatfield, E. (2004). Love types and subjective well-being: A cross-cultural study. *Social Behavior and Personality, 32*, 173–182.

Kim, J., Schallert, D. L., & Kim, M. (2010). An integrative cultural view of achievement motivation: Parental and classroom predictors of children's goal orientations when learning mathematics in Korea. *Journal Of Educational Psychology, 102*(2), 418–437. doi:10.1037/a0018676.

Kim, K. (2008). Meta-analyses of the relationship of creative achievement to both IQ and divergent thinking test scores. *The Journal of Creative Behavior, 42*(2), 106–130. doi:10.1002/j.2162-6057.2008.tb01290.x.

Kim, N. S., & Ahn, W.-K. (2002). Clinical psychologists' theory-based representations of mental disorders predict their diagnostic reasoning and memory. *Journal of Experimental Psychology: General, 131*, 451–476.

Kim, S., & Lee, D. (2011). Prefrontal cortex and impulsive decision making. *Biological Psychiatry, 69*(12), 1140–1146. doi:10.1016/j.biopsych.2010.07.005.

Kim, S. Y., Jeong, D. W., Jung, M. W., & Kim, J. M. (2011). Reduction of propofol injection pain by utilizing the gate control theory. *Korean Journal of Anesthesiology, 61*(4), 288–291.

Kimchi, R. (2003). Relative dominance of holistic and component properties in the perceptual organization of visual objects. In M. A. Peterson & G. Rhodes (Eds.), *Perception of faces, objects, and scenes* (pp. 235–268). New York: Oxford University Press.

Kim-Cohen, J., Arseneault, L., Caspi, A., Tomás, M. P., Taylor, A., & Moffitt, T. E. (2005). Validity of DSM-IV conduct disorder in 4 1/2–5-year-old children: A longitudinal epidemiological study. *American Journal of Psychiatry, 162*, 1108–1117.

Kim-Cohen, J., & Gold, A. L. (2009). Measured gene-environment interactions and mechanisms promoting resilient development. *Current Directions in Psychological Science, 18*, 138–142.

Kimura, M. & Higuchi, S. (2011). Genetics of alcohol dependence. *Psychiatry and Clinical Neurosciences, 65*(3), 213–25.

King, C. R., Knutson, K. L., Rathouz, P. J., Sidney, S., Liu, K., & Lauderdale, D. S. (2008). Short sleep duration and incident coronary artery calcification. *Journal of the American Medical Association, 300*, 2859–28566.

King, D. B., & DiCicco, T. L. (2007). The relationships between dream content and physical health, mood, and self-construal. *Dreaming, 17*, 127–139.

King, J. E., Weiss, A., & Farmer, K. H. (2005). A chimpanzee (*pan troglodytes*) analogue of cross-national generalization of personality structure: Zoological parks and an African sanctuary. *Journal of Personality, 73*, 389–410.

King, K. M., Karyadi, K. A., Luk, J. W., & Patock-Peckham, J. A. (2011). Dispositions to rash action moderate the associations between concurrent drinking, depressive symptoms, and alcohol problems during emerging adulthood. *Psychology of Addictive Behaviors, 25*(3), 446–454. doi:10.1037/a0023777

King, M., Nazareth, I., Levy, G., Walker, C., Morris, R., et al. (2008). Prevalence of common mental disorders in general practice attendees across Europe. *British Journal of Psychiatry, 192*, 362–367.

King, S., St-Hilaire, A., & Heidkamp, D. (2010). Prenatal factors in schizophrenia. *Current Directions in Psychological Science, 19*(4), 209–213. doi:10.1177/0963721410378360.

Kingdom, F. A. (2003). Color brings relief to human vision. *Nature Neuroscience, 6*, 641–644. Kingsbury, K., & McLeod, K. (2008, June 30). Postcard: Gloucester. *Time, 8.*

Kingston, D. A., Fedoroff, P., Firestone, P., Curry, S., & Bradford, J. (2008). Pornography use and sexual aggression: The impact of frequency and type of pornography use on recidivism among sexual offenders. *Aggressive Behavior, 34*, 341–351.

Kinley, D. J., Cox, B. J., Clara, I., Goodwin, R. D., & Sareen, J. (2009). Panic attacks and their relation to psychological and physical functioning in Canadians: Results from a nationally representative sample. *Canadian Journal of Psychiatry, 54*, 113–118.

Kinsbourne, M., & Cook, J. (1971). Generalized and lateralized effects of concurrent verbalization on a unimanual skill. *Quarterly Journal of Experimental Psychology, 23*, 341–345.

Kinsey, A. C., Pomeroy, W. B., & Martin, C. E. (1948). *Sexual behavior in the human male.* Philadelphia: Saunders.

Kinsey, A. C., Pomeroy, W. B., Martin, C. E., & Gebhard, P. H. (1953). *Sexual behavior in the human female.* Philadelphia: Saunders.

Kipps, C. M., Nestor, P. J., Acosta-Cabronero, J., Arnold, R., & Hodges, J. R. (2009). Understanding social dysfunction in the behavioural variant of frontotemporal dementia: The role of emotion and sarcasm processing. *Brain, 132*, 592–603.

Kircher, J. C., Horowitz, S. W., & Raskin, D. C. (1988). Meta-analysis of mock crime studies of the control question polygraph technique. *Law and Human Behavior, 12*, 79–90.

Kirkpatrick, B., Buchanan, R. W., Ross, D. E., & Carpenter, W. T., Jr. (2001). A separate disease within the syndrome of schizophrenia. *Archives of General Psychiatry, 58*, 165–171.

Kirkpatrick, B.; Fenton, W. S.; Carpenter, W. T., Jr.; & Marder, S. R. (2006). Consensus statement on negative symptoms. *Schizophrenia Bulletin, 32*, 214–219.

Kirsch, I. (2010). *The emperor's new drugs: Exploding the antidepressant myth.* New York: Basic Books.

Kirsch, I. (2009). Antidepressants and the placebo response. *Epidemiology and Psychiatric Sciences, 18*, 318–322.

Kirsch, I. (1994a). Clinical hypnosis as a nondeceptive placebo: Empirically derived techniques. *American Journal of Clinical Hypnosis, 37*(2), 95–106.

Kirsch, I. (1994b). Defining hypnosis for the public. *Contemporary Hypnosis, 11*(3), 142–143.

Kirsch, I., & Braffman, W. (2001). Imaginative suggestibility and hypnotizability. *Psychological Science, 10,* 57–61.

Kirsch, I., Moore, T. J., Scoboria, A., & Nicholls, S. S. (2002). The emperor's new drugs: An analysis of antidepressant medication data submitted to the U.S. Food and Drug Administration [Electronic version]. *Prevention and Treatment, 5,* np.

Kirsch, I., Scoboria, A., & Moore, T. J. (2002). Antidepressants and placebos: Secrets, revelations, and unanswered questions. *Prevention and Treatment, 5,* np.

Kirschenbaum, H., & Jourdan, A. (2005). The current status of Carl Rogers and the person-centered approach. *Psychotherapy: Theory, Research, Practice, Training, 42,* 37–51.

Kirsh, S. J. (2011). Children, Adolescents, and Media Violence: A Critical Look at the Research (2nd Edition). Sage: Washington, DC.

Kishi, T., & Elmquist, J. K. (2005). Body weight is regulated by the brain: A link between feeding and emotion. *Molecular Psychiatry, 10,* 132–146.

Kishi, T., Yoshimura, R., Fukuo, Y., Kitajima, T., Okochi, T., Matsunaga, S., Inada, T., Kunugi, H., Kato, T., Yoshikawa, T., Ujike, H., Umene-Nakano, W., Nakamura, J., Ozaki, N., Serretti, A., Correll, C. U., & Iwata, N. (2011). The CLOCK gene and mood disorders: A case-control study and meta-analysis. *Chronobiology International, 28*(9), 825–833.

Kishioka, S., Miyamoto, Y., Fukunaga, Y., Nishida, S., & Yamamoto, H. (1994). Effects of a mixture of peptidase inhibitors (Amastatin, Captopril and Phosphoramidon) on met enkephalin, beta-endorphin, dynorphin (1–13) and electroacupuncture induced antinociception in rats. *Japanese Journal of Pharmacology, 66,* 337–345.

Kisilevsky, B. S., Hains, S. M. J., Lee, K., Xie, X., Huang, H., Ye, H. H., et al. (2003). Effects of experience on fetal voice recognition. *Psychological Science, 14,* 220–224.

Kitano, H., Chi, I., Rhee, S., Law, C., & Lubben, J. (1992). Norms and alcohol consumption: Japanese in Japan, Hawaii, and California. *Journal of Studies on Alcohol, 53,* 33–39.

Kitayama, N., Vaccarino, V., Kutner, M., Weiss, P., & Bremner, J. D. (2005). Magnetic resonance imaging (MRI) measurement of hippocampal volume in posttraumatic stress disorder: A meta-analysis. *Journal of Affective Disorders, 88,* 79–86.

Kitayama, S., & Markus, H. R. (1992, May). *Construal of self as cultural frame: Implications for internationalizing psychology.* Paper presented to the Symposium on Internationalization and Higher Education, Ann Arbor, Michigan.

Kitayama, S., Park, H., Sevincer, A., T., Karasawa., M., & Uskul, A. K. (2009). A cultural task analysis of implicit independence: Comparing North America, Western Europe, and East Asia. *Journal of Personality and Social Psychology, 97,* 236–255.

Kitayama, S., Duffy, S., Kawamura, T., & Larsen, J. T. (2003). Perceiving an object and its context in different cultures: A cultural look at new look. *Psychological Science, 14,* 201–206.

Kitayama, S., Duffy, S., & Uchida, Y. (2007). Self as cultural mode of being. In S. Kitayama & D. Cohen (Eds.), *Handbook of cultural psychology.* New York: Guilford Press.

Kitayama, S., Snibbe, A. C., Markus, H. R., & Suzuki, T. (2004). Is there any "free" choice?: Self and dissonance in two cultures. *Psychological Science, 15,* 527–533.

Kitayama, S., & Uchida, Y. (2003). Explicit self-criticism and implicit self-regard: Evaluating self and friend in two cultures. *Journal of Experimental Social Psychology, 39,* 476–482.Olson, M. H., &

Kivimaki, M., Jussi, V., Elovainio, M., Helenius, H., et al. (2005). Optimism and pessimism as predictors of change in health aft er death or onset of severe illness in family. *Health Psychology, 24,* 413–421.

Kivimaki, M., Lawlor, D. A., Singh-Manoux, A., Batty, D., et al. (2009). Common mental disorder and obesity: Insight from four repeat measures over 19 years: Prospective Whitehall II cohort study. *British Medical Journal, 339,* b3765.

Kiviniemi, V. (2008). Endogenous brain fluctuations and diagnostic imaging. *Human Brain Mapping, 29,* 810–817.

Kjaer, T. W., Bertelsen, C., Piccini, P., Brooks, D., Alving, J., & Lou, H. C. (2002). Increased dopamine tone during meditation-induced change of consciousness. *Cognitive Brain Research, 13,* 255–259.

Klaczynski, P., Daniel, D. B., & Keller, P. S. (2009). Appearance idealization, body esteem, causal attributions, and ethnic variations in the development of obesity stereotypes. *Journal Of Applied Developmental Psychology, 30*(4), 537–551. doi:10.1016/j.appdev.2008.12.031.

Klahr, A. M., McGue, M., Iacono, W. G., & Burt, S. (2011). The association between parent–child conflict and adolescent conduct problems over time: Results from a longitudinal adoption study. *Journal of Abnormal Psychology, 120*(1), 46–56. doi:10.1037/a0021350.

Klahr, D., & Simon, H. (1999). Studies of scientific discovery: Complementary approaches and convergent findings. *Psychological Bulletin, 125,* 524–543.

Klaus, M. H., & Kennell, J. H. (1976). *Maternal infant bonding: The impact of early separation or loss on family development.* St. Louis: Mosby.

Kleber, B., Veit, R., Birbaumer, N., Gruzelier, J., & Lotze, M. (2009). The brain of opera singers: experience-dependent changes in functional activation. *Cerebral Cortex, 20*(5), 1144–1152.

Kleemola, P., Jousilahti, P., Pietinen, P., Vartiainen, E., & Tuomilehto, J. (2000). Coffee consumption and the risk of coronary heart disease and death. *Archives of Internal Medicine, 160,* 3393–3400.

Klein, D. N. (1993). False suff ocation alarms, spontaneous panics, and related conditions: An integrative hypothesis. *Archives of General Psychiatry, 50,* 306–316.

Klein, D. N. (2010). Chronic depression: Diagnosis and classifi cation. *Current Directions in Psychological Science, 19,* 96–100.Klein, D. C., & Seligman, M. E. P. (1976). Reversal of performance deficits and perceptual deficits in learned helplessness and depression. *Journal of Abnormal Psychology, 85,* 11–26.

Klein, D. N., Santiago, N. J., Vivian, D., Blalock, J. A., Kocsis, J. H., Markowitz, J. C., et al. (2004). Cognitive-behavioral analysis system of psychotherapy as a maintenance treatment for chronic depression. *Journal of Consulting and Clinical Psychology, 72,* 681–688.

Klein, F. (1990). The need to view sexual orientation as a multivariable dynamic process: A theoretical perspective. In McWhirter, D. P., Sanders, S. A., & Reinisch, J. M. (Eds.), *Homosexuality/heterosexuality: Concepts of sexual orientation. The Kinsey Institute series* (Vol. 2, pp. 277–282). New York, NY: Oxford University Press.

Klein, H. J., Noe, R. A., & Wang, C. (2006). Motivation to learn and course outcomes: The impact of delivery mode, learning goal orientation, and perceived barriers and enablers. *Personnel Psychology, 59,* 665–702.

Klein, M. (1975). *The writings of Melanie Klein: Vol. 3.* London: Hogarth Press.

Klein, P. D. (1997). Multiplying the problems of intelligence by eight: A critique of Gardner's theory. *Canadian Journal of Education, 22,* 377–394.

Kleingeld, A., van Mierlo, H., & Arends, L. (2011). The effect of goal setting on group performance: A meta-analysis. *Journal Of Applied Psychology, 96*(6), 1289–1304. doi:10.1037/a0024315.

Kleinknecht, R. A. (1991). *Mastering anxiety: The nature and treatment of anxious conditions.* New York: Plenum.

Kleinknecht, R. A. (1994). Acquisition of blood, injury, and needle fears and phobias. *Behaviour Research and Therapy, 32,* 817–823.

Kleinknecht, R. A. (2000). Social phobia. In M. Hersen & M. K. Biaggio (Eds.), *Effective brief therapies: A clinician's guide.* New York: Academic Press.

Kleinman, A. (1991, April). *Culture and DSM-IV: Recommendations for the introduction and for the overall structure.* Paper presented at the National Institute of Mental Health-sponsored Conference on Culture and Diagnosis, Pittsburgh, PA.

Kleinspehn-Ammerlahn, A., Kotter-Gruhn, D., & Smith, J. (2008). Self-perceptions of aging: Do subjective age and satisfaction with aging change during old age? *Journals of Gerontology, Series B: Psychological Sciences and Social Sciences, 63B,* P377–P385.

Klepp, K.-I., Kelder, S. H., & Perry, C. L. (1995). Alcohol and marijuana use among adolescents: Long-term outcomes of the class of 1989 study. *Annals of Behavioral Medicine, 17,* 19–24.

Kline, S., & Groninger, L. D. (1991). The imagery bizarreness effect as a function of sentence complexity and presentation time. *Bulletin of the Psychonomic Society, 29,* 25–27.

Klinesmith, J., Kasser, T., & McAndrew, F. T. (2006). Guns, testosterone, and aggression: An experimental test of a mediational hypothesis. *Psychological Science, 17,* 568–571.

Kling, K. C., Hyde, J. S., Showers, C. J., & Buswell, B. N. (1999). Gender differences in self-esteem: A meta-analysis. *Psychological Bulletin, 125,* 470–500.

Klintschar, M., & Heimbold, C. (2012). Association between a functional polymorphism in the MAOA gene and sudden infant death syndrome. *Pediatrics, 129*(3), e756–e761.

Klintsova, A. Y., & Greenough, W. T. (1999). Synaptic plasticity in cortical systems. *Current Opinion in Neurobiology, 9,* 203–208.

Kloep, M., & Hendry, L. B. (2010). Letting go or holding on? Parents' perceptions of their relationships with their children during emerging adulthood. *British Journal of Developmental Psychology, 28*(4), 817–834. doi:10.1348/026151009X480581.

Klossek, U. M. H., Russell, J., & Dickinson, A. (2008). The control of instrumental action following outcome devaluation in young children aged between 1 and 4 years. *Journal of Experimental Psychology: General, 137,* 39–51.

Kluger, A. N., & DeNisi, A. (1998). Feedback interventions: Toward the understanding of a double-edged sword. *Current Directions in Psychological Science, 7,* 67–72.

Klump, K. L., Suisman, J. L., Burt, S. A., McGue, M., & Iacono, W. G. (2009). Genetic and environmental infl uences on disordered eating: An adoption study. *Journal of Abnormal Psychology, 118,* 797–805.

Knafo, A., Zahn-Waxler, C., Van Hulle, C., Robinson, J. L., & Rhee, S. H. (2008). The developmental origins of a disposition toward empathy: Genetic and environmental contributions. *Emotion, 8,* 737–752.

Knack, W. A. (2009). Psychotherapy and Alcoholics Anonymous: An integrated approach. *Journal of Psychotherapy Integration, 19,* 86–109.

Knafo, A., Iervolino, A. C., & Plomin, R. (2005). Masculine girls and feminine boys: Genetic and environmental contributions to atypical gender development in early childhood. *Journal of Personality and Social Psychology, 88,* 400–412.

Knafo, A., & Spinath, F. M. (2011). Genetic and environmental influences on girls' and boys' gender-typed and gender-neutral values. *Developmental Psychology, 47*(3), 726–731. doi:10.1037/a0021910.

Knapp, S. J. (Ed.). (2011a). *APA handbook of ethics in psychology: Volume 1: Moral foundations and common themes.* Washington, DC: American Psychological Association.

Knapp, S. J. (Ed.). (2011b). *APA handbook of ethics in psychology: Volume 2: Practice, teaching, and research.* Washington, DC: American Psychological Association.

Knauper, B., McCollam, A., Rosen-Brown, A., Lacaille, J., Kelso, E., & Roseman, M. (2011). Fruitful plans: Adding targeted mental imagery to implementation intentions increases fruit consumption. *Psychology and Health, 26,* 601–617. doi: 10.1080/08870441003703218

Knoll, S., Bulik, C. M., & Hebebrand, J. (2011). Do the currently proposed DSM-5 criteria for anorexia nervosa adequately consider developmental aspects in children and adolescents? *European Child & Adolescent Psychiatry, 20*(2), 95–101. doi:10.1007/s00787-010-0141-5.

Knöpfel, T., Lin, M. Z., Levskaya, A., Lin, T., Lin, J. Y., & Boyden, E. S. (2010). Toward the second generation of optogenetic tools. *Journal Of Neuroscience, 30*(45), 14998–15004. doi:10.1523/JNEUROSCI.4190-10.2010.

Knopman, D. S. (2006). Dementia and cerebrovascular disease. *Mayo Clinic Proceedings, 81*(2), 223–230.

Kochanek, K.D., Xu, J., Murphy, S. L., Minino, A. M., Kung, H.-C. (2011). Deaths: Preliminary data for 2009. *National Vital Statistics Reports, Division of Vital Statistics, 4*(59).

Kochanska, G., Aksan, N., & Joy, M. E. (2007). Children's fearfulness as a moderator of parenting in early socialization: Two longitudinal studies. *Developmental Psychology, 43,* 222–237.

Koechlin, E., & Hyafil, A. (2007). Anterior prefrontal function and the limits of human decision-making. *Science, 318,* 594–598.

Koenen, K. C., Moffitt, T. E., Roberts, A. L., Martin, L. T., et al. (2009). Childhood IQ and adult mental disorders: A test of the cognitive reserve hypothesis. *American Journal of Psychiatry, 166,* 50–57.

Koenig, L. B., Haber, J., & Jacob, T. (2011). Childhood religious affiliation and alcohol use and abuse across the lifespan in alcohol-dependent men. *Psychology of Addictive Behaviors, 25*(3), 381–389. doi:10.1037/a0024774

Kogan, M. D., Blumberg, S. J., Schieve, L. A., Boyle, C. A., et al. (2009). Prevalence of parentreported diagnosis of autism spectrum disorder among children in the U.S., 2007. *Pediatrics, 124,* 1395–1403.

Koger, S. M., Schettler, T., & Weiss, B. (2005). Environmental toxicants and developmental disabilities: A challenge for psychologists. *American Psychologist, 60,* 243–255.

Kohlberg, L., & Gilligan, C. (1971). The adolescent as a philosopher: The discovery of the self in a postconventional world. *Daedalus, 100,* 1051–1086.

Köhler, W. (1924). *The mentality of apes.* New York: Harcourt Brace.

Kohli, M. A., Salyakina, D., Pfennig, A., Lucae, S., et al. (2010). Association of genetic variants in the neurotrophic receptor–encoding gene NTRK2 and a lifetime history of suicide attempts in depressed patients. *Archives of General Psychiatry, 67,* 348–359. doi:10.1001/archgenpsychiatry.2009.201

Kohn, A. (1993). *Punished by rewards: The trouble with gold stars, incentive plans, A's, praise, and other bribes.* Boston: Houghton Mifflin.

Kohn, N. W., Paulus, P. B., & Choi, Y. (2011). Building on the ideas of others: An examination of the idea combination process. *Journal of Experimental Social Psychology, 47*(3), 554–561. doi:10.1016/j.jesp.2011.01.004.

Kohn, N. W., Paulus, P. B., & Korde, R. M. (2011). Conceptual combinations and subsequent creativity. *Creativity Research Journal, 23*(3), 203–210. doi:10.1080/104 00419.2011.595659.

Kohn, N., & Smith, S. M. (2009). Partly versus completely out of your mind: Effects of incubation and distraction on resolving fixation. *The Journal of Creative Behavior, 43*(2), 102–118. doi:10.1002/j.2162-6057.2009.tb01309.x.

Kohn, N. W., & Smith, S. M. (2011). Collaborative fixation: Effects of others' ideas on brainstorming. *Applied Cognitive Psychology, 25*(3), 359–371. doi:10.1002/acp.1699.

Kohnert, K. (2004). Cognitive and cognate-based treatments for bilingual aphasia: A case study. *Brain and Language, 91,* 294–302.

Kohut, H. (1984). Selected problems of self-psychological theory. In J. D. Lichtenberg & S. Kaplan (Eds.), *Reflections on self psychology* (pp. 387–416). Hillsdale, NJ: Erlbaum.

Kolassa, I.-T., Kolassa, S., Bergmann, S., Lauche, R., Dilger, S., Miltner, W. H. R., & Musial, F. (2009). Interpretive bias in social phobia: An ERP study with morphed emotional schematic faces. *Cognition & Emotion, 23*(1), 69–95.

Kolassa, I.-T., Kolassa, S., Ertl, V., Papassotiropoulos, A., & De Quervain, D. J.-F. (2010). The risk of posttraumatic stress disorder after trauma depends on traumatic load and the catechol-o-methyltransferase val158 met polymorphism. *Biological Psychiatry, 67,* 304–308.

Kolata, G., & Markel, H. (2001, April 29). Baby not crawling? Reason seems to be less tummy time. *New York Times.*

Kolb, B., Gorny, G., Li, Y., Samaha, A.-N., & Robinson, T. E. (2003). Amphetamine or cocaine limits the ability of later experience to promote structural plasticity in the neocortex and nucleus accumbens. *Proceedings of the National Academy of Sciences, 100,* 10523–10528.

Kolgan, A., Impett, E. A., Oveis, C., Hui, B., Gordon, A. M., & Keltner, D. (2010). When giving feels good: The intrinsic benefits of sacrifice in romantic relationships for the communally motivated. *Psychological Science, 21,* 1918–1924. doi:10.1177/0956797610388815.

Kolonin, M. G., Saha, P. K., Chan, L., Pasqualini, R., & Arap, W. (2004). Reversal of obesity by targeted ablation of adipose tissue. *Nature Medicine, 10,* 625–632.

Komro, K. A., Flay, B. R., & Biglan, A. (2011). Creating nurturing environments: A science-based framework for promoting child health and development within high-poverty neighborhoods. *Clinical Child & Family Psychology Review, 14,* 111–134. doi:10.1007/s10567-011-0095-2

Komsi, N., Räikkönen, K., Heinonen, K., Pesonen, A.-K., Keskivaara, P., Järvenpää, A.-L., & Strandberg, T. (2008). Continuity of father-rated temperament from infancy to middle childhood. *Infant Behavior & Development, 31,* 239–254.

Konecná, M., Lhota, S., Weiss, A., Urbánek, T., Adamová, T., & Pluhácek, J. (2008). Personality in free-ranging Hanuman langur (Semnopithecus entellus) males: Subjective ratings and recorded behavior. *Journal of Comparative Psychology, 122*(4), 379–389.

Kong, L. L., Allen, J. J. B., & Gilsky, E. L. (2008). Interidentity memory transfer in dissociative identity disorder. *Journal of Abnormal Psychology, 117,* 686–692.

Konijn, E. A., Bijvank, M. N., & Bushman, B. J. (2007). I wish I were a warrior: The role of wishful identification in the effects of violent video games on aggression in adolescent boys. *Developmental Psychology, 43,* 1038–1044.

Konrad, K., Neufang, S., Hanisch, C., Fink, G. R., & Herpertz-Dahlmann, B. (2006). Dysfunctional attentional networks in children with attention deficit/hyperactivity disorder: Evidence from an event-related functional magnetic imaging study. *Biological Psychiatry, 59,* 643–651.

Kontoghiorghes, C. (2004). Reconceptualizing the learning transfer conceptual framework: Empirical validation of a new systemic model. *International Journal of Training and Development, 8,* 210–221.

Koob, G. F., & Bloom, F. E. (1988). Cellular and molecular mechanisms of drug dependence. *Science, 242,* 715–723.

Koob, G., & Kreek, M. J. (2007). Stress, dysregulation of drug reward pathways, and the transition to drug dependence. *American Journal of Psychiatry, 164,* 1149–1159.

Koob, G. F., & Volkow, N. D. (2010). Neurocircuitry of addiction. *Neuropsychopharmacology, 35,* 217–238.

Kop, W. J., Berman, D. S., Gransar, H., Wong, N. D., Miranda-Peats, R., White, M. D., et al. (2005). Social network and coronary artery calcification in asymptomatic individuals. *Psychosomatic Medicine, 67,* 343–352.

Koppenaal, L., & Glanzer, M. (1990). An examination of the continuous distractor task and the "long-term recency effect." *Memory & Cognition, 18,* 183–195.

Koppes, L. L. (1997). American female pioneers of industrial and organizational psychology during the early years. *Journal Of Applied Psychology, 82*(4), 500–515. doi:10.1037/0021-9010.82.4.500.

Kordower, J. H., Emborg, M. E., Bloch, J., Ma, S. Y., Chu, Y., Leventhal, L., et al. (2000). Neurodegeneration prevented by lentiviral vector delivery of GDNF in primate models of Parkinson's disease. *Science, 290,* 767–773.

Koretz, D., Lynch, P. S., & Lynch, C. A. (2000, June). The impact of score differences on the admission of minority students: An illustration. *Statements of the National Board on Educational Testing and Public Policy, 1,* 1–15.

Korman, M., Doyon, J., Doljansky, J., Carrier, J., Dagan, Y., & Karni, A. (2007). Daytime sleep condenses the time course of motor memory consolidation. *Nature Neuroscience, 10,* 1206–1213.

Korner, J., & Leibel, R. L. (2003). To eat or not to eat—How the gut talks to the brain. *The New England Journal of Medicine, 349,* 926–928.

Korochkin, L. I. (2000). New approaches in developmental genetics and gene therapy: Xenotransplantation of Drosophila embryonic nerve cells into the brain of vertebrate animals. *Genetika, 36,* 1436–1442.

Kossowsky, J., Wilhelm, F. H., Roth, W. T., & Schneider, S. (2012). Separation anxiety disorder in children: Disorder-specific responses to experimental separation from the mother. *Journal of Child Psychology and Psychiatry, 53*(2), 178–187. doi:10.1111/j.1469-7610.2011.02465.x

Kotani, N., Hashimoto, H., Sato, Y., Sessler, D. I., Yoshioka, H., Kitayama, M., et al. (2001). Preoperative intradermal acupuncture reduces postoperative pain, nausea and vomiting, analgesic requirement, and sympathoadrenal responses. *Anesthesiology, 95,* 349–356.

Kouider, S., & Dupoux, E. (2005). Subliminal speech priming. *Psychological Science, 16,* 617.

Kounios, J. Frymiare, J. L., Bowden, E. M., Fleck, J. L., Subramaniam, K., Parrish, T. B., & Jung-Beeman, M. (2006). The prepared mind: Neural activity prior to problem presentation predicts subsequent solution by sudden insight. *Psychological Science, 17,* 882–890.

Koustanaï, A., Van Elslande, P., & Bastien, C. (2012). Use of change blindness to measure different abilities to detect relevant changes in natural driving scenes. *Transportation Research: Part F, 15*(3), 233–242. doi:10.1016/j.trf.2011.12.012.

Kouyoumdjian, H. (2004). Influence of unannounced quizzes and cumulative exams on attendance and study behavior. *Teaching of Psychology, 31,* 110–111.

Kovacs, A. M., & Mehler, J. (2009). Flexible learning of multiple speech structures in bilingual infants. *Science, 325,* 611–612.

Kovács, Á., Teglas, E., & Endress, A. (2010). The social sense: Susceptibility to others' beliefs in human infants and adults. *Science, 330*(6012), 1830–1834. doi:10.1126/science.1190792.

Kozorovitskiy, Y., Gross, C. G., Kopil, C., Battaglia, L., McBreen, M., Stranahan, A. M., et al. (2005). Experience induces structural and biochemical changes in the adult primate brain. *Proceedings of the National Academy of Sciences, 102,* 17478–17482.

Krain, A. L., & Castellanos, F. X. (2006). Brain development and ADHD. *Clinical Psychology Review, 26,* 433–444.

Krakauer, J. (1997). *Into thin air.* New York: Villard.

Krakow, B., Hollifield, M., Johnston, L., Koss, M., et al. (2001). Imagery rehearsal therapy for chronic nightmares in sexual assault survivors with posttraumatic stress disorder: A randomized controlled trial. *Journal of the American Medical Association, 286,* 537–545.

Kramár, E., Babayan, A., Gavin, C., Cox, C., Jafari, M., Gall, C., & … Lynch, G. (2012). Synaptic evidence for the efficacy of spaced learning. *Proceedings Of The National Academy Of Sciences Of The United States Of America, 109*(13), 5121–5126.

Kramer, A. F., & Willis, S. (2002). Enhancing the cognitive vitality of older adults. *Current Directions in Psychological Science, 11,* 173–177.

Kramer, G. P., Bernstein, D. A., & Phares, V. (2013). *Introduction to clinical psychology* (8th ed.) Upper Saddle River, NJ: Prentice Hall.

Krantz, D., Contrada, R., Hill, D., & Friedler, E. (1988). Environmental stress and biobehavioral antecedents of coronary heart disease. *Journal of Consulting and Clinical Psychology, 56,* 333–341.

Krantz, D., & Durel, L. (1983). Psychobiological substrates of the Type A behavior pattern. *Health Psychology, 2,* 393–411.

Krantz, D. S., & McCeney, M. K. (2002). Effects of psychological and social factors on organic disease: A critical assessment of research on coronary heart disease. *Annual Review of Psychology, 53,* 341–369.

Kraus, W. E., Houmard, J. A., Duscha, B. D., Knetzger, K. J., Wharton, M. B., McCartney, J. S., et al. (2002). Effects of the amount and intensity of exercise on plasma lipoproteins. *The New England Journal of Medicine, 347,* 1483–1492.

Kraut, R., Olson, J., Banaji, M., Bruckman, A., Cohen, J., & Couper, M. (2004). Psychological research online: Report of board of scientific affairs' advisory group on the conduct of research on the Internet. *American Psychologist, 59,* 105–117.

Krauzlis, R. J. (2002). Reaching for answers. *Neuron, 34,* 673–674.

Krauzlis, R. J., & Lisberger, S. G. (1991). Visual motion commands for pursuit eye movements in the cerebellum. *Science, 253,* 568–571.

Kray, L. J., & Galinsky, A. D. (2003). The debiasing effect of counterfactual mind-sets: Increasing the search for disconfirmatory information in group decisions. *Organizational Behavior and Human Decision Processes, 91,* 69–81.

Krebs, D. (2011). How altruistic by nature? In S. Brown, M. Brown & L. Penner (Eds.) *Moving beyond self-interest* (pp. 25–38) New York, NY: Oxford.

Krebs, D. L., & Denton, K. (2005). Toward a more pragmatic approach to morality: A critical evaluation of Kohlberg's model. *Psychological Review, 112,* 629–649.

Kreek, M. J., Nielsen, D. A., Butelman, E. R., & LaForge, K. S. (2005). Genetic influences on impulsivity, risk taking, stress responsivity and vulnerability to drug abuse and addiction. *Nature Neuroscience, 8,* 1450–1457.

Kreek, M. J., Nielsen, D. A., Butelman, E. R., & LaForge, K. S. (2005). Genetic influences on impulsivity, risk taking, stress responsivity and vulnerability to drug abuse and addiction. *Nature Neuroscience, 8,* 1450–1457.

Kremen, W. S., & Lyons, M. J. (2011). Behavior genetics of aging. In K. W. Schaie & S. L. Willis (Eds.), *Handbook of the Psychology of Aging* (7th ed., pp. 93–108). San Diego, CA: Academic Press/Elsevier Science.

Kreppner, J. M., Rutter, M., Beckett, C., Castle, J., Colvert, E., Groothues, C., Hawkins, A., O'Connor, T. G., Stevens, S., & Sonuga-Barke, E. J. S. (2007). Normality and impairment following profound early institutional deprivation: A longitudinal follow-up into early adolescence. *Developmental Psychology, 43,* 931–946.

Kreuger, R. F., & Johnson, W. (2008). Behavioral genetics and personality: A new look at the integration of nature and nurture. In O. John, R. Robins, & L. Pervin (Eds.), *Handbook of personality: Theory and research* (3rd ed., pp. 287–310). New York: Guilford.

Krieger, N., Carney, D., Lancaster, K., Waterman, P. D., Kosheleva, A., & Banaji, M. (2010). Implicit measures reveal evidence of personal discrimination. *American Journal of Public Health, 100,* 1485–1492.

Krieglmeyer, R., Deutsch, R., De Houwer, J., & De Raedt, R. (2010). Being moved: Valence activates approach-avoidance behavior independently of evaluation and approach-avoidance intentions. *Psychological Science, 21*(4), 607–613. doi:10.1177/0956797610365131.

Kring, A. M., & Caponigro, J. M. (2010). Emotion in schizophrenia: Where feeling meets thinking. *Current Directions in Psychological Science, 19*(4), 255–259. doi:10.1177/0963721410377599.

Kring, A. M., Germans Gard, M., & Gard, D. E. (2011). Emotion deficits in schizophrenia: Timing matters. *Journal Of Abnormal Psychology, 120*(1), 79–87. doi:10.1037/a0021402.

Kring, A. M., & Gordon, A. H. (1998). Sex differences in emotion: Expression, experience, and physiology. *Journal of Personality & Social Psychology, 74,* 686–703.

Kristof, N. D. (1997, August 17). Where children rule. *New York Times Magazine.*

Krizman, J., Marian, V., Shook, A., Skoe, E., & Kraus, N. (2012). Subcortical encoding of sound is enhanced in bilinguals and relates to executive function advantages. *Proceedings of the National Academy of Sciences of the United States of America, 109*(20), 7877–7881. doi:10.1073/pnas.1201575109.

Krohne, H. W., & Slangen, K. E. (2005). Influence of social support on adaptation to surgery. *Health Psychology, 24,* 101–105.

Krosch, A. R., Figner, B., & Weber, E. U. (2012). Choice processes and their post-decisional consequences in morally conflicting decisions. *Judgment and Decision Making, 7*(3), 224–234.

Krosnick, J. A., Betz, A. L., Jussim, L. J., & Lynn, A. R. (1992). Subliminal conditioning of attitude. *Personality and Social Psychology Bulletin, 18,* 152–162.

Krueger, F., McCabe, K., Moll, J., Kriegeskorte, N., Zahn, R., Strenziok, M., Heinecke, A., & Grafman, J. (2007). Neural correlates of trust. *Proceedings of the National Academies of Science, 104*(50), 20084–20089.

Krueger, R. F., & Markon, K. E. (2006). Understanding psychopathology: Melding behavior genetics, personality, and quantitative psychology to develop an empirically based model. *Current Directions in Psychological Science 15,* 113–117.

Krueger, R. F., Watson, D., & Barlow, D. H. (2005). Introduction to the special section: Toward a dimensionally based taxonomy of psychopathology. *Journal of Abnormal Psychology, 114,* 491–493.

Kruger, J., Wirtz, D., & Miller, D. T. (2005). Counterfactual thinking and the first instinct fallacy. *Journal of Personality and Social Psychology, 88,* 725–735.

Kryger, M. H., Roth, T., & Dement, W. C. (2000). *Principles and practice of sleep medicine* (3rd ed.). Philadelphia: Saunders.

Krykouli, S. E., Stanley, B. G., Seirafi, R. D., & Leibowitz, S. F. (1990). Stimulation of feeding by galanin: Anatomical localization and behavioral specificity of this peptide's effects in the brain. *Peptides, 11*(5), 995–1001.

Kupfer, D. J., & Regier, D. A. (2011). Neuroscience, clinical evidence, and the future of psychiatric classification in DSM-5. *The American Journal Of Psychiatry, 168*(7), 672–674. doi:10.1176/appi.ajp.2011.11020219

Kupfer, D. J., & Regier, D. A. (2010). Why all of medicine should care about DSM-5. *Journal of the American Medical Association, 303,* 1974–1975.

Kurtz, L. F. (2004). Support and self-help groups. In C. D. Garvin, L. M. Gutierrez, & M. J. Galinsky (Eds.), *Handbook of social work with groups* (pp. 139–159). New York: Guilford Press.

Kubilius, J., Wagemans, J., & de Beeck, H. (2011). Emergence of perceptual Gestalts in the human visual cortex: The case of the configural-superiority effect. *Psychological Science, 22*(10), 1296–1303. doi:10.1177/0956797611417000.

Kubzansky, L. D., Davidson, K. W., & Rozanski, A. (2005). The clinical impact of negative psychological states: Expanding the spectrum of risk for coronary artery disease. *Psychosomatic Medicine, 67*(S1), S10–S14.

Kubzansky, L. D., Koenen, K. C., Jones, C., & Eaton, W. W. (2009). A prospective study of posttraumatic stress disorder symptoms and coronary heart disease in women. *Health Psychology, 28,* 125–130.

Kuhbandner, C., Spitzer, B., & Pekrun, R. (2011). Read-out of emotional information from iconic memory: The longevity of threatening stimuli. *Psychological Science, 22*(5), 695–700. doi:10.1177/0956797611406445.

Kuhl, B. A., Bainbridge, W. A., & Chun, M. M. (2012). Neural reactivation reveals mechanisms for updating memory. *The Journal of Neuroscience, 32*(10), 3453–3461. doi:10.1523/JNEUROSCI.5846-11.2012

Kuhl, E., Clifford, L., & Stark, L. (2012). Obesity in preschoolers: Behavioral correlates and directions for treatment. *Obesity (Silver Spring, Md.), 20*(1), 3–29. doi:10.1038/oby.2011.20

Kuhn, D., & Franklin, S. (2006). The second decade: What develops (and how)? In W. Damon & R. M. Lerner (Series Eds.) & D. Kuhn & R. Siegler (Vol. Eds.), *Handbook of child psychology: Vol. 2. Cognition, perception, and language* (6th ed.). New York: Wiley.

Kuhnen, C. M., & Knutson, B. (2005). The neural basis of financial risk taking. *Neuron, 47,* 763–770.

Kumanyika, S. K. (2008). Environmental influences on childhood obesity: Ethnic and cultural influences in context. *Physiology & Behavior, 94*(1), 61–70.

Kumar, N. (2010). Neurologic presentations of nutritional deficiencies. *Neurologic Clinics, 28,* 107–170.

Kumar, V. K., & Farley, F. (2009). Structural aspects of three hypnotizability scales: Smallest space analysis. *International Journal of Clinical and Experimental Hypnosis, 57,* 343–365.

Kuncel, N. R., & Hezlett, S. A. (2010). Fact and fiction in cognitive ability testing for admissions and hiring decisions. *Current Directions in Psychological Science, 19*(6), 339–345. doi:10.1177/0963721410389459.

Kuncel, N. R., Hezlett, S. A., & Ones, D. (2004). Academic performance, career potential, creativity, and job performance: Can one construct predict them all? *Journal of Personality and Social Psychology, 86,* 148–161.

Kuncel, N. R., Ones, D. S. & Sackett, P. R. (2010). Individual differences as predictors of work, educational, and broad life outcomes. *Personality and Individual Differences, 49,* 331–336.

Kunen, S., Niederhauser, R., Smith, P. O., Morris, J. A., & Marx, B. D. (2005). Race disparities in psychiatric rates in emergency departments. *Journal of Consulting and Clinical Psychology, 73,* 116–126.

Kunkel, D., Wilson, B. J., Linz, D., Potter, J., Donnerstein, E., Smith, S. L., et al. (1996). *The national television violence study.* Studio City, CA: Mediascope.

Kuo, L. E., Kitlinska, J. B., Tilan, J. U., Li, L., Baker, S. B., Johnson, M. D., Lee, E. W., Burnett, M. S., Fricke, S. T., Kvetnansky, R., Herzog, H., & Zukowska, Z. (2007). Neuropeptide Y acts directly in the periphery on fat tissue and mediates stress-induced obesity and metabolic syndrome. *Nature Medicine 13,* 803–811.

Kuo, Y.-L., Liao, H.-F., Chen, P.-C., Hsieh, W.-S., & Hwang, A.-W. (2008). The influence of wakeful prone positioning on motor development during the early life. *Journal of Developmental & Behavioral Pediatrics, 29*(5), 367–376.

Kurbat, M. A. (1997). Can the recognition of living things really be selectively impaired? *Neuropsychologia, 35*(6), 813–827.

Kurdek, L. A. (2005). What do we know about gay and lesbian couples? *Current Directions in Psychological Science, 14,* 251–254.

Kurita, H. (2012, March). Is recovery from a pervasive developmental disorder possible?. *Psychiatry & Clinical Neurosciences.* pp. 85–86. doi:10.1111/j.1440-1819.2011.02309.x.

Kush, J. C., Spring, M. B., & Barkand, J. (2012). Advances in the assessment of cognitive skills using computer-based measurement. *Behavior Research Methods, 44*(1), 125–134. doi:10.3758/s13428-011-0136-2.

Kutchins, H., & Kirk, S. A. (1997). *Making us crazy: The psychiatric bible and the creation of mental disorders.* New York: Free Press.

Kwan, M., Greenleaf, W. J., Mann, J., Crapo, L., & Davidson, J. M. (1983). The nature of androgen action on male sexuality: A combined laboratory-self-report study on hypogonadal men. *Journal of Clinical Endocrinology and Metabolism, 57,* 557–562.

Kwan, V. Y., Wojcik, S. P., Miron-shatz, T., Votruba, A. M., & Olivola, C. Y. (2012). Effects of symptom presentation order on perceived disease risk. *Psychological Science, 23*(4), 381–385. doi:10.1177/0956797611432177.

Kwate, N. O. A. (2001). Intelligence or misorientation? *Journal of Black Psychology, 27,* 221–238.

Kymalainen, J. A., Weisman, A. G., Resales, G. A., & Armesto, J. C. (2006). Ethnicity, expressed emotion, and communication deviance in family members of patients with schizophrenia. *Journal of Nervous and Mental Disease, 194,* 391–396.

Kyrios, M., Sanavio, E., Bhar, S., & Liguori, L. (2001). Associations between obsessive-compulsive phenomena, affect, and beliefs: Cross-cultural comparisons of Australian and Italian data. *Behavioural and Cognitive Psychotherapy, 29,* 409–422.

Labouvie-Vief, G. (1982). Discontinuities in development from childhood. In T. M. Field, A. Huston, H. C. Quay, L. Troll, & G. E. Finley (Eds.), *Review of human development.* New York: Wiley.

Labouvie-Vief, G. (1992). A new-Piagetian perspective on adult cognitive development. In R. J. Sternberg & C. A. Berg (Eds.), *Intellectual development.* New York: Cambridge University Press.

Lacayo, A. (1995). Neurologic and psychiatric complications of cocaine abuse. *Neuropsychiatry, Neuropsychology, and Behavioral Neurology, 8,* 53–60.

Lacor, P. N. (2007). Advances on the Understanding of the Origins of Synaptic Pathology in AD. *Current Genomics, 8*(8), 486–508.

Ladd, G. (2005). *Peer relationships and social competence of children and youth.* New Haven, CT: Yale University Press.

Laeng, B., Sirois, S., & Gredebäck, G. (2012). Pupillometry: A window to the preconscious? *Perspectives on Psychological Science, 7*(1) 18–27doi:10.1177/1745691611427305.

LaFrance, M., Hecht, M. A., & Paluck, E. L. (2003). The contingent smile: A meta-analysis of sex differences in smiling. *Psychological Bulletin, 129,* 305–334.

Lagerspetz, K. M. J., & Lagerspetz, K. Y. H. (1983). Genes and aggression. In E. C. Simmel, M. E. Hahn, & J. K. Walters (Eds.), *Aggressive behavior: Genetic and neural approaches.* Hillsdale, NJ: Erlbaum.

Lagopoulos, J., & Malhi, G. S. (2008). Transcranial magnetic stimulation. *Acta Neuropsychiatrica, 20*(6), 316–317.

Lahey, B., Rathouz, P., Lee, S., Chronis-Tuscano, A., Pelham, W., Waldman, I., & Cook, E. (2011). Interactions between early parenting and a polymorphism of the child's dopamine transporter gene in predicting future child conduct disorder symptoms. *Journal of Abnormal Psychology, 120*(1), 33–45.

Lahey, B. B., Loeber, R., Burke, J. D., & Applegate, B. (2005). Predicting future antisocial personality disorder in males from a clinical assessment in childhood. *Journal of Consulting and Clinical Psychology, 73,* 389–399.

Lahey, B. B., Loeber, R., Hart, E. L., Frick, P. J., & Applegate, B. (1995). Four-year longitudinal study of conduct disorder in boys: Patterns and predictors of persistence. *Journal of Abnormal Psychology, 104,* 83–93.

Lahey, B. B., Van Hulle, C. A., Keenan, K., Rathouz, P. J., D'Onofrio, B. M., Rodgers, J. L., & Waldman, I. D. (2008). Temperament and parenting during the first year of life predict future child conduct problems. *Journal of Abnormal Child Psychology, 36,* 1139–1158.

Lai, C. S. L., Fisher, S. E., Hurst, J. A., Vargha-Khadem, F., & Monaco, A. P. (2001). A forkhead-domain gene is mutated in severe speech and language disorder. *Nature, 413,* 519–523.

Laird, R. D., Jordan, K. Y., Dodge, K. A., Pettit, G. S., & Gates, J. E. (2001). Peer rejection in childhood, involvement with antisocial peers in early adolescence, and the development of externalizing behavior problems. *Development and Psychopathology, 13,* 337–354.

Lakin, J. L., & Chartrand, T. L. (2003). Using nonconscious behavioral mimicry to create affiliation and rapport. *Psychological Science, 14,* 334–339.

Lakshmikumar, S. T. (2009). Power line panic and mobile mania. *Skeptical Inquirer, 33,* 32–35.

Lally, P., van Jaarsveld,, C. H. M., Potts, H. W. W., & Wardle, J. (2010). How are habits formed: Modeling habit formation in the real world. *European Journal of Social Psychology, 40,* 998–1009. doi:10.1002/ejsp.674.

Lalumière, M. L., Blanchard, R., & Zucker, K. J. (2000). Sexual orientation and handedness in men and women: A meta-analysis. *Psychological Bulletin, 126,* 575–592.

Lam, D. H., Watkins, E. R., Hayward, P., Bright, J., Wright, K., Kerr, N., Parr-Davis, G., & Sham, P. (2003). A randomized controlled study of cognitive therapy for relapse prevention for bipolar affective disorder: outcome of the first year. *Archives of General Psychiatry, 60,* 145–152.

Lam, S. K., & Riedl, J. (2012). Are our online "friends" really friends? *Computer, 45,* 91–93. doi:10.1109/MC.2012.5.

Lamb, M. E. (1998). Assessments of children's credibility in forensic contexts. *Current Directions in Psychological Science, 7,* 43–46.

Lamb, M. E. (Ed.). (1997). *The role of the father in child development* (3rd ed.). New York: Wiley.

Lamb, M. E., & Ahnert, L. (2006). Nonparental child care. In W. Damon & R. M. Lerner (Series Eds.) & K. A. Renninger & I. E. Sigel (Vol. Eds.), *Handbook of child psychology: Vol. 4. Child psychology in practice* (6th ed.). New York: Wiley.

Lamb, M. E. & Lewis, C. (2010). The development and significance of father-child relationships in two-parent families. In M. E. Lamb (Ed.), *The role of the father in child development* (5th ed., pp. 94–153). Hoboken NJ: Wiley.

Lamberg, L. (2004). Impact of long working hours explored. *Journal of the American Medical Association, 292,* 25–26.

Lambert, M. J. (2011). Solving problems with randomized clinical trials is not enough to improve psychotherapy outcome: Comments on Krause. *Psychotherapy, 48,* 229–230. doi:10.1037/a0023132

Lambert, M. J., & Barley, D. E. (2001). Research summary on the therapeutic relationship and psychotherapy outcome. *Psychotherapy, 38,* 357–361.

Lambert, T., & Norman, T. R. (2008). Ethnic differences in psychotropic drug response and pharmacokinetics. In C. H. Ng, K. Lin, B. S. Singh, & E. Chiu (Eds.), *Ethnopsychopharmacology: Advances in current practice* (pp. 38–61). New York: Cambridge University Press.

Lamm, E., & Jablonka, E. (2008). The nurture of nature: Hereditary plasticity in evolution. *Philosophical Psychology, 21*(3), 305–319.

Landolt, A. S. & Milling, L. S. (2011). The efficacy of hypnosis as an intervention for labor and delivery pain: A comprehensive methodological review. *Clinical Psychology Review, 31*(6), 1022–1031.

Landgren, M., Svensson, L., Stromland, K., & Gronlund, M. A. (2010). Prenatal alcohol exposure and neurodevelopmental disorders in children adopted from eastern Europe. *Pediatrics, 125,* e1178–e1185.

Landrine, H. (1991). Revising the framework of abnormal psychology. In P. Bronstein & K. Quina (Eds.), *Teaching a psychology of people.* Washington, DC: American Psychological Association.

Landsdale, M., & Laming, D. (1995). Evaluating the fragmentation hypothesis: The analysis of errors in cued recall. *Acta Psychologica, 88,* 33–77.

Landy, F. J. (1992). Hugo Münsterberg: Victim or visionary? *Journal Of Applied Psychology, 77*(6), 787–802. doi:10.1037/0021-9010.77.6.787.

Laney, C., & Loftus, E. F. (2010). False memory In J. Brown & E. Campbell (Eds.) *The Cambridge handbook of forensic psychology* (pp. 187–194) New York, NY: Cambridge University Press.

Lang, A. R., Goeckner, D. J., Adesso, V. J., & Marlatt, G. A. (1975). Effects of alcohol on aggression in male social drinkers. *Journal of Abnormal Psychology, 84,* 508–518.

Lang, C., Barco, A., Zablow, L., Kandel, E. R., Siegelbaum, S. A., & Zakharenko, S. S. (2004). Transient expansion of synaptically connected dendritic spines upon induction of hippocampal long-term potentiation. *Proceedings of the National Academy of Sciences, 101,* 16665–16670.

Lang, J. W. B., & Lang, J. (2010). Priming competence diminishes the link between cognitive test anxiety and test performance: Implications for the interpretation of test scores. *Psychological Science, 21,* 811–819. Epub 2010 Apr 30.

Lang, P. J. (1995). The emotion probe: Studies of motivation and attention. *American Psychologist, 50*(5), 372–385.

Lang, P. J., & Melamed, B. G. (1969). Avoidance conditioning therapy of an infant with chronic ruminative vomiting. *Journal of Abnormal Psychology, 74,* 1–8.

Lang, T. J., Blackwell, S. E., Harmer, C. J., Davison, P., & Holmes, E. A. (2012). Cognitive bias modification using mental imagery for depression: Developing a novel computerized intervention to change negative thinking styles. *European Journal of Personality, 26*(2), 145–157. doi:10.1002/per.855.

Langan, C., & McDonald, C. (2009). Neurobiological trait abnormalities in bipolar disorder. *Molecular Psychiatry, 14,* 833–846.

Langan, M. (2011). Parental voices and controversies in autism. *Disability & Society, 26,* 193–205. doi:10.1080/09687599.2011.544059

Lange, C., & Byrd, M. (2002). Differences between students' estimated and attained grades in a first-year introductory psychology course as a function of identity development. *Adolescence, 37*(145), 93–108.

Langenbucher, J., & Nathan, P. E. (2006). Diagnosis and classification. In F. Andrasik (Ed.), *Comprehensive handbook of personality and psychopathology: Vol. 2. Adult psychopathology* (pp. 3–20). New York: Wiley.

Langens, T. A., & Schüler, J. (2007). Effects of written emotional expression: the role of positive expectancies. *Health Psychology, 26,* 174–182.

Langer, E., Djikic, M., Pirson, M., Madenci, A., & Donohue, R. (2010). Believing is seeing: Using mindlessness (mindfully) to improve visual acuity. *Psychological Science, 21*(5), 661–666. doi:10.1177/0956797610366543.

Langer, K. G. (2009). Babinski's anosognosia for hemiplegia in early-twentieth-century French neurology. *Journal of the History of Neuroscience, 18,* 387–405.

Lansford, J. E., Chang, L., Dodge, K. A., Malone, P. S., et al. (2005). Physical discipline and children's adjustment: Cultural normativeness as a moderator. *Child Development, 76,* 1234–1246.

Lansford, J. E., & Dodge, K. A. (2008). Cultural norms for adult corporal punishment of children and societal rates of endorsement and use of violence. *Parenting: Science & Practice, 8*(3), 257–270.

Lansky, D., & Wilson, G. T. (1981). Alcohol, expectations and sexual arousal in males: An information processing analysis. *Journal of Abnormal Psychology, 89,* 528–538.

Lantz, J. (2004). Research and evaluation issues in existential psychotherapy. *Journal of Contemporary Psychotherapy, 34,* 331–340.

Lanzenberger, R. R., Mitterhauser, M., Spindelegger, C., Wadsak, W., Klein, N., Mien, L. K., et al. (2007). Reduced serotonin-1a receptor binding in social anxiety disorder. *Biological Psychiatry, 61,* 1081–1089.

Lapierre, L. M., & Allen, T. D. (2006). Work-supportive family, family-supportive supervision, use of organizational benefits, and problem-focused coping: Implications for work-family conflict and employee well-being. *Journal of Occupational Health Psychology, 11,* 169–181.

Lapointe, L. (1990). *Aphasia and related neurogenic language disorders.* New York: Thieme Medical.

Larrick, R. P., Timmerman, T. A., Carton, A. M., & Abrevaya, J. (2011). Temper, temperature, and temptation: Heat—related retaliation in baseball. *Psychological Science, 22*(4), 423–428. doi:10.1177/0956797611399292.

Larsen, R. J., & Buss, D. M. (2010). *Personality psychology: Domains of knowledge about human nature* (4th ed) New York: McGraw-Hill.

Larsen, J. T., McGraw, A. P., Mellers, B. A., & Cacioppo, J. T. (2004). The agony of victory and thrill of defeat: Mixed emotional reactions to disappointing wins and relieving losses. *Psychological Science, 15,* 325–330.

Larsen, R., & Buss, D. M. (2005). *Personality psychology: Domains of knowledge about human nature* (2nd ed.). New York: McGraw-Hill.

Larson, E. B., Wang, L., Bowen, J. D., McCormick, W. C., Teri, L., Crane, P., & Kukull, W. (2006). Exercise is associated with reduced risk of incident dementia among persons 65 years of age and older. *Annals of Internal Medicine, 144,* 73–81.

Larson, J. R., Jr., Christensen, C., Franz, T. M., & Abbott, A. S. (1998). Diagnosing groups: The pooling, management, and impact of shared and unshared case information in team-based medical decision making. *Journal of Personality and Social Psychology, 75,* 93–108.

Larson, R. W., & Verma, S. (1999). How children and adolescents spend time across the world: Work, play, and developmental opportunities. *Psychological Bulletin, 125,* 701–736.

Larsson, H., Andershed, H., & Lichtenstein, P. (2006). A genetic factor explains most of the variation in the psychopathic personality. *Journal of Abnormal Psychology, 115,* 221–230.

Latané, B. (1981). The psychology of social impact. *American Psychologist, 36,* 343–356.

Latané, B., & Rodin, J. (1969). A lady in distress: Inhibiting effects of friends and strangers on bystander intervention. *Journal of Experimental Social Psychology, 5,* 189–202.

Latham, G. P. (2004). Motivate employee performance through goal-setting. In E. A. Locke (Ed.), *Handbook of principles of organizational behavior* (pp. 107–119). Malden, MA: Blackwell.

Latham, G. P., Skarlicki, D., Irvine, D., & Siegel, J. P. (1993). The increasing importance of performance appraisals to employee effectiveness in organizational settings in North America. In C. L. Cooper & I. T. Robertson (Eds.), *International review of industrial and organizational psychology 1993* (pp. 87–132). Chichester, UK: Wiley.

Lau, H., & Stotzer, R. L. (2011). Employment discrimination based on sexual orientation: A Hong Kong study. *Employee Responsibilities And Rights Journal, 23*(1), 17–35. doi:10.1007/s10672-010-9150-2

Lau, J., Molyneaux, E., Telman, M., & Belli, S. (2011). The plasticity of adolescent cognitions: Data from a novel cognitive bias modification training task. *Child Psychiatry and Human Development, 42*(6), 679–693.

Lau, M. A., Pihl, R. O., & Peterson, J. B. (1995). Provocation, acute alcohol intoxication, cognitive performance, and aggression. *Journal of Abnormal Psychology, 104,* 150–155.

Laudan, L. (2012). Eyewitness identifications: One more lesson on the costs of excluding relevant evidence. *Perspectives on Psychological Science, 7*(3), 272–274. doi:10.1177/1745691612443065.

Laughery, K. R. (1999). Modeling human performance during system design. In E. Salas (Ed.), *Human/technology interaction in complex systems* (Vol. 9, pp. 147–174). Stamford, CT: JAI Press.

Laughlin, P. L. (1999). Collective induction: Twelve postulates. *Organizational Behavior and Human Decision Processes, 80,* 50–69.

Laumann, E. O., Gagnon, J. H., Michael, R. T., & Michaels, S. (1994). *The social organization of sexuality: Sexual practices in the United States.* Chicago: University of Chicago Press.

Laumann, E. O., & Michael, R. T. (Eds.). (2000). *Sex, love, and health in America: Private choices and public policies.* Chicago: University of Chicago Press.

Laurenceau, J.-P., Stanley, S. M., Olmos-Gallo, A., Baucom, B., & Markman, H. J. (2004). Community-based prevention of marital dysfunction: Multilevel modeling of a randomized effectiveness study. *Journal of Consulting and Clinical Psychology, 72,* 933–943.

Laurin, K., Kay, A. C., & Fitzsimons, G. J. (2012). Reactance versus rationalization: Divergent responses to policies that constrain freedom. *Psychological Science, 23*(2), 205–209. doi:10.1177/0956797611429468.

Laursen, B., Bukowski, W. M., Aunola, K., & Nurmi, J.-E. (2007). Friendship moderates prospective associations between social isolation and adjustment problems in young children. *Child Development, 78,* 1395–1404.

Lavault, S., Dauvilliers, Y., Drouot , X., Leu-Semenescu, S., Golmard, J. L., Lecendreux, M., Franco, P., & Arnulf, I. (2011). Benefit and risk of modafinil in idiopathic hypersomnia vs. narcolepsy with cataplexy. *Sleep Medicine, 12*(6), 550–556.

Lavoie, M.-P., Lam, R. W., Bouchard, G., Sasseville, A., et al. (2009). Evidence of a biological eff ect of light therapy on the retina of patients with seasonal aff ective disorder. *Biological Psychiatry, 66,* 253–258.

Law, D. J., Pellegrino, J. W., & Hunt, E. B. (1993). Comparing the tortoise and the hare: Gender differences and experience in dynamic spatial reasoning tasks. *Psychological Science, 4,* 35–40.

Law, W., Elliot, A. J., & Murayama, K. (2012). Perceived competence moderates the relation between performance-approach and performance-avoidance goals. *Journal of Educational Psychology.* doi:10.1037/a0027179.

Lawder, R. R., Grant, I. I., Storey, C. C., Walsh, D. D., Whyte, B. B., & Hanlon, P. P. (2011). Epidemiology of hospitalization due to alcohol-related harm: Evidence from a Scottish cohort study. *Public Health, 125*(8), 533–539. doi:10.1016/j.puhe.2011.05.007

Lawless, H. T., & Engen, T. (1977). Associations to odors: Interference, memories and verbal learning. *Journal of Experimental Psychology, 3,* 52–59.

Lawson, C. A. (2004). Treating the borderline mother: Integrating EMDR with a family systems perspective. In M. M. MacFarlane (Ed.), *Family treatment of personality disorders: Advances in clinical practice* (pp. 305–334). Binghamton, NY: Haworth Clinical Practice Press.

Lazarus, A. A. (1971). *Behavior therapy and beyond.* New York: McGraw-Hill.

Lazarus, C. N., & Lazarus, A. A. (2002). EMDR: An elegantly concentrated multimodal procedure? In F. Shapiro (Ed.), *EMDR as an integrative psychotherapy approach: Experts of diverse orientations explore the paradigm prism* (pp. 209–223). Washington, DC: American Psychological Association.

Lazarus, R. S. (1966). *Psychological stress and the coping process.* New York: McGraw-Hill.

Lazarus, R. S. (1991). Progress on a cognitive-motivational-relational theory of emotion. *American Psychologist, 46,* 819–834.

Lazarus, R. S. (1999). *Stress and emotion: A new synthesis.* New York: Springer.

Lazarus, R. S., & Folkman, S. (1984). *Stress, appraisal, and coping.* New York: Springer-Verlag.

Lazarus, R. S., Opton, E. M., Nomikos, M. S., & Rankin, M. O. (1965). The principle of short-circuiting of threat: Further evidence. *Journal of Personality, 33,* 622–635.

Leal, S., & Vrij, A. (2010). The occurrence of eye blinks during a guilty knowledge test. *Psychology, Crime & Law, 16*(4), 349–357. doi:10.1080/10683160902776843.

Leal, S., Vrij, A., Mann, S., & Fisher, R. P. (2010). Detecting true and false opinions: The Devil's Advocate approach as a lie detection aid. *Acta Psychologica, 134*(3), 323–329. doi:10.1016/j.actpsy.2010.03.005.

Leamon, M. H., Wright, T. M., & Myrick, H. (2008). Substance-related disorders. In R. E. Hales, S. C. Yudofsky, & G. O. Gabbard (Eds.) *Textbook of psychiatry* (pp. 365–406). Washington, DC: American Psychiatric Publishing.

Leary, M. R. (2001).Shyness and the self: Attentional, motivational, and cognitive self-processes in social anxiety. In R. Crozier & L. Alden (Eds.), *International handbook of social anxiety: A handbook of concepts, research, and interventions relating to the self and shyness* (pp. 217–234). New York: John Wiley and Sons.

Leary, M. R. (2010). Affiliation, acceptance, and belonging: The pursuit of interpersonal connection. In S. T. Fiske, D. T. Gilbert, & G. Lindzey (Eds.), *Handbook of social psychology* (5th ed., Vol. 2, pp. 864–897). Hoboken, NJ: Wiley.

LeBlanc, M. M., & Barling, J. (2004). Workplace aggression. *Current Directions in Psychological Science, 13,* 9–12.

LeBlanc, M. M., Dupre, K. E., & Barling, J. (2006). Public-initiated violence. In K. E. Kelloway, J. Barling, & J. J. Hurrell (Eds.), *Handbook of workplace violence* (pp. 261–280). Thousand Oaks, CA: Sage.

Lederbogen, F., Kirsch, P., Haddad, L., Streit, F., Tost, H., Schuch, P., & Meyer-Lindenberg, A. (2011). City living and urban upbringing affect neural social stress processing in humans. *Nature, 474*(7352), 498–501. doi:10.1038/nature10190.

Leding, J. K. (2012). Working memory predicts the rejection of false memories. *Memory, 20*(3), 217–223. doi:10.1080/09658211.2011.653373.

LeDoux, J. E. (1995). Emotion: Clues from the brain. *Annual Review of Psychology, 46,* 209–235.

Lee, C. M., Ryan, J. J., & Kreiner, D. S. (2007). Personality in domestic cats. *Psychological Reports, 100*(1), 27–29.

Lee, C. W., Taylor, G., & Drummond, P. D. (2006). The active ingredient in EMDR: Is it traditional exposure or dual focus of attention? *Clinical Psychology & Psychotherapy, 13*(2), 97–107.

Lee, J. (2006). Human factors and ergonomics in automation design. In G. Salvendy (Ed.), *Handbook of human factors and ergonomics* (3rd ed., 1570–1596). Hoboken, NJ: John Wiley & Sons Inc.

Lee, J. L. C., Everitt, B. J., & Thomas, K. L. (2004). Independent cellular processes for hippocampal memory consolidation and reconsolidation. *Science, 304,* 839–843.

Lee, K., Ogunfowora, B., & Ashton, M. C. (2005). Personality traits beyond the big five: Are they within the HEXACO space? *Journal of Personality, 73,* 1437–1463.

Lee, M. S., Kim, J. I., Ha, J. Y., Boddy, K., & Ernst, E. (2009). Yoga for menopausal symptoms: A systematic review. *Menopause, 16,* 602–608.

Lee, S., Colditz, G., Berkman, L., & Kawachi, I. (2003). Caregiving to children and grandchildren and risk of coronary heart disease in women. *American Journal of Public Health, 93,* 1939–1944.

Lee, S., Rogge, R. D., & Reis, H. T. (2010). Assessing the seeds of relationship decay: Using implicit evaluations to detect the early stages of disillusionment. *Psychological Science, 21*(6), 857–864. doi:10.1177/0956797610371342.

Lee, S. S., Davis, B., & MacNeilage, P. (2010). Universal production patterns and ambient language influences in babbling: A cross-linguistic study of Korean- and English-learning infants. *Journal Of Child Language, 37*(2), 293–318. doi:10.1017/S0305000909009532.

Lee, S. W. S., & Schwarz, N. (2010, May 7). Washing away postdecisional dissonance. *Science, 328*(5979), 709. doi:10.1126/science.1186799.

Lee, T. M. C., Aua, R. K. C., Liud, H.-L., Tingf, K. H., Huangg, C.-M., & Chan, C. C. H. (2009). Are errors differentiable from deceptive responses when feigning memory impairment? An fMRI study. *Brain and Cognition, 69,* 406–412.

Lee, Y. S., & Silva, A. J. (2009). The molecular and cellular biology of enhanced cognition. *National Review of Neuroscience, 10*(2), 126–140.

Leeds, A. M. (2009). *A guide to the standard EMDR protocols for clinicians, supervisors, and consultants.* New York: Springer.

Leeman, R. F., Kulesza, M., Stewart, D. W., & Copeland, A. L. (2012). Cluster analysis of undergraduate drinkers based on alcohol expectancy scores. *Journal of Studies on Alcohol and Drugs, 73*(2), 238–249.

Leff, J. (2006). Whose life is it anyway? Quality of life for long-stay patients discharged from psychiatric hospitals. In H. Katschnig, H. Freeman, & N. Sartorius (Eds.), *Quality of life in mental disorders* (2nd ed., pp. 247–255). New York: Wiley.

Legare, C. H., & Gelman, S. A. (2008). Bewitchment, biology, or both: The co-existence of natural and supernatural explanatory frameworks across development. *Cognitive science, 32,* 607–642.

Legault, L., Gutsell, J. N., & Inzlicht, M. (2011). Ironic effects of antiprejudice messages: How motivational interventions can reduce (but also increase) prejudice. *Psychological Science, 22*(12), 1472–1477. doi:10.1177/0956797611427918.

Legerstee, M., Anderson, D., & Schaffer, A. (1998). Five- and eight-month-old infants recognize their faces and voices as familiar and social stimuli. *Child Development, 69,* 37–50.

le Grange, D., Crosby, R. D., Rathouz, P. J., & Leventhal, B. L. (2007). A randomized controlled comparison of family-based treatment and supportive psychotherapy for adolescent bulimia nervosa. *Archives of General Psychiatry, 64,* 1049–1056.

Lehman, B. J., Taylor, S. E., Keife, C. I., & Seeman, T. E. (2005). Relation of childhood socioeconomic status and family environment to adult metabolic functioning in the CARDIA study. *Psychosomatic Medicine, 67,* 846–854.

Lehman, H. E. (1967). Schizophrenia: IV. Clinical features. In A. M. Freedman, H. I. Kaplan, & H. S. Kaplan (Eds.), *Comprehensive textbook of psychiatry.* Baltimore: Williams & Wilkins.

Leibel, R. L., Rosenbaum, M., & Hirsch, J. (1995). Changes in energy expenditure resulting from altered body weight. *New England Journal of Medicine, 332*(10), 621–628.

Leibowitz, H. W., Brislin, R., Perlmutter, L., & Hennessy, R. (1969). Ponzo perspective illusion as a manifestation of space perception. *Science, 166,* 1174–1176.

Leibowitz, S. F. (1992). Neurochemical-neuroendocrine systems in the brain controlling macronutrient intake and metabolism. *TINS, 15,* 491–497.

Leigh, B. C., & Stacy, A. W. (2004). Alcohol expectancies and drinking in different age groups. *Addiction, 99,* 215–227.

Leiner, H. C., Leiner, A. L., & Dow, R. S. (1993). Cognitive and language functions of the human cerebellum. *Trends in Neuroscience, 16,* 444–447.

Leinhardt, G., & Knutson, K. (2004). *Listening in on museum conversations.* Walnut Creek, CA: AltaMira Press.

Leippe, M. R., Manion, A. P., & Romanczyk, A. (1992). Eyewitness persuasion: How and how well do fact finders judge the accuracy of adults' and children's memory reports? *Journal of Personality and Social Psychology, 63,* 181–197.

Leiser, D., & Azar, O. H. (2008). Behavioral economics and decision making: Applying insights from psychology to understand how people make economic decisions. *Journal of Economic Psychology, 29*(5), 613–618.

Leiser, D., Azar, O. H., & Hadar, L. (2008). Psychological construal of economic behavior. *Journal of Economic Psychology, 29*(5), 762–776.

Leising, D., & Zimmermann, J. (2011). An integrative conceptual framework for assessing personality and personality pathology. *Review of General Psychology.* Advance online publication. doi10.1037/a0025070.

Leitzmann MF, Park Y, Blair A, Ballard-Barbash R, Mouw T, Hollenbeck AR, Schatzkin A. Physical activity recommendations and decreased risk of mortality. *Archives of Internal Medicine, 167,* 2453–2460, 2007.

Lejuez, C. W., Hopko, D. R., Levine, S., Gholkar, R., & Collins, L. (2005). The therapeutic alliance in behavior therapy. *Psychotherapy: Theory, Research, Practice, and Training, 42,* 456–468.

Lemaire, P. (2010). Cognitive strategy variations during aging. *Current Directions in Psychological Science, 19*(6), 363–369. doi:10.1177/0963721410390354.

Lemmer, B., Kern, R. I., Nold, G., & Lohrer, H. (2002). Jet lag in athletes after eastward and westward time-zone transition. *Chronobiology International, 19,* 743–764.

Lemoine, P., Kermadi, I., Garcia-Acosta, S., Garay, R. P., & Dib, M. (2006). Double-blind, comparative study of cyamemazine vs. bromazepam in the benzodiazepine withdrawal syndrome. *Progress in Neuro-Psychopharmacology & Biological Psychiatry, 30,* 131–137.

Lemos, G. C., Almeida, L. S., & Colom, R. (2011). Intelligence of adolescents is related to their parents' educational level but not to family income. *Personality and Individual Differences, 50*(7), 1062–1067. doi:10.1016/j.paid.2011.01.025.

Lenneberg, E. H. (1967). *Biological foundations of language.* New York: Wiley.

Lent, M., Hill, T., Dollahite, J., Wolfe, W., & Dickin, K. (2012). Healthy children, healthy families: Parents making a difference! A curriculum integrating key nutrition, physical activity, and parenting practices to help prevent childhood obesity. *Journal of Nutrition, Education, and Behavior, 44*(1), 90–92.

Lenzenweger, M. F., McLachlan, G., & Rubin, D. B. (2007). Resolving the latent structure of schizophrenia endophenotypes using expectation-maximization-based finite mixture modeling. *Journal of Abnormal Psychology, 116,* 16–29.

Leon, D. A., Lawlor, D. A., Clark, H., Batty, G. D., & Macintyre, S. (2009). The association of childhood intelligence with mortality risk from adolescence to middle age: Findings from the Aberdeen Children of the 1950s cohort study. *Intelligence, 37,* 520–528.

Leonhardt, D. (2000, May 24). Management: On Testing for Common Sense; A Business School Thinks It Makes Sense. Yes? No? *New York Times,* p. C1.

Leotti, L. A., & Delgado, M. R. (2011). The inherent reward of choice. *Psychological Science, 22*(10), 1310–1318. doi:10.1177/0956797611417005.

Lepore, S. J. (1995). Cynicism, social support, and cardiovascular reactivity. *Health Psychology, 14,* 210–216.

Leppänen, J. M., & Nelson, C. A. (2012). Early development of fear processing. *Current Directions in Psychological Science, 21,* 200–204. doi:10.1177/0963721411435841.

Lepper, M. R. (1983). Social-control processes and the internalization of social values: An attributional perspective. In E. T. Higgins, D. N. Ruble, & W. W. Hartup (Eds.), *Social cognition and social development* (pp. 294–330). New York: Cambridge University Press.

Lepper, M. R., & Greene, D. (Eds.). (1978). *The hidden costs of reward.* Hillsdale, NJ: Erlbaum

Lepper, M. R., Greene, D., & Nisbett, R. E. (1973). Undermining children's intrinsic interest with extrinsic rewards: A test of the overjustification hypothesis. *Journal of Personality and Social Psychology, 28,* 129–137.

Lerner, J. S., Gonzalez, R. M., Small, D. A., & Fischhoff, B. (2003). Effects of fear and anger on perceived risks of terrorism: A national field experiment. *Psychological Science, 14,* 144–150.

Lesko, A. C., & Corpus, J. H. (2006). Discounting the difficult: How high math-identified women respond to stereotype threat. *Sex Roles, 54*(1–2), 113–125.

Leslie, K., Chan, M. T., Myles, P. S., Forbes, A., & McCulloch, T. J. (2010). Posttraumatic stress disorder in aware patients from the B-aware trial. *Anesthesia and Analgesia, 110*(30), 823–828.

Lettre, G. (2011). Recent progress in the study of the genetics of height. *Human Genetics, 129*(5), 465–472.

Leung, A. K.-y., Kim, S., Polman, E., Ong, L. S., Lin, Q., Goncalo, J. A., & Sanchez-Burks, J. (2012). Embodied metaphors and creative "acts." *Psychological Science.* Published online first. doi:10.1177/0956797611429801.

Leung, H. T., & Westbrook, F. R. (2008). Spontaneous recovery of extinguished fear responses deepens their extinction: A role for error-correction mechanisms. *Journal of Experimental Psychology: Animal Behavior Processes, 31,* 277–288.

Leung L. (2011). Cannabis and its derivatives: Review of medical use. *Journal of the American Board of Family Medicine, 24*(4), 452–462.

Levant, R. F. (2005). Evidence-based practice in psychology. *Monitor on Psychology, 36,* 5.

Leve, L. D., Kim, H. K., & Pears, K. C. (2005). Childhood temperament and family environment as predictors of internalizing and externalizing trajectories from ages 5 to 17. *Journal of Abnormal Child Psychology, 33,* 505–520.

Levenson, H. (2003). Time-limited dynamic psychotherapy: An integrationist perspective. *Journal of Psychotherapy Integration, 13,* 300–333.

Levenson, R. W., Ekman, P., & Friesen, W. V. (1990). Voluntary facial action generates emotion-specific autonomic nervous system activity. *Psychophysiology, 27*(4), 363–384.

Levenson, R. W., Ekman, P., Heider, K., & Friesen, W. V. (1992). Emotion and autonomic nervous system activity in the Minangkabau of West Sumatra. *Journal of Personality and Social Psychology, 62*(6), 972–988.

Levin, D. N., Xiaoping, H., Tan, K. K., Galhotra, S., Palizzare, C. A., Chen, G. T. Y., Beck, R. N., Chen, C. T., Cooper, M. D., Mullan, J. F., Mullan, Hekmatpanah, J., & Spire, J. P. (1989). The Brain: Integrated three-dimensional display of MR and PET images. *Radiology, 172:* 783–789.

Levin, L., Henderson, H. A., & Ehrenreich-May, J. (2012). Interpersonal predictors of early therapeutic alliance in a transdiagnostic cognitive-behavioral treatment for adolescents with anxiety and depression. *Psychotherapy, 49,* 218–230. doi:10.1037/a0028265

Levinthal, C. F. (2001). *Drugs, behavior, and modern society* (3rd ed.). Boston: Allyn & Bacon.

Levin, K. H., Copersino, M. L., Heishman, S. J., Liu, F., Kelly. D. L., Boggs, D. L., & Gorelick, D. A. (2010). Cannabis withdrawal symptoms in non-treatment-seeking adult cannabis smokers. *Drug and Alcohol Dependence, 111*(1–2), 120–127.

Levine, M. W., & Shefner, J. M. (1981). *Fundamentals of sensation and perception.* Reading, MA: Addison-Wesley.

Levine, R., Sato, S., Hashimoto, T., & Verna, J. (1995). Love and marriage in eleven cultures. *Journal of Cross-Cultural Psychology, 26,* 554–571.

Levine, R. V., Reysen, S., & Ganz, E. (2008). The kindness of strangers revisited: A comparison of 24 US cities. *Social Indicators Research, 85,* 461–481.

Levine, S. (1999, February 1). In a loud and noisy world, baby boomers pay the consequences. *International Herald Tribune.*

Levinson, D. F. (2006). The genetics of depression: A review. *Biological Psychiatry, 60,* 84–92.

Levinson, D. F., Evgrafov, O. V., Knowles, J. A., Potash, J. B., Weissman, M. M., Scheftner, W. A., et al. (2007). Genetics of recurrent early-onset major depression (GenRED): Significant linkage on chromosome 15q25-q26 after fine mapping with single nucleotide polymorphism markers. *American Journal of Psychiatry, 164,* 259–264.

Levinson, D. J., Darrow, C. N., Klein, E. B., Levinson, M. H., & McKee, B. (1978). *The seasons of a man's life.* New York: Knopf.

Levinthal, C. F. (2001). *Drugs, behavior, and modern society* (3rd ed.). Boston: Allyn & Bacon.

Levinthal, B. R., & Franconeri, S. L. (2011). Common-fate grouping as feature selection. *Psychological Science, 22*(9), 1132–1137. doi:10.1177/0956797611418346.

Levitsky, D. A., Iyer, S., & Pacanowski, C. R. (2012). Number of foods available at a meal determines the amount consumed. *Eating Behaviors, 13*(3), 183–187. doi:10.1016/j.eatbeh.2012.01.006.

Levitsky, D. A., & Pacanowski, C. R. (2011). Losing weight without dieting. Use of commercial foods as meal replacements for lunch produces an extended energy deficit. *Appetite, 57*(2), 311–317. doi:10.1016/j.appet.2011.04.015.

Levitsky, D. A., & DeRosimo, L. (2010). One day of food restriction does not result in an increase in subsequent daily food intake in humans. *Physiology & Behavior, 99*(4), 495–499. doi:10.1016/j.physbeh.2009.12.020.

Levy, B. R., Slade, M. D., Kunkel, S. R., & Kasl, S. V. (2002). Longevity increased by positive self-perceptions of aging. *Journal of Personality & Social Psychology, 83*(2), 261–270.

Levy, D. A., Bayley, P. J., & Squire L. R. (2004). The anatomy of semantic knowledge: Medial vs. lateral temporal lobe. *Proceedings of the National Academies of Science, 101,* 6710–6715.

Levy, R., & Ablon, J. S. (Eds.) (2009). *Handbook of evidence-based psychodynamic psychotherapy: Bridging the gap between science and practice.* Totowa, NJ: Humana Press.

Levy-Shiff, R. (1994). Individual and contextual correlates of marital change across the transition to parenthood. *Developmental Psychology, 30,* 591–601.

Lewicki, P. (1992). Nonconscious acquisition of information. *American Psychologist, 47,* 796–801.

Lewin, T. (2009, October 24). No Einstein in your crib? Get a refund. *New York Times,* p. A1.

Lewinsohn, P. M., Joiner, T. E., & Rohde, P. (2001). Evaluation of cognitive diathesis-stress models in preciting Major Depressive Disorder in adolescents. *Journal of Abnormal Psychology, 110,* 203–215.

Lewinsohn, P. M., & Rosenbaum, M. (1987). Recall of parental behavior by acute depressives, remitted depressives, and nondepressives. *Journal of Personality and Social Psychology, 52,* 611–619.

Lewis, B. A., Minnes, S., Short, E. J., Weishampel, P., Satayathum, S., Min, M. O., & Singer, L. T. (2011). The effects of prenatal cocaine on language development at 10 years of age. *Neurotoxicology and Teratology, 33*(1), 17–24. doi:10.1016/j.ntt.2010.06.006.

Lewis, G. J., & Bates, T. C. (2010). Genetic evidence for multiple biological mechanisms underlying in-group favoritism. *Psychological Science, 21*(11), 1263–1268. doi:10.1177/0956797610387439.

Lewis, J. E. (2008). Dream reports of animal rights activists. *Dreaming, 18,* 181–200.

Lewis, J. W., Brefczynski, J. A., Phinney, R. E., Janik, J. J., & DeYoe, E. A. (2005). Distinct cortical pathways for processing tool versus animal sounds. *Journal of Neuroscience, 25*(21), 5148–5158.

Lewis, K. L., Hodges, S. D., Laurent, S. M., Srivastava, S., & Biancarosa, G. (2012). Reading between the minds: The use of stereotypes in empathic accuracy. *Psychological Science,* DOI: 10.1177/0956797612439719 (published online first).

Lewis, T. T., Everson-Rose, S. A., Powell, L. H., Matthews, K. A., Brown, C., Karavolos, K., et al. (2006). Chronic exposure to everyday discrimination and coronary artery calcification in African-American women: The SWAN heart study. *Psychosomatic Medicine, 68*, 362–368.

Lewis-Fernández, R., Hinton, D. E., Laria, A. J., Patterson, E. H., Hofmann, S. G., Craske, M. G., & Liao, B. (2010). Culture and the anxiety disorders: Recommendations for DSM-V. *Depression & Anxiety (1091-4269), 27*(2), 212–229. doi:10.1002/da.20647.

Lewison, G. G., Roe, P. P., Wentworth, A. A., & Szmukler, G. G. (2012). The reporting of mental disorders research in British media. *Psychological Medicine, 42*(2), 435–441. doi:10.1017/S0033291711001012.

Lewkowicz, D. J., & Hansen-Tift, A. M. (2012). Infants deploy selective attention to the mouth of a talking face when learning speech. *Proceedings of the National Academy of Sciences of the United States of America, 109*(5), 1431–1436. doi:10.1073/pnas.1114783109.

Lewkowicz, D. J. (2011). The biological implausibility of the nature-nurture dichotomy and what it means for the study of infancy. *Infancy, 16*(4), 331–367. doi:10.1111/j.1532-7078.2011.00079.x.

Lewkowicz, D. J., & Ghazanfar, A. A. (2012). The development of the uncanny valley in infants. *Developmental Psychobiology, 54*(2), 124–132. doi:10.1002/dev.20583.

Lewy, A. J., Lefler, B. J., Emens, J. S., & Bauer, V. K. (2006). The circadian basis of winter depression. *Proceedings of the National Academy of Sciences, 103*, 7414–7419.

Ley, J. M., Bennett, P. C., & Coleman, G. J. (2009). A refinement and validation of the Monash Canine Personality Questionnaire (MCPQ). *Applied Animal Behaviour Science, 116*(2–4), 220–227.

Leyro, T. M.; Zvolensky, M. J., & Bernstein, A. (2010). Distress tolerance and psychopathological symptoms and disorders: A review of the empirical literature among adults. *Psychological Bulletin, 136*, 576–600.

Lezak, M. D., Loring, D. W., & Howieson, D. B. (2004). *Neuropsychological assessment* (4th ed.). New York: Oxford University Press.

Li, D.-K., Petitti, D. B., Willinger, M., McMahon, R., et al. (2003). Infant sleeping position and the risk of sudden infant death syndrome in California, 1997–2000. *American Journal of Epidemiology, 157*, 446–455.

Li, F., Harmer, P., McAuley, E., Duncan, T., Duncan, S. C., Chaumeton, N., & Fisher, K. J. (2001). An evaluation of the effects of Tai Chi exercise on physical function among older persons: A randomized controlled trial. *Annals of Behavioral Medicine, 23*, 139–146.

Li, J. (2005). Mind or virtue: Western and Chinese beliefs about learning. *Current Directions in Psychological Science, 14*, 190–194.

Li, L. C., & Kim, B. S. K. (2004). Effects of counseling style and client adherence to Asian cultural values on counseling process with Asian American college students. *Journal of Counseling Psychology, 51*, 158–167.

Li, N., Downey, J. E., Bar-Shir, A., Gilad, A. A., Walczak, P., Kim, H., & Pelled, G. (2011). Optogenetic-guided cortical plasticity after nerve injury. *Proceedings of the National Academy of Sciences of The United States Of America, 108*(21), 8838–8843. doi:10.1073/pnas.1100815108.

Li, N. P., & Kenrick, D. T. (2006). Sex similarities and differences in preferences for short-term mates: What, whether, and why. *Journal of Personality and Social Psychology, 90*, 468–489.

Li, S., Cullen, W., Anwyl, R., & Rowan, M. J. (2003). Dopamine-dependent facilitation of LTP induction in hippocampal CA1 by exposure to spatial novelty. *Nature Neuroscience, 6*, 526–531.

Li, S. C., Lindenberger, U., Hommel, B., Aschersleben, G., Prinz, W., & Baltes, P. B. (2004). Transformations in the couplings among intellectual abilities and constituent cognitive processes across the life span. *Psychological Science, 15*, 155–163.

Li, Y., Zheng, H., Witt, C. M., Roll, S., Yu, S. G., Yan, J., Sun, G., Zhao, L., Huang. W. J., Chang, X. R., Zhang, H. X., Wang, D. J., Lan, L., Zou, R., Liang, F. R. (2012). Acupuncture for migraine prophylaxis: a randomized controlled trial. *CMAJ*, Epub January 9, 2012.

Li Cavoli, G., Mulè, G., & Rotolo, U. (2011). Renal involvement in psychological eating disorders. *Nephron Clinical Practice, 119*(4), c338–c341. doi:10.1159/000333798.

Liang, C.-Y., Xu, Z.-Y., Mei, W., Wang, L.-L., Xue, L., Lu, D. J., & Zhao, H. (2012). Neural correlates of feigned memory impairment are distinguishable from answering randomly and answering incorrectly: An fMRI and behavioral study. *Brain and Cognition, 79*(1), 70–77. doi: http://dx.doi.org/10.1016/j.bandc.2012.01.009.

Liao, H., & Rupp, D. E. (2005). The impact of justice climate and justice orientation on work outcomes: A cross-level multifoci framework. *Journal of Applied Psychology, 90*, 242–256.

Liben, L. (1978). Perspective-taking skills in young children: Seeing the world through rose-colored glasses. *Developmental Psychology, 14*, 87–92.

Lichenstein, R., Smith, D. C., Ambrose, J. L., & Moody, L. A. (2012). Headphone use and pedestrian injury and death in the United States: 2004–2011. *Injury Prevention*. Advance online publication. doi: Inj Prev doi:10.1136/injuryprev-2011-040161.

Lichtenstein, E., Zhu, S.-H. , & Tedeschi, G. J. (2010). Smoking cessation quitlines: An underrecognized intervention success story. *American Psychologist, 65*(4), 252–261. doi:10.1037/a0018598.

Lichtman, J., & Denk, W. (2011). The big and the small: Challenges of imaging the brain's circuits. *Science, 334*(6056), 618–623.

Lickey, M., & Gordon, B. (1991). *Medicine and mental illness: The use of drugs in psychiatry.* San Francisco: Freeman.

Lickliter, R. (2008). The growth of developmental thought: Implications for a new evolutionary psychology. *New Ideas in Psychology, 26*(3), 353–369.

Liddle, J. R., Shackelford, T. K., & Weekes–Shackelford, V. A. (2012). Why can't we all just get along? Evolutionary perspectives on violence, homicide, and war. *Review of General Psychology, 16*, 24–36. doi:10.1037/a0026610.

Lidwall, U., & Marklund, S. (2011). Trends in long-term sickness absence in Sweden 1992–2008: The role of economic conditions, legislation, demography, work environment and alcohol consumption. *International Journal of Social Welfare, 20*(2), 167–179. doi:10.1111/j.1468-2397.2010.00744.x

Lieberman, J. A., Stroup, T. S., McEvoy, J. P., Swartz, M. S., Rosenheck, R. A., Perkins, D. O., et al. (2005). Effectiveness of antipsychotic drugs in patients with chronic schizophrenia. *New England Journal of Medicine, 353*, 1209–1223.

Lieberman, M. D. (2010). Social cognitive neuroscience In S. T. Fiske, D. T. Gilbert, & G. Lindzey (Eds.), *Handbook of social psychology* (5th ed., Vol. 1, pp. 143–193). Hoboken, NJ: Wiley.

Liebert, R. M., & Spiegler, M. D. (1994). *Personality: Strategies and issues.* Pacific Grove, CA: Brooks/Cole.

Liebeskind, D. S. (2010). Reperfusion for acute ischemic stroke: Arterial revascularization and collateral therapeutics. *Current Opinion in Neurology, 23*, 36–45.

Liechti, M. E., Gamma, A., & Vollenweider, F. X. (2001). Gender differences in the subjective effects of MDMA. *Psychopharmacology, 154*, 161–168.

Liechti, M. E. & Markou, A. (2008). Role of the glutamatergic system in nicotine dependence: implications for the discovery and development of new pharmacological smoking cessation therapies. *CNS Drugs, 22*(9), 705–724.

Liepert, J., Bauder, H., Miltner, W. H. R., Taub, E., & Weiller, C. (2000). Treatment-induced cortical reorganization after stroke in humans. *Stroke, 31*, 1210.

Lievens, F., Harris, M. M., Van Keer, E., & Bisqueret, C. (2003). Predicting cross-cultural training performance: The validity of personality, cognitive ability, and dimensions measured by an assessment center and a behavior description interview. *Journal of Applied Psychology, 88*, 476–489.

Lievens, F., Peeters, H., & Schollaert, E. (2008). Situational judgment tests: A review of recent research. *Personnel Review, 37*, 426–441.

Light, K. C., Girdler, S. S., Sherwood, A., Bragdon, E. E., Brownley, K. A., West, S. G., & Hinderliter, A. L. (1999). High stress responsivity predicts later blood pressure only in combination with positive family history and high life stress. *Hypertension, 33*, 1458–1464.

Light, K. J. (2008, August). Virtual fitness gets real. *BioMechanics Magazine*, 22–29.

Light, L. K., Grewen, K. M., Amico, J. A., Brownley, K. A., West, S. G., Hinderliter, A. L., et al. (2005). Oxytocinergic activity is linked to lower blood pressure and vascular resistance during stress in postmenopausal women on estrogen replacement. *Hormones and Behavior, 47*, 540–548.

Lilienfeld, S. O., Ammirati, R., & Landfi eld, K. (2009). Giving debiasing away: Can psychological research on correcting cognitive errors promote human welfare? *Perspectives on Psychological Science, 4*, 390–398.

Lilienfeld, S. O. (2011). Distinguishing scientific from pseudoscientific psychotherapies: Evaluating the role of theoretical plausibility, with a little help from Reverend Bayes. *Clinical Psychology: Science and Practice, 18*, 105–112.

Lilienfeld, S. O. (2007). Psychological treatments that cause harm. *Perspectives on Psychological Science, 2*, 53–70.

Lilienfeld, S. O. (2011). Public skepticism of psychology: Why many people perceive the study of human behavior as unscientific. *American Psychologist.* Advance online publication. doi:10.1037/a0023963.

Lilienfeld, S. O., & Arkowitz, H. (2007, December). EMDR: Taking a closer look. *Scientific American, 17*(4), 10–11.

Lilienfeld, S. O., & Lynn, S. J. (2003). Dissociative identity disorder: Multiple personalities, multiple controversies. In S. O. Lilienfeld & S. J. Lynn (Eds.), *Science and pseudoscience in clinical psychology* (pp. 109–142). New York: Guilford.

Lilienfeld, S. O., Lynn, S. J., Namy, L. L., & Wolff, N. J. (2009). *Psychology: From inquiry to understanding.* Boston, MA: Pearson.

Lim, J., & Dinges, D. F. (2010). A meta-analysis of the impact of short-term sleep deprivation on cognitive variables. *Psychological Bulletin, 136*, 375–389.

Lim, B.-C., & Ployhart, R. E. (2004). Transformational leadership: Relations to the five-factor model and team performance in typical and maximum contexts. *Journal of Applied Psychology, 89*, 610–621.

Lim, R. F. (Ed.). (2006). *Clinical manual of cultural psychiatry.* Washington, DC: American Psychiatric Publishing, Inc.

Lim, S.-L., & Kim, J.-H. (2005). Cognitive processing of emotional information in depression, panic, and somatoform disorder. *Journal of Abnormal Psychology, 114*, 50–61.

Lim, V. K. G., Teo, T. S. H., & Loo, G. L. (2003). Sex, financial hardship and locus of control: An empirical study of attitudes towards money among Singaporean Chinese. *Personality and Individual Differences, 34*, 411–429.

Lin, K. M., Smith, M. W., & Ortiz, V. (2001). Culture and psychopharmacology. *Psychiatric Clinics of North America, 24*, 523–538.

Lin, F., Graf, S., Kinshuk, & McGreal, R. (2009). Adaptive and intelligent web-based educational systems. *International Journal Of Web-Based Learning And Teaching Technologies, 4*(1), 1–3.

Lin, J. G., & Chen, W. L. (2008). Acupuncture analgesia: A review of its mechanisms of actions. *American Journal of Chinese Medicine, 36*(4), 635–645.

Lin, L., Umahara, M., York, D. A., & Bray, G. A. (1998). Beta-casomorphins stimulate and enterostatin inhibits the intake of dietary fat in rats. *Peptides, 19*, 325–331.

Lin, S., Thomas, T. C., Storlien, L. H., & Huang, X. F. (2000). Development of high fat diet-induced obesity and leptin resistance in C57Bl/6J mice. *International Journal of Obesity Related Metabolic Disorders, 24*, 639–646.

Lin, T., Chen, S., Huang, T., Chang, C., Chuang, J., Wu, F., & ... Jen, C. J. (2012). Different types of exercise induce differential effects on neuronal adaptations and memory performance. *Neurobiology of Learning and Memory, 97*(1), 140–147. doi:10.1016/j.nlm.2011.10.006.

Lin, Y., Wu, M., Yang, C., Chen, T., Hsu, C., Chang, Y., et al. (2008). Evaluation of assertiveness training for psychiatric patients. *Journal of Clinical Nursing, 17,* 2875–2883.

Lindau, S. T., & Gavrilova, N. (2010). Sex, health, and years of sexually active life gained due to good health: Evidence from two U.S. population based cross-sectional surveys of aging. *British Medical Journal, 340,* c810.

Lindau, S. T., Schumm, L. P., Laumann, E. O., Levinson, W., O'Muircheartaigh, C. A., & Waite, L. J. (2007). A study of sexuality and health among older adults in the United States. *The New England Journal of Medicine, 357,* 762–774.

Linde, K., Allais, G., Brinkhaus, B., Manheimer, E., Vickers, A., & White, A. R. (2009). Acupuncture for tension-type headache. *Cochrane Database Systematic Review,* 1, article no. CD007587. Retrieved March 25, 2009, from http://mrw.interscience.wiley.com/cochrane/clsysrev/articles/CD007587/frame.html.

Linden, D. J., Oosterhof, N. N., Klein, C., & Downing, P. E. (2012). Mapping brain activation and information during category-specific visual working memory. *Journal of Neurophysiology, 107*(2), 628–639. doi:10.1152/jn.00105.2011.

Lindner, I., Echterhoff, G., Davidson, P. R., & Brand, M. (2010). Observation inflation: Your actions become mine. *Psychological Science, 21*(9), 1291–1299. doi:10.1177/0956797610379860.

Lindsay, D. S., Hagen, L., Read, J. D., Wade, K., & Gary, M. (2004). True photographs and false memories. *Psychological Science, 15,* 149–154.

Lindvall, O., & Hagell, P. (2001). Cell therapy and transplantation in Parkinson's disease. *Clinical Chemistry and Laboratory Medicine, 39,* 356–361.

Lindvall, O., & Kokaia, Z. (2010). Stem cells in human neurodegenerative disorders: Time for clinical translation? *Journal of Clinical Investigation, 120,* 29–40. doi:10.1172/JCI40543.

Linnet, K. M., Dalsgaard, S., Obel, C., Wisborg, K., Henriksen, T. B., Rodriguez, A., et al. (2003). Maternal lifestyle factors in pregnancy risk of attention deficit hyperactivity disorder and associated behaviors: Review of the current evidence. *American Journal of Psychiatry, 160,* 1028–1040.

Linnet, K. M., Wisborg, K., Obel, C., Secher, N. J., Thomsen, P. H., Agerbo, E., & Henriksen, T. B. (2005). Smoking during pregnancy and the risk for hyperkinetic disorder in offspring. *Pediatrics, 116,* 462–467.

Linz, D., Donnerstein, E., & Penrod, S. (1987). The findings and recommendations of the Attorney General's Commission on Pornography: Do the psychological facts fit the political fury? *American Psychologist, 42,* 946–953.

Lippa, R. A. (2003). Are 2D:4D finger-length ratios related to sexual orientation? Yes for men, no for women. *Journal of Personality and Social Psychology, 85,* 179–188.

Lipscomb, S. T., Leve, L. D., Harold, G. T., Neiderhiser, J. M., Shaw, D. S., Ge, X., & Reiss, D. (2011). Trajectories of parenting and child negative emotionality during infancy and toddlerhood: A longitudinal analysis. *Child Development, 82,*1661–1675.

Lisanby, S. H. (Ed.). (2004). *Brain stimulation in psychiatric treatment.* Washington, DC: American Psychiatric Association.

Lisman, J., Yasuda, R., & Raghavachari, S. (2012). Mechanisms of CaMKII action in long-term potentiation. *Nature Reviews Neuroscience, 13*(3), 169–182.

Lisspers, J., Sundin, Ö., Öhman, A., Hofman-Bang, C., Rydén, L., & Nygren, Å. (2005). Long-term effects of lifestyle behavior change in coronary artery disease: Effects on recurrent coronary events after percutaneous coronary intervention. *Health Psychology, 24,* 41–48.

Liston, C., McEwen, B. S., & Casey, B. J. (2009). Psychosocial stress reversibly disrupts prefrontal processing and attentional control. *Proceedings of the National Academy of Sciences, 106,* 912–917.

Little, A. C., Saxton, T. K., Roberts, S., Jones, B. C., DeBruine, L. M., Vukovic, J., & .. Chenore, T. (2010). Women's preferences for masculinity in male faces are highest during reproductive age range and lower around puberty and post-menopause. *Psychoneuroendocrinology, 35*(6), 912–920. doi:10.1016/j.psyneuen.2009.12.006.

Littlewood, R. (1992). Psychiatric diagnosis and racial bias: Empirical and interpretative approaches. *Social Science & Medicine, 34,* 141–149.

Litwin, H., & Shiovitz-Ezra, S. (2006). The association between activity and well-being in later life: What really matters? *Aging and Society, 26,* 225–242.

Liu, Y. P., Lang, B. T., Baskaya, M. K., Dempsey, R. J., & Vemuganti, R. (2009). The potential of neural stem cells to repair stroke-induced brain damage. *Acta Neuropathologica, 117,* 469–480. Epub 2009 Mar 13.

Liu, G., & Akira, H. (1994). Basic principle of TCM. In Liu, G., Akira, H. (Eds.), *Fundamentals of acupuncture and moxibustion.* Tianjin, China: Tianjin Science and Technology Translation and Publishing Corporation.

Liu, G. F., Han, S., Liang, D. H., Wang, F. Z., Shi, X. Z., Yu, J., & Wu, Z. L. (2003), Driver sleepiness and risk of car crashes in Shenyang, a Chinese northeastern city: Population-based case-control study. *Biomedical and Environmental Sciences, 16*(3), 219–226.

Liu, J. (2011). Early health risk factors for violence: Conceptualization, evidence, and implications. *Aggression & Violent Behavior, 16*(1), 63–73. doi:10.1016/j.avb.2010.12.003.

Liuzza, M., Cazzato, V., Vecchione, M., Crostella, F., Caprara, G., & Aglioti, S. (2011). Follow my eyes: the gaze of politicians reflexively captures the gaze of ingroup voters. *Plos One, 6*(9), e25117.

Lively, W. M. (2001). Syncope and neurologic deficits in a track athlete: A case report. *Medicine and Science in Sports and Exercise, 33,* 345–347.

Liverence, B., & Scholl, B. (2011). Selective attention warps spatial representation: parallel but opposing effects on attended versus inhibited objects. *Psychological Science, 22*(12), 1600–1608.

Livianos-Aldana, L., Rojo-Moreno, L., & Sierra-Sanmiguel, P. (2007). F. J. Gall and the phrenological movement. *American Journal of Psychiatry, 164*(3), 414–414.

Livingston, R. W., Rosette, A., & Washington, E. F. (2012). Can an agentic Black woman get ahead? The impact of race and interpersonal dominance on perceptions of female leaders. *Psychological Science, 23,* 354–358. doi:10.1177/0956797611428079.

Lizardi, D., Oquendo, M. A., & Graver, R. (2009). Clinical pitfalls in the diagnosis of *ataque de nervios:* A case study. *Transcultural Psychiatry, 46,* 463–486.

Lleras, A., & Moore, C. M. (2006). What you see is what you get: Functional equivalence of a perceptually filled-in surface and a physically presented stimulus. *Psychological Science, 17,* 876–881.

Lobue, V., & Deloache, J. (2011). Pretty in pink: The early development of gender-stereotyped colour preferences. *The British Journal of Developmental Psychology, 29*(Pt 3), 656–667. doi:10.1111/j.2044-835X.2011.02027.x.

LoBue, V., & DeLoache, J. S. (2010). Superior detection of threat-relevant stimuli in infancy. *Developmental Science 13*(1), 221–228. doi:10.1111/j.1467-7687.2009.00872.x.

LoBue, V., Nishida, T., Cynthia, C., DeLoache, J. S., & Haidt, J. (2011). When getting something good is bad: even three-year-olds react to inequality. *Social Development, 20*(1), 154–170. doi:10.1111/j.1467-9507.2009.00560.x.

Lochman, J. E., & Wells, K.,C. (2004). The coping power program for preadolescent aggressive boys and their parents: Outcome effects at 1-year follow-up. *Journal of Consulting and Clinical Psychology, 72,* 571–578.

Lock, J. (2011). Evaluation of family treatment models for eating disorders. *Current Opinion In Psychiatry, 24*(4), 274–279. doi:10.1097/YCO.0b013e328346f71e.

Locke, E. A. (2000). Motivation, cognition, and action: An analysis of studies of task goals and knowledge. *Applied Psychology: An International Review, 49,* 408–429.

Locke, E. A., & Latham, G. P. (2002). Building a practically useful theory of goal setting and task motivation: A 35-year odyssey. *American Psychologist, 57,* 705–717.

Locke, E. A., & Latham G. P. (1990). *A theory of goal setting & task performance.* Englewood Cliffs, NJ: Prentice Hall.

Locke, K. D. (2010). Interpersonal moderators of the effects of upward comparisons on ability judgments. *Basic and Applied Social Psychology, 33,* 37–46.

Lockhart, R. S., & Craik, F. I. M. (1990). Levels of processing: A retrospective commentary on a framework for memory research. *Canadian Journal of Psychology, 44,* 87–112.

Lockley, S. W., Barger, L. K., Ayas, N. T., Rothschild, J. M., Czeisler, C. A., Landrigan, C. P. & the Harvard Work Hours, Health and Safety Group. (2007). Effects of health care provider work hours and sleep deprivation on safety and performance. *Joint Commission Journal on Quality and Patient Safety, 33*(11 Suppl), 7–18.

Loehlin, J. C. (2011). Genetic and environmental structures of personality: A cluster-analysis approach. *Personality and Individual Differences, 51,* 662–666.

Loehlin, J. C. (2010). Environment and the behavior genetics of personality: Let me count the ways. *Personality And Individual Differences, 49*(4), 302–305. doi:10.1016/j.paid.2009.10.035.

Loehlin, J. C. (1989). Partitioning environmental and genetic contributions to behavioral development. *American Psychologist, 44,* 1285–1292.

Loehlin, J. C. & Martin, N. G. (2011). The general factor of personality: Questions and elaboration. *Journal of Research in Personality, 45,* 44–49

Loehlin, J. C., McCrae, R. R., Costa, P. T., & John, O. P. (1998). Heritabilities of common and measure-specific components of the Big Five personality factors. *Journal of Research in Personality, 32*(4), 431–453.

Loewenstein, G. (1994). The psychology of curiosity: A review and reinterpretation. *Psychological Bulletin, 116*(1), 75–98.

Lofquist, D., Lugaila, T., O'Connell, M., & Feliz, S. (2012, April). Households and families: 2010 (2010 Census Briefs, No. C2010BR-14). Retrieved from http://www.census.gov/prod/cen2010/briefs/c2010br-14.pdf.

Loftus, E., & Guyer, M. (2002). Who abused Jane Doe? The hazards of the single case history (Part 1). *Skeptical Inquirer, 26,* 24–32.

Loftus, E. F. (1992). When a lie becomes memory's truth: Memory distortion after exposure to misinformation. *Psychological Science, 3,* 121–123.

Loftus, E. F. (1997a). Memory for a past that never was. *Current Directions in Psychological Science, 6,* 60–65.

Loftus, E. F. (1997b). Repressed memory accusations: Devastated families and devastated patients. *Applied Cognitive Psychology, 11,* 25–30.

Loftus, E. F. (1998). The price of bad memories. *Skeptical Inquirer, 22,* 23–24.

Loftus, E. F. (2003, January). *Illusions of memory.* Presentation at the 25th Annual National Institute on the Teaching of Psychology, St. Petersburg Beach, Florida.

Loftus, E. F. (2004). Memories of things unseen. *Current Directions in Psychological Science, 13,* 145–147.

Loftus, E. F., & Davis, D. (2006). Recovered memories. *Annual Review of Clinical Psychology, 2,* 469–498.

Loftus, E. F., & Hoffman, H. G. (1989). Misinformation and memory: The creation of new memories. *Journal of Experimental Psychology: General, 118,* 100–104.

Loftus, E. F., & Ketcham, K. (1994). *The myth of repressed memory: False memories and allegations of sexual abuse.* New York: St. Martin's Press.

Loftus, E. F., & Palmer, J. C. (1974). Reconstruction of automobile destruction: An example of the interaction between language and memory. *Journal of Verbal Learning and Verbal Behavior, 13,* 585–589.

Loftus, E. F., & Pickrell, J. E. (1995). The formation of false memories. *Psychiatric Annals, 25,* 720–725.

Loftus, T. M., Jaworsky, D. E., Frehywot, G. L., Townsend, C. A., Ronnett, G. V., Lane, M. D., & Kuhajda, F. P. (2000). Reduced food intake and body weight in mice treated with fatty acid synthase inhibitors. *Science, 288,* 2379–2381.

Logel, C., & Cohen, G. L. (2012). The role of the self in physical health: Testing the effect of a values-affirmation intervention on weight loss. *Psychological Science, 23,* 53–55. doi:10.1177/0956797611421936.

Logie, R. H. (2011). The functional organization and capacity limits of working memory. *Current Directions in Psychological Science, 20*(4), 240–245. doi:10.1177/0963721411415340.

Logue, A. W. (1985). Conditioned food aversion in humans. *Annals of the New York Academy of Sciences, 104,* 331–340.

Loher, B. T., Noe, R. A., Moeller, N. L., & Fitzgerald, M. P. (1985). A meta-analysis of the relation of job characteristics to job satisfaction. *Journal of Applied Psychology, 70,* 280–289.

Lohman, D. F. (2004). Aptitude for college: The importance of reasoning tests for minority admissions. In R. Zwick (Ed.), *Rethinking the SAT: The future of standardized testing in college admissions* (pp. 41–56). New York: RoutledgeFalmer.

Lohman, D. F. (2005). The role of non-verbal ability tests in identifying academically gifted students: An aptitude perspective. *Gifted Child Quarterly, 49,* 111–138.

Lohman, D. F., & Hagen, E. (2001). *Cognitive abilities test (Form 6): Interpretive guide for teachers and counselors.* Itasca, IL: Riverside.

Lohr, J. M., Hooke, W., Gist, R., & Tolin, D. F. (2003). Novel and controversial treatments for trauma-related stress disorders. In S. O. Lilienfeld, S. J. Lynn, & J. M. Lohr (Eds.), *Science and pseudoscience in clinical psychology* (pp. 243–272). New York: Guilford Press.

LoLordo, V. M. (2001). Learned helplessness and depression. In M. E. Carroll & J. B. Overmier (Eds.), *Animal research and human health: Advancing human welfare through behavioral science* (pp. 63–77). Washington, DC: American Psychological Association.

Lombard, C., Deeks, A., Jolley, D., Ball, K., & Teede, H. (2010). A low-intensity, community-based lifestyle programme to prevent weight gain in women with young children: Cluster randomised controlled trial. *British Medical Journal, 341,* c3215.

London Daily Telegraph. (1998, September 19). "'Cat' that turned out to be a clock." *London Daily Telegraph.*

Long, J. K., & Andrews, B. V. (2011). Fostering strength and resiliency in same-sex couples. In J. L. Wetchler (Ed.), *Handbook of clinical issues in couple therapy* (2nd ed.) (pp. 225–246). New York: Routledge/Taylor & Francis Group.

Longo, N., Klempay, S., & Bitterman, M. E. (1964). Classical appetitive conditioning in the pigeon. *Psychonomic Science, 1,* 19–20.

Longo, M. R., & Haggard, P. (2010). An implicit body representation underlying human position sense. *Proceedings Of The National Academy Of Sciences Of The United States Of America, 107*(26), 11727–11732.

Loos, R. J. F., Rankinen, T., Chagnon, Y., Tremblay, A., Pérusse, L., & Bouchard, C. (2006). Polymorphisms in the leptin and leptin receptor genes in relation to resting metabolic rate and respiratory quotient in the Québec Family Study. *International Journal of Obesity, 30,* 183–190.

Lopes, P. N., Salovey, P., Côté, S., & Beers, M. (2005). Emotion regulation abilities and the quality of social interaction. *Emotion, 5,* 113–118.

Lopez, S. R. (1989). Patient variable biases in clinical judgment: Conceptual overview and methodological considerations. *Psychological Bulletin, 106,* 184–203.

Lopez-Garcia, E., van Dam, R. M., Li, T. Y., Rodriguez-Artalejo, F., & Hu, F. B. (2008). The relationship of coffee consumption with mortality. *Annals of Internal Medicine, 148,* 904–914.

López-Ibor, J. J., López-Ibor, M.-I., & Pastrana, J. I. (2008). Transcranial magnetic stimulation. *Current Opinion in Psychiatry, 21*(6), 640–644.

Lopez-Moreno, J. A., Gonzalez-Cuevas, G., Moreno, G., & Navarro, M. (2008). The pharmacology of the endocannabinoid system: Functional and structural interactions with other neurotransmitter systems and their repercussions in behavioral addiction. *Addiction Biology, 13,* 160–187.

Lord, C. G. (1997). *Social psychology.* Fort Worth: Harcourt, Brace.

Lorenzo, G. L., Biesanz, J. C., & Human, L. J. (2010). What is beautiful is good and more accurately understood: Physical attractiveness and accuracy in first impressions of personality. *Psychological Science, 21*(12), 1777–1782. doi:10.1177/0956797610388048.

Lotze, M., Scheler, G., Tan, H.-R. M., Braun, C., & Birbaumer, N. (2003). The musician's brain: Functional imaging of amateurs and professionals during performance and imagery. *NeuroImage, 20*(3), 1817.

Loughnan, S., Kuppens, P., Allik, J., Balazs, K., de Lemus, S., Dumont, K., Gargurevich, R., Hidegkuti, I., Leidner, B., Matos, L., Park, J., Realo, A., Shi1, J., Sojo, V. E., Tong, Y.-Y., Vaes, J., Verduyn, P., Yeung, V., & Haslam, N. (2011). Economic inequality is linked to biased self-perception. *Psychological Science, 22*(10) 1254–1258. doi:10.1177/0956797611417003.

Lount, R. B., Jr.; Zhong, C. B.; Sivanathan, N.; & Murnighan, J. K. (2008). Getting off on the wrong foot: The timing of a breach and the restoration of trust. *Personality and Social Psychology Bulletin, 34,* 1601–1612.

Louzá, M. R., & Bassitt, D. P. (2005). Maintenance treatment of severe tardive dyskinesia with Clozapine: 5 years' follow-up. *Journal of Clinical Psychopharmacology, 25,* 180–182.

Lovallo, W. R., Yechiam, E., Sorocco, K. H., Vincent, A. S., & Collins, F. L. (2006). Working memory and decision-making biases in young adults with a family history of alcoholism: Studies from the Oklahoma Family Health Patterns Project. *Alcoholism: Clinical and Experimental Research, 30,* 763–773.

Love, J. M., Kisker, E. E., Ross, C., Raikes, H., Constantine, J., Boller, K., et al. (2005). The effectiveness of early head start for 3-year-old children and their parents: Lessons for policy and programs. *Developmental Psychology, 41,* 885–901.

Lovell, B., Moss, M., & Wetherell, M. (2012). The psychosocial, endocrine and immune consequences of caring for a child with autism or ADHD. *Psychoneuroendocrinology, 37*(4), 534–542. doi:10.1016/j.psyneuen.2011.08.003.

Lovibond, P. F., Mitchell, C. J., Minard, E., Brady, A., & Menzies, R. G. (2009). Safety behaviours preserve threat beliefs: Protection from extinction of human fear conditioning by an avoidance response. *Behaviour Research and Therapy, 47,* 716–720.

Low, C. A., Stanton, A. L., & Danoff-Burg, S. (2006). Expressive disclosure and benefit finding among breast cancer patients: Mechanisms for positive health effects. *Health Psychology, 25,* 181–189.

Löwe, B., Mundt, C., Herzog, W., Brunner, R., Backenstass, M., Kronmueller, K., & Henningsen, P. (2008). Validity of current somatoform disorder diagnoses: Perspective for classification in DSM-V and ICD-11. *Psychopathology, 41,* 4–9.

Lu, C., Chen, C., Ning, N., Ding, G., et al. (2009). Th e neural substrates for atypical planning and execution of word production in stuttering. *Experimental Neurology, 29,* 29.

Lubinski, D., Benbow, C. P., Webb, R. M., & Bleske-Rechek, A. (2006). Tracking exceptional human capital over two decades. *Psychological Science, 17*(3), 194–199.

Lubinski, D., Webb, R. M., Morelock, M. J., & Benbow, C. P. (2001). Top 1 in 10,000: A 10 year follow-up of the profoundly gifted. *Journal of Applied Psychology, 86,* 718–729.

Luborsky, L. (1972). Another reply to Eysenck. *Psychological Bulletin, 78,* 406–408.

Luborsky, L., Rosenthal, R., & Diguer, L. (2003). Are some psychotherapies much more effective than others? *Journal of Applied Psychoanalytic Studies, 5*(4), 455–460.

Luborsky, L., Rosenthal, R., Diguer, L., Andrusyna, T. P., Berman, J. S., Levitt, J. T., et al. (2002). The dodo bird verdict is alive and well–mostly. *Clinical Psychology: Science and Practice, 9,* 2–12.

Luborsky, L., Singer, B., & Luborsky, L. (1975). Comparative studies of psychotherapies: Is it true that everyone has won and all must have prizes? *Archives of General Psychiatry, 32,* 995–1008.

Luby, J. L. (2010). Preschool depression: Th e importance of identifi cation of depression early in development. *Current Directions in Psychological Science, 19,* 91–95.

Luby, J. L., Barch, D. M., Belden, A., Gaffrey, M. S., Tiliman, R., Babb, C., & .. Botteron, K. N. (2012). Maternal support in early childhood predicts larger hippocampal volumes at school age. *Proceedings of the National Academy of Sciences of the United States of America, 109*(8), 2854–2859. doi:10.1073/pnas.1118003109.

Lucas, J. A. (2005). Disorders of memory. *Psychiatric Clinics of North America, 28*(3), 581–597.

Lucas, R. E. (2007). Adaptation and the set-point model of subjective well-being: Does happiness change after major life events? *Current Directions in Psychological Science, 16,* 75–79.

Lucas-Thompson, R., & Clarke-Stewart, K. A. (2007). Forecasting friendship: How marital quality, maternal mood, and attachment security are linked to children's peer relationships. *Journal of Applied Developmental Psychology, 28,* 499–514.

Luders, E., Clark, K., Narr, K. L., & Toga, A. W. (2011). Enhanced brain connectivity in long-term meditation practitioners. *NeuroImage, 57*(4), 1308–1316

Ludwig-Rosenthal, R., & Neufeld, R. W. (1988). Stress management during noxious medical procedures: An evaluative review of outcome studies. *Psychological Bulletin, 104,* 326–342.

Luguri, J., Napier, J., & Dovidio, J. (2012). Reconstruing intolerance: Abstract thinking reduces conservatives' prejudice against nonnormative groups. *Psychological Science, 23,* 756–763.

Luhrmann, T. M. (2008). "The street will drive you crazy": Why homeless psychotic women in the institutional circuit in the United States often say no to offers of help. *American Journal of Psychiatry, 165,* 15–20.

Luk, G., Bialystok, E., Craik, F. M., & Grady, C. L. (2011). Lifelong bilingualism maintains white matter integrity in older adults. *The Journal of Neuroscience, 31*(46), 16808–16813. doi:10.1523/JNEUROSCI.4563-11.2011.

Lumley, M. A., Cohen, J. L., Borszcz, G. S., Cano, A., Radcliffe, A. M., Porter, L. S., Schubiner, H., & Keefe, F. J. (2011). Pain and emotion: A biopsychosocial review of recent research. *Journal of Clinical Psychology, 67*(9), 942–968.

Luna, D., Ringberg, T., & Peracchio, L. A. (2008). One individual, two identities: Frame switching among biculturals. *Journal of Consumer Research, 35*(2), 279–293.

Luna, K., & Martín-Luengo, B. (2012). Confidence–accuracy calibration with general knowledge and eyewitness memory cued recall questions. *Applied Cognitive Psychology, 26*(2), 289–295. doi:10.1002/acp.1822.

Lund, T., Labriola, M., Christensen, K. B., Bultmann, U., & Villadsen, E. (2006). Physical work environment risk factors for long-term sickness absence: Prospective findings among a cohort of 5357 employees in Denmark. *British Medical Journal, 332,* 449–452.

Lundy, R. F., Jr. (2008). Gustatory hedonic value: Potential function for forebrain control of brainstem taste processing. *Neuroscience & Biobehavioral Reviews, 32*(8), 1601–1606.

Luntz, B. K., & Widom, C. S. (1994). Antisocial personality disorder in abused and neglected children grown up. *American Journal of Psychiatry, 151,* 670–674.

Luria, Z. (1992, February). *Gender differences in children's play patterns.* Paper presented at University of Southern California, Los Angeles.

Lussier, J. P., Heil, S. H., Mongeon, J. A., Badger, G. J., & Higgins, S. T. (2006). A meta-analysis of voucher-based reinforcement therapy for substance use disorders. *Addiction, 101,* 192–203.

Lustig, R. H., Sen, S., Soberman, J. E., & Velasquez-Mieyer, P. A. (2004). Obesity, leptin resistance, and the effects of insulin reduction. *International Journal of Obesity, 28,* 1344–1348.

Luthar, S. S., & Latendresse, S. J. (2005). Children of the affluent. *Current Directions in Psychological Science, 14,* 49–53.

Lutz, D. J., & Sternberg, R. J. (1999). Cognitive development. In M. H. Bornstein & M. E. Lamb (Eds.), *Developmental psychology: An advanced textbook* (4th ed.). Mahwah, NJ: Erlbaum.

Lydon, J, Fitzsimons, G, & Naidoo, L. (2003). Devaluation versus enhancement of attractive alternatives: A critical test. *Personality and Social Psychology Bulletin, 29,* 349–359.

Lykken, D. T. (1998a). The genetics of genius. In A. Steptoe (Ed.) *Genius and mind: Studies of creativity and temperament* (pp. 15–37). New York, NY: Oxford University Press.

Lykken, D. T. (1998b). *A tremor in the blood: Uses and abuses of the lie detector*. Cambridge, MA: Perseus Publishing.

Lykken, D. T. (1999). *Happiness: What studies on twins show us about nature, nurture, and the happiness set point*. New York: Golden Books.

Lyman, D. R., & Gudonis, L. (2005). The development of psychopathy. *Annual Review of Clinical Psychology, 1,* 381–407.

Lyn, H., Greenfield, P. M., Savage-Rumbaugh, S., Gillespie-Lynch, K., & Hopkins, W. D. (2011). Nonhuman primates do declare! A comparison of declarative symbol and gesture use in two children, two bonobos, and a chimpanzee. *Language & Communication, 31*(1), 63–74. doi:10.1016/j.langcom.2010.11.001.

Lyn, H., Russell, J. L., & Hopkins, W. D. (2010). The impact of environment on the comprehension of declarative communication in apes. *Psychological Science, 21*(3), 360–365. doi:10.1177/0956797610362218.

Lynall, M.-E., Bassett, D. S., Kerwin, R., McKenna, P. J., et al. (2010). Functional connectivity and brain networks in schizophrenia. *Journal of Neuroscience, 30,* 9477–9487.

Lynam, D. R., & Widiger, T. A. (2001). Using the five-factor model to represent the *DSM-IV* personality disorders: An expert consensus approach. *Journal of Abnormal Psychology, 110,* 401–412.

Lynch, F. L., Hornbrook, M., Clarke, G. N., Perrin, N., Polen, M. R., O'Connor, E., et al. (2005). Cost-effectiveness of an intervention to prevent depression in at-risk teens. *Archives of General Psychiatry, 62,* 1241–1248.

Lynn, R. (2006). *Race differences in intelligence: An evolutionary analysis*. Augusta, GA: Washington Summit Publishers.

Lynn, R., & Mikk, J. (2007). National differences in intelligence and educational attainment. *Intelligence, 35,* 115–121.

Lynn, S. J., & Kirsch, I. (2006). *Essentials of clinical hypnosis: An evidence-based approach*. Washington, DC: American Psychological Association.

Lynn, S. J., Lilienfeld, S. O., Merckelbach, H., Giesbrecht, T., & Van Der Kloet, D. (2012). Dissociation and dissociative disorders: challenging conventional wisdom. *Current Directions in Psychological Science, 21,* 48–53. doi:10.1177/0963721411429457.

Lynn, S. J., Myers, B., & Malinoski, P. (1997). Hypnosis, pseudomemories, and clinical guidelines: A sociocognitive perspective. In J. D. Read & D. S. Lindsay (Eds.), *Recollections of trauma: Scientific evidence and clinical practice. NATO ASI series: Series A: Life sciences* (Vol. 291, pp. 305–336). New York: Plenum Press.

Lynn, S. J., & Rhue, J. W. (1986). The fantasy-prone person: Hypnosis, imagination, and creativity. *Journal of Personality and Social Psychology, 51,* 404–408.

Lynn, S. J., Vanderhoff, H., Shindler, K., & Stafford, J. (2002). Defining hypnosis as a trance vs. cooperation: Hypnotic inductions, suggestibility, and performance standards. *American Journal of Clinical Hypnosis, 44,* 231–240.

Lynskey, M. T., Heath, A. C., Bucholz, K. K., Slutske, W. S., Madden, P. A. F., Nelson, E. C., et al. (2003). Escalation of drug use in early-onset cannabis users vs. co-twin controls. *Journal of the American Medical Association, 289,* 427–433.

Lyon, L. (2009, May 8). 7 criminal cases that invoked the "sleepwalking defense." *U.S. News & World Report*. Retrieved from http://health.usnews.com.

Lyubomirsky, S. (2001). Why are some people happier than others? The role of cognitive and motivational processes in well-being. *American Psychologist, 56,* 239–249.

Lyubomirsky, S., King, L., & Diener, E. (2005). The benefits of frequent positive affect: Does happiness lead to success? *Psychological Bulletin, 131,* 803–855.

Lyubomirsky, S., & Nolen-Hoeksema, S. (1995). Effects of self-focused rumination on negative thinking and interpersonal problem solving. *Journal of Personality and Social Psychology, 69,* 176–190.

Ma, M. (2007). Encoding olfactory signals via multiple chemosensory systems. *Critical Reviews in Biochemistry and Molecular Biology, 42*(6), 463–480.

Ma, Y., Wang, C., & Han, S. (2011). Neural responses to perceived pain in others predict real-life monetary donations in different socioeconomic contexts. *Neuroimage, 57*(3), 1273–1280. doi:10.1016/j.neuroimage.2011.05.003.

Maandag, N. J., Coman, D., Sanganahalli, B. G., Herman, P., Smith, A. J., Blumenfeld, H., et al. (2007). Energetics of neuronal signaling and fMRI activity. *Proceedings of the National Academies of Sciences, 104*(51), 20546–20551.

MacAndrew, C., & Edgerton, R. B. (1969). *Drunken comportment*. Chicago: Aldine.

McCabe, D. P., Castel, A. D., & Rhodes, M. G. (2011). The influence of fMRI lie detection evidence on juror decision-making. *Behavioral Sciences & the Law, 29*(4), 566–577. doi:10.1002/bsl.993.

Maccoby, E. E., & Martin, J. A. (1983). Socialization in the context of the family: Parent-child interaction. In E. M. Hetherington (Ed.) and P. H. Mussen (Series Ed.), *Handbook of child psychology: Vol. 4. Socialization, personality, and social development* (pp. 1–101). New York: Wiley.

MacDonald, M., & Bernstein, D. A. (1974). Treatment of a spider phobia with in vivo and imaginal desensitization. *Journal of Behavior Therapy and Experimental Psychiatry, 5,* 47–52.

MacDonald, S.W. S., Hultsch, D. F., & Dixon, R. A. (2011). Aging and the shape of cognitive change before death: Terminal decline or terminal drop? *The Journals of Gerontology, 66B,* 292–301.

MacEvoy, S. P., & Paradiso, M. A. (2001). Lightness constancy in primary visual cortex. *Proceedings of the National Academy of Sciences, 98,* 8827–8831.

Macey, P. M., Henderson, L. A., Macey, K. E., Alger, J. R., Frysinger, R. C., Woo, M. A., et al. (2002). Brain morphology associated with obstructive sleep apnea. *American Journal of Respiratory and Critical Care Medicine, 166,* 1382–1387.

Machaalani, R., Say, M., & Waters, K. A. (2011). Effects of cigarette smoke exposure on nicotinic acetylcholine receptor subunits a7 and b2 in the sudden infant death syndrome (SIDS) brainstem. *Toxicology and Applied Pharmacology, 257*(3), 396–404.

Maciejewski, M. L., Livingston, E. H., Smith, V. A., Kavee, A. L., Kahwati, L. C., Henderson, W. G., & Arterburn, D. E. (2011). Survival among high-risk patients after bariatric surgery. *JAMA, 305*(23):2419–2426. doi:10.1001/jama.2011.817.

Mack, A. (2003). Inattentional blindness: Looking without seeing. *Current Directions in Psychological Science, 12,* 180–184.

Mack, A., & Rock, I. (1998). *Inattentional blindness*. Cambridge, MA: MIT Press.

Mackenzie, R., & Watts, J. (2011). Including emotionality in tests of competence: How does neurodiversity affect measures of free will and agency in medical decision making?. *AJOB Neuroscience, 2*(3), 27–36. doi:10.1080/21507740.2011.580491.

Mackinnon, S. P., Jordan, C. H., & Wilson, A. E. (2011). Birds of a feather sit together: Physical similarity predicts seating choice. *Personality And Social Psychology Bulletin, 37*(7), 879–892. doi:10.1177/0146167211402094.

Macleod, C., & Mathews, A. (2012). Cognitive bias modification approaches to anxiety. *Annual Review of Clinical Psychology,* 8189–8217.

MacLeod, C. M., Gopie, N., Hourihan, K. L., Neary, K. R., & Ozubko, J. D. (2010). The production effect: Delineation of a phenomenon. *Journal Of Experimental Psychology: Learning, Memory, And Cognition, 36*(3), 671–685. doi:10.1037/a0018785.

MacMillan, H. L., Fleming, J. E., Steiner, D. L., Lin, E., Boyle, M. H., Jamieson, E., et al. (2001). Childhood abuse and lifetime psychopathology in a community sample. *American Journal of Psychiatry, 158,* 1878–1883.

MacLean, K. A., Ferrer, E., Aichele, S. R., Bridwell, D. A., et al. (2010). Intensive meditation training improves perceptual discrimination and sustained attention. *Psychological Science, 21,* 829–839.

MacMillan, N. A., & Creelman, C. D. (2004). *Detection theory: A user's guide* (2nd ed.). Hillsdale, NJ: Erlbaum.

MacQuarrie, B., & Belkin, D. (2003, September 29). Franklin Park gorilla escapes, attacks 2. *Boston Globe*. Retrieved from http://www.boston.com.

MacQueen, G. M., Campbell, S., McEwen, B. S., Macdonald, K., et al. (2003). Course of illness, hippocampal function, and hippocampal volume in major depression. *Proceedings of the National Academy of Sciences, 100,* 1387–1392.

Macrae, C. N., & Quadflieg, S. (2010). Perceiving people. In S. T. Fiske, D. T. Gilbert, & G. Lindzey (Eds.), *Handbook of social psychology* (5th ed., Vol. 2, pp.428–464). Hoboken, NJ: Wiley.

Maddi, S. R., & Khoshaba, D. M. (2005). *Resilence at work*. New York: American Management Association.

Madhyastha, T. M., Hamaker, E, L. & Gottman, J. M (2011). Investigating spousal influence using moment-to-moment affect data from marital conflict *Journal of Family Psychology,* 25292–25300.

Madon, S., Willard, J., Guyll, M., & Scherr, K. C. (2011) Self-fulfilling prophecies: Mechanisms, power, and links to social problems. *Social and Personality Psychology Compass, 5,* 578–590

Madon, S., Willard, J., Guyll, M., Trudeau, L., & Spoth, R. (2006). Self-fulfilling prophecy effects of mothers' beliefs on children's alcohol use: Accumulation, dissipation, and stability over time. *Journal of Personality and Social Psychology, 90,* 911–926.

Magnavita, J. J. (2006). In search of unifying principles of psychotherapy: Conceptual, empirical, and clinical convergence. *American Psychologist, 61,* 882–892.

Maguire, E. A., & Hassabis, D. (2011). Role of the hippocampus in imagination and future thinking. *PNAS Proceedings of the National Academy of Sciences of The United States Of America, 108*(11), doi:10.1073/pnas.1018876108.

Mahler, S. V., Smith, K. S., & Berridge, K. C. (2007). Endocannabinoid hedonic hotspot for sensory pleasure: Anandamide in nucleus accumbens shell enhances 'liking' of a sweet reward. *Neuropsychopharmacology, 32*(11), 2267–2278.

Mahroo, O. A., & Lamb, T. D. (2004). Recovery of the human photopic electroretinogram after bleaching exposures: Estimation of pigment regeneration kinetics. *Journal of Physiology, 554,* 417–437.

Maier, S. F., & Watkins, L. R. (2000). The immune system as a sensory system: Implications for psychology. *Current Directions in Psychological Science, 9,* 98–102.

Mains, J. A., & Scogin, F. R. (2003). The effectiveness of self-administered treatments: A practice-friendly review of the research. *Journal of Clinical Psychology, 59,* 237–245.

Maio, G., Haddock, G., Manstead, A., & Spears, R. (In press.) Attitudes and intergroup relations. In J. F. Dovidio, M. Hewstone, P. Glick, & V. M. Esses (Eds.), *Handbook of prejudice, stereotyping, and discrimination*. London: Sage.

Maj, M., Gaebal, W., Lopez-Ibor, J. J., & Sartorius, N. (Eds.). (2002). *Psychiatric diagnosis and classification*. New York: Wiley.

Majid, A., Evans, N., Gaby, A., & Levinson, S. (2011). The grammar of exchange: a comparative study of reciprocal constructions across languages. *Frontiers in Psychology,* 234.

Major, B., Sciacchtinano, A. M., & Crocker, J. (1993). In-group versus out-group comparisons and self-esteem. *Personality and Social Psychology Bulletin, 19,* 711–721.

Makeover, R. B. (2004). *Treatment planning for psychotherapists* (2nd ed.). Washington, DC: American Psychiatric Publishing.

Makin, T. R., Holmes, N. P., & Ehrsson, H. H. (2008). On the other hand: Dummy hands and peripersonal space. *Behavioural Brain Research, 191*(1), 1–10.

Malamuth, N. M. (1998). The confluence model as an organizing framework for research on sexually aggressive men: Risk moderators, imagined aggression, and pornography consumption. In R. G. Geen & E. Donnerstein (Eds.), *Human aggression* (pp. 230–247). San Diego: Academic Press.

Malamuth, N., & Addison, T. (2001). Helping and altruism. In G. Fletcher & M. Clark (Eds.), *Blackwell handbook of social psychology: Interpersonal processes* (pp. 162–195). Oxford, UK: Blackwell.

Malamuth, N. M., Addison, T., & Koss, M. (2000). Pornography and sexual aggression: Are there reliable effects and can we understand them? *Annual Review of Sex Research, 11,* 26–91.

Malamuth, N. M., & Check, J. V. P. (1983). Sexual arousal to rape depictions: Individual differences. *Journal of Abnormal Psychology, 92,* 55–67.

Malarkey, W. B., Kiecolt-Glaser, J. K., Pearl, D., & Glaser, R. (1994). Hostile behavior during marital conflict alters pituitary and adrenal hormones. *Psychosomatic Medicine, 56,* 41–51.

Maldonado, J. R., & Spiegal, D. (2008). Dissociative disorders. In R. E. Hales, S. C. Yudofsky, & G. O. Gabbard (Eds.), *Textbook of psychiatry* (pp. 665–728). Washington, DC: American Psychiatric Publishing.

Maldonado, R., Valverde, O., & Berrendero, F. (2006). Involvement of the endocannabinoid system in drug addiction. *Trends in Neuroscience, 29,* 225–232.

Malenka, R. C. (1995). LTP and LTD: Dynamic and interactive processes of synaptic plasticity. *The Neuroscientist, 1,* 35–42.

Malenka, R. C., & Nicoll, R. A. (1999). Long-term potentiation—a decade of progress? *Science, 285,* 1870–1874.

Malgrange, B., Rigo, J. M., Van de Water, T. R., Staecker, H., Moonen, G., & Lefebvre, P. P. (1999). Growth factor therapy to the damaged inner ear: Clinical prospects. *International Journal of Pediatric Otorhinolaryngology, 49*(Suppl. 1), S19–S25.

Malhotra, S. (2008). Impact of the sexual revolution: Consequences of risky sexual behaviors. *Journal of American Physicians & Surgeons, 13*(3), 88–90.

Maljaars, P. W. J., Peters, H. P. F., Mela, D. J., & Masclee, A. A. M. (2008). Ileal brake: A sensible food target for appetite control. A review. *Physiology & Behavior, 95*(3), 271–281.

Mallick, B. N. & Singh, A. (2011). REM sleep loss increases brain excitability: Role of noradrenaline and its mechanism of action. *Sleep Medicine Reviews, 15*(3), 165–178.

Malone, D. A., Jr., Dougherty, D. D., Rezai, A. R., Carpenter, L. L., Friehsf, G. M., Eskandar, E. N., Rauch, S. L., Rasmussen, S. A., Machado, A. G., Kubu, C. S., Tyrka, A. R., Price, L. H., Stypulkowski, P. H., Giftakis, J. E., Rise, M. T., Malloy, P. F., Salloway, S. P., & Greenberg, B. D. (2009). Deep brain stimulation of the ventral capsule/ventral striatum for treatment-resistant depression. *Biological Psychiatry, 65,* 267–275.

Malouff, J. M., Rooke, S. E., & Schutte, N. S. (2008). The heritability of human behavior: Results of aggregating meta-analyses. *Current Psychology, 27*(3), 153–161.

Maltby, N., Kirsch, I., & Mayers, M. (2002). Virtual reality exposure therapy for the treatment of fear of flying: A controlled investigation. *Journal of Consulting and Clinical Psychology, 70*(5), 1112–1118.

Mamede, S., van Gog, T., van den Berge, K., Rikers, R. P., van Saase, J. M., van Guldener, C., & Schmidt, H. G. (2010). Effect of availability bias and reflective reasoning on diagnostic accuracy among internal medicine residents. *JAMA: Journal of the American Medical Association, 304*(11), 1198–1203. doi:10.1001/jama.2010.1276.

Mancinelli, R., Binetti, R., & Ceccanti, M. (2007). Woman, alcohol and environment: Emerging risks for health. *Neuroscience & Biobehavioral Reviews, 31*(2), 246–253.

Mandelid, L. J. (2003). Dodofugl-dommen og psykoterapeuters credo. [The Dodo-bird verdict and the beliefs of psychotherapists]. *Tidsskrift for Norsk Psykolog forening, 40*(4), 307–312.

Maner J. K., & Kenrick D. T (2010). Evolutionary social psychology In R. Baumeister & E. Finkel (Eds.) *Advanced social psychology: The state of the science* (pp. 613–654). New York, NY: Oxford.

Maner, J. K., Luce, C. L., Neuberg, S. L., Cialdini, R. B., Brown, S., & Sagarin, B. J. (2002). The effects of perspective taking on motivations for helping: Still no evidence for altruism. *Personality and Social Psychology Bulletin, 28,* 1601–1610.

Manfield, P., & Shapiro, F. (2004). Application of eye movement desensitization and reprocessing (EMDR) to personality disorders. In J. J. Magnavita (Ed.), *Handbook of personality disorders: Theory and practice* (pp. 304–328). New York: Wiley.

Mangels, J. A., Good, C., Whiteman, R. C., Maniscalco, B., & Dweck, C. S. (2012). Emotion blocks the path to learning under stereotype threat. *Social Cognitive and Affective Neuroscience, 7*(2), 230–241. doi:10.1093/scan/nsq100.

Manheimer, E., White, A., Berman, B., Forys, K., & Ernst, E. (2005). Meta-analysis: Acupuncture for low back pain. *Annals of Internal Medicine, 142,* 651–663.

Mann, J. J., Apter, A., Bertolote, J., Beautrais, A., Currier, D., Haas, A., et al. (2005). Suicide prevention strategies: A systematic review. *Journal of the American Medical Association, 294,* 2064–2074.

Mann, K., Roschke, J., Nink, M., Aldenhoff, J., Beyer, J., Benkert, O., & Lehnert, H. (1992). Effects of corticotropin-releasing hormone administration in patients suffering from sleep apnea syndrome. *Society for Neuroscience Abstracts, 22,* 196.

Manti, L., Braselmann, H., Calabrese, M. L., Massa, R., Pugliese, M., Scampoli, P., Sicignano, G., & Grossi, G. (2008). Effects of modulated microwave radiation at cellular telephone frequency (1.95 GHz) on X-ray-induced chromosome aberrations in human lymphocytes in vitro. *Radiation Research, 169*(5), 575–583.

Manto, M. (2008). The cerebellum, cerebellar disorders, and cerebellar research—Two centuries of discoveries. *Cerebellum, 7*(4), 505–516.

Manto, M. (2012). Toxic agents causing cerebellar ataxias. *Handbook of Clinical Neurology, 103,* 201–213.

Maraj, S., Figueredo, V. M., & Lynn, M. D. (2010). Cocaine and the heart. *Clinical Cardiology, 33*(5), 264–269.

March, J., Silva, S., Petrycki, S., Curry, J., Wells, K., Fairbank, J., et al. (2004). Fluoxetine, cognitive-behavioral therapy, and their combination for adolescents with depression: Treatment for Adolescents with Depression Study (TADS) randomized controlled trial. *Journal of the American Medical Association, 292,* 807–820.

Marchman, T. (2008, October 24). You Call That Bling? *Wall Street Journal—Eastern Edition, 252*(98).

Marcus, G. F. (1996). Why do children say "breaked"? *Current Directions in Psychological Science, 5,* 81–85.

Marcus, S. V. (2008). Phase 1 of integrated EMDR: An abortive treatment for migraine headaches. *Journal of EMDR Practice and Research, 2*(1), 15–25.

Marcy, B., Jian-Ping, H., Gabriela, K., Albano, A., Avenevoli, S., & Merikangas, K. R. (2011). Social phobia and subtypes in the National Comorbidity Survey-Adolescent Supplement: Prevalence, correlates, and comorbidity. *Journal of The American Academy of Child & Adolescent Psychiatry, 50*(9), 870–880. doi:10.1016/j.jaac.2011.06.005

Marenco, S., & Weinberger, D. R. (2000). The neurodevelopmental hypothesis of schizophrenia: Following a trail of evidence from cradle to grave. *Developmental Psychopathology, 12,* 501–527.

Marewski, J. N., & Schooler, L. J. (2011). Cognitive niches: An ecological model of strategy selection. *Psychological Review, 118*(3), 393–437. doi:10.1037/a0024143.

Margetic, S., Gazzola, C., Pegg, G. G., & Hill, R. A. (2002). Leptin: A review of its peripheral actions and interactions. *Obesity, 26,* 1407–1433.

Marich, J. (2010). Eye movement desensitization and reprocessing in addiction continuing care: A phenomenological study of women in recovery. *Psychology Of Addictive Behaviors, 24*(3), 498–507. doi:10.1037/a0018574.

Marin, S., Vinaixa, M., Brezmes, J., Llobet, E., Vilanova, X., Correig, X., Ramos, A. J., & Sanchez, V. (2007). Use of a MS-electronic nose for prediction of early fungal spoilage of bakery products. *International Journal of Food Microbiology, 114,* 10–16.

Markey, P. M., & Markey, C. N. (2010). Vulnerability to violent video games: A review and integration of personality research. *Review of General Psychology, 142*(2), 82–91. doi:10.1037/a0019000.

Markman, E. M. (1994). Constraints children place on word meanings. In P. Bloom (Ed.), *Language acquisition: Core readings* (pp. 154–173). Cambridge, MA: MIT Press.

Markon, K. E., Krueger, R. F., & Watson, D. (2005). Delineating the structure of normal and abnormal personality: An integrative hierarchical approach. *Journal of Personality and Social Psychology, 88,* 139–157.

Marks, D. F. (2011). IQ variations across time, race, and nationality: An artifact of differences in literacy skills. *Counselor Education And Supervision, 50*(3), 643–664.

Marks, I. M. (2002). Reduction of fear: Towards a unifying theory. *Psicoterapia Cognitivae Comportamentale, 8*(1), 63–66.

Markus, H. R., Kitayama, S., & Heiman, R. J. (1996). Culture and "basic" psychological principles. In E. T. Higgins & A. W. Kruglanski (Eds.), *Social psychology: Handbook of basic principles* (pp. 857–913). New York: Guilford.

Markus, H. R., & Kitayama, S. (1997). Culture and the self: Implications for cognition, emotion, and motivation. In L. A. Peplau & S. Taylor (Eds.), *Sociocultural perspectives in social psychology* (pp. 157–216). Upper Saddle River, NJ: Prentice Hall.

Markus, H. R. (2008). Pride, prejudice, and ambivalence: Toward a unified theory of race and ethnicity. *American Psychologist, 63*(8), 651–670.

Markus, H. R., & Kitayama, S. (2010). Cultures and selves: A cycle of mutual constitution. *Perspectives on Psychological Science, 54,* 420–430.

Marmarosh, C., Holtz, A., & Schottenbauer, M. (2005). Group cohesiveness, group-derived collective self-esteem, group-derived hope, and the well-being of group therapy members. *Group Dynamics: Theory, Research, and Practice, 9,* 32–44.

Maroda, K. J. (2010). *Psychodynamic techniques: Working with emotion in the therapeutic relationship.* New York: Guilford.

Marques, S., Batalha, V. L., Lopes, L. V., & Outeiro, T. F. (2011). Modulating Alzheimer's disease through caffeine: A putative link to epigenetics. *Journal of Alzheimer Disease, 24*(Suppl 2), 161–171.

Marsh, A. A., Ambady, N., & Kleck, R. E. (2005). The effects of fear and anger facial expressions on approach- and avoidance-related behaviors. *Emotion, 5,* 119–124.

Marshall, G. N., Miles, J. N. V., & Stewart, S. H. (2010). Anxiety sensitivity and PTSD symptom severity are reciprocally related: Evidence from a longitudinal study of physical trauma survivors. *Journal of Abnormal Psychology, 119,* 143–150.

Marshall, S. J., Biddle, S. J., Gorely, T., Cameron, N., & Murdey, I. (2004). Relationships between media use, body fatness and physical activity in children and youth: A meta-analysis. *International Journal of Obesity, 28,* 1238–1246.

Marshall, W. L. (1989). Pornography and sex offenders. In D. Zillmann & J. Bryant (Eds.), *Pornography: Research advances and policy considerations.* Hillsdale, NJ: Erlbaum.

Martens, M. H. (2011). Change detection in traffic: Where do we look and what do we perceive? *Transportation Research Part F: Traffic Psychology and Behaviour, 14*(3), 240–250. doi:10.1016/j.trf.2011.01.004.

Marti, P. R., Singleton, C. K., & Hiller-Sturmhofel, S. (2003). The role of thiamine deficiency in alcoholic brain disease. *Alcohol Research Health, 27*(2), 134–142.

Marti, S., Sackur, J., Sigman, M., & Dehaene, S. (2010). Mapping introspection's blind spot: Reconstruction of dual-task phenomenology using quantified introspection. *Cognition, 115*(2), 303–313. doi:10.1016/j.cognition.2010.01.003.

Martin, C. L., & Fabes, R. A. (2001). The stability and consequences of young children's same-sex peer interactions. *Developmental Psychology, 37,* 431–446.

Martin, G., & Pear, J., (2010) *Behavior Modification: What it is and how to do it.* (9th Edition) Pearson: San Francisco.

Martin, J. A., Hamilton, B. E., Sutton, P. D., Ventura, S. J., et al. (2009). Births: Final data for 2006. *National Vital Statistics Reports, 57*(7), 1–102.

Martin, J. A.; Hamilton, B. E.; Ventura, S. J., Osterman, M. J., K., Kirmeyer, S., Mathews, T.J., & Wilson, E. C. (2011). Births: Final data for 2009. *National Vital Statistics Reports, 60*(1). Washington, DC: U. S. Department of Health and Human Services, Centers for Disease Control and Prevention, National Center for Health Statistics, National Vital Statistics System. Retrieved from http://www.cdc.gov/nchs/data/nvsr/nvsr60/nvsr60_01.pdf.

Martin, J. G. A., & Réale, D. (2008). Temperament, risk assessment and habituation to novelty in eastern chipmunks, Tamias striatus. *Animal Behaviour, 75*(1), 309–318.

Martin, R., & Hewstone, M. (2003). Majority versus minority influence: When, not whether, source status instigates heuristic or systematic processing. *European Journal of Social Psychology, 33,* 313–330.

Martin, R. A. (2001). Humor, laughter, and physical health: Methodological issues and research findings. *Psychological Bulletin, 127,* 504–519.

Martinez, C. R., & Forgatch, M. S. (2001). Preventing problems with boys' noncompliance: Effects of a parent training intervention for divorcing mothers. *Journal of Consulting and Clinical Psychology, 69,* 416–428.

Martinez, D., Gil, R., Slifstein, M., Hwang, D.-R., Huang, Y., Perez, A., et al. (2005). Alcohol dependence is associated with blunted dopamine transmission in the ventral striatum. *Biological Psychiatry, 58,* 779–786.

Martinez, M. (2000). *Education as the cultivation of intelligence.* Mahwah, NJ: Erlbaum.

Martinez-Taboas, A. (2005). The plural world of culturally sensitive psychotherapy: A response to Castro-Blanco's (2005) comments. *Psychotherapy: Theory, Research, Practice, Training, 42,* 17–19.

Martinot, M.-L. P., Bragulat, V., Artiges, E., Dolle, F., Hinnen, F., Jouvent, R., et al. (2001). Decreased presynaptic dopamine function in the left caudate of depressed patients with affective flattening and psychomotor retardation. *American Journal of Psychiatry, 158,* 314–316.

Martin-Santos, R., Fagundo, A. B., Crippa, J. A., Atakan, Z., et al. (2010). Neuroimaging in cannabis use: A systematic review of the literature. *Psychological Medicine, 40,* 383–398.

Martiny, K., Lunde, M., & Bech, P. (2010). Transcranial low-voltage pulsed electromagnetic fields in patients with treatment-resistant depression. *Biological Psychiatry, 68,* 163–169.

Martiny, S. E., Roth, J., Jelenec, P., Steffens, M. C., & Croizet, J. (2012). When a new group identity does harm on the spot: Stereotype threat in newly created groups. *European Journal of Social Psychology, 42*(1), 65–71. doi:10.1002/ejsp.840.

Masand, P., Popli, A. P., & Welburg, J. B. (1995). Sleepwalking. *American Family Physician, 51*(3), 649–653.

Mash, E. J., & Wolfe, D. A. (2012). *Abnormal child psychology* (5th ed.). New York: Cengage.

Masi, C. M., Chen, H. Y., Hawkley, L. C., & Cacioppo, J. T. (2011). A meta-analysis of interventions to reduce loneliness. *Personality and Social Psychology Review, 15,* 219–266.

Maslach, C. (2003). Job burnout: New directions in research and intervention. *Current Directions in Psychological Science, 12,* 189–192.

Masland, R. H. (2001). Neuronal diversity in the retina. *Current Opinion in Neurobiology, 11,* 431–436.

Maslow, A. H. (1943). A theory of human motivation. *Psychological Review, 50,* 370–396.

Maslow, A. H. (1954). *Motivation and personality.* New York: Harper.

Maslow, A. H. (1970). *Motivation and personality* (2nd ed.). New York: Harper & Row.

Maslow, A. H. (1971). *Toward a psychology of being.* Princeton, NJ: Van Nostrand.

Mass, R., Hölldorfer, M., Moll, B., Bauer, R., & Wolf, K. (2008). Why we haven't died out yet: Changes in women's mimic reactions to visual erotic stimuli during their menstrual cycles. *Hormones and Behavior, 55*(2), 267–271.

Masson, M. E. J., & MacLeod, C. M. (1992). Reenacting the route to interpretation: Enhanced perceptual identification without prior perception. *Journal of Experimental Psychology: General, 121,* 145–176.

Mast, T. G., & Samuelsen, C. L. (2009). Human pheromone detection by the vomeronasal organ: Unnecessary for mate selection? *Chemical Senses, 34,* 529–531.

Master, S. L., Eisenberger, N. I., Taylor, S. E., Naliboff, B. D., et al. (2009). A picture's worth: Partner photographs reduce experimentally induced pain. *Psychological Science, 20,* 1316–1318.

Masters, J. C., Burish, T. G., Hollon, S. D., & Rimm, D. C. (1987). *Behavior therapy: Techniques and empirical findings* (3rd ed.). San Diego: Harcourt Brace Jovanovich.

Masters, W. H., & Johnson, V. E. (1966). *Human sexual response.* Boston: Little, Brown & Co.

Masuda, T., Gonzalez, R., Kwan, L., & Nisbett, R. E. (2008). Culture and aesthetic preference: Comparing the attention to context of East Asians and Americans. *Personality and Social Psychology Bulletin, 34*(9), 1260–1275.

Masudomi, I., Isse, K., Uchiyama, M., & Watanabe, H. (2004). Self-help groups reduce mortality risk: A 5-year follow-up study of alcoholics in the Tokyo metropolitan area. *Psychiatry and Clinical Neurosciences, 58,* 551–557.

Mataix-Cols, D., Frost, R. O., Pertusa, A., Clark, L. A., Saxena, S., Leckman, J. F. (2010). Hoarding disorder: A new diagnosis for DSM-V. *Depression and Anxiety, 27,* 556–572. doi:10.1002/da.20693.

Mather, M., & Carstensen, L. L. (2005). Aging and motivated cognition: The positivity effect in attention and memory. *Trends in Cognitive Sciences, 9,* 496–502.

Mather, M., & Lighthall, N. R. (2012). Risk and reward are processed differently in decisions made under stress. *Current Directions in Psychological Science, 21*(1) 36–41. doi:10.1177/0963721411429452.

Mathew, S. J., Amiel, J. M., & Sackeim, H. A. (2005). Electroconvulsive therapy in treatment-resistant depression. *Primary Psychiatry, 12,* 52–56.

Mathieu, M. T., & Gosling, S. D. (2012). The accuracy or inaccuracy of affective forecasts depends on how accuracy is indexed: A meta-analysis of past studies. *Psychological Science, 23,* 161–162.

Mathy, F., & Feldman, J. (2012). What's magic about magic numbers? Chunking and data compression in short-term memory. *Cognition, 122*(3), 346–362. doi:10.1016/j.cognition.2011.11.003.

Matlin, M. W. (1998). *Cognition* (4th ed.). Fort Worth, TX: Harcourt Brace.

Maton, K., Kohout, J. L., Wicherski, M., Leary, G. E., & Vinokurov, A. (2006). Minority students of color in the psychology graduate pipeline: Disquieting and encouraging trends, 1989–2003. *American Psychologist, 61,* 117–131.

Matson, J., Sevin, J., Fridley, D., & Love, S. (1990). Increasing spontaneous language in autistic children. *Journal of Applied Behavior Analysis, 23,* 227–223.

Matson, J. L., & Boisjoli, J. A. (2009). The token economy for children with intellectual disability and/or autism: A review. *Research in Developmental Disabilities, 30,* 240–248.

Matsumoto, D. (2000). *Culture and psychology: People around the world.* Belmont, CA: Wadsworth.

Matsumoto, D., & Ekman, P. (1989). American-Japanese cultural differences in intensity ratings of facial expressions of emotion. *Motivation and Emotion, 13,* 143–157.

Matsumoto, D., & Willingham, B. (2006). The thrill of victory and the agony of defeat: Spontaneous expressions of medal winners of the 2004 Athens Olympic games. *Journal of Personality and Social Psychology, 91,* 568–581.

Matsumoto, D., & Willingham, B. (2009). Spontaneous facial expressions of emotion of congenitally and noncongenitally blind individuals. *Journal of Personality and Social Psychology, 96,* 1–10.

Matsumoto, D., Yoo, S. H., Hirayama, S., & Petrova, G. (2005). Development and validation of a measure of display rule knowledge: The display rule assessment inventory. *Emotion, 5,* 23–40.

Matsumoto, D., Yoo, S. H., & Nakagawa, S. (2008). Multinational study of cultural display rules. Culture, emotion regulation, and adjustment. *Journal of Personality and Social Psychology, 94,* 925–937.

Matsumoto, H., & Matsumoto, I. (2008). Alcoholism: Protein expression profi les in a human hippocampal model. *Expert Review of Proteomics, 5,* 321–331.

Mattanah, J. F., Hancock, G. R., & Brand, B. L. (2004). Parental attachment, separation-individuation, and college student adjustment: A structural equation analysis of mediational effects. *Journal of Counseling Psychology, 51,* 213–225.

Mattar, A. A. G., & Gribble, P. L. (2005). Motor learning by observing. *Neuron, 46,* 153–160.

Matthews, C. A. (2009). Phenomenology of obsessive-compulsive disorder. In M. M. Antony & M. B. Stein (Eds.), *Oxford handbook of anxiety and related disorders* (pp. 56–64). New York: Oxford University Press.

Matthews, G. (2008). Reinforcement Sensitivity Theory: A critique from cognitive science. In P. J. Corr (Ed.) *The reinforcement sensitivity theory of personality* (pp. 482–507). Cambridge: Cambridge University Press.

Matthews, K. A., Katholi, C. R., McCreath, H., Whooley, M. A., Williams, D. R., Zhu, S., et al. (2004). Blood pressure reactivity to psychological stress predicts hypertension in the CARDIA study. *Circulation, 110,* 74–78.

Matthews, K. A., Salomon, K., Kenyon, K., & Zhou, F. (2005). Unfair treatment, discrimination, and ambulatory blood pressure in black and white adolescents. *Health Psychology, 24,* 258–265.

Matthies, E., Hoeger, R., & Guski, R. (2000). Living on polluted soil: Determinants of stress symptoms. *Environment and Behavior, 32,* 270–286.

Matute, H., Yarritu, I., & Vadillo, M. (2011). Illusions of causality at the heart of pseudoscience. *British Journal of Psychology (London, England: 1953), 102*(3), 392–405. doi:10.1348/000712610X532210.

Matyas, G. S. (2004). Using MMPI special scale configurations to predict police officer performance in New Jersey. *Applied HRM Research, 9,* 63–66.

Maurer, J. T. (2010). Surgical treatment of obstructive sleep apnea: standard and emerging techniques. *Current Opinion in Pulmonary Medicine, 16*(6), 552–8.

Maviel, T., Durkin, T. P., Menzaghi, F., & Bontempi, B. (2004). Sites of neocortical reorganization critical for remote spatial memory. *Science, 305,* 96–99.

Maxfield, M., Pyszczynski, T., Greenberg, J., Pepin, Renee, D., & Hasker, P. (2011) The moderating role of executive functioning in older adults' responses to a reminder of mortality.. *Psychology and Aging,* Jul 4, 2011.

May, E. R., & Zelikow, P. D. (Eds.). (1997). *The Kennedy tapes: Inside the White House during the Cuban Missile Crisis.* New York: Belknap Press.

May, G. L., & Kahnweiler, W. M. (2000). The effect of a mastery practice design on learning and transfer in behavior modeling training. *Personnel Psychology, 53,* 353–373.

Mayberry, R. I., & Lock, E. (2003). Age constraints on first versus second language acquisition. *Brain and Language, 87,* 369–384.

Mayberry, R. I., Lock, E., & Kazmi, H. (2002). Linguistic ability and early language exposure. *Nature, 417,* 38.

Maycock, G. (1997). Sleepiness and driving: the experience of U.K. car drivers. *Accident Analysis and Prevention, 29*(4), 453–462.

Mayer, D. J., & Price, D. D. (1982). A physiological and psychological analysis of pain: A potential model of motivation. In D. W. Pfaff (Ed.), *The physiological mechanisms of motivation.* New York: Springer-Verlag.

Mayer, F. S., & Sutton, K. (1996). *Personality: An integrative approach.* Upper Saddle River, NJ: Prentice Hall.

Mayer, J. D. (2005). A tale of two visions: Can a new view of personality help integrate psychology? *American Psychologist, 60,* 294–307.

Mayer, R. E. (1992). *Thinking, problem solving, and cognition* (2nd ed.). New York: Freeman.

Mayes, L., Cicchetti, D., Acharyya, S., & Zhang, H. (2003). Developmental trajectories of cocaine-and-other-drug-exposed and non-cocaine-exposed children. *Journal of Developmental Behavioral Pediatrics, 24,* 323–335.

Mayes, L. C., Molfese, D. L., Key, A. P. F., & Hunter, N. C. (2005). Event-related potentials in cocaine-exposed children during a Stroop task. *Neurotoxicology and Teratology, 27*(6), 797–813.

Mayet, A., Legleye, S., Chau, N., & Falissard, B. (2011). Transitions between tobacco and cannabis use among adolescents: A multi-state modeling of progression from onset to daily use. *Addictive Behaviors, 36*(11), 1101–1105.

Mayet, A., Legleye, S., Falissard, B., & Chau N. (2012). Cannabis use stages as predictors of subsequent initiation with other illicit drugs among French adolescents: Use of a multi-state model. *Addictive Behaviors, 37*(2), 160–166.

Mayeux, R. (2003). Epidemiology of neurodegeneration. *Annual Review of Neuroscience, 26,* 81–104.

Maynard, D. C., Joseph, T. A., & Maynard, A. M. (2006). Underemployment, job attitudes, and turnover intentions. *Journal of Organizational Behavior, 27,* 509–536.

Mayou, R., Kirmayer, L. J., Simon, G., Kroenke, K., & Sharpe, M. (2005). Somatoform disorders: Time for a new approach in DSM-V. *American Journal of Psychiatry, 162,* 847–855.

Mazerolle, M., Régner, I., Morisset, P., Rigalleau, F., & Huguet, P. (2012). Stereotype threat strengthens automatic recall and undermines controlled processes in older adults. *Psychological Science, 23*(7), 723–727. Epub 2012 May 18. Doi:10. 11770956797612437607.

Mazoyer, B., Tzouri-Mazoyer, N., Mazard, A., Denis, M., & Mellet, E. (2002). Neural basis of image and language interactions. *International Journal of Psychology, 37,* 204–208.

Mazzoccoli, G. (2011). The timing clockwork of life. *Journal of Biologic Regulators and Homeostatic Agents, 25*(1), 137–143.

Mazzoccoli, G., Panza, A., Valvano, M. R., Palumbo, O., Carella, M., Pazienza, V., Biscaglia, G., Tavano, F., Di Sebastiano, P., Andriulli, A., & Piepoli, A. (2011). Clock gene expression levels and relationship with clinical and pathological features in colorectal cancer patients. *Chronobiology International, 28*(10), 841–851.

Mazzoni, G., Rotriquenz, E., Carvalho, C., Vannucci, M., et al. (2009). Suggested visual hallucinations in and out of hypnosis. *Consciousness and Cognition, 18,* 494–499.

Mazzoni, G. A., & Loftus, E. F. (1996). When dreams become reality. *Consciousness and Cognition, 5,* 442–462.

McAdams, D. P., & Pals, J. L. (2006). A new big five: Fundamental principles for an integrative science of personality. *American Psychologist, 61,* 204–217.

McAllister-Williams, R. H. (2006). Relapse prevention in bipolar disorder: A critical review of current guidelines. *Journal of Psychopharmacology, 20*(Suppl. 2), 12–16.

McAuley, E. (1992). The role of efficacy cognitions in the prediction of exercise behavior in middle-aged adults. *Journal of Behavioral Medicine, 15,* 65–88.

McAuley, E., Kramer, A. F., & Colcombe, S. J. (2004). Cardiovascular fitness and neurocognitive function in older adults: A brief review. *Brain, Behavior, and Immunity, 18,* 214–220.

McAuliff, B. D., Kovera, M. B., & Nunez, G. (2008). Can jurors recognize missing control groups, confounds, and experimental bias in psychological science? *Law and Human Behavior, 33,* 247–257.

McCaffery, E. J., & Baron, J. (2006). Thinking about tax. *Psychology, Public Policy, and Law, 12,* 106–135.

McCaffrey, T. (2012). Innovation relies on the obscure: A key to overcoming the classic problem of functional fixedness. *Psychological Science, 23*(3), 215–218. doi:10.1177/0956797611429580.

McCarley, J. S., Kramer, A. F., Wickens, C. D., Vidoni, E. D., & Boot, W. R. (2004). Visual skills in airport-security screening. *Psychological Science, 15,* 302–306.

McCaul, K. D., Hockemeyer, J. R., Johnson, R. J., Zetocha, K., Quinlan, K., & Glasgow, R. E. (2006). Motivation to quit using cigarettes: A review. *Addictive Behaviors, 31,* 42–56.

McClain, M., & Foundas, A. (2004). Apraxia. *Current Neurology and Neuroscience Reports, 4*(6), 471–476.

McClelland, D. C. (1985). *Human motivation.* Glenview, IL: Scott, Foresman.

McClelland, D. C. (1958). Risk-taking in children with high and low need for achievement. In J. W. Atkinson (Ed.), *Motives in fantasy, action, and society* (pp. 306–321). Princeton, NJ: Van Nostrand.

McClelland, D. C., Atkinson, J. W., Clark, R. A., & Lowell, E. L. (1953). *The achievement motive.* New York: Appleton-Century-Crofts.

McCloskey, M. (1983). Naïve theories of motion. In D. Gentner & K. Stevens (Eds.), *Mental models* (pp. 299–324). Northvale, NJ: Erlbaum.

McCloskey, M. S., Ben-Zeev, D., Lee, R., Berman, M. E., & Coccaro, E. F. (2009). Acute tryptophan depletion and self-injurious behavior in aggressive patients and healthy volunteers. *Psychopharmacology (Berlin), 203,* 53–61. Epub 2008 Oct 23.

McClure, E. B. (2000). A meta-analytic review of sex differences in facial expression processing and their development in infants, children, and adolescents. *Psychological Bulletin, 126,* 424–453.

McConaghy, N., Hadzi-Pavlovic, D., Stevens, C., Manicavasagar, V., Buhrich, N., & Vollmer-Conna, U. (2006). Fraternal birth order and ratio of heterosexual/homosexual feelings in women and men. *Journal of Homosexuality, 51*(4), 161–174.

McCormick, D. A., & Thompson, R. F. (1984). Cerebellum essential involvement in the classically conditioned eyelid response. *Science, 223,* 296–299.

McCormick, E. J., Jeanneret, P. R., & Mecham, R. C. (1972). A study of job characteristics and job dimensions as based on the position analysis questionnaire (PAQ). *Journal of Applied Psychology, 56,* 347–368.

McCrae, R. R., & Costa, P. T., Jr. (2004). A contemplated revision of the NEO Five-Factor Inventory. *Personality and Individual Differences, 36,* 587–596.

McCrae, R. R., & Costa, P. T., Jr. (2006). Cross-cultural perspectives on adult personality trait development. In D. Mroczek, & T. Little (Eds.) *Handbook of personality development* (pp. 129–145). Mahwah, NJ: Lawrence Erlbaum Associates.

McCrae, R. R., & Costa, P. T., Jr. (2008). The Five-Factor theory of personality. In O. John, R. Robins, & L. Pervin (Eds.), *Handbook of personality: Theory and research* (3rd ed., pp. 159–181). New York: Guilford.

McCrae, R. R., Harwood, M. T., & Kelley, S. L. (2011). The NEO Inventories. In T. M. Harwood, L. E. Beutler, & G. Groth-Marnat (Eds.) *Integrative Assessment of Adult Personality* (pp. 252–275). New York, NY, US: Guilford.

McCrae, R. R., & John, O. (1992). An introduction to the five-factor model and its applications. *Journal of Personality, 60,* 175–215.

McCrae, R., Terracciano, A., & Personality Profiles of Cultures Project (2005). Personality profiles of cultures: Aggregate personality traits. *Journal of Personality and Social Psychology, 89,* 407–425.

McCullough M. E., & Tabak, B. A. (2010). Prosocial behavior In R. Baumeister & E. Finkel (Eds.) *Advanced social psychology: The state of the science.* (pp. 263–302). New York, NY: Oxford.

McCusker, R. R., Goldberger, B. A., & Cone, E. J. (2006). Caffeine content of decaffeinated coffee. *Journal of Analytical Toxicology, 30,* 611–613.

McDermott, K. B. (2002). Explicit and implicit memory. In V. S. Ramachandran (Ed.), *Encyclopedia of the human brain* (Vol. 2, pp. 773–781). New York: Academic Press.

McDermott, K. B., & Chan, J. C. K. (2006). Effects of repetition on memory for pragmatic inferences. *Memory and Cognition.*

McDermott, K. B., & Roediger, H. L. (1998). Attempting to avoid illusory memories: Robust false recognition of associates persists under conditions of explicit warnings and immediate testing. *Journal of Memory and Language, 39,* 508–520.

McDermott, K. B., Szpunar, K. K., & Christ, S. E. (2009). Laboratory-based and autobiographical retrieval tasks diff er substantially in their neural substrates. *Neuropsychologia, 47,* 2290–2298.

McDiarmid, M. A., & Condon, M. (2005). Organizational safety culture/climate and worker compliance with hazardous drug guidelines: Lessons from the blood-borne pathogen experience. *Journal of Occupational and Environmental Medicine, 47,* 740–749.

McDonald, G. (2010). The Flynn effect and the demography of schooling. *Teachers College Record, 112*(7), 1851–1870.

McDonald, R., & Siegel, S. (2004). The potential role of drug onset cues in drug dependence and withdrawal: Reply to Bardo (2004), Bossert and Shaham (2004), Bouton (2004), and Stewart (2004). *Experimental and Clinical Psychopharmacology, 12,* 23–26.

McDougall, W. (1908). *An introduction to social psychology.* London: Methuen.

McElvaney, C. (2011). Client evaluations and summaries: How person-centered planning is tainted by a diagnosis. Intellectual And Developmental Disabilities, 49(3), 203–205. doi:10.1352/1934-9556-49.3.203.

McElwain, N. L., Booth-LaForce, C., Lansford, J. E., Wu, X., & Dyer, W. J. (2008). A process model of attachment-friend linkages: Hostile attribution biases, language ability, and mother-child affective mutuality as intervening mechanisms. *Child Development, 79,* 1891–1906.

McElwain, N. L., Booth-LaForce, C., & Wu, X. (2011). Infant–mother attachment and children's friendship quality: Maternal mental-state talk as an intervening mechanism. *Developmental Psychology, 47*(5), 1295–1311. doi:10.1037/a0024094.

McEvoy, G. M., & Beatty, R. W. (1989). Assessment centers and subordinate appraisals of managers: A seven-year examination of predictive validity. *Personnel Psychology, 42,* 37–52.

McGarvey, C., McDonnell, M., Hamilton, K., O'Regan, M., & Matthews, T. (2006). An 8-year study of risk factors for SIDS: Bed-sharing versus non-bed-sharing. *Archives of Disease in Childhood, 91,* 318–323.

McGaugh, J. L. (2003). *Memory and emotion.* New York: Columbia University Press.

McGehee, D. S., Heath, M. J. S., Gelber, S., Devay, P., & Role, L. W. (1995). Nicotine enhancement of fast excitatory synaptic transmissions in CNS by presynaptic receptors. *Science, 269,* 1692–1696.

McGeown, W. J., Venneri, A., Kirsch, I., Nocetti, L., Roberts, K., Foan, L., & Mazzoni, G. (2012). Suggested visual hallucination without hypnosis enhances activity in visual areas of the brain. *Consciousness & Cognition, 21*(1), 100–116. doi:10.1016/j.concog. 2011.10.015.

McGilloway, S., Mhaille, G., Bywater, T., Furlong, M., Leckey, Y., Kelly, P., & Donnelly, M. (2012). A parenting intervention for childhood behavioral problems: A randomized controlled trial in disadvantaged community-based settings. *Journal of Consulting and Clinical Psychology, 80*(1), 116–127. doi:10.1037/a0026304.

McGlashan, T. H., & Hoffman, R. E. (2000). Schizophrenia as a disorder of reduced synaptic connectivity. *Archives of General Psychiatry, 57,* 637–648.

McGlynn, S. M., & Schacter, D. L. (1989). Unawareness of deficits in neuropsychological syndromes. *Journal of Clinical and Experimental Neuropsychology, 11*(2), 143–205.

McGorry, P. D., Purcell, R., Goldstone, S., & Amminger, G. P. (2011). Age of onset and timing of treatment for mental and substance use disorders: Implications for preventive intervention strategies and models of care. *Current Opinion in Psychiatry, 24,* 301–306.

McGorry, P. D., Yung, A. R., Phillips, L. J., Yuen, H. P., Francey, S., Cosgrave, E. M., et al. (2002). Randomized controlled trial of interventions designed to reduce the risk of progression to first-episode psychosis in a clinical sample with subthreshold symptoms. *Archives of General Psychiatry, 59,* 921–928.

McGrath, S. A., Nilsen, A., & Kerley, K. R. (2011). Sexual victimization in childhood and the propensity for juvenile delinquency and adult criminal behavior: A systematic review. *Aggression & Violent Behavior, 16*(6), 485–492. doi:10.1016/j.avb.2011.03.008.

McGraw, A., Larsen, J. T., Kahneman, D., & Schkade, D. (2010). Comparing gains and losses. *Psychological Science, 21*(10), 1438–1445. doi:10.1177/0956797610381504.

McGue, M., & Bouchard, T. J. (1998). Genetic and environmental influences on human behavioral differences. *Annual Review of Neuroscience, 21,* 1–24.

McGue, M., Elkins, I., Walden, B., & Iacono, W. G. (2005). Perceptions of the parent-adolescent relationship: A longitudinal investigation. *Developmental Psychology, 41,* 971–984.

McGue, M., Osler, M., & Christensen, K. (2010). Causal inference and observational research: The utility of twins. *Perspectives on Psychological Science, 5*(5), 546–556. doi:10.1177/1745691610383511.

McHale, S., & Hunt, N. (2008). Executive function deficits in short-term abstinent cannabis users. *Human Psychopharmacology, 23*, 409–415.

McHugh, P. R. (2005). Striving for coherence: Psychiatry's efforts over classification. *Journal of the American Medical Association, 293*, 2526–2528.

McHugh, P. R. (2009). *Try to remember: Psychiatry's clash over meaning, memory, and mind.* Chicago: Dana Press.

McHugh, R. K., & Barlow, D. H. (2010). The dissemination and implementation of evidence-based psychological treatments: A review of current efforts. *American Psychologist, 65*, 73–84.

McHugh, R. K., Murray, H. W., & Barlow, D. H. (2009). Balancing fidelity and adaptation in the dissemination of empirically-supported treatments: The promise of transdiagnostic interventions. *Behaviour Research and Therapy, 47*, 946–953.

McKay, M. T., Sumnall, H., Goudie, A. J., Field, M., & Cole, J. C. (2011). What differentiates adolescent problematic drinkers from their peers? Results from a cross-sectional study in Northern Irish school children. *Drugs: Education, Prevention & Policy, 18*(3), 187–199. doi:10.3109/09687637.2010.502160

McKone, E., Davies, A. A., Fernando, D., Aalders, R., Leung, H., Wickramariyaratne, T., & Platow, M. (2010). Asia has the global advantage: Race and visual attention. *Vision Research, 50*(16), 1540–1549.

McLaren, B. M., DeLeeuw, K. E., & Mayer, R. E. (2011). Polite web-based intelligent tutors: Can they improve learning in classrooms?. *Computers & Education, 56*(3), 574–584. doi:10.1016/j.compedu.2010.09.019.

McLaughlin, C., & Vitak, J. (2012). Norm evolution and violation on Facebook. *New Media & Society, 14*, 299–315. doi:10.1177/1461444811412712.

McLaughlin, K. A., Fox, N. A., Zeanah, C. H., & Nelson, C. A. (2011). Adverse rearing environments and neural development in children: The development of frontal electroencephalogram asymmetry. *Biological Psychiatry, 70*(11), 1008–1015. doi:10.1016/j.biopsych.2011.08.006.

McLaughlin, N. C. R., & Westervelt, H. J. (2008). Odor identification deficits in frontotemporal dementia: A preliminary study. *Archives of Clinical Neuropsychology, 23*(1), 119–123.

McLeod, J. D., Kessler, R. C., & Landis, K. R. (1992). Speed of recovery from major depressive episodes in a community sample of married men and women. *Journal of Abnormal Psychology, 101*, 277–286.

McLoyd, V. C. (1998). Socioeconomic disadvantage and child development. *American Psychologist, 53*, 185–204.

McMahon, F. J., Akula, N., Schulze, T. G., Muglia, P., et al. (2010). Meta-analysis of genomewide association data identifies a risk locus for major mood disorders on 3p21.1. *Nature Genetics, 42*, 128–131.

McMahon, P. (2000, January 31). Oregon man leads life without frills, leaves $9 million to charities, children. *USA Today*, p. 4A.

McMullan, J. L., & Miller, D. (2009). Wins, winning and winners: The commercial advertising of lottery gambling. *Journal of Gambling Studies, 25*(3), 273–295. doi:10.1007/s10899-009-9120-5.

McMurrich, S. L., & Johnson, S. L. (2008). Dispositional rumination in individuals with a depression history. *Cognitive Therapy and Research, 32*, 542–553.

McNally, R. J. (2003). Recovering memories of trauma: A view from the laboratory. *Current Directions in Psychological Science, 12*, 32–35.

McNally, R. J., Clancy, S. A., & Schacter, D. L. (2001). Directed forgetting of trauma cues in adults reporting repressed or recovered memories of childhood sexual abuse. *Journal of Abnormal Psychology, 110*, 151–156.

McNally, R. J., Clancy, S. A., Schacter, D. L., & Pittman, R. K. (2000a). Cognitive processing of trauma cues in adults reporting repressed, recovered, or continuous memories of childhood sexual abuse. *Journal of Abnormal Psychology, 109*, 355–359.

McNally, R. J., Clancy, S. A., Schacter, D. L., & Pittman, R. K. (2000b). Personality profiles, dissociation, and absorption in women reporting repressed, recovered, or continuous memories of childhood sexual abuse. *Journal of Consulting and Clinical Psychology, 68*, 1033–1037.

McNally, R. J., & Geraerts, E. (2009). A new solution to the recovered memory debate. *Perspectives on Psychological Science, 4*, 126–134.

McNay, E. C., McCarty, R. C., & Gold, P. E. (2001). Fluctuations in brain glucose concentration during behavioral testing: Dissociations between brain areas and between brain and blood. *Neurobiology of Learning and Memory, 75*, 325–337.

McNelis, P. D. (2004). Neural networks in finance: Gaining predictive edge in the market. San Diego, CA: Academic Press.

McNulty, J. K., & Karney, B. R. (2004). Positive expectations in the early years of marriage: Should couples expect the best or brace for the worst? *Journal of Personality and Social Psychology, 86*, 729–743.

McNulty, J. K., & Fincham, F. D. (2012). Beyond positive psychology? Toward a contextual view of psychological processes and well-being. *American Psychologist, 67*(2), 101–110. doi:10.1037/a0024572.

McTigue, K. M., Harris, R., Hemphill, B., Lux, L., Sutton, S., Bunton, A. J., & Lohr, K. N. (2003). Screening and interventions for obesity in adults: Summary of the evidence for the U.S. Preventive Services Task Force. *Annals of Internal Medicine, 139*, 933–949.

McWayne, C. M.; Cheung, K., Green Wright, L. E., Hahs-Vaughn, D. L. (2012). Patterns of school readiness among head start children: Meaningful within-group variability during the transition to kindergarten. *Journal of Educational Psychology, 104*(3), 862–878. doi:10.1037/a0028884.

Mealor, A., & Dienes, Z. (2012). No-loss gambling shows the speed of the unconscious. *Consciousness & Cognition, 21*(1), 228–237. doi:10.1016/j.concog.2011.12.001.

Meaney, D. F. & Smith, D. H. (2011). Biomechanics of concussion. *Clinics in Sports Medicine, 30*(1), 19–31.

Medin, D., Bennis, W., & Chandler, M. (2010). Culture and the home-field disadvantage. *Psychological Science, 5*(6), 708–713. doi:10.1177/1745691610388772.

Medin, D. L., Ross, B. H., & Markman, A. B. (2001). *Cognitive psychology* (3rd ed.). Fort Worth, TX: Harcourt.

Mednick, S., Nakayama, K., & Stickgold, R. (2003). Sleep-dependent learning: A nap is as good as a night. *Nature Neuroscience, 6*, 697–698.

Megreya, A. M., Memon, A., & Havard, C. (2012). The headscarf effect: Direct evidence from the eyewitness identification paradigm. *Applied Cognitive Psychology, 26*(2), 308–315. doi:10.1002/acp.1826.

Mehl, M. R., & Pennebaker, J. W. (2003a). The social dynamics of a cultural upheaval: Social interactions surrounding September 11, 2001. *Psychological Science, 14*, 579–585.

Mehl, M. R., & Pennebaker, J. W. (2003b). The sounds of social life: A psychometric analysis of students' daily social environments and natural conversations. *Journal of Personality and Social Psychology, 84*, 857–870.

Mehl, M. R., Vazire, S., Holleran, S. E., & Clark, C. (2010). Eavesdropping on happiness: Well-being is related to having less small talk and more substantive conversations. *Psychological Science, 21*(4), 539–541. doi:10.1177/0956797610362675.

Mehle, T. (1982). Hypothesis generation in an automobile malfunction inference task. *Acta Psychologica, 52*, 87–116.

Mehler, P. S. (2011). Medical complications of bulimia nervosa and their treatments. *International Journal of Eating Disorders, 44*(2), 95–104. doi:10.1002/eat.20825.

Mehta, P. H., & Beer, J. (2010). Neural mechanisms of the testosterone-aggression relation: The role of orbitofrontal cortex. *Journal of Cognitive Neuroscience, 22*, 2357–2368.

Meichenbaum, D. (1977). *Cognitive behavior modification: An integrative approach.* New York: Plenum.

Meichenbaum, D. (2009). Stress inoculation training. In W. T. O'Donohue & J. E. Fisher (Eds.), *General principles and empirically supported techniques of cognitive behavior therapy* (pp. 627–630). Hoboken, NJ: Wiley and Sons.

Meier, B. P., Moeller, S. K., Riemer-Peltz, M., & Robinson, M. D. (2011). Sweet taste preferences and experiences predict prosocial inferences, personalities, and behaviors. *Journal of Personality and Social Psychology*, doi:10.1037/a0025253.

Meiser, T., & Hewstone, M. (2006). Illusory and spurious correlations: Distinct phenomena or joint outcomes of exemplar-based category learning? *European Journal of Social Psychology, 36*, 315–336.

Melamed, S., Fried, Y., & Froom, P. (2001). The interactive effect of chronic exposure to noise and job complexity on changes in blood pressure and job satisfaction: A longitudinal study of industrial employees. *Journal of Occupational Health Psychology, 6*, 182–195.

Melby, T. (2008). The myth of teen promiscuity. *Contemporary Sexuality, 42*(9), 1–5.

Melcangi, R. C., Panzica, G., & Garcia-Segura, L. M. (2011) Neuroactive steroids: focus on human brain. *Neuroscience 191*:1–5.

Melchior, C. L. (1990). Conditioned tolerance provides protection against ethanol lethality. *Pharmacology, Biochemistry and Behavior, 37*, 205–206.

Mellon, R. C. (2009). Superstitious perception: Response-independent reinforcement and punishment as determinants of recurring eccentric interpretations. *Behaviour Research and Therapy, 47*, 868–875.

Melo, V., Garcia, M., Sandoval, H., Jiménez, H., & Calvo, C. (2011). Quality proteins from edible indigenous insect food of Latin America and Asia. *Emirates Journal of Food & Agriculture (EJFA), 23*(3), 283–289.

Meltzer, H. Y. (1997). Treatment-resistant schizophrenia: The role of clozapine. *Current Medical Research Opinion, 14*, 1–20.

Melzack, R., & Wall, P. D. (1965). Pain mechanisms: A new theory. *Science, 150*, 971–979.

Memon, A., Fraser, J., Colwell, K., Odinot, G., & Mastroberardino, S. (2010). Distinguishing truthful from invented accounts using reality monitoring criteria. *Legal & Criminological Psychology, 15*(2), 177–194. doi:10.1348/135532508X401382.

Memon, A., Vrij, A., & Bull, R. (2004). *Psychology and law: Truthfulness, accuracy and credibility* (2nd ed.). New York: Wiley.

Menaker, M., & Vogelbaum, M. A. (1993). Mutant circadian period as a marker of suprachiasmatic nucleus function. *Journal of Biological Rhythms, 8*, 93–98.

Mendel, R. R., Traut-Mattausch, E. E., Jonas, E. E., Leucht, S. S., Kane, J. M., Maino, K. K., & .. Hamann, J. J. (2011). Confirmation bias: why psychiatrists stick to wrong preliminary diagnoses. *Psychological Medicine, 41*(12), 2651–2659. doi:10.1017/S0033291711000808.

Mendez, I., Sanchez-Pernaute, R., Cooper, O., Vinuela, A., Ferrari, D., Bjorklund, L., et al. (2005). Cell type analysis of functional fetal dopamine cell suspension transplants in the striatum and substantia nigra of patients with Parkinson's disease. *Brain, 128*, 1498–1510.

Mendez, I., Viñuela, A., Astradsson, A., Mukhida, K., Hallett, P., Robertson, H., Tierney, T., Holness, R., Dagher, A., Trojanowski, J. Q., & Isacson, O. (2008). Dopamine neurons implanted into people with Parkinson's disease survive without pathology for 14 years. *Nature Medicine, 14*, 507–509.

Mendle, J., Turkheimer, E., & Emery, R. E. (2007). Detrimental psychological outcomes associated with early pubertal timing in adolescent girls. *Developmental Review, 27*, 151–171.

Menon, G. J., Rahman, I., Menon, S. J., & Dutton, G. N. (2003). Complex visual hallucinations in the visually impaired: The Charles Bonnet syndrome. *Survey Ophthalmology, 48*, 58–72.

Mente, A., de Koning, L., Shannon, H. S., & Anand, S. S. (2009). A systematic review of the evidence supporting a causal link between dietary factors and coronary heart disease. *Archives of Internal Medicine, 169*, 659–669.

Merchant, J. A., & Lundell, J. A. (2001). *Workplace violence: A report to the nation.* Iowa City: University of Iowa.

Merckelbach, H., Devilly, G. J., & Rassin, E. (2002). Alters in dissociative identity disorder: Metaphors or genuine entities? *Clinical Psychology Review, 22,* 481–497.

Meredith, E., & Baker, M. (2007). Factors associated with choosing a career in clinical psychology–Undergraduate minority ethnic perspectives. *Clinical Psychology and Psychotherapy, 14,* 475–487.

Meriac, J. P., Hoffman, B. J., Woehr, D. J., & Fleisher, M. S. (2008). Further evidence for the validity of assessment center dimensions: A meta-analysis of the incremental criterion-related validity of dimension ratings. *Journal of Applied Psychology, 93,* 1042–1052.

Merikangas, K. R., Akiskal, H. S., Angst, J., Greenberg, P. E., et al. (2007). Lifetime and 12-month prevalence of bipolar spectrum disorder in the national comorbidity survey replication. *Archives of General Psychiatry, 64,* 543–552.

Merikangas, K. R., He, J.-P., Body, D., Fisher, P. W., et al. (2010). Prevalence and treatment of mental disorders among U.S. children in the 2001–2004 NHANES. *Pediatrics, 125,* 75–81.

Merritt, M. M., Bennett, G. G., Jr, Williams, R. B., Edwards, C. L., & Sollers, J. J., III. (2006). Perceived racism and cardiovascular reactivity and recovery to personally relevant stress. *Health Psychology, 25,* 364–369.

Merry, T., & Brodley, B. T. (2002). The nondirective attitude in client-centered therapy: A response to Kahn. *Journal of Humanistic Psychology, 42,* 66–77.

Mesman, J., & Koot, H. M. (2000). Common and specific correlates of preadolescent internalizing externalizing psychopathology. *Journal of Abnormal Psychology, 109,* 428–437.

Mesquita, B., & Frijda, N. H. (1992). Cultural variations in emotions: A review. *Psychological Bulletin, 112,* 179–204.

Messer, S. B. (2004). Evidence-based practice: Beyond empirically supported treatments. *Professional Psychology: Research and Practice, 35,* 580–588.

Messer, S. B., & Kaplan, A. H. (2004). Outcomes and factors related to effi cacy of brief psychodynamic therapy. In D. P. Charman (Ed.), *Core processes in brief psychodynamic psychotherapy: Advancing effective practice* (pp. 103–118). Mahwah, NJ: Erlbaum.

Messick, S. (1989). Validity. In R. Linn (Ed.), *Educational measurement* (3rd ed., pp. 13–103). New York: American Council on Education/Macmillan.

Messinger, A., Squire, L. R., Zola, S. M., & Albright, T. D. (2001). Neuronal representations of stimulus associations develop in the temporal lobe during learning. *Proceedings of the National Academy of Sciences, 98,* 12239–12244.

Messinger, D. S., Bauer, C. R., Das, A., Seifer, R., Lester, B. M., Lagasse, L. L., et al. (2004). The maternal lifestyle study: Cognitive, motor, and behavioral outcomes of cocaine-exposed and opiate-exposed infants through three years of age. *Pediatrics, 113,* 1677–1685.

Meston, C. M., & Buss, D. M. (2007). Why humans have sex. *Archives of Sexual Behavior, 36,* 477–507.

Mesulam, M. M. (1990). Large-scale neurocognitive networks and distributed processing for attention, language, and memory. *Annals of Neurology, 28*(5), 597–613.

Metrik, J., Rohsenow, D. J., Monti, P. M., McGeary, J., Cook, T. A. R., de Wit, H., Haney, M., & Kahler, C. W. (2009). Effectiveness of a marijuana expectancy manipulation: Piloting the balanced-placebo design for marijuana. *Experimental and Clinical Psychopharmacology, 17*(4), 217–225.

Metzinger, T. (Ed.). (2000). Neural correlates of consciousness: Empirical and conceptual questions. Cambridge: MIT Press.

Meuret, A. E., Rosenfield, D., Wilhelm, F. H., Zhou, E., Conrad, A., Ritz, T., & Roth, W. T. (2011). Do unexpected panic attacks occur spontaneously? *Biological Psychiatry, 70*(10), 985–991. doi:10.1016/j.biopsych.2011.05.027

Meuret, A. E., Wolitzky-Taylor, K. B., Twohig, M. P., & Craske, M. G. (2011). Coping skills and exposure therapy in panic disorder and agoraphobia: Latest advances and future directions. *Behavior Therapy, 43,* 271–284.

Meyer, G. J., Finn, S. E., Eyde, L. D., Kay, G. G., Moreland, K. L., Dies, R. R., et al. (2001). Psychological testing and psychological assessment: A review of evidence and issues. *American Psychologist, 56,* 128–165.

Meyer, G. J., Mihura, J. L., & Smith, B. L. (2005). The interclinician reliability of Rorschach interpretation in four data sets. *Journal of Personality Assessment, 84,* 296–314.

Meyer, I. H. (2003). Prejudice, social stress, and mental health in lesbian, gay, and bisexual populations: Conceptual issues and research evidence. *Psychological Bulletin, 129,* 674–697.

Meyer, J. D., & Salovey, P. (1997). What is emotional intelligence? In P. Salovey & D. Sluyter (Eds.), *Emotional development and emotional intelligence* (pp. 3–31). New York: Basic Books.

Meyer, R. G. (1975). A behavioral treatment of sleepwalking associated with test anxiety. *Behavior Therapy and Experimental Psychiatry, 6,* 167–168.

Meyer-Bahlburg, H. F. L., Dolezal, C., Baker, S., & New, M. (2008). Sexual orientation in women with classical or non-classical congenital adrenal hyperplasia as a function of degree of prenatal androgen excess. *Archives of Sexual Behavior, 37*(1), 85–99.

Meyer-Lindenberg, A. (2010). From maps to mechanisms through neuroimaging of schizophrenia. *Nature, 468,* 194–202. doi:10.1038/nature09569.

Meyers, C., & Jones, T. B. (1993). *Promoting active learning: Strategies for the college classroom.* San Francisco: Jossey-Bass.

Mezey, E., Key, S., Vogelsang, G., Szalayova, I., Lange, G. D., & Crain, B. (2003). Transplanted bone marrow generates new neurons in human brains. *Proceedings of the National Academy of Sciences, 100,* 1364–1369.

Mezulis, A. H., Abramson, L. Y., Hyde, J. S., & Hankin, B. L. (2004). Is there a universal positivity bias in attributions? A meta-analytic review of individual, developmental, and cultural differences in the self-serving attributional bias. *Psychological Bulletin, 130,* 711–747.

Mezzacappa, E. S., Katkin, E. S., & Palmer, S. N. (1999). Epinephrine, arousal and emotion: A new look at two-factor theory. *Cognition and Emotion, 13,* 181–199.

Miceli, G., Fouch, E., Capasso, R., Shelton, J. R., Tomaiuolo, F., & Caramazza, A. (2001). The dissociation of color from form and function knowledge. *Nature Neuroscience, 4,* 662–667.

Michael, R. B., Garry, M., & Kirsch, I. (2012). Suggestion, cognition, and behavior. *Current Directions in Psychological Science, 21*(3), 151–156. doi:10.1177/0963721412446369.

Michael, R. T., Wadsworth, J., Feinleib, J., Johnson, A. M., Laumann, E. O., & Wellings, K. (1998). Private sexual behavior, public opinion, and public health policy related to sexually transmitted diseases: A US-British comparison. *American Journal of Public Health, 88,* 749–754.

Michalski, D., Kohout, J., Wicherski, M., & Hart, B. (2011). *2009 doctorate employment survey.* Washington, DC: American Psychological Association Center for Workforce Studies. Retrieved from http://www.apa.org/workforce/publications/09-doc-empl/index.aspx.

Michelena, P., Sibbald, A. M., Erhard, H. W., & McLeod, J. E. (2009). Effects of group size and personality on social foraging: The distribution of sheep across patches. *Behavioral Ecology, 20*(1), 145–152.

Mick, E., Biederman, J., Prince, J., Fischer, M. J., & Faraone, S. V. (2002). Impact of low birth weight on attention-deficit hyperactivity disorder. *Journal of Developmental and Behavioral Pediatrics, 23,* 16–22.

Middeldorp, C. M., Cath, D. C., Van Dyck, R., & Boomsma, D. I., (2005). The co-morbidity of anxiety and depression in the perspective of genetic epidemiology: A review of twin and family studies. *Psychological Medicine, 35,* 611–624.

Mikolajczak, M., Gross, J. J., Lane, A., Corneille, O., de Timary, P., & Luminet, O. (2010). Oxytocin makes people trusting, not gullible. *Psychological Science, 21,* 1072–1074. doi:10.1177/0956797610377343.

Miklowitz, D. J. (2008). Adjunctive psychotherapy for bipolar disorder: State of the evidence. *American Journal of Psychiatry, 165,* 1408–1419.

Miklowitz, D. J., Otto, M. W., Frank, E., Reilly Harrington, N. A., Wisniewski, S. R., Kogan, J. N., et al. (2007). Psychosocial treatments for bipolar depression. *Archives of General Psychiatry, 64,* 419–426.

Mikula, G., Riederer, B., & Bodi, O. (2011). Perceived justice in the division of domestic labor: Actor and partner effects. *Personal Relationships.* doi:10.1111/j.1475-6811.2011.01385.x.

Mikulincer, M., & Shaver, P. R. (2005). Mental representations of attachment security: Theoretical foundation for a positive social psychology. In M. W. Baldwin (Ed.), *Interpersonal cognition* (pp. 233–266). New York: Guilford Press.

Milan, G., Lamenza, F., Iavarone, A., Galeone, F., Lorè, E., De Falco, C., Correntino, P., & Postiglione, A. (2008). Frontal Behavioural Inventory in the differential diagnosis of dementia. *Acta Neurologica Scandinavica, 117*(4), 260–265.

Miles, K. S., & Cottle, J. L. (2011). Beyond Plain Language: A Learner-Centered Approach to Pattern Jury Instructions. *Technical Communication Quarterly, 20*(1), 92–112. doi:10.1080/10572252.2011.528345.

Milev, P., Ho, B. C., Arndt, S., & Andreasen, N. C. (2005). Predictive values of neurocognition and negative symptoms on functional outcome in schizophrenia: A longitudinal first-episode study with 7-year follow-up. *American Journal of Psychiatry, 162,* 495–506.

Milgram, S. (1963). Behavioral study of obedience. *Journal of Abnormal and Social Psychology, 67,* 371–378.

Milgram, S. (1965). Some conditions of obedience and disobedience to authority. *Human Relations, 18,* 57–76.

Milgram, S. (1974). *Obedience to authority.* New York: Harper & Row.

Milgram, S. (1977, October). Subject reaction: The neglected factor in the ethics of experimentation. *Hastings Center Report* (pp. 19–23).

Milisen, K., Braes, T., Fick, D. M., & Foreman, M. D. (2006). Cognitive assessment and differentiating the 3 Ds (dementia, depression, delirium). *Nursing Clinics of North America, 41*(1), 1–22.

Millar, H. R., Wardell, F., Vyvyan, J. P., Naji, S. A., Prescott, G. J., & Eagles, J. M. (2005). Anorexia nervosa mortality in Northeast Scotland, 1965–1999. *American Journal of Psychiatry, 162,* 753–757.

Miller, D. D., McEvoy, J. P., Davis, S. M., Caroff, S. N., et al. (2005). Clinical correlates of tardive dyskinesia in schizophrenia: Baseline data from the CATIE schizophrenia trial. *Schizophrenia Research, 80,* 33–43.

Miller, B. L. (2007). Frontotemporal dementia and semantic dementia: Anatomic variations on the same disease or distinctive entities?. *Alzheimer Disease & Associated Disorders, 21*(4), s19–s22.

Miller, E., Tancredi, D. J., McCauley, H. L., Decker, M. R., Virata, M. C. D., Anderson, H. A., Stetkevich, N., Brown, E. W., Moideen, F., & Silverman, J. G. (2012). "Coaching boys into men": A cluster-randomized controlled trial of a dating violence prevention program. *Journal of Adolescent Health Care.* doi:10.1016/j.jadohealth.2012.01.018.

Miller, G. (1956). The magical number seven, plus or minus two: Some limits on our capacity to process information. *Psychological Review, 63,* 81–97.

Miller, G. (2003). Spying on the brain, one neuron at a time. *Science, 300,* 78.

Miller, G. (2005a). Neuroscience: The dark side of glia. *Science, 308,* 778–781.

Miller, G., & Holden, C. (2010). Proposed revisions to psychiatry's canon unveiled. *Science, 327,* 770–771.

Miller, G., Lachman, M., Chen, E., Gruenewald, T., Karlamangla, A., & Seeman, T. (2011). Pathways to resilience: Maternal nurturance as a buffer against the effects of childhood poverty on metabolic syndrome at midlife. *Psychological Science, 22*(12), 1591–1599.

Miller, G., Tybur, J. M., & Jordan, B. D. (2007). Ovulatory cycle effects on tip earnings by lap dancers: Economic evidence for human estrus? *Evolution and Human Behavior, 28*, 375–381.

Miller, G. A. (1991). *The science of words*. New York: Scientific American Library.

Miller, G. A. (2010). Mistreating psychology in the decades of the brain. *Perspectives on Psychological Science, 5*(6), 716–743. doi:10.1177/1745691610388774.

Miller, G. A., Heise, G. A., & Lichten, W. (1951). The intelligibility of speech as a function of the context of the test materials. *Journal of Experimental Psychology, 41*, 329–335.

Miller, J. (2001). The cultural grounding of social psychological theory. In A. Tesser & N. Schwarz (Eds.), *Blackwell handbook of social psychology: Intraindividual processes* (pp. 22–43). Oxford, UK: Blackwell.

Miller, J. D., Lynam, D., Zimmerman, R. S., Logan, T. K., Leukefeld, C., & Clayton, R. (2004). The utility of the Five Factor Model in understanding risky sexual behavior. *Personality and Individual Differences, 36*, 1611–1626.

Miller, J. G., & Bersoff, D. M. (1994). Cultural influences on the moral status of reciprocity and the discounting of endogenous motivation. *Personality and Social Psychology Bulletin, 20*, 592–607.

Miller, K. F., Smith, C. M., Zhu, J., & Zhang, H. (1995). Preschool origins of cross-national differences in mathematical competence: The role of number-naming systems. *Psychological Science, 6*, 56–60.

Miller, L. C., Putcha-Bhagavatula, A., & Pedersen, W. C. (2002). Men's and women's mating preferences: Distinct evolutionary mechanisms? *Current Directions in Psychological Science, 11*, 88–93.

Miller, L. T., & Vernon, P. A. (1997). Developmental changes in speed of information processing in young children. *Developmental Psychology, 33*, 549–554.

Miller, N. E. (1959). Liberalization of basic S-R concepts: Extensions to conflict behavior, motivation, and social learning. In S. Koch (Ed.), *Psychology: A study of science* (Vol. 2, pp. 196–292). New York: McGraw-Hill.

Miller, R. R., & Laborda, M. A. (2011). Preventing recovery from extinction and relapse: A product of current retrieval cues and memory strengths. *Current Directions in Psychological Science, 20*(5), 325–329. doi:10.1177/0963721411418466.

Miller, S. L., & Maner, J. K. (2010). Ovulation as a male mating prime: Subtle signs of women's fertility influence men's mating cognition and behavior. *Journal of Personality and Social Psychology, 100*(2), 295–308. doi:10.1037/a0020930.

Miller, T. W., Nigg, J. T., & Miller, R. L. (2009). Attention deficit hyperactivity disorder in African American children: What can we conclude from the past ten years? *Clinical Psychology Review, 29*, 77–86.

Miller, W. R., & Rollnick, S. (2002). *Motivational interviewing: Preparing people for change* (2nd ed.). New York: Guilford.

Millon, T., & Davis, R. D. (1996). *Disorders of personality. DSM-IV and beyond* (2nd ed.). New York: Wiley.

Mills, P. E., Cole, K. N., Jenkins, J. R., & Dale, P. S. (1998). Effects of differing levels of inclusion on preschoolers with disabilities. *Exceptional Children, 65*, 79–90.

Milner, B. (1966). Amnesia following operation on temporal lobes. In C. W. M. Whitty & O. L. Zangwill (Eds.), *Amnesia*. London: Butterworth.

Milner, D. (1983). *Children and race*. Beverly Hills, CA: Sage.

Miltenberger, R. G. (2011). *Behavior modification: Principles and procedures* (5th ed.). New York: Cengage.

Mineka, S., & Zinbarg, R. (2006). A contemporary learning theory perspective on the etiology of anxiety disorders: It's not what you thought it was. *American Psychologist, 61*, 10–26.

Miner, J. L., & Clarke-Stewart, K. A. (2008). Trajectories of externalizing behavior from age 2 to age 9: Relations with gender, temperament, ethnicity, parenting, and rater. *Developmental Psychology, 44*, 771–786.

Ming, E. E., Adler, G. K., Kessler, R. C., Fogg, L. F., Matthews, K. A., Herd, J. A., & Rose, R. M. (2004). Cardiovascular reactivity to work stress predicts subsequent onset of hypertension: The air traffic controller health change study. *Psychosomatic Medicine, 66*, 459–465.

Minshew, N. J., & Williams, D. L. (2007). The new neurobiology of autism: Cortex, connectivity, and neuronal organization. *Archives of Neurology, 64*, 945–950.

Minsky, S., Vega, W., Miskimen, T., Gara, M., & Escobar, J. (2003). Diagnostic patterns in Latino, African American, and European American psychiatric patients. *Archives of General Psychiatry, 60*, 637–644.

Minson, J. A., & Mueller, J. S. (2012). The cost of collaboration: Why joint decision making exacerbates rejection of outside information. *Psychological Science, 23*(3), 219–224. doi:10.1177/0956797611429132.

Minuzzi, L., Nomikos, G. G., Wade, M. R., Jensen, S. B., et al. (2005). Interaction between LSD and dopamine D2/3 binding sites in pig brain. *Synapse, 56*, 198–204.

Minzenberg, M. J., Jong, H. Y., & Cameron, S. C. (2008). Schizophrenia. In R. E. Hales, S. C. Yudofsky, & G. O. Gabbard (Eds.), *Textbook of psychiatry* (pp. 407–456). Washington, DC: American Psychiatric Publishing.

Minzenberg, M. J., Watrous, A. J., Yoon, J. H., Ursu, S., & Carter, C. S. (2008). Modafinil shifts human locus coeruleus to low-tonic, high-phasic activity during functional MRI. *Science, 322*(5908), 1700–1702.

Miotto, K., Darakjian, J., Basch, J., Murray, S., Zogg, J., & Rawson, R. (2001). Gamma-hydroxybutyric acid: Patterns of use, effects and withdrawal. *American Journal on Addictions, 10*, 232–241.

Miranda, J., & Green, B. L. (1999). The need for mental health services research focusing on poor young women. *Journal of Mental Health Policy and Economics, 2*, 73–89.

Mischel, W. (2004a). *Introduction to personality: Toward an integration*. Hoboken, NJ: Wiley.

Mischel, W. (2004b). Toward an integrative science of the person. *Annual Review of Psychology, 55*, 1–22.

Mischel, W. (2009). From personality and assessment to personality science. *Journal of Research in Personality, 43*, 282–290.

Mischel, W., & Shoda, Y. (2008). Toward a unified theory of personality: Integrating dispositions and processing dynamics within the cognitive-affective processing system. In O. John, R. Robins, & L. Pervin (Eds.), *Handbook of personality: Theory and research* (3rd ed., pp. 208–241). New York: Guilford.

Mischel, W., Shoda, Y., & Smith, R. (2004). *Introduction to personality: Toward an integration* (7th ed.). New York: Wiley.

Mishna, F., Newman, P. A., Daley, A., & Solomon, S. (2009). Bullying of lesbian and gay youth: A qualitative investigation. *British Journal of Social Work, 39*(8), 1598–1614. doi:10.1093/bjsw/bcm148.

Mitchell, A. J., & Shiri-Feshki, M. (2009). Rate of progression of mild cognitive impairment to dementia: Meta-analysis of 41 robust inception cohort studies. *Acta Psychtrica Scandinavica, 119*, 252–265. Epub 2008 Feb 18.

Mitchell, D. B. (2006). Nonconscious priming after 17 years: Invulnerable implicit memory? *Psychological Science, 17*, 925–929.

Mitchell, K. J., & Zaragoza, M. S. (1996). Repeated exposure to suggestion and false memory: The role of contextual variability. *Journal of Memory and Learning, 35*, 246–260.

Mitka, M. (2011). Report weighs options for bulimia nervosa treatment. *JAMA: Journal of the American Medical Association, 305*(9), doi:10.1001/jama.2011.213.

Mitra, M., Wilber, N., Allen, D., & Walker, D. K. (2005). Prevalence and correlates of depression as a secondary condition among disabilities. *American Journal of Orthopsychiatry, 75*, 76–85.

Mitzner, G. B., Whelan, J. P., & Meyers, A. W. (2011). Comments from the trenches: Proposed changes to the DSM-V classification of pathological gambling. *Journal of Gambling Studies, 27*(3), 517–521. doi:10.1007/s10899-010-9225-x.

Miville, M. L., & Constantine, M. G. (2007). Cultural values, counseling stigma, and intentions to seek counseling among Asian American college women. *Counseling and Values, 52*(1), 2–11. doi:10.1002/j.2161-007X.2007.tb00083.x

Miyagawa, T., Kawashima, M. Nishida, N., Ohashi, J., Kimura, R., Fujimoto, A., Shimada, M., Morishita, S., Shigeta, T., Lin, L., Hong, S.-C., Faraco, J., Shin, Y.-K., Jeong, J.-H., Okazaki, Y. Tsuji, S., Honda, M., Honda, Y., Mignot, E., & Tokunaga, K. (2008). Variant between CPT1B and CHKB associated with susceptibility to narcolepsy. *Nature Genetics, 40*, 1324–1328.

Miyake, A., & Friedman, N. P. (2012). The nature and organization of individual differences in executive functions: Four general conclusions. *Current Directions in Psychological Science, 21*(1), 8–14. doi:10.1177/0963721411429458

Miyamoto, S., Duncan, G. E., Marx, C. E., & Lieberman, J. A. (2005). Treatments for schizophrenia: A critical review of pharmacology and mechanisms of action of antipsychotic drugs. *Molecular Psychiatry, 10*, 79–104.

Miyamoto, Y., & Kitayama, S. (2002). Cultural variation in correspondence bias: The critical role of attitude diagnosticity of socially constrained behavior. *Journal of Personality and Social Psychology, 83*, 1239–1248.

Miyamoto, Y. & Wilken, B. (2010). Culturally contingent situated cognition: Influencing other people fosters analytic perception in the United States but not in Japan. *Psychological Science, 21*(11), 1616–1622. doi:10.1177/0956797610385954.

Miyauchi, S., Misaki, M., Kan, S., Fukunaga, T., & Koike, T. (2009). Human brain activity time-locked to rapid eye movements during REM sleep. *Experimental Brain Research, 92*(4), 657–667.

Mochizuki-Kawai, H., Yamakawa, Y., Mochizuki, S., Anzai, S., & Arai, M. (2010). Structured floral arrangement programme for improving visuospatial working memory in schizophrenia. *Neuropsychological Rehabilitation, 20*(4), 624–636. doi:10.1080/09602011003715141.

Moen, P., Erickson, W. A., Agarwal, M., Fields, V., & Todd, L. (2000). *The Cornell Retirement and Well-Being Study. Final report*. Ithaca, NY: Bronfenbrenner Life Course Center, Cornell University.

Moffitt, T., Caspi, A., Taylor, A., Kokaua, J., Milne, B., Polanczyk, G., & Poulton, R. (2010). How common are common mental disorders? Evidence that lifetime prevalence rates are doubled by prospective versus retrospective ascertainment. *Psychological Medicine, 40*(6), 899–909.

Moffitt, T. E. (2002). Teen-aged mothers in contemporary Britain. *Journal of Child Psychology & Psychiatry & Allied Disciplines, 43*, 727–742.

Moffitt, T. E., Arseneault, L., Belsky, D., Dickson, N., Hancox, R. J., Harrington, H., & Caspi, A. (2011). A gradient of childhood self-control predicts health, wealth, and public safety. *Proceedings of the National Academy of Sciences of the United States of America, 108*(7), 2693–2698. doi:10.1073/pnas.1010076108.

Moffitt, T. E., Arseneault, L., Belsky, D., Dickson, N., Hancox, R. J., Harrington, H., McConnel, A. R., Brown, C. M., Shoda, T. M., Stayton, L. E., & Martin, C. E. (2011). Friends with benefits: On the positive consequences of pet ownership. *Journal of Personality & Social Psychology, 101*(6), 1239–1252. doi:10.1037/a0024506.

Moffitt, T. E., Caspi, A., & Rutter, M. (2005). Strategy for investigating interactions between measured genes and measured environments. *Archives of General Psychiatry, 62*, 473–481.

Mogenson, G. J. (1976). Neural mechanisms of hunger: Current status and future prospects. In D. Novin, W. Wyrwicka, & G. Bray (Eds.), *Hunger: Basic mechanisms and clinical applications*. New York: Raven.

Mogilner, C. (2010). The pursuit of happiness: Time, money, and social connection. *Psychological Science, 21*(9), 1348–1354. doi:10.1177/0956797610380696.

Mohr, C., Binkofski, F., Erdmann, C., Buchel, C., & Helmchen, C. (2005). The anterior cingulate cortex contains distinct areas dissociating external from self-administered painful stimulation: A parametric fMRI study. *Pain, 114*, 347–357.

Mohr, C., Rohrenbach, C. M., Landis, T., & Regard, M. (2001). Associations to smell are more pleasant than to sound. *Journal of Clinical and Experimental Neuropsychology, 23,* 484–489.

Mohtasib, R.S., Lumley, G., Goodwin, J. A., Emsley, H. C., Sluming, V., & Parkes, L. M. (2011) Calibrated fMRI during a cognitive Stroop task reveals reduced metabolic response with increasing age. *Neuroimage.*

Mojzisch, A., & Schulz-Hardt, S. (2010). Knowing others' preferences degrades the quality of group decisions. *Journal of Personality and Social Psychology, 98*(5), 794–808. doi:10.1037/a0017627.

Mokdad, A. H., Marks, J. S., Stroup, D. F., & Gerberding, J. L. (2004). Actual causes of death in the United States, 2000. *Journal of the American Medical Association, 291,* 1238–1245.

Molden, D. C., & Dweck, C. S. (2000). Meaning and motivation. In C. Sansone & J. M. Harackiewicz (Eds.), *Intrinsic and extrinsic motivation: The search for optimal motivation and performance.* San Diego: Academic Press.

Molenberghs, P., Cunnington, R., & Mattingley, J. B. (2012) Brain regions with mirror properties: A meta-analysis of 125 human fMRI studies. *Neurosci Biobehav Rev 36* (1):341–349.

Molsa, P. K., Marttila, R. J., & Rinne, U. K. (1995). Long-term survival and predictors of mortality in Alzheimer's disease and multi-infarct dementia. *Acta Neurologica Scandinavica, 91,* 159–164.

Monane, M., Leichter, D., & Lewis, O. (1984). Physical abuse in psychiatrically hospitalized children and adolescents. *Journal of the American Academy of Child and Adolescent Psychiatry, 23,* 653–658.

Moncrief, W. C., Babakus, E., Cravens, D. W., & Johnston, M. W. (2000). Examining gender differences in field sales organizations. *Journal of Business Research, 49,* 245–257.

Moncrieff, J., & Kirsch, I. (2005). Efficacy of antidepressants in adults. *British Medical Journal, 331,* 155–157.

Mongillo, G., Barak, O., & Tsodyks, M. (2008). Synaptic theory of working memory. *Science, 319,* 1543–1546.

Monroe, S., Thase, M., & Simons, A. (1992). Social factors and psychobiology of depression: Relations between life stress and rapid eye movement sleep latency. *Journal of Abnormal Psychology, 101,* 528–537.

Monroe, S. M., & Reid, M. W. (2009). Life stress and major depression. *Current Directions in Psychological Science, 18,* 68–72.

Monstad, K., Propper, C., & Salvanes, K. G. (2011). Is teenage motherhood contagious? Evidence from a natural experiment. *Working Paper No. 11/262.* Centre for Market and Public Organisation, Bristol Institute of Public Affairs. Bristol, UK: University of Bristol.

Montague, P. R., Hyman, S. E., & Cohen, J. D. (2004). Computational roles for dopamine in behavioural control. *Nature, 431,* 760–767.

Monteleone, P., & Maj, M. (2008). The circadian basis of mood disorders: Recent developments and treatment implications. *European Neuropsychopharmacology, 18,* 701–711.

Montgomery, S., Baldwin, D. S., Blier, P., Fineberg, N., Kasper, S., Lader, M., et al. (2007). Which antidepressants have demonstrated superior efficacy? A review of the evidence. *International Clinical Psychopharmacology, 22,* 323–329.

Moon, R., Calabrese, T., & Aird, L. (2008). Reducing the risk of sudden infant death syndrome in child care and changing provider practices: Lessons learned from a demonstration project. *Pediatrics, 122,* 788–798.

Moon, Y. (2003). Don't blame the computer: When self-disclosure moderates the self-serving bias. *Journal of Consumer Psychology, 13,* 125–137.

Moore, K. A. (2005). *Family strengths: Often overlooked, but real.* Washington, DC: Child Trends.

Moore, T. H. M., Zammit, S., Lingford-Hughes, A. Barnes, T. R. E., Jones, P. B., Burke, M., & Lewis, G. (2007). Cannabis use and risk of psychotic or affective mental health outcomes: A systematic review. *The Lancet, 370,* 319–328.

Moorman, R. H., & Byrne, Z. S. (2005). How does organizational justice affect organizational citizenship behavior? In J. Greenberg & J. A. Colquitt (Eds.), *Handbook of organizational justice* (pp. 355–380). Mahwah, NJ: Erlbaum.

Moran, C. C. (2002). Humor as a moderator of compassion fatigue. In C. R. Figley (Ed.), *Treating compassion fatigue* (pp. 139–154). New York: Brunner-Routledge.

Moran, D. R. (2000, June). *Is active learning for me?* Poster presented at APS Preconvention Teaching Institute, Denver.

Moran, R. (2006). Learning in high-tech and multimedia environments. *Current Directions in Psychological Science, 15,* 63–67.

Moreno, S., Bialystok, E., Barac, R., Schellenberg, E., Cepeda, N. J., & Chau, T. (2011). Short-term music training enhances verbal intelligence and executive function. *Psychological Science, 22*(11), 1425–1433. doi:10.1177/0956797611416999.

Morewedge, C. K., Gilbert, D. T., & Wilson, T. D. (2005). The least likely of times: How remembering the past biases forecasts of the future. *Psychological Science, 16*(8), 626–630.

Morgan, A. J., Jorm, A. F., & MacKinnon, A. J. (2012). Usage and reported helpfulness of self-help strategies by adults with sub-threshold depression. *Journal of Affective Disorders, 136,* 393–397.

Morgan, B. E., Horn, A. R., & Bergman, N. J. (2011). Should neonates sleep alone? *Biological Psychiatry, 70*(9), 817–825. doi:10.1016/j.biopsych.2011.06.018.

Morgan, C. A., Doran, A., Steffian, G., Hazlett, G., & Southwick, S. M. (2006). Stress-induced deficits in working memory and visuo-constructive abilities in special operations soldiers. *Biological Psychiatry, 60,* 722–729.

Morgan, E. M. (2011). Associations between young adults' use of sexually explicit materials and their sexual preferences, behaviors, and satisfaction. *Journal of Sex Research, 48*(6), 520–530. doi:10.1080/00224499.2010.543960.

Morgan, S. E., Stephenson, M. T., Harrison, T. R., Afifi, W. A., & Long, S. D. (2008). Facts versus "feelings": How rational is the decision to become an organ donor? *Journal of Health Psychology, 13*(5), 644–658.

Morgenthaler, T. I., Kapur, V. K., Brown, T., Swick, T. J., Alessi, C., Aurora, R. N., Boehlecke, B., Chesson, A. L. Jr, Friedman, L., Maganti, R., Owens, J., Pancer, J., Zak, R., & Standards of Practice Committee of the American Academy of Sleep Medicine. (2007). Practice parameters for the treatment of narcolepsy and other hypersomnias of central origin. *Sleep, 30*(12), 1705–1711.

Morikawa, H. & Morrisett, R. A. (2010). Ethanol action on dopaminergic neurons in the ventral tegmental area: Interaction with intrinsic ion channels and neurotransmitter inputs. *International Review of Neurobiology, 91,* 235–288.

Morillo, C., Belloch, A., & Garcia-Soriano, G. (2007). Clinical obsessions in obsessive-compulsive patients and obsession-relevant intrusive thoughts in non-clinical, depressed and anxious subjects: Where are the differences? *Behaviour Research and Therapy, 45,* 1319–1333.

Morin, C. (2011, March). Neuromarketing: The new science of consumer behavior. *Society.* pp. 131–135. doi:10.1007/s12115-010-9408-1.

Morin, C. M., Bélanger, L., LeBlanc, M., Ivers, H., Savard, J., Espie, C. A., Mérette, C., Baillargeon, L., & Grégoire, J.-P. (2009). The natural history of insomnia: A population-based 3-year longitudinal study. *Archives of Internal Medicine, 169,* 447–453.

Morino, M., Toppino, M., Forestieri, P., Angrisani, L., Allaix, M. E., Scopinaro, N. (2007). Mortality after bariatric surgery: Analysis of 13,871 morbidly obese patients from a national registry. *Annals of Surgery, 246,* 1002–1007.

Morisano, D., Hirsh, J. B., Peterson, J. B., Pihl, R. O., & Shore, B. M. (2010). Setting, elaborating, and reflecting on personal goals improves academic performance. *Journal of Applied Psychology, 95,* 255–264.

Morisky, D. E., Stein, J. A., Chiao, C., Ksobiech, K., & Malow, R. (2006). Impact of a social influence intervention on condom use and sexually transmitted infections among establishment-based female sex workers in the Philippines: A multilevel analysis. *Health Psychology, 25,* 595–603.

Morling, B., & Kitayama, S. (2008). Culture and motivation. In J. Y. Shah, & W. L. Gardner (Eds.), *Handbook of motivation science* (pp. 417–433). New York: Guilford Press.

Morris, M. C., Ciesla, J. A., & Garber, J. (2008). A prospective study of the cognitive-stress model of depressive symptoms in adolescents. *Journal of Abnormal Psychology, 117,* 719–734.

Morris, M. C., Evans, D. A., Tangney, C. C., Bienias, J. L., & Wilson, R. S. (2006). Associations of vegetable and fruit consumption with age-related cognitive change. *Neurology, 67,* 1370–1376.

Morrison, A., & Chein, J. (2011). Does working memory training work? The promise and challenges of enhancing cognition by training working memory. *Psychonomic Bulletin & Review, 18*(1), 46–60.

Morrison, A. P., French, P., Steward, S. L., K., Birchwood, M., Fowler, D., Guley, A. I., Jones, P. B., Bentall, R. P., Lewis, S. W., Murray, G. K., Patterson, P., Brunet, K., Conroy, J., Parker, S., Reilly, R., Byrne, R., Davies, L. M., & Dunn, G. (2012). Early detection and intervention evaluation for people at risk of psychosis: Multisite randomised controlled trial. *BMJ, 344.* doi:10.1136/bmj.e2233.

Morrison, I., Frangulyan, R., & Riha, R. L. (2011). Beta-blockers as a cause of violent rapid eye movement sleep behavior disorder: A poorly recognized but common cause of violent parasomnias. *American Journal of Medicine, 124*(1), e11.

Morrison, M., Tay, L., & Diener, E. (2011). Subjective well-being and national satisfaction: findings from a worldwide survey. *Psychological Science, 22*(2), 166–171. doi:10.1177/0956797610396224.

Mortimer, R. G., Goldsteen, K., Armstrong, R. W., & Macrina, D. (1988). *Effects of enforcement, incentives, and publicity on seat belt use in Illinois.* University of Illinois, Dept. of Health & Safety Studies, Final Report to Illinois Dept. of Transportation (Safety Research Report 88–11).

Morton, G. J., Cummings, D. E., Baskin, D. G., Barsh, G. S., & Schwartz, M. W. (2006). Central nervous system control of food intake and body weight. *Nature, 443,* 289–295.

Moscovici, S. (1985). Social influence and conformity. In G. Lindzey & E. Aronson (Eds.), *The handbook of social psychology* (Vol. 2, 3rd ed.). New York: Random House.

Moser, C. (2011). Hypersexual disorder: Just more muddled thinking. *Archives of Sexual Behavior, 40*(2), 227–229. doi:10.1007/s10508-010-9690-4.

Moses, E. B., & Barlow, D. H. (2006). A new unified treatment approach for emotional disorders based on emotion science. *Current Directions in Psychological Science, 15,* 146–150.

Moskowitz, G. B. (2005). *Social cognition: Understanding self and others.* New York: Guilford Press.

Moskowitz, J. T., Hult, J. R., Bussolari, C., & Acree, M. (2009). What works in coping with HIV? A meta-analysis with implications for coping with serious illness. *Psychological Bulletin, 135,* 121–141.

Moss, E., Bureau, J.-F., Cyr, C., Mongeau, C., & St.-Laurent, D. (2004). Correlates of attachment at age 3: Construct validity of the preschool attachment classification system. *Developmental Psychology, 40,* 323–334.

Motowidlo, S. J., Brownlee, A. L., & Schmit, M. J. (2008). Effects of personality characteristics on knowledge, skill, and performance in servicing retail customers. *International Journal of Selection and Assessment, 16,* 272–280.

Moussavi, S., Chatterji, S., Verdes, E., Tandon, A., Patel, V., & Ustun, B. (2007). Depression, chronic diseases, and decrements in health: Results from the World Health Surveys. *Lancet, 370,* 851–858.

Moyer, C. A., Donnelly, M. W., Anderson, J. C., Valek, K. C., Huckaby, S. J., Wiederholt, D. A., Doty, R. L., Rehlinger, A. S., & Rice, B. L. (2011). Frontal electroencephalographic asymmetry associated with positive emotion is produced by very brief meditation training. *Psychological Science, 22*(10), 1277–1279. doi:10.1177/0956797611418985.

Mozaffarian, D., Hao, T., Rimm, E. B., Willett, W. C., & Hu, F. B. (2011). Changes in diet and lifestyle and long-term weight gain in women and men. *New England Journal Of Medicine, 364*(25), 2392–2404. doi:10.1056/NEJMoa1014296.

Mozzachiodi, R., Lorenzetti, F. D., Baxter, D. A., & Byrne, J. H. (2008). Changes in neuronal excitability serve as a mechanism of long-term memory for operant conditioning. *Nature Neuroscience, 11*, 1146–1148.

Mroczek, D. K., & Spiro, A., III. (2005). Changing life satisfaction during adulthood: Findings from the Veterans Affairs normative aging study. *Journal of Personality and Social Psychology, 88*, 189–202.

Mucchi-Faina, A., & Pagliaro, S. (2008). Minority influence: The role of ambivalence toward the source. *European Journal of Social Psychology, 38*, 612–623.

Muchinsky, P. M. (2003). *Psychology applied to work* (7th ed.). Belmont, CA: Thomson.

Mudrick, L., Breska, A., Lamy, D., & Deouell, L. Y. (2011). Intergration without awareness: Expanding the limits of unconscious processing. *Psychological Science, 22*(6), 764–770.

Mueser, K. T., & Jeste, D. V. (Eds.) (2009). *Clinical handbook of schizophrenia*. New York: Guilford Press.

Mufson, L., Dorta, K. P. Moreau, D., & Weissman, M. M. (2004). *Interpersonal psychotherapy for depressed adolescents* (2nd ed.). New York: Guilford Press.

Muggleton, N. G., Chen, C. Y., Tzeng, O. J., Hung, D. L., & Juan, C. H. (2010). Inhibitory control and the frontal eye fields. *Journal of Cognitive Neuroscience* [Advance online publication]. doi:10.1162/jocn.2010.21416

Mühlberger, A., Wiedemann, G., Herrmann, M. J., & Pauli, P. (2006). Phylo- and ontogenetic fears and the expectation of danger: Differences between spider- and flight-phobic subjects in cognitive and physiological responses to disorder-specific stimuli. *Journal of Abnormal Psychology, 115*(3), 580–589.

Muir, J. L. (1997). Acetylcholine, aging, and Alzheimer's disease. *Pharmacological and Biochemical Behavior, 56*(4), 687–696.

Mukamel, R., Ekstrom, A. D., Kaplan, J., Iacoboni, M., & Fried, I. (2010). Single-neuron responses in humans during execution and observation of actions. *Current Biology, 20*(8), 750–756. doi:10.1016/j.cub.2010.02.045.

Mullen, B. (1986). Atrocity as a function of lynch mob composition: A self-attention perspective. *Personality and Social Psychology Bulletin, 12*, 187–197.

Müller, T. D., Föcker, M., Holtkamp, K., Herpertz-Dahlamnn, B., & Hebebrand, J. (2009). Leptin-mediated neuroendocrine alterations in anorexia nervosa: Somatic and behavioral implications. *Child and Adolescent Psychiatric Clinics of North America, 18*(1), 117–129.

Mulligan, N. W. (2012). Differentiating between conceptual implicit and explicit memory: A crossed double dissociation between category-exemplar production and category-cued recall. *Psychological Science.* Advance online publication. doi:10.1177/0956797611433335

Mulligan, N. W., & Picklesimer, M. (2012). Levels of processing and the cue-dependent nature of recollection. *Journal of Memory and Language, 66*(1), 79–92. doi:10.1016/j.jml.2011.10.001.

Mullin, R. E. (2000). *The new handbook of cognitive therapy techniques*. New York: Norton.

Mullins-Sweatt, S. N., Glover, N. G., Derefinko, K. J., Miller, J. D., & Widiger, T. A. (2010). The search for the successful psychopath. *Journal Of Research in Personality, 44*(4), 554–558. doi:10.1016/j.jrp.2010.05.010.

Mullis, I. V. S., Martin, M. O., Gonzales, E. J., & Chrostowski, S. J. (2004). *TIMSS 2003 international mathematics report: Findings from IEA's Trends in International Mathematics and Science Study at the fourth and eighth grades.* Chestnut Hill, MA: Boston College.

Mullis, I. V. S., Martin, M. O., Kennedy, A. M., & Foy, P. (2007). *PIRLS 2006 international report: IEA's Progress in International Reading Literacy Study in primary school in 40 countries.* Chestnut Hill, MA: Boston College.

Mumford, M. D., Connelly, M. S., Helton, W. B., Strange, J. M., & Osburn, H. K. (2001). On the construct validity of integrity tests: Individual and situational factors as predictors of test performance. *International Journal of Selection and Assessment, 9*, 240–257.

Mumme, D. L., & Fernald, A. (2003). The infant as onlooker: Learning from emotional reactions observed in a television scenario. *Child Development, 74*, 221–237.

Munafo, M. M. (2011). CS01-03 - Genetics of addiction. *European Psychiatry, 26*(Supplement 1), 1769. doi:10.1016/S0924-9338(11)73473-3

Munakata, Y. (2006). Information processing approaches to development. In W. Damon & R. M. Lerner (Series Eds.) & D. Kuhn & R. Siegler (Vol. Eds.), *Handbook of child psychology: Vol. 2. Cognition, perception, and language* (6th ed.). New York: Wiley.

Munakata, Y., Snyder, H. R., & Chatham, C. H. (2012). Developing cognitive control: Three key transitions. *Current Directions in Psychological Science, 21*(2), 71–77. doi:10.1177/0963721412436807.

Munn, M. A., Alexopoulos, J., Nishino, T., Babb, C. M., Flake, L. A., Singer, T., Ratnanather, J., Huang, H., Todd, R. D., Miller, M. I., Botteron, K. N. (2007). Amygdala volume analysis in female twins with major depression. *Biological Psychiatry, 62*(5), 415–422.

Muñoz, R. F., & Mendelson, T. (2005). Toward evidence-based interventions for diverse populations: The San Francisco General Hospital prevention and treatment manuals. *Journal of Consulting and Clinical Psychology, 73*, 790–799.

Munte, T. F., Altenmuller, E., & Jancke, L. (2002). The musician's brain as a model of neuroplasticity. *Nature Reviews: Neuroscience, 3*, 473–478.

Murayama, K., Matsumoto, M., Izuma, K., & Matsumoto, K. (2010). Neural basis of the undermining effect of monetary reward on intrinsic motivation. *Proceedings*

Of The National Academy Of Sciences Of The United States Of America, 107(49), 20911–20916. doi:10.1073/pnas.1013305107.

Murphy, M. C., Steele, C. M., & Gross, J. J. (2007). Signaling threat: How situational cues affect women in math, science, and engineering settings. *Psychological Science, 18*, 879–885.

Murphy, T. M., Ryan, M., Foster, T., Kelly, C., McClelland, R., O'Grady, J. (2011). Risk and protective genetic variants in suicidal behaviour: Association with SLC1A2, SLC1A3, 5-HTR1B & NTRK2 polymorphisms. *Behavioral and Brain Functions, 7*(22), 1–9.

Murray, B. (2000). Learning from real life. *APA Monitor, 31*, 72–73.

Murray, E. A., & Mishkin, M. (1985). Amygdalectomy impairs crossmodal association in monkeys. *Science, 228*, 604–606.

Murray, H. A. (1938). *Explorations in personality*. New York: Oxford University Press.

Murray, H. A. (1971). *Thematic Apperception Test*. Cambridge: Harvard University Press.

Murray, J. A., & Terry, D. (1999). Parental reactions to infant death: The effects of resources and coping strategies. *Journal of Social and Clinical Psychology, 18*, 341–369.

Murray, S. L., Griffin, D. W., Derrick, J. L., Harris, B., Aloni, M. & Leder, S. (2011). Tempting fate of inviting happiness? Unrealistic idealization prevents the decline of marital satisfaction. *Psychological Science, 22*(5), 619–626. doi:10.1177/0956797611403155.

Murayama et al., 2010 [cited in 6e motivation/emotion chapter]

Murrell, W., Feron, F., Wetzig, A., Cameron, N., Splatt, K., Bellette, B., et al. (2005). Multipotent stem cells from adult olfactory mucosa. *Developmental Dynamics, 233*, 496–515.

Murrough, J.W., Huang, Y., Hu, J., Henry, S., Williams, W., Gallezot, J. D., Bailey, C. R., Krystal, J. H., Carson, R. E., & Neumeister, A. (2011) Reduced amygdala serotonin transporter binding in posttraumatic stress disorder. *Biol Psychiatry 70* (11):1033–1038.

Muse, K., McManus, F., Leung, C., Meghreblian, B., & Williams, J. G. (2012). Cyberchondriasis: Fact or fiction? A preliminary examination of the relationship between health anxiety and searching for health information on the Internet. *Journal of Anxiety Disorders, 26*(1), 189–196. doi:10.1016/j.janxdis.2011.11.005.

Musser, E. D., Backs, R. W., Schmitt, C. F., Ablow, J. C., Measelle, J. R., & Nigg, J. T. (2011). Emotion regulation via the autonomic nervous system in children with attention-deficit/hyperactivity disorder (ADHD). *Journal of Abnormal Child Psychology, 39*(6), 841–852. doi:10.1007/s10802-011-9499-1.

Mustanski, B. S., Chivers, M. L., & Bailey, J. M. (2002). A critical review of recent biological research on human sexual orientation. *Annual Review of Sex Research, 13*, 89–140.

Myers, D. G. (2000). *The American paradox: Spiritual hunger in an age of plenty*. New Haven, CT: Yale University Press.

Myers, D. G. (2004). *Intuition: Its powers and perils*. New Haven, CT: Yale University Press.

Myers, K. M., & Davis, M. (2007). Mechanisms of fear extinction. *Molecular Psychiatry, 12*, 120–150.

Myers, S. L. (2001, March 12). Sub's crew may have hesitated to question a trusted captain. *New York Times*.

Nabeshima, T., & Yamada, K. (2000). Neurotrophic factor strategies for the treatment of Alzheimer disease. *Alzheimer Disease & Associated Disorders, 14*(Suppl. 1), S39–46.

Nadeau, S., & Crosson, B. (1995). A guide to the functional imaging of cognitive processes. *Neuropsychiatry, Neuropsychology, and Behavioral Neurology, 8*, 143–162.

Nader, K. & Hardt, O. (2009). A single standard for memory: The case for reconsolidation. *Nature Reviews Neuroscience, 10*, 224–234.

Nader, K., Schafe, G. E., & Le Doux, J. E. (2000). Fear memories require protein synthesis in the amygdala for reconsolidation after retrieval. *Nature, 406*, 722–726.

Nägerl, U. V., Willig, K. I., Hein, B., Hell, S. W., Bonhoeffer, T. (2008). Live-cell imaging of dendritic spines by STED microscopy. *Proceedings of the National Academy of Sciences, 105*, 18982–18987.

Naidoo, L. J., Scherbaum, C. A., Goldstein, H. W., & Graen, G. B. (2011). A longitudinal examination of the effects of LMX, ability, and differentiation on team performance. *Journal Of Business And Psychology, 26*(3), 347–357. doi:10.1007/s10869-010-9193-2.

Nairne, J. S. (2003). Sensory and working memory. In A. F. P. Healy, R. W. Proctor, & I. B. Weiner (Eds.), *Handbook of psychology: Vol. 4. Experimental psychology* (pp. 423–444). New York: Wiley.

Naito, M., & Miura, H. (2001). Japanese children's numerical competencies: Age-and schooling-related influences on the development of number concepts and addition skills. *Developmental Psychology, 37*, 217–230.

Najjar, M., Courtemanche, F., Hamam, H., & Mayers, A. (2010). DeepKover—An adaptive artificial intelligent assistance system for cognitively impaired people. *Applied Artificial Intelligence, 24*(5), 381–413. doi:10.1080/08839514.2010.481486.

Nakamura, J., & Csikszentmihalyi, M. (2001). Catalytic creativity. *American Psychologist, 56*, 337–341.

Nakano, K., & Kitamura, T. (2001). The relation of the anger subcomponent of Type A behavior to psychological symptoms in Japanese and foreign students. *Japanese Psychological Research, 43*, 50–54.

Nakao, M., & Yano, E. (2006). Prediction of major depression in Japanese adults: Somatic manifestations of depression in annual health examinations. *Journal of Affective Disorders, 90*, 29–35.

Naquin, C. E., Kurtzberg, T. R., & Belkin, L. Y. (2010). The finer points of lying online: E-mail versus pen and paper. *Journal Of Applied Psychology, 95*(2), 387–394. doi:10.1037/a0018627.

Narayan, V. M., Narr, K. L., Kumari, V., Woods, R. P., Thompson, P. M., Toga, A. W., & Sharma, T. (2007). Regional cortical thinning in subjects with violent antisocial personality disorder or schizophrenia. *American Journal of Psychiatry, 164,* 1418–1427.

Nardone, I. B., Ward, R., Fotopoulou, A., & Turnbull, O. H. (2007). Attention and emotion in anosognosia: Evidence of implicit awareness and repression? *Neurocase, 13*(5), 438–445.

Nash, A. J., & Fernandez, M. (1996). P300 and allocation of attention in dual-tasks. *International Journal of Psychophysiology, 23,* 171–180.

Nash, I. S., Mosca, L., Blumenthal, R. S., Davidson, M. H., Smith, S. C., Jr., & Pasternak, R. C. (2003). Contemporary awareness and understanding of cholesterol as a risk factor: Results of an American Heart Association national survey. *Archives of Internal Medicine, 163,* 1597–1600.

Nasoz, F., Lisetti, C. L., & Vasilakos, A. V. (2010). Affectively intelligent and adaptive car interfaces. *Information Sciences, 180*(20), 3817–3836. doi:10.1016/j.ins.2010.06.034.

Nathan, D. (2011). *Sybil exposed: The extraordinary story behind the famous multiple personality case.* New York, NY US: Free Press.

Nathan, P. E., & Gorman, J. M. (2007). *A guide to treatments that work* (3rd ed.). New York: Oxford University Press.

National Association of Anorexia Nervosa and Associated Disorders. (2002). *Facts about eating disorders.* Retrieved August 26, 2003, from http://www.altrue.net/site/anadweb/content.php?type=1&id=6982.

National Center for Chronic Disease Prevention and Health Promotion. (2002). Trends in Sexual Risk Behaviors Among High School Students—United States, 1991–2001. *Morbidity and Mortality Weekly Report, 51,* 856–859.

National Center for Education Statistics. (2000). *National assessment of education progress.* Washington, DC: NCES.

National Center for Education Statistics. (2002). *Digest of education statistics, 2001.* Washington, DC: Office of Educational Research & Improvement, U.S. Dept. of Education.

National Center for Health Statistics. (2001). *Births, marriages, divorces, and deaths: Provisional data for January–December 2000.* Hyattsville, MD: Public Health Service.

National Center for Health Statistics. (2007). *Sexual behavior and selected health measures: Men and women 15–44 years of age, United States, 2002.* Hyattsville, MD: U.S. Department of Health and Human Services.

National Center on Addiction and Substance Abuse. (2004). *National Survey of American Attitudes on Substance Abuse: IX. Teen dating practices and sexual activity.* New York: Author.

National Highway Traffic Safety Administration (2010). *Traffic Safety Facts 2009: Alcohol-Impaired Driving.* Washington, DC: NHTSA.

National Institute of Mental Health (2008b). Study probes environment-triggered genetic changes in schizophrenia. Retrieved March 6, 2009 from http://www.nimh.nih.gov/science-news/2008/study-probes-environment-triggered-genetic-changes-in-schizophrenia.shtml.

National Institute of Mental Health. (1995). *Medications.* Washington, DC: U.S. Department of Health and Human Services.

National Institute of Mental Health. (2004, April 23). *Statement on antidepressant medications for children: Information for parents and caregivers.* Retrieved April 24, 2004, from www.nimh.nih.gov/press/StmntAntidepmeds.cfm.

National Institute of Mental Health. (2006). *The numbers count: Mental disorders in America.* Retrieved August 8, 2006, from http://www.nimh.nih.gov.publicat/numbers.cfm.

National Institute of Mental Health. (2006). The numbers count: Mental disorders in America. Retrieved from http://www.nimh.nih.gov.

National Institute of Mental Health. (2009). Suicide in the U.S.: Statistics and prevention. Retrieved from http://www.nimh.nih.gov.

National Institute of Mental Health. (2012a).Any anxiety disorder among adults. Retrieved from http://www.nimh.nih.gov/statistics/1ANYANX_ADULT.shtml

National Institute of Mental Health. (2012b). Any anxiety disorder among children. Retrieved from http://www.nimh.nih.gov/statistics/1ANYANX_child.shtml

National Institute of Mental Health. (2012c). Specific phobia among adults. Retrieved from http://www.nimh.nih.gov/statistics/1SPEC_ADULT.shtml

National Institute of Mental Health. (2012d). Specific phobia among children. Retrieved from http://www.nimh.nih.gov/statistics/1SPECIFIC_CHILD.shtml

National Institute of Mental Health. (2012e). Agoraphobia among adults. Retrieved from http://www.nimh.nih.gov/statistics/1AGOR_ADULT.shtml

National Institute of Mental Health. (2012f). Agoraphobia among children. Retrieved from http://www.nimh.nih.gov/statistics/1AGOR_CHILD.shtml

National Institute of Mental Health. (2012g). Generalized anxiety disorder among adults. Retrieved from http://www.nimh.nih.gov/statistics/1GAD_ADULT.shtml

National Institute of Mental Health. (2012h). Panic disorder among adults. Retrieved from http://www.nimh.nih.gov/statistics/1PANIC_ADULT.shtml

National Institute of Mental Health. (2012i). Panic disorder among children. Retrieved from http://www.nimh.nih.gov/statistics/1PANIC_CHILD.shtml

National Institute of Mental Health. (2012j). Obsessive compulsive disorder among adults. Retrieved from http://www.nimh.nih.gov/statistics/1OCD_ADULT.shtml

National Institute of Mental Health. (2012k). Antisocial personality disorder. Retrieved from http://www.nimh.nih.gov/statistics/1Antisocial.shtml

National Institute of Mental Health. (2012l). Any mood disorder among adults. Retrieved from http://www.nimh.nih.gov/statistics/1ANYMOODDIS_ADULT.shtml

National Institute of Mental Health. (2012m). Schizophrenia. Retrieved from http://www.nimh.nih.gov/statistics/1SCHIZ.shtml

National Institute of Mental Health. (2012n). Any disorder among adults. Retrieved from http://www.nimh.nih.gov/statistics/1ANYDIS_ADULT.shtml

National Institute of Mental Health. (2012o). Any disorder among children. Retrieved from http://www.nimh.nih.gov/statistics/1ANYDIS_CHILD.shtml

National Institute on Alcohol Abuse and Alcoholism. (2000). *Tenth special report to the U.S. Congress on alcohol and health* (Publication No. 00–1583). Washington, DC: National Institutes of Health.

National Institute on Alcohol Abuse and Alcoholism [NIAAA], 2001 (from 9e)

National Institute on Alcohol Abuse and Alcoholism. (2001). *Alcoholism: Getting the facts.* Bethesda, MD: National Institute on Alcohol Abuse and Alcoholism.

National Institute on Drug Abuse. (2000). Facts about MDMA (Ecstasy). *NIDA Notes, 14.* Retrieved December 13, 2004, from http://drugabuse.gov/NIDA_Notes/NNVol14N4/tearoff.html.

National Institutes of Health. (2001). *Eating disorders: Facts about eating disorders and the search for solutions.* NIH Publication No. 01–4901. Washington, DC: U.S. Department of Health and Human Services.

National Safety Council. (2004). *Reports on injuries in America, 2003.* Itasca, IL: Author.

National Transportation Safety Board. (2011, December). *Highway accident report: Gray summit, MO: Collision involving two school buses, a bobtail and a passenger vehicle, August 5, 2010.* Retrieved from http://www.ntsb.gov/news/events/2011/gray_summit_mo/index.html.

Navarrete-Palacios, E., Hudson, R., Reyes-Guerrero, G., & Guevara-Guzman, R. (2003). Lower olfactory threshold during the ovulatory phase of the menstrual cycle. *Biological Psychology, 63,* 269–279.

Neff, L. A., & Karney, B. R. (2005). To know you is to love you: The implications of global adoration and specific accuracy for marital relationships. *Journal of Personality and Social Psychology, 88,* 480–497.

Neher, A. (1991). Maslow's theory of motivation: A critique. *Journal of Humanistic Psychology, 31,* 89–112.

Nehm, R., Ha, M., & Mayfield, E. (2012). Transforming biology assessment with machine learning: Automated scoring of written evolutionary explanations. *Journal of Science Education & Technology, 21*(1), 183–196. doi:10.1007/s10956-011-9300-9.

Nehm, R., & Haertig, H. (2012). Human vs. computer diagnosis of students' natural selection knowledge: Testing the efficacy of text analytic software. *Journal of Science Education & Technology, 21*(1), 56–73. doi:10.1007/s10956-011-9282-7.

Neighbors, H. W., Caldwell, C., Williams, D. R., Nesse, R., Taylor, R. J., Bullard, K. M., et al. (2007). Race, ethnicity, and the use of services for mental disorders. *Archives of General Psychiatry, 64,* 485–494.

Neighbors, H. W., Trierweiler, S. J., Fort, B. C., & Muroff, J. R. (2003). Racial differences in DSM diagnosis using a semi-structured instrument: The importance of clinical judgment in the diagnosis of African Americans. *Journal of Health and Social Behavior, 44,* 237–256.

Neil, A. L., & Christensen, H. (2009). Efficacy and effectiveness of school-based prevention and early intervention programs for anxiety. *Clinical Psychology Review, 29,* 208–215.

Neill, E., Rossell, S. L., McDonald, S., Joshua, N., Jansen, N., & Morgan, C. J. (2011). Using ketamine to model semantic deficits in schizophrenia. *Journal of Clinical Psychopharmacology, 31*(6), 690–697.

Neisser, U. (1998). *The rising curve: Long-term gains in I.Q. and related measures.* Washington, DC: American Psychological Association.

Neisser, U. (2000a). Memorists. In U. Neisser & I. E. Hyman, Jr. (Eds.), *Memory observed* (2nd ed., pp. 475–478). New York: Worth.

Neisser, U. (2000b). Snapshots or benchmarks? In U. Neisser & I. E. Hyman, Jr. (Eds.), *Memory observed* (2nd ed., pp. 68–74). New York: Worth.

Neisser, U., Boodoo, G., Bouchard, T. J., Boykin, A. W., Brody, N., Ceci, S. J., et al. (1996). Intelligence: Knowns and unknowns. *American Psychologist, 51,* 77–101.

Neitz, J. and Neitz, M. (2011). The genetics of normal and defective color vision. *Vision Research, 51*(7), 633–651.

Nelson, C. A. (1987). The recognition of facial expressions in the first two years of life: Mechanisms of development. *Child Development, 58,* 889–909.

Nelson, C. A. (1999). Neural plasticity and human development. *Current Directions in Psychological Science, 8,* 42–45.

Nelson, C. A. (2007). A neurobiological perspective on early human deprivation. *Child Development Perspectives, 1,* 13–18.

Nelson, G., & Prilleltensky, I. (2004). *Community psychology: In pursuit of liberation and wellbeing.* New York: Palgrave Macmillan.

Nelson, K. (1986). Event knowledge and cognitive development. In K. Nelson (Ed.), *Event knowledge: Structure and function in development* (pp. 1–19). Hillsdale, NJ: Erlbaum.

Nelson, P. T., Braak, H., & Markesbery, W. R. (2011). Neuropathology and cognitive impairment in Alzheimer disease: a complex but coherent relationship. *Journal of Neuropathology and Experimental Neurology, 68*(1), 1–14.

Nelson, T. D., & Steele, R. G. (2006). Beyond efficacy and effectiveness: A multifaceted approach to treatment evaluation. *Professional Psychology: Research and Practice, 37,* 389–397.

Nelson-LeGall, S., & Resnick, L. (1998). Help seeking, achievement motivation, and the social practice of intelligence in school. In S. A. Karabenick (Ed.), *Strategic help seeking* (pp. 39–60). Mahwah, NJ: Erlbaum.

Nemeroff, C. B., Heim, C. M., Thase, M. E., Klein, D. N., Rush, A. J., Schatzberg, A. F., et al. (2003). Differential responses to psychotherapy versus pharmacotherapy in patients with chronic forms of major depression and childhood trauma. *Proceedings of the National Academy of Sciences, 100,* 14293–14296.

Nemeth, C. J., Personnaz, B., Personnaz, M., & Goncalo, J. A. (2004). The liberating role of conflict in group creativity: A study in two countries. *European Journal of Social Psychology, 34,* 365–374.

Neovius, M., & Narbro, K. (2008). Cost-effectiveness of pharmacological anti-obesity treatments: a systematic review. *International Journal of Obesity, 32,* 1752–1763.

Nestadt, G., Hsu, F.-C., Samuels, J., Bienvenu, O. J., Reti, I. Costa, P. T., Jr., et al. (2005). Latent structure of the *Diagnostic and Statistical Manual of Mental Disorders, Fourth Edition,* personality disorder criteria. *Comprehensive Psychiatry, 47,* 54–62.

Nestler, E. J. (2001). Molecular basis of long-term plasticity underlying addiction. *National Review of Neuroscience, 2,* 119–128.

Nestler, S., & Egloff, B. (2009). When scary messages backfire: Influence of dispositional cognitive avoidance on the effectiveness of threat communications. *Journal Of Research In Personality, 44*(1), 137–141. doi:10.1016/j.jrp.2009.10.007.

Nestoriuc, Y., Rief, W., & Martin, A. (2008). Meta-analysis of biofeedback for tension-type headache: Efficacy, specificity, and treatment moderators. *Journal of Consulting and Clinical Psychology, 76,* 379–396.

Neuberg, S. L., Kenrick, D. T., & Schaller, M. (2010). Evolutionary social psychology. In S. T. Fiske, D. T. Gilbert, & G. Lindzey (Eds.), *Handbook of social psychology* (5th ed., Vol. 2, pp. 761–798). Hoboken, NJ: Wiley.

Neumann, C. S., Grimes, K., Walker, E. F., & Baum, K. (1995). Developmental pathways to schizophrenia: Behavioral subtypes. *Journal of Abnormal Psychology, 104,* 558–566.

Neumann, D. L., & Kitlertsirivatana, E. (2010). Exposure to a novel context after extinction causes a renewal of extinguished conditioned responses: Implications for the treatment of fear. *Behaviour Research and Therapy, 48,* 565–570. doi:10.1016/j.brat.2010.03.002.

Neumeister, A., Bain, E., Nugent, A. C., Carson, R. E., Bonne, O., Luckenbaugh, D. A., et al. (2004). Reduced serotonin type 1A receptor binding in panic disorder. *Journal of Neuroscience, 24,* 589–591.

Neves-Pereira, M., Cheung, J. K., Pasdar, A., Zhang, F., Breen, G., Yates, P., et al. (2005). BDNF gene is a risk factor for schizophrenia in a Scottish population. *Molecular Psychiatry, 10,* 208–212.

Nevicka, B., Velden, F. S. T., De Hoogh, A. H. B., & Van Vianen, A. E. M. (2011). Reality at odds with perceptions: Narcissistic leaders and group performance. *Psychological Science (Sage Publications Inc.), 22*(10), 1259–1264. doi:10.1177/0956797611417259.

Nevin, J.A., Grace, R., Holland S, & McLean A.P. (2001) Variable-ratio versus variable-interval schedules: response rate, resistance to change, and preference. *Journal of the Experimental Analysis of Behavior, 76,* 43–74.

Neville, L. (2012). Do economic equality and generalized trust inhibit academic dishonesty? Evidence from state-level search-engine queries. *Psychological Science, 23*(4), 339–345. doi:10.1177/0956797611435980.

New Israeli law bans underweight models in ads. (2012, 20 March). Retrieved from http://www.foxnews.com/health/2012/03/20/new-israeli-law-bans-underweight-models-in-ads/?test=latestnews.

Newberg, A., Alavi, A., Baime, M., Pourdehnad, M., Santanna, J., & d'Aquili, E. (2001). The measurement of regional cerebral blood flow during the complex cognitive task of meditation: A preliminary SPECT study. *Psychiatry Research, 106,* 113–122.

Newcombe, N., & Fox, N. A. (1994). Infantile amnesia: Through a glass darkly. *Child Development, 65,* 31–40.

Newcombe, N. S., Ambady, N., Eccles, J., Gomez, L., et al. (2009). Psychology's role in mathematics and science education. *American Psychologist, 64,* 538–550.

Newell, A., & Simon, H. A. (1972). *Human problem solving.* Englewood Cliffs, NJ: Prentice Hall.

Newhouse, P., Newhouse, C., & Astur, R. S. (2007). Sex differences in visual-spatial learning using a virtual water maze in pre-pubertal children. *Behavioural Brain Research, 183,* 1–7.

Newman, E. J., & Loftus, E. F. (2012). Clarkian logic on trial. *Perspectives on Psychological Science, 7*(3), 260–263. doi:10.1177/1745691612442907.

Newnam, S., Griffin, M. A., & Mason, C. (2008). Safety in work vehicles: A multilevel study linking safety values and individual predictors to work-related driving crashes. *Journal of Applied Psychology, 93,* 632–644.

Newpher, T. M., & Ehlers, M. D. (2008). Glutamate receptor dynamics in dendritic microdomains. *Neuron, 58*(4), 472–497.

Newsom, J. T., Mahan, T. L., Rook, K. S., & Krause, N. (2008). Stable negative social exchanges and health. *Health Psychology, 27,* 78–86.

Ng, C. H., Chong, S., Lambert, T., Fan, A., Hackett, L. P., Mahendran, R., et al. (2005). An inter-ethnic comparison study of clozapine dosage, clinical response, and plasma levels. *International Clinical Psychopharmacology, 20,* 163–168.

Ng, J. Y. Y., Ntoumanis, N., Thøgersen-Ntoumani, C., Deci, E. L., Ryan, R. M., Duda , J. L., & Williams, G. C. (2012). Self-determination theory applied to health contexts: A meta-analysis. *Perspectives on Psychological Science, 7.* Published online first. DOI: 10.1177/1745691612447309.

Ng, K.-Y., Ang, S., & Chan, K.-Yin. (2008). Personality and leader effectiveness: A moderated mediation model of leadership self-efficacy, job demands, and job autonomy. *Journal of Applied Psychology, 93,* 733–743.

Nguyen, B. H., Pérusse, D., Paquet, J., Petit, D., Boivin, M., Tremblay, R. E., & Montplaisir, J. (2008). Sleep terrors in children: A prospective study of twins. *Pediatrics, 122,* e1164–e1167.

Nguyen, N., Karipineni, F., Masoomi, H., Laugenour, K., Reavis, K., Hohmann, S., & Varela, E. (2011). Increasing utilization of laparoscopic gastric banding in the adolescent: data from academic medical centers, 2002–2009. *The American Surgeon, 77*(11), 1510–1514.

Nicassio, P. M., Meyerowitz, B. E., & Kerns, R. D. (2004). The future of health psychology interventions. *Health Psychology, 23,* 132–137.

NICHD Early Child Care Research Network. (2001, April). *Further explorations of the detected effects of quantity of early child care on socioemotional adjustment.* Paper presented at the biennial meetings of the Society for Research in Child Development, Minneapolis.

NICHD Early Child Care Research Network. (2006). Infant-mother attachment classification: Risk and protection in relation to changing maternal caregiving quality. *Developmental Psychology, 42,* 38–58.

NICHD Early Child Care Research Network. (2005). *Child care and child development: Results from the NICHD Study of Early Child Care and Youth Development.* New York: Guilford.

NICHD Early Child Care Research Network. (2006a). Infant-mother attachment classification: Risk and protection in relation to changing maternal caregiving quality. *Developmental Psychology, 42,* 38–58.

NICHD Early Child Care Research Network. (2006b). Child-care effect sizes for the NICHD study of early child care and youth development. *American Psychologist, 61,* 99–116.

Nichols, M. P. (2007). *Family therapy: Concepts and methods* (8th ed.). Boston, MA: Allyn & Bacon.

Nicholson, A., Fuhrer, R., & Marmot, M. (2005). Psychological distress as a predictor of CHD events in men: The effect of persistence and components of risk. *Psychosomatic Medicine, 67,* 522–530.

Nickell, J. (1997, January/February). Sleuthing a psychic sleuth. *Skeptical Inquirer, 21,* 18–19.

Nickell, J. (2011). First case of spontaneous human combustion? *Skeptical Inquirer, 36,* 6-7.

Nickerson, R. A., & Adams, M. J. (1979). Long-term memory for a common object. *Cognitive Psychology, 11,* 287–307.

Nicpon, M., & Pfeiffer, S. (2011). High-ability students: New ways to conceptualize giftedness and provide psychological services in the schools. *Journal of Applied School Psychology, 27*(4), 293–305. doi:10.1080/15377903.2011.616579.

Niederhoffer, K. G., & Pennebaker, J. W. (2002). Sharing one's story: On the benefits of writing or talking about emotional experience. In C. R. Snyder & S. J. Lopez (Eds.), *Handbook of positive psychology* (pp. 573–583). London: Oxford University Press.

Niederman, R., & Richards, D. (2005). Evidence-based dentistry: Concepts and implementation. *Journal of the American College of Dentistry, 72,* 37–41.

Nienhuys, J. W. (2001). Spontaneous human combustion: Requiem for Phyllis. *Skeptical Inquirer, 25,* 28–34.

Nieuwenhuis, I. L. & Takashima, A. (2011). The role of the ventromedial prefrontal cortex in memory consolidation. *Behavioural Brain Research, 218*(2), 325–334.

Nievar, M. A., & Becker, B. J. (2008). Sensitivity as a privileged predictor of attachment: A second perspective on De Wolff and Van IJzendoorn's meta-analysis. *Social Development, 17,* 102–114.

Nigg, J. T. (2001). Is ADHD a disinhibitory disorder? *Psychological Bulletin, 127,* 571–598.

Nigg, J., Nikolas, M., & Burt, S. (2010). Measured gene-by-environment interaction in relation to attention-deficit/hyperactivity disorder. *Journal of the American Academy of Child & Adolescent Psychiatry, 49*(9), 863–873. doi:10.1016/j.jaac.2010.01.025.

Nigg, J. T. (2010). Attention-deficit/hyperactivity disorder: Endophenotypes, structure, and etiological pathways. *Current Directions In Psychological Science, 19*(1), 24–29. doi:10.1177/0963721409359282.

Niiya, Y., Crocker, J., & Bartmess, E. N. (2004). From vulnerability to resilience: Learning orientations buffer contingent self-esteem from failure. *Psychological Science, 15,* 801–805.

Nijstad, B. A., Stroebe, W., & Lodewijkx, H. F. M. (2003). Production blocking and idea generation: Does blocking interfere with cognitive processes? *Journal of Experimental Social Psychology, 39,* 531–548.

Nikolas, M. A., & Burt, S. A. (2010). Genetic and environmental influences on ADHD symptom dimensions of inattention and hyperactivity: A meta-analysis. *Journal of Abnormal Psychology, 119,* 1–17.

Nikolas, M., Klump, K. L., & Burt, S. A. (2011). Youth appraisals of inter-parental conflict and genetic and environmental contributions to attention-deficit hyperactivity disorder: Examination of GxE effects in a twin sample. *Journal of Abnormal Child Psychology,* 1–12. doi:10.1007/s10802-011-9583-6

Nikulina, V., Widom, C., & Czaja, S. (2011). The role of childhood neglect and childhood poverty in predicting mental health, academic achievement and crime in adulthood. *American Journal of Community Psychology, 48,* 309–321. doi:10.1007/s10464-010-9385-y

Nilsson, G. (1996, November). Some forms of memory improve as people age. *APA Monitor, 27.*

Niparko, J. K., Tobey, E. A., Th al, D. J., Eisenberg, L. S., et al. (2010). Spoken language development in children following cochlear implantation. *Journal of the American Medical Association, 303,* 1498–1506.

Nir, Y. & Tononi. G. (2010). Dreaming and the brain: From phenomenology to neurophysiology. *Trends in Cognitive Science, 14*(2), 88–100.

Nisbett, R. E. (2005). Heredity, environment, and race differences in IQ: A commentary on Rushton and Jensen (2005). *Psychology, Public Policy, and Law, 11*(2), 302–310. doi:10.1037/1076-8971.11.2.302.

Nisbett, R. E., Aronson, J., Blair, C., Dickens, W., Flynn, J., Halpern, D. F., & Turkheimer, E. (2012). Intelligence: New findings and theoretical developments. *American Psychologist, 67*(2), 130–159. doi:10.1037/a0026699.

Nisbett, R. E. (2003). *The geography of thought.* New York: The Free Press.

Nisbett, R. E., & Masuda, T. (2007). Culture and point of view. *Intellectica, 46*(2), 153–172.

Nishio, Y., Hashimoto, M., Ishii, K., & Mori, E. (2011). Neuroanatomy of a neurobehavioral disturbance in the left anterior thalamic infarction. *Journal of Neurology, Neurosurgery, and Psychiatry, 82*(11), 1195–1200.

Nishino S. (2011). Hypothalamus, hypocretins/orexin, and vigilance control. *Handbook of Clinical Neurology, 99,* 765–82.

Noar, S. M., Crosby, R., Benac, C., Snow, G., & Troutman, A. (2011). Application of the attitude-social influence-efficacy model to condom use among African-American STD clinic patients: Implications for tailored health communication. *AIDS and Behavior, 15*(5), 1045–1057. doi:10.1007/s10461-009-9599-x.

Noble, H. B. (2000, January 25). Outgrowth of new field of tissue engineering. *New York Times.*

Nock, M. K., Kazdin, A. E., Hirpi, E., & Kessler, R. C. (2006). Prevalence, subtypes and correlates of DSM-IV conduct disorder in the National Comorbidity Survey Replication. *Psychological Medicine, 36,* 699–710.

Nock, M. K., & Kessler, R. C. (2006). Prevalence of and risk factors for suicide attempts versus suicide gestures: Analysis of the National Comorbidity Survey. *Journal of Abnormal Psychology, 115,* 616–623.

Noftle, E. E., & Robins, R. W. (2007). Personality predictors of academic outcomes: Big five correlates of GPA and SAT scores. *Journal of Personality and Social Psychology, 93,* 116–130.

Noftle, E. E., & Shaver, P. R. (2006). Attachment dimensions and the big five personality traits: Associations and comparative ability to predict relationship quality. *Journal of Research in Personality, 40,* 179–208.

Nolen-Hoeksema, S. (1990). *Sex differences in depression.* Stanford, CA: Stanford University Press.

Nolen-Hoeksema, S. (2001). Gender differences in depression. *Current Directions in Psychological Science, 10,* 173–176.

Nolen-Hoeksema, S. (2006). The etiology of gender differences in depression. In C. M. Mazure & G. P. Keita (Eds.), *Understanding depression in women: Applying empirical research to practice and policy* (pp. 9–43). Washington, DC: American Psychological Association.

Nolen-Hoeksma, S., Morrow, J., & Fredrickson, N. (1993). Response styles and the duration of episodes of depressed mood. *Journal of Abnormal Psychology, 102,* 20–28.

Nolen-Hoeksema, S., & Watkins, E. R. (2011). A heuristic for developing transdiagnostic models of psychopathology: Explaining multifinality and divergent trajectories. *Perspectives on Psychological Science, 6*(6), 589–609. doi:10.1177/1745691611419672.

Nolin, R. (2011). Heavier passengers force new guidelines on occupancy rates. *Palm Beach Post.* Retrieved from http://blogs.palmbeachpost.com/travelsmart/2011/04/05/heavier-passengers-force-new-guidelines-on-occupancy-rates/.

Noll, R. B. (1994). Hypnotherapy for warts in children and adolescents. *Journal of Developmental and Behavioral Pediatrics, 15*(3), 170–173.

Nomura, H., Inoue, S., Kamimura, N., Shimodera, S., Mino, Y., et al. (2005). A cross-cultural study on expressed emotion in careers of people with dementia and schizophrenia: Japan and England. *Social Psychiatry and Psychiatric Epidemiology, 40,* 564–570.

Norberg, M. M., Krystal, J. H., & Tolin, D. F. (2008). A meta-analysis of D-Cycloserine and the facilitation of fear extinction and exposure therapy. *Biological Psychiatry, 63,* 1118–1126.

Nørby, S., Lange, M., & Larsen, A. (2010). Forgetting to forget: On the duration of voluntary suppression of neutral and emotional memories. *Acta Psychologica, 133*(1), 73–80. doi:10.1016/j.actpsy.2009.10.002.

Norcross, J. C. (2006). Integrating self-help into psychotherapy: 16 practical suggestions. *Professional Psychology: Research and Practice, 37,* 683–693.

Norcross, J. C. (Ed.) (2011). *Psychotherapy relationships that work: Evidence-based responsiveness* (2nd ed.). New York: Oxford University Press.

Norcross, J. C. (2001). Purposes, processes and products of the task force on empirically supported therapy relationships. *Psychotherapy: Theory, Research, Practice, Training, 38*(4), 345–356.

Norcross, J. C. (2002). *Psychotherapy relationships that work.* New York: Oxford University Press.

Norcross, J. C., Beutler, L. E., & Levant, R. F. (2005). Prologue. In J. C. Norcross, L. E. Beutler, & R. F. Levant (Eds.), *Evidence-based practices in mental health: Debate and dialogue on the fundamental questions* (pp. 3–12). Washington, DC: American Psychological Association.

Norcross, J. C., Koocher, G. P., Fala, N. C., & Wexler, H. K. (2010). What does not work? Expert consensus on discredited treatments in the addictions. *Journal of Addiction Medicine, 4,* 174–180.

Norcross, J. C., Santrock, J. W., Campbell, L. F., Smith, T. P., et al. (2000). *Authoritative guide to self-help resources in mental health.* New York: Guilford Press.

Norcross, J. C., & Wampold, B. E. (2011). What works for whom: Tailoring psychotherapy to the person. *Journal of Clinical Psychology: In Session, 67,* 127–132.

Nordgren, L., & Chou, E. (2011). The push and pull of temptation: the bidirectional influence of temptation on self-control. *Psychological Science, 22*(11), 1386–1390.

Nordsletten, A. E., & Mataix-Cols, D. (2012). Hoarding versus collecting: Where does pathology diverge from play? *Clinical Psychology Review, 32*(3), 165–176. doi:10.1016/j.cpr.2011.12.003.

Norenzayan, A., & Lee, A. (2010). It was meant to happen: Explaining cultural variations in fate attributions. *Journal of Personality and Social Psychology, 98,* 702–720.

Norman, T., & Olver, J. S. (2004). New formulations of existing antidepressants: Advantages in the management of depression. *CNS Drugs, 18,* 505–520.

North, A. C. (2011). The effect of background music on the taste of wine. *British Journal of Psychology,* doi:10.1111/j.2044-8295.2011.02072.x.

North, M. M., North, S. M., & Burwick, C. B. (2008). Virtual reality therapy: A vision for a new paradigm. In L. L'Abate (Ed.), *Toward a science of clinical psychology: Laboratory evaluations and interventions* (pp. 307–320). Hauppauge, NY: Nova Science Publishers.

Norton, A., Zipse, L., Marchina, S., & Schlaug, G. (2009) Melodic intonation therapy: shared insights on how it is done and why it might help. *Ann N Y Acad Sci 1169:* 431–436.

Nosarti, C., Reichenberg, A., Murray, R. M., Cnattingius, S., Lambe, M. P., Yin, L., MacCabe, J., Rifkin, L., & Hultman, C. M. (2012). Preterm birth and psychiatric disorders in young adult life. *Archives of General Psychiatry, 69*(6), 610–617. doi:10.1001/archgenpsychiatry.2011.1374.

Nosko, A., Tieu, T.-T., Lawford, H., & Pratt, M. W. (2011). How do I love thee? Let me count the ways: Parenting during adolescence, attachment styles, and romantic narratives in emerging adulthood. *Developmental Psychology, 47,* 645–657.

Nourkova, V. V., Bernstein, D. M., & Loftus, E. F. (2004). Biography becomes autobiography: Distorting the subjective past. *American Journal of Psychology, 117,* 65–80.

Novick, K. K., & Novick, J. (2005). *Working with parents makes therapy work.* Northvale, NJ: Aronson.

Nowak, M. A., Komarova, N. L., & Niyogi, P. (2001). Evolution of universal grammar. *Science, 291,* 114–118.

Noyes, R., & Hoehn-Saric, R. (2006). *The anxiety disorders.* London: Cambridge University Press.

Nugent, N. R., Tyrka, A. R., Carpenter, L. L., & Price, L. H. (2011). Gene-environment interactions: Early life stress and risk for depressive and anxiety disorders. *Psychopharmacology, 214,* 175–196. doi:10.1007/s00213-010-2151-x.

Nunes, L. D., & Weinstein, Y. (2012). Testing improves true recall and protects against the build-up of proactive interference without increasing false recall. *Memory, 20*(2), 138–154. doi:10.1080/09658211.2011.648198.

Nurnberger, J. I., Jr., Foroud, T., Flury, L., Su, J., Meyer, E. T., Hu, K., et al. (2001). Evidence for a locus on chromosome 1 that influences vulnerability to alcoholism and affective disorder. *American Journal of Psychiatry, 158,* 718–724.

Nutt, D. J. (2005a). Death by tricyclic: The real antidepressant scandal? *Journal of Psychopharmacology, 19,* 123–124.

Nutt, D. J. (2005b). Overview of diagnosis and drug treatments of anxiety disorders. *CNS Spectrums, 10,* 49–56.

Nyberg, L., Petersson, K. M., Nilsson, L. G., Sandblom, J., Aberg, C., & Ingvar, M. (2001). Reactivation of motor brain areas during explicit memory for actions. *Neuroimage, 14,* 521–528.

Nye, C. D., Roberts, B. W., Saucier, G., & Zhou, X. (2008). Testing the measurement equivalence of personality adjective items across cultures. *Journal of Research in Personality, 42*(6), 1524–1536.

Nye, C. D., Su, R., Rounds, J., & Drasgow, F. (2012). Vocational interests and performance: A quantitative summary of over 60 years of research. *Perspectives on Psychological Science, 7,* 384–403. doi:10.1177/1745691612449021.

Oatley, K. (1993). Those to whom evil is done. In R. S. Wyer & T. K. Srull (Eds.), *Toward a general theory of anger and emotional aggression: Advances in social cognition* (Vol. 6). Hillsdale, NJ: Erlbaum.

Oberauer, K., & Hein, L. (2012). Attention to information in working memory. *Current Directions in Psychological Science, 21*(3), 164–169. doi:10.1177/0963721412444727.

Oberfeld, D., & Hecht, H. (2011). Fashion Versus Perception: The Impact of Surface Lightness on the Perceived Dimensions of Interior Space. *Human Factors, 53*(3), 284–298. doi:10.1177/0018720811407331.

O'Brien, E., & Ellsworth, P. C. (2012). Saving the last for best: A positivity bias for end experiences. *Psychological Science, 23*(2), 163–165. doi:10.1177/0956797611427408.

O'Brien, J. T. (2006). Depression and comorbidity. *American Journal of Psychiatry, 14,* 187–190.

O'Brien, R. J. (2011). Vascular dementia: atherosclerosis, cognition and Alzheimer's disease. *Current Alzheimer Research, 8*(4), 341–344.

O'Brien, T. L. (1991, September 2). Computers help thwart "groupthink" that plagues meetings. *Chicago Sun Times.*

Ocker, R., Huang, H., Benbunan-Fich, R., & Hiltz, S. (2011). Leadership dynamics in partially distributed teams: An exploratory study of the effects of configuration and distance. *Group Decision & Negotiation, 20*(3), 273–292. doi:10.1007/s10726-009-9180-z.

O'Connell, K. (2011). From black box to 'open' brain: Law, neuroimaging and disability discrimination. *Griffith Law Review, 20*(4), 883–904.

Oden, M. H. (1968). The fulfillment of promise: 40-year follow-up of the Terman gifted group. *Genetic Psychology Monographs, 17,* 3–93.

Odgers, C. L., Caspi, A., Nagin, D. S., Piquero, A. R., Slutske, W. S., Milne, B. J., Dickson, N., Poulton, R., & Moffitt, T. E. (2008). Is it important to prevent early exposure to drugs and alcohol among adolescents? *Psychological Science, 19,* 1037–1044.

O'Donohue, W., Fisher, J. E., & Hayes, S. C. (Eds.). (2003). *Cognitive behavior therapy: Applying empirically supported techniques in your practice.* New York: Wiley.

O'Driscoll, M., Brough, P., & Kalliath, T. (2006). Work-family conflict and facilitation. In F. Jones, R. J. Burke, & M. Westman (Eds.), *Work-life balance: A psychological perspective* (pp. 117–142). New York: Psychology Press.

Ogawa, N. & Ueki, H. (2007). Clinical importance of caffeine dependence and abuse. *Psychiatry and Clinical Neurosciences, 61*(3), 263–268.

Ogden, C. L., Carroll, M. D., Kitt, B., K., & Flegal, K. M. (2012). *Prevalence of obesity in the United States, 2009–2010.* (NCHS Data Brief No. 82). Retrieved from http://www.cdc.gov/nchs/data/databriefs/db82.pdf.

Oh, I., & Berry, C. M. (2009). The five-factor model of personality and managerial performance: Validity gains through the use of 360-degree performance ratings. *Journal of Applied Psychology, 94*, 1498–1513.

Ohayon, M. M., & Roth, T. (2003). Place of chronic insomnia in the course of depressive and anxiety disorders. *Journal of Psychiatric Research, 37*, 9–15.

Öhman, A., & Mineka, S. (2001). Fears, phobias, and preparedness: Toward an evolved module of fear and fear learning. *Psychological Review, 108*, 483–522.

Öhman, A., & Mineka, S. (2003). The malicious serpent: Snakes as a prototypical stimulus for an evolved module of fear. *Current Directions in Psychological Science, 12*, 5–9.

Öhman, A., & Soares, J. J. (1993). On the automatic nature of phobic fear: Conditioned electrodermal responses to masked fear-relevant stimuli. *Journal of Abnormal Psychology, 102*(1), 121–132.

Öhman, A., & Soares, J. J. (1994). "Unconscious anxiety": Phobic responses to masked stimuli. *Journal of Abnormal Psychology, 103*(2), 231–240.

Öhman, A., & Soares, J. J. F. (1998). Emotional conditioning to masked stimuli: Expectancies for aversive outcomes following nonrecognized fear-relevant stimuli. *Journal of Experimental Psychology: General, 127*(1), 69–82.

Öhman, A., Dimberg, U., & Öst, L. G. (1985). Animal and social phobias: A laboratory model. In S. Reiss & R. R. Bootzin (Eds.), *Theoretical issues in behavior therapy.* Orlando, FL: Academic Press.

Ohring, R., Graber, J. A., & Brooks-Gunn, J. (2002). Girls' recurrent and concurrent body dissatisfaction: Correlates and consequences over 8 years. *International Journal of Eating Disorders, 31*(4), 404–415.

Ohta, H., Yamazaki, S., & McMahon, D. G. (2005). Constant light desynchronizes mammalian clock neurons. *Nature Neuroscience, 8*, 267–269.

Oishi, S., Diener, E., Lucas, R. E., & Suh, E. M. (1999). Cross-cultural variations in predictors of life-satisfaction: Perspectives from needs and values. *Personality and Social Psychology Bulletin, 25*, 980–990.

Oishi, S., & Schimmack, U. (2010). Culture and well-being: A new inquiry into the psychological wealth of nations. *Perspectives On Psychological Science, 5*(4), 463–471. doi:10.1177/1745691610375561.

Oishi, S., Schimmack, U., & Diener, E. (2012). Progressive taxation and the subjective well-being of nations. *Psychological Science, 23*(1), 86–92.

Olatunji, B. O. (2006). Evaluative learning and emotional responding to fearful and disgusting stimuli in spider phobia. *Journal of Anxiety Disorders, 20*, 858–876.

Olatunji, B. O. (2008). New directions on research on health anxiety and hypochondriasis: Commentary on a timely special series. *Journal of Cognitive Psychotherapy, 22*, 183–190.

Oldenberg, P.-A., Zheleznyak, A., Fang, Y.-F., Lagenaur, C. F., Gresham, H. D., & Lindberg, F. P. (2000). Role of CD47 as a marker of self on red blood cells. *Science, 288*, 2051–2054.

Olds, J. (1973). Commentary on positive reinforcement produced by electrical stimulation of septal areas and other regions of rat brain. In E. S. Valenstein (Ed.), *Brain stimulation and motivation: Research and commentary.* Glenview, IL: Scott, Foresman.

Olds, J., & Milner, P. (1954). Positive reinforcement produced by electrical stimulation of septal areas and other regions of the rat brain. *Journal of Comparative and Physiological Psychology, 47*, 419–427.

O'Leary, D. S., Block, R. I., Koeppel, J. A., Flaum, M., Schulz, S. K., Andreason, N. C., et al. (2002). Effects of smoking marijuana on brain perfusion and cognition. *Neuropsychopharmacology, 26*, 802–816.

Olfson, M., Blanco, C., Liu, L., Moreno, C., & Laje, G. (2006). National trends in the outpatient treatment of children and adolescents with antipsychotic drugs. *Archives of General Psychiatry, 63*, 679–685.

Olfson, M., Marcus, S. C., & Shaffer, D. (2006). Antidepressant drug therapy and suicide in depressed children and adolescents: A case-control study. *Archives of General Psychiatry, 63*, 865–872.

Oliner, S. P., & Oliner, P. M. (1988). *The altruistic personality: Rescuers of Jews in Nazi Europe.* New York: Free Press.

Olio, K. A. (1994). Truth in memory. *American Psychologist, 49*, 442–443.

Oliver, R., Wright, G. & Kendall, E. (2011). Parental attachment and its relationship to contextualised trait expression and mean-corrected cross-context trait variability. *Personality and Individual Differences, 50*, 547–552.

Olshansky, S. J., Passaro, D. J., Hershow, R. C., Layden, J., Carnes, B. A., Brody, J., et al. (2005). A potential decline in life expectancy in the United States in the 21st century. *New England Journal of Medicine, 352*, 1138–1145.

Olson, I. R., Rao, H., Moore, K. S., Wang, J., Detre, J. A., & Aguirre, G. K. (2006). Using perfusion fMRI to measure continuous changes in neural activity with learning. *Brain and Cognition, 60*, 262–271.

Olson, J. M., & Stone, J. (2005). The influence of behavior on attitudes. In D. Albarracín, B. T. Johnson, & M. P. Zanna (Eds.), *Handbook of attitudes* (pp. 223–271). Mahwah, NJ: Erlbaum.

Olson, J. M., Vernon, P. A., Harris, J. A., & Jang, K. L. (2001). The heritability of attitudes: A study of twins. *Journal of Personality and Social Psychology, 80*, 845–860.

Olson, L. (1997). Regeneration in the adult central nervous system. *Nature Medicine, 3*, 1329–1335.

Olsson, A., Ebert, J. P., Banaji, M. R., & Phelps, E. A. (2005). The role of social groups in the persistence of learned fear. *Science, 309*, 785–787.

Olsson, C. J., Jonsson, B., Larsson, A., & Nyberg, L. (2008). Motor representations and practice affect brain systems underlying imagery: An FMRI study of internal imagery in novices and active high jumpers. *The Open Neuroimaging Journal, 2*, 5–13.

Oltmanns, T. F., & Turkheimer, E. (2009). Person perception and personality pathology. *Current Directions in Psychological Science, 18*, 32–36.

Ölveczky, B. P., Baccus, S. A., & Meister, M. (2003). Segregation of object and background motion in the retina. *Nature, 423*, 401–408.

Oman, D., Hedberg, J., & Thoreson, C. E. (2006). Passage meditation reduces perceived stress in health professionals: A randomized controlled trial. *Journal of Consulting and Clinical Psychology, 74*, 714–719.

O'Neill, H. (2000, September 24). After rape, jail—a friendship forms. *St. Petersburg Times*, pp. 1A, 14A.

Ones, D. S., Visweswaran, C., & Dilchert, S. (2005) Personality at Work: Raising awareness and correcting misconceptions. *Human Performance, 18*, 389–404.

Ones, D., & Visweswaran, C. (2001). Personality at work: Criterion focused occupational personality scales used in personnel selection. In R. Hogan & B. Roberts (Eds.), *Personality psychology in the workplace* (pp. 63–92). Washington, DC: American Psychological Association.

Ong, A. D. (2010). Pathways linking positive emotion and health in later life. *Current Directions in Psychological Science, 19*(6), 358–362. doi:10.1177/0963721410388805.

Onishi, K. H., & Baillargeon, R. (2005). Do 15-month-old infants understand false beliefs? *Science, 308*, 255–258.

Onyper, S. V., Carr, T. L., Farrar, J. S., & Floyd, B. R. (2011). Cognitive advantages of chewing gum. Now you see them, now you don't. *Appetite, 57*(2), 321–328. doi:10.1016/j.appet.2011.05.313.

Operario, D., & Fiske, S. T. (2001). Stereotypes: Processes, structures, content, and context. In R. Brown & S. Gaertner (Eds.), *Blackwell handbook in social psychology: Intergroup processes* (pp. 22–44). Oxford, UK: Blackwell.

Oppel, S. (2000, March 5). Managing ABCs like a CEO. *St. Petersburg Times*, 1A, 12–13A.

Oquendo, M. A., Ellis, S. P., Greenwald, S., Malone, K. M., Weissman, M. M., & Mann, J. J. (2001). Ethnic and sex differences in suicide rates relative to major depression in the United States. *American Journal of Psychiatry, 158*, 1652–1658.

Oquendo, M. A., & Mann, J. J. (2000). The biology of impulsivity and suicidality. *Psychiatric Clinics of North America, 23*, 11–25.

Orban, P., Rauchs, G., Balteau, E., Degueldre, C., Luxen, A., Maquet, P., et al. (2006). Sleep after spatial learning promotes covert reorganization of brain activity. *Proceedings of the National Academy of Sciences, 103*, 7124–7129.

O'Reardon, J. P., Fontecha, J. F., Cristancho, M. A., & Newman, S. (2007). Unexpected reduction in migraine and psychogenic headaches following rTMS treatment for major depression: A report of two cases. *CNS Spectrums, 12*, 921–925.

O'Reardon, J. P., Solvason, H. B., Janicak, P. G., Sampson, S., Isenberg, K. E., Nahas, Z., McDonald, W. M., Avery, D., Fitzgerald, P. B., Loo, C., Demitrack, M. A., George, M. S., & Sackeim, H. A. (2007). Efficacy and safety of transcranial magnetic stimulation in the acute treatment of major depression: A multisite randomized controlled trial. *Biological Psychiatry, 62*(11), 1208–1216.

O'Reilly, R. C. (2006). Biologically based computational models of high-level cognition. *Science, 314*, 91–94.

Organ, D. W., Podsakoff, P. M., & MacKenzie, S. B. (2006). *Organizational citizenship behavior: Its nature, antecedents, and consequences.* Thousand Oaks, CA: Sage.

Orgilés, M., Espada, J., García-Fernández, J., & Méndez, X. (2009). Relación entre miedos escolares y síntomas de ansiedad por separación infantil. *Revista Mexicana de Psicología, 26*(1), 17–25.

Orgilés, M., Espada, J., García-Fernández, J. M., Méndez, X., & Dolores Hidalgo, M. M. (2011). Most feared situations related to separation anxiety and characteristics by age and gender in late childhood. *Anales de Psicología, 27*(1), 80–85.

Oriña, M. M., W Collins, W. A., Simpson, J. A., Salvatore, J. E., Haydon, K. C., & Kim, J. S. (2011). Developmental and dyadic perspectives on commitment in adult romantic relationships. *Psychological Science, 22*, 908–915. doi:10.1177/0956797611410573.

Ormiston, M. E., & Wong, E. M. (2012). The gleam of the double-edged sword: The benefits of subgroups for organizational ethics. *Psychological Science, 23*, 400–403. doi:10.1177/0956797611431575.

Orne, M. T., & Evans, F. J. (1965). Social control in the psychological experiment: Antisocial behavior and hypnosis. *Journal of Personality and Social Psychology, 1*, 189–200.

Orne, M. T., Sheehan, P. W., & Evans, F. J. (1968). Occurrence of posthypnotic behavior outside the experimental setting. *Journal of Personality and Social Psychology, 9*, 189–196.

O'Rourke, M. (2011). The NFL fights concussions. *Risk Management* (00355593), *58*(3), 36.

Orth-Gomer, K., Schneiderman, N., Wang, H.-X., Walldin, C., et al. (2009). Stress reduction prolongs life in women with coronary disease: Th e Stockholm Women's Intervention Trial for Coronary Heart Disease (SWITCHD). *Circulation: Cardiovascular Quality and Outcomes, 2*, 25–32.

Oshima, N. (2008). Beneficial and adverse effects of pharmacotherapy with risperidone on behavioral and psychological symptoms of dementia (BPSD). *Psychogeriatrics, 8*(4), 175–177.

Öst, L.-G. (1978). Behavioral treatment of thunder and lightning phobia. *Behavior Research and Therapy, 16*, 197–207.

Öst, L.-G., Hellström, K., & Kåver, A. (1992). One- versus five-session exposure in the treatment of needle phobia. *Behavior Therapy, 23*, 263–282.

Öst, L.-G., Svensson, L., Hellström, K., & Lindwall, R. (2001). One-session treatment of specific phobias in youths: A randomized clinical trial. *Journal of Consulting and Clinical Psychology, 69*, 814–824.

Ostfeld, B. M., Perl, H., Esposito, L., Hempstead, K., et al. (2006). Sleep environment, positional, lifestyle, and demographic characteristics associated with bed sharing in sudden infant death syndrome cases: A population-based study. *Pediatrics, 118*, 2051–2059.

Ostrov, J. M. (2006). Deception and subtypes of aggression during early childhood. *Journal of Experimental Child Psychology, 93*, 322–336.

Ostrovsky, Y., Meyers, E., Ganesh, S., Mathur, U., & Sinha, P. (2009). Visual parsing after recovery from blindness. *Psychological Science, 20,* 1484–1491.

Otgaar, H., Peters, M., & Howe, M. L. (2012). Dividing attention lowers children's but increases adults' false memories. *Journal of Experimental Psychology: Learning, Memory, and Cognition, 38*(1), 204–210. doi:10.1037/a0025160.

Otgaar, H., Verschuere, B., Meijer, E. H., & van Oorsouw, K. (2012). The origin of children's implanted false memories: Memory traces or compliance? *Acta Psychologica, 139*(3), 397–403. doi:10.1016/j.actpsy.2012.01.002.

Otto, M. W., Bruce, S. E., & Deckersbach, T. (2005). Benzodiazepine use, cognitive impairment, and cognitive-behavioral therapy for anxiety disorders: Issues in the treatment of a patient in need. *Journal of Clinical Psychiatry, 66*(Suppl. 2), 34–38.

Oudiette, D., De Cock, V. C., Lavault, S., Leu, S., Vidailhet, M., & Arnulf, I. (2009). Nonviolent elaborate behaviors may also occur in REM sleep behavior disorder. *Neurology, 72,* 551–557.

Ouimet, A. J., Gawronski, B., & Dozois, D. J. A. (2009). Cognitive vulnerability to anxiety: A review and an integrative model. *Clinical Psychology Review, 29,* 459–470.

Overbeek, G., Stattin, H., Vermulst, A., Ha, T., & Engels, R. C. M. E. (2007). Parent-child relationships, partner relationships, and emotional adjustment: A birth-to-maturity prospective study. *Developmental Psychology, 43,* 429–437.

Overmier, J. B. (2002). On learned helplessness. *Integrative Physiological & Behavioral Science, 37,* 4–8.

Overmier, J. B., & Seligman, M. E. P. (1967). Effects of inescapable shock upon subsequent escape and avoidance learning. *Journal of Comparative and Physiological Psychology, 63,* 23–33.

Overton, D. A. (1984). State dependent learning and drug discriminations. In L. L. Iverson, S. D. Iverson, & S. H. Snyder (Eds.), *Handbook of psychopharmacology* (Vol. 18). New York: Plenum.

Ovsiew, F. (2006). An overview of the psychiatric approach to conversion disorder. In M. Hallet et al. (Eds.), *Psychogenic movement disorders: Neurology and neuropsychiatry* (pp. 112–121). New York: Lippincott Williams & Wilkins.

Owens, S. G., Garner, I. C., Loftin, J., van Blerk, N., & Ermin, K. (2011). Changes in physical activity and fitness after 3 months of home WII Fit use. *Journal of Strength & Conditioning Research, 25*(11), 3191–3197.

Pachankis, J. E., & Goldfried, M. R. (2004). Clinical issues in working with lesbian, gay, and bisexual clients. *Psychotherapy: Theory, Research, Practice, Training, 41,* 227–246.

Pacheco-Unguetti, A., Acosta, A., Callejas, A., & Lupiáñez, J. (2010). Attention and Anxiety: Different Attentional Functioning Under State and Trait Anxiety. *Psychological Science, 21*(2), 298–304. doi:10.1177/0956797609359624.

Packer, D. J. (2008). Identifying systematic disobedience in Milgram's obedience experiments: A meta-analytic review. *Perspectives on Psychological Science, 3,* 301–304.

Packer, D. J. (2009). Avoiding groupthink: Whereas weakly identifi ed members remain silent, strongly identifi ed members dissent about collective problems. *Psychological Science, 20,* 546–548

Page, L., Keshishian, C., Leonardi, G., Murray, V., Rubin, G., & Wessely, S. (2010). Frequency and predictors of mass psychogenic illness. *Epidemiology (Cambridge, Mass.), 21*(5), 744–747.

Paik, H., & Comstock, G. (1994). The effects of television violence on antisocial behavior: A meta-analysis. *Communication Research, 21,* 516–546.

Palkovitz, R., Copes, M. A., & Woolfolk, T. N. (2001). It's like . . . you discover a new sense of being: Involved fathering as an evoker of adult development. *Men & Masculinities, 4*(1), 49–69.

Palmer, S. E. (1999). *Vision science: Photons to phenomenology.* Cambridge, MA: MIT Press.

Palmisano, M., & Herrmann, D. (1991). The facilitation of memory performance. *Bulletin of the Psychonomic Society, 29,* 557–559.

Palmquist, C. M., & Jaswal, V. K. (2012). Preschoolers expect pointers (even ignorant ones) to be knowledgeable. *Psychological Science, 23*(3), 230–231. doi:10.1177/0956797611427043.

Paloski, W. H. (1998). Vestibulospinal adaptation to microgravity. *Otolaryngology and Head and Neck Surgery, 118,* S39–S44.

Pandharipande, P., Jackson, J., & Ely, E. W. (2005). Delirium: Acute cognitive dysfunction in the critically ill. *Current Opinion in Critical Care, 11*(4), 360–368.

Paoletti, M. G. (1995). Biodiversity, traditional landscapes and agroecosystem management. *Landscape and Urban Planning, 31*(1–3), 117–128.

Paolicelli, R. C., Bolasco, G., Pagani, F., Maggi, L., Scianni, M., Panzanelli, P., Giustetto, M., Ferreira, T. A., Guiducci, E., Dumas, L., Ragozzino, D., & Gross, C. T. (2011) Synaptic pruning by microglia is necessary for normal brain development. *Science* 333 (6048):1456–1458.

Paradise, A. (2007). *State of the Industry: ASTD's annual review of trends in workplace learning and performance.* Alexandria, VA: ASTD.

Parasuraman, R. (2011). Neuroergonomics: Brain, cognition, and performance at work. *Current Directions in Psychological Science* 20(3) 181–186. doi:10.1177/0963721411409176.

Pardini, D. A., Frick, P. J., & Moffitt, T. E. (2010). Building an evidence base for DSM-5 conceptualizations of oppositional defiant disorder and conduct disorder: Introduction to the special section. *Journal of Abnormal Psychology, 119*:4, 683–688. doi:10.1037/a0021441.

Parents Television Council. (2006). *TV bloodbath: Violence on primetime broadcast TV: A PTC state of the television industry report, March.* Retrieved May 24, 2006, from http://www.parentstv.org/PTC/publications/reports/stateindustryviolence/main.asp#_ftn.

Pariente, J., White, P., Frackowiak, R. S., & Lewith, G. (2005). Expectancy and belief modulate the neuronal substrates of pain treated by acupuncture. *NeuroImage, 25,* 1161–1167.

Parise, E., & Csibra, G. (2012). Electrophysiological evidence for the understanding of maternal speech by 9-month-old infants. *Psychological Science, 23,* 728–733. doi:10.1177/0956797612438734.

Parise, E., & Csibra, G. (2012). Electrophysiological evidence for the understanding of maternal speech by 9-month-old infants. *Psychological Science, 23,* 728–733.

Park, D. C. (2001, August). *The aging mind.* Paper presented at the annual convention of the American Psychological Association, San Francisco.

Park, D. C., & Huang, C. (2010). Culture wires the brain: A cognitive neuroscience perspective. *Perspectives on Psychological Science, 5*(4), 391–400. doi:10.1177/1745691610374591.

Park, D. C., Lautenschlager, G., Hedden, T., Davidson, N. S., Smith, A. D., & Smith, P. (2002). Models of visuospatial and verbal memory across the adult life span. *Psychology & Aging, 17*(2), 299–320.

Park, G., Lubinski, D., & Benbow, C. P. (2008). Ability differences among people who have commensurate degrees matter for scientific creativity. *Psychological Science, 19,* 957–961.

Park, H. J., Li, R. X., Kim, J., Kim, S. W., Moon, D. H., Kwon, M. H., & Kim, W. J. (2009). Neural correlates of winning and losing while watching soccer matches. *International Journal of Neuroscience, 119*(1), 76–87.

Park, I.-H., Zhao, R., West, J. A., Yabuuchi, A., Huo, H., Ince, T. A., Lerou, P. H., Lensch, M. W., & Daley, G. Q. (2008). Reprogramming of human somatic cells to pluripotency with defined factors. *Nature, 451,* 141–146.

Park, N., Peterson, C., & Seligman, M. E. P. (2004). Strengths of character and well-being. *Journal of Social and Clinical Psychology, 23,* 603–619.

Park, S., Lee, J., & Daily, J. (2011). Anti-obesity effects of Chang-Chul-Eui-Ee-In-Tang [see text] in female rats with diet-induced obesity. *Chinese Journal of Integrative Medicine, 17*(12), 925–932. doi:10.1007/s11655-011-0936-3.

Park, S., Shibusawa, T., Yoon, S., & Son, H. (2010). Characteristics of Chinese and Korean Americans in outpatient treatment for alcohol use disorders: Examining heterogeneity among Asian American subgroups. *Journal of Ethnicity In Substance Abuse, 9*(2), 128–142. doi:10.1080/15332641003772660

Parke, R. D., Gailey C., Coltrane, S., & DiMatteo, R. (2012). The pursuit of perfection: Transforming our construction of parenthood and family in the age of new reproductive technologies. In P. Essed & D. T. Goldberg (Eds.), *Clones, fakes and posthumans: Cultures of replication.* Amsterdam: Rodopi.

Parke, R. D., & Buriel, R. (2006). Child development and the family. In W. Damon & R. M. Lerner (Series Eds.) & N. Eisenberg (Vol. Ed.), *Handbook of child psychology: Vol. 3. Social, emotional, and personality development* (6th ed.). New York: Wiley.

Parker, E. S., Cahill, L., & McGaugh, J. L. (2006). A case of unusual autobiographical remembering. *Neurocase, 12,* 35–49.

Parker, G., Gladstone, G., & Chee, K. T. (2001). Depression in the planet's largest ethnic group: The Chinese. *American Journal of Psychiatry, 158,* 857–864.

Parker, J. G., Saxon, J. L., Asher, S. R., & Kovacs, D. M. (2001). Dimensions of children's friendship adjustment: Implications for understanding loneliness. In K. J. Rotenberg & S. Hymel (Eds.), *Loneliness in childhood and adolescence.* New York: Cambridge University Press.

Parkinson, B., Phiri, N., & Simons, G. (2012). Bursting with anxiety: Adult social referencing in an interpersonal Balloon Analogue Risk Task (BART). *Emotion.* doi:10.1037/a0026434.

Parolaro, D., Massi, P., Rubino, T., & Monti, E. (2002). Endocannabinoids in the immune system and cancer. *Prostaglandins Leukotrienes & Essential Fatty Acids, 66,* 319–332.

Parsons, J., Schoon, I., Rush, R., & Law, J. (2011). Long-term outcomes for children with early language problems: Beating the odds. *Children & Society, 25*(3), 202–214. doi:10.1111/j.1099-0860.2009.00274.x.

Parsons, T. J., Power, C., & Manor, O. (2005). Physical activity, television viewing and body mass index: A cross-sectional analysis from childhood to adulthood in the 1958 British cohort. *International Journal of Obesity, 29,* 1212–1221.

Pascual-Leone, A. (2001). The brain that plays music and is changed by it. *Annals of the New York Academy of Science, 930,* 315–329.

Pascual-Leone, A., & Torres, F. (1993). Plasticity of the sensorimotor cortex representation of the reading finger in Braille readers. *Brain, 116,* 39–52.

Pashler, H., Rohrer, D., & Cepeda, N. J. (2006). Temporal spacing and learning. *APS Observer, 19,* 30, 38.

Passie, T., Halpern, J. H., Stichtenoth, D. O., Emrich, H. M., & Hintzen, A. (2008). The pharmacology of lysergic acid diethylamide: A review. *CNS Neuroscience and Therapeutics, 14*(4), 295–314.

Pasztor, A. (2009, October 26). Pilots say they were distracted. *Wall Street Journal,* p. A4.

Pathela, P., Hajat, A., Schillinger, J., Blank, S., Sell, R., & Mostashari, F. (2006). Discordance between sexual behavior and self-reported sexual identity: A population-based survey of New York City men. *Annals of Internal Medicine, 145,* 416–425.

Pati, B. (2011). Inclusive education of children with intellectual disability under education for all (Sarva Shiksha Abhiyan) programme in Orissa. *Social Science International, 27*(1), 123–130.

Patkowski, M. (1994). The critical age hypothesis and interlanguage phonology. In M. Yavas (Ed.), *First and second language phonology* (pp. 205–221). San Diego: Singular Publishing Group.

Patten, S. B., Williams, J. V. A., Wang, J., Adair, C. E., Brant, C. E., Casebeer, A., et al. (2005). Antidepressant pharmacoepidemiology in a general population sample. *Journal of Clinical Psychopharmacology, 25,* 285–287.

Patterson, C. H. (2000). *Understanding psychotherapy: Fifty years of client-centered theory and practice.* Ross-on-Wye, UK: PCCS Books.

Patterson, C. J. (2002). Lesbian and gay parenthood. In M. H. Bornstein (Ed.), *Handbook of parenting* (2nd ed., pp. 255–274). Mahwah, NJ: Erlbaum.

Patterson, C. J. (2004). *Lesbian and gay parents and their children: Summary of research findings.* Washington, DC: American Psychological Association. Retrieved September 26, 2006, from http://www.apa.org/pi/parent.html.

Patterson, C. J. (2009). Children of lesbian and gay parents: Psychology, law, and policy. *American Psychologist, 64*(8), 727–736.

Patton, G. C., Coffey, C., Carlin, J. B., Degenhardt, L., Lynskey, M., & Hall, W. (2002). Cannabis use and mental health in young people: Cohort study. *British Medical Journal, 325,* 1195–1198.

Patton, G. C., McMorris, B. J., Toumbourou, J. W., Hemphill, S. A., Donath, S., & Catalano, R. F. (2004). Puberty and the onset of substance use and abuse [Electronic version]. *Pediatrics, 114*(3), e300–e306.

Pauk, W., & Owens, R. J. Q. (2010). *How to study in college* (10th ed.) Belmont, CA: Wadsworth.

Paul, G. L. (1969). Behavior modification research: Design and tactics. In C. M. Franks (Ed.), *Behavior therapy: Appraisal and status* (pp. 29–62). New York: McGraw-Hill.

Pauli, E., Hildebrandt, M., Romstöck, J., Stefan, H., & Blümcke, I. (2006). Deficient memory acquisition in temporal lobe epilepsy is predicted by hippocampal granule cell loss. *Neurology, 67*(8), 1383–1389.

Paul-Labrador, M., Polk, D., Dwyer, J. H., Velasquez, I., Nidich, S., Rainforth, M., et al. (2006). Effects of a randomized controlled trial of transcendental meditation on components on the metabolic syndrome in subjects with coronary heart disease. *Archives of Internal Medicine, 166,* 1218–1224.

Paulus, P. B., Kohn, N. W., & Arditti, L. E. (2011). Effects of quantity and quality instructions on brainstorming. *The Journal of Creative Behavior, 45*(1), 38–46. doi:10.1002/j.2162-6057.2011.tb01083.x.

Paulussen-Hoogeboom, M. C., Stams, G. J. J. M., Hermanns, J. M. A., Peetsma, T. T. D., & van den Wittenboer, G. L. H. (2008). Parenting style as a mediator between children's negative emotionality and problematic behavior in early childhood. *Journal of Genetic Psychology, 169,* 209–226.

Paus, T., Keshavan, M., & Giedd, J. N. (2008). Why do many psychiatric disorders emerge during adolescence? *Nature Reviews Neuroscience, 9*(12), 947–957.

Payne, J. D., & Kensinger, E. A. (2010). Sleep's role in the consolidation of emotional episodic memories. *Current Directions in Psychological Science, 19*(5), 290–295.

Payne, J. D., & Nadel, L. (2004). Sleep, dreams, and memory consolidation: The role of the stress hormone cortisol. *Learning and Memory, 11,* 671–678.

Payne, J. D., Tucker, M. A., Ellenbogen, J. M., Wamsley, E. J., Walker, M. P., Schacter, D. L., & Stickgold, R. (2012). Memory for semantically related and unrelated declarative information: The benefit of sleep, the cost of wake. *Plos ONE, 7*(3), doi:10.1371/journal.pone.0033079.

Payne, N. A., & Prudic, J. (2009). Electroconvulsive therapy: Part I. A perspective on the evolution and current practice of ECT. *Journal of Psychiatric Practice, 15,* 346–368.

Pea, R., Nass, C., Meheula, L., Rance, M., Kumar, A., Bamford, H., & .. Zhou, M. (2012). Media use, face-to-face communication, media multitasking, and social well-being among 8- to 12-year-old girls. *Developmental Psychology, 48*(2), 327–336. doi:10.1037/a0027030.

Pearsall, M. J., Christian, M. S., & Ellis, A. P. J. (2010). Motivating interdependent teams: Individual rewards, shared rewards, or something in between? *Journal of Applied Psychology, 95,* 183–191.

Pedersen, J., & Fields, W. M. (2009). Aspects of repetition in bonobo–human conversation: Creating cohesion in a conversation between species. *Integrative Psychological & Behavioral Science, 43*(1), 22–41. doi:10.1007/s12124-008-9067-6.

Pedersen, P. B., & Draguns, J. G. (2002). *Counseling across cultures.* Thousand Oaks, CA: Sage.

Pedrazzoli, A. (2010). OPUS One: An Intelligent Adaptive Learning Environment Using Artificial Intelligence Support. *AIP Conference Proceedings, 1247*(1), 215–227. doi:10.1063/1.3460231.

Pekrun, R., Elliot, A. J., & Maier, M. A. (2009). Achievement goals and achievement emotions: Testing a model of their joint relations with academic performance. *Journal of Educational Psychology, 101*(1), 115–135.

Peltola, M. S., Tamminen, H., Toivonen, H., Kujala, T., & Näätänen, R. (2012). Different kinds of bilinguals—Different kinds of brains: The neural organisation of two languages in one brain. *Brain & Language, 121*(3), 261–266. doi:10.1016/j.bandl.2012.03.007.

Peña, M., Pittaluga, E., & Mehler, J. (2010). Language acquisition in premature and full-term infants. *Proceedings of the National Academy of Sciences, 107,* 3823–3828.

Peña, M., Maki, A., Kovaci, D., Dehaene-Lambertz, G., Koizumi, H., Bouquet, F., & Mehler, J. (2003). Sounds and silence: An optical topography study of language recognition at birth. *Proceedings of the National Academy of Sciences, 100,* 11702–11705.

Pendergrast, M. (1996). A retractor's story. *Victims of memory: Sex abuse accusations and shattered lives.* Hinesburg, VT: Upper Access Books.

Penedo, F. J., & Dahn, J. (2004). Psychoneuroimmunology and aging. In M. Irwin & K. Vedhara (Eds.), *Psychoneuroimmunology.* New York: Kluwer.

Peng, W. (2009). Design and evaluation of a computer game to promote a healthy diet for young adults. *Health Communication, 24*(2), 115–127. doi:10.1080/10410230802676490.

Pengas, G., Hodges, J. R., Watson, P., & Nestor, P. J. (2010). Focal posterior cingulate atrophy in incipient Alzheimer's disease. *Neurobiology of Aging, 31,* 25–33.

Penko, A. L., & Barkley, J. E. (2010). Motivation and physiologic responses of playing a physically interactive video game relative to a sedentary alternative in children. *Annals of Behavioral Medicine, 39*(2), 162–169. doi:10.1007/s12160-010-9164-x.

Pennebaker, J. W. (1995). *Emotion, disclosure, and health.* Washington, DC: American Psychological Association.

Pennebaker, J. W. (2000). The effects of traumatic disclosure on physical and mental health: The values of writing and talking about upsetting events. In J. M. Violanti, D. Paton, & C. Dunning (Eds.), *Posttraumatic stress intervention: Challenges, issues, and perspectives* (pp. 97–114). Chicago: Charles C. Thomas.

Pennebaker, J. W., & Chew, C. H. (1985). Deception, electrodermal activity, and inhibition of behavior. *Journal of Personality and Social Psychology, 49,* 1427–1433.

Pennebaker, J. W., & O'Heeron, R. C. (1984). Confiding in others and illness rate among spouses of suicide and accidental death victims. *Journal of Abnormal Psychology, 93,* 473–476.

Penner, L., Brannick, M. T., Webb, S., & Connell, P. (2005). Effects on volunteering of the September 11, 2001 attacks: An archival analysis. *Journal of Applied Social Psychology, 35,* 1333–1360.

Penner, L. A. (2002). Dispositional and organizational influences on sustained volunteerism: An interactionist perspective. *Journal of Social Issues, 58,* 447–467.

Penner, L. A., & Craiger, J. P. (1992). The weakest link: The performance of individual group members. In R. W. Swezey & E. Salas (Eds.), *Teams: Their training and performance* (pp. 57–74). Norwood, NJ: Ablex.

Penner, L. A., & Finkelstein, M. A. (1998). Dispositional and structural determinants of volunteerism. *Journal of Personality and Social Psychology, 74,* 525–537.

Penner, L. A., Dovidio, J., & Albrecht, T. L. (2001). Helping victims of loss and trauma: A social psychological perspective. In J. Harvey & E. Miller (Eds.), *Loss and trauma: General and close relationship perspectives* (pp. 62–85). Philadelphia: Brunner Routledge.

Penner, L. A., Dovidio, J. F., Piliavin, J. A., & Schroeder, D. A. (2005). Prosocial behavior: Multilevel perspectives. *Annual Review of Psychology, 56,* 365–392.

Penner, L. A., & Orom, H. (2009). Enduring goodness: A person-by-situation perspective on prosocial behavior. In M. Mikulincer & P. Shaver (Eds.), *Prosocial motives, emotions, and behavior* (pp. 55–72). Washington, DC: American Psychological Association.

Penner, L. A., Fritzsche, B. A., Craiger, J. P., & Friefeld, T. R. (1995). Measuring the prosocial personality. In J. Butcher & C. D. Spielberger (Eds.), *Advances in personality assessment* (Vol. 10, pp. 147–163). Hillsdale, NJ: Erlbaum.

Penney, L. M., & Spector, P. E. (2005). Job stress, incivility, and counterproductive work behavior (CWB): The moderating role of negative affectivity. *Journal of Organizational Behavior, 26,* 777–796.

Pennington, J., & Knight, T. (2011). Through the lens of hetero-normative assumptions: Re-thinking attitudes towards gay parenting. *Culture, Health & Sexuality, 13*(1), 59–72. doi:10.1080/13691058.2010.519049.

Penninx, B. W., Beekman, A. T., Honig, A., Deeg, D. J., Schoevers, R. A., van Eijk, J. T., van Tilburg, W. (2001). Depression and cardiac mortality: Results from a community-based longitudinal study. *Archives of General Psychiatry, 58,* 221–227.

Penton, R. E., & Lester, R. A. (2009). Cellular events in nicotine addiction. *Seminars in Cell and Developmental Biology, 20,* 418–431.

Peplau, L. A. (2003). Human sexuality: How do men and women differ? *Current Directions in Psychological Science, 12,* 37–40.

Peretz, H., & Fried, Y. (2012). National cultures, performance appraisal practices, and organizational absenteeism and turnover: A study across 21 countries. *Journal of Applied Psychology, 97,* 448–459. doi:10.1037/a0026011.

Perfect, T. J., Andrade, J., & Syrett, L. (2012). Environmental visual distraction during retrieval affects the quality, not the quantity, of eyewitness recall. *Applied Cognitive Psychology, 26*(2), 296–300. doi:10.1002/acp.1823.

Perilloux, C., Easton, J., & Buss, D. (2012). The misperception of sexual interest. *Psychological Science, 23*(2), 146-151.

Perkins, T., Stokes, M., McGillivray, J., & Bittar, R. (2010) Mirror neuron dysfunction in autism spectrum disorders. *J Clin Neurosci 17* (10):1239-1243.

Perkonigg, A., Pfister, H., Stein, M. B., Hofler, M., Lieb, R., Maercker, A., et al. (2005). Longitudinal course of posttraumatic stress disorder and posttraumatic stress disorder symptoms in a community sample of adolescents and young adults. *American Journal of Psychiatry, 162,* 1320–1327.

Perlis, M, Aloia, M., & Kuhn, B. (2011). Behavioral Treatments for Sleep Disorders. Academic Press: London.

Perlis, M. L., Sharpe, M., Smith, M. T., Greenblatt, D., & Giles, D. (2001). Behavioral treatment of insomnia: Treatment outcomes and the relevance of medical and psychiatric morbidity. *Journal of Behavioral Medicine, 24,* 281–296.

Perlman, D. M., Salomons, T. V., Davidson, R. J., & Lutz, A. (2010). Diff erential effects on pain intensity and unpleasantness of two meditation practices. *Emotion, 10,* 65–71.

Perls, F. S. (1969). *Ego, hunger and aggression: The beginning of Gestalt therapy.* New York: Random House.

Perls, F. S., Hefferline, R. F., & Goodman, P. (1951). *Gestalt therapy.* New York: Julian Press.

Perovic, S., & Radenovic, L. (2011). Fine-tuning nativism: The 'nurtured nature' and innate cognitive structures. *Phenomenology And The Cognitive Sciences, 10*(3), 399–417. doi:10.1007/s11097-010-9180-0.

Perper, K., & Manlove, J. (2009). Estimated percentage of females who will become teen mothers: Diff erences across states. *Child Trends Research Brief.* Retrieved from http://www.childtrends.org/Files//Child_Trends-2009_03_19_RB_PercentTeenMothers.pdf.

Perper, K., Peterson, K., & Manlove, J. (2010). Diploma attainment among teen mothers. *Child Trends,* Fact Sheet Publication #2010-01. Washington, DC: Child Trends.

Perrin, J., Merz, S., Bennett, D., Currie, J., Steele, D., Reid, I., & Schwarzbauer, C. (2012). Electroconvulsive therapy reduces frontal cortical connectivity in severe depressive disorder. *Proceedings of the National Academy of Sciences of the United States of America, 109*(14), 5464–5468.

Perrin, M. A., DiGrande, L., Wheeler, K., Thorpe, L., Farfel, M., & Brackbill, R. (2007). Differences in PTSD prevalence and associated risk factors among World Trade Center disaster rescue and recovery workers. *American Journal of Psychiatry, 164,* 1385–1394.

Perry, B. L. (2011). The labeling paradox: Stigma, the sick role, and social networks in mental illness. *Journal of Health & Social Behavior, 52*(4), 460–477. doi:10.1177/0022146511408913.

Perry, E. K. (1980). The cholinergic system in old age and Alzheimer's disease. *Age and Ageing, 9*(1), 1–8.

Persons, J. B., Davidson, J., & Tompkins, M. A. (2001). *Essential components of cognitive-behavior therapy for depression.* Washington, DC: American Psychological Association.

Perthen, J. E., Lansing, A. E., Liau, J., Liu, T. T., & Buxton, R. B. (2008). Caffeine-induced uncoupling of cerebral blood flow and oxygen metabolism: A calibrated BOLD fMRI study. *NeuroImage, 40*(1), 237–247.

Pervin, L. A., Cervone, D., & John, O. P. (2005). *Personality: Theory and research.* New York: Wiley.

Pesonen, A.-K., Räikkönen, K., Heinonen, K., Komsi, N., Järvenpää, A.-L., & Strandberg, T. (2008). A transactional model of temperamental development: Evidence of a relationship between child temperament and maternal stress over five years. *Social Development, 17,* 326–340.

Pessiglione, M., Seymour, B., Flandin, G., Dolan, R. J., & Frith, C. D. (2006). Dopamine-dependent prediction errors underpin reward-seeking behaviour in humans. *Nature, 442,* 1042–1045.

Peters, E., Baker, D. P., Dieckmann, N. F., Leon, J., & Collins, J. (2010). Explaining the effect of education on health: A field study in Ghana. *Psychological Science, 21,* (10), 1369–1376. doi:10.1177/0956797610381506.

Peters, E., Hess, T. M., Västfjäll, D., & Auman, C. (2007). Adult age differences in dual information processes: Implications for the role of affective and deliberative processes in older adults' decision making. *Perspectives on Psychological Science, 2,* 1–23.

Petersen, J. L., & Hyde, J. S. (2010). A meta-analytic review of research on gender differences in sexuality, 1993–2007. *Psychological Bulletin, 136,* 21–38.

Petersen, R. C. (2011). Clinical practice. Mild cognitive impairment. *New England Journal of Medicine, 364*(23), 2227–2234.

Petersen, R. C., Smith, G. E., Waring, S. C., Ivnik, R. J., Tangalos, E., & Kokmen, E. (1999). Mild cognitive impairment: Clinical characterization and outcome. *Archives of Neurology, 56,* 303–308.

Peterson, C. (2006b). The Values in Action (VIA) Classification of Strengths: The un-DSM and the real DSM. In M. Csikszentmihalyi & I. Csikszentmihalyi (Eds.), *A life worth living: Contributions to positive psychology* (pp. 29–48). New York: Oxford University Press.

Peterson, C. (2006a). *A primer in positive psychology.* New York: Oxford University Press.

Peterson, C. (2006b). The Values in Action (VIA) Classification of Strengths: The un-DSM and the real DSM. In M. Csikszentmihalyi & I. Csikszentmihalyi (Eds.), *A life worth living: Contributions to positive psychology* (pp. 29–48). New York: Oxford University Press.

Peterson, C., Maier, S. F., & Seligman, M. E. (1993). *Learned helplessness: A theory for the age of personal control.* New York: Oxford University Press.

Peterson, C., & Seligman, M. E. P. (1984). Causal explanations as a risk factor for depression: Theory and evidence. *Psychological Review, 91,* 347–374.

Peterson, C., Seligman, M. E. P., Yurko, K. H., Martin, L. R., & Friedman, H. S. (1998). Catastrophizing and untimely death. *Psychological Science, 9,* 127–130.

Peterson, L. R., & Peterson, M. J. (1959). Short-term retention of individual verbal items. *Journal of Experimental Psychology, 58,* 193–198.

Peterson, N. G., Mumford, M. D., Borman, W. C., Jeanneret, P. R., Fleishman, E. A., Levin, K. Y., et al. (2001). Understanding work using the Occupational Information Network (O*NET): Implications for practice and research. *Personnel Psychology, 54,* 451–492.

Peterson, R. S., Smith, D. B., Martorana, P. V., & Owens, P. D. (2003). The impact of chief executive officer personality on top management team dynamics: One mechanism by which leadership affects organizational performance. *Journal of Applied Psychology, 88,* 795–808.

Petitclerc, A., & Tremblay, R. E. (2009). Childhood disruptive behaviour disorders: Review of their origin, development and prevention. *Canadian Journal of Psychiatry, 54,* 222–231.

Petrakis, I. L., Limoncelli, D., Gueorguieva, R., Jatlow, P., Boutros, N. N., Trevisan, L., et al. (2004). Altered NMDA glutamate receptor antagonist response in individuals with a family vulnerability to alcoholism. *American Journal of Psychiatry, 161,* 1776–1782.

Petrescu, N. (2008). Loud music listening. *McGill Journal of Medicine, 11*(2), 169–176.

Petrie K, Fontanilla I., Thomas M, Booth R, & Pennebaker JW. (2004) Effects of written emotional expression on immune function in patients with human immunodeficiency virus infection: a randomized trial. *Psychosomatic Medicine, 66,* 272–275, 2004.

Petrie, K. J., & Weinman, J. (2012). Patients' perceptions of their illness: The dynamo of volition in health care. *Current Directions in Psychological Science, 21*(1), 60–65. doi:10.1177/0963721411429456.

Petrill, S. A., Plomin, R., Berg, S., Johansson, B., Pederson, N. L., Ahern, F., & McClearn, G. E. (1998). The genetic and environmental relationship between general and specific cognitive abilities in twins age 80 and older. *Psychological Science, 9,* 183–189.

Petroski, H. (2008a). Scientists as inventors. *American Scientist, 96*(5), 368–371.

Petroski, H. (2008b). *Success through failure: The paradox of design.* Princeton, NJ: Princeton University Press.

Petrovic, P., Dietrich, T., Fransson, P., Andersson, J., Carlsson, K., & Ingvar, M. (2005). Placebo in emotional processing: Induced expectations of anxiety relief activate a generalized modulatory network. *Neuron, 46,* 957–969.

Pettigrew, T. F. (1979). The ultimate attribution error: Extending Allport's cognitive analysis of prejudice. *Personality and Social Psychology Bulletin, 5,* 461–476.

Pettigrew, T. F., Tropp, L. R., Wagner, U. & Christ, O. (2011) Recent advances in intergroup contact theory. *International Journal of Intercultural Relations, 35,* 271–280.

Pettit, D. L., Shao, Z., & Yakel, J. L. (2001). Beta-amyloid(1–42) peptide directly modulates nicotinic receptors in the rat hippocampal slice. *Journal of Neuroscience, 21,* RC120.

Petty, R. & Brinol, P. (2010). Attitude change In R. Baumeister & E. Finkel (Eds.) *Advanced social psychology: The state of the science* (pp. 217–262). New York, NY: Oxford.

Petzold, G. C., & Murthy, V. N. (2011) Role of astrocytes in neurovascular coupling. *Neuron 71* (5):782–797.

Pexman, P., Rostad, K., McMorris, C., Climie, E., Stowkowy, J., & Glenwright, M. (2011). Processing of ironic language in children with high-functioning autism spectrum disorder. *Journal of Autism and Developmental Disorders, 41,* 1097–1112.

Pfefferbaum, A., Rosenbloom, M., Deshmukkh, A., & Sullivan, E. (2001). Sex differences in the effects of alcohol on brain structure. *American Journal of Psychiatry, 158,* 188–197.

Pfister, J. A., Stegelmeier, B. L., Gardner, D. R., & James, L. F. (2003). Grazing of spotted locoweed (*Astragalus lentiginosus*) by cattle and horses in Arizona. *Journal of Animal Science, 81,* 2285–2293.

Pham, L. B., Taylor, S. E., & Seeman, T. E. (2001). Effects of environmental predictability and personal mastery on self-regulatory and physiological processes. *Personality & Social Psychology Bulletin, 27,* 611–620.

Phares, E. J. (1976). *Locus of control in personality.* Morristown, NJ: General Learning Press.

Phares, V. (2008). *Understanding abnormal child psychology* (2nd ed.). New York: Wiley & Sons.

Phelan, J. C., Link, B. G., Stueve, A., & Pescosolido, B. A. (2000). Public conceptions of mental illness in 1950 and 1996: What is mental illness and is it to be feared? *Journal of Health and Social Behavior, 41,* 188–207.

Phelps, E. A., & LeDoux, J. E. (2005). Contributions of the amygdala to emotion processing: From animal models to human behavior. *Neuron, 48,* 175–187.

Phelps, E. A., O'Connor, K. J., Cunningham, W. A., Funayama, E. S., Gatenby, J. C., Gore, J. C., & Banaji, M. R. (2000). Performance on indirect measures of race evaluation predicts amygdala activation. *Journal of Cognitive Neuroscience, 12,* 729–738.

Philibert, R. A., Gunter, T. D., Beach, S. H., Brody, G. H., Hollenbeck, N., Andersen, A., & Adams, W. (2009). Role of GABRA2 on risk for alcohol, nicotine, and cannabis dependence in the Iowa Adoption Studies. *Psychiatric Genetics, 19*(2), 91–98. doi:10.1097/YPG.0b013e3283208026

Philip, P., Vervialle, F., Le Breton, P., Taillard, J., & Horne, J. A. (2001). Fatigue, alcohol, and serious road crashes in France: Factorial study of national data. *British Medical Journal, 322,* 829–830.

Phillips, B., & Morse, E. (2011). Family child care learning environments: Caregiver knowledge and practices related to early literacy and mathematics. *Early Childhood Education Journal, 39*(3), 213–222. doi:10.1007/s10643-011-0456-y.

Phillips, K., Luk, A., Soor, G. S., Abraham, J. R., et al. (2009). Cocaine cardiotoxicity: A review of the pathophysiology, pathology, and treatment options. *American Journal of Cardiovascular Drugs, 9,* 177–196.

Phillips, K. M., Freund, B., Fordiani, J., Kuhn, R., & Ironson, G. (2009). EMDR treatment of past domestic violence: A clinical vignette. *Journal of EMDR Practice and Research, 3,* 192–197.

Phillips, P. E., Stuber, G. D., Heien, M. L., Wightman, R. M., & Carelli, R. M. (2003). Subsecond dopamine release promotes cocaine seeking. *Nature, 422,* 614–618.

Phinney, J. S., Ferguson, D. L., & Tate, J. D. (1997). Intergroup attitudes among ethnic minority adolescents: A causal model. *Child Development, 68,* 955–969.

Phinney, J. S., Jacoby, B., Silva, C. (2007). Positive intergroup attitudes: The role of ethnic identity. *International Journal of Behavioral Development, 31,* 478–490.

Phipps, M. G., Blume, J. D., & DeMonner, S. M. (2002). Young maternal age associated with increased risk of postneonatal death. *Obstetrics and Gynecology, 100,* 481–486.

Piaget, J. (1952). *The origins of intelligence in children.* New York: International Universities Press.

Pianta, R. C., Barnett, W., Burchinal, M., & Thornburg, K. R. (2009). The effects of preschool education: What we know, how public policy is or is not aligned with the evidence base, and what we need to know. *Psychological Science In The Public Interest, 10*(2), 49–88. doi:10.1177/1529100610381908.

Piasecki, T. M. (2006). Relapse to smoking. *Clinical Psychology Review, 26,* 196–215.

Pickering, A. D., & Gray, J. A. (1999). The neuroscience of personality. In L. Pervin & O. John (Eds.), *Handbook of personality: Theory and research* (2nd ed., pp. 277–299). New York: Guilford.

Pickler, N. (2002, November 19). *NTSB cites fatigue, sleep apnea in fatal train wreck.* Associated Press. Retrieved August 25, 2003, from http://newsobserver.com/24hour/nation/v-print/story/626769p-4807167c.html.

Pidsley, R., & Mill, J. (2011). Epigenetic studies of psychosis: Current findings, methodological approaches, and implications for postmortem research. *Biological Psychiatry, 69*(2), 146–156.

Pieterse, A. L., & Carter, R. T. (2010). The role of racial identity in perceived racism and psychological stress among Black American adults: Exploring traditional and alternative approaches. *Journal of Applied Social Psychology, 40*, 1028–1053. doi:10.1111/j.1559-1816.2010.00609.x

Pieterse, A. L., Todd, N. R., Neville, H. A., & Carter, R. T. (2012). Perceived racism and mental health among Black American adults: A meta-analytic review. *Journal of Counseling Psychology, 59*(1), 1–9. doi:10.1037/a0026208.

Pietro, P., Guazzeli, M., Basso, G., Jaffe, K., & Grafman, J. (2000). Neural correlates of imaginal aggressive behavior assessed by positron emission tomography in healthy subjects. *American Journal of Psychiatry, 157*, 1772–1781.

Pike, K. M., Walsh, B. T., Vitousek, K., Wilson, G. T., & Bauer, J. (2003). Cognitive behavior therapy in the posthospitalization treatment of anorexia nervosa. *American Journal of Psychiatry, 160*, 2046–2049.

Piko, B. F., Bak, J., Gibbons, F. X. (2007). Prototype perception and smoking: Are negative or positive social images more important in adolescents? *Addictive Behaviors, 32*, 1728–1732.

Piliavin, J. A., Dovidio, J. F., Gaertner, S. L., & Clark, R. D., III. (1981). *Emergency intervention.* New York: Academic Press.

Pillard, R. C., & Bailey, J. M. (1998). Human sexual orientation has a heritable component. *Human Biology, 70*, 347–365.

Pillemer, K., & Suitor, J. J. (2002). Explaining mothers' ambivalence towards their adult children. *Journal of Marriage and Family, 64*, 602–613.

Pillmann, F. (2009). Complex dream-enacting behavior in sleepwalking. *Psychosomatic Medicine, 71*, 231–234.

Pilon, M., Montplaisir, J., & Zadra, A. (2008). Precipitating factors of somnambulism: Impact of sleep deprivation and forced arousals. *Neurology, 70*, 2284–2290.

Pinel, J. P., Lehman, D. R., & Assanand, S. (2002). Eating for optimal health: How much should we eat? Comment. *American Psychologist, 57*, 372–373.

Pines, A., Neal, M. B., Hammer, L. B., & Icekson, T. (2011). Job burnout and couple burnout in dual-earner couples in the sandwiched generation. *Social Psychology Quarterly, 74*(4), 361–386. doi:10.1177/0190272511422452.

Pinker, S. (1994). *The language instinct: How the mind creates language.* New York: Morrow.

Pinto, J. M. (2011). Olfaction. *Proceedings of the American Thoracic Society, 8*(1), 46–52.

Pintrich, P. R. (2003). Motivation and classroom learning. In W. M. Reynolds & G. E. Miller (Eds.), *Handbook of psychology: Educational psychology, Vol. 7* (pp. 103–122). Hoboken, NJ: John Wiley & Sons Inc.

Pipes, R. B., Holstein, J. E., & Aguirre, M. G. (2005). Examining the personal-professional distinction: Ethics codes and the difficulty of drawing a boundary. *American Psychologist, 60*, 325–334.

Pipitone, R. N., & Gallup G. G., Jr. (2008). Women's voice attractiveness varies across the menstrual cycle. *Evolution and Human Behavior, 29*, 268–274.

Pittler, M. H., Verster, J. C., & Ernst, E. (2005). Interventions for preventing or treating alcohol hangover: Systematic review of randomised controlled trials. *British Medical Journal, 331*, 1515–1518.

Pizza, F., Contardi, S., Antognini, A. B., Zagoraiou, M., Borrotti, M., Mostacci, B., Mondini, S., & Cirignotta, F. (2010). Sleep quality and motor vehicle crashes in adolescents. *Journal of Clinical Sleep Medicine, 6*(1), 41–45.

Plaks, J. E., Malahy, L. W., Sedlins, M., & Shoda, Y. (2012). Folk beliefs about human genetic variation predict discrete versus continuous racial categorization and evaluative bias. *Social Psychological & Personality Science, 3*(1), 31–39.

Plant, E. A., & Peruche, B. M. (2005). The consequences of race for police officers' responses to criminal suspects. *Psychological Science, 16*, 180–183.

Plant, E. A., & Sachs-Ericsson, N. (2004). Racial and ethnic differences in depression: The roles of social support and meeting basic needs. *Journal of Consulting and Clinical Psychology, 72*, 41–52.

Plant, K. L., & Stanton, N. A. (2012). Why did the pilots shut down the wrong engine? Explaining errors in context using Schema Theory and the Perceptual Cycle Model. *Safety Science, 50*(2), 300–315. doi:10.1016/j.ssci.2011.09.005.

Platek, S. M., & Singh, D. (2010). Optimal Waist-to-Hip Ratios in Women Activate Neural Reward Centers in Men. *Plos ONE, 5*(2), 1–5. doi:10.1371/journal.pone.0009042.

Plomin, R., DeFries, J. C., McClearn, G. E., & McGuffin, P. (2008). *Behavioral genetics* (5th ed.). New York: Worth.

Plomin, R. (1994). *Genetics and experience: The developmental interplay between nature and nurture.* Newbury Park, CA: Sage.

Plomin, R. (2004). *Two views about the nurture assumption.* Retrieved June 15, 2005, from PsycCRITIQUES database.

Plomin, R., DeFries, J. C., Craig, I. W., & McGuffin, P. (2002). *Behavioral genetics in the postgenomic era.* Washington, DC: American Psychological Association.

Plomin, R., & McGuffin, P. (2003). Psychopathology in the postgenomic era. *Annual Review of Psychology, 54*, 205–228.

Plomin, R., & Spinath, F. M. (2004). Intelligence: Genetics, genes, and genomics. *Journal of Personality and Social Psychology, 86*, 112–129.

Ploner, M., Gross, J., Timmermann, L., & Schnitzler, A. (2002). Cortical representation of first and second pain sensation in humans. *Proceedings of the National Academy of Sciences, 99*, 12444–12448.

Plutchik, R., & Conte, H. R. (Eds.). (1997). *Circumplex models of personality and emotions.* Washington, DC: American Psychological Association.

Pogue-Geile, M. F., & Yokley, J. L. (2010). Current research on the genetic contributors to schizophrenia. *Current Directions in Psychological Science, 19*(4), 214–219. doi:10.1177/0963721410378490.

Polanczyk, G., Moffitt, T. E., Arseneault, L., Cannon, M., Ambler, A., Keefe, R. S. E. (2010). Etiological and clinical features of childhood psychotic symptoms. *Arch Gen Psychiatry, 67*:4, 328–338.

Poland, J., & Caplan, P. J. (2004). The deep structure of bias in psychiatric diagnosis. In P. J. Caplan & L. Cosgrove (Eds.), *Bias in psychiatric diagnosis: A project of the association for women in psychology* (pp. 9–23). New York: Aronson.

Poldrack, R. A. (2010). Mapping mental function to brain structure: How can cognitive neuroimaging succeed?. *Perspectives on Psychological Science, 5*(6), 753–761. doi:10.1177/1745691610388777.

Poldrack, R. A., Halchenko, Y. O., & Hanson, S. J. (2009). Decoding the large-scale structure of brain function by classifying mental states across individuals. *Psychological Science, 20*, 1364–1372.

Polivy, J., & Herman, C. P. (2002). If at first you don't succeed: False hopes of self-change. *American Psychologist, 57*, 677–689.

Pollack, I. (1953). The assimilation of sequentially coded information. *American Journal of Psychology, 66*, 421–435.

Pollack, V. (1992). Meta-analysis of subjective sensitivity to alcohol in sons of alcoholics. *American Journal of Psychiatry, 149*, 1534–1538.

Pollatsek, A., Romoser, M. E., & Fisher, D. L. (2011). Identifying and remediating failures of selective attention in older drivers. *Current Directions in Psychological Science 21*(1) 3–7. doi:10.1177/0963721411429459

Pollet, T. V., Roberts, S. B., & Dunbar, R. M. (2011). Use of social network sites and instant messaging does not lead to increased offline social network size, or to emotionally closer relationships with offline network members. *Cyberpsychology, Behavior, and Social Networking, 14*(4), 253–258. doi:10.1089/cyber.2010.0161.

Pollo, A., & Benedetti, F. (2009). The placebo response: Neurobiological and clinical issues of neurological relevance. *Progress in Brain Research, 175*, 283–294.

Polman, R., & Emich, K. J. (2011). Decisions for others are more creative than decisions for the self. *Personality and Social Psychology Bulletin, 37*(4), 492–501. doi:10.1177/0146167211398362.

Polman H., Orobio de Castro, B., & van Aken, M. A. G. (2008). Experimental study of the differential effects of playing versus watching violent video games on children's aggressive behavior. *Aggressive Behavior, 34*, 256–264.

Polusny, M. A., & Follette, V. M. (1995). Long-term correlates of child sexual abuse: Theory and review of the empirical literature. *Applied and Preventive Psychology, 4*, 143–166.

Pompili, M., Lester, D., De Pisa, E., Del Casale, A., et al. (2008). Surviving the suicides of significant others: A case study. *Crisis, 29*, 45–48.

Poole, D., Bruck, M., & Pipe, M. (2011). Forensic interviewing aids: Do props help children answer questions about touching?. *Current Directions In Psychological Science, 20*(1), 11–15. doi:10.1177/0963721410388804.

Poon, L. W. (2008). What can we learn from centenarians? In C. Y. Read, R. C. Green, & M. A. Smyer (Eds.), *Aging, biotechnology, and the future* (pp. 100–110). Baltimore: Johns Hopkins University Press.

Pope, H. G., Gruber, A. J., Hudson, J. I., Huestis, M. A., & Yurgelun-Todd, D. (2001). Neuropsychological performance in long-term cannabis users. *Archives of General Psychiatry, 58*, 909–915.

Pope, H. G., Jr., Hudson, J. I., Bodkin, J. A., & Oliva, P. (1998). Questionable validity of "dissociative amnesia" in trauma victims: Evidence from prospective studies. *British Journal of Psychiatry, 172*, 210–215.

Pope, H. G., Jr., & Yurgelun-Todd, D. (1996). The residual cognitive effects of heavy marijuana use in college students. *Journal of the American Medical Association, 275*, 521–527.

Popper, M. (2011). Toward a theory of followership. *Review of General Psychology, 15*(1), 29–36. doi:10.1037/a0021989.

Porges, S. W., Doussard, R. J. A., & Maita, A. K. (1995). Vagal tone and the physiological regulation of emotion. *Monographs of the Society for Research on Child Development, 59*(2–3), 167–186, 250–283.

Poropat, A. (2009). A meta-analysis of the five-factor model of personality and academic performance. *Psychological Bulletin, 135*, 322–338.

Port, C. L., Engdahl, B., & Frazier, P. (2001). A longitudinal and retrospective study of PTSD among older prisoners of war. *American Journal of Psychiatry, 158*, 1474–1479.

Porte, H. S., & Hobson, J. A. (1996). Physical motion in dreams: One measure of three theories. *Journal of Abnormal Psychology, 105*, 329–335.

Porter, J., Anand, T., Johnson, B., Khan, R. M., & Sobell, N. (2005). Brain mechanisms for extracting spatial information from smell. *Neuron, 47*, 581–592.

Porter, R. H. (1991). Human reproduction and the mother-infant relationship. In T. V. Getchell et al. (Eds.), *Taste and smell in health and disease.* New York: Raven Press.

Porter, R. H., Cernich, J. M., & McLaughlin, F. J. (1983). Maternal recognition of neonates through olfactory cues. *Physiology and Behavior, 30*, 151–154.

Porter, R. H., Makin, J. W., Davis, L. B., & Christensen, K. M. (1992). Breast-fed infants respond to olfactory cues from their own mother and unfamiliar lactating females. *Infant Behavior and Development, 15*, 85–93.

Porter, S., Birt, A. R., Yuille, J. C., & Lehman, D. R. (2000). Negotiating false memories: Interviewer and rememberer characteristics relate to memory distortion. *Psychological Science, 11*, 507–510.

Porter, S., & Brinke, L. (2010). The truth about lies: What works in detecting high-stakes deception?. *Legal & Criminological Psychology, 15*(1), 57–75. doi:10.1348/135532509X433151.

Porter, S., Brinke, L., Baker, A., & Wallace, B. (2011). Would I lie to you? "Leakage" in deceptive facial expressions relates to psychopathy and emotional intelligence. *Personality & Individual Differences, 51*(2), 133–137. doi:10.1016/j.paid.2011.03.031.

Porter, S., & Peace, K. A. (2007). The scars of memory: A prospective, longitudinal investigation of the consistency of traumatic and positive emotional memories in adulthood. *Psychological Science 18*, 435–441.

Porter, S., & ten Brinke, L. (2009). Dangerous decisions: A theoretical framework for understanding how judges assess credibility in the courtroom. *Legal & Criminological Psychology, 14*(1), 119–134. doi:10.1348/135532508X281520.

Porter, S., Yuille, J. C., & Lehman, D. R. (1999). The nature of real, implanted, and fabricated memories for emotional childhood events: Implications for the recovered memory debate. *Law & Human Behavior, 23,* 517–537.

Posener, J. A., DeBattista, C., Williams, G. H., Kraemer, H. C., Kalehzan, B. M., & Schatzberg, A. F. (2000). 24-hour monitoring of cortisol and corticotropin secretion in psychotic and nonpsychotic major depression. *Archives of General Psychiatry, 57,* 755–760.

Posner, J. B., Saper, C. B., Schiff, N. D., & Plum, F. (2007). *Plum and Posner's Diagnosis of Stupor and Coma. (Contemporary Neurology Series. 71.) Fourth edition.* New York, NY: Oxford University Press.

Posner, M. I., & Peterson, S. E. (1990). The attention system of the human brain. *Annual Review of Neurosciences, 13,* 24–42.

Posner, M. I., & Raichle, M. E. (1994). *Images of mind.* New York: Scientific American Books.

Posthuma, D., & deGeus, E. J. C. (2006). Progress in the molecular-genetic study of intelligence. *Current Directions in Psychological Science, 15,* 151–155.

Postuma, R. B., Gagnon, J. F., & Montplaisir, J. Y. (2011). REM sleep behavior disorder: From dreams to neurodegeneration. *Neurobiology of Disease,* October 14, 2011 [Epub ahead of print]

Poteat, V., O'Dwyer, L. M., & Mereish, E. H. (2012). Changes in how students use and are called homophobic epithets over time: Patterns predicted by gender, bullying, and victimization status. *Journal of Educational Psychology, 104*(2), 393–406. doi:10.1037/a0026437.

Potkin, S. G., Saha, A. R., Kujawa, M. J., Carson, W. H., Ali, M., Stock, E., et al. (2003). Aripiprazole, an antipsychotic with a novel mechanism of action, and risperidone vs placebo in patients with schizophrenia and schizoaffective disorder. *Archives of General Psychiatry, 60,* 681–690.

Potter, P. T., & Zautra, A. J. (1997). Stressful life events' effects on rheumatoid arthritis disease activity. *Journal of Consulting and Clinical Psychology, 65,* 319–323.

Pottick, K. J., Bilder, S., VanderStoep, A., Warner, L. A., & Alvarez, M. F. (2008). US patterns of mental health service utilization for transition-age youth and young adults. *Journal of Behavioral Health Services and Research, 35,* 373–389.

Pottick, K. J., Kirk, S. A., Hsieh, D. K., & Tian, X. (2007). Judging mental disorder in youths: Effects of client, clinician, and contextual differences. *Journal of Consulting and Clinical Psychology, 75,* 1–8.

Poulin, M. J., Holman, E., & Buffone, A. (2012). The neurogenetics of nice: Receptor genes for oxytocin and vasopressin interact with threat to predict prosocial behavior. *Psychological Science, 23,* 446–452. doi:10.1177/0956797611428471.

Poulin-Dubois, D., Blaye, A., Coutya, J., & Bialystok, E. (2011). The effects of bilingualism on toddlers' executive functioning. *Journal of Experimental Child Psychology, 108*(3), 567–579. doi:10.1016/j.jecp.2010.10.009.

Poulin-Dubois, D., Brooker, I., & Polonia, A. (2011). Infants prefer to imitate a reliable person. *Infant Behavior & Development, 34*(2), 303–309. doi:10.1016/j.infbeh.2011.01.006.

Pourtois, G., de Gelder, B., Bol, A., & Crommelinck, M. (2005). Perception of facial expressions and voices and of their combination in the human brain. *Cortex, 41,* 49–59.

Povinelli, D. J., & Bering, J. M. (2002). The mentality of apes revisited. *Current Directions in Psychological Science, 11,* 115–119.

Powch, I. G., & Houston, B. K. (1996). Hostility, anger-in, and cardiovascular activity in White women. *Health Psychology, 15,* 200–208.

Powell, A., Apovian, C., & Aronne, L. (2011). New drug targets for the treatment of obesity. *Clinical Pharmacology And Therapeutics, 90*(1), 40–51. doi:10.1038/clpt.2011.82.

Powell, L. H., Shahabi, L., & Thoresen, C. E. (2003). Religion and spirituality: Linkages to physical health. *American Psychologist, 58,* 36–52.

Power, C., & Rasko, J. J. (2011). Will cell reprogramming resolve the embryonic stem cell controversy? A narrative review. *Annals of Internal Medicine, 155*(2), 114–W43.

Powers, M. B., Halpern, J. M., Ferenschak, M. P., Gillihan, S. J., & Foa, E. B. (2010). A metaanalytic review of prolonged exposure for posttraumatic stress disorder. *Clinical Psychology Review, 30,* 635–641.

Powers, S. I., Pietromonaco, P. R., Gunlicks, M., & Sayer, A. (2006). Dating couples' attachment styles and patterns of cortisol reactivity and recovery in response to a relationship conflict. *Journal of Personality and Social Psychology, 90,* 613–628.

Powley, T. L., & Keesey, R. E. (1970). Relationship of body weight to the lateral hypothalamic feeding syndrome. *Journal of Comparative & Physiological Psychology, 70,* 25–36.

Poyares, D., Guilleminault, C., Ohayon, M. M., & Tufik, S. (2004). Chronic benzodiazepine usage and withdrawal in insomnia patients. *Journal of Psychiatric Research, 38,* 327–334.

Prabhudesai, S. G., Gould, S., Rekhraj, S., Tekkis, P. P., Glazer, G., & Ziprin, P. (2008). Artificial neural networks: Useful aid in diagnosing acute appendicitis. *World Journal of Surgery, 32*(2), 305–309.

Practice guidelines regarding psychologists' involvement in pharmacological issues. (2011). *American Psychologist, 66*(9), 835–849. doi:10.1037/a0025890.

Pratkanis, A., & Aronson, E. (2001). *The age of propaganda: The everyday use and abuse of propaganda.* New York: W. H. Freeman.

Pratkanis, A. R. (1992). The cargo-cult science of subliminal persuasion. *Skeptical Inquirer, 16,* 260–273.

Pratkanis, A. R., Eskenazi, J., & Greenwald, A. G. (1994). What you expect is what you believe (but not necessarily what you get): A test of the effectiveness of self-help audiotapes. *Basic and Applied Social Psychology, 15,* 251–276.

Prescott, J. W. (1996). The origins of human love and violence. *Pre- and Peri-Natal Psychology Journal, 10,* 143–188.

Preciado, P., Snijders, T. B., Burk, W. J., Stattin, H., & Kerr, M. (2012). Does proximity matter? Distance dependence of adolescent friendships. *Social Networks, 34,* 18–31.

President's New Freedom Commission on Mental Health. (2003). *Achieving the promise: Transforming mental health care in America.* Rockville, Maryland: U.S. Department of Health and Human Services.

Press, C., Heyes, C., Haggard, P., & Eimer, M. (2008). Visuotactile learning and body representation: An ERP study with rubber hands and rubber objects. *Journal of Cognitive Neuroscience, 20*(2), 312–323.

Press, Y., Margulin, T., Grinshpun, Y., Kagan, E., Snir, Y., Berzak, A., & Clarfield, A. M. (2009). The diagnosis of delirium among elderly patients presenting to the emergency department of an acute hospital. *Archives of Gerontology & Geriatrics, 48*(2), 201–204.

Pressman, M. R. (2007). Factors that predispose, prime and precipitate NREM parasomnias in adults: Clinical and forensic implications. *Sleep Medicine Reviews, 11*(1), 5–30. doi:10.1016/j.smrv.2006.06.003

Pressman, S. D., & Cohen, S. (2005). Does positive aff ect infl uence health? *Psychological Bulletin, 131,* 925–971.

Pressman, S. D., & Cohen, S. (2005). Does positive affect influence health? *Psychological Bulletin, 131,* 925–971.

Price, K. H., Harrison, D. A., & Gavin, J. H. (2006).Withholding inputs in team contexts: Member composition, interaction processes, evaluation structure, and social loafing. *Journal of Applied Psychology, 91,* 1375–1384.

Price, M., & Anderson, P. L. (2012). Outcome expectancy as a predictor of treatment response in cognitive behavioral therapy for public speaking fears within social anxiety disorder. *Psychotherapy, 49,* 173–179. doi:10.1037/a0024734.

Price, M., & Hyde, J. (2011). Perceived and observed maternal relationship quality predict sexual debut by age 15. *Journal of Youth & Adolescence, 40*(12), 1595–1606. doi:10.1007/s10964-011-9641-y.

Priego, T., Sanchez, J., Palou, A., & Pico, C. (2010). Leptin intake during the suckling period improves the metabolic response of adipose tissue to a high-fat diet. *International Journal of Obesity, 34,* 809–819.

Prigatano, G. P., Matthes, J., Hill, S. W., Wolf, T. R., & Heiserman, J. E. (2011). Anosognosia for hemiplegia with preserved awareness of complete cortical blindness following intracranial hemorrhage. *Cortex, 47*(10), 1219–1227.

Prikryl, R., Ceskova, E., Kasparek, T., & Kucerova, H. (2006). Neurological soft signs, clinical symptoms and treatment reactivity in patients suffering from first episode schizophrenia. *Journal of Psychiatric Research, 40,* 141–146.

Prinstein, M. J., & La Greca, A. M. (2002). Peer crowd affiliation and intrenalizing distress in childhood and adolescence: A longitudinal follow-back study. *Journal of Research on Adolescence, 12,* 35–351.

Prochaska, J. O. (1994). Strong and weak principles for progressing from precontemplation to action on the basis of twelve problem behaviors. *Health Psychology, 13,* 47–51.

Prochaska, J. O., DiClemente, C., & Norcross, J. (1992). In search of how people change: Application to addictive behaviors. *American Psychologist, 47,* 1102–1114.

Procopio, M., & Marriott, P. (2007). Intrauterine hormonal environment and risk of developing anorexia nervosa. *Archives of General Psychiatry, 64,* 1402–1407.

Program for International Student Assessment. (2004). *Learning for tomorrow's world: First results from PISA 2003.* Paris: OECD.

Program for International Student Assessment. (2005). *Learning for tomorrow's world: First results from PISA 2004.* Paris: OECD.

Pronin, E., Wegner, D. M., McCarthy, K., & Rodreguez, S. (2006). Everyday magical powers: The role of apparent causation in the overestimation of personal influence. *Journal of Personality and Social Psychology, 91,* 218–231.

Proske, E. (2006). Kinesthesia: The role of muscle receptors. *Muscle and Nerve, 34*(5), 545–558.

Przybylski, A. K., Weinstein, N., Murayama, K., Lynch, M. F., & Ryan, R. M. (2012). The Ideal self at play: The appeal of video games that let you be all you can be. *Psychological Science, 23*(1), 69–76. doi:10.1177/0956797611418676.

Puetz, A., & Ruenzi, S. (2011). Overconfidence among professional investors: Evidence from mutual fund managers. *Journal of Business Finance & Accounting, 38,* 684-712.

Pulakos, E. D., Schmitt, N., Dorsey, D. W., Arad, S., Hedge, J. W., & Borman, W. C. (2002). Predicting adaptive performance: Further tests of a model of adaptability. *Human Performance, 15,* 299–324.

Pulfrey, C., Buchs, C., & Butera, F. (2011). Why grades engender performance-avoidance goals: The mediating role of autonomous motivation. *Journal Of Educational Psychology, 103*(3), 683–700. doi:10.1037/a0023911.

Purdon, C. (2009). Psychological approaches to understanding obsessive-compulsive disorder. In M. M. Antony & M. B. Stein (Eds.), *Oxford handbook of anxiety and related disorders* (pp. 238–249). New York: Oxford University Press.

Putnam, F. W. (2003). Ten-year research update review: Child sexual abuse. *Journal of the American Academy of Child & Adolescent Psychiatry, 42,* 269–278.

Puvathingal, B. J., & Hantula, D. A. (2012). Revisiting the psychology of intelligence analysis: From rational actors to adaptive thinkers. *American Psychologist, 67*(3), 199–210. doi:10.1037/a0026640.

Pyc, M. A., & Rawson, K. A. (2010). Why testing improves memory: Mediator effectiveness hypothesis. *Science, 330*(6002), doi:10.1126/science.1191465.

Pyka, M., Burgmer, M., Lenzen, T., Pioch, R., Dannlowski, U., Pfleiderer, B., Ewert, A. W., Heuf, G., Arolt, V., & Konrad, C. (2011). Brain correlates of hypnotic paralysis—a resting-state fMRI study. *NeuroImage, 56,* 2173–2182.

Pyszczynski, T., Greenberg, J., Koole, S., & Solomon, S. (2010). Experimental existential psychology: Coping with the facts of life. In S. T. Fiske, D. T. Gilbert, & G. Lindzey (Eds.), *Handbook of social psychology* (5th ed., Vol. 2., pp. 724–760). Hoboken, NJ: Wiley.

Quinlivan, D. S., Neuschatz, J. S., Cutler, B. L., Wells, G. L., McClung, J., & Harker, D. L. (2012). Do pre-admonition suggestions moderate the effect of unbiased lineup instructions? *Legal and Criminological Psychology*, 17(1), 165–176. doi:10.1348/135532510X533554.

Quinn, P., & Liben, L. S. (2008). A sex difference in mental rotation in young infants. *Psychological Science*, 19, 1067–1070.

Quinn, P. C., & Bhatt, R. S. (2005). Learning perceptual organization in infancy. *Psychological Science*, 16, 511–515.

Quintana, S. M. (2011). Ethnicity, race, and children's social development. In P. K. Smith & C. H. Hart (Eds.), *Wiley-Blackwell handbook of childhood social development* (2nd ed). Hoboken, NJ: Wiley-Blackwell.

Quoidback, J., Dunn, E. W., Petrides, K. V., & Mikolajczak, M. (2010). Money giveth, money taketh away: The dual effect of wealth on happiness. *Psychological Science*, 21, 759–763.

Raaijmakers, Q. A. W., Engels, R. C. M. E., & Van Hoof, A. (2005). Delinquency and moral reasoning in adolescence and young adulthood. *International Journal of Behavioral Development*, 29, 247–258.

Rabaglia, C. D., & Salthouse, T. A. (2011). Natural and constrained language production as a function of age and cognitive abilities. *Language and Cognitive Processes*, 26(10), 1505–1531. doi:10.1080/01690965.2010.507489.

Rabasca, L. (1999, July/August). Behavioral interventions can cut the use of restraints. *APA Monitor*, p. 27.

Rabinowitz, J., De Smedt, G., Harvey, P. D., & Davidson, M. (2002). Relationship between premorbid functioning and symptom severity as assessed at first episode of psychosis. *American Journal of Psychiatry*, 159, 2021–2026.

Rabinowitz, J., Lichtenberg, P., Kaplan, Z., Mark, M., Nahon, D., & Davidson, M. (2001). Re-hospitalization rates of chronically ill schizophrenic patients discharged on a regimen of risperidone, olanzapine, or conventional antipsychotics. *American Journal of Psychiatry*, 158, 266–269.

Rabunal, J. R., & Dorado, J. (2006). *Artificial neural networks in real-life applications.* Hershey, PA: Idea Group.

Rachlin, H. (2000). *The science of self-control.* Cambridge, MA: Harvard University Press.

Rachlin, H., & Jones, B. A. (2008). Altruism among relatives and non-relatives. *Behavioural Processes*, 79, 120–123.

Racsmany, M., Conway, M. A., & Demeter, G. (2010). Consolidation of episodic memories during sleep: Long-term effects of retrieval practice. *Psychological Science*, 21, 80–85.

Rada, J. B., & Rogers, R. W. (1973). *Obedience to authority: Presence of authority and command strength.* Paper presented at the annual convention of the Southeastern Psychological Association.

Radcliffe, N. M., & Klein, W. M. (2002). Dispositional, unrealistic and comparative optimism: Differential relations with the knowledge and processing of risk information and beliefs about personal risk. *Personality & Social Psychology Bulletin*, 28, 836–846.

Radel, R., & Clément-Guillotin, C. (2012). Evidence of motivational influences in early visual perception: Hunger modulates conscious access. *Psychological Science*, 23(3), 232–234. doi:10.1177/0956797611427920.

Radford, B. (2005). Voice of reason: Exorcisms, fictional and fatal. *Skeptical Inquirer.* Retrieved August 1, 2005, from http://www.csicop.org/specialarticles/exorcist-rituals.html.

Radvansky, G. A. (1999). Aging, memory, and comprehension. *Current Directions in Psychological Science*, 8, 49–53.

Raffaelli, M., & Crockett, L. J. (2003). Sexual risk taking in adolescence: The role of self-regulation and attraction to risk. *Developmental Psychology*, 39, 1036–1046.

Raggatt, P. T. (1991). Work stress among long-distance coach drivers: A survey and correlational study. *Journal of Organizational Behavior*, 12, 565–579.

Rai, T., & Fiske, A. (2011). Moral psychology is relationship regulation: Moral motives for unity, hierarchy, equality, and proportionality. *Psychological Review*, 118(1), 57–75. doi:10.1037/a0021867.

Raij, T. T., Numminen, J., Narvanen, S., Hiltunen, J., & Hari, R. (2005). Brain correlates of subjective reality of physically and psychologically induced pain. *Proceedings of the National Academy of Sciences*, 102, 2147–2151.

Raikes, H., Pan, B. A., Luze, G., Tamis-LeMonda, C. S., Brooks-Gunn, J., Constantine, J., et al. (2006). Mother-child bookreading in low-income families: Correlates and outcomes during the first three years of life. *Child Development*, 77, 924–953.

Raine, A., Brennan, P., & Mednick, S. (1994). Birth complications combined with early maternal rejection at age 1 year predispose to violent crime at age 18 years. *Archives of General Psychiatry*, 51, 984–988.

Raine, A., & Liu, J. (1998). Biological predispositions to violence and their implications for biosocial treatment and prevention. *Psychology, Crime & Law*, 4(2), 107–125. doi:10.1080/10683169808401752.

Raine, A., Moffitt, T. E., Caspi, A., Loeber, R., Stouthamer-Loeber, M., & Lynam, D. (2005). Neurocognitive impairments in boys on the life-course persistent antisocial path. *Journal of Abnormal Psychology*, 114, 38–49.

Rains, G. C., Utley, S. L., & Lewis, W. J. (2006). Behavioral monitoring of trained insects for chemical detection. *Biotechnology Progress*, 22, 2–8.

Raisig, S., Welke, T., Hagendorf, H., & van der Meer, E. (2010). I spy with my little eye: Detection of temporal violations in event sequences and the pupillary response. *International Journal of Psychophysiology*, 76, 1–8.

Rajaram, S., & Barber, S. J. (2008). Retrieval processes in memory. In H. L. Roediger, III (Ed.), *Cognitive psychology of memory.* Oxford: Elsevier.

Rajaratnam, S. M. W., Barger, L. K., Lockley, S. W., Shea, S. A., Wang, W., Landrigan, C. P., O'Brien, C. S., Qadri, S., Sullivan, J. P., Cade, B. E.,

Epstein, L. J., White, D. P., Czeisler, C. A., for the Harvard Work Hours, Health and Safety Group. (2011). Sleep disorders, health, and safety in police officers. *JAMA*, 306(23), 2567–2578.

Rakic, P. (2002). Neurogenesis in adult primate neocortex: An evaluation of the evidence. *Nature Reviews Neuroscience*, 3, 65–71.

Ramachandran, V. S. (1988, August). Perceiving shape from shading. *Scientific American*, 76–83.

Ramachandran, V. S. (1998). Consciousness and body image: Lessons from phantom limbs, Capgras syndrome and pain asymbolia. *Philosophical Transactions of the Royal Society of London, B*, 353, 1851–1859.

Ramachandran, V. S. (2008). *The man with the phantom twin: Adventures in the neuroscience of the human brain.* New York: Dutton.

Ramey, C. T., Ramey, S. L., & Lanzi, R. G. (2006). Children's health and education. In W. Damon & R. M. Lerner (Series Eds.) & K. A. Renninger & I. E. Sigel (Vol. Eds.), *Handbook of child psychology: Vol. 4. Child psychology in practice* (6th ed.). New York: Wiley.

Randolph-Seng, B., & Mather, R. D. (2009). Does subliminal persuasion work? It depends on your motivation and awareness. *Skeptical Inquirer*, 33, 49–53.

Ranganath, C. (2010). Binding items and contexts: The cognitive neuroscience of episodic memory. *Current Directions in Psychological Science*, 19(3), 131–137. doi:10.1177/0963721410368805.

Rapaport, M. H., Clary, C., Fayyad, R., & Endicott, J. (2005). Quality-of-life impairment in depressive and anxiety disorders. *American Journal of Psychiatry*, 162, 1171–1178.

Rapee, R., Brown, T., Antony, M., & Barlow, D. (1992). Response to hyperventilation and inhalation of 5.5% carbon dioxide-enriched air across *DSM-III* anxiety disorders. *Journal of Abnormal Psychology*, 101, 538–552.

Rapee, R., Kennedy, S., Ingram, M., Edwards, S., & Sweeney, L. (2005). Prevention and early intervention of anxiety disorders in inhibited preschool children. *Journal of Consulting and Clinical Psychology*, 73, 488–497.

Rapoport, J. L., Addington, A. M., & Frangou, S. (2005). The neurodevelopmental model of schizophrenia: Update 2005. *Molecular Psychiatry*, 10, 434–449.

Rapp, S. R., Brenes, G., & Marsh, A. P. (2002). Memory enhancement training for older adults with mild cognitive impairment: A preliminary study. *Aging & Mental Health*, 6(1), 5–11.

Rasch, B., & Born, J. (2008). Reactivation and consolidation of memory during sleep. *Current Directions in Psychological Science*, 17, 188–192.

Rasinski, K. A., Kuby, A., Bzdusek, S. A., Silvestri, J. M., & Weese-Mayer, D. E. (2003). Effect of a sudden infant death syndrome risk reduction education program on risk factor compliance and information sources in primarily black urban communities. *Pediatrics*, 111, 347–354.

Raskin, D. C. (1986). The polygraph in 1986: Scientific, professional and legal issues surrounding applications and acceptance of polygraph evidence. *Utah Law Review*, 1, 29–74.

Raskin, N. J., & Rogers, C. R. (2001). Person-centered therapy. In R. J. Corsini & D. Wedding (Eds.), *Current psychotherapies* (6th ed.). Itasca, IL: Peacock.

Raskin, N. J., & Rogers, C. R. (2005). Person-centered therapy. In R. J. Corsini & D. Wedding (Eds.), *Current psychotherapies* (7th ed., pp. 130–165). Belmont, CA: Thomson Brooks/Cole.

Rasmussen, H., Erritzoe, D., Andersen, R., Ebdrup, B. H., et al. (2010). Decreased frontal serotonin 2A receptor binding in antipsychotic-naive patients with first-episode schizophrenia. *Archives of General Psychiatry*, 67, 9–16.

Ratcliff, R., & McKoon, G. (1989). Memory models, text processing, and cue-dependent retrieval. In H. L. Roediger & F. I. M. Craik (Eds.), *Varieties of memory and consciousness.* Hillsdale, NJ: Erlbaum.

Rattan, A., Good, C., & Dweck, C. S. (2012). "It's ok—Not everyone can be good at math": Instructors with an entity theory comfort (and demotivate) students. *Journal of Experimental Social Psychology*, 48(3), 731–737. doi:10.1016/j.jesp.2011.12.012.

Rattenborg, N., Lima, S. L., & Amlaner, C. J. (1999). Half-awake to the risk of predation. *Nature*, 397, 397–398.

Raudenbush, B., & Meyer, B. (2002). Effect of nasal dilators on pleasantness, intensity and sampling behaviors of foods in the oral cavity. *Rhinology*, 39, 80–83.

Rawson, K. A., & Dunlosky, J. (2011). Optimizing schedules of retrieval practice for durable and efficient learning: How much is enough? *Journal of Experimental Psychology: General*, 140(3), 283–302. doi:10.1037/a0023956.

Rawson, P. (2006). *Handbook of short-term psychodynamic psychotherapy.* London: Karnac Books. Ray, L. A.; Miranda, R., Jr.; Tidey, J. W.; McGeary, J. E.; et al. (2010). Polymorphisms of the m-opioid receptor and dopamine D4 receptor genes and subjective responses to alcohol in the natural environment. *Journal of Abnormal Psychology*, 119, 115–125.

Ray, L. A.; Miranda, R., Jr.; Tidey, J. W.; McGeary, J. E., et al. (2010). Polymorphisms of the μ-opioid receptor and dopamine D4 receptor genes and subjective responses to alcohol in the natural environment. *Journal of Abnormal Psychology*, 119, 115–125.

Raz, A., Fan, J., & Posner, M. I. (2005). Hypnotic suggestion reduces conflict in the brain. *Proceedings of the National Academy of Sciences*, 102, 9978–9983.

Razali, S. M., Aminah, K., & Umeed, A. (2002). Religious-cultural psychotherapy in the management of anxiety patients. *Transcultural Psychiatry*, 39, 130–136.

Read, S. J., Monroe, B. M., Brownstein, A. L., Yang, Y., et al. (2010). A neural network model of the structure and dynamics of human personality. *Psychological Review*, 117, 61–92.

Reber, A. S. (1992). The cognitive unconscious: An evolutionary perspective. *Consciousness and Cognition: An International Journal*, 1(2), 93–133.

Redd, M., & de Castro, J. M. (1992). Social facilitation of eating: Effects of social instruction on food intake. *Physiology and Behavior*, 52, 749–754.

Redmond, D. E., Jr., Bjugstad, K. B., Teng, Y. D., Ourednik, V., Ourednik, J., Wakeman, D. R., Parsons, X. H., Gonzalez, R., Blanchard, B. C., Kim, S. U., Gu, Z., Lipton, S. A., Markakis, E. A., Roth, R. H., Elsworth, J. D., Sladek, J. R., Jr., Sidman, R. L., & Snyder, E. Y. (2007). Behavioral improvement in a primate Parkinson's model is associated with multiple homeostatic effects of human neural stem cells. *Proceedings of the National Academy of Sciences, 104,* 12175–12180.

Reed, P. L., Anthony, J. C., & Breslau, N. (2007). Incidence of drug problems in young adults exposed to trauma and posttraumatic stress disorder: Do early life experiences and predispositions matter? *Archives of General Psychiatry, 64,* 1435–1442.

Reed, R. R. (2004). Aft er the holy grail: Establishing a molecular basis for mammalian olfaction. *Cell, 116,* 329–336.

Reed, S. K. (2000). *Cognition* (5th ed.). Belmont, CA: Wadsworth.

Reedy, M. N. (1983). Personality and aging. In D. S. Woodruff & J. E. Birren (Eds.), *Aging: Scientific perspectives and social issues* (2nd ed.). Monterey, CA: Brooks/Cole.

Rees, J., McKenna, P., Bell, V., Skucek, E., Nichols, E., & Fisher, P. (2008). The Rookwood Driving Battery: Normative older adult performance. *British Journal of Clinical Psychology, 47*(2), 139–151.

Reeve, J. (2009). Why teachers adopt a controlling motivating style toward students and how they can become more autonomy supportive. *Educational Psychologist, 44,* 159–175.

Reeve, J. M. (1996). *Understanding motivation and emotion.* New York: Harcourt, Brace, Jovanovich.

Reeves, G. K., Pirie, K., Beral, V., Green, J., Spencer, E., & Bull, D. (2007). Cancer incidence and mortality in relation to body mass index in the Million Women Study: Cohort study. *British Medical Journal, 335,* 1134.

Reeves, M. J., & Rafferty, A. P. (2005). Healthy lifestyle characteristics among adults in the United States, 2000. *Archives of Internal Medicine, 165,* 854–857.

Rehm, L. P., & DeMers, S. T. (2006). Licensure. *Clinical Psychology: Science and Practice, 13,* 249–253.

Reich, D. A. (2004). What you expect is not always what you get: The roles of extremity, optimism, and pessimism in the behavioral confirmation process. *Journal of Experimental Social Psychology, 40,* 199–215.

Reich, S. M., Subrahmanyam, K., & Espinoza, G. (2012). Friending, IMing, and hanging out face-to-face: Overlap in adolescents' online and offline social networks. *Developmental Psychology, 48*(2), 356–368. doi:10.1037/a0026980.

Reicher, S., Haslam, S.A., & Smith, J.R. (2012). Working toward the experimenter: Reconceptualizing obedience within the Milgram paradigm as identification-based followership. *Perspectives in Psychological Science, 7,* 315–324.

Reid, M. J., Webster-Stratton, C., & Baydar, N. (2004). Halting the development of conduct problems in Head Start children: The effects of parent training. *Journal of Clinical Child and Adolescent Psychology, 33,* 279–291.

Reijntjes, A., Thomaes, S., Bushman, B. J., Boelen, P. A., Orobio de Castro, B., & Telch, M. J. (2010). The outcast-lash-out effect in youth: Alienation increases aggression following peer rejection. *Psychological Science, 21*(10), 1394–1398. doi:10.1177/0956797610381509.

Reilly, T., Atkinson, G., Edwards, B., Waterhouse, J., Åkerstedt, T., Davenne, D., Lemmer, Björn, Wirz-Justice, A. (2007). Coping with jet-lag: A position statement for the European College of Sport Science. *European Journal of Sport Science, 7*(1), 1–7.

Reilly, T., Waterhouse, J., Burke, L. M., & Alonso, J. (2007). Nutrition for travel. *Journal of Sports Sciences, 25,* 125–134.

Reimer, B., Mehler, B. Coughlin, J. F., Roy, N., & Dusek, J. A. (2010). The impact of a naturalistic hands-free cellular phone task on heart rate and simulated driving performance in two age groups. *Transportation Research Part F: Traffic Psychology and Behaviour, 14*(1), 13–25. doi:10.1016/j.trf.2010.09.002.

Reingold, E. M., Charness, N., Pomplun, M., & Stampe, D. M. (2001). Visual span in expert chess players: Evidence from eye movements. *Psychological Science, 12,* 48–55.

Reinisch, J. M., Ziemba-Davis, M., & Sanders, S. A. (1991). Hormonal contributions to sexually dimorphic behavioral development in humans. *Psychoneuroendocrinology, 16,* 213–278.

Reinoso-Suárez, F., de Andrés, I., & Garzón, M. (2011). Functional anatomy of the sleep-wakefulness cycle: wakefulness. *Advances in Anatomy, Embryology, and Cell Biology, 208,* 1–128.

Reis, B. F., & Brown, L. G. (2006). Preventing therapy dropout in the real world: The clinical utility of videotape preparation and client estimate of treatment duration. *Professional Psychology: Research and Practice, 37,* 311–316.

Reis, H. T., & Aron, A. (2008). Love: What is it, why does it matter, and how does it operate? *Perspectives on Psychological Science 3,* 80–86.

Reis, H. T., Maniaci, M. R., Caprariello, P. A., Eastwick, P. W, & Finkel, E. J (2011). Familiarity does indeed promote attraction in live interaction. *Journal of Personality and Social Psychology, 101,* 557-570.

Reisenzein, R. (1983). The Schachter theory of emotion: Two decades later. *Psychological Bulletin, 94,* 239–264.

Reiss, A. J., & Roth, J. A. (1993). *Understanding and preventing violence.* Washington, DC: National Academy Press.

Reiss, D., Neiderhiser, J. M., Hetherington, E. M., & Plomin, R. (2000). *The relationship code: Deciphering genetic and social influences on adolescent development.* Cambridge, MA: Harvard University Press.

Reissig, C. J., Strain, E. C., & Griffiths, R. R. (2009). Caffeinated energy drinks—a growing problem.

Reitz, C., Brayne, C., & Mayeux, R. (2011). Epidemiology of Alzheimer disease. *Nature Reviews Neurology, 7*(3), 137–153. doi:10.1038/nrneurol.2011.2.

Reitz, C., Tang, M., Schupf, N., Manly, J., Mayeux, R., & Luchsinger, J. (2010). A summary risk score for the prediction of Alzheimer disease in elderly persons. *Archives of Neurology, 67*(7), 835–841.

Reivich, K. J., Seligman, M. P., & McBride, S. (2011). Master resilience training in the U.S. Army. *American Psychologist, 66*(1), 25–34. doi:10.1037/a0021897.

Remick, A. K., Polivy, J., & Pliner, P. (2009). Internal and external moderators of the effect of variety on food intake. *Psychological Bulletin, 135,* 434–451.

Ren, T. (2002). Longitudinal pattern of basilar membrane vibration in the sensitive cochlea. *Proceedings of the National Academy of Sciences, 99,* 17101–17106.

Rendall, D., Cheney, D. L., & Seyfarth, R. M. (2000). Proximate factors mediating "contact" calls in adult female baboons (*Papio cynocephalus ursinus*) and their infants. *Journal of Comparative Psychology, 114,* 36–46.

Reneman, L., Lavalaye, J., Schmand, B., de Wolff, F. A., van den Brink, W., den Heeten, G. J., & Booij, J. (2001). Cortical serotonin transporter density and verbal memory in individuals who stopped using 3, 4-methylenedioxymethamphetamine (MDMA or "ecstasy"). *Archives of General Psychiatry, 58,* 901–906.

Renner, K. H., & Beversdorf, D. Q. (2010). Effects of naturalistic stressors on cognitive flexibility and working memory task performance. *Neurocase, 16,* 293–300. doi:10.1080/13554791003463601

Rentfrow, P. J. (2010). Statewide differences in personality: Toward a psychological geography of the United States. *American Psychologist, 65*(6), 548–558. doi:10.1037/a0018194.

Rentz, D. M., Huh, T. J., Faust, R. R., Budson, A. E., Scinto, L. F. M., Sperling, R. A., & Daffner, K. R. (2004). Use of IQ-adjusted norms to predict progressive cognitive decline in highly intelligent older individuals. *Neuropsychology, 18,* 38–49.

Rescorla, L. A. (1981). Category development in early language. *Journal of Child Language, 8,* 225–238.

Rescorla, R. A. (1968). Probability of shock in the presence and absence of CS in fear conditioning. *Journal of Comparative and Physiological Psychology, 66,* 1–5.

Rescorla, R. A. (1988). Pavlovian conditioning: It's not what you think it is. *American Psychologist, 43,* 151–159.

Rescorla, R. A. (2004). Spontaneous recovery varies inversely with the training-extinction interval. *Learning and Behavior, 32,* 401–408.

Rescorla, R. A. (2005). Spontaneous recovery of excitation but not inhibition. *Journal of Experimental Psychology: Animal Behavior Processes, 31,* 277–288.

Rescorla, R. A., & Wagner, A. R. (1972). A theory of Pavlovian conditioning: Variations in the effectiveness of reinforcement and nonreinforcement. In A. H. Black & W. F. Prokasy (Eds.), *Classical conditioning II.* New York: Appleton Century Crofts.

Reuter, J., Raedler, T., Rose, M., Hand, I., Glascher, J., & Buchel, C. (2005). Pathological gambling is linked to reduced activation of the mesolimbic reward system. *Nature Neuroscience, 8,* 147–148.

Reuter, M., Schmitz, A., Corr, P., & Hennig, J. (2006). Molecular genetics support Gray's personality theory: The interaction of COMT and DRD2 polymorphisms predicts the behavioural approach system. *International Journal of Neuropsychopharmacology, 9,* 155–166.

Reuter, T. (2011). Fifty years of dark adaptation 1961-2011. *Vision Research, 51*(21–22), 2243–2262.

Revelle, W. (2008). The contribution of Reinforcement Sensitivity Theory to personality theory. In P. J. Corr (Ed)., *The reinforcement sensitivity theory of personality* (pp. 508–527). Cambridge, UK: Cambridge Press.

Reyes-Escogido, L, Gonzalez-Mondragon, E. G., and Vazquez-Tzompantzi, E. (2011). Chemical and pharmacological aspects of capsaicin. *Molecules, 16*(2), 1253–1270.

Reyna, V. F., & Farley, F. (2006). Risk and rationality in adolescent decision making: Implications for theory, practice, and public policy. *Psychological Science in the Public Interest, 7,* 1–44.

Reynolds, C. A., Finkel, D., McArdle, J. J., Gatz, M., Berg, S., & Pederson, N. L. (2005). Quantitative genetic analysis of latent growth curve models of cognitive abilities in adulthood. *Developmental Psychology, 41,* 3–16.

Reynolds, J. S., & Perrin, N. A. (2004). Mismatches in social support and psychosocial adjustment to breast cancer. *Health Psychology, 23,* 425–430.

Rhodes, R. E., Warburton, D. R., & Bredin, S. D. (2009). Predicting the effect of interactive video bikes on exercise adherence: An efficacy trial. *Psychology, Health & Medicine, 14*(6), 631–640. doi:10.1080/13548500903281088.

Ribases, M., Gratacos, M., Badia, A., Jimenez, L., Solano, R., Vallejo, J., et al. (2005). Contribution of NTRK2 to the genetic susceptibility to anorexia nervosa, harm avoidance and minimum body mass index. *Molecular Psychiatry, 10,* 851–860.

Ribchester, T., Yule, W., & Duncan, A. (2010). EMDR for childhood PTSD after road traffic accidents: Attentional, memory, and attributional processes. *Journal of EMDR Practice and Research, 4*(4), 138–147. doi:10.1891/1933-3196.4.4.138.

Riccio, D. C., Millin, P. M., & Gisquet-Verrier, P. (2003). Retrograde amnesia: Forgetting back. *Current Directions in Psychological science, 12,* 41–44.

Rice, F., Harold, G. T., Shelton, K. H., & Thaper, A. (2006). Family conflict interacts with genetic liability in predicting childhood and adolescent depression. *Journal of the American Academy of Child and Adolescent Psychiatry, 45,* 841–848.

Rice, G., Anderson, C., Risch, H., & Ebers, G. (1999). Male homosexuality: Absence of linkage to microsatellite markers at Xq28. *Science, 284,* 665–667.

Richards, D. (2011). Prevalence and clinical course of depression: A review. *Clinical Psychology Review, 31*(7), 1117–1125. doi:10.1016/j.cpr.2011.07.004.

Richards, D. A., & Schat, A. H. (2011). Attachment at (not to) work: Applying attachment theory to explain individual behavior in organizations. *Journal Of Applied Psychology, 96*(1), 169–182. doi:10.1037/a0020372.

Richards, J. M., & Gross, J. J. (2000). Emotion regulation and memory: The cognitive costs of keeping one's cool. *Journal of Personality and Social Psychology, 79,* 410–424.

Richards, K. C., Anderson, W. M., Chesson, A. L., Jr., & Nagel, C. L. (2002). Sleep-related breathing disorders in patients who are critically ill. *Journal of Cardiovascular Nursing, 17,* 42–55.

Richards, P. S., & Bergin, A. E. (Eds.). (2000). *Handbook of psychotherapy and religious diversity* (pp. 105–129). Washington, DC: American Psychological Association Press.

Richardson, G. A., Goldschmidt, L., & Larkby, C. (2007). Effects of prenatal cocaine exposure on growth: A longitudinal analysis. *Pediatrics, 120,* e1017–e1027.

Richardson, G. A., Goldschmidt, L., Leech, S., & Willford, J. (2011). Prenatal cocaine exposure: Effects on mother- and teacher-rated behavior problems and growth in school-age children. *Neurotoxicology and Teratology, 33*(1), 69–77. doi:10.1016/j.ntt.2010.06.003.

Richardson, M., Abraham, C., & Bond, R. (2012). Psychological correlates of university students' academic performance: A systematic review and meta-analysis. *Psychological Bulletin, 138,* 253–387. doi:10.1037/a0026838.

Richardson, R., & Hayne, R. (2007). You can't take it with you: The translation of memory across development. *Current Directions in Psychological Science, 16,* 223–227.

Richardson-Klavehn, A., & Bjork, R. A. (1988). Measures of memory. *Annual Review of Psychology, 39,* 475–543.

Richmond, J., & Nelson, C. A. (2007). Accounting for change in declarative memory: A cognitive neuroscience perspective. *Developmental Review, 27*(3), 349–373.

Rickels, K., & Rynn, M. (2002). Pharmocotherapy of generalized anxiety disorder. *Journal of Clinical Psychiatry, 63*(Suppl. 14), 9–16.

Rickels, K., Zaninelli, R., McCafferty, J., Bellew, K., Iyengar, M., & Sheehan, D. (2003). Paroxetine treatment of generalized anxiety disorder: A double-blind, placebo-controlled study. *American Journal of Psychiatry, 160,* 749–756.

Riddoch, M. J., Humphreys, G. W., Akhtar, N. A., Allen, H., Bracewell, R. M., & Schofield, A. J. (2008). A tale of two agnosias: Distinctions between form and integrative agnosia. *Cognitive Neuropsychology, 25*(1), 56–92.

Ridley, M. (2000). *Genome: The autobiography of a species in 23 chapters.* New York: HarperCollins. Rieber, R. W. (2006). *The bifurcation of the self: The history and theory of dissociation and its disorders.* New York: Springer.

Rieber, R. W. (2006). *The bifurcation of self: The history and theory of dissociation and its disorders.* New York: Springer.

Riggio, R. E. (1989). *Introduction to industrial/organizational psychology.* Glenview, IL: Scott, Foresman.

Riggs, K. J., McTaggart, J., Simpson, A., & Freeman, R. P. J. (2006). Changes in the capacity of visual working memory in 5- to 10-year-olds. *Journal of Experimental Child Psychology, 95*(1), 18–26.

Rihmer, Z. (2001). Can better recognition and treatment of depression reduce suicide rates? A brief review. *European Psychiatry, 16,* 406–409.

Riis, J., Loewenstein, G., Baron, J., Jepson, C., Fagerlin, A., & Ubel, P. A. (2005). Ignorance of hedonic adaptation to hemodialysis: A study using ecological momentary assessment. *Journal of Experimental Psychology: General, 134,* 3–9.

Rimes, K. A., & Watkins, E. (2005). The effects of self-focused rumination on global negative self-judgments in depression. *Behaviour Research and Therapy, 43,* 1673–1681.

Rimol, L. M., Hartberg, C. B., Nesvåg, R., Fennema-Notestine, C., Hagler, D. J., Pung, C. J., & Agartz, I. (2010). Cortical thickness and subcortical volumes in schizophrenia and bipolar disorder. *Biological Psychiatry, 68*(1), 41–50. doi:10.1016/j.biopsych.2010.03.036.

Rimol, L. M., Nesvåg, R., Hagler, D. J., Bergmann, Ø., Fennema-Notestine, C., Hartberg, C. B., & Dale, A. M. (2012). Cortical volume, surface area, and thickness in schizophrenia and bipolar disorder. *Biological Psychiatry, 71*(6), 552–560. doi:10.1016/j.biopsych.2011.11.026.

Rind, B., Tromovitch, P., & Bauserman, R. (1998). A meta-analytic examination of assumed properties of child sexual abuse using college samples. *Psychological Bulletin, 124,* 22–53.

Rindermann, H., & Ceci, S. J. (2009). Educational policy and country outcomes in international cognitive competence studies. *Perspectives on Psychological Science, 4,* 551–577.

Rinn, W. E. (1984). The neuropsychology of facial expressions: A review of the neurological and psychological mechanisms for producing facial expressions. *Psychological Bulletin, 95,* 52–77.

Rios, R., & Zautra, A. J. (2011). Socioeconomic disparities in pain: The role of economic hardship and daily financial worry. *Health Psychology, 30,* 58–66. doi:10.1037/a0022025.

Rioult-Pedotti, M.-S., Friedman, D., & Donoghue, J. P. (2000). Learning-induced LTP in neocortex. *Science, 290,* 533–536.

Ripple, C. H., Gilliam, W. S., Chanana, N., & Zigler, E. (1999). Will fifty cooks spoil the broth? The debate over entrusting Head Start to the states. *American Psychologist, 54,* 327–343.

Risen, J. (1998, July 7). CIA seeks "curmudgeon" to signal its mistakes. *New York Times.*

Rissman, J., Greely, H. T., & Wagner, A. D. (2010). Detecting individual memories through the neural decoding of memory states and past experience. *Proceedings of the National Academy of Sciences, 107,* 9849–9854.

Ritter, M. (2007). Experts link teen brains' immaturity, juvenile crime. *USA Today.* Retrieved from: http://www.usatoday.com/tech/science/2007-12-02-teenbrains_N.htm.

Rizzolatti, G., & Arbib, M. A. (1998). Language within our grasp. *Trends in Neuroscience, 21,* 188–194.

Rizzolatti, G., Fadiga, L., Gallese, V., & Fogassi, L. (1996). Premotor cortex and the recognition of motor actions. *Brain Research: Cognitive Brain Research, 3,* 131–141.

Ro, T., & Rafal, R. (2006). Visual restoration in cortical blindness: Insights from natural and TMS-induced blindsight. *Neuropsychology and Rehabilitation, 16,* 377–396.

Rob, L. (2012, January 6). Retailers beware shoplifters—and employees. *Colorado Springs Business Journal* (CO).

Robakis, T. K., & Hirsch, L. J. (2006). Literature review, case report, and expert discussion of prolonged refractory status epilepticus. *Neurocritical Care, 4*(1), 35–46.

Robbins, S. B., Lauver, K., Le, H., Davis, D., Langley, R., & Carlstrom, A. (2004). Do psychosocial and study skill factors predict college outcomes? A meta-analysis. *Psychological Bulletin, 130,* 261–288.

Robbins, R. A., Nishimura, M., Mondloch, C. J., Lewis, T. L., & Maurer, D. (2010). Deficits in sensitivity to spacing after early visual deprivation in humans: A comparison of human faces, monkey faces, and houses. *Developmental Psychobiology, 52*(8), 775–781.

Roberts, B.W., & Bogg, T. (2004). A longitudinal study of the relationships between conscientiousness and the social-environmental factors and substance use behaviors that influence health. *Journal of Personality, 72,* 325–353.

Roberts, B. W., Smith, J., Jackson, J. J., & Edmonds, G. (2009). Compensatory conscientiousness and health in older couples. *Psychological Science, 20,* 553–559.

Roberts, B. W., Wood, D., & Caspi, A. (2008). The development of personality traits in adulthood. In O. P. John, R. W. Robins, & L. A. Pervin (Eds.), *Handbook of personality: Theory and research* (3rd ed., pp. 375–398). New York: Guilford Press.

Roberts, B. W., Caspi, A., & Moffitt, T. E. (2001). The kids are alright: Growth and stability in personality development from adolescence to adulthood. *Journal of Personality & Social Psychology, 81*(4), 670–683.

Roberts, B. W., & DelVecchio, W. F. (2000). The rank-order consistency of traits from childhood to old-age: A quantitative review of longitudinal studies. *Psychological Bulletin, 126,* 3–25.

Roberts, B. W., Helson, R., & Klohnen, E. C. (2002). Personality development and growth in women across 30 years: Three perspectives. *Journal of Personality, 70,* 79–102.

Roberts, B. W., & Mroczek, D. (2008). Personality trait change in adulthood. *Current Directions in Psychological Science, 17,* 31–35.

Roberts, B. W., Smith, J., Jackson, J. J., & Edmonds, G. (2009). Compensatory conscientiousness and health in older couples. *Psychological Science, 20,* 553–559.

Roberts, B. W., Walton, K. E., & Viechtbauer, W. (2006). Patterns of mean-level change in personality traits across the life course: A meta-analysis of longitudinal studies. *Psychological Bulletin, 132,* 1–25.

Roberts, Y. H., Mitchell, M. J., Witman, M., & Taffaro, C. (2010). Mental health symptoms in youth affected by Hurricane Katrina. *Professional Psychology: Research and Practice, 41,* 10–18.

Robertson, E. M. (2012). New insights in human memory interference and consolidation. *Current Biology, 22*(2), R66–R71. doi:10.1016/j.cub.2011.11.051.

Robertson, J., & Robertson, J. (1971). Young children in brief separation: A fresh look. *Psychoanalytic Study of the Child, 26,* 264–315.

Robiner, W. N. (2006). The mental health professions: Workforce supply and demand, issues, and challenges. *Clinical Psychology Review, 26,* 600–625.

Robins, L. N., & Regier, D. A. (Eds.). (1991). *Psychiatric disorders in America: The Epidemiologic Catchment Area study.* New York: Free Press.

Robinson, G. E., Fernald, R. D., & Clayton, D. F. (2008). Genes and social behavior. *Science, 322,* 896–900.

Robinson, J. H., & Pritchard, W. S. (1995). "The scientific case that nicotine is addictive": Reply. *Psychopharmacology, 117*(1), 16–17.

Robinson, N. M., Zigler, E., & Gallagher, J. J. (2000). Two tails of the normal curve: Similarities and differences in the study of mental retardation and giftedness. *American Psychologist, 55,* 1413–1424.

Robinson, S., Sandstrom, S. M., Denenberg, V. H., & Palmiter, R. D. (2005). Distinguishing whether dopamine regulates liking, wanting, and/or learning about rewards. *Behavioral Neuroscience, 119,* 5–15.

Robinson, T. N., Borzekowski D. L. G., Matheson, D. M., Kraemer, H. C. (2009). Effects of fast food branding on young children's taste preferences. *Archives of Pediatric and Adolescent Medicine, 161*(8), 792–797.

Robinson, T. N., Wilde, M. L., Navracruz, L. C., Haydel, K. F., & Varady, A. (2001). Effects of reducing children's television and video game use on aggressive behavior: A randomized controlled trial. *Archives of Pediatrics and Adolescent Medicine, 155,* 17–23.

Robles, T. F., Glaser, R., & Kiecolt-Glaser, J. K. (2005). Out of balance: A new look at chronic stress, depression, and immunity. *Current Directions in Psychological Science, 14,* 111–115.

Rochon, P. A., Stukel, T. A., Sykora, K., Gill, S., Garfinkel, S., Anderson, G. M., et al. (2005). Atypical antipsychotics and Parkinsonism. *Archives of Internal Medicine, 165,* 1882–1888.

Rock, I. (1978). *An introduction to perception.* New York: Macmillan.

Rock, I. (1983). *The logic of perception.* Cambridge, MA: MIT Press.

Rodenburg, R., Benjamin, A., de Roos, C., Meijer, A. M., & Stams, G. J. (2009). Efficacy of EMDR in children: A meta-analytic review. *Clinical Psychology Review, 29,* 599–606.

Rodgers, J. (2000). Cognitive performance amongst recreational users of "ecstasy". *Psychopharmacology, 151,* 19–24.

Rodriguez, I., Greer, C. A., Mok, M. Y., & Mombaerts, P. (2000). A putative pheromone receptor gene expressed in human olfactory mucosa. *Nature Genetics, 26,* 18–19.

Roe, K. V. (2001). Relationship between male infants' vocal responses to mother and stranger at three months and self-reported academic attainment and adjustment measures in adulthood. *Psychological Reports, 89*(2), 255–258.

Roediger, H. L., III. (1990). Implicit memory: Retention without remembering. *American Psychologist, 45,* 1043–1056.

Roediger, H. L., III, & Karpicke, J. D. (2006). Test-enhanced learning: Taking memory tests improve long-term retention. *Psychological Science, 17,* 249–255.

Roediger, H.L., Agarwal, P.K., McDaniel, M.A., & McDermott, K.B. (2011). Test-enhanced learning in the classroom: Long-term improvements from quizzing. *Journal of Experimental Psychology: Applied, 17,* 382–395.

Roediger, H. L., & Gallo, D. A. (2001). Levels of processing: Some unanswered questions. In M. Naveh-Benjamin, M. Moscovitch, & H. L. Roediger (Eds.), *Perspectives on human memory and cognitive aging: Essays in hounour of Fergus Craik* (pp. 28–47). New York: Psychology Press.

Roediger, H. L., & McDermott, K. B. (2000). Tricks of memory. *Current Directions in Psychological Science, 9,* 123–127.

Roediger, H. L., Meade, M. L., & Bergman, E. T. (2001). Social contagion of memory. *Psychonomic Bulletin and Review, 8,* 365–371.

Roediger, H. L., Wixted, J. T. & DeSoto, K. A. (in press). The curious complexity between confidence and accuracy in reports from memory. In Nadel, Lynn, and Sinnott-Armstrong, Walter, (Eds.). *Memory and Law.* Oxford University Press, New York.

Roediger, H. L., III, Gallo, D. A., & Geraci, L. (2002). Processing approaches to cognition: The impetus from the levels-of-processing framework. *Memory, 10,* 319–332.

Roediger, H. L., III, Guynn, M. J., & Jones, T. C. (1995). Implicit memory: A tutorial review. In G. d'Ydewalle, P. Eelen, & P. Bertelson (Eds.), *International perspectives on psychological science: Vol. 2. The state of the art* (pp. 67–94). Hove, UK: Erlbaum.

Roediger, H. L., III, Jacoby, D., & McDermott, K. B. (1996). Misinformation effects in recall: Creating false memories through repeated retrieval. *Journal of Memory and Learning, 35,* 300–318.

Roediger, H. L., III, McDaniel, M., & McDermott, K. (2006). Test enhanced learning. *APS Observer, 19,* 28.

Roediger, H. L., III, & McDermott, K. B. (1995). Creating false memories: Remembering words not presented in lists. *Journal of Experimental Psychology: Learning, Memory, and Cognition, 21,* 803–814.

Roenneberg, T., Kuehnle, T., Juda, M., Kantermann, T., Allebrandt, K., Gordijn, M., & Merrow, M. (2007). Epidemiology of the human circadian clock. *Sleep Med Reviews, 11,* 429–438.

Roesch, R., Zapf, P., & Hart. S. (2010). *Forensic psychology and law.* Hoboken, NJ: John Wiley & Sons.

Roets, A., & Hiel, A. V. (2011). Allport's prejudiced personality today: Need for closure as the motivated cognitive basis of prejudice. *Current Directions in Psychological Science, 20*(6), 349–354. doi:10.1177/0963721411424894.

Roffman, J. L., & Gerber, A. J. (2008). Neural models of psychodynamic concepts and treatments: Implications for psychodynamic psychotherapy. In R. A. Levy & J. S. Ablon (Eds.), *Handbook of evidence-based psychodynamic psychotherapy* (pp. 305–339). Totowa, NJ: Humana Press.

Roffwarg, H. P., Muzio, J. N., & Dement, W. C. (1966). Ontogenetic development of the human sleep-dream cycle. *Science, 152,* 604–619.

Rog, D. J., Nurmikko, T. J., Friede, T., & Young, C. A. (2005). Randomized, controlled trial of cannabis-based medicine in central pain in multiple sclerosis. *Neurology, 65,* 812–819.

Rogers, C. E., Anderson, P. J., Thompson, D. K., Kidokoro, H., Wallendorf, M., Treyvaud, K., & Inder, T. E. (2012). Regional cerebral development at term relates to school-age social–emotional development in very preterm children. *Journal of the American Academy of Child & Adolescent Psychiatry, 51*(2), 181–191. doi:10.1016/j.jaac.2011.11.009.

Rogers, C. R. (1951). *Client-centered therapy.* Boston: Houghton Mifflin.

Rogers, C. R. (1961). *On becoming a person.* Boston: Houghton Mifflin.

Rogers, C. R. (1970). *Carl Rogers on encounter groups.* New York: Harper & Row.

Rogers, C. R. (1980). *A way of being.* Boston: Houghton Mifflin.

Rogers, J., Madamba, S. G., Staunton, D. A., & Siggins, G. R. (1986). Ethanol increases single unit activity in the inferior olivary nucleus. *Brain Research, 385,* 253–262.

Rogers, M. R., & Molina, L. E. (2006). Exemplary efforts in psychology to recruit and retain graduate students of color. *American Psychologist, 61,* 143–156.

Rogers, R. (1995). *Diagnostic and structured interviewing: A handbook for psychologists.* Odessa, FL: Psychological Assessment Resources.

Rogers, R. (2003). Standardizing DSM-IV diagnoses: The clinical application of structured interviews. *Journal of Personality Assessment, 81,* 220–225.

Rogoff, B., & Waddell, K. J. (1982). Memory for information organized in a scene by children from two cultures. *Child Development, 53,* 1224–1228.

Rohrer, D., & Pashier, H. (2007). Increasing retention without increasing study time. *Current Directions in Psychological Science, 16,* 183–186.

Roid, G. H. (2003). *Stanford-Binet Intelligence Scale* (5th ed.). Itasca, IL: Riverside.

Roisman, G. I. (2007). The psychophysiology of adult attachment relationships: Autonomic reactivity in marital and premarital interactions. *Developmental Psychology, 43,* 39–53.

Roisman, G. I., Masten, A. S., Coatsworth, J. D., & Tellegen, A. (2004). Salient and emerging developmental tasks in the transition to adulthood. *Child Development, 75,* 123–133.

Rokach, A. (2008). How do the homeless cope with loneliness? *Psychology Journal, 5*(4), 215–227.

Rolland, Y., Andrieu, S., Cantet, C., Morley, J. E., et al. (2007). Wandering behavior and Alzheimer disease: The REAL.FR prospective study. *Alzheimer Disease and Associated Disorders, 21,* 31–38.

Rolls, E. T. (2006). Brain mechanisms underlying fl avour and appetite. *Philosophical Transactions of the Royal Society of London, B, 361,* 1123–1136.

Rolls, E. T. (1997). Taste and olfactory processing in the brain and its relation to the control of eating. *Critical Review of Neurobiology, 11,* 263–287.

Rolls, E. T. (2009). Functional neuroimaging of umami taste: what makes umami pleasant? *American Journal of Clinical Nutrition, 90*(3), 804S–813S.

Romeo, R. D., Richardson, H. N., & Sisk, C. L. (2002). Puberty and the maturation of the male brain and sexual behavior: Recasting a behavioral potential. *Neuroscience and Biobehavioral Review, 26,* 381–391.

Roney, J. R., & Simmons, Z. L. (2008). Women's estradiol predicts preference for facial cues of men's testosterone. *Hormones & Behavior, 53*(1), 14–19. doi:10.1016/j.yhbeh.2007.09.008.

Ronnestad, M. H., & Ladany, N. (2006). The impact of psychotherapy training: Introduction to the special section. *Psychotherapy Research, 16,* 261–267.

Rooks, C., Veledar, E., Golberg, J., Bremner, J. D., & Vaccarino, V. (2012). Early trauma and inflammation: Role of familial factors in a study of twins. *Psychosomatic Medicine, 74*(2) 146–152. doi:10.1097/PSY.0b013e318240a7d8.

Roorda, A., & Williams, D. R. (1999). The arrangement of the three cone classes in the living human eye. *Nature, 397,* 520–522.

Root, J. C., Wong, P. S., & Kinsbourne, M. (2006). Left hemisphere specialization for response to positive emotional expressions: A divided output methodology. *Emotion, 6,* 473–483.

Rooy, D. L. V., Dilchert, S., Viswesvaran, C., & Ones, D. (2006). Multiplying intelligences: Are general, emotional, and practical intelligences equal? In K. R. Murphy (Ed.), *A critique of emotional intelligence: What are the problems and how can they be fixed?* (pp. 235–262). Mahwah, NJ: Erlbaum.

Rosch, E., Mervis, C. B., Gray, W. D., Johnson, D. M., & Boyes-Braem, P. (1976). Basic objects in natural categories. *Cognitive Psychology, 8,* 382–439.

Rose, A. J., & Rudolph, K. D. (2006). A review of sex differences in peer relationship processes: Potential trade-offs for the emotional and behavioral development of girls and boys. *Psychological Bulletin, 132,* 98–131.

Rose, S. A., & Feldman, J. F. (1995). Prediction of IQ and specific cognitive abilities at 11 years from infancy measures. *Developmental Psychology, 31,* 685–696.

Roseberry, S., Richie, R., Hirsh-Pasek, K., Golinkoff, R., & Shipley, T. F. (2011). Babies catch a break: 7- to 9-month-olds track statistical probabilities in continuous dynamic events. *Psychological Science, 22*(11), 1422–1424. doi:10.1177/0956797611422074.

Roseborough, D. J. (2006). Psychodynamic psychotherapy: An effectiveness study. *Research on Social Work Practice, 16,* 166–175.

Rosekind, M. R., Gregory, K. B., Mallis, M. M., Brandt, S. L., et al. (2010). The cost of poor sleep: Workplace productivity loss and associated costs. *Journal of Occupational and Environmental Medicine, 52,* 91–98.

Rosen, B. C., & D'Andrade, R. (1959). The psychosocial origins of achievement motivation. *Sociometry, 22,* 188–218.

Rosen, G. M. (1999). Treatment fidelity and research on eye movement desensitization and reprocessing (EMDR). *Journal of Anxiety Disorders, 13,* 173–184.

Rosen, H. J. (2011). Anosognosia in neurodegenerative disease. *Neurocase, 17*(3), 231–241.

Rosen, M. L., & López, H. H. (2009). Menstrual cycle shifts in attentional bias for courtship language. *Evolution and Human Behavior, 30*(2), 131–140.

Rosen, R. (1991). *The healthy company.* Los Angeles: Tarcher.

Rosen-Reynoso, M., Alegría, M., Chen, C., Laderman, M., & Roberts, R. (2011). The relationship between obesity and psychiatric disorders across ethnic and racial minority groups in the United States. *Eating Behaviors, 12*(1), 1–8. doi:10.1016/j.eatbeh.2010.08.008.

Rosenbaum, M., & Bennett, B. (1986). Homicide and depression. *American Journal of Psychiatry, 143,* 367–370.

Rosenbaum, R. S., Moscovitch, M., Foster, J. K., Schnyer, D. M., Gao, F., Kovacevic, N., Verfaellie, M., Black, S. E., & Levine, B. (2008). Patterns of autobiographical memory loss in medial-temporal lobe amnesic patients. *Journal of Cognitive Neuroscience, 20*(8), 1490–1506.

Rosenberg, R. N. (2009). Consciousness, coma, and brain death—2009. *Journal of the American Medical Association, 301*(11), 1172–1174.

Rosenfarb, I. S., Bellack, A. S., & Aziz, N. (2006). A sociocultural stress, appraisal, and coping model of subjective burden and family attitudes toward patients with schizophrenia. *Journal of Abnormal Psychology, 115,* 157–165.

Rosenfarb, I. S., Goldstein, M. J., Mintz, J., & Nuechterlein, K. H. (1995). Expressed emotion and subclinical psychopathology observable within the transactions between schizophrenic patients and their family members. *Journal of Abnormal Psychology, 104,* 259–267.

Rosenfeld, J. P. (1995). Alternative views of Bashore and Rapp's (1993) alternatives to traditional polygraphy: A critique. *Psychological Bulletin, 117*(1), 159–166.

Rosenkranz, M. A., Jackson, D. C., Dalton, K. M., Dolski, I., et al. (2003). Affective style and in vivo immune response: Neurobehavioral mechanisms. *Proceedings of the National Academy of Sciences, 100,* 11148–11152.

Rosenstock, I. M. (1974). Historical origins of the health belief model. *Health Education Monographs, 2,* 328–335.

Rosenthal, R. R. (1966). *Experimenter effects in behavioral research.* New York: Appleton-Century-Crofts.

Rösner, S., Hackl-Herrwerth, A., Leucht, S., Vecchi, S., Srisurapanont, M., & Soyka, M. (2010). Opioid antagonists for alcohol dependence. *Cochrane Database of Systematic Reviews, 8*(12), CD001867.

Ross, C. A. (1997). *Dissociative identity disorder: Diagnosis, clinical features, and treatment of multiple personality.* New York: Wiley.

Ross, E. D. (1981). The aprosodias: Functional-anatomic organization of the affective components of language in the right hemisphere. *Archives of Neurology, 38*(9), 561–569.

Ross, E. D., & Monnot, M. (2008). Neurology of affective prosody and its functional–anatomic organization in right hemisphere. *Brain & Language, 104*(1), 51–74.

Ross, M., & Wang, Q. (2010). Why we remember and what we remember: Culture and autobiographical memory. *Perspectives On Psychological Science, 5*(4), 401–409. doi:10.1177/1745691610375555.

Ross, M. W. (2002). Sexuality and health challenges: Responding to a public health imperative. *Journal of Sex Research, 39*, 7–9.

Ross, S., & Peselow, E. (2009). The neurobiology of addictive disorders. *Clinical Neuropharmacology, 32*, 269–276.

Ross, S. M., & Ross, L. E. (1971). Comparison of trace and delay classical eyelid conditioning as a function of interstimulus interval. *Journal of Experimental Psychology, 91*, 165–167.

Rost, K., Hsieh, Y. P., Xu, S., Menachemi, N., & Young, A. S. (2011). Potential disparities in the management of schizophrenia in the United States. *Psychiatric Services, 62*, 613–618.

Roth, G., Assor, A., Niemiec, C. P., Deci, E. L., & Ryan, R. M. (2009). The emotional and academic consequences of parental conditional regard. *Developmental Psychology, 45*, 1119–1142.

Roth, A., & Fonagy, P. (2005). *What works for whom: A critical review of psychotherapy research* (2nd ed.). New York: Guilford.

Roth, H. L., Lora, A. N., & Heilman, K. M. (2002). Effects of monocular viewing and eye dominance on spatial attention. *Brain, 125*, 2023–2035.

Roth, P. L., Huffcutt, A. I., & Bobko, P. (2003). Ethnic group differences in measures of job performance: A new meta-analysis. *Journal of Applied Psychology, 88*, 694–706.

Roth, S. P., Schmutz, P., Pauwels, S. L., Bargas-Avila, J. A., & Opwis, K. (2010). Mental models for web objects: Where do users expect to find the most frequent objects in online shops, news portals, and company web pages?. *Interacting with Computers, 22*(2), 140–152. doi:10.1016/j.intcom.2009.10.004.

Rothbart, M. (2011). *Becoming who we are: Temperament and personality in development.* New York: Guilford Press.

Rothbart, M. K., & Derryberry, D. (2002). Temperament in children. In C. von Hofsten & L. Baeckman (Eds.), *Psychology at the turn of the millennium: Vol. 2. Social, developmental, and clinical perspectives* (pp. 17–35). Florence, KY: Taylor & Frances/Routledge.

Rothbaum, B. O. (2006). Virtual reality in the treatment of psychiatric disorders. *CNS Spectrums, 11*, 34.

Rothbaum, B. O., Hodges, L. F., Kooper, R., & Opdyke, D. (1995). Effectiveness of computer-generated virtual reality graded exposure in the treatment of acrophobia. *American Journal of Psychiatry, 152*, 626–628.

Rothbaum, F., Morelli, G., & Rusk, N. (2010). Attachment, learning and coping: The interplay of cultural similarities and differences. In C.Y. Chiu, Y.Y. Hong, & M. Gelfand (Eds.), *Advances in Culture and Psychology*, Vol. 1, pp. 153–215.

Rothbaum, F., Pott, M., Azuma, H., Miyake, K., & Weisz, J. (2000). The development of close relationships in Japan and the United States: Paths of symbiotic harmony and generative tension. *Child Development, 71*, 1121–1142.

Rothschild, A. J. (2010). *Evidence-based guide to antipsychotic medications.* Arlington, VA: American Psychiatric Publishing.

Rothwell, P. M. (2003). Incidence, risk factors and prognosis of stroke and TIA: The need for high-quality, large-scale epidemiological studies and meta-analyses. *Cerebrovascular Disease, 16*(Suppl. 3), 2–10.

Rottenstreich, Y., & Tversky, A. (1997). Unpacking, repacking, and anchoring: Advances in support theory. *Psychological Review, 104*, 406–415.

Rotter, J. B. (1954). *Social learning and clinical psychology.* New York: Prentice Hall.

Rotter, J. B. (1982). *The development and application of social learning theory.* New York: Praeger.

Rotton, J., & Kelly, I. W. (1985). Much ado about the full moon: A meta-analysis of lunar-lunacy research. *Psychological Bulletin, 97*, 286–306.

Rouach, N., Koulakoff, A., Abudara, V., Willecke, K., & Giaume, C. (2008). Astro-glial metabolic networks sustain hippocampal synaptic transmission. *Science, 322*(5907), 1551–1555.

Rouch, I., Wild, P., Ansiau, D., & Marquie, J.-C. (2005). Shiftwork experience, age, and cognitive performance. *Ergonomics, 48*, 1282–1293.

Rouéché, B. (1986, December 8). Cinnabar. *New Yorker.*

Rouse, S. V. (2007). Using reliability generalization methods to explore measurement error: An illustration using the MMPI2 PSY-5 Scales. *Journal of Personality Assessment, 88*, 264–275.

Roussel, P., Elliot, A. J., & Feltman, R. (2011). The influence of achievement goals and social goals on help-seeking from peers in an academic context. *Learning & Instruction, 21*(3), 394–402. doi:10.1016/j.learninstruc.2010.05.003.

Roussotte, F. F., Sulik, K. K., Mattson, S. N., Riley, E. P., Jones, K. L., Adnams, C. M., & .. Sowell, E. R. (2012). Regional brain volume reductions relate to facial dysmor-phology and neurocognitive function in fetal alcohol spectrum disorders. *Human Brain Mapping, 33*(4), 920–937. doi:10.1002/hbm.21260.

Rovee-Collier, C., & Cuevas, K. (2009). The development of infant memory. In M. L. Courage & N. Cowan (Eds.), *The development of memory in infancy and childhood* (pp 11–41). New York: Psychology Press.

Rovee-Collier, C. (1999). The development of infant memory. *Current Directions in Psychological Science, 8*, 80–85.

Rowe, D. C. (2005). Under the skin: On the impartial treatment of genetic and environmental hypotheses of racial differences. *American Psychologist, 60*, 60–70.

Rowe, D. C., Jacobson, K. C., & Van den Oord, E. J. C. G. (1999). Genetic and environmental influences on vocabulary IQ: Parental education level as moderator. *Child Development, 70*, 1151–1162.

Rowe, M. L., & Goldin-Meadow, S. (2009). Differences in early gesture explain SES disparities in child vocabulary size at school entry. *Science, 323*, 951–953.

Roy, B., Diez-Roux, A. V., Seeman, T., Ranjit, N., et al. (2010). Association of optimism and pessimism with inflammation and hemostasis in the multiethnic study of atherosclerosis (MESA). *Psychosomatic Medicine, 72*, 134–140.

Roy, M., Piche, M., Chen, J.-I., Peretz, I., & Rainville, P. (2009). Cerebral and spinal modulation of pain by emotions. *Proceedings of the National Academy of Sciences, 106*, 20900–20905.

Roy, P.-M., Durieux, P., Gillaizeau, F., Legall, C., et al. (2009). A computerized handheld decision-support system to improve pulmonary embolism diagnosis: A randomized trial. *Annals of Internal Medicine, 151*, 677–686.

Roy-Byrne, P., Stang, P., Wittchen, H.-U., Ustun, B., Walters, E. E., & Kessler, R. (2000). Lifetime panic-depression comorbidity in the National Comorbidity Survey. *British Journal of Psychiatry, 176*, 229–235.

Roy-Byrne, P. P., Craske, M. G., Stein, M. B., Sullivan, G., Bystritsky, A., Katon, W., et al. (2005). A randomized effectiveness trial of cognitive-behavioral therapy and medication for primary care panic disorder. *Archives of General Psychiatry, 62*, 290–298.

Roye, A., Schröger, E., Jacobsen, T., & Gruber, T. (2010). Is my mobile ringing? Evidence for rapid processing of a personally significant sound in humans. *The Journal of Neuroscience, 30*(21):7310–7313; doi:10.1523/JNEUROSCI.1113-10.2010.

Rozin, P. (1982). "Taste-smell confusions" and the duality of the olfactory sense. *Perception and Psychophysics, 31*, 397–401.

Rozin, P. (2007). Food and eating. In S. Kitayama & D. Cohen (Eds.), *Handbook of cultural psychology* (pp. 391–416). New York, NY: Guilford Press.

Rubens, A. B., & Benson, D. F. (1971). Associative visual agnosia. *Archives of Neurology, 24*, 304–316.

Rubenwolf, B., & Spörrle, M. (2011). Intuitive decisions: the influence of phonetic and letter frequency recognition heuristics on brand selection decisions. *Neuropsychoeconomics Conference Proceedings, 43.*

Rubin, E. (1915). *Synsoplevede figure.* Copenhagen: Gyldendalske.

Rubin, K. H., Bukowski, W., & Parker, J. G. (2006). Peer interactions, relationships, and groups. In W. Damon & R. M. Lerner (Series Eds.) & N. Eisenberg (Vol. Ed.), *Handbook of child psychology: Vol. 3. Social, emotional, and personality development* (6th ed.). New York: Wiley.

Rubin, M. (2011). Social affiliation cues prime help-seeking intentions. *Canadian Journal Of Behavioural Science/Revue Canadienne Des Sciences Du Comportement, 43*(2), 138–141. doi:10.1037/a0022246.

Rubin, M., Paolini, S., & Crisp, R. J. (2010). A processing fluency explanation of bias against migrants. *Journal Of Experimental Social Psychology, 46*(1), 21–28. doi:10.1016/j.jesp.2009.09.006.

Rubin, R., Brown-Schmidt, S., Duff, M., Tranel, D., & Cohen, N. (2011). How do I remember that I know you know that I know? *Psychological Science, 22*(12), 1574–1582.

Rubinstein, S., & Caballero, B. (2000). Is Miss America an undernourished role model? *Journal of the American Medical Association, 283*, 1569.

Ruble, D. N., Martin, C. L., & Berenbaum, S. A. (2006). Gender development. In W. Damon & R. M. Lerner (Series Eds.) & N. Eisenberg (Vol. Ed.), *Handbook of child psychology: Vol. 3. Social, emotional, and personality development* (6th ed., pp. 858–932). New York: Wiley.

Rucker, D. D., Dubois, D., & Galinsky, A. D. (2011). Generous paupers and stingy princes: Power drives consumer spending on self versus others. *Journal of Consumer Research, 37*, doi:10.1086/657162.

Rudman, L. A., Greenwald, A. G., Mellott, D. S., & Schwartz, J. L. K. (1999). Measuring the automatic components of prejudice: Flexibility and generality of the Implicit Association Test. *Social Cognition, 17*, 437–465.

Rudolph, A. E., Jones, K. C., Latkin, C., Crawford, N. D., & Fuller, C. M. (2011). The association between parental risk behaviors during childhood and having high risk networks in adulthood. *Drug & Alcohol Dependence, 118*(2/3), 437–443. doi:10.1016/j.drugalcdep.2011.05.003

Rudolph, K. D., Lambert, S. F., Clark, A. G., & Kurlakowsky, K. D. (2001). Negotiat-ing the transition to middle school: The role of self-regulatory processes. *Child Development, 72*, 929–946.

Rudoy, J. D., Voss, J. L., Westerberg, C. E., & Paller, K. A. (2009). Strengthening individual memories by reactivating them during sleep. *Science, 326*(5956), 1079.

Rueckert, L., Baboorian, D., Stavropoulos, K., & Yasutake, C. (1999). Individual differences in callosal efficiency: Correlation with attention. *Brain and Cognition, 41*, 390–410.

Ruiz, J. M., Matthews, K. A., Scheier, M. F., & Schulz, R. (2006). Does who you marry matter for your health? Influence of patient's and spouses' personality on their partners' psychological well-being following coronary artery bypass surgery. *Journal of Personality and Social Psychology, 91*, 255–267.

Ruiz-Padial, E., & Vila, J. (2007). Fearful and sexual pictures not consciously seen modulate the startle reflex in human beings. *Biological Psychiatry, 61*, 996–1001.

Rule, N., Rosen, K., Slepian, M., & Ambady, N. (2011). Mating interest improves women's accuracy in judging male sexual orientation. *Psychological Science, 22*(7), 881–886.

Rumelhart, D. E., & McClelland, J. L. (1986). *Parallel distributed processing: Explorations in the microstructure of cognition: Vol. 1. Foundations.* Cambridge, MA: Bradford.

Runyan, D. K., Shankar, V., Hassan, F., Hunter, W. M., Jain, D., Paula, C. S., Bangdiwala, S. I., Ramiro, L. S., Munoz, S. R., Vizcarra, B., en Psic, L., & Bordin, I. A. (2010). International variations in harsh child discipline. *Pediatrics, 126*(3), e701–e711. doi:10.1542/peds.2008-2374.

Ruscio, A. M., Stein, D. J., Chiu, W. T., & Kessler, R. (2010). The epidemiology of obsessive-compulsive disorder in the National Comorbidity Survey Replication. *Molecular Psychiatry, 15,* 53–63.

Ruscio, J. (2005). Exploring controversies in the art and science of polygraph testing. *Skeptical Inquirer, 29,* 34–39.

Rushton, J. P., & Jensen, A. R. (2005). Thirty years of research on race differences in cognitive ability. *Psychology, Public Policy, and Law, 11(2),* 235–294. doi:10.1037/1076-8971.11.2.235.

Ruskin, P. E., Silver-Aylaian, M., Kling, M. A., Reed, S. A., Bradham, D. D., Hebel, J. R., et al. (2004). Treatment outcomes in depression: Comparison of remote treatment through telepsychiatry to in-person treatment. *American Journal of Psychiatry, 161,* 1471–1476.

Russ, S. (2006). Psychodynamic treatments. In R. T. Ammerman (Ed.), *Comprehensive handbook of personality and psychopathology* (Vol. 3, pp. 425–437). New York: Wiley.

Russell, J. A. (1994). Is there universal recognition of emotion from facial expression? A review of the cross-cultural studies. *Psychological Bulletin, 155(2),* 102–141.

Russell, J. A. (1995). Facial expressions of emotion: What lies beyond minimal universality? *Psychological Bulletin, 118,* 379–391.

Russell, M. C., Silver, S. M., Rogers, S., & Darnell, J. N. (2007). Responding to an identified need: A joint Department of Defense/Department of Veterans Affairs training program in eye movement desensitization and reprocessing (EMDR) for clinicians providing trauma services. *International Journal of Stress Management, 14(1),* 61–71.

Russo, P., Cesario, A., Rutella, S., Veronesi, G., Spaggiari, L., Galetta, D., Margaritora, S., Granone, P., & Greenberg, D. S. (2011). Impact of genetic variability in nicotinic acetylcholine receptors on nicotine addiction and smoking cessation treatment. *Current Medicinal Chemistry, 18(1),* 91–112.

Rusyniak, D. E. (2011). Neurologic manifestations of chronic methamphetamine abuse. *Neurologic Clinics, 29(3),* 641–655.

Rutkowski, G. K., Gruder, C. L., & Romer, D. (1983). Group cohesiveness, social norms, and bystander intervention. *Journal of Personality and Social Psychology, 44,* 545–552.

Rutkowski, L., Vasterling, J. J., Proctor, S. P., & Anderson, C. J. (2010). Posttraumatic stress disorder and standardized test-taking ability. *Journal Of Educational Psychology, 102(1),* 223–233. doi:10.1037/a0017287.

Rutland, A., Killen, M., & Abrams, D. (2010). A new social-cognitive developmental perspective on prejudice. *Perspectives on Psychological Science, 5,* 279–291.

Rutledge, T., Reis, S. E., Olson, M., Owens, J., Kelsey, S. F., Pepine, C. J., et al. (2004). Social networks are associated with lower mortality rates among women with suspected coronary disease: The National Heart, Lung, and Blood Institute-Sponsored Women's Ischemia Syndrome Evaluation study. *Psychosomatic Medicine, 66,* 882–888.

Rutter, M. (2007). Proceeding from observed correlation to causal inference: The use of natural experiments. *Perspectives on Psychological Science, 2,* 377–395.

Rutter, M., O'Connor, T. G., & ERA Study Team. (2004). Are there biological programming effects for psychological development? Findings from a study of Romanian adoptees. *Developmental Psychology, 40,* 81–94.

Ryan, C. S., Casas, J. F., Kelly-Vance, L., Ryalls, B. O., & Nero, C. (2010). Parent involvement and views of school success: The role of parents' Latino and White American cultural orientations. *Psychology in the Schools, 47(4),* 391–405.

Ryan, R., & Hout, M. (2011). Gateway transitions in rural Irish youth: Implications for culturally appropriate and targeted drug prevention. *Journal of Alcohol and Drug Education, 55(1),* 7–14.

Ryan, R. H., & Geiselman, R. E. (1991). Effects of biased information on the relationship between eyewitness confidence and accuracy. *Bulletin of the Psychonomic Society, 29,* 7–9.

Ryan, R. M. (1993). Agency and organization: Intrinsic motivation, autonomy, and the self in psychological development. In J. E. Jacobs (Ed.), *Nebraska symposium on motivation: Developmental perspectives on motivation* (Vol. 40, pp. 1–56). Lincoln: University of Nebraska Press.

Ryan, R. M., & Deci, E. L. (2000). Self-determination theory and the facilitation of intrinsic motivation, social development, and well-being. *American Psychologist, 55,* 68–78.

Rydell, R. J., Shiffrin, R. M., Boucher, K. L., Van Loo, K., & Rydell, M. T. (2010). Stereotype threat prevents perceptual learning. *PNAS Proceedings of the National Academy of Sciences of the United States of America, 107(32),* 14042–14047. doi:10.1073/pnas.1002815107.

Ryder, A. G., Yang, J., Zhu, X., Yao, S., Yi, J., Heine, S. J., & Bagby, R. M. (2008). The cultural shaping of depression: Somatic symptoms in China, psychological symptoms in North America? *Journal of Abnormal Psychology, 117,* 300–313.

Rymer, R. (1993). *Genie: A scientific tragedy.* New York: HarperCollins.

Rynders, J., & Horrobin, J. (1980). Educational provisions for young children with Down's syndrome. In J. Gottlieb (Ed.), *Educating mentally retarded persons in the mainstream* (pp. 109–147). Baltimore: University Park Press.

Rynes, S. L., Gerhart, B., & Parks, L. (2005). Performance evaluation and pay for performance. *Annual Review of Psychology, 56,* 571–600.

Saarni, C. (2006). Emotion regulation and personality development in childhood. In D. K. Mroczek & T. D. Little (Eds.), *Handbook of personality development* (pp. 245–262). Mahwah, NJ: Erlbaum.

Sabbagh, M. A., Xu, F., Carlson, S. M., Moses, L. J., & Lee, K. (2006). The development of executive functioning and theory of mind: A comparison of Chinese and U.S. preschoolers. *Psychological Science, 17,* 74–81.

Sachs, J. (1967). Recognition memory for syntactic and semantic aspects of connected discourse. *Perception and Psychophysics, 2,* 437–442.

Sackeim, H. A., Dillingham, E. M., Prudic, J., Cooper, T., et al. (2009). Effect of concomitant pharmacotherapy on electroconvulsive therapy outcomes. *Archives of General Psychiatry, 66,* 729–737.

Sackeim, H. A., Haskett, R. F., Mulsant, B. H., Thase, M. E., Mann, J. J., Pettinati, H. M., et al. (2001). Continuation pharmacotherapy in the prevention of relapse following electroconvulsive therapy: A randomized controlled trial. *Journal of the American Medical Association, 285,* 1299–1307.

Sackett, P. R., Borneman, M. J., & Connelly, B. S. (2008). High stakes testing in higher education and employment: Appraising the evidence for validity and fairness. *American Psychologist, 63,* 215–227.

Sackett, P. R., Hardison, C. M., & Cullen, M. J. (2004). On interpreting stereotype threat as accounting for African American-White differences on cognitive tests. *American Psychologist, 59,* 7–13.

Sackett, P. R., Kuncel, N. R., Arneson, J. J., Cooper, S. R., & Waters, S. D. (2009). Does socio-economic status explain the relationship between admissions tests and post-secondary academic performance? *Psychological Bulletin, 135,* 1–22.

Sackett, P. R., & Lievens, F. (2008). Personnel selection. *Annual Review of Psychology, 59,* 419–450.

Sackett, P. R., Schmitt, N., Ellington, J. E., & Kabin, M. B. (2001). High-stakes testing in employment, credentialing, and higher education: Prospects in a post-affirmative action world. *American Psychologist, 56,* 302–318.

Sacks, O. (1985). *The man who mistook his wife for a hat.* New York: Summit Books.

Sacks, O. (1992, July 27). The landscape of his dreams. *New Yorker.*

Sacks, O. (2002, October 7). The case of Anna H. *New Yorker,* pp. 62–73.

Sadeh, A. (2005). Cognitive-behavioral treatment for childhood sleep disorders. *Clinical Psychology Review, 25(5),* 612–628.

Sadetzki, S., Chetrit, A., Jarus-Hakak, A., Cardis, E., Deutch, Y., Duvdevani, S., Zultan, A., Novikov, I., Freedman, L., & Wolf, M. (2008). Cellular Phone use and risk of benign and malignant parotid gland tumors—A nationwide case-control study. *American Journal of Epidemiology, 167,* 457–467.

Sadler, L. S., Swartz, M. K., Ryan-Krause, P., Seitz, V., Meadows-Oliver, M., Grey, M., & Clemmens, D. A. (2007). Promising outcomes in teen mothers enrolled in a school-based parent support program and child care center. *Journal of School Health, 77(3),* 121–130.

Safir, M. P., & Wallach, H. S., & Bar-Zvi, M. (2012). Virtual reality cognitive-behavior therapy for public speaking anxiety: One-year follow-up. *Behavior Modification, 36,* 235–246.

Saffran, J. R., Senghas, A., & Trueswell, J. C. (2001). The acquisition of language by children. *Proceedings of the National Academy of Sciences, 98,* 12874–12875.

Safran, J. D. (2012). *Psychoanalysis and psychoanalytic therapies.* Washington, D.C.: American Psychological Association.

Safren, S. A., Gershuny, B. S., Marzol, P., Otto, M. W., Pollack, M. H. (2002). History of childhood abuse in panic disorder, social phobia, and generalized anxiety disorder. *Journal of Nervous and Mental Disease, 190,* 453–456.

Sagaspe, P., Taillard, J., Bayon, V., Lagarde, E., Moore, N., Boussuge, J., Chaumet, G., Bioulac, B., & Philip, P. (2010). Sleepiness, near-misses and driving accidents among a representative population of French drivers. *Journal of Sleep Research, 19(4):*578–584.

Saiz, P. A., Garcia-Portilla, M. P., Arango, C., Morales, B., Bascaran, M., et al. (2008). Association study between obsessive-compulsive disorder and serotonegic candidate genes. *Progress in Neuro-Psychopharmacology and Biological Psychiatry 32,* 765–770.

Sakairi, Y. (1992). Studies on meditation using questionnaires. *Japanese Psychological Review, 35(1),* 94–112.

Sakkalou, E., & Gattis, M. (2012). Infants infer intentions from prosody. *Cognitive Development, 27,* 1–16. doi:10.1016/j.cogdev.2011.08.003.

Sakuma, M., Endo, T., & Muto, T. (2000). The development of self-understanding in preschoolers and elementary school children: Analysis of self-descriptions and self-evaluations. *Japanese Journal of Developmental Psychology, 11,* 176–187.

Salas, C. R., Minakata, K., & Kelemen, W. L. (2011). Walking before study enhances free recall but not judgement-of-learning magnitude. *Journal Of Cognitive Psychology, 23(4),* 507–513. doi:10.1080/20445911.2011.532207.

Salas, E., Tannenbaum, S. I., Kraiger, K., & Smith-Jentsch, K. A. (2012). The science of training and development in organizations: What matters in practice. *Psychological Science in the Public Interest, 13,* 74–101. doi:10.1177/1529100612436661.

Salgado, J. F., Anderson, N., Moscoso, S., Bertua, C., de Fruyt, F., & Rolland, J. P. (2003). A meta-analytic study of general mental ability validity for different occupations in the European community. *Journal of Applied Psychology, 88,* 1068–1081.

Salgado-Pineda, P. P., Fakra, E. E., Delaveau, P. P., McKenna, P. J., Pomarol-Clotet, E. E., & Blin, O. O. (2011). Correlated structural and functional brain abnormalities in the default mode network in schizophrenia patients. *Schizophrenia Research, 125 (2–3),* 101–109. doi:10.1016/j.schres.2010.10.027

Salillas, E., & Wicha, N. Y. Y. Early learning shapes the memory networks for arithmetic: Evidence from brain potentials in bilinguals. *Psychological Science, 23,* 745–755. doi:10.1177/0956797612446347

Salin-Pascual, R., Gerashchenko, D., Greco, M., Blanco-Centurion, C., & Shiromani, P. J. (2001). Hypothalamic regulation of sleep. *Neuropsychopharmacology, 25(Suppl. 5),* S21.

Salisbury, A. L., Ponder, K. L., Padbury, J. F., & Lester, B. M. (2009). Fetal effects of psychoactive drugs. *Clinical Perinatology, 36,* 595–619.

Salmon, C. (2012). The pop culture of sex: An evolutionary window on the worlds of pornography and romance. *Review of General Psychology, 16,* 152–160. doi:10.1037/a0027910

Salo, R., Ravizza, S., & Fassbender, C. (2011). Overlapping cognitive patterns in schizophrenia and methamphetamine dependence. *Cognitive and Behavioral Neurology*, November 25, 2011 [Epub ahead of print]

Salokangas, R. K. R. (2004). Gender and the use of neuroleptics in schizophrenia. *Schizophrenia Research, 66*, 41–49.

Salovey, P., & Grewal, D. (2005). The science of emotional intelligence. *Current Directions in Psychological Science, 14*, 281–285.

Salovey, P., Mayer, J. D., & Rosenhan, D. L. (1991). Mood and helping: Mood as a motivator of helping and helping as a regulator of mood. In M. S. Clark (Ed.), *Review of personality and social psychology: Vol. 12. Prosocial behavior* (pp. 215–237). Newbury Park, CA: Sage.

Salthouse, T. A. (2012b). Does the level at which cognitive change occurs change with age? *Psychological Science, 23*(1), 18–23. doi:10.1177/0956797611421615.

Salthouse, T. A. (2012a). Does the direction and magnitude of cognitive change depend on initial level of ability? *Intelligence*, doi:10.1016/j.intell.2012.02.006.

Salvatore, J. E., Kuo, S., Steele, R. D., Simpson, J. A., & Collins, W. (2011). Recovering from conflict in romantic relationships: A developmental perspective. *Psychological Science, 22*(3), 376–383. doi:10.1177/0956797610397055.

Sambunaris, A., & Hyde, T. M. (1994). Stroke-related aphasias mistaken for psychotic speech: Two case reports. *Journal of Geriatric Psychiatry and Neurology, 7*(3), 144–147.

Samuel, D. B., & Widiger, T. A. (2006). Clinicians' judgments of clinical utility: A comparison of the DSM-IV and five-factor models. *Journal of Abnormal Psychology, 115*, 298–308.

Sanai, N., Tramontin, A. D., Quinones-Hinojosa, A., Barbaro, N. M., Gupta, N., Kunwar, S., et al. (2004). Unique astrocyte ribbon in adult human brain contains neural stem cells but lacks chain migration. *Nature, 427*, 740–744.

Sanders, M. R., Markie-Dadds, C., Tully, L. A., & Bor, W. (2000). The triple p-positive parenting program: A comparison of enhanced, standard, and self-directed behavioral family intervention for parents of children with early onset conduct problems. *Journal of Consulting and Clinical Psychology, 68*, 624–640.

Sanderson, C. A. (2010). *Social psychology.* Hoboken, NJ: Wiley.

Sanderson, W. C., Rapee, R. M., & Barlow, D. H. (1989). The influence of an illusion of control on panic attacks induced via inhalation of 5.5% carbon dioxide-enriched air. *Archives of General Psychiatry, 46*, 157–162.

Sanders Thompson, V. L., Bazile, A., & Akbar, M. (2004). African Americans' perceptions of psychotherapy and psychotherapists. *Professional Psychology: Research and Practice, 35*, 19–26.

Sandman, C. A., Davis, E. P., Buss, C., & Glynn, L. M. (2012). Exposure to prenatal psychobiological stress exerts programming influences on the mother and her fetus. *Neuroendocrinology, 95*(1), 8–21. doi:10.1159/000327017.

Sandman, C. A., Davis, E. P., Buss, C., & Glynn, L. M. (2011). Prenatal programming of human neurological function. *International Journal of Peptides*, 1–9. doi:10.1155/2011/837596.

Sandman, C. A., Davis, E., & Glynn, L. M. (2012). Prescient human fetuses thrive. *Psychological Science, 23*(1), 93–100. doi:10.1177/0956797611422073.

Sangwan, S. (2001). Ecological factors as related to I.Q. of children. *Psycho-Lingua, 31*(2), 89–92.

Santry, H. P., Gillen, D. L., & Lauderdale, D. S. (2005). Trends in bariatric surgical procedures. *Journal of the American Medical Association, 294*, 1909–1917.

Sansavini, A., Guarini, A., Savini, S., Broccoli, S., Justice, L., Alessandroni, R., & Faldella, G. (2011). Longitudinal trajectories of gestural and linguistic abilities in very preterm infants in the second year of life. *Neuropsychologia, 49*(13), 3677–3688. doi:10.1016/j.neuropsychologia.2011.09.023.

Saper, C. B., Chou, T. C., & Scammell, T. E. (2001). The sleep switch: Hypothalamic control of sleep and wakefulness. *Trends in Neurosciences, 24*, 726–731.

Sara, M., & Pistoia, F. (2009). Defining consciousness: Lessons from patients and modern techniques. *Journal of Neurotrauma, 27*, 771–773.

Saracino, J., Noseworthy, J., Steiman, M., Reisinger, L., & Fombonne, E. (2010). Diagnostic and assessment issues in autism surveillance and prevalence. *Journal Of Developmental & Physical Disabilities, 22*(4), 317–330. doi:10.1007/s10882-010-9205-1.

Sarafino, E. P., & Goehring, P. (2000). Age comparisons in acquiring biofeedback control and success in reducing headache pain. *Annals of Behavioral Medicine, 22*, 1–9.

Sarason, B. R., Sarason, I. G., & Gurung, R. A. R. (1997). Close personal relationships and health outcomes: A key to the role of social support. In S. Duck (Ed.), *Handbook of personal relationships* (pp. 547–573). New York: Wiley.

Sarason, I. G., Johnson, J., & Siegel, J. (1978). Assessing impact of life changes: Development of the life experiences survey. *Journal of Clinical and Consulting Psychology, 46*, 932–946.

Sarin, S., Abela, J. R. Z., & Auerbach, R. P. (2005). The response styles theory of depression: A test of specificity and causal mediation. *Cognition and Emotion, 19*, 751–761.

Sarkar, S. & Schmued, L. (2010). Neurotoxicity of ecstasy (MDMA): An overview. *Current Pharmaceutical Biotechnology, 11*(5), 460–469.

Sarrett, J. C. (2011). Trapped children: Popular images of children with autism in the 1960s and 2000s. *Journal of Medical Humanities, 32*(2), 141–153. doi:10.1007/s10912-010-9135-z.

Sarwer, D., & Dilks, R. (2012, January). Invited commentary: Childhood and adolescent obesity: Psychological and behavioral issues in weight loss treatment. *Journal of Youth & Adolescence.* pp. 98–104. doi:10.1007/s10964-011-9677-z.

Sasaki, Y., Jadjikhani, N., Fischl, B., Liu, A. K., Marret, S., Dale, A. M., & Tootell, R. B. H. (2001). Local and global attention are mapped retinotopically in human occipital cortex. *Proceedings of the National Academy of Sciences, 98*, 2077.

Sattler, C., Erickson, K. I., Toro, P., & Schröder, J. (2011). Physical fitness as a protective factor for cognitive impairment in a prospective population-based study in Germany. *Journal of Alzheimer's Disease, 26*(4), 709–718.

Sattler, D. N., Kaiser, C. F., & Hittner, J. B. (2000). Disaster preparedness: Relationships among prior experience, personal characteristics, and distress. *Journal of Applied Social Psychology, 30*, 1396–1420.

Saucier, G., Georgiades, S., Tsaousis, I., & Goldberg, L. R. (2005). The factor structure of Greek personality adjectives. *Journal of Personality and Social Psychology, 88*, 856–875.

Saunders, S. G., & Lynn, M. (2010). Why tip? An empirical test of motivations for tipping car guards. *Journal of Economic Psychology, 31*, 106–113. doi:10.1016/j.joep.2009.11.007.

Saurat, M.-T., Agbakou, M., Attigui, P., Golmard, J.-L., & Arnulf, I. (2011). Walking dreams in congenital and acquired paraplegia. *Consciousness and Cognition, 20*, 1425–1432.

Sauter, S., Murphy, L., Colligan, M., Swanson, N., Hurrell, J., Jr., Scharf, F., Jr., et al. (1999). *Stress at work* (DHHS [NIOSH] Publication No. 99–101). Washington, DC: National Institute on Occupational Health and Safety.

Savage, J., & Yancey, C. (2008). The effects of media violence exposure on criminal aggression: A meta-analysis. *Criminal Justice and Behavior, 35*, 772–791.

Saveliev, S. V., Lebedev, V. V., Evgeniev, M. B., & Korochkin, L. I. (1997). Chimeric brain: Theoretical and clinical aspects. *International Journal of Developmental Biology, 41*, 801–808.

Savelkoul, M., Post, M. W. M., de Witte, L. P., & van den Borne, H. B. (2000). Social support, coping, and subjective well-being in patients with rheumatic diseases. *Patient Education and Counseling, 39*, 205–218.

Savic, I., & Arver, S. (2011). Sex dimorphism of the brain in male-to-female transsexuals. *Cerebral Cortex (New York, N.Y.: 1991), 21*(11), 2525–2533.

Savic, I., Berglund, H., Gulyas, B., & Roland, P. (2001). Smelling of odorous sex hormone-like compounds causes sex-differentiated hypothalamic activations in humans. *Neuron, 31*, 661–668.

Savic, I., Berglund, H., & Lindstrom, P. (2005). Brain response to putative pheromones in homosexual men. *Proceedings of the National Academy of Sciences, 102*, 7356–7361.

Saville, B. K., Zinn, T. E., Neef, N. A., Van Norman, R., & Ferreri, S. J. (2006). A comparison of interteaching and lecture in the college classroom. *Journal of Applied Behavior Analysis, 39*, 49–61.

Savin-Williams, R. C. (2006). Who's gay? Does it matter? *Current Directions in Psychological Science, 15*, 40–44.

Savin-Williams, R. C., & Demo, D. H. (1984). Developmental change and stability in adolescent self-concept. *Developmental Psychology, 20*, 1100–1110.

Saxe, G. B. (2004). Practices of quantification from a sociocultural perspective. In K. A. Demetriou & A. Raftopoulos (Eds.), *Developmental change: Theories, models, and measurement* (pp. 241–263). New York: Cambridge University Press.

Saxe, L., & Ben-Shakhar, G. (1999). Admissibility of polygraph tests: The application of scientific standards post-Daubert. *Psychology, Public Policy, and Law, 5*, 203–223.

Saxe, R., Tzelnic, R., & Carey, S. (2007). Knowing who dunnit: Infants identify causal agent in an unseen causal interaction. *Developmental Psychology, 43*, 149–158.

Sayal, K., Heron, J., Golding, J., Alati, R., Smith, G. D., Gray, R., & Emond, A. (2009). Binge pattern of alcohol consumption during pregnancy and childhood mental health outcomes: Longitudinal population-based study. *Pediatrics, 123*, e289–e296.

Sayers, J. (1991). *Mother of psychoanalysis.* New York: Norton.

Sayim, B., Westheimer, & Herzog, M. H. (2010). Gestalt factors modulate basic spatial vision. *Psychological Science, 21*(5), 641–644. doi:10.1177/0956797610368811.

Sbarra, D. A., Law, R. W., & Portley, R. M. (2011). Divorce and death: A meta-analysis and research agenda for clinical, social, and health psychology. *Perspectives on Psychological Science, 6*(5) 454–474. doi:10.1177/1745691611414724.

Sbarra, D. A., Smith, H. L., & Mehl, M. R. (2012). When leaving your ex, love yourself: Observational ratings of self-compassion predict the course of emotional recovery following marital separation. *Psychological Science, 23*, 261–269. doi:10.1177/0956797611429466.

Scandura, T. A., & Lankau, M. J. (1997). Relationships of gender, family responsibility and flexible work hours to organizational commitment and job satisfaction. *Journal of Organizational Behavior, 18*, 377–391.

Scandura, T. A., & Schriesheim, C. A. (1994). Leader-member exchange and supervisor career mentoring as complementary constructs in leadership research. *Academy of Management Journal, 37*, 1588–1602.

Scarr, S. (1998). How do families affect intelligence? Social environmental and behavior genetic prediction. In J. J. McArdle & R. W. Woodcock (Eds.), *Human cognitive abilities in theory and practice* (pp. 113–136). Mahwah, NJ: Erlbaum.

Scarr, S., & Carter-Saltzman, L. (1982). Genetics and intelligence. In R. Sternberg (Ed.), *Handbook of human intelligence* (pp. 792–896). Cambridge, UK: Cambridge University Press.

Schabracq, M. J. (2003). Organizational culture, stress, and change. In M. J. Schabracq, J. A. M. Winnubst, & C. L. Cooper (Eds.), *Handbook of work and health psychology* (pp.37–62). West Sussex, UK: Wiley.

Schacter, D. L., Chiu, C.-Y. P., & Ochsner, K. N. (1993). Implicit memory: A selective review. *Annual Review of Neuroscience, 16*, 159–182.

Schacter, D. L., Cooper, L. A., Delaney, S. M., Peterson, M. A., & Tharan, M. (1991). Implicit memory for possible and impossible objects: Constraints on the construction of structural descriptions. *Journal of Experimental Psychology: Learning, Memory, and Cognition, 17*, 3–19.

Schacter, D. L., Norman, K. A., & Koutstaal, W. (1998). The cognitive neuroscience of constructive memory. *Annual Review of Psychology, 49*, 289–318.

Schachter, S., & Singer, J. (1962). Cognitive, social and physiological determinants of emotional state. *Psychological Review, 69,* 379–399.

Schaefer, J., Sykes, R., Rowley, R., & Baek, S. (1988, November). *Slow country music and drinking.* Paper presented at the 87th annual meeting of the American Anthropological Association, Phoenix, AZ.

Schaefer, M., Heinze, H. J., & Rotte, M. (2008). My third arm: Shifts in topography of the somatosensory homunculus predict feeling of an artificial supernumerary arm. *Human Brain Mapping, 6,* 6.

Schaefer, S., Lövdén, M., Wieckhorst, B., & Lindenberger, U. (2010). Cognitive performance is improved while walking: Differences in cognitive-sensorimotor couplings between children and young adults. *European Journal Of Developmental Psychology, 7*(3), 371–389. doi:10.1080/17405620802535666.

Schaie, K. W., & Willis, S. L. (in press). The Seattle Longitudinal Study of Adult Cognitive Development. *Bulletin of the International Society for the Study of Behavioral Development.*

Schalock, R. L., Borthwick-Duff y, S. A., Buntinx, W. H. E., Coulter, D. L., & Craig, E. M. (2009). *Intellectual disability: Definition, classification, and systems of supports* (11th ed.). Washington, DC: American Association of Intellectual and Developmental Disability.

Schanche, E., Stiles, T. C., McCullough, L., Svartberg, M., & Nielsen, G. (2011). The relationship between activating affects, inhibitory affects, and self-compassion in patients with Cluster C personality disorders. *Psychotherapy, 48*(3), 293–303. doi:10.1037/a0022012.

Schapiro, A. C., & McClelland, J. L. (2009). A connectionist model of a continuous developmental transition in the balance scale task. *Cognition, 110,* 395–411.

Schatzberg, A. F., Cole, J. O., & DeBattista, C. (2007). *Manual of clinical psychopharmacology* (6th ed.). Arlington, VA: American Psychiatric Publishing.

Schatzberg, A. F., Rush, A. J., Arnow, B. A., Banks, P. L., Blalock, J. A., Borian, F. E., et al. (2005). Chronic depression: Medication (nefazodone) or psychotherapy (CBASP) is effective when the other is not. *Archives of General Psychiatry, 62,* 513–520.

Schatzberg, A. F., Scully, J. H., Kupfer, D. J., & Regier, D. A. (2009). Setting the record straight: A response to Frances's commentary on DSM-V. *PsychiatricTimes, 26,* 1–10. Retrieved from http://psychiatrictimes.com/display/article/10168/1425806

Schaubroeck, J., Jones, J. R., & Xie, J. J. (2001). Individual differences in utilizing control to cope with job demands: Effects on susceptibility to infectious disease. *Journal of Applied Psychology, 86,* 265–278.

Schaufeli, W. B., & Buunk, B. P. (2003). Burnout: An overview of 25 years of research and theorizing. In M. J. Schabracq, J. A. M. Winnubst, & C. L. Cooper (Eds.), *Handbook of work and health psychology* (pp.383–428). West Sussex, UK: Wiley.

Scheerer, M., Rothmann, R., & Goldstein, K. (1945). A case of "idiot savant": An experimental study of personality organization. *Psychology Monograph, 58*(4), 1–63.

Scheibert, J., Leurent, S., Prevost, A., & Debrégeas, G. (2009). The role of fingerprints in the coding of tactile information probed with a biomimetic sensor. *Science, 323,* 1503–1506.

Scheidinger, S. (2004). Group psychotherapy and related helping groups today: An overview. *American Journal of Psychotherapy, 58,* 265–280.

Scheier, M. F., Matthews, K. A., Owens, J. F., Magovern, G. J., Lefebvre, R. C., Abbott, R. A., et al. (1989). Dispositional optimism and recovery from coronary artery bypass surgery: The beneficial effects on physical and psychological well-being. *Journal of Personality and Social Psychology, 57,* 1024–1040.

Scheier, M. F., Matthews, K. A., Owens, J. F., Schulz, R., Bridges, M. W., Magovern, G. J., et al. (1999). Optimism and rehospitalization after coronary artery bypass graft surgery. *Archives of Internal Medicine, 159,* 829–835.

Schell, T. L., Martino, S. C., Ellickson, P. L., Collins, R. L., & McCaffrey, D. (2005). Measuring developmental changes in alcohol expectancies. *Psychology of Addictive Behaviors, 19,* 217–220.

Schellenberg, E. (2011b). Music lessons, emotional intelligence, and IQ. *Music Perception, 29*(2), 185–194. doi:10.1525/MP.2011.29.2.185.

Schellenberg, E. (2011a). Examining the association between music lessons and intelligence. *British Journal of Psychology, 102*(3), 283–302. doi:10.1111/j.2044-8295.2010.02000.x.

Schellenberg, E. (2006). Long-term positive associations between music lessons and IQ. *Journal Of Educational Psychology, 98*(2), 457–468. doi:10.1037/0022-0663.98.2.457.

Schellenberg, E. (2005). Music and cognitive abilities. *Current Directions in Psychological Science, 14*(6), 317–320. doi:10.1111/j.0963-7214.2005.00389.x.

Schellenberg, E. G. (2004). Music lessons enhance IQ. *Psychological Science, 15,* 511–514. doi:10.1111/j.0956-7976.2004.00711.x.

Schenck, C. H. (2005). Rapid eye movement sleep parasomnias. *Neurology Clinics, 23,* 1107–1126.

Schenck, C. H., & Mahowald, M. W. (1992). Motor dyscontrol in narcolepsy: Rapid eye movement (REM) sleep without atonia and REM sleep behavior disorder. *Annals of Neurology, 32*(1), 3–10.

Schenk, S., Gittings, D., & Colussi-Mas, J. (2011). Dopaminergic mechanisms of reinstatement of MDMA-seeking behaviour in rats. *British Journal of Pharmacology, 162*(8), 1770–1780.

Scherbaum, C. A., Blanshetyn, V., Marshall-Wolp, E., McCue, E., & Strauss, R. (2011). Examining the effects of stereotype threat on test-taking behaviors. *Social Psychology of Education, 14*(3), 361–375. doi:10.1007/s11218-011-9154-2.

Scheufele, P. M. (2000). Effects of progressive relaxation and classical music on measurements of attention, relaxation, and stress responses. *Journal of Behavioral Medicine, 23,* 207–228.

Schiffman, S. S., Graham, B. G., Sattely-Miller, E. A., & Warwick, Z. (1999). Orosensory perception of dietary fat. *Current Directions in Psychological Science, 7,* 137–143.

Schirmer, A., Teh, K., Wang, S., Vijayakumar, R., Ching, A., Nithianantham, D., & .. Cheok, A. (2011). Squeeze me, but don't tease me: Human and mechanical touch enhance visual attention and emotion discrimination. *Social Neuroscience, 6*(3), 219–230. doi:10.1080/17470919.2010.507958.

Schleicher, D. J., Watt, J. D., & Greguras, G. J. (2004). Reexamining the job satisfaction–performance relationship: The complexity of attitudes. *Journal of Applied Psychology, 89,* 165–177.

Schlicht, E., Shimojo, S., Camerer, C., Battaglia, P., & Nakayama, K. (2010). Human wagering behavior depends on opponents' faces. *Plos One, 5*(7), e11663.

Schloss, P., & Williams, D. C. (1998). The serotonin transporter: A primary target for antidepressant drugs. *Journal of Psychopharmacology, 12,* 115–121.

Schlueter, N. N., Ganss, C. C., Pötschke, S. S., Klimek, J. J., & Hannig, C. C. (2012). Enzyme activities in the oral fluids of patients suffering from bulimia: A controlled clinical trial. *Caries Research, 46*(2), 130–139. doi:10.1159/000337105.

Schmader, T., Johns, M., & Forbes, C. (2008). An integrated process model of stereotype threat effects on performance. *Psychological Review, 115,* 336–356.

Schmader, T. (2010). Stereotype threat deconstructed. *Current Directions in Psychological Science, 19*(1), 14–18. doi:10.1177/0963721409359292.

Schmeichel, B. J., Gailliot, M. T., Filardo, E., McGregor, I., et al. (2009). Terror management theory and self-esteem revisited: The roles of implicit and explicit self-esteem in mortality salience effects. *Journal of Personality and Social Psychology, 96,* 1077–1087.

Schmid, M. C., Mrowka, S. W., Turchi, J. Saunders, R. C., Wilke, M., Peters, A. J., Ye, F. Q., & Leopold, D. A. (2010). Blindsight depends on the lateral geniculate nucleus. *Nature, 466*(7304), 373–377. doi:10.1038/nature09179.

Schmidt, F. L. (2011). A theory of sex differences in technical aptitude and some supporting evidence. *Perspectives on Psychological Science, 6*(6), 560–573. doi:10.1177/1745691611419670.

Schmidt, F. L., & Hunter, J. E. (2004). General mental ability in the world of work: Occupational attainment and job performance. *Journal of Personality and Social Psychology, 86,* 162–173.

Schmidt, M. F. H., & Tomasello, M. (2012) Young children enforce social norms. *Current Directions in Psychological Science, 21,* 232–236. doi: 10.1177/0963721412448659.

Schmidtke, A., & Hafner, H. (1988). The Werther effect after television films: New evidence for an old hypothesis. *Psychological Medicine, 18,* 665–676.

Schmitt, D. P. (2003). Universal sex differences in the desire for sexual variety: Tests from 52 nations, 6 continents, and 13 islands. *Journal of Personality and Social Psychology, 85,* 85–104.

Schmitt, D. P., Jonason, P. K., Byerley, G. J., Flores, S. D., Illbeck, B. E., O" Leary, K. N. O., & Qudrat, A. (2012). A reexamination of sex differences in sexuality: New studies reveal old truths. *Current Directions in Psychological Science 21*(2), 135–139. doi:10.1177/0963721412436808.

Schmolck, H., Buffalo, E. A., & Squire, L. R. (2000). Memory distortions over time: Recollections of the O. J. Simpson trial verdict after 15 and 32 months. *Psychological Science, 11,* 39–47.

Schnall, S., & Laird, J. D. (2003). Keep smiling: Enduring effects of facial expressions and postures on emotional experience and memory. *Cognition & Emotion, 17,* 787–797.

Schnee, M. E., Lawton, D. M., Furness, D. N., Benke, T. A., & Ricci, A. J. (2005). Auditory hair cell-afferent fiber synapses are specialized to operate at their best frequencies. *Neuron, 47,* 243–254.

Schneider, B. (1985). Organizational behavior. *Annual Review of Psychology, 36,* 573–611.

Schneider, B. H., Atkinson, L., & Tardif, C. (2001). Child-parent attachment and children's peer relations: A quantitative review. *Developmental Psychology, 37,* 86–100.

Schneider, K. T., Hitlan, R. T., & Radhakrishnan, P. (2000). The nature and correlates of ethnic harassment experiences in multiple contexts. *Journal of Applied Psychology, 85,* 3–12.

Schneider, T. R., Ring, C., & Katkin, E. S. (1998). A test of the validity of the method of constant stimuli as an index of heartbeat detection. *Psychophysiology, 35,* 86–89.

Schneider, W., & Bjorklund, D. F. (1998). Memory. In W. Damon, D. Kuhn, & R. Siegler (Eds.), *Handbook of child psychology: Vol. 2. Cognition, language and perception* (5th ed., pp. 467–521). New York: Wiley.

Schneiderman, N. (2004). Psychosocial, behavioral, and biological aspects of chronic diseases. *Current Directions in Psychological Science, 13,* 247–251.

Schneiderman, N., Antoni, M. H., Saab, P. G., & Ironson,G. (2001). Health psychology: Psychosocial and biobehavioral aspects of chronic disease management. *Annual Review of Psychology, 52,* 555–580.

Schnur, T. T., Schwartz, M. F., Kimberg, D. Y., Hirshorn, E., Coslett, H. B., & Thompson-Schill, S. L. (2009). Localizing interference during naming: Convergent neuroimaging and neuropsychological evidence for the function of Broca's area. *Proceedings of the National Academy of Sciences, 106*(1), 322–327.

Schnurr, P. P., Friedman, M. J., Engel, C. C., Foa, E. B., Shea, T., Chow, B. K., et al. (2007). Cognitive behavior therapy for posttraumatic stress disorder in women: A randomized controlled trial. *Journal of the American Medical Association, 297,* 820–830.

Schoebi, D., Karney, B. R., & Bradbury, T. N. (2011). Stability and change in the first 10 years of marriage: Does commitment confer benefits beyond the effects of satisfaction? *Journal of Personality and Social Psychology,* Nov 21, 2011.

Schoemaker, M. J., Swerdlow, A. J., Ahlbom, A., Auvinen, A., Blaasaas, K. G., Cardis, E., et al. (2005). Mobile phone use and risk of acoustic neuroma: Results of the Interphone case-control study in five North European countries. *British Journal of Cancer, 93,* 842–848.

Schoenbaum, M., Sherbourne, C., & Wells, K. (2005). Gender patterns in cost effectiveness of quality improvement for depression: Results of a randomized controlled trial. *Journal of Affective Disorders, 87,* 319.

Schofield, H.-L., Bierman, K. L., Heinrichs, B., & Nix, R. L. (2008). Predicting early sexual activity with behavior problems exhibited at school entry and in early adolescence. *Journal of Abnormal Child Psychology, 36*(8), 1175–1188.

Scholz, H., Franz, M., & Heberlein, U. (2005). The *hangover* gene defines a stress pathway required for ethanol tolerance development. *Nature, 436,* 845–847.

Schooler, C. (2007). Use it—and keep it, longer, probably: A reply to Salthouse (2006). *Perspectives on Psychological Science, 2,* 24–29.

Schoon, I., Parsons, S., Rush, R., & Law, J. (2010). Children's language ability and psychosocial development: A 29-year follow-up study. *Pediatrics, 126*(1), e73-e80. doi:10.1542/peds.2009-3282.

Schott, B. H., Henson, R. N., Richardson-Klavehn, A., Becker, C., Thoma, V., Heinze, H. J., & Duzel, E. (2005). Redefining implicit and explicit memory: The functional neuroanatomy of priming, remembering, and control of retrieval. *Proceedings of the National Academy of Sciences, 102,* 1257–1262.

Schredl, M. (2010). Characteristics and contents of dreams. *International Review of Neurobiology, 92,* 135–154.

Schredl, M. & Reinhard, I. (2011). Gender differences in nightmare frequency: A meta-analysis. *Sleep Medicine Reviews, 15*(2), 115–121.

Schreiber, G. B., Robins, M., Striegel-Moore, R., Obarzanek, E., Morrison, J. A., & Wright, D. J. (1996). Weight modification efforts reported by black and white preadolescent girls: National Heart, Lung, and Blood Institute Growth and Health Study. *Pediatrics, 98,* 63–70.

Schroeder, D. A. (1995). An introduction to social dilemmas. In D. Schroeder (Ed.), *Social dilemmas: Perspectives on individuals and groups* (pp. 1–13). Westport, CT: Praeger.

Schroeder, D. A., Penner, L. A., Dovidio, J. F., & Piliavin, J. A. (1995). *The psychology of helping and altruism: Problems and puzzles.* New York: McGraw-Hill.

Schuckit, M. A. (1998). Biological, psychological, and environmental predictors of alcoholism risk: A longitudinal study. *Journal of Studies in Alcoholism, 59,* 485–494.

Schulden, J., Chen, J., Kresnow, M., Arias, I., Crosby, A., Mercy, J., et al. (2006). Psychological responses to the sniper attacks: Washington DC area, October, 2002. *American Journal of Preventive Medicine, 31,* 324–327.

Schultheiss, O. (2008). Implicit motives. In O. John, R. Robins, & L. Pervin (Eds.), *Handbook of personality: Theory and research* (3rd ed., 603–633). New York: Guilford.

Schultheiss, O. C., & Rohde, W. (2002). Implicit power motivation predicts men's testosterone changes and implicit learning in a contest situation. *Hormones and Behavior, 41,* 195–202.

Schultz, D., & Schultz, S. E. (2002). *Psychology and work today: An introduction to industrial and organizational psychology* (8th ed.). Upper Saddle River, NJ: Prentice Hall.

Schultz, D. P., & Schultz, S. E. (2000). *A history of modern psychology* (7th ed.). Fort Worth, TX: Harcourt Brace.

Schultz, D. P., & Schultz, S. E. (2004). *A history of modern psychology* (8th ed.). Fort Worth, TX: Harcourt Brace.

Schultz, D. P., & Schultz, S. E. (2005). *Theories of personality* (8th ed.) Belmont, CA: Wadsworth.

Schultz, D. P., & Schultz, S. E. (2009). *Theories of personality* (9th ed.). Florence, KY: Cengage Learning.

Schultz, P. W., Nolan, J. M., Cialdini, R. B., Goldstein, N. J., & Griskevicius, V. (2007). The constructive, destructive, and reconstructive power of social norms. *Psychological Science, 18,* 429–434.

Schulz, R. (1978). *The psychology of death, dying, and bereavement.* Reading, MA: Addison-Wesley.

Schulz, R., Beach, S. R., Lind, B., Martire, L. M., Zdaniuk, B., Hirsch, C., et al. (2001). Involvement in caregiving and adjustment to death of a spouse: Findings from the caregiver health effects study. *Journal of the American Medical Association, 285,* 3123–3129.

Schulz-Hardt, S., Frey, D., Luthgens, C., & Moscovici, S. (2000). Biased information search in group decision making. *Journal of Personality and Social Psychology, 78,* 665–669.

Schuman-Olivier, Z., Vago, D. R., Ott, U., & Hopfer, C. (2011). Club drug, prescription drug, and over-the-counter medication abuse: Description, diagnosis, and intervention. In Kaminer, Y. & Winters, K. C. (Eds.), *Clinical manual of adolescent substance abuse treatment.* Arlington, VA, US: American Psychiatric Publishing, Inc.

Schumann, A., Meyer, C., Rumpf, H. J., Hannover, W., Hapke, U., & John, U. (2005). Stage of change transitions and processes of change, decisional balance, and self–efficacy in smokers: A transtheoretical model validation using longitudinal data. *Psychology of Addictive Behaviors, 19,* 3–9.

Schwabe, L., & Wolf, O. T. (2011). Stress increases behavioral resistance to extinction. *Psychoneuroendocrinology, 36*(9), 1287–1293. doi:10.1016/j.psyneuen.2011.02.002.

Schwarz, N., & Scheuring, B. (1992). Frequency reports of psychosomatic symptoms: What respondents learn from response alternatives. *Zeutschrift fur Klinische Psychologie, 22,* 197–208.

Schwartz, R. C., & Feisthamel, K. P. (2009). Disproportionate diagnosis of mental disorders among African American versus European American clients: Implications for counseling theory, research, and practice. *Journal of Counseling and Development, 87,* 295–301.

Schwartz, S. J., Weisskirch, R. S., Zamboanga, B. L., Castillo, L. G., Ham, L. S., Huynh, Q., & ... Cano, M. A. (2011). Dimensions of acculturation: Associations with health risk behaviors among college students from immigrant families. *Journal of Counseling Psychology, 58*(1), 27–41. doi:10.1037/a0021356

Schwarzer, R. (2001). Social-cognitive factors in changing health-related behaviors. *Current Directions in Psychological Science, 10,* 47–51.

Schwenck, C., Bjorklund, D. F., & Schneider, W. (2009). Developmental and individual differences in young children's use and maintenance of a selective memory strategy. *Developmental Psychology, 45,* 1034–1050.

Schwender, D., Klasing, D., Daunderer, M., Maddler, C., Poppel, E., & Peter, K. (1995). Awareness during general anesthetic: Definition, incidence, clinical relevance, causes, avoidance, and medicolegal aspects. *Anaesthetist, 44,* 743–754.

Schyns, B. (2006). Are group consensus in leader-member exchange (LMX) and shared work values related to organizational outcomes? *Small Group Research, 37,* 20–35.

Scoboria, A., Mazzoni, G., Jarry, J. L., & Bernstein, D. M. (2012). Personalized and not general suggestion produces false autobiographical memories and suggestion-consistent behavior. *Acta Psychologica, 139*(1), 225–232. doi:10.1016/j.actpsy.2011.10.008.

Scott, T. F. (2006). The neurological examination. In P. J. Snyder & P. D. Nussbaum (Eds.), *Clinical neuropsychology: A pocket handbook for assessment,* 2nd ed. (pp. 17–33). Washington, DC: American Psychological Association.

Scott, K. M., Bruffaerts, R., Simon, G. E., Alonso, J., Angermeyer, M., de Girolamo, G., Demyttenaere, K., Gasquet, I., Haro, J. M., Karam, E., Kessler, R. C., Levinson, D., Mora, M. E. M., Browne, M. A. O., Ormel, J., Villa, J. P., Uda, H., & Von Korff, M. (2008). Obesity and mental disorders in the general population: results from the world mental health surveys. *International Journal of Obesity, 32,* 192–200.

Scott, K. M., Smith, D. R., & Ellis, P. M. (2010). Prospectively ascertained child maltreatment and its association with DSM-IV mental disorders in young adults. *Archives of General Psychiatry, 67,* 712–719.

Scourfield, J., Van den Bree, M., Martin, N., & McGuffin, P. (2004). Conduct problems in children and adolescents: A twin study. *Archives of General Psychiatry, 61,* 489–496.

Scoville, W. B., & Milner, B. (1957). Loss of recent memory after bilateral hippocampal lesions. *Journal of Neurology, Neurosurgery, and Psychiatry, 20,* 11–21.

Scullin, M. K., & McDaniel, M. A. (2010). Remembering to execute a goal: Sleep on it!. *Psychological Science, 21*(7), 1028–1035. doi:10.1177/0956797610373373.

Seamon, J. G., Punjabi, P. V., & Busch, E. A. (2010). Memorising Milton's Paradise Lost: A study of a septuagenarian exceptional memoriser. *Memory, 18*(5), 498–503. doi:10.1080/09658211003781522.

Sears, R. (1977). Sources of satisfaction of the Terman gifted men. *American Psychologist, 32,* 119–128.

Sederberg, P. B., Schulze-Bonhage, A., Madsen, J. R., Bromfield, E. B., Litt, B., Brandt, A., & Kahana, M. J. (2007). Gamma oscillations distinguish true from false memories. *Psychological Science, 18,* 927–932.

Seegert, C. R. (2003). Token economies and incentive programs: Behavioral improvement in mental health inmates housed in state prisons. *Behavior Therapist, 26*(1), 208, 210–211.

Seeley, K. (2006). *Cultural psychotherapy: Working with culture in the clinical encounter.* Northvale, NJ: Aronson.

Seeman, M. V. (2004). Gender differences in the prescribing of antipsychotic drugs. *American Journal of Psychiatry, 161,* 1324–1333.

Seeman, M. V. (2011). Sleepwalking, a possible side effect of antipsychotic medication. *Psychiatric Quarterly, 82*(1), 59–67. doi:10.1007/s11126-010-9149-8.

Seeman, T., & Chen, X. (2002). Risk and protective factors for physical functioning in older adults with and without chronic conditions: MacArthur studies of successful aging. *Journals of Gerontology: Series B. Psychological Sciences & Social Sciences, 57*(3), S135–S144.

Segall, M. H., Dasen, P. R., Berry, J. W., & Poortinga, Y. H. (1990). *Human behavior in global perspective: An introduction to cross-cultural psychology.* Elmwood, NY: Pergamon Press.

Segerstrom, S. C., & Sephton, S. E. (2010). Optimistic expectancies and cell-mediated immunity. *Psychological Science, 21,* 448–455.

Segerstrom, S. C., Taylor, S. E., Kemeny, M. E., & Fahey, J. L. (1998). Optimism is associated with mood, coping, and immune change in response to stress. *Journal of Personality and Social Psychology, 74,* 1646–1655.

Seguin, J. R., & Zelazo, P. D. (2005). Executive function in early physical aggression. In R. E. Tremblay, W. W. Hartup, & J. Archer (Eds.), *Developmental origins of aggression* (pp. 307–329). New York: Guilford Press.

Seidler, G. H., & Wagner, F. E. (2006). Comparing the efficacy of EMDR and trauma-focused cognitive-behavioral therapy in the treatment of PTSD: A meta-analytic study. *Psychological Medicine, 36,* 1515–1522.

Seiger, A., Nordberg, A., Vonholst, H., Backman, L., Ebendal, T., Alafuzoff, I., et al. (1993). Intracranial infusion of purified nerve growth factor to an Alzheimer patient: The 1st attempt of a possible future treatment strategy. *Behavioral Brain Research, 57,* 255–261.

Sejnowski, T. J., Chattarji, S., & Stanton, P. K. (1990). Homosynaptic long-term depression in hippocampus and neocortex. *Seminars in the Neurosciences, 2,* 355–363.

Sejnowski, T. J., & Destexhe, A. (2000). Why do we sleep? *Brain Research, 886,* 208–223.

Selbom, M. & Bagby, M. R. (2010). Detection of overreported psychopathology with the MMPI-2 RF form validity scales. *Psychological Assessment: A Journal of Consulting and Clinical Psychology, 22,* 757–767.

Seligman, M. E. P. (1975). *Helplessness: On depression, development, and death.* San Francisco: Freeman.

Seligman, M. E. P. (1991). *Learned optimism.* New York: Knopf.

Seligman, M. E. P. (1996). Good news for psychotherapy: The *Consumer Reports* study. *Independent Practitioner, 16,* 17–20.

Seligman, M. E. P., Steen, T. A., Park, N., & Peterson, C. (2005). Positive psychology progress: Empirical validation of interventions. *American Psychologist, 60,* 410–421.

Seligman, M. E. P. (2011). *Flourish: A visionary new understanding of happiness and well-being.* New York: Free Press.

Seligman, M. E. P., Castellon, C., Cacciola, J., Shulman, P., Luborsky, L., Ollove, M., & Downing, R. (1988). Explanatory style change during cognitive therapy for unipolar depression. *Journal of Abnormal Psychology, 97,* 13–18.

Seligman, M. E. P., & Schulman, P. (1986). Explanatory style as a predictor of productivity and quitting among life insurance agents. *Journal of Personality and Social Psychology, 50,* 832–838.

Sell, R. L., Wells, J. A., & Wypij, D. (1995). The prevalence of homosexual behavior and attraction in the United States, the United Kingdom, and France: Results of national population-based samples. *Archives of Sexual Behavior, 24*(3), 235–248.

Selye, H. (1956). *The stress of life.* New York: McGraw-Hill.

Selye, H. (1975). *Stress without distress.* New York: Signet.

Selye, H. (1976). *The stress of life* (2nd ed.). New York: McGraw-Hill.

Semmler, C., Brewer, N., & Wells, G. L. (2004). Effects of postidentification feedback on eyewitness identification and nonidentification confidence. *Journal of Applied Psychology, 89,* 334–346.

Senghas, A., & Coppola, M. (2001). Children creating language: How Nicaraguan sign language acquired a spatial grammar. *Psychological Science, 12,* 323–328.

Senju, A., Southgate, V., Snape, C., Leonard, M., & Csibra, G. (2011). Do 18-month-olds really attribute mental states to others?: A critical test. *Psychological Science, 22*(7), 878–880. doi:10.1177/0956797611411584.

Seo, H., & Lee, D. (2009). Behavioral and neural changes after gains and losses of conditioned reinforcers. *Journal of Neuroscience, 29,* 3627–3641.

Seppa, N. (2010). Nearsightedness increasing in the United States. *Science News, 177,* 13.

Sergeant, J. A., Geurts, H., & Oosterlaan, J. (2001). How specific is a deficit of executive functioning for attention deficit/hyperactivity disorder? *Behavioural Brain Research, 130,* 3–28.

Serpell, R. (1994). The cultural construction of intelligence. In W. J. Lonner & R. S. Malpass (Eds.), *Psychology and culture* (pp. 157–164). Boston: Allyn & Bacon.

Serretti, A., Chiesa, A., Calati, R., Perma, G., Bellodi, L., & De Ronchi, D. (2009). Common genetic, clinical, demographic and psychosocial predictors of response to pharmacotherapy in mood and anxiety disorders. *International Clinical Psychopharmacology, 24,* 1–18.

Servan-Schreiber, D., Schooler, J., Dew, M. A., Carter, C., & Bartone, P. (2006). Eye movement desensitization and reprocessing for posttraumatic stress disorder: A pilot blinded, randomized study of stimulation type. *Psychotherapy and Psychosomatics, 75,* 290–297.

Servan-Schreiber, E., & Anderson, J. R. (1990). Learning artificial grammars with competitive chunking. *Journal of Experimental Psychology: Learning, Memory, and Cognition, 16,* 592–608.

Seto, M. C., Maric, A., & Barbaree, H. E. (2001). The role of pornography in the etiology of sexual aggression. *Aggression and Violent Behavior, 6,* 35–53.

Sewell, M. C., Goggin, K. J., Rabkin, J. G., Ferrando, S. J., McElhiney, M. C., & Evans, S. (2000). Anxiety syndromes and symptoms among men with AIDS: A longitudinal controlled study. *Psychosomatics, 41,* 294–300.

Seymour, N. E. (2008). VR to OR: A review of the evidence that virtual reality simulation improves operating room performance. *World Journal of Surgery, 32*(2), 182–188.

Shackman, A. J., Salomons, T. V., Slagter, H. A., Fox, A. S., Winter, J. J., Davidson, R. J. (2011). The integration of negative affect, pain and cognitive control in the cingulate cortex. *Nature Reviews Neuroscience, 12*(3), 154-167.

Shadish, W. R., & Baldwin, S. A. (2005). Effects of behavioral marital therapy: A meta-analysis of randomized controlled trials. *Journal of Counseling and Clinical Psychology, 73,* 6–14.

Shadish, W. R., Cook, T. D., & Campbell, D. T. (2002). *Experimental and quasi-experimental designs for generalized causal inference.* Boston: Houghton Mifflin.

Shadish, W. R., Matt, G. E., Navarro, A. M., & Phillips, G. (2000). The effects of psychological therapies under clinically representative conditions: A meta-analysis. *Psychological Bulletin, 126,* 512–529.

Shaffer, D. R. (1999). *Developmental psychology: Childhood and adolescence.* Pacific Grove, CA: Brooks/Cole.

Shafto, P., Goodman, N. D., & Frank, M. C. (2012). Learning from others: The consequences of psychological reasoning for human learning. *Perspectives on Psychological Science, 7,* 341–351. doi:10.1177/1745691612448481.

Shahar, G., Porcerelli, J. H, Kamoo, R., Czarkowski, K. A., Magriples, U., & Mayes, L. C. (2010). Defensive projection, superimposed on simplistic object relations, erodes patient-provider relationships in high-risk pregnancy: An empirical investigation. *Journal of the American Psychoanalytic Association, 58,* 953–974.

Shahin, A. J., Roberts, L. E., Chau, W., Trainor, L. J., & Miller, L. M. (2008). Music training leads to the development of timbre-specific gamma band activity. *NeuroImage, 41*(1), 113–122.

Shalev, A., Ankri, Y., Israeli-Shalev, Y., Peleg, T., Adessky, R., & Freedman, S. (2012). Prevention of posttraumatic stress disorder by early treatment: results from the jerusalem trauma outreach and prevention study. *Archives Of General Psychiatry, 69*(2), 166-176. doi:10.1001/archgenpsychiatry.2011.127.

Shalev, A. Y., & Freedman, S. (2005). PTSD following terrorist attacks: A prospective evaluation. *American Journal of Psychiatry, 162,* 1188–1191.

Shalev, A. Y., Tuval, R., Frenkiel-Fishman, S., Hadar, H., & Eth, S. (2006). Psychological responses to continuous terror: A study of two communities in Israel. *American Journal of Psychiatry, 163,* 667–673.

Shalvi, S., Moran, S., & Ritov, I. (2010). Overcoming initial anchors: The effect of negotiators' dispositional control beliefs., *Negotiation and Conflict Management Research, 3,* 232–248.

Shamah Levy, T., Morales Ruán, C., Amaya Castellanos, C., Salazar Coronel, A., Jiménez Aguilar, A., & Méndez Gómez Humarán, I. (2012). Effectiveness of a diet and physical activity promotion strategy on the prevention of obesity in Mexican school children. *BMC Public Health, 12,* 152.

Shamay-Tsoory, S. G., & Tomer, R. (2005). The neuroanatomical basis of understanding sarcasm and its relationship to social cognition. *Neuropsychology, 19,* 288–300.

Shand, M. A. (1982). Sign-based short-term memory coding of American Sign Language and printed English words by congenitally deaf signers. *Cognitive Psychology, 14,* 1–12.

Shankar, A., McMunn, A., Banks, J., & Steptoe, A. (2011). Loneliness, social isolation, and behavioral and biological health indicators in older adults. *Health Psychology: Official Journal of the Division of Health Psychology, American Psychological Association, 30*(4), 377–385.

Shankaran, S., Das, A., Bauer, C. R., Bada, H. S., Lester, B. M., Wright, L. L., & . Poole, W. (2011). Prenatal cocaine exposure and small-for-gestational-age status: Effects on growth at 6 years of age. *Neurotoxicology and Teratology, 33*(5), 575–581. doi:10.1016/j.ntt.2011.04.003.

Shankman, S. A., Klein, D. N., Tenke, C. E., & Bruder, G. E. (2007). Reward sensitivity in depression: A biobehavioral study. *Journal of Abnormal Psychology, 116,* 95–104.

Shanks, D. R. (1995). *The psychology of associative learning.* New York: Cambridge University Press.

Shapiro, A. F., Gottman, J. M., & Carrere, S. (2000). The baby and the marriage: Identifying factors that buffer against decline in marital satisfaction after the first baby arrives. *Journal of Family Psychology, 14,* 59–70.

Shapiro, F. (1989a). Efficacy of the eye movement desensitization procedure in the treatment of traumatic memories. *Journal of Traumatic Stress, 2,* 199–223.

Shapiro, F. (1989b). Eye movement desensitization: A new treatment for posttraumatic stress disorder. *Journal of Behavior Therapy and Experimental Psychiatry, 20,* 211–217.

Shapiro, F. (1991). Eye movement desensitization and reprocessing procedure: From EMD to EMD/R—A new treatment model for anxiety and related traumata. *Behavior Therapist, 15,* 133–135.

Shapiro, F., & Forrest, M. S. (2004). *EMDR: The breakthrough therapy for overcoming anxiety, stress, and trauma.* New York: Basic Books.

Shapiro, K. A., Moo, L. R., & Caramazza, A. (2006). Cortical signatures of noun and verb production. *Proceedings of the National Academy of Sciences, 103,* 1644–1649.

Shapiro, R. (2005). *EMDR solutions: Pathways to healing.* New York: Norton.

Shargorodsky, J., Curhan, S. G., Curhan, G. C., & Eavey, R. (2010). Change in Prevalence of Hearing Loss in US Adolescents. *JAMA: Journal Of The American Medical Association, 304*(7), 772–778.

Shariff, A. F., & Tracy, J. L. (2011). What are emotion expressions for? *Current Directions In Psychological Science, 20*(6), 395–399. doi:10.1177/0963721411424739.

Sharp, T., & Cowen, P. (2011). 5-HT and depression: is the glass half-full? *Current Opinion in Pharmacology, 11*(1), 45–51. doi:10.1016/j.coph.2011.02.003.

Shatzmiller, R. A. (2010, June 17). *Sleep stage scoring introduction/ Historical perspective.* Retrieved from http://emedicine.medscape.com/article/1188142-overview.

Shaunessy, E., Karnes, F. A., & Cobb, Y. (2004). Assessing potentially gifted students from lower socioeconomic status with nonverbal measures of intelligence. *Perceptual and Motor Skills, 98*(3, Pt 2), 1129–1138. doi:10.2466/PMS.98.4.1129-1138.

Shaver, P. R & Mikulincer, Mario (2011). An attachment-theory framework for conceptualizing interpersonal behavior. In L. Horowitz, & S. Strack, (Eds.), *Handbook of interpersonal psychology: Theory, research, assessment, and therapeutic interventions* (pp. 17–35). Hoboken, NJ: John Wiley & Sons Inc.

Shaw, D. S., Dishion, T. J., Supplee, L., Gardner, F., & Arnds, K. (2006). Randomized trial of a family-centered approach to the prevention of early conduct problems: 2-year effects of the family check-up in early childhood. *Journal of Consulting and Clinical Psychology, 74,* 1–9.

Shaw, D. S., Owens, E. B., Giovannelli, J., Winslow, E. B. (2001). Infant and toddler pathways leading to early externalizing disorders. *Journal of the American Academy of Child and Adolescent Psychiatry, 40,* 36–43.

Shayer, M. (2008). Intelligence for education: As described by Piaget and measured by psychometrics. *British Journal of Educational Psychology, 78*(1), 1–29.

Shaywitz, B. A., Shaywitz, S. E., Pugh, K. R., Constable, R. T., Skudlarski, P., Fulbright, R. K., et al. (1995). Sex differences in the functional organization of the brain for language. *Nature, 373,* 607–609.

Shechtman, Z. (1992). A group assessment procedure as a predictor of on-the-job performance of teachers. *Journal of Applied Psychology, 77,* 383–387.

Shedler, J. (2010). The efficacy of psychodynamic psychotherapy. *American Psychologist, 65,* 98–109.

Shedler, J., & Westen, D. (2004). Refining personality disorder diagnoses: Integrating science and practice. *American Journal of Psychiatry, 161,* 1350–1365.

Sheehy, R., & Horan, J. J. (2004). Effects of stress inoculation training for 1st-year law students. *International Journal of Stress Management, 11*(1), 41–55.

Sheer, V. C. (2011). Teenagers' use of MSN features, discussion topics, and online friendship development: The impact of media richness and communication control. *Communication Quarterly, 59,* 82–103. doi:10.1080/01463373.2010.525702.

Sheerin, C. M., Seim, R. W., & Spates, C. R. (2012). A new appraisal of combined treatments for PTSD in the era of psychotherapy adjunctive medications. *Journal of Contemporary Psychotherapy, 42,* 69–76.

Sheldon, K. M., & Kasser, T. (2001). Getting older, getting better? Personal striving and psychological maturity across the life span. *Developmental Psychology, 37,* 491–501.

Sheldon, K. M., & King, L. (2001). Why positive psychology is necessary. *American Psychologist, 56,* 216–217.

Sheldon, K. M., & King, L (2001). Why positive psychology is necessary. *American Psychologist, 56*, 216–217.

Shen, J., & Dicker, B. (2008). The impacts of shiftwork on employees. *International Journal of Human Resource Management, 19*, 392–405.

Shenker, J. I., Wylie, S. A., Fuchs, K., Manning, C. A., & Heilman, K. M. (2004). On-line anosognosia: Unawareness for chorea in real time but not on videotape delay. *Neurology, 63*(1), 159–160.

Shenker, J. I. (2010, February 19). The lady who didn't know she couldn't move, the vanishing mystery woman, and other broken brains that teach. Presentation to fifth annual Conference on Applied Learning in Higher Education, Missouri Western State University, Saint Joseph, MO.

Shepard, R. N., & Metzler, J. (1971). Mental rotation of three-dimensional objects. *Science, 171*, 701–703.

Shepherd, C., Kohut, J. J., & Sweet, R. (1989). *News of the weird*. New York: New American Library.

Shepherd, R. K., Coco, A., Epp, S. B., & Crook, J. M. (2005). Chronic depolarization enhances the trophic effects of brain-derived neurotrophic factor in rescuing auditory neurons following a sensorineural hearing loss. *Journal of Comparative Neurology, 486*, 145–158.

Shepherd, R. K., & McCreery, D. B. (2006). Basis of electrical stimulation of the cochlea and the cochlear nucleus. *Advances in Otorhinolaryngology, 64*, 186–205.

Shepperd, J., Malone, W., & Sweeny, K. (2008). Exploring causes of the self-serving bias. *Social and Personality Psychology Compass, 2*, 895–908.

Sheppes, G., Scheibe, S., Suri, G., & Gross, J. J. (2011). Emotion-regulation choice. *Psychological Science, 22*(11), 1391–1396. doi:10.1177/0956797611418350.

Sheppes, G., Scheibe, S., Suri, G., & Gross, J. J. (2011). Emotion-regulation choice. *Psychological Science, 22*, 1391–1396. doi:10.1177/0956797611418350.

Sher, K. J., Wood, M. D., Wood, P. K., & Raskin, G. (1996). Alcohol outcome expectancies and alcohol use: A latent variable cross-lagged panel study. *Journal of Abnormal Psychology, 105*, 561–574.

Shera, C. A., Guinan, J. J., & Oxenham, A. J. (2002). Revised estimates of human cochlear tuning from otoacoustic and behavioral measurements. *Proceedings of the National Academy of Sciences, 99*(5), 3318–3323.

Sherer, M. R., & Schreibman, L. (2005). Individual behavioral profiles and predictors of treatment effectiveness for children with autism. *Journal of Consulting and Clinical Psychology, 73*, 525–538.

Shergill, S. S., Brammer, M. J., Williams, S. C., Murray, R. M., & McGuire, P. K. (2000). Mapping auditory hallucinations in schizophrenia using functional magnetic resonance imaging. *Archives of General Psychiatry, 57*, 1033–1038.

Sherif, M. (1937). An experimental approach to the study of attitudes. *Sociometry, 1*, 90–98.

Sherman, S. M. (2007). The thalamus is more than just a relay. *Current Opinion in Neurobiology, 17*, 417–422.

Sherman, J. W., & Bessenoff, G. R. (1999). Stereotypes as source-monitoring cues: On the interaction between episodic and semantic memory. *Psychological Science, 10*, 106–110.

Sherman, R. T., & Thompson, R. A. (2004). The female athlete triad. *Journal of School Nursing, 20*, 197–202.

Sherman, S. J. (1980). On the self-erasing nature of errors of prediction. *Journal of Personality and Social Psychology, 39*, 211–221.

Sherwin, B. B., & Gelfand, M. M. (1987). The role of androgen in the maintenance of sexual functioning in oophorectomized women. *Psychosomatic Medicine, 49*, 397–409.

Sherwin, B. B., Gelfand, M. M., & Brender, W. (1985). Androgen enhances sexual motivation in females: A prospective crossover study of sex steroid administration in the surgical menopause. *Psychosomatic Medicine, 47*, 339–351.

Shidlovski, D., & Hassin, R. (2011). When pooping babies become more appealing: the effects of nonconscious goal pursuit on experienced emotions. *Psychological Science, 22*(11), 1381–1385.

Shields, L. B. E., Hunsaker, D. M., Muldoon, S., Corey, T. S., & Spivack, B. S. (2005). Risk factors associated with sudden unexplained infant death: A prospective study of infant care practices in Kentucky. *Pediatrics, 116*, e13–e20.

Shore, S. (2003). Life on and slightly to the right of the autistic spectrum: A personal account. *Exceptional Parent, 33*, 85–89.

Sieverding, M., Decker, S., & Zimmermann, F. (2010). Information about low participation in cancer screening demotivates other people. *Psychological Science, 21*(7), 941–943. doi:10.1177/0956797610373936.

Shiller, R. J. (2001). *Irrational exuberance*. Princeton, NJ: Princeton University Press.

Shimamura, A. P., Berry, J. M., Mangels, J. A., Rusting, C. L., & Jurica, P. J. (1995). Memory and cognitive abilities in university professors: Evidence for successful aging. *Psychological Science, 6*, 271–277.

Shimazu, T., Kuriyama1, S., Ohmori-Matsuda, K., Kikuchi, N., Nakaya, N., & Tsuji, I. (2009). Increase in body mass index category since age 20 years and all-cause mortality: A prospective cohort study (the Ohsaki Study). *International Journal of Obesity, 33*, 490–496.

Shin, M., Besser, L. M., Kucik, J. E., Lu, C., et al. (2009). Prevalence of Down syndrome among children and adolescents in 10 regions of the United States. *Pediatrics, 124*, 1565–1571.

Shin, L. M., Rauch, S. L., & Pitman, R. K. (2006). Amygdala, medial prefrontal cortex, and hippocampal function in PTSD. *Annals of the New York Academy of Sciences, 1071*, 67–79.

Shinskey, J. L., & Munakata, Y. (2005). Familiarity breeds searching. *Psychological Science, 16*, 596–600.

Shipstead, Z., Redick, T. S., & Engle, R. W. (2012). Is working memory training effective?. *Psychological Bulletin*, doi:10.1037/a0027473

Shiraev, E. B., & Levy, D. A. (2010). *Cross-cultural psychology: Critical thinking and contemporary applications* (4th ed.). Boston: Allyn & Bacon.

Shiwach, R. S., Reid, W. H., & Carmody, T. J. (2001). An analysis of reported deaths following electroconvulsive therapy in Texas, 1993–1998. *Psychiatric Services, 52*, 1095–1097.

Shneidman, E. S. (1987). A psychological approach to suicide. In G. VandenBos & B. K. Bryant (Eds.), *Cataclysms, crises, and catastrophes: Psychology in action. The master lectures* (Vol. 6, pp. 147–183). Washington, DC: American Psychological Association.

Shoda, Y., & LeeTiernan, S. (2002). What remains invariant? Finding order within a person's thoughts, feelings, and behavior across situations. In D. Cervone & W. Mischel (Eds.), *Advances in personality science* (pp. 241–270). New York: Guilford Press.

Shoda, Y., & Mischel, W. (2006). Applying meta-theory to achieve generalisability and precision in personality science: Comment. *Applied Psychology: An International Review, 55*, 439–452.

Shore, S. (2003). Life on and slightly to the right of the autistic spectrum: A personal account. *Exceptional Parent, 33*, 85–89.

Short, K. (2011, November). The research supplemental poverty measure: 2010. Washington, DC: U.S. Department of Commerce, Economics and Statistics Administration, U.S. Census Bureau. Retrieved from: http://www.census.gov/hhes/povmeas/methodology/supplemental/research/Short_ResearchSPM2010.pdf.

Shorter, E., & Healy, D. (2007). *Shock therapy: A history of electroconvulsive treatment in mental illness*. Piscataway, NJ: Rutgers University Press.

Shreeve, J. (1993, June). Touching the phantom. *Discover, 35*–42.

Shteynberg, G., & Galinsky, A. D. (2011). Implicit coordination: Sharing goals with similar others intensifies goal pursuit. *Journal of Experimental Social Psychology, 47*, 1291–1294. doi:10.1016/j.jesp.2011.04.012.

Shu, S. Y., Wu, Y. M., Bao, X. M., Wen, Z. B., Huang, F. H., Li, S. X., et al. (2002). A new area in the human brain associated with learning and memory: Immunohistochemical and functional MRI analysis. *Molecular Psychiatry, 7*, 1018–1022.

Shuffler, M. L., DiazGranados, D., & Salas, E. (2011). There's a science for that. *Current Directions in Psychological Science, 20*(6) 365–372. doi:10.1177/0963721411422054.

Shuffler, M. L., Wiese, C. W., Salas, E., & Burke, C. (2010). Leading one another across time and space: Exploring shared leadership functions in virtual teams. *Revista De Psicologia Del Trabajo Y De Las Organizaciones, 26*(1), 3–17.

Shultz, K. S., & Wang, M. (2011). Psychological perspectives on the changing nature of retirement. *American Psychologist, 66*(3), 170–179. doi:10.1037/a0022411.

Shweder, R. A., Much, N. C., Mahapatra, M., & Park, L. (1994). The "big three" of morality (autonomy, community, and divinity), and the "big three" explanations of suffering, as well. In A. Brandt & P. Rozin (Eds.), *Morality and health*. Stanford, CA: Stanford University Press.

Sibbald, M., Panisko, D., & Cavalcanti, R. B. (2011). Role of clinical context in residents' physical examination diagnostic accuracy. *Medical Education, 45*(4), 415–421. doi:10.1111/j.1365-2923.2010.03896.x.

Siber, K. (2005, December). Precious metal. *Skiing, 58*(4), 16E.

Siderowf, A., Jennings, D., Eberly, S., Oakes, D., Hawkins, K. A., Ascherio, A., Stern, M. B., Marek, K. and the PARS Investigators. (2012). Impaired olfaction and other prodromal features in the Parkinson At-Risk Syndrome study. *Movement Disorders*, Epub January 11, 2012

Sidney, S., Feng, L., & Kertesz, S. (2011). Association between marijuana exposure and pulmonary function over 20 years. *JAMA, 307*(2), 173–181. doi:10.1001/jama.2011.1961.

Siegel, J. M., & Rogawski, M. A. (1988). A function for REM sleep: Regulation of noradrenergic receptor sensitivity. *Brain Research Review, 13*, 213–233.

Siegel, J. M. (2005). Clues to the functions of mammalian sleep. *Nature, 437*, 1264–1271.

Siegal, M. (1997). *Knowing children: Experiments in conversation and cognition* (2nd ed.). Hove, UK: Psychology Press/Erlbaum/Taylor & Francis.

Siegel, S. (2005). Drug tolerance, drug addiction, and drug anticipation. *Current Directions in Psychological Science, 14*, 296–300.

Siegel, S., Hirson, R. E., Krank, M. D., & McCully, J. (1982). Heroin "overdose" death: The contribution of drug associated environmental cues. *Science, 216*, 430–437.

Siegler, R. S. (1994). Cognitive variability: A key to understanding cognitive development. *Current Directions in Psychological Science, 3*, 1–4.

Siegler, R. S. (2003). Thinking and intelligence. In M. H. Bornstein, L. Davidson, C. L. M. Keyes, & K. A. Moore (Eds.), *Well-being: Positive development across the life course. Crosscurrents in Contemporary Psychology* (pp. 311–320). Mahwah, NJ: Lawrence Erlbaum Associates Publishers.

Siegler, R. S. (2006). Microgenetic analysis of learning. In W. Damon & R. M. Lerner (Series Eds.) & D. Kuhn & R. Siegler (Vol. Eds.), *Handbook of child psychology: Vol. 2. Cognition, perception, and language* (6th ed.). New York: Wiley.

Siep, N., Roefs, A., Roebroeck, A., Havermans, R., Bonte, M. L., & Jansen, A. (2009). Hunger is the best spice: An fMRI study of the effects of attention, hunger and calorie content on food reward processing in the amygdala and orbitofrontal cortex. *Behavioural Brain Research, 198*(1), 149–158.

Siever, L. J. (2008). Neurobiology of aggression and violence. *American Journal of Psychiatry, 165*, 429–442.

Silber, M. H. (2001). Sleep disorders. *Neurology Clinics, 19*, 173–186. 857–868.

Silber, M. H., Ancoli-Israel, S., Bonnet, M. H., Chokroverty, S., Grigg-Damberger, M. M., Hirshkowitz, M., Kapen, S., Keenan, S. A., Kryger, M. H., Penzel, T., Pressman, M. R., & Iber, C. (2007). The visual scoring of sleep in adults. *Journal of Clinical Sleep Medicine, 3*(2), 121–131.

Silbert, M. H., & Pines, A. M. (1984). Pornography and sexual abuse of women. *Sex Roles, 10*, 857–868.

Silberhumer, G. R., Miller, K., Pump, A., Kriwanek, S., Widhalm, K., Gyoeri, G., & Prager, G. (2011). Long-term results after laparoscopic adjustable gastric banding in adolescent patients: follow-up of the Austrian experience. *Surgical Endoscopy, 25*(9), 2993–2999. doi:10.1007/s00464-011-1658-5.

Silver, E., Cirincione, C., & Steadman, H. J. (1994). Demythologizing inaccurate perceptions of the insanity defense. *Law and Human Behavior, 18*, 63–70.

Silverman, K., Evans, A. M., Strain, E. C., & Griffiths, R. R. (1992). Withdrawal syndrome after the double-blind cessation of caffeine consumption. *New England Journal of Medicine, 327*, 1109–1114.

Silverman, M. J. (2012). Effects of melodic complexity and rhythm on working memory as measured by digit-recall performance. *Music and Medicine, 4*(1), 22–27.

Silverthorne, C. (2001). Leadership effectiveness and personality: A cross cultural evaluation. *Personality & Individual Differences, 30*, 303–309.

Simcock, G., & Hayne, H. (2002). Breaking the barrier? Children fail to translate their preverbal memories into language. *Psychological Science, 13*, 225–231.

Simion, F., Cassia, V. M., Turati, C., & Valenza, E. (2003). Non-specific perceptual biases at the origins of face processing. In O. Pascalis & A. Slater (Eds.), *The development of face processing in infancy and early childhood* (pp. 13–25). Hauppauge, NY: Nova Science.

Simmons, A. L. (2012). Distributed practice and procedural memory consolidation in musicians' skill learning. *Journal of Research in Music Education, 59*(4), 357–368. doi:10.1177/0022429411424798.

Simon, G. E., Savarino, J., Operskalski, B., & Wang, P. S. (2006). Suicide risk during antidepressant treatment. *American Journal of Psychiatry, 163*, 41–47.

Simon, G. E., & von Korff, M. (2006). Medical co-morbidity and validity of DSM-IV depression criteria. *Psychological Medicine, 36*, 27–36.

Simon, S. R., Khateb, A., Darque, A., Lazeyras, F., Mayer, E., & Pegna, A. J. (2011). When the brain remembers, but the patient doesn't: converging fMRI and EEG evidence for covert recognition in a case of prosopagnosia. *Cortex, 47*(7), 825–838.

Simon, W., & Gagnon, J. H. (1986). Sexual scripts: Permanence and change. *Archives of Sexual Behavior, 15*, 97–120.

Simon-Thomas, E. R., Keltner, D. J., Sauter, D., Sinicropi-Yao, L., & Abramson, A. (2009). The voice conveys specific emotions: Evidence from vocal burst displays. *Emotion, 6*, 838–846.

Simons, C. J. P., Tracy, D. K., Sanghera, K. K., O'Daly, O., et al. (2010). Functional magnetic resonance imaging of inner speech in schizophrenia. *Biological Psychiatry, 67*, 232–237.

Simons, D. J., & Ambinder, M. S. (2005). Change blindness: Theory and consequences. *Current Directions in Psychological Science, 14*, 44–48.

Simons, D. J., & Chabris, C. F. (1999). Gorillas in our midst: Sustained inattentional blindness for dynamic events. *Perception, 28*, 1059–1074.

Simons, R., & Valk, P. J. L. (2009). Melatonin for commercial aircrew? *Biological Rhythm Research, 40*(1), 7–16.

Simons, T., & Roberson, Q. (2003). Why managers should care about fairness: The effects of aggregate justice perceptions on organizational outcomes. *Journal of Applied Psychology, 88*, 432–443.

Simonton, D. K. (1984). *Genius, creativity and leadership*. Cambridge, MA: Harvard University Press.

Simonton, D. K. (1999). Creativity and genius. In L. Pervin & O. John (Eds.), *Handbook of personality research* (2nd ed., pp. 629–652). New York: Guilford.

Simonton, D. K. (2002). In C. R. Snyder & J. Shane (Eds.), *Handbook of positive psychology* (pp. 189–201). London: Oxford University Press.

Simonton, D. K. (2004). *Creativity in science: Chance, logic, genius, and zeitgeist*. Cambridge, UK: Cambridge University Press.

Simonton, D. K. (2012). Teaching creativity: Current findings, trends, and controversies in the psychology of creativity. *Teaching of Psychology, 39*, 217–222.

Simonton, D. K., & Song, A. V. (2009). Eminence, IQ, physical and mental health, and achievement domain: Cox's 282 geniuses revisited. *Psychological Science, 20*, 429–434.

Simpson, J. A., Collins, W. A., & Salvatore, J. E. (2011). The impact of early interpersonal experience on adult romantic relationship functioning: Recent findings from the Simpson 10 Minnesota Longitudinal Study of Risk and Adaptation. *Current Directions in Psychological Science. 20*(6), 355–359. doi:10.1177/0963721411418468.

Simpson, J. A., & Kenrick, D. T. (1997). *Evolutionary social psychology*. Mahwah, NJ: Erlbaum.

Simpson, J. A., Rholes, W. S., & Winterheld, H. A. (2010). Attachment working models twist memories of relationship events. *Psychological Science, 21*(2), 252–259. doi:10.1177/0956797609357175.

Simpson, S., Hurtley, S. M., & Marx, J. (2000). Immune cell networks. *Science, 290*, 79.

Simpson, S. G., McMahon, F. J., McInnis, M. G., MacKinnon, D. F., Edwin, D., Folstein, S. E., et al. (2002). Diagnostic reliability of bipolar II disorder. *Archives of General Psychiatry, 59*, 736–740.

Simpson, S. H., Eurich, D. T., Majumdar, S. R., Padwal, R. S., Tsuyuki, R. T., et al. (2006). A meta-analysis of the association between adherence to drug therapy and mortality. *British Medical Journal, 333*.

Sinclair, R. C., Hoffman, C., Mark, M. M., Martin, L. L., & Pickering, T. L. (1994). Construct accessibility and the misattribution of arousal. *Psychological Science, 5*(1), 15–19.

Singer, L. T., Arendt, R., Minnes, S., Farkas, K., Salvator, A., Kirchner, L., & Kliegman, R. (2002). Cognitive and motor outcomes of cocaine-exposed infants. *Journal of the American Medical Association, 287*(15), 1952–1960.

Singer, L. T., Arendt, R., Minnes, S., Salvator, A., Siegel, C., & Lewis, B. A. (2001). Developing language skills of cocaine-exposed infants. *Pediatrics, 107*, 1057–1064.

Singer, L. T., Minnes, S., Short, E., Arendt, R., Farkas, K., Lewis, B., et al. (2004). Cognitive outcomes of preschool children with prenatal cocaine exposure. *Journal of the American Medical Association, 291*, 2448–2456.

Singh, H., & O'Boyle, M. W. (2004). Interhemispheric interaction during global-local processing in mathematically gifted adolescents, average-ability youth, and college students. *Neuropsychology, 18*, 371–377.

Singh, S. M., & O'Reilly, R. (2009). (Epi)genomics and neurodevelopment in schizophrenia: Monozygotic twins discordant for schizophrenia augment the search for disease-related (epi)genomic alterations. *Genome, 52*(1), 8–19.

Singh, V. S., Thornton, T., & Tonmyr, L. (2011). Determinants of substance abuse in a population of children and adolescents involved with the child welfare system. *International Journal of Mental Health and Addiction, 9*(4), 382–397. doi:10.1007/s11469-011-9320-y

Sinha, R., & Parsons, O. A. (1996). Multivariate response patterning of fear and anger. *Cognition and Emotion, 10*, 173–198.

Sirvio, J. (1999). Strategies that support declining cholinergic neurotransmission in Alzheimer's disease patients. *Gerontology, 45*, 3–14.

Siti, M. (2004). Hypochondriasis: Modern perspectives on an ancient malady. *Journal of Cognitive Psychotherapy, 18*, 369–370.

Sitzmann, T., Brown, K. G., Casper, W. D., Ely, K., & Zimmerman, R. D. (2008). A review and meta-analysis of the nomological network of trainee reactions. *Journal of Applied Psychology, 93*, 280–295.

Sivertsen, B., Øverland, S., Pallesen, S., Bjorvatn, B., Nordhus, I. H., Maeland, J. G., & Mykletun, A. (2009). Insomnia and long sleep duration are risk factors for later work disability. The Hordaland Health Study. *Journal of Sleep Research, 18*(1), 122–128.

Sjöström, L., Peltonen, M., Jacobson, P., Sjöström, C., Karason, K., Wedel, H., & Svensson, P. (2012). Bariatric surgery and long-term cardiovascular events. *JAMA: Journal Of The American Medical Association, 307*(1), 56–65.

Skarratt, P. A., Cole, G. G., & Kingstone, A. (2010). Social inhibition of return. *Acta Psychologica, 134*(1), 48–54. doi:10.1016/j.actpsy.2009.12.003.

Skeem, J. L., Polaschek, D. L., Patrick, C. J., & Lilienfeld, S. O. (2011). Psychopathic personality: Bridging the gap between scientific evidence and public policy. *Psychological Science in the Public Interest, 12*(3), 95–162. doi:10.1177/1529100611426706.

Skelton, J. A., Cook, S. R., Auinger, P., Klein, J. D., & Barlow, S. E. (2009). Prevalence and trends of severe obesity among U.S. children and adolescents. *Academic Pediatrics, 9*, 322–329.

Skinner, B. F. (1938). *The behavior of organisms*. New York: Appleton.

Skinner, B. F. (1961). *Cumulative record* (3rd ed.). Englewood Cliffs, NJ: Prentice Hall.

Skinner, N. F. (2009). Academic folk wisdom: Fact, fiction and falderal. *Psychology Learning & Teaching, 8*(1), 46–50.

Skitka, L. (2010) The psychology of moral conviction. *Social and Personality Psychology Compass, 4*, 267-28.

Skitka, L. J., Bauman, C. W., & Sargis, E. G. (2005). Moral conviction: Another contributor to attitude strength or something more? *Journal of Personality and Social Psychology, 88*, 895–917.

Skre, I., Onstad, S., Toregersen, S., Lyngren, S., & Kringlin, E. (2000). The heritability of common phobic fear: A twin study of a clinical sample. *Journal of Anxiety Disorders, 14*, 549–562.

Skrobik, Y. (2009). Delirium prevention and treatment. *Critical Care Clinics, 25*, 585–591.

Skroubis, G., Karamanakos, S., Sakellaropoulos, G., Panagopoulos, K., & Kalfarentzos, F. (2011). Comparison of early and late complications after various bariatric procedures: Incidence and treatment during 15 years at a single institution. *World Journal Of Surgery, 35*(1), 93–101.

Slade, E. P., & Wissow, L. S. (2004). Spanking in early childhood and later behavior problems: A prospective study of infants and young toddlers. *Pediatrics, 113*, 1321–1330.

Slamecka, N. J., & McElree, B. (1983). Normal forgetting of verbal lists as a function of their degree of learning. *Journal of Experimental Psychology: Learning, Memory, and Cognition, 9*, 384–397.

Slater, A., Mattock, A., Brown, E., & Bremner, J. G. (1991). Form perception at birth. *Journal of Experimental Child Psychology, 51*, 395–406.

Slavin, K. V. (2008). Peripheral nerve stimulation for neuropathic pain. *Neurotherapeutics, 5*(1), 100–106.

Slentz, C. A., Duscha, B. D., Johnson, J. L., Ketchum, K., Aiken, L. B., Samsa, G. P., et al. (2004). Effects of the amount of exercise on body weight, body composition, and measures of central obesity: STRRIDE—A randomized controlled study. *Archives of Internal Medicine, 164*, 31–39.

Sloan, D. M., Marx, B. P., & Epstein, E. M. (2005). Further examination of the exposure model underlying the efficacy of written emotional disclosure. *Journal of Consulting and Clinical Psychology, 73*, 549–554.

Sloan, D. M., Strauss, M. E., & Wisner, K. L. (2001). Diminished response to pleasant stimuli by depressed women. *Journal of Abnormal Psychology, 110*, 488–493.

Sloane, S., Baillargeon, R., & Premack, D. (2012). Do infants have a sense of fairness?. *Psychological Science, 23*(2), 196–204. doi:10.1177/0956797611422072.

Slomkowski, C., & Dunn, J. (1996). Young children's understanding of other people's beliefs and feelings and their connected communication with friends. *Developmental Psychology, 32*, 442–447.

Slotema, C. W., Blom, J. D., Hoek, H. W., & Sommer, I. E. (2010). Should we expand the toolbox of psychiatric treatment methods to include repetitive transcranial magnetic stimulation (rTMS)? A meta-analysis of the efficacy of rTMS in psychiatric disorder. *Journal of Clinical Psychiatry, 71*, 873–884.

Slotnick, S. D., & Schacter, D. L. (2004). A sensory signature that distinguishes true from fales memories. *Nature Neuroscience, 7,* 664–672.

Slutske, W. S., Moffitt, T. E., Poulton, R., & Caspi, A. (2012). Undercontrolled temperament at age 3 predicts disordered gambling at age 32: A longitudinal study of a complete birth cohort. *Psychological Science, 23,* 510–516. doi:10.1177/0956797611429708.

Small, D. M., Gregory, M. D., Mak, Y. E., Mesulam, M. M., & Parrish, T. (2003). Dissociation of neural representation of intensity and valuation in human gustation. *Neuron, 39,* 701–711.

Small, G., & Dubois, B. (2007). A review of compliance to treatment in Alzheimer's disease: potential benefits of a transdermal patch. *Current Medical Research & Opinion, 23*(11), 2705–2713.

Smillie, L. D., Pickering, A. D., & Jackson, C. J. (2006). The new Reinforcement Sensitivity Theory: Implications for personality measurement. *Personality and Social Psychology Review, 10,* 320–335.

Smit, Y., Huibers, M. H., Ioannidis, J. A., van Dyck, R., van Tilburg, W., & Arntz, A. (2012). The effectiveness of long-term psychoanalytic psychotherapy—A meta-analysis of randomized controlled trials. *Clinical Psychology Review, 32*(2), 81–92. doi:10.1016/j.cpr.2011.11.003.

Smith, A. M., Malo, S. A., Laskowski, E. R., Sabick, M., Cooney, W. P., III, Finnie, S. B., et al. (2000). A multidisciplinary study of the 'yips' phenomenon in golf: An exploratory analysis. *Sports Medicine, 30,* 423–437.

Smith, D. M., Loewenstein, G., Jankovic, A., & Ubel, P. A. (2009). Happily hopeless: Adaptation to a permanent, but not to a temporary, disability. *Health Psychology, 28,* 787–791.

Smith, E., & Quellar, S. (2001). Mental representations. In A. Tesser & N. Schwarz (Eds.), *Blackwell handbook of social psychology: Intraindividual processes* (pp. 499–517). Oxford, UK: Blackwell.

Smith, G. C. S., & White, I. R. (2006). Predicting the risk for sudden infant death syndrome from obstetric characteristics: A retrospective cohort study of 505,011 live births. *Pediatrics, 117,* 60–66.

Smith, G. T., Simmons, J. R., Flory, K., Annus, A. M., & Hill, K. K. (2007). Thinness and eating expectancies predict subsequent binge-eating and purging behavior among adolescent girls. *Journal of Abnormal Psychology, 116,* 188–197.

Smith, L. B., & Sera, M. D. (1992). A developmental analysis of the polar structure of dimensions. *Cognitive Psychology, 24,* 99–142.

Smith, M. L., Glass, G. V., & Miller, T. I. (1980). *The benefits of psychotherapy.* Baltimore: Johns Hopkins University Press.

Smith, P., Frank, J., Bondy, S., & Mustard, C. (2008). Do changes in job control predict differences in health status? Results from a longitudinal national survey of Canadians. *Psychosomatic Medicine, 70,* 85–91.

Smith, P. B., & Bond, M. H. (1999). *Social psychology across cultures: Analysis and perspectives* (2nd ed.). Boston: Allyn & Bacon.

Smith, P. C., & Kendall, L. M. (1963). Retranslation of expectations: An approach to the construction of unambiguous anchors for rating scales. *Journal of Applied Psychology, 47,* 149–155.

Smith, P. K., & Drew, L. M. (2002). Grandparenthood. In M. H. Bornstein (Ed.), *Handbook of parenting* (2nd ed.). Mahwah, NJ: Erlbaum.

Smith, R. E., Shoda, Y., Cumming, S. P. & Smoll, F. (2009). Behavioral signatures at the ballpark: Intraindividual consistency of adults' situation-behavior patterns and their interpersonal consequences. *Journal of Research in Personality, 43,* 187–195.

Smith, R. M., Tivarus, M., Campbell, H. L., Hillier, A., & Beversdorf, D. Q. (2006). Apparent transient effects of recent "ecstasy" use on cognitive performance and extrapyramidal signs in human subjects. *Cognitive & Behavioral Neurology, 19*(3), 157–164.

Smith, R. W., Uchino, B. N., Berg, C. A., Florsheim, P., Pearce, G., Hawkins, M., Henry, N. J. M., Beveridge, R. M., Skinner, M. A., Hopkins, P. N., & Yoon, H.-C. (2008). Associations of self-reports versus spouse ratings of negative affectivity, dominance, and affiliation with coronary artery disease: Where should we look and who should we ask when studying personality and health? *Health Psychology, 27,* 676–684.

Smith, S., & Freedman, D. G. (1983, April). *Mother-toddler interaction and maternal perception of child temperament in two ethnic groups: Chinese-American and European-American.* Paper presented at the meeting of the Society for Research in Child Development, Detroit, MI.

Smith, S., Weissman, N., Anderson, C., Sanchez, M., Chuang, E., Stubbe, S., & . Shanahan, W. (2010). Multicenter, placebo-controlled trial of lorcaserin for weight management. *The New England Journal Of Medicine, 363*(3), 245–256.

Smith, S. L., & Donnerstein, E. (1998). Harmful effects of exposure to media violence: Learning of aggression, emotional desensitization, and fear. In R. G. Geen & E. Donnerstein (Eds.), *Human aggression* (pp. 230–247). San Diego: Academic Press.

Smith, S. M., Dawson, D. A., Goldstein, R. B., & Grant, B. F. (2010). Examining perceived alcoholism stigma effect on racial-ethnic disparities in treatment and quality of life among alcoholics. *Journal of Studies on Alcohol and Drugs, 71*(2), 231–236.

Smith, S. M., & Vela, E. (2001). Environmental context-dependent memory: A review and meta-analysis. *Psychonomic Bulletin and Review, 8,* 203–220.

Smith, S. M., Vela, E., & Williamson, J. E. (1988). Shallow input processing does not induce environmental context-dependent recognition. *Bulletin of the Psychonomic Society, 26,* 537–540.

Smith, T. B., Constantine, M. G., Dunn, T. W., Dinehart, J. M., & Montoya, J. A. (2006). Multicultural education in the mental health professions: A meta-analytic review. *Journal of Counseling Psychology, 53,* 132–145.

Smith, T. E., & Sederer, L. I. (2009). A new kind of homelessness for individuals with serious mental illness? The need for a "mental health home." *Hospital and Community Psychiatry, 60,* 528–533.

Smith, T. W., Orleans, C. T., & Jenkins, C. D. (2004). Prevention and health promotion: Decades of progress, new challenges, and an emerging agenda. *Health Psychology, 23,* 126–131.

Smith, T. W., Uchino, B. N., Berg, C. A., Florsheim, P., Pearce, G., Hawkins, M., Hopkins, P. N., & Yoon, H.-C. (2007). Hostile personality traits and coronary artery calcification in middle-aged and older married couples: Different effects for self-reports versus spouse ratings. *Psychosomatic Medicine 69,* 441–448.

Smith-Crowe, K., Burke, M. J., & Landis, R. S. (2003). Organizational climate as a moderator of safety knowledge–safety performance relationships. *Journal of Organizational Behavior, 24,* 861–876.

Smither, J. W., London, M., & Reilly, R. R. (2005). Does performance improve following multisource feedback? A theoretical model, meta-analysis, and review of empirical findings. *Personnel Psychology, 58,* 33–66.

Smits, J. A. J., O'Cleirigh, C. M., & Otto, M. W. (2006). Combining cognitive-behavioral therapy and pharmacotherapy for the treatment of panic disorder. *Journal of Cognitive Psychotherapy, 20,* 75–84.

Smyth, C. L., & MacLachlan, M. (2005). Confirmatory factor analysis of the Trinity Inventory of Precursors to Suicide (TIPS) and its relationship to hopelessness and depression. *Death Studies, 29,* 333–350.

Smoller, J. W. (2008). Genetics of mood and anxiety disorder. In J. W. Smoller, B. R. Sheidley, & M. T. Tsaung (Eds.), *Psychiatric genetics: Applications in clinical practice* (pp. 131–176). Arlington: American Psychiatric Publishing.

Snarey, J. (1987). A question of morality. *Psychological Bulletin, 97,* 202–232.

Snarey, J., & Hooker, C. (2006). Lawrence Kohlberg. In E. M. Dowling & W. G. Scarlett (Eds.), *Encyclopedia of spiritual and religious development* (pp. 251–255). Thousand Oaks, CA: Sage.

Snarey, J. R. (1994). Cross-cultural universality of social-moral development: A critical review of Kohlbergian research. In B. Puka (Ed.), *New research in moral development* (pp. 268–298). New York: Garland.

Snel, J., & Lorist, M. M. (2011). Effects of caffeine on sleep and cognition. *Progress in Brain Research 190,* 105–117.

Snellingen, T., Evans, J. R., Ravilla, T., & Foster, A. (2002). Surgical interventions for age-related cataract. *Cochrane Database System Review, 2,* CD001323.

Snowden, L. R., & Cheung, F. (1990). Use of inpatient mental health services by members of ethnic minority groups. *American Psychologist, 45,* 347–355.

Snyder, C. R., & Lopez, S. J. (2006). *Handbook of positive psychology.* New York: Oxford University Press.

Snyder, C. R., & Lopez, S. J. (2007). *Positive psychology: The scientific and practical explorations of human strengths.* New York: Sage.

Snyder, C. R., & Lopez, S. J. (2009). *Oxford handbook of positive psychology* (2nd ed.). New York: Oxford University Press.

Snyder, D. M, Goodlin-Jones, B. L., Pionk, M. J., & Stein, M. T. (2008). Inconsolable night-time awakening: Beyond night terrors. *Journal of Developmental and Behavioral Pediatrics, 29*(4), 311–314.

Snyder, T. D., Dillow, S. A., & Hoffman, C. M. (2008). *Digest of Education Statistics: 2007* (Report No. NCES 2008-022). Washington, D. C.: National Center for Education Statistics, Institute of Education Sciences, U. S. Department of Education. Retrieved June 9, 2009, from http://nces.ed.gov/programs/digest/d07.

Snyderman, M., & Rothman, S. (1987). Survey of expert opinion on intelligence and aptitude testing. *American Psychologist, 42,* 137–144.

Sobel, D. M., & Kirkham, N. Z. (2006). Blickets and babies: The development of causal reasoning in toddlers and infants. *Developmental Psychology, 42,* 1103–1115.

Sohlberg, S., & Jansson, B. (2002). Unconscious responses to "mommy and I are one": Does gender matter? In R. F. Bornstein & J. M. Masling (Eds.), *The psychodynamics of gender and gender role. Vol. 10: Empirical studies in psychoanalytic theories* (pp. 165–201). Washington, DC: American Psychological Association.

Sohler, N., & Bromet, E. J. (2003). Does racial bias influence psychiatric diagnoses assigned at first hospitalization? *Social Psychiatry and Psychiatric Epidemiology, 38,* 463–472.

Soken, N. H., & Pick, A. D. (1992). Intermodal perception of happy and angry expressive behaviors by seven-month-old infants. *Child Development, 63,* 787–795.

Solfrizzi, V., Frisardi, V., Seripa, D., Logroscino, G., Imbimbo, B. P., D'Onofrio, G., Addante, F., Sancarlo, D., Cascavilla, L., Pilotto, A., & Panza, F. (2011). Mediterranean diet in predementia and dementia syndromes. *Current Alzheimer Research, 8*(5), 520–542.

Solomon, R. L. (1980). The opponent-process theory of acquired motivation: The costs of pleasure and the benefits of pain. *American Psychologist, 35,* 691–712.

Solomon, R. L., Kamin, L. J., & Wynne, L. C. (1953). Traumatic avoidance learning: The outcomes of several extinction procedures with dogs. *Journal of Abnormal and Social Psychology, 48,* 291–302.

Solomonson, A. L., & Lance, C. E. (1997). Examination of the relationship between true halo and halo error in performance ratings. *Journal of Applied Psychology, 82,* 665–674.

Solowij, N., Stephens, R. S., Roffman, R. A., Babor, T., Kadden, R., Miller, M., et al. (2002). Cognitive functioning of long-term heavy cannabis users seeking treatment. *Journal of American Medical Association, 287,* 1123–1131.

Son, J., & Wilson, J. (2011). Generativity and volunteering. *Sociological Forum, 26*(3), 644–667. doi:10.1111/j.1573-7861.2011.01266.x.

Song, H., & Baillargeon, R. (2008). Infants' reasoning about others' false perceptions. *Developmental Psychology, 44,* 1789–1795.

Song, H., Chui, T. Y., Zhong, Z., Elsner, A. E., and Burns, S. A. (2011). Variation of cone photoreceptor packing density with retinal eccentricity and age. *Investigative Ophthalmology and Visual Sciences, 52*(10), 7376–7384.

Song, Z., Li, W., & Arvey, R. D. (2011). Associations between dopamine and serotonin genes and job satisfaction: Preliminary evidence from the Add Health Study. *Journal of Applied Psychology, 96*(6), 1223–1233. doi:10.1037/a0024577.

Sonnentag, S. (2012). Psychological detachment from work during leisure time: The benefits of mentally disengaging from work. *Current Directions in Psychological Science, 21,* 114–118. doi:10.1177/0963721411434979.

Sonnentag, S., Binnewies, C., & Mojza, E. (2010). Staying well and engaged when demands are high: The role of psychological detachment. *The Journal of Applied Psychology, 95,* 965–976.

Sorce, J., Emde, R., Campos, J., & Klinnert, M. (1981, April). *Maternal emotional signaling: Its effect on the visual cliff behavior of one-year-olds.* Paper presented at the meeting of the Society for Research in Child Development, Boston, MA.

Sørensen, H. J., Mortensen, E. L., Reinisch, J. M., & Mednick, S. A. (2003). Do hypertension and diuretic treatment in pregnancy increase the risk of schizophrenia in offspring? *American Journal of Psychiatry, 160,* 464–468.

Sorrentino, R. M., & Roney, C. J. R. (2000). *The uncertain mind: Individual differences in facing the unknown.* Philadelphia: Psychology Press.

Soto, D., Funes, M. J., Guzmán-García, A., Warbrick, T., Rotshtein, P., & Humphreys, G. W. (2009). Pleasant music overcomes the loss of awareness in patients with visual neglect. *Proceedings of the National Academy of Sciences, 106*(14), 6011–6016.

South, S. C., & Krueger, R. F. (2008). An interactionist perspective on genetic and environmental contributions to personality. *Social and Personality Psychology Compass, 2*(2), 929–948.

Sowdon, J. (2001). Is depression more prevalent in old age? *Australian & New Zealand Journal of Psychiatry, 35,* 782–787.

Sowell, E. R., Delis, D., Stiles, J., & Jernigan, T. L. (2001). Improved memory functioning and frontal lobe maturation between childhood and adolescence: A structural MRI study. *Journal of the International Neuropsychological Society, 7,* 312–322.

Sowell, E. R., Peterson, B. S., Thompson, P. M., Welcome, S. E., Henkenius, A. L., & Toga, A. W. (2003). Mapping cortical change across the human life span. *Nature Neuroscience, 6,* 309–315.

Sowell, T. (2005). *Black rednecks and white liberals.* San Francisco: Encounter Books.

Spanagel, R., & Weiss, F. (1999). The dopamine hypothesis of reward: Past and current status. *Trends in Neuroscience, 22,* 521–527.

Spangler, G., Fremmer-Bombik, E., & Grossman, K. (1996). Social and individual determinants of infant attachment security and disorganization. *Infant Mental Health Journal, 17,* 127–139.

Spano, M. S., Ellgren, M., Wang, X., & Hurd, Y. L. (2007). Prenatal cannabis exposure increases heroin seeking with allostatic changes in limbic enkephalin systems in adulthood. *Biological Psychiatry, 61,* 554–563.

Spanos, N. P., Burnley, M. C. E., & Cross, P. A. (1993). Response expectancies and interpretations as determinants of hypnotic responding. *Journal of Personality and Social Psychology, 65*(6), 1237–1242.

Sparing, R., Dafotakis, M., Meister, I. G., Thirugnanasambandam, N., & Fink, G. R. (2008). Enhancing language performance with non-invasive brain stimulation—A transcranial direct current stimulation study in healthy humans. *Neuropsychologia, 46*(1), 261–268.

Sparks, K., Cooper, C., Fried, Y., & Shirom, A. (1997). The effects of hours of work on health: A meta-analytic review. *Journal of Occupational and Organizational Psychology, 70,* 391–408.

Sparks, K., Faragher, B., & Cooper, C. L. (2001). Well-being and occupational health in the 21st century workplace. *Journal of Occupational and Organizational Psychology, 74,* 489–509.

Sparrow, B., Liu, J., & Wegner, D. M. (2011). Google effects on memory: Cognitive consequences of having information at our fingertips. *Science, 333*(6043), 776–778. doi:10.1126/science.1207745.

Spear, L. P. (2000). Neurobiological changes in adolescence. *Current Directions in Psychological Science, 9,* 111–114.

Spears, R., Postmes, T., Lea, M., & Watt, S. E. (2001). A SIDE view of social influence. In J. P. Forgas & K. D. Williams (Eds.), *Social influence: Direct and indirect processes. The Sydney symposium of social psychology* (pp. 331–350). Philadelphia, PA: Psychology Press.

Speckhard, A. (2002). Voices from the inside: Psychological responses to toxic disasters. In J. M. Havenaar & J. G. Cwikel (Eds.), *Toxic turmoil: Psychological and societal consequences of ecological disasters* (pp. 217–236). New York: Plenum.

Specter, M. (2005, May 23). Higher risk. *New Yorker,* 38–45.

Spector, P. E. (1985). Measurement of human service staff satisfaction: Development of the Job Satisfaction Survey. *American Journal of Community Psychology, 13,* 693–713.

Spector, P. E. (2002). Employee control and occupational stress. *Current Directions in Psychological Science, 11,* 133–136.

Spector, P. E. (2003). *Industrial & organizational psychology: Research and practice* (3rd ed.). New York: Wiley.

Spector, P. E., Fox, S., & Domalgaski, T. (2006). Emotions, violence, and counterproductive work behavior. In E. K. Kelloway, J. Barling, & J. J. Hurrell (Eds.), *Handbook of workplace violence* (pp. 29–46). Thousand Oaks, CA: Sage.

Spelke, E. S., Breinlinger, K., Macomber, J., & Jacobson, K. (1992). Origins of knowledge. *Psychological Review, 99,* 605–632.

Spence, D. (2011). All a-Twitter. *BMJ: British Medical Journal (Overseas & Retired Doctors Edition), 343,* 1275.

Spence, I., & Feng, J. (2010). Video games and spatial cognition. *Review Of General Psychology, 14*(2), 92–104. doi:10.1037/a0019491.

Spence, S. H., Sheffield, J. K., & Donovan, C. L. (2005). Long-term outcome of a school-based, universal approach to prevention of depression in adolescents. *Journal of Consulting and Clinical Psychology, 73,* 160–167.

Sperry, R. W. (1968). Hemisphere deconnection and unity in conscious awareness. *American Psychologist, 23,* 723–733.

Spiegel, D. (Ed.). (1994). *Dissociation: Culture, mind, and body.* Washington, DC: American Psychiatric Press.

Spiegel, D. A., & Bruce, T. J. (1997). Benzodiazepines and exposure-based cognitive behavior therapies for panic disorder: Conclusions from combined treatment trials. *American Journal of Psychiatry, 151,* 876–881.

Spiegelman, B. M., & Flier, J. F. (2001). Obesity and the regulation of energy balance. *Cell, 104,* 531–543.

Spiegler, M. E., & Guevremont, D. C. (2009). *Contemporary behavior therapy* (5th ed.). New York: Cengage Learning.

Spillmann, L., Otte, T., Hamburger, K., & Magnussen, S. (2006). Perceptual filling-in from the edge of the blind spot. *Vision Research, 46,* 4252–4257.

Spinath, B., & Steinmayr, R. (2012). The roles of competence beliefs and goal orientations for change in intrinsic motivation. *Journal of Educational Psychology,* doi:10.1037/a0028115.

Spinath, F. M., Harlaar, N., Ronald, A., & Plomin, R. (2004). Substantial genetic influence on mild mental impairment in early childhood. *American Journal of Mental Retardation, 109,* 34–43.

Spinrad, T. L., Eisenberg, N., Cumberland, A., Fabes, R. A., et al. (2006). Relation of emotionrelated regulation to children's social competence: A longitudinal study. *Emotion, 6,* 498–510.

Spitzer, R. L. (2009, July 2). APA and DSM-V: Empty promises. *Psychiatric Times.* Retrieved from http://www.psychiatrictimes.com/display/article/10168/142584.

Spitzer, R. L., Gibbon, M., Skodol, A. E., & Williams, J. B. W., & First, M. B. (Eds.). (1994). *DSM-IV casebook: A learning companion to the Diagnostic and Statistical Manual of Mental Disorders* (4th ed.). Washington, DC: American Psychiatric Association.

Spörer, N., Brunstein, J. C., & Kieschke, U. (2009). Improving students' reading comprehension skills: Effects of strategy instruction and reciprocal teaching. *Learning And Instruction, 19*(3), 272–286. doi:10.1016/j.learninstruc.2008.05.003.

Springer, K., & Belk, A. (1994). The role of physical contact and association in early contamination sensitivity. *Developmental Psychology, 30*(6), 864–868.

Spychalski, A. C., Quinones, M. A., Gaugler, B. B., & Pohley, K. (1997). A survey of assessment center practices in organizations in the U.S. *Personnel Psychology, 50,* 71–90.

Squire, L. R. (1986). Mechanisms of memory. *Science, 232,* 1612–1619.

Squire, L. R. (1992). Memory and the hippocampus: A synthesis from findings with rats, monkeys, and humans. *Psychological Review, 99,* 195–231.

Squire, L. R. (2009). The legacy of patient H. M. for neuroscience. *Neuron, 61*(1), 6–9.

Srimathi, N. L., Kiran K., S. K. (2011). Self efficacy and psychological well-being among employed women. *Journal of Psychosocial Research, 6,* 95–102.

Srivastava, S., Guglielmo, S., & Beer, J. S. (2010). Perceiving others' personalities: Examining the dimensionality, assumed similarity to the self, and stability of perceiver effects. *Journal of Personality and Social Psychology, 98,* 520–534.

Srivastava, S., John, O. P., Gosling, S. D., & Potter, J. (2003). Development of personality in early and middle adulthood: Set like plaster or persistent change? *Journal of Personality and Social Psychology, 84,* 1041–1053.

Srivastava, S., Tamir, M., McGonigal, K. M., John, O. P., & Gross, J. J. (2009). The social costs of emotional suppression: A prospective study of the transition to college. *Journal of Personality and Social Psychology, 96,* 883–897.

Sroufe, L. A., Egeland, B., Carlson, E. A., & Collins, W. A. (2005). *The development of the person: The Minnesota study of risk and adaptation from birth to adulthood.* New York: Guilford Press.

St. John, W. (2003, September 28). In U.S. funeral industry, triple-wide isn't a trailer. *The New York Times,* p. 1.

Stacey, J., & Biblarz, T. J. (2001). (How) Does the sexual orientation of parents matter? *American Sociological Review, 66,* 159–183.

Stahl, S. M. (2002). Selective actions on sleep or anxiety by exploiting GABA-A/benzodiazepine receptor subtypes. *Journal of Clinical Psychiatry, 63,* 179–180.

Stahl, S. M. (2007). The genetics of schizophrenia converge upon the NMDA glutamate receptor. *CNS Spectrums, 12,* 583–588.

Staines, G. L., & Cleland, C. M. (2012). Observational studies versus randomized controlled trials of behavioral interventions in field settings. *Review of General Psychology, 16,* 37–58. doi:10.1037/a0026493

Staley, J. K., Sanacora, G., Tamagnan, G., Maciejewski, P. K., Malison, R. T., Berman, R. M., et al. (2006). Sex differences in diencephalon serotonin transporter availability in major depression. *Biological Psychiatry, 59,* 40–47.

Stanley, B. G., Willett, V. L., Donias, H. W., & Ha-Lyen, H. (1993). The lateral hypothalamus: A primary site mediating excitatory aminoacid-elicited eating. *Brain Research, 63*(1–2), 41–49.

Stansfeld, S. A., & Marmot, M. G. (Eds.). (2002). *Stress and the heart: Psychosocial pathways to coronary heart disease.* London: BMJ Books.

Stanton, A. L., & Low, C. A. (2012). Expressing emotions in stressful contexts: Benefits, moderators, and mechanisms. *Current Directions in Psychological Science, 21,* 124–128. doi:10.1177/0963721411434978.

Starkstein, S. E., Jorge, R. E., & Robinson, R. G. (2010). The frequency, clinical correlates, and mechanism of anosognosia after stroke. *Canadian Journal of Psychiatry, 55*(6), 355–361.

Starkstein, S. E., Fedoroff, J. P., Price, T. R., Leigguarda, R., & Robinson, R. G. (1992). Anosognosia in patients with cerebrovascular lesions: A study of causative factors. *Stroke, 23,* 1446–1453.

Stasser, G., Stewart, D., & Wittenbaum, G. M. (1995). Expert roles and information exchange during discussion: The importance of knowing who knows what. *Journal of Experimental Social Psychology, 31,* 244–265.

Staudt, M., Grodd, W., Niemann, G., Wildgruber, D., Erb, M., & Krageloh-Mann, I. (2001). Early left periventricular brain lesions induce right hemispheric organization of speech. *Neurology 2001, 57,* 122–125.

Stauffer, J. M., & Buckley, M. R. (2005). The existence and nature of racial bias in supervisory ratings. *Journal of Applied Psychology, 90,* 586–591.

Staw, B. M., Bell, N. E., & Clausen, J. A. (1986). The dispositional approach to job attitudes: A lifetime longitudinal test. *Administrative Science Quarterly, 31,* 56–77.

Staw, B. M., & Cohen-Charash, Y. (2005). The dispositional approach to job satisfaction: More than a mirage, but not yet an oasis. *Journal of Organizational Behavior, 26,* 59–78.

St. Claire, L., Hayward, R. C., & Rogers, P. J. (2010). Interactive Effects of Caffeine Consumption and Stressful Circumstances on Components of Stress: Caffeine Makes Men Less, But Women More Effective as Partners Under Stress. *Journal Of Applied Social Psychology, 40*(12), 3106–3129. doi:10.1111/j.1559-1816.2010.00693.x.

Steblay, N. K., Dysart, J. E., & Wells, G. L. (2011). Seventy-two tests of the sequential lineup superiority effect: A meta-analysis and policy discussion. *Psychology, Public Policy, and Law, 17*(1), 99–139. doi:10.1037/a0021650.

Steele, K., Schweitzer, M., Prokopowicz, G., Shore, A., Eaton, L., Lidor, A., & … Magnuson, T. (2011). The long-term risk of venous thromboembolism following bariatric surgery. *Obesity Surgery, 21*(9), 1371–1376.

Steele, T. D., McCann, U. D., & Ricaurte, G. A. (1994). 3,4-methylenedioxy-methamphetamine (MDMA, ecstasy): Pharmacology and toxicology in animals and humans. *Addiction, 89,* 539–551.

Steele, C. M. (1997). A threat in the air: How stereotypes shape intellectual identity and performance. *American Psychologist, 52,* 613–629.

Steele, C. M., & Aronson, J. (2000). Stereotype threat and the intellectual test performance of African Americans. In C. Stangor (Ed.), *Stereotypes and prejudice: Essential readings* (pp. 369–389). Philadelphia: Psychology Press/Taylor & Francis.

Steiger, H., Young, S. N., Ng Ying Kin, N. M. K., Koerner, N., Israel, M., Lageix, P., & Paris, J. (2001). Implications of impulsive and affective symptoms for serotonin function in bulimia nervosa. *Psychological Medicine, 31,* 85–95.

Stein, D. J. (2006). Specific phobia: A disorder of fear conditioning and extinction. *CNS Spectrums, 11,* 248–251.

Stein, D. J., Seedat, S., Herman, A., Moomal, H., Heeringa, S. G., Kessler, R. C., et al. (2008). Lifetime prevalence of psychiatric disorders in South Africa. *British Journal of Psyciatry, 192,* 112–117.

Stein, E. (1999). *The mismeasure of desire: The science, theory and ethics of sexual orientation.* New York: Oxford University Press.

Steinberg, L. (2007). Risk taking in adolescence: New perspectives from brain and behavioral science. *Current Directions in Psychological Science, 16*(2), 55–59.

Steinberg, L. (2008). A social neuroscience perspective on adolescent risk-taking. *Developmental Review, 28*(1), 78–106.

Steinberg, L., Dornbusch, S. M., & Brown, B. B. (1992). Ethnic differences in adolescent achievement: An ecological perspective. *American Psychologist, 47,* 723–729.

Steinberg, L., Lamborn, S. D., Darling, N., Mounts, N. S., & Dornbusch, S. M. (1994). Over-time changes in adjustment and competence among adolescents from authoritative, authoritarian, indulgent, and neglectful families. *Child Development, 65,* 754–770.

Steinberg, L., & Monahan, K. (2011). Adolescents' exposure to sexy media does not hasten the initiation of sexual intercourse. *Developmental Psychology, 47*(2), 562–576.

Steindler, D. A., & Pincus, D. W. (2002). Stem cells and neuropoiesis in the adult human brain. *Lancet, 359,* 1047–1054.

Steiner, J. E., Glaser, D., Hawilo, M. E., & Berridge, K. C. (2001). Comparative expression of hedonic impact: Affective reactions to taste by human infants and other primates. *Neuroscience and Biobehavioral Reviews, 25,* 53–74.

Steiner, J. M., & Fahrenberg, J. (2000). Authoritarianism and social status of former members of the Waffen-SS and SS and of the Wehrmacht: An extension and reanalysis of the study published in 1970. *Koelner Zeitschrift fuer Soziologie und Sozialpsychologie, 52,* 329–348.

Steinglass, J. E., Figner, B., Berkowitz, S., Simpson, H., Weber, E. U., & Walsh, B. (2012). Increased capacity to delay reward in anorexia nervosa. *Journal of the International Neuropsychological Society, 18*(4), 773–780. doi:10.1017/S1355617712000446.

Steinglass, J., Albano, A., Simpson, H., Carpenter, K., Schebendach, J., & Attia, E. (2012). Fear of food as a treatment target: Exposure and response prevention for anorexia nervosa in an open series. *International Journal Of Eating Disorders, 45*(4), 615–621. doi:10.1002/eat.20936.

Steinhausen, H.-C., & Weber, S. (2009). The outcome of bulimia nervosa: Findings from onequarter century of research. *American Journal of Psychiatry, 159,* 1284–1293.

Steinhauser, K. E., Alexander, S. C., Byock, I. R., George, L. K., et al. (2008). Do preparation and life completion discussions improve functioning and quality of life in seriously ill patients? Pilot randomized control trial. *Journal of Palliative Medicine, 11,* 1234–1240.

Stellar, J. E., Manzo, V. M., Kraus, M. W., & Keltner, D. (2011). Class and compassion: Socioeconomic factors predict responses to suffering. *Emotion,* doi:10.1037/a0026508.

Stenfelt, S. (2011). Acoustic and physiologic aspects of bone conduction hearing. *Advances in Otorhinolaryngology, 71,* 10-21.

Stepanikova, I., Nie, N. H., & He, X. (2010). Time on the Internet at home, loneliness, and life satisfaction: Evidence from panel time-diary data. *Computers In Human Behavior, 26*(3), 329–338. doi:10.1016/j.chb.2009.11.002.

Stepanikova, I., Triplett, J., & Simpson, B (2011). Implicit racial bias and prosocial behavior. *Social Science Research, 40,* 1186–1195.

Stepanski, E. J., & Perlis, M. L. (2000). Behavioral sleep medicine. An emerging subspecialty in health psychology and sleep medicine. *Journal of Psychosomatic Research, 49,* 343–347.

Stepanyants, A., & Escobar, G. (2011). Statistical traces of long-term memories stored in strengths and patterns of synaptic connections. *Journal Of Neuroscience, 31*(21), 7657–7669. doi:10.1523/JNEUROSCI.0255-11.2011.

Stephan, B. C. M., & Caine, D. (2009). Aberrant pattern of scanning in prosopagnosia reflects impaired face processing. *Brain and Cognition, 69,* 262–268.

Stephan, K. E., Marshall, J. C., Friston, K. J., Rowe, J. B., Ritzl, A., Zilles, K., & Fink, G. R. (2003). Lateralized cognitive processes and lateralized task control in the human brain. *Science, 301,* 384–386.

Stephan-Blanchard, E., Chardon, K., Leke, A., Delanaud, S., et al. (2010). In utero exposure to smoking and peripheral chemoreceptor function in preterm neonates. *Pediatrics, 125,* e592–e599.

Stephens, G. J., Silbert, L. J., & Hasson, U. (2010). Speaker–listener neural coupling underlies successful communication. *PNAS Proceedings of the National Academy of Sciences of the United States of America, 107*(32), 14425–14430. doi:10.1073/pnas.1008662107.

Stephens, R. S., Roffman, R. A., & Simpson, E. E. (1994). Treating adult marijuana dependence: A test of the relapse prevention model. *Journal of Consulting and Clinical Psychology, 62*(1), 92–99.

Stephenson, J. (2007, June 20). Jet lag relief? *Journal of the American Medical Association, 297*(23), 2578–2578.

Steptoe, A., Peacey, V., & Wardle, J. (2006). Sleep duration and health in young adults. *Archives of Internal Medicine, 166,* 1689–1692.

Steptoe, A., Wardle, J., & Marmot, M. (2005). Positive affect and health-related neuroendocrine, cardiovascular, and inflammatory processes. *Proceedings of the National Academy of Sciences, 102,* 6508–6512.

Steriade, M., & McCarley, R. W. (1990). *Brainstem control of wakefulness and sleep.* New York: Plenum.

Stern, K., & McClintock, M. K. (1998). Regulation of ovulation by human pheromones. *Nature, 392,* 177–179.

Stern, R. A, Riley, D. O., Daneshvar, D. H., Nowinski, C. J., Cantu, R. C., & McKee, A. C. (2011). Long-term consequences of repetitive brain trauma: chronic traumatic encephalopathy. *PM&R, 3*(10 Supplement 2), S460–2467.

Sternberg, D., & McClelland, J. (2012). Two mechanisms of human contingency learning. *Psychological Science, 23*(1), 59–68.

Sternberg, R. (2009). A duplex theory of love. In R. Sternberg & K. Weis (Eds.), *The new psychology of love* (pp. 184–199). New Haven, CT: Yale University Press.

Sternberg, R. J. (1985). *Beyond IQ: A triarchic theory of human intelligence.* Cambridge, England: Cambridge University Press.

Sternberg, R. J. (1988a). Triangulating love. In R. J. Sternberg & M. L. Barnes (Eds.), *The psychology of love* (pp. 500–520). New Haven: Yale University Press.

Sternberg, R. J. (1988b). *The triarchic mind.* Cambridge: Cambridge University Press.

Sternberg, R. J. (1989). Domain generality versus domain specificity: The life and impending death of a false dichotomy. *Merrill-Palmer Quarterly, 35,* 115–130.

Sternberg, R. J. (1996). *Successful intelligence.* New York: Simon & Schuster.

Sternberg, R. J. (1999). Ability and expertise: It's time to replace the current model of intelligence. *American Educator Spring 1999,* pp. 10–51.

Sternberg, R. J. (2001). What is the common thread of creativity? Its dialectical relation to intelligence and wisdom. *American Psychologist, 56,* 360–362.

Sternberg, R. J. (2004). Culture and intelligence. *American Psychologist, 59,* 325–338.

Sternberg, R. J. (2010). WICS: A new model for school psychology. *School Psychology International, 31*(6), 599–616. doi:10.1177/0143034310386534.

Sternberg, R. J., & Dess, N. K. (2001). Creativity for the new millennium. *American Psychologist, 56,* 332.

Sternberg, R. J., & Grigorenko, E. L. (Eds.). (2004a). *Creativity: From potential to realization.* Washington, DC: APA Books.

Sternberg, R. J., & Grigorenko, E. L. (Eds.). (2004b). *Culture and competence: Contexts of life success.* Washington, DC: APA Books.

Sternberg, R. J., & Kaufman, J. C. (1998). Human abilities. *Annual Review of Psychology, 49,* 479–502.

Sternberg, R. J., Lautrey, J., & Lubart, T. I. (2003). Where are we in the field of intelligence, how did we get here, and where are we going? In R. J. Sternberg, J. Lautrey, et al. (Eds.), *Models of intelligence: International perspectives* (pp. 3–25). Washington, DC: American Psychological Association.

Sternberg, R. J., & Lubart, T. I. (1992). Buy low and sell high: An investment approach to creativity. *Current Directions in Psychological Science, 1*(1), 1–5.

Sternberg, R. J., & O'Hara, L. A. (1999). Creativity and intelligence. In R. J. Sternberg, et al. (Eds.), *Handbook of creativity* (pp. 251–272). New York: Cambridge University Press.

Sternberg, R. J., & The Rainbow Project Coordinators. (2006). The Rainbow Project: Enhancing the SAT through assessments of analytical, practical, and creative skills. *Intelligence, 34,* 321–350.

Sternberg, R. J., Wagner, R. K., Williams, W. M., & Horvath, J. A. (1995). Testing common sense. *American Psychologist, 50,* 912–927.

Sternberg, R. J., & Williams, W. M. (1997). Does the graduate record examination predict meaningful success of graduate training of psychologists? A case study. *American Psychologist, 52,* 630–641.

Sternberg, S. (2011). Modular processes in mind and brain. *Cognitive Neuropsychology, 28*(3–4), 156–208.

Stettler, D. D., Yamahachi, H., Li, W., Denk, W., & Gilbert, C. D. (2006). Axons and synaptic boutons are highly dynamic in adult visual cortex. *Neuron, 49,* 877–887.

Steunenberg, B., Beekman, A. T. F., Deeg, D. J. H., & Kerkhof, A. J. F. M. (2006). Personality and the onset of depression in late life. *Journal of Affective Disorders, 92,* 243–251.

Stevens, A. (1996). *Private myths: Dreams and dreaming*. Cambridge, MA: Harvard University Press.

Stevens, A. A., & Weaver, K. E. (2009). Functional characteristics of auditory cortex in the blind. *Behavioural Brain Research, 196*, 134–138.

Stevens, J. C., & Pollack, M. H. (2005). Benzodiazepines in clinical practice: Consideration of their long-term use and alternative agents. *Journal of Clinical Psychiatry, 66*(Suppl. 2), 21–27.

Stevens, R. D., & Bhardwaj, A. (2006). Approach to the comatose patient. *Critical Care Medicine, 34*(1), 31–41.

Stevenson, H. (1992). *A long way from being number one: What we can learn from East Asia*. Washington, DC: Federation of Behavior, Psychological and Cognitive Sciences.

Stevenson, R. J., & Boakes, R. A. (2003). A mnemonic theory of odor perception. *Psychological Review, 110*, 340–364.

Stewart, G. L. (2006). A meta-analytic review of relationships between team design features and team performance. *Journal of Management, 32*, 29–55.

Stewart, J. G., & Harkness, K. L. (2012). Symptom specificity in the acute treatment of major depressive disorder: A re-analysis of the treatment of depression collaborative research program. *Journal of Affective Disorders, 137*, 87-97.

Stewart, J. H. (2005). Hypnosis in contemporary medicine. *Mayo Clinic Proceedings, 80*, 511–524.

Stewart, S. E., Platko, J., Fagerness, J., Birns, J., Jenike, E., Smoller, J. W., et al. (2007). A genetic family-based association study of OLIG2 in obsessive-compulsive disorder. *Archives of General Psychiatry, 64*, 209–214.

Stewart-Williams, S. (2004). The placebo puzzle: Putting together the pieces. *Health Psychology, 23*, 198–206.

Stewart-Williams, S., & Podd, J. (2004). The placebo effect: Dissolving the expectancy versus conditioning debate. *Psychological Bulletin, 130*(2), 324–340. doi:10.1037/0033-2909.130.2.324.

Stice, E., Marti, C., & Durant, S. (2011). Risk factors for onset of eating disorders: Evidence of multiple risk pathways from an 8-year prospective study. *Behaviour Research & Therapy, 49*(10), 622–627. doi:10.1016/j.brat.2011.06.009.

Stice, E. (2001). A prospective test of the dual-pathway model of bulimic pathology: Mediating effects of dieting and negative affect. *Journal of Abnormal Psychology, 110*, 124–135.

Stice, E., & Fairburn, C. G. (2003). Dietary and dietary-depressive subtypes of bulimia nervosa show differential symptom presentation, social impairment, comorbidity, and course of illness. *Journal of Consulting and Clinical Psychology, 71*, 1090–1094.

Stice, E., & Shaw, H. (2004). Eating disorder prevention programs: A meta-analytic review. *Psychological Bulletin, 130*, 206–227.

Stice, E., Ragan, J., & Randall, P. (2004). Prospective relations between social support and depression: Differential direction of effects for parent and peer support? *Journal of Abnormal Psychology, 113*, 155–159.

Stice, E., Shaw, H., & Nathan, C. (2006). A meta-analytic review of obesity prevention programs for children and adolescents: The skinny on interventions that work. *Psychological Bulletin, 132*, 667–691.

Stickgold, R., James, L., & Hobson, J. A. (2000). Visual discrimination learning requires sleep after training. *Nature Neuroscience, 3*, 1237–1238.

Stickgold, R., Rittenhouse, C. D., & Hobson, J. A. (1994). Dream splicing: A new technique for assessing thematic coherence in subjective reports of mental activity. *Consciousness and Cognition, 3*(1), 114–128.

Stiegler, M. P., Neelankavil, J. P., Canales, C. C., & Dhillon, A. A. (2012). Cognitive errors detected in anaesthesiology: A literature review and pilot study. *BJA: The British Journal of Anaesthesia, 108*(2), 229–235.

Stiles, W. B., Barkham, M., Twigg, E., Mellor-Clark, J., & Cooper, M. (2006). Effectiveness of cognitive-behavioural, person-centered and psychodynamic therapies as practised in UK national health service settings. *Psychological Medicine, 36*, 555–566.

Stillman, J. A. (2002). Gustation: Intersensory experience par excellence. *Perception, 31*, 1491–1500.

Stillwell, M. E. (2002). Drug-facilitated sexual assault involving gamma-hydroxybutyric acid. *Journal of Forensic Science, 47*, 1133–1134.

Stipek, D. J. (1983). A developmental analysis of pride and shame. *Human Development, 26*, 42–56.

Stirrat, M., & Perrett, D. I. (2010). Valid facial cues to cooperation and trust: Male facial width and trustworthiness. *Psychological Science, 21*(3) 349–354. doi:10.1177/0956797610362647.

Stoerig, P. & Cowey, A. (1997). "Blindsight in man and monkey". *Brain 120*(3): 535–559.

Stoet, G., & Geary, D. C. (2012). Can stereotype threat explain the gender gap in mathematics performance and achievement? *Review of General Psychology, 16*(1), 93–102. doi:10.1037/a0026617.

Stoff, D. M., Breiling, J., & Maser, J. D. (Eds.). (1997). *Handbook of antisocial behavior*. New York: Wiley.

Stone, A. A., Schwartz, J. E., Broderick, J. E., & Deaton, A. S. (2010). A snapshot of the age distribution of psychological well-being in the United States. *Proceedings of the National Academy of Sciences, 107*, 9985–9990.

Stone, M., Laughren, T., Jones, M. L., Levenson, M., et al. (2009). Risk of suicidality in clinical trials of antidepressants in adults: Analysis of proprietary data submitted to U.S. Food and Drug Administration. *British Medical Journal, 339*, b2880.

Stone, J., & Fernandez, N. C. (2008). To practice what we preach: The use of hypocrisy and cognitive dissonance to motivate behavior change. *Social and Personality Psychology Compass, 2*, 1024–1051.

Stoney, C. M., Hughes, J. W., Kuntz, K. K., West, S. G., & Thornton, L. M. (2002). Cardiovascular stress responses among Asian Indian and European American women and men. *Annals of Behavioral Medicine, 24*, 113–121.

Stoney, C. M., & Finney, M. L. (2000). Social support and stress: Influences on lipid reactivity. *International Journal of Behavioral Medicine, 7*, 111–126.

Stoney, C. M., & Hughes, J. W. (1999). Lipid reactivity among men with a parental history of myocardial infarction. *Psychophysiology, 36*, 484–490.

Stoney, C. M., & Matthews, K. A. (1988). Parental history of hypertension and myocardial infarction predicts cardiovascular responses to behavioral stressors in middle-aged men and women. *Psychophysiology, 25*, 269–277.

Stoney, C. M., Niaura, R., Bausserman, L., & Matacin, M. (1999). Lipid reactivity to stress: I. Comparison of chronic and acute stress responses in middle-aged airline pilots. *Health Psychology, 18*, 241–250.

Storch, E. A., Murphy, T. K., Goodman, W. K., Geffken, G. R., Lewin, A. B., Henin, A., et al. (2010). A preliminary study of d-cycloserine augmentation of cognitive-behavioral therapy in pediatric obsessive-compulsive disorder. *Biological Psychiatry, 68*, 1073–1076.

Storm, B. C. (2011). The benefit of forgetting in thinking and remembering. *Current Directions in Psychological Science, 20*(5) 291–295. doi:10.1177/0963721411418469.

Storm, B. C., & Angello, G. (2010). Overcoming fixation: Creative problem solving and retrieval-induced forgetting. *Psychological Science, 21*(9), 1263–1265. doi:10.1177/0956797610379864.

St. Pourcain, B., Wang, K., Glessner, J. T., Golding, J., Steer, C., Ring, S. M., Skuse, D. H., Grant, S.F.A., Hakonarson, H., & Smith, G. D. (2010). Association between a high-risk autism locus on 5p14 and social communication spectrum phenotypes in the general population. *American Journal of Psychiatry, xx*. Epub 2010 Jul 15. doi: 10.1176/appi.ajp.2010.09121789.

Strahan, E. J., Spencer, S. J., & Zanna, M. P. (2005). Subliminal priming and persuasion: How motivation affects the activation of goals and the persuasiveness of messages. In F. R. Kardes, P. Herr, & J. Nantel (Eds.), *Applying social cognition to consumer-focused strategy* (pp. 267–280). Mahwah, NJ: Erlbaum.

Strain, E. C., Mumford, G. K., Silverman, K., & Griffiths, R. R. (1994). Caffeine dependence syndrome: Evidence from case histories and experimental evaluations. *Journal of the American Medical Association, 272*(13), 1043–1048.

Strakowski, S. M., DelBello, M. P., & Adler, C. M. (2005). The functional neuroanatomy of bipolar disorder: A review of neuroimaging findings. *Molecular Psychiatry, 10*, 105–116.

Strauss, E., & Wada, J. (1983). Lateral preferences and cerebral speech dominance. *Cortex, 19*(2), 165–177.

Strauss, R. S., & Pollack, H. A. (2001). Epidemic increases in childhood overweight: 1986–1998. *Journal of the American Medical Association, 286*, 2845–2848.

Strayer, D. L., & Drews, F. A. (2007). Cell-phone-induced driver distraction. *Current Directions in Psychological Science, 16*(3), 128–131.

Strick, P. L., Dum, R. P., & Fiez, J. A. (2009). Cerebellum and nonmotor function. *Annual Review of Neuroscience, 32*, 413–434.

Stricker, L. J., & Ward, W. C. (2004). Stereotype threat, inquiring about test takers' ethnicity and gender, and standardized test performance. *Journal of Applied Social Psychology, 34*, 665–693.

Stright, A. D., Gallagher, K. C., & Kelley, K. (2008). Infant temperament moderates relations between maternal parenting in early childhood and children's adjustment in first grade. *Child Development, 79*, 186–200.

Stringhini, S., Sabia, S., Shipley, M., Brunner, E., et al. (2010). Association of socioeconomic position with health behaviors and mortality. *Journal of the American Medical Association, 303*, 1159–1166.

Stroebe, W., Papies, E. K., & Aarts, H. (2008). From homeostatic to hedonic theories of eating: Self-regulatory failure in food-rich environments. *Applied Psychology: An International Review, 57*(Suppl. 1), 172–193.

Strohmetz, D. B., Rind, B., Fisher, R., & Lynn, M. (2002). Sweetening the till: The use of candy to increase restaurant tipping. *Journal of Applied Social Psychology, 32*, 300–309.

Stroop, J. R. (1935). Studies of interference in serial verbal reactions. *Journal of Experimental Psychology, 18*, 643–662.

Strote, J., Lee, J. E., & Wechsler, H. (2002). Increasing MDMA use among college students: Results of a national survey. *Journal of Adolescent Health, 30*, 64–72.

Stroud, L. R., Paster, R. L., Goodwin, M. S., Shenassa, E., et al. (2009). Maternal smoking during pregnancy and neonatal behavior: A large-scale community study. *Pediatrics, 123*, e842–e848.

Strough, J., Karns, T. E., & Schlosnagle, L. (2011). Decision-making heuristics and biases across the life span. *Annals of the New York Academy of Sciences, 1235*(1), 57–74. doi:10.1111/j.1749-6632.2011.06208.x.

Stout, H. (2010, April 30). Antisocial networking. *The New York Times*. Retrieved from http://www.nytimes.com.

Studer-Luethi, B., Jaeggi, S. M., Buschkuehl, M., & Perrig, W. J. (2012). Influence of neuroticism and conscientiousness on working memory training outcome. *Personality and Individual Differences*, doi:10.1016/j.paid.2012.02.012.

Strunk, D. R., Lopez, H., & DeRubeis, R. J. (2006). Depressive symptoms are associated with unrealistic negative predictions of future life events. *Behaviour Research and Therapy, 44*, 875–896.

Stuart, R. B. (2004). Twelve practical suggestions for achieving multicultural competence. *Professional Psychology: Theory and Practice, 35*, 3–9.

Stuart, S., & Robertson, M. (2003). *Interpersonal psychotherapy: A clinician's guide*. London: Arnold Publishers.

Stürmer, T., Hasselbach, P., & Amelang, M. (2006). Personality, lifestyle, and risk of cardiovascular disease and cancer: Follow-up of population based cohort. *British Medical Journal, 332*, 1359.

Su, C. Y., Menuz, K., & Carlson, J. R. (2009). Olfactory perception: Receptors, cells, and circuits. *Cell, 139*, 45–59.

Su, J. C., Tran, A. G. T. T., Wirtz, J. G., Langteau, R. A., & Rothman, A. J. (2008). Driving under the influence (of stress): Evidence of a regional increase in impaired driving and traffic fatalities after the September 11 terrorist attacks. *Psychological Science, 20,* 59–65.

Suarez, M. & Mullins, S. (2008). Motivational interviewing and pediatric Health behavior interventions. *Journal of Developmental and Behavioral Pediatrics, 29,* 417–428.

Subotnik, K. L., Nuechterlein, K. H., Green, M. F., Horan, W. P., et al. (2006). Neurocognitive and social cognitive correlates of formal thought disorder in schizophrenia patients. *Schizophrenia Research, 85,* 84–95.

Subotnik, R. F., Olszewski-Kubilius, P., & Worrell, F. C. (2011). Rethinking giftedness and gifted education: A proposed direction forward based on psychological science. *Psychological Science in the Public Interest, 12*(1), 3–54. doi:10.1177/1529100611418056.

Substance Abuse and Mental Health Services Administration. (2007). *Results from the 2006 National Survey on Drug Use and Health: National findings.* Rockville, MD: Author.

Suddendorf, T. & Corballis, M. C. (2007) The evolution of foresight: What is mental time travel, and is it unique to humans? *Behavioral and Brain Sciences, 30,* 299–313.

Sue, D. W., & Sue, D. (2008). *Counseling the culturally diverse: Theory and practice* (5th ed.). Hoboken, NJ: Wiley.

Sue, S., & Okazaki, S. (1990). Asian-American educational achievements: A phenomenon in search of an explanation. *American Psychologist, 45,* 913–920.

Sue, S., Zane, N., Hall, G. C. N., & Berger, L. K. (2009). The case for cultural competency in psychotherapeutic interventions. *Annual Review of Psychology, 60,* 525–548.

Suh, E., Diener, E., & Fujita, F. (1996). Events and subjective well-being: Only recent events matter. *Journal of Personality and Social Psychology, 70,* 1091–1102.

Suinn, R. M. (2001). The terrible twos: Anger and anxiety. *American Psychologist, 56,* 27–36.

Sullivan, J. W., & Horowitz, F. D. (1983). The effects of intonation on infant attention: The role of the rising intonation contour. *Journal of Child Language, 10,* 521–534.

Sullivan, P. F., Kendler, K. S., & Neale, M. C. (2003). Schizophrenia as a complex trait: Evidence from a meta-analysis of twin studies. *Archives of General Psychiatry, 60,* 1187–1192.

Suls, J., & Bunde, J. (2005). Anger, anxiety, and depression as risk factors for cardiovascular disease: The problems and implications of overlapping affective dispositions. *Psychological Bulletin, 131,* 260–300.

Suls, J., & Howren, M. (2012). Understanding the physical-symptom experience: The distinctive contributions of anxiety and depression. *Current Directions in Psychological Science, 21*(2), 129–134. doi:10.1177/0963721412439298.

Suls, J., & Rothman, A. (2004). Evolution of the biopsychosocial model: Prospects and challenges for health psychology. *Health Psychology, 23,* 119–125.

Suls, J., & Wan, C. K. (1993). The relationship between trait hostility and cardiovascular reactivity: A quantitative review and analysis. *Psychophysiology, 30,* 1–12.

Sun, Q., Townsend, M. K., Okereke, O. I., Franco, O. H., et al. (2010). Physical activity at midlife in relation to successful survival in women at age 70 years or older. *Archives of Internal Medicine, 170,* 194–201.

Suomi, S. (1999). Attachment in rhesus monkeys. In J. Cassidy & P. Shaver (Eds.), *Handbook of attachment* (pp. 181–197). New York: Guilford.

Suomi, S. (2004). Aggression, serotonin, and gene-environment interactions in rhesus monkeys. In J. T. Cacioppo & G. G. Berntson (Eds.), *Essays in social neuroscience* (pp. 15–27). Cambridge, MA: MIT Press.

Suschinsky, K. D., & Lalumière, M. L. (2011). Prepared for anything? An investigation of female genital arousal in response to rape cues. *Psychological Science, 22*(2), 159–165. doi:10.1177/0956797610394660.

Suslow, T., Ohrmann, P., Bauer, J., Rauch, A. V., Schwindt, W., Arolt, V., et al. (2006). Amygdala activation during masked presentation of emotional faces predicts conscious detection of threat-related faces. *Brain and Cognition, 61,* 243–248.

Sussman, A. B., & Shafir, E. (2012). On assets and debt in the psychology of perceived wealth. *Psychological Science, 23*(1), 101–108. doi:10.1177/0956797611421484.

Sutcher, H. (2008). Hypnosis, hypnotizability, and treatment. *American Journal of Clinical Hypnosis, 51,* 57–67.

Suzdak, P. D., Glowa, J. R., Crawley, J. N., Schwartz, R. D., Skolnick, P., & Paul, S. M. (1986). A selective imidazobenzodiazepine antagonist of ethanol in the rat. *Science, 234,* 1243–1247.

Swaab, D. E., & Hofman, M. A. (1995). Sexual differentiation of the human hypothalamus in relation to gender and sexual orientation. *Trends in Neuroscience, 18*(6), 264–270.

Swan, G. E. (1996, December). Some elders thrive on working into late life. *APA Monitor,* 35.

Swan, G. E., & Carmelli, D. (1996). Curiosity and mortality in aging adults: A 5-year follow-up of the Western Collaborative Group Study. *Psychology and Aging, 11,* 449–453.

Swaney, W. T. & Keverne, E. B. (2009). The evolution of pheromonal communication. *Behavior and Brain Research, 200,* 239–247.

Swann, W. B., Jr., De la Ronde, C., & Hixon, J. G. (1994). Authenticity and positivity strivings in marriage and courtship. *Journal of Personality and Social Psychology, 66,* 857–869.

Swanson, S. A., Crow, S. J., Le Grange, D., Swendsen, J., & Merikangas, K. R. (2011). Prevalence and correlates of eating disorders in adolescents: Results from the national comorbidity survey replication adolescent supplement. *Archives of General Psychiatry, 68*(7), 714–723. doi:10.1001/archgenpsychiatry.2011.22.

Swarte, N. B., van der Lee, M. L., van der Bom, J. G., van den Bout, J., & Heintz, A. P. M. (2003). Effects of euthanasia on the bereaved family and friends: A cross sectional study. *British Medical Journal, 327,* 189.

Swartz, H. A., Zuckoff, A.,Grote, N. K., Spielvogle, H. N., Bledsoe, S. E., Shear, M. K., & Frank, E. (2007). Engaging depressed patients in psychotherapy: Integrating techniques from motivational interviewing and ethnographic interviewing to improve treatment. participation. *Professional Psychology: Research and Practice, 38,* 430–439.

Swartz, M. S., Perkins, D. O., Stroup, T. S., Davis, S. M., Capuano, G., Rosenheck, R. A., et al. (2007). Effects of antipsychotic medications on psychosocial functioning in patients with chronic schizophrenia: Findings from the NIMH CATIE study. *American Journal of Psychiatry, 164,* 428–436.

Sweet, M. A., Heyman, G. D., Genyue, F., & Lee, K. (2010). Are there limits to collectivism? Culture and children's reasoning about lying to conceal a group transgression. *Infant & Child Development, 19*(4), 422–442. doi:10.1002/icd.669.

Swendsen, J., Burstein, M., Case, B., Conway, K., Dierker, L., He, J., & Merikangas, K. (2012). Use and abuse of alcohol and illicit drugs in US adolescents: Results of the National Comorbidity Survey-Adolescent Supplement. *Archives Of General Psychiatry, 69*(4), 390–398.

Swerdlow, R., & Khan, S. M. (2009). The Alzheimer's disease mitochondrial cascade hypothesis: An update. *Experimental Neurology, 218,* 308–315.

Swerdlow, R. H. (2011). Brain aging, Alzheimer's disease, and mitochondria. *Biochimica et Biophysica Acta, 1812*(12), 1630–1639.

Swets, J. A. (1996). *Signal detection theory and ROC analysis in psychology and diagnostics.* New Jersey: Erlbaum.

Swets, J. A., Dawes, R. M., & Monahan, J. (2000). Psychological science can improve diagnostic decisions. *Psychological Science in the Public Interest, 1,* 1–26.

Swift, R. (2010). Medications acting on the dopaminergic system in the treatment of alcoholic patients. *Current Pharmaceutical Design, 16*(19), 2136–2140.

Swinburn, B. (2009). Obesity prevention in children and adolescents. *Child and Adolescent Psychiatric Clinics of North America, 18*(1), 209–223.

Swindle, R., Jr., Heller, K., Pescosolido, B., & Kikuzawa, S. (2000). Responses to nervous breakdowns in America over a 40-year period: Mental health policy implications. *American Psychologist, 55,* 740–749.

Swithers, S. E., & Hall, W. G. (1994). Does oral experience terminate ingestion? *Appetite, 23*(2), 113–138.

Symons, D. (1979). *The evolution of human sexuality.* Oxford, UK: Oxford University Press.

Symmonds, M., Emmanuel, J. J., Drew, M. E., Batterham, R. L., & Dolan, R. J. (2010). Metabolic state alters economic decision making under risk in humans. *PLoS ONE, 5*(6), e11090. doi:10.1371/journal.pone.0011090.

Szameitat, D. P., Kreifelts, B., Alter, K., Szameitat, A. J., Sterr, A., Grodd, W., & Wildgruber, D. (2010). It is not always tickling: Distinct cerebral responses during perception of different laughter types. *Neuroimage, 53*(4), 1264–1271. doi:10.1016/j.neuroimage.2010.06.028.

Szasz, T. (1972). *The myth of mental illness.* New York: Paladin.

Szasz, T. (2003). The psychiatric protection order for the "battered mental patient." *British Medical Journal, 327,* 1449–1451.

Szasz, T. (2009). *Coercion as cure.* Edison, NJ: Transaction Publishers.

Szegedi, A., Kohnen, R., Dienel, A., & Kieser, M. (2005). Acute treatment of moderate to severe depression with hypericum extract WS 5570 (St John's wort): Randomised controlled double blind non-inferiority trial versus paroxetine. *British Medical Journal, 330,* 503.

Szpunar, K. K. (2010). Episodic future thought: An emerging concept. *Perspectives on Psychological Science, 5,* 142–162.

Szpunar, K. K., Chan, J. C., & McDermott, K. B. (2009). Contextual processing in episodic future thought. *Cerebral Cortex, 19,* 1539–1548. doi:10.1093/cercor/bhn191.

Szpunar, K. K., Watson, J. M., & McDermott, K. B. (2007). Neural substrates of envisioning the future. *Proceedings of the National Academy of Sciences, 104,* 642–647.

Tabuchi, M., & Gondo, Y. (2011). How generativity affects motivation for altruistic behavior toward the young generation in elderly people. *Japanese Journal of Psychology, 82*(4), 392–398. doi:10.4992/jjpsy.82.392.

Taggar, S., Hackett, R., & Saha, S. (1999). Leadership emergence in autonomous work teams: Antecedents and outcomes. *Personnel Psychology, 52,* 899–926.

Tailby, C., Wright, L. L., Metha, A. B., & Calford, M. B. (2005). Activity-dependent maintenance and growth of dendrites in adult cortex. *Proceedings of the National Academy of Sciences, 102,* 4631–4636.

Takahashi, K., & Yamanaka, S. (2006). Induction of pluripotent stem cells from mouse embryonic and adult fibroblast cultures by defined factors. *Cell, 126*(4), 663–676.

Takashima, A., Petersson, K. M., Rutters, F., Tendolkar, I., Jensen, O., Zwarts, M. J., et al. (2006). Declarative memory consolidation in humans: A prospective functional magnetic resonance imaging study. *Proceedings of the National Academy of Sciences, 103,* 756–761.

Takeuchi, N., Uchimura, N., Hashizume, Y., Mukai, M., Etoh, Y., Yamamoto, K., et al. (2001). Melatonin therapy for REM behavior disorder. *Psychiatry and Clinical Neurosciences, 55,* 267–269.

Takkouche, B., Etminan, M., & Montes-Martinez, A. (2005). Personal use of hair dyes and risk of cancer. *Journal of the American Medical Association, 293,* 2516–2525.

Talarico, J. F., & Rubin, D. C. (2003). Confidence, not consistency, characterizes flashbulb memories. *Psychological Science, 14,* 455–461.

Talbott, J. A. (2004). Deinstitutionalization: Avoiding the disasters of the past. *Psychiatric Services, 55,* 1112–1115.

Tallman, B. A., Altmaier, E., & Garcia, C. (2007). Finding benefit from cancer. *Journal of Counseling Psychology, 54,* 481–487.

Talmi, D., Grady, C. L., Goshen-Gottstein, Y., & Moscovitch, M. (2005). Neuroimaging the serial position curve: A test of single-store versus dual-store models. *Psychological Science, 16,* 716–723.

Tam, K. P., Chiu, C. Y., Lau, I. Y. M. (2007). Terror managements among Chinese: Worldview defence and intergroup bias in resource allocation. *Asian Journal of Social Psychology 10*, 93–102.

Tamashiro, K. L. K., & Bello, N. T. (Eds.) (2008). Special issue on leptin. *Physiology & Behavior, 94*(5).

Tamir, D., & Mitchell, J. (2012). Disclosing information about the self is intrinsically rewarding. *Proceedings of the National Academy of Sciences of the United States of America, 109*, 8038–8043.

Tamir, M. (2009). What do people want to feel and why? Pleasure and utility in emotion regulation. *Current Directions in Psychological Science, 18*, 101–105.

Tan, G., Hammond, D. C., & Joseph, G. (2005). Hypnosis and irritable bowel syndrome: A review of efficacy and mechanism of action. *American Journal of Clinical Hypnosis, 47*, 161–178.

Tan, H.-Y., Chen, Q., Sust, S., Buckholtz, J. W., et al. (2007). Epistasis between catechol-Omethyltransferase and type II metabotropic glutamate receptor 3 genes on working memory brain function. *Proceedings of the National Academy of Sciences, 104*, 12536–12541.

Tanaka, A., Koizumi, A., Imai, H., Hiramatsu, S., Hiramoto, E., & de Gelder, B. (2010). I feel your voice: Cultural differences in the multisensory perception of emotion. *Psychological Science, 21*(9), 1259–1262. doi:10.1177/0956797610380698.

Tanaka, H., Black, J. M., Hulme, C., Stanley, L. M., Kesler, S. R., Whitfield-Gabrieli, S., & … Hoeft, F. (2011). The brain basis of the phonological deficit in dyslexia is independent of IQ. *Psychological Science, 22*(11), 1442–1451. doi:10.1177/0956797611419521

Tanaka, H., Taira, K., Arakawa, M., Toguti, H., Urasaki, C., Yamamoto, Y., et al. (2001). Effects of short nap and exercise on elderly people having difficulty sleeping. *Psychiatry and Clinical Neurosciences, 55*, 173–174.

Tanaka, K., & Miyake, Y. (2011). Association between prenatal and postnatal tobacco smoke exposure and allergies in young children. *Journal of Asthma, 48*(5), 458–463. doi:10.3109/02770903.2011.578314.

Tandon, R., Nasrallah, H. A., & Keshavan, M. S. (2009). Schizophrenia, "just the facts": 4. Clinical features and conceptualization, *Schizophrenia Research, 110*, 1–23.

Tandon, P. S., Zhou, C., Lozano, P., & Christakis, D. A. (2011). Preschoolers' total daily screen time at home and by type of child care. *The Journal Of Pediatrics, 158*(2), 297–300. doi:10.1016/j.jpeds.2010.08.005.

Tandon, R., Keshavan, M. S., & Nasrallah, H. A. (2008). Schizophrenia, "Just the facts" What we know in 2008: 2. Epidemiology and etiology. *Schizophrenia Research, 102*(1–3), 1–18.

Tang, S., Machaalani, R., & Waters, K. A. (2011). Expression of brain-derived neurotrophic factor and TrkB receptor in the sudden infant death syndrome brainstem. *Respiratory Physiology and Neurobiology*, Oct 14, 2011. [Epub ahead of print].

Tang, Y. Y., Ma, Y., Wang, J., Fan, Y., Feng, S., Lu, Q., Yu, Q., Sui, D., Rothbart, M. K., Fan, M., & Posner, M. I. (2007). Short-term meditation training improves attention and self-regulation. *Proceedings of the National Academies of Science, 104*, 17152–17156.

Tan-Laxa, M. A., Sison-Switala, C., Rintelman, W., & Ostrea, E. M. (2004). Abnormal auditory brainstem response among infants with prenatal cocaine exposure. *Pediatrics, 113*, 357–360.

Tannen, D. (2001). *You just don't understand: Women and men in conversation.* New York: HarperCollins.

Tanner, J. M. (1978). *Foetus into man: Physical growth from conception to maturity.* London: Open Books.

Targino, R. A., Imamura, M., Kaziyama, H. H., Souza, L. P., Hsing, W. T., Furland, A. D., Imamura, S. T., & Azevedo Neto, R. S. (2008). A randomized controlled trial of acupuncture added to usual treatment for fibromyalgia. *Journal of Rehabilitation Medicine, 40*(7), 582–588.

Task Force on Sudden Infant Death Syndrome. (2011). SIDS and other sleep-related infant deaths: Expansion of recommendations for a safe infant sleeping environment. *Pediatrics, 128*(5), 1030–1039.

Tasker, F., & Golombok, S. (1995). Adults raised as children in lesbian families. *American Journal of Orthopsychiatry, 65*(2), 203–215.

Tassi, P., & Muzet, A. (2001). Defining states of consciousness. *Neuroscience and Biobehavioral Reviews, 25*, 175–191.

Tavris, C. (2003). Mind games: Psychological warfare between therapists and scientists. *The Chronicle of Higher Education, 49*, B7–B9.

Tay, L., & Diener, E. (2011). Needs and subjective well-being around the world. *Journal Of Personality And Social Psychology, 101*(2), 354–365. doi:10.1037/a0023779.

Tayeb, H. O., Yang, H. D., Price, B. H., & Tarazi, F. I. (2011). Pharmacotherapies for Alzheimer's disease: Beyond cholinesterase inhibitors. *Pharmacology & Therapeutics.* Epub December 16, 2011.

Taylor, C. A., Manganello, J. A., Lee, S. J., & Rice, J. C. (2010). Mothers' spanking of 3-year-old children and subsequent risk of children's aggressive behavior. *Pediatrics, 125*(5), e1057–e1065. doi:10.1542/peds.2009-2678.

Taylor, H. A., & Tversky, B. (1992). Spatial mental models derived from survey and route descriptions. *Journal of Memory and Language, 31*, 261–292.

Taylor, J. C., & Downing, P. E. (2011). Division of labor between lateral and ventral extrastriate representation of faces, bodies, and objects. *Journal of Cognitive Neuroscience, 23*(12), 4122–4137.

Taylor, J. G. (2002). Paying attention to consciousness. *Trends in Cognitive Science, 6*, 206–210.

Taylor, R. L., & Richards, S. B. (1991). Patterns of intellectual differences of Black, Hispanic, and White children. *Psychology in the Schools, 28*, 5–8.

Taylor, S. (2004). Efficacy and outcome predictors for three PTSD treatments: Exposure therapy, EMDR, and relaxation training. In S. Taylor (Ed.), *Advances in the treatment of posttraumatic stress disorder: Cognitive-behavioral perspectives* (pp. 13–37). New York: Springer.

Taylor, S., & Asmundson, G. J. G. (2008). Hypochondriasis. In J. S. Abramowitz, D. McKay, & S. Taylor. *Clinical handbook of obsessive-compulsive disorder and related problems* (pp. 304–315). Baltimore, MD: Johns Hopkins University Press.

Taylor, S., Peplau, A., & Sears, D. (2006). *Social psychology* (12th ed.). Upper Saddle River, NJ: Pearson/Prentice Hall.

Taylor, S., Thordarson, D. S., Maxfield, L., Fedoroff, I. C., Lovell, K., & Ogrodniczuk, J. (2003). Comparative efficacy, speed, and adverse effects of three PTSD treatments: Exposure therapy, EMDR, and relaxation training. *Journal of Consulting and Clinical Psychology, 71*, 330–338.

Taylor, S. E. (2010). Mechanisms linking early life stress to adult health outcomes. *Proceedings of the National Academy of Sciences, 107*, 8507–8512.

Taylor, S. E. (2002). *Health psychology* (5th ed.). New York: McGraw-Hill.

Taylor, S. E. (1999). *Health psychology* (4th ed.). New York: McGraw-Hill.

Taylor, S. E., Dickerson, S. S., & Klein, L. C. (2002). Toward a biology of social support. In C. R. Snyder & S. L. Lopez (Eds.), *Handbook of positive psychology* (pp. 556–569). London: Oxford University Press.

Taylor, S. E., Gonzaga, G. C., Klein, L. C., Hu, P., Greendale, G. A., & Seeman, T. E. (2006). Relation of oxytocin to psychological stress responses and hypothalamic-pituitary-adrenocortical axis activity in older women. *Psychosomatic Medicine, 68*, 238–245.

Taylor, S. E., Kemeny, M. E., Aspinwall, L. G., Schneider, S. G., Rodriguez, R., & Herbert, M. (1992). Optimism, coping, psychological distress, and high-risk sexual behavior among men at risk for acquired immunodeficiency syndrome (AIDS). *Journal of Personality and Social Psychology, 63*, 460–473.

Taylor, S. E., Kemeny, M. E., Reed, G. M., Bower, J. E., & Gruenewald, T. L. (2000). Psychological resources, positive illusions, and health. *American Psychologist, 55*, 99–109.

Taylor, S. E., Klein, L. C., Lewis, B. P., Gruenewald, T. L., Gurung, R. A. R., & Updegraff, J. A. (2000). Biobehavioral responses to stress in females: Tend-and-befriend, not fight-or-flight. *Psychological Review, 107*, 411–429.

Taylor, S. E., Lerner, J. S., Sherman, K. D., Sage, R. M., & McDowell, N. K. (2003). Are self-enhancing cognitions associated with health or unhealthy biological profiles? *Journal of Personality and Social Psychology, 85*, 605–615.

Taylor, S. E., Lewis, B. P., Gruenewald, T. L., Gurung, R. A. R., Updegraff, J. A., & Klein, L. C. (2002). Sex differences in biobehavioral responses to threat: Reply to Geary and Flinn (2002). *Psychological Review, 109*, 751–753.

Taylor, V., & Walton, G. M. (2011). Stereotype threat undermines academic learning. *Personality And Social Psychology Bulletin, 37*(8), 1055–1067. doi:10.1177/0146167211406506.

Teachman, J. D. (2008). The living arrangements of children and their educational well-being. *Journal of Family Issues, 29*, 734–761.

Tedeschi, R. G., & McNally, R. J. (2011). Can We Facilitate Posttraumatic Growth in Combat Veterans?. *American Psychologist, 66*(1), 19–24. doi:10.1037/a0021896.

Téglás, E., Vul, E., Girotto, V., Gonzalez, M., Tenenbaum, J. B., & Bonatti, L. L. (2011). Pure Reasoning in 12-Month-Old Infants as Probabilistic Inference. *Science, 332*(6033), 1054–1059. doi:10.1126/science.1196404.

Teigen, K. H. (1994). Yerkes-Dodson: A law for all seasons. *Theory and Psychology, 4*(4), 525–547.

Telegraph Correspondent. (2005, April 18). Scratching your cars was art, says vandal. *Daily Telegraph*, p. 5.

Tellegen, A., Lykken, D. T., Bouchard, T. J., Wilcox, K. J., Segal, N. L., & Rich, S. (1988). Personality similarity in twins reared apart and together. *Journal of Personality and Social Psychology, 54*, 1031–1039.

Tellegen, A., Lykken, D. T., Bouchard, T. J., Wilcox, K. J., Segal, N. L., & Rich, S. (1988). Personality similarity in twins reared apart and together. *Journal of Personality and Social Psychology, 54*, 1031–1039.

ten Brummelhuis, L. L., & Bakker, A. B. (2012). A resource perspective on the work–home interface: The work-home resources model. *American Psychologist*, doi:10.1037/a0027974.

Tenenbaum, H. R. (2009). "You'd be good at that!" Gender patterns in parent-child talk about courses. *Social Development, 18*, 447–463.

Tenenbaum, H. R., & Leaper, C. (2003). Parent-child conversations about science: The socializations of gender inequities? *Developmental Psychology, 39*, 34–47.

Teng, Y. D., Lavik, E. B., Qu, X., Park, K. I., Ourednik, J., Zurakowski, D., et al. (2002). Functional recovery following traumatic spinal cord injury mediated by a unique polymer scaffold seeded with neural stem cells. *Proceedings of the National Academy of Sciences, 99*, 3024–3029.

Teper, R., Inzlicht, M., & Page-Gould, E. (2011). Are we more moral than we think?: Exploring the role of affect in moral behavior and moral forecasting. *Psychological Science, 22*(4), 553–558. doi:10.1177/0956797611402513.

Teplin, L. A., McClelland, G. M., Abram, K. M., & Weiner, D. A. (2005). Crime victimization in adults with severe mental illness. *Archives of General Psychiatry, 62*, 911–921.

Terburg, D., Aarts, H., & van Honk, J. (2012). Testosterone affects gaze aversion from angry faces outside of conscious awareness. *Psychological Science, 23*(5), 459–463. doi:10.1177/0956797611433336.

Terman, L. M. (1906). Genius and stupidity: A study of the intellectual process of seven "bright" and seven "stupid" boys. *Pedagogical Seminary, 13*, 307–373.

Terman, L. M. (1916). *The measurement of intelligence.* Boston: Houghton Mifflin.

Terman, L. M., & Oden, M. H. (1947). *The gifted child grows up: Vol. 4. Genetic studies of genius.* Stanford, CA: Stanford University Press.

Terman, L. M., & Oden, M. H. (1959). *The gifted group at midlife.* Stanford, CA: Stanford University Press.

Terman, M., & Terman, J. S. (2005). Light therapy for seasonal and nonseasonal depression: Efficacy, protocol, safety, and side effects. *CNS Spectrums, 10,* 647–663.

Terracciano, A., Löckenhoff, C. E., Zonderman, A. B., Ferrucci, L., & Costa, P. T. (2008). Personality predictors of longevity: Activity, emotional stability, and conscientiousness. *Psychosomatic Medicine, 70,* 621–627.

Terracciano, A., Sanna, S., Uda, M., Deiana, B., et al. (2010). Genome-wide association scan for five major dimensions of personality. *Molecular Psychiatry, 15,* 647–656.

Terracciano, A., Sutin, A. R., McCrae, R. R., Deiana, B., et al. (2009). Facets of personality linked to underweight and overweight. *Psychosomatic Medicine, 71,* 682–689.

Tessari, T., Rubaltelli, E., Tomelleri, S., Zorzi, C., Pietroni, D., Levorato, C., & Rumiati, R. (2011). €1 ≠ €1: Coins versus banknotes and people's spending behavior. *European Psychologist, 16*(3), 238–246. doi:10.1027/1016-9040/a000078.

Thakkar, R. R., Garrison, M. M., & Christakis, D. A. (2006). A systematic review for the effects of television viewing by infants and preschoolers. *Pediatrics, 118,* 2025–2031.

Thaler, E. R., Kennedy, D. W., & Hanson, C. W. (2001). Medical applications of electronic nose technology: Review of current status. *American Journal of Rhinology, 15,* 291–295.

Thase, M. E., Friedman, E. S., Biggs, M. M., Wisniewski, S. R., Trivedi, M. H., Luther, J. F., et al. (2007). Cognitive therapy versus medication in augmentation and switch strategies as second-step treatments: A STAR*D report. *American Journal of Psychiatry, 164,* 739–752.

Thelen, E. (1995). Motor development: A new synthesis. *American Psychologist, 50,* 79–95.

Theofilopoulos, S., Goggi, J., Riaz, S. S., Jauniaux, E., Stern, G. M., & Bradford, H. F. (2001). Parallel induction of the formation of dopamine and its metabolites with induction of tyrosine hydroxylase expression in foetal rat and human cerebral cortical cells by brain-derived neurotrophic factor and glial-cell derived neurotrophic factor. *Brain Research: Developmental Brain Research, 127,* 111–122.

Thiering, E., Brüske, I., Kratzsch, J., Thiery, J., Sausenthaler, S., Meisinger, C., & .. Heinrich, J. (2011). Prenatal and postnatal tobacco smoke exposure and development of insulin resistance in 10 year old children. *International Journal of Hygiene & Environmental Health, 214*(5), 361–368. doi:10.1016/j.ijheh.2011.04.004.

Thiessen, E. D., Hill, E. A., & Saffran, J. R. (2005). Infant-directed speech facilitates word segmentation. *Infancy, 7,* 53–71.

Thom, A., Sartory, G., & Jöhren, P. (2000). Comparison between one-session psychological treatment and benzodiazepine in dental phobia. *Journal of Consulting and Clinical Psychology, 68,* 378–387.

Thomas, A., & Chess, S. (1977). *Temperament and development.* New York: Brunner/Mazel.

Thomas, E. L., & Robinson, H. A. (1972). *Improving reading in every class: A sourcebook for teachers.* Boston: Allyn & Bacon.

Thomas, J. A., & Walton, D. (2007). Measuring perceived risk: Self-reported and actual hand positions of SUV and car drivers. *Traffic Psychology and Behavior, 10,* 201–207.

Thomas, R., & Forde, E. (2006). The role of local and global processing in the recognition of living and nonliving things. *Neuropsychologia, 44*(6), 982–986.

Thompson, D., Baranowski, T., Buday, R., Baranowski, J., Thompson, V., Jago, R., & Griffith, M. (2010). Serious video games for health: How behavioral science guided the development of a serious video game. *Simulation & Gaming, 41*(4), 587–606. doi:10.1177/1046878108328087.

Thompson, E. H., & Hampton, J. A. (2011). The effect of relationship status on communicating emotions through touch. *Cognition & Emotion, 25*(2), 295–306. doi:10.1080/02699931.2010.492957.

Thompson, V. B., Heiman, J., Chambers, J. B., Benoit, S. C., et al. (2009). Long-term behavioral consequences of prenatal MDMA exposure. *Physiology and Behavior, 96,* 593–601.

Thompson, C., Koon, E., Woodwell, W., Jr., & Beauvais, J. (2002). *Training for the next economy: An ASTD state of the industry report on trend in employer-provided training in the United States.* Washington, DC: American Society for Training and Development.

Thompson, D. S., & Pollack, B. G. (2001, August 26). Psychotropic metabolism: Gender-related issues. *Psychiatric Times, 14.* Available: http://www.mhsource.com/pt/p010147.html.

Thompson, E. M., & Morgan, E. M. (2008). "Mostly straight" young women: Variations in sexual behavior and identity development. *Developmental Psychology, 44,* 15–21.

Thompson, J. K. (1996). Introduction: Assessment and treatment of binge eating disorder. In J. K. Thompson (Ed.), *Body image, eating disorders, and obesity* (pp. 1–22). Washington, DC: American Psychological Association.

Thompson, R. A. (2006). The development of the person: Social understanding, relationships, self, conscience. In W. Damon & R. M. Lerner (Series Eds.) & N. Eisenberg (Vol. Ed.), *Handbook of child psychology: Vol. 3. Social, emotional, and personality development* (6th ed.). New York: Wiley.

Thompson, R. R., George, K., Walton, J. C., Orr, S. P., & Benson, J. (2006). Sex-specific influences of vasopressin on human social communication. *Proceedings of the National Academy of Sciences, 103,* 7889–7894.

Thompson-Brenner, H., Glass, S., & Westen, D. (2003). A multidimensional meta-analysis of psychotherapy for bulimia nervosa. *Clinical Psychology: Science and Practice, 10,* 269–287.

Thomsen, L., Green, E. G. T., & Sidanius, J. (2008).We will hunt them down: How social dominance orientation and right-wing authoritarianism fuel ethnic persecution of immigrants in fundamentally different ways. *Journal of Experimental Social Psychology, 44,* 1455–1464.

Thomson, C. P. (1982). Memory for unique personal events: The roommate study. *Memory & Cognition, 10,* 324–332.

Thomson Healthcare (2007). *PDR drug guide for mental health professionals* (3rd ed.). Washington, DC: Physician's Desk Reference.

Thorens, B. (2008). Glucose sensing and the pathogenesis of obesity and type 2 diabetes. *International Journal of Obesity, 32,* S62–S71.

Thorndike, E. L. (1898). Animal intelligence: An experienced study of the associative process in animals. *Psychological Monographs, 2*(Whole No. 8).

Thorndike, E. L. (1905). *The elements of psychology.* New York: Seiler.

Thorndike, R. L., & Hagen, E. P. (1996). *Form 5 CogAT interpretive guide of school administrators: All levels.* Chicago: Riverside.

Thornton, W. E. (2011). A rationale for space motion sickness. Aviation, Space, and Environmental Medicine, 82(4), 467–468.

Thurston, I. B., & Phares, V. (2008). Mental health service utilization in African American and Caucasian mothers and fathers. *Journal of Consulting and Clinical Psychology, 76,* 1058–1067.

Tienari, P., Wynne, L. C., Läksy, K., Moring, J., Nieminen, P., et al. (2003). Genetic boundaries of the schizophrenia spectrum: Evidence from the Finnish Adoptive Family Study of Schizophrenia. *American Journal of Psychiatry, 160,* 1587–1594.

Tierney, J. (2009, March 10). What do dreams mean? Whatever your bias says. *New York Times,* D2.

Tiihonen, J., Kuikka, J., Bergstrom, K., Hakola, P., Karhu, J., Ryynänen, O.-P., & Föhr, J. (1995). Altered striatal dopamine re-uptake site densities in habitually violent and non-violent alcoholics. *Nature Medicine, 1*(7), 654–657.

Tillfors, M., Carlbring, P., Furmark, T., Lewenhaupt, S., et al. (2008). Treating university students with social phobia and public speaking fears: Internet delivered self-help with or without live group exposure sessions. *Depression and Anxiety, 25,* 708–717.

Timko, C., Finney, J. W., & Moos, R. H. (2005). The 8-year course of alcohol abuse: Gender differences in social context and coping. *Alcoholism: Clinical and Experimental Research, 29,* 612–621.

Timms, P. (2005). Is there still a problem with homelessness and schizophrenia? *International Journal of Mental Health, 34,* 57–75.

Tinbergen, N. (1989). *The study of instinct.* Oxford, UK: Clarendon.

Tindale, R. S., & Kameda, T. (2000). "Social sharedness" as a unifying theme for information processing in groups. *Group Processes and Intergroup Relations, 3,* 123–140.

Tindle, H., Belnap, B. H., Houck, P. R., Mazumdar, S., Scheier, M. F., Matthews, K. A., He, F., & Rollman, B. L.(2012). Optimism, response to treatment of depression, and rehospitalization after coronary artery bypass graft surgery. *Psychosomatic Medicine, 74*(2), 200–207. doi:10.1097/PSY.0b013e318244903f.

Tippmann-Piekert, M., Park, J. G., Boeve, B. F., Shepard, J. W., & Silber, M. H. (2007). Pathologic gambling in patients with restless legs syndrome treated with dopaminergic agonists. *Neurology, 68,* 301–303.

Tobler, P. N., Fiorillo, C. D., & Schultz, W. (2005). Adaptive coding of reward value by dopamine neurons. *Science, 307,* 1642–1645.

Todd, A. R., Bodenhausen, G. V., & Galinsky, A. D. (2011). Perspective taking combats the denial of intergroup discrimination. *Journal of Experimental Social Psychology,* doi:10.1016/j.jesp.2011.12.011.

Todd, P. M., & Gigerenzer, G. (2007). Environments that make us smart: Ecological rationality. *Current Directions in Psychological Science, 16,* 167–171.

Toffolo, M. J., Smeets, M. M., & van den Hout, M. A. (2012). Proust revisited: Odours as triggers of aversive memories. *Cognition & Emotion, 26*(1), 83–92. doi:10.1080/02699931.2011.555475.

Tohen, M., Zarate, C. A., Jr., Hennen, J., Khalsa, H.-M. K., Strakowski, S. M., Gebre-Medhin, P., et al. (2003). The McLean-Harvard first-episode mania study: Prediction of recovery and first recurrence. *American Journal of Psychiatry, 160,* 2099–2107.

Tolin, D. F. (2010). Is cognitive-behavioral therapy better than other therapies? A metaanalytic review. *Clinical Psychology Review, 30,* 710–720.

Tolman, E. C., & Honzik, C. H. (1930). Introduction and removal of reward and maze performance in rats. *University of California Publication in Psychology, 4,* 257–265.

Tomasetto, C., Alparone, F., & Cadinu, M. (2011). Girls' math performance under stereotype threat: The moderating role of mothers' gender stereotypes. *Developmental Psychology, 47*(4), 943–949. doi:10.1037/a0024047.

Tomberlin, J. K., Rains, G. C., & Sanford, M. R. (2008). Development of Microplitis croceipes as a biological sensor. *Entomologia Experimentalis et Applicata, 128*(2), 249–257.

Tomes, H. (1999, April). The need for cultural competence. *APA Monitor,* p. 31.

Tomlinson, J. M., Carmichael, C. L., Reis, H. T., & Aron, A., (2010). Affective forecasting and individual differences: Accuracy for relational events and anxious attachment. *Emotion, 10,* 447–453.

Toni, N., Buchs, P. A., Nikonenko, I., Bron, C. R., & Muller, D. (1999). LTP promotes formation of multiple spine synapses between a single axon terminal and a dendrite. *Nature, 402,* 421–425.

Tonnesen, J., Sorensen, A. T., Deisseroth, K., Lundberg, C., & Kokaia, M. (2009). Optogenetic control of epileptiform activity. *Proceedings of the National Academy of Sciences, 106,* 12162–12167. doi:10.1073/pnas.0901915106.

Topakian, R., & Aichner, F. T. (2008). Vascular dementia: A practical update. *Current Medical Literature: Neurology, 24*(1), 1–8.

Topolinski, S. (2011). I 5683 You: Dialing phone numbers on cell phones activates key-concordant concepts. *Psychological Science, 22*(3), 355–360. doi:10.1177/0956797610397668.

Torges, C. M., Stewart, A. J., & Nolen-Hoeksema, S. (2008). Regret resolution, aging, and adapting to loss: Older adults are better than younger ones at resolving their bereavement-related regrets. *Psychology and Aging, 23,* 169–180.

Torry, Z. D., & Billick, S. B. (2010). Overlapping universe: Understanding legal insanity and psychosis. *Psychiatric Quarterly, 81*(3), 253–262. doi:10.1007/s11126-010-9134-2

Tosun, L. P. & Lajunen, T. (2010). Does Internet use reflect your personality? Relationship between Eysenck's personality dimensions and Internet use. *Computers in Human Behavior, 26,* 162–167. doi:10.1016/j.chb.2009.10.010.

Tosun, L. P. & Lajunen, T. (2009). Why do young adults develop a passion for Internet activities? The associations among personality, revealing "true self" on the Internet, and passion for the Internet. *CyberPsychology & Behavior, 12*(4), 401–406. doi:10.1089=cpb.2009.0006.

Touzani, K., Puthanveettil, S. V., & Kandel, E. R. (2007). Consolidation of learning strategies during spatial working memory taks requires protein synthesis in the prefrontal cortex. *Proceedings of the National Academy of Sciences, 104,* 5632–5637.

Trabasso, T. R., & Bower, G. H. (1968). *Attention in learning.* New York: Wiley.

Trachtenberg, F. L., Haas, E. A., Kinney, H. C., Stanley, C., & Krous, H. F. (2012). Risk factor changes for sudden infant death syndrome after initiation of back-to-sleep campaign. *Pediatrics, 129*(4), 630–638. doi:10.1542/peds.2011-1419.

Tramer, M. R., Carroll, D., Campbell, F. A., Reynolds, D. J., Moore, R. A., & McQuay, H. J. (2001). Cannabinoids for control of chemotherapy induced nausea and vomiting: quantitative systematic review. *British Medical Journal, 323,* 16–21.

Tranel, D., & Welsh-Bohmer, K. A. (2012). Pervasive olfactory impairment after bilateral limbic system destruction. *Journal Of Clinical & Experimental Neuropsychology, 34*(2), 117–125. doi:10.1080/13803395.2011.633897.

Tranter, L. J., & Koutstaal, W. (2008). Age and flexible thinking: An experimental demonstration of the beneficial effects of increased cognitively stimulating activity on fluid intelligence in healthy older adults. *Aging, Neuropsychology, and Cognition, 15*(2), 184–207.

Treat, T. A., & Viken, R. J. (2010). Cognitive processing of weight and emotional information in disordered eating. *Current Directions in Psychological Science, 19*(2), 81–85. doi:10.1177/0963721410364007.

Treboux, D., Crowell, J. A., & Waters, E. (2004). When "new" meets "old": Configurations of adult attachment representations and their implications for marital functioning. *Developmental Psychology, 40,* 295–314.

Tregear, S., Reston, J., Schoelles, K., & Phillips, B. (2009). Obstructive sleep apnea and risk of motor vehicle crash: Systematic review and meta-analysis. *Journal of Clinical Sleep Medicine, 5*(6), 573–581.

Treiber, F. A., Musante, L., Kapuku, G., Davis, C., Litaker, M., & Davis, H. (2001). Cardiovascular (CV) responsivity and recovery to acute stress and future CV functioning in youth with family histories of CV disease: A 4-year longitudinal study. *International Journal of Psychophysiology, 41,* 65–74.

Treisman, A. (1999). Feature binding, attention, and object perception. In G. W. Humphreys, J. Duncan., & A. Treisman (Eds.), *Attention, space, and action* (pp. 91–111). New York: Oxford University Press.

Tremblay, R. E., Pihl, R. O., Vitaro, F., & Dobkin, P. (1994). Predicting early onset of male antisocial behavior from preschool behavior. *Archives of General Psychiatry, 51,* 732–739.

Trevor, C. O. (2001). Interactions among actual ease-of-movement determinants and job satisfaction in the prediction of voluntary turnover. *Academy of Management Journal, 44,* 621–638.

Triandis, H. C., & Trafimow, D. (2001). Cross-national prevalence of collectivism. In C. Sedikides & M. B. Brewer (Eds.), *Individual self, relational self, collective self* (pp. 259–276). New York: Psychology Press.

Trickett, S., Trafton, J., & Schunn, C. D. (2009). How do scientists respond to anomalies? Different strategies used in basic and applied science. *Topics in Cognitive Science, 1*(4), 711–729. doi:10.1111/j.1756-8765.2009.01036.x.

Trierweiler, S. J., Muroff, J. R., Jackson, M. S., Neighbors, H. W., & Munday, C. (2005). Clinician race, situational attributions, and diagnoses of mood versus schizophrenia disorders. *Cultural Diversity & Ethnic Minority Psychology, 11,* 351–364.

Trierweiler, S. J., Neighbors, H. W., Munday, C., Thompson, E. E., Binion, V. J., & Gomez, J. P. (2000). Clinician attributions associated with the diagnosis of schizophrenia in African American and non-African American patients. *Journal of Consulting and Clinical Psychology, 68,* 171–175.

Trifiletti, L. B., Shields, W., McDonald, E., Reynaud, F., & Gielen, A. (2006). Tipping the scales: Obese children and child safety seats. *Pediatrics, 117,* 1197–1202.

Trillin, A. S. (2001, January 29). Betting your life. *New Yorker,* pp. 38–41.

Triscari, J. D., Faraci, P., D'Angelo, V., Urso, V., & Catalisano, D. (2011). Two treatments for fear of flying compared: Cognitive behavioral therapy combined with systematic desensitization or eye movement desensitization and reprocessing (EMDR). *Aviation Psychology and Applied Human Factors, 1*(1), 9–14. doi:10.1027/2192-0923/a00003.

Troisi, J. D., & Gabriel, S. (2011). "Chicken soup really is good for the soul: "Comfort food" fulfills the need to belong. *Psychological Science, 22*(6) 747–753. doi:10.1177/0956797611407931.

Tronick, E. Z., Messinger, D. S., Weinberg, M. K., Lester, B. M., LaGasse, L., Seifer, R., et al. (2005). Cocaine exposure is associated with subtle compromises of infants' and mothers' social-emotional behavior and dyadic features of their interaction in the face-to-face still-face paradigm. *Developmental Psychology, 41,* 711–722.

Trope, Y. (1983). Self-assessment in achievement behavior. In J. Suls & A. G. Greenwald (Eds.), *Psychological perspectives on the self* (Vol. 2, pp. 93–121). Hillsdale, NJ: Lawrence Erlbaum.

Trope, Y. (1975). Seeking information about one's own ability as a determinant of choice among tasks. *Journal of Personality and Social Psychology, 32,* 1004–1013.

Tropp, L. R., & Pettigrew, T. F. (2005). Relationships between intergroup contact and prejudice among minority and majority status groups. *Psychological Science, 16,* 951–957.

Trotter, M. I., & Morgan, D. W. (2008). Patients' use of the Internet for health related matters: A study of Internet usage in 2000 and 2006. *Health Informatics Journal, 14*(3), 175–181.

Trout, J., & Christie, B. (2007). Interactive Video Games in Physical Education. *JOPERD: The Journal of Physical Education, Recreation & Dance, 78*(5), 29–45.

Truelsen, T., & Bonita, R. (2003). Advances in ischemic stroke epidemiology. *Advances in Neurology, 92,* 1–12.

Trull, T. J., & Sher, K. J. (1994). Relationship between the five-factor model of personality and Axis I disorders in a nonclinical sample. *Journal of Personality and Social Psychology, 103,* 350–360.

Trumbetta, S. L., Seltzer, B. K., Gottsman, I. I., & McIntyre, K. M. (2010). Mortality predictors in a 60-year follow-up of adolescent males: Exploring delinquency, socioeconomic status, IQ, high school dropout status, and personality. *Psychosomatic Medicine, 72,* 46–52.

Trunko, M., Schwartz, T. A., Duvvuri, V., & Kaye, W. H. (2011). Aripiprazole in anorexia nervosa and low-weight bulimia nervosa: Case reports. *International Journal of Eating Disorders, 44*(3), 269–275. doi:10.1002/eat.20807.

Trunzo, J. J., & Pinto, B. M. (2003). Social support as a mediator of optimisim and distress in breast cancer survivors. *Journal of Consulting and Clinical Psychology, 71,* 805–811.

Tryon, W. W. (2005). Possible mechanisms for why desensitization and exposure therapy work. *Clinical Psychology Review, 25,* 67–95.

Tsai, J. L., Knutson, B., & Fung, H. H. (2006). Cultural variation in affect evaluation. *Journal of Personality and Social Psychology, 90,* 288–307.

Tsai, J. L., Levenson, R. W., & McCoy, K. (2006). Cultural and temperamental variation in emotional response. *Emotion, 6,* 484–497.

Tsang, J. S., Naughton, P. A., Leong, S., Hill, A. D. K., Kelly, C. J., & Leahy, A. L. (2008). Virtual reality simulation in endovascular surgical training. *Surgeon, 6*(4), 214–220.

Tsethlikai, M. (2011). An exploratory analysis of American Indian children's cultural engagement, fluid cognitive skills, and standardized verbal IQ scores. *Developmental Psychology, 47*(1), 192–202. doi:10.1037/a0020803.

Tsuang, M. T., Stone, W. S., & Faraone, S. V. (2000). Toward reformulating the diagnosis of schizophrenia. *American Journal of Psychiatry, 157,* 1041–1950.

Tuch, S. A., & Martin, J. K. (1991). Race in the workplace: Black/white differences in the sources of job satisfaction. *The Sociological Quarterly, 32,* 103–116.

Tucker, J. S., Green, H. D., Zhou, A. J., Miles, J. V., Shih, R. A., & D'Amico, E. J. (2011). Substance use among middle school students: Associations with self-rated and peer-nominated popularity. *Journal of Adolescence, 34*(3), 513–519. doi:10.1016/j.adolescence.2010.05.016

Tucker-Drob, E. M. (2012). Preschools reduce early academic-achievement gaps: A longitudinal twin approach. *Psychological Science, 23*(3), 310–319. doi:10.1177/0956797611426728.

Tucker-Drob, E. M. (2011). Global and domain-specific changes in cognition throughout adulthood. *Developmental Psychology, 47*(2), 331–343.

Tucker-Drob, E. M., & Harden, K. (2012b). Intellectual interest mediates gene × socioeconomic status interaction on adolescent academic achievement. *Child Development, 83*(2), 743–757. doi:10.1111/j.1467-8624.2011.01721.x.

Tucker-Drob, E. M., & Harden, K. (2012a). Early childhood cognitive development and parental cognitive stimulation: Evidence for reciprocal gene-environment transactions. *Developmental Science, 15*(2), 250–259. doi:10.1111/j.1467-7687.2011.01121.x.

Tucker-Drob, E. M., Rhemtulla, M., Harden, K., Turkheimer, E., & Fask, D. (2011). Emergence of a gene 3 socioeconomic status interaction on infant mental ability between 10 months and 2 years. *Psychological Science, 22*(1), 125–133. doi:10.1177/0956797610392926.

Tuller, D. (2004, January 27). Britain poised to approve medicine derived from marijuana. *New York Times,* p. F5.

Tulving, E. (1983). *Elements of episodic memory.* New York: Oxford University Press.

Tulving, E. (2000). Introduction to memory. In M. S. Gazzaniga (Ed.), *The new cognitive neurosciences* (pp. 727–732). Cambridge, MA: MIT Press.

Tulving, E. (2005). Episodic memory and autonoesis: Uniquely human? In H. S. Terrace and J. Metcalfe (Eds.), *The missing link in cognition: Origins of self-reflective consciousness* (pp. 3–56). New York: Oxford University Press.

Tulving, E., & Psotka, J. (1971). Retroactive inhibition in free recall: Inaccessibility of information available in the memory store. *Journal of Experimental Psychology, 87,* 1–8.

Turati, C. (2004). Why faces are not special to newborns: An alternative account of the face preference. *Current Directions in Psychological Science, 13,* 5–8.

Turiel, E. (2006). The development of morality. In W. Damon & R. M. Lerner (Series Eds.) & N. Eisenberg (Vol. Ed.), *Handbook of child psychology: Vol. 3. Social, emotional, and personality development* (6th ed.). New York: Wiley.

Turkheimer, E., Haley, A., Waldron, M., D'Onofrio, B., & Gottesman, I. I. (2003). Socioeconomic status modifies heritability of IQ in young children. *Psychological Science, 14,* 623–628.

Turkheimer, E., & Waldron M. (2000). Nonshared environment: A theoretical, methodological, and quantitative review. *Psychological Bulletin, 126,* 78–108.

Turkington, C. (1987). Special talents. *Psychology Today,* pp. 42–46.

Turnbull, C. (1961). Some observations regarding the experiences and behavior of the Bambuti Pygmies. *American Journal of Psychology, 74,* 304–308.

Turner, E. H., Matthews, A. M., Linardatos, E., Tell, R. A., & Rosenthal, R. (2008). Selective publication of antidepressant trials and its influence on apparent efficacy. *New England Journal of Medicine, 358,* 252–260.

Turner, R. J., & Lloyd, D. A. (2004). Stress burden and the lifetime incidence of psychiatric disorder in young adults: Racial and ethnic contrasts. *Archives of General Psychiatry, 61,* 481–488.

Turner, S. M., DeMers, S. T., Fox, H. R., & Reed, G. M. (2001). APA's guidelines for test user qualifications: An executive summary. *American Psychologist, 56,* 1099–1113.

Tuszynski, M. H., Thal, L., Pay, M., Salmon, D. P., U, H. S., Bakay, R., et al. (2005). A phase 1 clinical trial of nerve growth factor gene therapy for Alzheimer disease. *Nature Medicine, 11,* 551–555.

Tversky, A., & Kahneman, D. (1974). Judgment under uncertainty: Heuristics and biases. *Science, 185,* 1124–1131.

Tversky, A., & Kahneman, D. (1981). The framing of decisions and the psychology of choice. *Science, 211,* 453–458.

Tversky, A., & Kahneman, D. (1991). Loss aversion in riskless choice: A reference dependent model. *Quarterly Journal of Economics, 106,* 1039–1061.

Tversky, A., & Kahneman, D. (1993). Probabilistic reasoning. In A. Goldman (Ed.), *Readings in philosophy and cognitive science* (pp. 43–68). Cambridge: MIT Press.

Tversky, B., & Tuchin, M. (1989). A reconciliation of the evidence on eyewitness testimony: Comments on McCloskey and Zaragoza. *Journal of Experimental Psychology: General, 118,* 86–91.

Twenge, J. M., Gentile, B., DeWall, C. N., Ma, D., et al. (2010). Birth cohort increases in psychopathology among young Americans, 1938–2007: A cross-temporal meta-analysis of the MMPI. *Clinical Psychology Review, 30,* 145–154.

Tybur, J. M., Bryan, A. D., Magnan, R. E., & Caldwell Hooper, A. E. (2011). Smells like safe sex: Olfactory pathogen primes increase intentions to use condoms. *Psychological Science, 22*(4), 478–480. doi:10.1177/0956797611400096.

Tyler, K. L., & Malessa, R. (2000). The Goltz-Ferrier debates and the triumph of cerebral localizationist theory. *Neurology, 55*(7), 1015–1024.

Uchida, Y., & Kitayama, S. (2009). Happiness and unhappiness in East and West: Themes and variations. *Emotion, 9,* 441–456.

Uchida, Y., Kitayama, S., Mesquita, B., & Reyes, J. A. (2001, June). *Interpersonal sources of happiness: The relative significance in Japan, the Philippines, and the United States.* Paper presented at Annual Convention of American Psychological Society, Toronto, Canada.

Uddin, M., Aiello, A. E., Wildman, D. E., Koenen, K. C., et al. (2010). Epigenetic and immune function profiles associated with posttraumatic stress disorder. *Proceedings of the National Academy of Sciences, 107,* 9470. doi:10.1073/pnas.0910794107.

Udry, J. R., & Chantala, K. (2003). Masculinity-femininity guides sexual union formation in adolescents. *Personality and Social Psychology Bulletin, 30,* 44–55.

Ugajin, T., Hozawa, A., Ohkubo, T., Asayama, K., Kikuya, M., Obara, T., et al. (2005). White-coat hypertension as a risk factor for the development of home hypertension: The Ohasama study. *Archives of Internal Medicine, 165,* 1541–1546.

Ugwu, L. (2010). Employed "sandwich" generation women: Coping with work/family conflicts. *European Journal of Social Science, 15*(3), 396–410.

Uhl-Bien, M., Marion, R., & McKelvey, B. (2007). Complexity leadership theory: Shifting leadership from the Industrial Age to the Knowledge Era. *Leadership Quarterly, 18,* 298–318.

Uleman, J. S., Blader, S. L., & Todorov, A. (2005). Implicit impressions In R. Hassin, J. Uleman, & J. Bargh (Eds.), *The new unconscious* (pp. 362– 392). New York: Oxford University Press.

Ulett, G. A. (2003). Acupuncture, magic, and make-believe. *The Skeptical Inquirer, 27*(2), 47–50.

Um, E., Plass, J. L., Hayward, E. O., & Homer, B. D. (2011). Emotional design in multimedia learning. *Journal Of Educational Psychology,* doi:10.1037/a0026609.

Umbreit, J., Ferro, J., Liaupsin, C. J., & Lane, K. L. (2006). *Functional behavioral assessment and function-based intervention: An effective, practical approach.* Upper Saddle River, NJ: Prentice Hall.

Underdown, J. (2011). Power balance bracelets a bust in tests. *Skeptical Inquirer, 36,* 14–16.

Ungemach, C., Chater, N., & Stewart, N. (2009). Are probabilities overweighted or underweighted when rare outcomes are experienced (rarely)? *Psychological Science, 20,* 473–479.

Ungerleider, L. G., & Mishkin, M. (1982). Two cortical visual systems. In D. J. Ingle, M. A. Goodale, & R. J. W. Mansfield (Eds.), *Analysis of visual behavior.* Cambridge, MA: MIT Press.

Urbach, T. P., Windmann, S. S., Payne, D. G., & Kutas, M. (2005). Mismaking memories. *Psychological Science, 16,* 19–24.

Urquhart, B. L., & Kim, R. B. (2009). Blood-brain barrier transporters and response to CNS-active drugs. *European Journal of Clinical Pharmacology, 65,* 1063–1070.

Urry, H. L., & Gross, J. J. (2010). Emotion regulation in older age. *Current Directions in Psychological Science, 19,* 352–357.

Urry, H. L., Nitschke, J. B., Dolski, I., Jackson, D. C., Dalton, K. M., Mueller, C. J., et al. (2004). Making a life worth living: Neural correlates of well-being. *Psychological Science, 15,* 367–372.

Ursu, S., Kring, A. M., Gard, M., Minzenberg, M. J., Yoon, J. H., Ragland, J., & … Carter, C. S. (2011). Prefrontal cortical deficits and impaired cognition-emotion interactions in schizophrenia. *The American Journal Of Psychiatry, 168*(3), 279–285. doi:10.1176/appi.ajp.2010.09081215

U.S. Bureau of Labor Statistics. (2007). *Injuries, illnesses, and fatalities, 2005.* Washington, DC: U.S. Department of Labor. Retrieved May 9, 2007, from http://www.bls.gov/iif/home. htm#tables.

U.S. Census Bureau. (2012). Statistical Abstract of the United States. Retrieved from http://www.census.gov/compendia/statab/2012/tables/12s0133.pdf.

U.S. Department of Health and Human Services Office of Applied Studies. (2003). *Results from the 2002 National Survey on Drug Use and Health: Summary of national finding* (DHHS Publication No. SMA 03-3836, NHSDA Series H-22). Rockville, MD: Substance Abuse and Mental Health Services Administration.

U.S. Department of Justice. (1999). *Eyewitness evidence: A guide for law enforcement.* Washington, DC: National Institute of Justice.

U.S. Department of Justice. (2002). *Recidivism of prisoners released in 1994.* Washington, DC: U.S. Department of Justice, Bureau of Justice Statistics.

U.S. Department of Justice. (2007). *Crime characteristics.* Retrieved January 31, 2007, from http://www.ojp.usdoj.gov/bjs/cvict_c.htm#relate.

U.S. Department of Justice, Office of Justice Programs, Bureau of Justice Statistics. (2011). *Workplace violence, 1993-2009: National crime victimization survey and the census of fatal occupational injuries.* (DOJ Publication no. ncj 233231). Retrieved from http://bjs.gov/content/pub/pdf/wv09.pdf

Usher, A. (2011). *Annual yearly progress results for 2010–2011.* Washington, D.C.: Center on Education Policy.

U.S. Surgeon General. (1999). *Mental health: A report of the surgeon general.* Rockville, MD: U.S. Department of Health and Human Services.

Üstün B., & Kennedy, C. (2009). What is "functional impairment"? Disentangling disability from clinical significance. *World Psychiatry, 8,* 82–85.

Uther, M. M., & Haley, H. H. (2008). Back vs. stack: Training the correct mental model affects web browsing. *Behaviour & Information Technology, 27*(3), 211–218. doi:10.1080/01449290600956357.

Uttal, W. R. (2003). *The new phrenology: The limits of localizing cognitive processes in the brain.* Cambridge, MA: MIT Press.

Uvnas-Moberg, K., Arn, I., & Magnusson, D. (2005). The psychobiology of emotion: The role of the oxytocinergic system. *International Journal of Behavioral Medicine, 12,* 59–65.

Uwe, H. (2005). Therapeutic alliance: The best synthesizer of social influences on the therapeutic situation? On links to other constructs, determinants of its effectiveness, and its role for research in psychotherapy in general. *Psychotherapy Research, 15,* 9–23.

Uziel, L. (2007). Individual differences in the social facilitation effect: A review and metaanalysis. *Journal of Research in Personality, 41,* 579–601.

Uziel, L. (2010). Rethinking social desirability scales: From impression management to interpersonally oriented self-control. *Perspectives on Psychological Science, 5,* 243–262.

Vahia, I. V., & Cohen, C. I. (2009). Psychosocial factors. In K. T. Mueser & D. V. Jeste (Eds.), *Clinical handbook of schizophrenia.* (pp. 74–81). New York: Guilford Press.

Vaitl, D., Birbaumer, N., Gruzelier, J., Jamieson, G. A., Kotchoubey, B., Kubler, A., et al. (2005). Psychobiology of altered states of consciousness. *Psychological Bulletin, 131,* 98–127.

Valdés-Sosa, M., Bobes, M. A., Quiñones, I., Garcia, L., Valdes-Hernandez, P. A, Iturria, Y., Melie-Garcia, L., Lopera, F., & Asencio, J. (2011). Covert face recognition without the fusiform-temporal pathways. *Neuroimage, 57*(3), 1162–1176.

Valentine, T., & Maras, K. (2011). The effect of cross-examination on the accuracy of adult eyewitness testimony. *Applied Cognitive Psychology, 25*(4), 554–561. doi:10.1002/acp.1768.

Valenza, E., Simion, F., Assia, V. M., & Umilta, C. (1996). Face preference at birth. *Journal of Experimental Psychology: Human Perception and Performance, 22,* 892–903.

Valenza, E., & Bulf, H. (2007). The role of kinetic information in newborns' perception of illusory contours. *Developmental Science, 10*(4), 492-501.

Valkenburg, P. M., & Peter, J. (2007a). Preadolescents' and adolescents' online communication and their closeness to friends. *Developmental Psychology, 43*(2), 267–277.

Valkenburg, P. M., & Peter, J. (2009). Social consequences of the Internet for adolescents: A decade of research. *Current Directions in Psychological Science, 18,* 1–5.

Vallerand, R., Paquet, Y., Philippe, F., & Charest, J. (2010). On the role of passion for work in burnout: a process model. *Journal Of Personality, 78*(1), 289–312.

Vallotton, C. D. (2008). Signs of emotion: What can preverbal children "say" about internal states? *Infant Mental Health Journal, 29,* 234–258.

Valuck, R. J., Libby, A. M., Benton, T., D., & Evans, D. L. (2007). A descriptive analysis of 10,000 suicide attempters in the Unites States managed care plans, 1998–2005. *Primary Psychiatry, 14,* 52–60.

Van Allen, J., & Roberts, M. C. (2011). Critical incidents in the marriage of psychology and technology: A discussion of potential ethical issues in practice, education, and policy. *Professional Psychology: Research and Practice, 42*(6), 433–439. doi:10.1037/a0025278.

van Beek, J. A., Kendler, K. S., de Moor, M. M., Geels, L. M., Bartels, M., Vink, J. M., & … Boomsma, D. I. (2012). Stable genetic effects on symptoms of alcohol abuse and dependence from adolescence into early adulthood. *Behavior Genetics, 42*(1), 40–56. doi:10.1007/s10519-011-9488-8

Van Bezooijen, R., Otto, S. A., & Heenan, T. A. (1983). Recognition of vocal expression of emotion: A three-nation study to identify universal characteristics. *Journal of Cross-Cultural Psychology, 14,* 387–406.

van Dam, R. M., Li, T., Spiegelman, D., Franco, O. H., & Hu, F. B. (2008). Combined impact of lifestyle factors on mortality: prospective cohort study in US women. *British Medical Journal, 337,* a1440.

Vandello, J. A., & Cohen, D. (1999). Patterns of individualism and collectivism across the United States. *Journal of Personality and Social Psychology, 77,* 279–292.

van den Bos, W., van Dijk, E., Westenberg, M., Rombouts, S. B., & Crone, E. A. (2011). Changing brains, changing perspectives: The neurocognitive development of reciprocity. *Psychological Science, 6*(1), 60–70. doi:10.1177/0956797610391102.

van den Hout, M. A., Engelhard, I. M., Beetsma, D., Slofstra, C., Hornsveld, H., Houtveen, J., & Leer, A. (2011). EMDR and mindfulness. Eye movements and attentional breathing tax working memory and reduce vividness and emotionality of aversive ideation. *Journal of Behavior Therapy & Experimental Psychiatry, 42*(4), 423–431. doi:10.1016/j.jbtep.2011.03.004.

van der Kloet, D., Merckelbach, H., Giesbrecht, T., & Lynn, S. (2012). Fragmented sleep, fragmented mind: The role of sleep in dissociative symptoms. *Perspectives on Psychological Science, 7*(2), 159–175. doi:10.1177/1745691612437597.

van de Ven, N., Zeelenberg, M., & Pieters, R. (2011). Why envy outperforms admiration. *Personality And Social Psychology Bulletin, 37*(6), 784–795. doi:10.1177/0146167211400421.

van de Ven, N., Zeelenberg, M., & Pieters, R. (2010). Warding Off the Evil Eye: When the Fear of Being Envied Increases Prosocial Behavior. *Psychological Science (Sage Publications Inc.), 21*(11), 1671–1677. doi:10.1177/0956797610385352.

Van den Bergh, B. R., & Marcoen, A. (2004). High antenatal maternal anxiety is related to ADHD symptoms, externalizing problems, and anxiety in 8- and 9-year-olds. *Child Development, 75,* 1085–1097.

van der Does, W. (2006). Has everyone won, and must all have prizes? *Psycholoog, 41*(12), 650–657.

van der Hart, O., Bolt, H., & van der Kolk, B. A. (2005). Memory fragmentation in dissociative identity disorder. *Journal of Trauma & Dissociation, 6*(1), 55–70.

van der Kooy-Hofland, V. C., van der Kooy, J., Bus, A. G., van IJzendoorn, M. H., & Bonsel, G. J. (2012). Differential susceptibility to early literacy intervention in children with mild perinatal adversities: Short and long-term effects of a randomized control trial. *Journal of Educational Psychology, 104,* 337–349. doi:10.1037/a0026984

Van der Molen, J. H. W. (2004). Violence and suffering in television news: Toward a broader conception of harmful television content for children. *Pediatrics, 113,* 1771–1775.

Van Deusen, K. M. (2004). Bilateral stimulation in EMDR: A replicated single-subject component analysis. *Behavior Therapist, 27,* 79–86.

van Dick, R., Stellmacher, J., Wagner, U., Lemmer, G., & Tissington, P. A. (2009). Group membership salience and task performance. *Journal of Managerial Psychology, 24,* 609–626.

Van Durme, K., Goossens, L., & Braet, C. (2012). Adolescent aesthetic athletes: A group at risk for eating pathology? *Eating Behaviors, 13*(2), 119–122. doi:10.1016/j.eatbeh.2011.11.002.

Van Eerde, W., & Thierry, H. (1996). Vrooms's expectancy models and work-related criteria: A meta-analysis. *Journal of Applied Psychology, 81,* 575–586.

van Goozen, S. H. M., Fairchild, G., Snoek, H., & Harold, G. T. (2007). The evidence for a neurobiological model of childhood antisocial behavior. *Psychological Bulletin, 133,* 149–182.

van Haren, N.E.M., Rijsdijk, F., Schnack, H.G., Picchioni, M.M., Toulopoulou, T., Weisbrod, M., Sauer, H., van Erp, T.G., Cannon, T.D., Huttunen, M.O., Boomsma, D.I., Hulshoff Pol, H.E., Murray, R.M., & Kahn, R.S. (2012). The genetic and environmental determinants of the association between brain abnormalities and schizophrenia: The schizophrenia twins and relatives consortium. *Biological Psychiatry, 71,* 915–921.

Vanhaudenhuyse, A., Boly, M., Balteau, E., Schnakers, C., Moonen, G., Luxen, A., Lamy, M., Degueldre, C., Brichant, J. F., Maquet, P., Laureys, S., & Faymonville, M. E. (2009). Pain and non-pain processing during hypnosis: A thulium-YAG event-related fMRI study. *NeuroImage, 47*(3), 1047–1054.

Van Hiel, A., & Mervielde, I. (2004). Openness to experience and boundaries in the mind: Relationships with cultural and economic conservative beliefs. *Journal of Personality, 72,* 659–686.

van Hooft, E. J., & Born, M. h. (2012). Intentional response distortion on personality tests: Using eye-tracking to understand response processes when faking. *Journal of Applied Psychology, 97,* 301–316. doi:10.1037/a0025711.

Van Hulle, C. A., Waldman, I. D., D'Onofrio, B. M., Rogers, J. L., et al. (2009). Developmental structure of genetic influences on antisocial behavior across childhood and adolescence. *Journal of Abnormal Psychology, 118,* 711–721.

Van Hulst, A., Seguin, L., Zunzunegui, M., Velez, M. P., & Nikiema, B. (2011). The influence of poverty and social support on the perceived health of children born to minority migrant mothers. *Ethnicity & Health, 16,* 185–200. doi:10.1080/13557858.2011.559536

van IJzendoom, M. H., & Juffer, F. (2005). Adoption as a successful natural intervention enhancing adopted children's IQ and school performance. *Current Directions in Psychological Science, 14,* 326–330.

van IJzendoorn, M. H. (1995). Adult attachment representations, parental responsiveness, and infant attachment: A meta-analysis on the predictive validity of the Adult Attachment Interview. *Psychological Bulletin, 117,* 387–403.

Van Kleef, G. A., Homan, A. C., Beersma, B., & van Knippenberg, D. (2010). On angry leaders and agreeable followers: How leaders' emotions and followers' personalities shape motivation and team performance. *Psychological Science, 21*(12) 1827–1834. doi:10.1177/0956797610387438.

Vanman, E. J., Saltz, J. L., Nathan, L. R., & Warren, J. A. (2004). Racial discrimination by low-prejudiced whites. *Psychological Science, 15,* 711–714.

Van Meter, A. R., Youngstrom, E. A., & Findling, R. L. (2012). Cyclothymic disorder: A critical review. *Clinical Psychology Review, 32,* 229–243. doi:10.1016/j.cpr.2012.02.001

van Noorden, M. S., van Dongen, L. C., Zitman, F. G., & Vergouwen, T. A. (2009). Gammahydroxybutyrate withdrawal syndrome: Dangerous but not well known. *General Hospital Psychiatry, 31,* 394–396.

Van Oort, F. V. A., vanderEnde, J., Wadsworth, M. E., Verhulst, F. C., & Achenbach, T. M. (2011). Cross-national comparison of the link between socioeconomic status and emotional and behavioral problems in youths. *Social Psychiatry and Psychiatric Epidemiology, 46,* 167–172.

Van Orden, K. A., Witte, T. K., Cukrowicz, K. C., Braithwaite, S. R., et al. (2010). The interpersonal theory of suicide. *Psychological Review, 117,* 575–600.

van Os, J., Kenis, G., & Rutten, B. P. F. (2010). The environment and schizophrenia. *Nature, 468,* 203–212. doi:10.1038/nature09563.

van Rood, Y. R., & de Roos, C. (2009). EMDR in the treatment of medically unexplained symptoms: A systematic review. *Journal of EMDR Practice and Research, 3*(4), 248–263. doi:10.1891/1933-3196.3.4.248.

van Schijndel, T. P., Singer, E., van der Maas, H. J., & Raijmakers, M. J. (2010). A sciencing programme and young children's exploratory play in the sandpit. *European Journal of Developmental Psychology, 7*(5), 603–617. doi:10.1080/17405620903412344.

Vasconcellos-Silva, P., Castiel, L., Bagrichevsky, M., & Griep, R. (2010). New information technologies and health consumerism. *Cadernos De Saúde Pública / Ministério Da Saúde, Fundação Oswaldo Cruz, Escola Nacional De Saúde Pública, 26*(8), 1473–1482.

Vansteenkiste, M., Sierens, E., Soenens, B., Luyckx, K., & Lens, W. (2009). Motivational profiles from a self-determination theory perspective: Quality of motivation matters. *Journal of Educational Psychology, 101,* 671–688.

Vansteenkiste, M., Simons, J., Lens, W., Soenens, B., & Matos, L. (2005). Examining the Motivational impact of intrinsic versus extrinsic goal framing and autonomy-supportive versus internally-controlling communication style on early adolescents' academic achievement. *Child Development, 76,* 483–501.

van Wel, F., ter Bogt, T., & Raaijmakers, Q. (2002). Changes in the parental bond and the well-being of adolescents and young adults. *Adolescence, 37*(146), 317–333.

Varnum, M. W., Grossmann, I., Kitayama, S., & Nisbett, R. E. (2010). The origin of cultural differences in cognition: The social orientation hypothesis. *Current Directions in Psychological Science, 19*(1), 9–13. doi:10.1177/0963721409359301.

Varnum, M. E. W., Grossmann, I., Katunar, D., Nisbett, R. E., & Kitayama, S. (2008). Holism in a European cultural context: Differences in cognitive style between Central and East Europeans and westerners. *Journal of Cognition & Culture, 8*(3–4), 321–333.

Vartanian, O., Stewart, K., Mandel, D. R., Pavlovic, N., McLellan, L., & Taylor, P. J. (2012). Personality assessment and behavioral prediction at first impression. *Personality and Individual Differences, 52,* 250–254. doi:10.1016/j.paid.2011.05.024.

Vasconcellos-Silva, P., Castiel, L., Bagrichevsky, M., & Griep, R. (2010). New information technologies and health consumerism. *Cadernos De Saúde Pública / Ministério Da Saúde, Fundação Oswaldo Cruz, Escola Nacional De Saúde Pública, 26*(8), 1473–1482.

Vasey, P. L., & VanderLaan, D. P. (2007). Birth order and male androphilia in Samoan fa'afafine. *Proceedings of the Royal Society: Biological Sciences, 274*(1616), 1437–1442.

Vasilakopoulou, A., & le Roux, C. W. (2007). Could a virus contribute to weight gain? *International Journal of Obesity, 31,* 1350–1356.

Vasquez, M. J. T. (2007). Cultural difference and the therapeutic alliance: An evidence-based analysis. *American Psychologist, 62,* 878–885.

Vasquez, M. J. T., & Jones, J. M. (2006). Increasing the number of psychologists of color: Public policy issues for affirmative diversity. *American Psychologist, 61,* 132–142.

Veale, D. (2009). Body dysmorphic disorder. In M. M. Antony & M. B. Stein, (Eds.). *Oxford handbook of anxiety and related disorders* (pp. 541–550). New York: Oxford University Press USA.

Vecchione, M., Schoen, H., Castro, J. L. G., Cieciuch, J., Pavlopoulos, V. & Caprara, G. V. (2011). Personality correlates of party preference: The Big Five in five big European countries, *Personality and Individual Differences, 51,* 737–742.

Vecera, S. P., Vogel, E. K., & Woodman, G. F. (2002). Lower region: A new cue for figure-ground assignment. *Journal of Experimental Psychology: General, 131,* 194–205.

Velicer, C. M., Heckbert, S. R., Lampe, J. W., Potter, J. D., Robertson, C. A., & Taplin, S. H. (2004). Antibiotic use in relation to the risk of breast cancer. *Journal of the American Medical Association, 291,* 827–835.

Velik, R. (2010). Why machines cannot feel. *Minds and Machines, 20*(1), 1–18. doi:10.1007/s11023-010-9186-y.

Velligan, D. I., Bow-Thomas, C. C., Huntzinger, C., Ritch, J., Ledbetter, N., Prihoda, T. J., & Miller, A. L. (2000). Randomized controlled trial of the use of compensatory strategies to enhance adaptive functioning in outpatients with schizophrenia. *American Journal of Psychiatry, 157,* 1317–1328.

Vemuganti, R., Kalluri, H., Yi, J., Bowen, K. K., & Hazell, A. S. (2006). Gene expression changes in thalamus and inferior colliculus associated with inflammation, cellular stress, metabolism and structural damage in thiamine deficiency. *European Journal of Neuroscience, 23*(5), 1172–1188.

Vemuri, M., Kenna, H. A., Wang, P. W., Ketter, T. A., & Rasgon, N. L. (2011). Gender-specific lipid profiles in patients with bipolar disorder. *Journal of Psychiatry Research, 45,* 1036–1041.

Venâncio, C., Magalhães, A., Antunes, L., & Summavielle, T. (2011). Impaired spatial memory after ketamine administration in chronic low doses. *Current Neuropharmacology, 9*(1), 251–255.

Vennemann, M. M., Bajanowski, T., Brinkmann, B., Jorch, G., Sauerland, C., & Mitchell, E. A. (2009a). Sleep environment risk factors for sudden infant death syndrome: The German sudden infant death syndrome study. *Pediatrics, 123,* 1162–1170.

Vennemann, M. M., Bajanowski, T., Brinkmann, B., Jorch, G., Yücesan, K., Sauerland, C., & Mitchell, E. A. (2009b). Does breastfeeding reduce the risk of sudden infant death syndrome? *Pediatrics, 123,* e406–e410.

Venter, J. C., et al. (2001). The sequence of the human genome. *Science, 291,* 1304–1351.

Ventura, S. J., & Hamilton, B. E. (2011, February). U.S. Teenage birth rate resumes decline. (NCHS Data Brief No. 58). Washington, DC: U. S. Department of Health and Human Services, Centers for Disease Control and Prevention, National Center for Health Statistics. Retrieved from http://www.cdc.gov/nchs/data/databriefs/db58.pdf.

Verghese, J., LeValley, A., Derby, C., Kuslansky, G., Katz, M., Buschke, H., et al. (2006). Leisure activities and the risk of amnestic mild cognitive impairment in the elderly. *Neurology, 66,* 821–827.

Verghese, J., Lipton, R. B., Katz, M. J., Hall, C. B., Derby, C. A., Kuslansky, G., et al. (2003). Leisure activities and the risk of dementia in the elderly. *New England Journal of Medicine, 348,* 2508–2516.

Verhaeghen, P. (2011). Aging and executive control: Reports of a demise greatly exaggerated. *Current Directions in Psychological Science, 20,* 174–180.

Verhagen, E. A., ter Horst, H. J., Kooi, E. W., Keating, P., van den Berg, P. P., & Bos, A. F. (2011). Prenatal tobacco exposure influences cerebral oxygenation in preterm infants. *Early Human Development, 87*(6), 401–406. doi:10.1016/j.earlhumdev.2011.03.002.

Vernacchio, L., Corwin, M. J., Lesko, S. M., Vezina, R. M., Hunt, C. E., Hoffman, H. J., et al. (2003). Sleep position of low birth weight infants. *Pediatrics, 111,* 633–640.

Vernet, M. E., Robin, O., & Dittmar, A. (1995). The ohmic perturbation duration, an original temporal index to quantify electrodermal responses. *Behavioural Brain Research, 67*(1), 103–107.

Vernon, P. A., Villani, V. C., Vickers, L. C., & Harris, J. A. (2008). A behavioral genetic investigation of the Dark Triad and the Big 5. *Personality and Individual Differences, 44*(2), 445–452.

Verster, J. C., & Volkerts, E. R. (2004). Clinical pharmacology, clinical efficacy, and behavioral toxicity of alprazolam: A review of the literature. *CNS Drug Reviews, 10,* 45–76.

Vess, M. (2012). Warm thoughts: attachment anxiety and sensitivity to temperature cues. *Psychological Science, 23,* 472–474.

Vetter, M. L., Dumon, K. R., & Williams, N. N. (2011). Surgical treatments for obesity. *Psychiatric Clinics Of North America, 34*(4), 881–893. doi:10.1016/j.psc.2011.08.012

Vetter, M. L., Cardillo, S., Rickels, M. R., & Iqbal, N. (2009). Narrative review: effect of bariatric surgery on type 2 diabetes mellitus. *Annals of Internal Medicine, 150*(2), 94–103.

Vetter-O'Hagen, C., & Spear, L. (2012). Hormonal and physical markers of puberty and their relationship to adolescent-typical novelty-directed behavior. *Developmental Psychobiology, 54,* 523–535. doi:10.1002/dev.20610.

Vetter-O'Hagen, C., Varlinskaya, E., & Spear, L. (2009). Sex differences in ethanol intake and sensitivity to aversive effects during adolescence and adulthood. *Alcohol & Alcoholism, 44,* 547–554. doi:10.1093/alcalc/agp048

Vezzali, L., & Giovannini, D. (2011). Cross-group friendships, social dominance orientation and secondary transfer effect. *TPM-Testing, Psychometrics, Methodology in Applied Psychology, 18,* 181–194.

Vianello, M., Robusto, E., & Anselmi, P. (2010). Implicit conscientiousness predicts academic performance. *Personality & Individual Differences, 48,* 452–457. doi:10.1016/j.paid.2009.11.019

Vianello, R., & Lanfranchi, S. (2011). Positive effects of the placement of students with intellectual developmental disabilities in typical class. *Life Span and Disability, 14*(1), 75–84.

Vidmar, N. (2011). The psychology of trial judging. *Current Directions in Psychological Science, 20*(1), 58–62. doi:10.1177/0963721410397283.

Vidrine, J. I., Businelle, M. S., Cinciripini, P., Li, Y., et al. (2009). Associations of mindfulness with nicotine dependence, withdrawal, and agency. *Substance Abuse, 30,* 318–327.

Vierbuchen, T., Ostermeier, A., Pang, Z. P., Kokubu, Y., et al. (2010). Direct conversion of fibroblasts to functional neurons by defined factors. *Nature, 463,* 1035–1041. Epub 2010 Jan 27.

Vierikko, E., Pulkkinen, L., Kaprio, J., & Rose, R. J. (2006). Genetic and environmental sources of continuity and change in teacher–rated aggression during early adolescence. *Aggressive Behavior, 32,* 308–320.

Vieta, E., Gunter, O., Ekman, M., Miltenburger, C., Chatterton, M. & Astrom, M. (2011). Effectiveness of psychotropic medications in the maintenance phase of bipolar disorder: A meta-analysis of randomized controlled trials. *International Journal of Neuropsychopharmacology, 14,* 1029–1049.

Vieta, E., & Phillips, M. L. (2007). Deconstructing bipolar disorder: A critical review of its diagnostic validity and a proposal for DSM-V and ICD-11. *Schizophrenia Bulletin, 33,* 886–892.

Vignovic, J. A., & Thompson, L. F., J. A (2010). Computer-mediated cross-cultural collaboration: Attributing communication errors to the person versus the situation. *Journal of Applied Psychology, 95,* 265–276.

Vijayalaxmi, V. T. J. (2008). Genetic damage in mammalian somatic cells exposed to radiofrequency radiation: a meta-analysis of data from 63 publications (1990–2005). *Radiation Research, 169*(5), 561–574.

Villers-Sidani, E., Alzghoul, L., Xiaoming, Z., Simpson, K. L., Lin, R. S., & Merzenich, M. M. (2010). Recovery of functional and structural. age-related changes in the rat primary auditory cortex with operant training. *Proceedings of the National Academy of Sciences of the United States of America, 107*(31), 13900–13905. doi:10.1073/pnas.1007885107.

Vincent, C. A., & Richardson, P. H. (1986). The evaluation of therapeutic acupuncture: Concepts and methods. *Pain, 24,* 1–13.

Vines, B. W., Norton, A. C., & Schlaug, G. (2011). Non-invasive brain stimulation enhances the effects of melodic intonation therapy. *Front Psychol 2: article 230* pp. 1–10.

Vingerhoets, G., Berckmoes, C., & Stroobant, N. (2003). Cerebral hemodynamics during discrimination of prosodic and semantic emotion in speech studied by transcranial Doppler ultrasonography. *Neuropsychology, 17,* 93–99.

Vink, T., Hinney, A., van Elburg, A. A., van Goozen, S. H. M., Sandkuijl, L. A., Sinke, R. J., et al. (2001). Association between an agouti-related protein gene polymorphism and anorexia nervosa. *Molecular Psychiatry, 6,* 325–328.

Vinkhuyzen, A. E., van der Sluis, S., Maes, H. M., & Posthuma, D. (2012). Reconsidering the heritability of intelligence in adulthood: Taking assortative mating and cultural transmission into account. *Behavior Genetics, 42*(2), 187–198. doi:10.1007/s10519-011-9507-9.

Vinod, K. Y., Yalamanchili, R., Xie, S., Cooper, T. B., & Hungund, B. L. (2006). Effect of chronic ethanol exposure and its withdrawal on the endocannabinoid system. *Neurochemistry International, 49,* 619–625.

Virues-Ortega, J. (2010). Applied behavior analytic intervention for autism in early childhood: Meta-analysis, meta-regression and dose-response meta-analysis of multiple outcomes. *Clinical Psychology Review, 30,* 387–399. Epub 2010 Feb 11.

Visser, P. J., Krabbendam, L., Verhey, F. R., Hofman, P. A., Verhoeven, W. M., Tuinier, S., et al. (1999). Brain correlates of memory dysfunction in alcoholic Korsakoff 's syndrome. *Journal of Neurology, Neurosurgery, and Psychiatry, 67*(6), 774–778.

Visser, B. A., Bay, D., Cook, G. L., & Myburg, J. (2010). Psychopathic and antisocial, but not emotionally intelligent. *Personality and Individual Differences, 48,* 644–648.

Visser, P. S., Krosnick, J. A., & Lavrakas, P. J. (2000). Survey research. In H. T. Reis & C. Judd (Eds.), *Handbook of research methods in social and personality psychology* (pp. 223–252). Cambridge, UK: Cambridge University Press.

Vitaliano, P. P., Zhang, J. M., & Scanlan, J. M. (2003). Is caregiving hazardous to one's physical health? A meta-analysis. *Psychological Bulletin, 129,* 946–972.

Vlachou, S., & Markou, A. (2010). GABA receptors in reward processes. *Advances in Pharmacology, 58,* 315–371.

Vocat, R., Staub, F., Stroppini, T., & Vuilleumier, P. (2010). Anosognosia for hemiplegia: a clinical-anatomical prospective study. *Brain, 133*(Pt 12), 3578–3597.

Vocisano, C., Klein, D. N., Arnow, B., Rivera, C., Blalock, J. A., Rothbaum, B., et al. (2004). Therapist variables that predict symptom change in psychotherapy with chronically depressed outpatients. *Psychotherapy: Theory, Research, Training, Practice, 41,* 255–265.

Vogel, I., Brug, J., van der Ploeg, C. P. B., & Raat, H. (2009). Strategies for the prevention of mp3-induced hearing loss among adolescents: Expert opinions from a delphi study. *Pediatrics, 123,* 1257–1262.

Vokey, J. R. (2002). Subliminal messages. In J. R. Vokey & S. W. Allen (Eds.), *Psychological sketches* (6th ed., pp. 223–246). Lethbridge, Alberta, Canada: Psyence Ink.

Vokey, J. R., & Read, J. D. (1985). Subliminal messages: Between the devil and the media. *American Psychologist, 40,* 1231–1239.

Volk, H. E., Scherrer, J. F., Bucholz, K. K., Todorov, A., Heath, A. C., Jacob, T., & True, W. R. (2007). Evidence for specificity of transmission of alcohol and nicotine dependence in an offspring of twins design. *Alcohol Dependence, 87,* 225–232.

Volkow, N. D., Tomasi, D., Wang, G., Vaska, P., Fowler, J. S., Telang, F., & .. Wong, C. (2011). Effects of cell phone radiofrequency signal exposure on brain glucose metabolism. *JAMA: Journal of the American Medical Association, 305*(8), 808–814.

Vollset, S. E., Tverdal, A., & Gjessing, H. K. (2006). Smoking and deaths between 40 and 70 years of age in women and men. *Annals of Internal Medicine, 144,* 381–389.

Volz, J. (2000). Successful aging. The second 50. *APA Monitor, 31,* 24–28.

von Gontard, A. (2011). Elimination disorders: A critical comment on DSM-5 proposals. *European Child & Adolescent Psychiatry, 20*(2), 83–88. doi:10.1007/s00787-010-0152-2.

von Stumm, S., Hell, B., & Chamorro-Premuzic, T. (2011). The hungry mind: Intellectual curiosity is the third pillar of academic performance. *Perspectives on Psychological Science, 6*(6), 574–588. doi:10.1177/1745691611421204.

Von Wright, J. M., Anderson, K., & Stenman, U. (1975). Generalization of conditioned GSRs in dichotic listening. In P. M. A. Rabbitt & S. Dornic (Eds.), *Attention and performance V.* New York: Academic Press.

Voracek, M., & Fisher, M. L. (2002). Shapely centrefolds? Temporal change in body measures: trend analysis. *British Medical Journal, 325,* 1447–1448.

Vorstman, J. A. S., Staal, W. G., van Daalen, E., van Engeland, H., Hochstenbach, P. F. R., & Franke, L. (2006). Identification of novel autism candidate regions through analysis of reported cytogenetic abnormalities associated with autism. *Molecular Psychiatry, 11,* 18–28.

Voss, U., Tuin, I., Schermelleh-Engel, K., & Hobson, A. (2011). Waking and dreaming: Related but structurally independent. Dream reports of congenitally paraplegic and deaf-mute persons. *Consciousness and Cognition, 20*(3), 673–687.

Vouloumanos, A., Druhen, M. J., Hauser, M. D., & Huizink, A. T. (2009). Five-month-old infants' identification of the sources of vocalizations. *Proceedings of the National Academy of Sciences, 106,* 18867–18872.

Vrij, A., Granhag, P., & Porter, S. (2010). Pitfalls and opportunities in nonverbal and verbal lie detection. *Psychological Science in the Public Interest, 11*(3), 89–121. doi:10.1177/1529100610390861.

Vrij, A., Leal, S., Granhag, P., Mann, S., Fisher, R., Hillman, J., & Sperry, K. (2009). Outsmarting the liars: the benefit of asking unanticipated questions. *Law And Human Behavior, 33*(2), 159–166.

Vrij, A., Mann, S., Leal, S., & Fisher, R. (2010). 'Look into my eyes': Can an instruction to maintain eye contact facilitate lie detection?. *Psychology, Crime & Law, 16*(4), 327–348. doi:10.1080/10683160902740633.

Vrij, A., Leal, S., Mann, S., Warmelink, L., Granhag, P., & Fisher, R. P. (2010). Drawings as an innovative and successful lie detection tool. *Applied Cognitive Psychology, 24*(4), 587–594. doi:10.1002/acp.1627.

Vroling, M. S., & de Jong, P. J. (2010). Threat-confirming belief bias and symptoms of anxiety disorders. *Journal of Behavior Therapy and Experimental Psychiatry, 41,* 110–116.

Vroom, V. (1964). *Work and motivation.* New York: Wiley.

Vuoksimaa, E., Kaprio, J., Kremen, W. S., Hokkanen, L., et al. (2010). Having a male co-twin masculinizes mental rotation performance in females. *Psychological Science, 21,* 1069–1071.

Vuori, E., Tervo, T. M., & Holopainen, J. M. (2009). Laser refractive correction of myopia in visually impaired patients improves visual acuity. *Acta Ophthalmologica.* Epub 2009 Nov 7.

Vygotsky, L. S. (1991). Genesis of the higher mental functions. In P. Light, S. Sheldon, & M. Woodhead (Eds.), *Learning to think: Child development in social context* (Vol. 2, pp. 32–41). London: Routledge.

Vyse, S. A. (2000). *Believing in magic: The psychology of superstition* (Rep. ed.). New York: Oxford University Press.

Vyssoki, B., Praschak-Rieder, N., Sonneck, G., Blüml, V., Willeit, M., Kasper, S., & Kapusta, N. (2012). Effects of sunshine on suicide rates. *Comprehensive Psychiatry, 53,* 535–539.

Waagenaar, W. (1986). My memory: A study of autobiographical memory over six years. *Cognitive Psychology, 18,* 225–252.

Wadden, T. A., Berkowitz, R. I., Sarwer, D. B., Prus-Wisniewski, R., & Steinberg, C. (2001). Benefits of lifestyle modification in the pharmacologic treatment of obesity: A randomized trial. *Archives of Internal Medicine, 161,* 218–227.

Wadden, T. A., Berkowitz, R. I., Womble, L. G., Sarwer, D. B., Phelan, S., Cato, R. K., et al. (2005). Randomized trial of lifestyle modification and pharmacotherapy for obesity. *New England Journal of Medicine, 353,* 2111–2120.

Wadden, T. A., West, D. S., Neiberg, R. H., Wing, R. R., et al. (2009). One-year weight losses in the Look AHEAD study: Factors associated with success. *Obesity, 17,* 713–722.

Wade, C. (1988, April). *Thinking critically about critical thinking in psychology.* Paper presented at the annual meeting of the Western Psychological Association, San Francisco, CA.

Wade, J. B. (2004). Neuropsychologists diagnose traumatic brain injury. *Brain Injury, 18*(7), 629–643.

Wade-Benzoni, K. A., Tost, L., Hernandez, M., & Larrick, R. P. (2012). It's only a matter of time: Death, legacies, and intergenerational decisions. *Psychological Science 23,* 704–709. doi:10.1177/0956797612443967.

Waelti, P., Dickinson, A., & Schultz, W. (2001). Dopamine responses comply with basic assumptions of formal learning theory. *Nature, 412,* 43–48.

Wager, T. D., Atlas, L. Y., Leotti, L. A., & Rilling, J. K. (2011). Predicting Individual Differences in Placebo Analgesia: Contributions of Brain Activity during Anticipation and Pain Experience. *Journal Of Neuroscience, 31*(2), 439–452. doi:10.1523/JNEUROSCI.3420-10.2011.

Wagg, J. (2008, October 21). Yamaha Yakidding? Retrieved January 15, 2009, from http://www.randi.org/site/index.php/swift-blog/242-yamaha-yakidding.html.

Wagner, A. D. (1999). Working memory contributions to human learning and remembering. *Neuron, 22,* 19–22.

Wagner, K. D., Ambrosini, P., Rynn, M., Wohlberg, C., Yang, R., Greenbaum, M. S., et al. (2003). Efficacy of sertraline in the treatment of children and adolescents with major depressive disorder: Two randomized controlled trials. *Journal of the American Medical Association, 290,* 1033–1041.

Wagner, U., Hallschmid, M., Rasch, B., & Born, J. (2006). Brief sleep after learning keeps emotional memories alive for years. *Biological Psychiatry, 60,* 788–790.

Wahl, C., Svensson, Å., & Hydén, C. (2010). Effects of minor phrasing variations in traffic-related questionnaires—Comparison of objective equivalences and respondents' subjective statements. *Transportation Research: Part F, 13*(5), 315–328. doi:10.1016/j.trf.2010.06.002.

Wai, J., Lubinski, D., & Benbow, C. P. (2005). Creativity and occupational accomplishments among intellectually precocious youth: An age 13 to age 33 longitudinal study. *Journal of Educational Psychology, 97,* 484–492.

Wainryb, C. (2006). Moral development in culture: Diversity, tolerance, and justice. In M. Killen & J. G. Smetana (Eds.), *Handbook of moral development* (pp. 211–240). Mahwah, NJ: Erlbaum.

Wainryb, C., & Pasupathi, M. (2008). Developing moral agency in the midst of violence: Children, political conflict, and values. In I. A. Karawan, W. McCormack, & S. E. Reynolds (Eds.), *Values and violence: Intangible aspects of terrorism* (pp. 169–188). New York: Springer.

Wakefield, J. C. (1992). The concept of mental disorder: On the boundary between biological facts and social values. *American Psychologist, 47,* 373–388.

Wakimoto, R. (2006). Mortality salience effects on modesty and relative self-effacement. *Asian Journal of Social Psychology, 9,* 176–183.

Wakschlag, L. S., Briggs-Gowan, M. J., Hill, C., Danis, B., Leventhal, B. L., Keenan, K., Egger, H. L., Cicchetti, D., Burns, C., & Carter, A. S. (2008). Observational assessment of preschool disruptive behavior, Part II: Validity of the Disruptive Behavior Diagnostic Observation Schedule (DB-DOS). *Journal of the American Academy of Child & Adolescent Psychiatry, 47*(6), 632–641.

Wakschlag, L. S., Leventhal, B. L., Pine, D. S., Pickett, K. E., & Carter, A. S. (2006). Elucidating early mechanisms of developmental psychopathology: The case of prenatal smoking and disruptive behavior. *Child Development, 77,* 893–906.

Waldman, I. D., & Gizer, I. R. (2006). The genetics of attention deficit hyperactivity disorder. *Clinical Psychology Review, 26,* 396–432.

Walker, L. J. (2006). Gender and morality. In M. Killen & J. G. Smetana (Eds.), *Handbook of moral development* (pp. 93–118). Mahwah, NJ: Erlbaum.

Walker, E., Shapiro, D., Esterberg, M., & Trotman, H. (2010). Neurodevelopment and schizophrenia: Broadening the focus. *Current Directions In Psychological Science, 19*(4), 204–208. doi:10.1177/0963721410377744.

Walker, E. F., & Diforio, D. (1998). Schizophrenia: A neural diathesis-stress model. *Psychological Review, 104,* 667–685.

Walker, L. (1991). The feminization of psychology. *Psychology of Women Newsletter of Division, 35,* 1, 4.

Walker, M. P., & Stickgold, R. (2006). Sleep, memory, and plasticity. *Annual Review of Psychology, 57,* 139–166.

Walkup, J. T., Albano, A. M., Piacentini, J., Birmaher, B., Compton, S. N., Sherrill, J. T., Ginsburg, G. S., Rynn, M. A., McCracken, J., Waslick, B., Iyengar, S., March, J. S., & Kendall, P. C. (2008). Cognitive behavioral therapy, sertraline, or a combination in childhood anxiety. *The New England Journal of Medicine, 359,* 2753–2766.

Wall, T. L., Shea, S. H., Luczak, S. E., Cook, T. A., & Carr, L. G. (2005). Genetic associations of alcohol dehydrogenase with alcohol use disorders and endophenotypes in white college students. *Journal of Abnormal Psychology, 114,* 456–465.

Wallace, J. C., Popp, E., & Mondore, S. (2006). Safety climate as a mediator between foundation climates and occupational accidents: A group-level investigation. *Journal of Applied Psychology, 91,* 681–688.

Wallace, L. M., & vanRanson, K. M. (2011). Treatment manuals: Use in the treatment of bulimia nervosa. *Behaviour Research and Therapy, 49,* 815–820.

Wallace, R. K., & Benson, H. (1972). The physiology of meditation. *Scientific American, 226,* 84–90.

Wallen, K., & Lovejoy, J. (1993). Sexual behavior: Endocrine function and therapy. In J. Shulkin (Ed.), *Hormonal pathways to mind and brain.* New York: Academic Press.

Wallerstein, R. S. (2002). The growth and transformation of American ego psychology. *Journal of the American Psychoanalytic Association, 50,* 135–169.

Walling, S., Suvak, M. K., Howard, J. M., Taft, C. T., & Murphy, C. M. (2012). Race/ethnicity as a predictor of change in working alliance during cognitive behavioral therapy for intimate partner violence perpetrators. *Psychotherapy, 49,* 180–189. doi:10.1037/a0025751

Walsh, R. (2011). Lifestyle and mental health. *American Psychologist, 66*(7), 579–592. doi:10.1037/a0021769.

Walsh, R., & Shapiro, S. L. (2006). The meeting of meditative disciplines and Western psychology: A mutually enriching dialogue. *American Psychologist, 61,* 227–239.

Walther, E., & Langer, T. (2008). Attitude formation and change though association: An evaluative conditioning account. In R. Prislin & W. B. Crano (Eds.), *Attitudes and Persuasion* (pp. 87–110). New York: Psychology Press.

Walton, G. M., & Spencer, S. J. (2009). Latent ability: Grades and test scores systematically underestimate the intellectual ability of negatively stereotyped students. *Psychological Science, 20,* 1132–1139.

Walton, G. E., Bower, N. J. A., & Bower, T. G. R. (1992). Recognition of familiar faces by newborns. *Infant Behavior and Development, 15,* 265–269.

Wampold, B. E. (2001). Estimating variability in outcomes attributable to therapists: A naturalistic study of outcomes in managed care. *Journal of Consulting and Clinical Psychology, 73,* 914–923.

Wampold, B. E., Ahn, H., & Coleman, H. L. K. (2001). Medical model as metaphor: Old habits die hard. *Journal of Counseling Psychology, 48,* 263–273.

Wampold, B. E., Hollon, S. D., & Hill, C. E. (2011). Unresolved questions and future directions in psychotherapy research. In J. C. Norcross, G. R. VandenBos, & D. K. Freedheim (Eds.), *History of psychotherapy: Continuity and change* (pp. 333–356). Washington, D.C.: American Psychological Association.

Wampold, B. E., Minami, T., Tierney, S. C., Baskin, T. W., & Bhati, K. S. (2005). The placebo is powerful: Estimating placebo effects in medicine and psychotherapy from randomized clinical trials. *Journal of Clinical Psychology, 61,* 835–854.

Wan, X., Nakatani, H., Ueno, K., Asamizuya, T., Cheng, K., & Tanaka, K. (2011). The neural basis of intuitive best next-move generation in board game experts. *Science, 331*(6015), 341–346. doi:10.1126/science.1194732

Wanders, F., Serra, M., & de Jongh, A. (2008). EMDR versus CBT for children with self-esteem and behavioral problems: A randomized controlled trial. *Journal of EMDR Practice and Research, 2*(3), 180–189.

Wanek, J. E., Sackett, P. R., & Ones, D. S. (2003). Towards an understanding of integrity test similarities and differences: An item-level analysis of seven tests. *Personnel Psychology, 56,* 873–894.

Wang, C., Collet, J. P., & Lau, J. (2004). The effect of Tai Chi on health outcomes in patients with chronic conditions: A systematic review. *Archives of Internal Medicine, 164,* 493–501.

Wang, O. (2006). Earliest recollections of self and others in European American and Taiwanese young adults. *Psychological Science, 17,* 708–714.

Wang, P. S., Aguilar-Gaxiola, S., Alonso, J., Angermeyer, M. C., Borges, G., Bromet, E., et al. (2007). Use of mental health services for anxiety, mood, and substance disorders in 17 countries in the WHO world mental health surveys. *Lancet, 370,* 841–850.

Wang, P. S., Demler, O., Olfson, M., Pincus, H. A., Wells, K. B., & Kessler, R. C. (2006). Changing profiles of service sectors used in mental health care in the United States. *American Journal of Psychiatry, 163,* 1187–1198.

Wang, P. S., Lane, M., Olfson, M., Pincus, H. A., Wells, K. B., & Kessler, R. C. (2005). Twelve-month use of mental health services in the United States: Results from the National Comorbidity Survey Replication. *Archives of General Psychiatry, 62,* 629–640.

Wang, S., Kain, Z. N., & White, P. (2008). Acupuncture analgesia: I. The scientific basis. *Anesthesia and Analgesia, 106*(2), 602–610.

Wang, W., Chan, S. S., Heldman, D. A., & Moran, D. W. (2010). Motor cortical representation of hand translation and rotation during reaching. *Journal of Neuroscience, 30,* 958–962.

Wang, X., Merzenich, M. M., Sameshima, K., & Jenkins, W. M. (1995). Remodelling of hand representation in adult cortex determined by timing of tactile stimulation. *Nature, 378,* 71–75.

Wang, Y. (2007). Cognitive informatics: Exploring the theoretical foundations for natural intelligence, neural informatics, autonomic computing, and agent systems. *International Journal of Cognitive Informatics and Natural Intelligence, 1*(1), i–x.

Wanic, R. & Kulik, J. (2011) Toward an understanding of gender differences in the impact of marital conflict on health. *Sex Roles, 65,* 297–312.

Wann, J. P., Poulter, D. R., & Purcell, C. (2011). Reduced Sensitivity to Visual Looming Inflates the Risk Posed by Speeding Vehicles When Children Try to Cross the Road. *Psychological Science, 22*(4), 429–434. doi:10.1177/0956797611400917.

Wansink, B. (2010). From mindless eating to mindlessly eating better. *Physiology & Behavior, 100*(5), 454–463. doi:10.1016/j.physbeh.2010.05.003.

Wansink, B. B., & Wansink, C. S. (2010). The largest Last Supper: Depictions of food portions and plate size increased over the millennium. *International Journal Of Obesity, 34*(5), 943–944. doi:10.1038/ijo.2010.37.

Warburton, D. M. (1995). Effects of caffeine on cognition and mood without caffeine abstinence. *Psychopharmacology, 119,* 66–70.

Ward, C. (1994). Culture and altered states of consciousness. In W. J. Lonner & R. S. Malpass (Eds.), *Psychology and culture.* Boston: Allyn & Bacon.

Ward, L. M. (2011). The thalamic dynamic core theory of conscious experience, Consciousness and Cognition, 20, 464–486.

Wark, D. M. (2008). What we can do with hypnosis: A brief note. *American Journal of Clinical Hypnosis, 51,* 29–36.

Warmelink, L., Vrij, A., Mann, S., Leal, S., Forrester, D., & Fisher, R. (2011). Thermal imaging as a lie detection tool at airports. *Law And Human Behavior, 35*(1), 40–48.

Warmerdam, L., van Straten, A., Jongsma, J., Twisk, J., & Cuijpers, P. (2010). Online cognitive behavioral therapy and problem-solving therapy for depressive symptoms: Exploring mechanisms of change. *Journal of Behavior Th erapy and Experimental Psychiatry, 41,* 64–70.

Warneken, F., Lohse, K., Melis, A. P., & Tomasello, M. (2011). Young children share the spoils after collaboration. *Psychological Science, 22*(2), 267–273. doi:10.1177/0956797610395392.

Warner, B. (2010). Reducing suicidal ideation and depression in older primary care patients: The oldest old and pain. *American Journal of Psychiatry, 167,* 102.

Warner, L., Kessler, R., Hughes, M., Anthony, J., & Nelson, C. (1995). Prevalence and correlates of drug use and dependence in the United States. *Archives of General Psychiatry, 52,* 219–229.

Warren, S. (2011). The case of the malodorous infant: Food choices during pregnancy can have astounding effects. Retrieved from http://scienceline.org/2011/03/the-case-of-the-malodorous-infant/.

Warren, S. L., Bost, K. K., Roisman, G. I., Levin Silton, R., Spielberg, J. M., Engels, A. S., & .. Heller, W. (2010). Effects of adult attachment and emotional distractors on brain mechanisms of cognitive control. *Psychological Science, 21*(12), 1818–1826. doi:10.1177/0956797610388809.

Washburn, J. J., Romero, E. G., Welty, L. J., Abram, K. M., et al. (2007). Development of antisocial personality disorder in detained youths: Th e predictive value of mental disorders. *Journal of Consulting and Clinical Psychology, 75,* 221–231.

Wass, S., Porayska-Pomsta, K., & Johnson, M. (2011). Training attentional control in infancy. *Current Biology: CB, 21*(18), 1543–1547.

Wasserman, E. A. (1993). Comparative cognition: Beginning the second century of the study of animal intelligence. *Psychological Bulletin, 113,* 211–228.

Wasylkiw, L., MacKinnon, A., & MacLellan, A. (2012). Exploring the link between self-compassion and body image in university women. *Body Image, 9*(2), 236–245.

Wasylyshyn, C., Verhaeghen, P., & Sliwinski, M. J. (2011). Aging and task switching: A meta-analysis. *Psychology and Aging, 26,* 15–20.

Watanabe, S., Sakamoto, J., & Wakita, M. (1995). Pigeons' discrimination of paintings by Monet and Picasso. *Journal of Experimental Analysis of Behavior, 63,* 165–174.

Waterhouse, L. (2006a). Inadequate evidence for multiple intelligences, Mozart Effect, and emotional intelligence theories. *Educational Psychologist, 41*(4), 247–255.

Waterhouse, L. (2006b). Multiple Intelligences, the Mozart Effect, and emotional intelligence: A critical review. *Educational Psychologist, 41*(4), 207–225.

Waterman, A. S. (1982). Identity development from adolescence to adulthood: An extension of theory and a review of research. *Developmental Psychology, 18,* 341–358.

Waters, A. M., Henry, J., & Neumann, D. L. (2009). Aversive Pavlovian conditioning in childhood anxiety disorders: Impaired response inhibition and resistance to extinction. *Journal of Abnormal Psychology, 118,* 311–321.

Waters, E., Merrick, S., Treboux, D., Crowell, J., & Albersheim, L. (2000). Attachment security in infancy and early adulthood: A twenty-year longitudinal study. *Child Development, 71,* 684–689.

Watkins, K. E., Smith, S. M., Davis, S., & Howell, P. (2008). Structural and functional abnormalities of the motor system in developmental stuttering. *Brain, 131,* 50–59.

Watson, D., & Slack, A.K. (1993). General factors of affective temperament and their relation to job satisfaction over time. *Organizational Behavior and Human Decision Processes, 54,* 181–202.

Watson, J. B. (1913). Psychology as the behaviorist views it. *Psychological Review, 20,* 158–177.

Watson, J. B. (1919). *Psychology from the standpoint of a behaviorist.* Philadelphia: Lippincott.

Watson, J. B. (1925). *Behaviorism.* London: Kegan Paul, Trench, Trubner.

Watson, R. T., & Heilman, K. M. (1979). Thalamic neglect. *Neurology, 29*(5), 690–694.

Waugh, C. E., Fredrickson, B. L., & Taylor, S. F. (2008). Adapting to life's slings and arrows: Individual diff erences in resilience when recovering from an anticipated threat. *Journal of Research in Personality, 42,* 1031–1046.

Waugh, C. E., Wager, T. D., Fredrickson, B. L., Noll, D. C., & Taylor, S. F. (2008). The neural correlates of trait resilience when anticipating and recovering from threat. *Social Cognitive & Affective Neuroscience, 3*(4), 322–332. doi:10.1093/scan/nsn024.

Waytz, A., & Young, L. (2012). The group-member mind trade-off: Attributing mind to groups versus group members. *Psychological Science, 23,* 77–85. doi:10.1177/0956797611423546.

Wearden, A. J., Tarrier, N., Barrowclough, C., Zastowny, T. R., & Rahill, A. A. (2000). A review of expressed emotion research in health care. *Clinical Psychology Review, 20,* 633–666.

Weaver, F. M., Follett, K., Stern, M., Hur, K., Harris, C., Marks, W. J., Jr., et al. (2009). Bilateral deep brain stimulation vs best medical therapy for patients with advanced Parkinson disease: A randomized controlled trial. *Journal of the American Medical Association, 301*(1), 63–73.

Weaver, J. R., Vandello, J. A., & Bosson, Jennifer K. (2012). Intrepid, imprudent, or impetuous?: The effects of gender threats on men's financial decisions. *Psychology of Men & Masculinity.* doi:http://dx.doi.org/10.1037/a0027087.

Webb, T. L., & Sheeran, P. (2006). Does changing behavioral intentions engender behavior change? A meta-analysis of the experimental evidence. *Psychological Bulletin, 132,* 249–268.

Weber, E. U., & Morris, M. W. (2010). Culture and judgment and decision making: The constructivist turn. *Perspectives on Psychological Science, 5*(4), 410–419. doi:10.1177/1745691610375556.

Weber, M. A., Klein, N. J., Hartley, J. C., Lock, P. E., Malone, M., & Sebire, N. J. (2008). Infection and sudden unexpected death in infancy: A systematic retrospective case review. *The Lancet, 371,* 1848–1853.

Weber, R. J. (1992). *Forks, phonographs, and hot air balloons: A field guide to inventive thinking.* New York: Oxford University Press.

Wechsler, D. (1939). *The measurement of adult intelligence.* Baltimore: Williams & Wilkins.

Wechsler, D. (1949). *The Wechsler Intelligence Scale for Children.* New York: Psychological Corporation.

Wechsler, D. (2003). *Wechsler Intelligence Scale for Children* (4th ed.). San Antonio, TX: Psychological Corporation.

Wechsler, D. (2008). *Wechsler Adult Intelligence Scale—Fourth edition (WAIS-IV).* San Antonio, TX: Pearson Assessments.

Wecker, N. S., Kramer, J. H., Hallam, B. J., & Delis, D. C. (2005). Mental flexibility: Age effects on switching. *Neuropsychology, 19,* 345–352.

Weger, U. W., Hooper, N., Meier, B. P., & Hopthrow, T. (2012). Mindful maths: Reducing the impact of stereotype threat through a mindfulness exercise. *Consciousness and Cognition: An International Journal, 21*(1), 471–475. doi:10.1016/j.concog.2011.10.011.

Wegge, J., & Haslam, S. A. (2005). Improving work motivation and performance in brainstorming groups: The effects of three group goal-setting strategies. *European Journal of Work and Organizational Psychology, 14,* 400–430.

Wegner, D. M., Wenzlaff, R. M., & Kozak, M. (2004). Dream rebound: The return of suppressed thoughts in dreams. *Psychological Science, 15,* 232–236.

Weick, J. P., Liu, Y. & Zhang, S.-C. (2011). Human embryonic stem cell-derived neurons adopt and regulate the activity of an established neural network. *Proceedings of the National Academy of Sciences.* Retrieved from http://www.pnas.org/content/early/2011/11/14/1108487108.abstract?etoc. doi:10.1073/pnas.1108487108.

Weihs, K. L., Enright, T. M., & Simmens, S. J. (2008). Close relationships and emotional processing predict decreased mortality in women with breast cancer: Preliminary evidence. *Psychosomatic Medicine, 70,* 117–124.

Weiler, B. L., & Widom, C. S. (1996). Psychopathy and violent behavior in abused and neglected young adults. *Criminal Behaviour and Mental Health, 6,* 253–271.

Weinberg, R. A., Scarr, S., & Waldman, I. D. (1992). The Minnesota transracial adoption study: A follow-up of IQ test performance at adolescence. *Intelligence, 16,* 117–135.

Weiner, B. (1980). *Human motivation.* New York: Holt, Rinehart & Winston.

Weinfield, N. S., Sroufe, L. A., & Egeland, B. (2000). Attachment from infancy to early adulthood in a high-risk sample: continuity, discontinuity, and their correlates. *Child Development, 71,* 695–702.

Weinraub, M., Horvath, D. L., & Gringlas, M. B. (2002). Single parenthood. In M. H. Bornstein (Ed.), *Handbook of parenting: Vol. 3. Being and becoming a parent* (2nd ed., pp. 109–140). Mahwah, NJ: Erlbaum.

Weiner, R. D., & Falcone, G. (2011). Electroconvulsive therapy: How effective is it? *Journal of the American Psychiatric Nurses Association, 17,* 217–218.

Weinstein, D. (1999, July 24). Who are you? *Sunday Telegraph Magazine,* pp. 24–26.

Weinstein, E. A., & Kahn, R. L. (1955). *Denial of illness: Symbolic and physiological aspects.* Springfield, IL: Thomas.

Weis, R., & Cerankosky, B. C. (2010). Effects of video-game ownership on young boys' academic and behavioral functioning: A randomized, controlled study. *Psychological Science, 21*(4), 463–470. doi:10.1177/0956797610362670.

Weisbuch, M., Pauker, K., & Ambady, N. (2009). Th e subtle transmission of race bias via televised nonverbal behavior. *Science, 326,* 1711–1714.

Weiss, A., Gale, C. R., Batty, G. D., & Deary, I. J. (2009). Emotionally stable, intelligent men live longer: Th e Vietnam Experience Study cohort. *Psychosomatic Medicine, 71,* 385–394.

Weiss, L. A., & Arking, D. E. (2009). A genome-wide linkage and association scan reveals novel loci for autism. *Nature, 461,* 802–808.

Weiss, A., King, J. E., & Perkins, L. (2006). Personality and subjective well-being in orangutans (*pongo pygmaeus and pongo abelii*). *Journal of Personality and Social Psychology, 90,* 501–511.

Weiss, S., & Moore, M. (1990). Cultural differences in the perception of magazine alcohol advertisements by Israeli Jewish, Moslem, Druze, and Christian high school students. *Drug and Alcohol Dependence, 26,* 209–215.

Weiss, S. J., St. Jonn-Seed, M., & Harris-Muchell, C. (2007). The contribution of fetal drug exposure to temperament: Potential teratogenic effects on neuropsychiatric risk. *Journal of Child Psychology and Psychiatry, 48*(8), 773–784.

Weiss, V. (2007). Percentages of children living in poverty determine IQ averages of nations. *European Journal of Personality.* Special Issue: *European personality reviews, 21,* 761–763.

Weissman, M. M., Markowitz, J. C., & Kierman, G. L. (2007). *Clinician's quick guide to interpersonal psychotherapy.* New York: Oxford University Press.

Weisz, J. R., Doss, A. J., & Hawley, K. M. (2005). Youth psychotherapy outcome research: A review and critique of the evidence base. *Annual Review of Psychology, 56,* 337–363.

Weisz, J. R., McCarty, C. A., & Valeri, S. M. (2006). Effects of psychotherapy for depression in children and adolescents: A meta-analysis. *Psychological Bulletin, 132,* 132–149.

Weisz, R. R., & Kazdin, A. E. (2010). *Evidence-based psychotherapies for children and adolescents (2nd ed.).* New York: Guilford.

Weitzman, M., Rosenthal, D. G., & Liu, Y. (2011). Paternal depressive symptoms and child behavioral or emotional problems in the United States. *Pediatrics, 128*(6), 1126–1134. doi:10.1542/peds.2010-3034

Wells, A., & Matthews, G. (2006). Cognitive vulnerability to anxiety disorders: An integration. In L. B. Alloy & J. H. Ruskind (Eds.), *Cognitive vulnerability to emotional disorders* (pp. 303–325). New York: Erlbaum.

Wells, G. L., & Bradfield, A. L. (1999). Distortions in eyewitness' recollections: Can the postidentification-feedback effect be moderated? *Psychological Science, 10,* 138–144.

Wells, G. L., & Olson, E. A. (2003). Eyewitness testimony. *Annual Review of Psychology, 54,* 277–295.

Wells, G. L., & Quinnlivan, D. S. (2009). Suggestive eyewitness identification procedures and the Supreme Court's reliability test in light of eyewitness science: 30 years later. *Law and Human Behavior, 33*(1), 1–24.

Wells, G. L., Malpass, R. S., Lindsay, R. C. L., Fisher, R. P., Turtle, J. W., & Fulero, S. M. (2000). From the lab to the police station: A successful application of eyewitness research. *American Psychologist, 55,* 581–598.

Wells, G. L., Memon, A., & Penrod, S. D. (2006). Eyewitness evidence: Improving its probative value. *Psychological Science in the Public Interest, 7,* 45–75.

Wells, G. L., Olson, E. A., & Charman, S. D. (2002). The confidence of eyewitnesses in their identifications from lineups. *Current Directions in Psychological Science, 11,* 151–154.

Wells, G. L., Olson, E. A., & Charman, S. D. (2003). Distorted retrospective eyewitness reports as functions of feedback and delay. *Journal of Experimental Psychology: Applied, 9,* 42–52.

Wells, G. L., Steblay, N. K., & Dysart, J. E. (2012). Eyewitness identification reforms: Are suggestiveness-induced hits and guesses true hits? *Perspectives on Psychological Science, 7*(3), 264–271. doi:10.1177/1745691612443368.

Wells, J. C. K. (2009). Thrift : A guide to thrifty genes, thrifty phenotypes and thrifty norms. *International Journal of Obesity, 33,* 1331–1338.

Wells, S., Graham, K., & West, P. (2000). Alcohol-related aggression in the general population. *Journal of Studies on Alcohol, 61,* 626–632.

Welsh, J. A., Nix, R. L., Blair, C., Bierman, K. L., & Nelson, K. E. (2010). The development of cognitive skills and gains in academic school readiness for children from low-income families. *Journal of Educational Psychology, 102*(1), 43–53. doi:10.1037/a0016738.

Welsh, T. N., Ray, M. C., Weeks, D. J., Dewey, D., & Elliot, D. (2009). Does Joe influence Fred's action? Not if Fred has autism spectrum disorder. *Brain Research, 1248,* 141–148.

Weltzin, T. E., Bulik, C. M., McConaha, C. W., & Kaye, W. H. (1995). Laxative withdrawal and anxiety in bulimia nervosa. *International Journal of Eating Disorders, 17*(2), 141–146.

Wen, C. P, Wai, J. P. M., Tsai, M. K., Yang, T. Y. C., Cheng, T. Y. D., Lee, M.-C., Chan, H. T., Tsao, C. K., Tsai, S. P., & Wu, X. (2011). Minimum amount of physical activity for reduced mortality and extended life expectancy: A prospective cohort study. *The Lancet, 378,* 1244–1253.

Werner, E. (2003, January 28). Police: Sons kill mom, dismember her after seeing it done on "The Sopranos." *Naples Daily News.*

Wernig, M., Zhao, J. P., Pruszak, J., Hedlund, E., Fu, D., Soldner, F., et al. (2008). Neurons derived from reprogrammed fibroblasts functionally integrate into the fetal brain and improve symptoms of rats with Parkinson's disease. *Proceedings of the National Academy of Sciences, 105*(15), 5856–5861.

Wertheimer, M. (1923).Laws of organization in perceptual forms. First published as Untersuchungen zur Lehre von der Gestalt II in *Psycologische Forschung, 4,* 301-350. Translation published in Ellis, W. (1938). *A source book of Gestalt psychology* (pp. 71-88). London: Routledge & Kegan Paul.

West, C. P., Tan, A. D., Habermann, T. M., Sloan, J. A., & Shanafelt, T. D. (2009). Association of resident fatigue and distress with perceived medical errors. *Journal of the American Medical Association, 302,* 1294–1300.

West, G. L., Anderson, A. K., Bedwell, J. S., & Pratt, J. (2010). Red diffuse light suppresses the accelerated perception of fear. *Psychological Science, 21*(7), 992–999. doi:10.1177/0956797610371966.

West, M. A., Borrill, C. S., & Unsworth, K. L. (1998). Team effectiveness in organizations. In C. L. Cooper & I. T. Robertson (Eds.), *International review of industrial and organizational psychology 1998* (pp. 1–48). Chichester, UK: Wiley.

West, S. A., & Gardner, A. (2010). Altruism, spite, and greenbeards. *Science, 327,* 1341–1344.

Westen, D. (2005). Implications of research in cognitive neuroscience for psychodynamic psychotherapy. In G. Gabbard, J. Beck, & J. Holmes (Eds.), *Oxford textbook of psychotherapy* (pp. 447–454). Oxford: Oxford University Press.

Westen, D., & Bradley, R. (2005). Empirically supported complexity. *Current Directions in Psychological Science, 14,* 266–271.

Westen, D., Glen, O., Gabbard, G. O., & Ortigo, K. M. (2008). Psychoanalytic approaches to personality. In O. John, R. Robins, & L. Pervin (Eds.), *Handbook of personality: Theory and research* (3rd ed., pp. 61–113). New York: Guilford.

Westen, D., & Morrison, K. (2001). A multidimensional meta-analysis of treatments for depression, panic, and generalized anxiety disorder: An empirical examination of the status of empirically supported therapies. *Journal of Consulting and Clinical Psychology, 69,* 875–899.

Westen, D., Novotny, C. M., & Thompson-Brenner, H. (2004). The empirical status of empirically supported psychotherapies: Assumptions, findings, and reporting in controlled clinical trials. *Psychological Bulletin, 130,* 631–663.

Westen, D., Shedler, J., & Bradley, R. (2006). A prototype approach to personality disorder diagnosis. *American Journal of Psychiatry, 163,* 846–856.

Westra, H. A., Aviram, A., Connors, L., Kertes, A., & Ahmed, M. (2012). Therapist emotional reactions and client resistance in cognitive behavioral therapy. *Psychotherapy, 49,* 163–172. doi:10.1037/a0023200

Weuve, J., Kang, J. H., Manson, J. E., Breteler, M. M. B., Ware, J. H., & Grodstein, F. (2004). Physical activity, including walking, and cognitive function in older women. *Journal of the American Medical Association, 292,* 1454–1461.

Wexler, M. (2005). Anticipating the three-dimensional consequences of eye movements. *Proceedings of the National Academy of Sciences, 102,* 1246–1251.

Whalen, P. J., Kagan, J., Cook, R. G., Davis, F. C., Kim, H., Polis, S., et al. (2004). Human amygdala responsivity to masked fearful eye whites. *Science, 306,* 2061.

Whaley, A. L. (2011). Clinicians' competence in assessing cultural mistrust among African American psychiatric patients. *Journal of Black Psychology, 37*(4), 387–406. doi:10.1177/0095798410387133.

Whaley, A. L. (2001). Cultural mistrust: An important psychological construct for diagnosis and treatment of African-Americans. *Professional Psychology: Research and Practice, 32,* 555–562.

Whaley, A. L., & Hall, B. N. (2009). Cultural themes in the psychotic symptoms of African American psychiatric patients. *Professional Psychology: Research and Practice, 40,* 75–80.

Whang, W., Kubzansky, L. D., Kawachi, I., Rexrode, K. M., et al. (2009). Depression and risk of sudden cardiac death and coronary heart disease in women. *Journal of the American College of Cardiology, 53,* 950–958.

Wharton, C. M., Grafman, J., Flitman, S. S., Hansen, E. K., Brauner, J., Marks, A., & Honda, M. (2000). Toward neuroanatomical models of analogy: A positron emission tomography study of analogical mapping. *Cognitive Psychology, 40,* 173–197.

Wheaton, L. A., & Hallett, M. (2007). Ideomotor apraxia: A review. *Journal of the Neurological Sciences, 260*(1–2), 1–10.

Wheeler, L., & Suls, J. (2007). Social comparison: Can we agree on what it is? *Revue Internationale de Psychologie Sociale, 20,* 31–51.

Wheeler, B. W., Gunnell, D., Metcalfe, C., Stephens, P., & Martin, R. M. (2008). The population impact on incidence of suicide and non-fatal self harm of regulatory action against the use of selective serotonin reuptake inhibitors in under 18s in the United Kingdom: Ecological study. *British Medical Journal, 336,* 542–545.

Wheeler, M. E., & Fiske, S. T. (2005). Controlling racial prejudice. *Psychological Science, 16,* 56–63.

Whiffen, V. E. (2006). *A secret sadness: The hidden relationship patterns that make women depressed.* Oakland, CA: New Harbinger Publications.

Whimbey, A. (1976). *Intelligence can be taught.* New York: Bantam.

Whitaker, D. J., Morrison, S., Lindquist, C., Hawkins, S. R., O'Neil, J. A., Nesius, A. M., et al. (2006). A critical review of interventions for the primary prevention of perpetration of partner violence. *Aggression and Violent Behavior, 11,* 151–166.

Whitam, F. L., Diamond, M., & Martin, J. (1993). Homosexual orientation in twins: A report on 61 pairs and three triplet sets. *Archives of Sexual Behavior, 22*(3), 187–206.

Whitchurch, E. R., Wilson, T. D., & Gilbert, D. T. (2011). "He loves me, he loves me not . . ." Uncertainty can increase romantic attraction. *Psychological Science, 22*(2), 172–175. doi:10.1177/0956797610393745.

White, A. T., & Spector, P. E. (1987). An investigation of age-related factors in the age-job satisfaction relationship. *Psychology and Aging, 2,* 261–265.

White, F. J. (1998). Nicotine addiction and the lure of reward. *Nature Medicine, 4,* 659–660.

White, K. S., Brown, T. A., Somers, T. J., & Barlow, D. H. (2006). Avoidance behavior in panic disorder: The moderating influences of perceived control. *Behaviour Research and Therapy, 44,* 147–157.

White, R. W., & Horvitz, E. (2009). Cyberchondria: Studies of the escalation of medical concerns in Web search. *ACM Transactions on Information Systems, 27*(4), 23:1–23:37.

White, S. M. Talking genes. *Advances in Speech Language Pathology, 8,* 2–6.

Whitlock, J. R., Heynen, A. J., Shuler, M. G., & Bear, M. F. (2006). Learning induces long-term potentiation in the hippocampus. *Science, 313,* 1093–1097.

Whitman, D., Caleo, S., Carpenter, N., Horner, M., & Bernerth, J. (2012). Fairness at the collective level: A meta-analytic examination of the consequences and boundary conditions of organizational justice climate. *The Journal of Applied Psychology, 97,* 776–791.

Whitney, P. (2001). Schemas, frames, and scripts in cognitive psychology. In N. J. Smelser & P. B. Baltes (Eds.), *International encyclopedia of the social and behavioral sciences* (pp. 13522–13526). New York: Elsevier.

Whyte, E., Skidmore, E., Aizenstein, H., Ricker, J., & Butters, M. (2011). Cognitive impairment in acquired brain injury: a predictor of rehabilitation outcomes and an opportunity for novel interventions. *PM&R, 3*(6 Supplement 1), S45–S51

Wichers, M. C., Myin-Germeys, I., Jacobs, N., Kenis, G., Dermon, C., Vlietinck, R., et al. (2008). Susceptibility to depression expressed as alterations in cortisol day curve: A cross-twin, cross-trait study. *Biological Psychology, 79,* 80–90.

Wickens, C. D. (1989). Attention and skilled performance. In D. Holding (Ed.), *Human skills* (pp. 71–105). New York: Wiley.

Wickens, C. D. (1992). *Engineering psychology and human performance* (2nd ed.). New York: HarperCollins.

Wickens, C. D., & Carswell, C. M. (2006). Information processing. In G. Salvendy (Ed.), *Handbook of human factors and ergonomics* (3rd ed.). Hoboken, NJ: Wiley Interscience.

Wickens, C. D., Stokes, A., Barnett, B., & Hyman, F. (1992). The effects of stress on pilot judgment in a MIDIS simulator. In O. Svenson & J. Maule (Eds.), *Time pressure and stress in human judgment and decision making* (pp. 271–292). New York: Plenum.

Wicker, B., Keysers, C., Plailly, J., Royet, J. P., Gallese, V., & Rizzolatti, G. (2003). Both of us disgusted in My insula: The common neural basis of seeing and feeling disgust. *Neuron, 40,* 655–664.

Wickham, D. (2001, September 3). Castration often fails to halt offenders. *USA Today.*

Widiger, T. A. (2011). A shaky future for personality disorders. *Personality Disorders: Theory, Research, and Treatment, 2,* 54–67. doi:10.1037/a0021855.

Widiger, T. A. (2008). Personality disorders. In J. Hunsley, E. J. Mash (Eds.), *A guide to assessments that work* (pp. 413–435). New York: Oxford University Press.

Widiger, T. A., & Clark, L. A. (2000). Toward *DSM-V* and the classification of psychopathology. *Psychological Bulletin, 126,* 946–963.

Widiger, T. A., & Lowe, J. R. (2008). A dimensional model of personality disorder: Proposal for DSM-V. *Psychiatric Clinics of North America, 31,* 363–378.

Widiger, T. A., & Samuel, D. B. (2005). Diagnostic categories or dimensions? A question for the *Diagnostic and Statistical Manual of Mental Disorders—Fifth Edition. Journal of Abnormal Psychology, 114,* 494–504.

Widiger, T. A., & Sanderson, C. J. (1995). Assessing personality disorders. In J. N. Butcher (Ed.), Clinical personality assessment: Practical approaches (pp. 380–394). New York: Oxford University Press.

Widiger, T. A., Simonsen, E., Sirovatka, P., & Reiger, D. A. (2006). *Dimensional models of personality disorders: Refining the research agenda for DSM-V.* Washington, DC: American Psychiatric Publishing.

Widom, C. S. (1989). The cycle of violence. *Science, 244,* 160–166.

Widom, C. S. (2000). Childhood victimization: Early adversity, later psychopathology. *National Institute of Justice Journal, 19,* 2–9.

Widom, C. S., Czaja, S. J., & Dutton, M. A. (2008). Childhood victimization and lifetime revictimization. *Child Abuse and Neglect, 32,* 785–796.

Widom, C. S., Kahn, E. E., Kaplow, J. B., Sepulveda-Kozakowski, S., & Wilson, H. W. (2007). Child abuse and neglect: Potential derailment from normal developmental pathways. *NYS Psychologist, 19*(5), 2–6.

Wiederhold, B. K., & Wiederhold, M. D. (2005). *Virtual reality therapy for anxiety disorders: Advances in evaluation and treatment.* Washington, DC: American Psychological Association.

Wiens, S., Mezzacappa, E. S., & Katkin, E. S. (2000). Heartbeat detection and the experience of emotions. *Cognition & Emotion, 14,* 417–427.

Wiers, R. W., Eberl, C., Rinck, M., Becker, E. S., & Lindenmeyer, J. (2011). Retraining automatic action tendencies changes alcoholic patients' approach bias for alcohol and improves treatment outcome. *Psychological Science, 22*(4), 490–497. doi:10.1177/0956797611400615.

Wiesner, W. H., & Cronshaw, S. F. (1988). A meta-analytic investigation of the impact of interview format and degree of structure on the validity of the employment interview. *Journal of Occupational Psychology, 61,* 275–290.

Wigfield, A., & Eccles, J. S. (2000). Expectancy-value theory of achievement motivation. *Contemporary Educational Psychology, 25,* 68–81.

Wigfield, A., Eccles, J. S., Schiefele, U., Roeser, R. W., & Davis-Kean, P. (2006). Development of achievement motivation. In W. Damon & R. Lerner (Series Eds.), & N. Eisenberg (Vol. Ed.), *Handbook of child psychology: Vol. 3. Social, emotional, and personality development* (6th ed., pp. 933–1062). Hoboken, NJ: Wiley.

Wiik, K.L., Loman, M.M., Van Ryzin, M.J., Armstrong, J.M., Essex, M.J., Pollak, S.D., & Gunnar, M.R. (2011). Behavioral and emotional symptoms of post-institutionalized children in middle childhood. *Journal of Child Psychiatry and Psychology, 52,* 56–63

Wilcox, H. C., Grados, M., Samuels, J., Riddle, M. A., Beinvenu, O. J., III, Pinto, A., et al. (2008). The association between parental bonding and obsessive-compulsive disorder in offspring at high familial risk. *Journal of Affective Disorders, 111,* 31–39.

Wilcoxon, H. C., Dragoin, W. B., & Kral, P. A. (1971). Illness-induced aversions in rat and quail: Relative salience of visual and gustatory cues. *Science, 171,* 826–828.

Wilford, M. M., & Wells, G. L. (2010). Does Facial Processing Prioritize Change Detection? Change Blindness Illustrates Costs and Benefits of Holistic Processing. *Psychological Science, 21*(11), 1611–1615. doi:10.1177/0956797610385952.

Wilhelm, K., Mitchell, P. B., Niven, H., Finch, A., Wedgwood, L., et al. (2006). Life events, first depression onset, and the serotonin transporter gene. *British Journal of Psychiatry, 188,* 210–215.

Wilkowski, B. M., & Robinson, M. D. (2008). The cognitive basis of trait anger and reactive aggression: An integrative analysis. *Personality & Social Psychology Review, 12*(1), 3–21.

Wilksch, S. M., & Wade, T. D. (2010). Risk factors for clinically significant importance of shape and weight in adolescent girls. *Journal of Abnormal Psychology, 119,* 206–215.

Willemsen, R., & Vanderlinden, J. (2008). Hypnotic approaches for alopecia areata. *International Journal of Clinical and Experimental Hypnosis, 56,* 318–333.

Willford, J. A., Leech, S. L., & Day, N. L. (2006). Moderate prenatal alcohol exposure and cognitive status of children at age 10. *Alcoholism: Clinical and Experimental Research, 30,* 1051–1059.

Williams, C. L., & Pleil, K. E. (2008). Toy story: Why do monkey and human males prefer trucks? *Hormones and Behavior, 54,* 355–358.

Williams, E., Thomas, K., Sidebotham, H., & Emond, A. (2008). Prevalence and characteristics of autistic spectrum disorders in the ALSPAC cohort. *Developmental Medicine and Child Neurology, 50,* 672–677.

Williams, J. (2008). Working toward a neurobiological account of ADHD: Commentary on Gail Tripp and Jeff Wickens' dopamine transfer deficit. *Journal of Child Psychology and Psychiatry, 49,* 705–711.

Williams, J. E., & Best, D. L. (1990). *Measuring stereotypes: A multination study* (Rev. ed.). Newbury Park, CA: Sage.

Williams, J. H. G., Waiter, G. D., Gilchrist, A., Perrett, D. I., Murray, A. D., et al. (2006). Neural mechanisms of imitation and 'mirror neuron' functioning in autistic spectrum disorder. *Neuropsychologica, 44,* 610–621.

Williams, K. D., & Sommer, K. L. (1997). Social ostracism by coworkers: Does rejection lead to loafing or compensation? *Personality and Social Psychology Bulletin, 23,* 693–706.

Williams, L. E., Bargh, J. A., Nocera, C. C., & Gray, J. R. (2009). The unconscious regulation of emotion: Nonconscious reappraisal goals modulate emotional reactivity. *Emotion, 9,* 847–854.

Williams, L. M. (1994). What does it mean to forget child sexual abuse? A reply to Loftus, Garry, and Feldman (1994). *Journal of Consulting and Clinical Psychology, 62,* 1182–1186.

Williams, N. L., Reardon, J. M., Murray, K. T., & Cole, T. M. (2005). Anxiety disorders: A developmental vulnerability-stress perspective. In B. L. Hankin & J. R. Z. Abela (Eds.), *Development of psychopathology: A vulnerability-stress perspective* (pp. 289–327). Thousand Oaks, CA: Sage.

Williams, R. A. (2005). A short course in family therapy: Translating research into practice. *Family Journal: Counseling and Therapy for Couples and Families 13,* 188–194.

Williams, R. A. (2005). A short course in family therapy: Translating research into practice. *Family Journal: Counseling and Therapy for Couples and Families 13,* 188–194.

Williams, R. J., & Connolly, D. (2006). Does learning about the mathematics of gambling change gambling behavior? *Psychology of Addictive Behavior, 20,* 62–68.

Williams, T. & Williams, K. (2010). Self-efficacy and performance in mathematics: Reciprocal determinism in 33 nations. *Journal of Educational Psychology, 102*(2), 453–466. doi:10.1037/a0017271.

Williams, T. J., Pepitone, M. E., Christensen, S. E., Cooke, B. M., Huberman, A. D., Breedlove, N. J., et al. (2000). Finger-length ratios and sexual orientation. *Nature, 404,* 455–456.

Williams-Piehota, P., Pizarro, J., Schneider, T. R., Mowad, L., & Salovey, P. (2005). Matching health messages to monitor-blunter coping styles to motivate screening mammography. *Health Psychology, 24,* 58–67.

Willis, J., & Todorov, A. (2006). First impressions: Making up your mind after a 100-ms exposure to a face. *Psychological Science, 17,* 592–598.

Willmott L., Harris P, Gellaitry G, Cooper V., Horne R. The effects of expressive writing following first myocardial infarction: A randomized controlled trial. *Health Psychology, 30,* 642-650, 2011.

Wills, T. A., Sandy, J. M., Yaeger, A., & Shinar, O. (2001). Family risk factors and adolescent substance use: Moderation effects of temperament dimension. *Developmental Psychology, 37,* 283–297.

Wilson, G. T., Wilfley, D. E., Agras, W. S., & Bryson, S. W. (2010). Psychological treatments of binge eating disorder. *Archives of General Psychiatry, 67,* 94–101.

Wilson, A. D., & Baietto, M. (2011). Advances in electronic-nose technologies developed for biomedical applications. *Sensors, 11*(1), 1105–1176.

Wilson, B. S., & Dorman, M. F. (2008). Cochlear implants: A remarkable past and a brilliant future. *Hearing Research, 242*(1–2), 3–21.

Wilson, G. T., Nathan, P. E., O'Leary, K. D., & Clark, L. A. (1996). *Abnormal psychology.* Boston: Allyn & Bacon.

Wilson, J. M., Straus, S. G., & McEvily, B. (2006). All in due time: The development of trust in computer-mediated and face-to-face teams. *Organizational Behavior and Human Decision Processes, 99,* 16–33.

Wilson, K., & French, C. C. (2006). The relationship between susceptibility to false memories, dissociativity, and paranormal belief and experience. *Personality and Individual Differences, 41,* 1493–1502.

Wilson, R. E., Gosling, S. D., & Graham, L. T. (2012). A review of Facebook research in the social sciences. *Perspectives on Psychological Science, 7,* 203–220. doi:10.1177/1745691612442904.

Wilson, R. S., Beck, T. L., Bienias, J. L., & Bennett, D. A. (2007a). Terminal cognitive decline: Accelerated loss of cognition in the last years of life. *Psychosomatic Medicine, 69,* 131–137.

Wilson, R. S., Beckett, L. A. Barnes, L. L., Schneider, J. A., et al. (2002). Individual differences in rates of change in cognitive abilities of older persons. *Psychology & Aging, 17*(2), 179–193.

Wilson, R. S., Scherr, P. A., Schneider, J. A., Tang, Y., & Bennett, D. A. (2007b). Relation of cognitive activity to risk of developing Alzheimer disease. *Neurology, 69,* 1911–1920.

Wilson, R. S., Begeny, C. T., Boyle, P. A., Schneider, J. A., & Bennett, D. A. (2011). Vulnerability to stress, anxiety, and development of dementia in old age. *The American Journal of Geriatric Psychiatry, 19,* 327–334. doi:10.1097/ JGP.0b013e31820119da.

Wilson, R., Segawa, E., Boyle, P., & Bennett, D. (2012). Influence of late-life cognitive activity on cognitive health. *Neurology, 78*(15), 1123-1129.

Wilt, J., Cox, K. S., & McAdams, D. P. (2010). Exploring the relationships between Eriksonian

Wimo, A., Winblad, B., & Jonsson, L. (2010). The worldwide societal costs of dementia: Estimates for 2009. *Alzheimer's Dementia, 6,* 98–103.

Winer, G. A., Cottrell, J. E., Gregg, V., Fournier, J. S., & Bica, L. A. (2002). Fundamentally misunderstanding visual perception: Adults' belief in visual emissions. *American Psychologist, 57,* 417–424.

Winerman, L. (2005, July/August). A virtual cure. *Monitor on Psychology,* 87–89.

Winkelmayer, W. C., Stampfer, M. J., Willett, W. C., & Curhan, G. C. (2005). Habitual caffeine intake and the risk of hypertension in women. *Journal of the American Medical Association, 294,* 2330–2335.

Winkielman, P., & Berridge, K. C. (2004). Unconscious emotion. *Current Directions in Psychological Science, 13,* 120–123.

Winkielman, P., & Cacioppo J. T. (2004). Mind at ease puts a smile on the face: Psychophysiological evidence that processing facilitation elicits positive affect. *Journal of Personality and Social Psychology, 81,* 989–1000.

Winn, P. (1995). The lateral hypothalamus and motivated behavior: An old syndrome reassessed and a new perspective gained. *Current Directions in Psychological Science, 4,* 182–187.

Winner, E. (2000). Giftedness: Current theory and research. *Current Directions in Psychological Science, 9,* 153–156.

Winson, J. (1990, November). The meaning of dreams. *Scientific American,* pp. 86–96.

Winston, A., Been, H., & Serby, M. (2005). Psychotherapy and psychopharmacology: Different universes or an integrated future? *Journal of Psychotherapy Integration, 15,* 213–223.

Winter, D. G. (1996). *Personality: Analysis and interpretation of lives.* New York: McGraw-Hill.

Winterer, G. (2006). Cortical microcircuits in schizophrenia—The dopamine hypothesis re-visited. *Pharmacopsychiatry, 39,* S68–S71.

Wintersteen, M. B., Mensinger, J. L., & Diamond, G. S. (2005). Do gender and racial differences between patient and therapist affect therapeutic alliance and treatment retention in adolescents? *Professional Psychology: Research and Practice, 36,* 400–408.

Wise, R. A. & Kiyatkin, E. A. (2011). Differentiating the rapid actions of cocaine. Nature Reviews. *Neuroscience, 12*(8), 479–484.

Wiseman, R., West, D., & Stemman, R. (1996, January/February). Psychic crime detectives: A new test for measuring their successes and failures. *Skeptical Inquirer, 21,* 38–58.

Wismer Fries, A. B., Shirtcliff, E. A., & Pollak, S. D. (2008). Neuroendocrine dysregulation following early social deprivation in children. *Developmental Psychobiology, 50,* 588–599.

Wismer Fries, A. B., Ziegler, T. E., Kurian, J. R., Jacoris, S., & Pollak, S. D. (2005). Early experience in humans is associated with changes in neuropeptides critical for regulating social behavior. *Proceedings of the National Academy of Sciences, 102,* 17237–17240.

Witkamp, R. (2011). Current and future drug targets in weight management. *Pharmaceutical Research, 28*(8), 1792–1818.

Witt, C., Brinkhaus, B., Jena, S., Linde, K., Streng, A., Wagenpfeil, S., et al. (2005). Acupuncture in patients with osteoarthritis of the knee: A randomised trial. *Lancet, 366,* 136–143.

Witt, J. K., Linkenauger, S. A., & Proffitt, D. R. (2012). Get me out of this slump! Visual illusions improve sports performance. *Psychological Science, 23*(4), 397–399. doi:10.1177/0956797611428810.

Witt, J. K., Linkenauger, S. A., & Proffitt, D. R. (2012). Get me out of this slump! Visual illusions improve sports performance. *Psychological Science, 23*(4), 397–399. doi:10.1177/0956797611428810.

Wittchen, H. U., & Hoyer, J. (2001). Generalized anxiety disorder: Nature and course. *Journal of Clinical Psychiatry, 62,* 15–19.

Wixted, J. T. (2004). The psychology and neuroscience of forgetting. *Annual Review of Psychology, 55,* 235–269.

Wixted, J. T. (2005). A theory about why we forget what we once knew. *Current Directions in Psychological Science, 14,* 6–9.

Wixted, J. T., & Mickes, L. (2012). The field of eyewitness memory should abandon probative value and embrace receiver operating characteristic analysis. *Perspectives on Psychological Science, 7*(3), 275–278. doi:10.1177/1745691612442906.

Wohl, J. (1995). Traditional individual psychotherapy and ethnic minorities. In J. F. Aponte, R. Y. Rivers, & J. Wohl (Eds.), *Psychological interventions and cultural diversity* (pp. 74–91). Boston: Allyn & Bacon.

Wohlfarth, T., Storosum, J. G., Elferink, A. J. A., van Zweiten, B. J., Fouwels, A., & van den Brink, W. (2004). Response to tricyclic antidepressants: Independent of gender? *American Journal of Psychiatry, 161,* 370–372.

Wojcieszak, M., & Price, V. (2010). Bridging the divide or intensifying the conflict? How disagreement affects strong predilections about sexual minorities. *Political Psychology, 31,* 315–339. doi:10.1111/j.1467-9221.2009.00753.x

Woldt, A. L., & Toman, S. M. (Eds.). (2005). *Gestalt therapy: History, theory, and practice.* Newbury Park, CA: Sage.

Wolf, H., Angleitner, A., Spinath, F., Reimann, R., & Strelau, J. (2004). Genetic and environmental influences on the EPQ-RS scales: A twin study using self- and peer reports *Personality and Individual Differences. 37,* 579–590.

Wolf, P. A. (2003). Fifty years at Framingham: Contributions to stroke epidemiology. *Advances in Neurology, 92,* 165–172.

Wolfe, B. E. (2012). Healing the research–practice split: Let's start with me. *Psychotherapy, 49,* 101–108. doi:10.1037/a0027114

Wolfe, J. M., Horowitz, T. S., Van Wert, M., Kenner, N. M., Place, S. S., & Kibbi, N. (2007). Low target prevalence is a stubborn source of errors in visual search tasks. *Journal of Experimental Psychology, 136*(4), 623–638.

Wolfe, J. M., & Van Wert, M. J. (2010). Varying target prevalence reveals two dissociable decision criteria in visual search. *Current Biology, 20,* 121–124.

Wolitzky, D. L. (2011). Psychoanalytic theories of psychotherapy. In J. C. Norcross, G. R. VandenBos, & D. K. Freedheim (Eds.), *History of psychotherapy: Continuity and change* (pp. 65–100). Washington, D.C.: American Psychological Association.

Wolk, D. A., Dunfee, K. L., Dickerson, B. C., Aizenstein, H. J., & Dekosky, S. T. (2010). A medial temporal lobe division of labor: Insights from memory in aging and early Alzheimer disease. *Hippocampus.* Epub 2010 Mar 15.

Wollert, R. (2007). Poor diagnostic reliability, the Null-Bayes Logic Model, and their implications for sexually violent predator evaluations. *Psychology, Public Policy, and Law, 13,* 167–213.

Wolpaw, J. R., & Chen, X. Y. (2006). The cerebellum in maintenance of a motor skill: A hierarchy of brain and spinal cord plasticity underlies H-reflex conditioning. *Learning & Memory, 13,* 208–215.

Wolpe, J. (1958). *Psychotherapy by reciprocal inhibition.* Stanford, CA: Stanford University Press.

Wolpert, I. (1924). Die Simultanagnosie: Störung der Gesamtauffassung. Archiv für Psychiatrie und Nervenkrankheiten, vereinigt mit Zeitschrift für die gesamte Neurologie und Psychiatrie, 93, 397–413.

Wolraich, M. L., Wibbelsman, C. J., Brown, T. E., Evans, S. W., Gotlieb, E. M., Knight, J. R., et al. (2005). Attention-deficit/hyperactivity disorder among adolescents: A review of the diagnosis, treatment, and clinical implications. *Pediatrics, 115,* 1734–1746.

Wong, Q. J. J., & Moulds, M. L. (2009). Impact of rumination versus distraction on anxiety and maladaptive self-beliefs in socially anxious individuals. *Behaviour Research and Therapy, 47,* 861–867.

Wong, C. C., Mill, J., & Fernandes, C. (2011). Drugs and addiction: an introduction to epigenetics. *Addiction, 106*(3), 480–489.

Wong, C. G., Gibson, K. M., & Snead, O. C. (2004). From the street to the brain: Neurobiology of the recreational drug gamma-hydroxybutyric acid. *Trends in Pharmacological Science, 25,* 29–34.

Wong, K. F. E., & Kwong, J. Y. Y. (2005). Between-individual comparisons in performance evaluation: A perspective from prospect theory. *Journal of Applied Psychology, 90,* 284–294.

Wong, N., Ray, P., Stephens, G., & Lewis, L. (2012). Artificial immune systems for the detection of credit card fraud: An architecture, prototype and preliminary results. *Information Systems Journal, 22*(1), 53–76. doi:10.1111/j.1365-2575.2011.00369.x.

Wong, P. P. (2011). Positive psychology 2.0: Towards a balanced interactive model of the good life. *Canadian Psychology/Psychologie canadienne, 52*(2), 69–81. doi:10.1037/a0022511.

Wood, J. (2006). Effect of anxiety reduction on children's school performance and social adjustment. *Developmental Psychology, 42,* 345–349.

Wood, J. M., Lilienfeld, S. O., Nezworski, M. T., Garb, H. N., Allen, K. H., & Wildermuth, J. L. (2010). Validity of Rorschach inkblot scores for discriminating psychopaths from nonpsychopaths in forensic populations: A meta-analysis. *Psychological Assessment, 22,* 336–349.

Wood, N. D., Crane, D. R., Shaalje, G. B., & Law, D. D. (2005). What works for whom: A meta-analytic review of marital and couples therapy in reference to marital distress. *American Journal of Family Therapy, 33,* 273–287.

Wood, W., & Eagly, A. H. (2002). A cross-cultural analysis of the behavior of women and men: Implications for the origins of sex differences. *Psychological Bulletin, 128,* 699–727.

Wood, W., & Eagly, A. H. (2012). Chapter 2: Biosocial construction of sex differences and similarities in behavior. *Advances in Experimental Social Psychology, 46,* 55–123. doi: http://dx.doi.org/10.1016/B978-0-12-394281-4.00002-7.

Wood, W., Wong, F. Y., & Chachere, G. (1991). Effects of media violence on viewers' aggression in unconstrained social interaction. *Psychological Bulletin, 109,* 371–383.

Woods, B. T., Schoene, W., & Kneisley, L. (1982). Are hippocampal lesions sufficient to cause lasting amnesia? *Journal of Neurology, Neurosurgery, and Psychiatry, 45*(3), 243–247.

Woods, S. C., Schwartz, M. W., Baskin, D. G., & Seeley, R. J. (2000). Food intake and the regulation of body weight. *Annual Review of Psychology, 51,* 255–277.

Woodward, A. L. (2009). Infants' grasp of others' intentions. *Current Directions in Psychological Science, 18,* 53–57.

Woodward, T. S., Moritz, S., Cuttler, C., & Whitman, J. C. (2006). The contribution of a cognitive bias against disconfirmatory evidence (BADE) to delusions in schizophrenia. *Journal of Clinical and Experimental Neuropsychology, 28,* 605–617.

Woodworth, R. S., & Schlosberg, H. (1954). *Experimental psychology.* New York: Holt.

Woody, W. D., Daniel, D. B., & Baker, C. A. (2010). E-books or textbooks: Students prefer textbooks. *Computers & Education, 55,* 945–948. doi:10.1016/j.compedu.2010.04.005.

Woolley, J. D. (1997). Thinking about fantasy: Are children fundamentally different thinkers and believers from adults? *Child Development, 68,* 991–1011.

World Health Organization. (2002). *Nutrition: Controlling the global obesity epidemic.* Retrieved December 13, 2004, from http://www.who.int/nut/obs.htm

World Health Organization. (2003). *AIDS epidemic update.* Geneva, Switzerland: Author.

World Health Organization Mental Health Survey Consortium. (2004). Prevalence, severity, and unmet need for treatment of mental disorders in the World Health Organization World Mental Health Surveys. *Journal of the American Medical Association, 291,* 2581–2590.

World Health Organization. (2008). *World health report 2008: Primary health care now more than ever.* Geneva, Switzerland: World Health Organization. Retrieved June 11, 2009, from http://www.who.int/whr/2008/whr08_en.pdf.

World Health Organization. (2009). *World health organization mental health surveys.* Cambridge, MA: Cambridge University Press.

World Health Organization (2012). Depression: What is depression? Retrieved from http://www.who.int/mental_health/management/depression/definition/en/index.html.

Worley, J. R., Rogers, S. N., & Kraemer, R. R. (2011). Metabolic responses to Wii fit video games at different game levels. *Journal of Strength & Conditioning Research*, 25(3), 689–693.

Worthington, R. L., Navarro, R. L., Savoy, H. B., & Hampton, D. (2008). Development, reliability, and validity of the Measure of Sexual Identity Exploration and Commitment (MOSIEC). *Developmental Psychology, 44*, 22–33.

Worthy, D. A., Gorlick, M. A., Pacheco, J. L., Schnyer, D. M., & Maddox, W. (2011). With age comes wisdom: Decision making in younger and older adults. *Psychological Science*, 22(11), 1375–1380. doi:10.1177/0956797611420301.

Woythaler, M. A., McCormick, M. C., & Smith, V. C. (2011). Late preterm infants have worse 24-month neurodevelopmental outcomes than term infants. *Pediatrics*, 127(3), e622–e629. doi:10.1542/peds.2009-3598.

Wren, A. M., Seal, L. J., Cohen, M. A., Brynes, A. E., Frost, G. S., Murphy, K. G., Dhillo, W. S., Ghatei, M. A., & Bloom, S. R. (2001). Ghrelin enhances appetite and increases food intake in humans. *The Journal of Clinical Endocrinology and Metabolism, 86*, 5992.

Wren, C. S. (1999, February 24). U.N. drug board urges research on marijuana as medicine. *New York Times*. Retrieved December 13, 2004, from http://nytimes.com.

Wright, A. A., Katz, J. S., & Ma, W. (2012). How to be proactive about interference: Lessons from animal memory. *Psychological Science*, 23(5), 453–458. doi:10.1177/0956797611430096.

Wright, D. B., Memon, A., Skagerberg, E. M., & Gabber, F. (2009). When eyewitnesses talk. *Current Directions in Psychological Science, 18*, 174–178.

Wright, E. F., Voyer, D., Wright, R. D., & Roney, C. (1995). Supporting audiences and performance under pressure: The home-ice disadvantage in hockey championships. *Journal of Sport Behavior, 18*, 21–28.

Wright, G., Berry, C., & Bird, G. (2012). "You can't kid a kidder": Association between production and detection of deception in an interactive deception task. *Frontiers in Human Neuroscience, 6*, 87. doi: http://dx.doi.org/10.3389/fnhum.2012.00087.

Wu, C., Cui, B., He, L., Chen, L., & Mobley, W. C. (2009). The coming of age of axonal neurotrophin signaling endosomes. *Journal of Proteomics, 72*, 46–55. Epub 2008 Nov 6.

Wujcik, D. M. (2008, November). Are you part of the sandwich generation? *ONS Connect*, 23(11), 7.

Wupperman, P., & Neumann, C. S. (2006). Depressive symptoms as a function of sex-role, rumination, and neuroticism. *Personality and Individual Differences, 40*, 189–201.

Wyatt, T. D. (2009). Fifty years of pheromones. *Nature, 457*, 262–263.

Wynne, C. L. (2004). *Do animals think?* Princeton, NJ: Princeton University Press.

Xiao, Y., Seagull, F. J., Mackenzie, C. F., Klein, K. J., & Ziegert, J. (2008). Adaptation of team communication patterns. Exploring the effects of leadership at a distance (pp. 71–96). In S. Weisband (Ed.), *Leadership at a distance: Research in technologically-supported work*. New York: Erlbaum.

Xie, P., Kranzler, H. R., Poling, J., Stein, M. B., et al. (2009). Interactive eff ect of stressful life events and the serotonin transporter 5-HTTLPR genotype on posttraumatic stress disorder diagnosis in 2 independent populations. *Archives of General Psychiatry, 66*, 1201–1209.

Xie, Y. F., Huo, F. Q., & Tang, J. S. (2009). Cerebral cortex modulation of pain. *Acta Pharmacologica Sinica, 30*, 31–41.

Xu, L., Wu, A. S., & Yue, Y. (2009). The incidence of intraoperative awareness during general anesthesia in China: A multicenter observational study. *Acta Anaesthesioligica Scandinavica, 53*, 873–882.

Xue, Y., Leventhal, T., Brooks-Gunn, J., & Earls, F. J. (2005). Neighborhood residence and mental health problems of 5- to 11-year-olds. *Archives of General Psychiatry, 62*, 554–563.

Xue, Y., Luo, Y., Wu, P., Shi, H., Xue, L., Chen, C., & ... Lu, L. (2012). A memory retrieval-extinction procedure to prevent drug craving and relapse. *Science (New York, N.Y.), 336*(6078), 241–245.

Yaffe, K., Barnes, D., Nevitt, M., Lui, L.-Y., & Covinsky, K. (2001). A prospective study of physical activity and cognitive decline in elderly women. *Archives of Internal Medicine, 161*, 1703–1708.

Yaffe, K., Fiocco, A. J., Lindquist, K., Vittinghoff , E., et al. (2009). Predictors of maintaining cognitive function in older adults: The Health ABC Study. *Neurology, 72*, 2029–2035.

Yakimovich, D., & Saltz, E. (1971). Helping behavior: The cry for help. *Psychonomic Science, 23*, 427–428.

Yalom, E. D. (2005). *The theory and practice of group psychotherapy* (5th ed.). New York: Basic Books.

Yamagata, S., Suzuki, A., Ando, J., Ono, Y., Kijima, N., Yoshimura, K., Ostendorf, F., Angleitner, A., Riemann, R., Spinath, F. M., Livesley, W. J., Jang, K. L. (2006). Is the genetic structure of human personality universal? A cross-cultural twin study from North America, Europe, and Asia. *Journal of Personality and Social Psychology, 90*(6), 987–998.

Yan, Z., Chi, Y., Wang, P., Cheng, J., Wang, Y., Shu, Q., & Huang, G. (1992). Studies on the luminescence of channels in rats and its law of changes with "syndromes" and treatment of acupuncture and moxibustion. *Journal of Traditional Chinese Medicine, 12*(4), 283–287.

Yang, C.-M., & Spielman, A. J. (2001). The effect of delayed weekend sleep pattern on sleep and morning functioning. *Psychology and Health, 16*, 715–725.

Yang, C.-M., Spielman, A. J., & Glovinsky, P. (2006). Nonpharmacologic strategies in the management of insomnia. *Psychiatric Clinics of North America, 29*, 895–919.

Yang, J., Manolio, T., Pasquale, L., Boerwinkle, E., Caporaso, N., Cunningham, J., & .. Visscher, P. (2011). Genome partitioning of genetic variation for complex traits using common SNPs. *Nature Genetics, 43*(6), 519–525.

Yang, M. Y., Yang, W. C., Lin, P. M., Hsu, J. F., Hsiao, H. H., Liu, Y. C., Tsai, H. J., Chang, C. S., & Lin, S. F. (2011). Altered expression of circadian clock genes in human chronic myeloid leukemia. *Journal of Biological Rhythms, 26*(2), 136–148.

Yang, T., & Kubovy, M. (1999). Weakening the robustness of perspective: Evidence for a modified theory of compensation in picture perception. *Perception and Psychophysics, 61*, 456–467.

Yang, Y., Raine, A., Narr, K. L., Colletti, P., & Toga, A. W. (2009). Localization of deformations within the amygdala in individuals with psychopathy. *Archives of General Psychiatry, 66*, 986–994.

Yang, Y., & Wang, G. (2011). A novel emotion recognition method based on ensemble learning and rough set theory. *International Journal Of Cognitive Informatics And Natural Intelligence, 5*(3), 61–72. doi:10.4018/IJCINI.2011070104.

Yang-Teng, F., Decety, J., Chia-Yen, Y., Ji-Lin, L., & Yawei, C. (2010). Unbroken mirror neurons in autism spectrum disorders. *Journal Of Child Psychology & Psychiatry, 51*(9), 981–988. doi:10.1111/j.1469-7610.2010.02269.x.

Yanovski, S. Z., & Yanovski, J. A. (2002). Obesity. *New England Journal of Medicine, 346*(8), 591–602. doi:10.1056/NEJMra012586.

Yantis, S. (1993). Stimulus-driven attentional capture. *Current Directions in Psychological Science, 2*, 156–161.

Yarkoni, T. (2010). Personality in 100,000 words: A large-scale analysis of personality and word use among bloggers. *Journal of Research in Personality, 44*, 363–373. doi:10.1016/j.jrp.2010.04.001.

Yarlagadda, A., Helvink, B., Chou, C., Gladieux, K., Keller, A., & Clayton, A. (2008). Glutamic acid decarboxylase (GAD) antibodies in tardive dyskinesia (TD) as compared to patients with schizophrenia without TD and normal controls. *Schizophrenia Research, 105*, 287–288.

Yates, J. (2010). Culture and probability judgment. *Social and Personality Psychology Compass, 4*(3), 174–188. doi:10.1111/j.1751-9004.2009.00253.x.

Yearta, S. K., Maitlis, S., & Briner, R. B. (1995). An exploratory study of goal setting in theory and practice: A motivational technique that works? *Journal of Occupational and Organizational Psychology, 68*, 237–252.

Yee, E., Ahmed, S. Z., & Thompson-Schill, S. L. (2012). Colorless green ideas (can) prime furiously. *Psychological Science*. Advance online publication. doi:10.1177/0956797611430691.

Yeh, Y., Chen, C., Feng, H., Wang, S., Kuo, S., & Chen, C. (2009). New onset somnambulism associated with different dosage of mirtazapine: A case report. *Clinical Neuropharmacology, 32*(4), 232-233. doi:10.1097/WNF.0b013e318187bafc.

Yeomans, M. R., & Mobini, S. (2006). Hunger alters the expression of acquired hedonic but not sensory qualities of food-paired odors in humans. *Journal of Experimental Psychology: Animal Behavior Processes, 32*, 460–466.

Yerkes, R. M. (Ed.). (1921). Psychological examining in the U.S. Army. *Memoirs of the National Academy of Sciences*, No. 15.

Yesavage, J. A., Noda, A., Hernandez, B., Friedman, L., Cheng, J. J., Tinklenberg, J. R., Hallmayer, J., O'hara, R., David, R., Robert, P., Landsverk, E., Zeitzer, J. M. & the Alzheimer's Disease Neuroimaging Initiative. (2011). Circadian clock gene polymorphisms and sleep-wake disturbance in Alzheimer disease. *American Journal of Geriatric Psychiatry, 19*(7), 635–643.

Yeung, L. M., Linver, M. R., & Brooks-Gunn, J. (2002). How money matters for young children's development: Parental investment and family processes. *Child Development, 73*, 1861–1879.

Yip, T., Gee, G. C., & Takeuchi, D. T. (2008). Racial discrimination and psychological distress: The impact of ethnic identity and age among immigrant and United States-born Asian adults. *Developmental Psychology, 44*, 787–800.

Yonas, A., Arterberry, M. E., & Granrud, C. D. (1987). Space perception in infancy. In R. Vasta (Ed.), *Annals of child development* (Vol. 4, pp. 1–34). Greenwich, CT: JAI Press.

Yonke, A., & Barnett, M. (2001). Persistence of early psychoanalytic thought about women. *Gender & Psychoanalysis, 6*(1), 53–73.

Yoo, S.-S., Hu, P. T., Gujar, N., Jolesz, F. A., & Walker, M. P. (2007). A deficit in the ability to form new human memories without sleep. *Nature Neuroscience, 10*, 385–392.

York, J. L., & Welte, J. W. (1994). Gender comparisons of alcohol consumption in alcoholic and nonalcoholic populations. *Journal of Studies on Alcohol, 55*, 743–750.

Yoshikawa, H., Aber, J., & Beardslee, W. R. (2012). The effects of poverty on the mental, emotional, and behavioral health of children and youth. *American Psychologist, 67*, 272–284. doi:10.1037/a0028015.

Yoshimasu, K., Washio, M., Tokunaga, S., Tanaka, K., Liu, Y., Kodama, H., et al. (2002). Relation between Type A behavior pattern and the extent of coronary atherosclerosis in Japanese women. *International Journal of Behavioral Medicine, 9*, 77–93.

Youm, Y., & Laumann, E. O. (2002). Social network effects on the transmission of sexually transmitted diseases. *Sexually Transmitted Diseases, 29*, 689–697.

Youn, S., Kraus, D. R., & Castonguay, L. G. (2012). The treatment outcome package: Facilitating practice and clinically relevant research. *Psychotherapy, 49*, 115–22. doi:10.1037/a0027932

Young, C. B., Wu, S. S., & Menon, V. (2012). The neurodevelopmental basis of math anxiety. *Psychological Science, 23*, 492–501. doi:10.1177/0956797611429134

Young, K. (2009). Internet addiction: Diagnosis and treatment considerations. *Journal of Contemporary Psychotherapy, 39*, 241–246.

Young, K. A., Bonkale, W. L., Holcomb, L. A., Hicks, P. B., & German, D. C. (2008). Major depression, 5-HTTLPR genotype, suicide, and antidepressant infl uences on thalamic volume. *British Journal of Psychiatry, 192,* 285–289.

Young, M. S., Turner, J., Denny, G., & Young, M. (2004). Examining external and internal poverty as antecedents of teen pregnancy. *American Journal of Health Behavior, 28,* 361–373.

Young-Wolff, K. C., Enoch, M. A., & Prescott, C. A. (2011). The influence of gene-environment interactions on alcohol consumption and alcohol use disorders: A comprehensive review. *Clinical Psychology Review, 31,* 800–816.

Yousif, Y., & Korte, C. (1995). Urbanization, culture, and helpfulness: Cross-cultural studies in England and the Sudan. *Journal of Cross-Cultural Psychology, 26,* 474–489.

Yovel, I., & Mineka, S. (2005). Emotion-congruent attentional biases: The perspective of hierarchical models of emotional disorders. *Personality and Individual Differences, 38,* 785–795.

Yu, J., Vodyanik, M. A., Smuga-Otto, K., Antosiewicz-Bourget, J., Frane, J. L., Tian, S., Nie, J., Jonsdottir, G. A., Ruotti, V., Stewart, R., Slukvin, I. I., & Thomson, J. A. (2007). Induced pluripotent stem cell lines derived from human somatic cells. *Science, 318*(5858), 1917–1920.

Yu, X., Chen, D., Zhang, Y., Wu, X., Huang, Z., Zhou, H., Zhang, Y., and Zhang, Z. (2012). Overexpression of CXCR4 in mesenchymal stem cells promotes migration, neuroprotection and angiogenesis in a rat model of stroke. *Journal of the Neurological Science,* Epub. January 24.

Yuan, J., Kerr, D., Park, J., Liu, X. H., & McDonough, S. (2008). Treatment regimens of acupuncture for low back pain—A systematic review. *Complementary Therapies in Medicine, 16*(5), 295–304.

Yücel, M., Solowij, N., Respondek, C., Whittle, S., Fornito, A., Pantelis, C., & Lubman, D. I. (2008). Regional brain abnormalities associated with long-term heavy cannabis use. *Archives of General Psychiatry, 65,* 694–701.

Yuen, E. K., Goetter, E. M., Herbert, J. D., & Forman, E. M. (2012). Challenges and opportunities in internet-mediated telemental health. *Professional Psychology: Research and Practice, 43,* 1–8.

Yukl, G., & Van Fleet, D. D. (1992). Theory and research on leadership in organizations. In M. D. Dunnette & L. M. Hough (Eds.), *Handbook of industrial and organizational psychology* (Vol. 3, 2nd ed., pp. 147–198). Palo Alto, CA: Consulting Psychologists Press.

Yuma, Y. (2010). The effect of prison crowding on prisoners' violence in Japan: Testing with cointegration regressions and error correction models. *Japanese Journal of Psychology, 81,* 218–225.

Yun, S., Faraj, S., & Sims, H. P. (2005). Contingent leadership and effectiveness of trauma resuscitation teams. *Journal of Applied Psychology, 90,* 1288–1296.

Zabel, K. L., Christopher, A. N., Marek, P., Wieth, M. B., & Carlson, J. J. (2009). Mediational effects of sensation seeking on the age and financial risk-taking relationship. *Personality & Individual Differences, 47*(8), 917–921. doi:10.1016/j.paid.2009.07.016.

Zaccarco, S. J. (2007). Trait-based perspectives of leadership. *American Psychologist, 62,* 6–16.

Zadra, A., Desjardins, S., & Marcotte, E. (2006). Evolutionary function of dreams: A test of the threat simulation theory in recurrent dreams. *Consciousness and Cognition, 15,* 450–463.

Zadra, A., & Donderi, D. C. (2000). Nightmares and bad dreams: Their prevalence and relationship to well-being. *Journal of Abnormal Psychology, 109,* 273–281.

Zadra, A., Pilon, M., & Montplaisir, J. (2008). Polysomnographic diagnosis of sleepwalking: Effects of sleep deprivation. *Annals Of Neurology, 63*(4), 513–519. doi:10.1002/ana.21339.

Zahrani, S. S., & Kaplowitz, S. A. (1993). Attributional biases in individualistic and collectivist cultures: A comparison of Americans with Saudis. *Social Psychology Quarterly, 56*(3), 223–233.

Zajonc, R. B. (1965). Social facilitation. *Science, 149,* 269–274.

Zajonc, R. B. (1998). Emotions. In D. Gilbert, S. T. Fiske, & G. Lindzey (Eds.), *Handbook of social psychology* (Vol. 1, 4th ed., pp. 591–634). Boston: McGraw-Hill.

Zakhari, S. (2006). Overview: How is alcohol metabolized by the body? *Alcohol Research and Health, 29,* 245–254.

Zakriski, A. L., Wright, J. C., & Underwood, M. K. (2005). Gender similarities and differences in children's social behavior: Finding personality in contextualized patterns of adaptation. *Journal of Personality and Social Psychology, 88,* 844–855.

Zakzanis, K. K., & Young, D. A. (2001). Memory impairment in abstinent MDMA ("Ecstasy") users: A longitudinal investigation. *Neurology, 56,* 966–969.

Zald, D. H., & Pardo, J. V. (1997). Emotion, olfaction, and the human amygdala: Amygdala activation during aversive olfactory stimulation. *Proceedings of the National Academy of Sciences, 94*(8), 4119–4124.

Zalta, A. K., & Keel, P. K. (2006). Peer influence on bulimic symptoms in college students. *Journal of Abnormal Psychology, 115,* 185–189.

Zamani, R. (2010). An object-oriented view on problem representation as a search-efficiency facet: Minds vs. Machines. *Minds And Machines, 20*(1), 103–117. doi:10.1007/s11023-009-9160-8.

Zambelis, T., Paparrigopoulos, T., & Soldatos, C. R. (2002). REM sleep behaviour disorder associated with a neurinoma of the left pontocerebral angle. *Journal of Neurology, Neurosurgery, and Psychiatry, 72,* 821–822.

Zammit, G. K. (2007). Th e prevalence, morbidities, and treatments of insomnia. *CNS and Neurological Disorders—Drug Targets, 6,* 3–16.

Zammit, S., Allebeck, P., Andreasson, S., Lundberg, I., & Lewis, G. (2002). Self reported cannabis use as a risk factor for schizophrenia in Swedish conscripts of 1969: Historical cohort study. *British Medical Journal, 325,* 1199.

Zang, Y. (2008). Undergraduate students' mental models of the web as an information retrieval system. *Journal of the American Society for Information Science and Technology, 59,* 2087–2098.

Zapf, P. A., & Roesch, R. (2011). Future directions in the restoration of competency to stand trial. *Current Directions in Psychological Science, 20*(1), 43–47. doi:10.1177/0963721410396798.

Zarkadi, T., Wade, K. A., & Stewart, N. (2009). Creating fair lineups for suspects with distinctive features. *Psychological Science, 20*(12), 1448–1453. doi:10.1111/j.1467-9280.2009.02463.x.

Zaroff, C., & Uhm, S. (2012). Prevalence of autism spectrum disorders and influence of country of measurement and ethnicity. *Social Psychiatry & Psychiatric Epidemiology, 47*(3), 395–398. doi:10.1007/s00127-011-0350-3.

Zatorre, R. J. (2003). Music and the brain. *Annals of the New York Academy of Sciences, 999,* 4–14.

Zawilska, J. B., Skene, D. J., & Arendt, J. (2009). Physiology and pharmacology of melatonin in relation to biological rhythms. *Pharmacological Reports, 61*(3), 383–410.

Zeanah, C. H., Egger, H. L., Smyke, A. T., Nelson, C. A., et al. (2009). Institutional rearing and psychiatric disorders in Romanian preschool children. *American Journal of Psychiatry, 166,* 777–785.

Zeanah, C. H., Smyke, A. T., Koga, S. F., & Carlson, E. (2005). Attachment in institutionalized and community children in Romania. *Child Development, 76,* 1015–1028.

Zebrowitz, L., White, B., & Wieneke, K. (2008). Mere exposure and racial prejudice: Exposure to other-race faces increases liking for strangers of that race. *Social Cognition, 26,* 259–275.

Zeeck, A., Weber, S., Sandholz, A., Joos, A., & Hartmann, A. (2011). Stability of long-term outcome in bulimia nervosa: A 3-year follow-up. *Journal of Clinical Psychology, 67*(3), 318–327. doi:10.1002/jclp.20766

Zeman, A. (2001). Consciousness. *Brain, 124,* 1263–1289.

Zeman, A., Britton, T., Douglas, N., Hansen, A., Hicks, J., Howard, R., et al. (2004). Narcolepsy and excessive daytime sleepiness. *British Medical Journal, 329,* 724–728.

Zhai, F., Brooks-Gunn, J., & Waldfogel, J. (2011). Head Start and urban children's school readiness: A birth cohort study in 18 cities. *Developmental Psychology, 47*(1), 134–152. doi:10.1037/a0020784.

Zhai, F., Raver, C., & Jones, S. M. (2012). Academic performance of subsequent schools and impacts of early interventions: Evidence from a randomized controlled trial in head start settings. *Children and Youth Services Review,* doi:10.1016/j.childyouth.2012.01.026.

Zhang, J.-P., Lencz, T., & Malhotra, A. K. (2010). D2 receptor genetic variation and clinical response to antipsychotic drug treatment: A meta-analysis. *American Journal of Psychiatry, 167,* 763–772.

Zhang, L., Jones, C. R., Ptacek, L. J., & Fu, Y. H. (2011). The genetics of the human circadian clock. *Advances in Genetics, 74,* 231–47.

Zhang, P., Jiang, Y., & He, S. (2012). Voluntary attention modulates processing of eye-specific visual information. *Psychological Science, 23*(3), 254–260. doi:10.1177/0956797611424289

Zhang, N. R., & von der Heydt, R. (2010). Analysis of the context integration mechanisms underlying figure–ground organization in the visual cortex. *The Journal of Neuroscience, 30*(19):6482–6496; doi:10.1523/JNEUROSCI.5168-09.2010.

Zhang, Y., Hoon, M. A., Chandrashekar, J., Mueller, K. L., Cook, B., Wu, D., et al. (2003). Coding of sweet, bitter, and umami tastes: Different receptor cells sharing similar signaling pathways. *Cell, 112,* 293–301.

Zhang, Y., Proenca, R., Maffei, M., Barone, M., Leopold, L., & Friedman, J. M. (1994). Positional cloning of the mouse obese gene and its human homologue. *Nature, 372,* 425–432.

Zhang, Y., Qin, W., Liu, P., Tian, J., Liang, J., von Deneen, K. M., & Liu, Y. (2009). An fMRI study of acupuncture using independent component analysis. *Neuroscience Letter, 449*(1), 6–9.

Zhang, W., & Luck, S. J. (2011). The number and quality of representations in working memory. *Psychological Science, 22*(11), 1434–1441. doi:10.1177/0956797611417006.

Zhao, G., Ford, E. S., Dhingra, S., Li, C., Strine, T. W., & Mokdad, A. H. (2009). Depression and anxiety among US adults: Associations with body mass index. *International Journal of Obesity, 33,* 257–266.

Zhao, H., & Seibert, S. E. (2006). The big five personality dimensions and entrepreneurial status: A meta-analytical review. *Journal of Applied Psychology, 91,* 259–271.

Zhao, M., Momma, S., Delfani, K., Carlen, M., Cassidy, R. M., Johansson, C. B., et al. (2003). Evidence for neurogenesis in the adult mammalian substantia nigra. *Proceedings of the National Academy of Sciences, 100,* 7925–7930.

Zheng, H., Lenard, N. R., Shin, A. C., & Berthoud, H.-R. (2009). Appetite control and energy balance regulation in the modern world: Reward-driven brain overrides repletion signals. *International Journal of Obesity, 33,* S8–S13.

Zhong, C., & DeVoe, S. E. (2010). You are how you eat: Fast food and impatience. *Psychological Science, 21*(5), 619–622.

Zhong, C.-B., Bohns, V. K., & Gino, F. (2010). Good lamps are the best police: Darkness increases dishonesty and self-interested behavior. *Psychological Science, 21*(3), 311–314. doi:10.1177/0956797609360754.

Zhong, C.-B., Strejcek, B., & Sivanathan, N. (2010). A clean self can render harsh moral judgment. *Journal of Experimental Social Psychology, 46,* 859–862. doi:10.1016/j.jesp.2010.04.003.

Zhou, J.-N., Hofman, M. A., Gooren, L. J. G., & Swaab, D. F. (1995). A sex difference in the human brain and its relation to transsexuality. *Nature, 378,* 68–70.

Zhou, Q., Eisenberg, N., Wang, Y., & Reiser, M. (2004). Chinese children's effortful control and dispositional anger/frustration relations to parenting styles and children's social functioning. *Developmental Psychology, 40,* 352–366.

Zhou, W., Hou, P., Zhou, Y., & Chen, D. (2010). Reduced recruitment of orbito-frontal cortex to human social chemosensory cues in social anxiety. *Neuroimage,* doi:10.1016/j.neuroimage.2010.12.064.

Zhu, B., Chen, C., Loftus, E. F., He, Q., Chen, C., Lei, X., & … Dong, Q. (2012). Brief exposure to misinformation can lead to long-term false memories. *Applied Cognitive Psychology, 26*(2), 301–307. doi:10.1002/acp.1825.

Zhuang, S., Wixted, J. T., Hopkins, R. O., & Squire, L. R. (2011). Impaired capacity for familiarity after hippocampal damage. *Proceedings Of The National Academy Of Sciences Of The United States Of America, 108*(23), 9655–9660. doi:10.1073/pnas.1107247108.

Zickar, M. J., Gibby, R. E., & Robie, C. (2004). Uncovering faking samples in applicant, incumbent, and experimental data sets: An application of mixed-model item response theory. *Organizational Research Methods, 7,* 168–190.

Zigler, E., & Seitz, V. (1982). Social policy and intelligence. In R. J. Sternberg (Ed.), *Handbook of human intelligence* (pp. 586–641). Cambridge, UK: Cambridge University Press.

Zigurs, I. (2003). Leadership in virtual teams: Oxymoron or opportunity? *Organizational Dynamics, 31,* 339–351.

Zillmann, D. (1984). *Connections between sexuality and aggression.* Hillsdale, NJ: Erlbaum.

Zillmann, D. (1988). Cognition-excitation interdependencies in aggressive behavior. *Aggressive Behavior, 14,* 51–64.

Zillmann, D. (2003). Theory of affective dynamics: Emotions and moods. In J. Bryant & D. Roskos-Ewoldsen (Eds.), *Communication and emotion: Essays in honor of Dolf Zillmann* (pp. 533–567). Mahwah, NJ: Erlbaum.

Zillmann, D., Katcher, A. H., & Milavsky, B. (1972). Excitation transfer from physical exercise to subsequent aggressive behavior. *Journal of Experimental Social Psychology, 8,* 247–259.

Zimbardo, P. G. (1973). The psychological power and pathology of imprisonment. In E. Aronson & R. Helmreich (Eds.), *Social psychology.* New York: Van Nostrand.

Zimmerman, B. J., & Schunk, D. H. (2003). Albert Bandura: The scholar and his contributions to educational psychology. In B. J. Zimmerman (Ed.), *Educational psychology: A century of contributions* (pp. 431–457). Mahwah, NJ: Erlbaum.

Zimmerman, F. J., & Christakis, D. A. (2007). Associations between content types of early media exposure and subsequent attentional problems. *Pediatrics, 120*(5), 986–992.

Zimmerman, F. J., Christakis, D. A., & Meltzoff, A. N. (2007). Associations between media viewing and language development in children under age 2 years. *The Journal of Pediatrics, 151*(4), 364–368.

Zimmerman, F. J., Gilkerson, J., Richards, J. A., Christakis, D. A., et al. (2009). Teaching by listening: Th e importance of adult-child conversations to language development. *Pediatrics, 124,* 342–349.

Zimmerman, M., McDermut, W., & Mattia, J. I. (2000). Frequency of anxiety disorders in psychiatric outpatients with major depressive disorder. *American Journal of Psychiatry, 157,* 1337–1340.

Zimmerman, M., Posternak, M. A., Attiullah, N., Freidman, M., Michael, R. J., et al. (2005). Why isn't bupropion the most frequently prescribed antidepressant? *Journal of Clinical Psychiatry, 66,* 603–610.

Zimmerman, M. E., Pan, J. W., Hetherington, H. P., Katz, M. J., Verghese, J., Buschke, H., et al. (2008). Hippocampal neurochemistry, neuromorphometry, and verbal memory in nondemented older adults. *Neurology, 70*(18), 1594–1600.

Zinbarg, R. E., & Griffith, J. W. (2008). Behavior therapy. In J. L. Lebow (Ed.), *Twenty-first century psychotherapies: Contemporary approaches to theory and practice* (pp. 8–42). Hoboken, NJ: Wiley.

Zinbarg, R. E., & Mineka, S. (1991). Animal models of psychopathology: II. Simple phobia. *The Behavior Therapist, 14,* 61–65.

Zittoun, T., Gillespie, A., Cornish, F., & Psaltis, C. (2007). The metaphor of the triangle in theories of human development. *Human Development, 50*(4), 208–229.

Zoellner, L. A., Foa, E. B., Brigidi, B. D., & Przeworski, A. (2000). Are trauma victims susceptible to "false memories"? *Journal of Abnormal Psychology, 109,* 517–524.

Zoellner, T., & Maercker, A. (2006). Posttraumatic growth in clinical psychology: A critical review and introduction of a two component model. *Clinical Psychology Review, 26,* 626–653.

Zola-Morgan, S. (1995). Localization of brain function: The legacy of Franz Joseph Gall (1758–1828). *Annual Review of Neuroscience, 18,* 359–383.

Zolotor, A. J., Theodore, A. D., Chang, J. J., Berkoff, M. C., & Runyan, D. K. (2008). Speak softly—and forget the stick: Corporal punishment and child physical abuse. *American Journal of Preventive Medicine, 35,* 364–369.

Zonouzi M., Renzi M., Farrant M., & Cull-Candy S. G. (2011) Bidirectional plasticity of calcium-permeable AMPA receptors in oligodendrocyte lineage cells. Nat Neurosci 14 (11):1430–1438.

Zou, Z., & Buck, L. B. (2006). Combinatorial effects of odorant mixes in olfactory cortex. *Science, 311,* 1477–1481.

Zou, Z., Li, F., & Buck, L. B. (2005). Odor maps in the olfactory cortex. *Proceedings of the National Academy of Sciences, 102,* 7724–7729.

Zuberbühler, K. (2005). The phylogenetic roots of language. *Current Directions in Psychological Science, 14,* 126–130.

Zubieta, J. K. and Stohler, C. S. (2009). Neurobiological mechanisms of placebo responses. *Annals of the New York Academy of Sciences, 1156,* 198–210.

Zubin, J., & Spring, B. (1977). Vulnerability—A new view of schizophrenia. *Journal of Abnormal Psychology, 86,* 103–126.

Zucker, A. N., Ostrove, J. M., & Stewart, A. J. (2002). College-educated women's personality development in adulthood: Perceptions and age differences. *Psychology & Aging, 17*(2), 236–244.

Zuckerman, E. (2003). Finding, evaluating, and incorporating Internet self-help resources into psychotherapy practice. *Journal of Clinical Psychology: In Session, 59,* 217–227.

Zuckerman, M. (1984). Sensation seeking: A comparative approach to a human approach. *Behavioral and Brain Sciences, 7,* 413–471.

Zuckerman, M. (1990). Some dubious premises in research and theory on racial differences. *American Psychologist, 45,* 1297–1303.

Zuckerman, M. (1993). Out of sensory deprivation and into sensation seeking: A personal and scientific journey. In G. G. Brannigan & M. R. Merrens (Eds.), *The undaunted psychologist: Adventures in research* (pp. 45–57). Philadelphia: Temple University Press.

Zuckerman, M. (1996). "Conceptual clarification" or confusion in "The study of sensation seeking" by J. S. H. Jackson and M. Maraun. *Personality and Individual Differences, 21,* 111–114.

Zuroff, D. C., & Blatt, S. J. (2006). The therapeutic relationship in the brief treatment of depression: Contributions to clinical improvement and enhanced adaptive capacities. *Journal of Consulting and Clinical Psychology, 74,* 130–140.

Zuvekas, S. H., Vitiello, B., & Nordquist, G. S. (2006). Recent trends in stimulant medication use among U.S. children. *American Journal of Psychiatry, 163,* 579–585.

GLOSSARY

absolute threshold The minimum amount of stimulus energy that can be detected 50 percent of the time.

accessory structures Structures, such as the outer part of the ear, that modify a stimulus.

accommodation The process of modifying schemas when they do not work on new objects.

achievement motivation (need for achievement) The degree to which a person establishes specific goals, cares about meeting them, and experiences satisfaction by doing so.

acoustic nerve The bundle of axons that carries messages from the hair cells of the cochlea to the brain.

action potential The electrochemical impulse or message that is sent down an axon and stimulates the release of a neurotransmitter.

actor-observer effect The tendency to attribute other people's behavior to internal causes while attributing one's own behavior to external causes.

actualizing tendency An innate inclination toward growth and fulfillment that motivates all human behavior.

addiction Development of a physical need for a psychoactive drug.

affective disorder (mood disorder) A condition in which a person experiences extremes of moods for long periods, shifts from one extreme mood to another, and experiences moods that are inconsistent with events.

aggressive behavior (aggression) An act that is intended to harm another person.

agonists Drugs that bind to a receptor and mimic the effects of the neurotransmitter that normally fits that receptor.

agoraphobia A strong fear of being alone or away from the safety of home.

alcoholism A pattern of continuous or intermittent drinking that may lead to addiction and that almost always causes severe social, physical, and other problems.

algorithms Systematic procedures that cannot fail to produce a correct solution to a problem.

altered state of consciousness A condition that exists when changes in mental processes are extensive enough to produce noticeable differences in psychological and behavioral functioning.

altruism An unselfish concern for another's welfare.

Alzheimer's disease Dementia resulting from a neurodegenerative disease characterized by the loss of cognitive functions.

amnestic disorders Neuropsychological disorders that involve memory loss.

amplitude The distance between the peak and the baseline of a wave.

amygdala A forebrain structure that links information from various systems and plays a role in emotions.

anal stage The second of Freud's psychosexual stages, in which the focus of pleasure shifts from the mouth to the anus.

analgesia Reduction in the sensation of pain in the presence of a normally painful stimulus.

anchoring bias (anchoring heuristic) A shortcut in the thought process that involves adding new information to existing information to reach a judgment.

androgens Masculine hormones that circulate in the bloodstream.

anorexia nervosa An eating disorder characterized by self-starvation and dramatic weight loss.

antagonists Drugs that bind to a receptor and prevent the normal neurotransmitter from binding.

anterograde amnesia A loss of memory for events that occur after a brain injury.

antidepressant drugs Drugs that reduce symptoms of depression.

antisocial personality disorder A long-term, persistent pattern of impulsive, selfish, unscrupulous, even criminal behavior.

anxiety disorder A condition in which intense feelings of fear and dread are long-standing or disruptive.

arousal theory A theory that people are motivated to maintain what is an optimal level of arousal for them.

arousal: cost-reward theory A theory attributing people's prosocial behavior to their efforts to reduce unpleasant arousal in the face of someone's need or suffering, while also considering the costs involved.

artificial intelligence (AI) The field that studies how to program computers to imitate the products of human perception, understanding, and thought.

assertiveness training A set of methods for helping clients learn to express their feelings and stand up for their rights in social situations.

assessment center An extensive set of exercises designed to determine an individual's suitability for a particular job.

assimilation The process of taking in new information about objects by using existing schemas on objects that fit those schemas.

association cortex The parts of the cerebral cortex that integrate sensory and motor information and perform complex cognitive tasks.

attachment A deep, affectionate, close, and enduring relationship with a person with whom a baby has shared many experiences.

attachment behavior Actions such as crying, smiling, vocalizing, and gesturing that help bring an infant into proximity to its caretaker.

attachment theory [text obscured]

authoritarian parents Parents who are firm, punitive, and unsympathetic.

authoritative parents Parents who reason with their children and are firm but understanding.

autonomic nervous system The subsystem of the peripheral nervous system that carries messages between the central nervous system and the heart, lungs, and other organs and glands in the body.

autonomous work groups (AWGs) Self-managed employee groups that do not report to anyone for routine daily supervision.

availability heuristic A mental shortcut through which judgments are based on information that is most easily brought to mind.

aversion conditioning A method for reducing unwanted behaviors by using classical conditioning principles to create a negative response to some stimulus.

avoidance conditioning The process of learning particular responses that avoid an aversive stimulus.

axon A fiber that carries signals away from the cell body.

babblings Repetitions of syllables; the first sounds infants make that resemble speech.

basilar membrane The floor of the fluid-filled duct that runs through the cochlea.

behavior modification Treatments that use operant conditioning methods to change behavior.

behavior therapy Treatments that use classical conditioning principles to change behavior.

behavioral approach A view based on the assumption that human behavior is determined mainly by what a person has learned in life, especially through rewards and punishments.

behavioral genetics The study of how genes and environments interact to affect behavior and mental processes.

[behavioral] genetics The study of the effect of [genes o]n behavior.

[sampli]ng A group of research [subject]s selected from a population, [whos]e members did not have an [equal chance o]f being chosen.

[biological approach] The view that behavior [is related to phy]sical processes, [from genes] to the brain, to [other] chemicals.

[biological psy]chologists who [study fact]ors influencing [mental process]es.

[... o]f physical [...]in

biopsychosocial approach Viewing mental disorders as resulting from a combination of biological, psychological, and sociocultural factors.

bipolar disorder A condition in which a person alternates between the two emotional extremes of depression and mania.

bisexuality Sexual desire or behavior that is focused on members of both sexes.

blind spot The point at which the optic nerve exits the eyeball.

blood-brain barrier A characteristic of blood vessels in the brain that prevents some substances from entering brain tissue.

body dysmorphic disorder A somatoform disorder characterized by intense distress over imagined abnormalities of the skin, hair, face, or other areas of the body.

bottom-up processing Aspects of recognition that depend first on information about stimuli that come up to the brain from the sensory systems.

brightness The overall intensity of the wavelengths making up light.

Broca's aphasia A language disorder in which there is a loss of fluent speech.

Brown-Peterson distractor technique A method for determining how long unrehearsed information remains in short-term memory.

bulimia An eating disorder that involves eating massive quantities of food, then eliminating it by self-induced vomiting or laxatives.

burnout A pattern of physical and psychological dysfunctions in response to continuous stressors.

bystander effect A phenomenon in which the chances that someone will help in an emergency decrease as the number of people present increases.

case studies Research involving the intensive examination of some phenomenon in a particular individual, group, or situation.

central nervous system (CNS) The brain and spinal cord.

cerebellum The part of the hindbrain whose main functions include controlling finely coordinated movements and storing memories about movement; it may also be involved in impulse control, emotion, and language.

cerebral cortex The outer surface of the brain.

cerebrospinal fluid A clear liquid that surrounds and buffers the brain against vibration.

cerebrovascular accident (stroke) A loss of blood supply to some part of the brain,

resulting in disruption of some aspect of behavior or mental processes.

chromosomes Structures in every biological cell that contain genetic information in the form of genes.

chunking Organizing individual stimuli so that they will be perceived as larger units of meaningful information.

circadian rhythm (human biological rhythms) A cycle, such as waking and sleeping, that repeats about once a day.

classical conditioning A procedure in which a neutral stimulus is paired with a stimulus that triggers a reflexive response until the neutral stimulus alone comes to trigger a similar response.

client-centered therapy (person-centered therapy) A type of therapy in which the client decides what to talk about, and when, without direction, judgment, or interpretation from the therapist.

clinical, counseling, and community psychologists Psychologists who seek to assess, understand, modify, and prevent behavior disorders.

CNS depressant drugs Psychoactive drugs that inhibit the functioning of the central nervous system.

CNS stimulating drugs Psychoactive drugs that increase behavioral and mental activity.

cochlea A fluid-filled spiral structure in the inner ear in which auditory transduction occurs.

cognitive approach A view that emphasizes research on how the brain takes in information, creates perceptions, forms and retrieves memories, processes information, and generates integrated patterns of action.

cognitive behavior therapy Learning-based treatment methods that help clients change the way they think as well as the way they behave.

cognitive dissonance theory A theory that attitude change is driven by efforts to reduce tension caused by inconsistencies between attitudes and behaviors.

cognitive map A mental model that represents familiar parts of the environment.

cognitive psychologists Psychologists whose research focuses on analysis of the mental processes underlying judgment, decision making, problem solving, imagining, and other aspects of human thought or cognition.

cognitive therapy An organized problem-solving approach in which the therapist actively collaborates with clients to help them notice how certain negative thoughts precede anxiety and depression.

color saturation The purity of a color.

community psychology An approach to minimizing or preventing psychological disorders by promoting social change and community mental health programs.

competition Any type of behavior in which individuals try to attain a goal while denying others access to that goal.

compliance Adjusting one's behavior because of a direct request.

compulsions Repetitive behaviors that interfere with daily functioning but are performed in an effort to prevent dangers or events associated with obsessions.

concepts Categories of objects, events, or ideas that have common properties.

concrete operations According to Piaget, the third stage of cognitive development, during which children can learn to count, measure, add, and subtract.

conditioned response (CR) The response triggered by the conditioned stimulus.

conditioned stimulus (CS) An originally neutral stimulus that now triggers a conditioned response.

conditions of worth According to Rogers, circumstances in which an individual experiences positive regard from others only when displaying certain behaviors or attitudes.

cones Photoreceptors in the retina that are less light sensitive than rods but that can distinguish colors.

confabulation A characteristic of some neuropsychological disorders in which patients report false memories.

confirmation bias The tendency to pay more attention to evidence in support of one's hypothesis about a problem than to evidence that refutes that hypothesis.

conflict What occurs when a person or group believes that another person or group interferes with the attainment of a goal.

conformity Changing one's behavior or beliefs to match those of others, generally as a result of real or imagined (though unspoken) group pressure.

confound Any factor that affects the dependent variable along with, or instead of, the independent variable.

congruence In client-centered therapy, a consistency between the way therapists feel and the way they act toward clients.

conscious level The level of consciousness at which mental activities accessible to awareness occur.

consciousness The awareness of external stimuli and our own mental activity.

consciousness disturbances Neuropsychological disorders in which there are impairments in the ability to be conscious, or accurately aware, of the world.

consciousness state The characteristics of consciousness at any particular moment.

conservation The ability to recognize that the important properties of substances or objects, such as quantity, volume, or weight, remain constant despite changes in shape, length, or position.

contact hypothesis The idea that stereotypes and prejudice toward a group will diminish as contact with the group increases.

context-specific memory (context-specific learning) Memories that are helped or hindered by similarities or differences between the contexts in which they are learned and recalled.

control group The group that receives no treatment or provides some other baseline against which to compare the performance or response of the experimental group.

conventional level Moral reasoning that reflects a concern about other people as well as the belief that morality consists of following rules and conventions.

convergent thinking The ability to apply the rules of logic and what one knows about the world to narrow down the possible solutions to a problem.

conversion disorder A somatoform disorder in which a person appears to be (but actually is not) blind, deaf, paralyzed, or insensitive to pain.

cooperation Any type of behavior in which people work together to attain a goal.

cornea The curved, transparent, protective layer through which light rays enter the eye.

corpus callosum A bundle of fibers that connects the left and right cerebral hemispheres.

correlation The degree to which one variable is related to another.

correlational studies Research methods that examine relationships between variables in order to analyze trends, test predictions, evaluate theories, and suggest new hypotheses.

couples therapy A form of therapy that focuses on improving communication between partners.

creativity The capacity to produce original solutions or novel compositions.

critical period An interval during which certain kinds of growth must occur if development is to proceed normally.

critical thinking The process of assessing claims and making judgments based on well-supported evidence.

culture The accumulation of values, rules of behavior, forms of expression, religious beliefs, and occupational choices for a group of people who share a common language and environment.

cutaneous senses Senses including touch, temperature, pain, and kinesthetic perception that are spread throughout the body. Also called somatosensory systems.

cyclothymic personality (cyclothymic disorder) An affective disorder characterized by an alternating pattern of mood swings that is less extreme than that of bipolar disorder

dark adaptation The increasing ability to see in the dark as time passes.

data Numbers that represent research findings and provide the basis for conclusions.

decay theory A description of forgetting as the gradual disappearance of information from memory.

defense mechanisms Unconscious tactics that either prevent threatening material from surfacing or disguise it when it does.

deindividuation A psychological state occurring in group members that results in loss of individuality and a tendency to do things not normally done when alone.

delirium Periods of abnormally impaired and/or abnormally elevated levels of consciousness.

delusions False beliefs, such as those experienced by people suffering from schizophrenia or severe depression.

dementia Neuropsychological disorders in which there are significant and disruptive impairments in memory as well as in perceptual ability, language, or learned motor skills.

dendrites Fibers that receive signals from the axons of other neurons.

dependent variable In an experiment, the factor affected by the independent variable.

depth perception Perception of distance, allowing us to experience the world in three dimensions.

developmental psychologists Psychologists who seek to understand, describe, and explore how behavior and mental processes change over the course of a lifetime.

developmental psychology The psychological specialty that documents the course of people's social, emotional, moral, and intellectual development over the life-span.

diathesis-stress model The notion that psychological disorders arise when a predisposition for a disorder combines with sufficient amounts of stress to trigger symptoms.

discriminative conditioned stimuli Stimuli that signal whether reinforcement is available if a certain response is made.

diseases of adaptation Illnesses caused or worsened by stressors.

dissociative amnesia A psychological disorder marked by a sudden loss of memory for one's own name, occupation, or other identifying information.

dissociative disorders Conditions involving sudden and usually temporary disruptions in a person's memory, consciousness, or identity.

dissociative identity disorder (DID) A dissociative disorder in which a person appears to have more than one identity, each of which behaves in a different way.

distributed practice Learning new information in many study sessions that are spaced across time.

divergent thinking The ability to generate many different solutions to a problem.

DNA (deoxyribonucleic acid) The molecular structure of a gene that provides the genetic code.

double-blind design A research design in which neither the experimenter nor the participants know who is in the experimental group and who is in the control group.

dreaming The production during sleep of story-like sequences of images, sensations, and perceptions that last from several seconds to many minutes; it occurs mainly during REM sleep.

drive A psychological state that arises from an imbalance in homeostasis and prompts action to fulfill a need.

drive reduction theory A theory that motivation arises from imbalances in homeostasis.

drug abuse (substance abuse) The use of psychoactive drugs in ways that deviate from cultural norms and cause serious problems for the user.

drug tolerance A condition in which increasingly larger drug doses are needed to produce a given effect.

drug withdrawal A set of symptoms associated with ending the use of an addictive substance.

dysthymic disorder A pattern of depression in which the person shows the sad mood, lack of interest, and loss of pleasure associated with major depression but to a lesser degree and for a longer period.

educational psychologists Psychologists who study methods by which instructors teach and students learn and who apply their results to improve such methods.

ego According to Freud, the part of the personality that makes compromises and mediates conflicts between and among the demands of the id, the superego, and the real world.

elaboration likelihood model A model of attitude change suggesting that people can change their attitudes through a central route (by considering an argument's content) or through a peripheral route (by relying on irrelevant persuasion cues).

elaborative rehearsal A memorization method that relates new information to information already stored in memory.

Electra complex The notion that young girls develop an attachment to the father and compete with the mother for the father's attention.

electroconvulsive shock therapy (ECT) A brief electric shock administered to the brain, usually to reduce severe depression that does not respond to drug treatments.

embryo The developing individual from two weeks to two months after fertilization.

emotions Temporary positive or negative experiences that are felt as happening to the self, that are generated partly by interpretation of situations, and that are accompanied by learned and innate physical responses.

empathy In client-centered therapy, the therapist's attempt to appreciate how the world looks from the client's point of view.

empathy-altruism helping theory A theory suggesting that people help others because they feel empathy toward them.

empirically supported therapies (ESTs) Treatments for psychological disorders whose effectiveness has been validated by controlled experimental research.

empiricism The view that knowledge comes from experience and observation.

encoding The process of putting information into a form that the memory system can accept and use.

encoding Translation of the physical properties of a stimulus into a specific pattern of neural activity.

encoding specificity principle A principle stating that the ability of a cue to aid retrieval depends on how well it taps into information that was originally encoded.

endocrine system Cells that form organs called glands and that communicate with one another by secreting hormones.

engineering psychologists Psychologists who study and try to improve the relationships between human beings and the computers and other machines they use.

environmental psychologists Psychologists who study the relationship between people's physical environment and their behavior.

environmental psychology The study of the effects of the physical environment on people's behavior and mental processes.

epigenetics The study of potentially inheritable changes in gene expression that are caused by environmental factors that do not alter a cell's DNA.

episodic memory Memory of events in one's own past.

escape conditioning The process of learning responses that stop an aversive stimulus.

estrogens Feminine hormones that circulate in the bloodstream.

ethnic identity The part of a person's identity that reflects the racial, religious, or cultural group to which that person belongs.

evidence-based practice The selection of treatment methods based mainly on empirical evidence of their effectiveness.

evolutionary approach A view that emphasizes the inherited, adaptive aspects of behavior and mental processes.

excitation transfer theory The theory that physiological arousal stemming from one situation is carried over to and enhances emotional experience in an independent situation.

existence, relatedness, growth (ERG) theory A theory of motivation that focuses on employees' needs at the levels of existence, relatedness, and growth.

expectancy theory A theory of workplace motivation in which employees are seen as acting in accordance with expected results and with how much they value those results.

expected value The total benefit to be expected of a decision if it were repeated on several occasions.

experiment A situation in which the researcher manipulates one variable and observes the effect of that manipulation on another variable, while holding all other variables constant.

experimental group The group that receives the experimental treatment.

experimenter bias A confound that occurs when an experimenter unintentionally encourages participants to respond in a way that supports the hypothesis.

explicit memory Information retrieved through a conscious effort to remember something.

extinction The gradual disappearance of a conditioned response.

extrinsic motivation Engaging in behavior in order to obtain an external reward or avoid a penalty or other undesirable consequence.

eye convergence A depth cue that results when the eyes rotate to project the image of an object on each retina.

family therapy A type of treatment involving two or more clients from the same family.

feature detectors Cells in the cerebral cortex that respond to a specific feature of an object.

fetal alcohol syndrome A pattern of defects found in babies born to women who abused alcohol during pregnancy.

fetus The developing individual from the third month after conception until birth.

fiber tracts Bundles of axons that travel together.

fight-flight reaction (fight-or-flight syndrome) Physical reactions triggered by the sympathetic nervous system that prepare the body to fight or flee a threatening situation.

figure The part of the visual field that has meaning.

figure ground discrimination The ability to organize a visual scene so that it contains meaningful figures set against a less relevant ground.

five-factor personality model (Big Five model) A view based on studies using factor analysis that suggests the existence of five basic components of human personality: openness, conscientiousness, extraversion, agreeableness, and neuroticism.

flooding An exposure technique for reducing anxiety that keeps a client in a feared but harmless situation.

forebrain The part of the brain responsible for the most complex aspects of behavior and mental life.

forensic psychologists Psychologists who are involved in many aspects of psychology and law.

formal operations According to Piaget, the fourth stage of cognitive development, characterized by the ability to engage in hypothetical thinking.

formal reasoning A set of rigorous procedures for reaching valid conclusions.

fovea A region in the center of the retina.

frequency The number of complete waves, or cycles, that pass a given point per unit of time.

frustration-aggression hypothesis A proposition stating that frustration always leads to some form of aggressive behavior.

fugue reaction (dissociative fugue) A psychological disorder involving sudden loss of memory and the assumption of a new identity in a new locale.

functional fixedness The tendency to think about familiar objects in familiar ways.

fundamental attribution error A bias toward attributing the behavior of others to internal factors.

gate control theory of pain A theory suggesting the presence of a "gate" in the spinal cord that either permits or blocks the passage of pain impulses to the brain.

gender roles (sex roles) Patterns of work, appearance, and behavior that a society associates with being male or female.

general adaptation syndrome (GAS) A three-stage pattern of responses triggered by the effort to adapt to stressors.

generalized anxiety disorder A condition that involves long-lasting anxiety that is not focused on any particular object or situation.

generativity The concern of adults in midlife with generating something enduring.

genes Hereditary units, located on chromosomes, that contain biological instructions inherited from both parents, providing the blueprint for physical development.

genital stage The fifth and last of Freud's psychosexual stages, when sexual impulses reappear at the conscious level during adolescence.

Gestalt therapy An active form of humanistic treatment that seeks to create conditions in which clients can become more unified, more self-aware, and more self-accepting

glands Organs that secrete hormones into the bloodstream.

glial cells Nervous system cells that hold neurons together and help them communicate with each other.

goal-setting theory A theory of workplace motivation focused on the idea that employees' behavior is shaped by their intention to achieve specific goals.

grammar A set of rules for combining the symbols, such as words, used in a given language.

ground The contourless part of the visual field; the background.

group psychotherapy Psychotherapy involving six to twelve unrelated individuals.

groupthink A pattern of thinking that renders group members unable to evaluate realistically the wisdom of various options and decisions.

habituation Reduced responsiveness to a repeated stimulus.

hallucinations False or distorted perceptions of objects or events.

hallucinogenic drugs Psychoactive drugs that alter consciousness by producing a temporary loss of contact with reality and changes in emotion, perception, and thought.

health care psychology (health psychology) A field focused on understanding how psychological factors affect health and illness and which interventions help maintain health and combat illness.

health promotion The process of altering or eliminating behaviors that pose risks to health and, at the same time, fostering healthier behavior patterns.

health psychologists Psychologists who study the effects of behavior on health and the impact of illness on behavior and emotion.

heterosexuality Sexual desire or behavior that is focused on members of the opposite sex.

heuristics Mental shortcuts or rules of thumb.

higher order conditioning A process through which a conditioned stimulus comes to signal another conditioned stimulus that is already associated with an unconditioned stimulus.

hindbrain The portion of the brain that lies just inside the skull and is a continuation of the spinal cord.

hippocampus A forebrain structure associated with the formation of new memories.

histogram A pictorial presentation of how often each possible score on a dependent variable occurs in a set of research data.

homeostasis The tendency for physiological systems to remain stable by constantly adjusting themselves in response to change.

homosexuality Sexual desire or behavior that is focused on members of one's own sex.

hormones Chemicals secreted by glands into the bloodstream, which carries them throughout the body.

hue The essential color determined by the dominant wavelength of light.

humanistic approach A view of behavior as controlled by the decisions that people make about their lives based on their perceptions of the world.

humanistic psychology approach The view that personality develops in accordance with each person's unique perceptions of the world.

hunger The general state of wanting to eat.

hypnosis A phenomenon that is brought on by special techniques and is characterized by varying degrees of responsiveness to suggestions for changes in a person's behavior and experiences.

hypnotic susceptibility The degree to which a person responds to hypnotic suggestion.

hypochondriasis A strong, unjustified fear of physical illness.

hypothalamus A forebrain structure that regulates hunger, thirst, and sex drives and has many connections to and from the autonomic nervous system and other parts of the brain.

hypothesis In scientific research, a specific, testable proposition about a phenomenon.

iconic memory The sensory register for visual information.

id According to Freud, a personality component containing basic instincts, desires, and impulses with which all people are born.

identity crisis The phase during which an adolescent attempts to develop an integrated self-image as a unique person by pulling together self-knowledge acquired during childhood.

images Mental representations of visual information.

immediate memory span The maximum number of items a person can recall perfectly after one presentation of the items.

immune system The body's first line of biological defense against invading substances and microorganisms.

implicit memory The unintentional recollection and influence of prior experiences.

implosive therapy An exposure technique in which clients are helped to imagine being kept in a feared but harmless situation.

incentive theory A theory that people are pulled toward behaviors that offer positive incentives and pushed away from behaviors associated with negative incentives.

independent variable In an experiment, the variable manipulated by the researcher.

industrial and organizational (I/O) psychology The science of behavior and mental processes in the workplace.

industrial and organizational psychologists Psychologists who examine factors that influence people's performance in the workplace.

infant vocalizations Early sounds, such as babblings, made by babies.

inferential statistics A form of statistical analysis designed to provide a measure of confidence about how likely it is that a certain result appeared by chance.

inflammation An immune system response that combats infectious agents and helps to heal injuries.

informal reasoning The process of evaluating a conclusion based on the evidence available to support it.

information processing model A view of cognitive development which focuses on the processes of taking in, remembering or forgetting, and using information.

information-processing model of memory A model that suggests that information must pass through sensory memory, short-term memory, and long-term memory in order to become firmly embedded in memory.

information-processing system Mechanisms for receiving information, representing it with symbols, and manipulating it.

insight A sudden understanding of what is required to solve a problem.

insomnia A sleep disorder in which a person has trouble falling asleep or staying asleep at night.

instinct doctrine A view that behavior is motivated by automatic, involuntary, and unlearned responses.

instinctive behaviors Innate, automatic dispositions to respond in particular ways to specific stimuli.

intelligence The possession of knowledge, the ability to efficiently use that knowledge to reason about the world, and the ability to use that reasoning adaptively in different environments.

intelligence quotient (IQ) A number that was originally determined by dividing mental age by chronological age and multiplying the result by 100. It now reflects the degree to which a person's score on an intelligence test differs from the average score of others in his or her age group.

interference The process through which storage or retrieval of information is impaired by the presence of other information.

intrinsic motivation Engaging in behavior simply for the feelings of pleasure, satisfaction, or sense of competence or independence it brings.

iris The part of the eye that gives it its color and adjusts the amount of light entering it.

jet lag Fatigue, irritability, inattention, and sleeping problems caused by air travel across several time zones.

job analysis The process of collecting information about jobs and job requirements that is used to guide hiring and training decisions.

job performance A measure of how well employees are doing in various aspects of their work, usually recorded in an annual appraisal.

just-noticeable difference (JND) The smallest detectable difference in stimulus energy. Also called difference threshold.

kinesthetic perception The proprioceptive sense that tells us where the parts of the body are with respect to one another.

Korsakoff's psychosis An amnestic condition in people whose thiamine (vitamin B1) level is depleted by inadequate nutrition or alcoholism.

language Symbols (and a set of rules for combining them) that are used as a means of communicating.

language disorders (aphasias) Neuropsychological disorders in which there are disruptions in the ability to speak, read, write, and understand language.

latency period The fourth of Freud's psychosexual stages, in which sexual impulses become dormant and the child focuses on education and other matters.

latent learning Learning that is not demonstrated at the time it occurs.

law of effect A law stating that if a response made in the presence of a particular stimulus is rewarded, the same response is more likely to occur when that stimulus is encountered again.

leader-member exchange (LMX) theory A theory suggesting that leaders tend to supervise ingroup and outgroup employees in different ways.

learned helplessness A process in which a person or animal stops trying to exert control after experience suggests that no control is possible.

learning The modification of preexisting behavior and understanding.

lens The part of the eye directly behind the pupil.

lesion A damaged area in the brain.

levels-of-processing model of memory A model that suggests that memory depends on the degree or depth to which we mentally process information.

light intensity A physical dimension of light waves that refers to how much energy the light contains and that determines our experience of its brightness.

light wavelength A physical dimension of light waves that refers to their length and that produces sensations of different colors.

localization of function The idea that specific psychological functions can be affected by damage to specific brain areas.

locus coeruleus A small nucleus in the reticular formation that is involved in directing attention.

logic A system of formulas for drawing valid conclusions.

long-term memory (LTM) The stage of memory that researchers believe has an unlimited capacity to store new information.

looming A motion cue whereby rapid expansion in the size of an image fills the available space on the retina.

loudness A psychological dimension of sound determined by the amplitude of a sound wave.

lucid dreaming Being aware that a dream is a dream while it is occurring.

maintenance rehearsal A memorization method that involves repeating information over and over to keep it in memory.

major depression (major depressive disorder) A condition in which a person feels sad and hopeless for weeks or months, often losing interest in all activities and taking pleasure in nothing.

mania An elated, active emotional state.

massed practice Trying to learn complex new information in a single long study period.

matching hypothesis The notion that people are most likely to form committed relationships with those who are similar to themselves in physical attractiveness.

maturation Natural growth or change triggered by biological factors independent of the environment.

medulla oblongata The area of the hindbrain that controls vital autonomic functions such as heart rate, blood pressure, and breathing.

menopause The cessation of a woman's reproductive capacity.

mental age A score corresponding to the age level of the most-advanced items a child could answer correctly on Alfred Binet's first intelligence test.

mental models Sets of propositions that represent people's understanding of how things look and work.

mental set The tendency for old patterns of problem solving to persist.

midbrain A small region between the hindbrain and the forebrain that, among other things, helps produce smooth movements.

middle ear The part of the ear that contains the hammer, anvil, and stirrup, which transmit sound from the tympanic membrane to the oval window.

mnemonic strategies Methods for organizing information in order to remember it.

modeling A behavior therapy method in which desirable behaviors are demonstrated for clients.

moral development The growth of an individual's understanding of the concepts of right and wrong.

motivation The influences that account for the initiation, direction, intensity, and persistence of behavior.

motive A reason or purpose for behavior.

motor cortex The part of the cerebral cortex that controls voluntary movement.

motor neurons The neurons that influence muscles and other organs to respond to the environment in some way.

movement disorders (apraxias) Neuropsychological disorders in which there are impairments in the ability to perform or coordinate previously normal motor skills.

narcolepsy A daytime sleep disorder in which a person suddenly switches from an active waking state into REM sleep.

naturalistic observation The process of watching without interfering as a phenomenon occurs in the natural environment.

needs Biological requirements for well-being.

negative reinforcers The removal of unpleasant stimuli.

nervous system A network of billions of cells that detects what is going on inside or outside the body and guides appropriate responses.

neural networks Neurons that operate together to perform complex functions.

neural plasticity A property of the central nervous system that allows it to strengthen neural connections at synapses as well as to establish new connections.

neural receptors Cells that are specialized to detect certain types of energy and convert it into neural activity.

neurodegenerative diseases Conditions in the brain that result in the gradual loss of nerve cells and of the cognitive or other functions in which those cells are normally involved.

neuroleptic drugs Drugs that relieve the symptoms of schizophrenia and other severe psychological disorders.

neurons Specialized cells of the nervous system that send and receive messages.

neuropsychological assessment Testing a patient's intelligence, memory, reading, motor coordination, and other cognitive and sensory functions in an effort to locate problems in the brain responsible for neuropsychological symptoms.

neuropsychology The subfield of psychology whose goal is to explore and understand the relationship between brain processes, human behavior, and psychological functioning.

neurotransmitter A chemical that transfers messages across synapses.

nightmares Frightening dreams that take place during REM sleep.

noise The spontaneous random firing of nerve cells that occurs because the nervous system is always active.

nonconscious level The level of consciousness at which reside processes that are totally inaccessible to conscious awareness.

nonprojective personality measures Tests that list clear, specific questions, statements, or concepts to which people are asked to respond.

nonstate theories of hypnosis Theories, such as role theory, proposing that hypnosis does not create an altered state of consciousness.

normal distribution A smooth, bell-shaped curve representing a set of data in which most scores occur in the middle of the possible range, with fewer and fewer scores occurring toward the extremes of the range.

norms Descriptions of the frequency of particular scores on a test.

NREM (non-rapid eye movement) sleep Sleep stages N1, N2, and N3; they are accompanied by gradually slower and deeper breathing; a calm, regular heartbeat; reduced blood pressure; and slower brain waves. (Stage N3 is called slow-wave sleep.)

nuclei Clusters of nerve cell bodies in the central nervous system.

null hypothesis A testable statement that the independent variable manipulated by an experimenter will have no effect on the dependent variable being measured by the experimenter.

obedience Changing behavior in response to a demand from an authority figure.

obesity A condition in which a person is severely overweight.

object permanence The knowledge that an object exists even when it is not in view.

observational learning (social learning) Learning by watching the behavior of others.

observational methods Procedures for systematically watching behavior in order to summarize it for scientific analysis.

obsessions Persistent, upsetting, and unwanted thoughts that interfere with daily life and may lead to compulsions.

obsessive-compulsive disorder (OCD) An anxiety disorder in which a person becomes obsessed with certain thoughts or feels a compulsion to do certain things.

occupational health psychology A field concerned with psychological factors that affect the health, safety, and well-being of employees.

ocular accommodation The ability of the lens to change its shape and bend light rays so objects are in focus.

Oedipal complex The notion that young boys' impulses involve sexual feelings for the mother and the desire to eliminate the father.

olfactory bulb A brain structure that receives messages regarding smell.

olfactory perception (sense of smell) The sense that detects chemicals that are airborne. Also called olfaction.

one-word stage A stage of language development during which children tend to use one word at a time.

operant A response that has some effect on the world.

operant conditioning A process in which responses are learned on the basis of their rewarding or punishing consequences.

operational definitions Statements that define phenomena or variables by describing the exact research operations or methods used in measuring or manipulating them.

opiates Psychoactive drugs that produce both sleep-inducing and pain-relieving effects.

opponent-process theory A theory of color vision stating that the visual elements that are sensitive to color are grouped into red-green, blue-yellow, and black-white pairs.

optic nerve A bundle of fibers that carries visual information to the brain.

oral stage The first of Freud's psychosexual stages, in which the mouth is the center of pleasure.

organizational citizenship behavior (OCB) A willingness to go beyond formal job requirements in order to help co-workers and/or the organization.

panic disorder Anxiety in the form of severe panic attacks that come without warning or obvious cause.

papillae Structures in the mouth on which taste buds are grouped.

parallel distributed processing (PDP) models of memory Memory models in which new experiences are seen as changing one's overall knowledge base.

parasympathetic nervous system The subsystem of the autonomic nervous system that typically influences activity related to the protection, nourishment, and growth of the body.

parenting styles The varying patterns of behavior—ranging from permissive to authoritarian—that parents display as they interact with and discipline their children.

partial reinforcement effect A phenomenon in which behaviors learned under a partial reinforcement schedule are more difficult to extinguish than those learned on a continuous reinforcement schedule.

percentile A way of stating what percentage of scores in a data set fall at or below a certain score.

perception The process through which people take raw sensations from the environment and give them meaning using knowledge, experience, and understanding of the world.

perceptual constancy The perception that objects retain the same size, shape, color, and other properties despite changes in their retinal image.

perceptual disturbances Neuropsychological disorders in which there are impairments in the ability to organize, recognize, interpret, and make sense of incoming sensory information.

peripheral nervous system (PNS) The part of the nervous system that sends messages to and from the central nervous system.

permissive parents Parents who give their children complete freedom and lax discipline.

personality The pattern of psychological and behavioral characteristics by which each person can be compared and contrasted with other people.

personality disorders Long-standing, inflexible ways of behaving that become styles of life that create problems, usually for others.

personality psychologists Psychologists who focus on people's unique characteristics.

personality traits A set of stable characteristics that people display over time and across situations.

phallic stage The third of Freud's psychosexual stages, in which the focus of pleasure shifts to the genital area.

pheromones Chemicals that are released by one creature and detected by another, shaping the second creature's behavior or physiology.

phobia An anxiety disorder that involves strong, irrational fear of an object or situation that does not objectively justify such a reaction.

photoreceptors Specialized cells in the retina that convert light energy into neural activity.

physiological arousal A general level of activation reflected in several physiological systems.

pinna The crumpled part of the outer ear that collects sound waves.

pitch How high or low a tone sounds; pitch depends on the frequency of a sound wave.

place theory A theory of hearing that states that hair cells at a particular place on the basilar membrane respond most to a particular frequency of sound.

placebo A treatment that contains no active ingredient but produces an effect because the person receiving it believes it will.

pleasure principle The operating principle of the id, which guides people toward whatever feels good.

positive psychology A field of research that focuses on people's positive experiences and characteristics, such as happiness, optimism, and resilience.

positive reinforcement Presenting a positive reinforcer (reward) after a desired response.

positive reinforcers Stimuli that strengthen a response if they follow that response.

postconventional level Moral reasoning that reflects moral judgments based on personal standards or universal principles of justice, equality, and respect for human life.

posttraumatic stress disorder (PTSD) A pattern of adverse reactions following a traumatic event, commonly involving re-experiencing the event through nightmares or vivid memories.

preconscious level The level of consciousness at which reside mental events that are not currently conscious but can become conscious at will.

preconventional level Moral reasoning that is not based on the conventions or rules that guide social interactions in a society.

prejudice A positive or negative attitude toward people in certain groups.

preoperational stage According to Piaget, the second stage of cognitive development, during which children begin to understand, create, and use symbols that represent things that are not present.

primacy effect A characteristic of memory in which recall is particularly good for the first two or three items in a list.

primary drives Drives that arise from basic biological needs.

primary reinforcers Events or stimuli that satisfy physiological needs basic to survival.

proactive inhibition A cause of forgetting whereby previously learned information interferes with the ability to remember new information.

procedural knowledge (procedural memory) A type of memory containing information about how to do things.

progestational hormones (progestins) Feminine hormones that circulate in the bloodstream.

projective personality measures Tests made up of relatively unstructured stimuli in which responses are seen as reflecting the individuals' unconscious needs, fantasies, conflicts, thought patterns, and other aspects of personality.

proposition A mental representation that expresses a relationship between concepts.

proprioception The sensory processes that tell us about the location of our body parts and what each is doing.

proprioceptors Neural receptors that provide information about movement and body position.

prosocial behavior (helping behavior) Any act that is intended to benefit another person.

prototype A member of a natural concept that possesses all or most of its characteristic features.

psychiatrists Medical doctors who have completed special training in the treatment of mental disorders.

psychoactive drugs Chemical substances that act on the brain to create psychological effects.

psychoanalysis A method of psychotherapy that seeks to help clients gain insight into and work through unconscious thoughts and emotions presumed to cause psychological problems.

psychoanalytic theory Freud's view that human behavior and personality are determined largely by psychological factors, many of which are unconscious.

psychodynamic approach A view developed by Freud that emphasizes unconscious mental processes in explaining human thought, feelings, and behavior.

psychological model A view in which mental disorder is seen as arising from psychological processes.

psychologists Among therapists, those with advanced training in clinical or counseling psychology.

psychology The science that seeks to understand behavior and mental processes and to apply that understanding in the service of human welfare.

psychoneuroimmunology The field that examines the interaction of psychological and physiological processes affecting the body's ability to defend itself against disease.

psychopathology Patterns of thinking and behaving that are maladaptive, disruptive, or uncomfortable for the affected person or for others.

psychopharmacology The study of psychoactive drugs and their effects.

psychosexual development Periods of personality development in which, according to Freud, internal and external conflicts focus on particular issues.

psychosocial intellectual disability Cases of mild intellectual disability for which no environmental or genetic cause can be found.

psychotherapy The treatment of psychological disorders through talking and other psychological methods.

puberty The condition of being able, for the first time, to reproduce.

punishment The presentation of an aversive stimulus or the removal of a pleasant one following some behavior.

pupil An opening in the eye just behind the cornea through which light passes.

quantitative psychologists Psychologists who develop statistical methods for evaluating and analyzing data from psychological research.

random sampling A group of research participants selected from a population, each of whose members had an equal chance of being chosen.

random variables Uncontrolled or uncontrollable factors that affect the dependent variable along with, or instead of, the independent variable.

randomizing A procedure through which random variables are evenly distributed in an experiment by placing participants in experimental and control groups on the basis of a coin flip or some other random process.

rational-emotive behavior therapy (REBT) A treatment designed to identify and change illogical, self-defeating thoughts that lead to anxiety and other symptoms of disorder.

reality principle The operating principle of the ego, which takes into account the constraints of the social world.

reasoning The process by which people generate and evaluate arguments and reach conclusions about them.

recall Retrieving information stored in memory without much help from retrieval clues.

recency effect A characteristic of memory in which recall is particularly good for the last few items in a list.

recognition Retrieving information stored in memory with the help of retrieval clues.

reconditioning The relearning of a conditioned response following extinction.

reference groups Categories of people with whom individuals compare themselves.

reflexes Simple, involuntary, unlearned behaviors directed by the spinal cord without instructions from the brain.

refractory period A short recovery time after cell firing, during which the cell cannot fire again.

reinforcement The process through which a particular response is made more likely to recur.

reinforcement schedules In operant conditioning, rules that determine how and when certain responses will be reinforced.

reinforcer A stimulus event that increases the probability that the response immediately preceding it will occur again.

relationship-motivated leaders Leaders who provide loose supervision, ask for group members' ideas, and are generally concerned with subordinates' feelings.

relearning method A method for measuring forgetting.

REM (rapid eye movement) sleep The stage of sleep during which muscle tone decreases dramatically but the EEG resembles that of someone who is awake.

REM behavior disorder A sleep disorder in which the decreased muscle tone normally seen in REM sleep does not appear, thus allowing dreams to be acted out.

representative sampling A sample of research participants chosen from a larger population such that their age, gender, ethnicity, and other characteristics are typical of that larger population.

representativeness heuristic A mental shortcut that involves judging whether something belongs in a given class on the basis of its similarity to other members of that class.

repressed memory A painful memory that is said to be kept out of consciousness by psychological processes.

response bias (response criterion) The internal rule a person uses to decide whether or not to report a stimulus.

reticular formation A collection of cells and fibers in the hindbrain and midbrain that are involved in arousal and attention.

reticular formation A collection of cells and fibers in the hindbrain and midbrain that are involved in arousal and attention.

retina The surface at the back of the eye onto which the lens focuses light rays.

retinal disparity A depth cue based on the difference between the retinal images received by each eye.

retrieval The process of finding information stored in memory.

retrieval cues Stimuli that allow or help people to recall information.

retroactive inhibition A cause of forgetting whereby new information placed in memory interferes with the ability to recall information already in memory.

retrograde amnesia A loss of memory for events that occurred prior to a brain injury.

rods Photoreceptors in the retina that allow sight even in dim light but that cannot distinguish colors.

sampling The process of selecting participants who are members of the population that the researcher wishes to study.

satiation The satisfaction of a need such as hunger.

satiety The condition of no longer wanting to eat.

schemas Generalizations about categories of objects, places, events, and people, or mental representations of what we know and expect about the world.

schizophrenia A pattern of severely disturbed thinking, emotion, perception, and behavior that constitutes one of the most serious and disabling of all mental disorders.

school psychologists Psychologists who test cognitive abilities, diagnose students' academic problems, and set up programs to improve students' achievement.

scripts Mental representations of familiar sequences of activity.

secondary drives Stimuli that take on the motivational properties of primary drives through learning.

secondary reinforcers Rewards that people or animals learn to like.

selective attention The process of focusing mental resources on only part of the stimulus field.

self-actualization The reaching of one's fullest potential; the complete realization of a person's talents, faculties, and abilities.

self-concept The way one thinks of oneself.

self-efficacy According to Bandura, the learned expectation of success in given situations.

self-esteem The evaluations people make about their worth as human beings.

self-fulfilling prophecy A process in which an initial impression causes us to bring out behavior in another that confirms the impression.

self-serving bias The tendency to attribute one's successes to internal characteristics while blaming one's failures on external causes.

semantic memory Memory for generalized knowledge about the world.

sensations Raw information from the senses.

sense A system that translates data from outside the nervous system into neural activity.

sense of equilibrium (vestibular sense) The proprioceptive sense that provides information about the position of the head and its movements.

sensitivity The ability to detect a stimulus.

sensorimotor stage According to Piaget, the first stage of cognitive development, when the infant's mental activity is confined to sensory perception and motor skills.

sensory adaptation Decreasing responsiveness to an unchanging stimulus.

sensory cortex The parts of the cerebral cortex located in the parietal, occipital, and temporal lobes that receive stimulus information from the skin, eyes, and ears, respectively.

sensory memory A type of memory that is very brief but lasts long enough to connect one impression to the next.

sensory neurons The neurons that provide the brain with information about the environment.

sensory registers Memory systems that briefly hold incoming information.

sex hormones Chemicals in the blood that organize and motivate sexual behavior.

sexual arousal Physiological arousal that arises from sexual contact or erotic thoughts.

sexual response cycle The pattern of arousal before, during, and after sexual activity.

shaping The reinforcement of responses that come successively closer to some desired response.

short-term memory (STM) A stage of memory in which information normally lasts less than twenty seconds; a component of working memory.

signal detection theory A mathematical model of what determines a person's report of a near-threshold stimulus.

sleep apnea A sleep disorder in which a person briefly but repeatedly stops breathing during the night.

sleep deprivation A condition in which people do not get enough sleep; it may result in reduced cognitive abilities, inattention, and increased risk of accidents.

sleep terror disorder (night terrors) The occurrence of horrific dream images during N3 sleep, followed by a rapid awakening and a state of intense fear.

sleepwalking A phenomenon that starts primarily in NREM sleep, especially in stage N3, and involves walking while asleep.

social cognition Mental processes associated with people's perceptions of and reactions to other people.

social comparison Using other people as a basis of comparison for evaluating oneself.

social dilemmas Situations in which actions that produce rewards for one individual will produce negative consequences for all if they are adopted by everyone.

social discrimination Differential treatment of people in certain groups; the behavioral component of prejudice.

social facilitation A phenomenon in which the presence of others improves a person's performance.

social identity The beliefs we hold about the groups to which we belong.

social interference A reduction in performance due to the presence of other people.

social loafing Exerting less effort when performing a group task than when performing the same task alone.

social neuroscience A specialty that focuses on the influence of social processes on biological processes and on the influence of biological processes on social psychological phenomena.

social norms Learned, socially-based rules that prescribe what people should or should not do in various situations.

social perception The processes through which people interpret information about others, draw inferences about them, and develop mental representations of them.

social phobias Strong, irrational fears related to social situations.

social psychologists Psychologists who study how people influence one another's behavior and attitudes, especially in groups.

social psychology The subfield of psychology that explores the effects of the social world on the behavior and mental processes of individuals and groups.

social support The friends and social contacts on whom one can depend for help and support.

social-cognitive approach The view that personality reflects learned patterns of thinking and behavior.

socialization The process by which parents, teachers, and others teach children the skills and social norms necessary to be well-functioning members of society.

sociocultural factors Social identity and other background factors, such as gender, ethnicity, social class, and culture; also, characteristics or conditions that can influence the appearance and form of maladaptive behavior.

sociocultural perspective Explaining mental disorders in ways that emphasize the role of factors such as gender and age, physical situations, cultural values and expectations, and historical era.

somatic nervous system The subsystem of the peripheral nervous system that transmits information from the senses to the central nervous system and carries signals from the CNS to the muscles that move the skeleton.

somatization disorder A somatoform disorder in which there are numerous physical complaints without verifiable physical illness.

somatoform disorders Psychological problems in which a person shows the symptoms of a physical disorder for which there is no physical cause.

somatoform pain disorder A somatoform disorder marked by complaints of severe, often constant pain with no physical cause.

sound A repetitive fluctuation in the pressure of a medium such as air.

specific phobias Phobias that involve fear and avoidance of specific stimuli and situations such as heights, blood, and certain animals.

spinal cord The part of the central nervous system that receives information from the senses, passes these signals to the brain, and sends messages from the brain to the body.

spontaneous recovery The temporary reappearance of a conditioned response after extinction.

sport psychologists Psychologists whose research is aimed at maximizing athletic performance.

spreading activation In semantic network theories of memory, a principle that explains how information is retrieved.

standard score A way of stating how many standard deviations separate a particular score from the mean of all the scores in a data set.

Stanford-Binet Intelligence Scale A test for determining a person's intelligence quotient, or IQ.

state theories of hypnosis Theories proposing that hypnosis creates an altered state of consciousness.

state-dependent memory (state-dependent learning) Memory that is helped or hindered by similarities or differences in a person's internal state during learning versus recall.

statistical reliability The degree to which test results or other research evidence occurs repeatedly.

statistical significance Referring to a correlation or a difference between two groups that is larger than would be expected by chance.

statistical validity The degree to which evidence from a test or other research method measures what it is supposed to measure, is interpreted appropriately, and is used properly.

stereotypes False assumptions that all members of some group share the same characteristics.

stimulus discrimination A process through which people learn to differentiate among similar stimuli and respond appropriately to each one.

stimulus generalization A process in which a conditioned response is triggered by stimuli similar to the original conditioned stimulus.

storage The process of maintaining information in the memory system over time.

stress The process of adjusting to circumstances that disrupt or threaten to disrupt a person's daily functioning.

stress reactions Physical and psychological responses to stressors.

stressors Events or situations to which people must adjust.

stroboscopic illusion An illusion of motion that is created when we see slightly different images or slightly displaced lights flashed in rapid succession.

subconscious Another term that describes the mental level at which influential but normally inaccessible mental processes take place.

substance-related disorders Problems involving the use of psychoactive drugs for months or years in ways that harm the user or others.

sudden infant death syndrome (SIDS) A disorder in which a sleeping baby stops breathing, does not awaken, and dies.

superego According to Freud, the component of personality that tells people what they should and should not do.

surveys Research that involves giving people questionnaires or interviews designed to describe their attitudes, beliefs, opinions, and intentions.

sympathetic nervous system The subsystem of the autonomic nervous system that readies the body for vigorous activity.

synapse The tiny gap between the axon of one neuron and the dendrites of another, across which they communicate.

syndrome A pattern of symptoms associated with a particular neuropsychological disorder.

systematic desensitization therapy A behavioral method for treating anxiety in which clients visualize a graduated series of anxiety-provoking stimuli while remaining relaxed.

task-motivated leaders Leaders who provide close supervision, lead by giving directions, and generally discourage group discussion.

taste perception The sense that detects chemicals in solution that come into contact with receptors inside the mouth. Also called gustatory perception.

temperament An individual's basic, natural disposition that is evident from infancy.

teratogens Harmful substances, such as alcohol and other drugs, that can cause birth defects.

terminal drop A sharp decline in mental functioning that tends to occur in late adulthood, a few months or years before death.

test A systematic observation of behavior in a standard situation, described by a numerical scale or category.

thalamus A forebrain structure that relays messages from most sense organs to higher brain areas.

theory An integrated set of propositions used to explain certain phenomena, including behavior and mental processes.

thinking The manipulation of mental representations.

timbre The quality of a sound that identifies it.

token economy program A system for improving the behavior of clients in institutions by rewarding desirable behaviors with tokens that can be exchanged for various rewards

top-down processing Aspects of recognition guided by higher-level cognitive processes and by psychological factors such as expectations.

trait approach A perspective on personality that views it as the combination of stable characteristics that people display over time and across situations.

tranquilizing drugs (anxiolytics) Drugs that reduce tension and symptoms of anxiety.

transduction The process of converting incoming physical energy into neural activity.

transfer-appropriate processing model of memory A model that suggests that memory depends on how the encoding process matches up with what is later retrieved.

traumatic brain injury (trauma) An impact on the brain caused by a blow or sudden violent movement of the head.

trichromatic theory A theory of color vision stating that information from three types of visual elements combines to produce the sensation of color.

tympanic membrane (eardrum) A tightly stretched membrane in the middle ear that generates vibrations that match the sound waves striking it.

unconditional positive regard In client-centered therapy, the therapist's attitude that expresses caring for and acceptance of the client as a valued person.

unconditioned response (UCR) The automatic, unlearned, reflexive reaction to a stimulus.

unconditioned stimulus (UCS) A stimulus that triggers a response without conditioning.

unconscious The term used to describe a level of mental activity said by Freud to contain unacceptable sexual, aggressive, and other impulses of which an individual is unaware.

uninvolved parents (rejecting-neglecting parents) Parents who invest as little time, money, and effort in their children as possible.

utility In decision making, any subjective measure of value.

variables Specific factors or characteristics that can take on different numerical values in research.

vascular dementia A form of dementia caused by multiple restrictions of the brain's blood supply.

visual memory Mental representations of stimuli as pictures.

volley theory A theory of hearing that states that the firing rate of an acoustic nerve matches a sound wave's frequency. Also called frequency-matching theory.

wavelength The distance between peaks in a wave of light or sound.

Weber's law A law stating that the smallest detectable difference in stimulus energy (just-noticeable difference) is a constant fraction of the intensity of the stimulus.

well-being (subjective well-being) A cognitive judgment of satisfaction with life, the frequent experiencing of positive moods and emotions, and the relatively infrequent experiencing of unpleasant moods and emotions.

Wernicke's aphasia A language disorder in which there is a loss of ability to understand written or spoken language and to produce sensible speech.

work group At least two people who interact with one another as they perform the same or different workplace tasks.

work team A work group in which the members' specialized activities are coordinated and interdependent as they work toward a common goal.

working memory Memory that allows us to mentally work with, or manipulate, information being held in short-term memory.

NAME INDEX

SUBJECT INDEX